INDIAN
TREATIES
1778-1883

Nick Eggenhofer, for a picture which I hoped would capture the full essence of the times *AFTER* the treaties had been signed. Nick had only to step into his studio jammed with finished and half-finished paintings and drawings, Indian artifacts and various pieces of evidence of the old west, to find an already completed picture of Indians moving to the fort. This picture has never before been published and it was with deep gratitude that I accepted the picture for the frontispiece of this volume. The movement to the fort is symbolic of the time when Indians, in acceptance of terms stated in treaties, would move to the fort to collect the "largesse" due them according to the allowances stated categorically in the treaties. His picture is especially rewarding to view since it also is symbolic of a changing time, the period when most of the Indans attempted to make the difficult transition from a hunting society to an agricultural and sedentary one.

The complications, disappointments, anxieties, broken promises and treaties, the suffering and the deaths as well as all the other eventual happenings inherent in situations of this nature, are not a part of this volume; they have been the subjects of many books before this one. Rather, we are concerned only with the treaties as written and accepted, not in the execution of their terms or the lack of it. To this end this volume is dedicated to the entire American Indian population of the United States.

JOHN M. CARROLL
New Brunswick, New Jersey
Spring 1972

Introduction

In the republication of this most important resource book the general reading public, the student and the curious will have for the first time the opportunity to determine the justification of Indian and/or Federal disputes concerning the terms of Indian treaties. This volume in no way gives consideration to the historical moment when the treaties were signed, the pressures brought to bear, the legitimacy of the signers or the morality and/or legality of the treaties. These are just the treaties as they were written and signed and ratified by all parties concerned, and this rare information is now made available for the first time since 1903 when they were first compiled and published by the Government Printing Office and re-issued in 1904.

It was not enough just to reprint this volume. I felt that it should be presented with a scholarly endorsement and in such a way as to be aesthetically appealing. For the former I turned to one of the very few individuals in the United States who can be considered fully qualified to talk about Indian treaties, Commissioner Brantley Blue of the Indian Claims Commission in Washington, D. C. Commissioner Blue is a Lumbee Indian from North Carolina. Before his present responsibilities he practiced law for twenty years in Kingsport, Tennessee, during which time he served as Kingsport City Judge from 1955 to 1959. His degree as a Doctor of Jurisprudence, granted in 1969, qualified him for the all-important position in which he now functions. He is also the first Indian to serve as a Commissioner on the Indian Claims Commission; the appointment came from President Nixon in April, 1969. In his capacity, Commissioner Blue is constantly involved in the interpretation of these treaties as well as in all Indian claims. At present he is the National Chairman of American Indian Tribal Leaders' Conference on Scouting and a Member of the National Council of Boy Scouts of America. I sought his observations on the value of this volume of treaties and I was rewarded with a most insightful positional statement which I wholeheartedly share.

I then turned to one of America's greatest artists of the American West,

In 1871, the United States Congress enacted:

> That hereafter no Indian nation or tribe within the territory of the United States shall be acknowledged or recognized as an independent nation, tribe, or power with whom the United States may contract by treaty.

Thus the period of Indian treaties closed.

As the American nation became stronger, the Indians had declined. The old equality was over.

This is the story which this volume tells in detail.

BRANTLEY BLUE
Indian Claims Commissioner
Washington, D.C.
1972

Foreword

It is now sixty-eight years since publication of the second, and last, edition of Charles J. Kappler's compilation of Indian treaties. Only 3,000 copies were printed, half of them for official use and half for public sale. The first edition, printed for use of the Senate an even seventy years ago, was of a mere 500 copies. Kappler's Treaties, needless to say, have long been practically unobtainable, and the Indian Claims Commission has found its copies to be invaluable. This reprint will make them available for the first time to the many new libraries founded since 1904, and give a second chance to the older institutions not foresighted or lucky enough to get an original Kappler, or whose volume has fallen apart from three score and ten years of use.

But why reprint such a musty old document? The United States has not made a treaty with an Indian tribe since 1868 (there were later Agreements). What value does Kappler hold in the age of Aquarius?

The first part of the answer is that many Indian treaties are still in force. They must be referred to as the source, by legal standards, of existing Indian land titles and rights. A library without the Indian treaties lacks the complete body of living American law.

In my opinion, however, the greatest value of Kappler's *Treaties* is not as law but historical record. This chronological compilation reveals the course of relations between the United States of America and the Indians with an immediacy secondary sources can never attain.

The relationship started as one of relative equality. In the earliest treaty, made with the Delawares in 1778 (see page 3), the Indians, in return for help against the British in the Revolutionary War were invited to form a State of the Union. Their territorial rights were guaranteed "in the fullest and most ample manner."

Soon, however, the Indian treaties became little more than real estate conveyances, by which the Indians ceded almost any land the United States wanted for the price it was willing to pay. At the end, some of the tribes were signing away their rights to self-government.

Y.

O

Private Hermann Stieffel, present at the signing of the treaty at Medicine Lodge Creek, Kansas, in

Second printing 1973

Foreword and Introduction © 1972 by Interland Publishing, Inc.
Originally published as Indian Affairs: Laws and Treaties, Volume 2 (Treaties)
Reprinted from the edition of 1904, Washington, D.C.
First Interland Edition Published 1972
Manufactured in the United States of America

International Standard Book Number: 0-87989-025-8
Library of Congress Catalog Card Number: 72-75770

The illustration on the endpaper is used courtesy of The National Collection
of Fine Arts, Smithsonian Institution.

Frontispiece illustration reproduced from the original copyrighted by
Nick Eggenhofer, and used for this edition only, by permission of the artist.
The illustration on the last page is reproduced from the original drawing by
Brummett Echohawk, a Pawnee Indian, and used in this edition only,
by permission of the artist.

Map by courtesy of Sol Tax for Bruce Mac Lachlan, Samuel Stanley,
Robert K. Thomas, and the Smithsonian Institution.

The ornaments used on the binding and the Title Page are taken from
Decorative Art of the Southwestern Indians by Dorothy Smith Sides and
American Indian Design and Decoration by Le Roy H. Appleton and are
used with the permission of Dover Publications, Inc.

Binding design by Joan Stoliar

INTERLAND PUBLISHING, INC.
799 Broadway
New York, N.Y. 10003

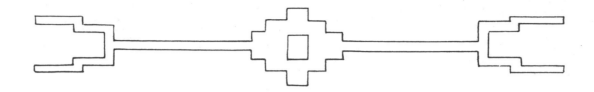

Indian Treaties
1778-1883

COMPILED AND EDITED BY Charles J. Kappler

WITH A NEW FOREWORD BY Brantley Blue
Indian Claims Commissioner

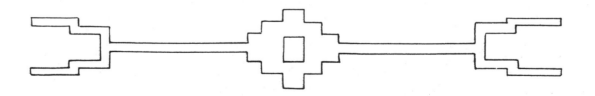

INTERLAND PUBLISHING INC.
NEW YORK, N.Y.

INDIAN
TREATIES
1778-1883

1867, painted the council as the great Kiowa Chief, Sa-tan-ti, was addressing the commissioners.

[see p. 977]

INDIAN AFFAIRS.

LAWS AND TREATIES.

Vol. II.
(TREATIES.)

COMPILED AND EDITED
BY
CHARLES J. KAPPLER, LL. M.,
CLERK TO THE SENATE COMMITTEE
ON INDIAN AFFAIRS.

WASHINGTON:
GOVERNMENT PRINTING OFFICE.
1904.

TREATIES.

TREATY WITH THE DELAWARES, 1778.

Articles of agreement and confederation, made and entered into by Andrew and Thomas Lewis, Esquires, Commissioners for, and in Behalf of the United States of North-America of the one Part, and Capt. White Eyes, Capt. John Kill Buck, Junior, and Capt. Pipe, Deputies and Chief Men of the Delaware Nation of the other Part.

ARTICLE I.

That all offences or acts of hostilities by one, or either of the contracting parties against the other, be mutually forgiven, and buried in the depth of oblivion, never more to be had in remembrance.

All offenses mutually forgiven.

ARTICLE II.

That a perpetual peace and friendship shall from henceforth take place, and subsist between the contracting parties aforesaid, through all succeeding generations: and if either of the parties are engaged in a just and necessary war with any other nation or nations, that then each shall assist the other in due proportion to their abilities, till their enemies are brought to reasonable terms of accommodation: and that if either of them shall discover any hostile designs forming against the other, they shall give the earliest notice thereof, that timeous measures may be taken to prevent their ill effect.

Peace and friendship perpetual.
In case of war, each party to assist the other.

ARTICLE III

And whereas the United States are engaged in a just and necessary war, in defence and support of life, liberty and independence, against the King of England and his adherents, and as said King is yet possessed of several posts and forts on the lakes and other places, the reduction of which is of great importance to the peace and security of the contracting parties, and as the most practicable way for the troops of the United States to some of the posts and forts is by passing through the country of the Delaware nation, the aforesaid deputies, on behalf of themselves and their nation, do hereby stipulate and agree to give a free passage through their country to the troops aforesaid, and the same to conduct by the nearest and best ways to the posts, forts or towns of the enemies of the United States, affording to said troops such supplies of corn, meat, horses, or whatever may be in their power for the accommodation of such troops, on the commanding officer's, &c. paying, or engageing to pay, the full value of whatever they can supply them with. And the said deputies, on the behalf of their nation, engage to join the troops of the United States aforesaid, with such a number of their best and most expert warriors as they can spare, consistent with their own safety, and act in concert with them; and for the better security of the old men, women and children of the aforesaid nation, whilst their warriors are engaged against the common enemy, it is agreed on the part of the United States, that a fort of suf-

United States to have free passage to forts or towns of their enemies.

Such warriors as can be spared, to join the troops of the United States.

3

ficient strength and capacity be built at the expense of the said States, with such assistance as it may be in the power of the said Delaware Nation to give, in the most convenient place, and advantageous situation, as shall be agreed on by the commanding officer of the troops aforesaid, with the advice and concurrence of the deputies of the aforesaid Delaware Nation, which fort shall be garrisoned by such a number of the troops of the United States,.as the commanding officer can spare for the present, and hereafter by such numbers, as the wise men of the United States in council, shall think most conducive to the common good.

ARTICLE IV.

Neither party to inflict punishment without an impartial trial.

For the better security of the peace and friendship now entered into by the contracting parties, against all infractions of the same by the citizens of either party, to the prejudice of the other, neither party shall proceed to the infliction of punishments on the citizens of the other, otherwise than by securing the offender or offenders by imprisonment, or any other competent means, till a fair and impartial trial can be had by judges or juries of both parties, as near as can be to the laws, customs and usages of the contracting parties and natural justice: The mode of such trials to be hereafter fixed by the wise men of the United States in Congress assembled, with the assistance of such deputies of the Delaware nation, as may be appointed to act in concert with them in adjusting this matter to their mutual liking. And it is further agreed between the parties aforesaid, that neither shall entertain or give countenance to the enemies of the other, or protect in their respective states, criminal fugitives, servants or slaves, but the same to apprehend, and secure and deliver to the State or States, to which such enemies, criminals, servants or slaves respectively belong.

Nor protect criminal fugitives, etc.

ARTICLE V.

Agent to be appointed by the United States to trade with the Delaware Nation.

Whereas the confederation entered into by the Delaware nation and the United States, renders the first dependent on the latter for all the articles of clothing, utensils and implements of war, and it is judged not only reasonable, but indispensably necessary, that the aforesaid Nation be supplied with such articles from time to time, as far as the United States may have it in their power, by a well-regulated trade, under the conduct of an intelligent, candid agent, with an adequate salary, one more influenced by the love of his country, and a constant attention to the duties of his department by promoting the common interest, than the sinister purposes of converting and binding all the duties of his office to his private emolument: Convinced of the necessity of such measures, the Commissioners of the United States, at the earnest solicitation of the deputies aforesaid, have engaged in behalf of the United States, that such a trade shall be afforded said nation, conducted on such principles of mutual interest as the wisdom of the United States in Congress assembled shall think most conducive to adopt for their mutual convenience.

ARTICLE VI.

United States guarantee to them all territorial rights as bounded by former treaties.

Whereas the enemies of the United States have endeavored, by every artifice in their power, to possess the Indians in general with an opinion, that it is the design of the States aforesaid, to extirpate the Indians and take possession of their country: to obviate such false suggestion, the United States do engage to guarantee to the aforesaid nation of Delawares, and their heirs, all their territorial rights in the fullest and most ample manner, as it hath been bounded by former treaties, as long as they the said Delaware nation shall abide by, and hold fast the chain of friendship now entered into.   And it is further agreed on between the contracting parties should it for the future be found conducive for the mutual interest of both parties to invite any other tribes who have been friends to the interest of the United States, to join the present confederation, and to form a state whereof the Delaware nation shall be the head, and have a representation in Congress: Provided, nothing contained in this article to be considered as conclusive until it meets with the approbation of Congress.   And it is also the intent and meaning of this article, that no protection or countenance shall be afforded to any who are at present our enemies, by which they might escape the punishment they deserve.

To have a representation in Congress on certain conditions.

In witness whereof, the parties have hereunto interchangeably set their hands and seals, at Fort Pitt, September seventeenth, anno Domini one thousand seven hundred and seventy-eight.

Andrew Lewis,	[L. s.]
Thomas Lewis,	[L. s.]
White Eyes, his x mark,	[L. s.]
The Pipe, his x mark,	[L. s.]
John Kill Buck, his x mark,	[L. s.]

In presence of—

Lach'n McIntosh, brigadier-general, commander the Western Department.
Daniel Brodhead, colonel Eighth Pennsylvania Regiment,
W. Crawford, colonel,
John Campbell,
John Stephenson,
John Gibson, colonel Thirteenth Virginia Regiment,
A. Graham, brigade major,
Lach. McIntosh, jr., major brigade,
Benjamin Mills,
Joseph L. Finley, captain Eighth Pennsylvania Regiment,
John Finley, captain Eighth Pennsylvania Regiment.

TREATY WITH THE SIX NATIONS, 1784.

Oct. 22, 1784.

7 Stat., 15.

Articles concluded at Fort Stanwix, on the twenty-second day of October, one thousand seven hundred and eighty-four, between Oliver Wolcott, Richard Butler, and Arthur Lee, Commissioners Plenipotentiary from the United States, in Congress assembled, on the one Part, and the Sachems and Warriors of the Six Nations, on the other.

The United States of America give peace to the Senecas, Mohawks, Onondagas and Cayugas, and receive them into their protection upon the following conditions:

ARTICLE I.

Six hostages shall be immediately delivered to the commissioners by the said nations, to remain in possession of the United States, till all the prisoners, white and black, which were taken by the said Senecas, Mohawks, Onondagas and Cayugas, or by any of them, in the late war, from among the people of the United States, shall be delivered up.

Hostages to be given till prisoners are delivered up.

ARTICLE II.

The Oneida and Tuscarora nations shall be secured in the possession of the lands on which they are settled.

Possession of lands secured.

ARTICLE III.

Boundaries.

A line shall be drawn, beginning at the mouth of a creek about four miles east of Niagara, called Oyonwayea, or Johnston's Landing-Place, upon the lake named by the Indians Oswego, and by us Ontario; from thence southerly in a direction always four miles east of the carrying-path, between Lake Erie and Ontario, to the mouth of Tehoseroron or Buffaloe Creek on Lake Erie; thence south to the north boundary of the state of Pennsylvania; thence west to the end of the said north boundary; thence south along the west boundary of the said state, to the river Ohio; the said line from the mouth of the Oyonwayea to the Ohio, shall be the western boundary of the lands of the Six Nations, so that the Six Nations shall and do yield to the United States, all claims to the country west of the said boundary, and then they shall be secured in the peaceful possession of the lands they inhabit east and north of the same, reserving only six miles square round the fort of Oswego, to the United States, for the support of the same.

ARTICLE IV.

Goods given to the Indians.

The Commissioners of the United States, in consideration of the present circumstances of the Six Nations, and in execution of the humane and liberal views of the United States upon the signing of the above articles, will order goods to be delivered to the said Six Nations for their use and comfort.

Oliver Wolcott,	[L. s.]	Oneidas:	
Richard Butler,	[L. s.]	Otyadonenghti, his x mark,	[L. s.]
Arthur Lee,	[L. s.]	Dagaheari, his x mark,	[L. s.]
Mohawks:		Cayuga:	
Onogwendahonji, his x mark,	[L. s.]	Oraghgoanendagen, his x mark,	[L. s.]
Touighnatogon, his x mark,	[L. s.]	Tuscaroras:	
Onondagas:		Ononghsawenghti, his x mark,	[L. s.]
Oheadarighton, his x mark,	[L. s.]	Tharondawagon, his x mark,	[L. s.]
Kendarindgon, his x mark,	[L. s.]	Seneka Abeal:	
Senekas:		Kayenthoghke, his x mark,	[L. s.]
Tayagonendagighti, his x mark,	[L. s.]		
Tehonwaeaghrigagi, his x mark,	[L. s.]		

Witnesses:

Sam. Jo. Atlee,
Wm. Maclay,
Fras. Johnston,
    Pennsylvania Commissioners.
Aaron Hill,
Alexander Campbell,
Saml. Kirkland, missionary,

James Dean,
Saml. Montgomery,
Derick Lane, captain,
John Mercer, lieutenant,
William Pennington, lieutenant,
Mahlon Hord, ensign,
Hugh Peebles.

TREATY WITH THE WYANDOT, ETC., 1785.

Jan. 21, 1785.
_____
7 Stat., 16.

Articles of a treaty concluded at Fort M'Intosh, the twenty-first day of January, one thousand seven hundred and eighty-five, between the Commissioners Plenipotentiary of the United States of America, of the one Part, and the Sachems and Warriors of the Wiandot, Delaware, Chippawa and Ottawa Nations of the other.

The Commissioners Plenipotentiary of the United States in Congress assembled, give peace to the Wiandot, Delaware, Chippewa and Ottawa nations of Indians, on the following conditions:

ARTICLE I.

Hostages to be given till prisoners are restored.

Three chiefs, one from among the Wiandot, and two from among the Delaware nations, shall be delivered up to the Commissioners of the United States, to be by them retained till all the prisoners, white and black, taken by the said nations, or any of them, shall be restored.

ARTICLE II.

The said Indian nations do acknowledge themselves and all their tribes to be under the protection of the United States and of no other sovereign whatsoever.

Indians acknowledge protection of United States.

ARTICLE III.

The boundary line between the United States and the Wiandot and Delaware nations, shall begin at the mouth of the river Cayahoga, and run thence up the said river to the portage between that and the Tuscarawas branch of Meskingum; then down the said branch to the forks at the crossing place above Fort Lawrence; then westerly to the portage of the Big Miami, which runs into the Ohio, at the mouth of which branch the fort stood which was taken by the French in one thousand seven hundred and fifty-two; then along the said portage to the Great Miami or Ome river, and down the south-east side of the same to its mouth; thence along the south shore of lake Erie, to the mouth of Cayahoga where it began.

Boundaries.

ARTICLE IV.

The United States allot all the lands contained within the said lines to the Wiandot and Delaware nations, to live and to hunt on, and to such of the Ottawa nation as now live thereon; saving and reserving for the establishment of trading posts, six miles square at the mouth of Miami or Ome river, and the same at the portage on that branch of the Big Miami which runs into the Ohio, and the same on the lake of Sanduske where the fort formerly stood, and also two miles square on each side of the lower rapids of Sanduske river, which posts and the lands annexed to them, shall be to the use and under the government of the United States.

Reserves.

ARTICLE V.

If any citizen of the United States, or other person not being an Indian, shall attempt to settle on any of the lands allotted to the Wiandot and Delaware nations in this treaty, except on the lands reserved to the United States in the preceding article, such person shall forfeit the protection of the United States, and the Indians may punish him as they please.

No citizen of United States to settle on Indian lands.

ARTICLE VI.

The Indians who sign this treaty, as well in behalf of all their tribes as of themselves, do acknowledge the lands east, south and west of the lines described in the third article, so far as the said Indians formerly claimed the same, to belong to the United States; and none of their tribes shall presume to settle upon the same, or any part of it.

Indians recognize title of United States to certain described lands.

ARTICLE VII.

The post of Detroit, with a district beginning at the mouth of the river Rosine, on the west end of lake Erie, and running west six miles up the southern bank of the said river, thence northerly and always six miles west of the strait, till it strikes the lake St. Clair, shall be also reserved to the sole use of the United States.

Post at Detroit reserved.

ARTICLE VIII.

Post at Michilli-machenac reserved.

In the same manner the post of Michillimachenac with its dependencies, and twelve miles square about the same, shall be reserved to the use of the United States.

ARTICLE IX

Robbers and murderers to be delivered to United States.

If any Indian or Indians shall commit a robbery or murder on any citizen of the United States, the tribe to which such offenders may belong, shall be bound to deliver them up at the nearest post, to be punished according to the ordinances of the United States.

ARTICLE X

Goods to be distributed.

The Commissioners of the United States, in pursuance of the humane and liberal views of Congress, upon this treaty's being signed, will direct goods to be distributed among the different tribes for their use and comfort.

SEPARATE ARTICLE.

It is agreed that the Delaware chiefs, Kelelamand or lieutenant-colonel Henry, Hengue Pushees or the Big Cat, Wicocalind or Captain White Eyes, who took up the hatchet for the United States, and their families, shall be received into the Delaware nation, in the same situation and rank as before the war, and enjoy their due portions of the lands given to the Wiandot and Delaware nations in this treaty, as fully as if they had not taken part with America, or as any other person or persons in the said nations.

Go. Clark,	[L. S.]	Talapoxic, his x mark,	[L. S.]
Richard Butler,	[L. S.]	Wingenum, his x mark,	[L. S.]
Arthur Lee,	[L. S.]	Packelant, his x mark,	[L. S.]
Daunghquat, his x mark,	[L. S.]	Gingewanno, his x mark,	[L. S.]
Abraham Kuhn, his x mark,	[L. S.]	Waanoos, his x mark,	[L. S.]
Ottawerreri, his x mark,	[L. S.]	Konalawassee, his x mark,	[L. S.]
Hobocan, his x mark,	[L. S.]	Shawnaqum, his x mark,	[L. S.]
Walendightun, his x mark,	[L. S.]	Quecookkia, his x mark,	[L. S.]

Witness:

Sam'l J. Atlee,
Fras. Johnston,
    Pennsylvania Commissioners.
Alex. Campbell,
Jos. Harmar, lieutenant-colonel commandant.
Alex. Lowrey,
Joseph Nicholas, interpreter.

I. Bradford,
George Slaughter,
Van Swearingen,
John Boggs,
G. Evans,
D. Luckett,

TREATY WITH THE CHEROKEE, 1785.

Nov. 28, 1785.
_____
7 Stat., 18.

Articles concluded at Hopewell, on the Keowee, between Benjamin Hawkins, Andrew Pickens, Joseph Martin, and Lachlan M'Intosh, Commissioners Plenipotentiary of the United States of America, of the one Part, and the Head-Men and Warriors of all the Cherokees of the other.

The Commissioners Plenipotentiary of the United States, in Congress assembled, give peace to all the Cherokees, and receive them into the favor and protection of the United States of America, on the following conditions:

ARTICLE I.

The Head-Men and Warriors of all the Cherokees shall restore all the prisoners, citizens of the United States, or subjects of their allies, to their entire liberty: They shall also restore all the Negroes, and all other property taken during the late war from the citizens, to such person, and at such time and place, as the Commissioners shall appoint.

Indians to restore all prisoners, etc.

ARTICLE II.

The Commissioners of the United States in Congress assembled, shall restore all the prisoners taken from the Indians, during the late war, to the Head-Men and Warriors of the Cherokees, as early as is practicable.

United States to re-store all prisoners.

ARTICLE III.

The said Indians for themselves and their respective tribes and towns do acknowledge all the Cherokees to be under the protection of the United States of America, and of no other sovereign whosoever.

Cherokees acknowl-edge protection of United States.

ARTICLE IV.

The boundary allotted to the Cherokees for their hunting grounds, between the said Indians and the citizens of the United States, within the limits of the United States of America, is, and shall be the follow-ing, viz. Beginning at the mouth of Duck river, on the Tennessee; thence running north-east to the ridge dividing the waters running into Cumberland from those running into the Tennessee; thence east-wardly along the said ridge to a north-east line to be run, which shall strike the river Cumberland forty miles above Nashville; thence along the said line to the river; thence up the said river to the ford where the Kentucky road crosses the river; thence to Campbell's line, near Cumberland gap; thence to the mouth of Claud's creek on Holstein; thence to the Chimney-top mountain; thence to Camp-creek, near the mouth of Big Limestone, on Nolichuckey; thence a southerly course six miles to a mountain; thence south to the North-Carolina line; thence to the South-Carolina Indian boundary, and along the same south-west over the top of the Oconee mountain till it shall strike Tugaloo river; thence a direct line to the top of the Currohee moun-tain; thence to the head of the south fork of Oconee river.

Boundaries.

ARTICLE V.

If any citizen of the United States, or other person not being an Indian, shall attempt to settle on any of the lands westward or south-ward of the said boundary which are hereby allotted to the Indians for their hunting grounds, or having already settled and will not remove from the same within six months after the ratification of this treaty, such person shall forfeit the protection of the United States, and the Indians may punish him or not as they please: Provided nevertheless, That this article shall not extend to the people settled between the fork of French Broad and Holstein rivers, whose particular situation shall be transmitted to the United States in Congress assembled for their decision thereon, which the Indians agree to abide by.

No citizen of United States to settle on In-dian lands.

ARTICLE VI.

If any Indian or Indians, or person residing among them, or who shall take refuge in their nation, shall commit a robbery, or murder, or other capital crime, on any citizen of the United States, or person

Indians to deliver up criminals.

under their protection, the nation, or the tribe to which such offender or offenders may belong, shall be bound to deliver him or them up to be punished according to the ordinances of the United States; Provided, that the punishment shall not be greater than if the robbery or murder, or other capital crime had been committed by a citizen on a citizen.

ARTICLE VII.

Citizens of United States committing crimes against Indians to be punished.

If any citizen of the United States, or person under their protection, shall commit a robbery or murder, or other capital crime, on any Indian, such offender or offenders shall be punished in the same manner as if the murder or robbery, or other capital crime, had been committed on a citizen of the United States; and the punishment shall be in presence of some of the Cherokees, if any shall attend at the time and place, and that they may have an opportunity so to do, due notice of the time of such intended punishment shall be sent to some one of the tribes.

ARTICLE VIII.

Retaliation prohibited.

It is understood that the punishment of the innocent under the idea of retaliation, is unjust, and shall not be practiced on either side, except where there is a manifest violation of this treaty; and then it shall be preceded first by a demand of justice, and if refused, then by a declaration of hostilities.

ARTICLE IX.

United States to regulate trade.

For the benefit and comfort of the Indians, and for the prevention of injuries or oppressions on the part of the citizens or Indians, the United States in Congress assembled shall have the sole and exclusive right of regulating the trade with the Indians, and managing all their affairs in such manner as they think proper.

ARTICLE X.

Special provision for trade.

Until the pleasure of Congress be known, respecting the ninth article, all traders, citizens of the United States, shall have liberty to go to any of the tribes or towns of the Cherokees to trade with them, and they shall be protected in their persons and property, and kindly treated.

ARTICLE XI.

Indians to give notice of designs against United States.

The said Indians shall give notice to the citizens of the United States, of any designs which they may know or suspect to be formed in any neighboring tribe, or by any person whosoever, against the peace, trade or interest of the United States.

ARTICLE XII.

Indians may send deputy to Congress.

That the Indians may have full confidence in the justice of the United States, respecting their interests, they shall have the right to send a deputy of their choice, whenever they think fit, to Congress.

ARTICLE XIII.

Peace and friendship perpetual.

The hatchet shall be forever buried, and the peace given by the United States, and friendship re-established between the said states on the one part, and all the Cherokees on the other, shall be universal;

and the contracting parties shall use their utmost endeavors to maintain the peace given as aforesaid, and friendship re-established.

In witness of all and every thing herein determined, between the United States of America and all the Cherokees, we, their underwritten Commissioners, by virtue of our full powers, have signed this definitive treaty, and have caused our seals to be hereunto affixed.

Done at Hopewell, on the Keowee, this twenty-eighth of November, in the year of our Lord one thousand seven hundred and eighty-five.

Benjamin Hawkins, [L. s.]	Chesecotetona, or Yellow Bird of the Pine Log, his x mark, [L. s.]
And'w Pickens, [L. s.]	Sketaloska, Second Man of Tillico,
Jos. Martin, [L. s.]	his x mark, [L. s.]
Lach'n McIntosh, [L. s.]	Chokasatahe, Chickasaw Killer Tasonta, his x mark, [L. s.]
Koatohee, or Corn Tassel of Toquo, his x mark, [L. s.]	Onanoota, of Koosoate, his x mark, [L. s.]
Scholauetta, or Hanging Man of Chota, his x mark, [L. s.]	Ookoseta, or Sower Mush of Kooloque, his x mark, [L. s.]
Tuskegatahu, or Long Fellow of Chistohoe, his x mark, [L. s.]	Umatooetha, the Water Hunter Choikamawga, his x mark, [L. s.]
Ooskwha, or Abraham of Chilkowa, his x mark, [L. s.]	Wyuka, of Lookout Mountain, his x mark, [L. s.]
Kolakusta, or Prince of Noth, his x mark, [L. s.]	Tulco, or Tom of Chatuga, his x mark, [L. s.]
Newota, or the Gritzs of Chicamaga, his x mark, [L. s.]	Will, of Akoha, his x mark, [L. s.]
Konatota, or the Rising Fawn of Highwassay, his x mark, [L. s.]	Necatee, of Sawta, his x mark, [L. s.]
Tuckasee, or Young Terrapin of Allajoy, his x mark, [L. s.]	Amokontakona, Kutcloa, his x mark, [L. s.]
Toostaka, or the Waker of Oostanawa, his x mark, [L. s.]	Kowetatahee, in Frog Town, his x mark, [L. s.]
Untoola, or Gun Rod of Seteco, his x mark, [L. s.]	Keukuck, Talcoa, his x mark, [L. s.]
	Tulatiska, of Chaway, his x mark, [L. s.]
Unsuokanail, Buffalo White Calf New Cussee, his x mark, [L. s.]	Wooaluka, the Waylayer, Chota, his x mark, [L. s.]
Kostayeak, or Sharp Fellow Wataga, his x mark, [L. s.]	Tatliusta, or Porpoise of Tilassi, his x mark, [L. s.]
Chonosta, of Cowe, his x mark, [L. s.]	John, of Little Tallico, his x mark, [L. s.]
Chescoonwho, Bird in Close of Tomotlug, his x mark, [L. s.]	Skelelak, his x mark, [L. s.]
Tuckasee, or Terrapin of Hightowa, his x mark, [L. s.]	Akonoluchta, the Cabin, his x mark, [L. s.]
	Cheanoka, of Kawetakac, his x mark, [L. s.]
Chesetoa, or the Rabbit of Tlacoa, his x mark, [L. s.]	Yellow Bird, his x mark, [L. s.]

Witness:

Wm. Blount,	Thos. Gregg,
Sam'l Taylor, Major.,	W. Hazzard.
John Owen,	James Madison,
Jess. Walton,	Arthur Cooley,
Jno. Cowan, capt. comm'd't,	Sworn interpreters.

TREATY WITH THE CHOCTAW, 1786.

Articles of a treaty concluded at Hopewell, on the Keowée, near Seneca Old Town, between Benjamin Hawkins, Andrew Pickens and Joseph Martin, Commissioners Plenipotentiary of the United States of America, of the one part; and Yockonahoma, great Medal Chief of Soonacoha; Yockehoopoie, leading Chief of Bugtoogoloo; Mingohoopoie, leading Chief of Hashooqua; Tobocoh, great Medal Chief of Congetoo; Pooshemastubie, Gorget Captain of Senayazo; and thirteen small Medal Chiefs of the first Class, twelve Medal and Gorget Captains, Commissioners Plenipotentiary of all the Choctaw Nation, of the other part.

Jan. 3, 1786

7 Stat., 21.

THE Commissioners Plenipotentiary of the United States of America give peace to all the Choctaw nation, and receive them into the favor and protection of the United States of America, on the following conditions:

ARTICLE I.

Indians to restore prisoners.

The Commissioners Plenipotentiary of all the Choctaw nation, shall restore all the prisoners, citizens of the United States, or subjects of their allies, to their entire liberty, if any there be in the Choctaw nation.   They shall also restore all the negroes, and all other property taken during the late war, from the citizens, to such person, and at such time and place as the Commissioners of the United States of America shall appoint, if any there be in the Choctaw nation.

ARTICLE II.

They acknowledge the protection of United States.

The Commissioners Plenipotentiary of all the Choctaw nation, do hereby acknowledge the tribes and towns of the said nation, and the lands within the boundary allotted to the said Indians to live and hunt on, as mentioned in the third article, to be under the protection of the United States of America, and of no other sovereign whosoever.

ARTICLE III.

Boundaries.

The boundary of the lands hereby allotted to the Choctaw nation to live and hunt on, within the limits of the United States of America, is and shall be the following, viz.   Beginning at a point on the thirty-first degree of north latitude, where the Eastern boundary of the Natches district shall touch the same; thence east along the said thirty-first degree of north latitude, being the southern boundary of the United States of America, until it shall strike the eastern boundary of the lands on which the Indians of the said nation did live and hunt on the twenty-ninth of November, one thousand seven hundred and eighty-two, while they were under the protection of the King of Great-Britain; thence northerly along the said eastern boundary, until it shall meet the northern boundary of the said lands; thence westerly along the said northern boundary, until it shall meet the western boundary thereof; thence southerly along the same to the beginning: saving and reserving for the establishment of trading posts, three tracts or parcels of land of six miles square each, at such places as the United [States] in Congress assembled shall think proper; which posts, and the lands annexed to them, shall be to the use and under the government of the United States of America.

ARTICLE IV.

No citizen of United States shall settle on Indian lands.

If any citizen of the United States, or other person not being an Indian, shall attempt to settle on any of the lands hereby allotted to the Indians to live and hunt on, such person shall forfeit the protection of the United States of America, and the Indians may punish him or not as they please.

ARTICLE V.

Indians to deliver criminals.

If any Indian or Indians, or persons, residing among them, or who shall take refuge in their nation, shall commit a robbery or murder or other capital crime on any citizen of the United States of America, or person under their protection, the tribe to which such offender may belong, or the nation, shall be bound to deliver him or them up to be punished according to the ordinances of the United States in Congress assembled: Provided, that the punishment shall not be greater than if the robbery or murder, or other capital crime, had been committed by a citizen on a citizen.

ARTICLE VI.

If any citizen of the United States of America, or person under their protection, shall commit a robbery or murder, or other capital crime, on any Indian, such offender or offenders shall be punished in the same manner as if the robbery or murder, or other capital crime, had been committed on a citizen of the United States of America; and the punishment shall be in presence of some of the Choctaws, if any will attend at the time and place; and that they may have an opportunity so to do, due notice, if practicable, of the time of such intended punishment, shall be sent to some one of the tribes.

Citizens of United States committing crimes against Indians to be punished.

ARTICLE VII.

It is understood that the punishment of the innocent, under the idea of retaliation, is unjust, and shall not be practiced on either side, except where there is a manifest violation of this treaty; and then it shall be preceded, first by a demand of justice, and if refused, then by a declaration of hostilities.

Retaliation restrained.

ARTICLE VIII.

For the benefit and comfort of the Indians, and for the prevention of injuries or oppressions on the part of the citizens or Indians, the United States in Congress assembled, shall have the sole and exclusive right of regulating the trade with the Indians, and managing all their affairs in such manner as they think proper.

United States to regulate trade.

ARTICLE IX.

Until the pleasure of Congress be known, respecting the eighth article, all traders, citizens of the United States of America, shall have liberty to go to any of the tribes or towns of the Choctaws, to trade with them, and they shall be protected in their persons and property, and kindly treated.

Special provision for trade.

ARTICLE X.

The said Indians shall give notice to the citizens of the United States of America, of any designs which they may know or suspect to be formed in any neighboring-tribe, or by any person whosoever, against the peace, trade or interest of the United States of America.

Indians to give notice of designs against United States.

ARTICLE XI.

The hatchet shall be forever buried, and the peace given by the United States of America, and friendship re-established between the said states on the one part, and all the Choctaw nation on the other part, shall be universal; and the contracting parties shall use their utmost endeavors to maintain the peace given as aforesaid, and friendship re-established.

Peace and friendship perpetual.

In witness of all and every thing herein determined, between the United States of America and all the Choctaws, we, their underwritten commissioners, by virtue of our full powers, have signed this definitive treaty, and have caused our seals to be hereunto affixed.

Done at Hopewell, on the Keowee, this third day of January, in the year of our Lord one thousand seven hundred and eighty-six.

Benjamin Hawkins,	[L. S.]	Yockenahoma, his x mark,	[L. S.]
Andrew Pickens,	[L. S.]	Yockehoopoie, his x mark,	[L. S.]
Jos. Martin,	[L. S.]	Mingohoopoie, his x mark,	[L. S.]

Tobocoh, his x mark,	[L. S.]	Cshecoopoohcomoch, his x mark,	[L. S.]
Pooshemastuby, his x mark,	[L. S.]	Stonakoohoopoie, his x mark,	[L. S.]
Pooshahooma, his x mark,	[L. S.]	Tushkoheegohta, his x mark,	[L. S.]
Tuscoonoohoopoie, his x mark,	[L. S.]	Teshuhenochloch, his x mark,	[L. S.]
Shinshemastuby, his x mark,	[L. S.]	Pooshonaltla, his x mark,	[L. S.]
Yoopahooma, his x mark,	[L. S.]	Okanconnooba, his x mark,	[L. S.]
Stoonokoohoopoie, his x mark,	[L. S.]	Autoonachuba, his x mark,	[L. S.]
Tehakuhbay, his x mark,	[L. S.]	Pangehooloch, his x mark,	[L. S.]
Pooshemastuby, his x mark,	[L. S.]	Steabee, his x mark,	[L. S.]
Tuskkahoomoih, his x mark,	[L. S.]	Tenetchenna, his x mark,	[L. S.]
Tushkahoomock, his x mark,	[L. S.]	Tushkementahock, his x mark,	[L. S.]
Yoostenochla, his x mark,	[L. S.]	Tushtallay, his x mark,	[L. S.]
Tootehooma, his x mark,	[L. S.]	Cshnaangchabba, his x mark,	[L. S.]
Toobenohoomoch, his x mark,	[L. S.]	Cunnopoie, his x mark,	[L. S.[

Witness:

    Wm. Blount,
    John Woods,
    Saml. Taylor,
    Robert Anderson,
    Benj. Lawrence.
    John Pitchlynn,
    James Cole,
            Interpreters.

TREATY WITH THE CHICKASAW, 1786.

Jan. 10, 1786.
7 Stat. 24.

Articles of a treaty, concluded at Hopewell, on the Keowée, near Seneca Old Town, between Benjamin Hawkins, Andrew Pickens, and Joseph Martin, Commissioners Plenipotentiary of the United States of America, of the one Part; and Piomingo, Head Warrior and First Minister of the Chickasaw Nation; Mingatushka, one of the leading Chiefs; and Latopoia, first beloved Man of the said Nation, Commissioners Plenipotentiary of all the Chickasaws, of the other Part.

THE Commissioners Plenipotentiary of the United States of America give peace to the Chickasaw Nation, and receive them into the favor and protection of the said States, on the following conditions:

ARTICLE I.

Indians to restore prisoners and property.

The Commissioners Plenipotentiary of the Chickasaw nation, shall restore all the prisoners, citizens of the United States, to their entire liberty, if any there be in the Chickasaw nation. They shall also restore all the negroes, and all other property taken during the late war, from the citizens, if any there be in the Chickasaw nation, to such person, and at such time and place, as the Commissioners of the United States of America shall appoint.

ARTICLE II.

Acknowledge protection of United States.

The Commissioners Plenipotentiary of the Chickasaws, do hereby acknowledge the tribes and the towns of the Chickasaw nation, to be under the protection of the United States of America, and of no other sovereign whosoever.

ARTICLE III.

Boundaries.

The boundary of the lands hereby allotted to the Chickasaw nation to live and hunt on, within the limits of the United States of America, is, and shall be the following, viz. Beginning on the ridge that divides the waters running into the Cumberland, from those running into the Tennessee, at a point in a line to be run north-east, which shall strike the Tennessee at the mouth of Duck river; thence running westerly along the said ridge, till it shall strike the Ohio; thence down the southern banks thereof to the Mississippi; thence down the same, to the Choctaw line or Natches district; thence along the said line, or the line of the district eastwardly as far as the Chickasaws claimed, and lived and hunted on, the twenty-ninth of November, one thousand seven hundred and eighty-two. Thence the said boundary, eastwardly, shall be the lands allotted to the Choctaws and Cherokees to live and hunt on, and the lands at present in the possession of the Creeks; saving and reserving for the establishment of a trading post, a tract or parcel of land to be laid out at the lower port of the Muscle shoals, at the mouth of Ocochappo, in a circle, the diameter of which shall be five miles on the[a]   river, which post, and the lands annexed thereto, shall be to the use and under the government of the United States of America.

Article IV.

If any citizen of the United States, or other person not being an Indian, shall attempt to settle on any of the lands hereby allotted to the Chickasaws to live and hunt on, such person shall forfeit the protection of the United States of America, and the Chickasaws may punish him or not as they please.

No citizen of United States shall settle on Indian lands.

Article V.

If any Indian or Indians, or persons residing among them, or who shall take refuge in their nation, shall commit a robbery or murder, or other capital crime, on any citizen of the United States, or person under their protection, the tribe to which such offender or offenders may belong, or the nation, shall be bound to deliver him or them up to be punished according to the ordinances of the United States in Congress assembled: Provided, that the punishment shall not be greater, than if the robbery or murder, or other capital crime, had been committed by a citizen on a citizen.

Indians to deliver up criminals.

Article VI.

If any citizen of the United States of America, or person under their protection, shall commit a robbery or murder, or other capital crime, on any Indian, such offender or offenders shall be punished in the same manner as if the robbery or murder or other capital crime had been committed on a citizen of the United States of America; and the punishment shall be in presence of some of the Chickasaws, if any will attend at the time and place, and that they may have an opportunity so to do, due notice, if practicable, of such intended punishment, shall be sent to some one of the tribes.

Citizens of United States committing crimes against Indians to be punished.

Article VII.

It is understood that the punishment of the innocent under the idea of retaliation is unjust, and shall not be practiced on either side, except where there is a manifest violation of this treaty; and then it shall be preceded, first by a demand of justice, and if refused, then by a declaration of hostilities.

Retaliation restrained.

Article VIII.

For the benefit and comfort of the Indians, and for the prevention of injuries or oppressions on the part of the citizens or Indians, the

United States to regulate trade.

---

[a] The name of the river is not in the original.

United States in Congress assembled shall have the sole and exclusive right of regulating the trade with the Indians, and managing all their affairs in such manner as they think proper.

ARTICLE IX.

Special provision for trade.

Until the pleasure of Congress be known respecting the eighth article, all traders, citizens of the United States, shall have liberty to go to any of the tribes or towns of the Chickasaws to trade with them, and they shall be protected in their persons and property, and kindly treated.

ARTICLE X.

Indians to give notice of designs against United States.

The said Indians shall give notice to the citizens of the United States of America, of any designs which they may know or suspect to be formed in any neighboring tribe, or by any person whosoever, against the peace, trade or interests of the United States of America.

ARTICLE XI.

Peace and friendship perpetual.

The hatchet shall be forever buried, and the peace given by the United States of America, and friendship re-established between the said States on the one part, and the Chickasaw nation on the other part, shall be universal, and the contracting parties shall use their utmost endeavors to maintain the peace given as aforesaid, and friendship re-established.

In witness of all and every thing herein contained, between the said States and Chickasaws, we, their underwritten commissioners, by virtue of our full powers, have signed this definitive treaty, and have caused our seals to be hereunto affixed.

Done at Hopewell, on the Keowee, this tenth day of January, in the year of our Lord one thousand seven hundred and eighty-six.

Benjamin Hawkins,	[L. S.]
And'w. Pickens,	[L. S.]
Jos. Martin,	[L. S.]
Piomingo, his x mark,	[L. S.]
Mingatushka, his x mark,	[L. S.]
Latopoia, his x mark,	[L. S.]

Witness:
    Wm. Blount,
    Wm. Hazard,
    Sam. Taylor,
    James Cole, Sworn Interpreter.

TREATY WITH THE SHAWNEE, 1786.

Jan. 31, 1786.
7 Stat., 26.

Articles of a Treaty concluded at the Mouth of the Great Miami, on the North-western Bank of the Ohio, the thirty-first day of January, one thousand seven hundred and eighty-six, between the Commissioners Plenipotentiary of the United States of America, of the one Part, and the Chiefs and Warriors of the Shawanoe Nation, of the other Part.

ARTICLE I.

Hostages delivered till prisoners are restored.

THREE hostages shall be immediately delivered to the Commissioners, to remain in the possession of the United States until all the prisoners, white and black, taken in the late war from among the citizens of the United States, by the Shawanoe nation, or by any other Indian or Indians residing in their towns, shall be restored.

ARTICLE II.

The Shawanoe nation do acknowledge the United States to be the sole and absolute sovereigns of all the territory ceded to them by a treaty of peace, made between them and the King of Great Britain, the fourteenth day of January, one thousand seven hundred and eighty-four. *(margin: Indians acknowledge the right of United States to territory ceded by Great Britain.)*

ARTICLE III.

If any Indian or Indians of the Shawanoe nation, or any other Indian or Indians residing in their towns, shall commit murder or robbery on, or do any injury to the citizens of the United States, or any of them, that nation shall deliver such offender or offenders to the officer commanding the nearest post of the United States, to be punished according to the ordinances of Congress; and in like manner, any citizen of the United States, who shall do an injury to any Indian of the Shawanoe nation, or to any other Indian or Indians residing in their towns, and under their protection, shall be punished according to the laws of the United States. *(margin: To deliver up criminals.)*

The Shawanoe nation having knowledge of the intention of any nation or body of Indians to make war on the citizens of the United States, or of their counselling together for that purpose, and neglecting to give information thereof to the commanding officer of the nearest post of the United States, shall be considered as parties in such war, and be punished accordingly: and the United States shall in like manner inform the Shawanoes of any injury designed against them. *(margin: To give notice of designs against United States.)*

ARTICLE V.

The United States do grant peace to the Shawanoe nation, and do receive them into their friendship and protection. *(margin: United States to give peace to the Shawanoe nation.)*

ARTICLE VI.

The United States do allot to the Shawanoe nation, lands within their territory to live and hunt upon, beginning at the south line of the lands allotted to the Wiandots and Delaware nations, at the place where the main branch of the Great Miami, which falls into the Ohio, intersects said line; then down the river Miami, to the fork of that river, next below the old fort which was taken by the French in one thousand seven hundred and fifty-two; thence due west to the river de la Panse; then down that river to the river Wabash, beyond which lines none of the citizens of the United States shall settle, nor disturb the Shawanoes in their settlement and possessions; and the Shawanoes do relinquish to the United States, all title, or pretence of title, they ever had to the lands east, west and south, of the east, west and south lines before described. *(margin: Allot to them certain lands.)*

ARTICLE VII.

If any citizen or citizens of the United States, shall presume to settle upon the lands allotted to the Shawanoes by this treaty, he or they shall be put out of the protection of the United States. *(margin: No citizen of United States to settle on Indian lands)*

In testimony whereof, the parties hereunto have affixed their hands and seals, the day and year first above mentioned.

G. Clark,	[L. S.]	Musquaconocah, his x mark,	[L. S.]
Richard Butler,	[L. S.]	Meanymsecah, his x mark,	[L. S.]
Samuel H. Parsons,	[L. S.]	Waupaucowela, his x mark,	[L. S.]
Aweecony, his x mark,	[L. S.]	Nihipeewa, his x mark,	[L. S.]
Kakawipilathy, his x mark,	[L. S.]	Nihinessicoe, his x mark,	[L. S.]
Malunthy, his x mark,	[L. S.]		

Attest:

      Alexander Campbell, Secretary Commissioners.

Witnesses:

W. Finney, Maj. B. B.
Thos. Doyle, Capt. B. B.
Nathan McDowell, Ensign
John Saffenger,
Henry Govy,
Kagy Galloway, his x mark,
John Boggs,
Samuel Montgomery,
Daniel Elliott,
James Rinker,
Nathaniel Smith,

Josep¹ Suffrein, his x mark, or Kemepemo
    Shawno,
Isaac Zane, (Wyandot) his x mark,
The Half King of the Wyandots, ⎰their x
The Crane of the Wyandots,   ⎱ mark,
Capt. Pipe, of the Delawares, his x mark,
Capt. Bohongehelas, his x mark,
Tetebockshicka, his x mark,
The Big Cat of the Delawares, his x mark,
Pierre Droullar.

TREATY WITH THE WYANDOT, ETC., 1789.

Jan. 9, 1789.

7 Stat., 28.
Proclamation, Sept. 27, 1789.

Articles of a Treaty Made at Fort Harmar, between Arthur St. Clair, Governor of the Territory of the United States North-West of the River Ohio, and Commissioner Plenipotentiary of the United States of America, for removing all Causes of Controversy, regulating Trade, and settling Boundaries, with the Indian Nations in the Northern Department, of the one Part; and the Sachems and Warriors of the Wiandot, Delaware, Ottawa, Chippewa, Pattawatima and Sac Nations, on the other Part.

ARTICLE I.

Two persons as hostages to be retained by United States until certain prisoners are restored.

WHEREAS the United States in Congress assembled, did, by their Commissioners George Rogers Clark, Richard Butler, and Arthur Lee, Esquires, duly appointed for that purpose, at a treaty holden with the Wiandot, Delaware, Ottawa and Chippewa nations, at Fort M'Intosh, on the twenty-first day of January, in the year of our Lord one thousand seven hundred and eighty-five, conclude a peace with the Wyandots, Delawares, Ottawas and Chippewas, and take them into their friendship and protection: And whereas at the said treaty it was stipulated that all prisoners that had been made by those nations, or either of them, should be delivered up to the United States. And whereas the said nations have now agreed to and with the aforesaid Arthur St. Clair, to renew and confirm all the engagements they had made with the United States of America, at the before mentioned treaty, except so far as are altered by these presents. And there are now in the possession of some individuals of these nations, certain prisoners, who have been taken by others not in peace with the said United States, or in violation of the treaties subsisting between the United States and them; the said nations agree to deliver up all the prisoners now in their hands (by what means soever they may have come into their possession) to the said Governor St. Clair, at Fort Harmar, or in his absence, to the officer commanding there, as soon as conveniently may be; and for the true performance of this agreement, they do now agree to deliver into his hands, two persons of the Wyandot Nation, to be retained in the hands of the United States as hostages, until the said prisoners are restored; after which they shall be sent back to their nation.

ARTICLE II.

Boundary line formerly fixed, renewed, and confirmed.

And whereas at the before mentioned treaty it was agreed between the United States and said nations, that a boundary line should be fixed between the lands of those nations and the territory of the

United States; which boundary is as follows, *viz.*—Beginning at the mouth of Cayahoga river, and running thence up the said river to the portage between that and the Tuscarawa branch of Muskingum, then down the said branch to the forks at the crossing-place above fort Lawrence, thence westerly to the portage on that branch of the Big Miami river which runs into the Ohio, at the mouth of which branch the fort stood which was taken by the French in the year of our Lord one thousand seven hundred and fifty-two, then along the said portage to the Great Miami or Omie river, and down the south-east side of the same to its mouth; thence along the southern shore of Lake Erie to the mouth of Cayahoga, where it began. And the said Wyandot, Delaware, Ottawa and Chippewa Nations, for and in consideration of the peace then granted to them by the said United States, and the presents they then received, as well as of a quantity of goods to the value of six thousand dollars, now delivered to them by the said Arthur St. Clair, the receipt whereof they do hereby acknowledge, do by these presents renew and confirm the said boundary line; to the end that the same may remain as a division line between the lands of the United States of America, and the lands of said nations, forever. And the undersigned Indians do hereby in their own names, *Lands ceded to United States.* and the names of their respective nations and tribes, their heirs and descendants, for the consideration above-mentioned, release, quit claim, relinquish and cede to the said United States, all the land east, south and west of the lines above described, so far as the said Indians formerly claimed the same; for them the said United States to have and to hold the same in true and absolute propriety forever.

ARTICLE III.

The United States of America do by these presents relinquish and *United States quit-claim to certain lands.* quit claim to the said nations respectively, all the lands lying between *Indians not at liberty to dispose of said lands, except, etc.* the limits above described, for them the said Indians to live and hunt upon, and otherwise to occupy as they shall see fit: But the said nations, or either of them, shall not be at liberty to sell or dispose of the same, or any part thereof, to any sovereign power, except the United States; nor to the subjects or citizens of any other sovereign power, nor to the subjects or citizens of the United States.

ARTICLE IV.

It is agreed between the said United States and the said nations, that *Indians at liberty to hunt on territory ceded to United States.* the individuals of said nations shall be at liberty to hunt within the territory ceded to the United States, without hindrance or molestation, so long as they demean themselves peaceably, and offer no injury or annoyance to any of the subjects or citizens of the said United States.

ARTICLE V.

It is agreed that if any Indian or Indians of the nations before men- *Individuals of one party committing murder or robbery on the other, to be delivered up for trial.* tioned, shall commit a murder or robbery on any of the citizens of the United States, the nation or tribe to which the offender belongs, on complaint being made, shall deliver up the person or persons complained of, at the nearest post of the United States; to the end that he or they may be tried, and if found guilty, punished according to the laws established in the territory of the United States north-west of the river Ohio, for the punishment of such offences, if the same shall have been committed within the said territory; or according to the laws of the State where the offence may have been committed, if the same has happened in any of the United States. In like manner, if any subject or citizen of the United States shall commit murder or robbery on any Indian or

Indians of the said nations, upon complaint being made thereof, he or they shall be arrested, tried and punished agreeable to the laws of the state or of the territory wherein the offence was committed; that nothing may interrupt the peace and harmony now established between the United States and said nations.

Article VI.

Persons to be severely punished for stealing horses; which may be reclaimed by the party to whom they belong.

And whereas the practice of stealing horses has prevailed very much, to the great disquiet of the citizens of the United States, and if persisted in, cannot fail to involve both the United States of America and the Indians in endless animosity, it is agreed that it shall be put an entire stop to on both sides; nevertheless, should some individuals, in defiance of this agreement, and of the laws provided against such offences, continue to make depredations of that nature, the person convicted thereof shall be punished with the utmost severity the laws of the respective states, or territory of the United States north-west of the Ohio, where the offence may have been committed, will admit of: And all horses so stolen, either by the Indians from the citizens or subjects of the United States, or by the citizens or subjects of the United States from any of the Indian nations, may be reclaimed, into whose possession soever they may have passed, and, upon due proof, shall be restored; any sales in market overt, notwithstanding. And the civil magistrates in the United States respectively, and in the territory of the United States north-west of the Ohio, shall give all necessary aid and protection to Indians claiming such stolen horses.

Article VII.

Trade to be opened with the Indians, and protection afforded to those licensed to reside among them.

Trade shall be opened with the said nations, and they do hereby respectively engage to afford protection to the persons and property of such as may be duly licensed to reside among them for the purposes of trade, and to their agents, factors and servants; but no person shall be permitted to reside at their towns, or at their hunting camps, as a trader, who is not furnished with a license for that purpose, under the hand and seal of the Governor of the territory of the United States north-west of the Ohio, for the time being, or under the hand and seal of one of his deputies for the management of Indian affairs; to the end

Persons intruding without license to be apprehended and given up.

that they may not be imposed upon in their traffic. And if any person or persons shall intrude themselves without such licence, they promise to apprehend him or them, and to bring them to the said Governor, or one of his deputies, for the purpose before mentioned, to be dealt with according to law: And that they may be defended against persons who might attempt to forge such licenses, they further engage to give information to the said Governor, or one of his deputies, of the names of all traders residing among them from time to time, and at least once in every year.

Article VIII.

Notice to be given of war or harm known to be meditated against either party.

Should any nation of Indians meditate a war against the United States, or either of them, and the same shall come to the knowledge of the before mentioned nations, or either of them, they do hereby engage to give immediate notice thereof to the Governor, or in his absence to the officer commanding the troops of the United States at the nearest post. And should any nation with hostile intentions against the United States, or either of them, attempt to pass through their country, they will endeavor to prevent the same, and in like manner give information of such attempt to the said Governor or commanding officer, as soon as possible, that all causes of mistrust and suspicion may be avoided between them and the United States: In like manner the United States shall give notice to the said Indian nations, of any harm that may be meditated against them, or either of them, that shall come to their knowledge; and do all in their power to hinder and prevent the same, that the friendship between them may be uninterrupted.

ARTICLE IX.

If any person or persons, citizens or subjects of the United States, or any other person not being an Indian, shall presume to settle upon the lands confirmed to the said nations, he and they shall be out of the protection of the United States; and the said nations may punish him or them in such manner as they see fit.

No citizen of United States shall settle on Indian lands.

ARTICLE X.

The United States renew the reservations heretofore made in the before mentioned treaty at Fort M'Intosh, for the establishment of trading posts, in manner and form following; that is to say: Six miles square at the mouth of the Miami or Omie river; six miles square at the portage upon that branch of the Miami which runs into the Ohio; six miles square upon the lake Sandusky where the fort formerly stood; and two miles square upon each side the Lower Rapids on Sandusky river, which posts, and the lands annexed to them, shall be for the use and under the government of the United States.

Reservations by United States for trading posts.

ARTICLE XI.

The post at Detroit, with a district of land beginning at the mouth of the river Rosine, at the west end of lake Erie, and running up the southern bank of said river six miles; thence northerly, and always six miles west of the strait, until it strikes the lake St. Clair, shall be reserved for the use of the United States.

The post at Detroit, etc., reserved.

ARTICLE XII.

In like manner the post at Michilimackinac, with its dependencies, and twelve miles square about the same, shall be reserved to the sole use of the United States.

The post at Michilimackinac, etc., reserved.

ARTICLE XIII.

The United States of America do hereby renew and confirm the peace and friendship entered into with the said nations, at the treaty before mentioned, held at Fort M'Intosh; and the said nations again acknowledge themselves, and all their tribes, to be under the protection of the said United States, and no other power whatever.

Peace and friendship renewed and confirmed.

ARTICLE XIV.

The United States of America do also receive into their friendship and protection, the nations of the Pattiwatimas and Sacs; and do hereby establish a league of peace and amity between them respectively; and all the articles of this treaty, so far as they apply to these nations, are to be considered as made and concluded in all, and every part, expressly with them and each of them.

The nations of Potawatomies and Sacs taken into protection of United States.

ARTICLE XV.

And whereas in describing the boundary before mentioned, the words, if strictly constructed, would carry it from the portage on that branch

Boundary line further explained.

of the Miami, which runs into the Ohio, over to the river Au Glaize; which was neither the intention of the Indians, nor of the Commissioners; it is hereby declared, that the line shall run from the said portage directly to the first fork of the Miami river, which is to the southward and eastward of the Miami village, thence down the main branch of the Miami river to the said village, and thence down that river to Lake Erie, and along the margin of the lake to the place of beginning.

Done at Fort Harmar, on the Muskingum, this ninth day of January, in the year of our Lord one thousand seven hundred and eighty-nine.

In witness whereof, the parties have hereunto interchangeably set their hands and seals.

Arthur St. Clair,	[L. S.]	Delawares:	
Peoutewatamie, his x mark,	[L. S.]	Captain Pipe, his x mark,	[L. S.]
Konatikina, his x mark,	[L. S.]	Wingenond, his x mark,	[L. S.]
		Pekelan, his x mark,	[L. S.]
Sacs:		Teataway, his x mark,	[L. S.]
Tepakee, his x mark,	[L. S.]	Chippewas:	
Kesheyiva, his x mark,	[L. S.]	Nanamakeak, his x mark,	[L. S.]
		Wetenasa, his x mark,	[L. S.]
Chippewas:		Soskene, his x mark,	[L. S.]
Mesass, his x mark,	[L. S.]	Pewanakum, his x mark,	[L. S.]
Paushquash, his x mark,	[L. S.]	Wyandots:	
Pawasicko, his x mark,	[L. S.]	Teyandatontec, his x mark,	[L. S.]
		Cheyawe, his x mark,	[L. S.]
Ottawas:		Doueyenteat, his x mark,	[L. S.]
Wewiskia, his x mark,	[L. S.]	Tarhe, his x mark,	[L. S.]
Neagey, his x mark,	[L. S.]	Terhataw, his x mark,	[L. S.]
		Datasay, his x mark,	[L. S.]
Pattawatimas:		Maudoronk, his x mark,	[L. S.]
Windigo, his x mark,	[L. S.]	Skahomat, his x mark,	[L. S.]
Wapaskea, his x mark,	[L. S.]		
Nequea, his x mark,	[L. S.]		

In presence of—

Jos. Harmar, lieutenant-colonel, commandant, First U. S. Regiment, and brigadier-general by brevet,
Richard Butler,
Jno. Gibson,
Will. McCurdey, captain,
E. Denny, ensign, First U. S. Regiment,
A. Hartshorn, ensign,

Robt. Thompson, ensign, First U. S. Regiment,
Frans. Muse, ensign,
J. Williams, jr.,
Wm. Wilson,
Joseph Nicholas,
James Rinkin.

Wyandots will dispossess the Shawanese, if the latter will not be at peace.

Be it remembered, That the Wyandots have laid claim to the lands that were granted to the Shawanese, at the treaty held at the Miami, and have declared, that as the Shawanese have been so restless, and caused so much trouble, both to them and to the United States, if they will not now be at peace, they will dispossess them, and take the country into their own hands; for that the country is theirs of right, and the Shawanese are only living upon it by their permission. They further lay claim to all the country west of the Miami boundary, from the village to the lake Erie, and declare that it is now under their management and direction.

SEPARATE ARTICLE.

Two Wyandot villages within the reservations not to be disturbed.

Whereas the Wyandots have represented, that within the reservation from the river Rosine along the Strait, they have two villages from which they cannot with any convenience remove; it is agreed, that they shall remain in possession of the same, and shall not be in any manner disturbed therein.

SEPARATE ARTICLE.

Should a robbery or murder be committed by an Indian or Indians of the said nations upon the citizens or subjects of the United States or any of them, or by the citizens or subjects of the United States or any of them, upon any Indian or Indians of the said nations, the parties accused of the same shall be tried, and, if found guilty, be punished according to the laws of the state, or of the territory of the United States, as the case may be, where the same was committed; and should any horses be stolen, either by the Indians of the said nations from the citizens or subjects of the United States or any of them, or by any of the said citizens and subjects from any of the said Indians, they may be reclaimed, into whose possession soever they may have come; and, upon due proof, shall be restored, any sales in open market notwithstanding. And the parties convicted shall be punished with the utmost severity the laws will admit; and the said nations engage to deliver the parties that may be accused of their nations of either of the before-mentioned crimes, at the nearest post of the United States, if the crime was committed within the territory of the United States, or to the civil authority of the States, if it shall have happened within any of the United States.

In case of robbery or murder, the offender to be delivered up, etc.

TREATY WITH THE SIX NATIONS, 1789.

Articles of a treaty made at Fort Harmar, the ninth day of January, in the year of our Lord one thousand seven hundred and eighty-nine, between Arthur St. Clair, esquire, governor of the territory of the United States of America, north-west of the river Ohio, and commissioner plenipotentiary of the said United States, for removing all causes of controversy, regulating trade, and settling boundaries, between the Indian nations in the northern department and the said United States, of the one part, and the sachems and warriors of the Six Nations, of the other part:

Jan. 9. 1789.

7 Stat., 33.

ART. 1. WHEREAS the United States, in congress assembled, did, by their commissioners, Oliver Wolcott, Richard Butler, and Arthur Lee, esquires, duly appointed for that purpose, at a treaty held with the said Six Nations, viz: with the Mohawks, Oneidas, Onondagas, Tuscaroras, Cayugas, and Senekas, at fort Stanwix, on the twenty-second day of October, one thousand seven hundred and eighty-four, give peace to the said nations, and receive them into their friendship and protection: And whereas the said nations have now agreed to and with the said Arthur St. Clair, to renew and confirm all the engagements and stipulations entered into at the beforementioned treaty at fort Stanwix: and whereas it was then and there agreed, between the United States of America and the said Six Nations, that a boundary line should be fixed between the lands of the said Six Nations and the territory of the said United States, which boundary line is as follows, viz: Beginning at the mouth of a creek, about four miles east of Niagara, called Ononwayea, or Johnston's Landing Place, upon the lake named by the Indians Oswego, and by us Ontario; from thence southerly, in a direction always four miles east of the carrying place, between lake Erie and lake Ontario, to the mouth of Tehoseroton, or Buffalo creek, upon lake Erie; thence south, to the northern boundary of the state of Pennsylvania; thence west, to the end of the said north boundary; thence south, along the west boundary of the said state to the river Ohio. The said line, from the mouth of Ononwayea to the Ohio, shall be the western boundary of the lands of the Six Nations, so that the Six Nations shall and do yield to the United States, all claim to the country west of the said boundary; and then they shall be secured in

Reference to the treaty of Fort Stanwix.

Renewal of engagements.

the possession of the lands they inhabit east, north, and south of the same, reserving only six miles square, round the fort of Oswego, for the support of the same.   The said Six Nations, except the Mohawks, none of whom have attended at this time, for and in consideration of the peace then granted to them, the presents they then received, as well as in consideration of a quantity of goods, to the value of three thousand dollars, now delivered to them by the said Arthur St. Clair, the receipt whereof they do hereby acknowledge, do hereby renew and confirm the said boundary line in the words beforementioned, to the end that it may be and remain as a division line between the lands of the said Six Nations and the territory of the United States, forever.   And the undersigned Indians, as well in their own names as in the name of their respective tribes and nations, their heirs and descendants, for the considerations beforementioned, do release, quit claim, relinquish, and cede, to the United States of America, all the lands west of the said boundary or division line, and between the said line and the strait, from the mouth of Ononwayea and Buffalo Creek, for them, the said United States of America, to have and to hold the same, in true and absolute propriety, forever.

The Mohawks excepted.

Old boundary confirmed.

Lands west of said line ceded forever to United States.

Art. 2. The United States of America confirm to the Six Nations, all the lands which they inhabit, lying east and north of the beforementioned boundary line, and relinquish and quit claim to the same and every part thereof, excepting only six miles square round the fort of Oswego, which six miles square round said fort is again reserved to the United States by these presents.

Certain lands confirmed to the Six Nations, etc.

Art. 3. The Oneida and Tuscarora nations, are also again secured and confirmed in the possession of their respective lands.

Lands of Oneidas and Tuscaroras confirmed to them anew.

Art. 4. The United States of America renew and confirm the peace and friendship entered into with the Six Nations, (except the Mohawks), at the treaty beforementioned, held at fort Stanwix, declaring the same to be perpetual.   And if the Mohawks shall, within six months, declare their assent to the same, they shall be considered as included.

Peace and friendship renewed.

Mohawks allowed six months to assent.

Done at Fort Harmar, on the Muskingum, the day and year first above written.

In witness whereof, the parties have hereunto, interchangeably, set their hands and seals.

Ar. St. Clair, [L. S.]	Owenewa, or Thrown in the Water, his x mark, [L. S.]
Cageaga, or Dogs Round the Fire, [L. S.]	Gyantwaia, or Cornplanter, his x mark, [L. S.]
Sawedowa, or The Blast, [L. S.]	
Kiondushowa, or Swimming Fish, [L. S.]	
Oncahye, or Dancing Feather, [L. S.]	Gyasota, or Big Cross, his x mark, [L. S.]
Sohaeas, or Falling Mountain, [L. S.]	Kannassee, or New Arrow, [L. S.]
Otachsaka, or Broken Tomahawk, his x mark, [L. S.]	Achiout, or Half Town, [L. S.]
	Anachout, or The Wasp, his x mark, [L. S.]
Tekahias, or Long Tree, his x mark, [L. S.]	Chishekoa, or Wood Bug, his x mark, [L. S.]
Onecnsetee, or Loaded Man, his x mark, [L. S.]	Sessewa, or Big Bale of a Kettle, [L. S.]
Kiahtulaho, or Snake, [L. S.]	Sciahowa, or Council Keeper, [L. S.]
Aqueia, or Bandy Legs, [L. S.]	Tewanias, or Broken Twig, [L. S.]
Kiandogewa, or Big Tree, his x mark, [L. S.]	Sonachshowa, or Full Moon, [L. S.]
	Cachunwasse, or Twenty Canoes, [L. S.]
	Hickonquash, or Tearing Asunder, [L. S.]

In presence of—
Jos. Harmar, lieutenant-colonel commanding First U. S. Regiment and brigadier-general by brevet,
Richard Butler,
Jno. Gibson,
Will. M'Curdy, captain,
Ed. Denny, ensign First U. S. Regiment,
A. Hartshorn, ensign,
Robt. Thompson, ensign, First U. S. Regiment,
Fran. Leile, ensign,
Joseph Nicholas.

SEPARATE ARTICLE.

Should a robbery or murder be committed by an Indian or Indians of the Six Nations, upon the citizens or subjects of the United States, or by the citizens or subjects of the United States, or any of them, upon any of the Indians of the said nations, the parties accused of the same shall be tried, and if found guilty, be punished according to the laws of the state, or of the territory of the United States, as the case may be, where the same was committed. And should any horses be stolen, either by the Indians of the said nations, from the citizens or subjects of the United States, or any of them, or by any of the said citizens or subjects from any of the said Indians, they may be reclaimed into whose possession soever they may have come; and, upon due proof, shall be restored, any sale in open market notwithstanding; and the persons convicted shall be punished with the utmost severity the laws will admit. And the said nations engage to deliver the persons that may be accused, of their nations, of either of the beforementioned crimes, at the nearest post of the United States, if the crime was committed within the territory of the United States; or to the civil authority of the state, if it shall have happened within any of the United States.

Ar. St. Clair.

Robberies and murders to be punished according to the law, etc.

Stolen horses to be restored.

Offenders to be delivered up.

TREATY WITH THE CREEKS, 1790.

A Treaty of Peace and Friendship made and concluded between the President of the United States of America, on the Part and Behalf of the said States, and the undersigned Kings, Chiefs and Warriors of the Creek Nation of Indians, on the Part and Behalf of the said Nation.

Aug. 7, 1790.

7 Stat., 35.
Proclamation, Aug. 13, 1790.

THE parties being desirous of establishing permanent peace and friendship between the United States and the said Creek Nation, and the citizens and members thereof, and to remove the causes of war by ascertaining their limits, and making other necessary, just and friendly arrangements: The President of the United States, by Henry Knox, Secretary for the Department of War, whom he hath constituted with full powers for these purposes, by and with the advice and consent of the Senate of the United States, and the Creek Nation, by the undersigned Kings, Chiefs and Warriors, representing the said nation, have agreed to the following articles.

ARTICLE I.

There shall be perpetual peace and friendship between all the citizens of the United States of America, and all the individuals, towns and tribes of the Upper, Middle and Lower Creeks and Semanolies composing the Creek nation of Indians.

Peace and friendship perpetual.

ARTICLE II.

The undersigned Kings, Chiefs and Warriors, for themselves and all parts of the Creek Nation within the limits of the United States, do acknowledge themselves, and the said parts of the Creek nation, to be under the protection of the United States of America, and of no other sovereign whosoever; and they also stipulate that the said Creek Nation will not hold any treaty with an individual State, or with individuals of any State.

Indians acknowledge protection of United States.

ARTICLE III.

The Creek Nation shall deliver as soon as practicable to the commanding officer of the troops of the United States, stationed at the Rock-Landing on the Oconee river, all citizens of the United States, white inhabitants or negroes, who are now prisoners in any part of the said nation. And if any such prisoners or negroes should not be so delivered, on or before the first day of June ensuing, the governor of Georgia may empower three persons to repair to the said nation, in order to claim and receive such prisoners and negroes.

ARTICLE IV.

The boundary between the citizens of the United States and the Creek Nation is, and shall be, from where the old line strikes the river Savannah; thence up the said river to a place on the most northern branch of the same, commonly called the Keowee, where a north east line to be drawn from the top of the Occunna mountain shall intersect; thence along the said line in a south-west direction to Tugelo river; thence to the top of the Currahee mountain; thence to the head or source of the main south branch of the Oconee river, called the Appalachee; thence down the middle of the said main south branch and river Oconee, to its confluence with the Oakmulgee, which form the river Altamaha; and thence down the middle of the said Altamaha to the old line on the said river, and thence along the said old line to the river St. Mary's.

And in order to preclude forever all disputes relatively to the head or source of the main south branch of the river Oconee, at the place where it shall be intersected by the line aforesaid, from the Currahee mountain, the same shall be ascertained by an able surveyor on the part of the United States, who shall be assisted by three old citizens of Georgia, who may be appointed by the Governor of the said state, and three old Creek chiefs, to be appointed by the said nation; and the said surveyor, citizens and chiefs shall assemble for this purpose, on the first day of October, one thousand seven hundred and ninety-one, at the Rock Landing on the said river Oconee, and thence proceed to ascertain the said head or source of the main south branch of the said river, at the place where it shall be intersected by the line aforesaid, to be drawn from the Currahee mountain. And in order that the said boundary shall be rendered distinct and well known, it shall be marked by a line of felled trees at least twenty feet wide, and the trees chopped on each side from the said Currahee mountain, to the head or source of the said main south branch of the Oconee river, and thence down the margin of the said main south branch and river Oconee for the distance of twenty miles, or as much farther as may be necessary to mark distinctly the said boundary. And in order to extinguish forever all claims of the Creek nation, or any part thereof, to any of the land lying to the northward and eastward of the boundary herein described, it is hereby agreed, in addition to the considerations heretofore made for the said land, that the United States will cause certain valuable Indian goods now in the state of Georgia, to be delivered to the said Creek nation; and the said United States will also cause the sum of one thousand and five hundred dollars to be paid annually to the said Creek nation. And the undersigned Kings, Chiefs and Warriors, do hereby for themselves and the whole Creek nation, their heirs and descendants, for the considerations above-mentioned, release, quit claim, relinquish and cede, all the land to the northward and eastward of the boundary herein described.

ARTICLE V.

The United States solemnly guarantee to the Creek Nation, all their lands within the limits of the United States to the westward and southward of the boundary described in the preceding article.

Guarantee.

ARTICLE VI.

If any citizen of the United States, or other person not being an Indian, shall attempt to settle on any of the Creeks lands, such person shall forfeit the protection of the United States, and the Creeks may punish him or not, as they please.

No citizen of United States to settle on Indian lands.

ARTICLE VII.

No citizen or inhabitant of the United States shall attempt to hunt or destroy the game on the Creek lands: Nor shall any such citizen or inhabitant go into the Creek country, without a passport first obtained from the Governor of some one of the United States, or the officer of the troops of the United States commanding at the nearest military post on the frontiers, or such other person as the President of the United States may, from time to time, authorize to grant the same.

Nor hunt on the same.

ARTICLE VIII.

If any Creek Indian or Indians, or person residing among them, or who shall take refuge in their nation, shall commit a robbery or murder, or other capital crime, on any of the citizens or inhabitants of the United States, the Creek nation, or town, or tribe to which such offender or offenders may belong, shall be bound to deliver him or them up, to be punished according to the laws of the United States.

Indians to deliver up criminals.

ARTICLE IX.

If any citizen or inhabitant of the United States, or of either of the territorial districts of the United States, shall go into any town, settlement or territory belonging to the Creek nation of Indians, and shall there commit any crime upon, or trespass against the person or property of any peaceable and friendly Indian or Indians, which if committed within the jurisdiction of any state, or within the jurisdiction of either of the said districts, against a citizen or white inhabitant thereof, would be punishable by the laws of such state or district, such offender or offenders shall be subject to the same punishment, and shall be proceeded against in the same manner, as if the offence had been committed within the jurisdiction of the state or district to which he or they may belong, against a citizen or white inhabitant thereof.

Citizens of United States committing crimes against Indians to be punished.

ARTICLE X.

In cases of violence on the persons or property of the individuals of either party, neither retaliation nor reprisal shall be committed by the other, until satisfaction shall have been demanded of the party, of which the aggressor is, and shall have been refused.

Retaliation restrained.

ARTICLE XI.

The Creeks shall give notice to the citizens of the United States of any designs, which they may know or suspect to be formed in any neighboring tribe, or by any person whatever, against the peace and interests of the United States.

Indians to give notice of designs against United States.

ARTICLE XII.

United States to make presents to them.

That the Creek nation may be led to a greater degree of civilization, and to become herdsmen and cultivators, instead of remaining in a state of hunters, the United States will from time to time furnish gratuitously the said nation with useful domestic animals and implements of husbandry. And further to assist the said nation in so desirable a pursuit, and at the same time to establish a certain mode of communication, the United States will send such, and so many persons to reside in said nation as they may judge proper, and not exceeding four in number, who shall qualify themselves to act as interpreters. These persons shall have lands assigned them by the Creeks for cultivation, for themselves and their successors in office; but they shall be precluded exercising any kind of traffic.

ARTICLE XIII.

Animosities to cease.

All animosities for past grievances shall henceforth cease; and the contracting parties will carry the foregoing treaty into full execution, with all good faith and sincerity.

ARTICLE XIV.

Ratification.

This treaty shall take effect and be obligatory on the contracting parties, as soon as the same shall have been ratified by the President of the United States, with the advice and consent of the Senate of the United States.

In witness of all and every thing herein determined, between the United States of America, and the whole Creek nation, the parties have hereunto set their hands and seals, in the city of New York, within the United States, this seventh day of August, one thousand seven hundred and ninety.

In behalf of the United States:

H. Knox, [L. s.]
Secretary of War and sole commissioner for treating with the Creek nation of Indians.

In behalf of themselves and the whole Creek nation of Indians:

Alexander McGillivray, [L. s.]
Cusetahs:
Fuskatche Mico, or Birdtail King, his x mark, [L. s.]
Neathlock, or Second Man, his x mark, [L. s.]
Halletemalthle, or Blue Giver, his x mark, [L. s.]
Little Tallisee:
Opay Mico, or the Singer, his x mark, [L. s.]
Totkeshajou, or Samoniac, his x mark, [L. s.]
Big Tallisee:
Hopothe Mico, or Tallisee King, his x mark, [L. s.]
Opototache, or Long Side, his x mark, [L. s.]
Tuckabatchy:
Soholessee, or Young Second Man, his x mark, [L. s.]
Ocheehajou, or Aleck Cornel, his x mark, [L. s.]
Natchez:
Chinabie, or the Great Natchez Warrior, his x mark, [L. s.]

Natsowachehee, or the Great Natchez Warrior's Brother, his x mark, [L. s.]
Thakoteehee, or the Mole, his x mark, [L. s.]
Oquakabee, his x mark, [L. s.]
Cowetas:
Tuskenaah, or Big Lieutenant, his x mark, [L. s.]
Homatah, or Leader, his x mark, [L. s.]
Chinnabie, or Matthews, his x mark, [L. s.]
Juleetaulematha, or Dry Pine, his x mark, [L. s.]
Of the Broken Arrow:
Chawookly Mico, his x mark, [L. s.]
Coosades:
Coosades Hopoy, or the Measurer, his x mark, [L. s.]
Muthtee, the Misser, his x mark, [L. s.]
Stimafutchkee, or Good Humor, his x mark, [L. s.]
Alabama Chief:
Stilnaleeje, or Disputer, his x mark, [L. s.]
Oaksoys:
Mumagechee, David Francis, his x mark, [L. s.]

Done in the presence of—
> Richard Morris, chief justice of the State of New York,
> Richard Varick, mayor of the city of New York,
> Marinus Willet,
> Thomas Lee Shippen, of Pennsylvania,
> John Rutledge, jun'r.
> Joseph Allen Smith,
> Henry Izard,
> Joseph Cornell, interpreter, his x mark.

TREATY WITH THE CHEROKEE, 1791.

A Treaty of Peace and Friendship made and concluded between the President of the United States of America, on the Part and Behalf of the said States, and the undersigned Chiefs and Warriors of the Cherokee Nation of Indians, on the Part and Behalf of the said Nation.

July 2, 1791.

7 Stat., 39.
Proclamation, Feb. 7, 1792.

The parties being desirous of establishing permanent peace and friendship between the United States and the said Cherokee Nation, and the citizens and members thereof, and to remove the causes of war, by ascertaining their limits and making other necessary, just and friendly arrangements: The President of the United States, by William Blount, Governor of the territory of the United States of America, south of the river Ohio, and Superintendant of Indian affairs for the southern district, who is vested with full powers for these purposes, by and with the advice and consent of the Senate of the United States: And the Cherokee Nation,. by the undersigned Chiefs and Warriors representing the said nation, have agreed to the following articles, namely:

ARTICLE I.

There shall be perpetual peace and friendship between all the citizens of the United States of America, and all the individuals composing the whole Cherokee nation of Indians.

Peace and friendship perpetual.

ARTICLE II.

The undersigned Chiefs and Warriors, for themselves and all parts of the Cherokee nation, do acknowledge themselves and the said Cherokee nation, to be under the protection of the said United States of America, and of no other sovereign whosoever; and they also stipulate that the said Cherokee nation will not hold any treaty with any foreign power, individual state, or with individuals of any state.

Indians acknowledge protection of United States.

ARTICLE III.

The Cherokee nation shall deliver to the Governor of the territory of the United States of America, south of the river Ohio, on or before the first day of April next, at this place, all persons who are now prisoners, captured by them from any part of the United States: And the United States shall on or before the same day, and at the same place, restore to the Cherokees, all the prisoners now in captivity, which the citizens of the United States have captured from them.

Prisoners to be restored.

ARTICLE IV.

The boundary between the citizens of the United States and the Cherokee nation, is and shall be as follows: Beginning at the top of the

Boundaries.

Currahee mountain, where the Creek line passes it; thence a direct line to Tugelo river; thence northeast to the Occunna mountain, and over the same along the South-Carolina Indian boundary to the North-Carolina boundary; thence north to a point from which a line is to be extended to the river Clinch, that shall pass the Holston at the ridge which divides the waters running into Little River from those running into the Tennessee; thence up the river Clinch to Campbell's line, and along the same to the top of Cumberland mountain; thence a direct line to the Cumberland river where the Kentucky road crosses it; thence down the Cumberland river to a point from which a south west line will strike the ridge which divides the waters of Cumberland from those of Duck river, forty miles above Nashville; thence down the said ridge to a point from whence a south west line will strike the mouth of Duck river.

And in order to preclude forever all disputes relative to the said boundary, the same shall be ascertained, and marked plainly by three persons appointed on the part of the United States, and three Cherokees on the part of their nation.

And in order to extinguish forever all claims of the Cherokee nation, or any part thereof, to any of the land lying to the right of the line above described, beginning as aforesaid at the Currahee mountain, it is hereby agreed, that in addition to the consideration heretofore made for the said land, the United States will cause certain valuable goods, to be immediately delivered to the undersigned Chiefs and Warriors, for the use of their nation; and the said United States will also cause the sum of one thousand dollars to be paid annually to the said Cherokee nation. And the undersigned Chiefs and Warriors, do hereby for themselves and the whole Cherokee nation, their heirs and descendants, for the considerations above-mentioned, release, quit-claim, relinquish and cede, all the land to the right of the line described, and beginning as aforesaid.

ARTICLE V.

Stipulation for a road.

It is stipulated and agreed, that the citizens and inhabitants of the United States, shall have a free and unmolested use of a road from Washington district to Mero district, and of the navigation of the Tennessee river.

ARTICLE VI.

United States to regulate trade.

It is agreed on the part of the Cherokees, that the United States shall have the sole and exclusive right of regulating their trade.

ARTICLE VII.

Guarantee.

The United States solemnly guarantee to the Cherokee nation, all their lands not hereby ceded.

ARTICLE VIII.

No citizen to settle on Indian lands.

If any citizen of the United States, or other person not being an Indian, shall settle on any of the Cherokees' lands, such person shall forfeit the protection of the United States, and the Cherokees may punish him or not, as they please.

ARTICLE IX.

Nor hunt on the same.

No citizen or inhabitant of the United States, shall attempt to hunt or destroy the game on the lands of the Cherokees; nor shall any citizen or inhabitant go into the Cherokee country, without a passport first obtained from the Governor of some one of the United States, or territorial districts, or such other person as the President of the United States may from time to time authorize to grant the same.

ARTICLE X.

If any Cherokee Indian or Indians, or person residing among them, or who shall take refuge in their nation, shall steal a horse from, or commit a robbery or murder, or other capital crime, on any citizens or inhabitants of the United States, the Cherokee nation shall be bound to deliver him or them up, to be punished according to the laws of the United States.

Indians to deliver up criminals.

ARTICLE XI.

If any citizen or inhabitant of the United States, or of either of the territorial districts of the United States, shall go into any town, settlement or territory belonging to the Cherokees, and shall there commit any crime upon, or trespass against the person or property of any peaceable and friendly Indian or Indians, which if committed within the jurisdiction of any state, or within the jurisdiction of either of the said districts, against a citizen or white inhabitant thereof, would be punishable by the laws of such state or district, such offender or offenders, shall be subject to the same punishment, and shall be proceeded against in the same manner as if the offence had been committed within the jurisdiction of the state or district to which he or they may belong, against a citizen or white inhabitant thereof.

Citizens of United States committing crimes in Indian territory to be punished.

ARTICLE XII.

In case of violence on the persons or property of the individuals of either party, neither retaliation or reprisal shall be committed by the other, until satisfaction shall have been demanded of the party of which the aggressor is, and shall have been refused.

Retaliation restrained.

ARTICLE XIII.

The Cherokees shall give notice to the citizens of the United States, of any designs which they may know, or suspect to be formed in any neighboring tribe, or by any person whatever, against the peace and interest of the United States.

Cherokees to give notice of designs against United States.

ARTICLE XIV.

That the Cherokee nation may be led to a greater degree of civilization, and to become herdsmen and cultivators, instead of remaining in a state of hunters, the United States will from time to time furnish gratuitously the said nation with useful implements of husbandry, and further to assist the said nation in so desirable a pursuit, and at the same time to establish a certain mode of communication, the United States will send such, and so many persons to reside in said nation as they may judge proper, not exceeding four in number, who shall qualify themselves to act as interpreters. These persons shall have lands assigned by the Cherokees for cultivation for themselves and their successors in office; but they shall be precluded exercising any kind of traffic.

United States to make presents.

ARTICLE XV.

All animosities for past grievances shall henceforth cease, and the contracting parties will carry the foregoing treaty into full execution with all good faith and sincerity.

Animosities to cease.

ARTICLE XVI.

Ratification.

This treaty shall take effect and be obligatory on the contracting parties, as soon as the same shall have been ratified by the President of the United States, with the advice and consent of the Senate of the United States.

In witness of all and every thing herein determined between the United States of America and the whole Cherokee nation, the parties have hereunto set their hands and seals, at the treaty ground on the bank of the Holston, near the mouth of the French Broad, within the United States, this second day of July, in the year of our Lord one thousand seven hundred and ninety-one.

William Blount, governor in and over the territory of the United States of America south of the river Ohio, and superintendent of Indian Affairs for the southern district, [L. S.]
Chuleoah, or the Boots, his x mark, [L. S.]
Squollecuttah, or Hanging Maw, his x mark, [L. S.]
Occunna, or the Badger, his x mark, [L. S.]
Enoleh, or Black Fox, his x mark, [L. S.]
Nontuaka, or the Northward, his x mark, [L. S.]
Tekakiska, his x mark, [L. S.]
Chutloh, or King Fisher, his x mark, [L. S.]
Tuckaseh, or Terrapin, his x mark, [L. S.]
Kateh, his x mark, [L. S.]
Kunnochatutloh, or the Crane, his x mark, [L. S.]
Cauquillehanah, or the Thigh, his x mark, [L. S.]
Chesquotteleneh, or Yellow Bird, his x mark, [L. S.]
Chickasawtehe, or Chickasaw Killer, his x mark, [L. S.]
Tuskegatehe, Tuskega Killer, his x mark, [L. S.]
Kulsatehe, his x mark, [L. S.]
Tinkshalene, his x mark, [L. S.]
Sawutteh, or Slave Catcher, his x mark, [L. S.]
Aukuah, his x mark, [L. S.]
Oosenaleh, his x mark, [L. S.]
Kenotetah, or Rising Fawn, his x mark, [L. S.]
Kanetetoka, or Standing Turkey, his x mark, [L. S.]

Yonewatleh, or Bear at Home, his x mark, [L. S.]
Long Will, his x mark, [L. S.]
Kunoskeskie, or John Watts, his x mark, [L. S.]
Nenetooyah, or Bloody Fellow, his x mark, [L. S.]
Chuquilatague, or Double Head, his x mark, [L. S.]
Koolaquah, or Big Acorn, his x mark, [L. S.]
Toowayelloh, or Bold Hunter, his x mark, [L. S.]
Jahleoonoyehka, or Middle Striker, his x mark, [L. S.]
Kinnesah, or Cabin, his x mark, [L. S.]
Tullotehe, or Two Killer, his x mark, [L. S.]
Kaalouske, or Stopt Still, his x mark, [L. S.]
Kulsatche, his x mark, [L. S.]
Auquotague, the Little Turkey's Son, his x mark, [L. S.]
Talohteske, or Upsetter, his x mark, [L. S.]
Cheakoneske, or Otter Lifter, his x mark, [L. S.]
Keshukaune, or She Reigns, his x mark, [L. S.]
Toonaunailoh, his x mark, [L. S.]
Teesteke, or Common Disturber, his x mark, [L. S.]
Robin McClemore, [L. S.]
Skyuka, [L. S.]
John Thompson, Interpreter.
James Cery, Interpreter.

Done in presence of—

Dan'l Smith, Secretary Territory United States south of the river Ohio.
Thomas Kennedy, of Kentucky.
Jas. Robertson, of Mero District.
Claiborne Watkins, of Virginia.
Jno. McWhitney, of Georgia.

Fauche, of Georgia.
Titus Ogden, North Carolina.
Jno. Chisolm, Washington District.
Robert King.
Thomas Gegg.

Feb. 17, 1792.

7 Stat., 42.
Proclamation, Feb. 17, 1792.

Additional Article To the Treaty made between the United States and the Cherokees on the second day of July, one thousand seven hundred and ninety-one.

IT is hereby mutually agreed between Henry Knox, Secretary of War, duly authorized thereto in behalf of the United States, on the one part, and the undersigned chiefs and warriors, in behalf of themselves and the Cherokee nation, on the other part, that the following article shall be added to and considered as part of the treaty made between the United States and the said Cherokee nation on the second day of July, one thousand seven hundred and ninety-one; to wit:

The sum to be paid annually by the United States to the Cherokee nation of Indians, in consideration of the relinquishment of land, as stated in the treaty made with them on the second day of July, one thousand seven hundred and ninety-one, shall be one thousand five hundred dollars instead of one thousand dollars, mentioned in the said treaty. *Increase of annual payment to Indians.*

In testimony whereof, the said Henry Knox, Secretary of War, and the said chiefs and warriors of the Cherokee nation, have hereunto set their hands and seals, in the city of Philadelphia, this seventeenth day of February, in the year of our Lord, one thousand seven hundred and ninety-two.

H. Knox, Secretary of War, [L. S.]
Iskagua, or Clear Sky, his x mark (formerly
    Nenetooyah, or Bloody Fellow), [L. S.]
Nontuaka, or the Northward, his x mark, [L. S.]
Chutloh, or King Fisher, his x mark, [L. S.]
Katigoslah, or the Prince, his x mark, [L. S.]
Teesteke, or Common Disturber, his x mark, [L. S.]
Suaka, or George Miller, his x mark, [L. S.]

In presence of—
Thomas Grooter.
Jno. Stagg, jr.
Leonard D. Shaw.
James Cery, sworn intrepreter to the Cherokee Nation.

TREATY WITH THE CHEROKEE, 1794.

June 26, 1794.

WHEREAS the treaty made and concluded on Holston river, on the second day of July, one thousand seven hundred and ninety-one, between the United States of America and the Cherokee nation of Indians, has not been fully carried into execution by reason of some misunderstandings which have arisen: *7 Stat., 43. Proclamation, Jan. 21, 1795. Ante, p. 29.*

ARTICLE I.

And whereas the undersigned Henry Knox, Secretary for the department of War, being authorized thereto by the President of the United States, in behalf of the said United States, and the undersigned Chiefs and Warriors, in their own names, and in behalf of the whole Cherokee nation, are desirous of re-establishing peace and friendship between the said parties in a permanent manner, Do hereby declare, that the said treaty of Holston is, to all intents and purposes, in full force and binding upon the said parties, as well in respect to the boundaries therein mentioned as in all other respects whatever. *Treaty of Holston binding.*

ARTICLE II.

It is hereby stipulated that the boundaries mentioned in the fourth article of the said treaty, shall be actually ascertained and marked in the manner prescribed by the said article, whenever the Cherokee nation shall have ninety days notice of the time and place at which the commissioners of the United States intend to commence their operation. *Boundaries to be marked.*

ARTICLE III.

Annual allowance
of goods.

The United States, to evince their justice by amply compensating the said Cherokee nation of Indians for all relinquishments of land made either by the treaty of Hopewell upon the Keowee river, concluded on the twenty-eighth of November, one thousand seven hundred and eighty-five, or the aforesaid treaty made upon Holston river, on the second of July, one thousand seven hundred and ninety-one, do hereby stipulate, in lieu of all former sums to be paid annually to furnish the Cherokee Indians with goods suitable for their use, to the amount of five thousand dollars yearly.

ARTICLE IV.

For every horse
stolen, a sum to be
deducted from the
annuity.

And the said Cherokee nation, in order to evince the sincerity of their intentions in future, to prevent the practice of stealing horses, attended with the most pernicious consequences to the lives and peace of both parties, do hereby agree, that for every horse which shall be stolen from the white inhabitants by any Cherokee Indians, and not returned within three months, that the sum of fifty dollars shall be deducted from the said annuity of five thousand dollars.

ARTICLE V.

These articles in
addition to the treaty
of Holston.

The articles now stipulated will be considered as permanent additions to the treaty of Holston, as soon as they shall have been ratified by the President of the United States and the Senate of the United States.

In witness of all and every thing herein determined between the United States of America and the whole Cherokee nation, the parties have hereunto set their hands and seals in the city of Philadelphia, within the United States, this twenty-sixth day of June, in the year of our Lord one thousand seven hundred and ninety-four.

H. Knox, Secretary of War, [L. s.]	John McCleemore, his x mark, [L. s.]
Tekakisskee, or Taken out of the Water, his x mark, [L. s.]	Walahue, or the Humming Bird, [L. s.]
Nontuaka, or the Northward, his x mark, [L. s.]	Chuleowee, his x mark, [L. s.]
	Ustanaqua, his x mark, [L. s.]
Cinasaw, or the Cabin, his x mark, [L. s.]	Kullusathee, his x mark, [L. s.]
Skyuka, his x mark, [L. s.]	Siteaha, his x mark, [L. s.]
Chuquilatague, or Double Head, his x mark, [L. s.]	Keenaguna, or the Lying Fawn, his x mark, [L. s.]
	Chatakaelesa, or the Fowl Carrier, [L. s.]

Done in presence of—

John Thompson,
Arthur Coodey, Interpreters,
Cantwell Jones, of Delaware.

William Wofford, of the State of Georgia.
W. McCaleb, of South Carolina.
Samuel Lewis, of Philadelphia.

TREATY WITH THE SIX NATIONS, 1794.

Nov. 11, 1794.
—————
7 Stat., 44.
Proclamation, Jan.
21, 1795.

A Treaty between the United States of America, and the Tribes of Indians called the Six Nations.

The President of the United States having determined to hold a conference with the Six Nations of Indians, for the purpose of removing from their minds all causes of complaint, and establishing a firm and permanent friendship with them; and Timothy Pickering being appointed sole agent for that purpose; and the agent having met and conferred with the Sachems, Chiefs and Warriors of the Six Nations, in a general council: Now, in order to accomplish the good design of this conference, the parties have agreed on the following articles; which, when ratified by the President, with the advice and consent of the Senate of the United States, shall be binding on them and the Six Nations.

ARTICLE I.

Peace and friendship are hereby firmly established, and shall be perpetual, between the United States and the Six Nations.

Peace and friendship perpetual.

ARTICLE II.

The United States acknowledge the lands reserved to the Oneida, Onondaga and Cayuga Nations, in their respective treaties with the state of New-York, and called their reservations, to be their property; and the United States will never claim the same, nor disturb them or either of the Six Nations, nor their Indian friends residing thereon and united with them, in the free use and enjoyment thereof: but the said reservations shall remain theirs, until they choose to sell the same to the people of the United States, who have the right to purchase.

Certain lands secured to Indians.

ARTICLE III.

The land of the Seneka nation is bounded as follows: Beginning on Lake Ontario, at the north-west corner of the land they sold to Oliver Phelps, the line runs westerly along the lake, as far as O-yōng-wong-yeh Creek, at Johnson's Landing-place, about four miles eastward from the fort of Niagara; then southerly up that creek to its main fork, then straight to the main fork of Stedman's creek, which empties into the river Niagara, above fort Schlosser, and then onward, from that fork, continuing the same straight course, to that river; (this line, from the mouth of O-yōng-wong-yeh Creek to the river Niagara, above fort Schlosser, being the eastern boundary of a strip of land, extending from the same line to Niagara river, which the Seneka nation ceded to the King of Great-Britain, at a treaty held about thirty years ago, with Sir William Johnson;) then the line runs along the river Niagara to Lake Erie; then along Lake Erie to the north-east corner of a triangular piece of land which the United States conveyed to the state of Pennsylvania, as by the President's patent, dated the third day of March, 1792; then due south to the northern boundary of that state; then due east to the south-west corner of the land sold by the Seneka nation to Oliver Phelps; and then north and northerly, along Phelps's line, to the place of beginning on Lake Ontario. Now, the United States acknowledge all the land within the aforementioned boundaries, to be the property of the Seneka nation; and the United States will never claim the same, nor disturb the Seneka nation, nor any of the Six Nations, or of their Indian friends residing thereon and united with them, in the free use and enjoyment thereof: but it shall remain theirs, until they choose to sell the same to the people of the United States, who have the right to purchase.

Boundary of lands belonging to the Seneca nation.

ARTICLE IV.

The United States having thus described and acknowledged what lands belong to the Oneidas, Onondagas, Cayugas and Senekas, and engaged never to claim the same, nor to disturb them, or any of the Six Nations, or their Indian friends residing thereon and united with them, in the free use and enjoyment thereof: Now, the Six Nations, and each of them, hereby engage that they will never claim any other lands within the boundaries of the United States; nor ever disturb the people of the United States in the free use and enjoyment thereof.

Six nations never to claim other lands in the United States.

ARTICLE V.

Right to make and use a road granted.

The Seneka nation, all others of the Six Nations concurring, cede to the United States the right of making a wagon road from Fort Schlosser to Lake Erie, as far south as Buffaloe Creek; and the people of the United States shall have the free and undisturbed use of this road, for the purposes of travelling and transportation. And the Six Nations, and each of them, will forever allow to the people of the United States, a free passage through their lands, and the free use of the harbors and rivers adjoining and within their respective tracts of land, for the passing and securing of vessels and boats, and liberty to land their cargoes where necessary for their safety.

ARTICLE VI.

Present and annuity.

In consideration of the peace and friendship hereby established, and of the engagements entered into by the Six Nations; and because the United States desire, with humanity and kindness, to contribute to their comfortable support; and to render the peace and friendship hereby established, strong and perpetual; the United States now deliver to the Six Nations, and the Indians of the other nations residing among and united with them, a quantity of goods of the value of ten thousand dollars. And for the same considerations, and with a view to promote the future welfare of the Six Nations, and of their Indian friends aforesaid, the United States will add the sum of three thousand dollars to the one thousand five hundred dollars, heretofore allowed them by an article ratified by the President, on the twenty-third day of April, 1792;[a] making in the whole, four thousand five hundred dollars; which shall be expended yearly forever, in purchasing clothing, domestic animals, implements of husbandry, and other utensils suited to their circumstances, and in compensating useful artificers, who shall reside with or near them, and be employed for their benefit. The immediate application of the whole annual allowance now stipulated, to be made by the superintendent appointed by the President for the affairs of the Six Nations, and their Indian friends aforesaid.

ARTICLE VII.

Retaliation restrained.

Lest the firm peace and friendship now established should be interrupted by the misconduct of individuals, the United States and Six Nations agree, that for injuries done by individuals on either side, no private revenge or retaliation shall take place; but, instead thereof, complaint shall be made by the party injured, to the other: By the Six Nations or any of them, to the President of the United States, or the Superintendent by him appointed: and by the Superintendent, or other person appointed by the President, to the principal chiefs of the Six Nations, or of the nation to which the offender belongs: and such prudent measures shall then be pursued as shall be necessary to preserve our peace and friendship unbroken; until the legislature (or great council) of the United States shall make other equitable provision for the purpose.

NOTE. It is clearly understood by the parties to this treaty, that the annuity stipulated in the sixth article, is to be applied to the benefit of such of the Six Nations and of their Indian friends united with them as aforesaid, as do or shall reside within the boundaries of the United States: For the United States do not interfere with nations, tribes or families, of Indians elsewhere resident.

---

[a] It appears that this treaty was never ratified by the Senate. See American State Papers, Indian Affairs, vol. 1, p. 232. Also, post 1027.

In witness whereof, the said Timothy Pickering, and the sachems and war chiefs of the said Six Nations, have hereto set their hands and seals.

Done at Konondaigua, in the State of New York, the eleventh day of November, in the year one thousand seven hundred and ninety-four.

Timothy Pickering, [L. S.]	Tauhoondos, his x mark, or Open
Onoyeahnee, his x mark, [L. S.]	the Way, [L. S.]
Konneatorteeooh, his x mark, or	Twaukewasha, his x mark, [L. S.]
Handsome Lake, [L. S.]	Sequidongquee, his x mark, alias
Tokenhyouhau, his x mark, alias	Little Beard, [L. S.]
Captain Key, [L. S.]	Kodjeote, his x mark, or Half
Oneshauee, his x mark, [L. S.]	Town, [L. S.]
Hendrick Aupaumut, [L. S.]	Kenjauaugus, his x mark, or
David Neesoonhuk, his x mark, [L. S.]	Stinking Fish, [L. S.]
Kanatsoyh, alias Nicholas Kusik, [L. S.]	Soonohquaukau, his x mark, [L. S.]
Sohhonteoquent, his x mark, [L. S.]	Twenniyana, his x mark, [L. S.]
Ooduhtsait, his x mark, [L. S.]	Jishkaaga, his x mark, or Green
Konoohqung, his x mark, [L. S.]	Grasshopper, alias Little Billy, [L. S.]
Tossonggaulolus, his x mark, [L. S.]	Tuggehshotta, his x mark, [L. S.]
John Skenendoa, his x mark, [L. S.]	Tehongyagauna, his x mark, [L. S.]
Oneatorleeooh, his x mark, [L. S.]	Tehongyoowush, his x mark, [L. S.]
Kussauwatau, his x mark, [L. S.]	Konneyoowesot, his x mark, [L. S.]
Eyootenyootauook, his x mark, [L. S.]	Tioohquottakauna, his x mark, or
Kohnyeaugong, his x mark, alias	Woods on Fire, [L. S.]
Jake Stroud, [L. S.]	Taoundaudeesh, his x mark, [L. S.]
Shaguiesa, his x mark, [L. S.]	Honayawus, his x mark, alias
Teeroos, his x mark, alias Captain	Farmer's Brother, [L. S.]
Prantup, [L. S.]	Soggooyawauthau, his x mark,
Sooshaoowau, his x mark, [L. S.]	alias Red Jacket, [L. S.]
Henry Young Brant, his x mark, [L. S.]	Konyootiayoo, his x mark, [L. S.]
Sonhyoowauna, his x mark, or Big	Sauhtakaongyees, his x mark, or
Sky, [L. S.]	Two Skies of a length, [L. S.]
Onaahhah, his x mark, [L. S.]	Ounnashattakau, his x mark, [L. S.]
Hotoshahenh, his x mark, [L. S.]	Kaungyanehquee, his x mark, [L. S.]
Kaukondanaiya, his x mark, [L. S.]	Sooayoowau, his x mark, [L. S.]
Nondiyauka, his x mark, [L. S.]	Kaujeagaonh, his x mark, or Heap
Kossishtowau, his x mark, [L. S.]	of Dogs, [L. S.]
Oojaugenta, his x mark, or Fish	Soonoohshoowau, his x mark, [L. S.]
Carrier, [L. S.]	Thaoowaunias, his x mark, [L. S.]
Toheonggo, his x mark, [L. S.]	Soonongjoowau, his x mark, [L. S.]
Ootaguasso, his x mark, [L. S.]	Kiantwhauka, his x mark, alias
Joonondauwaonch, his x mark, [L. S.]	Cornplanter, [L. S.]
Kiyauhaonh, his x mark, [L. S.]	Kaunehshonggoo, his x mark, [L. S.]
Ootaujeaugenh, his x mark, or	
Broken Axe, [L. S.]	

Witnesses:

Israel Chapin.	Israel Chapin, jr.
William Shepard, jr.	Horatio Jones,
James Smedley.	Joseph Smith,
John Wickham.	Jasper Parish,
Augustus Porter.	Interpreters.
James K. Garnsey.	Henry Abeele.
William Ewing.	

TREATY WITH THE ONEIDA, ETC., 1794.

A treaty between the United States and the Oneida, Tuscorora and Stockbridge Indians, dwelling in the Country of the Oneidas.

Dec. 2, 1794.

7 Stat., 47.
Proclamation, Jan. 21, 1795.

WHEREAS, in the late war between Great-Britain and the United States of America, a body of the Oneida and Tuscorora and the Stockbridge Indians, adhered faithfully to the United States, and assisted them with their warriors; and in consequence of this adherence and assistance, the Oneidas and Tuscororas, at an unfortunate period of the war, were driven from their homes, and their houses were burnt and their property destroyed: And as the United States in the time of their distress, acknowledged their obligations to these faithful friends, and promised to reward them: and the United States being now in a condition to fulfil the promises then made: the following articles are stipulated by the respective parties for that purpose; to be in force when ratified by the President and Senate.

ARTICLE I.

$5,000 to be distributed for past losses and services.

The United States will pay the sum of five thousand dollars, to be distributed among individuals of the Oneida and Tuscorora nations, as a compensation for their individual losses and services during the late war between Great-Britain and the United States. The only man of the Kaughnawaugas now remaining in the Oneida country, as well as some few very meritorious persons of the Stockbridge Indians, will be considered in the distribution.

ARTICLE II.

Mills to be erected by the United States.

For the general accommodation of these Indian nations, residing in the country of the Oneidas, the United States will cause to be erected a complete grist-mill and saw-mill, in a situation to serve the present principal settlements of these nations. Or if such one convenient situation cannot be found, then the United States will cause to be erected two such grist-mills and saw-mills, in places where it is now known the proposed accommodation may be effected. Of this the United States will judge.

ARTICLE III.

Millers to be provided.

The United States will provide, during three years after the mills shall be completed, for the expense of employing one or two suitable persons to manage the mills, to keep them in repair, to instruct some young men of the three nations in the arts of the miller and sawyer, and to provide teams and utensils for carrying on the work of the mills.

ARTICLE IV.

$1,000 given to build a church.

The United States will pay one thousand dollars, to be applied in building a convenient church at Oneida, in the place of the one which was there burnt by the enemy, in the late war.

ARTICLE V.

Indians relinquish further claims.

In consideration of the above stipulations to be performed on the part of the United States, the Oneida, Tuscorora and Stockbridge Indians afore-mentioned, now acknowledge themselves satisfied, and relinquish all other claims of compensation and rewards for their losses and services in the late war. Excepting only the unsatisfied claims of such men of the said nations as bore commissions under the United States, for any arrears which may be due to them as officers.

In witness whereof, the chiefs of those nations, residing in the country of the Oneidas, and Timothy Pickering, agent for the United States, have hereto set their hands and seals, at Oneida, the second day of December, in the year one thousand seven hundred and ninety-four.

Timothy Pickering, [L. S.]

Wolf Tribe:		Bear Tribe:	
Odotsaihte, his x mark,	[L. S.]	Lodowik Kohsauwetau, his x mark,	[L. S.]
Konnoquenyau, his x mark,	[L. S.]	Cornelius Kauhiktoton, his x mark,	[L. S.]
Head sachems of the Oneidas.			
John Skenendo, eldest war chief, his x mark,	[L. S.]	Thos. Osauhataugaunlot, his x mark,	[L. S.]
		War chiefs.	

Turtle Tribe:
Shonohleyo, war chief, his x mark, [L. S.]
Peter Konnauterlook, sachem, his x mark.   [L. S.]
Daniel Teouneslees, son of Skenendo, war chief, his x mark,   [L. S.]

Tuscaroras:
Thaulondauwaugon, sachem, his x mark,   [L. S.]
Kanatjogh, or Nicholas Cusick, war chief, his x mark,   [L. S.]

Witnesses to the signing and sealing of the agent of the United States, and of the chiefs of the Oneida and Tuscarora nations:

    S. Kirkland,
    James Dean, Interpreter.

Witnesses to the signing and sealing of the four chiefs of the Stockbridge Indians, whose names are below:

    Saml. Kirkland,
    John Sergeant.
Stockbridge Indians:

         Hendrick Aupaumut,   [L. S.]
         Joseph Quonney,   [L. S.]
         John Konkapot,   [L. S.]
         Jacob Konkapot,   [L. S.]

TREATY WITH THE WYANDOT, ETC., 1795.

A treaty of peace between the United States of America and the Tribes of Indians, called the Wyandots, Delawares, Shawanoes, Ottawas, Chipewas, Putawatimes, Miamis, Eel-river, Weea's, Kickapoos, Piankashaws, and Kaskaskias.

Aug. 3, 1795.

7 Stat., 49.
Proclamation, Dec. 2, 1795.

To put an end to a destructive war, to settle all controversies, and to restore harmony and a friendly intercourse between the said United States, and Indian tribes; Anthony Wayne, major-general, commanding the army of the United States, and sole commissioner for the good purposes above-mentioned, and the said tribes of Indians, by their Sachems, chiefs, and warriors, met together at Greeneville, the head quarters of the said army, have agreed on the following articles, which, when ratified by the President, with the advice and consent of the Senate of the United States, shall be binding on them and the said Indian tribes.

ARTICLE I.

Henceforth all hostilities shall cease; peace is hereby established, and shall be perpetual; and a friendly intercourse shall take place, between the said United States and Indian tribes.   *Peace established.*

ARTICLE II.

All prisoners shall on both sides be restored. The Indians, prisoners to the United States, shall be immediately set at liberty. The people of the United States, still remaining prisoners among the Indians, shall be delivered up in ninety days from the date hereof, to the general or commanding officer at Greeneville, Fort Wayne or Fort Defiance; and ten chiefs of the said tribes shall remain at Greeneville as hostages, until the delivery of the prisoners shall be effected.   *Prisoners on both sides to be restored.*

ARTICLE III.

The general boundary line between the lands of the United States, and the lands of the said Indian tribes, shall begin at the mouth of Cayahoga river, and run thence up the same to the portage between   *Boundary line established.*

that and the Tuscarawas branch of the Muskingum; thence down that branch to the crossing place above Fort Lawrence; thence westerly to a fork of that branch of the great Miami river running into the Ohio, at or near which fork stood Loromie's store, and where commences the portage between the Miami of the Ohio, and St. Mary's river, which is a branch of the Miami, which runs into Lake Erie; thence a westerly course to Fort Recovery, which stands on a branch of the Wabash; then south-westerly in a direct line to the Ohio, so as to intersect that river opposite the mouth of Kentucke or Cuttawa river. And in consideration of the peace now established; of the goods formerly received from the United States; of those now to be delivered, and of the yearly delivery of goods now stipulated to be made hereafter, and to indemnify the United States for the injuries and expenses they have sustained during the war; the said Indians tribes do hereby cede and relinquish forever, all their claims to the lands lying eastwardly and southwardly of the general boundary line now described; and these lands, or any part of them, shall never hereafter be made a cause or pretence, on the part of the said tribes or any of them, of war or injury to the United States, or any of the people thereof.

Cession of particular tracts of land by the Indians.

And for the same considerations, and as an evidence of the returning friendship of the said Indian tribes, of their confidence in the United States, and desire to provide for their accommodation, and for that convenient intercourse which will be beneficial to both parties, the said Indian tribes do also cede to the United States the following pieces of land; to-wit. (1.) One piece of land six miles square at or near Loromie's store before mentioned. (2.) One piece two miles square at the head of the navigable water or landing on the St. Mary's river, near Girty's town. (3.) One piece six miles square at the head of the navigable water of the Au-Glaize river. (4.) One piece six miles square at the confluence of the Au-Glaize and Miami rivers, where Fort Defiance now stands. (5.) One piece six miles square at or near the confluence of the rivers St. Mary's and St. Joseph's, where Fort Wayne now stands, or near it. (6.) One piece two miles square on the Wabash river at the end of the portage from the Miami of the lake, and about eight miles westward from Fort Wayne. (7.) One piece six miles square at the Ouatanon or old Weea towns on the Wabash river. (8.) One piece twelve miles square at the British fort on the Miami of the lake at the foot of the rapids. (9.) One piece six miles square at the mouth of the said river where it empties into the Lake. (10.) One piece six miles square upon Sandusky lake, where a fort formerly stood. (11.) One piece two miles square at the lower rapids of Sandusky river. (12.) The post of Detroit and all the land to the north, the west and the south of it, of which the Indian title has been extinguished by gifts or grants to the French or English governments; and so much more land to be annexed to the district of Detroit as shall be comprehended between the river Rosine on the south, lake St. Clair on the north, and a line, the general course whereof shall be six miles distant from the west end of lake Erie, and Detroit river. (13.) The post of Michillimackinac, and all the land on the island, on which that post stands, and the main land adjacent, of which the Indian title has been extinguished by gifts or grants to the French or English governments; and a piece of land on the main to the north of the island, to measure six miles on lake Huron, or the strait between lakes Huron and Michigan, and to extend three miles back from the water of the lake or strait, and also the island De Bois Blanc, being an extra and voluntary gift of the Chipewa nation. (14.) One piece of land six miles square at the mouth of Chikago river, emptying into the south-west end of Lake Michigan, where a fort formerly stood. (15.) One piece twelve miles square at or near the mouth of the Illinois river, emptying into the Mississippi. (16.) One

piece six miles square at the old Piorias fort and village, near the south
end of the Illinois lake on said Illinois river: And whenever the United
States shall think proper to survey and mark the boundaries of the
lands hereby ceded to them, they shall give timely notice thereof to
the said tribes of Indians, that they may appoint some of their wise
chiefs to attend and see that the lines are run according to the terms
of this treaty.

And the said Indian tribes will allow to the people of the United
States a free passage by land and by water, as one and the other shall
be found convenient, through their country, along the chain of posts
herein before mentioned; that is to say, from the commencement of
the portage aforesaid at or near Loromie's store, thence along said
portage to the St. Mary's, and down the same to Fort Wayne, and
then down the Miami to lake Erie: again from the commencement of
the portage at or near Loromie's store along the portage from thence
to the river Au-Glaize, and down the same to its junction with the
Miami at Fort Defiance: again from the commencement of the portage
aforesaid, to Sandusky river, and down the same to Sandusky bay and
lake Erie, and from Sandusky to the post which shall be taken at or
near the foot of the rapids of the Miami of the lake: and from thence
to Detroit. Again from the mouth of Chikago, to the commencement
of the portage, between that river and the Illinois, and down the Illinois river to the Mississippi, also from Fort Wayne along the portage
aforesaid which leads to the Wabash, and then down the Wabash to
the Ohio. And the said Indian tribes will also allow to the people of
the United States the free use of the harbors and mouths of rivers
along the lakes adjoining the Indian lands, for sheltering vessels and
boats, and liberty to land their cargoes where necessary for their
safety.

Cession of passages in certain places by the Indians.

ARTICLE IV.

In consideration of the peace now established and of the cessions
and relinquishments of lands made in the preceding article by the said
tribes of Indians, and to manifest the liberality of the United States,
as the great means of rendering this peace strong and perpetual; the
United States relinquish their claims to all other Indian lands northward of the river Ohio, eastward of the Mississippi, and westward and
southward of the Great Lakes and the waters uniting them, according
to the boundary line agreed on by the United States and the king of
Great-Britain, in the treaty of peace made between them in the year
1783. But from this relinquishment by the United States, the following tracts of land, are explicitly excepted. 1st. The tract of one hundred and fifty thousand acres near the rapids of the river Ohio, which
has been assigned to General Clark, for the use of himself and his
warriors. 2d. The post of St. Vincennes on the river Wabash, and
the lands adjacent, of which the Indian title has been extinguished.
3d. The lands at all other places in possession of the French people
and other white settlers among them, of which the Indian title has
been extinguished as mentioned in the 3d article; and 4th. The post
of fort Massac towards the mouth of the Ohio. To which several parcels of land so excepted, the said tribes relinquish all the title and
claim which they or any of them may have.

Relinquishment of certain lands by United States.

Exceptions.

And for the same considerations and with the same views as above
mentioned, the United States now deliver to the said Indian tribes a
quantity of goods to the value of twenty thousand dollars, the receipt
whereof they do hereby acknowledge; and henceforward every year
forever the United States will deliver at some convenient place northward of the river Ohio, like useful goods, suited to the circumstances
of the Indians, of the value of nine thousand five hundred dollars;
reckoning that value at the first cost of the goods in the city or place

Annual allowance to be made to the In-dians.

in the United States, where they shall be procured. The tribes to which those goods are to be annually delivered, and the proportions in which they are to be delivered, are the following.

1st. To the Wyandots, the amount of one thousand dollars. 2d. To the Delawares, the amount of one thousand dollars. 3d. To the Shawanese, the amount of one thousand dollars. 4th. To the Miamis, the amount of one thousand dollars. 5th. To the Ottawas, the amount of one thousand dollars. 6th. To the Chippewas, the amount of one thousand dollars. 7th. To the Putawatimes, the amount of one thousand dollars. 8th. And to the Kickapoo, Weea, Eel-river, Piankashaw and Kaskaskias tribes, the amount of five hundred dollars each.

Provided, That if either of the said tribes shall hereafter at an annual delivery of their share of the goods aforesaid, desire that a part of their annuity should be furnished in domestic animals, implements of husbandry, and other utensils convenient for them, and in compensation to useful artificers who may reside with or near them, and be employed for their benefit, the same shall at the subsequent annual deliveries be furnished accordingly.

Proviso.

ARTICLE V.

Indians have right to hunt on lands relinquished by United States, etc.

To prevent any misunderstanding about the Indian lands relinquished by the United States in the fourth article, it is now explicitly declared, that the meaning of that relinquishment is this: The Indian tribes who have a right to those lands, are quietly to enjoy them, hunting, planting, and dwelling thereon so long as they please, without any molestation from the United States; but when those tribes, or any of them, shall be disposed to sell their lands, or any part of them, they are to be sold only to the United States; and until such sale, the United States will protect all the said Indian tribes in the quiet enjoyment of their lands against all citizens of the United States, and against all other white persons who intrude upon the same. And the said Indian tribes again acknowledge themselves to be under the protection of the said United States and no other power whatever.

ARTICLE VI.

Indians may expel settlers from their lands.

If any citizen of the United States, or any other white person or persons, shall presume to settle upon the lands now relinquished by the United States, such citizen or other person shall be out of the protection of the United States; and the Indian tribe, on whose land the settlement shall be made, may drive off the settler, or punish him in such manner as they shall think fit; and because such settlements made without the consent of the United States, will be injurious to them as well as to the Indians, the United States shall be at liberty to break them up, and remove and punish the settlers as they shall think proper, and so effect that protection of the Indian lands herein before stipulated.

ARTICLE VII.

Indians may hunt on lands ceded to United States.

The said tribes of Indians, parties to this treaty, shall be at liberty to hunt within the territory and lands which they have now ceded to the United States, without hindrance or molestation, so long as they demean themselves peaceably, and offer no injury to the people of the United States.

ARTICLE VIII.

Trade to be opened with the Indians.

Trade shall be opened with the said Indian tribes; and they do hereby respectively engage to afford protection to such persons, with their property, as shall be duly licensed to reside among them for the purpose of trade, and to their agents and servants; but no person shall be permitted to reside at any of their towns or hunting camps as a trader, who is not furnished with a license for that purpose, under the hand and seal of the superintendent of the department north-west of the Ohio, or such other person as the President of the United States shall authorize to grant such licenses; to the end, that the said Indians may not be imposed on in their trade. And if any licensed trader shall abuse his privilege by unfair dealing, upon complaint and proof thereof, his license shall be taken from him, and he shall be further punished according to the laws of the United States. And if any person shall intrude himself as a trader, without such license, the said Indians shall take and bring him before the superintendent or his deputy, to be dealt with according to law. And to prevent impositions by forged licenses, the said Indians shall at least once a year give information to the superintendant or his deputies, of the names of the traders residing among them.

Article IX.

Lest the firm peace and friendship now established should be interrupted by the misconduct of individuals, the United States, and the said Indian tribes agree, that for injuries done by individuals on either side, no private revenge or retaliation shall take place; but instead thereof, complaint shall be made by the party injured, to the other: By the said Indian tribes, or any of them, to the President of the United States, or the superintendent by him appointed; and by the superintendent or other person appointed by the President, to the principal chiefs of the said Indian tribes, or of the tribe to which the offender belongs; and such prudent measures shall then be pursued as shall be necessary to preserve the said peace and friendship unbroken, until the Legislature (or Great Council) of the United States, shall make other equitable provision in the case, to the satisfaction of both parties. Should any Indian tribes meditate a war against the United States, or either of them, and the same shall come to the knowledge of the before-mentioned tribes, or either of them, they do hereby engage to give immediate notice thereof to the general or officer commanding the troops of the United States, at the nearest post. And should any tribe, with hostile intentions against the United States, or either of them, attempt to pass through their country, they will endeavor to prevent the same, and in like manner give information of such attempt, to the general or officer commanding, as soon as possible, that all causes of mistrust and suspicion may be avoided between them and the United States. In like manner the United States shall give notice to the said Indian tribes of any harm that may be meditated against them, or either of them, that shall come to their knowledge; and do all in their power to hinder and prevent the same, that the friendship between them may be uninterrupted.

Retaliation restrained.

Indians to give notice of designs against United States.

Article X.

All other treaties heretofore made between the United States and the said Indian tribes, or any of them, since the treaty of 1783, between the United States and Great Britain, that come within the purview of this treaty, shall henceforth cease and become void.

Former treaties void.

In testimony whereof, the said Anthony Wayne, and the sachems and war chiefs of the beforementioned nations and tribes of Indians, have hereunto set their hands and affixed their seals.

Done at Greenville, in the territory of the United States northwest of the river Ohio, on the third day of August, one thousand seven hundred and ninety-five.

Anthony Wayne, [L. S.]
Wyandots:
Tarhe, or Crane, his x mark, [L. S.]
J. Williams, jun. his x mark, [L. S.]
Teyyaghtaw, his x mark, [L. S.]
Haroenyou, or half king's son, his x mark, [L. S.]
Tehaawtorens, his x mark, [L. S.]
Awmeyeeray, his x mark, [L. S.]
Stayetah, his x mark, [L. S.]
Shateyyaronyah, or Leather Lips, his x mark, [L. S.]
Daughshuttayah, his x mark, [L. S.]
Shaawrunthe, his x mark, [L. S.]
Delawares:
Tetabokshke, or Grand Glaize King, his x mark, [L. S.]
Lemantanquis, or Black King, his x mark, [L. S.]
Wabatthoe, his x mark, [L. S.]
Maghpiway, or Red Feather, his x mark, [L. S.]
Kikthawenund, or Anderson, his x mark, [L. S.]
Bukongehelas, his x mark, [L. S.]
Peekeelund, his x mark, [L. S.]
Wellebawkeelund, his x mark, [L. S.]
Peekeetelemund, or Thomas Adams, his x mark, [L. S.]
Kishkopekund, or Captain Buffalo, his x mark, [L. S.]
Amenahehan, or Captain Crow, his x mark, [L. S.]
Queshawksey, or George Washington, his x mark, [L. S.]
Weywinquis, or Billy Siscomb, his x mark, [L. S.]
Moses, his x mark, [L. S.]
Shawanees:
Misquacoonacaw, or Red Pole, his x mark, [L. S.]
Cutthewekasaw, or Black Hoof, his x mark, [L. S.]
Kaysewaesekah, his x mark, [L. S.]
Weythapamattha, his x mark, [L. S.]
Nianymseka, his x mark, [L. S.]
Waytheah, or Long Shanks, his x mark, [L. S.]
Weyapiersenwaw, or Blue Jacket, his x mark, [L. S.]
Nequetaughaw, his x mark, [L. S.]
Hahgooseekaw, or Captain Reed, his x mark, [L. S.]
Ottawas:
Augooshaway, his x mark, [L. S.]
Keenoshameek, his x mark, [L. S.]
La Malice, his x mark, [L. S.]
Machiwetah, his x mark, [L. S.]
Thowonawa, his x mark, [L. S.]
Secaw, his x mark, [L. S.]
Chippewas:
Mashipinashiwish, or Bad Bird, his x mark, [L. S.]
Nahshogashe, (from Lake Superior,) his x mark, [L. S.]
Kathawasung, his x mark, [L. S.]
Masass, his x mark, [L. S.]
Nemekass, or Little Thunder, his x mark, [L. S.]
Peshawkay, or Young Ox, his x mark, [L. S.]
Nanguey, his x mark, [L. S.]
Meenedohgeesogh, his x mark, [L. S.]
Peewanshemenogh, his x mark, [L. S.]

Weymegwas, his x mark, [L. S.]
Gobmaatick, his x mark, [L. S.]
Ottawa:
Chegonickska, (an Ottawa from Sandusky,) his x mark, [L. S.]
Pattawatimas of the river St. Joseph:
Thupenebu, his x mark, [L. S.]
Nawac, (for himself and brother Etsimethe,) his x mark, [L. S.]
Nenanseka, his x mark, [L. S.]
Keesass, or Run, his x mark, [L. S.]
Kabamasaw, (for himself and brother Chisaugan,) his x mark, [L. S.]
Sugganunk, his x mark, [L. S.]
Wapmeme, or White Pigeon, his x mark, [L. S.]
Wacheness, (for himself and brother Pedagoshok,) his x mark, [L. S.]
Wabshicawnaw, his x mark, [L. S.]
La Chasse, his x mark, [L. S.]
Meshegethenogh, (for himself and brother Wawasek,) his x mark, [L. S.]
Hingoswash, his x mark, [L. S.]
Anewasaw, his x mark, [L. S.]
Nawbudgh, his x mark, [L. S.]
Missenogomaw, his x mark, [L. S.]
Waweegshe, his x mark, [L. S.]
Thawme, or Le Blanc, his x mark, [L. S.]
Geeque, (for himself and brother Shewinse,) his x mark, [L. S.]
Pattawatimas of Huron:
Okia, his x mark, [L. S.]
Chamung, his x mark, [L. S.]
Segagewan, his x mark, [L. S.]
Nanawme, (for himself and brother A. Gin,) his x mark, [L. S.]
Marchand, his x mark, [L. S.]
Wenameac, his x mark, [L. S.]
Miamis:
Nagohquangogh, or Le Gris, his x mark, [L. S.]
Meshekunnoghquoh, or Little Turtle, his x mark, [L. S.]
Miamis and Eel Rivers:
Peejeewa, or Richard Ville, his x mark, [L. S.]
Cochkepoghtogh, his x mark, [L. S.]
Eel River Tribe:
Shamekunnesa, or Soldier, his x mark, [L. S.]
Miamis:
Wapamangwa, or the White Loon, his x mark, [L. S.]
Weas, for themselves and the Piankeshaws:
Amacunsa, or Little Beaver, his x mark, [L. S.]
Acoolatha, or Little Fox, his x mark, [L. S.]
Francis, his x mark, [L. S.]
Kickapoos and Kaskaskias:
Keeawhah, his x mark, [L. S.]
Nemighka, or Josey Renard, his x mark, [L. S.]
Paikeekanogh, his x mark, [L. S.]
Delawares of Sandusky:
Hawkinpumiska, his x mark, [L. S.]
Peyamawksey, his x mark, [L. S.]
Reyntueco, (of the Six Nations, living at Sandusky,) his x mark, [L. S.]

In presence of (the word "goods" in the sixth line of the third article; the word "before" in the twenty-sixth line of the third article: the words "five hundred" in the tenth line of the fourth article, and the word "Piankeshaw" in the fourteenth line of the fourth article, being first interlined)—

H. De Butts, first aid de camp and secretary to Major General Wayne.
Wm. H. Harrison, aid de camp to Major General Wayne.
T. Lewis, aid de camp to Major General Wayne.
James O'Hara, quartermaster general.
John Mills, major of infantry and adjutant general.
Caleb Swan, P. M. T. U. S.
Geo. Demter, lieutenant artillery.
Vigo.
P. Frs. La Fontaine.
Ant. Lasselle.
H. Lasselle.
Jn. Beau Bien.

David Jones, chaplain U. S. S.
Lewis Beaufait.
R. Lachambre.
Jas. Pepen.
Baties Coutien.
P. Navarre.
    Sworn interpreters:
Wm. Wells.
Jacques Lasselle.
M. Morins.
Bt. Sans Crainte.
Christopher Miller.
Robert Wilson.
Abraham Williams, his x mark.
Isaac Zane, his x mark.

TREATY WITH THE SEVEN NATIONS OF CANADA, 1796.

At a treaty held at the city of New York, with the Nations or Tribes of Indians, denominating themselves the Seven Nations of Canada; Abraham Ogden, Commissioner, appointed under the authority of the United States, to hold the Treaty; Ohnaweio, alias Goodstream, Teharagwanegen, alias Thomas Williams, two Chiefs of the Caghnawagas; Atiatoharongwan, alias Colonel Lewis Cook, a Chief of the St. Regis Indians, and William Gray, Deputies, authorized to represent these Seven Nations or Tribes of Indians at the Treaty, and Mr. Gray, serving also as Interpreter; Egbert Benson, Richard Varick and James Watson, Agents for the State of New York; William Constable and Daniel M'Cormick, purchasers under Alexander Macomb:

May 31, 1796.

7 Stat., 55.
Proclamation, Jan. 31, 1797.

THE agents for the state, having, in the presence, and with the approbation of the commissioner, proposed to the deputies for the Indians, the compensation hereinafter mentioned, for the extinguishment of their claim to all lands within the state, and the said deputies being willing to accept the same, it is thereupon granted, agreed and concluded between the said deputies and the said agents, as follows: The said deputies do, for and in the name of the said Seven Nations or tribes of Indians, cede, release and quit claim to the people of the state of New-York, forever, all the claim, right, or title of them, the said Seven Nations or tribes of Indians, to lands within the said state: *Provided nevertheless*, That the tract equal to six miles square, reserved in the sale made by the commissioners of the land-office of the said state, to Alexander Macomb, to be applied to the use of the Indians of the village of St. Regis, shall still remain so reserved. The said agents do, for, and in the name of the people of the state of New-York, grant to the said Seven Nations or tribes of Indians, that the people of the state of New-York shall pay to them, at the mouth of the river Chazy, on Lake Champlain, on the third Monday in August next, the sum of one thousand two hundred and thirty-three pounds, six shillings and eight-pence, and the further sum of two hundred and thirteen pounds six shillings and eight-pence, lawful money of the said state, and on the third Monday in August, yearly, forever thereafter, the like sum of two hundred and thirteen pounds six shillings and eight-pence: *Provided nevertheless*, That the people of the state of New-York shall not

Cession of lands to State of New York.

Consideration paid therefor.

be held to pay the said sums, unless in respect to the two sums to be paid on the third Monday in August next, at least twenty, and in respect to the said yearly sum to be paid thereafter, at least five of the principal men of the said Seven Nations or tribes of Indians, shall attend as deputies to receive and to give receipts for the same: The said deputies having suggested, that the Indians of the village of St. Regis have built a mill on Salmon river, and another on Grass river, and that the meadows on Grass river are necessary to them for hay; in order, therefore, to secure to the Indians of the said village, the use of the said mills and meadows, in case they should hereafter appear not to be included within the above tract so to remain reserved; it is, therefore, also agreed and concluded between the said deputies, the said agents, and the said William Constable and Daniel M'Cormick, for themselves and their associates, purchasers under the said Alexander Macomb, of the adjacent lands, that there shall be reserved, to be applied to the use of the Indians of the said village of St. Regis, in like manner as the said tract is to remain reserved, a tract of one mile square, at each of the said mills, and the meadows on both sides of the said Grass river from the said mill thereon, to its confluence with the river St. Lawrence.

Indian reserve.

In testimony whereof, the said commissioner, the said deputies, the said agents, and the said William Constable and Daniel McCormick, have hereunto, and to two other acts of the same tenor and date, one to remain with the United States, another to remain with the State of New York, and another to remain with the said Seven Nations or tribes of Indians, set their hands and seals, in the city of New York, the thirty-first day of May, in the twentieth year of the independence of the United States, one thousand seven hundred and ninety-six.

Abraham Ogden,	[L. s.]
Egbert Benson,	[L. s.]
Richard Varick,	[L. s.]
James Watson,	[L. s.]
William Constable,	[L. s.]
Daniel McCormick,	[L. s.]
Ohaweio, alias Goodstream, his x mark,	[L. s.]
Otiatokarongwan, alias Col. Lewis Cook, his x mark,	[L. s.]
William Gray,	[L. s.]
Teharagwanegen, alias Thos. Williams, his x mark,	[L. s.]

Signed, sealed, and delivered, in the presence of

Samuel Jones, recorder of the city of New York,
John Tayler, recorder of the city of Albany,
Joseph Ogden Hoffman, attorney general of the State of New York.

TREATY WITH THE CREEKS, 1796.

June 29, 1796.

7 Stat., 56.
Proclamation, Mar. 18, 1797.

A treaty of peace and friendship made and concluded between the President of the United States of America, on the one Part, and Behalf of the said States, and the undersigned Kings, Chiefs and Warriors of the Creek Nation of Indians, on the Part of the said Nation.[a]

Subject to alterations of the third and fourth articles, as stated in the note.

The parties being desirous of establishing permanent peace and friendship between the United States and the said Creek nation, and the citizens and members thereof; and to remove the causes of war, by

---

[a] This treaty was ratified on condition that the third and fourth articles should be modified as follows:

The Senate of the United States, two-thirds of the Senators present concurring, did, by their resolution of the second day of March instant, "consent to, and advise

ascertaining their limits, and making other necessary, just and friendly arrangements; the President of the United States, by Benjamin Hawkins, George Clymer, and Andrew Pickens, Commissioners whom he hath constituted with powers for these purposes, by and with the advice and consent of the Senate; and the Creek Nation of Indians, by the undersigned Kings, Chiefs and Warriors, representing the whole Creek Nation, have agreed to the following articles:

ARTICLE I.

The Treaty entered into, at New-York, between the parties on the 7th day of August, 1790, is, and shall remain obligatory on the contracting parties, according to the terms of it, except as herein provided for.

Treaty at New York binding.

ARTICLE II.

The boundary line from the Currahee mountain, to the head, or source of the main south branch of the Oconeé river, called, by the white people, Appalatchee, and by the Indians, Tulapocka, and down the middle of the same, shall be clearly ascertained, and marked, at such time, and in such manner, as the President shall direct. And the Indians will, on being informed of the determination of the President, send as many of their old chiefs, as he may require, to see the line ascertained and marked.

Boundary line.

ARTICLE III.[a]

The President of the United States of America shall have full powers, whenever he may deem it advisable, to establish a trading or military post on the south side of the Alatamaha, on the bluff, about one mile above Beard's bluff; or any where from thence down the said river on

President may establish a trading or military post.

---

the President of the United States, to ratify the Treaty of Peace and Friendship, made and concluded at Coleraine, in the state of Georgia, on the 29th June, 1796, between the President of the United States of America, on the part and behalf of the said States, and the Kings, Chiefs and Warriors of the Creek nation of Indians, on the part of the said nation: *Provided, and on condition,* that nothing in the third and fourth articles of the said treaty, expressed in the words following, 'Article 3d, The President of the United States of America shall have full powers, whenever he may deem it advisable, to establish a trading or military post on the south side of the Altamaha, on the bluff, about one mile above Beard's bluff; or any where from thence down the said river on the lands of the Indians, to garrison the same with any part of the military force of the United States, to protect the post, and to prevent the violation of any of the provisions or regulations subsisting between the parties: And the Indians do hereby annex to the post aforesaid, a tract of land of five miles square, bordering one side on the river, which post and the lands annexed thereto, are hereby ceded to, and shall be to the use, and under the government of the United States of America.

" 'Art. 4th, as soon as the President of the United States has determined on the time and manner of running the line from the Currahee mountain, to the head or source of the main south branch of the Oconnee, and notified the Chiefs of the Creek land of the same, a suitable number of persons on their part shall attend, to see the same completed: And if the President should deem it proper, then to fix on any place or places adjoining the river, and on the Indian lands for military or trading posts: the Creeks who attend there, will concur in fixing the same, according to the wishes of the President. And to each post, the Indians shall annex a tract of land of five miles square, bordering one side on the river. And the said lands shall be to the use and under the government of the United States of America. *Provided always,* that whenever any of the trading or military posts mentioned in this treaty, shall, in the opinion of the President of the United States of America, be no longer necessary for the purposes intended by this cession, the same shall revert to, and become a part of the Indian lands,' shall be construed to affect any claim of the state of Georgia, to the right of preemption in the land therein set apart for military or trading posts; or to give to the United States without the consent of the said state, any right to the soil, or to the exclusive legislation over the same, or any other right than that of establishing, maintaining, and exclusively governing military and trading posts within the Indian territory mentioned in the said articles, as long as the frontier of Georgia may require these establishments."

[a] See note at the beginning of the treaty.

the lands of the Indians, to garrison the same with any part of the military force of the United States, to protect the posts, and to prevent the violation of any of the provisions or regulations subsisting between the parties: And the Indians do hereby annex to the post aforesaid, a tract of land of five miles square, bordering one side on the river; which post and the lands annexed thereto, are hereby ceded to, and shall be to the use, and under the government of the United States of America.

Article IV.[a]

Line to be run.

As soon as the President of the United States has determined on the time and manner of running the line from the Currahee mountain, to the head or source of the main south branch of the Oconee, and notified the chiefs of the Creek land of the same, a suitable number of persons on their part shall attend to see the same completed: And if the President should deem it proper, then to fix on any place or places adjoining *Trading or military* the river, and on the Indian lands for military or trading posts; the *posts to be established.* Creeks who attend there, will concur in fixing the same, according to the wishes of the President. And to each post, the Indians shall annex a tract of land of five miles square, bordering one side on the river. And the said lands shall be to the use and under the government of the United States of America. *Provided always*, that whenever any of the trading or military posts mentioned in this treaty, shall, in the opinion of the President of the United States of America, be no longer necessary for the purposes intended by this cession, the same shall revert to, and become a part of the Indian lands.

Article V.

Chiefs to attend the running the line with Spain.

Whenever the President of the United States of America, and the king of Spain, may deem it advisable to mark the boundaries which separate their territories, the President shall give notice thereof to the Creek chiefs, who will furnish two principal chiefs, and twenty hunters to accompany the persons employed on this business, as hunters and guides from the Chocktaw country, to the head of St. Mary's. The chiefs shall receive each half a dollar per day, and the hunters one quarter of a dollar each per day, and ammunition, and a reasonable value for the meat delivered by them for the use of the persons on this service.

Article VI.

Boundary line with Choctaws and Chickasaws.

The Treaties of Hopewell, between the United States and the Choctaws and Chickasaws, and at Holston between the Cherokees and the United States, mark the boundaries of those tribes of Indians. And the Creek nation do hereby relinquish all claims to any part of the territory inhabited or claimed by the citizens of the United States, in conformity with the said treaties.

Article VII.

Prisoners to be given up.

The Creek nation shall deliver, as soon as practicable, to the superintendent of Indian affairs, at such place as he may direct, all citizens of the United States; white inhabitants and negroes who are now prisoners in any part of the said nation, agreeably to the treaty at New-York, and also all citizens, white inhabitants, negroes and property taken since the signing of that treaty. And if any such prisoners, negroes or property should not be delivered, on or before the first day of January next, the governor of Georgia may empower three persons to repair to the said nation, in order to claim and receive such prisoners, negroes and property, under the direction of the President of the United States.

---

[a] See note at the beginning of the treaty.

ARTICLE VIII.

In consideration of the friendly disposition of the Creek nation towards the government of the United States, evidenced by the stipulations in the present treaty, and particularly the leaving it in the discretion of the President to establish trading or military posts on their lands; the commissioners of the United States, on behalf of the said states, give to the said nation, goods to the value of six thousand dollars, and stipulate to send to the Indian nation, two blacksmiths, with strikers, to be employed for the upper and lower Creeks with the necessary tools.

Presents to the Indians.

ARTICLE IX.

All animosities for past grievances shall henceforth cease, and the contracting parties will carry the foregoing treaty into full execution with all good faith and sincerity. *Provided nevertheless*, That persons now under arrest, in the state of Georgia, for a violation of the treaty at New-York, are not to be included in this amnesty, but are to abide the decision of law.

Animosities to cease.

ARTICLE X.

This treaty shall take effect and be obligatory on the contracting parties, as soon as the same shall have been ratified by the President of the United States, by and with the advise and consent of the senate.

Done at Colerain, the 29th of June, one thousand seven hundred and ninety-six.

When to take effect.

Benjamin Hawkins,	[L. S.]	Mico Opoey, his x mark,	[L. S.]
George Clymer,	[L. S.]	Tallessees:	
Andrew Pickens,	[L. S.]	Tallessee Mico, his x mark,	[L. S.]
Cowetas:		Othley Poey Mico, his x mark,	[L. S.]
Chruchateneah, his x mark,	[L. S.]	Little Oakjoys:	
Tusikia Mico, his x mark,	[L. S.]	Meeke Matla, his x mark,	[L. S.]
Inclenis Mico, his x mark,	[L. S.]	Hicory Ground:	
Tuskenah, his x mark,	[L. S.]	Opoey Mico, his x mark,	[L. S.]
Ookfuskee Tustuneka, his x mark,	[L. S.]	Kuyalegees:	
Clewalee Tustuneka, his x mark,	[L. S.]	Kelese Hatkie, his x mark,	[L. S.]
Cussitas:		Weakis:	
Tusikia Mico, his x mark,	[L. S.]	Nenehomotca Opoey, his x mark,	[L. S.]
Cussita Mico, his x mark,	[L. S.]	Tusikia Mico, his x mark,	[L. S.]
Fusateehee Mico, his x mark,	[L. S.]	Cleewallees:	
Opoey Mico, his x mark,	[L. S.]	Opoey-e-Matla, his x mark,	[L. S.]
Broken Arrows:		Coosis:	
Tustuneka Mico, his x mark,	[L. S.]	Hosonupe Hodjo, his x mark,	[L. S.]
Othley Opoey, his x mark,	[L. S.]	Tuckabathees:	
Opoey Tustuneka, his x mark,	[L. S.]	Holahto Mico, his x mark,	[L. S.]
Oboethly Tustuneka, his x mark,	[L. S.]	Tustunika Thlocco, his x mark,	[L. S.]
Euchees:		Oakfuskees:	
Euchee Mico, his x mark,	[L. S.]	Pashphalaha, his x mark,	[L. S.]
Usuchees:		Abacouchees:	
Osaw Enehah, his x mark,	[L. S.]	Spani Hodjo, his x mark,	[L. S.]
Ephah Tuskenah, his x mark,	[L. S.]	Tustonika, his x mark,	[L. S.]
Tusikia Mico, his x mark,	[L. S.]	Upper Euphaules:	
Chehaws:		Opoey, his x mark,	[L. S.]
Chehaw Mico, his x mark,	[L. S.]	Natchees:	
Talehanas:		Chinibe, his x mark,	[L. S.]
Othley Poey Mico, his x mark,	[L. S.]	Upper Cheehaws:	
Othley Poey Tustimiha, his x mark,	[L. S.]	Spokoi Hodjo, his x mark,	[L. S.]
Oakmulgees:		Tustunika, his x mark,	[L. S.]
Opoey Thlocco, his x mark,	[L. S.]	Mackasookos:	
Parachuckley, his x mark,	[L. S.]	Tuskeehenehaw, his x mark,	[L. S.]
Tuskenah, his x mark,	[L. S.]	Oconees:	
Euphales:		Knapematha Thlocco, his x mark,	[L. S.]
Pahose Mico, his x mark,	[L. S.]	Cusetahs:	
Tustunika Chopco, his x mark,	[L. S.]	Cusa Mico, his x mark,	[L. S.]
Ottassees:		Tusekia Mico Athee, his x mark,	[L. S.]
Fusatchee Hulloo Mico, his x mark,	[L. S.]	Halartee Matla, his x mark,	[L. S.]
Tusikia Mico, his x mark,	[L. S.]	Talahoua Mico, his x mark,	[L. S.]

Neathlocto, his x mark,	[L. S.]	Kialeegees:	
Nuckfamico, his x mark,	[L. S.]	Chuckchack Nincha, his x mark,	[L. S.]
Estechaco Mico, his x mark,	[L. S.]	Opoyo Matla, his x mark,	[L. S.]
Tuskegee Tuskinagee, his x mark,	[L. S.]	Lachlee Matla, his x mark,	[L. S.]
Cochus Mico, his x mark,	[L. S.]	Big Tallasees:	
Opio Hajo, his x mark,	[L. S.]	Chowostia Hajo, his x mark,	[L. S.]
Oneas Tustenagee, his x mark,	[L. S.]	Neathloco Opyo, his x mark,	[L. S.]
Alak Ajo, his x mark,	[L. S.]	Neathloco, his x mark,	[L. S.]
Stilcpeck Chatee, his x mark,	[L. S.]	Chowlactley Mico, his x mark,	[L. S.]
Tuchesee Mico, his x mark,	[L. S.]	Tocoso Hajo, his x mark,	[L. S.]
Kealeegees:		Hoochee Matla, his x mark,	[L. S.]
Cheea Hajo, his x mark,	[L. S.]	Howlacta, his x mark,	[L. S.]
Hitchetaws:		Tustinica Mico, his x mark,	[L. S.]
Talmasee Matla, his x mark,	[L. S.]	Opoy Fraico, his x mark,	[L. S.]
Tuckabatchees:		Big Talassee:	
Tustincke Hajo, his x mark,	[L. S.]	Houlacta, his x mark,	[L. S.]
Okolissa, his x mark,	[L. S.]	Etcatee Hajo, his x mark,	[L. S.]
Coweta Matla, his x mark,	[L. S.]	Chosolop Hajo, his x mark,	[L. S.]
Coosa Mico, his x mark,	[L. S.]	Coosa Hajo, his x mark,	[L. S.]
Fusatchee Mico, his x mark,	[L. S.]	Tuchabatchees:	
Pio Hatkee, his x mark,	[L. S.]	Chohajo, his x mark,	[L. S.]
Foosatchee Mico, his x mark,	[L. S.]	Weeokees:	
Neathlaco, his x mark,	[L. S.]	Tusticnika Hajo, his x mark,	[L. S.]
Tuchabatchee Howla, his x mark,	[L. S.]	Tuchabathees:	
Spoko Hajo, his x mark,	[L. S.]	Neamatoochee, his x mark,	[L. S.]
Coosis:		Cussitas:	
Tuskegee Tustinagee, his x mark,	[L. S.]	Telewa Othleopoya, his x mark,	[L. S.]
Talmasa Watalica, his x mark,	[L. S.]	Talmasse Matla, his x mark,	[L. S.]
Euphalees:		Niah Weathla, his x mark,	[L. S.]
Totkes Hago, his x mark,	[L. S.]	Emathlee-laco, his x mark,	[L. S.]
Otasees:		Ottesee Matla, his x mark,	[L. S.]
Opio Tustinagee, his x mark,	[L. S.]	Muclassee Matla, his x mark,	[L. S.]
Yafkee Mall Hajo, his x mark,	[L. S.]	Eufallee Matla, his x mark,	[L. S.]
Oboyethlee Tustinagee, his x mark,	[L. S.]	Tuckabatchees:	
Tustinagee Hajo, his x mark,	[L. S.]	Cunipee Howla, his x mark,	[L. S.]
Hillibee Tustinagee Hajo, his x mark,	[L. S.]	Cowetas:	
		Hospotak Tustinagee, his x mark,	[L. S.]
Effa Tuskeena, his x mark,	[L. S.]	Natchez:	
Emathlee Loco, his x mark,	[L. S.]	Spoko Hodjo, his x mark,	[L. S.]
Tustanagee Mico, his x mark,	[L. S.]	Uchees:	
Yaha Tustinagee, his x mark,	[L. S.]	Tustinagee Chatee, his x mark,	[L. S.]
Cunctastee Tustanagee, his x mark,	[L. S.]	Usuchees:	
Ottasees:		Spokoca Tustinagee, his x mark,	[L. S.]
Coosa Tustinagee, his x mark,	[L. S.]	Othley-poey-Tustinagee, his x mark,	[L. S.]
Neamatle Matla, his x mark,	[L. S.]	Tuskeeneah, his x mark,	[L. S.]

Witness:

J. Seagrove, superintendent Indian affairs, C. N.
Henry Gaither, lieutenant-colonel commandant,
Const. Freeman, A. W. D., major artillery and engineers,
Samuel Tinsley, captain, Third sub-legion.
Samuel Allison, ensign, Second sub-legion.
John W. Thompson, ensign, First U. S. legion.
Geo. Gillasspy, surgeon, L. U. S.

Tim. Barnard, D. A. and sworn interpreter.
James Burges, D. A. and sworn interpreter.
James Jordan.
Richard Thomas.
Alexander Cornels.
William Eaton, captain, Fourth U. S. sub-legion, commandant at Colerain, and secretary to the commission.

TREATY WITH THE MOHAWK, 1797.

Mar. 29, 1797.

7 Stat., 61.
Proclamation, Apr. 27, 1798.

Relinquishment to New York, by the Mohawk nation of Indians, under the sanction of the United States of America, of all claim to lands in that state.

AT a treaty held under the authority of the United States, with the Mohawk nation of Indians, residing in the province of Upper Canada, within the dominions of the king of Great Britain, present, the honorable Isaac Smith, commissioner appointed by the United States to hold this treaty; Abraham Ten Broeck, Egbert Benson, and Ezra L'Hommedieu, agents for the state of New York; captain Joseph Brandt, and captain John Deserontyon, two of the said Indians and deputies, to represent the said nation at this treaty.

The said agents having, in the presence, and with the approbation of the said commissioner, proposed to and adjusted with the said deputies, the compensation as hereinafter mentioned to be made to the said nation, for their claim, to be extinguished by this treaty, to all lands within the said state: it is thereupon finally agreed and done, between the said agents, and the said deputies, as follows, that is to say: the said agents do agree to pay to the said deputies, the sum of one thousand dollars, for the use of the said nation, to be by the said deputies paid over to, and distributed among, the persons and families of the said nation, according to their usages.　The sum of five hundred dollars, for the expenses of the said deputies, during the time they have attended this treaty: and the sum of one hundred dollars, for their expenses in returning, and for conveying the said sum of one thousand dollars, to where the said nation resides.　And the said agents do accordingly, for and in the name of the people of the state of New York, pay the said three several sums to the said deputies, in the presence of the said commissioner.　And the said deputies do agree to cede and release, and these presents witness, that they accordingly do, for and in the name of the said nation, in consideration of the said compensation, cede and release to the people of the state of New York, forever, all the right or title of the said nation to lands within the said state: and the claim of the said nation to lands within the said state, is hereby wholly and finally extinguished.

Agents of New York pay to the Mohawk deputies $1,000 and their expenses.

The Mohawks cede all right, etc., forever.

In testimony whereof, the said commissioner, the said agents, and the said deputies, have hereunto, and to two other acts of the same tenor and date, one to remain with the United States, one to remain with the said State, and one delivered to the said deputies, to remain with the said nation, set their hands and seals, at the city of Albany, in the said State, the twenty-ninth day of March, in the year one thousand seven hundred and ninety-seven.

Isaac Smith, [L. S.]
Abm. Ten Broeck, [L. S.]
Egbt. Benson, [L. S.]
Ezra L'Hommedieu, [L. S.]
Jos. Brandt, [L. S.]
John Deserontyon, [L. S.]

Witnesses:
　Robert Yates,
　John Tayler,
　Chas. Williamson,
　Thomas Morris,
　The mark of x John Abeel, alias the Cornplanter, a chief of the Senekas.

TREATY WITH THE CHEROKEE, 1798.

Articles of a Treaty between the United States of America, and the Cherokee Indians.

Oct. 2, 1798.
7 Stat., 62.

WHEREAS, the treaty made and concluded on Holston River, on the second day of July, in the year one thousand seven hundred and ninety-one, between the United States of America, and the Cherokee nation of Indians, had not been carried into execution, for some time thereafter, by reason of some misunderstandings which had arisen:—*And*

Preamble.
Ante 29.

whereas, in order to remove such misunderstandings, and to provide for carrying the said treaty into effect, and for re-establishing more fully the peace and friendship between the parties, another treaty was held, made and concluded by and between them, at Philadelphia, the twenty-sixth day of June, in the year one thousand seven hundred and ninety-four: In which, among other things, it was stipulated, that the boundaries mentioned in the fourth article of the said treaty of Holston, should be actually ascertained and marked, in the manner prescribed by the said article, whenever the Cherokee nation should have ninety days' notice of the time and place at which the commissioners of the United States intended to commence their operation: *And whereas* further delays in carrying the said fourth article into complete effect did take place, so that the boundaries mentioned and described therein, were not regularly ascertained and marked, until the latter part of the year, one thousand seven hundred and ninety-seven: before which time, and for want of knowing the direct course of the said boundary, divers settlements were made, by divers citizens of the United States, upon the Indian lands over and beyond the boundaries so mentioned and described in the said article, and contrary to the intention of the said treaties: but which settlers were removed from the said Indian lands, by authority of the United States, as soon after the boundaries had been so lawfully ascertained and marked as the nature of the case had admitted: *And whereas*, for the purpose of doing justice to the Cherokee nation of Indians, and remedying inconveniences arising to citizens of the United States from the adjustment of the boundary line between the lands of the Cherokees and those of the United States, or the citizens thereof, or from any other cause in relation to the Cherokees; and in order to promote the interests and safety of the said states, and the citizens thereof, the President of the United States, by and with the advice and consent of the Senate thereof, hath appointed George Walton, of Georgia, and the President of the United States hath also appointed Lieutenant-Colonel Thomas Butler, commanding the troops of the United States, in the state of Tennessee, to be commissioners for the purpose aforesaid: And who, on the part of the United States, and the Cherokee nation, by the undersigned chiefs and warriors, representing the said nation, have agreed to the following articles, namely:

ARTICLE I.

Peace and friendship perpetual.

The peace and friendship subsisting between the United States and the Cherokee people, are hereby renewed, continued, and declared perpetual.

ARTICLE II.

Subsisting treaties to operate.

The treaties subsisting between the present contracting parties, are acknowledged to be of full and operating force; together with the construction and usage under their respective articles, and so to continue.

ARTICLE III.

Limits to remain the same, etc.

The limits and boundaries of the Cherokee nation, as stipulated and marked by the existing treaties between the parties, shall be and remain the same, where not altered by the present treaty.

ARTICLE IV.

Cession of territory.

In acknowledgement for the protection of the United States, and for the considerations hereinafter expressed and contained, the Cherokee nation agree, and do hereby relinquish and cede to the United States, all the lands within the following points and lines, viz. From a point on the Tennessee river, below Tellico block-house, called the Wild-cat Rock, in a direct line to the Militia spring, near the Mary-ville road leading from Tellico. From the said spring to the Chill-howie mountain, by a line so to be run, as will leave all the farms on Nine-mile Creek to the northward and eastward of it; and to be continued along Chill-howie mountain, until it strikes Hawkins's line. Thence along the said line to the great Iron mountain; and from the top of which a line to be continued in a southeastwardly course to where the most southwardly branch of Little river crosses the divisional line to Tuggaloe river: From the place of beginning, the Wild-cat Rock, down the northeast margin of the Tennessee river (not including islands) to a point or place one mile above the junction of that river with the Clinch, and from thence by a line to be drawn in a right angle, until it intersects Hawkins's line leading from Clinch. Thence down the said line to the river Clinch; thence up the said river to its junction with Emmery's river; and thence up Emmery's river to the foot of Cumberland mountain. From thence a line to be drawn, northeastwardly, along the foot of the mountain, until it intersects with Campbell's line.

ARTICLE V.

To prevent all future misunderstanding about the line described in the foregoing article, two commissioners shall be appointed to superintend the running and marking the same, where not ascertained by the rivers, immediately after signing this treaty; one to be appointed by the commissioners of the United States, and the other by the Cherokee nation; and who shall cause three maps or charts thereof to be made out; one whereof shall be transmitted and deposited in the war office of the United States; another with the executive of the state of Tennessee, and the third with the Cherokee nation, which said line shall form a part of the boundary between the United States and the Cherokee nation.

Commissioners for running the line of the cession.

ARTICLE VI.

In consideration of the relinquishment and cession hereby made, the United States upon signing the present treaty, shall cause to be delivered to the Cherokees, goods, wares and merchandise, to the amount of five thousand dollars, and shall cause to be delivered, annually, other goods, to the amount of one thousand dollars, in addition to the annuity already provided for; and will continue the guarantee of the remainder of their country for ever, as made and contained in former treaties.

Consideration for the treaty.

ARTICLE VII.

The Cherokee nation agree, that the Kentucky road, running between the Cumberland mountain and the Cumberland river, where the same shall pass through the Indian land, shall be an open and free road for the use of the citizens of the United States in like manner as the road from Southwest point to Cumberland river. In consideration of which it is hereby agreed on the part of the United States, that until settlements shall make it improper, the Cherokee hunters shall be at liberty to hunt and take game upon the lands relinquished and ceded by this treaty.

Kentucky road to be kept open.

Indians may hunt on lands relinquished.

ARTICLE VIII.

Due notice shall be given to the principal towns of the Cherokees, of the time proposed for delivering the annual stipends; and sufficient supplies of provisions shall be furnished, by and at the expense of the United States, to subsist such reasonable number that may be sent, or shall attend to receive them during a reasonable time.

Notice of time for delivering annuities, etc.

Article IX.

Horses stolen to be paid for.

It is mutually agreed between the parties, that horses stolen and not returned within ninety days, shall be paid for at the rate of sixty dollars each; if stolen by a white man, citizen of the United States, the Indian proprietor shall be paid in cash; and if stolen by an Indian from a citizen, to be deducted as expressed in the fourth article of the treaty of Philadelphia.—This article shall have retrospect to the commencement of the first conferences at this place in the present year,

Oblivion of past aggressions.

and no further. And all animosities, aggressions, thefts and plunderings, prior to that day shall cease, and be no longer remembered or demanded on either side.

Article X.

The Cherokee agent to have a piece of ground.

The Cherokee nation agree, that the agent who shall be appointed to reside among them from time to time, shall have a sufficient piece of ground allotted for his temporary use.

And lastly, This treaty, and the several articles it contains, shall be considered as additional to, and forming a part of, treaties already subsisting between the United States and the Cherokee nation, and shall be carried into effect on both sides, with all good faith as soon as the same shall be approved and ratified by the President of the United States, and the Senate thereof.

In witness of all and every thing herein determined between the United States of America, and the whole Cherokee nation, the parties hereunto set their hands and seals in the council house, near Tellico, on Cherokee ground, and within the United States, this second day of October, in the year one thousand seven hundred and ninety-eight, and in the twenty-third year of the independence and sovereignty of the United States.

Thos. Butler,
Geo. Walton.

Nenetuah, or Bloody Fellow, his x mark, [L. S.]
Ostaiah, his x mark, [L. S.]
Jaunne, or John, his x mark, [L. S.]
Oortlokecteh, his x mark, [L. S.]
Chockonnistaller, or Stallion, his x mark, [L. S.]
Noothoietah, his x mark, [L. S.]
Kunnateelah, or Rising Fawn, his x mark, [L. S.]
Utturah, or Skin Worm, his x mark, [L. S.]
Weelee, or Will, his x mark, [L. S.]
Oolasoteh, his x mark, [L. S.]
Tlorene, his x mark, [L. S.]
Jonnurteekee, or Little John, [L. S.]
Oonatakoteekee, his x mark, [L. S.]
Kanow'surhee, or Broom, his x mark, [L. S.]
Yonah Oolah, Bear at Home, his x mark, [L. S.]
Tunksalenee, or Thick Legs, his x mark, [L. S.]
Oorkullaukee, his x mark, [L. S.]
Kumamah, or Butterfly, his x mark, [L. S.]
Chattakuteehee, his x mark, [L. S.]

Kanitta, or Little Turkey, his x mark, [L. S.]
Kettegiskie, his x mark, [L. S.]
Tauquotihee, or the Glass, his x mark, [L. S.]
Chuquilatague, his x mark, [L. S.]
Salleekookoolah, his x mark, [L. S.]
Tallotuskee, his x mark, [L. S.]
Chellokee, his x mark, [L. S.]
Tuskeegatee, or Long Fellow, his x mark, [L. S.]
Neekaanneah, or Woman Holder, his x mark, [L. S.]
Kulsateehee, his x mark, [L. S.]
Keetakeuskah, or Prince, his x mark, [L. S.]
Charley, his x mark, [L. S.]
Akooh, his x mark, [L. S.]
Sawanookeh, his x mark, [L. S.]
Yonahequah, or Big Bear, his x mark, [L. S.]
Keenahkunnah, his x mark, [L. S.]
Kaweesoolaskee, his x mark, [L. S.]
Teekakalohenah, his x mark, [L. S.]
Ookouseteeh, or John Taylor, his x mark, [L. S.]
Chochuchee, his x mark, [L. S.]

Witnesses:

Elisha I. Hall, secretary of the commission, [L. S.]
Silas Dinsmoor, Indian agent to the Cherokees, [L. S.]

John W. Hooker, United States factor, [L. S.]
Edw. Butler, captain commanding at Tellico, [L. S.]

Robert Purdy, lieutenant Fourth U. S. Regiment,	[L. S.]	Saml. Hanly,	[L. S.]
Ludwell Grymes,	[L. S.]	Michael McKinsey,	[L. S.]
Jno. McDonald,	[L. S.]	Chas. Hicks, interpreter,	[L. S.]
Daniel Ross,	[L. S.]	James Cazey, interpreter,	[L. S.]
Mattw. Wallace, esquire,	[L. S.]	John Thompson,	[L. S.]

TREATY WITH THE CHICKASAW, 1801.

A treaty, of reciprocal advantages and mutual convenience between the United States of America and the Chickasaws.

Oct. 24, 1801.

7 Stat. 65.
Ratified, May 1, 1802.
Proclaimed, May 4, 1802.

THE President of the United States of America, by James Wilkinson brigadier general in the service of the United States, Benjamin Hawkins of North Carolina, and Andrew Pickens of South Carolina, commissioners of the United States, who are vested with full powers, and the Mingco, principal men and warriors of the Chickasaw nation, representing the said nation, have agreed to the following articles.

ART. I. The Mingco, principal men and warriors of the Chickasaw nation of Indians, give leave and permission to the President of the United States of America, to lay out, open and make a convenient wagon road through their land between the settlements of Mero District in the state of Tennessee, and those of Natchez in the Mississippi Territory, in such way and manner as he may deem proper; and the same shall be a high way for the citizens of the United States, and the Chickasaws. The Chickasaws shall appoint two discreet men to serve as assistants, guides or pilots, during the time of laying out and opening the road, under the direction of the officer charged with that duty, who shall have a reasonable compensation for their service: Provided always, that the necessary ferries over the water courses crossed by the said road shall be held and deemed to be the property of the Chickasaw nation.

Right to make a road, etc., granted to United States.

ART. II. The commissioners of the United States give to the Mingco of the Chickasaws, and the deputation of that nation, goods to the value of seven hundred dollars, to compenstate him and them and their attendants for the expense and inconvenience they may have sustained by their respectful and friendly attention to the President of the United States of America, and to the request made to them in his name to permit the opening of the road. And as the persons, towns, villages, lands, hunting grounds, and other rights and property of the Chickasaws, as set forth in the treaties or stipulations heretofore entered into between the contracting parties, more especially in and by a certificate of the President of the United States of America, under their seal of the first of July 1794, are in the peace and under the protection of the United States, the commissioners of the United States do hereby further agree, that the President of the United States of America, shall take such measures from time to time, as he may deem proper, to assist the Chickasaws to preserve entire all their rights against the encroachments of unjust neighbors, of which he shall be the judge, and also to preserve and perpetuate friendship and brotherhood between the white people and the Chickasaws.

Present of goods to Indians.

ART. III. The commissioners of the United States may, if they deem it advisable, proceed immediately to carry the first article into operation; and the treaty shall take effect and be obligatory on the contracting parties, as soon as the same shall have been ratified by the President of the United States of America, by and with the advice and consent of the Senate of the United States.

Treaty, when to take effect.

In testimony whereof, we, the plenipotentiaries, have hereunto subscribed our names and affixed our seals, at Chickasaw Bluffs, the twenty-fourth of October, 1801.

James Wilkinson, Brigadier General,   [L. S.]
Benjamin Hawkins,   [L. S.]
Andw. Pickens,   [L. S.]
Chinmimbe Mingo, his x mark,   [L. S.]
Immuttauhaw, his x mark,   [L. S.]
Chumaube, his x mark,   [L. S.]
George Colbert, his x mark,   [L. S.]
William McGillivray, his x mark,   [L. S.]
Opiehoomuh, his x mark,   [L. S.]
Olohtohopoie, his x mark,   [L. S.]

Minkemattauhau, his x mark,   [L. S.]
Tuskkoopoie, his x mark,   [L. S.]
William Glover, his x mark,   [L. S.]
Thomas Brown, his x mark,   [L. S.]
William Colbert, W. C.   [L. S.]
Mooklushopoie, his x mark,   [L. S.]
Opoieolauhtau, his x mark,   [L. S.]
Teschoolauhtau, his x mark,   [L. S.]
Teschoolauptau, his x mark,   [L. S.]
James Underwood, his x mark,   [L. S.]

Samuel Mitchell, agent to the Chickasaws,
Malcolm McGee, his x signature, interpreter to the Chickasaws,
William R. Bootes, captain Third Regiment and aid de camp,
J. B. Wallach, lieutenant and aid de camp,
Jn. Wilson, lieutenant Third Regiment.

TREATY WITH THE CHOCTAW, 1801.

A treaty of friendship, limits and accommodation between the United States of America and the Chactaw nation of Indians.

Dec. 17, 1801.
7 Stat., 66.
Ratified April 30, 1802.
Proclaimed May 4, 1802.

THOMAS JEFFERSON, President of the United States of America, by James Wilkinson, of the state of Maryland, Brigadier-General in the army of the United States, Benjamin Hawkins, of North Carolina, and Andrew Pickens, of South Carolina, commissioners plenipotentiary of the United States on the one part, and the Mingos, principal men and warriors of the Chactaw nation, representing the said nation in council assembled, on the other part, have entered into the following articles and conditions, viz:

Peace and friendship.

ART. I. Whereas the United States in Congress assembled, did by their commissioners Plenipotentiary, Benjamin Hawkins, Andrew Pickens, and Joseph Martin, at a treaty held with the chiefs and head men of the Chactaw nation at Hopewell, on the Keowe, the third day of January, in the year of our Lord, one thousand seven hundred and eighty-six, give peace to the said nation, and receive it into the favor and protection of the United States of America; it is agreed by the parties to these presents respectively, that the Chactaw nation, or such part of it as may reside within the limits of the United States, shall be and continue under the care and protection of the said States; and that the mutual confidence and friendship which are hereby acknowledged to subsist between the contracting parties shall be maintained and perpetuated.

A wagon way to be made through Indian lands.

ART. II. The Mingos principal men and warriors of the Chactaw nation of Indians, do hereby give their free consent, that a convenient and durable wagon way may be explored, marked, opened and made under the orders and instructions of the President of the United States, through their lands to commence at the northern extremity of the settlements of the Mississippi Territory, and to be extended from thence, by such route as may be selected and surveyed under the authority of the President of the United States, until it shall strike the lands claimed by the Chickasaw nation; and the same shall be and continue for ever, a high-way for the citizens of the United States and the Chactaws; and the said Chactaws shall nominate two discreet men from their nation, who may be employed as assistants, guides or pilots, during the time of laying out and opening the said high-way, or so long as may be deemed expedient, under the direction of the officer charged with this duty, who shall receive a reasonable compensation for their services.

ART. III. The two contracting parties covenant and agree that the old line of demarkation heretofore established by and between the officers of his Britannic Majesty and the Chactaw nation, which runs in a parallel direction with the Mississippi river and eastward thereof, shall be retraced and plainly marked, in such way and manner as the President may direct, in the presence of two persons to be appointed by the said nation; and that the said line shall be the boundary between the settlements of the Mississippi Territory and the Chactaw nation. And the said nation does by these presents relinquish to the United States and quit claim for ever, all their right, title and pretension to the land lying between the said line and the Mississippi river, bounded south by the thirty-first degree of north latitude, and north by the Yazoo river, where the said line shall strike the same; and on the part of the commissioners it is agreed, that all persons who may be settled beyond this line, shall be removed within it, on the side towards the Mississippi, together with their slaves, household furniture, tools, materials and stock, and that the cabins or houses erected by such persons shall be demolished. *Boundary.*

ART. IV. The President of the United States may, at his discretion, proceed to execute the second article of this treaty; and the third article shall be carried into effect as soon as may be convenient to the government of the United States, and without unnecessary delay on the one part or the other, of which the President shall be the judge; the Chactaws to be seasonably advised, by order of the President of the United States, of the time when, and the place where, the re-survey and re-marking of the old line referred to in the preceding article, will be commenced. *Indians to be notified of the time, etc., of resurvey.*

ART. V. The commissioners of the United States, for and in consideration of the foregoing concessions on the part of the Chactaw nation, and in full satisfaction for the same, do give and deliver to the Mingos, chiefs and warriors of the said nation, at the signing of these presents, the value of two thousand dollars in goods and merchandise, net cost of Philadelphia, the receipt whereof is hereby acknowledged; and they further engage to give three sets of blacksmith's tools to the said nation. *$2,000 delivered to the Indians, etc.*

ART. VI. This treaty shall take effect and be obligatory on the contracting parties, so soon as the same shall be ratified by the President of the United States of America, by and with the advice and consent of the Senate thereof. *Treaty, when to take effect.*

In testimony whereof, the commissioners plenipotentiary of the United States, and the Mingos, principal men, and warriors, of the Choctaw nation, have hereto subscribed their names and affixed their seals, at Fort Adams, on the Mississippi, this seventeenth day of December, in the year of our Lord one thousand eight hundred and one, and of the Independence of the United States the twenty-sixth.

James Wilkinson,	[L. S.]	Shappa Homo, his x mark,	[L. S.]
Benjamin Hawkins,	[L. S.]	Hiupa Homo, his x mark,	[L. S.]
Andrew Pickens,	[L. S.]	Illatalla Homo, his x mark,	[L. S.]
Tuskona Hopoia, his x mark,	[L. S.]	Hoche Homo, his x mark,	[L. S.]
Toota Homo, his x mark,	[L. S.]	Tuspena Chaabe, his x mark,	[L. S.]
Mingo Hom Massatubby, his x mark,	[L. S.]	Muclusha Hopoia, his x mark,	[L. S.]
		Capputanne Thlucco, his x mark,	[L. S.]
Oak Shumme, his x mark,	[L. S.]	Robert McClure, his x mark,	[L. S.]
Mingo Pooscoos, his x mark,	[L. S.]	Poosha Homo, his x mark,	[L. S.]
Buckshun Nubby, his x mark,	[L. S.]	Baka Lubbe, his x mark,	[L. S.]

Witnesses present:

Alexander Macomb, jun. secretary to the commission,
John McKee, deputy superintendent, and agent to the Choctaws,
Henry Gaither, lieutenant colonel, commandant,
John H. Brull, major, Second Regiment Infantry,
Bw. Shaumburgh, captain, Second Regiment Infantry,
Frans. Jones, Assistant Quartermaster General]

Benjamin Wilkinson, lieutenant and paymaster, Third United States Regiment,
J. B. Walbach, aid-de-camp to the commanding general,
J. Wilson, lieutenant, Third Regiment Infantry,
Samuel Jeton, lieutenant, Second Regiment of Artillery and Engineers,
John F. Carmichael, surgeon, Third Regiment United States Army.

TREATY WITH THE CREEKS, 1802.

June 16, 1802.

7 Stat., 68.
Proclamation, Jan. 11, 1803.

A Treaty of Limits between the United States of America and the Creek Nation of Indians.

THOMAS JEFFERSON, President of the United States of America, by James Wilkinson, of the state of Maryland, Brigadier General in the army of the United States, Benjamin Hawkins, of North-Carolina, and Andrew Pickens of South-Carolina, Commissioners Plenipotentiary of the United States, on the one part, and the Kings, Chiefs, Head Men and Warriors of the Creek Nation, in council assembled, on the other part, have entered into the following articles and conditions, viz.

Cession of territory to United States.

ARTICLE I. The Kings, Chiefs, Head men and Warriors of the Creek nation, in behalf of the said nation, do by these presents cede to the United States of America, all that tract and tracts of land, situate, lying and being within and between the following bounds, and the lines and limits of the extinguished claims of the said nation, heretofore ascertained and established by treaty. That is to say—beginning at the upper extremity of the high shoals of the Appalachee river, the same being a branch of the Oconee river, and on the southern bank of the same—running thence a direct course to a noted ford of the south branch of Little river, called by the Indians Chat-to-chuc-co hat-chee—thence a direct line to the main branch of Commissioners' creek, where the same is intersected by the path leading from the rock-landing to the Ocmulgee Old Towns, thence a direct line to Palmetto Creek, where the same is intersected by the Uchee path, leading from the Oconee to the Ocmulgee river—thence down the middle waters of the said Creek to Oconee river, and with the western bank of the same to its junction with the Ocmulgee river, thence across the Ocmulgee river to the south bank of the Altamaha river, and down the same at low water mark to the lower bank of Goose Creek, and from thence by a direct line to the Mounts, on the Margin of the Okefinocau swamp, raised and established by the commissioners of the United States and Spain at the head of the St. Mary's river; thence down the middle waters of the said river, to the point where the old line of demarkation strikes the same, thence with the said old line to the Altamaha river, and up the same to Goose Creek: and the said Kings, Chiefs, Head men and Warriors, do relinquish and quit claim to the United States all their right, title, interest and pretensions, in and to the tract and tracts of land within and between the bounds and limits aforesaid, for ever.

Consideration for the foregoing concession.

ART. II. The commissioners of the United States, for and in consideration of the foregoing concession on the part of the Creek nation, and in full satisfaction for the same do hereby covenant and agree with the said nation, in behalf of the United States, that the said states shall pay to the said nation, annually, and every year, the sum of three thousand dollars, and one thousand dollars for the term of ten years, to the chiefs who administer the government, agreeably to a certificate under the hands and seals of the commissioners of the United States, of this date, and also twenty-five thousand dollars in the manner and form following, viz. Ten thousand dollars in goods and merchandise, the receipt of which is hereby acknowledged; ten thousand dollars to satisfy certain debts due from Indians and white persons of the Creek country to the factory of the United States; the said debts, after the payment aforesaid, to become the right and property of the Creek nation, and to be recovered for their use in such way and manner as the President of the United States may think proper to direct; five thousand dollars to satisfy claims for property taken by individuals of the said nation, from the citizens of the United States, subsequent to the treaty of Colerain, which has been or may be claimed and established agreeably to the provisions of the act for regulating trade and intercourse with the Indian tribes, and to preserve peace on the frontiers. And it is further agreed that the United States shall furnish to the said nation two sets of blacksmiths tools, and men to work them, for the term of three years.

ART. III. It is agreed by the contracting parties, that the garrison or garrisons which may be found necessary for the protection of the frontiers, shall be established upon the land of the Indians, at such place or places as the President of the United States may think proper to direct, in the manner and on the terms established by the treaty of Colerain. *Garrisons to be established on Indian lands.*

ART. IV. The contracting parties to these presents, do agree that this treaty shall become obligatory and of full effect so soon as the same shall be ratified by the President of the United States of America, by and with the advice and consent of the Senate thereof. *When to take effect*

In testimony whereof, the commissioners plenipotentiary of the United States, and the kings, chiefs, head men, and warriors, of the Creek nation, have hereunto subscribed their names and affixed their seals, at the camp of the commissioners of the United States, near fort Wilkinson, on the Oconee river, this sixteenth day of June, in the year of our Lord one thousand eight hundred and two, and of the independence of the United States the twenty-sixth.

James Wilkinson, [L. S.]	Yaufkee Emautla Haujo, his x mark,
Benjamin Hawkins, [L. S.]	Coosaudee Tustunnuggee, his x mark,
Andrew Pickens, [L. S.]	Nenehomohtau Tustunnuggee Micco, his x mark,
Efau Haujo, his x mark,	
1 Tustunnuggee Thlucco, his x mark,	Isfaunau Tustunnuggee, his x mark,
2 Hopoie Micco, his x mark,	Efaulau Tustunnuggee, his x mark,
3 Hopoie Olohtau, his x mark,	Tustunnuc Hoithlepoyuh, his x mark,
Tallessee Micco, his x mark,	Ishopei Tustunnuggee, his x mark,
Tussekia Micco, his x mark,	Cowetuh Tustunnuggee, his x mark,
Micco Thlucco, his x mark,	Hopoithle Haujo, his x mark,
Tuskenehau Chapco, his x mark,	Wocsee Haujo, his x mark,
Chouwacke le Micco, his x mark,	Uctijutchee Tustunnuggee, his x mark,
Toosce hatche Micco, his x mark,	Okelesau Hutkee, his x mark,
Hopoie Yauholo, his x mark,	Pahose Micco, his x mark,
Hoithlewau le Micco, his x mark,	Micke Emautlau, his x mark,
Efau Haujo, of Cooloome, his x mark,	Hoithlepoyau Haujo, his x mark,
Cussetuh Youholo, his x mark,	Cussetuh Haujo, his x mark,
Wewocau Tustunnuggee, his x mark,	Ochesee Tustunnuggee, his x mark,
Nehomahte Tustunnuggee, his x mark,	Toosehatchee Haujo, his x mark,
Tustunu Haujo, his x mark,	Isfaune Haujo, his x mark,
Hopoie Tustunnuggee, his x mark,	Hopoithle Hopoie, his x mark,
Talchischau Micco, his x mark,	Olohtuh Emautlau, his x mark,

Timothy Barnard,
Alexander Cornells, his x mark,
Joseph Islands, his x mark,

Interpreters,

Alexander Macomb, jr. secretary to the commission,
William R. Boote, captain Second Regiment Infantry,
T. Blackburn, lieutenant commanding Company G.
John B. Barnes, lieutenant U. S. Army.
Wm. Hill, Ast. C. D.
Olohtau Haujo, his x mark,
Tulmass Haujo, his x mark,
Auttossee Emautlaw, his x mark.

TREATY WITH THE SENECA, 1802.

June 30, 1802.

7 Stat., 70.
Ratified Jan. 12, 1803.
Proclaimed Jan. 12
1803.

This Indenture, made the thirtieth day of June, in the year of our Lord one thousand eight hundred and two, between the Sachems, Chiefs, and Warriors of the Seneca nation of Indians, of the first part, and Wilhem Willink, Pieter Van Eeghen, Hendrik Vollenhoven, W. Willink the younger, I. Willink the younger (son of Jan) Jan Gabriel Van Staphorst, Roelof Van Staphorst, the younger, Cornelis Vollenhoven, and Hendrik Seye, all of the city of Amsterdam, and republic of Batavia, by Joseph Ellicott, esquire, their agent and attorney, of the second part.

Preamble.

WHEREAS at a treaty held under the authority of the United States with the said Seneca nation of Indians, at Buffalo creek, in the county of Ontario, and state of New-York, on the day of the date of these présents, by the honorable John Taylor, esquire, a commissioner appointed by the President of the United States to hold the same, in pursuance of the constitution, and of the act of the Congress of the United States, in such case made and provided, a convention was entered into in the presence and with the approbation of the said commissioner, between the said Seneca nation of Indians and the said Wilhelm Willink, Pieter Van Eeghen, Hendrik Vollenhoven, W. Willink the younger, I. Willink the younger (son of Jan) Jan Gabiel Van Staphorst, Roelof Van Staphorst the younger, Cornelis Vollenhoven, and Hendrik Seye, by the said Joseph Ellicott, their agent and attorney, lawfully constituted and appointed for that purpose.

Cession of lands.

NOW THIS INDENTURE WITNESSETH, That the said parties of the first part, for and in consideration of the lands hereinafter described, do hereby exchange, cede, and forever quit claim to the said parties of the second part, their heirs and assigns, ALL those lands situate, lying and being in the county of Ontario and state of New-York, being part of the lands described and reserved by the said parties of the first part, in a treaty or convention held by the honorable Jeremiah Wadsworth, esquire, under the authority of the United States on the Genesee river the 15th day of September, one thousand seven hundred and ninety-seven, in words following, viz.

Boundary described.

"BEGINNING at the mouth of the eighteen mile or Kogh-quaw-gu creek, thence a line or lines to be drawn parallel to lake Erie, at the distance of one mile from the lake, to the mouth of Cataraugos creek, thence a line or lines extending twelve miles up the north side of said creek, at the distance of one mile therefrom, thence a direct line to the said creek, thence down the said creek to lake Erie, thence along the lake, to the first mentioned creek, and thence to the place of beginning. Also one other piece at Cataraugos, beginning at the shore of lake Erie, on the south side of Cataraugos creek, at the distance of one mile from the mouth thereof, thence running one mile from the lake, thence on a line parallel thereto, to a point within one mile from the Con-non-dau-we-gea creek, thence up the said creek one mile on a line parallel thereto, thence on a direct line to the said creek, thence down the same to lake Erie, thence along the lake to the place of beginning;" reference being thereunto had will fully appear. TOGETHER with all and singular the rights, privileges, hereditaments and appurtenances thereunto belonging, or in any wise appertaining. AND all the estate, right, title, and interest whatsoever, of them, the said parties of the first part, and their nation, of, in and to the said tracts of land, above described, TO HAVE AND TO HOLD all and singular the said granted premises, with the appurtenances, to the said parties of the second part, their heirs and assigns, to their only proper use, benefit and behoof forever.

AND in consideration of the said lands described and ceded as aforesaid, the said parties of the second part, by Joseph Ellicott, their agent and attorney as aforesaid, do hereby exchange, cede, release, and quit claim to the said parties of the first part, and their nation (the said parties of the second part, reserving to themselves the right of preemption) all that certain tract or parcel of land situate as aforesaid. BEGINNING at a post marked No. 0. standing on the bank of lake Erie, at the mouth of Cataraugos creek, and on the north bank thereof; thence along the shore of said lake N. 11° E. 21 chains; N. thirteen degrees east 45 chains; N. 19° E. 14 chains 65 links to a post; thence east 119 chains to a post; thence south 14 chains 27 links to a post; thence east 640 chains to a post standing in the meridian between the 8th and 9th ranges; thence along said meridian south 617 chains 75 links, to a post standing on the south bank of Cataraugos creek; thence west 160 chains to a post; thence north 290 chains 25 links to a post; thence west 482 chains 31 links to a post; thence north 219 chains 50 links to a post standing on the north bank of Cataraugos creek; thence down the same and along the several meanders thereof, to the place of beginning. To HOLD to the said parties of the first part in the same manner and by the same tenure as the lands reserved by the said parties of the first part in and by the said treaty or convention entered into on Genesee river, the 15th day of September, one thousand seven hundred and ninety-seven, as aforesaid, were intended to be held.

In testimony whereof, the parties to these presents have hereunto, and to two other indentures of the same tenor and date, one to remain with the United States, one to remain with the said parties of the first part, and one other to remain with the said parties of the second part, interchangeably set their hands and seals the day and year first above written.

Conneatiu, his x mark, [L. S.]
Koeentwahka, or Corn Planter, his x mark, [L. S.]
Wondongoohka, his x mark, [L. S.]
Tekonnondu, his x mark, [L. S.]
Tekiaindau, his x mark, [L. S.]
Sagooyes, his x mark, [L. S.]
Towyocauna, or Blue Sky, his x mark, [L. S.]
Koyingquautah, or Young King, his x mark, [L. S.]
Kaoundoowand, or Pollard, his x mark, [L. S.]
Connawaudeau, his x mark, [L. S.]
Soonoyou, his x mark, [L. S.]
Auwennausa, his x mark, [L. S.]
Soogooyawautau, or Red Jacket, his x mark, [L. S.]
Coshkoutough, his x mark, [L. S.]
Teyokaihossa, his x mark, [L. S.]

Onayawos, or Farmer's Brother, his x mark, [L. S.]
Sonaugoies, his x mark, [L. S.]
Gishkaka, or Little Billy, his x mark, [L. S.]
Sussaoowau, his x mark, [L. S.]
Wilhem Willink,
Pieter Van Eeghen,
Hendrik Vollenhoven,
W. Willink, the younger,
I. Willink, the younger, (son of Jan,)
Jan Gabriel Van Staphorst, [L. S.]
Roelof Van Staphorst, the younger,
Cornelis Vollenhoven, and
Hendrik Seye,
by their attorney, Joseph Ellicott,

Sealed and delivered in the presence of—
　　John Thomson,
　　Israel Chapin,
　　James W. Stevens.
　　Horatio Jones,
　　Jasper Parrish,
　　　　　　Interpreters.

Done at a full and general treaty of the Seneka nation of Indians, held at Buffalo creek, in the county of Ontario, and State of New York, on the thirteenth day of June, in the year of our Lord one thousand eight hundred and two, under the authority of the United States.

In testimony whereof, I have hereunto set my hand and seal, the day and year aforesaid.

　　　　　　　　　　John Tayler. [L. S.]

TREATY WITH THE SENECA, 1802.

June 30, 1802.

7 Stat., 72.
Ratified Feb. 7, 1803.
Proclaimed, Feb. 7, 1803.

At a treaty held under the authority of the United States, at Buffalo Creek in the county of Ontario, and state of New-York, between the Sachems, Chiefs and Warriors of the Seneca Nation of Indians, on behalf of said nation, and Oliver Phelps, Esq. of the county of Ontario, Isaac Bronson, Esq. of the city of New-York, and Horatio Jones, of the said county of Ontario, in the presence of John Tayler, Esq. Commissioner appointed by the President of the United States for holding said treaty.

Cession of certain lands.

KNOW ALL MEN by these presents, that the said Sachems, Chiefs and Warriors, for and in consideration of the sum of twelve hundred dollars, lawful money of the United States, unto them in hand paid by the said Oliver Phelps, Isaac Bronson and Horatio Jones, at or immediately before the sealing and delivery hereof, the receipt whereof is hereby acknowledged, HAVE and by these presents DO grant, remise, release and forever quit claim and confirm unto the said Oliver Phelps, Isaac Bronson and Horatio Jones, and to their heirs and assigns, ALL that tract of land commonly called and known by the name of Little Beard's Reservation, situate, lying and being in the said county of Ontario, BOUNDED on the East by the Genesee river and Little Beard's Creek, on the south and west by other lands of the said parties of the second part, and on the north by Big Tree Reservation—containing two square miles, or twelve hundred and eighty acres, together with all and singular, the hereditaments and appurtenances whatsoever thereunto belonging, or in any wise appertaining, to hold to them the said Oliver Phelps, Isaac Bronson and Horatio Jones, their heirs and assigns, to the only proper use and behoof of them the said Oliver Phelps, Isaac Bronson and Horatio Jones their heirs and assigns forever.

In testimony whereof, the said commissioner and the said parties have hereunto, and to two other instruments of the same tenor and date, one to remain with the United States, one to remain with the Seneka nation of Indians, and one to remain with the said Oliver Phelps, Isaac Bronson, and Horatio Jones, interchangeably set their hands and seals. Dated the 30th day of June, in the year of our Lord one thousand eight hundred and two.

Conneatiu, his x mark,   [L. S.]
Koeentwahka, or Corn Planter,
  his x mark,   [L. S.]
Wondongoohkta, his x mark,   [L. S.]
Tekonnondu, his x mark,   [L. S.]
Tekiaindau, his x mark,   [L. S.]
Sagooyes, his x mark,   [L. S.]
Touyocauna, or Blue Sky, his x
  mark,   [L. S.]

Koyingquautah, or Young King,
  his x mark,   [L. S.]
Soogooyawautau, or Red Jacket,
  his x mark,   [L. S.]
Onayawos, or Farmer's Brother,
  his x mark,   [L. S.]
Kaoundoowand, or Pollard, his
  x mark,   [L. S.]
Auwennausa, his x mark,   [L. S.]

Sealed and delivered in the presence of—
  John Thomson,
  James W. Stevens,
  Israel Chapin,
  Jasper Parrish, intrepreter.

TREATY WITH THE CHOCTAW, 1802.

A provisional convention entered into and made by brigadier general James Wilkinson, of the state of Maryland, commissioner for holding conferences with the Indians south of the Ohio River, in behalf of the United States, on the one part, and the whole Choctaw nation, by their chiefs, head men, and principal warriors, on the other part.

Oct. 17, 1802.

7 Stat., 73.
Ratified June 20, 1803.
Proclaimed Jan. 20, 1803.

Preamble. For the mutual accommodation of the parties, and to perpetuate that concord and friendship, which so happily subsists between them, they do hereby freely, voluntarily, and without constraint, covenant and agree,

ART. I. That the President of the United States may, at his discretion, by a commissioner or commissioners, to be appointed by him, by and with the advice and consent of the Senate of the United States, retrace, connect, and plainly remark the old line of limits, established by and between his Britannic majesty and the said Choctaw nation, which begins on the left bank of the Chickasawhay river and runs thence in an easterly direction to the right bank of the Tombigby river, terminating on the same, at a bluff well known by the name of Hach-a-Tig-geby, but it is to be clearly understood, that two commissioners, to be appointed by the said nation, from their own body, are to attend the commissioner or commissioners of the United States, who may be appointed to perform this service, for which purpose the said Choctaw nation shall be seasonably advised by the President of the United States, of the particular period at which the operation may be commenced, and the said Choctaw commissioners shall be subsisted by the United States, so long as they may be engaged on this business, and paid for their services, during the said term, at the rate of one dollar per day.

Boundary line to be re-marked, etc.

ART. II. The said line, when thus remarked and re-established, shall form the boundary between the United States and the said Choctaw nation, in that quarter, and the said Choctaw nation, for, and in consideration of one dollar, to them in hand paid by the said United States, the receipt whereof is hereby acknowledged, do hereby release to the said United States, and quit claim for ever, to all that tract of land which is included by the beforenamed line on the north, by the Chickasawhay river on the west, by the Tombigby and the Mobile rivers on the east, and by the boundary of the United States on the south.

Title to lands released to United States.

ART. III. The chiefs, head men, and warriors, of the said Choctaw nation, do hereby constitute, authorise and appoint, the chiefs and head men of the upper towns of the said nation, to make such alteration in the old boundary line near the mouth of the Yazou river, as may be found convenient, and may be done without injury to the said nation.

Alteration of old boundary.

ART. IV. This convention shall take effect and become obligatory on the contracting parties as soon as the President of the United States, by and with the advice and consent of the Senate, shall have ratified the same.

When to take effect.

In testimony whereof, the parties have hereunto set their hands and affixed their seals, at Fort Confederation, on the Tombigbee, in the Choctaw country, this 17th day of October, in the year of our Lord, one thousand eight hundred and two, and of the independence of the United States the twenty-seventh.

James Wilkinson,	[L. S.]
In behalf of the lower towns and Chicasawhay:	
Tuskona Hoopoio, his x mark,	[L. S.]
Mingo Pooskoos, his x mark,	[L. S.]
Mingo Pooskoos, 2d, his x mark,	[L. S.]
Poosha Mattahaw, his x mark,	[L. S.]

In behalf of the upper towns:
Oak Chummy, his x mark,　　　　　　　　　　　[L. S.]
Tuskee Maiaby, his x mark,　　　　　　　　　　[L. S.]
　　In behalf of the six towns and lower town:
Latalahomah, his x mark,　　　　　　　　　　　[L. S.]
Mooklahoosoopoieh, his x mark,　　　　　　　　[L. S.]
Mingo Hom Astubby, his x mark,　　　　　　　　[L. S.]
Tuskahomah, his x mark,　　　　　　　　　　　[L. S.]

Witnesses present:
　Silas Dinsmoor, Agent to the Choctaws.
　John Pitchlynn,
　Turner Brashears,
　Peter H. Naisalis,
　John Long,
　　　　　Interpreters.

TREATY WITH THE DELAWARES, ETC., 1803.

<table>
<tr><td>June 7, 1803.</td></tr>
<tr><td>7 Stat., 74.
Proclamation Dec.
26, 1803.</td></tr>
</table>

Articles of a treaty between the United States of America, and the Delawares, Shawanoes, Putawatimies, Miamies, Eel River, Weeas, Kickapoos, Piankashaws, and Kaskaskias nations of Indians.

ARTICLES of a treaty made at Fort Wayne on the Miami of the Lake, between William Henry Harrison, governor of the Indiana territory, superintendent of Indian affairs and commissioner plenipotentiary of the United States for concluding any treaty or treaties which may be found necessary with any of the Indian tribes north west of the Ohio, of the one part, and the tribes of Indians called the Delawares, Shawanoes, Putawatimies, Miamies and Kickapoos, by their chiefs and head warriors, and those of the Eel river, Weeas, Piankashaws and Kaskaskias by their agents and representatives Tuthinipee, Winnemac, Richerville and Little Turtle (who are properly authorized by the said tribes) of the other part.

Boundaries of a tract reserved to the United States described.

ARTICLE 1st. Whereas it is declared by the fourth article of the treaty of Greenville, that the United States reserve for their use the post of St. Vincennes and all the lands adjacent to which the Indian titles had been extinguished: *And whereas*, it has been found difficult to determine the precise limits of the said tract as held by the French and British governments: it is hereby agreed, that the boundaries of the said tract shall be as follow: Beginning at Point Coupee on the Wabash, and running thence by a line north seventy-eight degrees, west twelve miles, thence by a line parallel to the general course of the Wabash, until it shall be intersected by a line at right angles to the same, passing through the mouth of White river, thence by the last mentioned line across the Wabash and towards the Ohio, seventy-two miles, thence by a line north twelve degrees west, until it shall be intersected by a line at right angles to the same, passing through Point Coupee, and by the last mentioned line to the place of beginning.

United States give up all claim to adjoining lands.

ART. 2d. The United States hereby relinquish all claim which they may have had to any lands adjoining to or in the neighborhood of the tract above described.

Salt spring, etc., ceded to United States.

ART. 3d. As a mark of their regard and attachment to the United States, whom they acknowledge for their only friends and protectors, and for the consideration herein after mentioned, the said tribes do hereby relinquish and cede to the United States the great salt spring upon the Saline creek which falls into the Ohio below the mouth of the Wabash, with a quantity of land surrounding it, not exceeding four miles square, and which may be laid off in a square or oblong as the one or the other may be found most convenient to the United States: And the said United States being desirous that the Indian tribes should participate in the benefits to be derived from the said spring, hereby engage to deliver yearly and every year for the use of the said Indians, a quantity of salt not exceeding one hundred and fifty bushels, and which shall be divided among the several tribes in such manner as the general council of the chiefs may determine.

United States engage to deliver for the use of the Indians a certain quantity of salt yearly.

ART. 4th. For the considerations before mentioned and for the convenience which the said tribes will themselves derive from such establishments it is hereby agreed that as soon as the tribes called the Kickapoos, Eel River, Weeas, Piankashaws and Kaskaskias shall give their consent to the measure, the United States shall have the right of locating three tracts of lands (of such size as may be agreed upon with the last mentioned tribes) on the main road between Vincennes and Kaskaskias, and one other between Vincennes and Clarksville for the purpose of erecting houses of entertainment for the accommodation of travellers. But it is expressly understood that if the said locations are made on any of the rivers, which cross the said road, and ferries should be established on the same, that in times of high water any Indian or Indians belonging to either of the tribes who are parties to this treaty shall have the privilege of crossing such ferry toll free.

Grant to United States of sites for three houses of entertainment.

ART. 5th. Whereas there is reason to believe that if the boundary lines of the tract described in the first article should be run in the manner therein directed, that some of the settlements and locations of land made by the citizens of the United States will fall in the Indian country—It is hereby agreed that such alterations shall be made in the direction of these lines as will include them; and a quantity of land equal in quantity to what may be thus taken shall be given to the said tribes either at the east or the west end of the tract.

Provision for future alterations of the boundary.

In testimony whereof, the commissioner of the United States, and the chiefs and warriors of the Delawares, Shawanees, Pattawatimas, Miamis, and Kickapoos, and those of the Eel Rivers, Weas, Piankeshaws, and Kaskaskias, by their agents and representatives Tuthinipee, Winnemac, Richewille, and the Little Turtle, who are properly authorized, by the said tribes, have hereunto subscribed their names and affixed their seals, at fort Wayne, this seventh day of June, in the year of our Lord one thousand eight hundred and three, and of the independence of the United States the twenty-seventh.

William Henry Harrison, [L. S.]

Miamis:
Richewille, his x mark, [L. S.]
Meseekunnoghquoh, or Little Turtle, his x mark, [L. S.]
On behalf of themselves, Eel Rivers, Weas, Piankeshaws and Kaskaskias, whom they represent.
Kickapoos:
Nehmehtohah, or standing, his x mark, [L. S.]
Pashsheweha, or cat, his x mark, [L. S.]
Shawanees:
Neahmemsieeh, his x mark, [L. S.]
Pattawatimas:
Tuthinipee, his x mark, [L. S.]
Winnemac, his x mark, [L. S.]
On behalf of the Pattawatimas, and Eel Rivers, Weas, Piankeshaws, and Kaskaskias, whom they represent.

Wannangsea, or five medals, his x mark, [L. S.]
Keesas, or sun, his x mark, [L. S.]
Delawares:
Teta Buxike, his x mark, [L. S.]
Bukongehelas, his x mark, [L. S.]
Hockingpomskenn, his x mark, [L. S.]
Kechkawhanund, his x mark, [L. S.]
Shawanees:
Cuthewekasaw, or Black Hoof, his x mark, [L. S.]
Methawnasice, his x mark, [L. S.]

Signed, sealed, and delivered in the presence of—
J. R. Jones, secretary to commission,
John Gibson, secretary Indian Territory,
Tho. Pasteur, captain, First Regiment Infantry,
William Wells, interpreter,
John Johnson, United States factor,
H. Aupaumut, chief of Muhhecon,
Thomas Freeman.

The proceedings at the within treaty were faithfully interpreted by us, John Gibson and William Wells; that is, for the Delawares, John Gibson, and for the rest of the tribes, William Wells.

John Gibson,
William Wells.

TREATY WITH THE EEL RIVER, ETC., 1803.

Aug. 7, 1803.

7 Stat., 77.
Proclamation, Dec. 23, 1803.

At a council holden at Vincennes on the seventh day of August, one thousand eight hundred and three, under the direction of William Henry Harrison, governor of the Indiana territory, superintendent of Indian affairs, and commissioner plenipotentiary of the United States for concluding any treaty or treaties which may be found necessary with any of the Indian nations north west of the river Ohio, at which were present the chiefs and warriors of the Eel River, Wyandot, Piankashaw and Kaskaskia nations, and also the tribe of the Kikapoes, by their representatives, the chiefs of the Eel River nation.

Right given to United States of locating certain land.

THE fourth article of the treaty holden and concluded at Fort Wayne, on the seventh day of June, one thousand eight hundred and three, being considered, the chiefs and warriors of the said nations give their free and full consent to the same, and they do hereby relinquish and confirm to the United States the privilege and right of locating three several tracts of land of one mile square each, on the road leading from Vincennes to Kaskaskia, and also one other tract of land of one mile square on the road leading from Vincennes to Clarksville; which locations shall be made in such places on the aforesaid roads as shall best comport with the convenience and interest of the United States in the establishment of houses of entertainment for the accommodation of travellers.

In witness whereof, the said William Henry Harrison, and the said chiefs and warriors of the before-mentioned nations and tribe of Indians, have hereunto set their hands and affixed their seals, the day and year first above written.

William Henry Harrison.	[L. S.]	La Boussier, his x mark,	[L. S.]
Ka Tunga, or Charly, his x mark,	[L. S.]	Ducoigne, his x mark,	[L. S.]
Akaketa, or ploughman, his x mark,	[L. S.]	Pedagogue, his x mark,	[L. S.]
Gros Bled or big corn, his x mark,	[L. S.]	Saconquaneva, or tired legs, his x mark,	[L. S.]
Black Dog, his x mark,	[L. S.]	Little Eyes, his x mark,	[L. S.]
Puppequor, or gun, his x mark,	[L. S.]		

Signed, sealed, and delivered, in the presence of—
John Rice Jones,
B. Parke,
Joseph Barron, interpreter.

TREATY WITH THE KASKASKIA, 1803.

A treaty between the United States of America and the Kaskaskia Tribe of Indians.

Aug. 13, 1803.

7 Stat., 78.
Proclamation, Dec. 23, 1803.

ARTICLES of a treaty made at Vincennes in the Indiana territory, between William Henry Harrison, governor of the said territory, superintendent of Indian affairs and commissioner plenipotentiary of the United States for concluding any treaty or treaties which may be found necessary with any of the Indian tribes north west of the river Ohio of the one part, and the head chiefs and warriors of the Kaskaskia tribe of Indians so called, but which tribe is the remains and rightfully represent all the tribes of the Illinois Indians, originally called the Kaskaskia, Mitchigamia, Cahokia and Tamaroi of the other part:

ARTICLE 1st. Whereas from a variety of unfortunate circumstances the several tribes of Illinois Indians are reduced to a very small number, the remains of which have been long consolidated and known by the name of the Kaskaskia tribe, and finding themselves unable to occupy the extensive tract of country which of right belongs to them and which was possessed by their ancestors for many generations, the chiefs and warriors of the said tribe being also desirous of procuring the means of improvement in the arts of civilized life, and a more certain and effectual support for their women and children, have, for the considerations hereinafter mentioned, relinquished and by these presents do relinquish and cede to the United States all the lands in the Illinois country, which the said tribe has heretofore possessed, or which they may rightfully claim, reserving to themselves however the tract of about three hundred and fifty acres near the town of Kaskaskia, which they have always held and which was secured to them by the act of Congress of the third day of March, one thousand seven hundred and ninety-one, and also the right of locating one other tract of twelve hundred and eighty acres within the bounds of that now ceded, which two tracts of land shall remain to them forever. *(Cession to the United States.)*

ART. 2d. The United States will take the Kaskaskia tribe under their immediate care and patronage, and will afford them a protection as effectual against the other Indian tribes and against all other persons whatever as is enjoyed by their own citizens. And the said Kaskaskia tribe do hereby engage to refrain from making war or giving any insult or offence to any other Indian tribe or to any foreign nation, without having first obtained the approbation and consent of the United States. *(United States to take the Kaskaskias under their protection, etc.)*

ART. 3d. The annuity heretofore given by the United States to the said tribe shall be increased to one thousand dollars, which is to be paid to them either in money, merchandise, provisions or domestic animals, at the option of the said tribe: and when the said annuity or any part thereof is paid in merchandise, it is to be delivered to them either at Vincennes, Fort Massac or Kaskaskia, and the first cost of the goods in the sea-port where they may be procured is alone to be charged to the said tribe free from the cost of transportation, or any other contingent expense. Whenever the said tribe may choose to receive money, provisions or domestic animals for the whole or in part of the said annuity, the same shall be delivered at the town of Kaskaskia. The United States will also cause to be built a house suitable for the accommodation of the chief of the said tribe, and will enclose for their use a field not exceeding one hundred acres with a good and sufficient fence. *And whereas,* The greater part of the said tribe have been baptised and received into the Catholic church to which they are much attached, the United States will give annually for seven *(Former annuity to be increased; how to be paid.)* *(A house for the chief to be built, and a field for the tribe to be inclosed.)*

Annual sum to be paid to a Catholic priest, etc.

years one hundred dollars towards the support of a priest of that religion, who will engage to perform for the said tribe the duties of his office and also to instruct as many of their children as possible in the rudi-

A sum to be given by United States for erecting a church.

ments of literature. And the United States will further give the sum of three hundred dollars to assist the said tribe in the erection of a church. The stipulations made in this and the preceding article, together with the sum of five hundred and eighty dollars, which is now paid or assured to be paid for the said tribe for the purpose of procuring some necessary articles, and to relieve them from debts which they have heretofore contracted, is considered as a full and ample compensation for the relinquishment made to the United States in the first article.

Right of dividing annuity reserved to United States.

ART. 4th. The United States reserve to themselves the right at any future period of dividing the annuity now promised to the said tribe amongst the several families thereof, reserving always a suitable sum for the great chief and his family.

ART. 5th. And to the end that the United States may be enabled to fix with the other Indian tribes a boundary between their respective claims, the chiefs and head warriors of the said Kaskaskia tribe do

Boundaries fixed.

hereby declare that their rightful claim is as follows, viz: Beginning at the confluence of the Ohio and the Mississippi, thence up the Ohio to the mouth of the Saline creek, about twelve miles below the mouth of the Wabash, thence along the dividing ridge between the said creek and the Wabash until it comes to the general dividing ridge between the waters which fall into the Wabash, and those which fall into the Kaskaskia river; and thence along the said ridge until it reaches the waters which fall into the Illinois river, thence in a direct course to the mouth of the Illinois river, and thence down the Mississippi to the beginning.

Indians may hunt, etc., on ceded lands.

ART. 6th. As long as the lands which have been ceded by this treaty shall continue to be the property of the United States, the said tribe shall have the privilege of living and hunting upon them in the same manner that they have hitherto done.

When to take effect.

ART. 7th. This treaty is to be in force and binding upon the said parties, as soon as it shall be ratified by the President and Senate of the United States.

In witness whereof, the said commissioner plenipotentiary, and the head chiefs and warriors of the said Kaskaskia tribe of Indians, have hereunto set their hands and affixed their seals, the thirteenth day of August, in the year of our Lord one thousand eight hundred and three, and of the Independence of the United States the twenty-eighth.

William Henry Harrison,	[L. s.]	The mark x of Ocksinga, a Mitch-	
The mark x of Jean Baptiste Du-		igamian,	[L. s.]
coigne,	[L. s.]	The mark x of Keetinsa, a Cahok-	
The mark x of Pedagogue,	[L. s.]	ian,	[L. s.]
The mark x of Micolas or Nicholas,	[L. s.]	Louis Decoucigne,	[L. s.]

Sealed and delivered in the presence of—

    J. R. Jones, secretary to commission.
    H. Vanderburgh, judge of Indiana Territory.
    T. F. Rivet, Indian Miss.
    Vigo, colonel Knox County Militia.
    Cor. Lyman, Captain First Infantry Regiment.
    Jas. Johnson, of Indiana Territory.
    B. Parke, of the Indiana Territory.
    Joseph Barron, interpreter.

TREATY WITH THE CHOCTAW, 1803.

To whom these presents shall come,

KNOW YE, That the undersigned, commissioners plenipotentiary of the United States of America, of the one part, and of the whole Choctaw nation of the other part, being duly authorised by the President of the United States, and by the chiefs and headmen of the said nation, do hereby establish in conformity to the convention of Fort Confederation, for the line of demarkation recognized in the said convention, the following metes and bounds, viz.: Beginning in the channel of the Hatchee Comesa, or Wax river, at the point where the line of limits, between the United States and Spain crosseth the same, thence up the channel of said river to the confluence of the Chickasaw-Hay and Buckhatannee rivers, thence up the channel of the Buckhatannee to Bogue Hooma or Red creek, thence up the said creek to a Pine tree standing on the left bank of the same, and blazed on two of its sides, about twelve links southwest of an old trading path, leading from the town of Mobile to the Hewanee towns, much worn, but not in use at the present time:—From this tree we find the following bearings and distances, viz.: south fifty four degrees thirty minutes, west, one chain, one link a black gum, north thirty nine degrees east one chain seventy five links to a water oak; thence with the old British line of partition in its various inflections, to a Mulberry post, planted on the right bank of the main branch of Sintee Bogue or Snake creek, where it makes a sharp turn to the south east, a large broken top Cypress-tree standing near the opposite bank of the creek, which is about three poles wide, thence down the said creek to the Tombigby river, thence down the Tombigby and Mobile rivers, to the above mentioned line of limits between the United States and Spain, and with the same to the point of beginning: And we, the said commissioners plenipotentiary, do ratify and confirm the said line of demarkation, and do recognise and acknowledge the same to be the boundary which shall separate and distinguish the land ceded to the United States, between the Tombigby, Mobile and Pascagola rivers, from that which has not been ceded by the said Choctaw nation.

In testimony whereof, we hereunto affix our hands and seals, this thirty-first day of August, in the year of our Lord one thousand eight hundred and three, to triplicates of this tenor and date. Done at Hoe-Buckin-too-pa, the day and year above written, and in the twenty-seventh year of the independence of the United States.

Aug. 31, 1803.
7 Stat., 80.
Proclamation, Dec. 26, 1803.

James Wilkinson,	[L. S.]
Mingo Pooscoos, his x mark,	[L. S.]
Alatala Hooma, his x mark,	[L. S.]

Witnesses present:
　　Young Gains, interpreter,
　　John Bowyer, captain Second United States Regiment,
　　Joseph Chambers, United States factor.

We the commissioners of the Choctaw nation duly appointed and the chiefs of the said nation who reside on the Tombigby river, next to Sintee Bogue, do acknowledge to have received from the United States of America, by the hands of Brigadier General James Wilkinson, as a consideration in full for the confirmation of the above concession, the following articles, viz.: fifteen pieces of strouds, three rifles, one hundred and fifty blankets, two hundred and fifty pounds of powder, two hundred and fifty pounds of lead, one bridle, one man's saddle, and one black silk handkerchief.

> Mingo Pooscoos, his x mark,   [L. S.]
> Alatala Hooma, his x mark,   [L. S.]
>   Commissioners of the Choctaw nation.
>
> Pio Mingo, his x mark,   [L. S.]
> Pasa Mastubby Mingo, his x mark,   [L. S.]
> Tappena Oakchia, his x mark,   [L. S.]
> Tuskenung Cooche, his x mark,   [L. S.]
> Cussoonuckchia, his x mark,   [L. S.]
> Pushapia, his x mark,   [L. S.]
>   Chiefs residing on the Tombigbee near to St. Stephens.

Witnesses present:
   Young Gains, interpreter,
   John Bowyer, Captain Second United States Regiment,
   Joseph Chambers, United States factor.

TREATY WITH THE DELAWARES, 1804.

Aug. 18, 1804.

7 Stat., 81.
Ratified Jan. 21, 1805.
Proclaimed Feb. 14, 1805.

A treaty between the United States of America and the Delaware tribe of Indians.

THE Delaware tribe of Indians finding that the annuity which they receive from the United States, is not sufficient to supply them with the articles which are necessary for their comfort and convenience, and afford the means of introducing amongst them the arts of civilized life, and being convinced that the extensiveness of the country they possess, by giving an opportunity to their hunting parties to ramble to a great distance from their towns, is the principal means of retarding this desirable event; and the United States being desirous to connect their settlements on the Wabash with the state of Kentucky: therefore the said United States, by William Henry Harrison, governor of the Indiana territory, superintendent of Indian affairs, and their commissioner plenipotentiary for treating with the Indian tribes northwest of the Ohio river; and the said tribe of Indians, by their sachems, chiefs, and head warriors, have agreed to the following articles, which when ratified by the President of the United States, by and with the advice and consent of the Senate, shall be binding on the said parties.

Cession to the United States.

ARTICLE 1. The said Delaware tribe, for the considerations hereinafter mentioned, relinquishes to the United States forever, all their right and title to the tract of country which lies between the Ohio and Wabash rivers, and below the tract ceded by the treaty of Fort Wayne, and the road leading from Vincennes to the falls of Ohio.

Additional annuity to be paid to the Delawares.

Provision for teaching them agricultural and domestic arts, etc.

ART. 2. The said tribe shall receive from the United States for ten years, an additional annuity of three hundred dollars, which is to be exclusively appropriated to the purpose of ameliorating their condition and promoting their civilization. Suitable persons shall be employed at the expense of the United States to teach them to make fences, cultivate the earth, and such of the domestic arts as are adapted to their situation; and a further sum of three hundred dollars shall be appropriated annually for five years to this object. The United States will cause to be delivered to them in the course of the next spring, horses fit for draft, cattle, hogs and implements of husbandry to the amount of four hundred dollars. The preceding stipulations together with goods to the amount of eight hundred dollars which is now delivered to the said tribe, (a part of which is to be appropriated to the satisfying

Preceding stipulations, how to be considered.

certain individuals of the said tribe, whose horses have been taken by white people) is to be considered as full compensation for the relinquishment made in the first article.

ART. 3. As there is great reason to believe that there are now in the possession of the said tribe, several horses which have been stolen from citizens of the United States, the chiefs who represent the said tribe are to use their utmost endeavors to have the said horses forthwith delivered to the superintendent of Indian affairs or such persons as he may appoint to receive them. And as the United States can place the utmost reliance on the honor and integrity of those chiefs who have manifested a punctilious regard to the engagements entered into at the treaty of Grenville, it is agreed that in relation to such of the horses stolen as aforesaid, but which have died or been removed beyond the reach of the chiefs, the United States will compensate the owners for the loss of them without deducting from the annuity of the said tribe the amount of what may be paid in this way. But it is expressly understood that this provision is not to extend to any horses which have been stolen within the course of twelve months preceding the date hereof. *Stolen horses to be restored.*

ART. 4. The said tribe having exhibited to the above-named commissioner of the United States sufficient proof of their right to all the country which lies between the Ohio and White river, and the Miami tribe who were the original proprietors of the upper part of that country having explicitly acknowledged the title of the Delawares at the general council held at Fort Wayne in the month of June, 1803, the said United States will in future consider the Delawares as the rightful owners of all the country which is bounded by the white river on the north, the Ohio on the south, the general boundary line running from the mouth of the Kentucky river on the east, and the tract ceded by this treaty, and that ceded by the treaty of Fort Wayne, on the west and south west. *Right of the Delawares to lands, etc.*

ART. 5. As the Piankishaw tribe have hitherto obstinately persisted in refusing to recognize the title of the Delawares to the tract of country ceded by this treaty, the United States will negociate with them and will endeavor to settle the matter, in an amicable way; but should they reject the propositions that may be made to them on this subject, and should the United States not think proper to take possession of the said country without their consent; the stipulations and promises herein made on behalf the United States, shall be null and void. *Stipulation that the United States will treat with the Piankeshaws for an acknowledgment of the title of the Delawares, etc.*

ART. 6. As the road from Vincennes to Clark's grant will form a very inconvenient boundary, and as it is the intention of the parties to these presents that the whole of the said road shall be within the tract ceded to the United States, it is agreed that the boundary in that quarter shall be a straight line to be drawn parallel to the course of the said road from the eastern boundary of the tracts ceded by the treaty of Fort Wayne to Clark's grant; but the said line is not to pass at a greater distance than half a mile from the most northerly bend of said road. *Boundaries, etc.*

In witness whereof, the commissioner plenipotentiary of the United States, and the chiefs and head men of the said tribe, have hereunto set their hands and affixed their seals.

Done at Vincennes, the eighteenth day of August, in the year of our Lord one thousand eight hundred and four; and of the independence of the United States the twenty-ninth.

William Henry Harrison,	[L. S.]
Jeta Buxika, his x mark,	[L. S.]
Bokongehelas, his x mark,	[L. S.]
Alimee, or Geo. White Eyes, his x mark,	[L. S.]
Hocking Pomskann, his x mark,	[L. S.]
Tomaguee, or the beaver, his x mark,	[L. S.]

Signed, sealed, and delivered in the presence of—
John Gibson, secretary to commission.
Henry Vanderburg, judge of Indiana Territory.
Vigo, colonel of Knox County, I. T. Militia.
B. Parker, attorney-general of the Indiana Territory.
John Rice Jones, of Indiana Territory.
Robert Buntin, prothonotary of Knox County, Indiana Territory.
Geo. Wallace, jr., of Indiana Territory.
Antoine Marchal, of I. T.
Joseph Barron, interpreter.
Edward Hempstead, attorney at law.

I do certify, that each and every article of the foregoing treaty was carefully explained, and precisely interpreted, by me, to the Delaware chiefs who have signed the same.

John Gibson.

TREATY WITH THE PIANKESHAW, 1804.

Aug. 27, 1804.

7 Stat., 83.
Ratified Jan. 21, 1805.
Proclaimed Feb. 6, 1805.

A treaty between the United States of America, and the Piankeshaw tribe of Indians.

THE President of the United States, by William Henry Harrison, Governor of the Indiana territory, superintendent of Indian affairs; and commissioner plenipotentiary of the United States, for concluding any treaty or treaties which may be found necessary with any of the Indian tribes north west of the river Ohio; and the chiefs and head men of the Piankeshaw tribe, have agreed to the following articles, which when ratified by the President of the United States, by and with the advice and consent of the Senate, shall be binding upon the said parties.

Cession of land to the United States.

ARTICLE 1. The Piankeshaw tribe relinquishes, and cedes to the United States for ever, all that tract of country which lies between the Ohio and Wabash rivers, and below Clark's grant; and the tract called the Vincennes tract, which was ceded by the treaty of Fort Wayne, and a line connecting the said tract and grant, to be drawn parallel to the general course of the road leading from Vincennes to the falls of the Ohio, so as not to pass more than half a mile to the northward of the most northerly bend of said road.

Acknowledgment of the right of the Kaskaskias to sell certain lands.

ARTICLE 2. The Piankeshaw tribe acknowledges explicitly the right of the Kaskaskia tribe to sell the country which they have lately ceded to the United States, and which is separated from the lands of the Piankeshaws by the ridge or high land which divides the waters of the Wabash from the waters of the Saline creek; and by that which divides the waters of the said Wabash from those which flow into the Au-vase and other branches of the Mississippi.

Additional annuity to be paid to the Piankeshaws for ten years.

ARTICLE 3. An additional annuity of two hundred dollars shall be paid by the United States to the said tribe for ten years, in money, merchandise, provisions, or domestic animals, and implements of husbandry, at the option of the said tribe; and this annuity, together with goods to the value of seven hundred dollars, which are now delivered to them by the commissioner of the United States, is considered as a full compensation for the above-mentioned relinquishment.

Right reserved to United States of dividing the annuity, etc.

ARTICLE 4. The United States reserve to themselves the right of dividing the whole annuity which they pay to the said tribe amongst the families which compose the same; allowing always a due proportion for the chiefs: And the said chiefs whenever the President of the United States may require it, shall, upon proper notice being given, assemble their tribe, for the purpose of effecting this arrangement.

In witness whereof, the commissioner plenipotentiary of the United States, and the chiefs and head men of the said tribe, have hereunto set their hands and affixed their seals.

Done at Vincennes, in the Indiana territory, the twenty-seventh day of August, in the year of our Lord one thousand eight hundred and four, and of the independence of the United States the twenty-ninth.

William Henry Harrison,	[L. S.]
Wabochquinke, la gros bled, or big corn, his x mark,	[L. S.]
Swekania, trois fesse, or three thighs, his x mark,	[L. S.]
Makatewelama, chien noir, or black dog, his x mark,	[L. S.]
Alemoin, le chien, or the dog, his x mark,	[L. S.]
Kekelanquagoh, or lightning, his x mark,	[L. S.]

Signed, sealed and delivered in presence of—

John Gibson, secretary to the commission,
John Griffin, one of the judges of the Territory of Indiana,
Henry Vanderburg, one of the judges of Indiana Territory,
B. Parke, attorney general of the Territory of Indiana,
William Prince, sheriff of Knox county, Indiana Ter.,

George Wallace, jr., of the Indiana Territory,
Peter Jones, of Knox county, Indiana Ter.,
Edward Hempstead, attorney at law, Indiana Ter.,
Abraham F. Snapp,
Joseph Barron, interpreter.

I do certify, that each and every article of the foregoing treaty was carefully explained, and precisely interpreted, by me, to the Piankeshaw chiefs who have signed the same.

Joseph Barron, interpreter.

TREATY WITH THE CHEROKEE, 1804.

Articles of a treaty between the United States of America and the Cherokee Indians.

Oct. 24, 1804.
7 Stat., 228.
Proclamation, May 17, 1824.

DANIEL SMITH and Return J. Meigs, being commissioned by Thomas Jefferson, President of the United States, with powers of acting in behalf of the said United States, in arranging certain matters with the Cherokee nation of Indians; and the underwritten principal Chiefs, representing the said nation, having met the said Commissioners in a conference at Tellico, and having taken into their consideration certain propositions made to them by the said Commissioners of the United States; the parties aforesaid, have unanimously agreed and stipulated, as is definitely expressed in the following articles:

ARTICLE 1st. For the considerations hereinafter expressed, the Cherokee nation relinquish and cede to the United States, a tract of land bounding, southerly, on the boundary line between the State of Georgia and the said Cherokee nation, beginning at a point on the said boundary line northeasterly of the most northeast plantation, in the settlement known by the name of Wafford's Settlement, and running at right angles with the said boundary line four miles into the Cherokee land; thence at right angles southwesterly and parallel to the first mentioned boundary line, so far as that a line, to be run at right angles southerly to the said first mentioned boundary line, shall include, in this cession, all the plantations in Wafford's settlement, so called, as aforesaid.

Cession of land by Cherokees.

ARTICLE 2d. For, and in consideration of, the relinquishment and cession, as expressed in the first article, the United States, upon signing the present Treaty, shall cause to be delivered to the Cherokees, useful goods, wares, and merchandise, to the amount of five thousand dollars, or that sum in money, at the option (timely signified) of the

Useful goods to amount of $5,000 to be paid them as an annuity.

Cherokees, and shall, also, cause to be delivered, annually, to them, other useful goods to the amount of one thousand dollars, or money to that amount, at the option of the Cherokees, timely notice thereof being given, in addition to the annuity, heretofore stipulated, and to be delivered at the usual time of their receiving their annuity.

In witness of all and everything, herein determined, between the United States and the Cherokee nation, the parties have hereunto set their hands and seals, in the garrison of Tellico, on Cherokee ground, within the United States, this twenty-fourth day of October, in the year one thousand eight hundred and four, and in the twenty-ninth year of the independence and sovereignty of the United States.

Daniel Smith,	[L. s.]	Path Killer, his x mark,	[L. s.]
Return J. Meigs,	[L. s.]	Tagustiskee, his x mark,	[L. s.]
Tolluntuskie, his x mark,	[L. s.]	Tulio, his x mark,	[L. s.]
Broom, his x mark,	[L. s.]	Sour Mush, his x mark,	[L. s.]
J. McLamore, his x mark,	[L. s.]	Keatehee, his x mark,	[L. s.]
Quotequeskee, his x mark,	[L. s.]	James Vann.	[L. s.]

Witnesses:

Rob. Purdy, secretary,
John McKee,
Jno. Campbell, captain, second U. S. Regiment, Com.,
John Brahan, lieutenant, second Regiment, infantry,

Thos. J. Van Dyke, Sur. Mate.,
Wm. Charp,
Hinchey Pettway,
Wm. L. Lovely, assistant agent,
Ch. Hicks, interpreter.

TREATY WITH THE SAUK AND FOXES, 1804.

Nov. 3, 1804.

7 Stat., 84.
Ratified Jan. 25, 1805.
Proclaimed Feb. 21, 1805.

A treaty between the United States of America and the United tribes of Sac and Fox Indians.

ARTICLES of a treaty made at St. Louis in the district of Louisiana between William Henry Harrison, governor of the Indiana territory and of the district of Louisiana, superintendent of Indian affairs for the said territory and district, and commissioner plenipotentiary of the United States for concluding any treaty or treaties which may be found necessary with any of the north western tribes of Indians of the one part, and the chiefs and head men of the united Sac and Fox tribes of the other part.

Indians taken under protection of United States.

ARTICLE 1. The United States receive the united Sac and Fox tribes into their friendship and protection, and the said tribes agree to consider themselves under the protection of the United States, and of no other power whatsoever.

Boundaries.

ART. 2. The general boundary line between the lands of the United States and of the said Indian tribes shall be as follows, to wit: Beginning at a point on the Missouri river opposite to the mouth of the Gasconade river; thence in a direct course so as to strike the river Jeffreon at the distance of thirty miles from its mouth, and down the said Jeffreon to the Mississippi, thence up the Mississippi to the mouth of the Ouisconsing river and up the same to a point which shall be thirty-six miles in a direct line from the mouth of the said river, thence by a direct line to the point where the Fox river (a branch of the Illinois) leaves the small lake called Sakaegan, thence down the Fox river to the Illinois river, and down the same to the Mississippi. And the said tribes, for and in consideration of the friendship and protection of the United States which is now extended to them, of the goods (to the value of two thousand two hundred and thirty-four dollars and fifty cents) which are now delivered, and of the annuity hereinafter stipulated to be paid, do hereby cede and relinquish forever to the United States, all the lands included within the above-described boundary

ART. 3. In consideration of the cession and relinquishment of land made in the preceding article, the United States will deliver to the said tribes at the town of St. Louis or some other convenient place on the Mississippi yearly and every year goods suited to the circumstances of the Indians of the value of one thousand dollars (six hundred of which are intended for the Sacs and four hundred for the Foxes) reckoning that value at the first cost of the goods in the city or place in the United States where they shall be procured. And if the said tribes shall hereafter at an annual delivery of the goods aforesaid, desire that a part of their annuity should be furnished in domestic animals, implements of husbandry and other utensils convenient for them, or in compensation to useful artificers who may reside with or near them, and be employed for their benefit, the same shall at the subsequent annual delivery be furnished accordingly.

Goods to be delivered to the Indian tribes at St. Louis every year.

ART. 4. The United States will never interrupt the said tribes in the possession of the lands which they rightfully claim, but will on the contrary protect them in the quiet enjoyment of the same against their own citizens and against all other white persons who may intrude upon them. And the said tribes do hereby engage that they will never sell their lands or any part thereof to any sovereign power, but the United States, nor to the citizens or subjects of any other sovereign power, nor to the citizens of the United States.

Indians to be secured in their possessions, etc.

ART. 5. Lest the friendship which is now established between the United States and the said Indian tribes should be interrupted by the misconduct of individuals, it is hereby agreed that for injuries done by individuals no private revenge or retaliation shall take place, but, instead thereof, complaints shall be made by the party injured to the other—by the said tribes or either of them to the superintendent of Indian affairs or one of his deputies, and by the superintendent or other person appointed by the President, to the chiefs of the said tribes. And it shall be the duty of the said chiefs upon complaint being made as aforesaid to deliver up the person or persons against whom the complaint is made, to the end that he or they may be punished agreeably to the laws of the state or territory where the offence may have been committed; and in like manner if any robbery, violence or murder shall be committed on any Indian or Indians belonging to the said tribes or either of them, the person or persons so offending shall be tried, and if found guilty, punished in the like manner as if the injury had been done to a white man. And it is further agreed, that the chiefs of the said tribes shall, to the utmost of their power exert themselves to recover horses or other property which may be stolen from any citizen or citizens of the United States by any individual or individuals of their tribes, and the property so recovered shall be forthwith delivered to the superintendent or other person authorized to receive it, that it may be restored to the proper owner; and in cases where the exertions of the chiefs shall be ineffectual in recovering the property stolen as aforesaid, if sufficient proof can be obtained that such property was actually stolen by any Indian or Indians belonging to the said tribes or either of them, the United States may deduct from the annuity of the said tribes a sum equal to the value of the property which has been stolen. And the United States hereby guarantee to any Indian or Indians of the said tribes a full indemnification for any horses or other property which may be stolen from them by any of their citizens; provided that the property so stolen cannot be recovered and that sufficient proof is produced that it was actually stolen by a citizen of the United States.

Retaliation restrained.

Offenders on both sides to be apprehended and punished.

Stolen horses to be restored to the proper owner.

ART. 6. If any citizen of the United States or other white person should form a settlement upon lands which are the property of the Sac and Fox tribes, upon complaint being made thereof to the superintendent or other person having charge of the affairs of the Indians, such intruder shall forthwith be removed.

Intruders on Indian lands to be removed.

Indians may hunt on lands ceded to United States.

ART. 7. As long as the lands which are now ceded to the United States remain their property, the Indians belonging to the said tribes, shall enjoy the privilege of living and hunting upon them.

None but authorized traders to reside among the Saukes and Foxes.

ART. 8. As the laws of the United States regulating trade and intercourse with the Indian tribes, are already extended to the country inhabited by the Saukes and Foxes, and as it is provided by those laws that no person shall reside as a trader in the Indian country without a license under the hand [and] seal of the superintendent of Indian affairs, or other person appointed for the purpose by the President, the said tribes do promise and agree that they will not suffer any trader to reside amongst them without such license; and that they will from time to time give notice to the superintendent or to the agent for their tribes of all the traders that may be in their country.

Trading house or factory to be established.

ART. 9. In order to put a stop to the abuses and impositions which are practiced upon the said tribes by the private traders, the United States will at a convenient time establish a trading house or factory where the individuals of the said tribes can be supplied with goods at a more reasonable rate than they have been accustomed to procure them.

Peace to be made between certain tribes under the direction of United States.

ART. 10. In order to evince the sincerity of their friendship and affection for the United States and a respectful deference for their advice by an act which will not only be acceptable to them but to the common Father of all the nations of the earth; the said tribes do hereby solemnly promise and agree that they will put an end to the bloody war which has heretofore raged between their tribes and those of the Great and Little Osages. And for the purpose of burying the tomahawk and renewing the friendly intercourse between themselves and the Osages, a meeting of their respective chiefs shall take place, at which under the direction of the above-named commissioner or the agent of Indian affairs residing at St. Louis, an adjustment of all their differences shall be made and peace established upon a firm and lasting basis.

Cession of land for the establishment of a military post.

ART. 11. As it is probable that the government of the United States will establish a military post at or near the mouth of the Ouisconsing river; and as the land on the lower side of the river may not be suitable for that purpose, the said tribes hereby agree that a fort may be built either on the upper side of the Ouisconsing or on the right bank of the Mississippi, as the one or the other may be found most convenient; and a tract of land not exceeding two miles square shall be given

Traders, etc., to be free from any toll or exaction.

for that purpose. And the said tribes do further agree, that they will at all times allow to traders and other persons travelling through their country under the authority of the United States a free and safe passage for themselves and their property of every description. And that for such passage they shall at no time and on no account whatever be subject to any toll or exaction.

Treaty, when to take effect.

ART. 12. This treaty shall take effect and be obligatory on the contracting parties as soon as the same shall have been ratified by the President by and with the advice and consent of the Senate of the United States.

In testimony whereof, the said William Henry Harrison, and the chiefs and head men of the said Sac and Fox tribes, have hereunto set their hands and affixed their seals.

Done at Saint Louis, in the district of Louisiana, on the third day of November, one thousand eight hundred and four, and of the independence of the United States the twenty-ninth.

William Henry Harrison,	[L. S.]
Layauvois, or Laiyurva, his x mark,	[L. S.]
Pashepaho, or the giger, his x mark,	[L. S.]
Quashquame, or jumping fish, his x mark,	[L. S.]
Outchequaka, or sun fish, his x mark,	[L. S.]
Hahshequarhiqua, or the bear, his x mark,	[L. S.]

In presence of (the words "a branch of the Illinois," in the third line of the second article, and the word "forever," in the fifth line of the same article, being first interlined)—

Wm. Prince, secretary to the commissioner,
John Griffin, one of the judges of the Indiana Territory,
J. Bruff, major artillery, United States,
Amos Stoddard, captain, Corps Artillerists,
P. Chouteau,
Vigo,
S. Warrel, lieutenant, United States Artillery,
D. Delamay.
Joseph Barron,
Hypolite Bolen, his x mark,
     Sworn interpreters.

ADDITIONAL ARTICLE.

It is agreed that nothing in this treaty contained, shall affect the claim of any individual or individuals who may have obtained grants of land from the Spanish government, and which are not included within the general boundary line laid down in this treaty, provided that such grant have at any time been made known to the said tribes and recognized by them.

TREATY WITH THE WYANDOT, ETC., 1805.

A treaty between the United States of America, and the sachems, chiefs, and warriors of the Wyandot, Ottawa, Chipawa, Munsee and Delaware, Shawanee, and Pottawatima nations, holden at Fort Industry, on the Miami of the lake, on the fourth day of July, Anno Domini, one thousand eight hundred and five.

July 4, 1805.

7 Stat., 87.
Proclamation, Apr. 24, 1806.

ARTICLE I. The said Indian nations do again acknowledge themselves and all their tribes, to be in friendship with, and under the protection of the United States. — *Indians acknowledge protection of United States.*

ART. II. The boundary line between the United States, and the nations aforesaid, shall in future be a meridian line drawn north and south, through a boundary to be erected on the south shore of lake Erie, one hundred and twenty miles due west of the west boundary line of the state of Pennsylvania, extending north until it intersects the boundary line of the United States, and extending south it intersects a line heretofore established by the treaty of Grenville. — *Boundary line established.*

ART. III. The Indian nations aforesaid, for the consideration of friendship to the United States, and the sums of money hereinafter mentioned, to be paid annually to the Wyandot, Shawanee, Munsee and Delaware nations, have ceded and do hereby cede and relinquish to said United States for ever, all the lands belonging to said United States, lying east of the aforesaid line, bounded southerly and easterly by the line established by said treaty of Grenville, and northerly by the northernmost part of the forty first degree of north latitude. — *Cession from the Indians.*

ART. IV. The United States, to preserve harmony, manifest their liberality, and in consideration of the cession made in the preceding article, will, every year forever hereafter, at Detroit, or some other convenient place, pay and deliver to the Wyandot, Munsee, and Delaware nations, and those of the Shawanee and Seneca nations who reside with the Wyandots, the sum of eight hundred and twenty five dollars, current money of the United States, and the further sum of one hundred and seventy five dollars, making in the whole an annuity of one thousand dollars; which last sum of one hundred and seventy five dollars, has been secured to the President, in trust for said nations, by the Connecticut land company, and by the company incorporated by the name of "the proprietors of the half million acres of land lying — *Annuity stipulated to be paid by the United States.*

south of lake Erie, called Sufferer's Land," payable annually as aforesaid, and to be divided between said nations, from time to time, in such proportions as said nations, with the approbation of the President, shall agree.

Proportions to which the Indian tribes are entitled out of the purchase of the Connecticut land company, etc.

ART. V. To prevent all misunderstanding hereafter, it is to be expressly remembered, that the Ottawa and Chipawa nations, and such of the Pottawatima nation as reside on the river Huron of lake Erie, and in the neighborhood thereof, have received from the Connecticut land company, and the company incorporated by the name of "the proprietors of the half million acres of land lying south of Lake Erie, called Sufferer's Land," the sum of four thousand dollars in hand, and have secured to the President of the United States, in trust for them, the further sum of twelve thousand dollars, payable in six annual instalments of two thousand each; which several sums is the full amount of their proportion of the purchases effected by this treaty, and also by a treaty with said companies bearing even date herewith; which proportions were agreed on and concluded by the whole of said nations in their general council; which several sums, together with two thousand nine hundred and sixteen dollars and sixty seven cents, secured to the President, to raise said sum of one hundred and seventy five dollars annuity as aforesaid, is the amount of the consideration paid by the agents of the Connecticut Reserve, for the cession of their lands.

Indians at liberty to fish and hunt in ceded territories.

ART. VI. The said Indian nations, parties to this treaty, shall be at liberty to fish and hunt within the territory and lands which they have now ceded to the United States, so long as they shall demean themselves peaceably.

In witness whereof, Charles Jouett, esquire, a commissioner on the part of the United States, and the sachems, chiefs, and warriors, of the Indian nations aforesaid, have hereto set their hands and seals.

Charles Jouett,   [L. S.]
  Ottawa:
Nekeik, or Little Otter, his x mark,   [L. S.]
Kawachewan, or Eddy, his x mark,   [L. S.]
Mechimenduch, or Big Bowl, his x
  mark,   [L. S.]
Aubaway, his x mark,   [L. S.]
Ogonse, his x mark,   [L. S.]
Sawgamaw, his x mark,   [L. S.]
Tusquagan, or McCarty, his x mark, [L. S.]
Tondawganie, or the Dog, his x
  mark,   [L. S.]
Ashawet, his x mark,   [L. S.]
  Chippewa:
Macquettoquet, or Little Bear, his
  x mark,   [L. S.]
Quitchonequit, or Big Cloud, his x
  mark,   [L. S.]
Queoonequetwabaw, his x mark,   [L. S.]
Oscaquassanu, or Young Boy, his x
  mark,   [L. S.]
Monimack, or Cat Fish, his x mark, [L. S.]
Tonquish, his x mark,   [L. S.]
  Pattawatima:
Noname, his x mark,   [L. S.]
Mogawh, his x mark,   [L. S.]

Wyandot:
Tarhee, or the Crane, his x mark,   [L. S.]
Miere, or Walk in Water, his x
  mark,   [L. S.]
Thateyyanayoh, or Leather Lips,
  his x mark,   [L. S.]
Harrowenyou, or Cherokee Boy,
  his x mark,   [L. S.]
Tschauendah, his x mark,   [L. S.]
Tahunehawettee, or Adam Brown,
  his x mark,   [L. S.]
Shawrunthie, his x mark,   [L. S.]
  Munsee and Delaware:
Puckconsittond, his x mark,   [L. S.]
Paahmehelot, his x mark,   [L. S.]
Pamoxet, or Armstrong, his x
  mark,   [L. S.]
Pappellelond, or Beaver Hat, his x
  mark,   [L. S.]
  Shawanee:
Weyapurseawaw, or Blue Jacket,
  his x mark,   [L. S.]
Cutheaweasaw, or Black Hoff, his x
  mark,   [L. S.]
Auonasechla, or Civil Man, his x
  mark,   [L. S.]
Isaac Peters, his x mark,   [L. S.]

In presence of—
    Wm. Dean, C. F. L. C.
    J. B. Mower,
    Jasper Parrish,
    Whitmore Knaggs,
    William Walker,
              Interpreters.
    Israel Ruland,
    E. Brush.

TREATY WITH THE CHICKASAW, 1805.

Articles of arrangement made and concluded in the Chickasaw country, between James Robertson and Silas Dinsmoor, commissioners of the United States of the one part, and the Mingo chiefs and warriors of the Chickasaw nation of Indians on the other part.

July 23, 1805.

7 Stat., 89.
Ratified May 22, 1807.
Proclaimed May 23, 1807.

ART. I. WHEREAS the Chickasaw nation of Indians have been for some time embarrassed by heavy debts due to their merchants and traders, and being destitute of funds to effect important improvements in their country, they have agreed and do hereby agree to cede to the United States, and forever quit claim to the tract of country included within the following bounds, to wit: beginning on the left bank of Ohio, at the point where the present Indian boundary adjoins the same, thence down the left bank of Ohio to the Tennessee river, thence up the main channel of the Tennessee river to the mouth of Duck river; thence up the left bank of Duck river to the Columbian highway or road leading from Nashville to Natchez, thence along the said road to the ridge dividing the waters running into Duck river from those running into Buffaloe river, thence easterly along the said ridge to the great ridge dividing the waters running into the main Tennessee river from those running into Buffaloe river near the main source of Buffaloe river, thence in a direct line to the Great Tennessee river near the Chickasaw old fields or eastern point of the Chickasaw claim on that river; thence northwardly to the great ridge dividing the waters running into the Tennessee from those running into Cumberland river, so as to include all the waters running into Elk river, thence along the top of the said great ridge to the place of beginning: reserving a tract of one mile square adjoining to, and below the mouth of Duck river on the Tennessee, for the use of the chief O'Koy or Tishumastubbee. *[margin: Cession of territory to United States.]*

ART. II. The United States on their part, and in consideration of the above cession, agree to make the following payments, to wit: Twenty thousand dollars for the use of the nation at large, and for the payment of the debts due to their merchants and traders; and to George Colbert and O'Koy two thousand dollars, that is, to each one thousand dollars. This sum is granted to them at the request of the national council for services rendered their nation, and is to be subject to their individual order, witnessed by the resident agent; also to Chinubbee Mingo, the king of the nation, an annuity of one hundred dollars, during his natural life, granted as a testimony of his personal worth and friendly disposition. All the above payments are to be made in specie. *[margin: Consideration for said grant.]*

ART. III. In order to preclude for ever all disputes relative to the boundary mentioned in the first section, it is hereby stipulated, that the same shall be ascertained and marked by a commissioner or commissioners on the part of the United States, accompanied by such person as the Chickasaws may choose, so soon as the Chickasaws shall have thirty days' notice of the time and place, at which the operation is to commence: and the United States will pay the person appointed on the part of the Chickasaws two dollars per day during his actual attendance on that service. *[margin: Commissioner to be appointed to ascertain the boundary.]*

ART. IV. It is hereby agreed on the part of the United States, that from and after the ratification of these articles, no settlement shall be made by any citizen, or permitted by the government of the United States, on that part of the present cession included between the present Indian boundary and the Tennessee, and between the Ohio and a line drawn due north from the mouth of Buffaloe to the ridge dividing the waters of Cumberland from those of the Tennessee river, to the term of three years. *[margin: No citizen of United States allowed to settle on said tract.]*

These articles to be considered as permanent additions to former treaties.

ART. V. The articles now stipulated will be considered as permanent additions to the treaties now in force between the contracting parties, as soon as they shall have been ratified by the President of the United States of America, by and with the advice and consent of the Senate of the said United States.

In witness of all and every thing herein determined, the parties have hereunto interchangeably set their hands and seals, in the Chickasaw country, this twenty-third day of July, in the year of our Lord one thousand eight hundred and five, and of the independence of the United States of America the thirtieth.

Commissioners:	Tiphu Mashtubbee, his x mark, [L. S.]
James Robertson [L. S.]	Choomubbee, his x mark, [L. S.]
Silas Dinsmoor, [L. S.]	Mingo Mattaha, his x mark, [L. S.]
Chiefs and warriors:	E. Mattaha Meko, his x mark, [L. S.]
Chenubbee Mingo, the king, his x	Wm. McGillivry, his x mark, [L. S.]
mark, [L. S.]	Tisshoo Hooluhta, his x mark, [L. S.]
George Colbert, his x mark, [L. S.]	Levi Colbert, his x mark, [L. S.]
O Koy, his x mark, [L. S.]	

Signed, sealed, and interchanged, in presence of

Thomas Augustine Claiborne, secretary to the commissioners,
Samuel Mitchell, United States agent to the Chickasaw nation,
John McKee,
R. Chamberlin, second lieutenant Second Regiment Infantry,

W. P. Anderson, of Tennessee.
Malcolm McGee, his x mark,
John Pitchlynn,
Christopher Olney,
Wm. Tyrrell,
    Sworn interpreters.

TREATY WITH THE DELAWARES, ETC., 1805.

Aug. 21, 1805.

7 Stat., 91.
Proclamation, Apr. 24, 1806.

A treaty between the United States of America, and the tribes of Indians called the Delawares, Pottawatimies, Miames, Eel River, and Weas.

ARTICLES of a treaty made and entered into, at Grouseland, near Vincennes, in the Indiana territory, by and between William Henry Harrison, governor of said territory, superintendent of Indian affairs, and commissioner plenipotentiary of the United States, for treating with the north western tribes of Indians, of the one part, and the tribes of Indians called the Delewares, Putawatimis, Miamis, Eel River, and Weas, jointly and severally by their chiefs and head men, of the other part.

Delawares relinquish their claim.

ARTICLE I. Whereas, by the fourth article of a treaty made between the United States and the Delaware tribe, on the eighteenth day of August, eighteen hundred and four, the said United States engaged to consider the said Delewares as the proprietors of all that tract of country which is bounded by the White river on the north, the Ohio and Clark's grant on the south, the general boundary line running from the mouth of Kentucky river on the east, and the tract ceded by the treaty of fort Wayne, and the road leading to Clark's grant on the west and south west. And whereas, the Miami tribes, from whom the Delawares derived their claim, contend that in their cession of said tract to the Delewares, it was never their intention to convey to them the right of the soil, but to suffer them to occupy it as long as they thought proper, the said Delewares have, for the sake of peace and good neighborhood, determined to relinquish their claim to the said tract, and do by these presents release the United States from the guarantee made in the before-mentioned article of the treaty of August, eighteen hundred and four.

Cession of the Miamies, etc.

ART. II. The said Miami, Eel River, and Wea tribes, cede and relinquish to the United States forever, all that tract of country which lies to the south of a line to be drawn from the north east corner of the tract ceded by the treaty of fort Wayne, so as to strike the general boundary line, running from a point opposite to the mouth of the Kentucky river, to fort Recovery, at the distance of fifty miles from its commencement on the Ohio river.

ART. III. In consideration of the cession made in the preceding article, the United States will give an additional permanent annuity to said Miamis, Eel River, and Wea tribes, in the following proportions, viz: to the Miamis, six hundred dollars; to the Eel River tribe, two hundred and fifty dollars; to the Weas, two hundred and fifty dollars; and also to the Putawatemies, an additional annuity of five hundred dollars, for ten years, and no longer; which, together with the sum of four thousand dollars which is now delivered, the receipt whereof they do hereby acknowledge, is to be considered as a full compensation for the land now ceded. *An additional permanent annuity to be given to the Miamies, etc.*

ART. IV. As the tribes which are now called the Miamis, Eel River, and Weas, were formerly and still consider themselves as one nation, and as they have determined that neither of these tribes shall dispose of any part of the country which they hold in common; in order to quiet their minds on that head, the United States do hereby engage to consider them as joint owners of all the country on the Wabash and its waters, above the Vincennes tract, and which has not been ceded to the United States, by this or any former treaty; and they do farther engage that they will not purchase any part of the said country without the consent of each of the said tribes. *Provided always,* That nothing in this section contained, shall in any manner weaken or destroy any claim which the Kickapoos, who are not represented at this treaty, may have to the country they now occupy on the Vermillion river. *Miamies, etc., determine not to part with any of their territory without the consent of all parties.*

ART. V. The Putawatimies, Miami, Eel River, and Wea tribes, explicitly acknowledge the right of the Delawares to sell the tract of land conveyed to the United States by the treaty of the eighteenth day of August, eighteen hundred and four, which tract was given by the Piankashaws to the Delawares, about thirty-seven years ago. *Potawatomies, etc., acknowledge the right of the Delawares to sell, etc.*

ART. VI. The annuities herein stipulated to be paid by the United States, shall be delivered in the same manner, and under the same conditions as those which the said tribes have heretofore received. *Annuities, how to be paid.*

ART. VII. This treaty shall be in force and obligatory on the contracting parties as soon as the same shall have been ratified by the President, by, and with the advice and consent of the Senate of the United States. *Treaty, when to take effect.*

In testimony whereof, the said commissioner plenipotentiary of the United States, and the sachems, chiefs, and head men of the said tribes, have hereunto set their hands and affixed their seals.

Done at Grouseland, near Vincennes, on the twenty-first day of August, in the year eighteen hundred and five, and of the independence of the United States the thirtieth.

William Henry Harrison,   [L. s.]
Delawares:
Hocking Pomskan, his x mark,   [L. s.]
Kecklawhenund, or William Anderson, his x mark,   [L. s.]
Allime, or White Eyes, his x mark, [L. s.]
Tomague, or Beaver, his x mark, [L. s.]
Pattawatimas:
Topanepee, his x mark,   [L. s.]
Lishahecon, his x mark,   [L. s.]
Wenamech, his x mark,   [L. s.]
Miamis:
Kakonweconner, or Long Legs, his x mark,   [L. s.]
Missingguimeschan, or Owl, his x mark,   [L. s.]
Wabsier, or White Skin, his x mark,   [L. s.]

Mashekanochquah, or Little Turtle, his x mark,   [L. s.]
Richardville, his x mark,   [L. s.]
Eel Rivers:
Wanonecana, or Night Stander, his x mark,   [L. s.]
Metausauner, or Sam, his x mark, [L. s.]
Archekatauh, or Earth, his x mark, [L. s.]
Weas:
Assonnonquah, or Labossiere, his x mark,   [L. s.]
Misquaconaqua, or Painted Pole, his x mark,   [L. s.]
Ohequanah, or Little Eyes, his x mark,   [L. s.]
Delawares:
Missenewand, or Captain Bullet, his x mark,   [L. s.]

Done in the presence of—

B. Parke, secretary to the commissioner,
John Gibson, secretary Indiana Territory,
John Griffin, a judge of the Indiana Territory,
B. Chambers, president of the council,
Jesse B. Thomas, Speaker of the House
   of Representatives.
John Rice Jones,
Samuel Gwathmey,
Pierre Menard,
      Members legislative council
      Indiana Territory,

Davis Floyd,
Shadrach Bond,
William Biggs,
John Johnson,
      Members house of representatives Indiana Territory,
W. Wells, agent of Indian affairs,
Vigo, colonel of Knox County Militia,
John Conner,
Joseph Barron,
      Sworn interpreters.

ADDITIONAL ARTICLE.

It is the intention of the contracting parties, that the boundary line herein directed to be run from the north east corner of the Vincennes tract to the boundary line running from the mouth of the Kentucky river, shall not cross the Embarras or Drift Wood fork of White river, but if it should strike the said fork, such an alteration in the direction of the said line is to be made, as will leave the whole of the said fork in the Indian territory.

TREATY WITH THE CHEROKEE, 1805.

Oct. 25, 1805.

7 Stat., 93.
Proclamation, Apr. 24, 1806.

Articles of a treaty agreed upon between the United States of America, by their commissioners Return J. Meigs and Daniel Smith, appointed to hold conferences with the Cherokee Indians, for the purpose of arranging certain interesting matters with the said Cherokees, of the one part, and the undersigned chiefs and head men of the said nation, of the other part.

Former treaties recognized.

ARTICLE I. All former treaties, which provide for the maintenance of peace and preventing of crimes, are on this occasion recognized and continued in force.

Cession from the Cherokees.

Boundaries.

ART. II. The Cherokees quit claim and cede to the United States, all the land which they have heretofore claimed, lying to the north of the following boundary line: beginning at the mouth of Duck river, running thence up the main stream of the same to the junction of the fork, at the head of which fort Nash stood, with the main south fork; thence a direct course to a point on the Tennessee river bank opposite the mouth of Hiwassa river. If the line from Hiwassa should leave out Field's Settlement, it is to be marked round his improvement, and then continued the straight course; thence up the middle of the Tennessee river, (but leaving all the islands to the Cherokees,) to the mouth of Clinch river; thence up the Clinch river to the former boundary line agreed upon with the said Cherokees, reserving at the same time to the use of the Cherokees a small tract lying at and below the mouth of Clinch river; from the mouth extending thence down the Tennessee river, from the mouth of Clinch to a notable rock on the north bank of the Tennessee, in view from South West Point; thence a course at right angles with the river, to the Cumberland road; thence eastwardly along the same, to the bank of Clinch river, so as to secure the ferry landing to the Cherokees up to the first hill, and down the same to the mouth thereof, together with two other sections of one square mile each, one of which is at the foot of Cumberland mountain, at and near the place where the turnpike gate now stands; the other on the north bank of the Tennessee river, where the Cherokee Talootiske now lives. And whereas, from the present cession made by the Cherokees, and other circumstances, the site of the garrisons at South West Point and Tellico are become not the most convenient and suitable places for the accommodation of the said Indians, it may become expedient to remove the said garrisons and factory to some more suitable place; three other square miles are reserved for the particular disposal of the United States on the north bank of the Tennessee, opposite to and below the mouth of Hiwassa.

ART. III. In consideration of the above cession and relinquishment, the United States agree to pay immediately three thousand dollars in valuable merchandise, and eleven thousand dollars within ninety days after the ratification of this treaty, and also an annuity of three thousand dollars, the commencement of which is this day. But so much of the said eleven thousand dollars, as the said Cherokee may agree to accept in useful articles of, and machines for, agriculture and manufactures, shall be paid in those articles, at their option. *Payment for the above cession.* *Part of said payment to be machines for agriculture, etc.*

ART. IV. The citizens of the United States shall have the free and unmolested use and enjoyment of the two following described roads, in addition to those which are at present established through their country; one to proceed from some convenient place near the head of Stone's river, and fall into the Georgia road at a suitable place towards the southern frontier of the Cherokees. The other to proceed from the neighborhood of Franklin, on Big Harpath, and crossing the Tennessee at or near the Muscle Shoals, to pursue the nearest and best way to the settlements on the Tombigbee. These roads shall be viewed and marked out by men appointed on each side for that purpose, in order that they may be directed the nearest and best ways, and the time of doing the business the Cherokees shall be duly notified. *Citizens of United States to have the use of certain described roads.*

ART. V. This treaty shall take effect and be obligatory on the contracting parties, as soon as it is ratified by the President of the United States, by and with the advice and consent of the Senate of the same. *Treaty, when to take effect.*

In testimony whereof, the said commissioners, and the undersigned chiefs and head men of the Cherokees, have hereto set their hands and seals.

Done at Tellico, the twenty-fifth day of October, one thousand eight hundred and five.

Return J. Meigs,
Daniel Smith.

Fox, or Ennollee, his x mark, [L. S.]	John Jolly, or Eulatakee, his x mark, [L. S.]
Path Killer, or Nenohuttahe, his x mark, [L. S.]	Bark, or Eullooka, his x mark, [L. S.]
Glass, or Tauquatehee, his x mark, [L. S.]	John McLemore, or John Euskulacau, his x mark, [L. S.]
Double head, or Dhuqualutauge, his x mark, [L. S.]	Big Bear, or Yohanaqua, his x mark, [L. S.]
Dick Justice, his x mark, [L. S.]	Dreadfulwater, or Aumaudoskee, his x mark, [L. S.]
Tounhull, or Toonayeh, his x mark, [L. S.]	Challaugittihee, his x mark, [L. S.]
Turtle at Home, or Sullicooahwolu, his x mark, [L. S.]	Calliliskee, or Knife Sheath, his x mark, [L. S.]
Chenawee, his x mark, [L. S.]	Closenee, his x mark, [L. S.]
Slave Boy, or Oosaunabee, his x mark, [L. S.]	Challow, or Kingfisher, his x mark, [L. S.]
Tallotiskee, his x mark, [L. S.]	John Watts, jr., his x mark, [L. S.]
Broom, or Cunnaweesoskee, his x mark. [L. L.]	Sharp Arrow, or Costarauh, his x mark, [L. S.]
John Greenwood, or Sour Mush, his x mark, [L. S.]	John Dougherty, or Long John, his x mark, [L. S.]
Chulioah, his x mark, [L. S.]	Tuckasee, or Terrapin, his x mark, [L. S.]
Katigiskee, his x mark, [L. S.]	Tuskegittihee, or Long Fellow, his x mark, [L. S.]
William Shawry, or Eskaculiskee, his x mark, [L. S.]	Tochuwor, or Red Bird, his x mark, [L. S.]
Taochalar, his x mark, [L. S.]	Catihee, or Badgerson, his x mark, [L. S.]
James Davis, or Coowusaliskee, his x mark, [L. S.]	

Witnesses:

Rob. Purdy, secretary to the commissioner,
W. Yates, Lieutenant Artillerists,
Wm. L. Lovely, assistant agent,
Nicholas Byers, United States factor,

Go. W. Campbell,
Will. Polk,
James Blair,
Jno. Smith, T.
Thomas N. Clark,
Chas. Hicks, interpreter.

TREATY WITH THE CHEROKEE, 1805.

Oct. 27, 1805.

7 Stat., 95.
Proclamation, June
10, 1806.

Articles of a treaty between the United States of America, by their commissioners, Return J. Meigs and Daniel Smith, who are appointed to hold conferences with the Cherokees for the purpose of arranging certain interesting matters with the said Indians, of the one part, and the undersigned chiefs and head men of the Cherokees, of the other part, concluded at Tellico.

Cession of certain land to the United States.

ART. 1st. Whereas it has been represented by the one party to the other that the section of land on which the garrison of South West Point stands, and which extends to Kingston, is likely to be a desirable place for the assembly of the state of Tennessee to convene at (a committee from that body now in session having viewed the situation) now the Cherokees being possessed of a spirit of conciliation, and seeing that this tract is desired for public purposes, and not for individual advantages, (reserving the ferries to themselves,) quit claim and cede to the United States the said section of land, understanding at the same time, that the buildings erected by the public are to belong to the public, as well as the occupation of the same, during the pleasure of the government; we also cede to the United States the first island in the Tennessee, above the mouth of Clinch.

Cherokees grant the free use of a road through their country for the carriage of the mail.

ART. 2d. And whereas the mail of the United States is ordered to be carried from Knoxville to New-Orleans, through the Cherokee, Creek and Choctaw countries; the Cherokees agree that the citizens of the United States shall have, so far as it goes through their country, the free and unmolested use of a road leading from Tellico to Tombigbe, to be laid out by viewers appointed on both sides, who shall direct it the nearest and best way; and the time of doing the business the Cherokees shall be notified of.

Payment to Cherokees.

ART. 3d. In consideration of the above cession and relinquishment, the United States agree to pay to the said Cherokee Indians sixteen hundred dollars in money, or useful merchandise at their option, within ninety days after the ratification of this treaty.

Treaty, when to take effect.

ART. 4th. This treaty shall be obligatory between the contracting parties as soon as it is ratified by the President, by and with the advice and consent of the Senate of the United States.

In testimony whereof, the said commissioners, and the undersigned chiefs and head men of the Cherokees, have hereto set their hands and seals.

Done at Tellico, this twenty-seventh day of October, in the year of our Lord one thousand eight hundred and five.

Return J. Meigs,
Danl. Smith.

Black Fox, or Ennone, his x mark, [L. s.]
The Glass, or Tunnquetihee, his x
   mark,   [L. s.]
Kutigeskee, his x mark,   [L. s.]
Toochalar, his x mark,   [L. s.]
Turtle at Home, or Sullicookiewal-
   ar, his x mark,   [L. s.]
Dick Justice, his x mark,   [L. s.]
John Greenwood, or Eakosettas,
   his x mark,   [L. s.]
Chuleah, or Gentleman Tom, his x
   mark,   [L. s.]

Broom, or Cannarwesoske, his x
   mark,   [L. s.]
Bald Hunter, or Toowayullau, his x
   mark,   [L. s.]
John Melamere, or Euquellooka,
   his x mark,   [L. s.]
Closenie, or Creeping, his x mark, [L. s.]
Double Head, or Chuquacuttague,
   his x mark,   [L. s.]
Chickasawtihee, or Chickasawtihee
   Killer, his x mark,   [L. s.]

Witness:

Robert Purdy, secretary to the com-
   missioners.
William Yates, B. Com'g.
Nicholas Byers, United States fac-
   tor.
Wm. Lovely, assistant agent.

B. M'Ghee.
Saml. Love.
James Blair.
Hopkins Lacey.
Chs. Hicks, interpreter.

TREATY WITH THE CREEKS, 1805.

A convention between the United States and the Creek Nation of Indians, concluded at the City of Washington, on the fourteenth day of November, in the year of our Lord one thousand eight hundred and five.

Nov. 14, 1805.

7 Stat., 96.
Proclamation, June 2, 1806.

ARTICLES of a Convention made between Henry Dearborn, secretary of war, being specially authorized therefor by the President of the United States, and Oche Haujo, William M'Intosh, Tuskenehau Chapce, Tuskenehau, Enehau Thlucco, Checopeheke, Emantlau, chiefs and head men of the Creek nation of Indians, duly authorized and empowered by said nation.

ART. I. The aforesaid chiefs and head men do hereby agree, in consideration of certain sums of money and goods to be paid to the said Creek nation by the government of the United States as hereafter stipulated, to cede and forever quit claim, and do, in behalf of their nation, hereby cede, relinquish, and forever quit claim unto the United States all right, title, and interest, which the said nation have or claim, in or unto a certain tract of land, situate between the rivers Oconee and Ocmulgee (except as hereinafter excepted) and bounded as follows, viz: *Cession by the Creek Indians.*

Beginning at the high shoals of Apalacha, where the line of the treaty of fort Wilkinson touches the same, thence running in a straight line, to the mouth of Ulcofauhatche, it being the first large branch or fork of the Ocmulgee, above the Seven Islands: *Provided, however,* That if the said line should strike the Ulcofauhatche, at any place above its mouth, that it shall continue round with that stream so as to leave the whole of it on the Indian side; then the boundary to continue from the mouth of the Ulcofauhatche, by the water's edge of the Ocmulgee river, down to its junction with the Oconee; thence up the Oconee to the present boundary at Tauloohatche creek; thence up said creek and following the present boundary line to the first-mentioned bounds, at the high shoals of Apalacha, excepting and reserving to the Creek nation, the title and possession of a tract of land, five miles in length and three in breadth, and bounded as follows, viz: Beginning on the eastern shore of the Ocmulgee river, at a point three miles on a straight line above the mouth of a creek called Oakchoncoolgau, which empties into the Ocmulgee, near the lower part of what is called the old Ocmulgee fields—thence running three miles eastwardly, on a course at right angles with the general course of the river for five miles below the point of beginning;—thence, from the end of the three miles, to run five miles parallel with the said course of the river; thence westwardly, at right angles with the last-mentioned line to the river; thence by the river to the first-mentioned bounds.   *Boundaries.*

And it is hereby agreed, that the President of the United States, for the time being, shall have a right to establish and continue a military post, and a factory or trading house on said reserved tract; and to make such other use of the said tract as may be found convenient for the United States, as long as the government thereof shall think proper to continue the said military post or trading house. And it is also agreed on the part of the Creek nation, that the navigation and fishery of the Ocmulgee, from its junction with the Oconee to the mouth of the Ulcofauhatchee, shall be free to the white people; provided they use no traps for taking fish; but nets and scines may be used, which shall be drawn to the eastern shore only.   *A military post, etc., to be established.*

ART. II. It is hereby stipulated and agreed, on the part of the Creek nation that the government of the United States shall forever hereafter have a right to a horse path, through the Creek country, from the Ocmulgee to the Mobile, in such direction as shall, by the Presi-   *United States to have a right to the use of a road to the Mobile.*

dent of the United States, be considered most convenient, and to clear out the same, and lay logs over the creeks: And the citizens of said States, shall at all times have a right to pass peaceably cn said path, under such regulations and restrictions, as the government of the United States shall from time to time direct; and the Creek chiefs will have boats kept at the several rivers for the conveyance of men and horses, and houses of entertainment established at suitable places on said path for the accommodation of travellers; and the respective ferriages and prices of entertainment for men and horses, shall be regulated by the present agent, Col. Hawkins, or by his successor in office, or as is usual among white people.

An annuity to be paid to the Creek nation.

ART. III. It is hereby stipulated and agreed, on the part of the United States, as a full consideration for the land ceded by the Creek nation in the first article, as well as by permission granted for a horse path through their country, and the occupancy of the reserved tract, at the old Ocmulgee fields, that there shall be paid annually to the Creek nation, by the United States for the term of eight years, twelve thousand dollars in money or goods, and implements of husbandry, at the option of the Creek nation, seasonably signified from time to time, through the agent of the United States, residing with said nation, to the department of war; and eleven thousand dollars shall be paid in like manner, annually, for the term of the ten succeeding years, making in the whole, eighteen payments in the course of eighteen years, without interest: The first payment is to be made as soon as practicable after the ratification of this convention by the government of the United States, and each payment shall be made at the reserved tract, on the old Ocmulgee fields.

Blacksmiths to be provided at the expense of United States.

ART. IV. And it is hereby further agreed, on the part of the United States, that in lieu of all former stipulations relating to blacksmiths, they will furnish the Creek nation for eight years, with two blacksmiths and two strikers.

Line to be run at the time, etc., prescribed by the President.

ART. V. The President of the United States may cause the line to be run from the high shoals of Apalacha, to the mouth of Ulcofauhatche, at such time, and in such manner, as he may deem proper, and this convention shall be obligatory on the contracting parties as soon as the same shall have been ratified by the government of the United States.

Done at the place, and on the day and year above written.

H. Dearborn,	[L. S.]
Oche Haujo, his x mark,	[L. S.]
William McIntosh, his x mark,	[L. S.]
Tuskenehau Chapco, his x mark,	[L. S.]
Tuskenehau, his x mark,	[L. S.]
Enehau Thlucco, his x mark,	[L. S.]
Chekopeheke Emanthau, his x mark,	[L. S.]

Signed and sealed in presence of—
James Madison,
Rt. Smith,
Benjamin Hawkins,
Timothy Barnard,
Jno. Smith,
Andrew McClary.

The foregoing articles have been faithfully interpreted.

Timothy Barnard, interpreter.

TREATY WITH THE CHOCTAW, 1805.

A Treaty of Limits between the United States of America and the Chaktaw Nation of Indians.

Nov. 16, 1805.

7 Stat., 98.
Proclamation, Feb. 25, 1808.

THOMAS JEFFERSON, President of the United States of America, by James Robertson, of Tennessee, and Silas Dinsmoor, of New Hampshire, agent of the United States to the Chaktaws, commissioners plenipotentiary of the United States, on the one part, and the Mingoes, Chiefs and warriors of the Chaktaw nation of Indians, in council assembled, on the other part, have entered into the following agreement, viz:

ARTICLE I. The Mingoes, chiefs, and warriors of the Chaktaw nation of Indians in behalf of themselves, and the said nation, do by these presents cede to the United States of America, all the lands to which they now have or ever had claim, lying to the right of the following lines, to say. Beginning at a branch of the Humacheeto where the same is intersected by the present Chaktaw boundary, and also by the path leading from Natchez to the county of Washington, usually called M'Clarey's path, thence eastwardly along M'Clarey's path, to the east or left bank of Pearl river, thence on such a direct line as would touch the lower end of a bluff on the left bank of Chickasawhay river the first above the Hiyoowannee towns, called Broken Bluff, to a point within four miles of the Broken Bluff, thence in a direct line nearly parallel with the river to a point whence an east line of four miles in length will intersect the river below the lowest settlement at present occupied and improved in the Hiyoowannee town, thence still east four miles, thence in a direct line nearly parallel with the river to a point on a line to be run from the lower end of the Broken Bluff to Faluktabunnee on the Tombigbee river four miles from the Broken Bluff, thence along the said line to Faluktabunnee, thence east to the boundary between the Creeks and Chaktaws on the ridge dividing the waters running into the Alabama from those running into Tombigbee, thence southwardly along the said ridge and boundary to the southern point of the Chaktaw claim. Reserving a tract of two miles square run on meridians and parallels so as to include the houses and improvements in the town of Fuketcheepoonta, and reserving also a tract of five thousand one hundred and twenty acres, beginning at a post on the left bank of Tombigbee river opposite the lower end of Hatchatigbee Bluff, thence ascending the river four miles front and two back one half, for the use of Alzira, the other half for the use of Sophia, daughters of Samuel Mitchell, by Molly, a Chaktaw woman. The latter reserve to be subject to the same laws and regulations as may be established in the circumjacent country; and the said Mingoes of the Chaktaws, request that the government of the United States may confirm the title of this reserve in the said Alzira and Sophia.

Cession to the United States.

Reservation.

ART. II. For and in consideration of the foregoing cession on the part of the Chaktaw nation, and in full satisfaction for the same, the commissioners of the United States, do hereby covenant, and agree with the said nation in behalf of the United States, that the said States shall pay to the said nation fifty thousand five hundred dollars, for the following purposes, to wit:

Consideration.

Forty eight thousand dollars to enable the Mingoes to discharge the debt due to their merchants and traders; and also to pay for the depredations committed on stock, and other property by evil disposed persons of the said Chaktaw nation; two thousand five hundred dollars to be paid to John Pitchlynn, to compensate him for certain losses sustained in the Chaktaw country, and as a grateful testimonial of the nation's esteem. And the said States shall also pay annually to the said Chaktaws, for the use of the nation, three thousand dollars in such goods (at neat cost of Philadelphia) as the Mingoes may choose, they giving at least one year's notice of such choice.

ART. III. The commissioners of the United States, on the part of the said States, engage to give to each of the three great Medal Mingoes, Pukshunubbee-Mingo, Hoomastubbee, and Pooshamattaha, five hundred dollars in consideration of past services in their nation, and also to pay to each of them an annuity of one hundred and fifty dollars during their continuance in office. It is perfectly understood, that neither of those great Medal Mingoes is to share any part of the general annuity of the nation.

Payment to certain Indians for past services.

ART. IV. The Mingoes, chiefs, and warriors of the Chaktaws, certify that a tract of land not exceeding fifteen hundred acres, situated between the Tombigbee river and Jackson's creek, the front or river line extending down the river from a blazed white oak standing on the left bank of the Tombigbee near the head of the shoal, next above Hobukentoopa, and claimed by John M'Grew was in fact granted to the said M'Grew by Opiomingo Hesnitta, and others, many years ago, and they respectfully request the government of the United States to establish the claim of the said M'Grew to the said fifteen hundred acres.

Claim of John M'Grew.

ART. V. The two contracting parties covenant and agree that the boundary as described in the second [first] article shall be ascertained and plainly marked, in such way and manner as the President of the United States may direct, in the presence of three persons to be appointed by the said nation; one from each of the great medal districts, each of whom shall receive for this service two dollars per day during his actual attendance, and the Chaktaws shall have due and seasonable notice of the place where, and time when, the operation shall commence.

Boundaries.

ART. VI. The lease granted for establishments on the roads leading through the Chaktaw country, is hereby confirmed in all its conditions, and, except in the alteration of boundary, nothing in this instrument shall affect or change any of the pre-existing obligations of the contracting parties.

A certain former grant confirmed.

ART. VII. This treaty shall take effect and become reciprocally obligatory so soon as the same shall have been ratified by the President of the United States of America, by and with the advice and consent of the Senate of the United States.

When to take effect.

Done on Mount Dexter, in Pooshapukanuk, in the Choctaw country, this sixteenth day of November, in the year of our Lord one thousand eight hundred and five, and of the independence of the United States of America the thirtieth.

Commissioners:

James Robertson,	[L. S.]	John Carnes, his x mark,	[L. S.]
Silas Dinsmoor,	[L. S.]	Tooteehooma, his x mark,	[L. S.]
Great Medal Mingos:		Hoosheehooma, his x mark,	[L. S.]
Pukshunnubbee, his x mark,	[L. S.]	Tootuhooma, 2d. his x mark,	[L. S.]
Mingo Hoomastubbee, his x mark,	[L. S.]	George James, his x mark,	[L. S.]
Pooshamattaha, his x mark,	[L. S.]	Robert McClure, his x mark,	[L. S.]
Chiefs and warriors:		Tuskeamingo, his x mark,	[L. S.]
Ookchummee, his x mark,	[L. S.]	Hattukubbeehooluhta, his x mark,	[L. S.]
Tuskamiubbee, his x mark,	[L. S.]	Fishoommastubbee, his x mark,	[L. S.]
James Perry, his x mark,	[L. S.]	Anoguaiah, his x mark,	[L. S.]
Levi Perry, his x mark,	[L. S.]	Lewis Lucas, his x mark,	[L. S.]
Isaac Perry, his x mark,	[L. S.]	James Pitchlynn, his x mark,	[L. S.]
William Turnbull,	[L. S.]	Panshee Eenanhla, his x mark,	[L. S.]
		Pansheehoomubbu, his x mark,	[L. S.]

Witnesses present at signing and sealing:

Thomas Augustine Claiborn, secretary to the commissioners,
John M'Kee,
Samuel Mitchell, United States agent to the Chickasaws.
William Colbert, of the Chickasaws, his x mark,
Lewis Ward,
Charles Juzan,

Garrud E. Nelson,
David Chote,
Nathaniel Tolsom,
Mdl. Mackey,
Lewis Lefto,
John Pitchlynn, United States interpreter,
Will. Tyrrell, assistant interpreter.

TREATY WITH THE PIANKASHAW, 1805.

A treaty between the United States of America and the Piankishaw tribe of Indians.

Dec. 30, 1805.

7 Stat., 100.
Ratified May 22, 1807.
Proclaimed May 23, 1807.

ARTICLES of a treaty made at Vincennes, in the Indiana territory, between Willian Henry Harrison, governor of the said territory, superintendent of Indian affairs, and commissioner plenipotentiary of the United States, for concluding any treaty or treaties which may be found necessary with any of the Indian tribes north west of the Ohio, of the one part, and the chiefs and head men of the Piankishaw tribe, of the other part.

ART. I. The Piankishaw tribe cedes and relinquishes to the United States for ever, all that tract of country (with the exception of the reservation hereinafter made) which lies between the Wabash and the tract ceded by the Kaskaskia tribe, in the year one thousand eight hundred and three, and south of a line to be drawn from the north west corner of the Vincennes tract, north seventy eight degrees west, until it intersects the boundary line which has heretofore separated the lands of the Piankeshaws from the said tract ceded by the Kaskaskia tribe. *Cession to the United States.*

ART. II. The United States take the Piankishaw tribe under their immediate care and patronage, and will extend to them a protection as effectual as that which is enjoyed by the Kaskaskia tribe; and the said Piankishaw tribe will never commit any depredations or make war upon any of the other tribes without the consent of the United States. *United States take the Piankashaws under their protection.*

ART. III. The said United States will cause to be delivered to the Piankishaws yearly, and every year, an additional annuity of three hundred dollars, which is to be paid in the same manner, and under the same conditions as that to which they are entitled by the treaty of Greenville: *Provided always*, That the United States may, at any time they shall think proper, divide the said annuity amongst the individuals of the said tribe. *Additional annuity.* *Proviso.*

ART. IV. The stipulations made in the preceding articles, together with the sum of one thousand one hundred dollars, which is now delivered, the receipt whereof the said chiefs do hereby acknowledge, is considered a full compensation for the cession and relinquishment above mentioned. *Preceding stipulations, etc., to be considered a full compensation for the above cession.*

ART. V. As long as the lands now ceded, remain the property of the United States, the said tribe shall have the privilege of living and hunting upon them, in the same manner that they have heretofore done; and they reserve to themselves the right of locating a tract of two square miles, or twelve hundred and eighty acres, the fee of which is to remain with them for ever. *Indians to have the privilege of hunting, etc., on lands ceded.*

ART. VI. This treaty shall be in force as soon as it shall be ratified by the President of the United States, by and with the advice and consent of the Senate. *When to be in force.*

In testimony whereof, the said William Henry Harrison, and the chiefs and head men representing the said Piankeshaw tribe, have hereunto set their hands and affixed their seals.

Done at Vincennes, on the thirtieth day of December, in the year of our Lord, one thousand eight hundred and five, and of the independence of the United States the thirtieth.

William Henry Harrison,   [L. s.]
Wabakinklelia, or Gros Bled,   [L. s.]
Pauquia, or Montour,   [L. s.]
Macatiwaaluna, or Chien Noir,   [L. s.]

Signed, sealed, and executed, in presence of—

William Prince, secretary to the Commissioner,
John Griffin, one of the judges of the Indiana Territory,
John Gibson, secretary Indiana Territory,
John Badollet, register of the land office,
Nath'l Ewing, receiver public moneys,

John Rice Jones, of the Indiana Territory,
Dubois, of the Indiana Territory,
Wm. Bullett, of Vincennes,
Jacob Kingskedall, Vincennes,
H. Hurst, Vincennes, Ind. T.,
John Johnson,
Michel Brouillet, interpreter.

TREATY WITH THE CHEROKEE, 1806.

Jan. 7, 1806.

7 Stat., 101.
Ratified May 22, 1807.
Proclaimed May 23, 1807.

A convention between the United States and the Cherokee nation of Indians, concluded at the city of Washington, on the seventh day of January, in the year one thousand eight hundred and six.

ARTICLES of a Convention made between Henry Dearborn, secretary of war, being specially authorized thereto by the President of the United States, and the undersigned chiefs and head men of the Cherokee nation of Indians, duly authorized and empowered by said nation.

ARTICLE I.

Cession of territory.

The undersigned chiefs and head men of the Cherokee nation of Indians, for themselves and in behalf of their nation, relinquish to the United States all right, title, interest and claim, which they or their nation have or ever had to all that tract of country which lies to the northward of the river Tennessee and westward of a line to be run from the upper part of the Chickasaw Old Fields, at the upper point of an island, called Chickasaw island, on said river, to the most easterly head waters of that branch of said Tennessee river called Duck river, excepting the two following described tracts, viz. one tract bounded southerly on the said Tennessee river, at a place called the Muscle Shoals, westerly by a creek called Te Kee, ta, no-eh or Cyprus creek, and easterly by Chu, wa, lee, or Elk river or creek, and northerly by a line to be drawn from a point on said Elk river ten miles on a direct line from its mouth or junction with Tennessee river, to a point on the said Cyprus Creek, ten miles on a direct line from its junction with the Tennessee river.

The other tract is to be two miles in width on the north side of Tennessee river, and to extend northerly from that river three miles, and bounded as follows, viz. beginning at the mouth of Spring Creek, and running up said creek three miles on a straight line, thence westerly two miles at right angles with the general course of said creek, thence southerly on a line parallel with the general course of said creek to the Tennessee river, thence up said river by its waters to the beginning: which first reserved tract is to be considered the common property of the Cherokees who now live on the same; including John D. Chesholm, Au, tow, we and Cheh Chuh, and the other reserved tract on which Moses Melton now lives, is to be considered the property of said Melton and of Charles Hicks, in equal shares.

And the said chiefs and head men also agree to relinquish to the United States all right or claim which they or their nation have to what is called the Long Island in Holston river.

ARTICLE II.

Payment to Cherokees.

The said Henry Dearborn on the part of the United States hereby stipulates and agrees that in consideration of the relinquishment of title by the Cherokees, as stated in the preceding article, the United States will pay to the Cherokee nation two thousand dollars in money as soon as this convention shall be duly ratified by the government of the United States; and two thousand dollars in each of the four succeeding years, amounting in the whole to ten thousand dollars; and that a grist mill shall within one year from the date hereof, be built in the Cherokee country, for the use of the nation, at such place as shall be considered most convenient; that the said Cherokees shall be furnished with a machine for cleaning cotton; and also, that the old Cherokee chief, called the Black Fox, shall be paid annually one hundred dollars by the United States during his life.

ARTICLE III.

It is also agreed on the part of the United States, that the government thereof will use its influence and best endeavors to prevail on the Chickasaw nation of Indians to agree to the following boundary between that nation and the Cherokees to the southward of the Tennessee river, viz. beginning at the mouth of Caney Creek near the lower part of the Muscle Shoals, and to run up said creek to its head, and in a direct line from thence to the Flat Stone or Rock, the old corner boundary.

United States to use their influence with the Chickasaws in reference to a certain boundary.

But it is understood by the contracting parties that the United States do not engage to have the aforesaid line or boundary established, but only to endeavor to prevail on the Chickasaw nation to consent to such a line as the boundary beween the two nations.

ARTICLE IV.

It is further agreed on the part of the United States that the claims which the Chickasaws may have to the two tracts reserved by the first article of this convention on the north side of the Tennessee river, shall be settled by the United States in such manner as will be equitable, and will secure to the Cherokees the title to the said reservations.

Further agreement

Done at the place, and on the day and year first above written.

Henry Dearborn,	[L. S.]	Broom, his x mark,	[L. S.]
Double Head, his x mark,	[L. S.]	John Jolly, his x mark,	[L. S.]
James Vanu, his x mark,	[L. S.]	John Lowry, his x mark,	[L. S.]
Tallotiskee, his x mark,	[L. S.]	Red Bird, his x mark,	[L. S.]
Chulioa, his x mark,	[L. S.]	John Walker, his x mark,	[L. S.]
Sour Mush, his x mark,	[L. S.]	Young Wolf, his x mark,	[L. S.]
Turtle at home, his x mark,	[L. S.]	Skeuha, his x mark,	[L. S.]
Katihu, his x mark,	[L. S.]	Sequechu, his x mark,	[L. S.]
John McLemore, his x mark,	[L. S.]	Wm. Showry, his x mark,	[L. S.]

In presence of—
  Return J. Meigs,
  Benjamin Hawkins,
  Daniel Smith,
  John Smith,
  Andrew McClary,
  John McClarey.

I certify the foregoing convention has been faithfully interpreted.

Charles Hicks, Interpreter.

Elucidation of a convention with the Cherokee Nation.

Sept. 11, 1807.

7 Stat., 103.
Proclamation, Apr. 22, 1808.

WHEREAS, by the first article of a convention between the United States and the Cherokee nation, entered into at the city of Washington, on the seventh day of January, one thousand eight hundred and six, it was intended on the part of the Cherokee nation, and so understood by the Secretary of War, the commissioner on the part of the United States, to cede to the United States all the right, title and interest which the said Cherokee nation ever had to a tract of country contained between the Tennessee river and the Tennessee ridge (so called); which tract of country had since the year one thousand seven hundred and ninety four, been claimed by the Cherokees and Chickasaws: the eastern boundary whereof is limited by a line so to be run from the upper part of the Chickasaw Old Fields, as to include all the waters of Elk river, any thing expressed in said convention to the contrary notwithstanding. It is therefore now declared by James Robertson and Return J. Meigs, acting under the authority of the executive of the United States, and by a delegation of Cherokee chiefs, of whom Eunolee or Black Fox, the king or head chief of said Cherokee nation, acting on the part of, and in behalf of said nation, is one, that the eastern limits of said ceded tract shall be bounded by a line so to be run from the upper end of the Chickasaw Old Fields, a little above the upper point of an island, called Chickasaw Island, as will most directly intersect the first waters of Elk river, thence carried to the Great Cumberland mountain, in which the waters of Elk river have their source, then along the margin of said mountain until it shall intersect lands heretofore ceded to the United States, at the said Tennessee ridge. And in consideration of the readiness shown by the Cherokees to explain, and to place the limits of the land ceded by the said convention out of all doubt; and in consideration of their expenses in attending council, the executive of the United States will direct that the Cherokee nation shall receive the sum of two thousand dollars, to be paid to them by their agent, at such time as the said executive shall direct, and that the Cherokee hunters, as hath been the custom in such cases, may hunt on said ceded tract, until by the fullness of settlers it shall become improper. And it is hereby declared by the parties, that this explanation ought to be considered as a just elucidation of the cession made by the first article of said convention.

Eastern limits of the tract granted by the treaty of Jan. 7, 1806.

Done at the point of departure of the line at the upper end of the island opposite to the upper part of the said Chickasaw Oil Fields, the eleventh day of September, in the year one thousand eight hundred and seven.

> James Robertson,
> Return J. Meigs,
> Eunolee, or Black Fox, his x mark,
> Fauquitee, or Glass, his x mark,
> Fulaquokoko, or Turtle at home, his x mark,
> Richard Brown, his x mark,
> Sowolotoh, king's brother, his x mark.

Witnesses present:
Thomas Freeman,
Thomas Orme.

TREATY WITH THE OTTAWA, ETC., 1807.

Nov. 17, 1807.
———
7 Stat., 105.
Proclamation, Jan.
27, 1808.

Articles of a treaty made at Detroit, this seventeenth day of November, in the year of our Lord, one thousand eight hundred and seven, by William Hull, governor of the territory of Michigan, and superintendent of Indian affairs, and sole commissioner of the United States, to conclude and sign a treaty or treaties, with the several nations of Indians, north west of the river Ohio, on the one part, and the sachems, chiefs, and warriors of the Ottoway, Chippeway, Wyandotte, and Pottawatamie nations of Indians, on the other part. To confirm and perpetuate the friendship, which happily subsists between the United States and the nations aforesaid, to manifest the sincerity of that friendship, and to settle arrangements mutually beneficial to the

parties; after a full explanation and perfect understanding, the fol-
lowing articles are agreed to, which, when ratified by the President,
by and with the advice and consent of the Senate of the United States,
shall be binding on them, and the respective nations of Indians.

ARTICLE 1. The sachems, chiefs, and warriors of the nations afore- [Consideration.]
said, in consideration of money and goods, to be paid to the said
nations, by the government of the United States as hereafter stipulated; do hereby agree to cede and forever quit claim, and do in behalf
of their nations hereby cede, relinquish, and forever quit claim, unto [Cession.]
the said United States, all right, title, and interest, which the said
nations now have, or claim, or ever had, or claimed, in, or unto, the
lands comprehended within the following described lines and bound- [Boundaries.]
aries: Beginning at the mouth of the Miami river of the lakes, and
running thence up the middle thereof, to the mouth of the great Au
Glaize river, thence running due north, until it intersects a parallel of
latitude, to be drawn from the outlet of lake Huron, which forms the
river Sinclair; thence running north east the course, that may be found,
will lead in a direct line, to White Rock, in lake Huron, thence due
east, until it intersects the boundary line between the United States
and Upper Canada, in said lake, thence southwardly, following the
said boundary line, down said lake, through river Sinclair, lake St.
Clair, and the river Detroit, into lake Erie, to a point due east of the
aforesaid Miami river, thence west to the place of beginning.

ART. II. It is hereby stipulated and agreed on the part of the United [How the considera-]
States, as a consideration for the lands, ceded by the nations aforesaid, [tion is to be appor-]
in the preceding article, that there shall be paid to the said nations, at [tioned and paid.]
Detroit, ten thousand dollars, in money, goods, implements of hus-
bandry, or domestic animals, (at the option of the said nations, seasonably signified, through the superintendent of Indian affairs, residing
with the said nations, to the department of war,) as soon as practicable,
after the ratification of the treaty, by the President, with the advice
and consent of the Senate of the United States; of this sum, three
thousand three hundred and thirty three dollars thirty three cents and
four mills, shall be paid to the Ottoway nation, three thousand three
hundred and thirty three dollars thirty three cents and four mills, to
the Chippeway nation, one thousand six hundred sixty six dollars sixty
six cents and six mills, to the Wyandotte nation, one thousand six hundred sixty six dollars sixty six cents and six mills, to the Pottawatamie
nation, and likewise an annuity forever, of two thousand four hundred
dollars, to be paid at Detroit, in manner as aforesaid: the first payment to be made on the first day of September next, and to be paid to
the different nations, in the following proportions: eight hundred
dollars to the Ottoways, eight hundred dollars to the Chippeways,
four hundred dollars to the Wyandottes, and four hundred dollars to
such of the Pottawatamies, as now reside on the river Huron of lake
Erie, the river Raisin, and in the vicinity of the said rivers.

ART. III. It is further stipulated and agreed, if at any time here- [United States will]
after, the said nations should be of the opinion, that it would be more [agree to a reasonable]
for their interest, that the annuity aforesaid should be paid by instal- [commutation for the]
ments, the United States will agree to a reasonable commutation for [annuity, &c.]
the annuity, and pay it accordingly.

ART. IV. The United States, to manifest their liberality, and dispo- [United States to]
sition to encourage the said Indians, in agriculture, further stipulate, [supply the Indians]
to furnish the said Indians with two *blacksmiths*, one to reside with [with blacksmiths.]
the Chippeways, at Saguina, and the other to reside with the Otta-
ways, at the Miami, during the term of ten years; said blacksmiths
are to do such work for the said nations as shall be most useful to them.

ART. V. It is further agreed and stipulated, that the said Indian [Indians to have the]
nations shall enjoy the privilege of hunting and fishing on the lands [privilege of hunting,]
[&c., on lands ceded.]

ceded as aforesaid, as long as they remain the property of the United States.

ART. VI. It is distinctly to be understood, for the accommodation of the said Indians, that the following tracts of land within the cession aforesaid, shall be, and hereby are reserved to the said Indian nations, one tract of land six miles square, on the Miami of lake Erie, above *Roche dè Boeuf*, to include the village, where *Tondaganie*, (or the Dog) now lives. Also, three miles square on the said river, (above the twelve miles square ceded to the United States by the treaty of Greenville) including what is called *Presque Isle;* also four miles square on the Miami bay, including the villages where *Meshkemau* and *Waugau* now live; also, three miles square on the river *Raisin*, at a place called *Macon*, and where the river *Macon* falls into the river *Raizin*, which place is about fourteen miles from the mouth of said river *Raizin;* also, two sections of one mile square each, on the river *Rouge*, at *Seginsiwin's* village; also two sections of one mile square each, at *Tonquish's* village, near the river *Rouge;* also three miles square on lake St. Clair, above the river Huron, to include *Machonce's* village; also, six sections, each section containing one mile square, within the cession aforesaid, in such situations as the said Indians shall elect, subject, however, to the approbation of the President of the United States, as to the places of location. It is further understood and agreed, that whenever the reservations cannot conveniently be laid out in squares, they shall be laid out in *paralelograms*, or other figures, as found most practicable and convenient, so as to contain the *area* specified in miles, and in all cases they are to be located in such manner, and in such situations, as not to interfere with any improvements of the French or other white people, or any former cessions.

ART. VII. The said nations of Indians acknowledge themselves to be under the protection of the United States, and no other power, and will prove by their conduct that that are worthy of so great a blessing.

In testimony whereof, the said William Hull, and the sachems and war chiefs representing the said nations, have hereunto set their hands and seals.

Done at Detroit, in the territory of Michigan, the day and year first above written.

William Hull,	[L. S.]	Tonquish, his x mark,	[L. S.]
Chippewas:		Miott, his x mark,	[L. S.]
Peewanshemenogh, his x mark,	[L. S.]	Meuetugesheck, or the Little Cedar,	
Mamaushegauta, or Bad Legs, his x mark,	[L. S.]	his x mark,	[L. S.]
Pooquigauboawie, his x mark,	[L. S.]	Ottawas:	
Kiosk, his x mark,	[L. S.]	Aubauway, his x mark,	[L. S.]
Poquaquet, or the Ball, his x mark,	[L. S.]	Kawachewan, his x mark,	[L. S.]
Segangewan, his x mark,	[L. S.]	Sawgamaw, his x mark,	[L. S.]
Quitchonequit, or Big Cloud, his x mark,	[L. S.]	Ogouse, his x mark,	[L. S.]
		Wasagashick, his x mark,	[L. S.]
Quiconquish, his x mark,	[L. S.]	Pattawatimas:	
Puckenese, or the Spark of Fire,		Toquish, his x mark,	[L. S.]
his x mark,	[L. S.]	Noname, his x mark,	[L. S.]
Negig, or the Otter, his x mark,	[L. S.]	Nawme, his x mark,	[L. S.]
Measita, his x mark,	[L. S.]	Ninnewa, his x mark,	[L. S.]
Macquettequet, or Little Bear, his x mark,	[L. S.]	Skush, his x mark,	[L. S.]
		Wyandots:	
Nemekas, or Little Thunder, his x mark,	[L. S.]	Skahomet, his x mark,	[L. S.]
Sawanabenase, or Pechegabua, or		Miere, or Walk in the Water, his x mark,	[L. S.]
Grand Blanc, his x mark,	[L. S.]	Iyonayotha, his x mark,	[L. S.]

In presence of—

George McDougall, chief judge court D. H. and D.
C. Rush, attorney general.
Jacob Visger, associate judge of the D. court.
Jos. Watson, secretary to the legislature of Michigan.
Abijah Hull, surveyor for Michigan Territory.

Harris H. Hickman, counsellor at law.
Abraham Fuller Hull, counsellor at law and secretary to the
　Commission.
Whitmore Knaggs,
William Walker,
　　Sworn Interpreters.

TREATY WITH THE OSAGE, 1808.

Articles of a treaty made and concluded at Fort Clark, on the right bank of the Missouri, about five miles above the Fire Prairie, in the territory of Louisiana, the tenth day of November, in the year of our Lord one thousand eight hundred and eight, between Peter Chouteau, esquire, agent for the Osage, and specially commissioned and instructed to enter into the same by his excellency Meriwether Lewis, governor and superintendent of Indian affairs for the territory aforesaid, in behalf of the United States of America, of the one part, and the chiefs and warriors of the Great and Little Osage, for themselves and their nations respectively, on the other part.

Nov. 10, 1808.

7 Stat., 107.
Ratified Apr. 28, 1810.

ART. 1. The United States being anxious to promote peace, friendship and intercourse with the Osage tribes, to afford them every assistance in their power, and to protect them from the insults and injuries of other tribes of Indians, situated near the settlements of the white people, have thought proper to build a fort on the right bank of the Missouri, a few miles above the Fire Prairie, and do agree to garrison the same with as many regular troops as the President of the United States may, from time to time, deem necessary for the protection of all orderly, friendly and well disposed Indians of the Great and Little Osage nations, who reside at this place, and who do strictly conform to, and pursue the counsels or admonitions of the President of the United States through his subordinate officers.

A fort to be built.

ART. 2. The United States being also anxious that the Great and Little Osage, resident as aforesaid, should be regularly supplied with every species of merchandise, which their comfort may hereafter require, do engage to establish at this place, and permanently to continue at all seasons of the year, a well assorted store of goods, for the purpose of bartering with them on moderate terms for their peltries and furs.

A store of goods to be kept at the fort.

ART. 3. The United States agree to furnish at this place, for the use of the Osage nations, a black-smith, and tools to mend their arms and utensils of husbandry, and engage to build them a horse mill, or water mill; also to furnish them with ploughs, and to build for the great chief of the Great Osage, and for the great chief of the Little Osage, a strong block house in each of their towns, which are to be established near this fort.

A blacksmith, etc., to be furnished by United States.

ART. 4. With a view to quiet the animosities which at present exist between the inhabitants of the territory of Louisiana, and the Osage nations, in consequence of the lawless depredations of the latter, the United States do further agree to pay to their own citizens, the full value of such property as they can legally prove to have been stolen or destroyed by the said Osage, since the acquisition of Louisiana by the United States, provided the same does not exceed the sum of five thousand dollars.

Property stolen by the Osages before the acquisition of Louisiana to be paid for by the United States.

ART. 5. In consideration of the lands relinquished by the Great and Little Osage to the United States as stipulated in the sixth article of this treaty, the United States promise to deliver at Fire Prairie, or at St. Louis, yearly, to the Great Osage nation, merchandise to the

Merchandise to be delivered.

amount or value of one thousand dollars, and to the Little Osage nation, merchandise to the amount or value of five hundred dollars, reckoning the value of said merchandise at the first cost thereof, in the city or place in the United States, where the same shall have been procured.

Money paid.

And in addition to the merchandise aforesaid, the United States have, at and before the signature of these articles, paid to the Great Osage nation, the sum of eight hundred dollars, and to the Little Osage nation, the sum of four hundred dollars.

Boundary line established.

ART. 6. And in consideration of the advantages which we derive from the stipulations contained in the foregoing articles, we, the chiefs and warriors of the Great and Little Osage, for ourselves and our nations respectively, covenant and agree with the United States, that the boundary line between our nations and the United States shall be as follows, to wit: beginning at fort Clark, on the Missouri, five miles above Fire Prairie, and running thence a due south course to the river Arkansas, and down the same to the Mississippi; hereby ceding and relinquishing forever to the United States, all the lands which lie east of the said line, and north of the southwardly bank of the said river Arkansas, and all lands situated northwardly of the river Missouri. And we do further cede and relinquish to the United States forever, a tract of two leagues square, to embrace fort Clark, and to be laid off in such manner as the President of the United States shall think proper.

Lines to be run by United States.

ART. 7. And it is mutually agreed by the contracting parties, that the boundary lines hereby established, shall be run and marked at the expense of the United States, as soon as circumstances or their convenience will permit; and the Great and Little Osage promise to depute two chiefs from each of their respective nations, to accompany the commissioner, or commissioners who may be appointed on the part of the United States, to settle and adjust the said boundary line.

Hunting ground.

ART. 8. And the United States agree that such of the Great and Little Osage Indians, as may think proper to put themselves under the protection of fort Clark, and who observe the stipulations of this treaty with good faith, shall be permitted to live and to hunt, without molestation, on all that tract of country, west of the north and south boundary line, on which they, the said Great and Little Osage, have usually hunted or resided: *Provided*, The same be not the hunting grounds of any nation or tribe of Indians in amity with the United States; and on any other lands within the territory of Louisiana, without the limits of the white settlements, until the United States may think proper to assign the same as hunting grounds to other friendly Indians.

Injuries, how to be prevented and punished.

ART. 9. Lest the friendship which is now established between the United States and the said Indian nations should be interrupted by the misconduct of individuals, it is hereby agreed that for injuries done by individuals, no private revenge or retaliation shall take place, but instead thereof complaints shall be made by the party injured to the other, by the said nations or either of them, to the superintendent or other person appointed by the President to the chiefs of the said nation; and it shall be the duty of the said chiefs, upon complaints being made as aforesaid, to deliver up the person or persons against whom the complaint is made, to the end that he or they may be punished agreeably to the laws of the state or territory, where the offence may have been committed; and in like manner, if any robbery, violence or murder shall be committed on any Indian or Indians belonging to either of said nations, the person or persons so offending shall be tried, and if found guilty, shall be punished in like manner as if the injury had been done to a white man. And it is agreed that the chiefs of the Great and Little Osage, shall to the utmost of their power exert themselves to recover horses or other property which may be stolen from any citizen or citizens of the United States, by any individual or individuals of either of their nations; and the property so recovered shall be forthwith delivered to the superintendent or other person authorized to receive it, that it may be restored to the proper owner; and in cases where the exertions of the chiefs shall be ineffectual in recovering the property stolen as aforesaid, if sufficient proof can be adduced that such property was actually stolen by any Indian or Indians belonging to the said nations, or either of them, the superintendent, or other proper officer, may deduct from the annuity of the said nations respectively a sum equal to the value of the property which has been stolen. And the United States hereby guarantee to any Indian or Indians of the said nations respectively, a full indemnification for any horses or other property which may be stolen from them by any of their citizens: *Provided,* That the property so stolen cannot be recovered, and that sufficient proof is produced that it was actually stolen by a citizen of the United States. And the said nations of the Great and Little Osage engage, on the requisition or demand of the President of the United States, or of the superintendent, to deliver up any white man resident among them.

ART. 10. The United States receive the Great and Little Osage nations into their friendship and under their protection; and the said nations, on their part, declare that they will consider themselves under the protection of no other power whatsoever; disclaiming all right to cede, sell or in any manner transfer their lands to any foreign power, or to citizens of the United States or inhabitants of Louisiana, unless duly authorized by the President of the United States to make the said purchase or accept the said cession on behalf of the government. *(Osages received into the protection of the United States.)*

ART. 11. And if any person or persons, for hunting or other purpose, shall pass over the boundary lines, as established by this treaty, into the country reserved for the Great and Little Osage nations, without the license of the superintendent or other proper officer, they, the said Great and Little Osage, or either of them, shall be at liberty to apprehend such unlicensed hunters or other persons, and surrender them together with their property, but without other injury, insult or molestation, to the superintendent of Indian affairs, or to the agent nearest the place of arrest, to be dealt with according to law. *(Protection of the Indian hunting grounds.)*

ART. 12. And the chiefs and warriors as aforesaid, promise and engage that neither the Great nor Little Osage nation will ever, by sale, exchange or as presents, supply any nation or tribe of Indians, not in amity with the United States, with guns, ammunitions or other implements of war. *(Osages will not supply arms to Indians not in amity with the United States.)*

ART. 13. This treaty shall take effect and be obligatory on the contracting parties, as soon as the same shall have been ratified by the President, by and with the advice and consent of the Senate of the United States. *(Treaty, when to take effect.)*

In testimony whereof, the said Peter Chouteau, commissioned and instructed as aforesaid, and the chiefs and warriors of the Great and Little Osage nation of Indians, have hereunto set their hands and affixed their seals.

Done at fort Clark, the day above mentioned.

P. Chouteau, [L. S.]
E. B. Clemson, captain First Regiment Infantry, [L. S.]
L. Lorimer, lieutenant First Regiment Infantry, [L. S.]
Reazen Lewis, sub-agent Indian Affairs, [L. S.]
Papuisea, the grand chief of the Big Osage, his x mark, [L. S.]
Nichu Malli, the grand chief of the Little Osage, his x mark, [L. S.]
Voithe Voihe, the second chief of the Big Osage, his x mark, [L. S.]
Voithe Chinga, the second chief of the Little Osage, his x mark, [L. S.]
Ta Voingare, the little chief of the Big Osage, his x mark, [L. S.]
Osogahe, the little chief of the Little Osage, his x mark, [L. S.]
Voichinodhe, the little chief of the Big Osage, his x mark, [L. S.]
Voi Nache, the little chief of the Little Osage, his x mark, [L. S.]

Voi Nonpache, the little chief of the Big Osage, his x mark, [L. s.]
Quihi Ramaki, the little chief of the Little Osage, his x mark, [L. s.]
Voi Nache, the little chief of the Big Osage, his x mark, [L. s.]
Ponla Voitasuga, the little chief of the Little Osage, his x mark, [L. s.]
Caygache, the little chief of the Big Osage, his x mark, [L. s.]
Pahuroguesie, the little chief of the Little Osage, his x mark, [L. s.]
Miaasa, the little chief of the Big Osage, his x mark, [L. s.]
Manjaguida, the little chief of the Little Osage, his x mark, [L. s.]
Mantsa, the little chief of the Big Osage, his x mark, [L. s.]
Nicagaris, the little chief of the Big Osage, his x mark, [L. s.]
Dogachinga, the little chief of the Big Osage, his x mark, [L. s.]
Tavaingare, the little chief of the Little Osage, his x mark, [L. s.]
Tavainthere, the little chief of the Big Osage, his x mark, [L. s.]
Naguemani, the war chief of the Big Osage, his x mark, [L. s.]
Nicanauthe, the war chief of the Little Osage, his x mark, [L. s.]
Chonmelase, the war chief of the Big Osage, his x mark, [L. s.]
Nenonbas, the war chief of the Little Osage, his x mark, [L. s.]
The Pograngue, the war chief of the Big Osage, his x mark, [L. s.]
The Cayque, warrior, L. O. his x mark, [L. s.]
Nonpevoite, do. B. O. his x mark, [L. s.]
Vesasche, do. L. O. his x mark, [L. s.]
Tonchenanque, do. B. O. his x mark, [L. s.]
Caygache, do. L. O. his x mark, [L. s.]
Lihibi, do. B. O. his x mark, [L. s.]
Grinache, do. L. O. his x mark, [L. s.]
Ni Couil Bran, do. B. O. his x mark, [L. s.]
Chonnonsogue, do. L. O. his x mark, [L. s.]
Lisansandhe, do. B. O. his x mark, [L. s.]
Mequaque, do. L. O. his x mark, [L. s.]
Manhegare, do. B. O. his x mark, [L. s.]
Megahe, do. L. O. his x mark, [L. s.]
Meyhe, do. B. O. his x mark, [L. s.]
Nudhetavoi do. L. O. his x mark, [L. s.]
Thecayque, do. B. O. his x mark, [L. s.]
Voitasean, do. L. O. his x mark, [L. s.]
Cahapiche, do. B. O. his x mark, [L. s.]
Manhevoi, do. L. O. his x mark, [L. s.]
Talechiga, do. B. O. his x mark, [L. s.]
Pedhechiga, do. L. O. his x mark, [L. s.]
Cheganonsas, do. B. O. his x mark, [L. s.]
Nesaque, do. L. O. his x mark, [L. s.]
Lolechinga, do. B. O. his x mark, [L. s.]
Panevoiguanda, do. L. O. his x mark, [L. s.]
Tavoinhihi, do. B. O. his x mark, [L. s.]
Mithechinga, do. L. O. his x mark, [L. s.]
Voidhenache, do. B. O. his x mark, [L. s.]
Manquesi, do. L. O. his x mark, [L. s.]

Chingavoisa, do. B. O. his x mark, [L. s.]
Talevoile, do. L. O. his x mark, [L. s.]
Voiengran, do. B. O. his x mark, [L. s.]
Scamani, do. L. O. his x mark, [L. s.]
Nura Hague, do. B. O. his x mark, [L. s.]
Me Chinga, do. L. O. his x mark, [L. s.]
Pachigue, little chief, B. O. his x mark, [L. s.]
Rouda Nique, warrior, L. O. his x mark, [L. s.]
Ne Paste, do. B. O. his x mark, [L. s.]
Voibisandhe, do. L. O. his x mark, [L. s.]
Nehi Zanga, do. B. O. his x mark, [L. s.]
Nehudhe, warrior, L. O. his x mark, [L. s.]
The Pagranque, do. B. O. his x mark, [L. s.]
Chahetonga, do. L. O. his x mark, [L. s.]
Manguepee Mani, do. B. O. his x mark, [L. s.]
Voi Balune, do. L. O. his x mark, [L. s.]
Ponea Voitaniga, do. B. O. his x mark, [L. s.]
Taslondhe, do. L. O. his x mark, [L. s.]
Nendolagualui, warrior, B. O. his x mark, [L. s.]
Manguepu Mani, L. O. his x mark, [L. s.]
Ni Conil Bran, do. B. O. his x mark, [L. s.]
Voi Bahe, do. L. O. his x mark, [L. s.]
Onhehomani, do. B. O. his x mark, [L. s.]
Nuranin, do. L. O. his x mark, [L. s.]
Noguinilayque, do. B. O. his x mark, [L. s.]
Nanlatoho, do. L. O. his x mark, [L. s.]
Bashemindhe, do. B. O. his x mark, [L. s.]
Savoi, do. L. O. his x mark, [L. s.]
Chouquemonnon, do. B. O. his x mark, [L. s.]
Mandarihi, do. L. O. his x mark, [L. s.]
Manilourana, do. B. O. his x mark, [L. s.]
Nequevoile, do. L. O. his x mark, [L. s.]
Chonguehanga, do. B. O. his x mark, [L. s.]
Ponlachinga, do. L. O. his x mark, [L. s.]
Aguigueda, do. B. O. his x mark, [L. s.]
Manjaguida, do. L. O. his x mark, [L. s.]
Voidoguega, do. B. O. his x mark, [L. s.]
The Sindhe, do. L. O. his x mark, [L. s.]
Ninchagari, do. B. O. his x mark, [L. s.]
Voihadani, do. L. O. his x mark, [L. s.]
Voigaspache, do. B. O. his x mark, [L. s.]
Manyvoile, do. L. O. his x mark, [L. s.]
Quinihonigue, do. B. O. his mark, [L. s.]
Nognithe Chinga, do. L. O. his x mark, [L. s.]
Natanhi, do. B. O. his x mark, [L. s.]
Miasa, do. L. O. his x mark, [L. s.]
Ousabe, do. B. O. his x mark, [L. s.]
Voichinouthe, do. L. O. his x mark, [L. s.]
Amanpasse, do. B. O. his x mark, [L. s.]
Cutsagabe, do. L. O. his x mark, [L. s.]
Channahon, do. B. O. his x mark, [L. s.]
Non Basocri, do. L. O. his x mark, [L. s.]
Voichougras, do. B. O. his x mark, [L. s.]
Pedhechinga, do. L. O. his x mark, [L. s.]
Bassechinga, do. B. O. his x mark, [L. s.]

We, the undersigned chiefs and warriors of the band of Osages, residing on the river Arkansas, being a part of the Great Osage nation, having this day had the foregoing treaty read and explained to us, by his excellency Meriwether Lewis, esquire, do hereby acknowledge, consent to, and confirm all the stipulations therein contained, as fully and as completely as though we had been personally present at the signing, sealing, and delivering the same on the 10th day of November, 1808, the same being the day on which the said treaty was signed, sealed, and delivered, as will appear by a reference thereto.

In witness whereof, we have, for ourselves and our band of the Great Osage nation residing on the river Arkansas, hereunto set our hands and affixed our seals.

Done at St. Louis, in the territory of Louisiana, this thirty-first day of August, in the year of our Lord one thousand eight hundred and nine, and of the independence of the United States the thirty-fourth.

Gresdanmanses, or Clermond, first chief, his x mark,	[L. S.]	Hrulahtie, or Pipe Bird, his x mark,	[L. S.]
Couchesigres, or Big Tract, second chief, his x mark,	[L. S.]	Tawangahuh, or Builder of Towns, his x mark,	[L. S.]
Tales, or Straiting Deer, son of Big Tract, his x mark,	[L. S.]	Honencache, or the Terrible, his x mark,	[L. S.]
Aukickawakho, nephew of Big Tract, his x mark,	[L. S.]	Talahu, or Deer's Pluck, his x mark,	[L. S.]
Wachawahih, his x mark,	[L. S.]	Cahigiagreh, or Good Chief, his x mark,	[L. S.]
Pahelagren, or Handsome Hair, his x mark,	[L. S.]	Baughonghcheh, or Cutter, his x mark,	[L. S.]
Hombahagren, or Fine Day, his x mark,	[L. S.]	Basonchinga, or Little Pine, his x mark,	[L. S.]
Harachabe, or the Eagle, his x mark,	[L. S.]		

In presence of us, and before signature attached to the original:

John G. Comegys,
George Man,
John W. Honey,
Samuel Solomon, jun.

John P. Gates, Interpreter,
Noel Mongrain Marque, Indian Interpreter,
Bazil Nassier Marque, Indian Interpreter.

TREATY WITH THE CHIPPEWA, ETC., 1808.

Articles of a treaty made and concluded at Brownstown, in the territory of Michigan, between William Hull, governor of said territory, superintendant of Indian affairs, and commissioner plenipotentiary of the United States of America, for concluding any treaty or treaties, which may be found necessary, with any of the Indian tribes, North West of the river Ohio, of the one part, and the Sachems, Chiefs, and Warriors of the Chippewa, Ottawa, Pottawatamie, Wyandot, and Shawanoese nations of Indians, of the other part.

Nov. 25, 1808.

7 Stat., 112.
Ratified Mar. 1, 1809.
Proclaimed Mar. 3, 1809.

ARTICLE I. WHEREAS by a treaty concluded at Detroit, on the seventeenth day of November, in the year of our Lord one thousand eight hundred and seven, a tract of land lying to the West and North of the river Miami, of Lake Erie, and principally within the territory of Michigan, was ceded by the Indian nations, to the United States; and whereas the lands lying on the south eastern side of the said river Miami, and between said river, and the boundary lines established by the treaties of Greenville and Fort Industry, with the exception of a few small reservations to the United States, still belong to the Indian nations, so that the United States cannot, of right, open and maintain a convenient road from the settlements in the state of Ohio, to the settlements in the territory of Michigan, nor extend those settlements so as to connect them; in order therefore to promote this object, so desirable and evidently beneficial to the Indian nations, as well as to the United States, the parties have agreed to the following articles, which when ratified by the President of the United States, by and with the advice and consent of the Senate thereof, shall be reciprocally binding.

Preamble.

A tract of land granted for a road.

ARTICLE II. The several nations of Indians aforesaid, in order to promote the object mentioned in the preceding article, and in consideration of the friendship they bear towards the United States, for the liberal and benevolent policy, which has been practised towards them by the government thereof, do hereby give, grant, and cede, unto the said United States, a tract of land for a road, of one hundred and twenty feet in width, from the foot of the rapids of the river Miami of Lake Erie, to the western line of the Connecticut reserve, and all the land within one mile of the said road, *on each side thereof*, for the purpose of establishing settlements along the same; also a tract of land, for a *road only*, of one hundred and twenty feet in width, to run southwardly from what is called Lower Sandusky, to the boundary line established by the treaty of Greenville, with the privilege of taking at all times, such timber and other materials, from the adjacent lands as may be necessary for making and keeping in repair the said road, with the bridges that may be required along the same.

Lines to be run by United States.

ARTICLE III. It is agreed, that the lines embracing the lands, given and ceded by the preceding article, shall be run in such directions, as may be thought most advisable by the President of the United States for the purposes aforesaid.

Privilege of hunting and fishing on lands ceded.

ARTICLE IV. It is agreed that the said Indian nations shall retain the privilege of hunting and fishing on the lands given and ceded as above, so long as the same shall remain the property of the United States.

Indians acknowledge protection of United States.

ARTICLE V. The several nations of Indians aforesaid, do again acknowledge themselves to be under the protection of the United States, and of no other sovereign; and the United States on their part do renew their covenant, to extend protection to them according to the intent and meaning of stipulations in former treaties.

Done at Brownstown, in the territory of Michigan, this 25th day of November, in the year of our Lord one thousand eight hundred and eight, and of the independence of the United States of America the thirty-third.

William Hull, commissioner, [L. S.]
Chippewas:
Nemekas, or Little Thunder, his x mark, [L. S.]
Puckanese, or Spark of Fire, his x mark, [L. S.]
Macquettequet, or Little Bear, his x mark, [L. S.]
Shimnanaquette, his x mark, [L. S.]
Ottawas:
Kewachewan, his x mark, [L. S.]
Tondagane, his x mark, [L. S.]
Pattawatimas:
Mogau, his x mark, [L. S.]
Wapmeme, or White Pigeon, his x mark, [L. S.]
Mache, his x mark, [L. S.]

Wyandots:
Miere, or Walk in the Water, his x mark, [L. S.]
Iyonayotaha, or Joe, his x mark, [L. S.]
Skahomet, or Black Chief, his x mark, [L. S.]
Adam Brown, [L. S.]
Shawanees:
Makatewekasha, or Black Hoof, his x mark, [L. S.]
Koitawaypie, or Col. Lewis, his x mark, [L. S.]

Executed, after having been fully explained and understood, in presence of

Reuben Attwater, secretary of the Territory Michigan.
James Witherill, a judge of Michigan Territory.
Jacob Visger, judge of the district court.
Jos. Watson, secretary L. M. T.
Wm. Brown.
B. Campau.

Lewis Bond,
A. Lyons,
    As to the Ottawa chiefs.
Whitmore Knaggs,
William Walker,
F. Duchonquet,
Samuel Saunders,
    Sworn interpreters.

Attest:

Harris Hampden Hickman,
Secretary to the Commissioner.

TREATY WITH THE DELAWARES, ETC., 1809.

A treaty between the United States of America, and the tribes of Indians called the Delawares, Putawatimies, Miamies and Eel River Miamies.

Sept. 30, 1809.

7 Stat., 113.
Proclamation, Jan. 16, 1810.

JAMES MADISON, President of the United States, by William Henry Harrison, governor and commander-in-chief of the Indiana territory, superintendent of Indian affairs, and commissioner plenipotentiary of the United States for treating with the said Indian tribes, and the Sachems, Head men and Warriors of the Delaware, Putawatame, Miami and Eel River tribes of Indians, have agreed and concluded upon the following treaty; which, when ratified by the said President, with the advice and consent of the Senate of the United States, shall be binding on said parties.

ART. 1st. The Miami and Eel River tribes, and the Delawares and Putawatimies, as their allies, agree to cede to the United States all that tract of country which shall be included between the boundary line established by the treaty of Fort Wayne, the Wabash, and a line to be drawn from the mouth of a creek called Racoon Creek, emptying into the Wabash, on the south-east side, about twelve miles below the mouth of the Vermilion river, so as to strike the boundary line established by the treaty of Grouseland, at such a distance from its commencement at the north-east corner of the Vincennes tract, as will leave the tract now ceded thirty miles wide at the narrowest place. And also all that tract which shall be included between the following boundaries, viz: beginning at Fort Recovery, thence southwardly along the general boundary line, established by the treaty of Greenville, to its intersection with the boundary line established by the treaty of Grouseland; thence along said line to a point from which a line drawn parallel to the first mentioned line will be twelve miles distant from the same, and along the said parallel line to its intersection with a line to be drawn from Fort Recovery, parallel to the line established by the said treaty of Grouseland.

Cession of lands.

ART. 2d. The Miamies explicitly acknowledge the equal right of the Delawares with themselves to the country watered by the White river. But it is also to be clearly understood that neither party shall have the right of disposing of the same without the consent of the other: and any improvements which shall be made on the said land by the Delawares, or their friends the Mochecans, shall be theirs forever.

Equal right of the Delawares acknowledged.

ART. 3d. The compensation to be given for the cession made in the first article shall be as follows, viz: to the Delawares a permanent annuity of five hundred dollars; to the Miamies a like annuity of five hundred dollars; to the Eel river tribe a like annuity of two hundred and fifty dollars; and to the Putawatimies a like annuity of five hundred dollars.

Compensation.

ART. 4th. All the stipulations made in the treaty of Greenville, relatively to the manner of paying the annuities, and the right of the Indians to hunt upon the land, shall apply to the annuities granted and the land ceded by the present treaty.

Manner of paying annuities.

ART. 5th. The consent of the Wea tribe shall be necessary to complete the title to the first tract of land here ceded; a separate convention shall be entered into between them and the United States, and a reasonable allowance of goods given them in hand, and a permanent annuity, which shall not be less than three hundred dollars, settled upon them.

Consent of the Wea tribe required.

ART. 6th. The annuities promised by the third article, and the goods now delivered to the amount of five thousand two hundred dollars, shall be considered as a full compensation for the cession made in the first article.

Annuities, etc., to be considered full compensation.

Regulations to prevent trespasses.

ART. 7th. The tribes who are parties to this treaty being desirous of putting an end to the depredations which are committed by abandoned individuals of their own color, upon the cattle, horses, &c. of the more industrious and careful, agree to adopt the following regulations, viz: when any theft or other depredation shall be committed by any individual or individuals of one of the tribes above mentioned, upon the property of any individual or individuals of another tribe, the chiefs of the party injured shall make application to the agent of the United States, who is charged with the delivery of the annuities of the tribe to which the offending party belongs, whose duty it shall be to hear the proofs and allegations on either side, and determine between them: and the amount of his award shall be immediately deducted from the annuity of the tribe to which the offending party belongs, and given to the person injured, or to the chief of his village for his use.

Relinquishment by United States.

ART. 8th. The United States agree to relinquish their right to the reservation, at the old Ouroctenon towns, made by the treaty of Greenville, so far at least as to make no further use of it than for the establishment of a military post.

Kickapoos.

ART. 9th. The tribes who are parties to this treaty, being desirous to show their attachment to their brothers the Kickapoos, agree to cede to the United States the lands on the north-west side of the Wabash, from the Vincennes tract to a northwardly extention of the line running from the mouth of the aforesaid Raccoon creek, and fifteen miles in width from the Wabash, on condition that the United States shall allow them an annuity of four hundred dollars. But this article is to have no effect unless the Kickapoos will agree to it.

In testimony whereof, the said William Henry Harrison, and the sachems and war chiefs of the beforementioned tribes, have hereunto set their hands and affixed their seals, at fort Wayne, this thirtieth of September, eighteen hundred and nine.

William Henry Harrison,   [L. S.]
    Delawares:
Anderson, for Hockingpomskon,
    who is absent, his x mark,   [L. S.]
Anderson, his x mark,   [L. S.]
Petchekekapon, his x mark,   [L. S.]
The Beaver, his x mark,   [L. S.]
Captain Killbuck, his x mark,   [L. S.]
    Pattawatimas:
Winemac, his x mark,   [L. S.]
Five Medals, by his son, his x mark, [L. S.]
Mogawgo, his x mark,   [L. S.]
Shissahecon, for himself and his
    brother Tuthinipee, his x
    mark,   [L. S.]
Ossmeet, brother to Five Medals,
    his x mark,   [L. S.]
Nanousekah, Penamo's son, his x
    mark,   [L. S.]

Mosser, his x mark,   [L. S.]
Chequinimo, his x mark,   [L. S.]
Sackanackshut, his x mark,   [L. S.]
Conengee, his x mark,   [L. S.]
    Miamis:
Pucan, his x mark,
The Owl, his x mark,   [L. S.]
Meshekenoghqua, or the Little
    Turtle, his x mark,   [L. S.]
Wapemangua, or the Loon, his x
    mark,   [L. S.]
Silver Heels, his x mark,   [L. S.]
Shawapenomo, his x mark,
    Eel Rivers:
Charley, his x mark,   [L. S.]
Sheshangomequah, or Swallow, his
    x mark,   [L. S.]
The young Wyandot, a Miami of
    Elk Hart, his x mark,   [L. S.]

In presence of—

Peter Jones, secretary to the Commissioner,
John Johnson, Indian agent,
A. Heald, Capt. U. S. Army,
A. Edwards, surgeon's mate,
Ph. Ostrander, Lieut. U. S. Army,
John Shaw,
Stephen Johnston,

J. Hamilton, sheriff of Dearborn County,
Hendrick Aupaumut.
William Wells,
John Conner,
Joseph Barron,
Abraham Ash,
        Sworn Intepreters.

SUPPLEMENTARY TREATY WITH THE MIAMI, ETC., 1809.

A separate article entered into at fort Wayne, on the thirtieth day of September, in the year of our Lord one thousand eight hundred and nine, between William Henry Harrison, commissioner plenipotentiary of the United States for treating with the Indian tribes, and the Sachems and chief warriors of the Miami and Eel river tribes of Indians, which is to be considered as forming part of the treaty this day concluded between the United States and the said tribes, and their allies the Delawares and Putawatimies.

Sept. 30, 1809.

7 Stat., 115.
Proclamation Jan. 16, 1810.

As the greater part of the lands ceded to the United States, by the treaty this day concluded, was the exclusive property of the Miami nation and guaranteed to them by the treaty of Grouseland, it is considered by the said commissioner just and reasonable that their request to be allowed some further and additional compensation should be complied with. It is therefore agreed that the United States shall deliver for their use, in the course of the next spring at fort Wayne, domestic animals to the amount of five hundred dollars, and the like number for the two following years, and that an armoree shall be also maintained at fort Wayne for the use of the Indians as heretofore. It is also agreed that if the Kickapoos confirm the ninth article of the treaty to which this is a supplement, the United States will allow to the Meamies a further permanent annuity of two hundred dollars, and to the Wea and Eel river tribes a further annuity of one hundred dollars each.

Additional compensation to the Miamis.

Further allowance to the Miamis, Weas, and Eel Rivers.

In testimony whereof, the said William Henry Harrison, and the sachems and war chiefs of the said tribes, have hereunto set their hands and affixed their seals, the day and place abovementioned.

William Henry Harrison,	[L. s.]	Miamis:	
Charley, an Eel River, his x mark,	[L. s.]	The Owl, his x mark,	[L. s.]
Pacan, his x mark,	[L. s.]	Wafremanqua, or the Loon, his	
Sheshauqouoquah, or Swallow, an		x mark,	[L. s.]
Eel River, his x mark,	[L. s.]	Mushekeuoghqua, or the Little	
The young Wyandot, a Miami, or		Turtle, his x mark,	[L. s.]
Elk Hart, his x mark,	[L. s.]	Silver Heels, his x mark,	[L. s.]
Shywahbeanomo, his x mark,	[L. s.]		

In presence of—
    Peter Jones, secretary to the Commissioner.
    Joseph Barron,
    A. Edwards,
    William Wells,
    John Shaw.

TREATY WITH THE WEA, 1809.

A convention entered into at Vincennes, in the Indiana territory, between William Henry Harrison, commissioner plenipotentiary of the United States, for treating with the Indian tribes north-west of the Ohio and the Wea tribe.

Oct. 26, 1809.

7 Stat., 116.
Ratified Jan. 2, 1810.
Proclaimed Jan. 25, 1810.

The said tribe, by their Sachems and head warriors, hereby declare their full and free consent to the treaty concluded at fort Wayne, on the thirtieth ultimo, by the above mentioned commissioner, with the Delaware, Miami, Putawatimie, and Eel river tribes; and also to the separate article entered into on the same day with the Miami and Eel river tribes. And the said commissioner, on the part of the United States, agrees to allow the said Indian tribe an additional annuity of three hundred dollars, and a present sum of fifteen hundred dollars, in consideration of the relinquishment made in the first article of said treaty;

Weas consent to the treaty of Sept. 30, 1809.

and a further permanent annuity of one hundred dollars, as soon as the Kickapoos can be brought to give their consent to the ninth article of said treaty.

In testimony whereof, the said William Henry Harrison, and the sachems and head warriors of the said tribe, have hereunto set their hands and affixed their seals, this twenty-sixth day of October, eighteen hundred and nine.

William H. Harrison,	[L. s.]
Jacco, his x mark,	[L. s.]
Shawanee, his x mark,	[L. s.]
Tosania, his x mark,	[L. s.]
Cohona, his x mark,	[L. s.]
Lapousier, his x mark,	[L. s.]
Pequia, his x mark,	[L. s.]
Quewa, or Negro Legs, his x mark,	[L. s.]
Alengua, his x mark,	[L. s.]
Chequia, or Little Eyes, his x mark,	[L. s.]

In the presence of—

Peter Jones, secretary to the Commissioner,
B. Parke, one of the Judges of the Indiana Territory,
Thomas Randolph, A. G. of Indiana,
Will. Jones, of Vincennes,
Saml. W. Davis, lieutenant-colonel, Ohio State,
Shadrach Bond, jr., of the Illinois Territory,
Joseph Barron, sworn interpreter.

TREATY WITH THE KICKAPOO, 1809.

A treaty between the United States of America and the Kickapoo tribe of Indians.

Dec. 9, 1809.
───────
7 Stat., 117.
Ratified Mar. 5, 1810.
Proclaimed Mar. 8, 1810.

WILLIAM HENRY HARRISON, governor of the Indiana territory and commissioner plenipotentiary of the United States for treating with the Indian tribes north west of the Ohio, and the Sachems and war chiefs of the Kickapoo tribe, on the part of said tribe, have agreed on the following articles, which, when ratified by the President, by and with the advice of the Senate, shall be binding on said parties.

Kickapoos agree to second article of treaty of Sept. 30, 1809. ART. 1. The ninth article of the treaty concluded at Fort Wayne on the thirtieth of September last, and the cession it containes is hereby agreed to by the Kickapoos, and a permanent additional annuity of four hundred dollars, and goods to the amount of eight hundred dollars, now delivered, is to be considered as a full compensation for the said cession.

Cession to the United States. ART. 2. The said tribe further agrees to cede to the United States all that tract of land which lies between the tract above ceded, the Wabash, the Vermillion river, and a line to be drawn from the North corner of the said ceded tract, so as to strike the Vermilion river at the distance of twenty miles in a direct line from its mouth. For this cession a further annuity of one hundred dollars, and the sum of seven hundred dollars in goods now delivered, is considered as a full compensation. But if the Miamies should not be willing to sanction the latter cession, and the United States should not think proper to take possession of the land without their consent, they shall be released from the obligation to pay the additional annuity of one hundred dollars.

Manner of paying annuity. ART. 3. The stipulations contained in the treaty of Greenville, relatively to the manner of paying the annuity and of the right of the Indians to hunt upon the land, shall apply to the annuity granted and the land ceded by the present treaty.

In testimony whereof, the said William Henry Harrison, and the sachems and head war chiefs of the said tribe, have hereunto set their hands and affixed their seals, this ninth day of December, one thousand eight hundred and nine.

William Henry Harrison,	[L. S.]
Joe Renard, Nemahson, or a Man on his Feet, his x mark,	[L. S.]
Knoshania, or the Otter, his x mark,	[L. S.]
Wakoah, or Fox Hair, his x mark,	[L. S.]
Nonoah, or a Child at the Breast, his x mark,	[L. S.]
Moquiah, or the Bear Skin, his x mark,	[L. S.]

Signed in the presence of (the word "seven" in the second article being written upon an erasure)

Peter Jones, secretary to the Commissioner,
George Wallace, jun., justice of peace, K.
Jno. Gibson, secretary Indiana Territory,
Will. Jones, justice of peace,

E. Stout, justice of peace,
Charles Smith, of Vincennes,
Hyacinthe Lasselle, of Vincennes,
Dom. Lacroix, of Vincennes,
Joseph Barron, interpreter.

TREATY WITH THE WYANDOT, ETC., 1814.

A treaty of peace and friendship between the United States of America, and the tribes of Indians called the Wyandots, Delawares, Shawanoese, Senecas, and Miamies.

July 22, 1814.

7 Stat., 118.
Ratified, Dec. 13, 1814.
Proclaimed Dec. 21, 1814.

THE said United States of America, by William Henry Harrison, late a major general in the army of the United States, and Lewis Cass, governor of the Michigan territory, duly authorized and appointed commissioners for the purpose, and the said tribes, by their head men, chiefs, and warriors, assembled at Greenville, in the state of Ohio, have agreed to the following articles, which, when ratified by the president of the United States, by and with the advice and consent of the Senate thereof, shall be binding upon them and the said tribes.

ARTICLE I.

The United States and the Wyandots, Delawares, Shawanoese, and Senecas, give peace to the Miamie nation of Indians, formerly designated as the Miamie Eel River and Weea tribes; they extend this indulgence also to the bands of the Putawatimies, which adhere to the Grand Sachem Tobinipee, and to the chief Onoxa, to the Ottawas of Blanchard's creek, who have attached themselves to the Shawanoese tribe, and to such of the said tribe as adhere to the chief called the Wing, in the neighborhood of Detroit, and to the Kickapoos, under the direction of their chiefs who sign this treaty.

Peace given to the Miami nation, etc.

ARTICLE II.

The tribes and bands abovementioned, engage to give their aid to the United States in prosecuting the war against Great-Britain, and such of the Indian tribes as still continue hostile; and to make no peace with either without the consent of the United States. The assistance herein stipulated for, is to consist of such a number of their warriors from each tribe, as the president of the United States, or any officer having his authority therefor, may require.

Aid to be given to United States in the war with Great-Britain.

ARTICLE III.

The Wyandot tribe, and the Senecas of Sandusky and Stony Creek, the Delaware and Shawanoes tribes, who have preserved their fidelity

Protection of United States acknowledged.

to the United States throughout the war, again acknowledge themselves under the protection of the said states, and of no other power whatever; and agree to aid the United States, in the manner stipulated for in the former article, and to make no peace but with the consent of the said states.

ARTICLE IV.

United States will establish the boundaries, etc.

In the event of a faithful performance of the conditions of this treaty, the United States will confirm and establish all the boundaries between their lands and those of the Wyandots, Delawares, Shawanoese and Miamies, as they existed previously to the commencement of the war.

In testimony whereof, the said commissioners, and the said head men, chiefs, and warriors, of the beforementioned tribes of Indians, have hereunto set their hands and affixed their seals.

Done at Greenville, in the State of Ohio, this twenty-second day of July, in the year of our Lord one thousand eight hundred and fourteen, and of the independence of the United States the thirty-ninth.

William Henry Harrison, [L. S.]
Lewis Cass, [L. S.]
Wyandots:
Tarhe, or Crane, his x mark, [L. S.]
Harroneyough, or Cherokee Boy, his x mark, [L. S.]
Tearroneauou, or between the Legs, his x mark, [L. S.]
Menoucou, his x mark, [L. S.]
Rusharra, or Stookey, his x mark, [L. S.]
Senoshus, his x mark, [L. S.]
Zashuona, or Big Arm, his x mark, [L. S.]
Teanduttasooh, or Punch, his x mark, [L. S.]
Tapuksough, or John Hicks, his x mark, [L. S.]
Ronoinness, or Sky come down, his x mark, [L. S.]
Teendoo, his x mark, [L. S.]
Ronaiis, his x mark, [L. S.]
Omaintsiarnah, or Bowyers, his x mark, [L. S.]
Delawares:
Taiunshrah, or Charles, his x mark, [L. S.]
Tiundraka, or John Bolesle, his x mark, [L. S.]
Eroneniarah, or Shroneseh, his x mark, [L. S.]
Kicktohenina, or Captain Anderson, his x mark, [L. S.]
Lemottenuckques, or James Nanticoke, his x mark, [L. S.]
Laoponnichle, or Baube, his x mark, [L. S.]
Joon Queake, or John Queake, his x mark, [L. S.]
Kill Buck, his x mark, [L. S.]
Neachcomingd, his x mark, [L. S.]
Montgomery Montawe, his x mark, [L. S.]
Capt. Buck, his x mark, [L. S.]
Hooque, or Mole, his x mark, [L. S.]
Captain White Eyes, his x mark, [L. S.]
Captain Pipe, his x mark, [L. S.]
McDaniel, his x mark, [L. S.]
Captain Snap, his x mark, [L. S.]
Shawanees:
Cutewecusa, or Black Hoof, his x mark, [L. S.]
Tamenetha, or Butter, his x mark, [L. S.]
Piaseka, or Wolf, his x mark, [L. S.]

Pomtha, or Walker, his x mark, [L. S.]
Shammonetho, or Snake, his x mark, [L. S.]
Pemthata, or Turkey flying by, his x mark, [L. S.]
Wethawakasika, or Yellow Water, his x mark, [L. S.]
Quetawah, Sinking, his x mark, [L. S.]
Sokutchemah, or Frozen, his x mark, [L. S.]
Wynepuechsika, or Corn Stalk, his x mark, [L. S.]
Chiachska, or captain Tom, his x mark, [L. S.]
Quitawepeh, or captain Lewis, his x mark, [L. S.]
Teawascoota, or Blue Jacket, his x mark, [L. S.]
Tacomtequah, or Cross the water, his x mark, [L. S.]
Ottawas:
Watashnewa, or Bear's Legs, his x mark, [L. S.]
Wapachek, or White Fisher, his x mark, [L. S.]
Tootagen, or Bell, his x mark, [L. S.]
Aughquanahquose, or Stumptail Bear, his x mark, [L. S.]
Mcokenuh, or Bear King, his x mark, [L. S.]
Senekas:
Coontindnau, or Coffee Houn, his x mark, [L. S.]
Togwon, his x mark, [L. S.]
Endosquierunt, or John Harris, his x mark, [L. S.]
Cantareteroo, his x mark, [L. S.]
Cuntahtentuhwa, or Big Turtle, his x mark, [L. S.]
Renonnesa, or Wiping Stick, his x mark, [L. S.]
Corachcoonke, or Reflection, or Civil John, his x mark, [L. S.]
Coonautanahtoo, his x mark, [L. S.]
Seeistahe, Black, his x mark, [L. S.]
Tooteeandee, Thomas Brand, his x mark, [L. S.]
Haneusewa, his x mark, [L. S.]
Uttawuntus, his x mark, [L. S.]
Lutauqueson, his x mark, [L. S.]
Miamis:
Pecon, his x mark, [L. S.]

Lapassine, or Ashenonquah, his x mark, [L. s.]
Osage, his x mark, [L. s.]
Natoweesa, his x mark, [L. s.]
Meshekeleata, or the Big man, his x mark, [L. s.]
Sanamahhonga, or Stone Eater, his x mark, [L. s.]
Neshepehtah, or Double Tooth, his x mark, [L. s.]
Metoosania, or Indian, his x mark, [L. s.]
Chequia, or Poor Racoon, his x mark, [L. s.]
Wapepecheka, his x mark, [L. s.]
Chingomega Eboo, or Owl, his x mark, [L. s.]
Kewesekong, or Circular Travelling, his x mark, [L. s.]
Wapasabanah, or White Racoon, his x mark, [L. s.]
Chekemetine, or Turtle's Brother, his x mark, [L. s.]
Pocondoqua, or Crooked, his x mark, [L. s.]
Chequeah, or Poor Racoon, a Wea, or Little Eyes, his x mark, [L. s.]
Showilingeshua, or Open Hand, his x mark, [L. s.]
Okawea, or Porcupine, his x mark, [L. s.]
Shawanoe, his x mark, [L. s.]
Mawansa, or Young Wolf, his x mark, [L. s.]
Meshwawa, or Wounded, his x mark, [L. s.]
Sangwecomya, or Buffaloe, his x mark, [L. s.]
Pequia, or George, his x mark, [L. s.]

Keelswa, or Sun, his x mark, [L. s.]
Wabsea, or White Skin, his x mark, [L. s.]
Wanseea, or Sunrise, his x mark, [L. s.]
Angatoka, or Pile of Wood, his x mark, [L. s.]

Pattawatimas:
Toopinnepe, his x mark, [L. s.]
Onoxa, or Five Medals, his x mark, [L. s.]
Metea, his x mark, [L. s.]
Conge, or Bear's foot, his x mark, [L. s.]
Nanownseca, his x mark, [L. s.]
Chagobbe, or One who sees all over, his x mark, [L. s.]
Meshon, his x mark, [L. s.]
Penosh, his x mark, [L. s.]
Checanoe, his x mark, [L. s.]
Neshcootawa, his x mark, [L. s.]
Tonguish, his x mark, [L. s.]
Nebaughkua, his x mark, [L. s.]
Wesnanesa, his x mark, [L. s.]
Chechock, or Crane, his x mark, [L. s.]
Kepoota, his x mark, [L. s.]
Mackoota, or Crow, his x mark, [L. s.]
Papeketcha, or Flat Belly, his x mark, [L. s.]

Kickapoos:
Ketoote, or Otter, his x mark, [L. s.]
Makotanecote, or Black Tree, his x mark, [L. s.]
Sheshepa, or Duck, his x mark, [L. s.]
Wapekonnia, or White Blanket, his x mark, [L. s.]
Acooche, or the Man Hun, his x mark, [L. s.]
Chekaskagalon, his x mark, [L. s.]

In presence of (the words "and the Wyandots, Delawares, Shawanees, and Senekas," interlined in the first article before signing).

James Dill, secretary to the commissioners,
Jno. Johnston, Indian agent,
B. F. Stickney, Indian agent,
James J. Nisbet, associate judge of court of common pleas, Preble County,
Thos. G. Gibson.
Antoine Boindi,
Wm. Walker,
William Connor,

J. Bts. Chandonnai,
Stephen Ruddeed,
James Pelteir,
Joseph Bertrand, sworn interpreters,
Thos. Ramsey, captain First Rifle Regiment,
John Conner,
John Riddle, colonel First Regiment Ohio Militia.

TREATY WITH THE CREEKS, 1814.

Articles of agreement and capitulation, made and concluded this ninth day of August, one thousand eight hundred and fourteen, between major general Andrew Jackson, on behalf of the President of the United States of America, and the chiefs, deputies, and warriors of the Creek Nation.

Aug. 9, 1814.

7 Stat., 120.
Proclamation, Feb 16, 1815.

WHEREAS an unprovoked, inhuman, and sanguinary war, waged by the hostile Creeks against the United States, hath been repelled, prosecuted and determined, successfully, on the part of the said States, in conformity with principles of national justice and honorable warfare— And whereas consideration is due to the rectitude of proceeding dictated by instructions relating to the re-establishment of peace: Be it remembered, that prior to the conquest of that part of the Creek nation hostile to the United States, numberless aggressions had been committed against the peace, the property, and the lives of citizens of the

United States, and those of the Creek nation in amity with her, at the mouth of Duck river, Fort Mimms, and elsewhere, contrary to national faith, and the regard due to an article of the treaty concluded at New-York, in the year seventeen hundred ninety, between the two nations: That the United States, previously to the perpetration of such outrages, did, in order to ensure future amity and concord between the Creek nation and the said states, in conformity with the stipulations of former treaties, fulfil, with punctuality and good faith, her engagements to the said nation: that more than two-thirds of the whole number of chiefs and warriors of the Creek nation, disregarding the genuine spirit of existing treaties, suffered themselves to be instigated to violations of their national honor, and the respect due to a part of their own nation faithful to the United States and the principles of humanity, by impostures [impostors,] denominating themselves Prophets, and by the duplicity and misrepresentation of foreign emissaries, whose governments are at war, open or understood, with the United States.   Wherefore,

Cession of territory by the Creeks as equivalent to the expenses of the war.

1st—The United States demand an equivalent for all expenses incurred in prosecuting the war to its termination, by a cession of all the territory belonging to the Creek nation within the territories of the United States, lying west, south, and south-eastwardly, of a line to be run and described by persons duly authorized and appointed by the President of the United States—Beginning at a point on the eastern bank of the Coosa river, where the south boundary line of the Cherokee nation crosses the same; running from thence down the said Coosa river with its eastern bank according to its various meanders to a point one mile above the mouth of Cedar creek, at Fort Williams, thence east two miles, thence south two miles, thence west to the eastern bank of the said Coosa river, thence down the eastern bank thereof according to its various meanders to a point opposite the upper end of the great falls, (called by the natives Woetumka,) thence east from a true meridian line to a point due north of the mouth of Ofucshee, thence south by a like meridian line to the mouth of Ofucshee on the south side of the Tallapoosa river, thence up the same, according to its various meanders, to a point where a direct course will cross the same at the distance of ten miles from the mouth thereof, thence a direct line to the mouth of Summochico creek, which empties into the Chatahouchie river on the east side thereof below the Eufaulau town, thence east from a true meridian line to a point which shall intersect the line now dividing the lands claimed by the said Creek nation from those claimed and owned by the state of Georgia: Provided, nevertheless, that where any possession of any chief or warrior of the Creek nation, who shall have been friendly to the United States during the war, and taken an active part therein, shall be within the territory ceded by these articles to the United States, every such person shall be entitled to a reservation of land within the said territory of one mile square, to include his improvements as near the centre thereof as may be, which shall inure to the said chief or warrior, and his descendants, so long as he or they shall continue to occupy the same, who shall be protected by and subject to the laws of the United States; but upon the voluntary abandonment thereof, by such possessor or his descendants, the right of occupancy or possession of said lands shall devolve to the United States, and be identified with the right of property ceded hereby.

Guaranty of other territory of the Creeks.

2nd—The United States will guarantee to the Creek nation, the integrity of all their territory eastwardly and northwardly of the said line to be run and described as mentioned in the first article.

Intercourse with British or Spanish posts to cease.

3d—The United States demand, that the Creek nation abandon all communication, and cease to hold any intercourse with any British or Spanish post, garrison, or town; and that they shall not admit among them, any agent or trader, who shall not derive authority to hold commercial, or other intercourse with them, by licence from the President or authorized agent of the United States.

4th—The United States demand an acknowledgment of the right to establish military posts and trading houses, and to open roads within the territory, guaranteed to the Creek nation by the second article, and a right to the free navigation of all its waters.

Establishment of military posts.

5th—The United States demand, that a surrender be immediately made, of all the persons and property, taken from the citizens of the United States, the friendly part of the Creek nation, the Cherokee, Chickesaw, and Choctaw nations, to the respective owners; and the United States will cause to be immediately restored to the formerly hostile Creeks, all the property taken from them since their submission, either by the United States, or by any Indian nation in amity with the United States, together with all the prisoners taken from them during the war.

All property taken to be surrendered.

6th—The United States demand the caption and surrender of all the prophets and instigators of the war, whether foreigners or natives, who have not submitted to the arms of the United States, and become parties to these articles of capitulation, if ever they shall be found within the territory guaranteed to the Creek nation by the second article.

The prophets and instigators of the war to be given up.

7th—The Creek nation being reduced to extreme want, and not at present having the means of subsistance, the United States, from motives of humanity, will continue to furnish gratuitously the necessaries of life, until the crops of corn can be considered competent to yield the nation a supply, and will establish trading houses in the nation, at the discretion of the President of the United States, and at such places as he shall direct, to enable the nation, by industry and economy, to procure clothing.

Supplies of corn to be presented to the Creeks.

8th—A permanent peace shall ensue from the date of these presents forever, between the Creek nation and the United States, and between the Creek nation and the Cherokee, Chickasaw, and Choctaw nations.

Permanent peace.

9th—If in running east from the mouth of Summochico creek, it shall so happen that the settlement of the Kennards, fall within the lines of the territory hereby ceded, then, and in that case, the line shall be run east on a true meridian to Kitchofoonee creek, thence down the middle of said creek to its junction with Flint River, immediately below the Oakmulgee town, thence up the middle of Flint river to a point due east of that at which the above line struck the Kitchofoonee creek, thence east to the old line herein before mentioned, to wit: the line dividing the lands claimed by the Creek nation, from those claimed and owned by the state of Georgia.

Lines of the territory.

The parties to these presents, after due consideration, for themselves and their constituents, agree to ratify and confirm the preceding articles, and constitute them the basis of a permanent peace between the two nations; and they do hereby solemnly bind themselves, and all the parties concerned and interested, to a faithful performance of every stipulation contained therein.

In testimony whereof, they have hereunto, interchangeably, set their hands and affixed their seals, the day and date above written.

Andrew Jackson, major general commanding Seventh Military District,   [L. S.]

Tustunnuggee Thlucco, speaker for the Upper Creeks, his x mark, [L. S.]

Micco Aupoegau, of Toukaubatchee, his x mark,   [L. S.]

Tustunnuggee Hopoiee, speaker of the Lower Creeks, his x mark, [L. S.]

Micco Achulee, of Cowetau, his x mark,   [L. S.]

William McIntosh, jr., major of Cowetau, his x mark,   [L. S.]

Tuskee Eneah, of Cussetau, his x mark,   [L. S.]

Faue Emautla, of Cussetau, his x mark,   [L. S.]

Toukaubatchee Tustunnuggee, of Hitchetee, his x mark,   [L. S.]

Noble Kinnard, of Hitchetee, his x mark,   [L. S.]

Hopoiee Hutkee, of Souwagoolo,
his x mark,   [L. S.]
Hopoiee Hutkee, for Hopoie Yo-
holo, of Souwogoolo, his x mark, [L. S.]
Folappo Haujo, of Eufaulau, on
Chattohochee, his x mark,   [L. S.]
Pachee Haujo, of Apalachoocla,
his x mark,   [L. S.]
Timpoeechee Bernard, captain of
Uchees, his x mark,   [L. S.]
Uchee Micco, his x mark,   [L. S.]
Yoholo Micco, of Kialijee, his x
mark,   [L. S.]
Socoskee Emautla, of Kialijee, his
x mark,   [L. S.]
Choocchau Haujo, of Woccocoi,
his x mark,   [L. S.]
Esholoctee, of Nauchee, his x
mark,   [L. S.]
Yoholo Micco, of Tallapoosa Eu-
faulau, his x mark,   [L. S.]
Stinthellis Haujo, of Abecoochee,
his x mark,   [L. S.]
Ocfuskee Yoholo, of Toutacaugee,
his x mark,   [L. S.]
John O'Kelly, of Coosa,   [L. S.]
Eneah Thlucco, of Immookfau,
his x mark,   [L. S.]

Espokokoke Haujo, of Wewoko,
his x mark,   [L. S.]
Eneah Thlucco Hopoiee, of Tale-
see, his x mark,   [L. S.]
Efau Haujo, of Puccan Tallahassee,
his x mark,   [L. S.]
Talessee Fixico, of Ocheobofau,
his x mark,   [L. S.]
Nomatlee Emautla, or captain
Isaacs, of Cousoudee, his x mark, [L. S.]
Tuskegee Emautla, or John Carr,
of Tuskegee, his x mark,   [L. S.]
Alexander Grayson, of Hillabee,
his x mark,   [L. S.]
Lowee, of Ocmulgee, his x mark, [L. S.]
Nocoosee Emautla, of Chuskee
Tallafau, his x mark,   [L. S.]
William McIntosh, for Hopoiee
Haujo, of Ooseoochee, his x
mark,   [L. S.]
William McIntosh, for Chehahaw
Tustunnuggee, of Chehahaw, his
x mark,   [L. S.]
William McIntosh, for Spokokee
Tustunnuggee, of Otellewhoyon-
nee, his x mark   [L. S.]

Done at fort Jackson, in presence of—
    Charles Cassedy, acting secretary,
    Benjamin Hawkins, agent for Indian affairs,
    Return J. Meigs, A. C. nation,
    Robert Butler, Adjutant General U. S. Army,
    J. C. Warren, assistant agent for Indian affairs,
    George Mayfield,
    Alexander Curnels,
    George Lovett,
                Public interpreters.

TREATY WITH THE POTAWATOMI, 1815.

July 18, 1815.

7 Stat., 123.
Ratified, Dec. 26,
1815.

A treaty of peace and friendship, made and concluded at Portage des Sioux between William Clark, Ninian Edwards, and Auguste Chouteau, Commissioners Plenipotentiary of the United States of America, on the part and behalf of the said States, of the one part; and the undersigned Chiefs and Warriors of the Poutawatamie Tribe or Nation, residing on the river Illinois, on the part and behalf of the said Tribe or Nation, of the other part.

THE parties being desirous of re-establishing peace and friendship between the United States and the said tribe or nation, and of being placed in all things, and in every respect, on the same footing upon which they stood before the war, have agreed to the following articles:

Injuries, etc., forgiven.

ARTICLE 1. Every injury or act of hostility by one or either of the contracting parties against the other, shall be mutually forgiven and forgot.

Peace and friendship perpetual.

ART. 2. There shall be perpetual peace and friendship between all the citizens of the United States of America, and all the individuals composing the said Poutawatamie tribe or nation.

Prisoners to be delivered up.

ART. 3. The contracting parties hereby agree, promise, and bind themselves, reciprocally, to deliver up all the prisoners now in their hands, (by what means soever the same may have come into their possession,) to the officer commanding at Fort Clarke, on the Illinois river, as soon as it may be practicable.

ART. 4. The contracting parties, in the sincerity of mutual friend-ship, recognize, re-establish and confirm, all and every treaty, contract, and agreement, heretofore concluded between the United States and the Poutawatamie tribe or nation.

Former treaty recognized and confirmed.

In witness of all and every thing herein determined between the United States of America, and the said Poutawatamie tribe or nation, residing on the river Illinois: we, their underwritten commissioners and chiefs aforesaid, by virtue of our full powers, have signed this definitive treaty, and have caused our seals to be hereunto affixed. Done at Portage des Sioux, this eighteenth day of July, in the year of our Lord one thousand eight hundred and fifteen, and of the independence of the United States the fortieth.

William Clark,	[L. S.]
Ninian Edwards,	[L. S.]
Auguste Chouteau,	[L. S.]
Sunawchewome, his x mark,	[L. S.]
Mucketepoke, or Black Partridge, his x mark,	[L. S.]
Neggeneshkek, his x mark,	[L. S.]
Chawcawbeme, his x mark,	[L. S.]
Bendegakewa, his x mark,	[L. S.]
Wapewy, or White Hair, his x mark,	[L. S.]
Outawa, his x mark,	[L. S.]

In the presence of—

R. Wash, secretary of the commission,
Thomas Forsyth, Indian ag
N. Boilvin, agent,
T. Paul, C. M.
Maurice Blondeaux,
Manuel Lisa, agent,
John Miller, colonel Third Infantry,
Richard Chitwood, Major M.

Wm. Irvine Adair, captain Third Regiment U. S. Infantry,
Cyrus Edwards,
Samuel Solomon,
Jacques Mette,
Louis Decouagne,
John A. Camero,
   sworn interpreters.

TREATY WITH THE PIANKASHAW, 1815.

A treaty of peace and friendship, made and concluded at Portage des Sioux between William Clark, Ninian Edwards, and Auguste Chouteau, Commissioners Plenipotentiary of the United States of America, on the part and behalf of the said States, of the one part; and the undersigned Chiefs and Warriors of the Piankishaw Tribe or Nation, on the part and behalf of the said Tribe or Nation, of the other part.

July 18, 1815.

7 Stat., 124.
Ratified, Dec. 26, 1815.

THE parties being anxious of re-establishing peace and friendship between the United States and the said tribe or nation, and of being placed in all things, and in every respect, on the same footing upon which they stood before the war, have agreed to the following articles:

ARTICLE 1. Every injury or act of hostility by one or either of the contracting parties against the other, shall be mutually forgiven and forgot.

Injuries, etc., forgiven.

ART. 2. There shall be perpetual peace and friendship between all the citizens of the United States of America and all the individuals composing the Piankishaw tribe or nation.

Perpetual peace and friendship.

ART. 3. The contracting parties, in the sincerity of mutual friend-ship, recognize, re-establish, and confirm, all and every treaty, contract, or agreement, heretofore concluded between the United States and the said Piankishaw tribe or nation.

Former treaties recognized and confirmed.

In witness of all and every thing herein determined between the United States of America, and the said Piankeshaw tribe or nation: we, their underwritten commissioners, and chiefs aforesaid, by virtue of our full powers, have signed this definitive treaty, and have caused our seals to be hereunto affixed.

Done at Portage des Sioux, this eighteenth day of July, in the year of our Lord, one thousand eight hundred and fifteen, and of the independence of the United States of America the fortieth.

William Clark,	[L. S.]
Ninian Edwards,	[L. S.]
Auguste Choteau,	[L. S.]
La-ma-noan, or the Axe, his x mark,	[L. S.]
La-mee-pris-jeau, or Sea-wolf, his x mark,	[L. S.]
Mon-sai-raa, or Rusty, his x mark,	[L. S.]
Wa-pan-gia, or Swan, his x mark,	[L. S.]
Na-maing-sa, or the Fish, his x mark,	[L. S.]

Done at Portage des Sioux, in the presence of—

R. Wash, secretary to the commissioners,
Thomas Forsyth, Indian agent,
N. Boilvin, agent,
T. Paul, C. C. M.
Maurice Blondeaux,
John Hay,
John Miller, colonel Third Infantry,
Richard Chitwood, major mounted,
Wm. Irvine Adair, captain Third Regiment U. S. Infantry.
Cyrus Edwards,
Saml. Solomon,

Jacques Mette,
Louis Decouagne,
John A. Cameron,
    sworn interpr't'rs.
F. Duchouquet, United States interpreter,
W.
Louis Bufait, Indian interpreter,
J. Bts. Chandonnai, interpreter,
W. Knaggs,
Antoine Bondi,
Jean Bt. Massac, his x mark.

TREATY WITH THE TETON, 1815.

July 19, 1815.

7 Stat., 125.

Ratified, Dec. 26, 1815.

A treaty of peace and friendship made and concluded at Portage des Sioux, between William Clark, Ninian Edwards, and Auguste Chouteau, Commissioners Plenipotentiary of the United States of America, on the part and behalf of the said States, of the one part; and the undersigned Chiefs and Warriors of the Teeton Tribe of Indians, on the part and behalf of their said Tribe, of the other part.

THE parties being desirous of re-establishing peace and friendship between the United States and the said tribe, and of being placed in all things, and in every respect, on the same footing upon which they stood before the late war between the United States and Great Britain, have agreed to the following articles:

Injuries, etc., forgiven.

ARTICLE 1. Every injury, or act of hostility, committed by one or either of the contracting parties against the other, shall be mutually forgiven and forgot.

Perpetual peace and friendship, etc.

ART. 2. There shall be perpetual peace and friendship between all the citizens of the United States of America and all the individuals composing the said Teeton tribe; and the friendly relations that existed between them before the war, shall be, and the same are hereby, renewed.

Protection of United States acknowledged.

ART. 3. The undersigned chiefs and warriors, for themselves and their said tribe, do hereby acknowledge themselves and their aforesaid tribe to be under the protection of the United States of America, and of no other nation, power, or sovereign, whatsoever.

In witness whereof, the said William Clark, Ninian Edwards, and Auguste Chouteau, commissioners as aforesaid, and the chiefs and warriors of the said tribe, have hereunto subscribed their names, and affixed their seals this nineteenth day of July, one thousand eight hundred and fifteen, and of the independence of the United States the fortieth.

William Clark,	[L. S.]	Weechachamanza, the Man of Iron, his x mark,	[L. S.]
Ninian Edwards,	[L. S.]		
Auguste Chouteau,	[L. S.]	Ikmouacoulai, the Shooting Tiger, his x mark,	[L. S.]
Eskatapia, the Player, his x mark,	[L. S.]		
Tantanga, the True Buffaloe, his x mark,	[L. S.]	Uakahincoukai, the Wind that Passes, his x mark,	[L. S.]

Mazamanie, the Walker in Iron, his x mark, [L. S.]	Washeejonjrtga, the Left-handed Frenchman, his x mark, [L. S.]
Wanakagmamee, the Stamper, his x mark, [L. S.]	Monetowanari, the Bear's Soul, his x mark, [L. S.]

Done at Portage des Sioux, in the presence of—

R. Wash, secretary to the commission,
John Miller, colonel Third Infantry,
H. Dodge, brigadier-general Missouri Militia,
T. Paul, C. T. of the C.,
Manuel Lisa, agent,
Thomas Forsyth, Indian agent,

Maurice Blondeaux,
John A. Cameron,
Louis Decouagne,
Louis Dorion,
Cyrus Edwards,
John Hay.

TREATY WITH THE SIOUX OF THE LAKES, 1815.

A treaty of peace and friendship, made and concluded at Portage des Sioux between William Clark, Ninian Edwards, and Auguste Chouteau, Commissioners Plenipotentiary of the United States of America, on the part and behalf of the said States, of the one part; and the undersigned Chiefs and Warriors of the Siouxs of the Lakes, on the part and behalf of their Tribe, of the other part.

July 19, 1815.

7 Stat., 126.
Ratified Dec. 26, 1815.

THE parties being desirous of re-establishing peace and friendship between the United States and the said tribe, and of being placed in all things, and in every respect, on the same footing upon which they stood before the late war between the United States and Great Britain, have agreed to the following articles:

ARTICLE 1. Every injury, or act of hostility, committed by one or either of the contracting parties against the other, shall be mutually forgiven and forgot. *Injuries, etc., forgiven.*

ART. 2. There shall be perpetual peace and friendship between all the citizens of the United States of America and all the individuals composing the said tribe of the Lakes, and all the friendly relations that existed between them before the war, shall be, and the same are hereby, renewed. *Perpetual peace and friendship.*

ART. 3. The undersigned chiefs and warriors, for themselves and their said tribe, do hereby acknowledge themselves and their aforesaid tribe to be under the protection of the United States, and of no other nation, power, or sovereign, whatsoever. *Protection of United States acknowledged.*

In witness whereof, the said William Clark, Ninian Edwards, and Auguste Chouteau, commissioners aforesaid, and the chiefs and warriors of the aforesaid tribe, have hereunto subscribed their names and affixed their seals this nineteenth day of July, in the year of our Lord one thousand eight hundred and fifteen, and of the independence of the United States the fortieth.

William Clark,	[L. S.]
Ninian Edwards,	[L. S.]
Auguste Chouteau,	[L. S.]
Tatangamania, the Walking Buffaloe, his x mark,	[L. S.]
Haisanwee, the Horn, his x mark,	[L. S.]
Aampahaa, the Speaker, his x mark,	[L. S.]
Narcesagata, the Hard Stone, his x mark,	[L. S.]
Haibohaa, the Branching Horn, his x mark,	[L. S.]

Done at Portage des Sioux, in the presence of—

R. Wash, secretary to the commission,
John Miller, colonel Third Infantry,
T. Paul, C. T. of the C.,
Edmund Hall, lieutenant late Twenty-eighth Infantry,
J. B. Clark, adjutant Third Infantry,
Manuel Lisa, agent,
Thomas Forsyth, Indian agent,

Jno. W. Johnson, United States factor and Indian agent,
Maurice Blondeaux,
Lewis Decouagne,
Louis Dorion,
John A. Cameron,
Jacques Mette,
John Hay.

TREATY WITH THE SIOUX OF ST. PETER'S RIVER, 1815.

July 19, 1815.

7 Stat., 127.
Ratified Dec. 26, 1815.

A treaty of peace and friendship, made and concluded at Portage des Sioux, between William Clark, Ninian Edwards, and Auguste Chouteau, Commissioners Plenipotentiary of the United States of America, on the part and behalf of the said States, of the one part; and the Chiefs and Warriors of the Siouxs of the river St. Peter's, on the part and behalf of their said Tribe, on the other part.

THE parties being desirous of re-establishing peace and friendship between the United States and the said tribe, and of being placed in all things, and in every respect, on the same footing upon which they stood before the late war between the United States and Great Britain, have agreed to the following articles:

Injuries, etc., forgiven.

ARTICLE 1. Every injury or act of hostility committed by one or either of the contracting parties against the other, shall be mutually forgiven and forgot.

Perpetual peace and friendship, etc.

ART. 2. There shall be perpetual peace and friendship between all the citizens of the United States of America and all the individuals composing the tribe of the Siouxs of the river St. Peter's; and all the friendly relations that existed between them before the war, shall be, and the same are hereby, renewed.

Protection of United States acknowledged.

ART. 3. The undersigned chiefs and warriors, for themselves and their said tribe, do hereby acknowledge themselves and their tribe to be under the protection of the United States, and of no other power, nation, or sovereign, whatsoever.

In testimony whereof, the said William Clark, Ninian Edwards and Auguste Chouteau, commissioners as aforesaid, and the chiefs and warriors of the aforesaid tribe, have hereunto subscribed their names and affixed their seals, this nineteenth day of July, in the year of our Lord one thousand eight hundred and fifteen, and of the independence of the United States the fortieth.

William Clark,	[L. S.]
Ninian Edwards,	[L. S.]
Auguste Chouteau,	[L. S.]
Enigmanee, that Flies as he Walks, his x mark,	[L. S.]
Wasoukapaha, the Falling Hail, his x mark,	[L. S.]
Champisaba, the Black War Club, his x mark,	[L. S.]
Manpinsaba, the Black Cloud, his x mark,	[L. S.]
Tatarnaza, the Iron Wind, his x mark,	[L. S.]
Nankanandee, who puts his foot in it, his x mark,	[L. S.]

Done at Portage des Sioux, in the presence of—

R. Wash, secretary of the commission,
John Miller, colonel Third Infantry,
H. Paul, C. T. of the C.
John T. Chunn, brevet major of the U. S. Army,
Edmund Hall, lieutenant late Twenty-eighth Infantry,
Manuel Lisa, agent,
Thomas Forsyth, Indian agent,

J. W. Johnson, United States Factor and Indian agent.
Maurice Blondeaux,
Louis Decouagne,
John A. Cameron,
Louis Dorion,
Jacques Matte,
    sworn interpreters.

TREATY WITH THE YANKTON SIOUX, 1815.

A treaty of peace and friendship, made and concluded at Portage des Sioux between William Clark, Ninian Edwards, and Auguste Chouteau, Commissioners Plenipotentiary of the United States of America, on the part and behalf of the said States, of the one part; and the undersigned Chiefs and Warriors of the Yancton Tribe of Indians, on the part and behalf of their said Tribe, of the other part.

July 19, 1815.

7 Stat.. 128.
Ratified Dec. 26, 1815.

THE parties being desirous of re-establishing peace and friendship between the United States and the said tribe, and of being placed in all things, and in every respect, on the same footing upon which they stood before the late war between the United States and Great Britain, have agreed to the following articles:

ARTICLE 1. Every injury or act of hostility committed by one or either of the contracting parties against the other, shall be mutually forgiven and forgot.

Injuries, etc., forgiven.

ART. 2. There shall be perpetual peace and friendship between all the citizens of the United States of America, and all the individuals composing the said Yancton tribe, and all the friendly relations that existed between them before the war shall be, and the same are hereby, renewed.

Perpetual peace and friendship, etc.

ART. 3. The undersigned chiefs and warriors, for themselves and their said tribe, do hereby acknowledge themselves to be under the protection of the United States of America, and of no other nation, power, or sovereign, whatsoever.

Protection of United States acknowledged.

In witness whereof, the said William Clark, Ninian Edwards, and Auguste Chouteau, commissioners as aforesaid, and the chiefs aforesaid, have hereunto subscribed their names and affixed their seals, this nineteenth day of July, in the year of our Lord one thousand eight hundred and fifteen, and of the independence of the United States the fortieth.

Wm. Clark,	[L. s.]	Weopaatowechashla, or sun set,	[L. s.]
Ninian Edwards,	[L. s.]	Tokaymhominee, or the rock that	
Auguste Chouteau,	[L. s.]	turns, his x mark,	[L. s.]
Monlori, or white bear, his x mark,	[L. s.]	Keonorunco, or fast flyer, his x mark,	[L. s.]
Waskaijingo, or little dish, his x mark,	[L. s.]	Mazo, or the iron, his x mark,	[L. s.]
Padamape, or panis sticker, his x mark,	[L. s.]	Haiwongeeda, or one horn, his x mark,	[L. s.]
Chaponge, or musquitoe, his x mark,	[L. s.]	Mazehaio, or arrow sender, his x mark,	[L. s.]
Mindalonga, partisan, or war chief,	[L. s.]		

Done at the Portage des Sioux, in the presence of—

R. Wash, secretary to the commission,
John Miller, colonel, Third Infantry,
H. Dodge, brigadier-general Missouri Militia,
Manuel Lisa, agent,
Thomas Forsyth, Indian agent,
Maurice Blondeaux,

Jacques Mette,
John A. Cameron,
R. Paul, C. T. of the commission,
Louis Decouagne,
Cyrus Edwards,
Lewis Dorion,
John Hay, interpreter.

TREATY WITH THE MAKAH, 1815.

A treaty of peace and friendship, made and concluded between William Clark, Ninian Edwards, and Auguste Chouteau, Commissioners Plenipotentiary of the United States of America, on the part and behalf of the said States, of the one part; and the Chiefs and Warriors of the Mahas, on the part and behalf of said Tribe or Nation, of the other part.

July 20, 1815.

7 Stat., 129.
Ratified Dec. 26, 1815.

THE parties being desirous of re-establishing peace and friendship between the United States and the said tribe or nation, and of being placed in all things, and in every respect, on the same footing upon which they stood before the late war between the United States and Great Britain, have agreed to the following articles:

Injuries, etc., forgiven.

ARTICLE 1. Every injury or act of hostility committed by one or either of the contracting parties against the other, shall be mutually forgiven and forgot.

Perpetual peace and friendship, etc.

ART. 2. There shall be perpetual peace and friendship between all the citizens of the United States of America and all the individuals composing the tribe or nation of the Mahas, and all friendly relations that existed between them before the war, shall be, and the same are hereby, renewed.

Protection of United States acknowledged.

ART. 3. The undersigned chiefs and warriors, for themselves and their said tribe or nation, do hereby acknowledge themselves and their tribe or nation to be under the protection of the United States, and of no other nation, power, or sovereign, whatsoever.

In witness whereof, the said William Clark, Ninian Edwards, and Auguste Chouteau, commissioners as aforesaid, and the chiefs and warriors of the aforesaid tribe or nation, have hereunto subscribed their names and affixed their seals, this twentieth day of July, in the year of our Lord one thousand eight hundred and fifteen, and of the Independence of the United States the fortieth.

William Clark,	[L. S.]	Waanowrabai, or the blackbird's	
Ninian Edwards,	[L. S.]	grandson, his x mark,	[L. S.]
Auguste Chouteau,	[L. S.]	Osogagee, or the point maker, his x	
Oupaatanga, or the big elk, his x		mark,	[L. S.]
mark,	[L. S.]	Toireechee, or the cow's rib, his x	
Washcamanie, or the hard walker,		mark,	[L. S.]
his x mark,	[L. S.]	Manshaquita, or the little soldier,	
Kaaheeguia, or the old chief, his x		his x mark,	[L. S.]
mark,	[L. S.]	Pissinguai, or he who has no gall,	
		his x mark,	[L. S.]

Done at Portage des Sioux, in presence of—

R. Wash, secretary to the commission,
John Miller, colonel Third Infantry,
R. Paul, C. T. of the C.
Edw. Hall, lieutenant late Twenty-eighth Infantry,
John B. Clark, adjutant Third Infantry,
Manuel Lisa, agent,

Thos. Forsyth, Indian agent,
J. W. Johnson, Indian agent,
Louis Decouagne,
Louis Dorion,
John A. Cameron,
Jacques Mette.

TREATY WITH THE KICKAPOO, 1815.

Sept. 2, 1815.

7 Stat., 130.
Ratified Dec. 26, 1815.

A treaty of peace and friendship, made and concluded between William Clark, Ninian Edwards, and Auguste Chouteau, Commissioners Plenipotentiary of the United States of America, on the part and behalf of the said States, of the one part; and the undersigned Chiefs, Warriors, and Deputies, of the Kickapoo Tribe or Nation, on the part and behalf of the said Tribe or Nation, of the other part.

THE parties being desirous of re-establishing peace and friendship between the United States and the said tribe or nation, and of being placed in all things, and in every respect, on the same footing upon which they stood before the war, have agreed to the following articles:

Injuries, etc., forgiven.

ARTICLE 1. Every injury or act of hostility by one or either of the contracting parties towards the other, shall be mutually forgiven and forgot.

Perpetual peace and friendship.

ART. 2. There shall be perpetual peace and friendship between all the citizens of the United States of America, and all the individuals composing the said Kickapoo tribe or nation.

Prisoners to be delivered up.

ART. 3. The contracting parties do hereby agree, promise, and oblige themselves, reciprocally, to deliver up all the prisoners now in their hands (by what means soever the same may have come into their possession) to the officer commanding at Fort Clarke, on the Illinois river, to be by him restored to their respective nations as soon as it may be practicable.

ART. 4. The contracting parties, in the sincerity of mutual friendship, recognize, re-establish, and confirm, all and every treaty, contract, and agreement, heretofore concluded between the United States and the Kickapoo tribe or nation.

Former treaties recognized and confirmed.

In witness whereof, the said William Clark, Ninian Edwards, and Auguste Chouteau, commissioners as aforesaid, and the chiefs, warriors, and deputies of the said tribe, have hereunto subscribed their names and affixed their seals, this second day of September, in the year of our Lord one thousand eight hundred and fifteen, and of the independence of the United States the fortieth.

William Clark, [L. s.]	Cokecambaut, or elk looking back,
Ninian Edwards, [L. s.]	his x mark, [L. s.]
Auguste Chouteau, [L. s.]	Peywaynequa, or bear, his x mark, [L. s.]
Pauwoatam, by his representative,	Wettassa, or brave, his x mark, [L. s.]
Kenepaso, or the bond prisoner,	Weywaychecawbout, or meeter,
his x mark, [L. s.]	his x mark, [L. s.]
Kiteta, or Otter, his x mark, [L. s.]	Autuppehaw, or mover, his x
Kenepaso, or the bond prisoner,	mark, [L. s.]
his x mark, [L. s.]	Wesheown, or dirty face, his x
Teppema, or persuader, his x	mark, [L. s.]
mark, [L. s.]	

Done at Portage des Sioux in the presence of—

R. Wash, secretary to the commission,	Maurice Blondeaux,
T. A. Smith, brigadier-general, U. S.	Samuel Solomon, interpreter,
Army,	Samuel Brady, lieutenant Eighth U. S.
D'l. Bissell, brigadier-general,	Infantry,
Stephen Byrd, colonel M. N.,	Joseph C. Brown,
T. Paul, C. C. T.,	H. Battu,
A. McNair, district inspector,	Samuel Whiteside, captain Illinois Militia.
Thomas Forsyth, Indian agent,	
Pierre Menard, Indian agent,	
John W. Johnson, United States factor	
and Indian agent,	

TREATY WITH THE WYANDOT, ETC., 1815.

A Treaty between the United States of America and the Wyandot, Delaware, Seneca, Shawanoe, Miami, Chippewa, Ottawa, and Potawatimie, Tribes of Indians, residing within the limits of the State of Ohio, and the Territories of Indiana and Michigan.

Sept. 8, 1815.

7 Stat., 131.
Ratified Dec.26,1815.

WHEREAS the Chippewa, Ottawa, and Potawatimie, tribes of Indians, together with certain bands of the Wyandot, Delaware, Seneca, Shawanoe, and Miami tribes, were associated with Great Britain in the late war between the United States and that power, and have manifested a disposition to be restored to the relations of peace and amity with the said States; and the President of the United States having appointed William Henry Harrison, late a Major General in the service of the United States, Duncan M'Arthur, late a Brigadier in the service of the United States, and John Graham, Esquire, as Commissioners to treat with the said tribes; the said Commissioners and the Sachems, Headmen, and Warriors, of said tribes having met in Council at the Spring Wells, near the city of Detroit, have agreed to the following Articles, which, when ratified by the President, by and with the advice and consent of the Senate of the United States, shall be binding on them and the said tribes:

ARTICLE 1. The United States give peace to the Chippewa, Ottawa, and Potawatimie, tribes.

Peace given to certain tribes.

Said tribes restored to the pacific relations of 1811.

ART. 2. They also agree to restore to the said Chippewa, Ottawa, and Potawatimie tribes all the possessions, rights, and priviledges, which they enjoyed, or were entitled to, in the year one thousand eight hundred and eleven, prior to the commencement of the late war with Great Britain; and the said tribes, upon their part, agree again to place themselves under the protection of the United States, and of no other power whatsoever.

United States pardon the hostilities of the Wyandots, Delawares, etc.

ART. 3. In consideration of the fidelity to the United States which has been manifested by the Wyandot, Delaware, Seneca, and Shawanoe, tribes, throughout the late war, and of the repentance of the Miami tribe, as manifested by placing themselves under the protection of the United States, by the treaty of Greenville, in eighteen hundred and fourteen, the said States agree to pardon such of the chiefs and warriors of said tribes as may have continued hostilities against them until the close of the war with Great Britain, and to permit the chiefs of their respective tribes to restore them to the stations and property which they held previously to the war.

Treaty of Greenville, etc., ratified and confirmed.

ART. 4. The United States and the beforementioned tribes or nations of Indians, that is to say, the Wyandot, Delaware, Seneca, Shawanoe, Miami, Chippewa, Ottawa, and Potawatimies, agree to renew and confirm the treaty of Greenville, made in the year one thousand seven hundred and ninety-five, and all subsequent treaties to which they were, respectively, parties, and the same are hereby again ratified and confirmed in as full a manner as if they were inserted in this treaty.

Done at Spring Wells, the eighth day of September, in the year of our Lord one thousand eight hundred and fifteen, and of the independence of the United States, the fortieth.

In testimony whereof, they, the said commissioners, and the sachems, head men and warriors of the different tribes, have hereunto set their hands, and affixed their seals.

William Henry Harrison,	[L. S.]	Onqunogesh, or ugly fellow, his x mark, [L. S.]
Duncan McArthur,	[L. S.]	
John Graham,	[L. S.]	Menitugawboway, or the devil standing, his x mark, [L. S.]
Wyandot chiefs:		
Tarhee, or the crane, his x mark,	[L. S.]	Kelystum, or first actor, his x mark, [L. S.]
Harrouyeou, or Cherokee boy, his x mark,	[L. S.]	Ottawas from Mackinack:
		Kemenechagon, or the bastard, his x mark, [L. S.]
Sanohskee, or long house, his x mark,	[L. S.]	Karbenequane, or the one who went in front, his x mark, [L. S.]
Outoctutimoh, or cub, his x mark,	[L. S.]	
Myecruh, or walk in the water, his x mark,	[L. S.]	Ottawa from Grand River:
		Mechequez, his x mark, [L. S.]
Tyanumka, his x mark,	[L. S.]	A Winnebago from Mackinack:
Mymehamkee, or Barnett, his x mark,	[L. S.]	Wassachum, or first to start the whites, his x mark, [L. S.]
Shawanoe chiefs:		Chippewa chiefs:
Cutaweskeshah, or black hoof, his x mark,	[L. S.]	Papnescha, or turn round about, his x mark, [L. S.]
Nutsheway, or wolf's brother, his x mark,	[L. S.]	Nowgeschick, or twelve o'clock, his x mark, [L. S.]
Tamenatha, or butler, his x mark,	[L. S.]	Shamanetoo, or God Almighty, his x mark, [L. S.]
Shemenetoo, or big snake, his x mark,	[L. S.]	Wissenesoh, his x mark, [L. S.]
Outhowwaheshegath, or yellow plume, his x mark,		Cacheonquet, or big cloud, his x mark, [L. S.]
Quatawwepay, or capt. Lewis, his x mark,	[L. S.]	Pasheskiskaquashcum, [L. S.]
Mishquathree, or capt. Reid, his x mark,	[L. S.]	Menactome, or the little fly, his x mark, [L. S.]
Tecumtequah, his x mark,	[L. S.]	Enewame, or crow, his x mark, [L. S.]
Ottawa chiefs:		Nauaquaoto, his x mark, [L. S.]
Tontegenah, or the dog, his x mark,	[L. S.]	Paanassee, or the bird, his x mark, [L. S.]
Tashcuygon, or McArthur, his x mark,	[L. S.]	Delaware chiefs:
		Toctowayning, or Anderson, his x mark, [L. S.]
Okemas, or little chief, his x mark,	[L. S.]	Lamahtanoquez, his x mark, [L. S.]
Nashkemah, his x mark,	[L. S.]	Matahoopan, his x mark, [L. S.]
Watashnewah, his x mark,	[L. S.]	Aaheppan, or the buck, his x mark, [L. S.]

Jim Killbuck, his x mark,	[L. S.]	Kaitchaynee, his x mark,	[L. S.]
Captain Beaver, his x mark,	[L. S.]	Waymeego, or W. H. Harrison, his	
McDonald, his x mark,	[L. S.]	x mark,	[L. S.]
Seneca chiefs:		Louison, his x mark,	[L. S.]
Tahummindoyeh, or between		Osheouskeebee, his x mark,	[L. S.]
words, his x mark,	[L. S.]	Miami chiefs:	
Yonundankykueurent, or John		Pacan, his x mark,	[L. S.]
Harris, his x mark,	[L. S.]	Singomesha, or the owl, his x mark,	[L. S.]
Masomea, or Civil John, his x mark,	[L. S.]	Totanag, or the butterfly, his x	
Saccorawahtah, or wiping stick,		mark,	[L. S.]
his x mark,	[L. S.]	Osage, or the neutral, his x mark,	[L. S.]
Potawatimie chiefs:		Wabsioung, or the white skin, his	
Topeeneebee, his x mark,	[L. S.]	x mark,	[L. S.]
Noungeesai, or five medals, his x		Wapaassabina, or white racoon, his	
mark,	[L. S.]	x mark,	[L. S.]
Naynauawsekaw, his x mark,	[L. S.]	Otteutaqua, or a blower of his	
Joeeonce, his x mark,	[L. S.]	breath, his x mark,	[L. S.]
Cocneg, his x mark,	[L. S.]	Makatasabina, or black racoon, his	
Ohshawkeebee, his x mark,	[L. S.]	x mark,	[L. S.]
Waineamaygoas, his x mark,	[L. S.]	Wapeshesa, or white appearance in	
Meeksawbay, his x mark,	[L. S.]	the water, his x mark,	[L. S.]
Mongaw, his x mark,	[L. S.]	Motosamea, or Indian, his x mark,	[L. S.]
Nawnawmee, his x mark,	[L. S.]	Shacanbe, his x mark,	[L. S.]
Chay Chauk, or the crane, his x		Shequar, or the poor racoon, his x	
mark,	[L. S.]	mark,	[L. S.]
Wanaunaiskee, his x mark,	[L. S.]	Cartanquar, or the sky, his x mark,	[L. S.]
Pashapow, his x mark,	[L. S.]	Okemabenaseh, or the king bird,	
Honkemani, or the chief, his x		his x mark,	[L. S.]
mark,	[L. S.]	Wapenaseme, or the collector of	
Neesscatimeneemay, his x mark,	[L. S.]	birds, his x mark,	[L. S.]
Ponngeasais, his x mark,	[L. S.]	Mecinnabee, or the setting stone,	
Nounnawkeskawaw, his x mark,	[L. S.]	his x mark,	[L. S.]
Chickawno, his x mark,	[L. S.]	Annawba, his x mark,	[L. S.]
Mitteeay, his x mark,	[L. S.]	Mashepesheewingqua, or tiger's	
Messeecawee, his x mark,	[L. S.]	face, his x mark,	[L. S.]
Neepoashe, his x mark,	[L. S.]		

Signed in the presence of—

A. L. Langhan, secretary to the commission,
Lewis Cass,
James Miller, brig. general U. S. Army,
Willoughby Morgan, major U. S. Army,
A. B. Woodward,
Hy. B. Brevoort, late Major Forty-fifth Infantry,
John Bidder, Captain U. S. Corps Artillery,
James May, J. P.,
Peter Audrain, Reg. L. O. D.,
Jn. K. Walker, Wyandot interpreter,

Francis Jansen,
James Riley, interpreter,
William Kingg,
Francois Mouton,
John Kenzie, interpreter,
F. Duchouquet, United States interpreter, W.,
Louis Bufait, Indian interpreter,
J. Bts. Chandonnai, interpreter,
W. Knaggs,
Antoine Bondi,
Jean Bt. Massac, his x mark.

TREATY WITH THE OSAGE, 1815.

A treaty of peace and friendship, made and concluded between William Clark, Ninian Edwards, and Auguste Chouteau, Commissioners Plenipotentiary of the United States of America, on the part and behalf of the said States, of the one part; and the undersigned King, Chiefs, and Warriors, of the Great and Little Osage Tribes or Nations, on the part and behalf of their said Tribes or Nations, of the other part.

Sept. 12, 1815.

7 Stat., 133.
Ratified Dec. 26, 1815.

THE parties being desirous of re-establishing peace and friendship between the United States and the said tribes or nations, and of being placed in all things, and in every respect, on the same footing upon which they stood before the war, have agreed to the following articles:

ARTICLE 1. Every injury, or act of hostility, by one or either of the contracting parties against the other, shall be mutually forgiven and forgot.

Injuries, etc., forgiven.

ART. 2. There shall be perpetual peace and friendship between all the citizens of the United States of America and all the individuals composing the said Osage tribes or nations.

ART. 3. The contracting parties, in the sincerity of mutual friendship recognize, re-establish, and confirm, all and every treaty, contract, and agreement, heretofore concluded between the United States and the said Osage tribes or nations.

In witness whereof, the said William Clark, Ninian Edwards, and Auguste Chouteau, commissioners as aforesaid, and the king, chiefs, and warriors of the said tribes or nations have hereunto subscribed their names and affixed their seals, this twelfth day of September, in the year of our Lord one thousand eight hundred and fifteen, and of the independence of the United States the fortieth.

Wm. Clark,	[L. S.]	The Little Osages:	
Ninian Edwards,	[L. S.]	Caggatanagga, the great chief, his x	
Auguste Chouteau,	[L. S.]	mark,	[L. S.]
Teshuhimga, or white hair, his x mark,	[L. S.]	Nechoumanu, the walking rain, his x mark,	[L. S.]
Caygaywachepeche, or the bad chief, his x mark,	[L. S.]	Watashinga, he who has done little, his x mark,	[L. S.]
Couchestawasta, or the one who sees far, his x mark,	[L. S.]	Nehujamega, without ears, his x mark,	[L. S.]
Gradamnsa, or iron kite, his x mark,	[L. S.]	Ososhingga, the little point, his x mark,	[L. S.]
Mahsa, his x mark,	[L. S.]	Akidatangga, the big soldier, his x mark,	[L. S.]
Wanougpacha, or he who fears not, his x mark,	[L. S.]	Wabesongge, his x mark,	[L. S.]
Hurate, the piper bird, his x mark,	[L. S.]	Nehreegnegawachepecha, his x mark,	[L. S.]
Wasabatougga, big bear, his x mark,	[L. S.]	Grecnachee, he who arrives, his x mark,	[L. S.]
Nekagahre, he who beats the men, his x mark,	[L. S.]	Wahadanoe, of the Missouri tribe, his x mark,	[L. S.]
Mekewatanega, he who carries the sun, his x mark,	[L. S.]	Asooga, the little horn, his x mark,	[L. S.]
Nangawahagea, his x mark,	[L. S.]	Mathagrhra, the cutter, his x mark,	[L. S.]
Kemanha, the wind racer of the Arkinsaw band, his x mark,	[L. S.]		

Done at Portage des Sioux, in the presence of—

R. Wash, secretary of the commission,
Thomas Levers, lieutenant colonel, commanding First Regiment, I. T.,
P. Chouteau, agent Osages,
T. Paul, C. C. T.,
James B. Moore, captain.
Samuel Whiteside, captain.
Jno. W. Johnson, United States, factor and Indian agent,

Maurice Blondeaux.
Samuel Solomon,
Noel Mograine,
Interpreters.
P. L. Chouteau,
Daniel Converse, third lieutenant.

TREATY WITH THE SAUK, 1815.

A treaty of peace and friendship, made and concluded between William Clark, Ninian Edwards, and Auguste Chouteau, Commissioners Plenipotentiary of the United States of America, on the part and behalf of the said States, of the one part; and the undersigned Chiefs and Warriors of that portion of the Sac Nation of Indians now residing on the Missouri river, of the other part.

WHEREAS the undersigned chiefs and warriors, as well as that portion of the nation which they represent, have at all times been desirous of fulfilling their treaty with the United States, with perfect good faith; and for that purpose found themselves compelled, since the commencement of the late war, to separate themselves from the rest of their nation, and remove to the Missouri river, where they have continued to give proofs of their friendship and fidelity; and whereas the United States, justly appreciating the conduct of said Indians, are disposed to do them the most ample justice that is practicable; the said parties have agreed to the following articles:

ARTICLE 1. The undersigned chiefs and warriors, for themselves and that portion of the Sacs which they represent, do hereby assent to the treaty between the United States of America and the united tribes of Sacs and Foxes, which was concluded at St. Louis, on the third day of November, one thousand eight hundred and four; and they moreover promise to do all in their power to re-establish and enforce the same. The Sacs assent to treaty of Nov. 3, 1804, etc.

ART. 2. The said chiefs and warriors, for themselves and those they represent, do further promise to remain distinct and separate from the Sacs of Rock river, giving them no aid or assistance whatever, until peace shall also be concluded between the United States and the said Sacs of Rock river. The Sacs of Missouri promise to remain separate from Sacs of Rock River, etc,

ART. 3. The United States, on their part, promise to allow the said Sacs of the Missouri river all the rights and privileges secured to them by the treaty of St. Louis beforementioned, and also, as soon as practicable, to furnish them with a just proportion of the annuities stipulated to be paid by that treaty; provided they shall continue to comply with this and their former treaty. Allowance to Sacs of Missouri.

In witness whereof, the said William Clark, Ninian Edwards, and Auguste Chouteau, commissioners as aforesaid, and the aforesaid chiefs and warriors, have hereunto subscribed their names and affixed their seals, this thirteenth day of September, in the year of our Lord one thousand eight hundred and fifteen, and of the independence of the United States the fortieth.

Wm. Clark,	[L. S.]	Mecaitch, or the eagle, his x mark,	[L. S.]
Ninian Edwards,	[L. S.]	Neshota, or the twin, his x mark,	[L. S.]
Auguste Chouteau,	[L. S.]	Quashquammee, or the jumping	
Shamaga, or the lance, his x mark,	[L. S.]	fish, his x mark,	[L. S.]
Weesaka, or the Devil, his x mark,	[L. S.]	Chagasort, or the blues' son, his x	
Catchemackeseo, the big eagle, his		mark,	[L. S.]
x mark,	[L. S.]	Pecama, or the plumb, his x mark,	[L. S.]
Chekaqua, or he that stands by		Namachewana Chaha, or the	
the tree, his x mark,	[L. S.]	Sioux, his x mark,	[L. S.]
Kataka, or the sturgeon, his x		Nanochaatasa, or the brave by	
mark,	[L. S.]	hazard,	[L. S.]

Done at Portage des Sioux, in the presence of—

R. Wash, secretary of the commission,
Thomas Levers, lieutenant colonel commanding First Regiment I. T.
P. Chouteau, agent.
T. Paul, C. C. T.
James B. Moore, captain,
Samuel Whiteside, captain,

J. W. Johnson, United States factor and
  Indian agent,
Maurice Blondeaux.
Samuel Solomon,
Noel Mograine,
       Interpreters.
Daniel Converse, third lieutenant.

TREATY WITH THE FOXES, 1815.

A treaty of peace and friendship, made and concluded at Portage des Sioux between William Clark, Ninian Edwards, and Auguste Chouteau, Commissioners Plenipotentiary of the United States of America, on the part and behalf of the said States, of the one part; and the undersigned King, Chiefs, and Warriors, of the Fox Tribe or Nation, on the part and behalf of the said Tribe or nation, of the other part. Sept. 14, 1815.
7 Stat., 135.
Ratified Dec. 26, 1815.

The parties being desirous of re-establishing peace and friendship between the United States and the said tribe or nation, and of being placed in all things, and in every respect, on the same footing upon which they stood before the war, have agreed to the following articles:

ARTICLE 1. Every injury or act of hostility by one or either of the contracting parties against the other, shall be mutually forgiven and forgot. Injuries, etc., forgiven.

Perpetual peace and friendship.

ART. 2. There shall be perpetual peace and friendship between the citizens of the United States of America and all the individuals composing the said Fox tribe or nation.

Prisoners to be delivered up.

ART. 3. The contracting parties do hereby agree, promise, and oblige themselves, reciprocally, to deliver up all the prisoners now in their hands, (by what means soever the same may have come into their possession,) to the officer commanding at Fort Clark, on the Illinois river, to be by him restored to their respective nations as soon as it may be practicable.

Treaty of St. Louis of Nov. 3, 1804, confirmed.

ART. 4. The said Fox tribe or nation do hereby assent to, recognize, re-establish, and confirm, the treaty of St. Louis, which was concluded on the third day of November, one thousand eight hundred and four, to the full extent of their interest in the same, as well as all other contracts and agreements between the parties; and the United States promise to fulfil all the stipulations contained in the said treaty in favor of the said Fox tribe or nation.

In witness whereof, the said William Clark, Ninian Edwards, and Auguste Chouteau, commissioners as aforesaid, and the aforesaid king, chiefs and warriors of the Fox tribe or nation, aforesaid, have hereunto subscribed their names and affixed their seals this fourteenth day of September, in the year of our Lord one thousand eight hundred and fifteen, and of the independence of the United States the fortieth.

Wm. Clark, [L. s.]	Kechaswa, the sun, his x mark, [L. s.]
Ninian Edwards, [L. s.]	Mataqua, the medical woman, his x
Auguste Chouteau, [L. s.]	mark, [L. s.]
Pierremaskkin, the fox who walks	Paquampa, the bear that sits, his x
crooked, his x mark, [L. s.]	mark, [L. s.]
Muckkatawagout, black cloud, his	Aquoqua, the kettle, his x mark, [L. s.]
x mark, [L. s.]	Nemarqua, his x mark, [L. s.]
Namasosanamet, he who surpasses	Machenamau, the bad fish, his x
all others, his x mark, [L. s.]	mark, [L. s.]
Waapaca, his x mark, [L. s.]	Pesotaka, the flying fish, his x mark,
Mackkatananamakee, the black	[L. s.]
thunder, his x mark, [L. s.]	Mishecaqua, the hairy legs, his x
Pashechenene, the liar, his x mark,	mark, [L. s.]
[L. s.]	Capontwa, all at once, his x mark, [L. s.]
Wapasai, the white skin, his x mark,	Mowhinin, the wolf, his x mark, [L. s.]
[L. s.]	Omquo, his x mark, [L. s.]
Catchacommu, big lake, his x mark,	Wonakasa, the quick riser, his x
[L. s.]	mark, [L. s.]
Malasenokama, the war chief, his x	Nauatawaka, the scenting fox, his
mark, [L. s.]	x mark, [L. s.]

Done at Portage des Sioux, in the presence of—

R. Wash, secretary to the commission,
Thomas Levens, lieutenant colonel, commandant First Regiment, I. T.
P. Chouteau, agent,
T. Paul, C. C. T.
James B. Moore, captain,
Samuel Whiteside, captain,

Jno. W. Johnson, United States factor and Indian agent,
Maurice Blondeaux.
Samuel Solomon,
Noel Mograine,
          Interpreters.
Daniel Converse, third lieutenant.

TREATY WITH THE IOWA, 1815.

Sept. 16, 1815.

7 Stat., 136.
Ratified Dec. 26, 1815.

A treaty of peace and friendship, made and concluded at Portage des Sioux, between William Clark, Ninian Edwards, and Auguste Chouteau, Commissioners Plenipotentiary of the United States of America, on the part and behalf of the said States, of the one part; and the undersigned, King, Chiefs, and Warriors, of the Iaway Tribe or Nation, on the part and behalf of the said Tribe or Nation, of the other part.

The parties being desirous of re-establishing peace and friendship between the United States and the said tribe or nation, and of being placed in all things, and in every respect, on the same footing upon which they stood before the war, have agreed to the following articles:

ARTICLE 1. Every injury, or act of hostility, by one or either of the contracting parties against the other shall be mutually forgiven and forgot.

ART. 2. There shall be perpetual peace and friendship between all the citizens of the United States and all the individuals composing the said Iaway tribe or nation.

ART. 3. The contracting parties do hereby agree, promise, and oblige themselves, reciprocally to deliver up all the prisoners now in their hands, (by what means soever the same may have come into their possession,) to the officer commanding at St. Louis, to be by him restored to their respective nations, as soon as it may be practicable.

ART. 4. The contracting parties, in the sincerity of mutual friendship, recognize, re-establish, and confirm, all and every treaty, contract, and agreement, heretofore concluded between the United States and the said Iaway tribe or nation.

In witness whereof, the said William Clark, Ninian Edwards, and Auguste Chouteau, commissioners as aforesaid, and the aforesaid king, chiefs, and warriors, have hereunto subscribed their names and affixed their seals, this sixteenth day of September, in the year of our Lord one thousand eight hundred and fifteen, and of the independence of the United States the fortieth.

William Clark, [L. S.]	Ranoingga, the little pipe, his x mark, [L. S.]
Ninian Edwards, [L. S.]	
Auguste Chouteau, [L. S.]	Wohomppee, the broth, his x mark, [L. S.]
Wyingwaha, or hard heart, his x mark, [L. S.]	Shongatong, the horse jockey, his x mark, [L. S.]
Wongehehronyne, or big chief, his x mark, [L. S.]	Nahocheininugga, without ears, his x mark, [L. S.]
Wonehee, or the slave, his x mark, [L. S.]	Conja, the plumb, his x mark, [L. S.]
Hahraga, the forked horn, his x mark, [L. S.]	Chahowhrowpa, the dew-lap, his x mark, [L. S.]
Eniswahanee, the big axe, his x mark, [L. S.]	Manuhanu, the great walker, his x mark, [L. S.]
Washcommanee, the great marcher, his x mark, [L. S.]	Chapee, the pine buffaloe, his x mark,
Wyimppishcoonee, the ill-humoured man, his x mark, [L. S.]	Ckugwata, the roller, his x mark, [L. S.]
	Ishtagrasa, grey eyes, his x mark, [L. S.]

Done at Portage des Sioux, in the presence of---

R. Wash, secretary to the commission.
Dl. Bissel, brigadier-general.
R. Paul, C. C. T.
Samuel Brady, lieutenant.
Geo. Fisher, surgeon, Illinois regiment.
P. Chouteau, agent.
Jno. W. Johnson, United States factor and Indian agent.

Samuel Solomon, interpreter.
Maurice Blondeaux.
Louis Dorion.
Dennis Julien.
Jas. McCulloch, captain.

TREATY WITH THE KANSA, 1815.

A treaty of peace and friendship, made and concluded at St. Louis between Ninian Edwards and Auguste Chouteau, Commissioners Plenipotentiary of the United States of America, on the part and behalf of the said States, of one part; and the undersigned Chiefs and Warriors of the Kanzas Tribe of Indians, on the part and behalf of their said Tribe, of the other part.

Oct. 28, 1815.
7 Stat., 137.
Ratified Dec. 26, 1818.

THE parties being desirous of re-establishing peace and friendship between the United States and their said tribe, and of being placed, in all things, and in every respect, upon the same footing upon which they stood before the late war between the United States and Great Britain, have agreed to the following articles:

Injuries, etc., forgiven.

ARTICLE 1. Every injury or act of hostility by one or either of the contracting parties against the other, shall be mutually forgiven and forgot.

Perpetual peace and friendship.

ART. 2. There shall be perpetual peace and friendship between all the citizens of the United States of America and all the individuals composing the said Kanzas tribe, and all the friendly relations that existed between them before the war shall be, and the same are hereby, renewed.

Protection of United States acknowledged.

ART. 3. The undersigned chiefs and warriors, for themselves and their said tribe, do hereby acknowledge themselves to be under the protection of the United States of America, and of no other nation, power, or sovereign, whatsoever.

In witness whereof, the said Ninian Edwards and Auguste Chouteau, commissioners as aforesaid, and the chiefs aforesaid, have hereunto subscribed their names and affixed their seals, this twenty-eighth day of October, in the year of our Lord one thousand eight hundred and fifteen, and of the independence of the United States the fortieth.

Ninian Edwards,	[L. S.]	Washanzare, his x mark,	[L. S.]
Auguste Chouteau,	[L. S.]	Ezashabe, his x mark,	[L. S.]
Cayezettanzaw, or the big chief, his x mark,	[L. S.]	Kaehamony, or the floating down stream, his x mark,	[L. S.]
Needapy, his x mark,	[L. S.]	Opasheeza, his x mark,	[L. S.]
Hazeware, or the buck elk running after the doe, his x mark,	[L. S.]	Karahsheenzaw, or the little crow, his x mark,	[L. S.]
Wahanzasby, or the endless, his x mark,	[L. S.]	Metanezaw, or the foolish robe, his x mark,	[L. S.]
Cayebasneenzaw, or the little chief, his x mark,	[L. S.]	Wehurasudze, or the red eagle, his x mark,	[L. S.]
Manshenscaw, or the white plume, his x mark,	[L. S.]	Necolebran, or he who can smell a man, his x mark,	[L. S.]
Cayegettsazesheengaw, or the old chief, his x mark,	[L. S.]	Mannanedze, his x mark,	[L. S.]
Mocupamawny, or the walking cloud, his x mark,	[L. S.]	Watankezaw, his x mark,	[L. S.]
		Taritchu, or the cow's rib.	[L. S.]

Done at St. Louis, in presence of—

R. Wash, secretary to the commission.
R. Paul, C. T. of the C.
Ja. Kennerly, C. Indian Department.
Christian Witt,
Gabriel S. Chouteau, ensign M. M.

G. H. Kennerly,
Thomas Forsyth, Indian agent,
Taylor Berry.
Antoine Barada,
Paul Desjardins,
    Interpreters.

TREATY WITH THE CHEROKEE, 1816

Mar. 22, 1816.

7 Stat., 138.
Ratified Apr. 8, 1816.

Articles of a treaty made and concluded at the City of Washington, on the twenty-second day of March, one thousand eight hundred and sixteen, between George Graham, being specially authorized by the President of the United States thereto, and the undersigned Chiefs and Headmen of the Cherokee Nation, duly authorized and empowered by the said Nation.

Cession by Cherokees to South Carolina.

ARTICLE 1. Whereas the Executive of the State of South Carolina has made an application to the President of the United States to extinguish the claim of the Cherokee nation to that part of their lands which lie within the boundaries of the said State, as lately established and agreed upon between that State and the State of North Carolina; and as the Cherokee nation is disposed to comply with the wishes of their brothers of South Carolina, they have agreed and do hereby agree to cede to the State of South Carolina, and forever quit claim to, the tract

Bounds of the cession.

of country contained within the following bounds, viz.: beginning on the east bank of the Chattuga river, where the boundary line of the

Cherokee nation crosses the same, running thence, with the said boundary line, to a rock on the Blue Ridge, where the boundary line crosses the same, and which rock has been lately established as a corner to the States of North and South Carolina; running thence, south, sixty-eight and a quarter degrees west, twenty miles and thirty-two chains, to a rock on the Chattuga river at the thirty-fifth degree of north latitude, another corner of the boundaries agreed upon by the State of North and South Carolina; thence, down and with the Chattuga, to the beginning.

ART. 2. For and in consideration of the above cession, the United States promise and engage that the State of South Carolina shall pay to the Cherokee nation, or its accredited agent, the sum of five thousand dollars, within ninety days after the President and Senate shall have ratified this treaty: *Provided*, That the Cherokee nation shall have sanctioned the same in Council: *And provided also*, That the Executive of the State of South Carolina shall approve of the stipulations contained in this article. United States engage for the payment of $5,000 by South Carolina.

Proviso.

In testimony whereof, the said commissioner, and the undersigned chiefs and head men of the Cherokee nation, have hereto set their hands and seals.

George Graham,	[L. S.]
Colonel John Lowry, his x mark,	[L. S.]
Major John Walker, his x mark,	[L. S.]
Major Ridge, his x mark,	[L. S.]
Richard Taylor,	[L. S.]
John Ross,	[L. S.]
Cheucunsene, his x mark,	[L. S.]

Witnesses present at signing and sealing:
　Return J. Meigs,
　Jacob Laub,
　Gid. Davis.

TREATY WITH THE CHEROKEE, 1816.

Articles of a convention made and entered into between George Graham, specially authorized thereto by the President of the United States, and the undersigned Chiefs and Headmen of the Cherokee Nation, duly authorized and empowered by the said Nation. Mar. 22, 1816.
7. Stat., 139.
Ratified Apr. 8, 1816.

ARTICLE 1. Whereas doubts have existed in relation to the northern boundary of that part of the Creek lands lying west of the Coosa river, and which were ceded to the United States by the treaty held at Fort Jackson, on the ninth day of August, one thousand eight hundred and fourteen; and whereas, by the third article of the Treaty, dated the seventh of January, one thousand eight hundred and six, between the United States and the Cherokee nation, the United States have recognised a claim on the part of the Cherokee nation to the lands south of the Big Bend of the Tenessee river, and extending as far west as a place on the waters of Bear Creek, [a branch of the Tennessee river,] known by the name of the Flat Rock, or Stone; it is, therefore, now declared and agreed, that a line shall be run from a point on the west bank of the Coosa river, opposite to the lower end of the Ten Islands in said river, and above Fort Strother, directly to the Flat Rock or Stone, on Bear creek, [a branch of the Tennessee river;] which line shall be established as the boundary of the lands ceded by the Creek nation to the United States by the treaty held at Fort Jackson, on the ninth day of August, one thousand eight hundred and fourteen, and of the lands claimed by the Cherokee nation lying west of the Coosa and south of the Tennessee rivers. Doubts about boundary.

Boundary line designated and established.

ART. 2. It is expressly agreed on the part of the Cherokee nation that the United States shall have the right to lay off, open, and have the free use of, such road or roads, through any part of the Cherokee nation, lying north of the boundary line now established, as may be deemed necessary for the free intercourse between the States of Tennessee and Georgia and the Mississippi Territory. And the citizens of the United States shall freely navigate and use as a highway, all the rivers and waters within the Cherokee nation. The Cherokee nation further agree to establish and keep up, on the roads to be opened under the sanction of this article, such ferries and public houses as may be necessary for the accommodation of the citizens of the United States.

United States to have the right of opening and using roads, etc., in the Cherokee Nation.

Cherokees to keep up public houses, etc.

ART. 3. In order to preclude any dispute hereafter, relative to the boundary line now established, it is hereby agreed that the Cherokee nation shall appoint two commissioners to accompany the commissioners already appointed on the part of the United States, to run the boundary lines of the lands ceded by the Creek nation to the United States, while they are engaged in running that part of the boundary established by the first article of this treaty.

Commissioners to run the boundary line.

ART. 4. In order to avoid unnecessary expense and delay, it is further agreed that, whenever the President of the United States may deem it expedient to open a road through any part of the Cherokee nation, in pursuance of the stipulations of the second article of this Convention, the principal chief of the Cherokee nation shall appoint one commissioner to accompany the commissioners appointed by the President of the United States, to lay off and mark the road; and the said commissioner shall be paid by the United States.

Commissioners to lay off roads.

To be paid by the United States.

ART. 5. The United States agree to indemnify the individuals of the Cherokee nation for losses sustained by them in consequence of the march of the militia and other troops in the service of the United States through that nation; which losses have been ascertained by the agents of the United States to the amount of twenty-five thousand five hundred dollars.

Indemnity to Cherokees.

In testimony whereof, the said commissioner and the undersigned chiefs and head men of the Cherokee nation, have hereunto set their hands and seals. Done at the city of Washington, this twenty-second day of March, one thousand eight hundred and sixteen.

George Graham,	[L. S.]
Colonel John Lowry, his x mark,	[L. S.]
Major John Walker, his x mark,	[L. S.]
Major Ridge, his x mark,	[L. S.]
Richard Taylor,	[L. S.]
John Ross,	[L. S.]
Cheucunsene, his x mark,	[L. S.]

Witnesses present at signing and sealing:
Return J. Meigs,
Jacob Laub,
Gid. Davis.

TREATY WITH THE SAUK, 1816.

A treaty of peace and friendship made and concluded at St. Louis between William Clark, Ninian Edwards, and Auguste Chouteau, commissioners plenipotentiary of the United States of America, on the part and behalf of the said states, of the one part, and the undersigned chiefs and warriors of the Sacs of Rock river and the adjacent country, of the other part.

May 13, 1816.

7 Stat., 141.
Proclamation, Dec. 30, 1816.

WHEREAS by the ninth article of the treaty of peace, which was concluded on the twenty-fourth day of December, eighteen hundred and fourteen, between the United States and Great Britain, at Ghent, and

Preamble.

which was ratified by the president, with the advice and consent of the senate, on the seventeenth day of February, eighteen hundred and fifteen, it was stipulated that the said parties should severally put an end to all hostilities with the Indian tribes, with whom they might be at war, at the time of the ratification of said treaty; and to place the said tribes inhabiting their respective territories, on the same footing upon which they stood before the war: Provided, they should agree to desist from all hostilities against the said parties, their citizens or subjects respectively, upon the ratification of the said treaty being notified to them, and should so desist accordingly.

And whereas the United States being determined to execute every article of the treaty with perfect good faith, and wishing to be particularly exact in the execution of the article above alluded to, relating to the Indian tribes: The president, in consequence thereof, for that purpose, on the eleventh day of March, eighteen hundred and fifteen, appointed the undersigned William Clark, governor of Missouri territory, Ninian Edwards, governor of Illinois territory, and Auguste Chouteau, esq. of the Missouri territory, commissioners, with full power to conclude a treaty of peace and amity with all those tribes of Indians, conformably to the stipulations contained in the said article, on the part of the United States, in relation to such tribes.

And whereas the commissioners, in conformity with their instructions in the early part of last year, notified the Sacks of Rock river, and the adjacent country, of the time of the ratification of said treaty; of the stipulations it contained in relation to them; of the disposition of the American government to fulfil those stipulations, by entering into a treaty with them, conformably thereto; and invited the said Sacs of Rock river, and the adjacent country, to send forward a deputation of their chiefs to meet the said commissioners at Portage des Sioux, for the purpose of concluding such a treaty as aforesaid, between the United States and the said Indians, and the said Sacs of Rock river, and the adjacent country, having not only declined that friendly overture, but having continued their hostilities, and committed many depredations thereafter, which would have justified the infliction of the severest chastisement upon them; but having earnestly repented of their conduct, now imploring mercy, and being anxious to return to the habits of peace and friendship with the United States; and the latter being always disposed to pursue the most liberal and humane policy towards the Indian tribes within their territory, preferring their reclamation by peaceful measures, to their punishment, by the application of the military force of the nation—Now, therefore,

The said William Clark, Ninian Edwards, and Auguste Chouteau, commissioners as aforesaid, and the undersigned chiefs and warriors, as aforesaid, for the purpose of restoring peace and friendship between the parties, do agree to the following articles:

ART. 1. The Sacs of Rock river, and the adjacent country, do hereby unconditionally assent to recognize, re-establish, and confirm the treaty between the United States of America and the United tribes of Sacs and Foxes, which was concluded at St. Louis, on the third day of November, one thousand eight hundred and four; as well as all other contracts and agreements, heretofore made between the Sac tribe or nation, and the United States. *Treaty of St. Louis, of Nov. 3, 1804, confirmed.*

ART. 2. The United States agree to place the aforesaid Sacs of Rock river, on the same footing upon which they stood before the war; provided they shall, on or before the first day of July next, deliver up to the officer commanding at cantonment Davis, on the Mississippi, all the property they, or any part of their tribe, have plundered or stolen from the citizens of the United States, since they were notified, as aforesaid, of the time of the ratification of the late treaty between the United States and Great Britain. *Sacs placed on the same footing as before the war; provided, etc.*

Consequences of a failure or neglect to deliver up property.

ART. 3. If the said tribe shall fail or neglect to deliver up the property aforesaid, or any part thereof, on or before the first day of July aforesaid, they shall forfeit to the United States all right and title to their proportion of the annuities which, by the treaty of St. Louis, were covenanted to be paid to the Sac tribe; and the United States shall for ever afterwards be exonerated from the payment of so much of said annuities as, upon a fair distribution, would fall to the share of that portion of the Sacs who are represented by the undersigned chiefs and warriors.

When to take effect.

ART. 4. This treaty shall take effect and be obligatory on the contracting parties, unless the same shall be disapproved by the president and senate of the United States, or by the president only: and in the mean time all hostilities shall cease from this date.

In testimony whereof, the said William Clark, Ninian Edwards, and Auguste Chouteau, commissioners as aforesaid, and the undersigned chiefs and warriors as aforesaid, have hereunto set their hands and affixed their seals, this thirteenth day of May, one thousand eight hundred and sixteen.

Wm. Clark, [L. s.]	Wassekenequa, or Sharp-faced Bear, his x mark, [L. s.]
Ninian Edwards, [L. s.]	
Auguste Chouteau, [L. s.]	Sakeetoo, or the Thunder that Frightens, his x mark, [L. s.]
Anowart, or the One who speaks, his x mark, [L. s.]	Warpaloka, or the Rumbling Thunder, his x mark, [L. s.]
Namawenanu, or Sturgeon Man, his x mark, [L. s.]	Kemealosha, or the Swan that flies in the rain, his x mark, [L. s.]
Nasawarku, or the Forks, his x mark, [L. s.]	Pashekomack, or the Swan that flies low, his x mark, [L. s.]
Namatchesa, or the Jumping Sturgeon, his x mark, [L. s.]	Keotasheka, or the Running Partridge, his x mark, [L. s.]
Matchequawa, the Bad Axe, his x mark, [L. s.]	Wapalamo, or the White Wolf, his x mark, [L. s.]
Mascho, or Young Eagle, his x mark, [L. s.]	Caskupwa, or the Swan whose wings crack when he flies, his x mark, [L. s.]
Aquaosa, or a Lion coming out of the Water, his x mark, [L. s.]	Napetaka, or he who has a Swan's throat around his neck, his x mark, [L. s.]
Mucketamachekaka, or Black Sparrow Hawk, his x mark, [L. s.]	
Poinaketa, or the Cloud that don't stop, his x mark, [L. s.]	Mashashe, or the Fox, his x mark, [L. s.]
Mealeseta, or Bad Weather, his x mark, [L. s.]	Wapamukqua, or the White Bear, his x mark, [L. s.]
Anawashqueth, the Bad Root, his x mark, [L. s.]	

St. Louis, May 13th, 1816, Done in the presence of—

R. Wash, secretary to the commission,	B. G. Tavar,
R. Paul, C. T. of the C.	Charles Wm. Hunter,
J. Bt. Caron,	Cerre,
Samuel Solomon,	M. La Croix,
Interpreters.	Gayol de Guirano,
Joshua Norvell, Judge Advocate M. M.	Boon Ingels,
Joseph Perkins,	Moses Scott,
Joseph Charless,	James Sawyer.

TREATY WITH THE SIOUX, 1816.

June 1, 1816.

7 Stat., 143.
Proclamation, Dec. 30, 1816.

A treaty of peace and friendship made and concluded at St. Louis, between William Clark, Ninian Edwards, and Auguste Chouteau, commissioners plenipotentiary of the United States of America, on the part and behalf of the said states, of the one part, and the undersigned chiefs and warriors, representing eight bands of the Siouxs, composing the three tribes called the Siouxs of the Leaf, the Siouxs of the Broad Leaf, and the Siouxs who shoot in the Pine Tops, on the part and behalf of their said tribes, of the other part.

The parties being desirous of re-establishing peace and friendship between the United States and the said tribes, and of being placed in

all things, and in every respect, on the same footing upon which they Injuries, etc., for-
given.
stood before the late war between the United States and Great Britain,
have agreed to the following articles:

ART. 1. Every injury or act of hostility, committed by one or either Perpetual peace and
friendship, etc.
of the contracting parties against the other, shall be mutually forgiven
and forgot.

ART. 2. There shall be perpetual peace and friendship between all
the citizens of the United States, and all the individuals composing the
aforesaid tribes; and all the friendly relations that existed between Former cessions,
treaties, etc., con-
firmed.
them before the war shall be, and the same are hereby, renewed.

ART. 3. The undersigned chiefs and warriors, for themselves and
their tribes respectively, do, by these presents, confirm to the United
States all and every cession, or cessions, of land heretofore made by
their tribes to the British, French, or Spanish government, within the
limits of the United States or their territories; and the parties here Protection of United
States acknowledged
contracting do, moreover, in the sincerity of mutual friendship, recog-
nize, re-establish, and confirm, all and every treaty, contract, and
agreement, heretofore concluded between the United States and the
said tribes or nations.

ART. 4. The undersigned chiefs and warriors as aforesaid, for themselves and their said tribes, do hereby acknowledge themselves to be
under the protection of the United States, and of no other nation,
power, or sovereign, whatsoever.

In witness whereof, the commissioners aforesaid, and the undersigned
chiefs and warriors as aforesaid, have hereunto subscribed their names
and affixed their seals, this first day of June, in the year of our Lord
one thousand eight hundred and sixteen, and of the independence of
the United States the fortieth.

William Clark,	[L. S.]	Eoshark, the Belly-Ache, his x	
Ninian Edwards,	[L. S.]	mark,	[L. S.]
Auguste Chouteau,	[L. S.]	Tuquaacundup, the Doctor, his x	
Tatamanee, the Marching Wind,		mark,	[L. S.]
his x mark,	[L. S.]	Onudokea, the Fluttering Eagle,	
Warmadearwarup, the Man who		his x mark,	[L. S.]
looks at the Calumet Eagle, his		Tusarquarp, he that walks with a	
x mark,	[L. S.]	Cane, his x mark,	[L. S.]
Peneshon, his x mark,	[L. S.]	Markpeasena, the Black Cloud, his x	
Kanggawashecha, or French Crow,		mark,	[L. S.]
his x mark,	[L. S.]	Warksuamanee, the Man who is	
Eanggamanee, the Runner, his x		sick when he walks, his x mark,	[L. S.]
mark	[L. S.]	Otanggamanee, the Man with a	
Tatangascartop, the Playing Buf-		strong voice, his x mark,	[L. S.]
falo, his x mark,	[L. S.]	Hungkrehearpee, or the Half of his	
Tatangamarnee, the Walking Buf-		Body Gray, his x mark,	[L. S.]
falo, or Red Wing, his x mark,	[L. S.]	Warpearmusee, the Iron Cloud, his	
Warseconta, who shoots in the Pine		x mark,	[L. S.]
tops, his x mark,	[L. S.]	Etoagungamanee, the White Face,	
Weeshto, the Shoulder, his x mark,	[L. S.]	his x mark,	[L. S.]
Warmarnosa, the Thief, his x mark,	[L. S.]	Warchesunsapa, the Negro, his x	
Shutkaongka, the Bird on the		mark,	[L. S.]
Limb, his x mark,	[L. S.]	Ehaarp, the Climber, his x mark,	[L. S.]
Shakaska, White Nails, his x mark,	[L. S.]	Nahre, the Shifting Shadow, his x	
Shuskamanee, the Walking Bird,		mark,	[L. S.]
his x mark,	[L. S.]	Hapula, the fourth Son, his x mark,	[L. S.]
Manakohomonee, the Turning		Marcawachup, the Dancer, his x	
Iron, his x mark,	[L. S.]	mark,	[L. S.]
Oocus, the Watchman, his x mark,	[L. S.]	Shantanggaup, the Big Tree, his x	
Pahataka, the Humming Bird,		mark,	[L. S.]
his x mark,	[L. S.]	Shongkaska, the White Big-eared	
Eaohungko, the Man who marches		Dog, his x mark,	[L. S.]
quick, his x mark,	[L. S.]	Hasanee, the Buffalo with one	
Medermee, the Muddy Lake, his x		Horn, his x mark,	[L. S.]
mark,	[L. S.]	Narissakata, the Old Man who can	
Tatawaka, the Medicine Wind, his		hardly walk, his x mark,	[L. S.]
x mark,	[L. S.]	Aearpa, the Speaker, his x mark,	[L. S.]
Warshushasta, the Bad Hail, his x		Muckpeasarp, the Black Cloud,	
mark,	[L. S.]	his x mark,	[L. S.]

Done at St. Louis, in the presence of

R. Wash, secretary to the commission,	Henry Delorier, interpreter,
R. Paul, C. T. of the C.	Pierre Lapointe, interpreter,
Wm. O. Allen, captain U. S. Corps Artillery,	Samuel Solomon, interpreter,
	Jacques Mette, interpreter,
H. S. Geyer,	Cere,
Joshua Norvell, judge advocate M. M.	Richard Cave,
N. Boilvin, agent,	Willi Cave,
Thomas Forsyth, Indian agent,	Julius Pescay.
Maurice Blondeaux,	

TREATY WITH THE WINNEBAGO, 1816.

June 3, 1816.

7 Stat., 144.
Proclamation, Dec. 30, 1816.

A treaty of peace and friendship made and concluded between William Clark, Ninian Edwards, and Auguste Chouteau, commissioners plenipotentiary of the United States of America, on the part and behalf of the said states, of the one part, and the undersigned chiefs and warriors of that portion of the Winnebago tribe or nation residing on the Ouisconsin river, of the other part.

Injuries, etc., forgiven.

Whereas the undersigned chiefs and warriors, as well as that portion of the nation which they represent, have separated themselves from the rest of their nation, and reside in a village on the Ouisconsin river, and are desirous of returning to a state of friendly relations with the United States, the parties hereto have agreed to the following articles.

ART. 1. Every injury or act of hostility, committed by one or either of the contracting parties against the other, shall be mutually forgiven and forgot; and all the friendly relations that existed between them before the late war, shall be, and the same are hereby, renewed.

Former cessions, treaties, etc., confirmed.

ART. 2. The undersigned chiefs and warriors, for themselves and those they represent, do by these presents, confirm to the United States all and every cession of land heretofore made by their nation to the British, French, or Spanish government, within the limits of the United States, or their territories; and also, all and every treaty, contract, and agreement, heretofore concluded between the United States and the said tribe or nation, as far as their interest in the same extends.

Protection of United States acknowledged.

ART. 3. The undersigned chiefs and warriors as aforesaid, for themselves and those they represent, do hereby acknowledge themselves to be under the protection of the United States, and of no other nation, power, or sovereign, whatsoever.

Indians to remain distinct from the rest of their tribe.

ART. 4. The aforesaid chiefs and warriors, for themselves and those they represent, do further promise to remain distinct and separate from the rest of their tribe or nation, giving them no aid or assistance whatever, until peace shall also be concluded between the United States and the said tribe or nation.

Prisoners to be delivered up.

ART. 5. The contracting parties do hereby agree, promise, and oblige themselves, reciprocally, to deliver up all prisoners now in their hands (by what means soever the same may have come into their possession) to the officer commanding at Prairie du Chien, to be by him restored to the respective parties hereto, as soon as it may be practicable.

In witness whereof, the commissioners aforesaid, and the undersigned chiefs and warriors as aforesaid, have hereunto subscribed their names, and affixed their seals, this third day of June, in the year of our Lord one thousand eight hundred and sixteen, and of the independence of the United States, the fortieth.

William Clark,	[L. s.]	Achahouska, the White Sky, his x	
Ninian Edwards,	[L. s.]	mark,	[L. s.]
Aug. Chouteau,	[L. s.]	Chenapinka, the Good House, his	
Choukeka, or Dekare, the Spoon,		x mark,	[L. s.]
his x mark,	[L. s.]	Makamka, the Earth, his x mark,	[L. s.]
Onunaka, or Karamanu, his x mark,	[L. s.]		

Wechoka, the Green Feather, his
x mark,   [L. S.]
Shougkapar, the Dog, his x mark,   [L. S.]
Nekousaa, the Main Channel, his
x mark,   [L. S.]

Wapanoneker, the Bear, his mark, [L. S.]
Opwarchickwaka, the Rain, his x
mark,   [L. S.]
Chepurganika, the little Buffalo
Head, his x mark,   [L. S.]

Done at St. Louis, in the presence of—

R. Wash, secretary to the commission,
R. Paul, C. T. of the C.
Wm. O. Allen, captain U. S. Corps of
Artillery,
N. Boilvin, agent,
Thomas Forsyth, Indian agent,

Maurice Blondeaux, Indian agent,
Henry Delorier, interpreter,
Pierre Lapointe, interpreter,
Baptiste Pereault, interpreter,
Samuel Solomon, interpreter,
Jacques Mette, interpreter.

TREATY WITH THE WEA AND KICKAPOO, 1816.

Articles of a treaty made and entered into at Fort Harrison, in the Indiana Territory between Benjamin Parke, specially authorized thereto by the president of the United States, of the one part, and the tribes of Indians called the Weas and Kickapoos, by their chiefs and head men, of the other part.

June 4, 1816.

7 Stat., 145.
Proclamation, Dec. 30, 1816.

ART. 1. The Weas and Kickapoos again acknowledge themselves in peace and friendship with the United States. *Peace and friendship.*

ART. 2. The said tribes acknowledge the validity of, and declare their determination to adhere to, the treaty of Greenville, made in the year seventeen hundred and ninety-five, and all subsequent treaties which they have respectively made with the United States. *Treaty of Greenville confirmed.*

ART. 3. The boundary line, surveyed and marked by the United States, of the land on the Wabash and White rivers, ceded in the year eighteen hundred and nine, the said tribes do hereby explicitly recognize and confirm, as having been executed conformably to the several treaties they have made with the United States. *Boundary line confirmed.*

ART. 4. The chiefs and warriors of the said tribe of the Kickapoos acknowledge that they have ceded to the United States all that tract of country which lies between the aforesaid boundary line on the north west side of the Wabash—the Wabash, the Vermillion river, and a line to be drawn from the north west corner of the said boundary line, so as to strike the Vermillion river twenty miles in a direct line from its mouth, according to the terms and conditions of the treaty they made with the United States on the ninth day of December, in the year eighteen hundred and nine. *Kickapoos acknowledge a former cession.*

In testimony whereof, the said Benjamin Parke, and the chiefs and head men of the said tribes, have hereunto set their hands and affixed their seals, at fort Harrison, in the Indiana territory, the fourth day of June, in the year of our Lord, one thousand eight hundred and sixteen.

B. Parke.   [L. S.]
Weas:
Mesaupeekaunga, or Gamlan, his x
mark,   [L. S.]
Jacco, his x mark,   [L. S.]
Kesanguekamya, or Buffalo, his x
mark,   [L. S.]
Chequiha, or Little Eyes, his x
mark,   [L. S.]
Mahquakouonga, or Negro Legs,
his x mark,   [L. S.]
Pequaih, or George, his x mark,   [L. S.]
Kenokosetah, or Long Body, his x
mark,   [L. S.]
Owl, (a Miami) his x mark,   [L. S.]
Mahchekeleatah, or Big Man, (a
Miami,) his x mark,   [L. S.]
Kickapoos:
Sheshepah, or Little Duck, his x
mark,   [L. S.]

Kaanehkaka, or Drunkard's Son,
his x mark,   [L. S.]
Shekonah, or Stone, his x mark,   [L. S.]
Mahquah, or Bear, his x mark,   [L. S.]
Penashee, or Little Turkey, his x
mark,   [L. S.]
Mehtahkokeah, or Big Tree, his x
mark,   [L. S.]
Mauquasconiah, or Big Tree, his x
mark,   [L. S.]
Keetahtey, or Little Otter, his x
mark,   [L. S.]
Nepiseeah, or Blackberry, his x
mark,   [L. S.]
Pehsquonatah, or Blackberry
Flower, his x mark,   [L. S.]
Tecumthena, or Track in Prairie,
his x mark,   [L. S.]

Done in the presence of—

John L. McCollough, secretary to the commission,	Henry Gilham, of Vincennes,
	N. B. Baily, of Vincennes,
John T. Chunn, major, commanding Fort Harrison,	G. C. Copp,
	Michael Brouillet, interpreter, at Fort Harrison,
Gab. I. Floyd, lieutenant U. S. Army,	
Th. McCall, of Vincennes,	Joseph Barron, sworn interpret

TREATY WITH THE OTTAWA, ETC., 1816.

Aug. 24, 1816.

7 Stat., 146.
Proclamation, Dec. 30, 1816.

A treaty of Peace, Friendship, and Limits, made and concluded between Ninian Edwards, William Clark, and Auguste Chouteau, commissioners plenipotentiary of the United States of America, on the part and behalf of said states, of the one part, and the chiefs and warriors of the united tribes of Ottawas, Chipawas, and Pottowotomees, residing on the Illinois and Melwakee rivers, and their waters, and on the southwestern parts of Lake Michigan, of the other part.

WHEREAS a serious dispute has for some time past existed between the contracting parties relative to the right to a part of the lands ceded to the United States by the tribes of Sacs and Foxes, on the third day of November, one thousand eight hundred and four, and both parties being desirous of preserving a harmonious and friendly intercourse, and of establishing permanent peace and friendship, have, for the purpose of removing all difficulties, agreed to the following terms:

Cession to the United States.

ART. 1. The said chiefs and warriors, for themselves and the tribes they represent, agree to relinquish, and hereby do relinquish, to the United States, all their right, claim, and title, to all the land contained in the before-mentioned cession of the Sacs and Foxes, which lies south of a due west line from the southern extremity of Lake Michigan to the Mississippi river. And they moreover cede to the United States all the land contained within the following bounds, to wit: beginning on the left bank of the Fox river of Illinois, ten miles above the mouth of said Fox river; thence running so as to cross Sandy creek, ten miles above its mouth; thence, in a direct line, to a point ten miles north of the west end of the Portage, between Chicago creek, which empties into Lake Michigan, and the river Depleines, a fork of the Illinois; thence, in a direct line, to a point on Lake Michigan, ten miles northward of the mouth of Chicago creek; thence, along the lake, to a point ten miles southward of the mouth of the said Chicago creek; thence, in a direct line, to a point on the Kankakee, ten miles above its mouth; thence, with the said Kankakee and the Illinois river, to the mouth of Fox river, and thence to the beginning: *Provided, nevertheless,* That the said tribes shall be permitted to hunt and fish within the limits of the land hereby relinquished and ceded, so long as it may continue to be the property of the United States.

Proviso.

Consideration.

ART. 2. In consideration of the aforesaid relinquishment and cession, the United States have this day delivered to said tribes a considerable quantity of merchandise, and do agree to pay them, annually, for the term of twelve years, goods to the value of one thousand dollars, reckoning that value at the first cost of the goods in the city or place in which they shall be purchased, without any charge for transportation; which said goods shall be delivered to the said tribes at some place on the Illinois river, not lower down than Peoria. And the said United States do moreover agree to relinquish to the said tribes all the land contained in the aforesaid cession of the Sacs and Foxes, which lies north of a due west line, from the southern extremity of Lake Michigan to the Mississippi river, except three leagues square at the mouth of the Ouisconsing river, including both banks, and such other tracts,

Relinquishment by United States.

on or near to the Ouisconsing and Mississippi rivers, as the president of the United States may think proper to reserve: *Provided*, That such other tracts shall not in the whole exceed the quantity that would be contained in five leagues square. Proviso.

ART. 3. The contracting parties, that peace and friendship may be permanent, promise that in all things whatever, they will act with justice and correctness towards each other, and that they will, with perfect good faith, fulfill all the obligations imposed upon them by former treaties. Peace and friendship.

In witness whereof, the said Ninian Edwards, William Clark, and Auguste Chouteau, commissioners aforesaid, and the chiefs and warriors of the aforesaid tribes, have hereunto subscribed their names and affixed their seals, this twenty-fourth day of August, one thousand eight hundred and sixteen, and of the independence of the United States the forty-first.

Ninian Edwards,	[L. S.]	Cunnepepy, his x mark,	[L. S.]
William Clark,	[L. S.]	Wonesee, his x mark,	[L. S.]
Auguste Chouteau,	[L. S.]	Richeikeming, or Lake, his x mark,	[L. S.]
Mucketeypokee, or Black Partridge,		Cabenaw, his x mark,	[L. S.]
his x mark,	[L. S.]	Opaho, his x mark,	[L. S.]
Sinnowchewone, by his brother Ig-		Cowwesaut, his x mark,	[L. S.]
natius, his x mark,	[L. S.]	Chekinaka, his x mark,	[L. S.]
Mucketepennese, or Black Bird, his		Macheweskeaway, his x mark,	[L. S.]
x mark,	[L. S.]	Spanquissee, his x mark,	[L. S.]
Bendegakewa, his x mark,	[L. S.]	Ignatius, his x mark,	[L. S.]
Pemasaw, or Walker, his x mark,	[L. S.]	Takaonenee, his x mark,	[L. S.]
Ontawa,	[L. S.]	Ottawonce, his x mark,	[L. S.]
Nangesay, alias Stout, his x mark,	[L. S.]	Tawwaning, or Trader, his x mark,	[L. S.]
Chamblee, his x mark,	[L. S.]	Cashshakee, his x mark,	[L. S.]
Cacake, his x mark,	[L. S.]	Nigigwash, his x mark,	[L. S.]
Shawanoe, his x mark,	[L. S.]	Shesheburigge,	[L. S.]
Wapunsy, his x mark,	[L. S.]	Mowais, or Little Wolf, his x mark,	[L. S.]

Done at St. Louis, in the presence of—

R. Wash, secretary to the commission,
R. Graham, Indian agent for the Territory of Illinois,
Thomas Forsyth, Indian agent,
J. Maul, lieutenant Eighth Regiment of Infantry,

P. Provenchere, interpreter of the commissioners,
Maurice Blondeaux, Indian agent,
John Ruland.

TREATY WITH THE CHEROKEE, 1816.

Sept. 14, 1816.

7 Stat., 148.
Proclamation, Dec. 30, 1816.

To perpetuate peace and friendship between the United States and Cherokee tribe, or nation, of Indians, and to remove all future causes of dissension which may arise from indefinite territorial boundaries, the president of the United States of America, by major general Andrew Jackson, general David Meriwether, and Jesse Franklin, esquire, commissioners plenipotentiary on the one part, and the Cherokee delegates on the other, covenant and agree to the following articles and conditions, which, when approved by the Cherokee nation, and constitutionally ratified by the government of the United States, shall be binding on all parties:

ART. 1. Peace and friendship are hereby firmly established between the United States and Cherokee nation or tribe of Indians. Peace and friendship.

ART. 2. The Cherokee nation acknowledge the following as their western boundary: South of the Tennessee river, commencing at Camp Coffee, on the south side of the Tennessee river, which is opposite the Chickasaw Island, running from thence a due south course to the top of the dividing ridge between the waters of the Tennessee and Tombigby rivers, thence eastwardly along said ridge, leaving the head waters of the Black Warrior to the right hand, until opposed by the west branch of Well's Creek, down the east bank of said creek to the Coosa river, and down said river. Boundary line.

Relinquishment and cession by Cherokees.

ART. 3. The Cherokee nation relinquish to the United States all claim, and cede all title to lands laying south and west of the line, as described in the second article; and, in consideration of said relinquishment and cession, the commissioners agree to allow the Cherokee nation an annuity of six thousand dollars, to continue for ten successive years, and five thousand dollars, to be paid in sixty days after the ratification of the treaty, as a compensation for any improvements which the said nation may have had on the lands surrendered.

Line to be run by United States.

ART. 4. The two contracting parties covenant, and agree, that the line, as described in the second article, shall be ascertained and marked by commissioners, to be appointed by the president of the United States; that the marks shall be bold; trees to be blazed on both sides of the line, and the fore and aft trees to be marked with the letters U. S.; that the commissioners shall be accompanied by two persons, to be appointed by the Cherokee nation, and that said nation, shall have due and seasonable notice when said operation is to be commenced.

A council to be held.

ART. 5. It is stipulated that the Cherokee nation will meet general Andrew Jackson, general David Meriwether, and Jesse Franklin, esquire, in council, at Turkey's Town, Coosa river, on the 28th of September, (instant,) there and then to express their approbation, or not, of the articles of this treaty; and if they do not assemble at the time and place specified, it is understood that the said commissioners may report the same as a tacit ratification, on the part of the Cherokee nation, of this treaty.

In testimony whereof, the said commissioners and undersigned chiefs and delegates of the Cherokee nation, have hereto set their hands and seals. Done at the Chickasaw council house, this fourteenth day of September, in the year of our Lord one thousand eight hundred and sixteen.

Andrew Jackson,	[L. s.]	John Beuge,	[L. s.]
D. Meriwether,	[L. s.]	John Bawldridge,	[L. s.]
J. Franklin,	[L. s.]	Sallocooke Fields,	[L. s.]
Toochalar,	[L. s.]	George Guess,	[L. s.]
Oohulookee,	[L. s.]	Bark,	[L. s.]
Wososey,	[L. s.]	Campbell,	[L. s.]
Gousa,	[L. s.]	Spirit,	[L. s.]
Spring Frog,	[L. s.]	Young Wolf,	[L. s.]
Oowatata,	[L. s.]	Oolitiskee.	[L. s.]

Witness:

James Gadsden, secretary to the commissioners,

Arthur P. Hayne, inspector general, division of the South,

James C. Bronaugh, hospital surgeon, U. S. Army,

John Gordon,

John Rhea,

Thomas Wilson, interpreter for the Cherokees,

A. McCoy, interpreter for the Cherokees.

Ratified at Turkey Town, by the whole Cherokee nation in council assembled. In testimony whereof, the subscribing commissioners of of the United States, and the undersigned chiefs and warriors of the Cherokee nation, have hereto set their hands and seals, this fourth day of October, in the year of our Lord one thousand eight hundred and sixteen.

Andrew Jackson,	[L. s.]	Dick Justice, his x mark,	[L. s.]
D. Meriwether,	[L. s.]	Richard Brown, his x mark,	[L. s.]
Path Killer, his x mark,	[L. s.]	Bark, his x mark,	[L. s.]
The Glass, his x mark,	[L. s.]	The Boot, his x mark,	[L. s.]
Sour Mush, his x mark,	[L. s.]	Chickasawlua, his x mark,	[L. s.]
Chulioa, his x mark,	[L. s.]		

Witness:

James Gadsden, secretary.

Return J. Meigs,

Richard Taylor, interpreter,

A. McCoy, interpreter.

TREATY WITH THE CHICKASAW, 1816.

To settle all territorial controversies, and to perpetuate that peace and harmony which has long happily subsisted between the United States and Chickasaw nation, the president of the United States of America, by major general Andrew Jackson, general David Meriwether, and Jesse Franklin, esq. on the one part, and the whole Chickasaw nation, in council assembled, on the other, have agreed on the following articles, which when ratified by the president, with the advice and consent of the senate of the United States, shall be binding on all parties:

ART. 1. Peace and friendship are hereby firmly established, and perpetuated, between the United States of America and Chickasaw nation.

ART. 2. The Chickasaw nation cede to the United States (with the exception of such reservations as shall hereafter be specified) all right or title to lands on the north side of the Tennessee river, and relinquish all claim to territory on the south side of said river, and east of a line commencing at the mouth of Caney creek, running up said creek to its source, thence a due south course to the ridge path, or commonly called Gaines's road, along said road south westwardly to a point on the Tombigby river, well known by the name of the Cotton Gin port, and down the west bank of the Tombigby to the Chocktaw boundary.

ART. 3. In consideration of the relinquishment of claim, and cession of lands, made in the preceding article, the commissioners agree to allow the Chickasaw nation twelve thousand dollars per annum for ten successive years, and four thousand five hundred dollars to be paid in sixty days after the ratification of this treaty into the hands of Levi Colbert, as a compensation for any improvements which individuals of the Chickasaw nation may have had on the lands surrendered; that is to say, two thousand dollars for improvements on the east side of the Tombigby, and two thousand five hundred dollars for improvements on the north side of the Tennessee river.

ART. 4. The commissioners agree that the following tracts of land shall be reserved to the Chickasaw nation:

1. One tract of land for the use of Col. George Colbert and heirs, and which is thus described by said Colbert: "Beginning on the north bank of the Tennessee river, at a point that, running north four miles, will include a big spring, about half way between his ferry and the mouth of Cypress, it being a spring that a large cow-path crosses its branch near where a cypress tree is cut down; thence westwardly to a point, four miles from the Tennessee river, and standing due north of a point on the north bank of the river, three [four] miles below his ferry on the Tennessee river, and up the meanders of said river to the beginning point."

2. A tract of land two miles square on the north bank of the Tennessee river, and at its junction with Beach creek, for the use of Appassan Tubby and heirs.

3. A tract of land one mile square, on the north side of the Tennessee river, for the use of John M'Cleish and heirs, the said tract to be so run as to include the said M'Cleish's settlement and improvements on the north side of Buffalo creek.

4. Two tracts of land, containing forty acres each, on the south side of Tennessee river, and about two and a half miles below the Cotton Gin port, on the Tombigby river, which tracts of land will be pointed out by Major Levi Colbert, and for the use of said Colbert and heirs.

It is stipulated that the above reservations shall appertain to the Chickasaw nation only so long as they shall be occupied, cultivated, or used, by the present proprietors or heirs, and in the event of all or either of said tracts of land, so reserved, being abandoned by the present proprietors or heirs, each tract or tracts of land, so abandoned,

Sept. 20, 1816.

7 Stat., 150.
Proclamation, Dec. 30, 1816.

Peace and friendship.

Cession to the United States.

Allowance to Chickasaws.

Tracts reserved to the Chickasaw Nation.

shall revert to the United States as a portion of that territory ceded by the second article of this treaty.

Line on the south side of the Tennessee to be ascertained, etc.

ART. 5. The two contracting parties covenant and agree that the line on the south side of the Tennessee river, as described in the second article of this treaty, shall be ascertained and marked by commissioners to be appointed by the president of the United States; that the marks shall be bold; trees to be blazed on both sides of the line, and the fore and aft trees to be marked with the letters U. S. That the commissioners shall be attended by two persons to be designated by the Chickasaw nation, and that the said nation shall have due and seasonable notice when said operation is to be commenced.

Presents to certain Indians.

ART. 6. In consideration of the conciliatory disposition evinced, during the negotiation of this treaty, by the Chickasaw chiefs and warriors, but more particularly as a manifestation of the friendship and liberality of the president of the United States, the commissioners agree to give, on the ratification of this treaty, to Chinnubby, king of the Chickasaws, to Tishshominco, William M'Gilvery, Arpasarshtubby, Samuel Scely, James Brown, Levi Colbert, Ickaryoucullaha, George Pettygrove, Immartarharmicko, Chickasaw chiefs, and to Malcolm M'Gee, interpreter, one hundred and fifty dollars each, in goods or cash, as may be preferred, and to major William Glover, colonel George Colbert, capt. Rabbitt, Hoparyeahoummar, Immoukelourshsharhoparyea, Hoparyea, Houllartir, Tushkerhopoyyea, Hoparyeahoummar, jun. Immoukelusharhopoyyea, James Colbert, Coweamarthlar, and Iilnachouwarhopoyyea, military leaders, one hundred dollars each; and, as a particular mark of distinction and favor for his long services and faithful adherence to the United States government, the commissioners agree to allow to general William Colbert an annuity of one hundred dollars for and during his life.

No more pedlars to be licensed to traffic in the nation.

ART. 7. "Whereas the chiefs and warriors of the Chickasaw nation have found, from experience, that the crowd of pedlars, who are constantly traversing their nation from one end to the other, is of a serious disadvantage to the nation; that serious misunderstandings and disputes frequently take place, as well as frauds, which are often practised on the ignorant and uninformed of the nation, therefore it is agreed by the commissioners on the part of the government, and the chiefs of the nation, that no more licenses shall be granted by the agent of the Chickasaws to entitle any person or persons to trade or traffic merchandise in said nation; and that any person or persons, whomsoever, of the white people, who shall bring goods and sell them in the nation, contrary to this article, shall forfeit the whole of his or their goods, one half to the nation and the other half to the government of the United States; in all cases where this article is violated, and the goods are taken or seized, they shall be delivered up to the agent, who shall hear the testimony and judge accordingly."

This article was presented to the commissioners by the chiefs and warriors of the Chickasaw nation, and by their particular solicitation embraced in this treaty.

In testimony whereof, the said commissioners and undersigned chiefs and warriors have set their hands and seals.

Done at the Chickasaw council house, this twentieth day of September, in the year of our Lord one thousand eight hundred and sixteen.

Andrew Jackson,	[L. S.]	Levi Colbert, his x mark,	[L. S.]
D. Meriwether,	[L. S.]	Ickaryoucuttaha, his x mark,	[L. S.]
J. Franklin,	[L. S.]	George Pettygrove, his x mark,	[L. S.]
Chinnubby, King, his x mark,	[L. S.]	Immartarharmicco, his x mark,	[L. S.]
Tishshomingo, his x mark,	[L. S.]	Maj. Gen. Wm. Colbert, his x	
William McGilvery, his x mark,	[L. S.]	mark,	[L. S.]
Arpasarhtubby, his x mark,	[L. S.]	Major William Glover, his x mark,	[L. S.]
Samuel Seeley, his x mark,	[L. S.]	Major George Colbert, his x mark,	[L. S.]
James Brown, his x mark,	[L. S.]	Captain Rabbit, his x mark,	[L. S.]

Hopoyeahoummar, his x mark, [L. S.]   Hopoyeahoummar, jr., his x mark, [L. S.]
Immouklusharhopoyea, his x   Immouklusharhopyea, his x mark, [L. S.]
  mark, [L. S.]   James Colbert, his x mark, [L. S.]
Hopoyeahoullarter, his x mark, [L. S.]   Coweamarthtar, his x mark, [L. S.]
Tushkarhopoyea, his x mark, [L. S.]   Illachouwarhopoyea, his x mark, [L. S.]

Witness:
    James Gadsden, secretary,
    William Cocke,
    John Rhea,
    Malcum McGee,
    James Colbert, interpreter.

TREATY WITH THE CHOCTAW, 1816.

A treaty of cession between the United States of America and the Chactaw nation of Indians.

Oct. 24, 1816.

7 Stat., 152.
Proclamation, Dec. 30, 1816.

JAMES MADISON, president of the United States of America, by general John Coffee, John Rhea, and John M'Kee, esquires, commissioners on the part of the United States, duly authorized for that purpose, on the one part, and the mingoes, leaders, captains, and warriors, of the Chactaw nation, in general council assembled, in behalf of themselves and the whole nation, on the other part, have entered into the following articles, which, when ratified by the president of the United States, with the advice and consent of the senate, shall be obligatory on both parties:

ART. 1. The Chactaw nation, for the consideration hereafter mentioned, cede to the United States all their title and claim to lands lying east of the following boundary, beginning at the mouth of Ooktibbuha, the Chickasaw boundary, and running from thence down the Tombigby river, until it intersects the northern boundary of a cession made to the United States by the Chactaws, at Mount Dexter, on the 16th November, 1805. — *Cession.*

ART. 2. In consideration of the foregoing cession, the United States engage to pay to the Chactaw nation the sum of six thousand dollars annually, for twenty years; they also agree to pay them in merchandise, to be delivered immediately on signing the present treaty, the sum of ten thousand dollars. — *Consideration.*

Done and executed in full and open council, at the Choctaw trading house, this twenty-fourth day of October, in the year of our Lord one thousand eight hundred and sixteen, and of the independence of the United States the forty-first.

John Coffee, [L. S.]   General Humming Bird, his x mark, [L. S.]
John Rhea, [L. S.]   Talking warrior, his x mark, [L. S.]
John McKee, [L. S.]   David Folsom, [L. S.]
Mushoolatubbee, his x mark, [L. S.]   Bob Cole, his x mark, [L. S.]
Pooshamallaha, his x mark, [L. S.]   Oofuppa, his x mark, [L. S.]
Pukshunnubbu, his x mark, [L. S.]   Hoopoieeskitteenee, his x mark, [L. S.]
General Terror, his x mark, [L. S.]   Hoopoieemiko, his x mark, [L. S.]
Choctaw Eestannokee, his x mark, [L. S.] Hoopoieethoma, his x mark, [L. S.]

Witness:
    Tho. H. Williams, secretary to the commission,
    John Pitchlynn, interpreter,
    Turner Broshear, interpreter,
    M. Mackey, interpreter,
    Silas Dinsmoor,
    R. Chamberlin.

TREATY WITH THE MENOMINEE, 1817.

March 30, 1817.

7 Stat., 153.
Proclamation, Dec.
26, 1817.

A treaty of peace and friendship made and concluded at St. Louis by and between William Clark, Ninian Edwards, and Auguste Chouteau, commissioners on the part and behalf of the United States of America, of the one part, and the undersigned chiefs and warriors, deputed by the Menomenee tribe or nation of Indians, on the part and behalf of their said tribe or nation, of the other part.

THE parties, being desirous of re-establishing peace and friendship between the United States and the said tribe or nation, and of being placed in all things, and in every respect, on the same footing upon which they stood before the late war, have agreed to the following articles:

Injuries, etc., forgiven.

ART. 1. Every injury, or act of hostility, by one or either of the contracting parties, against the other, shall be mutually forgiven and forgot.

Perpetual peace and friendship.

ART. 2. There shall be perpetual peace and friendship between all the citizens of the United States and all the individuals composing the said Menomenee tribe or nation.

Former cessions and treaties confirmed.

ART. 3. The undersigned chiefs and warriors, on the part and behalf of their said tribe or nation, do, by these presents, confirm to the United States all and every cession of land heretofore made by their tribe or nation to the British, French, or Spanish, government, within the limits of the United States, or their territories; and also, all and every treaty, contract, and agreement, heretofore concluded between the said United States and the said tribe or nation.

Prisoners to be delivered up.

ART. 4. The contracting parties do hereby agree, promise, and oblige themselves, reciprocally, to deliver up all prisoners now in their hands (by what means soever the same may have come into their possession,) to the officer commanding at Prairie du Chien, to be by him restored to the respective parties hereto, as soon as it may be practicable.

Protection of United States acknowledged.

ART. 5. The undersigned chiefs and warriers as aforesaid, for themselves and those they represent, do hereby acknowledge themselves to be under the protection of the United States, and of no other nation, power, or sovereign, whatsoever.

In witness whereof, the commissioners aforesaid, and the undersigned chiefs and warriors, as aforesaid, have hereunto subscribed their names and affixed their seals, this thirtieth day of March, in the year of our Lord one thousand eight hundred and seventeen, and of the independence of the United States the forty-first.

William Clark,	[L. S.]	Wacaquon, or Shomin, his x mark, [L. S.]
Ninian Edwards,	[L. S.]	Warbano, the Dawn, his x mark, [L. S.]
Auguste Chouteau,	[L. S.]	Inemikee, Thunderer, his x mark, [L. S.]
Towanapee, Roaring Thunder, his x mark,	[L. S.]	Lebarnaco, the Bear, his x mark, [L. S.]
Weekay, the Calumet Eagle, his x mark,	[L. S.]	Karkundego, his x mark, [L. S.]
		Shashamanee, the Elk, his x mark, [L. S.]
Muequomota, the Fat of the Bear, his x mark,	[L. S.]	Penoname, the Running Wolf, his x mark, [L. S.]

Done at St. Louis, in the presence of—

R. Wash, secretary to the commissioners,
R. Graham, U. S. Indian agent for Illinois Territory,
T. Harrison,
Nimrod H. Moore,
S. Gantt, lieutenant U. S. Army,

C. M. Price,
Richard T. McKenney,
Amos Kibbe,
Nathaniel Mills,
Samuel Solomon.

TREATY WITH THE OTO, 1817.

A treaty of peace and friendship made and concluded between William Clark and Augusta Chouteau, commissioners on the part, and behalf of the United States of America, of the one part; and the undersigned chiefs and warriors, of the Ottoes tribe of Indians, on the part and behalf of their said tribe, of the other part.

June 24, 1817.

7 Stat., 154.
Proclamation, Dec. 26, 1817.

THE parties being desirous of re-establishing peace and friendship between the United States and their said tribe and of being placed, in all things, and in every respect, upon the same footing upon which they stood before the late war between the United States and Great Britain, have agreed to the following articles:

ART. 1. Every injury or act of hostility by one or either of the contracting parties against the other, shall be mutually forgiven and forgot.

Injuries, etc., forgiven.

ART. 2. There shall be perpetual peace and friendship between all the citizens of the United States of America and all the individuals composing the said Ottoes tribe, and all the friendly relations that existed between them before the war, shall be, and the same are hereby, renewed.

Perpetual peace and friendship, etc.

ART. 3. The undersigned chiefs and warriors, for themselves and their said tribe, do hereby acknowledge themselves to be under the protection of the United States of America, and of no other nation, power, or sovereign, whatsoever.

Protection of United States acknowledged.

In witness whereof, the said William Clark and Auguste Chouteau, commissioners as aforesaid, and the chiefs aforesaid, have hereunto subscribed their names and affixed their seals, this twenty-fourth day of June, in the year of our Lord one thousand eight hundred and seventeen, and of the independence of the United States the forty-first.

William Clark, [L. s.]	Mantoeignet, the Little Bow, his x
Auguste Choteau, [L. s.]	mark, [L. s.]
Ottoes:	Wapontraska, White Nostrils, his
Chongatonga, Big Horse, his x	x mark, [L. s.]
mark, [L. s.]	Missouries:
Histashone, Big Eyes, his x mark, [L. s.]	Tarposta, Son of the Priest, his x
Mihahande, Eldest Daughter, his x	mark, [L. s.]
mark, [L. s.]	Kahhehpah, Crow Head, his x
Kanseepa, the Kansee Head, his x	mark, [L. s.]
mark, [L. s.]	Harahkraton, the Sparrow Hawk,
Montistonga, Pewter, his x mark, [L. s.]	his x mark, [L. s.]
Pahagranga, Auguste, his x mark, [L. s.]	Tawequa, the Little Deer, his x
Watokieka, the Runner, his x mark, [L. s.]	mark, [L. s.]
Mantoeakiepa, Meeting of Bear, his	Chanohato, Buffalo Hump, his x
x mark, [L. s.]	mark, [L. s.]
Achieya, Broken Arm, his x mark, [L. s.]	
Wathapayignet, the Small Bear,	
his x mark, [L. s.]	

Witnesses present:

Lewis Bissell, acting secretary,	P. J. Nalsisor,
Manuel Lisa, United States Indian agent.	Sam. Solomon, interpreter,
Benjamin O'Fallon, United States Indian	Stephen Julien, United States Indian in-
agent,	terpreter,
W. Suigely,	Gabriel S. Chouteau, second lieutenant,
Geo. G. Taylor,	M. M.,
W. Tharp,	Joseph Lafleche, interpreter, his x mark.
Michl. E. Immell,	

TREATY WITH THE PONCA, 1817.

June 25, 1817.

7 Stat., 155.
Proclamation, Dec.
26, 1817.

A treaty of peace and friendship made and concluded between William Clark and Auguste Chouteau, commissioners on the part and behalf of the United States of America, of the one part, and the undersigned chiefs and warriors of the Poncarar tribe of Indians, on the [their] part and of their said tribe of the other part.

THE parties being desirous of re-establishing peace and friendship between the United States and their said tribe, and of being placed, in all things and every respect, upon the same footing upon which they stood before the late war between the United States and Great Britain, have agreed to the following articles:

Injuries, etc., forgiven.

ART. 1. Every injury or act of hostility by one or either of the contracting parties against the other, shall be mutually forgiven and forgot.

Perpetual peace and friendship, etc.

ART. 2. There shall be perpetual peace and friendship between all the citizens of the United States of America and all the individuals composing the said Poncarar tribe; and all the friendly relations that existed between them before the war shall be, and the same are hereby, renewed.

Protection of United States acknowledged.

ART. 3. The undersigned chiefs and warriors, for themselves and their said tribe, do hereby acknowledge themselves to be under the protection of the United States of America, and of no other nation, power, or sovereign, whatever.

In witness whereof, the said William Clark and Auguste Chouteau, commissioners as aforesaid, have hereunto subscribed their names and affixed their seals, this twenty-fifth day of June, in the year of our Lord one thousand eight hundred and seventeen, and of the independence of the United States the forty-first.

William Clark, [L. S.]	Necawcompe, the Handsome Man,
Auguste Chouteau, [L. S.]	his x mark, [L. S.]
Aquelaba, the Fighter, his x mark, [L. S.]	Ahahpah, the Rough Buffalo Horn,
Gradonga, Fork-tailed Hawk, his	his x mark, [L. S.]
x mark, [L. S.]	Showeno, the Comer, his x mark, [L. S.]
Shondagaha, Smoker, his x mark, [L. S.]	Bardegara, he who stands fire,
Kihegashinga, Little Chief, his x	his x mark, [L. S.]
mark, [L. S.]	

Witnesses present:

Lewis Bissel, acting secretary to the commissioners,	Dr. Wm. J. Clarke,
	B. Vasques,
Manual Lisa, United States Indian agent,	Saml. Solomon, interpreter,
Benja. O'Fallon, United States Indian agent,	Stephen Julien, United States Indian interpreter,
R. Graham, Indian agent for Illinois,	Joseph Lafleche, interpreter.

TREATY WITH THE CHEROKEE, 1817.

July 8, 1817.

7 Stat., 156.
Proclamation, Dec.
26, 1817.

Articles of a treaty concluded, at the Cherokee Agency, within the Cherokee nation, between major general Andrew Jackson, Joseph M'Minn, governor of the state of Tennessee, and general David Meriwether, commissioners plenipotentiary of the United States of America, of the one part, and the chiefs, head men, and warriors, of the Cherokee nation, east of the Mississippi river, and the chiefs, head men, and warriors, of the Cherokees on the Arkansas river, and their deputies, John D. Chisholm and James Rogers, duly authorized by the chiefs of the Cherokees on the Arkansas river, in open council, by written power of attorney, duly signed and executed, in presence of Joseph Sevier and William Ware.

Preamble.

WHEREAS in the autumn of the year one thousand eight hundred and eight, a deputation from the Upper and Lower Cherokee towns, duly authorized by their nation, went on to the city of Washington, the first named to declare to the President of the United States their anxious desire to engage in the pursuits of agriculture and civilized life, in the country they then occupied, and to make known to the President of the United States the impracticability of inducing the nation at large to do this, and to request the establishment of a division line between the upper and lower towns, so as to include all the waters of the Hiwassee river to the upper town, that, by thus contracting their society within narrow limits, they proposed to begin the establishment of fixed laws and a regular government: The deputies from the lower towns to make known their desire to continue the hunter life, and also the scarcity of game where they then lived, and, under those circumstances, their wish to remove across the Mississippi river, on some vacant lands of the United States. And whereas the President of the United States, after maturely considering the petitions of both parties, on the ninth day of January, A. D. one thousand eight hundred and nine, including other subjects, answered those petitions as follows: "The United States, my children, are the friends of both parties, and, as far as can be reasonably asked, they are willing to satisfy the wishes of both. Those who remain may be assured of our patronage, our aid, and good neighborhood. Those who wish to remove, are permitted to send an exploring party to reconnoitre the country on the waters of the Arkansas and White rivers, and the higher up the better, as they will be the longer unapproached by our settlements, which will begin at the mouths of those rivers. The regular districts of the government of St. Louis are already laid off to the St. Francis.

"When this party shall have found a tract of country suiting the emigrants, and not claimed by other Indians, we will arrange with them and you the exchange of that for a just portion of the country they leave, and to a part of which, proportioned to their numbers, they have a right. Every aid towards their removal, and what will be necessary for them there, will then be freely administered to them; and when established in their new settlements, we shall still consider them as our children, give them the benefit of exchanging their peltries for what they will want at our factories, and always hold them firmly by the hand."

And whereas the Cherokees, relying on the promises of the President of the United States, as above recited, did explore the country on the west side of the Mississippi, and made choice of the country on the Arkansas and White rivers, and settled themselves down upon United States' lands, to which no other tribe of Indians have any just claim, and have duly notified the President of the United States thereof, and of their anxious desire for the full and complete ratification of his promise, and, to that end, as notified by the President of the United States, have sent on their agents, with full powers to execute a treaty, relinquishing to the United States all the right, title, and interest, to all lands of right to them belonging, as part of the Cherokee nation, which they have left, and which they are about to leave, proportioned to their numbers, including, with those now on the Arkansas, those who are about to remove thither, and to a portion of which they have an equal right agreeably to their numbers.

Now, know ye, that the contracting parties, to carry into full effect the before recited promises with good faith, and to promote a continuation of friendship with their brothers on the Arkansas river, and for that purpose to make an equal distribution of the annuities secured to be paid by the United States to the whole Cherokee nation, have agreed and concluded on the following articles, viz:

ART. 1. The chiefs, head men, and warriors, of the whole Cherokee nation, cede to the United States all the lands lying north and east of the following boundaries, viz: Beginning at the high shoals of the Appalachy river, and running thence, along the boundary line between the Creek and Cherokee nations, westwardly to the Chatahouchy river; *Cession of lands to United States in exchange for other lands.*

thence, up the Chatahouchy river, to the mouth of Souque creek; thence, continuing with the general course of the river until it reaches the Indian boundary line, and, should it strike the Turrurar river, thence, with its meanders, down said river to its mouth, in part of the proportion of land in the Cherokee nation east of the Mississippi, to which those now on the Arkansas and those about to remove there are justly entitled.

Further cession of lands. ART. 2. The chiefs, head men, and warriors, of the whole Cherokee nation, do also cede to the United States all the lands lying north and west of the following boundary lines, viz: Beginning at the Indian boundry line that runs from the north bank of the Tennessee river, opposite to the mouth of Hywassee river, at a point on the top of Walden's ridge, where it divides the waters of the Tennessee river from those of the Sequatchie river; thence, along the said ridge, southwardly, to the bank of the Tennessee river, at a point near to a place called the Negro Sugar Camp, opposite to the upper end of the first island above Running Water Town; thence, westwardly, a straight line to the mouth of Little Sequatchie river; thence, up said river, to its main fork; thence, up its northernmost fork, to its source; and thence, due west, to the Indian boundary line.

A census of the Cherokee Nation to be taken. ART. 3. It is also stipulated by the contracting parties, that a census shall be taken of the whole Cherokee nation, during the month of June, in the year of our Lord one thousand eight hundred and eighteen, in the following manner, viz: That the census of those on the east side of the Mississippi river, who declare their intention of remaining, shall be taken by a commissioner appointed by the President of the United States, and a commissioner appointed by the Cherokees on the Arkansas river; and the census of the Cherokees on the Arkansas river, and those removing there, and who, at that time, declare their intention of removing there, shall be taken by a commissioner appointed by the President of the United States, and one appointed by the Cherokees east of the Mississippi river.

Annuity, how to be divided between the Cherokees. ART. 4. The contracting parties do also stipulate that the annuity due from the United States to the whole Cherokee nation for the year one thousand eight hundred and eighteen, is to be divided between the two parts of the nation in proportion to their numbers, agreeably to the stipulations contained in the third article of this treaty; and to be continued to be divided thereafter in proportion to their numbers; and the lands to be apportioned and surrendered to the United States agreeably to the aforesaid enumeration, as the proportionate part, agreeably to their numbers, to which those who have removed, and who declare their intention to remove, have a just right, including these with the lands ceded in the first and second articles of this treaty.

The United States to give as much land, etc., as they receive from the Cherokees. ART. 5. The United States bind themselves, in exchange for the lands ceded in the first and second articles hereof, to give to that part of the Cherokee nation on the Arkansas as much land on said river and White river as they have or may hereafter receive from the Cherokee nation east of the Mississippi, acre for acre, as the just proportion due that part of the nation on the Arkansas agreeably to their numbers; which is to commence on the north side of the Arkansas river, at the mouth of Point Remove or Budwell's Old Place; thence, by a straight line, northwardly, to strike Chataunga mountain, or the hill first above Shield's Ferry on White river, running up and between said rivers for complement, the banks of which rivers to be the lines; and to have the above line, from the point of beginning to the point on White river, run and marked, which shall be done soon after the ratification of this treaty; and all citizens of the United States, except Mrs. P. Lovely, who is to remain where she lives during life, removed **Former treaties in force.** from within the bounds as above named. And it is further stipulated, that the treaties heretofore between the Cherokee nation and the United States are to continue in full force with both parts of the nation, and both parts thereof entitled to all the immunities and privilege which the old nation enjoyed under the aforesaid treaties; the United States reserving the right of establishing factories, a military post, and roads, within the boundaries above defined.

ART. 6. The United States do also bind themselves to give to all the poor warriors who may remove to the western side of the Mississippi river, one rifle gun and ammunition, one blanket, and one brass kettle, or, in lieu of the brass kettle, a beaver trap, which is to be considered as a full compensation for the improvements which they may leave; which articles are to be delivered at such point as the President of the United States may direct: and to aid in the removal of the emigrants, they further agree to furnish flat bottomed boats and provisions sufficient for that purpose: and to those emigrants whose improvements add real value to their lands, the United States agree to pay a full valuation for the same, which is to be ascertained by a commissioner appointed by the President of the United States for that purpose, and paid for as soon after the ratification of this treaty as practicable. The boats and provisions promised to the emigrants are to be furnished by the agent on the Tennessee river, at such time and place as the emigrants may notify him of; and it shall be his duty to furnish the same. *Rifle guns, ammunition, etc., as compensation for Cherokee improvements.* *Full compensation for improvements of real value.*

ART. 7. And for all improvements which add real value to the lands lying within the boundaries ceded to the United States, by the first and second articles of this treaty, the United States do agree to pay for at the time, and to be valued in the same manner, as stipulated in the sixth article of this treaty; or, in lieu thereof, to give in exchange improvements of equal value which the emigrants may leave, and for which they are to receive pay. And it is further stipulated, that all these improvements, left by the emigrants within the bounds of the Cherokee nation east of the Mississippi river, which add real value to the lands, and for which the United States shall give a consideration, and not so exchanged, shall be rented to the Indians by the agent, year after year, for the benefit of the poor and decrepid of that part of the nation east of the Mississippi river, until surrendered by the nation, or to the nation. And it is further agreed, that the said Cherokee nation shall not be called upon for any part of the consideration paid for said improvements at any future period. *Payment for improvements which add real value to ceded lands, etc.*

ART. 8. And to each and every head of any Indian family residing on the east side of the Mississippi river, on the lands that are now, or may hereafter be, surrendered to the United States, who may wish to become citizens of the United States. the United States do agree to give a reservation of six hundred and forty acres of land, in a square, to include their improvements, which are to be as near the centre thereof as practicable, in which they will have a life estate, with a reversion in fee simple to their children, reserving to the widow her dower, the register of whose names is to be filed in the office of the Cherokee agent, which shall be kept open until the census is taken as stipulated in the third article of this treaty. Provided, That if any of the heads of families, for whom reservations may be made, should remove therefrom, then, in that case, the right to revert to the United States. And provided further, That the land which may be reserved under this article, be deducted from the amount which has been ceded under the first and second articles of this treaty. *Reservations for heads of Indian families.*

ART. 9. It is also provided by the contracting parties, that nothing in the foregoing articles shall be construed so as to prevent any of the parties so contracting from the free navigation of all the waters mentioned therein. *Free navigation of all the waters, etc.*

ART. 10. The whole of the Cherokee nation do hereby cede to the United States all right, title, and claim, to all reservations made to Doublehead and others, which were reserved to them by a treaty made and entered into at the city of Washington, bearing date the seventh of January, one thousand eight hundred and six.

ART. 11. It is further agreed that the boundary lines of the lands ceded to the United States by the first and second articles of this treaty, and the boundary line of the lands ceded by the United States in the fifth article of this treaty, is to be run and marked by a commissioner or commissioners appointed by the President of the United States, who shall be accompanied by such commissioners as the Cherokees may appoint; due notice thereof to be given to the nation.

ART. 12. The United States do also bind themselves to prevent the intrusion of any of its citizens within the lands ceded by the first and second articles of this treaty, until the same shall be ratified by the President and Senate of the United States, and duly promulgated.

ART. 13. The contracting parties do also stipulate that this treaty shall take effect and be obligatory on the contracting parties so soon as the same shall be ratified by the President of the United States, by and with the advice and consent of the Senate of the United States.

In witness of all and every thing herein determined, by and between the before recited contracting parties, we have, in full and open council, at the Cherokee Agency, this eighth day of July, A. D. one thousand eight hundred and seventeen, set our hands and seals.

Andrew Jackson,	[L. s.]	Young Davis, his x mark,	[L. s.]
Joseph McMinn,	[L. s.]	Souanooka, his x mark,	[L. s.]
D. Meriwether,	[L. s.]	The Locust, his x mark,	[L. s.]
United States Commis'rs.		Beaver Carrier, his x mark,	[L. s.]
Richard Brown, his x mark,	[L. s.]	Dreadful Water, his x mark,	[L. s.]
Cabbin Smith, his x mark,	[L. s.]	Chyula, his x mark,	[L. s.]
Sleeping Rabbit, his x mark,	[L. s.]	Ja. Martin,	[L. s.]
George Saunders, his x mark,	[L. s.]	John McIntosh, his x mark,	[L. s.]
Roman Nose, his x mark,	[L. s.]	Katchee of Cowee, his x mark,	[L. s.]
Currohe Dick, his x mark,	[L. s.]	White Man Killer, his x mark,	[L. s.]
John Walker, his x mark,	[L. s.]	Arkansas chiefs:	
George Lowry,	[L. s.]	Toochalar, his x mark,	[L. s.]
Richard Taylor,	[L. s.]	The Glass, his x mark,	[L. s.]
Walter Adair,	[L. s.]	Wassosee, his x mark,	[L. s.]
James Brown,	[L. s.]	John Jolly, his x mark,	[L. s.]
Kelachule, his x mark,	[L. s.]	The Gourd, his x mark,	[L. s.]
Sour Mush, his x mark,	[L. s.]	Spring Frog, his x mark,	[L. s.]
Chulioa, his x mark,	[L. s.]	John D. Chisholm,	[L. s.]
Chickasautchee, his x mark,	[L. s.]	James Rogers,	[L. s.]
The Bark of Chota, his x mark,	[L. s.]	Wawhatchy, his x mark,	[L. s.]
The Bark of Hightower, his x mark,	[L. s.]	Attalona, his x mark,	[L. s.]
Big Half Breed, his x mark,	[L. s.]	Kulsuttchee, his x mark,	[L. s.]
Going Snake, his x mark,	[L. s.]	Tuskekeetchee, his x mark,	[L. s.]
Leyestisky, his x mark,	[L. s.]	Chillawgatchee, his x mark,	[L. s.]
Ch. Hicks,	[L. s.]	John Smith, his x mark,	[L. s.]
		Toosawallata, his x mark,	[L. s.]

In presence of—

J. M. Glassel, secretary to the commission,
Thomas Wilson, clerk to the commissioners,
Walter Adair,
John Speirs, interpreter, his x mark,
A. McCoy, interpreter,

James C. Bronaugh, hospital surgeon, U. S. Army,
Isham Randolph, captain First Redoubtables,
Wm. Meriwether,
Return J. Meigs, agent Cherokee Nation.

TREATY WITH THE WYANDOT, ETC., 1817.

Articles of a treaty made and concluded, at the foot of the Rapids of the Miami of Lake Erie, between Lewis Cass and Duncan McArthur, commissioners of the United States, with full power and authority to hold conferences, and conclude and sign a treaty or treaties with all or any of the tribes or nations of Indians within the boundaries of the state of Ohio, of and concerning all matters interesting to the United States and the said nations of Indians on the one part; and the sachems, chiefs, and warriors, of the Wyandot, Seneca, Delaware, Shawanese, Potawatomees, Ottawas, and Chippeway, tribes of Indians.

Sept. 29, 1817.

7 Stat., 160.
Proclamation, Jan. 4, 1819.
Supplementary treaty, post, p. 162.

ART. 1. The Wyandot tribe of Indians, in consideration of the stipulations herein made on the part of the United States, do hereby forever cede to the United States the lands comprehended within the following lines and boundaries: Beginning at a point on the southern shore of lake Erie, where the present Indian boundary line intersects the same, between the mouth of Sandusky bay and the mouth of Portage river; thence, running south with said line, to the line established in the year one thousand seven hundred and ninety-five, by the treaty of Greenville, which runs from the crossing place above fort Lawrence to Loramie's store; thence, westerly, with the last mentioned line, to the eastern line of the reserve at Loramie's store; thence, with the lines of said reserve, north and west, to the northwestern corner thereof; thence to the northwestern corner of the reserve on the river St. Mary's, at the head of the navigable waters thereof; thence, east, to the western bank of the St. Mary's river aforesaid; thence, down on the western bank of the said river, to the reserve at fort Wayne; thence, with the lines of the last mentioned reserve, easterly and northerly, to the north bank of the river Miami of lake Erie; thence, down on the north bank of the said river, to the western line of the land ceded to the United States by the treaty of Detroit, in the year one thousand eight hundred and seven; thence, with the said line, south, to the middle of said Miami river, opposite the mouth of the Great Auglaize river; thence, down the middle of said Miami river, and easterly with the lines of the tract ceded to the United States by the treaty of Detroit aforesaid, so far that a south line will strike the place of beginning.

Cession of lands by the Wyandots.

ART. 2. The Potawatomy, Ottawas, and Chippeway, tribes of Indians, in consideration of the stipulations herein made on the part of the United States, do hereby forever cede to the United States the land comprehended within the following lines and boundaries: Beginning where the western line of the state of Ohio crosses the river Miami of lake Erie, which is about twenty-one miles above the mouth of the Great Auglaize river; thence, down the middle of the said Miami river, to a point north of the mouth of the Great Auglaize river; thence, with the western line of the land ceded to the United States by the treaty of Detroit, in one thousand eight hundred and seven, north forty-five miles; then, west, so far that a line south will strike the place of beginning; thence, south, to the place of beginning.

Cession of lands by Potawatomies, Ottawas, and Chippewas.

ART. 3. The Wyandot, Seneca, Delaware, Shawnese, Potawatomy, Ottawas, and Chippeway, tribes of Indians accede to the cessions mentioned in the two preceding articles.

Other tribes accede.

ART. 4. In consideration of the cessions and recognitions stipulated in the three preceding articles, the United States agree to pay to the Wyandot tribe, annually, forever, the sum of four thousand dollars, in specie, at Upper Sandusky: To the Seneca tribe, annually, forever,

Annual payments to certain tribes.

the sum of five hundred dollars, in specie, at Lower Sandusky: To the Shawnese tribe, annually, forever, the sum of two thousand dollars, in specie, at Wapaghkonetta: To the Potawatomy tribe, annually, for the term of fifteen years, the sum of one thousand three hundred dollars, in specie, at Detroit: To the Ottawas tribe, annually, for the term of fifteen years, the sum of one thousand dollars, in specie, at Detroit: To the Chippewa tribe, annually, for the term of fifteen years, the sum of one thousand dollars, in specie, at Detroit: To the Delaware tribe, in the course of the year one thousand eight hundred and eighteen, the sum of five hundred dollars, in specie, at Wapaghkonetta, but no annuity: And the United States also agree, that all annuities due by any former treaty to the Wyandot, Shawnese, and Delaware tribes, and the annuity due by the treaty of Greenville, to the Ottawas and Chippewas tribes, shall be paid to the said tribes, respectively, in specie.

Annuities under former treaties.

ART. 5. The schedule hereunto annexed, is to be taken and considered as part of this treaty; and the tracts herein stipulated to be granted to the Wyandot, Seneca, and Shawnese, tribes of Indians, are to be granted for the use of the persons mentioned in the said schedule, agreeably to the descriptions, provisions, and limitations, therein contained.

Schedule a part of the treaty.

ART. 6. The United States agree to grant, by patent, in fee simple, to Doanquod, Howoner, Rontondee, Tauyau, Rontayau, Dawatont, Manocue, Tauyaudautauson, and Haudaunwaugh, chiefs of the Wyandot tribe, and their successors in office, chiefs of the said tribe, for the use of the persons and for the purposes mentioned in the annexed schedule, a tract of land twelve miles square, at Upper Sandusky, the centre of which shall be the place where fort Ferree stands; and also a tract of one mile square, to be located where the chiefs direct, on a cramberry swamp, on Broken Sword creek, and to be held for the use of the tribe.

Grants in fee simple to the Wyandots.

The United States also agree to grant, by patent, in fee simple, to Tahawmadoyaw, captain Harris, Isahownusay, Joseph Tawgyou, captain Smith, Coffee-house, Running About, and Wiping stick, chiefs of the Seneca tribe of Indians, and their successors in office, chiefs of the said tribe, for the use of the persons mentioned in the annexed schedule, a tract of land to contain thirty thousand acres, beginning on the Sandusky river, at the lower corner of the section hereinafter granted to William Spicer; thence, down the said river, on the east side, with the meanders thereof at high water mark, to a point east of the mouth of Wolf creek; thence, and from the beginning, east, so far that a north line will include the quantity of thirty thousand acres aforesaid.

Grant to the Senecas.

The United States also agree to grant, by patent, in fee simple, to Catewekesa or Black Hoof, Byaseka or Wolf, Pomthe or Walker, Shemenetoo or Big Snake, Othawakeseka or Yellow Feather, Chakalowah or the Tail's End, Pemthala or John Perry, Wabepee or White Colour, chiefs of the Shawnese tribe, residing at Wapaghkonetta, and their successors in office, chiefs of the said tribe, residing there, for the use of the persons mentioned in the annexed schedule, a tract of land ten miles square, the centre of which shall be the council-house at Wapaghkonetta.

Grant to the Shawnees.

The United States also agree to grant, by patent, in fee simple, to Peeththa or Falling Tree, and to Onowaskemo or the Resolute Man, chiefs of the Shawnese tribes, residing on Hog Creek, and their successors in office, chiefs of the said tribe, residing there, for the use of the persons mentioned in the annexed schedule, a tract of land containing twenty-five square miles, which is to join the tract granted at Wapaghkonetta, and to include the Shawnese settlement on Hog creek. and to be laid off as near as possible in a square form.

Grant to the Shawnees on Hog Creek.

The United States also agree to grant, by patent, in fee simple, to Quatawape or Captain Lewis, Shekaghkela or Turtle, Skilowa or Robin, chiefs of the Shawnese tribe of Indians residing at Lewistown, and to Mesomea or Civil John, Wakawuxsheno or the White Man, Oquasheno or Joe, and Willaquasheno or When you are tired sit down, chiefs of the Seneca tribe of Indians residing at Lewistown, and to their successors in office, chiefs of the said Shawnese and Seneca tribes, for the use of the persons mentioned in the annexed schedule, a tract of land to contain forty-eight square miles, to begin at the intersection of the line run by Charles Roberts, in the year one thousand eight hundred and twelve, from the source of the Little Miami river to the source of the Sciota river, in pursuance of instructions from the commissioners appointed on the part of the United States, to establish the western boundary of the Virginia Military Reservation, with the Indian boundary line established by the treaty of Greenville, in one thousand seven hundred and ninety-five, from the crossings above fort Lawrence to Loramie's store, and to run from such intersection, northerly, with the first mentioned line, and westerly, with the second mentioned line, so as to include the quantity as nearly in a square form as practicable, after excluding the section of land hereinafter granted to Nancy Stewart.

Grants to the Shawnees and Senecas at Lewistown.

There shall also be reserved for the use of the Ottawas Indians, but not granted to them, a tract of land on Blanchard's fork of the Great Auglaize river, to contain five miles square, the centre of which tract is to be where the old trace crosses the said fork, and one other tract to contain three miles square, on the Little Auglaize river, to include Oquanoxa's village.

Reservations for the Ottawas.

ART. 7. And the said chiefs or their successors may, at any time they may think proper, convey to either of the persons mentioned in the said schedule, or his heirs, the quantity secured thereby to him, or may refuse so to do. But the use of the said land shall be in the said person; and after the share of any person is conveyed by the chiefs to him, he may convey the same to any person whatever. And any one entitled by the said schedule to a portion of the said land, may, at any time, convey the same to any person, by obtaining the approbation of the President of the United States, or of the person appointed by him to give such approbation. And the agent of the United States shall make an equitable partition of the said share when conveyed.

Power of conveyance in grantees.

Agent to make partition.

ART. 8. At the special request of the said Indians, the United States agree to grant, by patent, in fee simple, to the persons hereinafter mentioned, all of whom are connected with the said Indians, by blood or adoption, the tracts of land herein described:

Grants to Indian connections.

To Elizabeth Whitaker, who was taken prisoner by the Wyandots, and has ever since lived among them, twelve hundred and eighty acres of land, on the west side of the Sandusky river, below Croghansville, to be laid off in a square form, as nearly as the meanders of the said river will admit, and to run an equal distance above and below the house in which the said Elizabeth Whitaker now lives.

E. Whitaker.

To Robert Armstrong, who was taken prisoner by the Indians, and has ever since lived among them, and has married a Wyandot woman, one section, to contain six hundred and forty acres of land, on the west side of the Sandusky river, to begin at the place called Camp Ball, and to run up the river, with the meanders thereof, one hundred and sixty poles, and, from the beginning, down the river, with the meanders thereof, one hundred and sixty poles, and from the extremity of these lines west for quantity.

R. Armstrong.

To the children of the late William M'Collock, who was killed in August, one thousand eight hundred and twelve, near Maugaugon, and who are quarter-blood Wyandot Indians, one section, to contain six hundred and forty acres of land, on the west side of the Sandusky river, adjoining the lower line of the tract hereby granted to Robert

The children of Wm. M'Collock.

Armstrong, and extending in the same manner with and from the said river.

John Vanmeter and his wife's brothers.

To John Vanmeter, who was taken prisoner by the Wyandots, and who has ever since lived among them, and has married a Seneca woman, and to his wife's three brothers, Senecas, who now reside on Honey creek, one thousand acres of land, to begin north, forty-five degrees west, one hundred and forty poles from the house in which the said John Vanmeter now lives, and to run thence, south, three hundred and twenty poles, thence, and from the beginning, east for quantity.

Sarah and Joseph Williams and Rachel Nugent.

To Sarah Williams, Joseph Williams, and Rachel Nugent, late Rachel Williams, the said Sarah having been taken prisoner by the Indians, and ever since lived among them, and being the widow, and the said Joseph and Rachel being the children, of the late Isaac Williams, a half-blood Wyandot, one quarter section of land, to contain one hundred and sixty acres, on the east side of the Sandusky river, below Croghansville, and to include their improvements at a place called Negro Point.

C. Walker and her son John.

To Catharine Walker, a Wyandot woman, and to John R. Walker, her son, who was wounded in the service of the United States, at the battle of Mauguagon, in one thousand eight hundred and twelve, a section of six hundred and forty acres of land each, to begin at the northwestern corner of the tract hereby granted to John Vanmeter and his wife's brothers, and to run with the line thereof, south, three hundred and twenty poles, thence, and from the beginning, west for quantity.

Wm. Spicer.

To William Spicer, who was taken prisoner by the Indians, and has ever since lived among them, and has married a Seneca woman, a section of land, to contain six hundred and forty acres, beginning on the east bank of the Sandusky river, forty poles below the lower corner of said Spicer's cornfield, thence, up the river on the east side, with the meanders thereof, one mile, thence, and from the beginning, east for quantity.

Nancy Stewart.

To Nancy Stewart, daughter of the late Shawnese chief Blue Jacket, one section of land, to contain six hundred and forty acres, on the Great Miami river below Lewistown, to include her present improvements, three quarters of the said section to be on the southeast side of the river, and one quarter on the northwest side thereof.

The children of Captain Logan.

To the children of the late Shawnese chief captain Logan, or Spamagelabe, who fell in the service of the United States during the late war, one section of land, to contain six hundred and forty acres, on the east side of the Great Auglaize river, adjoining the lower line of the grant of ten miles at Wapaghkonetta and the said river.

A. Shane.

To Anthony Shane, a half blood Ottawas Indian, one section of land, to contain six hundred and forty acres, on the east side of the river St. Mary's, and to begin opposite the house in which said Shane now lives, thence, up the river, with the meanders thereof, one hundred and sixty poles, and from the beginning down the river, with the meanders thereof, one hundred and sixty poles, and from the extremity of the said lines east for quantity.

J. M'Pherson

To James M'Pherson, who was taken prisoner by the Indians, and has ever since lived among them, one section of land, to contain six hundred and forty acres, in a square form, adjoining the northern or western line of the grant of forty-eight miles at Lewistown, at such place as he may think proper to locate the same.

The Cherokee Boy.

To Horonu, or the Cherokee Boy, a Wyandot chief, a section of land, to contain six hundred and forty acres, on the Sandusky river, to be laid off in a square form, and to include his improvements.

A. D. and R. Godfroy.

To Alexander D. Godfroy and Richard Godfroy, adopted children of the Potawatomy tribe, and at their special request, one section of land, to contain six hundred and forty acres, in the tract of country herein ceded to the United States by the Potawatomy, Ottawas, and Chippewas, tribes, to be located by them, the said Alexander and Richard, after the said tract shall have been surveyed.

To Sawendebans, or the Yellow Hair, or Peter Minor, an adopted son of Tondaganie, or the Dog, and at the special request of the Ottawas, out of the tract reserved by the treaty of Detroit, in one thousand eight hundred and seven, above Roche de Bœuf, at the village of the said Dog, a section of land, to contain six hundred and forty acres, to be located in a square form, on the north side of the Miami, at the Wolf Rapid. **Yellow Hair.**

ART. 9. The United States engage to appoint an agent, to reside among or near the Wyandots, to aid them in the protection of their persons and property, to manage their intercourse with the government and citizens of the United States, and to discharge the duties which commonly appertain to the office of Indian agent; and the same agent is to execute the same duties for the Senecas and Delawares on the Sandusky river. And an agent for similar purposes, and vested with similar powers, shall be appointed, to reside among or near the Shawnese, whose agency shall include the reservations at Wapaghkonetta, at Lewistown, at Hog creek, and at Blanchard's creek. And one mile square shall be reserved at Malake for the use of the agent for the Shawnese. **Agent for the Wyandots, Senecas, and Delawares.** **Agent for the Shawnees.**

And the agent for the Wyandots and Senecas shall occupy such land in the grant at Upper Sandusky, as may be necessary for him and the persons attached to the agency. **Agent for the Wyandots and Senecas to occupy land.**

ART. 10. The United States engage to erect a saw-mill and a gristmill, upon some proper part of the Wyandot reservation, for their use, and to provide and maintain a blacksmith, for the use of the Wyandots and Senecas, upon the reservation of the Wyandots, and another blacksmith, for the use of the Indians at Wapaghkonetta, Hog creek, and Lewistown. **Sawmill, etc., for Indians.**

ART. 11. The stipulations contained in the treaty of Greenville, relative to the right of the Indians to hunt upon the land hereby ceded, while it continues the property of the United States, shall apply to this treaty; and the Indians shall, for the same term, enjoy the privilege of making sugar upon the same land, committing no unnecessary waste upon the trees. **Rights of hunting and making sugar.**

ART. 12. The United States engage to pay, in the course of the year one thousand eight hundred and eighteen, the amount of the damages which were assessed by the authority of the secretary of war, in favor of several tribes and individuals of the Indians, who adhered to the cause of the United States during the late war with great Britain, and whose property was, in consequence of such adherence, injured or destroyed. And it is agreed, that the sums thus assessed shall be paid in specie, at the places, and to the tribes or individuals, hereinafter mentioned, being in conformity with the said assessment; that is to say: **Payment to Indians for property destroyed during the war with Great Britain.**

To the Wyandots, at Upper Sandusky, four thousand three hundred and nineteen dollars and thirty-nine cents.

To the Senecas, at Lower Sandusky, three thousand nine hundred and eighty-nine dollars and twenty-four cents.

To the Indians at Lewis and Scoutashs towns, twelve hundred and twenty-seven dollars and fifty cents.

To the Delawares, for the use of the Indians who suffered losses at Greentown and at Jerome's town, three thousand nine hundred and fifty-six dollars and fifty cents, to be paid at Wapaghkonetta.

To the representatives of Hembis, a Delaware Indian, three hundred and forty-eight dollars and fifty cents, to be paid at Wapaghkonetta.

To the Shawnese, an additional sum of four hundred and twenty dollars, to be paid at Wapaghkonetta.

To the Senecas, an additional sum of two hundred and nineteen dollars, to be paid at Wapaghkonetta.

Payment under treaty of Fort Industry.

ART. 13. And whereas the sum of two thousand five hundred dollars has been paid by the United States to the Shawnese, being one half of five years' annuities due by the treaty of Fort Industry, and whereas the Wyandots contend that the whole of the annuity secured by that treaty is to be paid to them, and a few persons of the Shawnese and Senecas tribes; now, therefore, the commissioners of the United States, believing that the construction given by the Wyandots to the said treaty is correct, engage that the United States shall pay to the said Wyandot tribe in specie, in the course of the year one thousand eight hundred and eighteen, the said sum of two thousand five hundred dollars.

Roads, taverns, and ferries.

ART. 14. The United States reserve to the proper authority, the right to make roads through any part of the land granted or reserved by this treaty; and also to the different agents, the right of establishing taverns and ferries for the accommodation of travellers, should the same be found necessary.

Grants free from taxes.

ART. 15. The tracts of land herein granted to the chiefs, for the use of the Wyandot, Shawnese, Seneca, and Delaware Indians, and the reserve for the Ottawa Indians, shall not be liable to taxes of any kind so long as such land continues the property of the said Indians.

Grant for the education of Indian children.

ART. 16. Some of the Ottawa, Chippewa, and Potawatomy tribes, being attached to the Catholic religion, and believing they may wish some of their children hereafter educated, do grant to the rector of the Catholic church of St. Anne of Detroit, for the use of the said church, and to the corporation of the college at Detroit, for the use of the said college, to be retained or sold, as the said rector and corporation may judge expedient, each, one half of three sections of land, to contain six hundred and forty acres, on the river Raisin, at a place called Macon; and three sections of land not yet located, which tracts were reserved, for the use of the said Indians, by the treaty of Detroit, in one thousand eight hundred and seven; and the superintendent of Indian affairs, in the territory of Michigan, is authorized, on the part of the said Indians, to select the said tracts of land.

Improvements to be paid for.

ART. 17. The United States engage to pay to any of the Indians, the value of any improvements which they may be obliged to abandon in consequence of the lines established by this treaty.

Cession by the Delawares.

1807, ch. 49.

ART. 18. The Delaware tribe of Indians, in consideration of the stipulations herein made on the part of the United States, do hereby forever cede to the United States all the claim which they have to the thirteen sections of land reserved for the use of certain persons of their tribe, by the second section of the act of congress, passed March the third, one thousand eight hundred and seven, providing for the disposal of the lands of the United States between the United States Military Tract and the Connecticut Reserve, and the lands of the United States between the Cincinnati and Vincennes districts.

Grant to James and Silas Armstrong.

ART. 19. The United States agree to grant, by patent, in fee simple, to Jeeshawau, or James Armstrong, and to Sanondoyourayquaw, or Silas Armstrong, chiefs of the Delaware Indians, living on the Sandusky waters, and their successors in office, chiefs of the said tribe, for the use of the persons mentioned in the annexed schedule, in the same manner, and subject to the same conditions, provisions, and limitations, as is hereinbefore provided for the lands granted to the Wyandot, Seneca, and Shawnese, Indians, a tract of land, to contain nine square miles, to join the tract granted to the Wyandots of twelve miles square, to be laid off as nearly in a square form as practicable, and to include Captain Pipe's village.

Grant to the Ottawas.

ART. 20. The United States also agree to grant, by patent, to the chiefs of the Ottawas tribe of Indians, for the use of the said tribe, a tract of land, to contain thirty-four square miles, to be laid out as nearly in a square form as practicable, not interfering with the lines of the tracts reserved by the treaty of Greenville on the south side of the Miami river of Lake Erie, and to include Tushquegan, or M'Carty's village; which tracts, thus granted, shall be held by the said tribe, upon the usual conditions of Indian reservations, as though no patent were issued.

ART. 21. This treaty shall take effect, and be obligatory on the contracting parties, as soon as the same shall have been ratified by the President of the United States, by and with the advice and consent of the Senate thereof.

Treaty obligatory when ratified.

In testimony whereof, the said Lewis Cass and Duncan McArthur, commissioners as aforesaid, and the sachems, chiefs, and warriors, of the Wyandot, Seneca, Shawanee, Delaware, Pattawatima, Ottawa, and Chippewa tribes of Indians, have hereunto set their hands, at the foot of the Rapids of the Miami of lake Erie, this twenty-ninth day of September, in the year of our Lord one thousand eight hundred and seventeen.

Lewis Cass,
Duncan McArthur.

In presence of—

Wm. Turner, secretary to the commissioners,
John Johnson, Indian agent,
B. F. Stickney, Indian agent,

W. Knaggs, Indian agent,
G. Godfroy, Indian agent,
R. A. Forsyth, jr., secretary Indian department.

Sworn Interpreters:
William Conner,
H. W. Walker,
John R. Walker,
James McPherson,
F. Duchouquet,
A. Shane,
J. B. Beaugrand,

Peter Ryley,
Henry I. Hunt,
Jos. Vance,
Jonathan Leslie,
Alvan Coe,
John Gunn,
C. L. Cass, lieutenant U. S. Army.

Chippewas:
Wasonnezo, his x mark, [L. S.]
Okemance, or the Young Chief, his x mark, [L. S.]
Shinguax, or Cedar, his x mark, [L. S.]
Kinobee, his x mark, [L. S.]
Chinguagin, his x mark, [L. S.]
Sheganack, or Black Bird, his x mark, [L. S.]
Mintougaboit, or the Devil Standing, his x mark, [L. S.]
Wastuau, his x mark, [L. S.]
Penquam, his x mark, [L. S.]
Chemokcomon, or American his x mark, [L. S.]
Papecumegat, his x mark, [L. S.]
Matwaash, or Heard Fell Down, his x mark,
Potaquam, his x mark, [L. S.]
Pensweguesic, the Jay Bird, his x mark, [L. S.]
Weabskewen, or the White Man, his x mark, [L. S.]
Waynoce, his x mark, [L. S.]
Pattawatimas:
Metea, his x mark, [L. S.]
Wynemac, his x mark, [L. S.]
Wynemakons, or the Front, his x mark, [L. S.]
Ocheackabee, his x mark, [L. S.]
Conge, his x mark, [L. S.]
Wankeway, his x mark, [L. S.]
Perish, his x mark, [L. S.]
Tonguish, his x mark, [L. S.]
Papekitcha, or Flat Belly, his x mark, [L. S.]
Medomin, or Corn, his x mark, [L. S.]

Saguemai, or Musketo, his x mark, [L. S.]
Waweacee, or Full Moon, his x mark, [L. S.]
Ninwichemon, his x mark, [L. S.]
Missenonsai, his x mark, [L. S.]
Waysagua, his x mark, [L. S.]
Nannanmee, his x mark, [L. S.]
Nannanseku, his x mark, [L. S.]
Meanqueah, his x mark, [L. S.]
Wawenoke, his x mark, [L. S.]
Ashenekazo, his x mark, [L. S.]
Nanemucskuck, his x mark, [L. S.]
Ashkebee, his x mark, [L. S.]
Makotai, his x mark, [L. S.]
Wabinsheway, White Elk, his x mark, [L. S.]
Gabriel, or Gabiniai, his x mark, [L. S.]
Waishit, his x mark, [L. S.]
Naonquav, his x mark, [L. S.]
Meshawgonay, his x mark, [L. S.]
Nitchetash, his x mark, [L. S.]
Skewbicack, his x mark, [L. S.]
Chechalk, or Crane, his x mark, [L. S.]
Wyandots:
Dunquad, or Half King, his x mark, [L. S.]
Runtunda, or War Pole, his x mark, [L. S.]
Aronuc, or Cherokee Boy, his x mark, [L. S.]
T. Aruntue, or Between the legs, his x mark, [L. S.]
D. Wottondt, or John Hicks, his x mark, [L. S.]
T. Undetaso, or Geo. Punch, his x mark, [L. S.]
Menonkue, or Thomas, his x mark, [L. S.]

Undauwau, or Matthews, his x mark, [L. S.]
Delawares:
Kithtuwheland, or Anderson, his x mark, [L. S.]
Punchhuck, or Capt. Beaver, his x mark, [L. S.]
Tahunqeecoppi, or Capt. Pipe, his x mark, [L. S.]
Clamatonockis, his x mark, [L. S.]
Aweallesa, or Whirlwind, his x mark, [L. S.]
Shawanees:
Cateweekesa, or Black Hoof, his x mark, [L. S.]
Biaseka, or Wolf, his x mark, [L. S.]
Pomthe, or Walker, his x mark, [L. S.]
Shemenetu, or Big Snake, his x mark, [L. S.]
Chacalowa, or Tail's End, his x mark, [L. S.]
Pemthata, or Perry, his x mark, [L. S.]
Othawakeska; or Yellow Feather, his x mark, [L. S.]
Wawathethaka, or Capt. Reed, his x mark, [L. S.]
Tecumtequa, his x mark, [L. S.]
Quitewe, War Chief, his x mark, [L. S.]
Cheacksca, or Captain Tom, his x mark, [L. S.]

Quitawepea, or Captain Lewis, his x mark, [L. S.]
Senecas:
Methomea, or Civil John, his x mark, [L. S.]
Sacourewceeghta, or Whiping Stick, his x mark, [L. S.]
Shekoghkell, or Big Turtle, his x mark, [L. S.]
Aquasheno, or Joe, his x mark, [L. S.]
Wakenuceno, White Man, his x mark, [L. S.]
Samendue, or Captain Sigore, his x mark, [L. S.]
Skilleway, or Robbin, his x mark, [L. S.]
Dasquoerunt, his x mark, [L. S.]
Ottawas:
Tontagimi, or the Dog, his x mark, [L. S.]
Misquegin, McCarty, his x mark. [L. S.]
Pontiac, his x mark, [L. S.]
Oquenoxas, his x mark, [L. S.]
Tashmwa, his x mark, [L. S.]
Nowkesick, his x mark, [L. S.]
Wabekeighke, his x mark, [L. S.]
Kinewaba, his x mark, [L. S.]
Twaatum, his x mark, [L. S.]
Supay, his x mark, [L. S.]
Nashkema, his x mark, [L. S.]
Kuwashewon, his x mark, [L. S.]
Kusha, his x mark, [L. S.]

Schedule referred to in the foregoing treaty, and to be taken and considered as part thereof.

Appropriation of part of the lands granted to the Wyandots. Three sections, to contain six hundred and forty acres each, are to be reserved out of the tract of twelve miles square to be granted to the Wyandots. One of the said sections is to be appropriated to the use of a missionary, one for the support of schools, and one for the support of mechanics, and to be under the direction of the chiefs. Two sections, of six hundred and forty acres each, are to be granted to each of the following persons, being the chief of the Wyandot tribe, and his six counsellors, namely: Doouquod, or half king; Routoudu, or Warpole; Tauyaurontoyou, or Between the logs; Dawatout, or John Hicks; Manocue, or Thomas; Sauyoudautausaw, or George Ruuh; and Hawdowuwaugh, or Matthews.

Division of the remainder. And, after deducting the fifteen sections thus to be disposed of, the résidue of the said tract of twelve miles square is to be equally divided among the following persons, namely: Hoocue, Roudootouk, Mahoma, Naatoua, Mautanawto, Maurunquaws, Naynuhanky, Abrm. Williams, sen. Squautaugh, Tauyouranuta, Tahawquevouws, Dasharows, Trayhetou, Hawtooyou, Maydounaytove, Neudooslau, Deecalrautousay, Houtooyemaugh, Datoowawna, Matsaye-aanyourie, James Ranken, Sentumass, Tahautoshowweda, Madudara, Shaudauaye, Shamadeesay, Sommodowot, Moautaau, Nawsottomaugh, Maurawskinquaws, Tawtoolowme, Shawdouyeayourou, Showweno, Dashoree, Sennewdorow, Toayttooraw, Mawskattaugh, Tahawshodeuyea, Haunarawreudee, Shauromou, Tawyaurontoreyea, Roumelay, Nadocays, Carryumanduetaugh, Bigarms, Madonrawcays, Haurauoot, Syhrundash, Tahorowtsemdee, Roosayn, Dautoresay, Nashawtoomous, Skawduutoutee, Sanorowsha, Nautennee, Youausha, Aumatourow, Ohoutautoon, Tawyougaustayou, Sootonteeree, Dootooau, Hawreewaucudee, Yourahatsa, Towntoreshaw, Syuwewataugh, Cauyou, Omitztseshaw, Gausawaugh, Skashowayssquaw, Mawdovdoo, Narowayshaus, Nawcatay, Isuhowhayeato, Myatousha, Tauoodowma, Youhreo, George Williams, Oharvatoy, Saharossor, Isaac Williams, Squindatee, Mayeatohot, Lewis Coon, Isatouque or John Coon, Tawaumanocay or E. Wright, Owawtatuu, Isontraudee, Tomatsahoss, Sarrahoss, Tauyoureehoryeow, Saudotoss, Toworordu or Big Ears, Tauomatsarau, Tahoroudoyou or Two, Daureehau, Dauoreenu, Trautohauweetough, Yourowquains or the widow of the Crane, Caunaytoma, Hottomorrow, Taweesho, Dauquausay, Toumou, Hoogaudoorow, Newdeetoutow, Dawhowhouk, Daushouteehawk, Sawaronuis, Norrorow, Tawwass, Tawareroons, Neshaustay, Toharratough, Taurowtotucawaa, Youshindauyato, Tauosanays, Sadowerrais, Isanowtowtouk or Fox Widow, Sauratoudo or William Zane, Hayanoise or Ebenezer Zane, Mawcasharrow or widow M'Cullock, Susannah, Teshawtaugh, Bawews, Tamataurank, Razor, Rahisaus, Cudeetore, Shawnetaurew, Tatrarow, Cuqua, Yourowon, Sauyounaoskra, Tanorawayout, Howcuquawdorow, Gooyeamee, Dautsaqua, Maudamu, Sanoreeshoc, Hauleeyeatausay, Gearoohee, Matoskrawtouk, Dawweeshoe, Sawyourawot, Nacudseoranauaurayk, Youronurays, Scoutash, Serroymuch, Hoondeshotch, Ishuskeah, Dusharraw, Ondewaus, Duyewtale, Roueyoutacolo, Hoonorowyoutacob, Hownorowduro, Nawanaunonelo, Tolhomanona, Chiyamik, Tyyeakwheunohale, Aushewhowole, Schowondashres, Mondushawquaw, Tayoudrakele, Giveriahes, Sootreeshuskoh, Suyouturaw, Tiudee, Tahorroshoquaw, Irahkasquaw, Ishoreameusuwat, Curoweyottell, Noriyettete, Siyarech, Testeatete.

The thirty thousand acres for the Senecas upon the Sandusky river, Division of the lands granted to the Senecas. is to be equally divided among the following persons, namely: Syuwasautau, Nawwene, Joseph, Iseumetaugh or Picking up a club, Orawhaotodie or Turn over, Saudaurous or Split the river, Tahowtoorains or Jo Smee, Ispomduare Yellow-bay, Dashowrowramou or Drifting sand, Hauautounasquas, Hamyautuhow, Tahocayn, Howdautauyeao or King George, Standing Bones, Cyahaga or Fisher, Suthemoore, Red Skin, Mentauteehoore, Hyanashraman or Knife in his hand, Running About, John Smith, Carrying the Basket, Cauwauay or Striking, Rewauyeato or Carrying the news, Half up the Hill, Trowyoudoys or G. Hunter, Spike Buck, Caugooshow or Clearing up, Mark on his Hip, Captain Hams, Isetaune or Crying often, Taunerowyea or Two companies, Haudonwauays or Stripping the river, Isohauhasay or Tall chief, Tahowmandoyou, Howyouway or Paddling, Clouding up, Youwautowtoyou or Burnt his body, Shetouyouwee or Sweet foot, Tauhaugainstoany or Holding his hand about, Oharrawtodee or Turning over, Haucaumarout, Sarrowsauismatare or Striking sword, Sadudeto, Oshoutoy or Burning berry, Hard Hickery, Curetscetau, Youronocay or Isaac, Youtradowwonlee, Newtauyaro, Tayouonte or Old foot, Tauosanetee, Syunout or Give it to her, Doonstough or hunch on his forehead, Tyaudusout or Joshua Hendricks, Taushaushaurow or Cross the arms, Henry, Youwaydauyea or the Island, Armstrong, Shake the Ground, His Neck Down, Youheno, Towotoyoudo or Looking at her, Captain Smith, Tobacco, Standing Stone, Ronunaise or Wiping stick, Tarsduhatse or Large bones, Hamanchagave, House Fly or Maggot, Roudouma or Sap running, Big Belt, Cat Bone, Sammy, Taonganats or Round the point, Ramuye or Hold the sky, Mentoududu, Hownotant, Slippery nose, Tauslowquowsay or Twenty wives, Hoogaurow or Mad man, Coffee-house, Long Hair.

The tract of ten miles square at Wapaghkonetta is to be equally Division of the tract at Wapaghkonetta. divided among the following persons, namely: The Black Hoof, Pomthe or Walker, Piaseka or Wolf, Shemenutu or Snake, Othawakeseka or Yellow Feather, Penethata or Perry, Chacalaway or the End of the tail, Quitawee or War chief, Sachachewa, Wasewweela, Waseweela or Bright horn, Othawsa or Yellow, Tepetoseka, Caneshemo, Newabetucka, Cawawescucka, Thokutchema, Setakosheka, Topee or James Saunders, Meshenewa, Tatiape, Pokechaw, Alawaymotakah, Lalloway or Perry, Wabemee, Nemekoshe, Nenepemeshequa or Cornstalk, She-

she, Shawabaghke, Naneskaka, Thakoska or David M'Nair, Skapakake. Shapoquata, Peapakseka, Quaghquona, Quotowame, Nitaskeka, Thakaska or Spy buck, Pekathchseka, Tewaskoota or James Blue Jacket, Calawesa, Quaho, Kaketchheka or W. Perry, Swapee, Peektoo or Davy Baker, Skokapowa or George M'Dougall, Chepakosa, Shemay or Sam, Chiakoska or Captain Tom, General Wayne, Thaway, Othawee, Weeasesaka or Captain Reed, Lewaytaka, Tegoshea or George, Skekacumsheka, Wesheshemo, Mawenatcheka, Quashke, Thaswa, Baptieute, Waywalapee, Peshequkame, Chakalakee or Tom, Keywaypee, Egotacumshequa, Wabepee, Aquashequa, Pemotah, Nepaho, Takepee, Toposheka, Lathawanomo, Sowaghkota or Yellow clouds, Meenkesheka, Asheseka, Ochipway, Thapaeka, Chakata, Nakacheka, Thathouakata, Paytokothe, Palaske, Shesheloo, Quanaqua, Kalkoo, Toghshena, Capowa, Ethowakosee, Quaquesha, Capea, Thakatcheway, The man going up hill, Magotha, Tecumtequa, Setepakothe, Kekentha, Shiatwa, Shiabwasson, Koghkela, Akopee or a Heep of any thing, Lamatothe, Kesha, Pankoor, Peitehthator or Peter, Metchepelah, Capeah, Showagame, Wawaleepesheeka, Meewensheka, Nanemepahtoo or Trotter, Pamitchepetoo, Chalequa, Tetetee, Lesheshe, Nawabasheka or white feather, Skepakeskeshe, Tenakee, Shemaka, Pasheto, Thiatcheto, Metchemetche, Chacowa, Lawathska, Potchetee or the Man without a tail, Awabaneshekaw, Patacoma, Lamakesheka, Papashow, Weathaksheka, Pewaypee, Totah, Canaqua, Skepakutcheka, Welviesa, Kitahoe, Neentakoshe, Oshaishe, Chilosee, Quilaisha, Mawethaque, Akepee, Quelenee.

Division of the tract at Hog Creek. The tract of five miles square, at Hog creek, is to be equally divided among the following persons, namely: Peeththa, Onowashim, Pematheywa, Wabekesheke, Leeso, Pohcaywese, Shemagauashe, Nehquakahucka, Papaskootepa, Meamepetoo, Welawenaka, Petiska, Ketuckepe, Lawitchetee, Epaumee, Chanacke, Jose, Lanawytucka, Shawaynaka, Wawatashewa, Ketaksosa, Shashekopeah, Lakose, Quinaska.

Division of the tract including Lewistown. The tract of forty-eight square miles, including Lewistown, is to be equally divided among the following persons, namely: *Shawnoese*— Colonel Lewis, Polly Kizer, Theueteseepuah or Weed, Calossete, Vamauweke, Waucumsee, Skitlewa, Nayabepe, Wosheta, Nopamago, Willesque, Salock, Walathe, Silversmith, Siatha, Toseluo, Jemmy M'Donald, Jackson, Mohawk Thomas, Silverheels, John, Wewachee, Cassic, Atshena, Frenchman, Squesenau, Goohunt, Manwealte, Walisee, Billy, Thawwamee, Wopsquitty, Naywale, Big Turtle, Nolawat, Nawalippa, Razor, Blue, Tick, Nerer, Falling Star, Hale Clock, Hisoscock, Essquaseeto, Geore, Nuussome, Sauhanoe, Joseph, Scotowe, Battease, Crow, Shilling, Scotta, Nowpour, Nameawah, Quemauto, Snife, Captain, Taudeteso, Sonrise, Sowget, Deshau, Lettle Lewis, Jacquis, Tonaout, Swaunacou, General, Cussaboll, Bald, Crooked Stick, Wespata, Newasa, Garter, Porcupine, Pocaloche, Wocheque, Sawquaha, Enata, Panther, Colesetos, Joe. *Senecas*—Civil John, Wild Duck, Tall Man, Molasses, Ash, Nahanexa, Tasauk, Agusquenah, Roughleg, Quequesaw, Playful, Hairlip, Sieutinque, Hillnepewayatuska, Tauhunsequa, Nynoah, Suchusque, Leemutque, Treuse, Sequate, Caumecus, Scowneti, Tocondusque, Conhowdatwaw, Cowista, Nequatren, Cowhousted, Gillwas, Axtaea, Conawwehow, Sutteasee, Kiahoot, Crane, Silver, Bysaw, Crayfiste, Woolyhead, Conundahaw, Shacosaw, Coindos, Hutchequa, Nayau, Connodose, Coneseta, Nesluauta, Owl, Couauka, Cocheco, Couewash, Sinnecowacheckowe or Leek.

Division of the tract for the Delawares. The tract of three miles square for the Delaware Indians, adjoining the tract of twelve miles square upon the Sandusky river, is to be equally divided among the following persons, namely: Captain Pipe, Zeshauau or James Armstrong, Mahawtoo or John Armstrong, Sanowdoyeasquaw or Silas Armstrong, Teorow or Black Raccoon, Hawdorowwatistie or Billy Montour, Buck Wheat, William Dondee, Thomas

Lyons, Johnny Cake, Captain Wolf, Isaac Hill, John Hill, Tishata-
hoones or widow Armstrong, Ayenucere, Hoomaurow or John Ming,
Youdorast.

> Lewis Cass,
> Duncan McArthur,
>   Commissioners.

TREATY WITH THE CREEKS, 1818.

*A treaty of limits between the United States and the Creek nation of
Indians, made and concluded at the Creek Agency, on Flint river,
the twenty-second day of January, in the year of our Lord, one thousand eight hundred and eighteen.*

Jan. 22, 1818.

7 Stat., 171.
Proclamation, Mar.
28, 1818.

JAMES MONROE, President of the United States of America, by
David Brydie Mitchell, of the state of Georgia, agent of Indian affairs
for the Creek nation, and sole commissioner, specially appointed for
that purpose, on the one part, and the undersigned kings, chiefs, head
men, and warriors, of the Creek nation, in council assembled, on
behalf of the said nation, of the other part, have entered into the following articles and conditions, viz:

ART. 1. The said kings, chiefs, head men, and warriors, do hereby
agree, in consideration of certain sums of money to be paid to the said
Creek nation, by the government of the United States, as hereinafter
stipulated, to cede and forever quit claim, [and do, in behalf of their
said nation, hereby cede, relinquish, and forever quit claim,] unto the
United States, all right, title, and interest, which the said nation have,
or claim, in or unto, the two following tracts of land, situate, lying,
and being, within the following bounds; that is to say: 1st. Beginning
at the mouth of Goose Creek, on the Alatamahau river, thence, along
the line leading to the Mounts, at the head of St. Mary's river, to
the point where it is intersected by the line run by the commissioners
of the United States under the treaty of Fort Jackson, thence, along
the said last-mentioned line, to a point where a line, leaving the same,
shall run the nearest and a direct course, by the head of a creek called
by the Indians Alcasalekie, to the Ocmulgee river; thence, down the
said Ocmulgee river, to its junction with the Oconee, the two rivers
there forming the Alatamahau; thence, down the Alatamahau, to the
first-mentioned bounds, at the mouth of Goose creek. 2d. Beginning at
the high shoals of the Appalachee river, and from thence, along the line
designated by the treaty made at the city of Washington, on the fourteenth day of November, one thousand eight hundred and *five* [fifteen],
to the Ulcofouhatchie, it being the first large branch, or fork, of the
Ocmulgee, above the Seven Islands; thence, up the eastern bank of the
Ulcofouhatchie, by the water's edge, to where the path, leading from
the high shoals of the Appalachie to the shallow ford on the Chatahochie, crosses the same; and, from thence, along the said path, to the
shallow ford on the Chatahochie river; thence, up the Chatahochie
river, by the water's edge, on the eastern side, to Suwannee old town;
thence, by a direct line, to the head of Appalachie; and thence, down
the same, to the first-mentioned bounds at the high shoals of Appalachie.

ART. 2. It is hereby stipulated and agreed, on the part of the United
States, as a full consideration for the two tracts of land ceded by the
Creek nation in the preceding article, that there shall be paid to the
Creek nation by the United States, within the present year, the sum of
twenty thousand dollars, and ten thousand dollars shall be paid annually
for the term of ten succeeding years, without interest; making, in the
whole, eleven payments in the course of eleven years, the present year

Marginal notes: The Creeks cede two tracts of land to United States. Bounds of the first tract. Second tract. Payment for said cession.

inclusive; and the whole sum to be paid, one hundred and twenty thousand dollars.

Two blacksmiths and strikers to be furnished.

ART. 3. And it is hereby further agreed, on the part of the United States, that, in lieu of all former stipulations relating to blacksmiths, they will furnish the Creek nation for three years with two blacksmiths and strikers.

Line to be run by United States.

ART. 4. The President may cause any line to be run which may be necessary to designate the boundary of any part of both, or either, of the tracts of land ceded by this treaty, at such time, and in such manner, as he may deem proper. And this treaty shall be obligatory on the contracting parties as soon as the same shall be ratified by the government of the United States.

Treaty to be obligatory when ratified.

Done at the place, and on the day before written.

D. B. Mitchell.

Tustunnugee Thlucco, his x mark,	[L. S.]	Hopoethle Hauja, his x mark,	[L. S.]
Tustunnugee Hopoie, his x mark,	[L. S.]	Hopoie Hatkee, his x mark,	[L. S.]
William McIntosh,	[L. S.]	Yoholo Micco, his x mark,	[L. S.]
Tuskeenchaw, his x mark,	[L. S.]	Tustunnugee, his x mark,	[L. S.]
Hopoie Haujo, his x mark,	[L. S.]	Fatuske Henehau, his x mark,	[L. S.]
Cotchau Haujo, his x mark,	[L. S.]	Yauhau Haujo, his x mark,	[L. S.]
Inthlansis Haujo, his x mark,	[L. S.]	Tuskeegee Emautla, his x mark,	[L. S.]
Cowetau Micco, his x mark,	[L. S.]	Tustunnugee Hoithleloeo, his x	
Cusselau Micco, his x mark,	[L. S.]	mark,	[L. S.]
Eufaulu Micco, his x mark,	[L. S.]		

Present:

D. Brearly, colonel Seventh Infantry.
Wm. S. Mitchell, assistant agent, I. A. C. N.

M. Johnson, lieutenant corps of artillery.
Sl. Hawkins,
George [G. L.] Lovet,
    Interpreters.

TREATY WITH THE GRAND PAWNEE, 1818.

June 18, 1818.

**7 Stat., 172.
Proclamation, Jan. 7, 1819.**

A treaty of peace and friendship made and concluded, by and between, William Clark and Auguste Chouteau, Commissioners of the United States of America, on the part and behalf of the said States, of the one part, and the undersigned chiefs and warriors of the Grand Pawnee tribe, on the part and behalf of their said tribe, of the other part.

THE parties, being desirous of establishing peace and frienship between the United States and the said tribe, have agreed to the following articles:

Injuries, etc., forgiven.

ART. 1. Every injury, or act of hostility, by one or either of the contracting parties against the other, shall be mutually forgiven and forgot.

Perpetual peace and friendship.

ART. 2. There shall be perpetual peace and friendship between all the citizens of the United States of America, and all the individuals composing the said Grand Pawnee tribe.

Potection of United States acknowledged.

ART. 3. The undersigned chiefs and warriors, for themselves and their said tribe, do hereby acknowledge themselves to be under the protection of the United States of America, and of no other nation, power, or sovereign, whatsoever.

Violators of this treaty to be delivered up, etc.

ART. 4. The undersigned chiefs and warriors, for themselves and the tribe they represent, do moreover promise and oblige themselves to deliver up, or cause to be delivered up, to the authority of the United States, (to be punished according to law,) each and every individual of the said tribe, who shall, at any time hereafter, violate the stipulations of the treaty this day concluded between the said tribe and the said United States.

In witness whereof, the said William Clark and Auguste Chouteau, commissioners as aforesaid, and the said chiefs and warriors as aforesaid, have hereunto subscribed their names and affixed their seals, this eighteenth day of June, in the year of our Lord one thousand eight hundred and eighteen, and of the independence of the United States the forty-second.

Wm. Clark,	[L. S.]	Shakororishshara, Chief of the Sun, his x mark,	[L. S.]
Aug. Chouteau,	[L. S.]		
Teratuewit, the Bald Eagle, his x mark,	[L. S.]	Tarraecarwaa, the Wild Cat, his x mark,	[L. S.]
Taheerish, the Soldier, his x mark,	[L. S.]	Tarrarevetiishta, the Round Shield, his x mark,	[L. S.]
Petaperishta, Who wants to go to War, his x mark,	[L. S.]	Arorishhara, the Warrior, his x mark,	[L. S.]
Talawehouree, the Follower, his x mark,	[L. S.]	Telawaheartcarookot, the Fighter, his x mark,	[L. S.]
Tarraricarrawaa, the Grand Chief Big Hair, his x mark,	[L. S.]	Kagakereeouk, the Crow's Eye, his x mark,	[L. S.]
Shinggacahega, his x mark,	[L. S.]		
Aiuwechouoneeweeka, Chief of the Birds, his x mark,	[L. S.]	Latatorishhara, the Chief of the Shield, his x mark,	[L. S.]
Islacapee, his x mark,	[L. S.]		
Settulushaa, the Knife Chief, his x mark,	[L. S.]		

Done at St. Louis, in the presence of—

R. Wash, secretary to the commission.	Wm. Grayson,
R. Paul, colonel M. M.	I. T. Honore, interpreter.
John O'Fallon, R. R.	Stephin Julian, United States interpreter.
Jno. Rutland, sub-agent and trans., etc.	Josiah Ramsey,
A. L. Papin, interpreter.	Th. Robedout.

TREATY WITH THE NOISY PAWNEE, 1818.

A treaty of peace and friendship, made and concluded by, and between, William Clark and Auguste Chouteau, Commissioners of the United States of America, on the part and behalf of the said States, of the one part, and the undersigned, chiefs and warriors of the Pitavirate Noisy Pawnee tribe, on the part and behalf of their said tribe, of the other part.

June 19, 1818.

7 Stat., 173.
Proclamation, Jan. 7, 1819.

The parties, being desirous of establishing peace and friendship between the United States and the said tribe, have agreed to the following articles:

ART. 1. Every injury or act of hostility by one or either of the contracting parties, against the other, shall be mutually forgiven and forgot. *Injuries, etc., forgiven.*

ART. 2. There shall be perpetual peace and friendship between all the citizens of the United States of America, and all the individuals composing the said Noisy Pawnee tribe. *Perpetual peace and friendship.*

ART. 3. The undersigned chiefs and warriors, for themselves and their said tribe, do hereby acknowledge themselves to be under the protection of the United States of America, and of no other nation, power, or sovereign, whatsoever. *Protection of United States acknowledged.*

ART. 4. The undersigned chiefs and warriors, for themselves and the tribe they represent, do moreover promise and oblige themselves to deliver up, or cause to be delivered up, to the authority of the United States, (to be punished according to law,) each and every individual of the said tribe, who shall, at any time hereafter, violate the stipulations of the treaty this day concluded between the said Noisy Pawnee tribe and the said States. *Violators of this treaty to be delivered up, etc.*

In witness whereof, the said William Clark and Auguste Chouteau, commissioners as aforesaid, and the chiefs and warriors aforesaid, have hereunto subscribed their names, and affixed their seals, this nineteenth day of June, in the year of our Lord one thousand eight hundred and eighteen, and of the independence of the United States the forty-second.

Wm. Clark,	[L. S.]	Ishtataveeirou, the Discoverer, his	
Aug. Chouteau,	[L. S.]	x mark,	[L. S.]
Taretuushta, the First in War, his		Taarakarukaishta, the Handsome	
x mark,	[L. S.]	Bird, his x mark,	[L. S.]
Charuvaru, the Great Chief, his x		Lecoutswaroushtu, the Buffaloe	
mark,	[L. S.]	Doctor, his x mark,	[L. S.]
Skalavalacharo, the only Grand		Tacacatahekou, the Running Wolf,	
Chief. his x mark,	[L. S.]	his x mark,	[L. S.]
Pan kuhike, the Chief Man, his x		Kewatookoush, the Little Fox, his	
mark,	[L. S.]	x mark,	[L. S.]

Done at St. Louis, in the presence of—

R. Wash, secretary to the commission,	I. T. Honore, Indian Interpreter,
R. Paul, colonel M. M. C. Interpreter.	S. Julian, United States Indian Inter-
R. Graham, Indian agent, Illinois Terri-	preter,
tory,	Josiah Ramsey,
Jno. O'Fallon, captain R. Regiment.	Wm. Grayson,
Jno. Ruland, S. agent, Trans, etc.	John Robedout.
A. L. Papin, Interpreter, Indians,	

TREATY WITH THE PAWNEE REPUBLIC, 1818.

June 20, 1818.

7 Stat., 174.
Proclamation, Jan.
17, 1819.

A treaty of peace and friendship, made and concluded by, and between, William Clark and Auguste Chouteau, Commissioners of the United States of America, on the part and behalf of the said States, of the one part, and the undersigned, chiefs and warriors of the Pawnee Republic, on the part and behalf of their tribe, of the other part.

The parties, being desirous of establishing peace and friendship between the United States and the said tribe, have agreed to the following articles:

Injuries, etc., forgiven.

ART. 1. Every injury or act of hostility, by one or either of the contracting parties, against the other, shall be mutually forgiven and forgot.

Perpetual peace and friendship.

ART. 2. There shall be perpetual peace and friendship between all the citizens of the United States of America, and all the individuals composing the said Pawnee tribe.

Protection of United States acknowledged.

ART. 3. The undersigned, chiefs and warriors, for themselves and their said tribe, do hereby acknowledge themselves to be under the protection of the United States of America, and of no other nation, power, or sovereign, whatsoever.

Violators of this treaty to be delivered up, etc.

ART. 4. The undersigned chiefs and warriors, for themselves and the tribe they represent, do moreover promise and oblige themselves to deliver up, or to cause to be delivered up, to the authority of the United States, (to be punished according to law,) each and every individual of the said tribe who shall, at any time hereafter, violate the stipulations of the treaty this day concluded between the said Pawnee Republic and the said States.

In witness whereof, the said William Clark, and Auguste Chouteau, commissioners as aforesaid, and the chiefs and warriors aforesaid, have hereunto subscribed their names and affixed their seals, this twentieth day of June, in the year of our Lord one thousand eight hundred and eighteen, and of the independence of the United States the forty-second.

William Clark,	[L. S.]	Sheterahiate, the Partisan Discov-	
Aug. Chouteau,	[L. S.]	erer, his x mark,	[L. S.]
Petaheick, the Good Chief, his x		Tearekatacaush, the Brave, his x	
mark,	[L. S.]	mark,	[L. S.]
Rarnleshare, the Chief Man, his x		Pa, or the Elk, his x mark,	[L. S.]
mark,	[L. S.]	Tetawiouche, Wearer of Shoes, his	
Shernakitare, the First in the War		x mark,	[L. S.]
Party, his x mark,	[L. S.]		

Done at St. Louis, in the presence of—

R. Wash, secretary of the commission,
T. Paul, colonel M. M. C. Interpreter,
R. Graham, I. A. Illinois Territory,
John O'Fallon, captain R. Regiment,
John Ruland, S. agent Trans'r. etc.
A. L. Papin, interpreter,

J. T. Honore, Indian interpreter,
S. Julian, United States Indian interpreter,
Wm. Grayson,
Josiah Ramsey,
John Robedout.

TREATY WITH THE PAWNEE MARHAR, 1818.

A treaty of peace and friendship, made and concluded by, and between, William Clark and Auguste Chouteau, Commissioners of the United States of America, on the part and behalf of the said States, of the one part, and the undersigned, chiefs and warriors of the Pawnee Marhar tribe, on the part and behalf of their said tribe, of the other part.

June 22, 1818.

7 Stat., 175.
Proclamation, Jan. 5, 1819.

THE parties, being desirous of establishing peace and friendship between the United States and the said tribe, have agreed to the following articles:

ART. 1. Every injury or act of hostility, by one or either of the contracting parties, against the other, shall be mutually forgiven and forgot.   *Injuries, etc., forgiven.*

ART. 2. There shall be perpetual peace and friendship between all the citizens of the United States of America, and all the individuals composing the said Pawnee tribe.   *Perpetual peace and friendship.*

ART. 3. The undersigned chiefs and warriors, for themselves and their said tribe, do hereby acknowledge themselves to be under the protection of the United States of America, and of no other nation, power, or sovereign, whatsoever.   *Protection of United States acknowledged.*

ART. 4. The undersigned chiefs and warriors, for themselves and the tribe they represent, do moreover promise and oblige themselves to deliver up, or to cause to be delivered up, to the authority of the United States, (to be punished according to law,) each and every individual of the said tribe, who shall, at any time hereafter, violate the stipulations of the treaty this day concluded between the said Pawnee Marhar tribe and the said States.   *Violators of this treaty to be delivered up, etc.*

In witness whereof, the said William Clark, and Auguste Chouteau, commissioners as aforesaid, and the chiefs and warriors aforesaid, have hereunto subscribed their names and affixed their seals, this twenty-second day of June, in the year of our Lord one thousand eight hundred and eighteen, and of the independence of the United States the forty-second.

Wm. Clark,   [L. S.]
Aug. Chouteau,   [L. S.]
Tarahautacaw, White Bull, his x
    mark,   [L. S.]
Tearilari Sacki, Red Hawk, his x
    mark,   [L. S.]
Kakaletahaw, the Crow of other
    Nations, his x mark,   [L. S.]
Larapa Kouch, the soldier, his x
    mark,   [L. S.]
Tahorou, the Gun Flint, his x
    mark,   [L. S.]
Letereeshar, the Knife Chief, his x
    mark,   [L. S.]

Tearacheticktickspa, the Peace
    Maker, his x mark,   [L. S.]
Teakahore, the Divider of the Party,
    his x mark,   [L. S.]
Lahehozrashea, the Presence
    Striker, his x mark,   [L. S.]
Tarara, the Scalp Bearer, his x
    mark,   [L. S.]
Teripakoo, the First of Soldiers,
    his x mark,   [L. S.]
Irarikau, the White Cow, his x
    mark,   [L. S.]

Done at St. Louis, in the presence of—

R. Wash, secretary to the commission,
R. Graham, I. A. Illinois Territory,
John O'Fallon, captain rifle regiment,
R. Paul, Col. M. M. C. interpreter,
John Ruland, subagent, trans'r, etc.
A. L. Papin, interpreter,

J. T. Honore, Indian interpreter,
S. Julian, United States Indian interpreter,
Wm. Grayson,
Josiah Ramsey,
John Robedout.

TREATY WITH THE QUAPAW, 1818.

Aug. 24, 1818.

7 Stat., 176.
Proclamation Jan.5,
1819 [1818].

A treaty of friendship, cession, and limits, made and entered into, this twenty-fourth day of August, eighteen hundred and eighteen, by, and between, William Clark and Auguste Chouteau, Commissioners on the part and behalf of the United States, of the one part, and the undersigned, chiefs and warriors of the Quapaw tribe or nation, on the part and behalf of their said tribe or nation, of the other part.

Protection of United States acknowledged.

ART. 1. The undersigned chiefs and warriors, for themselves and their said tribe or nation, do hereby acknowledge themselves to be under the protection of the United States, and of no other state, power, or sovereignty, whatsoever.

Cession of lands.

ART. 2. The undersigned chiefs and warriors, for themselves and their said tribe or nation, do hereby, for, and in consideration of, the promises and stipulations hereinafter named, cede and relinquish to the United States, forever, all the lands within the following boundaries, viz: Beginning at the mouth of the Arkansaw river; thence extending up the Arkansaw, to the Canadian fork, and up the Canadian fork to its source; thence south, to Big Red river, and down the middle of that river, to the Big Raft; thence, a direct line, so as to strike the Mississippi river, thirty leagues in a straight line, below the mouth of Arkansaw; together with all their claims to land east of the Mississippi, and north of the Arkansaw river, included within the

(*A map accompanies the original treaty.)
Reservation.

coloured lines 1, 2, and 3, on the above map,* with the exception and reservation following, that is to say: the tract of country bounded as follows: Beginning at a point on the Arkansaw river, opposite the present post of Arkansaw, and running thence, a due southwest course, to the Washita river; thence, up that river, to the Saline fork; and up the Saline fork to a point, from whence a due north course would strike the Arkansaw river at the Little Rock; and thence, down the right bank of the Arkansaw, to the place of beginning: which said tract of land, last above designated and reserved, shall be surveyed and marked off, at the expense of the United States, as soon as the same can be done with convenience, and shall not be sold or disposed of, by the said Quapaw tribe or nation, to any individual whatever, nor to any state or nation, without the approbation of the United States first had and obtained.

The Quapaws may hunt in the ceded territory, until, etc.

ART. 3. It is agreed, between the United States and the said tribe or nation, that the individuals of the said tribe or nation shall be at liberty to hunt within the territory by them ceded to the United States, without hindrance or molestation, so long as they demean themselves peaceably, and offer no injury or annoyance to any of the citizens of the United States, and until the said United States may think proper to assign the same, or any portion thereof, as hunting grounds to other friendly Indians.

No persons to settle on lands reserved.

ART. 4. No citizen of the United States, or any other person, shall be permitted to settle on any of the lands hereby allotted to, and reserved for, the said Quapaw tribe or nation, to live and hunt on; yet it is expressly understood and agreed on, by, and between, the parties aforesaid, that, at all times, the citizens of the United States shall have the right to travel and pass freely, without toll or exaction, through the Quapaw reservation, by such roads or routes as now are, or hereafter may be, established.

Payment in goods for lands ceded.

ART. 5. In consideration of the cession and stipulations aforesaid, the United States do hereby promise and bind themselves to pay and deliver to the said Quapaw tribe or nation, immediately upon the execution of this treaty, goods and merchandise to the value of four thousand dollars, and to deliver, or cause to be delivered, to them, yearly, and every year, goods and merchandise to the value of one thousand dollars, to be estimated in the city or place, in the United States, where the same are procured or purchased.

ART. 6. Least the friendship which now exists between the United States and the said tribe or nation, should be interrupted by the misconduct of individuals, it is hereby agreed, that, for injuries done by individuals, no private revenge or retaliation shall take place; but, instead thereof, complaints shall be made by the party injured, to the other; by the tribe or nation aforesaid, to the governor, superintendent of Indian affairs, or some other person authorized and appointed for that purpose; and by the governor, superintendent, or other person authorized, to the chiefs of the said tribe or nation. And it shall be the duty of the said tribe or nation, upon complaint being made, as aforesaid, to deliver up the person or persons, against whom the complaint is made, to the end that he or they may be punished, agreeably to the laws of the state or territory where the offence may have been committed; and, in like manner, if any robbery, violence, or murder, shall be committed on any Indian or Indians, belonging to the said tribe or nation, the person or persons so offending shall be tried, and, if found guilty, punished in like manner as if the injury had been done to a white man. And it is further agreed, that the chiefs of the said tribe or nation shall, to the utmost of their power, exert themselves to recover horses, or other property, which may be stolen from any citizen or citizens of the United States, by any individual or individuals of the said tribe or nation; and the property so recovered, shall be forthwith delivered to the governor, superintendent, or other person authorized to receive the same, that it may be restored to the proper owner. And in cases where the exertions of the chief shall be ineffectual in recovering the property stolen, as aforesaid, if sufficient proof can be obtained that such property was actually stolen by an Indian or Indians, belonging to the said tribe or nation, a sum, equal to the value of the property which has been stolen, may be deducted, by the United States, from the annuity of said tribe or nation. And the United States hereby guaranty to the individuals of the said tribe or nation, a full indemnification for any horse or horses, or other property, which may be taken from them by any of their citizens: Provided, the property so stolen cannot be recovered, and that sufficient proof is produced that it was actually stolen by a citizen or citizens of the United States.

> *No private revenge for injuries by individuls.*

> *Offenders to be delivered up for punishment.*

> *Recovery of stolen property.*

> *Deduction for property stolen to be made from annuity.*

> *Indemnification for property stolen from Indians by citizens.*

ART. 7. This treaty shall take effect, and be obligatory on the contracting parties, as soon as the same shall have been ratified by the President of the United States, by and with the advice and consent of the Senate.

> *Treaty obligatory when ratified.*

William Clarke,	[L. s.]	Patongdi, or the Approaching Summer, his x mark,	[L. s.]
Aug. Chouteau,	[L. s.]		
Krakaton, or the Dry Man, his x mark,	[L. s.]	Tehonka, or the Tame Buffaloe, his x mark,	[L. s.]
Hradapaa, or the Eagle's Bill, his x mark,	[L. s.]	Hamonmini, or the Night Walker, his x mark,	[L. s.]
Mahraka, or Buck Wheat, his x mark,	[L. s.]	Washingteteton, or Mocking Bird's Bill, his x mark,	[L. s.]
Honkadagni, his x mark,	[L. s.]	Hontikani, his x mark,	[L. s.]
Wagonkedatton, his x mark,	[L. s.]	Tataonsa, or the Whistling Wind, his x mark,	[L. s.]
Hradaskamonmini, or the Pipe Bird, his x mark,	[L. s.]	Mozatete, his x mark,	[L. s.]

Done at St. Louis in the presence of—

R. Wash, Secretary to the commission,
R. Paul, Col. M. M. C. I.
Jn. Ruland, Sub. Agent, &c.
R. Graham, Indian Agent,
M. Lewis Clark,
J. T. Honore, Indian Interpreter,

Joseph Bonne, Interpreter,
Julius Pescay,
Stephen Julian, U. S. Indian Interpreter,
James Loper,
William P. Clark.

TREATY WITH THE WYANDOT, ETC., 1818.

Sept. 17, 1818.

7 Stat., 178.
Proclamation, Jan.
4, 1819.

Articles of a treaty made and concluded, at St. Mary's, in the state of Ohio, between Lewis Cass and Duncan McArthur, commissioners of the United States, with full power and authority to hold conferences, and conclude and sign a treaty or treaties, with all or any of the tribes or nations of Indians within the boundaries of the state of Ohio, of and concerning all matters interesting to the United States and the said nations of Indians, and the sachems, chiefs, and warriors, of the Wyandot, Seneca, Shawnese, and Ottawas, tribes of Indians; being supplementary to the treaty made and concluded with the said tribes, and the Delaware, Potawatamie, and Chippewa, tribes of Indians, at the foot of the Rapids of the Miami of Lake Erie, on the twenty-ninth day of September, in the year of our Lord one thousand eight hundred and seventeen.

The grants in the treaty of 29th Sept., 1817, to be considered only as reservations for the use of the Indians.

ART. 1. It is agreed, between the United States and the parties hereunto, that the several tracts of land, described in the treaty to which this is supplementary, and agreed thereby to be granted by the United States to the chiefs of the respective tribes named therein, for the use of the individuals of the said tribes, and also the tract described in the twentieth article of the said treaty, shall not be thus granted, but shall be excepted from the cession made by the said tribes to the United States, reserved for the use of the said Indians, and held by them in the same manner as Indian reservations have been heretofore held. But [it] is further agreed, that the tracts thus reserved shall be reserved for the use of the Indians named in the schedule to the said treaty, and held by them and their heirs forever, unless ceded to the United States.

Additional reservation for the Wyandots.

ART. 2. It is also agreed that there shall be reserved for the use of the Wyandots, in addition to the reservations before made, fifty-five thousand six hundred and eighty acres of land, to be laid off in two tracts, the first to adjoin the south line of the section of six hundred and forty acres of land heretofore reserved for the Wyandot chief, the Cherokee Boy, and to extend south to the north line of the reserve of twelve miles square, at Upper Sandusky, and the other to adjoin the east line of the reserve of twelve miles square, at Upper Sandusky, and to extend east for quantity.

Reservation for Wyandots at Solomon's town, etc.

There shall also be reserved, for the use of the Wyandots residing at Solomon's town, and on Blanchard's fork, in addition to the reservations before made, sixteen thousand acres of land, to be laid off in a square form, on the head of Blanchard's fork, the centre of which shall be at the Big Spring, on the trace leading from Upper Sandusky to fort Findlay; and one hundred and sixty acres of land, for the use of the Wyandots, on the west side of the Sandusky river, adjoining the said river, and the lower line of two sections of land, agreed, by the treaty to which this is supplementary, to be granted to Elizabeth Whitaker.

Additional reservation for the Shawnees and Senecas.

There shall also be reserved, for the use of the Shawnese, in addition to the reservations before made, twelve thousand eight hundred acres of land, to be laid off adjoining the east line of their reserve of ten miles square, at Wapaughkonetta; and for the use of the Shawnese and Senecas, eight thousand nine hundred and sixty acres of land, to be laid off adjoining the west line of the reserve of forty-eight square miles at Lewistown. And the last reserve hereby made, and the former reserve at the same place, shall be equally divided by an east and west line, to be drawn through the same. And the north half of the said tract shall be reserved for the use of the Senecas who reside there, and the south half for the use of the Shawnese who reside there.

Further reservation for the Senecas.

There shall also be reserved for the use of the Senecas, in addition to the reservations before made, ten thousand acres of land, to be laid off on the east side of the Sandusky river, adjoining the south line of their reservation of thirty thousand acres of land, which begins on the Sandusky river, at the lower corner of William Spicer's section, and excluding therefrom the said William Spicer's section.

ART. 3. It is hereby agreed that the tracts of land, which, by the eighth article of the treaty to which this is supplementary, are to be granted by the United States to the persons therein mentioned, shall never be conveyed, by them or their heirs, without the permission of the President of the United States. *Grants to certain persons not to be conveyed without permission.*

ART. 4. The United States agree to pay to the Wyandots an additional annuity of five hundred dollars, forever; to the Shawnese, and to the Senecas of Lewistown, an additional annuity of one thousand dollars, forever; and to the Senecas an additional annuity of five hundred dollars, forever; and to the Ottawas an additional annuity of one thousand five hundred dollars, forever. And these annuities shall be paid at the places, and in the manner, prescribed by the treaty to which this is supplementary. *Additional annuities to the Wyandots, etc.*

ART. 5. This treaty shall take effect, and be obligatory on the contracting parties, as soon as the same shall be ratified by the President of the United States, by and with the advice and consent of the Senate thereof. *When to take effect.*

In testimony whereof, the said Lewis Cass and Duncan McArthur, commissioners as aforesaid, and the sachems, chiefs, and warriors, of the Wyandot, Seneca, Shawanee, and Ottawa tribes of Indians, have hereunto set their hands, at St. Mary's, in the state of Ohio, this seventeenth day of September, in the year of our Lord one thousand eight hundred and eighteen.

Lewis Cass,
Duncan McArthur
   Ottawas:
Keueaghbon, or Bald Eagle, his x mark,
Peshekata, or Marked Legs, his x mark,
Shwanabe, or Muskrat, his x mark,
Toutogana, or The Dog, his x mark,
Tushquagon, or McCarty, his x mark,
Mushkema, his x mark,
   Shawanees:
Cuttewekasa, or Black Hoof, his x mark,
Shemenetu, or Big Snake, his x mark,
Biaseka, or Wolf, his x mark,
Pomthe, or Walker, his x mark,
Chacalawa, or Long Tail, his x mark,
Pemthata, or Perry, his x mark,
Red Man, or Capt. Reed, his x mark,
Chiakeska, or Captain Tom, his x mark,
Tecuntequa, or Elk in the Water, his x mark,
Quitawepa, or Colonel Lewis, his x mark,
Captain Pipe, his x mark,
James Armstrong, his x mark,
   Ottawas:
Metesheneiwa, or Bear's Man, his x mark,

Oquenoxe, his x mark,
Peneshaw, or Eagle, his x mark,
   Wyandots:
Douquad, or Half King, his x mark,
Rontondu, or War Pole, his x mark,
Tuayaurontoyou, or Between the Logs, his x mark,
Dauatout, or John Hicks his x mark,
Horonu, or Cherokee Boy, his x mark,
Teoudetosso, or George Punch, his x mark,
Hawdoro, or Matthews, his x mark,
Skoutous, his x mark,
Quouqua, his x mark,
   Senecas:
Methomea, or Civil John, his x mark,
Skekoghkell, or Big Turtle, his x mark,
Waghkonoxie, or White Bone, his x mark,
Tochequia, or Yellow Bone, his x mark,
Captain Togone, his x mark,
Cunneshohant, or Harris, his x mark,
Tousonecta, or his Blanket Down, his x mark,
Wiping Stick, his x mark,

In presence of—

Wm. Turner, secretary,
John Johnston, Indian agent,
B. F. Stickney, Indian agent,
B. Parke, district judge of Indiana,
Jonathan Jennings, governor of Indiana,
Wm. P. Rathbone, army contractor,
Alexander Wolcott, jr., Indian agent, Detroit,

John Conner,
J. T. Chunn, major of Third Infantry,
R. A. Forsyth, jr., secretary Indian Department,
G. M. Grosvenor, captain Eighth Infantry.

Sworn interpreters:

Henry I. Hunt,
John Kenzer, subagent,
F. Duchouquet,
W. Knaggs,

A. Shane,
John B. Walker,
L. Jouett, Indian agent.

TREATY WITH THE WYANDOT, 1818.

Sept. 20, 1818.
_____
7 Stat., 180.
Proclamation, Jan.
7, 1819.

Articles of a treaty made and concluded, at St. Mary's, in the state of Ohio, between Lewis Cass, Commissioner of the United States, thereto specially authorized by the President of the United States, and the chiefs and warriors of the Wyandot tribe of Indians.

Cession of lands.

ART. 1. The Wyandot tribe of Indians hereby cede to the United States all the right reserved to them in two tracts of land, in the territory of Michigan, one including the village called Brownstown, and the other the village called Maguagua, formerly in the possession of the Wyandot tribe of Indians, containing in the whole not more than five thousand acres of land; which two tracts of land were reserved for the use of the said Wyandot tribe of Indians, and their descendants, for the term of fifty years, agreeably to the provisions of the act of Congress, passed February 28, 1809, and entitled "An act for the relief of certain Alabama and Wyandot Indians."

1809, ch. 23.

Reservation for the use of the Wyandots south of the river Huron.

ART. 2. In consideration of the preceding cession, the United States will reserve, for the use of the said Wyandott Indians, sections numbered twenty-three, twenty-four, twenty-five, twenty-six, thirty-four, thirty-five, thirty-six, twenty-seven, and that part of section numbered twenty-two, which contains eight acres, and lies on the south side of the river Huron, being in the fourth township, south of the base line, and in the ninth range east of the first meridian, in the territory of Michigan, and containing four thousand nine hundred and ninety-six acres; and the said tract of land shall be reserved for the use of the said Wyandott Indians, and their descendants, and be secured to them in the same manner, and on the same terms and conditions, as is provided in relation to the Alabama Indians, by the first section of the beforementioned act of Congress, except that the said Wyandott Indians, and their descendants, shall hold the said land so long as they or their descendants shall occupy the same.

In testimony whereof, the said Lewis Cass, commissioner as aforesaid, and the chiefs and warriors of the said Wyandot tribe of Indians, have hereunto set their hands, at St. Mary's, in the State of Ohio, this twentieth day of September, in the year of our Lord one thousand eight hundred and eighteen.

> Lewis Cass,
> Ronesass, or Honas, his x mark,
> Haunsiaugh, or Boyer, his x mark,
> Ronaess, or Racer, his x mark,
> Ronioness, or Joseph, his x mark,
> Scoutash, his x mark,
> Dunquod, or Half King, his x mark,
> Aronne, or Cherokee Boy, his x mark,
> Taruntne, or Between the Logs, his x mark.

In presence of—
  R. A. Forsyth, jun. secretary to the commission,
  John Johnston, Indian agent,
  B. F. Stickney, S. I. A.
  W. W. Walker, interpreter,
  John Conner,
  Wm. Turner.

TREATY WITH THE PEORIA, ETC., 1818.

A treaty made and concluded by, and between, Ninian Edwards and Auguste Chouteau, Commissioners on the part and behalf of the United States of America, of the one part, and the undersigned, principal chiefs and warriors of the Peoria, Kaskaskia, Mitchigamia, Cahokia, and Tamarois, tribes of the Illinois nation of Indians, on the part and behalf of the said tribes, of the other part.

Sept. 25, 1818.

7 Stat., 181.
Proclamation, Jan. 5, 1819.

WHEREAS, by the treaty made at Vincennes, on the thirteenth day of August, in the year of our Lord one thousand eight hundred and three, between the United States, of the one part, and the head chiefs and warriors of the tribe of Indians commonly called the Kaskaskia tribe, but which was composed of, and rightfully represented, the Kaskaskia, Mitchigamia, Cahokia, and Tamarois, tribes of the Illinois nation of Indians, of the other part, a certain tract of land was ceded to the United States, which was supposed to include all the land claimed by those respective tribes, but which did not include, and was not intended to include, the land which was rightfully claimed by the Peoria Indians, a tribe of the Illinois nation, who then did, and still do, live separate and apart from the tribes abovementioned, and who were not represented in the treaty referred to above, nor ever received any part of the consideration given for the cession of land therein mentioned: And whereas the said tribe of Peoria are now also disposed to cede all their land to the United States, and, for the purpose of avoiding any dispute with regard to the boundary of their claim, are willing to unite with the Kaskaskia, Mitchigamia, Cahokia, and Tamarois, tribes, in confirming the cession of land to the United States, which was made by the treaty above referred to, and in extending the cession so as to include all the land claimed by those tribes, and themselves, respectively:

Preamble.

ART. 1. For which purpose the undersigned, head chiefs and warriors of the Peoria, Kaskaskia, Mitchigamia, Cahokia, and Tamarois, tribes of the Illinois nation of Indians, for the considerations hereinafter mentioned, do hereby relinquish, cede, and confirm, to the United States, all the land included within the following boundaries, viz: Beginning at the confluence of the Ohio and Mississippi rivers; thence, up the Ohio, to the mouth of Saline creek, about twelve miles below the mouth of the Wabash; thence, along the dividing ridge between the waters of said creek and the Wabash, to the general dividing ridge between the waters which fall into the Wabash and those which fall into the Kaskaskia river; thence, along the said ridge, until it reaches the waters which fall into the Illinois river; thence, a direct line to the confluence of the Kankakee and Maple rivers; thence, down the Illinois river, to its confluence with the Mississippi river, and down the latter to the beginning.

Cession by all the tribes, parties to this treaty.

ART. 2. It is mutually agreed, by the parties hereto, that all the stipulations contained in the treaty, above referred to, shall continue binding and obligatory on both parties.

Stipulations in treaty of Vincennes to continue obligatory.

ART. 3. The United States will take the Peoria tribe, as well as the other tribes herein abovementioned, under their immediate care and patronage, and will afford them a protection as effectual, against any other Indian tribes, and against all other persons whatever, as is enjoyed by the citizens of the United States. And the said Peoria tribe do hereby engage to refrain from making war, or giving any insult or offence, to any other Indian tribe, or to any foreign nation, without first having obtained the approbation and consent of the United States.

United States will protect the tribes, parties to this treaty.

Peorias not to make war without consent of United States.

ART. 4. In addition to two thousand dollars' worth of merchandize, this day paid to the abovementioned tribes of Indians, the receipt

Payment to the Peorias.

whereof is hereby acknowledged, the United States promise to pay to the said Peoria tribe, for the term of twelve years, an annuity of three hundred dollars, in money, merchandize, or domestic animals, at the option of the said tribe; to be delivered at the village of St. Genevieve, in the territory of Missouri.

The United States cede 640 acres of land to the Peorias.

ART. 5. The United States agree to cede, to the said Peoria tribe, six hundred and forty acres of land, including their village on Blackwater river, in the territory of Missouri; provided that the said tract is not included within a private claim; but should that be the case, then some other tract of equal quantity and value shall be designated for said tribe, at such place as the President of the United States may

Peorias accept the presents, etc., in full for all their claims.

direct. And the said Peoria tribe hereby agree to accept the same, together with the presents now given them, and the annuity hereby promised them, as a full equivalent for all and every tract of land to which they have any pretence of right or title.

In testimony whereof, the commissioners aforesaid, and the undersigned chiefs and warriors as aforesaid, have hereunto subscribed their names and affixed their seals. Done at Edwardsville, in the State of Illinois, this twenty-fifth day of September, in the year of our Lord one thousand eight hundred and eighteen, and of the independence of the United States the forty-third.

Ninian Edwards, [L. S.]
Aug. Chouteau, [L. S.]
  Peorias:
Waw Peeshawkawnan, Shield, his x mark, [L. S.]
Wassawcosangaw, Shine, his x mark, [L. S.]
Naynawwitwaw, Sentinel, his x mark, [L. S.]
Wissineeaw, the Eater, his x mark, [L. S.]
Rawmissawnoa, or Wind, his x mark, [L. S.]
Mawressaw, or Knife, his x mark, [L. S.]
Koongeepawtaw, his x mark, [L. S.]
Batticy, or Baptist, his x mark, [L. S.]
Keemawraneaw, or Seal, his x mark, [L. S.]
Wecomawkawnaw, his x mark, [L. S.]
Keeshammy, or Cut off a Piece, his x mark, [L. S.]
  Kaskaskias:
Louis Jefferson Decouagne, his x mark, [L. S.]
Wawpamahwhawaw, or White Wolf, his x mark, [L. S.]

Awrawmapingeaw, or Whale, his x mark, [L. S.]
Keemawassaw, of Little Chief, his x mark, [L. S.]
  Mitchigamias:
Wackshinggaw, or Crooked Moon, his x mark, [L. S.]
Keetawkeemawwaw, or Andrew, his x mark, [L. S.]
Manggonssaw, his x mark, [L. S.]
  Cahokias:
Mooyawkacke, or Mercier, his x mark, [L. S.]
Pemmeekawwattaw, or Henry, his x mark, [L. S.]
Papenegeesawwaw, his x mark, [L. S.]
Shopinnaw, or Pint, his x mark, [L. S.]
Maysheeweerattaw, or Big Horn, his x mark, [L. S.]
  Tamarois:
Mahkattamawweeyaw, Black Wolf, his x mark, [L. S.]
Queckkawpeetaw, or Round Seat, his x mark, [L. S.]

In presence of—

Pascal Cerre, secretary to the commissioners,
Abraham Prickett,
B. Stephenson,
John McKee,
Joseph Conway,
Josias Randle,
Ebenezer Baldwin,
Reuben H. Walworth,
William Swettaud,
John Kain,
R. Pulliam,
John Gaither,

N. Bucknett,
Jacob Prickett,
John Wilson,
William P. McKee,
James Watts,
John Howard,
Richard Brevoofield,
Robert Bogue,
James Mason,
John Shinn, jun.
John H. Randle,
Edmund Randle.

TREATY WITH THE OSAGE, 1818.

A treaty made and concluded by, and between, William Clark, governor of the Missouri Territory, superintendent of Indian affairs, and commissioner in behalf of the United States, of the one part; and a full and complete deputation of considerate men, chiefs, and warriors, of all the several bands of the Great and Little Osage nation, assembled in behalf of their said nation, of the other part; have agreed to the following articles:

Sept. 25, 1818.

7 Stat., 183.
Proclamation, Jan.
7, 1819.

ART. 1. WHEREAS the Osage nations have been embarrassed by the frequent demands for property taken from the citizens of the United States, by war parties, and other thoughtless men of their several bands, (both before and since their war with the Cherokees,) and as the exertions of their chiefs have been ineffectual in recovering and delivering such property, conformably with the condition of the ninth article of a treaty, entered into with the United States, at Fort Clark, the tenth of November, one thousand eight hundred and eight; and as the deductions from their annuities, in conformity to the said article, would deprive them of any for several years, and being destitute of funds to do that justice to the citizens of the United States which is calculated to promote a friendly intercourse, they have agreed, and do hereby agree, to cede to the United States, and forever quit claim to, the tract of country included within the following bounds, to wit: Beginning at the Arkansaw river, at where the present Osage boundary line strikes the river at Frog Bayou; then up the Arkansaw and Verdigris, to the falls of Verdigris river; thence, eastwardly, to the said Osage boundary line, at a point twenty leagues north from the Arkansaw river; and, with that line, to the place of beginning.

Cession to the United States of a tract of country within the bounds mentioned.

ART. 2. The United States, on their part, and in consideration of the above cession, agree, in addition to the amount which the Osage do now receive in money and goods, to pay their own citizens the full value of such property as they can legally prove to have been stolen or destroyed by the said Osage, since the year one thousand eight hundred and fourteen: provided the same does not exceed the sum of four thousand dollars.

United States to pay for certain losses sustained by their citizens.

ART. 3. The articles now stipulated will be considered as permanent additions to the treaties, now in force, between the contracting parties, as soon as they shall have been ratified by the President of the United States of America, by and with the advice and consent of the Senate of the said United States.

These articles to be considered as permanent additions to former treaties.

In witness whereof, the said William Clark, commissioner as aforesaid, and the considerate men and chiefs aforesaid, have hereunto subscribed their names, and affixed their seals, at St. Louis, this twenty-fifth day of September, in the year of our Lord one thousand eight hundred and eighteen, and of the independence of the United States the forty-third.

William Clark,		Thequalanan, his x mark,	[L. s.]
Canlenonpe, his x mark,	[L. s.]	Theoucoudhe, his x mark,	[L. s.]
Voibatice, his x mark,	[L. s.]	Nihecounache, his x mark,	[L. s.]
Thebonache, his x mark,	[L. s.]	Voidenoche, his x mark,	[L. s.]
Chonqueauga, his x mark,	[L. s.]	Conchestuvoilla, his x mark,	[L. s.]
Voipoqua, his x mark,	[L. s.]	Naquidatonga, his x mark,	[L. s.]
Mannansoudhe, his x mark,	[L. s.]	Voitanigau, his x mark,	[L. s.]
Nequivoire, his x mark,	[L. s.]	Huquevoire, his x mark,	[L. s.]
Nantagregre, his x mark,	[L. s.]	Hurathi, his x mark,	[L. s.]
Manshepogran, his x mark,	[L. s.]	Houneagon, or the Gentleman, his	
Pachique, his x mark,	[L. s.]	x mark,	[L. s.]
Tacindhe, his x mark,	[L. s.]	Hoquithevoico, his x mark,	[L. s.]
Voiletonchinga, his x mark,	[L. s.]	Voiscaudhe, his x mark,	[L. s.]
Voisabevoiquanddague, his x mark,	[L. s.]	Thedocavoichipiche, his x mark,	[L. s.]
Nanchache, his x mark.		Voithevoihe, his x mark,	[L. s.]

Mitaniga, his x mark,	[L. S.]	Tadhesajaudesor, or the Wind, his	
Thecanique, his x mark,	[L. S.]	x mark,	[L. S.]
Voibisonthe, his x mark,	[L. S.]	Nihuedheque, or Sans Oreillez, his	
Nicananthevoire, his x mark,	[L. S.]	x mark,	[L. S.]
Honhonquecon, his x mark,	[L. S.]	Caniquechaga, or the Little Chief,	
Tanhemonny, his x mark,	[L. S.]	his x mark,	[L. S.]
Sandhecaan, his x mark,	[L. S.]	Grinachie, or the Sudden Appear-	
Paheksaw, or the White Hairs, his		ance, his x mark,	[L. S.]
x mark,	[L. S.]	Voinasache, or the Raised Scalp,	
Kohesegre, or the Great Tract, his		his x mark,	[L. S.]
x mark,	[L. S.]	Dogachiga, his x mark,	[L. S.]
Nichenmanee, or the Walking		Tahechiga, his x mark,	[L. S.]
Rain, his x mark,	[L. S.]		

Signed, sealed, and delivered, in the presence of—

Pierre Chouteau,	Paul Loise, interpreter Osage,
Pierre Menard, Indian agent,	J. T. Honore, Indian interpreter,
John Ruland, sub-agent,	Meriwether Lewis Clark.
P. L. Chouteau, interpreter,	

TREATY WITH THE POTAWATOMI, 1818.

Oct. 2, 1818.

7 Stat., 185.
Proclamation, Jan, 15, 1819.

Articles of a treaty made and concluded at St. Mary's, in the state of Ohio, between Jonathan Jennings, Lewis Cass, and Benjamin Parke, commissioners of the United States, and the Potawatamie nation of Indians.

Cessions of land by the Pottawatomies.

ART. 1. The Potawatamie nation of Indians cede to the United States all the country comprehended within the following limits: Beginning at the mouth of the Tippecanoe river, and running up the same to a point twenty-five miles in a direct line from the Wabash river—thence, on a line as nearly parallel to the general course of the Wabash river as practicable, to a point on the Vermilion river, twenty-five miles from the Wabash river; thence, down the Vermilion river to its mouth, and thence, up the Wabash river, to the place of beginning. The Potawatamies also cede to the United States all their claim to the country south of the Wabash river.

United States agree to purchase Kickapoo claim.

ART. 2. The United States agree to purchase any just claim which the Kickapoos may have to any part of the country hereby ceded below Pine creek.

Perpetual annuity to Pottawatomies.

ART. 3. The United States agree to pay to the Potawatamies a perpetual annuity of two thousand five hundred dollars in silver; one half of which shall be paid at Detroit, and the other half at Chicago; and all annuities which, by any former treaty, the United States have engaged to pay to the Potawatamies, shall be hereafter paid in silver.

Grants not to be conveyed without consent of United States.

ART. 4. The United States agree to grant to the persons named in the annexed schedule, and their heirs, the quantity of land therein stipulated to be granted; but the land so granted shall never be conveyed by either of the said persons, or their heirs, unless by the consent of the President of the United States.

In testimony whereof, the said Jonathan Jennings, Lewis Cass, and Benjamin Parke, commissioners as aforesaid, and the sachems, chiefs, and warriors, of the Pattawatima tribe of Indians, have hereunto set their hands, at St. Mary's in the State of Ohio, this second day of October, in the year of our Lord one thousand eight hundred and eighteen, and of the independence of the United States the forty-third.

Jonathan Jennings,	Meetenwa, his x mark,
Lewis Cass,	Scomack, his x mark,
B. Parke,	Chewago, his x mark,
Tuthinepee, his x mark,	Jowish, his x mark,
Cheebaas, his x mark,	Checalk, his x mark,
Metamice, his x mark,	Eshcam, his x mark,
Winemakoos, his x mark,	Pesotem, his x mark,

Mescotnome, his x mark,
Wabmeshema, his x mark,
Shawano, his x mark,
Chacapma, his x mark,
Menomene, his x mark,
Wogaw, his x mark,
Metea, his x mark,
Metchepagiss, his x mark,
Nautchegno, his x mark,
Osheochebe, his x mark,
Keesis, his x mark,
Conge, his x mark,

Onoxas, his x mark,
Petcheco, his x mark,
Shepage, his x mark,
Sheackackabe, his x mark,
Peaneesh, his x mark,
Macota, his x mark,
Mona, or Moran, his x mark,
Mocksa, his x mark,
Nanouseka, his x mark,
Wistea, his x mark,
Mowa, or Black Wolf, his x mark.

In presence of—

James Dill, secretary to the commissioners,
William Turner, secretary,
Jno. Johnson, Indian agent,
B. F. Stickney, S. I. A.,
William Prince, Indian agent,
John Conner,
William Conner, interpreter,

R. A. Forsyth, secretary of Indian affairs,
Isaac Burnett,
Benedict Th. Flaget, Bishop of Bardstown,
G. Godfroy, Indian agent,
John T. Chunn, major Third Infantry.
P. Hackley, captain Third Infantry.

Schedule referred to in the foregoing treaty.

There shall be granted to James Burnett, Isaac Burnett, Jacob Burnett, and Abraham Burnett, two sections of land each; and to Rebecca Burnett and Nancy Burnett, one section of land each; which said James, John, Isaac, Jacob, Abraham, Rebecca, and Nancy, are children of Cakimi, a Potawatamie woman, sister of Topinibe, principal chief of the nation; and six of the sections herein granted, shall be located from the mouth of the Tippecanoe river, down the Wabash river, and the other six [five] sections shall be located at the mouth of Flint river. — Schedule of grantees.

There shall be granted to Perig, a Potawatamie chief, one section of land on the Flint river, where he now lives. There shall also be granted to Mary Chatalie, daughter of Neebosh, a Potawatamie chief, one section of land, to be located below the mouth of Pine river.

　　　　　　　　　　Jonathan Jennings,
　　　　　　　　　　Lewis Cass,
　　　　　　　　　　B. Parke.

TREATY WITH THE WEA, 1818.

Articles of a treaty made and concluded, at St. Mary's, between the United States of America, by their Commissioners, Jonathan Jennings, Lewis Cass, and Benjamin Park, and the Wea tribe of Indians. — Oct. 2, 1818.

7 Stat., 186.
Proclamation, Jan. 7, 1819.

ART. 1. The said Wea tribe of Indians agree to cede to the United State all the lands claimed and owned by the said tribe, within the limits of the states of Indiana, Ohio, and Illinois. — Cession of land by the Weas.

ART. 2. The said Wea tribe of Indians reserve to themselves the following described tract of land, viz: Beginning at the mouth of Raccoon creek; thence by the present boundary line, seven miles; thence, northeasterly, seven miles, to a point seven miles from the Wabash river; thence to the Wabash river, by a line parallel to the present boundary line aforesaid; and thence, by the Wabash river, to the place of beginning: to be holden by the said tribe as Indian reservations are usually held. — Reservation.

ART. 3. The United States agree to grant to Christmas Dageny and Mary Shields, formerly Mary Dageny, children of Mechinquamesha, sister of Jacco, a chief of the said tribe, and their heirs, one section — Grant to C. Dagemy and Mary Shields.

of land each; but the land hereby granted shall not be conveyed or transfered to any person or persons, by the grantees aforesaid, or their heirs, or either of them, but with the consent of the President of the United States.

The Weas sanction a cession of land by the Kickapoos in 1809.

ART. 4. The said Wea tribe of Indians accede to; and sanction, the cession of land made by the Kickapoo tribe of Indians, in the second article of a treaty concluded between the United States and the said Kickapoo tribe, on the ninth day of December, one thousand eight hundred and nine.

Payment to Weas.

ART. 5. In consideration of the cession made in the foregoing articles of this treaty, the United States agree to pay to the said Wea tribe of Indians, one thousand eight hundred and fifty dollars annually, in addition to the sum of one thousand one hundred and fifty dollars, (the amount of their former annuity,) making a sum total of three thousand dollars; to be paid in silver, by the United States, annually, to the said tribe, on the reservation described by the second article of this treaty.

In testimony whereof, the said Jonathan Jennings, Lewis Cass, and Benjamin Parke, commissioners as aforesaid, and the sachems, chiefs, and warriors, of the Wea tribe of Indians, have hereunto set their hands, at St. Mary's, in the State of Ohio, this second day of October, 'n the year of our Lord one thousand eight hundred and eighteen.

Jonathan Jennings,	Pequiah, his x mark,
Lewis Cass,	Shingonsa, or Mink, his x mark,
B. Parke,	Shepaqua, or Leaves, his x mark.
Jacco, his x mark,	Kickapoo chiefs:
Shamana, his x mark,	Metagekoka, or Big Tree, his x mark,
Shequiah, or Little Eyes, his x mark,	Wako or Fox, his x mark.
Quema, or Young Man, his x mark,	

In presence of—

John Dill, secretary to the commissioners,	John Conner,
William Turner, secretary,	Joseph Barron, interpreter,
John Johnson, Indian agent,	John T. Chunn, major, Third Infantry,
William Prince, Indian agent	J. Hackley, captain, Third Infantry,
B. F. Stickney, S. I. A.	Benedict Th. Flaget, Bishop of Bardstown.

TREATY WITH THE DELAWARES, 1818.

Oct. 3, 1818.
———
7 Stat., 188.
Proclamation, Jan. 15, 1819.

Articles of a treaty made and concluded at St. Mary's, in the state of Ohio, between Jonathan Jennings, Lewis Cass, and Benjamin Parke, commissioners of the United States, and the Delaware nation of Indians.

Delawares cede all claim to land in Indiana.

ART. 1. The Delaware nation of Indians cede to the United States all their claim to land in the state of Indiana.

United States to provide a country for them west of the Mississippi.

ART. 2. In consideration of the aforesaid cession, the United States agree to provide for the Delawares a country to reside in, upon the west side of the Mississippi, and to guaranty to them the peaceable possession of the same.

Full compensation for improvements of Delawares.

ART. 3. The United States also agree to pay the Delawares the full value of their improvements in the country hereby ceded: which valuation shall be made by persons to be appointed for that purpose by the President of the United States; and to furnish the Delawares with one hundred and twenty horses, not to exceed in value forty dollars each, and a sufficient number of perogues, to aid in transporting them to the west side of the Mississippi; and a quantity of provisions, proportioned to their numbers, and the extent of their journey.

Delawares allowed to occupy improvements for three years.

ART. 4. The Delawares shall be allowed the use and occupation of their improvements, for the term of three years from the date of this treaty if they so long require it.

ART. 5. The United States agree to pay to the Delawares a perpetual annuity of four thousand dollars; which, together with all annuities which the United States, by any former treaty, engaged to pay to them, shall be paid in silver, at any place to which the Delawares may remove.

ART. 6. The United States agree to provide and support a blacksmith for the Delawares, after their removal to the west side of the Mississippi.

ART. 7. One half section of land shall be granted to each of the following persons, namely; Isaac Wobby, Samuel Cassman, Elizabeth Petchaka, and Jacob Dick; and one quarter of a section of land shall be granted to each of the following persons, namely; Solomon Tindell, and Benoni Tindell; all of whom are Delawares; which tracts of land shall be located, after the country is surveyed, at the first creek above the old fort on White river, and running up the river; and shall be held by the persons herein named, respectively, and their heirs; but shall never be conveyed or transferred without the approbation of the President of the United States.

ART. 8. A sum, not exceeding thirteen thousand three hundred and twelve dollars and twenty-five cents, shall be paid by the United States, to satisfy certain claims against the Delaware nation; and shall be expended by the Indian agent at Piqua and Fort Wayne, agreeably to a schedule this day examined and approved by the commissioners of the United States.

ART. 9. This treaty, after the same shall be ratified by the President and Senate of the United States, shall be binding on the contracting parties.

In testimony whereof, the said Jonathan Jennings, Lewis Cass, and Benjamin Parke, commissioners as aforesaid, and the chiefs and warriors of the Delaware nation of Indians, have hereunto set their hands, at St. Mary's, in the State of Ohio, this third day of October, in the year of our Lord one thousand eight hundred and eighteen.

Margin notes:
- Perpetual annuity to Delawares.
- A blacksmith to be provided.
- Grants of land to individuals—not transferable without consent.
- United States to pay certain claims on the Delawares.
- Treaty binding when ratified.

Jonathan Jennings,	Captain Ketchum, his x mark,
Lew. Cass,	The Cat, his x mark
B. Parke,	Ben Beaver, his x mark,
Kithteeleland, or Anderson, his x mark,	The War Mallet, his x mark,
Lapahnihe, or Big Bear, his x mark,	Captain Caghkoo, his x mark,
James Nanticoke, his x mark,	The Buck, his x mark,
Apacahund, or White Eyes, his x mark,	Petchenanalas, his x mark,
Captain Killbuck, his x mark,	John Quake, his x mark,
The Beaver, his x mark,	Quenaghtoothmait, his x mark,
Netahopuna, his x mark,	Little Jack, his x mark.
Captain Tunis, his x mark,	

In the presence of—

James Dill, secretary to the commissioners,	John T. Chunn, major, Third U. S. Infantry,
William Turner, secretary,	J. Hackley, captain, Third Infantry,
Jno. Johnston, Indian agent,	William Oliver,
B. F. Stickney, S. I. A.	Hilary Brunot, lieutenant, Third Infantry,
John Conner,	David Oliver,
William Conner, interpreter,	R. A. Forsyth, jr., secretary Indian Department.
John Kinzie, sub-agent,	
G. Godfroy, sub-agent	

TREATY WITH THE MIAMI, 1818.

Articles of a treaty made and concluded, at St. Mary's, in the State of Ohio, between Jonathan Jennings, Lewis Cass, and Benjamin Parke, Commissioners of the United States, and the Miame nation of Indians.

Margin notes:
- Oct. 6, 1818.
- 7 Stats., 189.
- Proclamation Jan. 15, 1319.

ART. 1. The Miami nation of Indians cede to the United States the following tract of country: Beginning at the Wabash river, where the present Indian boundary line crosses the same, near the mouth of

Margin note: Cession of lands by the Miamis.

Raccoon creek; thence, up the Wabash river, to the reserve at its head, near Fort Wayne; thence, to the reserve at Fort Wayne; thence, with the lines thereof, to the St. Mary's river; thence, up the St. Mary's river, to the reservation at the portage; thence, with the line of the cession made by the Wyandot nation of Indians to the United States, at the foot of the Rapids of the Miami of Lake Erie, on the 29th day of September, in the year of our Lord one thousand eight hundred and seventeen, to the reservation at Loramie's store; thence, with the present Indian boundary line, to Fort Recovery; and, with the said line, following the courses thereof, to the place of beginning.

Reservations from the cession for the use of the Miamis.

ART. 2. From the cession aforesaid the following reservations, for the use of the Miami nation of Indians, shall be made; one reservation, extending along the Wabash river, from the mouth of Salamanie river to the mouth of Eel river, and from those points, running due south, a distance equal to a direct line from the mouth of Salamanie river to the mouth of Eel river. One other reservation, of two miles square, on the river Salamanie, at the mouth of Atchepongqwawe creek. One other reservation, of six miles square, on the Wabash river, below the forks thereof. One other reservation, of ten miles square, opposite the mouth of the river A Bouette. One other reservation, of ten miles square, at the village on Sugar Tree Creek. One other reservation, of two miles square, at the mouth of a creek, called Flat Rock, where the road to White river crosses the same.

Tracts granted by United States to J. B. Richardville.

ART. 3. The United States agree to grant, by patent, in fee simple, to Jean Bapt. Richardville, principal chief of the Miami nation of Indians, the following tracts of land: Three sections of land, beginning about twenty-five rods below his house, on the river St. Mary's, near Fort Wayne; thence, at right angles with the course of the river, one mile; and from this line, and the said river, up the stream thereof, for quantity. Two sections, upon the east side of the St. Mary's river, near Fort Wayne, running east one mile with the line of the military reservation; thence, from that line, and from the river, for quantity. Two sections, on the Twenty-seven mile creek, where the road from St. Mary's to Fort Wayne crosses it, being one section on each side of said creek.

Two sections on the left bank of the Wabash, commencing at the forks and running down the river.

Other grants to persons named.

The United States also agree to grant to each of the following persons, being Miami Indians by birth, and their heirs, the tracts of land herein described.

To Joseph Richardville and Joseph Richardville, jun. two sections of land, being one on each side of the St. Mary's river, and below the reservation made on that river by the treaty of Greenville, in 1795.

To Wemetche or the Crescent, one section, below and adjoining the reservation of Anthony Chesne, on the west side of the St. Mary's river, and one section immediately opposite to Macultamunqua or Black Loon.

To Keenquatakqua or Long Hair, Aronzon or Twilight, Peconbequa or a Woman striking, Aughquamauda or Difficulty, and to Miaghqua or Noon, as joint tenants, five sections of land upon the Wabash river, the centre of which shall be the Wyandot village, below the mouth of Tippecanoe river.

To François Godfroy, six sections of land, on the Salamanie river, at a place called La Petite Prairie.

To Louis Godfroy, six sections of land, upon the St. Mary's river, above the reservation of Anthony Shane.

To Charley, a Miamie chief, one section of land, on the west side of the St. Mary's river, below the section granted to Pemetche or the Crescent.

To the two eldest children of Peter Langlois, two sections of land, at a place formerly called Village du Puant, at the mouth of the river called Pauceaupichoux.

To the children of Antoine Bondie, two sections of land, on the border of the Wabash river, opposite a place called l'Esle a l'Aille.

To François Lafontaine and his son, two sections of land, adjoining and above the two sections granted to Jean Bapt. Richardville, near Fort Wayne, and on the same side of the St. Mary's river.

To the children of Antoine Rivarre, two sections of land, at the mouth of the Twenty-seven mile creek, and below the same.

To Peter Langlois' youngest child, one section of land, opposite the Chipaille, at the Shawnese village.

To Peter Labadie, one section of land, on the river St. Mary's, below the section granted to Charley.

To the son of George Hunt, one section of land, on the west side of the St. Mary's river, adjoining the two sections granted to François Lafontaine and his son.

To Meshenoqua or the Little Turtle, one section of land, on the south side of the Wabash, where the portage path strikes the same.

To Josette Beaubien, one section of land on the left bank of the St. Mary's, above and adjoining the three sections granted to Jean Bapt. Richardville.

To Ann Turner, a half-blooded Miami, one section of land on the northwest side of the Wabash river, to commence at the mouth of Fork creek, on the west bank of the said creek, and running up said creek one mile in a direct line, thence at right angles with this line for quantity.

To Rebecca Hackley, a half-blooded Miami, one section of land; to be located at the Munsey town, on White river, so that it shall extend on both sides to include three hundred and twenty acres of the prairie, in the bend of the river, where the bend assumes the shape of a horse shoe.

To William Wayne Wells, a half-blooded Miami, one section of land, at the mouth of the Fork creek, where the reservation for Ann Turner commences, running down the Wabash river on the northwest bank one mile; thence, back one mile; thence, east one mile, to the boundary line of the grant to Ann Turner.

To Mary Wells, a half-blooded Miami, one section of land, at the mouth of Stoney creek, on the southeast side of the Wabash river, the centre of which shall be at the mouth of said creek, running with the meanders thereof, up and down the Wabash river, one half mile, and thence back for quantity.

To Jane Turner Wells, a half-blooded Miami, one section of land, on the northwest side of the Wabash river, to commence on the west bank of said river, opposite the old lime kiln; thence, down the said river one mile and back for quantity.

ART. 4. The Miami nation of Indians assent to the cession made by the Kickapoos to the United States, by the treaty concluded at Vincennes, on the ninth day of December, one thousand eight hundred and nine. *Miami assent to the cession by the Kickapoo.*

ART. 5. In consideration of the cession and recognition aforesaid, the United States agree to pay to the Miami nation of Indians, a perpetual annuity of fifteen thousand dollars, which, together with all annuities which, by any former treaty, the United States have engaged to pay to the said Miami nation of Indians, shall be paid in silver. *Payment to Miami.*

The United States will cause to be built for the Miamis one grist-mill and one saw-mill, at such proper sites as the chiefs of the nation may select, and will provide and support one blacksmith and one gun-smith for them, and provide them with such implements of agriculture as the proper agent may think necessary. *A gristmill, sawmill, etc., for the Miami.*

160 bushels salt annually.

The United States will also cause to be delivered, annually, to the Miami nation, one hundred and sixty bushels of salt.

Tracts granted, except, etc., not transferable without consent.

ART. 6. The several tracts of land which, by the third article of this treaty, the United States have engaged to grant to the persons therein mentioned, except the tracts to be granted to Jean Bapt. Richardville, shall never be transferred by the said persons or their heirs, without the approbation of the President of the United States.

Treaty obligatory when ratified.

ART. 7. This treaty shall be obligatory on the contracting parties after the same shall be ratified by the President of the United States, by and with the advice and consent of the Senate thereof.

In testimony whereof, the said Jonathan Jennings, Lewis Cass, and Benjamin Parke, commissioners as aforesaid, and the chiefs and warriors of the Miami nation of Indians, have hereunto set their hands, at St. Mary's, the sixth day of October, in the year of our Lord one thousand eight hundred and eighteen.

Jonathan Jennings,	Papskeecha, or Flat Belly, his x mark,
Lewis Cass,	Metosma, his x mark,
B. Parke,	Sasakuthka, or Sun, his x mark,
Peshawa, or Richardville, his x mark,	Keosakunga, his x mark,
Osas, his x mark,	Koehenna, his x mark,
Ketauga, or Charley, his x mark,	Sinamahon, or Stone Eater, his x mark,
Metche Keteta, or Big Body, his x mark,	Cabma, his x mark,
Notawas, his x mark.	Ameghqua, his x mark,
Wapapeslea, his x mark,	Nawaushea, his x mark.
Tathtenouga, his x mark,	

In presence of—

James Dill, secretary to the commissioners,	John F. Swan, major Third U. S. Infantry,
William Turner, secretary,	Wm. Brunot, lieutenant Third Infantry,
John Johnson, Indian agent,	Wm. P. Rathbone, army contractor,
B. F. Stickney, S. I. A.	Wm. Oliver,
John Kenzie, sub-agent,	Joseph Benson, sworn interpreter,
G. Godfroy, sub-agent,	Wm. Conner, interpreter,
John Conner,	Antoine Pride, interpreter.

TREATY WITH THE CHICKASAW, 1818.

Oct. 19, 1818.

7 Stat., 192.
Proclamation, Jan. 7, 1819.

Treaty with the Chickasaws, to settle all territorial controversies, and to remove all ground of complaint or dissatisfaction, that might arise to interrupt the peace and harmony which have so long and so happily existed between the United States of America and the Chickasaw nation of Indians, James Monroe, President of the said United States, by Isaac Shelby and Andrew Jackson, of the one part, and the whole Chickasaw nation, by their chiefs, head men, and warriors, in full council assembled, of the other part, have agreed on the following articles; which, when ratified by the President and Senate of the United States of America, shall form a treaty binding on all parties.

Perpetual peace and friendship.

ART. 1. Peace and friendship are hereby firmly established and made perpetual, between the United States of America and the Chickasaw .nation of Indians.

Cession of land by the Chickasaws.

ART. 2. To obtain the object of the foregoing article, the Chickasaw nation of Indians cede to the United States of America, (with the exception of such reservation as shall be hereafter mentioned,) all claim or title which the said nation has to the land lying north of the south boundary of the state of Tennessee, which is bounded south by the thirty-fifth degree of north latitude, and which lands, hereby ceded, lies within the following boundary, viz: Beginning on the Tennessee river, about thirty-five miles, by water, below colonel George Colbert's ferry, where the thirty-fifth degree of north latitude strikes the same;

thence, due west, with said degree of north latitude, to where it cuts the Mississippi river at or near the Chickasaw Bluffs; thence, up the said Mississippi river, to the mouth of the Ohio; thence, up the Ohio river, to the mouth of Tennessee river; thence, up the Tennessee river, to the place of beginning.

ART. 3. In consideration of the relinquishment of claim and cession of lands in the preceding article, and to perpetuate the happiness of the Chickesaw nation of Indians, the commissioners of the United States, before named, agree to allow the said nation the sum of twenty thousand dollars per annum, for fifteen successive years, to be paid annually; and, as a farther consideration for the objects aforesaid, and at the request of the chiefs of the said nation, the commissioners agree to pay captain John Gordon, of Tennessee, the sum of one thousand one hundred and fifteen dollars, it being a debt due by general William Colbert, of said nation, to the aforesaid Gordon; and the further sum of two thousand dollars, due by said nation of Indians, to captain David Smith, now of Kentucky, for that sum by him expended, in supplying himself and forty-five soldiers from Tennessee, in the year one thousand seven hundred and ninety-five, when assisting them (at their request and invitation,) in defending their towns against the invasion of the Creek Indians; both which sums, (on the application of the said nation,) is to be paid, within sixty days after the ratification of this treaty, to the aforesaid Gordon and Smith. — *Payment to Chickasaws.*

ART. 4. The commissioners agree, on the further and particular application of the chiefs, and for the benefit of the poor and warriors of the said nation, that a tract of land, containing four miles square, to include a salt lick or springs, on or near the river Sandy, a branch of the Tennessee river, and within the land hereby ceded, be reserved, and to be laid off in a square or oblong, so as to include the best timber, at the option of their beloved chief Levi Colbert, and major James Brown, or either of them; who are hereby made agents and trustees for the nation, to lease the said salt lick or springs, on the following express conditions, viz: For the benefit of this reservation, as before recited, the trustees or agents are bound to lease the said reservation to some citizen or citizens of the United States, for a reasonable quantity of salt, to be paid annually to the said nation, for the use thereof; and that, from and after two years after the ratification of this treaty, no salt, made at the works to be erected on this reservation, shall be sold within the limits of the same for a higher price than one dollar per bushel of fifty pounds weight; on failure of which the lease shall be forfeited, and the reservation revert to the United States. — *Reservation for the Chickasaws.* *Terms on which the salt lick may be leased.*

ART. 5. The commissioners agree, that there shall be paid to Oppassantubby, a principal chief of the Chickasaw nation, within sixty days after the ratification of this treaty, the sum of five hundred dollars, as a full compensation for the reservation of two miles square, on the north side of Tennessee river, secured to him and his heirs by the treaty held, with the said Chickesaw nation, on the twentyeth day of September, 1816; and the further sum of twenty-five dollars to John Lewis, a half breed, for a saddle he lost while in the service of the United States; and, to shew the regard the President of the United States has for the said Chickasaw nation, at the request of the chiefs of the said nation, the commissioners agree that the sum of one thousand and eighty-nine dollars shall be paid to Maj. James Colbert, interpreter, within the period stated in the first part of this article, it being the amount of a sum of money taken from his pocket, in the month of June, 1816, at the theatre in Baltimore: And the said commissioners, as a further regard for said nation, do agree that the reservations made to George Colbert and Levi Colbert, in the treaty held at the council house of said nation, on the twenty-sixth [twentieth] day of September, 1816, the first to Col. George Colbert, on the north — *$500 to Oppassantubby, etc.* *The reservations of the Colberts to inure to them, their heirs and assigns, forever.*

side of Tennessee river, and those to Maj. Levi Colbert, on the east side of the Tombigby river, shall enure to the sole use of the said Col. George Colbert, and Maj. Levi Colbert, their heirs and assigns, forever, with their butts and bounds, as defined by said treaty, and agreeable to the marks and boundaries as laid off and marked by the surveyor of the United States, where that is the case, and where the reservations has not been laid off and marked by a surveyor of the United States, the same shall be so done as soon after the ratification of this treaty as practicable, on the application of the reservees, or their legally appointed agent under them, and agreeably to the definition in the before recited treaty. This agreement is made on the following express conditions: that the said land, and those living on it, shall be subject to the laws of the United States, and all legal taxation that may be imposed on the land or citizens of the United States inhabiting the territory where said land is situate. The commissioners further agree, that the reservation secured to John McCleish, on the north side of Tennessee river, by the before recited treaty, in consequence of his having been raised in the state of Tennessee, and marrying a white woman, shall enure to the sole use of the said John McCleish, his heirs and assigns, forever, on the same conditions attached to the lands of Col. George Colbert and Maj. Levi Colbert, in this article.

Reservation of J. McCleish to inure to him, his heirs and assigns, on the same terms.

The line of the south boundary of Tennessee to be marked.

ART. 6. The two contracting parties covenant and agree, that the line of the south boundary of the state of Tennessee, as described in the second article of this treaty, shall be ascertained and marked by commissioners appointed by the President of the United States; that the marks shall be bold; the trees to be blazed on both sides of the line, and the fore and aft •trees marked U. S.; and that the commissioners shall be attended by two persons, to be designated by the Chickasaw nation; and the said nation shall have due and seasonable notice when said operation is to be commenced. It is further agreed by the commissioners, that all improvements actually made by individuals of the Chickesaw nation, which shall be found within the lands ceded by this treaty, that a fair and reasonable compensation shall be paid therefor, to the respective individuals having made or owned the same.

Compensation for improvements in lands ceded by the Chickasaws.

Grants in cash to individuals named.

ART. 7. In consideration of the friendly and conciliatory disposition evinced during the negociation of this treaty, by the Chickesaw chiefs and warriors, but more particularly, as a manifestation of the friendship and liberality of the President of the United States, the commissioners agree to give, on the ratification of this treaty, to Chinnubby, King of the Chickesaws nation, to Teshuamingo, William M'Gilvery, Anpassantubby, Samuel Seely, James Brown, Levi Colbert, Ickaryoucuttaha, George Pettygrove, Immartarharmicco, Chickesaw chiefs, and to Malcum M'Gee, interpreter to this treaty, each, one hundred and fifty dollars, in cash; and to Major William Glover, Col. George Colbert, Hopoyeahaummar, Immauklusharhopoyea, Tushkarhopoye, Hopoyeahaummar, jun. Immauklusharhopyea, James Colbert, Coweamarthlar, Illachouwarhopoyea, military leaders, one hundred dollars each; and do further agree, that any annuity heretofore secured to the Chickesaw nation of Indians, by treaty, to be paid in goods, shall hereafter be paid in cash.

Annuities hereafter wholly in cash.

In testimony whereof the said commissioners, and undersigned chiefs and warriors, have set their hands and seals. Done at the treaty ground east of Old Town, this nineteenth day of October, in the year of our Lord one thousand eight hundred and eighteen.

Isaac Shelby,	[L. S.]	Arpasheushtubby, his x mark,	[L. S.]
Andrew Jackson.	[L. S.]	James Brown, his x mark,	[L. S.]
Levi Colbert, his x mark,	[L. S.]	Ickaryaucuttaha, his x mark,	[L. S.]
Samuel Seely, his x mark,	[L. S.]	Georgo Pettygrove, his x mark,	[L. S.]
Chinnubby, King, his x mark,	[L. S.]	Immartaharmico, his x mark,	[L. S.]
Teshuamingo, his x mark,	[L. S.]	Major General William Colbert,	
William McGilvery, his x mark,	[L. S.]	his x mark,	[L. S.]

Major William Glover, his x mark, [L. S.]	Immaaklusharhopoyea, his x mark, [L. S.]
Hopayahaummar, his x mark, [L. S.]	James Colbert, [L. S.]
Immouklusharhopoyea, his x mark, [L. S.]	Cowemarthlar, his x mark, [L. S.]
Tuskaehopoyea, his x mark, [L. S.]	Illackhanwarhopoyes, his x mark, [L. S.]
Hopoyahaummar, jun. his x mark, [L. S.]	Col. George Colbert, his x mark, [L. S.]

In the presence of—

Robert Butler, adjutant - general and secretary,
Th. J. Sherburne, agent for the Chickasaw nation of Indians,
Malcolm McGee, interpreter, his x mark,
Martin Colbert,
J. C. Bronaugh, assistant inspector-general S. D.,

Thos. H. Shelby, of Kentucky,
R. K. Call, Captain U. S. Army,
Benjamin Smith, of Kentucky,
Richard I. Easter, A. D. Q. M. General.
Ms. B. Winchester,
W. B. Lewis.

TREATY WITH THE CHEROKEE, 1819.

Articles of a convention made between John C. Calhoun, Secretary of War, being specially authorized therefor by the President of the United States, and the undersigned Chiefs and Head Men of the Cherokee nation of Indians, duly authorized and empowered by said nation, at the City of Washington, on the twenty-seventh day of February, in the year of our Lord one thousand eight hundred and nineteen.

Feb. 27, 1819.

7 Stat., 195.
Proclamation, Mar. 10, 1819.

Whereas a greater part of the Cherokee nation have expressed an earnest desire to remain on this side of the Mississippi, and being desirous, in order to commence those measures which they deem necessary to the civilization and preservation of their nation, that the treaty between the United States and them, signed the eighth of July, eighteen hundred and seventeen, might, without further delay, or the trouble or expense of taking the census, as stipulated in the said treaty, be finally adjusted, have offered to cede to the United States a tract of country at least as extensive as that which they probably are entitled to under its provisions, the contracting parties have agreed to and concluded the following articles.

Preamble.

Art. 1. The Cherokee nation cedes to the United States all of their lands lying north and east of the following line, viz: Beginning on the Tennessee river, at the point where the Cherokee boundary with Madison county, in the Alabama territory, joins the same; thence, along the main channel of said river, to the mouth of the Highwassee; thence, along its main channel, to the first hill which closes in on said river, about two miles above Highwassee Old Town; thence, along the ridge which divides the waters of the Highwassee and Little Tellico, to the Tennessee river, at Tallassee; thence, along the main channel, to the junction of the Cowee and Nanteyalee; thence, along the ridge in the fork of said river, to the top of the Blue Ridge; thence, along the Blue Ridge to the Unicoy Turnpike Road; thence, by a straight line, to the nearest main source of the Chestatee; thence, along its main channel, to the Chatahouchee; and thence to the Creek boundary; it being understood that all the islands in the Chestatee, and the parts of the Tennessee and Highwassee, (with the exception of Jolly's Island, in the Tennessee, near the mouth of the Highwassee,) which constitute a portion of the present boundary, belong to the Cherokee nation; and it is also understood, that the reservations contained in the second article of the treaty of Tellico, signed the twenty-fifth October, eighteen hundred and five, and a tract equal to twelve miles square, to be located by commencing at the point formed by the intersection of the

Cession of lands by the Cherokees.

boundary line of Madison county, already mentioned, and the north bank of the Tennessee river; thence, along the said line, and up the said river twelve miles, are ceded to the United States, in trust for the Cherokee nation as a school fund; to be sold by the United States, and the proceeds vested as is hereafter provided in the fourth article of this treaty; and, also, that the rights vested in the Unicoy Turnpike Company, by the Cherokee nation, according to certified copies of the instruments securing the rights, and herewith annexed, are not

The lands hereby ceded are in full satisfaction, etc.

to be affected by this treaty; and it is further understood and agreed by the said parties, that the lands hereby ceded by the Cherokee nation, are in full satisfaction of all claims which the United States have on them, on account of the cession to a part of their nation who have or may hereafter emigrate to the Arkansaw; and this treaty is a final adjustment of that of the eighth of July, eighteen hundred and seventeen.

United States to pay for improvements on ceded lands.

ART. 2. The United States agree to pay, according to the stipulations contained in the treaty of the eighth of July, eighteen hundred and seventeen, for all improvements on land lying within the country ceded by the Cherokees, which add real value to the land, and do agree to allow a reservation of six hundred and forty acres to each head of any Indian family residing within the ceded territory, those enrolled for the Arkansaw excepted, who choose to become citizens of the United States, in the manner stipulated in said treaty.

Grant of land to each person on the list annexed to this treaty, except Major Walker.

ART. 3. It is also understood and agreed by the contracting parties, that a reservation, in fee simple, of six hundred and forty acres square, with the exception of Major Walker's, which is to be located as is hereafter provided, to include their improvements, and which are to be as near the centre thereof as possible, shall be made to each of the persons whose names are inscribed on the certified list annexed to this treaty, all of whom are believed to be persons of industry, and capable of managing their property with discretion, and have, with few excep-

Notice to be given of intention to continue residence.

tions, made considerable improvements on the tracts reserved. The reservations are made on the condition, that those for whom they are intended shall notify, in writing, to the agent for the Cherokee nation, within six months after the ratification of this treaty, that it is their intention to continue to reside permanently on the land reserved.

Reservations.

The reservation for Lewis Ross, so to be laid off as to include his house, and out-buildings, and ferry adjoining the Cherokee agency, reserving to the United States all the public property there, and the continuance of the said agency where it now is, during the pleasure of the government; and **Major Walker's**, so as to include his dwelling house and ferry: for **Major Walker** an additional reservation is made of six hundred and forty acres square, to include his grist and saw

Additional reservations.

mill; the land is poor, and principally valuable for its timber. In addition to the above reservations, the following are made, in fee simple; the persons for whom they are intended not residing on the same: To Cabbin Smith, six hundred and forty acres, to be laid off in equal parts, on both sides of his ferry on Tellico, commonly called Blair's ferry; to John Ross, six hundred and forty acres, to be laid off so as to include the Big Island in Tennessee river, being the first below Tellico—which tracts of land were given many years since, by the Cherokee nation, to them; to Mrs. Eliza Ross, step daughter of Major Walker, six hundred and forty acres square, to be located on the river below and adjoining Major Walker's; to Margaret Morgan, six hundred and forty acres square, to be located on the west of, and adjoining, James Riley's reservation; to George Harlin, six hundred and forty acres square, to be located west of, and adjoining, the reservation of Margaret Morgan; to James Lowry, six hundred and forty acres square, to be located at Crow Mocker's old place, at the foot of Cumberland mountain; to Susannah Lowry, six hundred and forty acres, to be located at the Toll Bridge on Battle Creek; to Nicholas Byers, six hundred and forty acres, including the Toqua Island, to be located on the north bank of the Tennessee, opposite to said Island.

ART. 4. The United States stipulate that the reservations, and the tract reserved for a school fund, in the first article of this treaty, shall be surveyed and sold in the same manner, and on the same terms, with the public lands of the United States, and the proceeds vested, under the direction of the President of the United States, in the stock of the United States, or such other stock as he may deem most advantageous to the Cherokee nation. The interest or dividend on said stock, shall be applied, under his direction, in the manner which he shall judge best calculated to diffuse the benefits of education among the Cherokee nation on this side of the Mississippi. *The reservations, etc., to be sold, and proceeds vested in stock.*

Interest, how to be applied.

ART. 5. It is agreed that such boundary lines as may be necessary to designate the lands ceded by the first article of this treaty, may be run by a commissioner or commissioners to be appointed by the President of the United States, who shall be accompanied by such commissioners as the Cherokees may appoint, due notice thereof to be given to the nation; and that the leases which have been made under the treaty of the eighth of July, eighteen hundred and seventeen, of land lying within the portion of country reserved to the Cherokees, to be void; and that all white people who have intruded, or may hereafter intrude, on the lands reserved for the Cherokees, shall be removed by the United States, and proceeded against according to the provisions of the act passed thirtieth March, eighteen hundred and two, entitled "An act to regulate trade and intercourse with the Indian tribes, and to preserve peace on the frontiers." *Boundary lines to be run by commissioners.*

White intruders to be removed.

1802, ch. 13.

ART. 6. The contracting parties agree that the annuity to the Cherokee nation shall be paid, two-thirds to the Cherokees east of the Mississippi, and one-third to the Cherokees west of that river, as it is estimated that those who have emigrated, and who have enrolled for emigration, constitute one-third of the whole nation; but if the Cherokees west of the Mississippi object to this distribution, of which due notice shall be given them, before the expiration of one year after the ratification of this treaty, then the census, solely for distributing the annuity, shall be taken at such times, and in such manner, as the President of the United States may designate. *Division of annuity to Cherokee Nation.*

ART. 7. The United States, in order to afford the Cherokees who reside on the lands ceded by this treaty, time to cultivate their crop next summer, and for those who do not choose to take reservations, to remove, bind themselves to prevent the intrusion of their citizens on the ceded land before the first of January next. *Intrusion of citizens to be prevented.*

ART. 8. This treaty to be binding on the contracting parties so soon as it is ratified by the President of the United States, by and with the advice and consent of the Senate. *Treaty binding when ratified.*

Done at the place, and on the day and year, above written.

J. C. Calhoun.

Ch. Hicks,	[L. S.]	Gideon Morgan, jr.	[L. S.]
Jno. Ross,	[L. S.]	Cabbin Smith, his x mark,	[L. S.]
Lewis Ross,	[L. S.]	Sleeping Rabbit, his x mark,	[L. S.]
John Martin,	[L. S.]	Small Wood, his x mark,	[L. S.]
James Brown,	[L. S.]	John Walker, his x mark,	[L. S.]
Geo. Lowry,	[L. S.]	Currohee Dick, his x mark,	[L. S.]

Witnesses:
Return J. Meigs,
C. Vandeventer,
Elias Earle,
John Lowry.

List of persons referred to in the 3d article of the annexed Treaty.

Richard Walker, within the chartered limits of North Carolina.		John Brown,	do.	Tennessee.
Yonah, alias Big Bear,	do.	Elizabeth Lowry,	do. do.
John Martin,	do.	Georgia.	George Lowry,	do. do.
Peter Linch,	do. do.	John Benge,	do. do.
Daniel Davis,	do. do.	Mrs. Eliz. Peck,	do. do.
George Parris,	do. do.	John Walker, Sr.	do. do.
Walter S. Adair,	do. do.	John Walker, Jr. (unmarried,) do. do.
Thos. Wilson,	do.	Alab. Ter.	Richard Taylor,	do. do.
Richard Riley,	do. do.	John McIntosh,	do. do.
James Riley,	do. do.	James Starr,	do. do.
Edward Gunter,	do. do.	Samuel Parks,	do. do.
Robert McLemore,	do.	Tenn.	The Old Bark, (of Chota)	do. do.
John Baldridge,	do. do.	No. of reservees within the limits of
Lewis Ross,	do. do.	North Carolina,	2
Fox Taylor,	do. do.	Georgia,	5
Rd Timberlake,	do. do.	Alabama Terr.	4
David Fields, (to include his mill,)do. do.	Tennessee,	20
James Brown, (to include his field by the long pond,)	do. do.	Total No. of reservees,	31
William Brown,	do. do.	

I hereby certify, that I am, either personally, or by information on which I can rely, acquainted with the persons before named, all of whom I believe to be persons of industry, and capable of managing their property with discretion; and who have, with few exceptions, long resided on the tracts reserved, and made considerable improvements thereon.

RETURN J. MEIGS,
Agent in the Cherokee nation.

(COPY.)   *Cherokee Agency, Highwassee Garrison.*

Mar. 8, 1813.

We, the undersigned Chiefs and Councillors of the Cherokees in full council assembled, do hereby give, grant, and make over unto Nicholas Byers and David Russell, who are agents in behalf of the states of Tennessee and Georgia, full power and authority to establish a Turnpike Company, to be composed of them, the said Nicholas and David, Arthur Henly, John Lowry, Atto. and one other person, by them to be hereafter named, in behalf of the state of Georgia; and the above named persons are authorized to nominate five proper and fit persons, natives of the Cherokees, who, together with the white men aforesaid, are to constitute the company; which said company, when thus established, are hereby fully authorized by us, to lay out and open a road from the most suitable point on the Tennessee River, to be directed the nearest and best way to the highest point of navigation on the Tugolo River; which said road, when opened and established, shall continue and remain a free and public highway, unmolested by us, to the interest and benefit of the said company, and their successors, for the full term of twenty years, yet to come, after the same may be open and complete; after which time, said road, with all its advantages, shall be surrendered up, and reverted in, the said Cherokee nation. And the said company shall have leave, and are hereby authorized, to erect their public stands, or houses of entertainment, on said road, that is to say: one at each end, and one in the middle, or as nearly so as a good situation will permit: with leave also to cultivate one hundred acres of land at each end of the road, and fifty acres at the middle stand, with a privilege of a sufficiency of timber for the use and consumption of said stands. And the said Turnpike Company do hereby agree to pay the sum of one hundred and sixty dollars yearly to the Cherokee nation, for the aforesaid privilege, to commence after said road is opened and in complete operation. The said company are to have the benefit of one ferry on Tennessee river, and such other ferry or ferries as are necessary on said road; and, likewise, said company shall have the exclusive privilege of trading on said road during the aforesaid term of time.

In testimony of our full consent to all and singular the above named privileges and advantages, we have hereunto set our hands and affixed our seals, this eighth day of March, eighteen hundred and thirteen.

Outahelce, his x mark,	[L. S.]	Chulio,	[L. S.]
Naire, above, his x mark,	[L. S.]	Dick Justice,	[L. S.]
Theelagathahee, his x mark,	[L. S.]	Wausaway,	[L. S.]
The Raven, his x mark,	[L. S.]	Big Cabbin,	[L. S.]
Two Killers, his x mark,	[L. S.]	The Bark,	[L. S.]
Teeistiskee, his x mark,	[L. S.]	Nettle Carrier,	[L. S.]
John Boggs, his — mark,	[L. S.]	Seekeekee,	[L. S.]
Quotiquaskee, his — mark,	[L. S.]	John Walker,	[L. S.]
Currihee, Dick, his — mark,	[L. S.]	Dick Brown,	[L. S.]
Ooseekee, his — mark,	[L. S.]	Charles Hick,	[L. S.]
Toochalee,	[L. S.]		

Witnesses present:
> Wm. L. Lovely, assistant agent,
> William Smith,
> George Colville.
> James Carey,
> Richard Taylor,
> > Interpreters.

The foregoing agreement and grant was amicably negotiated and concluded in my presence.

> > Return J. Meigs.

I certify I believe the within to be a correct copy of the original.

> > Charles Hicks.

WASHINGTON CITY, *March 1, 1819.*

CHEROKEE AGENCY, *January 6, 1817.*

We, the undersigned Chiefs of the Cherokee nation, do hereby grant unto Nicholas Byers, Arthur H. Henly, and David Russell, proprietors of the Unicoy road to Georgia, the liberty of cultivating all the ground contained in the bend on the north side of Tennessee river, opposite and below Chota Old Town, together with the liberty to erect a grist mill on Four Mile creek, for the use and benefit of said road, and the Cherokees in the neighbourhood thereof; for them, the said Byers, Henly, and Russell, to have and to hold the above privileges during the term of lease of the Unicoy road, also obtained from the Cherokees, and sanctioned by the President of the United States.

Jan. 6, 1817.

In witness whereof, we hereunto affix our hands and seals, in presence of—

John McIntosh,	[L. S.]	The Gloss,	[L. S.]
Charles Hicks,	[L. S.]	John Walker,	[L. S.]
Path Killer,	[L. S.]	Path Killer, jr.	[L. S.]
Tuchalar,	[L. S.]	Going Snake.	[L. S.]

Witness:
> Return J. Meigs, United States agent.

The above instrument was executed in open Cherokee council, in my office, in January, 1817.

> > Return J. Meigs.

CHEROKEE AGENCY, *8th July, 1817.*

The use of the Unicoy road, so called, was for twenty years.

> > Return J. Meigs.

I certify I believe the within to be a correct copy of the original.

> > Ch. Hicks.

WASHINGTON CITY, *March 1, 1819.*

TREATY WITH THE KICKAPOO, 1 19.

July 30, 1819.

7 Stat., 200.
Proclamation, Jan.
13, 1821.

A treaty made and concluded at Edwardsville, in the State of Illinois, between Auguste Chouteau, and Benjamin Stephenson, Commissioners on the part and behalf of the United States of America, of the one part, and the undersigned principal Chiefs and Warriors of the Kickapoo Tribe of Indians, on the part and behalf of said Tribe, of the other part.

The tribe cede tracts of land.

ART. 1. The undersigned Chiefs and Warriors, for themselves and their said tribe, for, and in consideration of, the promises and stipulations hereinafter made, do hereby cede and relinquish to the United States for ever, all their right, interest, and title, of, in, and to, the following tracts of land, viz:

Land ceded.

All their land on the southeast side of the Wabash river, including the principal village in which their ancestors formerly resided, consisting of a large tract, to which they have had, from time immemorial, and now have, a just right; that they have never heretofore ceded, or otherwise disposed of, in any manner whatever.

Boundaries of other land ceded.

Also, all the land within the following boundaries, viz: Beginning on the Wabash river, at the upper point of their cession, made by the second article of their treaty at Vincennes, on the 9th December, 1809; running thence, northwestwardly, to the dividing line between the states of Illinois and Indiana; thence, along said line, to the Kankakee river; thence, with said river, to the Illinois river; thence, down the latter, to its mouth; thence, with a direct line, to the northwest corner of the Vincennes tract, as recognized in the treaty with the Piankeshaw tribe of Indians at Vincennes, on the 30th December, 1805; and thence, with the western and northern boundaries of the cessions heretofore made by the said Kickapoo tribe of Indians, to the beginning. Of which last described tract of land, the said Kickapoo tribe claim a large portion, by descent from their ancestors, and the balance by conquest from the Illinois nation, and uninterrupted possession for more than half a century.

Confirmation of former treaties, etc.

ART. 2. The said tribe hereby confirm all their former treaties with the United States, and relinquish to them all claim to every portion of their lands which may have been ceded by any other tribe or tribes, and all and every demand which they might have had, in consequence of the second article of the treaty made with the Pottawattamy nation of Indians at St. Mary's on the 2d October, 1818.

Protection of United States acknowledged.

ART. 3. The said tribe acknowledge themselves now to be, and promise to continue, under the protection of the United States of America, and of no other nation, power, or sovereign, whatever.

United States released from obligations.

ART. 4. The said tribe release the United States from all obligations imposed by any treaties heretofore made with them.

Annuity to Indians.

ART. 5. The United States, in lieu of all former stipulations, and in consideration of cessions of land heretofore made by the said tribe, promise to pay them, at their town on the waters of the Osage river, two thousand dollars in silver, annually, for fifteen successive years.

United States pay $3,000 worth of merchandise, and cede a tract of land in Missouri, etc.

ART. 6. In consideration of the cession made by the aforesaid tribe, in the first article of this treaty, the United States, in addition to three thousand dollars worth of merchandise this day paid to the said tribe, hereby cede to them, and their heirs for ever, a certain tract of land lying in the territory of Missouri, and included within the following boundaries, viz: Beginning at the confluence of the rivers Pommes de Terre and Osage; thence, up said river Pommes de Terre, to the dividing ridge which separates the waters of Osage and White rivers; thence, with said ridge, and westwardly, to the Osage line; thence due north with said line, to Nerve creek; thence, down the same, to a point due south of the mouth of White Clay, or Richard Creek; thence, north, to the Osage river; thence, down said river, to the beginning: *Provided, nevertheless,* That the said tribe shall never sell the said land without the consent of the President of the United States.

ART. 7. The United States promise to guaranty to the said tribe the peaceable possession of the tract of land hereby ceded to them, and to restrain and prevent all white persons from hunting, settling, or otherwise intruding upon it. But any citizen or citizens of the United States, being lawfully authorized for that purpose, shall be permitted to pass and repass through the said tract, and to navigate the waters thereof, without any hindrance, toll, or exaction, from the said tribe.

ART. 8. For the purpose of facilitating the removal of the said tribe to the tract of land hereby ceded to them, the United States will furnish them with two boats, well manned, to transport their property, from any point they may designate on the Illinois river, and some judicious citizen shall be selected to accompany them, in their passage through the white settlements, to their intended residence.

ART. 9. The United States will take the said Kickapoo tribe under their care and patronage, and will afford them protection against all persons whatever, provided they conform to the laws of the United States, and refrain from making war, or giving any insult or offence to any other Indian tribe, or to any foreign nation, without first having obtained the approbation and consent of the United States.

ART. 10. The said tribe, in addition to their above described cessions, do hereby cede and relinquish to the United States, generally, and without reservation, all other tracts of land to which they have any right or title on the left side of the Illinois and Mississippi rivers.

In testimony whereof, the commissioners aforesaid, and the undersigned chiefs and warriors as aforesaid, have hereunto subscribed their names and affixed their seals.

Done at Edwardsville, in the State of Illinois, this thirtieth day of July, in the year of our Lord one thousand eight hundred and nineteen, and of the independence of the United States the forty-fourth.

Aug. Chouteau,	[L. S.]	Anckoaw, his x mark,	[L. S.]
Ben. Stephenson,	[L. S.]	Namattsheekeeaw, his x mark,	[L. S.]
Pemoatam, his x mark,	[L. S.]	Sawkeema, his x mark,	[L. S.]
Little Thunder, by the White Elk,		Wawpeepoaw, his x mark,	[L. S.]
his x mark,	[L. S.]	Paneessa, his x mark,	[L. S.]
Keetatta, his x mark,	[L. S.]	Pawkonasheeno, his x mark,	[L. S.]
Tecko, his x mark,	[L. S.]	Ankwiskkaw, his x mark,	[L. S.]
Weesoetee, his x mark,	[L. S.]	Shekoan, his x mark,	[L. S.]
Meekasaw, his x mark,	[L. S.]	Pasheeto, his x mark,	[L. S.]
Neekawnakoa, his x mark,	[L. S.]	Wawpackeshaw, his x mark,	[L. S.]
Pacan, by Petshekosheek, his x		Awwatshee, his x mark,	[L. S.]
mark,	[L. S.]	Mawntoho, his x mark,	[L. S.]
Wawpeekonyaw, his x mark,	[L. S.]	Keetshay, his x mark,	[L. S.]
Peckoneea, his x mark,	[L. S.]		

Signed, sealed, and delivered, in presence of the following witnesses:

Pascal Cerre, secretary to the commissioners,
Jacques Mette, interpreter,
Ninian Edwards,
John Dew,
Thornton Peeples,
Tellery Merrick,
Dan. D. Smith,
Isaac A. Douglass,
Edmund Randle,
Palemon H. Wenchester,
N. Buckmaster,
Thomas Harcens,
Henry Head,
John Wilson,
Joseph Doer,

Elbert Perry,
Joseph Remington,
J. L. Barton,
David Roach,
William Head,
John Lee Williams,
Wm. W. Hickman,
Jacob Prickett,
James Watt,
Joseph B. Lewis,
Jona H. Pugh,
William P. McKee,
Stephen Johnson,
Nathan Clampet,
Reuben Hopkins,
Joseph Newman.

TREATY WITH THE KICKAPOO, 1819.

Aug. 30, 1819.

7 Stat., 202.
Proclamation, May
10, 1820.

A treaty made and concluded by Benjamin Parke, a commissioner on the part of the United States of America, of the one part, and the Chiefs, Warriors, and Head Men, of the tribe of Kickapoos of the Vermilion, of the other part.

Kickapoos cede all their lands on the Wabash, etc.

ART. 1. The Chiefs, Warriors, and Head Men, of the said tribe, agree to cede, and hereby relinquish, to the United States, all the lands which the said tribe has heretofore possessed, or which they may rightfully claim, on the Wabash river, or any of its waters.

Boundaries of the cession.

ART. 2. And to the end that the United States may be enabled to fix with the other Indian tribes a boundary between their respective claims, the Chiefs, Warriors, and Head Men, of the said tribe, do hereby declare, that their rightful claim is as follows, viz: beginning at the northwest corner of the Vincennes tract; thence, westwardly, by the boundary established by treaty with the Piankeshaws, on the thirtieth day of December, eighteen hundred and five, to the dividing ridge between the waters of the Embarras and the Little Wabash; thence, by the said ridge, to the source of the Vermilion river; thence, by the same ridge, to the head of Pine creek; thence, by the said creek, to the Wabash river; thence, by the said river, to the mouth of the Vermilion river, and thence by the Vermilion, and the boundary heretofore established, to the place of beginning.

Kickapoos relinquish annuity of $1,000.

ART. 3. The said Chiefs, Warriors, and Head Men, of the said tribe, agree to relinquish, and they do hereby exonerate and discharge the United States from, the annuity of one thousand dollars, to which they are now entitled.

Consideration for cession.

In consideration whereof, and of the cession hereby made, the United States agree to pay the said tribe two thousand dollars annually, in specie, for ten years; which, together with three thousand dollars now delivered, is to be considered a full compensation for the cession hereby made, as also of all annuities, or other claims, of the said tribe against the United States, by virtue of any treaty with the said United States.

Annuity, where to be paid.

ART. 4. As the said tribe contemplate removing from the country they now occupy, the annuity herein provided for shall be paid at such place as may be hereinafter agreed upon between the United States and said tribe.

Treaty binding when ratified.

ART. 5. This treaty, after the same shall be ratified by the President and Senate of the United States, shall be binding on the contracting parties.

In testimony whereof, the said Benjamin Parke, commissioner as aforesaid, and the chiefs, warriors, and head men, of the said tribe, have hereunto set their hands, at fort Harrison, the thirtieth day of August, in the year eighteen hundred and nineteen.

B. Parke,	La Ferine, his x mark,
Wagohaw, his x mark,	Macatewaket, his x mark,
Tecumcena, his x mark,	Pelecheah, his x mark,
Kaahna, his x mark,	Kechemaquaw, his x mark,
Macacanaw, his x mark,	Pacakinqua, his x mark.

In the presence of—

John Law, secretary to the commissioner,	James C. Turner,
William Prince, Indian agent,	Samuel L. Richardson,
William Markle,	Michael Brouillet, United States interpreter.
Andrew Brooks,	
Pierre Laplante,	

TREATY WITH THE CHIPPEWA, 1819.

Articles of a treaty made and concluded at Saginaw, in the Territory of Michigan, between the United States of America, by their Commissioner, Lewis Cass, and the Chippewa nation of Indians.

Sept. 24, 1819.

7 Stat., 203.
Proclamation, Mar. 25, 1820.

ART. 1. The Chippewa nation of Indians, in consideration of the stipulations herein made on the part of the United States, do hereby, forever, cede to the United States the land comprehended within the following lines and boundaries: Beginning at a point in the present Indian boundary line, which runs due north from the mouth of the great Auglaize river, six miles south of the place where the base line, so called, intersects the same; thence, west, sixty miles; thence, in a direct line, to the head of Thunder Bay River; thence, down the same, following the courses thereof, to the mouth; thence, northeast, to the boundary line between the United States and the British Province of Upper Canada; thence, with the same, to the line established by the treaty of Detroit, in the year one thousand eight hundred and seven; thence, with the said line, to the place of beginning.

The Chippewas cede land to United States.

Bounds of the cession.

ART. 2. From the cession aforesaid the following tracts of land shall be reserved, for the use of the Chippewa nation of Indians:

Reservations from the cession.

One tract, of eight thousand acres, on the east side of the river Au Sable, near where the Indians now live.

One tract, of two thousand acres, on the river Mesagwisk.

One tract, of six thousand acres, on the north side of the river Kawkawling, at the Indian village.

One tract, of five thousand seven hundred and sixty acres, upon the Flint river, to include Reaum's village, and a place called Kishkawbawee.

One tract, of eight thousand acres, on the head of the river Huron, which empties into the Saginaw river, at the village of Otusson.

One island in the Saginaw Bay.

One tract, of two thousand acres, where Nabobask formerly lived.

One tract, of one thousand acres, near the island in the Saginaw river.

One tract, of six hundred and forty acres, at the bend of the river Huron, which empties into the Saginaw river.

One tract, of two thousand acres, at the mouth of Point Augrais river.

One tract, of one thousand acres, on the river Huron, at Menoequet's village.

One tract, of ten thousand acres, on the Shawassee river, at a place called the Big Rock.

One tract, of three thousand acres, on the Shawassee river, at Ketchewaundaugenink.

One tract, of six thousand acres, at the Little Forks on the Tetabawasink river.

One tract, of six thousand acres, at the Black Bird's town, on the Tetabawasink river.

One tract, of forty thousand acres, on the west side of the Saginaw river, to be hereafter located.

ART. 3. There shall be reserved, for the use of each of the persons hereinafter mentioned and their heirs, which persons are all Indians by descent, the following tracts of land:

Reservations for persons named.

For the use of John Riley, the son of Menawcumegoqua, a Chippewa woman, six hundred and forty acres of land, beginning at the head of the first marsh above the mouth of the Saginaw river, on the east side thereof.

For the use of Peter Riley, the son of Menawcumegoqua, a Chippewa woman, six hundred and forty acres of land, beginning above and adjoining the apple trees on the west side of the Saginaw river, and running up the same for quantity.

For the use of James Riley, the son of Menawcumegoqua, a Chippewa woman, six hundred and forty acres, beginning on the east side of the Saginaw river, nearly opposite to Campeau's trading house, and running up the river for quantity.

For the use of Kawkawiskou, or the Crow, a Chippewa chief, six hundred and forty acres of land, on the east side of the Saginaw river, at a place called Menitegow, and to include, in the said six hundred and forty acres, the island opposite to the said place.

For the use of Nowokeshik, Metawanene, Mokitchenoqua, Nondashemau, Petabonaqua, Messawwakut, Checbalk, Kitchegeequa, Sagosequa, Annoketoqua, and Tawcumegoqua, each, six hundred and forty acres of land, to be located at and near the grand traverse of the Flint river, in such manner as the President of the United States may direct.

For the use of the children of Bokowtonden, six hundred and forty acres, on the Kawkawling river.

Payment to Chippewas. ART. 4. In consideration of the cession aforesaid, the United States agree to pay to the Chippewa nation of Indians, annually, for ever, the sum of one thousand dollars in silver; and do also agree that all annuities due by any former treaty to the said tribe, shall be hereafter paid in silver.

Right of hunting and making sugar on lands ceded, granted. ART. 5. The stipulation contained in the treaty of Greenville, relative to the right of the Indians to hunt upon the land ceded, while it continues the property of the United States, shall apply to this treaty; and the Indians shall, for the same term, enjoy the privilege of making sugar upon the same land, committing no unnecessary waste upon the trees.

United States to pay for Indian improvements. ART. 6. The United States agree to pay to the Indians the value of any improvements which they may be obliged to abandon, in consequence of the lines established by this treaty, and which improvements add real value to the land.

United States reserve right to make roads, ART. 7. The United States reserve to the proper authority the right to make roads through any part of the land reserved by this treaty.

United States to furnish a blacksmith, etc. ART. 8. The United States engage to provide and support a blacksmith for the Indians, at Saginaw, so long as the President of the United States may think proper, and to furnish the Chippewa Indians with such farming utensils and cattle, and to employ such persons to aid them in their agriculture, as the President may deem expedient.

Treaty to be obligatory when ratified. ART. 9. This treaty shall take effect, and be obligatory on the contracting parties, so soon as the same shall be ratified by the President of the United States, by and with the advice and consent of the Senate thereof.

In testimony whereof, the said Lewis Cass, commissioner as aforesaid, and the chiefs and warriors of the Chippewa nation of Indians, have hereunto set their hands, at Saginaw, in the territory of Michigan, this twenty-fourth day of September, in the year of our Lord one thousand eight hundred and nineteen.

Lewis Cass,	Anueemaycounbeeme, his x mark,
Pakenosega, his x mark,	Onewequa, his x mark,
Kekenutchega, his x mark,	Nayokeeman, his x mark,
Chimokemow, his x mark,	Peshquescum, his x mark,
Kekenutchegun, his x mark,	Muckcumcinau, his x mark,
Pashkobwis, his x mark,	Kitcheenoting, his x mark,
Muskobenense, his x mark,	Waubeekeenew, his x mark,
Waubonoosa, his x mark,	Pashkeekou, his x mark,
Wausaquanai, his x mark,	Mayto, his x mark,
Minequet, his x mark,	Sheemaugua, his x mark,
Otauson, his x mark,	Kauguest, his x mark,
Tussegua, his x mark,	Kitsheematush, his x mark,
Mixabee, his x mark,	Aneuwayba, his x mark,
Kitchewawashen, his x mark,	Walkcaykeejugo, his x mark,
Neebeenaquin, his x mark,	Autowaynabee, his x mark,

Nawgonissee, his x mark,
Owenisham, his x mark,
Wauweeyatam, his x mark,
Mooksonga, his x mark,
Noukonwabe, his x mark,
Shingwalk, his x mark,
Shingwalk, jun. his x mark,
Wawaubequak, his x mark,
Meewayson, his x mark,
Wepecumgegut, his x mark,
Markkenwuwbe, his x mark,
Fonegawne, his x mark,
Nemetetowwa, his x mark,
Kishkaukou, his x mark,
Peenaysee, his x mark,
Ogemaunkeketo, his x mark,
Reaume, his x mark,
Nowkeshuc, his x mark,
Mixmunitou, his x mark,
Wassau, his x mark,
Keneobe, his x mark,
Moksauba, his x mark,
Mutchwetau, his x mark,
Nuwagon, his x mark,
Okumanpinase, his x mark,
Meckseonne, his x mark,
Paupemiskobe, his x mark,
Kogkakeshik, his x mark,
Wauwassack, his x mark,
Misheneanonquet, his x mark,
Okemans, his x mark,
Nimeke, his x mark,
Maneleugobwawaa, his x mark,
Puckwash, his x mark,
Waseneso, his x mark,
Montons, his x mark,
Kennewobe, his x mark,
Shawshauwenaubais, his x mark,
Okooyousinse, his x mark,
Ondottowaugane, his x mark,
Amickoneena, nis x mark,
Kitcheonundeeyo, his x mark,
Saugassauway, his x mark,

Okeemanpeenaysee, his x mark,
Minggeeseetay, his x mark,
Waubishcan, his x mark,
Peaypaymanshee, his x mark,
Ocanauck, his x mark,
Ogeebouinse, his x mark,
Paymeenoting, his x mark,
Naynooautienishkoan, his x mark,
Kaujagonaygee, his x mark,
Mayneeseno, his x mark,
Kakagouryan, his x mark,
Kitchmokooman, his x mark,
Singgok, his x mark,
Maytwayaushing, his x mark,
Saguhosh, his x mark,
Saybo, his x mark,
Obwole, his x mark,
Aguagonabe, his x mark,
Sigonak, his x mark,
Kokoosh, his x mark,
Pemaw, his x mark,
Kawotoktame, his x mark,
Sabo, his x mark,
Kewageone, his x mark,
Metewa, his x mark,
Kawgeshequm, his x mark,
Keyacum, his x mark,
Atowagesek, his x mark,
Mawmawkens, his x mark,
Mamawsecuta, his x mark,
Penaysewaykesek, his x mark,
Kewaytinam, his x mark,
Sepewan, his x mark,
Shashebak, his x mark,
Shaconk, his x mark,
Mesnakrea, his x mark,
Paymusawtom, his x mark,
Endus, his x mark,
Aushetayawnekusa, his x mark,
Wawapenishik, his x mark,
Omikou, his x mark,
Leroy, his x mark.

Witnesses at signing:

John L. Leib, secretary,
D. G. Whitney, assistant secretary,
C. L. Cass, captain Third Infantry,
R. A. Forsyth, jun. acting commissioner,
Chester Root, captain U. S. Artillery,
John Peacock, lieutenant Third U. S. Infantry,
G. Godfroy, sub agent,
W. Knaggs, sub agent.
William Tucky,
Lewis Beufort,
John Hurson,
    Sworn interpreters.

James V. S. Riley,
B. Campau,
John Hill, army contractor,
J. Whipple,
Henry I. Hunt,
William Keith,
A. E. Lacock, M. S. K.
Richard Smyth,
Louis Dequindre,
B. Head,
John Smyth,
Conrad Ten Eyck.

TREATY WITH THE CHIPPEWA, 1820.

Articles of a treaty, made and concluded at the Sault de St. Marie, in the Territory of Michigan, between the United States, by their Commissioner Lewis Cass, and the Chippeway tribe of Indians.

June 16, 1820.

7 Stat., 206.
Proclamation, Mar. 2, 1821.

ART. 1. The Chippeway tribe of Indians cede to the United States the following tract of land: Beginning at the Big Rock, in the river St. Mary's, on the boundary line between the United States and the British Province of Upper Canada; and, running thence, down the said river, with the middle thereof, to the Little Rapid; and, from those

Cession by the Chippewas.

points, running back from the said river, so as to include sixteen square miles of land.

Receipt of goods acknowledged.

ART. 2. The Chippeway tribe of Indians acknowledge to have received a quantity of goods in full satisfaction of the preceding cession.

Perpetual right of fishing at the falls of St. Mary's secured to Indians.

ART. 3. The United States will secure to the Indians a perpetual right of fishing at the falls of St. Mary's, and also a place of encampment upon the tract hereby ceded, convenient to the fishing ground, which place shall not interfere with the defences of any military work which may be erected, nor with any private rights.

Treaty binding when ratified.

ART. 4. This treaty, after the same shall be ratified by the President of the United States, by and with the advice and consent of the Senate thereof, shall be obligatory on the contracting parties.

In witness whereof, the said Lewis Cass, commissioner as aforesaid, and the chiefs and warriors of the said Chippeway tribe of Indians, have hereunto set their hands, at the place aforesaid, this sixteenth day of June, in the year of our Lord one thousand eight hundred and twenty.

Lewis Cass,	Nabinois, his x mark,
Shingaubaywassin, his x mark,	Macadaywacwet, his x mark,
Kegeash, his x mark,	Shaiwabekaton, his x mark,
Sagishewayoson, his x mark,	Netaway, his x mark,
Wayishkey, his x mark,	Kaibayway, his x mark,
Nenowaiskam, his x mark,	Nawoquesequm, his x mark,
Wasawaton, his x mark,	Tawabit, his x mark,
Wemiguenacwanay, his x mark,	Augustin Bart, his x mark.

Witnesses present:

R. A. Forsyth, secretary,	Henry R. Schoolcraft, mineralogist to the expedition,
Alex. Wolcott, jr., Indian agent, Chicago,	
D. B. Douglass, captain U. S. Engineers,	James Duane Doty,
Æneas Mackay, lieutenant corps artillery,	Charles C. Trowbridge,
	Alex. R. Chase,
John J. Pearce, lieutenant artillery,	James Ryley, sworn interpreter.

TREATY WITH THE OTTAWA AND CHIPPEWA, 1820.

July 6, 1820.

7 Stat., 207.
Proclamation, Mar. 8, 1821.

Articles of a treaty, made and concluded at L'Arbre Croche and Michilimackinac, in the territory of Michigan, between the United States of America, by their Commissioner Lewis Cass, and the Ottawa and Chippewa nations of Indians.

St. Martin Islands ceded to the United States.

ART. 1. The Ottawa and Chippewa nations of Indians cede to the United States the Saint Martin Islands in Lake Huron, containing plaster of Paris, and to be located under the direction of the United States.

Goods in full satisfaction to the Indians.

ART. 2. The Ottawa and Chippewa nations of Indians acknowledge to have this day received a quantity of goods in full satisfaction of the above cession.

Treaty binding when ratified.

ART. 3. This treaty shall be obligatory on the contracting parties after the same shall be ratified by the President of the United States, by and with the advice and consent of the Senate thereof.

In testimony whereof, the said Lewis Cass, commissioner as aforesaid, and the chiefs and warriors of the Ottawa and Chippewa nations of Indians, have hereunto set their hands, at Michilimackinac and L'Arbre Croche, in the territory of Michigan, this 6th day of July, in the year of our Lord one thousand eight hundred and twenty.

Lewis Cass.	Chemogueman, or Big Knife, his x mark,
Skahjenini, his x mark,	Misesonguay, his x mark,
Pahquesegun, or Smoking Weed, his x mark,	Papametaby, his x mark,
	Ceitawa, his x mark

Shawanoe, his x mark,
Oninjuega, or Wing, Ottawa chief, his x mark,
Cuddimalmese, or Black Hawk, Ottawa chief, his mark,
Dionesau, his x mark,
Kojenoikoose, or Long, his x mark, Ottawa chiefs.
Kenojekum, or Pike, his x mark,

Cachetokee, his x mark,
Gimoewon, or Rain, his x mark,
Chiboisquisegun, or Big Gun, his x mark,
Skubinesse, or Red Bird, his x mark,
Weashe, his x mark,
Nebaguam, his x mark.
Ainse, his x mark,
Shaganash, or Englishman, his x mark, Chippewa chiefs.

Witnesses present:

Jed. Morse, D. D.
Gilbert Knapp,
Richard C. Morse,

H. G. Gravenant, sworn interpreter,
George Boyd, Indian agent.

TREATY WITH THE KICKAPOO, 1820.

A treaty made and concluded by, and between, Auguste Chouteau and Benjamin Stephenson, Commissioners of the United States of America, on the part and behalf of the said States, of the one part, and the undersigned Chiefs and Warriors, of the Kickapoo tribe of Indians, on the part and behalf of their said Nation, of the other part, the same being supplementary to, and amendatory of, the Treaty made and concluded at Edwardsville, on the 30th July, 1819, between the United States and the said Kickapoo nation.

July 19, 1820.

7 Stat., 208.
Proclamation, Jan. 13, 1821.

ART. 1. It is agreed, between the United States and the Kickapoo tribe of Indians, that the sixth article of the treaty, to which this is supplementary, shall be, and the same is hereby, altered and amended, so as to read as follows, viz:

Sixth article of treaty of Edwardsville altered and amended.

In consideration of, and exchange for, the cession made by the aforesaid tribe, in the first article of this treaty, the United States, in addition to three thousand dollars worth of merchandise, this day paid to the said tribe, hereby cede to the said tribe, to be by them possessed in like manner as the lands, ceded by the first article of this treaty by them to the United States, were possessed, a certain tract of land in the territory of Missiouri, and included within the following boundaries, viz: Beginning at the confluence of the rivers Pommes de Terre and Osage; thence, up said river Pommes de Terre, to the dividing ridge which separates the waters of Osage and White rivers; thence, with said ridge, and westwardly, to the Osage line; thence, due north with said line, to Nerve creek; thence, down the same, to a point due south of the mouth of White Clay, or Richard creek; thence, north, to the Osage river; thence, down said river, to the beginning.

Substitute for said sixth article.

In testimony whereof, the commissioners aforesaid, and the undersigned chiefs and warriors aforesaid, have hereunto subscribed their names and affixed their seals.

Done at St. Louis, in the territory of Missouri, the 19th of July, in the year of our Lord one thousand eight hundred and twenty, and of the independence of the United States the forty-fifth.

Aug. Chouteau,	[L. S.]	Paysheesaw, his x mark,	[L. S.]
Ben. Stephenson,	[L. S.]	Wawpee Konyaw, his x mark,	[L. S.]
Pemoatam, his x mark,	[L. S.]	Auckoaw, his x mark,	[L. S.]
Quitattay, his x mark,	[L. S.]	Namatchee, his x mark,	[L. S.]
Pawpaussapeeawaw, his x mark,	[L. S.]	Wakykapa, his x mark,	[L. S.]
Waysheeown, his x mark,	[L. S.]	Keechkakoy, his x mark,	[L. S.]
Paywaneckway, his x mark,	[L. S.]	Saw Koy, his x mark,	[L. S.]
Keeawnaw, his x mark,	[L. S.]	Namatt Shee Keeaw, his x mark,	[L. S.]
Shee Sheep, his x mark,	[L. S.]	Keesasway, his x mark,	[L. S.]
Keesawonaw, his x mark,	[L. S.]	Pemoatam Oseemin, his x mark.	[L. S.]
Mawkwawteppa, his x mark,	[L. S.]	Wawpeepoaw, his x mark,	[L. S.]
Waywetsheecawpaw, his x mark,	[L. S.]	Mentowta, his x mark,	[L. S.]
Keeotay, his x mark,	[L. S.]	Pawpaw Keemene, his x mark,	[L. S.]
Wawponashee, his x mark,	[L. S.]	Sheekeemakow, his x mark,	[L. S.]
Weepokothee, his x mark,	[L. S.]	Pawkonesheeno, his x mark,	[L. S.]

Signed, sealed, and delivered, in presence of the following witnesses:

Pascal Cerre, secretary to the commissioners,
Jacques Mette, interpreter,
Jn. Ruland, sub-agent,
Th. Estes,
Geo. Y. Bright,
J. Brand,
Mal. Detandebarat,
Gabriel G. Chouteau,
Henry P. Chouteau,

Felix St. Vrain,
G. P. Cerre,
F. Simon,
Peter Didier,
T. Goddard,
Gl. Paul,
R. Paul, colonel Mi. Mia.
Tho. T. Loury,
T. B. Mathurin,
B. Provinchere.

TREATY WITH THE WEA, 1820.

Aug. 11, 1820.

*7 Stat., 209.
Proclamation, Jan. 8, 1821.*

A treaty made and concluded by Benjamin Parke, a Commissioner for that purpose on the part of the United States, of the one part; and the Chiefs, Warriors, and Head Men, of the Wea tribe of Indians, of the other part.

Cession by the Weas.

ART. 1. The Chiefs, Warriors, and Head Men, of the said Tribe, agree to cede, and they do hereby cede and relinquish, to the United States all the lands reserved by the second article of the Treaty between the United States and the said Tribe, concluded at Saint Mary's, on the second day of October, eighteen hundred and eighteen.

$5,000 in money and goods, in full satisfaction to the tribe.

ART. 2. The sum of five thousand dollars, in money and goods, which is now paid and delivered by the United States, the receipt whereof the Chiefs, Warriors, and Head Men, of the said Tribe, do hereby acknowledge, is considered by the parties a full compensation for the cession and relinquishment above mentioned.

Annuity to be hereafter paid at Kaskaskia.

ART. 3. As it is contemplated by the said Tribe, to remove from the Wabash, it is agreed, that the annuity secured to the Weas, by the Treaty of Saint Mary's, above mentioned, shall hereafter be paid to them at Kaskaskia, in the state of Illinois.

Treaty binding when ratified.

ART. 4. This Treaty, as soon as it is ratified by the President and Senate of the United States, to be binding on the contracting parties.

In testimony whereof, the said Benjamin Parke, commissioner as aforesaid, and the said chiefs, warriors, and head men, of the said tribe, have hereunto set their hands, at Vincennes, this eleventh day of August, eighteen hundred and twenty.

B. Parke,
Maquakononga, or Negro Legs, his x mark,
Chequait, or Little Eyes, his x mark,
Me Tacoshia, the Frenchman, his x mark,
Gu Ta Shemi Tai, or Thunder, his x mark,
Kenacosah Ta, or Long Body, his x mark,
Wapou Kean, or Swan, his x mark,
Laushepate Ta, or Two Teeth, his x mark,
Meahanet, the Lean Man, his x mark,
Chekolcah, the Dipper, his x mark,

Ceholesehaquah, Bullet Mould, his x mark,
Samaquah, Yellow Beaver, his x mark,
Chasahwaha, or rifle, his x mark,
Go To paquah, or the Lone Tree, his x mark,
Chikousah, or Mink, his x mark,
Teche Pa Low, or Shirt, his x mark,
Pa Lon Swa, Francis.

In presence of—

John Law, secretary to the commission,
William Prince, Indian agent,
Nathl. Ewing,
W. E. Breading,

E. Boudinot,
Pr. Laplante,
Michael Brouillet, United States interpreter.

TREATY WITH THE KICKAPOO OF THE VERMILION 1820.

Articles of a convention made and concluded, between Benjamin Parke, a Commissioner on the part of the United States, for that purpose, of the one part, and the Chiefs, Warriors, and Head Men, of the Tribe of Kickapoos of the Vermilion, of the other part.

Sept. 5, 1820.

7 Stat., 210.
Proclamation, Jan. 8, 1821.

ART. 1. It is agreed, that the annuity secured to the said Tribe, by the Treaty of the thirtieth of August, eighteen hundred and nineteen, shall hereafter be paid to the said Tribe at Kaskaskias, in the state of Illinois.

Annuity to be hereafter paid at Kaskaskia.

ART. 2. As the said Tribe are now about leaving their settlements on the Wabash, and have desired some assistance to enable them to remove, the said Benjamin Parke, on behalf of the United States, has paid and advanced to the said Tribe, two thousand dollars, the receipt whereof is hereby acknowledged; which said sum of two thousand dollars, is to be considered as an equivalent, in full, for the annuity due the said Tribe, by virtue of the aforesaid Treaty, for the year eighteen hundred and twenty-one.

Two thousand dollars paid to enable them to remove; in full for annuity of 1821.

In testimony whereof, the said Benjamin Parke, commissioner as aforesaid, and the chiefs, warriors, and head men, of the said tribe, have hereunto set their hands, at Vincennes, the fifth day of September, eighteen hundred and twenty.

B. Parke,
Wagohaw, his x mark,
Tecumsena, his x mark,
Pelecheah, his x mark,

Kechemaqua, his x mark,
Paca Rinqua, her x mark,
Katewah, his x mark,
Nasa Reah, his x mark.

In presence of—

William Prince, Indian agent,
Samuel Jacobs,
R. S. Reynolds,

George R. C. Sullivan, Vincennes postmaster,
Toussaint Dubois,
Michael Brouillet, interpreter.

TREATY WITH THE CHOCTAW, 1820.

A treaty of friendship, limits, and accommodation, between the United States of America and the Choctaw nation of Indians, begun and concluded at the Treaty Ground, in said nation, near Doak's Stand, on the Natchez Road.

Oct. 18, 1820.

7 Stat., 210.
Proclamation, Jan. 8, 1821.

PREAMBLE.

WHEREAS it is an important object with the President of the United States, to promote the civilization of the Choctaw Indians, by the establishment of schools amongst them; and to perpetuate them as a nation, by exchanging, for a small part of their land here, a country beyond the Mississippi River, where all, who live by hunting and will not work, may be collected and settled together.—And whereas it is desirable to the state of Mississippi, to obtain a small part of the land belonging to said nation; for the mutual accommodation of the parties, and for securing the happiness and protection of the whole Choctaw nation, as well as preserving that harmony and friendship which so happily subsists between them and the United States, James Monroe, President of the United States of America, by Andrew Jackson, of the State of Tennessee, Major General in the Army of the United States, and General Thomas Hinds, of the State of Mississippi, Commissioners Plenipotentiary of the United States, on the one part, and the Mingoes, Head Men, and Warriors, of the Choctaw nation, in full Council assembled, on the other part, have freely and voluntarily entered into the following articles, viz:

Objects of the treaty.

Cession of lands by the Choctaws.

ART. 1. To enable the President of the United States to carry into effect the above grand and humane objects, the Mingoes, Head Men, and Warriors, of the Choctaw nation, in full council assembled, in behalf of themselves and the said nation, do, by these presents, cede to the United States of America, all the land lying and being within the boundaries following, to wit:—Beginning on the Choctaw boundary, East of Pearl River, at a point due South of the White Oak spring, on the old Indian path; thence north to said spring; thence northwardly to a black oak, standing on the Natchez road, about forty poles eastwardly from Doake's fence, marked A. J. and blazed, with two large pines and a black oak standing near thereto, and marked as pointers; thence a straight line to the head of Black Creek, or Bouge Loosa; thence down Black Creek or Bouge Loosa to a small Lake; thence a direct course, so as to strike the Mississippi one mile below the mouth of the Arkansas River; thence down the Mississippi to our boundary; thence around and along the same to the beginning.

Bounds of the cession.

United States cede a tract of country west of the Mississippi.

ART. 2. For and in consideration of the foregoing cession, on the part of the Choctaw nation, and in part satisfaction for the same, the Commissioners of the United States, in behalf of said States, do hereby cede to said nation, a tract of country west of the Mississippi River, situate between the Arkansas and Red River, and bounded as follows:— Beginning on the Arkansas River, where the lower boundary line of the Cherokees strikes the same; thence up the Arkansas to the Canadian Fork, and up the same to its source; thence due South to the Red River; thence down Red River, three miles below the mouth of Little River, which empties itself into Red River on the north side; thence a direct line to the beginning.

Boundaries.

Commissioners to ascertain the boundaries.

ART. 3. To prevent any dispute upon the subject of the boundaries mentioned in the 1st and 2d articles, it is hereby stipulated between the parties, that the same shall be ascertained and distinctly marked by a Commissioner, or Commissioners, to be appointed by the United States, accompanied by such person as the Choctaw nation may select; said nation having thirty days previous notice of the time and place at which the operation will commence. The person so chosen by the Choctaws, shall act as a pilot or guide, for which the United States will pay him two dollars per day, whilst actually engaged in the performance of that duty.

A Choctaw guile at $2 per day.

Boundaries east of the Mississippi to remain, until, etc.

ART. 4. The boundaries hereby established between the Choctaw Indians and the United States, on this side of the Mississippi river, shall remain without alteration until the period at which said nation shall become so civilized and enlightened as to be made citizens of the United States, and Congress shall lay off a limited parcel of land for the benefit of each family or individual in the nation.

A blanket, kettle, etc., to each warrior removing.

ART. 5. For the purpose of aiding and assisting the poor Indians, who wish to remove to the country hereby ceded on the part of the United States, and to enable them to do well and support their families, the Commissioners of the United States engage, in behalf of said States, to give to each warrior a blanket, kettle, rifle gun, bullet moulds and nippers, and ammunition sufficient for hunting and defence, for one year. Said warrior shall also be supplied with corn to support him and his family, for the same period, and whilst traveling to the country above ceded to the Choctaw nation.

An agent for the Choctaws, etc.

A blacksmith.

ART. 6. The Commissioners of the United States further covenant and agree, on the part of said States, that an agent shall be appointed, in due time, for the benefit of the Choctaw Indians who may be permanently settled in the country ceded to them beyond the Mississippi river, and, at a convenient period, a factor shall be sent there with goods, to supply their wants. A Blacksmith shall also be settled amongst them, at a point most convenient to the population; and a faithful person appointed, whose duty it shall be to use every reasonable exertion to collect all the wandering Indians belonging to the Choctaw nation, upon the land hereby provided for their permanent settlement.

ART. 7. Out of the lands ceded by the Choctaw nation to the United States, the Commissioners aforesaid, in behalf of said States, further covenant and agree, that fifty-four sections of one mile square shall be laid out in good land, by the President of the United States, and sold, for the purpose of raising a fund, to be applied to the support of the Choctaw schools, on both sides of the Mississippi river. Three-fourths of said fund shall be appropriated for the benefit of the schools here; and the remaining fourth for the establishment of one or more beyond the Mississippi; the whole to be placed in the hands of the President of the United States, and to be applied by him, expressly and exclusively, to this valuable object. *Land to be sold for support of Choctaw schools.*

ART. 8. To remove any discontent which may have arisen in the Choctaw Nation, in consequence of six thousand dollars of their annuity having been appropriated annually, for sixteen years, by some of the chiefs, for the support of their schools, the Commissioners of the United States oblige themselves, on the part of said States, to set apart an additional tract of good land, for raising a fund equal to that given by the said chiefs, so that the whole of the annuity may remain in the nation, and be divided amongst them. And in order that exact justice may be done to the poor and distressed of said nation, it shall be the duty of the agent to see that the wants of every deaf, dumb, blind, and distressed, Indian, shall be first supplied out of said annuity, and the balance equally distributed amongst every individual of said nation. *An additional tract of land for raising a fund for the nation, etc.*

ART. 9. All those who have separate settlements, and fall within the limits of the land ceded by the Choctaw nation to the United States, and who desire to remain where they now reside, shall be secured in a tract or parcel of land one mile square, to include their improvements. Any one who prefers removing, if he does so within one year from the date of this treaty, shall be paid their full value, to be ascertained by two persons, to be appointed by the President of the United States. *Provision for Indians who remain, etc.*

ART. 10. As there are some who have valuable buildings on the roads and elsewhere upon the lands hereby ceded, should they remove, it is further agreed by the aforesaid Commissioners, in behalf of the United States, that the inconvenience of doing so shall be considered, and such allowance made as will amount to an equivalent. For this purpose, there shall be paid to the Mingo, Puckshenubbee, five hundred dollars; to Harrison, two hundred dollars; to Captain Cobb, two hundred dollars; to William Hays, two hundred dollars; to O'Gleno, two hundred dollars; and to all others who have comfortable houses, a compensation in the same proportion. *An equivalent to such as have valuable buildings, if they remove, etc.*

ART. 11. It is also provided by the Commissioners of the United States, and they agree in behalf of said states, that those Choctaw Chiefs and Warriors, who have not received compensation for their services during the campaign to Pensacola, in the late war, shall be paid whatever is due them over and above the value of the blanket, shirt, flap, and leggins, which have been delivered to them. *Payment to Choctaws for services.*

ART. 12. In order to promote industry and sobriety amongst all classes of the Red people, in this nation, but particularly the poor, it is further provided by the parties, that the agent appointed to reside here, shall be, and he is hereby, vested with full power to seize and confiscate all the whiskey which may be introduced into said nation, except that used at public stands, or brought in by the permit of the agent, or the principal Chiefs of the three Districts. *Agent may seize and confiscate whiskey, unless, etc.*

ART. 13. To enable the Mingoes, Chiefs, and Head Men, of the Choctaw nation, to raise and organize a corps of Light-Horse, con- *Provision for raising a corps of light-horse, etc.*

sisting of ten in each District, so that good order may be maintained, and that all men, both white and red, may be compelled to pay their just debts, it is stipulated and agreed, that the sum of two hundred dollars shall be appropriated by the United States, for each district, annually, and placed in the hands of the agent, to pay the expenses incurred in raising and establishing said corps; which is to act as executive officers, in maintaining good order, and compelling bad men to remove from the nation, who are not authorized to live in it by a regular permit from the agent.

Annuity to Mushulatubbee.

ART. 14. Whereas the father of the beloved Chief Mushulatubbee, of the Lower Towns, for and during his life, did receive from the United States the sum of one hundred and fifty dollars, annually; it is hereby stipulated, that his son and successor Mushulatubbee, shall annually be paid the same amount during his natural life, to commence from the ratification of this Treaty.

Peace and harmony perpetual.

ART. 15. The peace and harmony subsisting between the Choctaw Nation of Indians and the United States, are hereby renewed, continued, and declared to be perpetual.

Treaty binding when ratified.

ART. 16. These articles shall take effect, and become obligatory on the contracting parties, so soon as the same shall be ratified by the President, by and with the advice and consent of the Senate of the United States.

In testimony whereof, the commissioners plenipotentiary of the United States and the Mingoes, head men, and warriors, of the Choctaw nation, have hereunto subscribed their names and affixed their seals, at the place above written, this eighteenth day of October, in the year of our Lord one thousand eight hundred and twenty, and of the independence of the United States the forty-fifth.

Andrew Jackson,	[L. s.]	Ticbehacubbee, his x mark,	[L. s.]
Thomas Hinds,	[L. s.]	Suttacanchihubbee, his x mark,	[L. s.]
Commissioners,		Capt. William Beams, his x mark,	[L. s.]
Medal Mingoes:		Captain James Pitchlynn,	[L. s.]
Puckshenubbee, his x mark,	[L. s.]	Capt. James Garland, his x mark,	[L. s.]
Pooshawattaha, his x mark,	[L. s.]	Tapanahomia, his x mark,	[L. s.]
Mushulatubbee, his x mark,	[L. s.]	Thlahomia, his x mark,	[L. s.]
Chiefs and warriors:		Tishotata, his x mark,	[L. s.]
General Humming Bird, his x mark,	[L. s.]	Inoquia, his x mark,	[L. s.]
James Hanizon, his x mark,	[L. s.]	Ultetoncubbee, his x mark,	[L. s.]
Talking Warrior, his x mark,	[L. s.]	Palochubbee, his x mark,	[L. s.]
Little Leader, his x mark,	[L. s.]	Jopannu, his x mark,	[L. s.]
Captain Bob Cole, his x mark,	[L. s.]	Captain Joel H. Vail,	[L. s.]
Red Fort, or Oolatahooma, his x mark,	[L. s.]	Tapanastonahamia, his x mark,	[L. s.]
Choctawistonocka, his x mark,	[L. s.]	Hoopihomia, his x mark,	[L. s.]
Oglano, his x mark,	[L. s.]	Chelutahomia, his x mark,	[L. s.]
Chuleta, his x mark,	[L. s.]	Tuskiamingo, his x mark,	[L. s.]
John Frazier, his x mark,	[L. s.]	Young Captain, his x mark,	[L. s.]
Oakchummia, his x mark,	[L. s.]	Chiefs and warriors:	
Nockestona, his x mark,	[L. s.]	Hakatubbee, his x mark,	[L. s.]
Chapahooma, his x mark,	[L. s.]	Tishoo, his x mark,	[L. s.]
Onanchahabee, his x mark,	[L. s.]	Capt. Bobb, his x mark,	[L. s.]
Copatanathoco, his x mark,	[L. s.]	Hopeanchahabee, his x mark,	[L. s.]
Atahobia, his x mark,	[L. s.]	Capt. Bradley, his x mark,	[L. s.]
Opehoola, his x mark,	[L. s.]	Capt. Daniel M'Curtain, his x mark,	[L. s.]
Chetantanchahubbee, his x mark,	[L. s.]	Mucklisahopia, his x mark,	[L. s.]
Captain Lapala, his x mark,	[L. s.]	Nuckpullachubbee, his x mark,	[L. s.]
Panchahabbee, his x mark,	[L. s.]	George Turnbull,	[L. s.]
Chuckahicka, his x mark,	[L. s.]	Captain Thomas M'Curtain, his x mark,	[L. s.]
Tallahomia, his x mark,	[L. s.]		
Totapia, his x mark,	[L. s.]	Oakehonahooma, his x mark,	[L. s.]
Hocktanlubbee, his x mark,	[L. s.]	Capt. John Cairns, his x mark,	[L. s.]
Tapawanchahubbee, his x mark,	[L. s.]	Topenastonahooma, his x mark,	[L. s.]
Capt. Red Bird, his x mark,	[L. s.]	Holatohamia, his x mark,	[L. s.]
Capt. Jerry Carney, his x mark,	[L. s.]	Col. Boyer, his x mark,	[L. s.]
Chapanchahabbee, his x mark,	[L. s.]	Holantachanshahubbee, his x mark,	[L. s.]
Tunnupnuia, his x mark,	[L. s.]	Chuckahabbee, his x mark,	[L. s.]
Ponhoopia, his x mark,	[L. s.]	Washaschahopia, his x mark,	[L. s.]

Chatamakaha, his x mark,	[L. S.]	Alex. Hamilton,	[L. S.]
Hapeahomia, his x mark,	[L. S.]	Capt. Red Knife, his x mark,	[L. S.]
William Hay, his x mark,	[L. S.]	Shapahroma, his x mark,	[L. S.]
Captain Samuel Cobb, his x mark,	[L. S.]	Capt. Tonnanpoocha, his x mark,	[L. S.]
Lewis Brashears, his x mark,	[L. S.]	Mechamiabbee, his x mark,	[L. S.]
Muckelehamia, his x mark,	[L. S.]	Tuskanohamia, his x mark,	[L. S.]
Capt. Sam. Magee, his x mark,	[L. S.]	Tookatubbetusea, his x mark,	[L. S.]
Ticbehamia, his x mark,	[L. S.]	William Frye, his x mark,	[L. S.]
Doctor Red Bird, his x mark,	[L. S.]	Greenwood Leflore, his x mark,	[L. S.]
Oontoola, his x mark,	[L. S.]	Archibald MaGee, his x mark,	[L. S.]
Pooshonshabbee, his x mark,	[L. S.]	Capt. Ben Burris, his x mark,	[L. S.]
Casania, his x mark,	[L. S.]	Tusconohicca, his x mark,	[L. S.]
Joseph Nelson, his x mark,	[L. S.]	Capt. Lewis Perry, his x mark,	[L. S.]
Unahubbee, his x mark,	[L. S.]	Henekachubbee, his x mark,	[L. S.]
Red Duck, his x mark,	[L. S.]	Tussashamia, his x mark,	[L. S.]
Muttahubbee, his x mark,	[L. S.]	Capt. Charles Durant, his x mark,	[L. S.]
Capt. Ihokahatubbee, his x mark,	[L. S.]	Piare Durant, his x mark.	[L. S.]

Witnesses present at sealing and signing:

Saml. R. Overton, secretary to the commission,
Eden Brashears,
J. C. Bronaugh, assistant sugeon-general, S. D., U. S. Army,
H. D. Downs,
Wm. F. Gangent,
Wm. M. Graham, first lieutenat, Corps of Artillery,
Andrew J. Donelson, brevet second lieutenant Corps of Engineers and aid-decamp to General Jackson,

P. A. Vandorn,
John H. Esty,
John Pitchlynn, United States interpreter,
M. Mackey, United States interpreter,
Edmund Falsome, interpreter, X,
James Hughes,
Geo. Fisher,
Jas. Jackson, jr.

TREATY WITH THE CREEKS, 1821.

Articles of a treaty entered into at the Indian Spring, in the Creek Nation, by Daniel M. Forney, of the State of North Carolina, and David Meriwether, of the State of Georgia, specially appointed for that purpose, on the part of the United States; and the Chiefs, Head Men, and Warriors, of the Creek Nation, in council assembled.

Jan. 8, 1821.

7 Stat., 215.
Proclamation, Mar. 2, 1821.

ART. 1. The Chiefs, Head Men, and Warriors, of the Creek Nation, in behalf of the said nation, do, by these presents, cede to the United States all that tract or parcel of land, situate, lying, and being, east of the following bounds and limits, viz: Beginning on the east bank of Flint river, where Jackson's line crosses, running thence, up the eastern bank of the same, along the water's edge, to the head of the principal western branch; from thence, the nearest and a direct line, to the Chatahooche river, up the eastern bank of the said river, along the water's edge, to the shallow Ford, where the present boundary line between the state of Georgia and the Creek nation touches the said river: *Provided, however,* That, if the said line should strike the Chatahooche river, below the Creek village Buzzard-Roost, there shall be a set-off made, so as to leave the said village one mile within the Creek nation; excepting and reserving to the Creek nation the title and possession, in the manner and form specified, to all the land hereafter excepted, viz: one thousand acres, to be laid off in a square, so as to include the Indian Spring in the centre thereof; as, also, six hundred and forty acres on the western bank of the Oakmulgee river, so as to include the improvements at present in the possession of the Indian Chief General M'Intosh.

Cession by the Creek.

Boundaries.

Proviso.

ART. 2. It is hereby stipulated, by the contracting parties, that the title and possession of the following tracts of land shall continue in the Creek nation so long as the present occupants shall remain in the personal possession thereof, viz: one mile square, each, to include, as

Title of certain tracts to be in the Creek nation, so long as the occupants remain, etc.

near as may be, in the centre thereof, the improvements of Michey Barnard, James Barnard, Buckey Barnard, Cussena Barnard, and Efauemathlaw, on the east side of Flint river; which reservations shall constitute a part of the cession made by the first article, so soon as they shall be abandoned by the present occupants.

Reservation for United States agency.

ART. 3. It is hereby stipulated, by the contracting parties, that, so long as the United States continue the Creek agency at its present situation on Flint river, the land included within the following boundary, viz: beginning on the east bank of Flint river, at the mouth of the Boggy Branch, and running out, at right angles, from the river, one mile and a half; thence up, and parallel with, the river, three miles: thence, parallel with the first line, to the river; and thence, down the river, to the place of beginning; shall be reserved to the Creek nation for the use of the United States' agency, and shall constitute a part of the cession made by the first article, whenever the agency shall be removed.

Payment for lands ceded.

ART. 4. It is hereby stipulated and agreed, on the part of the United States, as a consideration for the land ceded by the Creek nation by the first article, that there shall be paid to the Creek nation, by the United States, ten thousand dollars in hand, the receipt whereof is hereby acknowledged; forty thousand dollars as soon as practicable after the ratification of this convention; five thousand dollars, annually, for two years thereafter; sixteen thousand dollars, annually, for five years thereafter; and ten thousand dollars, annually, for six years thereafter; making, in the whole, fourteen payments in fourteen successive years, without interest, in money or goods and implements of husbandry, at the option of the Creek nation, seasonably signified, from time to time, through the agent of the United States residing with said nation, to the Department of War. And, as a further consideration for said cession,

United States to pay to the State of Georgia the balance due by the Creek Nation.

the United States do hereby agree to pay to the state of Georgia whatever balance may be found due by the Creek nation to the citizens of said state, whenever the same shall be ascertained, in conformity with the reference made by the commissioners of Georgia, and the chiefs, head men, and warriors, of the Creek nation, to be paid in five annual instalments without interest, provided the same shall not exceed the sum of two hundred and fifty thousand dollars; the commissioners of Georgia executing to the Creek nation a full and final relinquishment of all the claims of the citizens of Georgia against the Creek nation, for property taken or destroyed prior to the act of Congress of one thousand eight hundred and two, regulating the intercourse with the Indian tribes.

The President to cause the line to be run, etc.

ART. 5. The President of the United States shall cause the line to be run from the head of Flint river to the Chatahooche river, and the reservations made to the Creek nation to be laid off, in the manner specified in the first, second, and third, articles of this treaty, at such time and in such manner as he may deem proper, giving timely notice to the Creek nation; and this Convention shall be obligatory on the contracting parties, as soon as the same shall have been ratified by the government of the United States.

Done at the Indian Spring, this eighth day of January, A. D. eighteen hundred and twenty-one.

D. M. Forney,	[L. S.]	Taskagee Emauthlau, his x mark,	[L. S.]
D. Meriwether,	[L. S.]	Tuckle Luslee, his x mark,	[L. S.]
Wm. McIntosh,	[L. S.]	Tuckte Lustee Haujo, his x mark,	[L. S.]
Tustunnugee Hopoie, his x mark,	[L. S.]	Cunepee Emauthlau, his x mark,	[L. S.]
Efau Emauthlau, his x mark,	[L. S.]	Hethlepoie, his x mark,	[L. S.]
Holoughlan, or Col. Blue, his x mark,	[L. S.]	Tuskeenaheocki, his x mark,	[L. S.]
		Chaughle Micco, his x mark,	[L. S.]
Cussetau Micco, his x mark,	[L. S.]	Isfaune Tustunnuggee Haujo, his	
Sotetan Haujo, his x mark,	[L. S.]	x mark,	[L. S.]
Etomme Tustunnuggee, his x mark,	[L. S.]	Wau Thlucco Haujo, his x mark,	[L. S.]

Itchu Haujo, his x mark,	[L. S.]	Houpauthlee Tustunnuggee, his x mark,	[L. S.]
Alabama Tustunnuggee, his x mark,	[L. S.]	Nenehaumaughtoochie, his x mark,	[L. S.]
Holoughlan Tustunnuggee, his x mark,	[L. S.]	Henelau Tixico, his x mark,	[L. S.]
Auhauluck Yohola, his x mark,	[L. S.]	Tusekeagh Haujo, his x mark,	[L. S.]
Oseachee Tustunnuggee, his x mark,	[L. S.]	Joseph Marshall,	[L. S.]

In presence of—

I. McIntosh,
David Adams,
Daniel Newman,
     Commissioners of Georgia.
D. B. Mitchell, Agent for I. A.
William Meriwether, secretary U. S. C.

William Cook, secretary C. G.
William Hambly,
Sl. Hawkins,
George Levett,
     Interpreters.

TREATY WITH THE CREEKS, 1821.

Articles of agreement entered into, between the undersigned Commissioners, appointed by the Governor of the state of Georgia, for and on behalf of the citizens of the said state, and the Chiefs, Head Men, and Warriors, of the Creek nation of Indians.

Jan. 8, 1821.
_____
7 Stat., 217.
Proclamation, Mar. 2, 1821.

WHEREAS, at a conference opened and held at the Indian Spring, in the Creek nation, the citizens of Georgia, by the aforsaid commissioners, have represented that they have claims to a large amount against the said Creek nation of Indians: Now, in order to adjust and bring the same to a speedy and final settlement, it is hereby agreed by the aforesaid commissioners, and the chiefs, head men, and warriors, of the said nation, that all the talks had upon the subject of these claims at this place, together with all claims on either side, of whatever nature or kind, prior to the act of Congress of one thousand eight hundred and two, regulating the intercourse with the Indian tribes, with the documents in support of them, shall be referred to the decision of the President of the United States, by him to be decided upon, adjusted, liquidated, and settled, in such manner, and under such rules, regulations, and restrictions, as he shall prescribe: *Provided, however*, if it should meet the views of the President of the United States, it is the wish of the contracting parties, that the liquidation and settlement of the aforesaid claims shall be made in the state of Georgia, at such place as he may deem most convenient for the parties interested, and the decision and award, thus made and rendered, shall be binding and obligatory upon the contracting parties.

Claims on either side referred to decision of the President. 1802, ch. 13.

Proviso.

In witness whereof, we have hereunto set our hands and seals, this eighth day of January, one thousand eight hundred and twenty-one.

J. McIntosh,	[L. S.]
David Adams,	[L. S.]
Daniel Newman,	[L. S.]
William McIntosh,	[L. S.]
Tustunnuggee Hopoie, his x mark,	[L. S.]
Efau Emauthlau, his x mark,	[L. S.]

Present:
   D. M. Forney,
   D. Meriwether.

DISCHARGE FOR ALL CLAIMS ON THE CREEKS.

WHEREAS a treaty or convention has this day been made and entered into, by and between the United States and the Creek nation, by the provisions of which the United States have agreed to pay, and the commissioners of the state of Georgia have agreed to accept, for and on behalf of the citizens of the state of Georgia, having claims against the Creek nation, prior to the year one thousand eight hundred and two, the sum of two hundred and fifty thousand dollars:

Commissioners of Georgia release the Creeks from all claims prior to 1802., Now, know all men by these presents, that we, the undersigned, commissioners of the state of Georgia, for, and in consideration of, the aforesaid sum of two hundred and fifty thousand dollars, secured by the said treaty or convention to be paid to the state of Georgia, for the discharge of all bona fide and liquidated claims, which the citizens of the said state may establish against the Creek nation, do, by these presents, release, exonerate, and discharge, the said Creek nation from all and every claim and claims, of whatever description, nature, or kind, the same may be, which the citizens of Georgia now have, or may have had, prior to the year one thousand eight hundred and two, against *Claims transferred to United States.* the said nation. And we do hereby assign, transfer, and set over, unto the United States, for the use and benefit of the said Creek nation, for the consideration hereinbefore expressed, all the right, title, and interest, of the citizens of the said state, to all claims, debts, damages, and property, of every description and denomination, which the citizens of the said state have, or had, prior to the year one thousand eight hundred and two, as aforesaid, against the said Creek nation.

In witness whereof, we have hereunto affixed our hands and seals, at the Mineral Spring, in the said Creek nation, this eighth day of January, one thousand eight hundred and twenty-one.

J. McIntosh,   [L. s.]
David Adams,   [L. s.]
Daniel Newman, [L. s.]

Present:
    D. M. Forney,
    D. Meriwether,
    D. B. Mitchell, Agent for Indian Affairs.

TREATY WITH THE OTTAWA, ETC., 1821.

Aug. 29, 1821.

7 Stat., 218.
Proclamation, Mar. 25, 1822.

Articles of a treaty made and concluded at Chicago, in the State of Illinois, between Lewis Cass and Solomon Sibley, Commissioners of the United States, and the Ottawa, Chippewa, and Pottawatamie, Nations of Indians.

Cession of land within the boundaries described. ARTICLE I. The Ottawa, Chippewa, and Pottawatamie, Nations of Indians cede to the United States all the Land comprehended within the following boundaries: Beginning at a point on the south bank of the river St. Joseph of Lake Michigan, near the Parc aux Vaches, due north from Rum's Village, and running thence south to a line drawn due east from the southern extreme of Lake Michigan, thence with the said line east to the Tract ceded by the Pottawatamies to the United States by the Treaty of Fort Meigs in 1817, if the said line should strike the said Tract, but if the said line should pass north of the said Tract, then such line shall be continued until it strikes the western boundary of the Tract ceded to the United States by the Treaty of Detroit in 1807, and from the termination of the said line, following the boundaries of former cessions, to the main branch of the Grand River of Lake Michigan, should any of the said lines cross the said

River, but if none of the said lines should cross the said River, then to a point due east of the source of the said main branch of the said river, and from such point due west to the source of the said principal branch, and from the crossing of the said River, or from the source thereof, as the case may be, down the said River, on the north bank thereof, to the mouth; thence following the shore of Lake Michigan to the south bank of the said river St. Joseph, at the mouth thereof, and thence with the said south bank to the place of beginning.

ART. 2. From the cession aforesaid, there shall be reserved, for the use of the Indians, the following Tracts: *Reservations.*

One tract at Mang-ach-qua Village, on the river Peble, of six miles square.

One tract at Mick-ke-saw-be, of six miles square.

One tract at the village of Na-to-wa-se-pe, of four miles square.

One tract at the village of Prairie Ronde, of three miles square.

One tract at the village of Match-e-be narh-she-wish, at the head of the Kekalamazoo river.

ART. 3. There shall be granted by the United States to each of the following persons, being all Indians by descent, and to their heirs, the following Tracts of Land: *Grants to persons named.*

To John Burnet, two sections of land.

To James Burnet, Abraham Burnet, Rebecca Burnet, and Nancy Burnet, each one section of land; which said John, James, Abraham, Rebecca, and Nancy, are children of Kaw-kee-me, sister of Top-ni-be, principal chief of the Potwatamie nation.

The land granted to the persons immediately preceding, shall begin on the north bank of the river St. Joseph, about two miles from the mouth, and shall extend up and back from the said river for quantity. *Location of the preceding grants.*

To John B. La Lime, son of Noke-no-qua, one-half of a section of. land, adjoining the tract before granted, and on the upper side thereof. *Further grants.*

To Jean B. Chandonai, son of Chip-pe-wa-qua, two sections of land, on the river St. Joseph, above and adjoining the tract granted to J. B. La Lime.

To Joseph Dazé, son of Chip-pe-wa-qua, one section of land above and adjoining the tract granted to Jean B. Chandonai.

To Monguago, one-half of a section of land, at Mish-she-wa-ko-kink.

To Pierre Moran or Peeresh, a Potawatamie Chief, one section of land, and to his children two sections of land, at the mouth of the Elk-heart river.

To Pierre Le Clerc, son of Moi-qua, one section of land on the Elk-heart river, above and adjoining the tract granted to Moran and his children.

The section of land granted by the Treaty of St. Mary's, in 1818, to Peeresh or Perig, shall be granted to Jean B. Cicot, son of Pe-say-quot, sister of the said Peeresh, it having been so intended at the execution of the said Treaty.

To O-she-ak-ke-be or Benac, one-half of a section of land on the north side of the Elk-heart river, where the road from Chicago to Fort Wayne first crosses the said river.

To Me-naw-che, a Potawatamie woman, one-half of a section of land on the eastern bank of the St. Joseph, where the road from Detroit to Chicago first crosses the said river.

To Theresa Chandler or To-e-ak-qui, a Potawatamie woman, and to her daughter Betsey Fisher, one section of land on the south side of the Grand River, opposite to the Spruce Swamp.

To Charles Beaubien and Medart Beaubien, sons of Man-na-ben-a-qua, each one-half of a section of land near the village of Ke-wi-go-shkeem, on the Washtenaw river.

To Antoine Roland, son of I-gat-pat-a-wat-a-mie-qua, one-half of a section of land adjoining and below the tract granted to Pierre Moran.

To William Knaggs or Was-es-kuk-son, son of Ches-qua, one-half of a section of land adjoining and below the tract granted to Antoine Roland.

To Madeline Bertrand, wife of Joseph Bertrand, a Potawatamie woman, one section of land at the Parc aux Vaches, on the north side of the river St. Joseph.

To Joseph Bertrand, junior, Benjamin Bertrand, Laurent Bertrand, Theresa Bertrand, and Amable Bertrand, children of the said Madeline Bertrand, each one half of a section of land at the portage of the Kankakee river.

To John Riley, son of Me-naw-cum-a-go-quoi, one section of land, at the mouth of the river Au Foin, on the Grand River, and extending up the said River.

To Peter Riley, the son of Me-naw-cum-e-go-qua, one section of land, at the mouth of the river Au Foin, on the Grand River, and extending down the said river.

To Jean B. Le Clerc, son of Moi-qua, one half of a section of land, above and adjoining the tract granted to Pierre Le Clerc.

To Joseph La Framboise, son of Shaw-we-no-qua, one section of land upon the south side of the river St. Joseph, and adjoining on the upper side the land ceded to the United States, which said section is also ceded to the United States.

Grants not transferable without consent. The Tracts of Land herein stipulated to be granted, shall never be leased or conveyed by the grantees or their heirs to any persons whatever, without the permission of the President of the United States. **Tracts to be located after survey.** And such tracts shall be located after the said cession is surveyed, and in conformity with such surveys as near as may be, and in such manner as the President may direct.

Payment for said cession. ART. 4. In consideration of the cession aforesaid, the United States engage to pay to the Ottawa nation, one thousand dollars in specie annually forever, and also to appropriate annually, for the term of ten years, the sum of fifteen hundred dollars, to be expended as the President may direct, in the support of a Blacksmith, of a Teacher, and of a person to instruct the Ottawas in agriculture and in the purchase of cattle and farming utensils. And the United States also engage to pay to the Potawatamie nation five thousand dollars in specie, annually, for the term of twenty years, and also to appropriate annually, for the term of fifteen years, the sum of one thousand dollars, to be expended as the President may direct, in the support of a Blacksmith and a **Land to be reserved for blacksmiths and teachers.** Teacher. And one mile square shall be selected, under the direction of the President, on the north side of the Grand River, and one mile square on the south side of the St. Joseph, and within the Indian lands not ceded, upon which the blacksmiths and teachers employed for the said tribes, respectively, shall reside.

Right of Indians to hunt on land ceded. ART. 5. The stipulation contained in the treaty of Greenville, relative to the right of the Indians to hunt upon the land ceded while it continues the property of the United States, shall apply to this treaty.

United States may make a road through Indian country. ART. 6. The United States shall have the privilege of making and using a road through the Indian country, from Detroit and Fort Wayne, respectively, to Chicago.

Treaty binding when ratified. ART. 7. This Treaty shall take effect and be obligatory on the contracting parties, so soon as the same shall be ratified by the President of the United States, by and with the advice and consent of the Senate thereof.

In testimony whereof, the said Lewis Cass and Solomon Sibley, commissioners as aforesaid, and the chiefs and warriors of the said Ottawa, Chippewa, and Pattiwatima nations, have hereunto set their hands, at

Chicago aforesaid, this 29th day of August, in the year of our Lord one thousand eight hundred and twenty-one.

Lewis Cass,
Solomon Sibley.
 Ottawas:
Kewagoushcum, his x mark,
Nokawjegaun, his x mark,
Kee-o-to-aw-be, his x mark,
Ket-che-me-chi-na-waw, his x mark,
Ep-pe-san-se, his x mark,
Kay-nee-wee, his x mark,
Mo-a-put-to, his x mark,
Mat-che-pee-na-che-wish, his x mark,
 Chippewas:
Met-tay-waw, his x mark,
Mich-el, his x mark,
 Pattiwatimas:
To-pen-ne-bee, his x mark,
Mee-te-ay, his x mark,
Chee-banse, his x mark,
Loui-son, his x mark,
Wee-saw, his x mark,
Kee-po-taw, his x mark,
Shay-auk-ke-bee, his x mark,
Sho-mang, his x mark,
Waw-we-uck-ke-meck, his x mark,
Nay-ou-chee-mon, his x mark,
Kon-gee, his x mark,
Shee-shaw-gan, his x mark,
Aysh-cam, his x mark,
Meek-say-mank, his x mark,
May-ten-way, his x mark,
Shaw-wen-ne-me-tay, his x mark,
Francois, his x mark,
Mauk-see, his x mark,
Way-me-go, his x mark,
Man-daw-min, his x mark,

Quay-guee, his x mark,
Aa-pen-naw-bee, his x mark,
Mat-cha-wee-yaas, his x mark,
Mat-cha-pag-gish, his x mark,
Mongaw, his x mark,
Pug-gay-gaus, his x mark,
Ses-cobe-mesh, his x mark,
Chee-gwa-mack-gwa-go, his x mark,
Waw-seb-baw, his x mark,
Pee-chee-co, his x mark,
Quoi-quoi-taw, his x mark,
Pe-an-nish, his x mark,
Wy-ne-naig, his x mark,
Onuck-ke-méck, his x mark,
Ka-way-sin, his x mark,
A-meck-kose, his x mark,
Os-see-meet, his x mark,
Shaw-ko-to, his x mark,
No-shay-we-quat, his x mark,
Mee-gwun, his x mark,
Mes-she-ke-ten-now, his x mark,
Kee-no-to-go, his x mark,
Wa-baw-nee-she, his x mark,
Shaw-waw-nay-see, his x mark,
Atch-wee-muck-quee, his x mark,
Pish-she-baw-gay, his x mark,
Waw-ba-saye, his x mark,
Meg-ges-seese, his x mark,
Say-gaw-koo-nuck, his x mark,
Shaw-way-no, his x mark,
Shee-shaw-gun, his x mark,
To-to-mee, his x mark,
Ash-kee-wee, his x mark,
Shay-auk-ke-bee, his x mark,
Aw-be-tone, his x mark.

In presence of—

Alex. Wolcott, jr. Indian agent,
Jno. R. Williams, Adjutant-General, M.
 Ma.
G. Godfroy, Indian agent,
W. Knaggs, Indian agent,
Jacob Visget,
Henry I. Hunt,
A. Phillips, paymaster, U. S. Army,
R. Montgomery,

Jacob B. Varnum, United States factor
John B. Beaubien,
Conrad Ten Eyck,
J. Whipley,
George Miles, jun.
Henry Connor,
James Barnerd,
John Kenzie, subagent.

 The tract reserved at the village of Match-e-be-nash-she-wish, at the head of the Ke-kal-i-ma-zoo river, was by agreement to be three miles square. The extent of the reservation was accidentally omitted.

The tract at Match-ebenashshewish to be 3 miles square.

        Lewis Cass,
        Solomon Sibley.

TREATY WITH THE OSAGE, 1822.

Articles of a Treaty, entered into and concluded at the United States' Factory on the M. De Cigue Augt. by and between Richard Graham, Agent of Indian Affairs, authorized on the part of the United States for that purpose, and the Chiefs, Warriors, and Head Men, of the Tribes of Great and Little Osage Indians, for themselves and their respective Tribes, of the other part.

Aug. 31, 1822.

7 Stat., 222.
Proclamation, Feb. 13, 1823.

WHEREAS, by the second article of the Treaty made and entered into between the United States and the Great and Little Osage nation of Indians, concluded and signed at Fort Clark, on the Missouri, on the tenth day of November, one thousand eight hundred and eight, it

The second article of the treaty of Nov. 10, 1808. abrogated; consideration.

is stipulated that the United States shall establish at that place, and permanently continue, at all seasons of the year, a well assorted store of goods, for the purpose of bartering with them on moderate terms for their peltries and furs: Now, we, the said Chiefs, Warriors, and Head Men, in behalf of our said Tribes, for and in consideration of two thousand three hundred and twenty-nine dollars and forty cents, to us now paid in merchandise, out of the United States' Factory, by said Richard Graham, on behalf of the United States, the receipt whereof is hereby acknowledged, do exonerate, release, and forever discharge, the United States from the obligation contained in the said second article above mentioned; and the aforesaid second article is, from the date hereof, abrogated and of no effect.

In witness whereof, the said Richard Graham and the chiefs, warriors, and head men, of the Great and Little Osage tribes, have hereunto set their hands and affixed their seals, this thirty-first day of August, in the year of our Lord one thousand eight hundred and twenty-two.

R. Graham,	[L. S.]	Thinggahwassah, his x mark,	[L. S.]
Pahuska, his x mark, or White		Onnyago, his x mark,	[L. S.]
Hair, head chief, B. O.	[L. S.]	Wonopasheh, his x mark,	[L. S.]
Neshumoiny, his x mark, or Walk		Kehegethingah, his x mark,	[L. S.]
in Rain, head chief, L. O.	[L. S.]	Veheseheh, his x mark,	[L. S.]
Kahegewashinpisheh, his x mark,	[L. S.]	Thunkemono, his x mark,	[L. S.]
Big Soldier, his x mark,	[L. S.]	Ownakaheh, his x mark,	[L. S.]
Cothistwoshko, his x mark,	[L. S.]	Wahchewahheh, his x mark,	[L. S.]
Tocathingah, his x mark,	[L. S.]	Grenatheh, his x mark,	[L. S.]
Towakaheh, his x mark, chief of		Neocheninkeh, his x mark,	[L. S.]
the Crosse Cotte V.	[L. S.]	Tanwanhehe, his x mark,	[L. S.]
Kahegetankgah, his x mark,	[L. S.]	Wasabewangoudake, his x mark,	[L. S.]
Urattheheh, his x mark,	[L. S.]	Wathinsabbeh, his x mark,	[L. S.]

In presence of—
    Paul Baillio,
    Robert Dunlap,
    C. De La Croix.

TREATY WITH THE SAUK AND FOXES, 1822.

Sept. 3, 1822.
7 Stat., 223.
Proclamation, Feb. 13, 1823.

Articles of a Treaty entered into and concluded at Fort Armstrong, by and between Thomas Forsyth, Agent of Indian Affairs, authorized on the part of the United States for that purpose, of the one part, and the Chiefs, Warriors, and Head Men, of the United Sac and Fox Tribes, for themselves and their Tribes, of the other part.

Ninth article of treaty of Nov. 3, 1804, abrogated; consideration.

WHEREAS by the ninth article of the Treaty made and entered into between the United States and the Sac and Fox Tribes of Indians, concluded and signed at Saint Louis, in the District of Louisiana, on the third day of November, one thousand eight hundred and four, it is stipulated, in order to put a stop to the abuses and impositions which are practised upon the said Tribes by the private traders, the United States will, at a convenient time, establish a trading house or factory, where the individuals of the said Tribes can be supplied with goods at a more reasonable rate than they have been accustomed to procure them. Now, We, the said Chiefs, Warriors, and head men of the said Tribes, for and in consideration of the sum of one thousand dollars to us, now paid in merchandise out of the United States' Factory, by said Thomas Forsyth, on behalf of the United States, the receipt whereof is hereby acknowledged, do exonerate, release, and forever discharge, the United States from the obligation contained in the said ninth article above recited, and the aforesaid ninth article is, from the date hereof, abrogated and of no effect.

In witness whereof, the said Thomas Forsyth, and the chiefs, warriors, and head men, of the Sac and Fox tribes, have hereunto set their hands, and affixed their seals, this third day of September, in the year of our Lord one thousand eight hundred and twenty-two.

Thomas Forsyth, United States Indian Agent,	[L. S.]	Keeocuck, his x mark,	[L. S.]
Pushee Paho, his x mark,	[L. S.]	Wapulla, his x mark,	[L. S.]
Quash Quammee, his x mark,	[L. S.]	Themue, his x mark,	[L. S.]
Nesowakee, his x mark,	[L. S.]	Mucathaanamickee, his x mark,	[L. S.]
		Nolo, his x mark,	[L. S.]

In the presence of—

S. Burbank, major, U. S. Army,
P. Craig, assistant surgeon, U. S. Army,
J. M. Baxley, lieutenant, Fifth Infantry,
George Davenport,

Samuel C. Muir,
John Connelly,
Louis Betelle, interpreter.

TREATY WITH THE FLORIDA TRIBES OF INDIANS, 1823.

ARTICLE I. THE undersigned chiefs and warriors, for themselves and their tribes, have appealed to the humanity, and thrown themselves on, and have promised to continue under, the protection of the United States, and of no other nation, power, or sovereign; and, in consideration of the promises and stipulations hereinafter made, do cede and relinquish all claim or title which they may have to the whole territory of Florida, with the exception of such district of country as shall herein be allotted to them.

Sept. 18, 1823.

7 Stat., 224.
Proclamation, Jan. 2, 1824.

Said Indians to continue under the protection of United States.

ARTICLE II. The Florida tribes of Indians will hereafter be concentrated and confined to the following metes and boundaries: commencing five miles north of Okehumke, running in a direct line to a point five miles west of Setarky's settlement, on the waters of Amazura, (or Withlahuchie river,) leaving said settlement two miles south of the line; from thence, in a direct line, to the south end of the Big Hammock, to include Chickuchate; continuing, in the same direction, for five miles beyond the said Hammock—provided said point does not approach nearer than fifteen miles the sea coast of the Gulf of Mexico; if it does, the said line will terminate at that distance from the sea coast; thence, south, twelve miles; thence in a south 30° east direction, until the same shall strike within five miles of the main branch of Charlotte river; thence, in a due east direction, to within twenty miles of the Atlantic coast; thence, north, fifteen west, for fifty miles and from this last, to the beginning point.

Said Indians to be confined to the following metes and bounds.

ARTICLE III. The United States will take the Florida Indians under their care and patronage, and will afford them protection against all persons whatsoever; provided they conform to the laws of the United States, and refrain from making war, or giving any insult to any foreign nation, without having first obtained the permission and consent of the United States: And, in consideration of the appeal and cession made in the first article of this treaty, by the aforesaid chiefs and warriors, the United States promise to distribute among the tribes, as soon as concentrated, under the direction of their agent, implements of husbandry, and stock of cattle and hogs, to the amount of six thousand dollars, and an annual sum of five thousand dollars a year, for twenty successive years, to be distributed as the President of the United States shall direct, through the Secretary of War, or his Superintendents and Agent of Indian Affairs.

United States to take the Florida Indians under their care, etc.

ARTICLE IV. The United States promise to guaranty to the said tribes the peaceable possession of the district of country herein assigned them, reserving the right of opening through it such roads, as may, from time to time, be deemed necessary; and to restrain and prevent all white persons from hunting, settling, or otherwise intruding upon it. But any citizen of the United States, being lawfully

United States to guaranty peaceable possession of the district assigned them, on certain conditions.

authorized for that purpose, shall be permitted to pass and repass through the said district, and to navigate the waters thereof, without any hindrance, toll, or exaction, from said tribes.

Corn, meat, etc., to be allowed them for twelve months.

ARTICLE V. For the purpose of facilitating the removal of the said tribes to the district of country allotted them, and, as a compensation for the losses sustained, or the inconveniences to which they may be exposed by said removal, the United States will furnish them with rations of corn, meat, and salt, for twelve months, commencing on the first day of February next; and they further agree to compensate those individuals who have been compelled to abandon improvements on lands, not embraced within the limits allotted, to the amount of four thousand five hundred dollars, to be distributed among the sufferers, in a ratio to each, proportional to the value of the improvements abandoned. The United States further agree to furnish a sum, not exceeding two thousand dollars, to be expended by their agent, to facilitate the transportation of the different tribes to the point of concentration designated.

An agent, etc., to be appointed to reside among them.

ARTICLE VI. An agent, sub-agent, and interpreter, shall be appointed, to reside within the Indian boundary aforesaid, to watch over the interests of said tribes; and the United States further stipulate, as an evidence of their humane policy towards said tribes, who have appealed to their liberality, to allow for the establishment of a school at the agency, one thousand dollars per year for twenty successive years; and one thousand dollars per year, for the same period, for the support of a gun and blacksmith, with the expenses incidental to his shop.

Indians to prevent any fugitive slaves from taking shelter among them, etc.

ARTICLE VII. The chiefs and warriors aforesaid, for themselves and tribes, stipulate to be active and vigilant in the preventing the retreating to, or passing through, of the district of country assigned them, of any absconding slaves, or fugitives from justice; and further agree, to use all necessary exertions to apprehend and deliver the same to the agent, who shall receive orders to compensate them agreeably to the trouble and expenses incurred.

A commissioner and surveyor to be appointed.

ARTICLE VIII. A commissioner, or commissioners, with a surveyor, shall be appointed, by the President of the United States, to run and mark, (blazing fore and aft the trees) the line as defined in the second article of this treaty, who shall be attended by a chief or warrior, to be designated by a council of their own tribes, and who shall receive, while so employed, a daily compensation of three dollars.

Grounds on which the objections of said tribes to certain lands are founded.

ARTICLE IX. The undersigned chiefs and warriors, for themselves and tribes, having objected to their concentration within the limits described in the second article of this treaty, under the impression that the said limits did not contain a sufficient quantity of good land to subsist them, and for no other reason: it is, therefore, expressly understood, between the United States and the aforesaid chiefs and warriors, that, should the country embraced in the said limits, upon examination by the Indian agent and the commissioner, or commissioners, to be appointed under the 8th article of this treaty, be by them considered insufficient for the support of the said Indian tribes; then the north line, as defined in the 2d article of this treaty, shall be removed so far north as to embrace a sufficient quantity of good tillable land.

Said Indians request the grant in fee simple of certain lands to Colonel Humphreys and S. Richards.

ARTICLE X. The undersigned chiefs and warriors, for themselves and tribes, have expressed to the commissioners their unlimited confidence in their agent, Col. Gad Humphreys, and their interpreter, Stephen Richards, and, as an evidence of their gratitude for their services and humane treatment, and brotherly attentions to their wants, request that one mile square, embracing the improvements of Enehe Mathla, at Tallahassee (said improvements to be considered as the centre) be conveyed, in fee simple, as a present to Col. Gad Humphreys.—And they further request, that one mile square, at the Ochesee Bluffs, embracing Stephen Richard's field on said Bluffs, be conveyed in fee simple, as a present to said Stephen Richards. The commissioners accord in sentiment with the undersigned chiefs and warriors, and recommend a compliance with their wishes to the President and Senate of the United States; but the disapproval, on the part of the said authorities, of this article, shall, in no wise, affect the other articles and stipulations concluded on in this treaty.

In testimony whereof, the commissioners, William P. Duval, James Gadsden, and Bernard Segui, and the undersigned chiefs and warriors, have hereunto subscribed their names and affixed their seals. Done at camp on Moultrie creek, in the territory of Florida, this eighteenth day of September, one thousand eight hundred and twenty-three, and of the independence of the United States the forty-eighth.

William P. Duval,	[L. S.]	Wokse Holata, his x mark,	[L. S.]
James Gadsden,	[L. S.]	Amathla Ho, his x mark,	[L. S.]
Bernard Segui,	[L. S.]	Holatefiscico, his x mark,	[L. S.]
Nea Mathla, his x mark,	[L. S.]	Chefiscico Hajo, his x mark,	[L. S.]
Tokose Mathla, his x mark,	[L. S.]	Lathloa Mathla, his x mark,	[L. S.]
Ninnee Homata Tustenuky, his x mark,	[L. S.]	Senufky, his x mark,	[L. S.]
		Alak Hajo, his x mark,	[L. S.]
Miconope, his x mark,	[L. S.]	Fahelustee Hajo, his x mark,	[L. S.]
Nocosee Ahola, his x mark,	[L. S.]	Octahamico, his x mark,	[L. S.]
John Blunt, his x mark,	[L. S.]	Tusteneck Hajo, his x mark,	[L. S.]
Otlemata, his x mark,	[L. S.]	Okoskee Amathla, his x mark,	[L. S.]
Tuskeeneha, his x mark,	[L. S.]	Ocheeny Tustenuky, his x mark,	[L. S.]
Tuski Hajo, his x mark,	[L. S.]	Phillip, his x mark,	[L. S.]
Econchatimico, his x mark,	[L. S.]	Charley Amathla, his x mark,	[L. S.]
Emoteley, his x mark,	[L. S.]	John Hoponey, his x mark,	[L. S.]
Mulatto King, his x mark,	[L. S.]	Rat Head, his x mark,	[L. S.]
Chocholohano, his x mark,	[L. S.]	Holatta Amathla, his x mark,	[L. S.]
Ematlochee, his x mark,	[L. S.]	Foshatchimico, his x mark,	[L. S.]

Signed, sealed, and delivered, in the presence of—

George Murray, secretary to the commission,
G. Humphreys, Indian agent,
Stephen Richards, interpreter,
Isaac N. Cox,
J. Erving, captain, Fourth Artillery,
Harvey Brown, lieutenant, Fourth Artillery,

C. D'Espinville, lieutenant, Fourth Artillery,
Jno. B. Scott, lieutenant, Fourth Artillery,
William Travers,
Horatio S. Dexter.

ADDITIONAL ARTICLE.

Whereas Neo Mathla, John Blunt, Tuski Hajo, Mulatto King, Emathlochee, and Econchatimico, six of the principal Chiefs of the Florida Indians, and parties to the treaty to which this article has been annexed, have warmly appealed to the Commissioners for permission to remain in the district of country now inhabited by them; and, in consideration of their friendly disposition, and past services to the United States, it is, therefore, stipulated, between the United States and the aforesaid Chiefs, that the following reservations shall be surveyed, and marked by the Commissioner, or Commissioners, to be appointed under the 8th article of this Treaty: For the use of Nea Mathla and his connections, two miles square, embracing the Tuphulga village, on the waters of Rocky Comfort Creek. For Blunt and Tuski Hajo, a reservation, commencing on the Apalachicola, one mile below Tuski Hajo's improvements, running up said river four miles; thence, west, two miles; thence, southerly, to a point two miles due west of the beginning; thence, east, to the beginning point. For Mulatto King and Emathlochee, a reservation, commencing on the Apalachicola, at a point to include Yellow Hair's improvements; thence, up said river, for four miles; thence, west, one mile; thence, southerly, to a point one mile west of the beginning; and thence, east, to the beginning point. For Econ-

Sept. 18, 1823.

7 Stat., 226.

Additional article

chatimico, a reservation, commencing on the Chatahoochie, one mile below Econchatimico's house; thence, up said river, for four miles; thence, one mile, west; thence, southerly, to a point one mile west of the beginning; thence, east, to the beginning point.   The United States promise to guaranty the peaceable possession of the said reservations, as defined, to the aforesaid chiefs and their descendents *only*, so long as they shall continue to occupy, improve, or cultivate, the same; but in the event of the abandonment of all, or either of the reservations, by the chief or chiefs, to whom they have been allotted, the reservation, or reservations, so abandoned, shall revert to the United States, as included in the cession made in the first article of this treaty.   It is further understood, that the names of the individuals remaining on the reservations aforesaid, shall be furnished, by the chiefs in whose favor the reservations have been made, to the Superintendent or agent of Indian Affairs, in the territory of Florida; and that no other individuals shall be received or permitted to remain within said reservations, without the previous consent of the Superintendent or Agent aforesaid; And, as the aforesaid Chiefs are authorized to select the individuals remaining with them, so they shall each be separately held responsible for the peaceable conduct of their towns, or the individuals residing on the reservations allotted them.   It is further understood, between the parties, that this agreement is not intended to prohibit the voluntary removal, at any future period, of all or either of the aforesaid Chiefs and their connections, to the district of country south, allotted to the Florida Indians, by the second article of this Treaty, whenever either, or all may think proper to make such an election; the United States reserving the right of ordering, for any outrage or misconduct, the aforesaid Chiefs, or either of them, with their connections, within the district of country south, aforesaid.   It is further stipulated, by the United States, that, of the six thousand dollars, appropriated for implements of husbandry, stock, &c. in the third article of this Treaty, eight hundred dollars shall be distributed, in the same manner, among the aforesaid chiefs and their towns; and it is understood, that, of the annual sum of five thousand dollars, to be distributed by the President of the United States, they will receive their proportion.   It is further stipulated, that, of the four thousand five hundred dollars, and two thousand dollars, provided for by the 5th article of this Treaty, for the payment for improvements and transportation, five hundred dollars shall be awarded to Neo Mathla, as a compensation for the improvements abandoned by him, as well as to meet the expenses he will unavoidably be exposed to, by his own removal, and that of his connections.

In testimony whereof, the commissioners, William P. Duval, James Gadsden, and Bernard Segui, and the undersigned chiefs and warriors, have hereunto subscribed their names and affixed their seals.   Done at camp, on Moultrie creek, in the territory of Florida, this eighteenth day of September, one thousand eight hundred and twenty-three, and of the independence of the United States the forty-eighth.

Wm. P. Duval, his x mark,	[L. S.]
James Gadsden,	[L. S.]
Bernard Segui,	[L. S.]
Nea Mathla, his x mark,	[L. S.]
John Blunt, his x mark,	[L. S.]
Tuski Hajo, his x mark,	[L. S.]
Mulatto King, his x mark,	[L. S.]
Emathlochee, his x mark,	[L. S.]
Econchatimico, his x mark,	[L. S.]

Signed, sealed, delivered, in presence of–

George Murray, secretary to the commission
Ja. W. Ripley,
G. Humphreys, Indian agent,
Stephen Richards, interpreter.

The following statement shows the number of men retained by the Chiefs, who have reservations made them, at their respective villages:

	Number of Men.
Blount	43
Cochran	45
Mulatto King	30
Emathlochee	28
Econchatimico	38
Neo Mathia	30
Total	214

TREATY WITH THE SAUK AND FOXES, 1824.

To perpetuate peace and friendship between the United States and the Sock and Fox tribes or nations of Indians, and to remove all future cause of dissensions which may arise from undefined territorial boundaries, the President of the United States of America, by William Clark, Superintendent of Indian Affairs, and sole Commissioner specially appointed for that purpose, of the one part, and the undersigned Chiefs and Head Men of the Sock and Fox tribes or nations, fully deputized to act for and in behalf of their said nations, of the other part, have entered into the following articles and conditions, viz:

Aug. 4, 1824.

7 Stat., 229.
Proclamation, Jan. 18, 1825.

ARTICLE 1st. The Sock and Fox tribes or nations of Indians, by their deputations in council assembled, do hereby agree, in consideration of certain sums of money, &c. to be paid to the said Sock and Fox tribes, by the Government of the United States, as hereinafter stipulated, to cede and for ever quit claim, and do, in behalf of their said tribes or nations, hereby cede, relinquish, and forever quit claim, unto the United States, all right, title, interest, and claim, to the lands which the said Sock and Fox tribes have, or claim, within the limits of the state of Missouri, which are situated, lying, and being, between the Mississippi and Missouri rivers, and a line running from the Missouri, at the entrance of Kansas river, north one hundred miles to the Northwest corner of the state of Missouri, and from thence east to the Mississippi. It being understood, that the small tract of land lying between the rivers Desmoin and the Mississippi, and the section of the above line between the Mississippi and the Desmoin, is intended for the use of the half-breeds belonging to the Sock and Fox nations: they holding it, however, by the same title, and in the same manner, that other Indian titles are held.

Agreements entered into by said tribes.

ARTICLE 2d. The Chiefs and Head Men who sign this convention, for themselves and in behalf of their tribes, do acknowledge the lands east and south of the lines described in the first article, so far as the Indians claimed the same, to belong to the United States, and that none of their tribes shall be permitted to settle or hunt upon any part of it, after the first day of January, 1826, without special permission from the Superintendent of Indian Affairs.

Lands ceded, etc.

ARTICLE 3d. It is hereby stipulated and agreed, on the part of the United States, as a full consideration for the claims and lands ceded by the Sock and Fox tribes in the first article, there shall be paid to the Sock and Fox nations, within the present year, one thousand dollars in cash, or merchandize; and in addition to the annuities stipulated to be

Annuities, etc.

paid to the Sock and Fox tribes by a former treaty, the United States do agree to pay to the said Sock tribe, five hundred dollars, and to the Fox tribe five hundred dollars, annually, for the term of ten succeeding years; and, at the request of the Chiefs of the said Sock and Fox nations, the Commissioner agrees to pay to Morice Blondeau, a half Indian of the Fox tribe, the sum of five hundred dollars, it being a debt due by the said nation to the aforesaid Blondeaux, for property taken from him during the late war.

Assistance to be rendered them.

ARTICLE 4th. The United States engage to provide and support a Blacksmith for the Sock and Fox nations, so long as the President of the United States may think proper, and to furnish the said nations with such farming utensils and cattle, and to employ such persons to aid them in their agriculture, as the President may deem expedient.

Payment of the annuities.

ARTICLE 5th. The annuities stipulated to be paid by the 3d article, are to be paid either in money, merchandise, provisions, or domestic animals, at the option of the aforesaid tribes, and when the said annuities or part thereof is paid in merchandise, it is to be delivered to them at the first cost of the goods at St. Louis, free from cost of transportation.

Treaty obligatory when ratified.

ARTICLE 6th. This treaty shall take effect and be obligatory on the contracting parties so soon as the same shall be ratified by the President of the United States, by and with the advice and consent of the Senate thereof.

In testimony whereof, the said William Clark, commissioner as aforesaid, and the chiefs and head men of the Sock and Fox tribes of Indians as aforesaid, have hereunto set their hands, at Washington City, this fourth day of August, in the year of our Lord one thousand eight hundred and twenty-four.

William Clark, [L. s.]	Sah-col-o-quoit, or Rising Cloud, his
Socks:	x mark, [L. s.]
Pah-sha-pa-ha, or Stubbs, his x	Foxes:
mark, [L. s.]	Fai-mah, or the Bear, his x mark, [L. s.]
Kah-kee-kai-maik, or All Fish, his	Ka-pol-e-qua, or White Nosed Fox,
x mark, [L. s.]	his x mark, [L. s.]
Wash-kee-chai, or Crouching Eagle,	Pea-mash-ka, or the Fox winding
his x mark, [L. s.]	his horn, his x mark, [L. s.]
Kee-o-kuck, or Watchful Fox, his	Kee-sheswa, or the Sun, his x mark, [L. s.]
x mark, [L. s.]	
Kah-kee-kai-maik, or All Fish, his	
x mark, [L. s.]	

Witnesses at signing:

Thomas L. McKenney,	Maurice Blondeau,
Law. Taliaferro, Indian agent at St.	L. T. Honore.
Peter's,	Jno. W. Johnson,
G. W. Kennerly, Indian agent,	Meriwether Lewis Clark,
A. Baronet Vasques, acting S. I. A. and	Noal Dashnay.
Int.	

TREATY WITH THE IOWA, 1824.

Aug. 4, 1824.

7 Stat., 231.
Proclamation, Jan. 18, 1825.

Articles of a Treaty made and concluded at the City of Washington, on the fourth day of August, one thousand eight hundred and twenty-four, between William Clark, Superintendent of Indian Affairs, being specially authorized by the President of the United States thereto, and the undersigned Chiefs and Head men, of the Ioway Tribe or Nation, duly authorized and empowered by the said Nation.

Lands ceded to the United States.

ARTICLE 1st. THE Ioway Tribe or Nation of Indians by their deputies, Ma-hos-kah, (or White Cloud,) and Mah-ne-hah-nah, (or Great Walker,) in Council assembled, do hereby agree, in consideration of a certain sum of money, &c. to be paid to the said Ioway Tribe, by the government of the United States, as hereinafter stipulated, to cede and forever, quit claim, and do, in behalf of their said Tribe, hereby cede, relinquish, and forever quit claim, unto the United States, all right, title, interest, and claim, to the lands which the said Ioway Tribe have, or claim, within the State of Missouri, and situated between the Mississippi and Missouri rivers and a line running from the Missouri, at the mouth or entrance of Kanzas river, north one hundred miles, to the northwest corner of the limits of the state of Missouri, and, from thence, east to the Mississippi.

ARTICLE 2d. It is hereby stipulated and agreed, on the part of the United States, as a full compensation for the claims and lands ceded by the Ioway Tribe in the preceding article, there shall be paid to the said Ioway tribe, within the present year, in cash or merchandise, the amount of five hundred dollars, and the United States do further agree to pay to the Ioway Tribe, five hundred dollars, annually, for the term of ten succeeding years. *Payment for said cession.*

ARTICLE 3d. The Chiefs and Head Men who sign this Treaty, for themselves, and in behalf of their Tribe, do acknowledge that the lands east and south of the lines described in the first article, (which has been run and marked by Colonel Sullivan,) so far as the Indians claimed the same, to belong to the United States, and that none of their tribe shall be permitted to settle or hunt upon any part of it, after 1st day of January, one thousand eight hundred and twenty-six, without special permission from the Superintendent of Indian Affairs. *Acknowledgment of Indians.*

ARTICLE 4th. The undersigned Chiefs, for themselves, and all parts of the Ioway tribe, do acknowledge themselves and the said Ioway Tribe, to be under the protection of the United States of America, and of no other sovereign whatsoever; and they also stipulate, that the said Ioway tribe will not hold any treaty with any foreign powers, individual state, or with individuals of any state. *Protection of United States acknowledged.*

ARTICLE 5th. The United States engage to provide and support a blacksmith for the Ioway Tribe, so long as the President of the United States may think proper, and to furnish the said Tribe with such farming utensils and cattle, and to employ such persons to aid them in their agriculture, as the President may deem expedient. *Assistance to be rendered Indians.*

ARTICLE 6th. The annuities stipulated to be paid by the second article, to be. paid either in money, merchandise, provisions, or domestic animals, at the option of the aforesaid Tribe; and when the said annuities, or any part thereof, is paid in merchandise, it is to be delivered to them at the first cost of the goods at St. Louis, free from cost of transportation. *Payment of annuities.*

ARTICLE 7th. This Treaty shall take effect, and be obligatory on the contracting parties, so soon as the same shall be ratified by the President of the United States, by and with the advice and consent of the Senate thereof. *Treaty obligatory when ratified.*

In testimony whereof, the said William Clark, commissioner as aforesaid, and the chiefs and head men of the Ioway tribe of Indians, as aforesaid, have hereunto set their hands the day and year first before written.

Wm. Clark,
Ma-hos-kah, (White Cloud,) his x mark,
Mah-ne-hah-nah, (Great Walker,) his x mark.

Witnesses present:
Thos. L. McKenney,
G. W. Kennerly, Indian agent,
Law. Taliaferro, Indian agent at St. Peter's,
A. Baronet Vasques, acting subsistence agent and interpreter,
Meriwether Lewis Clark,
John W. Johnson,
William P. Clark,
William Radford.

TREATY WITH THE QUAPAW, 1824.

Articles of a treaty between the United States of America and the Quapaw Nation of Indians.

Nov. 15, 1824.

7 Stat., 232.
Proclamation, Feb. 19, 1825.

Lands ceded by the Quapaws.

ARTICLE 1. The Quapaw Nation of Indians cede to the United States of America, in consideration of the promises and stipulations hereinafter made, all claim or title which they may have to lands in the Territory of Arkansas, comprised in the following boundaries, to wit: Beginning at a point on the Arkansas river, opposite to the Post of Arkansas, and running thence a due south-west course to the Ouachita river; and thence, up the same, to the Saline Fork; and up the Saline Fork, to a point from whence a due north-east course will strike the Arkansas river at Little Rock: and thence down the right (or south bank) of the Arkansas river to the place of beginning.

$500 to be paid to the head chiefs, etc.

ART. 2. In consideration of the cession made in the first article of this Treaty, by the aforesaid Chiefs and Warriors, the United States engage to pay to the four head Chiefs of the Quapaw Nation, the sum of five hundred dollars each, in consideration of the losses they will sustain by removing from their farms and improvements. The payment to be made at the time they receive their annuity for the year 1825. And, also, to the said nation, the sum of four thousand dollars, to be paid in goods, at the signing of this Treaty. And the United States also engage to pay to the Quapaw Nation, one thousand dollars in specie, annually, for the term of eleven years, in addition to their present annuity.

Rights guarantied them.

ART. 3. The United States hereby guaranty to the said Nation of Indians, the same right to hunt on the lands by them hereby ceded, as was guarantied to them by a Treaty, concluded at St. Louis, on the 24th of August, 1818, between the said Quapaw Nation of Indians and WILLIAM CLARK and AUGUSTE CHOTEAU, Commissioners on the part of the United States.

To be confined to the district of country occupied by the Caddo Indians.

ART. 4. The Quapaw Tribe of Indians will hereafter be concentrated and confined to the district of country inhabited by the Caddo Indians, and form a part of said Tribe. The said nation of Indians are to commence removing to the district allotted them, before the twentieth day of January, one thousand eight hundred and twenty-six.

Assistance to be rendered to Quapaws.

ART. 5. For the purpose of facilitating the removal of the said Tribe, to the district of country allotted them, and as a compensation for the losses sustained, and the inconveniences to which they may be exposed by said removal, the United States will furnish them with corn, meat, and salt, for six months, from the first day of January, one thousand eight hundred and twenty-six. The United States further agree to furnish a sum not exceeding one thousand dollars, to be expended by their agent, to facilitate the transportation of the said Tribe to the district of country herein assigned them. An Agent, Sub Agent, or Interpreter, shall be appointed to accompany said tribe, and to reside among them.

$7,500 to be reserved to James Scull.

ART. 6. From the cession aforesaid, there shall be reserved to JAMES SCULL, in consideration of a debt of seven thousand five hundred dollars, due to him from the Quapaw Nation, and recognized in open Council, two sections of land commencing on the Arkansas river, opposite to Mrs. Embree's, and running up and back from said river for quantity. And the United States guaranty to the Quapaw Nation the payment of the said debt of seven thousand five hundred dollars, either by the ratification of the grant made in this article, or by the payment of said amount in money, exclusive of the amount stipulated to be paid to the said nation by this treaty.

Tracts of land granted to certain persons, Indians by descent.

ART. 7. There shall be granted by the United States, to the following persons, being Indians by descent, the following tracts of Land: To Francois Imbeau, one quarter section of land, commencing at a point on the Arkansas river, opposite the upper end of Wright Daniel's farm, and thence, up and back from said river, for quantity. To Joseph Duchassien, one quarter section of land, commencing at the lower corner of the quarter section granted to Francois Imbeau, and running down and back from said river for quantity. To Saracen, a half breed Quapaw, eighty acres of land, to be laid off so as to include his improvement, where he now resides, opposite Vaugine's. To Batiste Socie, eighty acres of land, laying above and adjoining Saracen's grant. To Joseph Bonne, eighty acres of land, lying above and adjoining Socie's grant. To Baptiste Bonne, eighty acres of land, lying above and adjoining Joseph Bonne's grant. To Lewis Bartelmi, eighty acres of land, lying above and adjoining Baptiste Bonne's grant. To Antoine Duchassin, eighty acres of land, lying above and adjoining Bartelmi's grant. To Baptiste Imbeau, eighty acres of land, lying above and adjoining A. Duchassin's grant. To Francois Coupot, eighty acres of land, lying above and adjoining Baptiste Imbeau's grant. To Joseph Valliere, eighty acres of land, lying above and adjoining Francois Coupot's grant. All the said tracts of land shall be laid off, so as to conform to the lines of the United States' surveys, and binding on the Arkansas river.

ART. 8. This treaty shall take effect, and be obligatory on the contracting parties, so soon as the same shall be ratified by the Senate of the United States. *When to take effect.*

In testimony whereof, the commissioner on the part of the United States, Robert Crittenden, and the undersigned chiefs and warriors of the said nation, have hereunto subscribed their names and affixed their seals.

Done at Harrington's, in the territory of Arkansas, on the fifteenth day of November, A. D. one thousand eight hundred and twenty-four, and of the independence of the United States the forty-ninth.

Robert Crittenden, Commissioner on the part of the United States, [L. S.]	Hunkatugonee, his x mark, [L. S.]
Hackehton, his x mark, [L. S.]	Hepahdagonneh, his x mark, [L. S.]
Tononseka, his x mark, [L. S.]	Wahehsonjekah, his x mark, [L. S.]
Kiahhacketady, his x mark, [L. S.]	Gratonjekah, his x mark, [L. S.]
Sarazen, his x mark, [L. S.]	Watuhtezka, his x mark, [L. S.]
Kakapah, his x mark, [L. S.]	Dohkuhnonjeshu, his x mark, [L. S.]
Hunkahkee, his x mark, [L. S.]	Kahtahkonku, his x mark, [L. S.]
Wahtonbeh, his x mark, [L. S.]	Hahcrontenah, his x mark, [L. S.]

Signed, sealed, and witnessed in presence of—

Thomas W. Newton, secretary to the commission,	D. Barber, S. Agt. to the Osages,
Robert C. Oden, lieutenant-colonel Second Regiment Arkansas Militia,	Gordon Neill,
F. Farrelly, adjutant-general of Arkansas Militia,	Edmund Hogan,
B. Harrington.	Thomas W. Johnston,
	Antoine Barrague,
	Etienne Vanyine, interpreter,
	Joseph Duchassin, interpreter.

TREATY WITH THE CHOCTAW, 1825.

Articles of a convention made between John C. Calhoun, Secretary of War, being specially authorized therefor by the President of the United States, and the undersigned Chiefs and Head Men of the Choctaw Nation of Indians, duly authorized and empowered by said Nation, at the City of Washington, on the twentieth day of January, in the year of our Lord one thousand eight hundred and twenty-five.

Jan. 20, 1825.

7 Stat., 234.
Proclamation, Feb. 19, 1825.

WHEREAS a Treaty of friendship, and limits, and accommodation, having been entered into at Doake's Stand, on the eighteenth of October, in the year one thousand eight hundred and twenty, between Andrew Jackson and Thomas Hinds, Commissioners on the part of the United States, and the Chiefs and Warriors of the Choctaw Nation *Preamble.*

of Indians; and whereas the second article of the Treaty aforesaid provides for a cession of lands, west of the Mississippi, to the Choctaw Nation, in part satisfaction for lands ceded by said Nation to the United States, according to the first article of said treaty: And whereas, it being ascertained that the cession aforesaid embraces a large number of settlers, citizens of the United States; and it being the desire of the President of the United States to obviate all difficulties resulting therefrom, and also, to adjust other matters in which both the United States and the Choctaw Nation are interested: the following articles have been agreed upon, and concluded, between John C. Calhoun, Secretary of War, specially authorized therefor by the President of the United States, on the one part, and the undersigned Delegates of the Choctaw Nation, on the other part:

Lands ceded to the United States. ARTICLE 1. The Choctaw Nation do hereby cede to the United States all that portion of the land ceded to them by the second article of the Treaty of Doak Stand, as aforesaid, lying east of a line beginning on the Arkansas, one hundred paces east of Fort Smith, and running thence, due south, to Red river: it being understood that this line shall constitute, and remain, the permanent boundary between the United States and the Choctaws; and the United States agreeing to remove such citizens as may be settled on the west side, to the east side of said line, and prevent future settlements from being made on the west thereof.

$6,000 to be paid to Choctaws annually, forever. ARTICLE 2. In consideration of the cession aforesaid, the United States do hereby agree to pay the said Choctaw Nation the sum of six thousand dollars, annually, forever; it being agreed that the said sum of six thousand dollars shall be annually applied, for the term of twenty years, under the direction of the President of the United States, to the support of schools in said nation, and extending to it the benefits of instruction in the mechanic and ordinary arts of life; when, at the expiration of twenty years, it is agreed that the said annuity may be vested in stocks, or otherwise disposed of, or continued, at the option of the Choctaw nation.

$6,000 to be paid them annually for 16 years. ARTICLE 3. The eighth article of the treaty aforesaid having provided that an appropriation of lands shall be made for the purpose of raising six thousand dollars a year for sixteen years, for the use of the Choctaw Nation; and it being desirable to avoid the delay and expense attending the survey and sale of said land; the United States do hereby agree to pay the Choctaw Nation, in lieu thereof, the sum of six thousand dollars, annually, for sixteen years, to commence with the present year. And the United States further stipulate and agree to take immediate measures to survey and bring into market, and sell, the fifty-four sections of land set apart by the seventh article of the treaty aforesaid, and apply the proceeds in the manner provided by the said article.

Provision for Choctaws who may desire to remain. ARTICLE 4. It is provided by the ninth section of the treaty aforesaid, that all those of the Choctaw Nation who have separate settlements, and fall within the limits of the land ceded by said Nation to the United States, and desire to remain where they now reside, shall be secured in a tract or parcel of land, one mile square, to include their improvements. It is, therefore, hereby agreed, that all who have reservations in conformity to said stipulation, shall have power, with the consent of the President of the United States, to sell and convey the same in fee simple. It is further agreed, on the part of the United States, that those Choctaws, not exceeding four in number, who applied for reservations, and received the recommendation of the Commissioners, as per annexed copy of said recommendation, shall have the privilege, and the right is hereby given to them, to select, each of them, a portion of land, not exceeding a mile square, any where within the limits of the cession of 1820, when the land is not occupied or disposed of by the United States;

and the right to sell and convey the same, with the consent of the President, in fee simple, is hereby granted.

ARTICLE 5. There being a debt due by individuals of the Choctaw Nation to the late United States' trading house on the Tombigby, the United States hereby agree to relinquish the same; the Delegation, on the part of their nation, agreeing to relinquish their claim upon the United States, to send a factor with goods to supply the wants of the Choctaws west of the Mississippi, as provided for by the 6th article of the treaty aforesaid. *A certain debt due by Choctaws relinquished.*

ARTICLE 6. The Choctaw nation having a claim upon the United States, for services rendered in the Pensacola Campaign, and for which it is stipulated, in the 11th article of the treaty aforesaid, that payment shall be made, but which has been delayed for want of the proper vouchers, which it has been found, as yet, impossible to obtain; the United States, to obviate the inconvenience of further delay, and to render justice to the Choctaw Warriors for their services in that campaign, do hereby agree upon an equitable settlement of the same, and fix the sum at fourteen thousand nine hundred and seventy-two dollars fifty cents; which, from the muster rolls, and other evidence in the possession of the Third Auditor, appears to be about the probable amount due, for the services aforesaid, and which sum shall be immediately paid to the Delegation, to be distributed by them to the Chiefs and Warriors of their nation, who served in the campaign aforesaid, as may appear to them to be just. *Payment for services rendered in the Pensacola campaign.*

ARTICLE 7. It is further agreed, that the fourth article of the treaty aforesaid, shall be so modified, as that the Congress of the United States shall not exercise the power of apportioning the lands, for the benefit of each family, or individual, of the Choctaw Nation, and of bringing them under the laws of the United States, but with the consent of the Choctaw Nation. *Fourth article of the aforesaid treaty to be modified.*

ARTICLE 8. It appearing that the Choctaws have various claims against citizens of the United States, for spoliations of various kinds, but which they have not been able to support by the testimony of white men, as they were led to believe was necessary, the United States, in order to a final settlement of all such claims, do hereby agree to pay to the Choctaw Delegation, the sum of two thousand dollars, to be distributed by them in such way, among the claimants, as they may deem equitable. It being understood that this provision is not to affect such claims as may be properly authenticated, according to the provision of the act of 1802. *Payment to satisfy claims due by United States.*

ARTICLE 9. It is further agreed that, immediately upon the Ratification of this Treaty, or as soon thereafter as may be, an agent shall be appointed for the Choctaws West of the Mississippi, and a Blacksmith be settled among them, in conformity with the stipulation contained in the 6th Article of the Treaty of 1820. *An agent and blacksmith for Choctaws west of the Mississippi.*

ARTICLE 10. The Chief Puck-she-nubbee, one of the members of the Delegation, having died on his journey to see the President, and Robert Cole being recommended by the Delegation as his successor, it is hereby agreed, that the said Robert Cole shall reserve the medal which appertains to the office of Chief, and, also, an annuity from the United States, of one hundred and fifty dollars a year, during his natural life, as was received by his predecessor. *Robert Cole to receive a medal.*

ARTICLE 11. The friendship heretofore existing between the United States and the Choctaw Nation, is hereby renewed and perpetuated. *Friendship perpetuated.*

ARTICLE 12. These articles shall take effect, and become obligatory on the contracting parties, so soon as the same shall be ratified by the President, by and with the advice and consent of the Senate of the United States. *When to take effect.*

In testimony whereof, the said John C. Calhoun, and the said delegates of the Choctaw nation, have hereunto set their hands, at the city of Washington, the twentieth day of January, one thousand eight hundred and twenty-five.

> J. C. Calhoun,
> Mooshulatubbee, his x mark,
> Robert Cole, his x mark,
> Daniel McCurtain, his x mark,
> Talking Warrior, his x mark,
> Red Fort, his x mark,
> Nittuckachee, his x mark,
> David Folsom, his x mark,
> J. L. McDonald.

In presence of—
> Thos. L. McKenney,
> Hezekiah Miller,
> John Pitchlynn, United States interpreter.

TREATY WITH THE CREEKS, 1825.

Feb. 12, 1825.

7 Stat., 237.
Proclamation, Mar. 7, 1825.

Articles of a convention, entered into and concluded at the Indian Springs, between Duncan G. Campbell, and James Meriwether, Commissioners on the part of the United States of America, duly authorised, and the Chiefs of the Creek Nation, in Council assembled.

Preamble.

WHEREAS the said Commissioners, on the part of the United States, have represented to the said Creek Nation that it is the policy and earnest wish of the General Government, that the several Indian tribes within the limits of any of the states of the Union should remove to territory to be designated on the west side of the Mississippi river, as well for the better protection and security of said tribes, and their improvement in civilization, as for the purpose of enabling the United States, in this instance, to comply with the compact entered into with the State of Georgia, on the twenty-fourth day of April, in the year one thousand eight hundred and two: And the said Commissioners having laid the late Message of the President of the United States, upon this subject, before a General Council of said Creek Nation, to the end that their removal might be effected upon terms advantageous to both parties:

And whereas the Chiefs of the Creek Towns have assented to the reasonableness of said proposition, and expressed a willingness to emigrate beyond the Mississippi, *those of Tokaubatchee excepted:*

These presents therefore witness, that the contracting parties have this day entered into the following Convention:

Cession by the Creek.

ART. 1. The Creek nation cede to the United States all the lands lying within the boundaries of the State of Georgia, as defined by the compact hereinbefore cited, now occupied by said Nation, or to which said Nation have title or claim; and also, all other lands which they now occupy, or to which they have title or claim, lying north and west of a line to be run from the first principal falls upon the Chatauhoochie river, above Cowetau town, to Ocfuskee Old Town, upon the Tallapoosa, thence to the falls of the Coosaw river, at or near a place called the Hickory Ground.

Further agreement between the contracting parties.

ART. 2. It is further agreed between the contracting parties, that the United States will give, in exchange for the lands hereby acquired, the like quantity, acre for acre, westward of the Mississippi, on the Arkansas river, commencing at the mouth of the Canadian Fork thereof, and running westward between said rivers Arkansas and Canadian Fork, for quantity. But whereas said Creek Nation have considerable improvements within the limits of the territory hereby ceded, and will moreover have to incur expenses in their removal, it is further stipulated, that, for the purpose of rendering a fair equivalent for the losses and inconveniences which said Nation will sustain by removal, and to enable them to obtain supplies in their new settlement, the United States agree to pay to the Nation emigrating from the lands herein ceded, the sum of four hundred thousand dollars, of which amount there shall be paid to said party of the second part, as soon as practicable after the ratification of this treaty, the sum of two hundred thousand dollars. And as soon as the said party of the second part shall notify the Government of the United States of their readiness to commence their removal, there shall be paid the further sum of one hundred thousand dollars. And the first year after said emigrating party shall have settled in their new country, they shall receive of the amount first above named, the further sum of twenty-five thousand dollars. And the second year, the sum of twenty-five thousand dollars. And annually, thereafter, the sum of five thousand dollars, until the whole is paid.

ART. 3. And whereas the Creek Nation are now entitled to annuities of thirty thousand dollars each, in consideration of cessions of territory heretofore made, it is further stipulated that said last mentioned annuities are to be hereafter divided in a just proportion between the party emigrating and those that may remain. *Annuities to be equally divided.*

ART. 4. It is further stipulated that a deputation from the said parties of the second part, may be sent out to explore the territory herein offered them in exchange; and if the same be not acceptable to them, then they may select any other territory, west of the Mississippi, on Red, Canadian, Arkansas, or Missouri Rivers—the territory occupied by the Cherokees and Choctaws excepted; and if the territory so to be selected shall be in the occupancy of other Indian tribes, then the United States will extinguish the title of such occupants for the benefit of said emigrants. *Territory offered said Indians to be explored, etc.*

ART. 5. It is further stipulated, at the particular request of the said parties of the second part, that the payment and disbursement of the first sum herein provided for, shall be made by the present Commissioners negotiating this treaty. *Payment of the first sum to be made by the commissioners.*

ART. 6. It is further stipulated, that the payments appointed to be made, the first and second years, after settlement in the West, shall be either in money, merchandise, or provisions, at the option of the emigrating party. *Other payments.*

ART. 7. The United States agree to provide and support a blacksmith and wheelwright for the said party of the second part, and give them instruction in agriculture, as long, and in such manner, as the President may think proper. *Provision to be made by United States.*

ART. 8. Whereas the said emigrating party cannot prepare for immediate removal, the United States stipulate, for their protection against the incroachments, hostilities, and impositions, of the whites, and of all others; but the period of removal shall not extend beyond the first day of September, in the year eighteen hundred and twenty-six. *Extension of the time of their removal, etc.*

ART. 9. This treaty shall be obligatory on the contracting parties, so soon as the same shall be ratified by the President of the United States, by and with the consent of the Senate thereof. *When to take effect.*

In testimony whereof, the commissioners aforesaid, and the chiefs and head men of the Creek nation, have hereunto set their hands and seals, this twelfth day of February, in the year of our Lord one thousand eight hundred and twenty-five.

Duncan G. Campbell,	[L. S.]	Etommee Tustunnuggee, of Cowe-	
James Meriwether,	[L. S.]	tau, his x mark,	[L. S.]
Commissioners on the part of the United States.		Holahtau, or Col. Blue, his x mark,	[L. S.]
		Cowetau Tustunnuggee, his x mark,	[L. S.]
William McIntosh, head chief of Cowetaus,	[L. S.]	Artus Mico, or Roby McIntosh, his x mark,	[L. S.]

Chilly McIntosh,	[L. S.]	
Joseph Marshall,	[L. S.]	
Athlan Hajo, his x mark,	[L. S.]	
Tuskenahah, his x mark,	[L. S.]	
Benjamin Marshall,	[L. S:]	
Coccus Hajo, his x mark,	[L. S.]	
Forshatepu Mico, his x mark,	[L. S.]	
Oethlamata Tustunnuggee, his x mark,	[L. S.]	
Tallasee Hajo, his x mark,	[L. S.]	
Tuskegee Tustunnuggee, his x mark,	[L. S.]	
Foshajee Tustunnuggee, his x mark,	[L. S.]	
Emau Chuccolocana, his x mark,	[L. S.]	
Abeco Tustunnuggee, his x mark,	[L. S.]	
Hijo Hajo, his x mark,	[L. S.]	
Thla Tho Hajo, his x mark,	[L. S.]	
Tomico Holueto, his x mark,	[L. S.]	
Yah Te Ko Hajo, his x mark,	[L. S.]	
No cosee Emautla, his x mark,	[L. S.]	
Col. Wm. Miller, Thleeatchca, his x mark,	[L. S.]	
Abeco Tustunnuggee, his x mark,	[L. S.]	
Hoethlepoga Tustunnuggee, his x mark,	[L. S.]	
Hepocokee Emautla, his x mark,	[L. S.]	
Samuel Miller, his x mark,	[L. S.]	
Tomoc Mico, his x mark,	[L. S.]	
Charles Miller, his x mark,	[L. S.]	
Tallasee Hoja, or John Carr, his x mark,	[L. S.]	
Otulga Emautla, his x mark,	[L. S.]	
Ahalaco Yoholo of Cusetau, his x mark,	[L. S.]	
Walucco Hajo, of New Yauco, his x mark,	[L. S.]	

Cohausee Ematla, of New Yauco, his x mark,	[L. S.]
Nineomau Tochee, of New Yauco, his x mark,	[L. S]
Konope Emautla, Sand Town, his x mark,	[L. S.]
Chawacala Mico, Sand Town, his x mark,	[L. S.]
Foctalustee Emaulta, Sand Town, his x mark,	[L. S.]
Josiah Gray, from Hitchatee, his x mark,	[L. S.]
William Kannard, from Hitchatee, his x mark,	[L. S.]
Neha Thlucto Hatkee, from Hitchatee, his x mark,	[L. S.]
Halathla Fixico, from Big Shoal, his x mark,	[L. S.]
Alex. Lasley, from Talledega, his x mark,	[L. S.]
Espokoke Hajo, from Talledega, his x mark,	[L. S.]
Emauthla Hajo, from Talledega, his x mark,	[L. S.]
Nincomatachee, from Talledega, his x mark,	[L. S].
Chuhah Hajo, from Talledega, his x mark,	[L. S.]
Efie Ematla, from Talledega, his x mark,	[L. S.]
Atausee Hopoie, from Talledega, his x mark,	[L. S:]
James Fife, from Talledega, his x mark,	[L. S.]

Executed on the day as above written, in presence of—
John Crowell, agent for Indian affairs,
Wm. F. Hay, secretary,
Wm. Meriwether,
Wm. Hambly, United States interpreter.

July 25, 1825.

Whereas, by a stipulation in the Treaty of the Indian Springs, in 1821, there was a reserve of land made to include the said Indian Springs for the use of General William M'Intosh, be it therefore known to all whom it may concern, that we, the undersigned chiefs and head men of the Creek nation, do hereby agree to relinquish all the right, title, and control of the Creek nation to the said reserve, unto him the said William M'Intosh and his heirs, forever, in as full and ample a manner as we are authorized to do.

Big B. W. Warrior,	[L. S.]
Yoholo Micco, his x mark,	[L. S.]
Little Prince, his x mark,	[L. S']
Hopoie Hadjo, his x mark,	[L. S.]
Tuskehenahau, his x mark,	[L. S.]
Oakefuska Yohola, his x mark,	[L. S.]
John Crowell, agent for Indian affairs,	[L. S.]

July 25, 1825.

Feb. 14, 1825.
Additional article.

Whereas the foregoing articles of convention have been concluded between the parties thereto: And, whereas, the Indian Chief, General William McIntosh, claims title to the Indian Spring Reservation (upon which there are very extensive buildings and improvements) by virtue of a relinquishment to said McIntosh, signed in full council of the nation: And, whereas the said General William McIntosh hath claim to another reservation of land on the Ocmulgee river, and by his lessee and tenant, is in possession thereof:

Now these presents further witness, that the said General William McIntosh, and also the Chiefs of the Creek Nation, in council assembled, do quit claim, convey, and cede to the United States, the reservations aforesaid, for, and in consideration of, the sum of twenty-five thousand dollars, to be paid at the time and in the manner as stipulated, for the first instalment provided for in the preceding treaty. Upon the ratification of these articles, the possession of said reservations shall be considered as passing to the United States, and the accruing rents of the present year shall pass also.

In testimony whereof, the said commissioners, on the part of the United States, and the said William McIntosh, and the chiefs of the Creek nation, have hereunto set their hands and seals, at the Indian Springs, this fourteenth day of February, in the year of our Lord one thousand eight hundred and twenty-five.

Duncan G. Campbell,	[L. S.]
James Meriwether,	[L. S.]

United States commissioners.

William McIntosh,	[L. S.]
Eetommee Tustunnuggee, his x mark,	[L. S.]
Tuskegoh Tustunnuggee, his x mark,	[L. S.]
Cowetau Tustunnuggee, his x mark,	[L. S.]
Col. Wm. Miller, his x mark,	[L. S.]
Josiah Gray, his x mark,	[L. S.]
Nehathlucco Hatchee, his x mark,	[L. S.]
Alexander Lasley, his x mark,	[L. S.]
William Canard, his x mark,	[L. S.]

Witnesses at execution:
   Wm. F. Hay, secretary,
   Wm. Hambly, United States interpreter.

TREATY WITH THE OSAGE, 1825.

Articles of a treaty made and concluded at St. Louis, in the State of Missouri, between William Clark, Superintendent of Indian Affairs, Commissioner on the part of the United States, and the undersigned, Chiefs, Head-Men, and Warriors, of the Great and Little Osage Tribes of Indians, duly authorized and empowered by their respective Tribes or Nations.

June 2, 1825.

7 Stat., 240.
Proclamation, Dec. 30, 1825.

In order more effectually to extend to said Tribes that protection of the Government so much desired by them, it is agreed as follows:

ARTICLE 1.

The Great and Little Osage Tribes or Nations do, hereby, cede and relinquish to the United States, all their right, title, interest, and claim, to lands lying within the State of Missouri and Territory of Arkansas, and to all lands lying West of the said State of Missouri and Territory of Arkansas, North and West of the Red River, South of the Kansas River, and East of a line to be drawn from the head sources of the Kansas, Southwardly through the Rock Saline, with such reservations, for such considerations, and upon such terms as are hereinafter specified, expressed, and provided for.

Cession by the Osages.

ARTICLE 2.

Tracts of land reserved for said Indians.

Within the limits of the country, above ceded and relinquished, there shall be reserved, to, and for, the Great and Little Osage Tribes or Nations, aforesaid, so long as they may choose to occupy the same, the following described tract of land: beginning at a point due East of White Hair's Village, and twenty-five miles West of the Western boundary line of the State of Missouri, fronting on a North and South line, so as to leave ten miles North, and forty miles South, of the point of said beginning, and extending West, with the width of fifty miles, to the Western boundary of the lands hereby ceded and relin-

Reservation by United States.

quished by said Tribes or Nations; which said reservations shall be surveyed and marked, at the expense of the United States, and upon which, the Agent for said Tribes or Nations and all persons attached to said agency, as, also, such teachers and instructors, as the President may think proper to authorize and permit, shall reside, and shall occupy, and cultivate, without interruption or molestation, such lands as may be necessary for them. And the United States do, hereby, reserve to themselves, forever, the right of navigating, freely, all water courses and navigable streams, within or running through, the tract of country above reserved to said Tribes or Nations.

ARTICLE 3.

Annuity to Indians.

In consideration of the cession and relinquishment, aforesaid, the United States do, hereby, agree to pay to the said tribes or nations, yearly, and every year, for twenty years, from the date of these presents, the sum of seven thousand dollars, at their Village, or at St. Louis, as the said tribes or nations may desire, either in money, merchandise, provisions, or domestic animals, at their option. And whenever the said annuity, or any part thereof, shall be paid in merchandise, the same is to be delivered to them at the first cost of the goods at St. Louis, free of transportation.

ARTICLE 4.

Cattle, farming utensils, etc., to be furnished them.

The United States shall, immediately, upon the ratification of this convention, or as soon thereafter as may be, cause to be furnished to the tribes or nations, aforesaid, six hundred head of cattle, six hundred hogs, one thousand domestic fowls, ten yoke of oxen, and six carts, with such farming utensils as the Superintendent of Indian Affairs may think necessary, and shall employ such persons, to aid them in their agricultural pursuits, as to the President of the United States may seem expedient, and shall, also, provide, furnish, and support for them, one blacksmith, that their farming utensils, tools, and arms, may be seasonably repaired; and shall build, for each of the four principal chiefs, at their respective villages, a comfortable and commodious dwelling house.

ARTICLE 5.

Reservations for half-breeds.

From the above lands ceded and relinquished, the following reservations, for the use of the half-breeds, hereafter named, shall be made, to wit: One section, or six hundred and forty acres, for Augustus Clermont, to be located and laid off so as to include Joseph Rivar's residence, on the East side of the Neosho, a short distance above the Grand Saline, and not nearer than within one mile thereof; one section for each of the following half-breeds: James, Paul, Henry, Rosalie, Anthony, and Amelia, the daughter of She-me-hunga, and Amelia, the daughter of Mi-hun-ga, to be located two miles below the Grand Saline, and extending down the Neosho, on the East side thereof; and one section for Noel Mongrain, the son of Wa-taw-nagres, and for each of his ten children, Baptiste, Noel, Francis, Joseph, Mongrain, Louis, Victoria, Sophia, Julia, and Juliet: and the like quantity for each of the following named grand-children, of the said Noel Mongrain, to wit: Charles, Francis, Louisson, and Wash, to commence on the Marias des Cygnes, where the Western boundary line of the State of Missouri crosses it at the fork of Mine river, and to extend up Mine river, for quantity: one section for Mary Williams, and one for Sarah Williams, to be located on the North side of the Marias des Cygnet, at the Double Creek, above Harmony; one section, for Francis T. Chardon; one section, for Francis C. Tayon; one section, for James G. Chouteau; one section, for Alexander Chouteau; one section, for Pelàgie Antaya; one section, for Celeste Antaya; one section, for Joseph Antaya; one section, for Baptiste St. Mitchelle, jr.; one section, for Louis St. Mitchelle; one section, for Victoria St. Mitchelle; one section, for Julia St. Mitchelle; one section, for Francis St. Mitchelle; one section, for Joseph Perra; one section, for Susan Larine; one section, for Marguerite Reneau; one section, for Thomas L. Balio; and one section, for Terese, the daughter of Paul Louise; which said several tracts are to be located on the North side of the Marias des Cygnes, extending up the river, above the reservations in favor of Mary and Sarah Williams, in the order in which they are herein above named.

Article 6.

And also fifty-four other tracts, of a mile square each, to be laid off under the direction of the President of the United States, and sold, for the purpose of raising a fund to be applied to the support of schools, for the education of the Osage children, in such manner as the President may deem most advisable to the attainment of that end.

Land to be sold for certain purposes.

Article 7.

Forasmuch as there is a debt due, from sundry individuals of the Osage tribes or nations, to the United States' trading houses, of the Missouri and Osage rivers, amounting in the whole, to about the sum of four thousand one hundred and five dollars and eighty cents, which the United States do hereby agree to release; in consideration thereof, the said tribes or nations do, hereby, release and relinquish their claim upon the United States, for regular troops to be stationed, for their protection, in garrison, at Fort Clark, and, also, for furnishing of a blacksmith, at that place, and the delivery of merchandise, at Fire Prairie, as is provided for in the first, third, and fifth, articles of the Treaty, concluded on the tenth day of November, one thousand eight hundred and eight.

Debts due by said tribes to United States trading houses, released.

Article 8.

It appearing that the Delaware nation have various claims against the Osages, which the latter have not had it in their power to adjust, and the United States being desirous to settle, finally and satisfactorily, all demands and differences between the Delawares and Osages, do hereby agree to pay to the Delawares, in full satisfaction of all their claims and demands against the Osages, the sum of one thousand dollars.

Claims of the Delawares against said tribes to be settled by United States.

Article 9.

With a view to quiet the animosities, which at present exist between a portion of the citizens of Missouri and Arkansas and the Osage tribes, in consequence of the lawless depredations of the latter, the United States do, furthermore, agree to pay, to their own citizens, the full

Animosities of citizens of Missouri, etc., to be quieted.

value of such property, as they can legally prove to have been stolen or destroyed, by the Osages, since the year eighteen hundred and eight, and for which payment has not been made under former treaties: *Provided*, The sum to be paid by the United States does not exceed the sum of five thousand dollars.

ARTICLE 10.

Land reserved to be disposed of as the President may direct.

It is furthermore agreed on, by and between the parties to these presents, that there shall be reserved two sections of land, to include the Harmony Missionary establishment, and their mill, on the Marias des Cygne; and one section, to include the Missionary establishment, above the Lick on the West side of Grand river, to be disposed of as the President of the United States shall direct, for the benefit of said Missions, and to establish them at the principal villages of the Great and Little Osage Nations, within the limits of the country reserved to them by this Treaty, and to be kept up at said villages, so long as said Missions shall be usefully employed in teaching, civilizing, and mproving, the said Indians.

ARTICLE 11.

Ninth article of treaty of Fort Clark to be in full force.

To preserve and perpetuate the friendship now happily subsisting between the United States and the said tribes or nations, it is hereby agreed, that the provisions contained in the ninth article of the Treaty concluded and signed at fort Clark, on the tenth day of November, one thousand eight hundred and eight, between the United States and the said tribes or nations, shall, in every respect, be considered as in full force and applicable to the provisions of this Treaty, and that the United States shall take and receive, into their friendship and protection, the aforesaid tribes or nations, and shall guaranty to them, forever, the right to navigate, freely, all water-courses, or navigable streams, within the tract of country hereby ceded, upon such terms as the same are or may be navigated by the citizens of the United States.

ARTICLE 12.

Merchandise to be delivered to Indians.

It is further agreed, that there shall be delivered as soon as may be, after the execution of this treaty, at the Osage villages, merchandise to the amount of four thousand dollars, first cost, in St. Louis, and two thousand dollars in merchandise, before their departure from this place; and horses and equipage, to the value of twenty-six hundred dollars; which, together with the sum of one hundred dollars, to be paid to Paul Loise, and the like sum to Baptiste Mongrain, in money, shall be in addition to the provisions and stipulations hereby above contained, in full satisfaction of the cession, hereinbefore agreed on.

ARTICLE 13.

Amount due A. P. Chouteau and others to be in part paid by the United States.

Whereas the Great and Little Osage tribes or nations are indebted to Augustus P. Chouteau, Paul Balio, and William S. Williams, to a large amount, for credits given to them, which they are unable to pay, and have particularly requested to have paid, or provided for, in the present negotiation; it is, therefore, agreed on, by and between the parties to these presents, that the United States shall pay to Augustus P. Chouteau, one thousand dollars; to Paul Balio, two hundred and fifty dollars, and to William S. Williams two hundred and fifty dollars, towards the liquidation of their respective debts due from the said tribes or nations.

ARTICLE 14.

These articles shall take effect, and become obligatory on the con- Treaty to be obligatory when ratified. tracting parties, so soon as the same shall be ratified by the President, by and with the advice and consent of the Senate of the United States.

In testimony whereof, the said William Clark, commissioner as aforesaid, and the deputation, chiefs, and head men, and warriors, of the Great and Little Osage nations of Indians, as aforesaid, have hereunto set their hands and seals, this second day of June, in the year of our Lord one thousand eight hundred and twenty-five, and of the independence of the United States the forty-ninth.

William Clark.

Clairmont, his x mark, [L. S.]	Vagasidda, his x mark, [L. S.]
Pahusca, or White Hair, his x mark, [L. S.]	Tawangahe, his x mark, [L. S.]
Chingawasa, or Handsome Bird, his x mark, [L. S.]	Paigaismanie, or Big Soldier, his x mark, [L. S.]
Wasabaistanga, or Big Bear, his x mark, [L. S.]	Tagawahais, or Town Maker, his x mark, [L. S.]
Waharsachais, his x mark, [L. S.]	Chongaismonnon, or Dog Thief, his x mark, [L. S.]
Cochestawasca, or He that sees far, his x mark, [L. S.]	Honiaigo, or Gentleman, his x mark, [L. S.]
Vanonpachais, or He that is not afraid, his x mark, [L. S.]	Hinchaacri, his x mark, [L. S.]
Khigaischinga, or Little Chief, his x mark, [L. S.]	Wakandaippahobi, his x mark, [L. S.]
Wataniga, or Fool, his x mark, [L. S.]	Saba, his x mark, [L. S.]
Jean Lafond, his x mark, [L. S.]	Nasa, his x mark, [L. S.]
Wachinsabais, or Black Spirit, his x mark, [L. S.]	Manchan, his x mark, [L. S.]
	Manchanginda, his x mark, [L. S.]
Hurachais, the War Eagle, his x mark, [L. S.]	Little Osages:
Huralu, his x mark, [L. S.]	Nichumani, or Walking Rain, his x mark, [L. S.]
Manchuhonga, his x mark, [L. S.]	Nihuchaisningaiswachinpichais, his x mark, [L. S.]
Chongaishonga, his x mark, [L. S.]	Waruhagais, his x mark, [L. S.]
Tawangahais, his x mark, [L. S.]	Mangaischis, his x mark, [L. S.]
Ponkchinga, his x mark, [L. S.]	Mances'tpogran, his x mark, [L. S.]
Nicohibran, his x mark, [L. S.]	Nonbaaheri, his x mark, [L. S.]
Panimonpachais, his x mark, [L. S.]	Howasabais, his x mark, [L. S.]
Wasissegaistango, or Big Broom, his x mark, [L. S.]	Nehuchaisningaischinga, his x mark, [L. S.]
Chonjaishengais, his x mark, [L. S.]	Aquidachinga, his x mark, [L. S.]
Wabachequand, his x mark, [L. S.]	Sanjaiskanha, his x mark, [L. S.]
Wastiagais, his x mark, [L. S.]	Manpumahi, his x mark, [L. S.]
Ishtassca, his x mark, [L. S.]	Manhinonba, his x mark, [L. S.]
Manchehamani, his x mark, [L. S.]	Khigaiswachinpichais, or Missouri chief, his x mark, [L. S.]
Hangaquechais, his x mark, [L. S.]	Ostiehingais, his x mark, [L. S.]
Hanhanmani, his x mark, [L. S.]	Hasachais, his x mark, [L. S.]
Walutacest, his x mark, [L. S.]	Hanhanpac'est, his x mark, [L. S.]
Niha, his x mark, [L. S.]	Manchaquida, his x mark, [L. S.]
Wanansonjais, his x mark, [L. S.]	Tiessinjais, his x mark, [L. S.]

Witnesses present:

R. Wash, secretary,	F. A. Chardon,
Edward Coles, governor of Illinois,	Antonie Leclaire, interpreter,
A. McNair, Osage agent,	James Coleman,
Pr. Chouteau,	Paul Louise, his x mark, interpreter,
W. B. Alexander, sub Indian agent,	(Osages,)
Theodore Hunt,	William Milburn,
Cerre,	Noel Dashnay, interpreter,
P. L. Chouteau, sub agent,	Mauchaugachau, his x mark,
L. T. Honorie, interpreter,	Thepogrenque, his x mark.

TREATY WITH THE KANSA, 1825.

June 3, 1825.
7 Stat., 244.
Proclamation, Dec. 30, 1825.

Articles of a treaty made and concluded at the City of Saint Louis, in the State of Missouri, between William Clark, Superintendent of Indian Affairs, Commissioner on the part of the United States of America, and the undersigned Chiefs, Head Men, and Warriors of the Kansas Nation of Indians, duly authorized and empowered by said Nation.

ARTICLE 1.

Cession by the Kansas.

THE Kansas do hereby cede to the United States all the lands lying within the State of Missouri, to which the said nation have title or claim; and do further cede and relinquish, to the said United States, all other lands which they now occupy, or to which they have title or claim, lying West of the said State of Missouri, and within the following boundaries: beginning at the entrance of the Kansas river into the Missouri river; from thence North to the North-West corner of the State of Missouri; from thence Westwardly to the Nodewa river, thirty miles from its entrance into the Missouri; from thence to the entrance of the big Nemahaw river into the Missouri, and with that river to its source; from thence to the source of the Kansas river, leaving the old village of the Pania Republic to the West; from thence, on the ridge dividing the waters of the Kansas river from those of the Arkansas, to the Western boundary of the State line of Missouri, and with that line, thirty miles, to the place of beginning.

ARTICLE 2.

Reservation for the use of the Kansas.

From the cession aforesaid, the following reservation for the use of the Kansas nation of Indians shall be made, of a tract of land, to begin twenty leagues up the Kansas river, and to include their village on that river; extending West thirty miles in width, through the lands ceded in the first Article, to be surveyed and marked under the direction of the President, and to such extent as he may deem necessary, and at the expense of the United States. The agents for the Kansas, and the persons attached to the agency, and such teachers and instructors as the President shall authorize to reside near the Kansas, shall occupy, during his pleasure, such lands as may be necessary for them within this reservation.

ARTICLE 3.

Payment to them for their cession.

In consideration of the cession of land and relinquishments of claims, made in the first Articles, the United States agree to pay to the Kansas nation of Indians, three thousand five hundred dollars per annum, for twenty successive years, at their villages, or at the entrance of the Kansas river, either in money, merchandise, provisions, or domestic animals, at the option of the aforesaid Nation; and when the said annuities, or any part thereof, is paid in merchandise, it shall be delivered to them at the first cost of the goods in Saint Louis, free of transportation.

ARTICLE 4.

Cattle, hogs, etc., to be furnished by United States.

The United States, immediately upon the ratification of this convention, or as soon thereafter as may be, shall cause to be furnished to the Kansas Nation, three hundred head of cattle, three hundred hogs, five hundred domestic fowls, three yoke of oxen, and two carts, with such implements of agriculture as the Superintendant of Indian Affairs may think necessary; and shall employ such persons to aid and instruct them in their agriculture, as the President of the United States may deem expedient; and shall provide and support a blacksmith for them.

ARTICLE 5.

Out of the lands herein ceded by the Kanzas Nation to the United States, the Commissioner aforesaid, in behalf of the said United States, doth further covenant and agree, that thirty-six sections of good lands, on the Big Blue river, shall be laid out under the direction of the President of the United States, and sold for the purpose of raising a fund, to be applied, under the direction of the President, to the support of schools for the education of the Kanzas children, within their Nation.

Land to be sold for support of schools.

ARTICLE 6.

From the lands above ceded to the United States, there shall be made the following reservations, of one mile square, for each of the half breeds of the Kanzas nation, viz: For Adel and Clement, the two children of Clement; for Josette, Julie, Pelagie, and Victoire, the four children of Louis Gonvil; for Marie and Lafleche, the two children of Baptiste of Gonvil; for Laventure, the son of Francis Laventure; for Elizabeth and Pierre Carbonau, the children of Pierre Brisa; for Louis Joncas; for Basil Joncas; for James Joncas; for Elizabeth Datcherute, daughter of Baptiste Datcherute; for Joseph Butler; for William Rodgers; for Joseph Coté; for the four children of Cicili Compáre, each one mile square; and one for Joseph James, to be located on the North side of the Kanzas river, in the order above named, commencing at the line of the Kanzas reservation, and extending down the Kanzas river for quantity.

Reservations for the use of half-breeds.

ARTICLE 7.

With the view of quieting all animosities which may at present exist between a part of the white citizens of Missouri and the Kanzas nation, in consequence of the lawless depredations of the latter, the United States do further agree to pay their own citizens, the full value of such property as they can legally prove to have been stolen or destroyed since the year 1815: *Provided*, The sum so to be paid by the United States shall not exceed the sum of three thousand dollars.

Agreement entered into by the United States for certain purposes.

Proviso.

ARTICLE 8.

And whereas the Kanzas are indebted to Francis G. Choteau, for credits given them in trade, which they are unable to pay, and which they have particularly requested to have included and settled in the present Treaty; it is, therefore, agreed on, by and between the parties to these presents, that the sum of five hundred dollars, towards the liquidation of said debt, shall be paid by the United States to the said Francois G. Choteau.

Payment to F. G. Choteau.

ARTICLE 9.

There shall be selected at this place such merchandise as may be desired, amounting to two thousand dollars, to be delivered at the Kanzas river, with as little delay as possible; and there shall be paid to the deputation now here, two thousand dollars in merchandise and horses, the receipt of which is hereby acknowledged; which, together with the amount agreed on in the 3d and 4th articles, and the provisions made in the other articles of this Treaty, shall be considered as a full compensation for the cession herein made.

Merchandise to amount of $2,000 to be delivered at the Kansas river.

ARTICLE 10.

Punishment of offenses.

Lest the friendship which is now established between the United States and the said Indian Nation should be interrupted by the misconduct of Individuals, it is hereby agreed, that for injuries done by individuals, no private revenge or retaliation shall take place, but instead thereof, complaints shall be made by the party injured, to the other by the said nation, to the Superintendent, or other person appointed by the President to the Chiefs of said nation. And it shall be the duty of the said Chiefs, upon complaints being made as aforesaid, to deliver up the person or persons against whom the complaint is made, to the end that he or they may be punished, agreeably to the laws of the State or Territory where the offence may have been committed; and in like manner, if any robbery, violence, or murder, shall be committed on any Indian or Indians belonging to said nation, the person or persons so offending shall be tried, and, if found guilty, shall be punished in

Chiefs to exert themselves to recover stolen property, etc.

like manner as if the injury had been done to a white man. And it is agreed, that the Chiefs of the Kanzas shall, to the utmost of their power, exert themselves to recover horses or other property which may be stolen from any citizen or citizens of the United States, by any individual or individuals of the Nation; and the property so recovered shall be forthwith delivered to the Superintendent, or other person authorized to receive it, that it may be restored to its proper owner; and in cases where the exertions of the Chiefs shall be ineffectual in recovering the property stolen as aforesaid, if sufficient proof can be adduced that such property was actually stolen, by any Indian or Indians belonging to the said nation, the Superintendent or other officer may deduct from the annuity of the said nation a sum equal to the value of the property which has been stolen. And the United States hereby guarantee, to any Indian or Indians, a full indemnification for any horses or other property which may be stolen from them by any

Proviso.

of their citizens: *Provided,* That the property so stolen cannot be recovered, and that sufficient proof is produced that it was actually stolen by a citizen of the United States. And the said Nation of Kanzas engage, on the requisition or demand of the President of the United States, or of the Superintendent, to deliver up any white man resident amongst them.

ARTICLE 11.

United States to enjoy the right of navigating the water courses, etc.

It is further agreed on, by and between the parties to these presents, that the United States shall forever enjoy the right to navigate freely all water courses or navigable streams within the limits of the tract of country herein reserved to the Kanzas Nation; and that the said Kanzas Nation shall never sell, relinquish, or in any manner dispose of the lands herein reserved, to any other nation, person or persons whatever, without the permission of the United States for that purpose first had and obtained. And shall ever remain under the protection of the United States, and in friendship with them.

ARTICLE 12.

Treaty binding when ratified.

This Treaty shall take effect, and be obligatory on the contracting parties, as soon as the same shall be ratified by the President, by and with the consent and advice of the Senate of the United States.

In testimony whereof, the said William Clark, commissioner as aforesaid, and the deputation, chiefs, head men, and warriors of the Kanzas nation of Indians, as aforesaid, have hereunto set their hands and seals, this third day of June, in the year of our Lord eighteen hundred and twenty-five, and of the independence of the United States of America the forty-ninth year.

William Clark,	[L. S.]	Hu-ru-ah-te, his x mark, or the Real Eagle,	[L. S.]
Nom-pa-wa-rah, or the White Plume, his x mark,	[L. S.]	Ca-she-se-gra, his x mark, or the track that sees far,	[L. S.]
Ky-he-ga-wa-ti-nin-ka, his x mark, or the Full Chief,	[L. S.]	Wa-can-da-ga-tun-ga, his x mark, or the Great Doctor,	[L. S.]
Ky-he-ga-wa-che-he, his x mark, or the Chief of great valor,	[L. S.]	O-pa-she-ga, his x mark, or the Cooper,	[L. S.]
Ky-he-ga-shin-ga, his x mark, or the Little Chief,	[L. S.]	Cha-ho-nush, his x mark,	[L. S.]
Ka-ba-ra-hu, his x mark,	[L. S.]	Ma-he-ton-ga, his x mark, or the American,	[L. S.]
Me-chu-chin-ga, his x mark, or the Little White Bear,	[L. S.]		

Witnesses present:

R. Wash, secretary,
W. B. Alexander, sub Indian agent,
John F. A. Sanford,
G. C. Sibley, United States Commissioner,
Baronet Vasquez, United States sale agent,
Russel Farnham,
Jno. K. Walker,
Jno. Simonds, Jr.

Sanderson Robert,
L. T. Honore, United States interpreter,
William Milburn,
Baptis Ducherut, interpreter for Kanzas,
Paul Louise, his x mark, Osage interpreter,
Noel Dashnay, interpreter,
Ant. Le Claire.

TREATY WITH THE PONCA, 1825.

For the purposes of perpetuating the friendship which has heretofore existed, as also to remove all future cause of discussion or dissension, as it respects trade and friendship between the United States and their citizens, and the Poncar tribe of Indians, the President of the United States of America, by Brigadier General Henry Atkinson, of the United States' Army, and Major Benjamin O'Fallon, Indian Agent, with full powers and authority, specially appointed and commissioned for that purpose of the one part, and the undersigned Chiefs, Headmen, and Warriors, of the Poncar tribe of Indians, on behalf of said tribe, of the other part, have made and entered into the following articles and conditions, which, when ratified by the President of the United States, by and with the advice and consent of the Senate, shall be binding on both parties—to wit:

June 9, 1825.

7 Stat., 247.
Proclamation, Feb 6, 1826.

ARTICLE 1.

It is admitted by the Poncar tribe of Indians, that they reside within the territorial limits of the United States, acknowledge their supremacy, and claim their protection. The said tribe also admit the right of the United States to regulate all trade and intercourse with them.

Supremacy of United States acknowledged.

ARTICLE 2.

The United States agree to receive the Poncar tribe of Indians into their friendship, and under their protection, and to extend to them, from time to time, such benefits and acts of kindness as may be convenient, and seem just and proper to the President of the United States.

United States will take the Poncars under their protection.

ARTICLE 3.

All trade and intercourse with the Poncar tribe shall be transacted at such place or places as may be designated and pointed out by the President of the United States, through his agents; and none but American citizens, duly authorized by the United States, shall be admitted to trade or hold intercourse with said tribe of Indians.

Trade, etc., to be transacted at such places as the President may designate.

ARTICLE 4.

Regulation of trade among the Indians.

That the Poncar tribe may be accommodated with such articles of merchandise, &c. as their necessities may demand, the United States agree to admit and license traders to hold intercourse with said tribe, under mild and equitable regulations: in consideration of which, the Poncar tribe bind themselves to extend protection to the persons and the property of the traders, and the persons legally employed under them, whilst they remain within the limits of the Poncar district of country. And the said Poncar tribe further agree, that if any foreigner, or other person not legally authorized by the United States, shall come into their district of country, for the purposes of trade or other views, they will apprehend such person or persons, and deliver him or them to some United States' superintendent, or agent of Indian Affairs, or to the Commandant of the nearest military post, to be dealt with according to law. And they further agree to give safe conduct to all persons who may be legally authorized by the United States to pass through their country; and to protect, in their persons and property, all agents or other persons sent by the United States to reside temporarily among them.

ARTICLE 5.

Course to be pursued in order to prevent injuries by individuals.

That the friendship which is now established between the United States and the Poncar tribe should not be interrupted by the misconduct of individuals, it is hereby agreed, that for injuries done by individuals, no private revenge or retaliation shall take place, but instead thereof, complaints shall be made, by the party injured, to the superintendent or agent of Indian affairs, or other person appointed by the President; and it shall be the duty of the said Chiefs, upon complaint being made as aforesaid, to deliver up the person or persons against whom the complaint is made, to the end that he or they may be punished agreeably to the laws of the United States. And, in like manner, if any robbery, violence, or murder, shall be committed on any Indian or Indians belonging to said tribe, the person or persons so offending shall be tried, and if found guilty shall be punished in like manner as

Chiefs to exert themselves to recover stolen property.

if the injury had been done to a white man. And it is agreed, that the Chiefs of said Poncar tribe shall, to the utmost of their power, exert themselves to recover horses or other property, which may be stolen or taken from any citizen or citizens of the United States, by any individual or individuals of said tribe; and the property so recovered shall be forthwith delivered to the agents or other person authorized to receive it, that it may be restored to the proper owner. And the United States hereby guaranty to any Indian or Indians of said tribe, a full indemnification for any horses or other property which may be stolen from

Proviso.

them by any of their citizens: *Provided,* That the property so stolen cannot be recovered, and that sufficient proof is produced that it was actually stolen by a citizen of the United States. And the said Poncar tribe engage, on the requisition or demand of the President of the United States, or of the agents, to deliver up any white man resident among them.

ARTICLE 6.

No guns, etc., to be furnished by them to any nation, etc., hostile to the United States.

And the Chiefs and Warriors, as aforesaid, promise and engage, that their tribe will never, by sale, exchange, or as presents, supply any nation or tribe of Indians, not in amity with the United States, with guns, ammunition, or other implements of War.

Done at the Poncar Village, at the mouth of White Paint creek, the first below the Qui Carre river, this 9th day of June, A. D. 1825, and of the independence of the United States the forty-ninth.

In testimony whereof, the said commissioners, Henry Atkinson and Benjamin O'Fallon, and the chiefs, head men, and warriors, of the Poncar tribe, have hereunto set their hands and affixed their seals.

H. Atkinson, brigadier-general, U. S. Army, [L. S.]
Benj. O'Fallon, United States agent Indian Affairs, [L. S.]
Shu-de-gah-he, or He who makes Smoke, his x mark, [L. S.]
Ish-ca-da-bee, or Child Chief, his x mark, [L. S.]
Wah-ha-nee-che, or He who hides something, his x mark, [L. S.]
Wah, or The Hoe, his x mark, [L. S.]
O-nam-ba-haa, or Lightning, his x mark, [L. S.]
Ti-e-kee-ree, or Big Head with tangled hair, his x mark, [L. S.]
Wa-we-shu-shee, or The Brave, his x mark, [L. S.]
Ou-de-cowee, or the one that has been wounded, his x mark, [L. S.]
Ne-ou-gree, or Prairie apple, his x mark, [L. S.]

Woh-ge-a-mussee, or The flying iron, his x mark, [L. S.]
Pee-la-ga, or Buffalo, his x mark, [L. S.]
Wah-buc-kee, or The bull that leads, his x mark, [L. S.]
Wah-ha-nega, or He that has no knife, his x mark, [L. S.]
Mah-shar-harree, or He that walks on land, his x mark, [L. S.]
Mach-souch-kee-na-pabee, or He that fears no bears, his x mark, [L. S.]
Ca-hee-tha-bee, or Black raven, his x mark, [L. S.]
Gah-he-ga, or The relative of the Chiefs, his mark, [L. S.]
Na-hee-tapee, or He that stamps, his x mark, [L. S.]
Na-ne-pa-shee, or One that knows, his x mark, [L. S.]

Witnesses:

H. Leavenworth, colonel, U. S. Army.
S. W. Kearny, brevet major First Infantry.
D. Ketchum, major, U. S. Army.
G. H. Kennerley, U. S. S. Indian agent.
John Gale, surgeon, U. S. Army.
J. Gantt, captain, Sixth Infanty.
Wm. Armstrong, captain, Sixth Regiment Infantry.
S. MacRee, lieutenant, First Infantry.
J. Rogers, lieutenant, Sixth Infantry.
Thomas Noel, lieutenant, Sixth Infantry.
S. Wragg, adjutant, First Regiment Infantry.
R. Holmes, lieutenant, Sixth Infantry.

Thos. P. Gwynn, lieutenant, First Infantry.
Levi Nute, lieutenant, Sixth Infantry.
Jas. W. Kingsbury, lieutenant, First Regiment Infantry.
M. W. Batman, lieutenant, Sixth Infantry.
Wm. L. Harris, First Infantry.
R. M. Coleman, assistant surgeon, U. S. Army.
Wm. Gordon,
A. Langman,
P. X. Promo,
A. L. Langham, Secretary to the Commission.

TREATY WITH THE TETON, ETC., SIOUX, 1825.

Treaty with the Teton, Yancton, and Yanctonies bands of the Sioux tribe of Indians.

June 22, 1825.

7 Stat., 250.
Proclamation, Feb. 6, 1826.

For the purposes of perpetuating the friendship which has heretofore existed, as also to remove all future cause of discussion or dissension, as it respects trade and friendship between the United States and their citizens, and the Teton, Yancton, and Yanctonies bands of the Sioux tribe of Indians, the President of the United States of America, by Brigadier-General Henry Atkinson, of the United States' army, and Major Benjamin O'Fallon, Indian Agent, with full powers and authority, specially appointed and commissioned for that purpose of the one part, and the undersigned Chiefs, head men and Warriors of the Teton, Yancton, and Yanctonies bands of the Sioux tribe of Indians, on behalf of said bands or tribe of the other part, have made and entered into the following Articles and Conditions; which, when ratified by the President of the United States, by and with the advice and consent of the Senate; shall be binding on both parties—to wit:

ARTICLE 1.

It is admitted by the Teton, Yancton and Yanctonies bands of Sioux Indians, that they reside within the territorial limits of the United

Supremacy of United States acknowledged.

States, acknowledge their supremacy, and claim their protection.   The said bands also admit the right of the United States to regulate all trade and intercourse with them.

ARTICLE 2.

Protection of United States extended to them.

The United States agree to receive the said Teton, Yancton, and Yanctonies band of Sioux Indians into their friendship, and under their protection, and to extend to them, from time to time, such benefits and acts of kindness as may be convenient, and seem just and proper to the President of the United States.

ARTICLE 3.

Places for trade to be designated by the President.

All trade and intercourse with the Teton, Yancton, and Yanctonies bands shall be transacted at such place or places as may be designated and pointed out by the President of the United States, through his agents; and none but American citizens, duly authorized by the United States, shall be admitted to trade or hold intercourse with said bands of Indians.

ARTICLE 4.

Regulation of trade with Indians.

That the Teton, Yancton, and Yanctonies bands may be accommodated with such articles of merchandise, &c. as their necessities may demand, the United States agree to admit and license traders to hold intercourse with said tribes or bands, under mild and equitable regulations: in consideration of which, the Teton, Yancton, and Yanctonies bands bind themselves to extend protection to the persons and the property of the traders, and the persons legally employed under them, whilst they remain within the limits of their particular district of country.   And the said Teton, Yancton, and Yanctonies bands further agree, that if any foreigner or other person, not legally authorized by the United States, shall come into their district of country, for the purposes of trade or other views, they will apprehend such person or persons, and deliver him or them to some United States' superintendent, or agent of Indian Affairs, or to the nearest military post, to be dealt with according to law.—And they further agree to give safe conduct to all persons who may be legally authorized by the United States to pass through their country: and to protect, in their persons and property, all agents or other persons sent by the United States to reside temporarily among them.

ARTICLE 5.

Course to be pursued in order to prevent injuries by individuals, etc.

That the friendship which is now established between the United States and the Teton, Yancton, and Yanctonies bands should not be interrupted by the misconduct of individuals, it is hereby agreed, that for injuries done by individuals, no private revenge or retaliation shall take place, but instead thereof, complaints shall be made, by the party injured, to the superintendent or agent of Indian affairs, or other person appointed by the President; and it shall be the duty of the said Chiefs, upon complaint being made as aforesaid, to deliver up the person or persons against whom the complaint is made, to the end that he or they may be punished agreeably to the laws of the United States.   And, in like manner, if any robbery, violence, or murder, shall be committed on any Indian or Indians belonging to said bands, the person or persons so offending shall be tried, and if found guilty, shall be punished in like manner as if the injury had been done to a white man.   And it is

Chiefs to exert themselves to recover stolen property.

agreed, that the chiefs of the said Teton, Yancton, and Yanctonies bands shall, to the utmost of their power, exert themselves to recover horses or other property, which may be stolen or taken from any citizen or citizens of the United States by any individual or individuals of said bands; and the property so recovered shall be forthwith delivered to the agents, or other person authorized to receive it, that it may be restored to the proper owner. And the United States hereby guaranty to any Indian or Indians of said bands, a full indemnification for any horses or other property which may be stolen from them by any of their citizens: *Provided*, That the property so stolen cannot be recovered, and that sufficient proof is produced that it was actually stolen by a citizen of the United States. And the said Teton, Yancton, and Yanctonies bands engage, on the requisition or demand of the President of the United States, or of the agents, to deliver up any white man resident among them.

Proviso.

ARTICLE 6.

And the Chiefs and Warriors, as aforesaid, promise and engage, their band or tribe will never, by sale, exchange, or as presents, supply any nation or tribe of Indians, not in amity with the United States, with guns, ammunition, or other implements of war.

No arms to be furnished by Indians to persons not in amity with United States.

Done at fort Look-out, near the three rivers of the Sioux pass, this 22d day of June, A. D. 1825, and of the independence of the United States the forty-ninth.

In testimony whereof the said commissioners, Henry Atkinson and Benjamin O'Fallon, and the chiefs, head men, and warriors, of the Teton, Yancton, and Yanctonies bands, of Sioux tribe, have hereunto set their hands, and affixed their seals.

H. Atkinson, brigadier general U. S. Army. [L. S.]
Benj. O'Fallon, United States Agent Indian Affairs, [L. S.]
Yanctons:
Maw-too-sa-be-kia, the black bear, his x mark, [L. S.]
Wacan-o-hi-gnan, the flying medicine, his x mark, [L. S.]
Wah-ha-ginga, the little dish, his x mark, [L. S.]
Cha-pon-ka, the musqueto, his x mark, [L. S.]
Eta-ke-nus-ke-an, the mad face, his x mark, [L. S.]
To-ka-oo, the one that kills, his x mark, [L. S.]
O-ga-tee, the fork, his x mark, [L. S.]
You-ia-san, the warrior, his x mark, [L. S.]
Wah-ta-ken-do, the one who comes from war, his x mark, [L. S.]
To-qui-in-too, the little soldier, his x mark, [L. S.]
Ha-sas-hah, the Ioway, his x mark, [L. S.]
Tétons:
Ta-tan-ka-guenish-qui-gnan, the mad buffalo, his x mark, [L. S.]
Mah-to-ken-do-ha-cha, the hollow bear, his x mark, [L. S.]

E-gue-mon-wa-con-ta, the one that shoots at the tiger, his x mark, [L. S.]
Jai-kan-kan-e, the child chief, his x mark, [L. S.]
Shawa-non, or O-e-te-kah, the brave, his x mark, [L. S.]
Man-to-dan-za, the running bear, his x mark, [L. S.]
Wa-can-guela-sassa, the black lightning, his x mark, [L. S.]
Wa-be-la-wa-con, the medicine war eagle, his x mark, [L. L.]
Cam-pes-cah-o-ran-co, the swift shell, his x mark, [L. S.]
Eh-ra-ka-che-ka-la, the little elk, his x mark, [L. S.]
Na-pe-a-mus-ka, the mad hand, his x mark, [L. S.]
J-a-pee, the soldier, his x mark, [L. S.]
Hoo-wa-gah-hak, the broken leg, his x mark, [L. S.]
Ce-cha-he, or the burnt thigh, his x mark, [L. S.]
O-caw-see-non-gea, or the spy, his x mark, [L. S.]
Ta-tun-ca-see-ha-hue-ka, the buffalo with the long foot, his x mark, [L. S.]
Ah-kee-che-ha-che-ga-la, the little soldier, his x mark, [L. S.]

In presence of—

A. L. Langham, secretary to the commission,
H. Leavenworth, colonel, U. S. Army,
S. W. Kearney, brevet major, First Infantry,
G. H. Kennerly, U. S. S. Indian agent,
P. Wilson, U. S. S. Indian agent,
Wm. Armstrong, captain, Sixth Regiment Infantry,
R. B. Mason, captain, First Infantry,

J. Gantt, captain, Sixth Infantry,
S. Mac Ree, lieutenant and aid de camp,
Wm. S. Harney, lieutenant, First Infantry,
Thomas Noel, lieutenant, Sixth Infantry.
B. Riley, captain, Sixth Infantry,
James W. Kingsbury, lieutenant, First Regiment,
S. Wragg, adjutant, First Regiment,
G. C. Spencer, captain, First Regiment,

A. S. Miller, lieutenant, First Infantry,
H. Swearingen, lieutenant, First Infantry,
Thos. P. Gwynn, lieutenant, First Infantry,
M. W. Batman, lieutenant, Sixth Infantry,
George C. Hutter, lieutenant, Sixth Infantry,

J. Rogers, lieutenant, Sixth Infantry,
Wm. Day, lieutenant, First Infantry,
John Gale, surgeon, U. S. Army,
D. Ketchum, major, U. S. Army,
R. H. Stuart, lieutenant, First Infantry,
Wm. Gordon,
Jean Baptiste Dorion.

July 5, 1825.

7 Stat., 252.
Proclamation, Feb.
6, 1826.

TREATY WITH THE SIOUNE AND OGLALA TRIBES, 1825.

For the purpose of perpetuating the friendship which has heretofore existed, as also to remove all future cause of discussion or dissension, as it respects trade and friendship between the United States and their citizens, and the Sioune and Ogallala bands of the Sioux tribe of Indians, the President of the United States of America, by Brigadier-General Henry Atkinson, of the United States' Army, and Major Benjamin O'Fallon, Indian Agent, with full powers and authority, specially appointed and commissioned for that purpose, of the one part, and the undersigned Chiefs, Head-men, and Warriors, of the said Sioune and Ogallala bands of Sioux Indians, on behalf of their bands, of the other part, have made and entered into the following articles and conditions, which, when ratified by the President of the United States, by and with the advice and consent of the Senate shall be binding on both parties,—to wit:

ARTICLE 1.

Supremacy of United States acknowledged.

It is admitted by the Sioune and Ogallala bands of Sioux Indians, that they reside within the territorial limits of the United States, acknowledge their supremacy, and claim their protection. The said bands also admit the right of the United States to regulate all trade and intercourse with them.

ARTICLE 2.

United States receive them under their protection.

The United States agree to receive the Sioune and Ogallala bands of Sioux into their friendship, and under their protection, and to extend to them, from time to time, such benefits and acts of kindness as may be convenient, and seem just and proper to the President of the United States.

ARTICLE 3.

Places for trade to be designated by the President.

All trade and intercourse with the Sioune and Ogallala bands shall be transacted at such place or places as may be designated and pointed out by the President of the United States, through his agents; and none but American citizens, duly authorized by the United States, shall be admitted to trade or hold intercourse with said bands of Indians.

ARTICLE 4.

Regulation of trade among the Indians.

That the Sioune and Ogallala bands may be accommodated with such articles of merchandise, &c. as their necessities may demand, the United States agree to admit and license traders to hold intercourse with said bands, under mild and equitable regulations: in consideration of which, the Sioune and Ogallala bands bind themselves to extend protection to the persons and the property of the traders, and the persons legally employed under them, whilst they remain within the limits of their particular district of country. And the said Sioune and Ogallala bands further agree, that if any foreigner or other persons, not legally authorized by the United States, shall come into their district of country, for the purposes of trade or other views, they will apprehend such person or persons, and deliver him or them to some United States' superintendent, or agent of Indian affairs, or to the commandant of the nearest military post, to be dealt with according to law.—And they further agree to give safe conduct to all persons who may be legally authorized by the United States to pass through their country; and to protect, in their persons and property, all agents or other persons sent by the United States to reside temporarily among them; nor will they, whilst on their distant excursions, molest or interrupt any American citizen or citizens who may be passing from the United States to New Mexico, or returning from thence to the United States.

ARTICLE 5.

That the friendship, which is now established between the United States and the Sioune and Ogallala bands should not be interrupted by the misconduct of individuals, it is hereby agreed, that for injuries done by individuals, no private revenge or retaliation shall take place, but instead thereof, complaints shall be made, by the injured party, to the superintendent or agent of Indian affairs, or other person appointed by the President; and it shall be the duty of said Chiefs, upon complaint being made as aforesaid, to deliver up the person or persons, against whom the complaint is made, to the end that he or they may be punished agreeably to the laws of the United States. And, in like manner, if any robbery, violence or murder, shall be committed on any Indian or Indians belonging to the said bands, the person or persons so offending shall be tried, and if found guilty shall be punished in like manner as if the injury had been done to a white man. And it is agreed, that the chiefs of said Sioune and Ogallala bands shall, to the utmost of their power, exert themselves to recover horses or other property, which may be stolen or taken from any citizen or citizens of the United States, by any individual or individuals of said bands; and the property so recovered shall be forthwith delivered to the agents or other person authorized to receive it, that it may be restored to the proper owner. And the United States hereby guaranty to any Indian or Indians of said bands, a full idemnification for any horses or other property which may be stolen from them by any of their citizens: *Provided*, The property stolen cannot be recovered, and that sufficient proof is produced that it was actually stolen by a citizen of the United States. And the said Sioune and Ogallala bands engage, on the requisition or demand of the President of the United States, or of the agents, to deliver up any white man resident among them.

Course to be pursued in order to prevent injuries by individuals, etc.

Chiefs to exert themselves to recover stolen property.

ARTICLE 6.

And the Chiefs and Warriors, as aforesaid, promise and engage, that their bands will never, by sale, exchange, or as presents, supply any nation, tribe, or band of Indians, not in amity with the United States, with guns, ammunition, or other implements of war.

No guns, etc., to be furnished by them to any tribe, etc., hostile to United States.

Done at the mouth of the Teton river, this 5th day of July, A. D. 1825, and of the independence of the United States the fiftieth.

In testimony whereof, the said commissioners, Henry Atkinson and Benjamin O'Fallon, and the chiefs, head men, and warriors, of the Sioune and Ogallala bands, have hereunto set their hands, and affixed their seals.

H. Atkinson, Brigadier-General, U. S. Army. [L. S.]	Ma-ra-sea, the White Swan, his x mark, [L. S.]
Benj. O'Fallon, United States agent Indian Affairs. [L. S.]	Chan-dee, the Tobacco, his x mark, [L. S.]
Siounes chiefs:	O-ke-ma, the Chief, his x mark, [L. S.]
Wah-e-ne-ta, the Rushing Man, his x mark, [L. S.]	Tow-cow-sa-no-pa, the Two Lance, his x mark, [L. S.]
Cah-re-we-ca-ca, the Crow Feather, his x mark, [L. S.]	Warriors:
	Chan-ta-wah-nee-cha, the No Heart, his x mark, [L. S.]

He-hum-pee, the one that has a voice in his neck, his x mark, [L. S.]
Num-cah-pay, the one that knocks down two, his x mark, [L. S.]
Ogallala chiefs:
Ta-tun-ca-nash-sha, the Standing Buffalo, his x mark, [L. S.]
He-a-long-ga, the Shoulder, his x mark, [L. S.]
Ma-to-weet-co, the Full White Bear, his x mark, [L. S.]

Wa-na-re-wag-she-go, the Ghost Boy, his x mark, [L. S.]
Warriors:
Ek-hah-ka-sap-pa, the Black Elk, his x mark, [L. S.]
Tah-tong-ish-nan-na, the One Buf- falo, his x mark, [L. S.]
Mah-to-ta-tong-ca, the Buffalo White Bear, his x mark, [L. S.]
Nah-ge-nish-ge-ah, the Mad Soul, his x mark, [L. S.]

Siounes of the Fire-hearts band, who sign at Camp Hidden Creek, on the 12th July, 1825:

Chiefs:
Chan-ta-pa-ta, the Fire-heart, his x mark, [L. S.]
Wah-con-ta-mon-ee, the one that shoots as he walks, his x mark, [L. S.]
Ke-ah-ash-sha-pa, the one that makes a noise as he flies, his x mark, [L. S.]
Warriors:
Mato-co-kee-pa, the one that is afraid of the White Bear, his x mark, [L. S.]

Warriors—Continued.
Ho-ton-co-kee-pa, the one that is afraid of his voice, his x mark, [L. S.]
Wom-dish-ki-a-ta, the Spotted War Eagle, his x mark, [L. S.]
Cha-lon-we-cha-ca-ta, the one that kills the buffalo, his x mark, [L. S.]
Ca-re-no-pa, the Two Crows, his x mark, [L. S.]
Ca-re-a-tun-ca, the Crow that sits down, his x mark, [L. S.]
To-ke-a-we-cha-ca-ta, the one that kills first, his x mark, [L. S.]

In the presence of—

P. Wilson, U. S. S. Indian agent,
John Gale, surgeon, U. S. Army,
D. Ketchum, major, U. S. Army,
Levi Nute, lieutenant, U. S. Army,
G. C. Spencer, captain, First Infantry,
M. W. Batman, lieutenant, Sixth In- fantry,
Wm. Armstrong, captain, Sixth Regiment Infantry,
Jas. W. Kingsbury, lieutenant, First Regi- ment Infantry,
R. Holmes, lieutenant, Sixth Infantry,

R. M. Coleman, U. S. Army,
W. L. Harris, lieutenant, First Infantry,
H. Leavenworth, colonel, U. S. Army,
B. Riley, captain, Sixth Infantry,
S. Wragg, adjutant, First Regiment In- fantry,
Wm. Day, lieutenant, U. S. Army,
C. Pentland, captain, Sixth Infantry,
G. H. Kennerly, U. S. S. Indian agent,
Thos. P. Gwynn, lieutenant, First In- fantry.

Witnesses to the signatures of the Fire-hearts band, as executed on the 12th July, 1825:

A. L. Langham, secretary to the Commis- sion,
G. H. Kennerly, U. S. S. Indian agent,
H. Leavenworth, colonel, U. S. Army,
S. W. Kearny, brevet major, First In- fantry,

P. Wilson, U. S. S. Indian agent,
R. M. Coleman, U. S. Army,
Wm. Armstrong, captain, Sixth Regi- ment Infantry,
J. Gantt, captain, Sixth Infantry.

TREATY WITH THE CHEYENNE TRIBE, 1825.

July 6, 1825.
_____
7 Stat., 255.
Proclamation, Feb. 6, 1826.

For the Purpose of perpetuating the friendship which has hereto- fore existed, as also to remove all future cause of discussion or dissen- sion, as it respects trade and friendship between the United States and their citizens, and the Chayenne tribe of Indians, the President of the United States of America, by Brigadier-General Henry Atkinson, of the United States' army, and Major Benjamin O'Fallon, Indian agent, with full powers and authority, specially appointed and commissioned for that purpose of the one part, and the undersigned Chiefs, Head- men and Warriors, of the Chayenne tribe of Indians, on behalf of said tribe, of the other part, have made and entered into the following Articles and Conditions; which, when ratified by the President of the United States, by and with the advice and consent of the Senate, shall be binding on both parties—to wit:

ARTICLE 1.

It is admitted by the Chayenne tribe of Indians, that they reside within the territorial limits of the United States, acknowledge their supremacy, and claim their protection,—The said tribe also admit the right of the United States to regulate all trade and intercourse with them.

Supremacy of United States acknowledged.

ARTICLE 2.

The United States agree to receive the Chayenne tribe of Indians into their friendship, and under their protection, and to extend to them, from time to time, such benefits and acts of kindness as may be convenient, and seem just and proper to the President of the United States.

United States receive them under their protection.

ARTICLE 3.

All trade and intercourse with the Chayenne tribe shall be transacted at such place or places as may be designated and pointed out by the President of the United States, through his agents; and none but American citizens, duly authorized by the United. States, shall be admitted to trade or hold intercourse with said tribe of Indians.

Places for trade to be designated by the President.

ARTICLE 4.

That the Chayenne tribe may be accommodated with such articles of merchandise, &c. as their necessities may demand, the United States agree to admit and license traders to hold intercourse with said tribe, under mild and equitable regulations: in consideration of which, the Chayenne tribe bind themselves to extend protection to the persons and the property of the traders, and the persons legally employed under them, whilst they remain within the limits of their particular district of country. And the said Chayenne tribe further agree, that if any foreigner or other person, not legally authorized by the United States, shall come into their district of country, for the purposes of trade or other views, they will apprehend such person or persons, and deliver him or them to some United States' superintendent or agent of Indian Affairs, or to the commandant of the nearest military post, to be dealt with according to law. And they further agree to give safe conduct to all persons who may be legally authorized by the United States to pass through their country, and to protect in their persons and property all agents or other persons sent by the United States to reside temporarily among them; nor will they, whilst on their distant excursions, molest or interrupt any American citizen or citizens, who may be passing from the United States to New Mexico, or returning from thence to the United States.

Regulation of trade.

ARTICLE 5.

That the friendship which is now established between the United States and the Chayenne tribe, should not be interrupted by the misconduct of individuals, it is hereby agreed, that for injuries done by individuals, no private revenge or retaliation shall take place, but instead thereof, complaints shall be made, by the party injured, to the superintendent or agent of Indian affairs, or other person appointed by the President; and it shall be the duty of the said chiefs, upon complaint being made as aforesaid, to deliver up the person or persons against whom the complaint is made, to the end that he or they may be punished, agreeably to the laws of the United States. And, in like manner, if any robbery, violence, or murder, shall be committed on any Indian or Indians belonging to said tribe, the person or persons

Course to be pursued in order to prevent injuries by individuals, etc.

Chiefs to exert themselves to recover stolen property.

so offending shall be tried, and, if found guilty, shall be punished in like manner as if the injury had been done to a white man. And it is agreed, that the Chiefs of said Chayenne tribe shall, to the utmost of their power, exert themselves to recover horses or other property, which may be stolen or taken from any citizen or citizens of the United States, by any individual or individuals of said tribe; and the property so recovered shall be forthwith delivered to the agents or other person authorized to receive it, that it may be restored to the proper owner. And the United States hereby guarranty to any Indian or Indians of said tribe, a full indemnification for any horses or other property which may be stolen from them by any of their citizens: *Provided*, That the property so stolen cannot be recovered, and that sufficient proof is produced that it was actully stolen by a citizen of the United States. And the said Chayenne tribe engage, on the requisition or demand of the President of the United States, or of the agents, to deliver up any white man resident among them.

ARTICLE 6.

No guns, etc., to be furnished to any tribe hostile to United States.

And the Chiefs and Warriors, as aforesaid, promise and engage that their tribe will never, by sale, exchange, or as presents, supply any nation or tribe of Indians, not in amity with the United States, with guns, ammunition, or other implements of war.

Done at the mouth of the Teton River, this sixth day of July, A. D. 1825, and of the independence of the United States the fiftieth.

In testimony whereof, the said commissioners, Henry Atkinson and Benjamin O'Fallon, and the chiefs, head men, and warriors, of the Chayenne tribe, have hereunto set their hands and affixed their seals.

H. Atkinson, brigadier general, U. S. Army, [L. S.]
Benj. O'Fallon, United States Agent Indian Affairs, [L. S.]
Chiefs:
Sho-e-mow-e-to-chaw-ca-we-wah-ca-to-we, or the wolf with the high back, his x mark, [L. S.]
We-che-gal-la, or the Little Moon, his x mark, [L. S.]
Ta-ton-ca-pa, or the Buffalo Head, his x mark, [L. S.]
J-a-pu, or the one who walks against the others, his x mark, [L. S.]
Warriors:
Ta-ke-che-sca, or the White Deer, his x mark, [L. S.]
Chah-pac-pah-ha, or the one that raises the War Club, his x mark, [L. S.]

Ta-ton-ca-hoo-oh-ca-la-eh-pa-ha, or the pile of Buffalo bones, his x mark, [L. S.]
Ma-te-wash-e-na, or the Little White Bear, his x mark, [L. S.]
Shong-ge-mon-e-to, or the Wolf, his x mark, [L. S.]
Shong-ge-mon-e-to-e-ah-ca, or the running Wolf, his x mark, [L. S.]
Nah-pa-ton-ca, or the Big Hand, his x mark, [L. S.]
Oh-kee-che-ta, or the Soldier, his x mark, [L. S.]
Tah-hi-o-ta, or the Lousy Man, his x mark, [L. S.]

In presence of—

G. H. Kennerly, U. S. special Indian agent,
John Gale, surgeon, U. S. Army,
D. Ketchum, major, U. S. Army,
B. Riley, captain, Sixth Infantry,
John Gantt, captain, Sixth Infantry,
C. Pentland, captain, Sixth Infantry,
R. B. Mason, captain, First Infantry,
R. M. Coleman, U. S. Army,
G. C. Spencer, captain, First Infantry,
R. Holmes, lieutenant, Sixth Infantry,
M. W. Batman, lieutenant, Sixth Infantry,
Levi Nute, lieutenant, U. S. Army,
Wm. S. Harney, lieutenant, First Infantry,
Jas. W. Kingsbury, lieutenant, First Regiment Infantry,

Wm. Armstrong, captain, Sixth Regiment Infantry,
S. W. Kearny, brevet major, First Infantry,
H. Leavenworth, brevet colonel, Sixth Infantry,
J. V. Swearengen, lieutenant, First Infantry,
R. M. Coleman, U. S. Army,
C. Harris, lieutenant, First Infantry,
Wm. Day, lieutenant, U. S. Army,
S. Wragg, adjutant, First Regiment Infantry,
Thos. P. Gwynn, lieutenant, First Infantry.

TREATY WITH THE HUNKPAPA BAND OF THE SIOUX TRIBE, 1825.

FOR the purpose of perpetuating the friendship which has heretofore existed, as also to remove all future cause of discussion or dissension, as it respects trade and friendship between the United States and their citizens, and the Hunkpapas band of the Sioux tribe of Indians, the President of the United States of America, by Brigadier-General Henry Atkinson, of the United States Army, and Major Benjamin O'Fallon, Indian agent, with full powers and authority, specially appointed and commissioned for that purpose, of the one part, and the undersigned Chiefs, Headmen, and Warriors of the said Hunkpapas band of Sioux Indians, on behalf of their band, of the other part, have made and entered into the following Articles and Conditions; which, when ratified by the President of the United States, by and with the advice and consent of the Senate, shall be binding on both parties, to wit:

July 16, 1825.

7 Stat., 257.
Proclamation, Feb. 6, 1826.

ARTICLE 1.

It is admitted by the Hunkpapas band of Sioux Indians that they reside within the territorial limits of the United States, acknowledge their supremacy, and claim their protection. The said band also admit the right of the United States to regulate all trade and intercourse with them.

Supremacy of United States acknowledged.

ARTICLE 2.

The United States agree to receive the Hunkpapas band of Sioux into their friendship, and under their protection, and to extend to them, from time to time, such benefits and acts of kindness as may be convenient, and seem just and proper to the President of the United States.

United States receive them under their protection.

ARTICLE 3.

All trade and intercourse with the Hunkpapas band shall be transacted at such place or places as may be designated and pointed out by the President of the United States, through his agents; and none but American citizens, duly authorized by the United States, shall be admitted to trade or hold intercourse with said band of Indians.

Places for trade to be designated by the President.

ARTICLE 4.

That the Hunkpapas band may be accommodated with such articles of merchandise, &c., as their necessaties may demand, the United States agree to admit and license traders to hold intercourse with said band under mild and equitable regulations: in consideration of which, the Hunkpapas band bind themselves to extend protection to the persons and the property of the traders, and the persons legally employed under them, whilst they remain within the limits of their particular district of country. And the said Hunkpapas band further agree, that if any foreigner, or other person not legally authorized by the United States, shall come into their district of country, for the purposes of trade or other views, they will apprehend such person or persons, and deliver him or them to some United States' superintendent or agent of Indian affairs, or to the commandant of the nearest military post, to be dealt with according to law. And they further agree to give safe conduct to all persons who may be legally authorized by the United States to pass through their country, and to protect in their persons and property all agents or other persons sent by the United States to reside temporarily among them.

Regulation of trade.

ARTICLE 5.

Course to be pursued in order to prevent injuries by individuals, etc.

That the friendship which is now established between the United States and the Hunkpapas band should not be interrupted by the misconduct of individuals, it is hereby agreed that, for injuries done by individuals, no private revenge or retaliation shall take place, but instead thereof, complaints shall be made, by the injured party, to the superintendent or agent of Indian affairs, or other person appointed by the President: and it shall be the duty of said Chiefs, upon complaint being made as aforesaid, to deliver up the person or persons against whom the complaint is made, to the end that he or they may be punished agreeably to the laws of the United States. And in like manner, if any robbery, violence, or murder, shall be committed on any Indian or Indians belonging to the said band, the person or persons so offending shall be tried, and if found guilty, shall be punished

Chiefs to exert themselves to recover stolen property, etc.

in like manner as if the injury had been done to a white man. And it is agreed, that the chiefs of said Hunkpapas band shall, to the utmost of their power, exert themselves to recover horses or other property, which may be stolen or taken from any citizen or citizens of the United States, by any individual or individuals of said band; and the property so recovered shall be forthwith delivered to the agents or other person authorized to receive it, that it may be restored to the proper owner. And the United States hereby guarranty to any Indian or Indians of said band, a full indemnification for any horses or other property which may be stolen from them by any of their citizens:

Proviso.

Provided, That the property stolen cannot be recovered, and that sufficient proof is produced that it was actually stolen by a citizen of the United States. And the said Hunkpapas band engage, on the requisition or demand of the President of the United States, or of the agents, to deliver up any white man resident among them.

ARTICLE 6.

No guns, etc., to be furnished by them to enemies of United States.

And the Chiefs and Warriors, as aforesaid, promise and engage that their band will never, by sale, exchange, or as presents, supply any nation or tribe of Indians, not in amity with the United States, with guns, ammunition, or other implements of war.

Done at the Auricara Village, this sixteenth day of July, A. D. 1825, and of the independence of the United States the fiftieth.

In testimony whereof, the said commissioners, Henry Atkinson, and Benjamin O'Fallon, and the chiefs, head men, and warriors of the Hunkpapas tribe of Indians, have hereunto set their hands and affixed their seals.

H. Atkinson, brigadier-general, U. S. Army, [L. s.]	Taw-ome-nee-o-tah, the Womb, his x mark, [L. s.]
Benj. O'Fallon, United States agent Indian affairs, [L. s.]	Mah-to-wee-tah, the White Bear's face, his x mark, [L. s.]
Mato-che-gal-lah, Little White Bear, his x mark, [L. s.]	Pah-sal-sa, the Auricara, his x mark, [L. s.]
Cha-sa-wa-ne-che, the one that has no name, his x mark, [L. s.]	Ha-hah-kus-ka, the White Elk, his x mark, [L. s.]
Tah-hah-nee-ah, the one that scares the game, his x mark, [L. s.]	

In presence of—

A. L. Langham, secretary to the commission,
H. Leavenworth, colonel, U. S. Army,
P. Wilson, U. S. S. Indian agent,
G. H. Kennerly, U. S. S. Indian agent,
G. C. Spencer, captain, First Infantry,
John Gale, surgeon, U. S. Army,
R. M. Coleman, U. S. Army,
John Gantt, captain, Sixth Infantry,

J. Rogers, lieutenant, Sixth Infantry,
D. Ketchum, major, U. S. Army,
Jas. W. Kingsbury, lieutenant, First Regiment Infantry,
Thomas Noel, lieutenant, Sixth Infantry,
R. H. Stuart, lieutenant, First Infantry.
Levi Nute, lieutenant, U. S. Army,
Collin Campbell.

TREATY WITH THE ARIKARA TRIBE, 1825.

July 18, 1825.

7 Stat., 259.
Proclamation, Feb. 6, 1826.

To put an end to an unprovoked hostility on the part of the Ricara Tribe of Indians against the United States, and to restore harmony between the parties, the President of the United States, by Brigadier-general Henry Atkinson, of the United States' Army, and Major Benjamin O'Fallon, Indian Agent, Commissioners duly appointed and commissioned to treat with the Indian tribes beyond the Mississippi river, give peace to the said Ricara Tribe; the Chiefs and Warriors thereof having first made suitable concessions for the offence. And, for the purpose of removing all further or future cause of misunderstanding as respects trade and friendly intercourse between the parties, the above named Commissioners on the part of the United States, and the undersigned Chiefs and Warriors of the Ricara Tribe of Indians on the part of said Tribe, have made and entered into the following articles and conditions, which, when ratified by the President of the United States, by and with the advice and consent of the Senate, shall be binding on both parties, to wit:

ARTICLE 1.

Henceforth there shall be a firm and lasting peace between the United States and the Ricara tribe of Indians; and a friendly intercourse shall immediately take place between the parties.

Peace and friendship.

ARTICLE 2.

It is admitted by the Ricara tribe of Indians, that they reside within the territorial limits of the United States, acknowledge their supremacy, and claim their protection. The said tribe also admit the right of the United States to regulate all trade and intercourse with them.

Supremacy of United States acknowledged.

ARTICLE 3.

The United States agree to receive the Ricara tribe of Indians into their friendship, and under their protection, and to extend to them, from time to time, such benefits and acts of kindness as may be convenient and seem just and proper to the President of the United States.

United States will take the Ricaras under their protection.

ARTICLE 4.

All trade and intercourse with the Ricara tribe shall be transacted at such place or places as may be designated and pointed out by the President of the United States, through his agents; and none but American citizens, duly authorized by the United States, shall be admitted to trade or hold intercourse with said tribe of Indians.

Regulation of trade among the Indians.

ARTICLE 5.

That the Ricara tribe may be accommodated with such articles of merchandise, &c. as their necessities may demand, the United States agree to admit and license traders to hold intercourse with said tribe, under mild and equitable regulations: in consideration of which, the Ricara tribe bind themselves to extend protection to the persons and the property of the traders, and the persons legally employed under them, while they remain within the limits of their district of country. And the said Ricara tribe further agree, that if any foreigner or other person, not legally authorized by the United States, shall come into their district of country for the purposes of trade or other views, they will apprehend such person or persons, and deliver him or them to some United States' superintendent or agent of Indian Affairs, or to the

Trade, etc., to be transacted at such places as the President may designate.

commandant of the nearest military post, to be dealt with according to law. And they further agree to give safe conduct to all persons who may be legally authorized by the United States to pass through their country, and to protect in their persons and property all agents or other persons sent by the United States to reside temporarily among them.

ARTICLE 6.

Course to be pursued in order to prevent injuries by individuals. That the friendship which is now established between the United States and the Ricara tribe, shall not be interrupted by the misconduct of individuals, it is hereby agreed, that for injuries done by individuals, no private revenge or retaliation shall take place, but instead thereof, complaints shall be made, by the party injured, to the superintendent or agent of Indian affairs or other person appointed by the President; and it shall be the duty of the said Chiefs, upon complaint being made as aforesaid, to deliver up the person or persons against whom the complaint is made, to the end that he or they may be punished, agreeably to the laws of the United States. And, in like manner, if any robbery, violence, or murder, shall be committed on any Indian or Indians belonging to said tribe, the person or persons so offending shall be tried, and, if found guilty, shall be punished in like manner as if the injury **Chiefs to exert themselves to recover stolen property.** had been done to a white man. And it is agreed, that the Chiefs of the said Ricara tribe shall, to the utmost of their power, exert themselves to recover horses or other property, which may be stolen or taken from any citizen or citizens of the United States, by any individual or individuals of said tribe; and the property so recovered shall be forthwith delivered to the agents or other person authorized to receive it, that it may be restored to the proper owner. And the United States hereby guaranty to any Indian or Indians of said tribe, a full indemnification for any horses or other property which may be stolen **Proviso.** from them by any of their citizens: *Provided*, That the property so stolen cannot be recovered, and that sufficient proof is produced that it was actually stolen by a citizen of the United States. And the said Ricara tribe engage, on the requisition or demand of the President of the United States, or of the agents, to deliver up any white man resident among them.

ARTICLE 7.

No guns, etc., to be furnished by them to any nation, etc., hostile to the United States. And the Chiefs and Warriors, as aforesaid, promise and engage that their tribe will never, by sale, exchange, or as presents, supply any nation, tribe, or bands of Indians, not in amity with the United States, with guns, ammunition, or other implements of war.

Done at the Ricara village, this eighteenth day of July, A. D. 1825, and of the independence of the United States the fiftieth.

In testimony whereof, the said commissioners, Henry Atkinson and Benjamin O'Fallon, and the chiefs, head men, and warriors of the Ricara tribe of Indians, have hereunto set their hands and affixed their seals.

H. Atkinson, brigadier-general U. S. Army, [L. S.]
Benj. O'Fallon, United States agent Indian affairs, [L. S.]
Chiefs:
Stan-au-pat, the bloody hand, his x mark, [L. S.]
Ca-car-we-ta, the little bear, his x mark, [L. S.]
Scar-e-naus, the skunk, his x mark, [L. S.]
Chan-son-nah, the fool chief, his x mark, [L. S.]
Chan-no-te-ne-na, the chief that is afraid, his x mark, [L. S.]

Coon-ca-ne-nos-see, the bad bear, his x mark, [L. S.]
Warriors:
En-hah-pe-tar, the two nights, his x mark, [L. S.]
Ca-ca-ne-show, the crow chief, his x mark, [L. S.]
Pah-can-wah, the old head, his x mark, [L. S.]
Wah-ta-an, the light in the night, his x mark, [L. S.]
Hon-eh-cooh, the buffalo that urinates and smells it, his x mark, [L. S.]

Ta-hah-son, the lip of the old buffalo, his x mark,   [L. s.]
Coo-wooh-war-e-scoon-hoon, the
 long haired bear, his x mark, [L. s.]
Ne-sha-non-nack, the chief by himself, his x mark,   [L. s.]
Ah-ree-squish, the buffalo that has
 horns, his x mark,   [L. s.]
Ou-cous-non-nair, the good buffalo,
 his x mark,   [L. s.]

Nack-sa-nou-wees, the dead heart,
 his x mark,   [L. s.]
Pah-too-car-rah, the man that
 strikes, his x mark,   [L. s.]
Toon-high-ouh, the man that runs,
 his x mark,   [L. s.]
Car-car-wee-as, the heart of the
 crow, his x mark,   [L. s.]

In the presence of—

A. L. Langham, secretary to the com-
 mission,
H. Leavenworth, colonel U. S. Army,
S. W. Kearny, brevet major First In-
 fantry,
D. Ketchum, major U. S. Army,
Wm. Armstrong, captain Sixth Regi-
 ment Infantry,
B. Riley, captain Sixth Infantry,
John Gantt, captain Sixth Infantry,
G. C. Spencer, captain First Infantry,
R. B. Mason, captain First Infantry,
W. S. Harney, lieutenant First Infantry,
John Gale, surgeon U. S. Army,
R. M. Coleman, U. S. Army,

S. Wragg, adjutant First Regiment In-
 fantry,
S. Mac Ree, lieutenant aid de camp,
R. Holmes, lieutenant Sixth Infantry,
R. H. Stuart, lieutenant First Infantry,
Jas. W. Kingsbury, lieutenant First Reg-
 iment Infantry,
Levi Nute, lieutenant U. S. Army,
W. L. Harris, lieutenant First Infantry,
G. H. Kennerly, U. S. special Indian
 agent,
P. Wilson, U. S. special Indian agent,
Antoine Garreau, his x mark, interpreter,
Joseph Garreau, his x mark, interpreter,
Pierre Garreau, his x mark.

TREATY WITH THE BELANTSE-ETOA OR MINITAREE TRIBE, 1825.

WHEREAS acts of hostility have been committed, by some restless men of the Belantse-etea or Minnetaree tribe of Indians, upon some of the citazens of the United States: therefore, to put a stop to any further outrages of the sort, and to establish a more friendly under-standing between the United States and the said Belantse-etea or Min-netaree tribe, the President of the United States, by Henry Atkinson, Brigadier-general of the United States' army, and Major Benjamin O'Fallon, Indian Agent, commissioners duly appointed and commis-sioned to treat with the Indian tribes beyond the Mississippi river, for-give the offences which have been committed, the Chiefs and Warriors having first made satisfactory explanations touching the same.   And, for the purpose of removing all future cause of misunderstanding, as respects trade and friendly intercourse, between the parties, the above-named Commissioners, on the part of the United States, and the under-signed chiefs and Warriors of the Belantse-etea or Minnetaree tribe of Indians, on the part of said tribe, have made and entered into the following Articles and Conditions; which, when ratified by the Presi-dent of the United States, by and with the advice and consent of the Senate, shall be binding on both parties—to wit:

July 30, 1825.

7 Stat., 261.
Proclamation, Feb-
6, 1826.

ARTICLE 1.

Henceforth there shall be a firm and lasting peace between the United States and the Belantse-etea or Minnetaree tribe of Indians; and a friendly intercourse shall immediately take place between the parties.

Peace and friend-
ship.

ARTICLE 2.

It is admitted by the Belantse-etea or Minnetaree tribe of Indians, that they reside within the territorial limits of the United States, acknowledge their supremacy, and claim their protection.—The said tribe also admit the right of the United States to regulate all trade and intercourse with them.

Supremacy of Unit-
ed States acknowl-
edged.

ARTICLE 3.

United States to receive them into their friendship.

The United States agree to receive the Belantse-etea or Minnetaree tribe of Indians into their friendship, and under their protection, and to extend to them, from time to time, such benefits and acts of kindness as may be convenient, and seem just and proper to the President of the United States.

ARTICLE 4.

Places of trade to be designated by the President.

All trade and intercourse with the Belantse-eta or Minnetaree tribe shall be transacted at such place or places as may be designated and pointed out, by the President of the United States, through his agents; and none but American citazens, duly authorized by the United States, shall be admitted to trade or hold intercourse with said tribe of Indians.

ARTICLE 5.

Regulation of trade.

That the Belantse-eta or Minnetaree tribe may be accommodated with such articles of merchandise, &c., as their necessities may demand, the United States agree to admit and license traders to hold intercourse with said tribe, under mild and equitable regulations: in consideration of which, the Belantse-eta or Minnetaree tribe bind themselves to extend protection to the persons and the property of the traders, and the persons legally employed under them, whilst they remain within the limits of their district of country. And the said Belantse-eta or Minnetaree tribe further agree, that if any foreigner or other person, not legally authorized by the United States, shall come into their district of country, for the purposes of trade or other views, they will apprehend such person or persons, and deliver him or them to some United States' superintendent or agent of Indian affairs, or to the commandant of the nearest military post, to be dealt with according to law. And they further agree to give safe conduct to all persons who may be legally authorized by the United States to reside temporarily among them.

ARTICLE 6.

Course to be pursued in order to prevent injuries by individuals, etc.

That the friendship which is now established between the United States and the Belantse-eta or Minnetaree tribe shall not be interrupted by the misconduct of individuals, it is hereby agreed, that for injuries done by individuals, no private revenge or retaliation shall take place, but instead thereof complaints shall be made, by the party injured, to the superintendent or agent of Indian affairs or other person appointed by the President; and it shall be the duty of the said Chiefs, upon complaint being made as aforesaid, to deliver up the person or persons against whom the complaint is made, to the end that he or they may be punished, agreeably to the laws of the United States. And, in like manner, if any robbery, violence, or murder, shall be committed on any Indian or Indians belonging to said tribe, the person or persons so offending shall be tried, and if found guilty, shall be punished in like manner as if the injury had been done to a white man. And it is agreed that the Chiefs of the said Belantse-eta or Minnetaree tribe shall, to the utmost of their power, exert themselves to recover horses or other property, which may be stolen or taken from any citizen or citizens of the United States, by any individual or individuals of said tribe; and the property so recovered shall be forthwith delivered to the agents or other person authorized to receive it, that it may be restored to the proper owner. And the United States hereby guarranty to any Indian or Indians of said tribe, a full indemnification for any horses or other property which may be stolen from them by any of their citizens:

Proviso.

Provided, That the property so stolen cannot be recovered, and that sufficient proof is produced that it was actually stolen by a citizen of

Chiefs to exert themselves to recover stolen property.

the United States. And the said Belantse-eta or Minnetaree tribe engage, on the requisition or demand of the President of the United States, or of the agents, to deliver up any white man resident among them.

ARTICLE 7.

And the Chiefs and Warriors, as aforesaid, promise and engage that their tribe will never, by sale, exchange, or as presents, supply any nation, tribe, or band of Indians, not in amity with the United States, with guns, ammunition, or other implements of war. No guns, etc., to be furnished by them to those hostile to United States.

Done at the Lower Mandan Village, this thirtieth day of July, A. D. 1825, and of the independence of the United States the fiftieth.

In testimony whereof, the commissioners, Henry Atkinson and Benjamin O'Fallon, and the chiefs and warriors of the said Belantse-etea or Minnetaree tribe of Indians, have hereunto set their hands and affixed their seals.

H. Atkinson, brigadier-general U. S. Army, [L. s.]
Benj. O'Fallon, United States agent, Indian affairs, [L. s.]
Chiefs:
Shan-sa-bat-say-e-see, the wolf chief, his x mark, [L. s.]
E-re-ah-ree, the one that make the road, his x mark, [L. s.]
Pas-ca-ma-e-ke-ree, the crow that looks, his x mark, [L. s.]
E-tah-me-nah-ga-e-she, the guard of the red arrows, his x mark, [L. s.]
Mah-shu-ca-lah-pah-see, the dog bear, his x mark, [L. s.]
Oh-sha-lah-ska-a-tee, his x mark, [L. s.]
Kah-re-pe-shu-pe-sha, the black buffalo, his x mark, [L. s.]
Ah-too-pah-she-pe-sha, the black mocasins, his x mark, [L. s.]
Mah-buk-sho-ok-oe-ah, the one that carries the snake, his x mark, [L. s.]
Warriors:
At-ca-chis, the black lodges, his x mark, [L. s.]
Nah-rah-ah-a-pa, the color of the hair, his x mark, [L. s.]
Pa-ta-e-she-as, the wicked cow, his x mark, [L. s.]

Kee-re-pee-ah-too, the buffalo head, his x mark, [L. s.]
Lah-pa-ta-see-e-ta, the bear's tail, his x mark, [L. s.]
Pa-ta-lah-kee, the white cow, his x mark, [L. s.]
Ah-sha-re-te-ah, the big thief, his x mark, [L. s.]
Bo-sah-nah-a-me, the three wolves, his x mark, [L. s.]
San-jah-oe-tee, the wolf that has no tail, his x mark, [L. s.]
Sa-ga-e-ree-shus, the finger that stinks, his x mark, [L. s.]
Me-a-cah-ho-ka, the woman that lies, his x mark, [L. s.]
Ah-mah-a-ta, the missouri, his x mark, [L. s.]
E-sha-kee-te-ah, the big fingers, his x mark, [L. s.]
Mah-shu-kah-e-te-ah, the big dog, his x mark, [L. s.]
Be-ra-ka-ra-ah, the rotten wood, his x mark, [L. s.]
E-ta-ro-sha-pa, the big brother, his x mark, [L. s.]

In the presence of—

A. L. Langham, secretary to the commission,
H. Leavenworth, colonel, U. S. Army,
G. H. Kennerly, United States sub-Indian agent,
John Gale, surgeon, U. S. Army,
D. Ketchum, major, U. S. Army,
John Gantt, captain, Sixth Infantry,
Wm. Day, lieutenant, First Infantry,
R. B. Mason, captain, First Infantry,
Jas. W. Kingbury, lieutenant, First Regiment Infantry,
R. Holmes, lieutenant, Sixth Infantry,
J. Rogers, lieutenant, Sixth Infantry,
W. S. Harney, lieutenant, First Infantry,

Levi Nute, lieutenant, Sixth Infantry,
B. Riley, captain, Sixth Infantry,
R. M. Coleman, assistant surgeon, U. S. Army,
George C. Hutter, lieutenant, Sixth Infantry,
Colin Campbell,
P. Wilson, United States sub-Indian agent,
Touissant Chaboneau, interpreter, his x mark,
S. W. Kearny, brevet major, First Infantry.
Wm. Armstrong, captain, Sixth Regiment Infantry.

TREATY WITH THE MANDAN TRIBE, 1825.

July 30, 1825.

7 Stat., 264.
Proclamation, Feb.
6, 1826.

WHEREAS acts of hostility have been committed by some restless men of the Mandan Tribe of Indians, upon some of the citizens of the United States: Therefore, to put a stop to any further outrages of the sort; and to establish a more friendly understanding between the United States and the said Mandan Tribe, the President of the United States, by Henry Atkinson, Brigadier General of the United States, Army, and Major Benjamin O'Fallon, Indian Agent, Commissioners duly appointed and commissioned to treat with the Indian Tribes beyond the Mississippi river, forgive the offences which have been committed; the Chiefs and Warriors having first made satisfactory explanations touching the same. And, for the purpose of removing all future cause of misunderstanding as respects trade and friendly intercourse between the parties, the above named Commissioners on the part of the United States, and the undersigned Chiefs and Warriors of the Mandan Tribe of Indians on the part of said Tribe, have made and entered into the following articles and conditions, which, when ratified by the President of the United States, by and with the advice and consent of the Senate, shall be binding on both parties—to wit:

ARTICLE 1.

Peace and friendship.

Henceforth there shall be a firm and lasting peace between the United States and the Mandan tribe of Indians; and a friendly intercourse shall immediately take place between the parties.

ARTICLE 2.

Supremacy of United States acknowledged.

It is admitted by the Mandan tribe of Indians, that they reside within the territorial limits of the United States, acknowledge their supremacy, and claim their protection.—The said tribe also admit the right of the United States to regulate all trade and intercourse with them.

ARTICLE 3.

United States agree to receive Indians into their friendship, etc.

The United States agree to receive the Mandan tribe of Indians into their friendship, and under their protection, and to extend to them, from time to time, such benefits and acts of kindness as may be convenient, and seem just and proper to the President of the United States.

ARTICLE 4.

Places for trade to be designated by the President.

All trade and intercourse with the Mandan tribe shall be transacted at such place or places as may be designated and pointed out by the President of the United States, through his agents; and none but American citizens, duly authorized by the United States, shall be admitted to trade or hold intercourse with said tribe of Indians.

ARTICLE 5.

Regulation of trade.

That the Mandan tribe may be accommodated with such articles of merchandise, &c., as their necessities may demand, the United States agree to admit and license traders to hold intercourse with said tribe, under mild and equitable regulations: in consideration of which, the Mandan tribe bind themselves to extend protection to the persons and the property of the traders, and the persons legally employed under them, whilst they remain within the limits of their district of country. And the said Mandan tribe further agree, that if any foreigner or other person, not legally authorized by the United States, shall come into their district of country, for the purposes of trade or other views, they will apprehend such person or persons, and deliver him or them to some United States' superintendent or agent of Indian Affairs, or to the commandant of the nearest military post, to be dealt with according to law. And they further agree to give safe conduct to all persons who may be legally authorized by the United States to pass through their country, and to protect in their persons and property all agents or other persons sent by the United States to reside temporarily among them.

ARTICLE 6.

That the friendship which is now established between the United States and the Mandan tribe, shall not be interrupted by the misconduct of individuals, it is hereby agreed, that for injuries done by individuals, no private revenge or retaliation shall take place, but instead thereof, complaints shall be made, by the party injured, to the superintendent or agent of Indian affairs, or other person appointed by the President; and it shall be the duty of the said Chiefs, upon complaint being made as aforesaid, to deliver up the person or persons against whom the complaint is made, to the end that he or they may be punished, agreeably to the laws of the United States. And, in like manner, if any robbery, violence, or murder, shall be committed on any Indian or Indians belonging to said tribe, the person or persons so offending shall be tried, and if found guilty, shall be punished in like manner as if the injury had been done to a white man. And it is agreed, that the Chiefs of the said Mandan tribe shall, to the utmost of their power, exert themselves to recover horses or other property, which may be stolen or taken from any citizen or citizens of the United States, by any individual or individuals of said tribe; and the property so recovered shall be forthwith delivered to the agents or other person authorized to receive it, that it may be restored to the proper owner. And the United States hereby guarranty to any Indian or Indians of said tribe, a full indemnification for any horses or other property which may be stolen from them by any of their citizens: *Provided,* That the property so stolen cannot be recovered, and that sufficient proof is produced that it was actually stolen by a citizen of the United States. And the said Mandan tribe engage, on the requisition or demand of the President of the United States, or of the agents, to deliver up any white man resident among them.

Course to be pursued in order to prevent injuries by individuals, etc.

Chiefs to exert themselves to recover stolen property.

ARTICLE 7.

And the Chiefs and Warriors as aforesaid, promise and engage that their tribe will never, by sale, exchange, or as presents, supply any nation, tribe, or band of Indians, not in amity with the United States, with guns, ammunition, or other implements of war.

No ammunition, etc., to be furnished by them to enemies of United States.

Done at the Mandan Village, this thirtieth day of July, A. D. 1825, and of the independence of the United States the fiftieth.

In testimony whereof, the commissioners, Henry Atkinson and Benjamin O'Fallon, and the chiefs and warriors of the Mandan tribe of Indians, have hereunto set their hands and affixed their seals.

H. Atkinson, brigadier-general U.
   S. Army, [L. S.]
Benj. O'Fallon, United States agent
   Indian affairs, [L. S.]
   Chiefs:
Mat-sa-to-pas-lah-hah-pah, the
   chiefs of four men, his x mark, [L. S.]
San-jah-mat-sa-eta, the wolf chiefs,
   his x mark, [L. S.]
Ah-ra-na-shis, the one that has no
   arm, his x mark, [L. S.]

Bot-sa-a-pa, the color of the wolf,
   his x mark, [L. S.]
Con-ke-sheesse, the good child, his
   x mark, [L. S.]
Lah-pa-see-ta-re-tah, the bear that
   does not walk, his x mark, [L. S.]
Par-res-kah-cah-rush-ta, the little
   crow, his x mark, [L. S.]
   Warriors—First village:
Obah-chash, the broken leg, his x
   mark, [L. S.]

La-pet-see-to-a-pus, the four bears,
his x mark, [L. s.]

Sah-cou-ga-rah-lah-pet-see, the bird
of the bears, his x mark, [L. s.]

She-ca-aga-mat-sa-et-see, the little
young man that is a chief, his x
mark, [L. s.]

Kee-re-pee-ah-pa-rush, the neck of
the buffalo, his x mark, [L. s.]

Bo-si-e-ree-bees, the little wolf that
sleeps, his x mark, [L. s.]

Second village:

San-jah-ca-ho-ka, the wolf that lies,
his x mark, [L. s.]

Ede-shu-bee, the fat of the paunch,
his x mark, [L. s.]

Pa-res-ca-a-huss, the band of crows,
his x mark, [L. s.]

Ba-rah-rah-ca-tah, the broken pot,
his x mark, [L. s.]

Me-ra-pa-sha-po, the five beavers,
his x mark, [L. s.]

Bout-sa-ca-ho-ka, the crouching
prairie wolf, his x mark, [L. s.]

In the presence of—

A. L. Langham, secretary to the commission,
H. Leavenworth, colonel U. S. Army,
S. W. Kearny, brevet major First Infantry,
D. Ketchum, major, U. S. Army,
B. Riley, captain, Sixth Infantry,
P. Wilson, United States S. Indian agent,
S. Mac Ree, lieutenant, aid-de-camp,
R. B. Mason, captain, First Infantry,
G. C. Spencer, captain, First Infantry,
John Gantt, captain, Sixth Infantry,
Thomas Noel, lieutenant, Sixth Infantry,
R. Holmes, lieutenant, Sixth Infantry,
J. Rogers, lieutenant, Sixth Infantry,
Jas. W. Kingsbury, lieutenant, First Regiment Infantry.
Levi Nute, lieutenant, Sixth Infantry.
S. Wragg, adjutant First Regiment Infantry,

M. W. Batman, lieutenant, Sixth Infantry,
Thomas P. Gwynne, lieutenant, First Infantry,
George C. Hutter, lieutenant, Sixth Infantry,
William Day, lieutenant, First Infantry,
John Gale, surgeon, U. S. Army,
R. M. Coleman, assistant surgeon, U. S. Army,
W. S. Harney, lieutenant, First Infantry,
J. C. Culbertson,
G. H. Kennerly, United States S. Indian agent,
A. S. Miller, lieutenant, First Infantry,
Colin Campbell,
Touissant Chaboneau, his x mark, interpreter.

TREATY WITH THE CROW TRIBE, 1825.

Aug. 4, 1825.

7 Stat., 266.
Proclamation, Feb.
6, 1826.

For the purpose of perpetuating the friendship which has heretofore existed, as also to remove all future cause of discussion or dissension, as it respects trade and friendship between the United States and their citizens, and the Crow tribe of Indians, the President of the United States of America, by Brigadier-General Henry Atkinson, of the United States' army, and Major Benjamin O'Fallon, Indian agent, with full powers and authority, specially appointed and commissioned for that purpose, of the one part, and the undersigned Chiefs, Head men and Warriors, of the said Crow tribe of Indians, on behalf of their tribe, of the other part, have made and entered into the following Articles and Conditions; which, when ratified by the President of the United States, by and with the advice and consent of the Senate, shall be binding on both parties—to wit:

ARTICLE 1.

Supremacy of United States acknowledged.

It is admitted by the Crow tribe of Indians, that they reside within the territorial limits of the United States, acknowledge their supremacy, and claim their protection.—The said tribe also admit the right of the United States to regulate all trade and intercourse with them.

ARTICLE 2.

Indians received into protection of United States.

The United States agree to receive the Crow tribe of Indians into their friendship, and under their protection, and to extend to them, from time to time, such benefits and acts of kindness as may be convenient, and seem just and proper to the President of the United States.

ARTICLE 3.

All trade and intercourse with the Crow tribe shall be transacted at such place or places as may be designated and pointed out by the President of the United States, through his agents; and none but American citizens, duly authorized by the United States, shall be admitted to trade or hold intercourse with said tribe of Indians.

Places for trade to be designated by the President.

ARTICLE 4.

That the Crow tribe may be accommodated with such articles of merchandise, &c. as their necessities may demand, the United States agree to admit and license traders to hold intercourse with said tribe, under mild and equitable regulations: in consideration of which, the Crow tribe bind themselves to extend protection to the persons and the property of the traders, and the persons legally employed under them, whilst they remain within the limits of their district of country. And the said Crow tribe further agree, that if any foreigner or other person, not legally authorized by the United States, shall come into their district of country, for the purposes of trade or other views, they will apprehend such person or persons, and deliver him or them to some United States' Superintendent or Agent of Indian Affairs, or to the commandant of the nearest military post, to be dealt with according to law. And they further agree to give safe conduct to all persons who may be legally authorized by the United States to pass through their country, and to protect in their persons and property all agents or other persons sent by the United States to reside temporarily among them; and that they will not, whilst on their distant excursions, molest or interrupt any American citizen or citizens, who may be passing from the United States to New Mexico, or returning from thence to the United States.

Regulation of trade.

ARTICLE 5.

That the friendship which is now established between the United States and the Crow tribe, should not be interrupted by the misconduct of individuals, it is hereby agreed, that for injuries done by individuals, no private revenge or retaliation shall take place, but instead thereof, complaints shall be made, by the party injured, to the superintendent or agent of Indian affairs, or other person appointed by the President; and it shall be the duty of said Chiefs, upon complaint being made as aforesaid, to deliver up the person or persons against whom the complaint is made, to the end that he or they may be punished, agreeably to the laws of the United States. And, in like manner, if any robbery, violence, or murder, shall be committed on any Indian or Indians belonging to the said tribe, the person or persons so offending shall be tried, and, if found guilty, shall be punished in like manner as if the injury had been done to a white man. And it is agreed, that the Chiefs of said Crow tribe shall, to the utmost of their power, exert themselves to recover horses or other property, which may be stolen or taken from any citizen or citizens of the United States, by any individual or individuals of said tribe; and the property so recovered shall be forthwith delivered to the agents or other person authorized to receive it, that it may be restored to the proper owner. And the United States hereby guarranty to any Indian or Indians of said tribe, a full indemnification for any horses or other property which may be stolen from them by any of their citizens: *Provided,* That the property stolen cannot be recovered, and that sufficient proof is produced that it was actually stolen by a citizen of the United States. And the said tribe engage, on the requisition or demand of the President of the United States, or of the agents, to deliver up any white man resident among them.

Course to be pursued in order to prevent injuries to individuals, etc.

Chiefs to exert themselves to recover stolen property.

Proviso.

ARTICLE 6.

No guns, etc., to be furnished by them to enemies of United States.

And the Chiefs and Warriors, as aforesaid, promise and engage that their tribe will never, by sale, exchange, or as presents, supply any nation, tribe, or band of Indians, not in amity with the United States, with guns, ammunition, or other implements of war.

Done at the Mandan Village, this fourth day of August, A. D. 1825, and of the independence of the United States the fiftieth.

In testimony whereof, the said commissioners, Henry Atkinson and Benjamin O'Fallon, and the chiefs and warriors of the said tribe, have hereunto set their hands and affixed their seals.

H. Atkinson, brigadier-general U. S. Army, [L. S.]
Benj. O'Fallon, U. S. agent Indian Affairs, [L. S.]
Chiefs:
E-she-huns-ka, or the long hair, his x mark, [L. S.]
She-wo-cub-bish, one that sings bad, his x mark, [L. S.]
Har-rar-shash, one that rains, his x mark, [L. S.]
Chay-ta-pah-ha, wolf's paunch, his x mark, [L. S.]
Huch-che-rach, little black dog, his x mark, [L. S.]
Mah-pitch, bare shoulder, his x mark, [L. S.]
Esh-ca-ca-mah-hoo, the standing lance, his x mark, [L. S.]
Che-rep-con-nes-ta-chea, the little white bull, his x mark, [L. S.]

Ah-mah-shay-she-ra, the yellow big belly, his x mark, [L. S.]
Co-tah-bah-sah, the one that runs, his x mark, [L. S.]
Bah-cha-na-mach, the one that sits in the pine, his x mark, [L. S.]
He-ran-dah-pah, the one that ties his hair before, his x mark, [L. S.]
Bes-ca-bar-ru-sha, the dog that eats, his x mark, [L. S.]
Nah-puch-kia, the little one that holds the stick in his mouth, his x mark, [L. S.]
Bah-da-ah-chan-dah, the one that jumps over every person, his x mark, [L. S.]
Mash-pah-hash, the one that is not right, [L. S.]

In presence of—

A. L. Langham, secretary to the commission,
H. Leavenworth, colonel U. S. Army,
S. W. Kearny, brevet major First Infantry,
D. Ketchum, major U. S. Army,
R. B. Mason, captain First Infantry,
G. C. Spencer, captain First Infantry,
John Gantt, captain Sixth Infantry,
Thos. P. Gwynne, lieutenant First Infantry,
S. MacRee, lieutenant and aid-de-camp,
Thomas Noel, lieutenant Sixth Infantry,
William L. Harris, First Infantry,
John Gale, surgeon U. S. Army,
J. V. Swearingen, lieutenant First Infantry,

R. Holmes, lieutenant Sixth Infantry,
M. W. Batman, lieutenant Sixth Infantry,
R. M. Coleman, U. S. Army,
J. Rogers, lieutenant Sixth Infantry,
Wm. Day, lieutenant First Infantry,
G. H. Kennerly, U. S. Indian agent,
B. Riley, captain Sixth Infantry,
Wm. S. Harney, lieutenant First Infantry,
James W. Kingsbury, lieutenant First Regiment Infantry,
George C. Hutter, lieutenant Sixth Infantry,
Wm. Armstrong, captain Sixth Regiment Infantry.

TREATY WITH THE GREAT AND LITTLE OSAGE, 1825.

Aug. 10, 1825.

7 Stat., 268.
Proclamation, May 3, 1826.

1825, ch. 50.

WHEREAS the Congress of the United States of America, being anxious to promote a direct commercial and friendly intercourse between the citizens of the United States and those of the Mexican Republic, and, to afford protection to the same, did, at their last session, pass an act, which was approved the 3d March, 1825, "to authorize the President of the United States to cause a road to be marked out from the Western frontier of Missouri to the confines of New Mexico," and which authorizes the President of the United States to appoint Commissioners to carry said act of Congress into effect, and enjoins on the Commissioners, so to be appointed, that they first obtain the consent of the intervening tribes of Indians, by treaty, to the marking of said road, and to the unmolested use thereof to the citizens of the United States and of the Mexican Republic; and Benjamin H. Reeves,

Geo. C. Sibley, and Thomas Mather, Commissioners duly appointed as aforesaid, being duly and fully authorized, have this day met the Chiefs and Head men of the Great and Little Osage Nations, who being all duly authorized to meet and negotiate with the said Commissioners upon the premises, and being specially met for that purpose, by the invitation of said Commissioners, at the place called the Council Grove, on the river Nee-o-zho, one hundred and sixty miles southwest from Fort Osage; have, after due deliberation and consultation, agreed to the following treaty, which is to be considered binding on the said Great and Little Osages, from and after this day:

ARTICLE 1.

The Chiefs and Head Men of the Great and Little Osages, for themselves and their nations, respectively, do consent and agree that the Commissioners of the United States shall and may survey and mark out a road, in such manner as they may think proper, through any of the territory owned or claimed by the said Great and Little Osage Nations.

Agreement.

ARTICLE 2.

The Chiefs and Head Men, as aforesaid, do further agree that the road authorized in article 1, shall, when marked, be forever free for the use of the citizens of the United States and of the Mexican Republic, who shall at all times pass and repass thereon, without any hindrance or molestation on the part of the said Great and Little Osages.

Further agreement.

ARTICLE 3.

The Chiefs and Head Men as aforesaid, in consideration of the friendly relations existing between them and the United States, do further promise, for themselves and their people, that they will, on all fit occasions, render such friendly aid and assistance as may be in their power, to any of the citizens of the United States, or of the Mexican Republic, as they may at any time happen to meet or fall in with on the road aforesaid.

Friendly relations.

ARTICLE 4.

The Chiefs and Head Men, as aforesaid, do further consent and agree that the road aforesaid shall be considered as extending to a reasonable distance on either side, so that travellers thereon may, at any time, leave the marked tract, for the purpose of finding subsistence and proper camping places.

Road.

ARTICLE 5.

In consideration of the privileges granted by the Chiefs of the Great and Little Osages in the three preceding articles, the said Commissioners on the part of the United States, have agreed to pay to them, the said Chiefs, for themselves and their people, the sum of five hundred dollars; which sum is to be paid them as soon as may be, in money or merchandise, at their option, at such place as they may desire.

Privileges.

ARTICLE 6.

And the said Chiefs and Head Men, as aforesaid, acknowledge to have received from the Commissioners aforesaid, at and before the signing of this Treaty, articles of merchandise to the value of three hundred dollars; which sum of three hundred dollars, and the payment

Merchandise, etc.

stipulated to be made to the said Osages in Article 5, shall be considered, and are so considered by said Chiefs, as full and complete compensation for every privilege herein granted by said Chiefs.

In testimony whereof, the said Benjamin H. Reeves, George C. Sibley, and Thomas Mather, commissioners as aforesaid, and the chiefs and head men of the Great and Little Osage tribes of Indians, have hereunto set their hands and seals, at Council Grove, this tenth day of August, in the year of our Lord one thousand eight hundred and twenty-five.

B. H. Reeves,	[L. S.]	Waw-bur-cou, warrior Little Osages, his x mark,	[L. S.]
G. C. Sibley,	[L. S.]	Maw-sho-hun-ga, warrior Great Osages, his x mark,	[L. S.]
Thomas Mather,	[L. S.]		
Pa-hu-sha, (white hair,) head chief of the G. O., his x mark,	[L. S.]	Waw-lo-gah, (Owl,) warrior Little Osages, his x mark,	[L. S.]
Ca-he-ga-wa-tonega, (foolish chief,) head chief of the L. O., his x mark,	[L. S.]	Maw-she-to-mo-nee, warrior Great Osages, his x mark,	[L. S.]
Shin-gawassa, (handsome bird,) chief of the G. O., his x mark,	[L. S.]	Che-he-kaw, warrior Little Osages, his x mark,	[L. S.]
Ta-ha-mo-nee, (swift walker,) chief L. O., his x mark,	[L. S.]	Ne-ha-wa-she-tun-ga, warrior Great Osages, his x mark,	[L. S.]
Ca-he-ga-wash-im-pee-she, (bad chief,) chief G. O., his x mark,	[L. S.]	Ho-no-posse, warrior Little Osages, his x mark,	[L. S.]
Wee-ho-je-ne-fare, (without ears,) chief L. O., his x mark,	[L. S.]	Waw-kun-chee, warrior Little Osages, his x mark,	[L. S.]
Ca-he-ga-shinga, (little chief,) chief G. O., his x mark,	[L. S.]	Pwa-ne-no-push-re, warrior Little Osages, his x mark,	[L. S.]

In the presence of—

Archibald Gamble, secretary,
Jos. C. Brown, surveyor,
W. S. Williams, interpreter,
Stephen Cooper,
Samuel Givens,
Richard Brannan,
Garrison Patrick,
Daniel J. Bahan,
I. R. Walker,

Singleton Vaughn,
Benjamin Jones,
Bradford Barbie,
Hendley Cooper,
John M. Walker,
Joseph Davis,
George West,
Thomas Adams,
James Brotherton.

TREATY WITH THE KANSA, 1825.

Aug. 16, 1825.

7 Stat., 270.
Proclamation, May 3, 1826.

1825, ch. 50.

WHEREAS the Congress of the United States of America being anxious to promote a direct commercial and friendly intercourse between the citizens of the United States and those of the Mexican Republic, and, to afford protection to the same, did, at their last session, pass an act, which was approved the 3d of March, 1825, "to authorize the President of the United States to cause a road to be marked out from the Western frontier of Missouri to the confines of New Mexico," and which authorizes the President of the United States to appoint Commissioners to carry said act of Congress into effect, and enjoins on the Commissioners, so to be appointed, that they first obtain the consent of the intervening tribes of Indians, by treaty, to the marking of said road and to the unmolested use thereof to the citizens of the United States and of the Mexican Republic; and Benjamin H. Reeves, Geo. C. Sibley, and Thomas Mather, being duly appointed Commissioners as aforesaid, and being duly and fully authorized, have this day met the Chiefs and Head Men of the Kansas tribe of Indians, who, being all duly authorized to meet and negotiate with the said Commissioners upon the premises, and being specially met for that purpose, by the invitation of said Commissioners, on the Sora Kansas Creek, two hundred and thirty-eight miles Southwestwardly from Fort Osage; have, after due deliberation and consultation, agreed to the following Treaty, which is to be considered binding on the said Kansas Indians, from and after this day:

ARTICLE 1.

The Chiefs and Head Men of the Kansas Nation, or tribe of Indians, for themselves and their nation, do consent and agree that the Commissioners of the United States shall, and may survey and mark out a road, in such manner as they may think proper, through any of the territory owned or claimed by the said Kansas Tribe or nation of Indians.

Road to be surveyed, etc.

ARTICLE 2.

The Chiefs and Head Men, as aforesaid, do further agree that the road authorized in article 1, shall, when marked, be forever free for the use of the citizens of the United States and of the Mexican Republic, who shall at all times pass and repass thereon, without any hindrance or molestation on the part of the said Kansas Indians.

Said road to be free, etc.

ARTICLE 3.

The Chiefs and Head Men as aforesaid, in consideration of the friendly relations existing between them and the United States, do further promise, for themselves and their people, that they will, on all fit occasions, render such friendly aid and assistance as may be in their power, to any of the citizens of the United States, or of the Mexican Republic, as they may at any time happen to meet or fall in with on the road aforesaid.

Kansas to render assistance to citizens of United States and of Mexico.

ARTICLE 4.

The Chiefs and Head Men, as aforesaid, do further consent and agree that the road aforesaid shall be considered as extending to a reasonable distance on either side, so that travellers thereon may, at any time, leave the marked track, for the purpose of finding subsistence and proper camping places.

Distance to which the road shall be considered to extend.

ARTICLE 5.

In consideration of the privileges granted by the Chiefs of Kansas Tribe in the three preceding articles, the said commissioners, on the part of the United States, have agreed to pay to them, the said Chiefs, for themselves and their people, the sum of five hundred dollars; which sum is to be paid them as soon as may be, in money or merchandise, at their option, at such place as they may desire.

Payment of indemnity by United States.

ARTICLE 6.

And the said Chiefs and Head Men, as aforesaid, acknowledge to have received from the Commissioners aforesaid, at and before the signing of this Treaty, articles of merchandise to the value of three hundred dollars; which sum of three hundred dollars. and the payment stipulated to be made to the said Kansas in article 5, shall be considered, and are so considered by said Chiefs, as full and complete compensation for every privilege herein granted by said Chiefs.

Acknowledgment of the chiefs, etc., of said tribe.

In testimony whereof, the said Benjamin H. Reeves, George C. Sibley, and Thomas Mather, commissioners as aforesaid, and the chiefs and head men of the Kanzas tribe or nation of Indians, have hereunto set their hands and seals, on the Sora Kanzas Creek aforesaid, this sixteenth day of August, in the year of our Lord one thousand eight hundred and twenty-five.

B. H. Reeves,	[L. S.]	Shone-gee-ne-gare—the great chief
G. C. Sibley,	[L. S.]	of the Kanzas nation—his x
Thomas Mather,	[L. S.]	mark, [L. S.]

Ke-hea-bash-ee—eldest son of the great chief, (a warrior and leader,) his x mark,   [L. S.]

Hu-ra-soo-gee, (the red eagle,) a chief and warrior, his x mark,   [L. S.]

Opa-she-ga, (the unready,) a warrior, his x mark,   [L. S.]

Nun-gee-saggy, (the hard heart,) a warrior and counsellor, his x mark,   [L. S.]

Nee-a-ke-shall—a chief, brother of the great chief, his x mark,   [L. S.]

Ee-be-seen-gee—a warrior, his x mark,   [L. S.]

Wa-rig-ni-ne-gare—a warrior, his x mark,   [L. S.]

Hah-ee-see-she (white plume's deputy,) warrior, his x mark,   [L. S.]

Nee-ha-wash-in-tun-ga (the passionate,) warrior, his x mark,   [L. S.]

Has-ska-mo-nee (white horns that walk,) warrior, his x mark,   [L. S.]

To-ka-mee-ra (the scalper,) warrior, his x mark,   [L. S.]

Mee-ra-ta-mo-nee (the midway walker,) warrior, his x mark,   [L. S.]

Mo-nee-ra-ta (he who walks off,) chief, his x mark,   [L. S.]

Mo-she-ha-mo-nee (the ridge walker,) warrior, his mark,   [L. S.]

Saw-nee-wah-ree (the striker of three,) warrior, his x mark,   [L. S.]

In presence of—

Archibald Gamble, secretary,
Jos. G. Brown, surveyor,
W. S. Williams, interpreter,
Stephen Cooper,
Daniel T. Bahan,
Benjamin Robertson,
David Murphy,
Singleton Vaughn,
John M. Walker,

Andrew Broaddies,
Benjamin Jones,
Hendley Cooper,
James Wells,
Joseph R. Walker,
Samuel Givens,
James Brotherton,
Harvy Clark.

TREATY WITH THE SIOUX, ETC., 1825.

Aug. 19, 1825.

7 Stat., 272.
Proclamation. Feb. 6, 1826.

Treaty with the Sioux and Chippewa, Sacs and Fox, Menominie, Ioway, Sioux, Winnebago, and a portion of the Ottawa, Chippewa, and Potawattomie, Tribes.

THE United States of America have seen with much regret, that wars have for many years been carried on between the Sioux and the Chippewas, and more recently between the confederated tribes of Sacs and Foxes, and the Sioux; and also between the Ioways and Sioux; which, if not terminated, may extend to the other tribes, and involve the Indians upon the Missouri, the Mississippi, and the Lakes, in general hostilities. In order, therefore, to promote peace among these tribes, and to establish boundaries among them and the other tribes who live in their vicinity, and thereby to remove all causes of future difficulty, the United States have invited the Chippewa, Sac, and Fox, Menominie, Ioway, Sioux, Winnebago, and a portion of the Ottowa, Chippewa and Potawatomie Tribes of Indians living upon the Illinois, to assemble together, and in a spirit of mutual conciliation to accomplish these objects; and to aid therein, have appointed William Clark and Lewis Cass, Commissioners on their part, who have met the Chiefs, Warriors, and Representatives of the said tribes, and portion of tribes, at Prairie des Chiens, in the Territory of Michigan, and after full deliberation, the said tribes, and portions of tribes, have agreed with the United States, and with one another, upon the following articles·

ARTICLE 1.

Firm and perpetual peace.

There shall be a firm and perpetual peace between the Sioux and Chippewas; between the Sioux and the confederated tribes of Sacs and Foxes; and between the Ioways and the Sioux.

ARTICLE 2.

Line between the respective countries.

It is agreed between the confederated Tribes of the Sacs and Foxes, and the Sioux, that the Line between their respective countries shall be as follows: Commencing at the mouth of the Upper Ioway River, on the west bank of the Mississippi, and ascending the said Ioway river, to its left fork; thence up that fork to its source; thence crossing the fork of Red Cedar River, in a direct line to the second or upper fork of the Desmoines river; and thence in a direct line to the lower fork of the Calumet river; and down that river to its juncture with the Missouri river. But the Yancton band of the Sioux tribe, being principally interested in the establishment of the line from the Forks of the Desmoines to the Missouri, and not being sufficiently represented to render the definitive establishment of that line proper, it is expressly declared that the line from the forks of the Desmoines to the forks of the Calumet river, and down that river to the Missouri, is not to be considered as settled until the assent of the Yancton band shall be given thereto. And if the said band should refuse their assent, the arrangement of that portion of the boundary line shall be void, and the rights of the parties to the country bounded thereby, shall be the same as if no provision had been made for the extension of the line west of the forks of the Desmoines. And the Sacs and Foxes relin- Relinquishment of quish to the tribes interested therein, all their claim to land on the east side of the Mississippi river.

Relinquishment of Sacs and Foxes.

ARTICLE 3.

The Ioways accede to the arrangement between the Sacs and Foxes, and the Sioux; but it is agreed between the Ioways and the confederated tribes of the Sacs and Foxes, that the Ioways have a just claim to a portion of the country between the boundary line described in the next preceding article, and the Missouri and Mississippi; and that the said Ioways, and Sacs and Foxes, shall peaceably occupy the same, until some satisfactory arrangement can be made between them for a division of their respective claims to country.

Iowas accede to the arrangement.

ARTICLE 4.

The Ottoes not being represented at this Council, and the Commissioners for the United States being anxious that justice should be done to all parties, and having reason to believe that the Ottoes have a just claim to a portion of the country upon the Missouri, east and south of the boundary line dividing the Sacs and Foxes and the Ioways, from the Sioux, it is agreed between the parties interested therein, and the United States, that the claim of the Ottoes shall not be affected by any thing herein contained; but the same shall remain as valid as if this treaty had not been formed.

Claim of the Ottoes not to be affected by this treaty.

ARTICLE 5.

It is agreed between the Sioux and the Chippewas, that the line dividing their respective countries shall commence at the Chippewa River, half a day's march below the falls; and from thence it shall run to Red Cedar River, immediately below the falls; from thence to the St. Croix River, which it strikes at a place called the standing cedar, about a day's paddle in a canoe, above the Lake at the mouth of that river; thence passing between two lakes called by the Chippewas "Green Lakes," and by the Sioux "the lakes they bury the Eagles in," and from thence to the standing cedar that "the Sioux Split;" thence to Rum River, crossing it at the mouth of a small creek called choaking creek, a long day's march from the Mississippi; thence to a point of woods that projects into the prairie, half a day's march from the Misissippi; thence in a straight line to the mouth of the first river which enters the Mississippi on its west side above the mouth of Sac river; thence ascending the said river (above the mouth of Sac river)

Agreement between the Sioux and Chippewas.

to a small lake at its source; thence in a direct line to a lake at the head of Prairie river, which is supposed to enter the Crow Wing river on its South side; thence to Otter-tail lake Portage; thence to said Otter-tail lake, and down through the middle thereof, to its outlet; thence in a direct line, so as to strike Buffalo river, half way from its source to its mouth, and down the said river to Red River; thence descending Red river to the mouth of Outard or Goose creek: The eastern boundary of the Sioux commences opposite the mouth of Ioway river, on the Mississippi, runs back two or three miles to the bluffs, follows the bluffs, crossing Bad axe river, to the mouth of Black river, and from Black river to half a day's march below the Falls of the Chippewa River.

ARTICLE 6.

Agreement between the Chippewas and the Winnebagoes.

It is agreed between the Chippewas and Winnebagoes, so far as they are mutually interested therein, that the southern boundary line of the Chippewa country shall commence on the Chippewa river aforesaid, half a day's march below the falls on that river, and run thence to the source of Clear Water river, a branch of the Chippewa; thence south to Black river; thence to a point where the woods project into the meadows, and thence to the Plover Portage of the Ouisconsin.

ARTICLE 7.

Agreement between the Winnebagoes and the Sioux, etc.

It is agreed between the Winnebagoes and the Sioux, Sacs and Foxes, Chippewas and Ottawas, Chippewas and Potawatomies of the Illinois, that the Winnebago country shall be bounded as follows: south easterly by Rock River, from its source near the Winnebago lake, to the Winnebago village, about forty miles above its mouth; westerly by the east line of the tract, lying upon the Mississippi, herein secured to the Ottawa, Chippewa and Potawatomie Indians, of the Illinois; and also by the high bluff, described in the Sioux boundary, and running north to Black river: from this point the Winnebagoes claim up Black river, to a point due west from the source of the left fork of the Ouisconsin; thence to the source of the said fork, and down the same to the Ouisconsin; thence down the Ouisconsin to the portage, and across the portage to Fox river; thence down Fox river to the Winnebago lake, and to the grand Kan Kanlin, including in their claim the whole of Winnebago lake; but, for the causes stated in the next article, this line from Black river must for the present be left indeterminate.

ARTICLE 8.

Agreement between the Menominees and the Sioux, etc.

The representatives of the Menominies not being sufficiently acquainted with their proper boundaries, to settle the same definitively, and some uncertainty existing in consequence of the cession made by that tribe upon Fox River and Green Bay, to the New York Indians, it is agreed between the said Menominie tribe, and the Sioux, Chippewas, Winnebagoes, Ottawa, Chippewa and Potawatomie Indians of the Illinois, that the claim of the Menominies to any portion of the land within the boundaries allotted to either of the said tribes, shall not be barred by any stipulation herein; but the same shall remain as valid as if this treaty had not been concluded. It is, however, understood that the general claim of the Menominies is bounded on the north by the Chippewa country, on the east by Green Bay and lake Michigan extending as far south as Millawaukee river, and on the West they claim to Black River.

ARTICLE 9.

Boundary of the Ottawas, Chippewas, and Potawatomies.

The country secured to the Ottawa, Chippewa, and Potawatomie tribes of the Illinois, is bounded as follows: Beginning at the Winnebago village, on Rock river, forty miles from its mouth and running thence down the Rock river to a line which runs from Lake Michigan to the Mississippi, and with that line to the Mississippi, opposite to Rock Island; thence up that river to the United States reservation, at the mouth of the Ouisconsin; thence with the south and east lines of the said reservation to the Ouisconsin; thence, southerly, passing the heads of the small streams emptying into the Mississippi, to the Rock river at the Winnebago village. The Illinois Indians have also a just claim to a portion of the country bounded south by the Indian boundary line aforesaid, running from the southern extreme of lake Michigan, east by lake Michigan, north by the Menominie country, and north-west by Rock river. This claim is recognized in the treaty concluded with the said Illinois tribes at St. Louis, August 24, 1816, but as the Millewakee and Manetoowalk bands are not represented at this Council, it cannot be now definitively adjusted.

ARTICLE 10.

All the tribes aforesaid acknowledge the general controlling power of the United States, and disclaim all dependence upon, and connection with, any other power. And the United States agree to, and recognize, the preceding boundaries, subject to the limitations and restrictions before provided. It being, however, well understood that the reservations at Fever River, at the Ouisconsin, and St. Peters, and the ancient settlements at Prairie des Chiens and Green Bay, and the land property thereto belonging, and the reservations made upon the Mississippi, for the use of the half breeds, in the treaty concluded with the Sacs and Foxes, August 24, 1824, are not claimed by either of the said tribes.

Said tribes acknowledge the supremacy of the United States.

ARTICLE 11.

The United States agree, whenever the President may think it necessary and proper, to convene such of the tribes, either separately or together, as are interested in the lines left unsettled herein, and to recommend to them an amicable and final adjustment of their respective claims, so that the work, now happily begun, may be consummated. It is agreed, however, that a Council shall be held with the Yancton band of the Sioux, during the year 1826, to explain to them the stipulations of this treaty, and to procure their assent thereto, should they be disposed to give it, and also with the Ottoes, to settle and adjust their title to any of the country claimed by the Sacs, Foxes, and Ioways.

A council to be held in 1826.

ARTICLE 12.

The Chippewa tribe being dispersed over a great extent of country, and the Chiefs of that tribe having requested, that such portion of them as may be thought proper, by the Government of the United States, may be assembled in 1826, upon some part of Lake Superior, that the objects and advantages of this treaty may be fully explained to them, so that the stipulations thereof may be observed by the warriors. The Commissioners of the United States assent thereto, and it is therefore agreed that a council shall accordingly be held for these purposes.

An assembly of the Chippewas to be convened.

ARTICLE 13.

It is understood by all the tribes, parties hereto, that no tribe shall hunt within the acknowledged limits of any other without their assent, but it being the sole object of this arrangement to perpetuate a peace among them, and amicable relations being now restored, the Chiefs of

No tribe to hunt within the acknowledged limits of any other without their assent.

all the tribes have expressed a determination, cheerfully to allow a reciprocal right of hunting on the lands of one another, permission being first asked and obtained, as before provided for.

ARTICLE 14.

In case of difficulty between the tribes.

Should any causes of difficulty hereafter unhappily arise between any of the tribes, parties hereunto, it is agreed that the other tribes shall interpose their good offices to remove such difficulties; and also that the government of the United States may take such measures as they may deem proper, to effect the same object.

ARTICLE 15.

When to take effect

This treaty shall be obligatory on the tribes, parties hereto, from and after the date hereof, and on the United States, from and after its ratification by the government thereof.

Done, and signed, and sealed, at Prairie des Chiens, in the territory of Michigan, this nineteenth day of August, one thousand eight hundred and twenty-five, and of the independence of the United States the fiftieth.

William Clark, [L. s.]
Lewis Cass, [L. s.]
Sioux:
Wa-ba-sha, x or the leaf, [L. s.]
Pe-tet-te x Corbeau, little crow, [L. s.]
The Little x of the Wappitong tribe, [L. s.]
Tartunka-nasiah x Sussitong, [L. s.]
Sleepy Eyes, x Sossitong, [L. s.]
Two faces x do [L. s.]
French Crow x Wappacoota, [L. s.]
Kee-jee x do [L. s.]
Tar-se-ga x do [L. s.]
Wa-ma-de-tun-ka x black dog, [L. s.]
Wan-na-ta x Yancton, or he that charges on his enemies, [L. s.]
Red Wing x [L. s.]
Ko-ko-ma-ko x [L. s.]
Sha-co-pe x the Sixth, [L. s.]
Pe-ni-si-on x [L. s.]
Eta-see-pa x Wabasha's band, [L. s.]
Wa-ka-u-hee, x Sioux band, rising thunder, [L. s.]
The Little Crow, x Sussetong, [L. s.]
Po-e-ha-pa x Me-da-we-con-tong, or eagle head, [L. s.]
Ta-ke-wa-pa x Wappitong, or medicine blanket, [L. s.]
Tench-ze-part, x his bow, [L. s.]
Masc-pu-lo-chas-tosh, x the white man, [L. s.]
Te-te-kar-munch, x the buffalo man, [L. s.]
Wa-sa-o-ta x Sussetong, or a great of hail, [L. s.]
Oeyah-ko-ca, x the crackling tract, [L. s.]
Mak-to-wah-ke-ark, x the bear, [L. s.]
Winnebagoes:
Les quatres jambes, x [L. s.]
Carimine, x the turtle that walks, [L. s.]
De-ca-ri, x [L. s.]
Wan-ca-ha-ga, x or snake's skin, [L. s.]
Sa-sa-ma-ni, x [L. s.]
Wa-non-che-qua, x the merchant, [L. s.]
Chon-que-pa, x or dog's head, [L. s.]
Cha-rat-chon, x the smoker, [L. s.]
Ca-ri-ca-si-ca, x he that kills the crow, [L. s.]
Watch-kat-o-que, x the grand canoe, [L. s.]

Ho-wa-mick-a, x the little elk, [L. s.]
Menominees:
Ma-can-me-ta, x medicine bear, [L. s.]
Chau-wee-nou-mi-tai, x medicine south wind, [L. s.]
Char-o-nee, x [L. s.]
Ma-wesh-a, x the little wolf, [L. s.]
A-ya-pas-mis-ai, x the thunder that turns, [L. s.]
Cha-ne-pau, x the riband, [L. s.]
La-me-quon, x the spoon, [L. s.]
En-im-e-tas, x the barking wolf, [L. s.]
Pape-at, x the one just arrived, [L. s.]
O-que-men-ce, x the little chief, [L. s.]
Chippewas:
Shinguaba x W'Ossin, 1st chief of the Chippewa nation, Saulte St. Marie, [L. s.]
Gitspee x Jiauba, 2d chief, [L. s.]
Gitspee x Waskee, or le bœuf of la pointe lake Superior, [L. s.]
Nain-a-boozhu, x of la pointe lake Superior, [L. s.]
Monga, x Zid or loon's foot of Fond du Lac, [L. s.]
Weescoup, x or sucre of Fond du Lac, [L. s.]
Mush-Koas, x or the elk of Fond du Lac, [L. s.]
Nau-bun x Aqeezhik, of Fond du Lac, [L. s.]
Kau-ta-waubeta, x or broken tooth of Sandy lake, [L. s.]
Pugisaingegen, x or broken arm of Sandy lake, [L. s.]
Kwee-weezaishish, x or grossguelle of Sandy lake, [L. s.]
Ba-ba-see-kundade, x or curling hair of Sandy lake, [L. s.]
Paashineep, x or man shooting at the mark of Sandy lake, [L. s.]
Pu-ga-a-gik, x the little beef, Leech lake, [L. s.]
Pee-see-ker, x or buffalo, St. Croix band, [L. s.]
Nau-din, x or the wind, St. Croix band, [L. s.]
Nau-quan-a-bee, x of Mille lac, [L. s.]

Tu-kau-bis-hoo, x or crouching lynx
  of Lac Courte Oreille,   [L. S.]
The Red Devil, x of Lac Courte
  Oreille,   [L. S.]
The Track, x of Lac Courte Oreille, [L. S.]
Ne-bo-na-bee, x the mermaid Lac
  Courte Oreille,   [L. S.]
Pi-a-gick, x the single man St.
  Croix,   [L. S.]
Pu-in-a-ne-gi, x, or the hole in the
  day, Sandy lake,   [L. S.]
Moose-o-mon-e, x plenty of elk, St.
  Croix band,   [L. S.]
Nees-o-pe-na, x or two birds of Up-
  per Red Cedar lake,   [L. S.]
Shaata, x the pelican of Leech lake, [L. S.]
Che-on-o-quet, x the great cloud
  of Leech lake,   [L. S.]
I-au-ben-see, x the little buck of
  Red lake,   [L. S.]
Kia-wa-tas, x the tarrier of Leech
  lake,   [L. S.]
Mau-ge-ga-bo, x the leader of Leech
  lake,   [L. S.]
Nan-go-tuck, x the flame of Leech
  lake,   [L. S.]
Nee-si-day-sish, x the sky of Red
  lake,   [L. S.]
Pee-chan-a-nim, x striped feather
  of Sandy lake,   [L. S.]
White Devil, x of Leech lake,   [L. S.]
Ka-ha-ka, x the sparrow, Lac
  Courte Oreille,   [L. S.]
I-au-be-ence, x little buck of Rice
  lake,
Ca-ba-ma-bee, x the assembly of
  St. Croix,   [L. S.]
Nau-gau-nosh, x the forward man
  lake Flambeau,   [L. S.]
Caw-win-dow, x he that gathers
  berries of Sandy Lake,   [L. S.]
On-que-ess, the mink, lake Supe-
  rior,   [L. S.]
Ke-we-ta-ke-pe, x all round the
  sky,   [L. S.]
The-sees, x   [L. S.]
    Ottawas:
Chaboner, x or Chambly,   [L. S.]
Shaw-fau-wick, x the mink,   [L. S.]
    Potawatomies:
Ignace, x   [L. S.]
Ke-o-kuk, x   [L. S.]
Che-chan-quose, x the little crane, [L. S.]
Taw-wa-na-nee, x the trader,   [L. S.]

Sacs:
Na-o-tuk, x the stabbing chief,   [L. S.]
Pish-ken-au-nee, x all fish,   [L. S.]
Po-ko-nau-qua, x or broken arm,   [L. S.]
Wau-kau-che, x eagle nose,   [L. S.]
Quash-kaume, x jumping fish,   [L. S.]
Ochaach, x the fisher,   [L. S.]
Ke-o-kuck, x the watchful fox,   [L. S.]
Skin-gwin-ee-see, the x ratler,   [L. S.]
Was-ar-wis-ke-no, x the yellow
  bird,   [L. S.]
Pau-ko-tuk, x the open sky,   [L. S.]
Au-kaak-wan-e-suk, x he that
  vaults on the earth,   [L. S.]
Mu-ku-taak-wan-wet, x   [L. S.]
Mis-ke-bee, x the standing hair,   [L. S.]

  Foxes:
Wan-ba-law, x the playing fox,   [L. S.]
Ti-a-mah, x the bear that makes
  the rocks shake,   [L. S.]
Pee-ar-maski, x the jumping stur-
  geon,   [L. S.]
Shagwa-na-tekwishu, x the thun-
  der that is heard all over the
  world,   [L. S.]
Mis-o-win, x moose deer horn,   [L. S.]
No-ko-wot, x the down of the fur,   [L. S.]
Nau-sa-wa-quot, x the bear that
  sleeps on the forks,   [L. S.]
Shin-quin-is, x the ratler,   [L. S.]
O-lo-pee-aau, x or Mache-paho-ta,
  the bear,   [L. S.]
Keesis, x the sun,   [L. S.]
No-wank, x he that gives too little, [L. S.]
Kan-ka-mote, x   [L. S.]
Neek-waa, x   [L. S.]
Ka-tuck-e-kan-ka, x the fox with a
  spotted breast,   [L. S.]
Mock-to-back-sa-gum, x black to-
  bacco,   [L. S.]
Wes-kesa, x the bear family,   [L. S.]

  Ioways:
Ma-hos-ka, x the white cloud,   [L. S.]
Pumpkin, x   [L. S.]
Wa-ca-nee, x the painted medi-
  cine,   [L. S.]
Tar-no-mun, x a great many deer,   [L. S.]
Wa-hoo-ga, x the owl,   [L. S.]
Ta-ca-mo-nee, x the lightning,   [L. S.]
Wa-push-a, x the man killer,   [L. S.]
To-nup-he-non-e, x the flea,   [L. S.]
Mon-da-tonga, x   [L. S.]
Cho-wa-row-a, x   [L. S.]

Witnesses:

Thomas Biddle, secretary,
R. A. McCabe, Captain Fifth Infantry,
R. A. Forsyth,
N. Boilvin, United States Indian agent,
C. C. Trowbridge, sub Indian agent,
Henry R. Schoolcraft, United States In-
  dian agent,
B. F. Harney, Surgeon U. S. Army,
W. B. Alexander, sub Indian agent,
Thomas Forsyth, agent Indian affairs,
Marvien Blondau,

David Bailey,
James M'Ilvaine, lieutenant U. S. Army,
Law. Taliaferro, Indian agent for Upper
  Mississippi,
John Holiday,
William Dickson,
S. Campbell, United States interpreter,
J. A. Lewis,
William Holiday,
Dunable Denejlevy,
Bela Chapman.

TREATY WITH THE OTO AND MISSOURI TRIBE, 1825.

Sept. 26, 1825.

7 Stat., 277.
Proclamation, Feb.
6, 1826.

For the purpose of perpetuating the friendship which has heretofore existed, as also to remove all future cause of discussion or dissension, as it respects trade and friendship between the United States and their citizens, and the Ottoe and Missouri tribe of Indians, the President of the United States of America, by Brigadier-General Henry Atkinson, of the United States' army, and Major Benjamin O'Fallon, Indian Agent, with full powers and authority, specially appointed and commissioned for that purpose, of the one part, and the undersigned Chiefs, Head-men, and Warriors, of the said Ottoe and Missouri tribe of Indians, on behalf of their tribe, of the other part, have made and entered into the following articles and conditions, which, when ratified by the President of the United States, by and with the advice and consent of the Senate, shall be binding on both parties—to wit:

ARTICLE 1.

Supremacy of United States acknowledged.

It is admitted by the Ottoe and Missouri tribe of Indians, that they reside within the territorial limits of the United States, acknowledge their supremacy, and claim their protection. The said tribe also admit the right of the United States to regulate all trade and intercourse with them.

ARTICLE 2.

Protection of United States extended to them.

The United States agree to receive the Ottoe and Missouri tribe of Indians into their friendship, and under their protection, and to extend to them, from time to time, such benefits and acts of kindness as may be convenient, and seem just and proper to the President of the United States.

ARTICLE 3.

Places for trade to be designated by the President.

All trade and intercourse with the Ottoe and Missouri tribe shall be transacted at such place or places as may be designated and pointed out by the President of the United States, through his agents; and none but American citizens, duly authorized by the United States, shall be admitted to trade or hold intercourse with said tribe of Indians.

ARTICLE 4.

Regulation of trade with Indians.

That the Ottoe and Missouri tribe may be accommodated with such articles of merchandise, &c. as their necessities may demand, the United States agree to admit and license traders to hold intercourse with said tribe, under mild and equitable regulations: in consideration of which, the said Ottoe and Missouri tribe bind themselves to extend protection to the persons and the property of the traders, and the persons legally employed under them, whilst they remain within the limits of their particular district of country. And the said Ottoe and Missouri tribe further agree, that if any foreigner or other person, not legally authorized by the United States, shall come into their district of country, for the purposes of trade or other views, they will apprehend such person or persons, and deliver him or them to some United States' superintendent, or agent of Indian Affairs, or to the Commandant of the nearest military post, to be dealt with according to law.— And they further agree to give safe conduct to all persons who may be legally authorized by the United States to pass through their country: and to protect, in their persons and property, all agents or other persons sent by the United States to reside temporarily among them; nor will they, whilst on their distant excursions, molest or interrupt any American citizen or citizens who may be passing from the United States to New Mexico, or returning from thence to the United States.

ARTICLE 5.

That the friendship which is now established between the United States and the Ottoe and Missouri tribe should not be interrupted by the misconduct of individuals, it is hereby agreed, that for injuries done by individuals, no private revenge or retaliation shall take place, but instead thereof, complaint shall be made, by the party injured, to the superintendent or agent of Indian affairs, or other person appointed by the President; and it shall be the duty of said Chiefs, upon complaint being made as aforesaid, to deliver up the person or persons against whom the complaint is made, to the end that he or they may be punished agreeably to the laws of the United States. And, in like manner, if any robbery, violence, or murder, shall be committed on any Indian or Indians belonging to said tribe, the person or persons so offending shall be tried, and if found guilty shall be punished in like manner as if the injury had been done to a white man. And it is agreed, that the Chiefs of said Ottoe and Missouri tribe shall, to the utmost of their power, exert themselves to recover horses or other property, which may be stolen or taken from any citizen or citizens of the United States, by any individual or individuals of said tribe; and the property so recovered shall be forthwith delivered to the agents or other person authorized to receive it, that it may be restored to the proper owner. And the United States hereby guarranty to any Indian or Indians of said tribe, a full indemnification for any horses or other property which may be stolen from them by any of their citizens: *Provided*, That the property stolen cannot be recovered, and that sufficient proof is produced that it was actually stolen by a citizen of the United States. And the said Ottoe and Missouri tribe engage, on the requisition or demand of the President of the United States, or of the agents, to deliver up any white man resident among them.

Course to be pursued in order to prevent injuries by individuals, etc.

Chiefs to exert themselves to recover stolen property.

Proviso.

ARTICLE 6.

And the Chiefs and Warriors, as aforesaid, promise and engage, that their tribe will never, by sale, exchange, or as presents, supply any nation, tribe, or band of Indians, not in amity with the United States, with guns, ammunition, or other implements of war.

No arms to be furnished by Indians to persons not in amity with United States.

Done at Fort Atkinson, Council Bluffs, this 26th day of September, A. D. 1825, and of the independence of the United States the fiftieth.

In testimony whereof, the said commissioners, Henry Atkinson and Benjamin O'Fallon, and the chiefs, head men, and warriors, of the Ottoe and Missouri tribe, have hereunto set their hands, and affixed their seals.

H. Atkinson, brigadier-general, U. S. Army, [L. s.]
Benj. O'Fallon, United States agent Indian Affairs, [L. s.]
Ish-na-wong-ge-ge-he, the only chief, his x mark, [L. s.]
Me-ha-hun-jah, the big female, his x mark, [L. s.]
Shunk-co-pe, his x mark, [L. s.]
Sho-mon-e-ka-sa, the prairie wolf, his x mark, [L. s.]
Wong-ge-ge-he, the chief, his x mark, [L. s.]
Waw-zob-e-ing-ge, the little black bear, his x mark, [L. s.]
Eho-che-nung-a, the mad man, his x mark, [L. s.]
E-ke-shaw-mon-ne, the walking bear, his x mark, [L. s.]

Waw-ne-sung-e, the one who bears down, his x mark, [L. s.]
Waw-ro-ne-sa, the bullet, his x mark, [L. s.]
Wa-do-ke-ga, his x mark, [L. s.]
Waw-paw-si-ae, his x mark, [L. s.]
Taw-ing-ee, the little deer, his x mark, [L. s.]
Gray-tan-in-ca, the sparrow hawk, his x mark, [L. s.]
Raw-no-way-braw, the broken pipe, his x mark, [L. s.]
Non-jah-ning-e, the no heart, his x mark, [L. s.]
Mon-to-ing-ge, the little white bear, his x mark, [L. s.]
Mosk-ca-gaw-ha, his x mark, [L. s.]

In presence of—

A. L. Langham, secretary to the commission,
A. R. Woolley, lieutenant-colonel, U. S. Army,
B. Riley, captain, Sixth Infantry,
J. Gantt, captain, Sixth Infantry,
John Gale, surgeon, U. S. Army,
Wm. N. Wickliffe, lieutenant, U. S. Army,
G. W. Folger, lieutenant, Sixth U. S. Infantry,
J. Rogers, lieutenant, Sixth Infantry,
Levi Nute, lieutenant, Sixth Infantry,

M. W. Batman, lieutenant, Sixth Infantry,
A. Richardson, lieutenant, Sixth Infantry,
J. Nichols, lieutenant, Sixth Infantry,
G. H. Crosman, lieutenant, Sixth Infantry,
G. H. Kennerly, U. S. S. Indian agent,
W. W. Eaton, lieutenant, Sixth Infantry,
Michael Burdeau, his x mark, Maha interpreter,
William Rogers.

TREATY WITH THE PAWNEE TRIBE, 1825.

Sept. 30, 1825.

7 Stat., 279.
Proclamation, Feb. 6, 1826.

FOR the purpose of perpetuating the friendship which has heretofore existed, as also to remove all future cause of discussion or dissension, as it respects trade and friendship between the United States and their citizens, and the Pawnee tribe of Indians, the President of the United States of America, by Brigadier General Henry Atkinson, of the United States' army, and Major Benjamin O'Fallon, Indian Agent, with full powers and authority, specially appointed and commissioned for that purpose, of the one part, and the undersigned Chiefs, head men and Warriors of said Pawnee tribe of Indians, on behalf of their tribe of the other part, have made and entered into the following Articles and Conditions; which, when ratified by the President of the United States, by and with the advice and consent of the Senate, shall be binding on both parties—to wit:

ARTICLE 1.

Supremacy of United States acknowledged.

It is admitted by the Pawnee tribe of Indians, that they reside within the territorial limits of the United States, acknowledge their supremacy, and claim their protection.—The said tribe also admit the right of the United States to regulate all trade and intercourse with them.

ARTICLE 2.

United States receive Pawnees under their protection.

The United States agree to receive the Pawnee tribe of Indians into their friendship, and under their protection, and to extend to them, from time to time, such benefits and acts of kindness as may be convenient, and seem just and proper to the President of the United States.

ARTICLE 3.

Places for trade to be designated by the President.

All trade and intercourse with the Pawnee tribe shall be transacted at such place or places as may be designated and pointed out by the President of the United States, through his agents; and none but American citizens, duly authorized by the United States, shall be admitted to trade or hold intercourse with said tribe of Indians.

ARTICLE 4.

Regulation of trade.

That the Pawnee tribe may be accommodated with such articles of merchandise, &c. as their necessities may demand, the United States agree to admit and license traders to hold intercourse with said tribe, under mild and equitable regulations: in consideration of which, the said Pawnee tribe bind themselves to extend protection to the persons and the property of the traders, and the persons legally employed under them, whilst they remain within the limits of their particular district of country. And the said Pawnee tribe further agree, that if any foreigner or other person, not legally authorized by the United States, shall come into their district of country, for the purpose of trade or other views, they will apprehend such person or persons, and deliver him or them to some United States' superintendent, or agent, of Indian Affairs, or to the commandant of the nearest military post, to be dealt with according to law. And they further agree to give safe conduct to all persons who may be legally authorized by the United States to pass through their country, and to protect in their persons and property all agents or other persons sent by the United States to reside temporarily among them; nor will they, whilst on their distant excursions, molest or interrupt any American citizen or citizens, who may be passing from the United States to New Mexico, or returning from thence to the United States.

ARTICLE 5.

That the friendship which is now established between the United States and the Pawnee tribe, shall not be interrupted by the misconduct of individuals, it is hereby agreed, that for injuries done by individuals, no private revenge or retaliation shall take place, but instead thereof, complaints shall be made, by the party injured, to the superintendent, or agent of Indian affairs, or other person appointed by the President; and it shall be the duty of said Chiefs, upon complaint being made as aforesaid, to deliver up the person or persons against whom the complaint is made, to the end that he or they may be punished, agreeably to the laws of the United States. And, in like manner, if any robbery, violence, or murder, shall be committed on any Indian or Indians belonging to said tribe, the person or persons so offending shall be tried, and if found guilty, shall be punished in like manner as if the injury had been done to a white man. And it is agreed, that the Chiefs of said Pawnee tribe shall, to the utmost of their power, exert themselves to recover horses or other property, which may be stolen or taken from any citizen or citizens of the United States, by any individual or individuals of said tribe; and the property so recovered shall be forthwith delivered to the agents or other person authorized to receive it, that it may be restored to the proper owner. And the United States hereby guaranty to any Indian or Indians of said tribe, a full indemnification for any horses or other property which may be stolen from them by any of their citizens: *Provided*, That the property stolen cannot be recovered, and that sufficient proof is produced that it was actually stolen by a citizen of the United States. And the said Pawnee tribe engage, on the requisition or demand of the President of the United States, or of the agents, to deliver up any white man resident among them.

Course to be pursued in order to prevent injuries by individuals, etc.

Chiefs to exert themselves to recover stolen property.

ARTICLE 6.

And the Chiefs and Warriors, as aforesaid, promise and engage that their tribe will never, by sale, exchange, or as presents, supply any nation, tribe, or band of Indians, not in amity with the United States, with guns, ammunition, or other implements of war.

No arms, etc., to be furnished by them to enemies of United States.

Done at Fort Atkinson, Council Bluffs, this thirtieth day of September, A. D. 1825, and of the independence of the United States the fiftieth.

In testimony whereof, the said commissioners, Henry Atkinson and Benjamin O'Fallon, and the chiefs, head men, and warriors, of the Pawnee tribe, have hereunto set their hands and affixed their seals.

H. Atkinson, brigadier-general, U. S. Army, [L. S.]
Benj. O'Fallon, United States agent Indian affairs, [L. S.]

Esh-ca-tar-pa, the bad chief, his x mark, [L. S.]
Shar-co-ro-la-shar, the sun chief, his x mark, [L. S.]

La-cota-ve-co-cho-la-shar, the eagle
  chief, his x mark,   [L. s.]
La-tah-carts-la-shar, the war eagle
  chief, his x mark,   [L. s.]
La-ta-le-shar, the knife chief, his x
  mark,   [L. s.]
Scar-lar-la-shar, the man chief, his
  x mark,   [L. s.]
La-ke-tar-la-shar, the partizan
  chief, his x mark,   [L. s.]
Lark-tar-ho-ra-la-shar, the pipe
  chief, his x mark,   [L. s.]
Esh-ca-tar-pa, the bad chief, republican band, his x mark,   [L. s.]
Co-rouch-la-shar, the bear chief,
  his x mark,   [L. s.]
Ah-sha-o-ah-lah-co, the dog chief,
  his x mark,   [L. s.]
La-ho-rah-sha-rete, the man who
  strikes men, his x mark,   [L. s.]
Tah-rah-re-tah-coh-sha, the singing
  crow, his x mark,   [L. s.]
Lah-ro-wah-go, the hill chief, his
  x mark,   [L. s.]
Ta-rah-re-tah-nash, the big horse
  stealer, his x mark,   [L. s.]

La-shar-pah-he, the tranquil chief,
  his x mark,   [L. s.]
Ah-re-cah-rah-co-chu, the mad elk,
  his x mark,   [L. s.]
Ta-lah-re-ta-ret, the partizan that
  strikes and carries his bird on
  his back, his x mark,   [L. s.]
Ta-lah-re-we-tail, the crow that
  strikes, his x mark,   [L. s.]
Lo-lah-re-wah, the horse stealer
  who suffers his prize to be re-
  taken, his x mark,   [L. s.]
Ta-hah-lah-re-esh-lah, the hand-
  some bird, his x mark,   [L. s.]
Ah-sho-cole, the rotten foot, his x
  mark,   [L. s.]
Ah-shar-o-ca-tah-co, the poor man,
  his x mark,   [L. s.]
Cha-nuck-cah-lah, the partizan
  that strikes, his x mark,   [L. s.]
Ta-lah-we-cah-wah-re, the man
  that is always at war, his x
  mark,   [L. s.]

In presence of—

A. L. Langham, secretary to the com-
  mission.
A. R. Woolley, lieutenant-colonel, U. S.
  Army.
John Gale, surgeon, U. S. Army.
John Gantt, captain, Sixth infantry.
S. MacRee, aide de camp.
Thomas Noel, adjutant, Sixth regiment.
J. Rogers, lieutentant, Sixth infantry.

R. Holmes, lieutenant, Sixth infantry.
M. W. Batman, lieutenant, Sixth infan-
  try.
J. Nichols, lieutenant, Sixth infantry.
W. W. Eaton, lieutenant, Sixth infantry.
G. H. Kennerly U. S. S. Indian agent.
A. L. Papin.
William Rodgers.

TREATY WITH THE MAKAH TRIBE, 1825.

Oct. 6, 1825.

7 Stat., 282.
Proclamation, Feb.
6, 1826.

FOR the purpose of perpetuating the friendship which has heretofore existed, as also to remove all future cause of discussion or dissension, as it respects trade and friendship between the United States and their citizens, and the Maha tribe of Indians, the President of the United States of America, by Brigadier General Henry Atkinson, of the United States' Army, and Major Benjamin O'Fallon, Indian Agent, with full powers and authority, specially appointed and commissioned for that purpose, of the one part, and the undersigned Chiefs, Head-men and Warriors, of the said Maha tribe of Indians, on behalf of their tribe, of the other part, ·have made and entered into the following articles and conditions, which, when ratified by the President of the United States, by and with the advice and consent of the Senate, shall be binding on both parties—to wit:

ARTICLE 1.

Supremacy of
United States ac-
knowledged.

It is admitted by the Maha tribe of Indians, that they reside within the territorial limits of the United States, acknowledge their supremacy, and claim their protection. The said tribe also admit the right of the United States to regulate all trade and intercourse with them.

ARTICLE 2.

United States re-
ceive them under
their protection.

The United States agree to receive the Maha tribe of Indians into their friendship, and under their protection, and to extend to them, from time to time, such benefits and acts of kindness as may be convenient, and seem just and proper to the President of the United States.

ARTICLE 3.

All trade and intercourse with the Maha tribe shall be transacted at such place or places as may be designated and pointed out by the President of the United States, through his agents: and none but American citizens, duly authorized by the United States, shall be admitted to trade or hold intercourse with said tribe of Indians.

Places for trade to be designated by the President.

ARTICLE 4.

That the Maha tribe may be accommodated with such articles of merchandise, &c. as their necessities may demand, the United States agree to admit and license traders to hold intercourse with said tribe, under mild and equitable regulations: in consideration of which, the Maha tribe bind themselves to extend protection to the persons and the property of the traders, and the persons legally employed under them, whilst they remain within the limits of their particular district of country. And the said Maha tribe further agree, that if any foreigner, or other person not legally authorized by the United States, shall come into their district of country, for the purposes of trade or other views, they will apprehend such person or persons, and deliver him or them to some United States' superintendent or agent of Indian Affairs, or to the Commandant of the nearest military post, to be dealt with according to law.—And they further agree to give safe conduct to all persons who may be legally authorized by the United States to pass through their country; and to protect in their persons and property, all agents or other persons sent by the United States to reside temporarily among them; nor will they, whilst on their distant excursions, molest or interrupt any American citizen or citizens who may be passing from the United States to New Mexico, or returning from thence to the United States.

Regulation of trade.

ARTICLE 5.

That the friendship which is now established between the United States and the Maha tribe should not be interrupted by the misconduct of individuals, it is hereby agreed, that, for injuries done by individuals, no private revenge or retaliation shall take place, but instead thereof, complaints shall be made by the party injured, to the superintendent or agent of Indian affairs, or other person appointed by the President; and it shall be the duty of said Chiefs, upon complaint being made as aforesaid, to deliver up the person or persons against whom the complaint is made, to the end that he or they may be punished agreeably to the laws of the United States. And, in like manner, if any robbery, violence, or murder, shall be committed on any Indian or Indians belonging to said tribe, the person or persons so offending shall be tried, and if found guilty shall be punished in like manner as if the injury had been done to a white man. And it is agreed, that the Chiefs of said Maha tribe shall, to the utmost of their power, exert themselves to recover horses or other property, which may be stolen or taken from any citizen or citizens of the United States, by any individual or individuals of said tribe; and the property so recovered shall be forthwith delivered to the agents or other person authorized to receive it, that it may be restored to the proper owner. And the United States hereby guarranty to any Indian or Indians of said tribe, a full indemnification for any horses or other property which may be stolen from them by any of their citizens: *Provided*, That the property stolen cannot be recovered, and that sufficient proof is produced that it was actually stolen by a citizen of the United States. And the said Maha tribe engage, on the requisition or demand of the President of the United States, or of the agents, to deliver up any white man resident among them.

Course to be pursued in order to prevent injuries by individuals, etc.

Chiefs to exert themselves to recover stolen property.

Proviso.

ARTICLE 6.

No guns, etc., to be furnished by them to those hostile to United States.

And the Chiefs and Warriors, as aforesaid, promise and engage, that their tribe will never, by sale, exchange, or as presents, supply any nation, tribe, or band of Indians, not in amity with the United States, with guns, ammunition, or other implements of war.

Done at fort Atkinson, Council Bluffs, this 6th day of October, A. D. 1825, and of the independence of the United States the fiftieth.

In testimony whereof, the said commissioners, Henry Atkinson and Benjamin O'Fallon, and the chiefs, head men, and warriors of the Maha tribe, have hereunto set their hands, and affixed their seals.

H. Atkinson, brigadier - general U. S. Army, [L. S.]	Ta-noh-ga, the buffalo bull, his x mark, [L. S.]
Benj. O'Fallon, U. S. agent Indian affairs, [L. S.]	Esh-sta-ra-ba, ——, his x mark, [L. S.]
Opa-ton-ga, the big elk, his x mark, [L. S.]	Ta-reet-tee, the side of a buffalo, his x mark, [L. S.]
Oho-shin-ga, the man that cooks little in a small kettle, his x mark, [L. S.]	Sa-da-ma-ne, he that arrives, his x mark, [L. S.]
Wash-ca-ma-nee, the fast walker, his x mark, [L. S.]	Mo-pe-ma-nee, the walking cloud, his x mark, [L. S.]
Shon-gis-cah, the white horse, his x mark, [L. S.]	Momee-shee, he who lays on the arrows from the number that pierce him, his x mark, [L. S.]
We-du-gue-noh, the deliberator, his x mark, [L. S.]	Ma-sha-ke-ta, the soldier, his x mark, [L. S.]
Wa-shing-ga-sabba, the black bird, his x mark, [L. S.]	Te-sha-va-gran, the door of the lodge, his x mark, [L. S.]

In the presence of—

A. L. Langham, secretary to the commission,	George C. Hutter, lieutenant Sixth Infantry,
A. R. Wooley, lieutenant-colonel U. S. Army,	M. W. Batman, lieutenant Sixth Infantry,
J. Gantt, captain Sixth Infantry,	G. H. Kennerly, U. S. S. Indian agent,
John Gale, surgeon U. S. Army,	Michael Burdeau, his x mark, interpreter,
	William Rodgers.

TREATY WITH THE SHAWNEE, 1825.

Nov. 7, 1825.

7 Stat., 284.
Proclamation, Dec. 30, 1825.

Articles of a convention made between William Clark, Superintendent of Indian Affairs, and the undersigned Chiefs and Head Men of the Shawonee Nation of Indians, residing within the State of Missouri, duly authorized and empowered by said Nation, at the City of St. Louis, on the seventh day of November, in the year of our Lord one thousand eight hundred and twenty-five.

Preamble.

WHEREAS the Shawnee Indians were in possession of a tract of land near Cape Geredeau, in the State of Missouri, settled under a permission from the Spanish Government, given to the said Shawnees and Delawares by the Baron De Carondelet, on the fourth day of January, one thousand seven hundred and ninety-three, and recorded in the office of Recorder of Land Titles at St. Louis, containing about (25) twenty-five miles square, which said tract of land was abandoned by the Delawares, in the year 1815: and from which the said Shawnees, under an assurance of receiving other lands in exchange, did remove, after having made valuable and lasting improvements on the same, which were taken possession of by the citizens of the United States: And it being the desire of the United States fully to indemnify said tribe for all losses and injuries sustained by them by reason of such removal—the following articles have been agreed upon, between WILLIAM CLARK, Superintendent of Indian Affairs, specially authorized on the one part, and the undersigned Delegates of the Shawnee tribe, residing within the State of Missouri, on the other part:

ARTICLE 1.

The Shawnee tribe, do, hereby, cede and relinquish to the United States, all their claim, interest and title, to the lands on which they settled, near Cape Geredeau, under an authority of the Spanish government as aforesaid, situate, lying, and being between the River St. Come and Cape Geredeau, and bounded on the east by the Mississippi, and westwardly by White Water.

Cession of land by the Shawnee.

ARTICLE 2.

It is further agreed by the contracting parties, that, in consideration of the cession aforesaid, the United States do, hereby, agree to give to the Shawnee tribe of Indians, within the State of Missouri for themselves and for those of the same nation, now residing in Ohio, who may hereafter emigrate to the west of the Mississippi, a tract of land equal to fifty (50) miles square, situated west of the State of Missouri, and within the purchase lately made from the Osages, by treaty bearing date the second day of June, one thousand eight hundred and twenty-five, and within the following boundaries: Commencing at a point (2) two miles north-west of the south-west corner of the State of Missouri; from thence, north, (25) twenty-five miles; thence, west, (100) one hundred miles; thence, south, (25) twenty-five miles; thence, east, (100) one hundred miles, to the place of beginning. But, whereas the said Shawnee tribe had valuable and lasting improvements within the tract of land hereby ceded, and moreover will have to incur expenses in their removal; it is further stipulated, that, for the purpose of rendering a fair equivalent for the losses and inconveniences which said tribe will sustain by removal, and to enable them to obtain supplies in their new settlements, the United States agree to pay to the tribe emigrating from the lands herein ceded, the sum of fourteen thousand dollars, which amount shall be paid to said party of the second part, as soon as practicable after the ratification of this treaty; five thousand dollars of which amount shall be furnished in domestic animals, implements of husbandry, and provisions, as soon as the said tribe remove upon the lands assigned them.

United States to give a certain tract in exchange.

Further stipulation.

ARTICLE 3.

It is further stipulated, that a deputation of the said parties of the second part may be sent to explore the lands assigned to them in the preceding article; and if the same be not acceptable to them, upon an examination of the same, which shall be had, and made known to the Superintendent of Indian affairs at St. Louis, on or before April next, who shall, in lieu thereof, assign to them an equal quantity of land, to be selected on the Kansas River, and laid off either south or north of that river, and west of the boundary of Missouri, not reserved or ceded to any other tribe.

A deputation to explore the lands.

ARTICLE 4.

It appearing that the Shawnee Indians have various claims against the citizens of the United States to a large amount, for spoliations of various kinds, but which they have not been able to support by the testimony of white men; the United States, in order to a final settlement of all such claims, do hereby agree to pay to the Shawnee nation, the sum of (11,000) eleven thousand dollars, to be distributed by them in such way as may be deemed equitable; and to support and keep a blacksmith for their use on the lands hereby assigned, for the term of five years, or as long as the President may deem advisable; and it is further stipulated, that the United States shall furnish for the use of the Shawnees,

Payment of claims against citizens of United States.

Tools, etc. for the use of a blacksmith, to be furnished.

the tools necessary for the blacksmith's shop, and (300) three hundred pounds of iron annually, to be furnished at the expense of the United States.

ARTICLE 5.

Friendship re-newed.

The friendship heretofore existing between the United States and the Shawnee Nation, is, hereby, renewed and perpetuated.

ARTICLE 6.

Treaty obligatory when ratified.

These articles shall take effect, and become obligatory on the contracting parties, so soon as the same shall be ratified by the President, by and with the advice and consent of the Senate of the United States.

In testimony whereof, the said William Clark, and the said delegates of the Shawanee nation, have hereunto set their hands, at the city of St. Louis, the seventh day of November, one thousand eight hundred and twenty-five.

William Clark,	Napawita, his x mark,
Wawelainni, his x mark,	Pepamousse, his x mark,
Kishkalwa, his x mark,	Pemitacamchika, his x mark,
Maywathekeha, his x mark,	Peter Cornstalk, or Wyawimon, interp.
Capt. Reed, or Pathecoussa, his x mark,	his x mark,
Nelawachika, his x mark,	Quamapea, his x mark,
Waquiwais, his x mark,	Pelmetachemo, his x mark.

Witnesses present:

A. McNair, United States Indian agent,	John F. A. Sandford,
R. Graham, United States Indian agent,	L. Valle,
Pierre Menard, sub-Indian agent,	John B. Saipy,
John Campbell, sub-Indian agent,	Quatwapea, or Col. Lewis, his x mark,
W. B. Alexander, sub-Indian agent,	Wysaosheka, his x mark.

TREATY WITH THE CREEKS, 1826.

Jan. 24, 1826.

7 Stat., 286.
Proclamation, Apr. 22, 1826.

Articles of a treaty made at the City of Washington, this twenty-fourth day of January, one thousand eight hundred and twenty-six, between James Barbour, Secretary of War, thereto specially authorized by the President of the United States, and the undersigned, Chiefs and Head Men of the Creek Nation of Indians, who have received full power from the said Nation to conclude and arrange all the matters herein provided for.

Preamble.

WHEREAS a treaty was concluded at the Indian Springs, on the twelfth day of February last, between Commissioners on the part of the United States, and a portion of the Creek Nation, by which an extensive district of country was ceded to the United States.

And whereas a great majority of the Chiefs and Warriors of the said Nation have protested against the execution of the said Treaty, and have represented that the same was signed on their part by persons having no sufficient authority to form treaties, or to make cessions, and that the stipulations in the said Treaty are, therefore, wholly void.

And whereas the United States are unwilling that difficulties should exist in the said Nation, which may eventually lead to an intestine war, and are still more unwilling that any cessions of land should be made to them, unless with the fair understanding and full assent of the Tribe making such cession, and for a just and adequate consideration, it being the policy of the United States, in all their intercourse with the Indians, to treat them justly and liberally, as becomes the relative situation of the parties.

Now, therefore, in order to remove the difficulties which have thus arisen, to satisfy the great body of the Creek Nation, and to reconcile the contending parties into which it is unhappily divided, the following articles have been agreed upon and concluded, between James Barbour, Secretary of War, specially authorized as aforesaid, and the said Chiefs and Head Men representing the Creek Nation of Indians:

ARTICLE 1.

The Treaty concluded at the Indian Springs, on the twelfth day of February, one thousand eight hundred and twenty-five, between Commissioners on the part of the United States and the said Creek Nation of Indians, and ratified by the United States on the seventh day of March, one thousand eight hundred and twenty-five, is hereby declared to be null and void, to every intent and purpose whatsoever; and every right and claim arising from the same is hereby cancelled and surrendered. *Treaty of Indian Springs declared null and void.*

ARTICLE 2.

The Creek Nation of Indians cede to the United States all the land belonging to the said Nation in the State of Georgia, and lying on the east side of the middle of the Chatahoochie river. And, also, another tract of land lying within the said State, and bounded as follows: Beginning at a point on the western bank of the said river, forty-seven miles below the point where the boundary line between the Creeks and Cherokees strikes the Chatahoochie river, near the Buzzard's Roost, measuring the said distance in a direct line, and not following the meanders of the said river; and from the point of beginning, running in a direct line to a point in the boundary line, between the said Creeks and the Cherokees, thirty miles west of the said Buzzard's Roost; thence to the Buzzard's Roost, and thence with the middle of the said river to the place of beginning. *Lands ceded to the United States.*

ARTICLE 3.

Immediately after the ratification of this Treaty, the United States agree to pay to the Chiefs of the said Nation the sum of two hundred and seventeen thousand six hundred dollars to be divided among the Chiefs and Warriors of the said Nation. *Payment to said nation.*

ARTICLE 4.

The United States agree to pay to the said Nation an additional perpetual annuity of twenty thousand dollars. *Perpetual annuity.*

ARTICLE 5.

The difficulties which have arisen in the said nation, in consequence of the Treaty of the Indian Springs, shall be amicably adjusted, and that portion of the Creek Nation who signed that treaty shall be admitted to all their privileges, as members of the Creek Nation, it being the earnest wish of the United States, without undertaking to decide upon the complaints of the respective parties, that all causes of dissatisfaction should be removed. *Difficulties to be adjusted, etc.*

ARTICLE 6.

That portion of the Creek Nation, known as the friends and followers of the late General William McIntosh, having intimated to the government of the United States their wish to remove west of the Mississippi, it is hereby agreed, with their assent, that a deputation of five persons shall be sent by them, at the expense of the United States, immediately after the ratification of this treaty, to examine the Indian *A deputation to examine the Indian country west of the Mississippi, etc.*

country west of the Mississippi, not within either of the States or Territories, and not possessed by the Choctaws or Cherokees. And the United States agree to purchase for them, if the same can be conveniently done upon reasonable terms, wherever they may select, a country, whose extent shall, in the opinion of the President, be proportioned to their numbers. And if such purchase cannot be thus made, it is then agreed that the selection shall be made where the President may think proper, just reference being had to the wishes of the emigrating party.

ARTICLE 7.

Emigrating party to remove within twenty-four months, etc.

The emigrating party shall remove within twenty-four months, and the expense of their removal shall be defrayed by the United States. And such subsistence shall also be furnished them, for a term not exceeding twelve months after their arrival at their new residence, as, in the opinion of the President, their numbers and circumstances may require.

ARTICLE 8.

An agent, etc., to be appointed to reside with them.

An agent, or sub-agent and Interpreter, shall be appointed to accompany and reside with them. And a blacksmith and wheelwright shall be furnished by the United States. Such assistance shall also be rendered to them in their agricultural operations, as the President may think proper.

ARTICLE 9.

Presents to Indians.

In consideration of the exertions used by the friends and followers of General McIntosh to procure a cession at the Indian Springs, and of their past difficulties and contemplated removal, the United States agree to present to the Chiefs of the party, to be divided among the Chiefs and Warriors, the sum of one hundred thousand dollars, if such party shall amount to three thousand persons, and in that proportion for any smaller number. Fifteen thousand dollars of this sum to be paid immediately after the ratification of this treaty, and the residue upon their arrival in the country west of the Mississippi.

ARTICLE 10.

Certain damages to be ascertained, etc.

It is agreed by the Creek Nation, that an agent shall be appointed by the President, to ascertain the damages sustained by the friends and followers of the late General McIntosh, in consequence of the difficulties growing out of the Treaty of the Indian Springs, as set forth in an agreement entered into with General Gains, at the Broken Arrow,[a] and which have been done contrary to the laws of the Creek Nation; and such damages shall be repaired by the said Nation, or the amount paid out of the annuity due to them.

ARTICLE 11.

Commissioners to value improvements.

All the improvements which add real value to any part of the land herein ceded shall be appraised by Commissioners, to be appointed by the President; and the amount thus ascertained shall be paid to the parties owning such improvements.

ARTICLE 12.

Possession of country ceded.

Possession of the country herein ceded shall be yielded by the Creeks on or before the first day of January next.

---

[a]This agreement, which is unratified, is set forth in the Appendix, post, p. 1034. The original can not be found, but a copy is among the files of the Indian Office, General Files, Creek, 1825–1826.—E. P. Gaines.

Article 13.

The United States agree to guarantee to the Creeks all the country, not herein ceded, to which they have a just claim, and to make good to them any losses they may incur in consequence of the illegal conduct of any citizen of the United States within the Creek country.

Guarantee by United States.

Article 14.

The President of the United States shall have authority to select, in some part of the Creek country, a tract of land, not exceeding two sections, where the necessary public buildings may be erected, and the persons attached to the agency may reside.

Authority of the President.

Article 15.

Wherever any stream, over which it may be necessary to establish ferries, forms the boundary of the Creek country, the Creek Indians shall have the right of ferriage from their own land, and the citizens of the United States from the land to which the Indian title is extinguished.

Liberty granted the Creeks.

Article 16.

The Creek Chiefs may appoint three Commissioners from their own people, who shall be allowed to attend the running of the lines west of the Chatahoochy river, and whose expenses, while engaged in this duty, shall be defrayed by the United States.

Commissioners to attend the running of the lines.

Article 17.

This treaty, after the same has been ratified by the President and Senate, shall be obligatory on the United States and on the Creek Nation.

Treaty binding when ratified.

In testimony whereof, the said James Barbour, Secretary of War, authorized as aforesaid, and the chiefs of the said Creek nation of Indians, have hereunto set their hands, at the City of Washington, the day and year aforesaid.

James Barbour,	Timpoochy Barnard, his x mark,
O-poth-le Yoholo, his x mark,	Apauly Tustunnuggee, his x mark,
John Stidham, his x mark,	Coosa Tustunnuggee, his x mark,
Mad Wolf, his x mark,	Nahetluc Hopie, his x mark,
Menawee, his x mark,	Selocta, his x mark,
Tuskeekee Tustunnuggee, his x mark,	Ledagi, his x mark,
Charles Cornells, his x mark,	Yoholo Micco, his x mark.

In presence of—

Thomas L. McKenney,	Hezekiah Miller,
Lewis Cass,	John Ridge, secretary Creek delegation,
John Crowell, agent for Indian Affairs,	David Vann.

Supplementary Article to the Creek Treaty of the Twenty-fourth January, 1826.

Mar. 31, 1826.

7 Stat., 289.

Whereas a stipulation in the second article of the Treaty of the twenty-fourth day of January, 1826, between the undersigned, parties to said Treaty, provides for the running of a line "beginning at a point on the western bank of the Chatahoochee river, forty-seven miles below the point where the boundary line between the Creeks and Cherokees strikes the said river, near the Buzzard's Roost, measuring the said distance in a direct line, and not following the meanders of the said river, and from the point of beginning, running in a direct line to a point in the boundary line between the said Creeks and the Cherokees, thirty miles west of the said Buzzard's Roost, thence to the Buzzard's Roost, and thence with the middle of said river to the place of beginning." And whereas it having been represented to the party to the said Treaty in behalf of the Creek Nation, that a certain extension of said lines might embrace in the cession all the lands which will be found to lie within the chartered limits of Georgia, and which are owned by the Creeks, the undersigned do hereby agree to the following extension of said lines, viz: In the place of "forty-seven miles," as stipulated in the second article of the Treaty aforesaid, as the point of beginning, the undersigned agree that it shall be *fifty* miles, in a direct line below the point designated in the second article of said Treaty; thence running in a direct line to a point in the boundary line between the Creeks and Cherokees, *forty-five miles* west of said Buzzard's Roost, in the place of "thirty miles," as stipulated in said Treaty; thence to the Buzzard's Roost, and thence to the place of beginning— it being understood that these lines are to stop at their intersection with the boundary line between Georgia and Alabama, wherever that may be, if that line shall cross them in the direction of the Buzzard's Roost, at a shorter distance than it is provided they shall run; and provided, also, that if the said dividing line between Georgia and Alabama shall not be reached by the extension of the two lines aforesaid, the one three, and the other fifteen miles, they are to run and terminate as defined in this supplemental article to the Treaty aforesaid.

Payment to Creeks.

It is hereby agreed, in consideration of the extension of said lines, on the part of the other party to the Treaty aforesaid, in behalf of the United States, to pay to the Creek Nation, immediately upon the ratification of said Treaty, the sum of thirty thousand dollars.

In witness whereof, the parties aforesaid have hereunto set their hands and seals, this thirty-first day of March, in the year of our Lord one thousand eight hundred twenty-six.

James Barbour,	[L. S.]	Charles Cornells, his x mark,	[L. S.]
Opothle Yoholo, his x mark,	[L. S.]	Apauly Tustunnuggee, his x mark,	[L. S.]
John Stidham, his x mark,	[L. S.]	Coosa Tustunnuggee, his x mark,	[L. S.]
Mad Wolf, his x mark,	[L. S.]	Nahetluc Hopie, his x mark,	[L. S.]
Tuskeekee Tustunnuggee, his x mark,	[L. S.]	Selocta, his x mark,	[L. S.]
Yoholo Micco, his x mark,	[L. S.]	Timpoochy Barnard, his x mark,	[L. S.]
Menawee, his x mark,	[L. S.]	Ledagi, his x mark,	[L. S.]

In presence of—
    Thomas L. McKenney,
    John Crowell, agent for Indian affairs,
    John Ridge, secretary,
    David Vann,
    Wm. Hambly.

TREATY WITH THE CHIPPEWA, 1826.

Aug. 5, 1826.

Stat. 7, 290.
Proclamation, Feb. 7, 1827.

Articles of a treaty made and concluded at the Font du Lac of Lake Superior, this fifth day of August, in the year of our Lord one thousand eight hundred and twenty-six, between Lewis Cass and Thomas L. McKenney, Commissioners on the part of the United States, and the Chippewa Tribe of Indians.

Preamble.

WHEREAS a Treaty was concluded at Prairie du Chien in August last, by which the war, which has been so long carried on, to their mutual distress, between the Chippewas and Sioux, was happily terminated by the intervention of the United States; and whereas, owing to the remote and dispersed situation of the Chippewas, full deputations of their different bands did not attend at Prairie du Chien, which circumstance, from the loose nature of the Indian government, would render the Treaty of doubtful obligation, with respect to the bands not represented; and whereas, at the request of the Chippewa Chiefs, a stipulation was inserted in the Treaty of Prairie du Chien, by which the United States agreed to assemble the Chippewa Tribe upon Lake Superior during the present year, in order to give full effect to the said Treaty, to explain its stipulations and to call upon the whole Chippewa tribe, assembled at their general council fire, to give their formal assent thereto, that the peace which has been concluded may be rendered permanent, therefore—

ARTICLE 1.

The Chiefs and Warriors of the Chippewa Tribe of Indians hereby fully assent to the Treaty concluded in August last at Prairie du Chien, and engage to observe and fulfil the stipulations thereof.

Indians agree to the treaty of Prairie du Chien.

ARTICLE 2.

A deputation shall be sent by the Chippewas to the Treaty to be held in 1827, at Green Bay, with full power to arrange and fix the boundary line between the Chippewas and the Winnebagoes and Menomonees, which was left incomplete by the treaty of Prairie du Chien, in consequence of the non-attendance of some of the principal Menomonee Chiefs.

A deputation to be sent to Green Bay.

ARTICLE 3.

The Chippewa tribe grant to the government of the United States the right to search for, and carry away, any metals or minerals from any part of their country. But this grant is not to affect the title of the land, nor the existing jurisdiction over it.

Metals or minerals.

ARTICLE 4.

It being deemed important that the half-breeds, scattered through this extensive country, should be stimulated to exertion and improvement by the possession of permanent property and fixed residences, the Chippewa tribe, in consideration of the affection they bear to these persons, and of the interest which they feel in their welfare, grant to each of the persons described in the schedule hereunto annexed, being half-breeds and Chippewas by descent, and it being understood that the schedule includes all of this description who are attached to the Government of the United States, six hundred and forty acres of land, to be located, under the direction of the President of the United States, upon the islands and shore of the St. Mary's river, wherever good land enough for this purpose can be found; and as soon as such locations are made, the jurisdiction and soil thereof are hereby ceded. It is the intention of the parties, that, where circumstances will permit, the grants be surveyed in the ancient French manner, bounding not less than six arpens, nor more than ten, upon the river, and running back for quantity; and that where this cannot be done, such grants be surveyed in any manner the President may direct. The locations for Oshauguscodaywayqua and her descendents shall be adjoining the lower part of the military reservation, and upon the head of Sugar Island. The persons to whom grants are made shall not have the privilege of conveying the same, without the permission of the President.

Location for the use of the half-breeds.

ARTICLE 5.

Annuity of $2,000 in money or goods to be paid them.

In consideration of the poverty of the Chippewas, and of the sterile nature of the country they inhabit, unfit for cultivation, and almost destitute of game, and as a proof of regard on the part of the United States, it is agreed that an annuity of two thousand dollars, in money or goods, as the President may direct, shall be paid to the tribe, at the Sault St. Marie. But this annuity shall continue only during the pleasure of the Congress of the United States.

ARTICLE 6.

Annual payment for the improvement of their children.

With a view to the improvement of the Indian youths, it is also agreed, that an annual sum of one thousand dollars shall be appropriated to the support of an establishment for their education, to be located upon some part of the St. Mary's river, and the money to be expended under the direction of the President; and for the accommodation of such school, a section of land is hereby granted. But the payment of the one thousand dollars stipulated for in this article, is subject to the same limitation described in the preceding article.

ARTICLE 7.

Rejection of certain articles not to affect the validity of the others.

The necessity for the stipulations in the fourth, fifth and sixth articles of this treaty could be fully apparent, only from personal observation of the condition, prospects, and wishes of the Chippewas, and the Commissioners were therefore not specifically instructed upon the subjects therein referred to; but seeing the extreme poverty of these wretched people, finding them almost naked and starving, and ascertaining that many perished during the last winter, from hunger and cold, they were induced to insert these articles. But it is expressly understood and agreed, that the fourth, fifth and sixth articles, or either of them, may be rejected by the President and Senate, without affecting the validity of the other articles of the treaty.

ARTICLE 8.

Authority of United States acknowledged.

The Chippewa tribe of Indians fully acknowledge the authority and jurisdiction of the United States, and disclaim all connection with any foreign power, solemnly promising to reject any messages, speeches, or councils, incompatible with the interest of the United States, and to communicate information thereof to the proper agent, should any such be delivered or sent to them.

ARTICLE 9.

Ratification.

This treaty, after the same shall be ratified by the President and Senate of the United States, shall be obligatory on the contracting parties.

Done at the Fond du Lac of lake Superior, in the territory of Michigan, the day and year above written, and of the independence of the United States the fifty-first.

Lewis Cass,	Noden, his x mark,
Thos. L. McKenney,	Nagwunabee, his x mark,
St. Marys:	Kaubemappa, his x mark,
Shingauba Wassin, his x mark,	Chaucopee, his x mark,
Shewaubeketoan, his x mark,	Jaubeance, his x mark,
Wayishkee, his x mark,	Ultauwau, his x mark,
Sheegud, his x mark.	Myeengunsheens, his x mark,
River St. Croix:	Moasomonee, his x mark,
Peezhickee, his x mark,	Muckuday peenaas, his x mark,

Sheeweetaugun, his x mark.
La Pointe:
Peexhickee, his x mark,
Keemeewun, his x mark,
Kaubuzoway, his x mark,
Wyauweenind, his x mark,
Peekwaukwotoansekay, his x mark.
Ottoway L:
Paybaumikoway, his x mark.
Lac de Flambeau:
Gitshee Waubeeshaans, his x mark,
Moazonee, his x mark,
Gitshee Migeezee, his x mark,
Mizhauquot, his x mark.
Ontonagon:
Keeshkeetowug, his x mark,
Peenaysee, his x mark,
Mautaugumee, his x mark,
Kweeweezaisish, his x mark.
Vermilion Lake:
Attickoans, his x mark,
Gyutsheeininee, his x mark,
Jaukway, his x mark,
Madwagkunageezhigwaab, his x mark,
Jaukogeezhigwaishkun, his x mark,
Neezboday, his x mark,
Nundocheeais, his x mark,
Ogeemaugeegid, his x mark,
Anneemeekees, his x mark.
Ontonagon:
Kauwaishkung, his x mark,
Mautaugumee, his x mark.
Snake River:
Waymittegoash, his x mark,
Iskquagwunaabee, his x mark,
Meegwunaus, his x mark.
Lac de Flambeau:
Pamoossay, his x mark,
Maytaukooseegay, his x mark.
Rainy Lake:
Aanubkumigishkunk, his x mark.
Sandy Lake:
Osaumemikee, his x mark,

Gitshee Waymirteegoost, his x mark.
Paashuninleel, his x mark,
Wauzhuskokok, his x mark,
Nitumogaubowee, his x mark,
Wattap, his x mark.
Fond du Lac:
Shingoop, his x mark,
Monetogeezisoans, his x mark,
Mongazid, his x mark.
Manetogeezhig, his x mark,
Ojauneemauson, his x mark,
Miskwautais, his x mark,
Naubunaygerzhig, his x mark,
Unnauwaubundaun, his x mark,
Pautaubay, his x mark,
Migeesee, his x mark.
Ontonagon:
Waubishkeepeenaas, his x mark,
Tweeshtweeshkeeway, his x mark,
Kundekund, his x mark,
Oguhbayaunuhquotwaybee, his x mark,
Paybaumausing, his x mark,
Keeshkeemun, his x mark.
River de Corbeau:
Maugugaubowie, his x mark,
Pudud, his x mark,
Naugdunosh, his x mark,
Ozhuskuckoen, his x mark,
Waubogee, his x mark,
Sawbanosh, his x mark,
Keewayden, his x mark,
Gitsheemeewininee, his x mark,
Wynunee, his x mark,
Obumaugeezhig, his x mark,
Payboumidgeewung, his x mark,
Maugeegaubou, his x mark,
Paybaumogeezhig, his x mark,
Kaubemappa, his x mark,
Waymittegoazhu, his x mark,
Oujupenaas, his x mark,
Madwayossin, his x mark.

In presence of—

A. Edwards, secretary to the commission;
E. Boardman, captain commanding detachment,
Henry R. Schoolcraft, United States Indian agent.
Z. Pitcher, assistant surgeon,
J. B. Kingsbury, lieutenant, Second Infantry,

E. A. Brush,
Daniel Dingley,
A. Morrison,
B. Champman,
Henry Connor,
W. A. Levake,
J. O. Lewis.

SUPPLEMENTARY ARTICLE.

As the Chippewas who committed the murder upon four American citizens, in June, 1824, upon the shores of Lake Pepin, are not present at this council, but are far in the interior of the country, so that they cannot be apprehended and delivered to the proper authority before the commencement of the next Summer; and, as the Commissioners have been specially instructed to demand the surrender of these persons, and to state to the Chippewa tribe the consequence of suffering such a flagitious outrage to go unpunished, it is agreed, that the persons guilty of the beforementioned murder shall be brought in, either to the Sault St. Marie, or Green Bay, as early next summer as practicable, and surrendered to the proper authority; and that, in the mean time, all further measures on the part of the United States, in relation to this subject, shall be suspended.

Lewis Cass,
Thomas L. McKenney.

Representing the bands to whom the persons guilty of the murder belong, for themselves and the Chippewa tribe:

> Gitshee Meegeesee, his x mark,
> Metaukoosegay, his x mark,
> Ouskunzheema, his x mark,
> Keenesteno, his x mark.

Witnesses:
> A. Edwards, secretary to the commission,
> E. Boardman, captain commanding detachment,
> Henry R. Schoolcraft, United States Indian agent.
> Henry Connor, interpreter.

Schedule referred to in the preceding Treaty.

To Oshauguscodaywagqua, wife of John Johnston, Esq., to each of her children, and to each of her grand children, one section.

To Saugemauqua, widow of the late John Baptiste Cadotte, and to her children, Louison, Sophia, Archangel, Edward, and Polly, one section each.

To Keneesequa, wife of Samuel Ashman, and to each of her children, one section.

To Teegaushau, wife of Charles H. Oakes, and to each of her children, one section.

To Thomas Shaw, son of Obimetunoqua, and to his wife Mary, being also of Indian descent, each one section.

To Fanny Levake, daughter of Meeshwauqua, and to each of her children, one section.

To Obayshaunoquotoqua, wife of Francis Goolay, Jr. one section.

To Omuckackeence, wife of John Holiday, and to each of her children, one section.

To Obimegeezhigoqua, wife of Joseph Due Chene, Jr. and to each of her children, one section.

To Monedoqua, wife of Charles Cloutier, one section.

To Susan Yarns, daughter of Odanbitogeezhigoqua, one section.

To Henry Sayer and John Sayer, sons of Obemau unoqua, each one section.

To each of the children of John Tanner, being of Chippewa descent, one section.

To Wassidjeewunoqua, and to each of her children, by George Johnston, one section.

To Michael Cadotte, senior, son of Equawaice, one section.

To Equaysayway, wife of Michael Cadotte, senior, and to each of her children living within the United States, one section.

To each of the children of Charlotte Warren, widow of the late Truman A. Warren, one section.

To Mary Chapman, daughter of Equameeg, and wife of Bela Chapman, and to each of her children, one section.

To Saganoshequa, wife of John H. Fairbanks, and to each of her children, one section.

To Shaughunomonee, wife of William Morrison, and to each of her children, one section.

To each of the children of the late Ingwaysuh, wife of Joseph Coté, one section.

To each of the children of Angelique Coté, late wife of Pierre Coté, one section.

To Pazhikwutoqua, wife of William Aitken, and to each of her children, one section.

To Susan Davenport, grand daughter of Misquabunoqua, and wife of Ambrose Davenport, and to each of her children, one section.

To Waubunequa, wife of Augustin Belanger, and to each of her children, one section.

To Charlotte Louisa Morrison, wife of Allan Morrison, and daughter of Manitowidjewung, and to each of her children, one section.

To each of the children of Eustace Roussain, by Shauwunaubunoqua, Wauwaussumoqua, and Payshaubunoqua, one section.

To Isabella Dingley, wife of Daniel Dingley and daughter of Pime geezhigoqua, and to each of her children, one section.

To George Birkhead, being a Chippewa by descent, one section.

To Susan Conner, wife of Thomas Conner, and daughter of Pime-geezhigoqua, and to each of her children, one section.

To the children of George Ermatinger, being of Shawnee extraction, two sections collectively.

To Ossinahjeeunoqua, wife of Michael Cadotte, Jr. and each of her children, one section.

To Minedemoeyah, wife of Pierre Duvernay, one section.

To Ogeemaugeezhigoqua, wife of Basil Boileau, one section.

To Wauneaussequa, wife of Paul Boileau, one section.

To Kaukaubesheequa, wife of John Baptiste Corbeau, one section.

To John Baptiste Du Chene, son of Pimegeizhigoqua, one section.

To each of the children of Ugwudaushee, by the late Truman A. Warren, one section.

To William Warren, son of Lyman M. Warren, and Mary Cadotte, one section.

To Antoine, Joseph, Louis, Chalot, and Margaret Charette, children of Equameeg, one section.

To the children of Francois Boutcher, by Waussequa, each one section.

To Angelique Brabent, daughter of Waussegundum, and wife of Alexis Brabent, one section.

To Odishqua, of Sault St. Marie, a Chippewa, of unmixed blood, one section.

To Pamidjeewung, of Sault St. Marie, a Chippewa, of unmixed blood, one section.

To Waybossinoqua, and John J. Wayishkee, children of Wayishkee, each one section.

Lewis Cass,
Thos. L. McKenney.

TREATY WITH THE POTAWATOMI, 1826.

Articles of a treaty made and concluded near the mouth of the Missis-sinewa, upon the Wabash, in the State of Indiana, this sixteenth day of October, in the year of our Lord one thousand eight hundred and twenty-six, between Lewis Cass, James B. Ray, and John Tipton, Commissioners on the part of the United States, and the Chiefs and Warriors of the Potawatamie Tribe of Indians.

Oct. 16, 1826.
7 Stat., 295.
Proclamation, Feb. 7, 1827.

ARTICLE 1.

The Potawatamie tribe of Indians cede to the United States their right to all the land within the following limits: Beginning on the Tippecanoe river, where the Northern boundary of the tract ceded by the Potawatamies to the United States by the treaty of St. Mary's, in the year of our Lord one thousand eight hundred and eighteen intersects the same; thence, in a direct line, to a point on Eel river, half way between the mouth of the said river and Pierish's village; thence up Eel River, to Seek's village, near the head thereof; thence, in a direct

Land ceded to United States.

line, to the mouth of a creek emptying into the St. Joseph's of the Miami, near Metea's village; thence, up the St. Joseph's, to the boundary line between the States of Indiana and Ohio; thence, South to the Miami; thence, up the same, to the reservation at Fort Wayne; thence, with the lines of the said reservation, to the boundary established by the treaty with the Miamies in one thousand eight hundred and eighteen; thence, with the said line, to the Wabash river; thence, with the same river, to the mouth of the Tippecanoe river; and thence, with the said Tippecanoe river, to the place of beginning. And the said tribe also cede to the United States, all their right to land within the following limits; Beginning at a point upon Lake Michigan, ten miles due north of the southern extreme thereof: running thence, due east, to the land ceded by the Indians to the United States by the treaty of Chicago; thence, south, with the boundary thereof, ten miles; thence, west, to the southern extreme of Lake Michigan; thence, with the shore thereof, to the place of beginning.

ARTICLE 2.

Further cession.

As an evidence of the attachment which the Potawatamie tribe feel towards the American people, and particularly to the soil of Indiana, and with a view to demonstrate their liberality, and benefit themselves by creating facilities for travelling and increasing the value of their remaining country, the said tribe do hereby cede to the United States, a strip of land, commencing at Lake Michigan, and running thence to the Wabash river, one hundred feet wide, for a road, and also, one section of good land contiguous to the said road, for each mile of the same, and also for each mile of a road from the termination thereof, through Indianapolis to the Ohio river, for the purpose of making a road aforesaid from Lake Michigan, by the way of Indianapolis, to some convenient point on the Ohio river. *And the General Assembly of the State of Indiana shall have a right to locate the said road, and to apply the said sections, or the proceeds thereof, to the making of the same, or any part thereof; and the said grant shall be at their sole disposal.*[a]

ARTICLE 3.

Annuity for twenty-two years.

In consideration of the cessions in the first article, the United States agree to pay to the Potawattamie tribe, an annuity of two thousand dollars in silver, for the term of twenty-two years, and also to provide and support a black-smith for them at some convenient point; to appropriate, for the purposes of education, the annual sum of two thousand dollars, as long as the Congress of the United States may think proper, to be expended as the President may direct; and also, to build for them a mill, sufficient to grind corn, on the Tippecanoe river, and to provide and support a miller; and to pay them annually one hundred and sixty bushels of salt; all of which annuities, herein specified, shall be paid by the Indian Agent at Fort Wayne.

ARTICLE 4.

Payment in goods.

The Commissioners of the United States have caused to be delivered to the Potawatamie tribe, goods to the value of thirty thousand five hundred and forty-seven dollars and seventy-one cents in goods, in consideration of the cessions in the first article of this treaty. Now, therefore, it is agreed, that, if this treaty should be ratified by the President and Senate of the United States, the United States shall pay to the persons named in the schedule this day transmitted to the War Department, and signed by the Commissioners, the sums affixed to

---

[a] These words in italics were struck out by the Senate.

their names respectively, for goods furnished by them, and amounting to the said sum of thirty thousand five hundred and forty-seven dollars and seventy-one cents, and also, to the persons who may furnish the said further sum, the amount of nine hundred dollars thus furnished. And it is also agreed, that payment for all these goods shall be made by the Potawatamie tribe out of their annuity, if this treaty should not be ratified by the United States.

ARTICLE 5.

The Potawatamie tribe being anxious to pay certain claims existing against them, it is agreed, as a part of the consideration for the cessions in the first article, that these claims, which are stated in a schedule this day signed by the Commissioners, and transmitted to the War Department, and amounting to the sum of nine thousand five hundred and seventy-three dollars. *United States agree to pay certain claims against Potawatomi.*

ARTICLE 6.

The United States agree to grant to each of the persons named in the schedule hereunto annexed, the quantity of land therein stipulated to be granted; but the land, so granted, shall never be conveyed by either of the said persons, or their heirs, without the consent of the President of the United States; and it is also understood, that any of these grants may be expunged from the schedule, by the President or Senate of the United States, without affecting any other part of the treaty. *Grants to persons named in the schedule annexed.*

ARTICLE 7.

The Potawatamie Indians shall enjoy the right of hunting upon any part of the land hereby ceded, as long as the same shall remain the property of the United States. *Hunting.*

ARTICLE 8.

The President and Senate of the United States may reject any article of this treaty, except those which relate to the consideration to be paid for the cessions of the land; and such rejection shall not affect any other part of the treaty. *Certain articles only may be rejected.*

ARTICLE 9.

This treaty, after the same shall be ratified by the President and Senate, shall be binding upon the United States. *Treaty binding when ratified.*

In testimony whereof, the said Lewis Cass, James B. Ray, and John Tipton, commissioners as aforesaid, and the chiefs and warriors of the said Potawatamie tribe have hereunto set their hands, at the Wabash, on the sixteenth day of October, in the year of our Lord one thousand eight hundred and twenty-six, and of the independence of the United States the fifty-first.

Lewis Cass,
J. Brown Ray,
John Tipton.
 Chiefs:
Topenibe, his x mark,
Gebaus, his x mark,
Toisoe, his x mark,
Metea, his x mark,
Aubenaube, his x mark,
Ashkom, his x mark,
Penashshees, his x mark,
Pecheco, his x mark,
Waupaukeeno, his x mark,
Pashpo, his x mark,

Kasha, his x mark,
Pierish, his x mark,
Penamo, his x mark,
Nasawauka, his x mark,
Mauxa, his x mark,
Makose, his x mark,
Shaupatee, his x mark,
Noshaweka, his x mark,
Menauquet, his x mark,
Wimeko, his x mark,
Saukena, his x mark,
Kepeaugun, his x mark,
Menomonie, his x mark,
Shokto, his x mark,

Shapeness, his x mark,	Squawbuk, his x mark,
Motiel, his x mark,	Maunis, his x mark,
Kauk, his x mark,	Jequaumkogo, his x mark,
Ackkushewa, his x mark,	Kewaune, his x mark,
Mukkose, his x mark,	Ahnowawausa, his x mark,
Shaquinon, his x mark,	Louison, his x mark,
Waupsee, his x mark,	Washeone, his x mark,
Jekose, his x mark,	Shakauwasee, his x mark,
Nequoquet, his x mark,	Paskauwesa, his x mark,
Waubonsa, his x mark,	Nauksee, his x mark,
Wasaushuck, his x mark,	Mukkose, his x mark,
Shaauquebe, his x mark,	Chechaukkose, his x mark,
Psakauwa, his x mark,	Louison, his x mark,
Kaukaamake, his x mark,	Meshekaunau, his x mark,
Shekomak, his x mark,	Menno, his x mark,
Makasess, his x mark,	Showaukau, his x mark,
No-ne, his x mark,	Kaukaukshee, his x mark,
Shepshauwano, his x mark,	Pashshepowo, his x mark,
Mesheketeno, his x mark,	Mowekatso, his x mark,

Done in presence of—

William Marshall, secretary to the commission,	D. G. Jones,
J. M. Ray, assistant secretary to the commission,	Samuel Hanna, member of the legislature,
Jno. Ewing, Senator, State of Indiana,	Martin M. Ray, member of the legislature.
Benj. B. Kercheval, sub-agent,	James Conner, interpreter,
William Conner, interpreter,	James Foster,
Joseph Barron, interpreter,	James Gregory, Senator of Indiana,
Henry Conner, interpreter,	O. L. Clark,
Josiah F. Polk,	C. W. Ewing,
Felix Hinchman,	J. D. Dorsey,
Isaac McCoy,	Lewis G. Thompson.

Schedule of grants referred to in the foregoing Treaty.

Land granted to each of the following persons by the sixth article. To Abraham Burnett, three sections of land; one to be located at and to include Wynemac's village, the centre of the line on the Wabash to be opposite that village, and running up and down the river one mile in a direct line, and back for quantity; the two other sections, commencing at the upper end of the Prairie, opposite the mouth of the Passeanong creek, and running down two miles in a direct line, and back, for quantity.

To Nancy Burnett, Rebecca Burnett, James Burnett, and William Burnett, each one section of land, to be located under the direction of the President of the United States; which said Abraham, Nancy, Rebecca and James, are the children, and the said William is the grandchild of Kaukeama, the sister of Topenibe, the principal Chief of the Potawatamie tribe of Indians.

To Eliza C. Kercheval, one section on the Miami river, commencing at the first place where the road from Fort Wayne to Defiance strikes the Miami on the north side thereof, about five miles below Fort Wayne, and from that point running half a mile down the river, and half a mile up the river, and back for quantity.

To James Knaggs, son of the sister of Okeos, Chief of the river Huron Potawatamies, one half section of land upon the Miami, where the boundary line between Indiana and Ohio crosses the same.

To the children of Joseph Barron, a relation of Richardville, principal Chief of the Miamies, three sections of land, beginning at the mouth of Eel River, running three miles down the Wabash in a direct line, thence back for quantity.

To Zachariah Cicott, who is married to an Indian woman, one section of land, below and adjoining Abraham Burnett's land, and to be located in the same way.

To Baptiste Cicott, Sophi Cicott, and Emelia Cicott, children of Zachariah Cicott, and an Indian woman, one half section each, adjoining and below the section granted to Zachariah Cicott.

To St. Luke Bertrand and Julia Ann Bertrand, children of Madeline Bertrand, a Potawatamie woman, one section of land, to be located under the direction of the President of the United States.

To the children of Stephen Johnson, killed by the Potawatamie Indians, one half section of land, to be located under the direction of the President of the United States.

To each of the following persons, Indians by birth, and who are now, or have been, scholars in the Carey Mission School, on the St. Joseph's, under the direction of the Rev. Isaac M'Coy, one quarter section of land, to be located under the direction of the President of the United States; that is to say: Joseph Bourissa, Noaquett, John Jones, Nuko, Soswa, Manotuk, Betsey Ash, Charles Dick, Susanna Isaacs, Harriet Isaacs, Betsey Plummer, Angelina Isaacs, Jemima Isaacs, Jacob Corbly, Konkapot, Celicia Nimham, Mark Bourissa, Jude Bourissa, Annowussau, Topenibe, Terrez, Sheshko, Louis Wilmett, Mitchel Wilmett, Lezett Wilmett, Esther Baily, Roseann Baily, Eleanor Baily, Quehkna, William Turner, Chaukenozwoh, Lazarus Bourissa, Achan Bourissa, Achemukquee, Wesauwau, Peter Moose, Ann Sharp, Joseph Wolf, Misnoqua, Pomoqua, Wymego, Cheekeh, Wauwossemoqua, Meeksumau, Kakautmo, Richard Clements, Louis M'Neff, Shoshqua, Nscotenama, Chikawketeh, Mnsheewoh, Saugana, Msonkqua, Mnitoqua, Okutcheek, Naomi G. Browning, Antoine, St. Antoine, Mary; being in all fifty-eight.

To Jane Martin and Betsey Martin, of Indian descent, each one section of land, to be located under the direction of the President of the United States.

To Mary St. Combe, of Indian descent, one quarter section of land, to be located under the direction of the President of the United States.

To Francois Duquindre, of Indian descent, one section of land, to be located under the direction of the President of the United States.

To Baptiste Jutreace, of Indian descent, one half section of land, to be located under the direction of the President of the United States.

To John B. Bourie, of Indian descent, one section of land, to be located on the Miami river, adjoining the old boundary line below Fort Wayne.

To Joseph Parks, an Indian, one section of land, to be located at the point where the boundary line strikes the St. Joseph's, near Metea's village.

To George Cicott, a Chief of the Potawatamies, three sections and a half of land; two sections and a half of which to be located on the Wabash, above the mouth of Crooked creek, running two miles and a half up the river, and back for quantity, and the remaining section at the Falls of Eel river, on both sides thereof.

To James Conner, one section of land; to Henry Conner, one section; and to William Conner, one section; beginning opposite the upper end of the Big Island, and running three miles in a direct line down the Wabash, and back for quantity.

To Hyacinth Lassel, two sections of land, to be located under the direction of the President of the United States.

To Louison, a half Potawatamie, two sections of land, to be located under the direction of the President of the United States.

Lewis Cass,
J. Brown Ray,
John Tipton.

October 16, 1826.

Note.—The Senate, in ratifying the foregoing treaty, excepted the words in Art. 2 which are printed in italics, and expressed their understanding that the meaning of Art. 5 is, that the money therein mentioned shall be paid by the United States to the individuals named in the schedule referred to therein.

TREATY WITH THE MIAMI, 1826.

Oct. 23, 1826.

7 Stat., 300.
Proclamation, Jan.
24, 1827.

*Articles of a treaty made and concluded, near the mouth of the Missis-
sinewa, upon the Wabash, in the State of Indiana, this twenty-third
day of October, in the year of our Lord one thousand eight hundred
and twenty-six, between Lewis Cass, James B. Ray, and John Tipton,
Commissioners on the part of the United States, and the Chiefs and
Warriors of the Miami Tribe of Indians.*

ARTICLE 1.

Lands ceded to the
United States.

The Miami Tribe of Indians cede to the United States all their claim
to land in the State of Indiana, north and west of the Wabash and
Miami rivers, and of the cession made by the said tribe to the United
States, by the treaty concluded at St. Mary's October 6, 1818.

ARTICLE 2.

Reservations for the
use of said tribe.

From the cession aforesaid, the following reservations, for the use
of the said tribe, shall be made:

Fourteen sections of Land at Seek's village;

Five sections for the Beaver, below and adjoining the preceding
reservation;

Thirty-six sections at Flat Belly's village;

Five sections for Little Charley, above the old village, on the North
side of Eel river;

One section for Laventure's daughter, opposite the Islands, about
fifteen miles below Fort Wayne;

One section for Chapine, above, and adjoining Seek's village;

Ten sections at the White Raccoon's village;

Ten sections at the mouth of Mud Creek, on Eel river, at the old
village;

Ten sections at the forks of the Wabash;

One reservation commencing two miles and a half below the mouth
of the Mississinewa, and running up the Wabash five miles, with the
bank thereof, and from these points running due north to Eel river.

Canal or road
through the reserva-
tions.

And it is agreed, that the State of Indiana may lay out a canal or a
road through any of these reservations, and for the use of a canal, six
chains along the same are hereby appropriated.

ARTICLE 3.

Land granted; not
to be conveyed with-
out the consent of the
President.

There shall be granted to each of the persons named in the schedule
hereunto annexed, and to their heirs, the tracts of land therein designated; but the land so granted shall never be conveyed without the
consent of the President of the United States.

ARTICLE 4.

Payment in goods.

The Commissioners of the United States have caused to be delivered
to the Miami tribe goods to the value of $31,040.53, in part considera-
tion for the cession herein made; and it is agreed, that if this treaty
shall be ratified by the President and Senate of the United States, the
United States shall pay to the persons, named in the schedule this day
signed by the Commissioners, and transmitted to the War Department, the sums affixed to their names respectively, for goods furnished by them, and amounting to the sum of $31,040.53. And it is

Further agreement.

further agreed, that payment for these goods shall be made by the
Miami tribe out of their annuity, if this treaty be not ratified by the
United States.

And the United States further engage to deliver to the said tribe, in the course of the next summer, the additional sum of $26,259.47 in goods.

Additional payment in goods.

And it is also agreed, that an annuity of thirty-five thousand dollars, ten thousand of which shall be in goods, shall be paid to the said tribe in the year one thousand eight hundred and twenty-seven, and thirty thousand dollars, five thousand of which shall be in goods, in the year one thousand eight hundred and twenty-eight; after which time a permanent annuity of twenty-five thousand dollars shall be paid to them, as long as they exist together as a tribe; which several sums are to include the annuities due by preceding treaties to the said tribe.

Annuity.

And the United States further engage to furnish a wagon and one yoke of oxen for each of the following persons: namely, Joseph Richardville, Black Raccoon, Flat Belly, White Raccoon, Francois Godfroy, Little Beaver, Mettosanea, Seek, and Little Huron; and one wagon and a yoke of oxen for the band living at the forks of the Wabash.

A wagon, etc., to be furnished certain persons.

And also to cause to be built a house, not exceeding the value of six hundred dollars for each of the following persons: namely, Joseph Richardville, Francois Godfroy, Louison Godfroy, Francis Lafontaine, White Raccoon, La Gros, Jean B. Richardville, Flat Belly, and Wauwe-as-see.

A house for certain persons.

And also to furnish the said tribe with two hundred head of cattle, from four to six years old, and two hundred head of hogs; and to cause to be annually delivered to them, two thousand pounds of iron, one thousand pounds of steel, and one thousand pounds of tobacco.

Cattle, etc., for said tribe.

And to provide five labourers to work three months in the year, for the small villages, and three labourers to work three months in the year, for the Mississinewa band.

Further provision.

ARTICLE 5.

The Miami tribe being anxious to pay certain claims existing against them, it is agreed, as a part of the consideration for the cession in the first article, that these claims amounting to $7,727.47, and which are stated in a schedule this day signed by the Commisioners, and transmitted to the War Department, shall be paid by the United States.

Claims against said tribe to be paid by United States.

ARTICLE 6.

The United States agree to appropriate the sum of two thousand dollars annually, as long as Congress may think proper, for the support of poor infirm persons of the Miami tribe, and for the education of the youth of the said tribe; which sum shall be expended under the direction of the President of the United States.

Appropriation for the support of the poor and infirm.

ARTICLE 7.

It is agreed, that the United States shall purchase of the persons, named in the schedule hereunto annexed, the land therein mentioned, which was granted to them by the Treaty of St. Mary's, and shall pay the price affixed to their names respectively; the payments to be made when the title to the lands is conveyed to the United States.

Further agreement.

ARTICLE 8.

The Miami tribe shall enjoy the right of hunting upon the land herein conveyed. so long as the same shall be the property of the United States.

Indians to enjoy the right of hunting, etc.

ARTICLE 9.

Treaty binding when ratified.   This treaty, after the same shall be ratified by the President and Senate, shall be binding upon the United States.

In testimony whereof, the said Lewis Cass, James B. Ray, and John Tipton, commissioners as aforesaid, and the chiefs and warriors of the said Miami tribe, have hereunto set their hands, at the Wabash, on the twenty-third day of October, in the year of our Lord one thousand eight hundred and twenty-six, and of the independence of the United States the fifty-first.

Lewis Cass,
J. Brown Ray,
John Tipton.
  Chiefs:
Wau-wa-aus-see, his x mark,
Flat Belly, his x mark,
La Gros, his x mark,
White Racoon, his x mark,
Black Loon, his x mark,
Chin-quin-sa, his x mark,
Jamas Abbot, his x mark,
Lon-gwa, his x mark,
Little Wolf, his x mark,
Pun-ge-she-nau, his x mark,
Wonse-pe-au, his x mark,
Francois Godfroy, his x mark,
Joseph Richardville, his x mark,
Francis Lafontaine,
Wau-no-sa, his x mark,
White Skin's Son, or the Popular, his x mark,
Seek, his x mark,

Mee-se-qua, his x mark,
Nota-wen-sa's Son, his x mark,
La-from-broise, his x mark,
Nego-ta-kaup-wa, his x mark,
Osage, his x mark,
Metto-sa-nea, his x mark,
Little Beaver, his x mark,
Black Racoon, his x mark,
Cha-pine, his x mark,
Pe-che-wau, or Jean B. Richardville, his x mark,
Chin-go-me-shau, his x mark,
Little Sun, his x mark,
W. Shin-gan-leau, his x mark,
Louis Godfroy, his x mark,
Ou-sane-de-au, his x mark,
Me-chane-qua, his x mark,
Un-e-cea-sa, his x mark,
She-qua-hau, his x mark,
Chin-qua-keau, his x mark,
Charley's Son, his x mark.

Done in presence of—

William Marshall, secretary to the commission,
J. M. Ray, assistant secretary to the commission,
Ben. B. Kercheval, subagent,
Wm. Conner, interpreter,
Joseph Barron,
C. W. Ewing,

J. B. Boure, interpreter,
James Foster,
John Ewing, Senator, State of Indiana,
James Gregory, Senator, State of Indiana,
Martin M. Ray, Representative, Indiana,
Sam. Hanna, Representative, Indiana,
George Hunt,
O. L. Clark.

Schedule of grants referred to the foregoing Treaty, Article 3d.

To John B. Richardville, one section of land, between the mouth of Pipe Creek and the mouth of Eel River, on the north side of the Wabash, and one section on the north-west side of the St. Joseph, adjoining the old boundary line; also, one half section on the east side of the St. Joseph's, below Cha-po-tee's village.

To John B. Boure, one section on the north side of the St. Joseph, including Chop-patees village.

To the wife and children of Charley, a Miami chief, one section where they live.

To Ann Hackley and Jack Hackley, one section each, between the Maumee and the St. Joseph's rivers.

To the children of Maria Christiana De Rome, a half blood Miami, one section between the Maumee and the St. Joseph's.

To Ann Turner, alias Hackley, Rebecca Hackley, and Jane S. Wells, each one half section of land, to be located under the direction of the President of the United States.

To John B. Richardville, one section of land upon the north side of the Wabash, to include a large spring nearly opposite the mouth of Pipe Creek.

To Francois Godfroy, one section above and adjoining said last grant to J. B. Richardville.

To Louison Godfroy, one section above and adjoining the grant to Francois Godfroy.

To Francis Lafontaine, one section above and adjoining the grant to Louison Godfroy.

To John B. Richardville, junior, one section on the Wabash, below and adjoining the reservation running from the Wabash to Eel River.

To Joseph Richardville, one section above and adjoining the reservation running from the Wabash to Eel River.

To La Gros, three sections, where he now lives, and one section adjoining the Cranberry in the Portage Prairie.

A quarter section of land to each of the following persons, namely: Charles Gouin, Purri Gouin, and Therese Gouin, to be located under the direction of the President of the United States.

Two sections of land at the old town on Eel River, to be reserved for the use of the Metchinequea.

OCTOBER 23D, 1826.

Lewis Cass.
J. Brown Ray,
John Tipton.

TREATY WITH THE CHIPPEWA, ETC., 1827.

Articles of a treaty made and concluded at the Butte des Morts, on Fox river, in the Territory of Michigan, between Lewis Cass and Thomas L. M'Kenney, Commissioners on the part of the United States, and the Chippewa, Menomonie, and Winebago tribes of Indians.

Aug. 11, 1827.

7 Stat., 303.
Proclamation, Feb. 23, 1829.

ARTICLE 1. Whereas, the southern boundary of the Chippewa country, from the Plover Portage of the Ouisconsin easterly, was left undefined by the treaty concluded at Prairie du Chien, August 19, 1825, in consequence of the non-attendance of some of the principal Menomonie chiefs; and, whereas it was provided by the said treaty, that, whenever the President of the United States might think proper, such of the tribes, parties to the said treaty, as might be interested in any particular line, should be convened, in order to agree upon its establishment; *Chippewa southern boundary left undefined by treaty of 1825.*

Therefore, in pursuance of the said provision, it is agreed between the Chippewas, Menomonies and Winebagoes, that the southern boundary of the Chippeway country shall run as follows, namely: From the Plover Portage of the Ouisconsin, on a northeasterly course, to a point on Wolf river, equidistant from the Ashawano and Post lakes of said river, thence to the falls of the Pashaytig river of Green Bay; thence to the junction of the Neesau Kootag or Burnt-wood river, with the Menomonie; thence to the big island of the Shoskinaubic or Smooth rock river; thence following the channel of the said river to Green Bay, which it strikes between the little and the great Bay de Noquet. *Southern boundary settled.*

ART. 2. Much difficulty having arisen from negotiations between the Menomonie and Winebago tribes and the various tribes and portions of tribes of Indians of the State of New York, and the claims of the respective parties being much contested, as well with relation to the tenure and boundaries of the two tracts, claimed by the said New York Indians, west of Lake Michigan, as to the authority of the persons who signed the agreement on the part of the Menomonies, and the whole subject having been fully examined at the Council this day concluded, and the allegations, proofs, and statements, of the respective parties having been entered upon the Journal of the Commissioners, so that the same can be decided by the President of the United States; it is agreed by the Menomonies and Winebagoes, that so far as respects their interest in the premises, the whole matter shall be referred to the President of the United States, whose decision shall be final. And *Territorial difficulties between certain tribes referred to the President of the United States.*

the President is authorized, on their parts, to establish such boundaries between them and the New York Indians as he may consider equitable and just.

Indian recognition of United States title to a certain tract of land. ART. 3. It being important to the settlement of Green Bay that definite boundaries should be established between the tract claimed by the former French and British governments, and the lands of the Indians, as well to avoid future disputes as to settle the question of jurisdiction—It is therefore agreed between the Menomonie tribe and the United States, that the boundaries of the said tracts, the jurisdiction and title of which are hereby acknowledged to be in the United **Boundaries thereof.** States, shall be as follows, namely:—Beginning on the shore of Green Bay, six miles due north from the parallel of the mouth of Fox river, and running thence in a straight line, but with the general course of the said river, and six miles therefrom to the intersection of the continuation of the westerly boundary of the tract at the Grand Kaukaulin, claimed by Augustin Grignion; thence on a line with the said boundary to the same; thence with the same to Fox river; thence on the same course, six miles; thence in a direct line to the southwestern boundary of the tract, marked on the plan of the claims at Green Bay, as the settlement at the bottom of the Bay; thence with the southerly boundary of the said tract to the southeasterly corner thereof; and thence with the easterly boundary of the said tract to Green Bay. **Proviso.** Provided, that if the President of the United States should be of opinion that the boundaries thus established interfere with any just claims of the New York Indians, the President may then change the said boundaries in any manner he may think proper, so that the quantity of land contained in the said tract be not greater than by the boundaries herein defined. And provided also, **Proviso.** that nothing herein contained shall be construed to have any effect upon the land claims at Green Bay; but the same shall remain as though this treaty had not been formed.

Distribution of goods among the Indians. ART. 4. In consideration of the liberal establishment of the boundaries as herein provided for, the Commissioners of the United States have this day caused to be distributed among the Indians, goods to the amount of fifteen thousand six hundred and eighty-two dollars, payment for which shall be made by the United States.

Annual appropriation for education of Indians. ART. 5. The sum of one thousand dollars shall be annually appropriated for the term of three years; and the sum of fifteen hundred dollars shall be annually thereafter appropriated as long as Congress think proper, for the education of the children of the tribes, parties hereto, and of the New York Indians, to be expended under the direction of the President of the United States.

Right of United States to punish certain Winnebagoes. ART. 6. The United States shall be at liberty, notwithstanding the Winebagoes are parties to this treaty, to pursue such measures as they may think proper for the punishment of the perpetrators of the recent outrages at Prairie du Chien, and upon the Mississippi, and for the prevention of such acts hereafter.

Treaty to be obligatory when ratified. ART. 7. This treaty shall be obligatory after its ratification by the President and Senate of the United States.

Done at the Butte des Morts, on Fox river, in the Territory of Michigan, this eleventh day of August, 1827.

Lewis Cass,
Thomas L. McKenney.
  Chippeways:
Shinguaba Wossin, his x mark,
Wayishkee, his x mark,
Sheewanbeketoan, his x mark,
Mozobodo, his x mark,
Gitshee Waubezhaas, his x mark,
Moazoninee, his x mark,
Mishaukewett, his x mark,
Monominee Cashee, his x mark,

Attikumaag, his x mark,
Umbwaygeezhig, his x mark,
Moneeto Penaysee, his x mark,
Akkeewaysee, his x mark,
Sheegad, his x mark,
Wauwaunishkau, his x mark,
Anamikee Waba, his x mark,
Ockewazee, his x mark.
  Menominies:
Oskashe, his x mark,
Josette Caron, his x mark,

Kominikey, jun. his x mark,
Kimiown, his x mark,
Kominikey, sen. his x mark,
Keshiminey, his x mark,
Woiniss-atte, his x mark,
Powoiysnoit, his x mark,
   Menominies:
Manbasseaux, his x mark,
Myanmechetnabewat, his x mark,
Pemabeme, his x mark,
Kegisse, his x mark,
L'Espagnol, his x mark,
Kichiaemtort, his x mark,
Hoo Tshoop, (or four legs,) his x mark,
Tshayro-tshoan Kaw, his x mark,
Karry-Man-nee, (walking turtle,) his x
   mark,

Sau-say-man-nee, his x mark,
Maunk-hay-raith, (tatood breast,) his x
   mark,
Shoank Skaw, (white dog,) his x mark,
Shoank-tshunksiap, (black wolf,) his x
   mark,
Kaw-Kaw-say-kaw, his x mark,
Wheank-Kaw, (big duck,) his x mark,
Shoank-ay-paw-kaw, (dog head), his x
   mark,
Sar-ray-num-nee, (walking mat,) his x
   mark,
Waunk-tshay-hee-sootsh, (red devil), his
   x mark.
Wau-kaun-hoa-noa-nick, (little snake,)
   his x mark,
Kaw-nee-shaw, (white crow,) his x mark.

Witnesses:

Philip B. Key, secretary,
E. Boardman, captain Second U. S. In-
   fantry,
Henry R. Schoolcraft, United States In-
   dian agent,
Henry B. Brevoort, United States Indian
   agent,
Thomas Rowland,

D. G. Jones,
R. A. Forsyth,
S. Conant,
E. A. Brush,
Jn. Bpt. Fcois Fauvel, clergyman,
Jesse Miner,
Henry Conner, interpreter,
John Kinzie, jun.

[NOTE.—This treaty was ratified with this proviso, contained in the resolution of
the Senate: "That the said treaty shall not impair or affect any right or claim which
the New York Indians or any of them have to the lands or any of the lands mentioned in the said treaty."]

TREATY WITH THE POTAWATOMI, 1827.

A treaty between the United States and the Potawatamie Tribe of
Indians.

Sept. 19, 1827.

7 Stat., 305.
Proclamation, Feb.
23, 1829.

IN order to consolidate some of the dispersed bands of the Potawatamie Tribe in the Territory of Michigan at a point removed from the
road leading from Detroit to Chicago, and as far as practicable from
the settlements of the Whites, it is agreed that the following tracts of
land, heretofore reserved for the use of the said Tribe, shall be, and
they are hereby, ceded to the United States.

Cession of land by the Indians.

Two sections of land on the river Rouge at Seginsairn's village.

Two sections of land at Tonguish's village, near the river Rouge.

That part of the reservation at Macon on the river Raisin, which yet
belongs to the said tribe, containing six sections, excepting therefrom
one half of a section where the Potawatamie Chief Moran resides,
which shall be reserved for his use.

One tract at Mang ach qua village, on the river Peble, of six miles
square.

One tract at Mickesawbe, of six miles square.

One tract at the village of Prairie Ronde, of three miles square.

One tract at the village of Match e be nash she wish, at the head of
the Kekalamazoo river, of three miles square, which tracts contain in
the whole ninety nine sections and one half section of land.

And in consideration of the preceding cession, there shall be
reserved for the use of the said tribe, to be held upon the same terms
on which Indian reservations are usually held, the following tracts of
land.

Sections numbered five, six, seven and eight, in the fifth township,
south of the base line, and in the ninth range west of the principal
meridian in the Territory of Michigan.

The whole of the fifth township, south, in the tenth range, west, not
already included in the Nottawa Sape reservation.

Sections numbered one, two, eleven, twelve, thirteen, fourteen, twenty-three, twenty-four, twenty-five, twenty-six, thirty-five, and thirty-six, in the fifth township, south, and eleventh range, west.

The whole of the fourth township, south, in the ninth range, west.

Sections numbered eight, seventeen, eighteen, nineteen, twenty, twenty-nine, thirty, thirty-one and thirty-two, in the fourth township, south, and ninth range, west.

Sections numbered one, two, eleven, twelve, thirteen, fourteen, twenty-three, twenty-four, twenty-five, twenty-six, thirty-five and thirty-six, in the fourth township, south, and eleventh range, west.

Which tracts of land will form a continuous reservation, and contain ninety-nine sections.

Treaty binding when ratified. — After this treaty shall be ratified by the President and Senate, the same shall be obligatory on the United States and the said tribe of Indians.

In testimony whereof, Lewis Cass, commissioner on the part of the United States, and the chiefs and warriors of the said tribe, have hereunto set their hands at St. Joseph, in the territory of Michigan, this nineteenth day of September, A. D. one thousand eight hundred and twenty-seven.

Lewis Cass,	Ma-tsai-bat-to, his x mark,
Mixs-a-bee, his x mark,	Ne-kee-quin-nish-ka, his x mark,
Shee-ko-maig, or marsh fish, his x mark,	Wa-kai-she-maus, his x mark,
Pee-nai-sheish, or little bird, his x mark,	Peerish Moran, his x mark,
Kne-o-suck-o-wah, his x mark,	Mee-she-pe-she-wa-non, his x mark,
Mais-ko-see, his x mark,	O-tuck-quen, his x mark,
A-bee-ta-que-zic, or half day, his x mark,	Que-quan, his x mark,
Ko-jai-waince, his x mark,	Wai-sai-gau, his x mark,
Sa-kee-maus, his x mark,	O-kee-yau, his x mark,
Mitch-e-pe-nain-she-wish, or bad bird, his x mark,	Me-shai-wais, his x mark.

In presence of—
    John L. Leib,
    R. A. Forsyth,
    Benj. B. Kercheval,
    Isaac McCoy,
    G. W. Silliman,
    James J. Godfroy,
    Joseph Bertrand,
    T. T. Smith.

TREATY WITH THE CREEKS, 1827.

Nov. 15, 1827.

7 Stat., 307.
Proclamation, Mar. 4, 1828.

Articles of agreement made and concluded at the Creek Agency, on the fifteenth day of November, one thousand eight hundred and twenty-seven, between Thomas L. McKenney, and John Crowell, in behalf of the United States, of the one part, and Little Prince and others, Chiefs and Head Men of the Creek Nation, of the other part.

Object of the treaty. — WHEREAS a Treaty of Cession was concluded at Washington City in the District of Columbia, by JAMES BARBOUR, Secretary of War, of the one part, and OPOTHLEOHOLO, JOHN STIDHAM, and OTHERS, of the other part, and which Treaty bears date the twenty-fourth day of January, one thousand eight hundred and twenty-six; and whereas, the object of said Treaty being to embrace a cession by the Creek Nation, of all the lands owned by them within the chartered limits of Georgia, and it having been the opinion of the parties, at the time when said Treaty was concluded, that all, or nearly all, of said lands were embraced in said cession, and by the lines as defined in said Treaty, and the supplemental article thereto: and whereas it having been since ascertained that the said lines in said Treaty, and the supplement thereto, do not embrace all the lands owned by the Creek Nation within the chartered limits of Georgia, and the President of the United States having urged the Creek Nation further to extend the limits as defined in the Treaty aforesaid, and the Chiefs and head men of the Creek Nation being desirous of complying with the wish of the President of the United States, therefore, they, the Chiefs and head men aforesaid, agree to cede, and they do hereby cede to the United States, all the remaining lands now owned or claimed by the Creek Nation, not heretofore ceded, and which, on actual survey, may be found to lie within the chartered limits of the State of Georgia

In consideration whereof, and in full compensation for the above cession, the undersigned, THOMAS L. MCKENNEY, and JOHN CROWELL, in behalf of the United States, do hereby agree to pay to the Chiefs and head men of the Creek Nation aforesaid, and as soon as may be after the approval and ratification of this agreement, in the usual forms, by the President and Senate of the United States, and its sanction by a council of the Creek Nation, to be immediately convened for the purpose, or by the subscription of such names, in addition to those subscribed to this instrument, of Chiefs and head men of the nation, as shall constitute it the act of the Creek Nation—the sum of twenty-seven thousand four hundred and ninety-one dollars. *United States agree to pay $27,491.*

It is further agreed by the parties hereto, in behalf of the United States, to allow, on account of the cession herein made, the additional sum of fifteen thousand dollars, it being the understanding of both the parties, that five thousand dollars of this sum shall be applied, under the direction of the President of the United States, towards the education and support of Creek children at the school in Kentucky, known by the title of the "*Chocktaw Academy*," and under the existing regulations; also, one thousand dollars towards the support of the Withington, and one thousand dollars towards the support of the Asbury stations, so called, both being schools in the Creek Nation, and under regulations of the Department of War; two thousand dollars for the erection of four horse mills, to be suitably located under the direction of the President of the United States; one thousand dollars to be applied to the purchase of cards and wheels, for the use of the Creeks, and the remaining five thousand dollars, it is agreed, shall be paid in blankets and other necessary and useful goods, immediately after the signing and delivery of these presents. *Further agreement.*

In witness whereof, the parties have hereunto set their hands and seals, this fifteenth day of November, one thousand eight hundred and twenty-seven.

Thomas L. McKenney,	[L. S.]
John Crowell,	[L. S.]
Little Prince, his x mark,	[L. S.]
Epau-emathla, his x mark,	[L. S.]
Timpouchoe Burnard, his x mark,	[L. S.]
Hathlan Haujo, his x mark,	[L. S.]
Oke-juoke Yau-holo, his x mark,	[L. S.]
Cassetaw Micco, his x mark,	[L. S.]

In presence of—
    Luther Blake, secretary,
    Andrew Hamill,
    Whitman C. Hill,
    Thomas Crowell.

Whereas, the above articles of agreement and cession were entered into at the Creek agency on the day and date therein mentioned, between the Little Prince, the head man of the nation, and five other chiefs, and Thomas L. McKenney and John Crowell, commissioners on the part of the United States, for the cession of all the lands owned or claimed by the Creek nation, and not heretofore ceded, and which, on actual survey, may be found to lie within the chartered limits of the State of Georgia, and which said agreement was made subject to the approval and ratification by the President and Senate of the United States, and the approval and sanction of the Creek nation, in general council of the said nation.

Now, these presents witnesseth, that we, the undersigned, chiefs and head men of the Creek nation in general council convened, at *Wetumph*, the third day of January, one thousand eight hundred and twenty-eight, have agreed and stipulated with John Crowell, commissioner on the part of the United States, for and in consideration of the additional sum of five thousand dollars, to be paid to us in blankets, and other necessary articles of clothing, immediately after the signing and sealing of these presents, to sanction, and by these presents do hereby approve, sanction, and ratify, the abovementioned and foregoing articles of agreement and session.

In witness whereof, the parties have hereunto set their hands and seals, the day and date above mentioned.

John Crowell,	[L. S.]	Arthlau Hayre, his x mark,	[L. S.]
Broken Arrow Town:		Cowetaw Micco, his x mark,	[L. S.]
Little Prince, his x mark,	[L. S.]	Oswichu Town:	
Tuskugu, his x mark,	[L. S.]	Halatta Tustinuggu, his x mark,	[L. S.]
Cotche Hayre, his x mark,	[L. S.]	Octiatchu Emartla, his x mark,	[L. S.]
Cusetau Town:		Charles Emartla, his x mark,	[L. S.]
Tukchenaw, his x mark,	[L. S.]	Uchee Town:	
Epi Emartla, his x mark,	[L. S.]	Timpoeche Barned, his x mark,	[L. S.]
Oakpushu Yoholo, his x mark,	[L. S.]	Chawaccola Hatchu Town:	
Cowetau Town:		Coe E. Hayo, his x mark,	[L. S.]
Neah Thleuco, his x mark,	[L. S.]	Powas Yoholo, his x mark,	[L. S.]
Tomasa Town:		Ema Hayre, his x mark,	[L. S.]
Colitchu Ementla, his x mark,	[L. S.]		

In presence of—
    Luther Blake, secretary,
    Andrew Hamill,
    Enoch Johnson,
    Thomas Crowell.
    Benjamin Marshall,
    Paddy Carr,
        interpreters.
    Joseph Marshall,
    John Winslett.

TREATY WITH THE MIAMI, 1828.

Feb. 11. 1828.

7 Stat., 309.
Proclamation, May 7, 1828.

Articles of a treaty made and concluded at the Wyandot village, near the Wabash in the State of Indiana between John Tipton, Commissioner for that purpose, on the part of the United States, and the Chiefs, Head Men and Warriors, of the Eel River, or Thorntown party of Miami Indians.

Cession of land to United States.

ART. 1. The Chiefs, Head Men, and Warriors of the Eel River or Thorntown party of Miami Indians, agree to cede, and by these presents do cede, and relinquish to the United States all their right, title, and claim to a reservation of land about ten miles square, at their village on Sugartree Creek in Indiana, which was reserved to said party by the second article of a Treaty between Commissioners of the United States, and the Miami nation of Indians, made and entered into at St. Mary's in the State of Ohio, on the sixth day of October, one thousand eight hundred and eighteen.

It is understood and agreed on by said Indians, that they will not burn or destroy the houses or fences on said reservation, and that they will leave them in as good condition as they now are; and remove to the five mile reservation on Eel River by the fifteenth day of October next. Indians not to burn-
houses, etc., on reser
vation.

ART. 2. The Commissioner of the United States has delivered to said party of Indians, goods to the value of two thousand dollars, in part consideration for the cession herein made, and it is agreed that in case this treaty should be ratified by the President and Senate of the United States, that the United States shall pay said party an additional sum of eight thousand dollars in goods next summer, build twelve log houses, ten on the five mile reservation, and two on the Wabash; clear and fence forty acres of land on the five mile reservation, furnish them one wagon and two yoke of oxen, furnish two hands to work three months in each year for two years, five hundred dollars worth of provisions delivered on the Wabash; furnish them five horses, five saddles and five bridles. Goods to amouut of
$2,000 delivered to In-
dians.

Provided however, that if this treaty should not be ratified by the President and Senate of the United States, that said party agree to pay for the goods this day received, two thousand dollars, to be deducted from their annuity for this present year. Proviso.

ART. 3. At the request of the Indians, and in part consideration for the cession aforesaid, the United States agree to pay to Peter Langlois, one thousand dollars in silver, and three thousand dollars in goods next summer, for provisions and goods heretofore delivered to said party. Payment to Peter
Langlois.

ART. 4. The United States agree to appropriate one thousand dollars per year for five years, and longer if Congress thinks proper, to be applied under the direction of the President, to the education of the youths of the Miami nation. Appropriation for
education of Indian
youths.

ART. 5. It is distinctly understood and agreed on by and between the contracting parties, that the President and Senate may, if they think proper, modify or expunge from this treaty, the fourth article, without affecting any other of its provisions. Fourth article may
be modified.

ART. 6. This treaty, after the same shall be ratified by the President and Senate of the United States, shall be binding on the contracting parties. Treaty obligatory
when ratified.

In testimony whereof, the said John Tipton, commissioner as aforesaid on the part of the United States, and the chiefs, head men, and warriors, of said party, have hereunto set their hand and seals at the Wyandot village, near the Wabash, this eleventh day of February, in the year of our Lord one thousand eight hundred and twenty-eight.

John Tipton, commissioner.	[L. S.]	Waw paw ko se aw, his x mark,	[L. S.]
Ne go ta kaup wa, his x mark,	[L. S.]	Mack kon zaw, his x mark,	[L. S.]
Shaw po to se aw, his x mark,	[L. S.]	Man je ne ki ah, his x mark,	[L. S.]
Ntah ko ke aw, his x mark,	[L. S.]	Naw waw pawm awn daw, his x	
Aw waw no zaw, his x mark,	[L. S.]	mark,	[L. S.]
Kaw koaw ma kau to aw, his x		Ne ah law naun daw, his x mark,	[L. S.]
mark,	[L. S.]	Ke pah naw mo aw, his x mark,	[L. S.]
Aw sawn zaw gaw, his x mark,	[L. S.]	Ke we kau law, his x mark,	[L. S.]
Shin go aw zaw, his x mark,	[L. S.]	Pierrish Constant, his x mark,	[L. S.]
Oh zau ke at tau, his x mark,	[L. S.]	Aw wawn saw peau, his x mark,	[L. S.]

Attest:
> Walter Wilson, secretary to the commissioner,
> J. B. Duret.
> Joseph Barron,
> J. B. Boure,
>> interpreters.
> Calvin Fletcher,
> Saml. Hanna,
> Allen Hamilton,
> Jordan Vigus,
> Pierre Langly,
> Joseph Holman.

TREATY WITH THE WESTERN CHEROKEE, 1828.

May 6, 1828.
_____
7 Stat., 311.
Proclamation, May
28, 1828.

Articles of a Convention, concluded at the City of Washington this sixth day of May, in the year of our Lord one thousand eight hundred and twenty-eight, between James Barbour, Secretary of War, being especially authorized therefor by the President of the United States, and the undersigned, Chiefs and Head Men of the Cherokee Nation of Indians, West of the Mississippi, they being duly authorized and empowered by their Nation.

Object of the treaty.

WHEREAS, it being the anxious desire of the Government of the United States to secure to the Cherokee nation of Indians, as well those now living within the limits of the Territory of Arkansas, as those of their friends and brothers who reside in States East of the Mississippi, and who may wish to join their brothers of the West, *a permanent* home, and which shall, under the most solemn guarantee of the United States, be, and remain, theirs forever—a home that shall never, in all future time, be embarrassed by having extended around it the lines, or placed over it the jurisdiction of a Territory or State, nor be pressed upon by the extension, in any way, of any of the limits of any existing Territory or State; and, Whereas, the present location of the Cherokees in Arkansas being unfavorable to their present repose, and tending, as the past demonstrates, to their future degradation and misery; and the Cherokees being anxious to avoid such consequences, and yet not questioning their right to their lands in Arkansas, as secured to them by Treaty, and resting also upon the pledges given them by the President of the United States, and the Secretary of War, of March, 1818, and 8th October, 1821, in regard to the outlet to the West, and as may be seen on referring to the records of the War Department, still being anxious to secure a permanent home, and to free themselves, and their posterity, from an embarrassing connexion with the Territory of Arkansas, and guard themselves from such connexions in future; and, Whereas, it being important, not to the Cherokees only, but also to the Choctaws, and in regard also to the question which may be agitated in the future respecting the location of the latter, as well as the former, within the limits of the Territory or State of Arkansas, as the case may be, and their removal therefrom; and to avoid the cost which may attend negotiations to rid the Territory or State of Arkansas whenever it may become a State, of either, or both of those Tribes, the parties hereto do hereby conclude the following Articles, viz:

Western boundary of Arkansas defined.

ART. 1. The Western boundary of Arkansas shall be, and the same is, hereby defined, viz: A line shall be run, commencing on Red River, at the point where the Eastern Choctaw line strikes said River, and run due North with said line to the River Arkansas, thence in a direct line to the South West corner of Missouri.

Territory guaranteed to Cherokees by United States.

ART. 2. The United States agree to possess the Cherokees, and to guarantee it to them forever, and that guarantee is hereby solemnly pledged, of seven millions of acres of land, to be bounded as follows, viz: Commencing at that point on Arkansas River where the Eastern Choctaw boundary line strikes said River, and running thence with the Western line of Arkansas, as defined in the foregoing article, to the South-West corner of Missouri, and thence with the Western boundary line of Missouri till it crosses the waters of Neasho, generally called Grand River, thence due West to a point from which a due South course will strike the present North West corner of Arkansas Territory, thence continuing due South, on and with the present Western boundary line of the Territory to the main branch of Arkansas River, thence down said River to its junction with the Canadian River, and thence up and between the said Rivers Arkansas and Canadian, to a point at which a line running North and South from River to River, will give the aforesaid seven millions of acres. In addition to the seven millions of acres thus provided for, and bounded, the United States further guarantee to the Cherokee Nation a perpetual outlet, West, and a free and unmolested use of all the Country lying West of the Western boundary of the above described limits, and as far West as the sovereignty of the United States, and their right of soil extend.

ART. 3. The United States agree to have the lines of the above cession run without delay, say not later than the first of October next, and to remove, immediately after the running of the Eastern line from the Arkansas River to the South-West corner of Missouri, all white persons from the West to the East of said line, and also all others, should there be any there, who may be unacceptable to the Cherokees, so that no obstacles arising out of the presence of a white population, or a population of any other sort, shall exist to annoy the Cherokees— and also to keep all such from the West of said line in future. *United States to run the lines.*

ART. 4. The United States moreover agree to appoint suitable persons whose duty it shall be, in conjunction with the Agent, to value all such improvements as the Cherokees may abandon in their removal from their present homes to the District of Country as ceded in the second Article of this agreement, and to pay for the same immediately after the assessment is made, and the amount ascertained. It is further agreed, that the property and improvements connected with the agency, shall be sold under the direction of the Agent, and the proceeds of the same applied to aid in the erection, in the country to which the Cherokees are going, of a Grist, and Saw Mill, for their use. The aforesaid property and improvements are thus defined: Commence at the Arkansas River opposite William Stinnetts, and run due North one mile, thence due East to a point from which a due South line to the Arkansas River would include the Chalybeate, or Mineral Spring, attached to or near the present residence of the Agent, and thence up said River (Arkansas) to the place of beginning. *Persons to be appointed to value Cherokee improvements.*

ART 5. It is further agreed, that the United States, in consideration of the inconvenience and trouble attending the removal, and on account of the reduced value of a great portion of the lands herein ceded to the Cherokees, as compared with that of those in Arkansas which were made theirs by the Treaty of 1817, and the Convention of 1819, will pay to the Cherokees, immediately after their removal which shall be within fourteen months of the date of this agreement, the sum of fifty thousand dollars; also an annuity, for three years, of two thousand dollars, towards defraying the cost and trouble which may attend upon going after and recovering their stock which may stray into the Territory in quest of the pastures from which they may be driven—also, eight thousand seven hundred and sixty dollars, for spoliations committed on them, (the Cherokees,) which sum will be in full of all demands of the kind up to this date, as well as those against the Osages, as those against citizens of the United States—this being the amount of the claims for said spoliations, as rendered by the Cherokees, and which are believed to be correctly and fairly stated.—Also, one thousand two hundred dollars for the use of Thomas Graves, a Cherokee Chief, for losses sustained in his property, and for personal suffering endured by him when confined as a prisoner, on a criminal, but false accusation; also, five hundred dollars for the use of George Guess, another Cherokee, for the great benefits he has conferred upon the Cherokee people, in the beneficial results which they are now experiencing from the use of the Alphabet discovered by him, to whom also, in consideration of his relinquishing a valuable saline, the privilege is hereby given to locate and occupy another saline on Lee's Creek. It is further agreed by the United States, to pay two thousand dollars, *Further agreement.*

annually, to the Cherokees, for ten years, to be expended under the direction of the President of the United States in the education of their children, in their own country, in letters and the mechanic arts; also, one thousand dollars towards the purchase of a Printing Press and Types to aid the Cherokees in the progress of education, and to benefit and enlighten them as a people, in their own, and our language. It is agreed further that the expense incurred other than that paid by the United States in the erection of the buildings and improvements, so far as that may have been paid by the benevolent society who have been, and yet are, engaged in instructing the Cherokee children, shall be paid to the society, it being the understanding that the amount shall be expended in the erection of other buildings and improvements, for like purposes, in the country herein ceded to the Cherokees. The United States relinquish their claim due by the Cherokees to the late United States Factory, provided the same does not exceed three thousand five hundred dollars.

Further agreement.

ART. 6. It is moreover agreed, by the United States, whenever the Cherokees may desire it, to give them a set of plain laws, suited to their condition—also, when they may wish to lay off their lands, and own them individually, a surveyor shall be sent to make the surveys at the cost of the United States.

Cherokees to surrender lands in Arkansas within fourteen months.

ART. 7. The Chiefs and Head Men of the Cherokee Nation, aforesaid, for and in consideration of the foregoing stipulations and provisions, do hereby agree, in the name and behalf of their Nation, to give up, and they do hereby surrender, to the United States, and agree to leave the same within fourteen months, as herein before stipulated, all the lands to which they are entitled in Arkansas, and which were secured to them by the Treaty of 8th January, 1817, and the Convention of the 27th February, 1819.

Cost of emigration, etc., to be borne by the United States.

ART. 8. The Cherokee Nation, West of the Mississippi having, by this agreement, freed themselves from the harassing and ruinous effects consequent upon a location amidst a white population, and secured to themselves and their posterity, under the solemn sanction of the guarantee of the United States, as contained in this agreement, a large extent of unembarrassed country; and that their Brothers yet remaining in the States may be induced to join them and enjoy the repose and blessings of such a State in the future, it is further agreed, on the part of the United States, that to each Head of a Cherokee family now residing within the chartered limits of Georgia, or of either of the States, East of the Mississippi, who may desire to remove West, shall be given, on enrolling himself for emigration, a good Rifle, a Blanket, and Kettle, and five pounds of Tobacco: (and to each member of his family one Blanket,) also, a just compensation for the property he may abandon, to be assessed by persons to be appointed by the President of the United States. The cost of the emigration of all such shall also be borne by the United States, and good and suitable ways opened, and provisions procured for their comfort, accommodation, and support, by the way, and provisions for twelve months after their arrival at the Agency; and to each person, or head of a family, if he take along with him four persons, shall be paid immediately on his arriving at the Agency and reporting himself and his family or followers, as emigrants and permanent settlers, in addition to the above, *provided he and they shall have emigrated from within the Chartered limits of the State of Georgia*, the sum of fifty dollars, and this sum in proportion to any greater or less number that may accompany him from within the aforesaid Chartered limits of the State of Georgia.

A certain tract of land to be reserved for the benefit of the United States.

ART. 9. It is understood and agreed by the parties to this Convention, that a Tract of Land, two miles wide and six miles long, shall be, and the same is hereby, reserved for the use and benefit of the

United States, for the accommodation of the military force which is now, or which may hereafter be, stationed at Fort Gibson, on the Neasho, or Grand River, to commence on said River half a mile below the aforesaid Fort, and to run thence due East two miles, thence Northwardly six miles, to a point which shall be two mile distant from the River aforesaid, thence due West to the said River, and down it to the place of beginning. And the Cherokees agree that the United States shall have and possess the right of establishing a road through their country for the purpose of having a free and unmolested way to and from said Fort.

ART. 10. It is agreed that Captain James Rogers, in consideration of his having lost a horse in the service of the United States, and for services rendered by him to the United States, shall be paid, in full for the above, and all other claims for losses and services, the sum of Five Hundred Dollars. Capt. J. Rogers to be paid in full for property lost in the service of United States.

ART. 11. This Treaty to be binding on the contracting parties so soon as it is ratified by the President of the United States, by and with the advice and consent of the Senate.

Done at the place, and on the day and year above written.

James Barbour.	[L. S.]
Black Fox, his x mark,	[L. S.]
Thomas Graves, his x mark,	[L. S.]
George Guess,[a]	[L. S.]
Thomas Maw,[a]	[L. S.]
George Marvis,[a]	[L. S.]
John Looney,[a]	[L. S.]
John Rogers,	[L. S.]
J. W. Flawey, counsellor of Del.	[L. S.]

Chiefs of the delegation.

Witnesses:
Thos. L. McKenney,
James Rogers, interpreter,
D. Kurtz,
H. Miller,
Thomas Murray,
D. Brown, secretary Cherokee delegation,
Pierye Pierya,
E. W. Duval, United States agent, etc.

Ratified with the following proviso:

"Provided, nevertheless, that the said convention shall not be so construed as to extend the northern boundary of the 'perpetual outlet west,' provided for and guaranteed in the second article of said convention, north of the thirty-sixth degree of north latitude, or so as to interfere with the lands assigned, or to be assigned, west of the Mississippi river, to the Creek Indians who have emigrated, or may emigrate, from the States of Georgia and Alabama, under the provisions of any treaty or treaties heretofore concluded between the United States and the Creek tribe of Indians; and provided further, That nothing in the said convention shall be construed to cede or assign to the Cherokees any lands heretofore ceded or assigned to any tribe or tribes of Indians, by any treaty now existing and in force, with any such tribe or tribes."

---

[a] Written by the signers in their language, and in the characters now in use among them, as discovered by George Guess.

DEPARTMENT OF WAR,
31st May, 1828.

To the Hon. HENRY CLAY,
Secretary of State:

SIR: I have the honor to transmit, herewith, **the acceptance of the terms**, by the Cherokees, upon which the recent **convention** with them was ratified. You will have the goodness to cause the same to be attached to the treaty, and published with it.

I have the honor to be, very respectfully, your obedient servant,

SAM'L. L. SOUTHARD.

———

COUNCIL ROOM, WILLIAMSON'S HOTEL,
Washington, May 31st, 1828.

To the SECRETARY OF WAR,
Washington City:

SIR: The undersigned, chiefs of the Cherokee nation, west of the Mississippi, for and in behalf of said nation, hereby agree to, and accept of, the terms upon which **the Senate of the United States** ratified the convention, concluded at Washington on the sixth day of May, 1828, between the United States and said nation.

In testimony whereof, they hereunto subscribe their names and affix their seals.

Thomas Graves, his x mark,	[L. S.]
George Maw, his x mark,	[L. S.]
George Guess, his x mark,	[L. S.]
Thomas Marvis, his x mark,	[L. S.]
John Rogers.	[L. S.]

Signed and sealed in the presence of—
E. W. Duval, United States agent, etc.
Thomas Murray,
James Rogers, interpreter.

———

TREATY WITH THE WINNEBAGO, ETC, 1828.

Aug. 25, 1828.
———
7 Stat., 315.
Proclamation, Jan.
7, 1829.

Preamble.

Articles of agreement with the Winnebago Tribe and the United Tribes of Potawatamie, Chippewa and Ottawa Indians.

THE Government of the United States having appointed Commissioners to treat with the Sac, Fox, Winebago, Potawatamie, Ottawa, and Chippewa, tribes of Indians, for the purpose of extinguishing their title to land within the State of Illinois, and the Territory of Michigan, situated between the Illinois river and the Lead Mines on Fever River, and in the vicinity of said Lead Mines, and for other purposes; and it having been found impracticable, in consequence of the lateness of the period when the instructions were issued, the extent of the country occupied by the Indians, and their dispersed situation, to convene them in sufficient numbers to justify a cession of land on their part; and the Chiefs of the Winnebago tribe, and of the united tribes of the Potawatamies, Chippewas, and Ottawas, assembled at Green Bay, having declined at this time to make the desired cession, the following temporary arrangement, subject to the ratification of the President and Senate of the United States, has this day been made, between Lewis Cass and Pierre Menard, Commissioners of the United States, and the said Winnebago tribe, and the United tribes of Potawatamie, Chippewa, and Ottawa, Indians, in order to remove the difficulties which have arisen in consequence of the occupation, by white persons, of that part of the mining country which has not been heretofore ceded to the United States.

ARTICLE 1. It is agreed that the following shall be the provisional boundary between the lands of the United States and those of the said Indians: The Ouisconsin river, from its mouth to its nearest approach to the Blue Mounds; thence southerly, passing east of the said mounds, to the head of that branch of the Pocatolaka creek which runs near the Spotted Arm's village; thence with the said branch to the main forks of Pocatolaka creek; thence southeasterly, to the ridge dividing the Winebago country from that of the Potawatamie, Chippewa, and Ottawa tribes; thence southerly, with the said ridge, to the line running from Chicago to the Mississippi, near Rock Island. And it is fully understood, that the United States may freely occupy the country between these boundaries and the Mississippi river, until a treaty shall be held with the Indians for its cession; which treaty, it is presumed, will be held in the year 1829. But it is expressly understood and agreed, that if any white persons shall cross the line herein described, and pass into the Indian country, for the purpose of mining, or for any other purpose whatever, the Indians shall not interfere with nor molest such persons, but that the proper measures for their removal shall be referred to the President of the United States. In the mean time, however, it is agreed, that any just compensation to which the Indians may be entitled for any injuries committed by white persons on the Indian side of the said line, shall be paid to the said Indians at the time such treaty may be held—It is also agreed by the Indians that a ferry may be established over the Rock River, where the Fort Clark road crosses the same; and, also, a ferry over the same river at the crossing of the Lewiston road.

Provisional boundary between lands of United States and those of the Indians.

Ferries to be established over Rock River.

ARTICLE 2. The United States agree to pay to the Winebago, Potawatamie, Chippewa, and Ottawa Indians, the sum of twenty thousand dollars, in goods, at the time and place when and where the said treaty may be held: which said sum shall be equitably divided between the said tribes, and shall be in full compensation for all the injuries and damages sustained by them, in consequence of the occupation of any part of the mining country by white persons, from the commencement of such occupation until the said treaty shall be held. Excepting, however, such compensation as the Indians may be entitled to, for any injuries hereafter committed on their side of the line hereby established.

Payment to Indians for trespasses on their mines, etc.

In testimony whereof, the said commissioners and the chiefs of the said tribes have hereunto set their hands at Green bay, in the territory of Michigan, this 25th day of August, in the year of our Lord one thousand eight hundred and twenty-eight.

Lewis Cass,
Pierre Menard.
  Winnebagoes:
Nan-kaw, or wood, his x mark,
Koan-kaw, or chief, his x mark,
Hoo-waun-ee-kaw, or little elk, his x mark,
Tshay-ro-tshoan-kaw, or smoker, his x mark,
Haump-ee-man-ne-kaw, or he who walks by day, his x mark,
Hoo-tshoap-kaw, or four legs, his x mark,
Morah-tshay-kaw, or little priest, his x mark,
Kau-ree-kau-saw-kaw, or white crow, his x mark,
Wau-kaun-haw-kaw, or snake skin, his x mark,
Man-ah-kee-tshump-kaw, or spotted arm, his x mark,
Wee-no-shee-kaw, his x mark,

Tshaw-wan-shaip-shootsh-kaw, his x mark,
Hoo-tshoap-kaw, or four legs, (senior) his x mark,
Nau-soo-ray-risk-kaw, his x mark,
Shoank-tshunsk-kaw, or black wolf, his x mark,
Wau-tshe-roo-kun-ah-kaw, or he who is master of the lodge, his x mark,
Kay-rah-tsho-kaw, or clear weather, his x mark,
Hay-ro-kaw-kaw, or he without horns, his x mark,
Wau-kaum-kam, or snake, his x mark,
Kan-kaw-saw-kaw, his x mark,
Man-kay-ray-kau, or spotted earth, his x mark,
Thaun-wan-kaw, or wild cat, his x mark,
Span-you-kaw, or Spaniard, his x mark,
Shoank-skaw-kaw, or white dog, his x mark,

Nee-hoo-kaw, or whirlpool, his x mark,
Nath-kay-saw-kaw, or fierce heart, his x mark,
Wheank-kaw, or duck, his x mark,
Saw-waugh-kee-wau, or he that leaves the yellow track, his x mark,
Sin-a-gee-wen, or ripple, his x mark,
Shush-que-nau, his x mark,
Sa-gin-nai-nee-pee, his x mark,
Nun-que-wee-bee, or thunder sitting, his x mark,

O-bwa-gunn, or thunder turn back, his x mark,
Tusk-que-gun, or last feather, his x mark,
Maun-gee-zik, or big foot, his x mark,
Way-meek-see-goo, or wampum, his x mark,
Meeks-zoo, his x mark,
Pay-mau-bee-mee, or him that looks over, his x mark.

Witnesses present:

W. B. Lee, secretary,
H. J. B. Brevoort, United States Indian agent,
R. A. Forsyth,
Jno. H. Kinzie,
John Marsh,
E. A. Brush,

G. W. Silliman,
C. Chouteau,
Peter Menard, jun., Indian subagent,
Henry Gratiot,
Pierre Paquet, Winnebago interpreter,
J. Ogee, Potawatamie interpreter.

TREATY WITH THE POTAWATOMI, 1828.

Sept, 20, 1828.

7 Stat., 317.
Proclamation, Jan. 7, 1829.

Articles of a treaty made and concluded at the Missionary Establishments upon the St. Joseph, of Lake Michigan, in the Territory of Michigan, this 20th day of September, in the year of our Lord one thousand eight hundred and twenty-eight, between Lewis Cass and Pierre Ménard, Commissioners, on the part of the United States, and the Potowatami tribe of Indians.

Potawatomies cede part of their lands.

ARTICLE 1st. The Potowatami tribe of Indians cede to the United States the tract of land included within the following boundaries:

1st. Beginning at the mouth of the St. Joseph, of Lake Michigan, and thence running up the said river to a point on the same river, half way between La-vache-qui-pisse and Macousin village: thence in a direct line, to the 19th mile tree, on the northern boundary line of the State Indiana; thence, with the same, west, to Lake Michigan; and thence, with the shore of the said Lake, to the place of beginning.

2. Beginning at a point on the line run in 1817, due east from the southern extreme of Lake Michigan, which point is due south from the head of the most easterly branch of the Kankekee river, and from that point running south ten miles; thence, in a direct line, to the northeast corner of Flatbelly's reservation; thence, to the northwest corner of the reservation at Seek's village; thence, with the lines of the said reservation, and of former cessions, to the line between the States of Indiana and Ohio; thence, with the same to the former described line, running due east from the southern extreme of Lake Michigan; and thence, with the said line, to the place of beginning.

Additional annuities.

ART. 2. In consideration of the cessions aforesaid, there shall be paid to the said tribe an additional permanent annuity of two thousand dollars; and also an additional annuity of one thousand dollars, for the term of twenty years; goods, to the value of thirty thousand dollars, shall be given to the said tribe, either immediately after signing this treaty, or as soon thereafter as they can be procured; an additional sum of ten thousand dollars, in goods, and another of five thousand dollars, in specie, shall be paid to them in the year 1829.

Purchase of domestic animals, etc.

The sum of seven thousand five hundred dollars shall be expended for the said tribe, under the direction of the President of the United States, in clearing and fencing land, erecting houses, purchasing domestic animals and farming utensils, and in the support of labourers to work for them.

Two thousand pounds of tobacco, fifteen hundred weight of iron, Tobacco, iron, and steel. and three hundred and fifty pounds of steel, shall be annually delivered to them.

One thousand dollars per annum shall be applied for the purposes Education. of education, as long as Congress may think the appropriation may be useful.

One hundred dollars, in goods, shall be annually paid to To-pen-i- Allowance of goods to principal chief. Blacksmith. be-the, principal chief of the said tribe, during his natural life. The blacksmith, stipulated by the treaty of Chicago to be provided for the term of fifteen years, shall be permanently supported by the United States.

Three labourers shall be provided, during four months of the year, Laborers. for ten years, to work for the band living upon the reservation South of the St. Joseph.

ART. 3. There shall be granted to the following persons, all of Grants of land to individual Indians, stipulated for. whom are Indians by descent, the tracts of land hereafter mentioned, which shall be located upon the second cession above described, where the President of the United States may direct, after the country may be surveyed, and to correspond with the surveys, provided that no location shall be made upon the Elkheart Prairie, nor within five miles of the same; nor shall the tracts there granted be conveyed by the grantees, without the consent of the President of the United States.

To Sah-ne-mo-quay, wife of Jean B. Dutrist, one-half section of land.

To Way-pe-nah-te-mo-quay, wife of Thomas Robb, one half section of land.

To Me-no-ka-mick-quay, wife of Edward McCarty, one half section of land.

To Ship-pe-shick-quay, wife of James Wyman, one half section of land.

To Assapo, wife of Antoine Gamlin, one half section of land.

To Moahquay, wife of Richard Chabert, one half section of land.

To Me-shaw-ke-to-quay, wife of George Cicot, two sections of land.

To Mary Préjean, wife of Louis St. Combe, one section of land.

To To-pe-naw-koung, wife of Peter Langlois, one section of land.

To Au-bee-nan-bee, a Potowatami chief, two sections of land.

To Me-che-hee, wife of Charles Minie, a half section of land.

To Louison, a Potowatamie, a reservation of one section, to include his house and cornfield.

To Kes-he-wa-quay, wife of Pierre F. Navarre, one section of land.

To Benac, a Potowatami, one section of land.

To Pe-pe-ne-way, a chief, one section of land.

To Pierre Le Clair, one section of land.

To Betsey Ducharme, one half section of land. The section of land granted by the treaty of Chicago to Nancy Burnett, now Nancy Davis, shall be purchased by the United States, if the same can be done for the sum of one thousand dollars.

To Madeleine Bertrand, wife of Joseph Bertrand, one section of land.

ART. 4. The sum of ten thousand eight hundred and ninety-five dol- Payment of claim against Indians. lars shall be applied to the payments of certain claims against the Indians, agreeably to a schedule of the said claims hereunto annexed.

ART. 5. Circumstances rendering it probable that the missionary Missionary establishments. establishment now located upon the St. Joseph, may be compelled to remove west of the Mississippi, it is agreed that when they remove, the value of their buildings and other improvements shall be estimated, and the amount paid by the United States. But, as the location is upon the Indian reservation, the Commissioners are unwilling to assume the responsibility, of making this provision absolute, and therefore its rejection is not to affect any other part of the treaty.

Treaty binding when ratified. ART. 6. This treaty shall be obligatory, after the same has been ratified by the President and Senate of the United States.

In testimony whereof, the commissioners, and the chiefs and warriors of the said tribe have hereunto set their hands, at the place and upon the day aforesaid.

Lewis Cass,
Pierre Menard,
To-pen-e-bee, his x mark,
A-bee-na-bee, his x mark,
Po-ka-gon, his x mark,
Ship-she-wa-non, his x mark,
Quai-quai-ta, his x mark,
Mixs-a-be, his x mark,
Mo-sack, his x mark,
Wa-ban-see, his x mark,
Pe-nan-shies, his x mark,
Mish-ko-see, his x mark,
Moran, his x mark,
Shaw-wa-nan-see, his x mark,
Mank-see, his x mark,
Shee-qua, his x mark,
Ash-kum, his x mark,
Louison, his x mark,
Che-chalk-koos, his x mark,
Pee-pee-nai-wa, his x mark,
Moc-conse, his x mark,
Kaush-quaw, his x mark,
Sko-mans, his x mark,
Au-tiss, his x mark,
Me-non-quet, his x mark,
Sack-a-mans, his x mark,
Kin-ne-kose, his x mark,
No-shai-e-quon, his x mark,
Pe-tee-nans, his x mark,
Jo-saih, his x mark,
Mo-teille, his x mark,
Wa-pee-kai-non, his x mark,
Pack-quin, his x mark,
Pash-po-oo, his x mark,
Mans-kee-os, his x mark,
Wash-e-on-ause, his x mark,

Pee-shee-wai, his x mark,
O-kee-au, his x mark,
Nau-kee-o-nuck, his x mark,
Me-she-ken-ho, his x mark,
Non-ai, his x mark.
Wa-shais-skuck, his x mark,
Pai-que-sha-bai, his x mark,
Mix-a-mans, his x mark,
Me-tai-was, his x mark,
Mis-qua-buck, his x mark,
A-bee-tu-que-zuck, his x mark,
Kee-ai-so-qua, his x mark,
A-bee-tai-que-zuck, his x mark,
Wau-shus-kee-zuck, his x mark,
Kee-kee-wee-nus-ka, his x mark,
Nichee-poo-sick, his x mark,
Wa-sai-ka, his x mark,
Mee-quen, his x mark,
Num-quai-twa, his x mark,
Mee-kee-sis, his x mark,
Sans-gen-ai, his x mark,
Wish-kai, his x mark,
She-she-gon, his x mark,
Pee-pee-au, his x mark,
O-tuck-quin, his x mark,
Moo-koos, his x mark,
Louison, his x mark,
Pchee-koo, his x mark,
Sha-wai-no-kuck, his x mark,
Zo-zai, his x mark,
Wai-za-we-shuck, his x mark,
Me-chee-pee-nai-she-insh, his x mark,
Com-o-zoo, his x mark,
Je-bause, his x mark,
Le Bœuf, his x mark.

Payment in goods. After the signature of the Treaty, and at the request of the Indians, it was agreed, that of the ten thousand, dollars stipulated to be delivered in goods, in 1829, three thousand dollars shall be delivered immediately, leaving seven thousand dollars in goods to be delivered in 1829.

Location of grants. The reservation of Pe. Langlois' wife to be located upon the north side of Eel river, between Peerish's village and Louison's reservation.

The reservation of Betsey Ducharme to be located at Louison's run.

Lewis Cass,
Pierre Menard.

Ratified, with the exception of the following paragraph in the third article: "To Joseph Barron, a white man, who has long lived with the Indians, and to whom they are much attached, two sections of land; but the rejection of this grant is not to affect any other part of the treaty."

Signed in the presence of—

Alex. Wolcott, Indian agent,
John Tipton, Indian agent,
Charles Noble, secretary to commissioners,
A. Edwards, president of the legislative council,
R. A. Forsyth,
D. G. Jones,
Walter Wilson, major general Indiana Militia,
Calvin Britain,
E. Reed.

APPENDIX II.

Schedule of claims referred to in the fourth article of the treaty of the 20th September, 1828, with the Pottawatamie Indians.

Sept. 20, 1828.

7 Stat., 603.

Thomas Robb $200, for goods heretofore sold to the Indians.
McGeorge $300, for provisions sold to the Indians.
Jno. B. Godfroy $200, for goods heretofore sold to the Indians.
Jno. P. Hedges $200, for goods heretofore delivered to the Indians.
Joseph Allen $145, for horses stolen from him by the Indians while he was surveying.
Jean B. Bourre $700, for goods furnished the Indians, a part of them in relation to this treaty.
Thomas Forsyth $200, for goods heretofore sold to the Indians.
S. Hanna & Co. $100, for goods heretofore sold to the Indians.
Gabriel Godfroy, jr., $500, for goods heretofore sold to the Indians.
Timothy S. Smith $100, for goods heretofore sold to the Indians.
W. G. and G. W. Ewings $200, for goods heretofore sold to the Indians.
Joseph Bertrand $2,000, for goods heretofore sold to the Indians.
To Eleanor Kinzie and her four children, by the late John Kinzie, $3,500, in consideration of the attachment of the Indians to her deceased husband, who was long an Indian trader, and who lost a large sum in the trade by the credits given to them, and also by the destruction of his property. The money is in lieu of a tract of land which the Indians gave the late John Kinzie long since, and upon which he lived.
Robert A. Forsyth $1,250, in consideration of the debts due from the Indians to his late father, Robert A. Forsyth, who was long a trader among them, and who was assisted by his son, the present R. A. Forsyth. The money is in lieu of a tract of land which the Indians gave to the late R. A. Forsyth, since renewed to the present R. A. Forsyth, upon which both of them heretofore lived.
Jean B. Comparet $500, for goods heretofore sold to the Indians.
C. and D. Dousseau $100, for goods heretofore sold to the Indians.
P. F. Navarre $100, for goods heretofore sold to the Indians.
Francis Paget $100, for goods heretofore sold to the Indians.
G. O. Hubbard $200, for goods heretofore sold to the Indians.
Alexis Coquillard $200, for goods heretofore sold to the Indians.
Amounting, in the whole, to the sum of ten thousand eight hundred and ninety-five dollars.

LEW. CASS,
PIERRE MENARD.

TREATY WITH THE CHIPPEWA, ETC., 1829.

Articles of a treaty made and concluded at Prairie du Chien, in the Territory of Michigan, between the United States of America, by their Commissioners, General John McNeil, Colonel Pierre Menard, and Caleb Atwater, Esq. and the United Nations of Chippewa, Ottawa, and Potawatamie Indians, of the waters of the Illinois, Milwaukee. and Manitoouck Rivers.

July 29, 1829.

7 Stat., 320.
Proclamation, Jan. 2, 1830.

ARTICLE I.

THE aforesaid nations of Chippewa, Ottawa, and Potawatamie Indians, do hereby cede to the United States aforesaid, all the lands comprehended within the following limits, to wit: Beginning at the Winnebago Village, on Rock river, forty miles from its mouth, and running thence down the Rock river, to a line which runs due west from the most southern bend of Lake Michigan to the Mississippi river, and with that line to the Mississippi river opposite to Rock Island; thence, up that river, to the United States' reservation at the mouth of the Ouisconsin; thence, with the south and east lines of said reservation, to the Ouisconsin river; thence, southerly, passing the heads of the small streams emptying into the Mississippi, to the Rock River aforesaid, at the Winnebago Village, the place of beginning. And, also, one other tract of land, described as follows, to wit: Beginning on the Western Shore of Lake Michigan, at the northeast corner of the field of Antoine Ouitmette, who lives near Gross Pointe, about twelve miles north of Chicago; thence, running due west, to the Rock River, aforesaid;

Certain lands ceded to United States.

thence, down the said river, to where a line drawn due west from the most southern bend of Lake Michigan crosses said river; thence, east, along said line, to the Fox River of the Illinois; thence, along the northwestern boundary line of the cession of 1816, to Lake Michigan; thence, northwardly, along the Western Shore of said Lake, to the place of beginning.

ARTICLE II.

Consideration therefor.

In consideration of the aforesaid cessions of land, the United States aforesaid agree to pay to the aforesaid nations of Indians the sum of sixteen thousand dollars, annually, forever, in specie: said sum to be paid at Chicago. And the said United States further agree to cause to be delivered to said nations of Indians, in the month of October next, twelve thousand dollars worth of goods as a present. And it is further agreed, to deliver to said Indians, at Chicago, fifty barrels of salt, annually, forever; and further, the United States agree to make permanent, for the use of the said Indians, the blacksmith's establishment at Chicago.

ARTICLE III.

Certain lands reserved.

From the cessions aforesaid, there shall be reserved, for the use of the undernamed Chiefs and their bands, the following tracts of land, viz:

For *Wau-pon-eh-see*, five sections of land at the Grand Bois, on Fox River of the Illinois, where *Shaytee's* Village now stands.

For *Shab-eh-nay*, two sections at his village near the Paw-paw Grove. For *Awn-kote*, four sections at the village of *Saw-meh-naug*, on the Fox River of the Illinois.

ARTICLE IV.

Certain tracts to be granted to certain descendants from the Indians.

There shall be granted by the United States, to each of the following persons, (being descendants from Indians,) the following tracts of land, viz: To Claude Laframboise, one section of land on the Riviere aux Pleins, adjoining the line of the purchase of 1816.

To François Bourbonné, Jr. one section at the Missionary establishment, on the Fox River of the Illinois. To Alexander Robinson, for himself and children, two sections on the Riviere aux Pleins, above and adjoining the tract herein granted to Claude Laframboise. To Pierre Leclerc, one section at the village of the As-sim-in-eh-Kon, or Paw-paw Grove. To Waish-kee-Shaw, a Potawatamie woman, wife of David Laughton, and to her child, one and a half sections at the old village of Nay-ou-Say, at or near the source of the Riviere aux Sables of the Illinois. To Billy Caldwell, two and a half sections on the Chicago River, above and adjoining the line of the purchase of 1816. To Victoire Pothier, one half section on the Chicago River, above and adjoining the tract of land herein granted to Billy Caldwell. To Jane Miranda, one quarter section on the Chicago River, above and adjoining the tract herein granted to Victoire Pothier. To Madeline, a Potawatamie woman, wife of Joseph Ogee, one section west of and adjoining the tract herein granted to Pierre Leclerc, at the Paw-paw Grove. To Archange Ouilmette, a Potawatamie woman, wife of Antoine Ouilmette, two sections, for herself and her children, on Lake Michigan, south of and adjoining the northern boundary of the cession herein made by the Indians aforesaid to the United States. To Antoine and François Leclerc, one section each, lying on the Mississippi River, north of and adjoining the line drawn due west from the most southern bend of Lake Michigan, where said line strikes the Mississippi River. To Mo-ah-way, one quarter section on the north side of and adjoining the tract herein granted to Waish-Kee-Shaw.

The tracts of land herein stipulated to be granted, shall never be leased or conveyed by the grantees, or their heirs, to any persons whatever, without the permission of the President of the United States.

ARTICLE V.

The United States, at the request of the Indians aforesaid, further agree to pay to the persons named in the schedule annexed to this treaty, the sum of eleven thousand six hundred and one dollars; which sum is in full satisfaction of the claims brought by said persons against said Indians, and by them acknowledged to be justly due.

United States to pay claims against Indians.

ARTICLE VI.

And it is further agreed, that the United [States] shall, at their own expense, cause to be surveyed, the northern boundary line of the cession herein made, from Lake Michigan to the Rock River, as soon as practicable after the ratification of this treaty, and shall also cause good and sufficient marks and mounds to be established on said line.

United States to survey boundary line of cession.

ARTICLE VII.

The right to hunt on the lands herein ceded, so long as the same shall remain the property of the United States, is hereby secured to the nations who are parties to this treaty.

Right to hunt reserved.

ARTICLE VIII.

This treaty shall take effect and be obligatory on the contracting parties, as soon as the same shall be ratified by the President of the United States, by and with the advice and consent of the Senate thereof.

Treaty binding when ratified.

In testimony whereof, the said John NcNiel, Pierre Menard, and Caleb Atwater, commissioners as aforesaid, and the chiefs and warriors of the said Chippewa, Ottawa, and Potawatamie nations, have hereunto set their hands and seals, at Prairie du Chein, as aforesaid, this twenty-ninth day of July, in the year of our Lord one thousand eight hundred and twenty-nine.

John McNiel, [L. S.]	Pooh-kin-eh-naw, his x mark, [L. S.]
Pierre Menard, [L. S.]	Waw-kay-zo, his x mark, [L. S.]
Caleb Atwater, [L. S.]	Sou-ka-mock, his x mark, [L. S.]
Commissioners.	Chee-chee-pin-quay, his x mark, [L. S.]
Sin-eh-pay-nim, his x mark, [L. S.]	Man-eh-bo-zo, his x mark, [L. S.]
Kawb-suk-we, his x mark, [L. S.]	Shah-way-ne-be-nay, his x mark, [L. S.]
Wau-pon-eh-see, his x mark, [L. S.]	Kaw-kee, his x mark, [L. S.]
Naw-geh-say, his x mark, [L. S.]	To-rum, his x mark, [L. S.]
Shaw-a-nay-see, his x mark, [L. S.]	Nah-yah-to-shuk, his x mark, [L. S.]
Naw-geh-to-nuk, his x mark, [L. S.]	Mee-chee-kee-wis, his x mark, [L. S.]
Meek-say-mauk, his x mark, [L. S.]	Es-kaw-bey-wis, his x mark, [L. S.]
Kaw-gaw-gay-shee, his x mark, [L. S.]	Wau-pay-kay, his x mark, [L. S.]
Maw-geh-set, his x mark, [L S.]	Michel, his x mark, [L. S.]
Meck-eh-so, his x mark, [L. S.]	Nee-kon-gum, his x mark, [L. S.]
Awn-kote, his x mark, [L. S.]	Mes-quaw-be-no-quay, her x mark, [L. S.]
Shuk-eh-nay-buk, his x mark, [L. S.]	Pe-i-tum, her x mark, [L. S.]
Sho-men, his x mark, [L. S.]	Kay-wau, her x mark, [L. S.]
Nay-a-mush, his x mark, [L. S.]	Wau-kaw-ou-say, her x mark, [L. S.]
Pat-eh-ko-zuk, his x mark, [L. S.]	Shem-naw, her x mark. [L. S.]
Mash-kak-suk, his x mark, [L. S.]	

In presence of—

Charles Hempstead, secretary to the commission,	Z. Taylor, Lieutenant-Colonel U. S. Army,
Alex. Wolcott, Indian agent,	John H. Kinzie, subagent Indian affairs,
Jos. M. Street, Indian agent,	R. B. Mason, captain, First Infantry,
Thomas Forsyth, Indian agent,	John Garland, major, U. S. Army,
	H. Dodge,

A. Hill,
Henry Gratiot,
Richard Gentry,
John Messersmith,
Wm. P. Smith,
C. Chouteau,
James Turney,

Jesse Benton, Jr.,
J. L. Bogardus,
Antoine Le Claire, Indian interpreter,
Jon. W. B. Mette, Indian interpreter,
Sogee,
John W. Johnson.

July 29, 1829.

7 Stat., 604.

Schedule of claims and debts to be paid by the United States for the Chippewa, Ottawa, and Pottawatamie Indians, under the fifth article of the treaty of the 29th July, 1829, with said tribe.

To Francis Laframboise, for a canoe-load of merchandise taken by the Chippewa and Ottowata Indians of Chab-way-way-gun and the neighboring villages, while frozen up in the lake in the winter of the year 1799, two thousand dollars	$2,000 00
To Antoine Ouilmett, for depredations committed on him by the Indians at the time of the massacre of Chicago and during the war, eight hundred dollars	800 00
To the heirs of the late John Kinzie, of Chicago, for depredations committed on him at the time of the massacre of Chicago and at St. Joseph's, during the winter of 1812, three thousand five hundred dollars	3,500 00
To Margaret Helm, for losses sustained at the time of the capture of Fort Dearborn, in 1812, by the Indians, eight hundred dollars	800 00
To the American Fur Company, for debts owed to them by the United Tribes of Chippewas, Ottowas, and Pottawatamies, three thousand dollars	3,000 00
To Bernardus Laughton, for debts owed to him by same tribes, ten hundred and sixteen dollars	1,016 00
To James Kinzie, for debts owed to him by same, four hundred and eighty-five dollars	485 00
	$11,601 00

TREATY WITH THE WINNEBAGO, 1829.

Aug. 1, 1829.

7 Stat., 323.
Proclamation, Jan. 2, 1830.

Articles of a treaty made and concluded at the Village of Prairie du Chien, Michigan Territory, on this first day of August, in the year one thousand eight hundred and twenty-nine, between the United States of America, by their Commissioners, General John M'Neil, Colonel Pierre Menard, and Caleb Atwater, Esq., for and on behalf of said States, of the one part, and the Nation of Winnebaygo Indians of the other part.

ARTICLE I.

Certain lands ceded to United States.

THE said Winnebaygo nation hereby, forever, cede and relinquish to the said United States, all their right, title, and claim, to the lands and country contained within the following limits and boundaries, to wit: beginning on Rock River, at the mouth of the *Pee-kee-tau-no* or *Pee-kee-tol-a-ka*, a branch thereof; thence, up the *Pee-kee-tol-a-ka*, to the mouth of Sugar Creek; thence, up the said creek, to the source of the Eastern branch thereof; thence, by a line running due North, to the road leading from the Eastern blue mound, by the most Northern of the four lakes, to the portage of the Wisconsin and Fox rivers; thence, along the said road, to the crossing of Duck Creek; thence, by a line running in a direct course to the most Southeasterly bend of Lake Puck-a-way, on Fox River; thence, up said Lake and Fox River, to the Portage of the Wisconsin; thence, across said portage, to the Wisconsin river; thence, down said river, to the Eastern line of the United States' reservation at the mouth of said river, on the south side thereof, as described in the second article of the treaty made at St. Louis, on the twenty-fourth day of August, in the year eighteen hundred and sixteen, with the Chippewas, Ottawas, and Potawatamies; thence, with the lines of a tract of country on the Mississippi river, (secured to the Chippewas, Ottawas, and Potawatamies, of the Illinois, by the ninth article of the treaty made at Prairie du Chien, on the nineteenth day of August, in the year eighteen hundred and twenty-five,) running Southwardly, passing the heads of the small streams emptying into the Mississippi to the Rock river, at the Winnebaygo village, forty miles above its mouth; thence, up Rock river, to the mouth of the *Pee-kee-tol-a-ka* river, the place of beginning.

ARTICLE II.

In consideration of the above cession, it is hereby stipulated, that the said United States shall pay to the said Winnebaygo nation of Indians the sum of eighteen thousand dollars in specie, annually, for the period of thirty years; which said sum is to be paid to said Indians at Prairie du Chien and Fort Winnebaygo, in proportion to the numbers residing within the most convenient distance of each place, respectively; and it is also agreed, that the said United States shall deliver immediately to said Indians, as a present, thirty thousand dollars in goods; and it is further agreed, that three thousand pounds of tobacco, and fifty barrels of salt, shall be annually delivered to the said Indians by the United States, for the period of thirty years; half of which articles shall be delivered at the Agency at Prairie du Chien, and the other half at the Agency of Fort Winnebaygo.

Consideration therefor.

ARTICLE III.

And it is further agreed between the parties, that the said United States shall provide and support three blacksmiths' shops, with the necessary tools, iron, and steel, for the use of the said Indians, for the term of thirty years; one at Prairie du Chien, one at Fort Winnebaygo, and one on the waters of Rock river; and furthermore, the said United States engage to furnish, for the use of the said Indians, two yoke of oxen, one cart, and the services of a man at the portage of the Wisconsin and Fox rivers, to continue at the pleasure of the Agent at that place, the term not to exceed thirty years.

United States to provide three blacksmiths' shops, etc.

ARTICLE IV.

The United States (at the request of the Indians aforesaid) further agree to pay to the persons named in the schedule annexed to this treaty, (and which forms part and parcel thereof,) the several sums as therein specified, amounting, in all, to the sum of twenty-three thousand five hundred and thirty-two dollars and twenty-eight cents; which sum is in full satisfaction of the claims brought by said persons against said Indians, and by them acknowledged to be justly due.

United States agree to pay certain claims against Winnebagoes.

ARTICLE V.

And it is further agreed, that, from the land hereinbefore ceded, there shall be granted by the United States to the persons herein named, (being descendants of said Indians,) the quantity of land as follows, to be located without the mineral country, under the direction of the President of the United States, that is to say: to Catherine Myott, two sections; to Mary, daughter of Catharine Myott, one section; to Michael St. Cyr, son of *Hee-no-kau*, (a Winnebaygo woman,) one section; to Mary, Ellen, and Brigitte, daughters of said *Hee-no-kau*, each one section; to Catherine and Olivier, children of Olivier Amelle, each one section; to François, Therese, and Joseph, children of Joseph Thibault, each one section; to Sophia, daughter of Joshua

United States to grant certain lands to descendants of Indians.

Palen, one section; to Pierre Pacquette, two sections; and to his two children, Therese and Moses, each one section; to Pierre Grignon L'Avoine, Amable, Margaret, Genevieve, and Mariette, children of said Pierre, each one section; to *Mauh-nah-tee-see*, (a Winnebaygo woman,) one section; and to her eight children, viz: Therese, Benjamin, James, Simeon, and Phelise Leciiyer, Julia and Antoine Grignon, and Alexis Peyet, each one section; to John Baptiste Pascal, Margaret, Angelique, Domitille, Therese, and Lisette, children of the late John Baptiste Pacquette, each one section; to Madeline Brisbois, daughter of the late Michel Brisbois, Jr. one section; to Therese Gagnier and her two children, François and Louise, two sections; to Mary, daughter of Luther Gleason, one section; and to Theodore Lupien, one section; all which aforesaid grants are not to be leased or sold by said grantees to any person or persons whatever, without the permission of the President of the United States; and it is further agreed, that the said United States shall pay to Therese Gagnier the sum of fifty dollars per annum, for fifteen years, to be deducted from the annuity to said Indians.

Annuity of $50 to Therese Gagnier.

ARTICLE VI. [Not ratified by Senate.]

ARTICLE VII.

Treaty binding when ratified.

This Treaty, after the same shall be ratified by the President of the United States, by and with the advice and consent of the Senate thereof, shall be obligatory on the contracting parties.

In testimony whereof, the said John McNiel, Pierre Menard, and Caleb Atwater, commissioners as aforesaid, and the chiefs and warriors of the said Winnebago nation of Indians, have hereunto set their hands and seals, at the time and place first herein above written.

John McNiel, [L. S.]	Koy-se-ray-kaw, his x mark, [L. S.]
Pierre Menard, [L. S.]	Nau-kaw-kary-maunie, wood, his
Caleb Atwater, [L. S.]	x mark, [L. S.]
Commissioners,	Hee-tshah-wau-shaip-soots-kau,
Hay-ray-tshon-sarp. black hawk,	red war eagle, his x mark, [L. S.]
his x mark, [L. S.]	Hee-tsha-wau-sharp-skaw-kau,
Tshay-o-skaw-tsho-kaw, who plays	white war eagle, his x mark, [L. S.]
with the ox, his x mark, [L. S.]	Tshu-o-nuzh-ee-kau, he who stands
Woank-shik-rootsh-kay, man	in the house, his x mark, [L. S.]
eater, his x mark, [L. S.]	Wau-kaun-hah-kaw, snake skin,
Kau-rah-kaw-see-kan, crow killer,	his x mark, [L. S.]
his x mark, [L. S.]	Hoo-wau-noo-kaw, little elk, his x
Maunk-shaw-ka, white breast, his	mark, [L. S.]
x mark, [L. S.]	Shoank-tshunk-saip-kau, black
Hah-pau-koo-see-kaw, his x mark, [L. S.]	wolf, his x mark, [L. S.]
Maun-kaw-kaw, earth, his x mark, [L. S.]	Kay-rah-tsho-kau, clear sky, his x
Ah-sheesh-kaw, broken arm, his x	mark, [L. S.]
mark, [L. S.]	Hee-tshaum-wau-kaw, wild cat, his
Waw-kaun-kaw, rattle snake, his x	x mark, [L. S.]
mark, [L. S.]	Hoo-tshoap-kau, four legs, Jr., his
Chey-skaw-kaw, white ox, his x	x mark, [L. S.]
mark, [L. S.]	Maunk-kay-ray-kau, crooked tail,
Nautch-kay-suck, the quick heart,	his x mark, [L. S.]
his x mark, [L. S.]	Wau-kaum-kaw, rattle snake, his
Wau-kaun-tshaw-way-kee-wen-	x mark, [L. S.]
kaw, whirling thunder, his x	Wau-tshee-roo-kun-o-kau, master
mark, [L. S.]	of the lodge, his x mark, [L. S.]
Thoap-nuzh-ee-kaw, four who	Menne-kam, the bear who
stand, his x mark, [L. S.]	scratches, his x mark, [L. S.]
Hay-nah-ah-ratsh-kay, left	Waun-kaun-tshaw-zee-kau, yellow
handed, his x mark, [L. S.]	thunder, his x mark, [L. S.]
Woan-knaw-hoap-ee-ne-kaw, big	Kay-ray-mau-nee, walking turtle,
medicine man, his x mark, [L. S.]	his x mark, [L. S.]
Pey-tshun-kaw, the crane, his x	Kaisn-kee-pay-kau, his x mark, [L. S.]
mark, [L. S.]	Ni-si-wau-roosh-kun, the bear, his
Jarot, or Jarrot, his x mark, [L. S.]	x mark, [L. S.]
Thay-hoo-kau-kaw, his x mark, [L. S.]	Kau-kau-saw-kaw, his x mark, [L. S.]

Maun-tsha-nig-ee-nig, little white
bear, his x mark, [L. S.]
Wau-kaun-tsha-nee-kau, deaf thunder, his x mark, [L. S.]
Chah-wau-saip-kau, black eagle,
his x mark, [L. S.]

Saun-tshah-mau-nee, his x mark, [L. S.]
Maunee-hat-a-kau, big walker, his
x mark, [L. S.]
Kaish-kee-pay-kau, his x mark, [L. S.]

In presence of—

Charles S. Hempstead, secretary to the
commission,
Joseph M. Street, Indian agent,
Thomas Forsyth, Indian agent,
Alex. Wolcott, Indian agent,
John H. Kenzie, subagent Indian affairs,
Z. Taylor, lieutenant-colonel, U. S. Army,
H. Dodge,
A. Hill,
Henry Gratiot,
Wm. Beaumont, surgeon, U. S. Army,
G. W. Garey,
Richard Gentry,
James Turner,
Richard H. Bell,
John W. Johnson,
Wm. M. Read,
G. H. Kennerly,
R. Holmes, U. S. Army,
John Dallam,
J. R. B. Gardenier, lieutenant, U. S. In-
fantry,

Charles Chouteau,
John Messersmith,
John L. Chastain,
Wm. D. Smith,
Charles K. Henshaw,
James B. Estis,
Jesse Benton, Jr.,
Jacob Hambleton,
John Quaill,
John Garland,
Henry Crossle,
J. L. Bogardus,
B. B. Kercheval,
Luther Gleason,
Pierre Paquet, his x mark, Winnebago
interpreter,
J. Palen,
Jacques Mette,
Antoine Le Claire,
Joge,
M. Brisbois.

TREATY WITH THE DELAWARES, 1829.

Articles of agreement made between John M'Elvain, thereto specially authorized by the President of the United States, and the band of Delaware Indians, upon the Sandusky River, in the State of Ohio, for the cession of a certain reservation of land in the said State.

Aug. 3, 1829.

7 Stat., 326.
Proclamation, Jan. 2, 1830.

ARTICLE I.

THE said band of Delaware Indians cede to the United States the tract of three miles square, adjoining the Wyandot reservation upon the Sandusky river, reserved for their use by the treaty of the Rapids of the Maumee, concluded between the United States and the Wyandots, Seneca, Delaware, Shawnees, Potawatamies, Ottawas, and Chippiwa tribes of Indians, on the twenty-ninth day of September, in the year of our Lord one thousand eight hundred and seventeen, and the said tribe of Delawares engage to remove to and join their nation on the west side of the Mississippi, on the land allotted to them, on or before the first day of January next, at which time peaceable possession of said reservation is to be given to the United States.

Certain land ceded to United States.

ARTICLE II.

In consideration of the stipulations aforesaid, it is agreed, that the United States shall pay to the said band the sum of three thousand dollars: two thousand dollars in hand, the receipt of which is hereby acknowledged by the undersigned Chiefs of said tribe, and the remaining balance of one thousand dollars to be appropriated to the purchase of horses, clothing, provisions, and other useful articles, to aid them on their journey so soon as they are prepared to remove.

In witness whereof, the said John McElvain, and the chiefs of the said band, have hereunto set their hands and seals at Little Sandusky,

Consideration therefor.

in the State of Ohio, this third day of August, in the year of our Lord one thousand eight hundred and twenty-nine.

John McElvain,	[L. S.]
Captain Pipe, his x mark,	[L. S.]
William Matacur, his x mark,	[L. S.]
Captain Wolf, his x mark,	[L. S.]
Eli Pipe, his x mark,	[L. S.]
Solomon Joneycake, his x mark,	[L. S.]
Joseph Armstrong, his x mark,	[L. S.]
George Williams, his x mark,	[L. S.]

In presence of—
    Nathaniel McLean,
    Cornelius Wilson,
    H. Barrett.

TREATY WITH THE DELAWARES, 1829.

Sept. 24, 1829.

7 Stat., 327.
Proclamation, Mar.
24, 1831.

Supplementary article to the Delaware Treaty, concluded at St. Mary's in the State of Ohio, on the 3d of October, 1818.

WHEREAS the foregoing Treaty stipulates that the United States shall provide for the Delaware Nation, a country to reside in, West of the Mississippi, as the permanent residence of their Nation; and whereas the said Delaware Nation, are now willing to remove, on the following conditions, from the country on James' fork of White river in the State of Missouri, to the Country selected in the fork of the Kansas and Missouri River, as recommended by the government, for the permanent residence of the whole Delaware Nation; it is hereby agreed upon by the parties, that the country in the fork of the Kansas and Missouri Rivers, extending up the Kansas River, to the Kansas Line, and up the Missouri River to Camp Leavenworth, and thence by a line drawn Westwardly, leaving a space ten miles wide, north of the Kansas boundary line, for an outlet; shall be conveyed and forever secured by the United States, to the said Delaware Nation, as their permanent residence: And the United States hereby pledges the faith of the government to guarantee to the said Delaware Nation forever, the quiet and peaceable possession and undisturbed enjoyment of the same, against the claims and assaults of all and every other people whatever.

Horses, wagons, etc., to be furnished for Delawares.

And the United States hereby agrees to furnish the Delaware Nation with forty horses, to be given to their poor and destitute people, and the use of six wagons and ox-teams, to assist the nation in removing their heavy articles to their permanent home; and to supply them with all necessary farming utensils and tools necessary for building houses, &c: and to supply them with provisions on their journey, and with one year's provisions after they get to their permanent residence; and to have a grist and saw mill erected for their use, within two years after their complete removal.

Additional permanent annuity.

And it is hereby expressly stipulated and agreed upon by the parties, that for and in consideration of the full and entire relinquishment by the Delaware Nation of all claim whatever to the country now occupied by them in the State of Missouri, the United States shall pay to the said Delaware Nation, an additional permanent annuity of one thousand dollars.

Reservation of land for school purposes.

And it is further stipulated that thirty-six sections of the best land within the limits hereby relinquished, shall be selected under the direction of the President of the United States, and sold for the purpose of raising a fund, to be applied under the direction of the President, to the support of schools for the education of Delaware children.

Country to be explored, etc.

It is agreed upon by the parties that this supplementary article shall be concluded in part only, at this time, and that a deputation of a Chief, or Warrior, from each town with their Interpretor shall proceed with the Agent to explore the country more fully, and if they approve of said country, to sign their names under ours, which shall be considered as finally concluded on our part; and after the same shall be ratified by the President and Senate of the United States, shall be binding on the contracting parties.

In testimony whereof the United States Indian agent, and the chiefs and warriors of the Delaware nation of Indians, have hereunto set their hands at Council camp, on James's fork of White river, in the State of Missouri, this 24th day of September, in the year of our Lord one thousand eight hundred and twenty-nine.

Geo. Vashon, United States Indian agent,	John Gray, his x mark,
Wm. Anderson, principal chief, his x mark,	George Guirty, his x mark,
	Capt. Beaver, his x mark,
Capt. Paterson, 2nd chief, his x mark,	Naunotetauxien, his x mark,
Pooshies, or the cat, his x mark,	Little Jack, his x mark,
Capt. Suwaunock, whiteman, his x mark,	Capt. Pipe, his x mark,
Jonny Quick, his x mark,	Big Island, his x mark.

Signed in presence of—
James Connor, Delaware interpreter.
Anth'y Shane, Shawanee interpreter.

These last six chiefs and warriors having been deputed to examine the country, have approved of it, and signed their names at Council camp in the fork of the Kansas and Missouri river, on the 19th October, 1829.

Nauochecaupauc, his x mark.
Nungailautone, his x mark,
James Gray, his x mark.
Sam Street, his x mark,
Aupaneek, his x mark,
Outhteekawshaweat, his x mark.

In presence of—
Anth'y Shane, interpreter,
James Conner, interpreter,
Baptiste Peoria, interpreter.

I hereby certify the above to be a true copy from the original in my possession,

Geo. Vashon,
United States Indian agent.

Indian agency, near Kansas river, 24th October, 1829.

TREATY WITH THE SAUK AND FOXES, ETC., 1830.

July 15, 1830.

7 Stat., 328.
Proclamation, Feb. 24, 1831.

Articles of a treaty made and concluded by William Clark Superintendent of Indian Affairs and Willoughby Morgan, Col. of the United States 1st Regt. Infantry, Commissioners on behalf of the United States on the one part, and the undersigned Deputations of the Confederated Tribes of the Sacs and Foxes; the Medawah-Kanton, Wahpacoota, Wahpeton and Sissetong Bands or Tribes of Sioux; the Omahas, Ioways, Ottoes and Missourias on the other part.

THE said Tribes being anxious to remove all causes which may hereafter create any unfriendly feeling between them, and being also anxious to provide other sources for supplying their wants besides those of hunting, which they are sensible must soon entirely fail them; agree with the United States on the following Articles.

Cession of lands.

ARTICLE I. The said Tribes cede and relinquish to the United States forever all their right and title to the lands lying within the following boundaries, to wit: Beginning at the upper fork of the Demoine River, and passing the sources of the Little Sioux, and Floyds Rivers, to the fork of the first creek which falls into the Big Sioux or Calumet on the east side; thence, down said creek, and Calumet River to the Missouri River; thence down said Missouri River to the Missouri State line, above the Kansas; thence along said line to the north west corner of the said State, thence to the high lands between the waters falling into the Missouri and Desmoines, passing to said high lands along the dividing ridge between the forks of the Grand River; thence along said high lands or ridge separating the waters of the Missouri from those of the Demoine, to a point opposite the source of Boyer River, and thence in a direct line to the upper fork of the Demoine, the place of beginning.

Purposes to which the lands are to be applied.

But it is understood that the lands ceded and relinquished by this Treaty, are to be assigned and allotted under the direction of the President of the United States, to the Tribes now living thereon, or to such other Tribes as the President may locate thereon for hunting, and other purposes.

Cession by the Sacs and Foxes.

ARTICLE II. The confederated Tribes of the Sacs and Foxes, cede and relinquish to the United States forever, a tract of Country twenty miles in width, from the Mississippi to the Demoine; situate south, and adjoining the line between the said confederated Tribes of Sacs and Foxes, and the Sioux; as established by the second article of the Treaty of Prairie du Chien of the nineteenth of August one thousand eight hundred and twenty-five.

Cession by the Medawah-Kanton, etc.

ARTICLE III. The Medawah-Kanton, Wah-pa-coota, Wahpeton and Sisseton Bands of the Sioux cede and relinquish to the United States forever, a Tract of Country twenty miles in width, from the Mississippi to the Demoine River, situate north, and adjoining the line mentioned in the preceding article.

Consideration.

ARTICLE IV. In consideration of the cessions and relinquishments made in the first, second, and third articles of this Treaty, the United States agree to pay to the Sacs, three thousand dollars,—and to the Foxes three thousand dollars; To the Sioux of the Mississippi two thousand dollars;—To the Yancton and Santie Bands of Sioux three thousand dollars;—To the Omahas, two thousand five hundred dollars;—To the Ioways two thousand five hundred dollars;—To the Ottoes and Missourias two thousand five hundred dollars, and to the Sacs of the Missouri River five hundred dollars; to be paid annually for ten successive years at such place, or places on the Mississippi or Missouri, as may be most convenient to said Tribes, either in money, merchandise, or domestic animals, at their option; and when said annuities or any portion of them shall be paid in merchandise, the same is to be delivered to them at the first cost of the goods at St. Louis free of transportation.

Annuities.

Further allowances.

And the United States further agree to make to the said Tribes and Bands, the following allowances for the period of ten years, and as long thereafter as the President of the United States may think necessary and proper, in addition to the sums herein before stipulated to be paid them; that is to say; To the Bands of the Sioux mentioned in the third article, one Blacksmith at the expense of the United States, and the necessary tools; also instruments for agricultural purposes, and iron and steel to the amount of seven hundred dollars;—To the Yancton and Santie Bands of Sioux, one Blacksmith at the expense of the United States, and the necessary tools, also instruments for agricultural purposes to the amount of four hundred dollars; To the Omahas one Blacksmith at the expense of the United States, and the necessary tools, also instruments for agricultural purposes to the amount of five hundred dollars;—To the Ioways an assistant Blacksmith at the expense of the United States, also instruments for agricultural purposes to the amount of six hundred dollars; To the Ottoes and Missourias one Blacksmith at the expense of the United States, and the necessary tools, also instruments for agricultural purposes to the amount of five hundred dollars; and to the Sacs of the Missouri River, one Blacksmith at the expense of the United States and the necessary tools; also instruments for agricultural purposes to the amount of two hundred dollars.

ARTICLE V. And the United States further agree to set apart three thousand dollars annually for ten successive years, to be applied in the discretion of the President of the United States, to the education of the children of the said Tribes and Bands, parties hereto. *Annuity for education.*

ARTICLE VI. The Yanckton and Santie Bands of the Sioux not being fully represented, it is agreed, that if they shall sign this Treaty, they shall be considered as parties thereto, and bound by all its stipulations. *Yanckton and Santie bands.*

ARTICLE VII. It is agreed between the parties hereto, that the lines shall be run, and marked as soon as the President of the United States may deem it expedient. *Lines to be run.*

ART. VIII. The United States agree to distribute between the several Tribes, parties hereto, five thousand, one hundred and thirty-two dollars worth of merchandise, the receipt whereof, the said Tribes hereby acknowledge; which, together with the amounts agreed to be paid, and the allowances in the fourth and fifth articles of this Treaty, shall be considered as a full compensation for the cession and relinquishments herein made. *Earnest.*

ARTICLE IX. The Sioux Bands in Council having earnestly solicited that they might have permission to bestow upon the half-breeds of their Nation, the tract of land within the following limits, to wit: Beginning at a place called the barn, below and near the village of the Red Wing Chief, and running back fifteen miles; thence in a parallel line with Lake Pepin and the Mississippi, about thirty-two miles to a point opposite Beef or O-Boeuf River; thence fifteen miles to the Grand Encampment opposite the River aforesaid; The United States agree to suffer said half Breeds to occupy said tract of country; they holding by the same title, and in the same manner that other Indian Titles are held. *Reservation for Sioux half-breeds.*

ARTICLE X. The Omahas, Ioways and Ottoes, for themselves, and in behalf of the Yanckton and Santie Bands of Sioux, having earnestly requested that they might be permitted to make some provision for their half-breeds, and particularly that they might bestow upon them the tract of country within the following limits, to wit; Beginning at the mouth of the Little Ne-mohaw River, and running up the main channel of said River to a point which will be ten miles from its mouth in a direct line; from thence in a direct line, to strike the Grand Ne-mohaw ten miles above its mouth, in a direct line (the distance between the two Ne-mohaws being about twenty miles)—thence down said River to its mouth; thence up, and with the Meanders of the Missouri River to the point of beginning, it is agreed that the half-breeds of said Tribes and Bands may be suffered to occupy said tract of land; holding it in the same manner, and by the same title that other Indian titles are held; but the President of the United States may hereafter assign to any of the said half-breeds, to be held by him or them in fee simple, any portion of said tract not exceeding a section, of six hundred and forty acres to each individual. And this provision shall extend to the cession made by the Sioux in the preceding Article. *Reservation for other half-breeds.*

ARTICLE XI. The reservation of land mentioned in the preceding Article having belonged to the Ottoes, and having been exclusively ceded by them; it is agreed that the Omahas, the Ioways and the Yanckton and Santie Bands of Sioux shall pay out of their annuities *Annuity to Ottoes from Omahas, etc.*

to the said Ottoe Tribe, for the period of ten years, Three hundred Dollars annually; of which sum the Omahas shall pay one hundred Dollars, the Ioways one hundred Dollars, and the Yanckton and Santie Bands one hundred dollars.

Saving of rights of the tribes.

ARTICLE XII. It is agreed that nothing contained in the foregoing Articles shall be so construed as to affect any claim, or right in common, which has heretofore been held by any Tribes, parties to this Treaty, to any lands not embraced in the cession herein made; but that the same shall be occupied and held by them as heretofore.

Treaty binding when ratified.

ARTICLE XIII. This Treaty, or any part thereof, shall take effect, and be obligatory upon the Contracting parties, so soon as the same shall be ratified by the President of the United States, by and with the advice and consent of the Senate thereof.

Done, and signed, and sealed at Prairie du Chien, in the Territory of Michigan, this fifteenth day of July, in the year of our Lord one thousand eight hundred and thirty, and of the independence of the United States, the fifty-fifth.

Wm. Clark, superintendent Indian affairs, [L. S.]
Willoughby Morgan, colonel First Infantry U. S. Army, [L. S.]
          commissioners.

Sacs:
Mash-que-tai-paw, or red head, his x mark, [L. S.]
Sheco-Calawko, or turtle shell, his x mark [L. S.]
Kee-o-cuck, the watchful fox, his x mark, [L. S.]
Poi-o-tahit, one that has no heart, his x mark, [L. S.]
Os-hays-kee, ridge, his x mark, [L. S.]
She-shee-quanince, little gourd, his x mark [L. S.]
O-saw-wish-canoe, yellow bird, his x mark, [L. S.]
I-onin, his x mark, [L. S.]
Am-oway, his x mark, [L. S.]
Niniwow-qua-saut, he that fears mankind, his x mark, [L. S.]
Chaukee Manitou, the little spirit, his x mark, [L. S.]
Moso-inn, the scalp, his x mark, [L. S.]
Wapaw-chicannuck, fish of the white marsh, his x mark, [L. S.]
Mesico, jic, his x mark, [L. S.]

Foxes:
Wapalaw, the prince, his x mark, [L. S.]
Taweemin, strawberry, his x mark, [L. S.]
Pasha-sakay, son of Piemanschie, his x mark, [L. S.]
Keewausette, he who climbs everywhere, his x mark, [L. S.]
Naw-mee, his x mark, [L. S.]
Appenioce, or the grand child, his x mark, [L. S.]
Waytee-mins, his x mark, [L. S.]
Nawayaw-cosi, his x mark, [L. S.]
Manquo-pwam, the bear's hip, (Morgan,) his x mark, [L. S.]
Kaw-Kaw-Kee, the crow, his x mark, [L. S.]
Mawcawtay-ee-quoiquenake, black neck, his x mark, [L. S.]
Watu-pawnonsh, his x mark, [L. S.]
Meshaw-nuaw-peetay, the large teeth, his x mark, [L. S.]
Cawkee-Kamack, always fish, his x mark, [L. S.]
Mussaw-wawquott, his x mark, [L. S.]

Sioux of the Mississippi, Medawakanton band:
Wabishaw, or red leaf, his x mark, [L. S.]
Tchataqua Manie, or little crow, his x mark, [L. S.]
Waumunde-tunkar, the great calumet eagle, his x mark, [L. S.]
Taco-coqui-pishnee, he that fears nothing, his x mark, [L. S.]
Wah-coo-ta, that shoots arrows, his x mark, [L. S.]
Pay-taw-whar, the fire owner, his x mark, [L. S.]
Kaugh-Mohr, the floating log, his x mark, [L. S.]
Etarz-e-pah, the bow, his x mark, [L. S.]
Teeah-coota, one that fires at the yellow, his x mark, [L. S.]
Toh-kiah-taw-kaw, he who bites the enemy, his x mark, [L. S.]
Nasiumpah, or the early riser, his x mark, [L. S.]
Am-pa-ta-tah-wah, his day, his x mark, [L. S.]
Wah-kee-ah-tunkar, big thunder, his x mark, [L. S.]
Tauchaw-cadoota, the red road, his x mark, [L. S.]
Tchaws-kesky, the elder, his x mark, [L. S.]
Mauzau-hautau, the grey iron, his x mark, [L. S.]
Wazee-o-monie, the walking pine, his x mark, [L. S.]
Tachaw-cooash-tay, the good road, his x mark, [L. S.]
Kie-ank-kaw, the mountain, his x mark, [L. S.]
Mah-peau-mansaw, iron cloud, his x mark, [L. S.]
E-taych-o-caw, half face, his x mark, [L. S.]
Anoug-genaje, one that stands on both sides, his x mark, [L. S.]
Hough-appaw, the eagle head, his x mark, [L. S.]
Hooka-mooza, the iron limb, his x mark, [L. S.]
Hoatch-ah-cadoota, the red voice, his x mark, [L. S.]
Wat-chu-da, the dancer. [L. S.]

Wah-pah-coota band:
Wiarh-hoh-ha, french crow, his x mark, [L. s.]
Shans-konar, moving shadow, his x mark, [L. s.]
Ah-pe-hatar, the grey mane, his x mark, [L. s.]
Wahmedecaw-cahn-bohr, one that prays for the land, his x mark, [L. s.]
Wah-con-de-kah-har, the one that makes the lightning, his x mark, [L. s.]
Mazo-manie, or the iron that walks, his x mark, [L. s.]
Mah-kah-ke-a-munch, one that flies on the land, his x mark, [L. s]
Mauzau-haut-amundee, the walking bell, his x mark, [L. s.]
Kah-hih, the Menominie, his x mark. [L. s.]
Sussiton band:
Ete-tahken-bah, the sleeping eyes, his x mark, [L. s.]
Ho-toh-monie, groans when he walks, his x mark. [L. s.]
Omahahs:
Opau-tauga, or the big elk, his x mark, [L. s.]
Chonques-kaw, the white horse, his x mark, [L. s.]
Tessan, the white crow, his x mark, [L. s.]
Ishtan-mauzay, iron-eye, chief's son, his x mark, [L. s.]
Waw-shin-ga-sau-bais, black bird, his x mark, [L. s.]
Waugh-pay-shan, the one who scalps but a small part from the crown of the head, his x mark, [L. s.]
Au-gum-an, the chief, his x mark, [L. s.]
Age-en-gaw, the wing, his x mark, [L. s.]
Non-bau-manie, the one that walks double, his x mark, [L. s.]
Way-cosh-ton, the frequent feast giver, his x mark, [L. s.]
Eh-que-naus-hus-kay, the second, his x mark, [L. s.]
Iosey, (the son of Kawsay,) his x mark. [L. s.]
Ioways:
Wassau-nie, or the medicine club, his x mark, [L. s.]
Mauhoos Kan, white cloud, his x mark, [L. s.]
Wo-hoompee, the broth, his x mark, [L. s.]
Tah-roh-na, a good many deer, his x mark, [L. s.]
Wa-nau-quash-coonie, without fear, his x mark, [L. s.]

Pah-a-manie, one who walks on the snow, his x mark, [L. s.]
Pie-kan-ha-igne, the little star, his x mark, [L. s.]
Niayoo Manie, walking rain, his x mark, [L. s.]
Nautah-hoo, burnt-wood, his x mark, [L. s.]
Pai-tansa, the white crane, his x mark. [L. s.]
Ottoes:
I-atan, or Shaumanie-Cassan, or prairie wolf, his x mark, [L. s.]
Mehah-hun-jee, second daughter, his x mark, [L. s.]
Wawronesan, the encircler, his x mark, [L. s.]
Kansa-tauga, the big Kansas, his x mark, [L. s.]
Noe-kee-sa-kay, strikes two, his x mark, [L. s.]
Tchai-au-grai, the shield, his x mark, [L. s.]
Mantoigne, the little bow, his x mark, [L. s.]
Thee-rai-tchai-neehgrai, wolf-tail at the heel, his x mark, [L. s.]
Oh-haw-kee-wano, that runs on the hills, his x mark, [L. s.]
Rai-grai-a, speckled turtle, his x mark, [L. s.]
Tchai-wah-tchee-ray, going by, his x mark, [L. s.]
Krai-taunica, the hawk, his x mark, [L. s.]
Mauto-a Kee-pah, that meets the bear, his x mark, [L. s.]
Kai-wan-igne, little turtle, his x mark. [L. s.]
Missourias:
Eh-shaw-manie, or the one who walks laughing, his x mark, [L. s.]
Ohaw-tchee-ke-sakay, one who strikes the Little Osages, his x mark, [L. s.]
Wamshe-katou-nat, the great man, his x mark, [L. s.]
Shoug-resh-kay, the horse fly, his x mark, [L. s.]
Tahmegrai-Soo-igne, little deer's dung, his x mark, [L. s.]
Missouri Sacs:
Sau-kis-quoi-pee, his x mark, [L. s.]
She-she-quene, the gourd, his x mark, [L. s.]
Nochewai-tasay, his x mark, [L. s.]
Mash-quaw-siais, his x mark, [L. s.]
Nawai-yak-oosee, his x mark, [L. s.]
Wee-tay-main, one that goes with the rest, his x mark, [L. s.]

The assent of the Yancton and Santie Bands of Sioux, to the foregoing treaty is given. In testimony whereof, the chiefs, braves, and principal men of said bands have hereunto signed their names and acknowledge the same, at St. Louis, this 13th October, 1830.

Yancton and Santie Bands of Siouxs:
Matto-Sa-Becha, the black bear, his x mark, [L. s.]
Pa-con-okra, his x mark, [L. s.]
Citta-eutapishma, he who dont eat buffalo, his x mark, [L. s.]
To-ki-e-ton, the stone with horns, his x mark, [L. s.]

Cha-pon-ka, or mosquitoe, his x mark, [L. s.]
To-ki-mar-ne, he that walks ahead, his x mark, [L. s.]
Wock-ta-ken-dee, kills and comes back, his x mark, [L. s.]
Ha Sazza, his x mark, [L. s.]
Chigga Wah-shu-she, little brave, his x mark, [L. s.]

Wah-gho-num-pa, cotton wood on the neck, his x mark, [L. S.]
Zuyesaw, warrior, his x mark, [L. S.]
Tokun Ohomenee, revolving stone, his x mark, [L. S.]
Eta-ga-nush-kica, mad face, his x mark, [L. S.]
Womendee Dooter, red war eagle, his x mark, [L. S.]
Mucpea A-har-ka, cloud elk, his x mark, [L. S.]
To-ka-oh, wounds the enemy, his x mark, [L. S.]
Pd-ta-sun eta womper, white buffalo with two faces, his x mark, [L. S.]

Cha-tun-kia, sparrow hawk, his x mark, [L. S.]
Ke-un-chun-ko, swift flyer, his x mark, [L. S.]
Ti-ha-uhar, he that carries his horn, his x mark, [L. S.]
Sin-ta-nomper, two tails, his x mark, [L. S.]
Wo-con Cashtaka, the whipt spirit, his x mark, [L. S.]
Ta Shena Pater, fiery blanket, his x mark, [L. S.]

In presence of—

Jno. Ruland, secretary to the commission.
Jon. L. Bean, special agent,
Law Taliaferro, Indian agent at St. Peters,
R. B. Mason, captain, First Infantry,
G. Loomis, captain, First Infantry,
James Peterson, lieutenant and adjutant, H. B. M., Thirty-third Regiment,
N. S. Harris, lieutenant and adjutant, regiment, U. S. Infantry,
Henry Bainbridge, lieutenant, U. S. Army,
John Gale, surgeon, U. S. Army,
J. Archer, lieutenant, U. S. Army,
J. Dougherty, Indian agent,
Thos. A. Davies, lieutenant, infantry,
Wm. S. Williamson, sub-Indian agent,
And. S. Hughes, sub-Indian agent,
A. G. Baldwin, lieutenant, Third Infantry,

David D. Mitchell,
H. L. Donsman,
Wynkoop Warner,
Geo. Davenport,
Wm. Hempstead,
Benjamin Mills,
Wm. H. Warfield, lieutenant, Third Infantry,
Sam. R. Throokmoor,
John Connelly,
Amos Farror,
Antoine Le Claire, interpreter of Sacs and Foxes,
Stephen Julian, United States interpreter,
Jacques Mette, interpreter,
Michel Berda, his x mark, Mohow interpreter,
S. Campbell, United States interpreter.

Witnesses to the signatures of the Yancton and Santie bands of Sioux, at Fort Tecumseh, Upper Missouri, on the fourth day of September, 1830:

Wm. Gordon,
James Archdale Hamilton,
David D. Mitchell,
Wm. Saidlau,
Jacob Halsey.

Witnesses present at the signing and acknowledgment of the Yancton and Santie Deputations:

Jno. Ruland, secretary to Commissioners.
Jon. L. Bean, sub-Indian agent for Upper Missouri,
Felix F. Wain, Indian agent for Sacs and Foxes,
John F. A. Sanford, United States Indian agent.

William C. Heyward, U. S. Army,
D. J. Royster, U. S. Infantry,
Samuel Kinney, U. S. Army,
Merewether Lewis Clark, Sixth Regiment Infantry,
Jacques Mette.

TREATY WITH THE CHOCTAW, 1830.

Sept. 27, 1830.

7 Stat., 333.
Proclamation, Feb. 24, 1831.

A treaty of perpetual friendship, cession and limits, entered into by John H. Eaton and John Coffee, for and in behalf of the Government of the United States, and the Mingoes, Chiefs, Captains and Warriors of the Choctaw Nation, begun and held at Dancing Rabbit Creek, on the fifteenth of September, in the year eighteen hundred and thirty.

WHEREAS the General Assembly of the State of Mississippi has extended the laws of said State to persons and property within the chartered limits of the same, and the President of the United States has said that he cannot protect the Choctaw people from the operation of these laws; Now therefore that the Choctaw may live under their own laws in peace with the United States and the State of Mississippi they have determined to sell their lands east of the Mississippi and have accordingly agreed to the following articles of treaty:[a]

ARTICLE I. Perpetual peace and friendship is pledged and agreed upon by and between the United States and the Mingoes, Chiefs, and Warriors of the Choctaw Nation of Red People; and that this may be considered the Treaty existing between the parties all other Treaties heretofore existing and inconsistent with the provisions of this are hereby declared null and void.

Peace and friendship.

ARTICLE II. The United States under a grant specially to be made by the President of the U. S. shall cause to be conveyed to the Choctaw Nation a tract of country west of the Mississippi River, in fee simple to them and their descendants, to inure to them while they shall exist as a nation and live on it, beginning near Fort Smith where the Arkansas boundary crosses the Arkansas River, running thence to the source of the Canadian fork; if in the limits of the United States, or to those limits; thence due south to Red River, and down Red River to the west boundary of the Territory of Arkansas; thence north along that line to the beginning. The boundary of the same to be agreeably to the Treaty made and concluded at Washington City in the year 1825. The grant to be executed so soon as the present Treaty shall be ratified.

Country to be conveyed to Choctaws.

ARTICLE III. In consideration of the provisions contained in the several articles of this Treaty, the Choctaw nation of Indians consent and hereby cede to the United States, the entire country they own and possess, east of the Mississippi River; and they agree to move beyond the Mississippi River, early as practicable, and will so arrange their removal, that as many as possible of their people not exceeding one half of the whole number, shall depart during the falls of 1831 and 1832; the residue to follow during the succeeding fall of 1833; a better opportunity in this manner will be afforded the Government, to extend to them the facilities and comforts which it is desirable should be extended in conveying them to their new homes.

Country ceded to United States.

ARTICLE IV. The Government and people of the United States are hereby obliged to secure to the said Choctaw Nation of Red People the jurisdiction and government of all the persons and property that may be within their limits west, so that no Territory or State shall ever have a right to pass laws for the government of the Choctaw Nation of Red People and their descendants; and that no part of the land granted them shall ever be embraced in any Territory or State; but the U. S. shall forever secure said Choctaw Nation from, and against, all laws except such as from time to time may be enacted in their own National Councils, not inconsistent with the Constitution, Treaties, and Laws of the United States; and except such as may, and which have been enacted by Congress, to the extent that Congress under the Constitution are required to exercise a legislation over Indian Affairs. But the Choctaws, should this treaty be ratified, express a wish that Congress may grant to the Choctaws the right of punishing by their own laws, any white man who shall come into their nation, and infringe any of their national regulations.

Self-government secured to Choctaws.

ARTICLE V. The United States are obliged to protect the Choctaws from domestic strife and from foreign enemies on the same principles that the citizens of the United States are protected, so that whatever would be a legal demand upon the U. S. for defence or for wrongs committed by an enemy, on a citizen of the U. S. shall be equally binding in favor of the Choctaws, and in all cases where the Choctaws shall be called upon by a legally authorized officer of the U. S. to fight an enemy, such Choctaw shall receive the pay and other emoluments,

United States to protect Choctaws, etc,

---

[a] This paragraph was not ratified.

which citizens of the U. S. receive in such cases, provided, no war shall be undertaken or prosecuted by said Choctaw Nation but by declaration made in full Council, and to be approved by the U. S. unless it be in self defence against an open rebellion or against an enemy marching into their country, in which cases they shall defend, until the U. S. are advised thereof.

Offences against citizens of United States, etc.

ARTICLE VI. Should a Choctaw or any party of Choctaws commit acts of violence upon the person or property of a citizen of the U. S. or join any war party against any neighbouring tribe of Indians, without the authority in the preceding article; and except to oppose an actual or threatened invasion or rebellion, such person so offending shall be delivered up to an officer of the U. S. if in the power of the Choctaw Nation, that such offender may be punished as may be provided in such cases, by the laws of the U. S.; but if such offender is not within the control of the Choctaw Nation, then said Choctaw Nation shall not be held responsible for the injury done by said offender.

Offences against Choctaws.

ARTICLE VII. All acts of violence committed upon persons and property of the people of the Choctaw Nation either by citizens of the U. S. or neighbouring Tribes of Red People, shall be referred to some authorized Agent by him to be referred to the President of the U. S. who shall examine into such cases and see that every possible degree of justice is done to said Indian party of the Choctaw Nation.

Delivery of offenders.

ARTICLE VIII. Offenders against the laws of the U. S. or any individual State shall be apprehended and delivered to any duly authorized person where such offender may be found in the Choctaw country, having fled from any part of U. S. but in all such cases application must be made to the Agent or Chiefs and the expense of his apprehension and delivery provided for and paid by the U. States.

Persons ordered from the nation, etc.

ARTICLE IX. Any citizen of the U. S. who may be ordered from the Nation by the Agent and constituted authorities of the Nation and refusing to obey or return into the Nation without the consent of the aforesaid persons, shall be subject to such pains and penalties as may be provided by the laws of the U. S. in such cases. Citizens of the U. S. travelling peaceably under the authority of the laws of the U. S. shall be under the care and protection of the nation.

Traders to require a written permit.

ARTICLE X. No person shall expose goods or other article for sale as a trader, without a written permit from the constituted authorities of the Nation, or authority of the laws of the Congress of the U. S. under penalty of forfeiting the Articles, and the constituted authorities of the Nation shall grant no license except to such persons as reside in the Nation and are answerable to the laws of the Nation. The U. S. shall be particularly obliged to assist to prevent ardent spirits from being introduced into the Nation.

Navigable streams, post-offices, and military posts.

ARTICLE XI. Navigable streams shall be free to the Choctaws who shall pay no higher toll or duty than citizens of the U. S. It is agreed further that the U. S. shall establish one or more Post Offices in said Nation, and may establish such military post roads, and posts, as they may consider necessary.

Intruders.

ARTICLE XII. All intruders shall be removed from the Choctaw Nation and kept without it. Private property to be always respected and on no occasion taken for public purposes without just compensation being made therefor to the rightful owner. If an Indian unlawfully take or steal any property from a white man a citizen of the U. S. the offender shall be punished. And if a white man unlawfully take or steal any thing from an Indian, the property shall be restored and the offender punished. It is further agreed that when a Choctaw shall be given up to be tried for any offence against the laws of the U. S. if unable to employ counsel to defend him, the U. S. will do it, that his trial may be fair and impartial.

Theft.

Agent.

ARTICLE XIII. It is consented that a qualified Agent shall be appointed for the Choctaws every four years, unless sooner removed by the President; and he shall be removed on petition of the constituted authorities of the Nation, the President being satisfied there is sufficient cause shown. The Agent shall fix his residence convenient to the great body of the people; and in the selection of an Agent immediately after the ratification of this Treaty, the wishes of the Choctaw Nation on the subject shall be entitled to great respect.

ARTICLE XIV. Each Choctaw head of a family being desirous to remain and become a citizen of the States, shall be permitted to do so, by signifying his intention to the Agent within six months from the ratification of this Treaty, and he or she shall thereupon be entitled to a reservation of one section of six hundred and forty acres of land, to be bounded by sectional lines of survey; in like manner shall be entitled to one half that quantity for each unmarried child which is living with him over ten years of age; and a quarter section to such child as may be under 10 years of age, to adjoin the location of the parent. If they reside upon said lands intending to become citizens of the States for five years after the ratification of this Treaty, in that case a grant in fee simple shall issue; said reservation shall include the present improvement of the head of the family, or a portion of it. Persons who claim under this article shall not lose the privilege of a Choctaw citizen, but if they ever remove are not to be entitled to any portion of the Choctaw annuity. *Choctaws wishing to become citizens of United States.*

ARTICLE XV. To each of the Chiefs in the Choctaw Nation (to wit) Greenwood Laflore, Nutackachie, and Mushulatubbe there is granted a reservation of four sections of land, two of which shall include and adjoin their present improvement, and the other two located where they please but on unoccupied unimproved lands, such sections shall be bounded by sectional lines, and with the consent of the President they may sell the same. Also to the three principal Chiefs and to their successors in office there shall be paid two hundred and fifty dollars annually while they shall continue in their respective offices, except to Mushulatubbe, who as he has an annuity of one hundred and fifty dollars for life under a former treaty, shall receive only the additional sum of one hundred dollars, while he shall continue in office as Chief; and if in addition to this the Nation shall think proper to elect an additional principal Chief of the whole to superintend and govern upon republican principles he shall receive annually for his services five hundred dollars, which allowance to the Chiefs and their successors in office, shall continue for twenty years. At any time when in military service, and while in service by authority of the U. S. the district Chiefs under and by selection of the President shall be entitled to the pay of Majors; the other Chief under the same circumstances shall have the pay of a Lieutenant Colonel. The Speakers of the three districts, shall receive twenty-five dollars a year for four years each; and the three secretaries one to each of the Chiefs, fifty dollars each for four years. Each Captain of the Nation, the number not to exceed ninety-nine, thirty-three from each district, shall be furnished upon removing to the West, with each a good suit of clothes and a broad sword as an outfit, and for four years commencing with the first of their removal, shall each receive fifty dollars a year, for the trouble of keeping their people at order in settling; and whenever they shall be in military service by authority of the U. S. shall receive the pay of a captain. *Reservations for chiefs.* *Annuities.* *Pay of chiefs, etc.*

ARTICLE XVI. In wagons; and with steam boats as may be found necessary—the U. S. agree to remove the Indians to their new homes at their expense and under the care of discreet and careful persons, who will be kind and brotherly to them. They agree to furnish them with ample corn and beef, or pork for themselves and families for twelve months after reaching their new homes. *Removal of Indians.*

It is agreed further that the U. S. will take all their cattle, at the valuation of some discreet person to be appointed by the President, and the same shall be paid for in money after their arrival at their *Cattle.*

new homes; or other cattle such as may be desired shall be furnished them, notice being given through their Agent of their wishes upon this subject before their removal that time to supply the demand may be afforded.

Annuities under former treaties.

ARTICLE XVII. The several annuities and sums secured under former Treaties to the Choctaw nation and people shall continue as though this Treaty had never been made.

Further annuity.

And it is further agreed that the U. S. in addition will pay the sum of twenty thousand dollars for twenty years, commencing after their removal to the west, of which, in the first year after their removal, ten thousand dollars shall be divided and arranged to such as may not receive reservations under this Treaty.

Survey of ceded lands, etc.

ART. XVIII. The U. S. shall cause the lands hereby ceded to be surveyed; and surveyors may enter the Choctaw Country for that purpose, conducting themselves properly and disturbing or interrupting none of the Choctaw people. But no person is to be permitted to settle within the nation, or the lands to be sold before the Choctaws shall remove. And for the payment of the several amounts secured in this Treaty, the lands hereby ceded are to remain a fund pledged to that purpose, until the debt shall be provided for and arranged. And further it is agreed, that in the construction of this Treaty wherever well founded doubt shall arise, it shall be construed most favorably towards the Choctaws.

Reservations of land, for—

ARTICLE XIX. The following reservations of land are hereby admitted. To Colonel David Fulsom four sections of which two shall include his present improvement, and two may be located elsewhere, on unoccupied, unimproved land.

Certain individuals.

To I. Garland, Colonel Robert Cole, Tuppanahomer, John Pytchlynn, Charles Juzan, Johokebetubbe, Eaychahobia, Ofehoma, two sections, each to include their improvements, and to be bounded by sectional lines, and the same may be disposed of and sold with the consent of the President. And that others not provided for, may be provided for, there shall be reserved as follows:

Heads of families.

First. One section to each head of a family not exceeding Forty in number, who during the present year, may have had in actual cultivation, with a dwelling house thereon fifty acres or more. Secondly, three quarter sections after the manner aforesaid to each head of a family not exceeding four hundred and sixty, as shall have cultivated thirty acres and less than fifty, to be bounded by quarter section lines of survey, and to be contiguous and adjoining.

Third; One half section as aforesaid to those who shall have cultivated from twenty to thirty acres the number not to exceed four hundred. Fourth; a quarter section as aforesaid to such as shall have cultivated from twelve to twenty acres, the number not to exceed three hundred and fifty, and one half that quantity to such as shall have cultivated from two to twelve acres, the number also not to exceed three hundred and fifty persons. Each of said class of cases shall be subject to the limitations contained in the first class, and shall be so located as to include that part of the improvement which contains the dwelling house. If a greater number shall be found to be entitled to reservations under the several classes of this article, than is stipulated for under the limitation prescribed, then and in that case the Chiefs separately or together shall determine the persons who shall be excluded in the respective districts.

Captains.

Fifth; Any Captain the number not exceeding ninety persons, who under the provisions of this article shall receive less than a section, he shall be entitled, to an additional quantity of half a section adjoining to his other reservation. The several reservations secured under this article, may be sold with the consent of the President of the U. S. but should any prefer it, or omit to take a reservation for the quantity he may be entitled to, the U. S. will on his removing pay fifty cents an acre, after reaching their new homes, provided that before the first of January next they shall adduce to the Agent, or some other authorized person to be appointed, proof of his claim and the quantity of it. Sixth; likewise children of the Choctaw Nation residing in the Nation, who have neither father nor mother a list of which, with satisfactory proof of Parentage and orphanage being filed with Agent in six months to be forwarded to the War Department, shall be entitled to a quarter section of Land, to be located under the direction of the President, and with his consent the same may be sold and the proceeds applied to some beneficial purpose for the benefit of said orphans. *Orphans.*

ARTICLE XX. The U. S. agree and stipulate as follows, that for the benefit and advantage of the Choctaw people, and to improve their condition, their shall be educated under the direction of the President, and at the expense of the U. S. forty Choctaw youths for twenty years. This number shall be kept at school, and as they finish their education others, to supply their places shall be received for the period stated. The U. S. agree also to erect a Council House for the Nation at some convenient central point, after their people shall be settled; and a House for each Chief, also a Church for each of the three Districts, to be used also as school houses, until the Nation may conclude to build others; and for these purposes ten thousand dollars shall be appropriated; also fifty thousand dollars (viz.) twenty-five hundred dollars annually shall be given for the support of three teachers of schools for twenty years. Likewise there shall be furnished to the Nation, three Blacksmiths one for each district for sixteen years, and a qualified Mill Wright for five years; Also there shall be furnished the following articles, twenty.one hundred blankets, to each warrior who emigrates a rifle, moulds, wipers and ammunition. One thousand axes, ploughs, hoes, wheels and cards each; and four hundred looms. There shall also be furnished, one ton of iron and two hundred weight of steel annually to each District for sixteen years. *Stipulations by United States for the benefit of the Choctaws.*

ARTICLE XXI. A few Choctaw Warriors yet survive who marched and fought in the army with General Wayne, the whole number stated not to exceed twenty. *Annuity to certain old warriors.*

These it is agreed shall hereafter, while they live, receive twenty-five dollars a year; a list of them to be early as practicable, and within six months, made out, and presented to the Agent, to be forwarded to the War Department.

ARTICLE XXII. The Chiefs of the Choctaws who have suggested that their people are in a state of rapid advancement in education and refinement, and have expressed a solicitude that they might have the privilege of a Delegate on the floor of the House of Representatives extended to them. The Commissioners do not feel that they can under a treaty stipulation accede to the request, but at their desire, present it in the Treaty, that Congress may consider of, and decide the application. *Delegate to Congress.*

Done, and signed, and executed by the commissioners of the United States, and the chiefs, captains, and head men of the Choctaw nation, at Dancing Rabbit creek, this 27th day of September, eighteen and thirty.

Jno. H. Eaton,	[L. S.]	Yobalarunehahubbee, his x mark,	[L. S.]
Jno. Coffee,	[L. S.]	Holubbee, his x mark,	[L. S.]
Greenwood Leflore,	[L. S.]	Robert Cole, his x mark,	[L. S.]
Musholatubbee, his x mark,	[L. S.]	Mokelareharhopin, his x mark,	[L. S.]
Nittucachee, his x mark,	[L. S.]	Lewis Perry, his x mark,	[L. S.]
Holarterhoomah, his x mark,	[L. S.]	Artonamarstubbe, his x mark,	[L. S.]
Hopiaunchahubbee, his x mark,	[L. S.]	Hopeatubbee, his x mark,	[L. S.]
Zishomingo, his x mark,	[L. S.]	Hoshahoomah, his x mark,	[L. S.]
Captainthalke, his x mark,	[L. S.]	Chuallahoomah, his x mark,	[L. S.]
James Shield, his x mark,	[L. S.]	Joseph Kincaide, his x mark,	[L. S.]
Pistiyubbee, his x mark,	[L. S.]	Eyarhocuttubbee, his x mark,	[L. S.]

Iyacherhopia, his x mark,	[L. S.]	Heshohomme, his x mark,	[L. S.]
Offahoomah, his x mark,	[L. S.]	John McKolbery, his x mark,	[L. S.]
Archalater, his x mark,	[L. S.]	Benjm. James, his x mark,	[L. S.]
Onnahubbee, his x mark,	[L. S.]	Tikbachahambe, his x mark,	[L. S.]
Pisinhocuttubbee, his x mark,	[L. S.]	Aholiktube, his x mark,	[L. S]
Tullarhacher, his x mark,	[L. S.]	Walking Wolf, his x mark,	[L. S.]
Little leader, his x mark,	[L. S.]	John Waide, his x mark,	[L. S.]
Maanhutter, his x mark,	[L. S.]	Big Axe, his x mark,	[L. S.]
Cowehoomah, his x mark,	[L. S.]	Bob, his x mark,	[L. S.]
Tillamoer, his x mark,	[L. S.]	Tushkochaubbee, his x mark,	[L. S.]
Imnullacha, his x mark,	[L. S.]	Ittabe, his x mark,	[L. S.]
Artopilachubbee, his x mark,	[L. S.]	Tishowakayo, his x mark,	[L. S.]
Shupherunchahubbee, his x mark,	[L. S.]	Folehommo, his x mark,	[L. S.]
Nitterhoomah, his x mark,	[L. S.]	John Garland, his x mark,	[L. S.]
Oaklaryubbee, his x mark,	[L. S.]	Koshona, his x mark,	[L. S.]
Pukumna, his x mark,	[L. S.]	Ishleyohamube, his x mark,	[L. S.]
Arpalar, his x mark,	[L. S.]	Jacob Folsom,	[L. S.]
Holber, his x mark,	[L. S.]	William Foster,	[L. S.]
Hoparmingo, his x mark,	[L. S.]	Ontioerharcho, his x mark,	[L. S.]
Isparhoomah, his x mark,	[L. S.]	Hugh A. Foster,	[L. S.]
Tieberhoomah, his x mark,	[L. S.]	Pierre Juzan,	[L. S.]
Tishoholarter, his x mark,	[L. S.]	Jno. Pitchlynn, jr.,	[L. S.]
Mahayarchubbee, his x mark,	[L. S.]	David Folsom,	[L. S]
Artooklubbetushpar, his x mark,	[L. S.]	Sholohommastube, his x mark,	[L. S.]
Metubbee, his x mark,	[L. S.]	Tesho, his x mark,	[L. S.]
Arsarkatubbee, his x mark,	[L. S.]	Lauwechubbee, his x mark,	[L. S.]
Issaterhoomah, his x mark,	[L. S.]	Hoshehammo, his x mark,	[L. S.]
Chohtahmatahah, his x mark,	[L. S.]	Ofenowo, his x mark,	[L. S.]
Tunnuppashubbee, his x mark,	[L. S.]	Ahekoche, his x mark,	[L. S.]
Okocharyer, his x mark,	[L. S.]	Kaloshoube, his x mark,	[L. S.]
Hoshhopia, his x mark,	[L. S.]	Atoko, his x mark,	[L. S.]
Warsharshahopia, his x mark,	[L. S.]	Ishtemeleche, his x mark,	[L. S.]
Maarshunchahubbee, his x mark,	[L. S.]	Emthtohabe, his x mark,	[L. S.]
Misharyubbee, his x mark,	[L. S.]	Silas D. Fisher, his x mark,	[L. S.]
Daniel McCurtain, his x mark,	[L. S.]	Isaac Folsom, his x mark,	[L. S.]
Tushkerharcho, his x mark,	[L. S.]	Hekatube, his x mark,	[L. S.]
Hoktoontubbee, his x mark,	[L. S.]	Hakseche, his x mark,	[L. S.]
Nuknacrahookmarhee, his x mark,	[L. S.]	Jerry Carney, his x mark,	[L. S.]
Mingo hoomah, his x mark,	[L. S.]	John Washington. his x mark,	[L. S.]
James Karnes, his x mark,	[L. S.]	Panshastubbee, his x mark,	[L. S.]
Tishohakubbee, his x mark,	[L. S.]	P. P. Pitchlynn, his x mark,	[L. S.]
Narlanalar, his x mark,	[L. S.]	Joel H. Nail, his x mark,	[L. S.]
Pennasha, his x mark,	[L. S.]	Hopia Stonakey, his x mark,	[L. S.]
Inharyarker, his x mark,	[L. S.]	Kocohomma, his x mark,	[L. S.]
Mottubbee, his x mark,	[L. S.]	William Wade, his x mark,	[L. S.]
Narharyubbee, his x mark,	[L. S.]	Panshstickubbee, his x mark,	[L. S.]
Ishmaryubbee, his x mark,	[L. S.]	Holittankchahubbee, his x mark,	[L. S.]
James McKing,	[L. S.]	Oklanowa, his x mark,	[L. S.]
Lewis Wilson, his x mark,	[L. S.]	Neto, his x mark,	[L. S.]
Istonarkerharcho, his x mark,	[L. S.]	James Fletcher, his x mark,	[L. S.]
Hohinshamartarher, his x mark,	[L. S.]	Silas D. Pitchlynn,	[L. S.]
Kinsulachubbee, his x mark,	[L. S.]	William Trahorn, his x mark,	[L. S.]
Emarhinstubbee, his x mark,	[L. S.]	Toshkahemmitto, his x mark,	[L. S.]
Gysalndalra, bm, his x mark,	[L. S.]	Tethetayo, his x mark,	[L. S.]
Thomas Wall,	[L. S.]	Emokloshahopie, his x mark,	[L. S.]
Sam. S. Worcester,	[L. S.]	Tishoimita, his x mark,	[L. S.]
Arlartar, his x mark,	[L. S.]	Thomas W. Foster, his x mark,	[L. S.]
Nittahubbee, his x mark,	[L. S.]	Zadoc Brashears, his x mark,	[L. S.]
Tishonouan, his x mark,	[L. S.]	Levi Perkins, his x mark,	[L. S.]
Warsharchahoomah, his x mark,	[L. S.]	Isaac Perry, his x mark,	[L. S.]
Isaac James, his x mark,	[L. S.]	Ishlonocka Hoomah, his x mark,	[L. S.]
Hopiaintushker, his x mark,	[L. S.]	Hiram King, his x mark,	[L. S.]
Aryoshkermer, his x mark,	[L. S.]	Ogla Enlah, his x mark,	[L. S.]
Shemotar, his x mark,	[L. S.]	Nultlahtubbee, his x mark,	[L. S.]
Hopiaisketina, his x mark,	[L. S.]	Tuska Hollattuh, his x mark,	[L. S.]
Thomas Leflore, his x mark,	[L. S.]	Kothoantchahubbee, his x mark,	[L. S.]
Arnokechatubbee, his x mark,	[L. S.]	Evarpulubbee, his x mark,	[L. S.]
Shokoperlukna, his x mark,	[L. S.]	Okentahubbe, his x mark,	[L. S.]
Posherhoomah, his x mark,	[L. S.]	Living War Club, his x mark,	[L. S.]
Robert Folsom, his x mark,	[L. S.]	John Jones, his x mark,	[L. S.]
Arharyotubbee, his x mark,	[L. S.]	Charles Jones, his x mark,	[L. S.]
Kushonolarter, his x mark,	[L. S.]	Isaac Jones, his x mark,	[L. S.]
James Vaughan, his x mark,	[L. S.]	Hocklucha, his x mark,	[L. S.]
Phiplip, his x mark,	[L. S.]	Muscogee, his x mark,	[L. S.]
Meshameye, his x mark,	[L. S.]	Eden Nelson, his x mark,	[L. S.]
Ishteheka, his x mark,	[L. S.]		

In presence of—

E. Breathitt, secretary to the Commission,	Luke Howard,
William Ward, agent for Choctaws,	Sam. S. Worcester,
John Pitchlyn, United States interpreter,	Jno. N. Byrn,
M. Mackey, United States interpreter,	John Bell,
Geo. S. Gaines, of Alabama,	Jno. Bond.
R. P. Currin,	

SUPPLEMENTARY ARTICLES TO THE PRECEDING TREATY.

Sept. 28, 1830.

7 Stat., 340.

Various Choctaw persons have been presented by the Chiefs of the nation, with a desire that they might be provided for. Being particularly deserving, an earnestness has been manifested that provision might be made for them. It is therefore by the undersigned commissioners here assented to, with the understanding that they are to have no interest in the reservations which are directed and provided for under the general Treaty to which this is a supplement.

As evidence of the liberal and kind feelings of the President and Government of the United States the Commissioners agree to the request as follows, (to wit) Pierre Juzan, Peter Pitchlynn, G. W. Harkins, Jack Pitchlynn, Israel Fulsom, Louis Laflore, Benjamin James, Joel H. Nail, Hopoynjahubbee, Onorkubbee, Benjamin Laflore, Michael Laflore and Allen Yates and wife shall be entitled to a reservation of two sections of land each to include their improvement where they at present reside, with the exception of the three first named persons and Benjamin Laflore, who are authorized to locate one of their sections on any other unimproved and unoccupied land, within their respective districts.

ARTICLE II. And to each of the following persons there is allowed a reservation of a section and a half of land, (to wit) James L. McDonald, Robert Jones, Noah Wall, James Campbell, G. Nelson, Vaughn Brashears, R. Harris, Little Leader, S. Foster, J. Vaughn, L. Durans, Samuel Long, T. Magagha, Thos. Everge, Giles Thompson, Tomas Garland, John Bond, William Laflore, and Turner Brashears, the two first named persons, may locate one section each, and one section jointly on any unimproved and unoccupied land, these not residing in the Nation; The others are to include their present residence and improvement.

Reservations.

Also one section is allowed to the following persons (to wit) Middleton Mackey, Wesley Train, Choclehomo, Moses Foster, D. W. Wall, Charles Scott, Molly Nail, Susan Colbert, who was formerly Susan James, Samuel Garland, Silas Fisher, D. McCurtain, Oaklahoma, and Polly Fillecuthey, to be located in entire sections to include their present residence and improvement, with the exception of Molly Nail and Susan Colbert, who are authorized to locate theirs, on any unimproved unoccupied land.

John Pitchlynn has long and faithfully served the nation in character of U. States Interpreter, he has acted as such for forty years, in consideration it is agreed, in addition to what has been done for him there shall be granted to two of his children, (to wit) Silas Pitchlynn, and Thomas Pitchlynn one section of land each, to adjoin the location of their father; likewise to James Madison and Peter sons of Mushulatubbee one section of land each to include the old house and improvement where their father formerly lived on the old military road adjoining a large Prerarie.

And to Henry Groves son of the Chief Natticache there is one section of land given to adjoin his father's land.

And to each of the following persons half a section of land is granted on any unoccupied and unimproved lands in the Districts where they respectively live (to wit) Willis Harkins, James D. Hamilton, William

Juzan, Tobias Laflore, Jo Doke, Jacob Fulsom, P. Hays, Samuel Worcester, George Hunter, William Train, Robert Nail and Alexander McKee.

And there is given a quarter section of land each to Delila and her five fatherless children, she being a Choctaw woman residing out of the nation; also the same quantity to Peggy Trihan, another Indian woman residing out of the nation and her two fatherless children; and to the widows of Pushmilaha, and Pucktshenubbee, who were formerly distinguished Chiefs of the nation and for their children four quarter sections of land, each in trust for themselves and their children.

All of said last mentioned reservations are to be located under and by direction of the President of the U. States.

Exploring party.   ARTICLE III. The Choctaw people now that they have ceded their lands are solicitous to get to their new homes early as possible and accordingly they wish that a party may be permitted to proceed this fall to ascertain whereabouts will be most advantageous for their people to be located.

It is therefore agreed that three or four persons (from each of the three districts) under the guidance of some discreet and well qualified person or persons may proceed during this fall to the West upon an examination of the country.

For their time and expenses the U. States agree to allow the said twelve persons two dollars a day each, not to exceed one hundred days, which is deemed to be ample time to make an examination.

If necessary, pilots acquainted with the country will be furnished when they arrive in the West.

Reservation.   ARTICLE IV. John Donly of Alabama who has several Choctaw grand children, and who for twenty years has carried the mail through the Choctaw Nation, a desire by the Chiefs is expressed that he may have a section of land, it is accordingly granted, to be located in one entire section, on any unimproved and unoccupied land.

Debts to Glover and Gaines.   Allen Glover and George S. Gaines licensed Traders in the Choctaw Nation, have accounts amounting to upwards of nine thousand dollars against the Indians who are unable to pay their said debts without distressing their families; a desire is expressed by the chiefs that two sections of land be set apart to be sold and the proceeds thereof to be applied toward the payment of the aforesaid debts. It is agreed that two sections of any unimproved and unoccupied land be granted to George S. Gaines who will sell the same for the best price he can obtain and apply the proceeds thereof to the credit of the Indians on their accounts due to the before mentioned Glover and Gaines; and shall make the application to the poorest Indian first.

Reservation.   At the earnest and particular request of th Chief, Greenwood Laflore there is granted to David Haley one half section of land to be located in a half section on any unoccupied and unimproved land as a compensation, for a journey to Washington City with dispatches to the Government and returning others to the Choctaw Nation.

The foregoing is entered into, as supplemental to the treaty concluded yesterday.

Done at Dancing Rabbit creek the 28th day of September, 1830.

Jno. H. Eaton,	[L. S.]	Robert Cole, his x mark,	[L. S.]
Jno. Coffee,	[L. S.]	Hopiaunchahubbee, his x mark,	[L. S.]
Greenwood Leflore,	[L. S.]	David Folsom,	[L. S.]
Nittucachee, his x mark,	[L. S.]	John Garland, his x mark,	[L. S.]
Mushulatubbee, his x mark,	[L. S.]	Hopiahoomah, his x mark,	[L. S.]
Offahoomah, his x mark,	[L. S.]	Captain Thalko, his x mark,	[L. S.]
Eyarhoeuttubbee, his x mark,	[L. S.]	Pierre Juzan,	[L. S.]
Iyaeherhopia, his x mark,	[L. S.]	Immarstarher, his x mark,	[L. S.]
Holubbee, his x mark,	[L. S.]	Hoshimhamartar, his x mark,	[L. S.]
Onarhubbee, his x mark,	[L. S.]		

In presence of—

E. Breathitt, Secretary to Commissioners,
W. Ward, Agent for Choctaws,
M. Mackey, United States Interpreter,
John Pitchlynn, United States Interpreter,

R. P. Currin,
Jno. W. Byrn,
Geo. S. Gaines.

TREATY WITH THE MENOMINEE, 1831.

Articles of agreement made and concluded at the City of Washington, this eighth day of February, one thousand eight hundred and thirty-one, between John H. Eaton, Secretary of War, and Samuel C. Stambaugh, Indian Agent at Green Bay, specially authorized by the President of the United States, and the undersigned chiefs and head men of the Menomonee nation of Indians, fully authorized and empowered by the said nation, to conclude and settle all matters provided for by this agreement.

Feb. 8, 1831.

7 Stat., 342.
Proclamation, July 9, 1832.

THE Menomonee Tribe of Indians, by their delegates in council, this day, define the boundaries of their country as follows, to wit;

Boundaries of Menomonee country.

On the *east* side of Green Bay, Fox river, and Winnebago lake; beginning at the south end of Winnebago lake; thence southeastwardly to the Milwauky or Manawauky river; thence down said river to its mouth at lake Michigan; thence north, along the shore of lake Michigan, to the mouth of Green Bay; thence up Green Bay, Fox river, and Winnebago lake, to the place of beginning. And on the *west* side of Fox river as follows: beginning at the mouth of Fox river, thence down the east shore of Green bay, and across its mouth, so as to include all the islands of the "Grand Traverse;" thence westerly, on the highlands between the lake Superior and Green bay, to the upper forks of the Menomonee river; thence to the Plover portage of the Wisconsin river; thence up the Wisconsin river, to the Soft Maple river; thence to the source of the Soft Maple river; thence west to the Plume river, which falls into the Chippeway river; thence down said Plume river to its mouth; thence down the Chippeway river thirty miles; thence easterly to the forks of the Manoy river, which falls into the Wisconsin river; thence down the said Manoy river to its mouth; thence down the Wisconsin river to the Wisconsin portage; thence across the said portage to the Fox river; thence down Fox river to its mouth at Green bay, or the place of beginning.

The country described within the above boundaries, the Menomonees claim as the exclusive property of their tribe. Not yet having disposed of any of their lands, they receive no annuities from the United States: whereas their brothers the Pootowottomees on the south, and the Winnebagoes on the west, have sold a great portion of their country, receive large annuities, and are now encroaching upon the lands of the Menomonees. For the purposes, therefore, of establishing the boundaries of their country, and of ceding certain portions of their lands to the United States, in order to secure great and lasting benefits to themselves and posterity, as well as for the purpose of settling the long existing dispute between themselves and the several tribes of the New York Indians, who claim to have purchased a portion of their lands, the undersigned, chiefs and headmen of the Menomonee tribe, stipulate and agree with the United States, as follows:

First. The Menomonee tribe of Indians declare themselves the friends and allies of the United States, under whose parental care and protection they desire to continue; and although always protesting that they are under no obligation to recognize any claim of the New York Indians to any portion of their country; that they neither sold nor received any value, for the land claimed by these tribes; yet, at the solicitation of their Great Father, the President of the United States, and as an evidence of their love and veneration for him, they agree that such part of the land described, being within the following boundaries, as he may direct, may be set apart as a home to the several tribes of the New York Indians, who may remove to, and settle upon the same, within three years from the date of this agreement, viz: beginning on the west side of Fox river, near the "Little Kackalin," at a point known as the "Old Mill Dam;" thence northwest forty miles; thence northeast to the Oconto creek, falling into Green bay; thence down said Oconto creek to Green bay; thence up and along Green bay and Fox river to the place of beginning; excluding therefrom all private land claims confirmed, and also the following reservation for military purposes; beginning on the Fox river, at the mouth of the first creek above Fort Howard; thence north sixty-four degrees west to Duck creek; thence down said Duck creek to its mouth; thence up and along Green bay and Fox river to the place of beginning. The Menomonee Indians, also reserve, for the use of the United States, from the country herein designated for the New York Indians, timber and firewood for the the United States garrison, and as much land as may be deemed necessary for public highways, to be located by the direction, and at the discretion of the President of the United States. The country hereby ceded to the United States, for the benefit of the New York Indians, contains by estimation about five hundred thousand acres, and includes all their improvements on the west side of Fox river. As it is intended for a home for the several tribes of the New York Indians, who may be residing upon the lands at the expiration of three years from this date, and for none others, the President of the United S'ates is hereby empowered to apportion the lands among the actual occupants at that time, so as not to assign to any tribe a greater number of acres than may be equal to one hundred for each soul actually settled upon the lands, and if, at the time of such apportionment, any lands shall remain unoccupied by any tribe of the New York Indians, such portion as would have belonged to said Indians, had it been occupied, shall revert to the United States. That portion, if any, so reverting, to be laid off by the President of the United States. It is distinctly understood, that the lands hereby ceded to the United States for the New York Indians, are to be held by those tribes, under such tenure as the Menomonee Indians now hold their lands, subject to such regulations and alteration of tenure, as Congress and the President of the United States shall, from time to time, think proper to adopt.

Second. For the above cession to the United States, for the benefit of the New York Indians, the United States consent to pay the Menomonee Indians, twenty thousand dollars; five thousand to be paid on the first day of August next, and five thousand annually thereafter; which sums shall be applied to the use of the Menomonees, after such manner as the President of the United States may direct.

Third. The Menomonee tribe of Indians, in consideration of the kindness and protection of the Government of the United States, and for the purpose of securing to themselves and posterity, a comfortable home, hereby cede and forever relinquish to the United States, all their country on the southeast side of Winnebago lake, Fox river, and Green bay, which they describe in the following boundaries, to wit: beginning at the south end of Winnebago lake, and running in a southeast direction to Milwauky or Manawauky river; thence down said river to its mouth; thence north, along the shore of lake Michigan, to the entrance of Green bay; thence up and along Green bay, Fox river, and Winnebago lake, to the place of beginning; excluding all private land claims which the United States have heretofore confirmed and

Margin notes:

Cession of land to United States for the benefit of the New York Indians.

Boundaries.

Consideration.

Further cession of lands to the United States.

sanctioned. It is also agreed that all the islands which lie in Fox river and Green bay, are likewise ceded; the whole comprising by estimation, two million five hundred thousand acres.

Fourth. The following described tract of land, at present owned and occupied by the Menomonee Indians, shall be set apart, and designated for their future homes, upon which their improvements as an agricultural people are to be made: beginning on the West side of Fox river, at the "Old Mill Dam" near the "Little Kackalin," and running up and along said river, to the Winnebago lake; thence along said lake to the mouth of Fox river; thence up Fox river to the Wolf river; thence up Wolf river to a point southwest of the west corner of the tract herein designated for the New York Indians; thence northeast to said west corner; thence southeast to the place of beginning. The above reservation being made to the Menomonee Indians for the purpose of weaning them from their wandering habits, by attaching them to comfortable homes, the President of the United States, as a mark of affection for his children of the Menomonee tribe, will cause to be employed five farmers of established character for capacity, industry, and moral habits, for ten successive years, whose duty it shall be to assist the Menomonee Indians in the cultivation of their farms, and to instruct their children in the business and occupation of farming. Also, five females shall be employed, of like good character, for the purpose of teaching young Menomonee women, in the business of useful housewifery, during a period of ten years.—The annual compensation allowed to the farmers, shall not exceed five hundred dollars, and that of the females three hundred dollars. And the United States will cause to be erected, houses suited to their condition, on said lands, as soon as the Indians agree to occupy them, for which ten thousand dollars shall be appropriated; also, houses for the farmers, for which three thousand dollars shall be appropriated; to be expended under the direction of the Secretary of War. Whenever the Menomonees thus settle their lands, they shall be supplied with useful household articles, horses, cows, hogs, and sheep, farming utensils, and other articles of husbandry necessary to their comfort, to the value of six thousand dollars; and they desire that some suitable device may be stamped upon such articles, to preserve them from sale or barter, to evil disposed white persons: none of which, nor any other articles with which the United States may at any time furnish them, shall be liable to sale, or be disposed of or bargained, without permission of the agent. The whole to be under the immediate care of the farmers employed to remain among said Indians, but subject to the general control of the United States' Indian Agent at Green Bay acting under the Secretary of War. The United States will erect a grist and saw mill on Fox river, for the benefit of the Menomonee Indians, and employ a good miller, subject to the direction of the agent, whose business it shall be to grind the grain, required for the use of the Menomonee Indians, and saw the lumber necessary for building on their lands, as also to instruct such young men of the Menomonee nation, as desire to, and conveniently can be instructed in the trade of a miller. The expenses of erecting such mills, and a house for the miller to reside in, shall not exceed six thousand dollars, and the annual compensation of the miller shall be six hundred dollars, to continue for ten years. And if the mills so erected by the United States, can saw more lumber or grind more grain, than is required for the proper use of said Menomonee Indians, the proceeds of such milling shall be applied to the payment of other expenses occurring in the Green bay agency, under the direction of the Secretary of War.

In addition to the above provision made for the Menomonee Indians, the President of the United States will cause articles of clothing to be distributed among their tribe at Green bay, within six months from

Reservation.

Farmers, etc.

Dwelling houses.

Grist and saw mill

Clothing and flour.

Annuity, etc.

the date of this agreement, to the amount of eight thousand dollars; and flour and wholesome provisions, to the amount of one thousand dollars, one thousand dollars to be paid in specie. The cost of the transportation of the clothing and provisions, to be included in the sum expended. There shall also be allowed annually thereafter, for the space of twelve successive years, to the Menomonee tribe, in such manner and form as the President of the United States shall deem most beneficial and advantageous to the Indians, the sum of six thousand dollars. As a matter of great importance to the Menomonees, there shall be one or more gun and blacksmith's shops erected, to be supplied with a necessary quantity of iron and steel, which, with a shop at Green bay, shall be kept up for the use of the tribe, and continued at the discretion of the President of the United States. There shall also be a house for an interpreter to reside in, erected at Green bay, the expenses not to exceed five hundred dollars.

Education of Menominees.

Fifth. In the treaty of Butte des Morts, concluded in August 1827, an article is contained, appropriating one thousand five hundred dollars annually, for the support of schools in the Menomonee country. And the representatives of the Menomonee nation, who are parties hereto, require, and it is agreed to, that said appropriation shall be increased five hundred dollars, and continued for ten years from this date, to be placed in the hands of the Secretary at War, in trust for the exclusive use and benefit of the Menomonee tribe of Indians, and to be applied by him to the education of the children of the Menomonee Indians, in such manner as he may deem most advisable.

Certain privileges reserved.

Sixth. The Menomonee tribe of Indians shall be at liberty to hunt and fish on the lands they have now ceded to the United States, on the east side of Fox river and Green bay, with the same privileges they at present enjoy, until it be surveyed and offered for sale by the President; they conducting themselves peaceably and orderly. The chiefs and Warriors of the Menomonee nation, acting under the authority and on behalf of their tribe, solemnly pledge themselves to preserve peace and harmony between their people and the Government of the United States forever. They neither acknowledge the power nor protection of any other State or people. A departure from this pledge by any portion of their tribe, shall be a forfeiture of the protection of the United States' Government, and their annuities will cease. In thus declaring their friendship for the United States, however, the Menomonee tribe of Indians, having the most implicit confidence in their great father, the President of the United States, desire that he will, as a kind and faithful guardian of their welfare, direct the provisions of this compact to be carried into immediate effect. The Menomonee

New York Indians.

chiefs request that such part of it as relates to the New York Indians, be immediately submitted to the representatives of their tribes. And if they refuse to accept the provision made for their benefit, and to remove upon the lands set apart for them, on the west side of Fox river, that he will direct their immediate removal from the Menomonee country; but if they agree to accept of the liberal offer made to them by the parties to this compact, then the Menomonee tribe as dutiful children of their great father the President, will take them by the hand as brothers, and settle down with them in peace and friendship.

The boundary, as stated and defined in this agreement, of the Menomonee country, with the exception of the cessions herein before made to the United States, the Menomonees claim as their country; that part of it adjoining the farming country, on the west side of Fox river, will remain to them as heretofore, for a hunting ground, until the President of the United States, shall deem it expedient to extinguish their title. In that case, the Menomonee tribe promise to surrender it immediately, upon being notified of the desire of Government to possess it. The additional annuity then to be paid to the Menomonee tribe, to be fixed by the President of the United States. It is conceded to the United States that they may enjoy the right of making such roads, and of establishing such military posts, in any part of the country now occupied by the Menomonee nation, as the President at any time may think proper.

As a further earnest of the good feeling on the part of their great father, it is agreed that the expenses of the Menomonee delegation to the city of Washington, and of returning, will be paid, and that a comfortable suit of clothes will be provided for each; also, that the United States will cause four thousand dollars to be expended in procuring fowling guns, and ammunition for them; and likewise, in lieu of any garrison rations, hereafter allowed or received by them, there shall be procured and given to said tribe one thousand dollars worth of good and wholesome provisions annually, for four years, by which time it is hoped their hunting habits may cease, and their attention be turned to the pursuits of agriculture.

Expenses of delegation, etc.

In testimony whereof, the respective parties to this agreement have severally signed the same, this 8th February, 1831.

John H. Eaton,	[L. S.]	Ah-ke-ne-pa-weh, earth standing,
S. C. Stambaugh,	[L. S.]	his x mark, [L. S.]
Kaush-kau-no-naive, grizzly bear,		Shaw-wan-noh, the south, his x
his x mark,	[L. S.]	mark, [L. S.]
A-ya-mah-taw, fish spawn, his x		Mash-ke-wet, his x mark, [L. S.]
mark,	[L. S.]	Pah-she-nah-sheu, his x mark, [L. S.]
Ko-ma-ni-kin, big wave, his x		Chi-mi-na-na-quet, great cloud, his
mark,	[L. S.]	x mark, [L. S.]
Ko-ma-ni-kee-no-shah, little wave,		A-na-quet-to-a-peh, setting in a
his x mark,	[L. S.]	cloud, his x mark, [L. S.]
O-ho-pa-shah, little whoop, his x		Sha-ka-cho-ka-mo, great chief, his
mark,	[L. S.]	x mark, [L. S.]

Signed, sealed, and delivered in presence of—

R. A. Forsyth,	William Wilkins, of Pennsylvania,
C. A. Grignon,	Samuel Swartwout, of N. York,
Interpreters,	John T. Mason, Michigan,
A. G. Ellis,	Rh. M. Johnson, Kentucky.
Richard Pricket, United States Interpreter, his x mark,	

TREATY WITH THE MENOMINEE, 1831.

WHEREAS certain articles of agreement were entered into and concluded at the city of Washington, on the 8th day of February instant, between the undersigned, Commissioners on behalf of the United States, and the chiefs and warriors, representing the Menomonee tribe of Indians, whereby a portion of the Menomonee country, on the northwest side of Fox river and Green bay, was ceded to the United States, for the benefit of the New York Indians, upon certain conditions and restrictions therein expressed: And whereas it has been represented to the parties to that agreement, who are parties hereto, that it would be more desirable and satisfactory to some of those interested that one or two immaterial changes be made in the *first* and *sixth* articles, so as not to limit the number of acres to one hundred for each soul who may be settled upon the land when the President apportions it, as also to make unlimited the time of removal and settlement upon these lands by the New York Indians, but to leave both these matters discretionary with the President of the United States.

Feb. 17, 1831.

7 Stat., 346.
Proclamation, July 9, 1832.

Now, therefore, as a proof of the sincerity of the professions made by the Menomonee Indians, when they declared themselves anxious to terminate in an amicable manner, their disputes with the New York Indians, and also as a further proof of their love and veneration for their great father, the President of the United States, the undersigned, representatives of the Menomonee tribe of Indians, unite and agree with the Commissioners aforesaid, in making and acknowledging the following supplementary articles a part of their former aforesaid agreement.

First. It is agreed between the undersigned, commissioners on behalf of the United States, and the chiefs and warriors representing the Menomonee tribe of Indians, that, for the reasons above expressed, such parts of the *first* article of the agreement, entered into between the parties hereto, on the eighth instant, as limits the removal and settlement of the New York Indians upon the lands therein provided for their future homes, to three years, shall be altered and amended, so as to read as follows: That the President of the United States shall prescribe the time for the removal and settlement of the New York Indians upon the lands thus provided for them; and, at the expiration of such reasonable time, he shall apportion the land among the actual settlers, in such manner as he shall deem equitable and just. And if, within such reasonable time, as the President of the United States shall prescribe for that purpose, the New York Indians, shall refuse to accept the provisions made for their benefit, or having agreed, shall neglect or refuse to remove from New York, and settle on the said lands, within the time prescribed for that purpose, that then, and in either of these events, the lands aforesaid shall be, and remain the property of the United States, according to said *first* article, excepting so much thereof, as the President shall deem justly due to such of the New York Indians, as shall actually have removed to, and settled on the said lands.

Second. It is further agreed that the part of the sixth article of the agreement aforesaid, which requires the removal of those of the New York Indians, who may not be settled on the lands at the end of three years, shall be so amended as to leave such removal discretionary with the President of the United States. The Menomonee Indians having full confidence, that, in making his decision, he will take into consideration the welfare and prosperity of their nation.

Done and signed at Washington, this 17th of February, 1831.

John H. Eaton,	[L. S.]	Ah-ke-ne-pa-weh, his x mark,	[L. S.]
S. C. Stambaugh,	[L. S.]	Shaw-wan-noh, his x mark,	[L. S.]
Kaush-kau-no-naive, his x mark,	[L. S.]	Mash-ke-wet, his x mark,	[L. S.]
A-ya-mah-taw, his x mark,	[L. S.]	Pah-she-nah-sheu, his x mark,	[L. S.]
Ko-ma-ni-kin, his x mark,	[L. S.]	Chi-mi-na-na-quet, his x mark,	[L. S.]
Ko-ma-ni-kee-no-shah, his x mark,	[L. S.]	A-na-quet-to-a-peh, his x mark,	[L. S.]
O-ho-pa-shah, his x mark,	[L. S.]	Sha-ka-cho-ka-mo, his x mark,	[L. S.]

Signed in presence of—

R. A. Forsyth,	John T. Mason,
C. A. Grignon,	P. G. Randolph,
Law. L. V. Kleeck,	A. G. Ellis.

[NOTE.—This treaty was ratified with the following Proviso contained in the Resolution of the Senate:

Provided, That for the purpose of establishing the rights of the New York Indians, on a permanent and just footing, the said treaty shall be ratified with the express understanding that two townships of land on the east side of the Winnebago lake, equal to forty-six thousand and eighty acres shall be laid off, (to commence at some

point to be agreed on,) for the use of the Stockbridge and Munsee tribes; and that the improvements made on the lands now in the possession of the said tribes, on the east side of the Fox river, which said lands are to be relinquished, shall, after being valued by a commissioner to be appointed by the President of the United States, be paid for by the Government: *Provided,* however, that the valuation of such improvements shall not exceed the sum of twenty-five thousand dollars; and that there shall be one township of land, adjoining the foregoing, equal to twenty-three thousand

and forty acres, laid off and granted for the use of the Brothertown Indians, who are to be paid, by the Government the sum of one thousand six hundred dollars for the improvements on the lands now in their possession, on the east side of Fox river, and which lands are to be relinquished by said Indians: Also, that a new line shall be run, parallel to the southwestern boundary line, or course of the tract of five hundred thousand acres described in the first article of this treaty, and set apart for the

New York Indians, to commence at a point on the west side of the Fox river, and one mile above the Grand Shute on Fox river, and at a sufficient distance from the said boundary line as established by the said first article, as shall comprehend the additional quantity of two hundred thousand acres of land, on and along the west side of Fox river, without including any of the confirmed private land claims on the Fox river, and which two hundred thousand acres shall be a part of the five hundred thousand acres intended to be set apart for the Six Nations of the New York Indians and the St. Regis tribe; and that an equal quantity to that which is added on the southwestern side shall be taken off from the northeastern side of the said tract, described in that article, on the Oconto Creek, to be determined by a Commissioner, to be appointed by the President of the United States; so that the whole number of acres to be granted to the Six Nations, and St. Regis tribe of Indians, shall not exceed the quantity originally stipulated by the treaty."]

TREATY WITH THE SENECA, 1831.

Articles of agreement and convention, made and concluded at the City of Washington, on the twenty-eighth day of February, in the year of our Lord, one thousand eight hundred and thirty-one, by and between James B. Gardiner, specially appointed Commissioner on the part of the United States, of the one part, and the undersigned, principal Chiefs and Warriors of the Seneca tribe of Indians, residing on the Sandusky river in the State of Ohio, on the part of said tribe, of the other part; for the cession of the lands now owned and occupied by the said tribe of Indians, lying on the waters of the Sandusky river, and situate within the territorial limits of the organized counties of Seneca and Sandusky, in said State of Ohio.

Feb. 28, 1831.

*7 Stat., 348.
Proclamation, Mar 24, 1831.*

WHEREAS the tribe of Seneca Indians, residing on Sandusky River, in the State of Ohio, have earnestly solicited the President of the United States to negotiate with them, for an exchange of the lands, now owned and occupied by them, for lands of the United States, west of the river Mississippi, and for the removal and permanent settlement of said tribe: Therefore, in order to carry into effect the aforesaid objects, the following articles have been agreed upon:

ART. 1. The Seneca tribe of Indians, in consideration of the stipulations herein made on the part of the United States, do forever cede, release and quit claim to the United States, the lands granted to them, by patent, in fee simple, by the sixth section of the Treaty, made at the foot of the Rapids of the Miami River of Lake Erie, on the twenty-ninth day of September, in the year 1817, containing thirty thousand acres, and described as follows: "beginning on the Sandusky river at the lower corner of the section granted to William Spicer; thence down the river on the east side, with the meanders thereof at high water mark, to a point east of the mouth of Wolf Creek; thence, and from the beginning, east, so far that a north line will include the quantity of thirty thousand acres." And said tribe also cede, as aforesaid, one other tract of land, reserved for the use of the said Senecas, by the second article of the treaty, made at St. Mary's, in the State of Ohio, on the seventeenth day of September, in the year 1818, which tract is described in said treaty as follows: "Ten thousand acres of land, to be laid off on the east side of the Sandusky river, adjoining the south side of their reservation of thirty thousand acres, which begins on the Sandusky river, at the lower corner of William Spicer's section, and excluding therefrom the said William Spicer's section:" making, in the whole of this cession, forty thousand acres.

Cession by the Senecas.

ART. 2. In consideration of the cessions stipulated in the foregoing article; the United States agree to cause the said tribe of Senecas, consisting of about four hundred souls, to be removed in a convenient and suitable manner, to the western side of the Mississippi river; and will grant them, by patent, in fee simple, as long as they shall exist as a nation and remain on the same, a tract of land, situate on, and adjacent to the northern boundary of the lands heretofore granted to the

Removal of Senecas.

Grant to them.

Cherokee nation of Indians, and adjoining the boundary of the State of Missouri; which tract shall extend fifteen miles from east to west, and seven miles from north to south, containing about sixty-seven thousand acres, be the same more or less; for which the President of the United States shall cause letters patent to be issued, in due form of law, agreeably to the Act of the last session of Congress.

One year's support.

ART. 3. The United States will defray the expenses of the removal of the said Senecas, and will moreover supply them with a sufficiency of wholesome provisions, to support them for one year, after their arrival at their new residence.

Gristmill, sawmill, etc.

ART. 4. Out of the first sales, to be made of the lands herein ceded by the Senecas, the United States will cause a grist mill, a saw mill, and a blacksmith shop to be erected on the lands herein granted to the Senecas, with all necessary tools, to be supported and kept in operation, at the expense of the United States, for the sole benefit of the said Senecas; and for these purposes, the United States will employ a miller and a blacksmith, for such term as the President of the United States, in his discretion, may think proper.

Advance of $6,000.

ART. 5. As the Seneca Indians, on their removal, will stand in need of funds to make farms and erect houses; it is agreed that the United States will advance them six thousand dollars, in lieu of the improvements which they have made on the lands herein ceded to the United States; which sum shall be reimbursed from the sales of the lands ceded. An equitable distribution of this sum shall be made by the Chiefs, with the consent of the tribe, in general council assembled, to such individuals of the tribe, as, having left improvements, may be properly entitled to receive the same.

Live stock, etc.

ART. 6. The live stock, farming utensils, and other chattel property, which the Senecas now own, and may not be able to take with them, shall be sold by some agent, to be appointed by the President; and the proceeds paid to the owners of such property, respectively.

Expenses of delegation.

ART. 7. The expenses of the Chiefs, in coming to and remaining at Washington, and returning to Ohio, as well as the expenses and *per diem* pay of the native Interpreter accompanying them, shall be paid by the United States.

Sale of lands.

ART. 8. The United States will expose to public sale, to the highest bidders, at such time and in such manner as the President may direct, the tracts of land herein ceded by the Seneca Indians: And, after deducting from the proceeds of such sale, the *minimum* price of the public lands; the cost of building the saw and grist mills and blacksmith shop for the Senecas; the cost of surveying the lands; and the sum of six thousand dollars, to be advanced in lieu of their present improvements: it is agreed that any balance which may remain, of the avails of the lands after sale as aforesaid, shall constitute a fund for the future exigencies of the tribe, on which the Government of the United States consent and agree to pay to the Chiefs of the nation, for the use and general benefit of the nation, annually, five per cent on said balance, as an annuity: And if, at any time hereafter, the Seneca Chiefs, by and with the advice and consent of their tribe in General Council assembled, shall make known to the President, their desire that the fund, thus to be created, should be dissolved and given to the tribe; the President shall cause the same to be paid over to them, in such manner as he may direct; provided he shall become satisfied of the propriety of so doing.

Annuity, etc.

Annuities by former treaties.

ART. 9. It is agreed that any annuity, accruing to the Senecas, by former treaties, shall be paid to them at their intended residence, west of the Mississippi, under the direction of the President.

Presents.

ART. 10. The United States hereby agree to give to the Senecas, as presents, one hundred rifles, as soon as practicable, and four hundred blankets, for the use of the tribe, to be delivered to them at such time and place as may be directed by the Secretary of War. Also fifty ploughs, fifty hoes and fifty axes, will be given to the tribe, as aforesaid, to assist them in commencing farming.

ART. 11. The Chiefs of the Senecas, being impressed with gratitude towards Henry C. Brish, their sub-agent, for his private advances of money and provisions, and numerous other acts of kindness towards them, as well as his extra services in coming with them to Washington; and having expressed a wish that a quarter section of a hundred and sixty acres of the lands ceded by them, should be granted to him in consideration thereof: the same is hereby granted to him and his heirs to be located under the direction of the President the United States. *Grant to H. C. Brish.*

ART. 12. The lands granted by this Agreement and Convention to the Seneca tribe of Indians shall not be sold or ceded by them, except to the United States. *Lands granted not to be sold.*

ART. 13. It is communicated by the Chiefs here, that, in Council, before they left home, it was agreed by the tribe, that, for their services in coming to the City of Washington, each should receive one hundred dollars, to be paid by said tribe: At the request of said Chiefs, it is agreed that the United States will advance the amount, to wit: five hundred dollars, to be hereafter reimbursed from the sale of their lands in Ohio. *Advances to chiefs.*

In testimony whereof, the parties respectively have this twenty-eighth of February signed the same and affixed their seals.

James B. Gardiner,	[L. S.]
Comstick, his x mark,	[L. S.]
Small Cloud Spicer, his x mark,	[L. S.]
Seneca Steel, his x mark,	[L. S.]
Hard Hickory, his x mark,	[L. S.]
Capt. Good Hunter, his x mark.	[L. S.]

Signed in presence of—

Henry C. Brish, Sub-agent,
George Herron, Interpreter,
W. B. Lewis,
Henry Toland,
P. G. Randolph.

TREATY WITH THE SENECA, ETC., 1831.

Articles of agreement and convention, made and concluded at Lewistown, in the county of Logan, and State of Ohio, on the twentieth day of July, in the year of our Lord one thousand eight hundred and thirty-one, by and between James B. Gardiner, specially appointed commissioner on the part of the United States, and John McElvain, Indian agent for the Wyandots, Senecas and Shawnees, on the one part, and the undersigned principal chiefs and warriors of the mixed band of Senecas and Shawnee Indians residing at and around the said Lewistown, of the other part; for the cession of the lands now owned and occupied by said band, lying on the waters of the Great Miami river, and within the territorial limits of the organized county of Logan, in said State of Ohio.

July 20, 1831.

7 Stat., 351.
Proclamation, Apr. 6, 1832.

WHEREAS the President of the United States, under the authority of the Act of Congress, approved May 28th, 1830, has appointed a special commissioner to confer with the different Indian tribes residing within the constitutional limits of the State of Ohio, and to offer for their acceptance the provisions contained in the before recited act. And whereas the mixed band or tribes of Seneca and Shawnee Indians residing at and around Lewistown in said State have expressed their perfect assent to the conditions of said act, and their willingness and anxiety to remove west of the Mississippi river, in order to obtain a more permanent and advantageous home for themselves and their posterity: Therefore, in order to carry into effect the aforesaid objects, the following articles have been agreed upon by the aforesaid contracting parties; which, when approved by the President and ratified by the Senate of the United States, shall be mutually binding upon the United States and the said Seneca and Shawnee Indians.

Cession of lands to United States.

ARTICLE I. The Seneca and Shawnee Indians, residing at and around Lewistown in the State of Ohio, in consideration of the stipulations herein made on the part of the United States, do for ever cede, release and quit claim to the United States, the lands granted to them by patent in fee simple by the sixth article of the treaty made at the foot of the rapids of the Miami river of Lake Erie, on the twenty-ninth day of September, in the year 1817, containing forty-eight square miles, and described in said treaty as follows:—"Beginning at the intersection of the line run by Charles Roberts in the year one thousand eight hundred and twelve, from the source of the Little Miami river, to the source of the Scioto river, in pursuance of instructions from the commissioners appointed on the part of the United States, to establish the western boundary of the Virginia military reservation, with the Indian boundary line established by the treaty of Greenville in one thousand seven hundred and ninety-five from the crossings above Fort Lawrence to Loramie's store, and to run from such intersection, northerly, with the first mentioned line, so as to include the quantity as nearly in a square form as practicable, after excluding the section of land granted to Nancy Stewart." And the said Senecas and Shawnees also cede to the United States, in manner aforesaid, one other tract of land, reserved for them by the second article of the treaty made at St. Mary's, in Ohio, on the seventeenth of September, in the year 1818, which tract is described in said treaty as follows:—"Eight thousand nine hundred and sixty acres, to be laid off adjoining the west line of the reserve of forty-eight square miles at Lewistown."

Removal of Senecas and Shawnees.

ARTICLE II. In consideration of the cessions stipulated in the foregoing article, the United States agree to cause the said band of Senecas and Shawnees, consisting of about three hundred souls, to be removed in a convenient and suitable manner to the western side of the Mississippi river, and will grant by patent, in fee simple to them and their heirs forever, as long as they shall exist as a nation and remain on the same, a tract of land to contain sixty thousand acres, to be located under the direction of the President of the United States, contiguous to the lands granted to the Senecas of Sandusky by the treaty made with them at the City of Washington, on the 28th of February 1831, and the Cherokee settlements—the east line of said tract shall be within two miles of the west line of the lands granted to the Senecas of Sandusky, and the south line shall be within two miles of the north line of the lands held by the Cherokees—and said two miles between the aforesaid lines, shall serve as a common passway between the before mentioned tribes to prevent them from intruding upon the lands of each other.

Grant of land.

One year's support, etc.

ARTICLE III. The United States will defray the expense of the removal of the said Senecas and Shawnees, and will moreover supply them with a sufficiency of good and wholesome provisions to support them for one year after their arrival at their new residence.

Sawmill and blacksmith's shop.

ARTICLE IV. Out of the first sales to be made of the lands herein ceded by the said Senecas and Shawnees, the United States will cause a saw-mill and a blacksmith shop to be erected on the lands granted to the said Indians west of the Mississippi, with all necessary machinery and tools, to be supported and kept in operation at the expense of the

United States, for the mutual and sole benefit of the said Senecas and Shawnees, and the United States will employ a blacksmith to execute the necessary work for the said Indians for such time as the President of the United States, in his discretion may think proper.

ARTICLE V. In lieu of the improvements which have been made on the lands herein ceded; it is agreed that the United States shall advance to the said Senecas and Shawnees the sum of six thousand dollars, to be reimbursed from the sales of the lands herein ceded by them to the United States. A fair and equitable distribution of this sum shall be made by the Chiefs of the said Senecas and Shawnees, with the consent of their tribes in general council assembled, to such individuals of the tribes as, having left improvements, may be properly entitled to the same. *$6,000 advanced for improvements.*

ARTICLE VI. The live stock, farming utensils, and other chattel property, which the said Senecas and Shawnees now own, and may not be able to carry with them, shall be sold under the superintendence of some suitable person appointed by the Secretary of War, and the proceeds paid over to owners of such property respectively. *Live stock, etc.*

ARTICLE VII. The said Senecas and Shawnees shall be removed to their new residence under the care and protection of some competent and proper person, friendly to them and acquainted with their habits, manners and customs; and the chiefs of the said tribes shall have the privilege of nominating such person to the President, who, if approved of by him, shall have charge of their conveyance. *Agent to superintend removal.*

ARTICLE VIII. The United States will expose to public sale to the highest bidders, in the manner of selling the public lands, the tracts of land herein ceded by the Senecas and Shawnees; and after deducting from the proceeds of such sale the sum of seventy cents per acre, exclusive of the cost of surveying the lands, the cost of the saw mill and blacksmith shop, and the sum of six thousand dollars to be advanced in lieu of the improvements on the ceded lands; it is agreed that any balance which may remain of the lands after sale as aforesaid, shall constitute a fund for the future necessities of said tribes, on which the Government of the United States agree and consent to pay to the chiefs for the use and general benefit of the said tribes annually, five per cent. on the amount of the said balance as an annuity. Said fund to be continued during the pleasure of Congress, unless the chiefs of the said tribes, by and with the consent of the whole of their people in general council assembled, should desire that the fund thus to be created, should be dissolved and paid over to them, in which case the President shall cause the same to be paid over, if in his discretion he shall think the happiness and prosperity of said tribes would be promoted thereby. *Sale of lands.* *Annuity, etc.*

ARTICLE IX. It is agreed that any annuities accruing to the said Senecas and Shawnees by former treaties shall be paid to them at their intended residence west of the Mississippi under the direction of the President. *Annuities by former treaties.*

ARTICLE X. In consideration of the former good conduct and friendly disposition of the aforesaid band of Senecas and Shawnees towards the American Government, and as an earnest of the kind feelings, and good wishes of their great father for the future welfare and happiness of themselves and their posterity, it is agreed that the United States will give them as presents, the following articles, to wit: one hundred blankets, twenty ploughs, one hundred hoes, fifty axes, ten rifles, twenty sets of horse gears, and Russia sheeting sufficient to make forty tents; the whole to be delivered to them as soon as practicable after their arrival at their new residence, except the blankets and the Russia sheeting for the tents, which shall be given at the time of their setting out on their journey; all of said articles to be distributed by the chiefs according to the just claims and necessities of their people. *Presents.*

Lands granted, not to be sold.

ARTICLE XI. The lands granted by this agreement and convention to the said band of Senecas and Shawnees, shall not be sold or ceded by

Guaranty by United States.

them except to the United States. And the United States guarantee that said lands shall never be within the bounds of any State or Territory, nor subject to the laws thereof; and further that the President of the United States will cause said tribe to be protected at their new residence against all interruption or disturbance from any other tribe or nation of Indians, or from any other person or persons whatever; and he shall have the same care and superintendence over them in the country to which they design to remove, that he has heretofore had over them at their present place of residence.

Grant to Jas. McPherson.

ARTICLE XII. At the request of the chiefs of the Senecas and Shawnees, there is granted to James McPherson, one half section of land to contain three hundred and twenty acres, to be laid off in such part of the lands here ceded as he may select, so that the said half section shall adjoin the land heretofore donated to him near the southeast corner of that part of the lands herein ceded which was assigned to the Shawnees by the second article of the treaty made at St. Mary's, on the 17th of September, 1818. And this grant is made in consideration of the sincere attachment of the said chiefs and their people for the said James McPherson, who has lived among them and near them for forty years, and from whom they have received numerous and valuable services and benefits; and also in consideration of the able and candid manner in which he has explained to the Indians the policy of the United States in regard to the future welfare and permanent settlement of the Indian tribes.

Grant to H. H. McPherson.

ARTICLE XIII. At the request of the aforesaid chiefs, there is hereby granted to Henry H. McPherson, an adopted son of their nation, a half section of land, to contain three hundred and twenty acres, to be added to a half section of land granted to him by the said chiefs on the 20th day of March 1821, and approved by the President of the United States, which is to be so laid off as to enlarge the last mentioned grant to a square section.

Grant to interpreter.

ARTICLE XIV. At the special request of the aforesaid chiefs, one quarter section of land, to contain one hundred and sixty acres, is hereby granted to Martin Lane their interpreter, who married a quarter blood Indian woman, and has lived a long time among the Senecas. The said quarter section is to be located under the direction of the President of the United States.

Explanatory.

ARTICLE XV. It is understood and agreed by the present contracting parties that the words, "the lands heretofore donated to him" in the twelfth article of this treaty, have direct and sole reference to a *verbal* donation heretofore made by the said Senecas and Shawnees to the said McPherson, and that the intention is that this treaty should confirm the former as well as the latter grant, so that the said McPherson is entitled to one whole section to be located in the southeast corner of the Shawnee part of the lands herein ceded as aforesaid.

In testimony hereof, the present contracting parties respectively have signed their hands, and affixed their seals, the day and year aforesaid, at Pleasant Plains, near Lewistown, in the State of Ohio.

James B. Gardiner,	[L. S.]	Quashacaugh, or Little Lewis, his	
John McElvain,	[L. S.]	x mark,	[L. S.]
Methomea, or Civil John, his x		James McDonnell, his x mark,	[L. S.]
mark,	[L. S.]	Honede, or Civil John's Son, his x	
Skilleway, or Robbin, his x mark,	[L. S.]	mark,	[L. S.]
Totala Chief, or John Young, his		Run Fast, his x mark,	[L. S.]
x mark,	[L. S.]	Yankee Bill, his x mark,	[L. S.]
Pewyache, his x mark,	[L. S.]	Cold Water, his x mark,	[L. S.]
Mingo Carpenter, his x mark,	[L. S.]	John Sky, his x mark,	[L. S.]
John Jackson, his x mark,	[L. S.]		

Signed, sealed, and delivered in presence of us—

David Robb, Sub-Agent,
James McPherson, United States Inter-
    preter,
H. E. Spencer,
Wm. Rianhard,
John Shelby,
Alexander Thomson,
H. B. Strother,
Benj. S. Brown,

Joseph Parks, his x mark, United States
    Interpreter,
N. Z. McCulloch,
D. M. Workman,
R. Patterson,
A. O. Spencer,
Jas. Stewart,
Stephen Giffin.

I do hereby certify that each and every article of the foregoing convention and agreement, was carefully explained and fully interpreted by me to the chiefs, head men and warriors who have signed the same.

Martin Lane, United States Interpreter. [L. S.]

TREATY WITH THE SHAWNEE, 1831.

Articles of agreement and convention, made and concluded at Wapagh-konnetta, in the county of Allen and State of Ohio on the 8th day of August in the year of our Lord one thousand eight hundred and thirty-one, by and between James B. Gardiner specially appointed commissioner on the part of the United States and John McElvain, Indian Agent for the Wyandots, Senecas and Shawnees residing in the State of Ohio, on the one part, and the undersigned, principal Chiefs, Headmen and Warriors of the tribe of Shawnee Indians residing at Wapaghkonnetta and Hog Creek, within the territorial limits of the organized county of Allen, in the State of Ohio.

Aug. 8, 1831.

7 Stat., 355.
Proclamation, Apr. 6, 1832.

Whereas the President of the United States under the authority of the Act of Congress, approved May 28, 1830, has appointed a special commissioner to confer with the different Indian tribes residing within the constitutional limits of the State of Ohio, and to offer for their acceptance the provisions of the before recited act:—And whereas the tribe or band of Shawnee Indians residing at Wapaghkonnetta and on Hog Creek in the said State, have expressed their perfect assent to the conditions of the said act, and their willingness and anxiety to remove west of the Mississippi river, in order to obtain a more permanent and advantageous home for themselves and their posterity. Therefore, in order to carry into effect the aforesaid objects, the following articles of Convention have been agreed upon by the aforesaid contracting parties, which, when ratified by the President of the United States, by and with the advice and consent of the Senate thereof, shall be mutually binding upon the United States and the said Shawnee Indians.

1830, ch. 148.

ARTICLE I. The tribe or band of Shawnee Indians residing at Wapaghkonnetta and on Hog Creek in the State of Ohio, in consideration of the stipulations herein made, on the part of the United States, do for ever cede, release and quit claim to the United States the lands granted to them by patent in fee simple by the sixth section of the treaty made at the foot of the Rapids of the Miami river of Lake Erie on the 29th day of September in the year of our Lord 1817, containing one hundred and twenty-five sections or square miles, and granted in two reservations and described in the said sixth section of the aforesaid treaty as follows:—"A tract of land ten miles square, the centre of which shall be the council house at Wahpaghkonnetta;" and "a tract of land containing twenty-five square miles, which is to join the tract granted at Wapaghkonnetta, and to include the Shawnee settlement on Hog creek, and to be laid off as nearly as possible in a square form," which said two tracts or reservations of land were

Cession of lands to United States.

granted as aforesaid to the said Shawnee Indians by the patents signed by the Commissioner of the General Land Office and certified by the Secretary of War dated the 20th day of April 1821. Also, one other tract of land, granted to the said Shawnees by the second article of the treaty made at St. Mary's in the state of Ohio, on the 17th day of September in the year 1818, and described therein as follows: "Twelve thousand eight hundred acres of land to be laid off adjoining the east line of their reserve of ten miles square at Wapaghkonnetta," making in the whole of the aforesaid cessions to the United States by the aforesaid Shawnees, one hundred and forty-five sections or square miles, which includes all the land now owned or claimed by the said band or tribe of Shawnees in the State of Ohio.

Removal of Shawnee.

Grant of land west of the Mississippi.

ARTICLE II. In consideration of the cessions stipulated in the foregoing article, the United States agree to cause the said tribe or band of Shawnees, consisting of about four hundred souls, to be removed in a convenient and suitable manner to the Western side of the Mississippi river, and will grant by patent in fee simple to them and their heirs for ever, as long as they shall exist as a nation and remain upon the same, a tract of land to contain one hundred thousand acres, to be located under the direction of the President of the United States, within the tract of land equal to fifty miles square, which was granted to the Shawnee Indians of the State of Missouri by the second article of a treaty made at the city of Saint Louis in said State, with the said Shawnees of Missouri by William Clark, Superintendent of Indian Affairs, on the 7th day of November in the year 1825; and in which it is provided that the grant aforesaid shall be for the Shawnee tribe of Indians within the State of Missouri, "and for those of the same nation now residing in Ohio, who may hereafter emigrate to the west of the Mississippi;" but if there should not be a sufficiency of good land unoccupied by the Shawnee Indians who have already settled on the tract granted as aforesaid by the said treaty of Saint Louis; then the tract of one hundred thousand acres, hereby granted to the said Shawnees of Ohio, parties to this compact, shall be located under the direction of the President of the United States on lands contiguous to the said Shawnees of Missouri, or on any other unappropriated lands within the district of country designed for the emigrating Indians of the United States.

One year's support, etc.

ARTICLE III. The United States will defray the expenses of the removal of the said band or tribe of Shawnees, and will moreover supply them with a sufficiency of good and wholesome provisions, to support them for one year after their arrival at their new residence.

Sawmill, gristmill, etc.

ARTICLE IV. Out of the first sales to be made of the lands herein ceded by the said Shawnees, the United States will cause a good and substantial saw mill, and a grist mill, built in the best manner, and to contain two pair of stones and a good bolting cloth, to be erected on the lands granted to the said Shawnees, west of the Mississippi; and said mills shall be solely for their use and benefit. The United States will, out of the sales of the ceded lands, as aforesaid, cause a blacksmith shop, (to contain all the necessary tools,) to be built for the said Shawnees, at their intended residence, and a blacksmith shall be employed by the United States, as long as the President thereof may deem proper, to execute all necessary and useful work for said Indians.

$13,000 advanced for improvements.

ARTICLE V. In lieu of the improvements which have been made on the lands herein ceded, it is agreed that the United States shall advance to the said Shawnees (for the purpose of enabling them to erect houses and open farms at their intended residence) the sum of thirteen thousand dollars, to be reimbursed from the sales of the lands herein ceded by them to the United States. A fair and equitable distribution of this sum shall be made by the chiefs of the said Shawnees; with the consent of the people, in general council assembled, to such individuals of their tribe who have made improvements on the lands herein ceded, and may be properly entitled to the same.

ARTICLE VI. The farming utensils, live stock and other chattel property, which the said Shawnees now own, and may not be able to carry with them, shall be sold, under the superintendance of some suitable person, appointed by the Secretary of War for that purpose, and the proceeds paid over to the owners of such property respectively.

Farming utensils, etc.

ARTICLE VII. The United States will expose to public sale to the highest bidder, in the manner of selling the public lands, the tracts of land herein ceded by the said Shawnees. And after deducting from the proceeds of such sales the sum of seventy cents per acre, exclusive of the cost of surveying, the cost of the grist mill, saw mill and blacksmith shop and the aforesaid sum of thirteen thousand dollars, to be advanced in lieu of improvements; it is agreed that any balance, which may remain of the avails of the lands, after sale as aforesaid, shall constitute a fund for the future necessities of said tribe, parties to this compact, on which the United States agree to pay to the chiefs, for the use and general benefit of their people, annually, five per centum on the amount of said balance, as an annuity. Said fund to be continued during the pleasure of Congress, unless the chiefs of the said tribe, or band, by and with the consent of their people, in general council assembled, should desire that the fund thus to be created, should be dissolved and paid over to them; in which case the President shall cause the same to be so paid, if in his discretion, he shall believe the happiness and prosperity of said tribe would be promoted thereby.

Sale of lands ceded by Shawnee.

Annuity, etc.

ARTICLE VIII. It is agreed that any annuities, accruing to the said band or tribe of Shawnees, by former treaties, shall be paid to them at their intended residence west of the Mississippi, under the direction of the President.

Annuities by former treaties.

ARTICLE IX. In consideration of the good conduct and friendly dispositions of the said band of Shawnees towards the American Government, and as an earnest of the kind feelings and good wishes of the people of the United States, for the future welfare and happiness of the said Shawnees, it is agreed that the United States, will give them, as presents, the following articles, to be fairly divided by the chiefs, among their people, according to their several necessities, to wit: two hundred blankets, forty ploughs, forty sets of horse gears, one hundred and fifty hoes, fifty axes, and Russia sheeting sufficient for fifty tents:—the whole to be delivered to them, as soon as practicable, after their arrival at their new residence, except the blankets and Russia sheeting, which shall be given previously to their removal.

Presents.

ARTICLE X. The lands granted by this agreement and convention to the said band or tribe of Shawnees, shall not be sold nor ceded by them, except to the United States. And the United States guarantee that said lands shall never be within the bounds of any State or territory, nor subject to the laws thereof; and further, that the President of the United States will cause said tribe to be protected at their intended residence, against all interruption or disturbance from any other tribe or nation of Indians, or from any other person or persons whatever, and he shall have the same care and superintendence over them, in the country to which they are to remove, that he has heretofore had over them at their present place of residence.

Lands granted, not to be sold.

Guarantee.

ARTICLE XI. It is understood by the present contracting parties, that any claims which Francis Duchouquet may have, under former treaties, to a section or any quantity of the lands herein ceded to the United States, are not to be prejudiced by the present compact; but to remain as valid as before.

Claims of F. Duchouquet.

ARTICLE XII. In addition to the presents given in the ninth article of this convention, it is agreed that there shall also be given to the

Additional presents.

said Shawnees, twenty-five rifle guns, to be distributed in the manner provided in said ninth article.

ARTICLE XIII. At the request of the chiefs, there is granted to Joseph Parks, a quarter blooded Shawnee, one section of land to contain six hundred and forty acres, and to include his present improvements at the old town near Wapaghkonnetta, in consideration of his constant friendship and many charitable and valuable services towards the said Shawnees:—and at the request of the chiefs, it is also stipulated that the price of an average section of the lands herein ceded, shall be reserved in the hands of the Government, to be paid to their friends, the Shawnees who now reside on the river Huron in the Territory of Michigan, for the purpose of bearing their expenses, should they ever wish to follow the Shawnees of Wapaghkonnetta and Hog creek to their new residence west of the Mississippi.

ARTICLE XIV. At the request of the chiefs it is agreed that they shall be furnished with two cross-cut saws for the use of their tribe; and also that they shall receive four grindstones annually, for the use of their people, to be charged upon the surplus fund, and they shall further receive, as presents, ten hand saws, ten drawing knives, twenty files, fifty gimblets, twenty augurs of different sizes, ten planes of different sizes, two braces and bits, four hewing axes, two dozen scythes, five frows and five grubbing hoes.

In testimony whereof, the said James B. Gardiner, specially appointed commissioner on the part of the United States, and John McElvain, Indian agent as aforesaid, and the said chiefs, warriors and head men of the said Shawnees of Wapaghkonnetta and Hog creek, have hereunto set their hands and seals at Wapaghkonnetta, this eighth day of August, in the year of our Lord one thousand eight hundred and thirty-one.

James B. Gardiner, [L. s.]
John McElvain, [L. s.]
Lauloway, or John Perry, his x
  mark, [L. s.]
Nolesimo, or Henry Clay, his x
  mark, [L. s.]
Peaghtucker, or McNear, his x
  mark, [L. s.]
P. H. Tha, his x mark, [L. s.]
Wiwelipea, his x mark, [L. s.]
Quarky, his x mark, [L. s.]
Letho, his x mark, [L. s.]
Naecimo, or little fox, his x mark, [L. s.]
Pamothaway, or George Williams,
  his x mark, [L. s.]
Squecawpowee, or Geo. McDougall,
  his x mark, [L. s.]

Lawathtucker, or John Wolf, his x
  mark, [L. s.]
Thothweillew, or bright horn, his
  x mark, [L. s.]
P. H. Thawtaw, or Peter Corn-
  stock, his x mark, [L. s.]
Saucothcaw, or spy buck, his x
  mark, [L. s.]
Chawwee, or ——, his x mark, [L. s.]
Thawquotsaway, or big man, his x
  mark, [L. s.]
Jakescaw, or Cap. Tom, his x mark, [L. s.]
Quelenee, his x mark, [L. s.]
Chissecaw, his x mark, [L. s.]
Chupehecaw, or old big knife, his x
  mark, [L. s.]
Be dee dee, or Big Jim, his x mark, [L. s.]

Signed and sealed in presence of us—

Wm. Walker, Secretary to the Commissioners,
David Robb, Sub. Agent,
John McLaughlin,
Alexander Thompson,
Henry Harvey,
John Elliott,
Amos Kenworthy,
John Armstrong,

Jeremiah A. Dooley,
Warpole, a Wyandot chief, his x mark,
Tashnewau, Ottoway chief, his x mark,
Francis Johnston,
John Gunn,
James S. Chewers,
A. D. Kinnard,
Pay ton quot, Ottoway chief, his x mark,

I hereby certify that the several articles in the foregoing treaty have been fairly interpreted and fully explained to the chiefs, head men and warriors of the Shawnee band or tribe, who have signed the same.

Joseph Parks, his x mark,
United States Interpreter.

TREATY WITH THE OTTAWA, 1831.

Articles of agreement and convention made and concluded this thirtieth day of August, in the year of our Lord one thousand eight hundred and thirty-one, by and between James B. Gardiner, specially appointed commissioner on the part of the United States, on the one part, and the chiefs, head men and warriors of the band of Ottoway Indians residing within the State of Ohio on the other part, for a cession of the several tracts of land now held and occupied by said Indians within said State, by reservations made under the treaty concluded at Detroit on the 17th day of November, 1807, and the treaty made at the foot of the rapids of the Miami river of Lake Erie, on the 29th of September, 1817.

Aug. 30, 1831.

7 Stat., 359.
Proclamation, April 6, 1832.

WHEREAS the President of the United States, under the authority of the act of Congress, approved May 28, 1830, has appointed a special commissioner to confer with the different Indian tribes residing within the constitutional limits of the State of Ohio, and to offer for their acceptance the provisions of the before mentioned act: And whereas the band of Ottoways residing on Blanchard's fork of the Great Auglaize river, and on the Little Auglaize river at Oquanoxie's village, have expressed their consent to the conditions of said act, and their willingness to remove west of the Mississippi, in order to obtain a more permanent and advantageous home for themselves and their posterity:

1830, ch. 148.

Therefore, in order to carry into effect the aforesaid objects, the following articles of convention have been agreed upon, by the aforesaid contracting parties, which, when ratified by the President of the United States, by and with the consent of the Senate thereof, shall be mutually binding upon the United States and the aforesaid band of Ottoway Indians.

ARTICLE I. The band of Ottoway Indians, residing on Blanchard's fork of the great Auglaize river, and at Oquanoxa's village on the Little Auglaize river, in consideration of the stipulations herein made on the part of the United States, do forever cede, release and quit claim to the United States, the lands reserved to them by the last clause of the sixth article of the treaty made at the foot of the Rapids of the Miami of the Lake on the 29th of September, 1817; which clause is in the following words: "There shall be reserved for the use of the Ottoway Indians, but not granted to them, a tract of land on Blanchard's fork of the Great Auglaize river, to contain five miles square, the center of which tract is to be where the old trace crosses the said fork; and one other tract, to contain three miles square on the Little Auglaize river, to include Oquanoxa's village," making in said cession twenty-one thousand seven hundred and sixty acres.

Cession of land to United States by Ottawa Indians.

ARTICLE II. The chiefs, head men and warriors of the band of Ottoway Indians, residing at and near the places called *Roche de Boeuf* and Wolf rapids, on the Miami river of Lake Erie, and within the State of Ohio, wishing to become parties to this convention, and not being willing, at this time, to stipulate for their removal west of the Mississippi; do hereby agree, in consideration of the stipulations herein made for them on the part of the United States, to cede, release and forever quit claim to the United States the following tracts of land, reserved to them by the treaty made at Detroit on the 17th day of November, 1807, to wit, the tract of six miles square above *Roche de Boeuf*, to include the village where Tondagonie (or Dog) formerly lived; and also three miles square at the Wolf rapids aforesaid, which was substituted for the three miles square granted by the said treaty of Detroit to the said Ottoways "to include *Presque Isle*," but which could not be granted as stipulated in said treaty of Detroit, in consequence of its collision with the grant of twelve miles square to the United States by the treaty of Greenville;

Cession by a certain other band of Ottawa.

making in the whole cession made by this article twenty-eight thousand one hundred and fifty-seven acres, which is exclusive of a grant made to Yellow Hair (or Peter Minor) by the 8th article of the treaty at the foot of the Rapids of Miami, on the 29th of September, 1817, and for which said Minor holds a patent from the General Land Office for 643 acres.

Removal of Ottawas residing at Blanchards Fork, etc,

Grant of land to said band.

ARTICLE III. In consideration of the cessions made in the first article of this convention, the United States agree to cause the band of Ottoways residing on Blanchard's fork, and at Oquanoxa's village, as aforesaid, consisting of about two hundred souls, to be removed, in a convenient and suitable manner, to the western side of the Mississippi river; and will grant, by patent in fee simple, to them and their heirs for ever, as long as they shall exist as a nation, and remain upon the same, a tract of land to contain thirty-four thousand acres, to be located adjoining the south or west line of the reservation equal to fifty miles square, granted to the Shawnees of Missouri and Ohio on the Kanzas river and its branches, by the treaty made at St. Louis, November 7th, 1825.

One year's support, etc.

ARTICLE IV. The United States will defray the expense of the removal of the said band of Ottoways, and will moreover supply them with a sufficiency of good and wholesome provisions to support them for one year after their arrival at their new residence.

$2,000 to be advanced for improvements.

ARTICLE V. In lieu of the improvements which have been made on the lands ceded by the first article of this convention, it is agreed that the United States shall advance to the Ottoways of Blanchard's fork and Oquanoxa's village, the sum of two thousand dollars, to be reimbursed from the sales of the lands ceded by the said first article. And it is expressly understood that this sum is not to be paid until the said Ottoways arrive at their new residence, and that it is for the purpose of enabling them to erect houses and open farms for their accommodation and subsistence in their new country. A fair and equitable distribution of this sum shall be made by the chiefs of the said Ottoways, with the consent of their people, in general council assembled, to such individuals of their band as may have made improvements on the lands ceded by the first article of this convention, and may be properly entitled to the same.

Farming utensils, live stock, etc.

ARTICLE VI. The farming untensils, live stock and other chattel property, which the said Ottoways of Blanchard's fork and Oquanoxa's village now own, shall be sold, under the superintendence of some suitable person appointed by the Secretary of War; and the proceeds paid to the owners of such property respectively.

Sale of lands ceded by said band.

ARTICLE VII. The United States will expose to sale to the highest bidder, in the manner of selling the public lands, the tracts ceded by the first article of this convention, and after deducting from the proceeds of such sales the sum of seventy cents per acre, exclusive of the cost of surveying, and the sum of two thousand dollars advanced in lieu of improvements; it is agreed that the balance, or so much thereof as may be necessary, shall be hereby guaranteed for the payment of the debts, which the said Ottoways of Blanchard's fork, and Oquanoxa's village may owe in the State of Ohio and the Territory of Michigan, and agree to be due by them, as provided in the sixteenth article of this convention; and any surplus of the proceeds of said lands, which may still remain, shall be vested by the President in Government stock, and five per cent. thereon shall be paid to the said Ottoways of Blanchard's fork and Oquanoxa's village, as an annuity during the pleasure of Congress.

Annuities by former treaties.

ARTICLE VIII. It is agreed that the said band of Ottoways of Blanchard's fork and Oquanoxa's village, shall receive, at their new residence, a fair proportion of the annuities due to their nation by former treaties, which shall be apportioned under the direction of the Secretary of War, according to their actual numbers.

ARTICLE IX. The lands granted by this agreement and convention to the said band of Ottoways residing at Blanchard's fork and Oquanoxa's village shall not be sold nor ceded by them, except to the United States. And the United States guarantee that said lands shall never be within the bounds of any State or territory, nor subject to the laws thereof, and further, that the President of the United States will cause said band to be protected at their new residence, against all interruption or disturbance from any other tribe or nation of Indians and from any other person or persons whatever: and he shall have the same care and superintendence over them in the country to which they design to remove, that he now has at their present residence. *Lands granted not to be sold.* *Guarantee.*

ARTICLE X. As an evidence of the good will and kind feeling of the people of the United States towards the said band of Ottoways of Blanchard's fork and Oquanoxa's village; it is agreed that the following articles shall be given them, as presents, to wit: eighty blankets, twenty-five rifle guns, thirty-five axes, twelve ploughs, twenty sets of horse gears, and Russian sheeting sufficient for tents for their whole band; the whole to be delivered according to the discretion of the Secretary of War. *Presents.*

ARTICLE XI. In consideration of the cessions made in the second article of this convention by the chiefs, head men and warriors of the band of Ottoways residing at *Roche de Bœuf* and Wolf rapids, it is agreed that the United States will grant to said band by patent in fee simple, forty thousand acres of land, west of the Mississippi, adjoining the lands assigned to the Ottoways of Blanchard's fork and Oquanoxa's village, or in such other situation as they may select, on the unappropriated lands in the district of country designed for the emigrating Indians of the United States. And whenever the said band may think proper to accept of the above grant, and remove west of the Mississippi, the United States agree that they shall be removed and subsisted by the Government in the same manner as is provided in this convention for their brethren of Blanchard's fork and Oquanoxa's village, and they shall receive like presents, in proportion to their actual numbers, under the direction of the Secretary of War. It is also understood and agreed that the said band, when they shall agree to remove west of the Mississippi, shall receive their proportion of the annuities due their nation by former treaties, and be entitled in every respect to the same privileges, advantages and protection, which are herein extended to their brethren and the other emigrating Indians of the State of Ohio. *Grant of land to Ottawas residing at Roche de Bœuf, etc.*

ARTICLE XII. The lands ceded by the second article of this convention shall be sold by the United States to the highest bidder, in the manner of selling the public lands, and after deducting from the avails thereof *seventy* cents per acre, exclusive of the cost of surveying, the balance is hereby guaranteed to discharge such debts of the Ottoways residing on the river and bay of the Miami of Lake Erie, as they may herein acknowledge to be due, and wish to be paid. And whatever overplus may remain of the avails of said lands, after discharging their debts as aforesaid, shall be paid to them in money, provided they shall refuse to remove west of the Mississippi, and wish to seek some other home among their brethren in the Territory of Michigan. But should the said band agree to remove west of the Mississippi, then any overplus which may remain to them, after paying their debts, shall be invested by the President, and five per centum paid to them as an annuity, as is provided for their brethren by this convention. *Sale of lands ceded by said band.* *Proceeds of sales.*

ARTICLE XIII. At the request of the chiefs residing at *Roche de Bœuf* and Wolf rapids, it is agreed that there shall be reserved for the use of Wau be ga kake (one of the chiefs) for three years only, from the signing of this convention, a section of land below and adjoining the section granted to and occupied by Yellow Hair or Peter Minor; and also there is reserved in like manner and for the term of three years, and no longer, for the use of Muck-qui-on-a, or Bearskin, one *Temporary reservations.*

section and a half, below Wolf rapids, and to include his present residence and improvements. And it is also agreed that the said Bearskin shall have the occupancy of a certain small island in the Maumee river, opposite his residence, where he now raises corn, which island belongs to the United States, and is now unsold; but the term of this occupancy is not guaranteed for three years; but only so long as the President shall think proper to reserve the same from sale. And it is further understood, that any of the temporary reservations made by this article, may be surveyed and sold by the United States, subject to the occupancy of three years, hereby granted to the aforesaid Indians.

Grants to H. Thebault and W. McNabb. ARTICLE XIV. At the request of the chiefs of *Roche de Boeuf* and Wolf rapids, there is hereby granted to Hiram Thebeault (a half blooded Ottoway,) a quarter section of land, to contain one hundred and sixty acres and to include his present improvements at the Bear rapids of the Miami of the Lake. Also, one quarter section of land, to contain like quantity, to William McNabb, (a half blooded Ottoway,) to adjoin the quarter section granted to Hiram Thebeault. In surveying the above reservations, no greater front is to be given on the river, than would properly belong to said quarter sections, in the common manner of surveying the public lands.

Grant to children of Peter Minor. ARTICLE XV. At the request of the chiefs of *Roche de Beouf* and Wolf rapids, there is granted to the children of Yellow Hair, (or Peter Minor,) one half section of land, to contain three hundred and twenty acres, to adjoin the north line of the section of land now held by said Peter Minor, under patent from the President of the United States, bearing date the 24th of November, 1827, and the lines are not to approach nearer than one mile to the Miami river of the Lake.

Claims against Ottawas recognized. ARTICLE XVI. It is agreed by the chiefs of Blanchard's fork and Oquanoxa's village, and the chiefs of *Roche de Boeuf* and Wolf rapids, jointly, that they are to pay out of the surplus proceeds of the several tracts herein ceded by them, equal proportions of the claims against them by John E. Hunt, John Hollister, Robert A. Forsythe, Payne C. Parker, Peter Minor, Theodore E. Phelps, Collister Haskins and S. and P. Carlan. The chiefs aforesaid acknowledge the claim of John E. Hunt to the amount of five thousand six hundred dollars; the claim of John Hollister to the amount of five thousand six hundred dollars; the claim of Robert A. Forsythe to the amount of seven thousand five hundred and twenty-four dollars, in which is included the claims assigned to said Forsythe by Isaac Hull, Samuel Vance, A. Peltier, Oscar White and Antoine Lepoint. They also allow the claim of Payne C. Parker to the amount of five hundred dollars; the claim of Peter Minor to the amount of one thousand dollars; the claim of Theodore E. Phelps to the amount of three hundred dollars; the claim of Collister Haskins to the amount of fifty dollars, but the said Haskins claims fifty dollars more as his proper demand: and the claim of S. and P. Carlan to the amount of three hundred and ninety-eight dollars and twenty-five cents. The aforesaid chiefs also allow the claim of Joseph Laronger to the amount of two hundred dollars, and the claim of Daniel Lakin to the amount of seventy dollars. Notwithstanding the above acknowledgments and allowances, it is expressly understood and agreed by the respective parties to this compact, that the several claims in this article, and the items which compose the same, shall be submitted to the strictest scrutiny and examination of the Secretary of War, and the accounting officers of the Treasury Department, and such amount only shall be allowed as may be found just and true.

Privileges by former treaties to cease. ARTICLE XVII. On the ratification of this convention, the privileges of every description, granted to the Ottoway nation within the State of Ohio, by the treaties under which they hold the reservations of land herein ceded, shall forever cease and determine.

ARTICLE XVIII. Whenever the deficiency of five hundred and eighty dollars, which accrued in the annuities of the Ottoways for 1830, shall be paid, the parties to this convention, residing on Blanchard's fork and Oquanoxa's village, shall receive their fair and equitable portion of the same, either at their present or intended residence.

Deficiency in annui-
ties for 1830.

ARTICLE XIX. The chiefs signing this convention, also agree, in addition to the claims allowed in the sixteenth article thereof, that they owe John Anderson two hundred dollars; and Francis Lavoy two hundred dollars.

Additional claims.

ARTICLE XX. It is agreed that there shall be allowed to Nau-on-quai-que-zhick, one hundred dollars, out of the surplus fund accruing from the sales of the lands herein ceded, in consequence of his not owing any debts, and having his land sold, to pay the debts of his brethren.

Allowance to Nau-
on-quai-que-zhick.

In testimony whereof, the aforesaid parties to this convention, have hereunto set their hands and seals at the Indian reserve on the Miami bay of lake Erie, the day and year above written.

James B. Gardiner,	[L. S.]	Cum-chaw, (Blanchard's fork,) his
Ar-taish-nai-wau, his x mark,	[L. S.]	x mark, [L. S.]
O-quai naas-a, his x mark,	[L. S.]	Cum-chaw, (Wolf rapids,) his x
Os-cha-no, or Charlo, his x mark,	[L. S.]	mark, [L. S.]
Quacint, his x mark,	[L. S.]	Sus-sain, his x mark, [L. S.]
Waw-ba-ga-cake, his x mark,	[L. S.]	Ca-ba-yaw, his x mark, [L. S.]
Che-cauk, his x mark,	[L. S.]	O-sho-quene, his x mark, [L. S.]
Peton-o-quet, his x mark,	[L. S.]	Muc-co-tai-pee-nai-see, his x mark, [L. S.]
Oshaw-wa-non, his x mark,	[L. S.]	O-sage, his x mark, [L. S.]
Pe-nais-we, his x mark.	[L. S.]	Pan-tee, his x mark, [L. S.]
Nau-qua-ga-sheek, his x mark,	[L. S.]	Me-sau-kee, his x mark, [L. S.]
Pe-nais-won-quet, his x mark,	[L. S.]	O-mus-se-nau, his x mark, [L. S.]
Pe-she-keinee, his x mark,	[L. S.]	Non-dai-wau, his x mark, [L. S.]
		E-au-vaince, his x mark, [L. S.]

Signed and sealed in presence of

Wm. Walker, Secretary to Commissioner,
R. A. Forsyth, Sub. Agent of Indian Affairs.
Levi S. Humphrey,
James H. Forsyth,
William Wilson,
Henry Conner, Sub-Agent,

John Anderson,
John McDouell,
Dan. B. Miller,
Lambert Cauchois,
Geo. B. Knaggs,
J. J. Godfroy.

I do hereby certify that each article of the foregoing convention was fairly interpreted and fully explained by me to the chiefs, head men, and warriors, who have signed the same.

Henry Conner, Interpreter.

TREATY WITH THE WYANDOT, 1832.

Articles of agreement and convention made and concluded at McCutch-eonsville, Crawford county, Ohio, on the nineteenth day of January, 1832, by and between James B. Gardiner, specially appointed commissioner on the part of the United States, and the Chiefs, Headmen and Warriors of the band of Wyandots, residing at the Big Spring in said county of Crawford, and owning a reservation of 16,000 acres at that place.

Jan. 19, 1832.

7 Stat., 364.
Proclamation, Apr.
6, 1832.

WHEREAS the said band of Wyandots have become fully convinced that, whilst they remain in their present situation in the State of Ohio, in the vicinity of a white population, which is continually increasing and crowding around them, they cannot prosper and be happy, and the morals of many of their people will be daily becoming more and more vitiated—And understanding that the Government of the United States is willing to purchase the reservation of land on which they reside, and for that purpose have deputed the said James B. Gardiner as special commissioner to treat for a cession for the same:—Therefore, to effect the aforesaid objects, the said Chiefs, Headmen and Warriors, and the said James B. Gardiner, have this day entered into and agreed upon the following articles of convention.

Cession of land to United States.

ARTICLE I. The band of Wyandots residing at the Big Spring in the county of Crawford, and State of Ohio, do hereby forever cede and relinquish to the United States the reservation of sixteen thousand acres of land, granted to them by the second article of the treaty made at St. Mary's, on the seventeenth day of September, eighteen hundred and eighteen, which grant is in the following words, to wit: "There shall be reserved for the use of the Wyandots residing at Solomon's town and on Blanchard's fork sixteen thousand acres of land, to be laid off in a square form, on the head of Blanchard's fork, the centre of which shall be at the Big spring, on the road leading from Upper Sandusky to Fort Findlay."

Sale of land.

ARTICLE II. The United States stipulate with the said band of Wyandots that, as soon as practicable after the ratification of this treaty, the aforesaid tract of sixteen thousand acres shall be surveyed into sections and put into market and sold in the ordinary manner of selling the public lands of the United States; and when the same shall be sold, or as soon as any part thereof shall be disposed of, (be the price received therefore more or less) there shall be paid to the chiefs, headmen and warriors, signing this treaty, for the benefit of all the said band of Wyandots, the sum of one dollar and twenty-five cents per acre for each and every acre so sold or for sale. The said price shall be paid in silver, and in the current coin of the United States.

United States agree to pay for improvements.

ARTICLE III. For the improvements now made upon said reservation the United States agree to pay a fair valuation in money, according to the appraisement of Joseph McCutcheon, Esq. (or such person as the Secretary of War may depute for that purpose) and an appraiser to be chosen by the said band of Wyandots. And in case the said appraisers shall not be able to agree upon any of their valuations, they shall call to their assistance some competent citizen of the county of Crawford.

Reservation for Roe-nu-nas.

ARTICLE IV. There shall [be] reserved for Roe-nu-nas, one of the oldest chiefs of said band, one half section, to contain three hundred and twenty acres, and to include the improvements where he now lives.

Removal.

ARTICLE V. It is expressly understood between the present contracting parties, that the said band of Wyandots may, as they think proper, remove to Canada, or to the river Huron in Michigan, where they own a reservation of land, or to any place they may obtain a right or privilege from others Indians to go.

ARTICLE VI. [Rejected.]

Special subagent.

ARTICLE VII. Inasmuch as the band of Wyandots, herein treating, have separated themselves from the Wyandots at Upper Sandusky and on the Sandusky plains, they ask of the General Government that there may be a special sub-agent and protector appointed for them whilst they remain in the State of Ohio, and they respectfully recommend Joseph McCutcheon, Esq. of the county of Crawford, as a fit and proper person to act in such capacity; and that he may have the power to employ such interpreter as he may think proper in his intercourse with said band.

Treaty binding when ratified.

The aforesaid articles of agreement shall be mutually binding upon the present contracting parties, when ratified by the President of the United States, by and with the consent of the Senate thereof.

J. B. Gardiner,   [L. S.]
Roe-nu-nas, his x mark,
Bear-skin, his x mark,
Shi-a-wa, or John Solomon, his x mark,
John McLean, his x mark,
Matthew Grey Eyes, his x mark,
Isaac Driver, his x mark,
John D. Brown,
Alex. Clarke.

Done in presence of—

C. Clarke, Secretary to the Commissioner,
Joseph McCutcheon, justice of the peace in the county of Crawford, Ohio,
John C. Dewit,
Richard Reynolds,
G. W. Sampson.

EXPLANATION.

In the first draft of this treaty, provision was made for the removal of the band west of the Mississippi, but they refused to accept of a grant of land, or to remove there, and the articles having relation thereto were accordingly omitted. It was therefore necessary to omit the 6th article; and circumstances did not admit of time to remodel and copy the whole treaty.

J. B. Gardiner,
Special Commissioner, &c.

TREATY WITH THE CREEKS, 1832.

Articles of a treaty made at the City of Washington between Lewis Cass, thereto specially authorized by the President of the United States, and the Creek tribe of Indians.

Mar. 24, 1832.

7 Stat., 366.
Proclamation, Apr. 4, 1832.

ARTICLE I. The Creek tribe of Indians cede to the United States all their land, East of the Mississippi river.

Cession of land by the Indians.

ARTICLE II. The United States engage to survey the said land as soon as the same can be conveniently done, after the ratification of this treaty, and when the same is surveyed to allow ninety principal Chiefs of the Creek tribe to select one section each, and every other head of a Creek family to select one half section each, which tracts shall be reserved from sale for their use for the term of five years, unless sooner disposed of by them. A census of these persons shall be taken under the direction of the President and the selections shall be made so as to include the improvements of each person within his selection, if the same can be so made, and if not, then all the persons belonging to the same town, entitled to selections, and who cannot make the same, so as to include their improvements, shall take them in one body in a proper form. And twenty sections shall be selected, under the direction of the President for the orphan children of the Creeks, and divided and retained or sold for their benefit as the President may direct. Provided however that no selections or locations under this treaty shall be so made as to include the agency reserve.

Land to be surveyed, etc.

ARTICLE III. These tracts may be conveyed by the persons selecting the same, to any other persons for a fair consideration, in such manner as the President may direct. The contract shall be certified by some person appointed for that purpose by the President, but shall not be valid 'till the President approves the same. A title shall be given by the United States on the completion of the payment.

Conveyances.

ARTICLE IV. At the end of five years, all the Creeks entitled to these selections, and desirous of remaining, shall receive patents therefor in fee simple, from the United States.

Land patents.

ARTICLE V. All intruders upon the country hereby ceded shall be removed therefrom in the same manner as intruders may be removed by law from other public land until the country is surveyed, and the selections made; excepting however from this provision those white persons who have made their own improvements, and not expelled the Creeks from theirs. Such persons may remain 'till their crops are gathered. After the country is surveyed and the selections made, this article shall not operate upon that part of it not included in such selections. But

Intruders.

intruders shall, in the manner before described, be removed from these selections for the term of five years from the ratification of this treaty, or until the same are conveyed to white persons.

Additional locations.

ARTICLE VI. Twenty-nine sections in addition to the foregoing may be located, and patents for the same shall then issue to those persons, being Creeks, to whom the same may be assigned by the Creek tribe. But whenever the grantees of these tracts possess improvements, such tracts shall be so located as to include the improvements, and as near as may be in the centre. And there shall also be granted by patent to Benjamin Marshall, one section of land, to include his improvements on the Chatahoochee river, to be bounded for one mile in a direct line along the said river, and to run back for quantity. There shall also be granted to Joseph Bruner a colored man, one half section of land, for his services as an interpreter.

Locations, how to be made.

ARTICLE VII. All the locations authorized by this treaty, with the exception of that of Benjamin Marshall shall be made in conformity with the lines of the surveys; and the Creeks relinquish all claim for improvements.

Additional annuity to Creeks.

ARTICLE VIII. An additional annuity of twelve thousand dollars shall be paid to the Creeks for the term of five years, and thereafter the said annuity shall be reduced to ten thousand dollars, and shall be paid for the term of fifteen years. All the annuities due to the Creeks shall be paid in such manner as the tribe may direct.

Consideration for improvements.

ARTICLE IX. For the purpose of paying certain debts due by the Creeks, and to relieve them in their present distressed condition, the sum of one hundred thousand dollars, shall be paid to the Creek tribe, as soon as may be after the ratification hereof, to be applied to the payment of their just debts, and then to their own relief, and to be distributed as they may direct, and which shall be in full consideration of all improvements.

Expenses of delegation.

ARTICLE X. The sum of sixteen thousand dollars shall be allowed as a compensation to the delegation sent to this place, and for the payment of their expenses, and of the claims against them.

United States to pay certain claims.

ARTICLE XI. The following claims shall be paid by the United States.

For ferries, bridges and causeways, three thousand dollars, provided that the same shall become the property of the United States.

For the payment of certain judgments obtained against the chiefs eight thousand five hundred and seventy dollars.

For losses for which they suppose the United States responsible, seven thousand seven hundred and ten dollars.

For the payment of improvements under the treaty of 1826 one thousand dollars.

Annuities.

The three following annuities shall be paid for life.

To Tuske-hew-haw-Cusetaw two hundred dollars.

To the Blind Uchu King one hundred dollars.

To Neah Mico one hundred dollars.

There shall be paid the sum of fifteen dollars, for each person who has emigrated without expense to the United States, but the whole sum allowed under this provision shall not exceed fourteen hundred dollars.

There shall be divided among the persons, who suffered in consequence of being prevented from emigrating, three thousand dollars.

The land hereby ceded shall remain as a fund from which all the foregoing payments except those in the ninth and tenth articles shall be paid.

Removal of Creeks.

ARTICLE XII. The United States are desirous that the Creeks should remove to the country west of the Mississippi, and join their countrymen there; and for this purpose it is agreed, that as fast as the Creeks are prepared to emigrate, they shall be removed at the expense of the

United States, and shall receive subsistence while upon the journey, and for one year after their arrival at their new homes—Provided however, that this article shall not be construed so as to compel any Creek Indian to emigrate, but they shall be free to go or stay, as they please.

Proviso.

ARTICLE XIII. There shall also be given to each emigrating warrior a rifle, moulds, wiper and ammunition and to each family one blanket. Three thousand dollars, to be expended as the President may direct, shall be allowed for the term of twenty years for teaching their children. As soon as half their people emigrate, one blacksmith shall be allowed them, and another when two-thirds emigrate, together with one ton of iron and two hundred weight of steel annually for each blacksmith.— These blacksmiths shall be supported for twenty years.

Presents to emigrants.

Blacksmiths.

ARTICLE XIV. The Creek country west of the Mississippi shall be solemnly guarantied to the Creek Indians, nor shall any State or Territory ever have a right to pass laws for the government of such Indians, but they shall be allowed to govern themselves, so far as may be compatible with the general jurisdiction which Congress may think proper to exercise over them.   And the United States will also defend them from the unjust hostilities of other Indians, and will also as soon as the boundaries of the Creek country West of the Mississippi are ascertained, cause a patent or grant to be executed to the Creek tribe; agreeably to the 3d section of the act of Congress of May 2d, [28,] 1830, entitled "An act to provide for an exchange of lands with the Indians residing in any of the States, or Territories, and for their removal West of the Mississippi."

Creek country west of the Mississippi.

1830, ch. 148.

ARTICLE XV. This treaty shall be obligatory on the contracting parties, as soon as the same shall be ratified by the United States.

Treaty obligatory when ratified.

In testimony whereof, the said Lewis Cass, and the undersigned chiefs of the said tribe, have hereunto set their hands at the city of Washington, this 24th day of March, A. D. 1832.

> Lewis Cass,
> Opothleholo, his x mark,
> Tuchebatcheehadgo, his x mark,
> Efiematla, his x mark,
> Tuchebatche Micco, his x mark,
> Tomack Micco, his x mark,
> William McGilvery, his x mark,
> Benjamin Marshall.

In the presence of—
 Samuel Bell,
 William R. King,
 John Tipton,
 William Wilkins,
 C. C. Clay,
 J. Speight,
 Samuel W. Mardis,
 J. C. Isacks,
 John Crowell, *I. A.*
 Benjamin Marshall,
 Thomas Carr,
 John H. Brodnax,
   Interpreters.

TREATY WITH THE SEMINOLE, 1832.

May 9, 1832.

7 Stat., 368.
Proclamation, April 12, 1834.

The Seminole Indians, regarding with just respect, the solicitude manifested by the President of the United States for the improvement of their condition, by recommending a removal to a country more suitable to their habits and wants than the one they at present occupy in the Territory of Florida, are willing that their confidential chiefs, Jumper, Fuck-a-lus-ti-had-jo, Charley Emartla, Coi-had-jo, Holati-Emartla, Ya-hadjo, Sam Jones, accompanied by their agent Major Phagan, and their faithful interpreter Abraham, should be sent at the expense of the United States as early as convenient to examine the country assigned to the Creeks west of the Mississippi river, and should they be satisfied with the character of that country, and of the favorable disposition of the Creeks to reunite with the Seminoles as one people; the articles of the compact and agreement, herein stipulated at Payne's landing on the Ocklewaha river, this ninth day of May, one thousand eight hundred and thirty-two, between James Gadsden, for and in behalf of the Government of the United States, and the undersigned chiefs and head-men for and in behalf of the Seminole Indians, shall be binding on the respective parties.

Cession to the United States of lands in Florida, etc.

ARTICLE I. The Seminole Indians relinquish to the United States, all claim to the lands they at present occupy in the Territory of Florida, and agree to emigrate to the country assigned to the Creeks, west of the Mississippi river; it being understood that an additional extent of territory, proportioned to their numbers, will be added to the Creek country, and that the Seminoles will be received as a constituent part of the Creek nation, and be re-admitted to all the privileges as members of the same.

$15,400 to be paid by United States.

ARTICLE II. For and in consideration of the relinquishment of claim in the first article of this agreement, and in full compensation for all the improvements, which may have been made on the lands thereby ceded; the United States stipulate to pay to the Seminole Indians, fifteen thousand, four hundred (15,400) dollars, to be divided among the chiefs and warriors of the several towns, in a ratio proportioned to their population, the respective proportions of each to be paid on their arrival in the country they consent to remove to; it being understood that their faithful interpreters Abraham and Cudjo shall receive two hundred dollars each of the above sum, in full remuneration for the improvements to be abandoned on the lands now cultivated by them.

Blankets, etc., to be supplied.

ARTICLE III. The United States agree to distribute as they arrive at their new homes in the Creek Territory, west of the Mississippi river, a blanket and a homespun frock, to each of the warriors, women and children of the Seminole tribe of Indians.

Blacksmith.

ARTICLE IV. The United States agree to extend the annuity for the support of a blacksmith, provided for in the sixth article of the treaty at Camp Moultrie for ten (10) years beyond the period therein stipulated, and in addition to the other annuities secured under that treaty;

Annuity.

the United States agree to pay the sum of three thousand (3,000) dollars a year for fifteen (15) years, commencing after the removal of the whole tribe; these sums to be added to the Creek annuities, and the whole amount to be so divided, that the chiefs and warriors of the Seminole Indians may receive their equitable proportion of the same as members of the Creek confederation—

Cattle to be valued.

ARTICLE V. The United States will take the cattle belonging to the Seminoles at the valuation of some discreet person to be appointed by the President, and the same shall be paid for in money to the respective owners, after their arrival at their new homes; or other cattle such as may be desired will be furnished them, notice being given through their agent of their wishes upon this subject, before their removal, that time may be afforded to supply the demand.

ARTICLE VI. The Seminoles being anxious to be relieved from repeated vexatious demands for slaves and other property, alleged to have been stolen and destroyed by them, so that they may remove unembarrassed to their new homes; the United States stipulate to have the same property investigated, and to liquidate such as may be satisfactorily established, provided the amount does not exceed seven thousand (7,000) dollars.— *Demands for slaves to be settled.*

ARTICLE VII. The Seminole Indians will remove within three (3) years after the ratification of this agreement, and the expenses of their removal shall be defrayed by the United States, and such subsistence shall also be furnished them for a term not exceeding twelve (12) months, after their arrival at their new residence; as in the opinion of the President, their numbers and circumstances may require, the emigration to commence as early as practicable in the year eighteen hundred and thirty-three (1833), and with those Indians at present occupying the Big Swamp, and other parts of the country beyond the limits as defined in the second article of the treaty concluded at Camp Moultrie creek, so that the whole of that proportion of the Seminoles may be removed within the year aforesaid, and the remainder of the tribe, in about equal proportions, during the subsequent years of eighteen hundred and thirty-four and five, (1834 and 1835.)— *Indians to remove within three years.*

In testimony whereof, the commissioner, James Gadsden, and the undersigned chiefs and head men of the Seminole Indians, have hereunto subscribed their names and affixed their seals. Done at camp at Payne's landing, on the Ocklawaha river in the territory of Florida, on this ninth day of May, one thousand eight hundred and thirty-two, and of the independence of the United States of America the fifty-sixth.

James Gadsden,	[L. S.]	Tokose-Emartla, or Jno. Hicks,	
Holati Emartla, his x mark,	[L. S.]	his x mark,	[L. S.]
Jumper, his x mark,	[L. S.]	Cat-sha-Tusta-nuck-i, his x mark,	[L. S.]
Fuch-ta-lus-ta-Hadjo, his x mark,	[L. S.]	Hola-at-a-Mico, his x mark,	[L. S.]
Charley Emartla, his x mark,	[L. S.]	Hitch-it-i-Mico, his x mark,	[L. S.]
Coa Hadjo, his x mark,	[L. S.]	E-ne-hah, his x mark,	[L. S.]
Ar-pi-uck-i, or Sam Jones, his x		Ya-ha-emartla Chup-ko, his x	
mark,	[L. S.]	mark,	[L. S.]
Ya-ha Hadjo, his x mark,	[L. S.]	Moke-his-she-lar-ni, his x mark,	[L. S.]
Mico-Noha, his x mark,	[L. S.]		

Witnesses:

Douglas Vass, Secretary to Commissioner,
John Phagan, Agent,
Stephen Richards, Interpreter,
Abraham, Interpreter, his x mark,

Cudjo, Interpreter, his x mark,
Erastus Rogers,
B. Joscan.

TREATY WITH THE WINNEBAGO, 1832.

Articles of a treaty made and concluded, at Fort Armstrong, Rock Island, Illinois, between the United States of America, by their Commissioners, Major General Winfield Scott of the United States' Army, and his Excellency John Reynolds, Governor of the State of Illinois, and the Winnebago nation of Indians, represented in general Council by the undersigned Chiefs, Headmen, and Warriors.

Sept. 15, 1832.

7 Stat., 370.
Proclamation, Feb. 13, 1833.

ARTICLE I. The Winnebago nation hereby cede to the United States, forever, all the lands, to which said nation have title or claim, lying to the south and east of the Wisconsin river, and the Fox river of Green Bay; bounded as follows, viz: beginning at the mouth of the Pee-kee-tol a-ka river; thence up Rock river to its source; thence, with a line dividing the Winnebago nation from other Indians east of the Winnebago lake, to the Grande Chûte; thence, up Fox river to the Winnebago lake, and with the northwestern shore of said lake, to the inlet of Fox river; thence, up said river to lake Puckaway, and with the east- *Cession to the United States.*

ern shore of the same to its most southeasterly bend; thence with the line of a purchase made of the Winnebago nation, by the treaty at Prairie du Chêne, the first day of August, one thousand eight hundred and twenty-nine, to the place of beginning.

Cession by the United States.

ARTICLE II. In part consideration of the above cession, it is hereby stipulated and agreed, that the United States grant to the Winnebago nation, to be held as other Indian lands are held, that part of the tract of country on the west side of the Mississippi, known, at present, as the Neutral ground, embraced within the following limits, viz: beginning on the west bank of the Mississippi river, twenty miles above the mouth of the upper Ioway river, where the line of the lands purchased of the Sioux Indians, as described in the third article of the treaty of Prairie du Chien, of the fifteenth day of July, one thousand eight hundred and thirty, begins; thence, with said line, as surveyed and marked, to the eastern branch of the Red Cedar creek, thence, down said creek, forty miles, in a straight line, but following its windings, to the line of a purchase, made of the Sac and Fox tribes of Indians, as designated in the second article of the before recited treaty; and thence along the southern line of said last mentioned purchase, to the Mississippi, at the point marked by the surveyor, appointed by the President of the United States, on the margin of said river; and thence, up said river, to the place of beginning. The exchange of the two tracts of country to take place on or before the first day of June next; that is to say, on or before that day, all the Winnebagoes now residing within the country ceded by them, as above, shall leave the said country, when, and not before, they shall be allowed to enter upon the country granted by the United States, in exchange.

Annuity for 27 years.

ARTICLE III. But, as the country hereby ceded by the Winnebago nation is more extensive and valuable than that given by the United States in exchange; it is further stipulated and agreed, that the United States pay to the Winnebago nation, annually, for twenty-seven successive years, the first payment to be made in September of the next year, the sum of ten thousand dollars, in specie; which sum shall be paid to the said nation at Prairie du Chien, and Fort Winnebago, in sums proportional to the numbers residing most conveniently to those places respectively.

School to be established and supported by the United States.

ARTICLE IV. It is further stipulated and agreed, that the United States shall erect a suitable building, or buildings, with a garden, and a field attached, somewhere near Fort Crawford, or Prairie du Chien, and establish and maintain therein, for the term of twenty-seven years, a school for the education, including clothing, board, and lodging, of such Winnebago children as may be voluntarily sent to it: the school to be conducted by two or more teachers, male and female, and the said children to be taught reading, writing, arithmetic, gardening, agriculture, carding, spinning, weaving, and sewing, according to their ages and sexes, and such other branches of useful knowledge as the President of the United States may prescribe: *Provided*, That the annual

Proviso.

cost of the school shall not exceed the sum of three thousand dollars. And, in order that the said school may be productive of the greatest benefit to the Winnebago nation, it is hereby subjected to the visits and inspections of his Excellency the Gouvernor of the State of Illinois for the time being; the United States' General Superintendents of Indian affairs; of the United States' agents who may be appointed to reside among the Winnebago Indians, and of any officer of the United States' Army, who may be of, or above the rank of Major: *Provided*, That the commanding officer of Fort Crawford shall make such visits and inspections frequently, although of an inferior rank.

Annual allowance for 27 years.

ARTICLE V. And the United States further agree to make to the said nation of Winnebago Indians the following allowances, for the period of twenty-seven years, in addition to the considerations herein before stipulated; that is to say: for the support of six agriculturists, and the purchase of twelve yokes of oxen, ploughs, and other agricultural implements, a sum not exceeding two thousand five hundred dollars per annum; to the Rock river band of Winnebagoes, one thousand five hundred pounds of tobacco, per annum; for the services and attendance of a physician at Prairie du Chien, and of one at Fort Winnebago, each, two hundred dollars, per annum.

ARTICLE VI. It is further agreed that the United States remove and maintain, within the limits prescribed in this treaty, for the occupation of the Winnebagoes, the blacksmith's shop, with the necessary tools, iron, and steel, heretofore allowed to the Winnebagoes, on the waters of the Rock river, by the third article of the treaty made with the Winnebago nation, at Prairie du Chien, on the first day of August, one thousand eight hundred and twenty-nine. *Blacksmith's shop.*

ARTICLE VII. And it is further stipulated and agreed by the United States, that there shall be allowed and issued to the Winnebagoes, required by the terms of this treaty to remove within their new limits, soldiers' rations of bread and meat, for thirty days: *Provided*, That the whole number of such rations shall not exceed sixty thousand. *Rations of bread, etc.*

ARTICLE VIII. The United States, at the request of the Winnebago nation of Indians, aforesaid, further agree to pay, to the following named persons, the sums set opposite their names respectively, viz: *Payment to be made by United States to certain individuals.*

To Joseph Ogee, two hundred and two dollars and fifty cents,

To William Wallace, four hundred dollars, and

To John Dougherty, four hundred and eighty dollars; amounting, in all, to one thousand and eighty-two dollars and fifty cents, which sum is in full satisfaction of the claims brought by said persons against said Indians, and by them acknowledged to be justly due.

ARTICLE IX. On demand of the United States' Commissioners, it is expressly stipulated and agreed, that the Winnebago nation shall promptly seize and deliver up to the commanding officer of some United States' military post, to be dealt with according to law, the following individual Winnebagoes, viz: Koo-zee-ray-Kaw, Moy-che-nun-Kaw, Tshik-o-ke-maw-kaw, Ah-hun-see-kaw, and Waw-zee-ree-kay-hee-wee-kaw, who are accused of murdering, or of being concerned in the murdering of certain American citizens, at or near the Blue mound, in the territory of Michigan; Nau-saw-nay-he-kaw, and Toag-ra-naw-koo-ray-see-ray-kaw; who are accused of murdering, or of being concerned in murdering, one or more American citizens, at or near Killogg's Grove, in the State of Illinois; and also Waw-kee-aun-shaw and his son, who wounded, in attempting to kill, an American soldier, at or near Lake Kosh-ke-nong, in the said territory; all of which offences were committed in the course of the past spring and summer. And till these several stipulations are faithfully complied with by the Winnebago nation, it is further agreed that the payment of the annuity of ten thousand dollars, secured by this treaty, shall be suspended. *Individuals to be delivered up to United States.*

ARTICLE X. At the special request of the Winnebago nation, the United States agree to grant, by patent, in fee simple, to the following named persons, all of whom are Winnebagoes by blood, lands as follows: To Pierre Paquette, three sections; to Pierre Paquette, junior, one section; to Therese Paquette one section; and to Caroline Harney, one section. The lands to be designated under the direction of the President of the United States, within the country herein ceded by the Winnebago nation. *Lands to be granted by United States.*

ARTICLE XI. In order to prevent misapprehensions that might disturb peace and friendship between the parties to this treaty, it is expressly understood that no band or party of Winnebagoes shall reside, plant, fish, or hunt after the first day of June next, on any portion of the country herein ceded to the United States. *Winnebagoes not to hunt, etc., in country ceded.*

Treaty binding when ratified. ARTICLE XII. This treaty shall be obligatory on the contracting parties, after it shall be ratified by the President and Senate of the United States.

Done at Fort Armstrong, Rock Island, Illinois, this fifteenth day of September, one thousand eight hundred and thirty-two.

Winfield Scott,
John Reynolds.

Prairie du Chien deputation:

Tshee-o-nuzh-ee-kaw, war chief, (Kar-ray-mau-nee,) his x mark,
Wau-kaun-hah-kaw, or snake skin, (Day-kan-ray,) his x mark,
Khay-rah-tshoan-saip-kaw, or black hawk, his x mark,
Wau-kaun-kaw, or snake, his x mark,
Sau-sau-mau-nee-kaw, or he who walks naked, his x mark,
Hoantsh-skaw-skaw, or white bear, his x mark,
Hoo-tshoap-kaw, or four legs, his x mark,
Mau-hee-her-kar-rah, or flying cloud, son of dog head, his x mark,
Tshah-shee-rah-wau-kaw, or he who takes the leg of a deer in his mouth, his x mark.
Mau-kee-wuk-kaw, or cloudy, his x mark,
Ho-rah-paw-kaw, or eagle head, his x mark,
Pash-kay-ray-kaw, or fire holder, his x mark,
Eezhook-hat-tay-kaw, or big gun, his x mark,
Mau-wau-ruck, or the muddy, his x mark,
Mau-shoatsh-kaw, or blue earth, his x mark,
Wee-tshah-un-kuk, or forked tail, his x mark,
Ko-ro-ko-ro-hee-kaw, or bell, his x mark,
Haun-heigh-kee-paw-kaw, or the night that meets, his x mark.

Fort Winnebago deputation:

Hee-tshah-wau-saip-skaw-skaw, or white war eagle, De-kaw-ray, sr., his x mark,

Hoo-wau-nee-kaw, or little elk, (orator,) one of the Kay-ra-men-nees, his x mark,
Wau-kaun-tshah-hay-ree-kaw, or roaring thunder, four legs nephew, his x mark,
Mau-nah-pey-kaw, or soldier, (black wolf's son,) his x mark,
Wau-kaun-tshah-ween-kaw, or whirling thunder, hix x mark,
Wau-nee-ho-no-nik, or little walker, son of firebrand, his x mark,
To-shun-uk-ho-no-nik, or little otter, son of sweet corn, his x mark,
Tshah-tshun-hat-tay-kaw, or big wave, son of clear sky, his x mark.

Rock River deputation:

Kau-ree-kaw-see-kaw, white crow, (the blind,) his x mark,
Wau-kaun-ween-kaw, or whirling thunder, his x mark,
Mo-rah-tshay-kaw, or little priest, his x mark,
Mau-nah-pey-kaw, or soldier, his x mark,
Ho-rah-hoank-kaw, or war eagle, his x mark,
Nautsh-kay-peen-kaw, or good heart, his x mark,
Keesh-koo-kaw, his x mark,
Wee-tshun-kaw, or goose, his x mark,
Wau-kaun-nig-ee-nik, or little snake, his x mark,
Hoo-way-skaw, or white elk, his x mark,
Hay-noamp-kaw, or two horns, his x mark,
Hauk-kay-kaw, or screamer, his x mark,
Ee-nee-wonk-shik-kaw, or stone man, his x mark.

Signed in presence of—

R. Bache, captain ordnance, secretary to the commission,
John H. Kinzie, subagent Indian affairs,
Abrm. Eustis,
H. Dodge, major U. S. Rangers,
Alexr. R. Thompson, major U. S. Army,
William S. Harney, captain First Infantry,
E. Kirby, paymaster U. S. Army,
Albion T. Crow,
J. R. Smith, first lieutenant Second Infantry,
H. Day, lieutenant Second Infantry,
William Maynadier, lieutenant and A. D. C.
P. G. Hambaugh,

S. Burbank, lieutenant First Infantry,
John Marsh,
Pierre Paquette, interpreter, his x mark,
P. H. Galt, assistant adjutant-general,
S. W. Wilson,
Benj. F. Pike,
J. B. F. Russell, captain Fifth Infantry,
S. Johnson, captain Second Infantry,
John Clitz, adjutant Second Infantry,
Jno. Pickell, lieutenant Fourth Artillery,
A. Drane, assistant quartermaster U. S. A,
J. H. Prentiss, lieutenant First Artillery,
E. Rose, lieutenant Third Artillery,
L. J. Beall, lieutenant First Infantry,
Antoine Le Claire.

TREATY WITH THE SAUK AND FOXES, 1832.

Articles of a Treaty of Peace, Friendship and Cession, concluded at Fort Armstrong, Rock Island, Illinois, between the United States of America, by their Commissioners, Major General Winfield Scott, of the United States Army, and his Excellency John Reynolds, Governor of the State of Illinois, and the confederated tribes of Sac and Fox Indians, represented, in general Council, by the undersigned Chiefs, Headmen and Warriors.

Sept. 21, 1832.

7 Stat., 374.
Proclamation. Feb. 13, 1833.

WHEREAS, under certain lawless and desperate leaders, a formidable band, constituting a large portion of the Sac and Fox nation, left their country in April last, and, in violation of treaties, commenced an unprovoked war upon unsuspecting and defenceless citizens of the United States, sparing neither age nor sex; and whereas, the United States, at a great expense of treasure, have subdued the said hostile band, killing or capturing all its principal Chiefs and Warriors—the said States, partly as indemnity for the expense incurred, and partly to secure the future safety and tranquillity of the invaded frontier, demand of the said tribes, to the use of the United States, a cession of a tract of the Sac and Fox country, bordering on said frontier, more than proportional to the numbers of the hostile band who have been so conquered and subdued.

ARTICLE I. Accordingly, the confederated tribes of Sacs and Foxes hereby cede to the United States forever, all the lands to which the said tribes have title, or claim, (with the exception of the reservation hereinafter made,) included within the following bounds, to wit: Beginning on the Mississippi river, at the point where the Sac and Fox northern boundary line, as established by the second article of the treaty of Prairie du Chien, of the fifteenth of July, one thousand eight hundred and thirty, strikes said river; thence, up said boundary line to a point fifty miles from the Mississippi, measured on said line; thence, in a right line to the nearest point on the Red Cedar of the Ioway, forty miles from the Mississippi river; thence, in a right line to a point in the northern boundary line of the State of Missouri, fifty miles, measured on said boundary, from the Mississippi river; thence, by the last mentioned boundary to the Mississippi river, and by the western shore of said river to the place of beginning. And the said confederated tribes of Sacs and Foxes hereby stipulate and agree to remove from the lands herein ceded to the United States, on or before the first day of June next; and, in order to prevent any future misunderstanding, it is expressly understood, that no band or party of the Sac or Fox tribes shall reside, plant, fish, or hunt on any portion of the ceded country after the period just mentioned.

Cession to the United States.

Agreement to remove, etc.

ARTICLE II. Out of the cession made in the preceding article, the United States agree to a reservation for the use of the said confederated tribes, of a tract of land containing four hundred square miles, to be laid off under the directions of the President of the United States, from the boundary line crossing the Ioway river, in such manner that nearly an equal portion of the reservation may be on both sides of said river, and extending downwards, so as to include Ke-o-kuck's principal village on its right bank, which village is about twelve miles from the Mississippi river.

Reservation.

ARTICLE III. In consideration of the great extent of the foregoing cession, the United States stipulate and agree to pay to the said confederated tribes, annually, for thirty successive years, the first payment to be made in September of the next year, the sum of twenty thousand dollars in specie.

Annuity.

ARTICLE IV. It is further agreed that the United States shall establish and maintain within the limits, and for the use and benefit of the

Blacksmith and gunsmith's shop, etc.

Sacs and Foxes, for the period of thirty years, one additional black and gun smith shop, with the necessary tools, iron and steel; and finally make a yearly allowance for the same period, to the said tribes, of forty kegs of tobacco, and forty barrels of salt, to be delivered at the mouth of the Ioway river.

Payment to Farnham & Davenport.

ARTICLE V. The United States, at the earnest request of the said confederated tribes, further agree to pay to Farnham and Davenport, Indian traders at Rock Island, the sum of forty thousand dollars without interest, which sum will be in full satisfaction of the claims of the said traders against the said tribes, and by the latter was, on the tenth day of July, one thousand eight hundred and thirty-one, acknowledged to be justly due, for articles of necessity, furnished in the course of the seven preceding years, in an instrument of writing of said date, duly signed by the Chiefs and Headmen of said tribes, and certified by the late Felix St. Vrain, United States' agent, and Antoine Le Claire, United States' Interpreter, both for the said tribes.

Grant to A. Le Claire.

ARTICLE VI. At the special request of the said confederated tribes, the United States agree to grant, by patent, in fee simple, to Antoine Le Claire, Interpreter, a part Indian, one section of land opposite Rock Island, and one section at the head of the first rapids above said Island, within the country herein ceded by the Sacs and Foxes.

Delivery of prisoners by the United States.

ARTICLE VII. Trusting to the good faith of the neutral bands of Sacs and Foxes, the United States have already delivered up to those bands the great mass of prisoners made in the course of the war by the United States, and promise to use their influence to procure the delivery of other Sacs and Foxes, who may still be prisoners in the hands of a band of Sioux Indians, the friends of the United States; but the following named prisoners of war, now in confinement, who were **Hostages.** Chiefs and Headmen, shall be held as hostages for the future good conduct of the late hostile bands, during the pleasure of the President of the United States, viz:— Muk-ka-ta-mish-a-ka-kaik (or Black Hawk) and his two sons; Wau-ba-kee-shik (the Prophet) his brother and two sons; Na-pope; We-sheet Ioway; Pamaho; and Cha-kee-pa-shi-pa-ho (the little stabbing Chief).

Hostile bands to be divided.

ARTICLE VIII. And it is further stipulated and agreed between the porties to this treaty, that there shall never be allowed in the confederated Sac and Fox nation, any separate band, or village, under any chief or warrior of the late hostile bands; but that the remnant of the said hostile bands shall be divided among the neutral bands of the said tribes according to blood—the Sacs among the Sacs, and the Foxes among the Foxes.

Peace and friendship.

ARTICLE IX. In consideration of the premises, peace and friendship are declared, and shall be perpetually maintained between the United States and the whole confederated Sac and Fox nation, excepting from the latter the hostages before mentioned.

Subsistence furnished by United States.

ARTICLE X. The United States, besides the presents, delivered at the signing of this treaty, wishing to give a striking evidence of their mercy and liberality, will immediately cause to be issued to the said confederated tribes, principally for the use of the Sac and Fox women and children, whose husbands, fathers and brothers, have been killed in the late war, and generally for the use of the whole confederated tribes, articles of subsistence as follows:—thirty-five beef cattle; twelve bushels of salt; thirty barrels of pork; and fifty barrels of flour, and cause to be delivered for the same purposes, in the month of April next, at the mouth of the lower Ioway, six thousand bushels of maize or Indian corn.

Present for discovery of mines.

ARTICLE XI. At the request of the said confederated tribes, it is agreed that a suitable present shall be made to them on their pointing out to any United States agent, authorized for the purpose, the position or positions of one or more mines, supposed by the said tribes to be of a metal more valuable than lead or iron.

ARTICLE XII. This treaty shall take effect and be obligatory on the contracting parties, as soon as the same shall be ratified by the President of the United States, by and with the advice and consent of the Senate thereof. Treaty binding
when ratified.

Done at Fort Armstrong, Rock Island, Illinois, this twenty-first day of September, in the year of our Lord one thousand eight hundred and thirty-two, and of the independence of the United States the fifty-seventh.

Winfield Scott,
John Reynolds.
  Sacs.
Kee-o-kuck, or he who has been every where, his x mark,
Pa-she-pa-ho, or the stabber, his x mark,
Pia-tshe-noay, or the noise maker, his x mark,
Wawk-kum-mee, or clear water, his x mark,
O-sow-wish-kan-no, or yellow bird, his x mark,
Pa-ca-tokee, or wounded lip, his x mark,
Winne-wun-quai-saat, or the terror of man, his x mark,
Mau-noa-tuck, or he who controls many, his x mark,
Wau-we-au-tun, or the curling wave, his x mark,
  Foxes.
Wau-pel-la, or he who is painted white, his x mark,
Tay-wee-mau, or medicine man, (strawberry,) his x mark,
Pow-sheek, or the roused bear, his x mark,
An-nau-mee, or the running fox, his x mark,
Ma-tow-e-qua, or the jealous woman, his x mark,
Me-shee-wau-quaw, or the dried tree, his x mark,

May-kee-sa-mau-ker, or the wampum fish, his x mark,
Chaw-co-saut, or the prowler, his x mark,
Kaw-kaw-kee, or the crow, his x mark,
Mau-que-tee, or the bald eagle, his x mark,
Ma-she-na, or cross man, his x mark,
Kaw-kaw-ke-monte, or the pouch, (running bear,) his x mark,
Wee-she-kaw-k-a-skuck, or he who steps firmly, his x mark.
Wee-ca-ma, or good fish, his x mark,
Paw-qua-nuey, or the runner, his x mark,
Ma-hua-wai-be, or the wolf skin, his x mark,
Mis-see-quaw-kaw, or hairy neck, his x mark,
Waw-pee-shaw-kaw, or white skin, his x mark,
Mash-shen-waw-pee-tch, or broken tooth, his x mark,
Nau-nah-que-kee-shee-ko, or between two days, his x mark,
Paw-puck-ka-kaw, or stealing fox, his x mark,
Tay-e-sheek, or the falling bear, his x mark,
Wau-pee-maw-ker, or the white loon, his x mark,
Wau-co-see-nee-me, or fox man, his x mark.

In presence of—

R. Bache, captain ordnance, secretary to the commission,
Abrm. Eustis,
Alex. Cummings, lieutenant-colonel Second Infantry,
Alex. R. Thompson, major U. S. Army,
Sexton G. Frazer,
P. H. Galt, Assistant Adjutant-General,
Benj. F. Pike,
Wm. Henry,
James Craig,
John Aukeney,
J. B. F. Russell,
Isaac Chambers,
John Clitz, adjutant infantry,
John Pickell, lieutenant Fourth Artillery,
A. G. Miller, lieutenant First Infantry,
Geo. Davenport, assistant quartermaster-general Illinois Militia,
A. Drane,
Æneas Mackay, captain U. S. Army,
J. R. Smith, first lieutenant Second Infantry,
Wm. Maynadier, lieutenant and aid-de-camp,
J. S. Gallagher, first lieutenant, acting commissary subsistence,
N. B. Bennett, lieutenant Third Artillery,

B. Riley, major U. S. Army,
H. Dodge, major,
W. Campbell,
Hy. Wilson, major Fourth U. S. Infantry,
Donald Ward,
Thos. Black Wolf,
Horatio A. Wilson, lieutenant Fourth Artillery,
H. Day, lieutenant Second Infantry,
Jas. W. Penrose, lieutenant Second Infantry,
J. E. Johnston, lieutenant Fourth Artillery,
S. Burbank, lieutenant First Infantry,
J. H. Prentiss, lieutenant First Artillery,
L. J. Beall, lieutenant First Infantry,
Addison Philleo,
Thomas L. Alexander, lieutenant Sixth Infantry,
Horace Beale, acting surgeon U. S. Army,
Oliver W. Kellogg,
Jona Leighton, acting surgeon U. S. Army,
Robt. C. Buchanan, lieutenant Fourth Infantry,
Jas. S. Williams, lieutenant Sixth Infantry,
John W. Spencer,
Antoine Le Claire, interpreter.

TREATY WITH THE APPALACHICOLA BAND, 1832.

Oct. 11, 1832.

7 Stat., 377.
Proclamation, Feb.
13, 1833.

Reservation relinquished to United States, etc. THE undersigned chiefs, for and in behalf of themselves and warriors, surrender to the United States, all their right, title and interest to a reservation of land made for their benefit, in the additional article of the treaty, concluded at Camp Moultrie, in the Territory of Florida, on the 18th of September, eighteen hundred and twenty-three, and which is described in said article, "as commencing on the Appalachicola, one mile below Tuski Hajo's improvements, running up said river four miles, thence west two miles, thence southerly to a point due west of the beginning, thence east to the beginning point," and agree to remove with their warriors and families, now occupying said reservation, and amounting in all to (256) two hundred and fifty-six souls, to the west of the Mississippi river, beyond the limits of the States and Territories of the United States of America.

Payments by United States. ARTICLE II. For, and in consideration of said surrender, and to meet the charges of a party to explore immediately the country west in search of a home more suitable to their habits, than the one at present occupied, and in full compensation for all the expenses of emigration, and subsistence for themselves and party: The United States agree to pay to the undersigned chiefs, and their warriors, thirteen thousand dollars; three thousand dollars in cash, the receipt of which is herewith acknowledged, and ten thousand dollars whenever they have completed their arrangements, and have commenced the removal of their whole party.

Time fixed for evacuation. ARTICLE III. The undersigned chiefs, with their warriors and families, will evacuate the reservation of land surrendered by the first article of this agreement, on or before the first of November, eighteen hundred and thirty-three; but should unavoidable circumstances prevent the conclusion of the necessary preparatory arrangements by that time, it is expected that the indulgence of the government of the United States will be reasonably extended for a term, not to exceed however another year.

Annuity to Blunt and Davy. ARTICLE IV. The United States further stipulate to continue to Blunt and Davy (formerly Tuski Hajo deceased) the Chiefs of the towns now consenting to emigrate, their proportion of the annuity of five thousand dollars which they at present draw, and to which they are entitled under the treaty of Camp Moultrie, so long as they remain in the Territory of Florida, and to advance their proportional amount of the said annuity for the balance of the term stipulated for its payment in the treaty aforesaid; whenever they remove in compliance of the terms of this agreement.

In testimony whereof, the commissioner, James Gadsden, in behalf of the United States, and the undersigned chiefs and warriors have hereunto subscribed their names and affixed their seals.

Done at Tallahassee, in the territory of Florida, this eleventh day of October one thousand eight hundred and thirty-two, and of the Independence of the United States the fifty-seventh.

James Gadsden, commissioner, &c.   [L. S.]
John Blunt, his x mark,   [L. S.]
O Saa-Hajo, or Davy, his x mark,   [L. S.]
Co-ha-thlock-co, or Cockrane, his x mark, [L. S.]

Witnesses:

Wm. P. Duval, superintendent,
Stephen Richards, interpreter,
Robt. W. Williams,
R. Lewis,
Tho. Brown,
James D. Westcott, jr.

TREATY WITH THE POTAWATOMI, 1832.

Articles of a treaty made and concluded at Camp Tippecanoe, in the State of Indiana, this twentieth day of October, in the year of our Lord one thousand eight hundred and thirty-two, between Jonathan Jennings, John W. Davis and Marks Crume, Commissioners on the part of the United States of the one part, and the Chiefs and Headmen of the Potawatamie Tribe of Indians of the Prairie and Kankakee, of the other part.

Oct. 20, 1832.

7 Stat., 378.
Proclamation, Jan. 21, 1833.

ARTICLE I. The said Potawatamie Tribe of Indians cede to the United States the tract of land included within the following boundary, viz: *Cession to the United States.*

Beginning at a point on Lake Michigan ten miles southward of the mouth of Chicago river; thence, in a direct line, to a point on the Kankakee river, ten miles above its mouth; thence, with said river and the Illinois river, to the mouth of Fox river, being the boundary of a cession made by them in 1816; thence, with the southern boundary of the Indian Territory, to the State line between Illinois and Indiana; thence, north with said line, to Lake Michigan; thence, with the shore of Lake Michigan, to the place of beginning.

ARTICLE II. From the cession aforesaid the following tracts shall be reserved, to wit: *Reservations.*

Five sections for Shaw-waw-nas-see, to include Little Rock village.

For Min-e-maung, one section, to include his village.

For Joseph Laughton, son of Wais-ke-shaw, one section, and for Ce-na-ge-wine, one section, both to be located at Twelve Mile Grove, or Na-be-na-qui-nong.

For Claude Laframboise, one section, on Thorn creek.

For Maw-te-no, daughter of Francois Burbonnois, jun. one section, at Soldier's village.

For Catish, wife of Francis Burbonnois, sen. one section, at Soldier's village.

For the children of Wais-ke-shaw, two sections, to include the small grove of timber on the river above Rock village.

For Jean B. Chevallier, one section, near Rock village; and for his two sisters, Angelique and Josette, one half section each, joining his.

For Me-she-ke-ten-o, two sections, to include his village.

For Francis Le Via, one section, joining Me-she-ke-ten-o.

For the five daughters of Mo-nee, by her last husband, Joseph Bailey, two sections.

For Me-saw-ke-qua and her children, two section, at Wais-us-kucks's village.

For Sho-bon-ier, two sections, at his village.

For Josette Beaubien and her children, two sections, to be located on Hickory creek.

For Therese, wife of Joseph Laframboise, one section; and for Archange Pettier, one section, both at Skunk Grove.

For Mau-i-to-qua and son, one half section each; for the children of Joseph Laframboise, one section, at Skunk Grove.

For Washington Burbonnois, one section, joining his mother's reservation (Calish Burbonnois).

For Ah-be-te-kezhic, one section, below the State line on the Kankakee river.

For Nancy, Sally, and Betsey Countreman, children of En-do-ga, one section, joining the reserves near Rock village.

For Jacque Jonveau, one section, near the reservation of Me-she-ke-ten-o.

For Wah-pon-seh and Qua-qui-to, five sections each, in the Prairie near Rock village.

The persons to whom the foregoing reservations are made, are all Indians and of Indian descent.

Annuities.

ARTICLE III. In consideration of the cession in the first article, the United States agree to pay to the aforesaid Potawatamie Indians, an annuity of fifteen thousand dollars for the term of twenty years. Six hundred dollars shall be paid annually to Billy Caldwell, two hundred dollars to Alexander Robinson, and two hundred dollars to Pierre Le Clerc, during their natural lives.

Payment of claims against Indians.

ARTICLE IV. The sum of twenty-eight thousand seven hundred and forty-six dollars, shall be applied to the payment of certain claims against the Indians, agreeably to a schedule of the said claims, hereunto annexed.

Merchandise.

The United States further agree to deliver to the said Indians, forty-five thousand dollars in merchandise immediately after signing this treaty; and also the further sum of thirty thousand dollars in merchandize is hereby stipulated to be paid to them at Chicago in the year 1833.

Payments for horses stolen.

There shall be paid by the United States, the sum of one thousand four hundred dollars to the following named Indians, for horses stolen from them during the late war, as follows, to wit:

To Pe-quo-no, for two horses, eighty dollars.	$80
To Pa-ca-cha-be, for two ditto, eighty dollars.	80
To Shaw-wa-nas-see, for one ditto, forty dollars.	40
To Francis Sho-bon-nier, for three ditto, one hundred and twenty dollars.	120
To Sho-bon-ier, or Cheval-ier, for one ditto, forty dollars.	40
To Naw-o-kee, for one ditto, forty dollars.	40
To Me-she-ke-ten-o, for one ditto, forty dollars.	40
To Aun-take, for two horses, eighty dollars.	80
To Che-chalk-ose, for one ditto, forty dollars.	40
To Naa-a-gue, for two ditto, eighty dollars.	80
To Pe-she-ka-of-le-beouf, one ditto, forty dollars.	40
To Naw-ca-a-sho, for four ditto, one hundred and sixty dollars.	160
To Nox-sey, for one ditto, forty dollars.	40
To Ma-che-we-tah, for three ditto, one hundred and twenty dollars.	120
To Masco, for one ditto, forty dollars.	40
To Wah-pou-seh, for one horse, forty dollars.	40
To Waub-e-sai, for three ditto, one hundred and twenty dollars.	$120
To Chi-cag, for one ditto, forty dollars.	40
To Mo-swah-en-wah, one ditto, forty dollars.	40
To She-bon-e-go, one ditto, forty dollars.	40
To Saw-saw-wais-kuk, for two ditto, eighty dollars.	80

Permission to hunt and fish.

The said tribe having been the faithful allies of the United States during the late conflict with the Sacs and Foxes, in consideration thereof, the United States agree to permit them to hunt and fish on the lands ceded, as also on the lands of the Government on Wabash and Sangamon rivers, so long as the same shall remain the property of the United States.

In testimony whereof, the commissioners, and the chiefs, head men, and warriors of the said tribe, have hereunto set their hands, at the place and on the day aforesaid.

Jonathan Jennings,
John W. Davis,
Marks Crume,
Ah-be-te-ke-zhic, his x mark,
Shaw-wa-nas-see, his x mark,
Wah-pon-seh, his x mark,
Caw-we-saut, his x mark,
Shab-e-neai, his x mark,

Pat-e-go-shuc, his x mark,
Aun-take, his x mark,
Me-she-ke-ten-o, his x mark,
Shay-tee, his x mark,
Ce-na-je-wine, his x mark,
Ne-swa-bay-o-sity, his x mark,
Ke-wah-ca-to, his x mark,
Wai-saw-o-ke-ah, his x mark,

Chi-cag, his x mark,
Te-ca-cau-co, his x mark,
Chah-wee, his x mark,
Mas-co, his x mark,
Sho-min, his x mark,
Car-bon-ca, his x mark,
O-gouse, his x mark,
Ash-ke-wee, his x mark,
Ka-qui-tah, his x mark,
She-mar-gar, his x mark,
Nar-ga-to-nuc, his x mark,
Puc-won, his x mark,
Ne-be-gous, his x mark,
E-to-wan-a-cote, his x mark,
Quis-e-wen, his x mark,
Wi-saw, his x mark,
Pierish, his x mark,
Cho-van-in, his x mark,
Wash-is-kuck, his x mark,
Ma-sha-wah, his x mark,
Capt. Heeld, his x mark,
Man-itoo, his x mark,
Ke-me-gu-bee, his x mark,
Pe-shuc-kee, his x mark,

No-nee, his x mark,
No-che-ke-se-qua-bee, his x mark,
She-bon-e-go, his x mark,
Mix-e-maung, his x mark,
Mah-che-wish-a-wa, his x mark,
Mac-a-ta-be-na, his x mark,
Ma-che-we-tah, his x mark,
Me-gis, his x mark,
Mo-swa-en-wah, his x mark,
Ka-che-na-bee, his x mark,
Wah-be-no-say, his x mark,
Mash-ca-shuc, his x mark,
A-bee-shah, his x mark,
Me-chi-ke-kar-ba, his x mark,
Nor-or-ka-kee, his x mark,
Pe-na-o-cart, his x mark,
Quar-cha-mar, his x mark,
Francois Cho-van-ier, his x mark,
Ge-toc-quar, his x mark,
Me-gwun, his x mark,
Ma-sha-ware, his x mark,
Che-co, his x mark,
So-wat-so, his x mark,
Wah-be-min, his x mark.

Signed in the presence of—

John Tipton,
Th. Jo. Owen, United States Indian agent,
J. B. Beaubien,
B. H. Laughton, interpreter,
G. S. Hubbard, interpreter,

William Conner, interpreter,
Thomas Hartzell,
Meadore B. Beaubien,
James Conner,
Henry B. Hoffman.

After the signing of this treaty, and at the request of the Indians, **Horses delivered.** three thousand dollars was applied to the purchasing of horses; which were purchased and delivered to the Indians by our direction, leaving the balance to be paid in merchandise at this time, forty-two thousand dollars.

> Jonathan Jennings,
> J. W. Davis,
> Marks Crume,
> 			Commissioners.

It is agreed, on the part of the United States, that the following **Claims to be paid.** claims shall be allowed, agreeably to the fourth article of the foregoing treaty, viz:

To Gurdon S. Hubbard, five thousand five hundred and seventy three dollars.

Samuel Miller, seven hundred and ninety dollars.
John Bt. Bobea, three thousand dollars.
Robert A. Kinzie, four hundred dollars.
Jacque Jombeaux, one hundred and fifty dollars.
Jacque Jombeaux, senior, fifteen hundred dollars.
Medad B. Bobeaux, five hundred and fifty dollars.
Noel Vasier, eighteen hundred dollars.
Joseph Balies, twelve hundred and fifty dollars.
Joseph Shawnier, one hundred and fifty dollars.
Thomas Hartzell, three thousand dollars.
Bernardus H. Lawton, three thousand five hundred dollars.
George Walker, seven hundred dollars.
Stephen J. Scott, one hundred dollars.
Cole Weeks, thirty eight dollars.
Timothy B. Clark, one hundred dollars.
George Pettijohn, fifty dollars.
Thomas Forsyth, five hundred dollars.
Antoine Le Clerc, fifty-five dollars.
James B. Campbell, fifty-three dollars.

John W. Blackstone, sixty dollars.
Alexander Robinson, ninety-one dollars.
Francis Bulbona, jr. one thousand dollars.
John Bt. Chevalier six hundred and sixty dollars.
Joseph La Frombois four hundred and forty-one dollars.
Leon Bourasau eight hundred dollars.
Peter Menard, jr. thirty-seven dollars.
Joseph Shoemaker, eighteen dollars.
Tunis S. Wendell one thousand dollars.
F. H. Countraman, forty dollars.
Samuel Morris, one hundred and forty dollars.
William Conner, two thousand dollars.
John B. Bourie, twelve hundred dollars.

> Jonathan Jennings,
> J. W. Davis,
> Marks Crume,
> Commissioners.

TREATY WITH THE CHICKASAW, 1832.

Oct. 20, 1832.

7 Stat., 381.
Proclamation Mar.
1, 1833.

Articles of a treaty made and entered into between Genl. John Coffee, being duly authorised thereto, by the President of the United States, and the whole Chickasaw Nation, in General Council assembled, at the Council House, on Pontitock Creek on the twentieth day of October, 1832.

Preamble.

THE Chickasaw Nation find themselves oppressed in their present situation; by being made subject to the laws of the States in which they reside. Being ignorant of the language and laws of the white man, they cannot understand or obey them. Rather than submit to this great evil, they prefer to seek a home in the west, where they may live and be governed by their own laws. And believing that they can procure for themselves a home, in a country suited to their wants and condition, provided they had the means to contract and pay for the same, they have determined to sell their country and hunt a new home. The President has heard the complaints of the Chickasaws, and like them believes they cannot be happy, and prosper as a nation, in their present situation and condition, and being desirous to relieve them from the great calamity that seems to await them, if they remain as they are—He has sent his Commissioner Genl. John Coffee, who has met the whole Chickasaw nation in Council, and after mature deliberation, they have entered into the following articles, which shall be binding on both parties, when the same shall be ratified by the President of the United States by and with the advice and consent of the Senate.

Cession of lands to United States.

ARTICLE I. For the consideration hereinafter expressed, the Chickasaw nation do hereby cede, to the United States, all the land which they own on the east side of the Mississippi river, including all the country where they at present live and occupy.

Ceded lands to be surveyed, etc.

ARTICLE II. The United States agree to have the whole country thus ceded, surveyed, as soon as it can be conveniently done, in the same manner that the public lands of the United States are surveyed in the States of Mississippi and Alabama, and as soon thereafter as may be practicable, to have the same prepared for sale. The President of the United States will then offer the land for sale at public auction, in the same manner and on the same terms and conditions as the other public lands, and such of the land as may not sell at the public sales shall be offered at private sale, in the same manner that other private sales are made of the United States lands.

ARTICLE III. As a full compensation to the Chickasaw nation, for the country thus ceded, the United States agree to pay over to the Chickasaw nation, all the money arising from the sale of the land which may be received from time to time, after deducting therefrom the whole cost and expenses of surveying and selling the land, including every expense attending the same.

Compensation to Chickasaws.

ARTICLE IV. The President being determined that the Chickasaw people shall not deprive themselves of a comfortable home, in the country where they now are, untill they shall have provided a country in the west to remove to, and settle on, with fair prospects of future comfort and happiness—It is therefore agreed to, by the Chickasaw nation, that they will endeavor as soon as it may be in their power, after the ratification of this treaty, to hunt out and procure a home for their people, west of the Mississippi river, suited to their wants and condition; and they will continue to do so during the progress of the survey of their present country, as is provided for in the second article of this treaty. But should they fail to procure such a country to remove to and settle on, previous to the first public sale of their country here then and in that event, they are to select out of the surveys, a comfortable settlement for every family in the Chickasaw nation, to include their present improvements, if the land is good for cultivation, and if not they may take it in any other place in the nation, which is unoccupied by any other person. Such settlement must be taken by sections. And there shall be allotted to each family as follows (to wit): To a single man who is twenty-one years of age, one section—to each family of five and under that number two sections—to each family of six and not exceeding ten, three sections, and to each family over ten in number, four sections—and to families who own slaves, there shall be allowed, one section to those who own ten or upwards and such as own under ten, there shall be allowed half a section. If any person shall now occupy two places and wish to retain both, they may do so, by taking a part at one place, and a part at the other, and where two or more persons are now living on the same section, the oldest occupant will be entitled to remain, and the others must move off to some other place if so required by the oldest occupant. All of which tracts of land, so selected and retained, shall be held, and occupied by the Chickasaw people, uninterrupted until they shall find and obtain a country suited to their wants and condition. And the United States will guaranty to the Chickasaw nation, the quiet possession and uninterrupted use of the said reserved tracts of land, so long as they may live on and occupy the same. And when they shall determine to remove from said tracts of land, the Chickasaw nation will notify the President of the United States of their determination to remove, and thereupon as soon as the Chickasaw people shall remove, the President will proclaim the said reserved tracts of land for sale at public auction and at private sale, on the same terms and conditions, as is provided for in the second article of this treaty, to sell the same, and the net proceeds thereof, to be paid to the Chickasaw nation, as is provided for in the third article of this treaty.

Chickasaws to seek a home west of the Mississippi.

In case they fail to procure such a home.

Allotments.

Guaranty by United States.

When Chickasaws determine to remove, they will give notice, etc.

ARTICLE V. If any of the Chickasaw families shall have made valuable improvements on the places where they lived and removed from, on the reservation tracts, the same shall be valued by some discreet person to be appointed by the President, who shall assess the real cash value of all such improvements, and also the real cash value of all the land within their improvements, which they may have cleared and actually cultivated, at least one year in good farming order and condition. And such valuation of the improvements and the value of the cultivated lands as before mentioned, shall be paid to the person who shall have made the same. To be paid out of the proceeds of the sales of the ceded lands. The person who shall value such land and improve-

Improvements to be valued, etc.

ments, shall give to the owner thereof, a certificate of the valuation, which shall be a good voucher for them to draw the money on, from the proper person, who shall be appointed to pay the same, and the money shall be paid, as soon as may be convenient, after the valuation, to enable the owner thereof to provide for their families on their journey to their new homes. The provisions of this article are intended to encourage industry and to enable the Chickasaws to move comfortably. But least the good intended may be abused, by designing persons, by hiring hands and clearing more land, than they otherwise would do for the benefit of their families—It is determined that no payment shall be made for improved lands, over and above one-eighth part of the tract allowed and reserved for such person to live on and occupy.

Surveyor-general to be appointed, etc. ARTICLE VI. The Chickasaw nation cannot receive any part of the payment for their land until it shall be surveyed and sold; therefore, in order to the greater facilitate, in surveying and preparing the land for sale, and for keeping the business of the nation separate and apart from the business and accounts of the United States, it is proposed by the Chickasaws, and agreed to, that a Surveyor General be appointed by the President, by and with the advice and consent of the Senate, to superintend alone the surveying of this ceded country or so much thereof as the President may direct, who shall appoint a sufficient number of deputy surveyors, as may be necessary to complete the survey, in as short a time as may be reasonable and expedient. That the said Surveyor General be allowed one good clerk, and one good draftsman to aid and assist him in the business of his office, in preparing the

Land office. lands for sale. It is also agreed that one land office be established for the sale of the lands, to have one Register and one Receiver of monies, to be appointed by the President, by and with the advice and consent of the Senate, and each Register and Receiver to have one good clerk to aid and assist them in the duties of their office. The Surveyor's office, and the office of the Register and Receiver of money, shall be kept somewhere central in the nation, at such place as the President of the United States may direct. As the before mentioned officers, and clerks, are to be employed entirely in business of the nation, appertaining to preparing and selling the land, they will of course be paid out of the proceeds of the sales of the ceded lands. That the Chickasaws, may now understand as near as may be, the expenses that will be incurred in the transacting of this business—It is proposed and

Salaries of surveyor-general, etc. agreed to, that the salary of the Surveyor General be fifteen hundred dollars a year, and that the Register and Receiver of monies, be allowed twelve hundred dollars a year each, as a full compensation for their services, and all expenses, except stationary and postages on their official business, and that each of the clerks and draftsman be allowed seven hundred and fifty dollars a year, for their services and all expenses.

No preemption rights to be granted by United States. ARTICLE VII. It is expressly agreed that the United States shall not grant any right of preference, to any person, or right of occupancy in any manner whatsoever, but in all cases, of either public or private sale, they are to sell the land to the highest bidder, and also that none of the lands be sold in smaller tracts than quarter sections or fractional sections of the same size as near as may be, until the Chickasaw nation

Combinations among purchasers to be prevented. may require the President to sell in smaller tracts. The Chiefs of the nation have heard that at some of the sales of the United States lands, the people there present, entered into combinations, and united in purchasing much of the land, at reduced prices, for their own benefit, to the great prejudice of the Government, and they express fears, that attempts will be made to cheat them, in the same manner when their lands shall be offered at public auction. It is therefore agreed that the President will use his best endeavours to prevent such combinations, or any other plan or state of things which may tend to prevent the land selling for its full value.

ARTICLE VIII. As the Chickasaws have determined to sell their country, it is desirable that the nation realize the greatest possible sum for their lands, which can be obtained. It is therefore proposed and agreed to that after the President shall have offered their lands for sale and shall have sold all that will sell for the Government price, then the price shall be reduced, so as to induce purchasers to buy, who would not take the land at the Government minimum price;—and it is believed, that five years from and after the date of the first sale, will dispose of all the lands, that will sell at the Government price. If then at the expiration of five years, as before mentioned, the Chickasaw nation may request the President to sell at such reduced price as the nation may then propose, it shall be the duty of the President to comply with their request, by first offering it at public and afterwards at private sale, as in all other cases of selling public lands.

Reduction of price, etc.

ARTICLE IX. The Chickasaw nation express their ignorance, and incapacity to live, and be happy under the State laws, they cannot read and understand them, and therefore they will always need a friend to advise and direct them. And fearing at some day the Government of the United States may withdraw from them, the agent under whose instructions they have lived so long and happy—They therefore request that the agent may be continued with them, while here, and wherever they may remove to and settle. It is the earnest wish of the United States Government to see the Chickasaw nation prosper and be happy, and so far as is consistent they will contribute all in their power to render them so—therefore their request is granted. There shall be an agent kept with the Chickasaws as heretofore, so long as they live within the jurisdiction of the United States as a nation, either within the limits of the States where they now reside, or at any other place. And whenever the office of agent shall be vacant, and an agent to be appointed, the President will pay due respect to the wishes of the nation in selecting a man in all respects qualified to discharge the responsible duties of that office.

Agent to be continued among Chickasaws.

ARTICLE X. Whenever the Chickasaw nation shall determine to remove from, and leave their present country, they will give the President of the United States timely notice of such intention, and the President will furnish them, the necessary funds, and means for their transportation and journey, and for one years provisions, after they reach their new homes, in such quantity as the nation may require, and the full amount of such funds, transportation and provisions, is to be paid for, out of the proceeds of the sales of the ceded lands. And should the Chickasaw nation remove, from their present country, before they receive money, from the sale of the lands, hereby ceded; then and in that case, the United States shall furnish them any reasonable sum of money for national purposes, which may be deemed proper by the President of the United States, which sum shall also be refunded out of the sales of the ceded lands.

Expenses of removal, etc.

ARTICLE XI. The Chickasaw nation have determined to create a perpetual fund, for the use of the nation forever, out of the proceeds of the country now ceded away. And for that purpose they propose to invest a large proportion of the money arising from the sale of the land, in some safe and valuable stocks, which will bring them in an annual interest or dividend, to be used for all national purposes, leaving the principal untouched, intending to use the interest alone. It is therefore proposed by the Chickasaws, and agreed to, that the sum to be laid out in stocks as above mentioned, shall be left with the government of the United States, until it can be laid out under the direction of the President of the United States, by and with the advice and consent of the Senate, in such safe and valuable stock as he may approve

Chickasaw fund.

of, for the use and benefit of the Chickasaw nation. The sum thus to be invested, shall be equal to, at least three-fourths of the whole net proceeds of the sales of the lands; and as much more, as the nation may determine, if there shall be a surplus after supplying all the national wants. But it is hereby provided, that if the reasonable wants of the nation shall require more than one fourth of the proceeds of the sales of the land, then they may, by the consent of the President and Senate, draw from the government such sum as may be thought reasonable, for valuable national purposes, out of the three-fourths reserved to be laid out in stocks. But if any of the monies shall be thus drawn out of the sum first proposed, to be laid out on interest, the sum shall be replaced, out of the first monies of the nation, which may come into the possession of the United States government, from the sale of the ceded lands, over and above the reasonable wants of the nation. At the expiration of fifty years from this date, if the Chickasaw nation shall have improved in education and civilization, and become so enlightened, as to be capable of managing so large a sum of money to advantage, and with safety, for the benefit of the nation, and the President of the United States, with the Senate, shall be satisfied thereof, at that time, and shall give their consent thereto, the Chickasaw nation may then withdraw the whole, or any part of the fund now set apart, to be laid out in stocks, or at interest, and dispose of the same, in any manner that they may think proper at that time, for the use and benefit of the whole nation; but no part of said fund shall ever be used for any other purpose, than the benefit of the whole Chickasaw nation. In order to facilitate the survey and sale of the lands now ceded, and to raise the money therefrom as soon as possible, for the foregoing purpose, the President of the United States is authorised to commence the survey of the land as soon as may be practicable, after the ratification of this treaty.

Annuities to chiefs, etc.

ARTICLE XII. The Chickasaws feel grateful to their old chiefs, for their long and faithful services, in attending to the business of the nation. They believe it a duty, to keep them from want in their old and declining age—with those feelings, they have looked upon their old and beloved chief Tish-o-mingo, who is now grown old, and is poor and not able to live, in that comfort, which his valuable life and great merit deserve. It is therefore determined to give him out of the national funds, one hundred dollars a year during the balance of his life, and the nation request him to receive it, as a token of their kind feelings for him, on account of his long and valuable services.

Annuity to Queen Puc-caun-la.

Our old and beloved Queen Puc-caun-la, is now very old and very poor. Justice says the nation ought not to let her suffer in her old age; it is therefore determined to give her out of the national funds, fifty dollars a year during her life, the money to be put in the hands of the agent to be laid out for her support, under his direction, with the advice of the chiefs.

Boundary line between Chickasaws and Choctaws.

ARTICLE XIII. The boundary line between the lands of the Chickasaws and Choctaws, has never been run, or properly defined, and as the Choctaws have sold their country to the United States, they now have no interest in the decision of that question. It is therefore agreed to call on the old Choctaw chiefs to determine the line to be run, between the Chickasaws and their former country. The Chickasaws, by a treaty made with the United States at Franklin in Tennessee, in Aug. 31, 1830, (a) declared their line to run as follows, to wit: Beginning at the mouth of Oak tibby-haw and running up said stream to a point, being a marked tree, on the old Natches road, one mile

---

(a) This treaty appears not to have been ratified. The original is on file in the Indian Office (Box 1, Treaties, 1802–1853) and a copy is found in the appendix, post p. 1035.

southwardly from Wall's old place. Thence with the Choctaw boundary, and along it, westwardly through the Tunicha old fields, to a point on the Mississippi river, about twenty-eight miles by water, below where the St. Francis river enter said stream on the west side. It is now agreed, that the surveys of the Choctaw country which are now in progress, shall not cross the line until the true line shall be decided and determined; which shall be done as follows, the agent of the Choctaws on the west side of the Mississippi shall call on the old and intelligent chiefs of that nation, and lay before them the line as claimed by the Chickasaws at the Franklin treaty, and if the Choctaws shall determine that line to be correct, then it shall be established and made the permanent line, but if the Choctaws say the line strikes the Mississippi river higher up said stream, then the best evidence which can be had from both nations, shall be taken by the agents of both nations, and submitted to the President of the United States for his decision, and on such evidence, the President will determine the true line on principles of strict justice.

ARTICLE XIV. As soon as the surveys are made, it shall be the duty of the chiefs, with the advice and assistance of the agent to cause a correct list to be made out of all and every tract of land, which shall be reserved, for the use and benefit of the Chickasaw people, for their residence, as is provided for in the fourth article of this treaty, which list, will designate the sections of land, which are set apart for each family or individual in the nation, shewing the precise tracts which shall belong to each and every one of them, which list shall be returned to the register of the land office, and he shall make a record of the same, in his office, to prevent him from offering any of said tracts of land for sale, and also as evidence of each person's lands. All the residue of the lands will be offered by the President for sale. *List of reservations.*

ARTICLE XV. The Chickasaws request that no persons be permitted to move in and settle on their country before the land is sold. It is therefore agreed, that no person, whatsoever, who is not Chickasaw or connected with the Chickasaws by marriage, shall be permitted to come into the country and settle on any part of the ceded lands until they shall be offered for sale, and then there shall not be any person permitted to settle on any of the land, which has not been sold, at the time of such settlement, and in all cases of a person settling on any of the ceded lands contrary to this express understanding, they will be intruders, and must be treated as such, and put off of the lands of the nation. *No settlement in Chickasaw country till land is sold.*

In witness of all and every thing herein determined, between the United States and the whole Chickasaw nation in general council assembled, the parties have hereunto set their hands and seals, at the council-house, on Pontitock creek, in the Chickasaw nation, on the twentieth day of October, one thousand eight hundred and thirty-two.

John Coffee,	[L. S.]	Im-mah-hoo-la-tubbe, his x mark,	[L. S.]
Ish-te-ho-to-pa, [king,] his x mark,	[L. S.]	Illup-pah-umba, his x mark,	[L. S.]
Tish-o-min-go, his x mark,	[L. S.]	Pitman Colbert,	[L. S.]
Levi Colbert, his x mark,	[L. S.]	Con-mush-ka-ish-kah, his x mark,	[L. S.]
George Colbert, his x mark,	[L. S.]	James Wolfe,	[L. S.]
William M'Gilvery, his x mark,	[L. S.]	Bah-ha-kah-tubbe, his x mark,	[L. S.]
Samuel Sely, his x mark,	[L. S.]	E. Bah-kah-tubbe, his x mark,	[L. S.]
To-pul-kah, his x mark,	[L. S.]	Captain Thompson, his x mark,	[L. S.]
Isaac Albertson, his x mark,	[L. S.]	New-berry, his x mark,	[L. S.]
Em-ub-by, his x mark,	[L. S.]	Bah-ma-hah-tubbe, his x mark,	[L. S.]
Pis-tah-lah-tubbe, his x mark,	[L. S.]	John Lewis, his x mark,	[L. S.]
Ish-tim-o-lut-ka, his x mark,	[L. S.]	I-yah-hou-tubbe, his x mark,	[L. S.]
James Brown, his x mark,	[L. S.]	Tok-holth-la-chah, his x mark,	[L. S.]
Im-mah-hoo-lo-tubbe, his x mark,	[L. S.]	Oke-lah-nah-nubbe, his x mark,	[L. S.]
Ish-ta-ha-chah, his x mark,	[L. S.]	Im-me-tubbe, his x mark,	[L. S.]
Lah-fin-hubbe, his x mark,	[L. S.]	In-kah-yea, his x mark,	[L. S.]
Shop-pow-me, his x mark,	[L. S.]	Ah-sha-cubbe, his x mark,	[L. S.]
Nin-uck-ah-umba, his x mark,	[L. S.]	Im-mah-ho-bah, his x mark,	[L. S.]

Fit-chah-pla, his x mark,	[L. S.]	Che-wut-ta-ha, his x mark,	[L. S.]
Unte-mi-ah-tubbe, his x mark,	[L. S.]	Fo-lut-ta-chah, his x mark,	[L. S.]
Oke-lah-hin-lubbe, his x mark,	[L. S.]	No-wo-ko, his x mark,	[L. S.]
John Glover, his x mark,	[L. S.]	Win-in-a-pa, his x mark,	[L. S.]
Bah-me-hubbe, his x mark,	[L. S.]	Oke-lah-shah-cubbe, his x mark,	[L. S.]
Hush-tah-tah-ubbe, his x mark,	[L. S.]	Ish-ta-ki-yu-ka-tubbe, his x mark,	[L. S.]
Un-ti-ha-kah-tubbe, his x mark,	[L. S.]	Mah-te-ko-shubbe, his x mark,	[L. S.]
Yum-mo-tubbe, his x mark,	[L. S.]	Tom-chick-ah, his x mark,	[L. S.]
Oh-ha-cubbe, his x mark,	[L. S.]	Ei-o-che-tubbe, his x mark,	[L. S.]
Ah-fah-mah, his x mark,	[L. S.]	Nuck-sho-pubbe, his x mark,	[L. S.]
Ah-ta-kin-tubbe, his x mark,	[L. S.]	Fah-lah-mo-tubbe, his x mark,	[L. S.]
Ah-to-ko-wah, his x mark,	[L. S.]	Co-chub-be, his x mark,	[L. S.]
Tah-ha-cubbe, his x mark,	[L. S.]	Thomas Sely, his x mark,	[L. S.]
Kin-hoi-cha, his x mark,	[L. S.]	Oke-lah-sha-pi-a, his x mark,	[L. S.]
Ish-te-ah-tubbe, his x mark,	[L. S.]		
Chick-ah-shah-nan-ubbe, his x mark,	[L. S.]		

Signed and sealed in the presence of—

Ben. Reynolds, Indian agent,
John L. Allen, subagent,
Nath. Anderson, secretary to the commissioner,
Benj. Love, United States interpreter,
Robert Gordon, Mississippi,

George Wightman, of Mississippi,
John Donley, Tennessee,
D. S. Parrish, Tennessee,
S. Daggett, Mississippi,
Wm. A. Clurm,
G. W. Long.

TREATY WITH THE CHICKASAW, 1832.

Oct. 22, 1832.
7 Stat., 388.

Articles supplementary to, and explanatory of, a Treaty which was entered into on the 20th instant, between General John Coffee on the part of the United States, and the whole Chickasaw nation in General Council assembled.

THE fourth article of the treaty to which this is a supplement, provides that each Chickasaw family, shall have a tract of land, reserved for the use of the family, to live on and occupy, so long as the nation resides in the country where they now are. And the fifth article of the treaty provides that each family or individual shall be paid for their improvements, and the value of their cleared lands, when the nation **Leases of reservations forbidden.** shall determine to remove and leave the said reserved tracts of land. It is now proposed and agreed to, that no family or person of the Chickasaw nation, who shall or may have tracts of land, reserved for their residence while here, shall ever be permitted to lease any of said land, to any person whatsoever, nor shall they be permitted to rent any of said land, to any person, either white, red, or black, or mixed blood of either. As the great object of the nation is to preserve the land, and timber, for the benefit of posterity, provided the nation shall continue to live here, and if they shall at any time determine to remove and sell the land, it will be more valuable, and will sell for more money, for the benefit of the nation, if the land and timber be preserved.

Reservations to be sold low for the benefit of the nation, etc. It is also expressly declared by the nation, that, whenever the nation shall determine to remove from their present country, that every tract of land so reserved in the nation, shall be given up and sold for the benefit of the nation. And no individual or family shall have any right to retain any of such reserved tracts of land, for their own use, any longer than the nation may remain in the country where they now are.

Minimum price. As the reserve tracts of land above alluded to, will be the first choice of land in the nation, it is determined that the minimum price of all the reserved tracts, shall be three dollars an acre, until the nation may determine to reduce the price, and then they will notify the President, of their wishes, and the price to which they desire to reduce it.

The Chiefs still express fears that combinations may be formed at the public sales, where their reserved tracts of land shall be offered for sale, and that they may not be sold so high as they might be sold, by judicious agents at private sale. They therefore suggest the propriety of the President determining on some judicious mode of selling the reserves at private sale. *Private sales.*

It is therefore agreed that the suggestion be submitted to the President, and if he and the Chiefs can agree on a plan of a sale, different from the one proposed in the treaty, to which this is a supplement, and which shall be approved of by both parties, then they may enter into such agreement and the President shall then be governed by the same, in the sale of the reserved tracts of land, whenever they may be offered for sale. *Plan for sales to be agreed upon.*

In the provisions of the fourth article of the treaty to which this is a supplement, for reserves to young men who have no families, it expresses that each young man, who is twenty-one years of age, shall have a reserve. But as the Indians mature earlier than white men, and generally marry younger, it is determined to extend a reserve, to each young man who is seventeen years of age. And as there are some orphan girls in the nation or whose families do not provide for them, and also some widows in the same situation, it is determined to allow to each of them a reservation of one section, on the same terms and conditions in all respects, with the other reservations for the nation generally, and to be allowed to the same ages, as to young men. *Reserves to young men, etc.*

Colbert Moore and family have always lived in the Chickasaw nation, and he requests the liberty to continue with the nation. The Chiefs and nation agree to his request, and they also agree to allow him and his family a reserve tract of land to live on and occupy in the same manner, and on the same terms and conditions as is provided for the Chickasaw families, in the nation generally, during his good behavior. *C. Moore.*

The Chiefs of the nation represent that they in behalf of the nation gave a bond to James Colbert for a debt due to him, of eighteen hundred and eleven dollars, ninety-three and three fourth cents principal, that James Colbert transferred said note to Robert Gordon and that said note, and the interest thereon is yet due and unpaid, and the said Robert Gordon has proposed to take a section of land for said note, and interest up to this date. It is therefore agreed by the nation to grant him a section of land, to be taken any where in the nation, so as not to interfere with any reserve which has been provided as a residence for the Chickasaws, which shall be in full for said note and interest. *Section of land to R. Gordon.*

The Treaty, to which this is a supplement provides that there shall be offices kept some where central in the nation, at such place as the President shall determine, for transacting the business of the nation in selling their lands &c. It is now agreed to by the nation, that the President may select a section of land, or four quarter sections adjoining, at such place as he may determine agreeably to that provision of the Treaty, to establish the said offices on, and for all the necessary uses thereto attached, and he is permitted to improve the said tract of land in any manner, whatsoever, but when it shall cease to be used for the purposes, for which it is set apart—for offices &c.—then the same shall be sold under the direction of the President—and the proceeds thereof shall be paid to the Chickasaw nation, after deducting therefrom the value of all the improvements on the land, which value shall be assessed by the President, and in no case shall it exceed one half the sale of the land. *Section of land for land office, etc.*

The Chickasaw nation request the Government to grant them a cross mail route through the nation as follows, one to pass from Tuscumbia in Alabama, by the Agency, and by the place to be selected for the offices to be kept and to Rankin in Mississippi on horse back, once a week each way. The other to run from Memphis in Tennessee, by the offices and to the Cotton Gin in Mississippi—to pass once a week each *Mail route.*

way. They conceive these mails would be useful to the nation, and indispensible to the carrying on the business of the nation when the offices are established, but they would respecfully solicit the mails to be started as soon as possible, to open the avenues of information into their country.

Section of land to
J. Donley. John Donley has long been known in this nation as a mail carrier; he rode on the mails through our nation when a boy and for many years after he was grown; we think he understands that business as well, if not better than any other man—and we should prefer him to carry our mails to any other person—and if he is given the contract, the nation will set apart a section of land for his use while we remain here in this country, which section he may select with the advice of the Chiefs any where that suits him best, so as not to interfere with any of the reserves, and he may use it in any manner to live on, or make such improvements as may be necessary for keeping his horses, or to raise forage for them. But when the nation shall move away and leave this country this tract of land must be sold for the benefit of the nation, in the same manner that the reserve tracts are sold &c. and he is not to claim of the nation any pay for improving said tract of land.

In witness of all and every thing herein determined between the United States and the whole Chickasaw nation, in general council assembled, the parties have hereunto set their hands and seals at the council house, on Pontitock creek, in the Chickasaw nation, on this twenty-second day of October one thousand eight hundred and thirty-two.

Jno. Coffee,	[L. S.]	Ah-shah-cubbe, his x mark,	[L. S.]
Ish-te-ho-to-pa, his x mark,	[L. S.]	Im-mah-ho-bah, his x mark,	[L. S.]
Tish-o-min-go, his x mark,	[L. S.]	Fit-chah-ple, his x mark,	[L. S.]
Levi Colbert, his x mark,	[L. S.]	Unte-mi-ah-tubbe, his x mark,	[L. S.]
George Colbert, his x mark,	[L. S.]	Oke-lah-hin-lubbe, his x mark,	[L. S.]
William McGilvery, his x mark,	[L. S.]	John Glover, his x mark,	[L. S.]
Samuel Sely, his x mark,	[L. S.]	Bah-me-hubbe, his x mark,	[L. S.]
To-pul-kah, his x mark,	[L. S.]	Ah-to-ko-wah, his x mark,	[L. S.]
Isaac Albertson, his x mark,	[L. S.]	Hush-tah-tah-hubbe, his x mark,	[L. S.]
Im-mubbe, his x mark,	[L. S.]	Un-ti-ha-kah-tubbe, his x mark,	[L. S.]
Pis-ta-la-tubbe, his x mark,	[L. S.]	Yum-me-tubbe, his x mark,	[L. S.]
Ish-tim-o-lut-ka, his x mark,	[L. S.]	Oh-ha-cubbe, his x mark,	[L. S.]
James Brown, his x mark,	[L. S.]	Ah-fah-mah, his x mark,	[L. S.]
Im-ma-hoo-lo-tubbe, his x mark,	[L. S.]	Ah-take-in-tubbe, his x mark,	[L. S.]
Ish-ta-ha-cha, his x mark,	[L. S.]	Tah-ha-cubbe, his x mark,	[L. S.]
Lah-fin-hubbe, his x mark,	[L. S.]	Kin-hoi-cha, his x mark,	[L. S.]
Shop-pow-we, his x mark,	[L. S.]	Ish-te-ah-tubbe, his x mark,	[L. S.]
Nin-uck-ah-umba, his x mark,	[L. S.]	Chick-ah-shah-nan-ubbe, his x mark,	[L. S.]
Im-mah-hoo-lo-tubbe, his x mark,	[L. S.]	Chee-wut-ta-ha, his x mark,	[L. S.]
Il-lup-pah-umba, his x mark,	[L. S.]	Fo-lut-ta-chah, his x mark,	[L. S.]
Pitman Colbert,	[L. S.]	No-wo-ko, his x mark,	[L. S.]
Con-nush-koish-kah, his x mark,	[L. S.]	Win-in-a-pa, his x mark,	[L. S.]
James Wolf,	[L. S.]	Oke-lah-shah-cubbe, his x mark,	[L. S.]
Bah-ha-kah-tubbe, his x mark,	[L. S.]	Ish-ta-ki-yu-ka-tubbe, his x mark,	[L. S.]
E-bah-kah-tubbe, his x mark,	[L. S.]	Mah-ta-ko-shubbe, his x mark,	[L S.]
Captain Thompson, his x mark,	[L. S.]	Tom-ah-chich-ah, his x mark,	[L. S.]
New-berry, his x mark,	[L. S.]	Ehi-o-che-tubbe, his x mark,	[L. S.]
Bah-me-hah-tubbe, his x mark,	[L. S.]	Nuck-sho-pubbe, his x mark,	[L. S.]
John Lewis, his x mark,	[L. S.]	Fah-lah-mo-tubbe, his x mark,	[L. S.]
I-yah-hou-tubbe, his x mark,	[L. S.]	Co-chub-be, his x mark,	[L. S.]
Tok-holth-la-chah, his x mark,	[L. S.]	Thomas Sely, his x mark,	[L. S.]
Oke-lah-nah-nubbe, his x mark,	[L. S.]	Oke-lah-sha-pi-a, his x mark,	[L. S.]
Im-me-tubbe, his x mark,	[I. S.]		
In-kah-yea, his x mark,	[L. S.]		

Signed and sealed in presence of—

Ben. Reynolds, Indian agent,
John L. Allen, subagent,
Nath. Anderson, secretary to commissioner,
Benjamin Love, United States interpreter,
Robt. Gordon, of Mississippi,
George Wightman,

John Donley,
D. S. Parrish,
S. Daggett, of Mississippi,
Wm. A. Clurm, of Mississippi,
G. W. Long,
W. D. King,
John H. McKennie.

TREATY WITH THE KICKAPOO, 1832.

Articles of a treaty made and entered into at Castor Hill, in the county of St. Louis, in the State of Missouri, this twenty-fourth day of October, one thousand eight hundred and thirty-two, between William Clark, Frank J. Allen, and Nathan Kouns, Commissioners on the part of the United States, of the one part, and the Chiefs, Warriors, and Counsellors of the Kickapoo tribe of Indians, on behalf of said tribe, on the other part.

Oct. 24, 1832.

7 Stat., 391.
Proclamation, Feb. 13, 1833.

ARTICLE I. The Kickapoo tribe of Indians, in consideration of the stipulations hereinafter made, do hereby cede to the United States, the lands assigned to them by the treaty of Edwardsville, and concluded at St. Louis, the nineteenth day of July, eighteen hundred and twenty [two] and all other claims to lands within the State of Missouri. *Cession of lands to United States.*

ARTICLE II. The United States will provide for the Kickapoo tribe, a country to reside in, southwest of the Missouri river, as their permanent place of residence as long as they remain a tribe. And whereas, the said Kickapoo tribe are now willing to remove on the following conditions, from the country ceded on Osage river, in the State of Missouri, to the country selected on the Missouri river, north of lands which have been assigned to the Delawares; it is hereby agreed that the country within the following boundaries shall be assigned, conveyed, and forever secured, and is hereby so assigned, conveyed, and secured by the United States to the said Kickapoo tribe, as their permanent residence, viz: Beginning on the Delaware line, six miles westwardly of Fort Leavenworth, thence with the Delaware line westwardly sixty miles, thence north twenty miles, thence in a direct line to the west bank of the Missouri, at a point twenty-six miles north of Fort Leavenworth, thence down the west bank of the Missouri river, to a point six miles nearly northwest of Fort Leavenworth, and thence to the beginning. *Cession by United States.*

ARTICLE III. In consideration of the cession contained in the first article, the United States agree to pay to the Kickapoo tribe, within one year after the ratification of this treaty, an annuity for one year of eighteen thousand dollars; twelve thousand dollars of which, at the urgent request of said Indians, shall be placed in the hands of the superintendent of Indian affairs at St. Louis, and be by him applied to the payment of the debts of the said tribe, agreeably to a schedule to be furnished by them to the said superintendent, stating as far as practicable, for what contracted, and to whom due; and the said superintendent shall, as soon as possible, after the said money comes into his hands, pay it over in a just apportionment, agreeably to their respective claims, to the creditors of the said tribe, as specified in the schedule furnished him. And should any balance remain in his hands after said apportionment and payment, it shall be by him paid over to the said Kickapoo tribe, for their use and benefit. *Annuity and payment of debts.*

ARTICLE IV. The United States further agree to pay to the Kickapoo tribe, an annuity of five thousand dollars per annum, in merchandize, at its cost in St. Louis, or in money, at their option, for nineteen successive years, commencing with the second year after the ratification of this treaty. *Annuity.*

ARTICLE V. The United States will pay one thousand dollars annually for five successive years, for the support of a blacksmith and strikers; purchase of iron, steel, tools, &c. for the benefit of said tribe, on the lands hereby assigned them. *Blacksmith, etc.*

ARTICLE VI. The United States agree to pay thirty-seven hundred dollars, for the erection of a mill and a church, for the use of said tribe, on the aforesaid lands. *Mill and church.*

School.

ARTICLE VII. The United States will pay five hundred dollars per annum, for ten successive years, for the support of a school, purchase of books, &c. for the benefit of said Kickapoo tribe on the lands herein ceded to them.

Farming utensils.

ARTICLE VIII. The United States agree to pay three thousand dollars for farming utensils, when such utensils may be required by said tribe, on their land.

Labor and improvements.

ARTICLE IX. The United States will pay four thousand dollars for labour and improvements on the lands herein ceded said Kickapoos.

Cattle.

ARTICLE X. The United States agree to pay four thousand dollars in cattle, hogs, and such other stock as may be required by the said tribe; to be also delivered on their land.

Payment in merchandise, etc.

ARTICLE XI. There shall be paid in merchandise and cash, to the Kickapoos now present, for the use and benefit of their tribe, six thousand dollars, the receipt of which is hereby acknowledged; which amount, together with the several stipulations contained in the preceding articles, shall be considered as a full compensation for the cession herein made by said Kickapoo tribe. The United States will furnish said Indians with some assistance when removing to the lands hereby assigned them, and supply them with one year's provisions after their arrival on said lands.

Boundary to be run.

ARTICLE XII. The United States agree to run and mark out the boundary lines of the lands hereby ceded to the said tribe, within three years from the date of the ratification of this treaty.

Removal of Indians.

ARTICLE XIII. The said Indians agree to remove with as little delay as possible, to the land hereby ceded to them.

Exploring party.

ARTICLE XIV. The United States agree, at the particular request of the Kickapoos, that a deputation of their tribe shall be sent, with one or two of the commissioners, to view the lands hereby ceded to them, which deputation and commissioners jointly agreeing, shall have power to alter the boundary lines so as to make a selection of a body of land not exceeding twelve hundred square miles, adjoining to, and lying between the Big Nemaha river and the Delaware lands, and of changing the lines of the land hereby ceded in the second article of this treaty, not exceeding half the front on the Missouri between the mouth of Big Nemaha and Fort Leavenworth, so as to include a suitable site for a mill seat, should it be desired by said tribe and appear necessary to the commissioners. And it is understood, that if the commissioners, on viewing the land ceded in the second article of this treaty, shall find it of good quality, and sufficient for said tribe, then the aforesaid second article to be as binding on the contracting parties, as if this article had not been inserted.

Treaty binding when ratified.

ARTICLE XV. This treaty to be binding when ratified by the President and Senate of the United States.

In testimony whereof, the commissioners aforesaid, and the undersigned chiefs, warriors and counsellors aforesaid, have hereunto subscribed their hands and affixed their seals, this twenty-fourth day of October, in the year of our Lord eighteen hundred and thirty-two, and of the independence of the United States, the fifty-seventh.

Wm. Clark, [L. s.]	Ma-she-nah, elk, his x mark, [L. s.]
Frank J. Allen, [L. s.]	Ma-cuta-we-she-kah, black fisher,
Nathan Kouns, [L. s.]	his x mark, [L. s.]
Pa-sha-cha-hah, jumping fish, his	Wah-co-haw, grey fox, his x mark, [L. s.]
x mark, [L. s.]	Pah-ta-kah-quoi, striking woman,
Ka-ana-kuck, the prophet, his x	his x mark, [L. s.]
mark, [L. s.]	Kitch-e-mah-quoi, big bear, his x
Pemo-quoi-ga, rolling thunder, his	mark, [L. s.]
x mark, [L. s.]	Ata-noi-tucka, gobling turkey, his
Pa-ana-wah-ha, elk shedding his	x mark, [L. s.]
hair, his x mark, [L. s.]	Kish-coe, guardian to Indians, his
Kick-a-poo-hor, Kickapoo, his x	x mark, [L. s.]
mark, [L. s.]	Ka-te-wah, bald eagle, his x mark, [L. s.]

Na-poi-teck, son of prophet, his x mark, [L. S.]

Na-na-co-wah, the bear, his x mark, [L. S.]

Pe-sha-ka-nah, the bear, his x mark, [L. S.]

Ah-nuck-quet-ta, the cloud, or black thunder, his x mark,` [L. S.]

Note-ta-noi, wind, his x mark, [L. S.]

Ma-cutta-mah-qui, black loon, his x mark, [L. S.]

Signed in presence of—

James Kemmly, secretary,
Meriwether Lewis Clark, lieutenant, Sixth Infantry,
Geo. Maguire, Indian Department,

A. Shane, United States interpreter,
William Marshall,
Jacques Mette, United States interpreter,
Pierre Cadue, interpreter, his x mark.

Supplemental article to the treaty with the Kickapoo tribe of Indians, of the twenty-fourth October, one thousand eight hundred and thirty-two.

Nov. 26, 1832.

7 Stat., 393.

The undersigned, commissioners, on the part of the United States, and a deputation of Kickapoos, on the part of the Kickapoo tribe of Indians, having visited the lands assigned to the said tribe by the second article of a treaty with the said tribe, concluded at Castor Hill, in the county of Saint Louis, and State of Missouri, on the twenty-fourth day of October, one thousand eight hundred and thirty-two, and by authority of the powers vested in the said commissioners, and the said deputation, by the fourteenth article of the aforesaid treaty, have agreed that the boundary lines of the lands assigned to the Kickapoos, shall begin on the Delaware line, where said line crosses the left branch of Salt creek, thence down said creek to the Missouri river, thence up the Missouri river thirty miles when measured on a straight line, thence westwardly to a point twenty miles from the Delaware line, so as to include in the lands assigned the Kickapoos, at least twelve hundred square miles.

Boundary as fixed by commissioners and deputation.

Done at fort Leavenworth, this twenty-sixth day of November, one thousand eight hundred and thirty-two.

Nathan Kouns, [L. S.]
Frank J. Allen, [L. S.]
Nam-a-co-wa-ha, the bear, his x mark, [L. S.]
Pe-sha-ka-nah, the bear, his x mark, [L. S.]
Na-poi-haw, the man asleep, his x mark, [L. S.]
Pam-a-saw, or walker, his x mark. [L. S.]

Signed and sealed in presence of—
James Kemmly, secretary,
Wm. N. Wickliffe, Captain Sixth Infantry,
J. Freeman, Lieutenant Sixth Infantry,
Winslow Turner,
And. L. Hughes, United States Indian agent.

TREATY WITH THE POTAWATOMI, 1832.

Articles of a treaty made and concluded on Tippecanoe River, in the State of Indiana, between Jonathan Jennings, John W. Davis and Marks Crume, Commissioners on the part of the United States, and the Chiefs, Headmen and Warriors, of the Pottawatimie Indians, this twenty-sixth day of October, in the year eighteen hundred and thirty-two.

Oct. 26, 1832.

7 Stat., 394.
Proclamation, Jan. 21, 1833.

ARTICLE I. The Chiefs, Headmen and Warriors, aforesaid, agree to cede to the United States their title and interest to lands in the State of Indiana, (to wit:) beginning at a point on Lake Michigan, where the line dividing the States of Indiana and Illinois intersects the same; thence with the margin of said Lake, to the intersection of the southern

Cession to the United States.

boundary of a cession made by the Pottawatimies, at the treaty of the Wabash, of eighteen hundred and twenty-six; thence east, to the northwest corner of the cession made by the treaty of St. Joseph's, in eighteen hundred and twenty-eight; thence south ten miles; thence with the Indian boundary line to the Michigan road; thence south with said road to the northern boundary line, as designated in the treaty of eighteen hundred and twenty-six, with the Pottawatimies; thence west with the Indian boundary line to the river Tippecanoe; thence with the Indian boundary line, as established by the treaty of eighteen hundred and eighteen, at St. Mary's to the line dividing the States of Indiana and Illinois; and thence north, with the line dividing the said States, to the place of beginning.

Reservations.

ARTICLE II. From the cession aforesaid, the following reservations are made, (to wit:)

For the band of Aub-be-naub-bee, thirty-six sections, to include his village.

For the bands of Men-o-mi-nee, No-taw-kah, Muck-kah-tah-mo-way and Pee-pin-oh-waw, twenty-two sections.

For the bands of O-kaw-wause, Kee-waw-nay and Nee-bosh, eight sections.

For J. B. Shadernah, one section of land in the Door Prairie, where he now lives.

For the band of Com-o-za, two sections.

For the band of Mah-che-saw, two sections.

For the band of Mau-ke-kose, six sections.

For the bands of Nees-waugh-gee and Quash-qua, three sections.

Annuities and payments.

ARTICLE III. In consideration of the cession aforesaid, the United States agree to pay to the Pottawatimie Indians, an annuity for the term of twenty years, of twenty thousand dollars; and will deliver to them goods to the value of one hundred thousand dollars, so soon after the signing of this treaty as they can be procured; and a further sum of thirty thousand dollars, in goods, shall be paid to them in the year eighteen hundred and thirty-three, by the Indian agent at Eel river.

Debts to be paid by United States.

ARTICLE IV. The United States agree to pay the debts due by the Pottawatimies, agreeably to a schedule hereunto annexed; amounting to sixty-two thousand four hundred and twelve dollars.

Provision for emigrating.

ARTICLE V. The United States agree to provide for the Pottawatimies, if they shall at any time hereafter wish to change their residence, an amount, either in goods, farming utensils, and such other articles as shall be required and necessary, in good faith, and to an extent equal to what has been furnished any other Indian tribe or tribes emigrating, and in just proportion to their numbers.

Sawmill to be built.

ARTICLE VI. The United States agree to erect a saw mill on their lands, under the direction of the President of the United States.

In testimony whereof, the said Jonathan Jennings, John W. Davis, and Marks Crume, commissioners as aforesaid, and the chiefs, head men, and warriors of the Pottawatimies, have hereunto set their hands at Tippecanoe river, on the twenty-sixth day of October, in the year eighteen hundred and thirty-two.

Jonathan Jennings,
John W. Davis,
Marks Crume.

Witness:
Geo. B. Walker.

Louison, his x mark,
Che-chaw-cose, his x mark,
Banack, his x mark,
Man-o-quett, his x mark,
Kin-kosh, his x mark,
Pee-shee-waw-no, his x mark,
Min-o-min-ee, his x mark,

Mis-sah-kaw-way, his x mark,
Kee-waw-nay, his x mark,
Sen-bo-go, his x mark,
Che-quaw-ma-caw-co, his x mark,
Muak-kose, his x mark,
Ah-you-way, his x mark,
Po-kah-kause, his x mark,

So-po-tie, his x mark,
Che-man, his x mark,
No-taw-kah, his x mark,
Nas-waw-kee, his x mark,
Pec-pin-a-waw, his x mark,
Ma-che-saw, his x mark,
O-kitch-chee, his x mark,
Pee-pish-kah, his x mark,
Com-mo-yo, his x mark,
Chick-kose, his x mark,
Mis-qua-buck, his x mark,
Mo-tie-ah, his x mark,
Muck-ka-tah-mo-way, his x mark,
Mah-quaw-shee, his x mark,
O-sheh-weh, his x mark,
Mah-zick, his x mark,
Queh-kah-pah, his x mark,

Quash-quaw, his x mark,
Louisor Perish, his x mark,
Pam-bo-go, his x mark,
Bee-yaw-yo, his x mark,
Pah-ciss, his x mark,
Mauck-co-paw-waw, his x mark,
Mis-sah-qua, his x mark,
Kawk, his x mark,
Miee-kiss, his x mark,
Shaw-bo, his x mark,
Aub-be-naub-bee, his x mark,
Mau-maut-wah, his x mark,
O-ka-mause, his x mark,
Pash-ee-po, his x mark,
We-wiss-lah, his x mark,
Ash-kum, his x mark,
Waw-zee-o-nes, his x mark.

Witnesses:

William Marshall, Indian agent,
Henry Hoover, secretary,
H. Lasselle, interpreter,
E. V. Cicott, Sint. interpreter,

J. B. Bourie, interpreter,
J. B. Jutra, Sint. interpreter,
Edward McCartney, interpreter,
Luther Rice, interpreter.

Horses delivered.

After the signing of this Treaty, and at the request of the Indians, five thousand one hundred and thirty-five dollars were applied to the purchase of horses, which were purchased and delivered to them, under our direction, leaving ninety-four thousand eight hundred and sixty-five dollars to be paid in merchandise.

Jonathan Jennings,
John W. Davis,
Marks Crume.

Claims to be paid.

It is agreed, that the United States will satisfy the claims mentioned in the following schedule, as provided for in the fourth article of the foregoing treaty, viz:

To Andrew Waymire, forty dollars.
Zacheriah Cicott, nine hundred and fifty dollars.
H. Lassell, senior, four thousand dollars.
Silas Atchinson, two hundred and twenty dollars.
Alexander McAllister, two hundred and twenty dollars.
Walker and Davis, fifteen hundred dollars.
Walker, Carter & Co. five thousand six hundred dollars.
Edward McCartney, one thousand dollars.
F. R. Kintner, six hundred and twenty dollars.
Joseph Trucky, one hundred dollars.
J. Vigus & C. Taber, eight hundred and fifty dollars.
James Burnit, six hundred dollars.
Samuel Hanna, executor of Abraham Burnet, three hundred and fifty dollars.
James Hickman, sixty dollars.
William Scott, two hundred and fifty dollars.
M. Harse, seventy dollars.
Emmerson and Huntington, assignees of Willis Fellows, four thousand five hundred dollars.
W. G. and G. W. Ewing, one thousand dollars.
Peter Barron, seventeen hundred and sixty-six dollars.
Hamilton & Taber, seven hundred and thirty-seven dollars.
Skelton & Scott, six hundred and fifty dollars.
Cyrus Taber, three hundred and fifty dollars.
G. S. Hubbard, one thousand dollars.
Moses Rice, one hundred dollars.
John E. Hunt, three thousand two hundred and sixteen dollars.
John Baldwin, one thousand dollars.
Louis Drouillard, sixty-eight dollars.

George Crawford, eighty dollars.
Thomas Hall, forty dollars.
John B. Duret, four hundred dollars.
Anthony Gambin, three hundred dollars.
Joseph Barron, seven hundred and ninety-six dollars.
James H. Kintner, three hundred and fifty-seven dollars.
John B. Bourie, five hundred dollars.
Henry Ossum, nine hundred dollars.
Samuel Hanna, fifteen hundred dollars.
Barnet & Hanna, three thousand five hundred dollars.
Todd & Vigus, six thousand five hundred and thirteen dollars.
Allen Hamilton, seven hundred dollars.
W. G. and G. W. Ewing, three thousand dollars.
George F. Turner, two hundred dollars.
Peter Longlois, two thousand five hundred dollars.
Thomas Robb, eight hundred and forty dollars.
The estate of George Cicott, deceased, fifteen hundred dollars.
George C. Spencer, one hundred and fifty-seven dollars.
John T. Douglass, one hundred dollars.
W. G. and G. W. Ewing, seven hundred and sixteen dollars.
H. B. M'Keen, six hundred dollars.
Joseph Bertrand, senior, fifteen hundred dollars.
George C. Spencer, three hundred dollars.
Jesse Buzann, three hundred and sixteen dollars.
Joseph Douglass, four hundred and fifty dollars.
John Smith, four hundred and eighty dollars.
Moses Barnett, eight hundred and forty-five dollars.
Harison Barnett, two hundred and sixty-seven dollars.
Lot Bozarth, ninety dollars.
Silas Alchison, two hundred and forty-four dollars.
Harison Barnett & Co. one hundred and seventy-eight dollars.
James Elliott, one hundred and nineteen dollars.
Alexander Smith, one hundred dollars.
Walker, Carter & Co. four hundred and four dollars.
John Forsyth, amr. &c. of Thomas Forsyth, four hundred and seventy-three dollars.
John Forsyth, six hundred dollars.

TREATY WITH THE SHAWNEE, ETC., 1832.

Oct. 26, 1832.
_____
7 Stat., 397.
Proclamation, Feb. 12, 1833.

Articles of a treaty made and entered into at Castor Hill, in the county of St. Louis, in the State of Missouri, this twenty-sixth day of October, one thousand eight hundred and thirty-two, between William Clark, Frank J. Allen and Nathan Kouns, Commissioners on the part of the United States, of the one part, and the Chiefs, Warriors and Counsellors of the Shawnoes and Delawares, late of Cape Girardeau, in behalf of their respective bands, of the other part.

Preamble.

WHEREAS parts of the Shawanoe and Delaware nations of Indians, did settle on lands near the town of Cape Girardeau, under a permission from the Spanish Government given to said Shawanoes and Delawares by the Baron de Carondelet, dated the fourth day of January one thousand seven hundred and ninety three, on which lands the Delawares resided until the year one thousand eight hundred and fifteen, at which period, from various causes, it became necessary for them to remove, leaving their fields and improvements: And whereas, lands have been assigned to the said Tribes by Treaties, viz: with the Shawanoes of the seventh November one thousand eight hundred and twenty-five, and with the Delawares of the twenty-fourth September one thousand eight hundred and twenty-nine, in which last named

Treaty no compensation was made to the Delawares late of Cape Girardeau, for their improvements or for their loss of stock, &c. and it being the desire of the United States to indemnify the said Delawares for all losses and injuries by them sustained in consequence of such removal, the following articles have been agreed upon by the contracting parties.

ARTICLE I. The Delawares and Shawanoes late of Cape Girardeau, hereby cede and relinquish to the United States all their lands within the State of Missouri, and also all claims which they may have against the United States for loss of property and for improvements which they have made up to the present time. *Cession of land to United States.*

ARTICLE II. In consideration of the foregoing cession and relinquishment, the United States agree to the following stipulations: There shall be paid and delivered to said Delawares as soon as possible after the ratification of this Treaty, horned cattle, hogs, and other stock, to the amount of two thousand dollars. *Stipulations on the part of the United States.*

For assistance in breaking up ground, and enclosing the same, one thousand dollars.

For pay of a person to attend their mill for five years, and for repairs of the same during the said period, two thousand five hundred dollars.

For support of a school for three years, one thousand five hundred dollars.

ARTICLE III. There shall be paid to the said Delawares on their lands, in merchandise suited to their wants, at the St. Louis cost prices, after the ratification of this treaty, the sum of five thousand dollars. There shall also be paid them the further sum of twelve thousand dollars, to be placed, at the request of said Indians, in the hands of the Superintendent of Indian affairs at St. Louis, to be by him applied to the payment of debts which the said Delawares have acknowledged to be due by their nation agreeably to a schedule presented in Council, and which sum they wish paid to Menard & Vallé of St. Genevieve, for the benefit of William Gillis and William Marshall.—The sum of one thousand dollars is also paid them in merchandise and cash, the receipt of which latter sum (of one thousand dollars) is hereby acknowledged. *Payment to Delawares.* *Payment of claims against Delawares.*

ARTICLE IV. To enable the Shawanoes who are parties to this Treaty, to remove immediately all the bands of their Tribe who are settled in the Territory of Arkansas, to the lands assigned their nation on the Kanzas river, the United States will pay them on the signing of this treaty, eight hundred dollars in cash, and four hundred dollars in clothing and horses, the receipt of which sums, amounting to twelve hundred dollars, is hereby acknowledged. And when they shall have removed to their lands, the further sum of five hundred dollars shall be paid them towards the expenses of said removal. The United States will moreover furnish the said Shawanoes with provisions on their land for one year after their removal, which, together with the preceding stipulations, will be considered in full of all their claims and demands against the United States, of whatever nature. *Payments to Shawnees.*

ARTICLE V. This treaty to be obligatory on the contracting parties when ratified by the President and Senate of the United States. *When to take effect.*

In testimony whereof, the commissioners aforesaid, and the undersigned chiefs, warriors, and counsellors aforesaid have hereunto subscribed their names and affixed their seals, at Castor Hill, in the county of St. Louis aforesaid, the date first above written.

William Clark,	[L. S.]	Nonon-da-qomon, his x mark,	[L. S.]
Frank J. Allen,	[L. S.]	Shawanoes:	
Nathan Kouns,	[L. S.]	Wah-wai-lainue, his x mark,	[L. S.]
Meh-shay-quo-wah, his x mark,	[L. S.]	La-lah-ow-che-ka, his x mark,	[L. S.]
Nah-ko-min, his x mark,	[L. S.]	Ki-ah-quah, his x mark,	[L. S.]
Ta-whe-la-len, his x mark,	L. S.]	Pee-tah-lah-wah, his x mark,	[L. S.]
Capt. Ketchum, his x mark,	L. S.]	Shot Pouch, his x mark,	[L. S.]

In presence of—

Jas. Kemmly, secretary,
Meriwether Lewis Clark, lieutenant, Sixth
    Infantry,
Geo. Maguire, Indian Depa´tment,
Sam. L. McKenny,
Pierre Menard,
Alex'r. Charles,

Pem-saw-taw, Capt. Perry, his x mark,
A. Shane, United States interpreter,
Jacques Mette, United States interpreter,
Geo. Catlin,
Pierre Cadue, his x mark, interpreter for
    Kickapoos and Pottawatamies.

Castor Hill, St. Louis County, Mo.
October 31st, 1832.

Annuities.

By an understanding had between the undersigned Commissioners on the part of the United States, and certain Chiefs of the Delaware Nation hereinafter named, and which was agreed to after the signing of the Treaty with said Tribe, it was stipulated by the said Chiefs and agreed to by the Commissioners, that an annuity for life to Meshe Kowhay, or Patterson, first Chief of the Delawares, Tah-whee-lalen, or Ketchum, Captain of a band; and Natcoming, also Captain of a band, should be paid to each of them by the United States, of one hundred dollars.

In testimony whereof, we have hereunto set our hands at Castor Hill, the date aforesaid.

William Clark,
Nathan Kouns,
Frank J. Allen.

TREATY WITH THE POTAWATOMI, 1832.

Oct. 27, 1832.

7 Stat., 399.
Proclamation, Jan. 21, 1833.

Articles of a Treaty, made and concluded on the Tippecanoe River, in the State of Indiana, on the twenty-seventh day of October, in the year of our Lord eighteen hundred and thirty-two, between Jonathan Jennings, John W. Davis and Marks Crume, Commissioners on the part of the United States, and the Chiefs and Warriors of the Potowatomies, of the State of Indiana and Michigan Territory.

Cession of land to United States.

ARTICLE I. The Chiefs and Warriors aforesaid cede to the United States, their title and interest to lands in the States of Indiana and Illinois, and in the Territory of Michigan, south of Grand river.

Reservations.

ARTICLE II. From the cession aforesaid, the following reservations are made, (to wit:) The reservation at Po-ca-gan's village for his band, and a reservation for such of the Potowatomies as are resident at the village of Notta-we-sipa, agreeably to the treaties of the nineteenth of September, eighteen hundred and twenty-seven, and twentieth of September, 1828.

For the band of Kin-Kash, four sections:
For O-ca-chee, one section:
For the band Mes-qua-buck, four sections, to include his village:
For the band of Che-kase, four sections, to include his village:
For the band of Che-Chaw-kose ten sections, to include his village:
For the Potowatomies, two sections, to include their mills on Tippecanoe river.
For the band of To-i-sas brother Me-mot-way, and Che-quam-ka-ko, ten sections to include their village:
For the band of Ma-sac, four sections:
For the band of Ash-kum and Wee-si-o-nas, sixteen sections, to include their village:
For the band of Wee-sau, five sections of land, including one section, granted to him by the Treaty of eighteen hundred and twenty-eight, and to include his present residence:
For the bands of Mo-ta and Men-o-quet. four sections, each, to include their villages:
For Be-si-ah, four sections.

ARTICLE III. The United States agree to grant to each of the following persons, the quantity of land annexed to their names, which lands shall be conveyed to them by patent:

For Mon-i-taw-quah, daughter of Swa-gaw, one section, to include Wi-me-gos village:

For Wee-saw, three sections:

For Po-quia, the sister of Jose, one section:

For Ben-ack, eight sections:

For Ursule Du-quin-dre, one section:

For Ge-neir, one section:

To To-pen-ne-bee, principal chief, one section:

To Poch-a-gan, second Chief, one section:

To Pet-chi-co, two sections:

To Sau-gana, one section:

To Louis Barnett, one section:

To Mam-qua, daughter of Sau-ga-na, one section:

To Mish-a-wa, adopted daughter of Pit-e-chew, one section:

To Kesis-Shadana, one section:

To Louis Chadana, one half section:

To Charles Chadana, one half section:

To John B. Chadana, one section:

To Pier Navarre's wife, one section:

To John B. Ducharm, one section:

To Mie-saw-bee, one quarter section:

To Baptiste L. Clare, one half section:

To Mary Lacombe's children, one half section:

To Joseph Bertrand's, jr. children, one half section jointly:

To Francis Page, jr. one half section:

To Alexander Rollane, a half blood, one half section:

To Re-re-mo-sau, (alias) Panish, one section and one half section, on the McCou, on the river Raison, in the Michigan Territory, which was reserved to his use at St. Joseph's treaty, of eighteen hundred and twenty-eight:

To Mary Nedeau, one quarter section:

To Saw-grets, son of Pier Moran, one half section:

To Isadore Mo-mence and Wa-be-ga, sons of Pier Morans, one quarter section each:

To Poch-a-gan's wife, one section:

To Pet-qua and Kee-see, sons of Ma-kee-sa-be, one half section:

To Pe-nem-chis, one half section:

To Neu-a-tau-naut, one half section:

To Francis de Jean, one section:

To Mary Ann Ben-ack, wife of Edward McCartney, three sections of land, to be located on the south side of the Turkey creek prairie:

For Francis Besion, one half section:

For Miss-no-qui, a chieftess, four sections:

For Luther Rice, one quarter section:

For Med-lin Aucharm, one quarter section:

For Sheaupo Truckey, one section:

For Ju-be Actrois, one section:

For Ash-kum, two sections:

For Pee-pees-kah one section:

For Po-ka-kause, one half section:

For Nas-wau-kee, one section:

For Man-me-nass, one half section:

For Paul Longlois, one half section:

For Peter Longlois, junr., one half section:

For Shaw-bo-wah-tuck, one quarter section:

For Betsey Rousau, one quarter section:

For John Davis, one half section:

For Nancy Cicott, one quarter section:

For Amelia Cicott, one quarter section:
For Lazette Allen, one quarter section:
For Polly Griffith, daughter of Ne-bosh, two sections:
For Chop-y-tuck, or John Payne, one section:
For Joe Borisau, one quarter section:
For Quash-mau, one quarter section:
For Mas-co, one quarter section:
For Mis-sink-qu-quah, six sections:
For Aub-e-naub-bee, ten sections:
For Nee-kaw Dizzardee, one quarter section:
For Mog-see, one half section:
To Kaubee, one half section:
To old Ann Mac-i-to, one half section:
To old Wee-saw, one half section:
To Pe-te-no-on, one half section:
To Tou-se-qua, the wife of Joe Baily, one section:
To Au-taw-co-num, daughter of the Crane, one section:
To Sen niss-quah and her daughter Nancy, two sections:
To James Burnett, one section:
To To-gah, a Potawatomie woman, one quarter section:
To Mary Ann Bruner, one quarter section.

The foregoing reservations shall be selected, under the direction of the President of the United States, after the lands shall have been surveyed, and the boundaries to correspond with the public surveys.

Annuities and payments. ARTICLE IV. In consideration of the aforesaid cession, the United States will pay fifteen thousand dollars annually for twelve years; Thirty-two thousand dollars, in goods, will be paid as soon after the signing of these articles, as they can be procured, and ten thousand dollars, in goods, will be paid next spring, at Notta-wa-si-pa, and to be paid to that band, and pay their just debts, agreeably to a schedule hereunto annexed, amounting to twenty thousand seven hundred and twenty-one dollars.

Tract to be bought by United States. The section of land granted by the treaty of St. Joseph to To-pe-nau-koung, wife of Peter Longlois, shall be purchased by the United States, if the same can be done for the sum of eight hundred dollars.

Education. The United States agree to appropriate, for the purpose of educating Indian youths, the annual sum of two thousand dollars, as long as the Congress of the United States may think proper, to be expended as the President may direct.

Treaty, when to take effect. This treaty shall take effect and be obligatory on the contracting parties, as soon as the same shall have been ratified, by the President of the United States, by and with the advice and consent of the Senate.

In testimony whereof, the said Jonathan Jennings, John W. Davis, and Marks Crume, commissioners as aforesaid, and the chiefs, head men, and warriors of the Potowatomies, have hereunto set their hands at Tippecanoe, on the twenty-seventh day of October, in the year eighteen hundred and thirty-two.

Jonathan Jennings,
J. W. Davis,
To-pe-ne-be, his x mark,
Po-ka-gou, his x mark,
Sa-ga-nah, his x mark,
Pe-che-co, his x mark,
We-is-saw, his x mark,
Che-shaw-gun, his x mark,
Ghe-bause, his x mark,
O-saw-o-wah-co-ne-ah, his x mark,
Mah-gah-guk, his x mark,
Sa-gue-na-nah, his x mark,
Louison Burnet, his x mark,
Shaw-wah-nuk-wuk, his x mark,
Mix-sau-bah, his x mark,
Ne-wah-ko-to, his x mark,

Che-bah, his x mark,
Wah-cose, his x mark,
Ship-she-wa-no, his x mark,
Kaw-kaw-bee, his x mark,
O-ge-mah-caw-so, his x mark,
Mash-kee, his x mark,
Saw-ge-maw, his x mark,
Nah-che-ke-zhie, his x mark,
Mis-ke-qua-tah, his x mark,
Now-o-le-naw, his x mark,
Tuck-e-now, his x mark,
Marks Crume.
Mo-nis, his x mark,
O-go-maw-be-tuk, his x mark,
Kaw-kaw-ke-moke, his x mark,
Ke-swah-bay, his x mark,

Win-keese, his x mark,
To-posh, his x mark,
Kawk-moc-a-sin, his x mark,
Sa-maw-cah, his x mark,
Ko-mack, his x mark,
O-guon-cote, his x mark,
Quis-sin, his x mark,
Chou-a-ma-see, his x mark,
Pat-e-ca-sha, his x mark,
Pe-nah-seh, his x mark,
Mix-e-nee, his x mark,

Pe-na-shee, his x mark,
So-wah-quen, his x mark,
Gib-e-nash-wish, his x mark,
Louison, his x mark,
Che-chaw-cose, his x mark,
Bee-zaw-yo, his x mark,
O-shah-yaw, his x mark,
Ash-kam, his x mark,
O-ketch-chee, his x mark,
Weh-zee-oness, his x mark,
Aub-bee-noub-bee, his x mark.

Witness:

H. Hoover, secretary,
Th. J. V. Owen, United States Indian
   agent,
Marius Willet,
J. Stewart, subagent,
J. Bt. Chandonnais,
J. E. Aunt,
Peter Godfroy,

G. A. Everts,
Robert Simerwell,
L. M. Taylor,
Francis Comparret,
E. N. Cicott, sint.
J. B. Baure, sint.
H. Lasselle,
Henry Ossem.

After the signing of this treaty, and at the request of the Indians, two thousand seven hundred dollars were applied to the purchasing of horses, which were purchased and delivered to the Indians under our direction, leaving the sum to be paid in merchandise, at this time, twenty-nine thousand three hundred dollars.

Horses delivered.

> Jonathan Jennings,
> J. W. Davis,
> Marks Crume,
> > Commissioners.

It is agreed on the part of the United States, that the following claims shall be allowed, agreeable to the fourth article of the foregoing treaty, viz:

Claims to be paid.

To Erasmus Winslow, three hundred dollars,
Squire Thompson, one hundred dollars,
L. Johnson, three hundred and seventy-five dollars,
Francis Comperret, two thousand four hundred and fifty dollars,
Ica Rice, fifteen hundred dollars,
T. P. and J. J. Godfroy, two hundred and fifty dollars,
Joseph Smith, twenty-six dollars,
James Aveline, ninety-eight dollars,
Edward Smith, forty-seven dollars,
Gustavus A. Everts, two hundred dollars,
Alexis Coquillard, five thousand one hundred dollars,
Lathrop M. Taylor, two thousand two hundred and eighty dollars,
Peter and J. J. Godfroy, three thousand five hundred dollars,
R. A. Forsyth, eighteen hundred dollars,
Louis Dupuis, forty dollars,
Timothy S. Smith, three hundred and ninety dollars,
William Huff, one hundred dollars,
Thomas Jones, two hundred and seventy-five dollars
Michael Cadieux, four hundred and ninety dollars,
Arthur Patterson, nine hundred dollars,
Samuel McGeorge, three hundred and fifty dollars,
D. H. Colerick, one hundred and fifty dollars,
James Conner, one thousand dollars.

> Jonathan Jennings,
> J. W. Davis,
> Marks Crume,
> > Commissioners.

TREATY WITH THE KASKASKIA, ETC., 1832.

Oct. 27, 1832.

7 Stat., 403.
Proclamation, Feb.
12, 1833.

Articles of a treaty made and entered into at Castor Hill, in the county of St. Louis in the State of Missouri, this twenty-seventh day of October, one thousand eight hundred and thirty-two, between William Clark, Frank J. Allen and Nathan Kouns, Commissioners on the part of the United States, of the one part; and the Kaskaskia and Peoria tribes, which, with the Michigamia, Cahokia and Tamarois bands, now united with the two first named tribes, formerly composed the Illinois nation of Indians, of the other part.

WHEREAS, the Kaskaskia tribe of Indians and the bands aforesaid united therewith, are desirous of uniting with the Peorias, (composed as aforesaid) on lands west of the State of Missouri, they have therefore for that purpose agreed with the commissioners aforesaid, upon the following stipulations:

Cession by Kaskaskia.

ARTICLE I. The Kaskaskia tribe of Indians and the several bands united with them as aforesaid, in consideration of the stipulations herein made on the part of the United States, do forever cede and release to the United States the lands granted to them forever by the first section of the treaty of Vincennes of 13th August 1803, reserving however to Ellen Decoigne the daughter of their late Chief who has married a white man, the tract of land of about three hundred and fifty acres near the town of Kaskaskia, which was secured to said tribe by the act of Congress of 3d March 1793.

Reservation.

ARTICLE II. The Kaskaskia tribe further relinquishes to the United States the permanent annuity of one thousand dollars which they receive under the third article of the aforesaid treaty, and their salt annuity due by treaty of Fort Wayne of 7th June 1803.

Annuity relinquished.

Cession by Peoria.

ARTICLE III. The Peoria tribe and the bands aforesaid, united therewith, cede and relinquish to the United States, all their claims to land heretofore reserved by, or assigned to them in former treaties, either in the State of Illinois or Missouri.

Cession by the United States.

ARTICLE IV. The United States cede to the combined tribes of Kaskaskias and Peorias, and the bands aforesaid united with them, one hundred and fifty sections of land forever, or as long as they live upon it as a tribe, to include the present Peoria village, west of the State of Missouri, on the waters of Osage river, to be bounded as follows, to wit: North by the lands assigned to the Shawanoes; west, by the western line of the reservation made for the Piankeshaws, Weas, and Peorias; and east by lands assigned the Piankeshaws and Weas.

Annuity.

ARTICLE V. In consideration of the foregoing cessions and relinquishments, the United [States] agree to pay to the said united Kaskaskia and Peoria tribes (composed as aforesaid) an annuity of three thousand dollars for ten successive years, to be paid on the lands assigned them in common, either in money, merchandise, or domestic stock, at their option; if in merchandise, to be delivered to them free of transportation.

Claims of Peoria to lands in Missouri.

ARTICLE VI. And whereas, the said Peoria tribe, and the bands united with them as aforesaid, assert in Council that they never understood the 5th article of the treaty of Edwardsville of 25th September *1818* [1825], as ceding to the United States their claims to lands in Missouri, on which they had been settled for a length of time previous to that treaty, and of which they had had possession for more than sixty years,—and now demand an equivalent for those claims. The Commissioners with a view of quieting forever the said claims and all demands of whatever nature which said Peoria tribe and the several bands united therewith as aforesaid, have against the government or citizens of the United States, agree to pay, viz:—To the Peorias in common with the Kaskaskias, the sum of sixteen hundred dollars; to the Kaskaskias alone, for seven horses lost by them, and for salt annuities due to them by the treaty of Fort Wayne aforesaid, three hundred and fifty dollars; to the Peorias alone for improvements on the lands they moved from, two hundred and fifty dollars; to the united Peorias and Kaskaskias, there shall be paid and delivered on their land as soon as practicable after the ratification of this treaty, cows and calves and other stock to the amount of four hundred dollars, three iron bound carts, three yoke of oxen, and six ploughs. There shall also be built for said tribes, four log houses;—for breaking up ground and fencing the same, three hundred dollars:—for agricultural implements, iron, and steel, fifty dollars per annum for four years. There shall also be paid to the said united tribes, on the signing of this treaty, eight hundred dollars in goods suited to their wants. Assistance shall also be given the Kaskaskias in moving to their lands, and provisions for one year after their removal, to the amount of one thousand dollars. It is understood that any stipulations in this or the preceding articles, for the benefit of the Peorias or Kaskaskias separately, or united, shall embrace, in either case the bands before mentioned, united with either, or both tribes, as the case may be.

ARTICLE VII. In consideration of the stipulations contained in the preceding articles, the Peoria and Kaskaskia tribes and the bands of Michigamia, Cahokia and Tamarois Indians united with them, hereby forever cede and relinquish to the United States, their claims to lands within the States of Illinois and Missouri, and all other claims of whatsoever nature which they have had or preferred against the United States or the citizens thereof, up to the signing of this treaty. *Relinquishment of claims by Peoria, etc.*

ARTICLE VIII. This treaty after the same shall be ratified by the President and Senate of the United States, shall be obligatory on the contracting parties. *Treaty binding when ratified.*

Done at Castor Hill, in the county of St. Louis in the State of Missouri, the day and year above written, and of the independence of the United States the fifty-seventh.

Wm. Clark,	Pa-me-kaw-wa-ta, man's track, his x mark,
Frank J. Allen,	Al-le-ne-pe-sh-en-sha, his x mark.
Nathan Kouns.	Kaskaskias:
Peorias:	Ke-mon-sah, little chief, his x mark,
Wah-pe-sha-ka-na, white skin, his x mark,	Wah-kah-pe-se-wah, round flyer,
Ken-mah-re-ne-ah, his x mark,	Wa-pe-sae, white, his x mark,
Pa-kee-sha-ma, cutter, his x mark,	Pe-me-ka-wai, man's track, his x mark.

In presence of—

James Kemmly, secretary,	Wm. Radford, U. S. Navy,
A. Shane, United States interpreter,	G. S. Rousseau, U. S. Army,
Jacques Mette, United States interpreter,	Meriwether Lewis Clark, lieutenant, Sixth
Jesse Oliver,	Infantry.
Pierre Menard.	

TREATY WITH THE MENOMINEE, 1832.

Oct. 27, 1832.

7 Stat., 405.
Proclamation, Mar. 13, 1833.

WHEREAS articles of agreement between the United States of America, and the Menominee Indians, were made and concluded at the city of Washington, on the eighth day of February A. D. one thousand eight hundred and thirty-one, by John H. Eaton, and Samuel C. Stambaugh, Commissioners on the part of the United States, and certain Chiefs and Headmen of the Menominee Nation, on the part of said nation; to which articles, an addition or supplemental article was afterwards made, on the seventeenth day of February in the same year, by which the said Menominee Nation agree to cede to the United States certain parts of their land; and that a tract of country therein defined shall be set apart for the New York Indians. All which with the many other stipulations therein contained will more fully appear, by refer- *Preamble.*

ence to the same. Which said agreements thus forming a *Treaty*, were laid before the Senate of the United States during their then session: but were not at said session acted on by that body. Whereupon a further agreement was on the fifteenth day of March, in the same year, entered into for the purpose of preserving the provisions of the treaty, made as aforesaid; by which it was stipulated that the said articles of agreement, concluded as aforesaid, should be laid before the next Senate of the United States, at their ensuing session; and if sanctioned and confirmed by them, that each and every article thereof should be as binding and obligatory upon the parties respectively, as if they had been sanctioned at the previous session. *And whereas* the Senate of the United States, by their resolution of the twenty-fifth day of June, one thousand eight hundred and thirty-two, did advise and consent to accept, ratify and confirm the same, and every clause and article thereof upon the *conditions* expressed in the proviso, contained in their said resolution: which proviso is as follows: "Provided that for the purpose of establishing the rights of the New York Indians, on a permanent and just footing, the said treaty shall be ratified, with the express understanding that two townships of land on the east side of Winnebago Lake, equal to forty-six thousand and eighty acres shall be laid off (to commence at some point to be agreed on) for the use of the Stockbridge and Munsee tribes; and that the improvements made on the lands now in the possession of the said tribes on the east side of the Fox river, which said lands are to be relinquished shall, after being valued by a commissioner to be appointed by the President of the United States, be paid for by the Government: Provided, however, that the valuation of such improvements shall not exceed the sum of twenty-five thousand dollars. And that there shall be one township of land adjoining the foregoing, equal to twenty-three thousand and forty acres laid off and granted for the use of the Brothertown Indians, who are to be paid by the Government the sum of one thousand six hundred dollars for the improvements on lands now in their possession, on the east side of Fox river, and which lands are to be relinquished by said Indians: also that a new line shall be run, parallel to the southwestern boundary line or course of the tract of five hundred thousand acres, described in the first article of this treaty, and set apart for the New York Indians, to commence at a point on the west side of the Fox river, and one mile above the Grand Shute, on Fox river, and at a sufficient distance from the said boundary line as established by the said first article, as shall comprehend the additional quantity of two hundred thousand acres of land on and along the west side of Fox river, without including any of the confirmed private land claims on the Fox river; and which two hundred thousand acres shall be a part of the five hundred thousand acres, intended to be set apart for the Six Nations of the New York Indians and the St. Regis tribe; and that an equal quantity to that which is added to the southwestern side shall be taken off from the northeastern side of the said tract described in that article, on the Oconto creek, to be determined by a commissioner to be appointed by the President of the United States; so that the whole number of acres to be granted to the Six Nations, and St. Regis tribe of Indians, shall not exceed the quantity originally stipulated by the treaty." And whereas, before the treaty aforesaid, *conditionally* ratified, according to the proviso to the resolution of the Senate, above recited, could be obligatory upon the said Menominee nation, their assent to the same must be had and obtained.

And whereas the honorable Lewis Cass, Secretary of the Department of War, by his letter of instructions of the eleventh day of September, A. D. 1832, did authorize and request George B. Porter, Governor of the Territory of Michigan, to proceed to Green Bay, and endeavor to procure the assent of the Menominees to the change proposed by the Senate, as above set forth; urging the necessity of directing his first efforts to an attempt to procure the unconditional assent of the Menominees to the said treaty, as ratified by the Senate. But should he fail in this object that he would then endeavor to procure their assent to the best practicable terms, short of those proposed by the Senate; giving them to understand that he merely received such proposition as they might make, with a view to transmit it for the consideration of the President and Senate of the United States. And if this course became necessary that it would be very desirable that the New York Indians should also signify their acceptance of the modifications required by the Menominees.

And whereas, in pursuance of the said instructions the said George B. Porter proceeded to Green Bay and having assembled all the chiefs and headmen of the Menominee nation, in council, submitted to them, on the twenty-second day of October A. D. one thousand eight hundred and thirty-two, the said proviso annexed to the resolution aforesaid of the Senate of the United States, for the ratification of the said treaty: and advised and urged on them the propriety of giving their assent to the same. And the said chiefs and headmen having taken time to deliberate and reflect on the proposition so submitted to them, and which they had been urged to assent to, did in the most positive and decided manner, refuse to give their assent to the same. (The many reasons assigned for this determination, by them, being reported in the journal of the said commissioner, which will be transmitted with this agreement.)

And whereas after failing in the object last stated, the said George B. Porter endeavored to procure the assent of the said chiefs and headmen of the Menominee nation to the best practicable terms short of those proposed by the Senate of the United States; and after much labor and pains, entreaty and persuasion, the said Menominees consented to the following, as the modifications which they would make; and which are reduced to writing, in the form of an agreement, as the best practicable terms which could be obtained from them, short of those proposed by the Senate of the United States, which they had previously positively refused to accede to. And as the modifications so made and desired, have been acceded to by the New York Indians, with a request that the treaty thus modified might be ratified and approved by the President and the Senate of the United States, it is the anxious desire of the *Objects.* Menominees also, that the treaty, with these alterations may be ratified and approved without delay, that they may receive the benefits and advantage secured to them by the several stipulations of the said treaty, of which they have so long been deprived.

The following is the article of agreement made between the said George B. Porter, commissioner on the part of the United States, specially appointed as aforesaid, and the said Menominee nation, through their chiefs and headmen on the part of their nation.

FIRST. The said chiefs and headmen of the Menominee nation of *Grant of land to the* Indians do not object to any of the matters contained in the proviso *Stockbridge, Munsee,* annexed to the resolution of the Senate of the United States, so far as *and Brothertown Indians.* the same relate to the granting of three townships of land on the east side of Winnebago Lake, to the Stockbridge, Munsee and Brothertown tribes; to the valuation and payment for their improvements, &c. (ending with the words "*and which lands are to be relinquished by said Indians.*") They therefore assent to the same.

SECOND. The said chiefs and headmen of the Menominee nation of Indians, objecting to all the matters contained in the said proviso annexed to the resolution of the Senate of the United States, so far as the same relate to the running of a new line parallel to the southwestern boundary line or course of the tract of five hundred thousand acres, described in the first article of the treaty, and set apart for the

New York Indians, to commence at a point on the southwestern side of Fox river, and one mile above the Grand Shute, on Fox river, and at a sufficient distance from the said boundary line, as established by the said first article, as shall comprehend the additional quantity of two hundred thousand acres of land, on and along the west side of the Fox river, without including any of the confirmed private land claims, on the Fox river, to compose a part of the five hundred thousand acres intended to be set apart for the Six Nations of the New York Indians and St. Regis tribe, *agree* in lieu of this proposition, to set off a like

Cession of land for New York Indians.

quantity of two hundred thousand acres as follows: The said Menominee nation hereby agree to cede for the benefit of the New York Indians along the southwestern boundary line of the present five hundred thousand acres described in the first article of the treaty as set apart for the New York Indians, a tract of land; bounded as follows.

Boundaries.

Beginning on the said treaty line, at the old mill dam on Fox river, and thence extending up along Fox river to the little *Rapid Croche;* from thence running a northwest course three miles; thence on a line running parallel with the several courses of Fox river, and three miles distant from the river, until it will intersect a line, running on a northwest course, commencing at a point one mile above the Grand Shute; thence on a line running northwest, so far as will be necessary to include, between the said last line and the line described as the southwestern boundary line of the five hundred thousand acres in the treaty aforesaid, the quantity of two hundred thousand acres; and thence running northeast until it will intersect the line, forming the southwestern boundary line aforesaid; and from thence along the said line to the old mill dam, or place of beginning, containing two hundred

Reservation.

thousand acres. Excepting and reserving therefrom the *privilege* of Charles A. Grignon, for erecting a mill on Apple creek, &c., as approved by the Department of War on the twenty-second day of April one thousand eight hundred and thirty-one and all confirmed private land claims on the Fox river. The lines of the said tract of land so granted to be run, marked and laid off without delay, by a commissioner to be appointed by the President of the United States. And that in exchange for the above, a quantity of land equal to that which is added to the southwestern side shall be taken off from the northeastern side of the said tract, described in that article, on the Oconto creek, to be run, marked and determined by the commissioner to be appointed by the President of the United States, as aforesaid, so that the whole number of acres to be granted to the Six Nations and St. Regis tribe of Indians, shall not exceed the quantity of five hundred thousand acres.

Treaty binding when ratified.

THIRD. The said chiefs and headmen of the Menominee nation agree, that in case the said original treaty, made as aforesaid, and the supplemental articles thereto, be ratified and confirmed at the ensuing session of the Senate of the United States, with the modifications contained in this agreement, that each and every article thereof shall be as binding and obligatory upon the parties respectively, as if they had been sanctioned at the times originally agreed upon.

In consideration of the above voluntary sacrifices of their interest, made by the said Menominee nation, and as evidence of the good feeling of their great father, the President of the United States, the said George B. Porter commissioner as aforesaid, has delivered to the said chiefs, headmen, and the people of the said Menominee nation here

Presents.

assembled, presents in clothing to the amount of one thousand dollars: five hundred bushels of corn, ten barrels of pork, and ten barrels of flour, &c. &c.

In witness whereof, we have hereunto set our hands and seals, at the Agency House, at Green Bay, this twenty-seventh day of October, in the year of our Lord one thousand eight hundred and thirty-two.

G. B. Porter, Commissioner of the United States, [L. S.]
Kausk-kan-no-naive, grizzly bear, his x mark, [L. S.]
Osh-rosh, the brave, (by his brother fully empowered to act,) [L. S.]
Osh-ke-e-na-neur, the young man, his x mark, [L. S.]
A-ya-mah-ta, fish spawn, his x mark, [L. S.]
Pe-wait-enaw, rain, his x mark, [L. S.]
Che-na-po-mee, one that is looked at, his x mark, [L. S.]
Ko-ma-ni-kin, big wave, his x mark, [L. S.]
Ke-shee-a-quo-teur, the flying cloud, his x mark, [L. S.]
Wain-e-saut, one who arranges the circle, (by his son, Wa-kee-che-on-a-peur,) his x mark, [L. S.]

Ke-shoh, the sun, (by his son, A-pa-ma-chao, shifting cloud,) his x mark, [L. S.]
Ma-concee-wa-be-no-chee, bear's child, his x mark, [L. S.]
Wa-bose, the rabbit, his x mark, [L. S.]
Shaw-e-no-ge-shick, south sky, his x mark, [L. S.]
Ac-camut, the prophet, his x mark, [L. S.]
Mas-ka-ma-gee, his x mark, [L. S.]
Sho-ne-on, silver, his x mark, [L. S.]
Maw-baw-so, pale color, his x mark, [L. S.]
Paw-a ko-neur, big soldier, (by his representative, Che-kaw-mah-kee-shen,) his x mark, [L. S.]

Sealed and delivered, in the presence of—

George Boyd, United States Indian agent,
Charles A. Grignon, interpreter,
Samuel Abbott,
Joshua Boyer, secretary,
James M. Boyd,

Richard Pricket, his x mark, interpreter,
Henry S. Baird,
R. A. Forsyth, paymaster U. S. Army,
B. B. Kercheval,
Ebenezer Childs.

APPENDIX.

Oct. 27, 1832.

7 Stat., 409.

To all to whom these presents shall come, the undersigned, Chiefs and Headmen of the sundry tribes of New York Indians, (as set forth in the specifications annexed to their signatures,) send greeting:

WHEREAS a tedious, perplexing and harassing dispute and controversy have long existed between the Menominee nation of Indians and the New York Indians, more particularly known as the Stockbridge, Munsee and Brothertown tribes, the Six Nations and St. Regis tribe. The treaty made between the said Menominee nation, and the United States, and the conditional ratification thereof by the Senate of the United States, being stated and set forth in the within agreement, entered into between the chiefs and headmen of the said Menominees, and George B. Porter, Governor of Michigan, commissioner specially appointed, with instructions referred to in the said agreement. And whereas the undersigned are satisfied, and believe that the best efforts of the said commissioner were directed and used to procure, if practicable, the unconditional assent of the said Menominees to the change proposed by the Senate of the United States in the ratification of the said treaty: but without success. And whereas the undersigned further believe that the terms stated in the within agreement are the best practicable terms, short of those proposed by the Senate of the United States, which could be obtained from the said Menominees; and being asked to signify our acceptance of the modifications proposed as aforesaid by the Menominees, we are compelled, by a sense of duty and propriety to say that we do hereby accept of the same. So far as the tribes to which we belong are concerned, we are perfectly satisfied, that the treaty should be ratified on the terms proposed by the Menominees. We further believe that the tract of land which the Menominees in the within agreement, are willing to cede, in exchange for an equal quantity on the northeast side of the tract of five hundred thousand acres,

Acceptance, on the part of the tribes interested, of the modifications proposed by the Menominee. contains a sufficient quantity of good land, favorably and advantageously situated, to answer all the wants of the New York Indians, and St. Regis tribe.   For the purpose, then, of putting an end to strife, and that we may all sit down in peace and harmony, we thus signify our acceptance of the modifications proposed by the Menominees: and we most respectfully request that the treaty as now modified by the agreement this day entered into with the Menominees, may be ratified and approved by the President and Senate of the United States.

In witness whereof, we have hereunto set our hands and seals, at the Agency House at Green Bay, this twenty-seventh day of October, in the year of our Lord one thousand eighteen hundred and thirty-two.

G. B. Porter, commissioner on behalf of the United States,   [L. s.]

For, and on behalf of, the Stockbridges and Munsees:

John Metoxen,   [L. s.]
John W. Quinny,   [L. s.]
Austin Quinny,   [L. s.]
Jacob Chicks,   [L. s.]
Robert Konkopa, his x mark,   [L. s.]
Thos. J. Hendrick,   [L. s.]
Benjamin Palmer, his x mark,   [L. s.]
Sampson Medyard,   [L. s.]
Capt. Porter, his x mark,   [L. s.]

For, and on behalf of, the Brothertowns:

William Dick,   [L. s.]
Daniel Dick,   [L. s.]
Elcanah Dick, his x mark,   [L. s.]

For, and on behalf of, the Six Nations and St. Regis tribe:

Daniel Bread,   [L. s.]
John Anthony Brant, his x mark,   [L. s.]
Henry Powles, his x mark,   [L. s.]
Nathaniel Neddy, his x mark,   [L. s.]
Cornelius Stevens, his x mark,   [L. s.]
Thomas Neddy, his x mark,   [L. s.]

Sealed, and delivered, in the presence of—

George Boyd, United States Indian agent,
R. A. Forsyth, paymaster U. S. Army,
Charles A. Grignon, interpreter,
Samuel Abbott,
Joshua Boyer, secretary,
B. B. Kercheval,

Eben. Childs,
Henry S. Baird,
Peter B. Grignon,
Hanson Johnson,
James M. Boyd,
Richard Pricket, his x mark, interpreter.

TREATY WITH THE PIANKASHAW AND WEA, 1832.

Oct. 29, 1832.

7 Stat., 410.
Proclamation, Feb. 12, 1833.

Articles of a treaty made and concluded at Castor Hill in the county of St. Louis and State of Missouri, between William Clark, Frank J. Allen, and Nathan Kouns, Commissioners on the part of the United States, of the one part, and the undersigned Chiefs, Warriors and Counsellors, of the Piankeshaw and Wea tribes of Indians, in behalf of their said tribes, of the other part.

Cession to United States, etc.

ARTICLE I. The undersigned Chiefs, Warriors, and considerate men, for themselves and their said tribes, for and in consideration of the stipulations hereinafter made, do hereby cede and relinquish to the United States forever, all their right, title and interest to and in lands within the States of Missouri and Illinois—hereby confirming all treaties heretofore made between their respective tribes and the United States, and relinquishing to them all claim to every portion of their lands which may have been ceded by any portion of their said tribes.

Cession by United States.

ARTCLE II. The United States cede to the Piankeshaw and Wea tribes, for their permanent residence, two hundred and fifty sections of land within the limits of the survey of the lands set apart for the Piankeshaws, Weas, and Peorias,—bounded east by the western boundary line of the State of Missouri for fifteen miles; north, by the southern boundary of the lands assigned to the Shawanoes; west by lands assigned to the Peorias and Kaskaskias, and south by the southern line of the original tract surveyed for the Piankeshaws, Weas and Peorias,—said tract being intended to include the present villages of the said Piankeshaws and Weas.

Payments to Piankashaw.

ARTICLE III. As a full equivalent to the said Piankeshaw tribe for their claim for salt annuities, for improvements on the lands they moved from within the State of Missouri, and for horses lost when moving, the United States agree to pay them after the ratification of this treaty, cattle, hogs, and such farming utensils as may be required by said tribe on their land, to the amount of five hundred dollars annually, for five years;—the sum of seven hundred and fifty dollars will also be expended in assistance to said tribe in agriculture, and improvements on the land hereby ceded to them, together with the sum of two hundred dollars in merchandise and cash paid at the signing of this treaty, the receipt whereof is hereby acknowledged by said tribe.

ARTICLE IV. As a full equivalent to the Wea tribe, for the improvements made by them on the lands of the United States which they removed from,—for horses lost in consequence of such removal, and for all other claims which they have preferred, the United States agree to pay them after the ratification of this treaty, cattle, hogs, and farming utensils on their land to the amount of five hundred dollars, together with two hundred dollars this day paid them in cash and merchandise, the receipt of which is hereby acknowledged. The United States will also afford some assistance to that part of the Wea tribe now residing in the State of Indiana, to enable them to join the rest of their tribe on the lands hereby assigned them, and will also furnish said portion of the tribe with provisions for one year after their arrival. *Payments to Wea.*

ARTICLE V. The United States will also support a blacksmith's shop for five years at a convenient place between the lands hereby ceded the said Piankeshaws and Weas, and the lands assigned to the Kaskaskias and Peorias; which shop is to be for the benefit of the said tribes of Piankeshaws, Weas, Peorias, and Kaskaskias, in common. *Blacksmith's shop.*

ARTICLE VI. This treaty to be obligatory on the contracting parties, when ratified by the President and Senate of the United States. *Treaty binding when ratified.*

Done at Castor Hill, in the county of St. Louis, in the State of Missouri, this twenty-ninth day of October, in the year of our Lord eighteen hundred and thirty-two, and of the independence of the United States the fifty-seventh.

Wm. Clark,	Weas—Continued.
Frank J. Allen,	Go-te-goh-pa, stands by himself, his x
Nathan Kouns.	mark.
Weas:	Piankeshaws:
Wa-pon-ke-ah, swan, his x mark,	Mah-son-shau, thunder, his x mark,
Shin-ga-rea, diving duck, his x mark,	Nah-he-comma, to do right, his x mark.

Signed in presence of—

James Kemmly, secretary,	Pierre Menard,
A. Shane, United States interpreter,	William Radford, U. S. Navy,
Jacques Mette, United States interpreter,	G. S. Rousseau, U. S. Army,
Jesse Elder,	Meriwether Lewis Clark, lieutenant,
Joseph Guion,	Sixth Infantry.
Baptiste Peoria, his x mark, interpreter,	

TREATY WITH THE SENECA AND SHAWNEE, 1832.

Articles of agreement, made and concluded at the Seneca agency, on the head waters of the Cowskin river, this 29th day of December, in the year of our Lord one thousand eight hundred and thirty-two, by and between Henry L. Ellsworth and John F. Schermerhorn, Commissioners, on behalf of the United States, and the Chiefs and Headmen of the " United Nation" of the Senecas and Shawnee Indians, on behalf of said Tribe or Nation. *Dec. 29, 1832.*

7 Stat., 411. Proclamation, Mar. 22, 1833.

WHEREAS certain articles of agreement and convention were concluded at Lewistown, Ohio, on the 20th day of July, A. D. 1831, by and between the United States and the Chiefs and Warriors of the mixed band of the Senecas and Shawnee Indians, residing at or near *Preamble.*

Lewistown, in the State of Ohio: And whereas, by the 2nd article of said agreement, the United States stipulated and agreed, with said Tribe, in the words following, to wit: "to *grant by patent, in fee simple*, to them, and their heirs forever, as long as they shall exist as a nation and remain on the same, a tract of land, to contain sixty thousand acres, to be located under the direction of the President of the United States, contiguous to the lands granted to the Senecas of Sandusky, by the treaty made with them at the City of Washington, on the 28th of February 1831, and the Cherokee settlements—the east line of said tract shall be within two miles of the west line of the lands granted to the Senecas of Sandusky; and the south line shall be within two miles of the north line of the lands held by the Cherokees— and said two miles between the aforesaid lines, shall serve as a common passway between the before-mentioned Tribes, to prevent them from intruding upon the lands of each other." And the treaty aforesaid was ratified and confirmed by the President and Senate of the United States, on the 6th day of April, A. D. 1832. And whereas, the said mixed Band of Senecas and Shawnees removed from their homes in Ohio to settle upon the lands assigned them west of the Mississippi, in pursuance of the provisions and stipulations of the treaty aforesaid: And whereas, the said Senecas from Sandusky, and the mixed Band of Senecas and Shawnees, have lately formed a confederacy, and have expressed their anxiety to unite as one Tribe or Nation, to be called the "United Nation of Senecas and Shawnees," to occupy their land as tenants in common—and have the whole of the country provided for them by the United States located on the east side of Ne-o-sho or Grand river, which runs through and now divides the same: For the purpose of affording a more convenient and satisfactory location to said United Nation, the parties aforesaid do, therefore, hereby stipulate and agree as follows:

Cession to the United States.

ARTICLE I. The United Tribe of Senecas and Shawnee Indians do hereby cede, relinquish and forever quit claim to the United States, all the land granted to them on the west side of Ne-o-sho or Grand river, by treaties made respectively with the Senecas of Sandusky and the mixed Band of Senecas and Shawnees of Lewistown, Ohio, on the 20th day of July, 1831, and on the 28th day of February, 1831.

Grant to Indians.

ARTICLE II. In consideration of said lands, described and ceded as aforesaid, the United States will grant, by letters patent, to the Tribe or Nation of Indians aforesaid, in manner as hereinafter mentioned, the following tract of land lying on the east side of Ne-o-sho or Grand river, viz: bounded on the east by the west line of the State of Missouri; south by the present established line of the Cherokee Indians; west by Ne-o-sho or Grand river; and north by a line running parallel with said south line, and extending so far from the present north line of the Seneca Indians from Sandusky, as to contain sixty thousand acres, exclusive of the land now owned by said Seneca Indians, which said boundaries include, however, all the land heretofore granted said Senecas of Sandusky, on the east side of Grand river. And the United States will grant said tract of land, by two letters patent; the north half, in quantity, to be granted to the mixed band of the Senecas and Shawnees of Ohio, and the south half to the Senecas from Sandusky, aforesaid: the whole to be occupied in common, so long as the said Tribes or Bands shall desire the same. The said patents shall be granted in fee simple; but the lands shall not be sold or ceded without the consent of the United States.

Grist and saw mill, etc.

ARTICLE III. The United States, at the request of said "United Nation," agree to erect immediately a grist mill, a saw mill and a blacksmith shop, and furnish the necessary tools and machinery in anticipation of a re-imbursement from sales of land, ceded to the United States, by the treaties aforesaid, of 28th of February, 1831, and July 20th, 1831, and so far in fulfilment of the same.

ARTICLE IV. The United Nation of Seneca and Shawnees having **Claims against the United States.** presented a claim for money advanced by them for forage while removing to their new homes in the west, and for horses and other property lost on the journey, the United States, in order to a final settlement of such claim, agree to pay one thousand dollars, as follows, viz:—six hundred dollars to the Seneca tribe of Indians from Sandusky; and the sum of four hundred dollars to the Senecas and Shawnees from Lewistown, Ohio, to be distributed by their respective tribes among the claimants, as they may deem just and equitable; and to be received by them in full payment and satisfaction of all the claims aforesaid.

ARTICLE V. Nothing in these articles of agreement shall be con- **Rights under existing treaties.** strued to affect the respective rights of the Seneca tribe of Indians from Sandusky, and the Senecas and Shawnees from Lewistown, Ohio, as secured by existing treaties, except so far as said treaties are inconsistent with the provisions of the articles aforesaid.

ARTICLE VI. This agreement or treaty shall be binding and obliga- **Treaty binding when ratified.** tory upon the contracting parties from and after its ratification by the President and Senate of the United States.

In testimony whereof, the said Henry L. Ellsworth and John F. Schermerhorn, commissioners, and the chiefs and head men of the United Nation of Seneca and Shawnee Indians, have hereunto signed their names and affixed their seals, on the day and year above written.

Henry L. Ellsworth,	[L. s.]	Chiefs of mixed band:
John F. Schermerhorn,	[L. s.]	Me-tho-mea, or Civil John, (first
Seneca chiefs:		chief Senecas and Shawnees,)
Comstick, (first chief Seneca nation,) his x mark,	[L. s.]	his x mark, [L. s.]
		Pe-wy-a-che, his x mark, [L. s.]
Seneca Steel, his x mark,	[L. s.]	Skilleway or Robbin, his x mark, [L. s.]
Small Cloud Spicer, his x mark,	[L. s.]	John Jackson, his x mark, [L. s.]
George Curly Hair, his x mark,	[L. s.]	Quash-acaugh or Little Lewis, his
Tall Chief, his x mark,	[L. s.]	x mark, [L. s.]
Captain Good Hunter, his x mark,	[L. s.]	To-ta-la or John Young, his x
Hard Hickory, his x mark,	[L. s.]	mark, [L. s.]
Wiping Stick, his x mark,	[L. s.]	Mingo Carpenter, his x mark, [L. s.]
Seneca John, his x mark,	[L. s.]	Jemmy McDaniel, his x mark, [L. s.]
John Johnson, his x mark,	[L. s.]	Civil John's son, his x mark, [L. s.]
John Sky, his x mark,	[L. s.]	Yankee Bill, his x mark, [L. s.]
Isaac White, his x mark,	[L. s.]	Big Ash, his x mark, [L. s.]
Joseph Smith, his x mark,	[L. s.]	Civil John's young son, his x
Captain Smith, his x mark,	[L. s.]	mark, [L. s.]

Signed, sealed, and delivered in the presence of us:
    S. C. Stambaugh, secretary to commissioners,
    St. John F. Sane, Indian agent,
    Augt. A. Chouteau,
    Wm. Young,
    George Herron, Seneca interpreter,
    Baptiste Peoria, Shawnee interpreter.

TREATY WITH THE WESTERN CHEROKEE, 1833.

Articles of agreement and convention made and concluded at Fort Gibson, on the Arkansas river on the fourteenth day of February one thousand eight hundred and thirty-three, by and between Montfort Stokes, Henry L. Ellsworth and John F. Schermerhorn duly appointed Commissioners on the part of the United States and the undersigned Chiefs and Head-men of the Cherokee nation of Indians west of the Mississippi, they being duly authorized and empowered by their nation. **Feb. 14, 1833.**

7 Stat., 414.
Proclamation, Apr. 12, 1834.

WHEREAS articles of convention were concluded at the city of Wash- **Preamble.** ington, on the sixth day of May one thousand eight hundred and twenty-eight, between James Barbour Secretary of War, being specially authorized therefor by the President of the United States, and the chiefs and head men of the Cheerokee nation of Indians west of the Mississippi, which articles of convention were duly ratified. And whereas it was agreed by the second article of said convention as follows " That the United States agree to possess the Cheerokees, and to guarantee it to them forever, and that guarantee is solemnly pledged, of seven millions of acres of land, said land to be bounded as follows; viz, commencing at a point on Arkansas river, where the eastern Choctaw boundary line strikes said river, and running thence with the western line of Arkansas Territory to the southwest corner of Missouri, and thence with the western boundary line of Missouri till it crosses the waters of Neasho, generally called Grand river, thence due west, to a point from which a due south course will strike the present northwest corner of Arkansas Territory, thence continuing due south on and with the present boundary line on the west of said Territory, to the main branch of Arkansas river, thence down said river to its junction with the Canadian, and thence up, and between said rivers Arkansas and Canadian to a point at which a line, running north and south, from river to river, will give the aforesaid seven millions of acres, thus provided for and bounded. The United States further guarantee to the Cherokee nation a perpetual outlet west, and a free and unmolested use of all the country lying west of the western boundary of the above-described limits; and as far west, as the sovereignty of the United States and their right of soil extend. And whereas there was to said articles of convention and agreement, the following proviso viz. " Provided nevertheless, that said convention, shall not be so construed, as to extend the northern boundary of said perpetual outlet west, provided for and guarantied in the second article of said convention, north of the thirty-sixth degree of north latitude, or so as to interfere with the lands assigned, or to be assigned, west of the Mississippi river, to the Creek Indians who have emigrated, or may emigrate, from the States of Georgia and Alabama, under the provision of any treaty, or treaties, heretofore concluded, between the United States, and the Creek tribe of Indians—and provided further, that nothing in said convention, shall be construed, to cede, or assign, to the Cheerokees any lands heretofore ceded, or assigned, to any tribe, or tribes of Indians, by any treaty now existing and in force, with any such tribe or tribes."—And whereas, it appears from the Creek treaty, made with the United States, by the Creek nation, dated twenty-fourth day of January eighteen hundred and twenty-six, at the city of Washington; that they had the right to select, and did select, a part of the country described within the boundaries mentioned above in said Cherokee articles of agreement—and whereas, both the Cheerokee and Creek nations of Indians west of the Mississippi, anxious to have their boundaries settled in an amicable manner, have met each other in council, and, after full deliberation mutually agreed upon the boundary lines between them—Now therefore, the United States on one part, and the chiefs and head-men of the Cherokee nation of Indians west of the Mississippi on the other part, agree as follows:

Land granted to Cherokees.

ARTICLE I. The United States agree to possess the Cheerokees, and to guarrantee it to them forever, and that guarrantee, is hereby pledged, of seven millions of acres of land, to be bounded as follows viz: Beginning at a point on the old western territorial line of Arkansas Territory, being twenty-five miles north from the point, where the Territorial line crosses Arkansas river—thence running from said north point, south, on the said Territorial line, to the place where said Territorial line crosses the Verdigris river—thence down said Verdigris river, to the Arkansas river—thence down said Arkansas to a point, where a stone is placed opposite to the east or lower bank of Grand river at its junction with the Arkansas—thence running south, forty-four degrees west, one mile—thence in a straight line to a point four miles northerly from the mouth of the north fork of the Canadian—thence along the said four miles line to the Canadian—thence down the Canadian to the Arkansas—thence, down the Arkansas, to that point on the Arkansas, where the eastern Choctaw boundary strikes, said river; and running thence with the western line of Arkansas Territory as now defined, to the southwest corner of Missouri—thence along the western Missouri line, to the land assigned the Senecas; thence, on the south line of the Senecas to Grand river; thence, up said Grand river, as far as the south line of the Osage reservation, extended if necessary— thence up and between said south Osage line, extended west if necessary and a line drawn due west, from the point of beginning, to a certain distance west, at which, a line running north and south, from said Osage line, to said due west line, will make seven millions of acres within the whole described boundaries. In addition to the seven millions of acres of land, thus provided for, and bounded, the United States, further guarrantee to the Cheerokee nation, a perpetual outlet west and a free and unmolested use of all the country lying west, of the western boundary of said seven millions of acres, as far west as the sovereignty of the United States and their right of soil extend—Provided however, that if the saline, or salt plain, on the great western prairie, shall fall within said limits prescribed for said outlet, the right is reserved to the United States to permit other tribes of red men, to get salt on said plain in common with the Cheerokees—and letters patent shall be issued by the United States as soon as practicable for the land hereby guarranteed.

Further guaranty.

ARTICLE II. The Cherokee nation hereby relinquish and quit claim to the United States all the right interest and title which the Cheerokees have, or claim to have in and to all the land ceded, or claimed to have been ceded to said Cheerokee nation by said treaty of sixth of May one thousand eight hundred and twenty-eight, and not embraced within the limits or boundaries fixed in this present supplementary treaty or articles of convention and agreement.

Quitclaim to the United States of former grant.

ARTICLE III. The Cherokee nation, having particularly requested the United States to annul and cancel the sixth article of said treaty of sixth May, one thousand eight hundred and twenty-eight, the United States, agree to cancel the same, and the same is hereby annulled—Said sixth article referred to, is in the following words—"It is moreover agreed by the United States, when the Cheerokees may desire it, to give them a plain set of laws, suited to their condition— also when they may wish to lay off their lands and own them individually, a surveyor shall be sent to survey them at the expense of the United States.

Sixth article of treaty of May 6, 1828, annulled.

ARTICLE IV. In consideration of the establishment of new boundaries in part, for the lands ceded to said Cheerokee nation, and in view of the improvement of said nation, the United States will cause to be erected, on land now guaranteed to the said nation, four blacksmith shops, one wagon maker shop, one wheelwright shop, and necessary tools and implements furnished for the same; together with one ton of iron, and two hundred and fifty pounds of steel, for each of said blacksmith shops, to be worked up, for the benefit of the poorer class of red men, belonging to the Cherokee nation—And the United States, will employ four blacksmiths, one wagon-maker, and one wheelwright, to work in said shops respectively, for the benefit of said Cheerokee nation; and said materials shall be furnished annually and said services continued, so long as the President may deem proper—And said United States, will cause to be erected on said lands, for the benefit of said Cheerokees, eight patent railway corn mills, in lieu of the mills to be erected according to the stipulation of the fourth article of said treaty, of sixth of May, one thousand eight hundred twenty-eight, from the avails of the sale of the old agency.

Blacksmiths and other workmen, materials and shops.

This supplementary to a former treaty.

ARTICLE V. These articles of agreement and convention are to be considered supplementary, to the treaty before mentioned between the United States, and the Cheerokee nation west of the Mississippi dated sixth of May one thousand eight hundred and twenty-eight, and not to vary the rights of the parties to said treaty, any further, than said treaty is inconsistent with the provisions of this treaty, now concluded, or these articles of convention or agreement.

One mile square for the agency.

ARTICLE VI. It is further agreed by the Cheerokee nation, that one mile square shall be reserved and set apart from the lands hereby guaranteed, for the accommodation of the Cheerokee agency; and the location of the same shall be designated by the Cheerokee nation, in conjunction with the agent of the Government of the United States.

Treaty binding when ratified.

ARTICLE VII. This treaty, or articles of convention, after the same have been ratified, by the President and Senate shall be obligatory on the United States and said Cheerokee nation.

In testimony whereof, the said Montfort Stokes, Henry L. Ellsworth, and John F. Schermerhorn, commissioners as aforesaid, and the chiefs and head men of the Cherokee nation aforesaid, have hereunto set their hands, at Fort Gibson on the Arkansas river, on the 14th day of February, one thousand eight hundred and thirty-three.

Montfort Stokes,	Walter Weller,
Henry L. Ellsworth,	Principal chiefs:
J. F. Schermerhorn,	John Rogers, president commissioners,
John Jolly, his x mark,	Glass, president council.
Black Coat, his x mark,	

Signed, sealed, and delivered in our presence:

S. C. Stambaugh, secretary commissioners,	Wilson Nesbitt,
	Peter A. Carns,
M. Arbuckle, colonel Seventh Infantry,	N. Young, major U. S. Army,
Geo. Vashon, agent Cherokees west,	W. Seawell, lieutenant Seventh Infantry,
Jno. Campbell, agent Creeks.	Wm. Thornton, clerk committee,
Alexander Brown, his x mark,	Charles Webber, clerk council.
Jno. Hambly,	

Interpreters,

TREATY WITH THE CREEKS, 1833.

Feb. 14, 1833.

7 Stat., 417.
Proclamation, Apr. 12, 1834.

Articles of agreement and convention, made and concluded at Fort Gibson, between Montfort Stokes, Henry L. Ellsworth and John F. Schermerhorn, Commissioners on the part of the United States, and the undersigned Chiefs and Head-men of the Muskogee or Creek nation of Indians, this 14th day of February, A. D. 1833.

Preamble.

WHEREAS, certain articles of a treaty were concluded at the City of Washington, on the 24th day of January one thousand eight hundred and twenty-six, by and between James Barbour, Secretary of War, on behalf of the United States, and the Chiefs and head-men of the Creek nation of Indians; by which it is agreed that the said Indians shall remove to a country west of the Mississippi river: and whereas the sixth article of said treaty provides as follows:—"that a deputation of five persons shall be sent by them, (the Creek nation) at the expense of the United States, immediately after the ratification of the treaty, to examine the country west of the Mississippi, not within the limits of the States or Territories, and not possessed by the Choctaws or Cherokees. And the United States agree to purchase for them, if the same can conveniently be done upon reasonable terms, wherever they may select, a country, whose extent shall in the opinion of the President, be proportioned to their numbers. And if such purchase can not be thus made, it is then agreed that the selection shall be made where the President may think proper, just reference being had to the wishes of the emigrating party." And whereas, the Creek Indians aforesaid, did send five persons as delegates, to explore the country pointed out to them by their treaty; which delegates selected a country west of the Territory of Arkansas, lying and being along and between the Verdi-gris, Arkansas, and Canadian rivers: and to the country thus selected, a party of the Creek Indians emigrated the following year.   And whereas certain articles of treaty or convention, were concluded at the city of Washington on the 6th day of May, A. D. one thousand eight hundred and twenty-eight, by and between James Barbour Secretary of War, on behalf of the United States, and certain chiefs and head-men of the Cherokee nation of Indians; by the second article of which convention, a country was assigned to the Cherokee Indians aforesaid, including within its boundaries some of the lands previously selected.and claimed by the Creek Indians, under their treaty aforesaid.   And whereas, the President and Senate of the United States, for the purpose of protect-ing the rights secured to the Creek Indians, by their treaty stipulations, and with a view to prevent collison and misunderstanding between the two nations, ratified and confirmed the Cherokee treaty, on the 28th day of May, 1828, with the following proviso: viz.—" *Provided, never-theless*, that the said convention shall not be so construed as to extend the northern boundary of the perpetual outlet west, provided for and guarranteed in the second article of said convention, north of the 36th deg. of north latitude, or so as to interfere with the lands assigned, or to be assigned, west of the Mississippi river to the Creek Indians, who have emigrated or may emigrate from the States of Georgia and Ala-bama, under the provisions of any treaty or treaties heretofore con-cluded between the United States and the Creek tribe of Indians: And provided further, that nothing in the said convention shall be construed to cede or assign to the Cherokees any lands heretofore ceded or assigned to any tribe or tribes of Indians, by any treaty now existing and in force, with any such tribe or tribes."   And whereas the said proviso and rati-fication of the Cherokee treaty, was accepted by the delegates of the nation, then at the City of Washington as satisfactory to them, as is shown in and by their certain instrument in writing, bearing date the 31st day of May 1828, appended to and published with their treaty aforesaid.   But, afterwards, the Cherokees of Arkansas and many of those residing east of the Mississippi at the time that treaty was con-cluded, removed to the country described in the second article of their treaty and settled upon a certain portion of the land claimed by the Creek Indians under their treaty provisions and stipulations.   And whereas difficulties and dissentions thus arose between the Cherokees and Creek tribes about their boundary lines, which occasioned an appeal to the President of the United States for his interposition, and final settlement of the question, which they were unable to settle between themselves.   And whereas the commissioners of the United States, whose names are signed hereto, in pursuance of the power and authority vested in them by the President of the United States, met the chiefs and head-men of the Cherokee and Creek nations of Indians, in council, on the 29th ultimo; and after a full and patient hearing and careful examination of all the claims, set up and brought forward by both the contending parties, they have this day effected an adjustment of all their difficulties, and have succeeded in defining and establishing bound-ary lines to their country west of the Mississippi, which have been acknowledged, in open council, this day, to be mutually satisfactory to both nations.

Difficulties subse-quent to former treaty.

Now, therefore, for the purpose of securing the great objects con-templated by an amicable settlement of the difficulties heretofore existing between the Cherokee and Muskogee or Creek Indians, so injurious to both parties; and in order to establish boundary lines which will secure a country and permanent home to the whole Creek

Objects.

nation of Indians, including the Seminole nation who are anxious to join them, the undersigned commissioners, duly authorized to act on behalf of the United States, and the chiefs and head-men of the said Muskogee or Creek Indians, having full power and authority to act for their people west of the Mississippi, hereby agree to the following articles:

Peace and friendship. ART. I. The Muskogee or Creek nation of Indians, west of the Mississippi declare themselves to be the friends and allies of the United States, under whose parental care and protection they desire to continue: and that they are anxious to live in peace and friendship not only with their near neighbors and brothers, the Cherokees, but with all the surrounding tribes of Indians.

Bounds of the grants to the Creeks. ART. II. The United States hereby agree, by and with the consent of the Creek and Cherokee delegates, this day obtained, that the Muskogee or Creek country west of the Mississippi, shall be embraced within the following boundaries, viz:—Beginning at the mouth of the north fork of the Canadian river, and run northerly four miles— thence running a straight line so as to meet a line drawn from the south bank of the Arkansas river opposite to the east or lower bank of Grand river, at its junction with the Arkansas, and which runs a course south, 44 deg. west, one mile, to a post placed in the ground— thence along said line to the Arkansas, and up the same and the Verdigris river, to where the old territorial line crosses it—thence along said line north to a point twenty-five miles from the Arkansas river where the old territorial line crosses the same—thence running a line at right angles with the territorial line aforesaid, or west to the Mexico line—thence along the said line southerly to the Canadian river or to the boundary of the Choctaw country—thence down said river to the place of beginning. The lines, hereby defining the country of the Muskogee Indians on the north and east, bound the country of the Cherokees along these courses, as settled by the treaty concluded this day between the United States and that tribe.

United States will convey in fee simple. ART. III. The United States will grant a patent, in fee simple, to the Creek nation of Indians for the land assigned said nation by this treaty or convention, whenever the same shall have been ratified by the President and Senate of the United States—and the right thus guaranteed by the United States shall be continued to said tribe of Indians, so long as they shall exist as a nation, and continue to occupy the country hereby assigned them.

The whole Creek nation and the Seminoles interested. ART. IV. It is hereby mutually understood and agreed between the parties to this treaty, that the land assigned to the Muskogee Indians, by the second article thereof, shall be taken and considered the property of the whole Muskogee or Creek nation, as well of those now residing upon the land, as the great body of said nation who still remain on the east side of the Mississippi: and it is also understood and agreed that the Seminole Indians of Florida, whose removal to this country is provided for by their treaty with the U. S. dated May 9th, 1832, shall also have a permanent and comfortable home on the lands hereby set apart as the country of the Creek nation: and they (the Seminoles) will hereafter be considered a constituent part of said nation, but are to be located on some part of the Creek country by themselves—which location will be selected for them by the commissioners who have signed these articles of agreement or convention.

Additional blacksmith, etc., to be furnished by United States. ART. V. As an evidence of the kind feeling of the United States towards the Muskogee Indians, and as a testimonial of the [their] gratification with the present amicable and satisfactory adjustment of their difficulties with the Cherokees, experienced by the commissioners, they agree on behalf of the United States, to furnish to the Creek Indians west of the Mississippi, one blacksmith and one wheelwright or wagon-maker, as soon as they may be required by the nation, in addition to those already employed—also, to erect shops and furnish tools for the same, and supply the smith shops with one ton of iron and two hundred and fifty pounds of steel each; and allow the said Creek Indians, annually, for education purposes, the sum of one thousand dollars, to be expended under the direction of the President of the United States— the whole of the above grants to be continued so long as the President may consider them conducive to the interest and welfare of the Creek Indians: And the United States will also cause to be erected, as soon as conveniently can be done, four patent railway mills, for grinding corn; and will immediately purchase for them twenty-four cross-cut saws. It being distinctly understood, however, that the grants thus made to the Creek Indians, by this article, are intended solely for the use and benefit of that portion of the Creek nation, who are now settled west of the Mississippi.

ART. VI. The United States agree that the improvements which the Creek Indians may be required to leave, in consequence of the boundary lines this day settled between their people and the Cherokees, shall be valued with as little delay as possible, and a fair and reasonable price paid for the same by the United States. _{Improvements left to be paid for.}

ART. VII. It is hereby agreed by the Creek nation, parties hereto, that if the saline or salt plains on the great western prairies, should come within the boundaries defined by this agreement, as the country of the Creek nation, then, and in that case the President of the United States, shall have the power to permit all other friendly Indian tribes to visit said salt plains and procure thereon and carry away salt sufficient for their subsistence, without hindrance or molestation from the said Creek Indians. *Friendly Indians may use the salt plains.*

ART. VIII. It is agreed by the parties to this convention, that the country hereby provided for the Creek Indians, shall be taken in lieu of and considered to be the country provided or intended to be provided, by the treaty made between the United States and the Creek nation on the 24th day of January, 1826, under which they removed to this country. *The land granted in lieu of former grant.*

ART. IX. This agreement shall be binding and obligatory upon the contracting parties, as soon as the same shall be ratified and confirmed by the President and Senate of the United States. *Treaty binding when ratified.*

Done in open council, at fort Gibson, this 14th day of February, A. D. one thousand eight hundred and thirty-three.

Montfort Stokes,	[L. S.]	Cowo-coogee, Maltha, his x mark,	[L. S.]
Henry L. Ellsworth,	[L. S.]	Holthimotty Tustonnucky, his x	
J. F. Schermerhorn,	[L. S.]	mark,	[L. S.]
Roly McIntosh, his x mark,	[L. S.]	Toatkah Haussie, his x mark,	[L. S.]
Fuss-hatchie Micoe, his x mark,	[L. S.]	Istauchoggo Harjoe, his x mark,	[L. S.]
Benj. Perryman, his x mark,	[L. S.]	Chocoatie Tustonnucky, his x mark,	[L. S.]
Hospottock Harjoe, his x mark,	[L. S.]	Chiefs of Creek nation.	

Signed, sealed, and delivered in our presence:

S. C. Stambaugh, secretary to comms,
M. Arbuckle, colonel Seventh Infantry,
Jno. Campbell, agent Creeks,
Geo. Vashon, agent Cherokee, west,
N. Young, major U. S. Army,
Wilson Nesbitt,

W. Seawell, lieutenant Seventh Infantry,
Peter A. Carns,
Jno. Hambly, interpreter,
Alex. Brown, his x mark, Cherokee interpreter.

TREATY WITH THE OTTAWA, 1833.

Feb. 18, 1833.
_____
7 Stat., 420.
Proclamation, Mar.
22, 1833.

Articles of a treaty made at Maumee in the State of Ohio, on the eight-eenth day of February in the year of our Lord one thousand eight hundred and thirty-three, between George B. Porter, Commissioner on the part of the United States, of the one part; and the undersigned Chiefs and Head men of the Band of Ottawa Indians, residing on the Indian Reserves, on the Miami of Lake Erie, and in the vicinity thereof, representing the whole of said band, of the other part:

Preamble.

WHEREAS, by the twentieth article of the treaty concluded at the foot of the Rapids of the Miami of Lake Erie, on the twenty-ninth day of September A. D. 1817, it is provided as follows: "The United States also agree to grant, by patent, to the Chiefs of the Ottawa tribe of Indians for the use of the said tribe, a tract of land, to contain thirty-four square miles, to be laid out as nearly in a square form as practicable, not interfering with the lines of the tracts reserved by the treaty of Greenville, on the south side of the Miami River of Lake Erie, and to include Tush-que-gan, or McCarty's village; which tracts, thus granted, shall be held by the said tribe, upon the usual conditions of Indian reservations, as though no patent were issued."

Objects.

And whereas by the sixth article of the treaty concluded at Detroit, on the seventeenth day of November A. D. 1807, it is provided, for the accommodation of the Indians named in the treaty, that certain tracts of land, within the cession then made, should be reserved to the said Indian nations, among which is a reservation described as follows:—"Four miles square on the Miami Bay, including the villages where Meskeman and Waugan now live," which reservation was expressly made for the Ottawa tribe.   By virtue of which stipulations and reservations the said Band of Ottawas are now in the occupancy and enjoyment of the two tracts of land therein described;—and for the consideration hereinafter stated, have agreed to cede the same to the United States; and bind themselves to each and all of the articles, and conditions which follow:

Cession to the United States.

ARTICLE I. The said Ottawa Band cede to the United States all their land on each or either side of the Miami River of Lake Erie, or on the Miami Bay, being all the lands mentioned or intended to be included in the two reservations aforesaid, or to which they have any claim. No claims to be made for improvements.

Reservations.

ARTICLE II. It is agreed that out of the lands hereby ceded, the following reservations shall be made: and that patents for each tract shall be granted by the United States to the individuals respectively and their heirs for the quantity hereby assigned to each, that is to say:—A tract of fifteen hundred and twenty acres shall be laid off at the mouth of the River, on the south side thereof, and to be so surveyed as to accommodate the following persons, for whose use respectively, each tract hereinafter described is reserved, viz: three hundred and twenty acres for Au-to-kee, a Chief, at the mouth of the river, to include Presque Isle:—eight hundred acres for Jacques, Robert, Peter, Antoine, Francis and Alexis Navarre, to include their present improvements:—one hundred and sixty acres for Way-say-on, the son of Tush-qua-guan, to include his father's old cabin:—the remaining two hundred and forty acres to be set off in the rear of these two sections:—eighty acres thereof for Pe-tau, and if practicable to include her cabin and field:—eighty acres more thereof for Che-no, a Chief, above, or higher up the little creek, and the other eighty acres thereof, for Joseph Le Cavalier Ranjard, in trust for himself, and the legal representatives of Albert Ranjard, deceased.   Also, the following tracts on the north side of said river:—one hundred and sixty acres for Wau-sa-on-o-quet, a Chief, to include the improvement where he now lives on Pike creek, and to front on the Bay:—eighty acres for Leon Guoin and his children, adjoining the last and on the south side thereof:—one hundred and sixty acres for Aush-cush and Ke-tuck-kee, Chiefs, to be laid off on the north side of Ottawa creek, fronting on the same, and above the place where the said Aush-cush now lives. One hundred and sixty acres for Robert A. Forsyth of Maumee, to be laid off on each side of the turnpike road where half-way creek crosses the same: and one hundred and sixty acres, fronting on the Maumee River, to include the place where Ke-ne-wau-ba formerly resided:— one hundred and sixty acres for John E. Hunt, fronting on the said river, immediately above and adjoining the last; and also one hundred and sixty acres, to adjoin the former tract, on the turnpike road. The said tracts to be surveyed and set off, under the direction of the President of the United States.   *Surveys.*

The said Au-to-kee, Wa-say-on, Pe-tau-che-no, Wau-sa-on-o-quet, Aush-cush, and Ke-tuck-kee, being Indians, the lands hereby reserved for them, are not to be alienated without the approbation of the President of the United States.

The said Leon Guoin has resided, for a long time among these Indians;—has subsisted them when they would otherwise have suffered, and they are greatly attached to him. They request that the grant be to him and his present wife, during their joint lives, and the life of the survivor, and to their children in fee.

The said Jacques, Robert, Peter, Antoine, Francis and Alexis Navarre have long resided among these Indians—intermarried with them, and been valuable friends.

The said Albert Ranjard, deceased, had purchased land of them previous to the late war, upon which, before he died, he had paid them three hundred dollars, for which his family have never received any equivalent.

The reservations to the said Robert A. Forsyth and John E. Hunt, being at the especial request of the said band, in consideration of their long residence among them, and the many acts of kindness they have extended to them.

ARTICLE III. In consideration of which it is agreed that the United States shall pay to the said band of Indians the sum of twenty-nine thousand four hundred and forty dollars, to be, by direction of the said band, applied in extinguishment of their debts, in manner following: that is to say, to John Hollister and Company, seven thousand three hundred and sixty-five dollars, which includes other claims, directed by the said Indians to be by him paid, amounting to thirteen hundred and nine-five dollars, as per schedule A. herewith:—To John E. Hunt, nine thousand nine hundred and twenty-nine dollars, which includes other claims, directed by the said Indians to be by him paid, amounting to two thousand six hundred and seventy-five dollars, and sixty-three cents, as per schedule B. herewith:—To Robert A. Forsyth of Maumee, ten thousand eight hundred and ninety dollars, which includes other claims directed by the said Indians to be by him paid, amounting to four thousand four hundred and ten dollars, as per schedule C. herewith.—To Louis Beaufit seven hundred dollars. To Pierre Menard four hundred dollars. To John King, one hundred dollars. To Louis King fifty-six dollars. (*a*)   *Consideration.*

Within six months after payment by the United States, of the said consideration money the said Indians agree to remove from all the lands herein ceded. And it is expressly understood that in the meantime no interruption shall be offered to the survey of the same by the United States.   *Removal of Indians from lands ceded.*

And whereas the said Band have represented to the said Commissioner that under the treaty, as interpreted to them, entered into with John B. Gardiner, Commissioner on the part of the United States, on   *Claims.*

_____

(*a*) These schedules are not on file at Washington.

the 30th day of August, 1831, for the cession of a part of their lands, there is due to them, jointly with that portion of the tribe that has emigrated, eighteen thousand dollars, and for which they have made claim: whenever this deficiency shall be paid, it is agreed that out of said fund there shall be paid to Joseph Leronger in full satisfaction of all his claim, four hundred dollars; and to Pierre Menard in like satisfaction, sixteen hundred dollars; to Gabriel· Godfroy, junior, in like satisfaction, two hundred dollars, to Waubee's daughter Nau-quesh-kum-o-qua, fifty dollars; to Charles Leway or Nau-way-nes, fifty dollars; to Dr. Horatio Conant, two hundred dollars in full satisfaction of all his claim; to Joseph F. Marsac, fifty dollars.

Treaty binding when ratified.

This treaty, after the same shall have been ratified by the President and Senate of the United States, shall be binding on the contracting parties.

In testimony whereof, the said George B. Porter, and the undersigned chiefs and head men of the said band, have hereunto set their hands, at Maumee, the said day and year.

G. B. Porter,	Nau-qua-gai-shik, his x mark,
Wau-see-on-o-quet, his x mark,	O-sage, his x mark,
An-to-kee, his x mark,	Me-sau-kee, his x mark,
She-no, his x mark,	Kin-je-way-no, his x mark,
Wau-be-gai-kek, his x mark,	An-ne-qua-to, his x mark,
Shaw-wa-no, his x mark,	Meesh-quet, his x mark.
Kee-tuk-kee, his x mark,	Sa-see-go-wa, his x mark,
Aush-cush, his x mark,	Pe-ton-o-quet, his x mark,
No-ten-o, his x mark,	Saw-ga-nosh, his x mark,
Way-say-on, his x mark,	Enne-me-kee, his x mark,
Sas-sain, his x mark,	Aish-qua-bee, his x mark.

In presence of—

E. A. Brush, secretary,	Chs. C. P. Hunt,
Kintzing Pritchette,	G. B. Knaggs,
Henry Conner,	John Hollister,
Louis Beaufait,	James H. Forsyth,
James Jackson, sub-agent,	J. D. Beaugrand.
John E. Hunt,	

Mar. 28, 1833.

7 Stat., 423.
Proclamation, Apr. 12, 1834.

TREATY WITH THE SEMINOLE, 1833.

Preamble.

WHEREAS, the Seminole Indians of Florida, entered into certain articles of agreement, with James Gadson, [Gadsden,] Commissioner on behalf of the United States, at Payne's landing, on the 9th day of May, 1832: the first article of which treaty or agreement provides, as follows: "The Seminoles Indians relinquish to the United States all claim to the land they at present occupy in the Territory of Florida, and agree to emigrate to the country assigned to the Creeks, west of the Mississippi river; it being understood that an additional extent of territory proportioned to their number will be added to the Creek country, and that the Seminoles will be received as a constituent part of the Creek nation, and be re-admitted to all the privileges as members of the same." And whereas, the said agreement also stipulates and provides, that a delegation of Seminoles should be sent at the expense of the United States to examine the country to be allotted them among the Creeks, and should this delegation be satisfied with the character of the country and of the favorable disposition of the Creeks to unite with them as one people, then the aforementioned treaty would be considered binding and obligatory upon the parties. And whereas

Treaty with the Creeks of Feb.14,1833.

a treaty was made between the United States and the Creek Indians west of the Mississippi, at Fort Gibson, on the 14th day of February 1833, by which a country was provided for the Seminoles in pursuance of the existing arrangements between the United States and that tribe. And whereas, the special delegation, appointed by the Seminoles on the 9th day of May 1832, have since examined the land designated for them by the undersigned Commissioners, on behalf of the United States, and have expressed themselves satisfied with the same, in and by their letter dated, March 1833, addressed to the undersigned Commissioners.

Now, therefore, the Commissioners aforesaid, by virtue of the power and authority vested in them by the treaty made with Creek Indians on the 14th day of February 1833, as above stated, hereby designate and assign to the Seminole tribe of Indians, for their separate future residence, forever, a tract of country lying between the Canadian river and the north fork thereof, and extending west to where a line running north and south between the main Canadian and north branch, will strike the forks of Little river, provided said west line does not extend more than twenty-five miles west from the mouth of said Little river. And the undersigned Seminole chiefs, delegated as aforesaid, on behalf of their nation hereby declare themselves well satisfied with the location provided for them by the Commissioners, and agree that their nation shall commence the removal to their new home, as soon as the Government will make arrangements for their emigration, satisfactory to the Seminole nation. *Commissioners designate land for the Seminole.*

And whereas, the said Seminoles have expressed high confidence in the friendship and ability of their present agent, Major Phagen, and desire that he may be permitted to remove them to their new homes west of the Mississippi; the Commissioners have considered their request, and cheerfully recommend Major Phagan as a suitable person to be employed to remove the Seminoles as aforesaid, and trust his appointment will be made, not only to gratify the wishes of the Indians but as conducive to the public welfare. *Major Phagan to superintend removal of Indians.*

In testimony whereof, the commissioners on behalf of the United States, and the delegates of the Seminole nation, have hereunto signed their names, this 28th day of March, A. D. 1833, at fort Gibson.

Montfort Stokes,
Henry L. Ellsworth,
John F. Schermerhorn.

Seminole Delegates:
   John Hick, representing Sam Jones, his x mark.
   Holata Emartta, his x mark.
   Jumper, his x mark.
   Coi Hadgo, his x mark.
   Charley Emartta, his x mark.
   Ya-ha-hadge, his x mark.
   Ne-ha-tho-clo, representing Fuch-a-lusti-hadgo, his x mark,
               On behalf of the Seminole nation.

TREATY WITH THE QUAPAW, 1833.

May 13, 1833.

7 Stat., 424.
Proclamation, Apr. 12, 1834.

Articles of agreement or a treaty between the United States and the Quapaw Indians entered into by John F. Schermerhorn, commissioner of Indian affairs west on the part of the United States and the chiefs and warriors of the Quapaw Indians.

WHEREAS, by the treaty between the United States and the Quapaw Indians, concluded November 15th, 1824, they ceded to the United States all their lands in the Territory of Arkansas, and according to which they were "*to be concentrated and confined to a district of country inhabited by the Caddo Indians and form a part of said tribe,*" and whereas they did remove according to the stipulations of said treaty, and settled on the Bayou Treache on the south side of Red River, on a tract of land given them by the Caddo Indians, but which was found *Preamble.*

subject to frequent inundations on account of the raft on Red River, and where their crops were destroyed by the water year after year, and which also proved to be a very sickly country and where in a short time, nearly one-fourth of their people died, and whereas they could obtain no other situation from the Caddoes and they refused to incorporate them and receive them as a constituent part of their tribe as contemplated by their treaty with the United States, and as they saw no alternative but to perish if they continued there, or to return to their old residence on the Arkansas, they therefore chose the latter; and whereas they now find themselves very unhappily situated in consequence of having their little improvements taken from them by the settlers of the country; and being anxious to secure a permanent and peaceable home the following articles or treaty are agreed upon between the United States and the Quapaw Indians by John F. Schermerhorn —— —— —— commissioners of Indian affairs west and the chiefs and warriors of said Quapaw Indians this (13th) thirteenth day of May 1833.——

Lands formerly given relinquished to United States.

ARTICLE I. The Quapaw Indians hereby relinquish and convey to the United States all their right and title to the lands given them by the Caddo Indians on the Bayou Treache of Red River.——

Other lands granted by United States.

ART. II. The United States hereby agree to convey to the Quapaw Indians one hundred and fifty sections of land west of the State line of Missouri and between the lands of the Senecas and Shawnees, not heretofore assigned to any other tribe of Indians, the same to be selected and assigned by the commissioners of Indian affairs west, and which is expressly designed to be [in] lieu of their location on Red River and to carry into effect the treaty of 1824, in order to provide a permanent home for their nation; the United States agree to convey the same by patent, to them and their descendants as long as they shall exist as a nation or continue to reside thereon, and they also agree to protect them in their new residence, against all interruption or disturbance from any other tribe or nation of Indians or from any other person or persons whatever.

Expenses of removal, etc.

ART. III. Whereas it is the policy of the United States in all their intercourse with the Indians to treat them liberally as well as justly, and to endeavour to promote their civilization and prosperity; it is further agreed that in consideration of the important and extensive cessions of lands made by the Quapaws to the United States and in view of their present impoverished and wretched condition, they shall be removed to their new homes at the expense of the United States and that they will supply them with one year's provision from the time of their removal, which shall be as soon as they receive notice of the ratification of this treaty by the President and Senate of the United States. The United States will also furnish and deliver to them, after their arrival at their new homes, one hundred cows, one hundred breeding hogs, one hundred sheep, ten yoke of working cattle, twenty-five ploughs, one hundred axes, one hundred hoes, four ox carts, and one wagon, with all their necessary rigging, twenty iron hand corn-mills, tools of different descriptions to the amount of two hundred dollars, also looms, wheels, reels and wool-cards to the amount of two hundred dollars, one hundred blankets, fifty rifles, and five shot guns all with flint locks, ten kegs of powder, and six hundred pounds of lead; The United States agree to provide a farmer to reside with them and to aid and instruct them in their agricultural pursuits and a blacksmith to do their necessary work, with a shop and tools and iron and steel not exceeding one ton per year. The United States also agree to appropriate one thousand dollars per year for education purposes to be expended under the direction of the President of the United States; the farmer and blacksmith and the above appropriation for education purposes to be continued only as long as the President of the United States deems necessary for the best interests of the Indians.

ART. IV. It is hereby mutually agreed upon between the parties respectively to this treaty, that in lieu of and in full consideration of their present annuities perpetual and limited, the United States will pay the debts of the Quapaw Indians according to the annexed schedule to the amount of four thousand one hundred and eighty dollars provided they can be discharged in full for that amount. They will also expend to the amount of one thousand dollars in hiring suitable labourers to build and aid them in erecting comfortable cabins and houses to live in; and also that they will pay them annually two thousand dollars for twenty years from the ratification of this treaty, and that out of said annuity there shall be allowed to their four principal chiefs, Hackatton, Sarassan, Tonnonjinka and Kaheketteda, and to their successors each, in addition to their distributive share of said annuity, the sum of fifty dollars per year. *[margin: Debts to be paid by United States. Other allowances.]*

ART. V. It is hereby agreed, and expressly understood, that this treaty is only supplementary to the treaty of 1824, and designed to carry into effect the views of the United States in providing a permanent and comfortable home for the Quapaw Indians; and also that all the stock and articles furnished the Indians by the United States as expressed in the fourth article shall be under the care and direction of the agent and farmer of said tribe, to see that the same is not squandered or sold, or any of the stock slain by the Indians, until such time as the natural increase of the stock will warrant the same to be done without destroying the whole, and thus defeating the benevolent views of the Government in making this provision for them. *[margin: Stock, etc., granted, to be under the care of the agent.]*

ART. VI. The United States also agrees to employ an interpreter to accompany them on their removal and the same to continue with them during the pleasure of the President of the United States—The above treaty shall be binding on the United States whenever ratified and approved by the President and Senate of the United States.— *[margin: Interpreter to accompany the Indians.]*

John F. Schermerhorn,
Hackatton chief, his x mark,
Sarrasin chief, his x mark,
Taunoujinka chief, his x mark,
Kaheketteda chief, his x mark,
Monehunka, his x mark,
Kunkadaquene, his x mark,
Wattekiane, his x mark,
Hadaskamonene, his x mark,
Hummonene, his x mark,
Hikaguedotton, his x mark,
Moussockane, his x mark.

The above treaty was signed in open council, in the presence of—

Richard M. Hannum, S. A.
Antoine Barraque,
James W. Walker,
Frederick Saugrain,
John D. Shaw,
Joseph Duchasin, interpreter.

The amount due from the Quapaw tribe of Indians to the following named persons—

Frederic Notrabe	$567 00
Joseph Dardene	300 00
Ignace Bogy	170 00
Alexander Dickerson	28 00
William Montgomery	350 00
Joseph Bonne	30 00
Joseph Duchasin	30 00
Baptiste Bonne	20 00
Antoine Barraque	2,235 00
George W. Boyer	50 00
Weylon King	400 00
	$4,180 00

TREATY WITH THE APPALACHICOLA BAND, 1833.

June 18, 1833.

7 Stat., 427.
Proclamation Apr,
12, 1834.

Relinquishment by
certain chiefs of land
reserved by the treaty
of Sept. 18, 1823.

THE undersigned Chiefs for and in behalf of themselves, and War-riors voluntarily relinquish all the privileges to which they are entitled as parties to a treaty concluded at Camp Moultrie on the 18th of September 1823, and surrender to the United States all their right, title and interest to a reservation of land made for their benefit in the additional article of the said Treaty and which is described in the said article as commencing " on the Appalachicola, at a point to include Yellow Hare's improvements, thence up said river four miles; thence, west, one mile; thence southerly to a point one mile west of the beginning; and thence, east, to the beginning point."

Other lands granted
by the United States,
etc.

ARTICLE II. For, and in consideration of said cession the U. States agree to grant, and to convey in three (3) years by patent to Mulatto King or Vacapasacy; and to Tustenuggy Hajo, head Chief of Ematlochees town, for the benefit of themselves, sub-Chiefs, and Warriors, a section and a half of land to each; or contiguous quarter and fractional sections containing a like quantity of acres; to be laid off hereafter under the direction of the President of the U. States so as to embrace the said Chiefs' fields and improvements, after the lands shall have been surveyed, and the boundaries to correspond with the public surveys; it being understood that the aforesaid Chiefs may with the consent and under the advisement of the Executive of the Territory of Florida, at any time previous to the expiration of the above three years, dispose of the said sections of land, and migrate to a country of their choice; but that should they remain on their lands, the U. States will so soon as Blunt's band and the Seminoles generally have migrated under the stipulations of the treaties concluded with them, withdraw the immediate protection hitherto extended to the aforesaid Chiefs and Warriors and that they thereafter become subject to the government and laws of the territory of Florida.

Annuity continued,
etc.

ARTICLE III. The U. States stipulate to continue to Mulato King and Tustenuggy Hadjo, their sub-Chiefs and Warriors their proportion of the annuity of (5000) five thousand dollars to which they are entitled under the treaty of Camp Moultrie, so long as the Seminoles remain in the Territory, and to advance their proportional amount of the said annuity for the balance of the term stipulated for its payment in the treaty aforesaid, whenever the Seminoles finally remove in compliance with the terms of the treaty concluded at Payne's Landing on 9th May 1832.

Provision in case of
future removal.

ARTICLE IV. If at any time hereafter the Chiefs and Warriors, parties to this agreement, should feel disposed to migrate from the Territory to Florida to the country allotted to the Creeks and Seminoles in Arkansas, should they elect to sell their grants of land as provided for in the first article of this treaty, they must defray from the proceeds of the sales of said land, or from their private resources all the expenses of their migration, subsistence, &c.—but if they prefer they may by surrendering to the U. States all the rights and privileges acquired under the provisions of this agreement, become parties to the obligations, provisions and stipulations of the treaty concluded at Payne's landing with the Seminoles on the 9th of May 1832, as a constituent part of said tribe, and re-unite with said tribe in their new abode on the Arkansas. The U. States, in that event, agreeing to pay (3,000) three thousand dollars for the reservation relinquished in the first article of this treaty, in addition to the rights and immunities the parties may acquire under the aforesaid treaty at Payne's landing.

In testimony whereof, the commissioner, James Gadsden, in behalf of the United States, and the undersigned chiefs and warriors, have hereunto subscribed their names, and affixed their seals.

Done at Pope's, Fayette county, in the territory of Florida, this eighteenth day of June, one thousand eight hundred and thirty-three, and of the independence of the United States, the fifty-eighth.

James Gadsden,	[L. S.]
Mulatto King, or Vacapachacy, his x mark,	[L. S.]
Tustenuggy Hajo, his x mark,	[L. S.]
Yellow Hare, his x mark,	[L. S.]
John Walker, his x mark,	[L. S.]
Yeo-lo-hajo, his x mark,	[L. S.]
Cath-a-hajo, his x mark,	[L. S.]
Lath-la-yahola, his x mark,	[L. S.]
Pa-hosta Tustenuckey, his x mark,	[L. S.]
Tuse-caia-hajo, his x mark,	[L. S.]

Witnesses:
  Wm. S. Pope, sub-agent,
  Robert Larance,
  Joe Miller, interpreter, his x mark,
  Jim Walker, interpreter, his x mark.

Relinquishment by certain chiefs, of land reserved by the treaty of 18th Sept. 1823.

June 18, 1833.

7 Stat., 428.

The undersigned Chiefs for and in behalf of themselves, and Warriors voluntarily reliquish all the privileges to which they are entitled as parties to a treaty concluded at Camp Moultrie on the 18th of September 1823, and surrender to the United States all their right, title and interest to a reservation of land made for their benefit in the additional article of the said treaty and which is described in said article as "commencing on the Chattahoochie, one mile below Econchatimico's house; thence up said river four miles; thence one mile west; thence southerly to a point, one mile west of the beginning; thence east to the beginning point."

ARTICLE II. For and in consideration of said cession the U. States agree to grant and to convey in three (3) years, by patent to Econchatimico for the benefit of himself, sub-Chiefs and Warriors three sections of land; (or contiguous quarter and fractional sections containing a like quantity of acres) to be laid off hereafter under the direction of the President of the U. States so as to embrace the said Chief's fields, improvements, &c., after the lands shall have been surveyed, and the boundaries to correspond with the public surveys; it being understood that the aforesaid Chief may with the consent and under the advisement of the Executive of the Territory of Florida, at any time previous to the expiration of the above three years dispose of the said sections of land, and migrate to a country of their choice; but that, should they remain on their lands, the U. States will, so soon as Blunt's band and the Seminoles generally have migrated under the stipulations of the treaty concluded with them, withdraw the immediate protection hitherto extended to the aforesaid Chief, his sub-Chiefs and Warriors, and that they thereafter become subject to the government and laws of the Territory of Florida.

Other lands granted by the United States, etc.

ARTICLE III. The United States stipulate to continue to Econchatimico, his sub-Chiefs and Warriors their proportion of the annuity of (5000) five thousand dollars to which they are entitled under the treaty of Camp Moultrie, so long as the Seminoles remain in the Territory, and to advance their proportional amount of said annuity for the balance of the term stipulated for its payment in the treaty aforesaid, whenever

Annuity continued.

the Seminoles finally remove in compliance with the terms of the treaty concluded at Payne's landing on 9th May 1832.—

Provision in case of future removal.

ARTICLE IV. If at any time hereafter, the Chiefs and Warriors, parties to this agreement, should feel disposed to migrate from the Territory of Florida to the country allotted to the Creeks and Seminoles in Arkansas; should they elect to sell their grants of land as provided for in the first article of this treaty, they must defray from the proceeds of the sales of said land, or from their private resources, all the expenses of their migration, subsistence, &c. But, if they prefer, they may, by surrendering to the U. States all the rights and privileges acquired under the provisions of this agreement, become parties to the obligations, provisions and stipulations of the treaty concluded at Payne's landing with the Seminoles on the 9th May 1832 as a constituent part of said tribe, and re-unite with said tribe in their new abode on the Arkansas, the United States, in that event agreeing to pay (3000) three thousand dollars for the reservation relinquished in the first article of this treaty; in addition to the rights and immunities the parties may acquire under the aforesaid treaty at Payne's landing.

In testimony whereof, the commissioner, James Gadsden, in behalf of the United States, and the undersigned chiefs and warriors, have hereunto subscribed their names and affixed their seals.

Done at Pope's Fayette county, in the territory of Florida, this eighteenth day of June, one thousand eight hundred and thirty-three, and of the independence of the United States, the fifty-eighth.

James Gadsden, [L. S.]
Econ-chati-mico, his x mark, [L. S.]
Billy Humpkin, his x mark, [L. S.]
Kaley Senehah, his x mark. [L. S.]
Elapy Tustenuckey, his x mark, [L. S.]
Vauxey Hajo, his x mark, [L. S.]
Fose-e-mathla, his x mark, [L. S.]
Lath-la-fi-cicio, his x mark, [L. S.]

Witnesses:

Wm. S. Pope, sub-agent,
Robert Larance,
Joe Miller, his x mark, interpreter.
Jim Walker, his x mark, interpreter.

TREATY WITH THE OTO AND MISSOURI, 1833.

Sept. 21, 1833.

7 Stat., 429.
Proclamation Apr. 12, 1834.

Articles of agreement and convention, made at the Otoe Village on the River Platte, between Henry L. Ellsworth, Commissioner, in behalf of the United States, and the united bands of Otoes, and Missourias dwelling on the said Platte this 21st day of September A. D. 1833.

Cession of land to United States.

ARTICLE I. The said Otoes, and Missourias, cede and relinquish to the United States, all their right and title, to the lands lying south of the following line viz.—Beginning, on the Little Nemohaw river, at the northwest corner of the land reserved by treaty at Prairie du Chien, on the 15th July 1830, in favor of certain half-breeds, of the Omahas, Ioways, Otoes, Yancton, and Santie bands of Sioux, and running westerly with said Little Nemohaw, to the head branches of the same; and thence running in a due west line as far west, as said Otoes and Missourias, have, or pretend to have any claim.

Annuity of $2,500 continued.

ARTICLE II. The United States agree, to continue the present annuity of twenty-five hundred dollars, granted by said treaty of Prairie du

Chien, to said Otoes and Missourias, ten years from the expiration of the same viz. ten years from 15th July 1840.

ARTICLE III. The United States agree to continue for ten years from said 15th July, 1840, the annuity of five hundred dollars, granted for instruments for agricultural purposes. *Annuity of $500 continued.*

ARTICLE IV. The United States agree, to allow annually five hundred dollars, for five years, for the purposes of education, which sum shall be expended under the direction of the President; and continued longer if he deems proper. The schools however, shall be kept within the limit of said tribe or nation. *$500 per annum for school purposes.*

ARTICLE V. The United States agree, to erect a horse-mill for grinding corn, and to provide two farmers to reside in the nation, to instruct and assist said tribe, for the term of five years, and longer if the President thinks proper. *Horse mill, etc.*

ARTICLE VI. The United States agree to deliver to said Otoes and Missourias, one thousand dollars value in stock, which shall be placed in the care of the agent, or farmer, until the President thinks the same can safely be intrusted to the Indians. *Stock to be delivered.*

ARTICLE VII. It is expressly agreed and understood, that the stipulations contained in the 3d 4th 5th and 6th articles are not to be fulfilled by the United States, until the Otoes and Missourias shall locate themselves in such convenient agricultural districts, as the President may think proper, nor shall the payments be continued, if the Otoes and Missourias shall abandon such location as the President shall think best for their agricultural interest. *Conditions of these stipulations.*

ARTICLE VIII. The Otoes and Missourias declare their entire willingness to abandon the chase for the agricultural life—their desire for peace with all other tribes, and therefore agree not to make war against any tribe with whom they now are, or shall be, at peace; but should any difficulty arise between them and any other tribe, they agree to refer the matter in dispute, to some arbiter, whom the President shall appoint to adjust the same. *Disputes to be referred to arbiter.*

ARTICLE IX. The United States agree to deliver the said Otoes and Missourias the value of four hundred dollars in goods and merchandise; which said Otoes and Missourias hereby acknowledge to have received. *Goods.*

ARTICLE X. This convention, or agreement, to be obligatory, when ratified by the President and Senate of the United States. *Treaty binding when ratified.*

In testimony whereof, the commissioners aforesaid, and the undersigned chiefs and warriors have hereunto subscribed their names, and affixed their seals, at the Otoe village on the said Platte river, the date first above written.

Henry L. Ellsworth,	[L. S.]	Pa-che-ga-he, his x mark,	[L. S.]
Jaton, his x mark,	[L. S.]	Wah-tcha-shing-a, his x mark,	[L. S.]
Big Kaw, his x mark,	[L. S.]	Mon-to-ni-a, his x mark,	[L. S.]
The Thief, his x mark,	[L. S.]	Gra-da-nia, his x mark,	[L. S.]
Wah-ro-ne-saw, his x mark,	[L. S.]	Mock-shiga-tona, his x mark,	[L. S.]
Rah-no-way-wah-ha-rah, his x mark,	[L. S.]	Wah-nah-sha, his x mark,	[L. S.]
Gra-tah-ni-kah, his x mark,	[L. S.]	Wash-kah-money, his x mark,	[L. S.]
Mah-skah-gah-ha, his x mark,	[L. S.]	Cha-ah-gra, his x mark,	[L. S.]
Nan-cha-si-zay, his x mark,	[L. S.]	To-he, his x mark,	[L. S.]
A-Sha-bah-hoo, his x mark,	[L. S.]	O-rah-kah-pe, his x mark,	[L. S.]
Kah-he-ga, his x mark,	[L. S.]	Wah-a-ge-hi-ru-ga-rah, his x mark,	[L. S.]
Wah-ne-min-nah, his x mark,	[L. S.]	O-ha-ah-che-gi-sug-a, his x mark,	[L. S.]
Cha-wa-che-ra, his x mark,	[L. S.]	Ish-kah-tap-a, his x mark,	[L. S.]
		Meh-say-way, his x mark,	[L. S.]

In presence of—

Edward A. Ellsworth, secretary pro tempore,
Jno. Dougherty, Indian agent,
Ward S. May, M. D.,
John Dunlop,

John T. Irving, jr.,
J. D. Blanchard,
Charlo Mobrien, his x mark,
Oloe, Interpreter.

TREATY WITH THE CHIPPEWA, ETC., 1833.

Sept. 26, 1833.
_____
7 Stat., 431.
Proclamation, Feb. 21, 1835.

See supplementary articles, post, 410.

Articles of a treaty made at Chicago, in the State of Illinois, on the twenty-sixth day of September, in the year of our Lord one thousand eight hundred and thirty-three, between George B. Porter, Thomas J. V. Owen and William Weatherford, Commissioners on the part of the United States of the one part, and the United Nation of Chippewa, Ottowa and Potawatamie Indians of the other part, being fully represented by the Chiefs and Head-men whose names are hereunto subscribed—which Treaty is in the following words, to wit:

Lands ceded to United States.

ARTICLE 1st.—The said United Nation of Chippewa, Ottowa, and Potawatamie Indians, cede to the United States all their land, along the western shore of Lake Michigan, and between this Lake and the land ceded to the United States by the Winnebago nation, at the treaty of Fort Armstrong made on the 15th September 1832—bounded on the north by the country lately ceded by the Menominees, and on the south by the country ceded at the treaty of Prairie du Chien made on the 29th July 1829—supposed to contain about five millions of acres.

Lands west of the Mississippi assigned to the Indians.

ARTICLE 2d—In part consideration of the above cession it is hereby agreed, that the United States shall grant to the said United Nation of Indians to be held as other Indian lands are held which have lately been assigned to emigrating Indians, a tract of country west of the Mississippi river, to be assigned to them by the President of the United States—to be not less in quantity than five millions of acres, and to be located as follows: beginning at the mouth of Boyer's river on the east side of the Missouri river, thence down the said river to the mouth of Naudoway river, thence due east to the west line of the State of Missouri, thence along the said State line to the northwest corner of the State, thence east along the said State line to the point where it is intersected by the western boundary line of the Sacs and Foxes—thence north along the said line of the Sacs and Foxes, so far as that when a straight line shall be run therefrom to the mouth of Boyer's river (the place of beginning) it shall include five millions of acres. And as it is the wish of the Government of the United States that the said nation of Indians should remove to the country thus assigned to them as soon as conveniently can be done; and it is deemed advisable on the part of their Chiefs and Headmen that a deputation should visit the said country west of the Mississippi and thus be assured that full justice has been done, it is hereby stipulated that the United States will defray the expenses of such deputation, to consist of not more than fifty persons, to be accompanied by not more than five individuals to be nominated by themselves, and the whole to be under the general direction of such officer of the United States Government as has been or shall be designated for the purpose.—And it is further agreed that as fast as the said Indians shall be prepared to emigrate, they shall be removed at the expense of the United States, and shall receive subsistence while upon the journey, and for one year after their arrival at their new homes.—It being understood, that the said Indians are to remove from all that part of the land now ceded, which is within the State of Illinois, immediately on the ratification of this treaty, but to be permitted to retain possession of the country north of the boundary line of the said State, for the term of three years, without molestation or interruption and under the protection of the laws of the United States.

Moneys to be paid by United States.

ARTICLE 3d—And in further consideration of the above cession, it is agreed, that there shall be paid by the United States the sums of money hereinafter mentioned: to wit.

One hundred thousand dollars to satisfy sundry individuals, in behalf of whom reservations were asked, which the Commissioners refused to grant: and also to indemnify the Chippewa tribe who are parties to this treaty for certain lands along the shore of Lake Michigan, to which they make claim, which have been ceded to the United States by the Menominee Indians—the manner in which the same is to be paid is set forth in Schedule "A" hereunto annexed.

One hundred and fifty thousand dollars to satisfy the claims made against the said United Nation which they have here admitted to be justly due, and directed to be paid, according to Schedule "B" hereunto annexed.

One hundred thousand dollars to be paid in goods and provisions, a part to be delivered on the signing of this treaty and the residue during the ensuing year.

Two hundred and eighty thousand dollars to be paid in annuities of fourteen thousand dollars a year, for twenty years.

One hundred and fifty thousand dollars to be applied to the erection of mills, farm houses, Indian houses and blacksmith shops, to agricultural improvements, to the purchase of agricultural implements and stock, and for the support of such physicians, millers, farmers, blacksmiths and other mechanics, as the President of the United States shall think proper to appoint.

Seventy thousand dollars for purposes of education and the encouragement of the domestic arts, to be applied in such manner, as the President of the United States may direct.—[The wish of the Indians being expressed to the Commissioners as follows: The united nation of Chippewa, Ottowa and Potawatamie Indians being desirous to create a perpetual fund for the purposes of education and the encouragement of the domestic arts, wish to invest the sum of seventy thousand dollars in some safe stock, the interest of which only is to be applied as may be necessary for the above purposes. They therefore request the President of the United States, to make such investment for the nation as he may think best. If however, at any time hereafter, the said nation shall have made such advancement in civilization and have become so enlightened as in the opinion of the President and Senate of the United States they shall be capable of managing so large a fund with safety they may withdraw the whole or any part of it.] *Fund for the purposes of education, etc.*

Four hundred dollars a year to be paid to Billy Caldwell, and three hundred dollars a year, to be paid to Alexander Robinson, for life, in addition to the annuities already granted them—Two hundred dollars a year to be paid to Joseph Lafromboise and two hundred dollars a year to be paid to Shabehnay, for life. *Annuities.*

Two thousand dollars to be paid to Wau-pon-eh-see and his band, and fifteen hundred dollars to Awn-kote and his band, as the consideration for nine sections of land, granted to them by the 3d Article of the Treaty of Prairie du Chien of the 29th of July 1829 which are hereby assigned and surrendered to the United States. *Payments for sections of land.*

Article 4th.—A just proportion of the annuity money, secured as well by former treaties as the present, shall be paid west of the Mississippi to such portion of the nation as shall have removed thither during the ensuing three years.—After which time, the whole amount of the annuities shall be paid at their location west of the Mississippi. *Where annuities shall be paid.*

Article 5th.—[Stricken out.]

This treaty after the same shall have been ratified by the President and Senate of the United States, shall be binding on the contracting parties. *Treaty binding when ratified.*

In testimony whereof, the said George B. Porter, Thomas J. V. Owen, and William Weatherford, and the undersigned chiefs and head men of the said nation of Indians, have hereunto set their hands at Chicago, the said day and year.

G. B. Porter,	Sau-ko-noek,
Th. J. V. Owen,	Che-che-bin-quay, his x mark,
William Weatherford,	Joseph, his x mark,
To-pen-e-bee, his x mark,	Wah-mix-i-co, his x mark,

Ob-wa-qua-unk, his x mark,
N-saw-way-quet, his x mark,
Puk-quech-a-min-nee, his x mark,
Nah-che-wine, his x mark,
Ke-wase, his x mark,
Wah-bou-seh, his x mark,
Mang-e-sett, his x mark,
Caw-we-saut, his x mark,
Ah-be-te-ke-zhic, his x mark,
Pat-e-go-shuc, his x mark,
E-to-wow-cote, his x mark,
Shim-e-nah, his x mark,
O-chee-pwaise, his x mark,
Ce-nah-ge-win, his x mark,
Shaw-waw-nas-see, his x mark,
Shab-eh-nay, his x mark,
Mac-a-ta-o-shic, his x mark,
Squah-ke-zic, his x mark,
Mah-che-o-tah-way, his x mark,
Cha-ke-te-ah, his x mark,
Me-am-ese, his x mark,
Shay-tee, his x mark,
Kee-new, his x mark,
Ne-bay-noc-scum, his x mark,
Naw-bay-caw, his x mark,
O'Kee-mase, his x mark,
Saw-o-tup, his x mark,
Me-tai-way, his x mark,
Na-ma-ta-way-shuc, his x mark,
Shaw-waw-nuk-wuk, his x mark,
Nah-che-wah, his x mark,
Sho-bon-nier, his x mark,
Me-nuk-quet, his x mark,
Chis-in-ke-bah, his x mark,
Mix-e-maung, his x mark,
Nah-bwait, his x mark,

Sen-e-bau-um, his x mark,
Puk-won, his x mark,
Wa-be-no-say, his x mark,
Mon-tou-ish, his x mark,
No-nee, his x mark,
Mas-quat, his x mark,
Sho-min, his x mark,
Ah-take, his x mark,
He-me-nah-wah, his x mark,
Che-pec-co-quah, his x mark,
Mis-quab-o-no-quah, his x mark,
Wah-be-Kai, his x mark,
Ma-ca-ta-ke-shic, his x mark,
Sho-min, (2d.) his x mark,
She-mah-gah, his x mark,
O'ke-mah-wah-ba-see, his x mark,
Na-mash, his x mark,
Shab-y-a-tuk, his x mark,
Ah-cah-o-mah, his x mark,
Quah-quah, tah, his x mark,
Ah-sag-a-mish-cum, his x mark,
Pa-mob-a-mee, his x mark,
Nay-o-say, his x mark,
Ce-tah-quah, his x mark,
Ce-ku-tay, his x mark,
Sauk-ee, his x mark,
Ah-quee-wee, his x mark,
Ta-cau-ko, his x mark,
Me-shim-e-nah, his x mark,
Wah-sus-kuk, his x mark,
Pe-nay-o-cat, his x mark,
Pay-maw-suc, his x mark,
Pe-she-ka, his x mark,
Shaw-we-mon-e-tay, his x mark,
Ah-be-nab, his x mark,
Sau-sau-quas-see, his x mark.

In presence of—

Wm. Lee D. Ewing, secretary to commission,
E. A. Brush,
Luther Rice, interpreter,
James Conner, interpreter,
John T. Schermerhorn, commissioner, etc. west,
A. C. Pepper, S. A. R. P.
Gho. Kercheval, sub-agent,
Geo. Bender, major, Fifth Regiment Infantry,
D. Wilcox, captain, Fifth Regiment,
J. M. Baxley, captain, Fifth Infantry,
R. A. Forsyth, U. S. Army,
L. T. Jamison, lieutenant, U. S. Army,
E. K. Smith, lieutenant, Fifth Infantry,
P. Maxwell, assistant surgeon,
J. Allen, lieutenant, Fifth Infantry,
I. P. Simonton, lieutenant, U. S. Army,
George F. Turner, assistant surgeon, U. S. Army,
Richd. J. Hamilton,
Robert Stuart,
Jona. McCarty,

Daniel Jackson, of New York,
Jno. H. Kinzie,
Robt. A. Kinzie,
G. S. Hubbard,
J. C. Schwarz, adjutant general M. M.
Jn. B. Beaubrier,
James Kinzie,
Jacob Beeson,
Saml. Humes Porter,
Andw. Porter,
Gabriel Godfroy,
A. H. Arndt,
Laurie Marsh,
Joseph Chaunier,
John Watkins,
B. B. Kercheval,
Jas. W. Berry,
Wm. French,
Thomas Forsyth,
Pierre Menard, Fils,
Edmd. Roberts,
Geo. Hunt,
Isaac Nash.

———

SCHEDULE "A."

(Referred to in the Treaty, containing the sums payable to Individuals in lieu of Reservations.)

	Dollars.
Jesse Walker	1500
Henry Cleveland	800
Rachel Hall	600
Sylvia Hall	600
Joseph Laframboise and children	1000

	Dollars.
Victoire Porthier and her children	700
Jean Bt. Miranda	300
Jane Miranda — For each of whom John H. Kinzie is Trustee	200
Rosetta Miranda	300
Thomas Miranda	400
Alexander Muller, Gholson Kercheval, trustee	800
Paschal Muller, do. do.	800
Margaret Muller	200
Socra Muller	200
Angelique Chevalier	200
Josette Chevallier	200
Joseph Chevalier	400
Fanny Leclare (Captain David Hunter, Trustee)	400
Daniel Bourassa's children	600
Nancy Contraman	
Sally Contraman — For each of whom J. B Campbell is Trustee	600
Betsey Contraman	
Alexis Laframboise	800
Alexis Laframbois' children	1200
Mrs. Mann's children	600
Mrs. Mann (daughter of Antoine Ouilmet)	400
Geo. Turkey's children (Fourtier) Th. J. V. Owen Trustee	500
Jacques Chapeau's children do. do	600
Antonie Roscum's children	750
Francois Burbonnais' Senrs. children	400
Francis Burbonnais' Jnr. children	300
John Bt. Cloutier's children, (Robert A. Kinsie Trustee)	600
Claude Lafromboise's children	300
Antoine Ouilmet's children	200
Josette Ouilmot (John H. Kinzie, Trustee)	200
Mrs. Welsh (daughter of Antoine Ouilmet)	200
Alexander Robinson's children	400
Billy Caldwell's children	600
Mo-ah-way	200
Medare B. Beaubien	300
Charles H. Beaubien	300
John K. Clark's Indian children, (Richard J. Hamilton, Trustee)	400
Josette Juno and her children	1000
Angelique Juno	300
Josette Beaubien's children	1000
Mah-go-que's child (James Kinzie, Trustee)	300
Esther, Rosene and Eleanor Bailly	500
Sophia, Hortense and Therese Bailly	1000
Rosa and Mary children of Hoo-mo-ni-gah wife of Stephen Mack	600
Jean Bt. Rabbu's children	400
Francis Chevallier's children	800
Mrs. Nancy Jamison and child	800
Co-pah, son of Archange	250
Martha Burnett (R. A. Forsyth, Trustee)	1000
Isadore Chabert's child (G. S. Hubbard Trustee)	400
Chee-bee-quai or Mrs. Allen	500
Luther Rice and children	2500
John Jones	1000
Pierre Corbonno's Children	800
Pierre Chalipeaux's children	1000
Phœbe Treat and children	1000
Robert Forsyth of St. Louis Mo	500
Alexander Robinson	5000
Billy Caldwell	5000
Joseph Laframboise	3000
Nis noan see (B. B. Kercheval Trustee)	200
Margaret Hall	1000
James, William, David and Sarah children of Margaret Hall	3200
Margaret Ellen Miller, Montgomery Miller and Finly Miller, grandchildren of Margaret Hall. — for each of whom Richard J. Hamilton of Chicago is Trustee	800
Jean Letendre's children	200
Bernard Grignon	100
Josette Polier	100
Joseph Vieux, Jacques Vieux, Louis Vieux, and Josette Vieux each $100.	400
Angelique Hardwick's children	1800
Joseph Bourassa and Mark Bourassa	200
Jude Bourassa and Therese Bourassa	200

	Dollars.
Stephen Bourassa and Gabriel Bourassa	200
Alexander Bourassa and James Bourassa	200
Elai Bourassa and Jerome Bourassa	200
M. D. Bourassa	100
Ann Rice and her Son William M. Rice and Nephew John Leib	1000
Agate Biddle and her children	900
Magdaline Laframboise and her son	400
Therese Schandler	200
Joseph Dailly's son and daughter Robert and Therese	500
Therese Lawe and George Lawe	200
David Lawe and Rachel Lawe	200
Rebecca Lawe and Maria Lawe	200
Polly Lawe and Jane Lawe	200
Appotone Lawe	100
Angelique Vieux and Amable Vieux	200
Andre Vieux and Nicholas Vieux	200
Pierre Vieux and Maria Vieux	200
Madaline Thibeault	100
Paul Vieux and Joseph Vieux	200
Susanne Vieux	100
Louis Grignon and his son Paul	200
Paul Grignon Sen'r. and Amable Grignon	200
Perish and Robert Grignon	200
Catist Grignon and Elizabeth Grignon	200
Ursal Grignon and Charlotte Grignon	200
Louise Grignon and Rachel Grignon	200
Agate Porlier and George Grignon	200
Amable Grignon and Emily Grignon	200
Therese Grignon and Simon Grignon	200
William Burnett (B. B. Kercheval Trustee)	1000
Shan-na-nees	400
Josette Beaubien	500
For the Chippewa, Ottawa, and Potawatamie Students at the Choctaw Academy. The Hon. R. M. Johnson to be the Trustee.	5000
James and Richard J. Connor	700
Pierre Duverney and Children	300
Joshua Boyd's Children (Geo. Boyd Esq to be the Trustee.)	500
Joseph Bailly	4000
R. A. Forsyth	3000
Gabriel Godfroy	2420
Thomas R. Covill	1300
George Hunt	750
James Kinzie	5000
Joseph Chaunier	550
John and Mark Noble	180
Alexis Provansalle	100
One hundred thousand dollars	$100,000

SCHEDULE "B."

(Referred to in the treaty containing the sums payable to individuals, on claims admitted to be justly due, and directed to be paid.)
[See Second Amendment, at end of this treaty.]

	Dollars.
Brewster Hogan & Co	343
John S. C. Hogan	50
Frederick H. Contraman	200
Brookfield & Bertrand	100
R. E. Heacock	100
George W. McClure, U. S. A	125
David McKee	180
Oliver Emmell	300
George Hollenbeck	100
Martha Gray	78
Charles Taylor	187
Joseph Naper	71
John Mann	200
James Walker	200
John Blackstone	100

	Dollars.
Harris & McCord	175
George W. Dole	133
George Haverhill	60
William Whistler, U. S. A	1000
Squire Thompson	100
C. C. Trowbridge	2000
Louis Druillard	350
Abraham Francis	25
D. R. Bearss & Co	250
Dr. E. Winslow	150
Nicholas Klinger	77
Joseph Porthier	200
Clark Hollenbeck	50
Henry Enslen	75
Robert A. Kinzie	1216
Joseph Ogie	200
Thomas Hartzell	400
Calvin Britain	46
Benjamin Fry	400
Pierre F. Navarre	100
C. H. Chapman	30
James Kinzie	300
G. S. Hubbard	125
Jacque Jenveaux	150
John B. Du Charme	55
John Wright	15
James Galloway	200
William Marquis	150
Louis Chevalier, Adm'r of J. B. Chevalier dec'd	112
Solomon McCullough	100
Joseph Curtis	50
Edward E. Hunter	90
Rachel Legg	25
Peter Lamseet	100
Robert Beresford	200
G. W. & W. Laird	150
M. B. Beaubien	440
Jeduthan Smith	60
Edmund Weed	100
Philip Maxwell, U. S. A	35
Henry Gratiot	116
Tyler K. Blodgett	50
Nehemiah King	125
S. P. Brady	188
James Harrington	68
Samuel Ellice	50
Peter Menard, Maumee	500
John W. Anderson	350
David Bailey	50
Wm. G. Knaggs	100
John Hively	150
John B. Bertrand, Sen'r	50
Robert A. Forsyth	3000
Maria Kercheval	3000
Alice Hunt	3000
Jane C. Forsyth	3000
John H. Kinzie	5000
Ellen M. Wolcott	5000
Maria Hunter	5000
Robert A. Kinzie	5000
Samuel Godfroy	120
John E. Schwarz	4800
Joseph Loranger	5000
H. B. and G. W. Hoffman	358
Phelps & Wendell	660
Henry Johns	270
Benjamin C. Hoyt	20
John H. Kinzie, in trust for the heirs of Jos. Miranda, dec'd	250
Francis Burbonnais, Senr	500
Francis Burbonnais, junr	200
R. A. Forsyth, in trust for Catherine McKenzie	1000
James Laird	50
Montgomery Evans	250
Joseph Bertrand, jr	300

	Dollars.
George Hunt	900
Benjamin Sherman	150
W. and F. Brewster, Assignees of Joseph Bertrand, Senr	700
John Forsyth, in trust for the heirs of Charles Peltier, dec'd	900
William Hazard	30
James Shirley	125
Jacob Platter	25
John B. Bourie	2500
B. B. Kercheval	1500
Charles Lucier	75
Mark Beaubien	500
Catharine Stewart	82
Francis Mouton	200
Dr. William Brown	40
R. A. Forsyth, in trust for he rs of Charles Guion	200
Joseph Bertrand, Senr	652
Moses Rice	800
James Connor	2250
John B. Du Charme	250
Coquillard & Comparet	5000
Richard J. Hamilton	500
Adolphus Chapin	80
John Dixon	140
Wm. Huff	81
Stephen Mack, in trust for the heirs of Stephen Mack, dec'd	500
Thomas Forsyth	1500
Felix Fontaine	200
Jacque Mette	200
Francis Boucher	250
Margaret Helm	2000
O. P. Lacy	1000
Henry and Richard J. Connor	1500
James W. Craig	50
R. A. Forsyth (Maumee)	1300
Antoine Peltier do.	200
R. A. Forsyth, in trust for Wau-se-on-o-quet	300
John E. Hunt	1450
Payne C. Parker	70
Isaac Hull	1000
Foreman Evans	32
Horatio N. Curtis	300
Ica Rice	250
Thomas P. Quick	35
George B. Woodcox	60
John Woodcox	40
George B. Knaggs	1400
Ebenezer Read	100
George Pomeroy	150
Thomas K. Green	70
William Mieure, in trust for Willis Fellows	500
Z. Cicott	1800
John Johnson	100
Antoine Antilla	100
John Baldwin	500
Isaac G. Bailey	100
James Cowen	35
Joseph D. Lane	50
T. E. Phelps	250
Edmund Roberts	50
Augustus Bona	60
E. C. Winter & Co	1850
Charles W. Ewing	200
Antoine Ouilmett	800
John Bt. Chandonai, ($1000 of this sum to be paid to Robert Stuart, agent of American Fur Company, by the particular request of Jno. B. Chandonai,)	2500
Lowrin Marsh	3290
P. & J. J. Godfroy	2000
David Hull	500
Andrew Drouillard	500
Jacob Beeson & Co	220
Jacob Beeson	900
John Anderson	600
John Green	100
James B. Campbell	600

	Dollars.
Pierre Menard, Jun. in right of G. W. Campbell	250
George E. Walker	1000
Joseph Thebault	50
Gideon Lowe, U. S. A	160
Pierre Menard, Jun	2000
John Tharp	45
Pierre Menard, Junr. in trust for Marie Tremblê	500
Henry B. Stillman	300
John Hamblin	500
Francois Pagê	100
George Brooks	20
Franklin McMillan	100
Lorance Shellhouse	30
Martin G. Shellhouse	35
Peter Bellair	150
Joseph Morass	200
John I. Wendell	2000
A. T. Hatch	300
Stephen Downing	100
Samuel Miller	100
Moses Hardwick	75
Margaret May	400
Frances Felix	1100
John B. Bourie	500
Harriet Ewing	500
Nancy Hedges	500
David Bourie	500
Caroline Ferry	500
Bowrie & Minie	500
Charles Minie	600
Francis Minie	700
David Bourie	150
Henry Ossum Reed	200
Françoise Bezion	2500
Dominique Rousseau	500
Hanna & Taylor	1570
John P. Hedges	1000
Francoise Chobare	1000
Isadore Chobare	600
Jacob Leephart	700
Amos Amsden	400
Nicholas Boilvin	350
Archibald Clyburn	200
William Conner (Michigan)	70
Tunis S. Wendall	500
Noel Vasseur	800
James Abbott, agent of the American Fur Company	2300
Robert Stewart, agent of the American Fur Company	17000
Solomon Jeauneau	2100
John Bt. Beaubien	250
Stephen Mack, Jnr	350
John Lawe	3000
Alexis Larose	1000
Daniel Whitney	1350
P. & A. Grignon	650
Louis Grignon	2000
Jacques Vieux	2000
Laframboise & Bourassa	1300
Heirs of N. Boilvin, deceased	1000
John K. Clark	400
William G. & G. W. Ewing	5000
Rufus Hitchcock	400
Reed and Coons	200
B. H. Laughton	1000
Rufus Downing	500
Charles Reed	200

One hundred and seventy-five thousand dollars $175,000

The above claims have been admitted and directed to be paid, only in case they be accepted in full of all claims and demands up to the present date.

G. B. Porter,
Th. J. V. Owen,
William Weatherford.

Goods purchased and delivered. Agreeably to the stipulations contained in the 3d Article of the Treaty, there have been purchased and delivered at the request of the Indians, goods, provisions and horses to the amount of sixty-five thousand dollars (leaving the balance to be supplied in the year one thousand eight hundred and thirty-four, thirty-five thousand dollars.)

As evidence of the purchase and delivery as aforesaid under the direction of the said Commissioners, and that the whole of the same have been received by the said Indians, the said George B. Porter, Thomas J. V. Owen and William Weatherford, and the undersigned Chiefs and Head-men on behalf of the said United Nation of Indians have hereunto set their hands the twenty-seventh day of September in the year of our Lord one thousand eight hundred and thirty-three.

G. B. Porter,	Tshee-Tshee-chin-be-quay, his x mark,
Th. J. V. Owen,	Joseph, his x mark,
William Weatherford,	Shab-e-nai, his x mark,
Jo-pen-e-bee, his x mark,	Ah-be-te-ke-zhic, his x mark,
We-saw, his x mark,	E-to-won-cote, his x mark,
Ne-kaw-nosh-kee, his x mark,	Shab-y-a-tuk, his x mark,
Wai-saw-o-ke-ne-aw, his x mark,	Me-am-ese, his x mark,
Ne-see-waw-bee-tuck, his x mark,	Wah-be-me-mee, his mark,
Kai-kaw-tai-mon, his x mark,	Shim-e-nah, his x mark,
Saw-ko-nosh,	We-in-co, his x mark.

In presence of—

Wm. Lee D. Ewing, secretary to the commission,	Andw. Porter,
	Joseph Bertrand, junr.
R. A. Forsyth, U. S. Army,	Jno. H. Kinzie,
Madn. F. Abbott,	James Conner, interpreter,
Saml. Humes Porter,	J. E. Schwarz, adjutant-general, M. M.

Articles supplementary, to the treaty made at Chicago, in the State of Illinois, on the 26th day of September, one thousand eight hundred and thirty-three, between George B. Porter, Thomas J. V. Owen and William Weatherford, Commissioners on the part of the United States, of the one part, and the United Nation of Chippewa, Ottowa, and Potawatamie Indians, of the other part, concluded at the same place on the twenty-seventh day of September, one thousand eight hundred and thirty-three, between the said Commissioners on the part of the United States of the one part, and the Chiefs and Head-men of the said United Nation of Indians, residing upon the reservations of land situated in the Territory of Michigan, south of Grand river, of the other part.

Cession of land to United States. ARTICLE 1st—The said chiefs and head-men cede to the United States, all their land situate in the Territory of Michigan south of Grand river being the reservation at Notawasepe of 4 miles square contained in the 3d clause of the 2d article of the treaty made at Chicago, on the 29th day of August 1821, and the ninety-nine sections of land contained in the treaty made at St. Joseph on the 19th day of Sept. 1827;—and also the tract of land on St. Joseph river opposite the town of Niles, and extending to the line of the State of Indiana, on which the villages of To-pe-ne-bee and Pokagon are situated, supposed to contain about 49 sections.

Chiefs and headmen parties to treaty. ARTICLE 2d—In consideration of the above cession, it is hereby agreed that the said chiefs and head-men and their immediate tribes shall be considered as parties to the said treaty to which this is supplementary, and be entitled to participate in all the provisions therein contained, as a part of the United Nation; and further, that there shall be paid by the United States, the sum of one hundred thousand dollars: to be applied as follows.

Ten thousand dollars in addition to the general fund of one hundred thousand dollars, contained in the said treaty to satisfy sundry individuals in behalf of whom reservations were asked which the Commissioners refused to grant;—the manner in which the same is to be paid being set forth in the schedule "A," hereunto annexed. *Moneys to be paid for lands relinquished.*

Twenty-five thousand dollars in addition to the sum of one hundred and fifty thousand dollars contained in the said Treaty, to satisfy the claims made against all composing the United Nation of Indians, which they have admitted to be justly due, and directed to be paid according to Schedule "B," to the Treaty annexed.

Twenty-five thousand dollars, to be paid in goods, provisions and horses, in addition to the one hundred thousand dollars contained in the Treaty. *Goods, provisions, etc.*

And forty thousand dollars to be paid in annuities of two thousand dollars a year for twenty years, in addition to the two hundred and eighty thousand dollars inserted in the Treaty, and divided into payments of fourteen thousand dollars a year. *Annuities.*

Article 3d—All the Indians residing on the said reservations in Michigan shall remove therefrom within three years from this date, during which time they shall not be disturbed in their possession, nor in hunting upon the lands as heretofore. In the mean time no interruption shall be offered to the survey and sale of the same by the United States. In case, however, the said Indians shall sooner remove the Government may take immediate possession thereof. *Indians to remove in three years.*

Article 4th—[Stricken out. See 4th Amendment at end of treaty.] *Obligatory when ratified.*

These supplementary articles after the same shall have been ratified by the President and Senate of the United States shall be binding on the contracting parties.

In testimony whereof, the said George B. Porter, Thomas J. V. Owen, and William Weatherford, and the undersigned chiefs and head men of the said United Nation of Indians, have hereunto set their hands at Chicago, the said day and year.

G. B. Porter,	Maatch-kee, his x mark,
Th. J. V. Owen,	Kaw-bai-me-sai, his x mark,
William Weatherford,	Wees-ke-qua-tap, his x mark,
To-pen-e-bee, his x mark,	Ship-she-wuh-no, his x mark,
We-saw, his x mark,	Wah-co-mah-o-pe-tuk, his x mark,
Ne-kaw-nosh-kee, his x mark,	Ne-so-wah-quet, his x mark,
Wai-saw-o-ko-ne-aw, his x mark,	Shay-o-no, his x mark,
Po-ka-gon, his x mark,	Ash-o-nees, his x mark,
Kai-kaw-tai-mon, his x mark,	Mix-i-nee, his x mark,
Pe-pe-ah, his x mark,	Ne-wah-ox-sec, his x mark,
Ne-see-waw-bee-tuck, his x mark,	Sauk-e-mau, his x mark,
Kitchee-bau, his x mark,	Shaw-waw-nuk-wuk, his x mark,
Pee-chee-ko, his x mark,	Mo-rah, his x mark,
Nai-gaw-geucke, his x mark,	Suk-see, his x mark,
Wag-maw-kan-so, his x mark,	Quesh-a-wase, his x mark,
Mai-go-sai, his x mark,	Pat-e-go-to, his x mark,
Nai-chee-wai, his x mark,	Mash-ke-oh-see, his x mark,
Aks-puck-sick, his x mark,	Mo-nase, his x mark,
Kaw-kai-mai, his x mark,	Wab-e-kaie, his x mark,
Mans-kai-sick, his x mark,	Shay-oh-new, his x mark,
Pam-ko-wuck, his x mark,	Mo-gua-go, his x mark,
No-taw-gai, his x mark,	Pe-qua-shuc, his x mark,
Kauk-muck-kisin, his x mark,	A-muwa-noc-sey, his x mark.
Wee-see-mon, his x mark,	Kau-ke-che-ke-to, his x mark,
Mo-so-ben-net, his x mark,	Shaw-waw-nuk-wuk, his x mark,
Kee-o-kum, his x mark,	

In presence of

Wm. Lee D. Ewing, secretary to the commission,	J. L. Thompson, lieutenant Fifth Infantry,
E. A. Brush,	J. Allen, lieutenant Fifth Infantry.
Luther Rice, interpreter,	P. Maxwell, assistant surgeon U. S. Army,
James Conner, interpreter,	Geo. F. Turner, assistant surgeon U. S. Army,
Joseph Bertrand, jr., interpreter,	
Geo. Kercheval, sub Indian agent,	

B. B. Kercheval,
Thomas Forsyth,
Daniel Jackson, of New York,
J. E. Schwarz, adjutant-general M. M.
Robt. A. Kinzie,
G. S. Hubbard,
Geo. Bender, major Fifth Regiment Infantry,
D. Wilcox, captain Fifth Regiment,
J. M. Baxley, captain Fifth Infantry,
R. A. Forsyth, U. S. Army,
L. T. Jamison, lieutenant U. S. Army,
O. K. Smith, lieutenant Fifth Infantry,

L. M. Taylor,
Pierre Menard, fils,
Jacob Beeson.
Samuel Humes Porter,
Edmd. Roberts,
Jno. H. Kinzie,
Jas. W. Berry,
Gabriel Godfroy, jr.
Geo. Hunt,
A. H. Arndt,
Andw. Porter,
Isaac Nash,
Richard J. Hamilton.

SCHEDULE "A,"

Referred to in the Article supplementary to the Treaty, containing the sums payable to Individuals, in lieu of Reservations of Land.

	Dollars.
Po-ka-gon	2000
Rebecca Burnett } Edward Brooks Trustee for each {	500
Mary Burnett	250
Martha Burnett (R. A. Forsyth Trustee)	250
Madaline Bertrand	200
Joseph Bertrand Junr	200
Luke Bertrand Junr	200
Benjamin Bertrand	200
Lawrence Bertrand	200
Theresa Bertrand	200
Amable Bertrand	200
Julianne Bertrand	200
Joseph H. Bertrand	100
Mary M. Bertrand	100
M. L. Bertrand	100
John B. Du Charme	200
Elizabeth Du Charme (R. A. Forsyth Trustee)	800
George Henderson	400
Mary Nado and children	400
John Bt. Chandonai	1000
Charles Chandonai } For each of whom R. A. Forsyth is Trustee {	400
Mary Chandonai	400
Mary St. Comb and children	300
Sa-gen-nais' daughter	200
Me-chain, daughter of Pe-che-co	200
Alexis Rolan	200
Polly Neighbush	200
Francois Page's wife and children	200
Pierre F. Navarre's children	100
Jarmont (half breed)	100
Ten thousand dollars	$10,000

Sept. 27, 1833.

Agreeably to the stipulations contained in the Articles supplementary to the Treaty, there have been purchased and delivered at the request of the Indians, Goods, Provisions and Horses to the amount of fifteen thousand dollars (leaving the balance to be supplied hereafter ten thousand dollars.)

As evidence of the purchase and delivery as aforesaid, under the direction of the said commissioners, and that the whole of the same been received by the said Indians, and the said George B. Porter, Thomas J. V. Owen, and William Weatherford, and the undersigned chiefs and head men on behalf of the said United Nation of Indians, have hereunto set their hands the twenty-seventh day of September, in the year of our Lord one thousand eight hundred and thirty-three.

G. B. Porter,
Th. J. V. Owen,
William Weatherford,

To-pen-e-bee, his x mark,
Wee-saw, his x mark,
Ne-kaw-nosh-kee, his x mark,

Wai-saw-o-ko-ne-aw, his x mark,
Ne-see-waw-be-tuk, his x mark,
Kai-kaw-tai-mon, his x mark,
Saw-Ka-Nosh, his x mark,
Tshee-tshee-chin-ke-bequay, his x mark,
Joseph, his x mark,
Shab-e-nai, his x mark,

Ah-be-to-ke-Zhic, his x mark,
E-to-wau-coto, his x mark,
Shab-y-a-tuk, his x mark,
Me-am-ese, his x mark,
Wah-be-me-mee, his x mark,
Shim-e-nah, his x mark,
We-in-co, his x mark.

In presence of—

Wm. Lee D. Ewing, secretary to the commission,
R. A. Forsyth, U. S. Army,
John H. Kinzie,
Madn. F. Abbott,

Saml. Humes Porter,
Joseph Bertrand, junr.
Andw. Porter,
J. E. Schwarz, adjutant-general M. M.
James Conner, interpreter.

———

On behalf of the Chiefs and Head men of the United Nation of Indians who signed the treaty to which these articles are supplementary we hereby, in evidence of our concurrence therein, become parties thereto.

And, as since the signing of the treaty a part of the band residing on the reservations in the Territory of Michigan, have requested, on account of their religious creed, permission to remove to the northern part of the peninsula of Michigan, it is agreed that in case of such removal the just proportion of all annuities payable to them under former treaties and that arising from the sale of the reservation on which they now reside shall be paid to them at, L'arbre, Croche.

Witness our hands, the said day and year.

Saw-ka-nosh, his x mark,
Che-ohe-bin-quay, his x mark,
Ah-be-te-ke-zhic, his x mark,
Shab-e-nay, his x mark,

O-cheep-pwaise, his x mark,
Maug-e-sett, his x mark,
Shim-e-nah, his x mark,
Ke-me-nah-wah, his x mark.

In the presence of—

Wm. Lee D. Ewing, secretary to the commission,
Jno. H. Kinzie,
Richd. J. Hamilton,
Robert Stuart,

R. A. Forsyth, U. S. Army,
Saml. Humes Porter,
J. E. Schwarz, adjutant-genera. M. M.
James Conner, interpreter.

———

The Commissioners certify that when these supplementary articles were ready for signature, the original paper of which the annexed is a copy was presented by Messrs. Peter and James J. Godfroy, and the due execution of it was made satisfactorily appear to the Commissioners, the subscribing witnesses R A Forsyth and Robert A Kinzie being present.—The Chiefs and Head men present recognizing this as a reservation, it was agreed that it shall be considered in the same light as though the purport of the instrument had been inserted in the body of the treaty;—with the understanding that the rejection of it by the President and Senate of the United States shall not affect the validity of the treaty.

> G. B. PORTER,
> TH. J. V. OWEN,
> WILLIAM WEATHERFORD.

———

(Copy of the instrument referred to in the above certificate.—)

Know all men by these presents that we the undersigned Chiefs and Young men of the Potawatamie tribe of Indians living at Na-to-wa-se-pe in the territory of Michigan, for and in consideration of the friendship and sundry services rendered to us by Peter and James J.   May 18, 1830.

Godfroy we do hereby by these presents give, grant, alien, transfer and convey unto the said Godfroys their heirs and assigns forever one entire section of land situate lying and being on our reserve of Na-to-wa-se-pe, in the Territory aforesaid to be located by said Godfroys wherever on said reserve they shall think it more to their advantage and benefit.

It is moreover the wishes of the undersigned Chiefs and Young men as aforesaid, that so soon as there shall be a treaty held between the United States and our said tribe of Pottawatamies, that our great father the President confirm and make good this our grant unto them, the said Godfroys by issuing a patent therefor to them and to their heirs forever.—In so doing our great father will accomplish the wishes of his children.

Done at Detroit, this eighteenth day of May, A. D. one thousand eight hundred and thirty.

In witness whereof, we have hereunto signed, sealed, and set our hands and seals, the day and year last above written.

Penenchese, his x mark,	[L. S.]
Pit-goit-ke-se, his x mark,	[L. S.]
Nah-o-te-nan, his x mark,	[L. S.]
Ke-a-sac-wa, his x mark,	[L. S.]
Sko-paw-ka, his x mark,	[L. S.]
Ce-ce-baw, his x mark,	[L. S.]
Na-wa-po-to, his x mark,	[L. S.]
To-ta-gas, his x mark,	[L. S.]
Pierre Morin, alias Perish, his x mark,	[L. S.]
We-say-gah, his x mark,	[L. S.]

Signed, sealed, and delivered in the presence of us—

R. A. Forsyth,
Robt. A. Kinzie,
G. Godfroy,
    Witnesses to the signature of Pierre Morin, alias Perish, and Wa-say-gah.
Richard Godfroy,
Francis Mouton.

Chicago, Illinois, Oct. 1, 1834.

Tho. J. V. Owen, Esqr. }
U. S. Indian Agent. }

Oct. 1, 1834.

FATHER: Feeling a disposition to comply with the resolution of Senate of the United States, and the views of the Government in relation to an alteration in the boundaries of the country ceded to the United nation of Chippewa, Ottawa, and Potawatamie Indians at the treaty at Chicago in the State of Illinois, concluded on the 26th and 27th days of September 1833:—we therefore propose as the chiefs of the said united nation, and for and on their behalf that we will accept of the following alteration in the boundaries of the said tract of country viz:—Beginning at the mouth of Boyer's river; thence down the Missouri river, to a point thereon; from which a due east line would strike the northwest corner of the State of Missouri; thence along the said east line, to the northwest corner of said State; then along the northern boundary line of the said State of Missouri, till it strikes the line of the lands of the Sac and Fox Indians; thence northwardly along said line to a point from which a west line would strike the sources of the Little Sioux river; thence along said west line, till it strikes the said sources of said river; then down said river to its mouth; thence down the Missouri river to the place of beginning: *Provided* the said boundary shall contain five million of acres; but should it contain more, then said boundaries are to be reduced so as to contain the said five millions of acres.

And, in consideration of the alteration of said boundary we ask that ten thousand dollars should be paid to such commissioner, as shall be designated by us to receive the same west of the Mississippi river, at such place on the tract of country ceded to the said united nation as we may designate, and to be applied, as we may direct for the use and benefit of the said nation. And the further sum of two thousand dollars to be paid to Gholson Kercheval, of Chicago, Ill.: for services rendered the said united nation of Indians during the late war, between the U. S. Government and the Sacs and Foxes; and the further sum of one thousand dollars to George E. Walker for services rendered the said United nation, in bringing Indian prisoners, from west of the Mississippi river to Ottawa, Lasalle county, Ill. for whose appearance at the circuit court of said county, the said nation was bound.

The foregoing propositions are made with the expectation, that with the exception of the alteration in the proposed boundary, and the indemnity herein demanded as an equivalent for said exchange, the whole of the treaty made and concluded at this place on the 26th and 27th days of September 1833, be ratified as made and concluded at that time, within the space of five months from the present date; otherwise it is our wish that the whole of the said treaty should be considered as cancelled.

In witness whereof, we, the undersigned chiefs of the said United Nation of Chippewa, Ottowa, and Pattawatamie Indians, being specially delegated with power and authority to effect this negotiation, have hereto set our hands and seals, at Chicago, in the State of Illinois, on the first day of October, A. D. 1834.

R. Caldwell,	[L. S.]
Kee-tshee-zhing-ee-beh, his x mark,	[L. S.]
Tshee-tshee-beeng-guay, his x mark,	[L. S.]
Joseph, his x mark,	[L. S.]
Ob-ee-tah-kee-zhik, his x mark,	[L. S.]
Wau-bon-see, his x mark,	[L. S.]
Kay-kot-ee-mo, his x mark,	[L. S.]

In presence of—

Richd. J. Hamilton,
Jno. H. Kenzie,
Dr. P. Maxwell, U. S. Army,
J. Grant, jr.,
E. M. Owen,
J. M. Baxley, captain Fifth Infantry.

[NOTE.—This Treaty and Supplementary Articles thereto, were ratified and confirmed, upon the conditions expressed in the two resolutions of the Senate in relation to the same; which conditions as contained in the first named resolution, are as follows:

"That the Senate do advise and consent to the ratification of the Treaty, made on the 26th day of September 1833, at Chicago, by George B. Porter and others, Commissioners on behalf of the United States, and the United Nation of Chippewas, Ottawas, and Pottawatamies Indians, and the supplementary articles thereto, dated on the 27th day of September, 1833, with the following amendments and provisions, to wit. 1st: amend the third article in Schedule A, by striking out the word "ten" and inserting the word *five* as to each of the sums to be paid to Billy Caldwell and Alexander Robinson; so that the sum of five thousand dollars *only* will be paid to each of them, and the sum of ten thousand dollars, thus deducted, to be paid to the Indians.—2d. All the debts, mentioned in schedule B, in the same article, and which are specified in exhibit E, to the report of the committee, to be examined by a commissioner to be appointed by the President, with the advice and consent of the Senate, and the individuals to be paid only the sums found by said commissioner, to have been justly due; in no instance increasing the sum agreed to be paid; and whatever sum is saved by deduction or disallowance of the debts in exhibit E, to be paid to the Indians, and the residue to the claimants respectively. 3d. Strike out article 5th in the Treaty. 4th. Strike out article 4th in the supplementary articles: and provided, that the lands

TREATY WITH THE PAWNEE, 1833.

Oct. 9, 1833.
_____
7 Stat., 448.
Proclamation, Apr. 12, 1834.

Articles of agreement and convention, made this ninth day of October, A. D. 1833, at the Grand Pawnee village, on the Platte river between Henry L. Ellsworth, commissioner in behalf of the United States, and the chiefs and head-men of the four confederated bands of Pawnees, viz.—Grand Pawnees, Pawnee Loups, Pawnee Republicans, and Pawnee Tappaye, residing on the Platte and the Loup fork.

Cession of land to United States.

ART. I. The confederated bands of Pawnees aforesaid hereby cede and relinquish to the United States all their right, interest, and title in and to all the land lying south of the Platte river.

Hunting ground.

ART. II. The land ceded and relinquished hereby, so far as the same is not and shall not be assigned to any tribe or tribes, shall remain a common hunting ground, during the pleasure of the President, for the Pawnees and other friendly Indians, who shall be permitted by the President to hunt on the same.

Amount of goods to be annually given.

ART. III. The United States, in consideration of said cession and for the purpose of advancing the welfare of the said Pawnees, agree to pay said bands annually, for the term of twelve years, the sum of forty-six hundred dollars in goods, at not exceeding St. Louis prices, as follows: to the Grand Pawnees and Republican villages, each thirteen hundred dollars, and to the Pawnee Loups and Tappaye Pawnee villages each one thousand dollars, and said annuity to said Grand Pawnees is in full remuneration for removal from the south to the north side of the Platte, and building again.

Agricultural implements.

ART. IV. The United States agree to pay to each of said four bands, for five years, the sum of five hundred dollars in agricultural implements; and to be continued longer if the President thinks proper.

Provision for schools.

ART. V. The United States agree to allow one thousand dollars a year for ten years, for schools to be established for the benefit of said four bands at the discretion of the President.

Blacksmiths, etc.

ART. VI. The United States agree to furnish two blacksmiths and two strikers, with shop, tools and iron, for ten years, for said four

---

given to the said Indians, in exchange, in place of being bounded in the manner described in the treaty be so changed, that the first line shall begin at the mouth of Boyer's river, and run down the river Missouri to a point thereon from which a line running due east will strike the northwestern corner of the State of Missouri; from that point due east till it strikes said northwest corner; then, along the northern boundary line of said State, till it strikes the line of the lands belonging to the Fox and Sac Indians; thence northwardly, so far as to make to the Indians full compensation for the quantity of land which will be thus taken from them on the southwestern part of the tract allowed them by the boundaries as at present described in the treaty; and provided, further, that this alteration of boundaries can be effected with the consent of the Indians. Also the said commissioner shall examine whether three thousand dollars, a part of the sum of seventeen thousand dollars directed to be paid to Robert Stuart agent of the American Fur Company, was to be paid and received in full discharge of all claims and demands which said company had against Gurdon S. Hubbard and James Kinzie; and if he finds it was to be so paid, that then the sum of fourteen thousand dollars, *only*, be paid, until said agent of said company give a receipt of all debts due, and demands which said company had against said Hubbard and Kinzie; and, upon giving such receipt, that then the said sum of three thousand dollars be likewise paid to said agent.''

And those contained in the second named resolution are as follows:

''That the Senate do advise and consent to the alteration proposed by the Chiefs of the United Nation of Chippewa, Ottawa and Pottawattamie Indians, concluded at Chicago, in the State of Illinois, on the first day of October 1834, to the treaty concluded between the Commissioners on the part of the United States and the chiefs of the said United Nation on the 26th of September, 1833:—it being expressly understood by the Senate that no other of the provisions of the resolution of the Senate of the 22d day of May 1834, ratifying the said treaty, shall be affected, or in any manner changed, by the said proposed alteration of 1st October, 1834, excepting the proposed alteration in the boundaries therein mentioned, and the sums of money therein stipulated to be paid.'']

bands, at an expense not exceeding two thousand dollars in the whole annually.

ART. VII. The United States agree to furnish each of said four tribes with a farmer for five years, and deliver to said farmers for the benefit of said nation, one thousand dollars value in oxen and other stock. But said stock is not to be delivered into the hands of the said Pawnees, until the President thinks the same can be done with propriety and safety. *Farmer, oxen, etc.*

ART. VIII. The United States agree to erect, for each of said four bands, a horse-mill for grinding corn. *Corn mill.*

ART. IX. The Pawnee nation renew their assurance of friendship for the white men, their fidelity to the United States, and their desire for peace with all neighboring tribes of red men. The Pawnee nation therefore agree not to molest or injure the person or property of any white citizen of the United States, wherever found, nor to make war upon any tribe with whom said Pawnee nation now are, or may be, at peace; but should any difficulty arise between said nation and any other tribe, they agree to refer the matter in dispute to such arbiter as the President shall appoint to settle the same. *Disputes with other tribes to arbiter.*

ART. X. It is agreed and understood that the United States shall not be bound to fulfil the stipulations contained in the fifth, seventh, and eighth articles, until said tribes shall locate themselves in convenient agricultural districts, and remain in these districts the whole year, so as to give protection to the teachers, the farmers, stock and mill. *Condition of these stipulations.*

ART. XI. The United States, desirous to show the Pawnees the advantages of agriculture, engage, in case the Pawnees cannot agree to remain to protect their domestic interest, to break up for each village a piece of land suitable for corn and potatoes for one season; and should either village at any time agree to give the protection required, said village shall be entitled to the benefits conferred in said fifth, seventh, and eighth articles. *To promote agriculture.*

ART. XII. In case the Pawnee nation will remain at home during the year, and give the protection specified, the United States agree to place twenty-five guns, with suitable ammunition, in the hands of the farmers of each village, to be used in case of an attack from hostile bands. *Guns and ammunition.*

ART. XIII. The United States further agree to deliver to said four bands collectively, on the execution of this treaty, the amount of sixteen hundred dollars in goods and merchandise, and the receipt of the same is hereby acknowledged by said bands. *Goods.*

ART. XIV. These articles of agreement and convention shall be obligatory and binding when ratified by the President and Senate of the United States. *Treaty binding when ratified.*

In testimony whereof the said Henry L. Ellsworth, commissioner, and the chiefs and head men of the four confederated bands of the Grand Pawnees, Pawnee Loups, Pawnee Republicans, and Tappaye Pawnees, have hereunto signed their names and affixed their seals on the day and year above written.

Henry L. Ellsworth.

Grand Pawnees:
Shah-re-tah-riche, his x mark, [L. S.]
Shon-gah-kah-he-gah, his x mark, [L. S.]
Pe-tah-lay-shah-rho, his x mark, [L. S.]
Ah-sha-kah-tah-kho, his x mark, [L. S.]

Pawnee Republicans:
Blue Coat, his x mark, [L. S.]
Lay-shah-rho-lah-re-ho-rho, his x mark, [L. S.]
Ah-shah-lay-kah-sah-hah, his x mark, [L. S.]
Lay-shah-ke-re-pahs-kay, his x mark, [L. S.]

Tappaye Pawnees:
Little Chief, his x mark, [L. S.]
Lah-ho-pah-go-lah-lay-shah-rho, his x mark, [L. S.]
Ah-ke-tah-we-he-kah-he-gay, his x mark, [L. S.]
Skah-lah-lay-shah-rho, his x mark, [L. S.]

Pawnee Loups:
Big Axe, his x mark, [L. S.]
Middle Chief, his x mark, [L. S.]
Spotted Horse, his x mark, [L. S.]
Big Soldier, his x mark, [L. S.]

Signed, sealed, and delivered in the presence of—

Edward A. Ellsworth, secretary pro tempore,	Ware S. May, M. D.
	John Dunlop,
Jno. Dougherty, Indian agent,	John T. Irving, jr.
A. L. Papin,	Lewis La Chapelle, interpreter.

TREATY WITH THE CHICKASAW, 1834.

May 24, 1834.

7 Stat., 450.
Proclamation, July 1, 1834.

Articles of convention and agreement proposed by the Commissioners on the part of the United States, in pursuance of the request made, by the Delegation representing the Chickasaw nation of Indians, and which have been agreed to.

Peace and friendship.

ART. I. It is agreed that perpetual amity, peace and friendship, shall exist between the United States, and the Chickasaw nation of Indians.

Indians about to remove are to be protected by United States.

ART. II. The Chickasaws are about to abandon their homes, which they have long cherished and loved; and though hitherto unsuccessful, they still hope to find a country, adequate to the wants and support of their people, somewhere west of the Mississippi and within the territorial limits of the United States; should they do so, the Government of the United States, hereby consent to protect and defend them against the inroads of any other tribe of Indians, and from the whites; and agree to keep them without the limits of any State or Territory. The Chickasaws pledge themselves never to make war upon any Indian people, or upon the whites, unless they are so authorized by the United States. But if war be made upon them, they will be permitted to defend themselves, until assistance, be given to them by the United States, as shall be the case.

United States to prevent intrusions on their lands.

ART. III. The Chickasaws are not acquainted with the laws of the whites, which are extended over them; and the many intruders which break into their country, interrupting their rights and disturbing their repose, leave no alternative whereby restraint can be afforded, other than an appeal to the military force of the country, which they are unwilling to ask for, or see resorted to; and therefore they agree to forbear such a request, for prevention of this great evil, with the understanding, which is admitted, that the agent of the United States, upon the application of the chiefs of the nation, will resort to every legal civil remedy, (at the expense of the United States,) to prevent intrusions upon the ceded country; and to restrain and remove trespassers from any selected reservations, upon application of the owner of the same. And it is also agreed, that the United States, will continue some discreet person as agent, such as they now have, to whom they can look for redress of wrongs and injuries which may be attempted against them; and it is consented, that if any of their property, be taken by persons of the United States, covertly or forcibly, the agent on satisfactory and just complaint being made, shall pursue all lawful civil means, which the laws of the State permit, in which the wrong is done, to regain the same, or to obtain a just remuneration; and on failure or inability to procure redress, for the offended, against the offending party; payment for the loss sustained, on production of the record, and certificate of the facts, by the agent, shall be made by the United States; but in all such cases, satisfactory proof, for the establishing of the claim, shall be offered.

Under what authority reservations may be sold.

ART. IV. The Chickasaws desire to have within their own direction and control, the means of taking care of themselves. Many of their people are quite competent to manage their affairs, though some are not capable, and might be imposed upon by designing persons; it is therefore agreed that the reservations hereinafter admitted, shall not be permitted to be sold, leased, or disposed of unless it appear by the certificate of at least two of the following persons, to wit: Ish-ta-ho-ta-pa the King, Levi Colbert, George Colbert, Martin Colbert, Isaac Alberson, Henry Love, and Benj. Love, of which five have affixed their names to this treaty, that the party owning or claiming the same, is capable to manage, and to take care of his or her affairs; which fact, to the best of his knowledge and information, shall be certified by the agent; and furthermore that a fair consideration has been paid; and thereupon, the deed of conveyance shall be valid provided the President of the United States, or such other person as he may designate shall approve of the same, and endorse it on the deed; which said deed and approval, shall be registered, at the place, and within the time, required by the laws of the State, in which the land may be situated; otherwise to be void. And where such certificate is not obtained; upon the recommendation of a majority of the Delegation, and the approval of the agent, at the discretion of the President of the United States, the same may be sold; but the consideration thereof, shall remain as part of the general Chickasaw fund in the hands of the Government, until such time as the chiefs in council shall think it advisable to pay it to the claimant or to those, who may rightfully claim under said claimant, and shall so recommend it. And as the King, Levi Colbert, and the Delegation, who have signed this agreement, and to whom certain important and interesting duties purtaining to the nation, are assigned, may die, resign, or remove, so that their people may be without the benefit of their services, it is stipulated, that as often as any vacancy happens, by death, resignation, or otherwise, the chiefs shall select some discrete person of their nation to fill the occurring vacancy, who, upon a certificate of qualification, discretion and capability, by the agent, shall be appointed by the Secretary of War; whereupon, he shall possess all the authority granted to those who are here named, and the nation will make to the person so appointed, such reasonable compensation, as they with the assent of the agent and the Secretary of War, may think right, proper and reasonable to be allowed.

ART. V. It is agreed that the fourth article of the "Treaty of Pontitock," be so changed, that the following reservations be granted in fee:—To heads of families, being Indians, or having Indian families, consisting of ten persons, and upwards, four sections of land are reserved. To those who have five and less than ten persons, three sections. Those who have less than five, two sections. Also those who own more than ten slaves, shall be entitled to one additional section; and those owning ten and less than ten to half a section. These reservations shall be confined, to the sections or fractional sections on which the party claiming lives, or to such as are contiguous or adjoining to the sections resided upon, subject to the following restrictions and conditions:— *Grants to be in fee; how determined.*

Firstly. In cases where there are interferences arising, the oldest occupant or settler, shall have the preference or,

Secondly. Where the land is adjudged unfit for cultivation, by the Agent, and three of the seven persons, named in the fourth article above, the party entitled, shall be, and is, hereby authorized, to locate his claim upon other lands, which may be unappropriated, and not subject to any other claim; and where two or more persons, insist upon the entry of the same unappropriated section or fractional section, the priority of right shall be determined by lot; and where a fractional section is taken, leaving a balance greater or less than the surveyed subdivision of a section, then the deficiency shall be made up, by connecting all the deficiencies so arising: and the Register and Receiver thereupon, shall locate full or fractional sections, fit for cultivation, in the names respectively of the different persons claiming which shall be held by them as tenants in common, according to the respective interests of those who are concerned; and the proceeds when sold by the parties claiming, shall be divided according to the interests, which each may have in said section or fractional section, so located, or the same may be divided agreeably to quality or quantity.

Reservations for persons not heads of families.

ART. VI. Also reservations of a section to each, shall be granted to persons male and female, not being heads of families, who are of the age of twenty-one years, and upwards, a list of whom, within a reasonable time shall be made out by the seven persons herein before mentioned, and filed with the Agent, upon whose certificate of its believed accuracy, the Register and Receiver, shall cause said reservations to be located upon lands fit for cultivation, but not to interfere with the settlement rights of others. The persons thus entitled, are to be excluded from the estimated numbers contained in any family enumeration, as is provided for in the fifth article preceding: and as to the sale, lease, or disposition of their reserves, they are to be subject to the conditions and restrictions, set forth in the fourth article. In these and in all other reserves where the party owning or entitled, shall die, the interest in the same shall belong to his wife, or the wife and children, or to the husband, or to the husband and children, if there be any; and in cases of death, where there is neither husband, wife, nor children left, the same shall be disposed of for the general benefit; and the proceeds go into the general Chickasaw fund. But where the estate as is prescribed in this article, comes to the children, and having so come, either of them die, the survivor or survivors of them, shall be entitled to the same. But this rule shall not endure longer than for five years, nor beyond the period when the Chickasaws may leave their present for a new home.

In case of marriage between a white man and an Indian woman.

ART. VII. Where any white man, before the date hereof has married an Indian woman, the reservation he may be entitled to under this treaty, she being alive, shall be in her name, and no right of alienation of the same shall purtain to the husband unless he divest her of the title, after the mode and manner that feme coverts, usually divest themselves of title to real estate, that is, by the acknowledgment of the wife which may be taken before the Agent, and certified by him, that she consents to the sale freely, and without compulsion from her husband, who shall at the same time certify that the head of such family is prudent, and competent to care of and manage his affairs; otherwise the proceeds of said sale shall be subject to the provisions and restrictions contained in the fourth article of this agreement. Rights to reservations as are herein, and in other articles of this agreement secured, will purtain to those who have heretofore intermarried with the Chickasaws and are residents of the nation.

Provision for orphans, etc.

ART. VIII. Males and females below the age of twenty-one years, whose father being dead, the mother again has married, or who have neither father nor mother, shall each be entitled to half a section of land, but shall not be computed as parts of families under the fifth article, the same to be located under the direction of the Agent, and under the supervision of the Secretary of War, so as not to interfere with any settlement right. These lands may be sold upon a recommendation of a majority of the seven persons, heretofore named in this agreement, setting forth that it will prove advantageous to the parties interested; subject however, to the approval of the President, or such other person as he shall designate. If sold, the funds arising shall be retained, in the possession of the Government, or if the President deem it advisable they shall be invested in stocks for the benefit of the parties interested, if there be a sufficient sum to be invested, (and it can be invested,) until said persons marry or come of age, when the amount shall be paid over to those who are entitled to receive it, provided a majority of the seven persons, with the Agent, shall certify, that in their opinion, it will be to their interest and advantage, then, and in that case, the proceeds shall be paid over to the party or parties entitled to receive them.

ART. IX. But, in running the sectional lines, in some cases it will Interfering sectional lines. happen, that the spring and the dwelling house, or the spring and the cleared land, or the cleared land and the dwelling house of settlers, may be separated by sectional lines, whereby manifest inconvenience and injury will be occasioned; it is agreed, that when any of these occurrences arise, the party shall be entitled as parts and portions of his reservations, to the adjoining section or fraction, as the case may be, unless there be some older occupant, claiming a preference; and in that event, the right of the party shall extend no farther than to give to the person, thus affected and injured, so much of his separated property, as will secure the spring; also, where a sectional line shall separate any improvement, dwelling house, kitchen or stable, so much of the section, which contains them, shall be added into the occupied section, as will secure them to their original owner; and then and in that case, the older occupant being deprived of preference, shall have his deficiency thus occasioned, made up to him by some fractional section, or after the mode pointed out in the latter part of the fifth article of this treaty.

ART. X. Reservations are admitted to the following persons, in Special reservations admitted. addition to those which may be claimed under the fifth article of this Treaty to wit:—Four sections to their beloved and faithful old Chief Levi Colbert; To George Colbert, Martin Colbert, Isaac Alberson, Henry Love and Benj. Love, in consideration of the trouble they have had in coming to Washington, and of the farther trouble hereafter to be encountered in taking care of the interests of their people, under the provisions of this treaty, one section of land to each. Also there is a fractional section, between the residence of George Colbert, and the Tennessee river, upon which he has a ferry, it is therefore consented, that said George Colbert, shall own and have so much of said fraction, as may be contained in the following lines, to wit.—begining near Smith's ferry at the point where the base meridian line and the Tennessee river come in contact,—thence south so far as to pass the dwelling-house, (and sixty yards beyond it,) within which is interred the body of his wife,—thence east of the river and down the same to the point of begining. Also there shall be reserved to him an island, in said river, nearly opposite to this fraction, commonly called Colberts Island. A reservation also of two sections is admitted to Ish-ta-ho-ta-pa the King of the Chickasaw nation. And to Min-ta-ho-yea the mother of Charles Colbert one section of land. Also one section, each, to the following persons:—Im-mub-bee, Ish-tim-o-lut-ka, Ah-to-ho-woh, Pis-tah-lah-tubbe, Capt. Samuel Seley and William McGilvery. To Col. Benj. Reynolds their long tried and faithful Agent, who has guarded their interests and twice travelled with their people far west, beyond the Mississippi, to aid them in seeking and finding a home, there is granted two sections of land. Jointly to William Cooper and John Davis, lawyers of Mississippi who have been faithful to the Indians, in giving them professional advice, and legal assistance, and who are to continue to do so, within the States of Tennessee, Alabama and Mississippi, while the Chickasaw people remain in said States, one section is granted. To Mrs. Margt. Allen wife of the subagent in her own right, half a section. These reservations to Benj. Reynolds, William Cooper, James Davis and Margt. Allen, are to be located so as not to interfere with the Indian reservations.

ART. XI. After the reservations are taken and located, which shall Disposal of the lands after the location of reservations. be the case as speedily as may be after the surveys are completed, of which the Register and Receiver shall give notice, the residue of the Chickasaw country shall be sold, as public lands of the United States are sold, with this difference; The lands as surveyed shall be offered at public sale at a price not less than one dollar and a quarter per acre; and thereafter for one year those which are unsold, and which shall have been previously offered at public sale, shall be liable to private entry and sale at that price; Thereafter, and for one year longer they shall be subject to entry and private sale, at one dollar per acre; Thereafter and during the third year, they shall be subject to sale and entry, at fifty cents per acre; Thereafter, and during the fourth year, at twenty-five cents per acre; and afterwards at twelve and a half cents per acre. But as it may happen, in the fourth and after years, that the expenses may prove greater than the receipts, it is agreed, that at any time after the third year, the Chickasaws may declare the residue of their lands abandoned to the United States, and if so, they shall be thenceforth acquitted of all and every expense on account of the sale of the same.

And that they may be advised of these matters it is stipulated, that the Government of the United States, within six months after any public sale takes place, shall advise them of the receipts and expenditures, and of balances in their favor; and also at regular intervals of six months, after the first report is made, will afford them information of the proceeds of all entries and sales. The funds thence resulting, after the necessary expenses of surveying and selling, and other advances which may be made, are repaid to the United States, shall from time to time be invested in some secure stocks, redeemable within a period of not more than twenty years; and the United States will cause the interest arising therefrom, annually to be paid to the Chickasaws.

Notice of sale to be given. ART. XII. When any portion of the country is fully surveyed, the President may order the same to be sold, but will allow six months, from the date of the first notice to the first sale; and three months' notice of any subsequent intended public sale, within which periods of time, those who can claim reservations, in the offered ranges of country, shall file their applications and entries with the Register and Receiver; that the name of the owner or claimant of the same, may be entered and marked on the general plat, at the office, whereby mistakes in the sales may be avoided, and injuries be prevented.

Provision for their removal. ART. XIII. If the Chickasaws shall be so fortunate as to procure a home, within the limits of the United States, it is agreed, that with the consent of the President and Senate so much of their invested stocks, as may be necessary to the purchase of a country for them to settle in, shall be permitted to them to be sold, or the United States will advance the necessary amount, upon a guarantee and pledge of an equal amount of their stocks; also, as much of them may be sold, with the consent of the President and Senate, as shall be adjudged necessary for establishing schools, mills, blacksmiths shops; and for the education of their children; and for any other needful purpose, which their situation and condition, may make, and by the President and Senate be considered, necessary; and on the happening of such a contingency, and information thereof being given of an intention of the whole or any portion of the nation to remove; the United States will furnish competent persons, safely to conduct them to their future destination, and also supplies necessary to the same, and for one year after their arrival at the west, provided the Indians shall desire supplies, to be furnished for so long a period; the supplies so afforded, to be chargeable to the general Chickasaw account, provided the funds of said nation shall be found adequate to the expenses which under this and other articles of this agreement may be required.

Certain articles of the treaty of Pontitock to remain in force. ART. XIV. It is understood and agreed, that articles twelve and thirteen of the "Treaty of Pontitock," of the twentieth day of October, one thousand, eight hundred and thirty-two, and which was concluded, with Genl. John Coffee shall be retained; all the other articles of said treaty, inconsistent in any respect with the provisions of this, are declared to be revoked. Also so much of the supplemental treaty as relates to Colbert Moore; to the bond of James Colbert transferred to Robert Gordon; to the central position of the Land Office; to the establishment of mail routes through the Chickasaw country; and as it respects the privilege given to John Donely; be, and the same are declared to be in full force.

ART. XV. By the sixth article of a treaty made with the Chickasaw nation, by Andrew Jackson and Isaac Shelby, on the nineteenth day of October, one thousand eight hundred and eighteen, it was provided that a Commissioner should be appointed, to mark the southern boundary of said cession; now it is agreed that the line which was run and marked by the Commissioner on the part of the United States, in pursuance of said treaty, shall be considered the true line to the extent that the rights and interests of the Chickasaws are conserned, and no farther. *Boundary under treaty of 1818, how considered.*

ART. XVI. The United States agree that the appropriation made by Congress, in the year one thousand eight hundred and thirty-three, for carrying into effect "the treaty with the Chickasaws," shall be applicable to this; to be reimbursed by them; and their agent may receive and be charged with the same, from time to time, as in the opinion of the Secretary of War, any portion may be wanted for national purposes, by the Chickasaws; of which nature and character, shall be considered their present visit to Washington City. *Appropriation made in 1833 to be applied. 1833, ch. 59.*

Done at the city of Washington, on the 24th day of May, one thousand eight hundred and thirty-four.

　　Jn. H. Eaton,
　　　　　commissioner on the part of the United States.

George Colbert, his x mark,
Isaac Albertson, his x mark,
Martin Colbert,　　　　　　　　　　　　　　　　　　[L. S.]
Henry Love,　　　　　　　　　　　　　　　　　　　[L. S.]
Benjamin Love,　　　　　　　　　　　　　　　　　　[L. S.]

Witnesses—
Charles F. Little, secretary to commissioner,
Ben. Reynolds, Indian agent,
G. W. Long,
James Standefer,
Thomas S. Smith,
Saml. Swartwout,
Wm. Gordon,
F. W. Armstrong, c. agent,
John M. Millard.

The undersigned, appointed by the Chickasaw nation of Indians in the two-fold capacity of a delegate and interpreter, hereby declares that in all that is set forth in the above articles of convention and agreement, have been by him fully and accurately interpreted and explained, and that the same has been approved by the entire delegation.
May 24, 1834.

　　　　Benjamin Love, delegate and interpreter.
　　　　Charles F. Little, secretary to commissioner.
　　　　Ben. Reynolds, Indian agent.

May 24, 1834.

7 Stat., 456.

Articles supplementary to those concluded and signed, by the United States Commissioner, and the Chickasaw delegation on the 24th day of May, one thousand eight hundred and thirty-four; which being agreed to by the President and Senate of the United States, are to stand as part of said treaty.

Provision in favor of Levi Colbert, etc.

ART. I. It is represented that the old chiefs Levi Colbert and Isaac Alberson, who have rendered many and valuable services to their nation, desire on account of their health, to visit some watering place, during the present year, for recovery and restoration; it is agreed that there be paid to the agent for these purposes, and to discharge some debts which are due and owing from the nation, the sum of three thousand dollars, out of the appropriation of one thousand eight hundred and thirty-three, for carrying into effect the "treaty of Pontitock," which said sum so far as used is to be hereafter reimbursed to the nation, by said Levi Colbert and Isaac Alberson, and by the nation to the United States, as other advances are to be reimbursed, from the sale of their lands.

Children to be educated in the United States.

ART. II. The Chickasaw people express a desire that the Government shall at the expense of the United States, educate some of their children, and they urge the justice of their application, on the ground, that they have ever been faithful and friendly to the people of this country,—that they have never raised the tomahawk, to shed the blood of an American, and have given up heretofore to their white brothers, extensive and valuable portions of their country, at a price wholly inconsiderable and inadequate; and from which the United States have derived great wealth and important advantages; therefore, with the advice and consent of the President and Senate of the United States, it is consented, that three thousand dollars for fifteen years, be appropriated and applied under the direction of the Secretary of War, for the education and instruction within the United States, of such children male and female or either, as the seven persons named in the treaty to which this is a supplement, and their successors, with the approval of the agent, from time to time may select and recommend.

A former reservation ceded to United States.

ART. III. The Chickasaw nation desire to close finally, all the business they have on the east side of the Mississippi, that their Great Father, may be no more troubled with their complaints, and to this end, they ask the Government to receive from them a tract of land, of four miles square, heretofore reserved under the 4th article of their "Treaty of 1818," and to pay them within three months, from the date of this arrangement, the Government price of one dollar and a quarter per acre, for said reserve; and accordingly the same is agreed to, provided a satisfactory relinquishment of title from the parties interested, be filed with the Secretary of War, previous to said payment being made.

Money stolen from the agent.

ART. IV. Benj. Reynolds, agent at the time of paying their last annuity, had stolen from him by a negro slave of the Chickasaws, a box containing one thousand dollars; the chiefs of the Chickasaw people satisfied of the fact, and hence unwilling to receive the lost amount from their agent, ask, and it is agreed, that the sum so stolen and lost, shall be passed to the credit of their nation by the United States, to be drawn on hereafter for their national purposes.

An additional clerk to be appointed.

ART. V. The Chickasaw people are aware that one clerk is insufficient to the bringing of their lands early into market; and rather than encounter the delay which must ensue, they prefer the increased expense of an additional one. It is therefore stipulated that the President shall appoint another clerk, at the same annual compensation, agreed upon by the "Treaty of Pontitock;" who shall be paid after the manner prescribed therein. But whenever the President shall be of opinion that the services of any officer employed under this treaty, for the sale of lands can be dispensed with; he will in justice to the Chickasaws, and to save them from unnecessary expenses, discontinue the whole, or such as can be dispensed with.

Signed the 24th of May, 1834.

Jn. H. Eaton, commissioner on the part of the United States.	Martin Colbert,	[L. S.]
George Colbert, his x mark,	Henry Love,	[L. S.]
Isaac Albertson, his x mark,	Benjamin Love,	[L. S.]

Witnesses:

Charles F. Little, secretary to commissioner,
Ben. Reynolds, Indian agent,
G. W. Long,
James Standefer,

Thomas S. Smith,
Saml. Swartwout,
Wm. Gordon,
F. W. Armstrong, C. agent,
John M. Millard.

TREATY WITH THE MIAMI, 1834.

Articles of a treaty between the United States and the Miami tribe of Indians, concluded at the Forks of the Wabash, in the State of Indiana, on the 23d day of October, 1834, by and between William Marshall, commissioner of the United States, and the chiefs and warriors of said tribe.

7 Stat., 458.
7 Stat., 463.
Proclamation, Dec. 22, 1837.

ARTICLE 1. The Miami tribe of Indians agree to cede to the United States the following described tracts of land within the State of Indiana, being a part of reservations made to said tribe from former cessions, now conveyed for and in consideration of the payments stipulated to be made to them in the 2d article of this treaty of cession.

The Indians cede the following tracts of land.

One tract of land, thirty-six sections, at Flat Belly's village, a reserve made by the treaty of Wabash of 1826.

Also, one tract of land, about twenty-three thousand acres more or less, a reserve made at Wabash treaty in 1826, of five miles in length on the Wabash river, extending back to Eel river.

Also, one other tract of ten sections at Racoon village, and a tract of ten sections at Mudd creek on Eel river, reserves made at Wabash treaty of 1826.

Also, one reserve of two miles square, on the Salamany river at the mouth of At-che-pong-quaw creek, reserve made at the treaty of St. Mary's of 1818.

Also, one other tract being a portion of the ten mile square reserve, made at the treaty of St. Mary's of 1818, opposite the mouth of the river Aboutte, commencing at the northeast corner of said reserve, thence south with the eastern boundary of the same ten miles to the southeast corner of the reserve, thence west with the southern boundary one mile, thence north nine miles, thence west nine miles, thence north one mile to the northwest corner of said reserve, thence to the place of beginning.

The Miamies also agree to cede a portion of their big reserve, made at the treaty of St. Mary's of 1818, situated southeast of the Wabash, extending along the Wabash river, from the mouth of Salamany river, to the mouth of Eel river. The part now ceded shall be embraced within the following bounds to wit: commencing on the Wabash river, opposite the mouth of Eel river, running up said Wabash river eight miles, thence south two miles, thence westerly one mile, thence south to the southern boundary of said reserve, thence along said boundary line seven miles to the southwest corner, thence northerly with the western boundary line to the place of beginning.

Consideration therefor.

ARTICLE 2. For and in consideration of the cession made in the first article of this treaty, the United States agree to pay the Miami tribe of Indians the sum of two hundred and eight thousand dollars; of this sum fifty-eight thousand dollars to be paid within six months from the ratification of this treaty, fifty thousand dollars to be applied to the payment of the debts of the tribe, and the remaining sum of one hundred thousand dollars in annual instalments of ten thousand dollars per year.

Grants to be made from the lands ceded.

ARTICLE 3. From the cession made in the first article of this treaty, there shall be granted to each of the persons named in the schedule hereunto annexed, and to their heirs and assigns, by patent from the President of the United States, the lands therein named.

A patent in fee simple to be issued to J. B. Richardville.

ARTICLE 4. It is agreed, between the parties to this treaty, that a patent in fee simple shall be issued by the President of the United States to John B. Richardville, principal chief of the Miami tribe, for a reserve of ten sections at the Forks of the Wabash, made to said tribe by treaty of twenty-third October, 1826, he having an Indian title to the same, a copy of which, marked A, accompanies this treaty.

A miller to be furnished.

ARTICLE 5. The United States agree to furnish a skilful miller, to superintend a mill for the Miamies, in lieu of the gunsmith promised by the 5th article of the treaty of St. Mary's of 1818.

Improvements.

ARTICLE 6. The United States agree to have the buildings and improvements on the lands ceded by the first article of this treaty valued. To cause a similar amount in value, laid out in building, clearing and fencing ground, for the use of the Indians, on such place or places as their chiefs may select, and that the Indians have peaceable possession of their houses and improvements, on the lands ceded in the first article of this treaty, until the improvements are made as provided for in this article.

United States to pay for horses stolen by the whites.

ARTICLE 7. The United States agree to pay the Miami Indians fifteen hundred dollars, for horses heretofore stolen from them by the whites.

Patents in fee simple to issue to persons named.

ARTICLE 8. The United States agree to cause patents in fee simple to issue to the following named persons, for the several tracts of land attached to their names, granted to them by former treaties, to wit:

To Little Charley, for five sections of land, above the old village on the north side of Eel river, granted to him by treaty of Wabash of 1826.

To Laronture's daughter, for one section of land on the Maumee river, granted to her by treaty of Wabash of 1826.

To To-pee ah, son of Francis Lafontain, for one section, granted him by treaty of St. Mary's of 1818.

To Met-chin-e-quea, for two sections of land granted him by treaty of Wabash of 1826, at the old town on Eel river.

To Francis Godfroy, for four sections of land on the Salamany river, granted him at treaty of St. Mary's of 1818, being the residue of what he now holds of said grant.

A quarter section of land to be granted to Hugh Hanna.

ARTICLE 9. There shall be granted to Hugh Hanna, one quarter section of land, in lieu of one selected and not approved on the grant made to Guire at the treaty of Wabash of 1826, (Hanna having purchased of Guire,) the selection to be made under the direction of the President of the United States.

Grants of land to persons named.

Schedule of grants referred to in the 3d Article.

To Francis Godfroy one section of land at the lower line of the five mile reserve on the Wabash river, to be located adjoining the town of Peru; one half section to be located on said Wabash river, opposite his trading house, and one half section to be located on that part of the big reserve southwest side the Wabash, above and adjoining the two sections granted to John B. Richardville; and one half section back and adjoining the one granted to said John B. Richardville, opposite the mouth of Eel river.

To To-pe-ah, one section of land, commencing one mile from the northeast corner of the ten mile reserve, opposite the mouth of Aboit river, (granted by treaty of St. Mary's of 1818,) thence south one mile, thence west one mile, thence north one mile, thence east to the place of beginning.

To Wa-pa-se-pah, son of Lafontain, one section of land west and adjoining the one to To-pee-ah.

To Ne-ah-long-quaw, two sections of land, west and adjoining the one to Wa-pa-se-pah.

To A-saw-som-ma-quah, or Susan, one section of land, west and adjoining the two to Ne-ah-long-quaw.

To Poqua, son of Francis Godfroy, one half section, west and adjoining the one to Susan.

To Francis Godfroy, one half section of land, west and adjoining the one to Poqua.

To Paul Longlois, one section of land on the Wabash river, to include his field.

To Chappene one section of land, to include Racoon village, commencing two poles west of the grave yard northwest of the village, thence on an easterly direction to river About, thence with said river until it strikes the reserve line, thence with said line for quantity to include within the bounds one section of land; also, one other section of land, west and adjoining the half section granted to Francis Godfroy on the ten mile reserve.

To John B. Richardville, principal chief of the Miami tribe, one section of land on the five mile reserve, opposite the mouth of the Mississineway river, to include the improvement made by Joseph Richardville, deceased; also, one quarter section of land on the Wabash river, at the upper part of the five mile reserve; also, two sections of land on the big reserve, commencing on the Wabash river, opposite the mouth of Eel river, running up said river two miles, thence back for quantity so as to include within the bounds two sections of land.

To Mac-keh-teh-maug-guaw, or Black Loon, one section of land to be located on the Wabash river, at the upper line of that part of the big reserve ceded by the first article of this treaty.

To Chin-gua-qua, or Duck, one section of land to be located on said Wabash river, below and adjoining the one granted to Black Loon.

To O-san-dear, one section of land back and adjoining the one granted to Black Loon.

To Wa-pa-pe-she, one section of land back and adjoining the one granted to Duck.

To Peter Longlois, one half section of land to be located at a point on Wildcat where the old trace from Mississineway to Thorntown crosses the same.

To the sons of Dupee, one half section of land to be located on the reserve at Racoon village, to be located under the direction of the President of the United States.

To Peter Guier, one half section of land, to be located back of the one granted to Wa-pa-pe-she.

To Waw-pee-mung-quah, one section of land on the ten mile reserve adjoining the one to Chappene.

To Ca-ta-ke-mon-gua, daughter of Godfroy and Angelique, one section of land to be located adjoining the one to Wau-pee-mung-guah.

To Rebecca Hackley, one quarter section of land, to be located under the direction of the President of the United States.

And whereas the assent of the Chiefs and Warriors of the said tribe of Indians, required by the aforesaid resolution of the Senate, has been given to the said amendment; which assent is as follows, viz:

We the chiefs and warriors of the Miami nation of Indians, residing in the State of Indiana, having assembled in general council and having seen and duly examined each and all of the amendments, made by the Senate in the treaty negotiated between said nation and Gen. William Marshall commissioner on the part of the United States, on the 23d of October, 1834, and the same having been fully and clearly explained to us, do hereby give our assent to each and all of them, in compliance with the requisition of the resolution of the Senate of the twelfth of October, 1837, advising and consenting to the ratification of said treaty.

In testimony whereof we have hereunto affixed our signatures this tenth day of November, A. D. 1837.

Me-shin-go-mask-a,	Wa-we-esse,
Wa-pa-pen-shaw,	Flat Belly,
Ne-con-saw,	Ne-con-sau,
Little Charley,	Ca-tah-ke-mun-quah,
Chen-qua-quah,	Ma-gure-ca,
Pe-wa-pe-ah,	Che-cho-wah,
O-san-dear,	Ne-con-saw,
Shappeen,	Ma-con-saw,
Keel-swa,	Little Maquri-ca,
Wa-pe-shin-wuah,	Shappen-do-ce-ah,
Ne-ah-lin-quah,	Ne-pa-wa,
Co-wy-sey,	Pin-daw-lin-shau,
To-pe-ah,	Men-na-tuo,
Ma-wuah-co-nah,	Poqua,
Me-ca-to-mun-quah,	Min-se-quah,
Wa-pe-mun-quah,	

In presence of—

A. C. Pepper, Indian agent.
Allen Hamilton.
F. Comparet, interpreter.
Lucien P. Ferny.

To the Indian names are subjoined marks.

TREATY WITH THE POTAWATOMI, 1834.

Dec. 4, 1834.

7 Stat., 467.
Proclamation, Mar. 16, 1835.

Articles of a Treaty, made and concluded at a camp, on Lake Max-ee-nie-kue-kee, in the State of Indiana, between William Marshall, Commissioner on the part of the United States, and Com-o-za, a Chief of the Potawattimie tribe of Indians and his band, on the fourth day of December, in the year eighteen hundred and thirty-four.

Cession to the United States.

ART. 1. The above named chief and his band hereby cede to the United States, the two sections of land reserved for them by the 2d article of the treaty between the United States and the Pottawattimie Indians on Tippecanoe river on the 26th day of October, in the year eighteen hundred and thirty-two.

Possession to be given within three years.

ART. 2. The above named chief and his band agree to yield peaceable possession of said sections within three years from the date of the ratification of said treaty of eighteen hundred and thirty-two.

Payment in goods.

ART. 3. In consideration of the cession aforesaid the United States stipulate to pay the above named chief and his band the sum of four hundred dollars in goods at the signing of this treaty, and an annuity of four hundred dollars for one year, the receipt of which former sum of (four hundred dollars in goods) is hereby acknowledged.

Treaty binding when ratified.

ART. 4. This treaty shall be binding upon both parties, from the date of its ratification by the President and Senate of the United States.

In testimony whereof, the said William Marshall, commissioner, on the part of the United States, and the above named chief and head men, for themselves and their band, have hereunto subscribed their names, the day and year above written.

William Marshall,
Com-o-za, his x mark,
Ah-ke-pah-am-sa, his x mark,
Nee-so-aw-quet, his x mark,
Paw-pee, his x mark.

Witnesses:
J. B. Duret, secretary to commission,
Cyrus Taber,
Joseph Barron, interpreter.

TREATY WITH THE POTAWATOMI, 1834.

Articles of a Treaty made and concluded at a camp on Tippecanoe river, in the State of Indiana, between William Marshall, Commissioner on the part of the United States and Muck Rose, a Chief of the Potawattamie tribe of Indians, and his band, on the tenth day of December, in the year eighteen hundred and thirty-four.

Dec. 10, 1834.

7 Stat., 467.
Proclamation, Mar. 16, 1835.

ART. 1. The above named chief and his band hereby cede to the United States, six sections of land reserved for them by the second article of the treaty between the United States and the Pottawattamie Indians on Tippecanoe river, on the twenty-sixth day of October, in the year, eighteen hundred and thirty-two. *Lands ceded to United States.*

ART. 2. The above named chief and his band agree to yield peaceable possession of the said sections of land to the United States within three years from the date of the ratification of said treaty of eighteen hundred and thirty-two. *Possession to be given within three years.*

ART. 3. In consideration of the cession aforesaid the United States stipulate to pay to the above named chief and his band, four hundred dollars in goods at the signing of this treaty, and an annuity of one thousand dollars for two years, the receipt of which former sum of (four hundred dollars in goods) is hereby acknowledged. *Consideration therefor.*

ART. 4. This treaty shall be binding upon both parties from the date of its ratification by the President and Senate of the United States. *Treaty binding when ratified.*

In testimony whereof, the said William Marshall, commissioner on the part of the United States, and the above named chief and his band, have hereunto subscribed their names the day and year above written.

William Marshall,
Muck Rose, his x mark,
Paw-tisse, his x mark,

Sis-see-yaw, his x mark,
Wau-pish-shaw, his x mark,
Koo-tah-waun-nay, his x mark.

Witnesses:

J. B. Duret, secretary,
Cyrus Taber,
Henry Ossem, interpreter,
J. B. Boure, interpreter,

John B. Intrais,
Joseph Barron, principal interpreter,
Jesse Vermilya.

TREATY WITH THE POTAWATOMI, 1834.

Dec. 16, 1834.

7 Stat., 468.
Proclamation, Mar.
16, 1835.

Articles of a treaty, made and concluded at the Potawattimie mills, in the State of Indiana, on the sixteenth day of December, in the year of our Lord one thousand eight hundred and thirty-four, between William Marshall Commissioner on the part of the United States and the Chiefs, headmen, and warriors of the Potawattamis Indians.

Land ceded to the United States.

ARTICLE 1st. The chiefs, head men and warriors aforesaid agree to cede to the United States their title and interest to a reservation made to them at the treaty on the Tippecanoe river on the 27th day of October 1832 of two sections of land to include their mills on said river.

Consideration therefor.

ART. 2nd. In consideration of the cession aforesaid the United States agree to pay the Potawattimie Indians, at the payment of their annuities in 1835, the sum of seven hundred dollars in cash, and pay their just debts agreeably to a schedule hereunto annexed, amounting to nine hundred dollars.

Miller to be discontinued.

ART. 3. The miller provided for by the 3rd article of the treaty with the Potawattimie tribe of Indians on the sixteenth day of October, in the year eighteen hundred and twenty-six, is not to be supported by the United States, and to cease from and after the signing of this treaty.

Treaty binding when ratified.

ART. 4. This treaty shall be binding upon both parties, from the date of its ratification by the President and Senate of the United States.

In testimony whereof, the said William Marshall, commissioner on the part of the United States, and the chiefs, head men, and warriors of the Potawatamie tribe of Indians, have hereunto subscribed their names, the day and year above written.

William Marshall,	Pam-bo-go, his x mark,
Ash-kum, his x mark,	Kaw-kawk-kay, his x mark,
Ku-waw-nay, his x mark,	Wi-aw-koos-say, his x mark,
Pash-po-ho, his x mark,	Te-kam-a-say, his x mark,
Che-quawm-a-kaw-ko, his x mark,	Sea-Coas, his x mark,
Nas-waw-kay, his mark,	Waw-paw-kue, his x mark,
Quaush-quaw, his x mark,	Mi-shaw-bo, his x mark,
Meno-quet, his x mark,	Te-quaw-kit, his x mark,
Kin-koash, his mark,	Waw-pe-no-quah, his x mark,
No-law-kah, his x mark,	We-wus-sah, his x mark,
Me-no-mi-nee, his x mark,	O-kah-maul, his x mark,
Mas-kah-tah-mo-ah, his x mark,	I-you-way, his x mark,
Pee-pis-kah, his x mark,	Mat-chis-saw, his mark.

Witnesses:
   J. B. Duret, secretary,
   Cyrus Taber,
   J. B. Boure, interpreter,
   Joseph Barron, principal interpreter.

It is agreed that the United States will satisfy the claims mentioned in the following schedule as provided for in the second article of the foregoing treaty.—viz:
   To J. B. Duret, four hundred dollars.
   To Cyrus Taber, one hundred dollars.
   To Ewing Walker & Co., three hundred dollars.
   To Cyrus Vigus, one hundred dollars.

TREATY WITH THE POTAWATOMI, 1834.

Articles of a treaty made and concluded at the Indian Agency, Logans-port, Indiana, between William Marshall, Commissioner on the part of the United States and Mota, a chief of the Potawattimie tribe of Indians, and his band on the 17th day of December, in the year eighteen hundred and thirty-four.

Dec. 17, 1834.

7 Stat., 469.
Proclamation, Mar. 16, 1835.

ART. 1. The above-named Chief and his band hereby cede to the United States the four sections of land reserved for them by the second article of the treaty between the United States and the Potawattimie Indians on the twenty-seventh day of October in the year eighteen hundred and thirty-two.

Land ceded to the United States.

ART. 2. The above named chief and head men and their band, do hereby agree to yield peaceable possession of said sections, and to remove, with their families, to a country provided for them by the United States, west of the Mississippi river, within three years or less from the date of the ratification of said treaty of eighteen hundred and thirty-two.

Possession to be given within three years.

ART. 3. The United States, in consideration of the cession, made in the first article of this treaty, do hereby stipulate to remove the above named chief and headmen and their bands to the new country provided for them, and to furnish them either goods, farming utensils or other articles necessary for them, agreeably to the provisions of the fifth article of the treaty of October twenty-sixth, eighteen hundred and thirty-two.

Consideration therefor.

ART. 4. The United States further stipulate to pay to the above named chief, and head men and their bands, the sum of six hundred and eighty dollars in goods, at the signing of this treaty, and the further sum of six hundred dollars in cash at the payment of their annuities in 1835, the receipt of which former sum of (six hundred and eighty dollars in goods) is hereby acknowledged.

$680 to be paid in goods.

ART. 5. This treaty shall be binding upon both parties, from the date of its ratification by the Senate of the United States.

Treaty binding when ratified.

In testimony whereof, the said William Marshall, commissioner on the part of the United States, and the above named chief and head men, for themselves and their bands, have hereunto subscribed their names, the day and year above written.

William Marshall,
Mo-ta, his x mark,
Ta-puck-koo-nee-nee, his x mark,
Shah-yauc-koo-pay, his x mark,
To-tauk-gaus, his x mark,
Poke-kee-to, his x mark,
Waus-no-guen, his x mark,
Ship-pe-she-waw-no, his x mark,
Mtaw-mah, his x mark,
Ship-pe-shick-quah, his x mark,

Aw-sho-kish-ko-quah, his x mark,
Pash-kum-ma-ko-quah, his x mark,
Me-naun-quah, his x mark,
Pee-nas-quah, his x mark,
Mee-shah-ke-to-quah, his x mark,
Waw-pee-shah-me-to-quah, his x mark,
Mat-che-ke-no-quah, his x mark,
Wau-waus-sa-mo-quah, his x mark,
Saw-moke-quaw, his x mark.

Witnesses:
　J. B. Duret, secretary to commissioner,
　Jesse Vermilya,
　Joseph Barron, interpreter.

TREATY WITH THE CADDO, 1835.

July 1, 1835.

7 Stat., 470.
Proclamation, Feb.
2, 1836.

Articles of a treaty made at the Agency-house in the Caddo nation and State of Louisiana, on the first day of July in the year of our Lord one thousand eight hundred and thirty-five, between Jehiel Brooks, Commissioner on the part of the United States, and the Chiefs, head men, and Warriors of the Caddo nation of Indians.

Lands ceded to the United States.

ARTICLE I. The chiefs, head men, and warriors of the said nation agree to cede and relinquish to the United States all their land contained in the following boundaries: to-wit—

Boundaries.

Bounded on the west by the north and south line which separates the said United States from the Republic of Mexico, between the Sabine and Red rivers wheresoever the same shall be defined and acknowledged to be by the two governments. On the north and east by the Red river from the point where the said north and south boundary line shall intersect the Red river whether it be in the Territory of Arkansas or the State of Louisiana, following the meanders of the said river down to its junction with the Pascagoula bayou. On the south by the said Pascagoula bayou to its junction with the Bayou Pierre, by said bayou to its junction with Bayou Wallace, by said bayou and Lake Wallace to the mouth of the Cypress bayou thence up said bayou to the point of its intersection with the first mentioned north and south line following the meanders of the said water-courses: But if the said Cypress bayou be not clearly definable so far then from a point which shall be definable by a line due west till it intersects the said first mentioned north and south boundary line, be the content of land within said boundaries more or less.

Indians to remove within one year.

ARTICLE II. The said chiefs head men and warriors of the said nation do voluntarily relinquish their possession to the territory of land aforesaid and promise to remove at their own expense out of the boundaries of the United States and the territories belonging and appertaining thereto within the period of one year from and after the signing of this treaty and never more return to live settle or establish themselves as a nation tribe or community of people within the same.

Money, etc., to be paid for cession.

ARTICLE III. In consideration of the aforesaid cession relinquishment and removal it is agreed that the said United States shall pay to the said nation of Caddo Indians the sums in goods, horses, and money hereinafter mentioned, to wit—

Thirty thousand dollars to be paid in goods, and horses, as agreed upon to be delivered on the signing of this treaty.

Ten thousand dollars in money to be paid within one year from the first day of September next.

Ten thousand dollars, *per annum* in money for the four years next following so as to make the whole sum paid and payable eighty thousand dollars.

An agent of the nation to be appointed by them.

ARTICLE IV. It is further agreed that the said Caddo nation of Indians shall have authority to appoint an agent or attorney in fact, resident within the United States for the purpose of receiving for them from the said United States all of the annuities stated in this treaty as the same shall become due to be paid to their said agent or attorney in fact at such place or places within the said United States as shall be agreed on between him and the proper Officer of the Government of the United States.

Treaty binding when ratified.

ARTICLE V. This treaty, after the same shall have been ratified and confirmed by the President and Senate of the United States, shall be binding on the contracting parties.

In testimony whereof, the said Jehiel Brooks, commissioner as aforesaid, and the chiefs, head men, and warriors of the said nation of

Indians, have hereunto set their hands, and affixed their seals at the place and on the day and year above written.

J. Brooks,	[L. S.]	Tiohtow, his x mark,	[L. S.]
Tarshar, his x mark,	[L. S.]	Tehowahinno, his x mark,	[L. S.]
Tsauninot, his x mark,	[L. S.]	Tooeksoach, his x mark,	[L. S.]
Satiownhown, his x mark,	[L. S.]	Tehowainia, his x mark,	[L. S.]
Tennehinum, his x mark,	[L. S.]	Sauninow, his x mark,	[L. S.]
Oat, his x mark,	[L. S.]	Saunivoat, his x mark,	[L. S.]
Tinnowin, his x mark,	[L. S.]	Highahidock, his x mark,	[L. S.]
Chowabah, his x mark,	[L. S.]	Mattan, his x mark,	[L. S.]
Kianhoon, his x mark,	[L. S.]	Towabinneh, his x mark,	[L. S.]
Tiatesum, his x mark,	[L. S.]	Aach, his x mark,	[L. S.]
Tehowawinow, his x mark,	[L. S.]	Sookiantow, his x mark,	[L. S.]
Tewinnum, his x mark,	[L. S.]	Sohone, his x mark,	[L. S.]
Kardy, his x mark,	[L. S.]	Ossinse, his x mark,	[L. S.]

In presence of—

T. J. Harrison, captain, Third Regiment Infantry, commanding detachment,
J. Bonnell, first lieutenant, Third Regiment U. S. Infantry,
J. P. Frile, brevet second lieutenant, Third Regiment U. S. Infantry,

D. M. Heard, M. D., acting assistant surgeon U. S. Army,
Isaac Williamson,
Henry Queen,
John W. Edwards, interpreter.

Agreeably to the stipulations in the third article of the treaty, there have been purchased at the request of the Caddo Indians, and delivered to them, goods and horses to the amount of thirty thousand dollars.

As evidence of the purchase and delivery as aforesaid, under the direction of the commissioner, and that the whole of the same have been received by the said Indians, the said commissioner, Jehiel Brooks, and the undersigned, chiefs and head men of the whole Caddo nation of Indians, have hereunto set their hands, and affixed their seals, the third day of July, in the year of our Lord one thousand eight hundred and thirty-five.

J. Brooks,	[L. S.]
Tarshar, his x mark,	[L. S.]
Tsauninot, his x mark,	[L. S.]
Satiownhown, his x mark,	[L. S.]
Oat, his x mark,	[L. S.]
Ossinse, his x mark,	[L. S.]
Tiohtow, his x mark,	[L. S.]
Chowawanow, his x mark,	[L. S.]

n presence of—
Larkin Edwards,
Henry Queen,
John W. Edwards, interpreter,
James Finnerty.

Articles supplementary to the treaty made at the agency house in the Caddo nation and State of Louisiana on the first day of July, one thousand eight hundred and thirty-five between Jehiel Brooks Commissioner on the part of the United States, and the Chiefs head men and Warriors of the Caddo nation of Indians concluded at the same place, and on the same day between the said Commissioner on the part of the United States and the Chiefs Head men and Warriors of the said nation of Indians, to wit—

July 1, 1835.

7 Stat., 472.

WHEREAS the said nation of Indians did in the year one thousand eight hundred and one, give to one François Grappe and to his three sons then born and still living, named Jacques, Dominique and Belthazar, for reasons stated at the time and repeated in a memorial which the said nation addressed to the President of the United States in the month of January last, one league of land to each, in accordance with the Spanish custom of granting land to individuals. That the chiefs

Preamble.

and head men, with the knowledge and approbation of the whole Caddo people did go with the said François Grappe, accompanied by a number of white men, who were invited by the said chiefs and head men to be present as witnesses, before the Spanish authority at Natchitoches, and then and there did declare their wishes touching the said donation of land to the said Grappe and his three sons, and did request the same to be written out in form and ratified and confirmed by the proper authorities agreeably to law.

And WHEREAS Larkin Edwards has resided for many years to the present time in the Caddo Nation—was a long time their true and faithful interpreter, and though poor he has never sent the Red man away from his door hungry. He is now old and unable to support himself by manual labor, and since his employment as their interpreter has ceased possesses no adequate means by which to live: Now therefore—

Grant by Indians to F. Grappe, confirmed. ARTICLE I. It is agreed that the legal representatives of the said François Grappe deceased and his three sons Jacques, Dominique, and Belthazar Grappe, shall have their right to the said four leagues of land reserved to them and their heirs and assigns for ever. The said land to be taken out of the lands ceded to the United States by the said Caddo Nation of Indians as expressed in the treaty to which this article is supplementary. And the said four leagues of land shall be laid off in one body in the southeast corner of their lands ceded as aforesaid, and bounded by the Red river four leagues and by the Pascagoula bayou one league, running back for quantity from each, so as to contain four square leagues of land, in conformity with the boundaries established and expressed in the original Deed of Gift made by the said Caddo nation of Indians to the said François Grappe and his three sons Jacques, Dominique, and Belthazar Grappe.

Reservation for Larkin Edwards. ARTICLE II. And it is further agreed that there shall be reserved to Larkin Edwards his heirs and assigns for ever one section of land to be selected out of the lands ceded to the United States by the said nation of Indians as expressed in the treaty to which this article is supplementary in any part thereof not otherwise appropriated by the provisions contained in these supplementary articles.

Articles binding when ratified. ARTICLE III. These supplementary articles, or either of them, after the same shall have been ratified and confirmed by the President and Senate of the United States, shall be binding on the contracting parties, otherwise to be void and of no effect upon the validity of the original treaty to which they are supplementary.

In testimony whereof, the said Jehiel Brooks, commissioner as aforesaid, and the chiefs, head men, and warriors of the said nation of Indians, have hereunto set their hands and affixed their seals at the place, and on the day and year above written.

J. Brooks,	[L. S.]	Tiohtow, his x mark,	[L. S.]
Tarshar, his x mark,	[L. S.]	Tehawahinno, his x mark,	[L. S.]
Tsauninot, his x mark,	[L. S.]	Toackooch, his x mark,	[L. S.]
Satiownhown, his x mark,	[L. S.]	Tchowainin, his x mark,	[L. S.]
Tinnehinan, his x mark,	[L. S.]	Sanninow, his x mark,	[L. S.]
Oat, his x mark,	[L. S.]	Sauninot, his x mark,	[L. S.]
Tinnowin, his x mark,	[L. S.]	Hiahidock, his x mark,	[L. S.]
Chowabah, his x mark,	[L. S.]	Mattan, his x mark,	[L. S.]
Kianhoon, his x mark,	[L. S.]	Towahinnek, his x mark,	[L. S.]
Tiatesun, his x mark,	[L. S.]	Aach, his x mark,	[L. S.]
Tehowawinow, his x mark,	[L. S.]	Soakiantow, his x mark,	[L. S.]
Tewinnun, his x mark,	[L. S.]	Sohone, his x mark,	[L. S.]
Kardy, his x mark,	[L. S.]	Ossinse, his x mark.	[L. S.]

In presence of—

T. J. Harrison, captain, Third Regiment, commanding detachment.
J. Bonnell, first lieutenant, Third Regiment U. S. Infantry.
G. P. Field, brevet second lieutenant, Third Regiment U. S. Infantry.

D. M. Heard, M. D., acting assistant surgeon, U. S. Army.
Isaac C. Williamson,
Henry Queen,
John W. Edwards, interpreter.

TREATY WITH THE COMANCHE, ETC., 1835.

Treaty with the Comanche and Witchetaw Indians and their associated Bands.

Aug. 24, 1835.

7 Stat., 474.
Proclamation, May 19, 1836.

For the purpose of establishing and perpetuating peace and friendship between the United States of America and the Comanche and Witchetaw nations, and their associated bands or tribes of Indians, and between these nations or tribes, and the Cherokee Muscogee, Choctaw, Osage, Seneca and Quapaw nations or tribes of Indians, the President of the United States has, to accomplish this desirable object, and to aid therein, appointed Governor M. Stokes, M. Arbuckle Brigdi.-Genl. United States army, and F. W. Armstrong, Actg. Supdt. Western Territory, commissioners on the part of the United States; and the said Governor M. Stokes and M. Arbuckle, Brigdi. Genl. United States army, with the chiefs and representatives of the Cherokee, Muscogee, Choctaw, Osage, Seneca, and Quapaw nations or tribes of Indians, have met the chiefs, warriors, and representatives of the tribes first above named at Camp Holmes, on the eastern border of the Grand Prairie, near the Canadian river, in the Muscogee nation, and after full deliberation, the said nations or tribes have agreed with the United States, and with one another upon the following articles:

ARTICLE 1. There shall be perpetual peace and friendship between all the citizens of the United States of America, and all the individuals composing the Comanche and Witchetaw nations and their associated bands or tribes of Indians, and between these nations or tribes and the Cherokee, Muscogee, Choctaw, Osage, Seneca and Quapaw nations or tribes of Indians. *Peace and friendship.*

ARTICLE 2. Every injury or act of hostility by one or either of the contracting parties on the other, shall be mutually forgiven and forever forgot. *Injuries, etc., forgiven.*

ARTICLE 3. There shall be a free and friendly intercourse between all the contracting parties hereto, and it is distinctly understood and agreed by the Comanche and Witchetaw nations and their associated bands or tribes of Indians, that the citizens of the United States are freely permitted to pass and repass through their settlements or hunting ground without molestation or injury on their way to any of the provinces of the Republic of Mexico, or returning therefrom, and that each of the nations or tribes named in this article, further agree to pay the full value for any injury their people may do to the goods or property of the citizens of the United States taken or destroyed, when peaceably passing through the country they inhabit, or hunt in, or elsewhere. And the United States hereby guaranty to any Indian or Indians of either of the said Comanche or Witchetaw nations, and their associated bands or tribes of Indians, a full indemnification for any horses or other property which may be stolen from them: *Provided*, that the property so stolen cannot be recovered, and that sufficient proof is produced that it was actually stolen by a citizen of the United States, and within the limits thereof. *Free passage through the Indian country. Indemnity for horses, etc., stolen. Proviso.*

ARTICLE 4. It is understood and agreed by all the nations or tribes of Indians parties to this treaty, that each and all of the said nations or tribes have free permission to hunt and trap in the Great Prairie west of the Cross Timber, to the western limits of the United States. *Hunting ground.*

ARTICLE 5. The Comanche and Witchetaw nations and their associated bands or tribes of Indians, severally agree and bind themselves to pay full value for any injury their people may do to the goods or other property of such traders as the President of the United States may place near to their settlements or hunting ground for the purpose of trading with them. *Injuries to goods, etc., to be paid for by Indians.*

Other Indians on their grounds not to be molested.

ARTICLE 6. The Comanche and Witchetaw nations and their associated bands or tribes of Indians, agree, that in the event any of the red people belonging to the nations or tribes residing south of the Missouri river and west of the State of Missouri, not parties to this treaty, should visit their towns or be found on their hunting ground, that they will treat them with kindness and friendship and do no injury to them in any way whatever.

Peace to be preserved.

ARTICLE 7. Should any difficulty hereafter unfortunately arise between any of the nations or tribes of Indians parties hereunto, in consequence of murder, the stealing of horses, cattle, or other cause, it is agreed that the other tribes shall interpose their good offices to remove such difficulties, and also that the Government of the United States may take such measures as they may deem proper to effect the same object, and see that full justice is done to the injured party.

Presents to be given to the Indians.

ARTICLE 8. It is agreed by the commissioners of the United States, that in consequence of the Comanche and Witchetaw nations and their associated bands or tribes of Indians having freely and willingly entered into this treaty, and it being the first they have made with the United States or any of the contracting parties, that they shall receive presents immediately after signing, as a donation from the United States; nothing being asked from these nations or tribes in return, except to remain at peace with the parties hereto, which their own good and that of their posterity require.

Relations with Mexico.

ARTICLE 9. The Commanche and Witchetaw nations and their associated bands or tribes, of Indians, agree, that their entering into this treaty shall in no respect interrupt their friendly relations with the Republic of Mexico, where they all frequently hunt and the Comanche nation principally inhabit; and it is distinctly understood that the Government of the United States desire that perfect peace shall exist between the nations or tribes named in this article and the said republic.

Obligatory when ratified.

ARTICLE 10. This treaty shall be obligatory on the nations or tribes parties hereto from and after the date hereof, and on the United States from and after its ratification by the Government thereof.

Done, and signed, and sealed at Camp Holmes, on the eastern border of the Grand Prairie, near the Canadian river, in the Muscogee nation, this twenty-fourth day of August, one thousand eight hundred and thirty-five, and of the independence of the United States the sixtieth.

Montfort Stokes, [L. S.]	Ettah, or the gun, his x mark, [L. S.]
M. Arbuckle, Brigadier-General U. S. Army, [L. S.]	Tennowikah, or the boy who was soon a man, his x mark, [L. S.]
Comanches:	Kumaquoi, or the woman who cuts buffalo meat, his x mark, [L. S.]
Ishacoly, or the wolf, his x mark, [L. S.]	Taqquanno, or the amorous man, his x mark, [L. S.]
Queenashano, or the war eagle, his x mark, [L. S.]	Kowa, or the stinking tobacco box, his x mark, [L. S.]
Tabaqueena, or the big eagle, his x mark, [L. S.]	Soko, or the old man, his x mark, [L. S.]
Pohowetowshah, or the brass man, his x mark, [L. S.]	Witchetaws:
Shabbakasha, or the roving wolf, his x mark, [L. S.]	Kanostowah, or the man who don't speak, his x mark, [L. S.]
Neraquassi, or the yellow horse, his x mark, [L. S.]	Kosharokah, or the man who marries his wife twice, his x mark, [L. S.]
Toshapappy, or the white hare, his x mark, [L. S.]	Terrykatowatix, the riding chief, his x mark, [L. S.]
Pahohsareya, or the broken arm, his x mark, [L. S.]	Tahdaydy, or the traveller, his x mark, [L. S.]
Pahkah, or the man who draws the bow, his x mark, [L. S.]	Hahkahpillush, or the drummer, his x mark, [L. S.]
Witsitony, or he who sucks quick, his x mark, [L. S.]	Lachkah, or the first man in four battles, his x mark; [L. S.]
Leahwiddikah, or one who stirs up water, his x mark, [L. S.]	Learhehash, or the man who weans children too soon, his x mark, [L. S.]
Esharsotsiki, or the sleeping wolf, his x mark, [L. S.]	Lachhardich, or the man who sees things done in the wrong way, his x mark, [L. S.]
Pahtrisula, or the dog, his x mark, [L. S.]	

Noccuttardaditch, or the man who tries to excel the head chief, his x mark, [L. S.]
Katardedwadick, or the man who killed an enemy in the water, his x mark, [L. S.]
Losshah, or the twin, his x mark, [L. S.]
Taytsaaytah, or the ambitious adulterer, his x mark, [L. S.]
Tokaytah, or the summer, his x mark, [L. S.]
Musshakratsatady, or the man with the dog skin cap, his x mark, [L. S.]
Kipsh, or the man with one side of his head shaved, his x mark, [L. S.]

Cherokees:
Dutch, his x mark, [L. S.]
David Melton, his x mark, [L. S.]
Muscogees:
Roley McIntosh, his x mark, [L. S.]
Chilly McIntosh, [L. S.]
Cho-co-te-tuston-nogu, or marshal of the Cho-co-te-clan, his x mark, [L. S.]
Tus-ca-ne-ha, or the marshal, his x mark, [L. S.]
Tusly Harjoe, or crazy town, his x mark, [L. S.]
Alexander Lasley, his x mark, [L. S.]
Neha Harjoe, or crazy marshal, his x mark, [L. S.]
Tustunucke Harjoe, or crazy warrior, his x mark, [L. S.]
Powes Emarlo, or marshal of Powes clan, his x mark, [L. S.]
Cosa Yehola, or marshal of Cosa clan, his x mark, [L. S.]
Powes Yehola, or marshal of Powes clan, his x mark, [L. S.]
Toma Yehola, or marshal of Toma clan, his x mark, [L. S.]
Cosado Harjoe, or crazy Cosada, his x mark, [L. S.]
Neha Harjoe, or crazy marshal, his x mark, [L. S.]
Cosada Tustonnogee, or the Cosada warrior, his x mark, [L. S.]
Octiyachee Yehola, or marshal of Octiyachee clan, his x mark, [L. S.]
Nulthcup Tustonnogee, or the middle warrior, his x mark, [L. S.]
Ufala Harjoe, or crazy Ufala, his x mark, [L. S.]
Cholafixico, or a fox without a heart, his x mark, [L. S.]
Joseph Miller, his x mark, [L. S.]
Samuel Brown, his x mark, [L. S.]
Archi Kennard, his x mark, [L. S.]
Towannay, or the slender man, his x mark, [L. S.]
Saccasumky, or to be praised, his x mark, [L. S.]
Siah Hardridge, his x mark, [L. S.]
Warrior Hardridge, his x mark, [L. S.]
George Stedham, his x mark, [L. S.]
Itchhas Harjoe, or crazy beaver, his x mark, [L. S.]
Itchofake Harjoe, or crazy deer's heart, his x mark, [L. S.]
Satockhaky, or the broad side, his x mark, [L. S.]
Semehechee, or hide it away, his x mark, [L. S.]
Hoyane, or passed by, his x mark, [L. S.]

Melola, or waving, his x mark, [L. S.]
Mateter, or the man who missed it, his x mark, [L. S.]
Billy, his x mark, [L. S.]
Tuskia Harjoe, or crazy brave, his x mark, [L. S.]
Aussy, or the pursuer, his x mark, [L. S.]
Tohoithla, or standing upon, his x mark, [L. S.]
John Hambly, [L. S.]
K. Lewis, [L. S.]
John Wynn, [L. S.]
David McKillap, [L. S.]

Choctaws:
Musha-la-tubbee, or the man killer, his x mark, [L. S.]
Na-tuck-a-chee, or fair day, his x mark, [L. S.]
Par-chee-ste-cubbee, or the scalpholder, his x mark, [L. S.]
To-pi-a-chee-hubbee, or the painted face, his x mark, [L. S.]
Ya-cha-a-o-pay, or the leader of the warriors, his x mark, [L. S.]
Tus-qui-hola-tah, or the travelling warrior, his x mark, [L. S.]
Tic-eban-jo-hubbee, or the first for war, his x mark, [L. S.]
Nucke Stubbee, or the bullet that has killed, his x mark, [L. S.]
Toqua, or what you say, his x mark, [L. S.]
Po-sha-ma-stubbee, or the killer, his x mark, [L. S.]
Nuck-ho-ma-harjoe, or the bloody bullet, his x mark, [L. S.]
Thomas Mickie, his x mark, [L. S.]
Halam-be-sha, or the bat, his x mark, [L. S.]
Ok-chia, or life, his x mark, [L. S.]
Tus-ca-homa-madia, or the red warrior, his x mark, [L. S.]
Tun-up-me-a-moma, or the red man who has gone to war, his x mark, [L. S.]
Par-homa, or the red hoop, his x mark, [L. S.]
No-wah-ba, the man who kills the enemy when he meets him, his x mark, [L. S.]
Hisho-he-meta, or a young waiter, his x mark, [L. S.]
Cho-ma-la-tubbee, or the man who is sure his enemy is dead, his x mark, [L. S.]
Hokla-no-ma, the traveller in the town, his x mark, [L. S.]
William, his x mark, [L. S.]
Neasho Nubbee, he who knows where the enemy is killed, his x mark, [L. S.]
Jim, his x mark, [L. S.]
Eu-eck Harma, or the man who is never tired, his x mark, [L. S.]
Nat-la Homa, or the bloody man, his x mark, [L. S.]
Pia-o-sta, or to whoop four times, his x mark, [L. S.]
Pa-sha-oa-cubbee, or the man who puts his foot on the scalp, his x mark, [L. S.]
La-po-na, or the man who killed the enemy, his x mark, [L. S.]
A-mo-na-tubbee, or lying in wait to kill, his x mark, [L. S.]

A-fa-ma-tubbee, or the man who kills every thing he meets, his x mark, [L. S.]
Osages:
Fah-ha-la, or the leaping deer, his x mark, [L. S.]
Shone-ta-sah-ba, or the black dog, his x mark, [L. S.]
Wah-shin-pee-sha, or the wicked man, his x mark, [L. S.]
Tun-wan-le-he, or the town mover, his x mark, [L. S.]
Whoa-har-tee, or the war eagle, his x mark, [L. S.]
Me-tah-ne-gah, or the crazy robe, his x mark, [L. S.]
Wah-she-sho-hee, or the smart spirit, his x mark, [L. S.]
Ah-ke-tah, or the soldier, his x mark, [L. S.]
Weir-sah-bah-sha, or the hidden black, his x mark, [L. S.]
Ne-ko-jah, or the man hunter, his x mark, [L. S.]
Hor-tea-go, or like night, his x mark, [L. S.]
Wah-hah-tah-nee, or the fast runner, his x mark, [L. S.]
Wah-nah-shee, or the taker away, his x mark, [L. S.]
Ces-sah-ba, or the man in black, his x mark, [L. S.]
Es-kah-mar-ne, or the white horn, his x mark, [L. S.]
Kou-sah-she-la, or walking together, his x mark, [L. S.]
Tcha-to-kah, or the buffalo, his x mark, [L. S.]
O-ke-sah, or the man aside, his x mark, [L. S.]
Wah-she-wah-ra, or the stopper, his x mark, [L. S.]
Wah-ho-ba-shungee, or the idolater, his x mark, [L. S.]
Tone-ba-wah-tcha-la, or hard to look at the sun rising, his x mark, [L. S.]
Shoe-chem-mo-nee, or the elk whistler, his x mark, [L. S.]
Wash-kah-cha, or the tumbler, his x mark, [L. S.]
Wah-ha, or the Pawnee chief's namesake, his x mark, [L. S.]
Wah-kee-bah-nah, or the hard runner, his x mark, [L. S.]
War-tcha-sheen-gah, or the scalp-carrier, his x mark, [L. S.]
O-shaun-ga-tun-ga, or the big path, his x mark, [L. S.]
Wah-hee-no-pee, or the bone necklace, his x mark, [L. S.]
Lee-sap-kah-pee, or the man who missed his enemy, his x mark, [L. S.]
Wah-to-ke-hak, or raw meat, his x mark, [L. S.]
Wah-wah-shee, or quick runner, his x mark, [L. S.]
Kah-he-ka-saree, or chief killer, his x mark, [L. S.]
O-lash-tah-ba, or plate-licker, his x mark, [L. S.]
Ma-ne-nah-shee, or the walker, his x mark, [L. S.]

Shaun-ga-mo-nee, or the fall chief, his x mark, [L. S.]
Tee-sha-wah-ra, or dry grass, his x mark, [L. S.]
Ne-kah-wah-shee-tun-gah, or the brave spirit, his x mark, [L. S.]
Senecas:
Thomas Brant, his x mark, [L. S.]
Small Crout Spicer, his x mark, [L. S.]
Isaac, his x mark, [L. S.]
Mingo Carpenter, his x mark, [L. S.]
John Sky, his x mark, [L. S.]
Henry Smith, his x mark, [L. S.]
Little Town Spicer, his x mark, [L. S.]
Young Henry, his x mark, [L. S.]
Peter Pork, his x mark, [L. S.]
William Johnston, his x mark, [L. S.]
Big Bone, his x mark, [L. S.]
Big Isaac, his x mark, [L. S.]
Civil Jack, his x mark, [L. S.]
Ya-ga-ha, or the water in the apple, his x mark, [L. S.]
Cau-ya-que-neh, or the snow drift, his x mark, [L. S.]
Ya-ta-ato, or the little lake, his x mark, [L. S.]
Douglass, his x mark, [L. S.]
George Herring, his x mark, [L. S.]
Quapaws:
Hi-ka-toa, or the dry man, his x mark, [L. S.]
Wa-ga-de-tone, or the maggot, his x mark, [L. S.]
Wa-to-va, or the spider, his x mark, [L. S.]
Ca-ta-hah, or the tortoise, his x mark, [L. S.]
Ma-towa-wah-cota, or the dug out, his x mark, [L. S.]
Wa-go-dah-hou-kah, or the plume, his x mark, [L. S.]
Ma-com-pa, or the doctor of the nose, his x mark, [L. S.]
Cas-sa, or the black tortoise, his x mark, [L. S.]
Haw-tez-chee-ka, or the little cedar, his x mark, [L. S.]
Ma-so-goda-toah, or the hawk, his x mark, [L. S.]
Wa-ka-toa-nosa, or the standing man, his x mark, [L. S.]
Motosa, or the black bear, his x mark, [L. S.]
Mor-bre-tone, or the little hawk, his x mark, [L. S.]
Mar-to-ho-ga, or the white bear, his x mark, [L. S.]
To-se-ca-da, or he who shows his track, his x mark, [L. S.]
Tah-tah-ho-so, or the wind, his x mark, [L. S.]
Hi-da-khe-da-sa, or the panther eagle, his x mark, [L. S.]
O-tene-cah-chee-ka, or he who struck the enemy, his x mark, [L. S.]
Me-ki-wah-kotah, or the star, his x mark, [L. S.]
Ka-ti-mo-ne, or clear weather, his x mark, [L. S.]
Vet-he-ka-ne, or thunder, his x mark, [L. S.]
Ne-to-sa-mo-ne, or the black freshet, his x mark. [L. S.]

In presence of—

R. B. Mason, major of dragoons,	Augustine A. Chouteau,
G. Birch, major, U. S. Army,	John Hambly, United States interpreter
Francis Lee, captain, Seventh Infantry,	to the Creeks,
Samuel G. I. DeCamp, surgeon,	George Herron,
W. Seawell, lieutenant and aid de camp;	Leonard C. McPhail, assistant surgeon,
secretary to the commissioners,	U. S. Army,
Thomas B. Ballard,	Robert M. French.

TREATY WITH THE CHEROKEE, 1835.

Articles of a treaty, concluded at New Echota in the State of Georgia on the 29th day of Decr. 1835 by General William Carroll and John F. Schermerhorn commissioners on the part of the United States and the Chiefs Head Men and People of the Cherokee tribe of Indians.

Dec. 29, 1835.

7 Stat., 478.
Proclamation, May 23, 1836.

Preamble

WHEREAS the Cherokees are anxious to make some arrangements with the Government of the United States whereby the difficulties they have experienced by a residence within the settled parts of the United States under the jurisdiction and laws of the State Governments may be terminated and adjusted; and with a view to reuniting their people in one body and securing a permanent home for themselves and their posterity in the country selected by their forefathers without the territorial limits of the State sovereignties, and where they can establish and enjoy a government of their choice and perpetuate such a state of society as may be most consonant with their views, habits and condition; and as may tend to their individual comfort and their advancement in civilization.

And whereas a delegation of the Cherokee nation composed of Messrs. John Ross Richard Taylor Danl. McCoy Samuel Gunter and William Rogers with full power and authority to conclude a treaty with the United States did on the 28th day of February 1835 stipulate and agree with the Government of the United States to submit to the Senate to fix the amount which should be allowed the Cherokees for their claims and for a cession of their lands east of the Mississippi river, and did agree to abide by the award of the Senate of the United States themselves and to recommend the same to their people for their final determination.

And whereas on such submission the Senate advised "that a sum not exceeding five millions of dollars be paid to the Cherokee Indians for all their lands and possessions east of the Mississippi river."

And whereas this delegation after said award of the Senate had been made, were called upon to submit propositions as to its disposition to be arranged in a treaty which they refused to do, but insisted that the same "should be referred to their nation and there in general council to deliberate and determine on the subject in order to ensure harmony and good feeling among themselves."

And whereas a certain other delegation composed of John Ridge Elias Boudinot Archilla Smith S. W. Bell John West Wm. A. Davis and Ezekiel West, who represented that portion of the nation in favor of emigration to the Cherokee country west of the Mississippi entered into propositions for a treaty with John F. Schermerhorn commissioner on the part of the United States which were to be submitted to their nation for their final action and determination:

And whereas the Cherokee people, at their last October council at Red Clay, fully authorized and empowered a delegation or committee of twenty persons of their nation to enter into and conclude a treaty with the United States commissioner then present, *at that place or elsewhere* and as the people had good reason to believe that a treaty would then and there be made or at a subsequent council at New Echota which the commissioners it was well known and understood, were authorized and instructed to convene for said purpose; and since the said delegation have gone on to Washington city, with a view to close negotiations there, as stated by them notwithstanding they were officially informed by the United States commissioner that they would not be received by the President of the United States; and that the Government would transact no business of this nature with them, and that if a treaty was made it must be done here in the nation, where the delegation at Washington last winter *urged that it should be done for the purpose of promoting peace and harmony among the people;* and since these facts have also been corroborated to us by a communication recently received by the commissioner from the Government of the United States and read and explained to the people in open council and therefore believing said delegation can effect nothing and since our difficulties are daily increasing and our situation is rendered more and more precarious uncertain and insecure in consequence of the legislation of the States; and seeing no effectual way of relief, but in accepting the liberal overtures of the United States.

And whereas Genl William Carroll and John F. Schermerhorn were appointed commissioners on the part of the United States, with full power and authority to conclude a treaty with the Cherokees east and were directed by the President to convene the people of the nation in general council at New Echota and to submit said propositions to them with power and authority to vary the same so as to meet the views of the Cherokees in reference to its details.

And whereas the said commissioners did appoint and notify a general council of the nation to convene at New Echota on the 21st day of December 1835; and informed them that the commissioners would be prepared to make a treaty with the Cherokee people who should assemble there and those who did not come they should conclude gave their assent and sanction to whatever should be transacted at this council and the people having met in couneil according to said notice.

Therefore the following articles of a treaty are agreed upon and concluded between William Carroll and John F. Schermerhorn commissioners on the part of the United States and the chiefs and head men and people of the Cherokee nation in general council assembled this 29th day of Decr 1835.

Cherokees relinquish to United States all their lands east of the Mississippi.

ARTICLE 1. The Cherokee nation hereby cede relinquish and convey to the United States all the lands owned claimed or possessed by them east of the Mississippi river, and hereby release all their claims upon the United States for spoliations of every kind for and in consideration of the sum of five millions of dollars to be expended paid and invested in the manner stipulated and agreed upon in the following articles But as a question has arisen between the commissioners and the Cherokees whether the Senate in their resolution by which they advised "that a sum not exceeding five millions of dollars be paid to the Cherokee Indians for all their lands and possessions east of the Mississippi river" have included and made any allowance or consideration for claims for spoliations it is therefore agreed on the part of the United States that this question shall be again submitted to the Senate for their consideration and decision and if no allowance was made for spoliations that then an additional sum of three hundred thousand dollars be allowed for the same.

Treaty of May, 1828, and Feb.,1833, referred to.

ARTICLE 2. Whereas by the treaty of May 6th 1828 and the supplementary treaty thereto of Feb. 14th 1833 with the Cherokees west of the Mississippi the United States guarantied and secured to be conveyed by patent, to the Cherokee nation of Indians the following tract of country "Beginning at a point on the old western territorial line of Arkansas Territory being twenty-five miles north from the point where the territorial line crosses Arkansas river, thence running from said north point south on the said territorial line where the said territorial line crosses Verdigris river; thence down said Verdigris river to the Arkansas river; thence down said Arkansas to a point where a stone is placed opposite the east or lower bank of Grand river at its junction with the Arkansas; thence running south forty-four degrees west one mile; thence in a straight line to a point four miles northerly, from the mouth of the north fork of the Canadian; thence along the said four mile line to the Canadian; thence down the Canadian to the Arkansas; thence down the Arkansas to that point on the Arkansas where the eastern Choctaw boundary strikes said river and running thence with the western line of Arkansas Territory as now defined, to the southwest corner of Missouri; thence along the western Missouri line to the land assigned the Senecas; thence on the south line of the Senecas to Grand river; thence up said Grand river as far as the south line of the Osage reservation, extended if necessary; thence up and between said south Osage line extended west if necessary, and a line drawn due west from the point of beginning to a certain distance west, at which a line running north and south from said Osage line to said due west line will make seven millions of acres within the whole described boundaries. In addition to the seven millions of acres of land thus provided for and bounded, the United States further guaranty to the Cherokee nation a perpetual outlet west, and a free and unmolested use of all the country west of the western boundary of said seven millions of acres, as far west as the sovereignty of the United States and their right of soil extend:

Provided however That if the saline or salt plain on the western Proviso. prairie shall fall within said limits prescribed for said outlet, the right is reserved to the United States to permit other tribes of red men to get salt on said plain in common with the Cherokees; And letters patent shall be issued by the United States as soon as practicable for the land hereby guarantied."

And whereas it is apprehended by the Cherokees that in the above Additional land conveyed to the nation, etc. cession there is not contained a sufficient quantity of land for the accommodation of the whole nation on their removal west of the Mississippi the United States in consideration of the sum of five hundred thousand dollars therefore hereby covenant and agree to convey to the said Indians, and their descendants by patent, in fee simple the following additional tract of land situated between the west line of the State of Missouri and the Osage reservation beginning at the southeast corner of the same and runs north along the east line of the Osage lands fifty miles to the northeast corner thereof; and thence east to the west line of the State of Missouri; thence with said line south fifty miles; thence west to the place of beginning; estimated to contain eight hundred thousand acres of land; but it is expressly understood that if any of the lands assigned the Quapaws shall fall within the aforesaid bounds the same shall be reserved and excepted out of the lands above granted and a pro rata reduction shall be made in the price to be allowed to the United States for the same by the Cherokees.

ARTICLE 3. The United States also agree that the lands above ceded Further agreement. by the treaty of Feb. 14 1833, including the outlet, and those ceded by this treaty shall all be included in one patent executed to the Cherokee nation of Indians by the President of the United States according to the provisions of the act of May 28 1830. It is, however, agreed that 1830, ch. 148. the military reservation at Fort Gibson shall be held by the United States. But should the United States abandon said post and have no further use for the same it shall revert to the Cherokee nation. The United States shall always have the right to make and establish such Right to establish forts, etc. post and military roads and forts in any part of the Cherokee country, as they may deem proper for the interest and protection of the same and the free use of as much land, timber, fuel and materials of all kinds for the construction and support of the same as may be necessary; provided that if the private rights of individuals are interfered with, a just compensation therefor shall be made.

Osage titles to reservations to be extinguished.

ARTICLE 4. The United States also stipulate and agree to extinguish for the benefit of the Cherokees the titles to the reservations within their country made in the Osage treaty of 1825 to certain half-breeds and for this purpose they hereby agree to pay to the persons to whom the same belong or have been assigned or to their agents or guardians whenever they shall execute after the ratification of this treaty a satisfactory conveyance for the same, to the United States, the sum of fifteen thousand dollars according to a schedule accompanying this treaty of the relative value of the several reservations.

Missionary reservations to be paid for.

And whereas by the several treaties between the United States and the Osage Indians the Union and Harmony Missionary reservations which were established for their benefit are now situated within the country ceded by them to the United States; the former being situated in the Cherokee country and the latter in the State of Missouri. It is therefore agreed that the United States shall pay the American Board of Commissioners for Foreign Missions for the improvements on the same what they shall be appraised at by Capt. Geo. Vashon Cherokee sub-agent Abraham Redfield and A. P. Chouteau or such persons as the President of the United States shall appoint and the money allowed for the same shall be expended in schools among the Osages and improving their condition. It is understood that the United States are to pay the amount allowed for the reservations in this article and not the Cherokees.

Lands permanently ceded to the nation.

ARTICLE 5. The United States hereby covenant and agree that the lands ceded to the Cherokee nation in the forgoing article shall, in no future time without their consent, be included within the territorial limits or jurisdiction of any State or Territory. But they shall secure to the Cherokee nation the right by their national councils to make and carry into effect all such laws as they may deem necessary for the government and protection of the persons and property within their own country belonging to their people or such persons as have connected themselves with them: provided always that they shall not be inconsistent with the constitution of the United States and such acts of Congress as have been or may be passed regulating trade and intercourse with the Indians; and also, that they shall not be considered as extending to such citizens and army of the United States as may travel or reside in the Indian country by permission according to the laws and regulations established by the Government of the same.

Peace to be preserved.

ARTICLE 6. Perpetual peace and friendship shall exist between the citizens of the United States and the Cherokee Indians. The United States agree to protect the Cherokee nation from domestic strife and foreign enemies and against intestine wars between the several tribes. The Cherokees shall endeavor to preserve and maintain the peace of the country and not make war upon their neighbors they shall also be protected against interruption and intrusion from citizens of the United States, who may attempt to settle in the country without their consent; and all such persons shall be removed from the same by order of the President of the United States. But this is not intended to prevent the residence among them of useful farmers mechanics and teachers for the instruction of Indians according to treaty stipulations.

Congress may allow a delegate from the Cherokee nation.

ARTICLE 7. The Cherokee nation having already made great progress in civilization and deeming it important that every proper and laudable inducement should be offered to their people to improve their condition as well as to guard and secure in the most effectual manner the rights guarantied to them in this treaty, and with a view to illustrate the liberal and enlarged policy of the Government of the United States towards the Indians in their removal beyond the territorial limits of the States, it is stipulated that they shall be entitled to a delegate in the House of Representatives of the United States whenever Congress shall make provision for the same.

ARTICLE 8. The United States also agree and stipulate to remove the Cherokees to their new homes and to subsist them one year after their arrival there and that a sufficient number of steamboats and baggage-wagons shall be furnished to remove them comfortably, and so as not to endanger their health, and that a physician well supplied with medicines shall accompany each detachment of emigrants removed by the Government. Such persons and families as in the opinion of the emigrating agent are capable of subsisting and removing themselves shall be permitted to do so; and they shall be allowed in full for all claims for the same twenty dollars for each member of their family; and in lieu of their one year's rations they shall be paid the sum of thirty-three dollars and thirty-three cents if they prefer it.

Expense of removal to be paid by United States.

Such Cherokees also as reside at present out of the nation and shall remove with them in two years west of the Mississippi shall be entitled to allowance for removal and subsistence as above provided.

ARTICLE 9. The United States agree to appoint suitable agents who shall make a just and fair valuation of all such improvements now in the possession of the Cherokees as add any value to the lands; and also of the ferries owned by them, according to their net income; and such improvements and ferries from which they have been dispossessed in a lawless manner or under any existing laws of the State where the same may be situated.

Agents to value improvements made by the Cherokee.

The just debts of the Indians shall be paid out of any monies due them for their improvements and claims; and they shall also be furnished at the discretion of the President of the United States with a sufficient sum to enable them to obtain the necessary means to remove themselves to their new homes, and the balance of their dues shall be paid them at the Cherokee agency west of the Mississippi. The missionary establishments shall also be valued and appraised in a like manner and the amount of them paid over by the United States to the treasurers of the respective missionary societies by whom they have been established and improved in order to enable them to erect such buildings and make such improvments among the Cherokees west of the Mississippi as they may deem necessary for their benefit. Such teachers at present among the Cherokees as this council shall select and designate shall be removed west of the Mississippi with the Cherokee nation and on the same terms allowed to them.

ARTICLE 10. The President of the United States shall invest in some safe and most productive public stocks of the country for the benefit of the whole Cherokee nation who have removed or shall remove to the lands assigned by this treaty to the Cherokee nation west of the Mississippi the following sums as a permanent fund for the purposes hereinafter specified and pay over the net income of the same annually to such person or persons as shall be authorized or appointed by the Cherokee nation to receive the same and their receipt shall be a full discharge for the amount paid to them viz: the sum of two hundred thousand dollars in addition to the present annuities of the nation to constitute a general fund the interest of which shall be applied annually by the council of the nation to such purposes as they may deem best for the general interest of their people. The sum of fifty thousand dollars to constitute an orphans' fund the annual income of which shall be expended towards the support and education of such orphan children as are destitute of the means of subsistence. The sum of one hundred and fifty thousand dollars in addition to the present school fund of the nation shall constitute a permanent school fund, the interest of which shall be applied annually by the council of the nation for the support of

The President to make investments in productive stock.

common schools and such a literary institution of a higher order as may be established in the Indian country. And in order to secure as far as possible the true and beneficial application of the orphans' and school fund the council of the Cherokee nation when required by the President of the United States shall make a report of the application of those funds and he shall at all times have the right if the funds have been misapplied to correct any abuses of them and direct the manner of their application for the purposes for which they were intended. The council of the nation may by giving two years' notice of their intention withdraw their funds by and with the consent of the President and Senate of the United States, and invest them in such manner as they may deem most proper for their interest. The United States also agree and stipulate to pay the just debts and claims against the Cherokee nation held by the citizens of the same and also the just claims of citizens of the United States for services rendered to the nation and the sum of sixty thousand dollars is appropriated for this purpose but no claims against individual persons of the nation shall be allowed and paid by the nation The sum of three hundred thousand dollars is hereby set apart to pay and liquidate the just claims of the Cherokees upon the United States for spoliations of every kind, that have not been already satisfied under former treaties.

Commutation of school fund.

ARTICLE 11. The Cherokee nation of Indians believing it will be for the interest of their people to have all their funds and annuities under their own direction and future disposition hereby agree to commute their permanent annuity of ten thousand dollars for the sum of two hundred and fourteen thousand dollars, the same to be invested by the President of the United States as a part of the general fund of the nation; and their present school fund amounting to about fifty thousand dollars shall constitute a part of the permanent school fund of the nation.

Provision respecting Cherokees averse to removal.

ARTICLE 12. Those individuals and families of the Cherokee nation that are averse to a removal to the Cherokee country west of the Mississippi and are desirous to become citizens of the States where they reside and such as are qualified to take care of themselves and their property shall be entitled to receive their due portion of all the personal benefits accruing under this treaty for their claims, improvements and *per capita;* as soon as an appropriation is made for this treaty.

Such heads of Cherokee families as are desirous to reside within the States of No. Carolina Tennessee and Alabama subject to the laws of the same; and who are qualified or calculated to become useful citizens shall be entitled, on the certificate of the commissioners to a pre-emption right to one hundred and sixty acres of land or one quarter section at the minimum Congress price; so as to include the present buildings or improvements of those who now reside there and such as do not live there at present shall be permitted to locate within two years any lands not already occupied by persons entitled to pre-emption privilege under this treaty and if two or more families live on the same quarter section and they desire to continue their residence in these States and are qualified as above specified they shall, on receiving their pre-emption certificate be entitled to the right of pre-emption to such lands as they may select not already taken by any person entitled to them under this treaty.

It is stipulated and agreed between the United States and the Cherokee people that John Ross James Starr George Hicks John Gunter George Chambers John Ridge Elias Boudinot George Sanders John Martin William Rogers Roman Nose Situwake and John Timpson shall be a committee on the part of the Cherokees to recommend such persons for the privilege of pre-emption rights as may be deemed entitled to the same under the above articles and to select the missionaries who shall be removed with the nation; and that they be hereby fully empowered and authorized to transact all business on the part of the Indians which may arise in carrying into effect the provisions of this treaty and settling the same with the United States. If any of the persons above mentioned should decline acting or be removed by death; the vacancies shall be filled by the committee themselves.

It is also understood and agreed that the sum of one hundred thousand dollars shall be expended by the commissioners in such manner as the committee deem best for the benefit of the poorer class of Cherokees as shall remove west or have removed west and are entitled to the benefits of this treaty. The same to be delivered at the Cherokee agency west as soon after the removal of the nation as possible.

ARTICLE 13. In order to make a final settlement of all the claims of the Cherokees for reservations granted under former treaties to any individuals belonging to the nation by the United States it is therefore hereby stipulated and agreed and expressly understood by the parties to this treaty—that all the Cherokees and their heirs and descendants to whom any reservations have been made under any former treaties with the United States, and who have not sold or conveyed the same by deed or otherwise and who in the opinion of the commissioners have complied with the terms on which the reservations were granted as far as practicable in the several cases; and which reservations have since been sold by the United States shall constitute a just claim against the United States and the original reservee or their heirs or descendants shall be entitled to receive the present value thereof from the United States as unimproved lands. And all such reservations as have not been sold by the United States and where the terms on which the reservations were made in the opinion of the commissioners have been complied with as far as practicable, they or their heirs or descendants shall be entitled to the same. They are hereby granted and confirmed to them—and also all persons who were entitled to reservations under the treaty of 1817 and who as far as practicable in the opinion of the commissioners, have complied with the stipulations of said treaty, although by the treaty of 1819 such reservations were included in the unceded lands belonging to the Cherokee nation are hereby confirmed to them and they shall be entitled to receive a grant for the same. And all such reservees as were obliged by the laws of the States in which their reservations were situated, to abandon the same or purchase them from the States shall be deemed to have a just claim against the United States for the amount by them paid to the States with interest thereon for such reservations and if obliged to abandon the same, to the present value of such reservations as unimproved lands but in all cases where the reservees have sold their reservations or any part thereof and conveyed the same by deed or otherwise and have been paid for the same, they their heirs or descendants or their assigns shall not be considered as having any claims upon the United States under this article of the treaty nor be entitled to receive any compensation for the lands thus disposed of. It is expressly understood by the parties to this treaty that the amount to be allowed for reservations under this article shall not be deducted out of the consideration money allowed to the Cherokees for their claims for spoliations and the cession of their lands; but the same is to be paid for independently by the United States as it is only a just fulfilment of former treaty stipulations.

ARTICLE 14. It is also agreed on the part of the United States that such warriors of the Cherokee nation as were engaged on the side of the United States in the late war with Great Britain and the southern tribes of Indians, and who were wounded in such service shall be entitled to such pensions as shall be allowed them by the Congress of the United States to commence from the period of their disability.

Settlement of claims for former reservations.

Pensions to certain warriors.

Funds to be divided among the Indians.

ARTICLE 15. It is expressly understood and agreed between the parties to this treaty that after deducting the amount which shall be actually expended for the payment for improvements, ferries, claims, for spoliations, removal subsistence and debts and claims upon the Cherokee nation and for the additional quantity of lands and goods for the poorer class of Cherokees and the several sums to be invested for the general national funds; provided for in the several articles of this treaty the balance whatever the same may be shall be equally divided between all the people belonging to the Cherokee nation east according to the census just completed; and such Cherokees as have removed west since June 1833 who are entitled by the terms of their enrolment and removal to all the benefits resulting from the final treaty between the United States and the Cherokees east they shall also be paid for their improvements according to their approved value before their removal where fraud has not already been shown in their valuation.

Indians to remove in two years.

ARTICLE 16. It is hereby stipulated and agreed by the Cherokees that they shall remove to their new homes within two years from the ratification of this treaty and that during such time the United States shall protect and defend them in their possessions and property and free use and occupation of the same and such persons as have been dispossessed of their improvements and houses; and for which no grant has actually issued previously to the enactment of the law of the State of Georgia, of December 1835 to regulate Indian occupancy shall be again put in possession and placed in the same situation and condition, in reference to the laws of the State of Georgia, as the Indians that have not been dispossessed; and if this is not done, and the people are left unprotected, then the United States shall pay the several Cherokees for their losses and damages sustained by them in consequence thereof. And it is also stipulated and agreed that the public buildings and improvements on which they are situated at New Echota for which no grant has been actually made previous to the passage of the above recited act if not occupied by the Cherokee people shall be reserved for the public and free use of the United States and the Cherokee Indians for the purpose of settling and closing all the Indian business arising under this treaty between the commissioners of claims and the Indians.

The United States, and the several States interested in the Cherokee lands, shall immediately proceed to survey the lands ceded by this treaty; but it is expressly agreed and understood between the parties that the agency buildings and that tract of land surveyed and laid off for the use of Colonel R. J. Meigs Indian agent or heretofore enjoyed and occupied by his successors in office shall continue subject to the use and occupancy of the United States, or such agent as may be engaged specially superintending the removal of the tribe.

Commissioners to settle claims.

ARTICLE 17. All the claims arising under or provided for in the several articles of this treaty, shall be examined and adjudicated by such commissioners as shall be appointed by the President of the United States by and with the advice and consent of the Senate of the United States for that purpose and their decision shall be final and on their certificate of the amount due the several claimants they shall be paid by the United States. All stipulations in former treaties which have not been superseded or annulled by this shall continue in full force and virtue.

United States to make advances for provisions, clothing, etc.

ARTICLE 18. Whereas in consequence of the unsettled affairs of the Cherokee people and the early frosts, their crops are insufficient to support their families and great distress is likely to ensue and whereas the nation will not, until after their removal be able advantageously to expend the income of the permanent funds of the nation it is therefore agreed that the annuities of the nation which may accrue under this treaty for two years, the time fixed for their removal shall be expended in provision and clothing for the benefit of the poorer class of the nation: and the United States hereby agree to advance the same for that purpose as soon after the ratification of this treaty as an appropriation for the same shall be made. It is however not intended in this article to interfere with that part of the annuities due the Cherokees west by the treaty of 1819.

ARTICLE 19. This treaty after the same shall be ratified by the President and Senate of the United States shall be obligatory on the contracting parties. *Treaty binding when ratified.*

ARTICLE 20. [Supplemental article. Stricken out by Senate.]

In testimony whereof, the commissioners and the chiefs, head men, and people whose names are hereunto annexed, being duly authorized by the people in general council assembled, have affixed their hands and seals for themselves, and in behalf of the Cherokee nation.

I have examined the foregoing treaty, and although not present when it was made, I approve its provisions generally, and therefore sign it.

Wm. Carroll,
J. F. Schermerhorn.

Major Ridge, his x mark,	[L. S.]	Te-gah-e-ske, his x mark,	[L. S.]
James Foster, his x mark,	[L. S.]	Robert Rogers,	[L. S.]
Tesa-ta-esky, his x mark,	[L. S.]	John Gunter,	[L. S.]
Charles Moore, his x mark,	[L. S.]	John A. Bell,	[L. S.]
George Chambers, his x mark,	[L. S.]	Charles F. Foreman,	[L. S.]
Tah-yeske, his x mark,	[L. S.]	William Rogers,	[L. S.]
Archilla Smith, his x mark,	[L. S.]	George W. Adair,	[L. S.]
Andrew Ross,	[L. S.]	Elias Boudinot,	[L. S.]
William Lassley,	[L. S.]	James Starr, his x mark,	[L. S.]
Cae-te-hee, his x mark,	[L. S.]	Jesse Half-breed, his x mark,	[L. S.]

Signed and sealed in presence of—

Western B. Thomas, secretary.
Ben. F. Currey, special agent.
M. Wolfe Batman, first lieutenant, sixth U. S. Infantry, disbursing agent.
Jon. L. Hooper, lieutenant, fourth Infantry.

C. M Hitchcock, M. D., assistant surgeon, U. S. A.
G. W. Currey,
Wm. H. Underwood,
Cornelius D. Terhune,
John W. H. Underwood.

In compliance with instructions of the council at New Echota, we sign this treaty.

Stand Watie,
John Ridge.

March 1, 1836.

Witnesses:

Elbert Herring,
Alexander H. Everett,
John Robb,
D. Kurtz,

Wm. Y. Hansell,
Samuel J. Potts,
Jno. Litle,
S. Rockwell.

Whereas the western Cherokees have appointed a delegation to visit the eastern Cherokees to assure them of the friendly disposition of their people and their desire that the nation should again be united as one people and to urge upon them the expediency of accepting the overtures of the Government; and that, on their removal they may be assured of a hearty welcome and an equal participation with them in all the benefits and privileges of the Cherokee country west and the undersigned two of said delegation being the only delegates in the eastern nation from the west at the signing and sealing of the treaty lately concluded at New Echota between their eastern brethren and the United States; and having fully understood the provisions of the same they agree to it in behalf of the western Cherokees. But it is expressly understood that nothing in this treaty shall affect any claims of the western Cherokees on the United States. *Dec. 31, 1835.* *7 Stat., 487.*

In testimony whereof, we have, this 31st day of December, 1835, hereunto set our hands and seals.

James Rogers,
John Smith,
Delegates from the western Cherokees.

Test:

    Ben. F. Currey, special agent.
    M. W. Batman, first lieutenant, Sixth Infantry,
    Jno. L. Hooper, lieutenant, Fourth Infantry,
    Elias Boudinot.

Schedule and estimated value of the Osage half-breed reservations within the territory ceded to the Cherokees west of the Mississippi, (referred to in article 5 on the foregoing treaty,) viz:

Augustus Clamont one section	$6,000
James " " "	1,000
Paul " " "	1,300
Henry " " "	800
Anthony " " "	1,800
Rosalie " " "	1,800
Emilia D, of Mihanga	1,000
Emilia D, of Shemianga	1,300
	$15,000

I hereby certify that the above schedule is the estimated value of the Osage reservations; as made out and agreed upon with Col. A. P. Choteau who represented himself as the agent or guardian of the above reservees.

J. F. Schermerhorn.

March 14, 1835.

March 1, 1836.

7 Stat., 488.
Proclamation, May 23, 1836.

Supplementary articles to a treaty concluded at New Echota, Georgia, December 29, 1835, between the United States and Cherokee people.

WHEREAS the undersigned were authorized at the general meeting of the Cherokee people held at New Echota as above stated, to make and assent to such alterations in the preceding treaty as might be thought necessary, and whereas the President of the United States has expressed his determination not to allow any pre-emptions or reservations his desire being that the whole Cherokee people should remove together and establish themselves in the country provided for them west of the Mississippi river.

Preemption rights declared void. ARTICLE 1. It is therefore agreed that all the pre-emption rights and reservations provided for in articles 12 and 13 shall be and are hereby relinquished and declared void.

ARTICLE 2. Whereas the Cherokee people have supposed that the sum of five millions of dollars fixed by the Senate in their resolution of —— day of March, 1835, as the value of the Cherokee lands and possessions east of the Mississippi river was not intended to include the amount which may be required to remove them, nor the value of certain claims which many of their people had against citizens of the United States, which suggestion has been confirmed by the opinion expressed to the War Department by some of the Senators who voted upon the question and whereas the President is willing that this subject should be referred to the Senate for their consideration and if it was not intended by the Senate that the above-mentioned sum of five millions of dollars should include the objects herein specified that in that case such further provision should be made therefor as might appear to the Senate to be just.

ARTICLE 3. It is therefore agreed that the sum of six hundred thousand dollars shall be and the same is hereby allowed to the Cherokee people to include the expense of their removal, and all claims of every nature and description against the Government of the United States not herein otherwise expressly provided for, and to be in lieu of the said reservations and pre-emptions and of the sum of three hundred thousand dollars for spoliations described in the 1st article of the above-mentioned treaty. This sum of six hundred thousand dollars shall be applied and distributed agreeably to the provisions of the said treaty, and any surplus which may remain after removal and payment of the claims so ascertained shall be turned over and belong to the education fund. *Allowance in lieu of preemptions, etc.*

But it is expressly understood that the subject of this article is merely referred hereby to the consideration of the Senate and if they shall approve the same then this supplement shall remain part of the treaty.

ARTICLE 4. It is also understood that the provisions in article 16, for the agency reservation is not intended to interfere with the occupant right of any Cherokees should their improvement fall within the same. *Provisions for agency reservations not to interfere, etc.*

It is also understood and agreed, that the one hundred thousand dollars appropriated in article 12 for the poorer class of Cherokees and intended as a set-off to the pre-emption rights shall now be transferred from the funds of the nation and added to the general national fund of four hundred thousand dollars so as to make said fund equal to five hundred thousand dollars.

ARTICLE 5. The necessary expenses attending the negotiations of the aforesaid treaty and supplement and also of such persons of the delegation as may sign the same shall be defrayed by the United States. *Expense of negotiations to be defrayed by the United States.*

In testimony whereof, John F. Schermerhorn, commissioner on the part of the United States, and the undersigned delegation have hereunto set their hands and seals, this first day of March, in the year one thousand eight hundred and thirty-six.

J. F. Schermerhorn.

Major Ridge, his x mark,	[L. S.]	John A. Bell,	[L. S.]
James Foster, his x mark,	[L. S.]	Jos. A. Foreman,	
Tah-ye-ske, his x mark,	[L. S.]	Robert Sanders,	[L. S.]
Long Shell Turtle, his x mark,	[L. S.]	Elias Boudinot,	[L. S.]
John Fields, his x mark,	[L. S.]	Johnson Rogers,	[L. S.]
James Fields, his x mark,	[L. S.]	James Starr, his x mark,	[L. S.]
George Welch, his x mark,	[L. S.]	Stand Watie,	[L. S.]
Andrew Ross,	[L. S.]	John Ridge,	[L. S.]
William Rogers,	[L. S.]	James Rogers,	[L. S.]
John Gunter,	[L. S.]	John Smith, his x mark.	[L. S.]

Witnesses:

Elbert Herring,
Thos. Glascock,
Alexander H. Everett,
Jno. Garland, Major, U. S. Army,
C. A. Harris,

John Robb,
Wm. Y. Hansell,
Saml. J. Potts,
Jno. Litle,
S. Rockwell.

TREATY WITH THE POTAWATOMI. 1836.

Mar. 26, 1836.

7 Stat., 490.
Proclamation, June
4, 1836.

Articles of a treaty made and concluded at camp in Turkey Creek Prairie, in the State of Indiana, between Abel C. Pepper commissioner of the United States and Mes-quaw-buck, a chief of the Pottawatamy tribe of Indians and his band, on twenty-sixth day of March, in the year eighteen hundred and thirty-six.

Cession of land to United States.

ART. 1. The above named chief and his band hereby cede to the United States the four sections of land reserved for them by the second article of the treaty between the United States and the Pottawatamy Indians, on Tippecanoe river on the twenty-seventh day of October 1832.

Payment therefor.

ART. 2. In consideration of the cession aforesaid the United States stipulate to pay the above named chief and his band the sum of twenty-five hundred and sixty dollars in specie at the next payment of annuity after the ratification of this treaty.

Expenses of this treaty to be paid by United States.

ART. 3. The United States stipulate to provide for the payment of the necessary expenses attending the making and concluding this treaty.

Indians to remove within two years.

ART. 4. The above named chief and his band agree to yield peaceable possession of the above sections of land and remove to the country west of the Mississippi provided for the Pottawatamy nation by the United States, within two years from this date.

Treaty binding when ratified.

ART. 5. This treaty shall be binding upon both parties from the date of its ratification by the President and Senate of the United States.

ART. 6. [Stricken out by Senate.]

In testimony whereof, the said A. C. Pepper, commissioner on the part of the United States, and the above named chief and head men for themselves and their band, hereunto subscribed their names, the day and year above written.

A. C. Pepper,
Mes-quaw-buck, his x mark,
Mess-Sett, his x mark,
Muck Rose, his x mark,

Waw-baw-que-ke-aw, his x mark,
Naush-waw-pi-tant, his x mark,
Che-qua-sau-quah, his x mark.

Witnesses:
 C. Carter, secretary,
 Edward McCartney, interpreter.

TREATY WITH THE OTTAWA, ETC., 1836.

Mar. 28, 1836.

7 Stat., 491.
Proclamation, May
27, 1836.

Articles of a treaty made and concluded at the city of Washington in the District of Columbia, between Henry R. Schoolcraft, commissioner on the part of the United States, and the Ottawa and Chippewa nations of Indians, by their chiefs and delegates.

Cession of land to the United States.

ARTICLE FIRST. The Ottawa and Chippewa nations of Indians cede to the United States all the tract of country within the following boundaries: Beginning at the mouth of Grand river of Lake Michigan on the north bank thereof, and following up the same to the line called for, in the first article of the treaty of Chicago of the 29th of August 1821, thence, in a direct line, to the head of Thunder-bay river, thence with the line established by the treaty of Saganaw of the 24th of September 1819, to the mouth of said river, thence northeast to the boundary line in Lake Huron between the United States and the British province of Upper Canada, thence northwestwardly, following the said line, as established by the commissioners acting under the treaty of Ghent, through the straits, and river St. Mary's, to a point in Lake Superior north of the mouth of *Gitchy Seebing*, or Chocolate river, thence south to the mouth of said river and up its channel to the source thereof, thence, in a direct line to the head of the *Skonawba* river of Green bay, thence down the south bank of said river to its mouth, thence, in a direct line, through the ship channel into Green bay, to the outer part thereof, thence south to a point in Lake Michigan west of the north cape, or entrance of Grand river, and thence east to the place of beginning, at the cape aforesaid, comprehending all the lands and islands, within these limits, not hereinafter reserved.

ARTICLE SECOND. From the cession aforesaid the tribes reserve for their own use, to be held in common the following tracts for the term of five years from the date of the ratification of this treaty, and no longer; unless the United States shall grant them permission to remain on said lands for a longer period, namely: One tract of fifty thousand acres to be located on Little Traverse bay: one tract of twenty thousand acres to be located on the north shore of Grand Traverse bay, one tract of seventy thousand acres to be located on, or, north of the *Pieire Marquetta* river, one tract of one thousand acres to be located by Chingassanoo,—or the Big Sail, on the Cheboigan. One tract of one thousand acres, to be located by Mujeekewis, on Thunder-bay river. Reservations in common.

ARTICLE THIRD. There shall also be reserved for the use of the Chippewas living north of the straits of Michilimackinac, the following tracts for the term of five years from the date of the ratification of this treaty, and· no longer, unless the United States shall grant them permission to remain on said lands for a longer period, that is to say: Two tracts of three miles square each, on the north shores of the said straits, between *Point-au-Barbe* and *Mille Coquin* river, including the fishing grounds in front of such reservations, to be located by a council of the chiefs. The Beaver islands of Lake Michigan for the use of the Beaver-island Indians. Round island, opposite Michilimackinac, as a place of encampment for the Indians, to be under the charge of the Indian department. The islands of the *Chenos*, with a part of the adjacent north coast of Lake Huron, corresponding in length, and one mile in depth. Sugar island, with its islets, in the river of St. Mary's. Six hundred and forty acres, at the mission of the Little Rapids. A tract commencing at the mouth of the *Pississowining* river, south of Point Iroquois, thence running up said stream to its forks, thence westward, in a direct line to the Red water lakes, thence across the portage to the Tacquimenon river, and down the same to its mouth, including the small islands and fishing grounds, in front of this reservation. Six hundred and forty acres, on Grand island, and two thousand acres, on the main land south of it. Two sections, on the northern extremity of Green bay, to be located by a council of the chiefs. All the locations, left indefinite by this, and the preceding articles, shall be made by the proper chiefs, under the direction of the President. It is understood that the reservation for a place of fishing and encampment, made under the treaty of St. Mary's of the 16th of June 1820, remains unaffected by this treaty. Reservations for Chippewas.

ARTICLE FOURTH. In consideration of the foregoing cessions, the United States engage to pay to the Ottawa and Chippewa nations, the following sums, namely. 1st. An annuity of thirty thousand dollars per annum, in specie, for twenty years; eighteen thousand dollars, to be paid to the Indians between Grand River and the Cheboigun; three thousand six hundred dollars, to the Indians on the Huron shore, between the Cheboigan and Thunder-bay river; and seven thousand four hundred dollars, to the Chippewas north of the straits, as far as the cession extends; the remaining one thousand dollars, to be invested in stock by the Treasury Department and to remain incapable of being Payments to be made to the Indians.

sold, without the consent of the President and Senate, which may, however, be given, after the expiration of twenty-one years. 2nd. Five thousand dollars per annum, for the purpose of education, teachers, school-houses, and books in their own language, to be continued twenty years, and as long thereafter as Congress may appropriate for the object. 3rd. Three thousand dollars for missions, subject to the conditions mentioned in the second clause of this article. 4th. Ten thousand dollars for agricultural implements, cattle, mechanics' tools, and such other objects as the President may deem proper. 5th. Three hundred dollars per annum for vaccine matter, medicines, and the services of physicians, to be continued while the Indians remain on their reservations. 6th. Provisions to the amount of two thousand dollars; six thousand five hundred pounds of tobacco; one hundred barrels of salt, and five hundred fish barrels, annually, for twenty years. 7th. One hundred and fifty thousand dollars, in goods and provisions, on the ratification of this treaty, to be delivered at Michilimackinac, and also the sum of two hundred thousand dollars, in consideration of changing the permanent reservations in article two and three to reservations for five years only, to be paid whenever their reservations shall be surrendered, and until that time the interest on said two hundred thousand dollars shall be annually paid to the said Indians.

Payment of claims against the Indians. ARTICLE FIFTH. The sum of three hundred thousand dollars shall be paid to said Indians to enable them, with the aid and assistance of their agent, to adjust and pay such debts as they may justly owe, and the overplus, if any, to apply to such other use as they may think proper.

Provision for half-breeds, etc. ARTICLE SIXTH. The said Indians being desirous of making provision for their half-breed relatives, and the President having determined, that individual reservations shall not be granted, it is agreed, hat in lieu thereof, the sum of one hundred and fifty thousand dollars shall be set apart as a fund for said half-breeds. No person shall be entitled to any part of said fund, unless he is of Indian descent and actually resident within the boundaries described in the first article of this treaty, nor shall any thing be allowed to any such person, who may have received any allowance at any previous Indian treaty. The following principles, shall regulate the distribution. A census shall be taken of all the men, women, and children, coming within this article. As the Indians hold in higher consideration, some of their half-breeds than others, and as there is much difference in their capacity to use and take care of property, and, consequently, in their power to aid their Indian connexions, which furnishes a strong ground for this claim, it is, therefore, agreed, that at the council to be held upon this subject, the commissioner shall call upon the Indian chiefs to designate, if they require it, three classes of these claimants, the first of which, shall receive one-half more than the second, and the second, double the third. Each man woman and child shall be enumerated, and an equal share, in the respective classes, shall be allowed to each. If the father is living with the family, he shall receive the shares of himself, his wife and children. If the father is dead, or separated from the family, and the mother is living with the family, she shall have her own share, and that of the children. If the father and mother are neither living with the family, or if the children are orphans, their share shall be retained till they are twenty-one years of age; provided, that such portions of it as may be necessary may, under the direction of the President, be from time to time applied for their support. All other persons at the age of twenty-one years, shall receive their shares agreeably to the proper class. Out of the said fund of one hundred and fifty thousand dollars, the sum of five thousand dollars shall be reserved to be applied, under the direction of the President, to the support of such of the poor half breeds, as may require assistance, to be expended in annual instalments for the term of ten years, commencing with the second year. Such of the half-breeds, as may be judged incapable of making a proper use of the money, allowed them by the commissioner, shall receive the same in instalments, as the President may direct.

ARTICLE SEVENTH. In consideration of the cessions above made, and Two additional blacksmiths, etc. as a further earnest of the disposition felt to do full justice to the Indians, and to further their well being, the United States engage to keep two additional blacksmith-shops, one of which, shall be located on the reservation north of Grand river, and the other at the *Sault Ste. Marie.* A permanent interpreter will be provided at each of these locations. It is stipulated to renew the present dilapidated shop at Michilimackinac, and to maintain a gunsmith, in addition to the present smith's establishment, and to build a dormitory for the Indians visiting the post, and appoint a person to keep it, and supply it with fire-wood. It is also agreed, to support two farmers and assistants, and two mechanics, as the President may designate, to teach and aid the Indians, in agriculture, and in the mechanic arts. The farmers and mechanics, and the dormitory, will be continued for ten years, and as long thereafter, as the President may deem this arrangement useful and necessary; but the benefits of the other stipulations of this article, shall be continued beyond the expiration of the annuities, and it is understood that the whole of this article shall stand in force, and inure to the benefit of the Indians, as long after the expiration of the twenty years as Congress may appropriate for the objects.

ARTICLE EIGHTH. It is agreed, that as soon as the said Indians Locations to be sought for; payment for improvements, etc. desire it, a deputation shall be sent to the southwest of the Missouri River, there to select a suitable place for the final settlement of said Indians, which country, so selected and of reasonable extent, the United States will forever guaranty and secure to said Indians. Such improvements as add value to the land, hereby ceded, shall be appraised, and the amount paid to the proper Indian. But such payment shall, in no case, be assigned to, or paid to, a white man. If the church on the Cheboigan, should fall within this cession, the value shall be paid to the band owning it. The net proceeds of the sale of the one hundred and sixty acres of land, upon the Grand River upon which the missionary society have erected their buildings, shall be paid to the said society, in lieu of the value of their said improvements. When the Indians wish it, the United States will remove them, at their expence, provide them a year's subsistence in the country to which they go, and furnish the same articles and equipments to each person as are stipulated to be given to the Pottowatomies in the final treaty of cession concluded at Chicago.

ARTICLE NINTH. Whereas the Ottawas and Chippewas, feeling a Payment to half-breeds in lieu of reservations. strong consideration for aid rendered by certain of their half-breeds on Grand river, and other parts of the country ceded, and wishing to testify their gratitude on the present occasion, have assigned such individuals certain locations of land, and united in a strong appeal for the allowance of the same in this treaty; and whereas no such reservations can be permitted in carrying out the special directions of the President on this subject, it is agreed, that, in addition to the general fund set apart for half-breed claims, in the sixth article, the sum of forty-eight thousand one hundred and forty-eight dollars shall be paid for the extinguishment of this class of claims, to be divided in the following manner: To Rix Robinson, in lieu of a section of land, granted to his Indian family, on the Grand river rapids, (estimated by good judges to be worth half a million,) at the rate of thirty-six dollars an acre: To Leonard Slater, in trust for Chiminonoquat, for a section of land above said rapids, at the rate of ten dollars an acre: To John A. Drew, for a tract of one section and three quarters, to his Indian family, at Cheboigan rapids, at the rate of four dollars; to Edward Biddle, for one section to his Indian family at the fishing grounds, at the rate of three dollars: To John Holiday, for five sections of land to five persons of his Indian family, at the rate of one dollar and twenty-five cents; to Eliza Cook, Sophia Biddle, and Mary Holiday, one section of land each, at two dollars and fifty cents: To Augustin Hamelin junr, being of Indian descent, two sections, at one dollar and twenty-five cents; to William Lasley, Joseph Daily, Joseph Trotier, Henry A. Levake, for two sections each, for their Indian families, at one dollar and twenty-five cents: To Luther Rice, Joseph Lafrombois, Charles Butterfield, being of Indian descent, and to George Moran, Louis Moran, G. D. Williams, for half-breed children under their care, and to Daniel Marsac, for his Indian child, one section each, at one dollar and twenty-five cents.

Payment to chiefs. ARTICLE TENTH. The sum of thirty thousand dollars shall be paid to the chiefs, on the ratification of this treaty, to be divided agreeably to a schedule hereunto annexed.

Annuities to two aged chiefs. ARTICLE ELEVENTH. The Ottawas having consideration for one of their aged chiefs, who is reduced to poverty, and it being known that he was a firm friend of the American Government, in that quarter, during the late war, and suffered much in consequence of his sentiments, it is agreed, that an annuity of one hundred dollars per annum shall be paid to Ningweegon or the Wing, during his natural life, in money or goods, as he may choose. Another of the chiefs of said nation, who attended the treaty of Greenville in 1793, and is now, at a very advanced age, reduced to extreme want, together with his wife, and the Government being apprized that he has pleaded a promise of Gen. Wayne, in his behalf, it is agreed that Chusco of Michilimackinac shall receive an annuity of fifty dollars per annum during his natural life.

Expenses of this treaty to be paid by United States. ARTICLE TWELFTH. All expenses attending the journeys of the Indians from, and to their homes, and their visit at the seat of Government, together with the expenses of the treaty, including a proper quantity of clothing to be given them, will be paid by the United States.

Right of hunting on lands ceded. ARTICLE THIRTEENTH. The Indians stipulate for the right of hunting on the lands ceded, with the other usual privileges of occupancy, until the land is required for settlement.

In testimony whereof, the said Henry R. Schoolcraft, commissioner on the part of the United States, and the chiefs and delegates of the Ottawa and Chippewa nation of Indians, have hereunto set their hands, at Washington the seat of Government, this twenty-eighth day of March, in the year one thousand eight hundred and thirty-six.

Henry R. Schoolcraft.
John Hulbert, secretary.
Oroun Aishkum, of Maskigo, his x mark,
Wassangaze, of Maskigo, his x mark,
Osawya, of Maskigo, his x mark,
Wabi Windego, of Grand river, his x mark,
Megiss Ininee, of Grand river, his x mark,
Nabun Ageezhig, of Grand river, his x mark,
Winnimissagee, of Grand river, his x mark,
Mukutaysee, of Grand river, his x mark,
Wasaw Bequm, of Grand river, his x mark,
Ainse, of Michilimackinac, his x mark,
Chabowaywa, of Michilimackinac, his x mark,
Jawba Wadiek, of Sault Ste. Marie, his x mark,
Waub Ogeeg, of Sault Ste. Marie, his x mark,

Kawgayosh, of Sault Ste. Marie, by Maidysage, his x mark,
Apawkozigun, of L'Arbre Croche, his x mark,
Keminitchagun, of L'Arbre Croche, his x mark,
Tawaganee, of L'Arbre Croche, his x mark,
Kinoshamaig, of L'Arbre Croche, his x mark,
Naganigobowa, of L'Arbre Croche, his x mark,
Onaisino, of L'Arbre Croche, his x mark,
Mukuday Benais, of L'Arbre Croche, his x mark,
Chingassamo, of L'Arbre Croche, his x mark,
Aishquagonabee, of Grand Traverse, his x mark,
Akosa, of Grand Traverse, his x mark,
Oshawun Epenaysse, of Grand Traverse, his x mark.

Lucius Lyon,
R. P. Parrott, captain, U. S. Army,
W. P. Zantzinger, purser, U. S. Navy,
Josiah F. Polk,
John Holiday,
John A. Drew,
Rix Bobinson,

Leonard Slater,
Louis Moran,
Augustin Hamelin, jr.,
Henry A. Lenake,
William Lasley,
George W. Woodward,
C. O. Ermatinger.

Schedule referred to, in the tenth article.

1. The following chiefs constitute the first class, and are entitled to receive five hundred dollars each, namely: On Grand river, Muccutay Osha, Namatippy, Nawequa Geezhig or Noon Day, Nabun Egeezhig son of Kewayguabowequa, Wabi Windego or the White Giant, Cawpemossay or the Walker, Mukutay Oquot or Black Cloud, Megis Ininee or Wampum-man, Winnimissagee: on the Maskigo, Osawya, and Owun Aishcum; at L'Arbre Croche, Apawkozigun, or Smoking Weed, Nisowakeout, Keminechawgun; at Grand Travers, Aishquagonabee, or the Feather of Honor, Chabwossun, Mikenok: on the Cheboigan, Chingassamo, or the Big Sail; at Thunder-bay; Mujeekiwiss; on the Manistic North, Mukons Ewyan; at Oak Point on the straits, Ains: at the Chenos, Chabowaywa: at Sault Ste. Marie, Iawba Wadick and Kewayzi Shawano; at Tac͏uimenon, Kawgayosh; at Grand Island, Oshawun Epenaysee, or the South Bird. **Chiefs entitled to $500 each.**

2. The following chiefs constitute the second class, and are entitled to receive two hundred dollars each, namely: On Grand river, Keeshaowash, Nugogikaybee, Kewaytowaby, Wapoos or the Rabbit, Wabitouguaysay, Kewatondo, Zhaquinaw, Nawiqua Geezhig of Flat river, Kenaytinunk, Weenonga, Pabawboco, Windecowiss, Muccutay Penay or Black Patridge, Kaynotin Aishcum, Boynashing, Shagwabeno son of White Giant, Tushetowun, Keway Gooshcum the former head chief, Pamossayga; at L'Arbre Croche, Sagitondowa, Ogiman Wininee, Megisawba, Mukuday Benais; at the Cross, Nishcajininee, Nawamushcota, Pabamitabi, Kimmewun, Gitchy Mocoman; at Grand Traverse, Akosa, Nebauquaum, Kabibonocca; at Little Traverse, Miscomamaingwa or Red Butterfly, Keezhigo Benais, Pamanikinong, Paimossega; on the Cheboigan, Chonees, or Little John, Shaweenossegay; on Thunder bay, Suganikwato; on Maskigo, Wassangazo; on Ossigomico or Platte river, Kaigwaidosay; at Manistee, Keway Gooshcum: on river Pierre Markette, Saugima: at Saulte Ste. Marie, Neegaubayun, Mukudaywacquot, Cheegud; at Carp river west of Grand island, Kaug Wyanais: at Mille Cocquin on the straits, Aubunway: at Michilimackinac, Missutigo, Saganosh, Akkukogeesh, Chebyawboas. **Chiefs entitled to $200 each.**

3. The following persons constitute the third class, and are entitled to one hundred dollars each, namely: Kayshewa, Penasee or Gun lake, Kenisoway, Keenabie of Grand river: Wasso, Mosaniko, Unwatin Oashcum, Nayogirna, Itawachkochi, Nanaw Ogomoo, Gitchy, Peendowan or Scabbard, Mukons, Kinochimaig, Tekamosimo, Pewaywitum, Mudji Keguabi, Kewayaum, Paushkizigun or Big Gun, Onaausino, Ashquabaywiss, Negaunigabowi, Petossegay, of L'Arbre Croche: Poiees or Dwarf and Pamossay of Cheboigan: Gitchy Ganocquot and Pamossegay of Thunder Bay: Tabusshy Geeshick and Mikenok, of Carp river south of Grand Traverse; Wapooso, Kaubinau, and Mudjeekee of river Pierre Markuette: Pubokway, Manitowaba, and Mishewatig, of White river: Shawun Epenaysee and Agausgee of Grand Traverse: Micqumisut, Chusco of Mackinac; Keeshkidjiwum, Waub Ojeeg, Aukudo, Winikis, Jaubeens, Maidosagee, Autya, Ishquagunaby, Shaniwaygwunabi son of Kakakee, Nittum Egabowi, Magisanikway, Ketekewegauboway, of Sault Ste. Marie: Chegauzehe and Waubudo of Grand island: Ashegons, Kinuwais, Misquaonaby and **Chiefs entitled to $100 each.**

Mongons of Carp and Chocolate rivers; Gitchy Penaisson of Grosse Tete, and Waubissaig of Bay de Nocquet: Kainwaybekis and Pazhikwaywitum of Beaver islands: Neezhick Epenais of the Ance: Ahdanima of Manistic: Mukwyon, Wahzahkoon, Oshawun, Oneshannocquot of the north shore of Lake Michigan: Nagauniby and Keway Gooshkum of the Chenos.

Henry R. Schoolcraft,
Commissioner.

SUPPLEMENTAL ARTICLE.

How certain provisions in preceding articles are to be construed.

To guard against misconstruction in some of the foregoing provisions, and to secure, by further limitations, the just rights of the Indians, it is hereby agreed: that no claims under the fifth article shall be allowed for any debts contracted previous to the late war with Great Britain, or for goods supplied by foreigners to said Indians, or by citizens, who did not withdraw from the country, during its temporary occupancy by foreign troops, for any trade carried on by such persons during the said period. And it is also agreed: that no person receiving any commutation for a reservation, or any portion of the fund provided by the sixth article of this treaty, shall be entitled to the benefit of any part of the annuities herein stipulated. Nor shall any of the half-breeds, or blood relatives of the said tribes, commuted with, under the provisions of the ninth article, have any further claim on the general commutation fund, set apart to satisfy reservation claims, in the said sixth article. It is also understood, that the personal annuities, stipulated in the eleventh article, shall be paid in specie, in the same manner that other annuities are paid. Any excess of the funds set apart in the fifth and sixth articles, shall, in lieu of being paid to the Indians, be retained and vested by the Government in stock under the conditions mentioned in the fourth article of this treaty.

In testimony whereof, the parties above recited, have hereunto set their hands, at Washington the seat of Government, this thirty-first day of March, in the year one thousand eight hundred and thirty-six.

Henry R. Schoolcraft.
John Hulbert, Secretary.

Owun Aaishkum, of Maskigo, his x mark,

Wassangazo, of Maskigo, his x mark,

Osawya, of Maskigo, his x mark,

Wabi Widego, of Grand river, his x mark,

Megiss Ininee, of Grand river, his x mark,

Nabun Ageezhig, of Grand river, his x mark,

Ainse, of Michilimackinac, his x mark,

Chabowaywa, of Michilimackinac, his x mark,

Jauba Wadic, of Sault Ste. Marie, his x mark,

Waub Ogeeg, of Sault Ste. Marie, his x mark,

Kawgayosh, of Sault Ste. Marie, by Maidosagee, his x mark,

Apawkozigun, of L'Arbre Croche, his x mark,

Keminitchagun, of L'Arbre Croche, his x mark,

Tawagnee, of L'Arbre Croche, his x mark,

Kinoshemaig, of L'Arbre Croche, his x mark,

Naganigabawi, of L'Arbre Croche, his x mark,

Oniasino, of L'Arbre Croche, his x mark,

Mukaday Benais, of L'Arbre Croche, his x mark,

Chingassamoo, of Cheboigan, his x mark,

Aishquagonabee, of Grand Traverse, his x mark,

Akosa, of Grand Traverse, his x mark,

Oshawun Epenaysee, of Grand Traverse, his x mark.

Robert Stewart,
Wm. Mitchell,
John A Drew,

Augustin Hamelin, jr.
Rix Robinson,
C. O. Ermatinger.

TREATY WITH THE POTAWATOMI, 1836.

Articles of a treaty made and concluded on Tippecanoe river in the State of Indiana between Abel C. Pepper commissioner on the part of the United States and Wau-ke-wa Che-cose's only son a Potta-watamy chief and his band, on the twenty-ninth day of March, eighteen hundred and thirty-six.

Mar. 29, 1836.

7 Stat., 498.
Proclamation, June 4, 1836.

ART. 1. The above named chief and his band hereby cede to the United States the four sections of land reserved for them by the second article of the treaty between the United States and the Pottawatamy Indians. Cession of land to United States.

ART. 2. The above named chief and his band agree to yield peaceable possession of said land within three months from this date, and to remove to the country provided for the Pottawatamy nation west of the Mississippi river within two years. Indians to remove within two years.

ART. 3. In consideration of the cession aforesaid the United States stipulate to pay the above named chief and his band twenty-five hundred and sixty dollars in specie at the first payment of annuity after the ratification of this treaty. Payment for land ceded.

ART. 4. The United States stipulate to provide for the payment of the necessary expenses attending the making and concluding this treaty. United States to pay expenses of this treaty.

ART. 5. This treaty shall be binding upon both the parties from the date of its ratification by the President and Senate of the United States. Treaty binding when ratified.

ART. 6. [Stricken out by Senate.]

In testimony whereof, the said Abel C. Pepper, commissioner on the part of the United States, and the above named chief and head men, have hereunto subscribed their names, the day and year above written.

Abel C. Pepper,
Wau-ke-wau, his x mark,
Waw-was-mo-queh, widow of Che-cose,
  her x mark,

Te-shaw-gen, his x mark,
Mes-quaw, her x mark,
Pah-Siss, his x mark,
She-aw-ke-pee, his x mark.

Witness:
  C. Carter, secretary.
  Henry Ossem, interpreter.

TREATY WITH THE POTAWATOMI, 1836.

Articles of a treaty made and concluded at a camp on Tippecanoe river, in the State of Indiana, between Abel C. Pepper commissioner on the part of the United States, and Pau-koo-shuck, Aub-ba-naub-ba's oldest son and the head men of Aub-ba-naub-ba's band of Potawattimie Indians, this eleventh day of April in the year, eighteen hundred and thirty-six.

Apr. 11, 1836

7 Stat., 499.
Proclamation, May 25, 1836.

ARTICLE 1. The aforesaid Pau-koo-shuck and the head men of Aub-ba-naub-ba's band, hereby cede to the United States the thirty-six sections of land reserved for them by the second article of the Treaty between the United States and the Potawattimie Indians on Tippecanoe river on the twenty-sixth day of October, in the year eighteen hundred and thirty-two, Cession of land to United States.

ART. 2. In consideration of the cession aforesaid, the United States stipulate to pay to the aforesaid band the sum of twenty-three thousand and forty dollars in specie, one half at the first payment of annuity, after the ratification of this Treaty, and the other half at the succeeding payment of annuity, Consideration therefor.

Indians to remove within two years.

ART. 3. The above-named Pau-koo-shuck and his band agree to remove to the country west of the Mississippi river, provided for the Potawattimie nation by the United States within two years,

ART. 4. [Stricken out by Senate.]

Treaty binding when ratified.

ART. 5. This Treaty, after the same shall be ratified by the President and Senate of the United States shall be binding upon both parties.

In testimony whereof, the said Abel C. Pepper, commissioner as aforesaid, and the said Pau-koo-shuck, and his band, have hereunto set their hands, this eleventh day of April, in the year of our Lord one thousand eight hundred and thirty-six.

Abel C. Pepper,	O-Sauk-kay, his x mark,
Pau-koo-shuck, his x mark,	Ke-waw-o-nuck, his x mark,
Taw-wah-quah, her x mark,	Aun-tuine, his x mark,
Shah-quaw-ko-shuck, Aub-ba-naub-ba's son, his x mark,	Sin-ba-nim, his x mark,
	Nees-se-ka-tah, his x mark,
Mat-taw-mim, his x mark,	Kaw-ke-me, her x mark,
Si-nis-quah, her x mark,	Pe-waw-ko, her x mark,
Dah-moosh-ke-keaw, her x mark,	O-ket-chee, her x mark,
Nan-wish-ma, his x mark,	Nan-cee, her x mark.

Witnesses:

E. O. Cicott, secretary,	Joseph Bamont, principal interpreter,
Henry Ossem,	Joseph Truckey,
Thos. Robb,	George W. Ewing,
Wm. Polke,	Cyrus Tober.

TREATY WITH THE POTAWATOMI, 1836.

Apr. 22, 1836.

7 Stat., 500.
Proclamation, May 25, 1836.

Articles of a treaty made and concluded at the Indian Agency, in the State of Indiana, between Abel C. Pepper, commissioner on the part of the United States and O-kah-mause, Kee-waw-nay, Nee-boash, and Mat-chis-jaw, chiefs and head men of the Patawattimie tribe of Indians and their bands, on the twenty-second day of April, in the year eighteen hundred and thirty-six.

Cession of land to the United States.

ART. 1. The above named chiefs and head men and their bands, hereby cede to the United States, ten sections of land, reserved for them by the second article of the treaty, between the United States and the Patawattimie tribe of Indians, on Tippecanoe river, on the 26th day of October, in the year 1832.

Payment therefor.

ART. 2. In consideration of the cession aforesaid, the United States stipulate to pay to the above-named chiefs and head men and their bands, the sum of six thousand four hundred dollars, at the first payment of annuity, after the ratification of this treaty.

Indians to remove within two years.

ART. 3. The above-named chiefs and head men and their bands agree to remove to the country west of the Mississippi river, provided for the Patawattimie nation by the United States, within two years.

ART. 4. [Stricken out by Senate.]

Expenses of treaty to be paid by United States.

ART. 5. The United States stipulate to provide for the payment of the necessary expenses attending the making and concluding this treaty.

Treaty binding when ratified.

ART. 6. This treaty, after the same shall be ratified by the President and Senate of the United States, shall be binding upon both parties.

In testimony thereof, the said Abel C. Pepper, commissioner as aforesaid, and the said chiefs and head men and their bands, have hereunto set their hands, this 22d day of April, A. D. 1836.

Abel C. Pepper,	Nee-boash, or twisted head, his x mark,
Pash-po-ho, his x mark,	I-o-weh, or nation's name, his x mark,
O-kaw-mause, his x mark,	Miss-no-qui, female fish, his x mark,
Kee-waw-nee, his x mark,	Kaw-che-noss, his x mark,

Cho-quiss, fishes entrails, his x mark,
Ma-che-saw, bleating fawn, his x mark,
Waw-po-ko-ne-aw, white night, his x mark,

Ah-muck, his x mark,
Kohe-kah-me, his x mark,
Que-que-nuk, his x mark.

Witnesses:

Geo. W. Ewing,
Cyrus Tober,
J. B. Duret, secretary,

Peter Barron,
Joseph Bamont, interpreter.

TREATY WITH THE POTAWATOMI, 1836.

Articles of a treaty made and concluded at the Indian agency, in the State of Indiana between Abel C. Pepper commissioner on the part of the United States, and Nas-waw-kee and Quash-quaw chiefs and head men of the Patawattimie tribe of Indians and their bands on the 22d day of April, 1836.

Apr. 22, 1836.

7 Stat., 501.
Proclamation, May 25, 1836.

ART. 1. The above named chiefs and head men and their bands hereby cede to the United States three sections of land reserved for them by the second article of the treaty between the United States and the Patawattimie tribe of Indians on Tippecanoe river on the 26th day of October, 1832.

Land ceded to the United States.

ART. 2. In consideration of the cession aforesaid the United States stipulate to pay the above chiefs and head men and their bands nineteen hundred and twenty dollars at the first payment of annuity after the ratification of this treaty.

Consideration therefor.

ART. 3. The above named chiefs and head men and their bands agree to give possession of the aforesaid three sections of land, and remove to the country west of the Mississippi river provided by the United States for the Potawattimie nation of Indians within two years from this date.

Indians to remove within two years.

ART. 4. [Stricken out by Senate.]

ART. 5. The United States stipulate to provide for the payment of the necessary expenses attending the making and concluding this treaty.

Expenses of this treaty to be paid by United States.

ART. 6. This treaty, after the same shall be ratified by the President and Senate of the United States, shall be binding upon both parties.

Treaty binding when ratified.

In testimony whereof, the said Abel C. Pepper, commissioner as aforesaid, and the said chiefs and head men and their bands, have hereunto set their hands, this 22d day of April, A. D. 1836.

A. C. Pepper,
Quash-quaw, his x mark,
Me-cos-ta, his x mark,
Nas-waw-kee, his x mark,
Wem-se-ko, his x mark,
Ah-quaush-she, his x mark.

Witnesses:
    J. B. Duret, secretary to commissioner,
    Joseph Bamont, interpreter,
    Cyrus Tober,
    Geo. W. Ewing,
    Peter Barron.

TREATY WITH THE WYANDOT, 1836.

Apr. 23, 1836.

7 Stat., 502.
Proclamation, May 16, 1836.

Articles of a treaty made and concluded between John A. Bryan, commissioner on the part of the United States, and William Walker, John Barnett, and Peacock, chiefs and principal men of the Wyandot tribe of Indians in Ohio, acting for and on behalf of the said tribe.

Land ceded to the United States.

ART. 1. The Wyandot tribe of Indians in Ohio cede to the United States a strip of land five miles in extent, on the east end of their reservation in Crawford county in said State—also, one section of land lying in Cranberry Swamp, on Broken Sword creek, being the one mile square specified and set forth in the treaty made with the said tribe on the twenty-ninth day of September in the year of our Lord one thousand eight hundred and seventeen—also, one hundred and sixty acres of land, which is to be received in the place and stead of an equal quantity set apart in a supplemental treaty made with the said Indians on the seventeenth day of September in the following year, all situate and being in the said county of Crawford.

To be surveyed and sold.

ART. 2. The said five mile tract, as also the additional quantities herein set forth, are each to be surveyed as other public lands are surveyed by the Surveyor General, and to be sold at such time and place, allowing sixty days' notice of the sale, as the President may direct.

A register and receiver to be appointed.

ART. 3. A Register and Receiver shall be appointed by the President and Senate, in accordance with the wishes of the delegation of chiefs, whose duties shall be similar to those of other Registers and Receivers.

They shall receive such compensation for services rendered, not exceeding five dollars per day for every day necessarily employed in the discharge of their duties, as the President may determine.

Expenses to be defrayed out of the sale of the land.

ART. 4. All expenses incurred in the execution of this treaty, and in the sale of the lands included in it, shall be defrayed out of the funds raised therefrom, including such expenses and disbursements as may have been incurred by the delegation to Washington—and such allowance to individuals who have assisted in the negotiation, as the chiefs in council, after a full and fair investigation, may adjudge to be reasonable and just, shall in all cases be made.

Roads, schools, etc.

ART. 5. Such portion of the monies not exceeding twenty thousand dollars, arising from the sales as the chiefs may deem necessary for the rebuilding of mills, repair and improvement of roads, establishing schools, and other laudable public objects for the improvement of their condition, shall be properly applied under their direction, and the remainder to be distributed among the individuals of said tribe as annuities are distributed.

Moneys, how payable.

ART. 6. The monies raised by the sales of the lands for all the above mentioned objects, except the last, shall be paid by the receiver on the order of the chiefs;—and such order, together with the receipt of the persons to whom payment shall be made, shall be the proper voucher for the final settlement of the accounts of the Receiver;—but the funds for the tribe shall be distributed by the Register and Receiver to each person entitled thereto.

Certain former reservations to be sold, and the amount paid to the owners.

ART. 7. By the 21st article of the treaty concluded at the foot of the rapids of the Miami of Lake Erie, dated the twenty-ninth day of September in the year one thousand eight hundred and seventeen, and the schedule thereunto attached, there was granted to Daonquot, or half King, Rontondee, or Warpole, Tayarrontoyea, or Between the Logs, Danwawtout, or John Hicks, Mononcue, or Thomas, Tayondottauseh, or George Punch, Hondaua-waugh, or Matthews, chiefs of the Wyandot nation, two sections of land each, within the Wyandot reservation—The aforesaid chiefs, their heirs or legal representatives, are entitled to, and allowed one section of land each, in the above designated tract of five miles, to be selected by them previous to sale, and the same shall be sold as the other lands are sold, and they allowed to receive the respective sums arising from said sale.

ART. 8. If during the progress of the sale, the Indians are not satisfied with the prices at which the lands sell, the Register and Receiver shall, on the written application of the chiefs, close the sale, and report the proceedings to the War Department—and the President may appoint such other time for the sale as he may deem proper. *Indians may close the sale.*

ART. 9. The President shall give such directions as he may judge necessary for the execution of this treaty, through the proper Departments of the Government. *Authority of the President.*

Signed this twenty-third day of April, in the year of our Lord one thousand eight hundred and thirty-six.

John A. Bryan,
Com'r. on the part of the United States,
Wm. Walker,
John Barnett, his x mark,
—— Peacock, his x mark.

In presence of us—
   Jn. McClene,
   John McElvain.

TREATY WITH THE CHIPPEWA, 1836.

Articles of a treaty made at Washington in the District of Columbia on the ninth day of May in the year of our Lord one thousand eight hundred and thirty-six, between Henry R. Schoolcraft, commissioner on the part of the United States and the chiefs of the Swan-creek and Black-river bands of the Chippewa nation, residing within the limits of Michigan. *May 9, 1836.*

7 Stat., 503.
Proclamation, May 25, 1836.

WHEREAS certain reservations of land were made to the said bands of Indians in the treaty concluded at Detroit on the 17th of November 1807, and these reservations after having been duly located, under the authority of the Government, have remained in their possession and occupancy to the present time: and whereas the said Indians actuated by considerations affecting their permanent improvement and happiness, are desirous of fixing their residence at some point more favorable to these objects, and have expressed their wishes to dispose of the same and authorized their chiefs to proceed to Washington for the purpose of making the necessary arrangement: It is therefore, after mature deliberation on their part, agreed as follows.

ARTICLE 1. The Swan-creek and Black-river bands of Chippewas cede to the United States the following tracts, namely: *Tracts ceded to the United States.*

One tract of three miles square, or five thousand seven hundred and sixty acres on Swan-creek of Lake St. Clair: One tract of one section and three quarters near Salt creek of said lake: One tract of one-fourth of a section at the mouth of the river Au Vaseau contiguous to the preceding cession: and one tract of two sections near the mouth of Black-river of the river St. Clair, estimated to contain, in the aggregate, eight thousand three hundred and twenty acres, be the same more or less.

ARTICLE 2. In consideration of the foregoing cessions, the United States agree to pay to the said Indians the net proceeds of the sale thereof, after deducting the cost of survey and sale and the contingent expenses attending the treaty. The lands shall be surveyed and offered for sale in the usual manner, at the land office in Detroit, as soon as practicable after the ratification of this treaty. A special account shall be kept at the Treasury of the amount of the sales of the said lands, and after deducting therefrom the sums hereafter stipulated, to be *Proceeds of sale to be paid to the Indians.*

advanced by the United States, ten thousand dollars shall be retained by the Treasury, and shall be paid to the said Indians in annuities of one thousand dollars a year for ten years; and the residue of the fund shall be vested by the Secretary of the Treasury in the purchase of some State stock, the interest of which shall be annually paid to the said Indians like other annuities: *Provided*, That if at any time hereafter the said Indians shall desire to have the said stock sold, and the proceeds paid over to them, the same may be done, if the President and Senate consent thereto.

Advance to be made by United States.

ARTICLE 3. The United States will advance to said Indians on the ratification of this treaty, to be deducted from the avails of the lands, the sum of two thousand five hundred dollars, and also goods to the value of four thousand dollars to be purchased in New York and delivered in bulk, at their expense, to the proper chiefs at Detroit, or at such point on Lake St. Clair as the chiefs may request: together with the expenses of the treaty, the journeys of the Indians to and from Washington and their subsistence and other expenses at the seat of Government.

Land west of the Mississippi to be furnished.

ARTICLE 4. The United States will furnish the said Indians, eight thousand three hundred and twenty acres or thirteen sections of land, west of the Mississippi or northwest of St. Anthony's Falls, to be located by an agent or officer of the Government, and the evidence of such location shall be delivered to the chiefs.

In testimony whereof, the said Henry R. Schoolcraft, commissioner as aforesaid, and the undersigned chiefs of the said bands of Chippewas, have hereunto set their hands, at Washington, the seat of Government, the day and year above expressed.

> Henry R. Schoolcraft,
> Esh-ton-o-quot, or clear sky, his x mark,
> Nay-gee-zhig, or driving clouds, his x mark,
> May-zin, or checkered, his x mark,
> Kee-way-gee-zhig, or returning sky, his x mark.

In presence of—
> Samuel Humes Porter, secretary,
> Stevens T. Mason, governor of Michigan,
> Lucius Lyon,
> John Holliday, interpreter,
> Joseph F. Murray,
> George Moran.

TREATY WITH THE POTAWATOMI, 1836.

Aug. 5, 1836.

7 Stat., 505.
Proclamation, Feb. 18, 1837.

Articles of a treaty made and concluded at a camp near Yellow river, in the State of Indiana, between Abel C. Pepper, commissioner on the part of the United States and Pe-pin-a-waw, No-taw-kah & Mac-kah-tah-mo-ah, chiefs and headmen of the Potawattimie tribe of Indians, and their bands on the fifth day of August in the year eighteen hundred and thirty-six.

Land ceded to the United States.

ART. 1st. The above named chiefs and headmen and their bands hereby cede to the United States twenty-two sections of land reserved for them by the second article of the treaty between the United States and the Potawattimie tribe of Indians on Tippecanoe river, on the twenty-sixth day of October in the year eighteen hundred and thirty-two.

Payment therefor.

ART. 2d. In consideration of the cession aforesaid, the United States stipulate to pay to the above named chiefs and headmen and their bands, the sum of fourteen thousand and eighty dollars in specie after the ratification of this treaty, and on or before the first day of May next ensuing the date hereof.

ART. 3d. The above named chiefs and headmen and their bands agree to remove to the country west of the Mississippi river, provided for the Potawattimic nation by the United States within two years.

Indians to remove within two years.

ART. 4th. At the request of the above named band it is stipulated that after the ratification of this treaty, the United States shall appoint a commissioner, who shall be authorized to pay such debts of the said band as may be proved to his satisfaction to be just, to be deducted from the amount stipulated in the second article of this treaty.

Payment of Indian debts.

ART. 5th. The United States stipulate to provide for the payment of the necessary expences attending the making and concluding this treaty.

United States to pay expenses of making treaty.

ART. 6th. This treaty, after the same shall be ratified by the President and Senate of the United States, shall be binding upon both parties.

Treaty binding when ratified.

In testimony whereof, the said Abel C. Pepper, commissioner as aforesaid, and the said chiefs, and headmen, and their bands, have hereunto set their hands, this fifth day of August, in the year of our Lord one thousand eight hundred and thirty-six.

A. C. Pepper,
Pee-pin-ah-waw, his x mark,
No-taw-kah, his x mark,
Te-cum-see, his x mark,
Pam-bo-go, his x mark,
Mup-paw-hue, his x mark,
See-co-ase, his x mark,
Co-quah-wah, his x mark,
Mack-kah-tah-mo-may, his x mark,
Wi-aw-koos-say, his x mark,
Quah-taw, his x mark,
Kaw-kawk-kay, his x mark,
Pis-saw, his x mark,
Nas-waw-kay, his x mark.

Proper chiefs of the Wabash Patawattamies:
Pash-pò-ho, his x mark,
I-o-wah, his x mark,
O-kah-maus, his x mark,
Jo-quiss, his x mark,
We-wis-sah, his x mark,
Nas-waw-wah, his x mark,
Ash-kum, his x mark,
Ku-waw-nay, his x mark,
Nu-bosh, his x mark,
Pah-siss, his x mark,
Mat-chis-saw, his x mark,
Mas-saw, his x mark,
Me-shaw-ki-to-quah, his x mark.

Witnesses:
    J. B. Duret, secretary,
    E. O. Cicott,
    Geo. W. Ewing,
    Jos. Barron, interpreter.

TREATY WITH THE MENOMINEE, 1836.

Articles of agreement made and concluded at Cedar Point, on Fox river, near Green bay, in the Territory of Wisconsin, this third day of September in the year of our Lord one thousand eight hundred and thirty-six between Henry Dodge, Governor of said Territory of Wisconsin, commissioner on the part of the United States, on the one part; and the chiefs and head men of the Menomonie nation of Indians, of the other part.

Sept. 3, 1836.

*7 Stat., 506.
Proclamation, Feb. 15, 1837.*

ARTICLE FIRST. The said Menomonie nation agree to cede to the United States, all of that tract or district of country included within the following boundaries, viz. Beginning at the mouth of Wolf river, and running up and along the same, to a point on the north branch of said river where it crosses the extreme north or rear line of the five hundred thousand acre tract heretofore granted to the New York Indians: thence following the line last mentioned, in a northeastwardly direction, three miles: thence in a northwardly course, to the upper

Lands ceded to the United States.

forks of the Menomonie river, at a point to intersect the boundary line between the Menomonie and Chippewa nation of Indians: thence following the said boundary line last mentioned, in an eastwardly direction as defined and established by the treaty of the Little Bute des Mort, in 1827, to the Smooth rock or Shos-kin-aubie river: thence down the said river to where it empties into Green bay, between the Little and Great bay de Noquet: thence up and along the west side of Green bay, (and including all the islands therein, not heretofore ceded) to the mouth of Fox river: thence up and along the said Fox river, and along the west side of Winnebago lake (including the islands therein) to the mouth of Fox river, where it empties into said lake: thence up and along said Fox river to the place of beginning, (saving and reserving out of the district of country above ceded and described, all that part of the five hundred thousand acre tract, granted by the treaties between the Menomonies and the United States, made on the eighth day of February A. D. 1831, and on the twenty-seventh day of October A. D. 1832, which may be situated within the boundaries hereinbefore described,) the quantity of land contained in the tract hereby ceded, being estimated at about four millions of acres.

Further cession.

And the said Menomonie nation do further agree to cede and relinquish to the United States all that tract or district of country lying upon the Wisconsin river, in said territory; and included within the following boundaries; viz—Beginning at a point upon said Wisconsin river two miles above the grant or privilege heretofore granted by said nation and the United States, to Amable Grignon; thence running up and along said river forty-eight miles in a direct line: and being three miles in width on each side of said river; this tract to contain eight townships or one hundred and eighty-four thousand three hundred and twenty acres of land.

Consideration therefor.

ARTICLE SECOND. In consideration of the cession of the aforesaid tract of land, the United States agree to pay to the said Menomonie nation, at the lower end of Wah-ne-kun-nah lake in their own country, or at such other place as may be designated by the President of the United States the sum of twenty thousand dollars, per annum for the term of twenty years.

Provisions, etc., to be supplied.

The United States further agree to pay and deliver to the said Indians, each and every year during the said term of twenty years, the following articles—Three thousand dollars worth of provisions; two thousand pounds of tobacco; thirty barrels of salt; also the sum of five hundred dollars, per year, during the same term, for the purchase of farming utensils, cattle, or implements of husbandry, to be expended under the direction of the superintendent or agent. Also to appoint and pay two blacksmiths to be located at such places as may be designated by the said superintendent or agent, to erect (and supply with the necessary quantity of iron, steel, and tools) two blacksmith shops; during the same term.

Blacksmiths.

Debts to be paid.

The United States shall also pay the just debts of the said Menomonie Indians, agreeably to the schedule hereunto annexed, amounting to the sum of ninety-nine thousand seven hundred and ten dollars and fifty cents. Provided, always, That no portion of said debts shall be paid until the validity and justice of each of them, shall have been inquired into by the Commissioner of Indian Affairs, who shall in no instance increase the amount specified in said schedule, but who shall allow the sum specified, reject it entirely, or reduce it as upon examination and proof may appear just, and if any part of said sum is left after paying said debts so adjudged to be just, then such surplus shall be paid to the said Indians for their own use.

Provision for persons of mixed blood.

And whereas the said Indians are desirous of making some provision and allowance to their relatives and friends of mixed blood; the United States do further agree to pay the sum of eighty thousand dollars, to be divided among all such persons of mixed blood as the chiefs shall hereafter designate: said sum to be apportioned and divided under the direction of a commissioner to be appointed by the President. Provided always, That no person shall be entitled to any part of said fund unless he is of Indian descent and actually resident within the boundaries described in the first article of this treaty, nor shall anything be allowed to any such person who may have received any allowance under any previous treaty. The portion of this fund allowed by the Commissioner to those half breeds who are orphans, or poor or incompetent to make a proper use thereof, shall be paid to them in installments or otherwise as the President may direct.

ARTICLE THIRD. The said Menomonie nation do agree to release the United States from all such provisions of the treaty of 1831 and 1832, aforesaid, as requires the payment of farmers, blacksmiths, millers &c. They likewise relinquish all their right under said treaty to appropriation for education, and to all improvements made or to be made upon their reservation on Fox river and Winnebago lake; together with the cattle, farming utensils or other articles furnished or to be furnish[ed] to them under said treaty. And in consideration of said release and relinquishment, the United States stipulate and agree that the sum of seventy-six thousand dollars, shall be allowed to the said Indians and this sum shall be invested in some safe stock and the interest thereof as it accrues shall also be so vested until such time as in the judgment of the President, the income of the aggregate sum can be usefully applied to the execution of the provisions in the said fourth article, or to some other purposes beneficial to the said Indians. *United States released from certain provisions of treaty of 1831 and 1832.*

ARTICLE FOURTH. The above annuities shall be paid yearly and every year, during the said term, in the month of June or July, or as soon thereafter as the amount shall be received; and the said Menomonie nation do agree to remove from the country ceded, within one year after the ratification of this treaty. *Annuities to be paid yearly.*

This treaty shall be binding and obligatory on the contracting parties, as soon as the same shall be ratified by the President and Senate of the United States. *Treaty binding when ratified.*

Done at Cedar Point, in said territory of Wisconsin, this third day of September, in the year of our Lord one thousand eight hundred and thirty-six, and in the year of the Independence of the United States the sixty-first.

H. Dodge,	[L. S.]
Osh-kosh, his x mark,	[L. S.]
Aya-ma-taw, his x mark,	[L. S.]
Ko-ma-ni-kin, his x mark,	[L. S.]
Wain-e-saut, his x mark,	[L. S.]
Kee-sis, his x mark,	[L. S.]
Carron-Glaude, his x mark,	[L. S.]
Say-ga-toke, his x mark,	[L. S.]
Shee-o-ga-tay, his x mark,	[L. S.]
Wah-pee-min, his x mark,	[L. S.]
Isk-ki-ninew, his x mark,	[L. S.]
Ko-ma-ni-kee-no-shah, his x mark,	
Wah-bee-ne-mickee, his x mark,	[L. S.]
Shee-pan-ago, his x mark,	[L. S.]
Maw-baw-so, his x mark,	[L. S.]
Chin-nay-pay-mawly, his x mark,	[L. S.]
Chee-chee-go-waw-way, his x mark,	[L. S.]
Shoneon, his x mark,	[L. S.]
Et-chee-kee, his x mark,	[L. S.]
Pee-a-tum, his x mark,	[L. S.]
Pay-maw-ba-may, his x mark,	[L. S.]
Ah-kah-mute, his x mark,	[L. S.]
Pah-mun-a-kut, his x mark,	[L. S.]
Chee-kah-ma-ke-shir, his x mark,	[L. S.]
Wah-kee-che-un, his x mark.	[L. S.]

Signed and sealed in the presence of—

Henry S. Baird, secretary to the commissioner.
George Boyd, United States Indian agent,
Charles A. Grignon, sworn interpreter,
William Powell, sworn interpreter,
George M. Brooke, brevet brigadier-general,
R. E. Clary, U. S. Army,
D. Jones,
John P. Arndt,

Charles R. Brush,
Louis Philipson,
L. Grignon,
Agt. Grignon,
Samuel Ryan,
William Bruce,
John Drake,
David Blish, jr.
J. Jourdain,
T. T. Porlier.

Schedule.

Claims to be paid
by United States. It is agreed on the part of the United States, that the following claims shall be allowed and paid, agreeably to the second article of the foregoing treaty, viz:

To John Lawe, twelve thousand five hundred dollars;
Augustine Grignon ten thousand dollars;
William Powell and Robert Grigon four thousand two hundred and fifty dollars;
Charles A. Grignon ten thousand dollars;
John Lawe & Co., six thousand dollars;
Walter T. Webster one hundred dollars;
John P. Arndt five hundred and fifty dollars;
William Farnsworth and Charles R. Brush two thousand five hundred dollars;
James Porlier, seven thousand five hundred dollars;
Heirs of Louis Beaupre one thousand five hundred dollars;
Dominick Brunette two hundred and thirty-one dollars and fifty cents;
Alexander J. Irwin, one thousand two hundred and fifty dollars;
American Fur Co. (western outfit) four hundred dollars;
Charles Grignon one thousand two hundred dollars;
Joseph Rolette one thousand seven hundred and fifty dollars;
Charles A. and Alexander Grignon seven hundred and fifty dollars;
James Reed seven hundred dollars;
Peter Powell one thousand seven hundred and fifty dollars;
Paul Grignon five thousand five hundred dollars;
William Dickinson three thousand dollars;
Robert M. Eberts seventy-four dollars;
Joseph Jourdain fifty dollars;
James Knaggs five hundred and fifty dollars ($550;)
Ebenezer Childs two hundred dollars;
Lewis Rouse five thousand dollars;
William Farnsworth two thousand five hundred dollars;
Saml. Irwin & Geo. Boyd jr. one hundred and five dollars;
Aneyas Grignon two thousand five hundred dollars;
Pierre Grignon decd. by Rob. & Peter B. Grignon six thousand dollars;
Stanislius Chappue one hundred dollars;
John Lawe one thousand two hundred dollars;
William Dickinson two hundred and fifty dollars;
Stanislius Chappue two thousand five hundred dollars;
Lewis Grignon seven thousand two hundred and fifty dollars.

H. Dodge, Commissioner.

All the above accts. were sworn to before me the 3d day of September, 1836.

John P. Arndt,
A Justice of the Peace.

TREATY WITH THE SIOUX, 1836.

Convention with the Sioux of Wa-ha-shaw's tribe.

Sept. 10, 1836.
───────
7 Stat., 510.
Proclamation, Feb.
15, 1837. In a convention held this tenth day of September 1836, between Col. Z. Taylor Indian Agent, and the chiefs, braves, and principal men of the Sioux of Wa-ha-shaw's tribe of Indians, it has been represented, that according to the stipulations of the first article of the treaty of Prairie du Chien, of the 15th July 1830, the country thereby ceded is "to be assigned and allotted under the direction of the President of the United States, to the tribes now living thereon, or to such other tribes as the President may locate thereon for hunting and other purposes," and, whereas, it is further represented to us, the chiefs, braves, and principal men of the tribe aforesaid, to be desirable that the lands lying between the State of Missouri and the Missouri river should be attached to and become a part of said State, and the Indian title thereto be extinguished but that, notwithstanding, as these lands compose a part of the country embraced by the provisions of said first article of the treaty aforesaid, the stipulations thereof will be strictly observed, until the assent of the Indians interested, is given to the proposed measure.

Now we, the chiefs, braves, and principal men of the above named tribe of Indians, fully understanding the subject, and well satisfied from the local position of the lands in question that they can never be made available for Indian purposes, and that an attempt to place an Indian population on them must inevitably lead to collisions with the citizens of the United States; and further believing that the extension of the State line in the direction indicated, would have a happy effect, by presenting a natural boundary between the whites and Indians: and, willing moreover, to give the United States a renewed evidence of our attachment & friendship, do hereby for ourselves, and on behalf of our respective tribes, (having full power and authority to this effect) forever cede, relinquish, and quit claim to the United States, all our right, title and interest of whatsoever nature in, and to, the lands lying between the State of Missouri and the Missouri river, and do freely and fully exonerate the United States from any guarantee, condition, or limitation, expressed or implied under the treaty of Prairie du Chien aforesaid or otherwise, as to the entire and absolute disposition of the said lands, fully authorizing the United States to do with the same whatever shall seem expedient or necessary. *Lands ceded to the United States.*

As a proof of the continued friendship and liberality of the United States towards the above named tribe of Indians, and as an evidence of the sense entertained for the good will manifested by said tribes to the citizens and Government of the United States, as evinced in the preceding cession or relinquishment, the undersigned agrees on behalf of the United States, to cause said tribes to be furnished with presents to the amount of four hundred dollars—in goods or in money. *Presents to be made by United States.*

In testimony whereof, we have hereunto set our hands and seals, the day and year above written.

> Sau-tabe-say, Wa-ba-shaw's son, his x mark, [L. S.]
> Wau-kaun-hendee-oatah, his x mark, [L. S.]
> Nau-tay-sah-pah, his x mark, [L. S.]
> Mauk-pee-au-cat-paun, his x mark, [L. S.]
> Hoo-yah, the eagle, his x mark, [L. S.]

Executed in presence of—

> H. L. Dousman,
> W. R. Jouett, captain, First Infantry,
> J. M. Scott, lieutenant, First Infantry,
> Geo. H. Pegram, lieutenant, First Infantry.

As a proof of the continued friendship and liberality of the United States towards the above named tribe of Indians, and as an evidence of the sense entertained for the good will manifested by said tribes to the citizens and Government of the United States, as evinced in the preceding cession or relinquishment, the undersigned agrees on behalf of the United States, to cause said tribes to be furnished with presents to the amount of four hundred dollars, in goods or in money.

In testimony whereof, I have hereunto set my hand and seal, this tenth day of September, 1836.   Z. Taylor,

> Colonel, U. S. Army,
> and Acting U. S. Indian Agent.   [L. S.]

TREATY WITH THE IOWA, ETC., 1836.

Sept. 17, 1836.

7 Stat., 511.
Proclamation, Feb. 15, 1837.

Articles of a treaty, made and concluded at Fort Leavenworth, on the Missouri river, between William Clark, Superintendent of Indian Affairs, on the part of the United States, of the one part, and the undersigned chiefs, warriors, and counsellors of the Ioway tribe and the band of Sacks and Foxes of the Missouri, (residing west of the State of Missouri,) in behalf of their respective tribes, of the other part.

Treaty of July 15, 1830.

ARTICLE 1. By the first article of the treaty of Prairie du Chien, held the fifteenth day of July eighteen hundred and thirty, with the confederated tribes of Sacks, Foxes, Ioways, Omahaws, Missourias, Ottoes, and Sioux, the country ceded to the United States by that treaty, is to be assigned and allotted under the direction of the President of the United States to the tribes living thereon, or to such other tribes as the President may locate thereon for hunting and other purposes.—And whereas it is further represented to us the chiefs, warriors, and counsellors of the Ioways and Sack and Fox band aforesaid, to be desirable that the lands lying between the State of Missouri and the Missouri river, should be attached to and become a part of said State, and the Indian title thereto, be entirely extinguished; but that. notwithstanding, as these lands compose a part of the country embraced by the provisions of said first article of the treaty aforesaid, the stipulations thereof will be strictly observed until the assent of the Indians interested is given to the proposed measures.

Lands ceded to the United States.

Now we the chiefs, warriors, and counsellors of the Ioways, and Missouri band of Sacks and Foxes, fully understanding the subject, and well satisfied from the local position of the lands in question, that they never can be made available for Indian purposes, and that an a tempt to place an Indian population on them, must inevitably lead to collisions with the citizens of the United States; and further believing that the extension of the State line in the direction indicated would have a happy effect, by presenting a natural boundary between the whites and Indians; and willing, moreover, to give the United States a renewed evidence of our attachment and friendship, do hereby for ourselves, and on behalf of our respective tribes, (having full power and authority to this effect,) forever cede, relinquish, and quit claim, to the United States, all our right, title, and interest of whatsoever nature in, and to, the lands lying between the State of Missouri and the Missouri river; and do freely and fully exonerate the United States from any guarantee; condition or limitation, expressed or implied, under the treaty of Prairie du Chien aforesaid, or otherwise, as to the entire and absolute disposition of the said lands, fully authorizing the United States to do with the same whatever shall seem expedient or necessary.

United States to pay as a present, $7,500.

As a proof of the continued friendship and liberality of the United States towards the Ioways and band of Sacks and Foxes of the Missouri, and as an evidence of the sense entertained for the good will manifested by said tribes to the citizens and Government of the United States, as evinced in the preceding cession or relinquishment, the undersigned, William Clark, agrees on behalf of the United States, to pay as a present to the said Ioways and band of Sacks and Foxes, seven thousand five hundred dollars in money, the receipt of which they hereby acknowledge.

Land assigned to Indians south of the Missouri river.

ARTICLE 2. As the said tribes of Ioways and Sacks and Foxes, have applied for a small piece of land, south of the Missouri, for a permanent home, on which they can settle, and request the assistance of the Government of the United States to place them on this land, in a situation at least equal to that they now enjoy on the land ceded by them: Therefore I, William Clark, Superintendent of Indian Affairs, do further agree on behalf of the United States, to assign to the Ioway tribe, and Missouri band of Sacks and Foxes, the small strip of land on the south side of the Missouri river, lying between the Kickapoo northern boundary line and the Grand Nemahar river, and extending from the Missouri back and westwardly with the said Kickapoo line and the Grand Nemahar, making four hundred sections; to be divided between the said Ioways and Missouri band of Sacks and Foxes, the lower half to the Sacks and Foxes, and the upper half to the Ioways.

ARTICLE 3. The Ioways and Missouri band of Sacks and Foxes further agree, that they will move and settle on the lands assigned them in the above article, as soon as arrangements can be made by them; and the undersigned William Clark, in behalf of the United States, agrees, that as soon as the above tribes have selected a site for their villages, and places for their fields, and moved to them, to erect for the Ioways five comfortable houses, to enclose and break up for them two hundred acres of ground; to furnish them with a farmer, a blacksmith, schoolmaster, and interpreter, as long as the President of the United States may deem proper; to furnish them with such agricultural implements as may be necessary, for five years; to furnish them with rations for one year, commencing at the time of their arrival at their new homes; to furnish them with one ferry-boat; to furnish them with one hundred cows and calves and five bulls, and one hundred stock hogs when they require them; to furnish them with a mill and assist in removing them, to the extent of five hundred dollars. And to erect for the Sacks and Foxes three comfortable houses; to enclose and break up for them two hundred acres of ground; to furnish them, with a farmer, blacksmith, schoolmaster, and interpreter, as long as the President of the United States may deem proper; to furnish them with such agricultural implements as may be necessary, for five years; to furnish them with rations for one year, commencing at the time of their arrival at their new home; to furnish them with one ferry-boat; to furnish them with one hundred cows and calves and five bulls, one hundred stock hogs when they require them; to furnish them with a mill; and to assist in moving them, to the extent of four hundred dollars.

United States to erect houses, inclose ground, furnish a farmer, etc.

ARTICLE 4. This treaty shall be obligatory on the tribes, parties hereto, from and after the date hereof, and on the United States from and after its ratification by the Government thereof.

Treaty binding when ratified.

Done, and signed, and sealed, at fort Leavenworth, on the Missouri, this seventeenth day of September, one thousand eight hundred and thirty-six, and of the independence of the United States the sixty-first.

Wm. Clark, Superintendent Indian Affairs.   [L. S.]
Ioways:
Mo-hos-ca, or white cloud, his x mark,   [L. S.]
Nau-che-ning, or no heart, his x mark,   [L. S.]
Wa-che-mo-ne, or the orator, his x mark,   [L. S.]
Ne-o-mo-ne, or raining cloud, his x mark,   [L. S.]
Mau-o-mo-ne, or pumpkin, his x mark,   [L. S.]
Congu, or plumb, his x mark,   [L. S.]
Wau-thaw-ca-be-chu, one that eats raw, his x mark,   [L. S.]
Ne-wau-thaw-chu, hair shedder, his x mark,   [L. S.]
Mau-hau-ka, bunch of arrows, his x mark,   [L. S.]
Cha-tau-the-ne, big bull, his x mark,   [L. S.]
Cha-tea-thau, buffalo bull, his x mark,   [L. S.]

Cha-ta-ha-ra-wa-re, foreign buffalo, his x mark,   [L. S.]
Sacks and Foxes:
Cau-ca-car-mack, rock bass, his x mark,   [L. S.]
Sea-sa-ho, sturgeon, his x mark,   [L. S.]
Pe-a-chin-a-car-mack, bald headed eagle, his x mark,   [L. S.]
Pe-a-chin-a-car-mack, jr., bald headed eagle, his x mark,   [L. S.]
Ca-ha-qua, red fox, his x mark,   [L. S.]
Pe-shaw-ca, bear, his x mark,   [L. S.]
Po-cau-ma, deer, his x mark,   [L. S.]
Ne-bosh-ca-wa, wolf, his x mark,   [L. S.]
Ne-squi-in-a, deer, his x mark,   [L. S.]
Ne-sa-au-qua, bear, his x mark,   [L. S.]
Qua-co-ou-si, wolf, his x mark,   [L. S.]
Se-quil-la, deer, his x mark,   [L. S.]
As-ke-pa-ke-ka-as-a, green lake, his x mark,   [L. S.]
Wa-pa-se, swan, his x mark,   [L. S.]
No-cha-taw-wa-ta-sa, star, his x mark,   [L. S.]

Witnesses:

S. W. Kearny, colonel First Regiment Dragoons,
Jno. Dougherty, Indian Agent,
Andrew S. Hughes, Sub-agent,
George R. H. Clark,
William Duncan, Indian farmer,
Jos. V. Hamilton, sutler Dragoons,
H. Robedou, jr.,

Wm. Bowman, sergeant-major First Dragoons,
Jeffrey Dorion, his x mark, sworn interpreter,
Peter Cadue, his x mark, sworn interpreter,
Jaques White, interpreter, United States,
Louis M. Darrion.

TREATY WITH THE POTAWATOMI, 1836.

Sept. 20, 1836.

7 Stat., 513.
Proclamation, Feb. 18, 1837.

Articles of a treaty made and concluded at Chippewanaung in the State of Indiana, between Abel C. Pepper, commissioner on the part of the United States, and To-i-sa's brother Me-mat-way and Che-quaw-ka-ko, chiefs and headmen of the Patawattimie tribe of Indians and their band on the twentieth day of September, in the year eighteen hundred and thirty-six.

Land ceded to the United States.

ART. 1. The above-named chiefs and headmen and their band hereby cede to the United States, ten sections of land reserved for them by the second article of the treaty between the United States, and the Patawattimie tribe of Indians, on Tippecanoe river, on the 27th day of October, in the year 1832.

Payment therefor.

ART. 2. In consideration of the cession aforesaid the United States stipulate to pay the above-named chiefs and headmen and their band the sum of eight thousand dollars on or before the first day of May next.

Indians to remove within two years.

ART. 3. The above-named chiefs and headmen and their band agree to remove to the country west of the Mississippi river, provided for the Patawattimie nation by the United States, within two years.

Payment of Indian debts.

ART. 4. At the request of the above-named band, it is stipulated that after the ratification of this treaty the United States shall appoint a commissioner who shall be authorized to pay such debts of the said band as may be proved to his satisfaction to be just, to be deducted from the amount stipulated in the second article of this treaty.

United States to pay expenses of making treaty.

ART. 5. The United States stipulate to provide for the payment of the necessary expenses attending the making and concluding this treaty.

Obligatory when ratified.

ART. 6. This treaty, after the same shall be ratified by the President and Senate of the United States, shall be binding upon both parties.

In testimony whereof, the said Abel C. Pepper, commissioner as aforesaid, and the said chiefs, and head men, and their band, have hereunto set their hands, this twentieth day of September, in the year eighteen hundred and thirty-six.

Abel C. Pepper,
We-we-sah, or To-i sa's brother, his x mark,
Me-mot-way, his x mark,
Che-quaw-ka-ko, his x mark,
Min-tom-in, his x mark,
Shaw-gwok-skuk, his x mark,
Mee-kiss, or Kawk's widow, her x mark.

Witnesses:
J. B. Duret, secretary.
Allen Hamilton,
Cyrus Taber,
Geo. W. Ewing,
James Moree,
Abram Burnett.

TREATY WITH THE POTAWATOMI, 1836.

*Articles of a treaty made and concluded at Chippewanaung—in the
State of Indiana between A. C. Pepper, commissioner on the part of
the United States and Mo-sack, chief of the Potawattimie tribe of
Indians and his band, on the twenty-second day of September, in the
year eighteen hundred and thirty-six.*

Sept. 22, 1836.

7 Stat., 514.
Proclamation, Feb.
16, 1837.

ART. 1. The above-named chief and his band hereby cede to the
United States four sections of land reserved for him and his band by
the 2nd article of the treaty between the United States, and the Potawattimie tribe of Indians, on Tippecanoe river, on the 27th day of
October, in the year eighteen hundred and thirty-two.

Land ceded to the
United States.

ART. 2nd. In consideration of the cession aforesaid, the United States
stipulate to pay the above-named chief and his band the sum of three
thousand two hundred dollars, on or before the first of May next.

Payment therefor.

ART. 3d. The above-named chief and his band agree to remove to
the country west of the Mississippi river provided for the Potawattimie nation by the United States within two years.

Indians to remove
within two years.

ART. 4. At the request of the above-named chief and his band, it is
stipulated that after the ratification of this treaty the United States
shall appoint a commissioner who shall be authorized to pay such debts
of the said band as may be proved to his satisfaction to be just, to be
deducted from the amount stipulated in the second article of this
treaty.

Payment of Indian
debts.

ART. 5. The United States stipulate to provide for the payment of
the necessary expenses attending the making and concluding this
treaty.

United States to pay
expenses of making
treaty.

ART. 6. This treaty after the same shall be ratified by the President and Senate of the United States, shall be binding upon both parties.

Treaty binding
when ratified.

In testimony whereof, the said A. C. Pepper, commissioner as
aforesaid, and the said chief and his band have hereunto set their
hands, the day and year first above written.

A. C. Pepper, commissioner,
Mo-sack, his x mark,
Nawb-bwitt, his x mark,
Skin-cheesh, her x mark,
Spo-tee, his x mark,
Naw-squi-base, her x mark,
Mose-so, his x mark.

Witnesses:
J. B. Duret, secretary,
Geo. W. Ewing,
Andrew Gosselin, his x mark,
Bennack, his x mark.

TREATY WITH THE POTAWATOMI, 1836.

*Articles of a treaty made and concluded at Chippe-way-naung in the
State of Indiana, on the twenty-third day of September in the year
one thousand eight hundred and thirty-six, between Abel C. Pepper
commissioner on the part of the United States, and the chiefs, warriors and headmen of the Potawattamie Indians of the Wabash.*

Sept. 23, 1836.

7 Stat., 515.
Proclamation, Feb.
18, 1837.

ART. 1. The chiefs, warriors and headmen of the Potawattamies of
the Wabash hereby cede to the United States, all the land belonging to
the said tribe, in the State of Indiana, and designated in the treaty of
1832, (between Jonathan Jennings, John W. Davis and Marks Crume,

Cession to the United
States.

commissioners of the United States, and the chiefs and warriors of the Potawattimies of the State of Indiana, and Michigan Territory) as reservations for the use of the following bands viz.

For the band of Kin-krash, four sections _____ 4 sec.
For the band of Che-chaw-kose, ten sections _____ 10 do.
For the band of Ash-kum and Wee-si-o-nas, sixteen sections_ 16 do.
For the band of We-saw, four sections _____ 4 do.
For the band of Mo-ta, four sections _____ 4 do.
For the bands of Mi-no-quet, four sections_____ 4 do.
_____
42

Payment therefor. ART. 2. In consideration of the cession aforesaid the United States stipulate to pay the above chiefs, warriors and headmen of the Potawattimie nation one dollar and twenty-five cents per acre or thirty-three thousand six hundred dollars, (33,600) in specie, on or before the first of May, in the year eighteen hundred and thirty-seven.

Indians to remove within two years. ART. 3. The above-named chiefs, warriors and headmen of the Potowattimies of the Wabash agree to remove to the country west of the Mississippi river, provided for the Potawattimie nation by the United States within two years.

Payment of Indian debts. ART. 4. At the request of the above-named chiefs, warriors and headmen of the Pottawattimies aforesaid, it is stipulated that after the ratification of this treaty, the United States shall appoint a commissioner who shall be authorized to pay such debts of said Wabash Potawattimies as may be proved to his satisfaction to be just, to be deducted from the amount stipulated in the 2d article of this treaty.

United States to pay expenses of making treaty. ART. 5. The United States stipulate to provide for the payment of the necessary expenses attending the making and concluding this treaty.

Treaty binding when ratified. ART. 6. This treaty shall be binding upon the parties aforesaid from the date of its ratification by the President and Senate of the United States.

In testimony whereof, the said Abel C. Pepper, commissioner as aforesaid, and the said chiefs, warriors, and head men of the Patawattamies of the Wabash, have hereunto set their hands, the day and year first above written.

Abel C. Pepper, commissioner,	Ash-kum, his x mark,
Pash-po-ho, his x mark,	Ke-waw-nay, his x mark,
O-koh-mause, his x mark,	Mat-che-saw, his x mark,
Jo-weh, his x mark,	Ne-boash, his x mark,
Mjo-quiss, his x mark,	Mee-shawk, his x mark,
We-wis-sah, his x mark,	Che-kaw-me, his x mark,
Pe-pin-a-waw, his x mark,	Kaw-te-nose, his x mark,
No-taw-kah, his x mark,	Saw-waw-quett, his x mark,
Po-kah-gause, his x mark,	W-daw-min, his x mark,
Nas-waw-ray, his x mark,	Kaw-we-saut, his x mark.

Witnesses:

J. B. Duret, secretary,	Allen Hamilton,
E. O. Cicott,	Cyrus Vigus,
I. P. Simonton, captain, First Regiment	Job B. Eldrige,
U. S. Dragoons,	Peter Barron.
Joseph Barron, interpreter,	

The above named chiefs acknowledge themselves to be justly indebted to Hamilton and Comperet, in the sum of eight hundred dollars, and request that it may be paid and deducted from the consideration named in the above treaty.

TREATY WITH THE SAUK AND FOX TRIBE, 1836.

In a convention held this twenty-seventh day of September 1836, between Henry Dodge Superintendent of Indian Affairs, and the chiefs, braves, and principal men of the Sac and Fox tribe of Indians, it has been represented, that according to the stipulations of the first article of the treaty of Prairie du Chien, of the 15th July 1830, the country thereby ceded, is "to be assigned and allotted under the direction of the President of the United States, to the tribes now living thereon, or to such other tribes as the President may locate thereon for hunting and other purposes." And, whereas, it is further represented to us, the chiefs, braves, and principal men of the tribe aforesaid, to be desirable that the lands lying between the State of Missouri and the Missouri river should be attached to, and become a part of said State, and the Indian title thereto be entirely extinguished; but that, notwithstanding, as these lands compose a part of the country embraced by the provisions of said first article of the treaty aforesaid, the stipulations thereof will be strictly observed until the assent of the Indians interested is given to the proposed measure.

Now, we the chiefs, braves, and principal men of the Sac and Fox tribes of Indians, fully understanding the subject, and well satisfied from the local position of the lands in question, that they can never be made available for Indian purposes, and that an attempt to place an Indian population on them must inevitably lead to collisions with the citizens of the United States; and further believing that the extension of the State line in the direction indicated, would have a happy effect, by presenting a natural boundary between the whites and Indians; and, willing moreover, to give the United States a renewed evidence of our attachment and friendship, do hereby, for ourselves, and on behalf of our respective tribes (having full power and authority to this effect) forever cede, relinquish, and quit claim to the United States, all our right, title, and interest of whatsoever nature in, and to, the lands lying between the State of Missouri and the Missouri river, and do freely and fully exonerate the United States from any guarantee, condition, or limitation, expressed or implied, under the treaty of Prairie du Chien aforesaid, or otherwise, as to the entire and absolute disposition of the said lands, fully authorizing the United States to do with the same whatever shall seem expedient or necessary.

In testimony whereof, we have hereunto set our hands and seals, the day and year first above written.

H. Dodge,	[L. s.]	Na-a-huck, his x mark,	[L. s.]
Wa-pa-ca, his x mark,	[L. s.]	Nau-a-wa-pit, his x mark,	[L. s.]
Po-we-seek, his x mark,	[L. s.]	Keo-kuck, his x mark,	[L. s.]
Qui-ya-ni-pe-na, his x mark,	[L. s.]	Pa-she-pa-ho, his x mark,	[L. s.]
Au-sa-wa-kuk, his x mark,	[L. s.]	We-she-oa-ma-quit, his x mark,	[L. s.]
Wa-ko-sa-see, his x mark,	[L. s.]	Ap-pi-nuis, his x mark,	[L. s.]
Sa-sa-pe-ma, his x mark,	[L. s.]	Pe-at-shin-wa, his x mark,	[L. s.]
Ma-wha-wi, his x mark,	[L. s.]	Wa-po-pa-nas-kuck, his x mark,	[L. s.]
Wa-pa-sa-kun, his x mark,	[L. s.]	Wa-ta-pe-naut, his x mark,	[L. s.]
Pa-ka-ka, his x mark,	[L. s.]	Pa-na-see, his x mark,	[L. s.]
We-se-au-ke-no-huck, his x mark,	[L. s.]	Ma-ke-no-na-see, his x mark,	[L. s.]
Ka-ha-kee, his x mark,	[L. s.]	Na-che-min, his x mark.	[L. s.]

In presence of us:

James W. Grimes, secretary of commission,
Jos. M. Street, Indian agent,
Ant. St. Clair, interpreter,
Frans. Labussir, interpreter,
James Craig,

Danniah Smith,
Nathl. Knapp,
Daniel Geire,
Erastus H. Bassett,
Geo. Catlin,
Robert Serrell Wood.

Sept. 27, 1836.

7 Stat., 516.
Proclamation, Feb. 15, 1837.

Lands ceded to United States.

TREATY WITH THE SAUK AND FOXES, 1836.

Sept. 28, 1836.

7 Stat., 517.
Proclamation, Feb. 27, 1837.

Articles of a treaty made and entered into at the treaty ground on the right bank of the Mississippi river in the county of Debuque and Territory of Wisconsin opposite Rock island, on the twenty-eighth day of September one thousand eight hundred and thirty-six, between Henry Dodge commissioner on the part of the United States, of the one part, and the confederated tribes of Sac and Fox Indians represented in general council by the undersigned chiefs headmen and warriors of the said tribes, of the other part.

Land ceded to the United States.

WHEREAS by the second article of the treaty made between the United States and the confederated tribes of Sac and Fox Indians on the twenty-first day of September one thousand eight hundred and thirty-two, a reservation of four hundred sections of land was made to the Sac and Fox Indians to be laid off under the direction of the President of the United States in conformity to the provisions of said article, and the same having been so subsequently laid out accordingly, and the confederated tribes of Sacs and Foxes being desirous of obtaining additional means of support, and to pay their just creditors have entered into this treaty, and make the following cession of land.

ARTICLE 1. The confederated tribes of Sacs and Foxes for the purposes above expressed, and for and in consideration of the stipulations and agreements hereinafter expressed, do hereby cede to the United States forever, the said reservation of four hundred sections of land as designated in the second article of the treaty made between the United States and the confederated tribes of Sacs and Foxes as the same has been surveyed and laid off by order of the President of the United States.

Payments by the United States.

ARTICLE 2. In consideration of the cession contained in the preceding article, the United States hereby agree as follows, to wit: To pay to the confederated tribes of the Sac and Fox Indians in the month of June one thousand eight hundred and thirty-seven, the sum of thirty thousand dollars, and for ten successive years thereafter the sum of ten thousand dollars each year in specie, to be paid at the treaty ground opposite Rock island or such other place as may be designated by the President of the United States; to pay to the widow and children of Felix St. Urain, deceased, former Indian agent who was killed by the Indians, one thousand dollars, and also to pay the sum of forty-eight thousand, four hundred and fifty-eight dollars, eighty-seven and a half cents to enable said Indians to pay such debts as may be ascertained by their superintendent to be justly due from them to individuals, and if such debts so ascertained to be just amount to more than said sum then the same shall be divided among said creditors pro rata; and if less, then the overplus to be paid to said Indians for their own use.

United States to furnish 200 horses.

ARTICLE 3. The United States further agree to deliver to the confederated tribes of Sacs and Foxes two hundred horses, as near that number as can be procured with the sum of nine thousand three hundred and forty-one dollars, to be delivered at the payment of the annuities in June one thousand eight hundred and thirty-seven.

Provision for half-breeds.

ARTICLE 4. At the special request of the Sac and Fox Indians aforesaid, the United States agree to make the following provision for the benefit and support of seven half-breeds of the Sac and Fox nation, to wit; The United States agree to pay to ———— Wayman for the use and benefit of his half-breed child by a Fox woman named Ni-an-no, one thousand dollars, to Wharton R. McPhearson, for the use and benefit of his half-breed child by To-to-qua, a Fox woman, one thousand dollars, to James Thorn for the use and benefit of his half-breed child by Ka-kee-o-sa-qua, a Fox woman, one thousand dollars, to Joseph

Smart for the use of his half-breed child by Ka-ti-qua a Fox woman one thousand dollars, to Nathan Smith for the use and benefit of his half-breed child by Wa-na-sa a Sac woman one thousand dollars, and to Joseph M. Street, Indian agent, two thousand dollars for the use and benefit of two half-breed children, one the child of Niwa-ka-kee a Fox woman, by one Mitchell, the other the child of Ni-an-na by Amos Farrar, the two thousand dollars to put at interest, and so much of said interest arising therefrom to be expended for the benefit of the children as said agent shall deem proper and necessary, and when each shall arrive at the age of twenty years, the said agent shall pay to each half breed one thousand dollars and any balance of interest remaining in his hands at the time.

ARTICLE 5. At the special request of the said confederated tribes of Sac and Fox Indians it is further agreed by the United States, to pay to Joseph M. Street, their agent, two hundred dollars for the use and benefit of Thompson Connoly and James Connoly children of their friend John Connoly deceased, to be by said agent put at interest and expended on the education of said Thompson and James Connoly, children of said John Connoly deceased.

Provision for the children of John Connoly, deceased.

ARTICLE 6. The said confederated tribes of Sac and Fox Indians hereby stipulate and agree to remove from off the lands herein in the first article of this treaty ceded to the United States, by the first day of November next ensuing the date hereof, and in order to prevent any future misunderstanding, it is expressly agreed and understood that no band or party of the said confederated tribes of Sac and Fox Indians, shall plant, fish or hunt on any portion of the country herein ceded after the period just mentioned.

Removal of Indians.

ARTICLE 6. This treaty shall be obligatory on the contracting parties after it shall be ratified by the President and Senate of the United States.

Treaty binding when ratified.

Done at the treaty ground on the right bank of the Mississippi, in Debuque county, Wisconsin Territory, opposite Rock island, this twenty-eighth day of September, one thousand eight hundred and thirty-six.

H. Dodge.

A-sho-wa-huk, his x mark,	[L. S.]	Wa-tup-a-waut, his x mark,	[L. S.]
Masha-na, his x mark,	[L. S.]	Me-kee-won-a-see, his x mark,	[L. S.]
Wa-ko-sha-she, his x mark,	[L. S.]	Ka-ka-no-an-na, his x mark,	[L. S.]
Sa-sa-pe-man, his x mark,	[L. S.]	Sacs:	
Na-wo-huck, his x mark,	[L. S.]	Kee-o-kuck, his x mark,	[L. S.]
Pa-na-see, his x mark,	[L. S.]	Pashapahoo, his x mark,	[L. S.]
Foxes:		We-she-ko-ma-quit, his x mark,	[L. S.]
Wa-pella, his x mark,	[L. S.]	Ap-a-noose, his x mark,	[L. S.]
Pow-a-sheek, his x mark,	[L. S.]	Pe-a-chin-wa, his x mark,	[L. S.]
Qua-qua-na-pe-qua, his x mark,	[L. S.]	Mo-wha-wi, his x mark,	[L. S.]
Wa-pak-onas-kuck, his x mark,	[L. S.]	Wa-pe-sha-kon, his x mark.	[L. S.]

In presence of us—

James W. Grimes, secretary of commission,
Jos. M. Street, Indian agent,
L. Dorsey Stockton, jr., attorney at law,
Ant. Leclaire, interpreter,
Frans. Labussir, interpreter,
James Craig,
P. R. Chouteau, jr.,
Geo. Davenport,
Nathl. Knapp,
W. R. McPherson,

Geo. W. Atchison,
Jeremiah Smith,
Nathan Smith,
Robt. Serrell Wood,
Geo. Catlin,
Richard J. Lockwood,
Enoch Gilbert,
Courtlandt Lawson,
George Miller, jr.,
Courtlandt Lawson.

TREATY WITH THE SAUK AND FOXES, 1836.

Sept. 28, 1836.
_____

7 Stat., 520.
Proclamation, Dec. 13, 1837.

Articles of a treaty made and entered into at the treaty ground on the right bank of the Mississippi river in the county of Debuque and Territory of Wisconsin opposite Rock island, on the twenty-eighth day of September one thousand eight hundred and thirty-six, between Henry Dodge commissioner on the part of the United States, of the one part, and the confederated tribes of Sac and Fox Indians represented in general council by the undersigned chiefs, headmen and warriors of the said tribes, of the other part:

WHEREAS by the second article of the treaty made between the United States and the confederate tribes of the Sac and Fox Indians on the twenty-first day of September one thousand eight hundred and thirty-two, a reservation of four hundred sections of land was made to the Sac and Fox Indians to be laid off under the directions of the President of the United States in conformity to the provisions of said article, and the same having been so subsequently laid out accordingly, and the confederated tribes of Sacs and Foxes being desirous of obtaining additional means of support, and to pay their just creditors, have entered into this treaty, and make the following cession of land.

Land ceded to the United States.

ARTICLE 1. The confederated tribes of Sacs and Foxes for the purposes above expressed, and for and in consideration of the stipulations and agreements hereinafter expressed, do hereby cede to the United States forever, the said reservation of four hundred sections of land as designated in the second article of the treaty made between the United States and the confederated tribes of Sacs and Foxes as the same has been surveyed and laid off by order of the President of the United States.

Consideration therefor.

ARTICLE 2. In consideration of the cession contained in the preceding article, the United States hereby agree as follows, to wit; To pay to the confederated tribes of the Sac and Fox Indians in the month of June one thousand eight hundred and thirty-seven, the sum of thirty thousand dollars, and for ten successive years thereafter the sum of ten thousand dollars each year in specie, to be paid at the treaty ground opposite Rock island or such other place as may be designated by the President of the United States, to pay to the widow and children of Felix St. Vrain deceased former Indian agent who was killed by the Indians, one thousand dollars; to pay to the following named persons the sums set opposite to their names respectively, being the one half of the amount agreed to be due and owing by the confederated tribes of Sacs and Foxes to their creditors, provided said creditors will wait for the other half untill the same can be paid out of their annuities, for which purpose the Sacs and Foxes will set apart the sum of five thousand dollars each year, beginning in one thousand eight hundred and thirty-eight, out of their annuities to be paid upon said debts in the proper proportion untill the whole amount is discharged; to wit: to John Campbell ten thousand dollars, to Jeremiah Smith six hundred and forty dollars, to Stephen Dubois three hundred and five dollars and twenty cents, to Nathaniel Knapp one hundred dollars, to Wharton R. McPhearson two hundred and fifty dollars, to S. S. Phelps & Co. four thousand dollars, to Jesse W. Shull five hundred dollars, to James Jordan one hundred and fifty dollars, to John R. Campbell fifteen dollars, to Amos Farrar one hundred dollars, to the owners of the S. boat Warrior, one hundred and sixty-two dollars and seventy-five cents, to George Davenport two thousand five hundred and sixty-three dollars and fifty cents, to Madame St. Ament five hundred dollars, to Madame Joseph Gunville five hundred dollars, to Madame Le Claire one hundred and twenty-five dollars, to Miss Blondeau one hundred and twenty-five dollars, to Antoine Le Claire two thousand four hundred and thirty-six dollars and fifty cents, to Francis Labachiere one thousand one hundred and sixty-seven dollars and seventy-five cents, to Pratte Chouteau & Co. twenty thousand three hundred and sixty-two dollars, and forty-two and a half cents, to Nathaniel Patterson four hundred and fifty-six dollars. The Iowa Indians having set up a claim to a part of the lands ceded by this treaty, it is therefore hereby provided, that the President of the United States shall cause the validity and extent of said claim to be ascertained, and upon a relinquishment of said claim to the United States, he shall cause the reasonable and fair value thereof to be paid to said Iowa Indians, and the same amount to be deducted from the sum stipulated to be paid to the Sacs and Foxes.

ARTICLE 3. The United States further agree to deliver to the confederated tribes of Sacs and Foxes two hundred horses, as near that number as can be procured with the sum of nine thousand three hundred and forty-one dollars, to be delivered at the payment of the annuities in June one thousand eight hundred and thirty-seven.

Two hundred horses to be furnished by the United States.

ARTICLE 4. At the special request of the Sac and Fox Indians aforesaid, the United States agree to make the following provisions for the benefit and support of seven half-breeds of the Sac and Fox nation, to wit; The United States agree to pay to —— Wayman for the use and benefit of his half-breed child by a Fox woman named Ni-an-no, one thousand dollars, to Wharton R. McPhearson for the use and benefit of his half-breed child by To-to-qua, a Fox woman, one thousand dollars, to James Thorn for the use and benefit of his half-breed child by Ka-kee-o-sa-qua, a Fox woman, one thousand dollars, to Joseph Smart for the use of his half-breed child by Ka-ti-qua a Fox woman one thousand dollars, to Nathan Smith for the use and benefit of his half-breed child by Wa-na-sa a Sac woman one thousand dollars, and to Joseph M. Street Indian agent, two thousand dollars for the use and benefit of two half-breed children, one the child of Niwa-ka-kee a Fox woman, by one Mitchell, the other the child of Ni-an-na by Amos Farrar, the two thousand dollars to be put at interest, and so much of said interest arising therefrom to be expended for the benefit of the children as said agent shall deem proper and necessary, and when each shall arrive at the age of twenty years, the said agent shall pay to each half-breed one thousand dollars and any balance of interest remaining in his hands at the time.

Provision for half-breeds.

ARTICLE 5. At the special request of the said confederated tribes of Sac and Fox Indians it is further agreed by the United States, to pay to Joseph M. Street their agent, two hundred dollars for the use and benefit of Thompson Connoly and James Connoly children of their friend John Connoly deceased, to be by said agent put at interest and expended on the education of said Thompson and James Connoly children of said John Connoly deceased.

Provision for the children of John Connoly, deceased.

ARTICLE 6. The said confederated tribes of Sac and Fox Indians hereby stipulate and agree to remove from off the lands herein in the first article of this treaty ceded to the United States, by the first day of November next ensuing the date hereof, and in order to prevent any future misunderstanding, it is expressly agreed and understood that no band or party of the said confederated tribes of Sac and Fox Indians, shall plant, fish or hunt on any portion of the country herein ceded after the period just mentioned.

Removal of Indians

ARTICLE 7. This treaty shall be obligatory on the contracting parties after it shall be ratified by the President and Senate of the United States.

Treaty binding when ratified.

Done at the treaty ground on the right bank of the Mississippe in Debuque county Wisconsin Territory opposite Rock island this twenty-eighth day of September one thousand eight hundred and thirty-six.

A. Dodge.

A-sho-wa-huk,
Ma-sha-na,
Wa-ko-sha-she,
Sa-sa-pe-man,
Na-wo-huck,
Pen-na-see
  Foxes:
Wa-pella,
Pow-a-sheek,
Qua-qua-na-pe-qua,
Wa-pak-onas-kuck,
Wa-tup-a-waut,
Ma-kee-won-a-see,
Ka-ka-no-an-na.
  Sacs:
Kee-o-kuck,
Pashapahoo,
We-she-ko-ma-quit,
Ap-a-noose,
Pe-a-chin-wa,
Mo-wha-wi,
Wa-pe-sha-kon.

In presence of us—

James W. Grimes, secretary of commission.
Jos. M. Street, Indian agent.
L. Dorsey Stockton, jr., attorney at law.
Ant. Leclaire, interpreter.
Frans. Labussar, interpreter.
James Craig.
P. R. Chouteau, jr.
Geo. Davenport.
Nathl. Knapp.
W. R. McPherson.
Geo. W. Atchison.
Jeremiah Smith.
Nathan Smith.
Robt. Serrell Wood.
Geo. Catlin.
Richard J. Lockwood.
Enoch Gilbert.
Courtlandt Lawson.
George Miller, jr.
Courtlandt Lawson.

To the Indian names are subjoined a mark and seal.

TREATY WITH THE OTO, ETC., 1836.

Articles of a convention entered into and concluded at Bellevue Upper Missouri the fifteenth day of October one thousand eight hundred and thirty-six, by and between John Dougherty U. S. agt. for Indian Affairs and Joshua Pilcher U. S. Ind. s. agt being specially authorized therefor; and the chiefs braves head men &c of the Otoes Missouries Omahaws and Yankton and Santee bands of Sioux, duly authorized by their respective tribes.

Oct. 15, 1836.

7 Stat., 524.
Proclamation, Feb. 15, 1837.

ARTICLE 1st. Whereas it has been represented that according to the stipulations of the first article of the treaty of Prairie du Chien of the fifteenth of July eighteen hundred and thirty, the country ceded is "to be assigned and allotted under the direction of the President of the United States to the tribes now living thereon or to such other tribes as the President may locate thereon for hunting and other purposes," and whereas it is further represented to us the chiefs, braves and head men of the tribes aforesaid, that it is desirable that the lands lying between the State of Missouri and the Missouri river, and south of a line running due west from the northwest corner of said State until said line strikes the Missouri river, should be attached to and become a part of said State, and the Indian title thereto be entirely extinguished; but that notwithstanding as these lands compose a part of the country embraced by the provisions of the said first article of the treaty aforesaid, the stipulations whereof will be strictly observed, until the assent of the Indians interested is given to the proposed measure. Now we the chiefs braves and principal men of the Otoes Missouries Omahaws Yankton and Santee bands of Sioux aforesaid fully understanding the subject and well satisfied from the local position of the lands in question, that they never can be made available for Indian purposes; and that an attempt to place an Indian population on them must inevitably lead to collisions with the citizens of the United States; and, further believing that the extension of the State line in the direction indicated, would have a happy effect by presenting a natural boundary between the whites and Indians; and willing moreover to give the United States a renewed evidence of our attachment and friendship; do hereby for ourselves and on behalf of our respective tribes (having full power and authority to this effect) for ever cede relinquish and quit claim to the United States all our right title and interest of whatsoever nature in and to the lands lying between the State of Missouri and the Missouri river, and south of a line running due west from the northwest corner of the State to the Missouri river, as herein before mentioned, and freely and fully exonerate the United States from any guarantee condition or limitation expressed or implied under the treaty of Prairie du Chien aforesaid or otherwise,

Treaty of July 15, 1830.

Cession of land to the United States.

as to the entire and absolute disposition of said lands, fully authorizing the United States to do with the same whatever shall seem expedient or necessary.

Present of $4,500 in merchandise.

ART. 2d. As a proof of the continued friendship and liberality of the United States towards the said Otoes Missouries Omahaws and Yankton and Santee bands of Sioux, and as an evidence of the sense entertained for the good will manifested by the said tribes to the citizens and Government of the United States as evinced in the preceding cession and relinquishment; and as some compensation for the great sacrifice made by the several deputations at this particular season, by abandoning their fall hunts and traveling several hundred miles to attend this convention the undersigned John Dougherty and Joshua Pilcher agrees on behalf of the United States to pay as a present to the tribes herein before named the sum of four thousand five hundred and twenty dollars in merchandise, the receipt of which they hereby acknowledge having been distributed among them in the proportions

Portions of each tribe.

following. To the Otoes twelve hundred and fifty dollars, to the Missouries one thousand dollars to the Omahaws twelve hundred and seventy dolls. to the Yankton and Santee bands of Sioux one thousand dollars.

Otoes and Missouries to be furnished with 500 bushels of corn.

ART. 3d. In consequence of the removal of the Otoes and Missouries from their former situation on the river Platte to the place selected for them, and of their having to build new habitations last spring at the time which should have been occupied in attending to their crops, it appears that they have failed to such a degree as to make it *certain* that they will lack the means of subsisting next spring, when it will be necessary for them to commence cultivating the lands now preparing for their use. It is therefore agreed that the said Otoes, and Missouries (in addition to the presents herein before mentioned) shall be furnished at the expense of the United States with five hundred bushels of corn to be delivered at their village in the month of April next. And

Omahas to have 100 acres of ground broke up, etc.

the same causes operating upon the Omahaws, they having also abandoned their former situation, and established at the place recommended to them on the Missouri river, and finding it difficult without the aid of ploughs to cultivate land near their village where they would be secure from their enemies, it is agreed as a farther proof of the liberality of the Government and its disposition to advance such tribes in the cultivation of the soil as may manifest a disposition to rely on it for the future means of subsistence; that they shall have one hundred acres of ground broke up and put under a fence near their village, so soon as it can be done after the ratification of this convention.

Obligatory when ratified.

ART. 5. This convention shall be obligatory on the tribes parties hereto, from and after the date hereof, and on the United States from and after its ratification by the Government thereof.

Done, signed, and sealed at Bellevue, Upper Missouri, this fifteenth day of October, one thousand eight hundred and thirty-six, and of the independence of the United States, the sixty-first.

Jno. Dougherty, Indian agent,	[L. S.]	Mon-nah-shu-jah, his x mark,	[L. S.]
Joshua Pilcher, United States In-		Missouries:	
dian subagent,	[L. S.]	Hah-che-ge-sug-a, his x mark,	[L. S.]
Otoes:		Black Hawk, his x mark,	[L. S.]
Jaton, his x mark,	[L. S.]	No Heart, his x mark,	[L. S.]
Big Kaw, his x mark,	[L. S.]	Wan-ge-ge-he-ru-ga-ror, his x mark,	[L. S.]
The Thief, his x mark,	[L. S.]	The Arrow Fender, his x mark,	[L. S.]
Wah-ro-ne-saw, his x mark,	[L. S.]	Wah-ne-min-er, his x mark.	[L. S.]
Buffalo Chief, his x mark,	[L. S.]	Big Wing, his x mark,	[L. S.]
Shaking Handle, his x mark,	[L. S.]	Omahaws:	
We-ca-ru-ton, his x mark,	[L. S.]	Big Elk, his x mark,	[L. S.]
Wash-shon-ke-ra, his x mark,	[L. S.]	Big Eyes, his x mark,	[L. S.]
Standing White Bear, his x mark,	[L. S.]	Wash-kaw-mony, his x mark,	[L. S.]
O-rah-car-pe, his x mark,	[L. S.]	White Horse, his x mark,	[L. S.]
Wah-nah-shah, his x mark,	[L. S.]	White Caw, his x mark,	[L. S.]
Wa-gre-ni-e, his x mark,	[L. S.]	Little Chief, his x mark,	[L. S.]

A-haw-paw, his x mark,	[L. S.]	Wash-ka-shin-ga, his x mark,	[L. S.]
Walking Cloud, his x mark,	[L. S.]	Mon-to-he, his x mark,	[L. S.]
Wah-see-an-nee, his x mark,	[L. S.]	Wah-kan-teau, his x mark,	[L. S.]
No Heart, his x mark,	[L. S.]	E-ta-ze-pa, his x mark,	[L. S.]
Wah-shing-gar, his x mark,	[L. S.]	Ha-che-you-ke-kha, his x mark,	[L. S.]
Standing Elk, his x mark,	[L. S.]	Wa-men-de-ah-wa-pe, his x mark,	[L. S.]
Ke-tah-an-nah, his x mark,	[L. S.]	E-chunk-ca-ne, his x mark,	[L. S]
Mon-chu-ha, his x mark,	[L. S.]	Chu-we-a-teau, his x mark,	[L. S.]
Pe-ze-nin-ga, his x mark,	[L. S.]	Mah-pe-a-tean, his x mark,	[L. S.]
Yankton and Santees,		Wah-mun-de-cha-ka, his x mark,	[L. S.]
Pitta-eu-ta-pishna, his x mark,	[L. S.]	Pah-ha-na-jie, his x mark,	[L. S.]

Witnesses:

J. Varnum Hamilton, sutler U. S. Dragoons and acting secretary,
William Steele,
John A. Ewell,
William J. Martin,
Martin Dorion, his x mark.

TREATY WITH THE SIOUX, 1836.

Convention with the Wahpaakootah, Susseton, and Upper Medawakanton tribes of Sioux Indians.

Nov. 30, 1836.

7 Stat., 527.
Proclamation, Feb 18, 1837.

In a convention held this thirtieth day of November 1836 between Lawrence Taliaferro, Indian Agent at St. Peters, and the chiefs, braves, and principal men of the Wahpaakootah, Susseton, and Upper Medawakanton tribes of Sioux Indians, it has been represented, that according to the stipulations of the first article of the treaty of Prairie du Chien of the 15th July, 1830, the country thereby ceded is "to be assigned and allotted under the direction of the President of the United States to the tribes now living thereon, or to such other tribes as the President may locate thereon for hunting and other purposes." And, whereas, it is further represented to us, the chiefs, braves and principal men of the tribes aforesaid, to be desirable, that the lands lying between the State of Missouri, and the Missouri river should be attached to, and become a part of said State, and the Indian title thereto be entirely extinguished; but that, notwithstanding, as these lands compose a part of the country embraced by the provisions of said first article of the treaty aforesaid, the stipulations thereof will be strictly observed until the assent of the Indians interested is given to the proposed measure.

Now we, the chiefs, braves, and principal men of the Wahpaakootah, Susseton and Upper Medawakanton tribes of Sioux Indians, fully understanding the subject, and well satisfied from the local position of the lands in question that they can never be made available for Indian purposes, and that an attempt to place an Indian population on them must inevitably lead to collisions with the citizens of the United States; and further believing that the extension of the State line in the direction indicated, would have a happy effect, by presenting a natural boundary between the whites and Indians; and willing, moreover, to give the United States a renewed evidence of our attachment and friendship, do hereby for ourselves, and on behalf of our respective tribes (having full power and authority to this effect) forever cede, relinquish and quit claim to the United States all our right, title and interest of whatsoever nature in, and to, the lands lying between the State of Missouri, and the Missouri river, and do freely and fully exonerate the United States from any guarantee, condition, or limitation, expressed or implied, under the treaty of Prairie du Chien aforesaid, or otherwise, as to the entire and absolute disposition of the said lands, fully authorizing the United States to do with the same whatever shall seem expedient or necessary.

Land ceded to the United States.

Presents to Indians.

As a proof of the continued friendship and liberality of the United States towards the Wahpaakootah, Susseton and Upper Medawakanton tribes of Sioux Indians, and as an evidence of the sense entertained for the good will manifested by said tribes to the citizens and Government of the United States, as evinced in the preceding session or relinquishment, the undersigned agrees, on behalf of the United States, to cause said tribes to be furnished with presents to the amount of five hundred and fifty dollars *in goods*, the receipt of which is hereby acknowledged.

In testimony whereof, we have hereunto set our hands and seals, the day and year first above written.

Law. Taliaferro, [L. S.]	Upper Medawakantons:
Sussetons:	Wahkon-Tunkah, or the big thunder, his x mark, [L. S.]
Ese-tah-ken-bah, or the sleepy eyes, his x mark, [L. S.]	Wahmadee-tunkah, or big eagle, his x mark, [L. S.]
Kahe-maa-doh-kah, or the male rover, his x mark, [L. S.]	Marcpeeah-mah-zah, or iron cloud, his x mark, [L. S.]
Tunkah-munnee, or the great walker, his x mark, [L. S.]	Koc-ko-moc-ko, or afloat, his x mark, [L. S.]
Hoh-wah-munnee, or the walking crier, his x mark, [L. S.]	Tah-chunk-pee-sappah, or the black tomahawk, his x mark, [L. S.]
Wahpaakootas:	Marc-pee-wee-chas-tah, or chiefs of the clouds, his x mark, [L. S.]
Tah-sau-ga, or the cane, his x mark, [L. S.]	Tah-chunk-washtaa, or the good road, his x mark, [L. S.]
Wahmaadee-sappah, or black eagle, his x mark, [L. S.]	Mah-zah-hoh-tah, or the gray iron, his x mark, [L. S.]
Skushkahnah, or moving shadow, his x mark, [L. S.]	Patah-eu-hah, or he that holds the five, his x mark, [L. S.]
Ahppaa-hoh-tah, or the gray mane, his x mark, [L. S.]	

Executed in presence of—

J. McClure, lieutenant, First Infantry,
S. M. Plummer, lieutenant, First Infantry,

J. N. Nicollet,
Scott Campbell, United States interpreter.

TREATY WITH THE CHIPPEWA, 1837.

Jan. 14, 1837.

7 Stat., 528.
Proclamation, July 2, 1838.

Articles of a treaty made and concluded at Detroit, in the State of Michigan, on the fourteenth day of January, in the year of our Lord eighteen hundred and thirty-seven, between the United States of America by their commissioner, Henry R. Schoolcraft, and the Saganaw tribe of the Chippewa nation, by their chiefs and delegates, assembled in council.

Cession of land to United States.

ART. 1st. The said tribe cede to the United States the following tracts of land, lying within the boundaries of Michigan; namely; One tract of eight thousand acres, on the river Au Sable. One tract of two thousand acres, on the *Misho-wusk* or Rifle river. One tract of six thousand acres, on the north side of the river *Kawkawling.* One tract of five thousand seven hundred and sixty acres upon Flint river, including the site of Reaums village, and a place called *Kishkawbawee.* One tract of eight thousand acres on the head of the Cass (formerly Huron) river, at the village of Otusson. One island in the Saganaw bay, estimated at one thousand acres, being the island called *Shaingwaukokaug,* on which *Mukokoosh* formerly lived. One tract of two thousand acres at *Nababish,* on the Saganaw river. One tract of one thousand acres, on the east side of the Saganaw river. One tract of six hundred and forty acres, at Great Bend, on Cass river. One tract of two thousand acres at the mouth of Point Augrais river. One tract of one thousand acres, on the Cass river at *Menoquet's* village. One tract of ten thousand acres on the *Shiawassee* river at *Ketchewaundauguminck* or Big Lick. One tract of six thousand acres at the Little Forks, on the

Tetabwasing river. One tract of six thousand acres at the Black-Birds' town, on the *Tetabwasing* river. One tract of forty thousand acres, on the west side of the Saganaw river. The whole containing one hundred and two thousand four hundred acres, be the same more or less.

Art. 2d. The said Indians shall have the right of living upon the tracts at the river Augrais, and Mushowusk or Rifle rivers, on the west side of Saganaw bay, for the term of five years, during which time no white man shall be allowed to settle on said tracts, under a penalty of five hundred dollars, to be recovered, at the suit of the informer; one half to the benefit of said informer, the other half to the benefit of the Indians.

Indians may live on certain tracts for five years.

Art. 3rd. The United States agree to pay to the said Indians, in consideration of the lands above ceded, the net proceeds of the sales thereof, after deducting the expense of survey and sale, together with the incidental expenses of this treaty. The lands shall be surveyed in the usual manner, and offered for sale, as other public lands, at the land offices of the proper districts, as soon as practicable after the ratification of this treaty. A special account of the sales shall be kept at the Treasury, indicating the receipts from this source, and after deducting therefrom the sums hereinafter set apart, for specified objects, together with all other sums, justly chargeable to this fund, the balance shall be invested, under the direction of the President, in some public stock, and the interest thereof shall be annually paid to the said tribe, in the same manner, and with the same precautions, that annuities are paid. *Provided*, That, if the said Indians shall, at the expiration of twenty years, or at any time thereafter, require the said stock to be sold, and the proceeds thereof distributed among the whole tribe, or applied to the advancement of agriculture, education, or any other useful object, the same may be done, with the consent of the President and Senate.

Payment for cession, etc.

Proviso.

Art. 4th. The said Indians hereby set apart, out of the fund, created by the sale of their lands, the following sums, namely;

Sums set apart by the Indians.

For the purchase of goods and provisions, to be delivered to them, as soon as practicable after the ratification of this treaty, forty thousand dollars.*

*Abrogated by art. 4 of treaty of Dec. 20, 1837.

For distribution among the heads of families, to be paid to them, as an annuity in 1837, ten thousand dollars.*

*Abrogated by art 4 of treaty of Dec. 20 1837.

For a special payment to each of the principal chiefs, agreeably to a schedule annexed, five thousand dollars.

For the support of schools, among their children, ten thousand dollars.

For the payment of their just debts, accruing since the treaty of Ghent, and before the signing of this treaty, forty thousand dollars.

For compensating American citizens, upon whose property this tribe committed depredations after the surrender of Detroit in 1812, ten thousand dollars.

For meeting the payment of claims which have been considered and allowed by the chiefs and delegates in council, as per schedule B hereunto annexed, twelve thousand two hundred and forty-three dollars, and seventy-five cents.

For vaccine matter, and the services of a physician, one hundred dollars per annum for five years.

For the purchase of tobacco to be delivered to them, two hundred dollars per annum for five years.

The whole of these sums shall be expended under the direction of the President, and the following principles shall govern the application. The goods and provisions shall be purchased by an agent, or officer of the Government, on contract, and delivered to them, at their expense, as early as practicable, after the ratification of the treaty. The annuity of ten thousand dollars shall be divided among the heads

To be expended under direction of the President.

of families, agreeably to a census, to be taken for the purpose. The school fund shall be put at interest, by investment in stocks, and the interest applied annually to the object, commencing in the year 1840, but the principal shall constitute a permanent fund for twenty years, nor shall the stock be sold, nor the proceeds diverted, at *that* period, without the consent of the President and Senate.

Payment of the moneys set apart for debts, etc.

The monies set apart for the liquidation of their debts, and for depredations, committed by them, shall be paid, under such precautions for ascertaining the justice of the indebtedness or claim, as the President may direct, but no payment shall be made, under either head, which is not supported by satisfactory proof, and sanctioned by the Indians: and if any balance of either sum remains, it shall be immediately divided by the disbursing officer, among the Indians. The other items of expenditure, mentioned in this article, shall be disbursed, under the usual regulations of the Indian Department, for insuring faithfulness and accountability in the application of the money.

The United States will advance the amount.
[See art. 3, treaty of Dec. 20, 1837.]

ART. 5th. The United States will advance the amount set apart in the preceding article for the purchase of goods and provisions, and the payment of debts, and depredations by the Indians, also the several sums stipulated to be paid to the chiefs, and distributed to the Indians as an annuity in 1837, and the amount set apart for claims allowed by the Indians, together with the expense of this negotiation.

Removal of Indians.

*See art. 2, treaty of Dec. 20, 1837.

ART. 6th. The said tribe agrees to remove from the State of Michigan, as soon as a proper location can be obtained. For this purpose, a deputation shall be sent, to view the country, occupied by their kindred tribes, west of the most westerly point of Lake Superior,* and if an arrangement for their future and permanent residence can be made in that quarter, which shall be satisfactory to them, and to the Government, they shall be permitted to form a reunion, with such tribes, and remove thereto. If such arrangement cannot be effected, the United States will afford its influence in obtaining a location for them at such place, west of the Mississippi, and southwest of the Missouri, as the legislation of Congress may indicate. The agency of the exploration, purchase, and removal will be performed by the United States, but the expenses attending the same shall be chargeable to said Indians at the Treasury, to be refunded out of the proceeds of their lands, at such time and in such manner as the Secretary of the Treasury shall deem proper.

The smith's shop, etc., to be continued, etc.

ART. 7th. It is agreed, that the smith's shop shall be continued among the Saganaws, together with the aid in agriculture, farming utensils, and cattle, secured to them under the treaty of September 24th 1819, as fixed, in amount, by the act of Congress of May 15th 1820. But the President is authorized to direct the discontinuance of the stated farmers should he deem proper, and the employment of a supervisor or overseer, to be paid out of this fund, who shall procure the services, and make the purchases required, under such instructions as may be issued by the proper department. And the services shall be rendered, and the shop kept, at such place or places, as may be most beneficial to the Indians. It shall be competent for the Government, at the request of the Indians, seasonably made, to furnish them agricultural products, or horses and saddlery, in lieu of said services, whenever the fund will justify it. *Provided*, That the whole annual expense, including the pay of the supervisor, shall not exceed the sum of two thousand dollars, fixed by the act herein above referred to.

Proviso.

Payment for two certain reservations.

ART. 8th. The United States, agree to pay to the said tribe, as one of the parties to the treaty, concluded at Detroit, on the 17th of November 1807, the sum of one thousand dollars, to quiet their claim, to two reservations of land, of two sections each, lying in Oakland county, in the State of Michigan, which were ceded to the Government by the Pottowatomies of St. Joseph's, on the nineteenth of September 1827. This sum will be paid to the chiefs, who are designated in the schedule referred to, in the fourth article, at the same time and place, that the annuities for the present year are paid to the tribe. And the said tribe hereby relinquish, and acknowledge full satisfaction, for any claim they now have, or have ever possessed, to the reservations aforesaid.

ART. 9th. Nothing in this treaty shall be construed to affect the payment of any annuity, due to the said tribe, by any prior treaty. But the same shall be paid as heretofore. *Annuities by former treaties not affected.*

ART. 10th. Should not the lands herein ceded, be sold, and the avails thereof, vested for said tribe, as provided in the third article, before the thirtieth day of September of the present year, so that the annual interest of such investment may be relied on, to constitute an annuity for said tribe in the year eighteen hundred and thirty-eight, the United States will, during the said year 1838, advance the same amount which is provided for that object in the fourth article of this treaty, which sum shall be refunded to the Treasury by said tribe with interest, out of any fund standing to their credit, at the discretion of the Secretary of the Treasury. *[Abrogated by art. 4, treaty of Dec. 20, 1837.]*

ART. 11th. The usual expenses, attending the formation of this treaty, will be paid by the United States, provided, that the Government may, in the discretion of the President, direct the one moiety thereof to be charged to the Indian fund, created by the third article of this treaty. *Expenses of treaty to be paid by United States.*

In testimony whereof, the said Henry R. Schoolcraft, commissioner on the part of the United States, and the chiefs and delegates of the said tribe, have hereunto set their hands, and affixed their marks, at the city of Detroit in Michigan, the day and year above written.

Henry R. Schoolcraft, Commissioner.

Ogima Keegido,	Monetogaubwee,
Naum Gitchigomee,	Aindunossega,
Osau Wauban,	Ugahbakwum,
Penayseewubee,	Shawun Epenaysee,
Washwa,	Waubredoaince,
Peenaysee Weegezhig,	Sheegunageezhig,
Mauk Esaut,	Etowanaquot,
Peetwayweetum,	Mukuday Ghenien,
Tontagonee,	Mukuckoosh,
Kaitchenoding,	Penayshee Weegezhig, the 2d,
Maishkoodagwana,	Mazinos,
Naishkayshig,	Pondiac,
Wasso,	Nawa Geezhig.
Pabaumosh,	

Francis Willett Shearman, secretary.	Douglass Houghton.
Henry Whiting, major, U. S. Army.	G. D. Williams.
J. P. Simonton, captain, U. S. Army.	William Johnston.
Z. Pitcher, surgeon, U. S. Army.	Joseph F. Menoy, interpreter.
Henry Connor, subagent.	John A. Drew.
Robert Stuart.	Darius Lawson.
Jno. Hulbert.	Charles H. Rodd.

(To the Indian names are subjoined marks.)

Schedule of the names of chiefs entitled to payments under the fourth and eighth articels of the foregoing treaty:

The following chiefs, representing the several bands of the tribe of the Saganaws, are entitled to receive the several sums of five hundred and one hundred dollars each, to wit:

1. Ogima Kegido
2. Shawun, Epenaysse
3. Naum Gitchegomee
4. Mauk Esaub
5. Muckuk, Kosh
6. Peteway, Weetum

7. Paypah, Monshee
8. Tontagonee
9. Wasse
10. Wahputo-ains.

HENRY R. SCHOOLCRAFT,
Commissioner.

Schedule B.

To Wawasso	$400 00
Ke-she-ah-be-no-qua, sister of Wawasso	400 00
Ke-wah-ne-quot	400 00
Peter Provencal	400 00
Leon, or Oge-ma-ge-ke-to	400 00
Moran, or Chemoquemont	200 00
Ke-she-go-qua	200 00
Wetonsaw, son of James Connor	400 00
Odis-pa-be-go-qua and children	800 00
Pen-a-see	400 00
Ozhe-me-ega	400 00
Bourissa's wife, at River au Sable	800 00
Nah-bwa-quo-una	400 00
Muttoway-bun-gee	400 00
Chonne	400 00
Mah-in-gun	800 00
Ma-conse	800 00
J. P. Simonton	800 00
Wabishkindib, or Henry Conner	3,243 75
Peepegauaince	200 00

Ogima Keegido,	Peteway, Weetum,
Shawun Epenaysee,	Pabaumoshee,
Naum Gitchegomee,	Tontagonee,
Mauk Esaub,	Wasse,
Muckuk, Kosh,	Waputo ains.

Signed in presence of—

Henry Whiting, major, U. S. Army.	Levi Cook, mayor of the city of Detroit.
E. Backus, U. S. Army.	Jno. Hulbert.
J. P. Simonton, captain, U. S. Army.	

Francis Willett Shearman, Secretary.

(To the Indian names are subjoined marks.)

TREATY WITH THE CHOCTAW AND CHICKASAW, 1837.

Jan. 17, 1837.

11 Stats., 573.
Proclamation Mar.
24, 1837.

Articles of convention and agreement made on the seventeenth day of January, 1837, between the undersigned chiefs and commissioners duly appointed and empowered by the Choctaw tribe of red people, and John McLish, Pitman Colbert, James Brown, and James Perry, delegates of the Chickasaw tribe of Indians, duly authorized by the chiefs and head-men of said people for that purpose, at Doaksville, near Fort Towson, in the Choctaw country.

Chickasaws may form a district in the Choctaw country.

ARTICLE 1. It is agreed by the Choctaws that the Chickasaws shall have the privilege of forming a district within the limits of their country, to be held on the same terms that the Choctaws now hold it, except the right of disposing of it, (which is held in common with the Choctaws and Chickasaws,) to be called the Chickasaw district of the Choctaw Nation; to have an equal representation in their general council, and to be placed on an equal footing in every other respect with any of the other districts of said nation, except a voice in the management of the consideration which is given for these rights and privileges; and the Chickasaw people to be entitled to all the rights and privileges of Choctaws, with the exception of participating in the Choctaw annuities and the consideration to be paid for these rights and privileges, and to be subject to the same laws to which the Choctaws are; but the Chickasaws reserve to themselves the sole right and privilege of controlling and managing the residue of their funds as far as is consistent with the late treaty between the said people and the Government of the United States, and of making such regulations and electing such officers for that purpose as they may think proper.

ARTICLE 2. The Chickasaw district shall be bounded as follows, viz: beginning on the north bank of Red River, at the mouth of Island Bayou, about eight or ten miles below the mouth of False Wachitta; thence running north along the main channel of said bayou to its source; thence along the dividing ridge between the Wachitta and Low Blue Rivers to the road leading from Fort Gibson to Fort Wachitta; thence along said road to the line dividing Musha-la-tubbee and Push-meta-haw districts; thence eastwardly along said district line to the source of Brushy Creek; thence down said creek to where it flows into the Canadian River, ten or twelve miles above the mouth of the south fork of the Canadian; thence west along the main Canadian River to its source, if in the limits of the United States, or to those limits; and thence due south to Red River, and down Red River to the beginning. *Boundaries of district.*

ARTICLE 3. The Chickasaws agree to pay the Choctaws, as a consideration for these rights and privileges, the sum of five hundred and thirty thousand dollars—thirty thousand of which shall be paid at the time and in the manner that the Choctaw annuity of 1837 is paid, and the remaining five hundred thousand dollars to be invested in some safe and secure stocks, under the direction of the Government of the United States, redeemable within a period of not less than twenty years—and the Government of the United States shall cause the interest arising therefrom to be paid annually to the Choctaws in the following manner: twenty thousand dollars of which to be paid as the present Choctaw annuity is paid, for four years, and the residue to be subject to the control of the general council of the Choctaws; and after the expiration of the four years the whole of said interest to be subject to the entire control of the said council. *Payment for these privileges.*

ARTICLE 4. To provide for the future adjustment of all complaints or dissatisfaction which may arise to interrupt the peace and harmony which have so long and so happily existed between the Choctaws and Chickasaws, it is hereby agreed by the parties that all questions relative to the construction of this agreement shall be referred to the Choctaw agent to be by him decided; reserving, however, to either party, should it feel itself aggrieved thereby, the rights of appealing to the President of the United States, whose decision shall be final and binding. But as considerable time might elapse before the decision of the President could be had, *in the mean time* the decision of the said agent shall be binding. *Differences as to the construction of this agreement to be referred to the Choctaw agent. Appeal to the President.*

ARTICLE 5. It is hereby declared to be the intention of the parties hereto; that equal rights and privileges shall pertain to both Choctaws and Chickasaws to settle in whatever district they may think proper, and to be eligible to all the different offices of the Choctaw Nation, and to vote on the same terms in whatever district they may settle, except that the Choctaws are not to vote *in anywise* for officers in relation to the residue of the Chickasaw fund. *Both to have equal rights and privileges. Excep*

In testimony whereof, the parties hereto have hereunto subscribed their names and affixed their seals, at Doaksville, near fort Towson in the Choctaw country, on the day and year first above written.

In the presence of—

Wm. Armstrong, Acting Superintendent Western Territory,
Henry R. Carter, Conductor of the Chickasaw Delegation
Josiah S. Doak,
Vincent B. Tims,
Daniel McCurtain, United States Interpreter,
P. J. Humphreys,
J. T. Sprague, Lieutenant U. S. Marine Corps,
Thomas Lafloor, his x mark, Chief of Oaklafalaya district,
Nituchachue, his x mark, Chief of Pushmatahaw district,
Joseph Kincaid, his x mark, Chief of Mushalatubbee district.

Commissioners of the Choctaw Nation:		Captains:
P. P. Pitchlynn,	[L. S.]	Oak-chi-a, his x mark,
George W. Haskins,	[L. S.]	Thomas Hays, his x mark,
Israel Folsom,	[L. S.]	Pis-tam-bee, his x mark,
R. M. Jones,	[L. S.]	Ho-lah-ta-ho-ma, his x mark,
Silas D. Fisher,	[L. S.]	E-yo-tah, his x mark,
Samuel Wowster,	[L. S.]	Isaac Perry, his x mark,
John McKenney, his x mark,		No-wah-ham-bee, his x mark.
Eyachahofaa, his x mark,		Chickasaw delegation:
Nathaniel Folsom, his x mark,		J. McLish,
Lewis Breashears, his x mark,		Pitman Colbert,
James Fletcher, his x mark,		James Brown, his x mark,
George Pusley, his x mark.		James Perry, his x mark.

TREATY WITH THE POTAWATOMI, 1837.

Feb. 11, 1837.

*7 Stat., 532.
Proclamation, Feb. 18, 1837.*

Articles of a treaty concluded in the city of Washington on the eleventh day of February eighteen hundred and thirty-seven between John T. Douglass, commissioner on the part of the United States and Chee-chaw-kose, Ash-kum Wee-saw or Louison, Muck-kose and Qui-qui-to, chiefs of the Potawatomie tribe of Indians.

Former treaties sanctioned.

ARTICLE 1. The chiefs and head men above named do, for themselves and their respective bands sanction and give their assent to the provisions of the treaties concluded between A. C. Pepper, commissioner on the part of the United States and certain chiefs and young men of the Potawatomie tribe of Indians, on the 5th day of August and 23d day of September 1836, in which were ceded to the United States certain lands in the State of Indiana, in which the chiefs and head men above named have an interest, the same having been reserved for them and their bands respectively in the treaties of October 26th and 27th 1832.

*Land ceded to the United States.
Indians to remove within two years.*

And the chiefs and head men above named, for themselves and their bands, do hereby cede to the United States all their interest in said lands, and agree to remove to a country that may be provided for them by the President of the United States, southwest of the Missouri river, within two years from the ratification of this treaty.

Payment by the United States.

ART. 2. The United States agree that the several sums, for the payment of which provision is made in the treaties of August and September 1836, referred to in the preceding article, shall be paid to the respective chiefs and bands, for whose benefit the lands, ceded by said treaties, were reserved.

United States to convey certain territory to Indians.

ART. 3. The United States further agree to convey by patent to the Potawatomies of Indiana, a tract of country, on the Osage river southwest of the Missouri river, sufficient in extent, and adapted to their habits and wants; remove them to the same; furnish them with one year's subsistence after their arrival there, and pay the expenses of this treaty, and of the delegation now in this city.

United States to purchase certain reserved land.

ART. 4. It is further stipulated, that the United States will purchase the "five sections in the prairie, near Rock Village" reserved for Qui-qui-to, in the second article of the treaty of October 20th 1832 for the sum of $4,000; to be paid to said chief at such times and places as the President of the United States may think proper.

Treaty binding when ratified.

ART. 5. This treaty to be obligatory upon the contracting parties when ratified by the President and Senate of the United States.

In witness whereof, the contracting parties have hereunto set their hands and seals, the day and year above written.

John T. Douglass, Commmissioner,	[L. S.]
Qui-qui-taw, his x mark,	[L. S.]
Che-chaw-kose, his x mark,	[L. S.]
Ash-kum, his x mark,	[L. S.]

We-saw, or Louison, his x mark,   [L. S.]
Muck-kose, his x mark,   [L. S.]
Sin-qui-waugh, his x mark,   [L. S.]
Po-ga-kose, his x mark.   [L. S.]
John C. Burnett,
Abram B. Burnett,
William Turner,
                    Interpreters.

Signed in presence of—
    G. C. Johnson,
    Isaac McCoy.

TREATY WITH THE KIOWA, ETC., 1837.

Treaty with the Kioway, Ka-ta-ka and Ta-wa-ka-ro, Nations of Indians.

Whereas a treaty of peace and friendship was made and signed on the 24th day of August 1835, between Montfort Stokes and Brigadier General Matthew Arbuckle, commissioners on behalf of the United States on the one part; and the chiefs, and head-men and representatives of the Comanche, Witchetaw, Cherokee Muscogee, Choctaw, Osage, Seneca and Quapaw nations or tribes of Indians on the other part: and whereas the said treaty has been duly ratified by the Government of the United States; now know all whom it may concern, that the President of the United States, by letter of appointment and instructions of the 7th day of April 1837, has authorized Col. A. P. Chouteau to make a convention or treaty between the United States and any of the nations or tribes of Indians of the Great Western Prairie; we the said Montfort Stokes, and A. P. Chouteau, commissioners of Indian treaties, have this day made and concluded a treaty of peace and friendship, between the United States of America, and the chiefs, headmen and representatives of the Kioway, Ka-ta-ka, and Ta-wa-ka-ro nations of Indians, on the following terms and conditions, that is to say:

ARTICLE 1st. There shall be perpetual peace and friendship between all the citizens of the United States of America and all the individuals composing the Kioway, Ka-ta-ka, and Ta-wa-ka-ro nations and their associated bands or tribes of Indians, and between these nations or tribes and the Muscogee and Osage nations or tribes of Indians.

ARTICLE 2d. Every injury or act of hostility by one or either of the contracting parties on the other, shall be mutually forgiven and for ever forgot.

ARTICLE 3d. There shall be a free and friendly intercourse between all the contracting parties hereto; and it is distinctly understood and agreed by the Kioway, Ka-ta-ka and Ta-wa-ka-ro nations, and their associated bands or tribes of Indians, that the citizens of the United States are freely permitted to pass and repass through their settlements or hunting ground without molestation or injury, on their way to any of the provinces of the Republics of Mexico or Texas, or returning therefrom, and that the nations or tribes named in this article further agree to pay the full value of any injury their people may do to the goods or property of the citizens of the United States, taken or destroyed when peaceably passing through the country they inhabit or hunt in, or elsewhere.—And the United States hereby guarantee to any Indian or Indians of the Kioway, Ka-ta-ka and Ta-wa-ka-ro nations, and their associated bands or tribes of Indians, a full indemnification for any horses or other property which may be stolen from them, *Provided* That the property so stolen cannot be recovered, and that sufficient proof is produced that it was actually stolen by a citizen of the United States, and within the limits thereof.

Margin notes:
May 26, 1837.

7 Stat., 533.
Proclamation, Feb. 21, 1838.

Peace and friendship.

Injuries mutually forgiven.

Friendly intercourse.

Payment for property stolen.

Proviso.

Hunting ground.

ARTICLE 4th. It is understood and agreed by all the nations or tribes of Indians, parties to this treaty, that each and all of the said nations or tribes have free permission to hunt and trap in the Great Prairie west of the Cross Timber to the western limits of the United States.

Payment for injuries to United States traders.

ARTICLE 5th. The Kioway, Ka-ta-ka and Ta-wa-ka-ro nations and their associated bands or tribes of Indians agree and bind themselves to pay full value for any injury their people may do to the goods or other property of such traders as the President of the United States may place near to their settlements or hunting ground for the purpose of trading with them.

Treatment of other Indians.

ARTICLE 6th. The Kioway, Ka-ta-ka and Ka-wa-ka-ro nations and their associated bands or tribes of Indians, agree, that in the event any of the red people belonging to the nations or tribes of Indians residing south of the Missouri river, and west of the States of Missouri and Arkansas, not parties to this treaty, should visit their towns, or be found on their hunting ground, that they will treat them with kindness and friendship, and do no injury to them in any way whatever.

In case of difficulties between any of the parties hereto.

ARTICLE 7th. Should any difficulty hereafter unfortunately arise between any of the nations or tribes of Indians, parties hereunto, in consequence of murder, the stealing of horses, cattle, or other cause, it is agreed that the other tribes shall interpose their good offices to remove such difficulties; and also that the Government of the United States may take such measures as they may deem proper to effect the same object, and see that full justice is done to the injured party.

Presents to Indians.

ARTICLE 8th. It is agreed by the commissioners of the United States that in consequence of the Kioway, Ka-ta-ka and Ta-wa-ka-ro nations and their associated bands or tribes of Indians having freely and willingly entered into this treaty, and it being the first they have made with the United States, or any of the contracting parties, that they shall receive presents immediately after signing, as a donation from the United States; nothing being asked from the said nations or tribes in return, except to remain at peace with the parties hereto, which their own good and that of their posterity require.

Relations with Mexico.

ARTICLE 9th. The Kioway, Ka-ta-ka and Ta-wa-ka-ro nations, and their associated bands or tribes of Indians, agree, that their entering into this treaty shall in no respect interrupt their friendly relations with the Republics of Mexico and Texas, where they all frequently hunt and the Kioway, Ka-ta-ka and Ta-wa-ka-ro nations sometimes visit; and it is distinctly understood that the Government of the United States desire that perfect peace shall exist between the nations or tribes named in this article, and the said Republics.

Treaty binding when ratified.

ARTICLE 10th. This treaty shall be obligatory on the nations or tribes, parties hereto, from and after the date hereof, and on the United States, from and after its ratification by the Government thereof.

Done and signed and sealed at Fort Gibson, this twenty-sixth day of May one thousand eight hundred and thirty-seven and of the independence of the United States the sixty-second.

M. Stokes,
Commissioner of Indian treaties.
A. P. Chouteau,
Commissioner Indian treaties.

Kioways:
Ta-ka-ta-couche, the Black Bird,
Cha-hon-de-ton, the Flying Squirrel,
Ta-ne-congais, the Sea Gull,
Bon-congais, the Black Cap,
To-ho-sa, the Top of the Mountain,
Sen-son-da-cat, the White Bird.
Con-a-hen-ka, the Horne Frog,
He-pan-ni-gais, the Night,
Ka-him-hi, the Prairie Dog,
Pa-con-ta, My Young Brother.

Ka-ta-kas:
Hen-ton-te, the Iron Shoe,
A-ei-kenda, the One who is Surrendered,
Cet-ma-ni-ta, the Walking Bear.
Ta-wa-ka-ros:
Ka-ta-ca-karo, He who receives the Word of God,
Ta-ce-hache, the One who Speaks to the Chief,
Ke-te-cara-con-ki, the White Cow,
Ta-ka, the Hunter of Men.

Muscogees:
Roly McIntosh,
Alex. Gillespie,
Samuel Miiler,
Samuel Perryman,
John Randam,
To-me-yo-hola,
Efi-emathla,
Chis-co-laco-mici,
Encotts Harjo,
Ufalila Harjo.
  Osages:
Clermont, the Principal Chief,
Ka-hi-gair-tanga, the Big Chief,
Ka-hi-gair-wa-chin-pi-chais, the Mad Chief,
Chan-gais-mon-non, the Horse Thief,

Wa-cri-cha, the Liberal,
Ta-lais, the Going Deer,
Chonta-sa-bais, the Black Dog,
Wa-clum-pi-chais, the Mad Warrior
Mi-ta-ni-ga, the Crazy Blanket,
Wa-ta-ni-ga, the Crazy,
Hec-ra-ti, the War Eagle,
Tan-wan-ga-hais, the Townmaker,
Ha-ha-ga-la, the One they Cry For,
Chongais-han-ga, the Learned Dog,
Man-pa-cha, the Brave Man,
Joseph Staidegais, the Tall Joseph,
Tais-ha-wa-gra-kim, the Chief Bearer,
Sa-wa-the, the Dreadful,
Ca-wa-wa-gu, the One Who Gives Horses,
U-de-gais-ta-wa-ta-ni-ga, the Crazy Osage.

Witnesses:

Wm. Whistler, Lieutenant-Colonel Seventh Infantry, commanding.
B. L. E. Bonneville, captain, Seventh Infantry.
Francis Lee, captain, Seventh Infantry.
Jas. R. Stephenson, captain, Seventh Infantry.
P. S. G. Bell, captain, First Dragoons.
W. Seawell, captain, Seventh Infantry. and secretary to the commissioners.
S. W. Moore, first lieutenant and adjutant, Seventh Infantry.
Th. H. Holmes, first lieutentant, Seventh Infantry.
R. H. Ross, first lieutenant, Seventh Infantry.

J. H. Bailey, assistant surgeon.
G. K. Paul, first lieutenant, Seventh Infantry.
S. G. Simmons, first lieutenant, Seventh Infantry.
J. G. Reed, second lieutenant, Seventh Infantry.
J. M. Wells, second lieutenant, Seventh Infantry.
R. L. Dodge.
F. Britton, lieutenant, Seventh, U. S. Army.
S. Hardage, Creek interpreter.

(To the Indian names are subjoined marks.)

TREATY WITH THE CHIPPEWA, 1837.

Articles of a treaty made and concluded at St. Peters (the confluence of the St. Peters and Mississippi rivers) in the Territory of Wisconsin, between the United States of America, by their commissioner, Henry Dodge, Governor of said Territory, and the Chippewa nation of Indians, by their chiefs and headmen.

July 29, 1837.

7 Stat., 536.
Proclamation, June 15, 1838.

ARTICLE 1. The said Chippewa nation cede to the United States all that tract of country included within the following boundaries: *Land ceded to the United States.*

Beginning at the junction of the Crow Wing and Mississippi rivers, between twenty and thirty miles above where the Mississippi is crossed by the forty-sixth parallel of north latitude, and running thence to the north point of Lake St. Croix, one of the sources of the St. Croix river; thence to and along the dividing ridge between the waters of Lake Superior and those of the Mississippi, to the sources of the Ocha-sua-sepe a tributary of the Chippewa river; thence to a point on the Chippewa river, twenty miles below the outlet of Lake De Flambeau; thence to the junction of the Wisconsin and Pelican rivers; thence on an east course twenty-five miles; thence southerly, on a course parallel with that of the Wisconsin river, to the line dividing the territories of the Chippewas and Menomonies; thence to the Plover Portage; thence along the southern boundary of the Chippewa country, to the commencement of the boundary line dividing it from that of the Sioux, half a days march below the falls on the Chippewa river; thence with said boundary line to the mouth of Wah-tap river, at its junction with the Mississippi; and thence up the Mississippi to the place of beginning.   *Boundaries.*

United States to make the following payments annually for twenty years.

ARTICLE 2. In consideration of the cession aforesaid, the United States agree to make to the Chippewa nation, annually, for the term of twenty years, from the date of the ratification of this treaty, the following payments.

1. Nine thousand five hundred dollars, to be paid in money.
2. Nineteen thousand dollars, to be delivered in goods.
3. Three thousand dollars for establishing three blacksmiths shops, supporting the blacksmiths, and furnishing them with iron and steel.
4. One thousand dollars for farmers, and for supplying them and the Indians, with implements of labor, with grain or seed; and whatever else may be necessary to enable them to carry on their agricultural pursuits.
5. Two thousand dollars in provisions.
6. Five hundred dollars in tobacco.

The provisions and tobacco to be delivered at the same time with the goods, and the money to be paid; which time or times, as well as the place or places where they are to be delivered, shall be fixed upon under the direction of the President of the United States.

The blacksmiths shops to be placed at such points in the Chippewa country as shall be designated by the Superintendent of Indian Affairs, or under his direction.

If at the expiration of one or more years the Indians should prefer to receive goods, instead of the nine thousand dollars agreed to be paid to them in money, they shall be at liberty to do so. Or, should they conclude to appropriate a portion of that annuity to the establishment and support of a school or schools among them, this shall be granted them.

Payment to half-breeds.

ARTICLE 3. The sum of one hundred thousand dollars shall be paid by the United States, to the half-breeds of the Chippewa nation, under the direction of the President. It is the wish of the Indians that their two sub-agents Daniel P. Bushnell, and Miles M. Vineyard, superintend the distribution of this money among their half-breed relations.

Payment of claims against Indians.

ARTICLE 4. The sum of seventy thousand dollars shall be applied to the payment, by the United States, of certain claims against the Indians; of which amount twenty-eight thousand dollars shall, at their request, be paid to William A. Aitkin, twenty-five thousand to Lyman M. Warren, and the balance applied to the liquidation of other just demands against them—which they acknowledge to be the case with regard to that presented by Hercules L. Dousman, for the sum of five thousand dollars; and they request that it be paid.

Hunting ground.

ARTICLE 5. The privilege of hunting, fishing, and gathering the wild rice, upon the lands, the rivers and the lakes included in the territory ceded, is guarantied to the Indians, during the pleasure of the President of the United States.

Treaty binding when ratified.

ARTICLE 6. This treaty shall be obligatory from and after its ratification by the President and Senate of the United States.

Done at St. Peters in the Territory of Wisconsin the twenty-ninth day of July eighteen hundred and thirty-seven.

Henry Dodge, Commissioner.

From Leech lake:
Aish-ke-bo-ge-koshe, or Flat Mouth,
R-che-o-sau-ya, or the Elder Brother.
Chiefs.

Pe-zhe-kins, the Young Buffalo,
Ma-ghe-ga-bo, or La Trappe,
O-be-gwa-dans, the Chief of the Earth,
Wa-bose, or the Rabbit,
Che-a-na-quod, or the Big Cloud.
Warriors.

From Gull lake and Swan river:
Pa-goo-na-kee-zhig, or the Hole in the Day,

Songa-ko-mig, or the Strong Ground.
Chiefs.

Wa-boo-jig, or the White Fisher,
Ma-cou-da, or the Bear's Heart.
Warriors.

From St. Croix river:
Pe-zhe-ke, or the Buffalo,
Ka-be-ma-be, or the Wet Month.
Chiefs.

Pa-ga-we-we-wetung, Coming Home Hollowing,
Ya-banse, or the Young Buck,
Kis-ke-ta-wak, or the Cut Ear.
Warriors.

From Lake Courteoville:
Pa-qua-a-mo, or the Wood Pecker.
Chief.

From Lac De Flambeau:
Pish-ka-ga-ghe, or the White Crow,
Na-wa-ge-wa, or the Knee,
O-ge-ma-ga, or the Dandy,
Pa-se-quam-jis, or the Commissioner,
Wa-be-ne-me, or the White Thunder.
Chiefs.

From La Pointe, (on Lake Superior):
Pe-zhe-ke, or the Buffalo,
Ta-qua-ga-na, or Two Lodges Meeting,
Cha-che-que-o.
Chiefs.

From Mille Lac:
Wa-shask-ko-kone, or Rats Liver,
Wen-ghe-ge-she-guk, or the First Day.
Chiefs.
Ada-we-ge-shik, or Both Ends of the Sky,
Ka-ka-quap, or the Sparrow.
Warriors.

From Sandy Lake:
Ka-nan-da-wa-win-zo, or Le Brocheux,
We-we-shan-shis, the Bad Boy, or Big
Mouth,
Ke-che-wa-me-te-go, or the Big French-
man.
Chiefs.

Na-ta-me-ga-bo, the Man that stands
First,
Sa-ga-ta-gun, or Spunk.
Warriors.

From Snake river:
Naudin, or the Wind,
Sha-go-bai, or the Little Six,
Pay-ajik, or the Lone Man,
Na-qua-na-bie, or the Feather.
Chiefs.
Ha-tau-wa,
Wa-me-te-go-zhins, the Little French-
man,
Sho-ne-a, or Silver.
Warriors.

From Fond du Lac, (on Lake Superior):
Mang-go-sit, or the Loons Foot,
Shing-go-be, or the Spruce.
Chiefs.

From Red Cedar lake:
Mont-so-mo, or the Murdering Yell.
From Red lake:
Francois Goumean (a half breed).
From Leech lake:
Sha-wa-ghe-zhig, or the Sounding Sky,
Wa-zau-ko-ni-a, or Yellow Robe.
Warriors.

Signed in presence of—

Verplanck Van Antwerp, Secretary to
the Commissioner.
M. M. Vineyard, U. S. Sub-Indian
Agent.
Daniel P. Bushnell.
Law. Taliaferro, Indian Agent at St.
Peters.
Martin Scott, Captain, Fifth Regiment
Infantry.
J. Emerson, Assistant Surgeon, U. S.
Army.
H. H. Sibley.

H. L. Dousman.
S. C. Stambaugh.
E. Lockwood.
Lyman M. Warren.
J. N. Nicollet.
Harmen Van Antwerp.
Wm. H. Forbes.
Jean Baptiste Dubay, Interpreter.
Peter Quinn, Interpreter.
S. Campbell, U. S. Interpreter.
Stephen Bonga, Interpreter.
Wm. W Coriell.

(To the Indian names are subjoined a mark and seal.)

TREATY WITH THE SIOUX, 1837.

Articles of a treaty, made at the City of Washington, between Joel R. Poinsett, thereto specially authorized by the President of the United States, and certain chiefs and braves of the Sioux nation of Indians.

Sept. 29, 1837.

7 Stat., 538.
Proclamation, June 15, 1838.

ARTICLE 1st. The chiefs and braves representing the parties having an interest therein, cede to the United States all their land, east of the Mississippi river, and all their islands in the said river. *(Cession of land to the United States.)*

ARTICLE 2d. In consideration of the cession contained in the preceding article, the United States agree to the following stipulations on their part. *(Consideration therefor.)*

First. To invest the sum of $300,000 (three hundred thousand dollars) in such safe and profitable State stocks as the President may direct, and to pay to the chiefs and braves as aforesaid, annually, forever, an income of not less than five per cent. thereon; a portion of said interest, not exceeding one third, to be applied in such manner as the President may direct, and the residue to be paid in specie, or in such other manner, and for such objects, as the proper authorities of the tribe may designate. *($300,000 to be invested for Indians.)*

Second. To pay to the relatives and friends of the chiefs and braves, as aforesaid, having not less than one quarter of Sioux blood, $110,000 *($110,000 for persons of mixed blood.)*

(one hundred and ten thousand dollars,) to be distributed by the proper authorities of the tribe, upon principles to be determined by the chiefs and braves signing this treaty, and the War Department.

Payment of Indian debts.

Third. To apply the sum of $90,000 (ninety thousand dollars) to the payment of just debts of the Sioux Indians, interested in the lands herewith ceded.

Annuity.

Fourth. To pay to the chiefs and braves as aforesaid an annuity for twenty years of $10,000 (ten thousand dollars) in goods, to be purchased under the direction of the President, and delivered at the expense of the United States.

Agricultural implements, etc.

Fifth. To expend annually for twenty years, for the benefit of Sioux Indians, parties to this treaty, the sum of $8,250 (eight thousand two hundred and fifty dollars) in the purchase of medicines, agricultural implements and stock, and for the support of a physician, farmers, and blacksmiths, and for other beneficial objects.

Improvement of lands.

Sixth. In order to enable the Indians aforesaid to break up and improve their lands, the United States will supply, as soon as practicable, after the ratification of this treaty, agricultural implements, mechanics' tools, cattle, and such other articles as may be useful to them, to an amount not exceeding $10,000, (ten thousand dollars.)

Provisions.

Seventh. To expend annually, for twenty years, the sum of $5.500 (five thousand five hundred dollars) in the purchase of provisions, to be delivered at the expense of the United States.

Goods.

Eighth. To deliver to the chiefs and braves signing this treaty, upon their arrival at St. Louis, $6,000 (six thousand dollars) in goods.

ARTICLE 3rd. [Stricken out by Senate.]

Treaty binding when ratified.

ARTICLE 4th. This treaty shall be binding on the contracting parties as soon as it shall be ratified by the United States.

In testimony whereof, the said Joel R. Poinsett, and the undersigned chiefs and braves of the Sioux nation, have hereunto set their hands, at the City of Washington, this 29th day of September A. D. 1837.

J. R. Poinsett.

Medawakantons:
Tah-tape-saah, The Upsetting Wind,
Wah-keah-tun-kah, Big Thunder,
Mah-zah-hoh-tah, Grey Iron,
Tautunga-munne, Walking Buffalo,
Eu-hah-kaakow, He that comes last,
Mah-kuah-pah, he that shakes the Earth,
Tah-mah-zah-hoh-wash-taa, The Iron of handsome voice,
Watt-chu-dah, The Dancer,
Mah-zah-tunkah, The Big Iron,
Mau-po-koah-munnee, He that runs after the clouds,

Tah-chunk-wash-taa, Good Road,
Mare-pu-ah-nasiah, Standing Cloud,
Koi-moko, Afloat,
Mau-pu-wee-chastah, White Man,
Mau-pu-ah-mah-zah, Iron Cloud,
Tah-chunek-oh-dutah, The Red Road,
Wasson-wee-chastish-nee, The Bad Hail,
Hoe-yah-pah, the Eagle Head
Annon-ge-nasiah, He that Stands on Both sides,
Chaudus-ka-mumee, the Walking Circle,
Tee-oh-du-tah, the Red Lodge.

In presence of—

Chauncy Bush, secretary.
Mahlon Dickerson, Secretary of the Navy.
W. J. Worth, lieutenant-colonel.
Geo. W. Jones, of Wisconsin.
Lau. Taliaferro, U. S. agent at St. Peters.
Wm. Hawley.

C. A. Harris, Commissioner of Indian Affairs.
S. Cooper, chief clerk War Department.
D. Kurtz, chief clerk Indian Office.
Charles Calvert.
S. Campbell, interpreter.

(To the Indian names are subjoined marks.)

TREATY WITH THE SAUK AND FOXES, 1837.

Articles of a treaty made at the city of Washington, between Carey A. Harris, Commissioner of Indian Affairs, thereto authorized by the President of the United States, and the confederated tribes of Sacs and Foxes, by their chiefs and delegates.

Oct. 21, 1837.

7 Stat., 540.
Proclamation, Feb. 21, 1838.

ARTICLE 1. The Sacs and Foxes make to the United States the following cessions:

Lands ceded to the United States.

First. Of a tract of country containing 1,250,000 (one million two hundred and fifty thousand) acres lying west and adjoining the tract conveyed by them to the United States in the treaty of September 21st, 1832. It is understood that the points of termination for the present cession shall be the northern and southern points of said tract as fixed by the survey made under the authority of the United States, and that a line shall be drawn between them, so as to intersect a line extended westwardly from the angle of said tract nearly opposite to Rock Island as laid down in the above survey, so far as may be necessary to include the number of acres hereby ceded, which last mentioned line it is estimated will be about twenty-five miles.

Second. Of all right or interest in the land ceded by said confederated tribes on the 15th of July 1830, which might be claimed by them, under the phraseology of the first article of said treaty.

ARTICLE 2d. In consideration of the cessions contained in the preceding article, the United States agree to the following stipulations on their part:

Consideration therefor.

First. To cause the land ceded to be surveyed at the expense of the United States, and permanent and prominent land marks established, in the presence of a deputation of the chiefs of said confederated tribes.

Land ceded to be surveyed, etc.

Second. To pay the debts of the confederated tribes, which may be ascertained to be justly due, and which may be admitted by the Indians, to the amount of one hundred thousand dollars ($100,000) provided, that if all their just debts amount to more than this sum, then their creditors are to be paid *pro rata* upon their giving receipts in full; and if said debts fall short of said sum, then the remainder to be paid to the Indians. *And provided also*, That no claim for depredations shall be paid out of said sum.

Payment of debts due by Indians.

Proviso.

Third. To deliver to them goods, suited to their wants, at cost, to the amount of twenty-eight thousand five hundred dollars ($28,500.)

Goods.

Fourth. To expend, in the erection of two grist mills, and the support of two millers for five years, ten thousand dollars ($10,000.)

Gristmills.

Fifth. To expend in breaking up and fencing in ground on the land retained by said confederated tribes, and for other beneficial objects, twenty-four thousand dollars ($24,000.)

Breaking up ground, etc.

Sixth. To expend in procuring the services of the necessary number of laborers, and for other objects connected with aiding them in agriculture, two thousand dollars ($2,000) a year, for five years.

Laborers.

Seventh. For the purchase of horses and presents, to be delivered to the chiefs and delegates on their arrival at St. Louis, four thousand five hundred dollars ($4,500,) one thousand dollars ($1,000) of which is in full satisfaction of any claim said tribe may have on account of the stipulation for blacksmiths in the treaty of 1832.

Horses and presents.

Eighth. To invest the sum of two hundred thousand dollars ($200,000) in safe State stocks, and to guarantee to the Indians, an annual income of not less than five per cent. the said interest to be paid to them each year, in the manner annuities are paid, at such time and place, and in money or goods as the tribe may direct. *Provided*, That it may be competent for the President to direct that a portion of the same may, with the consent of the Indians, be applied to education, or other purposes calculated to improve them.

$200,000 to be invested for Indians.

Proviso.

Blacksmiths' and gunsmith's establishments to be removed, etc.

ARTICLE 3d. The two blacksmith's establishments, and the gunsmith's establishment, to which the Sacs and Foxes are entitled under treaties prior to this, shall be removed to, and be supported in the country retained by them, and all other stipulations in former treaties, inconsistent with this, or with their residence, and the transaction of their business on their retained land are hereby declared void.

Removal of Indians.

ARTICLE 4th. The Sacs and Foxes agree to remove from the tract ceded, with the exception of Keokuck's village, possession of which may be retained for two years, within eight months from the ratification of this treaty.

United States to pay expenses of making treaty.

ARTICLE 5th. The expenses of this negotiation and of the chiefs and delegates signing this treaty to this city, and to their homes, to be paid by the United States.

Treaty binding when ratified.

ARTICLE 6th. This treaty to be binding upon the contracting parties when the same shall be ratified by the United States.

In witness whereof the said Carey A. Harris, and the undersigned chiefs and delegates of the said tribes, have hereunto set their hands at the city of Washington, this 21st October A. D. 1837.

C. A. Harris.

Sacs or Saukes:
Kee-o-kuck, The Watchful Fox, principal chief of the confederated tribes,
Wau-cai-chai, Crooked Sturgeon, a chief,
A-shee-au-kon, Sun Fish, a chief,
Pa-nau-se, Shedding Elk,
Wau-wau-to-sa, Great Walker,
Pa-sha-ka-se, The Deer,
Appan-oze-o-ke-mar, The Hereditary Chief, (or He who was a Chief when a Child,)
Waa-co-me, Clear Water, a chief,
Kar-ka-no-we-nar, The Long-horned Elk,
Nar-nar-he-keit, the Self-made Man,
As-ke-puck-a-wau, The Green Track,
Wa-pella, the Prince, a principal chief,

Qua-qua-naa-pe-pua, the Rolling Eyes, a chief,
Paa-ka-kar, the Striker,
Waa-pa-shar-kon, the White Skin,
Wa-pe-mauk, White Lyon,
Nar-nar-wau-ke-hait, the Repenter, (or the Sorrowful,)
Po-we-sheek, Shedding Bear, a (principal chief,)
Con-no-ma-co, Long Nose Fox, a chief, (wounded,)
Waa-co-shaa-shee, Red Nose Fox, a principal chief Fox tribe, (wounded,)
An-non-e-wit, The Brave Man,
Kau-kau-kee, The Crow,
Kish-kee-kosh, The Man with one leg off.

Signed in presence of—

Chauncey Bush, Secretary.
Joseph M. Street, U. S. Indian Agent.
Joshua Pilcher, Indian Agent.
Geo. Davenport.
J. F. A. Sanford.

S. C. Stambaugh.
P. G. Hambaugh.
Antoine Le Claire, U. S. Indian Interpreter.

(To the Indian names are subjoined marks.)

TREATY WITH THE YANKTON SIOUX, 1837.

Oct. 21, 1837.
7 Stat., 542.
Proclamation, Feb. 21, 1838.

Articles of a treaty made at the city of Washington, between Carey A. Harris, thereto specially authorized by the President of the United States, and the Yankton tribe of Sioux Indians, by their chiefs and delegates.

Indians cede all their right in land ceded by treaty of 15th July, 1830.

ARTICLE 1st. The Yankton tribe of Sioux Indians cede to the United States all the right and interest in the land ceded by the treaty, concluded with them and other tribes on the fifteenth of July, 1830, which they might be entitled to claim, by virtue of the phraseology employed in the second article of said treaty.

Consideration therefor.

ARTICLE 2d. In consideration of the cession contained in the preceding article, the United States stipulate to pay them four thousand dollars ($4,000.)

How to be expended.

It is understood and agreed, that fifteen hundred dollars ($1,500) of this sum shall be expended in the purchase of horses and presents, upon the arrival of the chiefs and delegates at St. Louis; two thousand dollars ($2,000) delivered to them in goods, at the expense of the United States, at the time their annuities are delivered next year; and five hundred dollars ($500) be applied to defray the expense of removing the agency building and blacksmith shop from their present site.

ARTICLE 3d. The expenses of this negotiation, and of the chiefs and delegates signing this treaty to this city and to their homes, to be paid by the United States.

United States to pay expenses of this treaty.

ARTICLE 4th. This treaty to be binding upon the contracting parties, when the same shall be ratified by the United States.

Treaty binding when ratified.

In witness whereof, the said Carey A. Harris, and the undersigned chiefs and delegates of said tribe, have hereunto set their hands at the city of Washington, this 21st day of October A. D. 1837.

C. A. Harris.

Ha-sa-za (The Elk's Horn)	Mau-ka-ush-can (The Trembling Earth)
Ha-sha-ta (The Forked Horn)	Mon-to-he (White crane)
Za-ya-sa (Warrior)	Ish-ta-ap-pi (Struck in the eye)
Pa-la-ni-a-pa-pi (Struck by a Riccara)	E-mo-ne.
To-ka-can (He that gives the First Wound)	

In presence of—

Chauncey Bush, Secretary.
Joshua Pilcher, Indian agent.
W. Thompson.

(To the Indian names are subjoined marks.)

TREATY WITH THE SAUK AND FOXES, 1837.

Articles of a treaty made at the City of Washington, between Carey A. Harris, thereto specially authorized by the President of the United States, and the Sacs and Foxes of Missouri, by their Chiefs and Delegates.

Oct. 21, 1837.
7 Stat., 543.
Proclamation, Feb. 21, 1838.

ARTICLE 1st. The Missouri Sac and Fox Indians make the following cessions to the United States:

Cessions to the United States.

First. Of all right or interest in the country between the Missouri and Mississippi rivers and the boundary line between the Sac and Fox and the Sioux Indians, described in the second article of the treaty made with these and other tribes on the 19th of August 1825, to the full extent to which said claim was recognized in the third article of said treaty; and of all interest or claim by virtue of the provisions of any treaties since made by the United States with the Sacs and Foxes.

Second. Of all the right to locate, for hunting or other purposes, on the land ceded in the first article of the treaty of July 15th 1830, which, by the authority therein conferred on the President of the United States they may be permitted by him to enjoy.

Third. Of all claims or interest under the treaties of November 3d, 1804, August 4th, 1824, July 15th, 1830, and September 17th, 1836, for the satisfaction of which no appropriations have been made.

ARTICLE 2d. In consideration of the cession contained in the preceding article, the United States agree to the following stipulations on their part:

Consideration therefor.

First. To pay to the said Sacs and Foxes of the Missouri, the sum of one hundred and sixty thousand dollars ($160,000.)

Payment of $160,000 to Indians.

It is understood and agreed that of the said sum of one hundred and sixty thousand dollars, ($160,000,) there shall be expended in the purchase of merchandise to be delivered whenever in the judgment of the President it may be best for them twenty-five hundred dollars, ($2,500;) and there shall be paid to Jacques Mettez, their interpreter, for services rendered, and at their request, one hundred dollars, ($100.)

$2,500 to be expended for merchandise.

Balance to be invested.

Second. To invest the balance of said sum amounting to one hundred and fifty-seven thousand four hundred dollars ($157,400,) and to guaranty them an annual income of not less than five per cent. thereon.

Interest, how to be applied.

Third. To apply the interest herein guaranteed, in the following manner:

For the support of a blacksmith's establishment, one thousand dollars ($1,000) per annum.

For the support of a farmer, the supply of agricultural implements and assistance, and other beneficial objects, sixteen hundred dollars ($1,600) per annum.

For the support of a teacher and the incidental expenses of a school, seven hundred and seventy dollars ($770) per annum.

The balance of the interest, amounting to forty-five hundred dollars ($4,500,) shall be delivered at the cost of the United States, to said Sac and Fox Indians, in money or merchandise, at the discretion of the President, and at such time and place as he may direct.

Expenses of this treaty to be paid by United States.

ARTICLE 3d. The expenses of this negotiation and of the chiefs and delegates signing this treaty to this city and to their homes to be paid by the United States.

Treaty binding when ratified.

ARTICLE 4th. This treaty to be binding upon the contracting parties, when the same shall be ratified by the United States.

In witness whereof, the said Carey A. Harris and the undersigned chiefs and delegates of said tribe, have hereunto set their hands at the city of Washington, this 21st day of October A. D. 1837.

C. A. Harris.

Sacs:
Po-ko-mah (The Plum)
Nes-mo-ea (The Wolf)
Au-ni-mo-ni (The Sun Fish)

Foxes:
Sa-ka-pa (son of Quash-qua-mi)
A-ka-ke (The Crow)

In presence of—

Chauncey Bush, Secretary.
Joshua Pilcher, Indian Agent.
W. Thompson.

(To the Indian names are subjoined marks.)

TREATY WITH THE WINNEBAGO, 1837.

Nov. 1, 1837.

7 Stat., 544.
Proclamation, June 15, 1838.

Articles of a treaty made at the city of Washington, between Carey A. Harris, thereto specially directed by the President of the United States, and the Winnebago nation of Indians, by their chiefs and delegates.

Lands ceded to the United States.

ARTICLE 1st. THE Winnebago nation of Indians cede to the United States all their land east of the Mississippi river.

Indians relinquish their right to occupy, except for hunting, certain land.

ARTICLE 2d. The said Indians further agree to relinquish the right to occupy, except for the purpose of hunting a portion of the land held by them west of the Mississippi, included between that river and a line drawn from a point twenty miles distant therefrom on the southern boundary of the neutral ground to a point, equidistant from the said river, on the northern boundary thereof.

Their title not to be invalidated.

But this stipulation shall not be so construed, as to invalidate their title to the said tract.

Indians to remove within eight months.

ARTICLE 3d. The said Indians agree to remove within eight months from the ratification of this treaty, to that portion of the neutral ground west of the Mississippi, which was conveyed to them in the second article of the treaty of September *15th,* [21st] 1832, and the United States agree that the said Indians may hunt upon the western part of said neutral ground until they shall procure a permanent settlement.

Consideration for said cession.

ARTICLE 4th. In consideration of the cession and relinquishment contained in the preceding articles, the United States agree to the following stipulations on their part.

First. To set apart the sum of two hundred thousand dollars ($200,000) for the following purposes:

To pay to the individuals herein named the sum specified for each; To Nicholas Boilvin, six thousand dollars ($6,000); to the other four children of Nicholas Boilvin, formerly agent for said nation, four thousand dollars ($4,000) each; to Catherine Myott, one thousand dollars, ($1,000); to Hyancinthe St. Cyr one thousand dollars ($1,000); to the widow of Henry Gratiot, late sub-agent of the nation, in trust for her eight children, ten thousand dollars ($10,000); to H. L. Dousman, in trust for the children of Pierre Paquette, late interpreter for the nation three thousand dollars ($3,000); to Joseph Brisbois, two thousand dollars ($2,000); to Satterlee Clark, junior, two thousand dollars ($2,000;) to John Roy, two thousand dollars ($2,000); to Antoine Grignon, two thousand dollars ($2,000); to Jane F. Rolette, two thousand dollars ($2,000); to George Fisher, one thousand dollars ($1,000); to Therese Roy, one thousand dollars ($1,000); to Domitille Brisbois, one thousand dollars ($1,000). These sums are allowed, at the earnest solicitation of the chiefs and delegates, for supplies and services to the nation, afforded by these individuals.

The balance of the above sum of two hundred thousand dollars ($200,000) shall be applied to the debts of the nation, which may be ascertained to be justly due, and which may be admitted by the Indians: *Provided,* That if all their just debts shall amount to more than this balance, their creditors shall be paid *pro rata,* upon their giving receipts in full; and if the just debts shall fall short of said balance, the residue of it shall be invested for the benefit of the nation; *And provided, also,* That no claim for depredations shall be paid out of said balance.

Second. To pay, under the direction of the President, to the relations and friends of said Indians, having not less than one quarter of Winnebago blood, one hundred thousand dollars ($100,000).

Third. To expend, for their removal to the lands assigned them, a sum not exceeding seven thousand dollars ($7,000).

Fourth. To deliver to the chiefs and delegates on their arrival at St. Louis, goods and horses to the amount of three thousand dollars ($3,000); and, also, to deliver to them, as soon as practicable after the ratification of this treaty, and at the expense of the United States goods to the amount of forty-seven thousand dollars ($47,000).

Fifth. To deliver to them provisions to the amount of ten thousand dollars, ($10,000); and horses to the same amount.

Sixth. To apply to the erection of a grist-mill, three thousand dollars, ($3,000).

Seventh. To expend, in breaking up and fencing in ground, after the removal of the said Indians, ten thousand dollars ($10,000).

Eighth. To set apart the sum of ten thousand dollars ($10,000) to defray contingent and incidental expenses in the execution of this treaty, and the expenses of an exploring party, when the said Indians shall express a willingness to send one to the country southwest of the Missouri river.

Ninth. To invest the balance of the proceeds of the lands ceded in the first article of the treaty, amounting to eleven hundred thousand dollars (1,100,000,) and to guaranty to them an interest of not less than five per cent.

Of this interest amounting to fifty-five thousand dollars ($55,000,) it is agreed the following disposition shall be made;

For purposes of education, twenty-eight hundred dollars ($2,800).

For the support of an interpreter for the school, five hundred dollars, ($500.)

For the support of a miller, six hundred dollars ($600.)

For the supply of agricultural implements and assistance, five hundred dollars, ($500.)

For medical services and medicines, six hundred dollars ($600.)

The foregoing sums to be expended for the objects specified, for the term of twenty-two years, and longer at the discretion of the President. If at the expiration of that period, or any time thereafter, he shall think it expedient to discontinue either or all of the above allowances, the amount so discontinued shall be paid to the said Winnebago nation. The residue of the interest, amounting to fifty thousand dollars ($50,000,) shall be paid to said nation, in the following manner; Ten thousand dollars ($10,000) in provisions, twenty thousand dollars ($20,000) in goods, and twenty thousand dollars ($20,000) in money.

So much of existing treaties as requires services, etc., to be null and void.

ARTICLE 5th. It is understood and agreed that so much of the stipulations in existing treaties with said Winnebago nation, as requires services to be performed, supplies furnished, or payments made, at designated times and places, shall be henceforth null and void; and those stipulations shall be carried into effect at such times and at such points in the country to which they are about to remove, as the President may direct.

Treaty binding when ratified.

ARTICLE 6th. This treaty to be binding on the contracting parties when it shall be ratified by the United States.

In witness whereof, the said Carey A. Harris and the undersigned chiefs and delegates of the said Winnebago nation, have hereunto set their hands at the City of Washington, this first day of November, A. D. 1837.

C. A. Harris.

Watch-hat-ty-kan, (Big Boat,)	Mai-ta-sha-hay-ma-ne-kah, (Young Kar-i-mo-nee,)
Keesh-kee-pa-kah, (Kar-i-mo-nee,)	Wa-kaun-ho-no-nic-kah, (Little Snake,)
Mo-ra-chay-kah, (Little Priest,)	Hoong-kah, (Old Chief,)
Ma-na-pay-kah, (Little Soldier,)	To-shun-uc-kah, (Little Otter,)
Wa-kaun-ha-kah, (Snake Skin,)	Sho-go-nic-kah, (Little Hill,)
Ma-hee-koo-shay-nuz-he-kah, (Young Decori,)	Homp-ska-kah, (Fine Day,)
Wa-kun-cha-koo-kah, (Yellow Thunder,)	Chow-walk-saih-e-nic, (The Plover,)
Wa-kaun-kah, (The Snake,)	Ah-oo-shush-kah, (Red Wing,)
Wa-kun-cha-nic-kah, (Little Thunder,)	Shoog-hat-ty-kah, (Big Gun,)
Nautch-kay-suck-kah, (Quick Heart,)	Ha-kah-kah, (Little Boy Child.)

In presence of—

Thos. A. B. Boyd, U. S. S. Indian agent.	Alexis Bailly.
N. Boilvin,	H. H. Sibley, agent Am. Fur. Co.
Antoine Grinion,	John Lowe.
Jean Roy,	John M'Farlane.
Interpreters.	W. Gunton.
Joseph Moore,	T. R. Cruttenden.
J. Brisbois,	Charles E. Mix.
Sat. Clark, jr.,	A. R. Potts.
Conductors.	Rd. L. Mackall.

(To the Indian names are subjoined a mark.)

TREATY WITH THE IOWA, 1837.

Nov. 23, 1837.

7 Stat., 547. Proclamation, Feb. 21, 1838.

Articles of a treaty made at the city of Saint Louis, between Joshua Pilcher, thereto specially authorized by the President of the United States, and the Ioway Indians, by their chiefs and delegates.

Cession to the United States.

ARTICLE 1st. THE Ioway Indians cede to the United States all the right and interest in the land ceded by the treaty, concluded with them and other tribes on the 15th of July 1830, which they might be entitled to claim, by virtue of the phraseology employed in the second article of said treaty.

Consideration therefor.

ARTICLE 2d. In consideration of the cession contained in the preceding article, the United States stipulate to pay them two thousand five hundred dollars ($2,500) in horses, goods and presents, upon their signing this treaty in the city of Saint Louis.

ARTICLE 3d. The expenses of this negotiation and of the chiefs and *United States to pay expenses of making treaty.* delegates signing this treaty to the city of Washington and to their homes to be paid by the United States.

ARTICLE 4th. This treaty to be binding upon the contracting parties *Treaty binding when ratified.* when the same shall be ratified by the United States.

In witness whereof the said Joshua Pilcher and the undersigned chiefs and delegates of said Indians have hereunto set their hands at the city of Saint Louis, this twenty-third day of November A. D. 1837.

Joshua Pilcher,
U. S. Indian agent.
Ne-o-mon-ni,
Non-che-ning-ga,
Wat-che-mon-ne,
Tah-ro-hon.

Signed in presence of—

E. A. Hitchcock, Captain U. S. Army
John B Farpy.
L. G. C. Bliss.

(To the Indian names are subjoined marks.)

TREATY WITH THE CHIPPEWA, 1837.

Articles of a treaty, made and concluded at Flint river, in the State of *Dec. 20, 1837,* *Michigan, on the twentieth day of December, eighteen hundred and* *7 Stat., 547.* *thirty-seven, between the United States, by Henry R. Schoolcraft* *Proclamation, July 2, 1838.* *commissioner duly authorized for that purpose, and acting super-intendent of Indian affairs, and the Saganaw tribe of Chippewas.*

ARTICLE 1. It is agreed, that the sum of fifty cents per acre shall *Fifty cents per acre to be retained, etc.* be retained out of every acre of land ceded by said tribe, by the treaty of the 14th of January 1837, as an indemnification for the location to be furnished for their future permanent residence and to constitute a fund for emigrating thereto.

ARTICLE 2d. The United States agree to reserve a location for said *A location to be reserved for said tribe, etc.* tribe on the head waters of the Osage river, in the country visited by a delegation of the said tribe during the present year, to be of proper extent, agreeably to their numbers, embracing a due proportion of wood and water, and lying contiguous to tribes of kindred language. Nor shall anything contained in the sixth article of the treaty of the 14th January 1837, entitle them, at this time, to a location in the country west of Lake Superior.

ARTICLE 3d. Nothing embraced in the fifth article of said treaty *The United States not obliged to advance the money required by 5th article, treaty 14th Jan., 1837.* shall obligate the United States, at the present time, to advance from the Treasury, the entire amount appropriated by the said tribe in the fourth article of said treaty; but the President shall have authority to direct such part of the said moneys to be paid for the objects indicated, so far as the same are not hereinafter modified, as he may deem proper: *Provided,* That the whole sum so advanced, shall not exceed *Proviso.* seventy-five thousand dollars. And the reduction shall be made upon the several items ratably, or in any other manner he may direct; *Pro-* *Proviso.* *vided,* That the balance of said appropriations, or of any item or items thereof, shall be paid out of the proceeds of the ceded lands, as soon as the fund will permit, and the President may direct.

ARTICLE 4th. The first and second clauses of the fourth article of *Parts of treaty of 14th Jan., 1837, abrogated.* the treaty of the 14th of January 1837, and the tenth article of said treaty, are hereby abrogated; and in lieu thereof, it is agreed, that the United States shall pay to said tribe in each of the years 1838 and 1839, respectively, an annuity of five thousand dollars, and goods to the amount of ten thousand dollars, to be advanced by the Treasury, and to be refunded out of the first proceeds of their lands. But no further annuity, nor in any higher amounts, shall be paid to them, by virtue of the treaty aforesaid, until the same shall be furnished by the interest of the proceeds of their lands, vested in conformity with the provisions of the third article of said treaty.

Division of payments due certain chiefs.
ARTICLE 5th. Several of the chiefs entitled to payments by schedule A, affixed to the treaty aforesaid, having died within the year, it is agreed, that the proportion of the fund, to which they would have been entitled, may be redivided in such manner as the President may direct.

No preemption right to be granted, etc.
ARTICLE 6th. No act of Congress shall confer upon any citizen, or other person, the right of pre-emption to any lands ceded to the United States by the treaty of the 14th of January 1837, herein above referred to. Nor shall any construction be put upon any existing law, respecting the public lands, granting this right to any lands ceded by said treaty.

Expenses to be paid of this and prior negotiations.
ARTICLE 7th. The United States will pay the expenses of this negotiation, together with the unpaid expenses of the prior negotiations, with said tribe, of the 24th of May 1836, and of the 14th of January 1837.

In testimony whereof, the commissioner above named, and the chiefs and headmen of said tribe, have hereunto affixed their signatures at the time and place above recited, and of the independence of the United States the sixty-second year.

Henry R. Schoolcraft,
Commissioner.

Ogisna Kegido, (The Chief Speaker), 1st chief of the tribe.
Tondagonee, (A dog rampant or furious.)
Mukkukoosh, (The Broken Chest, Keg, or Box.)
Ogimaus, (The Little Chief, or chief of subordinate authority.)
Ottawaus, (The Little Ottawa.)
Peetwaweetam, (The Coming Voice.)

Mushkootagwìma, (The Meadow Sparrow, or Feather in the Meadow or Plain.)
Acqueweezais, (The Expert Boy, i. e. wickedly expert.)
Kaugaygeezhig, (The Everlasting Sky.)
Wasso, (The Bright Light, or light falling on a distant object.)

Signed in presence of—

Jno. Garland, Major, U. S. Army.
Henry Connor, sub-agent.
T. B. W. Stockton.
G. D. Williams, commission of internal improvements, South Michigan.
Jonathan Beach.
Chas. C. Hascall, receiver of public moneys.

Albert J. Smith.
Robt. J. S. Page.
Wait Beach.
Rev. Luther D. Whitney.
T. R. Cumings.

(To the Indian names are subjoined marks.)

TREATY WITH THE NEW YORK INDIANS, 1838.

Jan. 15, 1838.

7 Stat., 550.
Proclamation, Apr. 4, 1840.

Articles of a treaty made and concluded at Buffalo Creek in the State of New York, the fifteenth day of January in the year of our Lord one thousand eight hundred and thirty-eight, by Ransom H. Gillet, a commissioner on the part of the United States, and the chiefs, head men and warriors of the several tribes of New York Indians assembled in council witnesseth:

Preamble.

WHEREAS, the six nations of New York Indians not long after the close of the war of the Revolution, became convinced from the rapid increase of the white settlements around, that the time was not far distant when their true interest must lead them to seek a new home among their red brethren in the West: And whereas this subject was agitated in a general council of the Six nations as early as 1810, and resulted in sending a memorial to the President of the United States, inquiring whether the Government would consent to their leaving their habitations and their removing into the neighborhood of their western brethren, and if they could procure a home there, by gift or purchase, whether the Government would acknowledge their title to the lands so obtained in the same manner it had acknowledged it in those from whom they might receive it; and further, whether the existing treaties would, in such a case remain in full force, and their annuities be paid as heretofore: And whereas, with the approbation of the President of the United States, purchases were made by the New York Indians from the Menomonie and Winnebago Indians of certain lands at Green Bay in the Territory of Wisconsin, which after much difficulty and contention with those Indians concerning the extent of that purchase, the whole subject was finally settled by a treaty between the United States and the Menomonie Indians, concluded in February, 1831, to which the New York Indians gave their assent on the seventeenth day of October 1832: And whereas, by the provisions of that treaty, five hundred thousand acres of land are secured to the New York Indians of the Six Nations and the St. Regis tribe, as a future home, on condition that they all remove to the same, within three years, or such reasonable time as the President should prescribe: And whereas, the President is satisfied that various considerations have prevented those still residing in New York from removing to Green Bay, and among other reasons, that many who were in favour of emigration, preferred to remove at once to the Indian territory, which they were fully persuaded was the only permanent and peaceful home for all the Indians. And they therefore applied to the President to take their Green Bay lands, and provide them a new home among their brethren in the Indian territory. And whereas, the President being anxious to promote the peace, prosperity and happiness of his red children, and being determined to carry out the humane policy of the Government in removing the Indians from the east to the west of the Mississippi, within the Indian territory, by bringing them to see and feel, by his justice and liberality, that it is their true policy and for their interest to do so without delay.

Therefore, taking into consideration the foregoing premises, the following articles of a treaty are entered into between the United States of America and the several tribes of the New York Indians, the names of whose chiefs, head men and warriors are hereto subscribed, and those who may hereafter give their assent to this treaty in writing, within such time as the President shall appoint.

GENERAL PROVISIONS.

ARTICLE 1. The several tribes of New York indians, the names of whose chiefs, head men, warriors and representatives are hereunto annexed, in consideration of the premises above recited, and the covenants hereinafter contained, to be performed on the part of the United States, hereby cede and relinquish to the United States all their right, title and interest to the lands secured to them at Green Bay by the Menomonie treaty of 1831, excepting the following tract, on which a part of the New York Indians now reside: beginning at the southwesterly corner of the French grants at Green Bay, and running thence southwardly to a point on a line to be run from the Little Cocaclin, parallel to a line of the French grants and six miles from Fox River; from thence on said parallel line, northwarely six miles; from thence eastwardly to a point on the northeast line of the Indian lands, and being at right angles to the same.

Indians relinquish their right to lands at Green Bay.

United States set apart other lands for Indians.

ARTICLE 2. In consideration of the above cession and relinquishment, on the part of the tribes of the New York Indians, and in order to manifest the deep interest of the United States in the future peace and prosperity of the New York Indians, the United States agree to set apart the following tract of country, situated directly west of the State of Missouri, as a permanent home for all the New York Indians, now residing in the State of New York, or in Wisconsin, or elsewhere in the United States, who have no permanent homes, which said country is described as follows, to wit: Beginning on the west line of the State of Missouri, at the northeast corner of the Cherokee tract, and running thence north along the west line of the State of Missouri twenty-seven miles to the southerly line of the Miami lands; thence west so far as shall be necessary, by running a line at right angles, and parallel to the west line aforesaid, to the Osage lands, and thence easterly along the Osage and Cherokee lands to the place of beginning to include one million eight hundred and twenty-four thousand acres of land, being three hundred and twenty acres for each soul of said Indians as their numbers are at present computed. To have and to hold the same in fee simple to the said tribes or nations of Indians, by patent from the President of the United States, issued in conformity with the provisions of the third section of the act, entitled "An act to provide for an exchange of lands, with the Indians residing in any of the States or Territories, and for their removal west of the Mississippi," approved on the 28th day of May, 1830, with full power and authority in the said Indians to divide said lands among the different tribes, nations, or bands, in severalty, with the right to sell and convey to and from each other, under such laws and regulations as may be adopted by the respective tribes, acting by themselves, or by a general council of the said New York Indians, acting for all the tribes collectively. It is understood and agreed that the above described country is intended as a future home for the following tribes, to wit: The Senecas, Onondagas, Cayugas, Tuscaroras, Oneidas, St. Regis, Stockbridges, Munsees, and Brothertowns residing in the State of New York, and the same is to be divided equally among them, according to their respective numbers, as mentioned in a schedule hereunto annexed.

1830, ch. 148.

Tribes that do not agree to remove, etc., to forfeit all interest in said lands.

ARTICLE 3. It is further agreed that such of the tribes of the New York Indians as do not accept and agree to remove to the country set apart for their new homes within five years, or such other time as the President may, from time to time, appoint, shall forfeit all interest in the lands so set apart, to the United States.

Peace and friendship.

ARTICLE 4. Perpetual peace and friendship shall exist between the United States and the New York Indians; and the United States hereby guaranty to protect and defend them in the peaceable possession and enjoyment of their new homes, and hereby secure to them, in said country, the right to establish their own form of government, appoint their own officers, and administer their own laws; subject, however, to the legislation of the Congress of the United States, regulating trade and intercourse with the Indians. The lands secured to them by patent under this treaty shall never be included in any State or Territory of this Union. The said Indians shall also be entitled, in all respects, to the same political and civil rights and privileges, that are granted and secured by the United States to any of the several tribes of emigrant Indians settled in the Indian Territory.

Land set apart for the Oneida.

ARTICLE 5. The Oneidas are to have their lands in the Indian Territory, in the tract set apart for the New York Indians, adjoining the Osage tract, and that hereinafter set apart for the Senecas; and the same shall be so laid off as to secure them a sufficient quantity of timber for their use. Those tribes, whose lands are not specially designated in this treaty, are to have such as shall be set apart by the President.

ARTICLE 6. It is further agreed that the United States will pay to those who remove west, at their new homes, all such annuities, as shall properly belong to them. The schedules hereunto annexed shall be deemed and taken as a part of this treaty. *Annuities, where to be paid.*

ARTICLE 7. It is expressly understood and agreed, that this treaty must be approved by the President and ratified and confirmed by the Senate of the United States, before it shall be binding upon the parties to it. It is further expressly understood and agreed that the rejection, by the President and Senate, of the provisions thereof, applicable to one tribe, or distinct branch of a tribe, shall not be construed to invalidate as to others, but as to them it shall be binding, and remain in full force and effect. *Treaty binding when ratified.*

ARTICLE 8. It is stipulated and agreed that the accounts of the Commissioner, and expenses incurred by him in holding a council with the New York Indians, and concluding treaties at Green Bay and Duck Creek, in Wisconsin, and in the State of New York, in 1836, and those for the exploring party of the New York Indians, in 1837, and also the expenses of the present treaty, shall be allowed and settled according to former precedents. *The accounts of the commissioner, etc., how to be paid.*

SPECIAL PROVISIONS FOR THE ST. REGIS.

ARTICLE 9. It is agreed with the American party of the St. Regis Indians, that the United States will pay to the said tribe, on their removal west, or at such time as the President shall appoint, the sum of five thousand dollars, as a remuneration for monies laid out by the said tribe, and for services rendered by their chiefs and agents in securing the title to the Green Bay lands, and in removal to the same, the same to be aportioned out to the several claimants by the chiefs of the said party and a United States' Commissioner, as may be deemed by them equitable and just. It is further agreed, that the following reservation of land shall be made to the Rev. Eleazor Williams, of said tribe, which he claims in his own right, and in that of his wife, which he is to hold in fee simple, by patent from the President, with full power and authority to sell and dispose of the same, to wit: beginning at a point in the west bank of Fox River thirteen chains above the old milldam at the rapids of the Little Kockalin; thence north fifty-two degrees and thirty minutes west, two hundred and forty chains; thence north thirty-seven degrees and thirty minutes east, two hundred chains, thence south fifty-two degrees and thirty minutes east, two hundred and forty chains to the bank of Fox river; thence up along the bank of Fox river to the place of beginning. *Payment to St. Regis Indians on their removal.*

SPECIAL PROVISIONS FOR THE SENECAS.

ARTICLE 10. It is agreed with the Senecas that they shall have for themselves and their friends, the Cayugas and Onondagas, residing among them, the easterly part of the tract set apart for the New York Indians, and to extend so far west, as to include one half-section (three hundred and twenty acres) of land for each soul of the Senecas, Cayugas and Onandagas, residing among them; and if, on removing west, they find there is not sufficient timber on this tract for their use, then the President shall add thereto timber land sufficient for their accommodation, and they agree to remove; to remove from the State of New York to their new homes within five years, and to continue to reside there. And whereas at the making of this treaty, Thomas L. Ogden and Joseph Fellows the assignees of the State of Massachusetts, have purchased of the Seneca nation of Indians, in the presence and with the approbation of the United States Commissioner, appointed *Land set apart for the Seneca, Cayuga, and Onondaga.* *Money due to the Seneca by Massachusetts to be paid to United States, etc.*

by the United States to hold said treaty, or convention, all the right, title, interest, and claim of the said Seneca nation, to certain lands, by a deed of conveyance a duplicate of which is hereunto annexed; and whereas the consideration money mentioned in said deed, amounting to two hundred and two thousand dollars, belongs to the Seneca nation, and the said nation agrees that the said sum of money shall be paid to the United States, and the United States agree to receive the same, to be disposed of as follows: the sum of one hundred thousand dollars is to be invested by the President of the United States in safe stocks, for their use, the income of which is to be paid to them at their new homes, annually, and the balance, being the sum of one hundred and two thousand dollars, is to be paid to the owners of the improvements on the lands so deeded, according to an appraisement of said improvements and a distribution and award of said sum of money among the owners of said improvements, to be made by appraisers, hereafter to be appointed by the Seneca nation, in the presence of a United States Commissioner, hereafter to be appointed, to be paid by the United States to the individuals who are entitled to the same, according to said apprisal and award, on their severally relinquishing their respective possessions to the said Ogden and Fellows.

SPECIAL PROVISIONS FOR THE CAYUGAS.

Moneys to be invested for the Cayuga, etc. ARTICLE 11. The United States will set apart for the Cayugas, on their removing to their new homes at the west, two thousand dollars, and will invest the same in some safe stocks, the income of which shall be paid them annually, at their new homes. The United States further agree to pay to the said nation, on their removal west, two thousand five hundred dollars, to be disposed as the chiefs shall deem just and equitable.

SPECIAL PROVISIONS FOR THE ONONDAGAS RESIDING ON THE SENECA RESERVATIONS.

Investment for the Onondagas, etc. ARTICLE 12. The United States agree to set apart for the Onondagas, residing on the Seneca reservations, two thousand five hundred dollars, on their removing west, and to invest the same in safe stocks, the income of which shall be paid to them annually at their new homes. And the United States further agree to pay to the said Onondagas, on their removal to their new homes in the west, two thousand dollars, to be disposed of as the chiefs shall deem equitable and just.

SPECIAL PROVISIONS FOR THE ONEIDAS RESIDING IN THE STATE OF NEW YORK.

Payment to certain persons for services, etc. ARTICLE 13. The United States will pay the sum of four thousand dollars, to be paid to Baptista Powlis, and the chiefs of the first Christian party residing at Oneida, and the sum of two thousand dollars shall be paid to William Day, and the chiefs of the Orchard party residing there, for expenses incurred and services rendered in securing the Green Bay country, and the settlement of a portion thereof; and they hereby agree to remove to their new homes in the Indian territory, as soon as they can make satisfactory arrangements with the Governor of the State of New York for the purchase of their lands at Oneida.

SPECIAL PROVISIONS FOR THE TUSCARORAS.

Tuscaroras agree to remove in five years, etc. ARTICLE 14. The Tuscarora nation agree to accept the country set apart for them in the Indian territory, and to remove there within five years, and continue to reside there. It is further agreed that the Tuscaroras shall have their lands in the Indian country, at the forks of the Neasha river, which shall be so laid off as to secure a sufficient quantity of timber for the accommodation of the nation. But if on examination they are not satisfied with this location, they are to have their lands at such place as the President of the United States shall designate. The United States will pay to the Tuscarora nation, on their settling at the West, three thousand dollars, to be disposed of as the chiefs shall deem most equitable and just. Whereas the said nation owns, in fee simple, five thousand acres of land, lying in Niagara county, in the State of New York which was conveyed to the said nation by Henry Dearborn and they wish to sell and convey the same before they remove West: Now therefore, in order to have the same done in a legal and proper way, they hereby convey the same to the United States and to be held in trust for them, and they authorize the President to sell and convey the same, and the money which shall be received for the said lands, exclusive of the improvements, the President shall invest in safe stocks for their benefit, the income from which shall be paid to the nation, at their new homes, annually; and the money which shall be received for improvements on said lands shall be paid to the owners of the improvements when the lands are sold. The President shall cause the said lands to be surveyed, and the improvements shall be appraised by such persons as the nation shall appoint; and said lands shall also be appraised, and shall not be sold at a less price than the appraisal, without the consent of James Cusick, William Mountpleasant and William Chew, or the survivor, or survivors of them; and the expenses incurred by the United States in relation to this trust are to be deducted from the moneys received before investment. *Tuscaroras convey certain land to United States, in trust, etc.*

Proceeds of improvements to be paid to the owners thereof.

And whereas, at the making of this treaty, Thomas L. Ogden and Joseph Fellows, the assignees of the State of Massachusetts, have purchased of the Tuscarora nation of Indians, in the presence and with the approbation of the commissioner appointed on the part of the United States to hold said treaty or convention, all the right, title, interest, and claim of the Tuscarora nation to certain lands, by a deed of conveyance, a duplicate of which is hereunto annexed: And whereas, the consideration money for said lands has been secured to the said nation to their satisfaction, by Thomas L. Ogden and Joseph Fellows; therefore the United States hereby assent to the said sale and conveyance and sanction the same.

ARTICLE 15. The United States hereby agree that they will appropriate the sum of four hundred thousand dollars, to be applied from time to time, under the direction of the President of the United States, in such proportions, as may be most for the interest of the said Indians, parties to this treaty, for the following purposes, to wit: To aid them in removing to their homes, and supporting themselves the first year after their removal; to encourage and assist them in education, and in being taught to cultivate their lands; in erecting mills and other necessary houses; in purchasing domestic animals, and farming utensils and acquiring a knowledge of the mechanic arts. *$400,000 to be applied for the benefit of Indians, how.*

In testimony whereof, the commissioner and the chiefs, head men, and people, whose names are hereto annexed, being duly authorized, have hereunto set their hands, and affixed their respective seals, at the time and place above mentioned.

R. H. Gillet, Commissioner.

Senecas:
Dao-nepho-gah, or Little Johnson,
Da-ga-o-geas, or Daniel Twoguns,
Gee-odow-neh, or Captain Pollard,
Joh-nes-ha-dih, or James Stevenson,
Hure-hau-stock, or Captain Strong,
So-ne-a-ge, or Captain Snow,
Hau-neh-hoy's-oh, or Blue Eyes,

Haw-naw-wah-es, or Levi Halftown,
Goat-hau-oh, or Billy Shanks,
Hau-sa-nea-nes, or White Seneca,
Howah-do-goh-deh, or George Bennet,
Hays-tah-jih, or Job Pierce,
Sho-nan-do-wah, or John Gordon,
Noh-sok-dah, or Jim Jonas,
Shaw-neh-dik, or William Johnson,

Gaw-neh-do-au-ok, or Reuben Pierce,
Shaw-go-nes-goh-sha-oh, or Morris Half-
town,
Shaw-go-za-sot-hoh, or Jacob Jameson,
Gua-wa-no-oh, or George Big Deer,
Joh-que-ya-suse, or Samuel Gordon,
Gua-ne-oh-doh, or Thompson S. Harris,
Gau-geh-queh-doh, or George Jimeson,
Hon-non-de-uh, or Nathaniel T. Strong,
Nuh-joh-gau-eh, or Tall Peter,
Sho-nauk-ga-nes, or Tommy Jimmy,
So-joh-gwa-us, or John Tall Chief,
Shau-gau-nes-es-tip, or George Fox,
Go-na-daw-goyh, or Jabez Stevenson,
Tit-ho-yuh, or William Jones,
Juneah-dah-glence, or George White, by
his agent White Seneca,
Gau-nu-su-goh, or Walter Thompson, by
his agent Daniel Twoguns,
Dau-ga-se, or Long John,
Gua-sa-we-dah, or John Bark,
Gau-ni-dough, or George Lindsay,
Ho-ma-ga-was, or Jacob Bennet,
On-di-heh-oh, or John Bennet,
Nis-ha-nea-nent, or Seneca White,
Ha-dya-no-doh, or Maris Pierce,
Yoh-dih-doh, or David White,
James Shongo,
Ka-non-da-gyh, or William Cass,
Ni-ge-jos-a, or Samuel Wilson,
Jo-on-da-goh, or John Seneca.

Tuscaroras:

Ka-nat-soyh, or Nicholas Cusick,
Sacharissa, or William Chew,
Kaw-we-ah-ka, or William Mt. Pleasant,
Kaw-re-a-roek-ka, or John Fox,
Gee-me, or James Cusick,
Ju-hu-ru-at-kak, or John Patterson,
O-tah-guaw-naw-wa, or Samuel Jacobs,
Ka-noh-sa-ta, or James Anthony,
Gou-ro-quan, or Peter Elm,
Tu-nak-she-a-han, or Daniel Peter.

Oneidas residing in the State of New-
York, for themselves and their parties:
Baptiste Powlis,
Jonathan Jordan.
Oneidas at Green Bay:
John Anthony,
Honjoit Smith,
Henry Jordan,
Thomas King.
St. Regis:
Eleazer Williams, chief and agent.
Oneidas residing on the Seneca Reser-
vation:
Hon-no-ne-ga-doh, or Silversmith, (For
himself and in behalf of his nation.)
Hoge-wayhtah, or William Jacket,
Sah-hu-gae-ne, or Button George.
Principal Onondaga Warriors, in behalf
of themselves and the Onondaga War-
riors:
Ka-noh-qua-sa, or William John,
Dah-gu-o-a-dah, or Noah Silversmith.
Cayugas:
Skok-no-eh, or King William,
Geh-da-or-loh, or James Young,
Gay-on-wek, or Jack Wheelbarrow,
D'yo-ya-tek, or Joseph Isaac, For them-
selves and in behalf of the nation.
Principal Cayuga Warriors, in behalf
of themselves and the Cayuga Warriors:
Hah-oh-u, or John Crow,
Ho-na-e-geh-dah, or Snow Darkness,
Gone-ah-ga-u-do, or Jacob G. Seneca,
Di-i-en-use, or Ghastly Darkness,
Hon-ho-gah-dyok, or Thomas Crow,
Wau-wah-wa-na-onk, or Peter Wilson,
So-en-dagh, or Jonathan White,
Sago-gan-e-on-gwus, or Harvey Rowe,
To-ga-ne-ah-doh, or David Crow,
Soh-win-dah-neh, or George Wheeler,
Do-goh-no-do-nis, or Simon Isaac,
He-dai-ses, or Joseph Peter,
Sa-go-di-get-ka, or Jacob Jackson.

Witnesses:

James Stryker, Sub-agent, Six Nations,
New York Indians.
Nathaniel T. Strong, United States' In-
terpreter, New York agency.
H. B. Potter.
Orlando Allen.
H. P. Wilcox.

Charles H. Allen.
Horatio Jones.
Spencer H. Cone.
W. W. Jones.
J. F. Schermerhorn.
Josiah Trowbridge.

(To the Indian names are subjoined a mark and seal.)

SCHEDULE A.

CENSUS OF THE NEW YORK INDIANS AS TAKEN IN 1837.

Number residing on the Seneca reservations.

Senecas	2,309
Onondagas	194
Cayugas	130
	2,633
Onondagas, at Onondaga	300
Tuscaroras	273
St. Regis, in New York	350
Oneidas, at Green Bay	600
Oneidas, in New York	620
Stockbridges	217
Munsees	132
Brothertowns	360

The above was made before the execution of the treaty.

R. H. Gillet, Commissioner.

SCHEDULE B.

The following is the disposition agreed to be made of the sum of three thousand dollars provided in this treaty for the Tuscaroras, by the chiefs, and assented to by the commissioner, and is to form a part of the treaty: Disposition of the $3,000 provided for Tuscaroras by fourteenth article of this treaty.

To Jonathan Printess, ninety-three dollars.
To William Chew, one hundred and fifteen dollars.
To John Patterson, forty-six dollars.
To William Mountpleasant, one hundred and seventy-one dollars.
To James Cusick, one hundred and twenty-five dollars.
To David Peter, fifty dollars.
The rest and residue thereof is to be paid to the nation.
The above was agreed to before the execution of the treaty.

R. H. Gillet, Commissioner.

———

SCHEDULE C.

Schedule applicable to the Onondagas and Cayugas residing on the Seneca reservations. It is agreed that the following disposition shall be made of the amount set apart to be divided by the chiefs of those nations, in the preceding parts of this treaty, any thing therein to the contrary notwithstanding. Disposition of the $4,000 provided for the Onondagas and Cayugas.

To William King, one thousand five hundred dollars.
Joseph Isaacs, seven hundred dollars.
Jack Wheelbarrow, three hundred dollars.
Silversmith, one thousand dollars.
William Jacket, five hundred dollars.
Buton George, five hundred dollars.
The above was agreed to before the treaty was finally executed.

R. H. Gillet, Commissioner.

At a treaty held under the authority of the United States of America, at Buffalo Creek in the county of Erie, and State of New York, between the chiefs and head men of the Seneca nation of Indians, duly assembled in council, and representing and acting for the said nation, on the one part, and Thomas Ludlow Ogden of the city of New York and Joseph Fellows of Geneva, in the county of Ontario, on the other part, concerning the purchase of the right and claim of the said Indians in and to the lands within the State of New York remaining in their occupation: Ransom H. Gillet, Esquire, a commissioner appointed by the President of the United States to attend and hold the said treaty, and also Josiah Trowbridge, Esquire, the superintendent on behalf of the Commonwealth of Massachusetts, being severally present at the said treaty, the said chiefs and head men, on behalf of the Seneca nation did agree to sell and release to the said Thomas Ludlow Ogden and Joseph Fellows, and they the said Thomas Ludlow Ogden and Joseph Fellows did agree to purchase all the right, title and claim of the said Seneca nation of, in and to the several tracts, pieces, or parcels of land mentioned, and described in the instrument of writing next hereinafter set forth, and at the price or sum therein specified, as the consideration, or purchase money for such sale and release; which instrument being read and explained to the said parties and mutually agreed to, was signed and sealed by the said contracting parties, and is in the words following: Jan. 15, 1838.
In relation to the sale of lands by the Senecas to the State of Massachusetts, referred to in tenth article.

This indenture, made this fifteenth day of January in the year of our Lord one thousand eight hundred and thirty-eight, between the chiefs and head men of the Seneca nation of Indians, duly assembled in council, and acting for and on behalf of the said Seneca nation, of the first The deed of conveyance.

part, and Thomas Ludlow Ogden, of the city of New York, and Joseph Fellows of Geneva, in the county of Ontario, of the second part witnesseth: That the said chiefs and head men of the Seneca nation of Indians, in consideration of the sum of two hundred and two thousand dollars to them in hand paid by the said Thomas Ludlow Ogden and Joseph Fellows, the receipt whereof is hereby acknowledged, have granted, bargained, sold, released and confirmed, and by these presents do grant, bargain, sell, release and confirm unto the said Thomas Ludlow Ogden and Joseph Fellows, and to their heirs and assigns, all that certain tract, or parcel of land situate, lying and being in the county of Erie and State of New York commonly called and known by the name of Buffalo Creek reservation, containing, by estimation forty-nine thousand nine hundred and twenty acres be the contents thereof more or less. Also, all that certain other tract, or parcel of land, situate, lying and being in the counties of Erie, Chatauque, and Cattaraugus in said State commonly called and known by the name of Cattaraugus reservation, containing by estimation twenty-one thousand six hundred and eighty acres, be the contents thereof more or less. Also, all that certain other tract, or parcel of land, situate, lying and being in the said county of Cattaraugus, in said State, commonly called and known by the name of the Allegany reservation, containing by estimation thirty thousand four hundred and sixty-nine acres, be the contents more or less. And also, all that certain other tract or parcel of land, situate, lying and being partly in said county of Erie and partly in the county of Genesee, in said State, commonly called and known by the name of the Tonawando reservation, and containing by estimation twelve thousand, eight hundred acres, be the same more or less; as the said several tracts of land have been heretofore reserved and are held and occupied by the said Seneca nation of Indians, or by individuals thereof, together with all and singular the rights, privileges, hereditaments and appurtenances to each and every of the said tracts or parcels of land belonging or appertaining; and all the estate, right, title, interest, claim, and demand of the said party of the first part, and of the said Seneca nation of Indians, of, in, and to the same, and to each and every part and parcel thereof: to have and to hold all and singular the above described and released premises unto the said Thomas Ludlow Ogden and Joseph Fellows, their heirs and assigns, to their proper use and behoof for ever, as joint tenants, and not as tenants in common.

In witness whereof, the parties to these presents have hereunto and to three other instruments of the same tenor and date one to remain with the United States, one to remain with the State of Massachusetts, one to remain with the Seneca nation of Indians, and one to remain with the said Thomas Ludlow Ogden and Joseph Fellows, interchangeably set their hands and seals the day and year first above written.

Little Johnson,	William Johnson,
Daniel Two Guns,	Reuben Pierce,
Captain Pollard,	Morris Halftown,
James Stevenson,	Jacob Jimeson,
Captain Strong,	Samuel Gordon,
Captain Snow,	Thompson S. Harris,
Blue Eyes,	George Jemison,
Levi Halftown,	Nathaniel T. Strong,
Billy Shanks,	Tall Peter,
White Seneca,	Tommy Jimmy,
George Bennet,	John Tall Chief,
John Pierce,	George Fox,
John Gordon,	Jabez Stevenson,
Jim Jonas,	William Jones.

I have attended a treaty of the Seneca Nation of Indians, held at Buffalo Creek, in the county of Erie, in the State of New York, on the fifteenth day of January in the year of our Lord one thousand eight hundred and thirty-eight, when the within instrument was duly executed, in my presence, by the chiefs of the Seneca Nation, being fairly and properly understood by them. I do, therefore, certify and approve the same.

R. H. Gillet, Commissioner.

———

At a treaty held under and by the authority of the United States of America, at Buffalo Creek, in the county of Erie, and State of New York, between the sachems, chiefs and warriors of the Tuscarora nation of Indians, duly assembled in council and representing and acting for the said nation, on the one part and Thomas Ludlow Ogden of the city of New York and Joseph Fellows of Geneva in the county of Ontario, on the other part, concerning the purchase of the right and claim of the said nation of Indians in and to the lands within the State of New York, remaining in their occupation: Ransom H. Gillet, Esquire, a commissioner appointed by the President of the United States to attend and hold the said treaty, and also Josiah Trowbridge, Esquire, the superintendent on behalf of the Commonwealth of Massachusetts, being severally present at the said treaty, the said sachems, chiefs and warriors, on behalf of the said Tuscarora nation, did agree to sell and release to the said Thomas Ludlow Ogden and Joseph Fellows, and they, the said Thomas Ludlow Ogden and Joseph Fellows did agree to purchase all the right, title and claim of the said Tuscarora nation of, in and to the tract, piece, or parcel of land mentioned and described in the instrument of writing next hereinafter set forth, and at the price, or sum therein specified, as the consideration or purchase money for such sale and release; which instrument being read and explained to the said parties, and mutually agreed to, was signed and sealed by the said contracting parties, and is in the words following:

Jan. 15, 1838.

In relation to the sale of lands by the Tuscaroras to the State of Massachusetts, referred to in the fourteenth article.

This indenture, made this fifteenth day of January in the year of our Lord one thousand eight hundred and thirty-eight, between the sachems, chiefs, and warriors of the Tuscarora nation of Indians, duly assembled in council, and acting for and on behalf of the said Tuscarora nation of the first part, and Thomas Ludlow Ogden of the city of New York, and Joseph Fellows of Geneva, in the county of Ontario, of the second part witnesseth: That the said sachems, chiefs and warriors of the Tuscarora nation, in consideration of the sum of nine thousand six hundred dollars, to them in hand paid by the said Thomas Ludlow Ogden and Joseph Fellows, the receipt whereof is hereby acknowledged, have granted, bargained, sold released, and confirmed, and by these presents do grant, bargain, sell, release and confirm to the said Thomas Ludlow Ogden and Joseph Fellows, and to their heirs and assigns, all that tract or parcel of land situate, lying and being in the county of Niagara and State of New York, commonly called and known by the name of the Tuscarora reservation or Seneca grant, containing nineteen hundred and twenty acres, be the same more, or less, being the lands in their occupancy, and not included in the land conveyed to them by Henry Dearborn, together with all and singular the rights, the rights, privileges, hereditaments, and appurtenances to the said tract or parcel of land belonging, or appertaining, and all the estate, right, title, interest, claim and demand of the said party of the first part, and of the said Tuscarora nation of Indians of, in and to the same, and to every part and parcel thereof: To have and to hold all and singular the above described and released premises unto the said Thomas Ludlow Ogden and Joseph Fellows, and their heirs and assigns, to their proper use and behoof for ever, as joint tenants and not as tenants in common.

The deed of conveyance.

In witness whereof, the parties to these presents have hereunto and to three other instruments of the same tenor and date, one to remain with the United States, one to remain with the State of Massachusetts, one to remain with the Tuscarora nation of Indians and one to remain with the said Thomas Ludlow Ogden and Joseph Fellows, interchangeably set their hands and seals, the day and year first above written.

Nicholas Cusick,	John Patterson,
William Chew,	Samuel Jacobs,
William Mountpleasant,	James Anthony,
John Fox,	Peter Elm,
James Cusick,	Daniel Peter.

Sealed and delivered in presence of—

James Stryker.
R. H. Gillet.
Charles H. Allen.
J. F. Schermerhorn.
Nathaniel T. Strong, U. S. interpreter.
H. B. Potter.
Orlando Allen.

(To the Indian names are subjoined a mark and seal.)

At the abovementioned treaty, held in my presence, as superintendent on the part of the Commonwealth of Massachusetts, and this day concluded, the foregoing instrument was agreed to by the contracting parties therein named, and was in my presence executed by them; and being approved by me, I do hereby certify and declare such my approbation thereof.

Witness my hand and seal, at Buffalo Creek, this 15th day of January, in the year 1838.

J. Trowbridge, Superintendent.

I have attended a treaty of the Tuscarora nation of Indians, held at Buffalo Creek, in the county of Erie in the State of New York, on the fifteenth day of January in the year of our Lord one thousand eight hundred and thirty-eight, when the within instrument was duly executed in my presence, by the sachems, chiefs, and warriors of the said nation, being fairly and properly understood and transacted by all the parties of Indians concerned and declared to be done to their full satisfaction. I do therefore certify and approve the same.

R. H. Gillet, Commissioner.

———

Feb. 13, 1838.

7 Stat., 561.

Supplemental article to the treaty concluded at Buffalo Creek, in the State of New York, on the 15th of January 1838, concluded between Ransom H. Gillet, commissioner on the part of the United States, and chiefs and head men of the St. Regis Indians, concluded on the 13th day of February 1838.

Supplemental article to the treaty concluded at Buffalo Creek in the State of New York, dated January 15 1838.

Assent of the St. Regis Indians to the treaty. The undersigned chiefs and head men of the St. Regis Indians residing in the State of New York having heard a copy of said treaty read by Ransom H. Gillet, the commissioner who concluded that treaty on the part of the United States, and he having fully and publicly explained the same, and believing the provisions of the said treaty to be very liberal on the part of the United States and calculated to be highly beneficial to the New York Indians, including the St. Regis, who are embraced in its provisions do hereby assent to every part of the said treaty and approve the same. And it is further agreed, that any of the St. Regis Indians who wish to do so, shall be at liberty to remove to the said country at any time hereafter within the time specified in this treaty, but under it the Government shall not compel them to remove. The United States will, within one year after the ratification of this treaty, pay over to the American party of said Indians one thousand dollars, part of the sum of five thousand dollars mentioned in the special provisions for the St. Regis Indians, any thing in the article contained to the contrary notwithstanding.

$1,000 to be paid to them within one year after the ratification of this treaty.

Done at the council house at St. Regis, this thirteenth day of February in the year of our Lord one thousand eight hundred and thirty-eight. Witness our hands and seals.

R. H. Gillet, Commissioner.

Lover-taie-enve,	Tier-sgane-kor-hapse-e,
Louis-taio-rorio-te,	Ennios-anas-ota-ka,
Michael Gaveault,	Louis-te-ganota-to-ro,
Lose-sori-sosane,	Wise-atia-taronne,
Louis-tioonsate,	Tomas-outa-gosa,
Jok-ta-nen-shi-sa,	Sose-te-gaomsshke,
Ermoise-gana-saien-to,	Louis-orisake-wha,
Tomos-tataste,	Sosatis-atis-tsiaks,
Tier-te-gonotas-en,	Tier-anasaken-rat,
Tier-sokoia-ni-saks,	Louis-tar-oria-keshon,
Sa-satis-otsi-tsia-ta-gen,	Jasen-karato-on.

The foregoing was executed in our presence—

A. K. Williams, Agent on the part of New York for St. Regis Indians.
W. L. Gray, Interpreter:
Owen C. Donnelly.
Say Saree.
(To the Indian names are subjoined a mark and seal.)

We the undersigned chiefs of the Seneca tribe of New York Indians, residing in the State of New York, do hereby give our free and voluntary assent to the foregoing treaty as amended by the resolution of the Senate of the United States on the eleventh day of June 1838, and to our contract therewith, the same having been submitted to us by Ransom H. Gillet, a Commissioner on the part of the United States, and fully and fairly explained by him, to our said tribe, in council assembled.

Dated Buffalo Creek September 28 1838.

Captain Pollard,	N. T. Strong,
Captain Strong,	Thompson S. Harris,
White Seneca,	Samuel Gordon,
Blue Eyes,	Jacob Jimeson,
George Bennett,	John Gordon,
Job Pierce,	Tall Peter,
Tommy Jimmy,	Billy Shanks,
William Johnson,	James Stevenson,
Reuben Pierce,	Walter Thompson,
Morris Halftown,	John Bennett,
Levi Halftown,	John Seneca,
George Big Deer,	John General,
Jim Jonas,	Major Jack Berry,
George Jimeson,	John Tall Chief,
Thomas Jimeson,	Jabez Stevenson.
George Fox,	

(To the Indian names are subjoined marks.)

The above signatures were freely and voluntarily given after the treaty and amendments had been fully and fairly explained in open council.

R. H. Gillet, Commissioner.

Witness:

H. A. S. Dearborn, Superintendent of Massachusetts.	Long John,
	Sky Carrier,
James Stryker, U. S. Agent.	Charles Greybeard,
Little Johnson,	John Hutchinson,
Samuel Wilson,	Charles F. Pierce,
John Buck,	John Snow.
William Cass,	

(To the Indian names are subjoined marks.)

These ten chiefs signed in my presence except the last John Snow.

H. A. S. Dearborn,
Superintendent of Massachusetts.

Signed in presence of—

Nathl. T. Strong, U. S. Interpreter.
James Stryker, U. S. Agent.
George Kenququide, by his attorneys.
N. T. Strong.
White Seneca.

The signature of George Kenququide was added by his attorneys in our presence.

R. H. Gillet,
James Stryker.

18th January 1839.

We the undersigned chiefs of the Oneida tribe of New York Indians do hereby give our free and voluntary assent to the foregoing treaty as amended by the resolution of the Senate of the United States on the eleventh day of June 1838, the same having been submitted to us by Ransom H. Gillet, a commissioner on the part of the United States and fully and fairly explained by him to our said tribe in council assembled. Dated August 9th 1838 at the Oneida Council House.

Executed in the presence of—

Timothy Jenkins.

First Christian Party:
Baptista Powlis,
Anthony Big Knife,
Peter Williams,
Jacob Powlis,
Anthony Anthony,
Peter Martin,
Cornelius Summer,
Isaac Wheelock,
Thomas Doxtater,
William Hill,
Baptiste Denny.

Orchard Party:
Jonathan Jordon,
Thomas Scanado,
Henry Jordon,
William Day.
    Second Christian Party:
Abraham Denny,
Adam Thompson,
Peter Elm,
Lewis Denny,
Martin Denny.

(To the Indian names are subjoined marks.)

The above assent was voluntarily freely and fairly given in my presence, after being fully and fairly explained by me.

R. H. Gillet, Commissioner, &c.

We the undersigned sachems chiefs and head men of the Tuscarora nation of Indians residing in the State of New York, do hereby give our free and voluntary assent to the foregoing treaty as amended by the resolution of the Senate of the United States on the eleventh day of June 1838, and to our contract connected therewith, the same having been submitted to us by Ransom H. Gillet, a commissioner on the part of the United States, and fully and fairly explained by him to our said tribe in council assembled.

Dated August 14th, 1838.

Nicholas Cusick,
William Chew,
William Mountpleasant,
John Patterson,
Matthew Jack,

George L. Printup,
James Cusick,
Jonathan Printup,
Mark Jack,
Samuel Jacobs.

Executed in presence of—

J. S. Buckingham,
D. Judson,
Leceister S. Buckingham,
Orlando Allen.

(To the Indian names are subjoined marks.)

The above assent was freely and voluntarily given after being fully and fairly explained by me.

R. H. Gillet, Commissioner.

We the undersigned chiefs and head men of the tribe of Cayuga Indians residing in the State of New York do hereby give our free and voluntary assent to the foregoing treaty as amended by the resolution of the Senate of the United States on the eleventh day of June 1838, the same having been submitted to us by Ransom H. Gillet, a commissioner on the part of the United States, and fully and fairly explained by him to our said tribe in council assembled.

Dated August 30th 1838.

Thomas Crow,   Ghastly Darkness,
John Crow,   Jacob G. Seneca.

Executed in presence of—

James Young.

(To the Indian names are subjoined marks.)

The above four signatures were freely given in our presence.

R. H. Gillet, Commissioner,
H. A. S. Dearborn,
Superintendent of Massachusetts.

We the undersigned sachems, chiefs and head men of the American party of the St. Regis Indians residing in the State of New York, do hereby give our free and voluntary assent to the foregoing treaty as amended by the Senate of the United States on the eleventh day of June 1838, the same having been submitted to us by Ransom H. Gillet a commissioner on the part of the United States, and fully and fairly explained by him to our said tribe in council assembled. The St. Regis Indians shall not be compelled to remove under the treaty or amendments.

Dated October 9th, 1838.

Lorenn-taie-enne,   Sa-ga-tis-asi-kgar-a-tha,
Sase-sori-hogane,   Simon-sa-he-rese,
Louis-taw-roniate,   Resis-tsis-kako,
Thomas-talsete,   Ennias-kar-igiio,
Saro-sako-ha-gi-tha,   Sak-tsior-ak-gisen,
Louis-te-ka-nota-tiron,   Tier-kaien-take-ron,
Michael Gareault,   Kor-ari-hata-ko,
W. L. Gray, Int.   Tomas-te-gaki-gasen,
Louis-tio-on-sate,   Saro-thar-on-ka-tha,
Tier-ana-sa-ker-rat,   Ennias-anas-ota-ko,
Tomas-ska-en-to-gane,   Wishe-te-ka-nia-tasoken,
Tier-sa-ko-eni-saks,   Tomas-tio-nata-kgente,
Saro-tsio-her-is-en,   Wishe-aten-en-rahes,
Sak-tho-te-ras-en,   Tomas-ioha-hiio,
Saro-saion-gese,   Ennias-kana-gaien-ton,
Louis-onia-rak-ete,   Louis-taro-nia-ke-thon,
Louis-aion-gahes,   Louis-ari-ga-ke-wha,
Sak-tha-nen-ris-hon,   Sak-tsio-ri-te-ha,
Sa-ga-tis-ania-ta-ri-co,   Louis-te-ga-ti-rhon,
Louis-sa-ka-na-tie,   Tier-atsi-non-gis-aks.

The foregoing assent was signed in our presence.

R. H. Gillet, Commissioner.

Witnesses:

James B. Spencer.
Heman W. Tucker.
A. K. Williams, Agent St. Regis Indians.
Frs. Marcoux Dictre.

(To the Indian names are subjoined marks.)

We the undersigned, chiefs, head men and warriors of the Onondaga tribe of Indians residing on the Seneca reservations in the State of New-York, do hereby give our free and voluntary assent to the fore-going treaty as amended by the Senate of the United States on the eleventh day of June, 1838, the same having been submitted to us, by Ransom H. Gillet, a commissioner on the part of the United States and fully and fairly explained by him to our said tribe in council assembled.

Dated August 31st, 1838.

Silversmith,
Noah Silversmith,
William Jacket.

(To the Indian names are subjoined marks.)

The above signatures were freely given in our presence.

R. H. Gillet, Commissioner.
H. A. S. Dearborn,
Superintendent of Massachusetts.

TREATY WITH THE CHIPPEWA, 1838.

Jan. 23, 1838.

7 Stat., 565.
Proclamation, July 2, 1838.

Articles of a treaty concluded at the city of Saganaw in Michigan, on the twenty-third day of January eighteen hundred and thirty-eight, between the United States of America, by the undersigned commissioner, and the several bands of the Chippewa nation comprehended within the district of Saganaw.

Preamble.

WHEREAS the chiefs of said bands have represented, that combinations of purchasers may be formed, at the sale of their lands for the purpose of keeping down the price thereof, both at the public and private sales, whereby the proceeds would be greatly diminished; and whereas, such a procedure would defeat some of the primary objects of the cession of the lands to the United States, and thereby originate difficulties to their early removal and expatriation to the country west of the Mississippi; and whereas, full authority has been given to the undersigned, respectively, on the part of the United States, and the said bands, to conclude and settle every question connected with the sale and cession aforesaid; Now therefore, to the end, that justice may completely ensue, the objects of both the contracting parties be attained, and peace and friendship be preserved with said tribes, it is mutually agreed as follows:

Lands ceded by treaty of 14th Jan., 1837, to be offered for sale by proclamation, etc.
Proviso.

ARTICLE 1st. The lands ceded by the treaty of the 14th of January 1837, shall be offered for sale, by proclamation of the President, and the sale shall be conducted in the same manner, as the laws require other lands to be sold. *But it is provided,* That all lands brought into market, under the authority of said treaty, shall be put up for sale by the register and receiver of the respective land office, at five dollars per acre, which is hereby declared to be the minimum price thereof; and if this price is not bid the sales shall be stopped; nor shall any such lands be disposed of, either at public or private sales, for a sum less than five dollars per acre, for, and during the term of two years from the commencement of the sale. Should any portion of said lands remain unsold at the expiration of this time, the minimum price shall be diminished to two dollars and fifty cents per acre, at which price they shall be subject to entry until the whole quantity is sold: *Provided,* That if any part of said lands remain unsold at the expiration of five years from the date of the ratification of this treaty, such lands shall fall under the provision of third article of this treaty.

Proviso.

Provision in case any of said lands remain unsold.

ARTICLE 2nd. To provide against the contingency of any of said lands remaining unsold, and to remove any objections to emigrating, on the part of the Indians, based on such remainder, it is hereby agreed, that every such section, fractional section, or other unsold remainder, shall, at the expiration of five years from the ratification of this treaty, be sold for such sum as it will command, *Provided*, That no such sale shall be made for less than seventy-five cents per acre.

Proviso.

ARTICLE 3rd. This treaty shall be binding from the date of its constitutional ratification; but its validity shall not be affected by any modification, or non-concurrence of the President and Senate, in the third and fourth articles thereof.

Treaty binding when ratified.

In testimony whereof, the undersigned, Superintendent of Indian Affairs and commissioner on the part of the United States, and the chiefs and delegates of said bands, have hereunto set their hands, and affixed their seals, at the city of Saganaw on this twenty-third day of January, in the year of our Lord one thousand eight hundred and thirty-eight, and of the independence of the United States, the sixty-second year.

Henry R. Schoolcraft, commissioner.

Ogima Keegido,	Saw-wur-bon,
Mo-cuck-koosh,	Show-show-o-nu-bee-see,
Oe-quee-wee-sance,	Ar-ber-too-quet.

Signed and executed in presence of—

Jeremiah Riggs, overseer farmers I. D.	Leon Tremble,
E. S. Williams,	Jas. La-Schoolcraft,
Sam'l G. Watson,	Joseph F. Marsac,
Wm. F. Mosely,	William S. Lee.
D. E. Corbin,	

(To the Indian names are subjoined a mark and seal.)

TREATY WITH THE ONEIDA, 1838.

Articles of a treaty made at the City of Washington between Carey A. Harris, thereto specially directed by the President of the United States and the First Christian and Orchard parties of the Oneida Indians residing at Green Bay, by their chiefs and representatives.

Feb. 3, 1838.

7 Stat., 566.
Proclamation, May 17, 1838.

ART. 1. THE First Christian and Orchard parties of Indians cede to the United States all their title and interest in the land set apart for them in the 1st article of the treaty with the Menomonies of February 8th, 1831, and the 2d article of the treaty with the same tribe of October 27th, 1832.

Cession to the United States.

ART. 2. From the foregoing cession there shall be reserved to the said Indians to be held as other Indian lands are held a tract of land containing one hundred (100) acres, for each individual, and the lines of which shall be so run as to include all their settlements and improvements in the vicinity of Green Bay.

Reservations to be made from said cession.

ART. 3. In consideration of the cession contained in the 1st article of this treaty, the United States agree to pay to the Orchard party of the Oneida Indians three thousand (3000) dollars, and to the First Christian party of Oneida Indians thirty thousand five hundred (30,500) dollars, of which last sum three thousand (3,000) dollars may be expended under the supervision of the Rev. Solomon Davis, in the erection of a church and parsonage house, and the residue apportioned, under the direction of the President among the persons having just claims thereto; it being understood that said aggregate sum of thirty-three thousand five hundred (33,500) dollars is designed to be in reimbursement of monies expended by said Indians and in remuneration of the services of their chiefs and agents in purchasing and securing a title to the land ceded in the 1st article. The United States further

Consideration for said cession.

agree to cause the tracts reserved in the 2d article to be surveyed as soon as practicable.

Relinquishment by John Denny.

ART. 4. In consideration of the sum of five hundred (500) dollars to be paid to him by the chiefs and representatives of the said parties of Oneida Indians, John Denny (alias John Sundown,) their interpreter agrees to relinquish to them all his title and interest in the tract reserved in the 2d article of this treaty.

Expenses of this treaty to be paid by United States.

ART. 5. It is understood and agreed that the expenses of this treaty and of the chiefs and representatives signing it, in coming to and returning from this city, and while here, shall be paid by the United States.

Treaty binding when ratified.

ART. 6. This treaty to be binding upon the contracting parties when the same shall be ratified by the United States.

In witness whereof, the said Carey A. Harris and the undersigned chiefs and representatives of the said parties of Oneida Indians have hereunto set their hands at the City of Washington, this third day of February 1838.

C. A. Harris.

First Christians:
  Henry Powles,
  John Denny, alias John Sundown,
  Adam Swamp,
  Daniel Bread.
Orchard:
  Jacob Cornelius.

In presence of—

  Geo. W. Jones, Delegate Wisconsin Territory.
  Solomon Davis.
  Alfred Iverson.
  O. S. Hall.
  Jas. P. Maury.
  Charles E. Mix.
  Charles J. Love.
  John Denny, alias John Sundown, Interpreter
(To the Indian names are subjoined marks.)

TREATY WITH THE IOWA, 1838.

Oct. 19, 1838.

7 Stat., 568.
Proclamation, Mar. 2, 1839.

Articles of a treaty made at the Great Nemowhaw sub-agency between John Dougherty Agent of Indian Affairs on the part of the United States, being specially authorized, and the chiefs and headmen of the Ioway tribe of Indians for themselves, and on the part of their tribe.

Cession to United States by the Iowa.

ARTICLE 1st. The Ioway tribe of Indians cede to the United States,
  First. All right or interest in the country between the Missouri and Mississippi rivers, and the boundary between the Sacs and Foxes, and Sioux, described in the second article of the treaty made with these and other tribes, on the 19th of August 1825, to the full extent to which said claim is recognized in the third article of said treaty, and all interest or claim by virtue of the provisions of any treaties since made by the United States with the Sacs and Foxes of the Mississippi.
  Second. All claims or interest under the treaties of August 4th 1824, July 15th 1830, and September 17th 1836, except so much of the last mentioned treaty as secures to them two hundred sections of land the erection of five comfortable houses, to enclose and break up for them two hundred acres of ground to furnish them with a ferry boat, one hundred cows and calves, five bulls, one hundred head of stock hogs a mill and interpreter.

Consideration therefor.

ARTICLE 2d. In consideration of the cession contained in the preceding article, the United States agree to the following stipulations on their part.

First. To pay to the said Ioway tribe of Indians the sum of one hundred and fifty-seven thousand five hundred ($157,500) dollars.

Second. To invest said sum of one hundred and fifty-seven thousand five hundred (157,500) dollars, and to guaranty them an annual income of not less than five per cent. thereon during the existence of their tribe.

Third. To set apart annually such amount of said income as the chiefs and headmen of said tribe may require, for the support of a blacksmith shop agricultural assistance, and education to be expended under the direction of the President of the United States.

Fourth. To pay out of said income to Jeffrey Derroin interpreter for said tribe for services rendered, the sum of fifty dollars annually during his natural life the balance of said income shall be delivered, at the cost of the United States, to said tribe of Ioway Indians in money or merchandise, at their own discretion, at such time and place as the President may direct, *Provided always* That the payment shall be made each year in the month of October.

ARTICLE 3d. The United States further agree in addition to the above consideration to cause to be erected ten houses at such place or places on their own land as said Ioways may select, of the following description (viz) each house to be ten feet high from bottom sill to top plate eighteen by twenty feet in the clear the roof to be well sheeted and shingled, the gable ends to be weather boarded a good floor above and below, one door and two windows complete, one chimney of stone or brick, and the whole house to be underpined. *United States to erect ten houses at such places as the Indians may direct.*

ARTICLE 4th. This treaty to be binding upon the contracting parties when the same shall be ratified by the United States. *Treaty binding when ratified.*

In witness whereof the said John Dougherty agent of Indian affairs and the undersigned chiefs and headmen of the Ioway tribe of Indians have hereunto set their hands this 19th day of October A. D. 1838.

Jno. Dougherty, Indian Agent.

Frank White Cloud,	Rahno way ing ga, or Little Pipe,
Non-gee-ninga, or No Heart,	Thraw ing ga, or Little War Eagle,
Kon-gee, or the Plum,	Pak she ing ga, or the Cocked Nose,
Mock Shig a ton-ah, or the Great Man,	O yaw tche a, or Heard to Load,
Wah nun gua schoo ny, or He that has no Fear,	Ro to gra zey, or Speckled Rib,
	Mah za, or the Iron,
Seenah ty yaa, or the Blistered Foot,	Ta-ro-hah, or Pile of Meat.

Done in presence of—

Anthony L. Davis, Indian sub-agent.
Vance M. Campbell.
James M. Crope.
Jeffrey Deroin, interpreter.

(To the Indian names are subjoined marks.)

TREATY WITH THE MIAMI, 1838.

Articles of a treaty made and concluded at the Forks of the Wabash in the State of Indiana, between the United States of America, by her Commissioner Abel C. Pepper, and the Miami tribe of Indians on the sixth day of November in the year of our Lord eighteen hundred and thirty-eight. *Nov. 6, 1838.*

7 Stat., 569.
Proclamation, Feb. 8, 1839.

ART. 1. The Miami tribe of Indians hereby cede to the United States all that tract of land lying south of the Wabash river and included within the following bounds to wit: Commencing at a point on said river where the western boundary line of the Miami reserve intersects the same, near the mouth of Pipe creek; thence south two miles; *Land ceded to the United States.*

thence west one mile; thence south along said boundary line, three miles; thence east to the Mississinnewa river; thence up the said river with the meanders thereof to the eastern boundary line of the said Miami reserve; thence north along said eastern boundary line to the Wabash river; thence down the said last named river with the meanders thereof to the place of beginning.

Cession of certain reservations. The said Miami tribe of Indians do also hereby cede to the United States, the three following reservations of land made for the use of the Miami nation of Indians by the 2d article of a treaty made and concluded at St. Mary's in the State of Ohio, on the 6th of October 1818 to wit:

The reservation on the Wabash river, below the forks thereof:

The residue of the reservation opposite the mouth of the river Abouette:

The reservation at the mouth of a creek called Flat Rock, where the road to White river crosses the same.

Also one other reservation of land made for the use of said tribe at Seeks village on Eel river, by the 2d article of a treaty made and concluded on the 23d October 1826.

Reservation for the band of Me-to-sin-ia. ART. 2. From the cession aforesaid, the Miami tribe reserve for the band of Me-to-sin-ia, the following tract of land to wit: Beginning on the eastern boundary line of the big reserve, where the Mississinnewa river crosses the same; thence down said river with the meanders thereof to the mouth of the creek called Forked Branch; thence north two miles; thence in a direct line to a point on the eastern boundary line two miles north of the place of beginning; thence south to the place of beginning, supposed to contain ten square miles.

Consideration for said cession. ART. 3. In consideration of the cession aforesaid, the United States agree to pay the Miami tribe of Indians three hundred and thirty-five thousand six hundred and eighty dollars; sixty thousand dollars of which to be paid immediately after the ratification of this treaty and the appropriation to carry its provisions into effect; and the residue of said sum after the payment of claims hereinafter stipulated to be paid, in ten yearly instalments of twelve thousand five hundred and sixty-eight dollars per year.

Payments to J. B. Richardville and F. Godfroy. ART. 4. It is further stipulated that the sum of six thousand eight hundred dollars, be paid John B. Richardville; and the sum of two thousand six hundred and twelve dollars be paid Francis Godfroy; which said sums are their respective claims against said tribe prior to October 23, 1834, excluded from investigation by the late commissioner of the United States, by reason of their being Indians of said tribe.

Commissioner to investigate claims, etc. ART. 5. The said Miami tribe of Indians being anxious to pay all their just debts, at their request it is stipulated, that immediately after the ratification of this treaty, the United States shall appoint a commissioner or commissioners, who shall be authorized to investigate all claims against said tribe which have accrued since the 23d day of October 1834, without regard to distinction of blood in the claimants; and to pay such debts as, having accrued since the said period, shall be proved to his or their satisfaction, to be legal and just.

$150,000 to be set apart for the payment of certain claims. ART. 6. It is further stipulated that the sum of one hundred and fifty thousand dollars out of the amount agreed to be paid said tribe in the third article of this treaty, shall be set apart for the payment of the claims under the provisions of the fourth and fifth articles of this treaty, as well as for the payment of any balance ascertained to be due from said tribe by the investigation under the provisions of the treaty of 1834; and should there be an unexpended balance in the hands of said commissioner or commissioners after the payment of said claims, the same shall be paid over to the said tribe at the payment of their next subsequent annuity; but should the said sum so set apart for the purpose aforesaid, be found insufficient to pay the same, then the ascertained balance due on said claims shall be paid in three equal instalments from the annuities of said tribe.

And the said Miami tribe of Indians through this public instrument proclaim to all concerned, that no debt or debts that any Indian or Indians of said tribe may contract with any person or persons, shall operate as a lien on the annuity or annuities, nor on the land of the said tribe for legal enforcement. Nor shall any person or persons other than the members of said Miami tribe, who may by sufferance live on the land of, or intermarry in, said tribe, have any right to the land or any interest in the annuities of said tribe, until such person or persons shall have been by general council adopted into their tribe. *Debts of Indians not to operate as a lien on their annuities or lands.*

ART. 7. It is further stipulated, that the United States will cause the buildings and improvements on the land hereby ceded, to be appraised, and have buildings and improvements of a corresponding value made at such places as the chiefs of said tribe may designate: and the Indians of said tribe are to remain in the peaceable occupation of their present improvements, until the United States shall make the said corresponding improvements. *Buildings, etc., to be appraised, etc.*

ART. 8. It is further stipulated that the United States patent to Beaver, the five sections of land, and to Chapine the one section of land, reserved to them respectively in the second article of the treaty made Anno Domino 1826, between the parties to the present treaty. *Patent for certain land to issue to Beaver and Chapine.*

ART. 9. The United States agree to cause the boundary lines of the land of said tribe in the State of Indiana, to be surveyed and marked within the period of one year after the ratification of this treaty. *Boundary to be surveyed and marked.*

ART. 10. The United States stipulate to possess, the Miami tribe of Indians of, and guarranty to them forever, a country west of the Mississippi river, to remove to and settle on, *when the said tribe may be disposed to emigrate from their present country*, and that guarranty is hereby pledged: And the said country shall be sufficient in extent, and suited to their wants and condition and be in a region contiguous to that in the occupation of the tribes which emigrated from the States of Ohio and Indiana. And when the said tribe shall have emigrated, the United States shall protect the said tribe and the people thereof, in their rights and possessions, against the injuries, encroachments and oppressions of any person or persons, tribe or tribes whatsoever. *United States to provide Indians with a country west of the Mississippi, etc.*

ART. 11. It is further stipulated, that the United States will defray the expenses of a deputation of six chiefs or headmen, to explore the country to be assigned to said tribe, west of the Mississippi river. Said deputation to be selected by said tribe in general council. *Exploring party.*

ART. 12. The United States agree to grant by patent to each of the Miami Indians named in the schedule hereunto annexed, the tracts of land therein respectively designated. *United States to grant patents to Indians named in schedule annexed.*

And the said tribe in general council request, that the patents for the grants in said schedule contained, shall be transmitted to the principal chief of said tribe, to be by him distributed to the respective grantees.

ART. 13. It is further stipulated, that should this treaty not be ratified at the next session of the Congress of the United States, then it shall be null and void to all intents and purposes between the parties. *If not ratified at next session, etc., to be null and void.*

ART. 14. And whereas John B. Richardville, the principal chief of said tribe, is very old and infirm, and not well able to endure the fatigue of a long journey, it is agreed that the United States will pay to him and his family the proportion of the annuity of said tribe which their number shall indicate to be due to them, at Fort Wayne whenever the said tribe shall emigrate to the country to be assigned them west, as a future residence. *J. B. Richardville's portion to be paid him at Fort Wayne.*

ART. 15. It is further stipulated that as long as the Congress of the United States shall in its discretion make an appropriation under the sixth article of the treaty made between the United States and said tribe in the year 1826 for the support of the infirm and the education *Support of the infirm, etc.*

of the youth of said tribe one half of the amount so appropriated shall be paid to the chiefs, to be by them applied to the support of the poor and infirm of said tribe, in such manner as shall be most beneficial.

Treaty binding when ratified. ART. 16. This treaty after the same shall be ratified by the President and Senate of the United States, shall be binding on the contracting parties.

In testimony whereof the said Abel C. Pepper commissioner as aforesaid, and the chiefs, headmen and warriors of the Miami tribe of Indians, have hereunto set their hands at the forks of the Wabash the sixth day of November in the year of our Lord one thousand eight hundred and thirty eight.

Abel C. Pepper, Commissioner.

J. B. Richardville,	Nac-kon-zaw,
Minjenickeaw,	Ne-kon-zaw,
Paw-lawn-zo-aw,	Waw-pe-maung-guaw,
Ne-we-lang-guaung-gaw,	Ching-guaw-ke-aw,
O-zan-de-ah,	Aw-koo-te-aw,
Waw-pa-pin-shaw,	Ke-mo-te-aw,
Nac-kaw-guaung-gaw,	Kil-so-aw,
Kaw-tah-maung-guaw,	Taw-we-ke-juc,
Kah-wah-zay,	Waw-paw-ko-se-aw,
To-pe-yaw,	Mac-quaw-ko-naung,
Pe-waw-pe-yaw,	Maw-yauc-que-yaw.
Me-shing-go-me-jaw,	

Signed in presence of—

John T. Douglass, Sub-Agent.
Allen Hamilton, Secretary to Commissioner.
Danl. D. Pratt, Assistant Secretary to Commissioner.

J. B. Duret,
H. Lasselle,
Wm. Hulbert, Indian Agent.

(To the Indian names are subjoined marks.)

———

Schedule of grants referred to in the foregoing treaty article twelve.

Grants of land to persons named. To John B. Richardville, principal chief.

Two sections of land, to include and command the principal falls of Pipe creek.

Three sections of land, commencing at the mouth of the Salamania river, thence running three miles down the Wabash river, and one mile up the Salamania river.

Two sections of land, commencing at the mouth of the Mississinnewa river, thence down the Wabash river two miles and up the Mississinnewa river, one mile.

One and one half section of land on the Wabash river at the mouth of Flat Rock (creek) to include his mills and the privileges thereof.

One section of land on the Wabash river opposite the town of Wabash:

All of which said tracts of land are to be surveyed as directed by the said grantee.

To Francis Godfroy a chief one section of land opposite the town of Peru and on the Wabash river.

One section of land on Little Pipe creek, to include his mill and the privileges thereof.

Four sections of land where he now lives.

All which said tracts of land are to be surveyed as directed by the said grantee.

To Po-qua Godfroy one section of land to run one mile on the Wabash river and to include the improvements where he now lives.

To Catherine Godfroy, daughter of Francis Godfroy and her children one section of land to run one mile on the Wabash river, and to include the improvement where she now lives.

To Kah-tah-mong-quah, son of Susan Richardville one half section of land on the Wabash river below and adjoining the three sections granted to John B. Richardville.

To Mong-go-sah, son of La Blonde one-half section of land on the Wabash river below and adjoining the half section granted to Kah-tah-mong-quah.

To Peter Gouin one section of land on the Sixth mile reserve, commencing where the northern line of said reserve intersects the Wabash river; thence down said river one mile and back for quantity.

To Mais-shil-gouin-mi-zah, one section of land to include the "Deer Lick," *alias* La Saline, on the creek that enters the Wabash river nearly opposite the town of Wabash.

To O-zah-shin-quah and the wife of Bronilette, daughters of the "Deaf Man" as tenants in common one section of land on the Mississinnewa river to include the improvements where they now live.

To O-san-di ah one section of land where he now lives on the Mississinnewa river, to include his improvements.

To Wah-pi-pin-cha one section of land on the Mississinnewa river, directly opposite the section granted to O-san-di-ah.

To Mais-zi-quah one section of land on the Wabash river, commencing at the lower part of the improvement of Old Sally, thence up said river one mile and back for quantity.

To Tah-ko-nong one section of land where he now lives on the Mississinnewa river.

To Cha-pine one section of land where he now lives on the Ten mile reserve.

To White Loon one section of land, at the crossing of Longlois's creek, on the Ten mile reserve, to run up said creek.

To Francis Godfroy one section of land, to be located where he shall direct.

To Neh-wah-ling-quah one section of land where he now lives on the Ten mile reserve.

To La Fountain one section of land south of the section he now lives on and adjoining the same, on the Ten mile reserve.

To Seek one section of land south of the section of land granted to Wa-pa-se-pah by the treaty of 1834 on the Ten mile reserve.

To Black Loon one section of land on the Six mile reserve, commencing at a line which will divide his field on the Wabash river, thence up the river one mile and back for quantity.

To Duck one section of land on the Wabash river below and adjoining the section granted to Black Loon, and one mile down said river, and back for quantity.

To Me-cha-ne-qua a chief, *alias* Gros-mis one section of land where he now lives;

One section to include his field on the Salamania river;

One and one-half section commencing at the Wabash river where the road crosses the same from John B. Richardville, jr.'s; thence down the said river to the high bank on Mill creek; thence back so as to include a part of the prairie, to be surveyed as directed by said chief.

To Tow-wah-keo-shee, wife of Old Pish-a-wa one section of land on the Wabash river below and adjoining the half section granted to Mon-go-sah.

To Ko-was-see a chief one section of land now Seeks reserve, to include his orchard and improvements.

To Black Loon one section of land on the Six mile reserve and on the Salamania river, to include his improvements.

To the wife of Benjamin, Ah-mac-kon-zee-quah one section of land where she now lives, near the prairie and to include her improvements, she being commonly known as Pichoux's sister.

Grants of land to persons named.

To Pe-she-wah one section of land above and adjoining the section and a half granted to John B. Richardville on Flat Rock (creek) and to run one mile on the Wabash river.

To White Raccoon one section of land on the Ten mile reserve where he may wish locate the same.

To La Blonde, the chiefs daughter one section of land on the Wabash river below and adjoining the section of land granted to Francis God-froy, to be surveyed as she may direct.

To Ni-con-zah one section of land on the Mississinnewa river a little above the section of land granted to the Deaf Man's daughters, and on the opposite side of the river, to include the pine or evergreen tree, and to be surveyed as he may direct.

To John B. Richardville one section of land to include the Osage village on the Mississinewa river as well as the burying ground of his family, to be surveyed as he may direct.

To Kee-ki-lash-e-we-ah *alias* Godfroy one half section of land back of the section granted to the principal chief opposite the town of Wa-bash, to include the creek;

One-half section of land commencing at the lower corner of the section granted to Mais-zi-quah, thence half a mile down the Wabash river.

To Al-lo-lah one section of land above and adjoining the section granted to Mais-shie-gouin-mi-zah and on the same creek.

To John B. Richardville, jr. one section of land on Pipe creek above and adjoining the two sections of land granted to the principal chief, to be surveyed as he may direct.

To John B. Richardville, one section of land wherever he may choose to have the same located.

It is understood that all the foregoing grants are to be located and surveyed so as to correspond with the public surveys as near as may be to include the points designated in each grant respectively.

TREATY WITH THE CREEKS, 1838.

Nov. 23, 1838.

7 Stat., 574.
Proclamation, Mar. 2, 1839.

Articles of a treaty, made and concluded at Fort Gibson west of Arkansas between Captain William Armstrong act superintendent Western Territory, and Brevt Brig Gen Arbuckle commissioners on the part of the United States and the undersigned chiefs being a full delegation of the Creek chiefs duly authorized and empowered by their nation to adjust " their claims for property and improvements aban-doned, or lost, in consequence of their emigration west of the Missis-sippi.

Certain claims relinquished by Creeks.

ART. 1st. The Creek nation do hereby relinquish all "claims for property and improvements abandoned or lost, in consequence of their emigration west of the Mississippi," in consideration of the sums stipu lated in the following articles.

Payment for said claims.

ART. 2d. The United States agree to pay the Creek nation for prop-erty &c. as set forth in the preceding article the sum of fifty thousand dollars in stock animals as soon as practicable after the ratification of this treaty. These animals to be furnished and distributed to the people of each town in proportion to their loss, as set forth by the accompany-ing schedule under the direction of their chiefs and an agent of the Government.

Investment for certain Creeks.

ART. 3d. The United States further agrees to invest for the benefit of the individuals of the Creek nation referred to in the preceding article, the sum of three hundred and fifty thousand dollars and secure to them the interest of five per cent. thereon, to be paid annually, the interest for the first year to be paid in money, the interest thereafter to be paid in money, stock animals, blankets, domestics or such articles of a similar nature as the President of the United States may direct, to be distributed as set forth in the preceding article.

ART. 4th. It is further agreed that the sum invested by the preceeding article shall at the expiration of twenty-five years be appropriated under the direction of the President of the United States for the common benefit of the Creek nation. *Said investment, after 25 years, how to be appropriated.*

ART. 5th. The United States further agrees to pay the sum of twenty-one thousand one hundred and three dollars and thirty-three cents, to satisfy claims of the early Creek emigrants to the west, of the McIntosh party as set forth in the accompanying schedule marked (A.) *Payment to satisfy claims of the McIntosh party.*

ART. 6th. In consideration of the suffering condition of about two thousand five hundred of the Creek nation who were removed to this country as hostiles and that are not provided for by this treaty, and the representation of the chiefs of the nation, that their extreme poverty has, and will cause them to commit depredations on their neighbours, it is therefore agreed on the part of the United States that the Creek Indians referred to in this article shall receive ten thousand dollars in stock animals for one year, as soon as convenience will permit after the ratification of this treaty. *Supplies for hostile Creeks.*

It is however understood by the contracting parties that the rejection of this article will not effect the other provisions of this treaty. *Rejection of the last article not to affect etc.*

In testamony whereof the commissioners on behalf of the United States and the delegates of the Creek nation have hereunto signed their names, this 23d day of November A. D. 1838 at Fort Gibson.

Wm. Armstrong,
Acting Superintendent Western Territory,
M. Arbuckle,
Brevet Brigadier-General, U. S. Army.

Rowly McIntosh,	Yargu,
O Poth-le Yoholo,	Yar Dicker Tustannugga,
Little Doctor,	Charlo Hadjo,
Tus kem haw,	Kusseter Micco,
Ufawala Hadjo,	Lotti Fixico,
Fur-hutche-micco,	Tom Marth Micco,
Cotchy Tustannuggee,	David Barnett,
Chilby McIntosh,	Bob Tiger,
Co-wock-co-ge Emarthlar,	Tuckabatche Hadjo,
Jas. Islands,	Cho Coater Tustannugga,
Tin Thlannis Hadjo,	Echo Hadjo,
Jim Boy,	Tal Mars Hadjo,
Cotchay Emarta,	Emarth Ea Hadjo.
Jimmy Chopco,	

Witnesses:

J. S. McIntosh, major, Seventh Infantry,
B. Riley, major, Fourth Infantry,
S. W. Moore, captain, Seventh Infantry,
W. K. Hanson, lieutenant, Seventh Infantry,
G. K. Paul, first lieutenant, Seventh Infantry, acting commissary sergeant,
D. J. Whiting, first lieutenant, Seventh Infantry,
G. J. Rains, captain, Seventh Infantry,
M. Stokes, agent for Cherokee nation,
James Logan, agent for Creek nation,
S. G. Simmons, first lieutenant, Seventh Infantry, secretary to the Commission.

(To the Indian names are subjoined marks.)

TREATY WITH THE OSAGE, 1839.

Articles of a treaty made and concluded at Fort Gibson, west of Arkansas between Brig. General M. Arbuckle, Commissioner on the part of the United States, and the chiefs, headmen and warriors of the Great and Little Osage Indians, duly authorized by their respective bands. *Jan. 11, 1839.*

7 Stat., 576. Proclamation, Mar. 2, 1839

ARTICLE 1st. The Great and Little Osage Indians make the following cessions to the United States. *Cessions by the Osage.*

First, Of all titles or interest in any reservation heretofore claimed by them within the limits of any other tribe.

Second, Of all claims or interests under the treaties of November tenth, one thousand eight hundred and eight and June second, one thousand eight hundred and twenty-five, except so much of the latter as is contained in the sixth article thereof and the said Indians bind themselves to remove from the lands of other tribes, and to remain within their own boundaries.

Consideration there-for.

ARTICLE 2d. In consideration of the cessions and obligations contained in the preceding article, the United States agree to the following stipulations on their part.

Annuity.

First, To pay to the said Great and Little Osage Indians, for the term of twenty years an annuity of twenty thousand dollars to be paid in the Osage nation, twelve thousand in money and eight thousand in goods, stock, provisions, or money as the President may direct.

Blacksmiths.

Second, To furnish the Osage nation, for the term of twenty years, two blacksmiths and two assistants, the latter to be taken from the Osage nation, and receive two hundred and twenty-five dollars each, per year; each smith to be furnished with a dwelling house shop and tools, and five hundred pounds of iron, and sixty pounds of steel annually.

Grist and saw mills.

Third, To furnish the Osage nation with a grist and saw mill, a miller to each for fifteen years, and an assistant to each for eleven years, the latter to be taken from the Osage nation and receive each two hundred and twenty-five dollars per year; each miller to be furnished with a dwelling house, and the necessary tools.

Cows, calves, hogs, etc.

Fourth, To supply the said Great and Little Osage Indians within their country with one thousand cows and calves, two thousand breeding hogs, one thousand ploughs; one thousand sets of horse gear; one thousand axes, and one thousand hoes; to be distributed under the direction of their agent, and chiefs, as follows, viz: to each family who shall form an agricultural settlement, one cow and calf, two breeding hogs, one plough, one set of horse gear, one axe, and one hoe. The stock tools &c. to be in readiness for delivery, as soon as practicable after the ratification of this treaty, and the Osages shall have complied with the stipulations herein contained.

Houses, wagons, etc., for certain chiefs.

Fifth, To furnish the following named chiefs, viz: Pa-hu-sca, Clermont, Chiga-wa-sa, Ka-he-gais-tanga, Tawan-ga-hais, Wa-cho chais, Ni-ka-wa-chin-tanga, Tally, Gui-hira-ba-chais, Baptisté Mongrain, each with a house worth two hundred dollars; and the following named chiefs, viz: Chi-to-ka-sa-bais, Wa-ta-ni-ga, Wa-tier-chi-ga, Chon-ta-sa-bais, Nan-gais-wa-ha-qui hais, Ka-hi-gais-stier-de-gais, Man-haie-spais-we-te-chis, Chow-gais-mo-non, Gre-tan-man-sais, Kan-sais-ke-cris, Cho-mi-ka-sais, Man-cha-ki-da-chi-ga, each with a house worth one hundred dollars, and to furnish the above named chiefs with six good wagons, sixteen carts, and twenty-eight yoke of oxen, with a yoke and log chain to each yoke of oxen, to be delivered to them in their own country, as soon as practicable after the ratification of this treaty.

Payment of claims against Indians.

Sixth, To pay all claims against said Osages, for depredations committed by them against other Indians or citizens of the United States, to an amount not exceeding thirty thousand dollars, provided that the said claims shall be previously examined under the direction of the President.

Purchase of certain reservations.

Seventh, To purchase the reservations provided for individuals in the fifth article of the treaty of June second, one thousand eight hundred and twenty-five, at not exceeding two dollars per acre, to be paid to the respective reservees, excepting however from this provision, the tracts that were purchased in the fourth article of the treaty with the Cherokees of December twenty-ninth one thousand eight hundred and thirty-five.

Reimbursement of $3,000 deducted from their annuity.

Eighth, To reimburse the sum of three thousand dollars deducted from their annuity in one thousand eight hundred and twenty-five, to pay for property taken by them, which they have since returned.

Ninth, To pay to Clermont's band, their portion of the annuity for one thousand eight hundred and twenty-nine, which was wrongfully withheld from them, by the agent of the Government, amounting to three thousand dollars.   Payment to Clermont's band.

ART. 3d. This treaty shall be binding on both parties when ratified by the United States Senate.   Treaty binding when ratified.

In testimony whereof the said Brig. General M. Arbuckle, commissioner as aforesaid, and the chiefs, headmen, and warriors, of the Great and Little Osage nation of Indians, have hereunto set their hands this eleventh day of January, in the year of our Lord one thousand eight hundred and thirty-nine.

M. Arbuckle,
Brevet Brigadier General, U. S. Army.

Wa-tier-chi-ga,	Chi-to-ka-sa-bais,
Chon-ta-sa-bais,	Wa-ta-ni-ga,
Nan-gais-wa-ha-qui-hais,	Ka-hi-gais-wa-tier-hais,
Ka-hi-gais-stier-de-gais,	Man-hi-han-ga,
Man-haie-spais-we-te-chis,	Wa-non-pa-chais,
Chou-gais-mo-non,	Owa-sa-bais,
Gre-tan-man-sais,	Ti-cho-wa-ta-ni-ga,
Kan-sais-ke-cris,	Wa-kan-da-hi-pa-on-be,
Cho-mi-ka-sais,	Hi-hi-tanga,
Man-cha-ki-da-chi-ga,	Ka-wa-tan-ga,
Hu-car-ti,	Chon-ta-sais-bais-chiga,
Cha-bais-chiga,	Mon-ka-sa-bais,
Pa-hu-sca,	Han-ber-la-que-ni,
Clermont,	Hais-wa-tier-hai,
Chiga-wa-sa,	Ma-non-po-chais,
Ka-hi-gais-tanga,	We-ha-sa-chais,
Ta-wan-ga-hais,	Hude-gais-ta-wa-ta-nige,
Wa-cho-chais,	Ti-cho-han-ga,
Ni-ka-wa-chin-tanga,	Non-de-gais-tan-ga,
Tally,	Mi-ta-ni-ga,
Gui-hira-ba-chais,	Wa-ka-non-te-si-rais,
Baptisti Mongrain,	Ka-hi-gais-ka-cris,
Wa-cha-our-ta-sa,	Wa-chin-o-ti,
Wa-chin-pi-chais,	Equi-has,
Tier-to-ha,	To-wan-li-hi,
Ka-wa-ho-de-gais-ha-gue-ni,	Opa-chi-gais,
Ni-ko-hi-bran,	Ta-wan-te-se-rais,
Hi-cha-ha-cris,	Hi-bi-son-de-gais,
Wa-chin-pi-chais-la-ta,	Man-cha-ki-dais,
Hai-sca-ma-ni,	Ta-bais-ki-hais,
Wa-kan-da-gais-chi-ga,	Pani-wa-we-tas,
Pon-ka-wa-ta-ni-ga,	Ko-chi-wa-tier,
Sa-tan-wa-cris,	Wa-cha-chais-wo-chin-oti,
Ha-ha-ga-be,	Tier-pa-ga-hais,
Wa-la-ni,	Wa-han-ga-tier Econ-Chais,
Hi-wa-ha-ga-chi-ga,	Ni-ka-ha-cris.

Witnesses:

B. Riley, Major fourth, Infantry.	C. Hanson, lieutenant, Seventh Infantry.
James R. Stephenson, captain, Seventh Regiment Infantry.	P. Z. Chouteau.
W. Seawell, captain, Seventh Infantry.	Frank Ritchie.
D. P. Whiting, lieutenant, Seventh Infantry.	M. Giraud.
R. C. Gatlin, adjutant, Seventh Infantry.	Danl. Boyd.
P. S. G. Cooke, captain, First Dragoons.	Geo. R. Beard.
Jno. B. Shepherd, lieutenant, Seventh Infantry.	Leo. Wetmore.
	Baptiste Mongrain, Osage interpreter.
	Lieut. S. G. Simmons, Seventh Infantry, secretary to the commission.

(To the Indian names are subjoined marks.)

TREATY WITH THE CHIPPEWA, 1839.

Feb. 7, 1839.

7 Stat., 578.
Proclamation, Mar.
2, 1839.

Preamble.

Articles supplementary to certain treaties between the United States and the Saganaw tribes of Chippewa.

Indians agree to sell certain lands.

ART. 1. Whereas the said tribe have, by the treaty of the 14th January, 1837, ceded to the United States, all their reserves of land in the State of Michigan, on the principle of said reserves being sold at the public land offices for their benefit, and the actual proceeds being paid to them, as farther defined by stipulations contained in the amendments to said treaty of the 20th December 1837, and of the 23d January 1838. And whereas it is required by a subsequent law of Congress, to erect a light-house on one of said reserves, called Na-bo-bish tract, lying at the mouth of the Saganaw river, and to reserve so much of the same from sale as may be necessary; it is therefore hereby agreed, by the said tribe, that for, and in consideration of the sum of eight dollars per acre, one sixteenth of a section of said tract, situated as aforesaid, shall be, and the same is hereby appropriated and set apart, to be located and disposed of in any manner the President may direct. And the same shall be reserved from sale, and all claim to any proceeds therefrom, except the sum herein before stipulated, is fully, completely and forever relinquished by said tribe.

This compact to be submitted to the Senate for approval, etc.

ART. 2. This compact shall be submitted to the President and Senate of the United States, to be approved by them, whereupon possession of the land may be immediately taken, and the usufructory right of the Indians thereto shall cease.

In testimony whereof, the Acting Superintendent pro tem. of Indian Affairs for the State of Michigan, duly authorized for this purpose, and the chiefs of said tribe, have hereunto set their hands and seals at Lower Saginaw, in Michigan, this seventh day of February, in the year eighteen hundred and thirty-nine.

John Hulbert,
Acting Superintendent of Indian Affairs pro tem.

Ogima Kegido,
Waubredoaince,
Muckuk Kosh,
Osaw Wauban,

Sheegunageezhig,
Penayseewabee,
Caw-ga-ke-seh-sa,
Shawun Epenaysee.

In presence of—

J. E. Schwarz, adjutant-general M. M.
Henry Connor, subagent.
Leon Tremble, jr., U. S. interpreter.
B. C. Tremble.
Joseph Tremble.

(To the Indian names are subjoined a mark and seal.)

Feb. 7, 1839.

7 Stat., 579.
Proclamation, Mar.
2, 1839.

Supplementary article to a certain treaty between the United States and the Chippewa chiefs of Saganaw, concluded at Lower Saganaw on the seventh day of February eighteen hundred and thirty-nine.

Preamble

ART. 1st. Whereas by the first article of the aforesaid treaty, the chiefs stipulate to sell to the United States forty acres of land to be located on the Na-bo-bish tract at the mouth of Saganaw river, for the purpose of erecting thereon a light-house.

President may change a certain location.

Now provided the President of the U. S. should prefer forty acres, on the tract, known as the forty thousand acre reservation, at the mouth of the aforesaid river, he is fully authorized by these presents to change the location from the Na-bo-bish tract, to the said forty thousand acre reservation.

Signed and sealed at Lower Saganaw this seventh day of February, 1839.

John Hulbert,
Acting Superintendent of Indian Affairs pro tem.

Ogima Kegido,
Waubredoaince,
Muckuk Kosk,
Osau Wauban,

Sheeguanageezhig
Penayseewabee,
Caw-ga-ke-seh-sa,
Shawun Epenaysee.

In presence of—

J. Schwarz, adjutant general M. M.
Henry Connor, subagent.
Leon Tremble, jr., U. S. interpreter.
B. C. Tremble.
Joseph Tremble.

(To the Indian names are subjoined a mark and seal.)

TREATY WITH THE STOCKBRIDGE AND MUNSEE, 1839.

Articles of a treaty made at Stockbridge in the Territory of Wisconsin, on the third day of September in the year of our Lord one thousand eight hundred and thirty-nine, between the United States of America, by their commissioner Albert Gallup, and the Stockbridge and Munsee tribes of Indians, who reside upon Lake Winnebago in the territory of Wisconsin.

Sept. 3, 1839.

7 Stat., 580.
11 Stat., 577.
Proclamation; May 16, 1840.

ARTICLE 1. The Stockbridge and Munsee tribes of Indians (formerly of New York) hereby cede and relinquish to the United States, the east half of the tract of forty-six thousand and eighty acres of land, which was laid off for their use, on the east side of Lake Winnebago, in pursuance of the treaty made by George B. Porter commissioner on the part of the United States, and the Menominee nation of Indians, on the twenty-seventh day of October eighteen hundred and thirty-two. The said east half hereby ceded, to contain twenty-three thousand and forty acres of land; to be of equal width at the north and south ends, and to be divided from the west half of said tract of forty-six thousand and eighty acres, by a line to be run parallel to the east line of said tract. The United States to pay therefor, one dollar per acre at the time and in the manner hereinafter provided.

Land ceded to the United States.

Payment therefor.

ART. 2. Whereas a portion of said tribes, according to a census or roll taken, and hereunto annexed, are desirous to remove west and the others to remain where they now are; and whereas the just proportion of the emigrating party in the whole tract of forty-six thousand and eighty acres is eight thousand seven hundred and sixty-seven and three-fourths acres of land; it is agreed that the United States pay to the said emigrating party, the sum of eight thousand seven hundred and sixty-seven dollars and seventy-five cents, as a full compensation for all their interest in the lands held by the party who remain, as well as in the lands hereby ceded to the United States.

Payment to the emigrating party.

ART. 3. Whereas the improvements of the emigrating party are all on that part of the original tract which is reserved and still held by the party who remain in Stockbridge, and it is but equitable that those who remain should pay those who emigrate for such improvements; it is agreed that the United States shall pay to the emigrating party the sum of three thousand eight hundred and seventy-nine dollars and thirty cents, the appraised value of said improvements; and it is hereby agreed and expressly understood, that the monies payable to the emigrating party shall be distributed among the heads of families according to the schedule hereunto annexed, the whole amount to be paid to the emigrating party under this and the preceding article being the sum of twelve thousand six hundred and forty-seven dollars and five cents.

Improvements of emigrating party to be paid for.

S. Doc. 319, 58–2, vol 2——34

Balance of the consideration money to be invested, etc.

ART. 4. The balance of the consideration money for the lands hereby ceded, (after deducting the sums mentioned in the second and third articles,) amounting to the sum of ten thousand three hundred and ninety-two dollars and ninety-five cents, is to be paid to, and invested for the benefit of such of the Stockbridge and Munsee tribes of Indians (numbering three hundred and forty-two souls) as remain at their present place of residence at Stockbridge on the east side of Winnebago lake, as follows. Six thousand dollars of said sum to be invested by the United States in public stocks at an interest of not less than five per cent. per annum as a permanent school fund; the interest of which shall be paid annually to the sachem and counsellors of their tribes, or such other person as they may appoint to receive the same, whose receipt shall be a sufficient voucher therefor; and the balance thereof amounting to four thousand three hundred and ninety-two dollars and ninety-five cents, shall be paid to the said sachem and counsellors, or to such person as they may appoint to receive the same, whose receipt shall be a sufficient voucher therefor.

The moneys to be paid in one year.

ART. 5. The monies herein secured to be paid by the United States to the Stockbridge and Munsee tribes amounting in all to twenty-three thousand and forty dollars, are to be paid in manner aforesaid, in one year from the date hereof, or sooner if practicable.

Exploring party.

ART. 6. It is agreed that an exploring party not exceeding three in number may visit the country west, if the Indians shall consider it necessary, and that whenever those who are desirous of emigrating shall signify their wish to that effect, the United States will defray the expenses of their removal west of the Mississippi and furnish them with subsistence for one year after their arrival at their new homes. The expenses of the exploring party to be borne by the emigrants.

Mode of settling claims between Indians.

ART. 7. Whereas there are certain unliquidated claims and accounts existing between the emigrating party, and those who remain where they now are, which it is now impossible to liquidate and adjust; it is hereby agreed that the same shall be submitted to the agent of the United States who shall be appointed to make the payments under this treaty, and that his decision shall be final thereon.

In witness whereof we have hereunto set our hands and seals this third day of September in the year of our Lord one thousand eight hundred and thirty-nine.

Albert Gallup,
Commissioner on the part of the United States.

Austin E. Quinny, Sachem,
Thomas T. Hendrick,
John Metoxen,
Jacob Chicks,
Robert Konkapot,
Captain Porter, Munsee chief,
James Rain, Munsee war chief.
  Stockbridges:
Timothy Jourdan,
Benjamin Palmer,
Jno. N. Chicks,
Jno. W. Quinney,
John P. Quinney,
John W. Newcom,
Thomas S. Branch,
Levi Konkapot,
John Littlemon,
Peter Sherman,
J. L. Chicks.

  Munsee:
John Killsnake.
  Stockbridges:
Jeremiah Singerland,
Jonas Thompson,
Eli Hendrick,
Elisha Konkapot,
Henry Skicket,
Simon S. Metoxen,
Samuel Miller,
Gerret Thompson,
Daniel David,
Ziba T. Peters,
Simeon Konkapot,
David Abrams,
Jonas Konkapot,
David Calvin,
Benjamin Pye, sen.
Aaron Ninham.

Signed and sealed in presence of—

A. S. Kellogg,
Cutting Marsh,
Clark Whitney,
John Deen,
John Wilber.

(To the Indian names are subjoined a mark and seal.)

Roll and schedule referred to in articles two and three of the treaty hereunto annexed.

Names of heads of families of emigrating party.	No. of each family.	No. of acres of land to each family.	Value of lands in dollars and cents.	Appraised value of improvements.	Total value of lands and improvements and amount to be paid to head of each family.
Thomas T. Hendrick	6	713	$713 00	$480 50	$1,193 50
Robert Konkapot	4	490¼	490 50	939 00	1,429 50
Timothy Tousse	6	642	642 00	135 00	777 00
Elisha Konkapot	6	642	642 00	67 50	709 50
Cornelius Charles	7	686	686 00	....	686 00
Jonas Konkapot	3	321	321 00	56 25	377 25
Levi Konkapot	1	107	107 00	384 00	491 00
David Abrams	2	214	214 00	....	214 00
Dolly Dockstader	5	597	597 50	168 75	766 25
Eli Hendrick	3	321	321 00	238 25	559 25
Simeon Konkapot	3	321	321 00	....	321 00
Lydia Hendrick	1	107	107 00	305 00	412 00
Thomas S. Branch	1	131½	131 50	....	131 50
John Baldwin	1	107	107 00	....	107 00
John W. Newcom	5	535	535 00	....	535 00
Jonas Littleman	1	107	107 00	....	107 00
Henry Skickett	3	321	321 00	....	321 00
Betsy Bennet	1	107	107 00	....	107 00
Peter Sherman	1	107	107 00	390 00	497 00
David Calvin	1	44½	44 50	....	44 50
Eli Williams	1	107	107 00	....	107 00
Catherine Littleman	6	642	642 00	....	642 00
James Rain	6	642	642 00	40 00	682 00
Big Deer	1	107	107 00	....	107 00
Ziba T. Peters	3	246¼	246 25	144 30	390 55
Cornelius Chemaucum	2	214	214 00	....	214 00
And other heirs of Phebe Ducham	......	187½	187 50	530 75	718 25
	80	8,767¾	8,767 75	3,879 30	12,647 05

TREATY WITH THE MIAMI, 1840.

Articles of a treaty made and concluded at the Forks of the Wabash, in the State of Indiana, this twenty-eighth day of November in the year of our Lord one thousand eight hundred and forty, between Samuel Milroy and Allen Hamilton, acting (unofficially) as commissioners on the part of the United States, and the chiefs, warriors and headmen of the Miami tribe of Indians.

Nov. 28, 1840.

7 Stat., 582.
Proclamation, June 7, 1841.

ART. 1. THE Miami tribe of Indians, do hereby cede to the United States all that tract of land on the south side of the Wabash river, not heretofore ceded, and commonly known as "the residue of the Big Reserve." Being all of their remaining lands in Indiana.

Lands ceded to the United States.

ART. 2. For and in consideration of the cession aforesaid, the United States agree to pay to the Miami tribe of Indians the sum of five hundred and fifty thousand dollars. Three hundred thousand dollars of which sum to be set apart, and applied immediately after the ratification of this treaty and an appropriation is made by Congress to carry its provisions into effect, to the payment of the debts of the tribe, as hereinafter stipulated. And the residue, two hundred and fifty thousand dollars, to be paid in twenty equal yearly instalments.

Consideration therefor.

ART. 3. The Miamies, being desirous that their just debts shall be fully paid; it is hereby, at their request stipulated, that immediately on the ratification of this treaty, the United States shall appoint a commissioner or commissioners, who shall be authorized to investigate all claims against any and every member of the tribe, which have accrued since the 6th day of November, 1838, or which may accrue before the date of the ratification of this treaty, without regard to distinction of blood in the claimant or claimants. And whose duty it shall be to enquire into the equity and legality of the original cause of indebtedness, whether the same now is, or may then be in the form of

Commissioners to investigate claims.

judgments, notes, or other evidence of debt, and report for payment out of the money set apart by this treaty for that purpose, such claims only, or parts of claims, as shall be both legal and just. And his or their award when approved by the President of the United States shall be final. Two hundred and fifty thousand dollars of the sum set apart in the second article of this treaty shall be applied to the payment of debts contracted before the twenty-eighth day of November, 1840; and the residue of said sum, after such debts are satisfied, being fifty thousand dollars, to the payment of debts contracted between the last named date and the time of the ratification of this treaty by the Senate of the United States; giving preference, in the application of said sum of fifty thousand dollars, to debts contracted for provisions and subsistence.

Payments to J. B. Richardville and the executor of F. Godfroy. ART. 4. It is further stipulated that the sum of twenty-five thousand dollars be paid to John B. Richardville. And the sum of fifteen thousand dollars to the acting executor of Francis Godfroy deceased, being the amount of their respective claims against the tribe; out of the money set apart for the payment of their debts by the second article of this treaty.

Payments to the family of F. Godfroy. ART. 5. And whereas the late war chief, (Francis Godfroy,) bequeathed to his children a large estate, to remain unsold until the youngest of said children shall arrive at the age of twenty-one years. It is therefore stipulated, that the United States shall pay to the family of said deceased chief their just proportion of the annuities of said tribe, at Fort Wayne, from and after the time the tribe shall emigrate to the country assigned to them west of the Mississippi.

Payments in lieu of labor. ART. 6. It is further stipulated, that the sum of two hundred and fifty dollars shall be paid annually by the United States, and accepted by the Miamies in lieu of the labour stipulated to be furnished by the fourth article of the treaty of the 23d of October 1826, for the purpose of preventing the dissatisfaction, occasioned heretofore, in the distribution of said labour amongst the different bands.

United States to convey certain land to Me-shing-go-me-zia. ART. 7. It is further stipulated, that the United States convey by patent, to Me-shing-go-me-sia, son of Ma-to-sin-ia, the tract of land reserved by the 2d article of the treaty of the 6th of November 1838, to the band of Ma-to-sin-ia to be held by the said Me-shin-go-me-zia, for his band; and the proceeds thereof, when the same shall be alienated, shall be equitably distributed to said band, under the direction of the President. And the same provision made in favour of John B. Richardville and family, in the 14th article of the treaty of the 6th of November 1838, is hereby granted and extended to the above named Me-shing-go-me-sia, and to his brothers.

Removal of Indians. ART. 8. It is hereby stipulated, that the Miami tribe of Indians shall remove to the country assigned them west of the Mississippi, within five years from this date; the United States paying every expense attending such removal, and to furnish rations to said tribe for twelve months after their arrival at said country. And the United States shall also cause four thousand dollars to be expended to the best advantage in supplying good merchantable pork and flour to said tribe, during the second year of their residence at their new homes. Which sum is to be deducted from their annuity of that year.

In case of the sum set apart for the payment of debts being too great. ART. 9. It is further stipulated, that should there be an unexpended ballance of the "three hundred thousand dollars," after the payment of the debts of the tribe as provided in the second article of this treaty; such balance to be paid over to the Miamies at the next payment of annuities after the amount of said balance shall have been ascertained.

Reservations of land to J. B. Richardville and F. Lafountain. ART. 10. It is stipulated and agreed between the contracting parties, that there shall be, and hereby is granted and reserved to John B. Richardville, principal chief, seven sections of land, from the land ceded in the first article of this treaty; at such point or points as he may select (not less than one section at any one point,) to be conveyed to him by patent from the United States. And also, in like manner, one section of land to Francis Lafountain, at the rapids of Wildcat, to be surveyed under his direction.

Art. 11. Nothing in this treaty shall be so construed as to impair the force or validity of former treaty stipulations, existing between the United States and the Miami tribe of Indians, not altered by nor coming within the purview of any of the provisions of this treaty.

Provisions of former treaties not altered except, etc.

Art. 12. The United States hereby stipulate to set apart and assign to the Miamies, for their occupancy west of the Mississippi, a tract of country bounded on the east by the State of Missouri, on the north by the country of the Weas and Kaskaskias, on the west by the Potawatomies of Indiana, and on the south by the land assigned to the New York Indians, estimated to contain five hundred thousand acres.

Expenses of this treaty to be paid by United States.

Art. 13. It is hereby stipulated, that the United States provide for the payment of the expense which may be necessarily incurred in the negotiation of this treaty.

Art. 14. This treaty shall be binding on the United States, and on the Miami tribe of Indians, from and after the date of its ratification by the President by and with the advice and consent of the Senate of the United States. But, if the same shall not be so ratified before the 4th day of March next, it shall be of no binding force or validity.

Treaty binding when ratified.

Art. 15. We the chiefs warriors, and headmen of the Miami tribe of Indians, having examined and considered the foregoing articles, after the same had been interpreted and explained to us to our satisfaction, do hereby agree and request, that the said articles shall be taken and held as a treaty between the parties thereto; and when ratified as provided in the last preceding article, be binding on our tribe, and on the United States, as fully to all intents and purposes as though the same had been officially and formally made on the part of the United States.

Assent of the Indians to this treaty.

In testimony whereof, we, Samuel Milroy, and Allen Hamilton, on behalf of the United States, (as aforesaid,) and the chiefs, warriors, and headmen of the Miami tribe of Indians, have hereunto set our hands.

Done at the Forks of the Wabash, in the State of Indiana, this twenty-eighth day of November, one thousand eight hundred and forty.

Samuel Milroy,
Allen Hamilton.

John B. Richardville, principal chief.
Wau-pa-pin-shaw,
O-zan-de-ah,
Cha-pine,
Me-shing-go-me-zia,
Wauk-a-shing-guah,
To-pe-ah,
Te-moo-te-oh,
Ma-qua-co-nong,
Mon-go-sou,

Pe-wan-pe-oh,
Ma-ze-qua,
Ma-gou-zah,
Peshe-a-wauh,
Po-qua-Godfroy,
Na-kun-sah,
Ko-es-say,
Shin-go-me-zia,
Tuc-ke-mun-guagh,
Bo-wa-wah.

Signed in the presence of—

H. B. Milroy, secretary.
David Carrier.
Geo. M. Maxwell.
Robert H. Milroy.
Peter Andre, interpreter.

We the undersigned chiefs headmen and warriors of the Miami tribe of Indians residing in the State of Indiana, do hereby give our free and voluntary assent to the amendments made by the Senate of the United States on the 25th day of February last, to the treaty concluded by us with the United States on the 28th day of November 1840; the same having been submitted and fully explained to us by Samuel Milroy and Allen Hamilton, commissioners on the part of the United States for that purpose, in full council assembled at the Forks of the Wabash in the State of Indiana.

In testimony whereof we have hereunto set our hands, and affixed our seals respectively this fifteenth day of May 1841.

Na-wa-lin-guah,	Mah-gon-zah,
Pe-she-wah,	Con-o-cot-wah,
O-yan-de-ah,	Shau-cot-to-wah,
Na-kan-yah,	Sha-pen-do-zia,
Shin-go-me-zia,	Cant-ah-chin-guah,
Pe-wau-pe-ah,	Ma-ze-quah,
Te-moo-te-ah,	Cant-au-seep-au,
Wau-pe-mun-guah,	To-pe-ah,
Sha-pen-do-ziah,	Ma-con-zah,
Wan-pe-pin-ce-ah,	Maun-go-zah,
Co-i-sey,	Ka-lah-ca-mic,
Mah-con-zah,	Keel-son-sauh,
Pa-cong-ye-ah,	Keel-swah,
Mah-qui-e-cah,	Benjamin,
Cau-te-mon-guah,	John B. Richardville,
Mong-gon-zah,	Poqua Godfroy.

Done in presence of—

Samuel Milroy,
Allen Hamilton,
    Commissioners.
H. B. Milroy, secretary to commission.
Peter Andrie,
Grigway Boudie,
    Interpreters.
(To the Indian names are subjoined a mark and seal.)

TREATY WITH THE WYANDOT, 1842.

Mar. 17, 1842.

11 Stat., 581.
Proclamation Oct. 5, 1842.

John Tyler, President of the United States of America, by John Johnston, formerly agent for Indian affairs, now a citizen of the State of Ohio, commissioner duly authorized and appointed to treat with the Wyandott Nation of Indians for a cession of all their lands lying and being in the States of Ohio and Michigan; and the duly constituted chiefs, counsellors, and head-men, of the said Wyandott Nation, in full council assembled, on the other part, have entered into the following articles and conditions, viz:

Cession of lands to the United States.

ARTICLE 1. The Wyandott Nation of Indians do hereby cede to the United States all that tract of land situate, lying, and being in the county of Crawford and State of Ohio, commonly known as the residue of the large reserve, being all of their remaining lands within the State of Ohio, and containing one hundred and nine thousand one hundred and forty-four acres, more or less. The said nation also hereby cedes to the United States all their right and title to the Wyandotte Reserve, on both sides of the river Huron, in the State of Michigan, containing four thousand nine hundred and ninety-six acres, be the same more or less, being all the remaining lands claimed or set apart for the use of the Wyandotts within the State of Michigan; and the United States hereby promises to pay the sum of five hundred dollars towards the expenses of removing the Indians of the river Huron to Upper Sandusky, but before the latter clause of this article is binding on the contracting parties, the consent of the head-men of the river Huron Wyandotts is to be had in writing.

Grant by the United States to the Wyandotts.

ARTICLE 2. In consideration of the foregoing cession, the United States hereby grant to the aforesaid Wyandott Nation a tract of land west of the Mississippi River, to contain one hundred and forty-eight thousand acres, and to be located upon any lands owned by the United States, now set apart, or may in future be set apart for Indian use, and not already assigned to any other tribe or nation.

ARTICLE 3. The United States agree to pay the Wyandott Nation a perpetual annuity of seventeen thousand five hundred dollars in specie, the first payment to be made within the present year, 1842, to enable the nation the more speedily to remove to their new home in the West; this includes all former annuities.

Annuity.

ARTICLE 4. The United States agree to make a permanent provision of five hundred dollars per annum, for the support of a school, to be under the direction of the chiefs, and for no other purpose whatever, the first payment to be made three years hence, and afterwards at the payment of the annuity in each succeeding year.

School.

ARTICLE 5. The United States agree to pay the Wyandotts the full value of their improvements in the country hereby ceded by them in Ohio and Michigan, which valuation shall be made by two persons to be appointed by the President of the United States, who shall be sworn faithfully to do justice to the parties, the amount of such valuation to be paid at any time after the 1st day of April, 1843, as shall be acceptable to the Wyandott chiefs, to meet their arrangements for emigrating.

Value of improvements to be paid the Wyandot.

ARTICLE 6. The United States hereby agree to pay the debts due by members of the Wyandott Nation to citizens of the United States, amounting to twenty-three thousand eight hundred and sixty dollars, in conformity to a schedule hereto annexed.

Debts.

ARTICLE 7. The Wyandotts shall be allowed the use and occupancy of their improvements until the 1st of April, 1844, on the condition that they nor any persons claiming or occupying under them by lease or otherwise shall not commit waste or damage on the premises hereby ceded, but this is not to prevent the United States from surveying and selling the land at any time previous to the said 1st day of April, 1844.

Improvements to be used on conditions.

ARTICLE 8. The United States engage to provide and support a blacksmith and an assistant blacksmith for the Wyandott Nation, and to furnish annually a sufficient quantity of iron, steel, coal, files, tools, and all other things necessary and proper in such on establishment, and to erect a suitable shop and house or houses for the residence of the blacksmith and his assistant.

Blacksmith.

ARTICLE 9. The United States engage to maintain and support a sub-agent and interpreter to reside among the Wyandotts to aid them in the protection of their persons and property, and to manage their intercourse with the Government and citizens of the United States.

Subagent and interpreter.

ARTICLE 10. The buildings and farm occupied by the mission of the Methodist Episcopal Church shall remain in possession of the present incumbents until the 1st day of April, 1844, and permission is hereby given to harvest and remove the crop of fall-grain which may be then sown.

Mission and buildings to remain.

ARTICLE 11. All persons identified as members of the Wyandott Nation, and their heirs, and who may emigrate to the west, shall participate equally in the benefits of the annuity, and all other national privileges, and it is expressly understood that those who do not emigrate, and any that may hereafter cease to remain with the nation, will not be entitled to the benefits and privileges aforesaid.

Who may share the annuity.

ARTICLE 12. Whereas by the 8th article of the treaty of Miami Rapids of September 29th, 1817, (proclaimed January 4, 1819,) there was granted unto Horonu, or Cherokee Boy, a Wyandott chief, one section of land, to contain six hundred and forty acres; and whereas the said Horonu did during his life-time sell and convey to James Whitaker one quarter-section of said land, containing 160 acres, which sale was confirmed by the President of the United States. The said Horonu died in the month of March, 1826, having by his last will bequeathed the remaining three quarter-sections, containing 480 acres, to Squeendehtee and Sooharress, or Isaac Williams, they being the nearest of kin to the deceased, now to the intent that the purposes of

Heirs of Horonu.

the testator may be fully complied with, it is hereby agreed the 480 acres of land, as aforesaid, shall be immediately sold under the directions of the President of the United States, and the net proceeds, after deducting all expenses, be paid over to the heirs aforesaid.

Removal.

ARTICLE 13. The chiefs of the Wyandott Nation hereby agree to remove their whole people to the west of the Mississippi River without any other cost to the United States than the sum of ten thousand dollars; five thousand dollars of which is to be paid the said chiefs when the first detachment of their people sets out on their journey to the west, and the remaining five thousand dollars on the arrival of the whole nation at the place of their destination in the west.

Grant to certain persons.

ARTICLE 14. The United States agree to grant by patent in fee-simple to each of the following-named persons, and their heirs all of whom are Wyandotts by blood or adoption, one section of land of six hundred and forty acres each, out of any lands west of the Missouri River set apart for Indian use, not already claimed or occupied by any person or tribe, viz: Silas Armstrong, John M. Armstrong, Matthew R. Walker, William Walker, Joel Walker, Charles B. Garrett, George Garrett, George J. Clark, Irwin P. Long, Ethan A. Long, Joseph L. Tennery, Robert Robertaile, Jared S. Dawson, Joseph Newell, John T. Walker, Peter D. Clark, James Rankin, Samuel McCulloch, Elliott McCulloch, Isaiah Walker, William M. Tennery, Henry Clay Walker, Ebenezer Z. Reed, and Joel Walker Garrett, and to the following chiefs and councillors one section each: Francis A. Hicks, James Washington, Squeendehtee, Henry Jaques, Tauroonee, Doctor Grey Eyes, George Armstrong, Warpole, John Hicks, Peacock, and George Punch. The lands hereby granted to be selected by the grantees, surveyed and patented at the expense of the United States, but never to be conveyed by them or their heirs without the permission of the President of the United States.

Payment for services.

ARTICLE 15. The United States agree to pay to William Walker and Joel Walker, each, the sum of two hundred and fifty dollars, and to John M. Armstrong the sum of one hundred and fifty dollars, for services rendered as interpreters in the progress of the negotiation; and to Warpole, a former chief of the Wyandott Nation, one hundred and fifty dollars, money expended by him as one of the party who accompanied Joseph McCutchen, a former commissioner of the United States, to the city of Washington in September, 1839.

Grant to Catharine Walker.

ARTICLE 16. In the year 1812 the houses, barns, stables, fences, horses, cattle, and hogs, with farming utensils and household furniture, to a large amount, the property of the late William Walker, of Brownstown, in the Territory of Michigan, was destroyed by the enemy while in the occupancy of the United States forces; and by reason of his attachment to the cause of his country, being a native citizen, taken prisoner in early life by the Wyandott Indians, intermarried, and ever afterward living among them, the evidence of all which is ample and conclusive. There is therefore granted unto Catharine Walker, widow of the said William Walker, and to his heirs, the sum of three thousand dollars, in full satisfaction of their claim, to be paid by the United States to her or them after the ratification of this treaty.

Reservations.

ARTICLE 17. There shall be reserved from sale, and forever devoted to public use, two acres of ground as near as can be in a square form, to include the stone meeting-house and burying-ground near to and north of Upper Sandusky, one acre to include the burying-ground on the bank near the council-house at Upper Sandusky, and one-half acre to include the burying-ground on the farm of Silas Armstrong, which several lots of ground shall forever remain open and free to all persons for the purpose of interment and houses of worship, and for no other purposes whatever.

When to take effect.

ARTICLE 18. This treaty shall take effect and be obligatory on the contracting parties as soon as the same shall be ratified by the President of the United States, by and with the advice and consent of the Senate thereof.

In testimony whereof the said John Johnston, commissioner as aforesaid, and the chiefs and councillors and headmen of the Wyandott nation in open council, at the council-house at Upper Sandusky in the county of Crawford, and the State of Ohio, on the seventeenth day of March, in the year of our Lord one thousand eight hundred and forty-two, have set their names.

[SEAL]   John Johnston.

Fran. A. Hicks, Principal Chief.   Tauroone (x)
James Washington (x)   George Armstrong (x)
Squeendehtee (x)   Doctor Grey Eyes (x)
Henry Jaquis (x)

Signed in the presence of—

John W. Bear, Sub. Indian Agent   Charles Graham
James Rankin, U. S. Interpreter   John Walker
G. C. Worth   Chester Wells
John Cary   I. Duddleson
Samuel Newell   Andrew Gardner, jur.,
Stephen Fowler   John Justus

We, the undersigned, chiefs and counsellors of the Wyandott nation of Indians, residing in the State of Ohio, and representing also the Wyandotts of the River Huron, in Michigan, do hereby give our free and voluntary assent to the amendments made by the Senate of the United States on the 17th day of August, one thousand eight hundred and forty-two, to the treaty concluded by us with the United States on the 17th day of March, 1842, the same having been submitted and fully explained to us by John Johnston, commissioner on the part of the United States for that purppose, in full council assembled.

In testimony whereof, we have hereunto set our hands and affixed our seals, respectively, at Upper Sandusky, Ohio, the sixteenth day of September, one thousand eight hundred and forty-two, 1842.

Henry Jacques, Principal Chief this   Geroge Punch, sen., his x mark,   [L. S.]
  year, his x mark,   [L. S.]   Tauroomee, his x mark,   [L. S.]
James Washington, his x mark,   [L. S.]   James Big Tree, his x mark,   [L. S.]
Doctor Grey Eyes, his x mark,   [L. S.]   Franccis A. Hicks,   [L. S.]

In the presence of—

John Johnston, U. S. Commissioner   James Wheeler, Missionary to the Meth-
James Rankin, U. S. Interpreter   odist Episcopal Church, Wyandotts.
John Cary   William M. Buell
Joseph Chaffee   Chas. Graham
                                          H. J. Starr

TREATY WITH THE SENECA, 1842.

Articles of a treaty made and concluded at Buffalo Creek, in the State of New York, on the twentieth day of May in the year one thousand eight hundred and forty-two, between the United States of America, acting herein by Ambrose Spencer their Commissioner, thereto duly authorized, on the one part, and the chiefs, headmen and warriors of the Seneca nation of Indians, duly assembled in council, on the other part.

May 20, 1842.
_____
7 Stat., 586.
Proclamation, Aug
26, 1842.

Preamble.

WHEREAS a treaty was heretofore concluded, and made between the said United States, and the chiefs, headmen, and warriors of the several tribes of New York Indians, dated the fifteenth day of January in the year one thousand eight hundred and thirty-eight, which treaty having been afterwards amended, was proclaimed by the President of the United States, on the fourth of April one thousand eight hundred and forty, to have been duly ratified.

And whereas on the day of making this treaty, and bearing even date herewith, a certain indenture was made executed and concluded by and between the said Seneca nation of Indians and Thomas L. Ogden, and Joseph Fellows, assignees under the State of Massachusetts, in the presence, and with the approbation of a Commissioner appointed by the United States, and in the presence and with the approbation of Samuel Hoare, a superintendent on the part of the commonwealth of Massachusetts, which indenture is in the words and figures following to wit:

Indenture between Ogden and Fellows and the Seneca Indians.

"THIS INDENTURE made and concluded between Thomas Ludlow Ogden of the city of New York, and Joseph Fellows of Geneva, in the county of Ontario of the one part, and the chiefs and headmen of the Seneca nation of Indians, on the other part at a council duly assembled and held at Buffalo Creek in the State of New York on the twentieth day of May in the year one thousand eight hundred and forty-two in the presence of Samuel Hoare, the superintendent thereto authorized and appointed by and on the part of the commonwealth of Massachusets, an of Ambrose Spencer a Commissioner thereto duly appointed and authorized on the part of the United States.

"Whereas at a council held at Buffalo Creek on the fifteenth day of January in the year one thousand eight hundred and thirty eight, an indenture of that date was made and executed by and between the parties to this agreement, whereby the chiefs and headmen of the Seneca nation of Indians for the consideration of two hundred and two thousand dollars did grant, bargain, release and confirm unto the said Thomas Ludlow Ogden and Joseph Fellows, all those four several tracts of land, situate within the State of New York, then and yet occupied by the said nation, or the people thereof, severally described in the said indenture, as the Buffalo Creek Reservation, containing by estimation forty-nine thousand nine hundred and twenty acres of land, the Cattaraugus Reservation containing by estimation twenty-one thousand six hundred and eighty acres of land, the Allegany Reservation, containing by estimation thirty thousand four hundred and sixty-nine acres of land, and the Tonnewanda Reservation containing by estimation twelve thousand eight hundred acres of land; a duplicate of which indenture was annexed to a treaty of the same date made between the United States of America and the chiefs, headmen, and warriors of the several tribes of New York Indians assembled in council; which treaty was amended and proclaimed by the President of the United States on the fourth of April one thousand eight hundred and forty, as having been duly ratified; as by the said indenture, treaty and proclamation more fully appear.

"And whereas divers questions and differences having arisen between the chiefs and headmen of the Seneca nation of Indians or some of them, and the said Thomas Ludlow Ogden and Joseph Fellows in relation to the said indenture, and the rights of the parties thereto, and the provisions contained in the said indenture being still unexecuted, the said parties have mutually agreed to settle, compromise and finally terminate all such questions and differences on the terms and conditions hereinafter specified.

"Now therefore it is hereby mutually declared, and agreed, by and between the said parties as follows.

"ARTICLE FIRST. The said Thomas Ludlow Ogden, and Joseph Fellows in consideration of the release and agreements hereinafter contained, on the part of the said Seneca nation do on their part consent. covenant and agree that they the said nation (the said indenture notwithstanding) shall and may continue in the occupation and enjoyment of the whole of the said two several tracts of land, called the Cattaraugus Reservation, and the Allegany Reservation with the same right and title in all things, as they had and possessed therein immediately before the date of the said indenture, saving and reserving to the said Thomas Ludlow Ogden, and Joseph Fellows the right of pre-emption, and all other the right and title which they then had or held in or to the said tracts of land.

"ARTICLE SECOND. The chiefs and headmen of the Seneca nation of Indians in consideration of the foregoing, and of the agreement next hereinafter contained, do on their part grant, release and confirm unto the said Thomas Ludlow Ogden, and Joseph Fellows, and to their heirs and assigns, in joint tenancy, the whole of the said two tracts of land severally called the Buffalo Creek Reservation, and the Tonnewanda Reservation, and all the right and interest therein of the said nation.

Indenture between Ogden and Fellows and the Seneca Indians.

"ARTICLE THIRD. It is mutually agreed, between the parties hereto that in lieu of the sum expressed in the said indenture, as the consideration of the sale, and release of the said four tracts of land, there shall be paid to the said nation a just consideration sum, for the release of the two tracts, hereby confirmed to the said Ogden and Fellows, to be estimated and ascertained as follows.

"The present value of the Indian title to the whole of the said four tracts of land including the improvements thereon, shall for all the purposes of this present compact, be deemed and taken to be two hundred and two thousand dollars, of which sum one hundred thousand dollars shall be deemed to be the value of such title in and to all the lands within the said four tracts exclusive of the improvements thereon, and one hundred and two thousand dollars to be the value of all the improvements within the said four tracts, and of the said sum of one hundred thousand dollars the said Ogden and Fellows shall pay to the Seneca nation such proportion as the value of all the lands within the said two tracts called the Buffalo Creek, and Tonnewanda Reservations shall bear to the value of all the lands within all the said four tracts—and of the said sum of one hundred and two thousand dollars, the said Ogden and Fellows shall pay such proportion as the value of the improvements on the same two tracts, shall bear to the value of the improvements on all the said four tracts.

"ARTICLE FOURTH. The amount of the consideration monies to be paid in pursuance of the last preceding article, shall be determined by the judgment and award of arbitrators, one of whom shall be named by the Secretary of the War Department of the United States, and one by the said Ogden and Fellows, which arbitrators in order to such judgment and award, and to the performance of the other duties hereby imposed on them, may employ suitable surveyors to explore examine and report on the value of the said lands and improvements, and also to ascertain the contents of each of the said four tracts, which contents shall govern the arbitrators as to quantity in determining the amount of the said consideration money.

"The same arbitrators shall also award and determine the amount to be paid to each individual Indian out of the sum which on the principles above stated, they shall ascertain and award to be the proportionate value of the improvements on the said two tracts called the Buffalo Creek Reservation and the Tonnewanda Reservation, and in case the said arbitrators shall disagree as to any of the matters hereby submitted to them, they may choose an umpire whose decision thereon shall be final and conclusive, and the said arbitrators shall make a report in writing of their proceedings in duplicate, such reports to be acknowledged or proved according to the laws of the State of New York, in order to their being recorded, one of such reports to be filed in the office of the Secretary of the Department of War, and the other thereof to be delivered to the said Thomas L. Ogden and Joseph Fellows.

"ARTICLE FIFTH. It is agreed, that the possession of the two pa.. s hereby confirmed, to the said Ogden and Fellows, shall be surrendered and delivered up to them, as follows, viz: The forest or unimproved lands on the said tracts, within one month after the report of the said arbitrators shall be filed, in the office of the Department of War, and he improved lands within two years after the said report shall have been so filed; Provided always that the amount to be so ascertained and awarded, as the proportionate value of the said improvements, shall on the surrender thereof be paid to the President of the United States, to be distributed among the owners of the said improvements, according to the determination and award of the said arbitrators, in this behalf, and provided further that the consideration for the release and conveyance of the said lands shall at the time of the surrender thereof be paid or secured to the satisfaction of the said Secretary of the War Department, the income of which is to be paid to the said Seneca Indians annually.

Indenture between Ogden and Fellows and the Seneca Indians.

"But any Indian having improvements may surrender the same, and the land occupied by him and his family at any time prior to the expiration of the said two years, upon the amount awarded to him for such improvements being paid to the President of the United States, or any agent designated by him for that purpose by the said Ogden and Fellows, which amount shall be paid over to the Indian entitled to the same, under the direction of the War Department.

"ARTICLE SIXTH. It is hereby agreed and declared to be the understanding and intent of the parties hereto, that such of the said Seneca nation, as shall remove from the State of New York, under the provisions of any treaty, made or to be made, between the United States and the said Indians, shall be entitled in proportion to their relative numbers to the funds of the Seneca nation, and that the interest and income of such their share and proportion of the said funds, including the consideration money to be paid to the said nation in pursuance of this Indenture, and of all annuities belonging to the said Nation shall be paid to the said Indians so removing at their new homes, and whenever the said tracts called the Allegheny and the Cattaraugus Reservations, or any part thereof shall be sold and conveyed by the Indians remaining in the State of New York, the Indians so removing shall be entitled to share in the proceeds of said sales in the like proportion. And it is further agreed and declared, that such Indians owning improvements in the Cattaraugus and Alleghany tracts as may so remove from the State of New York, shall be entitled on such removal, and on surrendering their improvements to the Seneca nation, for the benefit of the nation to receive the like compensation for the same, according to their relative values, as in the third and fourth articles of this treaty are stipulated to be paid, to the owners of improvements in the Buffalo Creek and Tonnewanda Tracts, on surrendering their improvements; which compensations may be advanced by the President of the United States, out of any funds in the hands of the Government of the United States, belonging to the Seneca nation, and the value of these improvements shall be ascertained and reported by the Arbitrators, to be appointed in pursuance of the fourth article.

"ARTICLE SEVENTH. This Indenture is to be deemed to be in lieu of, and as a substitute for the above recited Indenture made and dated the fifteenth day of January, one thousand eight hundred and thirty eight, so far as the provisions of the two instruments may be inconsistent, or contradictory, and the said Indenture so far as the same may be inconsistent with the provisions of this compact, is to be regarded and is hereby declared to be rescinded and released.

"ARTICLE EIGHTH. All the expenses attending the execution of this Indenture and compact including those of the arbitration and surveys hereinbefore referred to, and also those of holding the treaty now in negotiation between the United States and the said Seneca Nation, except so far as may be provided for by the United States, shall be advanced and paid by the said Ogden and Fellows.

"ARTICLE NINTH. The parties to this compact mutually agree to solicit the influence of the Government of the United States to protect such of the lands of the Seneca Indians, within the State of New York, as may from time to time remain in their possession from all taxes, and assessments for roads, highways, or any other purpose until such lands shall be sold and conveyed by the said Indians, and the possession thereof shall have been relinquished by them.

"In witness whereof, the parties to these presents have hereunto, and to three other instruments of the same tenor and date, one to remain with the United States, one to remain with the State of Massachusetts, one to remain with the Seneca Nation of Indians, and one to remain with the said Thomas Ludlow Ogden and Joseph Fellows, interchangeably set their hands and seals the day and year first above written."

THEREFORE taking into consideration the premises it is agreed and stipulated by and between the United States of America and the Seneca nation of Indians, as follows, to wit:

First, The United States of America consent to the several articles and stipulations contained in the last recited Indenture between the said nation, and the said Thomas Ludlow Ogden and Joseph Fellows, above set forth. United States agree to said indenture.

Second, The United States further consent and agree that any number of the said nation, who shall remove from the State of New York, under the provisions of the above mentioned Treaty proclaimed as aforesaid, on the fourth day of April one thousand eight hundred and forty, shall be entitled in proportion to their relative numbers to all the benefits of the said Treaty. Indians who remove under treaty of April 4, 1840, entitled to benefits thereof.

Third, The United States of America further consent and agree, that the tenth article of said Treaty proclaimed as aforesaid on the fourth day of April one thousand eight hundred and forty, be deemed, and considered as modified, in conformity with the provisions of the Indenture hereinabove set forth, so far as that the United States will receive and pay the sum stipulated to be paid as the consideration money of the improvements therein specified, and will receive hold and apply the sum to be paid, or the securities to be given for the lands therein mentioned, as provided for in such Indenture. Tenth article of treaty proclaimed April 4, 1840, modified

In testimony whereof the undersigned Ambrose Spencer Commissioner on the part of the United States of America, and the undersigned chiefs and headmen of the Seneca nation of Indians, have to two parts of this treaty, one thereof to remain with the United States, and the other thereof with the Seneca nation of Indians, set their hands and affixed their seals the day and year first above mentioned.

Ambrose Spencer.

Tit-ho-yah, or William Jones,	Samuel Goudon,
Saul Lagure,	Tunis Halftown,
Gau-geh-gruh-doh, or George Jimison,	Hau-sa-nea-nes, or White Seneca,
N. T. Strong,	Gah-nang-ga-eot, or Young Chief,
Hau-neh-hoys-soh, or Blue Eyes,	Thomas Jimeson,
Jabez Stevenson,	Moses Stevenson,
William Krouse,	Jonah Armstrong,
Samuel Wilson, or Ni-ge-jos-a,	Joseph Silverheels,
William Krouse,	Da-o-as-sah-au, or Jo. Hunlock,
Thompson S. Harris,	George Fox,
Sah-go-en-toh, or Morris Halftown,	Yaw-sau-ge, or Peter Johnson,
Ten-wan-ne-us, or Governor Black Snake,	Noh-sok-dah, or Jim Jonas,
Doa-ne-pho-gah, or Little Johnson,	Dih-no-se-du, or Jacob Shongo,
Joh-nesh-ha-dih, or James Stevenson,	John Seneca, or Jo-on-da-goh,
Ho-wah-tan-eh-goh, or John Pierce,	Ho-no-yea-os, or Jocob Bennett,
Da-gon-on-de, or William Patterson,	George Turkey,

Daniel Fau Guns,	David Snow,
Goat-hau-oh, or Billy Shanks,	John Bark,
Daniel Fau Guns,	George Killbuck,
Goat-hau-oh, or Billy Shanks,	George Dennis,
James Pierce,	John Kennedy, sen.,
Gi-eut-twa-geh, or Robert Watt,	Abram John,
Seneca White,	Job Pierce,
Gesh-u-aw, or James Shongo,	Saw-da-ne, or George Deer,
Jarvis Spraing,	Ga-na-waw, or John Cook,
Ti-at-tah-co, or Adam Dextador,	Jaw-ne-es, or John Dickey,
Moris B. Pierce,	George Big Deer,
So-gooh-quas, or John Tallchief,	Nah-joh-gau-eh, or Tall Peter,
Isaac Halftown,	John Kennedy, jr.

Signed sealed and delivered in the presence of ——. (The words "and Allegany" in the sixth page being interlined.)

A. Dixon, Commissioner on the part of New York.	O. H. Marshall,
	Elam R. Jewett,
Benj. Ferris,	Cortland B. Stebbins,
Orlando Allen,	Joseph S. Wasson.
Asher Wright,	

(To the Indian names are subjoined a mark and seal.)

TREATY WITH THE CHIPPEWA, 1842.

Oct. 4, 1842.

7 Stat., 591.
Proclamation, Mar.
23, 1843.

Articles of a treaty made and concluded at La Pointe of Lake Superior, in the Territory of Wisconsin, between Robert Stuart commissioner on the part of the United States, and the Chippewa Indians of the Mississippi, and Lake Superior, by their chiefs and headmen.

ARTICLE I.

Land ceded to the United States.

THE Chippewa Indians of the Mississippi and Lake Superior, cede to the United States all the country within the following bounderies; viz: beginning at the mouth of Chocolate river of Lake Superior; thence northwardly across said lake to intersect the boundery line between the United States and the Province of Canada; thence up said Lake Superior, to the mouth of the St. Louis, or Fond du Lac river (including all the islands in said lake); thence up said river to the American Fur Company's trading post, at the southwardly bend thereof, about 22 miles from its mouth; thence south to intersect the line of the treaty of 29th July 1837, with the Chippewas of the Mississippi; thence along said line to its southeastwardly extremity, near the Plover portage on the Wisconsin river; thence northeastwardly, along the boundery line, between the Chippewas and Menomonees, to its eastern termination, (established by the treaty held with the Chippewas, Menomonees, and Winnebagoes, at Butte des Morts, August 11th 1827) on the Skonawby river of Green Bay; thence northwardly to the source of Chocolate river; thence down said river to its mouth, the place of beginning; it being the intention of the parties to this treaty, to include in this cession, all the Chippewa lands eastwardly of the aforesaid line running from the American Fur Company's trading post on the Fond du Lac river to the intersection of the line of the treaty made with the Chippewas of the Mississippi July 29th 1837.

ARTICLE II.

Hunting ground.

The Indians stipulate for the right of hunting on the ceded territory, with the other usual privileges of occupancy, until required to remove by the President of the United States, and that the laws of the United

States shall be continued in force, in respect to their trade and inter course with the whites, until otherwise ordered by Congress.

Article III.

It is agreed by the parties to this treaty, that whenever the Indians shall be required to remove from the ceded district, all the unceded lands belonging to the Indians of Fond du Lac, Sandy Lake, and Mississippi bands, shall be the common property and home of all the Indians, party to this treaty. Unceded lands to be common property of the Indians.

Article IV.

In consideration of the foregoing cession, the United States, engage to pay to the Chippewa Indians of the Mississippi, and Lake Superior, annually, for twenty-five years, twelve thousand five hundred (12,500) dollars, in specie, ten thousand five hundred (10,500) dollars in goods, two thousand (2,000) dollars in provisions and tobacco, two thousand (2,000) dollars for the support of two blacksmiths shops, (including pay of smiths and assistants, and iron steel &c.) one thousand (1,000) dollars for pay of two farmers, twelve hundred (1,200) for pay of two carpenters, and two thousand (2,000) dollars for the support of schools for the Indians party to this treaty; and further the United States engage to pay the sum of five thousand (5,000) dollars as an agricultural fund, to be expended under the direction of the Secretary of War. And also the sum of seventy-five thousand (75,000) dollars, shall be allowed for the full satisfaction of their debts within the ceded district, which shall be examined by the commissioner to this treaty, and the amount to be allowed decided upon by him, which shall appear in a schedule hereunto annexed. The United States shall pay the amount so allowed within three years. Sums to be paid by United States for cession.

Indian debts to be paid by United States.

Whereas the Indians have expressed a strong desire to have some provision made for their half breed relatives, therefore it is agreed, that fifteen thousand (15,000) dollars shall be paid to said Indians, next year, as a present, to be disposed of, as they, together with their agent, shall determine in council. Provision for half breeds.

Article V.

Division of annuity.

Whereas the whole country between Lake Superior and the Mississippi, has always been understood as belonging in common to the Chippewas, party to this treaty; and whereas the bands bordering on Lake Superior, have not been allowed to participate in the annuity payments of the treaty made with the Chippewas of the Mississippi, at St. Peters July 29th 1837, and whereas all the unceded lands belonging to the aforesaid Indians, are hereafter to be held in common, therefore, to remove all occasion for jealousy and discontent, it is agreed that all the annuity due by the said treaty, as also the annuity due by the present treaty, shall henceforth be equally divided among the Chippewas of the Mississippi and Lake Superior, party to this treaty, so that every person shall receive an equal share.

Article VI.

The Indians residing on the Mineral district, shall be subject to removal therefrom at the pleasure of the President of the United States. Indians on mineral districts subject to removal.

Article VII.

This treaty shall be obligatory upon the contracting parties when ratified by the President and Senate of the United States. Obligatory when ratified.

In testimony whereof the said Robert Stuart commissioner, on the part of the United States, and the chiefs and headmen of the Chippewa Indians of the Mississippi and Lake Superior, have hereunto set their hands, at La Pointe of Lake Superior, Wisconsin Territory this fourth day of October in the year of our Lord one thousand eight hundred and forty-two.

Robert Stuart, Commissioner.
Jno. Hulbert, Secretary.

Crow wing River,	Po go ne gi shik,	1st chief.
Do.	Son go com ick,	2d do.
Sandy Lake,	Ka non do ur uin zo,	1st do.
Do.	Na tum e gaw bon,	2d do.
Gull Lake,	Ua bo jig,	1st do.
Do.	Pay pe si gon de bay,	2d do.
Red Ceder Lake,	Kui ui sen shis,	1st do.
Do.	Ott taw wance,	2d do.
Po ke gom maw,	Bai ie jig,	1st do.
Do.	Show ne aw,	2d do.
Wisconsin River,	Ki uen zi,	1st do.
`Do.	Wi aw bis ke kut te way,	2d do.
Lac de Flambeau,	A pish ka go gi,	1st do.
Do.	May tock cus e quay,	2d do.
Do.	She maw gon e,	2d do.
Lake Bands,	Ki ji ua be she shi,	1st do.
Do.	Ke kon o tum,	2d do.
Fon du Lac,	Shin goob,	1st do.
Do.	Na gan nab,	2d do.
Do.	Mong o zet,	2d do.
La Pointe,	Gitchi waisky,	1st do.
Do.	Mi zi,	2d do.
Do.	Ta qua gone e,	2d do.
Onlonagan,	O kon di kan,	1st do.
Do.	Kis ke taw wac,	2d do.
Ance,	Pe na shi,	1st do.
Do.	Guck we san sish,	2d do.
Vieux Desert,	Ka she osh e,	1st do.
Do.	Medge waw gwaw wot,	2d do.
Mille Lac,	Ne qua ne be,	1st do.
Do.	Ua shash ko kum,	2d do.
Do.	No din,	2d do.
St. Croix,	Be zhi ki,	1st do.
Do.	Ka bi na be,	2d do.
Do.	Ai aw bens,	2d do.
Snake River,	Sha go bi,	1st do.
Chippewa River,	Ua be she shi,	1st do.
	Que way zhan sis,	2d do.
Lac Courtulle,	Ne na nang eb,	1st do.
Do.	Be bo kon uen,	2d do.
Do.	Ki uen zi.	2d do.

In presence of—

Henry Blanchford, interpreter.	Z. Platt.
Samuel Ashmun, interpreter.	C. H. Beaulieau.
Justin Rice.	L. T. Jamison.
Charles H. Oakes.	James P. Scott.
William A. Aitkin.	Cyrus Mendenhall.
William Brewster.	L. M. Warren.
Charles M. Borup.	

(To the Indian names are subjoined marks.)

Schedule of claims examined and allowed by Robert Stuart, commissioner, under the treaty with the Chippewa Indians of the Mississippi and Lake Superior, concluded at La Pointe, October 4th 1842, setting forth the names of claimants, and their proportion of allowance of the seventy-five thousand dollars provided in the fourth article of the aforesaid treaty, for the full satisfaction of their debts, as follows:

Schedule of debts of Indians to be paid.

No. of claim.	Name of claimant.	Proportion of $75,000, set apart in 4th article of treaty.
1	Edward F. Ely	$50 80
2	Z. Platt, esq., attorney for George Berkett	484 67
3	Cleveland North Lake Co	1,485 67
4	Abraham W. Williams	75 03
5	William Brewster	2,052 67
	This claim to be paid as follows, viz:	
	William Brewster, or order ... $1,929 77	
	Charles W. Borup, or order ... 122 90	
	$2,052 67	
6	George Copway	61 67
7	John Kahbege	57 55
8	Alixes Carpantier	28 58
9	John W. Bell	186 16
10	Antoine Picard	6 46
11	Michael Brisette	182 42
12	François Dejaddon	301 48
13	Pierre C. Duvernay	1,101 00
14	Jean Bts. Bazinet	325 46
15	John Hotley	69 00
16	François Charette	234 92
17	Clement H. Beaulieu, agent for the estate of Bazil Beaulieu, dec'd	596 84
18	François St. Jean and George Bonga	366 84
19	Louis Ladebauche	322 52
20	Peter Crebassa	499 27
21	B. T. Kavanaugh	516 82
22	Augustin Goslin	169 05
23	American Fur Company	13,365 30
	This claim to be paid as follows, viz:	
	American Fur Company ... 12,565 10	
	Charles W. Borup ... 800 20	
	$13,365 30	
24	William A. Aitken	935 67
25	James P. Scott	73 41
26	Augustin Bellanger	192 35
27	Louis Corbin	12 57
28	Alexes Corbin	596 03
29	George Johnston	35 24
30	Z. Platt, esq., attorney for Sam'l Ashman	1,771 63
31	Z. Platt, esq., attorney for Wm. Johnson	390 27
32	Z. Platt, esq., attorney for estate of Dan'l Dingley	1,991 62
33	Lyman M. Warren	1,566 65
34	Estate of Michael Cadotte, *disallowed.*	
35	Z. Platt, esq., attorney for estate of E. Roussain	959 13
36	Joseph Dufault	144 32
37	Z. Platt, esq., attorney for Antoine Mace	170 35
38	Michael Cadotte	205 60
39	Z. Platt, esq., att'y for François Gauthier	167 05
40	Z. Platt, esq., att'y for Joseph Gauthier	614 30
41	Z. Platt, esq., attorney for J. B. Uoulle	64 78
42	Jean Bts. Corbin	531 50
43	John Hulbert	209 18
44	Jean Bts. Couvellion	18 80
45	Nicholas Da Couteau, *withdrawn.*	
46	Pierre Cotté	732 50
47	W. H. Brockway and Henry Holt, executors to the estate of John Holliday, dec'd.	3,157 10
48	John Jacob Astor	37,994 98
	This claim to be paid as follows, viz:	
	Charles W. Borup ... 1,676 90	
	Z. Platt, esq ... 2,621 80	
	John Jacob Astor ... 23,696 28	
	$27,994 98	
49	Z. Platt, esq., attorney for Thos. Connor	1,118 60
50	Charles H. Oakes	4,309 21
51	Z. Platt, esq., attorney for Wm. Morrison	1,074 70
52	Z. Platt, esq., att'y for Isaac Butterfield	1,275 56
53	J. B. Van Rensselaer	62 00
54	William Brewster and James W. Abbot	2,067 10
	The parties to this claim request no payment be made to either without their joint consent, or until a decision of the case be had, in a court of justice.	
55	William Bell	17 62
		$75,000 00

Robert Stuart, Commissioner.
Jno. Hulbert, Secretary.

TREATY WITH THE SAUK AND FOXES, 1842.

Oct. 11, 1842.

7 Stat., 596.
Proclamation, Mar.
23, 1843.

Articles of a treaty made and concluded at the agency of the Sac and Fox Indians in the Territory of Iowa, between the United States of America, by John Chambers their commissioner thereto specially authorized by the President, and the confederated tribes of Sac and Fox Indians represented by their chiefs, headmen and braves:

ARTICLE I.

Lands ceded to United States.

THE confederated tribes of Sacs and Foxes cede to the United States, forever, all the lands west of the Mississippi river, to which they have any claim or title, or in which they have any interest whatever; reserving a right to occupy for the term of three years from the time of signing this treaty, all that part of the land hereby ceded which lies west of a line running due north and south from the painted or red rocks on the White Breast fork of the Des Moines river, which rocks will be found about eight miles, when reduced to a straight line, from the junction of the White Breast with the Des Moines.

ARTICLE II.

Payment by United States for cession.

In consideration of the cession contained in the preceding article, the United States agree to pay annually to the Sacs and Foxes, an interest of five per centum upon the sum of eight hundred thousand dollars, and to pay their debts mentioned in the schedule annexed to and made part of this treaty, amounting to the sum of two hundred and fifty-eight thousand, five hundred and sixty-six dollars and thirty-four cents; and the United States also agree,

Lands to be assigned to Indians for permanent residence.

First. That the President will as soon after this treaty is ratified on their part as may be convenient, assign a tract of land suitable and convenient for Indian purposes, to the Sacs and Foxes for a permanent and perpetual residence for them and their descendants, which tract of land shall be upon the Missouri river, or some of its waters.

Blacksmiths' and gunsmiths' shops, etc.

Second. That the United States will cause the blacksmiths and gunsmiths' tools, with the stock of iron and steel on hand at the present agency of the Sacs and Foxes, to be removed, as soon after their removal as convenient, to some suitable point at or near their residences west of the north and south line mentioned in the first article of this treaty; and will establish and maintain two blacksmiths and two gunsmiths' shops convenient to their agency, and will employ two blacksmiths, with necessary assistance, and two gunsmiths to carry on the said shops for the benefit of the Sacs and Foxes; one blacksmiths and one gunsmiths' shop to be employed exclusively for the Sacs, and one of each to be employed exclusively for the Foxes, and all expenses attending the removal of the tools, iron and steel, and the erection of new shops, and the purchase of iron and steel, and the support and maintenance of the shops, and wages of the smiths and their assistants, are to be paid by the tribe, except such portion thereof as they are now entitled to have paid by the United States, under the 4th article of the treaty made with them on the 4th of August 1824, and the 4th article of the treaty of the 21st of September 1832. And when the said tribes shall remove to the land to be assigned them by the President of the United States, under the provisions of this treaty, the smiths' shops above stipulated for shall be re-established and maintained at their new residence, upon the same terms and conditions as are above provided for their removal and establishment west of the north and south line mentioned in the first article of this treaty.

Boundary to be run and marked.

Third. That the President of the United States will as soon as convenient after the ratification of this treaty, appoint a commissioner for the purpose, and cause a line to be run north from the painted or red rocks on the White Breast, to the southern boundary of the neutral ground, and south from the said rocks to the northern boundary of Missouri; and will have the said lines so marked and designated, that the Indians and white people may know the boundary which is to separate their possessions.

ARTICLE III.

The Sacs and Foxes agree that they will remove to the west side of the line running north and south from the painted or red rocks on the White Breast, on or before the first of May next, and that so soon after the President shall have assigned them a residence upon the waters of the Missouri, as their chiefs shall consent to do so, the tribe will remove to the land so assigned them; and that if they do not remove before the expiration of the term of three years, they will then remove at their own expense; and the United States agree, that whenever the chiefs shall give notice to the Commissioner of Indian Affairs of the time at which they will commence their removal to the land to be assigned them by the President, a quantity of provisions sufficient for their subsistence while removing, shall be furnished them at their agency, and an additional quantity, not exceeding one years supply shall be delivered to them upon their arrival upon the lands assigned them; the cost and expenses of which supplies shall be retained out of any money payable to them by the United States.

Removal of Indians

Provisions for removal.

ARTICLE IV.

It is agreed that each of the principal chiefs of the Sacs and Foxes, shall hereafter receive the sum of five hundred dollars annually, out of the annuities payable to the tribe, to be used and expended by them for such purposes as they may think proper, with the approbation of their agent.

Each principal chief to receive $500 annually.

ARTICLE V.

It is further agreed that there shall be a fund amounting to thirty thousand dollars retained at each annual payment to the Sacs and Foxes, in the hands of the agent appointed by the President for their tribe, to be expended by the chiefs, with the approbation of the agent, for national and charitable purposes among their people; such as the support of their poor, burying their dead, employing physicians for the sick, procuring provisions for their people in cases of necessity, and such other purposes of general utility as the chiefs may think proper, and the agent approve. And if at any payment of the annuities of the tribe, a balance of the fund so retained from the preceding year shall remain unexpended, only so much shall be retained in addition as will make up the sum of thirty thousand dollars.

$30,000 to be retained at each annual payment.

How to be expended.

ARTICLE VI.

It is further agreed that the Sacs and Foxes may, at any time, with the consent of the President of the United States, direct the application of any portion of the annuities payable to them, under this or any former treaty, to the purchase of goods or provisions, or to agricultural purposes, or any other object tending to their improvement, or calculated to increase the comfort and happiness of their people.

Application of any portion of annuities.

ARTICLE VII.

The United States agree, that the unexpended balance of the fund created by the seventh paragraph of the second article of the treaty of the twenty-first of October, 1837, for agricultural purposes, or so much thereof as may be necessary, shall be used and employed in the cultivation of the pattern farm near the present Sac and Fox agency, in the

Certain funds for agricultural purposes.

year 1843, for the exclusive use and benefit of the tribe. And they further agree, that such portion of the fund for erecting mills, and supporting millers, specified in the fourth paragraph of the second article of the aforesaid treaty of October 21st, 1837, as may be and remain unexpended on the 1st day of May next, shall be transferred to and made part of the sum designated in the fifth paragraph (as amended) of the article and treaty above named, for breaking up land and other beneficial objects, and become thereafter applicable to the same purposes, as were in the said fifth paragraph, originally intended.

ARTICLE VIII.

Remains of the late Chief Wa-pel-lo to be buried, etc.

The Sacs and Foxes have caused the remains of their late distinguished chief Wa-pel-lo to be buried at their agency, near the grave of their late friend and agent General Joseph M. Street, and have put into the hands of their agent the sum of one hundred dollars to procure a tombstone to be erected over his grave, similar to that which has been erected over the grave of General Street; and because they wish the graves of their friend and their chief to remain in the possession of the family of General Street, to whom they were indebted in his life-time for many acts of kindness, they wish to give to his widow Mrs. Eliza M. Street one section of land to include the said graves, and the agency-house and enclosures around and near it; and as the agency house was built at the expense of the United States, the Sacs and Foxes agree to pay them the sum of one thousand dollars the value of said building, assessed by gentlemen appointed by them, and Governor Chambers commissioner on the part of the United States, to be deducted from the first annuity payable to them under the provisions of this treaty. And the United States agree to grant to the said Eliza M. Street by one or more patents, six hundred and forty acres of land in such legal subdivisions, as will include the said burial ground, the agency house, and improvements around, and near it, in good and convenient form, to be selected by the said E. M. Street or her duly authorized agent.

Patent to issue to E. M. Street for 640 acres.

ARTICLE IX.

Treaty binding when ratified.

Proviso.

It is finally agreed that this treaty shall be binding on the two contracting parties, so soon as it shall have been ratified by the President and Senate of the United States: *Provided always*, That should the Senate disagree to and reject, alter or amend any portion or stipulation thereof, the same must be again submitted to the Sacs and Foxes, and assented to by them, before it shall be considered valid and obligatory upon them, and if they disagree to such alteration or amendment, the treaty shall be returned to the Senate for ratification or rejection, in the form in which it was signed.

In witness whereof, the said John Chambers, commissioner on the part of the United States, and the undersigned chiefs, braves, and headmen of the Sac and Fox nation of Indians, have hereunto set their hands, at the Sac and Fox agency, in the Territory of Iowa, this eleventh day of October, Anno Domini one thousand eight hundred and forty-two.

John Chambers.

Sacs:	Foxes:
Ke o kuk,	Pow a shick,
Ke o kuk, Jr.,	Wa co sha she,
Wa ca cha,	An au e wit,
Che kaw que,	Ka ka ke,
Ka pon e ka,	Ma wha why,
Pa me kow art,	Ma che na ka me quat,
Ap pe noose,	Ka ka ke mo,
Wa pe,	Kish ka naqua hok,
Wa sa men,	Pe a tau a quis,
Wis ko pe,	Ma' ne ni sit,
As ke po ka won,	Mai con ne,

I o nah,	Pe she she mone,
Wish e co ma que,	Pe shaw koa,
Pash e pa ho,	Puck aw koa,
Ka pe ko ma,	Qua co ho se,
Tuk quos,	Wa pa sha kon,
Wis co sa,	Kis ke kosh,
Ka kon we na,	Ale mo ne qua,
Na cote e we na,	Cha ko kow a,
Sho wa ke,	Wah ke mo wa ta pa,
Mean ai to wa,	Muk qua gese,
Muk e ne	Ko ko etch.

Signed in presence of—

John Beach, U. S. Indian agent and secretary.
Antoine Le Claire, U. S. interpreter.
Josiah Swart, U. S. interpreter.
J. Allen, captain, First Dragoons.

C. F. Ruff, lieutenant, First U. S. Dragoons.
Arthur Bridgman.
Alfred Hebard.
Jacob O. Phister.

(To the Indian names are subjoined marks.)

Schedule of debts due from the confederated tribes of the Sac and Fox Indians to be paid by the United States under the provisions of a treaty made and concluded at the Sac and Fox agency in the Territory of Iowa on the eleventh day of October in the year 1842; to which this schedule is annexed as a part thereof.

Schedule of debts of Indians to be paid.

Name of claimant.	Place of residence.	Amount.
Pierre Chouteau, jr. & Co.	St. Louis, Missouri, licensed traders	$112,109 47
W. G. & G. W. Erving	Indiana, do do	66,371 83
J. P. Eddy & Co.	Ioway, do do	52,332 78
Thomas Charlton	Van Buren c'ty, Ioway	76 69
R. B. Willoughby	Do do	25 00
Francis Withington	Lincoln county, Missouri	4,212 58
Jesse B. Webber	Burlington, Ioway	116 60
J. C. Wear	Jefferson county, Ioway	50 00
W. C. Cameron, assignee of A. M. Bissel (bankrupt)	Burlington	283 14
David Bailey	Lincoln c'ty, Missouri	75 00
Thomas W. Bradley	Ioway	20 00
John J. Grimes	Lincoln c'ty, Missouri	625 00
William Settles	Do do	320 00
John S. David	Burlington, Ioway	20 00
F. Hancock	Van Buren, do	20 00
C. G. Pelton	Burlington, do	34 00
J. Tolman	Van Buren, do	115 00
J. L. Burtiss	Lee county, do	715 00
Isaac A. Lefevre	Van Buren, do	348 00
Jeremiah Smith, jr	Burlington, do	4,000 00
William & Sampson Smith	Jefferson county, do	60 00
John Koontz		6 50
Robert Moffet	New Lexington, Ioway	129 63
Antoine Leclair	Davenport, do	1,375 00
Margaret Price	Lee county, do	9 00
Jesse Sutton	Van Buren, do	22 00
Jefferson Jordon	Do do	175 00
Jeremiah Wayland	St. Francisville, Missouri	15 00
Robert Brown, assignee of Cutting & Gordon	Van Buren c'ty, Ioway	73 25
William Rowland	Do do	460 32
Edward Kilbourne	Lee county, do	10,411 80
Perry & Best	Do	22 75
P. Chouteau, jr. & Co.	St. Louis, Missouri	26 00
Job Carter	Van Buren c'ty	28 00
Francis Bosseron	St. Louis, Mo	26 00
James Jordon	Van Buren, Ioway	1,775 00
Sampson Smith	do	54 00
Louis Laplant	Ioway	122 00
William Phelps	Clark county, Missouri	310 00
William B. Street	Ioway	300 00
Julia Ann Goodell	Do	855 00
George L. Davenport	Davenport, Ioway	320 00
G. C. R. Mitchell	Do do	100 00
David Noggle	Van Buren, do	20 00
	Amount,	$258,566 34

John Chambers,
Commissioner on the part of the U. S.

Alfred Hebard,
Arthur Bridgman,
Commissioners appointed by the commission
on the part of the U. S. for examining and adjusting claims.

TREATY WITH THE CREEKS AND SEMINOLE, 1845.

Jan. 4, 1845.

9 Stat., 821.
Proclamation, July 18, 1845.

Articles of a treaty made by William Armstrong, P. M. Butler, James Logan, and Thomas L. Judge, commissioners in behalf of the United States, of the first part; the Creek tribe of Indians, of the second; and the Seminole tribe of Indians, of the third part.

Preamble.

WHEREAS it was stipulated, in the fourth article of the Creek treaty of 1833, that the Seminoles should thenceforward be considered a constituent part of the Creek nation, and that a permanent and comfortable home should be secured for them on the lands set apart in said treaty as the country of the Creeks; and whereas many of the Seminoles have settled and are now living in the Creek country, while others, constituting a large portion of the tribe, have refused to make their homes in any part thereof, assigning as a reason that they are unwilling to submit to Creek laws and government, and that they are apprehensive of being deprived, by the Creek authorities, of their property; and whereas repeated complaints have been made to the United States government, that those of the Seminoles who refused to go into the Creek country have, without authority or right, settled upon lands secured to other tribes, and that they have committed numerous and extensive depredations upon the property of those upon whose lands they have intruded:

Now, therefore, in order to reconcile all difficulties respecting location and jurisdiction, to settle all disputed questions which have arisen, or may hereafter arise, in regard to rights of property, and especially to preserve the peace of the frontier, seriously endangered by the restless and warlike spirit of the intruding Seminoles, the parties to this treaty have agreed to the following stipulations:

ARTICLE 1.

The Seminoles to settle in any part of the Creek country. To be subject generally to the Creek council. No distinction between them except in pecuniary affairs.

The Creeks agree that the Seminoles shall be entitled to settle in a body or separately, as they please, in any part of the Creek country; that they shall make their own town regulations, subject, however, to the general control of the Creek council, in which they shall be represented; and, in short, that no distinctions shall be made between the two tribes in any respect, except in the management of their pecuniary affairs, in which neither shall interfere with the other.

ARTICLE 2.

Seminoles who have not removed to Creek country to do so immediately.

The Seminoles agree that those of their tribe who have not done so before the ratification of this treaty, shall, immediately thereafter, remove to and permanently settle in the Creek country.

ARTICLE 3.

Certain contested cases concerning the right of property to be subject to the decision of the President.

It is mutually agreed by the Creeks and Seminoles, that all contested cases between the two tribes, concerning the right of property, growing out of sales or transactions that may have occurred previous to the ratification of this treaty, shall be subject to the decision of the President of the United States.

ARTICLE 4.

Additional annuity of $3,000 for education allowed the Creeks for twenty years.

The Creeks being greatly dissatisfied with the manner in which their boundaries were adjusted by the treaty of 1833, which they say they did not understand until after its execution, and it appearing that in said treaty no addition was made to their country for the use of the Seminoles, but that, on the contrary, they were deprived, without adequate compensation, of a considerable extent of valuable territory: And, moreover, the Seminoles, since the Creeks first agreed to receive them, having been engaged in a protracted and bloody contest, which has naturally engendered feelings and habits calculated to make them troublesome neighbors: The United States in consideration of these circumstances, agree that an additional annuity of three thousand dollars for purposes of education shall be allowed for the term of twenty years; that the annuity of three thousand dollars provided in the treaty of 1832 for like purposes shall be continued until the determination of the additional annuity above mentioned. It is further agreed that all the education funds of the Creeks, including the annuities above named, the annual allowance of one thousand dollars, provided in the treaty of 1833, and also all balances of appropriations for education annuities that may be due from the United States, shall be expended under the direction of President of the United States, for the purpose of education aforesaid.

Education fund, annuities, etc., of the Creeks to be expended in their own country in support of certain schools.

ARTICLE 5.

The Seminoles having expressed a desire to settle in a body on Little River, some distance westward of the present residence of the greater portion of them, it is agreed that rations shall be issued to such as may remove while on their way to their new homes; and that, after their emigration is completed, the whole tribe shall be subsisted for six months, due notice to be given that those who do not come into the Creek country before the issues commence shall be excluded. And it is distinctly understood that all those Seminoles who refuse to remove to, and settle in, the Creek Country, within six months after this treaty is ratified, shall not participate in any of the benefits it provides: Except those now in Florida, who shall be allowed twelve months from the date of the ratification of this treaty for their removal.

Rations to be issued to such Seminoles as remove during removal, and the whole tribe to be subsisted for six months after emigration.

Those refusing to remove in six months after ratification of this treaty not to participate in its benefits.

ARTICLE 6.

The sum of fifteen thousand four hundred dollars, provided in the second article of the treaty of Payne's Landing, shall be paid in the manner therein pointed out, immediately after the emigration of those Seminoles who may remove to the Creek country is completed; also, as soon after such emigration as practicable, the annuity of three thousand dollars for fifteen years, provided in the fourth article of said treaty, and, in addition thereto, for the same period, two thousand dollars per annum in goods suited to their wants, to be equally divided among all the members of the tribe.

The sum of $15,400 provided for in the treaty of Payne's Landing, and the $3,000 provided for in said treaty, when to be paid.

ARTICLE 7.

In full satisfaction and discharge of all claims for property left or abandoned in Florida at the request of the officers of the United States, under promise of remuneration, one thousand dollars per annum, in agricultural implements, shall be furnished the Seminoles for five years.

$1,000 per annum for five years to be furnished in agricultural implements.

ARTICLE 8.

To avoid all danger of encroachment, on the part of either Creeks or Seminoles, upon the territory of other nations, the northern and western boundary lines of the Creek country shall be plainly and distinctly marked.

The northern and western boundary line of the Creeks to be marked.

In witness whereof, the said Commissioners and the undersigned Chiefs and Head Men of the Creek and Seminole tribes, have hereunto set their hands, at the Creek Agency, this fourth day of January, 1845.

Wm. Armstrong,
Acting Superintendent Western Territory.
P. M. Butler,
Cherokee Agent.
James Logan,
Creek Agent.
Thomas L. Judge,
Seminole Sub-Agent.

Creeks:
Roly McIntosh,
To-marth-le Micco,
Eu-faula Harjo,
O-poeth-le Yoholo,
Yargee,
Samuel Miller,
Cot-char Tustunnuggee,
*K. Lewis,
Tuskunar Harjo,
Tinthlanis Harjo,
To-cose Fixico,
*Samuel C. Brown,
Ho-tul-gar Harjo,
Oak-chun Harjo,
Art-tis Fixico,
Joseph Carr,
Ar-ar-te Harjo,
Samuel Perryman,
O-switchee Emarthlar,
Talloaf Harjo,
David Barnett,
Jim Boy,
*B. Marshall,
Tinthlanis Harjo,
Co-ah-coo-che Emarthlar,
Thlathlo Harjo,
E-cho Harjo,
Co-ah-thlocco,
Ke-sar-che Harjo,
No cose Harjo,
Yar-dick-ah Harjo,
Yo-ho-lo Chop-ko,

Phil Grayson,
Chu-ille,
E-cho Emarthla,
Pol-lot-ke,
Kot-che Harjo,
To-cose Micco,
Henry Marshall,
Matthew Marshall,
Che-was-tiah Fixico,
Tom Carr.
Seminoles:
Miccanope,
Coah-coo-che, or Wild Cat,
Alligator,
Nocose Yoholo,
Halleck Tustunnuggee,
Emah-thloo-chee,
Octi-ar-chee,
Tus-se-kiah,
Pos-cof-far,
E-con-chat-te-micco,
Black Dirt,
Itch-hos-se Yo-ho-lo,
Kap-pe-chum-e-coo-che,
O-tul-ga Harjo,
Yo-ho-lo Harjo,
O-switchee Emarthla,
Kub-bit-che,
An-lo-ne,
Yah-hah Fixico,
Fus-hat-chee, Micco,
O-chee-see Micco,
Tus-tun-nug-goo-chee.

In the presence of—

J. B. Luce, secretary to commissioners.
Samuel C. Brown, U. S. interpreter.
B. Marshall, Creek Nation interpreter.
Abraham, U. S. interpreter for Seminoles.
J. P. Davis, captain U. S. Army.

A. Cady, captain Sixth Infantry.
J. B. S. Todd, captain Sixth Infantry.
George W. Clarke.
Jno. Dillard.
J. L. Alexander.
J. H. Heard.

(To the names of Indians, except those marked with an asterisk, are subjoined their marks.)

TREATY WITH KANSA TRIBE, 1846.

Jan. 14, 1846.

9 Stat., 842.
Ratified Apr. 13, 1846.
Proclaimed, Apr. 15, 1846.

Articles of a treaty made and concluded at the Methodist Mission, in the Kansas country, between Thomas H. Harvey and Richard W. Cummins, commissioners of the United States, and the Kansas tribe of Indians.

Lands ceded to the United States.

ARTICLE 1. The Kansas tribe of Indians cede to the United States two millions of acres of land on the east part of their country, embracing the entire width, thirty miles, and running west for quantity.

ARTICLE 2. In consideration of the foregoing cession, the United States agree to pay to the Kansas Indians two hundred and two thousand dollars, two hundred thousand of which shall be funded at five per cent., the interest of which to be paid annually for thirty years, and thereafter to be diminished and paid *pro rata*, should their numbers decrease, but not otherwise—that is: the Government of the United States shall pay them the full interest for thirty years on the amount funded, and at the end of that time, should the Kansas tribe be less than at the first payment, they are only to receive *pro rata* the sums paid them at the first annuity payment. One thousand dollars of the interest thus accruing shall be applied annually to the purposes of education in their own country; one thousand dollars annually for agricultural assistance, implements, &c.; but should the Kansas Indians at any time be so far advanced in agriculture as to render the expenditure for agricultural assistance unnecessary, then the one thousand dollars above provided for that purpose shall be paid them in money with the balance of their annuity; the balance, eight thousand dollars, shall be paid them annually in their own country. The two thousand dollars not to be funded shall be expended in the following manner: first, the necessary expenses in negotiating this treaty; second, four hundred dollars shall be paid to the Missionary Society of the Methodist Episcopal Church for their improvements on the land ceded in the first article; third, six hundred dollars shall be applied to the erection of a mill in the country in which the Kansas shall settle for their use, it being in consideration of their mill on the land ceded in the first article. The balance to be placed in the hands of their agent, as soon after the ratification of this treaty as practicable, for the purpose of furnishing the said Kansas Indians with provisions for the present year. {.marginal Sums to be paid by the United States for the cession of lands; how disposed of.} {.marginal Educational.} {.marginal Agricultural.} {.marginal Methodist Episcopal Church.} {.marginal Provisions.}

ARTICLE 3. In order that the Kansas Indians may know the west line of the land which they have ceded by this treaty, it is agreed that the United States shall, as soon as may be convenient in the present year, cause the said line to be ascertained and marked by competent surveyors. {.marginal West line of land ceded by this treaty to be ascertained and marked.}

ARTICLE 4. The Kansas Indians are to move from the lands ceded to the United States, by the first article of this treaty, by the first day of May, 1847. {.marginal To move from lands ceded by May 1, 1847.}

ARTICLE 5. As doubts exist whether there is a sufficiency of timber on the land remaining to the Kansas, after taking off the land ceded in the first article of this treaty, it is agreed by the contracting parties, that after the western line of the said cession shall be ascertained, [and] the President of the United States shall be satisfied that there is not a sufficiency of timber, he shall cause to be selected and laid off for the Kansas a suitable country, near the western boundary of the land ceded by this treaty, which shall remain for their use forever. In consideration of which, the Kansas nation cede to the United States the balance of the reservation under the treaty of June 3, 1825, and not ceded in the first article of this treaty. {.marginal The President, on being satisfied that there is not a sufficiency of timber on lands remaining to the Kansas, to select and lay off a suitable country, etc.} {.marginal Additional cession by the Kansas.}

ARTICLE 6. In consideration of the great distance which the Kansas Indians will be removed from the white settlements and their present agent, and their exposure to difficulties with other Indian tribes, it is agreed that the United States shall cause to reside among the Kansas Indians a sub-agent, who shall be especially charged with the direction of their farming operations, and general improvement, and to be continued as long as the President of the United States should consider it advantageous to the Kansas. {.marginal A subagent to reside among them.}

ARTICLE 7. Should the Government of the United States be of opinion that the Kansas Indians are not entitled to a smith under the fourth article of the treaty of June 3, 1825, it is agreed that a smith shall be supported out of the one thousand dollars provided in the fourth article for agricultural purposes. {.marginal Provisions for a smith.}

In testimony whereof, Thomas H. Harvey and Richard W. Cummins, Commissioners, [and] the Chiefs and Principal Men of the Kansas tribe of Indians have, this the 14th day of January one thousand eight hundred and forty-six, set their hands and seals at the Methodist Kansas Mission.

Th. H. Harvey,
Rich. W. Cummins,
Commissioners.

Ki-hi-ga-wah-chuffe, or Hard Chief,
Me-cho-shin-gah, or Broken Thigh,
Pi-is-cah-cah,
Ish-tal-a-sa, or Speckled Eyes,
Mah-gah-ha,
Shin-gah-ki-hi-ga,
Ca-ho-nah-she,
Wa-shon-ge-ra,
Ne-qui-bra,
Ke-bucco-mah-e,

No-pa-war-ra,
Was-sol-ba-shinga,
Ke-hi-ga-wat-ti-in-ga,
Big-no-years,
Wah-pug-ja,
Ah-ke-is-tah,
Chi-ki-cah-rah,
Ke-hah-ga-cha-wah-go,
Wah-hah-hah.

Witnesses:

James M. Simpson, secretary,
Clement Lesserts, interpreter,
John T. Peery,
John D. Clark,

Chs. Choteau,
Seth M. Hays,
Nelson Henrys,
R. M. Parrett.

(To the names of the Indians are added their marks.)

TREATY WITH THE COMANCHE, AIONAI, ANADARKO, CADDO, ETC., 1846.

May 15, 1846.

9 Stat., 844.
Proclamation, Mar. 8, 1847.

Treaty with the Comanches and other tribes. Articles of a treaty made and concluded at Council Springs, in the county of Robinson, Texas, near the Brazos River, this 15th day of May, A. D. 1846, between P. M. Butler and M. G. Lewis, commissioners on the part of the United States, of the one part, and the undersigned chiefs, counsellors, and warriors of the Comanche, I-on-i, Ana-da-ca, Cadoe, Lepan, Long-wha, Keechy, Tah-wa-carro, Wi-chita, and Wacoe tribes of Indians, and their associate bands, in behalf of their said tribes, on the other part.

Said tribes or nations to be under the sole protection of the United States.

ARTICLE 1. The undersigned chiefs, warriors, and counsellors, for themselves and their said tribes or nations, do hereby acknowledge themselves to be under the protection of the United States, and of no other power, state, or sovereignty whatever.

United States to have the sole and exclusive right to regulate trade and intercourse with said tribes.

ARTICLE 2. It is stipulated and agreed by the said tribes or nations, and their associate bands, that the United States shall have the sole and exclusive right of regulating trade and intercourse with them, and they do hereby respectively engage to afford protection to such persons, with their property, as shall be duly licensed to reside among them for the purpose of trade and intercourse, and to their agents and

No person to reside among them as a trader who is not furnished with a license for that purpose.

servants, but no person shall be permitted to reside among them as a trader who is not furnished with a license for that purpose, under the hand and seal of the superintendent to be appointed by the President of the United States or such other person as the President shall authorize to grant such licenses, to the end that said Indians may not

Unfair dealing; how punished.

be imposed on in their trade; and if any licensed trader shall abuse his privilege by unfair dealing, upon complaint by the chiefs to their agents and proof thereof, his license shall be taken from him, and he shall be further punished according to the laws of the United States; and if any person shall intrude himself as a trader without such license, upon complaint he shall be dealt with according to law.

ARTICLE 3. [Stricken out.]

ARTICLE 4. The said tribes and their associate bands agree to deliver, by the first day of November next, to the superintendent of Indian affairs to be appointed by the President, at such place as he may direct, due notice of which shall be given to the said tribes, all white persons and negroes who are now prisoners among any of the said tribes or nations, for which the United States agree to make them a fair compensation; and the United States further agree *to make* [that] all the prisoners taken from said tribes by Texas or the United States, shall be delivered up to the said tribes, at the same time and place, without charge. And when any member of any of said tribes or nations, and their associate bands, having in his possession an American prisoner or prisoners, white or black, shall refuse to give them up, the President of the United States shall have the privilege of sending among said tribes or nations such force as he may think necessary to take them; and the chiefs of the nations or tribes, parties to this treaty, pledge themselves to give protection and assistance to such persons as may be sent among them for this purpose.

All white persons and negroes now prisoners with said Indians to be delivered up.

Persons taken from said tribes by Texas to be delivered up.

Force may be used.

ARTICLE 5. [Stricken out.]

ARTICLE 6. The said tribes and their associate bands pledge themselves to give notice to the agent of the United States residing near them of any designs which they may know or suspect to [be] formed in any neighboring tribe, or by any person whatever, against the peace and interests of the United States.

The said tribes to give notice of any designs against the peace and interest of the United States.

ARTICLE 7. It is agreed that, if any Indian or Indians shall commit a murder or robbery on any citizen of the United States, the tribe or nation to which the offender belongs shall deliver up the person or persons so complained of, on complaint being made to their chief, to the nearest post of the United States, to the end that he or they may be tried, and, if found guilty, punished, according to the law of the State or Territory where such offence may have been committed. In like manner, if any subject or citizen of the United States shall commit murder or robbery on any Indian or Indians of the said tribes or nations, upon complaint thereof to the agent residing near them, he or they shall be arrested, tried, and punished according to the law of the State or Territory where such offence may have been committed.

Indians guilty of murder or robbery to be delivered up.

Citizens of the United States guilty of murder or robbery to be punished according to law.

ARTICLE 8. The practice of stealing horses has prevailed very much to the great disquiet of the citizens of the United States, and, if persisted in, cannot fail to involve both the United States and the Indians in endless strife. It is therefore agreed that it shall be put an entire stop to on both sides. Nevertheless, should bad men, in defiance of this agreement, continue to make depredations of that nature, the person convicted thereof shall be punished with the utmost severity, according to the laws of the State or Territory where the offence may have been committed; and all horses so stolen, either by the Indians from the citizens of the United States or by the citizens of the United States from any of the said tribes or nations, into whose possession soever they may have passed, upon due proof of rightful ownership, shall be restored; and the chiefs of said tribes or nations shall give all necessary aid and protection to citizens of the United States in reclaiming and recovering such stolen horses; and the civil magistrates of the United States, respectively, shall give all necessary aid and protection to Indians in claiming and recovering such stolen horses.

Horse stealing.

How punished.

All stolen horses to be restored.

ARTICLE 9. For the protection of said Indians and for the purpose of carrying out the stipulations of this treaty more effectually, the President shall, at his discretion, locate upon their borders trading-houses, agencies, and posts. In consideration of the friendly disposition of said tribes, evidenced by the stipulations in the present treaty, the commissioners of the United States, in behalf of the said States, agree to give to the said tribes or nations goods, as presents, at this time, and agree to give presents in goods to them, to the amount of

Trading houses, agencies, and posts to be located on the borders.

ten thousand dollars, at such time as the President of the United States may think proper, at the Council Springs, on the Brazos, where this council is now held, or at some other point to be designated, and of which due notice shall be given to said tribes.

Perpetual peace between the United States and said tribes. ARTICLE 10. The said tribes or nations and their associate bands are now, and forever agree to remain, at peace with the United States. All animosities for past offences are hereby mutually forgiven and forgotten, and the parties to this treaty pledge themselves to carry it into full execution, in good faith and sincerity.

Said tribes to remain at peace with Indians friendly to the United States. ARTICLE 11. And the said tribes and their associate bands are now, and agree to remain, friendly with such tribes as are now at peace with the United States, residing upon the waters of the Arkansas, Missouri, and Red Rivers.

Penalty for the introduction of ardent spirits or intoxicating liquors into the Indian country. ARTICLE 12. If any person or persons shall introduce ardent spirits or intoxicating liquors of any kind among said tribes or nations, such person or *person* [persons] shall be punished according to the laws of the United States, and the said tribes or nations agree to give immediate notice to the agent of the United States residing near them, and to prevent by any means in their power the violation of this article of treaty.

Blacksmiths to be sent to reside among said tribes. ARTICLE 13. It is further agreed that blacksmiths shall be sent to reside among the said tribes or nations, to keep their guns and farming-utensils in order, as long and in such manner as the President may **School-teachers to be sent among said tribes; and preachers of the gospel may travel and reside among them.** think proper. It is further agreed that school-teachers, at the discretion of the President, shall be sent among the said tribes or nations for the purpose of instructing them; and the said tribes or nations agree that preachers of the gospel may travel or reside among them by permission of the President or his agents to be appointed, and that ample protection shall be afforded them in the discharge of their duties.

The President to use his exertions to preserve peace between said tribes and all other Indian tribes. ARTICLE 14. The said tribes or nations, parties to this treaty, are anxious to be at peace with all other tribes or nations, and it is agreed that the President shall use his exertions, in such manner as he may think proper, to preserve friendly relations between the different tribes or nations parties to this treaty, and all other tribes of Indians under his jurisdiction.

Given under our hands and seals this day and date above.

P. M. Butler,
M. G. Lewis,
U. S. Commissioners.

Comanches:
Pah-ha-u-ca, (or the Amorous Man,)
Mo-pe-chu-co-pe, (or Old Owl,)
Cush-un-a-rah-ah, (or Ravisher,)
Ka-bah-ha-moo, (or Won't Smoke,)
O-ka-art-su, (or Rope Cutter,)
Moo-ra-que-top, (or Nasty Mule,)
Ta-bup-pua-ta, (or the Winner,)·
Kai-tia-tah, (or Little,)
Kai-he-na-mou-rah, (Blind Man,)
Ho-chu-cah, (Birdshouse,)
Pah-moo-wah-tah, (No Tobacco,)
Mon-ne-con-nah-heh, (Ring,)
Po-che-na-qua-heip, (Buffalo Hump,)
Santa Anna,
Sa-ba-heit, (Small Wolf,)
Quarah-ha-po-e, (Atelope Road,)
Ka-nah-u-mah-ka, (Nearly Dead,)
Ish-a-me-a-qui, (Travelling Wolf,)
Mo-he-ka, (Polecat,.)
A-ka-chu-a-ta, (No Horn,)
Ka-he-na-bo-ne, (Blind Man,)
Ma-war-ra, (The Lost,)
Ke-wid-da-wip-pa, (Tall Woman,)
Pa-na-che, (Mistletoe.)

Wacoes:
We-ar-ras, (Big Dog,)
Hed-e-cok-isk, (Double-Barrelled,)
Keeches:
Sa-sed-da-qua, (Dead Man,)
A-ko-ha-rai-at, (Pursuer,)
Hens-ke-da-hick, (Long Frock,)
Uks-que-ra-qua-ar-da, (House Keeper,)
Ha-wi-da-sai-kish, (Man Killer,)
No-cur-ra-oh-to-a-wa, (Loud Talker,)
To-ka-rah, (Black House,)
Ken-di-ash-ush-sa, (Narrow Escape.)
Tonkaways:
Ha-set-ta, (Sitting by a River,) Campo,
Ha-shu-ka-nah, (Can't Kill Him,) Place-don,
Cha-al-lah, (Strong Man,) Jose,
Ka-sa, (A Worshipper,)
Tron-ke-la, (Thunder,)
Nic-co-na-nah, (Killed an Indian on the Hill,)
Hose-Marea, (or Aish,)
Be-cin-ta,
Shell Chief, (or Tow-a-ash,)
Bin-chah,
Chick-a-saw-che.

Wichetas:
To-sa-quas, (White Tail,)
Cho-wash-ta-ha-da, (Runner,)
Kow-wah, (Shirt Tail,)
'Wich-qua-sa-is, (Contrary,)
His-si-da-wah, (Stubborn.)
　Towa-karroes:
Ke-chi-ko-ra-ko, (Stubborn,)
Nes-ho-chil-lash, (Traveller,)
Na-co-ah, (Dangerfield,)
Ka-ra-ko-ris, (Deceiver,)
Ha-ke-di-ad-ah, (Gallant Man,)
Wha-cha-ash-da, (Looker-on,)
Wash-le-doi-ro-ka, (Don't you do so,)
Te-ah-kur-rah, (Lightman,)
Sar-rah-de-od-a-sa, (Straight Looker.)
　Wacoes:
A-qua-gosh, (Short Tail,)

Ho-hed-orah, (Long Ways over the
　River,)
Chos-toch-ka-a-wah, (Charger,)
Cha-to-wait, (Ghost.)
　Secretaries:
Thomas J. Wilson,
Isaac H. Du Val.
　Witnesses:
Robt. S. Neighbsor,
Hugh Rose,
Jno. H. Rollins,
Thomas J. Smith,
E. Morehouse.
　Interpreters:
Louis Sanches,
John Conner,
Jim Shaw.

(To each of the names of the Indians is affixed his mark.)

TREATY WITH THE POTAWATOMI NATION, 1846.

Whereas the various bands of the Pottowautomie Indians, known as the Chippewas, Ottawas, and Pottowautomies, the Pottowautomies of the Prairie, the Pottowautomies of the Wabash, and the Pottowautomies of Indiana, have, subsequent to the year 1828, entered into separate and distinct treaties with the United States, by which they have been separated and located in different countries, and difficulties have arisen as to the proper distribution of the stipulations under various treaties, and being the same people by kindred, by feeling, and by language, and having, in former periods, lived on and owned their lands in common; and being desirous to unite in one common country, and again become one people, and receive their annuities and other benefits in common, and to abolish all minor distinctions of bands by which they have heretofore been divided, and are anxious to be known only as the Pottowautomie Nation, thereby reinstating the national character; and

Whereas the United States are also anxious to restore and concentrate said tribes to a state so desirable and necessary for the happiness of their people, as well as to enable the Government to arrange and manage its intercourse with them:

Now, therefore, the United States and the said Indians do hereby agree that said people shall hereafter be known as a nation, to be called the Pottowautomie Nation; and to the following

Articles of a treaty made and concluded at the Agency on the Missouri River, near Council Bluffs, on the fifth day of June, and at Pottawatomie Creek, near the Osage River, south and west of the State of Missouri, on the seventeenth day of the same month, in the year of our Lord one thousand eight hundred and forty-six, between T. P. Andrews, Thomas H. Harvey, and Gideon C. Matlock, commissioners on the part of the United States, on the one part, and the various bands of the Pottowautomie, Chippewas, and Ottowas Indians on the other part:

ARTICLE 1. It is solemnly agreed that the peace and friendship which so happily exist between the people of the United States and the Pottowautomie Indians shall continue forever; the said tribes of Indians giving assurance, hereby, of fidelity and friendship to the Government and people of the United States; and the United States giving, at the same time, promise of all proper care and parental protection.

Margin notes:

June 5 and 17, 1846.

9 Stat., 853.
Ratified, July 22, 1846.
Proclaimed, July 23, 1846.

Preamble.

Peace and friendship to continue forever.

Potawatomi cede certain lands to United States.

ARTICLE 2. The said tribes of Indians hereby agree to sell and cede, and do hereby sell and cede, to the United States, all the lands to which they have claim of any kind whatsoever, and especially the tracts or parcels of lands ceded to them by the treaty of Chicago, and subsequent thereto, and now, in whole or in part, possessed by their people, lying and being north of the river Missouri, and embraced in the limits of the Territory of Iowa; and also all that tract of country lying and being on or near the Osage River, and west of the State of Mis-

These cessions not to affect title of said Indians to former grants and reservations.

souri; it being understood that these cessions are not to affect the title of said Indians to any grants or reservations made to them by former treaties.

Consideration to be paid by the United States for cession.

ARTICLE 3. In consideration of the foregoing cessions or sales of land to the United States, it is agreed to pay to said tribes of Indians the sum of eight hundred and fifty thousand dollars, subject to the conditions, deductions, and liabilities provided for in the subsequent articles of this treaty.

Grant by the United States of a tract of land to said Indians.

ARTICLE 4. The United States agree to grant to the said united tribes of Indians possession and title to a tract or parcel of land containing five hundred and seventy-six thousand acres, being thirty miles square, and being the eastern part of the lands ceded to the United States by the Kansas tribe or Indians, by treaty concluded on the 14th day of January, and ratified on the 15th of April of the present year, lying adjoining the Shawnees on the south, and the Delawares and Shawnees on the east, on both sides of the Kansas River, and to guarantee the full and complete possession of the same to the Pottowauto-

Consideration to be paid by said Indians for grants.

mie Nation, parties to this treaty, as their land and home forever; for which they are to pay the United States the sum of eighty-seven thousand dollars, to be deducted from the gross sum promised to them in the 3d article of this treaty.

The United States to pay said Indians $50,000 out of sum granted in third article—when, and for what purpose.

ARTICLE 5. The United States agree to pay said nation of Indians, at the first annuity payment after the ratification of this treaty, and after an appropriation shall have been made by Congress, the sum of fifty thousand dollars, out of the aggregate sum granted in the third article of this treaty to enable said Indians to arrange their affairs, and pay their just debts, before leaving their present homes; to pay for their improvements; to purchase wagons, horses, and other means of transportation, and pay individuals for the loss of property necessarily sacrificed in moving to their new homes; said sum to be paid, in open council, by the proper agents of the United States, and in such just proportions to each band as the President of the United States may direct.

Said tribes to remove to new homes within two years from ratification of treaty. Provisions for expenses of removal and subsistence.

ARTICLE 6. The said tribes of Indians agree to remove to their new homes on the Kansas River, within two years from the ratification of this treaty; and further agree to set apart the sum of twenty thousand dollars to the upper bands, (being ten dollars per head,) and ten thousand dollars to the lower bands, (being five dollars per head,) to pay the actual expenses of removing; and the sum of forty thousand dollars for all the bands, as subsistence money, for the first twelve months after their arrival at their new homes; to be paid to them so soon as their arrival at their new homes is made known to the Government, and convenient arrangements can be made to pay the same between the parties to this treaty; the aforesaid sums to be also deducted from the aggregate sum granted by the United States to said tribes of Indians by the 3d article of this treaty.

Balance of $850,000 to remain with United States as trust fund, at interest of 5 per cent.

ARTICLE 7. The balance of the said sum of eight hundred fifty thousand dollars, after deducting the cost of removal and subsistence, &c., it is agreed shall remain with the United States, *in trust* for said Indians, and an interest of five per cent. annually paid thereon, commencing at the expiration of one year after the removal of said Indians, and continuing for thirty years, and until the nation shall be reduced below one thousand souls.   If, after the expiration of thirty years, or any period thereafter, it shall be ascertained that the nation is reduced below that number, the said annuity shall thenceforth be paid *pro rata* so long as they shall exist as a separate and distinct nation, in proportion as the present number shall bear to the number then in existence.

ARTICLE 8.   It is agreed upon by the parties to this treaty that, after the removal of the Pottowautomie Nation to the Kansas country, the annual interest of their "improvement fund" shall be paid out promptly and fully, for their benefit at their new homes.   If, however, at any time thereafter, the President of the United States shall be of opinion that it would be advantageous to the Pottowautomie Nation, and they should request the same to be done, to pay them the interest of said money in lieu of the employment of persons or purchase of machines or implements, he is hereby authorized to pay the same, or any part thereof, in money, as their annuities are paid at the time of the general payments of annuities.   It is also agreed that, after the expiration of two years from the ratification of this treaty, the school-fund of the Pottowautomies shall be expended entirely in their own country, unless their people, in council, should, at any time, express a desire to have any part of the same expended in a different manner. *After removal of said Indians the annual interest of their improvement fund to be paid at new homes.*

The President may pay in money in lieu of employing persons or purchase of machines, etc.

After two years, school fund to be expended in their own country.

ARTICLE 9.   It is agreed by the parties to this treaty that the buildings occupied as a missionary establishment, including twenty acres of land now under fence, shall be reserved for the use of the Government agency; also the houses used for blacksmith house and shop shall be reserved for the use of the Pottowautomie smith; but should the property cease to be used for the aforementioned purposes, then it shall revert to the use of the Pottowautomie Nation. *Buildings now occupied as missionary establishment to be reserved for the agency. The blacksmith house and shop to be reserved for the Potawatomi smith.*

ARTICLE 10.   It is agreed that hereafter there shall be paid to the Pottowautomie Nation, annually, the sum of three hundred dollars, in lieu of the two thousand pounds of tobacco, fifteen hundred pounds of iron, and three hundred and fifty pounds of steel, stipulated to be paid to the Pottowautomies under the third article of the treaty of September 20, 1828. *Money to be paid in lieu of tobacco, iron, and steel, stipulated in treaty of Sept. 20, 1828.*

In testimony whereof, T. P. Andrews, Thomas H. Harvey, and Gideon C. Matlock, aforesaid Commissioners, and the Chiefs and Principal Men of the Pottowautomie, Ottowa, and Chippewas tribes of Indians, have set their hands, at the time and place first mentioned.

T. P. Andrews,
Th. H. Harvey,
G. C. Matlock,
Commissioners.

Mi-au-mise, (the Young Miami,)
Op-te-gee-shuck, (or Half Day,)
Wa-sow-o-ko-uck, (or the Lightning,)
Kem-me-kas, (or Bead,)
Mi-quess, (or the Wampum,)
Wab-na-ne-me, or White Pigeon,
Na-no-no-uit, (or Like the Wind,)
Patt-co-shuck, junior,
Catte-nab-mee, (the Close Observer,)
Wap-que-shuck, (or White Cedar,)
Sah-ken-na-ne-be,
Etwa-gee-shuck,
Saass-pucks-kum, (or Green Leaf,)
Ke-wa-ko-to, (Black Cloud Turning,)
Meek-sa-mack, (the Wampum,)
Chau-cose, (Little Crane,)
Co-shae-wais, (Tree Top,)
Patt-qui,
Me-shuk-to-no,
Ween-co,
Joseph Le Frambeau, Interpreter,
Pierre or Perish Le Clerk,
M. B. Beaubien, Interpreter,

Pes-co-unk, (Distant Thunder,)
Naut-wish-cum,
Ob-nob, (or He Looks Back,)
Pam-wa-mash-kuck,
Pacq-qui-pa-chee,
Ma-shaus, (the Cutter,)
Ci-co,
Puck-quon, (or the Rib,)
Sena-tche-wan, (or Swift Current,)
Shaub-poi-tuck, (the Man goes through,)
Wab-sai, (or White Skin,)
Shaum-num-teh, (or Medicine Man,)
Nah-o-sah, (the Walker,)
Keahh,
Ne-ah-we-quot, (the Four Faces,)
Wa-sash-kuck, (or the Grass Turner,)
Ke-ton-ne-co, (or the Kidneys,)
*Francois Bourbonnai,
*Chas. H. Beaubien,
*Shau-on-nees,
*Paskal Miller,
*Joseph Glaudeau,
*Joseph Laughton,

Ca-ta-we-num, (the Black Dog,)
Sine-pe-num,
Chatt-tee, (the Pelican,)
Me-shik-ke-an,
Teh-cah-co, (Spotted Fawn,)
Ca-shaw-kee, (the Craw Fish,)
Shem-me-nah,

Nah-kee-shuck, (In the Air,)
Mich-e-wee-tah, (Bad Name,)
Patte-co-to,
Shau-bon-ni-agh,
Kah-bon-cagh,
Wock-quet.

Witnesses.

R. B. Mitchell, Indian sub-agent,
Richard Pearson,
A. G. Wilson,
S. W. Smith,
Edward Pore,
John H. Whitehead,

John Copeland,
T. D. S. McDonnell,
W. R. English,
S. E. Wicks,
Lewis Kennedy,
L. T. Tate.

(To the names of the Indians, except where there is an asterisk, are added their marks.)

We, the undersigned, Chiefs and Head Men, and Repesentatives of the Wabash, St. Joseph, and Prairie bands of the Ottowa, Chippewas, and Pottowautomie Indians, do hereby accept, ratify, and confirm the foregoing articles of a treaty, in all particulars. Done at Pottowautomie Creek, near the Osage River, west and south of the State of Missouri, this seventeenth day of June, A. D., 1846.

To-pen-e-be,
We-we-say,
Gah-gah-amo,
I-o-way,
Mah-go-quick,
Zhah-wee,
Louison,
Mash-kum-me,
Crane,
Esk-bug-ge,
Noa-ah-kye,
Abraham Burnet,
Ma-gis-gize,
Nas-wah-gay,
Pok-to,
Little Bird,
Shim-nah,
Ma-kda-wah,
Black Wolf,
Root,
Niena-kto,
Ma-je-sah,
Mah-suck,
Bade-je-zha,
Kah-shqua,
Little American,
Match-kay,
Wane-mage,
Wah-wah-suck 2d,
Black Bird,
Wah-wah-suck 1st,
Wab-mack, (Henry Clay,)
T-buck-kc,
Zah-gna,
N. D. Grover,
Big Snake,
En-ne-byah,

Jau-ge-mage,
Sin-be-nim,
No-clah-Koshig,
Os-me-at,
Wah-bah-koze,
I-o-wa 2d,
Wah-we-sueah,
Mowa,
Moses H. Scott,
Kah-kee,
Andrew Jackson,
Ke-sis,
Pame-qe-yah,
Peme-nuek,
Be-to-quah,
Mesha-de,
Wm. Hendricks,
Nma-quise,
Mas-co,
Peter Moose,
Kah-dot,
Za-k-ta,
Ah-bdah-sqa,
Wah-nuck-ke,
Wah-be-een-do,
At-yah-she,
Qua-qua-tah,
Nah-nim-muck-shuck,
Antoine,
No-zha-kum,
Na-che-wa,
Ahn-quot,
*Jos. N. Bourassa,
Kka-mage,
*Jude W. Bourassa,
Bossman,
Joel Barrow.

(To the names of the Indians, except where there is an asterisk. are added their marks.)

Witnesses.

Joseph Bertrand, Jr.,
R. W. Cummins, Indian Agent,
Leonidas A. Vaughan,
Robert Simerwell,
Thomas Hurlburt,
J. W. Polk,
J. Lykins,

M. H. Scott,
Washn. Bossman,
John T. Jones,
James A. Poage,
Joseph Clymer, Jr.,
W. W. Cleghorn.

TREATY WITH THE CHEROKEE, 1846.

Articles of a treaty made and concluded at Washington, in the District of Columbia, between the United States of America, by three commissioners, Edmund Burke, William Armstrong, and Albion K. Parris; and John Ross, principal chief of the Cherokee Nation; David Vann, William S. Coody, Richard Taylor, T. H. Walker, Clement V. McNair, Stephen Foreman, John Drew, and Richard Field, delegates duly appointed by the regularly constituted authorities of the Cherokee Nation; George W. Adair, John A. Bell, Stand Watie, Joseph M. Lynch, John Huss, and Brice Martin, a delegation appointed by, and representing that portion of the Cherokee tribe of Indians known and recognized as the "Treaty Party;" John Brown, Captain Dutch, John L. McCoy, Richard Drew, and Ellis Phillips, delegates appointed by, and representing, that portion of the Cherokee Tribe of Indians known and recognized as "Western Cherokees," or "Old Settlers."

Aug. 6, 1846.

9 Stat., 871.
Ratified Aug. 8, 1846.
Proclaimed Aug. 17, 1846.

WHEREAS serious difficulties have, for a considerable time past, existed between the different portions of the people constituting and recognized as the Cherokee Nation of Indians, which it is desirable should be speedily settled, so that peace and harmony may be restored among them; and whereas certain claims exist on the part of the Cherokee Nation, and portions of the Cherokee people, against the United States; Therefore, with a view to the final and amicable settlement of the difficulties and claims before mentioned, it is mutually agreed by the several parties to this convention as follows, viz:

Preamble.

ARTICLE 1. That the lands now occupied by the Cherokee Nation shall be secured to the whole Cherokee people for their common use and benefit; and a patent shall be issued for the same, including the eight hundred thousand acres purchased, together with the outlet west, promised by the United States, in conformity with the provisions relating thereto, contained in the third article of the treaty of 1835, and in the third section of the act of Congress, approved May twenty-eighth, 1830, which authorizes the President of the United States, in making exchanges of lands with the Indian tribes, "to assure the tribe or nation with which the exchange is made, that the United States will forever secure and guarantee to them, and their heirs or successors, the country so exchanged with them; and if they prefer it, that the United States will cause a patent or grant to be made and executed to them for the same: *Provided, always*, That such lands shall revert to the United States if the Indians become extinct or abandon the same."

Lands occupied by Cherokee Nation to be secured to whole people, and a patent to be issued.

1830, Ch. 148.

Reversion to be in United States.

ARTICLE 2. All difficulties and differences heretofore existing between the several parties of the Cherokee Nation are hereby settled and adjusted, and shall, as far as possible, be forgotten and forever buried in oblivion. All party distinctions shall cease, except so far as they may be necessary to carry out this convention or treaty. A general amnesty is hereby declared. All offences and crimes committed by a citizen or citizens of the Cherokee Nation against the nation, or against an individual or individuals, are hereby pardoned. All Cherokees who are now out of the nation are invited and earnestly requested to return to their homes, where they may live in peace, assured that they shall not be prosecuted for any offence heretofore committed against the Cherokee Nation, or any individual thereof. And this pardon and amnesty shall extend to all who may now be out of the nation, and who shall return thereto on or before 1st day of December next. The several parties agree to unite in enforcing the laws against all future offenders. Laws shall be passed for equal protection, and for the security of life, liberty, and property; and full authority shall be given by law, to all or any portion of the Cherokee

All difficulties and disputes adjusted, and a general amnesty declared.

Laws to be passed for equal protection, and for the security of life, liberty, and property.

people, peaceably to assemble and petition their own government, or the Government of the United States, for the redress of grievances, and to discuss their rights. All armed police, light horse, and other military organization, shall be abolished, and the laws enforced by the civil authority alone.

No one to be punished for any crime, except on conviction by a jury.

No one shall be punished for any crime or misdemeanor except on conviction by a jury of his country, and the sentence of a court duly authorized by law to take cognizance of the offence. And it is further agreed, all fugitives from justice, except those included in the general amnesty herein stipulated, seeking refuge in the territory of the United States, shall be delivered up by the authorities of the United States to the Cherokee Nation for trial and punishment.

Fugitives from justice.

Certain claims paid out of the $5,000,000 fund to be reimbursed by the United States.

ARTICLE 3. Whereas certain claims have been allowed by the several boards of commissioners heretofore appointed under the treaty of 1835, for rents, under the name of improvements and spoliations, and for property of which the Indians were dispossessed, provided for under the 16th article of the treaty of 1835; and whereas the said claims have been paid out of the $5,000,000 fund; and whereas said claims were not justly chargeable to that fund, but were to be paid by the United States, the said United States agree to re-imburse the said fund the amount thus charged to said fund, and the same shall form a part of the aggregate amount to be distributed to the Cherokee people, as provided in the 9th article of this treaty; and whereas a further amount has been allowed for reservations under the provisions of the 13th article of the treaty of 1835, by said commissioners, and has been paid out of the said fund, and which said sums were properly chargeable to, and should have been paid by, the United States, the said United States further agree to re-imburse the amounts thus paid for reservations to said fund; and whereas the expenses of making the treaty of New Echoto were also paid out of said fund, when they should have been borne by the United States, the United States agree to re-imburse the same, and also to re-imburse all other sums paid to any agent of the government, and improperly charged to said fund; and the same also shall form a part of the aggregate amount to be distributed to the Cherokee people, as provided in the 9th article of this treaty.

Provisions for the equitable interest of the Western Cherokees in lands ceded by treaty of 1828.

ARTICLE 4. And whereas it has been decided by the board of commissioners recently appointed by the President of the United States to examine and adjust the claims and difficulties existing against and between the Cherokee people and the United States, as well as between the Cherokees themselves, that under the provisions of the treaty of 1828, as well as in conformity with the general policy of the United States in relation to the Indian tribes, and the Cherokee Nation in particular, that that portion of the Cherokee people known as the "Old Settlers," or "Western Cherokees," had no exclusive title to the territory ceded in that treaty, but that the same was intended for the use of, and to be the home for, the whole nation, including as well that portion then east as that portion then west of the Mississippi; and whereas the said board of commissioners further decided that, inasmuch as the territory before mentioned became the common property of the whole Cherokee Nation by the operation of the treaty of 1828, the Cherokees then west of the Mississippi, by the equitable operation of the same treaty, acquired a common interest in the lands occupied by the Cherokees east of the Mississippi river, as well as in those occupied by themselves west of that river, which interest should have been provided for in the treaty of 1835, but which was not, except in so far as they, as a constituent portion of the nation, retained, in proportion to their numbers, a common interest in the country west of the Mississippi, and in the general funds of the nation; and therefore they have an equitable claim upon the United States for the value of that interest, whatever it may be. Now, in order to ascertain the How the value of said interest shall be ascertained. value of that interest, it is agreed that the following principle shall be adopted, viz: All the investments and expenditures which are properly chargeable upon the sums granted in the treaty of 1835, amounting in the whole to five millions six hundred thousand dollars, (which investments and expenditures are particularly enumerated in the 15th article of the treaty of 1835,) to be first deducted from said aggregate sum, thus ascertaining the residuum or amount which would, under such marshalling of accounts, be left for *per capita* distribution among the Cherokees emigrating under the treaty of 1835, excluding all extravagant and improper expenditures, and then allow to the Old Settlers (or Western Cherokees) a sum equal to one third part of said residuum, to be distributed *per capita* to each individual of said party of "Old Settlers," or "Western Cherokees." It is further agreed that, so far as the Western Cherokees are concerned, in estimating the expense of removal and subsistence of an Eastern Cherokee, to be charged to the aggregate fund of five million six hundred thousand dollars above mentioned, the sums for removal and subsistence stipulated in the 8th article of the treaty of 1835, as commutation money in those cases in which the parties entitled to it removed themselves, shall be adopted. And as it affects the settlement with the Western Cherokees, there shall be no deduction from the fund before mentioned in consideration of any payments which may hereafter be made out of said fund; and it is hereby further understood and agreed, that the principle above defined shall embrace all those Cherokees west of the Mississippi, who emigrated prior to the treaty of 1835.

Release by Western Cherokees to United States. In the consideration of the foregoing stipulation on the part of the United States, the "Western Cherokees," or "Old Settlers," hereby release and quit-claim to the United States all right, title, interest, or claim they may have to a common property in the Cherokee lands east of the Mississippi River, and to exclusive ownership to the lands ceded to them by the treaty of 1833 west of the Mississippi, including the outlet west, consenting and agreeing that the said lands, together with the eight hundred thousand acres ceded to the Cherokees by the treaty of 1835, shall be and remain the common property of the whole Cherokee people, themselves included.

Per capita allowance for Western Cherokees to be held in trust by United States, etc. ARTICLE 5. It is mutually agreed that the *per capita* allowance to be given to the "Western Cherokees," or "Old Settlers," upon the principle above stated, shall be held in trust by the Government of the United States, and paid out to each individual belonging to that party or head of family, or his legal representatives. And it is further agreed that the *per capita* allowance to be paid as aforesaid shall not be Not assignable. assignable, but shall be paid directly to the persons entitled to it, or to his heirs or legal representatives, by the agent of the United States, authorized to make such payments.

Committee of five from "Old Settlers." And it is further agreed that a committee of five persons shall be appointed by the President of the United States, from the party of "Old Settlers," whose duty it shall be, in conjunction with an agent of the United States, to ascertain what persons are entitled to the *per capita* allowance provided for in this and the preceding article.

Indemnity for "Treaty Party." ARTICLE 6. And whereas many of that portion of the Cherokee people known and designated as the "Treaty Party" have suffered losses and incurred expenses in consequence of the treaty of 1835, therefore, Provisions for heirs of Major Ridge, John Ridge, and Elias Boudinot. to indemnify the treaty party, the United States agree to pay to the said treaty party the sum of one hundred and fifteen thousand dollars, of which the sum of five thousand dollars shall be paid by the United States to the heirs or legal representatives of Major Ridge, the sum of five thousand dollars to the heirs or legal representatives of John Ridge, and the sum of five thousand dollars to the heirs or legal representatives of Elias Boudinot, and the balance, being the sum of one hundred thousand dollars, which shall be paid by the United States, in such amounts and to such persons as may be certified by a committee to be appointed by the treaty party, and which committee shall consist of not exceeding five persons, and approved by an agent of the United States, to be entitled to receive the same for losses and damages sustained by them, or by those of whom they are the heirs or legal representatives: *Provided*, That out of the said balance of one hundred thousand dollars, the present delegation of the treaty party may receive the sum of twenty-five thousand dollars, to be by them applied to the payment of claims and other expenses. And it is further provided that, if the said sum of one hundred thousand dollars should not be sufficient to pay all the claims allowed for losses and damages, that then the same shall be paid to the said claimants *pro rata*, and which payments shall be in full of all claims and losses of the said treaty party.

Proviso.

Values of salines to be ascertained and paid to individuals dispossessed of them.

ARTICLE 7. The value of all salines which were the private property of individuals of the Western Cherokees, and of which they were dispossessed, provided there be any such, shall be ascertained by the United States agent, and a commissioner to be appointed by the Cherokee authorities; and, should they be unable to agree, they shall select an umpire, whose decision shall be final; and the several amounts found due shall be paid by the Cherokee Nation, or the salines returned to their respective owners.

Payment for a printing press, arms, etc.

ARTICLE 8. The United States agree to pay to the Cherokee Nation the sum of two thousand dollars for a printing-press, materials, and other property destroyed at that time; the sum of five thousand dollars to be equally divided among all those whose arms were taken from them previous to their removal West by order of an officer of the United States; and the further sum of twenty thousand dollars, in lieu of all claims of the Cherokee Nation, as a nation, prior to the treaty of 1835, except all lands reserved, by treaties heretofore made, for school funds.

A fair and just settlement of all moneys due the Cherokees under the treaty of 1835 to be made.

ARTICLE 9. The United States agree to make a fair and just settlement of all moneys due to the Cherokees, and subject to the *per capita* division under the treaty of 29th December, 1835, which said settlement shall exhibit all money properly expended under said treaty, and shall embrace all sums paid for improvements, ferries, spoliations, removal, and subsistence, and commutation therefor, debts and claims upon the Cherokee Nation of Indians, for the additional quantity of land ceded to said nation; and the several sums provided in the several articles of the treaty, to be invested as the general funds of the nation; and also all sums which may be hereafter properly allowed and paid under the provisions of the treaty of 1835. The aggregate of which said several sums shall be deducted from the sum of six millions six hundred and forty-seven thousand and sixty-seven dollars, and the balance thus found to be due shall be paid over, *per capita*, in equal amounts, to all those individuals, heads of families, or their legal representatives, entitled to receive the same under the treaty of 1835, and the supplement of 1836, being all those Cherokees residing east at the date of said treaty and the supplement thereto.

Rights under treaty of Aug. 1, 1835, not affected.

ARTICLE 10. It is expressly agreed that nothing in the foregoing treaty contained shall be so construed as in any manner to take away or abridge any rights or claims which the Cherokees now residing in States east of the Mississippi River had, or may have, under the treaty of 1835 and the supplement thereto.

Certain questions to be submitted to Senate of United States.

ARTICLE 11. Whereas the Cherokee delegations contend that the amount expended for the one year's subsistence, after their arrival in the west, of the Eastern Cherokees, is not properly chargeable to the treaty fund: it is hereby agreed that that question shall be submitted to the Senate of the United States for its decision, which shall decide whether the subsistence shall be borne by the United States or the Cherokee funds, and if by the Cherokees, then to say, whether the subsistence shall be charged at a greater rate than thirty-three, $\frac{33}{100}$ dollars per head; and also the question, whether the Cherokee Nation shall be allowed interest on whatever sum may be found to be due the nation, and from what date and at what rate per annum.

ARTICLE 12. [Stricken out.]

ARTICLE 13. This treaty, after the same shall be ratified by the President and Senate of the United States, shall be obligatory on the contracting parties.

In testimony whereof, the said Edmund Burke, William Armstrong, and Albion K. Parris, Commissioners as aforesaid, and the several delegations aforesaid, and the Cherokee nation and people, have hereunto set their hands and seals, at Washington aforesaid, this sixth day of August, in the year of our Lord one thousand eight hundred and forty-six.

Edmund Burke.
Wm. Armstrong.
Albion K. Parris.

Delegation of the Government Party:
Jno. Ross,
W. S. Coody,
R. Taylor,
C. V. McNair,
Stephen Foreman,
John Drew,
Richard Fields.
Delegation of the Treaty Party:
Geo. W. Adair,
J. A. Bell,

S. Watie,
Joseph M. Lynch,
John Huss,
Brice Martin (by J. M. Lynch, his attorney).
Delegation of the Old Settlers:
Jno. Brown,
Wm. Dutch,
John L. McCoy,
Richard Drew,
Ellis F. Phillips.

(To each of the names of the Indians a seal is affixed.)

In presence of—

Joseph Bryan, of Alabama.
Geo. W. Paschal.
John P. Wolf, (Secretary of Board.)
W. S. Adair.
Jno. F. Wheeler.

TREATY WITH THE WINNEBAGO, 1846.

Articles of a treaty made and concluded at the city of Washington, on the thirteenth day of October, in the year one thousand eight hundred and forty-six, between the United States, of the one part, by their commissioners, Albion K. Parris, John J. Abert, and T. P. Andrews, and the Winnebago tribe of Indians, of the other part, by a full delegation of said tribe, specially appointed by the chiefs, head-men, and warriors thereof.

Oct. 13, 1846.

9 Stat., 878.
Proclamation, Feb. 4, 1847.

ARTICLE 1. It is solemnly agreed that the peace and friendship which exist between the people of the United States and the Winnebago Indians shall be perpetual; the said tribe of Indians giving assurance, hereby, of fidelity and friendship to the Government and people of the United States, and the United States giving to them, at the same time, promise of all proper care and parental protection.

Peace and friendship to be perpetual.

ARTICLE 2. The said tribe of Indians hereby agree to cede and sell, and do hereby cede and sell, to the United States, all right, title, interest, claim, and privilege, to all lands, wherever situated, now or heretofore occupied or claimed by said Indians, within the States and Territories of the United States, and especially to the country now occupied, inhabited, or in any way used by them, called the "neutral ground," which tract of country was assigned to said Indians by the

Lands ceded to the United States.

second article of the treaty of Fort Armstrong, concluded on the fifteenth day of September, 1832, and ratified on the thirteenth day of February following.

ARTICLE 3. In consideration of the foregoing purchase from, or cession by, the said Indians, the United States hereby agree to purchase and give to the said Indians, as their home, to be held as all Indians' lands are held, a tract of country north of St. Peter's and west of the Mississippi Rivers, of not less than eight hundred thousand acres, which shall be suitable to their habits, wants, and wishes: *Provided*, Such land can be obtained on just and reasonable terms.

ARTICLE 4. The United States agree to pay to said tribe of Indians the sum of one hundred and fifty thousand dollars for the land, and the sum of forty thousand dollars for release of hunting privileges, on the lands adjacent to their present home, making the sum of one hundred and ninety thousand dollars, being in further consideration of the cession or sale made to the United States by the second article of this treaty; to be paid as follows: Forty thousand dollars to enable them to comply with their present just engagements, and to cover the expenses of exploring and selecting (by their own people, or by an agent of their own appointment) their new home; twenty thousand dollars in consideration of their removing themselves, and twenty thousand dollars in consideration of their subsisting themselves the first year after their removal; ten thousand dollars to be expended for breaking up and fencing lands, under the direction of the President of the United States, at their new home; ten thousand dollars to be set apart and applied, under the direction of the President, to the creation and carrying on of one or more manual-labor schools for the benefit of said tribe of Indians; and five thousand dollars for building a saw and grist mill. The balance of said sum of one hundred and ninety thousand

dollars, viz, eighty-five thousand dollars, to remain *in trust* with the United States, and five per cent. interest thereon to be paid annually to said tribe, or applied for their benefit, as the President of the United States may from time to time direct, for the period of thirty years, which shall be in full payment of the said balance: *Provided*, That no

part of the said consideration moneys shall be paid until after the arrival of said tribe of Indians at their new home, and appropriations shall have been made by Congress; and that the sums for meeting their present engagements, for removal and subsistence, and for exploring their new home, shall be paid to the chiefs in open council, in such a manner as they in said council shall request.

ARTICLE 5. It is further agreed by the parties to this treaty that the said tribe of Indians shall remove to their new home within one year after the ratification of this treaty, and their new home shall have been procured for them, and they duly notified of the same.

ARTICLE 6. It is further agreed by the parties to this treaty, that the President may, at his discretion, (should he at any time be of opinion that the interest of the Indians would be thereby promoted,) direct that any portion of the money, not exceeding ten thousand dollars per annum, now paid in goods, as provided for by the last clause of the fourth article of the treaty of the first of November, 1837, be applied to the purchase of additional provisions, or to other purposes.

In testimony whereof, the Commissioners, Albion K. Parris, John J. Abert, and T. P. Andrews, and the undersigned Chiefs, Head Men, and Delegates, of the Winnebago Tribe of Indians, have hereunto subscribed their names and affixed their seals, at the City of Washington, this thirteenth day of October, one thousand eight hundred and forty-six.

Albion K. Parris,
John J. Abert,
T. P. Andrews,
Commissioners.

Hoong-ho-no-kaw,
Is-jaw-go-bo-kaw,
Co-no-ha-ta-kaw,
Naw-hoo-skaw-kaw,
Shoong-skaw-kaw,
Kooz-a-ray-kaw,
Waw-ma-noo-ka-kaw,
Ha-naw-hoong-per-kaw,
Wo-gie-qua-kaw,
Waw-kon-chaw-she-shick-kaw,
Chas-chun-kaw,
Naw-hey-kee-kaw,
Ah-hoo-zheb-kaw,

Waw-roo-jaw-hee-kaw,
Baptist-Lasalica,
Waw-kon-chaw-per-kaw,
Kaw-how-ah-kaw,
Hakh-ee-nee-kaw,
Waw-kon-chaw-ho-no-kaw,
Maw-hee-ko-shay-naw-zhee-kaw,
Maw-nee-ho-no-nic,
Maw-ho-kee-wee-kaw,
Sho-go-nee-kaw,
Watch-ha-ta-kaw, (by Henry M. Rice, his delegate).

Witnesses:

John C. Mullay, secretary to board of commissioners.
J. E. Fletcher, subagent.
S. B. Lowry,
Peter Mananaige,
Antoine Grignon, } interpreters.
Simeon Lecure,

H. L. Dousman,
Richard Chute,
John Haney,
George Cahn,
James Maher.

(To each of the names of the Indians are affixed a seal and mark.)

TREATY WITH THE CHIPPEWA OF THE MISSISSIPPI AND LAKE SUPERIOR, 1847.

Articles of a treaty made and concluded at the Fond du Lac of Lake Superior, on the second day of August, in the year one thousand eight hundred and forty-seven, between the United States, by their commissioners, Isaac A. Verplank and Henry M. Rice, and the Chippewa Indians of the Mississippi and Lake Superior, by their chiefs and head-men.

Aug. 2, 1847.

9 Stat., 904.
Ratified Apr. 3, 1848.
Proclaimed, Apr. 7, 1848.

ARTICLE 1. It is agreed that the peace and friendship which exists between the people of the United States and the Chippewa Indians shall be perpetual.

Peace and friendship to be perpetual.

ARTICLE 2. The Chippewa Indians of the Mississippi and Lake Superior cede and sell to the United States all the land within the following boundaries, viz: Beginning at the junction of the Crow Wing and Mississippi Rivers, thence up the Crow Wing River to the junction of that river with the Long Prairie River, thence up the Long Prairie River to the boundary-line between the Sioux and Chippewa Indians, thence southerly along the said boundary-line to a lake at the head of Long Prairie River, thence in a direct line to the sources of the Watab River, thence down the Watab to the Mississippi River, thence up the Mississippi to the place of beginning; and also all the interest and claim which the Indians, parties to this treaty, have in a tract of land lying upon and north of Long Prairie River, and called One-day's Hunt; but, as the boundary-line between the Indians, parties to this treaty, and the Chippewa Indians, commonly called "Pillagers," is indefinite, it is agreed that before the United States use or occupy the said tract of land north of Long Prairie River, the boundary-line between the said tract and the Pillager lands shall be defined and settled to the satisfaction of the Pillagers.

Cession of lands by the Chippewa of the Mississippi and Lake Superior to the United States.

Boundary between the Indians, parties to this treaty, and the "Pillager" band, to be settled to the satisfaction of the latter.

ARTICLE 3. In consideration of the foregoing cession, the United States agree to pay to the Chippewas of Lake Superior seventeen thousand dollars in specie, and to the Chippewas of the Mississippi seventeen thousand dollars in specie; the above sums to be paid at such place or places, and in such manner, as the President shall direct, and to be paid within six months after this treaty shall be ratified by the Presi-

In consideration of the foregoing cession, the United States to pay the Chippewa $17,000.

And further to pay to the Mississippi Indians the sum of $1,000 for 46 years.

dent and Senate of the United States; and the United States further agree to pay to the Mississippi Indians the sum of one thousand dollars annually for forty-six years; but it is agreed that whenever the Chippewas of the Mississippi shall agree as to the schools to be established, and the places at which they shall be located, the number of blacksmiths and laborers to be employed for them, and shall request the United States to expend, from year to year, the annual payments remaining unpaid, in the support of schools, blacksmiths, and labor- ers, the same shall be expended by the United States for such purposes; and that Chippewas of full or mixed blood shall be employed as teach- ers, blacksmiths, and laborers, when such persons can be employed who are competent to perform the duties required of them under this and all former treaties.

How to be expended.

Half or mixed blood of the Chippewa to be considered as Chippewa.

ARTICLE 4. It is stipulated that the half or mixed bloods of the Chippewas residing with them shall be considered Chippewa Indians, and shall, as such, be allowed to participate in all annuities which shall hereafter be paid to the Chippewas of the Mississippi and Lake Supe- rior, due them by this treaty, and by the treaties heretofore made and ratified.

ARTICLE 5. [Stricken out.]

ARTICLE 6. This treaty shall be obligatory upon the contracting parties when ratified by the President and Senate of the United States.

In testimony whereof, the said Isaac A. Verplank and Henry M. Rice, commissioners as aforesaid, and the chiefs, headmen and warriors of the Chippewas of the Mississippi and Lake Superior, have hereunto set their hands, at the Fond du Lac of Lake Superior, this second day of August, in the year one thousand eight hundred and forty-seven.

Isaac A. Verplank.
Henry M. Rice.

Kai-ah-want-eda, 2d chief, his x mark, Crow-wing.

Waub-o-jceg, 1st chief, his x mark, Gull Lake.

Uttom-auh, 1st warrior, his x mark, Crow-wing.

Shen-goob, 1st warrior, his x mark, Crow-wing.

Que-wish-an-sish, 1st warrior, his x mark, Gull Lake.

Maj-c-gah-bon, 2d warrior, his x mark, Crow-wing.

Kag-gag-c-we guon, warrior, his x mark, Crow-wing.

Mab uk-um-ig, warrior, his x mark, Crow-wing.

Nag aun cg-a bon, 2d chief, his x mark, Sandy Lake.

Wan jc-ke-shig-uk, chief, his x mark, Sandy Lake.

Kow-az-rum-ig-ish-kung, warrior, his x mark, Sandy Lake.

Ke-che-wask keenk, 1st chief, his x mark, Lapointe.

Gab im ub-be, chief, his x mark, St. Croix Lake.

Kee che-waub-ish-ash, 1st chief, his x mark, Pelican Lakes.

Nig-gig, 2d chief, his x mark, Pelican Lakes.

Ud-c-kum-ag, 2d chief, his x mark, Lac flambeau.

Ta-che-go-onk, 3d chief, his x mark, La- pointe.

Muk-no-a-wuk-und, warrior, his x mark, Lapointe.

O-sho-gaz, warrior, his x mark, St. Croix.

A-dow-c-re-shig, warrior, his x mark, La- pointe.

Keesh-ri-tow-ng, 1st warrior, his x mark, Lapointe.

I-aub-ans, chief, his x mark, Rice Lake.

Tug-wany-am-az, 2d chief, his x mark, Lapointe.

O-rum-de-kun, chief, his x mark, Ontona- gin.

Keesh-re-tow-no, 2d chief, his x mark, Ontonagin.

Maj-c-wo-we-clung, 2d chief, his x mark, Puckaguno.

Ke-che-wa-mibco-osk, 1st chief, his x mark, Puckaguno.

Mongo-o-sit, 3d chief, his x mark, Fond- du-lac.

Mug-un-ub, 2d chief, his x mark, Fond- du-lac.

An-im-as-ung, 1st warrior, his x mark, Fond-du-lac.

Waub-ish-ashe, 1st chief, his x mark, Chippeway River.

Make-cen-gun, 2d chief, his x mark, Chippeway River.

Kee-wan-see, chief. his x mark, Lac Con- tereille.

Ten-as-see, chief, his x mark, Puk-wa- wun.

Nag-an-is, 2d chief, his x mark, Lac Con- tereille.

Ke-chi-in-in-e, 1st warrior. his x mark, Puk-wa-wun.

Ke-che-now-uj-c-nim, chief, his x mark, Turtle Portage.

Bus-e-guin-jis, warrior, his x mark, Lac flambeau.

Shin-goob, 1st chief, his x mark, Fond- du-lac.

Shay-u-ash-cens, 1st chief. his x mark, Grand Portage.

Ud-ik-ons, 2d chief, his x mark, Grand Portage.
Me-zye, 4th chief, his x mark, Lapointe.
David King, 1st chief, his x mark, Ance.
Ma-tak-o-se-ga, 1st warrior, his x mark, Ance.
Assurcens, 2d warrior, his x mark, Ance.
Peter Marksman, chief.
Alexander Corbin, chief.
William W. W. Warren, 1st chief.
Jno. Pta. Rellenger, his x mark.

Charles Charlo, his x mark.
Chief, Battiste Gauthier, his x mark.
   Half-breeds—Lapointe Band:
Chief, Vincent Roy, his x mark.
Warrior, John Btse. Cadotte, his x mark.
Second Chief, Lemo Sayer, his x mark.
Warrior, Jhn. Btse. Roy, his x mark.
Michel Bas-he-na, his x mark.
Lueson Godin, his x mark.
John Sayer, his x mark.
Chief, Lueson Corbin, his x mark.

Witnesses—

Wm. W. Warren, interpreter.
Chas. H. Oakes, Lapointe.
Roswell Hart, Rochester, New York.
Henry Evans, Batavia, New York.
A. Morrison.

S. Hovers.
Mamoci M. Samuel.
Henry Blatchford, interpreter.
William A. Aitken.
Julius Ombrian.

The following signatures are those of chiefs and headmen parties to this treaty:

Ke-nesh-te-no, chief, Trout Lake, his x mark.
Mah-shah, 1st warrior, his x mark, Lac flambeau.
I-oush-ou-c-ke-shik, chief, his x mark, Red Cedar Lake.
Mah-ko-dah, 1st warrior, his x mark, Mille Lac.
Pe-tud, 1st chief, his x mark, Mille Lac.
Aunch-e-be-nas, 2d warrior, his x mark, Mille Lac.
Mish-in-nack-in-ugo, warrior, his x mark, Red Cedar Lake.

Gah-nin-dum-a-win-so, 1st chief, his x mark, Sandy Lake.
Mis-quod-ase, warrior, his x mark, Sandy Lake.
Na-tum-e-gaw-bow, 2d chief, his x mark, Sandy Lake.
I-ah-be-dua-we-dung, warrior, his x mark, Sandy Lake.
Bi-a-jig, 1st chief, his x mark, Pukaguno.
Joseph Montre, 1st chief, Mississippi half-breeds.

Witnesses—
   Wm. W. Warren,
   Peter Marksman,
               Interpreters.
   Smith Hovers.

The signature of No-din, or The Wind, written by his request on the 3d day of August, 1847, and with the consent of the commissioners—
                    No-din, or The Wind, his x mark.

In presence of—
   William A. Aitkin,
   R. B. Carlton.

I approve of this treaty, and consent to the same, August 3d, 1847. Fond-du-lac.
                    Po-go-ne-gi-shik, or Hole-in-the-day, his x mark.

Witness—
   William Aitkin,
   D. T. Sloan.

TREATY WITH THE PILLAGER BAND OF CHIPPEWA INDIANS, 1847.

Articles of a treaty made and concluded at Leech Lake on the twenty-first day of August, in the year one thousand eight hundred and forty-seven, between the United States, by their commissioners, Isaac A. Verplank and Henry M. Rice, and the Pillager Band of Chippewa Indians, by their chiefs, head-men, and warriors.

Aug. 21, 1847.

9 Stat., 908.
Proclamation Apr. 7, 1848.

ARTICLE 1. It is agreed that the peace and friendship which exists between the United States and the Indians, parties to this treaty, shall be perpetual.

Peace and friendship to be perpetual.

Cession of lands to the United States.

ARTICLE 2. The Pillager band of Chippewa Indians hereby sell and cede to the United States all the country within the following boundaries, viz: Beginning at the south end of Otter-Tail Lake; thence southerly on the boundary-line between the Sioux and Chippeway Indians to Long Prairie River; thence up said river to Crow Wing River; thence up Crow Wing River to Leaf River; thence up Leaf River to the head of said river; and from thence in a direct line to the place of beginning.

Country ceded to be held as Indian land until otherwise ordered.

ARTICLE 3. It is stipulated that the country hereby ceded shall be held by the United States as Indian land, until otherwise ordered by the President.

Annuity in goods for five years, in consideration of the foregoing cession.

ARTICLE 4. In consideration of the foregoing cession, the United States agree to furnish to the Pillager band of Chippewa Indians annually, for five years, the following articles: Fifty three-point Mackinaw blankets, three hundred two and a half point Mackinaw blankets, fifty one and a half point Mackinaw blankets, three hundred and forty yards of gray list-cloth, four hundred and fifty yards of white list scarlet cloth, eighteen hundred yards of strong dark prints, assorted colors, one hundred and fifty pounds three-thread gray gilling-twine, seventy-five pounds turtle-twine, fifty bunches sturgeon-twine, twenty-five pounds of linen thread, two hundred combs, five thousand assorted needles, one hundred and fifty medal looking-glasses, ten pounds of vermilion, thirty nests (fourteen each) heavy tin kettles, five hundred pounds of tobacco, and five barrels of salt. And the United States further agree that at the first payment made under this treaty, the Indians, parties to this treaty, shall receive as a present two hundred warranted beaver-traps and seventy-five north-west guns.

Treaty to be obligatory when ratified by the President.

ARTICLE 5. This treaty shall be obligatory upon the parties thereto when ratified by the President and Senate of the United States.

In testimony whereof, the said Isaac A. Verplank and Henry M. Rice, commissioners, as aforesaid, and the chiefs, headmen, and warriors of the Pillager band of Chippewa Indians, have hereunto set their hands at Leech Lake, this twenty-first day of August, one thousand eight hundred and forty-seven.

> Isaac A. Verplank.
> Henry M. Rice.
> George Bonja, Interpreter.

Aish-ke-bo-ge-Koshe, or Flat Mouth, first chief, his x mark.
Ca-pe-ma-be, or Elder Brother's Son, second chief, his x mark.
Nia-je-ga-boi, or La Trappe, head warrior, his x mark.
Ca-gouse, or Small Porcupine, headman, his x mark.
Pe-ji-ke, or the Buffalo, second warrior, his x mark.
Ca-ken-ji-wi-nine, or Charcoal, third warrior, his x mark.
Na-bi-ne-ashe, or the Bird that flies on one side, second headman, his x mark.
Ne-ba-coim, or Night Thunder, warrior, his x mark.
Chang-a-so-ning, or Nine Fingers, third headman, his x mark.

Witness: George Bonja, Interpreter.
A. Morrison,
A. R. McLeod,
J. W. Lynde.

TREATY WITH THE PAWNEE—GRAND, LOUPS, REPUBLICANS, ETC., 1848.

Treaty with the Pawnees; articles of agreement and convention made this sixth day of August, A. D. 1848, at Fort Childs, near the head of Grand Island, on the south side of the Nebraska or Great Platte River, between Lieutenant-Colonel Ludwell E. Powell, commanding battalion Missouri Mounted Volunteers, en route to Oregon, in behalf of the United States, and the chiefs and head-men of the four confederated bands of Pawnees, viz: Grand Pawnees, Pawnee Loups, Pawnee Republicans, and Pawnee Tappage, at present residing on the south side of the Platte River.

Aug. 6, 1848.

9 Stat., 949.
Ratified Jan. 8, 1849.

ARTICLE 1. The confederated bands of the Pawnees hereby cede and relinquish to the United States all their right, title, and interest in and to all that tract of land described as follows, viz: Commencing on the south side of the Platte River, five miles west of this post, "Fort Childs;" thence due north to the crest of the bluffs north of said Platte River; thence east and along the crest of said bluffs to the termination of Grand Island, supposed to be about sixty miles distant; thence south to the southern shore of said Platte River; and thence west and along the southern shore of the said Platte River to the place of beginning. *[margin: Land ceded to the United States.]*

The land hereby conveyed is designated within the red lines of the following plat:

[NOTE.—*The red lines in the original plat are designated by dotted lines in this copy.*]

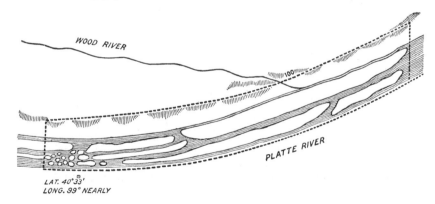

ARTICLE 2. In consideration of the land hereby ceded and relinquished, the United States has this day paid, through Captain Stewart Van Vliet, assistant quartermaster United States Army, under an order from Lieutenant-Colonel Ludwell E. Powell, commanding battalion Missouri Mounted Volunteers, to the said four bands collectively, on the execution of this treaty, the amount of two thousand dollars in goods and merchandise, the receipt of which is hereby acknowledged. *[margin: Payment of goods, etc., in consideration of foregoing cession.]*

ARTICLE 3. The United States shall have the privilege of using any hard timber that may at any time be needed, situate upon Wood River, immediately north of the land hereby conveyed. *[margin: United States to use timber on Wood River.]*

ARTICLE 4. The Pawnee Nation renew their assurance of friendship for the white men, their fidelity to the United States, and their desire for peace with all the neighboring tribes of Indians. *[margin: Friendship and fidelity pledged.]*

The Pawnee Nation, therefore, faithfully promise not to molest or injure the property or person of any white citizen of the United States, wherever found, nor to make war upon any tribes with whom said Pawnee tribes now are, or may hereafter be, at peace; but, should any *[margin: Disputes to be arbitrated.]*

difficulty arise, they agree to refer the matter in dispute to such arbitration as the President of the United States may direct.

ARTICLE 5. These articles of agreement and convention shall be binding and obligatory from this sixth day of August, A. D. 1848.

In testimony whereof, the said Lieutenant-Colonel Ludwell E. Powell, commanding battalion Missouri mounted volunteers, and the chiefs and headmen of the four confederated bands of Grand Pawnees, Pawnee Loups, Pawnee Republicans, and Pawnee Tappage, have hereunto signed their names, and affixed their seals, on the day and year aforesaid.

Ludwell E. Powell,
Lieutenant-Colonel Commanding Battalion
Missouri Mounted Volunteers.
Chef Ma-laigne,
Principal Chief of the Four Confederated Bands.

Chiefs of—

Grand Pawnees:
Sha-re-ta-riche,
Ah-tah-ra-scha.
    Pawnee Loups:
Ish-Ka-top-pa,
French Chief,
Big Chief.

Pawnee Republicans:
La-lo-che-la-sha-ro,
A-sha-la-la-cot-sha-lo,
American Chief.
    Pawnee Tappage:
La-pa-ko-lo-lo-ho-la-sha,
La-sha-pit-ko,
Ta-ra-re-tappage.

(To each of the Indian names is affixed his mark.)

Executed and delivered in the presence of—

Thomas J. Todd, adjutant, battalion Missouri Mounted Volunteers, secretary.
A. W. Sublette, captain, Company A.
J. Walker, A. S., U. S. Army.
W. H. Rodgers, captain, Company L.
David McCausland, captain, Company B.
Stewart Van Vliet, captain and acting quartermaster, U. S. Army.

D. P. Woodbury, lieutenant, Engineers.
J. W. Kelly, second lieutenant, commanding Company C.
Saml. J. Lingenfelter.
Ant. Le Faivre.
Peter A. Carnes, forage master.
J. B. Small, A. S., U. S. Army.
F. Jeffrey Deroine, interpreter.

TREATY WITH THE MENOMINEE, 1848.

Oct. 18, 1848.

9 Stat., 952.
Ratified Jan.23,1849.

Articles of a treaty made and concluded at Lake Pow-aw-hay-kon-nay, in the State of Wisconsin, on the eighteenth day of October, one thousand eight hundred and forty-eight, between the United States of America, by William Medill, a commissioner duly appointed for that purpose, and the Menomonee tribe of Indians, by the chiefs, headmen, and warriors of said tribe.

Peace perpetual.

ARTICLE 1. It is stipulated and solemnly agreed that the peace and friendship now so happily subsisting between the Government and people of the United States and the Menomonee Indians shall be perpetual.

Cession of lands.

ARTICLE 2. The said Menomonee tribe of Indians agree to cede, and do hereby cede, sell, and relinquish to the United States all their lands in the State of Wisconsin, wherever situated.

Home provided for said tribe.

ARTICLE 3. In consideration of the foregoing cession, the United States agree to give, and do hereby give, to said Indians for a home, to be held as Indians' lands are held, all that country or tract of land ceded to the said United States by the Chippewa Indians of the Mississippi and Lake Superior, in the treaty of August 2, 1847, and the Pillager band of Chippewa Indians, in the treaty of August 21, 1847, which may not be assigned to the Winnebago Indians, under the treaty with that tribe of October 13, 1846, and which is guarantied to contain not less than six hundred thousand acres.

ARTICLE 4. In further and full consideration of said cession, the United States agree to pay the sum of three hundred and fifty thousand dollars, at the several times, in the manner, and for the purposes following, viz: Payment of $350,000 by United States.

To the chiefs, as soon after the same shall be appropriated by Congress as may be convenient, to enable them to arrange and settle the affairs of their tribe preparatory to their removal to the country set apart for and given to them as above, thirty thousand dollars. To chiefs, for preparation for removal.

To such person of mixed blood, and in such proportion to each as the chiefs in council, and a commissioner to be appointed by the President, shall designate and determine, and as soon after the appropriation thereof as may be found practicable and expedient, forty thousand dollars. To mixed bloods.

In such manner and at such times as the President shall prescribe, in consideration of their removing themselves, which they agree to do, without further cost or expense to the United States, twenty thousand dollars. Expenses of removal.

In such manner and at such times as the President shall prescribe, in consideration of their subsisting themselves the first year after their removal, which they agree to do, without further cost or expense on the part of the United States, twenty thousand dollars. Subsistence after removal.

To be laid out and applied, under the direction of the President, in the establishment of a manual-labor school, the erection of a grist and saw mill, and other necessary improvements in their new country, fifteen thousand dollars. Manual-labor school, mill, etc., in new country.

To be laid out and applied, under the direction of the President, in procuring a suitable person, to attend and carry on the said grist and saw mill for a period of fifteen years, nine thousand dollars. Person to direct mill.

To be laid out and applied, under the direction of the President, in continuing and keeping up a blacksmith's shop, and providing the usual quantity of iron and steel for the use and benefit of said tribe, for a period of twelve years, commencing with the year one thousand eight hundred and fifty-seven, and when all provision for blacksmiths' shops under the treaty of 1836 shall cease, eleven thousand dollars. Blacksmith shop, iron, etc.

To be set apart, applied, and distributed under the direction of the President, in payment of individual improvements of the tribe upon the lands above ceded to the United States, five thousand dollars. Individual improvements on ceded land.

And the balance, amounting to the sum of two hundred thousand dollars, to be paid over to the tribe, as Indian annuities are required to be paid, in ten equal annual instalments, commencing with the year one thousand eight hundred and fifty-seven, and when their annuities or annual instalments under the treaty of 1836 shall have ceased. Balance in ten annual installments.

ARTICLE 5. It is stipulated and agreed, that the sum now invested in stocks, under the Senate's amendment to the treaty of 1836, with the interest due thereon at this time, shall be and remain invested, under the direction of the President, and that the interest hereafter arising therefrom shall be disposed of as follows: that is to say, so much thereof as may be necessary to the support and maintenance of the said manual-labor school, and other means of education, and the balance be annually paid over in money as other annuities, or applied for the benefit and improvement of said tribe, as the President, on consultation with the chiefs, may, from time to time, determine. Sum invested in stocks under treaty of 1836, how applied.

ARTICLE 6. To enable the said Indians to explore and examine their new country, and as an inducement to an early removal thereto, it is agreed that the United States will pay the necessary expenses of a suitable delegation, to be selected for that purpose, under the direction of the President. Exploration of new country.

ARTICLE 7. It is alleged that there were less goods delivered to the said Indians at the annuity payment of 1837 than were due and required to be paid and delivered to them under the stipulations of their treaties Deficit in goods delivered in 1837 to be made up.

with the United States then in force; and it is therefore agreed that the subject shall be properly investigated, and that full indemnity shall be made to them for any loss which they may be shown to have sustained.

To remain on ceded lands for two years. ARTICLE 8. It is agreed that the said Indians shall be permitted, if they desire to do so, to remain on the lands hereby ceded for and during the period of two years from the date hereof, and until the President shall notify them that the same are wanted.

Robert Grignon to preempt certain land. ARTICLE 9. It is stipulated that Robert Grignon, who has erected a saw-mill upon the Little Wolf River, at his own expense, for the benefit and at the request of said Indians, shall have the right of a pre-emptor to the lands upon which such improvements are situated, not exceeding in quantity on both sides of said river one hundred and sixty acres.

Treaty to be binding as soon as ratified by the President and Senate. ARTICLE 10. This treaty to be binding on the contracting parties as soon as it is ratified by the President and Senate of the United States.

In testimony whereof, the said William Medill, Commissioner as aforesaid, and the chiefs, headmen, and warriors of the said Menomonee tribe of Indians, have hereunto set their hands and seals, at the place and on the day and year aforesaid.

W. Medill, [SEAL.]
Commissioner on the Part of the United States.

Signed and sealed in the presence of us—

Albert G. Ellis, Sub-Agent,
Chas. A. Grignon, U. S. Interpreter,
F. J. Bonduel, Missionary Priest among the Menomonee Indians.
M. L. Martin,
P. B. Grignon,
Samuel Ryan,
A. G. Grignon,
John B. Jacobs.

Osh, Kush,	Sho-na-new, Jr.,
Jau-ma-tau,	Pah-maw-po-may,
Waw-kee-che-un,	Naw-kaw-chis-ka,
Sage-toke,	Show-anno-penessee,
Wy-tah-sauh,	Tah-ko,
Kee-chee-new,	Osh-kish-he-nay-new,
Chee-cheequon-away,	Little Wave,
Corron Glaude,	Muck-atah-penesse,
Sho-nee-nieu,	Wa-pee-men-shaw,
Lamotte,	Ah-ke-na-pe-new,
Che-quo-tum,	Ah-kaw-mut,
Shaw-wan-on,	Kee-she-teu-ke-tau,
Ah-ko-no-may,	She-pau-na-ko,
Shaw-poa-tuk,	Naw-kaw-nish-kau-wa.
Wau-po-nan-ah,	

(To each of the names of the Indians is affixed his mark.)

Witnesses:

William Powell,	Antoine Gotheiu,
John B. Dube,	F. Desnoyers,
John G. Kittson,	Louis G. Porhir,
Robt. Grignon,	O. W. F. Bruce.
Charles Caron,	

TREATY WITH THE STOCKBRIDGE TRIBE, 1848.

Nov. 24, 1848.

9 Stat., 955.
Ratified Mar. 1, 1849.

Preamble.

WHEREAS by an act of Congress entitled "An act for the relief of the Stockbridge tribe of Indians, in the Territory of Wisconsin," approved on the third day of March, A. D. 1843, it was provided that the township of land on the east side of Winnebago Lake, secured to said tribe by the treaty with the Menomonee Indians of February 8th,

1831, as amended by the Senate of the United States, and not heretofore ceded by said tribe to the United States, should be divided and allotted among the individual members of said tribe, by commissioners to be elected for that purpose, who were to make report of such division and allotment, and thereupon the persons composing said tribe were to become citizens of the United States.

And whereas a portion of said tribe refused to recognize the validity of said act of Congress, or the proceedings which were had under it, or to be governed by its provisions, and upon their petition a subsequent act was passed by the Congress of the United States, on the 6th day of August, 1846, repealing the said act of March 3d, 1843, and providing, among other things, that such of said tribe as should enroll themselves with the subagent of Indian affairs at Green Bay, should be and remain citizens of the United States, and the residue of said tribe were restored to their ancient form of government as an Indian tribe. It was also provided that the said township of land should be divided into two districts, one of which was to be known as the "Indian district," the other as the "citizen district;" the former to be held in common by the party who did not desire citizenship, and the latter to be divided and allotted among such as were citizens and desired to remain so.

And whereas it has been found impracticable to carry into full effect the provisions of the act of August 6th, 1846, by dividing the said township of land in the manner specified in said act, without infringing upon private rights acquired in good faith under the act of 1843 hereinbefore referred to, with a view of relieving both the Indian and citizen parties of said Stockbridge tribe of Indians from their present embarrassments, and to secure to each their just rights, articles of agreement and compromise have been entered into, as follows:

Articles of agreement and treaty made and concluded at Stockbridge, in the State of Wisconsin, on the 24th day of November, in the year of our Lord one thousand eight hundred and forty-eight, by and between the undersigned, acting commissioners on the part of the United States of America, and the Stockbridge tribe of Indians.

ARTICLE 1. The said Stockbridge tribe of Indians renounce all participation in any of the benefits or privileges granted or conferred by the act of Congress entitled "An act for the relief of the Stockbridge tribe of Indians, in the Territory of Wisconsin," approved March 3, 1843, and relinquish all rights secured by said act; and they do hereby acknowledge and declare themselves to be under the protection and guardianship of the United States, as other Indian tribes.

Renunciation of rights under act of 1843, ch. 101.

Acknowledge guardianship of United States.
Census of tribe.

ARTICLE 2. That no misunderstanding may exist, now or hereafter, in determining who compose said tribe and are parties hereto, it is agreed that a roll or census shall be taken and appended to this agreement, and in like manner taken annually hereafter, and returned to the Secretary of the War Department of the United States, containing the names of all such as are parties hereto, and to be known and recognized as the Stockbridge tribe of Indians, who shall each be entitled to their due proportion of the benefits to be derived from the provisions made for their tribe by this and former agreements; and whenever any of them shall separate themselves from said tribe, or abandon the country which may be selected for their future home, the share or portion of such shall cease, and they shall forfeit all claims to be recognized as members of said tribe.

ARTICLE 3. The said Stockbridge tribe of Indians hereby sell and relinquish to the United States the township of land on the east side of Lake Winnebago, (granted and secured to said tribe by the treaty with the Menomonee tribe of Indians of February 8, 1831, as amended

Cession to United States.

by the resolution of the Senate of the United States,) and situated in the State of Wisconsin.

Survey of land ceded and patents to issue for land allotted under act of 1843, ch. 101.

ARTICLE 4. The said township of land shall be surveyed into lots, in conformity with the plan adopted by the commissioners elected under the act of March 3, 1843, and such of said lands as were allotted by said commissioners to members of said tribe who have become citizens of the United States (a schedule of which is hereunto annexed) are hereby confirmed to such individuals respectively, and patents therefor shall be issued by the United States. The residue of said lands belonging to the United States shall be brought into market but shall not be sold at less than the appraised value, unless the Senate of the United States shall otherwise determine.

Sale of residue.

Payment to tribe for necessaries, etc.

ARTICLE 5. In consideration of the cession and relinquishment hereinbefore made by the said Stockbridge tribe of Indians, it is agreed that the United States shall pay to said tribe, within six months after the ratification of this agreement, the sum of sixteen thousand five hundred dollars, to enable them to settle their affairs, obtain necessaries, and make provision for establishing themselves in a new home.

Payment for improvements on ceded land.

ARTICLE 6. The United States shall also pay to said tribe, within six months after the ratification of this agreement, the sum of fourteen thousand five hundred and four dollars and eighty-five cents, being the appraised value of their improvements upon the lands herein ceded and relinquished to the United States, and to be paid to the individuals claiming said improvements according to the schedule and assessment herewith transmitted.

Tribe to remain on ceded lands for one year.

ARTICLE 7. It is further stipulated and agreed that the said Stockbridge tribe may remain upon the lands they now occupy for one year after the ratification of this agreement, and that they will remove to the country set apart for them, or such other west of the Mississippi River as they may be able to secure, where all their treaty stipulations with the Government shall be carried into effect.

Expenses of removal and subsistence.

ARTICLE 8. Whenever the said Stockbridge tribe shall signify their wish to emigrate, the United States will defray the expenses of their removal west of the Mississippi and furnish them with subsistence for one year after their arrival at their new home.

Investment in stock fund.

ARTICLE 9. It is further stipulated and agreed, that, for the purpose of making provision for the rising generation of said tribe, the sum of sixteen thousand five hundred dollars shall be invested by the United States in stock, bearing an interest of not less than five per cent. per annum, the interest of which shall be paid annually to said tribe, as other annuities are paid by the United States.

Surveys.

ARTICLE 10. It is agreed that nothing herein shall prevent a survey of said lands, at any time after the ratification of this agreement, and that said tribe shall commit no waste or do unnecessary damage upon the premises occupied by them.

United States to pay expenses of chiefs since 1843.

ARTICLE 11. The United States will pay the expenses incurred by the sachem and head-men, amounting to three thousand dollars, in attending to the business of said tribe since the year 1843.

ARTICLE 12. This agreement to be binding and obligatory upon the contracting parties from and after its ratification by the Government of the United States.

In witness whereof, the said commissioners, and the sachem, councillors, and headmen of said tribe, have hereunto set their hands and seals, the day and year above written.

Morgan L. Martin,	[L. S.]	Jeremiah Slingerland,	[L. S.]
Albert G. Ellis,	[L. S.]	*Benjamin Pye, 2d,	[L. S.]
Augustin E. Quinney, sachem,	[L. S.]	Simon S. Metoxen,	[L. S.]
Zeba T. Peters, ⎫	[L. S.]	Daniel Metoxen,	[L. S.]
Peter D. Littleman, ⎬ Councillors.	[L. S.]	*Moses Charles,	[L. S.]
*Abram Pye, ⎭	[L. S.]	*Benjamin Pye, 3d,	[L. S.]
Joseph M. Quinney,	[L. S.]	*Jacob Jehoiakim,	[L. S.]
Samuel Stephens,	[L. S.]		

John Metoxen, ⎫	[L. S.]	*Laurens Yocron,	[L. S.]
John W. Quinney, ⎬ Councillors.	[L. S.]	*Thomas Schanandoah,	[L. S.]
Samuel Miller, ⎭	[L. S.]	*John W. Quinney, jr.,	[L. S.]
*David Palmer,	[L. S.]	*Nicolas Palmer,	[L. S.]
Ezekiel Robinson,	[L. S.]	John P. Quinney,	[L. S.]
*James Joshua,	[L. S.]	*Washington Quinney,	[L. S.]
*Garrett Thompson,	[L. S.]	*Aaron Turkey.	[L. S.]

To each of the names of the Indians marked with an asterisk is affixed his mark.

In presence of—
Charles A. Grignon, U. S. Interpreter.
Lemuel Goodell,
Eleazer Williams,
Charles Poreuninozer.

SUPPLEMENTAL ARTICLE.

Whereas the Stockbridge and Munsee Indians consider that they *Claims.* have a claim against the United States for indemnity for certain lands on White River in the State of Indiana, and for certain other lands in the State of Wisconsin, which they allege they have been deprived of by treaties entered into with the Miamies and Delawares, or to the lands claimed by them in Indiana, and with the Menomonees and Winnebagoes, or to the lands in Wisconsin, without their consent; and whereas the said Stockbridge and Munsee Indians, by their chiefs and agents, have continued to prosecute their said claims during the last twenty years at their own expense, except the sum of three thousand dollars paid them in 1821; and whereas it is desirable that all ground of discontent on the part of said Indians shall be removed, the United *Payment for relin-* States do further stipulate, in consideration of the relinquishment by *quishment of certain* them of said claims, and all others, except as provided in this treaty, *claims.* to pay the sachems or chiefs of said Indians, on the ratification of this article by them, with the assent of their people, the sum of five thousand dollars, and the further sum of twenty thousand dollars, to be paid in ten annual instalments, to commence when the said Indians shall have selected and removed to their new homes, as contemplated by the seventh article of this treaty.

The President of the United States, within two years from the ratification of this treaty, shall procure for the use of said Stockbridge Indians a quantity of land west of the Mississippi River, upon which they shall reside, not less than seventy-two sections, said Indians to be consulted as to the location of said land, and to be holden by the same tenure as other Indian lands.

Roll or census of the Stockbridge tribe of Indians, taken in conformity with the provisions of the second article of the within agreement.

Heads of families.	Male.	Female.	Boys.	Girls.	Total
Austin E. Quinney	1	1	3	4	9
John Metoxen	1	---	---	2	1
Benjamin Pye, sen	1	1	---	1	3
Garret Thompson	1	1	2	---	4
Elisha Konkapot	1	1	1	---	3
John W. Quinney	1	---	---	---	1
John P. Quinney	1	1	1	---	3
Peter D. Littleman	1	1	1	2	5
Jonas Thompson	1	1	1	1	4
James Joshua	1	---	---	---	1
Joseph M. Quinney	1	1	2	1	5
Simon L. Metoxen	1	1	2	5	9
Benjamin Pye, 2d	1	1	1	3	6
Thomas Schenandoah	1	1	---	---	2
Aaron Turkey	1	1	2	2	6

Roll or census of the Stockbridge tribe of Indians, etc.—Continued.

Heads of families.	Male.	Female.	Boys.	Girls.	Total.
Abram Pye	1	1	4	1	7
Benjamin Pye, 4th	1	1	...	1	3
Benjamin Doxtater	1	1	1	1	4
Moses Charles	1	1	1	1	4
Benjamin Pye, 3d	1	1	1	1	4
Eli Williams	1	...	...	...	1
David Palmer	1	1	1	...	3
Jacob Konkapot	1	1	...	1	3
Daniel Metoxen	1	1	...	...	2
Elizabeth Palmer (widow)	...	1	1	1	3
Elizabeth Aaron	...	1	1	2	4
Catharine Butterfield	...	1	...	1	2
Samuel Miller	1	1	4	2	8
Louisa Jamison	...	1	...	...	1
Jacob Jahoicum	1	...	...	...	1
Anna Turkey	...	1	...	...	1
Jeremiah Slingerland	1	...	3	...	4
John Yocum	1	1	...	2	4
Elizabeth Wilber	...	1	1	3	5
John W. Quinney, jr., and sister	1	1	...	...	2
Clarissa Miller and son	1	1	...	...	2
Elizabeth Pye	...	1	...	1	2
Phœbe S. Ricket	...	1	...	...	1
Josiah Abrams, wife, and sister	1	2	...	...	3
Jeremiah Bennet	1	2	...	2	5
Paul Pye	1	1	1	...	3
Peter Bennet	1	...	...	...	1
Ziba T. Peters	1	1	2	...	4
Ezekiel Robinson and brother	...	...	2	...	2
Lawrence Yocum	1	...	...	...	1
Moses Doxtater	1	...	...	1	2
Lucinda Quinney	...	1	2	1	4
Jemima Doxtater	...	1	...	...	1
Amelia Quinney	...	1	1	...	2
Peter Bennet, sen	1	1	1	3	6
John Bennet	1	1	1	1	4
Levi Konkapot	1	...	...	...	1
Samuel Stevens	1	...	...	...	1
John Killsnake	1	...	...	...	1
Lewis Hendricks	1	...	...	...	1
Diana Davids	...	1	...	...	1

177

M. L. Martin,
Albert G. Ellis,
Austin E. Quinney.

Stockbridge, November 24, 1848.

John Metoxen,	Benjamin Pye, 3d,
John W. Quinney,	Jacob Jehoiakim,
Samuel Miller,	David Palmer,
Ziba T. Peters,	Ezekiel Robinson,
Peter D. Littleman,	James Joshua,
Abram Pye,	Garret Thompson,
Joseph M. Quinney,	Laurens Yocum,
Samuel Stephens,	Thomas Schanandoah,
Jeremiah Slingerland,	Joshua W. Quinney, jr.,
Benjamin Pye, 2d,	Nicholas Palmer,
Simon S. Metoxen,	John P. Quinney,
Daniel Metoxen,	Washington Quinney,
Moses Charles,	Aaron Turkey.

Schedule of lands to be patented to individuals under the 4th article of the above agreement.

Names.	No. of lot.	No. of acres.
Josiah Chicks	1	
Nancy Chicks	2	
John N. Chicks	4	
Jacob Davids	5	
Harvey Johnson	8	
Hannah P. Chicks	10	
Dindemia, Big Deer ⅓ E. end	14	22. 66
Puella Jourdain	16	
Jacobs Chicks	17	
John N. Chicks	18	
Josiah Chicks	20	
Jacob Chicks	21	
Jos. L. Chicks	22	
Jacob Chicks	23	
John N. Chicks	24	
Moses E. Merrill	25, 26, 27	
John N. Chicks	28, 29	
Jane Dean	30	
Mariette Abrams	31	
Catharine Mills N. ½	32	30. 62
Joseph L. Chicks	33	
John Dick	37	
John More	38	
Isaac Jacobs	40	
Benjamin Welch	31	
Lucy Jacobs	44	
Daniel Davids	47	
Daniel Davids N. ½	48	
John W. Abrams S. ½	48	
Louisa Davids	50	
Harry E. Eastman	51	
Eunice Abrams	52	
Daniel Davids	53	
John N. Chicks	54	
Hoel S. Wright S. part of	55	5
Oscar Wright N. part of	55	57½
John Littleman S ½	56	
Daniel Davids N ½	56	
Darius Davids	57	
Margaret Davids	58	
Daniel Davids	60	
Erastus Welch, (a strip E. of road)	65	6 chains 25 lks. wide off S. side of lot.
Richard Fiddler E. of road	65	Balance of the lot.
Henry Modlin part	65	W. of road, 54⅜
Henry Jacobs	63	
Lucy Jacobs frac'l part of	66	W. of road, 50.50
John W. Abrams E ½	68	
John Dick	70	
Eunice Abrams N. ½	76	
Mary Hendrick E. ½	78	
Isaac Jacobs and George Bennet	79	
John N. Chicks	81	
John N. Chicks and Jacob Davids.	82	
Nancy Hunt W. ½	83	31¼

Schedule of lands to be patented to individuals under the 4th article of the above agreement—Continued.

Names.	No. of lot.	No. of acres.
James Menagre and Betsy Menagre	part of 84 E. end	15½
Betsy Wyatt	W. ½ 85 & 86	62½
William Gardner	87	
Timothy Jourdain	90	
Timothy Jourdain	S. ½ 91	31. 25
Charles Stevens	92 & 94	
Nancy Homm	98	
Joseph L. Chicks	102	
John N. Chicks	103	
John Moore	105	
Josiah Chicks	106	
John N. Chicks	110	
Timothy Jourdain	111, 112	
John Littleman	113	
Nathan Goodell	115	
Charles Stevens	S. part 119	50
Catharine Littleman	E. part 128	54. 60
John Moore	129	
John W. Abrams	130	
Jacob Davids	131	
Adam Sheriff	W. ½ 132	31. 25
Jacob Davids	133	
Joseph L. Chicks	134	
Catharine Mills	W. ½ 136	
Joseph Doxtater	144 & 145	
Isaac Jacobs	151	
Alexander Abrams	154	
Jacob Davids	155	
Darius Davids	156	
John Littleman	157	
Isaac Jacobs	158	
Hannah W. Chicks	159	
Catharine Mills	160	
Nathan Goodell	170	
John N. Chicks	173	
James N. Lane	174	
Jacob Davids	175	
Job Moore	176	
Thomas J. Chicks	179	
Harvey Johnson	180	
Nancy Gardner	181	
Abagail Jourdain	182	
Abram Chicks	184	
Bartholomew Bowman	186	
Harriet Jourdain	187	
Andrew Chicks	188	
Sarah Davids	189	
Job Moore	191	
William Gardner	S. part of 192, and 221	50
Mordy Mann	N. part of 192, and 221	70
Mary N. Chicks	194	
William Gardner	220	
Triphane E. Jourdain	222	
Caleb Moors	223	
Isaac Simons	224	

Schedule of lands to be patented to individuals under the 4th article of the above agreement—Continued.

Names.	No. of lot.
Isabel Chicks	225
Sophia M. Jourdain	226
Jesse Bownan	227
Catharine Franks	228
Jonathan Chicks	229
Jonas Davids	231
Adam Davids	232
Linke Jourdain	233
Elizabeth Moore	234
Joseph Doxtater	235
George Bennet	237
Isaac Simmons	240
Abigail Moore	263
Henry Moore	264
William Scott	265
William Scott	S. ½ 266
George Bennet	N. ½ 266
Reuben Johnson	267
Silas Jourdain	268
Jesse M. Jourdain	271
Simon Gardner	274
Hannah Moore	276
Solomon Davids	277
Edward Howell	279
Harriet Johnson	280
Lucinda Gardner	282
Hope Moore	284
Jemison C. Chicks	308
Obadiah Gardner	309
Rachael Davids	313
Julius Davids	314
Elizabeth Bowman	315
Jeremiah Gardner	316
Mary Jane Bowman	317
Nancy Johnson	319
Jason Simmons	320
Betsy Menagre	321
Darius Davids	323
Humble M. Jourdain	325
Stephen Gardner	326
Francis T. Davids	327
Mary McAllister	328
Mary Hendrick	335
Susannah Hendrick	349
Jacob Moore	355
David Gardner	357
George Gardner	359
Catharine Bowman	360
Serepta Johnson	361
Thankful Stephens	362
William Gardner	364
Joseph Chicks	365
John Chicks	366
Charles Stephens	367, 368
Timothy Jourdain	369, 370, 371
Jacob Chicks	372, 373

Schedule of lands to be patented to individuals under the 4th article of the above agreement—Continued.

Names.	No. of lot.	
Paul D. Hayward	375	
State of Wisconsin	383	School purposes.
Timothy Jourdain	384	
Jeremiah Johnson	385, 389	
American Board of Commissioners for Foreign Missions.	386, 390	
Jacob Chick	387, 391	
Timothy Jourdain	388	
John N. Chicks	392, 396	
William Gardner	393, 394, 397, 398	
Lemuel Goodell	N. end 395 2 acres.	

M. L. Martin.
Albert G. Ellis.

Valuation of improvements, (vide Art. 6.)

	Acres.	Dollars.	
Austin E. Quinney	163.38	2,760	63
	49.50	718	25
Joseph M. Quinney	30.90	617	15
Samuel Stevens	38.76	703	26
Moses Chicks	43.00	980	50
Elizabeth Palmer	29.06	512	41
Samuel Miller	55.62	880	87
Elisha Konkapot	5.00	142	50
Peter D. Littleman	3.25	168	88
John P. Quinney	15.50	267	50
Heirs of J. Yocum	5.78	78	03
Aaron Turkey	6.00	311	00
Benjamin Pye, 2d	40.00	640	00
John Metoxen	50.00	825	00
Mrs. B. Wright	5.00	67	50
Abraham Pye	30.00	495	00
Benjamin Pye, 4th		40	00
Benjamin Pye, sr		40	00
Benjamin Pye, 3d	20.00	350	00
Garrett Thompson	30.00	485	00
Ziba T. Peters	10.00	215	00
Betsy T. Aaron	3.00	85	00
Thomas Skenandoah	17.00	349	50
Simon S. Metoxen	30.00	535	00
Elizabeth Wilber	41.62	711	87
Ezekiel Robinson	4.00	60	00
J. W. Quinney	60.00	1,315	00
School-house		150	00

$14,504 85

M. L. Martin,
Albert G. Ellis.

TREATY WITH THE NAVAHO, 1849.

Sept. 9, 1849.

9 Stat., 974.
Ratified Sept. 9, 1850.
Proclaimed Sept. 24, 1850.

THE following acknowledgements, declarations, and stipulations have been duly considered, and are now solemnly adopted and proclaimed by the undersigned; that is to say, John M. Washington, governor of New Mexico, and lieutenant-colonel commanding the troops of the United States in New Mexico, and James S. Calhoun, Indian agent, residing at Santa Fé, in New Mexico, representing the United States of America, and Mariano Martinez, head chief, and Chapitone, second chief, on the part of the Navajo tribe of Indians:

I. The said Indians do hereby acknowledge that, by virtue of a treaty entered into by the United States of America and the United Mexican States, signed on the second day of February, in the year of our Lord eighteen hundred and forty-eight, at the city of Guadalupe Hidalgo, by N. P. Trist, of the first part, and Luis G. Cuevas, Bernardo Couto, and Mgl Atristain, of the second part, the said tribe was lawfully placed under the exclusive jurisdiction and protection of the Government of the said United States, and that they are now, and will forever remain, under the aforesaid jurisdiction and protection. *Navaho under jurisdiction of the United States.*

II. That from and after the signing of this treaty, hostilities between the contracting parties shall cease, and perpetual peace and friendship shall exist; the said tribe hereby solemnly covenanting that they will not associate with, or give countenance or aid to, any tribe or band of Indians, or other persons or powers, who may be at any time at enmity with the people of the said United States; that they will remain at peace, and treat honestly and humanely all persons and powers at peace with the said States; and all cases of aggression against said Navajoes by citizens or others of the United States, or by other persons or powers in amity with the said States, shall be referred to the Government of said States for adjustment and settlement. *Perpetual peace to exist.*

III. The Government of the said States having the sole and exclusive right of regulating the trade and intercourse with the said Navajoes, it is agreed that the laws now in force regulating the trade and intercourse, and for the preservation of peace with the various tribes of Indians under the protection and guardianship of the aforesaid Government, shall have the same force and efficiency, and shall be as binding and as obligatory upon the said Navajoes, and executed in the same manner, as if said laws had been passed for their sole benefit and protection; and to this end, and for all other useful purposes, the government of New Mexico, as now organized, or as it may be by the Government of the United States, or by the legally constituted authorities of the people of New Mexico, is recognized and acknowledged by the said Navajoes; and for the due enforcement of the aforesaid laws, until the Government of the United States shall otherwise order, the territory of the Navajoes is hereby annexed to New Mexico. *Laws now in force regulating trade and peace to be binding upon the Navaho.*

IV. The Navajo Indians hereby bind themselves to deliver to the military authority of the United States in New Mexico, at Sante Fé, New Mexico, as soon as he or they can be apprehended, the murderer or murderers of Micente Garcia, that said fugitive or fugitives from justice may be dealt with as justice may decree. *The Navaho to deliver to the United States murderer or murderers of M. Garcia.*

V. All American and Mexican captives, and all stolen property taken from Americans or Mexicans, or other persons or powers in amity with the United States, shall be delivered by the Navajo Indians to the aforesaid military authority at Jemez, New Mexico, on or before the 9th day of October next ensuing, that justice may be meted out to all whom it may concern; and also all Indian captives and stolen property of such tribe or tribes of Indians as shall enter into a similar reciprocal treaty, shall, in like manner, and for the same purposes, be turned over to an authorized officer or agent of the said States by the aforesaid Navajoes. *Captives and stolen property to be delivered to United States, by the 9th Oct., 1850.*

Citizens of the United States committing outrages upon Navaho to be subjected to the penalties of law.

VI. Should any citizen of the United States, or other person or persons subject to the laws of the United States, murder, rob, or otherwise maltreat any Navajo Indian or Indians, he or they shall be arrested and tried, and, upon conviction, shall be subjected to all the penalties provided by law for the protection of the persons and property of the people of the said States.

Free passage through their territory.

VII. The people of the United States of America shall have free and safe passage through the territory of the aforesaid Indians, under such rules and regulations as may be adopted by authority of the said States.

Military posts and agencies to be established.

VIII. In order to preserve tranquility, and to afford protection to all the people and interests of the contracting parties, the Government of the United States of America will establish such military posts and agencies, and authorize such trading-houses, at such time and in such places as the said Government may designate.

The United States to adjust territorial boundaries.

IX. Relying confidently upon the justice and the liberality of the aforesaid Government, and anxious to remove every possible cause that might disturb their peace and quiet, it is agreed by the aforesaid Navajoes that the Government of the United States shall, at its earliest convenience, designate, settle, and adjust their territorial boundaries, and pass and execute in their territory such laws as may be deemed conducive to the prosperity and happiness of said Indians.

Donations, presents, and implements to be given.

X. For and in consideration of the faithful performance of all the stipulations herein contained by the said Navajo Indians, the Government of the United States will grant to said Indians such donations, presents, and implements, and adopt such other liberal and humane measures, as said Government may deem meet and proper.

To be binding after signed, and to receive a liberal construction.

XI. This treaty shall be binding upon the contracting parties from and after the signing of the same, subject only to such modifications and amendments as may be adopted by the Government of the United States; and, finally, this treaty is to receive a liberal construction, at all times and in all places, to the end that the said Navajo Indians shall not be held responsible for the conduct of others, and that the Government of the United States shall so legislate and act as to secure the permanent prosperity and happiness of said Indians.

In faith whereof, we, the undersigned, have signed this treaty, and affixed thereunto our seals, in the valley of Cheille, this the ninth day of September, in the year of our Lord one thousand eight hundred and forty-nine.

J. M. Washington, [L. s.]
    Brevet Lieutenant-Colonel Commanding.
James S. Calhoun, [L. s.]
    Indian Agent, residing at Santa Fe.
Mariano Martinez, Head Chief, his x mark, [L. s.]
Chapitone, Second Chief, his x mark, [L. s.]
J. L. Collins.
James Conklin.
Lorenzo Force.
Antonio Sandoval, his x mark.
Francisco Josto, Governor of Jemez, his x mark.

Witnesses—
H. L. Kendrick, Brevet Major U. S. Army.
J. N. Ward, Brevet First Lieutenant Third Infantry.
John Peck, Brevet Major U. S. Army.
J. F. Hammond, Assistant Surgeon U. S. Army.
H. L. Dodge, Captain commanding Eut. Regulars.
Richard H. Kern.
J. H. Nones, Second Lieutenant Second Artillery.
Cyrus Choice.

John H. Dickerson, Second Lieutenant First Artillery.
W. E. Love.
John G: Jones.
J. H. Simpson, First Lieutenant Corps Topographic Engineers.

TREATY WITH THE UTAH, 1849.

THE following articles have been duly considered and solemnly adopted by the undersigned, that is to say, James S. Calhoun, Indian agent, residing at Santa Fé, acting as commissioner on the part of the United States of America, and Quixiachigiate, Nanito, Nincocunachi, Abaganixe, Ramahi, Subleta, Rupallachi, Saguasoxego, Paguisachi, Cobaxanor, Amuche, Puigniachi, Panachi, Sichuga, Uvicaxinape, Cuchuticay, Nachitope, Pueguate, Guano Juas, Pacachi, Saguanchi, Acaguate nochi, Puibuquiacte, Quixache tuate, Saxiabe, Pichiute, Nochichigue, Uvive, principal and subordinate chiefs, representing the Utah tribe of Indians.

Dec. 30, 1849.

9 Stats., 984.
Ratified, Sept. 9, 1850.
Proclaimed, Sept. 9, 1850.

I. The Utah tribe of Indians do hereby acknowledge and declare they are lawfully and exclusively under the jurisdiction of the Government of said States: and to its power and authority they now unconditionally submit.

Utah Indians acknowledge themselves under jurisdiction of the United States.

II. From and after the signing of this treaty, hostilities between the contracting parties shall cease, and perpetual peace and amity shall exist, the said tribe hereby binding themselves most solemnly never to associate with, or give countenance or aid to, any tribe or band of Indians, or other persons or powers, who may be, at any time, at enmity with the people or Government of said States; and that they will, in all future time, treat honestly and humanely every citizen of the United States, and all persons and powers at peace with the said States, and all cases of aggression against the said Utahs shall be referred to the aforesaid Government for adjustment and settlement.

Cessation of hostilities and peace to exist.

III. All American and Mexican captives, and others, taken from persons or powers at peace with the said States shall be restored and delivered by said Utahs to an authorized officer or agent of said States, at Abiquin, on or before the first day of March, in the year of our Lord one thousand eight hundred and fifty. And, in like manner, all stolen property, of every description, shall be restored by or before the aforesaid first day of March, 1850. In the event such stolen property shall have been consumed or destroyed, the said Utah Indians do agree and are hereby bound to make such restitution and under such circumstances as the Government of the United States may order and prescribe. But this article is not to be so construed or understood, as to create a claim against said States, for any losses or depredations committed by said Utahs.

Captives to be restored to the United States before Mar. 1, 1850.

Stolen property to be returned or restitution made.

IV. The contracting parties agree that the laws now in force, and such others as may be passed, regulating the trade and intercourse, and for the preservation of peace with the various tribes of Indians under the protection and guardianship of the Government of the United States, shall be as binding and obligatory upon the said Utahs as if said laws had been enacted for their sole benefit and protection. And that said laws may be duly executed, and for all other useful purposes, the territory occupied by the Utahs is hereby annexed to New Mexico as now organized or as it may be organized or until the Government of the United States shall otherwise order.

Laws now in force regulating trade and peace with Indians to be extended over the Utahs, and territory occupied by them is annexed to New Mexico.

V. The people of the United States, and all others in amity with the United States, shall have free passage through the territory of said Utahs, under such rules and regulations as may be adopted by authority of said States.

Free passage through their territory.

Military posts and agencies to be established.

VI. In order to preserve tranquility, and to afford protection to all the people and interests of the contracting parties, the Government of the United States will establish such military posts and agencies, and authorize such trading-houses, at such time and in such places as the said Government may designate.

The United States to limit boundaries and provide laws.

VII. Relying confidently upon the justice and liberality of the United States, and anxious to remove every possible cause that might disturb their peace and quiet, it is agreed by the Utahs that the aforesaid Government shall, at its earliest convenience, designate, settle, and adjust their territorial boundaries, and pass and execute such laws, in their territory, as the Government of said States may deem conducive to the happiness and prosperity of said Indians. And the said Utahs, further, bind themselves not to depart from their accustomed homes or localities unless specially permitted by an agent of the aforesaid Government; and so soon as their boundaries are distinctly defined, the said Utahs are further bound to confine themselves to said limits, under such rules as the said Government may prescribe, and to build up pueblos, or to settle in such other manner as will enable them most successfully to cultivate the soil, and pursue such other industrial pursuits as will best promote their happiness and prosperity: and they now deliberately and considerately, pledge their existence as a distinct tribe, to abstain, for all time to come, from all depredations; to cease the roving and rambling habits which have hitherto marked them as a people; to confine themselves strictly to the limits which may be assigned them; and to support themselves by their own industry, aided and directed as it may be by the wisdom, justice, and humanity of the American people.

The Utahs to live within their limits, and cultivate the soil.

The United States to grant presents, donations, and implements.

VIII. For, and in consideration of the faithful performance of all the stipulations contained in this treaty by the said Utahs, the Government of the United States will grant to said Indians such donations, presents, and implements, and adopt such other liberal and humane measures, as said Government may deem meet and proper.

Obligations of this treaty.

IX. This treaty shall be binding upon the contracting parties from and after the signing of the same, subject, in the first place, to the approval of the civil and military governor of New Mexico, and to such other modifications, amendments, and orders as may be adopted by the Government of the United States.

In faith whereof, the undersigned have signed this treaty, and affixed thereunto their seals, at Abiquin, in New Mexico, this the thirtieth day of December, in the year of our Lord one thousand eight hundred and forty-nine.

James S. Calhoun, [L. S.]
Indian Agent, Commissioner, U. S.
Quixiachigiate, his x mark, [L. S.]
Principal Chief.

Nanito, his x mark,	[L. S.]	Cuchuticay, his x mark,	[L. S.]
Nincocunachi, his x mark,	[L. S.]	Nachitope, his x mark,	[L. S.]
Abaganixe, his x mark,	[L. S.]	Pueguate, his x mark,	[L. S.]
Ramahi, his x mark,	[L. S.]	Guano Juas, his x mark,	[L. S.]
Subleta, his x mark,	[L. S.]	Pacachi, his x mark,	[L. S.]
Rupallachi, his x mark,	[L. S.]	Saguanchi, his x mark,	[L. S.]
Saguasoxego, his x mark,	[L. S.]	Acaguate nochi, his x mark,	[L. S.]
Paguishachi, his x mark,	[L. S.]	Puibuquiacte, his x mark,	[L. S.]
Cobaxanor, his x mark,	[L. S.]	Quixache tuate, his x mark,	[L. S.]
Amuche, his x mark,	[L. S.]	Saxiabe his x mark,	[L. S.]
Puigniachi, his x mark.	[L. S.]	Pichiute, his x mark,	[L. S.]
Panachi, his x mark,	[L. S.]	Nochichigue, his x mark,	[L. S.]
Sichuga, his x mark,	[L. S.]	Uvive, his x mark,	[L. S.]
Uvicaxinape, his x mark,	[L. S.]		Subordinates.

Witnesses:

Anto. Jesus Solosa,
Franco Tomas Baco,
Vicente Vilarde, his x mark, Interpreter.
Antonio Leroux, Interpreter.
James Conklin, Interpreter.

J. H. Whittlesey, First Lieutenant First
    Dragoons.
Edward M. Kern,
George W. Martin,
Wm. H. Mitchell.

Approved:

John Munroe,
Brevet Colonel U. S. Army, Civil and Military Governor.

TREATY WITH THE WYANDOT, 1850.

Articles of a convention concluded in the city of Washington, this first day of April, one thousand eight hundred and fifty, by and between Ardavan S. Loughery, commissioner especially appointed by the President of the United States, and the undersigned head chief and deputies of the Wyandot tribe of Indians, duly authorized and empowered to act for their tribe.

Apr. 1, 1850.

9 Stat., 987.
Ratified Sept. 24, 1850.
Proclaimed Sept. 30, 1850.

WHEREAS, By the treaty of March 17, 1842, between the United States and the Wyandot nation of Indians, then chiefly residing within the limits of the State of Ohio, the said nation of Indians agreed to sell and transfer, and did thereby sell and transfer, to the United States their reservations of land, one hundred and nine thousand acres of which was in the State of Ohio, and Six thousand acres were in the State of Michigan, and to remove to the west of the Mississippi River: And whereas, among other stipulations it was agreed that the United States should convey to said Indians a tract of country for their permanent settlement in the Indian territory west of the Mississippi River, to contain one hundred an [and] forty-eight thousand acres of land: And whereas, The said Indians never did receive the said one hundred and forty-eight thousand acres of land from the United States, but were forced to purchase lands from the Delaware nation of Indians, which purchase was agreed to and ratified by the United States: Now, in order to settle the claim of the Wyandot tribe of Indians to said land, the United States having appointed A. S. Loughery a commissioner on their part, who, with the undersigned delegates from the Wyandot nation, have agreed to the following treaty:

Preamble.

ARTICLE 1.

The United States, in consideration that the Wyandot nation of Indians shall and do hereby release, relinquish, and give up all claim to the said one hundred and forty-eight thousand acres of land agreed to be assigned and given to them by the treaty of March 17, 1842, hereby stipulate and agree to pay to the said Wyandot tribe of Indians the sum of one hundred and eighty-five thousand dollars, being at and after the rate of one dollar and twenty-five cents per acre, in the manner and form following, to wit: One hundred thousand dollars to be invested in United States Stocks, bearing five per cent. interest per annum, which interest shall be paid to them at the time and in the manner in which their present annuities are paid—and for the purpose of enabling the Wyandot Indians to pay and extinguish all their just debts, as well what is now due to the Delawares for the purchase of their lands as to others, the balance of said sum, being the sum of eighty-five thousand dollars, shall be paid to the Wyandot nation, or on their drafts, specifically describing for what the drafts are given.

In consideration that the Wyandots relinquish all claim to certain lands, the United States agree to pay to them $100,000, to be invested in Government stocks at 5 per cent per annum, and $85,000 shall be paid to them or on their drafts.

ARTICLE 2.

Expenses of negotiating this treaty to be paid by the United States.

All the reasonable expenses attending the negotiation of this treaty, including a reasonable allowance for the expenses of the delegation, signers hereto, in coming to Washington, whilst here on the business connected herewith, and in returning to their nation, shall be defrayed by the United States.

In testimony whereof, the said commissioners on the part of the United States, and the said head chief and deputies, delegates on the part of the Wyandot tribe or nation of Indians, have hereunto set their hands, at the city of Washington, D. C., this first day of April, in the year of our Lord eighteen hundred and fifty.

Ardavan S. Loughery,   [L. S.]
United States Commissioner.
F. A. Hick,   [L. S.]
Geo. J. Clark,   [L. S.]
Joel Walker,   [L. S.]
William B. Waugh, Secretary.

In presence of—
    R. W. Johnson,
    James X. MacLanahan
    Geo. F. Wood,
    James Myer,
    A. M. Mitchell,
    Jno. G. Camp,
    Richard Fields,
    S. C. Stambaugh,
    Sam. J. Potts.

TREATY WITH THE SIOUX—SISSETON AND WAHPETON BANDS, 1851.

July 23, 1851.

10 Stats., 949.
Proclamation, Feb. 24, 1853.

Articles of a treaty made and concluded at Traverse des Sioux, upon the Minnesota River, in the Territory of Minnesota, on the twenty-third day of July, eighteen hundred and fifty-one, between the United States of America, by Luke Lea, Commissioner of Indian Affairs, and Alexander Ramsey, governor and ex-officio superintendent of Indian affairs in said Territory, commissioners duly appointed for that purpose, and See-see-toan and Wah-pay-toan bands of Dakota or Sioux Indians.

Peace to exist.

ARTICLE 1. It is stipulated and solemnly agreed that the peace and friendship now so happily existing between the United States and the aforesaid bands of Indians, shall be perpetual.

Cession of lands to the United States.

ARTICLE 2. The said See-see-toan and Wah-pay-toan bands of Dakota or Sioux Indians, agree to cede, and do hereby cede, sell, and relinquish to the United States, all their lands in the State of Iowa; and, also all their lands in the Territory of Minnesota, lying east of the following line, to wit: Beginning at the junction of the Buffalo River with the Red River of the North; thence along the western bank of said Red River of the North, to the mouth of the Sioux Wood River; thence along the western bank of said Sioux Wood River to Lake Traverse; thence, along the western shore of said lake, to the southern extremity thereof; thence in a direct line, to the junction of Kampeska Lake with the Tchan-kas-an-data, or Sioux River; thence along the western bank of said river to its point of intersection with the northern line of the State of Iowa; including all the islands in said rivers and lake.

ARTICLE 3. [Stricken out.]

Payment to said Indians.

ARTICLE 4. In further and full consideration of said cession, the United States agree to pay to said Indians the sum of one million six hundred and sixty-five thousand dollars ($1,665,000,) at the several times, in the manner and for the purposes following, to wit:

1st. To the chiefs of the said bands, to enable them to settle their affairs and comply with their present just engagement; and in consideration of their removing themselves to the country set apart for them as above, which they agree to do within two years, or sooner, if required by the President, without further cost or expense to the United States, and in consideration of their subsisting themselves the first year after their removal, which they agree to do without further cost or expense on the part of the United States, the sum of two hundred and seventy-five thousand dollars, ($275,000): *Provided*, That said sum shall be paid to the chiefs in such manner as they, hereafter, in open council shall request, and as soon after the removal of said Indians to the home set apart for them, as the necessary appropriation therefor shall be made by Congress.

Proviso.

2d. To be laid out under the direction of the President for the establishment of manual-labor schools; the erection of mills and blacksmith shops, opening farms, fencing and breaking land, and for such other beneficial objects as may be deemed most conducive to the prosperity and happiness of said Indians, thirty thousand dollars, ($30,000.)

The balance of said sum of one million six hundred and sixty-five thousand dollars, ($1,665,000,) to wit: one million three hundred and sixty thousand dollars ($1,360,000) to remain in trust with the United States, and five per cent. interest thereon to be paid, annually, to said Indians for the period of fifty years, commencing the first day of July, eighteen hundred and fifty-two (1852,) which shall be in full payment of said balance, principal and interest, the said payment to be applied under the direction of the President, as follows, to wit:

3d. For a general agricultural improvement and civilization fund, the sum of twelve thousand dollars, ($12,000.)

4th. For educational purposes, the sum of six thousand dollars, ($6,000.)

5th. For the purchase of goods and provisions, the sum of ten thousand dollars, ($10,000.)

6th. For money annuity, the sum of forty thousand dollars, ($40,000.)

ARTICLE 5. The laws of the United States prohibiting the introduction and sale of spirituous liquors in the Indian country shall be in full force and effect throughout the territory hereby ceded and lying in Minnesota until otherwise directed by Congress or the President of the United States.

Laws respecting liquors to remain in force.

ARTICLE 6. Rules and regulations to protect the rights of persons and property among the Indians, parties to this treaty, and adapted to their condition and wants, may be prescribed and enforced in such manner as the President or the Congress of the United States, from time to time, shall direct.

Rules may be prescribed.

In testimony whereof, the said Commissioners, Luke Lea and Alexander Ramsey, and the undersigned Chiefs and Headmen of the aforesaid See-see-toan and Wah-pay-toan bands of Dakota or Sioux Indians, have hereunto subscribed their names and affixed their seals, in duplicate, at Traverse des Sioux, Territory of Minnesota, this twenty-third day of July, one thousand eight hundred and fifty-one.

L. Lea,   [SEAL.]

Alex. Ramsey, [SEAL.]

Een-yang-ma-nee, (Running Walker or "the Gun,")

Wee-tchan-h'pee-ee-tay-toan, (the Star face or the "Orphan,")

Ee-tay-wa-keen-yan, ("Limping Devil" or "Thunder Face,")

Eesh-ta-hum-ba, ("Sleepy Eyes,")

Oo-pee-ya-hen-day-a, (Extending his train,)

Hoak-shee-dan-wash-tay, (Good Boy,)

Ee-tay-tcho-ka, (Face in the midst,)

Hay-ha-hen-day-ma-za, (Metal Horn,)

Am-pay-too-sha, (Red Day,)

Eesh-ta-humba-koash-ka, (Sleepy Eyes young,)

A na-wang-ma-nee, (Who goes galloping on,)

Ma-h'pee-wee-tchash-ta, (Cloud man,)

Tan-pa-hee-da, (Sounding Moccasin,)	Ta-pe-ta-tan-ka, (His Big fire,)
Eenk-pa, (the upper end,)	Ma-h'pee-ya-h'na-shkan-shkan, (Moving Cloud,)
Wee-yoa-kee-yay, (Standard,)	
Wa-kan-ma-nee, (Walking Spirit,)	Wa-na-pay-a, (The pursuer,)
Ee-tay-sha, (the one that reddens his face,)	Ee-tcha-shkan-shkan-ma-nee, (Who walks shaking,)
Ta-ka-ghay, (Elk maker,)	Ta-wa-kan-he-day-ma-za, (His Metal Lightning,)
Wa-ma-ksoon-tay, ("Walnut," or Blunt headed arrow,)	Ee-tay doo-ta, (Red Face,)
Ma-za-sh'a, (Metal Sounding,)	Henok-marpi-yahdi-nape, (Reappearing Cloud,)
Ya-shoa-pee, (The wind instrument,)	
Noan-pa keen-yan, (Twice Flying,)	Tchan-hedaysh-ka-ho-toan-ma-nee, (the moving sounding Harp)
Wash-tay-da, (Good, a little,)	
Wa-keen-yan-ho-ta, (Grey Thunder,)	Ma-zaku-te-ma-ni, (Metal walks shooting,)
Wa-shee-tchoon-ma-za, (Iron Frenchman,)	A-kee-tchee-ta, (Standing Soldier.)

Signed in presence of Thomas Foster, Secretary. Nathaniel McLean, Indian Agent. Alexander Faribault, Stephen R. Riggs, Interpreters. A. S. H. White; Thos. S. Williamson; W. C. Henderson; A. Jackson; James W. Boal; W. G. Le Duc; Alexis Bailly; H. L. Dousman; Hugh Tyler.

To the Indian names are subjoined marks.

SUPPLEMENTAL ARTICLE.

Payment for land ceded.

1st. The United States do hereby stipulate to pay the Sioux bands of Indians, parties to this treaty, at the rate of ten cents per acre, for the lands included in the reservation provided for in the third article of the treaty as originally agreed upon in the following words:

"ARTICLE 3. In part consideration of the foregoing cession, the United States do hereby set apart for the future occupancy and home of the Dakota Indians, parties to this treaty, to be held by them as Indian lands are held, all that tract of country on either side of the Minnesota River, from the western boundary of the lands herein ceded, east, to the Tchay-tam-bay River on the north, and to Yellow Medicine River on the south side, to extend, on each side, a distance of not less than ten miles from the general course of said river; the boundaries of said tract to be marked out by as straight lines as practicable, whenever deemed expedient by the President, and in such manner as he shall direct:" which article has been stricken out of the treaty by the Senate, the said payment to be in lieu of said reservation: the amount when ascertained under instructions from the Department of the Interior, to be added to the trust-fund provided for in the fourth article.

Land to be set apart for said Indians.

2d. It is further stipulated, that the President be authorized, with the assent of the said band of Indians, parties to this treaty, and as soon after they shall have given their assent to the foregoing *article*, as may be convenient, to cause to be set apart by appropriate landmarks and boundaries, such tracts of country without the limits of the cession made by the first [2d] article of the treaty as may be satisfactory for their future occupancy and home: *Provided*, That the President may, by the consent of these Indians, vary the conditions aforesaid if deemed expedient.

Proviso.

TREATY WITH THE SIOUX—MDEWAKANTON AND WAHPAKOOTA BANDS, 1851.

Articles of a treaty made and concluded at Mendota, in the Territory of Minnesota, on the fifth day of August, eighteen hundred and fifty-one, between the United States of America, by Luke Lea, Commissioner of Indian Affairs, and Alexander Ramsey, governor and ex-officio superintendent of Indian affairs in said Territory, commissioners duly appointed for that purpose, and the Med-ay-wa-kan-toan and Wah-pay-koo-tay bands of Dakota and Sioux Indians.

Aug. 5, 1851.

10 Stats., 954.
Proclamation Feb. 24, 1853.

ARTICLE 1. The peace and friendship existing between the United States and the Med-ay-wa-kan-toan and Wah-pay-koo-tay bands of Dakota or Sioux Indians shall be perpetual.

Peace and friendship.

ARTICLE 2. The said Med-ay-wa-kan-toan and Wah-pay-koo-tay bands of Indians do hereby cede and relinquish all their lands and all their right, title and claim to any lands whatever, in the Territory of Minnesota, or in the State of Iowa.

Cession of lands in Minnesota and Iowa.

ARTICLE 3. [Stricken out.]

ARTICLE 4. In further and full consideration of said cession and relinquishment, the United States agree to pay to said Indians the sum of one million four hundred and ten thousand dollars, ($1,410,000,) at the several times, in the manner and for the purposes following, to wit:

Payment for said cession.

1st. To the chiefs of the said bands, to enable them to settle their affairs and comply with their present just engagements; and in consideration of their removing themselves to the country set apart for them as above, (which they agree to do within one year after the ratification of this treaty, without further cost or expense to the United States,) and in consideration of their subsisting themselves the first year after their removal, (which they agree to do without further cost or expense on the part of the United States,) the sum of two hundred and twenty thousand dollars ($220,000.) *Provided*, That said sum shall be paid, one-half to the chiefs of the Med-ay-wa-kan-toan band, and one-half to the chief and headmen of the Wah-pay-koo-tay band, in such manner as they, hereafter, in open council, shall respectively request, and as soon after the removal of said Indians to the home set apart for them as the necessary appropriations therefor shall be made by Congress.

2d. To be laid out, under the direction of the President, for the establishment of manual-labor schools; the erection of mills and blacksmith shops, opening farms, fencing and breaking land, and for such other beneficial objects as may be deemed most conducive to the prosperity and happiness of said Indians, thirty thousand dollars ($30,000.)

The balance of said sum of one million four hundred and ten thousand dollars, ($1,410,000,) to wit: one million, one hundred and sixty thousand dollars ($1,160,000) to remain in trust with the United States, and five per cent. interest thereon to be paid annually to said Indians for the period of fifty years, commencing on the first day of July, eighteen hundred and fifty-two (1852,) which shall be in full payment of said balance, principal and interest: said payments to be made and applied, under the direction of the President as follows, to wit:

3d. For a general agricultural improvement and civilization fund, the sum of twelve thousand dollars, ($12,000.)

4th. For educational purposes, the sum of six thousand dollars, ($6,000.)

5th. For the purchase of goods and provisions, the sum of ten thousand dollars, ($10,000.)

6th. For money annuity, the sum of thirty thousand dollars, ($30,000.)

The annuity provided in treaty to be paid in money.

ARTICLE 5. The entire annuity, provided for in the first section of the second article of the treaty of September twenty-ninth, eighteen hundred and thirty-seven, (1837,) including an unexpended balance that may be in the Treasury on the first of July, eighteen hundred and fifty-two, (1852,) shall thereafter be paid in money.

Spirituous liquors.

ARTICLE 6. The laws of the United States prohibiting the introduction and sale of spirituous liquors in the Indian country shall be in full force and effect throughout the territory hereby ceded and lying in Minnesota until otherwise directed by Congress or the President of the United States.

Rules and regulations.

ARTICLE 7. Rules and regulations to protect the rights of persons and property among the Indian parties to this Treaty, and adapted to their condition and wants, may be prescribed and enforced in such manner as the President or the Congress of the United States, from time to time, shall direct.

In witness whereof, the said Luke Lea and Alexander Ramsey, Commissioners on the part of the United States and the undersigned Chiefs and Headmen of the Med-ay-wa-kan-toan and Wah-pay-koo-tay bands of Dakota or Sioux Indians, have hereunto set their hands, at Mendota, in the Territory of Minnesota, this fifth day of August, Anno Domini, one thousand eight hundred and fifty-one.

L. Lea.
Alex. Ramsey.

Med-ay-wa-kan-toans.

Chief Ta-oya-te-duta, (his scarlet people, or "Little Crow,")

Headmen Wa-kan-o-zhan, (Sacred Light, or Medicine Bottle,)
Tee-tchay, (Top of the Lodge or "Jim," or "Old Thad,")
Ta-tchan-h'pee-sa-pa, (His "Black Tomahawk,")
Ma-ka-na-ho-toan-ma-nee, (At whose tread the earth resounds,)
H'-da-ee-yan-kay, (he runs rattling,)
Too-kan-a-hena-ma-nee, (Walker on the Medicine Boulders or Stones,)
Wa-m'dee-doo-ta, (Scarlet War Eagle,)
Na-ghee-yoo-shkan, (He moves the Ghosts or Shadows,)
Shoank'-a-ska, ("White Dog,")
Hoo-sa-nee-ghee, (one leg yellow or orange colored,)
Wa-keen-yan-wash-tay, ("Good Thunder,")

Chief Wa-pa-sha, (The Standard, or "Red Leaf,")

Headmen Wa-kan-hendee-o-ta, (Many Lightnings,)
Tchan-h'pee-yoo-ka, (He has a war club,)
Heen-han-doo-ta, (Red Owl,)
Ma ka-ka-ee-day, (He sets the Earth on fire,)
Ee-a-hee-herday, (He bursts out speaking,)

Chief Wa-koo-tay, (The "Shooter,")

Headmen Ma-h'pee-ya-ma za, (Metal cloud,)
Ta-ma-za-ho-wash-tay, (his good iron voice,)
Ma-ka ta-na-zheen, (He stands on the earth,)

Ee-wan-kam-ee-na-zhan, (He stands above,)
Wa-kan-ta-pay-ta, (The Spirit's Fire,)
Na-ghee-mee-tcha-keetay, (He kills the Ghosts,)
Een-yan-sha-sha, (Red Stones,)
Ee-day-wa-kan, (Sacred Blaze,)
Ta-sag-yay-ma-za, (His metal Staff,)

Chief Ma-h'pee mee-tchash-tay, (man of the sky,)

Headmen Wee-tchan-h'pee, (The Star,)
Ta-tay-na-zhee-na, (Little standing Wind,)

Headmen Hoak-shee-dan-doo-ta, (Scarlet Boy,)
Am-pay-sho-ta, (Smoky Day,)
Ha-ha-ka-ma-za, (Metal Elk,)
Ta-tay-h'moo-he-ya-ya, ("Whistling Wind,")
Wa-pa-ma-nee, (He strikes walking,)
Ma-h'pee-ya-wa-kan, (Sacred Cloud,)
Ta-tchan-h'pee-ma-za, (His Iron War Club,)

Chief Ma-za-ho-ta, (Gray Metal,)

Headmen Wa-soo-mee-tchash-ta-shnee, (Wicked or "Bad Hail,")
Oan-ketay-hee-dan, (Little Water-God or "Little Whale,")
Tcha-noon-pay-sa, (The Smoker,)
Ta-tay-to-kay-tcha, (Other wind,)
Ka-ho, (The Rambler about,)

Chief Ta-tchan-koo-wash-tay, (Good Road,)

Headmen Ta-tay-o-wo-teen-ma-nee, (Roaring Wind that walks,)
O-yay-tchan-ma-nee, (Track Maker,)

	Ta-shoark-ay, (His Dog,)	Headmen	Pay-pay, (Sharp,)
Chief	Sha-k'pay, ("Six,")		Ta-wo-ta-way-doo-ta, (His Scarlet Armor,)
Headmen	A-no-ghee-ma-zheen, (He that stands on both sides,)		Hay-pee, (Third Son,)
	Hoo-ya-pa, (Eagle Head,)		A-pay-ho-ta, (Grey mane or crest,)
	Ta-tay-mee-na, (Round Wind,)		Ho-tan-een, (His voice can be heard,)
	Ka-t'pan-t'pan-oo, (He comes pounding to pieces,)		Ma-h'pee-ya-shee-tcha, (Bad Cloud,)
	Ma-h'pee-ya-henda-keen-yan, (Walking across a cloud,)		Ta-wa-tcheen, (His mind,)
	Wa-pee-ghee, (The orange red speckled cloud,)		Han-yay-too-ko-kee-pa-pee, (Night which is feared,)
	Ma-za-wa-menoo-ha, (Gourd shell metal medicine rattle,)		
Chief	Hay-ee-tcha-h'moo-ma-nee, (Horn whistling walking,)		

In presence of Thomas Foster, Secretary. Nathaniel McLean, Indian Agent. Alexander Fairboult, P. Prescott, G. H. Pond, Interpreters. David Olmstead; W. C. Henderson; Alexis Bailly; Richard Chute; A. Jackson; A. L. Larpenteur; W. H. Randall, Sr.; A. S. H. White; H. L. Dousman; Frederic B. Sibley; Marten McLeod; Geo. H. Faribault.

To the Indian names are subjoined marks.

SUPPLEMENTAL ARTICLE.

1st. The United States do hereby stipulate to pay the Sioux bands of Indians, parties to this treaty, at the rate of ten cents per acre, for the lands included in the reservation provided for in the third article of the treaty as originally agreed upon in the following words: *Payment for said cession.*

"ARTICLE 3. In part consideration of the foregoing cession and relinquishment, the United States do hereby set apart for the future occupancy and home of the Dakota Indians, parties to this treaty, to be held by them as Indian lands are held, a tract of country of the average width of ten miles on either side of the Minnesota River, and bounded on the west by the Tchaytam-bay and Yellow Medicine Rivers, and on the east by the Little Rock River and a line running due south from its mouth to the Waraju River; the boundaries of said tract to be marked out by as straight lines as practicable, whenever and in such manner as the President of the United States shall direct: *Provided,* That said tract shall be held and occupied by said bands in common, and that they shall hereafter participate equally and alike, in all the benefits derived from any former treaty between said bands, or either of them, and the United States," which article has been stricken out of the treaty by the Senate. The said payment to be in lieu of said reservation; the amount, when ascertained under instructions from the Department of the Interior, to be added to the trust fund provided for in the fourth article. *Tract of land to be set apart.* *To be occupied in common.*

2d. It is further stipulated that the President be authorized, with the assent of the said bands of Indians, parties to this treaty, and as soon after they shall have given their assent to the foregoing article, as may be convenient, to cause to be set apart by appropriate landmarks and boundaries, such tracts of country without the limits of the cession made by the first article of the treaty as may be satisfactory for their future occupancy and home: *Provided,* That the President may, by the consent of these Indians, vary the conditions aforesaid if deemed expedient.

TREATY OF FORT LARAMIE WITH SIOUX, ETC., 1851.

Sept. 17, 1851.

11 Stats., p. 749.

Articles of a treaty made and concluded at Fort Laramie, in the Indian Territory, between D. D. Mitchell, superintendent of Indian affairs, and Thomas Fitzpatrick, Indian agent, commissioners specially appointed and authorized by the President of the United States, of the first part, and the chiefs, headmen, and braves of the following Indian nations, residing south of the Missouri River, east of the Rocky Mountains, and north of the lines of Texas and New Mexico, viz, the Sioux or Dahcotahs, Cheyennes, Arrapahoes, Crows, Assinaboines, Gros-Ventre Mandans, and Arrickaras, parties of the second part, on the seventeenth day of September, A. D. one thousand eight hundred and fifty-one.[a]

Peace to be observed.

ARTICLE 1. The aforesaid nations, parties to this treaty, having assembled for the purpose of establishing and confirming peaceful relations amongst themselves, do hereby covenant and agree to abstain in future from all hostilities whatever against each other, to maintain good faith and friendship in all their mutual intercourse, and to make an effective and lasting peace.

Roads may be established.

ARTICLE 2. The aforesaid nations do hereby recognize the right of the United States Government to establish roads, military and other posts, within their respective territories.

Indians to be protected.

ARTICLE 3. In consideration of the rights and privileges acknowledged in the preceding article, the United States bind themselves to protect the aforesaid Indian nations against the commission of all depredations by the people of the said United States, after the ratification of this treaty.

Depredations on whites to be satisfied.

ARTICLE 4. The aforesaid Indian nations do hereby agree and bind themselves to make restitution or satisfaction for any wrongs committed, after the ratification of this treaty, by any band or individual of their people, on the people of the United States, whilst lawfully residing in or passing through their respective territories.

Boundaries of lands.

ARTICLE 5. The aforesaid Indian nations do hereby recognize and acknowledge the following tracts of country, included within the metes and boundaries hereinafter designated, as their respective territories, viz:

Sioux.

The territory of the Sioux or Dahcotah Nation, commencing the mouth of the White Earth River, on the Missouri River; thence in a southwesterly direction to the forks of the Platte River; thence up the north fork of the Platte River to a point known as the Red Bute, or where the road leaves the river; thence along the range of mountains known as the Black Hills, to the head-waters of Heart River; thence down Heart River to its mouth; and thence down the Missouri River to the place of beginning.

Grosventre, etc.

The territory of the Gros Ventre, Mandans, and Arrickaras Nations, commencing at the mouth of Heart River; thence up the Missouri River to the mouth of the Yellowstone River; thence up the Yellowstone River to the mouth of Powder River in a southeasterly direction, to the head-waters of the Little Missouri River; thence along the Black Hills to the head of Heart River, and thence down Heart River to the place of beginning.

Assiniboin.

The territory of the Assinaboin Nation, commencing at the mouth of Yellowstone River; thence up the Missouri River to the mouth of the Muscle-shell River; thence from the mouth of the Muscle-shell River in a southeasterly direction until it strikes the head-waters of

---

[a] This treaty as signed was ratified by the Senate with an amendment changing the annuity in Article 7 from fifty to ten years, subject to acceptance by the tribes. Assent of all tribes except the Crows was procured (see Upper Platte C., 570, 1853, Indian Office) and in subsequent agreements this treaty has been recognized as in force (see post p. 776).

Big Dry Creek; thence down that creek to where it empties into the Yellowstone River, nearly opposite the mouth of Powder River, and thence down the Yellowstone River to the place of beginning.

The territory of the Blackfoot Nation, commencing at the mouth of Muscle-shell River; thence up the Missouri River to its source; thence along the main range of the Rocky Mountains, in a southerly direction, to the head-waters of the northern source of the Yellowstone River; thence down the Yellowstone River to the mouth of Twenty-five Yard Creek; thence across to the head-waters of the Muscle-shell River, and thence down the Muscle-shell River to the place of beginning. *Blackfoot.*

The territory of the Crow Nation, commencing at the mouth of Powder River on the Yellowstone; thence up Powder River to its source; thence along the main range of the Black Hills and Wind River Mountains to the head-waters of the Yellowstone River; thence down the Yellowstone River to the mouth of Twenty-five Yard Creek; thence to the head waters of the Muscle-shell River; thence down the Muscle-shell River to its mouth; thence to the head-waters of Big Dry Creek, and thence to its mouth. *Crow.*

The territory of the Cheyennes and Arrapahoes, commencing at the Red Bute, or the place where the road leaves the north fork of the Platte River; thence up the north fork of the Platte River to its source; thence along the main range of the Rocky Mountains to the head-waters of the Arkansas River; thence down the Arkansas River to the crossing of the Santa Fé road; thence in a northwesterly direction to the forks of the Platte River, and thence up the Platte River to the place of beginning. *Cheyenne and Arapaho.*

It is, however, understood that, in making this recognition and acknowledgement, the aforesaid Indian nations do not hereby abandon or prejudice any rights or claims they may have to other lands; and further, that they do not surrender the privilege of hunting, fishing, or passing over any of the tracts of country heretofore described. *Rights in other lands.*

ARTICLE 6. The parties to the second part of this treaty having selected principals or head-chiefs for their respective nations, through whom all national business will hereafter be conducted, do hereby bind themselves to sustain said chiefs and their successors during good behavior. *Head chiefs of said tribes.*

ARTICLE 7. In consideration of the treaty stipulations, and for the damages which have or may occur by reason thereof to the Indian nations, parties hereto, and for their maintenance and the improvement of their moral and social customs, the United States bind themselves to deliver to the said Indian nations the sum of fifty thousand dollars per annum for the term of ten years, with the right to continue the same at the discretion of the President of the United States for a period not exceeding five years thereafter, in provisions, merchandise, domestic animals, and agricultural implements, in such proportions as may be deemed best adapted to their condition by the President of the United States, to be distributed in proportion to the population of the aforesaid Indian nations. *Annuities.*

ARTICLE 8. It is understood and agreed that should any of the Indian nations, parties to this treaty, violate any of the provisions thereof, the United States may withhold the whole or a portion of the annuities mentioned in the preceding article from the nation so offending, until, in the opinion of the President of the United States, proper satisfaction shall have been made. *Annuities suspended by violation of treaty.*

In testimony whereof the said D. D. Mitchell and Thomas Fitzpatrick commissioners as aforesaid, and the chiefs, headmen, and braves, parties hereto, have set their hands and affixed their marks, on the day and at the place first above written.

D. D. Mitchell
Thomas Fitzpatrick
Commissioners.

Sioux:
Mah-toe-wha-you-whey, his x mark.
Mah-kah-toe-zah-zah, his x mark.
Bel-o-ton-kah-tan-ga, his x mark.
Nah-ka-pah-gi-gi, his x mark.
Mak-toe-sah-bi-chis, his x mark.
Meh-wha-tah-ni-hans-kah, his x mark.
  Cheyennes:
Wah-ha-nis-satta, his x mark.
Voist-ti-toe-vetz, his x mark.
Nahk-ko-me-ien, his x mark.
Koh-kah-y-wh-cum-est, his x mark.
  Arrapahoes:
Bè-ah-té-a-qui-sah, his x mark.
Neb-ni-bah-seh-it, his x mark.
Beh-kah-jay-beth-sah-es, his x mark.

Crows:
Arra-tu-ri-sash, his x mark.
Doh-chepit-seh-chi-es, his x mark.
  Assinaboines:
Mah-toe-wit-ko, his x mark.
Toe-tah-ki-eh-nan, his x mark.
  Mandans and Gros Ventres:
Nochk-pit-shi-toe-pish, his x mark.
She-oh-mant-ho, his x mark.
  Arickarees:
Koun-hei-ti-shan, his x mark.
Bi-atch-tah-wetch, his x mark.

In the presence of—

A. B. Chambers, secretary.
S. Cooper, colonel, U. S. Army.
R. H. Chilton, captain, First Drags.
Thomas Duncan, captain, Mounted Riflemen.
Thos. G. Rhett, brevet captain R. M. R.
W. L. Elliott, first lieutenant R. M. R.
C. Campbell, interpreter for Sioux.
John S. Smith, interpreter for Cheyennes.
Robert Meldrum, interpreter for the Crows.

H. Culbertson, interpreter for Assiniboines and Gros Ventres.
Francois L'Etalie, interpreter for Arickarees.
John Pizelle, interpreter for the Arrapahoes.
B. Gratz Brown.
Robert Campbell.
Edmond F. Chouteau.

TREATY WITH THE CHICKASAW, 1852.

June 22, 1852.

10 Stat., 974.
Ratified Aug. 13, 1852.
Proclaimed, Feb. 24, 1853.

Articles of a treaty concluded at Washington, on the 22nd day of June, 1852, between Kenton Harper, commissioner on the part of the United States, and Colonel Edmund Pickens, Benjamin S. Love, and Sampson Folsom, commissioners duly appointed for that purpose, by the Chickasaw tribe of Indians.

Agent to reside among the Chickasaws.

ARTICLE 1. The Chickasaw tribe of Indians acknowledge themselves to be under the guardianship of the United States, and as a means of securing the protection guaranteed to them by former treaties, it is agreed that an Agent of the United States shall continue to reside among them.

Sale of Chickasaw lands.

ARTICLE 2. That the expenses attending the sale of the land ceded by the Chickasaws to the United States, under the treaty of 1832, having, for some time past, exceeded the receipts, it is agreed that the remnant of the lands so ceded and yet unsold, shall be disposed of as soon as practicable, under the direction of the President of the United States in such manner and in such quantities, as, in his judgment, shall be least expensive to the Chickasaws, and most conducive to their benefit: Provided, That a tract of land, including the grave-yard near the town of Pontotoc, where many of the Chickasaws and their white friends are buried, and not exceeding four acres in quantity, shall be, and is hereby set apart and conveyed to the said town of Pontotoc to be held sacred for the purposes of a public burial-ground forever.

Burial ground in Pontotoc.

Settlement of title of Chickasaws to a tract in Tennessee.

ARTICLE 3. It is hereby agreed that the question of the right of the Chickasaws, so long contended for by them, to a reservation of four miles square on the River Sandy, in the State of Tennessee, and particularly described in the 4th article of the treaty concluded at Oldtown, on the 19th day of October, 1818, shall be submitted to the Secretary of the Interior who shall decide, what amount, if any thing, shall be paid to the Chickasaws for said reservation: Provided, however, That the amount so to be paid shall not exceed one dollar and twenty-five cents per acre.

Proviso.

ARTICLE 4. The Chickasaws allege that in the management and disbursement of their funds by the government, they have been subjected to losses and expenses which properly should be borne by the United States.   With the view, therefore, of doing full justice in the premises, it is hereby agreed that there shall be, at as early a day as practicable, an account stated, under the direction of the Secretary of the Interior, exhibiting in detail all the moneys which, from time to time, have been placed in the Treasury to the credit of the Chickasaw nation, resulting from the treaties of 1832, and 1834, and all the disbursements made therefrom.   And said account as stated, shall be submitted to the Chickasaws, who shall have the privilege, within a reasonable time, of filing exceptions thereto, and any exceptions so filed shall be referred to the Secretary of the Interior, who shall adjudicate the same according to the principles of law and equity, and his decisions shall be final and conclusive on all concerned.

It is also alleged by the Chickasaws that there are numerous cases in which moneys held in trust by the United States for the benefit of orphans and incompetent Chickasaws, have been wrongfully paid out to persons having no right to receive the same.   It is therefore further agreed, that all such cases shall be investigated by the Agent of the United States under the direction of the Secretary of the Interior. And if it shall appear to the satisfaction of said Secretary, that any of the orphans and incompetents have been defrauded by such wrongful payments, the amount thus misapplied shall be accounted for by the United States, as if no such payment had been made: *Provided*, That the provisions of this article shall not be so construed as to impose any obligations on the United States to reimburse any expenditures heretofore made in conformity with the stipulations contained in the treaties of 1832 and 1834: *And provided further*, That the United States shall not be liable to repay moneys held in trust for the benefit of orphans and incompetent Chickasaws, in any case in which payment of such moneys has been made upon the recommendation or certificate of the persons appointed for that purpose in the Fourth Article of the Treaty of 1834, or of their successors, and in other respects in conformity with the provisions of that article: *And provided further*, That the United States shall not be held responsible for any reservation of land or of any sale, lease, or other disposition of the same, made, sold, leased, or otherwise disposed of, in conformity with the several provisions of said treaties of 1832 and 1834.

ARTICLE 5. The Chickasaws are desirous that the whole amount of their national fund shall remain with the United States, in trust for the benefit of their people, and that the same shall on no account be diminished.   It is, therefore, agreed that the United States shall continue to hold said fund, in trust, as aforesaid, and shall constantly keep the same invested in safe and profitable stocks, the interest upon which shall be annually paid to the Chickasaw nation: *Provided*, That so much of said funds as the Chickasaws may require for the purpose of enabling them to effect the permanent settlement of their tribe as contemplated by the treaty of 1834, shall be subject to the control of their General Council.

ARTICLE 6. The powers and duties confered on certain persons particularly mentioned in the 4th article of the treaty of 1834, and their successors in office, shall hereafter be vested in and performed by the General Council of the Chickasaws, or such officers as may be by said council appointed for that purpose; and no certificate or deed given or executed by the persons aforesaid, from which the approval of the President of the United States has once been withheld, shall be hereafter approved unless the same shall first receive the sanction of the Chickasaw Council, or the officers appointed as aforesaid, and of the agent of the United States for said Chickasaw nation.

Marginal notes:

Settlement of Chickasaw claims.

Chickasaw fund to be held in trust.

Proviso.

Payment of the
Chickasaw funds re-
stricted.
ARTICLE 7. No claim or account shall hereafter be paid by the Government of the United States out of the Chickasaw fund, unless the same shall have first been considered and allowed by the Chickasaw General Council: *Provided, however*, That this clause shall not effect payment upon claims existing contracts made by authority of the Chickasaw General Council, or interfere with the due administration of the acts of Congress, regulating trade and intercourse with the Indian tribes.

Proviso.

Accounts.
ARTICLE 8. It is further agreed, that regular semiannual accounts of the receipts and disbursements of the Chickasaw fund shall be furnished the Chickasaw Council by the Government of the United States.

Expenses of the
treaty.
ARTICLE 9. The sum of fifteen hundred dollars shall be paid the Chickasaw nation, in full of expenses incurred by their commissioners in negotiating this treaty.

Payments: to whom
to be made.
ARTICLE 10. And it is further stipulated, That in no case hereafter, shall any money due or to be paid under this treaty or any former treaty between the same contracting parties be paid to any agent or attorney; but shall in all cases be paid directly to the party or parties primarily entitled thereto.

In witness whereof the contracting parties have hereto set their hands and seals, the day and year above written.

Kenton Harper,
Commissioner for the United States. [SEAL.]
Edmund Pickens, his x mark [SEAL.]
Benjamin S. Love, [SEAL.]
Sampson Folsom, [SEAL.]
Commissioners for the Chickasaws.

In presence of—
    Charles E. Mix, chief clerk, Office Indian Affairs,
    L. R. Smoot,
    T. R. Cruttenden,
    H. Miller,
    Aaron V. Brown, interpreter.

TREATY WITH THE APACHE, 1852.

July 1, 1852.

10 Stat., 979.
Ratified Mar. 23, 1853.
Proclaimed Mar. 25, 1853.
Articles of a treaty made and entered into at Santa Fe, New Mexico, on the first day of July in the year of our Lord one thousand eight hundred and fifty-two, by and between Col. E. V. Sumner, U. S. A., commanding the 9th Department and in charge of the executive office of New Mexico, and John Greiner, Indian agent in and for the Territory of New Mexico, and acting superintendent of Indian affairs of said Territory, representing the United States, and Cuentas, Azules, Blancito, Negrito, Capitan Simon, Capitan Vuelta, and Mangus Colorado, chiefs, acting on the part of the Apache Nation of Indians, situate and living within the limits of the United States.

Authority of the
United States ac-
knowledged.
ARTICLE 1. Said nation or tribe of Indians through their authorized Chiefs aforesaid do hereby acknowledge and declare that they are lawfully and exclusively under the laws, jurisdiction, and government of the United States of America, and to its power and authority they do hereby submit.

Peace to exist.
ARTICLE 2. From and after the signing of this Treaty hostilities between the contracting parties shall forever cease, and perpetual peace and amity shall forever exist between said Indians and the The Apaches not to
assist other tribes in
hostilities. Government and people of the United States; the said nation, or tribe of Indians, hereby binding themselves most solemnly never to asso-

ciate with or give countenance or aid to any tribe or band of Indians, or other persons or powers, who may be at any time at war or enmity with the government or people of said United States.

ARTICLE 3. Said nation, or tribe of Indians, do hereby bind themselves for all future time to treat honestly and humanely all citizens of the United States, with whom they have intercourse, as well as all persons and powers, at peace with the said United States, who may be lawfully among them, or with whom they may have any lawful intercourse. *Good treatment of citizens of the United States and nations at peace with them.*

ARTICLE 4. All said nation, or tribe of Indians, hereby bind themselves to refer all cases of aggression against themselves or their property and territory, to the government of the United States for adjustment, and to conform in all things to the laws, rules, and regulations of said government in regard to the Indian tribes. *Cases of aggression on them to be referred to Government. Laws to be conformed to.*

ARTICLE 5. Said nation, or tribe of Indians, do hereby bind themselves for all future time to desist and refrain from making any "incursions within the Territory of Mexico" of a hostile or predatory character; and that they will for the future refrain from taking and conveying into captivity any of the people or citizens of Mexico, or the animals or property of the people or government of Mexico; and that they will, as soon as possible after the signing of this treaty, surrender to their agent all captives now in their possession. *Provisions against incursions into Mexico.*

ARTICLE 6. Should any citizen of the United States, or other person or persons subject to the laws of the United States, murder, rob, or otherwise maltreat any Apache Indian or Indians, he or they shall be arrested and tried, and upon conviction, shall be subject to all the penalties provided by law for the protection of the persons and property of the people of the said States. *Persons injuring the Apaches to be tried and punished.*

ARTICLE 7. The people of the United States of America shall have free and safe passage through the territory of the aforesaid Indians, under such rules and regulations as may be adopted by authority of the said States. *Free passage over the Apache territory.*

ARTICLE 8. In order to preserve tranquility and to afford protection to all the people and interests of the contracting parties, the government of the United States of America will establish such military posts and agencies, and authorize such trading houses at such times and places as the said government may designate. *Military posts, agencies, and trading houses to be established.*

ARTICLE 9. Relying confidently upon the justice and the liberality of the aforesaid government, and anxious to remove every possible cause that might disturb their peace and quiet, it is agreed by the aforesaid Apache's that the government of the United States shall at its earliest convenience designate, settle, and adjust their territorial boundaries, and pass and execute in their territory such laws as may be deemed conducive to the prosperity and happiness of said Indians. *Territorial boundaries to be established.*

ARTICLE 10. For and in consideration of the faithful performance of all the stipulations herein contained, by the said Apache's Indians, the government of the United States will grant to said Indians such donations, presents, and implements, and adopt such other liberal and humane measures as said government may deem meet and proper. *Presents to the Apaches.*

ARTICLE 11. This Treaty shall be binding upon the contracting parties from and after the signing of the same, subject only to such modifications and amendments as may be adopted by the government of the United States; and, finally, this treaty is to receive a liberal construction, at all times and in all places, to the end that the said Apache Indians shall not be held responsible for the conduct of others, and that the government of the United States shall so legislate and act as to secure the permanent prosperity and happiness of said Indians. *When treaty to be binding.*

How construed.

In faith whereof we the undersigned have signed this Treaty, and affixed thereunto our seals, at the City of Santa Fé, this the first day of July in the year of our Lord one thousand eight hundred and fifty-two.

E. V. Sumner,   [SEAL.]
Bvt. Col. U. S. A. commanding Ninth Department
In charge of Executive Office of New Mexico.
John Greiner,   [SEAL.]
Act. Supt. Indian Affairs, New Mexico.
Capitan Vuelta, his x mark   [SEAL.]
Cuentas Azules, his x mark   [SEAL.]
Blancito ———, his x mark   [SEAL.]
Negrito ———, his x mark   [SEAL.]
Capitan Simon, his x mark   [SEAL.]
Mangus Colorado, his x mark   [SEAL.]

Witnesses:
F. A. Cunningham,
Paymaster, U. S. A.
J. C. McFerran,
1st Lt. 3d Inf. Act. Ast. Adj. Gen.
Caleb Sherman.
Fred. Saynton.
Chas. McDougall,
Surgeon, U. S. A.
S. M. Baird.

Witness to the signing of Mangus Colorado:
John Pope,
Bvt. Capt. T. E.

TREATY WITH THE COMANCHE, KIOWA, AND APACHE, 1853.

<table>
<tr>
<td>

July 27, 1853.

10 Stats., 1013.
Ratified Apr. 12, 1854.
Proclaimed Feb. 12, 1855 [4].

</td>
<td>

Articles of a treaty, made and concluded at Fort Atkinson, in the Indian Territory, of the United States of America, on the 27th day of July, anno Domini eighteen hundred and fifty-three, between the United States of America, by Thomas Fitzpatrick, Indian agent, and sole commissioner, duly appointed for that purpose, and the Camanche, and Kiowa, and Apache tribes or nations of Indians, inhabiting the said territory south of the Arkansas River.

</td>
</tr>
</table>

Peace and friendship to exist with United States.

ARTICLE 1. Peace, friendship, and amity shall hereafter exist between the United States and the Camanche and Kiowa, and Apache tribes of Indians, parties to this treaty, and the same shall be perpetual.

Peace to exist between the tribes.

ARTICLE 2. The Camanche, Kiowa, and Apache tribes of Indians do hereby jointly and severally covenant that peaceful relations shall likewise be maintained amongst themselves in future; and that they will abstain from all hostilities whatsoever against each other, and cultivate mutual good-will and friendship.

Certain rights of United States acknowledged.

ARTICLE 3. The aforesaid Indian tribes do also hereby fully recognize and acknowledge the right of the United States to lay off and mark out roads or highways—to make reservations of land necessary thereto—to locate depots—and to establish military and other posts within the territories inhabited by the said tribes; and also to prescribe and enforce, in such manner as the President or the Congress of the United States shall from time to time direct, rules and regulations to protect the rights of persons and property among the said Indian tribes.

Restitution for injuries by Indians.

ARTICLE 4. The Camanche, Kiowa, and Apache tribes, parties as before recited, do further agree and bind themselves to make restitution or satisfaction for any injuries done by any band or any individuals of their respective tribes to the people of the United States who may be lawfully residing in or passing through their said territories; and to abstain hereafter from levying contributions from, or molesting them in any manner; and, so far as may be in their power, to render assistance to such as need relief, and to facilitate their safe passage.

ARTICLE 5. The Camanche, and Kiowa, and Apache tribes of Indians, parties to this treaty, do hereby solemnly covenant and agree to refrain in future from warlike incursions into the Mexican provinces, and from all depredations upon the inhabitants thereof; and they do likewise bind themselves to restore all captives that may hereafter be taken by any of the bands, war-parties, or individuals of the said several tribes, from the Mexican provinces aforesaid, and to make proper and just compensation for any wrongs that may be inflicted upon the people thereof by them, either to the United States or to the Republic of Mexico, as the President of the United States may direct and require.

ARTICLE 6. In consideration of the foregoing agreements on the part of the Camanche, and Kiowa, and Apache tribes, parties to this treaty— of the losses which they may sustain by reason of the travel of the people of the United States through their territories—and for the better support, and the improvement of the social condition of the said tribes— the United States do bind themseles, and by these presents stipulate to deliver to the Camanche, Kiowa, and Apache tribes aforesaid, the sum of eighteen thousand dollars per annum, for and during the term of ten years next ensuing from this date, and for the additional term of five years, if, in the opinion of the President of the United States, such extension shall be advisable;—the same to be given to them in goods, merchandise, provisions, or agricultural implements, or in such shape as may be best adapted to their wants, and as the President of the United States may designate, and to be distributed amongst the said several tribes in proportion to the respective numbers of each tribe.

ARTICLE 7. The United States do moreover bind themselves, in consideration of the covenants contained in the preceding articles of this treaty, to protect and defend the Indian tribes, parties hereto, against the committal of any depredations upon them, and in their territories, by the people of the United States, for and during the term for which this treaty shall be in force, and to compensate them for any injuries that may result therefrom.

ARTICLE 8. It is also stipulated and provided, by and between the parties to this treaty, that should any of the Indian tribes aforesaid violate any of the conditions, provisions, or agreements herein contained, or fail to perform any of the obligations entered into on their part, then the United States may withhold the whole or a part of the annuities mentioned in the sixth article of this treaty, from the tribe so offending, until, in the opinion of the President or the Congress of the United States, proper satisfaction shall have been made, or until persons amongst the said Indians offending against the laws of the United States shall have been delivered up to justice.

ARTICLE 9. It is also consented to and determined between the parties hereto, that the annuities to be given on the part of the United States, as provided in the sixth article of this treaty, shall be delivered to the said Indian tribes collectively, at or in the vicinity of Beaver Creek, yearly, during the month of July in each year, until some other time and place shall have been designated by the President of the United States, in which event the said Indian tribes shall have due notice thereof, and the place of distribution which may be selected shall always be some point within the territories occupied by the said tribes.

ARTICLE 10. It is agreed between the United States and the Camanche, Kiowa, and Apache tribes of Indians, that, should it at any time hereafter be considered by the United States as a proper policy to

Conduct to persons passing through the Indian country.

Provisions against invasion of Mexican Territory.

Captives to be restored.

Compensation to be made.

Eighteen thousand dollars per annum to be paid said tribes, in such mode as the President shall prescribe.

Protection of Indians.

Annuities may be withheld for violation of this treaty.

Annuities, when and where to be paid.

Annuities may be changed into farms.

establish farms among and for the benefit of said Indians, it shall be discretionary with the President, by and with the advice and consent of the Senate, to change the annuities herein provided for, or any part thereof, into a fund for that purpose.

In witness whereof, the said Thomas Fitzpatrick, Indian Agent, and sole commissioner on the part of the United States, and the undersigned chiefs and headmen of the Camanche and Kiowa, and Apache tribes or nations, have hereunto set their hands, at Fort Atkinson, in the Indian Territory of the United States, this twenty-seventh day of July, A. D. eighteen hundred and fifty-three.

Thomas Fitzpatrick,
Indian Agent, and Commissioner on behalf of the United States.

B. Gratz Brown, Secretary.
R. H. Chilton.
B. T. Moylero.

Wulea-boo, his x mark (Shaved Head) chief Camanche
Wa-ya-ba-tos-a, his x mark (White Eagle) chief of band
Hai-nick-seu, his x mark (The Crow) chief of band
Paro-sa-wa-no, his x mark (Ten Sticks) chief of band
Wa-ra-kon-alta, his x mark (Poor Cayote Wolf) chief of band
Ka-na-re-tah, his x mark (One that Rides the Clouds) chief of the southern Camanches.
To-hau-sen, his x mark (Little Mountain) chief Kiowas
Si-tank-ki, his x mark (Sitting Bear) war chief

Tah-ka-eh-bool, his x mark (The Bad Smelling Saddle) headman
Che-koon-ki, his x mark (Black Horse) headman
On-ti-an-te, his x mark (The Snow Flake) headman
El-bo-in-ki, his x mark (Yellow Hair) headman
Si-tah-le, his x mark (Poor Wolf) chief Apache
Oh-ah-te-kah, his x mark (Poor Bear) headman
Ah-zaah, his x mark (Prairie Wolf) headman
Kootz-zah, his x mark (The Cigar) headman

Witness:
B. B. Dayton,
Geo. M. Alexander,
T. Polk,
Geo. Collier, jr.

We do hereby accept and consent to the *Senate* amendments to the treaty aforesaid, and agree that the same may be considered as a part thereof.

In testimony whereof we have hereunto set our hands and affixed our seals, this 21st day of July, A. D. 1854.

Camanches:
To-che-ra-nah-boo, (Shaved Head,) his x mark.
Wa-ya-ba-to-sa, (White Eagle,) his x mark.
Hai-nick-seu, (Crow,) his x mark.
Ty-har-re-ty, (One who runs after women,) his x mark.
Para-sar-a-man-no, (Ten Bears,) his x mark.

Kiowas:
To-han-seu, (Little Mountain,) his x mark.
Ti-sank-ki, (Sitting Bear,) his x mark.
Ko-a-ty-ka, (Wolf outside,) his x mark.

Executed in presence of—
Aquilla T. Ridgely, assistant surgeon, U. S. Army.
A. H. Plummer, brevet second lieutenant, Sixth Infantry.
Paul Carrey.
John Kinney, United States interpreter.
H. E. Nixon, clerk.

I certify that the foregoing amendments to the treaty of 27th day of July, 1853, was read and explained to the chiefs, and that they consented to, and signed the same on the 21st day of July, 1854.

J. W. Whitfield, Indian Agent.

TREATY WITH THE ROGUE RIVER, 1853.

Whereas a treaty was made and entered into at Table Rock, near Rogue River, in the Territory of Oregon, this 10th day of September, A. D. 1853, by and between Joel Palmer, superintendent of Indian affairs, and Samuel H. Culver, Indian agent, on the part of the United States; and Jo-aps-er-ka-har, principal chief, Sam To-qua-he-ar, and Jim Ana-cha-a-rah, subordinate chiefs, and others, head-men of the bands of the Rogue River tribe of Indians, on the part of said tribe.

Sept. 10, 1853.

10 Stats., 1018.
Ratified Apr. 12, 1854.
Proclaimed Feb. 5, 1855.

ARTICLE 1. The Rogue River tribe of Indians do hereby cede and relinquish, for the considerations hereinafter specified, to the United States, all their right, title, interest, and claim to all the lands lying in that part of the Territory of Oregon, and bounded by lines designated as follows, to wit:

Cession of lands in Oregon.

Commencing at a point one mile below the mouth of Applegate Creek, on the south side of Rogue River, running thence southerly to the highlands dividing the waters of Applegate Creek from those of Althouse Creek, thence along said highlands to the summit of the Siskiyon range of mountains, thence easterly to Pilot Rock, thence northeasterly to the summit of the Cascade range, thence northerly along the said Cascade range to Pitt's Peak, continuing northerly to Rogue River, thence westerly to the head-waters of Jump-off-jo Creek, thence down said creek to the intersection of the same with a line due north from the place of beginning, thence to the place of beginning.

ARTICLE 2. It is agreed on the part of the United States that the aforesaid tribe shall be allowed to occupy temporarily that portion of the above-described tract of territory bounded as follows, to wit: Commencing on the north side of Rogue River, at the mouth of Evan's Creek; thence up said creek to the upper end of a small prairie bearing in a northwesterly direction from Table Mountain, or Upper Table Rock, thence through the gap to the south side of the cliff of the said mountain, thence in a line to Rogue River, striking the southern base of Lower Table Rock, thence down said river to the place of beginning. It being understood that this described tract of land shall be deemed and considered an Indian reserve, until a suitable selection shall be made by the direction of the President of the United States for their permanent residence and buildings erected thereon, and provision made for their removal.

Indians to occupy a portion of the ceded land temporarily.

Permanent home to be selected.

ARTICLE 3. For and in consideration of the cession and relinquishment contained in article 1st, the United States agree to pay to the aforesaid tribe the sum of sixty thousand dollars, fifteen thousand of which sum to be retained, (according to the stipulations of article 4th of a "treaty of peace made and entered into on the 8th day of September, 1853,[a] between Gen'l Jo. Lane, commanding forces of Oregon Territory, and Jo., principal chief, Sam and Jim, subordinate chiefs, on the part of the Rogue River tribe of Indians,") by the superintendent of Indian affairs, to pay for the property of the whites destroyed by them during the late war, the amount of property so destroyed to be estimated by three disinterested commissioners, to be appointed by the superintendent of Indian affairs, or otherwise, as the President may direct. Five thousand dollars to be expended in the purchase of agricultural implements, blankets, clothing, and such other goods as may be deemed by the superintendent, or agent most conducive to the comfort and necessities of said tribe, on or before the 1st day of September, 1854; and for the payment of such permanent improvements as may have been made by land claimants on the aforesaid reserve, the

Payment for said cession.

---

[a] This agreement is unratified and a copy of the original agreement on file in the Indian Office (Oregon, 1844–1858, Ore. Sup. L., 323) has been included in the Appendix, post, p. 1049.

value of which to be ascertained by three persons appointed by the said superintendent.

The remaining forty thousand dollars to be paid in sixteen equal annual instalments, of two thousand five hundred dollars each, (commencing on or about the 1st day of September, 1854,) in blankets, clothing, farming-utensils, stock, and such other articles as may be deemed most conducive to the interests of said tribe.

Buildings to be erected.

ARTICLE 4. It is further agreed that there shall be erected, at the expense of the United States, one dwelling-house for each of the three principal chiefs of the aforesaid tribe, the cost of which shall not exceed five hundred dollars each, the aforesaid buildings to be erected as soon after the ratification of this treaty as possible. And when the tribe may be removed to another reserve, buildings and other improvements shall be made on such reserve of equal value to those which

Additional payments on removal.

may be relinquished; and upon such removal, in addition to the before-mentioned sixty thousand dollars, the United States agree to pay the further sum of fifteen thousand dollars, in five equal annual instalments, commencing at the expiration of the before-named instalments.

Protection of travelers.

ARTICLE 5. The said tribe of Indians further agree to give safe-conduct to all persons who may be authorized to pass through their reserve, and to protect, in their person and property, all agents or other persons sent by the United States to reside among them; they further agree not to molest or interrupt any white person passing through their reserve.

Redress for individual grievances.

ARTICLE 6. That the friendship which is now established between the United States and the Rogue River tribe of Indians shall not be interrupted by the misconduct of individuals, it is hereby agreed that for injuries done by individuals no private revenge or retaliation shall take place; but instead thereof, complaint shall be made by the party injured to the Indian agent; and it shall be the duty of the chiefs of the said tribe, that upon complaint being made as aforesaid, to deliver up the person or persons against whom the complaint is made, to the end that he or they may be punished agreeably to the laws of the United States; and in like manner if any violation, robbery, or murder shall be committed on any Indian or Indians belonging to said tribe, the person or persons so offending shall be tried, and if found guilty, shall be punished according to the laws of the United States.

Restitution of stolen property.

And it is agreed that the chiefs of the said tribe shall, to the utmost of their power, exert themselves to recover horses or other property, which has or may be stolen or taken from any citizen or citizens of the United States, by any individual of said tribe; and the property so recovered shall be forthwith delivered to the Indian agent or other person authorized to receive the same, that it may be restored to the proper owner.

Guaranty for property stolen from Indians.

And the United States hereby guarantee to any Indian or Indians of the said tribe a full indemnification for any horses or other property which may be stolen from them by any citizens of the United States: *Provided,* That the property stolen or taken cannot be recovered, and that sufficient proof is produced that it was actually stolen or taken by a citizen of the United States. And the chiefs and head-men of the said tribe engage, on the requisition or demand of the President of the United States, superintendent of Indian affairs, or Indian agent, to deliver up any white person or persons resident among them.

Farms may be established.

ARTICLE 7. It is agreed between the United States and the Rogue River tribe of Indians, that, should it at any time hereafter be considered by the United States as a proper policy to establish farms among and for the benefit of said Indians, it shall be discretionary with the President, by and with the advice and consent of the Senate, to change the annuities herein provided for, or any part thereof, into a fund for that purpose.

ARTICLE 8. This treaty shall take effect and be obligatory on the contracting parties as soon as the same shall have been ratified by the President of the United States by and with the advice and consent of the Senate.

In testimony whereof the said Joel Palmer and Samuel H. Culver, on the part of the United States, and the chiefs and headmen of the Rogue River Indians aforesaid, have hereunto set their hands and seals, the day and year aforesaid.

Joel Palmer,	[L. S.]
Superintendent Indian Affairs.	
Samuel H. Culver,	[L. S.]
Indian Agent.	
Jo, his x mark,	[L. S.]
Aps-er-ka-har,	
Sam, his x mark,	[L. S.]
To-qua-he-ar,	
Jim, his x mark,	[L. S.]
Ana-chah-a-rah,	
John, his x mark,	[L. S.]
Lympe, his x mark,	[L. S.]

Signed in presence of—
  J. W. Nesmith, Interpreter,
  R. B. Metcalf,
  John, his x mark,
  J. D. Mason, Secretary,
  T. T. Tierney.

Witness,
  Joseph Lane,
  August V. Kautz.

We the undersigned principal chief, subordinate chiefs and headmen of the bands of the Rogue River tribe of Indians, parties to the treaty concluded at Table Rock, near Rogue River, in the Territory of Oregon, on the 10th day of September, A. D. 1853, having had fully explained to us the amendment made to the same by the Senate of the United States, on the 12th day of April, 1854, do hereby accept and consent to the said amendment to the treaty aforesaid, and agree that the same shall be considered as a part thereof.

In testimony whereof we have hereunto set our hands and affixed our seals, this 11th day of November, A. D. 1854.

Aps-so-ka-hah, Horse-rider, or Jo, his x mark.	[L. S.]
Ko-ko-ha-wah, Wealthy, or Sam, his x mark.	[L. S.]
Te-cum-tom, Elk Killer, or John, his x mark.	[L. S.]
Chol-cul-tah, Joquah Trader, or George, his x mark.	[L. S.]

Executed in presence of—
  Edward H. Geary, Secretary
  Cris. Taylor,
  John Flett,
  R. B. Metcalf, Interpreter,
  Joel Palmer, Superintendent.

TREATY WITH THE UMPQUA—COW CREEK BAND, 1853.

Sept. 19, 1853.

10 Stats., 1027.
Ratified Apr. 12, 1854.
Proclaimed Feb. 5, 1855.

Stipulations of a treaty made and entered into on Cow Creek, Umpqua Valley, in the Territory of Oregon, this 19th day of September, A. D. 1853, by and between Joel Palmer, superintendent of Indian Affairs, on the part of the United States, and Quin-ti-oo-san, or Bighead, principal chief, and My-n-e-letta, or Jackson; and Tom, son of Quin-ti-oo-san, subordinate chiefs, on the part of the Cow Creek band of Umpqua tribe of Indians.

Cession of land.

ARTICLE 1. The Cow Creek band of Indians do hereby cede and relinquish, for the consideration hereinafter specified, to the United States, all their right, title, interest, and claim to all the lands lying in that part of the Territory of Oregon bounded by lines designated as follows, to wit:

Commencing on the north bank of the south fork of Umpqua River, at the termination of the high-lands, dividing the waters of Myrtle Creek from those of Day's Creek, thence running easterly along the summit of said range to the headwaters of Day's Creek, thence southerly, crossing the Umpqua River to the headwaters of Cow Creek, thence to the dividing ridge between Cow Creek and Grave Creek, thence southwesterly along the said divide to its junction with the ridge dividing the waters of Cow Creek from those of Rogue River, thence westerly and northerly around on said ridge to its connection with the spur terminating opposite the mouth of Myrtle Creek, thence along said spur to a point on the same northwest of the eastern line of Isaac Baily's land-claim, thence southeast to Umpqua River, thence up said river to place of beginning.

Temporary occupation of part of said cession.

ARTICLE 2. It is agreed on the part of the United States that the aforesaid tribe shall be allowed to occupy temporarily that portion of the above-described tract of territory bounded as follows, to wit: Commencing on the south side of Cow Creek, at the mouth of Council Creek, opposite Wm. H. Riddle's land-claim, thence up said creek to the summit of Cañon Mountain, thence westerly along said summit two miles, thence northerly to Cow Creek, at a point on the same one mile above the falls; thence down said creek to place of beginning. It being understood that this last-described tract of land shall be deemed and considered an Indian reserve until a suitable selection

Permanent homes to be selected.

shall be made by the direction of the President of the United States for their permanent residence, and buildings erected thereon and other improvements made of equal value of those upon the above reserve at the time of removal.

Payment for said cession.

ARTICLE 3. For and in consideration of the cession and relinquishment contained in article first, the United States agree to pay to the aforesaid band of Indians, the sum of twelve thousand dollars, in manner to wit: one thousand dollars to be expended in the purchase of twenty blankets, eighteen pairs pants, eighteen pairs shoes, eighteen hickory shirts, eighteen hats or caps, three coats, three vests, three pairs socks, three neckhandkerchiefs, forty cotton flags, one hundred and twenty yards prints, one hundred yards domestic, one gross buttons, two lbs. thread, ten papers needles, and such other goods and provisions as may be deemed by the superintendent or agent most conducive to the comfort and necessities of said Indians, on or before the first day of October, A. D. 1854. The remaining eleven thousand dollars to be paid in twenty equal annual instalments of five hundred and fifty dollars each, commencing on or about the first day of October, 1854, in blankets, clothing, provisions, stock, farming-implements, or such other articles, and in such manner as the President of the United States may deem best for the interests of said tribe.

Houses to be erected.

ARTICLE 4. In addition to the aforesaid twelve thousand dollars there shall be erected for the use of said tribe, at the expense of the United States, two dwelling-houses, the cost of which shall not exceed two hundred dollars each, and a field of five acres fenced and ploughed, and suitable seed furnished for planting the same.

ARTICLE 5. The said band of Indians agree to give safe conduct to all persons passing through their reserve, and to protect in their person and property all agents or other persons sent by authority of the United States to reside among them. *Protection to travelers.*

ARTICLE 6. That the friendship which is now established between the United States and the Cow Creek band of Indians, shall not be interrupted by the misconduct of individuals, it is hereby agreed that for injuries done, no private revenge or retaliation shall take place; but instead thereof complaint shall be made by the party injured to the Indian agent; and it shall be the duty of the chiefs of said band of Indians, upon complaint being made as aforesaid, to deliver up the person against whom the complaint is made, to the end that he may be punished, agreeably to the laws of the United States; and in like manner if any violation, robbery, or murder shall be committed on any Indian belonging to said band, the person so offending shall be tried, and if found guilty, shall be punished according to the laws of the United States. And it is further agreed that the chiefs shall, to the utmost of their ability, exert themselves to recover horses or other property which has or may hereafter be stolen from any citizen of the United States, by any individual of said tribe, and deliver the same to the agent or other person authorized to receive it; and the United States hereby guarantee to any Indian or Indians of said band, a full indemnification for any horses or other property which may be stolen or taken from them by any citizen of the United States, provided, the property stolen cannot be recovered, and that sufficient proof is produced that it was actually stolen or taken by a citizen of the U. S. And the chiefs further agree, that upon the requsition of the President of the U. S., superintendent of Indian affairs, or Indian agent, to deliver up any person resident among them. *Redress for private grievances.* *Restitution of stolen property.* *Indemnification for property stolen from Indians.*

ARTICLE 7. It is agreed between the United States and the Cow Creek band of the Umpqua tribe of Indians, that, should it at any time hereafter be considered by the United States as a proper policy to establish farms among and for the benefit of said Indians, it shall be discretionary with the President, by and with the advice and consent of the Senate, to change the annuities herein provided for, or any part thereof, into a fund for that purpose. *Farms may be established.*

ARTICLE 8. This treaty shall take effect and be obligatory on the contracting parties as soon as the same shall be ratified by the President of the United States, by and with the advice and consent of the Senate.

In testimony whereof the said Joel Palmer, Superintendent of Indian Affairs, on the part of the United States, and chiefs of the Cow Creek band of Umpqua Indians, before named, have hereunto set their hands and seals, the day and year aforesaid.

Joel Palmer,   [L. s.]
Superintendent Indian Affairs, O. T.

Bighead, Quin-ti-oo-san, his x mark,   [L. s.]
Jackson, My-n-e-letta, his x mark,   [L. s.]
Tom, son of Quin-ti-oo-san, his x mark,   [L. s.]
Tom, Tal-sa-pe-er, his x mark,   [L. s.]

Signed in presence of—
    J. B. Nichols,
    E. Catching,
            Interpreters.
    Theodore Tierney,
            Secretary.
    John D. Bown,
    W. Starr,
            Witnesses.

TREATY WITH THE OTO AND MISSOURI, 1854.

Mar. 15, 1854.

10 Stats., 1038.
Ratified Apr. 17, 1854.
Proclaimed June 21, 1854.

Articles of agreement and convention made and concluded at the city of Washington, this fifteenth day of March, one thousand eight hundred and fifty-four, by George W. Manypenny, as commissioner on the part of the United States, and the following-named Chiefs of the confederate tribes of the Ottoe and Missouria Indians, viz: Ar-ke-kee-tah, or Stay by It; Heh-cah-po, or Kickapoo; Shaw-ka-haw-wa, or Medicine Horse; Mi-ar-ke-tah-hun-she, or Big Soldier; Cha-won-a-ke, or Buffalo Chief; Ah-hah-che-ke-saw-ke, or Missouria Chief; and Maw-thra-ti-ne, or White Water; they being thereto duly authorized by said confederate tribes.

Cession of land to the United States.

ARTICLE 1. The confederate tribes of Ottoe and Missouria Indians cede to the United States all their country west of the Missouri River, excepting a strip of land on the waters of the Big Blue River, ten miles in width and bounded as follows: Commencing at a point in the middle of the main branch of the Big Blue River, in a west or southwest direction from Old Fort Kearney, at a place called by the Indians the "Islands;" thence west to the western boundary of the country hereby ceded; thence in a northerly course with said western boundary, ten miles; thence east to a point due north of the starting point and ten miles therefrom; thence to the place of beginning: *Provided*, That in case the said initial point is not within the limits of the country hereby ceded, or that the western boundary of said country is not distant twenty-five miles or more from the initial point, in either case, there shall be assigned by the United States to said Indians, for their future home, a tract of land not less than ten miles wide by twenty-five miles long, the southeast corner of which tract shall be the initial point above named. And such portion of such tract, if any, as shall prove to be outside of the ceded country, shall be and the same is hereby granted and ceded to the confederate tribes of Ottoe and Missouria Indians by the United States, who will have said tract properly set off by durable monuments as soon after the ratification of this instrument as the same can conveniently be done.

Reserve for the Indians.
See treaty of Dec. 9, 1854, post, p. 660.

Indians to vacate the ceded lands.

ARTICLE 2. The said confederate tribes agree, that as soon after the United States shall make the necessary provision for fulfilling the stipulations of this instrument, as they can conveniently arrange their affairs, and not to exceed one year after such provision is made, they will vacate the ceded country, and remove to the lands herein reserved for them.

Relinquishment of former claims.

ARTICLE 3. The said confederate tribes relinquish to the United States, all claims, for money or other thing, under former treaties, and all claim which they may have heretofore, at any time, set up, to any land on the east side of the Missouri River; *Provided*, That said confederate tribes shall receive the unexpended balances of former appropriations now in the United States Treasury, of which, four thousand dollars shall at once be applied for the purchase of provisions and to farming purposes.

Payment to the Indians.

ARTICLE 4. In consideration of, and payment for the country herein ceded, and the relinquishments herein made, the United States agree to pay to the said confederate tribes of Ottoe and Missouria Indians, the several sums of money following, to wit:

1st. Twenty thousand dollars, per annum, for the term of three years, commencing on the first day of January, one thousand eight hundred and fifty-five.

2d. Thirteen thousand dollars, per annum, for the term of ten years, next succeeding the three years.

3d. Nine thousand dollars, per annum, for the term of fifteen years, next succeeding the ten years.

4th. Five thousand dollars, per annum, for the term of twelve years, next succeeding the fifteen years.

All which several sums of money shall be paid to the said confederate tribes, or expended for their use and benefit under the direction of the President of the United States, who may, from time to time, determine, at his discretion, what proportion of the annual payments, in this article provided for, if any, shall be paid to them in money, and what proportion shall be applied to and expended, for their moral improvement and education; for such beneficial objects as in his judgment will be calculated to advance them in civilization; for buildings, opening farms, fencing, breaking land, providing stock, agricultural implements, seeds, &c., for clothing, provisions, and merchandise; for iron, steel, arms and ammunition; for mechanics, and tools; and for medical purposes.

ARTICLE 5. In order to enable the said confederate tribes to settle their affairs, and to remove, and subsist themselves for one year at their new home, (and which they agree to do without further expense to the United States,) and to break up and fence one hundred and fifty acres of land at their new home, they shall receive from the United States the further sum of twenty thousand dollars, to be paid out and expended under the direction of the President, and in such manner as he shall approve. *Further payment.*

ARTICLE 6. The President may, from time to time, at his discretion, cause the whole of the land herein reserved or appropriated west of the Big Blue River, to be surveyed off into lots, and assign to such Indian or Indians of said confederate tribes, as are willing to avail of the privilege, and who will locate on the same as a permanent home, if a single person over twenty-one years of age, one-eighth of a section; to each family of two, one-quarter section; to each family of three and not exceeding five, one-half section; to each family of six and not exceeding ten, one section; and to each family exceeding ten in number, one quarter section for every additional five members. And he may prescribe such rules and regulations as will secure to the family, in case of the death of the head thereof, the posession and enjoyment of such permanent home and the improvements thereon. And the President may, at any time in his discretion, after such person or family has made a location on the land assigned for a permanet home, issue a patent to such person or family for such assigned land, conditioned that the tract shall not be aliened or leased for a longer term than two years; and shall be exempt from levy, sale, or forfeiture, which conditions shall continue in force, until a State constitution embracing such land within its boundaries shall have been formed, and the legislature of the State shall remove the restrictions. And if any such person or family shall at any time neglect or refuse to occupy and till a portion of the land assigned, and on which they have located, or shall rove from place to place, the President may, if the patent shall have been issued, revoke the same, or, if not issued, cancel the assignment, and may also withhold from such person or family, their proportion of the annuities or other moneys due them, until they shall have returned to such permanent home, and resumed the pursuits of industry; and in default of their return, the tract may be declared abandoned, and thereafter assigned to some other person or family of such confederate tribes, or disposed of as is provided for the disposal of the excess of said land. And the residue of the land hereby reserved, after all the Indian persons or families of such confederate tribes shall have had assigned to them permanent homes, may be sold for their benefit, under such laws, rules, or regulations as may hereafter be prescribed by the Congress or President of the United States. No State legislature shall remove the restriction herein provided for, without the consent of Congress. *Disposition of the Indian reserves.*

Grist and saw mills.

ARTICLE 7. The United States will erect for said confederate tribes at their new home a grist and saw mill, and keep the same in repair, and provide a miller for a term of ten years; also erect a good blacksmith shop, supply the same with tools, and keep it in repair for the term of ten years, and provide a good blacksmith for a like period, and employ an experienced farmer, for ten years, to instruct the Indians in agriculture.

Blacksmith.

Annuities not to be taken for debts.

ARTICLE 8. The annuities of the Indians shall not be taken to pay the debts of individuals.

Peace and friendship.

Conduct of Indians; depredations.

ARTICLE 9. The said confederate tribes acknowledge their dependence on the Government of the United States, and promise to be friendly with all the citizens thereof, and pledge themselves to commit no depredations on the property of such citizens. And should any one or more of the Indians violate this pledge, and the fact be satisfactorily proven before the agent, the property taken shall be returned, or in default thereof, or if injured or destroyed, compensation may be made by the Government out of their annuities. Nor will they make war on any other tribe except in self-defence, but will submit all matters of difference between them and other Indians, to the Government of the United States, or its agent, for decision, and abide thereby. And if any of the said Indians commit any depredations on any other Indians, the same rule shall prevail as that prescribed in this article in cases of depredations against citizens.

Provision against the introduction of liquor.

ARTICLE 10. The Ottoes and Missourias are desirous to exclude from their country the use of ardent spirits, and to prevent their people from drinking the same; and therefore it is provided that any one of them who is guilty of bringing liquor into their country, or who drinks liquor, may have his or her proportion of the annuities withheld from him or her for such time, as the President may determine.

Roads through Indian lands.

ARTICLE 11. The said confederate tribes agree, that all the necessary roads and highways, and railways, which may be constructed as the country improves, and the lines of which may run through their land west of the Big Blue River, shall have a right of way through the reservation, a just compensation being made therefor in money.

Payment to Lewis Barnard.

ARTICLE 12. The United States will pay to Lewis Barnard the sum of three hundred dollars, he having been in the service of the said tribes and they being unable to pay him.

Ratifications.

ARTICLE 13. This treaty shall be obligatory on the contracting parties as soon of the same shall be ratified by the President and Senate of the United States.

In testimony whereof the said George W. Manypenny, commissioner as aforesaid, and the undersigned, chiefs of the said confederate tribes of Ottoes and Missourias, have hereunto set their hands and seals, at the place and on the day and year hereinbefore written.

George W. Manypenny, Commissioner. [L. s.]
Ar-ke-kee-tah, his x mark, Or Stay By It. [L. s.]
Heh-cah-po, his x mark, Or Kickapoo. [L. s.]
Shaw-ka-haw-wa, his x mark, Or Medicine Horse. [L. s.] } Ottoes.
Mi-ar-ke-tah-hun-she, his x mark, Or Big Soldier. [L. s.]
Cha-won-a-ke, his x mark, Or Buffalo Chief. [L. s.]
Ah-hah-che-ke-saw-ke, his x mark, Or Missouria Chief. [L. s.] } Missourias.
Maw-thra-ti-ne, his x mark, Or White Water. [L. s.]

Executed in the presence of us:

James M. Gatewood, Indian agent.
Thomas Maxfield.
H. N. Tabb.
Charles Calvert.
Jno. D. McPherson.
Hezekiah Miller.
Alfred Chapman.
Henry Beard.
Lewis Bernard, interpreter, his x mark.

TREATY WITH THE OMAHA, 1854.

Articles of agreement and convention made and concluded at the city of Washington this sixteenth day of March, one thousand eight hundred and fifty-four, by George W. Manypenny, as commissioner on the part of the United States, and the following-named chiefs of the Omaha tribe of Indians, viz: Shon-ga-ska, or Logan Fontenelle; E-sta-mah-za, or Joseph Le Flesche; Gra-tah-nah-je, or Standing Hawk; Gah-he-ga-gin-gah, or Little Chief; Ta-wah-gah-ha, or Village Maker; Wah-no-ke-ga, or Noise; So-da-nah-ze, or Yellow Smoke; they being thereto duly authorized by said tribe.

March 16, 1854.

10 Stats., 1043.
Ratified Apr. 17, 1854.
Proclaimed June 21, 1854.

ARTICLE 1. The Omaha Indians cede to the United States all their lands west of the Missouri River, and south of a line drawn due west from a point in the centre of the main channel of said Missouri River due east of where the Ayoway River disembogues out of the bluffs, to the western boundary of the Omaha country, and forever relinquish all right and title to the country south of said line: *Provided, however,* That if the country north of said due west line, which is reserved by the Omahas for their future home, should not on exploration prove to be a satisfactory and suitable location for said Indians, the President may, with the consent of said Indians, set apart and assign to them, within or outside of the ceded country, a residence suited for and acceptable to them. And for the purpose of determining at once and definitely, it is agreed that a delegation of said Indians, in company with their agent, shall, immediately after the ratification of this instrument, proceed to examine the country hereby reserved, and if it please the delegation, and the Indians in counsel express themselves satisfied, then it shall be deemed and taken for their future home; but if otherwise, on the fact being reported to the President, he is authorized to cause a new location, of suitable extent, to be made for the future home of said Indians, and which shall not be more in extent than three hundred thousand acres, and then and in that case, all of the country belonging to the said Indians north of said due west line, shall be and is hereby ceded to the United States by the said Indians, they to receive the same rate per acre for it, less the number of acres assigned in lieu of it for a home, as now paid for the land south of said line.

Cession of lands to the United States.

Reserve for the Indians.

ARTICLE 2. The Omahas agree, that so soon after the United States shall make the necessary provision for fulfilling the stipulations of this instrument, as they can conveniently arrange their affairs, and not to exceed one year from its ratification, they will vacate the ceded country, and remove to the lands reserved herein by them, or to the other lands provided for in lieu thereof, in the preceding article, as the case may be.

Removal of the Indians.

ARTICLE 3. The Omahas relinquish to the United States all claims, for money or other thing, under former treaties, and likewise all claim

Relinquishment of former claims.

which they may have heretofore, at any time, set up, to any land on the east side of the Missouri River: *Provided*, The Omahas shall still be entitled to and receive from the Government, the unpaid balance of the twenty-five thousand dollars appropriated for their use, by the act of thirtieth of August, 1851.

ARTICLE 4. In consideration of and payment for the country herein ceded, and the relinquishments herein made, the United States agree to pay to the Omaha Indians the several sums of money following, to wit;

1st. Forty thousand dollars, per annum, for the term of three years, commencing on the first day of January, eighteen hundred and fifty-five.

2d. Thirty thousand dollars per annum, for the term of ten years, next succeeding the three years.

3d. Twenty thousand dollars per annum, for the term of fifteen years, next succeeding the ten years.

4th. Ten thousand dollars per annum, for the term of twelve years, next succeeding the fifteen years.

All which several sums of money shall be paid to the Omahas, or expended for their use and benefit, under the direction of the President of the United States, who may from time to time determine at his discretion, what proportion of the annual payments, in this article provided for, if any, shall be paid to them in money, and what proportion shall be applied to and expended, for their moral improvement and education; for such beneficial objects as in his judgment will be calculated to advance them in civilization; for buildings, opening farms, fencing, breaking land, providing stock, agricultural implements, seeds, &c.; for clothing, provisions, and merchandise; for iron, steel, arms, and ammunition; for mechanics, and tools; and for medical purposes.

ARTICLE 5. In order to enable the said Indians to settle their affairs and to remove and subsist themselves for one year at their new home, and which they agree to do without further expense to the United States, and also to pay the expenses of the delegation who may be appointed to make the exploration provided for in article first, and to fence and break up two hundred acres of land at their new home, they shall receive from the United States, the further sum of forty-one thousand dollars, to be paid out and expended under the direction of the President, and in such manner as he shall approve.

ARTICLE 6. The President may, from time to time, at his discretion, cause the whole or such portion of the land hereby reserved, as he may think proper, or of such other land as may be selected in lieu thereof, as provided for in article first, to be surveyed into lots, and to assign to such Indian or Indians of said tribe as are willing to avail of the privilege, and who will locate on the same as a permanent home, if a single person over twenty-one years of age, one-eighth of a section; to each family of two, one quarter section; to each family of three and not exceeding five, one half section; to each family of six and not exceeding ten, one section; and to each family over ten in number, one quarter section for every additional five members. And he may prescribe such rules and regulations as will insure to the family, in case of the death of the head thereof, the possession and enjoyment of such permanent home and the improvements thereon. And the President may, at any time, in his discretion, after such person or family has made a location on the land assigned for a permanent home, issue a patent to such person or family for such assigned land, conditioned that the tract shall not be aliened or leased for a longer term than two years; and shall be exempt from levy, sale, or forfeiture, which conditions shall continue in force, until a State constitution, embracing such lands within its boundaries, shall have been formed, and the legislature of the State shall remove the restrictions. And if any such person or family shall at any time neglect or refuse to occupy and till a portion of the lands assigned and on which they have located, or shall rove from place to place, the President may, if the patent shall have been issued, cancel the assignment, and may also withhold from such person or family, their proportion of the annuities or other moneys due them, until they shall have returned to such permanent home, and resumed the pursuits of industry; and in default of their return the tract may be declared abandoned, and thereafter assigned to some other person or family of such tribe, or disposed of as is provided for the disposition of the excess of said land. And the residue of the land hereby reserved, or of that which may be selected in lieu thereof, after all of the Indian persons or families shall have had assigned to them permanent homes, may be sold for their benefit, under such laws, rules or regulations, as may hereafter be prescribed by the Congress or President of the United States. No State legislature shall remove the restrictions herein provided for, without the consent of Congress.

ARTICLE 7. Should the Omahas determine to make their permanent home north of the due west line named in the first article, the United States agree to protect them from the Sioux and all other hostile tribes, as long as the President may deem such protection necessary; and if other lands be assigned them, the same protection is guaranteed. *Protection from hostile tribes.*

ARTICLE 8. The United States agree to erect for the Omahas, at their new home, a grist and saw mill, and keep the same in repair, and provide a miller for ten years; also to erect a good blacksmith shop, supply the same with tools, and keep it in repair for ten years; and provide a good blacksmith for a like period; and to employ an experienced farmer for the term of ten years, to instruct the Indians in agriculture. *Grist and sawmill.* *Blacksmith.*

ARTICLE 9. The annuities of the Indians shall not be taken to pay the debts of individuals. *Annuities not to be taken for debts.*

ARTICLE 10. The Omahas acknowledge their dependence on the Government of the United States, and promise to be friendly with all the citizens thereof, and pledge themselves to commit no depredations on the property of such citizens. And should any one or more of them violate this pledge, and the fact be satisfactorily proven before the agent, the property taken shall be returned, or in default thereof, or if injured or destroyed, compensation may be made by the Government out of their annuities. Nor will they make war on any other tribe, except in self-defence, but will submit all matters of difference between them and other Indians to the Government of the United States, or its agent, for decision, and abide thereby. And if any of the said Omahas commit any depredations on any other Indians, the same rule shall prevail as that prescribed in this article in cases of depredations against citizens. *Conduct of the Indians.* *Depredations.*

ARTICLE 11. The Omahas acknowledge themselves indebted to Lewis Sounsosee, (a half-breed,) for services, the sum of one thousand dollars, which debt they have not been able to pay, and the United States agree to pay the same. *Payment to Lewis Sounsosee.*

ARTICLE 12. The Omahas are desirous to exclude from their country the use of ardent spirits, and to prevent their people from drinking the same, and therefore it is provided that any Omaha who is guilty of bringing liquor into their country, or who drinks liquor, may have his or her proportion of the annuities withheld from him or her for such time as the President may determine. *Provision against introduction of ardent spirits.*

ARTICLE 13. The board of foreign missions of the Presbyterian Church have on the lands of the Omahas a manual-labor boarding-school, for the education of the Omaha, Ottoe, and other Indian youth, which is now in successful operation, and as it will be some time before *Grant to the missions of the Presbyterian Church.*

the necessary buildings can be erected on the reservation, and [it is] desirable that the school should not be suspended, it is agreed that the said board shall have four adjoining quarter sections of land, so as to include as near as may be all the improvements heretofore made by them; and the President is authorized to issue to the proper authority of said board, a patent in fee-simple for such quarter sections.

Construction of roads.

ARTICLE 14. The Omahas agree that all the necessary roads, highways, and railroads, which may be constructed as the country improves, and the lines of which may run through such tract as may be reserved for their permanent home, shall have a right of way through the reservation, a just compensation being paid therefor in money.

ARTICLE 15. This treaty shall be obligatory on the contracting parties as soon as the same shall be ratified by the President and Senate of the United States.

In testimony whereof, the said George W. Manypenny, commissioner as aforesaid, and the undersigned chiefs, of the Omaha tribe of Indians, have hereunto set their hands and seals, at the place and on the day and year hereinbefore written.

George W. Manypenny, Commissioner. [L. s.]
Shon-ga-ska, or Logan Fontenelle, his x mark. [L. s.]
E-sta-mah-za, or Joseph Le Flesche, his x mark. [L. s.]
Gra-tah-mah-je, or Standing Hawk, his x mark. [L. s.]
Gah-he-ga-gin-gah, or Little Chief, his x mark. [L. s.]
Tah-wah-gah-ha, or Village Maker, his x mark. [L. s.]
Wah-no-ke-ga, or Noise, his x mark. [L. s.]
So-da-nah-ze, or Yellow Smoke, his x mark. [L. s.]

Executed in the presence of us:
James M. Gatewood, Indian agent.
James Goszler.
Charles Calvert.
James D. Kerr.
Henry Beard.
Alfred Chapman.
Lewis Saunsoci, interpreter.

TREATY WITH THE DELAWARES, 1854.

May 6, 1854.

10 Stats., 1048.
Ratified July 11, 1854.
Proclaimed July 17, 1854.

Articles of agreement and convention made and concluded at the city of Washington this sixth day of May, one thousand eight hundred and fifty-four, by George W. Manypenny, as commissioner on the part of the United States, and the following-named delegates of the Delaware tribe of Indians, viz: Sarcoxey; Ne-con-he-cond; Kock-ka-to-wha; Qua-cor-now-ha, or James Segondyne; Ne-sha-pa-na-cumin, or Charles Journeycake; Que-sha-to-wha, or John Ketchem; Pondoxy, or George Bullet; Kock-kock-quas, or James Ketchem; Ah-lah-a-chick, or James Conner, they being thereto duly authorized by said tribe.

Cession to the United States.

Ante, p. 170.

ARTICLE 1. The Delaware tribe of Indians hereby cede, relinquish, and quit-claim to the United States all their right, title, and interest in and to their country lying west of the State of Missouri, and situate in the fork of the Missouri and Kansas Rivers, which is described in the article supplementary to the treaty of October third, one thousand eight hundred and eighteen, concluded, in part, on the twenty-fourth September, one thousand eight hundred and twenty-nine, at Council Camp, on James' Fork of White River, in the State of Missouri; and finally concluded at Council Camp, in the fork of the Kansas and Missouri Rivers, on the nineteenth October, one thousand eight hundred and twenty-nine; and also their right, title, and interest in and to the "outlet" mentioned and described in said supplementary article, excepting that portion of said country sold to the Wyandot tribe of Indians, by instrument sanctioned by act of Congress approved July twenty-fifth, one thousand eight hundred and forty-eight, and also excepting that part of said country lying east and south of a line beginning at a point on the line between the land of the Delawares and the half-breed Kanzas, forty miles, in a direct line, west of the boundary between the Delawares and Wyandots, thence north ten miles, thence in an easterly course to a point on the south bank of Big Island Creek, which shall also be on the bank of the Missouri River where the usual high-water line of said creek intersects the high-water line of said river.

Reservation.

1848, ch. 118.

ARTICLE 2. The United States hereby agree to have the ceded country (excepting the said "outlet") surveyed, as soon as it can be conveniently done, in the same manner that the public lands are surveyed—such survey to be commenced and prosecuted as the President of the United States may deem best. And the President will, so soon as the whole or any portion of said lands are surveyed, proceed to offer such surveyed lands for sale, at public auction, in such quantities as he may deem proper, being governed in all respects, in conducting such sales, by the laws of the United States respecting the sales of the public lands; and such of the lands as may not be sold at the public sales, shall thereafter be subject to private entry, in the same manner that private entries are made of United States lands; and any, or all, of such lands as remain unsold, after being three years subject to private entry, at the minimum Government price, may, by act of Congress, be graduated and reduced in price, until all said lands are sold; regard being had in said graduation and reduction to the interests of the Delawares, and also to the speedy settlement of the country.

Disposition of ceded country.

ARTICLE 3. The United States agree to pay to the Delaware tribe of Indians the sum of ten thousand dollars; and, in consideration thereof, the Delaware tribe of Indians hereby cede, release, and quit-claim to to the United States, the said tract of country hereinbefore described as the "outlet." And as a further and full compensation for the cession made by the first article, the United States agree to pay to said tribe all the moneys received from the sales of the lands provided to be surveyed in the preceding article, after deducting therefrom the cost of surveying, managing, and selling the same.

Payment to the Indians.

ARTICLE 4. The Delaware Indians have now, by treaty stipulation, the following permanent annuities, to wit: One thousand dollars per fourth article of the treaty of third August, one thousand seven hundred and ninety-five. Five hundred dollars, per third article of the treaty of thirtieth of September, one thousand eight hundred and nine. Four thousand dollars per fifth article of the treaty of the third October, one thousand eight hundred and eighteen. One thousand dollars per supplemental treaty of twenty-fourth September, one thousand eight hundred and twenty-nine. One hundred dollars for salt annuity, per third article of the treaty of June seventh, one thousand eight hundred and three. Nine hundred and forty dollars, for blacksmith annuity, per sixth article of the treaty of third October, one thousand eight hundred and eighteen. All which several permanent annuities they hereby relinquish and forever absolve the United States from the further payment thereof; in consideration whereof the United States agree to pay to them, under the direction of the President, the sum of one hundred and forty-eight thousand dollars, as follows: seventy-four thousand dollars in the month of October, one thousand eight hundred and fifty-four, and seventy-four thousand dollars in the month of October, one thousand eight hundred and fifty-five. The object of converting the permanent annuities into these two payments being to aid the Delawares in making improvments on their present

Payment in lieu of annuities.

farms, and opening new ones on the land reserved, building houses, buying necessary household furniture, stock, and farming-utensils, and such other articles as may be necessary to their comfort.

The value of the school land to remain at interest as heretofore.

ARTICLE. 5. It is agreed that the sum of forty-six thousand and eighty dollars, being the value of the thirty-six sections of land set apart for school purposes by the supplemental treaty of one thousand eight hundred and twenty-nine, remain for the present at five per cent. interest, as stipulated by the resolution of the Senate of the nineteenth January, one thousand eight hundred and thirty-eight.

Payment to chiefs.

ARTICLE 6. The Delawares feel now, as heretofore, grateful to their old chiefs for their long and faithful services. In former treaties, when their means were scanty, they provided, by small life-annuities, for the wants of these chiefs, some of whom are now receiving them. These chiefs are poor, and the Delawares believe it their duty to keep them from want in their old and declining age. It is the wish of the Delawares, and hereby stipulated and agreed, that the sum of ten thousand dollars, the amount provided in the third article as a consideration for the "outlet," shall be paid to their five chiefs, to wit: Captain Ketchem, Sarkoxey, Segondyne, Neconhecond, and Kock-ka-to-wha, in equal shares of two thousand dollars each, to be paid as follows: to each of said chiefs, annually, the sum of two hundred and fifty dollars, until the whole sum is paid: *Provided*, That if any one or more of said chiefs die before the whole or any part of the sum is paid, the annual payments remaining to his share shall be paid to his male children, and, in default of male heirs, then to the legal representatives of such deceased chief or chiefs; and it is understood that the small life-annuities stipulated for by former treaties, shall be paid as directed by said treaties.

Investment of surplus from sales, and appropriation of the income.

ARTICLE 7. It is expected that the amount of moneys arising from the sales herein provided for will be greater than the Delawares will need to meet their current wants; and as it is their duty, and their desire also, to create a permanent fund for the benefit of the Delaware people, it is agreed that all the money not necessary for the reasonable wants of the people, shall from time to time be invested by the President of the United States, in safe and profitable stocks, the principal to remain unimpaired, and the interest to be applied annually for the civilization, education, and religious culture of the Delaware people, and such other objects of a beneficial character, as in his judgment, are proper and necessary.

Same subject.

ARTICLE 8. As the annual receipts from the sales of the lands cannot now be determined, it is agreed that the whole subject be referred to the judgment of the President, who may, from time to time, prescribe how much of the net proceeds of said sales shall be paid out to the Delaware people, and the mode and manner of such payment, also how much shall be invested, and in distributing the funds to the people, due regard and encouragement shall be given to that portion of the Delawares who are competent to manage their own affairs, and who know and appreciate the value of money; but Congress may, at any time, and from time to time, by law, make such rules and regulations in relation to the funds arising from the sale of said lands, and the application thereof for the benefit and improvement of the Delaware people, as may in the wisdom of that body, seem just and proper.

Private debts not to be paid from the general fund.

ARTICLE 9. The debts of Indians, contracted in their private dealings as individuals, whether to traders or otherwise, shall not be paid from the general fund.

Ardent spirits.

ARTICLE 10. The Delawares promise to renew their efforts to suppress the introduction and the use of ardent spirits in their country and among their people, and to encourage industry, integrity, and virtue, so that every one may become civilized, and, as many now are, competent to manage their business affairs; but should some of them unfortunately continue to refuse to labor, and remain or become dissipated and worthless, it shall be discretionary with the President to give such direction to the portion of funds, from time to time, due to such persons, as will prevent them from squandering the same, and secure the benefit thereof to their families.

ARTICLE 11. At any time hereafter, when the Delawares desire it, and at their request and expense, the President may cause the country reserved for their permanent home to be surveyed in the same manner as the ceded country is surveyed, and may assign such portion to each person or family as shall be designated by the principal men of the tribe: *Provided,* Such assignment shall be uniform. *Divisions of lands reserved for a home.*

ARTICLE 12. In the settlement of the country adjacent to the Delaware reservation, roads and highways will become necessary, and it is agreed that all roads and highways laid out by authority of law, shall have a right of way through the reserved lands, on the same terms that the law provides for their location through the lands of citizens of the United States; and railroad companies, when the lines of their roads necessarily pass through the said reservation, shall have the right of way, on payment of a just compensation therefor in money. *Construction of roads.*

ARTICLE 13. The Christian Indians live in the country herein ceded, and have some improvements. They desire to remain where they are, and the Delawares are willing, provided the Christian Indians can pay them for the land. It is therefore agreed that there shall be confirmed by patent to the said Christian Indians, subject to such restrictions as Congress may provide, a quantity of land equal to four sections, to be selected in a body from the surveyed lands, and to include their present improvements: *Provided,* The said Christian Indians, or the United States for them, pay to the Secretary of the Interior for the use of the Delaware Indians, within one year from the date of the ratification of this treaty, the sum of two dollars and fifty cents per acre therefor: *And provided further,* That the provisions of article twelve, in relation to roads, highways, and railroads, shall be applicable to the land thus granted to the Christian Indians. *Provisions respecting the lands occupied by the Christian Indians.*

ARTICLE 14. The Delawares acknowledge their dependence on the Government of the United States, and invoke its protection and care. They desire to be protected from depredations and injuries of every kind, and to live at peace with all the Indian tribes; and they promise to abstain from war, and to commit no depredations on either citizens or Indians; and if, unhappily, any difficulty should arise, they will at all times, as far as they are able, comply with the law in such cases made and provided, as they will expect to be protected and their rights vindicated by it, when they are injured. *Conduct of the Indians.* *Submission to United States Government.*

ARTICLE 15. A primary object of this instrument being to advance the interests and welfare of the Delaware people, it is agreed, that if it prove insufficient to effect these ends, from causes which cannot now be foreseen, Congress may hereafter make such further provision, by law, not inconsistent herewith, as experience may prove to be necessary to promote the interests, peace, and happiness of the Delaware people. *Laws may be passed to carry out the objects of this treaty.*

ARTICLE 16. It is agreed by the parties hereto, that the provisions of the act of Congress, approved third of March, one thousand eight hundred and seven, in relation to lands ceded to the United States, shall, so far as applicable, be extended to the lands herein ceded. *Act of 1807, ch. 46, applicable to the ceded land.*

ARTICLE 17. It is further stipulated, that should the Senate of the United States reject the thirteenth article hereof, such rejection shall in no wise affect the validity of the other articles.

ARTICLE 18. This instrument shall be obligatory on the contracting parties as soon as the same shall be ratified by the President, and the Senate, of the United States.

In testimony whereof the said George W. Manypenny, commissioner as aforesaid, and the said delegates of the Delaware tribe of Indians, have hereunto set their hands and seals, at the place and on the day and year hereinbefore written.

George W. Manypenny, Commissioner. [L. S.]

Sarcoxey, his x mark. [L. S.]

Ne-con-he-cond, his x mark. [L. S.]

Kock-ka-to-wha, his x mark. [L. S.]

Qua-cor-now-ha, or James Segondyne, his x mark. [L. S.]

Ne-sha-pa-na-cumin, or Charles Journeycake. [L. S.]

Que-sha-to-wha, or John Ketchem, his x mark. [L. S.]

Pondoxy, or George Bullet, his x mark. [L. S.]

Kock-kock-quas, or James Ketchem. [L. S.]

Ah-lah-a-chick, or James Conner, his x mark. [L. S.]

Executed in the presence of:

Thos. Johnson.
Charles Calvert.
Douglas H. Cooper.
Wm. B. Waugh.
Henry Beard.
B. F. Robinson, Indian agent.
Henry Tiblow, United States interpreter.

TREATY WITH THE SHAWNEE, 1854.

May 10, 1854.

10 Stat., 1053.
Ratified Aug. 2, 1854.
Proclaimed Nov. 2, 1854.

Articles of agreement and convention made and concluded at the city of Washington, this tenth day of May, one thousand eight hundred and fifty-four, by George W. Manypenny, as commissioner on the part of the United States, and the following-named delegates, representing the bands of Shawnees who were parties to the treaties of seventh of November, one thousand eight hundred and twenty-five, and eighth of August, one thousand eight hundred and thirty-one, viz: Joseph Parks, Black Hoof, George McDougal, Longtail, George Blue Jacket, Graham Rogers, Wa-wah-che-pa-e-kar, or Black Bob, and Henry Blue Jacket, they being thereto duly authorized by the now united tribe of said Shawnee Indians.

Cession to the United States of reserve.

ARTICLE 1. The Shawnee tribe of Indians hereby cede and convey to the United States, all the tract of country lying west of the State of Missouri, which was designated and set apart for the Shawnees in fulfilment of, and pursuant to, the second and third articles of a convention made between William Clark, superintendent of Indian affairs, and the chiefs and head-men of the Shawnee Nation of Indians, at St. Louis, on the seventh day of November, one thousand eight hundred and twenty-five, which said tract was conveyed to said tribe, (subject to the right secured by the second article of the treaty made at Wapaghkonetta, on the eighth day August, one thousand eight hundred and thirty-one,) by John Tyler, President of the United States, by deed bearing date the eleventh day of May, one thousand eight hundred and forty-four—said tract being described by metes and bounds as follows: "Beginning at a point in the western boundary of the State of Missouri, three miles south of where said boundary crosses the mouth of Kansas River, thence continuing south and coinciding with said boundary for twenty-five miles; thence due west one hundred and twenty miles; thence due north, until said line shall intersect the southern boundary of the Kansas reservation; thence due east, coinciding with the southern boundary of said reservation, to the termination thereof; thence due north, coinciding with the eastern boundary

Ante, p. 262.

Ante, p. 331.

Boundaries of said reserve.

of said reservation, to the southern shore of the Kansas River; thence Cession to Shawnee.
along said southern shore of said river, to where a line from the place
of beginning drawn due west, shall intersect the same"—estimated to
contain sixteen hundred thousand acres, more or less.

ARTICLE 2. The United States hereby cede to the Shawnee Indians
two hundred thousand acres of land, to be selected between the Missouri State line, and a line parallel thereto, and west of the same,
thirty miles distant; which parallel line shall be drawn from the Kansas River, to the southern boundary-line of the country herein ceded;
Provided, however, That the few families of Shawnees who now reside
on their own improvements in the ceded country west of said parallel
line, many, if they desire to remain, select there, the same quantity of Lands of Methodist Missionary Society.
land for each individual of such family, which is hereinafter provided
for those Shawnees residing east of said parallel line—the said selection,
in every case, being so made as to include the present improvement of Friends' Shawnee Labor School.
each family or individual. Of the lands lying east of the parallel
line aforesaid, there shall firs_ _e set apart to the Missionary Society of American Baptist Missionary Union.
the Methodist Episcopal Church South, to include the improvements
of the Indian manual-labor school, three sections of land; to the Friends'
Shawnee labor-school, including the improvements there, three hun- Shawnee Methodist Church.
dred and twenty acres of land; and to the American Baptist Missionary Shawnee Baptist Church.
Union, to include the improvements where the superintendent of their
school now resides, one hundred and sixty acres of land; also five acres
of land to the Shawnee Methodist Church, including the meeting-house
and graveyard; and two acres of land to the Shawnee Baptist Church,
including the meeting-house and graveyard. All the land selected, as
herein provided, west of said parallel line, and that set apart to the How the lands selected are to be divided.
respective societies for schools, and to the churches before named,
shall be considered as part of the two hundred thousand acres reserved
by the Shawnees.

All Shawnees residing east of said parallel line shall be entitled to,
out of the residue of said two hundred thousand acres, if a single person, two hundred acres, and if the head of a family, a quantity equal
to two hundred acres for each member of his or her family—to include,
in every case, the improvement on which such person or family now
resides; and if two or more persons or families occupy the same
improvement, or occupy different improvements in such close proximity, that all of such persons or families cannot have the quantity of
land (to include their respective improvements) which they are entitled
to, and if in such cases the parties should be unable to make an amicable arrangement among themselves, the oldest occupant or settler
shall have the right to locate his tract so as to include said improvements, and the others must make a selection elsewhere, adjoining some
Shawnee settlement; and in every such case, the person or family retaining the improvement shall pay those leaving it for the interest of the
latter therein—the value of the same to be fixed, when the parties cannot agree thereupon, by such tribunal, and in such mode, as may be
prescribed by the Shawnee council, with the consent of the United
States agent for that tribe.

The privilege of selecting lands, under this provision, shall extend
to every head of a family, who, although not a Shawnee, may have
been legally married to a Shawnee, according to the customs of that
people, and adopted by them; and to all minor orphan children of
Shawnees, and of persons who have been adopted as Shawnees, who
shall not have received their shares with any family; and all incompetent persons shall have selections made for them adjacent, or as near
as practicable, to their friends or relatives, which selections shall be
made by some disinterested person or persons, appointed by the
Shawnee council, and approved by the United States agent. In the

Provision for Black
Bob's settlement and
Long Tail's settle-
ment. settlement known as Black Bob's settlement, in which he has an improvement, whereon he resides; and in that known as Long Tail's settlement, in which he has an improvement whereon he resides, there are a number of Shawnees who desire to hold their lands in common; it is therefore agreed that all Shawnees, including the persons adopted as aforesaid, and incompetent persons, and minor orphan children, who reside in said settlements respectively, and all who shall, within sixty days after the approval of the surveys hereinafter provided for, signify to the United States agent their election to join either of said communities and reside with them, shall have a quantity of land assigned and set off to them, in a compact body, at each of the settlements aforesaid, equal to two hundred acres to every individual in each of said communities. A census of the Shawnees residing at each of these settlements, and of the minor orphan children of their kindred, and of those electing to reside in said communities, shall be taken by the United States agent for the Shawnees, in order that a quantity of land equal to two hundred acres for each person may be set off and

Provision for absent
Shawnees. allotted them, to hold in common as aforesaid. After all the Shawnees, and other persons herein provided for, shall have received their shares of the two hundred thousand acres of land reserved, it is anticipated that there will still be a residue; and as there are some Shawnees who have been for years separated from the tribe, it is agreed that whatever surplus remains, after provision is made for all present members of the tribe, shall be set apart, in one body of land, in compact form, under the direction of the President of the United States; and all such Shawnees as return to, and unite with the tribe, within five years from the proclamation of this instrument, shall be entitled to the same quantity of lands, out of said surplus, and in the same manner, and subject to the same limitations and provisions, as are hereinbefore made for those now members of the said tribe; and whatever portion of said surplus remains unassigned, after the expiration of said five years, shall be sold as hereinafter provided,—the proceeds of all such sales shall be retained in the Treasury of the United States until the expiration of ten years from the proclamation of this instrument, after which time, should said absent Shawnees not have returned and united with the tribe, all the moneys then in the Treasury, or that may thereafter be received therein, as proceeds of the sales of such surplus land, shall be applied to, or invested for, such beneficial or benevolent objects among the Shawnees, as the President of the United States, after consulting with the Shawnee council, shall determine,—and should any such absent Shawnees return and unite with said tribe, after the expiration of the period of five years hereinbefore mentioned, and before the expiration of the said period of ten years, the proper portion of any of said residue of lands that then may remain unsold shall be assigned to such persons; and if all said lands have been disposed of, an equitable payment in money shall be made to them out of the pro-

Assignments and
selections—how
made. ceeds of the said sales. The aforesaid assignments and selections of lands in the tract lying between the Missouri State-line and the said parallel line, shall be made within ninety days after the approval of the survey of said tract, and if there be any individuals recognized as at present entitled to lands therein, under the provisions of this article, who shall not have selected, or had selected for them, within said ninety days, their proper shares of land, the Shawnee council shall select one or more disinterested persons, who shall, immediately after the expiration of such ninety days, make selections of lands for them, in the same manner, and subject to the same restrictions, as hereinbefore provided for minor orphan children, not members of a family, and for incompetent persons. And those residing on improvements west of the said parallel line, shall, within sixty days after the approval

of the survey of the lands on which they live, make the selections of lands as, and to the amount, they are hereinbefore authorized to do. It is agreed that all the tracts of land in this article assigned, or provided to be assigned or selected, shall be assigned and selected according to the legal subdivisions of United States lands, and according to the laws of the United States respecting the entry of public lands, so far as said laws are applicable; and no portion of this instrument shall be so construed as to nullify or impair this stipulation. And the said Indians hereby cede, relinquish, and convey to the United States, all tracts or parcels of land which may be sold, or are required to be sold in pursuance of any article of this instrument.

ARTICLE 3. In consideration of the cession and sale herein made, the United States agree to pay to the Shawnee people, the sum of eight hundred and twenty-nine thousand dollars, in manner as follows, viz: Forty thousand dollars to be invested by the United States, at a rate of interest not less than five per centum per annum, which, as it accrues, is to be applied to the purposes of education; that amount, with the addition of the three thousand dollars of perpetual annuities provided by the treaties of August third, one thousand seven hundred and ninety-five, and September twenty-ninth, one thousand eight hundred and seventeen, and now hereby agreed to be likewise so applied, together with the sum to be paid by the Missionary Society of the Methodist Episcopal Church South, as hereinafter provided, being deemed by the Shawnees as sufficient, for the present, for such purposes. Seven hundred thousand dollars, to be paid in seven equal annual installments, during the month of October of each year, commencing with the year one thousand eight hundred and fifty-four; and the residue of eighty-nine thousand dollars, to be paid within the same month of the year, after the termination of that period. *(margin: Payments in consideration of said cession. Ante, p. 39. Ante, p. 145.)*

ARTICLE 4. Those of the Shawnees who may elect to live in common shall hereafter be permitted, if they so desire, to make separate selections within the bounds of the tract which may have been assigned to them in common; and such selections shall be made in all respects in conformity with the rule herein provided to govern those who shall, in the first instance, make separate selections. *(margin: Provision for Shawnees electing to live in common.)*

ARTICLE 5. The lands heretofore described lying between the Missouri State-line, and the parallel line thirty miles west of it, as soon after the ratification of this instrument as can conveniently be done, shall be surveyed, in the same manner as the public lands of the United States are surveyed, the expenses thereof to be borne by the Shawnees and the United States in due proportion; and no white persons or citizens shall be permitted to make locations or settlements within said limits, until after all the lands shall have been surveyed, and the Shawnees shall have made their selections and locations, and the President shall have set apart the surplus. *(margin: Sale of said lands. Locations and settlements forbidden until, etc.)*

ARTICLE 6. The grants of land above made to missionary societies and churches, shall be subject to these conditions: The grant to the Missionary Society of the Methodist Episcopal Church South, at the Indian manual-labor school, shall be confirmed to said society, or to such person or persons as may be designated by it, by patent, from the President of the United States, upon the allowance to the Shawnees, by said society, of ten thousand dollars, to be applied to the education of their youth; which it has agreed to make. The grants for the schools established by the Baptists and Friends, shall be held by their respective boards of missions, so long as those schools shall be kept by them—when no longer used for such purpose by said boards, the lands, with the improvements, shall, under the direction of the President, be sold at public sale, to the highest bidder, upon such terms as he may prescribe, the proceeds to be applied by the Shawnees to such general beneficial and charitable purposes as they may wish: *Provided,* That *(margin: Conditions of the above grants to societies and schools.)*

the improvements shall be valued, and the valuation deducted from the proceeds of sale, and returned to said boards respectively.

Share of Joseph Parks and Black Hoof. ARTICLE 7. Inasmuch as Joseph Parks and Black Hoof, who have in times past rendered important services to the Shawnee Nation, would not, by reason of the small number of persons in their families, be entitled under the provisions of Article 2 to a quantity of land equal to that which will be generally received by the other members of the tribe, it is agreed, at the request of the Shawnees, that Joseph Parks, in lieu of the land which he would have a right to select under the provisions of Article 2, shall have a quantity of land equal to two sections, or twelve hundred and eighty acres, to include his present residence and improvement; and Black Hoof, in lieu of that which he would have a right to select as aforesaid, shall have a quantity of land equal to one section, or six hundred and forty acres, to include his present residence and improvement; and they shall make selections of the land hereby granted them in the same manner and subject to the same limitations as are prescribed in Article 2, for such as shall make separate selections, in severalty, under the provisions thereof.

How money shall be paid. ARTICLE 8. Such of the Shawnees as are competent to manage their affairs shall receive their portions of the aforementioned annual instalments in money. But the portions of such as shall be found incompetent to manage their affairs, whether from drunkenness, depravity, or other cause, shall be disposed of by the President in that manner deemed by him best calculated to promote their interests and the comfort of their families, the Shawnee council being first consulted with respect to such persons, whom it is expected they will designate to their agent. The portions of orphan children shall be appropriated by the President in the manner deemed by him best for their interests.

Land patents to issue. ARTICLE 9. Congress may hereafter provide for the issuing, to such of the Shawnees as may make separate selections, patents for the same, with such guards and restrictions as may seem advisable for their protection therein.

Said payments not to be stopped for debts. ARTICLE 10. No portion of the money stipulated by this instrument to be paid to the Shawnees, shall be taken by the Government of the United States, by its agent or otherwise, to pay debts contracted by the Shawnees, as private individuals; nor any part thereof for the payment of national debts or obligations contracted by the Shawnee chiefs or council; *Provided*, That this article shall not be construed to prohibit the council from setting apart a portion of any annual payment, for purposes strictly national in their character, and for the payment of national or tribal debts, first to be approved by the President.

Payment in full satisfaction of all claims. ARTICLE 11. It being represented that many of the Shawnees have sustained damage in the loss and destruction of their crops, stock, and other property, and otherwise, by reason of the great emigration which has for several years passed through their country, and of other causes, in violation, as they allege, of guaranties made for their protection by the United States, it is agreed that there shall be paid, in consideration thereof, to the Shawnees, the sum of twenty-seven thousand dollars, which shall be taken and considered in full satisfaction, not only of such claim, but of all others of what kind soever, and in release of all demands and stipulations arising under former treaties, with the exception of the perpetual annuities, amounting to three thousand dollars, hereinbefore named, and which are set apart and appropriated in **Proof of claims.** the third article hereof. All Shawnees who have sustained damage by the emigration of citizens of the United States, or by other acts of such citizens, shall, within six months after the ratification of this treaty, file their claims for such damages with the Shawnee agent, to be submitted by him to the Shawnee council for their action and decision and the amount in each case approved shall be paid by said agent: *Provided*, The whole amount of claims thus approved, shall not exceed the said sum stipulated for in this article: *And provided*, That if such amount shall exceed that sum then a reduction shall be made, *pro rata*, from each claim until the aggregate is lowered to that amount. If less than that amount be adjudged to be due, the residue, it is agreed, shall be appropriated as the council shall direct.

ARTICLE 12. If, from causes not now foreseen, this instrument should prove insufficient for the advancement and protection of the welfare and interest of the Shawnees, Congress may hereafter, by law make such further provision, not inconsistent herewith, as experience may prove to be necessary to promote the interests, peace, and happiness of the Shawnee people. *Congress may make further provisions to effectuate the objects of this treaty.*

ARTICLE 13. It is agreed that all roads and highways, laid out by authority of the law, shall have a right of way through any of the reserved, assigned, and selected lands, on the same terms that the law provides for their location through the lands of citizens of the United States; and railroad companies, when the lines of their roads necessarily pass through any of said lands, shall have the right of way, on payment of a just compensation therefor in money *Right of way over selected lands.*

ARTICLE 14. The Shawnees acknowledge their dependence on the Government of the United States, and invoke its protection and care. They will abstain from the commission of depredations, and comply, as far as they are able, with the laws in such cases made and provided, as they will expect to be protected, and to have their rights vindicated. *Conduct of Indians.*

ARTICLE 15. The Shawnees agree to suppress the use of ardent spirits among their people, and to resist, by all prudent means, its introduction into their settlements. *Provision against ardent spirits.*

ARTICLE 16. The United States reserve, at the site of the agency-house in the Shawnee country, including the improvements, one hundred and sixty acres of land. *Reservation at the agency house.*

ARTICLE 17. The foregoing instrument shall be obligatory on the contracting parties, as soon as the same shall be ratified by the President and the Senate of the United States.

In testimony whereof, the said George W. Manypenny, commissioner aforesaid, and the undersigned delegates representing the bands of Shawnees who were parties to the treaties of seventh November, one thousand eight hundred and twenty-five, and eighth of August, one thousand eight hundred and thirty-one, have hereunto set their hands and seals, at the place, and on the day and year, first hereinbefore written.

George W. Manypenny, Commissioner.	[L. S.]
Joseph Parks, his x mark.	[L. S.]
Black Hoof, his x mark.	[L. S.]
George McDougal, his x mark.	[L. S.]
Longtail, his x mark.	[L. S.]
George Blue Jacket, his x mark.	[L. S.]
Grayham Rogers,	[L. S.]
Wa-wah-che pa-e-kar,	
Or Black Bob, his x mark.	[L. S.]
Henry Blue Jacket, his x mark.	[L. S.]

Executed in presence of—

Charles Calvert,
Benjamin S. Love,
Holmes Colbert,
James Lindsey,
Alfred Chapman,
Wm. B. Waugh,
B. F. Robinson, Indian agent,
Chas. Blue Jacket, United States interpreter.

*   *   *   *   *   *

We the undersigned chiefs, Councillors, and head men of the United tribe of Shawnee Indians, on behalf of said united tribe, now in full council assembled, having had fully explained to us the amendments made on the 2d of August, 1854, by the Senate of the United States, to the articles of agreement and convention which were concluded at the City of Washington, on the 10th day of May, 1854, between George W. Manypenny, as Commissioner on the part of the United States, and Joseph Parks, Black Hoof, George McDougal, Longtail, George Blue Jacket, Graham Rogers, Wa-wah-che-pa-e-kar,-or Black Bob, and Henry Blue Jacket, delegates representing the bands of Skawnees who were parties to the treaties of Nov. 7th, 1825, and of August 8th, 1831, and which bands compose the now united band assembled,

Which are in the following words, viz:

AMENDMENTS.

ARTICLE 1. Strike out the following words:

"Excepting and reserving therefrom two hundred thousand acres for homes for the Shawnee people, which said two hundred thousand acres is retained, as well for the benefit of those Shawnees, parties to the treaty of August 8th, 1831, as for those parties to the treaty of November 7, 1825."

ARTICLE 2. Strike out the following words where the[y] first occur:

"The two hundred thousand acres of land reserved by the Shawnees, shall" and insert the following in lieu thereof:

The United States hereby cede to the Shawnee Indians two hundred thousand acres of land to be

ARTICLE 10. Strike out the word "small," and after the word "character" insert the following:

And for the payment of national or tribal debts —— do hereby accept and consent to the said amendments to the articles of agreement and convention aforesaid, and agree that the same shall be considered as a part thereof. But this assent is given on the condition that neither the present, or any future council, shall ever make provision for the pretended claims of R. W. Thompson, of Indiana, George C. Johnson, of Ohio, or Ewing and Clymer: and upon the further condition that no national or tribal obligations shall ever be made by the council to pay the debts of individual Shawnees to traders or other persons.

In testimony whereof, we have hereunto set our hands and affixed our seals, this 21st day of August, A. D. 1854.

Joseph Parks, his x mark	[L. S.]	John Flint, his x mark	[L. S.]
Henry Blue Jacket, his x mark	[L. S.]	Tucker, his x mark	[L. S.]
Graham Rogers, his x mark	[L. S.]	James Sucket, his x mark	[L. S.]
Matthew King, his x mark	[L. S.]	Tooly, his x mark	[L. S.]
Paschal Fish, his x mark	[L. S.]	Silas Dougherty, his x mark	[L. S.]
Joseph Flint, his x mark	[L. S.]	Jackson Rogers, his x mark	[L. S.]
Lewis Dougherty, his x mark	[L. S.]	Joseph White, his x mark	[L. S.]
Joseph Day, his x mark	[L. S.]	John Parks, his x mark	[L. S.]
Silverheels, his x mark	[L. S.]	David Dushane, his x mark	[L. S.]
Black Wolf, his x mark	[L. S.]	Levi Flint, his x mark	[L. S.]
Greyfeather, his x mark	[L. S.]	Neona, his x mark	[L. S.]
Joseph Dougherty, his x mark	[L. S.]	William Shoto, his x mark	[L. S.]
George Francis, his x mark	[L. S.]	George Flint, his x mark	[L. S.]
Wilson Rogers, his x mark	[L. S.]	John Shane, his x mark	[L. S.]
Pacutsekah, his x mark	[L. S.]	Jackson Wheeler, his x mark	[L. S.]
Kakwekah, his x mark	[L. S.]		
David Deshane, his x mark,	[L. S.]	Bill Littletail, his x mark,	[L. S.]
Morris, his x mark,	[L. S.]	George McDougal, his x mark,	[L. S.]

Executed in presence of us, Augt. 21, 1854—
    Richard C. Meek,
    A. S. Johnson,
    Thomas S. Lewis,
    Luther M. Carter,
    Charles Blue Jacket, United States interpreter.

I do hereby certify that the foregoing instrument of writing was fully explained by me to the Shawnee tribe of Indians, in council assembled, on the day and year last above written, and that they did accept and consent to the said foregoing instrument of writing, and subscribed their names and affixed their seals thereto, in my presence.

Given under my hand this 22d day of Aug., 1854.

B. F. Robinson,
Indian Agent for the Kansas Agency.

Whereas the Shawnee Indians in full council assembled did, on the 21st day of August, 1854, assent to the amendments of the Senate of the 2d of August, 1854, to the Articles of Agreement and Convention, concluded between them and the United States on the 10th of May, 1854, which assent was coupled with conditions as follows: "But this assent is given on the condition that neither the present or any future council shall ever make provision for the pretended claims of R. W. Thompson of Indiana, George C. Johnson of Ohio, or Ewing and Clymer; and upon the further condition, that no national or tribal obligations shall ever be made by the council to pay the debts of individual Shawnees to traders or other persons." And whereas the Secretary of the Department of the Interior, having in his letter of September 12th, 1854, to the Superintendent of Indian Affairs at St. Louis, expressed the opinion that the above-named conditions were of such a character as to require the constitutional action of the Senate, before the treaty could be proclaimed or executed. And whereas the said Shawnee Indians are now in full council assembled to take into consideration the suggestion or advice of the Secretary of the Interior that the assent to said amendments should be unconditional. Therefore, we the chiefs, councillors, and head men of said tribe, in their behalf, and by their direction, and in review of the suggestions in the letter of the Secretary of the Interior, do rescind the said conditions, and hereby assent to the said amendments, and unconditionally accept and consent to the same.

In testimony whereof we have hereunto set our hands and affixed our seals, this 28th day of September, 1854.

Joseph Parks, his x mark,	[L. S.]	George Flint, his x mark,	[L. S.]
George McDougal, his x mark,	[L. S.]	John Shane, his x mark,	[L. S.]
Black Hoof, his x mark,	[L. S.]	David Deshane, his x mark,	[L. S.]
Henry Blue Jacket, his x mark,	[L. S.]	Morris, his x mark,	[L. S.]
Graham Rogers, his x mark,	[L. S.]	Little Tom, his x mark,	[L. S.]
Mathew King, his x mark,	[L. S.]	John Ham, his x mark,	[L. S.]
Paschal Fish, his x mark,	[L. S.]	William Barber, his x mark,	[L. S.]
Joseph Flint, his x mark,	[L. S.]	White Deer, his x mark,	[L. S.]
Joseph Hay, his x mark,	[L. S.]	Big Jim, his x mark,	[L. S.]
Wilson Rogers, his x mark,	[L. S.]	James McLane, his x mark,	[L. S.]
Longtail, his x mark,	[L. S.]	Qwaper, his x mark,	[L. S.]
George Blue Jacket, his x mark,	[L. S.]	Ka-ka, his x mark,	[L. S.]
Pa-ket-se-cha, his x mark,	[L. S.]	John Whitefeather, his x mark,	[L. S.]
John Flint, his x mark,	[L. S.]	Qwelena, his x mark,	[L. S.]
Tucker, his x mark,	[L. S.]	Simon Harvey, his x mark,	[L. S.]
James Sucket, his x mark,	[L. S.]	George Big Knife, his x mark,	[L. S.]
Toola, his x mark,	[L. S.]	Charles Fish, his x mark,	[L. S.]
Jackson Rogers, his x mark,	[L. S.]	Possum, his x mark,	[L. S.]
Joseph White, his x mark,	[L. S.]	James Kizen, his x mark,	[L. S.]
John Parks, his x mark,	[L. S.]	Te-la-so, his x mark.	[L. S.]
David Deshane, his x mark,	[L. S.]	John Teenmosa, his x mark,	[L. S.]
Levi Flint, his x mark,	[L. S.]	John Francis, his x mark,	[L. S.]
Neona, his x mark,	[L. S.]		

Executed in presence of us, this 28th September, 1854—

J. W. Whitfield, Indian agent Upper Platte,
A. S. Johnson,
Charles Blue Jacket, United States interpreter.

I do hereby certify that the foregoing instrument of writing was fully explained by me, to the Shawnee tribe of Indians in council assembled, on the 28th day of September, 1854, and that they did accept and consent to the said foregoing instrument of writing, and subscribed their names and affixed their seals thereto, in my presence, on the day and year last aforesaid.

Given under my hand this 11th day of October, 1854.

B. F. Robinson,
Indian Agent.

TREATY WITH THE MENOMINEE, 1854.

May 12, 1854.

10 Stats., p. 1064.
Proclamation Aug. 2, 1854.

Articles of agreement made and concluded at the Falls of Wolf River, in the State of Wisconsin, on the twelfth day of May, one thousand eight hundred and fifty-four, between the United States of America, by Francis Huebschmann, superintendent of Indian affairs, duly authorized thereto, and the Menomonee tribe of Indians, by the chiefs, headmen, and warriors of said tribe—such articles being supplementary and amendatory to the treaty made between the United States and said tribe on the eighteenth day of October, one thousand eight hundred and forty-eight.

Preamble

Whereas, among other provisions contained in the treaty in the caption mentioned, it is stipulated that for and in consideration of all the lands owned by the Menomonees, in the State of Wisconsin, wherever situated, the United States should give them all that country or tract of land ceded by the Chippewa Indians of the Mississippi and Lake Superior, in the treaty of the second of August, eighteen hundred and forty-seven, and by the Pillager band of Chippewa Indians in the treaty of the twenty-first of August, eighteen hundred and forty-seven, which had not been assigned to the Winnebagoes, guarantied not to contain less than six hundred thousand acres; should pay them forty thousand dollars for removing and subsisting themselves; should give them fifteen thousand dollars for the establishment of a manual-labor school, the erection of a grist and saw mill, and for other necessary improvements in their new country; should cause to be laid out and expended in the hire of a miller, for the period of fifteen years, nine thousand dollars; and for continuing and keeping up a blacksmith shop and providing iron and steel for twelve years, commencing on the first of January, eighteen hundred and fifty-seven, eleven thousand dollars.

And whereas, upon manifestation of great unwillingness on the part of said Indians to remove to the country west of the Mississippi River, upon Crow Wing, which had been assigned them, and a desire to remain in the State of Wisconsin, the President consented to their locating temporarily upon the Wolf and Oconto Rivers.

Now, therefore, to render practicable the stipulated payments herein recited, and to make exchange of the lands given west of the Mississippi for those desired by the tribe, and for the purpose of giving them the same for a permanent home, these articles are entered into.

Cession to United States.

ARTICLE 1. The said Menomonee tribe agree to cede, and do hereby cede, sell, and relinquish to the United States, all the lands assigned to them under the treaty of the eighteenth of October, eighteen hundred and forty-eight.

Home provided in lieu of such cession.

ARTICLE 2. In consideration of the foregoing cession the United States agree to give, and do hereby give, to said Indians for a home, to be held as Indian lands are held, that tract of country lying upon the Wolf River, in the State of Wisconsin, commencing at the southeast corner of township 28 north of range 16 east of the fourth principal meridian, running west twenty-four miles, thence north eighteen miles, thence east twenty-four miles, thence south eighteen miles, to the place of beginning—the same being townships 28, 29, and 30, of ranges 13, 14, 15, and 16, according to the public surveys.

ARTICLE 3. The United States agree to pay, to be laid out and applied under the direction of the President, at the said location, in the establishment of a manual-labor school, the erection of a grist and saw mill, and other necessary improvements, fifteen thousand dollars; in procuring a suitable person to attend and carry on the said grist and saw mill, for a period of fifteen years, nine thousand dollars, in continuing and keeping up a blacksmith shop, and providing the usual quantity of iron and steel for the use of said tribe, for a period of twelve years, commencing with the year eighteen hundred and fifty-seven, eleven thousand dollars; and the United States further agree to pay the said tribe, to be applied under the direction of the President, in such manner and at such times as he may deem advisable, for such purposes and uses as in his judgment will best promote the improvement of the Menomonees, the forty thousand dollars stipulated to be applied to their removal and subsistence west of the Mississippi. It being understood that all other beneficial stipulations in said treaty of 1848 are to be fulfilled as therein provided. *Payments.*

ARTICLE 4. In consideration of the difference in extent between the lands hereby ceded to the United States, and the lands given in exchange, and for and in consideration of the provisions hereinbefore recited, and of the relinquishment by said tribe of all claims set up by or for them, for the difference in quantity of lands supposed by them to have been ceded in the treaty of eighteenth of October, eighteen hundred and forty-eight, and what was actually ceded, the United States agree to pay said tribe the sum of two hundred and forty-two thousand six hundred and eighty-six dollars, in fifteen annual instalments, commencing with the year 1867; each instalment to be paid out and expended under the direction of the President of the United States, and for such objects, uses, and purposes, as he shall judge necessary and proper for their wants, improvement, and civilization. *Further payments.*

ARTICLE 5. It is further agreed that all expense incurred in negotiating this treaty shall be paid by the United States. *Expenses of this treaty.*

ARTICLE 6. This treaty to be binding on the contracting parties as soon as it is ratified by the President and Senate of the United States, and assented to by Osh-kosh and Ke-she-nah, chiefs of said tribe.

In testimony whereof, the said Francis Huebschmann, superintendent as aforesaid, and the chiefs, headmen, and warriors of the said Menomonee tribe, have hereunto set their hands and seals, at the place and on the day and year aforesaid.

Francis Huebschmann,   [L. S.]
Superintendent of Indian affairs.

Wau-ke-chon, his x mark.	[L. S.]	Ta-ko, his x mark.	[L. S.]
Wis-ke-no, his x mark.	[L. S.]	Ko-man-ne-kin-no-shah, his x	
Way-tan-sah, his x mark.	[L. S.]	mark.	[L. S.]
Carron, his x mark.	[L. S.]	Wau-pa-mah-shaew, his x mark.	[L. S.]
Sho-ne-niew, his x mark.	[L, S.]	Auck-ka-na-pa-waew, his x mark.	[L. S.]
Lamotte, his x mark.	[L. S.]	Ah-way-sha-shah, his x mark.	[L. S.]
Pe-quo-quon-ah, his x mark.	[L. S.]	Chech-e-quon-o-way, his x mark.	[L. S.]
Shaw-poa-tuk, his x mark.	[L. S.]	Nah-pone, his x mark.	[L. S.]
Wau-pen-na-nosh, his x mark.	[L. S.]	Mo-sha-hat, his x mark.	[L. S.]
Sho-ne-on, his x mark.	[L. S.]	I-yaw-shiew, his x mark.	[L. S.]
Shaw-wan-na-penasse, his x mark.	[L. S.]	Kah way-sot, his x mark.	[L. S.]

Signed and sealed in the presence of us:

John V. Suydam, sub-agent,
Chas. A. Grignon, United States
  interpreter,
H. W. Jones, secretary to the commissioner,
Chas. H. White, deputy United States marshal,

Heman M. Cady, United States
  timber agent,
William Powell,
John Wiley,
H. L. Murray.

TREATY WITH THE IOWA, 1854.

May 17, 1854.

10 Stats., p. 1069.
Proclamation July
17, 1854.

Articles of agreement and convention made and concluded at the city of Washington, this seventeenth day of May, one thousand eight hundred and fifty-four, by George W. Manypenny, commissioner on the part of the United States, and the following-named delegates of the Ioway tribe of Indians, viz: Nan-chee-ning-a, or No Heart; Shoonty-ing-a, or Little Wolf; Wah-moon-a-ka, or the Man who Steals; and Nar-ge-ga-rash, or British; they being thereto duly authorized by said tribe.

Cession to the United States.

ARTICLE 1. The Ioway tribe of Indians hereby cede, relinguish, and convey to the United States, all their right, title, and interest in and to the country, with the exception hereinafter named, which was assigned to them by the treaty concluded with their tribe and the Missouri band of Sacs and Foxes, by William Clark, superintendent of Indian affairs, on the seventeenth of September, one thousand eight hundred and thirty-six, being the upper half of the tract described in the second article thereof, as " the small strip of land on the south side of the Missouri River, lying between the Kickapoo northern boundary-line and the Grand Nemahaw River, and extending from the Missouri back and westwardly with the said Kickapoo line and the Grand Nemahaw, making four hundred sections; to be divided between the said Ioways and Missouri band of Sacs and Foxes; the lower half to the Sacs and Foxes, the upper half to the Ioways," but they except and reserve of said country, so much thereof as is embraced within and designated by the following metes and bounds, viz: Beginning at the mouth of the Great Nemahaw River where it empties into the Missouri; thence down the Missouri River to the mouth of Noland's Creek; thence due south one mile; thence due west to the south fork of the Nemahaw River; thence down the said fork with its meanders to the Great Nemahaw River, and thence with the meanders of said river to the place of beginning, which country, it is hereby agreed, shall be the future and permanent home of the Ioway Indians.

Reservation.

Proceeds of sale to be paid over to the Indians.

ARTICLE 2. In consideration of the cession made in the preceding article, the United States agree to pay in the manner hereinafter prescribed, to the Ioway Indians, all the moneys received from the sales of the lands which are stipulated in the third article hereof, to be surveyed and sold—after deducting therefrom the costs of surveying, managing, and selling the same.

Disposition of the ceded lands.

ARTICLE 3. The United States agree to have surveys made of the country ceded by the Ioways in article first in the same manner that the public lands are surveyed, and as soon as it can conveniently be done; and the President, after the surveys shall have been made and approved, shall proceed to offer said surveyed land for sale, at public auction, being governed therein by the laws of the United States respecting sales of public lands; and such of said lands as may not be sold at public sales, shall be subject to private entry in the manner that private entries are made of United States land; and all the land remaining unsold after being for three years subject to private entry at the minimum Government price, may, by act of Congress, be graduated and reduced in price until the whole is disposed of, proper regard being had, in making such reduction, to the interests of the Ioways and the speedy settlement of the country. Until after the said land shall have been surveyed, and the surveys approved, no white persons or citizens shall be permitted to make thereon any location or settlement; and the provisions of the act of Congress, approved on the third day of March, one thousand eight hundred and seven, relating to lands ceded to the United States, shall, so far as they are applicable, be extended over the lands herein ceded.

ARTICLE 4. It being understood that the present division-line between the Ioways and the Sacs and Foxes of Missouri, as run by Isaac McCoy, will, when the surveys are made, run diagonally through many of the sections, cutting them into fractions; it is agreed that the sections thus cut by said line, commencing at the junction of the Wolf with the Missouri River, shall be deemed and taken as part of the land hereinbefore ceded and directed to be sold for the benefit of the Ioways, until the quantity thus taken, including the before-recited reservation, and all the full sections north of said line, shall amount to two hundred sections of land. And should the Sacs and Foxes of Missouri consent to a change of their residence and be so located by the United States as to occupy any portion of the land herein ceded and directed to be sold for the benefit of the Ioways, west of the tract herein reserved, the Ioways hereby agree to the same, and consent to such an arrangement, upon the condition that a quantity of land equal to that which may be thus occupied by the Sacs and Foxes, and of as good quality, shall be set apart for them out of the country now occupied by the last-named tribe, contiguous to said division-line, and sold for their benefit as hereinbefore provided.

Provision respecting the Sacs and Foxes.

ARTICLE 5. As the receipts from the sales of the lands cannot now be determined, it is agreed that the whole subject shall be referred to the President of the United States, who may, from time to time, prescribe how much of the proceeds thereof shall be paid out to the Ioway people, and the time and mode of such payments, and also how much shall be invested in safe and profitable stocks, the principal of which to remain unimpaired, and the interest to be applied annually for the civilization, education, and religious culture of the Ioways and such other objects of a beneficial character as may be proper and essential to their well-being and prosperity: provided, that if necessary, Congress may, from time to time, by law, make such regulations in regard to the funds arising from the sale of said lands, and the application thereof for the benefit of the Ioways, as may in the wisdom of that body seem just and expedient.

Investment of the surplus sales and appropriation of the income.

ARTICLE 6. The President may cause the country the Ioways have reserved for their future home, to be surveyed, at their expense, and in the same way as the public lands are surveyed, and assign to each person or family such portion thereof as their industry and ability to manage business affairs may, in his opinion, render judicious and proper; and Congress may hereafter provide for the issuing to such persons, patents for the same, with guards and restrictions for their protection in the possession and enjoyment thereof.

Division of the reserved lands.

ARTICLE 7. Appreciating the importance and the benefit derived from the mission established among them by the board of foreign missions of the Presbyterian Church, the Ioways hereby grant unto the said board a tract of three hundred and twenty acres of land, to be so located as to include the improvements at the mission, and also a tract of one hundred and sixty acres of timbered land, to be selected by some agent of the board from the legal subdivisions of the surveyed land; and the President shall issue a patent or patents for the same, to such person or persons as said board may direct. They further grant to John B. Roy, their interpreter, a tract of three hundred and twenty acres of land, to be selected by him in "Wolf's Grove," for which the President shall also issue a patent.

Grant to the board of missions.

Grant to John B. Roy.

ARTICLE 8. The debts of Indians contracted in their private dealings as individuals, whether to traders or otherwise, shall not be paid out of the general fund.

Private debts not to be paid out of the general fund.

ARTICLE 9. As some time must elapse before any benefit can be derived from the proceeds of the sale of their land, and as it is desir-

Part of the fund set apart by treaty of Oct. 19, 1838, may be spent.

able that the Ioways should at once engage in agricultural pursuits and in making improvements on the tract hereinbefore reserved for them, it is hereby agreed that, of the fund of one hundred and fifty-seven thousand five hundred dollars, set apart to be invested by the second clause of the second article of the treaty concluded on the nineteenth day of October, one thousand eight hundred and thirty-eight, a sum not exceeding one hundred thousand dollars shall be paid to the Indians, or expended under the direction of the President for the erection of houses, breaking and fencing lands, purchasing stock, farming utensils, seeds, and such other articles as may be necessary for their comfort. Fifty thousand dollars, or so much thereof as may be deemed expedient, to be paid during the year commencing on the first of October, one thousand eight hundred and fifty-four; and the other fifty thousand dollars, or so much thereof as shall be deemed expedient, to be paid during the year commencing on the first of October, one thousand eight hundred and fifty-five. The residue of said fund of one hundred and fifty-seven thousand five hundred dollars on hand after the payments herein provided for have been made shall remain as a trust fund, the interest upon which, as well as the interest that may have accrued on the portion drawn out, shall be applied, under the direction of the President, to educational or other beneficial purposes among the Ioways.

The remainder to be held in trust.

Construction of roads.

ARTICLE 10. It is agreed that all roads and highways laid out by authority of law shall have a right of way through the lands herein reserved, on the same terms as are provided by law when roads and highways are made through the lands of citizens of the United States; and railroad companies, when the lines of their roads necessarily pass through the lands of the Ioways, shall have right of way on the payment of a just compensation therefor in money.

Provisions against use of ardent spirits.

Friendly conduct.

ARTICLE 11. The Ioways promise to renew their efforts to suppress the introduction and use of ardent spirits in their country, to encourage industry, thrift, and morality, and by every possible effort to promote their advancement in civilization. They desire to be at peace with all men, and they bind themselves to commit no depredation or wrong upon either Indians or citizens; and whenever difficulties arise they will abide by the laws of the United States, in such cases made and provided, as they expect to be protected and to have their rights vindicated by them.

Release of claims under former treaties.

ARTICLE 12. The Ioway Indians release the United States from all claims and demands of every kind and description arising under former treaties, and agree to remove themselves within six months after the ratification of this instrument, to the lands herein reserved for their homes; in consideration whereof, the United States agree to pay to said Indians five thousand dollars—two thousand of which with such portion of balances of former appropriations of interest-fund as may not now be necessary under specific heads, may be expended in the settlement of their affairs preparatory to removal.

ARTICLE 13. The object of this instrument being to advance the interests of the Ioway people, it is agreed, if it prove insufficient, from causes which cannot now be foreseen, to effect these ends, that the President may, by and with the advice and consent of the Senate, adopt such policy in the management of their affairs as, in his judgment, may be most beneficial to them; or Congress may hereafter make such provision by law as experience shall prove to be necessary.

ARTICLE 14. This instrument shall be obligatory on the contracting parties whenever the same shall be ratified by the President and the Senate of the United States.

In testimony whereof, the said George W. Manypenny, commissioner as aforesaid, and the delegates of the Ioway tribe of Indians, have hereunto set their hands and seals, at the place and on the day and in the year hereinbefore written.

George W. Manypenny, Commissioner.	[L. S.]
Nan-chee-ning-a, or No Heart, his x mark.	[L. S.]
Shoon-ty-ing-a, or Little Wolf, his x mark.	[L. S.]
Wah-moon-na-ka, or The Man who Steals, his x mark.	[L. S.]
Nar-ge-ga-rash, or British, his x mark.	[L. S.]

Executed in the presence of—

Jas. D. Kerr.
Jas. T. Wynne.
N. Quackenbush.
Wm. B. Waugh.
D. Vanderslice, Indian agent.
John B. Roy, his x mark, United States interpreter.
Wm. B. Waugh, witness to signing of John B. Roy.

TREATY WITH THE SAUK AND FOXES OF MISSOURI, 1854.

Articles of agreement and convention made and concluded at the city of Washington this eighteenth day of May, one thousand eight hundred and fifty-four, by George W. Manypenny, commissioner on the part of the United States, and the following-named delegates of the Sacs and foxes of Missouri, viz: Pe-to-o-ke-mah, or Hard Fish; Mo-less or Wah-pe-nem-mah, or Sturgeon; Ne-son-quoit, or Bear; Mo-ko-ho-ko, or Jumping Fish; and No-ko-what, or Fox; they being thereto duly authorized by the said Sac and Fox Indians.

May 18, 1854.

10 Stat., 1074.
Ratified July 11, 1854.
Proclaimed July 17, 1854.

ARTICLE 1. The Sacs and Foxes of Missouri hereby cede, relinquish and convey to the United States all their right, title and interest in and to the country assigned to them by the treaty concluded on the seventeenth day of September, one thousand eight hundred and thirty-six, between William Clark, superintendent of Indian affairs, on the part of the United States, and the Ioways and Missouri Sacs and Foxes, being the lower half of the country described in the second article thereof as "the small strip of land on the south side of the Missouri River, lying between the Kickapoo northern boundary-line and the Grand Nemahaw River, and extending from the Missouri back and westwardly with the said Kickapoo line and the Grand Nemahaw, making four hundred sections; to be divided between the said Ioways and Missouri band of Sacs and Foxes; the lower half to the Sacs and Foxes, the upper half to the Ioways;" saving and reserving fifty sections, of six hundred and forty acres each, which shall be selected in the western part of the cession by the delegates, parties hereto, and the agent for the tribe, after their return home, and which shall be located in one body and set off by metes and bounds: *Provided,* That the delegates and agent can find such an amount of land in one body within said specified section of country suitable to the wants and wishes of the Indians. *And it is further provided,* That should a suitable location, upon examination, to the full extent of fifty sections not be found within said western part of this cession, then the said delegates a d agent shall be permitted to extend the location west or northwest of the country herein ceded and south of the Great Nemahaw River, over so much of the public domain, otherwise unappropriated, as shall make up the deficiency; or to make a selection entirely beyond the limits of the country herein ceded upon any lands of the United States, not otherwise appropriated, lying as aforesaid west or northwest of the ceded country and south of the Great Nemahaw. And in either

Cession of lands to the United States.

Reservation.

case they shall describe their selection, which must be made within six months from the date hereof, by metes and bounds, and transmit the description thereof signed by said delegates and agent, to the Commissioner of Indian Affairs; and thereupon the selection so made, shall be taken and deemed as the future permanent home of the Sacs and Foxes of Missouri. It is expressly understood that these Indians shall claim under this article, no more than fifty sections of land, and if that quantity or any portion thereof shall be selected, as provided above, outside of the reservation herein made, then said reservation or a quantity equal to that which may be selected outside thereof, shall be and the same is hereby, ceded, relinquished, and conveyed to the United States.

Payment for said cession.

ARTICLE 2. In consideration of the cession and relinquishment made in the preceding article, the United States agree to pay to the Sacs and Foxes of Missouri, the sum of forty-eight thousand dollars, in manner following, viz: Fifteen thousand dollars in the month of October in each of the years one thousand eight hundred and fifty-four and one thousand eight hundred and fifty-five; ten thousand dollars in the same month of the year one thousand eight hundred and fifty-six, and eight thousand dollars in the same month of the year one thousand eight hundred and fifty-seven; which several sums shall be paid directly to the Indians, or otherwise, as the President may deem advisable, for building houses, breaking and fencing lands, purchasing stock, farming-implements, seeds, and such other articles as may be necessary for their comfort and prosperity,

Disposition of said reservation.

ARTICLE 3. The President may cause to be surveyed, in the same manner in which the public lands are surveyed, the reservation herein provided for the Sacs and Foxes of Missouri, and may assign to each person or family desiring it such quantity of land as, in his opinion, will be sufficient for such person or family, with the understanding that he or they will occupy, improve, and cultivate the same, and comply with such other conditions as the President may prescribe. The land thus assigned may hereafter be confirmed by patent to the parties, or their representatives, under such regulations and restrictions as Congress may prescribe.

Reserve of their farm and mill.

ARTICLE 4. The said Indians reserve a tract of one section of land at the site of their present farm and mill, and to include the same; and if they desire it, said farm may be cultivated for them for a term not exceeding two years—at the end of which time, or sooner if the Indians request it, the said tract and mill may be sold by the President to the highest bidder, and upon payment being made a patent to issue to the purchaser; the proceeds of the sale to be paid over to the Indians with their other moneys.

Grant to the board of missions.

ARTICLE 5. At the request of the Indians, it is hereby agreed that the Board of Foreign Missions of the Presbyterian Church shall have a tract of one hundred and sixty acres of land, to be selected by said board at a distance not exceeding two miles in a westerly direction from the grant made to said board at their misson by the Ioway Indians—and the President is authorized to issue a patent for the same to such person or persons as said board may designate.

Release of claims under former treaties.

ARTICLE 6. The said Indians release the United States from all claims or demands of any kind whatsoever arising, or which may hereafter arise, under former treaties, and agree to remove within six months after the ratification of this instrument, and to subsist themselves, without cost to the United States. In consideration of which release and agreement, the United States agree to pay them the sum of five thousand dollars—three thousand of which may be applied to the settlement of their affairs preparatory to removal.

Provisions respecting the fund invested under treaty of Oct. 21, 1837.

ARTICLE 7. The invested fund provided by the second clause of the second article of the treaty of twenty-first day of October, one thousand eight hundred and thirty-seven, (being one hundred and fifty-seven thousand four hundred dollars,) shall remain with the United States at an annual interest of five per cent., which interest as it accumulates, shall be expended under the direction of the President in such manner as he may deem best for the interests of the Indians—and a like disposition may be made of any unexpended balance of interest now on hand.

ARTICLE 8. No part of the moneys hereby stipulated to be paid to the Indians or for their benefit, or of their invested fund, shall be applied to the payment of debts contracted by them in their private dealings, as individuals, whether with traders or otherwise. *Private debts not to be charged on the fund.*

ARTICLE 9. It is agreed by said Indians that all roads and highways laid out by authority of law, shall have right of way through their reservation on the same terms as are provided by law when roads and highways are made through lands of citizens of the United States; and railroad companies, when the lines of their roads necessarily pass through the lands of these Indians, shall have right of way on the payment of a just compensation therefor in money. *Construction of roads.*

ARTICLE 10. The said Indians promise to use their best efforts to prevent the introduction and use of ardent spirits in their country; to encourage industry, thrift and morality; and by every possible means to promote their advancement in civilization. They desire to be at peace with all men, and therefore bind themselves to commit no depredation or wrong upon either Indians or citizens, and whenever difficulties arise, to abide by the laws of the United States in such cases made and provided, as they expect to be protected and to have their own rights vindicated by them. *Ardent spirits.* *Conduct of Indians.*

ARTICLE 11. The object of these articles of agreement and convention being to advance the true interests of the Sac and Fox Indians, it is agreed should they prove insufficient, from causes which cannot now be foreseen, to effect these ends, that the President may, by and with the advice and consent of the Senate, adopt such policy in the management of their affairs, as in his judgment may be most beneficial to them; or Congress may hereafter make such provisions by law, as experience shall prove to be necessary. *Future arrangements to effectuate the objects of this treaty.*

ARTICLE 12. This instrument shall be obligatory on the contracting parties whenever the same shall be ratified by the President and the Senate of the United States.

In testimony whereof the said George W. Manypenny, commissioner aforesaid and the delegates of the Sacs and Foxes of Missouri, have hereunto set their hands and seals at the place, and on the day and year first above written.

George W. Manypenny, Commissioner.	[L. S.]
Pe-to-o-ke-mah, or Hard Fish, his x mark.	[L. S.]
Mo-less or Wah-pe-nem-mah, or Sturgeon, his x mark.	[L. S.]
Ne-son-quoit, or Bear, his x mark.	[L. S.]
Mo-ko-ho-ko, or Jumping Fish, his x mark.	[L. S.]
No-ko-what, or Fox, his x mark.	[L. S.]

Executed in presence of—

Charles Calvert.
John West.
Wm. B. Waugh.
D. Vanderslice, Indian agent.
Peter Cadue, his x mark, United States interpreter.
Wm. B. Waugh, witness to signing of Peter Cadue.

TREATY WITH THE KICKAPOO, 1854.

May 18, 1854.

10 Stat., 1078.
Ratified, July 11, 1854.
Proclaimed July 17, 1854.

Articles of agreement and convention made and concluded at the city of Washington this eighteenth day of May, one thousand eight hundred and fiifty-four, by George W. Manypenny, commissioner on the part of the United States, and the following-named delegates of the Kickapoo tribe of Indians, viz: Pah-kah-kah or John Kennekuk, Kap-i-o-mah or the Fox Carrier, No-ka-wat or the Fox Hair; Pe-sha-gon or Tug made of Bear Skin, and Ke-wi-sah-tuk or Walking Bear or Squire, thereto duly authorized by said tribe.

Cession of land to the United States.

ARTICLE 1. The Kickapoo tribe of Indians hereby cede, sell, and convey unto the United States all that country southwest of the Missouri River, which was provided as a permanent home, for them in the treaty of Castor Hill, of the twenty-fourth of October, one thousand eight hundred and thirty-two, and described in the supplemental article thereto, entered into at Fort Leavenworth, on the 26th of November, one thousand eight hundred and thirty-two, as follows: Beginning "on the Delaware line, where said line crosses the left branch of Salt Creek, thence down said creek to the Missouri River, thence up the Missouri River thirty miles when measured on a straight line, thence westwardly to a point twenty miles from the Delaware line, so as to include

Reservation for a permanent home.

in the lands assigned to the Kickapoos, at least twelve hundred square miles;" saving and reserving, in the western part thereof, one hundred and fifty thousand acres for a future and permanent home, which shall be set off for, and assigned to, them by metes and bounds. *Provided,* That upon the return home of the delegates here contracting, and upon consultation with their people, and after an exploration if required by them, in company with their agent, a location to that extent can be found within said specified section of country suited to their wants and wishes. *And it is also further provided,* That should a suitable location, upon examination and consultation, to the full extent of one hundred and fifty thousand acres, not be found within said western part of this cession, then the said delegates and agents shall be permitted to extend the location beyond the western line of the country herein ceded and north of the recent Delaware line over so much of the public domain, otherwise unappropriated, as shall make up the deficiency— or to make a selection entirely beyond the limits of the country at present occupied by the Kickapoos upon any lands of the United States, not otherwise appropriated, lying within the limits bounded by the said western line, by the recent Delaware northern line, and the waters of the Great Nemahaw River; and in either case they shall describe their selection, which must be made within six months from the date hereof, by metes and bounds, and transmit the description thereof, signed by said delegates and agent, to the Commissioner of Indian Affairs; and thereupon, the selection so made, shall be taken and deemed as the future permanent home of the Kickapoo Indians. It is expressly understood that the Kickapoos shall claim under this article no more thon one hundred and fifty thousand acres of land; and if that quantity, or any portion thereof shall be selected, as provided above, outside of the reservation herein made, then said reservation, or a quantity equal to that which may be selected outside thereof, shall be, and the same is hereby, ceded and relinquished to the United States.

Payment for said cession.

ARTICLE 2. In consideration whereof the United States agree to pay to the said Indians, under the direction of the President, and in such manner as he shall from time to time prescribe, the sum of three hundred thousand dollars, as follows: one hundred thousand dollars to be invested at an interest of five per centum per annum; the interest of which shall be annually expended for educational and other beneficial purposes. The remaining two hundred thousand dollars to be paid thus: Twenty-five thousand dollars in the month of October, one thousand eight hundred and fifty-four; twenty thousand dollars during the same month in each of the years one thousand eight hundred and fifty-five and one thousand eight hundred and fifty-six; fourteen thousand dollars during the same month in each of the years one thousand eight hundred and fifty-seven and one thousand eight hundred and fifty-eight; nine thousand dollars in the same month of each of the six years next succeeding that of one thousand eight hundred and fifty-eight; seven thousand dollars in the same month of each of the four years next succeeding the expiration of the last-named period of six years; and five thousand dollars in the same month of each of the five years next succeeding the last-named four years. And as the Kickapoos will remove to a new home, and will, therefore, require the principal portion of the annual payments for several years to aid in building houses, in breaking and fencing land, in buying stock, agricultural implements, and other articles needful for their comfort and civilization, it is understood that such portion of said annual payments as may be necessary, will be appropriated to and expended for such purposes. *How expended.*

ARTICLE 3. The President may cause to be surveyed, in the same manner in which the public lands are surveyed, the reservation herein provided for the Kickapoos; and may assign to each person, or family desiring it, such quantity of land as, in his opinion, will be sufficient for such person, or family, with the understanding that he, or they, will occupy, improve, and cultivate the same, and comply with such other conditions as the President may prescribe. The land thus assigned may hereafter be confirmed by patent to the parties, or their representatives, under such regulations and restrictions as Congress may impose. *Disposition of the reservation.*

ARTICLE 4. It is agreed that the United States shall pay to such of the Kickapoos, as have improvement upon the lands hereby ceded a fair compensation for the same—the value to be ascertained in such mode as shall be prescribed by the President. *Payment for improvements.*

ARTICLE 5. The debts of Indians contracted in their private dealings as individuals, whether to traders or others, shall not be paid out of the general fund. *Private debts not to be paid from general fund.*

ARTICLE 6. It is the desire of the Kickapoo Indians that their faithful friend and interpreter, Peter Cadue, should have a home provided for him and his family. It is therefore agreed that there shall be assigned to him a tract of land equal to one section, to be taken from the legal subdivisions of the surveyed land, and to include his present residence and improvement on Cadue's Creek, and the President is authorized to issue a patent to him for the same. *Grant to Peter Cadue.*

ARTICLE 7. It is agreed that all roads and highways laid out by authority of law shall have right of way through the reservation on the same terms as are provided by law when roads and highways are made through lands of citizens of the United States; and railroad companies, when the lines of their roads necessarily pass through the lands of the Kickapoos, shall have right of way on the payment of a fair compensation therefor in money. *Construction of roads.*

ARTICLE 8. The Kickapoos release the United States from all claims or demands of any kind whatsoever, arising or which may hereafter arise under former treaties, and agree within twelve months after the ratification of this instrument, to remove and subsist themselves, without cost to the United States; in consideration of which release and agreement the United States agree to pay them the sum of twenty thousand dollars. *Release from former treaties.*

ARTICLE 9. The Kickapoos promise to use their best efforts to prevent the introduction and use of ardent spirits in their country, to encourage industry, thrift, and morality, and by every possible means to promote their advancement in civilization. They desire to be at *Provisions against use of ardent spirits.*

Conduct of the In-
dians.

peace with all men, and therefore bind themselves to commit no depredation or wrong upon Indians or citizens, and whenever difficulties
arise to abide by the laws of the United States in such cases made and
provided, as they expect to be protected and to have their own rights
vindicated by them.

Future arrange-
ments to effectuate
the objects of this
treaty.

ARTICLE 10. The object of these articles of agreement and convention being to advance the true interests of the Kickapoo people, it is
agreed, should they prove insufficient, from causes which cannot now
be foreseen, to effect these ends, that the President may, by and with
the advice and consent of the Senate, adopt such policy in the management of their affairs as in his judgment may be most beneficial to
them; or Congress may hereafter make such provision by law, as
experience shall prove to be necessary.

ARTICLE 11. This instrument shall be obligatory on the contracting
parties whenever the same shall be ratified by the President and the
Senate of the United States.

In testimony whereof the said George W. Manypenny, commissioner as aforesaid, and the delegates of the Kickapoo tribe of Indians,
have hereunto set their hands and seals, at the place and on the day
and in the year first herein written.

George W. Manypenny, Commissioner.   [L. S.]
Pah-kah-kah, or John Kennekuk, his x mark.   [L. S.]
Kap-i-o-ma, or the Fox Carrier, his x mark.   [L. S.]
No-ka-wat, or the Fox Hair, his x mark.   [L. S.]
Pe-sha-gon, or Tug made of Bear Skin, his x mark.   [L. S.]
Ke-wi-sah-tuk, or Walking Bear or Squire, his x mark.   [L. S.]

Executed in presence of
James D. Kerr.
Charles Calvert.
Wm. B. Waugh.
D. Vanderslice, Indian agent.
Peter Cadue, his x mark, United States interpreter.
Wm. B. Waugh, witness to signing of Peter Cadue.

TREATY WITH THE KASKASKIA, PEORIA, ETC., 1854.

May 30, 1854.

10 Stats., 1082.
Ratified August 2,
1854.
Proclaimed Aug. 10,
1854.

*Articles of agreement and convention made and concluded at the city of
Washington, this thirtieth day of May, one thousand eight hundred
and fifty-four, by George W. Manypenny, commissioner on the part
of the United States, and the following-named delegates representing
the united tribes of Kaskaskia and Peoria, Piankeshaw and Wea
Indians, viz: Kio-kaw-mo-zan, David Lykins; Sa-wa-ne-ke-ah, or
Wilson; Sha-cah-quah, or Andrew Chick; Ta-ko-nah, or Mitchel;
Che-swa-wa, or Rogers; and Yellow Beaver, they being duly authorized thereto by the said Indians.*

Consent of the
United States to union
of tribes.

ARTICLE 1. The tribes of Kaskaskia and Peoria Indians, and of
Piankeshaw and Wea Indians, parties to the two treaties made with
them respectively by William Clark, Frank J. Allen, and Nathan
Kouns, commissioners on the part of the United States, at Castor Hill,
on the twenty-seventh and twenty-ninth days of October, one thousand
eight hundred and thirty-two, having recently in joint council assembled, united themselves into a single tribe, and having expressed a
desire to be recognized and regarded as such, the United States hereby
assent to the action of said joint council to this end, and now recognize
the delegates who sign and seal this instrument as the authorized
representatives of said consolidated tribe.

ARTICLE 2. The said Kaskaskias and Peorias, and the said Pianke- Cession to the United States. shaws and Weas, hereby cede and convey to the United States, all their right, title, and interest in and to the tracts of country granted and assigned to them, respectively, by the fourth article of the treaty of October twenty-seventh, and the second article of the treaty of Octo- Ante, p. 376. Ante, p. 382. ber twenty-ninth, one thousand eight hundred and thirty-two, for a particular description of said tracts, reference being had to said arti- cles; excepting and reserving therefrom a quantity of land equal to Reservation. one hundred and sixty acres for each soul in said united tribe, accord- ing to a schedule attached to this instrument, and ten sections additional, to be held as the common property of the said tribe—and also the grant to the American Indian Mission Association, hereinafter specifically set forth.

ARTICLE 3. It is agreed that the United States, shall as soon as it Disposition of ceded lands. can conveniently be done, cause the lands hereby ceded to be surveyed as the public lands are surveyed; and, that the individuals and heads of families shall, within ninety days after the approval of the surveys, Selection of lots. select the quantity of land therefrom to which they may be respec- tively entitled as specified in the second article hereof; and that the selections shall be so made, as to include in each case, as far as possible, the present residences and improvements of each—and where that is not practicable, the selections shall fall on lands in the same neighbor- hood; and if by reason of absence or otherwise the above-mentioned selections shall not all be made before the expiration of said period, the chiefs of the said united tribe shall proceed to select lands for those in default; and shall also, after completing said last-named selections, choose the ten sections reserved to the tribe; and said chiefs in the execu- tion of the duty hereby assigned them, shall select lands lying adjacent to or in the vicinity of those that have been previously chosen by indi- viduals. All selections in this article provided for, shall be made in conformity with the legal subdivisions of the United States lands, and shall be reported immediately in writing, with apt descriptions of the same, to the agent for the tribe. Patents for the lands selected by or for individuals or families may be issued subject to such restrictions respecting leases and alienation as the President or Congress of the United States may prescribe. When selections are so made or attempted to be made as to produce injury to, or controversies between individuals, which cannot be settled by the parties, the matters of dif- ficulty shall be investigated, and decided on equitable terms by the council of the tribe, subject to appeal to the agent, whose decision shall be final and conclusive.

ARTICLE 4. After the aforesaid selections shall have been made, the Sale of residue. President shall immediately cause the residue of the ceded lands to be offered for sale at public auction, being governed in all respects in conducting such sale by the laws of the United States for the sale of public lands, and such of said lands as may not be sold at public sale, shall be subject to private entry at the minimum price of United States lands, for the term of three years; and should any thereafter remain unsold, Congress may, by law, reduce the price from time to time, until the whole of said lands are disposed of, proper regard being had in making the reduction to the interests of the Indians and to the set- tlement of the country. And in consideration of the cessions herein- Proceeds of sale. before made, the United States agree to pay to the said Indians, as hereinafter provided, all the moneys arising from the sales of said lands after deducting therefrom the actual cost of surveying, manag- ing, and selling the same.

ARTICLE 5. The said united tribes appreciate the importance and Grant to the American Indian Mission Association. usefulness of the mission established in their country by the board of the American Indian Mission Association, and desiring that it shall continue with them, they hereby grant unto said board a tract of one section of six hundred and forty acres of land, which they, by their chiefs, in connection with the proper agent of the board, will select; and it is agreed that after the selections shall have been made, the President shall issue to such person or persons as the aforesaid board may designate, a patent for the same.

Relinquishment of present annuities and of all claims under former treaties. ARTICLE 6. The said Kaskaskias and Peorias, and the said Piankeshaws and Weas, have now, by virtue of the stipulations of former treaties, permanent annuities amounting in all to three thousand eight hundred dollars per annum, which they hereby relinquish and release, and from the further payment of which they forever absolve the United States; and they also release and discharge the United States from all claims or damages of every kind by reason of the non-fulfilment of former treaty stipulations, or of injuries to or losses of stock or other property by the wrongful acts of citizens of the United **Payment for such releases.** States; and in consideration of the relinquishments and releases aforesaid, the United States agree to pay to said united tribe, under the direction of the President, the sum of sixty-six thousand dollars, in six annual instalments, as follows: In the month of October, in each of the years one thousand eight hundred and fifty-four, one thousand eight hundred and fifty-five, and one thousand eight hundred and fifty-six, the sum of thirteen thousand dollars, and in the same month in each of the years one thousand eight hundred and fifty-seven, one thousand eight hundred and fifty-eight, and one thousand eight hundred and fifty-nine, nine thousand dollars, and also to furnish said tribe with an interpreter and a blacksmith for five years, and supply the smith-shop with iron, steel, and tools, for a like period.

Disposition of payments. ARTICLE 7. The annual payments provided for in article six are designed to be expended by the Indians, chiefly in extending their farming operations, building houses, purchasing stock, agricultural implements, and such other things as may promote their improvement and comfort, and shall so be applied by them. But at their request it is agreed that from each of the said annual payments the sum of five hundred dollars shall be reserved for the support of the aged and infirm, and the sum of two thousand dollars shall be set off and applied to the education of their youth; and from each of the first three there shall also be set apart and applied the further sum of two thousand dollars, to enable said Indians to settle their affairs. And as the amount of the annual receipt from the sales of their lands, cannot now be ascertained, it is agreed that the President may, from time to time, and upon consultation with said Indians, determine how much of the net proceeds of said sales shall be paid them, and how much shall be invested in safe and profitable stocks, the interest to be annually paid to them, or expended for their benefit and improvement.

Settlements by others not permitted till after selection by Indians. ARTICLE 8. Citizens of the United States, or other persons not members of said united tribe, shall not be permitted to make locations or settlements in the country herein ceded, until after the selections provided for, have been made by said Indians; and the provisions of the act of Congress approved March third, one thousand eight hundred and seven, in relation to lands ceded to the United States, shall, so far as the same are applicable, be extended to the lands herein ceded.

Debt of individuals not a charge on the fund. ARTICLE 9. The debts of individuals of the tribe, contracted in their private dealings, whether to traders or otherwise, shall not be paid **Provision for those intemperate, etc.** out of the general funds. And should any of said Indians become intemperate or abandoned, and waste their property, the President may withhold any moneys due or payable to such, and cause them to be paid, expended or applied, so as to ensure the benefit thereof to their families.

Provision against the use of ardent spirits. ARTICLE 10. The said Indians promise to renew their efforts to prevent the introduction and use of ardent spirits in their country, to encourage industry, thrift, and morality, and by every possible means to promote their advancement in civilization. They desire to be at peace with all men, and they bind themselves not to commit depredation or wrong upon either Indians or citizens; and, should difficulties at any time arise, they will abide by the laws of the United States in such cases made and provided, as they expect to be protected and to have their rights vindicated by those laws. *Conduct of Indians.*

ARTICLE 11. The object of the instrument being to advance the interests of said Indians, it is agreed if it prove insufficient, from causes which cannot now be foreseen, to effect these ends, that the President may, by and with the advice and consent of the Senate, adopt such policy in the management of their affairs, as, in his judgment, may be most beneficial to them; or, Congress may hereafter make such provisions by law as experience shall prove to be necessary. *Future arrangements to effectuate the objects of this treaty.*

ARTICLE 12. It is agreed that all roads and highways, laid out by authority of law, shall have right of way through the lands herein ceded and reserved, on the same terms as are provided by law, when roads and highways are made through lands of citizens of the United States; and railroad companies, when the lines of their roads necessarily pass through the lands of the said Indians, shall have right of way, on the payment of a just compensation therefor in money. *Construction of roads.*

ARTICLE 13. It is believed that all the persons and families of the said combined tribe are included in the annexed schedule, but should it prove otherwise, it is hereby stipulated that such person or family shall select from the ten sections reserved as common property, the quantity due, according to the rules hereinbefore prescribed, and the residue of said ten sections or all of them, as the case may be, may hereafter, on the request of the chiefs, be sold by the President, and the proceeds applied to the benefit of the Indians. *Provisions for persons omitted in schedule.*

ARTICLE 14. This instrument shall be obligatory on the contracting parties whenever the same shall be ratified by the President and the Senate of the United States.

In testimony whereof the said George W. Manypenny, commissioner as aforesaid, and the delegates of the said combined tribe, have hereunto set their hands and seals, at the place and on the day and year first above written.

George W. Manypenny, Commissioner. [L. S.]
Kio-kaw-mo-zan, his x mark. [L. S.]
Ma-cha-ko-me-ah, or David Lykins. [L. S.]
Sa-wa-ne-ke-ah, or Wilson, his x mark. [L. S.]
Sha-cah-quah, or Andrew Chick, his x mark. [L. S.]
Ta-ko-nah, or Mitchel, his x mark. [L. S.]
Che-swa-wa, or Rogers, his x mark. [L. S.]
Yellow Beaver, his x mark. [L. S.]

Executed in the presence of—
Charles Calvert,
Jas. T. Wynne,
Robert Campbell,
Wm. B. Waugh,
Ely Moore, Indian agent.
Baptiste Peoria, his x mark, U. S. interpreter.
Wm. B. Waugh, witness to signing of Baptiste Peoria.

Schedule of persons or families composing the united tribes of Weas,
Piankeshaws, Peorias, and Kaskaskias, with the quantity of land to
be selected in each case as provided in the second and third articles.

Persons or families.	Males.	Females.	Total.	Number of acres.
Mash-she-we-lot-ta, or Joe Peoria	2	2	4	640
Marcus Lindsay	3	3	6	960
Sam Slick	5	1	6	960
Wah-ka-ko-nah, or Billy	1	0	1	160
Wah-kah-ko-se-ah	1	1	2	320
Luther Pascal	2	2	4	640
Lewis Pascal	1	1	2	320
John Pascal	1	0	1	160
Edward Black	3	2	5	800
Sha-cah-quah, or Andrew Chick	3	4	7	1,120
Che-swa-wa, or Rodgers	2	4	6	960
John Westley	1	1	2	320
Ma-co-se-tah, or F. Valley	3	1	4	640
Ma-cha-co-me-yah, or David Lykins	3	2	5	800
Sa-wa-na-ke-keah, or Wilson	1	2	3	480
Na-me-quah-wah	2	0	2	320
Pun-gish-e-no-qua	1	3	4	640
Ma-cen-sah	1	1	2	320
Yellow Beaver	3	3	6	960
John Charly	3	3	6	960
Bam-ba-cap-wa, or Battiste Charly	2	3	5	800
Pah-to-cah	2	2	4	640
Lee-we-ah, or Lewis	1	2	3	480
Mah-kon-sah, junior	2	2	4	640
Baptiste Peoria	3	5	8	1,280
Ma-qua-ko-non-ga, or Lewis Peckham	5	2	7	1,120
Captain Mark	2	2	4	640
Te-com-se, or Edward Dajexat	3	1	4	640
Thomas Hedges	1	1	2	320
Pah-ka-ko-se-qua	0	1	1	160
En-ta-se-ma-qua	0	1	1	160
Yon-za-na-ke-sa-gah	2	1	3	480
Aw-sap-peen-qua-zah	4	0	4	640
Kio-kaw-mo-zaw	4	2	6	960
Chin-qua-ke-ah	2	3	5	800
Peter Cloud	3	–	3	480
Au-see-pan-nah, or Coon	2	1	3	480
My-he-num-ba	3	3	6	960
Kish-e-koon-sah	1	2	3	480
Kish-e-wan-e-sah	3	1	4	640
Sho-cum-qua	–	2	2	320
Pe-ta-na-ke-ka-pa	2	0	2	320
Pa-kan-giah	2	1	3	480
Se-pah-ke-ah	1	1	2	320
Ngo-to-kop-wa	1	1	2	320
Kil-so-qua	2	2	4	640
Be-zio, or Ben	1	2	3	480
Kil-son-zah	1	2	3	480
Shaw-lo-lee	2	1	3	480
Ke-she-kon-sah, or Wea	1	2	3	480
Ah-shaw-we-se-wah	2	–	2	320
George Clinton	2	–	2	320
Ke-kaw-ke-to-qua	2	2	4	640
Sa-saw-kaw-qua-ga, or Kain Tuck	2	3	5	800
Wah-sah-ko-le-ah	1	3	4	640
Kin-ge-ton-no-zah, or Red Bird	1	1	2	320
Paw-saw-qua, or Jack Booei	3	1	4	640
No-wa-ko-se-ah	2	–	2	320
Me-shin-qua-me-saw	1	3	4	640
Chen-gwan-zaw	3	–	3	480
Ke-che-kom-e-ah	2	–	2	320
Na-me-qua-wah, junior	2	–	2	320
Ta-pah-con-wah	1	1	2	320
Pa-pee-ze-sa-wah	1	1	2	320
Ta-ko-nah, or Mitchel	2	3	5	800
Pe-la-she	1	1	2	320
Wah-ke-shin-gah	2	2	4	640
Waw-pon-ge-quah, or Mrs. Ward	3	3	6	960

Persons or families.	Males.	Fe-males.	To-tal.	Number of acres.
Paw-saw-kaw-kaw-maw	–	2	2	320
Ke-maw-lan-e-ah	2	3	5	800
Qua-kaw-me-kaw-trua, or J. Cox	2	2	4	640
Cow-we-shaw	2	–	2	320
Tah-wah-qua-ke-mon-ga	3	1	4	640

TREATY WITH THE MIAMI, 1854.

Articles of agreement and convention made and concluded at the city of Washington, this fifth day of June, one thousand eight hundred and fifty-four, between George W. Manypenny, commissioner on the part of the United States, and the following-named delegates representing the Miami tribe of Indians, viz: Nah-we-lan-quah, or Big Legs; Ma-cat-a-chin-quah, or Little Doctor; Lan-a-pin-cha, or Jack Hackley; So-ne-lan-gish-eah, or John Bowrie; and Wan-zop-e-ah; they being thereto duly authorized by said tribe—and Me-shin-go-me-zia, Po-con-ge-ah, Pim-yi-oh-te-mah, Wop-pop-pe-tah, or Bondy, and Ke-ah-cot-woh, or Buffalo, Miami Indians, residents of the State of Indiana, being present, and assenting, approving, agreeing to, and confirming said articles of agreement and convention.

June 5, 1854.

10 Stats., 1093.
Ratified Aug. 4, 1854.
Proclaimed Aug. 4, 1854.

ARTICLE 1. The said Miami Indians hereby cede and convey to the United States, all that certain tract of country set apart and assigned to the said tribe, by the article added by the Senate of the United States, by resolution of the date of February twenty-fifth, one thousand eight hundred and forty-one, to the treaty of November twenty-eighth, one thousand eight hundred and forty, and denominated among the amendments of the Senate as "Article 12," which was assented to by said Indians, on the fifteenth day of May, one thousand eight hundred and forty-one; which tract is designated in said article as "bounded on the east by the State of Missouri, and on the north by the country of the Weas and Piankeshaws, on the west by the Pottowatomies of Indiana, and on the south by the land assigned to the New York Indians, estimated to contain five hundred thousand acres," excepting and reserving therefrom seventy thousand acres for their future homes, and also a section of six hundred and forty acres for school purposes, to be selected and assigned to said tribe as hereinafter provided. *(margin: Cession to the United States. / Reservation for homes and schools.)*

ARTICLE 2. The United States shall, as soon as it can conveniently be done, cause the lands herein ceded and reserved, to be surveyed, as the Government lands are surveyed, the Miamis bearing the expense of survey of the reserved lands; and within four months after the approval of such surveys, each individual or head of a family of the Miami tribe, now residing on said lands, shall select, if a single person, two hundred acres; and if the head of a family, a quantity equal to two hundred acres for each member of the family; which selections shall be so made as to include in each case, as far as practicable, the present residences and improvements of each person or family, and, where it is not practicable, the selection shall fall on lands in the same neighborhood. And if, by reason of absence or otherwise, any single person, or head of a family, entitled to lands as aforesaid, shall fail to make his or her selection within the period prescribed, the chiefs of the tribe shall proceed to select the lands for those thus in default. The chiefs shall also select the six hundred and forty acres hereinbefore reserved for their school, to include the buildings erected for school purposes, and to embrace a sufficient portion of timber-land. After all of the before-named selections shall have been made, the said chiefs shall further proceed to select, in a compact body, and contiguous to the individual reservations, the residue of the seventy thou- *(margin: Disposition of the ceded lands.)*

sand acres accepted and reserved by the preceding article, which body
of land shall be held as the common property of the tribe, but may, at
any time, when the chiefs and a majority of the tribe request it, be
sold by the President, in the manner that public lands of the United
States are sold, and the proceeds, after deducting the expense of such
sale, be paid to the tribe, under the direction of the President, and in
such mode as he may prescribe: *Provided*, That if any single person or
family entitled to land, shall have been overlooked, or wrongfully
excluded, and shall make the fact appear to the satisfaction of the
chiefs, such person or family may, with the approbation of the Commissioner of Indian Affairs, receive their quantity, by the rule prescribed in this article, out of the tract to be thus selected and held as
the common property of the tribe.   All the selections herein provided
for, shall, as far as practicable, be made in conformity with the legal
subdivisions of United States lands, and immediately reported to the
agent of the tribe, with apt descriptions of the same, and the President
may cause patents to issue to single persons or heads of families for
the lands selected by or for them, subject to such restrictions respecting leases and alienation as the President or Congress of the United
States may impose; and the lands so patented shall not be liable to
levy, sale, execution, or forfeiture: *Provided*, That the legislature of
a State within which the ceded country may be hereafter embraced
may, with the assent of Congress, remove these restrictions.   When
selections are so made, or attempted to be made, as to produce injury
to, or controversies between, individuals, which cannot be settled by
the parties, the matters of difficulty shall be investigated and decided
on equitable terms, by the chiefs of the tribe, subject to appeal to the
agent, whose decision shall be final.

*Sale of the reserva-
tion.* (margin note)

*Payment for said
cession.* (margin note)

ARTICLE 3. In consideration of the cession hereinbefore made, the
United States agree to pay to the Miami tribe of Indians the sum of
two hundred thousand dollars, in manner as follows, viz: Twenty
annual instalments of seven thousand five hundred dollars each, the
first payable on the first day of October, one thousand eight hundred
and sixty, and the remainder to be paid respectively on the first day
of October of each succeeding year, until the whole shall have been
paid; and the remaining fifty thousand dollars shall be invested by
the President in safe and profitable stocks, the interest thereon to be
applied, under his direction, for educational purposes, or such objects
of a beneficial character, for the good of the tribe, as may be considered necessary and expedient; and hereafter, whenever the President
shall think proper, the sum thus provided to be invested, may be converted into money, and the same paid to the tribe in such manner as
he may judge to be best for their interests.   No part of the moneys
in this or the preceding article mentioned shall ever be appropriated
or paid to the persons, families, or bands, who, by the fourteenth
article of the treaty of November sixth, one thousand eight hundred
and thirty-eight, by the fifth and seventh articles of the treaty of
November twenty-eight, one thousand eight hundred and forty, or by
virtue of two resolutions of Congress, approved March third, one
thousand eight hundred and forty-five, and May first, one thousand
eight hundred and fifty, or otherwise, are permitted to draw or have
drawn, in the State of Indiana, their proportion of the annuities of
the Miami tribe.

*Mode of payments
of the remaining in-
stallments under
treaty of Nov. 28, 1840.* (margin note)

ARTICLE 4. It is agreed that the remaining instalments of the limited
annuity of twelve thousand five hundred dollars, stipulated to be paid
by the second article of the treaty of November twenty-eight, one
thousand eight hundred and forty, shall be divided and paid to the
said Indians hereafter as follows: to the Indiana Miamis, six thousand
eight hundred and sixty-three dollars and sixty-four cents, and to the
Western Miamis, five thousand six hundred and thirty-six dollars and

thirty-six cents, per annum; subject, however, to the deductions provided for in the sixth article of this instrument; and that the permanent annuity stipulated in the fifth article of the treaty of October sixth, one thousand eight hundred and eighteen, as modified by the fifth article of the treaty of October twenty-third, one thousand eight hundred and thirty-four, for a blacksmith and miller, shall be continued for the benefit of said Western Miamis; but the said Miami Indians hereby relinquish and forever absolve the United States from the payment of the permanent annuity of twenty-five thousand dollars, stipulated in the fourth article of the treaty of October twenty-third, one thousand eight hundred and twenty-six, of the permanent provisions for money in lieu of laborers, for agricultural assistance, for tobacco, iron, steel, and salt, and from the payment of any and all other annuities of every kind or description, if any there be, to which said Indians may now be entitled by virtue of the stipulations of any former treaty or treaties; and they also release and discharge the United States from all claims or damages on account of the non-fulfilment of the stipulations of any former treaties, or of injuries to, or destruction or loss of property by the wrongful acts of citizens or agents of the United States or otherwise; and in consideration of the relinquishments and releases aforesaid, the United States agree to pay to the said Miami Indians, the sum of four hundred and twenty-one thousand four hundred and thirty-eight dollars and sixty-eight cents, in manner as follows, viz: one hundred and ninety thousand four hundred and thirty-four dollars and sixty-eight cents, to the Miami Indians residing on the ceded land; and two hundred and thirty-one thousand and four dollars, to the Miami Indians in the State of Indiana; to be paid under the direction of the President, and in such manner and for such objects as he may prescribe, in six equal annual instalments, the first of which shall be paid in the month of October, one thousand eight hundred and fifty-four. And in full payment and satisfaction of a balance of eight thousand dollars and sixty-eight cents, heretofore appropriated by Congress to pay for the valuation of certain improvements, or to make others in lieu of them, but which, not having been expended, has gone to the surplus fund; and of the accumulation of the appropriations for the support of the poor and infirm, and the education of the youth of the tribe, as provided by the treaties of October twenty-third, one thousand eight hundred and twenty-six, and November sixth, one thousand eight hundred and thirty-eight, amounting to fourteen thousand two hundred and twenty-three dollars and fifty cents; and of the claims of the Miamis who live on the ceded land, for damages and loss of stock and other property, caused by their removal west, and their subsequent loss by removal from Sugar Creek—it is agreed that the United States will pay to the Miami Indians residing on said ceded lands, the sum of thirty thousand dollars, to be paid as follows, viz: fourteen thousand two hundred and twenty-three dollars and fifty cents, in three equal annual instalments, the first of which shall be paid in the month of October, one thousand eight hundred and fifty-four; and the sums of eight thousand dollars and sixty-eight cents, in lieu of the improvement money referred to, and seven thousand seven hundred and seventy-five dollars and eighty-two cents, being the residue of said amount of thirty thousand dollars, shall be paid immediately after the requisite appropriation shall have been made: *Provided*, That the said sum of eight thousand dollars and sixty-eight cents, shall be paid to the persons who are entitled to the same, as far as that may be practicable; and the seven thousand seven hundred and seventy-five dollars and eighty-two cents shall be paid to such of the Miamis west as have lost stock or other property by wrongful acts of citizens of the United States, while in the Indian country, and to those who were injured by the loss of improvements in their

Blacksmith and miller.

Ante, p. 425.

Release of claims under other treaties.

Ante, p. 278.

Payment for such release.

Ante, p. 278.

Claims.

removal from Sugar Creek to their present home. The claimants, in all cases, to file their demands with the chiefs within six months after the ratification of this instrument; and if the aggregate sum of the lawful claims exceeds the amount of the fund, the claims shall be reduced by a uniform rule, so that each claimant shall receive his pro rata; but if it fall within the amount of said fund, the excess shall be paid to the tribe as annuities are paid. Any person aggrieved by the decision of the chiefs may appeal to the agent.

The sum of two hundred and thirty-one thousand and four dollars hereby stipulated to be paid to Miami Indians of Indiana shall be held by the United States for said last-named Indians, and by the Government invested, as the President may direct, at an interest of five per cent. per annum, and which interest shall be paid annually, for the period of twenty-five years, to the said Miami Indians of Indiana, and at the expiration of that time, or sooner if required by them and approved by the President, the principal sum to be paid in full, the United States being directly responsible therefor; said investment to be made and the interest thereon to commence accruing the first day of July, eighteen hundred and fifty-five, and thence to continue: *Provided*, That no persons other than those embraced in the corrected list agreed upon by the Miamis of Indiana, in the presence of the Commissioner of Indian Affairs, in June, eighteen hundred and fifty-four, comprising three hundred and two names as Miami Indians of Indiana, and the increase of the families of the persons embraced in said corrected list, shall be recipients of the payments, annuities, commutation moneys and interest hereby stipulated to be paid to the Miami Indians of Indiana, unless other persons shall be added to said list by the consent of the said Miami Indians of Indiana, obtained in

Mode of payment.

council, according to the custom of Miami tribe of Indians: *Provided*, That the sum of nine thousand seven hundred and forty-six dollars and fourteen cents shall immediately be paid out of said sum of two hundred and thirty-one thousand and four dollars (and deducted from the same) to the following persons, who are a portion of the Miami tribe of Indians residing in Indiana, and in the following manner; seven thousand six hundred and eighty-nine dollars and twenty-two cents to the family of Jane T. Griggs, consisting of herself and six children, to wit, Warren A—, Charles F—, Anthony W—, Ann Eliza—, Martha Jane, and Maria Elizabeth Griggs, which sum may be paid to the said Jane T. Griggs, and her husband John H. Griggs, the father of said children, or to either of them; and the sum of two thousand and fifty-six dollars and ninety-two cents to Sash-o-quash and his wife, E-len-e-pish-o-quash, which may be paid to the said Sash-o-quash, it being understood that the said Griggs family have drawn but one annuity for the last eight years, the others having been paid to the balance of the tribe; which sum of nine thousand seven hundred and forty-six dollars and fourteen cents is to be in full payment and satisfaction of all sums of money that may be due, owing or coming to said two families, by virtue of this and all former treaties on account of their being of the Miami tribe of Indians or otherwise.

The Miami Indians of Indiana, being now represented in Washington by a fully authorized deputation, and having requested the foregoing amendments, the same are binding on them; but these amendments are in no way to affect or impair the stipulations in said treaty contained as to the Miamis west of the Mississippi, the said amendments being final, and not required to be submitted to the Miamis for their consent:

And the sum of two thousand two hundred dollars is hereby directed to be paid to the said Indians residing in the State of Indiana, for time employed and money expended in assisting to make this treaty, which may be paid to James T. Miller, their interpreter, and Tyn-yi-oh-te-mah, or to either of them, to be divided among said Indians according to justice and equity.

ARTICLE 5. It is hereby understood and agreed, respecting the permanent annuity of twenty-five thousand dollars, that the said Indians shall receive the same for the years eighteen hundred and fifty-four and eighteen hundred and fifty-five, but no longer. It is also understood and agreed (the Miamis west consenting) that as the Miamis of Indiana have had no share of the iron, steel, salt, tobacco, and so forth, given under treaty stipulations, and that as there is now in the Treasury under those heads of appropriation an unexpended balance of four thousand and fifty-nine dollars and eight cents, they shall have and receive said amount—and that the said annuity of twenty-five thousand dollars for said two years shall be divided between the Miamis of Indiana and those west of Missouri, in the same proportion as the annuity of twelve thousand five hundred dollars is divided in the preceding article.

The annuity of $25,000 to be paid for 1854 and 1855, and no longer.

Division of the money.

ARTICLE 6. The United States having advanced, in pursuance of a provision of the act of Congress approved August thirtieth, one thousand eight hundred and fifty-two, entitled "An act making appropriations for the current and contingent expenses of the Indian Department," &c., the sum of twelve thousand four hundred and thirty-seven dollars and six cents to the Miami Indians, for the payment of an amount due to the Eel River band that had been erroneously paid to the "Miami Nation;" and the sum of one thousand five hundred and fifty-four dollars and sixty-three cents only, having, since said advance, been withheld by the United States, as a re-imbursement in part therefor, and there being still due to the United States, on account thereof, the sum of ten thousand eight hundred and eighty-two dollars and forty-three cents, it is hereby agreed that said balance shall be re-imbursed fully to the United States out of the limited annuity of twelve thousand five hundred dollars, before mentioned in this instrument, in the manner and proportions following; that is to say, out of said annuity for the year one thousand eight hundred and fifty-four, and each of the five consecutive years, there shall be retained from the portion to be paid in those years to the Miamis of Indiana, the sum of eight hundred and fifty-three dollars and sixty-three cents, and from the portion to be paid to the Miamis west, the sum of seven hundred dollars and ninety-nine cents, and in the year one thousand eight hundred and sixty, from the portion due the Miamis of Indiana, the sum of eight hundred and fifty-three· dollars and sixty-eight cents, and from the portion due those west, the sum of seven hundred and one dollars and three cents.

Repayment to the United States of amount advanced under act of 1852, ch. 103.

ARTICLE 7. Citizens of the United States or other persons not members of said tribe, shall not be permitted to make locations or settlements in the ceded country, until after the selections hereinbefore provided for have been made; and the provisions of the act of Congress approved March third, one thousand eight hundred and seven, in relation to lands ceded to the United States, shall, so far as the same are applicable, be extended to the lands herein ceded.

Settlement of the ceded lands.

ARTICLE 8. The debts of Indians contracted in their private dealings as individuals, whether to traders or otherwise, shall not be paid out of the general fund. And should any of said Indians become intemperate or abandoned, and waste their property, the President may withhold any moneys due or payable to such, and cause them to be paid, expended or applied, so as to ensure the benefit thereof to their families.

Private debts not a charge on the general fund.

Provisions respecting the idle and intemperate.

ARTICLE 9. The said Indians promise to renew their efforts to prevent the introduction and use of ardent spirits in their country, to encourage industry, thrift, and morality, and by every possible means to promote their advancement in civilization. They desire to be at peace with all men, and they bind themselves not to commit depredations or wrong upon either Indians or citizens; and should difficulties at any time arise, they will abide by the laws of the United States in such cases made and provided, as they expect to be protected, and to have their rights vindicated by those laws.

Conduct of the Indians.

Construction of roads.

ARTICLE 10. It is agreed that all roads and highways, laid out by authority of law, shall have right of way through the lands herein reserved, on the same terms as are provided by law when roads and highways are made through lands of citizens of the United States; and railroad companies, when the lines of their roads necessarily pass through the lands of the said Indians, shall have right of way on the payment of a just compensation therefor in money.

Future arrangements to effectuate the objects of this treaty.

ARTICLE 11. The object of this instrument being to advance the interests of said Indians, it is agreed, if it prove insufficient, from causes which cannot now be foreseen, to effect these ends, that the President may, by and with the advice and consent of the Senate, adopt such policy in the management of their affairs, as, in his judgment, may be most beneficial to them; or Congress may, hereafter, make such provision by law, as experience shall prove to be necessary.

Application of the first installment of one of the above payments.

ARTICLE 12. It is agreed that the first instalment of the fourteen thousand two hundred and twenty-three dollars and fifty cents, mentioned in the fourth article, being the accumulation of the poor, infirm, and education fund, shall be applied, under the direction of the President, to purposes of education; and that a sufficient sum shall annually be set apart out of the payments to the Miamis west of Missouri, so long as any of the annuities herein provided for shall continue, to be expended under the direction of the chiefs, for the support of the poor and infirm, and for defraying any expenses of the tribe of a civil nature.

Application of part of the annual payments to the Miamis west.

ARTICLE 13. It is hereby agreed that the sum of six thousand five hundred dollars may be set apart from each of the first four annual payments to be made to the Miamis west, and applied as far as it may be necessary, to the settlement of their affairs. It is also agreed that

Mill and school-house.

so much as may be necessary for the repair of their mill and school-house, shall be set apart from any fund now on hand belonging to said Indians, or be taken from any of the first instalments in this instrument provided for.

ARTICLE 14. This instrument shall be obligatory on the contracting parties whenever the same shall be ratified by the President and the Senate of the United States.

In testimony whereof the said George W. Manypenny, Commissioner as aforesaid, and the said delegates representing the Miami tribe of Indians, and also the said Miami Indians residents of the State of Indiana, have hereunto set their hands and seals, at the place, and on the day and year first above written.

George W. Manypenny, commissioner. [L. S.]
Nah-we-lan-quah, or Big Legs, his x mark. [L. S.]
Ma-cat-a-chin-quah, or Little Doctor, his x mark. [L. S.]
Lan-a-pin-chah, or Jack Hackley. [L. S.]
So-ne-lan-gish-eah, or John Bowrie, his x mark. [L. S.]
Wan-zop-e-ah, his x mark. [L. S.]

Miamis of Indiana:
Me-shin-go-me-zia, his x mark. [L. S.]
Po-con-ge-ah, his x mark. [L. S.]
Pim-yi-oh-te-nah, his x mark. [L. S.]
Wop-pop-pe-tah, or Bondy. [L. S.]
Ke-ah-cot-woh, or Buffalo, his x mark. [L. S.]

Executed in presence of—
Nathan Rice,
Joseph F. Brown,
Robert Campbell,
James T. Miller,
Wm. B. Waugh,
Ely Moore, Indian agent.
Baptiste Peoria, his x mark, U. S. interpreter.
W. B. Waugh, witness to signing of Baptiste Peoria.

TREATY WITH THE CREEKS, 1854.

Supplementary article to the treaty with the Creek tribe of Indians made and concluded at Fort Gibson on the twenty-third day of November, in the year eighteen hundred and thirty-eight.

June 13, 1854.

11 Stats., 599.
Ratified July 21, 1854.

Whereas the third article of said treaty provided for the investment by the United States of the sum of three hundred and fifty thousand dollars for the benefit of certain individuals of the Creek nation, but which sum remains uninvested; and the fourth article of the same treaty further provides that at the expiration of twenty-five years from the date thereof, the said sum of three hundred and fifty thousand dollars shall be appropriated for the common benefit of the Creek nation; which provision has caused great dissatisfaction, the individuals to whom the fund rightfully belongs never having authorized or assented to such a future disposition thereof; and whereas the chiefs and people of the Creek nation recognize and consider the said fund as the exclusive property of said individuals, and are opposed to their hereafter being deprived thereof; and whereas the annual interest thereon is of no advantage to the great body of the persons to whom it is payable, and the distribution of the principal of the fund would be far more beneficial for them and prevent probable contest and difficulty hereafter; and such distribution has been requested by the chiefs representing both the nation and the individual claimants of said fund, the following supplementary article to the aforesaid treaty of 1838, has this day been agreed to and entered into, by and between William H. Garrett, United States agent for the Creeks and Tuckabatche Micco, Hopoithle Yoholo, Benjamin Marshall, and George W. Stidham, chiefs and delegates of the Creek nation duly empowered to represent and act for the same and the individuals thereof to wit:

ARTICLE. It is hereby agreed and stipulated by and between the aforementioned parties, that the third and fourth articles of the treaty with the Creek nation of November 23, 1838, shall be and the same are hereby annulled; and the fund of three hundred and fifty thousand dollars therein mentioned and referred to shall be divided and paid out to the individuals of said nation for whose benefit the same was originally set apart, according to their respective and proportionate interests therein, as exemplified and shown by the schedule mentioned in the second article of said treaty; the said division and payment to be made by the United States so soon as the necessary appropriation for that purpose can be obtained from Congress.

Third and fourth articles of treaty of Nov. 23, 1838, annulled and fund to be divided.

In testimony whereof the said parties have hereunto set their hands and seals on this thirteenth day of June in the year of our Lord one thousand eight hundred and fifty-four.

W. H. Garrett, United States agent for the Creeks.	[L. S.]
Tuckabatche Micco, his x mark,	[L. S.]
Hopothlegoholo, his x mark,	[L. S.]
B. Marshall,	[L. S.]
G. W. Stidham,	[L. S.]

Signed and sealed in the presence of—
James Abercrombie, Sen.
Andrew R. Potts,
Robert A. Allen,
Philip H. Raiford.

TREATY WITH THE CHIPPEWA, 1854.

Sept. 30, 1854.

10 Stats., 1109.
Ratified Jan. 10, 1855.
Proclaimed Jan. 29,
1855.

Articles of a treaty made and concluded at La Pointe, in the State of Wisconsin, between Henry C. Gilbert and David B. Herriman, commissioners on the part of the United States, and the Chippewa Indians of Lake Superior and the Mississippi, by their chiefs and head-men.

Cession to the United States by the Chippewa of Lake Superior.

ARTICLE 1. The Chippewas of Lake Superior hereby cede to the United States all the lands heretofore owned by them in common with the Chippewas of the Mississippi, lying east of the following boundary-line, to wit: Beginning at a point, where the east branch of Snake River crosses the southern boundary-line of the Chippewa country, running thence up the said branch to its source, thence nearly north, in a straight line, to the mouth of East Savannah River, thence up the St. Louis River to the mouth of East Swan River, thence up the East Swan River to its source, thence in a straight line to the most westerly bend of Vermillion River, and thence down the Vermillion River to its mouth.

Relinquishment to Chippewa of Mississippi by Chippewa of Lake Superior.

The Chippewas of the Mississippi hereby assent and agree to the foregoing cession, and consent that the whole amount of the consideration money for the country ceded above, shall be paid to the Chippewas of Lake Superior, and in consideration thereof the Chippewas of Lake Superior hereby relinquish to the Chippewas of the Mississippi, all their interest in and claim to the lands heretofore owned by them in common, lying west of the above boundry-line.

Reservation for Chippewa of Lake Superior.

ARTICLE 2. The United States agree to set apart and withhold from sale, for the use of the Chippewas of Lake Superior, the following-described tracts of land, viz:

1st. For the L'Anse and Vieux De Sert bands, all the unsold lands in the following townships in the State of Michigan: Township fifty-one north range thirty-three west; township fifty-one north range thirty-two west; the east half of township fifty north range thirty-three west; the west half of township fifty north range thirty-two west, and all of township fifty-one north range thirty-one west, lying west of Huron Bay.

2d. For the La Pointe band, and such other Indians as may see fit to settle with them, a tract of land bounded as follows: Beginning on the south shore of Lake Superior, a few miles west of Montreal River, at the mouth of a creek called by the Indians Ke-che-se-be-we-she, running thence south to a line drawn east and west through the centre of township forty-seven north, thence west to the west line of said township, thence south to the southeast corner of township forty-six north, range thirty-two west, thence west the width of two townships, thence north the width of two townships, thence west one mile, thence north to the lake shore, and thence along the lake shore, crossing Shag-waw-me-quon Point, to the place of beginning. Also two hundred acres on the northern extremity of Madeline Island, for a fishing ground.

3d. For the other Wisconsin bands, a tract of land lying about Lac De Flambeau, and another tract on Lac Court Orielles, each equal in extent to three townships, the boundaries of which shall be hereafter agreed upon or fixed under the direction of the President.

4th. For the Fond Du Lac bands, a tract of land bounded as follows: Beginning at an island in the St. Louis River, above Knife Portage, called by the Indians Paw-paw-sco-me-me-tig, running thence west to the boundary-line heretofore described, thence north along said boundary-line to the mouth of Savannah River, thence down the St. Louis River to the place of beginning. And if said tract shall contain less than one hundred thousand acres, a strip of land shall be added on the south side thereof, large enough to equal such deficiency.

5th. For the Grand Portage band, a tract of land bounded as follows: Beginning at a rock a little east of the eastern extremity of Grand Portage Bay, running thence along the lake shore to the mouth of a small stream called by the Indians Maw-ske-gwaw-caw-maw-se-be, or Cranberry Marsh River, thence up said stream, across the point to Pigeon River, thence down Pigeon River to a point opposite the starting-point, and thence across to the place of beginning.

6th. The Ontonagon band and that subdivision of the La Pointe band of which Buffalo is chief, may each select, on or near the lake shore, four sections of land, under the direction of the President, the boundaries of which shall be defined hereafter. And being desirous to provide for some of his connections who have rendered his people important services, it is agreed that the chief Buffalo may select one section of land, at such place in the ceded territory as he may see fit, which shall be reserved for that purpose, and conveyed by the United States to such person or persons as he may direct.

7th. Each head of a family, or single person over twenty-one years of age at the present time of the mixed bloods, belonging to the Chippewas of Lake Superior, shall be entitled to eighty acres of land, to be selected by them under the direction of the President, and which shall be secured to them by patent in the usual form.

ARTICLE 3. The United States will define the boundaries of the reserved tracts, whenever it may be necessary, by actual survey, and the President may, from time to time, at his discretion, cause the whole to be surveyed, and may assign to each head of a family or single person over twenty-one years of age, eighty acres of land for his or their separate use; and he may, at his discretion, as fast as the occupants become capable of transacting their own affairs, issue patents therefor to such occupants, with such restrictions of the power of alienation as he may see fit to impose. And he may also, at his discretion, make rules and regulations, respecting the disposition of the lands in case of the death of the head of a family, or single person occupying the same, or in case of its abandonment by them. And he may also assign other lands in exchange for mineral lands, if any such are found in the tracts herein set apart. And he may also make such changes in the boundaries of such reserved tracts or otherwise, as shall be necessary to prevent interference with any vested rights. All necessary roads, highways, and railroads, the lines of which may run through any of the reserved tracts, shall have the right of way through the same, compensation being made therefor as in other cases. *Survey and patents of reservation.*

ARTICLE 4. In consideration of and payment for the country hereby ceded, the United States agree to pay to the Chippewas of Lake Superior, annually, for the term of twenty years, the following sums, to wit: five thousand dollars in coin; eight thousand dollars in goods, household furniture and cooking utensils; three thousand dollars in agricultural implements and cattle, carpenter's and other tools and building materials, and three thousand dollars for moral and educational purposes, of which last sum, three hundred dollars per annum shall be paid to the Grand Portage band, to enable them to maintain a school at their village. The United States will also pay the further sum of ninety thousand dollars, as the chiefs in open council may direct, to enable them to meet their present just engagements. Also the further sum of six thousand dollars, in agricultural implements, household furniture, and cooking utensils, to be distributed at the next annuity payment, among the mixed bloods of said nation. The United States will also furnish two hundred guns, one hundred rifles, five hundred beaver-traps, three hundred dollars' worth of ammuni- *Payments for said cession.*

tion, and one thousand dollars' worth of ready-made clothing, to be distributed among the young men of the nation, at the next annuity payment.

Blacksmiths and assistants.

ARTICLE 5. The United States will also furnish a blacksmith and assistant, with the usual amount of stock, during the continuance of the annuity payments, and as much longer as the President may think proper, at each of the points herein set apart for the residence of the Indians, the same to be in lieu of all the employees to which the Chippewas of Lake Superior may be entitled under previous existing treaties.

Annuities not to be withheld for debt, but may be for depredations.

ARTICLE 6. The annuities of the Indians shall not be taken to pay the debts of individuals, but satisfaction for depredations committed by them shall be made by them in such manner as the President may direct.

Spirituous liquors.

ARTICLE 7. No spirituous liquors shall be made, sold, or used on any of the lands herein set apart for the residence of the Indians, and the sale of the same shall be prohibited in the Territory hereby ceded, until otherwise ordered by the President.

Division between Chippewa of Mississippi and of Lake Superior of benefits of former treaties.

ARTICLE 8. It is agreed, between the Chippewas of Lake Superior and the Chippewas of the Mississippi, that the former shall be entitled to two-thirds, and the latter to one-third, of all benefits to be derived from former treaties existing prior to the year 1847.

Arrearages.

ARTICLE 9. The United States agree that an examination shall be made, and all sums that may be found equitably due to the Indians, for arrearages of annuity or other thing, under the provisions of former treaties, shall be paid as the chiefs may direct.

Preemption.

ARTICLE 10. All missionaries, and teachers, and other persons of full age, residing in the territory hereby ceded, or upon any of the reservations hereby made by authority of law, shall be allowed to enter the land occupied by them at the minimum price whenever the surveys shall be completed to the amount of one quarter-section each.

Annuities, how paid.

ARTICLE 11. All annuity payments to the Chippewas of Lake Superior, shall hereafter be made at L'Anse, La Pointe, Grand Portage, and on the St. Louis River; and the Indians shall not be required to remove from the homes hereby set apart for them. And such of them as reside in the territory hereby ceded, shall have the right to hunt and fish therein, until otherwise ordered by the President.

Stipulations for Bois Forte Indians.

ARTICLE 12. In consideration of the poverty of the Bois Forte Indians who are parties to this treaty, they having never received any annuity payments, and of the great extent of that part of the ceded country owned exclusively by them, the following additional stipulations are made for their benefit. The United States will pay the sum of ten thousand dollars, as their chiefs in open council may direct, to enable them to meet their present just engagements. Also the further sum of ten thousand dollars, in five equal annual payments, in blankets, cloth, nets, guns, ammunition, and such other articles of necessity as they may require.

They shall have the right to select their reservation at any time hereafter, under the direction of the President; and the same may be equal in extent, in proportion to their numbers, to those allowed the other bands, and be subject to the same provisions.

They shall be allowed a blacksmith, and the usual smithshop supplies, and also two persons to instruct them in farming, whenever in the opinion of the President it shall be proper, and for such length of time as he shall direct.

It is understood that all Indians who are parties to this treaty, except the Chippewas of the Mississippi, shall hereafter be known as the Chippewas of Lake Superior. *Provided,* That the stipulation by which the Chippewas of Lake Superior relinquishing their right to land west of the boundary-line shall not apply to the Bois Forte band who are parties to this treaty.

ARTICLE 13. This treaty shall be obligatory on the contracting parties, as soon as the same shall be ratified by the President and Senate of the United States.

In testimony whereof, the said Henry C. Gilbert, and the said David B. Herriman, commissioners as aforesaid, and the undersigned chiefs and headmen of the Chippewas of Lake Superior and the Mississippi, have hereunto set their hands and seals, at the place aforesaid, this thirtieth day of September, one thousand eight hundred and fifty-four.

Henry C. Gilbert,
David B. Herriman,
Commissioners.

Richard M. Smith, Secretary.

La Pointe Band:

Ke-che-waish-ke, or the Buffalo, 1st chief, his x mark. [L. S.]

Chay-che-que-oh, 2d chief, his x mark. [L. S.]

A-daw-we-ge-zhick, or Each Side of the sky, 2d chief, his x mark. [L. S.]

O-ske-naw-way, or the Youth, 2d chief, his x mark. [L. S.]

Maw-caw-day-pe-nay-se, or the Black Bird, 2d chief, his x mark. [L. S.]

Naw-waw-naw-quot, headman, his x mark. [L. S.]

Ke-wain-zeence, headman, his x mark. [L. S.]

Waw-baw-ne-me-ke, or the White Thunder, 2d chief, his x mark. [L. S.]

Pay-baw-me-say, or the Soarer, 2d chief, his x mark. [L. S.]

Naw-waw-ge-waw-nose, or the Little Current, 2d chief, his x mark. [L. S.]

Maw-caw-day-waw-quot, or the Black Cloud, 2d chief, his x mark. [L. S.]

Me-she-naw-way, or the Disciple, 2d chief, his x mark. [L. S.]

Key-me-waw-naw-um, headman, his x mark. [L. S.]

She-gog headman, his x mark. [L. S.]

Ontonagon Band:

O-cun-de-cun, or the Buoy 1st chief, his x mark. [L. S.]

Waw-say-ge-zhick, or the Clear Sky, 2d chief, his x mark. [L. S.]

Keesh-ke-taw-wug, headman, his x mark. [L. S.]

L'Anse Band:

David King, 1st chief, his x mark. [L. S.]

John Southwind, headman, his x mark. [L. S.]

Peter Marksman, headman, his x mark. [L. S.]

Naw-taw-me-ge-zhick, or the First Sky, 2d chief, his x mark. [L. S.]

Aw-se-neece, headman, his x mark. [L. S.]

Vieux De Sert Band:

May-dway-aw-she, 1st chief, his x mark. [L. S.]

Posh-quay-gin, or the Leather, 2d chief, his x mark. [L. S.]

Grand Portage Band:

Shaw-gaw-naw-sheence, or the Little Englishman, 1st chief, his x mark. [L. S.]

May-mosh-caw-wosh, headman, his x mark. [L. S.]

Aw-de-konse, or the Little Reindeer, 2d chief, his x mark. [L. S.]

Way-we-ge-wam, headman, his x mark. [L. S.]

Fond Du Lac Band:

Shing-goope, or the Balsom, 1st chief, his x mark. [L. S.]

Mawn-go-sit, or the Loon's Foot, 2d chief, his x mark. [L. S.]

May-quaw-me-we-ge-zhick, headman, his x mark. [L. S.]

Keesh-kawk, headman, his x mark. [L. S.]

Caw-taw-waw-be-day, headman, his x mark. [L. S.]

O-saw-gee, headman, his x mark. [L. S.]

Ke-che-aw-ke-wain-ze, headman, his x mark. [L. S.]

Naw-gaw-nub, or the Foremost Sitter, 2d chief, his x mark. [L. S.]

Ain-ne-maw-sung, 2d chief, his x mark. [L. S.]

Naw-aw-bun-way, headman, his x mark. [L. S.]

Wain-ge-maw-tub, headman, his x mark. [L. S.]

Aw-ke-wain-zeence, headman, his x mark. [L. S.]

Shay-way-be-nay-se, headman, his x mark. [L. S.]

Paw-pe-oh, headman, his x mark. [L. S.]

Lac Court Oreille Band:

Aw-ke-wain-ze, or the Old Man, 1st chief, his x mark. [L. S.]

Key-no-zhance, or the Little Jack Fish, 1st chief, his x mark. [L. S.]

Key-che-pe-nay-se, or the Big Bird, 2d chief, his x mark. [L. S.]

Ke-che-waw-be-shay-she, or the Big Martin, 2d chief, his x mark. [L. S.]

Waw-be-shay-sheence, headman, his x mark. [L. S.]

Quay-quay-cub, headman, his x mark. [L. S.]

Shaw-waw-no-me-tay, headman, his x mark. [L. S.]

Nay-naw-ong-gay-be, or the Dressing Bird, 1st chief, his x mark. [L. S.]

O-zhaw-waw-sco-ge-zhick, or the Blue Sky, 2d chief, his x mark. [L. S.]

I-yaw-banse, or the Little Buck, 2d chief, his x mark. [L. S.]

Ke-che-e-nin-ne, headman, his x mark. [L. s.]

Haw-daw-gaw-me, headman, his x mark. [L. s.]

Way-me-te-go-she, headman, his x mark. [L. s.]

Pay-me-ge-wung, headman, his x mark. [L. s.]

Lac Du Flambeau Band:

Aw-mo-se, or the Wasp, 1st chief, his x mark. [L. s.]

Ke-nish-te-no, 2d chief, his x mark. [L. s.]

Me-gee-see, or the Eagle, 2d chief, his x mark. [L. s.]

Kay-kay-co-gwaw-nay-aw-she, headman, his x mark. [L. s.]

O-che-chog, headman, his x mark. [L. s.]

Nay-she-kay-gwaw-nay-be, headman, his x mark. [L. s.]

O-scaw-bay-wis, or the Waiter, 1st chief, his x mark. [L. s.]

Que-we-zance, or the White Fish, 2d chief, his x mark. [L. s.]

Ne-gig, or the Otter, 2d chief, his x mark. [L. s.]

Nay-waw-che-ge-ghick-may-be, headman, his x mark. [L. s.]

Quay-quay-ke-cah, headman, his x mark. [L. s.]

Bois Forte Band:

Kay-baish-caw-daw-way, or Clear Round the Prairie, 1st chief, his x mark. [L. s.]

Way-zaw-we-ge-zhick-way-sking, headman, his x mark. [L. s.]

O-saw-we-pe-nay-she, headman, his x mark. [L. s.]

The Mississippi Bands:

Que-we-san-se, or Hole in the Day, head chief, his x mark. [L. s.]

Caw-nawn-daw-waw-win-zo, or the Berry Hunter, 1st chief, his x mark. [L. s.]

Waw-bow-jieg, or the White Fisher, 2d chief, his x mark. [L. s.]

Ot-taw-waw, 2d chief, his x mark. [L. s.]

Que-we-zhan-cis, or the Bad Boy, 2d chief, his x mark. [L. s.]

Bye-a-jick, or the Lone Man, 2d chief, his x mark. [L. s.]

I-yaw-shaw-way-ge-zhick, or the Crossing Sky, 2d chief, his x mark. [L. s.]

Maw-caw-day, or the Bear's Heart, 2d chief, his x mark. [L. s.]

Ke-way-de-no-go-nay-be, or the Northern Feather, 2d chief, his x mark. [L. s.]

Me-squaw-dace, headman, his x mark. [L. s.]

Naw-gaw-ne-gaw-bo, headman, his x mark. [L. s.]

Wawm-be-de-yea, headman, his x mark. [L. s.]

Waish-key, headman, his x mark. [L. s.]

Caw-way-caw-me-ge-skung, headman, his x mark. [L. s.]

My-yaw-ge-way-we-dunk, or the One who carries the Voice, 2d chief, his x mark. [L. s.]

John F. Godfroy,
Geo. Johnston,
S. A. Marvin,
Louis Codot,   } Interpreters.
Paul H. Beaulieu,
Henry Blatchford,
Peter Floy,

Executed in the presence of—

Henry M. Rice,
J. W. Lynde,
G. D. Williams,
B. H. Connor,
E. W. Muldough,
Richard Godfroy,

D. S. Cash,
H. H. McCullough,
E. Smith Lee,
Wm. E. Vantassel,
L. H. Wheeler.

TREATY WITH THE CHOCTAW AND CHICKASAW, 1854.

Nov. 4, 1854.

10 Stat., 1116.
Ratified Feb. 28, 1855.
Proclaimed Apr. 10, 1855.

Preamble.

Whereas a convention and agreement was made and entered into by the Choctaw and Chickasaw Indians, at Doaksville, near Fort Towson, in the Choctaw country, on the seventeenth day of January, A. D. one thousand eight hundred and thirty-seven; and, whereas, difficulties have arisen between said tribes in regard to the line of boundary, between the Chickasaw district and other districts of the Choctaw nation, described in article second of said convention and agreement; and, whereas, it is the desire of the said tribes, that there shall no longer exist any dispute in regard to the boundary of the Chickasaw district, the undersigned, Thomas J. Pitchlynn, Edmund McKenny, R. M. Jones, Daniel Folsom, and Samuel Garland, commissioners duly appointed and empowered by the Choctaw tribe of red people; and Edmund Pickens, Benjamin S. Love, James T. Gaines, Sampson Folsom, and Edmund Perry, commissioners duly appointed and empowered by the Chickasaw tribe of Indians, to settle all matters in dispute between their respective tribes, which require new articles of agreement between them, have solemnly made the following articles of convention and agreement, on the fourth day of November, A. D. one thousand eight hundred and fifty-four, at Doaksville, near Fort Towson, in the Choctaw country, subject to the approval of the President and the Senate of the United States.

ARTICLE 1. It is agreed by the Choctaw and Chickasaw tribes of Indians, in lieu of the boundaries established under article second of the convention and agreement entered into between said tribes, January 17th, A. D. 1837, the Chickasaw district of the Choctaw nation shall be bounded as follows, viz: Beginning on the north bank of the Red River, at the mouth of Island Bayou, where it empties into the Red River, about twenty-six miles on a straight line, below the mouth of False Wachitta, thence running a northwesterly course, along the main channel of said bayou to the junction of three prongs of said bayou nearest the dividing ridge between Wachitta and Low Blue rivers, as laid down upon Capt. R. L. Hunter's map; thence, northerly along the eastern prong of Island Bayou to its source; thence, due north to the Canadian River, thence west, along the main Canadian, to one hundred degrees of west longitude; thence south to Red River, and down Red River to the beginning: *Provided, however*, if the line running due north from the eastern source of Island Bayou to the main Canadian shall not include Allen's or Wa-pa-nacka academy within the Chickasaw district, then an offset shall be made from said line so as to leave said academy two miles within the Chickasaw district, north, west, and south from the lines of boundary.

Boundaries of the Chickasaw district of the Choctaws.

ARTICLE 2. It is agreed by the Choctaws, that the Chickasaws employ a surveyor or engineer to run out and mark the eastern line of the Chickasaw district, and by the Chickasaws that they will pay all expenses incurred in running out and marking said line; and it is mutually agreed that the chiefs of each district of the Choctaw nation shall appoint one commissioner to attend and supervise the running and marking of said line; the chief of the Chickasaw district giving them at least thirty days' notice of the time when the surveyor or engineer will proceed to run out and mark the line agreed upon; which shall be plainly marked upon trees, where there is timber, and by permanent monuments of stone, at every mile, where there is not sufficient timber upon which the line can be marked in a permanent manner, before the first day of August, A. D. one thousand eight hundred and fifty-five.

Line, how to be run and marked.

In testimony whereof, the parties to this convention and agreement have hereunto subscribed their names and affixed their seals.

Done in triplicate at Doaksville, near Fort Towson, Choctaw Nation, the day and year first above written.

Thos. J. Pitchlynn,	[L. S.]
Edmund McKenny,	[L. S.]
R. M. Jones,	[L. S.]
Daniel Folsom,	[L. S.]
Samuel Garland,	[L. S.]

Commissioners on the part of Choctaws.

Edmund Pickens	[L. S.]
Benjamin S. Love,	[L. S.]
James T. Gaines,	[L. S.]
Sampson Folsom,	[L. S.]
Edmund Perry,	[L. S.]

Commissioners on the part of the Chickasaws.

In presence of—
Geo. W. Harkins,
Peter Folsom,
Nicholas Cochnaner,
Jackson Frazier,
    Chiefs of the Choctaw Nation.

Douglas H. Cooper, United States Indian agent.
William K. McKean.

TREATY WITH THE ROGUE RIVER, 1854.

Nov. 15, 1854.

10 Stats., 1119.
Ratified Mar. 3, 1855.
Proclaimed Apr. 7,
1855.

Articles of an agreement entered into and concluded this fifteenth day of November, one thousand eight hundred and fifty-four, between Joel Palmer, superintendent of Indian affairs, on the part of the United States, and the chiefs and headmen of the Rogue River tribe of Indians, on the part of said tribe.

Other Indians may be settled on the Table Rock Reserve.

ARTICLE 1. It is agreed on the part of said tribe, that the Table Rock reserve, described in the treaty of the 10th September, 1853, between the United States and the Rogue River tribe, shall be possessed and occupied jointly by said tribe and such other tribes and bands of Indians as the United States shall agree with by treaty stipulations, or the President of the United States shall direct, to reside thereupon, the place of residence of each tribe, part of tribe, or band on said reserve, to be designated by the superintendent of Indian affairs or Indian agent; that the tribes and bands hereafter to be settled on said reserve shall enjoy equal rights and privileges with the Rogue River tribe; and that the annuities paid to the Indians now residing, or hereafter to reside on said reserve, shall be shared by all alike, from and after said residence thereon: *Provided*, That the annuity of the Rogue River tribe, as agreed on in the treaty of the 10th September, 1853, shall not be diminished or in any way impaired thereby. It is also agreed, that the United States shall have the right to make such roads, highways, and railroads through said reserve as the public good may from time to time require, a just compensation being made therefor.

Ante, p. 603.

Annuities.

Roads may be made.

Payment and stipulations in consideration of the foregoing article.

ARTICLE 2. In consideration of the foregoing stipulations, it is agreed on the part of the United States to pay to the Rogue River tribe, as soon as practicable after the signing of this agreement, two thousand one hundred and fifty dollars, in the following articles: twelve horses, one beef, two yokes of oxen, with yokes and chains, one wagon, one hundred men's coats, fifty pairs of pantaloons, and fifty hickory shirts; also, that in the treaties to be made with other tribes and bands, hereafter to be located on said reserve, that provision shall be made for the erection of two smith-shops; for tools, iron, and blacksmiths for the same; for opening farms and employing farmers; for a hospital, medicines, and a physician; and for one or more schools; the uses and benefits of all which shall be secured to said Rogue River tribe, equally with the tribes and bands treated with; all the improvements made, and schools, hospital, and shops erected, to be conducted in accordance with such laws, rules, and regulations as the Congress or the President of the United States may prescribe.

Provision in case of removal from said reservation.

ARTICLE 3. It is further agreed, that when at any time hereafter the Indians residing on this reserve shall be removed to another reserve, or shall be elsewhere provided for, that the fifteen thousand dollars thereafter to be paid to said Rogue River tribe, as specified in the treaty of the 10th September, 1853, shall be shared alike by the members of all the tribes and bands that are, or hereafter shall be located on the said Table Rock reserve.

Provision in case treaty is not ratified or no Indians are removed to said reserve.

ARTICLE 4. It is also further provided that in the event that this agreement shall not be ratified by the President and Senate of the United States, or that no other tribe or band shall be located on said reserve, the two thousand one hundred and fifty dollars stipulated in article second of this agreement to be paid said Rogue River tribe, shall be deducted from their annuities hereafter to be paid said Indians.

In testimony whereof, the said Joel Palmer, superintendent as aforesaid, and the undersigned chiefs and headmen of the Rogue River Tribe of Indians, have hereunto set their hands and seals, at Even's

Creek, on the Table Rock Reserve, on the day and year herein before written.

Joel Palmer, superintendent	[L. S.]
Ap-sa-ka-hah, or Joe, first chief, his x mark,	[L. S.]
Ko-ko-ha-wah, or Sam, second chief, his x mark,	[L. S.]
Sambo, third chief, his x mark,	[L. S.]
Te-cum-tum, or John, fourth chief, his x mark,	[L. S.]
Te-wah-hait, or Elijah, his x mark,	[L. S.]
Cho-cul-tah, or George, his x mark,	[L. S.]
Telum-whah, or Bill, his x mark,	[L. S.]
Hart-tish, or Applegate John, his x mark,	[L. S.]
Qua-chis, or Jake, his x mark,	[L. S.]
Tom, his x mark,	[L. S.]
Henry, his x mark,	[L. S.]
Jim, his x mark,	[L. S.]

Executed in presence of—
    Edward R. Geary, secretary.
    Cris. Taylor,
    John Flett, interpreter.
    R. B. Metcalfe.

TREATY WITH THE CHASTA, ETC., 1854.

Articles of a convention and agreement made and concluded at the council-ground, opposite the mouth of Applegate Creek, on Rogue River, in the Territory of Oregon, on the eighteenth day of November, one thousand eight hundred and fifty-four, by Joel Palmer, superintendent of Indian affairs, on the part of the United States, and the chiefs and head-men of the Quil-si-eton and Na-hel-ta bands, of the Chasta tribe of Indians, the Cow-nan-ti-co, Sa-cher-i-ton, and Na-al-ye bands of Scotons, and the Grave Creek band of Umpquas, to wit, Jes-tul-tut, or Little Chief, Ko-ne-che-quot, or Bill, Se-sel-che-tel, or Salmon Fisher, Kul-ki-am-i-na, or Bush-head, Te-po-kon-ta, or Sam, and Jo, they being duly authorized thereto by said united bands.

Nov. 18, 1854.

10 Stats., 1122.
Ratified Mar. 3, 1855.
Proclaimed Apr. 10, 1855.

Preamble.

ARTICLE 1. The aforesaid united bands cede to the United States all their country, bounded as follows:

Cession to the United States.

Commencing at a point in the middle of Rogue River, one mile below the mouth of Applegate Creek; thence northerly, on the western boundary of the country heretofore purchased of the Rogue River tribe by the United States, to the head-waters of Jump-Off-Jo Creek; thence westerly to the extreme northeastern limit of the country purchased of the Cow Creek band of Umpquas; thence along that boundary to its extreme southwestern limit; thence due west to a point from which a line running due south would cross Rogue River, midway between the mouth of Grave Creek and the great bend of Rogue River; thence south to the southern boundary of Oregon; thence east along said boundary to the summit of the main ridge of the Siskiou Mountains, or until this line reaches the boundary of the country purchased of the Rogue River tribe; thence northerly along the western boundary of said purchase to the place of beginning.

ARTICLE 2. The said united bands agree that as soon after the ratification of this convention as practicable, they will remove to such portion of the Table Rock reserve as may be assigned them by the superintendent of Indian affairs or agent, or to whatsoever other reserve the President of the United States may at any time hereafter direct.

Removal to Table Rock reserve.

ARTICLE 3. In consideration of and payment for the country herein ceded, the United States agree to pay to the said united bands the sum

Payment for said cession.

of two thousand dollars annually for fifteen years, from and after the first day of September, one thousand eight hundred and fifty-five, which annuities shall be added to those secured to the Rogue River tribe by the treaty of the 10th September, 1853, and the amount shared by the members of the united bands and of the Rogue River tribe, jointly and alike; said annuities to be expended for the use and benefit of said bands and tribe in such manner as the President may from time to time prescribe; for provisions, clothing, and merchandise; for buildings, opening and fencing farms, breaking land, providing stock, agricultural implements, tools, seeds, and such other objects as will in his judgment promote the comfort and advance the prosperity and civilization of said Indians. The United States also agree to appropriate the additional sum of five thousand dollars, for the payment of the claims of persons whose property has been stolen or destroyed by any of the said united bands of Indians since the first day of January, 1849; such claims to be audited and adjusted in such manner as the President may prescribe.

Provision in case of removal from said reserve. ARTICLE 4. When said united bands shall be required to remove to the Table Rock reserve or elsewhere, as the President may direct, the further sum of six thousand five hundred dollars shall be expended by the United States for provisions to aid in their subsistence during the first year they shall reside thereon; for the erecting of necessary buildings, and the breaking and fencing of fifty acres of land, and providing seed to plant the same, for their use and benefit, in common with the other Indians on the reserve.

Stipulations for all Indians on said reserve. ARTICLE 5. The United States engage that the following provisions, for the use and benefit of all Indians residing on the reserve, shall be made:

An experienced farmer shall be employed to aid and instruct the Indians in agriculture for the term of fifteen years.

Two blacksmith-shops shall be erected at convenient points on the reserve, and furnished with tools and the necessary stock, and skilful smiths employed for the same for five years.

A hospital shall be erected, and proper provision made for medical purposes, and the care of the sick for ten years.

School-houses shall be erected, and qualified teachers employed to instruct children on the reserve, and books and stationery furnished for fifteen years.

All of which provisions shall be controlled by such laws, rules, or regulations as Congress may enact or the President prescribe.

Survey and allotment of said reserve. ARTICLE 6. The President may, from time to time, at his discretion, direct the surveying of a part or all of the agricultural lands on said reserve, divide the same into small farms of from twenty to eighty acres, according to the number of persons in a family, and assign them to such Indians as are willing to avail themselves of the privilege and locate thereon as a permanent home, and to grant them a patent therefor under such laws and regulations as may hereafter be enacted or prescribed.

Annuities not to be taken for debt. ARTICLE 7. The annuities of the Indians shall not be taken to pay the debts of individuals.

Conduct of said tribes. ARTICLE 8. The said united bands acknowledge themselves subject to the Government of the United States, and engage to live in amity with the citizens thereof, and commit no depredations on the property of said citizens; and should any Indian or Indians violate this pledge, and the fact be satisfactorily proven, the property shall be returned, or if not returned, or if injured or destroyed, compensation may be made therefor out of their annuities. They also pledge themselves to live peaceably with one another, and with other Indians, to abstain from war and private acts of revenge, and to submit all matters of difference between themselves and Indians of other tribes and bands to the decision of the United States or the agent, and to abide thereby.

It is also agreed that if any individual shall be found guilty of bringing liquor into their country, or drinking the same, his or her annuity may be withheld during the pleasure of the President.

ARTICLE 9. This convention shall be obligatory on the contracting parties from and after its ratification by the President and Senate of the United States.

In testimony whereof, Joel Palmer, superintendent aforesaid, and the undersigned chiefs and headmen of said united bands, have hereunto set their hands and seals at the place and on the day and year herein written.

(Signed in duplicate)

Joel Palmer, Superintendent.   [L. S.]
Jes-tul-tut, or Little Chief, his x mark.   [L. S.]
Ko-ne-che-quot, or Bill, his x mark.   [L. S.]
Se-sel-chetl, or Salmon Fisher, his x mark.   [L. S.]
Bas-ta-shin, his x mark,   [L. S.]
    For Kul-ke-am-ina, or Bushland.
Te-po-kon-ta, or Sam, his x mark,   [L. S.]
Jo (Chief of Grave Creeks), his x mark.   [L. S.]

Executed in presence of us—
    Edward R. Geary, Secretary.
    John Flett, Interpreter.
    Cris. Taylor.

TREATY WITH THE UMPQUA AND KALAPUYA, 1854.

Articles of agreement and convention made and concluded at Calapooia Creek, Douglas County, Oregon Territory, this twenty-ninth day of November, one thousand eight hundred and fifty-four, by Joel Palmer, superintendent of Indian affairs, on the part of the United States, and the following-named chiefs and heads of the confederated bands of the Umpqua tribe of Indians, and of the Calapooias residing in Umpqua Valley, to wit: Napesa, or Louis, head chief; Peter, or Injice; Tas-yah, or General Jackson; Bogus; Nessick; Et-na-ma or William, Cheen-len-ten or George, Nas-yah or John, Absaquil or Chenook, Jo, and Tom, they being assembled in council with their respective bands.

Nov. 29, 1854.

10 Stats., 1125.
Ratified Mar. 3, 1855.
Proclaimed Mar. 30, 1855.

ARTICLE 1. The confederated bands of Umpqua and Calapooia Indians cede to the United States all their country included within the following limits, to wit: Commencing at the northwest corner of the country purchased of the Galeese Creek and Illinois River Indians on the 18th day of November, 1854, and running thence east to the boundary of the Cow Creek purchase, thence northerly along said boundary to its northeastern extremity; thence east to the main ridge of the Cascade Mountains; thence northerly to the main falls of the North Umpqua River; thence to Scott's Peak, bearing easterly from the head-waters of Calapooia Creek; thence northerly to the connection of the Calapooia Mountains with the Cascade range; thence westerly along the summit of the Calapooia Mountains to a point whence a due south line would cross Umpqua River at the head of tide-water; thence on that line to the dividing ridge between the waters of Umpqua and Coose Rivers; thence along that ridge, and the divide between Coquille and Umpqua Rivers, to the western boundary of the country purchased of the Galeese Creek Indians, or of the Cow Creek Indians, as the case may be, and thence to the place of beginning.

Cession to the United States.

Provided, however, That so much of the lands as are embraced within the following limits, shall be held by said confederated bands, and such other bands as may be designated to reside thereupon, as an Indian

Reservation for a residence.

reservation. To wit: Commencing at a point three miles due south of the mouth of a small creek emptying into the Umpqua River, near the western boundary of John Churchell's land-claim, at the lower end of Cole's Valley; thence north to the middle of the channel of Umpqua River; thence u·) said river to a point due south of the highest peak of the ridge, immediately west of Allan Hubbard's land-claim; thence to said peak, thence along the summit of the ridge dividing the waters, to its termination at or near the mouth of Little Canyon Creek; thence, crossing the Umpqua River in a westerly direction to the high-lands opposite the mouth of said creek; thence following the divide until it reaches a point whence a line drawn to the place of beginning will run three miles south of the extreme southern bend in the Umpqua River between these two points: and thence to the place *Removal from said reserve if it should become expedient.* of beginning. And should the President at any time believe it demanded by the public good and promotive of the best interests of said Indians to be located elsewhere, the said Indians agree peaceably, and without additional expense to the Government of the United States, to remove to such reserve as may be selected; provided that a delegation of three or more of the principal men of said bands selected by them, shall concur with the authorized agent or agents of the United States in the selection of said new reserve. And when said removal shall take place, the particular tracts then actually occupied by said Indians, on the reserve herein described, according to the provisions of this treaty, and those occupied by Indians of other bands that may be located thereon, shall be sold by order of the President of the United States, and the proceeds of such sales expended in permanent improvements on the new reserve, for the use and benefit of the holders of said tracts respectively.

Removal from the ceded lands. ARTICLE 2. The confederated bands agree that as soon after the United States shall make the necessary provision for fulfilling the stipulations of this treaty as they conveniently can, and not to exceed one year after such provision is made, they will vacate the ceded territory and remove to the lands herein reserved for them.

Payment for said cession. ARTICLE 3. In consideration of and payment for the country herein ceded, the United States agree to pay the said confederated bands the several sums of money following, to wit: First, three thousand dollars per annum for the term of five years, commencing on the first day of September, 1855. Second, two thousand three hundred dollars per annum for the term of five years next succeeding the first five. Third, one thousand seven hundred dollars per annum for the term of five years next succeeding the second five years. Fourth, one thousand dollars per annum for the term of five years next succeeding the third five years.

All of which several sums of money shall be expended for the use and benefit of the confederated bands, under the direction of the President of the United States, who may from time to time, at his discretion, determine ·what proportion shall be expended for such beneficial objects as in his judgment will be calculated to ,advance them in civilization; for their moral improvement and education; for buildings, opening farms, fencing, breaking land, providing stock, agricultural implements, seeds, &c.; for clothing, provisions, and merchandise; for iron, steel, arms, and ammunition; for mechanics and tools, and for medical purposes.

Payment for expense of removal. ARTICLE 4. In order to enable the said Indians to remove to their new home, and subsist themselves for one year thereafter, (and which they agree to do without further expense to the United States,) and to provide for the breaking up and fencing of fifty acres of land, and the erection of buildings on the reserve, the purchase of teams, farming-utensils, tools, &c., and for other purposes necessary to their comfort and subsistence, they shall receive from the United States the further sum of ten thousand dollars, to be paid out and expended under the direction of the President, and in such manner as he shall approve.

ARTICLE 5. The President may from time to time, at his discretion, cause the whole or such portion of the land hereby reserved as he may think proper, or of such other land as may be selected in lieu thereof, as provided for in the first article, to be surveyed into lots, and assigned to such Indian or Indians of said confederated bands as are willing to avail themselves of the privilege, and who will locate thereon as a permanent home, if a single person over twenty-one years of age, twenty acres; to each family of two persons, forty acres; to each family of three and not exceeding five persons, sixty acres; to each family of six and not exceeding ten persons, eighty acres; and to each family over ten in number, forty acres for each additional five members. And the President may provide such rules and regulations as will secure to the family, in case of the death of the head thereof, the possession and enjoyment of such permanent home, and the improvements thereon; and he may at any time, at his discretion, after such person or family has made location on the land assigned for a permanent home, issue a patent to such person or family for such assigned land, conditioned that the tract shall not be aliened or leased for a longer term than two years, and shall be exempt from levy, sale, or forfeiture, which conditions shall continue in force until a State constitution, embracing such lands within its boundaries, shall have been formed, and the legislature of the State shall remove the restrictions. And if any such family shall at any time neglect or refuse to occupy or till a portion of the land assigned, and on which they have located, or shall rove from place to place, the President may, if the patent shall have been issued, revoke the same, or, if not issued, cancel the assignment, and may also withhold from such person or family their proportion of the annuities or other moneys due them, until they shall have returned to such permanent home, and resume the pursuits of industry; and in default of their return, the tract may be declared abandoned and thereafter assigned to some other person or family of the Indians residing on the reserve.

Survey and allotment of the reserve.

No State legislature shall remove the restrictions herein provided for, without the consent of Congress.

Power of future States over restrictions limited.

ARTICLE 6. The United States agree to erect for said Indians a good blacksmith-shop, furnish it with tools, and keep it in repair for ten years, and provide a competent blacksmith for the same period; to erect suitable buildings for a hospital, supply medicines, and provide an experienced physician for fifteen years; to provide a competent farmer to instruct the Indians in agriculture for ten years; and to erect a school-house, and provide books, stationery, and a properly qualified teacher for twenty years.

Blacksmith's shop, etc.

ARTICLE 7. The annuities of the Indians shall not be taken to pay the debts of individuals.

Annuities not to be taken for debt.

ARTICLE 8. The said confederated bands acknowledge their dependence on the Government of the United States, and promise to be friendly with all the citizens thereof, and pledge themselves to commit no depredations on the property of such citizens. And should any one or more of the Indians violate this pledge, and the fact be satisfactorily proven before the agent, the property shall be returned, or in default thereof, or if injured or destroyed, compensation may be made by the Government out of their annuities. Nor will they make war on any other tribe except in self-defense, but will submit all matters of difference between them and other Indians to the Government of the United States or its agent, for decision, and abide thereby. And if any of the said Indians commit any depredations on any other Indians, the same rule shall prevail as that prescribed in this article in case of any depredations against citizens. Said Indians further engage

Submission and conduct of Indians.

to submit to, and observe all laws, rules, and regulations which may be prescribed by the United States for the government of said Indians.

Provision against intemperance.

ARTICLE 9. It is hereby provided, in order to prevent the evils of intemperance among said Indians, that any one of them who shall be guilty of bringing liquor into their reserve, or shall drink liquor, may have his or her proportion of the annuities withheld from him or her for such time as the President may determine.

Roads, etc., may be constructed.

ARTICLE 10. The said confederate bands agree, that all the necessary roads, highways, and railroads which may be constructed as the country improves, the lines of which may run through the reservation of said Indians, shall have the right of way therein, a just compensation being made therefor.

Merchandise to be part payment of annuities.

ARTICLE 11. The merchandise distributed to the members of the said confederate bands at the nogotiation of this treaty shall be considered as in part payment of the annuities herein provided.

ARTICLE 12. This treaty shall be obligatory on the contracting parties as soon as the same shall be ratified by the President and Senate of the United States.

In testimony whereof, the said Joel Palmer, on the part of the United States as aforesaid, and the undersigned chiefs and heads of the said confederated bands of Umpquas and Calapooias, have hereunto set their hands and seals, at the place and on the day and year heretofore written.

Joel Palmer, superintendent.
Na-pe-sa, or Louis, his x mark.   [L. S.]
Injice, or Peter, his x mark.   [L. S.]
Tas-yah, or General Jackson, his x mark.   [L. S.]
Bogus, his x mark.   [L. S.]
Nessick, his x mark.   [L. S.]
Et-na-ma, or William, his x mark.   [L. S.]
Cheen-len-ten, or George, his x mark.   [L. S.]
Nas-yah, or John, his x mark.   [L. S.]
Absaquil, or Chenook, his x mark.   [L. S.]
Jo, his x mark.   [L. S.]
Tom, his x mark.   [L. S.]

Executed in the presence of us—
Edward R. Geary, secretary.
Cris. Taylor.
John Flett, interpreter.

TREATY WITH THE CONFEDERATED OTO AND MISSOURI, 1854.

Dec. 9, 1854.

10 Stat., 1130.
11 Stat., 605.
Ratified, Feb. 28, 1855.
Proclaimed Apr. 10, 1855.

Article of agreement and convention made and concluded at Nebraska City, in the Territory of Nebraska, on the ninth day of December, one thousand eight hundred and fifty-four, between the United States of America, by George Hepner, United States' Indian agent, duly authorized thereto, and the chiefs and headmen of the confederate tribes of the Ottoe and Missouria Indians, to be taken and considered as a supplement to the treaty made between the United States and said confederate tribes, on the fifteenth day of March, one thousand eight hundred and fifty-four.

Preamble.

Whereas, by the first article of the treaty in the caption mentioned, it is stipulated that the confederate tribes of the Ottoe and Missouria Indians cede to the United States all their country west of the Missouri River, excepting a strip of land on the waters of the Big Blue River, ten miles in width, and bounded as follows: commencing at a point in the middle of the main branch of the Big Blue River, in a west or southwest direction from old Fort Kearney, at a place called by the Indians the "Islands;" thence west to the western boundary of the country hereby ceded; thence in a northerly course with said western boundary ten miles; thence east to a point due north of the starting point, and ten miles therefrom; thence to the place of beginning.

And whereas, upon exploration of said reservation by the said confederate tribes, it was found that they had been mistaken as to the location thereof, much the larger portion, or nearly the entirety of it, being to the west of the Big Blue River, and without sufficiency of timber, and they being dissatisfied therewith, and the United States being desirous of removing all cause of complaint, this article is entered into.

ARTICLE. It is agreed and stipulated, between the United States and the said confederate tribes of Ottoe and Missouria Indians, that the initial point of their reservation, in lieu of that stated in the treaty, in the caption hereof mentioned, shall be a point five miles due east thereof, thence west twenty-five miles, thence north ten miles, thence east to a point due north of the starting point and ten miles therefrom, thence to the place of beginning; and the country embraced within said boundaries shall be taken and considered as the reservation and home of said confederate tribes, in lieu of that provided for them and described in the first article of said treaty. *Boundary of their reservation.*

In witness whereof the said George Hepner and the undersigned chiefs and head men of the said Confederate tribes of Ottoes and Missourias, have hereunto set their hands and seals, at the place and on the day and year above written.

George Hepner, United States Indian agent.	[SEAL.]
Hick Kapoo, his x mark.	[SEAL.]
Bil Soldier, his x mark.	[SEAL.]
Chi-an-a-ka, or Buffalo Chief, his x mark.	[SEAL.]
Missouri Chief, his x mark.	[SEAL.]
White Water, his x mark.	[SEAL.]

Executed in the presence of—
   Lewis Bernard, his x mark,
                 U. S. interpreter.
   H. P. Downs.
   John Baulware.

TREATY WITH THE NISQUALLI, PUYALLUP, ETC., 1854.

Articles of agreement and convention made and concluded on the She-nah-nam, or Medicine Creek, in the Territory of Washington, this twenty-sixth day of December, in the year one thousand eight hundred and fifty-four, by Isaac I. Stevens, governor and superintendent of Indian affairs of the said Territory, on the part of the United States, and the undersigned chiefs, head-men, and delegates of the Nisqually, Puyallup, Steilacoom, Squawskin, S'Homamish, Stehchass, T'Peek-sin, Squi-aitl, and Sa-heh-wamish tribes and bands of Indians, occupying the lands lying round the head of Puget's Sound and the adjacent inlets, who, for the purpose of this treaty, are to be regarded as one nation, on behalf of said tribes and bands, and duly authorized by them. Dec. 26, 1854.

10 Stat., 1132.
Ratified Mar. 3, 1855.
Proclaimed Apr. 10, 1855.

ARTICLE 1. The said tribes and bands of Indians hereby cede, relinquish, and convey to the United States, all their right, title, and interest in and to the lands and country occupied by them, bounded and described as follows, to wit: Commencing at the point on the eastern side of Admiralty Inlet, known as Point Pully, about midway between Commencement and Elliott Bays; thence running in a south- *Cession to United States.*

easterly direction, following the divide betweeen the waters of the Puyallup and Dwamish, or White Rivers, to the summit of the Cascade Mountains; thence southerly, along the summit of said range, to a point opposite the main source of the Skookum Chuck Creek; thence to and down said creek, to the coal mine; thence northwesterly, to the summit of the Black Hills; thence northerly, to the upper forks of the Satsop River; thence northeasterly, through the portage known as Wilkes's Portage, to Point Southworth, on the western side of Admiralty Inlet; thence around the foot of Vashon's Island, easterly and southeasterly, to the place of beginning.

Reservation for said tribes.

ARTICLE 2. There is, however, reserved for the present use and occupation of the said tribes and bands, the following tracts of land, viz: The small island called Klah-che-min, situated opposite the mouths of Hammersley's and Totten's Inlets, and separated from Hartstene Island by Peale's Passage, containing about two sections of land by estimation; a square tract containing two sections, or twelve hundred and eighty acres, on Puget's Sound, near the mouth of the She-nah-nam Creek, one mile west of the meridian line of the United States land survey, and a square tract containing two sections, or twelve hundred and eighty acres, lying on the south side of Commencement Bay; all which tracts shall be set apart, and, so far as necessary, surveyed and marked out for their exclusive use; nor shall any white man be permitted to reside upon the same without permission of the

Removal thereto.

tribe and the superintendent or agent. And the said tribes and bands agree to remove to and settle upon the same within one year after the ratification of this treaty, or sooner if the means are furnished them. In the mean time, it shall be lawful for them to reside upon any ground not in the actual claim and occupation of citizens of the United States, and upon any ground claimed or occupied, if with the permission of the owner or claimant. If necessary for the public convenience, roads

Roads to be constructed.

may be run through their reserves, and, on the other hand, the right of way with free access from the same to the nearest public highway is secured to them.

Rights to fish.

ARTICLE 3. The right of taking fish, at all usual and accustomed grounds and stations, is further secured to said Indians in common with all citizens of the Territory, and of erecting temporary houses for the purpose of curing, together with the privilege of hunting, gathering roots and berries, and pasturing their horses on open and unclaimed lands: *Provided, however*, That they shall not take shell-fish from any beds staked or cultivated by citizens, and that they shall alter all stallions not intended for breeding-horses, and shall keep up and confine the latter.

Payments for said cession.

ARTICLE 4. In consideration of the above session, the United States agree to pay to the said tribes and bands the sum of thirty-two thousand five hundred dollars, in the following manner, that is to say: For the first year after the ratification hereof, three thousand two hundred and fifty dollars; for the next two years, three thousand dollars each year; for the next three years, two thousand dollars each year; for the next four years fifteen hundred dollars each year; for the next five years twelve hundred dollars each year; and for the next five years one thousand dollars each year; all which said sums of money shall be

How applied.

applied to the use and benefit of the said Indians, under the direction of the President of the United States, who may from time to time determine, at his discretion, upon what beneficial objects to expend the same. And the superintendent of Indian affairs, or other proper officer, shall each year inform the President of the wishes of said Indians in respect thereto.

Expenses of removal.

ARTICLE 5. To enable the said Indians to remove to and settle upon their aforesaid reservations, and to clear, fence, and break up a sufficient quantity of land for cultivation, the United States further agree to pay the sum of three thousand two hundred and fifty dollars, to be laid out and expended under the direction of the President, and in such manner as he shall approve.

ARTICLE 6. The President may hereafter, when in his opinion the interests of the Territory may require, and the welfare of the said Indians be promoted, remove them from either or all of said reservations to such other suitable place or places within said Territory as he may deem fit, on remunerating them for their improvements and the expenses of their removal, or may consolidate them with other friendly tribes or bands. And he may further, at his discretion, cause the whole or any portion of the lands hereby reserved, or of such other land as may be selected in lieu thereof, to be surveyed into lots, and assign the same to such individuals or families as are willing to avail themselves of the privilege, and will locate on the same as a permanent home, on the same terms and subject to the same regulations as are provided in the sixth article of the treaty with the Omahas, so far as the same may be applicable. Any substantial improvements heretofore made by any Indian, and which he shall be compelled to abandon in consequence of this treaty, shall be valued under the direction of the President, and payment be made accordingly therefor.

Removal from said reservation.

Ante, p. 612.

ARTICLE 7. The annuities of the aforesaid tribes and bands shall not be taken to pay the debts of individuals.

Annuities not to be taken for debt.

ARTICLE 8. The aforesaid tribes and bands acknowledge their dependence on the Government of the United States, and promise to be friendly with all citizens thereof, and pledge themselves to commit no depredations on the property of such citizens. And should any one or more of them violate this pledge, and the fact be satisfactorily proved before the agent, the property taken shall be returned, or in default thereof, or if injured or destroyed, compensation may be made by the Government out of their annuities. Nor will they make war on any other tribe except in self-defence, but will submit all matters of difference between them and other Indians to the Government of the United States, or its agent, for decision, and abide thereby. And if any of the said Indians commit any depredations on any other Indians within the Territory, the same rule shall prevail as that prescribed in this article, in cases of depredations against citizens. And the said tribes agree not to shelter or conceal offenders against the laws of the United States, but to deliver them up to the authorities for trial.

Stipulations respecting conduct of Indians.

ARTICLE 9. The above tribes and bands are desirous to exclude from their reservations the use of ardent spirits, and to prevent their people from drinking the same; and therefore it is provided, that any Indian belonging to said tribes, who is guilty of bringing liquor into said reservations, or who drinks liquor, may have his or her proportion of the annuities withheld from him or her for such time as the President may determine.

Intemperance.

ARTICLE 10. The United States further agree to establish at the general agency for the district of Puget's Sound, within one year from the ratification hereof, and to support, for a period of twenty years, an agricultural and industrial school, to be free to children of the said tribes and bands, in common with those of the other tribes of said district, and to provide the said school with a suitable instructor or instructors, and also to provide a smithy and carpenter's shop, and furnish them with the necessary tools, and employ a blacksmith, carpenter, and farmer, for the term of twenty years, to instruct the Indians in their respective occupations. And the United States further agree to employ a physician to reside at the said central agency, who shall furnish medicine and advice to their sick, and shall vaccinate them; the expenses of the said school, shops, employées, and medical attendance, to be defrayed by the United States, and not deducted from the annuities.

Schools, shops, etc

Slaves to be freed.

ARTICLE 11. The said tribes and bands agree to free all slaves now held by them, and not to purchase or acquire others hereafter.

Trade out of the limits of the United States forbidden.

Foreign Indians not to reside on reservation.

Treaty, when to take effect.

ARTICLE 12. The said tribes and bands finally agree not to trade at Vancouver's Island, or elsewhere out of the dominions of the United States; nor shall foreign Indians be permitted to reside in their reservations without consent of the superintendent or agent.

ARTICLE 13. This treaty shall be obligatory on the contracting parties as soon as the same shall be ratified by the President and Senate of the United States.

In testimony whereof, the said Isaac I. Stevens, governor and superintendent of Indian Affairs, and the undersigned chiefs, headmen, and delegates of the aforesaid tribes and bands, have hereunto set their hands and seals at the place and on the day and year hereinbefore written.

Isaac I. Stevens, [L. S.]
Governor and Superintendent Territory of Washington.

Qui-ee-metl, his x mark.	[L. S.]	Klo-out, his x mark.	[L. S.]
Sno-ho-dumset, his x mark.	[L. S.]	Se-uch-ka-nam, his x mark.	[L. S.]
Lesh-high, his x mark.	[L. S.]	Ske-mah-han, his x mark.	[L. S.]
Slip-o-elm, his x mark.	[L. S.]	Wuts-un-a-pum, his x mark.	[L. S.]
Kwi-ats, his x mark.	[L. S.]	Quuts-a-tadm, his x mark.	[L. S.]
Stee-high, his x mark.	[L. S.]	Quut-a-heh-mtsn, his x mark.	[L. S.]
Di-a-keh, his x mark.	[L. S.]	Yah-leh-chn, his x mark.	[L. S.]
Hi-ten, his x mark.	[L. S.]	To-lahl-kut, his x mark.	[L. S.]
Squa-ta-hun, his x mark.	[L. S.]	Yul-lout, his x mark.	[L. S.]
Kahk-tse-min, his x mark.	[L. S.]	See-ahts-oot-soot, his x mark.	[L. S.]
Sonan-o-yutl, his x mark.	[L. S.]	Ye-takho, his x mark.	[L. S.]
Kl-tehp, his x mark.	[L. S.]	We-po-it-ee, his x mark.	[L. S.]
Sahl-ko-min, his x mark.	[L. S.]	Kah-sld, his x mark.	[L. S.]
T'bet-ste-heh-bit, his x mark.	[L. S.]	La'h-hom-kan, his x mark.	[L. S.]
Tcha-hoos-tan, his x mark.	[L. S.]	Pah-how-at-ish, his x mark.	[L. S.]
Ke-cha-hat, his x mark.	[L. S.]	Swe-yehm, his x mark.	[L. S.]
Spee-peh, his x mark.	[L. S.]	Sah-hwill, his x mark.	[L. S.]
Swe-yah-tum, his x mark.	[L. S.]	Se-kwaht, his x mark.	[L. S.]
Cha-achsh, his x mark.	[L. S.]	Kah-hum-klt, his x mark.	[L. S.]
Pich-kehd, his x mark.	[L. S.]	Yah-kwo-bah, his x mark.	[L. S.]
S'Klah-o-sum, his x mark.	[L. S.]	Wut-sah-le-wun, his x mark.	[L. S.]
Sah-le-tatl, his x mark.	[L. S.]	Sah-ba-hat, his x mark.	[L. S.]
See-lup, his x mark.	[L. S.]	Tel-e-kish, his x mark.	[L. S.]
E-la-kah-ka, his x mark.	[L. S.]	Swe-keh-nam, his x mark.	[L. S.]
Slug-yeh, his x mark.	[L. S.]	Sit-oo-ah, his x mark.	[L. S.]
Hi-nuk, his x mark.	[L. S.]	Ko-quel-a-cut, his x mark.	[L. S.]
Ma-mo-nish, his x mark.	[L. S.]	Jack, his x mark.	[L. S.]
Cheels, his x mark.	[L. S.]	Keh-kise-bel-lo, his x mark.	[L. S.]
Knutcanu, his x mark.	[L. S.]	Go-yeh-hn, his x mark.	[L. S.]
Bats-ta-kobe, his x mark.	[L. S.]	Sah-putsh, his x mark.	[L. S.]
Win-ne-ya, his x mark.	[L. S.]	William, his x mark.	[L. S.]

Executed in the presence of us—

M. T. Simmons, Indian agent.
James Doty, secretary of the commission.
C. H. Mason, secretary Washington Territory.
W. A. Slaughter, first lieutenant, Fourth Infantry.
James McAlister,
E. Giddings, jr.
George Shazer,
Henry D. Cock,

S. S. Ford, jr.,
John W. McAlister,
Clovington Cushman,
Peter Anderson,
Samuel Klady,
W. H. Pullen,
P. O. Hough,
E. R. Tyerall,
George Gibbs,
Benj. F. Shaw, interpreter,
Hazard Stevens.

TREATY WITH THE KALAPUYA, ETC., 1855.

Articles of agreement and convention made and concluded at Dayton, Oregon Territory, by Joel Palmer, superintendent of Indian affairs, on the part of the United States, and the following-named chiefs of the confederated bands of Indians residing in the Willamette Valley, they being duly authorized thereto by their respective bands, to-wit: Ki-a-kuts, Le Medecin, and Yat-Skaw, or Dave, chiefs of the Tualatin band of Calapooias; Shap-h, or William, Shel-ke-ah, or David, and Cha-ah, or Jesse, chiefs of the Yam Hill band; Dabo, or Jim, Sco-la-quit, or John, and Yah-kow or Kompetine, chiefs of the Che-luk-i-ma-uke band; Ah-mo, or George, Himpher, or Hubbard, and Oh-no, or Tim, chiefs of the Chep-en-a-pho or Marysville band; Ma-mah-mo, or Charley Peter, Cha-che-clue, or Tom, and Quineflat, or Ben, chiefs of the Chem-a-pho or Maddy band; Luck-a-ma-foo, or Antoine, and Hoo-til, or Charley, chief of the Che-lam-e-la or Long Tom band, all of the Calapooias; Qui-a-qua-ty, Yalkus, and Kow-ka-ma, or Long Hair, chiefs of the Mo-lal-la band of Mo-lal-las; Kiles, or Jim, and Kow-ah-tough, or John, chiefs of the Calapooia band of Calapooias; Anta-quil-al-la, or John, and Mequah, of the Winnefelly and Mohawk bands; Yack-a-tee, or Sam, To-phor, or Jim Brown, and Hal-la-be, or Doctor, of the Tekopa band; Pulk-tah, of the Chafan band of the Calapooia tribe; Tum-walth and O-ban-a-hah, chiefs of the Wah-lal-la band of Tum-waters; Watch-a-no, Te-ap-i-nick, and Wal-lah-pi-coto, chiefs of the Clack-a-mas tribe; Lallak and Cuck-a-man-na, or David, of the Clow-we-wal-la or Willamette Tum-water band; Tow-ye-col-la, or Louis; Yelk-ma, or Jo, La-ham, or Tom, Joseph Sanegertta, Pullican, Te-na, or Kiles, Pul-kup-li-ma, or John, Sallaf, or Silas, Hoip-ke-nek, or Jack, Yepta, and Sat-invose or James, chiefs and head-men o'the Santiam bands of Calapooias.

Jan. 22, 1855.

10 Stats., 1143.
Ratified, Mar. 3, 1855.
Proclaimed, Apr. 10, 1855.

ARTICLE 1. The above-named confederated bands of Indians cede to the United States all their right, title, and claim to all and every part of the country included in the following boundaries, to wit:

Commencing in the middle of the main channel of the Columbia River, opposite the mouth of the first creek emptying into said river from the south below Oak Point, thence south to the first standard parallel north of the base-line in the Government survey, thence west to the summit of the Coast Range of mountains, thence southerly along the summit of said range to the Calapooia Mountains, thence easterly along the summit of said mountains to the summit of the Cascade Mountains, thence along said summit northerly, to the middle of the Columbia River, at the Cascade Falls, and thence down the middle of said river to the place of beginning.

Provided, however, That said bands be permitted to remain within the limits of the country ceded, and on such temporary reserves as may be made for them by the superintendent of Indian affairs, until a suitable district of country shall be designated for their permanent home, and proper improvements made thereon: *And provided,* That the United States make proper provision for the security of their persons and property from the hostile attacks of Indians of other tribes and bands. At which time, or when thereafter directed by the superintendent of Indian affairs, or agent, said confederated bands engage peaceably, and without expense to the United States other than that provided for in this treaty, to vacate the country hereby ceded, and remove to the district which shall be designated for their permanent occupancy.

ARTICLE 2. In consideration of, and payment for the country herein described, the United States agree to pay to the bands and tribes of

Cession to the United States.

Temporary reservation.

Protection.

Removal to a home to be assigned.

Payment to said Indians.

Indians claiming territory and residing in said country, the several sums of money following, to wit:

Ten thousand dollars per annum for the first five years, commencing on the first day of September, 1855.

Eight thousand dollars per annum for the term of five years next succeeding the first five.

Six thousand five hundred dollars per annum for the term of five years next succeeding the second five.

Five thousand five hundred dollars per annum for the term of five years next succeeding the third five.

How expended.

All of which several sums of money shall be expended for the use and benefit of the confederated bands, under the direction of the President of the United States, who may, from time to time, at his discretion, determine what proportion thereof shall be expended for such objects as in his judgment will promote their well-being, and advance them in civilization, for their moral improvement and education, for buildings, opening and fencing farms, breaking land, providing stock, agricultural implements, seeds, &c.; for clothing, provisions, and tools; for medical purposes; providing mechanics and farmers, and for arms and ammunition.

Further payment.
How expended.

The United States agree to pay said Indians the additional sum of fifty thousand dollars, a portion wherefore shall be expended for such articles as the superintendent of Indian affairs shall furnish the Indians, as soon as practicable after the signing of this treaty; and in providing, after the ratification thereof, and while the Indians shall reside on the temporary reserves that may be assigned them, horses, oxen, and other stock, wagons, agricultural implements, clothing, and provisions, as the President may direct; and for erecting on the tract that may be selected as their permanent homes, mills, shops, school-houses, a hospital, and other necessary buildings, and making improvements; for seeds, stock, and farming operations thereon; for paying for the permanent improvements of settlers, should any such be on said tract at the time of its selection; to pay the expenses of the removal of the Indians thereto, and in providing for their subsistence thereon for the

Provision if any refuse to sign this treaty.

first year after their removal. *Provided, however,* That if any band or bands of Indians, residing on or claiming any portion or portions of the country described in article first, shall not accede to the terms of this treaty, then the bands becoming parties hereunto agree to receive such part of the several annual and other payments herein named, as a consideration for the entire country described as aforesaid, as shall be in the proportion that their aggregate number may bear to the whole number of Indians residing in and claiming the entire country aforesaid, as consideration and payment in full for the tracts in said country claimed by them. *And, provided,* Any of the bands becoming parties

Provision if any claim to territory north of the Columbia is established.

to this treaty establish a legitimate claim to any portion of the country north of the Columbia River, that the amount to which they may be entitled as a consideration for such country, in any treaties hereafter entered into with the United States, shall be added to the annuities herein provided for.

Physician, etc.

ARTICLE 3. In addition to the considerations specified, the United States agree to provide for the employment, for the term of five years from and after the removal of said Indians to their permanent reserve, of a physician, a school-teacher, a blacksmith, and a superintendent of farming operations.

Reservation and home may be surveyed and allotted.

ARTICLE 4. The President may, from time to time, at his discretion, cause the whole, or such portion as he may think proper, of the tract that may hereafter be set apart as the permanent home of these Indians, to be surveyed into lots, and assign them to such Indians of the confederated bands as may wish to enjoy the privilege, and locate thereon permanently; to a single person, over twenty-one years of age, twenty acres; to a family of two persons, forty acres; to a family of three, and not exceeding five persons, fifty acres; to a family of six persons, and not exceeding ten, eighty acres; and to each family over ten in number, twenty acres for each additional three members. And the President may provide such rules and regulations as will secure to the family, in case of the death of the head thereof, the possession and enjoyment of such permanent home, and the improvements thereon; and he may, at any time, at his discretion, after such person or family has made location on the land assigned as a permanent home, issue a patent to such person or family, for such assigned land, conditioned that the tract shall not be aliened or leased for a longer time than two years, and shall be exempt from levy, sale, or forfeiture; which conditions shall continue in force until a State constitution, embracing such lands within its boundaries, shall have been formed, and the legislature of the State shall remove the restrictions: *Provided, however*, That no state legislature shall remove the restrictions herein provided for, without the consent of Congress. And if any such family shall, at any time neglect or refuse to occupy or till a portion of the land assigned, and on which they have located, or shall rove from place to place, the President may, if the patent shall have been issued, revoke the same; or, if not issued, cancel the assignment; and may also withhold from such person or family their proportion of the annuities or other moneys due them, until they shall have returned to such permanent home, and resume the pursuits of industry; and in default of their return, the tract may be declared abandoned, and thereafter assigned to some other person or family of the Indians residing on the reserve.

ARTICLE 5. The annuities of the Indians shall not be taken to pay the debts of individuals.

Annuities not to be taken for debt.

ARTICLE 6. The confederated bands acknowledge their dependence on the government of the United States, and promise to be friendly with all the citizens thereof, and pledge themselves to commit no depredations on the property of such citizens. And should any one or more of the Indians violate this pledge, and the fact be satisfactorily proven before the agent, the property taken shall be returned, or in default thereof, or if injured or destroyed, compensation may be made by the Government out of their annuities. Nor will they make war on any other band or tribe of Indians, except in self-defence, but will submit all matters of difference between them and other Indians to the Government of the United States, or its agent, for decision, and abide thereby. And if any of said Indians commit any depredations on any other Indians, the same rule shall prevail as that prescribed in this article in case of depredations against citizens. Said Indians further engage to submit to and observe all laws, rules, and regulations which may be prescribed by the United States for the government of said Indians.

Stipulations as to conduct of said Indians.

ARTICLE 7. In order to prevent the evils of intemperance among said Indians, it is hereby provided that any one of them who shall drink liquor, or procure it for other Indians to drink, may have his or her proportion of the annuities withheld from him or her for such time as the President may determine.

Intemperance.

ARTICLE 8. The said confederated bands agree that when a permanent reserve shall be assigned them, all roads, highways, and railroads, demanded at any time by the public convenience, shall have the right of way therein, a just compensation being made therefor.

Roads may be constructed.

ARTICLE 9. This treaty shall be obligatory on the contracting parties as soon as the same shall be ratified by the President and Senate of the United States.

Treaty, when obligatory.

In testimony whereof the said Joel Palmer, on the part of the United States as aforesaid, and the undersigned chiefs of the said confederated bands, have hereunto set their hands and seals this fourth day of January, eighteen hundred and fifty-five, at Dayton, in Oregon Territory.

Joel Palmer, superintendent of Indian Affairs. [L. S.]
Ki-ac-kuts, first chief, his x mark. [L. S.]
Le Medecin or Doctor, second chief, his x mark. [L. S.]
Yats-kow, or Dave, third chief, his x mark. [L. S.]
Shap-h, or William, first chief, his x mark. [L. S.]
Shel-ke-ah, or David, second chief, his x mark. [L. S.]
Che-ah, or Jesse, third chief, his x mark. [L. S.]
Dabo, or Jim, first chief, his x mark. [L. S.]
Sco-la-quit, or John, second chief, his x mark. [L. S.]
Yah-kow, or Kompetine, third chief, his x mark. [L. S.]

Ah-mo, or George, first chief, his x mark. [L. S.]
Hinc-phor, or Hubbard, second chief, his x mark. [L. S.]
Oh-no, or Tim, third chief, his x mark. [L. S.]
Ma-mah-mo, or Charley Peter, first chief, his x mark. [L. S.]
Cha-che-clue, or Tom, second chief, his x mark. [L. S.]
Quineflat, or Ben, third chief, his x mark. [L. S.]
Luck-a-moo-foo, or Antoine, first chief, his x mark. [L. S.]
Hoo-til, or Charley, second chief, his x mark. [L. S.]

Executed in the presence of us—

Edward R. Geary, secretary.
John Flett, interpreter.
George Dorsey.
Phillip A. Decker.
Lorenzo Palmer.

We, the chiefs of the Molalla band of Molallas, and of the Calapooia band of Calapooias, give our assent unto and agree to the provisions of the foregoing treaty.

In testimony whereof we have hereunto set our hands and seals, at Dayton, this ninth day of January, eighteen hundred and fifty-five.

Quia-quaty, first chief, his x mark. [L. S.]
Yalkus, second chief, his x mark. [L. S.]
Kaw-ka-ma, or Long Hair, third chief, his x mark. [L. S.]
Kiles, or Jim, first chief, his x mark. [L. S.]
Kowah-tough, or John, second chief, his x mark. [L. S.]

Executed in the presence of us—

Edward R. Geary, secretary.
Cris. Taylor, assistant secretary.
John Flett, interpreter.
Phillip A. Decker.
Lorenzo Palmer.

We, the chiefs and headmen of the Nin-ne-felly, Mohawk, Chapen, and Te-co-pa bands of Calapooias, Wal-lal-lah band of Tum-waters, and the Clockamus tribe of Indians, being duly authorized by our respective bands, give our assent unto, and agree to the provisions of the foregoing treaty.

In testimony whereof we have hereunto set our hands and seals, at Dayton, Oregon Territory, this tenth day of January, eighteen hundred and fifty-five.

An-ta, first chief, his x mark. [L. S.]
Quil-al-la, or John, second chief, his x mark. [L. S.]
Me-quah, or Dick, his x mark. [L. S.]
Yack-a-tee, or Sam, first chief, his x mark. [L. S.]
To-phor, or Jim Brown, second chief, his x mark. [L. S.]
Hal-la-le, or Doctor, his x mark. [L. S.]
Pulk-tah, second chief, his x mark. [L. S.]
Tum-walth, first chief, his x mark. [L. S.]
O-ban-a-hah, second chief, his x mark. [L. S.]
Watch-a-no, first chief, his x mark. [L. S.]
Te-ap-i-nick, second chief, his x mark. [L. S.]
Wal-lah-pi-cate, third chief, his x mark. [L. S.]

Executed in the presence of us—

Cris. Taylor, assistant secretary.
Andrew Smith.
John Flett, interpreter.

We, the chiefs and headmen of the Clow-we-wal-la, or Willamette Tum-water band of Indians, being assembled in council, give our assent unto, and agree to the provisions of the foregoing treaty.

In testimony whereof we have hereunto set our hands and seals, at Linn city, Oregon Territory, this nineteenth day of January, eighteen hundred and fifty-five.

Lal-bick, or John, his x mark.   [L. S.]
Cuck-a-man-na, or David, his x mark.   [L. S.]

Executed in the presence of us—

Cris. Taylor, assistant secretary.
John Flett, interpreter.

We, the chiefs and headmen of the Santam bands of Calapooia Indians, being duly authorized by our respective bands, give our assent unto, and agree to the provisions of the foregoing treaty.

In testimony whereof we have hereunto set our hands and seals, at Dayton, Oregon Territory, this twenty-second day of January, eighteen hundred and fifty-five.

Tow-ye-colla, or Louis, first chief, his x mark.   [L. S.]
La-ham, or Tom, third chief, his x mark.   [L S.]
Senegertta, his x mark.   [L. S.]
Pul-i-can, his x mark.   [L. S.]
Te-na, or Kiles, his x mark.   [L. S.]
Pul-kup-ti-ma, or John, his x mark.   [L. S.]
Sal-laf, or Silas, his x mark.   [L. S.]
Hoip-ke-nek, or Jack, his x mark.   [L. S.]
Yep-tah, his x mark.   [L. S.]
Satinvose, or James, his x mark.   [L. S.]

Executed in the presence of us—

Edward R. Geary, secretary.
Cris. Taylor.
Andrew Smith.
John Flett, interpreter.

TREATY WITH THE DWAMISH, SUQUAMISH, ETC., 1855.

Articles of agreement and convention made and concluded at Múckl-te-óh, or Point Elliott, in the Territory of Washington, this twenty-second day of January, eighteen hundred and fifty-five, by Isaac I. Stevens, governor and superintendent of Indian affairs for the said Territory, on the part of the United States, and the undersigned chiefs, head-men and delegates of the Dwámish, Suquámish, Sk-táhl-mish, Sam-áhmish, Smalh-kamish, Skope-áhmish, St-káh-mish, Snoquálmoo, Skai-wha-mish, N'Quentl-má-mish, Sk-táh-le-jum, Stoluck-whá-mish, Sno-ho-mish, Skágit, Kik-i-állus, Swin-á-mish, Squin-áh-mish, Sah-ku-méhu, Noo-whá-ha, Nook-wa-cháh-mish, Mee-sée-qua-guilch, Cho-bah-áh-bish, and other allied and subordinate tribes and bands of Indians occupying certain lands situated in said Territory of Washington, on behalf of said tribes, and duly authorized by them.

ARTICLE 1. The said tribes and bands of Indians hereby cede, relinquish, and convey to the United States all their right, title, and interest in and to the lands and country occupied by them, bounded and described

Jan. 22, 1855.

12 Stat. 927.
Ratified Mar. 8, 1859.
Proclaimed Apr. 11, 1859.

Cession of lands to the United States.

as follows: Commencing at a point on the eastern side of Admiralty Inlet, known as Point Pully, about midway between Commencement and Elliott Bays; thence eastwardly, running along the north line of lands heretofore ceded to the United States by the Nisqually, Puyallup, and other Indians, to the summit of the Cascade range of mountains; thence northwardly, following the summit of said range to the 49th parallel of north latitude; thence west, along said parallel to the middle of the Gulf of Georgia; thence through the middle of said gulf and the main channel through the Canal de Arro to the Straits of Fuca, and crossing the same through the middle of Admiralty Inlet to Suquamish Head; thence southwesterly, through the peninsula, and following the divide between Hood's Canal and Admiralty Inlet to the portage known as Wilkes' Portage; thence northeastwardly, and following the line of lands heretofore ceded as aforesaid to Point Southworth, on the western side of Admiralty Inlet, and thence around the foot of Vashon's Island eastwardly and southeastwardly to the place of beginning, including all the islands comprised within said boundaries, and all the right, title, and interest of the said tribes and bands to any lands within the territory of the United States.

Boundaries.

ARTICLE 2. There is, however, reserved for the present use and occupation of the said tribes and bands the following tracts of land, viz: the amount of two sections, or twelve hundred and eighty acres, surrounding the small bight at the head of Port Madison, called by the Indians Noo-sohk-um; the amount of two sections, or twelve hundred and eighty acres, on the north side Hwhomish Bay and the creek emptying into the same called Kwilt-seh-da, the peninsula at the southeastern end of Perry's Island, called Shais-quihl, and the island called Chah-choo-sen, situated in the Lummi River at the point of separation of the mouths emptying respectively into Bellingham Bay and the Gulf of Georgia. All which tracts shall be set apart, and so far as necessary surveyed and marked out for their exclusive use; nor shall any white man be permitted to reside upon the same without permission of the said tribes or bands, and of the superintendent or agent, but, if necessary for the public convenience, roads may be run through the said reserves, the Indians being compensated for any damage thereby done them.

Reservation.

Whites not to reside thereon unless, etc.

ARTICLE 3. There is also reserved from out the lands hereby ceded the amount of thirty-six sections, or one township of land, on the northeastern shore of Port Gardner, and north of the mouth of Snohomish River, including Tulalip Bay and the before-mentioned Kwilt-seh-da Creek, for the purpose of establishing thereon an agricultural and industrial school, as hereinafter mentioned and agreed, and with a view of ultimately drawing thereto and settling thereon all the Indians living west of the Cascade Mountains in said Territory. *Provided, however*, That the President may establish the central agency and general reservation at such other point as he may deem for the benefit of the Indians.

Further reservation for schools.

ARTICLE 4. The said tribes and bands agree to remove to and settle upon the said first above-mentioned reservations within one year after the ratification of this treaty, or sooner, if the means are furnished them. In the mean time it shall be lawful for them to reside upon any land not in the actual claim and occupation of citizens of the United States, and upon any land claimed or occupied, if with the permission of the owner.

Tribes to settle on reservation within one year.

ARTICLE 5. The right of taking fish at usual and accustomed grounds and stations is further secured to said Indians in common with all citizens of the Territory, and of erecting temporary houses for the purpose of curing, together with the privilege of hunting and gathering roots and berries on open and unclaimed lands. *Provided, however,*

Rights and privileges secured to Indians.

That they shall not take shell-fish from any beds staked or cultivated by citizens.

ARTICLE 6. In consideration of the above cession, the United States Payment by the United States. agree to pay to the said tribes and bands the sum of one hundred and fifty thousand dollars, in the following manner—that is to say: For the first year after the ratification hereof, fifteen thousand dollars; for the next two year, twelve thousand dollars each year; for the next three years, ten thousand dollars each year; for the next four years, seven thousand five hundred dollars each years; for the next five years, six thousand dollars each year; and for the last five years, four thousand two hundred and fifty dollars each year. All which said sums of money How to be applied. shall be applied to the use and benefit of the said Indians, under the direction of the President of the United States, who may, from time to time, determine at his discretion upon what beneficial objects to expend the same; and the superintendent of Indian affairs, or other proper officer, shall each year inform the President of the wishes of said Indians in respect thereto.

ARTICLE 7. The President may hereafter, when in his opinion the Indians may be removed to reservation, etc. interests of the Territory shall require and the welfare of the said Indians be promoted, remove them from either or all of the special reservations hereinbefore made to the said general reservation, or such other suitable place within said Territory as he may deem fit, on remunerating them for their improvements and the expenses of such removal, or may consolidate them with other friendly tribes or bands; and he may further at his discretion cause the whole or any portion of the lands hereby reserved, or of such other land as may be selected in lieu thereof, to be surveyed into lots, and assign the same to such Lots may be assigned to individuals. individuals or families as are willing to avail themselves of the privilege, and will locate on the same as a permanent home on the same Ante, p. 612. terms and subject to the same regulations as are provided in the sixth article of the treaty with the Omahas, so far as the same may be applicable. Any substantial improvements heretofore made by any Indian, and which he shall be compelled to abandon in consequence of this treaty, shall be valued under the direction of the President and payment made accordingly therefor.

ARTICLE 8. The annuities of the aforesaid tribes and bands shall not be taken to pay the debts of individuals.

ARTICLE 9. The said tribes and bands acknowledge their dependence Tribes to preserve friendly relations. on the Government of the United States, and promise to be friendly with all citizens thereof, and they pledge themselves to commit no depredations on the property of such citizens. Should any one or more of them violate this pledge, and the fact be satisfactorily proven before the agent, the property taken shall be returned, or in default thereof, of if injured or destroyed, compensation may be made by the Govern- To pay for depredations, not to make war, etc. ment out of their annuities. Nor will they make war on any other tribe except in self-defence, but will submit all matters of difference between them and the other Indians to the Government of the United States or its agent for decision, and abide thereby. And if any of the said Indians commit depredations on other Indians within the Territory the same rule shall prevail as that prescribed in this article in cases of depredations against citizens. And the said tribes agree not to shelter or To surrender offenders. conceal offenders against the laws of the United States, but to deliver them up to the authorities for trial.

ARTICLE 10. The above tribes and bands are desirous to exclude Annuities to be withheld from those who drink, etc., ardent spirits. from their reservations the use of ardent spirits, and to prevent their people from drinking the same, and therefore it is provided that any Indian belonging to said tribe who is guilty of bringing liquor into said reservations, or who drinks liquor, may have his or her proportion of the annuities withheld from him or her for such time as the President may determine.

Tribes to free all slaves and not to acquire others.

ARTICLE 11. The said tribes and bands agree to free all slaves now held by them and not to purchase or acquire others hereafter.

Not to trade out of the United States.

ARTICLE 12. The said tribes and bands further agree not to trade at Vancouver's Island or elsewhere out of the dominions of the United States, nor shall foreign Indians be permitted to reside in their reservations without consent of the superintendent or agent.

$15,000 appropriated for expenses of removal and settlement.

ARTICLE 13. To enable the said Indians to remove to and settle upon their aforesaid reservations, and to clear, fence, and break up a sufficient quantity of land for cultivation, the United States further agree to pay the sum of fifteen thousand dollars to be laid out and expended under the direction of the President and in such manner as he shall approve.

United States to establish school and provide instructors, furnish mechanics, shops, physicians, etc.

ARTICLE 14. The United States further agree to establish at the general agency for the district of Puget's Sound, within one year from the ratification hereof, and to support for a period of twenty years, an agricultural and industrial school, to be free to children of the said tribes and bands in common with those of the other tribes of said district, and to provide the said school with a suitable instructor or instructors, and also to provide a smithy and carpenter's shop, and furnish them with the necessary tools, and employ a blacksmith, carpenter, and farmer for the like term of twenty years to instruct the Indians in their respective occupations. And the United States finally agree to employ a physician to reside at the said central agency, who shall furnish medicine and advice to their sick, and shall vaccinate them; the expenses of said school, shops, persons employed, and medical attendance to be defrayed by the United States, and not deducted from the annuities.

Treaty, when to take effect.

ARTICLE 15. This treaty shall be obligatory on the contracting parties as soon as the same shall be ratified by the President and Senate of the United States.

In testimony whereof, the said Isaac I. Stevens, governor and superintendent of Indian affairs, and the undersigned chiefs, headmen, and delegates of the aforesaid tribes and bands of Indians, have hereunto set their hands and seals, at the place and on the day and year hereinbefore written.

Isaac I. Stevens, Governor and Superintendent. [L. S.]

Seattle, Chief of the Dwamish and Suquamish tribes, his x mark. [L. S.]

Pat-ka-nam, Chief of the Snoqualmoo, Snohomish and other tribes, his x mark. [L. S.]

Chow-its-hoot, Chief of the Lummi and other tribes, his x mark. [L. S.]

Goliah, Chief of the Skagits and other allied tribes, his x mark. [L. S.]

Kwallattum, or General Pierce, Sub-chief of the Skagit tribe, his x mark. [L. S.]

S'hootst-hoot, Sub-chief of Snohomish, his x mark. [L. S.]

Snah-talc, or Bonaparte, Sub-chief of Snohomish, his x mark. [L. S.]

Squush-um, or The Smoke, Sub-chief of the Snoqualmoo, his x mark. [L. S.]

See-alla-pa-han, or The Priest, Sub-chief of Sk-tah-le-jum, his x mark. [L. S.]

He-uch-ka-nam, or George Bonaparte, Sub-chief of Snohomish, his x mark. [L. S.]

Tse-nah-talc, or Joseph Bonaparte, Sub-chief of Snohomish, his x mark. [L. S.]

Ns'ski-oos, or Jackson, Sub-chief of Snohomish, his x mark. [L. S.]

Wats-ka-lah-tchie, or John Hobtst-hoot, Sub-chief of Snohomish, his x mark. [L. S.]

Smeh-mai-hu, Sub-chief of Skai-wha-mish, his x mark. [L. S.]

Slat-eah-ka-nam, Sub-chief of Snoqualmoo, his x mark. [L. S.]

St'hau-ai, Sub-chief of Snoqualmoo, his x mark. [L. S.]

Lugs-ken, Sub-chief of Skai-wha-mish, his x mark. [L. S.]

S'heht-soolt, or Peter, Sub-chief of Snohomish, his x mark. [L. S.]

Do-queh-oo-satl, Snoqualmoo tribe, his x mark. [L. S.]

John Kanam, Snoqualmoo sub-chief, his x mark. [L. S.]

Klemsh-ka-nam, Snoqualmoo, his x mark. [L. S.]

Ts'huahntl, Dwa-mish sub-chief, his x mark. [L. S.]

Kwuss-ka-nam, or George Snatelum, Sen., Skagit tribe, his x mark. [L. S.]

Hel-mits, or George Snatelum, Skagit sub-chief, his x mark. [L. S.]

S'kwai-kwi, Skagit tribe, sub-chief, his x mark. [L. S.]

Seh-lek-qu, Sub-chief Lummi tribe, his x mark. [L. S.]

S'h'-cheh-oos, or General Washington, Sub-chief of Lummi tribe, his x mark.   [L. s.]

Whai-lan-hu, or Davy Crockett, Sub-chief of Lummi tribe, his x mark.   [L. s.]

She-ah-delt-hu, Sub-chief of Lummi tribe, his x mark.   [L. s.]

Kwult-seh, Sub-chief of Lummi tribe, his x mark.   [L. s.]

Kwull-et-hu, Lummi tribe, his x mark.   [L. s.]

Kleh-kent-soot, Skagit tribe, his x mark.   [L. s.]

Sohn-heh-ovs, Skagit tribe, his x mark.   [L. s.]

S'deh-ap-kan, or General Warren, Skagit tribe, his x mark.   [L. s.]

Chul-whil-tan, Sub-chief of Suquamish tribe, his x mark.   [L. s.]

Ske-eh-tum, Skagit tribe, his x mark.   [L. s.]

Patchkanam, or Dome, Skagit tribe, his x mark.   [L. s.]

Sats-Kanam, Squin-ah-nush tribe, his x mark.   [L. s.]

Sd-zo-mahtl, Kik-ial-lus band, his x mark.   [L. s.]

Dahtl-de-min, Sub-chief of Sah-ku-meh-hu, his x mark.   [L. s.]

Sd'zek-du-num, Me-sek-wi-guilse sub-chief, his x mark.   [L. s.]

Now-a-chais, Sub-chief of Dwamish, his x mark.   [L. s.]

Mis-lo-tche, or Wah-hehl-tchoo, Sub-chief of Suquamish, his x mark.   [L. s.]

Sloo-noksh-tan, or Jim, Suquamish tribe, his x mark.   [L. s.]

Moo-whah-lad-hu, or Jack, Suquamish tribe, his x mark.   [L. s.]

Too-leh-plan, Suquamish tribe, his x mark.   [L. s.]

Ha-seh-doo-an, or Keo-kuck, Dwamish tribe, his x mark.   [L. s.]

Hoovilt-meh-tum, Sub-chief of Suquamish, his x mark.   [L. s.]

We-ai-pah, Skaiwhamish tribe, his x mark.   [L. s.]

S'ah-an-hu, or Hallam, Snohomish tribe, his x mark.   [L. s.]

She-hope, or General Pierce, Skagit tribe, his x mark.   [L. s.]

Hwn-lah-lakq, or Thomas Jefferson, Lummi tribe, his x mark.   [L. s.]

Cht-simpt, Lummi tribe, his x mark.   [L. s.]

Tse-sum-ten, Lummi tribe, his x mark.   [L. s.]

Klt-hahl-ten, Lummi tribe, his x mark.   [L. s.]

Kut-ta-kanam, or John, Lummi tribe, his x mark.   [L. s.]

Ch-lah-ben, Noo-qua-cha-mish band, his x mark.   [L. s.]

Noo-heh-oos, Snoqualmoo tribe, his x mark.   [L. s.]

Hweh-uk, Snoqualmoo tribe, his x mark.   [L. s.]

Peh-nus, Skai-whamish tribe, his x mark.   [L. s.]

Yim-ka-dam, Snoqualmoo tribe, his x mark.   [L. s]

Twooi-as-kut, Skaiwhamish tribe, his x mark.   [L. s.]

Luch-al-kanam, Snoqualmoo tribe, his x mark.   [L. s.]

S'hoot-kanam, Snoqualmoo tribe, his x mark.   [L. s.]

Sme-a-kanam, Snoqualmoo tribe, his x mark.   [L. s.]

Sad-zis-keh, Snoqualmoo, his x mark.   [L. s.]

Heh-mahl, Skaiwhamish band, his x mark.   [L. s.]

Charley, Skagit tribe, his x mark.   [L. s.]

Sampson, Skagit tribe, his x mark.   [L. s.]

John Taylor, Snohomish tribe, his x mark.   [L. s.]

Hatch-kwentum, Skagit tribe, his x mark.   [L. s.]

Yo-i-kum, Skagit tribe, his x mark.   [L. s.]

T'kwa-ma-han, Skagit tribe, his x mark.   [L. s.]

Sto-dum-kan, Swinamish band, his x mark.   [L. s.]

Be-lole, Swinamish band, his x mark.   [L. s.]

D'zo-lole-gwam-hu, Skagit tribe, his x mark.   [L. s.]

Steh-shail, William, Skaiwhamish band, his x mark.   [L. s.]

Kel-kahl-tsoot, Swinamish tribe, his x mark.   [L. s.]

Pat-sen, Skagit tribe, his x mark.   [L. s.]

Pat-teh-us, Noo-wha-ah sub-chief, his x mark.   [L. s.]

S'hoolk-ka-nam, Lummi sub-chief, his x mark.   [L. s.]

Ch-lok-suts, Lummi sub-chief, his x mark.   [L. s.]

Executed in the presence of us—

M. T. Simmons, Indian agent.
C. H. Mason, Secretary of Washington Territory.
Benj. F. Shaw, Interpreter.
Chas. M. Hitchcock.
H. A. Goldsborough.
George Gibbs.
John H. Scranton.
Henry D. Cock.

S. S. Ford, jr.
Orrington Cushman.
Ellis Barnes.
R. S. Bailey.
S. M. Collins.
Lafayetee Balch.
E. S. Fowler.
J. H. Hall.
Rob't Davis.

TREATY WITH THE S'KLALLAM, 1855.

Jan. 26, 1855.

12 Stats., 933.
Ratified Mar. 8, 1859.
Proclaimed Apr. 29,
1859.

Articles of agreement and convention made and concluded at Hahdskus, or Point no Point, Suquamish Head, in the Territory of Washington, this twenty-sixth day of January, eighteen hundred and fifty-five, by Isaac I. Stevens, governor and superintendent of Indian affairs for the said Territory, on the part of the United States, and the undersigned chiefs, headmen, and delegates of the different villages of the S'Klallams, viz: Kah-tai, Squah-quaihtl, Tch-queen, Ste-tehtlum, Tsohkw, Yennis, Elh-wa, Pishtst, Hunnint, Klat-la-wash, and Oke-ho, and also of the Sko-ko-mish, To-an-hooch, and Chem-a-kum tribes, occupying certain lands on the Straits of Fuca and Hood's Canal, in the Territory of Washington, on behalf of said tribes, and duly authorized by them.

Cession of lands to the United States.

ARTICLE 1. The said tribes and bands of Indians hereby cede, relinquish, and convey to the United States all their right, title, and interest in and to the lands and country occupied by them, bounded and described as follows, viz: Commencing at the mouth of the Okeho River, on the Straits of Fuca; thence southeastwardly along the westerly line of territory claimed by the Makah tribe of Indians to the summit of the Cascade Range; thence still southeastwardly and southerly along said summit to the head of the west branch of the Satsop River, down that branch to the main fork; thence eastwardly and following the line of lands heretofore ceded to the *the* United States by the Nisqually and other tribes and bands of Indians, to the summit of the Black Hills, and northeastwardly to the portage known as Wilkes' Portage; thence northeastwardly, and following the line of lands heretofore ceded to the United States by the Dwamish, Suquamish, and other tribes and bands of Indians, to Suquamish Head; thence northerly through Admiralty Inlet to the Straits of Fuca; thence westwardly through said straits to the place of beginning; including all the right, title, and interest of the said tribes and bands to any land in the Territory of Washington.

Boundaries.

Reservation.

ARTICLE 2. There is, however, reserved for the present use and occupation of the said tribes and bands the following tract of land, viz: The amount of six sections, or three thousand eight hundred and forty acres, situated at the head of Hood's Canal, to be hereafter set apart, and so far as necessary, surveyed and marked out for their exclusive use; nor shall any white man be permitted to reside upon the same without permission of the said tribes and bands, and of the superintendent or agent; but, if necessary for the public convenience, roads may be run through the said reservation, the Indians being compensated for any damage thereby done them. It is, however, understood that should the President of the United States hereafter see fit to place upon the said reservation any other friendly tribe or band, to occupy the same in common with those above mentioned, he shall be at liberty to do so.

Whites not to reside thereon.

Tribes to settle on reservation.

ARTICLE 3. The said tribes and bands agree to remove to and settle upon the said reservation within one year after the ratification of this treaty, or sooner if the means are furnished them. In the mean time, it shall be lawful for them to reside upon any lands not in the actual claim or occupation of citizens of the United States, and upon any land claimed or occupied, if with the permission of the owner.

Privileges to Indians.

ARTICLE 4. The right of taking fish at usual and accustomed grounds and stations is further secured to said Indians, in common with all citizens of the United States; and of erecting temporary houses for the purpose of curing; together with the privilege of hunting and gathering roots and berries on open and unclaimed lands. *Provided, however,*

That they shall not take shell-fish from any beds staked or cultivated by citizens.

ARTICLE 5. In consideration of the above cession the United States agree to pay to the said tribes and bands the sum of sixty thousand dollars, in the following manner, that is to say: during the first year after the ratification hereof, six thousand dollars; for the next two years, five thousand dollars each year; for the next three years, four thousand dollars each year; for the next four years, three thousand dollars each year; for the next five years, two thousand four hundred dollars each year; and for the next five years, one thousand six hundred dollars each year. All which said sums of money shall be applied to the use and benefit of the said Indians under the direction of the President of the United States, who may from time to time determine at his discretion upon what beneficial objects to expend the same. And the superintendent of Indian affairs, or other proper officer, shall each year inform the President of the wishes of said Indians in respect thereto.

Payments by the United States.

How to be applied.

ARTICLE 6. To enable the said Indians to remove to and settle upon their aforesaid reservations, and to clear, fence, and break up a sufficient quantity of land for cultivation, the United States further agree to pay the sum of six thousand dollars, to be laid out and expended under the direction of the President, and in such manner as he shall approve.

Appropriations for removal, etc.

ARTICLE 7. The President may hereafter, when in his opinion the interests of the Territory shall require, and the welfare of said Indians be promoted, remove them from said reservation to such other suitable place or places within said Territory as he may deem fit, on remunerating them for their improvements and the expenses of their removal; or may consolidate them with other friendly tribes or bands. And he may further, at his discretion, cause the whole or any portion of the lands hereby reserved, or of such other lands as may be selected in lieu thereof, to be surveyed into lots, and assign the same to such individuals or families as are willing to avail themselves of the privilege, and will locate thereon as a permanent home, on the same terms and subject to the same regulations as are provided in the sixth article of the treaty with the Omahas, so far as the same may be applicable. Any substantial improvements heretofore made by any Indian, and which he shall be compelled to abandon in consequence of this treaty, shall be valued under the direction of the President, and payment made therefor accordingly.

Indians may be removed to other reservation.

Lands may be surveyed and assigned.

Ante, p. 612.

ARTICLE 8. The annuities of the aforesaid tribes and bands shall not be taken to pay the debts of individuals.

Annuities not to be taken for debts of individuals.

ARTICLE 9. The said tribes and bands acknowledge their dependence on the Government of the United States, and promise to be friendly with all citizens thereof; and they pledge themselves to commit no depredations on the property of such citizens. And should any one or more of them violate this pledge, and the fact be satisfactorily proven before the agent, the property taken shall be returned, or in default thereof, or if injured or destroyed, compensation may be made by the Government out of their annuities. Nor will they make war on any other tribe, except in self-defence, but will submit all matters of difference between them and other Indians to the Government of the United States, or its agent, for decision, and abide thereby. And if any of the said Indians commit any depredations on any other Indians within the Territory, the same rule shall prevail as that prescribed in this article in cases of depredations against citizens. And the said tribes agree not to shelter or conceal offenders against the United States, but to deliver them up for trial by the authorities.

Tribes to preserve friendly relations.

To pay for depredations.

Not to make war but in self-defense.

To surrender offenders.

ARTICLE 10. The above tribes and bands are desirous to exclude from their reservation the use of ardent spirits, and to prevent their people from drinking the same, and therefore it is provided that any

Annuities may be withheld from those drinking ardent spirits.

an Indian agent in their vicinity, for such a limited period or periods of time, according to the circumstances of the case, as shall be determined by the Commissioner of Indian Affairs; and on the expiration of such period or periods, the said exemption, protection, and assistance shall cease; and said persons shall then, also, become citizens of the United States, with all the rights and privileges, and subject to the obligations, above stated and defined.

Cession by Wyandot of land purchased of the Delawares.

9 Stat., 337.

Partition of said lands among the Wyandot.

ARTICLE 2. The Wyandott Nation hereby cede and relinquish to the United States, all their right, title, and interest in and to the tract of country situate in the fork of the Missouri and Kansas Rivers, which was purchased by them of the Delaware Indians, by an agreement dated the fourteenth day of December, one thousand eight hundred and forty-three, and sanctioned by a joint resolution of Congress approved July twenty-fifth, one thousand eight hundred and forty-eight, the object of which cession is, that the said lands shall be subdivided, assigned, and reconveyed, by patent, in fee-simple, in the manner hereinafter provided for, to the individuals and members of the Wyandott Nation, in severalty; except as follows, viz: The portion now enclosed and used as a public burying-ground, shall be permanently reserved and appropriated for that purpose; two acres, to include the church-building of the Methodist Episcopal Church, and the present burying-ground connected therewith, are hereby reserved, granted, and conveyed to that church; and two acres, to include the church-building of the Methodist Episcopal Church South, are hereby reserved, granted, and conveyed to said church. Four acres, at and adjoining the Wyandott ferry, across and near the mouth of the Kansas River, shall also be reserved, and, together with the rights of the Wyandotts in said ferry shall be sold to the highest bidder, among the Wyandott people, and the proceeds of sale paid over to the Wyandotts. On the payment of purchase-money in full, a good and sufficient title to be secured and conveyed to the purchaser, by patent from the United States.

Same subject.

ARTICLE 3. As soon as practicable after the ratification of this agreement, the United States shall cause the lands ceded in the preceding article to be surveyed into sections, half and quarter sections, to correspond with the public surveys in the Territory of Kansas; and three commissioners shall be appointed—one by the United States, and two by the Wyandott council—whose duty it shall be to cause any additional surveys to be made that may be necessary, and to make a fair and just division and distribution of the said lands among all the individuals and members of the Wyandott tribe; so that those assigned to or for each shall, as nearly as possible, be equal in quantity, and also in value, irrespective of the improvements thereon; and the division and assignment of the lands shall be so made as to include the houses, and, as far as practicable, the other improvements, of each person or family; be in as regular and compact a form as possible, and include those for each separate family all altogether. The judgment and decision of said commissioners, on all questions connected with the division and assignment of said lands, shall be final.

On the completion of the division and assignment of the lands as aforesaid, said commissioners shall cause a plat and schedule to be made, showing the lands assigned to each family or individual, and the quantity thereof. They shall also make up carefully prepared lists of all the individuals and members of the Wyandott tribe—those of each separate family being arranged together—which lists shall exhibit, separately, first, those families the heads of which the commissioners, after due inquiry and consideration, shall be satisfied are sufficiently intelligent, competent, and prudent to control and manage their affairs and interests, and also all persons without families.

Second, those families the heads of which are not competent and proper persons to be entrusted with their shares of the money, payable under this agreement; and, third, those who are orphans, idiots, or insane. Accurate copies of the lists of the second and third of the above classes, shall be furnished by the commissioners to the Wyandott council; whereupon said council shall proceed to appoint or designate the proper person or persons to be recognized as the representatives of those of the second class, for the purpose of receiving and properly applying the sums of money due and payable to or for them, as hereinafter provided, and also those who are to be entrusted with the guardianship of the individuals of the third class, and the custody and management of their rights and interests; the said acts or proceedings of the council, duly authenticated, to be forwarded to the Commissioner of Indian Affairs, and filed in his office; and the same shall be annually revised by the said council, until the payment of the last instalment of the moneys payable to the Wyandotts, under this agreement, and such change or changes made therein as may, from casualties or otherwise, become necessary; such revisions and changes, duly authenticated, to be communicated to, and subject to the approval of, the Commissioner of Indian Affairs.

The said commissioners shall likewise prepare a list of all such persons and families among the Wyandott people as may apply to be temporarily exempted from citizenship and for continued protection and assistance from the United States and an Indian agent, as provided for in the first article of this agreement. The agent through and by whom such protection and assistance is to be furnished, shall be designated by the Commissioner of Indian Affairs.

The aforesaid plat and schedule, and lists of persons, duly authenticated by the commissioners, shall be forwarded to the Commissioner of Indian Affairs, and filed in his office, and copies of the said plat and schedule, and of the list of persons temporarily exempted from citizenship and entitled to the continued protection and assistance of the United States and an Indian agent, duly attested by the commissioners, shall be filed by them in each of the offices of the secretary of the Territory of Kansas, and the clerk of the county in which the Wyandott lands are situated.

ARTICLE 4. On the receipt, by the Commissioner of Indian Affairs, of the plat and schedule, lists of persons, and of the first proceedings of the Wyandott council, mentioned in the next preceding article, patents shall be issued by the General Land-Office of the United States, under the advisement of the Commissioner of Indian Affairs, to the individuals of the Wyandott tribe, for the lands severally assigned to them, as provided for in the third article of this agreement, in the following manner, to wit: To those reported by the commissioners to be competent to be entrusted with the control and management of their affairs and interests, the patents shall contain an absolute and unconditional grant in fee-simple; and shall be delivered to them by the Commissioner of Indian Affairs, as soon as they can be prepared and recorded in the General Land-Office: but to those not so competent, the patents shall contain an express condition, that the lands are not to be sold or alienated for a period of five years; and not then, without the express consent of the President of the United States first being obtained; and the said patents may be withheld by the Commissioner of Indian Affairs, so long as, in his judgment, their being so withheld may be made to operate beneficially upon the character and conduct of the individuals entitled to them.

Patents to issue.

None of the lands to be thus assigned and patented to the Wyandotts, shall be subject to taxation for a period of five years from and after the organization of a State government over the territory where they reside; and those of the incompetent classes shall not be aliened or released for a longer period than two years, and shall be exempt from levy, sale, or forfeiture, until otherwise provided by State legislation, with the assent of Congress.

Appraisement of the improvements of the Methodist Episcopal Church and Methodist Episcopal Church South.
ARTICLE 5. Disinterested persons, not to exceed three, shall be appointed by the Commissioner of Indian Affairs, to make a just and fair appraisement of the parsonage houses, and other improvements connected therewith, on the Wyandott lands, belonging to the Methodist Episcopal Church, and the Methodist Episcopal Church South, the amounts of which appraisements shall be paid to the said churches, respectively, by the individual or individuals of the Wyandott tribe, to whom the lands on which said houses and improvements are, shall have been assigned under the provisions of this agreement; said payments to be made within a reasonable time, in one or more instalments, to be determined by said appraisers; and until made in full, no patent or other evidence of title to the lands so assigned to said individual or individuals, shall be issued or given to them.

Release of claims under treaties.
ARTICLE 6. The Wyandott Nation hereby relinquish, and release the United States from all their rights and claims to annuity, school moneys, blacksmith establishments, assistance and materials, employment of an agent for their benefit, or any other object or thing, of a national character, and from all the stipulations and guarantees of that character, provided for or contained in former treaties, as well as from any and all other claims or demands whatsoever, as a nation, arising under any treaty or transaction between them and the Government of the United States; in consideration of which release and relinquishment, the United States hereby agree to pay to the Wyandott Payment in lieu thereof. Nation, the sum of three hundred and eighty thousand dollars, to be equally distributed and paid to all the individuals and members of the said nation, in three annual instalments, payable in the months of October, commencing the present year; the shares of the families whose heads the commissioners shall have decided not to be competent or proper persons to receive the same, and those of orphans, idiots, and insane persons, to be paid to and receipted for by the individuals designated or appointed by the Wyandott council to act as their representatives and guardians.

Such part of the annuity, under the treaty of one thousand eight hundred and forty-two, as shall have accrued, and may remain unpaid, at the date of the payment of the first of the above-mentioned instalments, shall then be paid to the Wyandotts, and be in full, and a final discharge of, said annuity.

Additional payments.
ARTICLE 7. The sum of one hundred thousand dollars, invested under the treaty of one thousand eight hundred and fifty, together with any accumulation of said principal sum, shall be paid over to the Wyandotts, in like manner with the three hundred and eighty thousand dollars mentioned in the next preceding article; but in two equal annual instalments, commencing one year after the payment of the last instalment of said above-mentioned sum. In the mean time, the interest on the said invested fund, and on any accumulation thereof, together with the amount which shall be realized from the disposition of the ferry and the land connected therewith, the sale of which is provided for in the second article of this agreement, shall be paid over to the Wyandott council, and applied and expended, by regular appropriation of the legislative committee of the Wyandott Nation, for the support of schools, and for other purposes of a strictly national or public character.

Persons entitled to land and money.
ARTICLE 8. The persons to be included in the apportionment of the lands and money, to be divided and paid under the provisions of this agreement, shall be such only as are actual members of the Wyandott Nation, their heirs and legal representatives, at the date of the ratification hereof, and as are entitled to share in the property and funds of said nation, according to the laws, usages, and customs thereof.

ARTICLE 9. It is stipulated and agreed, that each of the individuals, to whom reservations were granted by the fourteenth article of the treaty of March seventeenth, one thousand eight hundred and forty-two, or their heirs or legal representatives, shall be permitted to select and locate said reservations, on any Government lands west of the States of Missouri and Iowa, subject to pre-emption and settlement, said reservations to be patented by the United States, in the names of the reservees, as soon as practicable after the selections are made; and the reservees, their heirs or proper representatives, shall have the unrestricted right to sell and convey the same, whenever they may think proper; but, in cases where any of said reservees may not be sufficiently prudent and competent to manage their affairs in a proper manner, which shall be determined by the Wyandott council, or where any of them have died, leaving minor heirs, the said council shall appoint proper and discreet persons to act for such incompetent persons and minor heirs in the sale of the reservations, and the custody and management of the proceeds thereof—the persons so appointed, to have full authority to sell and dispose of the reservations in such cases, and to make and execute a good and valid title thereto.

Grantees under former treaty of 1842 permitted to locate elsewhere.

The selections of said reservations, upon being reported to the surveyor-general of the district in which they are made, shall be entered upon the township plats, and reported, without delay, to the Commissioner of the General Land-Office, and patents issued to the reservees, accordingly. And any selection of, settlement upon, or claim to, land included in any of said reservations, made by any other person or persons, after the same shall have been selected by the reservees, their heirs or legal representatives, shall be null and void.

ARTICLE 10. It is expressly understood, that all the expenses connected with the subdivision and assignment of the Wyandott lands, as provided for in the third article hereof, or with any other measure or proceeding, which shall be necessary to carry out the provisions of this agreement, shall be borne and defrayed by the Wyandotts, except those of the survey of the lands into sections, half and quarter sections, the issue of the patents, and the employment of the commissioner to be appointed by the United States; which shall be paid by the United States.

Expenses; how to be borne.

ARTICLE 11. This instrument shall be obligatory on the contracting parties whenever the same shall be ratified by the President and the Senate of the United States.

In testimony whereof, the said George W. Manypenny, commissioner as aforesaid, and the said chiefs and delegates of the Wyandott tribe of Indians, have hereunto set their hands and seals, at the place and on the day and year hereinbefore written.

Geo. W. Manypenny,	[L. S.]
Tan-roo-mee, his x mark.	[L. S.]
Mathew Mudeater,	[L. S.]
John Hicks, his x mark.	[L. S.]
Silas Armstrong,	[L. S.]
Geo. J. Clark,	[L. S.]
Joel Walker,	[L. S.]

Executed in presence of—

A. Cumming, superintendent Indian affairs,
Robert S. Neighbors, special agent,
Will. P. Ross, Cherokee delegate,
J. T. Cochrane.

TREATY WITH THE MAKAH, 1855.

Jan. 31, 1855.

12 Stat., 939.
Ratified Mar. 8, 1859.
Proclaimed Apr. 18, 1859.

Articles of agreement and convention, made and concluded at Neah Bay, in the Territory of Washington, this thirty-first day of January, in the year eighteen hundred and fifty-five, by Isaac I. Stevens, governor and superintendent of Indian affairs for the said Territory, on the part of the United States, and the undersigned chiefs, head-men, and delegates of the several villages of the Makah tribe of Indians, viz: Neah Waatch, Tsoo-Yess, and Osett, occupying the country around Cape Classett or Flattery, on behalf of the said tribe and duly authorized by the same.

Surrender of lands to the United States.

ARTICLE 1. The said tribe hereby cedes, relinquishes, and conveys to the United States all their right, title, and interest in and to the lands and country occupied by it, bounded and described as follows, viz: Commencing at the mouth of the Oke-ho River, on the Straits *Boundaries.* of Fuca; thence running westwardly with said straits to Cape Classett or Flattery; thence southwardly along the coast to Osett, or the Lower Cape Flattery; thence eastwardly along the line of lands occupied by the Kwe-déh-tut or Kwill-eh-yute tribe of Indians, to the summit of the coast-range of mountains, and thence northwardly along the line of lands lately ceded to the United States by the S'Klallam tribe to the place of beginning, including all the islands lying off the same on the straits and coast.

Reservation.
Boundaries.

ARTICLE 2. There is, however, reserved for the present use and occupation of the said tribe the following tract of land, viz: Commencing on the beach at the mouth of a small brook running into Neah Bay next to the site of the old Spanish fort; thence along the shore round Cape Classett or Flattery, to the mouth of another small stream running into the bay on the south side of said cape, a little above the Waatch village; thence following said brook to its source; thence in a straight line to the source of the first-mentioned brook, and thence following the same down to the place of beginning; which said tract shall be set apart, and so far as necessary surveyed and marked out for their *Whites not to reside* exclusive use; nor shall any white man be permitted to reside upon the *thereon unless, etc.* same without permission of the said tribe and of the superintendent or *Roads may be made.* agent; but if necessary for the public convenience, roads may be run through the said reservation, the Indians being compensated for any *Other friendly* damage thereby done them. It is, however, understood that should *bands may be placed* the President of the United States hereafter see fit to place upon the *thereon.* said reservation any other friendly tribe or band to occupy the same in common with those above mentioned, he shall be at liberty to do so.

Indians to settle on reservation within a year.

ARTICLE 3. The said tribe agrees to remove to and settle upon the said reservation, if required so to do, within one year after the ratification of this treaty, or sooner, if the means are furnished them. In the mean time it shall be lawful for them to reside upon any land not in the actual claim and occupation of citizens of the United States, and upon any land claimed or occupied, if with the permission of the owner.

Rights and privileges secured to Indians.

ARTICLE 4. The right of taking fish and of whaling or sealing at usual and accustomed grounds and stations is further secured to said Indians in common with all citizens of the United States, and of erecting temporary houses for the purpose of curing, together with the privilege of hunting and gathering roots and berries on open and *Proviso.* unclaimed lands: *Provided, however,* That they shall not take shell-fish from any beds staked or cultivated by citizens.

Payments by the United States.

ARTICLE 5. In consideration of the above cession the United States agree to pay to the said tribe the sum of thirty thousand dollars, in the following manner, that is to say: During the first year after the ratification hereof, three thousand dollars; for the next two years, twenty-five hundred dollars each year; for the next three years, two thousand dollars each year; for the next four years, one thousand five hundred dollars each year; and for the next ten years, one thousand dollars each year; all which said sums of money shall be applied to the use and benefit of the said Indians, under the direction of the President of the United States, who may from time to time determine at his discretion upon what beneficial objects to expend the same. And the superintendent of Indian affairs, or other proper officer, shall each year inform the President of the wishes of said Indians in respect thereto.

How to be applied.

ARTICLE 6. To enable the said Indians to remove to and settle upon their aforesaid reservation, and to clear, fence, and break up a sufficient quantity of land for cultivation, the United States further agree to pay the sum of three thousand dollars, to be laid out and expended under the direction of the President, and in such manner as he shall approve. And any substantial improvements heretofore made by any individual Indian, and which he may be compelled to abandon in consequence of this treaty, shall be valued under the direction of the President and payment made therefor accordingly.

Appropriation for removal and for clearing and fencing land, etc.

ARTICLE 7. The President may hereafter, when in his opinion the interests of the Territory shall require, and the welfare of said Indians be promoted thereby, remove them from said reservation to such suitable place or places within said Territory as he may deem fit, on remunerating them for their improvements and the expenses of their removal, or may consolidate them with other friendly tribes or bands; and he may further, at his discretion, cause the whole, or any portion of the lands hereby reserved, or such other land as may be selected in lieu thereof, to be surveyed into lots, and assign the same to such individuals or families as are willing to avail themselves of the privilege, and will locate thereon as a permanent home, on the same terms and subject to the same regulations as are provided in the sixth article of the treaty with the Omahas, so far as the same may be practicable.

Indians may be removed from the reservation.

Tribes may be consolidated.

Ante, p. 612.

ARTICLE. 8. The annuities of the aforesaid tribe shall not be taken to pay the debts of individuals.

Annuities of tribe not to pay individual debts.

ARTICLE 9. The said Indians acknowledge their dependence on the Government of the United States, and promise to be friendly with all citizens thereof, and they pledge themselves to commit no depredations on the property of such citizens. And should any one or more of them violate this pledge, and the fact be satisfactorily proven before the agent, the property taken shall be returned, or in default thereof, or if injured or destroyed, compensation may be made by the Government out of their annuities. Nor will they make war on any other tribe except in self-defence, but will submit all matters of difference between them and other Indians to the Government of the United States or its agent for decision and abide thereby. And if any of the said Indians commit any depredations on any other Indians within the Territory, the same rule shall prevail as that prescribed in this article in case of depredations against citizens. And the said tribe agrees not to shelter or conceal offenders against the United States, but to deliver up the same for trial by the authorities.

Indians to preserve friendly relations.

To pay for depredations.

Not to make war, except.

To surrender offenders.

ARTICLE 10. The above tribe is desirous to exclude from its reservation the use of ardent spirits, and to prevent its people from drinking the same, and therefore it is provided that any Indian belonging thereto who shall be guilty of bringing liquor into said reservation, or who drinks liquor, may have his or her proportion of the annuities withheld from him or her for such time as the President may determine.

Annuities to be withheld from those drinking ardent spirits.

ARTICLE 11. The United States further agree to establish at the general agency for the district of Puget's Sound, within one year from the ratification hereof, and to support for the period of twenty years, an agricultural and industrial school, to be free to children of the said tribe in common with those of the other tribes of said district and to

United States to establish an agricultural, etc., school for the Indians; to provide tools and employ mechanics, etc.

provide a smithy and carpenter's shop, and furnish them with the necessary tools and employ a blacksmith, carpenter and farmer for the like term to instruct the Iindians in their respective occupations. *Provided, however,* That should it be deemed expedient a separate school may be established for the benefit of said tribe and such others as may be associated with it, and the like persons employed for the same purposes at

some other suitable place. And the United States further agree to employ a physician to reside at the said central agency, or at such other school should one be established, who shall furnish medicine and advice to the sick, and shall vaccinate them; the expenses of the said school, shops, persons employed, and medical attendance to be defrayed by the United States and not deducted from the annuities.

ARTICLE 12. The said tribe agrees to free all slaves now held by its people, and not to purchase or acquire others hereafter.

ARTICLE 13. The said tribe finally agrees not to trade at Vancouver's Island or elsewhere out of the dominions of the United States, nor shall foreign Indians be permitted to reside in its reservation without consent of the superintendent or agent.

ARTICLE 14. This treaty shall be obligatory on the contracting parties as soon as the same shall be ratified by the President of the United States.

In testimony whereof, the said Isaac I. Stevens, governor and superintendent of Indian affairs, and the undersigned, chiefs, headmen and delegates of the tribe aforesaid have hereunto set their hands and seals at the place and on the day and year hereinbefore written.

Isaac I. Stevens, governor and superintendent. [L. S.]

Tse-kauwtl, head chief of the Makah tribe, his x mark. [L. S.]
Kal-chote, subchief of the Makahs, his x mark. [L. S.]
Tah-a-howtl, subchief of the Makahs, his x mark. [L. S.]
Kah-bach-sat, subchief of the Makahs, his x mark. [L. S.]
Kets-kus-sum, subchief of the Makahs, his x mark. [L. S.]
Haatse, subchief of the Makahs, his x mark. [L. S.]
Keh-chook, subchief of the Makahs, his x mark. [L. S.]
It-an-da-ha, subchief of the Makahs, his x mark. [L. S.]
Klah-pe-an-hie, or Andrew Jackson, subchief of the Makahs, his x mark. [L. S.]
Tsal-ab-oos, or Peter, Neah village, his x mark. [L. S.]
Tahola, Neah village, his x mark. [L. S.]
Kleht-li-quat-stl, Waatch village, his x mark. [L. S.]
Too-whaii-tan, Waatch village, his x mark. [L. S.]
Tahts-kin, Neah village, his x mark. [L. S.]
Nenchoop, Neah village, his x mark. [L. S.]
Ah-de-ak-too-ah, Osett village, his x mark. [L. S.]
William, Neah village, his x mark. [L. S.]
Wak-kep-tup, Waatch village, his x mark. [L. S.]
Klaht-te-di-yuke, Waatch village, his x mark. [L. S.]
Oobick, Waatch village, his x mark. [L. S.]
Bich-took, Waatch village, his x mark. [L. S.]

Baht-se-ditl, Neah village, his x mark. [L. S.]
Wack-shie, Neah village, his x mark. [L. S.]
Hah-yo-hwa, Waatch village, his x mark. [L. S.]
Daht-leek, or Mines, Osett village, his x mark. [L. S.]
Pah-hat, Neah village, his x mark. [L. S.]
Pai-yeh, Osett village, his x mark. [L. S.]
Tsah-weh-sup, Neah village, his x mark. [L. S.]
Al-is-kah, Osett village, his x mark. [L. S.]
Kwe-tow'tl, Neah village, his x mark. [L. S.]
Kaht-saht-wha, Neah village, his x mark. [L. S.]
Tchoo-quut-lah, or Yes Sir, Neah village, his x mark. [L. S.]
Klatts-ow-sehp, Neah village, his x mark. [L. S.]
Kai-kl-chis-sum, Neah village, his mark. [L. S.]
Kah-kwt-lit-ha, Waatch village, his x mark. [L. S.]
He-dah-titl, Neah village, his x mark. [L. S.]
Sah-dit-le-uad, Waatch village, his x mark. [L. S.]
Klah-ku-pihl, Tsoo-yess village, his x mark. [L. S.]
Billuk-whtl, Tsoo-yess village, his x mark. [L. S.]
Kwah-too-qualh, Tsoo-yess village, his x mark. [L. S.]
Yooch-boott, Tsoo-yess village, his x mark. [L. S.]
Swell, or Jeff. Davis, Neah village, his x mark. [L. S.]

Executed in the presence of us. The words "five hundred" being first interlined in the 5th article, and erasures made in the 8th and 9th articles.

    M. T. Simmons, Indian agent.
    George Gibbs, secretary.
    B. F. Shaw, interpreter.
    C. M. Hitchcock, M. D.
    E. S. Fowler.
    Orrington Cushman.
    Robt. Davis.

TREATY WITH THE CHIPPEWA, 1855.

Articles of agreement and convention made and concluded at the city of Washington, this twenty-second day of February, one thousand eight hundred and fifty-five, by George W. Manypenny, commissioner, on the part of the United States, and the following-named chiefs and delegates, representing the Mississippi bands of Chippewa Indians, viz: Pug-o-na-ke-shick, or Hole-in-the-day; Que-we-sans-ish, or Bad Boy; Wand-e-kaw, or Little Hill; I-awe-showe-we-ke-shig, or Crossing Sky; Petud-dunce, or Rat's Liver; Mun-o-min-e-kay-shein, or Rice-Maker; Mah-yah-ge-way-we-durg, or the Chorister; Kay-gwa-daush, or the Attempter; Caw-caug-e-we-goon, or Crow Feather; and Show-baush-king, or He that passes under Everything, and the following-named chiefs and delegates representing the Pillager and Lake Winnibigoshish bands of Chippewa Indians, viz: Aish-ke-bug-e-koshe, or Flat Mouth; Be-sheck-kee, or Buffalo; Nay-bun-a-caush, or Young Man's Son; Maug-e-gaw-bow, or Stepping Ahead; Mi-gi-si, or Eagle, and Kaw-be-mub-bee, or North Star, they being thereto duly authorized by the said bands of Indians respectively.

Feb. 22, 1855.

10 Stat., 1165.
Ratified Mar. 3, 1855.
Proclaimed Apr. 7, 1855.

ARTICLE 1. The Mississippi, Pillager, and Lake Winnibigoshish bands of Chippewa Indians hereby cede, sell, and convey to the United States all their right, title, and interest in, and to, the lands now owned and claimed by them, in the Territory of Minnesota, and included within the following boundaries, viz: Beginning at a point where the east branch of Snake River crosses the southern boundary-line of the Chippewa country, east of the Mississippi River, as established by the treaty of July twenty-ninth, one thousand eight hundred and thirty-seven, running thence, up the said branch, to its source; thence, nearly north in a straight line, to the mouth of East Savannah River; thence, up the St. Louis River, to the mouth of East Swan River; thence, up said river, to its source; thence, in a straight line, to the most westwardly bend of Vermillion River; thence, northwestwardly, in a straight line, to the first and most considerable bend in the Big Fork River; thence, down said river, to its mouth; thence, down Rainy Lake River, to the mouth of Black River; thence, up that river, to its source; thence, in a straight line, to the northern extremity of Turtle Lake; thence, in a straight line, to the mouth of Wild Rice River; thence, up Red River of the North, to the mouth of Buffalo River; thence, in a straight line, to the southwestern extremity of Otter-Tail Lake; thence, through said lake, to the source of Leaf River; thence down said river, to its junction with Crow Wing River; thence down Crow Wing River, to its junction with the Mississippi River; thence to the commencement on said river of the southern boundary-line of the Chippewa country, as established by the treaty of July twenty-ninth, one thousand eight hundred and thirty-seven; and thence, along said line, to the place of beginning. And the said Indians do further fully and entirely relinquish and convey to the United States, any and all right, title, and

Cession to the United States.

interest, of whatsoever nature the same may be, which they may now have in, and to any other lands in the Territory of Minnesota or elsewhere.

Reservations for permanent homes.

ARTICLE 2. There shall be, and hereby is, reserved and set apart, a sufficient quantity of land for the permanent homes of the said Indians; the lands so reserved and set apart, to be in separate tracts, as follows, viz:

For the Mississippi bands of Chippewa.

For the Mississippi bands of Chippewa Indians: The first to embrace the following fractional townships, viz: forty-two north, of range twenty-five west; forty-two north, of range twenty-six west; and forty-two and forty-three north, of range twenty-seven west; and, also, the three islands in the southern part of Mille Lac. Second, beginning at a point half a mile east of Rabbit Lake; thence south three miles; thence westwardly, in a straight line, to a point three miles south of the mouth of Rabbit River; thence north to the mouth of said river; thence up the Mississippi River to a point directly north of the place of beginning; thence south to the place of beginning. Third, beginning at a point half a mile southwest from the most southwestwardly point of Gull Lake; thence due south to Crow Wing River; thence down said river, to the Mississippi River; thence up said river to Long Lake Portage; thence, in a straight line, to the head of Gull Lake; thence in a southwestwardly direction, as nearly in a direct line as practicable, but at no point thereof, at a less distance than half a mile from said lake, to the place of beginning. Fourth, the boundaries to be, as nearly as practicable, at right angles, and so as to embrace within them Pokagomon Lake; but nowhere to approach nearer said lake than half a mile therefrom. Fifth, beginning at the mouth of Sandy Lake River; thence south, to a point on an east and west line, two miles south of the most southern point of Sandy Lake; thence east, to a point due south from the mouth of West Savannah River; thence north, to the mouth of said river; thence north to a point on an east and west line, one mile north of the most northern point of Sandy Lake; thence west, to Little Rice River; thence down said river to Sandy Lake River; and thence down said river to the place of beginning. Sixth, to include all the islands in Rice Lake, and also half a section of land on said lake, to include the present gardens of the Indians. Seventh, one section of land for Pug-o-na-ke-shick, or Hole-in-the-day, to include his house and farm; and for which he shall receive a patent in fee-simple.

For the Pillager and Lake Winnibigoshish bands.

For the Pillager and Lake Winnibigoshish bands, to be in three tracts, to be located and bounded as follows, viz: First, beginning at mouth of Little Boy River; thence up said river to Lake Hassler; thence through the center of said lake to its western extremity; thence in a direct line to the most southern point of Leech Lake; and thence through said lake, so as to include all the islands therein, to the place of beginning. Second, beginning at the point where the Mississippi River leaves Lake Winnibigoshish; thence north, to the head of the first river; thence west, by the head of the next river, to the head of the third river, emptying into said lake; thence down the latter to said lake; and thence in a direct line to the place of beginning. Third, beginning at the mouth of Turtle River; thence up said river to the first lake; thence east, four miles; thence southwardly, in a line parallel with Turtle River, to Cass Lake; and thence, so as to include all the islands in said lake, to the place of beginning; all of which said tracts shall be distinctly designated on the plats of the public surveys.

Reservations may be surveyed and allotted.

And at such time or times as the President may deem it advisable for the interests and welfare of said Indians, or any of them, he shall cause the said reservation, or such portion or portions thereof as may be necessary, to be surveyed; and assign to each head of a family, or single person over twenty-one years of age, a reasonable quantity of land, in one body, not to exceed eighty acres in any case, for his or their separate use; and he may, at his discretion, as the occupants thereof become capable of managing their business and affairs, issue patents to them for the tracts so assigned to them, respectively; said tracts to be exempt from taxation, levy, sale, or feiture; and not to be aliened or leased for a longer period than two years, at one time, until otherwise provided by the legislature of the State in which they may be situate, with the assent of Congress. They shall not be sold, or alienated, in fee, for a period of five years after the date of the patents; and not then without the assent of the President of the United States being first obtained. Prior to the issue of the patents, the President shall make such rules and regulations as he may deem necessary and expedient, respecting the disposition of any of said tracts in case of the death of the person or persons to whom they may be assigned, so that the same shall be secured to the families of such deceased person; and should any of the Indians to whom tracts may be assigned thereafter abandon them, the President may make such rules and regulations, in relation to such abandoned tracts, as in his judgment may be necessary and proper.

ARTICLE 3. In consideration of, and in full compensation for, the cessions made by the said Mississippi, Pillager, and Lake Winnibigoshish bands of Chippewa Indians, in the first article of this agreement, the United States hereby agree and stipulate to pay, expend, and make provision for, the said bands of Indians, as follows, viz: For the Mississippi bands:

Payment to the Mississippi band for the above cessions.

Ten thousand dollars ($10,000) in goods, and other useful articles, as soon as practicable after the ratification of this instrument, and after an appropriation shall be made by Congress therefor, to be turned over to the delegates and chiefs for distribution among their people.

Fifty thousand dollars ($50,000) to enable them to adjust and settle their present engagements, so far as the same, on an examination thereof, may be found and decided to be valid and just by the chiefs, subject to the approval of the Secretary of the Interior; and any balance remaining of said sum not required for the above-mentioned purpose shall be paid over to said Indians in the same manner as their annuity money, and in such instalments as the said Secretary may determine; *Provided*, That an amount not exceeding ten thousand dollars ($10,000) of the above sum shall be paid to such full and mixed bloods as the chiefs may direct, for services rendered heretofore to their bands.

Twenty thousand dollars ($20,000) per annum, in money, for twenty years, provided, that two thousand dollars ($2,000) per annum of that sum, shall be paid or expended, as the chiefs may request, for purposes of utility connected with the improvement and welfare of said Indians, subject to the approval of the Secretary of the Interior.

Five thousand dollars ($5,000) for the construction of a road from the mouth of Rum River to Mille Lac, to be expended under the direction of the Commissioner of Indian Affairs.

A reasonable quantity of land, to be determined by the Commissioner of Indian Affairs, to be ploughed and prepared for cultivation in suitable fields, at each of the reservations of the said bands, not exceeding, in the aggregate, three hundred acres for all the reservations, the Indians to make the rails and inclose the fields themselves.

For the Pillager and Lake Winnibigoshish bands:

Payment to the Pillager and Lake Winnibigoshish bands for said cessions.

Ten thousand dollars ($10,000) in goods, and other useful articles, as soon as practicable, after the ratification of this agreement, and an appropriation shall be made by Congress therefor; to be turned over to the chiefs and delegates for distribution among their people.

Forty thousand dollars ($40,000) to enable them to adjust and settle their present engagements, so far as the same, on an examination thereof, may be found and decided to be valid and just by the chiefs, subject to the approval of the Secretary of the Interior; and any balance remaining of said sum, not required for that purpose, shall be paid over to said Indians, in the same manner as their annuity money, and in such instalments as the said Secretary may determine; provided that an amount, not exceeding ten thousand dollars ($10,000) of the above sum, shall be paid to such mixed-bloods as the chiefs may direct, for services heretofore rendered to their bands.

Ten thousand six hundred and sixty-six dollars and sixty-six cents ($10,666.66) per annum, in money, for thirty years.

Eight thousand dollars ($8,000) per annum, for thirty years, in such goods as may be requested by the chiefs, and as may be suitable for the Indians, according to their condition and circumstances.

Four thousand dollars ($4,000) per annum, for thirty years, to be paid or expended, as the chiefs may request, for purposes of utility connected with the improvement and welfare of said Indians; subject to the approval of the Secretary of the Interior: *Provided*, That an amount not exceeding two thousand dollars thereof, shall, for a limited number of years, be expended under the direction of the Commissioner of Indian Affairs, for provisions, seeds, and such other articles or things as may be useful in agricultural pursuits.

Such sum as can be usefully and beneficially applied by the United States, annually, for twenty years, and not to exceed three thousand dollars, in any one year, for purposes of education; to be expended under the direction of the Secretary of the Interior.

Three hundred dollars' ($300) worth of powder, per annum, for five years.

One hundred dollars' ($100) worth shot and lead, per annum, for five years.

One hundred dollars' ($100) worth of gilling twine, per annum, for five years.

One hundred dollars' ($100) worth of tobacco, per annum, for five years.

Hire of three laborers at Leech Lake, of two at Lake Winnibigoshish, and of one at Cass Lake, for five years.

Expense of two blacksmiths, with the necessary shop, iron, steel, and tools, for fifteen years.

Two hundred dollars ($200) in grubbing-hoes and tools, the present year.

Fifteen thousand dollars ($15,000) for opening a road from Crow Wing to Leech Lake; to be expended under the direction of the Commissioner of Indian Affairs.

To have ploughed and prepared for cultivation, two hundred acres of land, in ten or more lots, within the reservation at Leech Lake; fifty acres, in four or more lots, within the reservation at Lake Winnibigoshish; and twenty-five acres, in two or more lots within the reservation at Cass Lake: *Provided*, That the Indians shall make the rails and inclose the lots themselves.

A saw-mill, with a portable grist-mill attached thereto, to be established whenever the same shall be deemed necessary and advisable by the Commissioner of Indian Affairs, at such point as he shall think best; and which, together, with the expense of a proper person to take charge of and operate them, shall be continued during ten years: *Provided*, That the cost of all the requisite repairs of the said mills shall be paid by the Indians, out of their own funds.

Payment to the Mississippi bands under former treaties may be made in cash.

ARTICLE 4. The Mississippi bands have expressed a desire to be permitted to employ their own farmers, mechanics, and teachers; and it is therefore agreed that the amounts to which they are now entitled, under former treaties, for purposes of education, for blacksmiths and assistants, shops, tools, iron and steel, and for the employment of farmers and carpenters, shall be paid over to them as their annuities are paid: *Provided, however*, That whenever, in the opinion of the

Commissioner of Indian Affairs, they fail to make proper provision for the above-named purposes, he may retain said amounts, and appropriate them according to his discretion, for their education and improvement.

ARTICLE 5. The foregoing annuities, in money and goods, shall be paid and distributed as follows: Those due the Mississippi bands, at one of their reservations; and those due the Pillager and Lake Winnibigoshish bands, at Leech Lake; and no part of the said annuities shall ever be taken or applied, in any manner, to or for the payment of the debts or obligations of Indians contracted in their private dealings, as individuals, whether to traders or other persons. And should any of said Indians become intemperate or abandoned, and waste their property, the President may withhold any moneys or goods, due and payable to such, and cause the same to be expended, applied, or distributed, so as to insure the benefit thereof to their families. If, at any time, before the said annuities in money and goods of either of the Indian parties to this convention shall expire, the interests and welfare of said Indians shall, in the opinion of the President, require a different arrangement, he shall have the power to cause the said annuities, instead of being paid over and distributed to the Indians, to be expended or applied to such purposes or objects as may be best calculated to promote their improvement and civilization. *How the above annuities shall be paid.*

ARTICLE 6. The missionaries and such other persons as are now, by authority of law, residing in the country ceded by the first article of this agreement, shall each have the privilege of entering one hundred and sixty acres of the said ceded lands, at one dollar and twenty-five cents per acre; said entries not to be made so as to interfere, in any manner, with the laying off of the several reservations herein provided for. *Preemption rights in said cession.*

And such of the mixed bloods as are heads of families, and now have actual residences and improvements in the ceded country, shall have granted to them, in fee, eighty acres of land, to include their respective improvements. *Grants of land to mixed bloods.*

ARTICLE 7. The laws which have been or may be enacted by Congress, regulating trade and intercourse with the Indian tribes, to continue and be in force within the several reservations provided for herein; and those portions of said laws which prohibit the introduction, manufacture, use of, and traffic in, ardent spirits, wines, or other liquors, in the Indian country, shall continue and be in force, within the entire boundaries of the country herein ceded to the United States, until otherwise provided by Congress. *Laws extended to said reservations.*

ARTICLE 8. All roads and highways, authorized by law, the lines of which shall be laid through any of the reservations provided for in this convention, shall have the right of way through the same; the fair and just value of such right being paid to the Indians therefor; to be assessed and determined according to the laws in force for the appropriation of lands for such purposes. *Roads may be constructed.*

ARTICLE 9. The said bands of Indians, jointly and severally, obligate and bind themselves not to commit any depredations or wrong upon other Indians, or upon citizens of the United States; to conduct themselves at all times in a peaceable and orderly manner; to submit all difficulties between them and other Indians to the President, and to abide by his decision in regard to the same, and to respect and observe the laws of the United States, so far as the same are to them applicable. And they also stipulate that they will settle down in the peaceful pursuits of life, commence the cultivation of the soil, and appropriate their means to the erection of houses, opening farms, the education of their children, and such other objects of improvement and convenience, as are incident to well-regulated society; and that they will abstain from the use of intoxicating drinks and other vices to which they have been addicted. *Stipulations as to conduct of the Indians.*

ARTICLE 10. This instrument shall be obligatory on the contracting parties as soon as the same shall be ratified by the President and the Senate of the United States.

In testimony whereof the said George W. Manypenny, commissioner as aforesaid, and the said chiefs and delegates of the Mississippi, Pillager and Lake Winnibigoshish bands of Chippewa Indians have hereunto set their hands and seals, at the place and on the day and year hereinbefore written.

George W. Manypenny, commissioner.   [L. S.]

Tug-o-na-ke-shick, or Hole in the the Day, his x mark. [L. S.]	Mah-yah-ge-way-we-durg, or The Chorister, his x mark. [L. S.]
Que-we-sans-ish, or Bad Boy, his x mark. [L. S.]	Kay-gwa-daush, or The Attempter, his x mark. [L. S.]
Waud-e-kaw, or Little Hill, his x mark. [L. S.]	Caw-cang-e-we-gwan, or Crow Feather, his x mark. [L. S.]
I-awe-showe-we-ke-shig, or Crossing Sky, his x mark. [L. S.]	Show-baush-king, or He that Passeth Under Everything, his x mark. [L. S.]
Petud-dunce, or Rat's Liver, his x mark. [L. S.]	
Mun-o-min-e-kay-shein, or Rice Maker, his x mark. [L. S.]	

Chief delegates of the Mississippi bands.

Aish-ke-bug-e-koshe, or Flat Mouth, his x mark. [L. S.]	Maug-e-gaw-bow, or Stepping Ahead, his x mark. [L. S.]
Be-sheck-kee, or Buffalo, his x mark. [L. S.]	Mi-gi-si, or Eagle, his x mark. [L. S.]
Nay-bun-a-caush, or Young Man's Son, his x mark. [L. S.]	Kaw-be-mub-bee, or North Star, his x mark. [L. S.]

Chiefs and delegates of the Pillager and Lake Winnibigoshish bands.

Executed in the presence of—

Henry M. Rice.	Paul H. Beaulieu, interpreter.
Geo. Culver.	Edward Ashman, interpreter.
D. B. Herriman, Indian agent.	C. H. Beaulieu, interpreter.
J. E. Fletcher.	Peter Roy, interpreter.
John Dowling.	Will P. Ross, Cherokee Nation.
T. A. Warren, United States interpreter.	Riley Keys.

TREATY WITH THE WINNEBAGO, 1855.

Feb. 27, 1855.

10 Stat., 1172.
Ratified Mar. 3, 1855.
Proclaimed Mar. 23, 1855.

Articles of agreement and convention, made and concluded at Washington City on the twenty-seventh day of February, eighteen hundred and fifty-five, between George W. Manypenny, commissioner on the part of the United States, and the following-named chiefs and delegates representing the Winnebago tribe of Indians, viz: Waw-konchaw-koo-kaw, The Coming Thunder, or Kinnoshik; Sho-go-nik-kaw, or Little Hill; Maw-he-coo-shah-naw-zhe-kaw, One that Stands and Reaches the Skies, or Little Decorie; Waw-kon-chaw-hoo-no-kaw, or Little Thunder; Hoonk-hoo-no-kaw, Little Chief, or Little Priest; Honch-hutta-kaw, or Big Bear; Wach-ha-ta-kaw, or Big Canoe; Ha-zum-kee-kaw, or One Horn; Ha-zee-kaw, or Yellow Bank; and Baptiste Lassallier, they being thereto duly authorized by said tribe:

Cession to the United States of the land granted pursuant to treaty of Oct. 13, 1846.

ARTICLE 1. The Winnebago Indians hereby cede, sell, and convey to the United States all their right, title, and interest in, and to, the tract of land granted to them pursuant to the third article of the treaty concluded with said tribe, at Washington City, on the thirteenth day of October, one thousand eight hundred and forty-six, lying north of St. Peter's River and west of the Mississippi River, in the Territory of Minnesota, and estimated to contain about eight hundred and ninety-seven thousand and nine hundred (897,900) acres; the boundary-lines of which are thus described, in the second article of the treaty concluded between the United States and the Chippewa Indians of the Mississippi and Lake Superior, on the second day of August, one thousand eight hundred and forty seven, viz: "Beginning at the junction of the Crow

Wing and Mississippi Rivers; thence, up the Crow Wing River, to the junction of that river with the Long Prairie River; thence, up the Long Prairie River, to the boundary line between the Sioux and Chippewa Indians; thence, southerly, along the said boundary-line, to a lake at the head of Long Prairie River; thence, in a direct line, to the sources of the Watab River; thence, down the Watab to the Mississippi River; thence, up the Mississippi, to the place of beginning:" *Provided, however,* That the portions of said tract embracing the improved lands of the Indians, the grist and saw mill, and all other improvements made for or by them, shall be specially reserved from pre-emption, sale, or settlement until the said mills and improvements, including the improvements to the land, shall have been appraised and sold, at public sale, to the highest bidder, for the benefit of the Indians, but no sale thereof shall be made for less than the appraised value. And the President may prescribe such rules and regulations in relation to said sale as he may deem proper; and the person or persons purchasing said mills and improvements, shall have the right, when the land is surveyed, to enter the legal subdivisions thereof, including the improvements purchased by them, at one dollar and twenty-five cents per acre. *[Certain parts of said cession to be sold for benefit of said tribe.]*

ARTICLE 2. In consideration of the cessions aforesaid, and in full compensation therefor, the United States agree to pay to the said Indians, the sum of seventy thousand dollars, ($70,000,) and to grant them, as a permanent home, a tract of land equal to eighteen miles square, on the Blue Earth River, in the Territory of Minnesota, which shall be selected and located by the agent of the Government and a delegation of the Winnebagoes, immediately after the ratification of this instrument, and after the necessary appropriations to carry it into effect shall have been made; and a report of such selection and location, shall be made in writing, to the superintendent of Indian affairs for the Territory of Minnesota, who shall attach his official signature to the same, and forward it to the Commissioner of Indian Affairs; and the country thus selected shall be the permanent home of the said Indians; *Provided,* Said tract shall not approach nearer the Minnesota River than the mouth of the La Serrer fork of the Blue Earth River. *[Payment for the above cession. Provision for permanent home.]*

ARTICLE 3. It is agreed, that the moneys received from the sale of the Indian improvements, as provided for in the first article, and the sum stipulated to be paid by the second article of this instrument, shall be expended under the direction of the President, in removing the Indians to their new homes, including those who are now severed from the main body of the tribe, living in Kansas Territory, Wisconsin, or elsewhere; in subsisting them a reasonable time after their removal; in making improvements, such as breaking and fencing land, and building houses; in purchasing stock, agricultural implements and household furniture, and for such other objects as may tend to promote their prosperity and advancement in civilization. And the said Winnebago Indians agree to remove to their new homes immediately after the selection of the tract hereinbefore provided for, is made. *[How payments and proceeds of sale shall be expended.]*

ARTICLE 4. In order to encourage the Winnebago Indians to engage in agriculture, and such other pursuits as will conduce to their well-being and improvement, it is agreed: that, at such time or times as the President may deem advisable, the land herein provided to be selected as their future home, or such portions thereof as may be necessary, shall be surveyed; and the President shall, from time to time, as the Indians may desire it, assign to each head of a family, or single persons over twenty-one years of age, a reasonable quantity of land, in one body, not to exceed eighty acres in any case, for their separate use; and he may, at his discretion, as the occupants thereof become capable of managing their business and affairs, issue patents to them for the tract so assigned to them, respectively; said tracts to be exempt from taxation, levy, sale, or forfeiture, until otherwise provided by the legislature of the State in which they may be situated, with the *[Survey and allotment of the permanent home.]*

assent of Congress; nor shall they be sold or alienated, in fee, within fifteen years after the date of the patents, and not then, without the assent of the President of the United States being first obtained. Prior to the patents being issued, the President shall make such rules and regulations as he may deem necessary and expedient, respecting the disposition of any of said tracts, in case of the death of the person or persons to whom they may be assigned, so that the same shall be secured to the families of such deceased persons; and should any of the Indians to whom tracts may be assigned, thereafter abandon them, the President may take such action in relation to such abandoned tracts, as in his judgment may be necessary and proper.

Payments under former treaties, how to be made.

ARTICLE 5. All unexpended balances now in the hands of the agent of the tribe, arising under former treaties, for schools, pay of interpreter therefor, support of blacksmiths and assistants; and also of the sum of ten thousand dollars set apart by the treaty of October thirteenth eighteen hundred and forty-six, for manual-labor schools, shall be expended and applied, in the opening of farms, building and furnishing of houses, and the purchase of stock for said Indians. And the stipulations in former treaties providing for the application or expenditure of particular sums of money for specific purposes, are hereby so far modified and changed, as to confer upon the President the power, in his discretion, to cause such sums of money, in whole or in part, to be expended for, or applied to such other objects and purposes and in such manner as he shall deem best calculated to promote the welfare and improvement of said Indians.

Payments not to be taken for debt.

ARTICLE 6. No part of the moneys stipulated to be paid to the Winnebago Indians by these articles of agreement and convention, nor any of the future instalments due and payable under former treaties between them and the United States, shall ever be taken, by direction of the chiefs, to pay the debts of individual Indians, contracted in their private dealings, known as national or tribal debts.

Preemption rights in said cession.

ARTICLE 7. The missionaries, or other persons who are, by authority of law, now residing on the lands ceded by the first article of this agreement, shall each have the privilege of entering one hundred and sixty acres of the said ceded lands, to include any improvements they may *Grant of land to the mixed-blood Indians.* have, at one dollar and twenty-five cents per acre: and such of the mixed-bloods, as are heads of families, and now have actual residences and improvements of their own, in the ceded country, shall each have granted to them, in fee, eighty acres of land, to include their improvements: *Provided, however,* That said entries and grants shall in no case be upon, or in any manner interfere with, any of the lands improved by the Government, or by or for the Indians, or on which the agency building, saw and grist mill, or other public or Indian improvements have been erected or made.

Laws extended to said home.

ARTICLE 8. The laws which have been or may be enacted by Congress, regulating trade and intercourse with the Indian tribes, shall continue and be in force within the country herein provided to be selected as the future permanent home of the Winnebago Indians; and those portions of said laws which prohibit the introduction, manufacture, use of, and traffic in, ardent spirits in the Indian country, shall continue and be in force within the country herein ceded to the United States, until otherwise provided by Congress.

Roads may be constructed.

ARTICLE 9. All roads and highways authorized by law, the lines of which may be required to be laid through any part of the country herein provided as the future permanent home of the Winnebago Indians, shall have right of way through the same; a fair and just value of such right being paid to the Indians, in money, to be assessed and determined according to the laws in force for the appropriation of land for such purposes.

Provisions as to conduct of said tribe.

ARTICLE 10. The said tribe of Indians, jointly and severally, obligate and bind themselves, not to commit any depredation or wrong upon other Indians, or upon citizens of the United States; to conduct themselves at all times in a peaceable and orderly manner; to submit all difficulties between them and other Indians to the President, and to abide by his decision; to respect and observe the laws of the United States, so far as the same are to them applicable; to settle down in the peaceful pursuits of life; to commence the cultivation of the soil; to educate their children, and to abstain from the use of intoxicating drinks and other vices to which many of them have been addicted. And the President may withhold from such of the Winnebagoes as abandon their homes, and refuse to labor, and from the idle, intemperate, and vicious, the benefits they may be entitled to under these articles of agreement and convention, or under articles of former treaties, until they give evidences of amendment and become settled, and conform to, and comply, with the stipulations herein provided; or, should they be heads of families, the same may be appropriated, under the direction of the President, to the use and enjoyment of their families.

Payments may be withheld from the ill-behaved.

ARTICLE 11. These articles of agreement and convention, shall be in lieu of the "Articles of a convention made and concluded between Willis A. Gorman and Jonathan E. Fletcher, on the part of the United States, and the chiefs and head-men of the Winnebago tribe of Indians, on the 6th day of August, A. D. 1853," and the amendments of the Senate thereto, as expressed in its resolution of July twenty-first, eighteen hundred and fifty-four; to which amendments the said Winnebago Indians refused to give their assent, which refusal was communicated to the Commissioner of Indian Affairs, by the governor of Minnesota Territory, on the twenty-fourth of January, eighteen hundred and fifty-five.

This treaty to be in lieu of an unratified one.

ARTICLE 12. The United States will pay the necessary expenses incurred by the Winnebago delegates in making their present visit to Washington, while here, and in returning to their homes.

Expenses of a visit to Washington to be paid.

ARTICLE 13. This instrument shall be obligatory on the contracting parties as soon as the same shall be ratified by the President and the Senate of the United States.

In testimony whereof the said George W. Manypenny, commissioner as aforesaid, and the said chiefs and delegates of the Winnebago tribe of Indians, have hereunto set their hands and seals, at the place and on the day and year hereinbefore written.

George W. Manypenny, commissioner,   [L. S.]
Waw-koṅ-chaw-koo-haw, the Coming Thunder, or
    Win-no-shik, his x mark   [L. S.]
Sho-go-nik-kaw, or Little Hill his x mark   [L. S.]
Maw-he-coo-shaw-naw-zhe-kaw, One that Stands and
    Reaches the Skies, or Little Decorie, his x mark   [L. S.]
Waw-kon-chaw-hoo-no-kaw, or Little Thunder, his
    x mark   [L. S.]
Hoonk-hoo-no-kaw, Little Chief or Little Priest his
    x mark   [L. S.]
Honch-hutta-kaw, or Big Bear, his x mark   [L. S.]
Watch-ha-ta-kaw, or Big Canoe, his x mark   [L. S.]
Ha-zhun-kee-kaw, or One Horn, his x mark   [L. S.]
Ha-zee-kaw, or Yellow Bank, His x mark,   [L. S.]
Baptiste Lasallier.

In presence of—
    Geo. Culver,
    Asa White,
    John Dowling,
    J. E. Fletcher,
    Peter Manaiy, United States interpreter.

TREATY WITH THE WALLAWALLA, CAYUSE, ETC., 1855.

June 9, 1855.

12 Stats., 945.
Ratified Mar. 8, 1859.
Proclaimed Apr. 11,
1859.

Articles of agreement and convention made and concluded at the treaty-ground, Camp Stevens, in the Walla-Walla Valley, this ninth day of June, in the year one thousand eight hundred and fifty-five, by and between Isaac I. Stevens, governor and superintendent of Indian affairs for the Territory of Washington, and Joel Palmer, superintendent of Indian affairs for Oregon Territory, on the part of the United States, and the undersigned chiefs, head-men, and delegates of the Walla-Wallas, Cayuses, and Umatilla tribes, and bands of Indians, occupying lands partly in Washington and partly in Oregon Territories, and who, for the purposes of this treaty, are to be regarded as one nation acting for and in behalf of their respective bands and tribes, they being duly authorized thereto; it being understood that Superintendent I. I. Stevens assumes to treat with that portion of the above-named bands and tribes residing within the Territory of Washington, and Superintendent Palmer with those residing within Oregon.

Cession of lands to
the United States.

Boundaries.

ARTICLE 1. The above-named confederated bands of Indians cede to the United States all their right, title, and claim to all and every part of the country claimed by them included in the following boundaries, to wit: Commencing at the mouth of the Tocannon River, in Washington Territory, running thence up said river to its source; thence easterly along the summit of the Blue Mountains, and on the southern boundaries of the purchase made of the Nez Percés Indians, and easterly along that boundary to the western limits of the country claimed by the Shoshonees or Snake Indians; thence southerly along that boundary (being the waters of Powder River) to the source of Powder River, thence to the head-waters of Willow Creek, thence down Willow Creek to the Columbia River, thence up the channel of the Columbia River to the lower end of a large island below the mouth of Umatilla River, thence northerly to a point on the Yakama River, called Tomah-luke, thence to Le Lac, thence to the White Banks on the Columbia below Priest's Rapids, thence down the Columbia River to the junction of the Columbia and Snake Rivers, thence up the Snake

Boundaries.

River to the place of beginning: *Provided, however,* That so much of the country described above as is contained in the following boundaries shall be set apart as a residence for said Indians, which tract for the purposes contemplated shall be held and regarded as an Indian reservation; to wit: Commencing in the middle of the channel of Umatilla River opposite the mouth of Wild Horse Creek, thence up the middle of the channel of said creek to its source, thence southerly to a point in the Blue Mountains, known as Lee's Encampment, thence in a line to the head-waters of Howtome Creek, thence west to the divide between Howtome and Birch Creeks, thence northerly along said divide to a point due west of the southwest corner of William C.

Reservation.

McKay's land-claim, thence east along his line to his southeast corner, thence in a line to the place of beginning; all of which tract shall be set apart and, so far as necessary, surveyed and marked out for their

Whites not to reside
thereon, unless, etc.

exclusive use; nor shall any white person be permitted to reside upon the same without permission of the agent and superintendent. The said tribes and bands agree to remove to and settle upon the same

Tribes to settle
thereon in a year.

within one year after the ratification of this treaty, without any additional expense to the Government other than is provided by this treaty, and until the expiration of the time specified, the said bands shall be permitted to occupy and reside upon the tracts now possessed by them, guaranteeing to all citizen[s] of the United States, the right to enter upon and occupy as settlers any lands not actually enclosed by said

Rights and privileges secured to the
Indians.

Indians: *Provided, also,* That the exclusive right of taking fish in the streams running through and bordering said reservation is hereby secured to said Indians, and at all other usual and accustomed stations in common with citizens of the United States, and of erecting suitable buildings for curing the same; the privilege of hunting, gathering roots and berries and pasturing their stock on unclaimed lands in common with citizens, is also secured to them. *And provided, also,* That if any band or bands of Indians, residing in and claiming any portion or portions of the country described in this article, shall not accede to the terms of this treaty, then the bands becoming parties hereunto agree to reserve such part of the several and other payments herein named, as a consideration for the entire country described as aforesaid, as shall be in the proportion that their aggregate number may have to the whole number of Indians residing in and claiming the entire country aforesaid, as consideration and payment in full for the tracts in said country claimed by them. *And provided, also,* That when substantial improvements have been made by any member of the bands being parties to this treaty, who are compelled to abandon them in consequence of said treaty, [they] shall be valued under the direction of the President of the United States, and payment made therefor.

Proviso in case any tribe does not accede to this treaty.

Allowance for improvements, if, etc.

ARTICLE 2. In consideration of and payment for the country hereby ceded, the United States agree to pay the bands and tribes of Indians claiming territory and residing in said country, and who remove to and reside upon said reservation, the several sums of money following, to wit: eight thousand dollars per annum for the term of five years, commencing on the first day of September, 1856; six thousand dollars per annum for the term of five years next succeeding the first five; four thousand dollars per annum for the term of five years next succeeding the second five, and two thousand dollars per annum for the term of five years next succeeding the third five; all of which several sums of money shall be expended for the use and benefit of the confederated bands herein named, under the direction of the President of the United States, who may from time to time at his discretion, determine what proportion thereof shall be expended for such objects as in his judgment will promote their well-being, and advance them in civilization, for their moral improvement and education, for buildings, opening and fencing farms, breaking land, purchasing teams, wagons, agricultural implements and seeds, for clothing, provision and tools, for medical purposes, providing mechanics and farmers, and for arms and ammunition.

Payments by the United States.

How to be expended.

ARTICLE 3. In addition to the articles advanced the Indians at the time of signing this treaty, the United States agree to expend the sum of fifty thousand dollars during the first and second years after its ratification, for the erection of buildings on the reservation, fencing and opening farms, for the purchase of teams, farming implements, clothing, and provisions, for medicines and tools, for the payment of employés, and for subsisting the Indians the first year after their removal.

United States to expend $50,000 for buildings, etc.

ARTICLE 4. In addition to the consideration above specified, the United States agree to erect, at suitable points on the reservation, one saw-mill, and one flouring-mill, a building suitable for a hospital, two school-houses, one blacksmith shop, one building for wagon and plough maker and one carpenter and joiner shop, one dwelling for each, two millers, one farmer, one superintendent of farming operations, two school-teachers, one blacksmith, one wagon and plough maker, one carpenter and joiner, to each of which the necessary out-buildings. To purchase and keep in repair for the term of twenty years all necessary mill fixtures and mechanical tools, medicines and hospital stores, books and stationery for schools, and furniture for employés.

To erect sawmills, schools, mechanics' shops, etc.

The United States further engage to secure and pay for the services and subsistence, for the term of twenty years, [of] one superintendent of farming operations, one farmer, one blacksmith, one wagon and plough maker, one carpenter and joiner, one physician, and two school-teachers.

To employ mechanics, teachers, etc.

ARTICLE 5. The United States further engage to build for the head chiefs of the Walla-Walla, Cayuse, and Umatilla bands each one dwelling-house, and to plough and fence ten acres of land for each, and to pay to each five hundred dollars per annum in cash for the term of twenty years. The first payment to the Walla-Walla chief to commence upon the signing of this treaty. To give to the Walla-Walla chief three yoke of oxen, three yokes and four chains, one wagon, two ploughs, twelve hoes, twelve axes, two shovels, and one saddle and bridle, one set of wagon-harness, and one set of plough-harness, within three months after the signing of this treaty.

To build for the son of Pio-pio-mox-mox one dwelling-house, and plough and fence five acres of land, and to give him a salary for twenty years, one hundred dollars in cash per annum, commencing September first, eighteen hundred and fifty-six.

The improvement named in this section to be completed as soon after the ratification of this treaty as possible.

It is further stipulated that Pio-pio-mox-mox is secured for the term of five years, the right to build and occupy a house at or near the mouth of Yakama River, to be used as a trading-post in the sale of his bands of wild cattle ranging in that district: *And provided, also,* That in consequence of the immigrant wagon-road from Grand Round to Umatilla, passing through the reservation herein specified, thus leading to turmoils and disputes between Indians and immigrants, and as it is known that a more desirable and practicable route may be had to the south of the present road, that a sum not exceeding ten thousand dollars shall be expended in locating and opening a wagon-road from Powder River or Grand Round, so as to reach the plain at the western base of the Blue Mountain, south of the southern limits of said reservation.

ARTICLE 6. The President may, from time to time at his discretion cause the whole or such portion as he may think proper, of the tract that may now or hereafter be set apart as a permanent home for those Indians, to be surveyed into lots and assigned to such Indians of the confederated bands as may wish to enjoy the privilege, and locate thereon permanently, to a single person over twenty-one years of age, forty acres, to a family of two persons, sixty acres, to a family of three and not exceeding five, eighty acres; to a family of six persons and not exceeding ten, one hundred and twenty acres; and to each family over ten in number, twenty acres to each additional three members; and the President may provide for such rules and regulations as will secure to the family in case of the death of the head thereof, the possession and enjoyment of such permanent home and improvement thereon; and he may at any time, at his discretion, after such person or family has made location on the land assigned as a permanent home, issue a patent to such person or family for such assigned land, conditioned that the tract shall not be aliened or leased for a longer term than two years, and shall be exempt from levy, sale, or forfeiture, which condition shall continue in force until a State constitution, embracing such land within its limits, shall have been formed and the legislature of the State shall remove the restriction: *Provided, however*, That no State legislature shall remove the restriction herein provided for without the consent of Congress: *And provided, also,* That if any person or family, shall at any time, neglect or refuse to occupy or till a portion of the land assigned and on which they have located, or shall roam from place to place, indicating a desire to abandon his home, the President may if the patent shall have been issued, cancel the assignment, and may also withhold from such person or family their portion of the annuities or other money due them, until they shall have returned to such permanent home, and resumed the pursuits of industry, and in default of their return the tract may be declared

(marginal notes)
To build dwelling houses, etc., for head chiefs.

Pio-pio-mox-mox.

$10,000 to be expended for opening wagon road from Powder River.

Allotments of land may be made to individual Indians.

Patents may issue therefor.
Conditions.

Restrictions not to be removed, unless, etc.

Assignments of patents may be canceled.

abandoned, and thereafter assigned to some other person or family of Indians residing on said reservation: *And provided, also,* That the head chiefs of the three principal bands, to wit, Pio-pio-mox-mox, Weyatenatemany, and Wenap-snoot, shall be secured in a tract of at least one hundred and sixty acres of land. Certain head chiefs to have 160 acres.

ARTICLE 7. The annuities of the Indians shall not be taken to pay the debts of individuals. Annuities of Indians not to pay debts of individuals.

ARTICLE 8. The confederated bands acknowledge their dependence on the Government of the United States and promise to be friendly with all the citizens thereof, and pledge themselves to commit no depredation on the property of such citizens, and should any one or more of the Indians violate this pledge, and the fact be satisfactorily proven before the agent, the property taken shall be returned, or in default thereof, or if injured or destroyed, compensation may be made by the Government out of their annuities; nor will they make war on any other tribe of Indians except in self-defense, but submit all matter of difference between them and other Indians, to the Government of the United States or its agents for decision, and abide thereby; and if any of the said Indians commit any depredations on other Indians, the same rule shall prevail as that prescribed in the article in case of depredations against citizens. Said Indians further engage to submit to and observe all laws, rules, and regulations which may be prescribed by the United States for the government of said Indians. Bands to preserve friendly relations.
To pay for depredations.
Not to make war, except, etc.
To submit to regulations.

ARTICLE 9. In order to prevent the evils of intemperance among said Indians, it is hereby provided that if any one of them shall drink liquor, or procure it for others to drink, [such one] may have his or her proportion of the annuities withheld from him or her for such time as the President may determine. Annuities withheld from those drinking liquor.

ARTICLE 10. The said confederated bands agree that, whenever in the opinion of the President of the United States the public interest may require it, *that* all roads highways and railroads shall have the right of way through the reservation herein designated or which may at any time hereafter be set apart as a reservation for said Indians. Right of way reserved for roads through reservation.

ARTICLE 11. This treaty shall be obligatory on the contracting parties as soon as the same shall be ratified by the President and Senate of the United States. When treaty to take effect.

In testimony whereof, the said I. I. Stevens and Joel Palmer, on the part of the United States, and the undersigned chiefs, headmen, and delegates of the said confederated bands, have hereunto set their hands and seals, this ninth day of June, eighteen hundred and fifty-five.

Isaac I. Stevens,   [L. S.]

Governor and Superintendent Washington Territory.

Joel Palmer,   [L. S.]

Superintendent Indian Affairs, O. T.

Pio-pio-mox-mox, his x mark, head chief of Walla-Wallas. [L. S.]	U-wait-quaick, his x mark.	[L. S.]
Meani-teat or Pierre, his x mark. [L. S.]	Tilch-a-waix, his x mark.	[L. S.]
Weyatenatemany, his x mark, head chief of Cayuses. [L. S.]	La-ta-chin, his x mark.	[L. S.]
Wenap-snoot, his x mark, head chief of Umatilla. [L. S.]	Kacho-rolich, his x mark.	[L. S.]
Kamaspello, his x mark. [L. S.]	Kanocey, his x mark.	[L. S.]
Steachus, his x mark. [L. S.]	Som-na-howlish, his x mark.	[L. S.]
Howlish-wampo, his x mark. [L. S.]	Ta-we-way, his x mark.	[L. S.]
Five Crows, his x mark. [L. S.]	Ha-hats-me-cheat-pus, his x mark.	[L. S.]
Stocheania, his x mark. [L. S.]	Pe-na-cheanit, his x mark.	[L. S.]
Mu-howlish, his x mark. [L. S.]	Ha-yo-ma-kin, his x mark.	[L. S.]
Lin-tin-met-cheania, his x mark. [L. S.]	Ya-ca-lox, his x mark.	[L. S.]
Petamyo-mox-mox, his x mark. [L. S.]	Na-kas, his x mark.	[L. S.]
Watash-te-waty, his x mark. [L. S.]	Stop-cha-yeou, his x mark.	[L. S.]
She-yam-na-kon, his x mark. [L. S.]	He-yeau-she-keaut, his x mark.	[L. S.]
Qua-chim, his x mark. [L. S.]	Sha-wa-way, his x mark.	[L. S.]
Te-walca-temany, his x mark. [L. S.]	Tam-cha-key, his x mark.	[L. S.]
Keantoan, his x mark. [L. S.]	Te-na-we-na-cha, his x mark.	[L. S.]
	Johnson, his x mark.	[L. S.]
	Whe-la-chey, his x mark.	[L. S.]

Signed in the presence of—

James Doty, secretary treaties.
Wm. C. McKay, secretary treaties.
C. Chirouse, O. M. I.
A. D. Pamburn, interpreter.
John Whitford, his x mark, interpreter.
Mathew Dofa, his x mark, interpreter.
William Craig, interpreter.
James Coxey, his x mark, interpreter.
Patrick McKenzie, interpreter.
Arch. Gracie, jr., brevet second lieutenant, Fourth Infantry.
R. R. Thompson, Indian agent.
R. B. Metcalfe, Indian sub-agent.

TREATY WITH THE YAKIMA, 1855.

June 9, 1855.

12 Stat., 951.
Ratified Mar. 8, 1859.
Proclaimed Apr. 18, 1859.

Articles of agreement and convention made and concluded at the treaty-ground, Camp Stevens, Walla-Walla Valley, this ninth day of June, in the year one thousand eight hundred and fifty-five, by and between Isaac I. Stevens, governor and superintendent of Indian affairs for the Territory of Washington, on the part of the United States, and the undersigned head chiefs, chiefs, head-men, and delegates of the Yakama, Palouse, Pisquouse, Wenatshapam, Klikatat, Klinquit, Kow-was-say-ee, Li-ay-was, Skin-pah, Wish-ham, Shyiks, Oche-chotes, Kah-milt-pah, and Se-ap-cat, confederated tribes and bands of Indians, occupying lands hereinafter bounded and described and lying in Washington Territory, who for the purposes of this treaty are to be considered as one nation, under the name of "Yakama," with Kamaiakun as its head chief, on behalf of and acting for said tribes and bands, and being duly authorized thereto by them.

Cession of lands to the United States.

ARTICLE 1. The aforesaid confederated tribes and bands of Indians hereby cede, relinquish, and convey to the United States all their right, title, and interest in and to the lands and country occupied and claimed by them, and bounded and described as follows, to wit:

Boundaries.

Commencing at Mount Ranier, thence northerly along the main ridge of the Cascade Mountains to the point where the northern tributaries of Lake Che-lan and the southern tributaries of the Methow River have their rise; thence southeasterly on the divide between the waters of Lake Che-lan and the Methow River to the Columbia River; thence, crossing the Columbia on a true east course, to a point whose longitude is one hundred and nineteen degrees and ten minutes, (119° 10',) which two latter lines separate the above confederated tribes and bands from the Oakinakane tribe of Indians; thence in a true south course to the forty-seventh (47°) parallel of latitude; thence east on said parallel to the main Palouse River, which two latter lines of boundary separate the above confederated tribes and bands from the Spokanes; thence down the Palouse River to its junction with the Moh-hah-ne-she, or southern tributary of the same; thence in a southesterly direction, to the Snake River, at the mouth of the Tucannon River, separating the above confederated tribes from the Nez Percé tribe of Indians; thence down the Snake River to its junction with the Columbia River; thence up the Columbia River to the "White Banks" below the Priest's Rapids; thence westerly to a lake called "La Lac;" thence southerly to a point on the Yakama River called Toh-mah-luke; thence, in a southwesterly direction, to the Columbia River, at the western extremity of the "Big Island," between the mouths of the Umatilla River and Butler Creek; all which latter boundaries separate the above confederated tribes and bands from the Walla-Walla, Cayuse, and Umatilla tribes and bands of Indians; thence down the Columbia River to midway between the mouths of White Salmon and Wind Rivers; thence along the divide between said rivers to the main ridge of the Cascade Mountains; and thence along said ridge to the place of beginning.

ARTICLE 2. There is, however, reserved, from the lands above ceded for the use and occupation of the aforesaid confederated tribes and bands of Indians, the tract of land included within the following boundaries, to wit: Commencing on the Yakama River, at the mouth of the Attah-nam River; thence westerly along said Attah-nam River to the forks; thence along the southern tributary to the Cascade Mountains; thence southerly along the main ridge of said mountains, passing south and east of Mount Adams, to the spur whence flows the waters of the Klickatat and Pisco Rivers; thence down said spur to the divide between the waters of said rivers; thence along said divide to the divide separating the waters of the Satass River from those flowing into the Columbia River; thence along said divide to the main Yakama, eight miles below the mouth of the Satass River; and thence up the Yakama River to the place of beginning. *Reservation.* *Boundaries.*

All which tract shall be set apart and, so far as necessary, surveyed and marked out, for the exclusive use and benefit of said confederated tribes and bands of Indians, as an Indian reservation; nor shall any white man, excepting those in the employment of the Indian Department, be permitted to reside upon the said reservation without permission of the tribe and the superintendent and agent. And the said confederated tribes and bands agree to remove to, and settle upon, the same, within one year after the ratification of this treaty. In the mean time it shall be lawful for them to reside upon any ground not in the actual claim and occupation of citizens of the United States; and upon any ground claimed or occupied, if with the permission of the owner or claimant. *Reservations to be set apart, etc., and Indians to settle thereon.* *Whites not to reside thereon.*

Guaranteeing, however, the right to all citizens of the United States to enter upon and occupy as settlers any lands not actually occupied and cultivated by said Indians at this time, and not included in the reservation above named.

And provided, That any substantial improvements heretofore made by any Indian, such as fields enclosed and cultivated, and houses erected upon the lands hereby ceded, and which he may be compelled to abandon in consequence of this treaty, shall be valued, under the direction of the President of the United States, and payment made therefor in money; or improvements of an equal value made for said Indian upon the reservation. And no Indian will be required to abandon the improvements aforesaid, now occupied by him, until their value in money, or improvements of an equal value shall be furnished him as aforesaid. *Improvements on ceded lands.*

ARTICLE 3. *And provided,* That, if necessary for the public convenience, roads may be run through the said reservation; and on the other hand, the right of way, with free access from the same to the nearest public highway, is secured to them; as also the right, in common with citizens of the United States, to travel upon all public highways. *Roads may be made.*

The exclusive right of taking fish in all the streams, where running through or bordering said reservation, is further secured to said confederated tribes and bands of Indians, as also the right of taking fish at all usual and accustomed places, in common with the citizens of the Territory, and of erecting temporary buildings for curing them; together with the privilege of hunting, gathering roots and berries, and pasturing their horses and cattle upon open and unclaimed land. *Privileges secured to Indians.*

Payments by the United States.

ARTICLE 4. In consideration of the above cession, the United States agree to pay to the said confederated tribes and bands of Indians, in addition to the goods and provisions distributed to them at the time of signing this treaty, the sum of two hundred thousand dollars, in the following manner, that is to say: Sixty thousand dollars, to be expended under the direction of the President of the United States, the first year after the ratification of this treaty, in providing for their removal to the reservation, breaking up and fencing farms, building houses for them, supplying them with provisions and a suitable outfit, and for such other objects as he may deem necessary, and the remainder in annuities, as follows: For the first five years after the ratification of the treaty, ten thousand dollars each year, commencing September first, 1856; for the next five years, eight thousand dollars each year; for the next five years, six thousand dollars per year; and for the next five years, four thousand dollars per year.

How to be applied.

All which sums of money shall be applied to the use and benefit of said Indians, under the direction of the President of the United States, who may from time to time determine, at his discretion, upon what beneficial objects to expend the same for them. And the superintendent of Indian affairs, or other proper officer, shall each year inform the President of the wishes of the Indians in relation thereto.

United States to establish schools.

ARTICLE 5. The United States further agree to establish at suitable points within said reservation, within one year after the ratification hereof, two schools, erecting the necessary buildings, keeping them in repair, and providing them with furniture, books, and stationery, one of which shall be an agricultural and industrial school, to be located at the agency, and to be free to the children of the said confederated tribes and bands of Indians, and to employ one superintendent of teaching and two teachers; to build two blacksmiths' shops, to one of which shall be attached a tin-shop, and to the other a gunsmith's shop; one carpenter's shop, one wagon and plough maker's shop, and to keep the same in repair and furnished with the necessary tools; to employ one superintendent of farming and two farmers, two blacksmiths, one tinner, one gunsmith, one carpenter, one wagon and plough maker, for the instruction of the Indians in trades and to assist them in the same; to erect one saw-mill and one flouring-mill, keeping the same in repair and furnished with the necessary tools and fixtures; to erect a hospital, keeping the same in repair and provided with the necessary medicines and furniture, and to employ a physician; and to erect, keep in repair, and provided with the necessary furniture, the building required for the accommodation of the said employees. The said buildings and establishments to be maintained and kept in repair as aforesaid, and the employees to be kept in service for the period of twenty years.

Mechanics' shops.

Sawmill and flouring mill.
Hospital.

Salary to head chief; house, etc.

And in view of the fact that the head chief of the said confederated tribes and bands of Indians is expected, and will be called upon to perform many services of a public character, occupying much of his time, the United States further agree to pay to the said confederated tribes and bands of Indians five hundred dollars per year, for the term of twenty years after the ratification hereof, as a salary for such person as the said confederated tribes and bands of Indians may select to be their head chief, to build for him at a suitable point on the reservation a comfortable house, and properly furnish the same, and to plough and fence ten acres of land. The said salary to be paid to, and the said house to be occupied by, such head chief so long as he may continue to hold that office.

Kamaiakun is the head chief.

And it is distinctly understood and agreed that at the time of the conclusion of this treaty Kamaiakun is the duly elected and authorized head chief of the confederated tribes and bands aforesaid, styled the Yakama Nation, and is recognized as such by them and by the commissioners on the part of the United States holding this treaty; and all the expenditures and expenses contemplated in this article of this treaty shall be defrayed by the United States, and shall not be deducted from the annuities agreed to be paid to said confederated tribes and band of Indians. Nor shall the cost of transporting the goods for the annuity payments be a charge upon the annuities, but shall be defrayed by the United States.

ARTICLE 6. The President may, from time to time, at his discretion, cause the whole or such portions of such reservation as he may think proper, to be surveyed into lots, and assign the same to such individuals or families of the said confederated tribes and bands of Indians as are willing to avail themselves of the privilege, and will locate on the same as a permanent home, on the same terms and subject to the same regulations as are provided in the sixth article of the treaty with the Omahas, so far as the same may be applicable. *[sidenote: Reservation may be surveyed into lots and assigned to individuals or families.]*

ARTICLE 7. The annuities of the aforesaid confederated tribes and bands of Indians shall not be taken to pay the debts of individuals. *[sidenote: Annuities not to pay for debts of individuals.]*

ARTICLE 8. The aforesaid confederated tribes and bands of Indians acknowledge their dependence upon the Government of the United States, and promise to be friendly with all citizens thereof, and pledge themselves to commit no depredations upon the property of such citizens. *[sidenote: Tribes to preserve friendly relations.]*

And should any one or more of them violate this pledge, and the fact be satisfactorily proved before the agent, the property taken shall be returned, or in default thereof, or if injured or destroyed, compensation may be made by the Government out of the annuities. *[sidenote: To pay for depredations.]*

Nor will they make war upon any other tribe, except in self-defence, but will submit all matters of difference between them and other Indians to the Government of the United States or its agent for decision, and abide thereby. And if any of the said Indians commit depredations on any other Indians within the Territory of Washington or Oregon, the same rule shall prevail as that provided in this article in case of depredations against citizens. And the said confederated tribes and bands of Indians agree not to shelter or conceal offenders against the laws of the United States, but to deliver them up to the authorities for trial. *[sidenote: Not to make war but in self-defense.]* *[sidenote: To surrender offenders.]*

ARTICLE 9. The said confederated tribes and bands of Indians desire to exclude from their reservation the use of ardent spirits, and to prevent their people from drinking the same, and, therefore, it is provided that any Indian belonging to said confederated tribes and bands of Indians, who is guilty of bringing liquor into said reservation, or who drinks liquor, may have his or her annuities withheld from him or her for such time as the President may determine. *[sidenote: Annuities may be withheld from those who drink ardent spirits.]*

ARTICLE 10. *And provided*, That there is also reserved and set apart from the lands ceded by this treaty, for the use and benefit of the aforesaid confederated tribes and bands, a tract of land not exceeding in quantity one township of six miles square, situated at the forks of the Pisquouse or Wenatshapam River, and known as the "Wenatshapam Fishery," which said reservation shall be surveyed and marked out whenever the President may direct, and be subject to the same provisions and restrictions as other Indian reservations. *[sidenote: Wenatshapam fishery reserved.]*

ARTICLE 11. This treaty shall be obligatory upon the contracting parties as soon as the same shall be ratified by the President and Senate of the United States. *[sidenote: When treaty to take effect.]*

In testimony whereof, the said Isaac I. Stevens, governor and superintendent of Indian affairs for the Territory of Washington, and the undersigned head chief, chiefs, headmen, and delegates of the aforesaid confederated tribes and bands of Indians, have hereunto set their hands and seals, at the place and on the day and year hereinbefore written.

ISAAC I. STEVENS,
Governor and Superintendent. [L. S.]

Kamaiakun, his x mark.	[L. S.]	Wish-och-kmpits, his x mark.	[L. S.]
Skloom, his x mark.	[L. S.]	Koo-lat-toose, his x mark.	[L. S.]
Owhi, his x mark.	[L. S.]	Shee-ah-cotte, his x mark.	[L. S.]
Te-cole-kun, his x mark.	[L. S.]	Tuck-quille, his x mark.	[L. S.]
La-hoom, his x mark.	[L. S.]	Ka-loo-as, his x mark.	[L. S.]
Me-ni-nock, his x mark.	[L. S.]	Scha-noo-a, his x mark.	[L. S.]
Elit Palmer, his x mark.	[L. S.]	Sla-kish, his x mark.	[L. S.]

Signed and sealed in the presence of—

James Doty, secretary of treaties,
Mie. Jles. Pandosy, O. M. T.,
Wm. C. McKay,
W. H. Tappan, sub Indian agent, W. T.,
C. Chirouse, O. M. T.,
Patrick McKenzie, interpreter,
A. D. Pamburn, interpreter,
Joel Palmer, superintendent Indian affairs, O. T.,
W. D. Biglow,
A. D. Pamburn, interpreter.

TREATY WITH THE NEZ PERCÉS, 1855.

June 11, 1855.

12 Stats., 957.
Ratified Mar. 8, 1859.
Proclaimed Apr. 29, 1859.

Articles of agreement and convention made and concluded at the treaty ground, Camp Stevens, in the Walla-Walla Valley, this eleventh day of June, in the year one thousand eight hundred and fifty-five, by and between Isaac I. Stevens, governor and superintendent of Indian affairs for the Territory of Washington, and Joel Palmer, superintendent of Indian affairs for Oregon Territory, on the part of the United States, and the undersigned chiefs, head-men, and delegates of the Nez Percé tribe of Indians occupying lands lying partly in Oregon and partly in Washington Territories, between the Cascade and Bitter Root Mountains, on behalf of, and acting for said tribe, and being duly authorized thereto by them, it being understood that Superintendent Isaac I. Stevens assumes to treat only with those of the above-named tribe of Indians residing within the Territory of Washington, and Superintendent Palmer with those residing exclusively in Oregon Territory.

Cession of lands to the United States.

Boundaries.

ARTICLE 1. The said Nez Percé tribe of Indians hereby cede, relinquish and convey to the United States all their right, title, and interest in and to the country occupied or claimed by them, bounded and described as follows, to wit: Commencing at the source of the Wo-na-ne-she or southern tributary of the Palouse River; thence down that river to the main Palouse; thence in a southerly direction to the Snake River, at the mouth of the Tucanon River; thence up the Tucanon to its source in the Blue Mountains; thence southerly along the ridge of the Blue Mountains; thence to a point on Grand Ronde River, midway between Grand Ronde and the mouth of the Woll-low-how River; thence along the divide between the waters of the Woll-low-how and Powder River; thence to the crossing of Snake River, at the mouth of Powder River; thence to the Salmon River, fifty miles above the place known [as] the " crossing of the Salmon River;" thence due north to the summit of the Bitter Root Mountains; thence along the crest of the Bitter Root Mountains to the place of beginning.

Reservation.

ARTICLE 2. There is, however, reserved from the lands above ceded for the use and occupation of the said tribe, and as a general reservation for other friendly tribes and bands of Indians in Washington Territory, not to exceed the present numbers of the Spokane, Walla-Walla, Cayuse, and Umatilla tribes and bands of Indians, the tract of land included within the following boundaries, to wit: Commencing where *Boundaries.* the Moh ha-na-she or southern tributary of the Palouse River flows from the spurs of the Bitter Root Mountains; thence down said tributary to the mouth of the Ti-nat-pan-up Creek; thence southerly to the crossing of the Snake River ten miles below the mouth of the Al-po-wa-wi River; thence to the source of the Al-po-wa-wi River in the Blue Mountains; thence along the crest of the Blue Mountains; thence to the crossing of the Grand Ronde River, midway between the Grand Ronde and the mouth of the Woll-low-how River; thence along the divide between the waters of the Woll-low-how and Powder Rivers; thence to the crossing of the Snake River fifteen miles below the mouth of the Powder River; thence to the Salmon River above the crossing; thence by the spurs of the Bitter Root Mountains to the place of beginning.

All which tract shall be set apart, and, so far as necessary, surveyed *Reservation to be set apart, and Indians to settle thereon.* and marked out for the exclusive use and benefit of said tribe as an Indian reservation; nor shall any white man, excepting those in the *Whites not to reside thereon without, etc.* employment of the Indian Department, be permitted to reside upon the said reservation without permission of the tribe and the superintendent and agent; and the said tribe agrees to remove to and settle upon the same within one year after the ratification of this treaty. In the mean time it shall be lawful for them to reside upon any ground not in the actual claim and occupation of citizens of the United States, and upon any ground claimed or occupied, if with the permission of the owner or claimant, guarantying, however, the right to all citizens of the United States to enter upon and occupy as settlers any lands not actually occupied and cultivated by said Indians at this time, and not included in the reservation above named. And provided that any *Improvements to be paid for by the United States.* substantial improvement heretofore made by any Indian, such as fields enclosed and cultivated, and houses erected upon the lands hereby ceded, and which he may be compelled to abandon in consequence of this treaty, shall be valued under the direction of the President of the United States, and payment made therefor in money, or improvements of an equal value be made for said Indian upon the reservation, and no Indian will be required to abandon the improvements aforesaid, now occupied by him, until their value in money or improvements of equal value shall be furnished him as aforesaid.

ARTICLE 3. And provided that, if necessary for the public conven- *Roads may be made.* ience, roads may be run through the said reservation, and, on the other hand, the right of way, with free access from the same to the nearest public highway, is secured to them, as also the right, in common with citizens of the United States, to travel upon all public highways. The use of the Clear Water and other streams flowing through the reservation is also secured to citizens of the United States for rafting purposes, and as public highways.

The exclusive right of taking fish in all the streams where running *Privileges secured to Indians.* through or bordering said reservation is further secured to said Indians; as also the right of taking fish at all usual and accustomed places in common with citizens of the Territory; and of erecting temporary buildings for curing, together with the privilege of hunting, gathering roots and berries, and pasturing their horses and cattle upon open and unclaimed land.

ARTICLE 4. In consideration of the above cession, the United States *Payments by the United States.* agree to pay to the said tribe in addition to the goods and provisions distributed to them at the time of signing this treaty, the sum of two hundred thousand dollars, in the following manner, that is to say, sixty thousand dollars, to be expended under the direction of the President of the United States, the first year after the ratification of this treaty, in providing for their removal to the reserve, breaking up and fencing farms, building houses, supplying them with provisions and a suitable outfit, and for such other objects as he may deem necessary, and the remainder in annuities, as follows: for the first five years after the ratification of this treaty, ten thousand dollars each year, commencing September 1, 1856; for the next five years, eight thousand dollars each year; for the next five years, six thousand each year, and for the next five years, four thousand dollars each year.

Payments, how to be applied.

All which said sums of money shall be applied to the use and benefit of the said Indians, under the direction of the President of the United States, who may from time to time determine, at his discretion, upon what beneficial objects to expend the same for them. And the superintendent of Indian affairs, or other proper officer, shall each year inform the President of the wishes of the Indians in relation thereto.

The United States to establish schools, etc.

ARTICLE 5. The United States further agree to establish, at suitable points within said reservation, within one year after the ratification hereof, two schools, erecting the necessary buildings, keeping the same in repair, and providing them with furniture, books, and stationery, one of which shall be an agricultural and industrial school, to be located at the agency, and to be free to the children of said tribe, and to employ one superintendent of teaching and two teachers; to build two blacksmiths' shops, to one of which shall be attached a tin-shop and to the other a gunsmith's shop; one carpenter's shop, one wagon and plough maker's shop, and to keep the same in repair, and furnished with the necessary tools; to employ one superintendent of farming and two farmers, two blacksmiths, one tinner, one gunsmith, one carpenter, one wagon and plough maker, for the instruction of the Indians in trades, and to assist them in the same; to erect one saw-mill and one flouring-mill, keeping the same in repair, and furnished with the necessary tools and fixtures, and to employ two millers; to erect a hospital, keeping the same in repair, and provided with the necessary medicines and furniture, and to employ a physician; and to erect, keep in repair, and provide with the necessary furniture the buildings required for the accommodation of the said employees. The said buildings and establishments to be maintained and kept in repair as aforesaid, and the employees to be kept in service for the period of twenty years.

To build mechanics' shops, etc.

Sawmill.

Hospital.

Salary to head chief; house, etc.

And in view of the fact that the head chief of the tribe is expected, and will be called upon, to perform many services of a public character, occupying much of his time, the United States further agrees to pay to the Nez Percé tribe five hundred dollars per year for the term of twenty years, after the ratification hereof, as a salary for such person as the tribe may select to be its head chief. To build for him, at a suitable point on the reservation, a comfortable house, and properly furnish the same, and to plough and fence for his use ten acres of land. The said salary to be paid to, and the said house to be occupied by, such head chief so long as he may be elected to that position by his tribe, and no longer.

And all the expenditures and expenses contemplated in this fifth article of this treaty shall be defrayed by the United States, and shall not be deducted from the annuities agreed to be paid to said tribe; nor shall the cost of transporting the goods for the annuity-payments be a charge upon the annuities, but shall be defrayed by the United States.

Reservation may be surveyed into lots and assigned to individuals or families.

ARTICLE 6. The President may from time to time, at his discretion, cause the whole, or such portions of such reservation as he may think proper, to be surveyed into lots, and assign the same to such individuals or families of the said tribe as are willing to avail themselves of the privilege, and will locate on the same as a permanent home, on the same terms and subject to the same regulations as are provided in the sixth article of the treaty with the Omahas in the year 1854, so far as the same may be applicable.

ARTICLE 7. The annuities of the aforesaid tribe shall not be taken to pay the debts of individuals. *Annuities not to pay debts of individuals.*

ARTICLE 8. The aforesaid tribe acknowledge their dependence upon the Government of the United States, and promise to be friendly with all citizens thereof, and pledge themselves to commit no depredations on the property of such citizens; and should any one or more of them violate this pledge, and the fact be satisfactorily proved before the agent, the property taken shall be returned, or in default thereof, or if injured or destroyed, compensation may be made by the Government out of the annuities. Nor will they make war on any other tribe except in self-defence, but will submit all matters of difference between them and the other Indians to the Government of the United States, or its agent, for decision, and abide thereby; and if any of the said Indians commit any depredations on any other Indians within the Territory of Washington, the same rule shall prevail as that prescribed in this article in cases of depredations against citizens. And the said tribe agrees not to shelter or conceal offenders against the laws of the United States, but to deliver them up to the authorities for trial. *Tribes to preserve friendly relations.* *To pay for depredations.* *Not to make war except in self-defense.* *Offenders to be delivered up.*

ARTICLE 9. The Nez Percés desire to exclude from their reservation the use of ardent spirits, and to prevent their people from drinking the same; and therefore it is provided that any Indian belonging to said tribe who is guilty of bringing liquor into said reservation, or who drinks liquor, may have his or her proportion of the annuities withheld from him or her for such time as the President may determine. *Annuities may be withheld from those who drink ardent spirits.*

ARTICLE 10. The Nez Percé Indians having expressed in council a desire that William Craig should continue to live with them, he having uniformly shown himself their friend, it is further agreed that the tract of land now occupied by him, and described in his notice to the register and receiver of the land-office of the Territory of Washington, on the fourth day of June last, shall not be considered a part of the reservation provided for in this treaty, except that it shall be subject in common with the lands of the reservation to the operations of the intercourse act. *Land of William Craig.*

ARTICLE 11. This treaty shall be obligatory upon the contracting parties as soon as the same shall be ratified by the President and Senate of the United States. *When treaty to take effect.*

In testimony whereof, the said Isaac I. Stevens, governor and superintendent of Indian affairs for the Territory of Washington, and Joel Palmer, superintendent of Indian affairs for Oregon Territory, and the chiefs, headmen, and delegates of the aforesaid Nez Percé tribe of Indians, have hereunto set their hands and seals, at the place, and on the day and year hereinbefore written.

Isaac I. Stevens,   [L. S.]
Governor and Superintendent Washington Territory.
Joel Palmer,   [L. S.]
Superintendent Indian Affairs.

Aleiya, or Lawyer, Head-chief of the Nez Percés,	[L. S.]	Tippelanecbupooh, his x mark.	[L. S.]
Appushwa-hite, or Looking-glass, his x mark.	[L. S.]	Hah-hah-stilpilp, his x mark.	[L. S.]
		Cool-cool-shua-nin, his x mark.	[L. S.]
Joseph, his x mark.	[L. S.]	Silish, his x mark.	[L. S.]
James, his x mark.	[L. S.]	Toh-toh-molewit, his x mark.	[L. S.]
Red Wolf, his x mark.	[L. S.]	Tuky-in-lik-it, his x mark.	[L. S.]
Timothy, his x mark.	[L. S.]	Te-hole-hole-soot, his x mark.	[L. S.]
U-ute-sin-male-cun, his x mark.	[L. S.]	Ish-coh-tim, his x mark.	[L. S.]
Spotted Eagle, his x mark.	[L. S.]	Wee-as-cus, his x mark.	[L. S.]
Stoop-toop-nin or Cut-hair, his x mark.	[L. S.]	Hah-hah-stoore-tee, his x mark.	[L. S.]
		Eee-maht-sin-pooh, his x mark.	[L. S.]
		Tow-wish-au-il-pilp, his x mark.	[L. S.]
Tah-moh-moh-kin, his x mark.	[L. S.]	Kay-kay-mass, his x mark.	[L. S.]

Speaking Eagle, his x mark.	[L. S.]	Kole-kole-til-ky, his x mark.	[L. S.]
Wat-ti-wat-ti-wah-hi, his x mark.	[L. S.]	In-mat-tute-kah-ky, his x mark.	[L. S.]
Howh-no-tah-kun, his x mark.	[L. S.]	Moh-see-chee, his x mark.	[L. S.]
Tow-wish-wane, his x mark.	[L. S.]	George, his x mark.	[L. S.]
Wahpt-tah-shooshe, his x mark.	[L. S.]	Nicke-el-it-may-ho, his x mark.	[L. S.]
Bead Necklace, his x mark.	[L. S.]	Say-i-ee-ouse, his x mark.	[L. S.]
Koos-koos-tas-kut, his x mark.	[L. S.]	Wis-tasse-cut, his x mark.	[L. S.]
Levi, his x mark.	[L. S.]	Ky-ky-soo-te-lum, his x mark.	[L. S.]
Pee-oo-pe-whi-hi, his x mark.	[L. S.]	Ko-ko-whay-nee, his x mark.	[L. S.]
Pee-oo-pee-iecteim, his x mark.	[L. S.]	Kwin-to-kow, his x mark.	[L. S.]
Pee-poome-kah, his x mark.	[L. S.]	Pee-wee-au-ap-tah, his x mark.	[L. S.]
Hah-hah-stlil-at-me, his x mark.	[L. S.]	Wee-at-tenat-il-pilp, his x mark.	[L. S.]
Wee-yoke-sin-ate, his x mark.	[L. S.]	Pee-oo-pee-u-il-pilp, his x mark.	[L. S.]
Wee-ah-ki, his x mark.	[L. S.]	Wah-tass-tum-mannee, his x mark.	[L. S.]
Necalahtsin, his x mark.	[L. S.]	Tu-wee-si-ce, his x mark.	[L. S.]
Suck-on-tie, his x mark.	[L. S.]	Lu-ee-sin-kah-koose-sin, his x mark.	[L. S.]
Ip-nat-tam-moose, his x mark.	[L. S.]	Hah-tal-ee-kin, his x mark.	[L. S.]
Jason, his x mark.	[L. S.]		

Signed and sealed in presence of us—

James Doty, secretary of treaties, W. T.
Wm. C. McKay, secretary of treaties, O. T.
W. H. Tappan, sub-Indian agent,
William Craig, interpreter,
A. D. Pamburn, interpreter,

Wm. McBean,
Geo. C. Bomford,
C. Chirouse, O. M. T.
Mie. Cles. Pandosy,
Lawrence Kip,
W. H. Pearson.

TREATY WITH THE CHOCTAW AND CHICKASAW, 1855.

June 22, 1855.
11 Stats., 611.
Ratified Feb. 21, 1856.
Proclaimed Mar. 4, 1856.

Articles of agreement and convention between the United States and the Choctaw and Chickasaw tribes of Indians, made and concluded at the city of Washington, the twenty-second day of June, A. D. one thousand eight hundred and fifty-five, by George W. Manypenny, commissioner on the part of the United States, Peter P. Pitchlynn, Israel Folsom, Samuel Garland, and Dixon W. Lewis, commissioners on the part of the Choctaws; and Edmund Pickens and Sampson Folsom, commissioners on the part of the Chickasaws:

Preamble.

Whereas, the political connection heretofore existing between the Choctaw and the Chickasaw tribes of Indians, has given rise to unhappy and injurious dissensions and controversies among them, which render necessary a re-adjustment of their relations to each other and to the United States: and

Whereas the United States desire that the Choctaw Indians shall relinquish all claim to any territory west of the one hundredth degree of west longitude, and also to make provision for the permanent settlement within the Choctaw country, of the Wichita and certain other tribes or bands of Indians, for which purpose the Choctaws and Chickasaws are willing to lease, on reasonable terms, to the United States, that portion of their common territory which is west of the ninety-eighth degree of west longitude: and

Ante, p. 310.

Whereas, the Choctaws contend, that, by a just and fair construction of the treaty of September 27, 1830, they are, of right, entitled to the net proceeds of the lands ceded by them to the United States, under said treaty, and have proposed that the question of their right to the same, together with the whole subject-matter of their unsettled claims, whether national or individual, against the United States, arising under the various provisions of said treaty, shall be referred to the Senate of the United States for final adjudicatiion and adjustment, and whereas, it is necessary for the simplification and better understanding of the relations between the United States and the Choctaw Indians, that all their subsisting treaty stipulations be embodied in one comprehensive instrument:

Now, therefore, the United States of America, by their commissioner, George W. Manypenny, the Choctaws, by their commissioners, Peter P. Pitchlynn, Israel Folsom, Samuel Garland, and Dickson W. Lewis, and the Chickasaws, by their commissioners, Edmund Pickens and Sampson Folsom do hereby agree and stipulate as follows, viz:

ARTICLE 1. The following shall constitute and remain the boundaries of the Choctaw and Chickasaw country, viz: Beginning at a point on the Arkansas River, one hundred paces east of old Fort Smith, where the western boundary-line of the State of Arkansas crosses the said river, and running thence due south to Red River; thence up Red River to the point where the meridian of one hundred degrees west longitude crosses the same; thence north along said meridian to the main Canadian River; thence down said river to its junction with the Arkansas River; thence down said river to the place of beginning. *[Future boundaries of the Choctaw and Chickasaw country.]*

And pursuant to an act of Congress approved May 28, 1830, the United States do hereby forever secure and guarantee the lands embraced within the said limits, to the members of the Choctaw and Chickasaw tribes, their heirs and successors, to be held in common; so that each and every member of either tribe shall have an equal, undivided interest in the whole: *Provided, however,* No part thereof shall ever be sold without the consent of both tribes, and that said land shall revert to the United States if said Indians and their heirs become extinct or abandon the same. *[The lands in those limits guaranteed to them. 1830, ch. 148. 4 Stat., 411. Proviso as to sales, and as to the reversion of said lands.]*

ARTICLE 2. A district for the Chickasaws is hereby established, bounded as follows, to wit: Beginning on the north bank of Red River, at the mouth of Island Bayou, where it empties into Red River, about twenty-six miles in a straight line, below the mouth of False Wachitta; thence running a northwesterly course, along the main channel of said bayou, to the junction of the three prongs of said bayou, nearest the dividing ridge between Wachitta and Low Blue Rivers, as laid down on Capt. R. L. Hunter's map; thence northerly along the eastern prong of Island Bayou to its source; thence due north to the Canadian River; thence west along the main Canadian to the ninety-eighth degree of west longitude; thence south to Red River; and thence down Red River to the beginning: *Provided, however,* If the line running due north, from the eastern source of Island Bayou, to the main Canadian shall not include Allen's or Wa-pa-nacka Academy, within the Chickasaw District, then, an offset shall be made from said line, so as to leave said academy two miles within the Chickasaw district, north, west and south from the lines of boundary. *[District established for the Chickasaw.]*

ARTICLE 3. The remainder of the country held in common by the Choctaws and Chickasaws, shall constitute the Choctaw district, and their officers and people shall at all times have the right of safe conduct and free passage through the Chickasaw district. *[Choctaw district.]*

ARTICLE 4. The government and laws now in operation and not incompatible with this instrument, shall be and remain in full force and effect within the limits of the Chickasaw district, until the Chickasaws shall adopt a constitution, and enact laws, superseding, abrogating, or changing the same. And all judicial proceedings within said district, commenced prior to the adoption of a constitution and laws by the Chickasaws, shall be conducted and determined according to existing laws. *[Present laws and government to remain in force until altered.]*

ARTICLE 5. The members of either the Choctaw or the Chickasaw tribe, shall have the right, freely, to settle within the jurisdiction of the other, and shall thereupon be entitled to all the rights, privileges, and immunities of citizens thereof; but no member of either tribe *[Either tribe may settle within the limits of the other, and sue in courts.]*

shall be entitled to participate in the funds belonging to the other tribe. Citizens of both tribes shall have the right to institute and prosecute suits in the courts of either, under such regulations as may, from time to time, be prescribed by their respective legislatures.

Extradition of criminals between said districts.

ARTICLE 6. Any person duly charged with a criminal offence against the laws of either the Choctaw or the Chickasaw tribe, and escaping into the jurisdiction of the other, shall be promptly surrendered, upon the demand of the proper authorities of the tribe, within whose jurisdiction the offence shall be alleged to have been committed.

So far as lawful the said tribes to have self-government.

ARTICLE 7. So far as may be compatible with the Constitution of the United States and the laws made in pursuance thereof, regulating trade and intercourse with the Indian tribes, the Choctaws and Chickasaws shall be secured in the unrestricted right of self-government, and full jurisdiction, over persons and property, within their respective limits; excepting, however, all persons, with their property, who are not by birth, adoption, or otherwise citizens or members of either the Choctaw

Intruders to be removed.

or Chickasaw tribe, and all persons, not being citizens or members of either tribe, found within their limits, shall be considered intruders, and be removed from, and kept out of the same, by the United States agent, assisted if necessary by the military, with the following exceptions, viz: Such individuals as are now, or may be in the employment of the Government, and their families; those peacefully travelling, or temporarily sojourning in the country or trading therein, under license from the proper authority of the United States, and such as may be permitted by the Choctaws or Chickasaws, with the assent of the United States agent, to reside within their limits, without becoming citizens or members of either of said tribes.

Payment to Choctaws out of the Chickasaw funds.

ARTICLE 8. In consideration of the foregoing stipulations, and immediately upon the ratification of this convention, there shall be paid to the Choctaws, in such manner as their national council shall direct, out of the national fund of the Chickasaws held in trust by the United States, the sum of one hundred and fifty thousand dollars.

Cession of land by the Choctaws.

ARTICLE 9. The Choctaw Indians do hereby absolutely and forever quit-claim and relinquish to the United States all their right, title, and interest in, and to any and all lands, west of the one hundredth degree of

Lease by the Choctaws and Chickasaws for the use of other Indians.

west longitude; and the Choctaws and Chickasaws do hereby lease to the United States all that portion of their common territory west of the ninety-eighth degree of west longitude, for the permanent settlement of the Wichita and such other tribes or bands of Indians as the Government may desire to locate therein; excluding, however, all the Indians of New Mexico, and also those whose usual ranges at present are north of the Arkansas River, and whose permanent locations are north of the Canadian River, but including those bands whose permanent ranges are south of the Canadian, or between it and the Arkansas; which Indians shall be subject to the exclusive control of the United States, under such rules and regulations, not inconsistent with the rights and interests of the Choctaws and Chickasaws, as may from time to time be prescribed by the President for their government: *Provided, however*, The territory so leased shall remain open to settlement by Choctaws and Chickasaws as heretofore.

Payment to each of said tribes.

ARTICLE 10. In consideration of the foregoing relinquishment and lease, and as soon as practicable after the ratification of this convention, the United States will pay to the Choctaws the sum of six hundred thousand dollars, and to the Chickasaws the sum of two hundred thousand dollars, in such manner as their general councils shall respectively direct.

Certain questions to be submitted to the Senate for decision.

ARTICLE 11. The Government of the United States, not being prepared to assent to the claim set up under the treaty of September the twenty-seventh, eighteen hundred and thirty and so earnestly contended for by the Choctaws as a rule of settlement, but justly appreciating the sacrifices, faithful services, and general good conduct of the Choctaw people, and being desirous that their rights and claims against the United States shall receive a just, fair, and liberal consideration, it is therefore stipulated that the following questions be submitted for adjudication to the Senate of the United States.

First. Whether the Choctaws are entitled to, or shall be allowed, the proceeds of the sale of the lands ceded by them to the United States, by the treaty of September the twenty-seventh, eighteen hundred and thirty, deducting therefrom the cost of their survey and sale, and all just and proper expenditures and payments under the provisions of said treaty; and if so, what price per acre shall be allowed to the Choctaws for the lands remaining unsold, in order that a final settlement with them may be promptly effected.   Or,

Second. Whether the Choctaws shall be allowed a gross sum in further and full satisfaction of all their claims national and individual against the United States; and, if so, how much.

ARTICLE 12. In case the Senate shall award to the Choctaws the net proceeds of the lands, ceded as aforesaid, the same shall be received by them in full satisfaction of all their claims against the United States, whether national or individual, arising under any former treaty; and the Choctaws shall thereupon become liable and bound to pay all such individual claims as may be adjudged by the proper authorities of the tribe to be equitable and just—the settlement and payment to be made with the advice and under the direction of the United States agent for the tribe; and so much of the fund, awarded by the Senate to the Choctaws, as the proper authorities thereof shall ascertain and determine to be necessary for the payment of the just liabilities of the tribe, shall on their requisition be paid over to them by the United States. But should the Senate allow a gross sum, in further and full satisfaction of all their claims, whether national or individual, against the United States, the same shall be accepted by the Choctaws, and they shall thereupon become liable for, and bound to pay, all the individual claims as aforesaid; it being expressly understood that the adjudication and decision of the Senate shall be final.

If sums are awarded, how to be paid.

ARTICLE 13. The amounts secured by existing treaty stipulations—viz: permanent annuity of three thousand dollars, under the second article of the treaty of eighteen hundred and five; six hundred dollars per annum for the support of light-horse men under the thirteenth article of the treaty of eighteen hundred and twenty; permanent annuity of six thousand dollars for education; under the second article of the treaty of eighteen hundred and twenty-five; six hundred dollars per annum permanent provision for the support of a blacksmith, under the sixth article of the treaty of eighteen hundred and twenty; and three hundred and twenty dollars permanent provision for iron and steel, under the ninth article of the treaty of eighteen hundred and twenty-five—shall continue to be paid to, or expended for the benefit of, the Choctaws as heretofore; or the same may be applied to such objects of general utility as may, from time to time, be designated by the general council of the tribe, with the approbation of the Government of the United States.   And the funds now held in trust by the United States for the benefit of the Choctaws under former treaties, or otherwise, shall continue to be so held; together with the sum of five hundred thousand dollars out of the amount payable to them under articles eighth and tenth of this agreement, and also whatever balance shall remain, if any, of the amount that shall be allowed the Choctaws, by the Senate, under the twelfth article hereof, after satisfying the just liabilities of the tribe.   The sums so to be held in trust shall constitute a general Choctaw fund, yielding an annual interest of not less

Sum due under present treaties to be still paid.

Funds held in trust.

than five per centum; no part of which shall be paid out as annuity, but shall be regularly and judiciously applied, under the direction of the general council of the Choctaws, to the support of their government for purposes of education, and such other objects as may be best calculated to promote and advance the improvement, welfare, and happiness of the Choctaw people and their descendants.

Protection of said Indians. ARTICLE 14. The United States shall protect the Choctaws and Chickasaws from domestic strife, from hostile invasion, and from aggression by other Indians and white persons not subject to their jurisdiction and laws; and for all injuries resulting from such invasion or aggression, full indemnity is hereby guaranteed to the party or parties injured, out of the Treasury of the United States, upon the same principle and according to the same rules upon which white persons are entitled to indemnity for injuries or aggressions upon them, committed by Indians.

Extradition of criminals to United States or particular States. ARTICLE 15. The Choctaws and Chickasaws shall promptly apprehend and deliver up all persons accused of any crime or offence against the laws of the United States, or of any State thereof, who may be found within their limits, on demand of any proper officer of a State, or of the United States.

Payments by licensed traders. ARTICLE 16. All persons licensed by the United States to trade with the Choctaws or Chickasaws shall be required to pay to the respective tribes a moderate annual compensation for the land and timber used by them; the amount of such compensation, in each case, to be assessed by the proper authorities of said tribe, subject to the approval of the United States agent.

Military posts, post-roads, and agencies may be established. ARTICLE 17. The United States shall have the right to establish and maintain such military posts, post-roads, and Indian agencies, as may be deemed necessary within the Choctaw and Chickasaw country, but no greater quantity of land or timber shall be used for said purposes, than shall be actually requisite; and if, in the establishment or maintenance of such posts, post-roads, and agencies, the property of any Choctaw or Chickasaw shall be taken, injured, or destroyed, just and adequate compensation shall be made by the United States. Only such persons as are, or may be in the employment of the United States, or subject to the jurisdiction and laws of the Choctaws, or Chickasaws, shall be permitted to farm or raise stock within the limits of any of said military posts or Indian agencies. And no offender against the laws of either of said tribes, shall be permitted to take refuge therein.

Right of way for railroads and telegraphs. ARTICLE 18. The United States, or any incorporated company, shall have the right of way for railroads, or lines of telegraphs, through the Choctaw and Chickasaw country; but for any property taken or destroyed in the construction thereof, full compensation shall be made to the party or parties injured, to be ascertained and determined in such manner as the president of the United States shall direct.

Boundary to be run and marked. ARTICLE 19. The United States shall, as soon as practicable, cause the eastern and western boundary lines of the tract of country described in the 1st article of this convention, and the western boundary of the Chickasaw district, as herein defined, to be run and permanently marked.

General amnesty between said tribes. ARTICLE 20. That this convention may conduce as far as possible to the restoration and preservation of kind and friendly feeling among the Choctaws and Chickasaws, a general amnesty of all past offences, committed within their country, is hereby declared.

Only one agent to be appointed. And in order that their relations to each other and to the United States may hereafter be conducted in a harmonious and satisfactory manner, there shall be but one agent for the two tribes.

ARTICLE 21. This convention shall supersede and take the place of all former treaties between the United States and the Choctaws, and also, of all treaty stipulations between the United States and the Chickasaws, and between the Choctaws and Chickasaws, inconsistent with this agreement, and shall take effect and be obligatory upon the contracting parties, from the date hereof, whenever the same shall be ratified by the respective councils of the Choctaw and Chickasaw tribes, and by the President and Senate of the United States.

This treaty to supersede all former treaties with the Choctaw, and all inconsistent treaties with Chickasaw, or between said tribes.

When to take effect.

ARTICLE 22. It is understood and agreed that the expenses of the respective commissioners of the two tribes, signing these articles of agreement and convention, in coming to, and returning from this city, and while here, shall be paid by the United States.

United States to pay the commissioners.

In testimony whereof, the said George W. Manypenny, commissioner on the part of the United States, and the said commissioners on the part of the Choctaws and of the Chickasaws, have hereunto set their hands and seals.

Done in triplicate at the city of Washington, on this twenty-second day of June, in the year of our Lord one thousand eight hundred and fifty-five.

<blockquote>
George W. Manypenny, United States Commissioner.   [L. S.]
P. P. Pitchlynn,   [L. S.]
Israel Folsom,   [L. S.]
Sam'l Garland,   [L. S.]
Dickson W. Lewis,   [L. S.]
    Choctaw Commissioners.
Edmund Pickens, his x mark,   [L. S.]
Sampson Folsom,   [L. S.]
    Chickasaw Commissioners.
</blockquote>

Executed in presence of—

A. O. P. NICHOLSON,
JAMES G. BERRET,
DOUGLAS H. COOPER, United States Indian agent.

And whereas the said treaty having been submitted to the general council of the Chickasaw tribe, the general council did, on the third day of October, A. D. one thousand eight hundred and fifty-five, assent to, ratify, and confirm the same, with the following amendment: "Add to the 19th article, By commissioners to be appointed by the contracting parties hereto" by an instrument in writing, in the words and figures following, to wit:—

Whereas articles of agreement and convention were made and concluded on the twenty-second day of June, A. D. one thousand eight hundred and fifty-five, by and between George W. Manypenny, commissioner on the part of the United States; Peter P. Pitchlynn, Israel Folsom, Samuel Garland, and Dickson W. Lewis, commissioners on the part of the Choctaws; and Edmund Pickens, and Sampson Folsom, commissioners on the part of the Chickasaws, at the city of Washington, in the District of Columbia, the preamble whereof is in the words and figures following, "to wit:" Whereas, the political connection heretofore existing between the Choctaw and Chickasaw tribes of Indians, has given rise to unhappy and injurious dissensions and controversies among them, which render necessary a readjustment of their relations to each other and to the United States; and whereas, the United States desire that the Choctaw Indians shall relinquish all claim to any territory west of the one hundredth degree of west longitude, and also to make provision for the permanent settlement within the Choctaw country of the Wichita and certain other tribes or bands of Indians, for which purpose the Choctaws and Chickasaws are willing

Assent of Chickasaws.

to lease, on reasonable terms, to the United States, that portion of their common territory which is west of the ninety-eighth degree of west longitude; and whereas the Choctaws contend that, by a just and fair construction of the treaty of September 27, 1830, they are of right entitled to the net proceeds of the lands ceded by them to the United States, under said treaty, and have proposed that the question of their right to the same, together with the whole subject-matter of their unsettled claims, whether national or individual, against the United States, arising under the various provisions of said treaty, shall be referred to the Senate of the United States for final adjudication and adjustment; and whereas it is necessary, for the simplification and better understanding of the relations between the United States and the Choctaw Indians, that all their subsisting treaty stipulations be embodied in one comprehensive instrument; and whereas, in the twenty-first article thereof, it is, among other things, recited that said agreement "shall take effect and be obligatory upon the contracting parties from the date hereof, whenever the same shall be ratified by the respective councils of the Choctaw and Chickasaw tribes of Indians and by the President and Senate of the United States."

Now, therefore, be it known, that the Chickasaws, in general council assembled, having duly considered said articles of agreement and convention, and each and every clause thereof, and being satisfied therewith, do, upon their part, hereby assent to, ratify, and confirm the same, as stipulated and required, with the following amendment: "Add to the nineteenth article, "By commissioners to be appointed by the contracting parties hereto."

Done and approved at Tishomingo, in the Chickasaw district of the Choctaw nation, this third day of October, in the year of our Lord, one thousand eight hundred and fifty-five.

Joel Kemp, President.
D. Colbert, F. C.

Passed the council.
Attest—
Cyrus Harris, clerk of the council.

And whereas the Chickasaws, in general council assembled, did, on the 13th day of December, A. D. 1855, recede from and rescind the said amendment, and did ratify and confirm the said treaty, and every part thereof, by an instrument in writing, in the words and figures following, to wit:—

Whereas the Chickasaws, in general council assembled, after having duly considered the stipulations contained in a certain convention and agreement, made and entered into at the city of Washington, on the 22d day of June, A. D. 1855, between George W. Manypenny, commissioner on the part of the United States; Peter P. Pitchlynn, Israel Folsom, Samuel Garland, and Dickson W. Lewis, commissioners on the part of the Choctaws; Edmund Pickens and Sampson Folsom, commissioners on the part of the Chickasaws, did, on the third day of October, A. D. 1855, at Tisho-mingo, in the Chickasaw district, Choctaw nation, assent to, ratify, and confirm each and every part of said convention and agreement, with the following amendment, viz: "Add to the 19th article, 'By commissioners to be appointed by the contracting parties hereto.'" And whereas, said amendment was not duly considered and concurred in by the Choctaws in general council assembled; but said agreement and convention, and every part thereof, was assented to, ratified, and confirmed by said council without amendment. Now, therefore, be it known, that the Chickasaws, in general council assembled, having reconsidered said proposed amendment, do hereby recede from, and rescind the same, hereby assenting to, rati-

Amendment.

Amendment of Chickasaws rescinded by them.

fying, and confirming said agreement and convention, and every part thereof.

Done and approved at the council-house at Tisho-mingo, Chickasaw district, Choctaw nation, this 13th day of December, A. D. 1855.

Approved December 13, 1855.

> J. McCoy, President of the Council.
> Dougherty Colbert, F. C.

Attest—

Cyrus Harris, Secretary.

Signed in presence of—

Jackson Frazier, Chief Chickasaw district, Choctaw nation.
Douglas H. Cooper, United States Indian agent.

And whereas the said treaty having been submitted to the general council of the Choctaw tribe, the said general council did, on the 16th day of November, A. D. one thousand eight hundred and fifty-five, consent to and ratify the same by an instrument in the words and figures following, to wit:

Whereas articles of agreement and convention were made and concluded on the twenty-second day of June, A. D. one thousand eight hundred and fifty-five, by and between George W. Manypenny, commissioner on the part of the United States; Peter P. Pitchlynn, Israel Folsom, Samuel Garland, and Dickson W. Lewis, commissioners on the part of the Choctaws; and Edmund Pickens and Sampson Folsom, commissioners on the part of the Chickasaws, at the city of Washington, in the District of Columbia, the preamble whereof is in the words and figures following, viz: "Whereas the political connection heretofore existing between the Choctaw and the Chickasaw tribes of Indians, has given rise to unhappy and injurious dissensions and controversies among them, which render necessary a readjustment of their relations to each other and to the United States; and whereas the United States desire that the Choctaw Indians shall relinquish all claim to any territory west of the one hundredth degree of west longitude, and also to make provision for the permament settlement within the Choctaw country, of the Wichita and certain other tribes or bands of Indians, for which purpose the Choctaws and Chickasaws are willing to lease, on reasonable terms, to the United States, that portion of their common territory which is west of the ninety-eighth degree of west longitude; and whereas, the Choctaws contend that, by a just and fair construction of the treaty of September 27, 1830, they are, of right, entitled to the net proceeds of the lands ceded by them to the United States, under said treaty, and have proposed that the question of their right to the same, together with the whole subject-matter of their unsettled claims, whether national or individual, against the United States arising under the various provisions of said treaty, shall be referred to the Senate of the United States, for final adjudication and adjustment; and whereas it is necessary, for the simplification and better understanding of the relations between the United States and the Choctaw Indians, that all their subsisting treaty stipulations be embodied in one comprehensive instrument;" and whereas, in the twenty-first article thereof, it is, among other things, recited that said agreement "shall take effect and be obligatory upon the contracting [parties] from the date hereof, whenever the same shall be ratified by the respective councils of the Choctaw and Chickasaw tribes and by the President and Senate of the United States."

Now, therefore, be it known, that the Choctaws, in general council assembled, having duly considered said articles of agreement and convention, and each and every clause thereof, and being satisfied therewith, do, upon their part, hereby assent to, ratify, and confirm the same as stipulated and required.

Assent of Choctaws.

Done and approved at the council-house, at Fort Towson, in the Choctaw nation, this sixteenth day of November, in the year of our Lord one thousand eight hundred and fifty-five.

Tandy Walker,
President of the Senate.
Kennedy M. Curtain,
Speaker of the House of Representatives.

Approved:

Geo. W. Harkins,
Chief of Ahpuck District.
N. Cochnaner,
Chief of Pushematahn District.
Adam Christy,
Speaker, and Acting Chief of Moosholatubbee District.

Signed in presence of—
Douglas H. Cooper, U. S. Indian Agent for Choctaw Tribe.

TREATY WITH THE TRIBES OF MIDDLE OREGON, 1855.

June 25, 1855.

12 Stats., 963.
Ratified Mar. 8, 1859.
Proclaimed Apr. 18, 1859.

Articles of agreement and convention made and concluded at Wasco, near the Dalles of the Columbia River, in Oregon Territory, by Joel Palmer, superintendent of Indian affairs, on the part of the United States, and the following-named chiefs and head-men of the confederated tribes and bands of Indians, residing in Middle Oregon, they being duly authorized thereto by their respective bands, to wit: Symtustus, Locks-quis-sa, Shick-a-me, and Kuck-up, chiefs of the Taih or Upper De Chutes band of Walla-Wallas; Stocket-ly and Iso, chiefs of the Wyam or Lower De Chutes band of Walla-Wallas; Alexis and Talkish, chiefs of the Tenino band of Walla-Wallas; Yise, chief of the Dock-Spus or John Day's River band of Walla-Wallas; Mark, William Chenook, and Cush-Kella, chiefs of the Dalles band of the Wascoes; Toh-simph, chief of the Ki-gal-twal-la band of Wascoes; and Wal-la-chin, chief of the Dog River band of Wascoes.

Cession of lands to the United States.

ARTICLE 1. The above-named confederated bands of Indians cede to the United States all their right, title, and claim to all and every part of the country claimed by them, included in the following boundaries, to wit:

Boundaries.

Commencing in the middle of the Columbia River, at the Cascade Falls, and running thence southerly to the summit of the Cascade Mountains; thence along said summit to the forty-fourth parallel of north latitude; thence east on that parallel to the summit of the Blue Mountains, or the western boundary of the Sho-sho-ne or Snake country; thence northerly along that summit to a point due east from the head-waters of Willow Creek; thence west to the head-waters of said creek; thence down said stream to its junction with the Columbia River; and thence down the channel of the Columbia River to the place of beginning. *Provided, however,* that so much of the country described above as is contained in the following boundaries, shall, until otherwise directed by the President of the United States, be set apart as a residence for said Indians, which tract for the purposes contemplated shall be held and regarded as an Indian reservation, to wit:

Reservation.

Boundaries.

Commencing in the middle of the channel of the De Chutes River opposite the eastern termination of a range of high lands usually known as the Mutton Mountains; thence westerly to the summit of said range, along the divide to its connection with the Cascade Mountains;

thence to the summit of said mountains; thence southerly to Mount Jefferson; thence down the main branch of De Chutes River; heading in this peak, to its junction with De Chutes River; and thence down the middle of the channel of said river to the place of beginning. All of which tract shall be set apart, and, so far as necessary, surveyed and marked out for their exclusive use; nor shall any white person be permitted to reside upon the same without the concurrent permission of the agent and superintendent.

Whites not to reside thereon unless, etc.

The said bands and tribes agree to remove to and settle upon the same within one year after the ratification of this treaty, without any additional expense to the United States other than is provided for by this treaty; and, until the expiration of the time specified, the said bands shall be permitted to occupy and reside upon the tracts now possessed by them, guaranteeing to all white citizens the right to enter upon and occupy as settlers any lands not included in said reservation, and not actually inclosed by said Indians. *Provided, however,* That prior to the removal of said Indians to said reservation, and before any improvements contemplated by this treaty shall have been commenced, that if the three principal bands, to wit: the Wascopum, Tiah, or Upper De Chutes, and the Lower De Chutes bands of Walla-Wallas shall express in council, a desire that some other reservation may be selected for them, that the three bands named may select each three persons of their respective bands, who with the superintendent of Indian affairs or agent, as may by him be directed, shall proceed to examine, and if another location can be selected, better suited to the condition and wants of said Indians, that is unoccupied by the whites, and upon which the board of commissioners thus selected may agree, the same shall be declared a reservation for said Indians, instead of the tract named in this treaty. *Provided, also,* That the exclusive right of taking fish in the streams running through and bordering said reservation is hereby secured to said Indians; and at all other usual and accustomed stations, in common with citizens of the United States, and of erecting suitable houses for curing the same; also the privilege of hunting, gathering roots and berries, and pasturing their stock on unclaimed lands, in common with citizens, is secured to them. *And provided, also,* That if any band or bands of Indians, residing in and claiming any portion or portions of the country in this article, shall not accede to the terms of this treaty, then the bands becoming parties hereunto agree to receive such part of the several and other payments herein named as a consideration for the entire country described as aforesaid as shall be in the proportion that their aggregate number may have to the whole number of Indians residing in and claiming the entire country aforesaid, as consideration and payment in full for the tracts in said country claimed by them. *And provided, also,* That where substantial improvements have been made by any members of the bands being parties to this treaty, who are compelled to abandon them in consequence of said treaty, the same shall be valued, under the direction of the President of the United States, and payment made therefor; or, in lieu of said payment, improvements of equal extent and value at their option shall be made for them on the tracts assigned to each respectively.

Bands to settle thereon within a year.
Another reservation to be selected in lieu of this, if, etc.
Rights and privileges secured to Indians.
See Art. 1, treaty of Nov. 1, 1865.
Proviso in case any band does not accede to this treaty.
Allowance for improvements if, etc.

ARTICLE 2. In consideration of, and payment for, the country hereby ceded, the United States agree to pay the bands and tribes of Indians claiming territory and residing in said country, the several sums of money following, to wit:

Payments by the United States.

Eight thousand dollars per annum for the first five years, commencing on the first day of September, 1856, or as soon thereafter as practicable.

Six thousand dollars per annum for the term of five years next succeeding the first five.

Four thousand dollars per annum for the term of five years next succeeding the second five; and

Two thousand dollars per annum for the term of five years next succeeding the third five.

How to be expended. All of which several sums of money shall be expended for the use and benefit of the confederated bands, under the direction of the President of the United States, who may from time to time, at his discretion determine what proportion thereof shall be expended for such objects as in his judgment will promote their well-being and advance them in civilization; for their moral improvement and education; for building, opening and fencing farms, breaking land, providing teams, stock, agricultural implements, seeds, &c.; for clothing, provisions, and tools; for medical purposes, providing mechanics and farmers, and for arms and ammunition.

$50,000 additional to be expended for buildings, etc. ARTICLE 3. The United States agree to pay said Indians the additional sum of fifty thousand dollars, a portion whereof shall be applied to the payment for such articles as may be advanced them at the time of signing this treaty, and in providing, after the ratification thereof and prior to their removal, such articles as may be deemed by the President essential to their want; for the erection of buildings on the reservation, fencing and opening farms; for the purchase of teams, farming implements, clothing and provisions, tools, seeds, and for the payment of employees; and for subsisting the Indians the first year after their removal.

United States to erect sawmills, school-house, etc. ARTICLE 4. In addition to the considerations specified the United States agree to erect, at suitable points on the reservation, one sawmill and one flouring-mill; suitable hospital buildings; one school-house; one blacksmith-shop with a tin and a gunsmith-shop thereto attached; one wagon and ploughmaker shop; and for one sawyer, one miller, one superintendent of farming operations, a farmer, a physician, a school-teacher, a blacksmith, and a wagon and ploughmaker, a dwelling house and the requisite outbuildings for each; and to purchase and keep in repair for the time specified for furnishing employees all necessary mill-fixtures, mechanics' tools, medicines and hospital stores, books and stationery for schools, and furniture for employees.

To furnish farmer, mechanics, physician, etc. The United States further engage to secure and pay for the services and subsistence, for the term of fifteen years, of one farmer, one blacksmith, and one wagon and plough maker; and for the term of twenty years, of one physician, one sawyer, one miller, one superintendent of farming operations, and one school teacher.

To erect dwelling houses, etc., for head chiefs. The United States also engage to erect four dwelling-houses, one for the head chief of the confederated bands, and one each for the Upper and Lower De Chutes bands of Walla-Wallas, and for the Wascopum band of Wascoes, and to fence and plough for each of the said chiefs ten acres of land; also to pay the head chief of the confederated bands a salary of five hundred dollars per annum for twenty years, commencing six months after the three principal bands named in this treaty shall have removed to the reservation, or as soon thereafter as a *Successor of head chief to take them.* head chief should be elected: *And provided, also,* That at any time when by the death, resignation, or removal of the chief selected, there shall be a vacancy and a successor appointed or selected, the salary, the dwelling, and improvements shall be possessed by said successor, so long as he shall occupy the position as head chief; so also with reference to the dwellings and improvements provided for by this treaty for the head chiefs of the three principal bands named.

Lands may be allotted to individual Indians for permanent homes. ARTICLE 5. The President may, from time to time, at his discretion, cause the whole, or such portion as he may think proper, of the tract that may now or hereafter be set apart as a permanent home for these Indians, to be surveyed into lots and assigned to such Indians of the confederated bands as may wish to enjoy the privilege, and locate thereon permanently. To a single person over twenty-one years of age, forty acres; to a family of two persons, sixty acres; to a family of three and not exceeding five, eighty acres; to a family of six persons, and not exceeding ten, one hundred and twenty acres; and to each family over ten in number, twenty acres for each additional three members. And the President may provide such rules and regulations as will secure to the family in case of the death of the head thereof the possession and enjoyment of such permanent home and the improvement thereon; and he may, at any time, at his discretion, after such person or family has made location on the land assigned as a permanent home, issue a patent to such person or family for such assigned land, conditioned that the tract shall not be aliened or leased for a longer term than two years and shall be exempt from levy, sale, or forfeiture, which condition shall continue in force until a State constitution embracing such lands within its limits shall have been formed, and the legislature of the State shall remove the restrictions. *Provided, however*, That no State legislature shall remove the restrictions herein provided for without the consent of Congress. *And provided, also*, That if any person or family shall at any time neglect or refuse to occupy or till a portion of the land assigned and on which they have located, or shall roam from place to place indicating a desire to abandon his home, the President may, if the patent shall have been issued, revoke the same, and if not issued, cancel the assignment, and may also withhold from such person, or family, their portion of the annuities, or other money due them, until they shall have returned to such permanent home and resumed the pursuits of industry, and in default of their return the tract may be declared abandoned, and thereafter assigned to some other person or family of Indians residing on said reservation. *(Patents to issue therefor; conditions thereof. Restrictions not to be removed without, etc. Patent may be cancelled.)*

ARTICLE 6. The annuities of the Indians shall not be taken to pay the debts of individuals. *(Annuities of Indians not to pay debt of individuals.)*

ARTICLE 7. The confederated bands acknowledge their dependence on the Government of the United States, and promise to be friendly with all the citizens thereof, and pledge themselves to commit no depredation on the property of said citizens; and should any one or more of the Indians violate this pledge, and the fact be satisfactorily proven before the agent, the property taken shall be returned, or in default thereof, or if injured or destroyed, compensation may be made by the Government out of their annuities; nor will they make war on any other tribe of Indians except in self-defence, but submit all matters of difference between them and other Indians to the Government of the United States, or its agents for decision, and abide thereby; and if any of the said Indians commit any depredations on other Indians, the same rule shall prevail as that prescribed in the case of depredations against citizens; said Indians further engage to submit to and observe all laws, rules, and regulations which may be prescribed by the United States for the government of said Indians. *(Bands to preserve friendly relations. To pay for depredations. Not to make war, except, etc.)*

ARTICLE 8. In order to prevent the evils of intemperance among said Indians, it is hereby provided, that if any one of them shall drink liquor to excess, or procure it for others to drink, his or her proportion of the annuities may be withheld from him or her for such time as the President may determine. *(Annuities to be withheld from those drinking liquor to excess.)*

ARTICLE 9. The said confederated bands agree that whensoever, in the opinion of the President of the United States, the public interest may require it, that all roads, highways, and railroads shall have the right of way through the reservation herein designated, or which may at any time hereafter be set apart as a reservation for said Indians. *(Roads, etc., may be made through reservation.)*

This treaty shall be obligatory on the contracting parties as soon as the same shall be ratified by the President and Senate of the United States. *(When treaty to take effect.)*

In testimony whereof, the said Joel Palmer, on the part of the United States, and the undersigned, chiefs, headmen, and delegates of the said confederated bands, have hereunto set their hands and seals, this twenty-fifth day of June, eighteen hundred fifty-five.

Joel Palmer, Superintendent of Indian Affairs, O. T. [L. S.]

Wasco:
Mark, his x mark. [L. S.]
William Chenook, his x mark. [L. S.]
Cush Kella, his x mark. [L. S.]
Lower De Chutes:
Stock-etley, his x mark. [L. S.]
Iso, his x mark. [L. S.]
Upper De Chutes:
Simtustus, his x mark. [L. S.]
Locksquissa, his x mark. [L. S.]
Shick-ame, his x mark. [L. S.]
Kuck-up, his x mark. [L. S.]
Tenino:
Alexsee, his x mark. [L. S.]
Talekish, his x mark. [L. S.]
Dog River Wasco:
Walachin, his x mark. [L. S.]
Tah Symph, his x mark. [L. S.]
Ash-na-chat, his x mark. [L. S.]
Che-wot-nleth, his x mark. [L. S.]
Te-cho, his x mark. [L. S.]
Sha-qually, his x mark. [L. S.]
Louis, his x mark. [L. S.]
Yise, his x mark. [L. S.]
Stamite, his x mark. [L. S.]
Ta-cho, his x mark. [L. S.]
Penop-teyot, his x mark. [L. S.]
Elosh-kish-kie, his x mark. [L. S.]
Am. Zelic, his x mark. [L. S.]
Ke-chac, his x mark. [L. S.]
Tanes Salmon, his x mark. [L. S.]
Ta-kos, his x mark. [L. S.]
David, his x mark. [L. S.]
Sowal-we, his x mark. [L. S.]
Postie, his x mark. [L. S.]
Yawan-shewit, his x mark. [L. S.]
Own-aps, his x mark. [L. S.]
Kossa, his x mark. [L. S.]
Pa-wash-ti-mane, his x mark. [L. S.]
Ma-we-nit, his x mark. [L. S.]
Tipso, his x mark. [L. S.]
Jim, his x mark. [L. S.]
Peter, his x mark. [L. S.]
Na-yoct, his x mark. [L. S.]
Wal-tacom, his x mark. [L. S.]
Cho-kalth, his x mark. [L. S.]
Pal-sta, his x mark. [L. S.]
Mission John, his x mark. [L. S.]
Le Ka-ya, his x mark. [L. S]
La-wit-chin, his x mark. [L. S.]
Low-las, his x mark. [L. S.]
Thomson, his x mark. [L. S.]
Charley, his x mark. [L. S.]
Copefornia, his x mark. [L. S.]
Wa-toi-mettla, his x mark. [L. S.]
Ke-la, his x mark. [L. S.]
Pa-ow-ne, his x mark. [L. S.]
Kuck-up, his x mark. [L. S.]
Poyet, his x mark. [L. S.]
Ya-wa-clax, his x mark. [L. S.]
Tam-cha-wit, his x mark. [L. S.]
Tam-mo-yo-cam, his x mark. [L. S.]
Was-ca-can, his x mark. [L. S.]
Talle Kish, his x mark. [L. S.]
Waleme Toach, his x mark. [L. S.]
Site-we-loch, his x mark. [L. S.]
Ma-ni-nect, his x mark. [L. S.]
Pich-kan, his x mark. [L. S.]

Pouh-que, his x mark. [L. S.]
Eye-eya, his x mark. [L. S.]
Kam-kus, his x mark. [L. S,]
Sim-yo, his x mark. [L. S.]
Kas-la-chin, his x mark. [L. S.]
Pio-sho-she, his x mark. [L. S.]
Mop-pa-man, his x mark. [L. S.]
Sho-es, his x mark. [L. S.]
Ta-mo-lits, his x mark. [L. S.]
Ka-lim, his x mark. [L. S.]
Ta-yes, his x mark. [L. S.]
Was-en-was, his x mark. [L. S.]
E-yath Kloppy, his x mark. [L. S.]
Paddy, his x mark. [L. S.]
Sto-quin, his x mark. [L. S.]
Charley-man, his x mark. [L. S.]
Ile-cho, his x mark. [L. S.]
Pate-cham, his x mark. [L. S.]
Yan-che-woc, his x mark. [L. S.]
Ya-toch-la-le, his x mark. [L. S.]
Alpy, his x mark. [L. S.]
Pich, his x mark. [L. S.]
William, his x mark. [L. S.]
Peter, his x mark. [L. S.]
Ischa Ya, his x mark. [L. S.]
George, his x mark. [L. S.]
Jim, his x mark. [L. S.]
Se-ya-las-ka, his x mark. [L. S.]
Ha-lai-kola, his x mark. [L. S.]
Pierro, his x mark. [L. S.]
Ash-lo-wash, his x mark. [L. S.]
Paya-tilch, his x mark. [L. S.]
Sae-pa-waltcha, his x mark. [L. S.]
Shalquilkey, his x mark. [L. S.]
Wa-qual-lol, his x mark. [L. S.]
Sim-kui-kui, his x mark. [L. S.]
Wacha-chiley, his x mark. [L. S.]
Chi-kal-kin, his x mark. [L. S.]
Squa-yash, his x mark. [L. S.]
Sha Ka, his x mark. [L. S.]
Keaui-sene, his x mark. [L. S.]
Che-chis, his x mark. [L. S.]
Sche-noway, his x mark. [L. S.]
Scho-ley, his x mark. [L. S.]
We-ya-thley, his x mark. [L. S.]
Pa-leyathley, his x mark. [L. S.]
Keyath, his x mark. [L. S.]
I-poth-pal, his x mark. [L. S.]
S. Kolps, his x mark. [L. S.]
Walimtalin, his x mark. [L. S.]
Tash Wick, his x mark. [L. S.]
Hawatch-can, his x mark. [L. S.]
Ta-wait-cla, his x mark. [L. S.]
Patoch Snort, his x mark. [L. S.]
Tachins, his x mark. [L. S.]
Comochal, his x mark. [L. S.]
Passayei, his x mark. [L. S.]
Watan-cha, his x mark. [L. S.]
Ta-wash, his x mark. [L. S.]
A-nouth-shot, his x mark. [L. S.]
Hanwake, his x mark. [L. S.]
Pata-la-set, his x mark. [L. S.]
Tash-weict, his x mark. [L. S.]
Wescha-matolla, his x mark. [L. S.]
Chle-mochle-mo, his x mark. [L. S.]
Quae-tus, his x mark. [L. S.]
Skuilts, his x mark. [L. S.]
Panospam, his x mark. [L. S.]

Stolameta, his x mark.	[L. S.]	Ash-ka-wish, his x mark.	[L. S.]
Tamayechotote, his x mark.	[L. S.]	Pasquai, his x mark.	[L. S.]
Qua-losh-kin, his x mark.	[L. S.]	Wasso-kui, his x mark.	[L. S.]
Wiska Ka, his x mark.	[L. S.]	Quaino-sath, his x mark.	[L. S.]
Che-lo-tha, his x mark.	[L. S.]	Cha-ya-tema, his x mark.	[L. S.]
Wetone-yath, his x mark.	[L. S.]	Wa-ya-lo-chol-wit, his x mark.	[L. S.]
We-ya-lo-cho-wit, his x mark.	[L. S.]	Flitch Kui Kui, his x mark.	[L. S.]
Yoka-nolth, his x mark.	[L. S.]	Walcha Kas, his x mark.	[L. S.]
Wacha-ka-polle, his x mark.	[L. S.]	Watch-tla, his x mark.	[L. S.]
Kon-ne, his x mark.	[L. S.]	Enias, his x mark.	[L. S.]

Signed in presence of—

Wm. C. McKay, secretary of treaty, O. T.
R. R. Thompson, Indian agent.
R. B. Metcalfe, Indian sub-agent.
C. Mespotie.
John Flett, interpreter.
Dominick Jondron, his x mark, interpreter.
Mathew Dofa, his x mark, interpreter.

TREATY WITH THE QUINAIELT, ETC., 1855.

Articles of agreement and convention made and concluded by and between Isaac I. Stevens, governor and superintendent of Indian affairs of the Territory of Washington, on the part of the United States, and the undersigned chiefs, headmen, and delegates of the different tribes and bands of the Qui-nai-elt and Quil-leh-ute Indians, on the part of said tribes and bands, and duly authorized thereto by them.

July 1, 1855.
Jan. 25, 1856.

12 Stats., 971.
Ratified Mar. 8, 1859.
Proclaimed, Apr. 11, 1859.

ARTICLE 1. The said tribes and bands hereby cede, relinquish, and convey to the United States all their right, title, and interest in and to the lands and country occupied by them, bounded and described as follows: Commencing at a point on the Pacific coast, which is the southwest corner of the lands lately ceded by the Makah tribe of Indians to the United States, and running easterly with and along the southern boundary of the said Makah tribe to the middle of the coast range of mountains; thence southerly with said range of mountains to their intersection with the dividing ridge between the Chehalis and Quiniatl Rivers; thence westerly with said ridge to the Pacific coast; thence northerly along said coast to the place of beginning.

Surrender of lands to the United States.

Boundaries.

ARTICLE 2. There shall, however, be reserved, for the use and occupation of the tribes and bands aforesaid, a tract or tracts of land sufficient for their wants within the Territory of Washington, to be selected by the President of the United States, and hereafter surveyed or located and set apart for their exclusive use, and no white man shall be permitted to reside thereon without permission of the tribe and of the superintendent of Indian affairs or Indian agent. And the said tribes and bands agree to remove to and settle upon the same within one year after the ratification of this treaty, or sooner if the means are furnished them. In the meantime it shall be lawful for them to reside upon any lands not in the actual claim and occupation of citizens of the United States, and upon any lands claimed or occupied, if with the permission of the owner or claimant. If necessary for the public convenience, roads may be run through said reservation, on compensation being made for any damage sustained thereby.

Reservation within the Territory of Washington.

Whites not to reside thereon, unless, etc.

Indians agree to move and settle there.

Roads may be made.

ARTICLE 3. The right of taking fish at all usual and accustomed grounds and stations is secured to said Indians in common with all citizens of the Territory, and of erecting temporary houses for the purpose of curing the same; together with the privilege of hunting, gathering roots and berries, and pasturing their horses on all open and unclaimed lands. *Provided, however,* That they shall not take

Rights and privileges secured to the Indians.

shell-fish from any beds staked or cultivated by citizens; and provided, also, that they shall alter all stallions not intended· for breeding, and keep up and confine the stallions themselves.

Payment by the United States. ARTICLE 4. In consideration of the above cession, the United States agree to pay to the said tribes and bands the sum of twenty-five thousand dollars, in the following manner, that is to say: For the first year after the ratification hereof, two thousand five hundred dollars; for the next two years, two thousand dollars each year; for the next three years, one thousand six hundred dollars each year; for the next four years, one thousand three hundred dollars each year; for the next five years, one thousand dollars each year; and for the next five **How to be applied.** years, seven hundred dollars each year. All of which sums of money shall be applied to the use and benefit of the said Indians under the directions of the President of the United States, who may from time to time, determine at his discretion upon what beneficial objects to expend the same; and the superintendent of Indian affairs, or other proper officer, shall each year inform the President of the wishes of said Indians in respect thereto.

Appropriation for removal, for clearing and fencing lands, etc. ARTICLE 5. To enable the said Indians to remove to and settle upon such reservation as may be selected for them by the President, and to clear, fence, and break up a sufficient quantity of land for cultivation, the United States further agree to pay the sum of two thousand five hundred dollars, to be laid out and expended under the direction of the President, and in such manner as he shall approve.

Indians may be removed from the reservation, etc. ARTICLE 6. The President may hereafter, when in his opinion the interests of the Territory shall require, and the welfare of the said Indians be promoted by it, remove them from said reservation or reservations to such other suitable place or places within said Territory as he may deem fit, on remunerating them for their improvements and the expenses of their removal, or may consolidate them with other friendly **Tribe annuities may be consolidated.** tribes or bands, in which latter case the annuities, payable to the consolidated tribes respectively, shall also be consolidated; and he may further, at his discretion, cause the whole or any portion of the lands to be reserved, or of such other land as may be selected in lieu thereof, to be surveyed into lots, and assign the same to such individuals or families as are willing to avail themselves of the privilege, and will locate on the same as a permanent home, on the same terms and subject to the same regulations as are provided in the sixth article of the treaty with the Omahas, so far as the same may be applicable. Any substantial improvements heretofore made by any Indians, and which they shall be compelled to abandon in consequence of this treaty, shall be valued under the direction of the President, and payment made accordingly therefor.

Annuities of tribes not to pay debts of individuals. ARTICLE 7. The annuities of the aforesaid tribes and bands shall not be taken to pay the debts of individuals.

Tribes to preserve friendly relations, etc. ARTICLE 8. The said tribes and bands acknowledge their dependence on the Government of the United States, and promise to be friendly with all citizens thereof, and pledge themselves to commit no depredations on the property of such citizens; and should any one or more of them violate this pledge, and the fact be satisfactorily proven before the agent, the property taken shall be returned, or in default thereof, **To pay for depredations.** or if injured or destroyed, compensation may be made by the Government out of their annuities. **Not to make war, except, etc.** ment out of their annuities. Nor will they make war on any other tribe except in self-defence, but will submit all matters of difference between them and other Indians to the Government of the United States, or its agent, for decision and abide thereby; and if any of the said Indians commit any depredations on any other Indians within the Territory, the same rule shall prevail as is prescribed in this article in **To surrender offenders.** case of depredations against citizens. And the said tribes and bands agree not to shelter or conceal offenders against the laws of the United States, but to deliver them to the authorities for trial.

ARTICLE 9. The above tribes and bands are desirous to exclude from their reservations the use of ardent spirits, and to prevent their people from drinking the same, and therefore it is provided that any Indian belonging to said tribes who is guilty of bringing liquor into said reservations, or who drinks liquor, may have his or her proportion of the annuities withheld from him or her, for such time as the President may determine.

ARTICLE 10. The United States further agree to establish at the general agency for the district of Puget Sound, within one year from the ratification hereof, and to support for a period of twenty years, an agricultural and industrial school, to be free to the children of the said tribes and bands in common with those of the other tribes of said district, and to provide the said school with a suitable instructor or instructors, and also to provide a smithy and carpenter's shop, and furnish them with the necessary tools, and to employ a blacksmith, carpenter, and farmer for a term of twenty years, to instruct the Indians in their respective occupations. And the United States further agree to employ a physician to reside at the said central agency, who shall furnish medicine and advice to their sick, and shall vaccinate them; the expenses of the said school, shops, employees, and medical attendance to be defrayed by the United States, and not deducted from their annuities.

United States to establish agricultural schools, etc.

To employ mechanics, etc., a physician, etc.

ARTICLE 11. The said tribes and bands agree to free all slaves now held by them, and not to purchase or acquire others hereafter.

The tribes are to free all slaves and not to acquire others.

ARTICLE 12. The said tribes and bands finally agree not to trade at Vancouver's Island or elsewhere out of the dominions of the United States, nor shall foreign Indians be permitted to reside on their reservations without consent of the superintendent or agent.

Not to trade out of the United States. Foreign Indians not to reside on reservation.

ARTICLE 13. This treaty shall be obligatory on the contracting parties as soon as the same shall be ratified by the President and Senate of the United States.

When treaty to take effect.

In testimony whereof, the said Isaac I. Stevens, governor and superintendent of Indian affairs, and the undersigned chiefs, headmen, and delegates of the aforesaid tribes and bands of Indians, have hereunto set their hands and seals, at Olympia, January 25, 1856, and on the Qui-nai-elt River, July 1, 1855.

Isaac I. Stevens, Governor and Sup't of Indian Affairs.

Tah-ho-lah, Head Chief Qui-nite-'l tribe, his x mark. [L. S.]	Hay-nee-si-oos, his x mark. [L. S.]
How-yat'l, Head Chief Quil-ley-yute tribe, his x mark. [L. S.]	Hoo-e-yas'lsee, his x mark. [L. S.]
Kal-lape, Sub-chief Quil-ley-hutes, his x mark. [L. S.]	Quilt-le-se-mah, his x mark. [L. S.]
	Qua-lats-kaim, his x mark. [L. S.]
Tah-ah-ha-wht'l, Sub-chief Quil-ley-hutes, his x mark. [L. S.]	Yah-le-hum, his x mark. [L. S.]
Lay-le-whash-er, his x mark. [L. S.]	Je-tah-let-shin, his x mark. [L. S.]
E-mah-lah-cup, his x mark. [L. S.]	Ma-ta-a-ha, his x mark. [L. S.]
Ash-chak-a-wick, his x mark. [L. S.]	Wah-kee-nah, Sub-chief Qui-nite'l tribe, his x mark. [L. S.]
Ay-a-quan, his x mark. [L. S.]	Yer-ay-let'l, Sub-chief, his x mark. [L. S.]
Yats-see-o-kop, his x mark. [L. S.]	Silley-mark'l, his x mark. [L. S.]
Karts-so-pe-ah, his x mark. [L. S.]	Cher-lark-tin, his x mark. [L. S.]
Quat-a-de-tot'l, his x mark. [L. S.]	How-yat-'l, his x mark. [L. S.]
Now-ah-ism, his x mark. [L. S.]	Kne-she-guartsh, Sub-chief, his x mark. [L. S.]
Cla-kish-ka, his x mark. [L. S.]	Klay-sumetz, his x mark. [L. S.]
Kler-way-sr-hun, his x mark. [L. S.]	Kape, his x mark. [L. S.]
Quar-ter-heit'l, his x mark. [L. S.]	Hay-et-lite-'l, or John, his x mark. [L. S.]

Executed in the presence of us; the words "or tracts," in the II. article, and "next," in the IV. article, being interlined prior to execution.

M. T. Simmons, special Indian agent.
H. A. Goldsborough, commissary, &c.
B. F. Shaw, interpreter.

James Tilton, surveyor-general Washington Territory.
F. Kennedy.
J. Y. Miller.
H. D. Cock.

TREATY WITH THE FLATHEADS, ETC., 1855.

July 16, 1855.

12 Stats., 975.
Ratified Mar. 8, 1859.
Proclaimed Apr. 18, 1859.

Articles of agreement and convention made and concluded at the treaty-ground at Hell Gate, in the Bitter Root Valley, this sixteenth day of July, in the year one thousand eight hundred and fifty-five, by and between Isaac I. Stevens, governor and superintendent of Indian affairs for the Territory of Washington, on the part of the United States, and the undersigned chiefs, head-men, and delegates of the confederated tribes of the Flathead, Kootenay, and Upper Pend d'Oreilles Indians, on behalf of and acting for said confederated tribes, and being duly authorized thereto by them. It being understood and agreed that the said confederated tribes do hereby constitute a nation, under the name of the Flathead Nation, with Victor, the head chief of the Fleathead tribe, as the head chief of the said nation, and that the several chiefs, head-men, and delegates, whose mames are signed to this treaty, do hereby, in behalf of their respective tribes, recognise Victor as said head chief.

Cession of lands to the United States.

ARTICLE 1. The said confederated tribe of Indians hereby cede, relinquish, and convey to the United States all their right, title, and interest in and to the country occupied or claimed by them, bounded and described as follows, to wit:

Boundaries.

Commencing on the main ridge of the Rocky Mountains at the forty-ninth (49th) parallel of latitude, thence westwardly on that parallel to the divide between the Flat-bow or Kootenay River and Clarke's Fork, thence southerly and southeasterly along said divide to the one hundred and fifteenth degree of longitude, (115°,) thence in a southwesterly direction to the divide between the sources of the St. Regis Borgia and the Cœur d'Alene Rivers, thence southeasterly and southerly along the main ridge of the Bitter Root Mountains to the divide between the head-waters of the Koos-koos-kee River and of the southwestern fork of the Bitter Root River, thence easterly along the divide separating the waters of the several tributaries of the Bitter Root River from the waters flowing into the Salmon and Snake Rivers to the main ridge of the Rocky Mountains, and thence northerly along said main ridge to the place of beginning.

Reservation.

ARTICLE 2. There is, however, reserved from the lands above ceded, for the use and occupation of the said confederated tribes, and as a general Indian reservation, upon which may be placed other friendly tribes and bands of Indians of the Territory of Washington who may agree to be consolidated with the tribes parties to this treaty, under the common designation of the Flathead Nation, with Victor, head chief of the Flathead tribe, as the head chief of the nation, the tract of land included within the following boundaries, to wit:

Boundaries.

Commencing at the source of the main branch of the Jocko River; thence along the divide separating the waters flowing into the Bitter Root River from those flowing into the Jocko to a point on Clarke's Fork between the Camash and Horse Prairies; thence northerly to, and along the divide bounding on the west the Flathead River, to a point due west from the point half way in latitude between the northern and southern extremities of the Flathead Lake; thence on a due east course to the divide whence the Crow, the Prune, the So-ni-el-em and the Jocko Rivers take their rise, and thence southerly along said divide to the place of beginning.

Whites not to reside thereon unless, etc.

All which tract shall be set apart, and, so far as necessary, surveyed and marked out for the exclusive use and benefit of said confederated tribes as an Indian reservation. Nor shall any white man, excepting those in the employment of the Indian department, be permitted to reside upon the said reservation without permission of the confederated tribes, and the superintendent and agent. And the said confederated tribes agree to remove to and settle upon the same within one year after the ratification of this treaty. In the meantime it shall be lawful for them to reside upon any ground not in the actual claim and occupation of citizens of the United States, and upon any ground claimed or occupied, if with the permission of the owner or claimant.

Guaranteeing however the right to all citizens of the United States to enter upon and occupy as settlers any lands not actually occupied and cultivated by said Indians at this time, and not included in the reservation above named. *And provided*, That any substantial improvements heretofore made by any Indian, such as fields enclosed and cultivated and houses erected upon the lands hereby ceded, and which he may be compelled to abandon in consequence of this treaty, shall be valued under the direction of the President of the United States, and payment made therefor in money, or improvements of an equal value be made for said Indian upon the reservation; and no Indian will be required to abandon the improvements aforesaid, now occupied by him, until their value in money or improvements of an equal value shall be furnished him as aforesaid. *Indians to be allowed for improvements on land ceded.*

ARTICLE 3. *And provided*, That if necessary for the public convenience roads may be run through the said reservation; and, on the other hand, the right of way with free access from the same to the nearest public highway is secured to them, as also the right in common with citizens of the United States to travel upon all public highways. *Roads may be made through reservation.*

The exclusive right of taking fish in all the streams running through or bordering said reservation is further secured to said Indians; as also the right of taking fish at all usual and accustomed places, in common with citizens of the Territory, and of erecting temporary buildings for curing; together with the privilege of hunting, gathering roots and berries, and pasturing their horses and cattle upon open and unclaimed land. *Rights and privileges of Indians:*

ARTICLE 4. In consideration of the above cession, the United States agree to pay to the said confederated tribes of Indians, in addition to the goods and provisions distributed to them at the time of signing this treaty the sum of one hundred and twenty thousand dollars, in the following manner—that is to say: For the first year after the ratification hereof, thirty-six thousand dollars, to be expended under the direction of the President, in providing for their removal to the reservation, breaking up and fencing farms, building houses for them, and for such other objects as he may deem necessary. For the next four years, six thousand dollars each year; for the next five years, five thousand dollars each year; for the next five years, four thousand dollars each year; and for the next five years, three thousand dollars each year. *Payments by the United States.*

All which said sums of money shall be applied to the use and benefit of the said Indians, under the direction of the President of the United States, who may from time to time determine, at his discretion, upon what beneficial objects to expend the same for them, and the superintendent of Indian affairs, or other proper officer, shall each year inform the President of the wishes of the Indians in relation thereto. *How to be applied.*

ARTICLE 5. The United States further agree to establish at suitable points within said reservation, within one year after the ratification hereof, an agricultural and industrial school, erecting the necessary buildings, keeping the same in repair, and providing it with furniture, books, and stationery, to be located at the agency, and to be free to the children of the said tribes, and to employ a suitable instructor or instructors. To furnish one blacksmith shop, to which shall be attached a tin and gun shop; one carpenter's shop; one wagon and ploughmaker's shop; and to keep the same in repair, and furnished with the *United States to establish schools.* *Mechanics' shop.*

necessary tools. To employ two farmers, one blacksmith, one tinner, one gunsmith, one carpenter, one wagon and plough maker, for the instruction of the Indians in trades, and to assist them in the same. To erect one saw-mill and one flouring-mill, keeping the same in repair and furnished with the necessary tools and fixtures, and to employ two millers. To erect a hospital, keeping the same in repair, and provided with the necessary medicines and furniture, and to employ a physician; and to erect, keep in repair, and provide the necessary furniture the buildings required for the accommodation of said employees. The said buildings and establishments to be maintained and kept in repair as aforesaid, and the employees to be kept in service for the period of twenty years.

And in view of the fact that the head chiefs of the said confederated tribes of Indians are expected and will be called upon to perform many services of a public character, occupying much of their time, the United States further agree to pay to each of the Flathead, Kootenay, and Upper Pend d'Oreilles tribes five hundred dollars per year, for the term of twenty years after the ratification hereof, as a salary for such persons as the said confederated tribes may select to be their head chiefs, and to build for them at suitable points on the reservation a comfortable house, and properly furnish the same, and to plough and fence for each of them ten acres of land. The salary to be paid to, and the said houses to be occupied by, such head chiefs so long as they may be elected to that position by their tribes, and no longer.

And all the expenditures and expenses contemplated in this article of this treaty shall be defrayed by the United States, and shall not be deducted from the annuities agreed to be paid to said tribes. Nor shall the cost of transporting the goods for the annuity payments be a charge upon the annuities, but shall be defrayed by the United States.

ARTICLE 6. The President may from time to time, at his discretion, cause the whole, or such portion of such reservation as he may think proper, to be surveyed into lots, and assign the same to such individuals or families of the said confederated tribes as are willing to avail themselves of the privilege, and will locate on the same as a permanent home, on the same terms and subject to the same regulations as are provided in the sixth article of the treaty with the Omahas, so far as the same may be applicable.

ARTICLE 7. The annuities of the aforesaid confederated tribes of Indians shall not be taken to pay the debts of individuals.

ARTICLE 8. The aforesaid confederated tribes of Indians acknowledge their dependence upon the Government of the United States, and promise to be friendly with all citizens thereof, and pledge themselves to commit no depredations upon the property of such citizens. And should any one or more of them violate this pledge, and the fact be satisfactorily proved before the agent, the property taken shall be returned, or, in default thereof, or if injured or destroyed, compensation may be made by the Government out of the annuities. Nor will they make war on any other tribe except in self-defence, but will submit all matters of difference between them and other Indians to the Government of the United States, or its agent, for decision, and abide thereby. And if any of the said Indians commit any depredations on any other Indians within the jurisdiction of the United States, the same rule shall prevail as that prescribed in this article, in case of depredations against citizens. And the said tribes agree not to shelter or conceal offenders against the laws of the United States, but to deliver them up to the authorities for trial.

ARTICLE 9. The said confederated tribes desire to exclude from their reservation the use of ardent spirits, and to prevent their people from drinking the same; and therefore it is provided that any Indian belonging to said confederated tribes of Indians who is guilty of bringing

Hospital.

To pay salary to head chiefs.

Certain expenses to be borne by the United States and not charged on annuities.

Lots may be assigned to individuals.

Ante, p. 612.

Annuities not to pay individuals' debts.

Indians to preserve friendly relations.

Indians to pay for depredations, not to make war except, etc.

To surrender offenders.

Annuities to be reserved from those who drink, etc., ardent spirits.

liquor into said reservation, or who drinks liquor, may have his or her proportion of the annuities withheld from him or her for such time as the President may determine.

ARTICLE 10. The United States further agree to guaranty the exclusive use of the reservation provided for in this treaty, as against any claims which may be urged by the Hudson Bay Company under the provisions of the treaty between the United States and Great Britain of the fifteenth of June, eighteen hundred and forty-six, in consequence of the occupation of a trading-post on the Pru-in River by the servants of that company.

Guaranty of reservation against certain claims of Hudson Bay Company.

ARTICLE 11. It is, moreover, provided that the Bitter Root Valley, above the Loo-lo Fork, shall be carefully surveyed and examined, and if it shall prove, in the judgment of the President, to be better adapted to the wants of the Flathead tribe than the general reservation provided for in this treaty, then such portions of it as may be necessary shall be set apart as a separate reservation for the said tribe. No portion of the Bitter Root Valley, above the Loo-lo Fork, shall be opened to settlement until such examination is had and the decision of the President made known.

Bitter Root Valley to be surveyed, and portions may be set apart for reservation.

Meanwhile not to be opened for settlement.

ARTICLE 12. This treaty shall be obligatory upon the contracting parties as soon as the same shall be ratified by the President and Senate of the United States.

When treaty to take effect.

In testimony whereof, the said Isaac I. Stevens, governor and superintendent of Indian affairs for the Territory of Washington, and the undersigned head chiefs, chiefs and principal men of the Flathead, Kootenay, and Upper Pend d'Oreilles tribes of Indians, have hereunto set their hands and seals, at the place and on the day and year hereinbefore written.

Isaac I. Stevens, [L. S.]
Governor and Superintendent Indian Affairs W. T.

Victor, head chief of the Flathead Nation, his x mark. [L. S.]	Big Canoe, his x mark. [L. S.]
Alexander, chief of the Upper Pend d'Oreilles, his x mark. [L. S.]	Kootel Chah, his x mark. [L. S.]
	Paul, his x mark. [L. S.]
Michelle, chief of the Kootenays, his x mark. [L. S.]	Andrew, his x mark. [L. S.]
	Michelle, his x mark. [L. S.]
Ambrose, his x mark. [L. S.]	Battiste, his x mark. [L. S.]
Pah-soh, his x mark. [L. S.]	*Kootenays.*
Bear Track, his x mark. [L. S.]	Gun Flint, his x mark. [L. S.]
Adolphe, his x mark. [L. S.]	Little Michelle, his x mark. [L. S.]
Thunder, his x mark. [L. S.]	Paul See, his x mark. [L. S.]
	Moses, his x mark. [L. S.]

James Doty, secretary.
R. H. Lansdale, Indian Agent.
W. H. Tappan, sub Indian Agent.

Henry R. Crosire,
Gustavus Sohon, Flathead Interpreter.
A. J. Hoecken, sp. mis.
William Craig.

TREATY WITH THE OTTAWA AND CHIPPEWA, 1855.

Articles of agreement and convention made and concluded at the city of Detroit, in the State of Michigan, this the thirty-first day of July, one thousand eight hundred and fifty-five, between George W. Manypenny and Henry C. Gilbert, commissioners on the part of the United States, and the Ottawa and Chippewa Indians of Michigan, parties to the treaty of March 28, 1836.

July 31, 1855.

11 Stat., 621.
Ratified April 15, 1856.
Proclaimed Sept. 10, 1856.

In view of the existing condition of the Ottowas and Chippewas, and of their legal and equitable claims against the United States, it is agreed between the contracting parties as follows:

ARTICLE 1. The United States will withdraw from sale for the benefit of said Indians as hereinafter provided, all the unsold public lands

Certain lands in Michigan to be withdrawn from sale.

within the State of Michigan embraced in the following descriptions, to wit:

For use of the six bands at and near Sault Ste. Marie. First. For the use of the six bands residing at and near Saulte Ste. Marie, sections 13, 14, 23, 24, 25, 26, 27, and 28, in township 47 north, range 5 west; sections 18, 19, and 30, in township 47 north, range 4 west; sections 11, 12, 13, 14, 15, 22, 23, 25, and 26, in township 47 north, range 3 west, and section 29 in township 47 north, range 2 west; sections 2, 3, 4, 11, 14, and 15 in township 47 north, range 2 east, and section 34 in township 48 north, range 2 east; sections 6, 7, 18, 19, 20, 28, 29, and 33 in township 45 north, range 2 east; sections 1, 12, and 13, in township 45 north, range 1 east, and section 4 in township 44 north, range 2 east.

For the use of the bands north of the Straits of Mackinac. Second. For the use of the bands who wish to reside north of the Straits of Macinac townships 42 north, ranges 1 and 2 west; township 43 north, range 1 west, and township 44 north, range 12 west.

For the Beaver Island band. Third. For the Beaver Island Band—High Island, and Garden Island, in Lake Michigan, being fractional townships 38 and 39 north, range 11 west—40 north, range 10 west, and in part 39 north, range 9 and 10 west.

For certain other bands. Fourth. For the Cross Village, Middle Village, L'Arbrechroche and Bear Creek bands, and of such Bay du Noc and Beaver Island Indians as may prefer to live with them, townships 34 to 39, inclusive, north, range 5 west—townships 34 to 38, inclusive, north, range 6 west—townships 34, 36, and 37 north, range 7 west, and all that part of township 34 north, range 8 west, lying north of Pine River.

For bands who are usually paid at Grand Traverse Township. Fifth. For the bands who usually assemble for payment at Grand Traverse, townships 29, 30, and 31 north, range 11 west, and townships 29, 30, and 31 north, range 12 west, and the east half of township 29 north, range 9 west.

For the Grand River bands. Sixth. For the Grand River bands, township 12 north, range 15 west, and townships 15, 16, 17 and 18 north, range 16 west.

For the Cheboygan band. Seventh. For the Cheboygan band, townships 35 and 36 north, range 3 west.

For the Thunder Bay band. Eighth. For the Thunder Bay band, section 25 and 36 in township 30 north, range 7 east, and section 22 in township 30 north, range 8 east.

Purchase for bands who wish to locate near the missionary lands at Iroquois Point. Should either of the bands residing near Sault Ste. Marie determine to locate near the lands owned by the missionary society of the Methodist Episcopal Church at Iroquois Point, in addition to those who now reside there, it is agreed that the United States will purchase as much of said lands for the use of the Indians as the society may be willing to sell at the usual Government price.

Grant of lands to each Indian. The United States will give to each Ottawa and Chippewa Indian being the head of a family, 80 acres of land, and to each single person over twenty-one years of age, 40 acres of land, and to each family of orphan children under twenty-one years of age containing two or more persons, 80 acres of land, and to each single orphan child under twenty-one years of age, 40 acres of land to be selected and located within the several tracts of land hereinbefore described, under the following rules and regulations:

Selection, how made. Each Indian entitled to land under this article may make his own selection of any land within the tract reserved herein for the band to which he may belong—*Provided,* That in case of two or more Indians claiming the same lot or tract of land, the matter shall be referred to the Indian agent, who shall examine the case and decide between the parties.

List of those entitled to be prepared. For the purpose of determining who may be entitled to land under the provisions of this article, lists shall be prepared by the Indian agent, which lists shall contain the names of all persons entitled, designating them in four classes. Class 1st, shall contain the names of heads of families; class 2d, the names of single persons over twenty-one years of age; class 3d, the names of orphan children under twenty-one years of age, comprising families of two or more persons, and class 4th, the names of single orphan children under twenty-one years of age, and no person shall be entered in more than one class.   Such lists shall be made and closed by the first day of July, 1856, and thereafter no applications for the benefits of this article will be allowed.

At any time within five years after the completion of the lists, selections of lands may be made by the persons entitled thereto, and a notice thereof, with a description of the land selected, filed in the office of the Indian agent in Detroit, to be by him transmitted to the Office of Indian Affairs at Washington City. *Selections may be made within five years.*

All sections of land under this article must be made according to the usual subdivisions; and fractional lots, if containing less than 60 acres, may be regarded as forty-acre lots, if over sixty and less than one hundred and twenty acres, as eighty-acre lots.   Selections for orphan children may be made by themselves or their friends, subject to the approval of the agent. *To be according to usual subdivisions.*

After selections are made, as herein provided, the persons entitled to the land may take immediate possession thereof, and the United States will thenceforth and until the issuing of patents as hereinafter provided, hold the same in trust for such persons, and certificates shall be issued, in a suitable form, guaranteeing and securing to the holders their possession and an ultimate title to the land.   But such certificates shall not be assignable and shall contain a clause expressly prohibiting the sale or transfer by the holder of the land described therein. *Possession may be taken at once.* *Sale within ten years forbidden.*

After the expiration of ten years, such restriction on the power of sale shall be withdrawn, and a patent shall be issued in the usual form to each original holder of a certificate for the land described therein, *Provided* That such restriction shall cease only upon the actual issuing of the patent; *And provided further* That the President may in his discretion at any time in individual cases on the recommendation of the Indian agent when it shall appear prudent and for the welfare of any holder of a certificate, direct a patent to be issued.   *And provided also,* That after the expiration of ten years, if individual cases shall be reported to the President by the Indian agent, of persons who may then be incapable of managing their own affairs from any reason whatever, he may direct the patents in such cases to be withheld, and the restrictions provided by the certificate, continued so long as he may deem necessary and proper. *After ten years a patent shall issue and restrictions on sales cease.*

Should any of the heads of families die before the issuing of the certificates or patents herein provided for, the same shall issue to the heirs of such deceased persons. *Provision for case of death.*

The benefits of this article will be extended only to those Indians who are at this time actual residents of the State of Michigan, and entitled to participate in the annuities provided by the treaty of March 28, 1836; but this provision shall not be construed to exclude any Indian now belonging to the Garden River band of Sault Ste. Marie. *To whom this treaty shall extend.*

All the land embraced within the tracts hereinbefore described, that shall not have been appropriated or selected within five years shall remain the property of the United States, and the same shall thereafter, for the further term of five years, be subject to entry in the usual manner and at the same rate per acre, as other adjacent public lands are then held, by Indians only; and all lands, so purchased by Indians, shall be sold without restriction, and certificates and patents shall be issued for the same in the usual form as in ordinary cases; and all lands remaining unappropriated by or unsold to the Indians after the expiration of the last-mentioned term, may be sold or disposed of by the United States as in the case of all other public lands. *After five years the remaining lands may be entered in the usual manner by Indians for five years, and then by anyone.*

Nothing contained herein shall be so construed as to prevent the appropriation, by sale, gift, or otherwise, by the United States, of any tract or tracts of land within the aforesaid reservations for the location of churches, school-houses, or for other educational purposes, and *Grants for churches, schools, etc., may be made.*

for such purposes purchases of land may likewise be made from the Indians, the consent of the President of the United States, having, in every instance, first been obtained therefor.

It is also agreed that any lands within the aforesaid tracts now occupied by actual settlers, or by persons entitled to pre-emption thereon, shall be exempt from the provisions of this article; provided, that such pre-emption claims shall be proved, as prescribed by law, before the 1st day of October next.

Any Indian who may have heretofore purchased land for actual settlement, under the act of Congress known as the Graduation Act, may sell and dispose of the same; and, in such case, no actual occupancy or residence by such Indians on lands so purchased shall be necessary to enable him to secure a title thereto.

In consideration of the benefits derived to the Indians on Grand Traverse Bay by the school and mission established in 1838, and still continued by the Board of Foreign Missions of the Presbyterian Church, it is agreed that the title to three separate pieces of land, being parts of tracts Nos. 3 and 4, of the west fractional half of section 35, township 30 north, range 10 west, on which are the mission and school buildings and improvements, not exceeding in all sixty-three acres, one hundred and twenty-four perches, shall be vested in the said board on payment of $1.25 per acre; and the President of the United States shall issue a patent for the same to such person as the said board shall appoint.

The United States will also pay the further sum of forty thousand dollars, or so much thereof as may be necessary, to be applied in liquidation of the present just indebtedness of the said Ottawa and Chippewa Indians; provided, that all claims presented shall be investigated under the direction of the Secretary of the Interior, who shall prescribe such rules and regulations for conducting such investigation, and for testing the validity and justness of the claims, as he shall deem suitable and proper; and no claim shall be paid except upon the certificate of the said Secretary that, in his opinion, the same is justly and equitably due; and all claimants, who shall not present their claims within such time as may be limited by said Secretary within six months from the ratification of the treaty, or whose claims, having been presented, shall be disallowed by him, shall be forever precluded from collecting the same, or maintaining an action thereon in any court whatever; and provided, also, that no portion of the money due said Indians for annuities, as herein provided, shall ever be appropriated to pay their debts under any pretence whatever; provided, that the balance of the amount herein allowed, as a just increase of the amount due for the cessions and relinquishments aforesaid, after satisfaction of the awards of the Secretary of the Interior, shall be paid to the said Chippewas or expended for their benefit, in such manner as the Secretary shall prescribe, in aid of any of the objects specified in the second article of this treaty.

ARTICLE 2. The United States will also pay to the said Indians the sum of five hundred and thirty-eight thousand and four hundred dollars, in manner following, to wit:

First. Eighty thousand dollars for educational purposes to be paid in ten equal annual instalments of eight thousand dollars each, which sum shall be expended under the direction of the President of the United States; and in the expenditure of the same, and the appointment of teachers and management of schools, the Indians shall be consulted, and their views and wishes adopted so far as they may be just and reasonable.

Second. Seventy-five thousand dollars to be paid in five equal annual instalments of fifteen thousand dollars each in agricultural implements and carpenters' tools, household furniture and building materials, cattle, labor, and all such articles as may be necessary and useful for them in removing to the homes herein provided and getting permanently settled thereon.

Third. Forty-two thousand and four hundred dollars for the support of four blacksmith-shops for ten years. Forty-two thousand four hundred dollars for blacksmith shops.

Fourth. The sum of three hundred and six thousand dollars in coin, as follows: ten thousand dollars of the principal, and the interest on the whole of said last-mentioned sum remaining unpaid at the rate of five per cent. annually for ten years, to be distributed *per capita* in the usual manner for paying annuities. And the sum of two hundred and six thousand dollars remaining unpaid at the expiration of ten years, shall be then due and payable, and if the Indians then require the payment of said sum in coin the same shall be distributed *per capita* in the same manner as annuities are paid, and in not less than four equal annual instalments. Three hundred and six thousand dollars "to be paid per capita."

Fifth. The sum of thirty-five thousand dollars in ten annual instalments of three thousand and five hundred dollars each, to be paid only to the Grand River Ottawas, which is in lieu of all permanent annuities to which they may be entitled by former treaty stipulations, and which sum shall be distributed in the usual manner *per capita*. Thirty-five thousand dollars in ten annual installments.

ARTICLE 3. The Ottawa and Chippewa Indians hereby release and discharge the United States from all liability on account of former treaty stipulations, it being distinctly understood and agreed that the grants and payments hereinbefore provided for are in lieu and satisfaction of all claims, legal and equitable on the part of said Indians jointly and severally against the United States, for land, money or other thing guaranteed to said tribes or either of them by the stipulations of any former treaty or treaties; excepting, however, the right of fishing and encampment secured to the Chippewas of Sault Ste. Marie by the treaty of June 16, 1820. Liabilities under former treaties released.

ARTICLE 4. The interpreters at Sault Ste. Marie, Mackinac, and for the Grand River Indians, shall be continued, and another provided at Grand Traverse, for the term of five years, and as much longer as the President may deem necessary. Interpreters.

ARTICLE 5. The tribal organization of said Ottawa and Chippewa Indians, except so far as may be necessary for the purpose of carrying into effect the provisions of this agreement, is hereby dissolved; and if at any time hereafter, further negotiations with the United States, in reference to any matters contained herein, should become necessary, no general convention of the Indians shall be called; but such as reside in the vicinity of any usual place of payment, or those only who are immediately interested in the questions involved, may arrange all matters between themselves and the United States, without the concurrence of other portions of their people, and as fully and conclusively, and with the same effect in every respect, as if all were represented. Tribal organization dissolved in most respects.
Future treaties; how made.

ARTICLE 6. This agreement shall be obligatory and binding on the contracting parties as soon as the same shall be ratified by the President and Senate of the United States. Treaty· when to be binding.

In testimony whereof the said George W. Manypenny and the said Henry C. Gilbert, commissioners as aforesaid, and the undersigned chiefs and headmen of the Ottawas and Chippewas, have hereto set their hands and seals, at the city of Detroit the day and year first above written.

Geo. W. Manypenny, [L. S.]

Henry C. Gilbert,   [L. S.]

Commissioners on the part of the United States.

J. Logan Chipman,
Rich'd M. Smith,
   Secretaries.

Sault Ste. Marie Bands:
O-shaw-waw-no-ke-wain-ze, chief, his x mark. [L. s.]
Waw-bo-jieg, chief, his x mark. [L. s.]
Kay-bay-no-din, chief, his x mark. [L. s.]
O-maw-no-maw-ne, chief, his x mark. [L. s.]
Shaw-wan, chief, his x mark. [L. s.]
Pi-aw-be-daw-sung, chief, his x mark. [L. s.]
Waw-we-gun, headman, his x mark. [L. s.]
Pa-ne-gwon, headman, his x mark. [L. s.]
Bwan, headman, his x mark. [L. s.]
Taw-meece, headman, his x mark. [L. s.]
Naw-o-ge-zhick, headman, his x mark. [L. s.]
Saw-gaw-giew, headman, his x mark. [L. s.]
Grand River Bands:
Ne-baw-nay-ge-zhick, chief, his x mark. [L. s.]
Shaw-gwaw-baw-no, chief, his x mark. [L. s.]
Aish-ke-baw-gosh, 2d chief, his x mark. [L. s.]
Nay-waw-goo, chief, his x mark. [L. s.]
Ne-be-ne-seh, chief, his x mark. [L. s.]
Waw-be-gay-kake, chief, his x mark. [L. s.]
Ke-ne-we-ge-zhick, chief, his x mark. [L. s.]
Men-daw-waw-be, chief, his x mark. [L. s.]
Maish-ke-aw-she, chief, his x mark. [L. s.]
Pay-shaw-se-gay, chief, his x mark. [L. s.]
Pay-baw-me, headman, his x mark. [L. s.]
Pe-go, chief, his x mark. [L. s.]
Ching-gwosh, chief, his x mark. [L. s.]
Shaw-be-quo-ung, chief, his x mark. [L. s.]
Andrew J. Blackbird, headman, his x mark. [L. s.]
Ke-sis-swaw-bay, headman, his x mark. [L. s.]

Naw-te-naish-cum, headman, his x mark. [L. s.]
Grand Traverse Bands:
Aish-quay-go-nay-be, chief, his x mark. [L. s.]
Ah-ko-say, chief, his x mark. [L. s.]
Kay-quay-to-say, chief, his x mark. [L. s.]
O-naw-maw-nince, chief, his x mark. [L. s.]
Shaw-bwaw-sung, chief, his x mark. [L. s.]
Louis Mick-saw-bay, headman, his x mark. [L. s.]
May-dway-aw-she, headman, his x mark. [L. s.]
Me-tay-o-meig, chief, his x mark. [L. s.]
Me-naw-quot, headman, his x mark. [L. s.]
Little Traverse Bands:
Waw-so, chief, his x mark. [L. s.]
Mwaw-ke-we-naw, chief, his x mark. [L. s.]
Pe-taw-se-gay, headman, his x mark. [L. s.]
Ke-ne-me-chaw-gun, chief, his x mark. [L. s.]
May-tway-on-daw-gaw-she, headman, his x mark. [L. s.]
Me-ge-se-mong, headman, his x mark. [L. s.]
Pi-a-zhick-way-we-dong, headman, his x mark. [L. s.]
Key-way-ken-do, headman, his x mark. [L. s.]
Mackinac Bands:
O-saw-waw-ne-me-ke, chief, his x mark. [L. s.]
Ke-no-zhay, headman, his x mark. [L. s.]
Peter Hanse, headman, his x mark. [L. s.]
Shaw-be-co-shing, chief, his x mark. [L. s.]
Shaw-bway-way, chief, his x mark. [L. s.]
Pe-ane, headman, his x mark. [L. s.]
Saw-gaw-naw-quaw-do, headman, his x mark. [L. s.]
Nay-o-ge-maw, chief, (Little Traverse,) his x mark. [L. s.]

* * * * * * *

Executed in the presence of—

Jno. M. D. Johnston,
John F. Godfroy,
Gbt. Johnston,
Aug. Hamlin,
    Interpreters.

L. Campau,
Joseph F. Mursul,
G. D. Williams,
P. B. Barbeau,
A. M. Fitch,
W. H. Godfroy.

We, the undersigned chiefs and headmen of the Chippewa Indians living near Sault Ste. Marie, Mich., having had the amendments adopted by the Senate of the United States to the treaty concluded at Detroit on the 31st day of July, 1855, fully explained to us and being satisfied therewith, do hereby assent to and ratify the same.

In witness whereof we have hereunto set our hands this 27th day of June, A. D. 1856.

Pi-aw-be-daw-sung, his x mark.
Te-gose, his x mark.
Saw-gaw-jew, his x mark.
Shaw-ano, his x mark.
Waw-bo-jick, his x mark.
Ray-bay-no-din, his x mark.
Shaw-wan, his x mark.

O-me-no-mee-ne, his x mark.
Pay-ne-gown, his x mark.
Waw-we-gown, his x mark.
Ma-ne-do-scung, his x mark.
Naw-we-ge-zhick, his x mark.
Yaw-mence, his x mark.
Bawn, his x mark.

Signed in presence of—

Ebenzr Warner,
Jno. M. Johnston, United States Indian Interpreter.
Placidus Ord.

We, the undersigned chiefs and headmen of the Ottawa and Chippewa nation, having heard the foregoing amendments read and explained to us by our agent, do hereby assent to and ratify the same.

In witness whereof we have hereto affixed our signatures this 2d day of July, A. D. 1856, at Little Traverse, Mich.

Waw-so, his x mark.	Pe-taw-se-gay, his x mark.
Mwaw-ke-we-naw, his x mark.	Ke-ne-me-chaw-gun, his x mark.
Ne-saw-waw-quot, his x mark.	May-tway-on-day-gaw-she, his x mark.
Aw-se-go, his x mark.	Me-ge-se-mong, his x mark.
Ke-zhe-go-ne, his x mark.	Key-way-ken-do, his x mark.
Kain-waw-be-kiss-se, his x mark.	Nay-o-ge-maw, his x mark.
Pe-aine, his x mark.	

In the presence of—

Henry C. Gilbert, Indian Agent,
Aug. Hamlin, Interpreter,
John F. Godfroy, Interpreter,
G. T. Wendell,
A. J. Blackbird.

We, the chiefs and headmen of the Ottowa and Chippewa Indians residing near Grand Traverse Bay, having heard the foregoing amendments adopted by the Senate of the United States to the treaty of July 31, 1855, read, and the same having been fully explained to us by our agent, do hereby assent to and ratify the same.

Done at Northport on Grand Traverse Bay, Mich., this 5th day of July, A. D. 1856.

> Aish-quay-go-nay-be, his x mark.
> Ah-ko-say, his x mark.
> O-naw-mo-neece, his x mark.
> Kay-qua-to-say, his x mark.
> Peter-waw-ka-zoo, his x mark.
> Shaw-bwaw-sung, his x mark.
> Louis-mick-saw-bay, his x mark

In presence of—

H. C. Gilbert, Indian agent,
J. F. Godfroy, interpreter,
Geo. N. Smith,
Peter Dougherty,
Normon Barnes.

We, the undersigned, chiefs and headmen of the Grand River bands of the Ottowa and Chippewa Indians of Michigan having heard the amendments of the Senate to the treaty of the 31st of July, 1855, read, and the same having been fully explained to us, do hereby assent to and ratify the same.

Done at Grand Rapids in the State of Michigan this 31st day of July, A. D. 1856.

Caw-ba-mo-say, his x mark.	Gaw-ga-gaw-bwa, his x mark.
Shaw-gwaw-baw-no, his x mark.	Note-eno-kay, his x mark.
Aish-ke-baw-gosh, his x mark.	Ne-baw-nay-ge-zhick, his x mark.
Waw-be-gay-kake, his x mark.	Pay-baw-me, his x mark.
Ne-ba-ne-seh, his x mark.	Shaw-be-quo-ung, his x mark.
Ching-gwosh, his x mark.	Men-daw-waw-be, his x mark.
Mash-caw, his x mark.	

In presence of—

John F. Godfroy, United States interpreter.
Wm. Cobmosy,
F. N. Gonfry.

TREATY WITH THE CHIPPEWA OF SAULT STE. MARIE, 1855.

Aug. 2, 1855.

11 Stat. 631.
Ratified Apr. 15, 1856.
Proclaimed Apr. 24, 1856.

Articles of agreement made and concluded at the city of Detroit, in the State of Michigan, the second day of August, 1855, between George W. Manypenny and Henry C. Gilbert, commissioners on the part of the United States, and the Chippewa Indians of Sault Ste. Marie.

Rights of fishing surrendered.

Ante, p. 187.

ARTICLE 1. The said Chippewa Indians surrender to the United States the right of fishing at the falls of St. Mary's and of encampment, convenient to the fishing-ground, secured to them by the treaty of June 16, 1820.

Payment to Indians.

ARTICLE 2. The United States will appoint a commissioner who shall, within six months after the ratification of this treaty, personally visit and examine the said fishery and place of encampment, and determine the value of the interest of the Indians therein as the same originally existed. His award shall be reported to the President, and shall be final and conclusive, and the amount awarded shall be paid to said Indians, as annuities are paid, and shall be received by them in full satisfaction for the right hereby surrendered: *Provided,* That one-third of said award shall, if the Indians desire it, be paid to such of their half-breed relations as they may indicate.

Grant to Oshaw-wawno.

ARTICLE 3. The United States also give to the chief, O-shaw-waw-no, for his own use, in fee-simple, a small island in the river St. Mary's, adjacent to the camping-ground hereby surrendered, being the same island on which he is now encamped, and said to contain less than half an acre: *Provided,* That the same has not been heretofore otherwise appropriated or disposed of; and in such case, this grant is to be void, and no compensation is to be claimed by said chief or any of the Indians, parties hereto, in lieu thereof.

ARTICLE 4. This agreement shall be obligatory and binding on the contracting parties as soon as the same shall be ratified by the President and Senate of the United States.

In testimony whereof, the said George W. Manypenny and the said Henry C. Gilbert, commissioners as aforesaid, and the undersigned chiefs and headmen of the Chippewa Indians of Sault. Ste. Marie, have hereto set their hands and seals at the city of Detroit the day and year first above written.

Geo. W. Manypenny, [L. s.]
Henry C. Gilbert,   [L. s.]
                        Commissioners.
Richard M. Smith,
                        Secretary.

O-shaw-waw-no, chief, his x mark. [L. s.]	Pay-ne-gwon, headman, his x mark. [L. s.]
Waw-bo-jieg, chief, his x mark. [L. s.]	Taw-meece, headman, his x mark. [L. s.]
Kay-bay-no-din, chief, his x mark. [L. s.]	Bwan, headman, his x mark. [L. s.]
O-maw-no-maw-ne, chief, his x mark. [L. s.]	Saw-gaw-jew, headman, his x mark. [L. s.]
Shaw-wan, chief, his x mark. [L. s.]	Naw-we-ge-zhick, headman, his x mark. [L. s.]
Pi-aw-be-daw-sung, chief, his x mark. [L. s.]	
Wa-we-gun, headman, his x mark. [L. s.]	

Executed in the presence of—
    J. Logan Chipman,
    George Smith,
    W. H. Collins,
    Jno. M. Johnston, } Interpreters.
    Geo. Johnston,

TREATY WITH THE CHIPPEWA OF SAGINAW, ETC., 1855.

Articles of agreement and convention, made and concluded at the city of Detroit, in the State of Michigan, this second day of August, one thousand eight hundred and fifty-five, between George W. Manypenny and Henry C. Gilbert, commissioners on the part of the United States, and the Chippewa Indians of Saginaw, parties to the treaty of January 14, 1837, and that portion of the band of Chippewa Indians of Swan Creek and Black River, parties to the treaty of May 9, 1836, and now remaining in the State of Michigan.

Aug. 2, 1855.

11 Stat., 633.
Ratified   Apr.   15, 1856.
Proclaimed June 21, 1856.

In view of the existing condition of the Indians aforesaid, and of their legal and equitable claims against the United States, it is agreed between the contracting parties as follows, viz:

ARTICLE 1. The United States will withdraw from sale, for the benefit of said Indians, as herein provided, all the unsold public lands within the State of Michigan embraced in the following description, to wit: *Certain lands in Michigan to be withdrawn from sale.*

First. Six adjoining townships of land in the county of Isabella, to be selected by said Indians within three months from this date, and notice thereof given to their agent.

Second. Townships Nos. 17 and 18 north, ranges 3, 4, and 5 east.

The United States will give to each of the said Indians, being a head of a family, eighty acres of land; and to each single person over twenty-one years of age, forty acres of land; and to each family of orphan children under twenty-one years of age, containing two or more persons, eighty acres of land; and to each single orphan child under twenty-one years of age, forty acres of land; to be selected and located within the several tracts of land hereinbefore described, under the same rules and regulations, in every respect, as are provided by the agreement concluded on the 31st day of July, A. D. 1855, with the Ottawas and Chippewas of Michigan, for the selection of their lands. *Grant of land to each of said Indians.*

And the said Chippewas of Saginaw and of Swan Creek and Black River, shall have the same exclusive right to enter lands within the tracts withdrawn from sale for them for five years after the time limited for selecting the lands to which they are individually entitled, and the same right to sell and dispose of land entered by them, under the provisions of the Act of Congress known as the Graduation Act, as is extended to the Ottawas and Chippewas by the terms of said agreement.

And the provisions therein contained relative to the purchase and sale of land for school-houses, churches, and educational purposes, shall also apply to this agreement.

ARTICLE 2. The United States shall also pay to the said Indians the sum of two hundred and twenty thousand dollars, in manner following, to wit: *Payment to said Indians.*

First. Thirty thousand dollars for educational purposes, to be paid in five equal annual instalments of four thousand dollars each, and in five subsequent equal annual instalments of two thousand dollars each, to be expended under the direction of the President of the United States.

Second. Forty thousand dollars, in five equal annual instalments of five thousand dollars each, and in five subsequent equal annual instalments of three thousand dollars each, in agricultural implements and carpenters' tools, household furniture and building materials, cattle, labor, and all such articles as may be necessary and useful for them in removing to the homes herein provided, and getting permanently settled thereon.

Third. One hundred and thirty-seven thousand and six hundred dollars in coin, in ten equal instalments of ten thousand dollars each, and in two subsequent equal annual instalments of eighteen thousand and eight hundred dollars each, to be distributed *per capita* in the usual manner for paying annuities.

Fourth. Twelve thousand and four hundred dollars for the support of one blacksmith-shop for ten years.

The United States will also build a grist and saw mill for said Indians at some point in the territory, to be selected by them in said county of Isabella, provided, a suitable water-power can be found, and will furnish and equip the same with all necessary fixtures and machinery, and will construct such dam, race, and other appurtenances as may be necessary to render the water-power available: *Provided* That the whole amount for which the United States shall be liable under this provision, shall not exceed the sum of eight thousand dollars.

The United States will also pay the further sum of four thousand dollars for the purpose of purchasing a saw-mill, and in repair of the same, and in adding thereto the necessary machinery and fixtures for a run of stone for grinding grain—the same to be located on the tract described in clause "second," Article 1.

The United States will also pay the further sum of twenty thousand dollars, or so much thereof as may be necessary, to be applied in liquidation of the present just indebtedness of the said Indians; *Provided*, That all claims presented shall be investigated under the direction of the Secretary of the Interior within six months, who shall prescribe such rules and regulations for conducting such investigation, and for testing the validity and justice of the claims as he shall deem suitable and proper. And no claim shall be paid except on the certificate of the said Secretary that, in his opinion, the same is justly and equitably due; and all claimants, who shall not present their claims within such time as may be limited by said Secretary, or, whose claims having been presented, shall be disallowed by him, shall be forever precluded from collecting the same, or maintaining an action thereon in any court whatever; *And, provided, also,* That no portion of the money due said Indians for annuities, as herein provided, shall ever be appropriated to pay their debts under any pretence whatever; *Provided* That the balance of the amount herein allowed as a just increase for the cessions and relinquishments aforesaid, after satisfaction of the awards of the Secretary of the Interior, shall be paid to the said Indians, or expended for their benefit in such manner as the Secretary shall prescribe, in aid of any of the objects specified in this treaty.

Cession of all the lands heretofore owned by said Indians.

ARTICLE 3. The said Chippewas of Saginaw, and of Swan Creek and Black River, hereby cede to the United States all the lands within the State of Michigan heretofore owned by them as reservations, and whether held for them in trust by the United States or otherwise; and

Release of liability.

they do hereby, jointly and severally, release and discharge the United States from all liability to them, and to their, or either of their said tribes, for the price and value of all such lands, heretofore sold, and the proceeds of which remain unpaid.

Surrender of annuities.

And they also hereby surrender all their, and each of their permanent annuities, secured to them, or either of them by former treaty stipulations, including that portion of the annuity of eight hundred

Ante, p. 92.

dollars payable to "the Chippewas," by the treaty of November 17, 1807, to which they are entitled, it being distinctly understood and agreed, that the grants and payments hereinbefore provided for, are in

Said grants and payments to be in full of claims.

lieu and satisfaction of all claims, legal and equitable on the part of said Indians, jointly and severally, against the United States for land, money, or other thing guaranteed to said tribes, or either of them, by the stipulations of any former treaty or treaties.

ARTICLE 4. The entries of land heretofore made by Indians and by the Missionary Society of the Methodist Episcopal Church for the benefit of the Indians, on lands withdrawn from sale in townships 14 north, range 4 east, and 10 north, range 5 east, in the State of Michigan, are hereby confirmed, and patents shall be issued therefor as in other cases.

ARTICLE 5. The United States will provide an interpreter for said Indians for five years, and as much longer as the President may deem necessary.

ARTICLE 6. The tribal organization of said Indians, except so far as may be necessary for the purpose of carrying into effect the provisions of this agreement, is hereby dissolved.

ARTICLE 7. This agreement shall be obligatory and binding on the contracting parties as soon as the same shall be ratified by the President and Senate of the United States.

In testimony whereof, the said George W. Manypenny and the said Henry C. Gilbert, commissioners as aforesaid, and the undersigned, chiefs and headmen of the Chippewas of Saginaw, and of Swan Creek and Black River, have hereto set their hands and seals at the city of Detroit, the day and year first above written.

> Geo. W. Manypenny, [L. S.]
> Henry C. Gilbert, [L. S.]
> Commissioners.

Richard M. Smith,
J. Logan Chipman,
   Secretaries.

Saginaw Bands:

Ot-taw-ance, chief, his x mark. [L. S.]
O-saw-waw-bun, chief, his x mark. [L. S.]
Nanck-che-gaw-me, chief, his x mark. [L. S.]
Kaw-gay-ge-zhick, chief, his x mark. [L. S.]
Shaw-shaw-way-nay-beece, chief, his x mark. [L. S.]
Pe-nay-se-waw-be, chief, his x mark. [L. S.]
Naw-we-ge-zhick, chief, his x mark. [L. S.]
Saw-gaw-che-way-o-say, chief, his x mark. [L. S.]
Naw-taw-way, chief, his x mark. [L. S.]
Wain-ge-ge-zhick, chief, his x mark. [L. S.]

Caw-me-squaw-bay-no-kay, chief, his x mark. [L. S.]
Pe-tway-we-tum, headman, his x mark. [L. S.]
Kay-bay-guo-um, headman, his x mark. [L. S.]
Pay-baw-maw-she, headman, his x mark. [L. S.]
Aw-be-taw-quot, headman, his x mark. [L. S.]
Aish-quay-go-nay-be, headman, his x mark. [L. S.]
Pay-me-saw-aw, headman, his x mark. [L. S.]
Aw-taw-we-go-nay-be, headman, his x mark. [L. S.]
Pay-she-nin-ne, headman, his x mark. [L. S.]

Swan Creek and Black River Band:

Pay-me-quo-ung, chief, his x mark. [L. S.]
Nay-ge-zhick, headman, his x mark. [L. S.]

Maw-che-che-won, headman, his x mark. [L. S.]

Executed in the presence of—

G. D. Williams.
George Smith.
W. H. Collins.
Manasseh Hickey.
P. O. Johnson.

Joseph F. Marsal.
Jno. M. D. Johnston,
Chas. H. Rodd,   } Interpreters.
L. M. Moran,

TREATY WITH THE BLACKFEET, 1855.

Oct. 17, 1855.

11 Stat., 657.
Ratified Apr.15,1856.
Proclaimed Apr. 25, 1856.

Articles of agreement and convention made and concluded at the council-ground on the Upper Missouri, near the mouth of the Judith River, in the Territory of Nebraska, this seventeenth day of October, in the year one thousand eight hundred and fifty-five, by and between A. Cumming and Isaac I. Stevens, commissioners duly appointed and authorized, on the part of the United States, and the undersigned chiefs, headmen, and delegates of the following nations and tribes of Indians, who occupy, for the purposes of hunting, the territory on the Upper Missouri and Yellowstone Rivers, and who have permanent homes as follows: East of the Rocky Mountains, the Blackfoot Nation, consisting of the Piegan, Blood, Blackfoot, and Gros Ventres tribes of Indians. West of the Rocky Mountains, the Flathead Nation, consisting of the Flathead, Upper Pend d'Oreille, and Kootenay tribes of Indians, and the Nez Percé tribe of Indians, the said chiefs, headmen and delegates, in behalf of and acting for said nations and tribes, and being duly authorized thereto by them.

Peace to exist with the United States.

ARTICLE 1. Peace, friendship and amity shall hereafter exist between the United States and the aforesaid nations and tribes of Indians, parties to this treaty, and the same shall be perpetual.

Peace to exist with each other and with certain other tribes.

ARTICLE 2. The aforesaid nations and tribes of Indians, parties to this treaty, do hereby jointly and severally covenant that peaceful relations shall likewise be maintained among themselves in future; and that they will abstain from all hostilities whatsoever against each other, and cultivate mutual good-will and friendship. And the nations and tribes aforesaid do furthermore jointly and severally covenant, that peaceful relations shall be maintained with and that they will abstain from all hostilities whatsoever, excepting in self-defense, against the following-named nations and tribes of Indians, to wit: the Crows, Assineboins, Crees, Snakes, Blackfeet, Sans Arcs, and Auncepa-pas bands of Sioux, and all other neighboring nations and tribes of Indians.

Blackfoot territory recognized as common hunting ground.

ARTICLE 3. The Blackfoot Nation consent and agree that all that portion of the country recognized and defined by the treaty of Laramie as Blackfoot territory, lying within lines drawn from the Hell Gate or Medicine Rock Passes in the main range of the Rocky Mountains, in an easterly direction to the nearest source of the Muscle Shell River, thence to the mouth of Twenty-five Yard Creek, thence up the Yellowstone River to its northern source, and thence along the main range of the Rocky Mountains, in a northerly direction, to the point of beginning, shall be a common hunting-ground for ninety-nine years, where all the nations, tribes and bands of Indians, parties to this treaty, may enjoy equal and uninterupted privileges of hunting, fishing and gathering fruit, grazing animals, curing meat and dressing robes. They further agree that they will not establish villages, or in any other way exercise exclusive rights within ten miles of the northern line of the common hunting-ground, and that the parties to this treaty may hunt on said northern boundary line and within ten miles thereof.

Provided, That the western Indians, parties to this treaty, may hunt on the trail leading down the Muscle Shell to the Yellowstone; the Muscle Shell River being the boundary separating the Blackfoot from the Crow territory.

No settlements to be made thereon.

And provided, That no nation, band, or tribe of Indians, parties to this treaty, nor any other Indians, shall be permitted to establish permanent settlements, or in any other way exercise, during the period above mentioned, exclusive rights or privileges within the limits of the above-described hunting-ground.

And provided further, That the rights of the western Indians to a Vested rights not affected. whole or a part of the common hunting-ground, derived from occupancy and possession, shall not be affected by this article, except so far as said rights may be determined by the treaty of Laramie.

ARTICLE 4. The parties to this treaty agree and consent, that the Certain territory to belong to the Blackfoot Nation. tract of country lying within lines drawn from the Hell Gate or Medicine Rock Passes, in an easterly direction, to the nearest source of the Muscle Shell River, thence down said river to its mouth, thence down the channel of the Missouri River to the mouth of Milk River, thence due north to the forty-ninth parallel, thence due west on said parallel to the main range of the Rocky Mountains, and thence southerly along said range to the place of beginning, shall be the territory of the Blackfoot Nation, over which said nation shall exercise exclusive control, excepting as may be otherwise provided in this treaty. Subject, however, to the provisions of the third article of this treaty, giving the right to hunt, and prohibiting the establishment of permanent villages and the exercise of any exclusive rights within ten miles of the northern line of the common hunting-ground, drawn from the nearest source of the Muscle Shell River to the Medicine Rock Passes, for the period of ninety-nine years.

Provided also, That the Assiniboins shall have the right of hunting, in common with the Blackfeet, in the country lying between the aforesaid eastern boundary line, running from the mouth of Milk River to the forty-ninth parallel, and a line drawn from the left bank of the Missouri River, opposite the Round Butte north, to the forty-ninth parallel.

ARTICLE 5. The parties to this treaty, residing west of the main How to enter and leave the common hunting ground. range of the Rocky Mountains, agree and consent that they will not enter the common hunting ground, nor any part of the Blackfoot territory, or return home, by any pass in the main range of the Rocky Mountains to the north of the Hell Gate or Medicine Rock Passes. And they further agree that they will not hunt or otherwise disturb the game, when visiting the Blackfoot territory for trade or social intercourse.

ARTICLE 6. The aforesaid nations and tribes of Indians, parties to Indians to remain in their respective territories except, etc. this treaty, agree and consent to remain within their own respective countries, except when going to or from, or whilst hunting upon, the "common hunting ground," or when visiting each other for the purpose of trade or social intercourse.

ARTICLE 7. The aforesaid nations and tribes of Indians agree that Citizens may pass through and live in the Indian Territory. citizens of the United States may live in and pass unmolested through the countries respectively occupied and claimed by them. And the Protection against depredations. United States is hereby bound to protect said Indians against depredations and other unlawful acts which white men residing in or passing through their country may commit.

ARTICLE 8. For the purpose of establishing travelling thoroughfares Roads, telegraph lines, and military posts, etc., may be established. through their country, and the better to enable the President to execute the provisions of this treaty, the aforesaid nations and tribes do hereby consent and agree, that the United States may, within the countries respectively occupied and claimed by them, construct roads of every description; establish lines of telegraph and military posts; use materials of every description found in the Indian country; build houses for agencies, missions, schools, farms, shops, mills, stations, and for any other purpose for which they may be required, and permanently occupy as much land as may be necessary for the various purposes above enumerated, including the use of wood for fuel and land for grazing, and that the navigation of all lakes and streams shall be forever free to citizens of the United States.

ARTICLE 9. In consideration of the foregoing agreements, stipula- Annual payment for benefit of Blackfoot Nation. tions, and cessions, and on condition of their faithful observance, the

United States agree to expend, annually, for the Piegan, Blood, Blackfoot, and Gros Ventres tribes of Indians, constituting the Blackfoot Nation, in addition to the goods and provisions distributed at the time of signing the treaty, twenty thousand dollars, annually, for ten years, to be expended in such useful goods and provisions, and other articles, as the President, at his discretion, may from time to time determine; and the superintendent, or other proper officer, shall each year inform the President of the wishes of the Indians in relation thereto: *Provided, however,* That if, in the judgment of the President and Senate, this amount be deemed insufficient, it may be increased not to exceed the sum of thirty-five thousand dollars per year.

Same object. ARTICLE 10. The United States further agree to expend annually, for the benefit of the aforesaid tribes of the Blackfoot Nation, a sum not exceeding fifteen thousand dollars annually, for ten years, in establishing and instructing them in agricultural and mechanical pursuits, and in educating their children, and in any other respect promoting their civilization and Christianization: *Provided, however,* That to accomplish the objects of this article, the President may, at his discretion, apply any or all the annuities provided for in this treaty: *And provided, also,* That the President may, at his discretion, determine in what proportions the said annuities shall be divided among the several tribes.

Provisions to secure peace, and indemnity against Indian depredations. ARTICLE 11. The aforesaid tribes acknowledge their dependence on the Government of the United States, and promise to be friendly with all citizens thereof, and to commit no depredations or other violence upon such citizens. And should any one or more violate this pledge, and the fact be proved to the satisfaction of the President, the property taken shall be returned, or, in default thereof, or if injured or destroyed, compensation may be made by the Government out of the annuities. The aforesaid tribes are hereby bound to deliver such offenders to the proper authorities for trial and punishment, and are held responsible, in their tribal capacity, to make reparation for depredations so committed.

War not to be made on other tribes except in self-defense. Nor will they make war upon any other tribes, except in self-defense, but will submit all matter of difference, between themselves and other Indians, to the Government of the United States, through its agents, **Provision against depredations of other Indians.** for adjustment, and will abide thereby. And if any of the said Indians, parties to this treaty, commit depredations on any other Indians within the jurisdiction of the United States, the same rule shall prevail as that **Criminals to be surrendered.** prescribed in this article in case of depredations against citizens. And the said tribes agree not to shelter or conceal offenders against the laws of the United States, but to deliver them up to the authorities for trial.

Annuities may be stopped in case of violation of this treaty. ARTICLE 12. It is agreed and understood, by and between the parties to this treaty, that if any nation or tribe of Indians aforesaid, shall violate any of the agreements, obligations, or stipulations, herein contained, the United States may withhold, for such length of time as the President and Congress may determine, any portion or all of the annuities agreed to be paid to said nation or tribe under the ninth and tenth articles of this treaty.

Provision against intoxication or the introduction of ardent spirits. ARTICLE 13. The nations and tribes of Indians, parties to this treaty, desire to exclude from their country the use of ardent spirits or other intoxicating liquor, and to prevent their people from drinking the same. Therefore it is provided, that any Indian belonging to said tribes who is guilty of bringing such liquor into the Indian country, or who drinks liquor, may have his or her proportion of the annuities withheld from him or her, for such time as the President may determine.

This treaty to be in full for compensation. ARTICLE 14. The aforesaid nations and tribes of Indians, west of the Rocky Mountains, parties to this treaty, do agree, in consideration of the provisions already made for them in existing treaties, to accept the guarantees of the peaceful occupation of their hunting-grounds, east of the Rocky Mountains, and of remuneration for depredations made by the other tribes, pledged to be secured to them in this treaty out of the annuities of said tribes, in full compensation for the concessions which they, in common with the said tribes, have made in this treaty.

The Indians east of the mountains, parties to this treaty, likewise recognize and accept the guarantees of this treaty, in full compensation for the injuries or depredations which have been, or may be committed by the aforesaid tribes, west of the Rocky Mountains.

ARTICLE 15. The annuities of the aforesaid tribes shall not be taken to pay the debts of individuals. *Annuities not to be taken for debt.*

ARTICLE 16. This treaty shall be obligatory upon the aforesaid nations and tribes of Indians, parties hereto, from the date hereof, and upon the United States as soon as the same shall be ratified by the President and Senate.

In testimony whereof the said A. Cumming and Isaac I. Stevens, commissioners on the part of the United States, and the undersigned chiefs, headmen, and delegates of the aforesaid nations and tribes of Indians, parties to this treaty, have hereunto set their hands and seals at the place and on the day and year hereinbefore written.

A. Cumming. [L. S.]
Isaac I. Stevens. [L. S.]

Piegans:
Nee-ti-nee, or "the only chief," now called the Lame Bull, his x mark. [L. S.]
Mountain Chief, his x mark. [L. S.]
Low Horn, his x mark. [L. S.]
Little Gray Head, his x mark. [L. S.]
Little Dog, his x mark. [L. S.]
Big Snake, his x mark. [L. S.]
The Skunk, his x mark. [L. S.]
The Bad Head, his x mark. [L. S.]
Kitch-eepone-istah, his x mark. [L. S.]
Middle Sitter, his x mark. [L. S.]
Bloods:
Onis-tay-say-nah-que-im, his x mark. [L. S.]
The Father of All Children, his x mark. [L. S.]
The Bull's Back Fat, his x mark. [L. S.]
Heavy Shield, his x mark. [L. S.]
Nah-tose-onistah, his x mark. [L. S.]
The Calf Shirt, his x mark. [L. S.]
Gros Ventres:
Bear's Shirt, his x mark. [L. S.]
Little Soldier, his x mark. [L. S.]
Star Robe, his x mark. [L. S.]
Sitting Squaw, his x mark. [L. S.]
Weasel Horse, his x mark. [L. S.]
The Rider, his x mark. [L. S.]
Eagle Chief, his x mark. [L. S.]
Heap of Bears, his x mark. [L. S.]
Blackfeet:
The Three Bulls, his x mark. [L. S.]
The Old Kootomais, his x mark. [L. S.]
Pow-ah-que, his x mark. [L. S.]
Chief Rabbit Runner, his x mark. [L. S.]
Nez Percés:
Spotted Eagle, his x mark. [L. S.]
Looking Glass, his x mark. [L. S.]

The Three Feathers, his x mark. [L. S.]
Eagle from the Light, his x mark. [L. S.]
The Lone Bird, his x mark. [L. S.]
Ip-shun-nee-wus, his x mark. [L. S.]
Jason, his x mark. [L. S.]
Wat-ti-wat-ti-we-hinck, his x mark. [L. S.]
White Bird, his x mark. [L. S.]
Stabbing Man, his x mark. [L. S.]
Jesse, his x mark. [L. S.]
Plenty Bears, his x mark. [L. S.]
Flathead Nation:
Victor, his x mark. [L. S.]
Alexander, his x mark. [L. S.]
Moses, his x mark. [L. S.]
Big Canoe, his x mark. [L. S.]
Ambrose, his x mark. [L. S.]
Kootle-cha, his x mark. [L. S.]
Michelle, his x mark. [L. S.]
Francis, his x mark. [L. S.]
Vincent, his x mark. [L. S.]
Andrew, his x mark. [L. S.]
Adolphe, his x mark. [L. S.]
Thunder, his x mark. [L. S.]
Piegans:
Running Rabbit, his x mark, [L. S.]
Chief Bear, his x mark. [L. S.]
The Little White Buffalo, his x mark. [L. S.]
The Big Straw, his x mark. [L. S.]
Flathead:
Bear Track, his x mark. [L. S.]
Little Michelle, his x mark. [L. S.]
Palchinah, his x mark. [L. S.]
Bloods:
The Feather, his x mark. [L. S.]
The White Eagle, his x mark. [L. S.]

Executed in presence of—

James Doty, secretary.
Alfred J. Vaughan, jr.
E. Alw. Hatch, agent for Blackfeet.
Thomas Adams, special agent Flathead Nation.
R. H. Lansdale, Indian agent Flathead Nation.
W. H. Tappan, sub-agent for the Nez Percés.
James Bird, ⎫
A. Culbertson, ⎬ Blackfoot interpreters.
Benj. Deroche, ⎭
Benj. Kiser, his x mark, ⎫
Witness, James Doty, ⎬ Flat Head interpreters.
Gustavus Sohon, ⎭

W. Craig, ⎫ Nez Percé
Delaware Jim, his x mark, ⎬ interpreters.
Witness, James Doty, ⎭
A Cree Chief (Broken Arm,) his mark.
Witness, James Doty.
A. J. Hoeekeorsg,
James Croke,
E. S. Wilson,
A. C. Jackson,
Charles Shucette, his x mark.
Christ. P. Higgins,
A. H. Robie,
S. S. Ford, jr.

TREATY WITH THE MOLALA, 1855.

Dec. 21, 1855.

12 Stat., 981.
Ratified Mar. 8, 1859.
Proclaimed Apr. 27, 1859.

Articles of convention and agreement entered into this 21st day of December, 1855, between Joel Palmer, superintendent of Indian affairs, acting for and in behalf of the United States, and the chiefs and head-men of the Mo-lal-la-las or Molel tribe of Indians, they being authorized by their respective bands in council assembled.

Cession of lands to the United States.

ARTICLE 1. The above-named tribe of Indians hereby cede to the United States all their right, title, interest and claim to all that part of Oregon Territory situated and bounded as hereinafter described, the

Boundaries.

same being claimed by them. To wit: Beginning at Scott's Peak, being the northeastern termination of the purchase made of the Umpaquah, and Calapooias of Umpaquah Valley on the 29th day of November, 1854; thence running southernly on the eastern boundary line of that purchase and the purchase of the Cow Creeks, on the 19th day of September, 1853, and the tract purchased of the Scotens, Chestas and Grave Creeks, on the *nineteenth* [eighteenth] day of November, 1854, to the boundary of the Rogue River purchase made on the tenth day of September, 1853; thence along the northern boundary of that purchase to the summit of the Cascade Mountains; thence northerly along the summit of said mountains to a point due east of Scott's Peak; thence west to the place of beginning.

Payments, etc., by the United States.

ARTICLE 2. In consideration of the cession and relinquishment herein made, the United States agree to make the following provisions for said Indians and pay the sums of money as follows:

Privileges of former treaties secured.

1st. To secure to the members of said tribe all the rights and privileges guaranteed by treaty to the Umpaquah and Calapooias, of the Umpaquah Valley, jointly with said tribes, they hereby agreeing to confederate with those bands.

Flouring and saw mill.

2d. To erect and keep in repair and furnish suitable persons to attend the same for the term of ten years, the benefits of which to be shared alike by all the bands confederated, one flouring-mill and one saw-mill.

Smith's and tin shop, etc.

3d. To furnish iron, steel, and other materials for supplying the smith's shop and tin-shop stipulated in the treaty of 29th November, 1854, and pay for the services of the necessary mechanics for that service for five years in addition to the time specified by that treaty.

Manual-labor schools.

4th. To establish a manual-labor school, employ and pay teachers, furnish all necessary materials and subsistence for pupils, of sufficient capacity to accommodate all the children belonging to said confederate bands, of suitable age and condition to attend said school.

Carpenter and joiner.

5th. To employ and pay for the services of a carpenter and joiner for the term of ten years to aid in erecting buildings and making furniture for said Indians, and to furnish tools for use in said service.

6th. To employ and pay for the services of an additional farmer for the term of five years.

Additional farmer.

ARTICLE 3. In consequence of the existence of hostilities between the whites and a portion of the Indian tribes in Southern Oregon and Northern California, and the proximity of the Umpaquah reservation to the mining district, and the consequent fluctuating and transient population, and the frequent commission by whites and Indians of petty offences, calculated to disturb the peace and harmony of the settlement, it is hereby agreed, the Umpaquahs and Calapooias agreeing, that the bands thus confederated shall immediately remove to a tract of land selected on the head-waters of the Yamhill River adjoining the coast reservation, thereon to remain until the proper improvements are made upon that reservation, for the accommodation of said confederate bands, in accordance with the provisions of this and the treaty of 29th November, 1854, and when so made, to remove to said coast reservation, or such other point as may, by direction of the President of the United States, be designated for the permanent residence of said Indians.

Indians to remove to reservation.

ARTICLE 4. For the purpose of carrying out in good faith the objects expressed in the preceding article, it is hereby agreed on the part of the United States, that the entire expense attending the removal of the bands named, including transportation and subsistence, and the erection of temporary buildings at the encampment designated, as well as medical attendance on the sick, shall be paid by the United States.

Expense of removal to be borne by the United States.

ARTICLE 5. It is further agreed that rations, according to the Army regulations, shall be furnished the members of the said confederated bands, and distributed to the heads of families, from the time of their arrival at the encampment on the head-waters of Yamhill River until six months after their arrival at the point selected as their permanent residence.

Rations to be furnished the Indians.

ARTICLE 6. For the purpose of insuring the means of subsistence for said Indians, the United States engage to appropriate the sum of twelve thousand dollars for the extinguishment of title and the payment of improvements made thereon by white settlers to lands in the Grand Round Valley, the point of encampment referred to, to be used as wheat-farms, or other purposes, for the benefit of said Indians, and for the erection of buildings upon the reservation, opening farms, purchasing of teams, tools and stock; the expenditure of which amounts, and the direction of all the provisions of this convention, shall be in accordance with the spirit and meaning of the treaty of 29th November, 1854, with the Umpaquah and Calapooia tribes aforesaid.

Appropriation to extinguish title, etc., of white settlers to lands in Grand Round Valley.

In witness whereof, we, the several parties, hereto set our hands and seals, the day and date before written.

Joel Palmer, [L. S.]
Superintendent Indian Affairs.

Steencoggy, his x mark. [L. S.]
Lattchie, his x mark. [L. S.]
Dugings, his x mark. [L. S.]
Counisnase, his x mark. [L. S.]

Done in presence of the undersigned witnesses—

    C. M. Walker,
    T. R. Magruder,
    John Flett, interpreter.

We, the chiefs and headmen of the Umpaquah and Calapooia tribes, treated with in the Umpaquah Valley, on the 29th day of November, 1854, referred to in the foregoing treaty, to the provisions of this treaty, this day in convention, accede to all the terms therein expressed.

In witness whereof, we do severally hereto set our names and seals, the day and date written in the foregoing treaty.

Louis la Pe Cinque, his x mark.	[L. S.]
Peter, his x mark.	[L. S.]
Tom, his x mark.	[L. S.]
Billy, his x mark.	[L. S.]
Nessick, his x mark.	[L. S.]
George, his x mark.	[L. S.]
Bogus, his x mark.	[L. S.]
Cars, his x mark.	[L. S.]

Done in the presence of the undersigned witnesses—

C. M. Walker,
T. R. Magruder,
John Flett, interpreter.

TREATY WITH THE STOCKBRIDGE AND MUNSEE, 1856.

Feb. 5, 1856.

*11 Stat., 663.
Ratified Apr. 18, 1856.
Proclaimed Sept. 8, 1856.
Ante, p. 325.*

Whereas by Senate amendment to the treaty with the Menomonees of February [*twenty*] eighth, one thousand eight hundred and thirty-one, two townships of land on the east side of Winnebago Lake, Territory of Wisconsin, were set aside for the use of the Stockbridge and Munsee tribes of Indians, all formerly of the State of New York, but a part of whom had already removed to Wisconsin; and

Whereas said Indians took possession of said lands, but dissensions existing among them led to the treaty of September third, one thousand eight hundred and thirty-nine, by which the east half of said two townships was retroceded to the United States, and in conformity to which a part of said Stockbridges and Munsees emigrated west of the Mississippi; and

1843, ch. 101, 5 Stat. 645.

Whereas to relieve them from dissensions still existing by "An act for the relief of the Stockbridge tribe of Indians in the Territory of Wisconsin," approved March third, one thousand eight hundred and forty-three, it was provided, that the remaining townships of land should be divided into lots and allotted between the individual members of said tribe; and

1846, ch. 85, 9 Stat. 55.

Whereas a part of said tribe refused to be governed by the provisions of said act, and a subsequent act was passed on the sixth day of August, one thousand eight hundred and forty-six, repealing the aforementioned act, but without making provision for bona fide purchasers of lots in the townships subdivided in conformity to the said first-named act; and

Whereas it was found impracticable to carry into effect the provisions of the last-mentioned act, and to remedy all difficulties, a treaty was entered into on the twenty-fourth of November, one thousand eight hundred and forty-eight, wherein among other provisions, the tribe obligated itself to remove to the country west of the Mississippi set apart for them by the amendment to said treaty; and

Whereas dissensions have yet been constantly existing amongst them, and many of the tribe refused to remove, when they were offered a location in Minnesota, and applied for a retrocession to them of the township of Stockbridge, which has been refused by the United States; and

Whereas a majority of the said tribe of Stockbridges and the Munsees are averse to removing to Minnesota and prefer a new location in Wisconsin, and are desirous soon to remove and to resume agricultural pursuits, and gradually to prepare for citizenship, and a number of other members of the said tribe desire at the present time to sever their tribal relations and to receive patents for the lots of land at Stockbridge now occupied by them; and

Whereas the United States are willing to exercise the same liberal policy as heretofore, and for the purpose of relieving these Indians from the complicated difficulties, by which they are surrounded, and to establish comfortably together all such Stockbridges and Munsees—wherever they may be now located, in Wisconsin, in the State of New York, or west of the Mississippi—as were included in the treaty of September third, one thousand eight hundred and thirty-nine, and desire to remain for the present under the paternal care of the United States Government; and for the purpose of enabling such individuals of said tribes as are now qualified and desirous to manage their own affairs, to exercise the rights and to perform the duties of the citizen, these articles of agreement have been entered into:

Articles of agreement and convention made and concluded at Stockbridge in the State of Wisconsin, on the fifth day of February, in the year of our Lord one thousand eight hundred and fifty-six, between Francis Huebschmann, commissioner on the part of the United States, and the Stockbridge and Munsee tribes of Indians assembled in general council, and such of the Munsees who were included in the treaty of September third, one thousand eight hundred and thirty-nine, but are yet residing in the State of New York, by their duly authorized delegates, William Mohawk and Joshua Willson.

ARTICLE 1. The Stockbridge and Munsee tribes, who were included in the treaty of September third, one thousand eight hundred and thirty-nine, and all the individual members of said tribes, hereby jointly and severally cede and relinquish to the United States all their remaining right and title in the lands at the town of Stockbridge, State of Wisconsin, the seventy-two sections of land in Minnesota set aside for them by the amendment to the treaty of November twenty-fourth, one thousand eight hundred and forty-eight, the twenty thousand dollars stipulated to be paid to them by the said amendment, the sixteen thousand five hundred dollars invested by the United States in stocks for the benefit of the Stockbridge tribe in conformity to Article 9 of the said treaty, and all claims set up by and for the Stockbridge and Munsee tribes, or by and for the Munsees separately, or by and for any individuals of the Stockbridge tribe who claim to have been deprived of annuities since the year one thousand eight hundred and forty-three, and all such and other claims set up by or for them or any of them are hereby abrogated, and the United States released and discharged therefrom. *Cession of lands at Stockbridge, Wis., and in Minnesota.*

Relinquishment of certain payments and claims.

ARTICLE 2. In consideration of such cession and relinquishment by said Stockbridges and Munsees, the United States agree to select as soon as practicable and to give them a tract of land in the State of Wisconsin, near the southern boundary of the Menomonee reservation, of sufficient extent to provide for each head of a family and others lots of land of eighty and forty acres, as hereinafter provided; every such lot to contain at least one-half of arable land, and to pay to be expended for improvements for the said Stockbridges and Munsees as provided in article 4, the sum of forty-one thousand one hundred dollars, and a further sum of twenty thousand five hundred and fifty dollars to enable them to remove, and the further sum of eighteen thousand dollars, (twelve thousand for the Stockbridges and six thousand for the Munsees,) to be expended, at such time, and in such manner, as may be prescribed by the Secretary of the Interior, in the purchase of stock and necessaries, the discharge of national or tribal debts, and to enable them to settle their affairs. *Another tract to be selected by them and payment made.*

ARTICLE 3. As soon as practicable after the selection of the lands set aside for these Indians by the preceding article, the United States shall cause the same to be surveyed into sections, half and quarter sections, to correspond with the public surveys, and the council of the Stockbridges and Munsees shall under the direction of the superintendent of Indian affairs for the northern superintendency, make a fair and just allotment among the individuals and families of their tribes. Each head of a family shall be entitled to eighty acres of land, and in case his or her family consists of more than four members, if thought expedient by the said council, eighty acres more may be allotted to him or her; each single male person above eighteen years of age shall be entitled to eighty acres; and each female person above eighteen years of age, not belonging to any family, and each orphan child, to forty acres; and sufficient land shall be reserved for the rising generation.

After the said allotment is made, the persons entitled to land may take immediate possession thereof, and the United States will thenceforth and until the issuing of the patents, as hereinafter provided, hold the same in trust for such persons, and certificates shall be issued, in a suitable form, guaranteeing and securing to the holders their possession and an ultimate title to the land; but such certificates shall not be assignable, and shall contain a clause expressly prohibiting the sale or transfer by the holder of the land described therein. After the expiration of ten years upon the application of the holder of such certificate, made with the consent of the said Stockbridge and Munsee council, and when it shall appear prudent and for his or her welfare, the President of the United States may direct, that such restriction on the power of sale shall be withdrawn and a patent issued in the usual form.

Should any of the heads of families die before the issuing of the certificates or patents herein provided for, the same shall issue to their heirs; and if the holder of any such certificate shall die without heirs, his or her land shall not revert to the United States, unless on petition of the Stockbridge and Munsee council for the issuing of a new certificate for the land of such deceased person, to the holder of any other certificate for land, and on the surrendering to the United States of such other certificate, by the holder thereof, the President shall direct the issuing of a new certificate for such land; and in like manner new certificates, may be given for lots of land, the prior certificates for which have been surrendered by the holders thereof.

ARTICLE 4. Of the monies set aside for improvements by the second of these articles, not exceeding one-fourth shall be applied to the building of roads leading to, and through said lands: to the erection of a school-house, and such other improvements of a public character, as will be deemed necessary by the said Stockbridge and Munsee council, and approved by the superintendent of the northern superintendency. The residue of the said fund shall be expended for improvements to be made by and for the different members and families composing the said tribes, according to a system to be adopted by the said council, under the direction of the superintendent aforesaid, and to be first approved by the Commissioner of Indian Affairs.

ARTICLE 5. The persons to be included in the apportionment of the land and money to be divided and expended under the provisions of this agreement, shall be such only, as are actual members of the said Stockbridge and Munsee tribes, (a roll or census of whom shall be taken and appended to this agreement,) their heirs, and legal representatives; and hereafter, the adoption of any individual amongst them shall be null and void, except it be first approved by the Commissioner of Indian Affairs.

Marginal notes:

Survey of such tract and allotment thereof.

Immediate possession given after allotment.

Certificates not assignable to issue.

Provision in case of death of person entitled.

How moneys are to be expended.

Who are entitled to lot.

ARTICLE 6. In case the United States desire to locate on the tract of land to be selected as herein provided, the Stockbridges and Munsees emigrated to the west of the Mississippi in conformity to the treaty of September third, one thousand eight hundred and thirty-nine, the Stockbridges and Munsees, parties to this treaty, agree to receive them as brethren: *Provided,* That none of the said Stockbridges and Munsees, whether now residing at Stockbridge, in the State of Wisconsin, in the State of New York, or west of the Mississippi, shall be entitled to any of these lands or the money stipulated to be expended by these articles, unless they remove to the new location within two years from the ratification hereof. Emigrated Indians may be located on said tract.

ARTICLE 7. The said Stockbridges and Munsees hereby set aside, for educational purposes exclusively, their portion of the annuities under the treaties of November the eleventh, one thousand seven hundred and ninety-four; August eleventh, one thousand eight hundred and twenty-seven; and September third, one thousand eight hundred and thirty-nine. Payments for educational purposes. Ante pp. 34 and 281.

ARTICLE 8. One hundred and fifty dollars valuation of the schoolhouse at Stockbridge made in conformity to article 6 of the treaty of November twenty-fourth, one thousand eight hundred and forty-eight, and remaining unpaid, shall be expended in the erection of a schoolhouse, with the other funds set aside for the same purpose by article 4 of this agreement. Schoolhouse.

ARTICLE 9. About seven and two-fifths acres bounded as follows: Beginning at the northeast corner of lot eighty-nine, in the centre of the military road; thence west, along the north line of said lot, fifty-four and a quarter rods; thence south, thirty-eight and a quarter rods; thence east twenty-eight and a quarter rods; thence north thirty four and a quarter rods; thence east twenty-six rods; thence north, four rods, to the place of beginning, comprising the ground heretofore used by the Stockbridges to bury their dead, shall be patented to the supervisors of the town of Stockbridge, to be held by them and their successors in trust for the inhabitants of said town, to be used by them as a cemetery, and the proceeds from cemetery lots and burial-places to be applied in fencing, clearing, and embellishing the grounds. Grounds for a cemetery.

ARTICLE 10. It is agreed that all roads and highways laid out by authority of law shall have right of way through the lands set aside for said Indians, on the same terms as are provided by law for their location through lands of citizens of the United States. Right of way of roads.

ARTICLE 11. The object of this instrument being to advance the welfare and improvement of said Indians, it is agreed, if it prove insufficient from causes which cannot now be foreseen, to effect these ends, that the President of the United States may, by and with the advice and consent of the Senate, adopt such policy in the management of their affairs, as in his judgment may be most beneficial to them; or Congress may, hereafter, make such provision by law, as experience shall prove to be necessary. President and Senate or Congress may regulate affairs.

ARTICLE 12. The said Stockbridges and Munsees agree to suppress the use of ardent spirits among their people and to resist by all prudent means, its introduction in their settlements. Provision against ardent spirits.

ARTICLE 13. The Secretary of the Interior, if deemed by him expedient and proper, may examine into the sales made by the Stockbridge Indians, to whom lots of land were allotted in conformity to the acts of Congress, entitled "An act for the relief of the Stockbridge tribe of Indians in the Territory of Wisconsin," approved March third, one thousand eight hundred and forty-three; and if it shall be found that any of the said sales have been improperly made, or that a proper consideration has not been paid, the same may be disapproved or set aside. By the direction of the said Secretary, patents to such lots of Sales of allotment under act of 1843, ch. 101, may be examined into, set aside, or confirmed.

5 Stat., 645.

land shall be issued to such persons as shall be found to be entitled to the same.

Sales of sundry lots. ARTICLE 14. The lots of land the equitable title to which shall be found not to have passed by valid sales from the Stockbridge Indians to purchasers, and such lots as have, by the treaty of November twenty-fourth, one thousand eight hundred and forty-eight, been receded to the United States, shall be sold at the minimum price of ten dollars per acre for lots fronting on Lake Winnebago, on both sides of the military road, and all the lands in the three tiers of lots next to Lake Winnebago, and at five dollars per acre for the residue of the lands in said township of Stockbridge. Purchasers of lots, on which improvements were made by Stockbridge Indians shall pay, in addition to the said minimum price, the appraised value of such improvements. To actual settlers on any of said lots possessing the qualifications requisite to acquire pre-emption rights, or being civilized persons of Indian descent, not members of any tribe, who shall prove, to the satisfaction of the register of the land district to which the township of Stockbridge shall be attached, that he or she has made improvements to the value of not less than fifty dollars on such lot, and that he or she is actually residing on it; the time of paying the purchase-price may be extended for a term not exceeding three years from the ratification hereof, as shall be deemed advisable by the President of the United States, provided, that no such actual settler shall be permitted to pre-empt, in the manner aforesaid, more than one lot, or two contiguous lots, on which he has proved to have made improvements exceeding the value of one hundred dollars. The residue of said lots shall be brought into market as other Government lands are offered for sale, and shall not be sold at a less price than the said minimum price; and all said sales shall be made, and the patents provided for in these articles shall be issued in accordance with the survey made in conformity to said act of March third, one thousand eight hundred and forty-three, unless, in the opinion of the Secretary of the Interior, a new survey shall be deemed necessary and proper.

Appraised value of improvements on the ceded land to be paid. ARTICLE 15. The United States agree to pay, within one year after the ratification of this agreement, the appraised value of the improvements upon the lands herein ceded and relinquished to the United States, to the individuals claiming the same, the valuation of such improvements, to be made by a person to be selected by the superintendent of Indian affairs for the northern superintendency, and not to exceed, in the aggregate, the sum of five thousand dollars.

Certain persons to have patents in fee of certain lots in full of all claims. ARTICLE 16. The hereinafter named Stockbridge Indians, having become sufficiently advanced in civilization, and being desirous of separating from the Stockbridge tribe, and of enjoying the privileges granted to persons of Indian descent by the State of Wisconsin, and in consideration of ceding and relinquishing to the United States all their rights in the lands and annuities of the Stockbridge tribe of Indians, and in the annuities, money, or land, to which said Indians now are or may hereafter be entitled, the United States agree to issue patents in fee-simple to the said Stockbridge Indians to the lots of land, at the town of Stockbridge, described and set opposite their names.

Names of persons.	Lots to be patented to them.	Lots, the privilege of entering which on the same terms of payment as prescribed for actual settlers in article 14 is granted.
John Moore	9, 38, and 105	226 and 187
Job Moore	69, 176 and 191	280
Sopha Moore	177	

Names of persons	Lots to be patented to them.	Lots, the privilege of entering which on the same terms of payment as prescribed for actual settlers in article 14 is granted.
Caleb Moore	223	
Elizabeth Moore	234	
Henry Moore	264	233
Daniel Davids' heirs	47, N. half 48, 60	
John Littleman's heirs	113	
Jane Dean's heirs	30	
A. Miller's heirs	14	
Mary McAllister	N. half 280	S. half 280
Hope Welch	284	
Catharine Mills	S. half 194	N. half 194
Nancy Hom	N. half 270	S. half 270
Margaret Beaulieu	N. half 238	S. half 238
Sally Shenandoah	76	
Jacob Moore	233	190
Martha Moore, wife of Jacob Moore	253	
Betsey Manague	N. half 349	S. half 349
Levy Konkapot	61, 152	
Mary Hendrick	78	
John W. Abrams	59	

The said Mary Hendrick, and Levy Konkapot, John W. Abrams to have the privilege of joining again the said Stockbridges and Munsees in their new location.

ARTICLE 17. So much of the treaties of September third, one thousand eight hundred and thirty-nine, and of November twenty-fourth, one thousand eight hundred and forty-eight, as is in contravention or in conflict with the stipulations of this agreement, is hereby abrogated and annulled.

Inconsistent treaties annulled.

ARTICLE 18. This instrument shall be binding upon the contracting parties whenever the same shall be ratified by the President and the Senate of the United States.

In testimony whereof, the said Francis Huebschmann, commissioner as aforesaid, and the chiefs, headmen, and members of the said Stockbridge and Munsee tribes, and the said delegates of the Munsees of New York, have hereunto set their hands and seals at the place and on the day and year hereinbefore written.

Francis Huebschmann,   [L. S.]
Commissioner on the part of the United States.

Ziba T. Peters, sachem,	[L. S.]	James Joshua, his x mark.	[L. S.]
John N. Chicks,	[L. S.]	Benjamin Pye, 2d, his x mark.	[L. S.]
Jeremiah Slingerland, } Counsellors.	[L. S.]	John Hendricks,	[L. S.]
John W. Abrams, }	[L. S.]	Eli Williams, his x mark.	[L. S.]
Levi Konkapot,	[L. S.]	Cornelius Anthony,	[L. S.]
Joshua Willson, his x mark.	[L. S.]	Lewis Hendrick,	[L. S.]
Delegate of Munsees of New York.		Adam Davids,	[L. S.]
Thomas S. Branch,	[L. S.]	Elias Konkapot, his x mark.	[L. S.]
Jacob Davids, his x mark.	[L. S.]	Jediehal Wilber,	[L. S.]
John W. Quinney, jr. his x mark.	[L. S.]	William Gardner,	[L. S.]
Timothy Jourden, his x mark.	[L. S.]	Stephen Gardner,	[L. S.]
John Yoccom, his x mark.	[L. S.]	Simeon Gardner, his x mark.	[L. S.]
William Mohawk, his x mark.	[L. S.]	Polly Bennett, her x mark.	[L. S.]
Delegate of Munsees of New York.		Eleanor Charles, her x mark.	[L. S.]
George T. Bennett,	[L. S.]	Mary Hendrick, her x mark.	[L. S.]
Jacob Konkapot,	[L. S.]	Susan Hendrick, her x mark.	[L. S.]
Jessee Jourden, his x mark.	[L. S.]	Joseph Doxtator, his x mark.	[L. S.]
Jeremiah Bennett, his x mark.	[L. S.]	Joseph L. Chicks,	[L. S.]
Isaac Jacobs, his x mark.	[L. S.]	Solomon Davids, his x mark.	[L. S.]

Job Moore, his x mark.	[L. S.]	Cornelius Yoccom, his x mark.	[L. S.]
Sophia Moore, her x mark.	[L. S.]	Harriet Jourden, her x mark.	[L. S.]
Caleb Moore, his x mark.	[L. S.]	Peter D. Littleman, his x mark.	[L. S.]
Elizabeth Moore, her x mark.	[L. S.]	Lovina Pye, her x mark.	[L. S.]
Henry Moore, his x mark.	[L. S.]	Charlotte Palmer, her x mark.	[L. S.]
Elizabeth Boman, her x mark.	[L. S.]	Ramona Miller, her x mark.	[L. S.]
Humble Jourden,	[L. S.]	Hannah Turkey, her x mark.	[L. S.]
Phebe Pye, her x mark.	[L. S.]	Didema Miller,	[L. S.]
Jacob Jacobs,	[L. S.]	Dr. Big Deer, his x mark.	[L. S.]
Aaron Konkapot,	[L. S.]	Elizabeth Wilber, her x mark.	[L. S.]
Jeremiah Gardner, his x mark.	[L. S.]	Darius Davids, his x mark.	[L. S.]
Andrew Wilber, his x mark.	[L. S.]	Harvy Johnston, his x mark.	[L. S.]
Prudence Quinney, her x mark.	[L. S.]	Mary Eliza Butler, her x mark.	[L. S.]
Bersheba Wright,	[L. S.]	Thomas Tousey,	[L. S.]
Alonzo Quinney, his x mark.	[L. S.]	Chester Tousey,	[L. S.]
Rebecca Thompson, her x mark.	[L. S.]	Daniel Tousey,	[L. S.]
Dianah Davids,	[L. S.]	Sarah Tousey, her x mark.	[L. S.]
Mary Ann Littleman, her x mark.	[L. S.]	Philena Pye, 1st, her x mark.	[L. S.]
Peter Bennett, sr., his x mark.	[L. S.]	Lucinda Quinney, her x mark.	[L. S.]
Peter Bennett, jr., his x mark.	[L. S.]	Sally Schanandoah, her x mark.	[L. S.]
Daniel Gardner,	[L. S.]	Mary McAllister, her x mark.	[L. S.]
Bashiba Brown, her x mark.	[L. S.]	Hope Welch, her x mark.	[L. S.]
Dennis T. Turkey,	[L. S.]	Catharine Mills, her x mark.	[L. S.]
Benjamin Pye, 3d, his x mark.	[L. S.]	Nancy Hom, her x mark.	[L. S.]
Abram Pye, sr., his x mark.	[L. S.]	Margaret Bolrew, her x mark.	[L. S.]
Abram Pye, jr., his x mark.	[L. S.]	Eliza Franks, her x mark.	[L. S.]
David Pye, his x mark.	[L. S.]	Lucinda Gardner, her x mark.	[L. S.]
Elizabeth Doxtator, her x mark.	[L. S.]	Mary Jane Boman, her x mark.	[L. S.]
Margaret Davids, her x mark.	[L. S.]	Debby Baldwin, her x mark.	[L. S.]
Cornelius Aaron, his x mark.	[L. S.]	Edward Boman, his x mark.	[L. S.]
Anna Turkey, her x mark.	[L. S.]	Hannah Smith, her x mark.	[L. S.]
Louisa Konkapot, her x mark.	[L. S.]	Moses Smith, his x mark.	[L. S.]
Phebe Shicket, her x mark.	[L. S.]	Betsy Manague, her x mark.	[L. S.]
Elizabeth Aaron, her x mark.	[L. S.]	Dolly Doxtator, her x mark.	[L. S.]
Rebecca Aaron, her x mark.	[L. S.]	Aaron Smith, his x mark.	[L. S.]
Benjamin Pye, 4th, his x mark.	[L. S.]	Polly Smith, her x mark.	[L. S.]
Paul Pye, his x mark.	[L. S.]	Mary Thebeant, her x mark.	[L. S.]
Jackson Chicks, and 2 heirs of Josiah Chicks,	[L. S.]	Jacob Moore,	[L. S.]
		Abigail Moore,	[L. S.]
Electa W. Candy, sister of the late John W. Quinney,	[L. S.]	Clarissa Miller, her x mark.	[L. S.]
		Polly Konkapot, her x mark.	[L. S.]
Mary Jane Dean, } heirs of Jane Dean.	[L. S.]	John Lewis, his x mark.	[L. S.]
Daniel P. Dean,	[L. S.]	James Chicks, his x mark.	[L. S.]
John W. Dean,	[L. S.]		

Signed and sealed in presence of—
Theodore Koven, Secretary to Commissioner.
Saml. W. Beall,
Adam Scherff,
James Christie,
Lemuel Goodell,
Enos McKenzie,
Elam C. Pease.

Roll and census made in conformity to Article 5 of the foregoing treaty.

Names.—Census of the Munsees of New York, included in the treaty of September 3, 1839.	Men.	Women.	Children.	Total.
Isaac Durkee	1	1	2	4
William Mohawk	1	1	2	4
Titus Mohawk	--	--	1	1
Thomas Snake's widow	--	1	1	2
Austin Half White	--	--	1	1
Clarissa Spragg	--	1	7	8
George Moses	1	1	2	4
Jonathan Waterman	1	1	5	7
Jonathan Titus	1	--	--	1
Levy Halftown	1	1	7	9
Jefferson Halftown	1	1	--	2
Eunice Red Eye	--	1	5	6
John Wilson	1	1	3	5
Joshua Wilson	1	1	2	4

Names.—Census of Stockbridges and Munsees at Stockbridge, Wisconsin.	Men.	Women.	Children.	Total.
John N. Chicks	1	--	3	4
Jeremiah Slingerland	1	1	3	5
John W. Abrams	1	1	4	6
Ziba T. Peters	1	1	2	4
Levy Konkapot	1	--	--	1
Thomas S. Branch	1	1	2	4
Jacob Davids	1	1	4	6
John W. Quinney, jr	1	1	2	4
Timothy Jourdan	1	1	3	5
John Yoccum	1	1	4	6
George T. Bennet	1	1	3	5
Jacob Konkapot	1	1	3	5
Jesse Jourdan	1	1	2	4
Jeremiah Bennet	1	1	2	4
Isaac Jacobs	1	1	1	3
James Joshua	1	--	--	1
Benjamin Pye, 2d	1	2	4	7
John P. Hendricks	1	1	2	4
Eli Williams	1	1	3	5
Cornelius Anthony	1	1	2	4
Lewis Hendrick	1	--	--	1
Adam Davids	1	1	2	4
Elias Konkapot	1	--	--	1
Jedediah Wilber	1	--	--	1
William Gardner	1	1	3	5
Stephen Gardner	1	1	1	3
Simeon Gardner	1	1	1	3
Polly Bennett	--	1	2	3
Eleanor Charles	--	1	--	1
Mary Hendrick	--	1	--	1
Susannah Hendrick	--	1	--	1
Joseph Doxtater	1	1	--	2
Joseph L. Chicks	1	-	3	4
James Chicks	--	--	1	1
Solomon Davids	1	1	1	3
Elizabeth Bowman	--	1	3	4
Humble Jourdan	1	1	--	2
Phebe Pye	--	1	--	1
Jacob Jacobs	1	--	--	1
Aaron Konkapot	1	--	--	1
Jeremiah Gardiner	1	--	--	1
Andrew Wilber	1	--	--	1
Prudence Quinney	--	1	--	1
Bethseba Wright	--	1	--	1
Alonzo Quinney	1	--	--	1
Rebecca Thompson	--	1	--	1
Peter Bennett, sen	1	1	4	6
Peter Bennett, jr	1	1	--	2
Daniel Gardner	1	--	--	1
Bathseba Brown	--	1	--	1
Dennis T. Turkey	1	1	--	2
Benjamin Pye, 3d	1	1	4	6
Abram Pye, sen	1	--	2	3
Abram Pye, jr	1	--	--	1
David Pye	1	--	--	1
Elizabeth Doxtater	--	1	4	5
Margaret Davids	--	1	1	2
Cornelius Aaron	1	1	1	3
Anna Turkey	--	1	--	1

Names.—Census of Stockbridges and Munsees at Stockbridge, Wisconsin.	Men.	Women	Children.	Total.
Phebe Skicket	--	1	--	1
Louisa Konkapot	--	1	--	1
Elizabeth Aaron	--	1	--	1
Rebecca Aaron	--	1	--	1
Benjamin Pye, 4th	1	1	3	5
Paul Pye	1	--	--	1
Jackson Chicks and one other orphan, heirs of Josiah Chicks	--	--	2	2
Electa W. Candy	1	1	4	6
Cornelius Yoccum	1	1	3	5
Harriet Jourdan	--	1	--	1
Levina Pye	--	1	--	1
Charlotte Palmer	--	1	3	4
Remona Miller	--	1	2	3
Hannah Turkey	--	1	3	4
Bigdeer	1	--	--	1
Elizabeth Wilber	--	1	2	3
Harvey Johnson	1	1	7	9
Mary Eliza Butler	--	1	3	4
Thomas Tousey	1	1	6	8
Chester Tousey	1	1	5	7
Daniel Tousey	1	--	--	1
Sarah Tousey	--	1	--	1
Philena Pye, 1st	--	1	--	1
Lucinda Quinney	--	1	2	3
Eliza Franks	--	1	1	2
Lucinda Gardner	--	1	1	2
Mary Jane Bowman	--	1	--	1
Debby Baldwin	--	1	2	3
Edward Bowman	1	1	1	3
Moses Smith	1	1	2	4
Dolly Doxtater	--	1	1	2
Polly Smith	--	1	--	1
Aaron Smith, (Hannah Smith)	1	1	2	4
Polly Konkapot	--	1	--	1
John Lewis	1	--	--	1
Peter D. Littleman	1	1	4	6
Clarissa Miller	--	1	--	1
John P. Quinney, (absent)	1	1	--	2
Paul Quinney, (absent)	1	1	1	3
Charles Stevens	1	--	--	1
Samuel Stevens	1	1	--	2
Samuel Miller	--	1	4	5
John Metoxen, sen	1	1	--	2
Simeon S. Metoxen	1	1	4	6
Nicholas Palmer	1	1	2	4
Daniel Metoxen	1	--	--	1
Moses Doxtator	1	1	2	4
Darius Charles	1	--	2	3
Catharine Butterfield	--	1	1	2
Washington Quinney	1	1	3	5
Ezekiel Robinson	1	--	--	1
Sally Pye	--	1	2	3
James Palmer	1	--	2	3
Jonas Thompson	1	1	3	5
William Thompson	1	--	--	1
Austin E. Quinney	1	1	3	5
John Beaman	1	--	--	1
Simeon Quinney	1	1	1	3
Elizabeth Palmer	--	1	--	1

Names.—Census of Stockbridges and Munsees at Stockbridge, Wisconsin.	Men.	Women.	Children.	Total.
Margaret Miller	--	1	2	3
William Miller	1	--	--	1
Zachariah Miller	1	1	--	2
Solomon Duchamp	1	--	--	1
John Metoxen, jr	1	--	--	1
Joseph M. Quinney	1	1	1	3
Mary Quinney	--	1	--	1
Frelinghuysen Quinney	1	--	--	1
Bartholomew Bowman	1	--	--	1
Lewis Bowman	1	--	--	1

FRANCIS HUEBSCHMANN,
Commissioner on the part of the United States.
ZIBA T. PETERS, *Sachem.*

Roll and census of Stockbridges and Munsees who prefer to remain at Stockbridge according to article 16.

Names.	Men.	Women.	Children.	Total.
John Moore	1	--	--	1
Job Moore	1	1	6	8
Sophia Moore	--	1	--	1
Caleb Moore	--	--	--	--
Elizabeth Moore	--	--	--	--
Henry Moore	1	--	1	2
Diana Davids	--	1	--	1
Mary Ann Littleman	--	1	1	2
Mary Jane Dean — {Children	--	--	1	1
Daniel P. Dean — of Jane	--	--	1	1
John W. Dean — Dean. }	--	--	1	1
Dideema Miller	--	1	--	1
Darius Davids	1	--	--	1
Mary McAllister	--	--	1	1
Hope Welch	--	1	--	1
Catharine Mills	--	1	--	1
Nancy Hom	--	1	--	1
Margaret Beaulieu	--	1	5	6
Sally Schenandoah	--	1	2	3
Betsey Manague	--	1	5	6
Jacob Moore	1	1	2	4

FRANCIS HUEBSCHMANN,
Commissioner on the part of the United States.
ZIBA T. PETERS, *Sachem.*

DEPARTMENT OF THE INTERIOR,
Office of Indian Affairs, March 3, 1856.

SIR: Referring to my last two annual reports, where the embarrassed condition of the Stockbridge and Munsee Indians is discussed, and to the paragraph of the general Indian appropriation bill, of the 3d March, 1855, Stat. at Large, vol. x, p. 699, where there is appropriated, "for the purpose of enabling the President to treat with, and arrange the difficulties existing among the Stockbridge and Munsee Indians, of Lake Winnebago, in the State of Wisconsin, arising out of the acts of Congress of third March, eighteen hundred and forty-three, and August sixth, eighteen hundred and forty-six, and the treaty of twenty-fourth of November, eighteen hundred and forty-eight, in such manner as may be just to the Indians, and with their assent, and not inconsistent with the legal rights of white persons who may reside on the Stockbridge reserve, of the claim of the United States under the treaty of eighteen hundred and forty-eight, the sum of fifteen hundred dollars;" and also to the treaty which was made between these Indians and Superintendent Francis Huebschmann, during the last

Letter of Geo. W. Manypenny, Indian Commissioner.

summer, which, for reasons then given you, was disapproved of, I have now the honor to send up a treaty concluded with them on the 5th ultimo, by Superintendent Huebschmann, the provisions of which are approved by me, and would recommend, if you agree, that it may be laid before the President, to the end, if approved by him, that it may be sent to the Senate for its constitutional action thereon.

And I herewith transmit a copy of the letter of the superintendent sending on said treaty, together with a copy of a power of attorney from certain Munsees to Isaac Durkee, William Mohawk, and Joshua Wilson, for purposes therein indicated.

I would merely remark that, by locating the Stockbridges in Wisconsin instead of Minnesota about $20,000 of expense would be saved in removal, while a location in Minnesota could not be more out of the way of the whites, and the lands there would be worth to the Government at least as much as the price to be paid the Menomonees.

Very respectfully, your obedient servant,

GEO. W. MANYPENNY *Commissioner.*

Hon. ROBERT McCLELLAND,
  Secretary of the Interior.

NORTHERN SUPERINTENDENCY,
Milwaukie, February 23, 1856.

Letter of Francis Huebschmann, superintendent.

SIR: I have the honor to enclose a treaty with the Stockbridges and Munsees, concluded in conformity to your instructions. In consequence of the complicated difficulties at Stockbridge, and the factious spirit ruling among the Indians, the task imposed upon me was not an easy one, and required extraordinary patience and forbearance. I believe I have used all proper means to make the arrangement contemplated by the treaty as acceptable to all parties interested as could be expected under the circumstances. However, about one-fifth of the Indians, headed by Austin E. Quinney, and mostly consisting of members of the Quinney family, did not sign the treaty, but without giving any sensible reason. The only two objections raised by Austin E. Quinney to the draft of the treaty were: *First*, That the issuing of patents to lands, to be apportioned to the individuals of the tribe, was contemplated. This objection was virtually obviated by amending the treaty, so that the application for a patent to be made after ten years, has first to be consented to by the general council of the Stockbridges and Munsees.

His second objection was, that there was no provision made for the payment of a claim he himself has against the tribe. Though I invited him to submit the claim to me for examination, he did not do so, and, from what I learned from himself and others, it appears that it would, if submitted, not bear very accurate examination, as about half of it is made up of high charges for meals furnished councillors of the Stockbridges, and the other half for funds advanced to one certain Chandler, on his share of the twenty thousand dollars to be paid under the amendment to the treaty of 1848 for procuring the adoption of the said amendment.

The real objection on the part of the Quinneys to the re-organization of the Stockbridges and Munsees under this treaty is, no doubt, the certainty staring them in the face, that their rule over the tribe will be at an end if the treaty is ratified. To show what use this family has made of their power over the tribe, I will only mention a few instances. Though claiming to hold their lands again in commonalty in consequence of the law of August 6, 1846, Austin E. Quinney, by barter and trade carried on with widows and other Indians, and by advancing to them a few provisions, pretended to have bought their lots of land, and, under the treaty of 1848, he not only received pay for the improvements on all these lands, (1,440 acres,) $2,760.63, but of the sixteen thousand five hundred dollars paid under V article of treaty of 1848 he received $3,083, while under a proper per capita apportionment, the share of his family would not have been much more than about three hundred dollars. The interest of the $16,500, to be paid "as other annuities are paid by the United States," has been apportioned in direct violation of the said treaty until the Stockbridge affairs came under my superintendence, in the same manner as the $16,500 under article 5 had peen paid; and for the benefit of Sam'l Miller, even that illegal apportionment was falsified so as to pay him one-half of $1,662.50, and the interest on the other half instead of $412.50, the proportion to which he would have been entitled by the quantity of land held by him at the treaty of 1848. Austin E. Quinney realized about a thousand dollars more by selling his pretended right of occupancy to lots, so that it appears, that he has received about seven thousand dollars in addition to what he has received of the money paid to his tribe by the State of New York, and it is no doubt mortifying to him that his share of moneys hereafter, is to be no larger than that of any other member of the tribe. A great part of the funds received from the State of New York has been used by the Quinney family for their own aggrandizement and the sending of delegations to Washington; and the wishes of a majority of the Stockbridges in relation to the application of those funds, have been frequently disregarded, and at the present time Sam'l Miller has been sent by Austin E. Quinney as delegate to Washington with a part of those funds, in direct opposition to the wishes of the majority.

I proposed to Austin E. Quinney and his followers to patent to them lands at Stockbridge, and to make other stipulations favorable to them, if they preferred to remain there and to separate from the tribe; but as they would not declare their willingness to accept of such provisions, and as Quinney declared that he would probably desire to remove with the others if the lands to be selected were of good quality, and deeming it more beneficial to them that they should remove with the others and be settled by themselves, if they preferred it, in some corner of the new reservation, I did not feel prompted to provide for their remaining at Stockbridge, and increased the sums to be paid in proportion to their number.

I had made no secret, since my visit to Stockbridge during the fore part of December last, of the arrangement contemplated in relation to lands and land-titles at Stockbridge, (articles 13 and 14,) and it appeared generally satisfactory to white settlers; yet there will be always found meddlesome individuals, and it appears that, at the request of a resident of Stockbridge, who, however, has no land himself, a lawyer of Green Bay had drawn up a petition or memorial asking the treaty to be amended.

When I saw the document no names were attached to it, and I have not inquired afterwards if it has been signed by anybody and forwarded. I read it very hastily, but it left the impression upon my mind that little legal knowledge was displayed by its author. Since the authority to issue patents, given by the law of 1843, was destroyed by the repealing act of 1846, and the list of patents to lots to be granted under the treaty of 1848 is imperfect and incorrect, the settlers at Stockbridge, if they understand it, will be the last to object to authority being granted to the proper officer to issue patents; and the investigation of sales made by Indians provided for, I think, will not be seriously objected to, except by such who are afraid that the consideration paid by them would be found to have consisted of whiskey.

The minimum price fixed in the treaty for the land to be sold by the United States Government is not too high nor unjust to any class of the settlers of Stockbridge. Those who settled there shortly after the treaty of 1848, and bought out, for a small consideration, the right of occupancy of Indians, to their houses, clearings, and fields, have since mostly confined themselves to cultivating the fields already made and raised fine crops, without paying any taxes or bearing any of the hardships of a new settlement. It has not been so much by their labor that these lands have become valuable, as by the settlements and improvements made in the surrounding country and the general prosperity of the State. The settlers who have recently squatted on lots of land at Stockbridge, have gone there with the perfect knowledge of the price which was expected to be fixed on those lands, and since it has become known that the treaty was signed, that part of the State has been under great excitement, and many have flocked to Stockbridge to make claims and to avail themselves of the privileges contemplated to be extended to actual settlers by the treaty. It is feared that there are even more settlers and claimants than lots of land, and if the price should be reduced the excitement would, no doubt, become more intense, and the land-officers would find it more difficult to settle the conflicting claims. The privilege of entering lands at the terms of payment as prescribed for actual settlers in article 14, granted to a number of Indians by article 16, was considered by all as very valuable, which seems to prove beyond a doubt that the price is considered very moderate. If the petition above referred to has been signed generally by the settlers at Stockbridge, they have done so in consequence of its being represented to them that it could do no harm to try to get the lands from the Government at a less price, and not because the price is too high or unjust to any one of them. A power of attorney of the Munsees of New York to their delegate is herewith enclosed.

Very respectfully, your obedient servant,

FRANCIS HUEBSCHMANN,
Superintendent.

Hon. GEORGE W. MANYPENNY,
Commissioner of Indian Affairs, Washington, D. C.

Know all men that by these presents we make, constitute, and appoint Isaac Durkee, William Mohawk, and Joshua Wilson, or either two of them in the absence of the other, to receive from the commissioner of the United States the share of us, and each of us, and our families in money, which, in consideration of annuities due us from the United States, or by virtue and effect of a treaty which it is understood, is about to be made between the United States and the Stockbridge and Munsee tribes of Indians, we are informed will be our due, and will be paid to us by the said commissioner, or by the superintendent of Indian affairs for Wisconsin. And we hereby authorize our attorneys as aforesaid to give receipts and vouchers to the said commissioner or superintendent, as may be right, or he may require; our intention being that our said attorneys shall transmit to us, in the State of New York, said moneys, to enable us immediately to remove to, improve and subsist in our new homes in the State of Wisconsin.

Hereby ratifying the acts of our attorneys in the premises.

In witness whereof, we have hereunto set our hands and seals, this, ———— day of January, A. D. 1856.

ISAAC DURKEE.	
WILLIAM MOHAWK.	
TITUS MOHAWK,	his x mark.
AUSTIN HALF WHITE,	his x mark.
CLARISSA SPRAGG,	his x mark.
GEORGE MOSES,	his x mark.
JONATHAN WATERMAN,	his x mark.
JONATHAN TITUS,	his x mark.
LEVY HALF TOWN,	his x mark.
JEFFERSON HALF TOWN,	his x mark.

In presence of—
SAM'L W. BEALL,
JOHN ARMSTONG.

STATE OF NEW YORK, *Cattaraugus County, ss.*

On this 19th day of January, A. D. 1856, came before me Isaac Durkee, William Mohawk, Titus Mohawk, Austin Half White, Clarissa Spragg, George Moses, Jonathan Watersnake, Jonathan Titus, Levy Half Town, Jefferson Half Town, proven to me by the oath of George Jamison, to me well known, to be the individuals who signed and executed the within instrument of attorney, and acknowledged that they executed it freely.

GEORGE JAMISON, his x mark.

Sworn and subscribed before me, this 19th day of January, 1856.

ELISHA BROWN,
Justice of the Peace.

TREATY WITH THE MENOMINEE, 1856.

Whereas a treaty was entered into at Stockbridge, in the State of Wisconsin, on the fifth of the present month, between the United States of America on the one part, and the Stockbridge and Munsee tribes of Indians on the other, stipulating that a new home shall be furnished to the said Stockbridge and Munsee Indians, near the south line of the Menomonee reservation; and

Feb. 11, 1856.
11 Stat., 679.
Ratified Apr. 18, 1856.
Proclaimed Apr. 24, 1856.

Whereas the United States desire to locate said Stockbridges and Munsees near the said line in the western part of the said reservation, on lands on which no permanent settlements have been made by the Menomonees; and

Whereas there is no objection on the part of the Menomonees to the location of the Stockbridges and Munsees in their neighborhood, therefore this agreement and convention has been entered into.

Articles of agreement made and concluded at Keshena, State of Wisconsin, on the eleventh day of February, in the year of our Lord eighteen hundred and fifty-six, between Francis Huebschmann, commissioner on the part of the United States, and the Menomonee tribe of Indians, assembled in general council. — *Title*

ARTICLE 1. The Menomonee tribe of Indians cede to the United States a tract of land, not to exceed two townships in extent, to be selected in the western part of their present reservation on its south line, and not containing any permanent settlements made by any of their number, for the purpose of locating thereon the Stockbridge and Munsee Indians, and such others of the New York Indians as the United States may desire to remove to the said location within two years from the ratification hereof. — *Cession of land to the United States.*

ARTICLE 2. The United States agree to pay for the said cession, in case the said New York Indians will be located on the said lands, at the rate of sixty cents per acre; and it is hereby stipulated, that the monies so to be paid shall be expended in a like manner, to promote the improvement of the Menomonees, as is stipulated by the third article of the treaty of May twelfth, eighteen hundred and fifty-four, for the expenditure of the forty thousand dollars which had been set aside for their removal and subsistence, west of the Mississippi, by the treaty of October eighteenth, eighteen hundred and forty-eight. — *Payment for said cession.*

ARTICLE 3. To promote the welfare and the improvement of the said Menomonees, and friendly relations between them and the citizens of the United States, it is further stipulated—

1. That in case this agreement and the treaties made previously with the Menomonees should prove insufficient, from causes which cannot now been [be] foreseen, to effect the said objects, the President of the United States may, by and with the advice and consent of the Senate, adopt such policy in the management of the affairs of the Menomonees — *Laws may be made for the affairs of the Menomonees.*

as in his judgment may be most beneficial to them; or Congress may, hereafter, make such provision by law as experience shall prove to be necessary.

Suppression of use of ardent spirits.

2. That the Menomonees will suppress the use of ardent spirits among their people, and resist, by all prudent means, its introduction in their settlements.

Annuities may be paid semiannually or quarterly.

3. That the President of the United States, if deemed by him conducive to the welfare of the Menomonees, may cause their annuity monies to be paid to them in semi-annual or quarterly instalments.

Right of way of roads.

4. That all roads and highways, laid out by authority of law, shall have right of way through the lands of the said Indians on the same terms as are provided by law for their location through lands of citizens of the United States.

ARTICLE 4. This instrument shall be binding upon the contracting parties whenever the same shall be ratified by the President and Senate of the United States.

In testimony whereof, the said Francis Huebschmann, commissioner as aforesaid, and the chiefs and headmen of the said Menomonee tribe, in presence and with the consent of the warriors and young men of the said tribe, assembled in general council, have hereunto set their hands and seals at the place and on the day and year hereinbefore written.

Francis Huebschmann, [L. S.]
Commissioner on the part of the United States.

Osh-kosh, his x mark.	[L. S.]	Naw-no-ha-toke, his x mark.	[L. S.]
Sho-ne-niew, his x mark.	[L. S.]	Match-a-kin-naew, his x mark.	[L. S.]
Ke-she-na, his x mark.	[L. S.]	Mah-mah-ke-wet, his x mark.	[L. S.]
La-motte, his x mark.	[L. S.]	Ko-man-e-kim, his x mark.	[L. S.]
Pe-quah-kaw-nah, his x mark.	[L. S.]	Shaw-puy-tuck, his x mark.	[L. S.]
Car-ron, his x mark.	[L. S.]	Oken-a-po-wet, his x mark.	[L. S.]
Wau-ke-chon, his x mark.	[L. S.]	Way-taw-say, his x mark.	[L. S.]
Ah-kamote, his x mark.	[L. S.]	Naw-kaw-chis-ka, his x mark.	[L. S.]
Ah-yah-metah, his x mark.	[L. S.]	Wa-ta-push, his x mark.	[L. S.]
Osh-ke-he-na-niew, his x mark.	[L. S.]	Py-aw-wah-say, his x mark.	[L. S.]
Kotch-kaw-no-naew, his x mark.	[L. S.]	Way-aich-kiew, his x mark.	[L. S.]
Sho-ne-on, his x mark.	[L. S.]	Ay-oh-sha, his x mark.	[L. S.]
Wa-pa-massaew, his x mark.	[L. S.]	Mo-sha-hart, his x mark.	[L. S.]

Signed and sealed in presence of—

Benja Hunkins, Indian agent.
Talbot Pricket, United States interpreter.
Theodore Koven, secretary to commissioner.
John Wiley.
R. Otto Skolla.

H. L. Murny.
Benjamin Rice.
John Werdchaff.
Stephen Canfield.
Thomas Heaton.

TREATY WITH THE CREEKS, ETC., 1856.

Aug. 7, 1856.

11 Stats., 699.
Ratified Aug. 16, 1856.
Proclaimed Aug. 28, 1856.

Articles of agreement and convention between the United States and the Creek and Seminole Tribes of Indians, made and concluded at the city of Washington the seventh day of August, one thousand eight hundred and fifty-six, by George W. Manypenny, commissioner on the part of the United States, Tuck-a-batchee-Micco, Echo-Harjo, Chilly McIntosh, Benjamin Marshall, George W. Stidham, and Daniel N. McIntosh, commissioners on the part of the Creeks; and John Jumper, Tuste-nuc-o-chee, Pars-co-fer, and James Factor, commissioners on the part of the Seminoles:

Preamble.

Whereas the convention heretofore existing between the Creek and Seminole tribes of Indians west of the Mississippi River, has given rise to unhappy and injurious dissensions and controversies among them, which render necessary a readjustment of their relations to each other and to the United States; and

Whereas the United States desire, by providing the Seminoles remaining in Florida with a comfortable home west of the Mississippi River, and by making a liberal and generous provision for their welfare, to induce them to emigrate and become one people with their brethren already west, and also to afford to all the Seminoles the means of education and civilization, and the blessings of a regular civil government; and

Whereas the Creek Nation and individuals thereof, have, by their delegation, brought forward and persistently urged various claims against the United States, which it is desirable shall be finally adjusted and settled; and

Whereas it is necessary for the simplification and better understanding of the relations between the United States and said Creek and Seminole tribes of Indians, that all their subsisting treaty stipulations shall, as far as practicable, be embodied in one comprehensive nstrument;

Now, therefore, the United States, by their commissioner, George W. Manypenny, the Creek tribe of Indians, by their commissioners, Tuck-a-batchee-Micco, Echo-Harjo, Chilly McIntosh, Benjamin Marshall, George W. Stidham, and Daniel N. McIntosh; and the Seminole tribe of Indians, by their commissioners, John Jumper, Tuste-nuc-o-chee, Pars-co-fer, and James Factor, do hereby agree and stipulate as follows, viz:

ARTICLE 1. The Creek Nation doth hereby grant, cede, and convey to the Seminole Indians, the tract of country included within the following boundaries, viz: beginning on the Canadian River, a few miles east of the ninety-seventh parallel of west longitude, where Ock-hi-appo, or Pond Creek, empties into the same; thence, due north to the north fork of the Canadian; thence up said north fork of the Canadian to the southern line of the Cherokee country; thence, with that line, west, to the one hundredth parallel of west longitude; thence, south along said parallel of longitude to the Canadian River, and thence down and with that river to the place of beginning.

Cession by Creeks to Seminoles.

ARTICLE 2. The following shall constitute and remain the boundaries of the Creek country, viz: beginning at the mouth of the north fork of the Canadian River, and running northerly four miles; thence running a straight line so as to meet a line drawn from the south bank of the Arkansas River, opposite to the east or lower bank of Grand River, at its junction with the Arkansas, and which runs a course, south, forty-four degrees, west, one mile, to a post placed in the ground; thence along said line to the Arkansas and up the same and the Verdigris River, to where the old territorial line crosses it; thence along said line, north, to a point twenty-five miles from the Arkansas River, where the old territorial line crosses the same; thence running west with the southern line of the Cherokee country, to the north fork of the Canadian River, where the boundary of the session to the Seminoles defined in the preceding article, first strikes said Cherokee line; thence down said north fork, to where the eastern boundary-line of the said cession to the Seminoles strikes the same; thence, with that line, due south to the Canadian River, at the mouth of the Ock-hi-appo, or Pond Creek; and thence down said Canadian River to the place of beginning.

Boundaries of Creek country.

ARTICLE 3. The United States do hereby solemnly guarantee to the Seminole Indians the tract of country ceded to them by the first article of this convention; and to the Creek Indians, the lands included within the boundaries defined in the second article hereof; and likewise that the same shall respectively be secured to and held by said Indians by the same title and tenure by which they were guaranteed and secured to the Creek Nation by the fourteenth article of the treaty of March twenty-fourth, eighteen hundred and thirty-two, the third article of

Seminole and Creek countries to be fixed, guaranteed to them.

Ante, p. 341.

Ante, p. 3
the treaty of February fourteenth, eighteen hundred and thirty-three, and by the letters-patent issued to the said Creek Nation, on the eleventh day of August, eighteen hundred and fifty-two, and recorded in volume four of records of Indian deeds in the Office of Indian Affairs, pages 446 and 447. *Provided however,* That no part of the tract of country so ceded to the Seminole Indians, shall ever be sold, or otherwise disposed of without the consent of both tribes legally given.

No State or Territory to pass laws for said tribes.

Said countries not to be included in any State or Territory without their consent.

ARTICLE 4. The United States do hereby, solemnly agree and bind themselves, that no State or Territory shall ever pass laws for the government of the Creek or Seminole tribes of Indians, and that no portion of either of the tracts of country defined in the first and second articles of this agreement shall ever be embraced or included within, or annexed to, any Territory or State, nor shall either, or any part of either, ever be erected into a Territory without the full and free consent of the legislative authority of the tribe owning the same.

Release by Creeks of all title to other lands, and all claims against the United States, except, etc.

ARTICLE 5. The Creek Indians do hereby absolutely and forever quit-claim and relinquish to the United States all their right, title, and interest in and to any lands heretofore owned or claimed by them, whether east or west of the Mississippi River, and any and all claim for or on account of any such lands, except those embraced within the boundaries described in the second article of this agreement; and it doth also, in like manner, release and fully discharge the United States from all other claims and demands whatsoever, which the Creek Nation or any individual thereof may now have against the United States, excepting only such as are particularly or in terms provided for and secured to them by the provisions of existing treaties and laws; and which are as follows, viz: permanent annuities in money

Ante, p. 26.
amounting to twenty-four thousand five hundred dollars, secured to them by the fourth article of the treaty of seventh August, seventeen hundred and ninety, the second article of the treaty of June

Ante, p. 38.
sixteenth, eighteen hundred and two, and the fourth article of the treaty of January twenty-fourth, eighteen hundred and twenty-six; permanent provision for a wheelwright, for a blacksmith and assistant; blacksmith-shop and tools, and for iron and steel under the eighth article of the last-mentioned treaty; and costing annually one thousand seven hundred and ten dollars; two thousand dollars per annum, during the pleasure of the President, for assistance in agricultural operations under the same treaty and article; six thousand dollars per annum for education for seven years, in addition to the estimate for present fiscal year, under the fourth article of the treaty of January

Ante, p. 388.
fourth, eighteen hundred and forty-five; one thousand dollars per annum during the pleasure of the President, for the same object, under the fifth article of the treaty of February fourteenth, eighteen hundred and thirty-three; services of a wagon-maker, blacksmith and assistant, shop and tools, iron and steel, during the pleasure of the President, under the same treaty and article, and costing one thousand seven hundred and ten dollars annually; the last instalment of two thousand two hundred and twenty dollars for two blacksmiths and assistants, shops and tools, and iron and steel, under the thirteenth

Ante, p. 343.
article of the treaty of March twenty-fourth, eighteen hundred and thirty-two, and which last it is hereby stipulated shall be continued for seven additional years. The following shall also be excepted from the foregoing quit-claim, relinquishment, release, and discharge, viz: the fund created and held in trust for Creek orphans under the second article of the treaty of March twenty-fourth, eighteen hundred and

Ante, p. 341.
thirty-two; the right of such individuals among the Creeks as have not received it, to the compensation in money provided for by the act of

1837, ch. 41.
Congress of March third, eighteen hundred and thirty-seven, in lieu of reservations of land to which they were entitled, but which were

not secured to them, under the said treaty of eighteen hundred and thirty-two; the right of the reservees under the same treaty, who did not dispose of their reservations to the amounts for which they have been or may be sold by the United States; and the right of such members of the tribe to military-bounty lands, as are entitled thereto under existing laws of the United States. The right and interest of the Creek Nation and people in and to the matters and things so excepted, shall continue and remain the same as though this convention had never been entered into.

ARTICLE 6. In consideration of the foregoing quit-claim, relinquishment, release, and discharge, and of the cession of a country for the Seminole Indians contained in the first article of this agreement, the United States do hereby agree and stipulate to allow and pay the Creek Nation the sum of one million of dollars, which shall be invested and paid as follows, viz: two hundred thousand dollars to be invested in some safe stocks, paying an interest of at least five per cent. per annum; which interest shall be regularly and faithfully applied to purposes of education among the Creeks; four hundred thousand dollars to be paid *per capita*, under the direction of the general council of the Creek Nation to the individuals and members of said nation, except such portion as they shall, by order of said national council, direct to be paid to the treasurer of said nation for any specified national object not exceeding ($100,000) one hundred thousand dollars, as soon as practicable after the ratification of this agreement; and two hundred thousand dollars shall be set apart to be appropriated and paid as follows, viz: ten thousand dollars to be equally distributed and paid to those individuals and their heirs, who, under act of Congress of March third, eighteen hundred and thirty-seven, have received money in lieu of reservations of land to which they were entitled, but which were not secured to them under the treaty of March twenty-fourth, eighteen hundred and thirty-two; one hundred and twenty thousand dollars to be equally and justly distributed and paid, under the direction of the general council, to those Creeks, or their descendants, who emigrated west of the Mississippi River prior to said treaty of eighteen hundred and thirty two, and to be in lieu of and in full compensation for the claims of such Creeks to an allowance equivalent to the reservations granted to the eastern Creeks by that treaty, and seventy thousand dollars for the adjustment and final settlement of such other claims of individual Creek Indians, as may be found to be equitable and just by the general council of the nation: *Provided however*, That no part of the three last-mentioned sums shall be allowed or paid to any other person or persons, whatsoever, than those who are actual and *bona-fide* members of the Creek Nation and belonging respectively to the three classes of claimants designated; said sums to be remitted and paid as soon as practicable after the general council shall have ascertained and designated the persons entitled to share therein. *And provided further*, That any balance of the said sum of seventy thousand dollars, which may be found not to be actually necessary for the adjustment and settlement of the claims for which it is set apart, shall belong to the nation, and be applied to such object or objects of utility or necessity as the general council shall direct. The remaining sum of two hundred thousand dollars shall be retained by the United States, until the removal of the Seminole Indians, now in Florida, to the country west of the Mississippi River herein provided for their tribe; whereupon the same, with interest thereon, at five per cent., from the date of the ratification of this agreement, shall be paid over to, or invested for the benefit of the Creek Nation, as may then be requested by the proper authorities thereof. *Provided however*, That if so paid over, it shall be equally divided and paid *per capita* to all the individuals and members of the Creek Nation, or be used and applied only for

Payment to the Creeks for said cession and release of $1,000,000.

Two hundred thousand dollars to be invested.

Four hundred thousand dollars to be paid per capita.

Ten thousand dollars for arrears under act of 1837, ch. 41.

One hundred and twenty thousand dollars for Creeks who emigrated before 1832.

Two hundred thousand dollars to be retained till the Seminoles remove, and then paid or invested.

such objects or purposes of a strictly national or beneficial character as the interests and welfare of the Creek people shall actually require.

Educational, etc., funds to be paid to treasurer. ARTICLE 7. It being the desire of the Creeks to employ their own teachers, mechanics, and farmers, all of the funds secured to the nation for educational, mechanical, and agricultural purposes, shall as the same become annually due, be paid over by the United States to the treasurer of the Creek Nation. And the annuities in money due the nation under former treaties, shall also be paid to the same officer, whenever the general council shall so direct.

Release of Seminole claims. ARTICLE 8. The Seminoles hereby release and discharge the United States from all claims and demands which their delegation have set up against them, and obligate themselves to remove to and settle in the new country herein provided for them as soon as practicable. In consideration of such release, discharge, and obligation, and as the Indians must abandon their present improvements, and incur considerable expense in re-establishing themselves, and as the Government desires to secure their assistance in inducing their brethren yet in Florida to emigrate and settle with them west of the Mississippi River, and is willing to offer liberal inducements to the latter peaceably so to do, the **Payment for such release.** United States do therefore agree and stipulate as follows, viz: To pay to the Seminoles now in the west the sum of ninety thousand dollars, which shall be in lieu of their present improvements, and in full for the expenses of their removal and establishing themselves in their new country; to provide annually for ten years the sum of three thousand dollars for the support of schools; two thousand dollars for agricultural assistance; and two thousand two hundred dollars for the support of smiths and smith-shops among them, said sums to be applied to these objects in such manner as the President shall direct. Also to invest for them the sum of two hundred and fifty thousand dollars, at five per cent. per annum, the interest to be regularly paid over to them *per capita* as annuity; the further sum of two hundred and fifty thousand dollars shall be invested in like manner whenever the Seminoles now remaining in Florida shall have emigrated and joined their brethren in the west, whereupon the two sums so invested, shall constitute a fund belonging to the united tribe of Seminoles, and the interest on which, at the rate aforesaid, shall be annually paid over to them *per capita* as an annuity; but no portion of the principal thus invested, or the interest thereon annually due and payable, shall ever be taken to pay claims or demands against said Indians, except such as may hereafter arise under the intercourse laws.

United States to remove Seminoles who will emigrate, and give them certain supplies. ARTICLE 9. The United States agree to remove comfortably to their new country west, all those Seminoles now in Florida who can be induced to emigrate thereto; and to furnish them with sufficient rations of wholesome subsistence during their removal and for twelve months after their arrival at their new homes; also, to provide each warrior of eighteen years of age and upwards, who shall so remove, with one rifle-gun, if he shall not already possess one; with two blankets, a supply of powder and lead, a hunting-shirt, one pair of shoes, one and a half yards of strouding, and ten pounds of good tobacco; and each woman, youth, and child with a blanket, pair of shoes, and other necessary articles of comfortable clothing, and to expend for them in improvements, after they shall all remove, the sum of twenty thousand dollars. And to encourage the Seminoles to devote themselves to the cultivation of the soil, and become a sober, settled, industrious, and independent people, the United States do further agree to expend three thousand dollars in the purchase of ploughs and other agricultural implements, axes, seeds, looms, cards, and wheels; the same to be proportionately distributed among those now west, and those who shall emigrate from Florida.

ARTICLE 10. The Seminoles west do hereby agree and bind themselves to furnish, at such time or times as the President may appoint, a delegation of such members of their tribe as shall be selected for the purpose, to proceed to Florida, under the direction of an agent of the Government, to render such peaceful services as may be required of them, and otherwise to do all in their power to induce their brethren remaining in that State to emigrate and join them in the west; the United States agreeing to pay them and such members of the Creek tribe as may voluntarily offer to join them and be accepted for the same service, a reasonable compensation for their time and services, as well as their travelling and other actual and necessary expenses.

Seminoles west to send a delegation to Florida.

ARTICLE 11. It is further hereby agreed that the United States shall pay Foc-te-lus-te-harjo, his heirs or assigns, the sum of four hundred dollars, in consideration of the unpaid services of said Foc-te-luc-te-harjoe, or Black Dirt, rendered by him as chief of the friendly band of Seminole warriors who fought for the United States during the Florida war.

Payment to certain Indians.

ARTICLE 12. So soon as the Seminoles west shall have removed to the new country herein provided for them, the United States will then select a site and erect the necessary buildings for an agency, including a council-house for the Seminoles.

Agency for Seminoles.

ARTICLE 13. The officers and people of each of the tribes of Creeks and Seminoles shall, at all times, have the right of safe conduct and free passage through the lands and territory of the other. The members of each shall have the right freely to settle within the country of the other, and shall thereupon be entitled to all the rights, privileges, and immunities of members thereof, except that no member of either tribe shall be entitled to participate in any funds belonging to the other tribe. Members of each tribe shall have the right to institute and prosecute suits in the courts of the other, under such regulations as may, from time to time, be prescribed by their respective legislatures.

Rights of Creeks and Seminoles in each other's countries.

ARTICLE 14. Any person duly charged with a criminal offense against the laws of either the Creek or Seminole tribe, and escaping into the jurisdiction of the other, shall be promptly surrendered upon the demand of the proper authority of the tribe within whose jurisdiction the offense shall be alleged to have been committed.

Extradition of criminals between said Indian countries.

ARTICLE 15. So far as may be compatible with the Constitution of the United States, and the laws made in pursuance thereof, regulating trade and intercourse with the Indian tribes, the Creeks and Seminoles shall be secured in the unrestricted right of self-government, and full jurisdiction over persons and property, within their respective limits; excepting, however, all white persons, with their property, who are not, by adoption or otherwise, members of either the Creek or Seminole tribe; and all persons not being members of either tribe, found within their limits, shall be considered intruders, and be removed from and kept out of the same by the United States agents for said tribes, respectively; (assisted, if necessary, by the military;) with the following exceptions, viz: such individuals with their families as may be in the employment of the Government of the United States; all persons peaceably travelling, or temporarily sojourning in the country, or trading therein under license from the proper authority of the United States; and such persons as may be permitted by the Creeks or Seminoles, with the assent of the proper authorities of the United States, to reside within their respective limits without becoming members of either of said tribes.

Government of Creeks and Seminoles.

ARTICLE 16. The Creeks and Seminoles shall promptly apprehend and deliver up all persons accused of any crime against the laws of the United States, or of any State thereof, who may be found within their

Extradition of criminals to the United States or States.

limits, on demand of any proper officer of a State or of the United States.

Traders to pay for use of land and timber.

ARTICLE 17. All persons licensed by the United States to trade with the Creeks or Seminoles shall be required to pay to the tribe within whose country they trade, a moderate annual compensation for the land and timber used by them, the amount of such compensation, in each case, to be assessed by the proper authorities of said tribe, subject to the approval of the United States agent therefor.

Protection of said Creeks and Seminoles.

ARTICLE 18. The United States shall protect the Creeks and Seminoles from domestic strife, from hostile invasion, and from aggression by other Indians and white persons, not subject to their jurisdiction and laws; and for all injuries resulting from such invasion or aggression, full indemnity is hereby guaranteed to the party or parties injured out of the Treasury of the United States, upon the same principle and according to the same rules upon which white persons are entitled to indemnity for injuries or aggressions upon them, committed by Indians.

Right to establish posts, roads, and agencies reserved to the United States.

ARTICLE 19. The United States shall have the right to establish and maintain such military posts, military and post-roads and Indian agencies as may be deemed necessary within the Creek and Seminole country, but no greater quantity of land or timber shall be used for said purposes than shall be actually requisite; and if, in the establishment or maintenance of such posts, roads, or agencies, the property of any Creek or Seminole be taken, destroyed, or injured, or any property of either nation, other than land and timber, just and adequate compensation shall be made by the United States. Such persons

Regulations respecting the same.

only as are or may be in the employment of the United States, in any capacity, civil or military, or subject to the jurisdiction and laws of the Creeks and Seminoles, shall be permitted to farm or raise stock within the limits of any of said military posts or Indian agencies. And no offender against the laws of either of said tribes shall be permitted to take refuge therein.

Right of way for railroads and telegraphs.

ARTICLE 20. The United States, or any incorporated company, shall have the right of way for railroads, or lines of telegraphs, through the Creek and Seminole countries; but in the case of any incorporated company, it shall have such right of way only upon such terms, and payment of such amount to the Creeks and Seminoles, as the case may be, as may be agreed upon between it and the national council thereof: or, in case of disagreement by making full compensation, not only to individual parties injured, but also to the tribe for the right of way, all damage and injury done to be ascertained and determined in such manner as the President of the United States shall direct. And the right of way granted by either of said tribes for any railroad shall be perpetual or for such shorter term as the same may be granted, in the same manner as if there were no reversion of their lands to the United States provided for, in case of abandonment by them, or of extinction of their tribe.

Survey of boundaries.

ARTICLE 21. The United States will cause such portions of the boundaries of the Creek and Seminole countries, as do not consist of well-defined natural boundaries, to be surveyed and permanently marked and established. The Creek and Seminole general councils may each appoint a commissioner from their own people to attend the running of their respective boundaries, whose expenses and a reasonable allowance for their time and services, while engaged in such duty, shall be paid by the United States.

Amnesty declared.

ARTICLE 22. That this convention may conduce, as far as possible, to the restoration and preservation of kind and friendly feelings among the Creeks and Seminoles; a general amnesty of all past offences committed within their country, either west or east of the Mississippi, is hereby declared.

ARTICLE 23. A liberal allowance shall be made to each of the delegations signing this convention; including, with the Seminole delegation, George W. Brinton, the interpreter, as a compensation for their travelling and other expenses in coming to and remaining in this city and returning home.

Allowances to delegation.

ARTICLE 24. Should the Seminoles in Florida desire to have a portion of the country described in the first article of this agreement, set apart for their residence, it is agreed that the Seminoles west may make such arrangement, not inconsistent with this instrument, as may be satisfactory to their brethren in Florida.

Seminoles may set a tract apart for Florida Seminoles.

ARTICLE 25. The Creek laws shall be in force and continue to operate in the country herein assigned to the Seminoles, until the latter remove thereto; when they shall cease and be of no effect.

Creek laws, force of, in Seminole country.

ARTICLE 26. This convention shall supersede and take the place of all former treaties, between the United States and the Creeks, between the United States and the Florida Indians and Seminoles, and between the Creeks and Seminoles, inconsistent herewith; and shall take effect and be obligatory on the contracting parties from the date hereof, whenever it shall be ratified by the Senate and President of the United States.

This treaty to supersede former inconsistent ones; when to take effect.

ARTICLE 27. And it is further agreed, that nothing herein contained shall be so construed as to release the United States from any liability other than those in favor of said nations or individuals thereof.

In testimony whereof, the said George W. Manypenny, commissioner on the part of the United States, and the said commissioners on the part of the Creeks and Seminoles, have hereunto set their hands and seals.

Done in triplicate at the city of Washington, on the day and year first above written.

Geo. W. Manypenny, [L. S.]
   United States Commissioner.
Tuck-a-batchee-micco, his x mark, [L. S.]
Echo-harjo, his x mark, [L. S.]
Chilly McIntosh, [L. S.]
Benjamin Marshall, [L. S.]
George W. Stidham, [L. S.]
Daniel N. McIntosh, [L. S.]
   Creek Commissioners.
John Jumper, his x mark, [L. S.]
Tus-te-nuc-o-chee, his x mark, [L. S.]
Pars-co-fer, his x mark, [L. S.]
James Factor, his x mark, [L. S.]
   Seminole Commissioners.

Executed in presence of—
 John W. Allen,
 Edward Hanrick,
 W. H. Garrett, Creek agent,
 J. W. Washbourne, Seminole agent,
 G. W. Stidham, United States interpreter,
 Geo. W. Brinton, interpreter,
 James R. Roche,
 Chs. O. Joline.

TREATY WITH THE PAWNEE, 1857.

Sept. 24, 1857.

11 Stats., 729.
Ratified, Mar. 31,
1858.
Proclaimed May 26,
1858.

Articles of agreement and convention made this twenty-fourth day of September, A. D. 1857, at Table Creek, Nebraska Territory, between James W. Denver, commissioner on behalf of the United States, and the chiefs and head-men of the four confederate bands of Pawnee Indians, viz: Grand Pawnees, Pawnee Loups, Pawnee Republicans, and Pawnee Tappahs, and generally known as the Pawnee tribe.

Lands hereby ceded by the Pawnees to the United States.

ARTICLE 1. The confederate bands of the Pawnees aforesaid, hereby cede and relinquish to the United States all their right, title, and interest in and to all the lands now owned or claimed by them, except as hereinafter reserved, and which are bounded as follows, viz: On the east by the lands lately purchased by the United States from the Omahas; on the south by the lands heretofore ceded by the Pawnees to the United States; on the west by a line running due north from the junction of the North with the South Fork of the Platte River, to the Keha-Paha River; and on the north by the Keha-Paha River to its junction with the Niobrara, L'eauqi Court, or Running-Water River, and thence, by that river, to the western boundary of the late Omaha cession. Out of this cession the Pawnees reserve a tract of country, thirty miles long from east to west, by fifteen miles wide from north to south, including both banks of the Loup Fork of the Platte River; the east line of which shall be at a point not further east than the mouth of Beaver Creek. If, however, the Pawnees, in conjunction with the United States agent, shall be able to find a more suitable locality for their future homes, within said cession, then, they are to have the privilege of selecting an equal quantity of land there, in lieu of the reservation herein designated, all of which shall be done as soon as practicable; and the Pawnees agree to remove to their new homes, thus reserved for them, without cost to the United States, within one year from the date of the ratification of this treaty by the Senate of the United States, and, until that time, they shall be permitted to remain where they are now residing, without molestation.

Reservation.

Payment to Pawnee.

ARTICLE 2. In consideration of the foregoing cession, the United States agree to pay to the Pawnees the sum of forty thousand dollars per annum, for five years, commencing on the first day of January, A. D. eighteen hundred and fifty-eight; and, after the end of five years, thirty thousand dollars per annum, as a perpetual annuity, at least one-half of which annual payments shall be made in goods, and such articles as may be deemed necessary for them.

And it is further agreed that the President may, at any time, in his discretion, discontinue said perpetuity, by causing the value of a fair commutation thereof to be paid to, or expended for the benefit of, said Indians, in such manner as to him shall seem proper.

United States to establish manual labor schools.

ARTICLE 3. In order to improve the condition of the Pawnees, and teach them the arts of civilized life, the United States agree to establish among them, and for their use and benefit, two manual-labor schools, to be governed by such rules and regulations as may be prescribed by the President of the United States, who shall also appoint the teachers, and, if he deems it necessary, may increase the number of schools to four. In these schools, there shall be taught the various branches of a common-school education, and, in addition, the arts of agriculture, the most useful mechanical arts. and whatever else the President may direct. The Pawnees, on their part, agree that each and every one of their children, between the ages of seven and eighteen years, shall be kept constantly at these schools for, at least, nine months in each year; and if any parent or guardian shall fail, neglect, or refuse to so keep the child or children under his or her control at such school, then, and in that case, there shall be deducted from the

Children to be kept at school.

annuities to which such parent or guardian would be entitled, either individually or as parent or guardian, an amount equal to the value, in time, of the tuition thus lost; but the President may at any time change or modify this clause as he may think proper. The chiefs shall be held responsible for the attendance of orphans who have no other guardians; and the United States agree to furnish suitable houses and farms for said schools, and whatever else may be necessary to put them in successful operation; and a sum not less than five thousand dollars per annum shall be applied to the support of each school, so long as the Pawnees shall, in good faith, comply with the provisions of this article; but if, at any time, the President is satisfied they are not doing so, he may, at his discretion, discontinue the schools in whole or in part.

ARTICLE 4. The United States agree to protect the Pawnees in the possession of their new homes. The United States also agree to furnish the Pawnees: *Pawnees to be protected in their new homes.*

First, with two complete sets of blacksmith, gunsmith, and tinsmith tools, not to exceed in cost seven hundred and fifty dollars; and erect shops at a cost not to exceed five hundred dollars; also five hundred dollars annually, during the pleasure of the President, for the purchase of iron, steel, and other necessaries for the same. The United States are also to furnish two blacksmiths, one of whom shall be a gunsmith and tinsmith; but the Pawnees agree to furnish one or two young men of their tribe to work constantly in each shop as strikers or apprentices, who shall be paid a fair compensation for their labor. *To supply certain tools, etc.*

Second. The United States agree to furnish farming utensils and stock, worth twelve hundred dollars per annum, for ten years, or during the pleasure of the President, and for the first year's purchase of stock, and for erecting shelters for the same, an amount not exceeding three thousand dollars, and also to employ a farmer to teach the Indians the arts of agriculture. *Farming utensils and stock.*

Third. The United States agree to have erected on said reservation a steam-mill, suitable to grind grain and saw lumber, which shall not exceed in cost six thousand dollars, and to keep the same in repair for ten years; also, to employ a miller and engineer for the same length of time, or longer, at the discretion of the President; the Pawnees agreeing to furnish apprentices, to assist in working the mill, who shall be paid a fair compensation for their services. *To erect and run a mill.*

Fourth. The United States agree to erect dwelling-houses for the interpreter, blacksmiths, farmer, miller and engineer, which shall not exceed in cost five hundred dollars each; and the Pawnees agree to prevent the members of their tribe from injuring or destroying the houses, shops, machinery, stock farming utensils, and all other things furnished by the Government, and if any such shall be carried away, injured, or destroyed, by any of the members of their tribe, the value of the same shall be deducted from the tribal annuities. Whenever the President shall become satisfied that the Pawnees have sufficiently advanced in the acquirement of a practical knowledge of the arts and pursuits to which this article relates, then, and in that case, he may turn over the property to the tribe, and dispense with the services of any or all of the employees herein named. *Dwellings for interpreter, etc.*

ARTICLE 5. The Pawnees acknowledge their dependence on the Government of the United States, and promise to be friendly with all the citizens thereof, and pledge themselves to commit no depredations on the property of such citizens, nor on that of any other person belonging to any tribe or nation at peace with the United States. And should any one or more of them violate this pledge, and the fact be satisfactorily proven before the agent, the property taken shall be returned, or in default thereof, or if injured or destroyed, compensation may be made by the Government out of their annuities. Nor will *Pawnees to be friendly, and not to make war, except, etc.*

they make war on any other tribe, except in self-defence, but will submit all matters of difference between them and other Indians to the Government of the United States, or its agent, for decision, and abide thereby.

United States may build forts on lands of Pawnees.

ARTICLE 6. The United States agent may reside on or near the Pawnee reservation; and the Pawnees agree to permit the United States to build forts and occupy military posts on their lands, and to allow the whites the right to open roads through their territories; but

White persons not to reside thereon unless licensed.

no white person shall be allowed to reside on any part of said reservation unless he or she be in the employ of the United States, or be licensed to trade with said tribe, or be a member of the family of such employé or licensed trader; nor shall the said tribe, or any of them,

Pawnees not to alienate any part thereof.

alienate any part of said reservation, except to the United States; but, if they think proper to do so, they may divide said lands among themselves, giving to each person, or each head of a family, a farm, subject to their tribal regulations, but in no instance to be sold or disposed of to persons outside, or not themselves of the Pawnee tribe.

United States to furnish six laborers.

ARTICLE 7. The United States agree to furnish, in addition to the persons heretofore mentioned, six laborers for three years, but it is expressly understood that while these laborers are to be under the control, and subject to the orders, of the United States agent, they are employed more to teach the Pawnees how to manage stock and use the implements furn shed, than as merely laboring for their benefit; and for every laborer thus furnished by the United States, the Pawnees engage to furnish at least three of their tribe to work with them, who shall also be subject to the orders of the agent, and for whom the chiefs shall be responsible.

Offenders against United States laws, etc., to be surrendered.

ARTICLE 8. The Pawnees agree to deliver up to the officers of the United States all offenders against the treaties, laws, or regulations of the United States, whenever they may be found within the limits of their reservation; and they further agree to assist such officers in discovering, pursuing, and capturing any such offender or offenders, anywhere, whenever called on so to do; and they agree, also, that, if they violate any of the stipulations contained in this treaty, the President may, at his discretion, withhold a part, or the whole, of the annuities herein provided for.

Provision for the half-breeds of the tribe.

ARTICLE 9. The Pawnees desire to have some provision made for the half-breeds of their tribe. Those of them who have preferred to reside, and are now residing, in the nation, are to be entitled to equal rights and privileges with other members of the tribes, but those who have chosen to follow the pursuits of civilized life, and to reside among the whites, viz: Baptiste Bayhylle, William Bayhylle, Julia Bayhylle, Frank Tatahyee, William Nealis, Julia Nealis, Catharine Papan, Politte Papan, Rousseau Papan, Charles Papan, Peter Papan, Emily Papan, Henry Geta, Stephen Geta, James Cleghorn, Eliza Deroine, are to be entitled to scrip for one hundred and sixty acres, or one quarter section, of land for each, provided application shall be made for the same within five years from this time, which scrip shall be receivable at the United States land-offices, the same as military bounty-land warrants, and be subject to the same rules and regulations.

Two thousand dollars to be paid Samuel Allis.

ARTICLE 10. Samuel Allis has long been the firm friend of the Pawnees, and in years gone by has administered to their wants and necessities. When in distress, and in a state of starvation, they took his property and used it for themselves, and when the small-pox was destroying them, he vaccinated more than two thousand of them; for all these things, the Pawnees desire that he shall be paid, but they think that the Government should pay a part. It is, therefore, agreed that the Pawnees will pay to said Allis one thousand dollars, and the United States agree to pay him a similar sum of one thousand dollars, as a full remuneration for his services and losses.

ARTICLE 11. Ta-ra-da-ka-wa, head-chief of the Tappahs band, and four other Pawnees, having been out as guides for the United States troops, in their late expedition against the Cheyennes, and having to return by themselves, were overtaken and plundered of everything given them by the officers of the expedition, as well as their own property, barely escaping with their lives; and the value of their services being fully acknowledged, the United States agree to pay to each of them one hundred dollars, or, in lieu thereof, to give to each a horse worth one hundred dollars in value. Acknowledgment of certain services by United States.

ARTICLE 12. To enable the Pawnees to settle any just claims at present existing against them, there is hereby set apart, by the United States, ten thousand dollars, out of which the same may be paid, when presented, and proven to the satisfaction of the proper department; and the Pawnees hereby relinquish all claims they may have against the United States under former treaty stipulations. Contingent claims against the Pawnees.

In testimony whereof, the said James W. Denver, Commissioner, as aforesaid, and the undersigned, chiefs and head-men of the four confederate bands of Pawnee Indians, have hereunto set their hands and seals, at the place and on the day and year hereinbefore written.

James W. Denver,
U. S. Commissioner.

Grand Pawnees:
Pe-ta-na-sharo, or the Man and the Chief, his x mark. [L. s.]
Sa-ra-cherish, the Cross Chief, his x mark. [L. s.]
Te-ra-ta-puts, he who Steals Horses, his x mark. [L. s.]
Le-ra-kuts-a-nasharo, the Grey Eagle Chief, his x mark. [L. s.]
  Pawnee Loups:
La-le-ta-ra-nasharo, the Comanche Chief, his x mark. [L. s.]
Te-ste-de-da-we-tel, the Man who Distributes the Goods, his x mark. [L. s.]
Le-ta-kuts-nasharo, the Grey Eagle Chief, his x mark. [L. s.]
A-sa-na-sharo, the Horse Chief, his x mark. [L. s.]

Pawnee Republicans:
Na-sharo-se-de-ta-ra-ko, the one the Great Spirit smiles on, his x mark. [L. s.]
Na-sharo-cha-hicko, a Man, but a Chief, his x mark. [L. s.]
Da-lo-le-kit-ta-to-kah, the Man the Enemy steals from, his x mark. [L. s.]
Da-lo-de-na-sharo, the Chief like an Eagle, his x mark. [L. s.]
  Pawnee Tappahs:
Ke-we-ko-na-sharo, the Buffalo Bull Chief, his x mark. [L. s.]
Na-sharo-la-da-hoo, the Big Chief, his x mark. [L. s.]
Na-sharo, the Chief, his x mark. [L. s.]
Da-ka-to-wa-kuts-o-ra-na-sharo, the Hawk Chief, his x mark. [L. s.]

Signed and sealed in presence of—

Wm. W. Dennison, United States Indian Agent.
A. S. H. White, secretary to commissioner.
N. W. Tucker,

Will. E. Harvey,
O. H. Irish,
Samuel Allis, interpreter
J. Sterling Morton.

TREATY WITH THE SENECA, TONAWANDA BAND, 1857.

Articles of agreement and convention made this fifth day of November, in the year one thousand eight hundred and fifty seven, at the meeting house on the Tonawanda reservation, in the county of Genesee, and State of New York, between Charles E. Mix, commissioner on behalf of the United States, and the following persons, duly authorized thereunto by the Tonawanda band of Seneca Indians, viz: Jabez Ground, Jesse Spring, Isaac Shanks, George Sky, and Ely S. Parker. Nov. 5, 1857.
11 Stat., 735.
12 Stat., 991.
Ratified June 4, 1858.
Proclaimed Mar. 31, 1859.

Whereas a certain treaty was heretofore made between the Six Nations of New York Indians and the United States on the 15th day of January, 1838, and another between the Seneca Nation of Indians and the United States on the 20th day of May, 1842, by which, among other things, the Seneca Nation of Indians granted and conveyed to Former treaties.

Ante, p. 502.

Thomas Ludlow Ogden and Joseph Fellows the two certain Indian reservations in the State of New York known as the Buffalo Creek and the Tonawanda reservations, to be surrendered to the said Ogden and Fellows, on the performance of certain conditions-precedent defined in said treaties; and

Terms of said treaties.

Whereas in and by the said treaties there were surrendered and relinquished to the United States 500,000 acres of land in the then Territory of Wisconsin; and

Whereas the United States, in and by said treaties, agreed to set apart for said Indians certain lands in the Indian Territory immediately west of the Missouri, and to grant the same to them, to be held and enjoyed in fee-simple, the quantity of said lands being computed to afford 320 acres to each soul of said Indians, and did agree that any individual, or any number of said Indians, might remove to said Territory, and thereupon be entitled to hold and enjoy said lands, and all the benefits of said treaties, according to numbers, respectively; and

Whereas the United States did further agree to pay the sum of $400,000 for the removal of the Indians of New York to the said Territory, and for their support and assistance during the first year of their residence in said Territory; and

Whereas the said Ogden and Fellows did agree to pay to the said Seneca Nation of Indians, as the consideration of the surrender and relinquishment of the said two reservations, known as the Buffalo Creek and Tonawanda reservations, certain sums of money, one part of which was to be paid to the individual Indians residing upon said reservations, for the improvements held and owned by them in severalty, the amount of which "improvement money" heretofore apportioned to those residing upon the Tonawanda reservation, being $15,018$\frac{36}{100}$, which money has been paid into, and still remains in the Treasury of the United States; and

Whereas, for divers reasons and differences, the said treaties remain unexecuted as to the said Tonawanda reservation, and the band of Senecas residing thereon; and

Whereas it is ascertained, at the date of these articles, that the Seneca Indians, composing the Tonawanda band and residing upon the Tonawanda reservation, amount to 650 souls in number; and

Whereas the United States are willing to exercise the liberal policy which has heretofore been exercised in regard to the Senecas, and for the purpose of relieving the Tonawandas of the difficulties and troubles under which they labor,

These articles are entered into:

Certain claims under former treaties relinquished.

ARTICLE 1. The said persons, authorized as in the caption hereof stated, hereby surrender and relinquish to the United States all claims severally and in common as a band of Indians, and as a part of the Seneca Nation, to the lands west of the State of Missouri, and all right and claim to be removed thither, and for support and assistance after such removal, and all other claims against the United States under the aforesaid treaties of 1838 and 1842, except, however; such moneys as they may be entitled to under said treaties, paid or payable by the said Ogden and Fellows.

Pay for such surrender.

ARTICLE 2. In consideration of which aforesaid surrender and relinquishment, the United States agree to pay and invest, in the manner hereinafter specified, the sum of $256,000 for the said Tonawanda band of Indians.

Tonawandas may purchase reservation.

ARTICLE 3. It is hereby agreed that the Tonawanda band may purchase of the said Ogden and Fellows, of the survivor of them, or of their heirs or assigns, the entire Tonawanda reservation, or such portions thereof as they may be willing to sell and said band may be willing to purchase; and the United States undertake and agree to pay for the same out of the said sum of $256,000, upon the express condition that the rate of purchase shall not exceed, on an average, $20 per acre.

United States will pay therefor not exceeding $20 per acre.

The land so purchased shall be taken by deed of conveyance to the Secretary of the Interior of the United States, and his successors in office, in fee, to be held by him in trust for the said Tonawanda band of Indians and their exclusive use, occupation, and enjoyment, until the legislature of the State of New York shall pass an act designating some persons, or public officer of that State, to take and hold said land upon a similar trust for said Indians; whereupon they shall be granted by the said Secretary to such persons or public officer. *Deed to run to Secretary of the Interior in trust.*

ARTICLE 4. And the said Tonawanda band of Indians hereby agree to surrender, relinquish, and give up to the said Ogden and Fellows, the survivor of them, or their assigns—provided the whole reservation shall not be purchased—the unimproved lands which they shall not purchase, as aforesaid, within thirty days after this treaty shall be proclaimed by the President of the United States, and the improved lands which they shall not purchase, as aforesaid, on the 1st day of June, 1859. *Unimproved lands surrendered.*

ARTICLE 5. For the purpose of contracting for and making purchase of the lands contemplated herein, a majority of the chiefs and head-men of said Tonawanda band, in council assembled, may appoint one or more attorneys with adequate powers, which appointment must be approved by the Secretary of the Interior before such attorney or attorneys can have power to act in the premises. *Tonawandas may appoint one or more attorneys.*

ARTICLE 6. Whenever a quantity of said lands, amounting to 6,500 acres, at the least, upon the terms hereinbefore provided, may be purchased, written notice, executed by the chiefs and head-men in council, and acknowledged before a justice of the supreme court of New York, or judge of the superior court of the city of Buffalo, shall be given to the Secretary of the Interior, whereupon the portion of said sum of $256,000, not expended in the purchase of lands, as aforesaid, shall be invested by the said Secretary of the Interior in stocks of the United States, or in stocks of some of the States, at his discretion; and the increase arising from such investment shall be paid to the said Tonawanda Indians, at the time and in the manner that the annuities are paid which said Indians are now entitled to receive from the United States. *Part of purchase money to be invested in stocks.*

ARTICLE 7. It is hereby agreed that the sum of $15,018\frac{36}{100}$ "improvement money," heretofore apportioned to the Indians upon the Tonawanda reservation, shall be again apportioned by an agent, to be appointed by the chiefs and head-men in council assembled, to be approved by the Secretary of the Interior, which agent shall make a report of such apportionment to the said Secretary of the Interior, and if he concur therein, the shares so ascertained shall be paid to the individual Indians entitled thereto, who shall surrender and relinquish to the said Ogden and Fellows, or the survivor of them, or their assigns, their improvements, and any balance remaining shall be paid to the chiefs and head-men of the band, to be disbursed by them in payment of the debts or for the use of the band. The services of the agent to be thus appointed, and all other expenses attending the execution of these articles, are to be paid by the United States out of any moneys coming to the Tonawandas. *Improvement money to be apportioned.*

In testimony whereof the said Charles E. Mix, commissioner, as aforesaid, and the undersigned persons, representing the Tonawanda band of Seneca Indians, have hereunto set their hands and seals the day and year first above written.

Charles E. Mix, commissioner. [L. s.]
Isaac x Shanks, [L. s.]
George x Sky, [L. s.]
Jabez x Ground, [L. s.]
Jesse x Spring, [L. s.]
Ely S. Parker. [L. s.]

The foregoing instrument was, on the day of the date thereof, executed in our presence, and we have hereunto at the same time affixed our names as subscribing witnesses.

John H. Martindale,
Frederick Follett,
William G. Bryan,
C. B. Rich,
Leander Mix,
Henry Bittinger,
Nicholson H. Parker, United States interpreter.

Also, the following chiefs and headmen heartily concur in the foregoing articles in behalf of themselves and their people:—

Jesse x Spring,
Wm. x Parker,
Jabez x Ground,
John x Wilson,
John x Bigfire,
Thomson x Blinkey,
James x Mitten,
John x Joshua,
James x Williams,

George x Sky,
Snow x Cooper,
Isaac x Doctor,
Isaac x Shanks,
William x Moses,
David x Printup,
Benj. x Jonas,
Addison x Charles,
John x Hatch.

Headmen:

John x Smith,
Small x Peter,
John x Beaver,
John x Farmer,
Tommy x White,
John x Griffin,
Geo. x Moses,
Henry x Moses,
Saml. x Blue Sky,
James x Scroggs,
Monroe x Jonas,
Wm. x Johnson,
Jackson x Ground,
Harrison x Scrogg,

Wm. x Alick,
Wm. x Stewart,
Andrew x Blackchief,
John x Infant,
Wm. x Taylor,
James x Billy,
Danl. x Peter,
John x Hill,
John x Jones,
John x Shanks,
Levi x Parker,
John x Jemison,
Chauncey x Abram.

Signed in open council, in presence of—

Frederick Follett,
Nicholson H. Parker, United States interpreter.

Supplemental articles.

Supplemental articles of agreement and convention, made this fifth day of November, in the year one thousand eight hundred and fifty-seven, at the meeting-house on the Tonawanda reservation, in the county of Genesee, State of New York, between Charles E. Mix, commissioner on behalf of the United States, of the first part, and the following persons, duly authorized thereunto by the Tonawanda band of Seneca Indians, viz: Jabez Ground, Jesse Spring, Isaac Shanks, George Sky, and Ely S. Parker, of the second part.

Whereas, at the date hereof and concurrent with the execution of this instrument, articles of agreement and convention have been entered into between the parties aforesaid, in and by which articles it is provided that the said Tonawanda band of Seneca Indians may purchase portions of the Tonawanda reservation, "upon the express condition that the rate of purchase shall not exceed $20 per acre on an average."

And whereas the President of the United States may deem it discreet and expedient that certain portions of said reservations, held in severalty by the assigns of said Ogden and Fellows, should be purchased by said Indians if it shall be necessary so to do, at a rate exceeding $20 per acre on an average.

Now, therefore, the said parties of the second part agree, that por- Portions of reserva-
tion may be bought
for more than $20 per
acre, if, etc.
tions of said reservation may be purchased by the authorized agents
of said Indians for them, and paid for out of said sum of $256,000,
at a rate exceeding $20 per acre on an average, provided the contract
or contracts therefor shall be first submitted to and approved by the
President, or some public officer to be designated by him.

And the said parties of the second part solicit the President to
accept and adopt this supplement as a part of the said articles of agreement and convention entered into concurrent with the execution of
this agreement.

In testimony whereof the said Charles E. Mix, commissioner as Signatures.
aforesaid, and the undersigned persons representing the Tonawanda
band of Seneca Indians, have hereunto set their hands and seals the
day and year first above written.

Charles E. Mix, Commissioner.	[L. s.]
Isaac x Shanks,	[L. s.]
George x Sky,	[L. s.]
Jabez x Ground,	[L. s.]
Jesse x Spring,	[L. s.]
Ely S. Parker.	[L. s.]

The foregoing instrument was, on the day of the date thereof, executed in our presence, and we have hereunto, at the same time, affixed
our names as subscribing witnesses.

John H. Martindale,
Frederick Follett,
William G. Bryan,
C. B. Rich,
Leander Mix,
Henry Bittinger,
Nicholson H. Parker, United States interpreter.

Also, the following chiefs and headmen heartily concur in the foregoing supplemental articles in behalf of themselves and their people:—

Lewis x Poodry,	John x Farmer,
Jesse x Spring,	Tommy x White,
Wm. x Parker,	John x Griffin,
Jabez x Ground,	George x Moses,
John x Wilson,	Henry x Moses,
Isaac x Shanks,	John x Hill,
Snow x Cooper,	John x Jones,
Isaac x Doctor,	Monroe x Jonas,
John x Bigfire,	Wm. x Johnson,
William x Moses,	Jackson x Ground,
Thomson x Blinkey,	Harrison x Scrogg,
James x Mitten,	Wm. x Alick,
John x Joshua,	Wm. x Stewart,
James x Williams,	Andrew x Blackchief,
Samuel x Parker,	John x Infant,
George x Sky,	Wm. x Taylor,
David x Printup,	James x Billy,
Benj. x Jonas,	Danl. x Peter,
Addison x Charles,	Saml. x Blue Sky,
John x Hatch.	James x Scrogg,
Headmen:	John x Shanks,
John x Smith,	Levi x Parker,
Small x Peter,	John x Jemison,
John x Beaver,	Chauncey x Abram

Signed in open council, in presence of—

Frederick Follett,
Nicholson H. Parker, United States interpreter.

TREATY WITH THE PONCA, 1858.

Mar. 12, 1858.

12 Stats., 997.
Ratified Mar. 8, 1859.
Proclaimed Apr. 11, 1859.

Articles of agreement and convention made and concluded at the city of Washington, on the twelfth day of March, one thousand eight hundred and fifty-eight, by Charles E. Mix, commissioner on the part of the United States, and Wa-gah-sah-pi, or Whip; Gish-tah-wah-gu, or Strong Walker; Mitchell P. Cera, or Wash-kom-moni; A-shno-ni-kah-gah-hi, or Lone Chief; Shu-kah-bi, or Heavy Clouds; Tah-tungah-nushi, or Standing Buffalo, on the part of the Ponca tribe of Indians; they being thereto duly authorized and empowered by said tribe.

Cession of all lands to the United States.

Reservation. Boundaries.

ARTICLE 1. The Ponca tribe of Indians hereby cede and relinquish to the United States all the lands now owned or claimed by them, wherever situate, except the tract bounded as follows, viz: Beginning at a point on the Neobrara River and running due north, so as to intersect the Ponca River twenty-five miles from its mouth; thence from said point of intersection, up and along the Ponca River, twenty —— miles; thence due south to the Neobrara River; and thence down and along said river to the place of beginning; which tract is hereby reserved for the future homes of said Indians; and to which they agree and bind themselves to remove within one year from the date of the ratification of this agreement by the Senate and President of the United States.

Stipulations on the part of the United States.
To protect the Ponca.

ARTICLE 2. In consideration of the foregoing cession and relinquishment, the United States agree and stipulate as follows, viz:

First. To protect the Poncas in the possession of the tract of land reserved for their future homes, and their persons and property thereon, during good behavior on their part.

To pay them annuities for thirty years.

Second. To pay to them, or expend for their benefit, the sum of twelve thousand dollars ($12,000) per annum for five years; commencing with the year in which they shall remove to and settle upon the tract reserved for their future homes; ten thousand dollars ($10,000) per annum for ten years, from and after the expiration of the said five years; and thereafter eight thousand dollars ($8,000) per annum, for

How to be paid.

fifteen years; of which sums the President of the United States shall, from time to time, determine what proportion shall be paid to the Poncas in cash, and what proportion shall be expended for their benefit; and also in what manner or for what objects such expenditure shall be made. He shall likewise exercise the power to make such provision out of the same, as he may deem to be necessary and proper for the support and comfort of the aged and infirm members of the tribe.

In case of any material decrease of the Poncas in number, the said amounts shall be reduced and diminished in proportion thereto, or they may, at the discretion of the President, be discontinued altogether should said Indians fail to make satisfactory efforts to advance and improve their condition; in which case such other provision shall be made for them as the President and Congress may judge to be suitable and proper.

United States to expend $20,000 for subsistence building houses, etc.

Third. To expend the sum of twenty thousand dollars ($20,000) in maintaining and subsisting the Poncas during the first year after their removal to their new homes, purchasing stock and agricultural implements, breaking up and fencing land, building houses, and in making such other improvements as may be necessary for their comfort and welfare.

To maintain schools. Children to be kept at school or payment discontinued.

Fourth. To establish, and to maintain for ten years, at an annual expense not to exceed five thousand dollars, ($5,000,) one or more manual-labor schools for the education and training of the Ponca youth in letters, agriculture, the mechanic arts, and housewifery; which school or schools shall be managed and conducted in such manner as the President of the United States shall direct; the Poncas hereby stipulating to constantly keep thereat, during at least nine months in every year, all their children between the ages of seven and eighteen years; and that, if this be not done, there shall be deducted from the shares of the annuities due to the parents, guardians, or other persons having control of the children, such amounts as may be proportioned to the deficiency in their time of attendance, compared with the said nine months, and the cost of maintaining and educating the children during that period. It is further agreed that such other measures may be adopted, to compel the attendance of the children at the school or schools as the President may think proper and direct; and whenever he shall be satisfied of a failure to fulfil the aforesaid stipulation on the part of the Poncas, he may, at his discretion, diminish or wholly discontinue the allowance and expenditure of the sum herein set apart for the support and maintenance of said school or schools.

Fifth. To provide the Poncas with a mill suitable for grinding grain and sawing timber, one or more mechanic shops, with the necessary tools for the same, and dwelling-houses for an interpreter, miller, engineer for the mill, if one be necessary, farmer, and the mechanics that may be employed for their benefit, the whole not to exceed in cost the sum of ten thousand five hundred dollars, ($10,500;) and also to expend annually, for ten years, or during the pleasure of the President, an amount not exceeding seven thousand five hundred dollars, ($7,500,) for the purpose of furnishing said Indians with such aid and assistance in agricultural and mechanical pursuits, including the working of said mill, as the Secretary of the Interior may consider advantageous and necessary for them; the Poncas hereby stipulating to furnish from their tribe the number of young men that may be required as apprentices and assistants in the mill and mechanic shops, and at least three persons to work constantly with each laborer employed for them in agricultural pursuits, it being understood that such laborers are to be employed more for the instruction of the Indians than merely to work for their benefit. The persons so to be furnished by the tribe shall be allowed a fair and just compensation for their services, to be fixed by the Secretary of the Interior. *(To provide saw and grist mills, mechanics' shop, etc.)* *(Ponca to furnish apprentices, etc.)*

The Poncas further stipulate and bind themselves to prevent any of the members of their tribe from destroying or injuring the said houses, shops, mill, machinery, stock, farming utensils, or any other thing furnished them by the Government; and in case of any such destruction or injury, or of any of the things so furnished being carried off by any member or members of their tribe, the value of the same shall be deducted from the tribal annuities. And whenever the President shall be satisfied that the Poncas have become sufficiently confirmed in habits of industry, and advanced in acquiring a practical knowledge of agriculture and the mechanic arts, he may, at his discretion, cause to be turned over to the tribe all of the said houses and other property furnished them by the United States, and dispense with the services of any or all of the persons hereinbefore stipulated to be employed for their benefit and assistance. *(To prevent injury to mills, etc.)* *(Ponca to have houses, etc., given them, when, etc.)*

Sixth. To provide and set apart the sum of twenty thousand dollars ($20,000) to enable the Poncas to adjust and settle their existing obligations and engagements, including depredations committed by them on property of citizens of the United States prior to the date of the ratification of this agreement, so far as the same may be found and decided by their agent to be valid and just, subject to the approval of the Secretary of the Interior; and in consideration of the long-continued friendship and kindness of Joseph Hollman and William G. Crawford toward the Poncas, of their furnishing them, when in distress, with large quantities of goods and provisions, and of their good counsel and advice, in consequence of which peace has often been pre- *(United States to pay $20,000 to settle existing obligations for the Ponca.)* *(Payment to Joseph Hollman and to William G. Crawford.)*

served between the Poncas and other Indians and the whites, it is agreed that out of the above-mentioned amount they shall be paid the sum of three thousand five hundred dollars, ($3,500,) and the sum of one thousand dollars ($1,000) shall in like manner be paid to Jesse Williams. of Iowa, in full for his claim, as such has been admitted by the Poncas for depredations committed by them on his property.

To Jesse Williams.

Provisions for half-breeds.

ARTICLE 3. The Poncas being desirous of making provision for their half-breed relatives, it is agreed that those who prefer and elect to reside among them shall be permitted to do so, and be entitled to and enjoy all the rights and privileges of members of the tribe; but to those who have chosen and left the tribe to reside among the whites and follow the pursuits of civilized life, viz: Charles Leclaire, Fort Piere, N. T.; Cillaste Leclaire, Pottowattomie, K. T.; Ciprian Leclaire, St. Louis, Missouri; Julia Harvey, Omaha, N. T.; Jenny Ruleau, Sioux City, Iowa; David Leclaire, Amelia Deloge, and Laura Deloge, at the Omaha mission, there shall be issued scrip for one hundred and sixty acres of land each, which shall be receivable at the United States land-offices in the same manner, and be subject to the same rules and regulations as military bounty-land warrants. And in consideration of the faithful services rendered to the Poncas by Francis Roy, their interpreter, it is agreed that scrip shall, in the like manner and amount, be issued to his wife and to each of his six children now living, without their being required to leave the nation. *Provided*, That application for the said scrip shall be made to the Commissioner of Indian Affairs within five years from and after the date of the ratification of this agreement.

Scrip for 160 acres of land to issue to each.

And to Francis Roy.

Scrip to be applied for in five years.

United States may maintain military posts, road, etc.

ARTICLE 4. The United States shall have the right to establish and maintain such military posts, roads, and Indian agencies as may be deemed necessary within the tract of country hereby reserved for the Poncas, but no greater quantity of land or timber shall be used for said purposes than shall be actually requisite; and if, in the establishment or maintenance of such posts, roads, and agencies, the property of any Ponca shall be taken, injured, or destroyed, just and adequate compensation shall be made therefor by the United States. And all roads or highways authorized by competent authority, other than the United States, the lines of which shall lie through said tract, shall have the right of way through the same; the fair and just value of such right being paid to the Poncas therefor by the party or parties authorizing the same or interested therein; to be assessed and determined in such manner as the President of the United States shall direct.

Whites not to reside on reservation, unless, etc.

ARTICLE 5. No white person, unless in the employment of the United States, or duly licensed to trade with the Poncas, or members of the family of such persons, shall be permitted to reside, or to make any settlement, upon any part of the tract herein reserved for said Indians, nor shall the latter alienate, sell, or in manner dispose of any portion thereof, except to the United States; but, whenever they may think proper, they may divide said tract among themselves, giving to each head of a family or single person a farm, with such rights of possession, transfer to any other member of the tribe, or of descent to their heirs and representatives, as may be in accordance with the laws, customs, and regulations of the tribe.

Lawful residents of lands hereby ceded may enter 160 acres at $1.25 per acre.

ARTICLE 6. Such persons as are now lawfully residing on the lands herein ceded by the Poncas shall each have the privilege of entering one hundred and sixty acres thereof, to include any improvements they may have, at one dollar and twenty-five cents per acre.

Ponca to maintain friendly relations.

ARTICLE 7. The Poncas acknowledge their dependence upon the Government of the United States, and do hereby pledge and bind themselves to preserve friendly relations with the citizens thereof, and to commit no injuries or depredations on their persons or property, nor on those of members of any other tribe; but, in case of any such injury or depredation, full compensation shall, as far as practicable, be made therefor out of their tribal annuities; the amount in all cases to be determined by the Secretary of the Interior. They further pledge themselves not to engage in hostilities with any other tribe, unless in self-defence, but to submit, through their agent, all matters of dispute and difficulty between themselves and other Indians for the decision of the President of the United States, and to acquiesce in and abide thereby. They also ageee, whenever called upon by the proper officer, to deliver up all offenders against the treaties, laws, or regulations of the United States, who may be within the limits of their reservation, and to assist in discovering, pursuing, and capturing all such offenders, whenever required to do so by such officer.

To pay for depredations.

Not to make war, except, etc.

To surrender offenders.

ARTICLE 8. To aid in preventing the evils of intemperance, it is hereby stipulated that if any of the Poncas shall drink, or procure for others, intoxicating liquor, their proportion of the tribal annuities shall be withheld from them for at least one year; and for a violation of any of the stipulations of this agreement on the part of the Poncas, they shall be liable to have their annuities withheld, in whole or in part, and for such length of time as the President of the United States shall direct.

Annuities to be withheld from those drinking, etc., intoxicating liquor.

ARTICLE 9. No part of the annuities of the Poncas shall be taken to pay any claims or demands against them, except such as may arise under this agreement, or under the trade and intercourse laws of the United States; and the said Indians do hereby fully relinquish and release the United States from all demands against them on the part of the tribe or any individuals thereof, except such as are herein stipulated and provided for.

Annuities of Indians not to pay individual debts.

Release of claims.

ARTICLE 10. The expenses connected with the negotiation of this agreement shall be paid by the United States.

In testimony whereof, the said Charles E. Mix, commissioner, as aforesaid, and the undersigned delegates and representatives of the Ponca tribes of Indians, have hereunto set their names and seals, at the place and on the day hereinbefore written.

Expenses of negotiation, how borne.

Charles E. Mix, Commissioner.	[L. S.]
Wah-gah-sah-pi, or Whip, his x mark.	[L. S.]
Gish-tah-wah-gu, or Strong Walker, his x mark.	[L. S.]
Mitchell P. Cera, or Wash-kom-mo-ni, his x mark.	[L. S.]
A-shno-ni-kah-gah-hi, or Lone Chief, his x mark.	[L. S.]
Shu-kah-bi, or Heavy Clouds, his x mark.	[L. S.]
Tah-tungah-nushi, or Standing Buffalo, his x mark.	[L. S.]

Executed in the presence of—
    Edward Hanrick,
    E. B. Grayson,
    James R. Roche,
    Moses Kelly,
    Joseph Hollman,
    Jno. Wm. Wells,
    J. B. Robertson, United States Indian agent,
    Henry Fontenelle, United States interpreter,
    Francis Roy, his x mark.

TREATY WITH THE YANKTON SIOUX, 1858.

Apr. 19. 1858.

11 Stat., 743.
Ratified Feb.16,1859.
Proclaimed Feb. 26,
1859.

Articles of agreement and convention made and concluded at the city of Washington, this nineteenth day of April, A. D. one thousand eight hundred and fifty-eight, by Charles E. Mix, commissioner on the part of the United States, and the following-named chiefs and delegates of the Yancton tribe of Sioux or Dacotah Indians, viz:

Pa-la-ne-a-pa-pe, the man that was struck by the Ree.
Ma-to-sa-be-che-a, the smutty bear.
Charles F. Picotte, Eta-ke-cha.
Ta-ton-ka-wete-co, the crazy bull.
Pse-cha-wa-kea, the jumping thunder.
Ma-ra-ha-ton, the iron horn.
Mombe-kah-pah, one that knocks down two.
Ta-ton-ka-e-yah-ka, the fast bull.
A-ha-ka-ma-ne, the walking elk.
A-ha-ka-na-zhe, the standing elk.
A-ha-ka-ho-che-cha, the elk with a bad voice.
Cha-ton-wo-ka-pa, the grabbing hawk.
E-ha-we-cha-sha, the owl man.
Pla-son-wa-kan-na-ge, the white medicine cow that stands.
Ma-ga-scha-che-ka, the little white swan.
Oke-che-la-wash-ta, the pretty boy.
(The three last names signed by their duly-authorized agent and representative, Charles F. Picotte,) they being thereto duly authorized and empowered by said tribe of Indians.

ARTICLE 1. The said chiefs and delegates of said tribe of Indians do hereby cede and relinquish to the United States all the lands now owned, possessed, or claimed by them, wherever situated, except four hundred thousand acres thereof, situated and described as follows, to wit—Beginning at the mouth of the Naw-izi-wa-koo-pah or Chouteau River and extending up the Missouri River thirty miles; thence due north to a point; thence easterly to a point on the said Chouteau River; thence down said river to the place of beginning, so as to include the said quantity of four hundred thousand acres. They, also, hereby relinquish and abandon all claims and complaints about or growing out of any and all treaties heretofore made by them or other Indians, except their annuity rights under the treaty of Laramie, of September 17, A. D. 1851.

Lands relinquished to the United States, except, etc.

ARTICLE 2. The land so ceded and relinquished by the said chiefs and delegates of the said tribe of Yanctons is and shall be known and described as follows, to wit—

"Beginning at the mouth of the Tchan-kas-an-data or Calumet or Big Sioux River; thence up the Missouri River to the mouth of the Pa-hah-wa-kan or East Medicine Knoll River; thence up said river to its head; thence in a direction to the head of the main fork of the Wan-dush-kah-for or Snake River; thence down said river to its junction with the Tchan-san-san or Jaques or James River; thence in a direct line to the northern point of Lake Kampeska; thence along the northern shore of said lake and its outlet to the junction of said outlet with the said Big Sioux River; thence down the Big Sioux River to its junction with the Missouri River."

Boundaries of land ceded.

And they also cede and relinquish to the United States all their right and title to and in all the islands of the Missouri River, from the mouth of the Big Sioux to the mouth of the Medicine Knoll River.

Islands in the Missouri River.

And the said chiefs and delegates hereby stipulate and agree that all the lands embraced in said limits are their own, and that they have full and exclusive right to cede and relinquish the same to the United States.

Title.

ARTICLE 3. The said chiefs and delegates hereby further stipulate and agree that the United States may construct and use such roads as may be hereafter necessary across their said reservation by the consent and permission of the Secretary of the Interior, and by first paying the said Indians all damages and the fair value of the land so used for said road or roads, which said damages and value shall be determined in such manner as the Secretary of the Interior may direct. And the said Yanctons hereby agree to *remove* and *settle* and *reside* on said reservation within one year from this date, and, until they do so remove, (if within said year,) the United States guarantee them in the quiet and undisturbed possession of their present settlements.

Necessary roads may be built across the lands reserved, paying damages therefor.

ARTICLE 4. In consideration of the foregoing cession, relinquishment, and agreements, the United States do hereby agree and stipulate as follows, to wit:

Indians to settle etc., on reservation within a year.

Agreements on part of the United States.

1st. To protect the said Yanctons in the quiet and peaceable possession of the said tract of four hundred thousand acres of land so reserved for their future home, and also their persons and property thereon during good behavior on their part.

Protection on the reserved lands.

2d. To pay to them, or expend for their benefit, the sum of sixty-five thousand dollars per annum, for ten years, commencing with the year in which they shall remove to, and settle and reside upon, their said reservation—forty thousand dollars per annum for and during ten years thereafter—twenty-five thousand dollars per annum for and during ten years thereafter—and fifteen thousand dollars per annum for and during twenty years thereafter; making *one million and six hundred thousand dollars in annuities in the period of fifty years*, of which sums the President of the United States shall, from time to time, determine what proportion shall be paid to said Indians, in cash, and what proportion shall be expended for their benefit, and, also, in what manner and for what objects such expenditure shall be made, due regard being had in making such determination to the best interests of said Indians. He shall likewise exercise the power to make such provision out of said sums as he may deem to be necessary and proper for the support and comfort of the aged or infirm, and helpless orphans of the said Indians. In case of any material decrease of said Indians, in number, the said amounts may, in the discretion of the President of the United States, be diminished and reduced in proportion thereto—or they may, at the discretion of the President of the United States, be discontinued entirely, should said Indians fail to make reasonable and satisfactory efforts to advance and improve their condition, in which case, such other provisions shall be made for them as the President and Congress may judge to be suitable and proper.

Payment of annuities.

3d. In addition to the foregoing sum of one million and six hundred thousand dollars as annuities, to be paid to or expended for the benefit of said Indians, during the period of fifty years, as before stated, the United States hereby stipulate and agree to expend for their benefit the sum of fifty thousand dollars more, as follows, to wit: Twenty-five thousand dollars in maintaining and subsisting the said Indians during the first year after their removal to and permanent settlement upon their said reservation; in the purchase of stock, agricultural implements, or other articles of a beneficial character, and in breaking up and fencing land; in the erection of houses, store-houses, or other needful buildings, or in making such other improvements as may be necessary for their comfort and welfare.

Subsistence.

Purchase of stock, etc.

4th. To expend ten thousand dollars to build a school-house or school-houses, and to establish and maintain one or more normal-labor schools (so far as said sum will go) for the education and training of the children of said Indians in letters, agriculture, the mechanic arts, and housewifery, which school or schools shall be managed and conducted in such manner as the Secretary of the Interior shall direct. The said

Schools and school-houses.

Indians hereby stipulating to keep constantly thereat, during at least nine months in the year, all their children between the ages of seven and eighteen years; and if any of the parents, or others having the care of children, shall refuse or neglect to send them to school, such parts of their annuities as the Secretary of the Interior may direct, shall be withheld from them and applied as he may deem just and proper; and such further sum, in addition to the said ten thousand dollars, as shall be deemed necessary and proper by the President of the United States, shall be reserved and taken from their said annuities, and applied annually, during the pleasure of the President to the support of said schools, and to furnish said Indians with assistance and aid and instruction in agricultural and mechanical pursuits, including the working of the mills, hereafter mentioned, as the Secretary of the Interior may consider necessary and advantageous for said Indians; and all instruction **Indians to furnish apprentices for mills, etc.** in reading shall be in the English language. And the said Indians hereby stipulate to furnish, from amongst themselves, the number of young men that may be required as apprentices and assistants in the mills and mechanic shops, and at least three persons to work constantly with each white laborer employed for them in agriculture and mechanical pursuits, it being understood that such white laborers and assistants as may be so employed *are* thus employed more for the instruction of the said Indians than merely to work for their benefit; and that the laborers so to be furnished by the Indians may be allowed a fair and just compensation for their services, to be fixed by the Secretary of the Interior, and to be paid out of the shares of annuity of such Indians as **President may discontinue allowance for school.** are able to work, but refuse or neglect to do so. And whenever the President of the United States shall become satisfied of a failure, on the part of said Indians, to fulfil the aforesaid stipulations, he may, at his discretion, discontinue the allowance and expenditure of the sums so provided and set apart for said school or schools, and assistance and instruction.

United States to furnish mills, mechanic shops, etc. 5th. To provide the said Indians with a mill suitable for grinding grain and sawing timber; one or more mechanic shops, with the necessary tools for the same; and dwelling-houses for an interpreter, mi ler, engineer for the mill, (if one be necessary,) a farmer, and the mech lnics that may be employed for their benefit, and to expend therefor aa sum not exceeding fifteen thousand dollars.

Mills, etc., not to be injured. ARTICLE 5. Said Indians further stipulate and bind themselves to prevent any of the members of their tribe from destroying or injuring the said houses, shops, mills, machinery, stock, farming-utensils, or any other thing furnished them by the Government, and in case of any **If injured value to be deducted from annuity.** such destruction or injury of any of the things so furnished, or their being carried off by any member or members of their tribe, the value of the same shall be deducted from their general annuity; and whenever the Secretary of the Interior shall be satisfied that said Indians have become sufficiently confirmed in habits of industry and advanced in the acquisition of a practical knowledge of agriculture and the mechanic arts to provide for themselves, he may, at his discretion, **Houses, etc., to be given to the Indians when, etc.** cause to be turned over to them all of the said houses and other property furnished them by the United States, and dispense with the services of any or all persons hereinbefore stipulated to be employed for their benefit, assistance, and instruction.

Portion of annuities may be paid for debts, etc. ARTICLE 6. It is hereby agreed and understood that the chiefs and head-men of said tribe may, at their discretion, in open council, authorize to be paid *out of their said annuities* such a sum or sums as may be found to be necessary and proper, not exceeding in the aggregate one hundred and fifty thousand dollars, to satisfy their just debts and obligations, and to provide for such of their half-breed relations as do not live with them, or draw any part of the said annuities of said Indians: **Proviso.** *Provided, however*, That their said determinations shall be approved by their agent for the time being, and the said payments authorized by the Secretary of the Interior: *Provided, also,* That there shall not Proviso. be so paid out of their said annuities in any one year, a sum exceeding fifteen thousand dollars.

ARTICLE 7. On account of their valuable services and liberality to Grants of land to Charles F. Picotte, Zephyr Rencontre, Paul Dorian, and others. the Yanctons, there shall be granted in fee to Charles F. Picotte and Zephyr Rencontre, each, one section of six hundred and forty acres of land, and to Paul Dorian one-half a section; and to the half-breed Yancton, wife of Charles Reulo, and her two sisters, the wives of Eli Bedaud and Augustus Traverse, and to Louis Le Count, each, one-half a section. The said grants shall be selected in said ceded territory, and shall not be within said reservation, nor shall they interfere in any way with the improvements of such persons as are on the lands ceded above by authority of law; and all other persons (other than Indians, Persons other than Indians or mixed bloods may enter 160 acres at $1.25 per acre. or mixed-bloods) who are now residing within said ceded country, by authority of law, shall have the privilege of entering one hundred and sixty acres thereof, to include each of their residences or improvements, at the rate of one dollar and twenty-five cents per acre.

ARTICLE 8. The said Yancton Indians shall be secured in the free Yankton to be secure in the use of the red pipestone quarry. and unrestricted use of the red pipe-stone quarry, or so much thereof as they have been accustomed to frequent and use for the purpose of procuring stone for pipes; and the United States hereby stipulate and agree to cause to be surveyed and marked so much thereof as shall be necessary and proper for that purpose, and retain the same and keep it open and free to the Indians to visit and procure stone for pipes so long as they shall desire.

ARTICLE 9. The United States shall have the right to establish and United States may maintain military posts, etc. maintain such military posts, roads, and Indian agencies as may be deemed necessary within the tract of country herein reserved for the use of the Yanctons; but no greater quantity of land or timber shall be used for said purposes than shall be actually requisite; and if, in the establishment or maintenance of such posts, roads, and agencies, the property of any Yancton shall be taken, injured, or destroyed, just and adequate compensation shall be made therefor by the United States.

ARTICLE 10. No white person, unless in the employment of the No trade with Indians unless licensed. United States, or duly licensed to trade with the Yanctons, or members of the families of such persons, shall be permitted to reside or make any settlement upon any part of the tract herein reserved for said Indians, nor shall said Indians alienate, sell, or in any manner dispose Land not to be alienated except, etc. of any portion thereof, except to the United States. Whenever the Secretary of the Interior shall direct, said tract shall be surveyed and divided as he shall think proper among said Indians, so as to give to each head of a family or single person a separate farm, with such rights of possession or transfer to any other member of the tribe or of descent to their heirs and representatives as he may deem just.

ARTICLE 11. The Yanctons acknowledge their dependence upon the The Yankton to preserve friendly relations. Government of the United States, and do hereby pledge and bind themselves to preserve friendly relations with the citizens thereof, and to commit no injuries or depredations on their persons or property, nor on those of members of any other tribe or nation of *of* Indians; and in case of any such injuries or depredations by said Yanctons, full compensation shall, as far as possible, be made therefor out of their tribal annuities, the amount in all cases to be determined by the Secretary of the Interior. They further pledge themselves not to engage in hostilities with any other tribe or nation, unless in self-defence, but to submit, through their agent, all matters of dispute and difficulty between themselves and other Indians for the decision of the President of the United States, and to acquiesce in and abide thereby. They Surrender of offenders. also agree to deliver, to the proper officer of the United States all offenders against the treaties, laws, or regulations of the United States, and to assist in discovering, pursuing, and capturing all such offenders, who may be within the limits of their reservation, whenever required to do so by such officer.

Tribal annuities to be withheld if intemperate, etc.

ARTICLE 12. To aid in preventing the evils of intemperance, it is hereby stipulated that if any of the Yanctons shall drink, or procure for others, intoxicating liquor, their proportion of the tribal annuities shall be withheld from them for at least one year; and for a violation of any of the stipulations of this agreement on the part of the Yanctons they shall be liable to have their annuities withheld, in whole or in part, and for such length of time as the President of the United States shall direct.

Annuities not to be subject to debts, except, etc.

ARTICLE 13. No part of the annuities of the Yanctons shall be taken to pay any debts, claims, or demands against them, except such existing claims and demands as have been herein provided for, and except such as may arise under this agreement, or under the trade and intercourse laws of the United States.

Release of all demands, etc.

ARTICLE 14. The said Yanctons do hereby fully acquit and release the United States from all demands against them on the part of said tribe, or any individual thereof, except the beforementioned right of the Yanctons to receive an annuity under said treaty of Laramie, and except, also, such as are herein stipulated and provided for.

Indian agent for Yankton.

ARTICLE 15. For the special benefit of the Yanctons, parties to this agreement, the United States agree to appoint an agent for them, who shall reside on their said reservation, and shall have set apart for his sole use and occupation, at such a point as the Secretary of the Interior may direct, one hundred and sixty acres of land.

Expenses hereof to be borne by the United States.

ARTICLE 16. All the expenses of the making of this agreement, and of surveying the said Yancton reservation, and of surveying and marking said pipe-stone quarry, shall be paid by the United States.

When to take effect.

ARTICLE 17. This instrument shall take effect and be obligatory upon the contracting parties whenever ratified by the Senate and the President of the United States.

In testimony whereof, the said Charles E. Mix, commissioner, as aforesaid, and the undersigned chiefs, delegates, and representatives of the said tribe of Yancton Indians, have hereunto set their hands and seals at the place and on the day first above written.

Charles E. Mix, Commissioner. [L. S.]

Pa-la-ne-apa-pe, or the Man that was struck by the Ree, his x mark. [L. S.]

Ma-to-sa-be-che-a, or the Smutty Bear, his x mark. [L. S.]

Charles F. Picotte, or Eta-ke-cha. [L. S.]

Ta-ton-ka-wete-co, or the Crazy Bull, his x mark. [L. S.]

Pse-cha-wa-kea, or the Jumping Thunder, his x mark. [L. S.]

Ma-ra-ha-ton, or the Iron Horn, his x mark. [L. S.]

Nombe-kah-pah, or One that knocks down two, his x mark. [L. S.]

Ta-ton-ka-e-yah-ka, or the Fast Bull, his x mark. [L. S.]

A-ha-ka Ma-ne, or the Walking Elk, his x mark. [L. S.]

A-ha-ka-na-zhe, or the Standing Elk, his x mark. [L. S.]

A-ha-ka-ho-che-cha, or the Elk with a bad voice, his x mark. [L. S.]

Cha-ton-wo-ka-pa, or the Grabbing Hawk, his x mark. [L. S.]

E-ha-we-cha-sha, or the Owl Man, his x mark. [L. S.]

Pla-son-wa-kan-na-ge, or the White Medicine Cow that stands, by his duly authorized delegate and representative, Charles F. Picotte. [L. S.]

Ma-ga-scha-che-ka, or the Little White Swan, by his duly authorized delegate and representative, Charles F. Picotte. [L. S.]

O-ke-che-la-wash-ta, or the Pretty Boy, by his duly authorized delegate and representative, Chas. F. Picotte. [L. S.]

Executed in the presence of—

A. H. Redfield, agent.
J. B. S. Todd.
Theophile Bruguier.
John Dowling.
Fr. Schmidt.
John W. Wells
D. Walker.

E. B. Grayson.
S. J. Johnson.
George P. Mapes.
H. Bittinger.
D. C. Davis.
Zephier Roncontre, his x mark, United States interpreter.

Witness:

    J. B. S. Todd,
    Paul Dorain, his x mark.
    Charles Rulo, his x mark.

Witness:

    J. B. S. Todd.

TREATY WITH THE SIOUX, 1858.

Articles of agreement and convention made and concluded at the city of Washington, on the nineteenth day of June, one thousand eight hundred and fifty-eight, by Charles E. Mix, commissioner on the part of the United States, and the following-named chiefs and headmen of the Mendawakanton and Wahpahoota bands of the Dakota or Sioux tribe of Indians, viz, Wabashaw, Chetanakooamonee, Washuhiyahidan, Shakopee, Wamindeetonkee, Muzzaojanjan, and Makawto, chiefs, and Hinhanduta, Ha-raka-Muzza, Wakanojanjan, Tachunrpee-muz-za, Wakinyantowa, Chunrpiyuha, Onkeeterhidan, and Wamouisa, braves, on the part of the Mendawakantons, and Hushawshaw, chief, and Pa-Pa and Tataebomdu, braves, on the part of the Wahpakootas, they being duly authorized and empowered to act for said bands.

June 19, 1858.

12 Stats., 1031.
Ratified Mar, 9, 1859.
Proclaimed Mar. 31, 1859.

ARTICLE 1. It is hereby agreed and stipulated that, as soon as practicable after the ratification of this agreement, so much of that part of the reservation or tract of land now held and possessed by the Mendawakanton and Wahpakoota bands of the Dakota or Sioux Indians, and which is described in the third article of the treaty made with them on the fifth day of August, one thousand eight hundred and fiftyone, which lies south or southwestwardly of the Minnesota River, shall constitute a reservation for said bands, and shall be surveyed, and eighty acres thereof, as near as may be in conformity with the public surveys, be allotted in severalty to each head of a family, or single person over the age of twenty-one years, in said band of Indians, said allotments to be so made as to include a proper proportion of timbered land, if the same be practicable, in each of said allotments. The residue of said part of said reservation not so allotted, shall be held by said bands in common, and as other Indian lands are held: *Provided, however,* That eighty acres, as near as may be, shall, in like manner as above provided for, be allotted to each of the minors of said bands on his or her attaining their majority, or on becoming heads of families by contracting marriage, if neither of the parties shall have previously received land.

Eighty acres of reservation to be allotted to each head of a family or, etc.

Residue to be held in common.

Further allotment.

All the necessary expenses of the surveys, and allotments thus provided, for shall be defrayed out of the funds of said bands of Indians in the hands of the Government of the United States.

Expenses of survey and allotments, how borne.

As the members of said bands become capable of managing their business and affairs, the President of the United States may, at his discretion, cause patents to be issued to them, for the tracts of land allotted to them, respectively, in conformity with this article; said tracts to be exempt from levy, taxation, sale or forfeiture, until otherwise provided for by the legislature of the State in which they are situated with the assent of Congress; nor shall they be sold or alienated in fee, or be in any other manner disposed of except to the United States or to members of said bands.

Patents to issue to them for said lands.

Lands to be exempt from taxes, etc.

And not to be alienated except.

ARTICLE 2. Whereas by the treaty with the Mendawakanton and Wahpakoota bands of Sioux Indians, concluded at Mendota on the fifth day of August, one thousand eight hundred and fifty-one, said bands retained for their "future occupancy and home," "to be held by them as Indian lands are held, a tract of country of the average width of

Preamble.
Provisions of treaty of Aug. 5, 1851.

ten miles on either side of the Minnesota River," extending from Little Rock River to the Tchatamba and Yellow Medicine Rivers, which land was to "be held by said bands in common."

Amended by the Senate.

And whereas the Senate of the United States so amended said treaty as to strike therefrom the provision setting apart said land as a home for said bands, and made provision for the payment to said bands "at the rate of ten cents per acre for the lands included in the" said tract so reserved and set apart for the "occupancy and home" of said bands, and also provided in addition thereto, that there should be "set apart, by appropriate landmarks and boundaries, such tracts of country without the limits of the cession made by the first article of the" said treaty as should "be satisfactory for their future occupancy and home," said Senate amendment providing also "that the President may, with the consent of these Indians, vary the conditions aforesaid, if deemed expedient;" all of which provisions in said amendment were assented to by said Indians.

And whereas the President so far varied the conditions of said Senate amendment, as to permit said bands to locate for the time being, upon the tract originally reserved by said bands for a home, and no "tracts of country without the limits of the cession" made in the said treaty *has* [have] ever been provided for, or offered to, said bands:

Act of 1854, ch. 167, 10 Stat. 326.

And whereas by the "act making appropriations for the current and contingent expenses of the Indian Department and for fulfilling treaty stipulations with various Indian tribes," approved July 31, 1854, the President was authorized to confirm to the Sioux of Minnesota forever, the reserve on the Minnesota River now occupied by them, upon such conditions as he may deem just:

And whereas, although the President has not directly confirmed said reserve to said Indians, they claim that as they were entitled to receive "such tracts of country" as should "be satisfactory for their future occupancy and home," and as no such country has been provided for,

Question of title of the bands to certain lands to be submitted to the Senate, and what allowance to be made if decision is in their favor.

or offered to, said bands, it is agreed and stipulated that the question shall be submitted to the Senate for decision whether they have such title: and if they have, what compensation shall be made to them for that part of said reservation or tract of land lying on the north side of the Minnesota River—whether they shall be allowed a specific sum of money therefor, and if so, how much; or whether the same shall be sold for their benefit, they to receive the proceeds of such sale, deducting the necessary expenses incident thereto. Such sale, if decided in favor of by the Senate, shall be made under and according to regulations to be prescribed by the Secretary of the Interior, and in such manner as will secure to them the largest sum it may be practicable to obtain for said land.

From proceeds of sale not over $70,000 may be paid chiefs and headmen.

ARTICLE 3. It is also agreed that if the Senate shall authorize the land designated in article two of this agreement to be sold for the benefit of the said Mendawakanton and Wahpakoota bands, or shall prescribe an amount to be paid said bands for their interest in said tract, provision shall be made by which the chiefs and head-men of said bands may, in their discretion, in open council, authorize to be paid out of the proceeds of said tract, such sum or sums as may be found necessary and proper, not exceeding seventy thousand dollars, to satisfy their just debts and obligations, and to provide goods to be taken by said chiefs and head-men to the said bands upon their return:

Proviso.

Provided, however, That their said determinations shall be approved by the superintendent of Indian affairs for the northern superintendency for the time being, and the said payments be authorized by the Secretary of the Interior.

Lands retained under the first article to be deemed an Indian reservation.

ARTICLE 4. The lands retained and to be held by the members of the Mendawakanton and Wahpakoota bands of the Dakota or Sioux Indians, under and by virtue of the first article of this agreement, shall, to all intents and purposes whatever, be deemed and held to be an Indian reservation; and the laws which have been, or may hereafter be enacted by Congress, to regulate trade and intercourse with the Indian tribes, shall have full force and effect over and within the limits of the same; and no person other than the members of the said bands, to be ascertained and defined under such regulations as the Secretary of the Interior shall prescribe, unless such as may be duly licensed to trade with said bands, or employed for their benefit, or members of the family of such persons, shall be permitted to reside or make any settlement upon any part of said reservation; and the timbered land allotted to individuals, and also that reserved for subsequent distribution as provided in the first article of this agreement, shall be free from all trespass, use, or occupation, except as hereinafter provided.

ARTICLE 5. The United States shall have the right to establish and maintain upon said reservation such military posts, agencies, schools, mills, shops, roads, and agricultural or mechanical improvements, as may be deemed necessary, but no greater quantity of land or timber shall be taken and used for said purposes than shall be actually requisite therefor. And if in the establishment or maintenance of such posts, agencies, roads or other improvements, the timber or other property of any individual Indian shall be taken, injured, or destroyed, just and adequate compensation shall be made therefor by the United States. Roads or highways authorized by competent authority other than the United States, the lines of which shall lie through said reservation, shall have the right of way through the same, upon the fair and just value of such right being paid to the said Mendawakanton and Wapakoota bands by the party or parties authorizing or interested in the same, to be assessed and determined in such manner as the Secretary of the Interior shall direct.

The United States may maintain military posts, roads, etc., on reservation.

Compensation to be made for damages caused thereby to any Indian.

ARTICLE 6. The Mendawakanton and Wahpakoota bands of Dakota or Sioux Indians acknowledge their dependence on the Government of the United States, and do hereby pledge and bind themselves to preserve friendly relations with the citizens thereof, and to commit no injuries or depredations on their persons or property, nor on those of the members of any other tribe; but in case of any such injury or depredation, full compensation shall, as far as practicable be made therefor out of their moneys in the hands of the United States; the amount in all cases to be determined by the Secretary of the Interior. They further pledge themselves not to engage in hostilities with the Indians of any other tribe unless in self-defence, but to submit, through their agent, all matters of dispute and difficulty between themselves and other Indians, for the decision of the President of the United States, and to acquiesce in and abide thereby. They also agree to deliver to the proper officers all persons belonging to their said bands who may become offenders against the treaties, laws, or regulations of the United States, or the laws of the State of Minnesota, and to assist in discovering, pursuing, and capturing all such offenders whenever required so to do by such officers, through the agent or other proper officer of the Indian Department.

The bands to preserve friendly relations, etc.

To pay for depredations.

Not to engage in hostilities unless, etc.

Bands to surrender offenders.

ARTICLE 7. To aid in preventing the evils of intemperance, it is hereby stipulated that if any of the members of the said Mendawakanton and Wahpakoota bands of Sioux Indians shall drink, or procure for others, intoxicating liquors, their proportion of the annuities of said bands shall, at the discretion of the Secretary of the Interior, be withheld from them for the period of at least one year; and for a violation of any of the stipulations of this agreement on the part of any members of said bands, the persons so offending shall be liable to have their annuities withheld and to be subject to such other punishment as the Secretary of the Interior may prescribe.

Annuities to be withheld from those drinking, etc., intoxicating liquors.

ARTICLE 8. Such of the stipulations of former treaties as provided for the payment of particular sums of money to the said Mendawakanton and Wahpakoota bands, or for the application or expenditure

Secretary of the Interior to have discretion over manner and object of annual expenditure.

of specific amounts for particular objects or purposes, shall be, and hereby are, so amended and changed as to invest the Secretary of the Interior with discretionary power in regard to the manner and objects of the annual expenditure of all such sums or amounts which have accrued and are now due to said bands, together with the amount the said bands shall become annually entitled to under and by virtue of the provisions of this agreement: *Provided*, The said sums or amounts shall be expended for the benefit of said bands at such time or times and in such manner as the said Secretary shall deem best calculated to promote their interests, welfare, and advance in civilization. And it is further agreed, that such change may be made in the stipulations of former treaties which provide for the payment of particular sums for specified purposes, as to permit the chiefs and braves of said bands or any of the subdivisions of said bands, with the sanction of the Secretary of the Interior, to authorize such payment or expenditures of their annuities, or any portion thereof, which are to become due hereafter, as may be deemed best for the general interests and welfare of the said bands or subdivisions thereof.

Senate to decide whether $10,000 to be paid to A. J. Campbell.
Ante, p. 493.

ARTICLE 9. As the Senate struck from the treaty with the Mendawakanton band of Sioux on the twenty-ninth day of September, one thousand eight hundred and thirty-seven, the ninth clause of the second article and the whole of the third article of said treaty, which provided for the payment of four hundred and fifty (450) dollars annually, for twenty years, to Scott Campbell, and confirmed to the said Scott Campbell a title to five hundred (500) acres of land which he then occupied, said payment and land being deemed by said Indians to form a part of the consideration for which they ceded to the United States a certain tract of land in said treaty specified, which reduction, in the consideration for said land, has never been sanctioned by said Indians, the said Mendawakantons and Wahpakoota bands now request that provision be made for the payment of the sum of ten thousand (10,000) dollars to A. J. Campbell, the son of said Scott Campbell, now deceased, in full consideration of the money stipulated to be paid and land confirmed to said Scott Campbell in the original draft of said treaty aforesaid; which subject is hereby submitted to the Senate for its favorable consideration.

United States to pay expenses of negotiation.

ARTICLE 10. The expenses attending the negotiation of this agreement shall be defrayed by the United States.

In testimony whereof, the said Charles E. Mix, Commissioner, as aforesaid, and the undersigned chiefs and headmen of the said Mendawakanton and Wahpakoota bands, have hereunto set their hands and seals at the place and on the day first above written.

Charles E. Mix, Commissioner, [L. S.]

Wa-bash-aw, his x mark. [L. S.]	Wu-ka-no-jan-jan, (Medicine Light,) his x mark. [L. S.]
Che-tan-a-koo-a-mo-nee, (Little Crow,) his x mark. [L. S.]	Ta-chunr-pee-muzza, (His Iron War Club,) his x mark. [L. S.]
Wa-su-hi-ya-hi-dan, his x mark. [L. S.]	Wa-kin-yan-to-wa, (Owns the Thunder,) his x mark. [L. S.]
Sha-ko-pee, (Six,) his x mark. [L. S.]	
Wa-min-dee-ton-kee, (Large War Eagle,) his x mark. [L. S.]	Chunr-pi-you-ha, (Has a War Club,) his x mark. [L. S.]
Muz-za-o-jan-jan, (Iron Light,) his x mark. [L. S.]	On-kee-ter-hi-dan, (Little Whale,) his x mark. [L. S.]
Ma-kaw-to, (Blue Earth,) his x mark. [L. S.]	Wa-mo-u-i-sa, (The Thief,) his x mark. [L. S.]
Hu-shaw-shaw, (Red Legs,) his x mark. [L. S.]	Pa-pa, (Sharp,) his x mark. [L. S.]
Hin-han-du-ta, (Scarlet Owl,) his x mark. [L. S.]	Ta-ta-i-bom-du, (Scattering Wind,) his x mark. [L. S.]
Ha-raka-muz-za, (Iron Elk,) his x mark. [L. S.]	

Signed, sealed and delivered in presence of—

Joseph R. Brown, Sioux agent
A. J. Campbell, interpreter.
N. R. Brown.
A. Robertson.
John Dowling.

James R. Roche.
B. D. Hyam.
H. J. Myrick.
Thos. A. Robertson.
Fr. Schmidt.

[N. B.—By the first section of the act of February 16, 1863, 12th Statutes at Large, page 652, it is provided as follows: That all treaties heretofore made and entered into by the Sisseton, Wahpaton, Medawakanton, and Wahpakoota bands of Sioux or Dakota Indians, or any of them, with the United States, are hereby declared to be abrogated and annulled, so far as said treaties or any of them purport to impose any future obligation on the United States, and all lands and rights of occupancy within the State of Minnesota, and all annuities and claims heretofore accorded to said Indians, or any of them, to be forfeited to the United States.]

TREATY WITH THE SIOUX, 1858.

Articles of agreement and convention made and concluded at the city of Washington on the nineteenth day of June, one thousand eight hundred and fifty-eight, by Charles E. Mix, commissioner on the part of the United States, and the following-named chiefs and head-men of the Sisseeton and Wahpaton bands of the Dakota or Sioux tribe of Indians, viz: Maz-zah-shaw, Wamdupidutah, Ojupi, and Hahutanai, on the part of the Sisseetons, and Maz-zomanee, Muz-zakoote-manee, Upiyahideyaw, Umpedutokechaw, and Tachandupahotanka, on the part of the Wahpatons, they being duly authorized and empowered to act for said bands.

June 19, 1858.

12 Stats., p. 1037.
Ratified Mar. 9, 1859.
Proclaimed Mar. 31, 1859.

ARTICLE 1. It is hereby agreed and stipulated that as soon as practicable after the ratification of this agreement, so much of that part of the reservation or tract of land now held and possessed by the Sisseeton and Wahpaton bands of the Dakota or Sioux Indians, and which is described in the third article of the treaty made with them on the twenty-third day of July, one thousand eight hundred and fifty-one, which lies south or southwestwardly of the Minnesota River, shall constitute a reservation for said bands, and shall be surveyed, and eighty acres thereof, as near as may be in conformity with the public surveys, be allotted in severalty to each head of a family or single person over the age of twenty-one years, in said bands of Indians; said allotments to be so made as to include a proper proportion of timbered land, if the same be practicable, in each of said allotments. The residue of said part of said reservation not so allotted shall be held by said bands in common, and as other Indian lands are held: *Provided, however*, That eighty acres thereof, as near as may be, shall in like manner, as above provided for, be allotted to each of the minors of said bands on his or her attaining their majority, or on becoming heads of families, by contracting marriage, if neither of the parties shall have previously received land. All the necessary expenses of the surveys and allotments thus provided for shall be defrayed out of the funds of said bands of Indians in the hands of the Government of the United States.

As the members of said bands become capable of managing their business and affairs, the President of the United States may at his discretion, cause patents to be issued to them for the tracts of lands allotted to them respectively, in conformity with this article; said tracts to be exempt from levy, taxation, sale, or forfeiture, until otherwise provided for by the legislature of the State in which they are situated, with the assent of Congress; nor shall they be sold or alienated in fee, or be in any other manner disposed of, except to the United States or to members of said bands.

Eighty acres of reservation to be allotted each head of a family or, etc.

Residue to be held in common.

Further allotment.

Expenses of surveys and allotments, how borne.

Patents to issue to them for said lands.

Lands to be exempt from taxes, and not to be alienated, except, etc.

Preamble.
Provisionsofatreaty
of July 23, 1851.

ARTICLE 2. Whereas, by the treaty with the Sisseeton and Wahpaton bands of Sioux Indians, concluded at Traverse des Sioux on the twenty-third day of July, one thousand eight hundred and fifty-one, said bands retained for their "future occupancy and home," "to be held by them as Indian lands are held, all that tract of country on the Minnesota River, from the western boundary" of the cession therein made "east to the Tcha-tam-ba   iver on the north, and to the Yellow Medicine River on the south side, to extend on each side a distance of not less than ten miles from the general course of said Minnesota River;"

Amended by the
Senate.

And whereas the Senate of the United States so amended said treaty as to strike therefrom the provision setting apart the said land as a home for said bands, and made provision for the payment to said bands, "at the rate of ten cents per acre for the land included in the said tract so retained and set apart for the occupancy and home" of said bands, and also provided, in addition thereto, that there should be "set apart by appropriate landmarks and boundaries such tracts of country without the limits of the cession made by the first article of the said treaty as shall be satisfactory for their future occupancy and home;" said Senate amendment providing also "that the President may, with the consent of these Indians, vary the conditions aforesaid, if deemed expedient;" all of which provisions in said amendment were assented to by said Indians;

And whereas the President so far varied the conditions of said Senate amendment as to permit said bands to locate for the time being upon the tract originally reserved by said bands for a home, and " no tract of country, without the limits of the cession " made in the said treaty, has ever been provided for or offered to said bands;

Provisions of act of
1854, ch. 167.

And whereas, by the act making appropriations for the current and contingent expenses of the Indian Department, and for fulfilling treaty stipulations with various Indian tribes, approved July 31, 1854, the President was authorized " to confirm to the Sioux of Minnesota, forever, the reserve on the Minnesota River now occupied by them, upon such conditions as he may deem just;"

And whereas, although the President has not directly confirmed said reserve to said Indians, they claim that, as they were entitled to receive " such tracts of country " as should " be satisfactory for their future occupancy and home," and as no other country than this reservation was ever provided for or offered to them, and as valuable improvements

Question of title of
the bands to certain
lands to be submitted
to the Senate and
what allowance is to
be made if the deci-
sion is in their favor.

have been made on said reservation with the moneys belonging to said bands, it is agreed and stipulated that the question shall be submitted to the Senate for decision whether they have such title, and if they have, what compensation shall be made to them for that part of said reservation or tract of land lying on the north side of the Minnesota River; whether they shall be allowed a specific sum of money therefor, and if so, how much; or whether the same shall be sold for their benefit, they to receive the proceeds of such sale, deducting the necessary expenses incident thereto. Such sale, if decided in favor of by the Senate, shall be made under and according to regulations to be prescribed by the Secretary of the Interior, and in such manner as will secure to them the largest sum it may be practicable to obtain for said land.

From proceeds of
sale not over $70,000
to be paid chiefs and
headmen.

ARTICLE 3. It is also agreed that if the Senate shall authorize the land designated in article two of this agreement to be sold for the benefit of the said Sisseeton and Wahpaton bands, or shall prescribe an amount to be paid to said bands for their interest in said tract, provision shall be made by which the chiefs and head-men of said bands may, in their discretion, in open council, authorize to be paid out of the proceeds of said tract such sum or sums as may be found necessary and proper, not exceeding seventy thousand dollars, to satisfy their just debts and obligations, and to provide goods to be taken by said chiefs and head-men to the said bands on their return: *Provided, however*, That their said determinations shall be approved by the superintendent of Indian affairs for the northern superintendency for the time being, and the said payments be authorized by the Secretary of the Interior. Proviso.

ARTICLE 4. The lands retained and to be held by the members of the Sisseeton and Wahpaton bands of Dakota or Sioux Indians, under and by virtue of the first article of this agreement, shall, to all intents and purposes whatever be deemed and held to be an Indian reservation, and the laws which have been or may hereafter be enacted by Congress to regulate trade and intercourse with the Indian tribes, shall have full force and effect over and within the limits of the same; and no person other than the members of said bands, to be ascertained and defined under such regulations as the Secretary of the Interior shall prescribe—unless such as may be duly licensed to trade with said bands, or employed for their benefit, or members of the family of such persons—shall be permitted to reside or make any settlement upon any part of said reservation; and the timbered land allotted to individuals, and also that reserved for subsequent distribution, as provided in the first article of this agreement, shall be free from all trespass, use or occupation, except as hereinafter provided. *Lands retained under the first article to be deemed an Indian reservation.*

ARTICLE 5. The United States shall have the right to establish and maintain upon said reservation such military posts, agencies, schools, mills, shops, roads, and agricultural or mechanical improvements as may be deemed necessary; but no greater quantity of land or timber shall be taken and used for said purposes than shall be actually requisite therefor. And if in the establishment or maintenance of such posts, agencies, roads, or other improvements, the timber or other property of any individual Indian shall be taken, injured, or destroyed, just and adequate compensation shall be made therefor by the United States. Roads or highways authorized by competent authority other than the United States, the lines of which shall lie through said reservation, shall have the right of way through the same upon the fair and just value of such right being paid to the said Sisseeton and Wahpaton bands by the party or parties authorizing or interested in the same, to be assessed and determined in such manner as the Secretary of the Interior shall direct. *United States may maintain military posts, roads, etc., in reservation.* *Compensation to be paid for damages caused thereby to any Indian.*

ARTICLE 6. The Sisseeton and Wahpaton bands of Dakota or Sioux Indians acknowledge their dependence on the Government of the United States, and do hereby pledge and bind themselves to preserve friendly relations with the citizens thereof, and to commit no injuries or depredations on their persons or property, nor on those of the members of any other tribe; but in case of any such injury or depredation, full compensation shall, as far as practicable, be made therefor out of their moneys in the hands of the United States, the amount in all cases to be determined by the Secretary of the Interior. They further pledge themselves not to engage in hostilities with the Indians of any other tribe, unless in self-defence, but to submit, through their agent, all matters of dispute and difficulty between themselves and other Indians for the decision of the President of the United States, and to acquiesce in and abide thereby. They also agree to deliver to the proper officers all persons belonging to their said bands who may become offenders against the treaties, laws, or regulations of the United States, or the laws of the State of Minnesota, and to assist in discovering, pursuing, and capturing all such offenders whenever required so to do by such officers, through the agent or other proper officer of the Indian Department. *The bands to preserve friendly relations.* *To pay for depredations.* *Not to engage in hostilities except, etc.* *To surrender offenders.*

ARTICLE 7. To aid in preventing the evils of intemperance, it is hereby stipulated that if any of the members of the said Sisseeton and Wahpaton bands of Sioux Indians shall drink or procure for others intoxicating liquors, their proportion of the annuities of said bands *Annuities to be withheld from those drinking, etc., intoxicating liquors.*

shall, at the discretion of the Secretary of the Interior, be withheld from them for the period of at least one year; and for a violation of any of the stipulations of this agreement on the part of any member of said bands, the persons so offending shall be liable to have their annuities withheld, and to be subject to such other punishment as the Secretary of the Interior may prescribe.

Members of the bands may dissolve tribal connections, etc.

ARTICLE 8. Any members of said Sisseeton and Wahpaton bands who may be desirous of dissolving their tribal connection and obligations, and of locating beyond the limits of the reservation provided for said bands, shall have the privilege of so doing, by notifying the United States agent of such intention, and making an actual settlement beyond the limits of said reservation; shall be vested with all the rights, privileges, and immunities, and be subject to all the laws, obligations, and duties, of citizens of the United States; but such procedure shall work no forfeiture on their part of the right to share in the annuities of said bands.

Secretary of Interior to have discretion over manner and objects of annual expenditure.

ARTICLE 9. Such of the stipulations of the former treaties as provide for the payment of particular sums of money to the said Sisseeton and Wahpaton bands, or for the application or expenditure of specific amounts for particular objects or purposes, shall be, and hereby are, so amended and changed as to invest the Secretary of the Interior with discretionary power in regard to the manner and objects of the annual expenditure of all such sums or amounts which have accrued and are now due to said bands, together with the amount the said bands shall become annually entitled to under and by virtue of the provisions of this agreement: *Provided,* The said sums or amounts shall be expended for the benefit of said bands at such time or times and in such manner as the said Secretary shall deem best calculated to promote their interests, welfare, and advance in civilization. And it is further agreed that such change may be made in the stipulations of former treaties, which provide for the payment of particular sums for specified purposes, as to permit the chiefs and braves of said bands, or any of the subdivisions of said bands, with the sanction of the Secretary of the Interior, to authorize such payment or expenditure of their annuities, or any portion thereof, which are to become due hereafter, as may be deemed best for the general interests and welfare of the said bands or subdivisions thereof.

United States to pay expenses of negotiation.

ARTICLE 10. The expenses attending the negotiation of this agreement shall be defrayed by the United States.

In testimony whereof, the said Charles E. Mix, Commissioner, as aforesaid, and the undersigned chiefs and headmen of the said Sisseeton and Wahpaton bands, have hereunto set their hands and seals at the place and on the day first above written.

Charles E. Mix, Commissioner. [SEAL.]

Muz-zah-shaw, (Red Iron,) his x mark. [SEAL.]
Wam-du-pi-du-tah, (War Eagle's Scarlet Tail,)
  his x mark. [SEAL.]
Ojupi, (The Planter,) his x mark. [SEAL.]
Ha-hu-ta-nai, (The Stumpy Horn,) his x mark. [SEAL.]
Maz-zo-ma-nee, (Walking Iron,) his x mark. [SEAL.]
Maz-za-koote-manee, (Shoots Iron as he Walks,)
  his x mark. [SEAL.]
Upi-ya-hi-de-yaw, (Chief of Lac qui Parle,) his
  x mark. [SEAL.]
Umpe-du-to-ke-chaw, (Other Day,) his x mark. [SEAL.]
Ta-chan-du-pa-ho-tan-ka, (His Pipe with Strong
  Voice,) his x mark. [SEAL.]

Signed, sealed and delivered in presence of—

Joseph R. Brown, Sioux agent.
A. J. Campbell, interpreter.
A. Robertson.
John Dowling.
N. R. Brown.
Friedrich Schmidt.
M. Smitser.
B. D. Hyam.
P. F. Wood.
Charles Crawford.
James R. Roche.

RESOLUTION OF THE SENATE OF THE UNITED STATES.

Right and title of certain bands of Sioux Indians, to the lands embraced in reservation on the Minnesota River.

June 27, 1860.

12 Stat., 1042.

IN THE SENATE OF THE UNITED STATES,
June 27th, 1860.

Whereas by the second articles of the treaties of June 19, 1858, with the Med-a-wa-kanton and Wah-pa-koo-ta, and the Sisseeton and Wah-pa-ton bands of the Dacotah or Sioux Indians, it is submitted to the Senate to decide as to the right or title of said bands of Indians to the lands embraced in the reservation occupied by them on the Minnesota River, in the State of Minnesota, and what compensation shall be made to them for those portions of said reservation lying on the north side of that river, which they agreed by said treaties to surrender and relinquish to the United States; "whether they shall be allowed a specified sum in money therefor, and if so, how much, or whether the same shall be sold for their benefit, they to receive the proceeds of such sale, deducting the necessary expenses incident thereto;" and whereas said Indians were permitted to retain and occupy said reservations in lieu of other lands which they were entitled to under the amendments of the Senate to the treaties made with them in the year 1851, and large amounts of the money of said Indians have been expended by the government in improvements and otherwise upon the lands contained in said reservations; and whereas by act of Congress of July 31, 1854, said reservations were authorized to be confirmed to those Indians:

Preamble.

1854, ch. 167, 10 Stat., 326.

Resolved, That said Indians possessed a just and valid right and title to said reservations, and that they be allowed the sum of thirty cents per acre for the lands contained in that portion thereof lying on the north side of the Minnesota River, exclusive of the cost of survey and sale, or any contingent expense that may accrue whatever, which by the treaties of June, 1858, they have relinquished and given up to the United States,—

Right of Indians determined, and allowance to them.

Resolved, further, That all persons who have in good faith settled and made improvements upon any of the lands contained in said reservations, believing the same to be government lands, shall have the right of preemption to one hundred and sixty acres thereof, to include their improvements, on paying the sum of one dollar and twenty-five cents per acre therefor: *Provided,* That when such settlements have been made on the lands of the Indians on the south side of the Minnesota River, the assent of the Indians shall first be obtained, in such a manner as the Secretary of the Interior shall prescribe, and that the amount which shall be so paid for their lands, shall be paid into the treasury of the United States.

Settlers in good faith on said reservations may preempt, etc.

Proviso.

TREATY WITH THE WINNEBAGO, 1859.

Apr. 15, 1859.

12 Stats., 1101.
Ratified Mar. 16,
1861.
Proclaimed Mar. 23,
1861.

Articles of agreement and convention made and concluded at Washington City on the fifteenth day of April, eighteen hundred and fifty-nine, by and between Charles E. Mix, commissioner on the part of the United States, and the following-named chiefs and delegates, representing the Winnebago tribes of Indians, viz: Baptiste Lassalleur. Little Hill, Little De-Corie, Prophet, Wakon, Conohutta-kau, Big Bear, Rogue, Young Frenchman, One Horn, Yellow Banks, and O-o-kau, they being thereto duly authorized by said tribe.

Eastern portion of reservation to be set apart and assigned in severalty to members of tribe.

ARTICE 1. The Winnebago Indians having now more lands than are necessary for their occupancy and use, and being desirous of promoting settled habits of industry and enterprise amongst themselves by abolishing the tenure in common by which they now hold their lands, and by assigning limited quantities thereof, in severalty, to the members of the tribe, including their half or mixed blood relatives now residing with them, to be cultivated and improved for their own individual use and benefit, it is hereby agreed and stipulated that the eastern portion of their present reservation, embracing townships one hundred and six, (106) and one hundred and seven, (107,) range twenty-four (24) and one hundred and six (106) and one hundred and seven, (107,) range twenty-five (25) and the two strips of land immediately adjoining them on the east and north, shall be set apart and retained by them for said purposes; and that out of the same there shall be assigned to each head of a family not exceeding eighty acres, and to each male person eighteen years of age and upwards, without family, not exceeding forty acres of land, to include, in every case, as far as practicable, a reasonable proportion of timber; one hundred and sixty acres of said retained lands in a suitable locality shall also be set apart and appropriated to the occupancy and use of the agency for said Indians. The lands to be so assigned, including those for the use of the agency, shall be in as regular and compact a body as possible, and so as to admit of a distinct and well-defined exterior boundary, embracing the whole of them and any intermediate portions or parcels of land or water not included in or made part of the tracts assigned in severalty. Any such intermediate parcels of land and water shall be owned by the Winnebagoes in common; but in case of increase in the tribe, or other cause, rendering it necessary or expedient, the said intermediate parcels of land shall be subject to distribution and assignment, in severalty, in such manner as the Secretary of the Interior shall prescribe and direct. The whole of the lands assigned or unassigned in severalty, embraced within the said exterior boundary, shall constitute and be known as the Winnebago reservation, within and over which all laws passed or which may be passed by Congress regulating trade and intercourse with the Indian tribes shall have full force and effect. And no white person, except such as shall be in the employment of the United States, shall be allowed to reside or go upon any portion of said reservation, without the written permission of the superintendent of Indian affairs, or of the agent for the tribe. Said division and assignment of lands to the Winnebagoes in severalty shall be made under the direction of the Secretary of the Interior, and when approved by him shall be final and conclusive. Certificates shall be issued by the Commissioner of Indian Affairs for the tracts so assigned, specifying the names of the individuals to whom they have been assigned, respectively, and that they are for the exclusive use and benefit of themselves, their heirs, and descendants. And said tracts shall not be alienated in fee, leased, or otherwise disposed of, except to the United States, or to other members of the tribe, under such rules and regulations as may be prescribed by the Secretary of the

Assignments of land.

Whole to be known as the Winnebago Reservation.

Whites not to reside thereon.

Division, etc., to be under the direction of Secretary of Interior.

Certificates to issue.

Not to be assigned unless, etc.

Interior; and they shall be exempt from taxation, levy, sale, or forfeiture until otherwise provided for by Congress. Prior to the issue of said certificates, the Secretary of the Interior shall make such rules and regulations as he may deem necessary and expedient respecting the disposition of any of said tracts, in case of the death of the person, or persons to whom they may be assigned, so that the same shall be secured to the families of such deceased persons; and should any of the Indians to whom tracts shall be assigned abandon them, the said Secretary may take such action in relation to the proper disposition thereof as in his judgment may be necessary and proper.

ARTICLE 2. For the purpose of procuring the means of comfortably establishing the Winnebagoes upon the lands to be assigned to them in severalty, by building them houses, and by furnishing them with agricultural implements, stock-animals, and other necessary aid and facilities for commencing agricultural pursuits under favorable circumstances, the lands embraced in that portion of their reservation not stipulated to be retained and divided, as aforesaid, shall be sold, under the direction of the Secretary of the Interior, in parcels not exceeding one hundred and sixty acres each, to the highest bidder, for cash; the sales to be made upon sealed proposals to be duly invited by public advertisement. And should any of the tracts so to be sold have upon them improvements of any kind which were made by or for the Indians, or for Government purposes, the proposals therefor must state the price for both the land and improvements. And if, after assigning to all the members of the tribe entitled thereto their proportions of land in severalty, there shall remain a surplus of that portion of the reservation retained for that purpose, outside of the exterior boundary-line of the lands assigned in severalty, the Secretary of the Interior shall be authorized and empowered, whenever he shall think proper, to cause such surplus to be sold in the same manner as the other lands to be so disposed of, and the proceeds thereof to be paid over to the Winnebagoes, or used and applied for their benefit in such manner as he shall deem to be best for them.

Certain lands may be sold.

Mode of sale.

ARTICLE 3. The Winnebagoes being anxious to relieve themselves from the burden of their present liabilities, and it being essential to their welfare and best interests that they shall be enabled to commence their new mode of life and pursuits free from the annoyance and embarrassment thereof, or which may be occasioned thereby, it is agreed that the same shall be liquidated and paid out of the fund arising from the sale of their surplus lands, so far as found valid and just on an examination thereof, to be made by their agent and the superintendent of Indian affairs for the northern superintendency, subject to revision and confirmation by the Secretary of the Interior.

Debts of Winnebago to be paid out of proceeds of sale.

ARTICLE 4. Should the proceeds of the surplus lands of the Winnebagoes not prove to be sufficient to carry out the purposes and stipulations of this agreement, and some further aid be, from time to time, requisite, to enable said Indians to sustain themselves successfully in agricultural and other industrial pursuits, such additional means as may be necessary therefor shall be taken from the moneys due and belonging to them under the provisions of former treaties; and so much thereof as may be required to furnish them further aid, as aforesaid, shall be applied in such manner, under the direction of the Secretary of the Interior, as he shall consider best calculated to promote and advance their improvement and welfare; and, in order to render unnecessary any further treaty engagements or arrangements hereafter with the United States, it is hereby agreed and stipulated that the President, with the assent of Congress, shall have full power to modify or change any of the provisions of former treaties with the Winnebagoes in such manner and to whatever extent he may judge to be necessary and expedient for their welfare and best interest.

Provision in case proceeds of sale are insufficient to pay debts.

All members of tribe
to be notified of this
agreement.

ARTICLE 5. The Winnebagoes, parties to this agreement, are anxious that all the members of their tribe shall participate in the advantages herein provided for respecting their permanent settlement and their improvement and civilization, and to that end, to induce all that are now separated from, to rejoin and unite with them. It is therefore agreed that, as soon as practicable, the Commissioner of Indian Affairs shall cause the necessary proceeding to be adopted to have them notified of this agreement and its advantages, and to induce them to come in and unite with their brethren; and, to enable them to do so and to sustain themselves for a reasonable time thereafter, such assistance shall be provided for them, at the expense of the tribe, as may be

Proviso.

actually necessary for those purposes: *Provided, however,* That those who do not rejoin and permanently re-unite themselves with the tribe within one year from the date of the ratification of this agreement shall not be entitled to the benefit of any of its stipulations.

Expenses to be paid
from funds of Winne-
bago.

ARTICLE 6. All the expenses connected with, and incident to, the making of this agreement, and the carrying out of its provisions, shall be defrayed out of the funds of the Winnebagoes.

Signatures.

In testimony whereof, the said Charles E. Mix, commissioner as aforesaid, and the said chiefs and delegates of the Winnebago tribe of Indians, have hereunto set their hands and seals at the place and on the day and year hereinbefore written.

Charles E. Mix, Commissioner. [L. S.]

Baptiste Lassalleur, his x mark.	[L. S.]	Big Bear, his x mark.	[L. S.]
Little Hill, his x mark.	[L. S.]	Rogue, his x mark.	[L. S.]
Little De-Corrie, his x mark.	[L. S.]	Young Frenchman, his x mark.	[L. S.]
Prophet, (being sick, by his representative, Big Bear,) his x mark.	[L. S.]	One Horn, his x mark.	[L. S.]
Wakon, his x mark.	[L. S.]	Yellow Banks, his x mark.	[L. S.]
Cono-hutta-kau, his x mark.	[L. S.]	O-o-kau, his x mark.	[L. S.]

In presence of—

W. J. Cullen, superintendent Indian affairs.	Joseph R. Brown, Sioux agent.
	George H. Holtzman.
Charles H. Mix, United States Indian agent for the Winnebagoes.	George L. Otis.
	George Culver.
Peter Manaize, United States interpreter.	Nathan Myrick.
John Dowling.	Harry H. Young.
S. B. Loury, interpreter.	Henry Foster.
D. Crawford.	Asa White.

TREATY WITH THE CHIPPEWA, ETC., 1859.

July 16, 1859.

12 Stat., 1105.
Ratified Apr. 19,
1860.
Proclaimed July 9,
1860.

Articles of agreement and convention made and concluded at the Sac and Fox agency on this sixteenth day of July, one thousand eight hundred and fifty-nine, by David Crawford, commissioner on the part of the United States, and the following-named delegates representing the Swan Creek and Black River Chippewas and the Munsee or Christian Indians, they being duly authorized thereto by said Indians, viz: Eshton-quit, or Francis McCoonse, Edward McCoonse, William Turner, Antwine Gokey, Henry Donohue, Ignatius Caleb, and John Williams.

Whereas the Swan Creek and Black River band of Chippewas, of Kansas Territory, who were parties to the treaty of May 9, 1836, claim to be entitled to participate in the beneficial provisions of the subsequent treaty of August 2, 1855, under a misapprehension of the terms and conditions of said instrument, the provisions of which were only designed to embrace the Chippewas of Saginaw and that portion of the Chippewas of Swan Creek and Black River who were then residing in Michigan; and whereas a reservation of eight thousand three hundred and twenty acres, or thirteen sections of land, was set apart in Kansas Territory for the use of the Swan Creek and Black River band of Chippewas, in consideration of the cession and relinquishment of certain lands in the State of Michigan which were reserved for said band of Indians by the 6th article of the treaty of November 17, 1807; and in view of the fact that a part of the aforesaid band, who now reside in the Territory of Kansas, have not received their full proportion of the benefits designed to have been conferred upon them by the provisions of the second article of the treaty of May 9, 1836, it is understood to be the intention of the United States, in the execution of these articles of agreement and convention, to manifest their liberality and disposition to encourage said Indians in agricultural pursuits, and, with a view to remove from their minds all erroneous impressions respecting the non-fulfilment of the stipulations of former treaties, a liberal provision will be made for their benefit as hereinafter expressed. It is further understood to be the intention of this instrument to unite the Munsee or Christian Indians with the aforesaid band of Chippewas, in order to provide them with a suitable and permanent home, as contemplated by the act of Congress entitled "An act to confirm the sale of the reservation held by the Christian Indians, and to provide a permanent home for said Indians," approved June 8, 1858.

Intention of this treaty.

1858, chap. 122. 11 Stat., 312.

ARTICLE 1. The United States agree that the reservation of eight thousand three hundred and twenty acres, or thirteen sections of land, in Franklin County, Kansas Territory, set apart for the entire band of Swan Creek and Black River Chippewas, shall inure to the benefit of that portion of said band now residing thereon, and the United States shall cause said reservation to be surveyed into sections, half, quarter, and quarter-quarter sections, in harmony with the public-land system. For the purpose of securing a permanent home thereon for the band of Munsee or Christian Indians who have expressed a desire to unite with said band of Chippewas, it is agreed between the contracting parties to this instrument that the aforesaid bands of Indians are hereby united for their mutual advantage as herein indicated. And within said reservation there shall be assigned, in severalty, to the members of said united bands, not exceeding forty acres of land to each head of a family, and not exceeding forty acres to each child or other member of said family; forty acres to each orphan child, and eighty acres to each unmarried person of the age of twenty-one years and upwards, not connected with any family, to include in each case, so far as practicable, a reasonable proportion of timber; and the selections shall be so made as to respect the present improvements of the aforesaid Chippewas, so far as the same can be done consistently with the rights of the Christian Indians, and when it is found expedient to select lands for one Indian, embracing part of the improvements made by another, then, in such case, a reasonable compensation shall be made for such improvements by the Indian to whom they may be assigned by the party entitled to the same, to be determined by the Secretary of the Interior, upon an investigation of the facts in the case. At a suitable point within said reservation there shall be set apart for the establishment of a manual-labor school and educational and missionary purposes a quarter section of land, or one hundred and sixty acres, and the land so set apart, together with the tracts which may be assigned to the members of said united bands, shall be in as regular and compact a body as possible, and so as to admit of a distinct and well-defined exterior boundary, embracing the whole of them, and also any intermediate portions or parcels of land or water not included in or made part of the tracts assigned in severalty. Any such intermediate parcels of land and water shall be held by said united bands in common, but in case of increase in the bands of said Indians, or other cause rendering it necessary or expedient, the said intermediate parcels of land

Former reservation to inure to benefit of that part of band now residing thereon and to be surveyed.

Munsee and Swan Creeks, etc. Chippewa united.

Portions of land to be assigned in severalty.

Manual-labor school, etc.

Lands held in common.

shall be subject to distribution and assignment in severalty, in such manner as the Secretary of the Interior shall prescribe and direct.

Amount of lands in reservation. The whole of the lands assigned or unassigned in severalty embraced within said exterior boundary to include in the aggregate not exceeding seven sections, or four thousand eight hundred and eighty acres of land, shall constitute and be known as the Chippewa and Christian **Laws thereon.** Indian reservation, within and over which all laws passed or which may be passed by Congress, regulating trade and intercourse with the **Whites not permitted, etc.** Indian tribes, shall have full force and effect. And no white person, except such as may be in the employ of the United States, shall be allowed to reside or go upon any portion of said reservation without the written permission of the superintendent of Indian affairs, or agent, or other person who may be intrusted with the management and con- **Division and assignment, how made.** trol thereof. The aforesaid division and assignment of lands to the Indians shall be made under the direction of the Secretary of the Interior, and when approved by him shall be final and conclusive. **Certificates.** Certificates shall be issued by the Commissioner of Indian Affairs for the tracts so assigned, specifying the names of the individuals to whom they have been assigned respectively, and that they are for the exclusive use and benefit of themselves, their heirs, and descendants; and said tracts shall not be alienated in fee, leased, or otherwise disposed of, except to the United States, or to the members of said bands of Indians, under such rules and regulations as may be prescribed by the Secretary of the Interior; and said lands shall be exempt from taxation, levy, sale, or forfeiture, until otherwise provided for by Congress. Prior to the issue of said certificates, the Secretary of the Interior shall make such rules and regulations as he may deem necessary and expedient, respecting the disposition of any of said tracts in case of the death of the person or persons to whom they may be assigned, so that the same shall be secured to the families of such deceased persons; and should any of the Indians to whom tracts shall be assigned abandon them, the said Secretary may take such action in relation to the proper disposition thereof as in his judgment may be necessary and expedient.

Residue of land to be sold. ARTICLE 2. After all the selections and assignments hereinbefore specified shall have been made and approved, the residue of the land in the tract set apart for the use of the Swan Creek and Black River **Ante, p. 462.** Chippewas, under the provisions of the fourth article of the treaty of May ninth, eighteen hundred and thirty-six, which may not be embraced by the exterior boundary of the reduced reservation, shall be appraised at a reasonable value, and the same shall be sold at public auction to the highest bidder, but no bid shall be received for a sum less than the appraised value, and the proceeds of sale, after deducting therefrom the expenses incident thereto, shall be regarded as belonging to the aforesaid band of Chippewas. The said band of Indians **Allowance of money; how to be raised.** shall be allowed the sum of three thousand dollars out of the funds of the Christian Indians, as a consideration for the tracts of land which shall be assigned to the members of said band of Indians, and also the sum of six thousand dollars, (to be taken from the Treasury of the United States,) in full satisfaction of all claims and demands, legal, equitable, or otherwise, which the aforesaid band of Chippewas may have against the United States under the stipulations and provisions of former treaties, and these sums of money, together with the proceeds of the sales of the lands before mentioned, shall be invested in the manner hereinafter provided. And to enable the Secretary of the Interior to liquidate the allowance of the aforesaid sum of six thousand dollars, he is authorized, at his discretion, to dispose of the stock of the State of Missouri, purchased from avails of land sold under the treaty of eighteen hundred and thirty-six, and such a sum from interest accruing thereon, and of any balance of annuities now in the Treasury of the United States, resulting from other treaties with said Indians.

ARTICLE 3. For the purpose of comfortably establishing the Christian Indians upon the lands which shall be assigned to them in severalty, by building them houses, and furnishing them with agricultural implements, stock animals, and other necessary aid and facilities for commencing agricultural pursuits under favorable circumstances, there shall be expended, under the direction of the Secretary of the Interior, (out of the aggregate sum of forty-three thousand four hundred dollars deposited in the Treasury of the United States by A. J. Isacks, to the credit of said Secretary for the use of the Christian Indians,) a sum not exceeding twenty-three thousand dollars, and the balance of the aforesaid aggregate sum shall be mingled with the funds of the aforesaid band of Chippewas, and the moneys so mingled together shall constitute a joint fund, subject to the direction and control of the Secretary of the Interior. Two thousand dollars thereof shall be expended for the benefit of said united bands of Indians, in providing them with a schoolhouse, church building, and blacksmith-shop, and necessary fixtures, and the residue of said joint fund, after deducting therefrom all the expenses incident to the negotiation of this treaty, the survey and assignment of the lands, the concentration of the Indians thereon, and all other necessary expenses, shall be invested in safe and profitable stocks, yielding an interest of not less than five per centum per annum; and said interest, as it becomes due, shall be applied, under the direction of the Secretary of the Interior, from time to time, for educational purposes, for the support of a blacksmith-shop, and such other beneficial objects as he may adjudge to be necessary and expedient for the general prosperity and advancement of the aforesaid bands of Indians in the arts of civilized life.

> *Appropriation for stock, agricultural implements, etc.*

> *Schoolhouse and shops.*

ARTICLE 4. In consideration of the provisions contained in the several articles of this treaty, the aforesaid band of Swan Creek and Black River Chippewas hereby relinquish all claims and demands which they may have against the United States, under the stipulations of the treaty of November 17, 1807, and the treaty of May 9, 1836; and they hereby abandon and renounce any and all claims to participate in the provisions of the subsequent treaty of August 2, 1855, and they receive the stipulations and provisions contained in these articles of agreement and convention, in full satisfaction of the terms and conditions of all former treaties, and release the United States from the payment of all claims of every character whatsoever.

> *Relinquishment of claims by the Indians.*

> *Ante, pp. 92, 361.*

ARTICLE 5. It is agreed that all roads and highways, laid out by authority of law, shall have right of way through the lands within the reservation hereinbefore specified, on the same terms as are provided by law, when roads and highways are made through lands of citizens of the United States; and railroad companies, when the lines of their roads necessarily pass through the lands of said Indians, shall have right of way on the payment of just compensation therefor in money.

> *Right of way.*

ARTICLE 6. This instrument shall be obligatory on the contracting parties whenever the same shall be ratified by the President and the Senate of the United States.

> *When this treaty takes effect.*

In testimony whereof, the said David Crawford, commissioner as aforesaid, and the undersigned delegates of the united bands of Swan Creek and Black River Chippewas, and the Munsee or Christian Indians, have hereunto set their hands and seals, at the place and on the day and year hereinbefore written.

> *Signature.*

David Crawford, United States commissioner.		[L. S.]
Esh-ton-quit, or Francis McCoonse,	his x mark.	[L. S.]
Edward McCoonse,	his x mark.	[L. S.]
William Turner,		[L. S.]
Antwine Gokey,	his x mark.	[L. S.]
Henry Donohoe,		[L. S.]
Ignatius Caleb,	his x mark.	[L. S.]
John Williams.		[L. S.]

Signed and sealed in the presence of—
    Hugh S. Walsh, secretary of Kansas Territory.
    Perry Fuller, United States agent.
    Cyrus F. Currier.
    Thos. J. Connolly, United States interpreter.

TREATY WITH THE SAUK AND FOXES, 1859.

Oct. 1, 1859.

15 Stats., 467.
Ratified, June 27, 1860.
Proclaimed, July 9, 1860.

Articles of agreement and convention made and concluded at the Sac and Fox agency, in the Territory of Kansas, on the first day of October, in the year of our Lord one thousand eight hundred and fifty-nine, by and between Alfred B. Greenwood, commissioner on the part of the United States, and the following-named chiefs and delegates, representing the confederated tribes of Sacs and Foxes of the Mississippi, viz: Ke-o-kuk, Mack-a-sah-pee, Sha-bah-caw-kah, Mat-tah-tah, My-ah-pit, Kaw-ah-kee, Kah-sha-moh-mee, Maw-mee-won-e-kah, and Che-ko-skuk, they being thereto duly authorized by said confederated tribes.

Part of present reservation to be set apart.

ARTICLE 1. The Sacs and Foxes of the Mississippi having now more lands than are necessary for their occupancy and use, and being desirous of promoting settled habits of industry and enterprise amongst themselves by abolishing the tenure in common by which they now hold their lands, and by assigning limited quantities thereof, in severalty, to the individual members of the tribe, to be cultivated and improved for their individual use and benefit, it is hereby agreed and stipulated that the portion of their present reservation contained within

Boundaries.

the following boundaries, that is to say: beginning at a point on the northern boundary-line of their reservation, six miles west of the northeastern corner of the same; running thence due south, to the southern boundary of the same, twenty miles; thence west, and along said southern boundary, twelve miles; thence due north, to the northern boundary of said reservation, twenty miles; and thence east, along said boundary-line, twelve miles, to the place of beginning—estimated to contain about one hundred and fifty-three thousand and six hundred acres—shall be set apart and retained by them for the purposes aforesaid.

Assignment to each member of the confederated tribes.

ARTICLE 2. Out of the lands so set apart and retained there shall be assigned to each member of said confederated tribe, without distinction of age or sex, a tract of eighty acres, to include, in every case, as far as practicable, a reasonable portion of timber. One hundred and

For agent.

sixty acres of said retained lands shall also be set apart and appropriated to the use and occupancy of the agent for the time being of said

For school location.

confederated tribe; and one hundred and sixty acres shall also be reserved for the establishment and support of a school for the education of the youth of the tribe. The location of the tracts, the assignment of which is provided for in this article, shall be made in as regular and compact a manner as possible, and so as to admit of a distinct and well-defined exterior boundary, embracing the whole of them and any

Intermediate parcels.

intermediate portions or parcels of land or water not included in or made part of the tracts assigned in severalty. All such intermediate parcels of land and water shall be owned by the Sacs and Foxes of the Mississippi in common; but, in case of increase in the tribe, or other cause, rendering it necessary or expedient, the said intermediate parcels of land shall be subject to distribution and assignment in such

Lands to be known as, etc.

manner as the Secretary of the Interior may prescribe and direct. The whole of the lands, assigned or unassigned, embraced within said exterior boundary, shall constitute and be known as the reservation of

Laws.

the Sacs and Foxes of the Mississippi; and all laws which have been, or may be, passed by the Congress of the United States regulating trade and intercourse with Indian tribes shall have full force and effect over the same, and no white person, except such as shall be in the employment of the United States, shall be allowed to reside or go upon any portion of said reservation, without the written permission of the superintendent of the central superintendency, or of the agent of the tribe.

White persons not to reside thereon, except, etc.

ARTICLE 3. The division and assignment in severalty among the Sacs and Foxes of the Mississippi of the land hereinbefore reserved for that purpose shall be made under the direction of the Secretary of the Interior, and his decision of all questions arising thereupon shall be final and conclusive. Certificates shall be issued by the Commissioner of Indian Affairs for the tracts assigned in severalty, specifying the names of the individuals to whom they have been assigned, respectively, and that the said tracts are set apart for the exclusive use and benefit of the assignees and their heirs. And said tracts shall not be alienated in fee, leased, or otherwise disposed of, except to the United States, or to members of the Sac and Fox tribe, and under such rules and regulations as may be prescribed by the Secretary of the Interior. And said tracts shall be exempt from taxation, levy, sale, or forfeiture, until otherwise provided by Congress. Prior to the issue of the certificates aforesaid, the Secretary of the Interior shall make such rules and regulations as he may deem necessary or expedient respecting the disposition of any of said tracts, in case of the death of the person or persons to whom they may be assigned, so that the same shall be secured to the families of such deceased persons; and should any of the Indians to whom tracts shall be assigned abandon them, the said Secretary may take such action in relation to the proper disposition thereof as, in his judgment, may be necessary and proper.

Division and assignment. how made.

Certificates for tracts.

Tracts not to be disposed of. etc.

To be exempt, etc.

ARTICLE 4. For the purpose of establishing the Sacs and Foxes of the Mississippi comfortably upon the lands to be assigned to them in severalty, by building them houses, and by furnishing them with agricultural implements, stock-animals, and other necessary aid and facilities for commencing agricultural pursuits under favorable circumstances, the lands embraced in that portion of their present reservation, not stipulated to be retained and divided as aforesaid, shall be sold, under the direction of the Secretary of the Interior, in parcels not exceeding one hundred and sixty acres each, to the highest bidder, for cash; the sale to be made upon sealed proposals, to be duly invited by public advertisement, and the proceeds thereof to be expended, for the purposes hereinbefore recited, in such manner as the Secretary of the Interior may think proper. And should any of the tracts so to be sold have upon them improvements of any kind which were made by or for the Indians, or for Government purposes, the proposals therefor must state the price for both the land and the improvements. And if, after assigning to all the members of the tribe entitled thereto their proportion of land in severalty, there shall remain a surplus of that portion of the reservation retained for that purpose, outside of the exterior boundaries of the lands assigned in severalty, the Secretary of the Interior shall be authorized and empowered, whenever he shall think proper, to cause such surplus to be sold in the same manner as the other lands to be so disposed of, and to apply the proceeds of such sale to the purposes and in the mode hereinbefore provided with respect to that portion of their present reservation not retained for distribution.

Certain lands of present reservation to be sold and proceeds how applied.

Sales, how made.

Improvements.

ARTICLE 5. The Sacs and Foxes of the Mississippi being anxious to relieve themselves from the burden of their present liabilities, and it being essential to their best interests that they should be allowed to commence their new mode of life, free from the embarrassments of debt, it is stipulated and agreed that debts which may be due and

Debts of the Indians to be paid, etc.

owing at the date of the signing and execution hereof, either by the said confederated tribes of Sacs and Foxes, or by individual members thereof, shall be liquidated, and paid out of the fund arising from the sale of their surplus lands, so far as the same shall be found to be just and valid on an examination thereof, to be made by their agent and the superintendent of Indian affairs for the central superintendency, subject to revision and correction by the Secretary of the Interior.

If proceeds of lands are insufficient, other moneys to be taken. ARTICLE 6. Should the proceeds of the surplus lands aforesaid prove insufficient to carry out the purposes and stipulations of this agreement, and further aid be, from time to time, requisite to enable the Sacs and Foxes of the Mississippi to sustain themselves successfully in agricultural or other industrial pursuits, such additional means as may be necessary therefor shall be taken from the moneys due and belonging to them under the provisions of former treaties; and so much of said moneys as may be required to furnish them further aid as aforesaid shall be applied in such manner, under the direction of the Secretary of the Interior, as he shall consider best calculated *Provisions of former treaties may be changed.* to improve and promote their welfare. And, in order to render unnecessary any further treaty engagements or arrangements hereafter with the United States, it is hereby agreed and stipulated that the President, with the assent of Congress, shall have full power to modify or change any of the provisions of former treaties with the Sacs and Foxes of the Mississippi in such manner and to whatever extent he may judge to be necessary and expedient for their welfare and best interests.

All members of the tribe to share herein. ARTICLE 7. The Sacs and Foxes of the Mississippi, parties to this agreement, are anxious that all the members of their tribe shall participate in the advantages herein provided for respecting their improvement and civilization, and to that end to induce all that are now separated to rejoin and reunite with them. It is therefore agreed that, as soon as practicable, the Commissioner of Indian Affairs shall cause the necessary proceedings to be adopted to have them notified of this agreement and its advantages, and to induce them to come in and unite with their brethren; and to enable them to do so, and to sustain themselves for a reasonable time thereafter, such assistance shall be provided for them at the expense of the tribe as may be actually necessary *To come in within one year.* for that purpose: *Provided, however,* That those who do not rejoin and permanently re-unite themselves with the tribe within one year from the date of the ratification of this treaty shall not be entitled to the benefit of any of its stipulations.

Expenses of the treaty, etc. ARTICLE 8. All the expenses connected with and incident to the making of this agreement, and the carrying out of its provisions, shall be defrayed out of the funds of the Sacs and Foxes of the Mississippi.

Roads and highways. ARTICLE 9. It is agreed that all roads and highways laid out by authority of law shall have right of way through the lands within the reservation hereinbefore specified, on the same terms as are provided by law when roads and highways are made through lands of citizens of *Railroads.* the United States; and railroad companies, when the lines pass through the lands of said Indians, shall have right of way on the payment of a just compensation therefor in money.

Mixed and half bloods and whole bloods intermarried with white men. ARTICLE 10. The Sacs and Foxes of the Mississippi being anxious to make some suitable provision for their mixed and half bloods, and such of their women (whole-bloods) who have intermarried with white men, it is agreed that there shall be assigned to the mixed and half bloods of their tribe, and to such whole-blood females as have intermarried with white men, at the date of this agreement, three hundred and twenty acres each; the location and allotments of said lands to be made out of that portion relinquished by this treaty to the United States in trust, provided the mixed or half bloods, and such females of their tribes as have intermarried with white men, desire to do so. The allotments to such of the mixed or half bloods as may be minors to be made by the agent of the tribe, subject to the confirmation and approval of the Secretary of the Interior; and in allotting lands to those provided for in this article, said allotments shall be made so as to include their improvements, (if any,) provided it can be done, and at the same time make said allotments conform to the public surveys. And it is further Thomas Connelly. agreed between the parties to this agreement, that Thomas Connelly, a half-breed, and a member of the tribe who has been uniformly kind to his people, shall be permitted to so locate his three hundred and twenty acres as to include Randal's dwelling and trading-house, if it can be done so as to harmonize with the public surveys; and provided the said Connelly shall pay to the owner of said improvements a fair valuation therefor. The lands granted by this article shall remain inalienable except to the United States or members of the tribe, nor shall the mixed or half bloods, or such females as have intermarried with white men, participate in the proceeds of the lands herein ceded.

ARTICLE 11. The United States also agree to cause to be paid to the tribe any funds that may have heretofore been withheld under the provisions of the fifth article of the treaty of one thousand eight hundred and forty-two, the same to be expended for their benefit, or paid in money, as the Secretary may direct.

Funds withheld to be paid.

ARTICLE 12. This instrument shall be obligatory on the contracting parties whenever the same shall be ratified by the President and the Senate of the United States.

Treaty when to take effect.

In testimony whereof, the said Alfred B. Greenwood, commissioner as aforesaid, and the said chiefs and delegates of the Sacs and Foxes of the Mississippi, have hereunto set their hands and seals at the place and on the day and year hereinbefore written.

Execution.

Alfred B. Greenwood.		[L. S.]

Sacs:

Ke-o-kuk,	his x mark.	[L. S.]
Mack-ah-sah-pee,	his x mark.	[L. S.]
Shaw-pah-caw,	his x mark.	[L. S.]
Mat-tah-tah,	his x mark.	[L. S.]
My-ah-pit,	his x mark.	[L. S.]
Kaw-ah-kee,	his x mark.	[L. S.]

Foxes:

Ka-sha-mah-me,	his x mark.	[L. S.]
Maw-me-wone-cah,	his x mark.	[L. S.]
Che-co-skuk,	his x mark.	[L. S.]

In presence of—
    Perrey Fuller, United States agent.
    Thos. J. Connolly, United States interpreter.
    G. Bailey, secretary to commissioner.
    J. M. Luce.
    H. S. Randall.
    John Goodell.

TREATY WITH THE KANSA TRIBE, 1859.

Oct. 5, 1859.

12 Stat., 1111.
Ratified June 27,
1860.
Proclaimed Nov. 17,
1860.

Articles of agreement and convention made and concluded at the Kansas agency, in the Territory of Kansas, on the fifth day of October, eighteen hundred and fifty-nine, by and between Alfred B. Greenwood, commissioner, on the part of the United States, and the following-named chiefs and headmen representing the Kansas tribe of Indians, to wit: Ke-hi-ga-wah Chuffe, Ish-tal-a-sa, Ne-hoo-ja-in-gah, Ki-hi-ga-wat-te-in-gah, Ki-he-gah-cha, Al-li-ca-wah-ho, Pah-hous-ga-tun-gah, Ke-hah-lah-la-hu, Ki-ha-gah-chu, Ee-le-sun-gah, Wah-pah-jah, Ko-sah-mun-gee, Oo-ga-shama, Wah-Shumga, Wah-ti-inga, Wah-e-la-ga, Pa-ha-ne-ga-la, Pa-ta-go, Cahulle, Ma-she-tum, Wa-no-ba-ga-ha, She-ga-wa-sa, Ma-his-pa-wa-cha, Ma-shon-o-pusha, Ja-ha-sha-watanga, Ki-he-ga-tussa, and Ka-la-sha-wat-lumga, they being thereto duly authorized by said tribe.

Portion of reservation to be set apart and assigned in severalty to members of tribe.

ARTICLE 1. The Kansas Indians having now more lands than are necessary for their occupation and use, and being desirous of promoting settled habits of industry amongst themselves by abolishing the tenure in common by which they now hold their lands, and by assigning limited quantities thereof in severalty to the members of their tribe, owning an interest in their present reservation, to be cultivated and improved for their individual use and benefit, it is agreed and stipulated that that portion of their reservation commencing at the *Boundaries.* southwest corner of said reservation, thence north with the west boundary nine miles, thence east fourteen miles, thence south nine miles, thence west with the south boundary fourteen miles to the place of beginning, shall be set apart and retained by them for said purposes; and that out of the same there shall be assigned to each head *Assignments.* of a family not exceeding forty acres, and to each member thereof not exceeding forty acres, and to each single male person of the age of twenty-one years and upwards not exceeding forty acres of land, to include in every case, as far as practicable, a reasonable proportion of *Indian agency and schools.* timber. One hundred and sixty acres of said retained lands, in a suitable locality, shall also be set apart and appropriated to the occupancy and use of the agency of said Indians, and one hundred and sixty acres of said lands shall also be reserved for the establishment of a school for the education of the youth of the tribe.

Land assigned to be in compact form, etc.

ARTICLE 2. The lands to be so assigned, including those for the use of the agency, and those reserved for school purposes, shall be in as regular and compact a body as possible, and so as to admit of a distinct and well-defined exterior boundary, embracing the whole of them, and any intermediate portions or parcels of land or water not included in or made part of the tracts assigned in severalty. Any such intermediate parcels of land and water shall be owned by the Kansas tribe of Indians in common; but in case of increase in the tribe, or other cause rendering it necessary or expedient, the said intermediate parcels of land shall be subject to distribution and assignment in such manner as the Secretary of the Interior shall prescribe and direct. *To be called the Kansas reservation.* The whole of the lands assigned or unassigned in severalty, embraced within the said exterior boundary, shall constitute and be known as the Kansas reservation, within and over which all laws passed, or which may be passed by Congress, regulating trade and intercourse *Whites not to reside thereon.* with the Indian tribes, shall have full force and effect. And no white person, except such as shall be in the employment of the United States, shall be allowed to reside or go upon any portion of said reservation without the written permission of the superintendent of Indian affairs, or of the agent for the tribe.

ARTICLE 3. Said division and assignment of lands to the Kansas tribe of Indians in severalty shall be made under the direction of the Secretary of the Interior, and when approved by him shall be final and conclusive. Certificates shall be issued by the Commissioner of Indian Affairs for the tracts so assigned, specifying the names of the individuals to whom they have been assigned respectively and that they are for the exclusive use and benefit of themselves, their heirs and descendants, and said tracts shall not be alienated in fee, leased or otherwise disposed of, except to the United States or to other members of the tribe, under such rules and regulations as may be prescribed by the Secretary of the Interior; and they shall be exempt from taxation, levy, sale, or forfeiture, until otherwise provided by Congress. Prior to the issue of said certificates, the Secretary of the Interior shall make such rules and regulations, as he may deem necessary and expedient respecting the disposition of any of said tracts, in case of the death of the person or persons to whom they may be assigned, so that the same shall be secured to the families of such deceased persons; and should any of the Indians to whom tracts shall be assigned abandon them, the said Secretary may take such action in relation to the proper disposition thereof as in his judgment may be necessary and proper.

Assignment, etc., to be under the direction of the Secretary of the Interior.

Certificates to issue.

Lands not to be alienated, etc.

Secretary of the Interior to make rules and regulations.

ARTICLE 4. For the purpose of procuring the means of comfortably establishing the Kansas tribe of Indians upon the lands to be assigned to them in severalty, by building them houses, and by furnishing them with agricultural implements, stock animals, and other necessary aid and facilities for commencing agricultural pursuits under favorable circumstances, the lands embraced in that portion not stipulated to be retained and divided as aforesaid shall be sold, under the direction of the Secretary of the Interior, in parcels not exceeding one hundred and sixty acres each, to the highest bidder for cash, the sale to be made upon sealed proposals to be duly invited by public advertisement, and should any of the tracts so to be so sold have upon them improvements of any kind, which were made by or for the Indians, or for Government purposes, the proposals therefor must state the price for both the land and improvements, and if, after assigning to all the members of the tribe entitled thereto, their proportions in severalty, there shall remain a surplus of that portion of the reservation retained for that purpose, outside of the exterior boundary-line of the lands assigned in severalty, the Secretary of the Interior shall be authorized and empowered, whenever he shall think proper, to cause such surplus to be sold in the same manner as the other lands to be so disposed of, and the proceeds thereof to be expended for their benefit in such manner as the Secretary of the Interior may deem proper: *Provided*, That all those who had in good faith settled and made improvements upon said reservation prior to the second day of December, eighteen hundred and fifty-six, (that being the day when the survey was certified by the agent of the tribe), and who would have been entitled to enter their improvements under any general or special pre-emption law, (had their improvements not fallen within the reservation,) such settlers shall be permitted to enter their improvements at the sum of one dollar and seventy-five cents per acre, in cash; said entries to be made in legal subdivisions and in such quantities as the pre-emption laws under which they may claim entitle them to locate: payments to be made on or before a day to be named by the Secretary of the Interior: *And provided, further*, That all those who had in good faith settled upon that portion of the reservation retained by this treaty for the future homes of the Kansas tribe of Indians, and had made *bona-fide* improvements thereon prior to the second day of December, eighteen hundred and fifty-six, aforesaid, and who would have been entitled to enter their lands, under the general pre-emption law, at one dollar and

Certain lands may be sold.

Mode of sale.

Proceeds, how expended.

twenty-five cents per acre, had their improvements not fallen upon the reservation, such settlers shall be entitled to receive a fair compensation for their improvements, to be ascertained by the Commissioner of Indian Affairs, under the direction of the Secretary of the Interior; such compensation to be paid out of the proceeds of the lands sold in trust for said tribe of Indians. All questions growing out of this amendment, and rights claimed in consequence thereof, shall be determined by the Commissioner of Indian Affairs, to be approved by the Secretary of the Interior. And in all cases where licensed traders, or others lawfully there, may have made improvements upon said reservation, the Secretary of the Interior shall have power to adjust the claims of each upon fair and equitable terms, they paying a fair value for the lands awarded to such persons, and shall cause patents to issue in pursuance of such award.

Debts to be paid from proceeds of sales.

ARTICLE 5. The Kansas tribe of Indians being anxious to relieve themselves from the burden of their *present* liabilities, and it being very essential to their welfare that they shall be enabled to commence their new mode of life and pursuits free from the annoyance and embarrassment thereof, or which may be occasioned thereby, it is agreed that the same shall be liquidated and paid out of the fund arising from the sale of their surplus lands so far as found valid and just, (if they have the means,) on an examination thereof, to be made by their agent and the superintendent of Indian affairs for the central superintendency, subject to revision and confirmation by the Secretary of the Interior.

Provision in case proceeds of sales are insufficient.

ARTICLE 6. Should the proceeds of the surplus lands of the Kansas tribe of Indians not prove to be sufficient to carry out the purposes and stipulations of this agreement, and some further aid be necessary, from time to time, to enable said Indians to sustain themselves successfully in agricultural and other industrial pursuits, such additional means may be taken, so far as may be necessary, from the moneys due and belonging to them under the provisions of former treaties, and so much thereof as may be required to furnish further aid as aforesaid shall be applied in such manner, under the direction of the Secretary of the Interior, as he shall consider best calculated to promote and advance their improvement and welfare.

President, with assent of Congress, may modify treaties with the Kansas Indians.

ARTICLE 7. In order to render unnecessary any further treaty engagements or arrangements hereafter with the United States, it is hereby agreed and stipulated that the President, with the assent of Congress, shall have full power to modify or change any of the provisions of former treaties with the Kansas tribes of Indians in such manner and to whatever extent he may judge to be necessary and expedient for their welfare and best interest.

Expenses to be paid out of funds of Kansas Indians.

ARTICLE 8. All the expenses connected with and incident to the making of this agreement, and the carrying out its provisions, shall be defrayed out of the funds of the Kansas tribe of Indians.

Assignments to children of Julia Pappan and others.

ARTICLE 9. The Kansas tribe of Indians being desirous of manifesting their good-will towards the children of their half-breed relatives now residing upon the half-breed tract on the north side of the Kansas River, agree that out of the tract retained by this agreement there shall also be assigned, in severalty, to the eight children of Julia Pappan forty acres each, to the three children of Adel Bellmard, to the four children of Jasette Gouville, to the child of Lewis Pappan, to the four children of Pelagia Obrey, to the child of Acaw Pappan, to the two children of Victoria Pappan, to the two children of Elizabeth Carboneau, to the child of Victoria Williams, to the child of Joseph Butler, to the child of Joseph James, to the two children of Pelagia Pushal, Frank James, and Batest Gouville, forty acres each, but the

Lands not to be alienated.

land so to be assigned under this article shall not be alienated in fee, leased, or otherwise disposed of, except to the United States, or to other members of the tribe, under such regulations as may be prescribed by the Secretary of [the] Interior.

ARTICLE 10. It is agreed that all roads and highways laid out by authority of law shall have right of way through the lands within the reservation hereinbefore specified, on the same terms as are provided by law when roads and highways are made through lands of citizens of the United States; and railroad companies, when the lines pass through the lands of said Indians, shall have right of way on the payment of a just compensation therefor in money. Right of way for roads.

ARTICLE 11. This instrument shall be obligatory on the contracting parties whenever the same shall be ratified by the President and Senate of the United States. Agreement, when to be obligatory.

In testimony whereof the said Alfred B. Greenwood, commissioner as aforesaid, and the said chiefs and headmen of the Kansas tribe of Indians, have hereunto set their hands and seals, at the place and on the day and year hereinbefore written.

In presence of (the words "upon the lands" and the word "pursuits," upon fifth page, interlined before signing)—

Milton C. Dickney, United States Indian agent,
Joseph James, United States interpreter,
John Goodell,
Frank Lecompte.

Alfred B. Greenwood. [L. S.]

Ki-he-ga-wah-chuffee, his x mark. [L. S.]	Sha-kep-pah, his x mark. [L. S.]
Ish-tal-a-sa, his x mark. [L. S.]	Oo-ga-sha-ma, his x mark. [L. S.]
Nee-hoo-ja-in-ga, his x mark. [L. S.]	Wah-e-lah-ga, his x mark. [L. S.]
Ki-hi-ga-wat-te-in-ga, his x mark. [L. S.]	Pa-ha-ne-ga-li, his x mark. [L. S.]
Ki-he-gah-cha, his x mark. [L. S.]	Pa-ta-go-hulle, his x mark. [L. S.]
Al-li-cah-wah-ho, his x mark. [L. S.]	Ma-she-tum-wa, his x mark. [L. S.]
Pah-hous-ga-tun-gah, his x mark. [L. S.]	No-ba-ga-ha, his x mark. [L. S.]
Ke-hah-lah-la-hu, his x mark. [L. S.]	She-ga-wa-sa, his x mark. [L. S.]
Ee-he-sun-gah, his x mark. [L. S.]	Ma-his-pa-wa-cha, his x mark. [L. S.]
Ko-sah-mungee, his x mark. [L. S.]	Ma-shon-o-pusha, his x mark. [L. S.]
Wah-pa-jah, his x mark. [L. S.]	Ja-ha-sha-watunga, his x mark. [L. S.]
Oo-gah-sha-ma, his x mark. [L. S.]	Ki-he-ga-tussa, his x mark. [L. S.]
Wah-shun-ga, his x mark. [L. S.]	Ka-la-sha, his x mark. [L. S.]
Wah-ti-in-ga, his x mark. [L. S.]	

TREATY WITH THE DELAWARES, 1860.

Articles of agreement and convention made and concluded at Sarcoxieville, on the Delaware reservation, this thirtieth day of May, one thousand eight hundred and sixty, by Thomas B. Sykes, as a commissioner on the part of the United States, and following named chiefs of the Delaware tribe of Indians, viz: John Conner, head chief of the whole tribe; Sar-cox-ie, chief of the Turtle band; Necon-he-con, chief of the Wolf band; Rock-a-to-wha, chief of the Turkey band, and assistants to the said head chief, chosen and appointed by the people, and James Connor, chosen by the said chief as delegate. May 30, 1860.
12 Stat., 1129.
Ratified July 27, 1860.
Proclaimed Aug. 22, 1860.

ARTICLE 1. By the first article of the treaty made and concluded at the city of Washington, on the sixth day of May, one thousand eight hundred and fifty-four, between George W. Manypenny, commissioner on the part of the United States, and certain delegates of the Delaware tribe of Indians, which treaty was ratified by the Senate of the United States on the eleventh day of July, one thousand eight hundred and fifty-four, there was reserved, as a permanent home for the said tribe, that part of their country lying east and south of a line beginning at a point on the line between the Delawares and Half-breed Kansas, forty miles in a direct line west of the boundary between the Delawares and Provisions of treaty of May 6, 1854.

Wyandottes; thence north ten miles; thence in a easterly course to a point on the south bank of Big Island Creek, which shall also be on the bank of the Missouri river, where the usual high-water line of said creek intersects the high-water line of said river. And by the eleventh article of said treaty it was stipulated that "at any time hereafter when the Delawares desire it, and at their request and expense, the President may cause the country reserved for their permanent home, to be surveyed in the same' manner as the ceded country is surveyed, and may assign such portion to each person or family as shall be designated by the principal men of the tribe: *Provided*, such assignments shall be uniform."

Reservation shall be surveyed.

The Delawares having represented to the government that it is their wish that a portion of the lands reserved for their home may be divided among them in the manner contemplated by the eleventh article of the treaty aforesaid, it is hereby agreed by the parties hereto, that the said reservation shall be surveyed as early as practicable after the ratification of these articles of agreement and convention, in the same manner that the public lands are surveyed; and to each member of the Delaware tribe there shall be assigned a tract of land containing eighty acres, to include in every case, as far as practicable, a reasonable portion of timber, to be selected according to the legal subdivisions of survey.

Eighty acres to be assigned to each member of the tribe.

Mode of division.

ARTICLE 2. The division and assignment in severalty among the Delawares of the land shall be made in a compact body, under the direction of the Secretary of the Interior, and his decision of all questions arising thereupon shall be final and conclusive.

Certificates to issue, etc.

Certificates shall be issued by the Commissioner of Indian Affairs, for the tracts assigned in severalty, specifying the names of the individuals to whom they have been assigned respectively, and that the said tracts are set apart for the exclusive use and benefit of the assignees and their heirs.

Land not alienable except, etc.

And said tracts shall not be alienable in fee, leased, or otherwise disposed of, except to the United States or to members of the Delaware tribe, and under such rules and regulations as may be prescribed by the Secretary of the Interior; and the said tracts shall be exempt from levy, taxation, sale, or forfeiture, until otherwise provided by Congress.

Certificates to be secured to family, etc.

Prior to the issue of the certificates aforesaid, the Secretary of the Interior shall make such rules and regulations as he may deem necessary or expedient, respecting the disposition of any of said tracts, in case of the death of the person or persons to whom they may be assigned, so that the same shall be secured to the families of such deceased persons. And should any of the Indians to whom tracts shall be assigned, abandon them, the said Secretary may take such action in relation to the proper disposition thereof, as, in his judgment, may be necessary and proper.

Abandonment of land assigned.

Improvements.

The improvements of the Indians residing on the lands to be sold shall be valued by the United States, and the individual owners thereof shall receive the amount realized from the sale of the same, to be expended in building other improvements for them on the lands retained.

Leavenworth, Pawnee and Western Railroad Company to have a preference in the purchase of land remaining.

ARTICLE 3. The Delaware tribe of Indians, entertaining the belief that the value of their lands will be enhanced by having a railroad passing through their present reservation, and being of the opinion that the Leavenworth, Pawnee, and Western Railroad Company, incorporated by an act of the legislative assembly of Kansas Territory, will have the advantage of travel and general transportation over every other company proposed to be formed, which will run through their lands, have expressed a desire that the said Leavenworth, Pawnee, and Western Railroad Company shall have the preference of purchasing the remainder of their lands after the tracts in severalty and those for the special objects herein named shall have been selected and set apart, upon the payment into the United States treasury, which payment shall be made within six months after the quantity shall have been ascertained, in gold or silver coin, of such a sum as three commissioners, to be appointed by the Secretary of the Interior, shall appraise to be the value of said land: *Provided*, in no event shall the value be placed below the sum of one dollar and twenty-five cents per acre, exclusive of the cost of the survey of the same. (And that the United States will issue a patent in fee-simple to said company, upon the payment as aforesaid, for all the land remaining in Kansas.) It is, therefore, agreed by the United States that the wishes of the Delawares shall be granted; that they will accept of the trust reposed upon them; and that the money resulting from such disposition of the lands shall be disposed of and applied in the manner provided for by the seventh and eighth articles of the Delaware treaty of sixth May, one thousand eight hundred and fifty-four, after expending a sufficient sum to enable them to commence agricultural pursuits under favorable circumstances. It is also agreed that the said railroad company shall have the perpetual right of way over any portion of the lands allotted to the Delawares in severalty, upon payment of a just compensation therefor, in money, to the respective parties whose lands are crossed by the line of railroad. It being the intent and meaning of the Delawares, in consenting to the sale of their surplus lands to said company, that they should, in good faith, and within a reasonable time, construct a railroad through their reservation, and to carry out this intent as well as to secure so great a public convenience, it is agreed that no patent shall issue for any of these lands, nor shall the sale be binding upon the Delaware Indians or the United States, until the Secretary of the Interior shall be fully satisfied that a line of twenty-five miles of the road from Leavenworth City shall have been completed and equipped, when a patent shall issue for one-half of the ascertained quantity. The patent for the residue shall issue only when the said Secretary shall be satisfied that the road has been, in like manner, completed and equipped to the western boundary of the Delaware reservation. And if the said company shall fail or neglect to construct either the first or second section of the road, or having constructed the first section and fail to complete the second section within a reasonable time they shall forfeit to the United States all right to the lands not previously patented, and the certificate of purchase shall be deemed and considered cancelled. *And provided further*, That in case the said company shall fail to make payment for the lands or fail to construct the road, as hereinbefore stipulated, within a reasonable time, the surplus lands shall be disposed of by the Secretary of the Interior, at public auction, in quantities not exceeding one hundred and sixty acres; but, in no case for a sum less than the appraised value, the net proceeds to be applied in the same manner as hereinbefore specified: *And provided further*, That the said railroad company shall, finally, and in good faith, sell and dispose of all said lands within seven years after receiving the patent therefor, except what may be necessary for railroad purposes; and in default thereof so much thereof as may remain undisposed of shall revert to the Delaware nation, to be disposed of as herein provided for other forfeited lands.

ARTICLE 4. Whereas some years ago a good many of the Delawares went down among the Southern Indians, and as there are still about two hundred of them there, and as they have reason to believe they will return soon, it is hereby agreed that eighty acres each be set apart for them, to be allotted to them as they return, and certificates to be then issued to them, in the same manner as to those now within the reservation, and in every respect to be governed by the same rules and regulations prescribed for the government of the lands reserved

Marginal notes:

Minimum price $1.25 per acre.

Railroad company to have perpetual right of way.

Conditions on which patents shall issue to railroad.

In case of failure, etc., surplus lands to be disposed of.

Railroad to sell lands within seven years.

Provision for Delawares who are absent.

by the preceding articles, that until they return the allotments set apart for belong to the nation in common.

ARTICLE 5. There shall be reserved three hundred and twenty acres of ground where the mill, and school-house, and Ketchum's store now stand; three hundred and twenty acres where the council-house now is; one hundred and sixty acres where the Baptist mission now is; one hundred and sixty acres where the agency house now is; forty acres where the Methodist Episcopal Church South now is; forty acres

where the Methodist Episcopal Church North now is; which several tracts, with the improvements thereupon, shall be disposed of when the objects for which they have been reserved shall have been accomplished. in such manner and for such purposes as the Secretary of the Interior shall determine to be just and equitable, for the benefit of the Delawares.

ARTICLE 6. By article fourteen of the treaty between the Delawares and the United States, of May six, eighteen hundred and fifty-four, ratified by the Senate July eleven, eighteen hundred and fifty-four, the United States bound herself to protect them and their rights: and that whereas, that depredations of various kinds have been committed

upon them and their lands, it is hereby agreed that the United States shall pay them, within twelve months from the ratification of these articles of treaty and convention, thirty thousand dollars as indemnity for timber that has been cut off their reservation by the whites, and nine thousand five hundred dollars as indemnity for ponies and cattle that have been stolen from them by the whites since their last treaty

with the United States. It is further stipulated that should the Senate of the United States refuse this article, it shall in no wise effect the validity of the other articles, or prejudice the right of the Delawares to appeal to the Congress of the United States for the indemnities hereby agreed upon.

It is further understood that, at the treaty between the Delawares and the United States, made September twenty-four, eighteen hundred and twenty-nine, the boundary of the reservation then set apart for them included the Half-breed Kansas lands; but it afterwards proved that the United States had previously set apart these lands for the Half-breed Kaws, and by that means they have been kept out of the use and

benefit of said lands; it is, therefore, hereby agreed that a fair valuation shall be made by the United States upon such lands, under the direction of the Secretary of the Interior, and that the amount of said valuation shall be paid the Delawares.

ARTICLE 7. In consideration of the long and faithful services of the chiefs of the Delaware nation, and of the interpreter, who is also a member of the nation, it is further agreed that the said chiefs and interpreter shall have allotted to each a tract of land, to be selected by themselves, and shall receive a patent in fee-simple therefor from the

President of the United States, viz: John Conner, principal chief, six hundred and forty acres; Sar-cox-ie, chief of the Turtle band, three hundred and twenty acres; Rock-a-to-wha, chief of the Turkey band, three hundred and twenty acres; Ne-con-he-con, chief of the Wolf band, three hundred and twenty acres; and Henry Tiblow, interpreter, three hundred and twenty acres; the lines of each tract to conform to the legal subdivisions of survey. It is further agreed that, from the money as paid the Delaware tribe of Indians, in accordance with article

number ten of this treaty, the chiefs of said tribe of Indians shall appropriate one thousand five hundred dollars as the annual salary of the councilmen of the said tribe of Indians.

ARTICLE 8. Any stipulation in former treaties inconsistent with those embraced in the foregoing articles shall be of no force or effect.

ARTICLE 9. As these articles are entered into for the sole use and benefit of the Delaware Indians, it is understood that the expenses incident to carrying them into effect shall be defrayed from the funds of said Indians, held in trust for them by the United States.

ARTICLE 10. The interest accruing to the Delawares under the former treaties, and that which may accrue under this, shall be paid on the first of April and October in each year. Interest to be paid Apr. 1 and Oct. 1.

In testimony whereof, the said Thomas B. Sykes, commissioner as aforesaid, and the said delegates of the Delaware tribe of Indians have hereunto set their hands and seals, at the place and on the day and year hereinbefore written. Signature.

Thomas B. Sykes, Commissioner,   [SEAL.]
John Connor, Head Chief, his x mark.   [SEAL.]
Sar-cox-ie, or The Highest, Assistant Chief, his x mark.   [SEAL.]
Ne-con-he-con, or Bounding Ahead, Assistant Chief, his x mark.   [SEAL.]
Rock-a-to-wha, or Sun Rise, Assistant Chief, his x mark.   [SEAL.]
James Connor, or Ah-la-a-chick, his x mark.   [SEAL.]

Signed in the presence of—
    Henry Tiblow, United States interpreter.
    James Findlay.
    William G. Bradshaw.
    Samuel Priestley.
    Thomas S. Gladding.

TREATY WITH THE ARAPAHO AND CHEYENNE, 1861.

Articles of agreement and convention made and concluded at Fort Wise, in the Territory of Kansas, on the eighteenth day of February, in the year of our Lord one thousand eight hundred and sixty-one, by and between Albert G. Boone and F. B. Culver, commissioners on the part of the United States, and the following named chiefs and delegates, representing the confederated tribes of Arapahoe and Cheyenne Indians of the Upper Arkansas River, viz: Little Raven, Storm, Shave-Head, and Big-Mouth, (on the part of the Arapahoes), and Black Kettle, White Antelope, Lean Bear, Little Wolf, and Left Hand, or Namos (on the part of the Cheyennes), they being thereto duly authorized by said confederated tribes of Indians. Feb. 18, 1861.
12 Stat., 1163.
Ratified, Aug. 6, 1861.
Proclaimed Dec. 5, 1861.

ARTICLE 1. The said chiefs and delegates of said Arapahoe and Cheyenne tribes of Indians do hereby cede and relinquish to the United States all lands now owned, possessed, or claimed by them, wherever situated, except a tract to be reserved for the use of said tribes located within the following described boundaries, to wit: Beginning at the mouth of the Sandy Fork of the Arkansas River and extending westwardly along the said river to the mouth of Purgatory River; thence along up the west bank of the Purgatory River to the northern boundary of the Territory of New Mexico; thence west along said boundary to a point where a line drawn due south from a point on the Arkansas River, five miles east of the mouth of the Huerfano River, would intersect said northern boundary of New Mexico; thence due north from that point on said boundary of the Sandy Fork to the place of the beginning. Cession of lands.

Boundaries.

The Arapahoe and Cheyennes, being desirous of promoting settled habits of industry and enterprise among themselves, by abolishing the tenure in common by which they now hold their lands, and by assigning limited quantities thereof in severalty to the individual members of the respective tribes, to be cultivated and improved for their individual use and benefit, it is hereby agreed and stipulated that the tract of country contained within the boundary above described shall be set apart and retained by them for the purposes aforesaid. Tenure of lands.

According to the understanding among themselves, it is hereby agreed between the United States and the said tribes that the said reservation shall be surveyed and divided by a line to be run due north from a point on the northern boundary of New Mexico, fifteen miles west of Purgatory River, and extending to the Sandy Fork of the Arkansas River, which said line shall establish the eastern boundary of that portion of the reservation, to be hereafter occupied by the Cheyennes, and the western boundary of portion of said reservation to be hereafter occupied by the Arapahoes.

Reservation to be surveyed and divided.

ARTICLE 2. Out of the lands so set apart and retained there shall be assigned to each member of said tribes, without distinction of age or sex, a tract of forty acres, to include in every case, as far as practicable, a reasonable portion of timber and water; one hundred and sixty acres of said retained lands shall also be set apart and appropriated to the use and occupancy of the agent, for the time being, of said tribes; and one hundred and sixty acres shall also be reserved out of each division of the retained tract for the establishment and support of schools for the education of the youth of the tribe. The location of the tracts, the assignment of which is provided for in this article, shall be made in as regular and compact a manner as possible, and so as to admit of a distinct and well-defined exterior boundary, embracing the whole of them, and any intermediate portions or parcels of land or water not included in or made part of the tracts assigned in severalty. All such intermediate parcels of land and water shall be owned in common by the tribe occupying that portion of the reservation within the limits of which said parcels of land and water may be included; but in case of increase in the tribe, or other causes rendering it necessary or expedient, the said intermediate parcels of land shall be subject to distribution and assignment in such manner as the Secretary of the Interior may prescribe and direct. The whole of the lands, assigned and unassigned, embraced within the exterior boundary herein designated, shall constitute and be known as the Reservation of the Arapahoes and Cheyennes of the Upper Arkansas; and all laws which have been or may be passed by the Congress of the United States regulating trade and intercourse with Indian tribes, shall have full force and effect over the same, and no white person, except as shall be in the employment of the United States, shall be allowed to reside or go upon any portion of said reservation without the written permission of the superintendent of the central superintendency, or of the agent of the tribes.

Assignment in severalty of lands to members of tribe.

To agent of tribes.

For schools. Location of land.

Lands owned in common.

Name of reservation. Laws.

ARTICLE 3. The division and assignment in severalty among the Arapahoes and Cheyennes of the land hereinbefore reserved for that purpose, shall be made under the direction of the Secretary of the Interior, and his decision of all questions arising thereupon shall be final and conclusive. Certificates shall be issued by the Commissioner of Indian Affairs for the tracts assigned in severalty, specifying the names of the individuals to whom they have been assigned respectively, and that the said tracts are set apart for the exclusive use and benefit of the assignees and their heirs. And said tracts shall not be alienated in fee, leased, or otherwise disposed of, except to the United States, or to members of the respective bands of Arapahoes and Cheyennes, and under such rules and regulations as may be prescribed by the Secretary of the Interior. And said tracts shall be exempt from taxation, levy, sale, or forfeiture, until otherwise provided by Congress. Prior to the issue of the certificates aforesaid, the Secretary of the Interior shall make such rules and regulations as he may deem necessary or expedient respecting the disposition of any of said tracts, in the case of the death of the person or persons to whom they may be assigned, so that the same shall be secured to the families of such deceased persons; and should any of the Indians to whom tracts shall

Assignment to be under the direction of the Secretary of the Interior.

Certificates.

Lands not to be alienated, except, etc.

To be exempt, etc.

Disposition in case of death, etc.

be assigned, abandon them, the said Secretary may take such action in relation to the proper disposition thereof as, in his judgment, may be necessary and proper.

ARTICLE 4th. In consideration of the foregoing cession, relinquishment, and agreements, and for the purpose of establishing the Arapahoes and Cheyennes comfortably upon the lands to be assigned to them in severalty, by building them houses, and by furnishing them with agricultural implements, stock animals, and other necessary aid and facilities for commencing agricultural pursuits under favorable circumstances, the United States do hereby agree and stipulate as follows, to wit: 1st. To protect the said Arapahoes and Cheyennes in the quiet and peaceful possession of the said tract of land so reserved for their future home, and also their persons and property thereon, during good behavior on their part. 2d. To pay to them, or expend for their benefit the sum of thirty thousand dollars per annum for fifteen years; that is to say, fifteen thousand dollars per annum for each tribe for that number of years, commencing with the year in which they shall remove to and settte and reside upon their said reservation; making four hundred and fifty thousand dollars in annuities in the period of fifteen years, of which sum the Secretary of the Interior shall, from time to time, determine what proportion shall be expended for their benefit, and for what object such expenditure shall be made, due regard being had, in making such determination, to the best interests of said Indians. He shall likewise exercise the power to make such provision out of said sums as he may deem to be necessary and proper for the support and comfort of the aged or infirm and helpless orphans of the said Indians. Their annuities may, at the discretion of the President of the United States, be discontinued entirely, should said Indians fail to make reasonable and satisfactory efforts to advance and improve their condition; in which case such other provision shall be made for them as the President and Congress may judge to be suitable and proper. 3d. It is hereby agreed that the expenses to be incurred in the purchase of agricultural implements, stock animals, etc., referred to in this article, as also the cost and expenses of breaking up and fencing land, building houses, store-houses, and other needful buildings, or in making such other improvements as may be necessary for their comfort and welfare, shall be defrayed out of the aforesaid sum of four hundred and fifty thousand dollars, to be paid to or expended for the benefit of the Arapahoes and Cheyennes as annuities.

ARTICLE 5th. To provide the said Indians with a mill suitable for sawing timber and grinding grain, one or more mechanic shops, with necessary tools for the same, and dwelling-houses for an interpreter, miller, engineer for the mill, (if one be necessary,) farmers, and the mechanics that may be employed for their benefit, the United States agree to expend therefor a sum not exceeding five thousand dollars per annum for five years; and it is agreed that all articles of goods and provisions, stock, implements, lumber, machinery, &c., referred to in this treaty, shall be transported to the respective tribes of Arapahoes and Cheyennes, at the cost and expense of the United States.

ARTICLE 6th. The Arapahoes and Cheyennes of the Upper Arkansas, parties to this Agreement, are anxious that all the members of their tribe shall participate in the advantages herein provided for respecting their improvements and civilization, and, to that end, to induce all that are now separated to rejoin and reunite with them. It is therefore agreed that, as soon as practicable, the Commissioner of Indian affairs shall cause the necessary proceedings to be adopted to have them notified of this agreement and its advantages; and to induce them to come in and unite with their brethren; and to enable them to do so, and to sustain themselves for a reasonable time thereafter, such assistance

Stipulations on part of the United States.

Protection of persons and property.

Annuities.

Aged and infirm.

Annuities may be discontinued.

Purchase of stock, agricultural implements, etc.

Mills and mechanic shops.

All members of the tribe to participate.

·To come in within one year.

shall be provided for them, at the expense of the tribe as may be actually necessary for that purpose: *Provided, however,* That those who did not rejoin and permanently reunite themselves with the tribe within one year from the date of the ratification of this treaty, shall not be entitled to the benefit of any of its stipulations.

Further aid.

ARTICLE 7th. Should any further aid from time to time be necessary to enable the Arapahoes and Cheyennes of the Upper Arkansas to sustain themselves successfully in agricultural or other industrial pursuits, such additional means as may be required therefor shall be taken from the moneys due and belonging to them under the provisions of former treaties or articles of agreement and convention, and so much of said moneys as may be required to furnish them further aid as aforesaid shall be applied in such manner, under the direction of the Secretary of the Interior, as he shall consider best calculated to improve and promote their welfare. And, in order to render unnecessary any further treaty engagements or arrangements hereafter with the United

President and Congress may modify, etc., former treaties.

States, it is hereby agreed and stipulated that the President, with the assent of Congress, shall have full power to modify or change any of the provisions of former treaties with the Arapahoes and Cheyennes of the Upper Arkansas, in such manner and to whatever extent he may judge to be necessary and expedient for their best interests.

Expenses of this treaty.

ARTICLE 8th. All the expenses connected with and incident to the making of this agreement and carrying out its provisions shall be defrayed by the United States, except as otherwise herein provided.

Roads, etc., to have right of way.

ARTICLE 9th. It is agreed that all roads and highways, laid out by authority of law, shall have right of way through the lands within the reservation hereinbefore specified, on the same terms as are provided by law when roads and highways are made through lands of citizens of the United States.

Existing annuities to be continued, etc.

ARTICLE 10th. It is also agreed by the United States that the annuities now paid to the Arapahoes and Cheyennes, under existing treaties or articles of agreement and convention, shall be continued to them until the stipulations of said treaties or articles of agreement and convention relating to such annuities shall be fulfilled.

ARTICLE 11th. [Stricken out.]

Instrument, when to be obligatory.

ARTICLE 12th. This instrument shall be obligatory on the contracting parties whenever the same shall be ratified by the President and the Senate of the United States.

In testimony whereof, the said Commissioner[s] as aforesaid, and the said Chiefs and Delegates of the Arapahoes and Cheyennes of the Upper Arkansas, have hereunto set their hands and seals, at the place and on the day and year hereinbefore written.

A. G. Boone,
United States Indian Agent and Commissioner.

F. B. Culver,
Commissioner and Special Agent.

On the part of the Arapahoes:
Ho-ha-ca-che, his x mark, or Little Raven.
Ac-ker-ba-the, his x mark, or Storm.
Che-ne-na-e-te, his x mark, Shave-Head.
Ma-na-sa-te, his x mark, Big Mouth.
On the part of the Cheyennes:
Mo-ta-va-to, his x mark, Black Kettle.
Vo-ki-vokamast, his x mark, White Antelope.

Avo-na-co, his x mark, Lean Bear.
O-ne-a-ha-ket, his x mark, Little Wolf.
Na-ko-hais-tah, his x mark, Tall Bear.
A-am-a-na-co, his x mark, Left Hand, or Namos.
John S. Smith, United States interpreter.
Robert Bent, United States interpreter.

Witnesses to the signatures:
John Sedgwick, major of Cavalry.
R. Ransom, jr., lieutenant of Cavalry.
J. E. B. Stuart, first lieutenant First Cavalry.
John White, clerk to the Indian signatures.

P. S.—And it is further understood, before signing the above treaty, that it was the particular request and wish of the Chiefs and Councillors in general convention, in consideration of Robert Bent being one of their half-breed tribe, that he should have, as a gift from the nation, six hundred and forty acres of land, covering the valley and what is called the Sulphur Spring, lying on the north side of the Arkansas River and about five miles below the Pawnee Hills, and they wish the general government to recognize and confirm the same; and that Jack Smith, son of John S. Smith, who is also a half-breed of said nation, shall have six hundred and forty acres of land, lying seven miles above Bent's Old Fort, on the north side of the Arkansas River, including the valley and point of rock, and respectfully recommend the general government to confirm and recognize the same.

Gift to Robert Bent.

To Jack Smith.

TREATY WITH THE SAUK AND FOXES, ETC., 1861.

Articles of agreement and convention made and concluded at the office of the Great Nemaha agency, Nebraska Territory, on the sixth day of March, A. D. one thousand eight hundred and sixty-one, by and between Daniel Vanderslice, U. S. Indian agent, on the part of the United States, and the following-named delegates of the Sacs and Foxes of Missouri, viz: Pe-ta-ok-a-ma, Ne-sour-quoit, Mo-less, and Se-se-ah-kee; and the following-named delegates of the Iowa tribe, viz: No-heart, Nag-ga-rash, Mah-hee, To-hee, Tah-ra-kee, Thur-o-mony, and White Horse; they being duly authorized thereto by their respective tribes.

Mar. 6, 1861.

12 Stat., 1171.
Ratified Feb. 6, 1863.
Proclaimed Mar. 26, 1863.

ARTICLE 1. The Sacs and Foxes of Missouri hereby cede, relinquish, and convey to the United States all their right, title, and interest in and to lands within their present reservation, described as follows, viz: beginning at the mouth of the south fork of the Great Nemaha River, and thence up the southwest bank of the Great Nemaha, with its meanders, to the mouth of the west fork; thence up the west fork, with its meanders, to the line of the 40° of parallel on the west bank of creek or fork where is established the southwest corner of the Sac and Fox reserve, by erecting a stone monument, from which the following references bear, viz: A large cottonwood tree, three feet in diameter, bears S. 44° 00′ E. 1.05 chains; a rock bears N. 30° 00′ W. 50 links; another rock bears N. 50° 00′ west 50 links; and another rock bears due north one chain; thence east along the line of the 40° of parallel to the west bank of the south fork of the Great Nemaha River, distance fourteen miles twenty-seven chains and sixty links, where is established the southeast corner of the Sac and Fox reserve, by erecting a stone pile with a black walnut post in the center of it, from which a white elm, two feet in diameter, bears S. 33° 00′ E. 22 links, and marked with the letters S. E. Cor. for the southeast corner, and another elm, 18 inch[e]s in diameter, bears S. 39° 00′ E. 1.05 chains, and marked SE C B SE., for the southeast corner, bearing, and distance; and another black walnut, 9 inch[e]s in diameter, bears S. 15° 00′ E. 85 links, and thence down the south fork, with its meanders, to the point of beginning, estimated to contain 32,098 acres, 3 roods and 35 perches.

Cession of reservation to the United States.

Boundaries.

ARTICLE 2. The aforesaid lands shall be surveyed in conformity with the system governing the survey of the public lands; and the same shall be sold, under the direction of the Secretary of the Interior, in parcels not exceeding one hundred and sixty acres each, to the highest bidder for cash; the sale to be made upon sealed proposals, to be duly invited by public advertisement, provided, no bid shall be favorably considered which may be less than one dollar and twenty-five cents per acre. And should any of the tracts so to be sold have upon them improvements of any kind which were made by or for the Indians, or for Government purposes, the proposals therefor must state the price for both the land and improvements. The proceeds of the sales thereof, after deducting therefrom the expenses of surveying the lands and all

Lands to be surveyed and sold at auction.

Improvements.

Proceeds of sale.

other expenses incident to the negotiation of these articles of convention and the proper execution thereof, the balance shall be applied as follows, viz: One half shall be held in trust by the United States for the benefit of the Sacs and Foxes of Missouri, and interest thereon, at the rate of five per centum per annum, shall be paid annually, with the other funds to be paid said tribe, in the same manner as stipulated in the treaty of May 18th, 1854; and the other half of said balance shall be applied as hereinafter specified.

Iowas cede to the United States lands for the Sacs and Foxes.

ARTICLE 3. The Iowa tribe of Indians, parties to this agreement, hereby cede, relinquish, and convey to the United States, for the use and benefit of the Sacs and Foxes of Missouri, for their permanent home, all that part of their present reservation lying and being west of Nohearts Creek, and bounded as follows, viz: Beginning at a point where the southern line of the present Iowa reserve crosses Nohearts Creek; thence with said line to the south fork of the Nemaha, (commonly known as Walnut Creek;) thence down the middle of said south fork, with the meanders thereof, to its mouth, and to a point in the middle of the Great Nemaha River; thence down the middle of said river to a point opposite the mouth of Nohearts Creek; and thence, in a southerly direction with the middle of said Nohearts Creek, to the place of beginning. And it is hereby understood and agreed that, in full consideration for said cession, the United States shall hold in trust, for the use and benefit of the Iowas, the one-half of the net proceeds of the sales of the lands described in the second article of this agreement, and interest thereon, at the rate of five per centum per annum, shall be paid to the Iowa tribe in the same manner as their annuities are paid under the treaty of May 17, 1854. The reservation herein described shall be surveyed and set apart for the exclusive use and benefit of the Sacs and Foxes of Missouri, and the remainder of the Iowa lands shall be the tribal reserve of said Iowa Indians for their exclusive use and benefit.

Boundaries.

Joseph Tesson to select a quarter section of land.

ARTICLE 4. The Sacs and Foxes of Missouri being anxious to make full satisfaction for a just claim which Joseph Tesson holds against said tribe, it is hereby agreed by the parties to this convention that said claimant shall select a quarter section or one hundred and sixty acres of land, to include his present residence and improvements, to be located in one body, in conformity with the legal subdivisions of the public surveys, which tract of land shall be received by him in full payment of said claim, estimated at about eight hundred dollars, and all other claims or rights of every character whatsoever against said tribe; and when a relinquishment shall have been executed by said claimant in favor of said tribe for all claims that he may have against them, a patent shall be issued to him for said tract of land in fee-simple.

Certain chiefs may select each a quarter section of land.

The following chiefs shall be entitled to select each a quarter section or one hundred and sixty acres of land in one body, in conformity with the public surveys, to include their present residences and improvements, viz: Pe-te-ok-a-ma, Ne-sour-quoit, and Mo-less: and George Gomess, a member of the Sac and Fox tribe, shall select in like manner one-eighth of a section or eighty acres of land in one body, to include his improvements, and patents shall be issued therefor in favor of said persons in fee-simple.

Grant for purposes of education.

ARTICLE 5. In order to encourage education among the aforesaid tribes of Indians, it is hereby agreed that the United States shall expend the sum of one thousand dollars for the erection of a suitable school-house, and dwelling-house for the school teacher, for the benefit of the Sacs and Foxes, and also the additional sum of two hundred dollars per annum for school purposes, so long as the President of the United States may deem advisable. And for the benefit of the Iowa tribe of Indians there shall be expended, in like manner, at the discretion of the President, the sum of three hundred dollars per annum, for school purposes, which two last-mentioned sums shall be paid out of the funds to be appropriated for the civilization of Indians.

ARTICLE 6. There shall be set apart in one body, under the direction of the Commissioner of Indian Affairs, one section, or six hundred and forty acres of land, in harmony with the public survey, so as to include the agency-dwelling, agency-office, council-house, school-house, teachers' dwelling, blacksmith's dwelling and shops, and such farming land as may be necessary for the use of the school, agency, and employees thereat.

ARTICLE 7. No person not a member of either of the tribes, parties to this convention, shall go upon the reservations or sojourn among the Indians without a license or written permit from the agent or superintendent of Indian affairs, except Government employees or persons connected with the public service. And no mixed-blood Indians, except those employed at some mission, or such as may be sent there to be educated, or other members of the aforesaid tribes, shall participate in the beneficial provisions of this agreement or former treaties, unless they return to and unite permanently with said tribes, and reside upon the respective reservations within six months from the date of this convention. *Persons not to reside on the reservation without permit.*

ARTICLE 8. It is hereby understood and agreed by the contracting parties hereto that the stipulations of the treaty with the Sacs and Foxes of Missouri of May 18th, 1854, and the treaty with the Iowa Indians of the 17th of May, 1854, which may not be inconsistent with these articles of convention, shall have full force and effect upon the contracting parties hereto. *Former treaty stipulations.*

ARTICLE 9. This instrument shall be obligatory upon the respective parties hereto, whenever the same shall be ratified by the President and the Senate of the United States. *When this treaty to be obligatory.*

ARTICLE 10. The Secretary of the Interior may expend a sum not exceeding three thousand five hundred dollars, ($3,500,) out of the proceeds of the sales of said lands, at any time he may deem it advisable, for the purpose of erecting a toll-bridge across the Great Nemaha River, at or near Roy's Ferry, for the use of the Iowa Indians; and a like sum of three thousand five hundred dollars, ($3,500,) out of the proceeds of the sales of said lands, for the purpose of erecting a toll-bridge across the Great Nemaha River, at or near Wolf Village, for the use of the Sacs and Foxes of Missouri. *Toll bridge.*

Toll shall be charged and collected for the use of said bridges at such rates and under such rules and regulations as may be established by the Commissioner of Indian Affairs, with the approval of the Secretary of the Interior, the proceeds of such tolls to be expended as follows: 1st, in making necessary repairs on said bridges; 2d, for the use of said tribes, respectively. *Tolls.*

ARTICLE 11. It is further stipulated that, whenever Congress shall by law so provide, all annuities due and to become due and payable to the said tribes of Indians under this treaty, and under all other previous treaties, may be paid in specific articles, clothing, agricultural implements, and such other articles as Congress shall direct. *Annuities.*

In testimony whereof, the said commissioner as aforesaid, and the said chiefs and delegates of the Sacs and Foxes of Missouri, and [of the] Iowa tribe of Indians, have hereunto set their hands and seals at the place and on the day and year hereinbefore written.

D. Vanderslice, United States Indian agent.		[L. S.]
Pe-te-ok-a-ma,	his x mark.	[L. S.]
Ne-sour-quoit,	his x mark.	[L. S.]
Mo-less,	his x mark.	[L. S.]
Se-se-ah-kee.	his x mark.	[L. S.]

Sac[s] and Foxes of Mo.

No-heart,	his x mark.	[L. S.]
Nag-ga-rash,	his x mark.	[L. S.]
Mah-hee,	his x mark.	[L. S.]
To-hee,	his x mark.	[L. S.]
Tah-ra-kee,	his x mark.	[L. S.]
Thur-o-mony,	his x mark.	[L. S.]
White-horse,	his x mark.	[L. S.]

Iowa Indians.

Signed in the presence of—

George Gomess, his x mark, United States interpreter for Sac[s] and Foxes of Mo.

Harvey W. Forman, witness to signing by George Gomess.

Kirwan Murray, United States interpreter for Iowa Indians.

Harvey W. Forman.

John W. Forman.

Josephus Utt.

TREATY WITH THE DELAWARES, 1861.

July 2, 1861.

12 Stats., 1177.
Ratified.Aug.6,1861.
Proclaimed, Oct. 4, 1861.

Preamble.

Whereas a treaty or agreement was made and concluded at Leavenworth City, Kansas, on the second day of July, one thousand eight hundred and sixty-one, between the United States of America and the Delaware tribe of Indians, relative to certain lands of that tribe conveyed to the Leavenworth, Pawnee, and Western Railroad Company, and to bonds executed to the United States by the said company for the payment of the said Indians, which treaty or agreement, with the preliminary and incidental papers necessary to the full understanding of the same, is in the following words, to wit:

Whereas, by the treaty of May 30, 1860, between the United States and the Delaware tribe of Indians, it is provided that the surplus lands of said Delawares, not included in their "home reserve," should be surveyed and appraised under direction of the Secretary of the Interior:

Certain lands pledged by railroad company to secure its bonds. and that in order to aid in the construction of a railroad near and through their said "home reserve," the Leavenworth, Pawnee, and Western Railroad Company of Kansas, duly organized and incorporated under the laws of said Territory, should have the right to purchase such surplus lands at such appraised value—on condition, however, that after paying for said lands, said company should only receive title to one-half of them on completing and equipping, within a reasonable time, twenty-five (25) miles of said railroad from Leavenworth City westward; and should only receive title to the remaining half of said lands on completing and equipping said road, within a reasonable time, to the western boundary of the "Delaware Reserve;" and that in case said company should fail to pay for said lands, or having paid, should forfeit the same, or any part thereof, before receiving title, by failing to construct either the first or the second section of said road within such reasonable time, then the lands so forfeited, or not paid for, should be sold in quantities not exceeding one hundred and sixty (160) acres, at not less than such appraised value; the proceeds of such sale, subject to a certain contingent deduction, to be invested by the President of the United States in "safe and profitable stocks," for the benefit of said Delaware Indians: and

Whereas said surplus lands, to the amount of $223,966\frac{78}{100}$ acres, have been duly surveyed and appraised at an aggregate valuation of two hundred and eighty-six thousand seven hundred and forty-two and $\frac{15}{100}$ ($286,742\frac{15}{100}$) dollars: and

Whereas the said Leavenworth, Pawnee, and Western Railroad Company has executed, under their corporate seal, and by the hand of Thomas Ewing, jr., their agent, their twenty-nine (29) several bonds.

all of even date herewith, and numbered from one to twenty-nine, inclusive, for sums amounting in the aggregate to $286,742$\frac{15}{100}$, being the amount of the valuation of said surplus lands as above stated, twenty eight (28) of which said bonds are for the sum of ten thousand ($10,000) dollars each, and one is for the sum of six thousand and seven hundred and forty-two and $\frac{15}{100}$ ($6,742$\frac{15}{100}$) dollars, and payable in ten (10) years after their date, at the office of the assistant treasurer of the United States, in the city of New York, to the Commissioner of Indian Affairs of the United States or bearer, with interest at the rate of six per cent. per annum, payable annually at the same place on interest-warrants attached to said bonds, which said bonds have been delivered by said company to Archibald Williams, judge of the United States court for the district of Kansas, and have been by him received and receipted for as agent of the United States for that purpose specially appointed, in accordance with the instructions of the President of the United States of June 10, 1861, hereto attached and made part hereof, and for the consideration and use in said instructions set forth:

Now, therefore, to secure the payment of said bonds and every part thereof, and of all interest to become due thereon, according to the terms thereof, the Leavenworth, Pawnee, and Western Railroad Company by its agent hereto specially authorized by resolution of the board of directors of said company of April 11, 1861, a certified copy of which said resolution is hereto attached, hereby agrees with the United States, as trustee for said Delaware tribe of Indians, that in case said company shall at any time hereafter neglect or fail to pay the whole or any part of the interest on all or any one of said bonds, or shall neglect or fail to pay the whole or any part of the principal of all or any one of said bonds, when any such payment, either of principal or of interest, shall become due and payable, then the said railroad company shall be deemed and held to have forfeited all right and title of any kind whatever to the one hundred thousand (100,000) acres of land herein described, to wit:

Description.	Section.	Township.	Range.	Meridian. P. M.	
Southeast quarter	2	10	17 E.	6th.	List of lands.
Section	12	10	17 E.	6th.	
West half	13	10	17 E.	6th.	
East half	14	10	17 E.	6th.	
Section	24	10	17 E.	6th.	
West half	25	10	17 E.	6th.	
Section	36	10	17 E.	6th.	
South half	3	10	18 E.	6th.	
South half	4	10	18 E.	6th.	
Section	9	10	18 E.	6th.	
South half	25	10	19 E.	6th.	
Section	26	10	19 E.	6th.	
Section	28	10	19 E.	6th.	
West half	30	10	19 E.	6th.	
Section	32	10	19 E.	6th.	
Section	34	10	19 E.	6th.	
Section	36	10	19 E.	6th.	
South half	2	10	20 E.	6th.	
South half	4	10	20 E.	6th.	
S. W. quarter	5	10	20 E.	6th.	
East half	19	10	18 E.	6th.	
East half	24	10	18 E.	6th.	
North half	25	10	18 E.	6th.	
East half	26	10	18 E.	6th.	
West half	28	10	18 E.	6th.	
East half	30	10	18 E.	6th.	

Description.	Section.	Township.	Range.	Meridian. P. M.
West half	32	10	18 E.	6th.
Section	35	10	18 E.	6th.
South half	1	10	19 E.	6th.
South half	3	10	19 E.	6th.
South half	5	10	19 E.	6th.
East half	7	10	19 E.	6th.
Section	9	10	19 E.	6th.
Section	11	10	19 E.	6th.
Section	13	10	19 E.	6th.
Section	15	10	19 E.	6th.
Section	17	10	19 E.	6th.
East half	19	10	19 E.	6th.
West half	20	10	19 E.	6th.
Section	22	10	19 E.	6th.
East half	23	10	19 E.	6th.
Section	24	10	19 E.	6th.
S. E. quarter	6	10	20 E.	6th.
Section	8	10	20 E.	6th.
Section	10	10	20 E.	6th.
Section	12	10	20 E.	6th.
Section	14	10	20 E.	6th.
West half	15	10	20 E.	6th.
Section	17	10	20 E.	6th.
East half	19	10	20 E.	6th.
East half	20	10	20 E.	6th.
West half	21	10	20 E.	6th.
Section	22	10	20 E.	6th.
Section	24	10	20 E.	6th.
Section	26	10	20 E.	6th.
Section	28	10	20 E.	6th.
Section	30	10	20 E.	6th.
Section	32	10	20 E.	6th.
Section	34	10	20 E.	6th.
Section	36	10	20 E.	6th.
Section	8	10	21 E.	6th.
Section	10	10	21 E.	6th.
Section	12	10	21 E.	6th.
Section	13	10	21 E.	6th.
Section	15	10	21 E.	6th.
Section	17	10	21 E.	6th.
Section	19	10	21 E.	6th.
Section	21	10	21 E.	6th.
Section	23	10	21 E.	6th.
Section	25	10	21 E.	6th.
Section	27	10	21 E.	6th.
Section	29	10	21 E.	6th.
Section	31	10	21 E.	6th.
Section	33	10	21 E.	6th.
Section	35	10	21 E.	6th.
Section	7	10	22 E.	6th.
Section	9	10	22 E.	6th.
Section	11	10	22 E.	6th.
Section	13	10	22 E.	6th.
Section	15	10	22 E.	6th.
Section	17	10	22 E.	6th.
Section	19	10	22 E.	6th.
Section	21	10	22 E.	6th.
Section	23	10	22 E.	6th.
Section	25	10	22 E.	6th.

Description.	Section.	Township.	Range.	Meridian. P.M.
Section	27	10	21 E.	6th.
Section	29	10	22 E.	6th.
Section	31	10	22 E.	6th.
Section	33	10	22 E.	6th.
Section	35	10	22 E.	6th.
Section	7	10	23 E.	6th.
Section	9	10	23 E.	6th.
Section	11	10	23 E.	6th.
Section	19	10	23 E.	6th.
South half	1	11	17 E.	6th.
South half	12	11	17 E.	6th.
North half	13	11	17 E.	6th.
South half	24	11	17 E.	6th.
South half	2	11	18 E.	6th.
South half	4	11	18 E.	6th.
East half	6	11	18 E.	6th.
East half	7	11	18 E.	6th.
Section	8	11	18 E.	6th.
Section	10	11	18 E.	6th.
Section	12	11	18 E.	6th.
Section	14	11	18 E.	6th.
West half	15	11	18 E.	6th.
East half	17	11	18 E.	6th.
East half	18	11	18 E.	6th.
West half	20	11	18 E.	6th.
East half	22	11	18 E.	6th.
West half	23	11	18 E.	6th.
West half	24	11	18 E.	6th.
East half	25	11	18 E.	6th.
South half	1	11	19 E.	6th.
South half	3	11	19 E.	6th.
South half	5	11	19 E.	6th.
East half	7	11	19 E.	6th.
Section	9	11	19 E.	6th.
Section	11	11	19 E.	6th.
Section	13	11	19 E.	6th.
Section	15	11	19 E.	6th.
Section	17	11	19 E.	6th.
East half	18	11	19 E.	6th.
East half	19	11	19 E.	6th.
Section	21	11	19 E.	6th.
Section	23	11	19 E.	6th.
Section	25	11	19 E.	6th.
East half	24	11	19 E.	6th.
Section	27	11	19 E.	6th.
Section	29	11	19 E.	6th.
East half	30	11	19 E.	6th.
East half	33	11	19 E.	6th.
West half	34	11	19 E.	6th.
North half	35	11	19 E.	6th.
Section	36	11	19 E.	6th.
South half	1	11	20 E.	6th.
South half	2	11	20 E.	6th.
South half	3	11	20 E.	6th.
South half	4	11	20 E.	6th.
East half	7	11	20 E.	6th.
South half	8	11	20 E.	6th.
South half	9	11	20 E.	6th.
N. W. quarter	13	11	20 E.	6th.

Description.	Section.	Township.	Range.	Meridian. P. M.
S. W. quarter	15	11	20 E.	6th.
North half	17	11	20 E.	6th.
East half	18	11	20 E.	6th.
East half	19	11	20 E.	6th.
North half	20	11	20 E.	6th.
West half	21	11	20 E.	6th.
East half	22	11	20 E.	6th.
South half	23	11	20 E.	6th.
South half	24	11	20 E.	6th.
Section	25	11	20 E.	6th.
South half	26	11	20 E.	6th.
East half	27	11	20 E.	6th.
East half	33	11	20 E.	6th.
Section	34	11	20 E.	6th.
Section	36	11	20 E.	6th.
South half	1	11	21 E.	6th.
South half	3	11	21 E.	6th.
South half	5	11	21 E.	6th.
East half	7	11	21 E.	6th.
Section	8	11	21 E.	6th.
Section	10	11	21 E.	6th.
Section	12	11	21 E.	6th.
South half	13	11	21 E.	6th.
Section	14	11	21 E.	6th.
West half	15	11	21 E.	6th.
Section	17	11	21 E.	6th.
East half	18	11	21 E.	6th.
East half	19	11	21 E.	6th.
East half	20	11	21 E.	6th.
West half	21	11	21 E.	6th.
Section	22	11	21 E.	6th.
South half	27	11	21 E.	6th.
Section	28	11	21 E.	6th.
West half	29	11	21 E.	6th.
East half	30	11	21 E.	6th.
East half	31	11	21 E.	6th.
Section	32	11	21 E.	6th.
Section	34	11	21 E.	6th.
Section	3	11	22 E.	6th.
Section	5	11	22 E.	6th.
East half	7	11	22 E.	6th.
West half	8	11	22 E.	6th.
Section	9	11	22 E.	6th.
Section	15	11	22 E.	6th.
Section	17	11	22 E.	6th.
East half	18	11	22 E.	6th.
Section	1	12	19 E.	6th.
East half	2	12	19 E.	6th.
South half	12	12	19 E.	6th.
N. E. quarter	13	12	19 E.	6th.
Section	1	12	20 E.	6th.
Section	3	12	20 E.	6th.
Section	5	12	20 E.	6th.
East half	6	12	20 E.	6th.
East half	7	12	20 E.	6th.
Section	9	12	20 E.	6th.
Section	11	12	20 E.	6th.
Section	12	12	20 E.	6th.
Section	14	12	20 E.	6th.

Description.	Section.	Township.	Range.	Meridian. P. M.
East half	15	12	20 E.	6th.
East half	18	12	20 E.	6th.
East half	19	12	20 E.	6th.
Section	21	12	20 E.	6th.
North half	29	12	20 E.	6th.
S. E. quarter	21	12	20 E.	6th.
Section	16	12	20 E.	6th.

156¼ sections, or 100,000 acres.

And immediately on such failure, the United States may take possession of and sell said lands for the exclusive benefit of said Delaware Indians.

And in case said company shall forfeit the one hundred thousand (100,000) acres above described, it shall thereupon also forfeit all its right and title to all the lands purchased by it from said Indians, not earned and patented at the date of such forfeiture.

And said company further agree that, on the completion of the first section of said road, it shall only be entitled to a patent for one-half of the lands not pledged for the payment of said bonds; and on the completion of said second section it shall have a patent for only the remaining half; and that no patent shall issue to it for any of the lands so pledged, until after said bonds and the interest warrants attached shall all and every part of them have been fully and promptly paid and cancelled.

In witness whereof, the said Leavenworth, Pawnee, and Western Railroad Company, by Thomas Ewing, jr., their agent aforesaid, have executed this instrument and attached thereto the seal of said company, this 2d day of July, 1861.

The Leavenworth, Pawnee, and Western Railroad Company, by their agent,

[SEAL.]   THOMAS EWING, JR.

Marginal note: When United States may take possession.

Marginal note: Company entitled to patent.

———

State of Kansas, Leavenworth County, ss:

On this second day of July, A. D. 1861, before me, the undersigned authority, a notary public in and for the county aforesaid, in the State aforesaid, personally came Thomas Ewing, jr., agent of the Leavenworth, Pawnee, and Western Railroad Company, to me personally known to be the identical person who signed the foregoing instrument of writing, and whose name is thereto affixed as grantor, and he acknowledged the same to be his own voluntary act and deed.

Witness my hand and notarial seal, this 2d day of July, A. D. 1861.

[SEAL.]   W. S. VAN DOREN,
Notary Public, Leavenworth County, Kansas.

Marginal note: Acknowledgment.

———

At a called meeting of the board of directors of the Leavenworth, Pawnee, and Western Railway Company, on Monday, July 1st, 1861, at the office of A. J. Isacks, in Leavenworth City, Kansas, was present Jas. C. Stone, Amos Rees, Thomas Ewing, jr., and Thomas S. Gladding.

Resolved, That Thomas Ewing, jr., be authorized and directed, as agent of the company, to make, execute, and deliver to Archibald Williams, as agent of the United States, the bonds and interest-warrants of the company for $286,742$\frac{15}{100}$, payable in ten years from their date, with 6 per cent. interest, payable annually, payable to the Commissioner of Indian Affairs, or bearer, at the office of the assistant treasurer of the United States in the city of New York; and also to make and execute to the United States, and cause to be recorded and

Marginal note: Authority of agent of road to make conveyance.

delivered to said Williams, as such agent, a mortgage of the company on the one hundred thousand acres of Delaware Indian lands, described in the letter of the Commissioner of Indian Affairs to the Secretary of the Interior, on May 29th, 1861; such mortgage to contain all the conditions prescribed in the paper signed by the President of the United States, of June 10th, 1861, the terms of which are hereby accepted by the company.

I hereby certify that at a meeting of the board of directors of the Leavenworth, Pawnee, and Western Railroad Company, held at the office of A. J. Isacks, in the city of Leavenworth, in the State of Kansas, on the 1st day of July, 1861, the foregoing proceedings were had and recorded on the journal of the company; and that the same is a true and correct transcript of the same from the journal of said company.

In testimony whereof I hereunto sign my name and affix the official seal of the company.

[SEAL.]   THOS. S. GLADDING,
                                          Secretary L. P. & W. R. R. Co.

Railroad company to execute bonds and mortgage. Whereas, by the treaty of Sarcoxieville, amended by the United States Senate, and finally ratified by the President of the United States on the 22d day of August, 1860, a principal object of both parties was the construction of a certain contemplated railroad therein named; and to that end the Leavenworth, Pawnee, and Western Railroad Company were to pay into the United States Treasury, in gold or silver coin, a sum of money, afterwards ascertained to be $286,742.15, as the appraised value of certain lands in Kansas belonging to the Delaware tribe of Indians; which sum of money, after expending a sufficient part of it to enable the Indians to commence agricultural pursuits under favorable circumstances, was to be, by the President, for said Indians, invested in safe and profitable stocks; and

Whereas the said railroad company is not able to pay said sum of money within time, according to said treaty; and

Whereas the President is of opinion that it is not for the interest of either party that said object of the treaty shall fail, but not knowing what would be the desire of said Indians on this point, nor knowing whether any part of said sum would be needed to enable the Indians to commence agricultural pursuits under favorable circumstances, but supposing it probable that no part of it would be so needed, as said Indians now have over fifty thousand dollars lying idle in the United States Treasury; Therefore—

It is directed by the President that said Railroad Company may execute their bonds, with interest-warrants or coupons attached, according to the forms hereto annexed, the principal of which bonds shall amount to the aggregate sum of $286,742.15, and deposit the same with Archibald Williams, of Kansas, hereby appointed to receive and receipt for the same, to be by him transmitted to the Commissioner of Indian Affairs for the use of said Indians; and also shall, in due and proper form, execute a mortgage upon one hundred thousand acres of the land contemplated in and by said treaty to aid in the construction of said railroad, the said one hundred thousand acres to be the lands designated in the letter of the Commissioner of Indian Affairs to the Secretary of the Interior, dated May 29, 1861; said mortgage to be conditioned for the full payment of said bonds, both as to interest and principal, and that on any failure to pay either when due all right and interest of said railroad company in and to said mortgaged land, and also to all such of said land not mortgaged as shall not at that time be earned and patented according to said treaty, shall be forfeited, and said land again become the absolute property of the United States in trust for said Indians; and said mortgaged lands to be in no event patented to said   until said bonds, principal and interest, shall be fully paid.   And upon said bonds being so made and deposited, and said mortgage being so executed and duly recorded in Leavenworth County, Kansas, all matters, so far as not necessarily varied by this arrangement, shall proceed in conformity to said treaty, as if the money had been paid by said railroad company and had been invested by the President in said railroad bonds: *Provided always*, That this arrangement shall be of no effect until Archibald Williams, judge of the United States court for the district of Kansas, shall have endorsed a certificate upon this paper that he has carefully examined the same, and also the bonds and mortgage offered in compliance with its provisions, and has found that bonds and mortgage do in fact comply with and fulfil said provisions; and also that he has had before him the chiefs and headmen named in said treaty, as John Connor, Sar-cox-ie, Necon-he-con, and Rock-a-to-wha, and has fully explained to them the nature and effect of this departure from the terms of said treaty, and that they freely assented to the same.

ABRAHAM LINCOLN.

JUNE 10, 1861.

Form of Bond.

$10,000.   No. 1.

Form of bond.

Know all men by these presents: That the Leavenworth, Pawnee, and Western Railroad Company is held and bound to the United States, as trustee for the Delaware tribe of Indians, in the sum of ten thousand dollars, to be paid to the Commissioner of Indian Affairs, or bearer, at the office of the assistant treasurer of the United States, in the city of New York, in ten years from the date hereof, on the surrender of this bond, with interest on said sum from the same date, at six per cent. per annum, payable annually at the same office, on the surrender, as they severally fall due, of the annexed interest-warrants.   This bond being one of twenty-nine bonds for sums amounting in the aggregate to $290,560, the payment of which, with the interest-warrants attached, is secured by mortgage of even date herewith on one hundred thousand acres of the land acquired by said company, under the conditions and provisions of the treaty between the United States and the Delaware tribe of Indians of May 30, 1860.

In witness whereof the Leavenworth, Pawnee, and Western Railroad Company, by Thomas Ewing, jr., their agent, have signed this obligation, and have attached thereto their corporate seal this 14th day of May, 1861.

The Leavenworth, Pawnee, and Western Railroad Company by

[SEAL.]   THOMAS EWING, JR.,
Their Agent.

———

Form of Warrant.

The Leavenworth, Pawnee, and Western Railroad Company promises to pay to the Commissioner of Indian Affairs of the United States or bearer, on the 14th day of May, 1862, at the office of the assistant treasurer of the United States, in the city of New York, six hundred dollars, interest due that day on their bond No. 1.

Of warrant.

The Leavenworth, Pawnee, and Western Railroad Company, by

THOMAS EWING, Jr.,
Their Agent.

OFFICE OF REGISTER OF DEEDS,
County of Leavenworth, State of Kansas, ss:

Certificate of register of deeds.

I, W. S. Van Doren, register of deeds within and for the county aforesaid, do hereby certify that the within and foregoing instruments of writing were received by me for record this second day of July. A. D. 1861, at 3½ o'clock p. m., and that the same are duly recorded in Book P, for recording mortgages, at page 230, &c.

In testimony whereof I have hereunto set my hand and official seal of office, the day and year aforesaid.

[SEAL.]

W. S. VAN DOREN,
Register of Deeds.

———

Of judge of district court.

I, Archibald Williams, judge of the United States court for the district of Kansas, do hereby certify that I have carefully examined the within paper signed by the President of the United [States,] and have also examined and approved the bonds and mortgage offered by the Leavenworth, Pawnee, and Western Railroad Company in compliance with its provisions, and have accepted said bonds and mortgage, and receipted to said company for the same, as agent of the United States, and caused said mortgage to be duly recorded in the office of the recorder of deeds for Leavenworth County, Kansas.

And I do further certify, that I have had before me the chiefs and head-men therein named, as John Connor, Sar-cox-ie, and Ne-con-he-con, and also James Connor, who was the delegate at large of said tribe, in making the treaty of 1860, and read to them the said paper signed by the President, and fully explained to them the nature and effect of the proposition set forth in said paper; and that, after they had fully discussed the proposition, John Connor, in English, and James Connor, Sar-cox-ie, and Ne-con-he-con, through the said John Connor and other interpreters, declared that they understood it thoroughly, and each freely assented to the same; and that evidence has been presented to me by John Connor and other chiefs of said tribe, by which I am satisfied that Rock-a-to-wha died several months ago, and that no chief has been appointed in his place.

Given under my hand at Leavenworth city, Kansas, this 2d day of July, 1861.

Archibald Williams.

Ratification.

And whereas the said treaty or agreement having been submitted to the Senate of the United States for its constitutional action thereon, the Senate did, on the sixth of August, one thousand eight hundred and sixty-one, advise and consent to the ratification of the same by a resolution, and with amendments. in the words and figures following. to wit:

"IN EXECUTIVE SESSION,
"*Senate of the United States, August 6, 1861.*

"*Resolved,* (two-thirds of the Senators present concurring,) That the Senate advise and consent to the ratification of the treaty or agreement between the United States of America and the Delaware tribe of Indians relative to certain lands of that tribe conveyed to the Leavenworth, Pawnee, and Western Railroad Company, and to bonds executed to the United States by the said company for the payment of the said Indians, done the second day of July, eighteen hundred and sixty-one:

"*Provided,* That the provisions of this treaty shall not be held to apply to any lands not heretofore surveyed and appraised and not included within the limits of said reserve, nor any lands included in any fort or reservation for military purposes:

"*Provided further,* That if twenty-five miles of said railroad, from Leavenworth city westwardly, is not completed and equipped within *five* years from the ratification hereof, said company shall thereupon forfeit all right, title, and interest, legal and equitable, in and to all and every part of said lands; and if the remaining section to the western boundary of the said reserve be not completed and equipped within *three years* from the date fixed for the completion of said first section, said company shall thereupon forfeit all right, title, and interest, legal and equitable, in and to all of said lands not theretofore earned and patented.

"*Provided further*, That in the event of a failure of the said Railroad Company to pay the annual interest accruing upon the bonds, secured as above, within thirty days after the same falls due at the end of any year, then and in such case the contract included in this treaty shall be rescinded and shall be of no binding efficacy upon either party thereto.

"*Provided further*, That no part of said lands shall be patented to said Railroad Company until the money price for such part shall have been fully paid therefor.

"*And provided*, That this treaty shall not go into operation and be binding on them until accepted by the Indians thus amended.

"Attest: J. W. Forney, Secretary.

And whereas William P. Dole, commissioner of Indian affairs, was designated by the Executive to present the treaty, as above amended, to the Indians, through their chiefs and headmen, for their acceptance, and to take such acceptance, if freely given, with the signatures of said Indian chiefs and headmen, and to certify his proceedings therein to the Executive; and the foregoing amendments having been fully interpreted and explained to the cheifs and headmen of the Delaware tribe aforesaid, they did thereunto, on the second day of September, one thousand eight hundred and sixty-one, give their free and voluntary assent in the words and figures following, to wit:

We, the undersigned, chiefs, councillors, and headmen of the Delaware tribe of Indians, acting for and on behalf of said tribe, this day in full council assembled, having had read and carefully explained and interpreted to us the within and foregoing treaty or agreement between the United States of America and the Delaware tribe of Indians, concluded on [the] 2d day of July, 1861, together with the within and foregoing amendments thereto, made by the Senate of the United States on the 6th day of August, 1861, do hereby accept and consent to said treaty as so amended.

In witness whereof, we have hereunto set our hands and affixed our seals this 2d day of September, 1861.

John Connor, head chief, his x mark.	[L. S.]
Ne-con-he-con, chief of the Wolf Band, his x mark.	[L. S.]
Sar-cox-ie, chief of the Turtle Band, his x mark.	[L. S.]
James Connor, delegate, his x mark.	[L. S.]
Charles Journeycake.	[L. S.]

Signed and sealed in presence of—

Isaac Golmarke, United States interpreter.

F. Johnson.

H. B. Branch, } (As to Sar-cox-ie.)
W. G. Coffin, }

I hereby certify that the foregoing treaty or agreement between the United States and the Delaware tribe of Indians, concluded on the 2d day of July, 1861, together with the foregoing amendments thereto, made by the Senate of the United States on the 6th day of August, 1861, were read and fully explained by me to said Indians, except Sar-cox-ie, through Isaac Journeycake, the United States interpreter, and to Sar-cox-ie through Charles Journeycake; and that the delegate, chiefs, councillors, and headmen above named, on behalf of said tribe, this day, in council assembled, did freely accept and consent to said treaty, together with said amendments, and subscribed their names and affixed their seals thereto in my presence.

Given under my hand this 2d September, 1861.

Wm. P. Dole, Commissioner Indian Affairs.

Now, therefore, be it known that I, Abraham Lincoln, President of the United States of America, do, in pursuance of the advice and consent of the Senate, as expressed in their resolution of the sixth of August, one thousand eight hundred and sixty-one, accept, ratify, and confirm said treaty, with the amendments, as aforesaid.

In testimony whereof, I have caused the seal of the United States to be hereto affixed, having signed the same with my hand.

Done at the city of Washington, this fourth day of October, in the year of our Lord one thousand eight hundred and sixty-one, and of the Independence of the United States the eighty-sixth.

[L. s.]					Abraham Lincoln.

By the President:

William H. Seward, Secretary of State.

TREATY WITH THE POTAWATOMI, 1861.

Nov. 15, 1861.

12 Stats., 1191.
Ratified Apr. 15, 1862.
Proclaimed Apr. 19, 1862.

Articles of a treaty made and concluded at the agency on the Kansas River, on the fifteenth day of November, in the year of our Lord one thousand eight hundred and sixty-one, by and between Wm. W. Ross, commissioner on the part of the United States, and the undersigned chiefs, braves, and head-men of the Pottawatomie Nation, on behalf of said nation.

Potawatomi reservation in Kansas to be disposed of.

ARTICLE 1. The Pottawatomie tribe of Indians believing that it will contribute to the civilization of their people to dispose of a portion of their present reservation in Kansas, consisting of five hundred and seventy-six thousand acres, which was acquired by them for the sum of $87,000, by the fourth article of the treaty between the United States and the said Pottawatomies, proclaimed by the President of the United States on the 23d day of July, 1846, and to allot lands in severalty to those of said tribe who have adopted the customs of the whites and desire to have separate tracts assigned to them, and to assign a portion of said reserve to those of the tribe who prefer to hold their lands in common: it is therefore agreed by the parties hereto that the Commissioner of Indian Affairs shall cause the whole of said reservation to be surveyed in the same manner as the public lands are surveyed, the expense whereof shall be paid out of the sales of lands hereinafter provided for, and the quantity of land hereinafter provided to be set apart to those of the tribe who desire to take their lands in severalty, and the quantity hereinafter provided to be set apart for the rest of the tribe in common; and the remainder of the land, after the special reservations hereinafter provided for shall have been made, to be sold for the benefit of said tribe.

To be surveyed.

Reservation to be set apart in severalty.

Remainder.

Census of the tribe to be taken.

ARTICLE 2. It shall be the duty of the agent of the United States for said tribe to take an accurate census of all the members of the tribe, and to classify them in separate lists, showing the names, ages, and numbers of those desiring lands in severalty, and of those desiring lands in common, designating chiefs and head-men, respectively; each adult choosing for himself or herself, and each head of a family for the minor children of such family, and the agent for orphans and persons of an unsound mind. And thereupon there shall be assigned, under the direction of the Commissioner of Indian Affairs, to each chief at

Assignments of land.

the signing of the treaty, one section; to each head-man, one half section; to each other head of a family, one quarter section; and to each other person eighty acres of land, to include, in every case, as far as practicable, to each family, their improvements and a reasonable portion of timber, to be selected according to the legal subdivision of survey. When such assignments shall have been completed, certificates shall be issued by the Commissioner of Indian Affairs for the tracts assigned in severalty, specifying the names of the individuals to whom they have been assigned, respectively, and that said tracts are set apart for the perpetual and exclusive use and benefit of such assignees and their heirs. Until otherwise provided by law, such tracts shall be exempt from levy, taxation, or sale, and shall be alienable in fee or leased or otherwise disposed of only to the United States, or to persons then being members of the Pottawatomie tribe and of Indian blood, with the permission of the President, and under such regulations as the Secretary of the Interior shall provide, except as may be hereinafter provided. And on receipt of such certificates, the person to whom they are issued shall be deemed to have relinquished all right to any portion of the lands assigned to others in severalty, or to a portion of the tribe in common, and to the proceeds of sale of the same whensoever made. *Certificates to issue.*

Exemption from levy, etc.

Receipts of certificates to be relinquished, etc.

ARTICLE 3. At any time hereafter when the President of the United States shall have become satisfied that any adults, being males and heads of families, who may be allottees under the provisions of the foregoing article, are sufficiently intelligent and prudent to control their affairs and interests, he may, at the request of such persons, cause the lands severally held by them to be conveyed to them by patent in fee-simple, with power of alienation; and may, at the same time, cause to be paid to them, in cash or in the bonds of the United States, their proportion of the cash value of the credits of the tribe, principal and interest, then held in trust by the United States, and also, as the same may be received, their proportion of the proceeds of the sale of lands under the provisions of this treaty. And on such patents being issued and such payments ordered to be made by the President, such competent persons shall cease to be members of said tribe, and shall become citizens of the United States; and thereafter the lands so patented to them shall be subject to levy, taxation, and sale, in like manner with the property of other citizens: *Provided*, That, before making any such application to the President, they shall appear in open court in the district court of the United States for the district of Kansas, and make the same proof and take the same oath of allegiance as is provided by law for the naturalization of aliens, and shall also make proof to the satisfaction of said court that they are sufficiently intelligent and prudent to control their affairs and interests, that they have adopted the habits of civilized life, and have been able to support, for at least five years, themselves and families. *The President may cause lands to be granted in fee to certain male adults.*

And payments to be made.

Such persons to become citizens and cease to be members of tribe.

To take oath of allegiance.

ARTICLE 4. To those members of said tribe who desire to hold their lands in common there shall be set apart an undivided quantity sufficient to allow one section to each chief, one half section to each headman, and one hundred and sixty acres to each other head of a family, and eighty acres of land to each other person, and said land shall be held by that portion of the tribe for whom it is set apart by the same tenure as the whole reserve has been held by all of said tribe under the treaty of one thousand eight hundred and forty-six. And upon such land being assigned in common, the persons to whom it is assigned shall be held to have relinquished all title to the lands assigned in severalty and in the proceeds of sales thereof whenever made. *Undivided quantities to be set out to those, etc.*

ARTICLE 5. The Pottawatomies believing that the construction of the Leavenworth, Pawnee, and Western Railroad from Leavenworth City to the western boundary of the former reserve of the Delawares, *The Leavenworth, Pawnee and Western Railroad may purchase certain land.*

is now rendered reasonably certain, and being desirous to have said railroad extended through their reserve in the direction of Fort Riley, so that the value of the lands retained by them may be enhanced, and the means afforded them of getting the surplus product of their farms to market, it is provided that the Leavenworth, Pawnee, and Western Railroad Company shall have the privilege of buying the remainder of their lands within six months after the tracts herein otherwise disposed of shall have been selected and set apart, provided they purchase the whole of said surplus lands at the rate of one dollar and twenty-five cents per acre.

Price.

And if said company make such purchase it shall be subject to the considerations following, to wit: They shall construct and fully equip a good and efficient railroad from Leavenworth City to a point half way between the western boundary of the said former Delaware reserve and the western boundary of the said Pottawatomie reserve, (being the first section of said road,) within six years from the date of such purchase, and shall construct and fully equip such road from said last-named point to the western boundary of said Pottawatomie reserve, (being the second section of said road,) within three years from the date fixed for the completion of said first section; and no patent or patents shall issue to said company or its assigns for any of said lands purchased until the first section of said railroad shall have been completed and equipped, and then for not more than half of said lands, and no patent or patents shall issue to said company or its assigns for any of the remaining portion of said lands until said second section of said railroad shall have been completed and equipped as aforesaid; and before any patents shall issue for any part of said lands payment shall be made for the lands to be patented at the rate of one dollar and twenty-five cents per acre; and said company shall pay the whole amount of the purchase-money for said lands in gold or silver coin, to the Secretary of the Interior of the United States, in trust for said Pottawatomie Indians, within nine years from the date of such purchase, and shall also in like manner pay to the Secretary of the Interior of the United States, in trust as aforesaid, each and every year, until the whole purchase-money shall have been paid, interest from date of purchase, at six per cent. per annum, on all the purchase-money remaining unpaid.

Terms of purchase.

And if said company shall fail to complete either section of such railroad in a good and efficient manner, or shall fail to pay the whole of the purchase-money for said land within the times above prescribed, or shall fail to pay all or any part of the interest upon said purchase-money each year as aforesaid within thirty days from the date when such payment of interest shall fall due, then the contract or purchase shall be deemed and held absolutely null and void, and shall cease to be binding on either of the parties thereto, and said company and its assigns shall forfeit all payments of principal and interest made on such purchase, and all right and title, legal and equitable, of any kind whatsoever, in and to all and every part of said lands which shall not have been before the date of such forfeiture earned and patented pursuant to the provisions of this treaty.

Patents to contain condition.

And whenever any patent shall issue to said railroad company for any part of said lands, it shall contain the condition that the said company shall sell the land described in such patent, except so much as shall be necessary for the working of the road, within five years from the issuing of such patent.

Right of way.

And said company shall have the perpetual right of way over the lands of the Pottawatomies not sold to it for the construction and operation of said railroad, not exceeding one hundred feet in width, and the right to enter on said lands and take and use such gravel, stone, earth, water, and other material, except timber, as may be necessary for the construction and operation of said road, making compensation for any damages to improvements done in obtaining such material, and for any damages arising from the location or running of said road to improvements made before the road is located. Such damages and compensation, in cases where said company and the persons whose improvements are injured or property taken cannot agree, to be ascertained and adjusted under the direction of the Commissioner of Indian Affairs. And in case said company shall not promptly pay the amount of such damages and compensation, the Secretary of the Interior may withhold patents for any part of the lands purchased by them until payment be made of the amount of such damages, with six per cent. interest thereon from the date when the same shall have been ascertained and demanded. *Damages.*

And in case said company shall not purchase said surplus lands, or, having purchased, shall forfeit the whole or any part thereof, the Secretary of the Interior shall thereupon cause the same to be appraised at not less than one dollar and twenty-five cents per acre, and shall sell the same, in quantities not exceeding one hundred and sixty acres, at auction to the highest bidder for cash, at not less than such appraised value. *In case the railroad company shall forfeit any lands, etc.*

ARTICLE 6. There shall be selected by the Commissioner of Indian Affairs three hundred and twenty acres of land, including the church, school-houses, and fields of the St. Mary's Catholic Mission, but not including the buildings and enclosures occupied and used by persons other than those connected with the mission, without the consent of such persons, which shall be conveyed by the Secretary of the Interior to John F. Diel, John Summaker, and M. Gerillain, as trustees for the use of the society under whose patronage and control the church and school have been conducted within the last fourteen years; on condition, however, that, so long as the Pottawatomie Nation shall continue to occupy its present reservation, or any portion thereof, the said land shall be used and its products devoted exclusively to the maintenance of a school and church for their benefit. And there shall be reserved and conveyed in like manner, and upon like conditions, three hundred and twenty acres of land, including the Baptist Mission buildings and enclosures, such conveyances to be made to such persons as may be designated by the Baptist Board of Missions. *Conveyance of land to John F. Diel. John Summaker, and M. Gerillain, in trust for school and church purposes for Catholic mission.* *Condition.* *Reservation for Baptist mission.*

ARTICLE 7. By article eight of the treaty of June 5th, 1846, between the United States and the Pottawatomie Indians, it is stipulated "that the annual interest of their improvement fund shall be paid out promptly and fully for their benefit at their new homes. If, however, at any time thereafter, the President of the United States shall be of opinion that it would be advantageous to the Pottawatomie Nation, and they should request the same to be done, to pay them the interest of said money in lieu of the employment of persons, or the purchase of implements or machines, he is hereby authorized to pay the same, or any part thereof, in money, as their annuities are paid, at the time of the general payment of annuities." *Annual interest of improvement fund.*

It is hereby agreed that the interest arising from said improvement-fund shall, in all cases hereafter, be paid in such machines and implements as will be useful to the people in their agricultural pursuits, as long as the nation shall desire it to be done, except that the shops and mechanics and physicians, now sustained by the funds of the nation, shall continue to be maintained, as at this time, for one year after this treaty shall have been ratified. *How hereafter to be paid.*

ARTICLE 8. If at any time hereafter any band or bands of the Pottawatomie Nation shall desire to remove from the homes provided for them in this treaty, it shall be the duty of the Secretary of the Interior to have their proportionate part of the lands which may be assigned to the tribe appraised and sold, and invest such portion of the pro- *Provision if any bands desire to remove.*

ceeds thereof as may be necessary in the purchase of a new home for such band or bands, leaving the remainder, should any remain after paying the expense of their removal, to be invested in six per cent. bonds of the United States, for the benefit of such band or bands. Such band or bands so removed shall continue to receive their proportion of the annuities of the tribe.

Former claims to hold good.

ARTICLE 9. No provision of this treaty shall be so construed as to invalidate any claim heretofore preferred by the Pottawatomies against the United States arising out of previous treaties.

Agricultural purposes.

ARTICLE 10. It is hereby agreed that the Commissioner of Indian Affairs shall set apart, for the benefit of said allottees, their equal pro rata share of the improvement-fund of the tribe, which sum so set apart may be expended, in whole or in part, by the said Commissioner, and under his direction, for agricultural purposes, as he shall from time to time deem expedient and for the welfare of the said Indians.

When articles of treaty to take effect.

ARTICLE 11. Should the Senate reject or amend any of the above articles, such rejection or amendment shall not affect the other provisions of this treaty, but the same shall go into effect when ratified by the Senate and approved by the President.

Wm. W. Ross,
Commissioner on behalf of United States.

Shaw-guee, (chief,) his x mark.	Thos. L. McKenney.
We-we-say, (chief,) his x mark.	Za-gah-knuk, his x mark.
Jos. Lafromboise, (chief,) his x mark.	Che-gueah-mkuh-go, (brave,) his x mark.
Mu-zhe, (chief,) his x mark.	Ain-waish-ke, his x mark.
Mkome-da, (chief,) his x mark.	Msquah-mke, his x mark.
Myean-ko, (speaker,) his x mark.	Mko-nuih, his x mark.
A. B. Burnett.	Oketch-gum-me, his x mark.
N-wą-kto, (brave,) his x mark.	We-zos, his x mark.
Wah-bea-shkuk, his x mark.	A-sah-sahng-gah, his x mark.
Sho-nim, (brave,) his x mark.	Buck, his x mark.
Pauce-je-yah, (chief,) his x mark.	M. B. Beaubien.
Ka-pshkuh-wid, (brave,) his x mark.	L. H. Ogee.
Muis-no-ogih-mah, his x mark.	Lewis View, his x mark.
Ka-me-gas, his x mark.	B. H. Bertrand.
Mo-zo-ba-net, his x mark.	Shop-kuk, (speaker,) his x mark.
Wah-sah-to, (chief,) his x mark.	George Fortier, his x mark.
Shaw-we, (chief,) his x mark.	Odah-wahs, his x mark.
Bourie, his x mark.	Little American, his x mark.
Nah-neam-nuk-shkuk, his x mark.	Puk-ke, his x mark.
Pa-mah-me, his x mark.	Nah-ge-zhick, his x mark.
Kah-dot, his x mark.	Oketch-gum-me, his x mark.
Mink, his x mark.	Je-gueah-kyah, his x mark.
Peter The Great, his x mark.	Bapt. LeClere, his x mark.
M-tom-ma, (brave,) his x mark.	Leon Bertrand, his x mark.
Za-kto, his x mark.	Bzug-nah, his x mark.
Ain-na-by-ah, his x mark.	Beau-mo, his x mark.
Wah-sha, his x mark.	Ke-yo-kum, his x mark.
White, his x mark.	Muk-kose, his x mark.
Wah-nuk-ke, his x mark.	Wa-me-go, his x mark.
Bah-be-jmah, his x mark.	Ka-beame-sa, his x mark.
Onak-sa, (second,) his x mark.	Onak-sa, his x mark.
Nom-mah-kshkuk, his x mark.	Frank Bourbonnie, his x mark.
Thomas Evans.	Bescue Bourbonnie, his x mark.
Peter Moose, his x mark.	Eli G. Nadeau.
Jas. Levia, his x mark.	Charles Viean.
Tquah-ket, his x mark.	To-to-qua, her x mark.
Wahs-meg-guea, his x mark.	Messah, her x mark.
Pame-bo-go, his x mark.	Otter-woman, her x mark.
A-yea-nah-be, his x mark.	Mary Jutions, her x mark.
Nah-duea, his x mark.	Pnah-zuea, her x mark.
Nau-wah-ga, his x mark.	Louis Blackbird, his x mark.
Pahs-kah-we, his x mark.	Jos. N. Bourassa, United States Interpreter.
Wahb-na-mid, his x mark.	
Moz-wa-nwah, his x mark.	

Signed in presence of—

L. R. Palmer.
S. M. Ferguson.
C. N. Gray.
John D. Lusby.

TREATY WITH THE KANSA INDIANS, 1862.

Mar. 13, 1862.

12 Stats., 1221.
Ratified Feb, 6, 1863.
Proclaimed Mar. 16, 1863.

Whereas a treaty was made and concluded at the Kansas agency, in the then Territory, but now State, of Kansas, on the fifth day of October, A. D. 1859, by and between Alfred B. Greenwood, commissioner on the part of the United States, and the chiefs and head-men representing the Kansas tribe of Indians, and authorized by said tribe for that purpose; which treaty, after having been submitted to the Senate of the United States for its constitutional action thereon, was duly accepted, ratified, and confirmed by the President of the United States, on the seventeenth day of November, A. D. 1860, with an amendment to the fourth article thereof, which amendment, first proposed and made by the Senate on the twenty-seventh day of June, A. D. 1860, was afterwards agreed to and ratified by the aforesaid chiefs and head-men of the Kansas tribe of Indians on the fourth day of October of the same year:

Former treaty.

Now, therefore, it is further agreed and concluded on this thirteenth day of March, A. D. 1862, by and between H. W. Farnsworth, a commissioner on the part of the United States, and the said Kansas tribe of Indians, by their authorized representatives, the chiefs and headmen thereof, to wit:

Contracting parties.

ARTICLE 1. That the said treaty and the amendment thereof be further amended so as to provide that a fair and reasonable value of the improvements made by persons who settled on the diminished reserve of said Kansas Indians between the second day of December, A. D. 1856, and the fifth day of October, A. D. 1859, shall be ascertained by the Secretary of the Interior, and certificates of indebtedness by said tribe shall be issued by him to each of such persons for an amount equal to the appraisement of his or her improvements, as aforesaid, not exceeding in the aggregate the sum of fifteen thousand dollars; and that like certificates shall be issued to the class of persons who settled on said diminished reservation prior to the second day of December, A. D. 1856, for the amounts of the respective claims as provided for and ascertained under the provisions of the amendment of said treaty, not exceeding in the aggregate the sum of fourteen thousand four hundred and twenty-one dollars; and that like certificates be issued to the owners of the same for the amounts of claims which have been examined and approved by the agent and superintendent, and revised and confirmed by the Secretary of the Interior, under the provisions of the 5th article of said treaty, not exceeding in the aggregate the sum of thirty-six thousand three hundred and ninety-four dollars and forty-seven cents, and that all such certificates shall be receivable as cash, to the amount for which they may be issued, in payment for lands purchased or entered on that part of the first assigned reservation outside of said diminished reservation.

The value of improvements by certain settlers to be ascertained and certificates of indebtedness issued therefor.

ARTICLE 2. The Kansas tribe of Indians, being desirous of making a suitable expression of the obligations the said tribe are under to Thomas S. Huffaker, for the many services rendered by said Huffaker as missionary, teacher, and friendly counsellor of said tribe of Indians, hereby authorize and request the Secretary of the Interior to convey to the said Thomas S. Huffaker the half-section of land on which he has resided and improved and cultivated since the year A. D. 1851, it being the south half of section eleven, (11,) in township numbered sixteen (16) south, range numbered eight (8) east, of the sixth principal meridian, Kansas, on the payment by said Huffaker of the appraised value of said lands, at a rate not less than one dollar and seventy-five cents per acre.

Half-section of land to Thomas S. Huffaker.

In testimony whereof, the said H. W. Farnsworth, commissioner, as aforesaid, and the said chiefs and headmen of the Kansas tribe of Indians, have hereunto set their hands and seals, at the Kansas agency, in the State of Kansas, on the said thirteenth day of March, in the year of our Lord one thousand eight hundred and sixty-two.

In presence of—

    T. S. Huffaker.
    A. G. Barnett.
    Edward Wolcott.
    A. N. Blocklidge.
    Joseph James, his x mark.

                        H. W. Farnsworth.   [SEAL.]

Ish-tah-les-ice, his x mark.	[SEAL.]	Wah-pah-gah, his x mark.	[SEAL.]
No-pa-wy, his x mark.	[SEAL.]	Wah-ti-in-gah, his x mark.	[SEAL.]
Ne-hu-gah-in-ka, his x mark.	[SEAL.]	Pah-hah-nah-gah-le, his x mark.	[SEAL.]
Kah-he-ga-wah-ti-in-ga, his x mark.	[SEAL.]	Shun-gah-wah-sa, his x mark.	[SEAL.]
Wak-shun-ge-a, his x mark.	[SEAL.]	Ke-wah-les-is, his x mark.	[SEAL.]
Alle-gah-wah-ho, his x mark.	[SEAL.]	Ke-ah-hah-wa-cu, his x mark.	[SEAL.]
Cah-ke-ges-cha, his x mark.	[SEAL.]	Kah-he-gah-she, his x mark.	[SEAL.]
E. B. Sun-gah, his x mark.	[SEAL.]	O-me-sia, his x mark.	[SEAL.]
Ke-bah-lah-he, his x mark.	[SEAL.]	Wy-e-lah-in-gah, his x mark.	[SEAL.]
Wah-hah-nah-sha, his x mark.	[SEAL.]	Les-ya, his x mark.	[SEAL.]
Kah-he-gah-wah-chehhe, his x mark.	[SEAL.]	Ke-hah-ga-cha-wah-go, his x mark.	[SEAL.]
		Wah-ho-bec-ca, his x mark.	[SEAL.]

Whereas, the amendments of the Senate having been fully interpreted and explained to us, the undersigned, chiefs and headmen of the Kansas tribe of Indians, we do hereby agree to and ratify the same.

Done at Kansas agency, this twenty-sixth day of February. A. D. eighteen hundred and sixty-three.

Signed in the presence of—

    H. W. Farnsworth, United States Indian agent.
    Joseph James, United States interpreter, his x mark.
    Joseph Dunlap, witness to signature of interpreter.
    Christopher Mooney.
    Thomas C. Hill.

No-pa-wi, his x mark.	[SEAL.]	Mo-shon-no-pussa, his x mark.	[SEAL.]
Kai-he-gah-wa-ti-in-ka, his x mark.	[SEAL.]	Ho-yuh-ne-ka, his x mark.	[SEAL.]
Kai-he-gah-shin-gah, his x mark.	[SEAL.]	Wy-a-hog-gy, his x mark.	[SEAL.]
E-be-sungah, his x mark.	[SEAL.]	Uts-ah-gah-ba, his x mark.	[SEAL.]
O-gor-she-nor-sha, his x mark.	[SEAL.]	Sah-ya, his x mark.	[SEAL.]
Wah-pah-gah, his x mark.	[SEAL.]	Ge-no-in-ga, his x mark.	[SEAL.]
Ke-wah-lezhe, his x mark.	[SEAL.]	Me-ho-je, his x mark.	[SEAL.]
Pah-du-ca-golle, his x mark.	[SEAL.]	Mah-ku-sa-ba, his x mark.	[SEAL.]
Mo-she-tumvia, his x mark.	[SEAL.]	Me-o-tum-wa, his x mark.	[SEAL.]
Wi-e-lon-ge, his x mark.	[SEAL.]	Tah-se-hah, his x mark.	[SEAL.]

TREATY WITH THE OTTAWA OF BLANCHARD'S FORK AND ROCHE DE BŒUF, 1862.

June 24, 1862.

12 Stats., 1237.
Ratified July 16, 1862.
Proclaimed July 28, 1862.

Articles of agreement and convention, made and concluded at Washington City, on the twenty-fourth day of June, eighteen hundred and sixty-two, by and between William P. Dole, commissioner, on the part of the United States, and the following-named chief and councilmen of the Ottawa Indians of the united bands of Blanchard's Fork and of Roche de Bœuf, now in Franklin County, Kansas, viz: Pem-ach-wung, chief; John T. Jones, William Hurr, and James Wind, councilmen, they being thereto duly authorized by said tribe.

Certain Ottawa Indians to become citizens of the United States in five years.

ARTICLE 1. The Ottawa Indians of the united bands of Blanchard's Fork and of Roche de Bœuf, having become sufficiently advanced in civilization, and being desirous of becoming citizens of the United States, it is hereby agreed and stipulated that their organization, and their relations with the United States as an Indian tribe shall be dissolved and terminated at the expiration of five years from the ratification of this treaty; and from and after that time the said Ottawas, and each and every one of them, shall be deemed and declared to be citizens of the United States, to all intents and purposes, and shall be entitled to all the rights, privileges, and immunities of such citizens, and shall, in all respects, be subject to the laws of the United States, and of the State or States thereof in which they may reside.

ARTICLE 2. It is hereby made the duty of the Secretary of the Interior to cause a survey of the reservation of the said Ottawas to be made as soon as practicable after the ratification of this treaty, dividing it into eighty-acre tracts, with marked stones set at each corner; and said Ottawas having already caused their reservation to be surveyed, and quarter-section stones set, it is hereby stipulated that such survey shall be adopted, in so far as it shall be found correct. *Reservation of Ottawa to be surveyed.*

ARTICLE 3. It being the wish of said tribe of Ottawas to remunerate several of the chiefs, councilmen, and head-men of the tribe, for their services to them many years without pay, it is hereby stipulated that five sections of land is [are] reserved and set apart for that purpose, to be apportioned among the said chiefs, councilmen, and head-men as the members of the tribes shall in full council determine; and it shall be the duty of the Secretary of the Interior to issue patents, in fee-simple, of said lands, when located and apportioned, to said Indians. In addition thereto, said last-named persons, and each and every head of a family in said tribe, shall receive 160 acres of land, which shall include his or her house and all improvements, so far as practicable; and all other members of the tribe shall receive 80 acres of land each, and all the locations for the heads of families, made in accordance with this treaty, shall be made adjoining, and in as regular and compact form as possible, and with due regard to the rights of each individual and of the whole tribe. *Sections of land reserved to remunerate chiefs, etc.* *Patents to issue.* *Heads of families to receive 160 acres of land; others to have 80 acres.*

ARTICLE 4. To enable said tribe to establish themselves more fully in agriculture, and gradually to increase their preparations for assuming the responsibilities and duties of citizenship, it is stipulated that, subject to the limitations hereinafter mentioned, the sum of eighteen thousand ($18,000) dollars shall be paid to said tribe in the manner of annuities, out of their moneys now in the hands of the United States, in September, 1862, and subject to the limitations of this treaty. There shall be paid to them in four equal annual payments thereafter, as near as may be, all the moneys which the United States hold, or may hold, in any wise for them, with accruing interest on all moneys remaining with the United States. *Annuities.*

ARTICLE 5. It being the desire of the tribe to pay all lawful and just debts against them contracted since they were removed to Kansas, it is agreed that such demands as the council of the tribe and the agent shall approve, when confirmed by the Secretary of the Interior, may be received in payment for the lands hereinafter provided to be sold, or otherwise such debts shall be paid out of the funds of said Ottawas, but in no case shall more than $15,000 be allowed and paid for such debts. *Debts*

ARTICLE 6. The Ottawas deeming this a favorable opportunity to provide for the education of their posterity, and feeling that they are able to do so by the co-operation of the United States, now, in pursuance of this desire of the Ottawas, after the selections and allotments herein provided have been made, there shall be set apart, under the direction of the Secretary of the Interior, twenty thousand acres of average lands for the purpose of endowing a school for the benefit of said Ottawas; also one section of land, upon which said school shall be located, which section of land shall be inalienable, and upon which, and all the appurtenances and property for school purposes thereon, no tax shall ever be laid by any authority whatever. *Lands to be set apart for endowing a school.* *Locating school.* *No tax.*

Management of school lands.

Five thousand acres of said land may be sold by the trustees hereinafter named, the proceeds of which may be devoted to the erection of proper buildings and improvements upon said section for reception of the pupils; and the residue of the school-lands may, in like manner, be sold from time to time, as full prices can be obtained for the same. The money received therefor shall be loaned upon good real estate security, to be improved farms in the county of the reservation, the same not to be a security for more than half the appraised value of the land as returned by the county assessor, and no land to be taken as security for such loan or loans which shall be encumbered in any manner, or the title to which shall have been derived from or held by any judicial, administrator, or executor's sale, or by the sale of any person acting in a fiduciary capacity. The security shall never be avoided on account of any rate of interest reserved, and the interest only shall be applied to the support of the school, so that the principal sum shall never be diminished.

What to be taught in the school.

And to the end that the Ottawas may derive the greatest advantage from said school, the pupils shall be instructed and practiced in industrial pursuits suitable to their age and sex, as well as in such branches of learning as the means of the institution and the capacity of the pupils will permit.

Lands not subject to taxation until, etc.

The lands hereby set apart shall not be subject to taxation until they are sold. They may be sold upon such credit as the trustees may think most for the interest of the enterprise. Security for the payment shall be taken with interest, the interest to be paid annually, but no title shall be made until the purchase money is all paid.

Trustees to manage the property.

John T. Jones, James Wind, William Hurr, Joseph King, who are Ottawas, and John G. Pratt, and two other citizens of Kansas, who shall be elected by the said Ottawa Indians, are, by the parties agreed, to be trustees to manage the funds and property by this article set apart. They and their successors shall have the control and management of the school, and the funds arising from the sales of lands set apart therefor, and also the reserved section whereon the school is situated. Upon the death, resignation, or refusal to act, by either of them, the vacancy shall be filled by the survivors, provided that the board of trustees shall always have three white citizens members of said board.

Majority to form quorum.

Records.

A majority of the trustees shall form a quorum to transact business, but there shall be two of the white trustees present at the transaction of business. All acts of the trustees shall be recorded in a book or books to be by them kept for that purpose, and the proceedings of each meeting shall be signed by the president, to be by them elected out of their number. They shall also elect a treasurer and secretary from their number. All contracts of the trustees shall be in the name of their treasurer, who shall be competent to sue and be sued in all matters affecting the trust; he shall give bond conditioned for the faithful discharge of his duty, and the proper accounting for all money or property of the trust coming to his hands, with at least two good freehold sureties, in the penalty of ten thousand dollars, to be approved by a judge of a court of record in Kansas.

Treasurer and secretary.
Contracts.

Bond of treasurer.

Upon sales, the United States to give patent to purchaser.

And the secretary and treasurer may be allowed, from time to time, such sum, from the proceeds of the trust, as the trustees in their judgment shall think just. Upon a sale of any of the lands by the trustees, upon their request, the same shall be conveyed by the United States, by patent, to the purchaser.

Who may enjoy the privileges of the school.

And it is hereby expressly provided and agreed that the children of the Ottawas and their descendants, no matter where they may emigrate, shall have the right to enter said school and enjoy all the privileges thereof, the same as though they had remained upon the lands by this treaty allotted.

ARTICLE 7. There shall be set apart ten acres of land for the benefit of the Ottawa Baptist church, and said land shall include the church buildings, mission-house, and graveyard, and the title to said property shall be vested in a board of five trustees, to be appointed by said church, in accordance with the laws of the State of Kansas. <sub/> *Land set apart for the Ottawa Baptist Church, etc.*

And in respect for the memory of Rev. J. Meeker, deceased, who labored with unselfish zeal for nearly twenty years among said Ottawas, greatly to their spiritual and temporal welfare, it is stipulated that 80 acres of good land shall be, and hereby is, given, in fee-simple, to each of the two children of said Meeker, viz, Emmeline and Eliza; their lands to be selected and located as the other allotments herein provided are to be selected and located, which lands shall be inalienable to the same as the lands allotted to the Ottawas. *Land to each of the children of Rev. J. Meeker.*

And all the above-mentioned selections of lands shall be made by the agent of the tribe, under the direction of the Secretary of the Interior. And plats and records of all the selections and locations shall be made, and upon their completion and approval proper patents by the United States shall be issued to each individual member of the tribe and person entitled for the lands selected and allotted to them, in which it shall be stipulated that no Indian, except as herein provided, to whom the same may be issued, shall alienate or encumber the land allotted to him or her in any manner, until they shall, by the terms of this treaty, become a citizen of the United States; and any conveyance or encumbrance of said lands, done or suffered, except as aforesaid, by any Ottawa Indian, of the lands allotted to him or her, made before they shall become a citizen, shall be null and void. *Lands, how selected.* *Plats and records.* *Not alienable.*

And forty acres, including the houses and improvements of the allottee, shall be inalienable during the natural lifetime of the party receiving the title: *Provided*, That such of said Indians as are not under legal disabilities by the local laws may sell to each other such portions of their lands as are subject to sale, with the consent of the Secretary of the Interior, at any time. *Census.*

ARTICLE 8. That upon the ratification of this treaty a census of all the Ottawas entitled to land or money under the treaty shall be taken under the direction of the Secretary of the Interior.

The principal to be paid to the minors shall be paid to their parents, unless the council of the tribe shall object because of the incompetency of the parent, growing out of ignorance, profligacy, or any other good cause; the council may also object to the payment of the money to any such incompetent which may be coming to himself or herself; and in all such cases the principal sum shall be withheld, and only the annuity paid, until such minor comes of age, or the disability is removed by the action of the council: *Provided further*, That the money of minors may, in all cases, be paid to guardians appointed by the local laws. *Money of minors.*

ARTICLE 9. It being the desire of the said Ottawas, in making this treaty, to insure, as far as possible, the settlement of their reservation by industrious whites, whose example shall be of benefit to the tribe at large, it is stipulated that after all the above-mentioned locations, assignments, and sales are made, the remainder of the land shall be sold to actual settlers at not less than $1.25 per acre, in the following manner: Any white person desiring to obtain any unsold, unlocated tract of the land, may file his proposition, in writing, with the agent of the Ottawas, for the purchase of the tract, stating the price which he proposes to pay for said tract, not less than $1.25 per acre, a copy of which proposition, as well as all others herein contemplated, shall be posted for thirty days, dating from the first posting at the agency, in some conspicuous place; and if no person will propose a better price therefor within thirty days next after the first posting, in which further proposition the first person may join, he, or such other person as shall have offered the best price, shall, upon the payment of one-quarter *After locations, etc., are made, the rest of the land may be sold to actual settlers.* *Mode of sale.*

of the price offered, be taken and deemed the purchaser of said tract, and shall be entitled to a patent therefor from the United States at the end of one year, if he shall pay the remainder of the price offered, have occupied the land, and placed lasting and valuable improvements upon said tract to the extent and value of two hundred dollars to each quarter section entered: *Provided*, That if said Ottawas, by their council, shall, at any time before any person shall become the purchaser of any tract of land, file their protest in writing against such purchaser, he shall not be permitted to enter upon said lands or become the purchaser thereof, and white persons not purchasers shall not be permitted to settle upon said lands, it being the duty of the agent to prevent such settlement, or their occupancy by the whites who are not purchasers, and only to the extent of their purchase: *And provided, further*, That if any purchaser shall fail to pay for the land by him purchased under this treaty at the time stipulated, it shall be the duty of the agent to dispossess him as an intruder upon the lands, and his advances, payments, and all his improvements, shall enure to the benefit of the Ottawas, and the land shall be sold for their benefit, as herein provided. But no person under this article shall be entitled to enter more than 320 acres.

And all the lands which are not thus entered with the agent within two years from the ratification of this treaty may, upon the request of the council, be offered for sale at not less than $1.25 per acre, upon a credit of one year, under the direction of the Secretary of the Interior; and if any lands thereafter remain unsold, they may be sold upon such terms as the council of said tribe and the Secretary of the Interior shall mutually agree upon. And all the moneys derived from the sales of the above-described lands shall be paid at the time and place where the Secretary of the Interior may direct.

Ottawas to be paid claims allowed for stolen ponies, cattle, etc.

ARTICLE 10. And it is stipulated that the United States shall pay to the said Ottawas the claims for stolen ponies, cattle, and timber, already reported and approved by the Secretary of the Interior, amounting to $13,005\frac{95}{100}$. And also other claims for damages within two years, or since the taking of testimony for the above-mentioned damages, upon the presentation of sufficient proof: *Provided*, Such last-mentioned claims shall not exceed $3,500.

Interpreter.

ARTICLE 11. It is hereby made the duty of the Indian Department to appoint an interpreter for said tribe, in the customary manner, to be continued during the pleasure of the Secretary of the Interior. And it is expressly understood that all expenses incurred by the stipulations of this treaty shall be paid out of the funds of the aforementioned tribe of Ottawas, and their annuities shall be paid semi-annually.

In testimony whereof, the said Wm. P. Dole, commissioner, as aforesaid, and the undersigned chief and councilman of the United Bands of Blanchard's Fork and of Roche de Bœuf, in Franklin county, Kansas, have hereunto set their hands and seals at the place and on the day and year hereinbefore written.

Wm. P. Dole, commissioner.	[SEAL.]
Pem-ach-wung, his x mark.	[SEAL.]
John T. Jones.	[SEAL.]
William Hurr.	[SEAL.]
James Wind.	[SEAL.]

Interpreted by John T. Jones, and signed by the respective parties in presence of—

Clinton C. Hutchinson, Indian agent.

Charles E. Mix.

Antoine Gokey, his x mark, United States interpreter.

TREATY WITH THE KICKAPOO, 1862.

Articles of a treaty made and concluded at the agency of the Kickapoo tribe of Indians, on the 28th day of June, in the year of our Lord one thousand eight hundred and sixty-two, by and between Charles B. Keith, commissioner, on the part of the United States, and the undersigned chiefs, headmen, and delegates of the Kickapoo Nation, on behalf of said nation.

June 28, 1862.

13 Stats., 623.
Ratified Mar. 13, 1863.
Proclaimed May 28, 1863.

ARTICLE 1. The Kickapoo tribe of Indians, believing that it will contribute to the civilization of their people to dispose of a portion of their present reservation in Kansas, consisting of one hundred and fifty thousand acres of land, to allot land in severalty to those members of said tribe who desire to have separate tracts of lands, and have adopted the customs of the whites, and to set apart for the others of said tribe a portion of said reservation, to be held by them in common, or (if a majority of them so elect) provide for them a suitable home elsewhere, to be held by them in common, it is therefore hereby agreed that the Secretary of the Interior shall cause the whole of said reservation to be surveyed in the same manner as the public lands are surveyed, and the quantity of land hereinafter mentioned to be set apart to those of said tribe who desire to have their land in severalty; and, if so elected by a majority of the others of said tribe, the quantity of land hereinafter mentioned to be by such others held in common, and the remainder of the land, after the special reservations hereinafter provided for shall have been made, to be sold for the benefit of said tribe.

Reservation to be surveyed.

Portion to be set apart.

Remainder to be sold.

ARTICLE 2. It shall be the duty of the Secretary of the Interior to cause to be made an accurate census of all the members of the tribe, and to classify them in separate lists, showing the names, ages, and numbers of those desiring lands in severalty, and of those desiring lands in common, designating chiefs and heads of families respectively; each adult choosing for himself or herself, and each head of a family for the minor children of such family, and the agent for orphans and persons of an unsound mind and otherwise incompetent, as to which of these classes they will belong. And thereupon shall be assigned, under the direction of the Commissioner of Indian Affairs, to each chief, at the signing of the treaty, one half section; to each other head of a family, one quarter section; and to each other person, forty acres of land; to include in every case as far as practicable, to each family, their improvements and a reasonable portion of timber, to be selected according to the legal subdivision of survey. When such assignments shall have been completed, certificates shall be issued by the Commissioner of Indian Affairs for the tracts assigned in severalty, specifying the names of the individuals to whom they have been assigned respectively, and that said tracts are set apart for the perpetual and exclusive use and benefit of such assignees and their heirs. Until otherwise provided by law, such tracts shall be exempt from levy, taxation, or sale, and shall be alienable in fee, or leased, or otherwise disposed of only to the United States, or to persons then being members of the Kickapoo tribe, and of Indian blood, with the permission of the President, and under such rules and regulations as the Secretary of the Interior shall provide, except as may be hereinafter provided. And on receipt of such certificates, the person[s] to whom they are issued shall be deemed to have relinquished all right to any portion of the lands assigned to others in severalty, or to a portion of the tribe in common, and to the proceeds of sale of the same whensoever made.

Census to be taken.

Separate lists to be made.

Assignments of land.

Certificates to issue.

Lands to be exempt from taxation, etc.

Persons receiving certificates to relinquish, etc.

ARTICLE 3. At any time hereafter, when the President of the United States shall have become satisfied that any adults, being males and

Patents in fee simple; when to issue to allottees.

heads of families, who may be allottees under the provision of the foregoing article, are sufficiently intelligent and prudent to control their affairs and interests, he may, at the request of such persons, cause the lands severally held by them to be conveyed to them by patent in fee-simple, with power of alienation; and may, at the same time, cause to be set apart and placed to their credit severally, their

Their shares of credits to be paid them.

proportion of the cash value of the credits of the tribe, principal and interest, then held in trust by the United States, and also, as the same may be received, their proportion of the proceeds of the sale of lands under the provisions of this treaty. And on such patents being issued, and such payments ordered to be made by the President, such compe-

They to become citizens of the United States.

tent persons shall cease to be members of said tribe, and shall become citizens of the United States; and thereafter the lands so patented to them shall be subject to levy, taxation, and sale, in like manner with the property of other citizens: *Provided*, That, before making any such application to the President, they shall appear in open court, in the district court of the United States for the district of Kansas, and

Oath of allegiance and proof.

make the same proof and take the same oath of allegiance as is provided by law for the naturalization of aliens; and shall also make proof, to the satisfaction of said court, that they are sufficiently intelligent and prudent to control their affairs and interests; that they have adopted the habits of civilized life, and have been able to support, for at least five years, themselves and families.

Provision for those members who wish to hold their lands in common.

ARTICLE 4. To those members of said tribe who desire to hold their lands in common, there shall be set apart from the present reservation of the tribe an undivided quantity, sufficient to allow one half section to each chief, one quarter section to each other head of family, and forty acres to each other person, and said land shall be held by that portion of the tribe for whom it is set apart by the same tenure as the whole reserve has been held by all of said tribe under the treaty of

Effect of assignment in common.

1854. And upon such land being assigned in common, the persons to whom it is assigned shall be held to have relinquished all title to lands assigned in severalty, and in the proceeds of sales thereof whenever made; or should a majority of the adult males of said class decide to remove to the Indian country south of Kansas, then, and in that case, their new home shall not be limited to the quantity above designated, but shall be as large as can be purchased with the proceeds of the sale of the tract to which they would have been entitled had they determined to remain upon the present reservation, computing the same at the rate of at least one dollar and twenty-five cents per acre: *Provided*,

New home to be purchased, etc.

That the purchase of such new home shall be made by the Commissioner of Indian Affairs, under the direction of the Secretary of the Interior, and at such locality within said Indian country as he may select: *And provided also*, That such new home shall be purchased and the Indians entitled removed thereto, within the period of two years after the completion of the survey herein provided for. And such Indians shall be entitled to the benefits of their full proportionate share of all assets belonging to said tribe, in the same manner that they would have been entitled had such removal not been made, deducting therefrom the necessary expenses of their removal.

Atchison and Pike's Peak Railroad may buy certain lands.

ARTICLE 5. The Kickapoo tribe of Indians, entertaining the opinion that it is the desire of the Government and the people of the United States to extend railroad communication as far west as possible in the shortest possible time, and believing that it will greatly enhance the value of their lands reserved in severalty by having a railroad built, connecting with the eastern railroads running from the city of Atchison, in the State of Kansas, westerly in the direction of the gold mines in Colorado Territory; and entertaining the opinion that the Atchison and Pike's Peak Railroad Company, incorporated by an act of the legislative assembly of the Territory of Kansas, approved February 11,

1859, has advantages for travel and transportation over all other companies, it is therefore provided that the Atchison and Pike's Peak Railroad Company shall have the privilege of buying the remainder of their land within six months after the tracts herein otherwise disposed of shall have been selected and set apart, provided said railroad company purchase the whole of such surplus lands at the rate of one dollar and twenty-five cents per acre; and when the selections shall have been made and assigned as aforesaid, it shall be the duty of the Commissioner of Indian Affairs to notify the president of said railroad company thereof; and if said railroad company signifies its consent to purchase said surplus lands within sixty days thereafter, and shall make, execute, and deliver to the Secretary of the Interior the bonds of the said company in a penal sum equal to double the value of said surplus lands as heretofore ascertained, with the condition that the said bonds shall become void whenever the said company shall comply with the conditions of the treaty, the Secretary of the Interior shall issue to said railroad company certificates of purchase, and such certificates shall be deemed and held in all courts as evidence of the right of possession in said railroad company to all or any part of said lands, unless the same shall be forfeited as hereinafter provided. And if said railroad company make such purchase, it shall be subject to the following considerations, viz: They shall construct and fully equip a good and efficient railroad from the city of Atchison, in the State of Kansas, westerly, within six years, and as follows: The first section of fifteen miles of said road to be completed within three years from the date of said purchase, and the second section to a point as far west as the western boundary of said reservation within three years thereafter; and no patent or patents shall issue to said company or its assigns for any portion of said lands until the first section of said road shall be completed, and then for not more than one-half of said lands; and no patent or patents shall issue to said company or its assigns for any of the remaining portion of said lands until said second section of said railroad shall be completed as aforesaid; and before any patents shall issue for any part of said lands, payments shall be made for the lands to be patented at the rate of one dollar and twenty-five cents per acre. And said company shall pay the whole amount of the purchase-money for said lands in the securities of the United States to the Secretary of the Interior, in trust for said Kickapoo tribe of Indians, within six years from the date of such purchase; and when so paid the president is authorized hereby to issue patents therefor. Said company shall, in like manner, pay to the Secretary of the Interior, in trust as aforesaid, each and every year, until the whole purchase-money shall have been paid, interest from date of purchase, at six per cent. per annum, on all the purchase-money remaining unpaid. Said interest, and the interest due on the purchase-money after it is paid to the United States, shall be held in trust and paid to said Indians on the first day of April of each and every year; and in ten years from the ratification of this treaty there shall be paid by the United States to said tribe of Indians ten thousand dollars, as their first instalment upon the amount of said purchase-money, and ten thousand dollars each and every year thereafter until all is paid.

ARTICLE 6. In case said railroad company shall fail to complete either section of said railroad in a good and efficient manner, or shall fail to pay the whole of the purchase-money for said lands within the time herein prescribed, or shall fail to pay all or any part of the interest upon the same each year as aforesaid, within thirty days from the date when such payment of interest may fall due, then the contract or purchase shall be deemed and held absolutely null and void, if the Secretary of the Interior shall so determine, and said company or its assigns shall forfeit all payments of principal and interest made on such pur-

[margin notes:] Proviso.

Conditions of purchase.

Contract or purchase, when to be null and void.

chase, and all right and title, legal and equitable, of any kind whatsoever, in and to all and every part of said lands which shall not have been before the date of such forfeiture earned and paid for pursuant to the provisions of this treaty. And whenever any patents shall issue to said railroad company for any part of said lands, it shall contain the condition that the said company shall sell the lands described in such patent, except so much as shall be necessary for the working of the road, within five years from the issuing of such patent. And said company shall have the perpetual right of way over the lands of the Kickapoos not sold to it for the construction and operation of said railroad, not exceeding one hundred feet in width, and the right to enter on said lands and take and use such gravel, stone, earth, water, and other material, except timber, as may be necessary for the construction and operation of the said road, making compensation for any damages to improvements caused by obtaining such material, and for any damages arising from the location or running of said road, to improvements made before the road was located; such damages and compensation, in cases where said company and the persons whose improvements are injured or the property taken cannot agree, to be ascertained and adjusted under the direction of the Commissioner of Indian Affairs. And in case said company shall not promptly pay the amount of such damages and compensation, the Secretary of the Interior may withhold patents for any part of the lands purchased by them until payment be made of the amount of such damages, with six per cent. interest thereon from the date when the same, not including improvements, shall have been ascertained and demanded; and in case said company shall not purchase said surplus lands, or having purchased, shall forfeit the whole or any part thereof, the Secretary of the Interior shall thereupon cause the same to be appraised at not less than one dollar and twenty-five cents per acre, and shall sell the same in quantities not exceeding one hundred and sixty acres at auction, to the highest bidder for cash, at not less than [the] appraised value: *Provided, however,* In case any of said lands have been conveyed to bona-fide purchasers by said railroad company, such purchasers shall be entitled to a patent for said lands so purchased by them on payment to the United States in trust for said Kickapoos of the appraised value thereof, (exclusive of their improvements,) and not less than one dollar and twenty-five cents per acre therefor, under such rules and regulations as may be prescribed by the Secretary of the Interior. On the purchase of said lands by the said railroad company the same shall become a part of the State of Kansas, but none of said lands shall be subject to taxation until the patents have been issued therefor.

ARTICLE 7. [Stricken out.]

ARTICLE 8. [Stricken out.]

ARTICLE 9. [Stricken out.]

ARTICLE 10. Whereas some years since a portion of the Kickapoos went down among the Southern Indians, and there is reason to believe that but few, if any, of them will ever return, and they having been notified of the provisions of this treaty, it is hereby agreed that they shall receive no benefits arising therefrom, unless they return to the present reservation of the Kickapoos within one year from the ratification of this treaty, in which case it is hereby agreed that forty acres each be allotted to them, with the understanding that they will occupy, improve, and cultivate the same, and in every respect to be governed by the same rules and regulations as is prescribed for the government of the lands reserved by the preceding articles.

ARTICLE 11. There shall be reserved six hundred and forty acres of land to be selected by the chiefs of said tribe of Kickapoos as a site for a saw and grist mill, three hundred and twenty acres where the mission-house now is, and one hundred and sixty acres where the house built for the agency now is, which, with the improvements thereupon,

Patents to contain what conditions.

Provisions as to Kickapoo who heretofore went South.

Reservation for saw and grist mills.

shall be disposed of when the objects for which they have been reserved shall have been accomplished, in such a manner and for such purposes as may be provided by law.

ARTICLE 12. [Stricken out.]

ARTICLE 13. Inasmuch as it was provided by the treaty between the United States and said Kickapoos, entered into on the 18th day of May, A. D. 1854, that the President may cause to be surveyed, in the same manner that the public lands are surveyed, the reservation provided for the Kickapoos, it is agreed that the expense of said surveys shall be paid by the United States out of the proceeds of sales of said lands, and all expenses incident to the negotiation and execution of this treaty, and not otherwise provided for, shall be defrayed by the Kickapoos; the same to be deducted from any funds applicable to that purpose now or hereafter held for them in trust by the United States. *Expenses of surveys to be paid by the United States.*

ARTICLE 14. It is further agreed that all rights, title, and interest of the Kickapoos in their present reservation shall cease, and the same is hereby ceded to and vested in the United States, subject to the limitations and for the purposes herein expressed and provided for. *Reservation ceded to the United States.*

ARTICLE 15. Any stipulation in former treaties inconsistent with those embraced in the foregoing articles shall be of no force or effect. *Inconsistent stipulations of no effect.*

ARTICLE 16. Should the Senate reject or amend any of the foregoing articles, such rejection or amendment shall not affect the other provisions of this treaty, but the same shall go into effect when ratified and approved. *Effect of rejection, etc., of any article of this treaty.*

In testimony whereof, the said Charles B. Keith, commissioner as aforesaid, and the undersigned chiefs, headmen, and delegates of the Kickapoo Tribe of Indians, have hereunto set their hands and seals, at the place, on the day, and in the year hereinbefore written.

Charles B. Keith, [SEAL.]
Commissioner on behalf of the United States.

Chief Par-thee, or the Elk Chief, his x mark.   [SEAL.]
Chief Pah-kah-kah, or John Kennekuk, his x mark.   [SEAL.]
Chief Mack-a-tair-chee-qua, or Black Thunder, his x mark.   [SEAL.]
Ken-ne-kuk, or Stephen Pen-sion-eau, his x mark.   [SEAL.]
Mah-mah-she-cow-ah, or Bear Track, her x mark.   [SEAL.]
Pet-ti-quauk, or Rolling Thunder, his x mark.   [SEAL.]
John C. Anderson,   [SEAL.]
Toth-way, or Frank Cadue, his x mark.   [SEAL.]

Executed in presence of—
   John E. Badger.
   H. C. Pursel.
   Nelson S. Shaler.
   Paschall Pensioneau, his x mark, United States interpreter.
   W. D. Barnett, witness to signature of Paschall Pensioneau.

TREATY WITH THE CHIPPEWA OF THE MISSISSIPPI AND THE PILLAGER AND LAKE WINNIBIGOSHISH BANDS, 1863.

Articles of agreement and convention, made and concluded at the city of Washington, this eleventh day of March, A. D. one thousand eight hundred and sixty-three, between William P. Dole, Commissioner of Indian Affairs, and Clark W. Thompson, superintendent of Indian affairs of the northern superintendency, on the part of the United States, and Henry M. Rice, of Minnesota, for and on behalf of the Chippewas of the Mississippi and the Pillager and Lake Winnibigoshish bands of Chippewa Indians in Minnesota. Mar. 11, 1863.

12 Stats., 1249.
Ratified, Mar. 13, 1863.
Proclaimed Mar. 19, 1863.

ARTICLE 1. The reservations known as Gull Lake, Mille Lac, Sandy Lake, Rabbit Lake, Pokagomin Lake, and Rice Lake, as described in *Certain reservations ceded to the United States, except, etc.*

the second clause of the second article of the treaty with the Chippe-was of the 22d February, 1855, are hereby ceded to the United States, excepting one-half section of land, including the mission-buildings at Gull Lake, which is hereby granted in fee simple to the Reverend John Johnson, missionary.

Reservation set apart in lieu thereof.

ARTICLE 2. In consideration of the foregoing cession, the United States agree to set apart for the future homes of the Chippewas of the Mississippi, all the lands embraced within the following-described bound-aries, excepting the reservations made and described in the third clause of the second article of the said treaty of February 22, 1855, for the Pillager and Lake Winnibigoshish bands; that is to say, beginning at a point one mile south of the most southerly point of Leech Lake, and running thence in an easterly course to a point one mile south of the most southerly point of Goose Lake; thence due east to a point due south from the intersection of the Pokagomin reservation and the Mis-sissippi River; thence on the dividing-line between " Deer River and Lakes " and " Mashkorden's River and Lakes," until a point is reached north of the first-named river and lakes; thence in a direct line north-westwardly to the outlet of " Two-Routes Lake;" thence in a south-westerly direction to the northwest corner of the " Cass Lake " reser-vation; thence in a southwesterly direction to "Karbekaun " River: thence down said river to the lake of the same name; thence due south to a point due west from the beginning; thence to the place of begin-ning.

Boundaries.

Annuities.

ARTICLE 3. In consideration of the foregoing cession to the United States, and the valuable improvements thereon, the United States further agree: 1st. To extend the present annuities of the Indians, par-ties to this treaty, for ten years beyond the periods respectively named in existing treaties; 2nd. And to pay toward the settlement of the claims for depredations committed by said Indians in 1862, the sum of twenty thousand dollars, or so much thereof as may be necessary, pro-vided that no money shall be paid under this item, except upon claims which have been duly adjudicated and found to be due under existing treaties, from said Indians, and allowed by the Secretary of the Inte-rior, or under his direction; 4th. To the chiefs of the Chippewas of the Mississippi, sixteen thousand dollars, (provided they shall pay to the chiefs of the Pillager and Lake Winnibigoshish bands one thousand dollars,) to be paid upon the signing of this treaty, out of the arrear-ages due under the 9th article of the treaty concluded at La Pointe, in the State of Wisconsin, on the 30th of September, 1854; 5th. And to pay the expenses incurred by the legislature of the State of Minnesota. in the month of September, 1862, in sending commissioners to visit the Chippewa Indians, amounting to thirteen hundred and thirty-eight dollars and seventy-five cents.

Reservation to be cleared. etc., in lots.

ARTICLE 4. The United States further agree to clear, stump, grub. and break in, the reservation hereby set apart for the Chippewas of the Mississippi, in lots of not less than ten acres each, at such point or points as the chiefs of each band may select, as follows, viz: For the Gull Lake band, seventy acres; for the Mille Lac band, seventy acres: for the Sandy Lake band, fifty acres; for the Pokagomin band, fifty acres; for the Rabbit Lake band, forty acres; for the Rice Lake band. twenty acres; and to build for the chiefs of said bands one house each. of the following description: to be constructed of hewn logs; to be sixteen by twenty feet each, and two stories high; to be roofed with good shaved pine shingles; the floors to be of seasoned pine-plank. jointed; stone or brick fire-places and chimneys; three windows in lower story and two in the upper story, with good substantial shutters to each, and suitable doors; said houses to be pointed with lime mor-tar: provided, that the amount expended under this article shall not exceed the sum of three thousand six hundred dollars.

Houses for chiefs.

ARTICLE 5. The United States agree to furnish to said Indians, parties to this treaty, ten yoke of good, steady, work oxen, and twenty log-chains, annually, for ten years, provided the Indians shall take proper care of, and make proper use of the same; also, for the same period, annually, two hundred grubbing-hoes, ten ploughs, ten grindstones, one hundred axes, handled, not to exceed in weight three and one-half pounds each; twenty spades. Also two carpenters and two blacksmiths, and four farm laborers, and one physician—not exceeding, in the aggregate, one thousand dollars. *Oxen and tools.* *Carpenters, blacksmiths, etc.*

ARTICLE 6. The United States further agree to remove the saw-mill from Gull Lake reservation; to such point on the new reservation hereby set apart as may be selected by the agent, and to keep the same in good running order, and to employ a competent sawyer, so long as the President of the United States may deem it necessary; and to extend the road between Gull Lake and Leech Lake, from the last-named lake to the junction of the Mississippi and Leech Lake Rivers; and to remove the agency to said junction, or as near thereto as practicable; but not more than three thousand dollars shall be expended for this purpose. *Sawmill.*

ARTICLE 7. The President shall appoint a board of visitors, to consist of not less than two nor more than three persons, to be selected from such Christian denominations as he may designate, whose duty it shall be to attend the annuity payments to the Indians, and to inspect the fields and other improvements of the Indians, and to report annually thereon, on or before the first of November; and also as to the qualifications and moral deportment of all persons residing upon the reservation under the authority of law; and they shall receive for their services five dollars per day for the time actually employed, and ten cents per mile for travelling expenses: *Provided,* That no one shall be paid in any one year for more than twenty days' service, or for more than three hundred miles' travel. *Board of visitors to be present at annuity payments.*

ARTICLE 8. No person shall be recognized as a chief whose band numbers less than fifty persons; and to encourage and aid the said chiefs in preserving order, and inducing by their example and advice the members of their respective bands to adopt the pursuits of civilized life, there shall be paid to each of said chiefs, annually, out of the annuities of said bands, a sum not exceeding one hundred and fifty dollars, to be determined by the Commissioner of Indian Affairs, according to their respective merits. *Who to be recognized as chiefs.*

ARTICLE 9. To improve the morals and industrial habits of said Indians, it is agreed that no agent, teacher, interpreter, traders, or their employés, shall be employed, appointed, licensed, or permitted to reside within the reservations belonging to the Indians, parties to this treaty, missionaries excepted, who shall not have a lawful wife residing with them at their respective places of employment or trade within the agency, and no person of full or mixed blood, educated or partially educated, whose fitness, morally or otherwise, is not conducive to the welfare of said Indians, shall receive any benefits from this or any former treaties. *Agents, teachers, etc., to have families, and to be of good moral character.*

ARTICLE 10. All annuities under this or former treaties shall be paid as the chiefs in council may request, with the approval of the Secretary of the Interior, until otherwise altered or amended: *Provided,* That not less than one-half of said annuities shall be paid in necessary clothing, provisions, and other necessary and useful articles. *Payment of annuities.*

ARTICLE 11. Whenever the services of laborers are required upon the reservation, preference shall be given to full or mixed bloods, if they shall be found competent to perform them. *Laborers to be full or mixed bloods, where competent.*

ARTICLE 12. It shall not be obligatory upon the Indians, parties to this treaty, to remove from their present reservations until the United States shall have first complied with the stipulations of Articles 4 and *Indians not to remove from present reservations, until, after, etc.*

6 of this treaty, when the United States shall furnish them with all necessary transportation and subsistence to their new homes, and subsistence for six months thereafter: *Provided,* That owing to the heretofore good conduct of the Mille Lac Indians, they shall not be compelled to remove so long as they shall not in any way interfere with or in any manner molest the persons or property of the whites.

ARTICLE 13. Female members of the family of any Government employé residing on the reservation, who shall teach Indian girls domestic economy, shall be allowed and paid a sum not exceeding ten dollars per month while so engaged: *Provided,* That not more than one thousand dollars shall be so expended during any one year, and that the President of the United States may suspend or annul this article whenever he may deem it expedient to do so.

ARTICLE 14. It is distinctly understood and agreed that the clearing and breaking of land for the Chippewas of the Mississippi, as provided for in the fourth article of this treaty, shall be in lieu of all former engagements of the United States as to the breaking of lands for those bands.

In testimony whereof, the said William P. Dole and Clark W. Thompson, on behalf of the United States, and Henry M. Rice and the undersigned chiefs and headmen, on behalf of the Indians, parties to this treaty, have hereunto set their hands and affixed their seals this eleventh day of March, A. D. one thousand eight hundred and sixty-three.

Side notes: Mille Lac Indians. — Female teachers. — Clearing and breaking, in lieu of former engagements. — Signature.

Wm. P. Dole, Commissioner of Indian Affairs.   [SEAL.]

Clark W. Thompson, superintendent of Indian affairs for the northern superintendency. [SEAL.]	Te-daw-kaw-mo-say, Walking to and fro, his x mark. [SEAL.]
Henry M. Rice. [SEAL.]	Mose-o-man-nay, or Moose, his x mark. [SEAL.]
Gull Lake band:	Way-sa-wa-gwon-aib, Yellow Feather, his x mark. [SEAL.]
Qui-we-shen-shish, or Bad Boy, his x mark. [SEAL.]	Me-no-ke-shick, or Fine Day, his x mark. [SEAL.]
Wa-bo-geeg, or White Fisher, his x mark. [SEAL.]	Pillager band of Leech Lake:
J. Johnson, [SEAL.]	Be-she-kee, or Buffalo, his x mark. [SEAL.]
Rabbitt Lake band:	Naw-bon-e-aush, Young Man's Son, his x mark. [SEAL.]
Me-jaw-ke-ke-shick, or Sky that Touches the Ground, his x mark. [SEAL.]	O-ge-ma-way-che-waib, Chief of the Mountain, his x mark. [SEAL.]
Ah-ah-jaw-wa-ke-shick, Crossing Sky, his x mark. [SEAL.]	Ke-me-wen-aush, Raining Wind, his x mark. [SEAL.]
Naw-gaw-ne-gaw-bow, or One Standing Ahead, his x mark. [SEAL.]	Keh-beh-naw-gay, the Winner, his x mark. [SEAL.]
Sandy Lake and Rice Lake bands:	Winne-pe-go-shish band:
Aw-aw-bedway-we-dung, or Returning Echo, his x mark. [SEAL.]	Kob-mub-bey, or North Star, his x mark. [SEAL.]
Po-ke-ga-ma band:	Mis-co-pe-nen-shey, Red Bird, his x mark. [SEAL.]
Ma-ya-je-way-we-dung, or Chorrister, his x mark. [SEAL.]	Cass Lake band:
Mille Lac band:	Maw-je-ke-shick, Travelling Sky, his x mark. [SEAL.]
Shob-osh-kunk, or Passes under Everything, his x mark. [SEAL.]	Ma-ne-to-ke-shick, Spirit of the Day, his x mark. [SEAL.]
Me-no-min-e-ke-shen, or Ricemaker, his x mark. [SEAL.]	O-Gee-tub, the Trader, his x mark. [SEAL.]
Pe-dud-ence, Rat's Liver, his x mark. [SEAL.]	

Executed in presence of—

E. A. C. Hatch,	Paul H. Beaubien, United States interpreter,
Geo. C. Whiting,	Peter Roy, interpreter,
A. S. H. White,	J. G. Morrison, interpreter,
George Fuller,	James Thompson.
James Whitehead,	
D. Geo. Morrison,	

TREATY WITH THE NEZ PERCÉS, 1863.

Articles of agreement made and concluded at the council-ground, in the valley of the Lapwai, W. T., on the ninth day of June, one thousand eight hundred and sixty-three, between the United States of America, by C. H. Hale, superintendent of Indian affairs, and Charles Hutchins and S. D. Howe, U. S. Indian agents for the Territory of Washington, acting on the part and in behalf of the United States, and the Nez Percé Indians, by the chiefs, head-men, and delegates of said tribe, such articles being supplementary and amendatory to the treaty made between the United States and said tribe on the 11th day of June, 1855.

June 9, 1863.

14 Stats., 647.
Ratified Apr.17,1867.
Proclaimed Apr. 20, 1867.

ARTICLE 1. The said Nez Percé tribe agree to relinquish, and do hereby relinquish, to the United States the lands heretofore reserved for the use and occupation of the said tribe, saving and excepting so much thereof as is described in Article II for a new reservation.

Cession of lands to the United States.

ARTICLE 2. The United States agree to reserve for a home, and for the sole use and occupation of said tribe, the tract of land included within the following boundaries, to wit: Commencing at the northeast corner of Lake Wa-ha, and running thence, northerly, to a point on the north bank of the Clearwater River, three miles below the mouth of the Lapwai, thence down the north bank of the Clearwater to the mouth of the Hatwai Creek; thence, due north, to a point seven miles distant; thence, eastwardly, to a point on the north fork of the Clearwater, seven miles distant from its mouth; thence to a point on Oro Fino Creek, five miles above its mouth; thence to a point on the north fork of the south fork of the Clearwater, five miles above its mouth; thence to a point on the south fork of the Clearwater, one mile above the bridge, on the road leading to Elk City, (so as to include all the Indian farms now within the forks;) thence in a straight line, westwardly, to the place of beginning.

Reservation.

Boundaries.

All of which tract shall be set apart, and the above-described boundaries shall be surveyed and marked out for the exclusive use and benefit of said tribe as an Indian reservation, nor shall any white man, excepting those in the employment of the Indian Department, be permitted to reside upon the said reservation without permission of the tribe and the superintendent and agent; and the said tribe agrees that so soon after the United States shall make the necessary provision for fulfilling the stipulations of this instrument as they can conveniently arrange their affairs, and not to exceed one year from its ratification, they will vacate the country hereby relinquished, and remove to and settle upon the lands herein reserved for them, (except as may be hereinafter provided.) In the meantime it shall be lawful for them to reside upon any ground now occupied or under cultivation by said Indians at this time, and not included in the reservation above named. And it is provided, that any substantial improvement heretofore made by any Indian, such as fields inclosed and cultivated, or houses erected upon the lands hereby relinquished, and which he may be compelled to abandon in consequence of this treaty, shall be valued under the direction of the President of the United States, and payment therefor shall be made in stock or in improvements of an equal value for said Indian upon the lot which may be assigned to him within the bounds of the reservation, as he may choose, and no Indian will be required to abandon the improvements aforesaid, now occupied by him, until said payment or improvement shall have been made. And it is further provided, that if any Indian living on any of the land hereby relinquished should prefer to sell his improvements to any white man, being a loyal citizen of the United States, prior to the same being valued as aforesaid, he shall be allowed so to do, but the sale or transfer of said improvements shall be made in the presence of, and with the consent

Reservation to be for the sole use of the tribe, who shall settle thereon within a year.

Improvements on lands ceded to be paid for.

May be sold to loyal whites.

Certificates of sale.

and approval of, the agent or superintendent, by whom a certificate of sale shall be issued to the party purchasing, which shall set forth the amount of the consideration in kind. Before the issue of said certificate, the agent or superintendent shall be satisfied that a valuable consideration is paid, and that the party purchasing is of undoubted loyalty to the United States Government. No settlement or claim made upon the improved lands by any Indian will be permitted, except as herein provided, prior to the time specified for their removal. Any sale or transfer thus made shall be in the stead of payment for improvements from the United States.

Boundary lines to be marked and lands surveyed into lots.

Heads of families may locate on lot.

ARTICLE 3. The President shall, immediately after the ratification of this treaty, cause the boundary-lines to be surveyed, and properly marked and established; after which, so much of the lands hereby reserved as may be suitable for cultivation shall be surveyed into lots of twenty acres each, and every male person of the tribe who shall have attained the age of twenty-one years, or is the head of a family, shall have the privilege of locating upon one lot as a permanent home for such person, and the lands so surveyed shall be allotted under such rules and regulations as the President shall prescribe, having such reference to their settlement as may secure adjoining each other the location of the different families pertaining to each band, so far as the same may be practicable. Such rules and regulations shall be prescribed by the President, or under his direction, as will insure to the family, in case of the death of the head thereof, the possession and enjoyment of such permanent home, and the improvements thereon.

Certificates therefor.

When the assignments as above shall have been completed, certificates shall be issued by the Commissioner of Indian Affairs, or under his direction, for the tracts assigned in severalty, specifying the names of the individuals to whom they have been assigned respectively, and that said tracts are set apart for the perpetual and exclusive use and benefit of such assignees and their heirs.

These lots to be exempt from levy, taxes, etc.

Until otherwise provided by law, such tracts shall be exempt from levy, taxation, or sale, and shall be alienable in fee, or leased, or otherwise disposed of, only to the United States, or to persons then being members of the Nez Percé tribe, and of Indian blood, with the permission of the President, and under such regulations as the Secretary of the Interior or the Commissioner of Indian Affairs shall prescribe; and if any such person or family shall at any time neglect or refuse to occupy and till a portion of the land so assigned, and on which they have located, or shall rove from place to place, the President may cancel the assignment, and may also withhold from such person or family their proportion of the annuities or other payments due them until they shall have returned to such permanent home, and resumed the pursuits of industry; and in default of their return, the tract may be declared abandoned, and

Residue to be held in common.

thereafter assigned to some other person or family of such tribe. The residue of the land hereby reserved shall be held in common for pasturage for the sole use and benefit of the Indians: *Provided, however,* That from time to time, as members of the tribe may come upon the reservation, or may become of proper age, after the expiration of the time of one year after the ratification of this treaty, as aforesaid, and claim the privileges granted under this article, lots may be assigned from the lands thus held in common, wherever the same may be suitable for cultivation.

Restriction not to be removed without the consent of Congress.

No State or territorial legislature shall remove the restriction herein provided for, without the consent of Congress, and no State or territorial law to that end shall be deemed valid until the same has been specially submitted to Congress for its approval.

Payments to the tribe.

ARTICLE 4. In consideration of the relinquishment herein made the United States agree to pay to the said tribe, in addition to the annuities provided by the treaty of June 11, 1855, and the goods and provisions distributed to them at the time of signing this treaty, the sum of two hundred and sixty-two thousand and five hundred dollars, in manner following, to wit:

First. One hundred and fifty thousand dollars, to enable the Indians to remove and locate upon the reservation, to be expended in the ploughing of land, and the fencing of the several lots, which may be assigned to those individual members of the tribe who will accept the same in accordance with the provisions of the preceding article, which said sum shall be divided into four annual instalments, as follows: For the first year after the ratification of this treaty, seventy thousand dollars; for the second year, forty thousand dollars; for the third year, twenty-five thousand dollars; for the fourth year, fifteen thousand dollars.

Second. Fifty thousand dollars to be paid the first year after the ratification of this treaty in agricultural implements, to include wagons or carts, harness, and cattle, sheep, or other stock, as may be deemed most beneficial by the superintendent of Indian affairs, or agent, after ascertaining the wishes of the Indians in relation thereto.

Third. Ten thousand dollars for the erection of a saw and flouring mill, to be located at Kamia, the same to be erected within one year after the ratification hereof.

Fourth. Fifty thousand dollars for the boarding and clothing of the children who shall attend the schools, in accordance with such rules or regulations as the Commissioner of Indian Affairs may prescribe, providing the schools and boarding-houses with necessary furniture, the purchase of necessary wagons, teams, agricultural implements, tools, &c., for their use, and for the fencing of such lands as may be needed for gardening and farming purposes, for the use and benefit of the schools, to be expended as follows: The first year after the ratification of this treaty, six thousand dollars; for the next fourteen years, three thousand dollars each year; and for the succeeding year, being the sixteenth and last instalment, two thousand dollars.

Fifth. A further sum of two thousand five hundred dollars shall be paid within one year after the ratification hereof, to enable the Indians to build two churches, one of which is to be located at some suitable point on the Kamia, and the other on the Lapwai. *Churches.*

ARTICLE 5. The United States further agree, that in addition to a head chief the tribe shall elect two subordinate chiefs, who shall assist him in the performance of his public services, and each subordinate chief shall have the same amount of land ploughed and fenced, with comfortable house and necessary furniture, and to whom the same salary shall be paid as is already provided for the head chief in article 5 of the treaty of June 11, 1855, the salary to be paid and the houses and land to be occupied during the same period and under like restrictions as therein mentioned. *Subordinate chiefs*

And for the purpose of enabling the agent to erect said buildings, and to plough and fence the land, as well as to procure the necessary furniture, and to complete and furnish the house, &c., of the head chief, as heretofore provided, there shall be appropriated, to be expended within the first year after the ratification hereof, the sum of two thousand five hundred dollars.

And inasmuch as several of the provisions of said art. 5th of the treaty of June 11, 1855, pertaining to the erection of school-houses, hospital, shops, necessary buildings for employe[e]s and for the agency, as well as providing the same with necessary furniture, tools, &c., have not yet been complied with, it is hereby stipulated that there shall be appropriated, to be expended for the purposes herein specified during the first year after the ratification hereof, the following sums, to wit: *Further appropriation.*

First. Ten thousand dollars for the erection of the two schools, including boarding-houses and the necessary out-buildings; said schools to be conducted on the manual-labor system as far as practicable. *Schools.*

Hospital.

Second. Twelve hundred dollars for the erection of the hospital, and providing the necessary furniture for the same.

Blacksmith's shop, tools, etc.

Third. Two thousand dollars for the erection of a blacksmith's shop, to be located at Kamia, to aid in the completion of the smith's shop at the agency, and to purchase the necessary tools, iron, steel, &c.; and to keep the same in repair and properly stocked with necessary tools and materials, there shall be appropriated thereafter, for the fifteen years next succeeding, the sum of five hundred dollars each year.

Houses, mills, etc.

Fourth. Three thousand dollars for erection of houses for employe[e]s, repairs of mills, shops, &c., and providing necessary furniture, tools, and materials. For the same purpose, and to procure from year to year the necessary articles—that is to say, saw-logs, nails, glass, hardwaie, &c.—there snall be appropriated thereafter, for the twelve years next succeeding, the sum of two thousand dollars each year; and for the next three years, one thousand dollars each year.

Matrons, teachers, mechanics, millers.

And it is further agreed that the United States shall employ, in addition to those already mentioned in art. 5th of the treaty of June 11, 1855, two matrons to take charge of the boarding-schools, two assistant teachers, one farmer, one carpenter, and two millers.

All the expenditures and expenses contemplated in this treaty, and not otherwise provided for, shall be defrayed by the United States.

Payment to the chief, Timothy.

ARTICLE 6. In consideration of the past services and faithfulness of the Indian chief, Timothy, it is agreed that the United States shall appropriate the sum of six hundred dollars, to aid him in the erection of a house upon the lot of land which may be assigned to him, in accordance with the provisions of the third article of this treaty.

Claims for services and for horses to be paid.

ARTICLE 7. The United States further agree that the claims of certain members of the Nez Percé tribe against the Government for services rendered and for horses furnished by them to the Oregon mounted volunteers, as appears by certificate issued by W. H. Fauntleroy, A. R. Qr. M. and Com. Oregon volunteers, on the 6th of March, 1856, at Camp Cornelius, and amounting to the sum of four thousand six hundred and sixty-five dollars, shall be paid to them in full, in gold coin.

Authority, etc., of the United States acknowledged.

ARTICLE 8. It is also understood that the aforesaid tribe do hereby renew their acknowledgments of dependence upon the Government of the United States, their promises of friendship, and other pledges, as set forth in the eighth article of the treaty of June 11, 1855; and further, that all the provisions of said treaty which are not abrogated or specifically changed by any article herein contained, shall remain the same to all intents and purposes as formerly,—the same obligations resting upon the United States, the same privileges continued to the Indians outside of the reservation, and the same rights secured to citizens of the U. S. as to right of way upon the streams and over the roads which may run through said reservation, as are therein set forth.

Roads and highways.

But it is further provided, that the United States is the only competent authority to declare and establish such necessary roads and highways, and that no other right is intended to be hereby granted to citizens of the United States than the right of way upon or over such roads as may thus be legally established: *Provided, however,* That the roads now usually travelled shall, in the mean time, be taken and deemed as within the meaning of this article, until otherwise enacted by act of Congress or by the authority of the Indian Department.

Hotels and stage stands.

And the said tribe hereby consent, that upon the public roads which may run across the reservation there may be established, at such points as shall be necessary for public convenience, hotels, or stage-stands, of the number and necessity of which the agent or superintendent shall be the sole judge, who shall be competent to license the same, with the privilege of using such amount of land for pasturage and other purposes connected with such establishment as the agent or superintendent shall deem necessary, it being understood that such lands for pasturage are to be enclosed, and the boundaries thereof described in the license.

And it is further understood and agreed that all ferries and bridges within the reservation shall be held and managed for the benefit of said tribe.

Such rules and regulations shall be made by the Commissioner of Indian Affairs, with the approval of the Secretary of the Interior, as shall regulate the travel on the highways, the management of the ferries and bridges, the licensing of public houses, and the leasing of lands, as herein provided, so that the rents, profits, and issues thereof shall inure to the benefit of said tribe, and so that the persons thus licensed, or necessarily employed in any of the above relations, shall be subject to the control of the Indian Department, and to the provisions of the act of Congress "to regulate trade and intercourse with the Indian tribes, and to preserve peace on the frontiers."

All timber within the bounds of the reservation is exclusively the property of the tribe, excepting that the U. S. Government shall be permitted to use thereof for any purpose connected with its affairs, either in carrying out any of the provisions of this treaty, or in the maintaining of its necessary forts or garrisons.

The United States also agree to reserve all springs or fountains not adjacent to, or directly connected with, the streams or rivers within the lands hereby relinquished, and to keep back from settlement or entry so much of the surrounding land as may be necessary to prevent the said springs or fountains being enclosed; and, further, to preserve a perpetual right of way to and from the same, as watering places, for the use in common of both whites and Indians.

ARTICLE 9. Inasmuch as the Indians in council have expressed their desire that Robert Newell should have confirmed to him a piece of land lying between Snake and Clearwater Rivers, the same having been given to him on the 9th day of June, 1861, and described in an instrument of writing bearing that date, and signed by several chiefs of the tribe, it is hereby agreed that the said Robert Newell shall receive from the United States a patent for the said tract of land.

ARTICLE 10. This treaty shall be obligatory upon the contracting parties as soon as the same shall be ratified by the President and Senate of the United States.

In testimony whereof the said C. H. Hale, superintendent of Indian affairs, and Charles Hutchins and S. D. Howe, United States Indian agents in the Territory of Washington, and the chiefs, headmen, and delegates of the aforesaid Nez Perce tribe of Indians, have hereunto set their hands and seals at the place and on the day and year hereinbefore written.

Calvin H. Hale,
    Superintendent Indian Affairs, Wash. T.   [SEAL.]
Chas. Hutchins,
    United States Indian agent, Wash. T.   [SEAL.]
S. D. Howe,
    United States Indian agent, Wash. T.   [SEAL.]

Fa-Ind-7-1803 Lawyer,		We-as-cus, x	[SEAL.]
Head Chief Nez Perces Nation.	[SEAL.]	Pep-hoom-kan, (Noah,) x	[SEAL.]
Ute-sin-male-e-cum, x	[SEAL.]	Shin-ma-sha-ho-soot, x	[SEAL.]
Ha-harch-tuesta, x	[SEAL.]	Nie-ki-lil-meh-hoom, (Jacob,) x	[SEAL.]
Tip-ulania-timecca, x	[SEAL.]	Stoop-toop-nin, x	[SEAL.]
Es-coatum, x	[SEAL.]	Su-we-cus, x	[SEAL.]
Timothy, x	[SEAL.]	Wal-la-ta-mana, x	[SEAL.]
Levi, x	[SEAL.]	He-kaikt-il-pilp, x	[SEAL.]
Jason, x	[SEAL.]	Whis-tas-ket, x	[SEAL.]
Ip-she-ne-wish-kin, (Capt.		Neus-ne-keun, x	[SEAL.]
John,) x	[SEAL.]	Kul-lou-o-haikt, x	[SEAL.]
Weptas-jump-ki, x	[SEAL.]	Wow-en-am-ash-il-pilp, x	[SEAL.]

Marginal notes: Ferries and bridges. Timber. Springs or fountains. Robert Newell to receive a patent for a tract of land. Treaty, when to take effect.

Kan-pow-e-een, x	[SEAL.]	Tuck-e-tu-et-as, x	[SEAL.]
Watai-watai-wa-haikt, x	[SEAL.]	Nic-a-las-in, x	[SEAL.]
Kup-kup-pellia, x	[SEAL.]	Was-atis-il-pilp, x	[SEAL.]
Wap-tas-ta-mana, x	[SEAL.]	Wow-es-en-at-im, x	[SEAL.]
Peo-peo-ip-se-wat, x	[SEAL.]	Hiram, x	[SEAL.]
Louis-in-ha-cush-nim, x	[SEAL.]	Howlish-wampum, x	[SEAL.]
Lam-lim-si-lilp-nim, x	[SEAL.]	Wat-ska-leeks, x	[SEAL.]
Tu-ki-lai-kish, x	[SEAL.]	Wa-lai-tus, x	[SEAL.]
Sah-kan-tai, (Eagle,) x	[SEAL.]	Ky-e-wee-pus, x	[SEAL.]
We-ah-se-nat, x	[SEAL.]	Ko-ko-il-pilp, x	[SEAL.]
Hin-mia-tun-pin, x	[SEAL.]	Reuben, Tip-ia-la-na-uy-kala-	
Ma-hi-a-kim, x	[SEAL.]	tsekin, x	[SEAL.]
Shock-lo-turn-wa-haikt, (Jo-		Wish-la-na-ka-nin, x	[SEAL.]
nah,) x	[SEAL.]	Me-tat-ueptas,(Three Feathers,)x	[SEAL.]
Kunness-tak-mal, x	[SEAL.]	Ray-kay-mass, x	[SEAL.]
Tu-lat-sy-wat-kin, x	[SEAL.]		

Signed and sealed in presence of—

George F. Whitworth, Secretary.
Justus Steinberger, Colonel U. S. Volunteers.
R. F. Malloy, Colonel Cavalry, O. V.
J. S. Rinearson, Major First Cavalry Oregon Volunteers.
William Kapus, First Lieutenant and Adjutant First W. T. Infantry U. S. Volunteers.

Harrison Olmstead.
Jno. Owen, (Bitter Root.)
James O'Neill.
J. B. Buker, M. D.
George W. Elber.
A. A. Spalding, assistant interpreter.
Perrin B. Whitman, interpreter for the council.

TREATY WITH THE EASTERN SHOSHONI, 1863.

July 2, 1863.

18 Stats., 685.
Ratified Mar. 7, 1864.
Proclaimed June 7, 1869.

Articles of Agreement made at Fort Bridger, in Utah Territory, this second day of July, A. D. one thousand eight hundred and sixty-three, by and between the United States of America, represented by its Commissioners, and the Shoshone nation of Indians, represented by its Chiefs and Principal Men And Warriors of the Eastern Bands, as follows:

ARTICLE 1.

Friendly relations reestablished; perpetual peace.

Friendly and amically relations are hereby re-established between the bands of the Shoshonee nation, parties hereto, and the United States; and it is declared that a firm and perpetual peace shall be henceforth maintained between the Shoshonee nation and the United States.

ARTICLE 2.

Routes of travel; safety of travelers; settlements and posts; offenders.

The several routes of travel through the Shoshonee country, now or hereafter used by white men, shall be and remain forever free and safe for the use of the government of the United States, and of all emigrants and travellers under its authority and Protection, without molestation or injury from any of the people of the said nation. And if depredations should at any time be committed by bad men of their nation, the offenders shall be immediately seized and delivered up to the proper officers of the United States, to be punished as their offences shall deserve; and the safety of all travellers passing peaceably over said routes is hereby guaranteed by said nation. Military agricultural settlements and military posts may be established by the President of the United States along said routes; ferries may be maintained over the rivers wherever they may be required; and houses erected and settlements formed at such points as may be necessary for the comfort and convenience of travellers.

ARTICLE 3.

The telegraph and overland stage lines having been established and operated through a part of the Shoshonee country, it is expressly agreed that the same may be continued without hindrance, molestation, or injury from the people of said nation; and that their property, and the lives of passengers in the stages, and of the employes of the respective companies, shall be protected by them. *Telegraph and overland stage lines.*

And further, it being understood that provision has been made by the Government of the United States for the construction of a railway from the plains west to the Pacific ocean, it is stipulated by said nation that said railway, or its branches, may be located, constructed, and operated, without molestation from them, through any portion of the country claimed by them. *Railway.*

ARTICLE 4.

It is understood the boundaries of the Shoshonee country, as defined and described by said nation, is as follows: On the north, by the mountains on the north side of the valley of Shoshonee or Snake River; on the east, by the Wind River mountains, Peenahpah river, the north fork of Platte or Koo-chin-agah, and the north Park or Buffalo House; and on the south, by Yampah river and the Uintah mountains. The western boundary is left undefined, there being no Shoshonees from that district of country present; but the bands now present claim that their own country is bounded on the west by Salt Lake. *Boundaries of Shoshoni country.*

ARTICLE 5.

The United States being aware of the inconvenience resulting to the Indians in consequence of the driving away and destruction of game along the routes travelled by whites, and by the formation of agricultural and mining settlements, are willing to fairly compensate them for the same; therefore, and in consideration of the preceding stipulations, the United States promise and agree to pay to the bands of the Shoshonee nation, parties hereto, annually for the term of twenty years, the sum of ten thousand dollars, in such articles as the President of the United States may deem suitable to their wants and condition, either as hunters or herdsmen. And the said bands of the Shoshonee nation hereby acknowledge the reception of the said stipulated annuities, as a full compensation and equivalent for the loss of game, and the rights and privileges hereby conceded. *Annuity: acceptance as a compensation for loss of game.*

ARTICLE 6.

The said bands hereby acknowledge that they have received from said Commissioners provisions and clothing amounting to six thousand dollars, as presents, at the conclusion of this treaty. *Presents acknowledged.*

ARTICLE 7.

Nothing herein contained shall be construed or taken to admit any other or greater title or interest in the lands embraced within the territories described in said Treaty with said tribes or bands of Indians than existed in them upon the acquisition of said territories from Mexico by the laws thereof. *Amendment.*

S. Doc. 319, 58–2, vol 2——54

Done at Fort Bridger the day and year above written.

James Duane Doty,
Luther Mann, jr.,
   Commissioners.
Washakee, his x mark.
Wanapitz, his x mark.
Toopsapowet, his x mark.
Pantoshiga, his x mark.
Ninabitzee, his x mark.
Narkawk, his x mark.
Taboonshea, his x mark.
Weerango, his x mark.
Tootsahp, his x mark.
Weeahyukee, his x mark.
Bazile, his x mark.

In the presence of—
 Jack Robertson, interpreter.
 Samuel Dean.

TREATY WITH THE SHOSHONI—NORTHWESTERN BANDS, 1863.

July 30, 1863.

13 Stats., 663.
Ratified Mar. 7, 1864.
Proclaimed Jan. 17, 1865.

Articles of agreement made at Box Elder, in Utah Territory, this thirtieth day of July, A. D. one thousand eight hundred and sixty-three, by and between the United States of America, represented by Brigadier-General P. Edward Connor, commanding the military district of Utah, and James Duane Doty, commissioner, and the northwestern bands of the Shoshonee Indians, represented by their chiefs and warriors:

Peace and friendship. ARTICLE 1. It is agreed that friendly and amicable relations shall be re-established between the bands of the Shoshonee Nation, parties hereto, and the United States, and it is declared that a firm and perpetual peace shall be henceforth maintained between the said bands and the United States.

Treaty of Fort Bridger assented to. ARTICLE 2. The treaty concluded at Fort Bridger on the 2nd day of July, 1863, between the United States and the Shoshonee Nation, being read and fully interpreted and explained to the said chiefs and warriors, they do hereby give their full and free assent to all of the provisions of said treaty, and the same are hereby adopted as a part of this agreement, and the same shall be binding upon the parties hereto.

Annuity increased. ARTICLE 3. In consideration of the stipulations in the preceding articles, the United States agree to increase the annuity to the Shoshonee Nation five thousand dollars, to be paid in the manner provided in said treaty. And the said northwestern bands hereby acknowledge **Receipt.** to have received of the United States, at the signing of these articles, provisions and goods to the amount of two thousand dollars, to relieve their immediate necessities, the said bands having been reduced by the war to a state of utter destitution.

Boundary of Pokatello's country. ARTICLE 4. The country claimed by Pokatello, for himself and his people, is bounded on the west by Raft River and on the east by the Porteneuf Mountains.

ARTICLE 5. Nothing herein contained shall be construed or taken to admit any other or greater title or interest in the lands embraced within the territories described in said treaty in said tribes or bands of Indians than existed in them upon the acquisition of said territories from Mexico by the laws thereof.

Done at Box Elder, this thirtieth day of July, A. D. 1863.

  James Duane Doty,
     Governor and acting superintendent of Indian
      affairs in Utah Territory.

  P. Edw. Connor,
     Brigadier-General U. S. Volunteers, commanding
      District of Utah.

  Pokatello, his x mark, chief.
  Toomontso, his x mark, chief.
  Sanpitz, his x mark, chief.
  Tosowitz, his x mark, chief.
  Yahnoway, his x mark, chief.
  Weerahsoop, his x mark, chief.
  Pahragoosahd, his x mark, chief.
  Tahkwetoonah, his x mark, chief.
  Omashee, (John Pokatello's brother,) his x mark, chief.

Witnesses:
  Robt. Pollock, colonel Third Infantry, C. V.
  M. G. Lewis, captain Third Infantry, C. V.
  S. E. Jocelyn, first lieutenant Third Infantry, C. V.
  Jos. A. Gebone, Indian interpreter.
  John Barnard, jr., his x mark, special interpreter.
  Willis H. Boothe, special interpreter.
  Horace Wheat.

TREATY WITH THE WESTERN SHOSHONI, 1863.

Treaty of Peace and Friendship made at Ruby Valley, in the Territory of Nevada, this first day of October, A. D. one thousand eight hundred and sixty-three, between the United States of America, represented by the undersigned commissioners, and the Western Bands of the Shoshonee Nation of Indians, represented by their Chiefs and Principal Men and Warriors, as follows:

Oct. 1, 1863.

18 Stats., 689.
Ratified June 26, 1866.
Proclaimed Oct. 21, 1869.

ARTICLE 1.

Peace established; depredations to cease.

Peace and friendship shall be hereafter established and maintained between the Western Bands of the Shoshonee nation and the people and Government of the United States; and the said bands stipulate and agree that hostilities and all depredations upon the emigrant trains, the mail and telegraph lines, and upon the citizens of the United States within their country, shall cease.

ARTICLE 2.

Routes of travel; offenders; safety of travelers.

The several routes of travel through the Shoshonee country, now or hereafter used by white men, shall be forever free, and unobstructed by the said bands, for the use of the government of the United States, and of all emigrants and travellers under its authority and protection, without molestation or injury from them. And if depredations are at any time committed by bad men of their nation, the offenders shall be immediately taken and delivered up to the proper officers of the United States, to be punished as their offences shall deserve; and the safety of all travellers passing peaceably over either of said routes is hereby guarantied by said bands.

Military posts; stations.

Military posts may be established by the President of the United States along said routes or elsewhere in their country; and station houses may be erected and occupied at such points as may be necessary for the comfort and convenience of travellers or for mail or telegraph companies.

ARTICLE 3.

Telegraph and overland stage lines. The telegraph and overland stage lines having been established and operated by companies under the authority of the United States through a part of the Shoshonee country, it is expressly agreed that the same may be continued without hindrance, molestation, or injury from the people of said bands, and that their property and the lives and property of passengers in the stages and of the employes of the respective companies, shall be protected by them. And further, it being understood that provision has been made by the government of the United *Railway.* States for the construction of a railway from the plains west to the Pacific ocean, it is stipulated by the said bands that the said railway or its branches may be located, constructed, and operated, and without molestation from them, through any portion of country claimed or occupied by them.

ARTICLE 4.

Explorations, mines, settlements, use of timber. It is further agreed by the parties hereto, that the Shoshonee country may be explored and prospected for gold and silver, or other minerals; and when mines are discovered, they may be worked, and mining and agricultural settlements formed, and ranches established whenever they may be required. Mills may be erected and timber taken for their use, as also for building and other purposes in any part of the country claimed by said bands.

ARTICLE 5.

Boundaries of western bands of Shoshoni. It is understood that the boundaries of the country claimed and occupied by said bands are defined and described by them as follows: On the north by Wong-goga-da Mountains and Shoshonee River Valley; on the west by Su-non-to-yah Mountains or Smith Creek Mountains; on the south by Wi-co-bah and the Colorado Desert; on the east by Po-ho-no-be Valley or Steptoe Valley and Great Salt Lake Valley.

ARTICLE 6.

Reservations may be established. The said bands agree that whenever the President of the United States shall deem it expedient for them to abandon the roaming life, which, they now lead, and become herdsmen or agriculturalists, he is hereby authorized to make such reservations for their use as he may deem necessary within the country above described; and they do also hereby agree to remove their camps to such reservations as he may indicate, and to reside and remain therein.

ARTICLE 7.

Annuity, acceptance of, as compensation for loss of game. The United States, being aware of the inconvenience resulting to the Indians in consequence of the driving away and destruction of game along the routes travelled by white men, and by the formation of agricultural and mining settlements, are willing to fairly compensate them for the same; therefore, and in consideration of the preceding stipulations, and of their faithful observance by the said bands, the United States promise and agree to pay to the said bands of the Shoshonee nation parties hereto, annually for the term of twenty years, the sum of five thousand dollars in such articles, including cattle for herding or other purposes, as the President of the United States shall deem suitable for their wants and condition, either as hunters or herdsmen. And the said bands hereby acknowledge the reception of the said stipulated annuities as a full compensation and equivalent for the loss of game and the rights and privileges hereby conceded.

ARTICLE 8.

The said bands hereby acknowledge that they have received from Presents acknowledged. said commissioners provisions and clothing amounting to five thousand dollars as presents at the conclusion of this treaty.

Done at Ruby Valley the day and year above written.

James W. Nye.
James Duane Doty.

Te-moak, his x mark.	Po-on-go-sah, his x mark.
Mo-ho-a.	Par-a-woat-ze, his x mark.
Kirk-weedgwa, his x mark.	Ga-ha-dier, his x mark.
To-nag, his x mark.	Ko-ro-kout-ze, his x mark.
To-so-wee-so-op, his x mark.	Pon-ge-mah, his x mark.
Sow-er-e-gah, his x mark.	Buck, his x mark.

Witnesses:

    J. B. Moore, lieutenant-colonel Third Infantry California Volunteers.
    Jacob T. Lockhart, Indian agent Nevada Territory.
    Henry Butterfield, interpreter.

TREATY WITH THE CHIPPEWA—RED LAKE AND PEMBINA BANDS, 1863.

Articles of a treaty made and concluded at the Old Crossing of Red Lake River, in the State of Minnesota, on the second day of October, in the year eighteen hundred and sixty-three, between the United States of America, by their commissioners, Alexander Ramsey and Ashley C. Morrill, agent for the Chippewa Indians, and the Red Lake and Pembina bands of Chippewas; by their chiefs, head-men, and warriors.

Oct. 2. 1863.

13 Stats., 667.
Ratified Mar. 1, 1864.
Proclaimed May 5, 1864.

ARTICLE 1. The peace and friendship now existing between the Perpetual peace and friendship. United States and the Red Lake and Pembina bands of Chippewa Indians shall be perpetual.

ARTICLE 2. The said Red Lake and Pembina bands of Chippewa Lands ceded to the United States. Indians do hereby cede, sell, and convey to the United States all their right, title, and interest in and to all the lands now owned and claimed by them in the State of Minnesota and in the Territory of Dakota within the following described boundaries, to wit: Beginning at the Boundaries point where the international boundary between the United States and the British possessions intersects the shore of the Lake of the Woods; thence in a direct line southwesterly to the head of Thief River; thence down the main channel of said Thief River to its mouth on the Red Lake River; thence in a southeasterly direction, in a direct line toward the head of Wild Rice River, to the point where such line would intersect the northwestern boundary of a tract ceded to the United States by a treaty concluded at Washington on the 22d day of February, in the year eighteen hundred and fifty-five, with the Mississippi, Pillager, and Lake Winnebigoshish bands of Chippewa Indians; thence along the said boundary-line of the said cession to the mouth of Wild Rice River; thence up the main channel of the Red River to the mouth of the Shayenne; thence up the main channel of the Shayenne River to Poplar Grove; thence in a direct line to the Place of Stumps, otherwise called Lake Chicot; thence in a direct line to the head of the main branch of Salt River; thence in a direct line due north to the point where such line would intersect the international boundary aforesaid; thence eastwardly along said boundary to the place of beginning.

ARTICLE 3. In consideration of the foregoing cession, the United Payment for lands ceded. States agree to pay to the said Red Lake and Pembina bands of Chippewa Indians the following sums, to wit: Twenty thousand dollars per annum for twenty years; the said sum to be distributed among the

Chippewa Indians of the said bands in equal amounts per capita, and for this purpose an accurate enumeration and enrollment of the members of the respective bands and families shall be made by the officers of the United States: *Provided*, That so much of this sum as the President of the United States shall direct, not exceeding five thousand dollars per year, may be reserved from the above sum, and applied to agriculture, education, the purchase of goods, powder, lead, &c., for their use, and to such other beneficial purposes, calculated to promote the prosperity and happiness of the said Chippewa Indians, as he may prescribe.

Proviso.

Amount reserved.

Amnesty for past offenses.

ARTICLE 4. And in further consideration of the foregoing cession, and of their promise to abstain from such acts in future, the United States agree that the said Red Lake and Pembina bands of Chippewa Indians shall not be held liable to punishment for past offences. And in order to make compensation to the injured parties for the depredations committed by the said Indians on the goods of certain British and American traders at the mouth of Red Lake River, and for exactions forcibly levied by them on the proprietors of the steamboat plying on the Red River, and to enable them to pay their just debts, the United States agree to appropriate the sum of one hundred thousand dollars, it being understood and agreed that the claims of individuals for damages or debt under this article shall be ascertained and audited, in consultation with the chiefs of said bands, by a commissioner or commissioners appointed by the President of the United States; furthermore, the sum of two thousand dollars shall be expended for powder, lead, twine, or such other beneficial purposes as the chiefs may request, to be equitably distributed among the said bands at the first payment: *Provided*, That no part of the sum of one hundred thousand dollars shall be appropriated or paid to make compensation for damages or for the payment of any debts owing from said Indians until the said commissioner or commissioners shall report each case, with the proofs thereof, to the Secretary of the Interior, to be submitted to Congress, with his opinion thereon, for its action; and that, after such damages and debts shall have been paid, the residue of said sum shall be added to the annuity funds of said Indians, to be divided equally upon said annuities.

Appropriation for former depredations.

Claims, how to be audited.

Appropriation for powder, lead, etc.

ARTICLE 5. To encourage and aid the chiefs of said bands in preserving order and inducing, by their example and advice, the members of their respective bands to adopt the habits and pursuits of civilized life, there shall be paid to each of the said chiefs annually, out of the annuities of the said bands, a sum not exceeding one hundred and fifty dollars, to be determined by their agents according to their respective merits. And for the better promotion of the above objects, a further sum of five hundred dollars shall be paid at the first payment to each of the said chiefs to enable him to build for himself a house. Also, the sum of five thousand dollars shall be appropriated by the United States for cutting out a road from Leach Lake to Red Lake.

Appropriation to encourage the adoption of habits of civilized life.

For road from Leach Lake to Red Lake.

ARTICLE 6. The President shall appoint a board of visitors, to consist of not less than two nor more than three persons, to be selected from such Christian denominations as he may designate, whose duty it shall be to attend at all annuity payments of the said Chippewa Indians, to inspect their field and other improvements, and to report annually thereon on or before the first day of November, and also as to the qualifications and moral deportment of all persons residing upon the reservation under the authority of law; and they shall receive for their services five dollars a day for the time actually employed, and ten cents per mile for travelling expenses: *Provided*, That no one shall be paid in any one year for more than twenty days' service or for more than three hundred miles' travel.

Board of visitors, their appointment; duty, pay.

ARTICLE 7. The laws of the United States now in force, or that may hereafter be enacted, prohibiting the introduction and sale of spirituous

Spirituous liquors prohibited.

liquors in the Indian country, shall be in full force and effect throughout the country hereby ceded, until otherwise directed by Congress or the President of the United States.

ARTICLE 8. In further consideration of the foregoing cession, it is hereby agreed that the United States shall grant to each male adult half-breed or mixed-blood who is related by blood to the said Chippewas of the said Red Lake or Pembina bands who has adopted the habits and customs of civilized life, and who is a citizen of the United States, a homestead of one hundred and sixty acres of land, to be selected at his option, within the limits of the tract of country hereby ceded to the United States, on any land not previously occupied by actual settlers or covered by prior grants, the boundaries thereof to be adjusted in conformity with the lines of the official surveys when the same shall be made, and with the laws and regulations of the United States affecting the location and entry of the same: *Provided*, That no scrip shall be issued under the provisions of this article, and no assignments shall be made of any right, title, or interest at law or in equity until a patent shall issue, and no patent shall be issued until due proof of five years' actual residence and cultivation, as required by the act entitled "An act to secure homesteads on the public domain."

Grant of 160 acres of land to certain of these Indians.

ARTICLE 9. Upon the urgent request of the Indians, parties to this treaty, there shall be set apart from the tract hereby ceded a reservation of (640) six hundred and forty acres near the mouth of Thief River for the chief "Moose Dung," and a like reservation of (640) six hundred and forty acres for the chief "Red Bear," on the north side of Pembina River.

Reservations of 640 acres each for the chiefs Moose Dung and Red Bear.

In witness whereof, the said Alexander Ramsey and Ashley C. Morrill, commissioners on the part of the United States, and the chiefs, headmen, and warriors of the Red Lake and Pembina bands of Chippewa Indians, have hereunto set their hands, at the Old Crossing of Red Lake River, in the State of Minnesota, this second day of October, in the year of our Lord one thousand eight hundred and sixty-three.

Alex. Ramsey,
Ashley C. Morrill,
Commissioners.

Mons-o-mo, his x mark, Moose Dung, Chief of Red Lake.

Kaw-wash-ke-ne-kay, his x mark, Crooked Arm, Chief of Red Lake.

Ase-e-ne-wub, his x mark, Little Rock, Chief of Red Lak(e).

Mis-co-muk-quoh, his x mark, Red Bear, Chief of Pembina.

Ase-anse, his x mark, Little Shell, Chief of Pembina.

Mis-co-co-noy-a, his x mark, Red Rob, Warrior of Red Lake.

Ka-che-un-ish-e-naw-bay, his x mark, The Big Indian, Warrior of Red Lake.

Neo-ki-zhick, his x mark, Four Skies, Warrior of Red Lake.

Nebene-quin-gwa-hawegaw, his x mark, Summer Wolverine, Warrior of Pembina.

Joseph Gornon, his x mark, Warrior of Pembina.

Joseph Montreuil, his x mark, Warrior of Pembina.

Teb-ish-ke-ke-shig, his x mark, Warrior of Pembina.

May-shue-e-yaush, his x mark, Dropping Wind, Head Warrior of Red Lake.

Min-du-wah-wing, his x mark, Berry Hunter, Warrior of Red Lake.

Naw-gaun-e-gwan-abe, his x mark, Leading Feather, Chief of Red Lake.

Signed in presence of—

Paul H. Beaulieu, special interpreter.

Peter Roy,

T. A. Warren, United States interpreter.

J. A. Wheelock, secretary.

Reuben Ottman, secretary.

George A. Camp, major Eighth Regiment Minnesota Volunteers.

William T. Rockwood, Captain Company K, Eighth Regiment Minnesota Volunteers.

P. B. Davy, Captain Company L, First Regiment Minnesota Mounted Rangers.

G. M. Dwelle, Second Lieutenant Third Minnesota Battery.

F. Rieger, Surgeon Eighth Regiment Minnesota Volunteers.

L. S. Kidder, First Lieutenant Company L, First Minnesota Mounted Rangers.

Sam. B. Abbe.

C. A. Kuffer.

Pierre x Bottineau.

TREATY WITH THE UTAH—TABEGUACHE BAND, 1863.

Oct. 7, 1863.

13 Stat., 673.
Ratified Mar. 25, 1864.
Proclaimed Dec. 14, 1864.

Whereas the Tabeguache band of Utah Indians claim as against all other Indian tribes an exclusive right to the following-described country as their lands and hunting grounds within the territory of the United States of America, being bounded and described as follows, to wit:

Boundaries of land, etc.

"Beginning on the 37th degree of north latitude, at the eastern base of the Sierra Madre Mountain; running thence northerly with the base of the Rocky Mountains to the forty-first parallel of north latitude: thence west with the line of said forty-first parallel of north latitude to its intersection with the summit of the Snowy range northwest of the North Park; thence with the summit of the Snowy range southerly to the Rabbit-Ear Mountains; thence southerly with the summit of said Rabbit-Ear range of Mountains, west of the Middle Park, to the Grand River; thence with the said Grand River to its confluence with the Gunnison River; thence with the said Gunnison River to the mouth of the Uncompahgre River; thence with the said Uncompahgre River to its source in the summit of the Snowy range, opposite the source of the Rio Grande del Norte; thence in a right line south to the summit of the Sierra La Plata range of mountains, dividing the waters of the San Juan River from those of the Rio Grande del Norte; thence with the summit of said range southeasterly to the thirty-seventh parallel of north latitude; thence with the line of said parallel of latitude to the place of beginning:"

The President of the United States of America, by John Evans, governor of Colorado Territory, and *ex-officio* superintendent of Indian affairs for the same; Michael Steck, superintendent of Indian affairs for the Territory of New Mexico; Simeon Whiteley and Lafayette Head, Indian agents, duly authorized and appointed as commissioners for the purpose, of the one part, and the undersigned chiefs and warriors of the Tabeguache band of Utah Indians, of the other part, have made and entered into the following treaty, which, when ratified by the President of the United States, by and with the advice and consent of the Senate, shall be binding on both parties, to wit:

Authority of the United States admitted.

ARTICLE 1. It is admitted by the Tabeguache band of Utah Indians that they reside within the territorial limits of the United States, acknowledging their supremacy, and claim their protection. The said band also admits the right of the United States to regulate all trade and intercourse with them.

Cession of lands.

ARTICLE 2. Said Tabeguache band of Utah Indians hereby cede, convey, and relinquish all of their claims, right, title, and interest in and to any and all lands within the territory of the United States, wherever situated, excepting that which is included within the following boundaries, which are hereby reserved as their hunting-grounds, viz:

Boundary.

Beginning at the mouth of the Uncompahgre River; thence down Gunnison River to its confluence with Bunkara River; thence up the Bunkara River to the Roaring Fork of the same; thence up the Roaring Fork to its source; thence along the summit of the range dividing the waters of the Arkansas from those of the Gunnison River to its intersection with the range dividing the waters of the San Luis Valley from those of the Gunnison's Fork of the Great Colorado River; thence along the summit of said range to the source of the Uncompahgre River; thence from said source and down the main channel of said Uncompahgre River to its mouth, the place of beginning. Nothing contained in this treaty shall be construed or taken to admit on the part of the United States any other or greater title or interest in the lands above excepted and reserved in said tribe or band of Indians than existed in them upon the acquisition of said Territory from Mexico by the laws thereof.

ARTICLE 3. And it is further agreed that the United States shall have the right to establish one or more military posts, with their needful reservations, upon the lands and hunting-grounds not ceded by the Tabeguache band in this treaty; also the right to locate, construct, and maintain railroads and other roads and highways through the same, and along routes of United States mail-lines, at suitable points, to establish and maintain stations. *Military posts may be established on lands not ceded.*

Any citizen of the United States may mine, without interference or molestation, in any part of the country hereby reserved to said Indians where gold or other metals or minerals may be found. *Mining.*

ARTICLE 4. And the said Tabeguache band hereby gives its consent that the Mohuache band of Utah Indians may also be settled with them upon the lands and hunting-grounds reserved in this treaty. *Mohuache band of Utahs.*

ARTICLE 5. And the said Tabeguache band further agrees to give safe-conduct to all persons who may be legally authorized by the United States to pass through their reservation, and to protect in their persons and property all agents or other persons sent by the United States to reside temporarily among them. *Protection to be given to certain persons.*

ARTICLE 6. That the friendship which is now established between the United States and the Tabeguache band of Utah Indians should not be interrupted by the misconduct of individuals, it is hereby agreed that for injuries done no private revenge or retaliation shall take place, but, instead thereof, complaint shall be made by the party injured to the superintendent or agent of Indian affairs, or other person appointed by the President. And it shall be the duty of the chiefs of said Tabeguache band, upon complaint being made as aforesaid, to deliver up the person or persons against whom the complaint is made, to the end that he or they may be punished agreeably to the laws of the United States. And in like manner, if any robbery, violence, or murder shall be committed on any Indian or Indians belonging to said band, the person or persons so offending shall be tried, and if found guilty, shall be punished in like manner as if the injury had been done to a white man. And it is agreed that the chiefs of said Tabeguache band shall, to the utmost of their power, exert themselves to recover horses or other property which may be stolen or taken from any citizen or citizens or white residents of the United States by any individual or individuals of said band; and the property so recovered shall be forthwith delivered to the agents or other persons authorized to receive it, that it may be restored to the proper owner. And for such property as any Indian or Indians belonging to said band may have taken from citizens or white residents of the United States which cannot be restored, payment shall be reserved from the annuities which the said band is to receive, upon sufficient proof of the fact. And the United States hereby guarantee to any Indian or Indians of said band a full indemnification for any horses or other property which may be stolen from them by any of their citizens or white residents: *Provided,* That the property so stolen cannot be recovered, and that sufficient proof is produced that it was actually stolen by a citizen or white resident of the United States. And the said Tabeguache band engages, on the requisition or demand of the President of the United States, or of the agents, to deliver up any white man resident among them. *Redress of injuries.* *Delivery of offenders.* *Recovery of stolen property.* *Surrender of white men.*

ARTICLE 7. And the chiefs and warriors as aforesaid promise and engage their band will never, by sale, exchange, or as presents, supply any nation or tribe of Indians, not in amity with the United States, with guns, ammunition, or other implements of war. *Munitions of war.*

ARTICLE 8. For the period of ten years the said band shall receive, annually, by such distribution as the Secretary of the Interior may direct, ten thousand dollars' worth of goods, and also ten thousand dollars' worth of provisions. *Annuity.*

Horses.

ARTICLE 9. For the purpose of improving their breed of horses, the band shall receive five American stallions the first year after the ratification of this treaty.

Donations of stock.

ARTICLE 10. That in case the chiefs of said band shall announce to the agent a willingness and determination on their part, and on the part of their people, to begin and follow agricultural or pastoral pursuits by farming or raising stock, and growing wool upon such lands to be selected and set apart within said reservation, and according to such regulations as the Secretary of the Interior may prescribe, they shall receive the following donations of stock to aid them in their endeavor to gain a livelihood by such new pursuits, viz:

Of cattle, not exceeding one hundred and fifty head annually during five years, beginning with the ratification of this treaty.

Of sheep, not exceeding one thousand head annually during the first two years after the ratification of this treaty, and five hundred head annually during the three years thereafter.

The Secretary of the Interior may also direct that their share of annuity goods and provisions shall be of a character suited to such change of life: *Provided, however,* That such stock shall only be donated as long as such chiefs shall in good faith keep and use the same for the purpose indicated in this article, and provided that the amount expended under this article shall not exceed ten thousand dollars annually.

All the Indians of said band who may adopt and conform to the provisions of this article shall be protected in the quiet and peaceable possession of their said lands and property.

Blacksmith and shop.

The Government also agrees to establish and maintain a blacksmith-shop, and employ a competent blacksmith, for the purpose of repairing the guns and agricultural implements which may be used by said band of Indians.

Signatures.

In testimony whereof, the said commissioners, as aforesaid, and the said chiefs and warriors of the Tabeguache band of Utah Indians, have hereunto set their hands and seals, at the Tabeguache agency, at Conejos, Colorado Territory, on this the seventh day of October, in the year of our Lord one thousand eight hundred and sixty-three.

> Jno. Evans,　　　　[SEAL.]
> Governor C. T., Superintendent Indian
> Affairs, and Commissioner.
>
> M. Steck,　　　　[SEAL.]
> Superintendent Indian Affairs New Mexico
> and Commissioner.
>
> Simeon Whiteley,　　[SEAL.]
> U. S. Agent to the Grand River and Uintah
> Bands of Utah Indians and Commissioner.
>
> Lafayette Head,　　[SEAL.]
> U. S. Indian Agent and Commissioner.

Un-cow-ra-gut, or Red Color, his x mark.　　[SEAL.]
Sha-wa-she-yet, or Blue Flower, his x mark.　[SEAL.]
Colorado, his x mark.　　　　　　　　　　[SEAL.]
U-ray, or Arrow, his x mark.　　　　　　　[SEAL.]
No-va-ve-tu quar-et, or One that Slides under
　the Snow, his x mark.　　　　　　　　　[SEAL.]
Sa-wa-wat-se-wich, or Blue River, his x mark.　[SEAL.]
A-ca-mu-che-ne, or Red Wind, his x mark.　　[SEAL.]
Mu-chu-chop, or Lock of Hair, his x mark.　　[SEAL.]
Sa-patch, or White Warm, his x mark.　　　[SEAL.]
Cinche, or Left Hand.　　　　　　　　　　[SEAL.]

Witnesses to the treaty:

Jno. G. Nicolay, Secretary to the Commission.

Chas. E. Phillips, Assistant Secretary to Commission.

J. W. Chroughton, Colonel First Cavalry of Colorado, Commanding District.

Samuel F. Tappan, Lieutenant-Colonel First Cavalry of Colorado.

Charles Kerber, Captain, First Cavalry of Colorado.

J. P. Benesteel, Captain, First Cavalry of Colorado.

Interpreters:

Juan V. Valdes.

Bernardo Sanchez, his x mark.

Amador Sanchez, his x mark.

TREATY WITH THE SHOSHONI-GOSHIP, 1863.

Treaty of peace and friendship made at Tuilla Valley, in the Territory of Utah, this twelfth day of October, A. D. one thousand eight hundred and sixty-three, between the United States of America, represented by the undersigned commissioners, and the Shoshonee-Goship bands of Indians, represented by their chiefs, principal men, and warriors, as follows:

Oct. 12, 1863.

13 Stats., 681.
Ratified Mar. 7, 1864
Proclaimed Jan. 17, 1865.

ARTICLE 1. Peace and friendship is hereby established and shall be hereafter maintained between the Shoshonee-Goship bands of Indians and the citizens and Government of the United States; and the said bands stipulate and agree that hostilities and all depredations upon the emigrant trains, the mail and telegraph lines, and upon the citizens of the United States, within their country, shall cease. *Peace and friendship.*

ARTICLE 2. It is further stipulated by said bands that the several routes of travel through their country now or hereafter used by white men shall be forever free and unobstructed by them, for the use of the Government of the United States, and of all emigrants and travellers within it under its authority and protection, without molestation or injury from them. And if depredations are at any time committed by bad men of their own or other tribes within their country, the offenders shall be immediately taken and delivered up to the proper officers of the United States, to be punished as their offences may deserve; and the safety of all travellers passing peaceably over either of said routes is hereby guaranteed by said bands. *Routes through their country to be free and peaceful.* *Surrender of offenders.*

Military posts may be established by the President of the United States along said routes, or elsewhere in their country; and station-houses may be erected and occupied at such points as may be necessary for the comfort and convenience of travellers or for the use of the mail or telegraph companies. *Military posts and station houses.*

ARTICLE 3. The telegraph and overland stage lines having been established and operated by companies under the authority of the United States through the country occupied by said bands, it is expressly agreed that the same may be continued without hindrance, molestation, or injury from the people of said bands, and that their property, and the lives and property of passengers in the stages, and of the employees of the respective companies, shall be protected by them. *Telegraph and overland stage lines.*

And further, it being understood that provision has been made by the Government of the United States for the construction of a railway from the plains west to the Pacific Ocean, it is stipulated by said bands that the said railway or its branches may be located, constructed, and operated, and without molestation from them, through any portion of the country claimed or occupied by them. *Railway and branches.*

Mines, mills, and ranches.

ARTICLE 4. It is further agreed by the parties hereto that the country of the Goship tribe may be explored and prospected for gold and silver, or other minerals and metals; and when mines are discovered they may be worked, and mining and agricultural settlements formed and ranchos established wherever they may be required. Mills may be erected and timber taken for their use, as also for building and other purposes, in any part of said country.

Timber.

Boundaries.

ARTICLE 5. It is understood that the boundaries of the country claimed and occupied by the Goship tribe, as defined and described by said bands, are as follows: On the north by the middle of the Great Desert; on the west by Steptoe Valley; on the south by Tooedoe or Green Mountains; and on the east by Great Salt Lake, Tuilla, and Rush Valleys.

Reservations.

ARTICLE 6. The said bands agree that whenever the President of the United States shall deem it expedient for them to abandon the roaming life which they now lead, and become settled as herdsmen or agriculturists, he is hereby authorized to make such reservations for their use as he may deem necessary; and they do also agree to remove their camps to such reservations as he may indicate, and to reside and remain thereon.

Residence thereon.

Annuities.

ARTICLE 7. The United States being aware of the inconvenience resulting to the Indians, in consequence of the driving away and destruction of game along the routes travelled by white men, and by the formation of agricultural and mining settlements, are willing to fairly compensate them for the same. Therefore, and in consideration of the preceding stipulations, and of their faithful observance by said bands, the United States promise and agree to pay to the said Goship tribe, or to the said bands, parties hereto, at the option of the President of the United States, annually, for the term of twenty years, the sum of one thousand dollars, in such articles, including cattle for herding or other purposes, as the President shall deem suitable for their wants and condition either as hunters or herdsmen. And the said bands, for themselves and for their tribe, hereby acknowledge the reception of the said stipulated annuities as a full compensation and equivalent for the loss of game and the rights and privileges hereby conceded; and also one thousand dollars in provisions and goods at and before the signing of this treaty.

Cattle.

Receipt.

ARTICLE 8. Nothing herein contained shall be construed or taken to admit any other or greater title or interest in the lands embraced within the territories described in said treaty in said tribes or bands of Indians than existed in them upon the acquisition of said territories from Mexico by the laws thereof.

James Duane Doty, commissioner.
P. Edw. Connor,
        Brigadier-General U. S. Volunteers,
               Commanding District of Utah.

Tabby,   his x mark.
Adaseim,   his x mark.
Tintsa-pa-ġin, his x mark.
Harray-nup,   his x mark.

Witnesses:—
  Amos Reed.
  Chas. H. Hempstead,
    captain and chief commissary district of Utah.
  William Lee, interpreter.
  Jos. A. Gebon, interpreter.

TREATY WITH THE CHIPPEWA—RED LAKE AND PEMBINA BANDS, 1864.

Articles supplementary to the treaty made and concluded at the Old Crossing of Red Lake River, in the State of Minnesota, on the second day of October, in the year eighteen hundred and sixty-three, between the United States of America, by their commissioners, Clark W. Thompson and Ashley C. Morrill, and the Red Lake and Pembina bands of Chippewa Indians, by their chiefs, head-men, and warriors, concluded at the city of Washington, District of Columbia, on the twelfth day of April, in the year eighteen hundred and sixty-four, between the United States, by the said commissioners, of the one part, and the said bands of the Chippewa Indians, by their chiefs, head-men, and warriors, of the other part.

Apr. 12, 1864.

13 Stat., 689.
Ratified Apr. 21, 1864.
Proclaimed Apr. 25, 1864.

ARTICLE 1. The said Red Lake and Pembina bands of Chippewa Indians do hereby agree and assent to the provisions of the said treaty, concluded at the Old Crossing of Red Lake River, as amended by the Senate of the United States by resolution bearing date the first of March, in the year eighteen hundred and sixty-four.

Assent to treaty of Oct. 2, 1863, as amended.

ARTICLE 2. In consideration of the cession made by said treaty, concluded at the Old Crossing of Red Lake River, and in lieu of the annuity payment provided for by the third article of said last-mentioned treaty, the United States will pay annually, during the pleasure of the President of the United States, to the Red Lake band of Chippewas the sum of ten thousand dollars, and to the Pembina band of Chippewas the sum of five thousand dollars, which said sums shall be distributed to the members of said bands, respectively, in equal amounts per capita, for which purpose an accurate enumeration and enrollment of the members of the respective bands shall be made by the officers of the United States.

Payment in lieu of annuity by former treaty.

ARTICLE 3. The United States will also expend annually, for the period of fifteen years, for the Red Lake band of Chippewas, for the purpose of supplying them with gilling-twine, cotton mater, calico, linsey, blankets, sheeting, flannels, provisions, farming-tools, and for such other useful articles, and for such other useful purposes as may be deemed for their best interests, the sum of eight thousand dollars; and will expend in like manner, and for a like period, and for like purposes, for the Pembina band of Chippewas, the sum of four thousand dollars.

Annual expenditures for blankets, provisions. etc.

ARTICLE 4. The United States also agree to furnish said bands of Indians, for the period of fifteen years, one blacksmith, one physician, one miller, and one farmer; and will also furnish them annually, during the same period, with fifteen hundred dollars' worth of iron, steel, and other articles for blacksmithing purposes, and one thousand dollars for carpentering, and other purposes.

Blacksmith, physician, miller, farmer, iron, steel. etc.

ARTICLE 5. The United States also agree to furnish for said Indians at some suitable point, to be determined by the Secretary of the Interior, a saw-mill with a run of millstones attached.

Sawmill and millstones.

ARTICLE 6. It is further agreed, by and between the parties hereto, that article four of the said treaty, concluded at the Old Crossing of Red Lake River, and the amendment to said article, shall be modified as follows: that is to say, twenty-five thousand dollars of the amount thereby stipulated shall be paid to the chiefs of said bands, through their agent, upon the ratification of these articles, or so soon thereafter as practicable, to enable them to purchase provisions and clothing, presents to be distributed to their people upon their return to their homes; of which amount five thousand dollars shall be expended for the benefit of their chief, May-dwa-gwa-no-nind; and that from the remaining seventy-five thousand dollars the claims of injured parties for depredations committed by said Indians on the goods of certain

Modification of article 4 of former treaty.

British and American traders at the mouth of Red Lake River, and for exactions forcibly levied by them on the proprietors of the steamboat plying on the Red River, shall have priority of payment, and be paid in full, and the remainder thereof shall be paid pro rata upon the debts of said tribe incurred since the first day of January, in the year eighteen hundred and fifty-nine, to be ascertained by their agent in connection with the chiefs, in lieu of the commissioner or commissioners provided for in the fourth article of said treaty concluded at the Old Crossing of Red Lake River.

Scrip to issue to mixed bloods in lieu of lands.

ARTICLE 7. It is further agreed by the parties hereto, that, in lieu of the lands provided for the mixed-bloods by article eight of said treaty, concluded at the Old Crossing of Red Lake River, scrip shall be issued to such of said mixed-bloods as shall so elect, which shall entitle the holder to a like amount of land, and may be located upon any of the lands ceded by said treaty, but not elsewhere, and shall be accepted by said mixed-bloods in lieu of all future claims for annuities.

In testimony whereof, the said commissioners, on behalf of the United States, and the said chiefs, headmen, and war[r]iors, on behalf of the Red Lake and Pembina bands of Chippewa Indians, have hereunto affixed their hands and seals this twelfth day of April, in the year eighteen hundred and sixty-four.

Clark W. Thompson, [SEAL.]
Ashley C. Morrill, [SEAL.]
Commissioners.

Principal Red Lake chief, May-dwa-gua-no-nind (He that is spoken to), his x mark, [SEAL.]
Red Lake chief, Mons-o-mo (Moose-dung), his x mark, [SEAL.]
Red Lake chief, Ase-e-ne-wub (Little Rock), his x mark, [SEAL.]
Principal Pembina chief, Mis-co-muk-quah (Red Bear), his x mark, [SEAL.]
Red Lake headman, Naw-gon-e-gwo-nabe (Leading Feather), his x mark, [SEAL.]
Red Lake war[r]ior, Que-we-zance (The Boy), his x mark, [SEAL.]
Red Lake headman, May-zha-ke-osh (Dropping Wind), his x mark, [SEAL.]
Red Lake headman, Bwa-ness (Little Shoe), his x mark, [SEAL.]
Red Lake headman, Wa-bon-e-

qua-osh (White Hair), his x mark, [SEAL.]
Pembina headman, Te-bish-co-ge-shick (Equal Sky), his x mark, [SEAL.]
Red Lake warrior, Te-besh-co-be-ness (Straight Bird), his x mark, [SEAL.]
Red Lake warrior, Osh-shay-o-sick (no interpretation), his x mark, [SEAL.]
Red Lake warrior, Sa-sa-goh-cum-ick-ish-cum (He that makes the ground tremble), his x mark, [SEAL.]
Red Lake warrior, Kay-tush-ke-wub-e-tung (no interpretation), his x mark, [SEAL.]
Pembina warrior, I-inge-e-gaun-abe, (Wants Feathers), his x mark, [SEAL.]
Red Lake warrior, Que-we-zance-ish (Bad Boy), his x mark, [SEAL.]

Signed in presence of—

P. H. Beaulieu, special interpreter.
J. G. Morrison, special interpreter.
Peter Roy, special interpreter.

T. A. Warren, United States interpreter.
Chas. E. Gardell.
Charles Botteneau.

TREATY WITH THE CHIPPEWA, MISSISSIPPI, AND PILLAGER AND LAKE WINNIBIGOSHISH BANDS, 1864.

May 7, 1864.

13 Stat., 693.
Ratified Feb. 9, 1865.
Proclaimed Mar. 20. 1865.

Articles of agreement and convention made and concluded at the city of Washington this seventh day of May, A. D. 1864, between William P. Dole, Commissioner of Indian Affairs, and Clark W. Thompson, superintendent of Indian affairs for the northern superintendency, on the part of the United States, and the Chippewa chief Hole-in-the-day, and Mis-qua-dace, for and on behalf of the Chippewas of the Mississippi, and Pillager and Lake Winnebagoshish bands of Chippewa Indians in Minnesota.

Gull Lake and other reservations ceded to the United States, except, etc.

ARTICLE 1. The reservations known as Gull Lake, Mille Lac, Sandy Lake, Rabbit Lake, Pokagomin Lake, and Rice Lake, as described in the second clause of the second article of the treaty with the Chippewas of the twenty-second of February, 1855, are hereby ceded to the United States, excepting one half section of land, including the mission buildings at Gull Lake, which is hereby granted in fee simple to the Reverend John Johnson, missionary, and one section of land, to be located by the Secretary of the Interior on the southeast side of Gull Lake, and which is hereby granted in fee simple to the chief Hole-in-the-day, and a section to chief Mis-qua-dace, at Sandy Lake, in like manner, and one section to chief Shaw-vosh-kung, at Mille Lac, in like manner.

Hole-in-the-day- Mis-qua-dace, Shaw, vosh-kung.

ARTICLE 2. In consideration of the foregoing cession, the United States agree to set apart, for the future home of the Chippewas of the Mississippi, all the lands embraced within the following-described boundaries, excepting the reservations made and described in the third clause of the second article of the said treaty of February 22d, 1855, for the Pillager and Lake Winnebagoshish bands; that is to say, beginning at a point one mile south of the most southerly point of Leach Lake, and running thence in an easterly course to a point one mile south of the most southerly point of Goose Lake, thence due east to a point due south from the intersection of the Pokagomin reservation and the Mississippi River, thence on the dividing-line between Deer River and lakes and Mashkordens River and lakes, until a point is reached north of the first-named river and lakes; thence in a direct line northwesterly to the outlet of Two Routs Lake, then in a southwesterly direction to Turtle Lake, thence southwesterly to the headwater of Rice River, thence northwesterly along the line of the Red Lake reservation to the mouth of Thief River, thence down the centre of the main channel of Red Lake River to a point opposite the mouth of Black River, thence southeasterly in a direct line with the outlet of Rice Lake to a point due west from the place of beginning, thence to the place of beginning.

Reservation for the Chippewa of the Mississippi.

Boundaries.

ARTICLE 3. In consideration of the foregoing cession to the United States, and the valuable improvements thereon, the United States further agree, first, to extend the present annuities of the Indians, parties to this treaty, for ten years beyond the periods respectively named in existing treaties; second, and to pay towards the settlement of the claims for depredations committed by said Indians in 1862, the sum of twenty thousand dollars; third, to the chiefs of the Chippewas of the Mississippi, ten thousand dollars, to be paid upon the ratification of this treaty; and five thousand dollars to the chief Hole-in-the-day, for depredations committed in burning his house and furniture in 1862.

Annuities to be extended for ten years.

Payment toward settlement for depredations, and to the chiefs.

ARTICLE 4. The United States further agree to pay seven thousand five hundred ($7,500) dollars for clearing, stumping, grubbing, breaking, and planting, on the reservation hereby set apart for the Chippewas of the Mississippi, in lots of not less than ten acres each, at such point or points as the Secretary of the Interior may select, as follows, viz: For the Gull Lake band, seventy (70) acres; for the Mille Lac band, seventy (70) acres; for the Sandy Lake band, fifty (50) acres; for the Pokagomin band, fifty (50) acres; for the Rabbit Lake band, forty (40) acres; for the Rice Lake band, twenty (20) acres; and to expend five thousand dollars ($5,000) in building for the chiefs of said bands one house each, under the direction of the Secretary of the Interior.

Payments for clearing, etc., lots in reservation.
See art. 14.

Houses for chiefs.

ARTICLE 5. The United States agree to furnish to said Indians, parties to this treaty, ten (10) yoke of good steady work oxen, and twenty log-chains annually for ten years, provided the Indians shall take proper care of and make proper use of the same; also for the same period annually two hundred (200) grubbing-hoes, ten (10) ploughs, ten (10) grindstones, one hundred (100) axes, handled, not to exceed in weight three and one-half pounds each, twenty (20) spades, and other farming implements, provided it shall not amount to more

Oxen, plows, and agricultural implements to be furnished.

Carpenters, blacksmiths, laborers, and physician.

than fifteen hundred dollars in one year; also two carpenters, and two blacksmiths, and four farm-laborers, and one physician.

Sawmill.

ARTICLE 6. The United States further agree to pay annually one thousand dollars ($1,000) towards the support of a sawmill to be built for the common use of the Chippewas of the Mississippi and the Red Lake and Pembina bands of Chippewa Indians, so long as the President of the United States may deem it necessary; and to expend in

Road, bridges, etc.
Buildings.

building a road, bridges, &c., to their new agency seven thousand five hundred dollars ($7,500;) and to expend for new agency buildings, to be located by the Secretary of the Interior for the common use of the Chippewas of the Mississippi, Red Lake, and Pembina, and Pillager and Lake Winnebagoshish bands of Chippewa Indians, twenty-five thousand dollars ($25,000.)

Board of visitors to be present at annuity payment, make inspection, and report annually.

ARTICLE 7. There shall be a board of visitors, to consist of not less than two nor more than five persons, to be selected from such Christian denomination or denominations as the chiefs in council may designate, whose duty it shall be to be present at all annuity payments to the Indians, whether of goods, moneys, provisions, or other articles, and to inspect the fields, buildings, mills, and other improvements made or to be made, and to report annually thereon, on or before the first day of November; and also as to the qualifications and moral deportment of all persons residing upon the reservation under the sanction of law or regulation, and they shall receive for their services five dollars per

Pay.

day for the time actually employed, and ten cents per mile for travelling expenses; *Provided*, That no one shall be paid in any one year for more than twenty days' service, or for more than three hundred miles' travel.

Chiefs with bands of less than fifty not to be recognized.

ARTICLE 8. No person shall be recognized as a chief whose band numbers less than fifty persons; and to encourage and aid the said chiefs in preserving order, and inducing by their example and advice, the members of their respective bands to adopt the pursuits of civilized life, there shall be paid to each of said chiefs annually out of the

Gratuities.

annuities of said bands, a sum not exceeding one hundred and fifty dollars, ($150,) to be determined by their agent according to their respective merits.

Agent, teachers, etc., to have families.

ARTICLE 9. To improve the morals and industrial habits of said Indians, it is agreed that no agent, teacher, interpreter, trader, or other employees shall be employed, appointed, licensed, or permitted to reside within the reservations belonging to the Indians, parties to this treaty, missionaries excepted, who shall not have a family residing with them at their respective places of employment or trade within the agency, whose moral habits and fitness shall be reported upon

Improper persons not to have benefits of treaties.

annually by the board of visitors; and no person of full or mixed blood, educated or partially educated, whose fitness, morally or otherwise, is not conducive to the welfare of said Indians, shall receive any benefit from this or any former treaties, and may be expelled from the reservation.

Payment of annuities.

ARTICLE 10. All annuities under this or former treaties shall be paid as the chiefs in council may request, with the approval of the Secretary of the Interior, until otherwise altered or amended, which shall be done whenever the board of visitors, by the requests of the chiefs, may recommend it: *Provided* That no change shall take place oftener than once in two years.

Preference given to full or mixed bloods as laborers.

ARTICLE 11. Whenever the services of laborers are required upon the reservation, preference shall be given to full or mixed bloods, if they shall be found competent to perform them.

Indians not to remove from present reservations until, etc.

ARTICLE 12. It shall not be obligatory upon the Indians, parties to this treaty, to remove from their present reservations until the United States shall have first complied with the stipulations of Articles IV and VI of this treaty, when the United States shall furnish them with all necessary transportation and subsistence to their new homes and subsistence for six months thereafter: *Provided*, That, owing to the heretofore good conduct of the Mille Lac Indians, they shall not be compelled to remove so long as they shall not in any way interfere with or in any manner molest the persons or property of the whites: *Provided*, That those of the tribe residing on the Sandy Lake reservation shall not be removed until the President shall so direct.

ARTICLE 13. Female members of the family of any government employe[e] residing on the reservation, who shall teach Indian girls domestic economy, shall be allowed and paid a sum not exceeding ten dollars per month while so engaged: *Provided*, That not more than one thousand dollars shall be so expended during any one year, and that the President of the United States may suspend or annul this article whenever he may deem it expedient to do so.

Certain females may be paid as teachers.

Proviso.

ARTICLE 14. It is distinctly understood and agreed that the clearing and breaking of land for the Chippewas of the Mississippi, as provided for in the fourth article of this treaty, shall be in lieu of all former engagements of the United States as to the breaking of lands for those bands, and that this treaty is in lieu of the treaty made by the same tribes, approved March 11th, 1863.

Provisions for clearing, etc., lands to be in lieu of former provisions.

In testimony whereof the said Wm. P. Dole and Clark W. Thompson, on behalf of the United States, and Chippewa chiefs, Hole-in-the-day and Mis-qua-dace, on behalf of Indians parties to this treaty, have hereunto set their hands and affixed their seals this seventh day of May, A. D. one thousand eight hundred and sixty-four.

  W. P. Dole, Commissioner Indian Affairs.   [SEAL.]
  Clark W. Thompson, Superintendent Indian Affairs. [SEAL.]
  Que-ze-zance, or Hole-in-the-day, his x mark.   [SEAL.]
  Mis-qua-dace, or Turtle, his x mark.   [SEAL.]

Signed in presence of
  Peter Roy, special interpreter.
  Benjn. Thompson.

TREATY WITH THE KLAMATH, ETC., 1864.

Articles of agreement and convention made and concluded at Klamath Lake, Oregon, on the fourteenth day of October, A. D. one thousand eight hundred and sixty-four, by J. W. Perit Huntington, superintendent of Indian affairs in Oregon, and William Logan, United States Indian agent for Oregon, on the part of the United States, and the chiefs and head-men of the Klamath and Moadoc tribes, and Yahooskin band of Snake Indians, hereinafter named, to wit, La-Lake, Chil-o-que-nas, Kellogue, Mo-ghen-kas-kit, Blow, Le-lu, Palmer, Jack, Que-as, Poo-sak-sult, Che-mult, No-ak-sum, Mooch-kat-allick, Toon-tuck-tee, Boos-ki-you, Ski-a-tic, Shol-las-loos, Ta-tet-pas, Muk-has, Herman-koos-mam, chiefs and head-men of the Klamaths; Schon-chin, Stat-it-ut, Keint-poos, Chuck-e-i-ox, chiefs and head-men of the Moadocs, and Kile-to-ak and Sky-te-ock-et, chiefs of the Yahooskin band of Snakes.

Oct. 14, 1864.
16 Stats., 707.
Ratified, July 2, 1866.
Proclaimed Feb. 17, 1870.

ARTICLE 1. The tribes of Indians aforesaid cede to the United States all their right, title, and claim to all the country claimed by them, the same being determined by the following boundaries, to wit: Beginning at the point where the forty fourth parallel of north latitude crosses the summit of the Cascade Mountains; thence following the main dividing-ridge of said mountains in a southerly direction to the ridge which separates the waters of Pitt and McCloud Rivers from the waters on the north; thence along said dividing-ridge in an easterly direction to the southern end of Goose Lake; thence northeasterly to the north-

Cession of lands to the United States.

Boundaries.

ern end of Harney Lake; thence due north to the forty-fourth parallel
of north latitude; thence west to the place of beginning: *Provided*,
That the following-described tract, within the country ceded by this
treaty, shall, until otherwise directed by the President of the United
States, be set apart as a residence for said Indians, [and] held and
regarded as an Indian reservation, to wit: Beginning upon the eastern
shore of the middle Klamath Lake, at the Point of Rocks, about twelve
miles below the mouth of Williamson's River; thence following up
said eastern shore to the mouth of Wood River; thence up Wood River
to a point one mile north of the bridge at Fort Klamath; thence due
east to the summit of the ridge which divides the upper and middle
Klamath Lakes; thence along said ridge to a point due east of the north
end of the upper lake; thence due east, passing the said north end of
the upper lake, to the summit of the mountains on the east side of the
lake; thence along said mountain to the point where Sprague's River
is intersected by the Ish-tish-ea-wax Creek; thence in a southerly
direction to the summit of the mountain, the extremity of which forms
the Point of Rocks; thence along said mountain to the place of beginning. And the tribes aforesaid agree and bind themselves that, immediately after the ratification of this treaty, they will remove to said
reservation and remain thereon, unless temporary leave of absence be
granted to them by the superintendent or agent having charge of the
tribes.

It is further stipulated and agreed that no white person shall be
permitted to locate or remain upon the reservation, except the Indian
superintendent and agent, employés of the Indian department, and
officers of the Army of the United States, and that in case persons
other than those specified are found upon the reservation, they shall
be immediately expelled therefrom; and the exclusive right of taking
fish in the streams and lakes, included in said reservation, and of
gathering edible roots, seeds, and berries within its limits, is hereby
secured to the Indians aforesaid: *Provided, also*, That the right of
way for public roads and railroads across said reservation is reserved
to citizens of the United States.

ARTICLE 2. In consideration of, and in payment for the country ceded
by this treaty, the United States agree to pay to the tribes conveying
the same the several sums of money hereinafter enumerated, to wit:
Eight thousand dollars per annum for a period of five years, commencing on the first day of October, eighteen hundred and sixty-five, or as
soon thereafter as this treaty may be ratified; five thousand dollars
per annum for the term of five years next succeeding the first period
of five years; and three thousand dollars per annum for the term of
five years next succeeding the second period; all of which several
sums shall be applied to the use and benefit of said Indians by the
superintendent or agent having charge of the tribes, under the direction of the President of the United States, who shall, from time to
time, in his discretion, determine for what objects the same shall be
expended, so as to carry out the design of the expenditure, [it] being
to promote the well-being of the Indians, advance them in civilization,
and especially agriculture, and to secure their moral improvement
and education.

ARTICLE 3. The United States agree to pay said Indians the additional sum of thirty-five thousand dollars, a portion whereof shall be
used to pay for such articles as may be advanced to them at the time
of signing this treaty, and the remainder shall be applied to subsisting
the Indians during the first year after their removal to the reservation, the purchase of teams, farming implements, tools, seeds, clothing,
and provisions, and for the payment of the necessary employés.

ARTICLE 4. The United States further agree that there shall be erected
at suitable points on the reservation, as soon as practicable after the

ratification of this treaty, one saw-mill, one flouring-mill, suitable buildings for the use of the blacksmith, carpenter, and wagon and plough maker, the necessary buildings for one manual-labor school, and such hospital buildings as may be necessary, which buildings shall be kept in repair at the expense of the United States for the term of twenty years; and it is further stipulated that the necessary tools and material for the saw-mill, flour-mill, carpenter, blacksmith, and wagon and plough maker's shops, and books and stationery for the manual-labor school, shall be furnished by the United States for the period of twenty years.

Schoolhouse and hosp.tal.

Tools, books, and stationery

ARTICLE 5. The United States further engage to furnish and pay for the services and subsistence, for the term of fifteen years, of one superintendent of farming operations, one farmer, one blacksmith, one sawyer, one carpenter, and one wagon and plough maker, and for the term of twenty years of one physician, one miller, and two school-teachers.

Farmer, mechanics, and teachers.

ARTICLE 6. The United States may, in their discretion, cause a part or the whole of the reservation provided for in Article 1 to be surveyed into tracts and assigned to members of the tribes of Indians, parties to this treaty, or such of them as may appear likely to be benefited by the same, under the following restrictions and limitations, to wit: To each head of a family shall be assigned and granted a tract of not less than forty nor more than one hundred and twenty acres, according to the number of persons in such family; and to each single man above the age of twenty-one years a tract not exceeding forty acres. The Indians to whom these tracts are granted are guaranteed the perpetual possession and use of the tracts thus granted and of the improvements which may be placed thereon; but no Indian shall have the right to alienate or convey any such tract to any person whatsoever, and the same shall be forever exempt from levy, sale, or forfeiture: *Provided*, That the Congress of the United States may hereafter abolish these restrictions and permit the sale of the lands so assigned, if the prosperity of the Indians will be advanced thereby: *And provided further*, If any Indian, to whom an assignment of land has been made, shall refuse to reside upon the tract so assigned for a period of two years, his right to the same shall be deemed forfeited.

Reservation may be surveyed into tracts and assigned to heads of families and single persons.

Not to be alienated nor subject to levy, etc.

Restrictions may be removed.

Forfeiture.

ARTICLE 7. The President of the United States is empowered to declare such rules and regulations as will secure to the family, in case of the death of the head thereof, the use and possession of the tract assigned to him, with the improvements thereon.

Regulations as to successions.

ARTICLE 8. The annuities of the tribes mentioned in this treaty shall not be held liable or taken to pay the debts of individuals.

Annuities not liable for debts.

ARTICLE 9. The several tribes of Indians, parties to this treaty, acknowledge their dependence upon the Government of the United States, and agree to be friendly with all citizens thereof, and to commit no depredations upon the person or property of said citizens, and to refrain from carrying on any war upon other Indian tribes; and they further agree that they will not communicate with or assist any persons or nation hostile to the United States, and, further, that they will submit to and obey all laws and regulations which the United States may prescribe for their government and conduct.

Peace and friendship.

ARTICLE 10. It is hereby provided that if any member of these tribes shall drink any spirituous liquor, or bring any such liquor upon the reservation, his or her proportion of the benefits of this treaty may be withheld for such time as the President of the United States may direct.

Members drinking, etc., spirituousliquors, not to have the benefits of this treaty.

ARTICLE 11. It is agreed between the contracting parties that if the United States, at any future time, may desire to locate other tribes upon the reservation provided for in this treaty, no objection shall be made thereto; but the tribes, parties to this treaty, shall not, by such

Other tribes may be located on reservation.

Proviso

Treaty, when to take effect.

Execution.

location of other tribes, forfeit any of their rights or privileges guaranteed to them by this treaty.

ARTICLE 12. This treaty shall bind the contracting parties whenever the same is ratified by the Senate and President of the United States.

In witness of which, the several parties named in the foregoing treaty have hereunto set their hands and seals at the place and date above written.

J. W. Perit Huntington, [SEAL.]
Superintendent Indian Affairs.
William Logan, [SEAL.]
United States Indian Agent.

La-lake, his x mark.	[SEAL.]	Boss-ki-you, his x mark.	[SEAL.]
Chil-o-que-nas, his x mark.	[SEAL.]	Ski-at-tic, his x mark.	[SEAL.]
Kellogue, his x mark.	[SEAL.]	Shol-lal-loos, his x mark.	[SEAL.]
Mo-ghen-kas-kit, his x mark.	[SEAL.]	Tat-tet-pas, his x mark.	[SEAL.]
Blow, his x mark.	[SEAL.]	Muk-has, his x mark.	[SEAL.]
Le-lu, his x mark.	[SEAL.]	Herman-kus-mam, his x mark.	[SEAL.]
Palmer, his x mark.	[SEAL.]	Jackson, his x mark.	[SEAL.]
Jack, his x mark.	[SEAL.]	Schon-chin, his x mark.	[SEAL.]
Que-ass, his x mark	[SEAL.]	Stak-it-ut, his x mark.	[SEAL.]
Poo-sak-sult, his x mark.	[SEAL.]	Keint-poos, his x mark.	[SEAL.]
Che-mult, his x mark.	[SEAL.]	Chuck-e-i-ox, his x mark.	[SEAL.]
No-ak-sum, his x mark.	[SEAL.]	Kile-to-ak, his x mark.	[SEAL.]
Mooch-kat-allick, his x mark.	[SEAL.]	Sky-te-ock-et, his x mark.	[SEAL.]
Toon-tuc-tee, his x mark.	[SEAL.]		

Signed in the presence of—

R. P. Earhart, secretary.
Wm. Kelly, captain First Cavalry, Oregon Volunteers.
James Halloran, second lieutenant First Infantry, W. T. Volunteers.
William C. McKay, M. D.
Robert (his x mark) Biddle.

TREATY WITH THE CHIPPEWA OF SAGINAW, SWAN CREEK, AND BLACK RIVER, 1864.

Oct. 18, 1864.

14 Stats., 657.
Ratified May 22, 1866.
Proclaimed Aug. 16, 1866.

Articles of agreement and convention made and concluded at the Isabella Indian Reservation, in the State of Michigan, on the eighteenth day of October, in the year one thousand eight hundred and sixty-four, between H. J. Alvord, special commissioner of the United States, and D. C. Leach, United States Indian agent, acting as commissioners for and on the part of the United States, and the Chippewas of Saginaw, Swan Creek, and Black River, in the State of Michigan aforesaid, parties to the treaty of August 2d, 1855, as follows, viz:

Released to the United States of reservation and right to locate and purchase certain lands.

ARTICLE 1. The said Chippewas of Saginaw, Swan Creek, and Black River, for and in consideration of the conditions hereinafter specified, do hereby release to the United States the several townships of land reserved to said tribe by said treaty aforesaid, situate and being upon Saginaw Bay, in said State.

The said Indians also agree to relinquish to the United States all claim to any right they may possess to locate lands in lieu of lands sold or disposed of by the United States upon their reservation at Isabella, and also the right to purchase the unselected lands in said reservation, as provided for in the first article of said treaty.

Certain lands set apart for the Indians in Isabella County.

ARTICLE 2. In consideration of the foregoing relinquishments, the United States hereby agree to set apart for the exclusive use, ownership, and occupancy of the said *of the said* Chippewas of Saginaw, Swan Creek, and Black River, all of the unsold lands within the six townships in Isabella County, reserved to said Indians by the treaty of August 2, 1855, aforesaid, and designated as follows, viz:

The north half of township fourteen, and townships fifteen and sixteen north, of range three west; the north half of township fourteen and township fifteen north, of range four west, and townships fourteen and fifteen north, of range five west.

ARTICLE 3. So soon as practicable after the ratification of this treaty, the persons who have heretofore made selections of lands within the townships upon Saginaw Bay, hereby relinquished, may proceed to make selections of lands upon the Isabella reservation in lieu of their selections aforesaid, and in like quantities. *Mode and order of selections of lands in lieu of those relinquished.*

After a reasonable time shall have been given for the parties aforesaid to make their selections in lieu of those relinquished, the other persons entitled thereto may then proceed to make their selections, in quantities as follows, viz:

For each chief of said Indians who signs this treaty, eighty acres in addition to their selections already made, and to patents in fee-simple. *Chiefs.*

For one head-man in each band into which said Indians are now divided, forty acres, and to patents in fee simple. *Headmen.*

For each person being the head of a family, eighty acres. *Heads of families.*

For each single person over the age of twenty-one years, forty acres. *Single persons.*

For each orphan child under the age of twenty-one years, forty acres. *Orphans and children.*

For each married female who has not heretofore made a selection of land, forty acres. *Married women.*

And for each other person now living, or who may be born hereafter, when he or she shall have arrived at the age of twenty-one years, forty acres, so long as any of the lands in said reserve shall remain unselected, and no longer. *Other persons.*

In consideration of important services rendered to said Indians during many years past, by William Smith, John Collins 1st, Andrew J. Campeau, and Thomas Chatfield, it is hereby agreed that they shall each be allowed to select eighty acres in addition to their previous selections, and receive patents therefor in fee simple; and to Charles H. Rodd, eighty acres, and a patent therefor in fee simple, to be received by said Rodd as a full consideration and payment of all claims he may have against said Indians, except claims against individuals for services rendered or money expended heretofore by said Rodd for the benefit of said Indians. *William Smith and others may select lands and receive patents therefor.*

It is understood and agreed that those Ottawas and Chippewas and Pottawatomies now belonging to the bands of which Metayomeig, May-me-she-gaw-day, Keche-kebe-me-mo-say, and Waw-be-maw-ing-gun are chiefs, who have heretofore made selections upon said reservations, by permission of said Chippewas of Saginaw, Swan Creek, and Black River, who now reside upon said reservation in Isabella County, or who may remove to said reservation within one year after the ratification of this treaty, shall be entitled to the same rights and privileges to select and hold land as are contained in the third article of this agreement. *Certain Ottawa, Chippewa, and Pottawatomie may select and hold lands.*

So soon as practicable after the ratification of this treaty, the agent for the said Indians shall make out a list of all those persons who have heretofore made selections of lands under the treaty of August 2d, 1855, aforesaid, and of those who may be entitled to selections under the provisions of this treaty, and he shall divide the persons enumerated in said list into two classes, viz: "competent" and "those not so competent." *Agent to make lists.*

Two classes.

Those who are intelligent, and have sufficient education, and are qualified by business habits to prudently manage their affairs, shall be set down as "competents," and those who are uneducated, or unqualified in other respects to prudently manage their affairs, or who are of idle, wandering, or dissolute habits, and all orphans, shall be set down as "those not so competent." *Competents.*

Those not so competent.

The United States agrees to issue patents to all persons entitled to selections under this treaty, as follows, viz: To those belonging to the class denominated "competents," patents shall be issued in fee simple, *Patents to those of both classes.*

but to those belonging to the class of "those not so competent," the patent shall contain a provision that the land shall never be sold or alienated to any person or persons whomsoever, without the consent of the Secretary of the Interior for the time being.

Manual-labor school.

ARTICLE 4. The United States agress to expend the sum of twenty thousand dollars for the support and maintenance of a manual-labor school upon said reservation: *Provided*, That the Missionary Society of the Methodist Episcopal Church shall, within three years after the ratification of this treaty, at its own expense, erect suitable buildings for school and boarding-house purposes, of a value of not less than three thousand dollars, upon the southeast quarter of section nine, township fourteen north, of range four west, which is hereby set apart for that purpose.

Buildings.

Board of visitors or such schools.

The superintendent of public instruction, the lieutenant governor of the State of Michigan, and one person, to be designated by said missionary society, shall constitute a board of visitors, whose duty it shall be to visit said school once during each year, and examine the same, and investigate the character and qualifications of its teachers and all other persons connected therewith, and report thereon to the Commissioner of Indian Affairs.

Control, etc., of school and farm.

Annual appropriation.

The said Missionary Society of the Methodist Episcopal Church shall have full and undisputed control of the management of said school and the farm attached thereto. Upon the approval and acceptance of the school and boarding-house buildings by the board of visitors, the United States will pay to the authorized agent of said missionary society, for the support and maintenance of the school, the sum of two thousand dollars, and a like sum annually thereafter, until the whole sum of twenty thousand dollars shall have been expended.

May be suspended.

The United States reserves the right to suspend the annual appropriation of two thousand dollars for said school, in part or in whole, whenever it shall appear that said missionary society neglects or fails to manage the affairs of said school and farm in a manner acceptable to the board of visitors aforesaid; and if, at any time within a period of ten years after the establishment of said school, said missionary society shall abandon said school or farm for the purposes intended in this treaty, then, and in such case, said society shall forfeit all of its rights in the lands, buildings, and franchises under this treaty, and it shall then be competent for the Secretary of the Interior to sell or dispose of the land hereinbefore designated, together with the buildings and improvements thereon and expend the proceeds of the same for the educational interests of the Indians in such manner as he may deem advisable.

If school and farm are abandoned, the rights under this treaty are lost.

Land and buildings may be sold.

At the expiration of ten years after the establishment of said school, if said missionary society shall have conducted said school and farm in a manner acceptable to the board of visitors during said ten years, the United States will convey to said society the land before mentioned by patent in trust for the benefit of said Indians.

Lands to be conveyed in fee simple, if, etc.

If society does not accept trust, etc.

In case said missionary society shall fail to accept the trust herein named within one year after the ratification of this treaty, then, and in that case, the said twenty thousand dollars shall be placed to the credit of the educational fund of said Indians, to be expended for their benefit in such manner as the Secretary of the Interior may deem advisable.

Present school-house.

It is understood and agreed that said missionary society may use the school-house now standing upon land adjacent to the land hereinbefore set apart for a school-farm, where it now stands, or move it upon the land so set apart.

Blacksmith shop, stock, tools, etc.

ARTICLE 5. The said Indians agree that, of the last two payments of eighteen thousand eight hundred dollars each, provided for by the said treaty of August second, eighteen hundred and fifty-five, the sum of seventeen thousand six hundred dollars may be withheld, and the same shall be placed to the credit of their agricultural fund, to be expended for their benefit in sustaining their blacksmith-shop, in stock, animals, agricultural implements, or in such other manner as the Secretary of the Interior may deem advisable.

ARTICLE 6. The Commissioner of Indian Affairs may, at the request of the chiefs and head-men, sell the mill and land belonging thereto at Isabella City, on said reservation, and apply the proceeds thereof for such beneficiary objects as may be deemed advisable by the Secretary of the Interior. Mill and land at Isabella City may be sold.

ARTICLE 7. Inasmuch as the mill belonging to said Indians is partly located upon land heretofore selected by James Nicholson, it is hereby agreed that upon a relinquishment of ten acres of said land by said Nicholson, in such form as may be determined by the agent for said Indians, he, the said Nicholson, shall be entitled to select eighty acres of land, subject to the approval of the Secretary of the Interior, and to receive a patent therefor in fee simple. James Nicholson may select 80 acres, upon, etc.

ARTICLE 8. It is hereby expressly understood that the eighth article of the treaty of August second, eighteen hundred and fifty-five, shall in no wise be affected by the terms of this treaty. Eighth article of former treaty not affected.

In testimony whereof, the said H. J. Alvord and the said D. C. Leach, Commissioners as aforesaid, and the undersigned chiefs and headmen of the Chippewas of Saginaw, Swan Creek, and Black River, have hereto set their hands and seals at Isabella, in the State of Michigan, the day and year first above written. Execution

H. J. Alvord,   [SEAL.]
D. C. Leach,   [SEAL.]
Special Commissioners.

In the presence of—

Richd. M. Smith,
Charles H. Rodd, United States interpreter,
George Bradley.

S. D. Simonds, chief, his x mark. [SEAL.]
Lyman Bennett, headman, his x mark. [SEAL.]
Jno. Pay-me-quo-ung, chief, his x mark. [SEAL.]
William Smith, headman, his x mark. [SEAL.]
Nauck-che-gaw-me, chief, his x mark. [SEAL.]
Me-squaw-waw-naw-quot, headman, his x mark. [SEAL.]
Thomas Dutton, chief, his x mark. [SEAL.]
Paim-way-we-dung, headman, his x mark. [SEAL.]
Elliott Kaybay, chief, his x mark. [SEAL.]
Solomon Ottawa, headman, his x mark. [SEAL.]
Andw. O-saw-waw-bun, chief, his x mark. [SEAL.]
Thos. Wain-daw-naw-quot, headman, his x mark. [SEAL.]
Naw-taw-way, chief, his x mark. [SEAL.]
I-kay-che-no-ting, headman, his x mark. [SEAL.]

William Smith, chief, his x mark. [SEAL.]
Naw-gaw-nevay-we-dung, headman, his x mark. [SEAL.]
Naw-we-ke-zhick, chief, his x mark. [SEAL.]
I-yalk, headman, his x mark. [SEAL.]
Nay-aw-be-tung, chief, his x mark. [SEAL.]
Jos. Waw-be-ke-zhick, headman, his x mark. [SEAL.]
Saml. Mez-haw-quaw-naw-um, chief, his x mark. [SEAL.]
John P. Williams, headman, his x mark. [SEAL.]
L. Pay-baw-maw-she, chief, his x mark. [SEAL.]
Ne-gaw-ne-quo-um, headman, his x mark. [SEAL.]
David Fisher, chief, his x mark. [SEAL.]
Waw-be-man-i-do, headman, his x mark. [SEAL.]
Ne-be-nay-aw-naw-quot-way-be, chief, his x mark. [SEAL.]
Key-o-gwaw-nay-be, headman, his x mark. [SEAL.]

In the presence of—

Richd. M. Smith,
Charles H. Rodd, United States interpreter.
Amos F. Albright, superintendent mills.

Marcus Grinnell, United States blacksmith.
M. D. Bourassa,
F. C. Babbitt,
George Bradley.

TREATY WITH THE OMAHA, 1865.

Mar. 6, 1865.

14 Stats., 667.
Ratified, Feb. 13, 1866.
Proclaimed Feb. 15, 1866.

Articles of treaty made and concluded at Washington, D. C., on the sixth day of March, A. D. 1865, between the United of America, by their commissioners, Clark W. Thompson, Robert W. Furnas, and the Omaha tribe of Indians by their chiefs, E-sta-mah-za, or Joseph La Flesche, Gra-ta-mah-zhe, or Standing Hawk; Ga-he-ga-zhinga, or Little Chief; Tah-wah-gah-ha, or Village Maker; Wah-no-ke-ga, or Noise; Sha-da-na-ge, or Yellow Smoke; Wastch-com-ma-nu, or Hard Walker; Pad-a-ga-he, or Fire Chief; Ta-su, or White Cow; Ma-ha-nin-ga, or No Knife.

Cession of lands to the United States.

Boundaries.

ARTICLE 1. The Omaha tribe of Indians do hereby cede, sell, and convey to the United States a tract of land from the north side of their present reservation, defined and bounded as follows, viz: commencing at a point on the Missouri River four miles due south from the north boundary line of said reservation, thence west ten miles, thence south four miles, thence west to the western boundary line of the reservation, thence north to the northern boundary line, thence east to the Missouri River, and thence south along the river to the place of beginning: and that the said Omaha tribe of Indians will vacate and give possession of the lands ceded by this treaty immediately after its ratification:

Proviso.

Provided, That nothing herein contained shall be construed to include any of the lands upon which the said Omaha tribe of Indians have now improvements, or any land or improvements belonging to, connected with, or used for the benefit of the Missouri school now in existence upon the Omaha reservation.

Payments to the Omaha, and how to be expended.

ARTICLE 2. In consideration of the foregoing cession, the United States agree to pay to the said Omaha tribe of Indians the sum of fifty thousand dollars, to be paid upon the ratification of this treaty, and to be expended by their agent, under the direction of the Commissioner of Indian Affairs, for goods, provisions, cattle, horses, construction of buildings, farming implements, breaking up lands, and other improvements on their reservation.

Articles of former treaty to be extended.

ARTICLE 3. In further consideration of the foregoing cession, the United States agree to extend the provisions of article 8 of the treaty between the Omaha tribe of Indians and the United States, made on the 16th day of March, A. D. 1854, for a term of ten years from and after the ratification of this treaty; and the United States further agree to pay to the said Omaha tribe of Indians, upon the ratification

Damages.

of this treaty, the sum of seven thousand dollars as damages in consequence of the occupancy of a portion of the Omaha reservation not hereby ceded, and use and destruction of timber by the Winnebago tribe of Indians while temporarily residing thereon.

Present reservation to be divided among members of the tribe in severalty.

ARTICLE 4. The Omaha Indians being desirous of promoting settled habits of industry and enterprise amongst themselves by abolishing the tenure in common by which they now hold their lands, and by assigning limited quantities thereof in severalty to the members of the tribe, including their half or mixed blood relatives now residing with them, to be cultivated and improved for their own individual use and benefit, it is hereby agreed and stipulated that the remaining portion of their present reservation shall be set apart for said purposes; and

How assigned.

that out of the same there shall be assigned to each head of a family not exceeding one hundred and sixty acres, and to each male person, eighteen years of age and upwards, without family, not exceeding forty acres of land—to include in every case, as far as practicable, a reasonable proportion of timber; six hundred and forty acres of said

Agency.

lands, embracing and surrounding the present agency improvements, shall also be set apart and appropriated to the occupancy and use of the agency for said Indians. The lands to be so assigned, including those for the use of the agency, shall be in as regular and compact a body as possible, and so as to admit of a distinct and well-defined exterior boundary. The whole of the lands, assigned or unassigned, in severalty, shall constitute and be known as the Omaha reservation, *Omaha Reservation.* within and over which all laws passed or which may be passed by Congress, regulating trade and intercourse with the Indian tribes shall have full force and effect, and no white person, except such as *Whites not to go or reside thereon unless, etc.* shall be in the employ of the United States, shall be allowed to reside or go upon any portion of said reservation without the written permission of the superintendent of Indian affairs or the agent for the tribe. Said division and assignment of lands to the Omahas in severalty shall be made under the direction of the Secretary of the Interior, and when approved by him, shall be final and conclusive. Certificates *Certificates to be issued for tracts assigned.* shall be issued by the Commissioner of Indian Affairs for the tracts so assigned, specifying the names of individuals to whom they have been assigned respectively, and that they are for the exclusive use and benefit of themselves, their heirs, and descendants; and said tracts shall not *Not to be alienated or leased, etc.* be alienated in fee, leased, or otherwise disposed of except to the United States or to other members of the tribe, under such rules and regulations as may be prescribed by the Secretary of the Interior, and they shall be exempt from taxation, levy, sale, or forfeiture, until otherwise provided for by Congress.

ARTICLE 5. It being understood that the object of the Government *Omaha may repurchase this land if the* in purchasing the land herein described is for the purpose of locating *location of the Winnebago affect their* the Winnebago tribe thereon, now, therefore, should their location *peace.* there prove detrimental to the peace, quiet, and harmony of the whites as well as of the two tribes of Indians, then the Omahas shall have the privilege of repurchasing the land herein ceded upon the same terms they now sell.

In testimony whereof, the said Clark W. Thompson and Robert W. Furnas, Commissioners as aforesaid, and the said chiefs and delegates of the Omaha tribe of Indians, have hereunto set their hands and seals at the place and on the day and year hereinbefore written.

Clark W. Thompson,
R. W. Furnas,
Commissioners.

E-sta-mah-zha, or Joseph La Flesche, his x mark.	[SEAL.]
Gra-ta-mah-zhe, or Standing Hawk, his x mark.	[SEAL.]
Ga-he-ga-zhin-ga, or Little Chief, his x mark.	[SEAL.]
Tah-wah-ga-ha, or Village Maker, his x mark.	[SEAL.]
Wah-no-ke-ga, or Noise, his x mark.	[SEAL.]
Sha-da-na-ge, or Yellow Smoke, his x mark.	[SEAL.]
Wastch-com-ma-nu, or Hard Walker, his x mark.	[SEAL.]
Pad-a-ga-he, or Fire Chief, his x mark.	[SEAL.]
Ta-su, or White Cow, his x mark.	[SEAL.]
Ma-ha-nin-ga, or No Knife, his x mark.	[SEAL.]

In presence of—

    H. Chase, United States interpreter.
    Lewis Saunsoci, interpreter.
    St. A. D. Balcombe, United States Indian agent.
    Geo. N. Propper.
    J. N. H. Patrick.

TREATY WITH THE WINNEBAGO, 1865.

Articles of treaty made and concluded at Washington, D. C., between the United States of America, by their commissioners, Wm. P. Dole, C. W. Thompson, and St. A. D. Balcombe, and the Winnebago tribe of Indians, by their chiefs, Little Hill, Little Decoria, Whirling Thunder, Young Prophet, Good Thunder, and White Breast, on the 8th day of March, 1865.

Mar. 8, 1865.

14 Stats., 671.
Ratified Feb. 13, 1866.
Proclaimed Mar. 28, 1866.

Cession of lands to the United States.

ARTICLE 1. The Winnebago tribe of Indians hereby cede, sell, and convey to the United States all their right, title, and interest in and to their present reservation in the Territory of Dakota, at Usher's Landing, on the Missouri River, the metes and bounds whereof being on file in the Indian Department.

Reservation for the Winnebago.

ARTICLE 2. In consideration of the foregoing cession, and the valuable improvements thereon, the United States agree to set apart for the occupation and future home of the Winnebago Indians, forever, all that certain tract or parcel of land ceded to the United States by the Omaha tribe of Indians on the sixth day of March, A. D. 1865, situated in the Territory of Nebraska, and described as follows, viz:

Boundaries.

Commencing at a point on the Missouri River four miles due south from the north boundary-line of said reservation; thence west ten miles; thence south four miles; thence west to the western boundary-line of the reservation; thence north to the northern boundary-line; thence east to the Missouri River, and thence south along the river to the place of beginning.

The United States to erect mills, to break, etc., lands, to furnish seeds, tools, etc.

ARTICLE 3. In further consideration of the foregoing cession, and in order that the Winnebagos may be as well situated as they were when they were moved from Minnesota, the United States agree to erect on their reservation, hereby set apart, a good steam saw-mill with a grist-mill attached, and to break and fence one hundred acres of land for each band, and supply them with seed, to sow and plant the same, and shall furnish them with two thousand dollars' worth of guns, four hundred horses, one hundred cows, twenty yoke of oxen and wagons, two chains each, and five hundred dollars' worth of agricultural implements, in addition to those on the reserve hereby ceded.

Agency and other buildings and houses for chiefs.

ARTICLE 4. The United States further agree to erect on said reservation an agency building, school-house, warehouse, and suitable buildings for the physician, interpreter, miller, engineer, carpenter, and blacksmith, and a house 18 by 24 feet, one and a half story high, well shingled and substantially finished, for each chief.

Expenses of removal, etc.

ARTICLE 5. The United States also stipulate and agree to remove the Winnebago tribe of Indians and their property to their new home, and to subsist the tribe one year after their arrival there.

In testimony whereof, the said Wm. P. Dole, Clark W. Thompson, and St. A. D. Balcombe, Commissioners as aforesaid, and the undersigned chiefs and delegates of the Winnebago Tribe of Indians, have hereunto set their hands and seals, at the place and on the day hereinbefore written.

W. P. Dole,
Clark W. Thompson,
St. A. D. Balcombe,
Commissioners.

Little Hill, his x mark.   [SEAL.]
Little Dacoria, his x mark.   [SEAL.]
Whirling Thunder, his x mark.   [SEAL.]
Young Prophet, his x mark,   [SEAL.]
Good Thunder, his x mark,   [SEAL.]
Young Crane, his x mark,   [SEAL.]
White Breast, his x mark,   [SEAL.]

In presence of—
    Mitchell St. Cyr, United State[s] interpreter.
    Alexander Payn, United State[s] interpreter.
    R. W. Furnas, United States agent for Omahas.
    Benj. F. Lushbaugh, United States Indian agent.
    Augustus Kountze.
    C. Hazlett.

TREATY WITH THE PONCA, 1865.

Supplementary treaty between the United States of America and the Ponca tribe of Indians, made at the city of Washington on the tenth day of March, A. D. 1865, between William P. Dole, commissioner on the part of the United States, and Wah-gah-sap-pi, or Iron Whip; Gist-tah-wah-gu, or Strong Walker; Wash-com-mo-ni, or Mitchell P. Cerre; Ash-nan-e-kah-gah-he, or Lone Chief; Tah-ton-ga-nuz-zhe, or Standing Buffalo; on the part of the Ponca tribe of Indians, they being duly authorized and empowered by the said tribe, as follows, viz:

Mar. 10, 1865.

14 Stat., 675.
Ratified Mar. 2. 1867.
Proclaimed Mar. 28. 1867.

ARTICLE 1. The Ponca tribe of Indians hereby cede and relinquish to the United States all that portion of their present reservation as described in the first article of the treaty of March 12th, 1858, lying west of the range line between townships numbers (32) thirty-two and (33) thirty-three north, ranges (10) ten and (11) eleven west of the (6) sixth principal meridian, according to the Kansas and Nebraska survey; estimated to contain thirty thousand acres, be the same more or less. *[Cession of lands to the United States. Boundaries.]*

ARTICLE 2. In consideration of the cession or release of that portion of the reservation above described by the Ponca tribe of Indians to the Government of the United States, the Government of the United States, by way of rewarding them for their constant fidelity to the Government and citizens thereof, and with a view of returning to the said tribe of Ponca Indians their old burying-grounds and corn-fields, hereby cede and relinquish to the tribe of Ponca Indians the following-described fractional townships, to wit: township (31) thirty-one north, range (7) seven west; also, fractional township (32) thirty-two north, ranges (6,) six, (7,) seven, (8,) eight, (9,) nine, and (10) ten west; also, fractional township (33) thirty-three north, ranges (7) seven and (8) eight west; and also all that portion of township (33) thirty-three north, ranges (9) nine and (10) ten west, lying south of Ponca Creek; and also all the islands in the Niobrara or Running Water River, lying in front of lands or townships above ceded by the United States to the Ponca tribe of Indians. But it is expressly understood and agreed that the United States shall not be called upon to satisfy or pay the claims of any settlers for improvements upon the lands above ceded by the United States to the Poncas, but that the Ponca tribe of Indians shall, out of their own funds, and at their own expense, satisfy said claimants, should any be found upon said lands above ceded by the United States to the Ponca tribe of Indians. *[Certain fractional townships of land ceded by the United States to the Poncas. Claims of settlers for improvements, how to be settled.]*

ARTICLE 3. The Government of the United States, in compliance with the first paragraph of the second article of the treaty of March 12th, 1858, hereby stipulate and agree to pay to the Ponca tribe of Indians for indemnity for spoliation committed upon them, satisfactory evidence of which has been lodged in the office of the Commissioner of Indian Affairs, and payment recommended by that officer, and also by the Secretary of the Interior, the sum of fifteen thousand and eighty dollars. *[Indemnity for spoliation.]*

ARTICLE 4. The expenses attending the negotiation of this treaty or agreement shall be paid by the United States. *[Expenses of this treaty to be paid by United States.]*

In testimony whereof, the said Wm. P. Dole, Commissioner as aforesaid, and the undersigned, chiefs of the Ponca tribe of Indians, have hereunto set their hands and seals at the place and on the day hereinbefore written.

Wm. P. Dole.

Wah-gah-sap-pi, or Iron Whip, his x mark.   [SEAL.]
Gist-tah-wah-gu, or Strong Walker, his x mark.   [SEAL.]
Wash-com-mo-ni, or Mitchell P. Cerre, his x mark.   [SEAL.]
Ash-nan-e-kah-gah-he, or Lone Chief, his x mark.   [SEAL.]
Tah-ton-ga-nuz-zhe, or Standing Buffalo, his x mark. [SEAL.]

Executed in the presence of—
Chas. Sims.
Stephen A. Dole.
Newton Edmunds.
J. Shaw Gregory.
George N. Propper.

TREATY WITH THE SNAKE, 1865.

Aug. 12, 1865.

14 Stat., 683.
Ratified July 5, 1866.
Proclaimed July 10, 1866.

Articles of agreement and convention made and concluded at Sprague River Valley, on this twelfth day of August, in the year one thousand eight hundred and sixty-five, by J. W. Perit Huntington, superintendent of Indian affairs in Oregon, on the part of the United States, and the undersigned chiefs and head-men of the Woll-pah-pe tribe of Snake Indians, acting in behalf of said tribe, being duly authorized so to do.

Peace.

Prisoners and slaves.

ARTICLE 1. Peace is declared henceforth between the United States and the Woll-pah-pe tribe of Snake Indians, and also between said tribe and all other tribes in amity with the United States. All prisoners and slaves held by the Woll-pah-pe tribe, whether the same are white persons or members of Indian tribes in amity with the United States, shall be released; and all persons belonging to the said Woll-pah-pe tribe now held as prisoners by whites, or as slaves by other Indian tribes, shall be given up.

Cession of lands to the United States.

Boundaries.

ARTICLE 2. The said tribe hereby cedes and relinquishes to the United States all their right, title, and interest to the country occupied by them, described as follows, to wit: Beginning at the Snow Peak in the summit of the Blue Mountain range, near the heads of the Grande Ronde River and the north fork of John Day's River; thence down said north fork of John Day's River to its junction with the south fork; thence due south to Crooked River; thence up Crooked River and the south fork thereof to its source; thence southeasterly to Harney Lake; thence northerly to the heads of Malheur and Burnt Rivers; thence continuing northerly to the place of beginning.

Indians to remove to reservation.

ARTICLE 3. The said tribe agree to remove forthwith to the reservation designated by the treaty concluded on the *14th* [15th] of October, 1864, with the Klamath, Moadoc, and Yahooskiu Snake Indians, there to remain under the authority and protection of such Indian agent, or other officer, as the Government of the United States may assign to such duty, and no member of said tribe shall leave said reservation for any purpose without the written consent of the agent or superintendent having jurisdiction over said tribe.

To submit to the United States and not depredate.

Offenders to be given up.

ARTICLE 4. The said Woll-pah-pe tribe promise to be friendly with the people of the United States, to submit to the authority thereof, and to commit no depredations upon the persons or property of citizens thereof, or of other Indian tribes; and should any member of said tribe commit any such depredations, he shall be delivered up to the agent for punishment, and the property restored. If after due notice the tribe neglect or refuse to make restitution, or the property is injured or destroyed, compensation may be made by the Government out of the annuities hereinafter provided. In case of any depredation being committed upon the person or property of any member of the aforesaid Woll-pah-pe tribe, it is stipulated that no attempt at revenge, retaliation, or reclamation shall be made by said tribe; but the case shall be reported to the agent or superintendent in charge, and the United States guarantee that such depredation shall be punished in the same manner as if committed against white persons, and that the property shall be restored to the owner. *Wrongs upon Indians, how redressed.*

ARTICLE 5. The said tribe promise to endeavor to induce the Hoo-ne-boo-ey and Wa-tat-kah tribes of Snake Indians to cease hostilities against the whites; and they also agree that they will, in no case, sell any arms or ammunition to them nor to any other tribe hostile to the United States. *Hostile tribes, sale of arms, etc.*

ARTICLE 6. The United States agree to expend, for the use and benefit of said tribe, the sum of five thousand dollars to enable the Indians to fence, break up, and cultivate a sufficient quantity of land for their use, to supply them with seeds, farming-implements, domestic animals, and such subsistence as may be necessary during the first year of their residence upon the reservation. *Fencing and cultivating lands. Seeds, tools, etc.*

ARTICLE 7. The United States also agree to expend, for the use and benefit of said tribe, the sum of two thousand dollars per annum for five years next succeeding the ratification of this treaty, and twelve hundred dollars per annum for the next ten years following, the same to be expended under the direction of the President of the United States for such objects as, in his judgment, will be beneficial to the Indians, and advance them in morals and knowledge of civilization. *Beneficial expenditures.*

ARTICLE 8. The said tribe, after their removal to the reservation, are to have the benefit of the services of the physician, mechanics, farmers, teachers, and other employés provided for in the treaty of the 15th October, 1864, in common with the Klamaths, Moadocs, and Yahooskiu Snakes, and are also to have the use of the mills and school-houses provided for in said treaty, so far as may be necessary to them, and not to the disadvantage of the other tribes; and, in addition, an interpreter who understands the Snake language shall be provided by the Government. Whenever, in the judgment of the President, the proper time shall have arrived for an allotment of land in severalty to the Indians upon the said reservation, a suitable tract shall be set apart for each family of the said Woll-pah-pe tribe, and peaceable possession of the same is guaranteed to them. *Physician, mechanics, etc. Mill and school houses. Interpreter.*

ARTICLE 9. The tribe are desirous of preventing the use of ardent spirits among themselves, and it is therefore provided that any Indian who brings liquor on to the reservation, or who has it in his possession, may in addition to the penalties affixed by law, have his or her proportion of the annuities withheld for such time as the President may determine. *Possession of ardent spirits on reservation, how punished.*

ARTICLE 10. This treaty shall be obligatory upon the contracting parties as soon as the same shall be ratified by the Senate of the United States. *Treaty, when to be obligatory.*

In testimony whereof, the said J. W. Perit Huntington, superintendent of Indian affairs, and the undersigned chiefs and headmen of the tribe aforesaid, have hereunto set their signatures and seals, at the place and on the day and year above written.

J. W. Perit Huntington,
Superintendent Indian Affairs in Oregon. [SEAL.]

Pah-ni-ne,	his x mark.	[SEAL.]
Hau-ni-noo-ey,	his x mark.	[SEAL.]
Ki-nau-ney,	his x mark.	[SEAL.]
Wa-ak-chau,	his x mark.	[SEAL.]

Chok-ko-si,	his x mark.	[SEAL.]
She-zhe,	his x mark.	[SEAL.]
Che-em-ma,	his x mark.	[SEAL.]
Now-hoop-a-cow-.c..,	his x mark.	[SEAL.]
Ki-po-weet-ka,	his x mark.	[SEAL.]
Hau-ne, or Shas-took,	his x mark.	[SEAL.]
Sah-too-too-we,	his x mark.	[SEAL.]

Executed in our presence—

W. V. Rinehart, major First Oregon Infantry.
Wm. Kelly, captain First Cavalry, Oregon Volunteers.
Lindsay Applegate.
Wm. C. McKay, M. D., acting interpreter.
Albert Applegate, second lieutenant, First Oregon Infantry,
    commanding escort.
F. B. Chase.

TREATY WITH THE OSAGE, 1865.

Sept. 29, 1865.

14 Stat., 687.
Ratified June 26, 1866.
Proclaimed, Jan. 21, 1867.

Articles of treaty and convention, made and concluded at Canville Trading Post, Osage Nation, within the boundary of the State of Kansas, on the twenty-ninth day of September, eighteen hundred and sixty-five, by and between D. N. Cooley, Commissioner of Indian Affairs, and Elijah Sells, superintendent of Indian Affairs for the southern superintendency, commissioners on the part of the United States, and the chiefs of the tribe of Great and Little Osage Indians, the said chiefs being duly authorized to negotiate and treat by said tribes.

Sale of lands to the United States.

ARTICLE 1. The tribe of the Great and Little Osage Indians, having now more lands than are necessary for their occupation, and all payments from the Government to them under former treaties having ceased, leaving them greatly impoverished, and being desirous of improving their condition by disposing of their surplus lands, do hereby grant and sell to the United States the lands contained within the following boundaries, that is to say: Beginning at the southeast corner of their present reservation, and running thence north with the eastern boundary thereof fifty miles to the northeast corner; thence west with the northern line thirty miles; thence south fifty miles, to the southern boundary of said reservation; and thence east with said southern boundary to the place of beginning: *Provided,* That the western boundary of said land herein ceded shall not extend further westward than upon a line commencing at a point on the southern boundary of said Osage country one mile east of the place where the Verdigris River crosses the southern boundary of the State of Kansas. And, in consideration of the grant and sale to them of the above-described lands, the United States agree to pay the sum of three hundred thousand dollars, which sum shall be placed to the credit of said tribe of Indians in the Treasury of the United States, and interest thereon at the rate of five per centum per annum shall be paid to said tribes semi-annually, in money, clothing, provisions, or such articles of utility as the Secretary of the Interior may, from time to time, direct. Said lands shall be surveyed and sold, under the direction of the Secretary of the Interior, on the most advantageous terms, for cash, as public lands are surveyed and sold under existing laws, including any act granting lands to the State of Kansas in aid of the construction of a railroad through said lands; but no preemption claim or homestead settlement shall be recognized: and after re-imbursing the United States the cost of said survey and sale, and the said sum of three hundred thousand dollars placed to the credit of

Boundaries.

Proviso.

Payment for lands purchased, and in what.

Lands to be surveyed and sold.

said Indians, the remaining proceeds of sales shall be placed in the Proceeds Treasury of the United States to the credit of the "civilization fund," to be used, under the direction of the Secretary of the Interior, for the education and civilization of Indian tribes residing within the limits of the United States.

ARTICLE 2. The said tribe of Indians also hereby cede to the United States a tract of land twenty miles in width from north to south, off the north side of the remainder of their present reservation, and extending its entire length from east to west; which land is to be held in trust for said Indians, and to be surveyed and sold for their benefit under the direction of the Commissioner of the General Land-Office, at a price not less than one dollar and twenty-five cents per acre, as other lands are surveyed and sold, under such rules and regulations as the Secretary of the Interior shall from time to time prescribe. The proceeds of such sales, as they accrue, after deducting all expenses incident to the proper execution of the trust, shall be placed in the Treasury of the United States to the credit of said tribe of Indians; and the interest thereon, at the rate of five per centum per annum, shall be expended annually for building houses, purchasing agricultural implements and stock animals, and for the employment of a physician and mechanics, and for providing such other necessary aid as will enable said Indians to commence agricultural pursuits under favorable circumstances: *Provided*, That twenty-five per centum of the net proceeds arising from the sale of said trust lands, until said percentage shall amount to the sum of eighty thousand dollars, shall be placed to the credit of the school fund of said Indians; and the interest thereon, at the rate of five per centum per annum, shall be expended semi-annually for the boarding, clothing, and education of the children of said tribe.

Margin notes: Cession of other lands to the United States to be held in trust. Proceeds of the sale thereof; how to be executed. Proviso. School fund.

ARTICLE 3. The Osage Indians, being sensible of the great benefits they have received from the Catholic mission, situate in that portion of their reservation herein granted and sold to the United States, do hereby stipulate that one section of said land, to be selected by the Commissioner of Indian Affairs so as to include the improvements of said mission, shall be granted in fee-simple to John Shoenmaker, in trust, for the use and benefit of the society sustaining said mission, with the privilege to said Shoenmaker, on the payment of one dollar and twenty-five cents per acre, of selecting and purchasing two sections of land adjoining the section above granted; the said selection to be held in trust for said society, and to be selected in legal subdivisions of surveys, and subject to the approval of the Secretary of the Interior.

Margin note: One section granted to John Shoenmaker, in trust, and with privileges, etc.

ARTICLE 4. All loyal persons, being heads of families and citizens of the United States, or members of any tribe at peace with the United States, having made settlements and improvements as provided by the pre-emption laws of the United States, and now residing on the lands provided to be sold by the United States, in trust for said tribe, as well as upon the said lands herein granted and sold to the United States, shall have the privilege, at any time within one year after the ratification of this treaty, of buying a quarter section each, at one dollar and twenty-five cents per acre; such quarter section to be selected according to the legal subdivisions of surveys, and to include, as far as practicable, the improvements of the settler.

Margin note: Certain loyal persons, heads of families, etc., may buy a quarter section each at, etc.

ARTICLE 5. The Osages being desirous of paying their just debts to James N. Coffey and A. B. Canville, for advances in provisions, clothing, and other necessaries of life, hereby agree that the superintendent of Indian affairs for the southern superintendency and the agent of the tribe shall examine all claims against said tribe, and submit the same to the tribe for approval or disapproval, and report the same to the Secretary of the Interior, with the proofs in each case, for his concurrence or rejection; and the Secretary may issue to the claimants

Margin note: James N. Coffey and A. B. Canville to be paid their claims.

Proviso.

scrip for the claims thus allowed, which shall be receivable as cash in payment for any of the lands sold in trust for said tribe: *Provided,* The aggregate amount thus allowed by the Secretary of the Interior shall not exceed five thousand dollars.

Heirs of Charles Mograin may select a section of land, etc.

ARTICLE 6. In consideration of the long and faithful services rendered by Charles Mograin, one of the principal chiefs of the Great Osages, to the people, and in consideration of improvements made and owned by him on the land by this treaty sold to the United States, and in lieu of the provision made in article fourteen for the half-breed Indians, the heirs of the said Charles Mograin, dec[ease]d, may select one section of land, including his improvements, from the north half of said land, subject to the approval of the Secretary of the Interior, and upon his approval of such selection it shall be patented to the heirs of the said Mograin, dec[ease]d, in fee-simple.

$500 to be paid to the chiefs annually.

ARTICLE 7. It is agreed between the parties hereto that the sum of five hundred dollars shall be set apart each year from the moneys of said tribe, and paid by the agent to the chiefs.

One section of land to be selected, etc., for purposes of education.

ARTICLE 8. The Osage Indians being anxious that a school should be established in their new home, at their request it is agreed and provided that John Shoenmaker may select one section of land within their diminished reservation, and upon the approval of such selection by the Secretary of the Interior, such section of land shall be set apart to the said Shoenmaker and his successors, upon condition that the same shall be used, improved, and occupied for the support and education of the children of said Indians during the occupancy of said reser-

Proviso.

vation by said tribe: *Provided,* That said lands shall not be patented, and upon the discontinuance of said school shall revert to said tribe and to the United States as other Indian lands.

Patents to issue to Darius Rogers for 160 acres, and he may purchase other land at, etc.

ARTICLE 9. It is further agreed that, in consideration of the services of Darius Rogers to the Osage Indians, a patent shall be issued to him for one hundred and sixty acres of land, to include his mill and improvements, on paying one dollar and twenty-five cents per acre; and said Rogers shall also have the privilege of purchasing, at the rate of one dollar and twenty-five cents per acre, one quarter section of land adjoining the tract above mentioned, which shall be patented to him in like manner; said lands to be selected subject to the approval of the Secretary of the Interior.

Dependence on the United States acknowledged.

ARTICLE 10. The Osages acknowledge their dependence on the Government of the United States, and invoke its protection and care; they desire peace, and promise to abstain from war, and commit no depredations on either citizens or Indians; and they further agree to use their best efforts to suppress the introduction and use of ardent spirits in their country.

Right of way through reservations for highways and railroads.

ARTICLE 11. It is agreed that all roads and highways laid out by the State or General Government shall have right of way through the remaining lands of said Indians, on the same terms as are provided by law, when made through lands of citizens of the United States; and railroad companies, when the lines of their roads necessarily pass through the lands of said Indians, shall have right of way upon the payment of fair compensation therefor.

Indians to remove from ceded lands, etc.

ARTICLE 12. Within six months after the ratification of this treaty the Osage Indians shall remove from the lands sold and ceded in trust, and settle upon their diminished reservation.

United States to advance expenses of survey and sale; to be reimbursed.

ARTICLE 13. The Osage Indians having no annuities from which it is possible for them to pay any of the expenses of carrying this treaty into effect, it is agreed that the United States shall appropriate twenty thousand dollars, or so much thereof as may be necessary, for the purpose of defraying the expense of survey and sale of the lands hereby ceded in trust, which amount so expended shall be re-imbursed to the

Treasury of the United States from the proceeds of the first sales of said lands.

ARTICLE 14. The half-breeds of the Osage tribe of Indians, not to exceed twenty-five in number, who have improvements on the north half of the lands sold to the United States, shall have a patent issued to them, in fee-simple, for eighty acres each, to include, as far as practicable, their improvements, said half-breeds to be designated by the chiefs and head-men of the tribe; and the heirs of Joseph Swiss, a half-breed, and a former interpreter of said tribe, shall, in lieu of the above provision, receive a title, in fee-simple, to a half section of land, including his house and improvements, if practicable, and also to a half section of the trust lands; all of said lands to be selected by the parties, subject to the approval of the Secretary of the Interior.

Patents to issue to half-breeds for 80 acres, including their improvements.

Heirs of Joseph Swiss.

ARTICLE 15. It is also agreed by the United States that said Osage Indians may unite with any tribe of Indians at peace with the United States, residing in said Indian Territory, and thence afterwards receive an equitable proportion, according to their numbers, of all moneys, annuities, or property payable by the United States to said Indian tribe with which the agreement may be made; and in turn granting to said Indians, in proportion to their numbers, an equitable proportion of all moneys, annuities, and property payable by the United States to said Osages.

Osage may unite with other Indians, and receive portion of annuities.

ARTICLE 16. It is also agreed by said contracting parties, that if said Indians should agree to remove from the State of Kansas, and settle on lands to be provided for them by the United States in the Indian Territory on such terms as may be agreed on between the United States and the Indian tribes now residing in said Territory or any of them, then the diminished reservation shall be disposed of by the United States in the same manner and for the same purposes as hereinbefore provided in relation to said trust lands, except that 50 per cent. of the proceeds of the sale of said diminished reserve may be used by the United States in the purchase of lands for a suitable home for said Indians in said Indian Territory.

If Indians remove from Kansas, their diminished reservation to be sold, and proceeds, how applied.

ARTICLE 17. Should the Senate reject or amend any of the above articles, such rejection or amendment shall not affect the other provisions of this treaty, but the same shall go into effect when ratified by the Senate and approved by the President.

Rejection of some articles not to affect others, etc.

D. N. Cooley,
Commissioner of Indian Affairs.

Elijah Sells,
Superintendent Indian Affairs Southern Superintendency, and Commissioner.

Me-tso-shin-ca, (Little Bear.) his x mark.
Chief Little Osages.
No-pa-wah-la, his x mark.
Second Chief to Little Bear.
Pa-tha-hun-kah, his x mark.
Little Chief L. B. Band.
White Hair, his x mark.
Principal Chief Osage Nation.
Ta-wah-she-he, his x mark.
Chief Big Hill Band.
Beaver, his x mark.
Second Chief White Hair's Band.
Clermont, his x mark.
Chief Clermont Band.
O-po-ton-koh, his x mark.
Wa-she-pe-she, his x mark.
Little Chief W. H. Band.

Witnesses:
    Ma-sho-hun-ca, counsellor Little Bear Band, his x mark.
    Wa-sha-pa-wa-ta-ne-ca, his x mark.
    Wa-du-ha-ka, his x mark.
    Shin-ka-wa-ta-ne-kah, his x mark.
    She-weh-teh, his x mark.
    Gra-ma, his x mark.
    Hu-la-wah-sho-sha, his x mark.
    Na-ta-ton-ca-wa-ki, his x mark.
    Num-pa-wah-cu, his x mark.
    Ha-ska-mon-ne, his x mark.

Attest:
    G. C. Snow, U. S. Neosho Indian agent.
    Milton W. Reynolds, acting clerk.
    Theodore C. Wilson, phonographic reporter.
    Alexander Beyett, interpreter Osage Nation.

Witnesses, Little Bear's Band:
    Ka-wah-ho-tza, his x mark.
    O-ke-pa-hola, his x mark.
    Me-he-tha, his x mark.

White Hair's band of witnesses:
    Shin-ka-wa-sha, councillor of White Hair's, his x mark.
    Wa-sha-wa, his x mark.
    Ka-he-ka-stza-jeh, his x mark.
    Ka-he-ka-wa-shin-pe-she, his x mark.
    Saw-pe-ka-la, his x mark.
    Wa-tza-shim-ka, his x mark.
    Wa-no-pa-she, his x mark.
    Shin-be-ka-shi, his x mark.
    Ne-koo-le-blo, his x mark.
    O-ke-pa-ka-loh, his x mark.
    Ke-nu-in-ca, his x mark.
    Pa-su-mo-na, his x mark.

We the undersigned, chiefs and headmen of the Clermont and Black Dog Band of the Great Osage nation, in council at Fort Smith, Ark., have had the foregoing treaty read and explained in full by our interpreter, L. P. Chouteau, and fully approve the provisions of said treaty made by our brothers the Osages, and by this signing make it our act and deed.

    Clermont, chief of Clermont Band, his x mark.
    Palley, second chief of Clermont Band, his x mark.
    Hah-ti-in-gah, (Dry Feather,) counsellor, his x mark.
    Kah-ha-che-la-ton, brave, his x mark.
    Do-tah-cah-she, brave, his x mark.
    Black Dog, chief Black Dog Band, his x mark.
    William Penn, second chief Black Dog Band, his x mark.
    Broke Arm, counsellor, his x mark.
    Ne-kah-ke-pon-nah, brave, his x mark.
    Ne-kah-gah-hee, brave, his x mark.

Witnesses:
    Wah-skon-mon-ney, his x mark.
    Wah-kon-che-la, his x mark.
    Wah-sha-sha-wah-ti-in-gah, his x mark.
    Pah-cha-hun-gah, his x mark.
    Long Bow, his x mark.

Wah-she-wah-la, his x mark.
War Eagle, his x mark.
Pon-hon-gle-gah-ton, his x mark.
Sun Down, his x mark.
Ton-won-ge-hi, his x mark.
Wah-cha-o-nau-she, his x mark.

TREATY WITH THE SIOUX—MINICONJOU BAND, 1865.

Articles of a treaty made and concluded at Fort Sully, in the Territory of Dakota, by and between Newton Edmunds, governor and ex-officio superintendent of Indian affairs of Dakota Territory; Edward B. Taylor, superintendent of Indian affairs for the northern superintendency; Major-General S. R. Curtis, Brigadier-General H. H. Sibley, Henry W. Reed, and Orin Guernsey, commissioners on the part of the United States, duly appointed by the President, and the undersigned chiefs and head-men of the Minneconjon band of Dakota or Sioux Indians.

Oct. 10, 1865.

14 Stats., 695.
Ratified Mar. 5, 1866.
Proclaimed Mar. 17, 1866.

ARTICLE 1. The Minneconjon band of Dakota or Sioux Indians, represented in council, hereby acknowledge themselves to be subject to the exclusive jurisdiction and authority of the United States, and hereby obligate and bind themselves individually and collectively, not only to cease all hostilities against the persons and property of its citizens, but to use their influence, and, if requisite, physical force, to prevent other bands of the Dakota or Sioux, or other adjacent tribes, from making hostile demonstrations against the Government or people of the United States. *{Jurisdiction and authority of the United States acknowledged, etc.}*

ARTICLE 2. Inasmuch as the Government of the United States is desirous to arrest the effusion of blood between the Indian tribes within its jurisdiction hitherto at war with each other, the Minneconjon band of Dakotas or Sioux, represented in council, anxious to respect the wishes of the Government, hereby agree and bind themselves to discontinue for the future all attacks upon the persons or property of other tribes, unless first assailed by them, and to use their influence to promote peace everywhere in the region occupied or frequented by them. *{Persons and property of other tribes not to be first attacked.}*

ARTICLE 3. All controversies or differences arising between the Minneconjon band of Dakotas or Sioux, represented in council, and other tribes of Indians, involving the question of peace or war, shall be submitted to the arbitrament of the President, or such person or persons as may be designated by him, and the decision or award faithfully observed by the said band represented in council. *{Controversies between tribes to be submitted to the President for arbitrament, etc.}*

ARTICLE 4. The said band, represented in council, shall withdraw from the routes overland already established or hereafter to be established through their country; and in consideration thereof the Government of the United States agree to pay the said band the sum of ten thousand dollars annually for twenty years, in such articles as the Secretary of the Interior may direct: *Provided,* That said band, so represented in council, shall faithfully conform to the requirements of this treaty. *{Indians to withdraw from overland routes.}* *{Payment to the Indians.}*

ARTICLE 5. Should any individual or individuals or portion of the band of the Minneconjon band of Dakotas or Sioux, represented in council, desire hereafter to locate permanently upon any part of the lands claimed by the said band for the purpose [of] agricultural or other pursuits, it is hereby agreed by the parties to this treaty that such individual or individuals shall be protected in such location against any annoyance or molestation on the part of whites or Indians. *{Individual Indians locating on lands to be protected.}*

Amendments to be binding. ARTICLE 6. Any amendment or modification of this treaty by the Senate of the United States shall be considered final and binding upon the said band, represented in council, as a part of this treaty, in the same manner as if it had been subsequently presented and agreed to by the chiefs and head-men of said band.

In testimony whereof, the Commissioners on the part of the United States, and the chiefs and headmen of the said Minneconjon band of Dakota or Sioux, have hereunto set their hands, this tenth day of October, one thousand eight hundred and sixty-five, after the contents had previously been read, interpreted, and explained to the said chiefs and headmen.

> Newton Edmunds,
> Edward B. Taylor,
> S. R. Curtis, Major-General,
> H. H. Sibley, Brigadier-General,
> Henry W. Reed,
> Orrin Guernsey,
> Commissioners on the part of the United States.

Ha-wah-zee-dan, The Lone Horn, his x mark, 1st chief.

Tah-ke-chah-hoosh-tay, The Lame Deer, his x mark, 1st chief.

Kee-yam-e-i-a, One that flies when going, his x mark, chief.

Ha-il-o-kah-chah-skah, White Young Bull, his x mark, chief.

Ke-yar-cum-pee, Give him Room, his x mark, chief.

Ha-har-skah-kah, Long Horn, his x mark, chief.

He-han-we-chak-chah, The Old Owl, his x mark, chief.

Wah-chee-ha-skah, White Feather, his x mark, chief.

Tah-ton-kah-wak-kanto, The High Bull, his x mark, soldier.

Mah-to-chat-kah, The Left-handed Bear, his x mark, soldier.

Chan-wah-pa, The Tree in Leaf, his x mark, soldier.

To-kalla-doo-tah, The Red Fox, his x mark, soldier.

Cha-tan-sappah, The Black Hawk, his x mark, soldier.

Muck-a-pee-ah-to, The Blue Cloud, his x mark.

Signed by the Commissioners on the part of the United States, and by the chiefs and headmen, after the treaty had been fully read, interpreted, and explained in our presence:

A. W. Hubbard, M. C. Sixth district Iowa.

S. S. Curtis, Major Second Colorado Cavalry, Brevet Lieutenant-Colonel U. S. Volunteers.

Chas. C. G. Thornton, Lieutenant-Colonel Fourth U. S. Volunteers.

E. F. Ruth, Secretary of Commission.

R. R. Hitt, Reporter of Commission.

Thos. D. Maurice, Late Major First Missouri Light Artillery.

W. Mott, Captain and C. S.

Zephier Rencontre, his x mark, interpreter.

Charles Degres, his x mark, interpreter.

The following chiefs came into council on the 20th Oct. and desired to sign the treaty. They are represented as always friendly to the whites, and have, therefore, been away from most of the tribe.

> Hah-sah-ne-na-maza, One Iron Horse, his x mark.
> To-kio-wi-chack-a-ta, The One that Kills the First on Hand, his x mark.

Attest:

> S. S. Curtis, Brevet Lieutenant-Colonel U. S. Volunteers.
> Hez. L. Hosmer, Chief Justice of Montana Territory.
> Charles Degres, his x mark.

TREATY WITH THE SIOUX—LOWER BRULÉ BAND, 1865.

Articles of a treaty made and concluded at Fort Sully, in the Territory of Dakota, by and between Newton Edmunds, governor and ex-officio superintendent of Indian affairs of Dakota Territory; Edward B. Taylor, superintendent of Indian affairs for the northern superintendency; Major-General S. R. Curtis, Brigadier-General H. H. Sibley, Henry W. Reed, and Orrin Guernsey, commissioners on the part of the United States, duly appointed by the President, and the undersigned chiefs and head-men of the Lower Brulé band of Dakota or Sioux Indians.

Oct. 14, 1865.

14 Stats., 699.
Ratified Mar. 5, 1866.
Proclaimed Mar. 17, 1866.

ARTICLE 1. The Lower Brulé band of Dakota or Sioux Indians, represented in council, hereby acknowledge themselves to be subject to the exclusive jurisdiction and authority of the United States, and hereby obligate and bind themselves individually and collectively, not only to cease all hostilities against the persons and property of its citizens, but to use their influence, and, if necessary, physical force, to prevent other bands of the Dakota or Sioux, or other adjacent tribes, from making hostile demonstrations against the Government of the United States or its people.

Jurisdiction and authority of the United States acknowledged.

ARTICLE 2. Inasmuch as the Government of the United States is desirous to arrest the effusion of blood between the Indian tribes within its jurisdiction hitherto at war with each other, the Lower Brulé band of Dakotas or Sioux, represented in council, anxious to respect the wishes of the Government, hereby agree and bind themselves to discontinue for the future all attacks upon the persons or property of other tribes, unless first assailed by them, and to use their influence to promote peace everywhere in the region occupied or frequented by them.

Persons and property of other tribes not to be first attacked.

ARTICLE 3. All controversies or differences arising between the Lower Brulé band of Dakotas or Sioux, represented in council, and other tribes of Indians, involving the question of peace or war, shall be submitted for the arbitrament of the President, or such person or persons as may be designated by him, and the decision or award faithfully observed by the said band represented in council.

Controversies between the tribes to be submitted to the President for arbitrament, etc.

ARTICLE 4. The said band represented in council shall withdraw from the routes overland already established, or hereafter to be established through their country; and in consideration thereof the Government of the United States agree to pay to the said band the sum of six thousand dollars annually, for twenty years, in such articles as the Secretary of the Interior may direct: *Provided*, That said band so represented in council shall faithfully conform to the requirements of this treaty.

Indians to withdraw from overland routes.

Payments.

Proviso.

ARTICLE 5. Should any individual, or individuals, or portion of the Lower Brulé band of Dakotas, or Sioux, represented in council, desire hereafter to locate permanently upon any part of the lands claimed by the said band, for the purpose of agricultural or other pursuits, it is hereby agreed by the parties to this treaty that such individual or individuals shall be protected in such location against any annoyance or molestation on the part of whites or Indians.

Individual Indians locating on lands to be protected.

ARTICLE 6. It is hereby agreed upon the part of the Government of the United States that the said band of Lower Brulés shall locate on a permanent reservation at or near the mouth of the White River, to include Fort Lookout, twenty miles in a straight line along the Missouri River, and ten miles in depth; and that upon the actual occupation of not less than fifty lodges or families of said reservation, and their engaging permanently in agricultural and other kindred pursuits, the Government of the United States agree to furnish at its own cost the sum of twenty-five dollars for each and every lodge or family so

Reservation for Lower Brulé.

Boundaries.

Payment for agricultural and other purposes.

engaged, as a common fund, to be expended in stock, agricultural and other implements and general improvements as shall be directed by the Secretary of the Interior; the said sum to be furnished annually **Stock, etc., to be the property of the United States.** for five years. It being understood that the said stock, agricultural and other implements shall be and remain the property of the United States, to be used and employed for the exclusive benefit of the lodges or families so located, and in no case to be sold or alienated by the said band or any member thereof; and the United States further **Blacksmith and farmer.** engage to employ at its own cost a blacksmith and farmer for the benefit of the said lodges or families.

Roads. The United States reserve the right to construct a road or roads through the said reservation.

Whites not to go, etc., thereon. No white person, other than officers, agents or employés of the United States, shall be permitted to go on or remain on the said reservation, unless previously admitted as a member of the said band according to their usages.

Schools. Whenever the Secretary of the Interior may so direct, schools for the instruction of the said band may be opened on the said reservation.

Two Kettles band may be located adjoining Brulé. ARTICLE 7. The undersigned chiefs of the Brulés, hereby further agree that should the Two Kettles band of the Dakota or Sioux Indians be located adjoining them, they will cheerfully allow them to do so, and also agree that the employés secured to the Brulés may be used also for the joint benefit of the said Two Kettles, at the discretion of the Government.

Amendments to be binding. ARTICLE 8. Any amendment or modification of this treaty by the Senate of the United States shall be considered final and binding upon the said band, represented in council, as a part of this treaty, in the same manner as if it had been subsequently presented and agreed to by the chiefs and head-men of said band.

In testimony whereof, the Commissioners on the part of the United States, and the chiefs and headmen of the said Lower Brulé band of Dakota or Sioux, have hereunto set their hands, this fourteenth day of October, one thousand eight hundred and sixty-five, after the contents had previously been read, interpreted, and explained to the said chiefs and headmen.

> Newton Edmunds,
> Edward B. Taylor,
> S. R. Curtis, major-general,
> H. H. Sibley, brigadier-general,
> Henry W. Reed,
> Orrin Guernsey,
> Commissioners on the part of the United States.

Chiefs:

Muz-zah-wy-ah-tay, The Iron Nation, his x mark.

Tah-ton-kah-wak-kon, Medicine Ball, his x mark.

Pta-son-we-chak-tay, The One who Killed the White Buffalo Cow, his x mark.

She-o-tche-kah, Little Pheasant, his x mark.

Pta-san-man-nee, White Buffalo Cow that walks, his x mark.

Chon-tay-o-kit-e-kah, The Brave Heart, his x mark.

Tah-o-pee, The Wounded Man, his x mark.

Wag-ah-mo-ah-win, The Gourd Ear Rings, his x mark.

E-chap-sin-ta-muz-zah, The Iron Whip, his x mark.

Chief soldiers:

Ze-te-kah-dan-sap-pah, The Blackbird, his x mark.

Wah-hah-chunki-e-un-ka, The Shield that Runs, his x mark.

Muck-a-pee-e-chash-nah, The Cloud that Rattles, his x mark.

Is-to-o-pee, The Wounded Arm, his x mark.

Min-do-ton-kah-che-kah, The Little Partisan, his x mark.

Wah-min-dee-shon-ton-kah, The War Eagle with Large Feathers, his x mark.

Signed by the Commissioners on the part of the United States, and by the chiefs and headmen, after the treaty had been fully read, interpreted, and explained in our presence:—

A. W. Hubbard, M. C., Sixth district Iowa.
S. S. Curtis, major, Second Colorado Cavalry, brevet lieutenant-colonel.
W. S. Woods, surgeon, U. S. Volunteers.
E. F. Ruth, secretary to Commission.
R. R. Hitt, reporter of Commission.
Zephier Recontre, his x mark, interpreter.
Charles Degre, his x mark, interpreter.

TREATY WITH THE CHEYENNE AND ARAPAHO, 1865.

Articles of a treaty made and concluded at the camp on the Little Arkansas River, in the State of Kansas, on the fourteenth day of October, in the year of our Lord one thousand eight hundred and sixty-five, by and between John B. Sanborn, William S. Harney, Thomas Murphy, Kit Carson, William W. Bent, Jesse H. Leavenworth, and James Steele, commissioners on the part of the United States, and the undersigned, chiefs and head-men of and representing the confederate tribes of Arrapahoe and Cheyenne Indians of the Upper Arkansas River, they being duly authorized by their respective tribes to act in the premises.

Oct. 14, 1865.

14 Stats., 703.
Ratified May 22, 1866.
Proclaimed Feb. 2, 1867.

ARTICLE 1. It is agreed by the parties to this treaty that hereafter perpetual peace shall be maintained between the people and Government of the United States and the Indians parties hereto, and that the Indians parties hereto, shall forever remain at peace with each other, and with all other Indians who sustain friendly relations with the Government of the United States. For the purpose of enforcing the provisions of this article it is agreed that in case hostile acts or depredations are committed by the people of the United States, or by Indians on friendly terms with the United States, against the tribe or tribes, or the individual members of the tribe or tribes, who are parties to this treaty, such hostile acts or depredations shall not be redressed by a resort to arms, but the party or parties aggrieved shall submit their complaints through their agent to the President of the United States, and thereupon an impartial arbitration shall be had, under his direction, and the award thus made shall be binding on all parties interested, and the Government of the United States will in good faith enforce the same. And the Indians, parties hereto, on their part, agree, in case crimes or other violations of law shall be committed by any person or persons, members of their tribe, such person or persons shall, upon complaint being made, in writing, to their agent, superintendent of Indian affairs, or to other proper authority, by the party injured, and verified by affidavit, be delivered to the person duly authorized to take such person or persons into custody, to the end that such person or persons may be punished according to the laws of the United States.

Perpetual peace.

Hostile acts to be settled by arbitration.

Members of tribes committing depredations to be surrendered.

ARTICLE 2. The United States hereby agree that the district of country embraced within the following limits, or such portion of the same as may hereafter be designated by the President of the United States for that purpose, viz: commencing at the mouth of the Red Creek or Red Fork of the Arkansas River; thence up said creek or fork to its source; thence westwardly to a point on the Cimarone River, opposite the mouth of Buffalo Creek; thence due north to the Arkansas River; thence down the same to the beginning, shall be, and is hereby, set apart for the absolute and undisturbed use and occupation of the tribes who are parties to this treaty, and of such other friendly tribes as they

Reservation for Indians who are parties hereto.

Boundaries.

No whites except.
etc., to settle thereon,
unless.
may from time to time agree to admit among them, and that no white person, except officers, agents, and employees of the Government,
Indians not required
to settle thereon, un-
til, etc.
shall go upon or settle within the country embraced within said limits, unless formerly admitted and incorporated into some one of the tribes lawfully residing there, according to its laws and usages: *Provided, however*, That said Indians shall not be required to settle upon said reservation until such time as the United States shall have extinguished all claims of title thereto on the part of other Indians, so that the Indians parties hereto may live thereon at peace with all other tribes:
Provided, however, That as soon as practicable, with the assent of said tribe, the President of the United States shall designate for said tribes a reservation, no part of which shall be within the State of Kansas, and cause them as soon as practicable to remove to and settle thereon, but no such reservation shall be designated upon any reserve belonging to any other Indian tribe or tribes without their consent.

To remove thereto
and not leave unless,
etc.
The Indians parties hereto, on their part, expressly agree to remove to and accept as their permanent home the country embraced within said limits whenever directed so to do by the President of the United States, in accordance with the provisions of this treaty, and that they will not go from said country for hunting or other purposes without the consent in writing of their agent or other authorized person, such written consent in all cases specifying the purpose for which such leave is granted, and shall be borne with them upon their excursions as evidence that they are rightfully away from their reservation, and shall be respected by all officers, employees, and citizens of the United States as their sufficient safeguard and protection against injury or damage in person or property by any and all persons whomsoever.

It is further agreed by the Indians parties hereto that when absent from their reservation they will refrain from the commission of any depredations or injuries to the person or property of all persons sustaining friendly relations with the Government of the United States:
that they will not, while so absent, encamp by day or night within ten miles of any of the main traveled routes or roads through the country to which they go, or of the military posts, towns, or villages therein, without the consent of the commanders of such military posts, or of
Claims to other
lands relinquished,
and especially to cer-
tain thus bounded.
the civil authorities of such towns or villages; and that henceforth they will, and do hereby, relinquish all claims or rights in and to any portion of the United States or Territories, except such as is embraced within the limits aforesaid, and more especially their claims and rights in and to the country bounded as follows, viz: beginning at the junction of the north and south forks of the Platte River; thence up the north fork to the top of the principal range of the Rocky Mountains, or to the Red Buttes; thence southwardly along the summit of the Rocky Mountains to the headwaters of the Arkansas River; thence down the Arkansas River to the Cimarone crossing of the same; thence to the place of beginning; which country they claim to have originally owned, and never to have relinquished the title thereto.

Until removed to
reservation, Indians
to be where.
ARTICLE 3. It is further agreed that until the Indians parties hereto have removed to the reservation provided for by the preceding article in pursuance of the stipulations thereof, said Indians shall be, and they are hereby, expressly permitted to reside upon and range at pleasure throughout the unsettled portions of that part of the country they claim as originally theirs, which lies between the Arkansas and Platte Rivers; and that they shall and will not go elsewhere, except upon the terms and conditions prescribed by the preceding article in
relation to leaving the reservation thereby provided for: *Provided*, That the provisions of the preceding article in regard to encamping within ten miles of main travelled routes, military posts, towns, and

villages shall be in full force as to occupancy of the country named and permitted by the terms of this article: *Provided, further*, That they, the said Indians, shall and will at all times during such occupancy, without delay, report to the commander of the nearest military post the presence in or approach to said country of any hostile bands of Indians whatsoever.

Proviso.

ARTICLE 4. It is further agreed by the parties hereto that the United States may lay off and build through the reservation, provided for by Article 2 of this treaty, such roads or highways as may be deemed necessary; and may also establish such military posts within the same as may be found necessary in order to preserve peace among the Indians, and in order to enforce such laws, rules, and regulations as are now, or may from time to time be, prescribed by the President and Congress of the United States for the protection of the rights of persons and property among the Indians residing upon said reservation; and further, that in time of war such other military posts as may be considered essential to the general interests of the United States may be established: *Provided, however*, That upon the building of such roads, or establishment of such military posts, the amount of injury sustained by reason thereof by the Indians inhabiting said reservation shall be ascertained under direction of the President of the United States, and thereupon such compensation shall be made to said Indians as in the judgment of the Congress of the United States may be deemed just and proper.

United States may build roads through reservation and establish military posts.

Damages therefor to be ascertained and paid.

ARTICLE 5. At the special request of the Cheyenne and Arrapahoe Indians, parties to this treaty, the United States agree to grant, by patent in fee-simple, to the following-named persons, all of whom are related to the Cheyennes or Arrapahoes by blood, to each an amount of land equal to one section of six hundred and forty acres, viz: To Mrs. Margaret Wilmarth and her children, Virginia Fitzpatrick, and Andrew Jackson Fitzpatrick; to Mrs. Mary Keith and her children, William Keith, Mary J. Keith, and Francis Keith; to Mrs. Matilda Pepperdin and her child, Miss Margaret Pepperdin; to Robert Poisal and John Poisal; to Edmund Guerrier, Rosa Guerrier, and Julia Guerrier; to William W. Bent's daughter, Mary Bent Moore, and her three children, Adia Moore, William Bent Moore, and George Moore; to William W. Bent's children, George Bent, Charles Bent, and Julia Bent; to A-ma-che, the wife of John Prowers, and her children, Mary Prowers and Susan Prowers; to the children of Ote-se-ot-see, wife of John Y. Sickles, viz: Margaret, Minnie, and John; to the children of John S. Smith, interpreter, William Gilpin Smith, and daughter Armama; to Jenny Lind Crocker, daughter of Ne-souhoe, or Are-you-there, wife of Lieutenant Crocker; to —— Winsor, daughter of Tow-e-nah, wife of A. T. Winsor, sutler, formerly at Fort Lyon. Said lands to be selected under the direction of the Secretary of the Interior, from the reservation established by the 1st article of their treaty of February 18, A. D. 1861: *Provided*, That said locations shall not be made upon any lands heretofore granted by the United States to any person, State, or corporation, for any purpose.

Patents for 640 acres in fee simple to certain persons.

ARTICLE 6. The United States being desirous to express its condemnation of, and, as far as may be, repudiate the gross and wanton outrages perpetrated against certain bands of Cheyenne and Arrapahoe Indians, on the twenty-ninth day of November, A. D. 1864, at Sand Creek, in Colorado Territory, while the said Indians were at peace with the United States, and under its flag, whose protection they had by lawful authority been promised and induced to seek, and the Government being desirous to make some suitable reparation for the injuries then done, will grant three hundred and twenty acres of land by patent to each of the following-named chiefs of said bands, viz: Moke-

Grants of lands in reparation for outrages against certain bands, to certain chiefs of bands.

ta-ve-to, or Black Kettle; Oh-tah-ha-ne-so-weel, or Seven Bulls; Alik-ke-home-ma, or Little Robe; Moke-tah-vo-ve-hoe, or Black White Man; and will in like manner grant to each other person of said bands made a widow, or who lost a parent upon that occasion, one hundred and sixty acres of land, the names of such persons to be ascertained **Conditions of grants.** under the direction of the Secretary of the Interior: *Provided*, That said grants shall be conditioned that all devises, grants, alienations, leases, and contracts relative to said lands, made or entered into during the period of fifty years from the date of such patents, shall be **Lands, how to be selected.** unlawful and void.   Said lands shall be selected under the direction of the Secretary of the Interior within the limits of country hereby set apart as a reservation for the Indians parties to this treaty, and shall be free from assessment and taxation so long as they remain inalien- **Further compensation for property lost.** able.   The United States will also pay in United States securities, animals, goods, provisions, or such other useful articles as may, in the discretion of the Secretary of the Interior, be deemed best adapted to the respective wants and conditions of the persons named in the schedule hereto annexed, they being present and members of the bands who suffered at Sand Creek, upon the occasion aforesaid, the sums set opposite their names, respectively, as a compensation for property belonging to them, and then and there destroyed or taken from them by the United States troops aforesaid.

Annuities for forty years. ARTICLE 7. The United States agree that they will expend annually during the period of forty years, from and after the ratification of this treaty, for the benefit of the Indians who are parties hereto, and of such others as may unite with them in pursuance of the terms hereof, in such manner and for such purposes as, in the judgment of the Secretary of the Interior, for the time being, will best subserve their wants and interests as a people, the following amounts, that is to say, until such time as said Indians shall be removed to their reservation, **Amount.** as provided for by Article 2 of this treaty, an amount which shall be equal to twenty dollars per capita for each person entitled to participate in the beneficial provisions of this treaty, and from and after the time when such removal shall have been accomplished, an amount which shall be equal to forty dollars per capita for each person entitled **When to be delivered.** as aforesaid.   Such proportion of the expenditure provided for by this article as may be considered expedient to distribute in the form of annuities shall be delivered to said Indians as follows, viz: one-third thereof during the spring, and two-thirds thereof during the autumn of each year.

Present number of Indians. For the purpose of determining from time to time the aggregate amount to be expended under the provisions of this article, it is agreed that the number entitled to its beneficial provisions the coming year is two thousand eight hundred, and that an accurate census of the Indians entitled shall be taken at the time of the annuity payment in the spring of each year by their agent or other person designated for that purpose by the Secretary of the Interior, which census shall be the basis on which the amount to be expended the next ensuing year shall be determined.

Other portion of tribe to be urged to join in this treaty. ARTICLE 8. The Indians parties to this treaty expressly covenant and agree that they will use their utmost endeavor to induce that portion of the respective tribes not now present to unite with them and acceed to the provisions of this treaty, which union and accession shall be evidenced and made binding on all parties whenever such absentees shall have participated in the beneficial provisions of this treaty.

ARTICLE 9. Upon the ratification of this treaty all former treaties are hereby abrogated.

In testimony whereof, the said Commissioners as aforesaid, and the undersigned chiefs and headmen of the confederated tribes of the Arrapahoes and Cheyennes of the Upper Arkansas, have hereunto set their hands and seals, at the place and on the day and year first hereinbefore written.

John B. Sanborn,	[SEAL.]
Wm. S. Harney,	[SEAL.]
Thos. Murphy,	[SEAL.]
Kit Carson,	[SEAL.]
Wm. W. Bent,	[SEAL.]
J. H. Leavenworth,	[SEAL.]
James Steele,	[SEAL.]

Commissioners on the part of the United States.

Moke-ta-ve-to, or Black Kettle, head chief, his x mark. [SEAL.]

Oh-to-ah-ne-so-to-wheo, or Seven Bulls, chief, his x mark. [SEAL.]

Hark-kah-o-me, or Little Robe, chief, his x mark. [SEAL.]

Moke-tah-vo-ve-ho, or Black White Man, chief, his x mark. [SEAL.]

Mun-a-men-ek, or Eagle's Head, headman, his x mark. [SEAL.]

O-to-ah-nis-to, or Bull that Hears, headman, his x mark. [SEAL.]

On the part of the Cheyennes.

Oh-has-tee, or Little Raven, head chief, his x mark. [SEAL.]

Oh-hah-mah-hah, or Storm, chief, his x mark. [SEAL.]

Pah-uf-pah-top, or Big Mouth, chief, his x mark. [SEAL.]

Ah-cra-kah-tau-nah, or Spotted Wolf, chief, his x mark. [SEAL.]

Ah-nah-wat-tan, or Black Man, headman, his x mark. [SEAL.]

Nah-a-nah-cha, or Chief in Everything, headman, his x mark. [SEAL.]

Chi-e-nuk, or Haversack, headman, his x mark. [SEAL.]

On the part of the Arrapahoes.

Signed and sealed in the presence of—

John S. Smith, United States interpreter.
W. R. Irwin, ⎫
O. T. Atwood, ⎬ secretaries.
S. A. Kingman,⎭
D. C. McNeil,

E. W. Wynkoop,
Bon. H. Van Havre,
J. E. Badger,
W. W. Rich.

N. B.—The Apache tribe was brought into the provisions of the above treaty by the second article of the treaty with the Apaches, Cheyennes and Arrapahoes, proclaimed May 26, 1866.

TREATY WITH THE APACHE, CHEYENNE, AND ARAPAHO, 1865.

Oct. 17, 1865.

14 Stat., 713.
Ratified May 22, 1866.
Proclaimed May 26, 1866.

Preamble.

Whereas a treaty was made and concluded, by and between the undersigned commissioners on the part of the United States, and the undersigned chiefs and head-men of the Cheyenne and Arrapahoe tribes of Indians, on the part of said tribes, on the fourteenth day of October, A. D. 1865, at the council-grounds on the Little Arkansas River, in the State of Kansas; and, whereas, the Apache Indians, who have been heretofore confederated with the Kiowa and Comanche tribes of Indians, are desirous of dissolving said confederation and uniting their fortunes with the said Cheyennes and Arrapahoes; and whereas the said last-named tribes are willing to receive among themselves on an equal footing with the members of their own tribes, the said Apache Indians; and the United States, by their said commissioners, having given their assent thereto; it is therefore hereby agreed by and between the United States, by their said commissioners, and the said Cheyenne, Arrapahoe, and Apache Indians, by the undersigned chiefs and head-men of said tribes respectively, as follows, viz:

ARTICLE 1. The said Cheyenne, Arrapahoe, and Apache tribes, henceforth shall be and they are hereby united, and the United States will hereafter recognize said tribes as the confederated bands or tribes of Cheyenne, Arrapahoe, and Apache Indians.

Cheyenne, Arapaho, and Apache tribes are united and recognized as confederated tribes by the United States.

ARTICLE 2. The several terms, stipulations and agreements to be done and performed on the part of the United States for and with the said Cheyenne and Arrapahoe tribes of Indians, and by the said Cheyenne

Stipulations of former treaty to be binding upon the parties hereto.

and Arrapahoe tribes of Indians, for and with the United States, by the provisions of said treaty of October 14th, A. D. 1865, shall be done and performed by the United States for and on behalf of the said confederated tribes or bands of Cheyenne, Arrapahoe, and Apache Indians, and on their part shall be done, observed and performed to, with and for the United States in the same manner, to the same extent, and for like objects, to all intents and purposes, as would have been the case had said treaty been originally made and executed with the said confederated tribes of Cheyenne, Arrapahoe, and Apache Indians.

In testimony whereof, the undersigned, Commissioners on the part of the United states, and the chiefs and headmen of said tribes, have hereunto set their hands and seals at the council-ground on the Little Arkansas, in the State of Kansas, this 17th day of October, A. D. 1865.

John B. Sanborn,   [SEAL.]
Wm. S. Harney,   [SEAL.]
James Steele,   [SEAL.]
Wm. W. Bent,   [SEAL.]
Kit Carson,   [SEAL.]
Thos. Murphy,   [SEAL.]
J. H. Leavenworth,   [SEAL.]
Commissioners on the part of the United States.

Kou-zhon-ta-co, or Poor Bear, head chief, his x mark. [SEAL.]
Ba-zhe-ech, or Iron Shirt, his x mark. [SEAL.]
Az-che-om-a-te-ne, or the Old Fool Man, chief, his x mark. [SEAL.]
Karn-tin-ta, or the Crow, chief, his x mark. [SEAL.]
Mah-vip-pah, or The Wolf Sleeve, chief, his x mark. [SEAL.]
Nahn-tan, or The Chief, his x mark. [SEAL.]
On the part of the Apaches.
Moke-ta-ve-to, or Black Kettle, head chief, his x mark. [SEAL.]
Oh-to-ah-ne-so-to-wheo, or Seven Bulls, chief, his x mark. [SEAL.]
Hark-kah-o-me, or Little Robe, chief, his x mark. [SEAL.]
Moke-tah-vo-ve-ho, or Black White Man, chief, his x mark. [SEAL.]

Mun-a-men-ek, or Eagle's Head, headman, his x mark. [SEAL.]
O-to-ah-nis-to, or Bull that Hears, headman, his x mark. [SEAL.]
On the part of the Cheyennes.
Oh-has-tee, or Little Raven, head chief, his x mark. [SEAL.]
Oh-hah-mah-hah, or Storm, chief, his x mark. [SEAL.]
Pah-uf-pah-top, or Big Mouth, chief, his x mark. [SEAL.]
Ah-cra-ka-tau-nah, or Spotted Wolf, chief, his x mark. [SEAL.]
Ah-nah-wat-tan, or Black Man, headman, his x mark. [SEAL.]
Nah-a-nah-cha, Chief in Everything, headman, his x mark. [SEAL.]
Chi-e-nuk, or Haversack, headman, his x mark. [SEAL.]
On the part of the Arrapahoes.

Signed and sealed in presence of—
W. R. Irwin, Secretary.
D. C. McNeil.

TREATY WITH THE COMANCHE AND KIOWA, 1865.

Oct. 18, 1865.

14 Stat., 717.
Ratified May 22, 1866.
Proclaimed May 26, 1866.

Articles of a treaty made and concluded at the council-ground on the Little Arkansas River eight miles from the mouth of said river, in the State of Kansas, on the eighteenth day of October, in the year of our Lord one thousand eight hundred and sixty-five, by and between John B. Sanborn, William S. Harney, Thomas Murphy, Kit Carson, William W. Bent, Jesse H. Leavenworth, and James Steele, Commissioners on the part of the United States, and the undersigned chiefs and head-men of the several bands of Comanche Indians specified in connection with their signatures, and the chiefs and head-men of the Kiowa tribe of Indians, the said chiefs and head-men by the said bands and tribes being thereunto duly authorized.

Perpetual peace.

ARTICLE 1. It is agreed by the parties to this treaty that hereafter perpetual peace shall be maintained between the people and Government of the United States and the Indians parties hereto, and that the

Indians parties hereto shall forever remain at peace with each other and with all other Indians who sustain friendly relations with the Government of the United States.

For the purpose of enforcing the provisions of this article, it is agreed that in case hostile acts or depredations are committed by the people of the United States, or by the Indians on friendly terms with the United States, against the tribe or tribes or the individual members of the tribe or tribes who are parties to this treaty, such hostile acts or depredations shall not be redressed by a resort to arms, but the party or parties aggrieved shall submit their complaints, through their agent, to the President of the United States, and thereupon an impartial arbitration shall be had under his direction, and the award thus made shall be binding on all parties interested, and the Government of the United States will in good faith enforce the same. *Hostile acts to be settled by arbitration.*

And the Indians parties hereto, on their part, agree, in case crimes or other violations of law shall be committed by any person or persons members of their tribe, such person or persons shall, upon complaint being made in writing to their agent, superintendent of Indian affairs, or to other proper authority, by the party injured, and verified by affidavit, be delivered to the person duly authorized to take such person or persons into custody, to the end that such person or persons may be punished according to the laws of the United States. *Members of the tribe committing crimes to be surrendered.*

ARTICLE 2. The United States hereby agree that the district of country embraced within the following limits, or such portion of the same as may hereafter from time to time be designated by the President of the United States for that purpose, viz: commencing at the northeast corner of New Mexico, thence south to the southeast corner of the same: thence northeastwardly to a point on main Red River opposite the mouth of the North Fork of said river: thence down said river to the 98th degree of west longitude: thence due north on said meridian to the Cimarone river: thence up said river to a point where the same crosses the southern boundary of the State of Kansas: thence along said southern boundary of Kansas to the southwest corner of said State: thence west to the place of beginning, shall be and is hereby set apart for the absolute and undisturbed use and occupation of the tribes who are parties to this treaty, and of such other friendly tribes as have heretofore resided within said limits, or as they may from time to time agree to admit among them, and that no white person except officers, agents, and employés of the Government shall go upon or settle within the country embraced within said limits, unless formally admitted and incorporated into some one of the tribes lawfully residing there, according to its laws and usages. The Indians parties hereto on their part expressly agree to remove to and accept as their permanent home the country embraced within said limits, whenever directed so to do by the President of the United States, in accordance with the provisions of this treaty, and that they will not go from said country for hunting purposes without the consent in writing of their agent or other authorized person, specifying the purpose for which such leave is granted, and such written consent in all cases shall be borne with them upon their excursions, as evidence that they are rightfully away from their reservation, and shall be respected by all officers, employés, and citizens of the United States, as their sufficient safeguard and protection against injury or damage in person or property, by any and all persons whomsoever. It is further agreed by the Indians parties hereto, that when absent from their reservation, they will refrain from the commission of any depredations or injuries to the person or property of all persons sustaining friendly relations with the Government of the United States; that they will not while so absent encamp, by day or night, within ten miles of any of the main travelled routes or roads through the country to which they go, or of the military posts, *Reservation for Indians who are parties hereto.* *Boundaries, no whites except, etc., to settle thereon unless, etc.* *Indians to remove thereto and not leave, unless, etc.* *To refrain from depredations.* *Not to encamp within ten miles of, etc.*

towns, or villages therein, without the consent of the commanders of such military posts, or of the civil authorities of such towns or villages, and that henceforth they will and do hereby, relinquish all claims or rights in and to any portion of the United States or territories, except such as is embraced within the limits aforesaid, and more especially their claims and rights in and to the country north of the Cimarone River and west of the eastern boundary of New Mexico.

ARTICLE 3. It is further agreed that until the Indians parties hereto have removed to the reservation provided for by the preceding article, in pursuance of the stipulations thereof, said Indians shall be and they are hereby, expressly permitted to reside upon and range at pleasure throughout the unsettled portions of that part of the country they claim as originally theirs, which lies south of the Arkansas River, as well as the country embraced within the limits of the reservation provided for by the preceding article, and that they shall and will not go elsewhere, except upon the terms and conditions prescribed by the preceding article in relation to leaving said reservation: *Provided*, That the provisions of the preceding article in regard to encamping within ten miles of main travelled routes, military posts, towns, and villages, shall be in full force as to the privileges granted by this article: *And provided further*, That they, the said Indians, shall and will at all times, and without delay, report to the commander of the nearest military post the presence in or approach to said country of any hostile band or bands of Indians whatever.

ARTICLE 4. It is further agreed by the parties hereto that the United States may lay off and build through the reservation, provided for by Article 2 of this treaty, roads or highways as may be deemed necessary, and may also establish such military posts within the same as may be found necessary, in order to preserve peace among the Indians, and in order to enforce such laws, rules, and regulations as are now or may from time to time be prescribed by the President and Congress of the United States for the protection of the rights of persons and property among the Indians residing upon said reservation, and further, that in time of war such other military posts as may be considered essential to the general interests of the United States may be established: *Provided, however*, That upon the building of such roads, or establishment of such military posts, the amount of injury sustained by reason thereof by the Indians inhabiting said reservation shall be ascertained under direction of the President of the United States, and thereupon such compensation shall be made to said Indians as, in the judgment of the Congress of the United States, may be deemed just and proper.

ARTICLE 5. The United States agree that they will expend annually, during the period of forty years, from and after the ratification of this treaty, for the benefit of the Indians who are parties hereto, and of such others as may unite with them in pursuance of the terms hereof, in such manner and for such purposes as, in the judgment of the Secretary of the Interior for the time being, will best subserve their wants and interests as a people, the following amounts, that is to say, until such time as said Indians shall be removed to their reservations, as provided for by article two of this treaty, an amount which shall be equal to ten dollars per capita for each person entitled to participate in the beneficial provisions of this treaty; and from and after the time when such removal shall have been accomplished, an amount which shall be equal to fifteen dollars per capita for each person entitled as aforesaid. Such proportion of the expenditure provided for by this article as may be considered expedient to distribute in the form of annuities shall be delivered to said Indians as follows, viz: One-third thereof during the spring, and two-thirds thereof during the autumn of each year.

Marginal notes:

Claims to other lands relinquished.

Until removal to reservation Indians to be where.

Proviso.

Proviso.

United States may build roads through reservation and establish military posts.

Damages therefor to be ascertained and paid.

Annuities. See post, Art. 10, treaty of Oct. 21, 1867.

For the purpose of determining from time to time the aggregate amount to be expended under the provisions of this article, it is agreed that the number entitled to its beneficial provisions the coming year is four thousand, and that an accurate census of the Indians entitled shall be taken at the time of the annuity payment in the spring of each year by their agent or other person designated by the Secretary of the Interior, which census shall be the basis on which the amount to be expended the next ensuing year shall be determined.

Payment of annuities.

ARTICLE 6. The Indians parties to this treaty expressly covenant and agree that they will use their utmost endeavors to induce that portion of the respective tribes not now present to unite with them and accede to the provisions of this treaty, which union and accession shall be evidenced and made binding on all parties whenever such absentees shall have participated in the beneficial provisions of this treaty.

Other portions of tribes to be urged to join in this treaty.

In testimony whereof, the said Commissioners on the part of the United States, and the chiefs and headmen of the said bands of Camanche Indians and of the Kiowa tribe of Indians, hereinbefore referred to, and designated in connection with their signatures, have hereunto subscribed their names and affixed their seals on the day and year first above written.

Execution.

John B. Sanborn,	[SEAL.]
Wm. S. Harney,	[SEAL.]
Kit Carson,	[SEAL.]
Wm. W. Bent,	[SEAL.]
James Steele,	[SEAL.]
Thos. Murphy,	[SEAL.]
J. H. Leavenworth,	[SEAL.]

Commissioners on the part of the United States.

Signed and sealed in presence of—
W. R. Irwin, secretary.
Wm. T. Kittridge.
D. C. McNeil.
Jas. S. Boyd.

Tab-e-nan-i-kah, or Rising Sun, chief of Yampirica, or Root Eater band of Camanches, for Paddy-wah-say-mer and Ho-to-yo-koh-wat's bands, his x mark. [SEAL.]

Esh-e-tave-pa-rah, or Female Infant, headman of Yampirica band of Camanches, his x mark. [SEAL.]

A-sha-hab-beet, or Milky Way, chief Penne-taha, or Sugar Eater band of Camanches, and for Co-che-te-ka, or Buffalo Eater band, his x mark. [SEAL.]

Queen-ah-e-vah, or Eagle Drinking, head chief of No-co-nee or Go-about band of Camanches, his x mark. [SEAL.]

Ta-ha-yer-quoip, or Horse's Back, second chief of No-co-nee or Go-about band of Camanches, his x mark. [SEAL.]

Pocha-naw-quoip, or Buffalo Hump, third chief of Penne-taka, or Sugar Eater band of Camanches, his x mark. [SEAL.]

Ho-to-yo-koh-wot, or Over the Buttes, chief of Yampirica band, his x mark. [SEAL.]

Parry-wah-say-mer, or Ten Bears, chief of Yampirica band, his x mark. [SEAL.]

Bo-yah-wah-to-yeh-be, or Iron Mountain, chief of Yampirica band of Camanches, his x mark. [SEAL.]

Bo-wah-quas-suh, or Iron Shirt, chief of De-na-vi band, or Liver Eater band of Camanches, his x mark. [SEAL.]

To-sa-wi, or Silver Brooch, head chief of Pennetaka band of Camanches, his x mark. [SEAL.]

Queil-park, or Lone Wolf, his x mark. [SEAL.]

Wah-toh-konk, or Black Eagle, his x mark. [SEAL.]

Zip-ki-yah, or Big Bow, his x mark. [SEAL.]

Sa-tan-ta, or White Bear, his x mark. [SEAL.]

Ton-a-en-ko, or Kicking Eagle, his x mark. [SEAL.]

Settem-ka-yah, or Bear Runs over a Man, his x mark. [SEAL.]

Kaw-pe-ah, or Plumed Lance, his x mark. [SEAL.]

To-hau-son, or Little Mountain, his x mark. [SEAL.]

Sa-tank, or Sitting Bear, his x mark. [SEAL.]

Pawnee, or Poor Man, his x mark. [SEAL.]

Ta-ki-bull, or Stinking Saddle Cloth, chief of the Kiowa tribe, his x mark. [SEAL.

TREATY WITH THE SIOUX—TWO-KETTLE BAND, 1865.

Oct. 19, 1865.

14 Stats., 723.
Ratified Mar. 5, 1866.
Proclaimed Mar. 17, 1866.

Articles of a treaty made and concluded at Fort Sully, in the Territory of Dakota, by and between Newton Edmunds, governor and ex-officio superintendent of Indian affairs of Dakota Territory, Edward B. Taylor, superintendent of Indian affairs for the northern superintendency, Major-General S. R. Curtis, Brigadier-General H. H. Sibley, Henry W. Reed, and Orrin Guernsey, commissioners on the part of the United States, duly appointed by the President, and the undersigned, chiefs and head-men of the Two-Kettles band of Dakota or Sioux Indians.

Authority and jurisdiction of the United States acknowledged.

ARTICLE 1. The Two-Kettles band of Dakota or Sioux Indians represented in council, hereby acknowledge themselves to be subject to the exclusive jurisdiction and authority of the United States, and hereby obligate and bind themselves individually and collectively, not only to cease all hostilities against the persons and property of its citizens, but to use their influence, and, if necessary, physical force, to prevent other bands of the Dakota or Sioux, or other adjacent tribes, from making hostile demonstrations against the Government of the United States, or its people.

Persons and property of other tribes not to be first attacked.

ARTICLE 2. Inasmuch as the Government of the United States is desirous to arrest the effusion of blood between the Indian tribes within its jurisdiction, hitherto at war with each other, the Two-Kettles band of Dakota or Sioux, represented in council, anxious to respect the wishes of the Government, hereby agree and bind themselves to discontinue, for the future, all attacks upon the persons or property of other tribes, unless first assailed by them, and to use their influence to promote peace everywhere in the region occupied or frequented by them.

Controversies to be submitted to the arbitrament of the President.

ARTICLE 3. All controversies or differences arising between the Two-Kettles band of Dakota or Sioux, represented in council, and other tribes of Indians, involving the question of peace or war, shall be submitted for the arbitrament of the President, or such person or persons as may be designated by him, and the decision or award faithfully observed by the said band, represented in council.

Indians to withdraw from overland routes.

ARTICLE 4. The said band, represented in council, shall withdraw from the routes overland already established, or hereafter to be established, through their country; and, in consideration thereof, the Government of the United States agree to pay to the said band the sum of six thousand dollars annually, for twenty years, in such articles as the Secretary of the Interior may direct: *Provided*, That the said bands so represented in council shall faithfully conform to the requirements of this treaty.

Individual Indians locating upon lands to be protected.

ARTICLE 5. Should any individual or individuals, or portion of the band of the Two-Kettles band of Dakota and Sioux Indians, represented in council, desire hereafter to locate permanently upon any part of the land claimed by the said band, for the purpose of agricultural or other pursuits, it is hereby agreed by the parties to this treaty that such individual or individuals shall be protected in such location against any annoyance or molestation on the part of whites or Indians: and where twenty lodges or families of the Two-Kettles band shall have located on lands for agricultural purposes, and signified the same

Payments for agricultural, etc., implements.

to their agent or superintendent, they as well as other families so locating shall receive the sum of twenty-five dollars annually, for five years, for each family, in agricultural implements and improvements; and when one hundred lodges or families shall have so engaged in

Farmer and blacksmith.
Teachers.

agricultural pursuits, they shall be entitled to a farmer and blacksmith, at the expense of the Government, also teachers, at the option of the Secretary of the Interior, when deemed necessary.

ARTICLE 6. Soldiers in the United States service having killed Ish- Indemnity for kill-
ing a chief.
tah-chah-ne-aha, (Puffing Eyes,) a friendly chief of the Two-Kettles band of Dakota or Sioux Indians, it is hereby agreed that the Government of the United States shall cause to be paid to the surviving widow of the deceased and his children, seventeen in number, the sum of five hundred dollars; and to the said tribe or band, in common, as indemnity for killing said chief, the sum of five hundred dollars, said payment to be made under the direction of the Secretary of the Interior.

ARTICLE 7. Any amendment or modification of this treaty by the Amendments to be
binding.
Senate of the United States shall be considered final and binding upon the said band, represented in council, as a part of this treaty, in the same manner as if it had been subsequently presented and agreed to by the chiefs and head-men of said band.

In testimony whereof, the Commissioners on the part of the United Execution.
States, and the chiefs and headmen of the said Two Kettles band of Dakota or Sioux, have hereunto set their hands, this nineteenth day of October, one thousand eight hundred and sixty-five, after the contents had previously been read, interpreted, and explained to the said chiefs and headmen.

Newton Edmunds,
Edward B. Taylor,
S. R. Curtis, major-general,
H. H. Sibley, brigadier-general,
Henry W. Reed,
Orrin Guernsey,
Commissioners on the part of the United States.

Cha-tan-skah, The White Hawk, chief, his x mark.

E-to-ke-ah, The Hump, chief, his x mark.

Shon-kah-wak-kon-ke-desh-kah, The Spotted Horse, chief, his x mark.

Mah-to-ke-desh-kah, The Spotted Bear, chief, his x mark.

Mah-to-to-pah, The Four Bears, his x mark.

Chan-tay-o-me-ne-o-me-ne, The Whirling Heart, his x mark.

Mah-to-a-cha-chah, The Bear that is like him, his x mark.

Tah-hoo-ka-zah-nom-pub, The Two Lances, his x mark.

Mah-to-ton-kah, The Big Bear, his x mark.

To-ke-chi-wy-a, He that Catches the Enemy, his x mark.

Mah-to-nan-gee, the Bear that Stands, his x mark.

Shon-kah-doo-tah, The Red Dog, his x mark.

Chon-nom-pah-pa-ge-nan-kah, He that wears the Pipe on his head, his x mark.

Tah-shon-kah-muz-zah, His Iron Dog, his x mark.

Ho-po-e-muz-zah, The Iron Wing, his x mark.

Chah-ge-lesh-kah-wak-ke-an, The Thunder Spotted Hoop, his x mark.

Hak-kah-doo-sah, The Fast Elk, his x mark.

Wy-ah-tah-ton-kah, The Big Nation, his x mark.

We-kee-pah, The One that Calls the Women, his x mark.

Fa-je-to, Green Grass, his x mark.

Chief Chon-ka-has-ka, Stinking Dog, his x mark.

Chief Pa-ta-sea-wah-bel-lu, White Cow Eagle, his x mark.

Signed by the Commissioners on the part of the United States, and by the chiefs and headmen, after the treaty had been fully read, interpreted, and explained, in our presence:—

A. W. Hubbard, M. C. Sixth district Iowa.

Hez. L. Hosmer, chief justice of Montana Territory.

Chas. C. G. Thornton, lieutenant-colonel Fourth U. S. Volunteers.

E. F. Ruth, secretary of commission.

O. D. Barrett, special agent Indian Affairs.

Zephier Recontere, his x mark, interpreter.

Charles Degre, his x mark, interpreter.

The foregoing signatures in this handwriting (that of Gen. Curtis) were made in presence of the undersigned.

Maj. A. P. Shreve, paymaster U. S. Army.

John Pattee, lieutenant-colonel Seventh Iowa Cavalry.

TREATY WITH THE BLACKFEET SIOUX, 1865.

Oct. 19, 1865.

14 Stat., 727.
Ratified Mar. 5, 1866.
Proclaimed Mar. 17, 1866.

Articles of a treaty made and concluded at Fort Sully, in the Territory of Dakota, by and between Newton Edmunds, governor and ex-officio superintendent of Indian affairs, of Dakota Territory, Edward B. Taylor, superintendent of Indian affairs for the northern superintendency, Major-General S. R. Curtis, Brigadier-General H. H. Sibley, Henry W. Reed, and Orrin Guernsey, commissioners on the part of the United States, duly appointed by the President, and the undersigned chiefs and headmen of the Blackfeet band of Dakota or Sioux Indians.

Jurisdiction of authority of the United States acknowledged, etc.

ARTICLE 1. The Blackfeet band of Dakota or Sioux Indians, represented in council, hereby acknowledge themselves to be subject to the exclusive jurisdiction and authority of the United States, and hereby obligate and bind themselves, individually and collectively, not only to cease all hostilities against the persons and property of its citizens, but to use their influence, and, if necessary, physical force to prevent other bands of the Dakota or Sioux, or other adjacent tribes from making hostile demonstrations against the Government of the United States, or its people.

Persons and property of other tribes not to be first attacked.

ARTICLE 2. Inasmuch as the Government of the United States is desirous to arrest the effusion of blood between the Indian tribes within its jurisdiction hitherto a[t] war with each other, the Blackfeet band of Dakota or Sioux, represented in council, anxious to respect the wishes of the Government, hereby agree and bind themselves to discontinue for the future all attacks upon the persons or property of other tribes, unless first assailed by them, and to use their influence to promote peace everywhere in the region occupied or frequented by them.

Controversies to be submitted to the arbitrament of the President.

ARTICLE 3. All controversies or differences arising between the Blackfeet band of Dakota or Sioux, represented in council, and other tribes of Indians, involving the question of peace or war, shall be submitted for the arbitrament of the President, or such person or persons as may be designated by him, and the decision or award faithfully observed by the said band represented in council.

Indians to withdraw from overland routes.

Payments.

Proviso.

ARTICLE 4. The said band, represented in council, shall withdraw from the routes overland already established or hereafter to be established, through their country, and in consideration thereof, the Government of the United States agree to pay to the said band the sum of seven thousand dollars annually, for twenty years, in such articles as the Secretary of the Interior may direct: *Provided*, That said band, so represented in council, shall faithfully conform to the requirements of this treaty.

Amendments to be binding.

ARTICLE 5. Any amendment or modification of this treaty by the [Senate of the United States shall be considered final and binding upon the] said band represented in council, as a part of this treaty, in the same manner as if it had been subsequently presented and agreed to by the chiefs and headmen of said nation.

In testimony whereof the commissioners on the part of the United States, and the chiefs and headmen of the said Blackfeet band of the Dakota or Sioux, have hereunto set their hands, this nineteenth day of October, one thousand eight hundred and sixty-five, after the contents had previously been read, interpreted, and explained to the said chiefs and headmen.

Newton Edmunds,
Edward B. Taylor,
S. R. Curtis, major-general,
H. H. Sibley, brigadier-general,
Henry W. Reed,
Orrin Guernsey.

Chiefs:

Wah-hah-chunk-i-ah-pee, The One that is used as a Shield, his x mark.

Wah-mun-dee-wak-kon-o, The War Eagle in the Air, his x mark.

Principal braves or soldiers:

Mah-to-ko-ke-pah, He that Fears the Bear, his x mark.

A-hack-ah-sap-pah, The Black Stag, his x mark.

A-hack-ah-we-chash-tah, The Stag Man, his x mark.

Mah-to-wash-tay, The Good Bear, his x mark.

Tah-ton-kah-ho-wash-tay, The Buffalo with a Fine Voice, his x mark.

Oya-hin-di-a-man-nee, The Track that Rings as it Walks, his x mark.

Shon-kah-hon-skah, The Long Dog, his x mark.

Shon-kah-wah-mun-dee, The Dog War Eagle, his x mark.

Wah-mun-dee-you-hah, He that has the War Eagle, his x mark.

Muz-zah-to-yah, The Blue Iron, his x mark.

Chief Chan-ta-pa-ta, Fire Heart, his x mark.

Chief Chan-ta-non-pas, Two Hearts, his x mark.

Signed by the Commissioners on the part of the United States, and by the chiefs and headmen after the treaty had been fully read, interpreted, and explained, in our presence:—

A. W. Hubbard, M. C. Sixth District Iowa.

E. F. Ruth, secretary to Commission.

O. D. Barrett, special agent Indian Affairs.

S. S. Curtis, major, Second Colorado Cavalry.

R. R. Hitt, reporter of the Commission.

Zephier Recontre, his x mark,

Charles Degres, his x mark,

Interpreter[s]

Soldiers:

Ce-ha-pa-chi-ke-la, Little Blackfoot, his x mark.

Chan-ta-pe-a, Strong Heart, his x mark.

Non-pa-ge-gu-mugama, Round Hand, his x mark.

TREATY WITH THE SIOUX—SANS ARCS BAND, 1865.

Articles of a treaty made and concluded at Fort Sully, in the Territory of Dakota, by and between Newton Edmunds, governor and ex-officio superintendent of Indian affairs of Dakota Territory, Edward B. Taylor, superintendent of Indian affairs for the northern superintendency, Major-General S. R. Curtis, Brigadier-General H. H. Sibley, Henry W. Reed, and Orrin Guernsey, commissioners on the part of the United States, duly appointed by the President, and the undersigned chiefs and head-men of the Sans Arcs band of Dakota or Sioux Indians.

Oct. 20, 1865.

14 Stat., 731.
Ratified Mar. 5, 1866.
Proclaimed Mar. 17, 1866.

ARTICLE 1. The Sans Arcs band of Dakota or Sioux Indians, represented in council, hereby acknowledge themselves to be subject to the exclusive jurisdiction and authority of the United States, and hereby obligate and bind themselves, individually and collectively, not only to cease all hostilities against the persons and property of its citizens, but to use their influence, and, if requisite, physical force, to prevent other bands of Dakota Indians, or other adjacent tribes, from making hostile demonstrations against the Government or people of the United States.

Authority and jurisdiction of the United States acknowledged.

ARTICLE 2. Inasmuch as the Government of the United States is desirous to arrest the effusion of blood between the Indian tribes within its jurisdiction hitherto at war with each other, the Sans Arcs band of Dakota or Sioux Indians, represented in council, anxious to respect the wishes of the Government, hereby agree to discontinue for the future all attacks upon the persons or property of other tribes, unless first attacked by them, and to use their influence to promote peace everywhere in the region occupied or frequented by them.

Persons and property of other tribes not to be first attacked.

Controversies to be submitted to the arbitrament of the President.

ARTICLE 3. All controversies or differences arising between the Sans Arcs band of Dakota or Sioux Indians, involving the question of peace or war, shall be submitted for the arbitrament of the President, or such person or persons as may be designated by him, and the decision or award shall be faithfully observed by the said band represented in council.

Indians to withdraw from overland routes.

Payments.

Proviso.

ARTICLE 4. The said band represented in council shall withdraw from the route overland already established, or hereafter to be established, through their country; and in consideration thereof the Government of the United States agree to pay the said band the sum of thirty dollars for each lodge or family, annually, for twenty years, in such articles as the Secretary of the Interior may direct: *Provided*, That said band so represented in council shall faithfully conform to the requirements of this treaty.

Individual Indians locating upon the lands to be protected.

Payments for agricultural, etc., implements.

Farmer and blacksmith.
Teachers.

ARTICLE 5. Should any individual or individuals or portion of the band of the Sans Arcs band of Dakota or Sioux Indians, represented in council, desire hereafter to locate permanently upon any land claimed by said band for the purposes of agricultural or other similar pursuits, it is hereby agreed by the parties to this treaty, that such individuals shall be protected in such location against any annoyance or molestation on the part of whites or Indians; and whenever twenty lodges or families of the Sans Arcs band shall have located on land for agricultural purposes, and signified the same to their agent or superintendent, they, as well as other families so locating, shall receive the sum of twenty-five dollars annually, for five years, for each family, in agricultural implements and improvements; and when one hundred lodges or families shall have so engaged in agricultural pursuits they shall be entitled to a farmer and blacksmith, at the expense of the Government; as also teachers, at the option of the Secretary of the Interior, whenever deemed necessary.

Amendments to be binding.

ARTICLE 6. Any amendment or modification of this treaty, by the Senate of the United States, shall be considered final and binding upon the said band represented in council as a part of this treaty, in the same manner as if it had been subsequently presented and agreed to by the chiefs and head-men of said band.

In testimony whereof, the Commissioners on the part of the United States, and the chiefs and headmen of the said Sans Arcs band of Dakota or Sioux Indians, have hereunto set their hands this twentieth day of October, eighteen hundred and sixty-five, after the contents had previously been read, interpreted, and explained to the chiefs and headmen.

> Newton Edmunds,
> Edward B. Taylor,
> S. R. Curtis, major-general,
> Henry H. Sibley, brigadier-general,
> Henry W. Reed,
> Orrin Guernsey.

Chiefs:

Wah-mun-dee-o-pee-doo-tah, The War Eagle with the Red Tail, his x mark.

Cha-tau-'hne, Yellow Hawk, his x mark.

Shon-kah-we-to-ko, The Fool Dog, his x mark.

Chief soldiers:

Chan-tay-mah-to, The Bear's Heart, his x mark.

Tah-ko-ko-ke-pish-nee, The Man that Fears Nothing, his x mark.

Nup-che-unk, The Nine, his x mark.

Mah-to-nuk-kah, The Bear's Ears, his x mark.

Chan-desh-kah-sappah, The Black Hoop, his x mark.

Ze-te-kah-nah-sappee, The Bird Necklace, his x mark.

Signed by the Commissioners on the part of the United States, and by the chiefs and headmen after the treaty had been fully read, interpreted, and explained, in our presence:

Hez. L. Hosmer, chief justice of Montana Territory.
S. S. Curtis, brevet lieutenant-colonel, U. S. Volunteers.
E. F. Ruth, secretary of Commission.
W. S. Woods, surgeon, U. S. Volunteers.
C. S. Morrison,
O. E. Guernsey,
Charles Degre, his x mark, interpreter.
Chief Crow Feather, Con-ge-we-a-ka, his x mark.
Gray Hair, Pa-he-sa, his x mark.
Red Hair, Pa-he-sha, his x mark.
The Shield Eagle, Wa-chan-ka-wam-ba-lee, his x mark.
Black Bear, Ma-to-sapa, his x mark.

TREATY WITH THE SIOUX—HUNKPAPA BAND, 1865.

Articles of a treaty made and concluded at Fort Sully, in the Territory of Dakota, by and between Newton Edmunds, governor and ex-officio superintendent of Indian affairs of Dakota Territory, Edward B. Taylor, superintendent of Indian Affairs for the northern superintendency, Major-General S. R. Curtis, Brigadier-General H. H. Sibley, Henry W. Reed, and Orrin Guernsey, commissioners on the part of the United States, duly appointed by the President, and the undersigned chiefs and head-men of the Onkpahpah band of Dakota or Sioux Indians.

Oct. 20, 1865.

14 Stat., 739.
Ratified Mar. 5, 1866.
Proclaimed, Mar. 17, 1866.

ARTICLE 1. The Onkpahpah band of Dakota or Sioux Indians, represented in council, hereby acknowledge themselves to be subject to the exclusive jurisdiction and authority of the United States, and hereby obligate and bind themselves, individually and collectively, not only to cease all hostilities against the persons and property of its citizens, but to use their influence, and, if requisite, physical force, to prevent other bands of Dakota Indians, or other adjacent tribes, from making hostile demonstrations against the Government or people of the United States.

Jurisdiction and authority of the United States acknowledged.

ARTICLE 2. Inasmuch as the Government of the United States is desirous to arrest the effusion of blood between the Indian tribes within its jurisdiction hitherto at war with each other, the Onkpahpah band of Dakota or Sioux Indians, represented in council, anxious to respect the wishes of the Government, hereby agree to discontinue for the future all attacks upon the persons or property of other tribes, unless first attacked by them, and to use their influence to promote peace everywhere in the region occupied or frequented by them.

Persons and property of other tribes not to be first attacked.

ARTICLE 3. All controversies or differences arising between the Onkpahpah band of Dakota or Sioux Indians involving the question of peace or war shall be submitted for the arbitrament of the President, or such person or persons as may be designated by him, and the decision or award shall be faithfully observed by the said band represented in council.

Controversies to be submitted to the arbitrament of the President.

ARTICLE 4. The said band represented in council shall withdraw from the routes overland already established, or hereafter to be established, through their country; and in consideration thereof the Government of the United States agree to pay the said band the sum of thirty dollars for each lodge or family, annually, for twenty years, in

Indians to withdraw from overland routes.

Payments.

Proviso.

such articles as the Secretary of the Interior may direct: *Provided*. That said band so represented in council shall faithfully conform to the requirements of this treaty.

Individual Indians locating on lands to be protected.

ARTICLE 5. Should any individual or individuals, or portion of the band of the Onkpahpah band of Dakota or Sioux Indians, represented in council, desire hereafter to locate permanently upon any land claimed by said band for the purposes of agricultural or other similar pursuits, it is hereby agreed by the parties to this treaty that such individuals shall be protected in such location against any annoyance or molestation on the part of whites or Indians, and whenever twenty lodges or families of the Onkpahpah band shall have located on land for agricultural purposes, and signified the same to their agents or superintendent, they as well as other families so locating shall receive the sum of twenty-five dollars annually for five years, for each family, in agricultural implements and improvements; and when one hundred lodges or families shall have so engaged in agricultural pursuits, they shall be entitled to a farmer and blacksmith, at the expense of the Government, as also teachers, at the option of the Secretary of the Interior, whenever deemed necessary.

Payments for agricultural, etc., purposes.

Farmer, blacksmith, and teachers.

Amendments to be binding.

ARTICLE 6. Any amendment or modification of this treaty by the Senate of the United States shall be considered final and binding upon the said band, represented in council, as a part of this treaty, in the same manner as if it had been subsequently presented and agreed to by the chiefs and head-men of said band.

In testimony whereof, the Commissioners on the part of the United States, and the chiefs and headmen of the said Yanktonai band of Dakota or Sioux Indians, have hereunto set their hands, this twentieth day of October, eighteen hundred and sixty-five, after the contents had previously been read, interpreted, and explained to the chiefs and headmen.

> Newton Edmunds,
> Edward B. Taylor,
> S. R. Curtis, major-general,
> H. H. Sibley, brigadier-general,
> Henry Reed,
> Orrin Guernsey.

Chiefs:
> M'doka, or The Buck, his x mark.
> Mah-to-wak-kouah, He that Runs the Bear, his x mark.
> Shon-kah-we-te-ko, The Fool Dog, his x mark.

Chief soldiers:
> Tah-chonk-pee-sappah, The Black Tomahawk, his x mark.
> Wah-doo-tah-wak-kean, The Red Thunder, his x mark.
> Ton-kon-ha-ton, The Rock with a Horn, his x mark.

Chiefs:
> Two Bears, Mato-non-pa, his x mark.
> White Bear, Ma-to-sea, his x mark.
> Bone Necklace, Ho-hoo-non-pee, his x mark.

Soldier:
> Dog Cloud, his x mark.

In presence of—
> Hez L. Hosmer, chief justice of Montana Territory.
> S. S. Curtis, brevet lieutenant-colonel U. S. Volunteers.
> A. W. Hubbard, M. C. Sixth District Iowa.
> E. F. Ruth, secretary of commission.
> R. R. Hitt, reporter of commission.
> Zephier Re[n]contre, his x mark, interpreter.
> Charles Degres, his x mark, interpreter.
> The Man that Runs in His Tracks, O-yea-ke-pa, his x mark.
> The Man Surrounded, Na-je-om-pee, his x mark.

The Medicine White Man, Wa-se-che-wa-kon, his x mark.
The Man that Stirs, Skin-ich-e-a, his x mark.
Fast Walker, Mon-ne-loo-sa, his x mark.
Red Bull, Taw-ton, his x mark.

The foregoing signatures in this handwriting (that of General Curtis) were made in presence of the undersigned on the 28th and 29th October, 1865, at Fort Sully.

Maj. A. P. Shreve, paymaster U. S. Army.
John Pattie, lieutenant-colonel Seventh Iowa Cavalry.

TREATY WITH THE SIOUX—YANKTONAI BAND, 1865.

Articles of a treaty made and concluded at Fort Sully, in the Territory of Dakota, by and between Newton Edmunds, governor and ex-officio superintendent of Indian affairs of Dakota Territory, Edward B. Taylor, superintendent of Indian affairs for the northern superintendency, Major-General S. R. Curtis, Brigadier-General H. H. Sibley, Henry W. Reed, and Orrin Guernsey, commissioners on the part of the United States, duly appointed by the President, and the undersigned chiefs and head-men of the Yanktonai band of Dakota or Sioux Indians.

Oct. 20, 1865.

14 Stat., 735.
Ratified, Mar. 5, 1866.
Proclaimed, Mar. 17, 1866.

ARTICLE 1. The Yanktonai band of Dakota or Sioux Indians, represented in council, hereby acknowledge themselves to be subject to the exclusive jurisdiction and authority of the United States, and hereby obligate and bind themselves, individually and collectively, not only to cease all hostilities against the persons and property of its citizens, but to use their influence, and, if requisite, physical force, to prevent other bands of Dakota Indians, or other adjacent tribes, from making hostile demonstrations against the Government or people of the United States.

Authority and jurisdiction of the United States acknowledged.

ARTICLE 2. Inasmuch as the Government of the United States is desirous to arrest the effusion of blood between the Indian tribes within its jurisdiction hitherto at war with each other, the Yanktonai band of Dakota or Sioux Indians represented in council, anxious to respect the wishes of the Government, hereby agree to discontinue, for the future all attacks upon the persons or property of other tribes, unless first attacked by them, and to use their influence to promote peace everywhere in the region occupied or frequented by them.

Persons and property of other tribes not to be first attacked.

ARTICLE 3. All controversies or differences arising between the Yanktonai band of Dakota or Sioux Indians, represented in council, and other tribes of Indians, involving the question of peace or war, shall be submitted for the arbitrament of the President, or such person or persons as may be designated by him, and the decision or award shall be faithfully observed by the said band represented in council.

Controversies to be submitted to the arbitrament of the President.

ARTICLE 4. The said band, represented in council shall withdraw from the routes overland already established, or hereafter to be established, through their country; and in consideration thereof, the Government of the United States agree to pay the said band the sum of thirty dollars for each lodge or family, annually, for twenty years, in such articles as the Secretary of the Interior may direct: *Provided,* That said band, so represented in council, shall faithfully conform to the requirements of this treaty.

Indians to withdraw from overland routes.

Payments.

Proviso.

ARTICLE 5. Should any individual or individuals, or portion of the band of the Yanktonai band of Dakota or Sioux Indians represented in council, desire hereafter to locate permanently upon any land claimed by said band for the purposes of agricultural or other similar pursuits, it is hereby agreed by the parties to this treaty that such

Individual Indians locating on lands to be protected.

individuals shall be protected in such location against any annoyance or molestation on the part of whites or Indians; and whenever twenty lodges or families of the Yanktonai band shall have located on lands for agricultural purposes, and signified the same to their agents or superintendent, they, as well as other families so locating, shall **Payments for agricultural, etc., purposes.** receive the sum of twenty-five dollars annually, for five years, for each family, in agricultural implements and improvements; and when one hundred lodges or families shall have so engaged in agricultural pur- **Farmer, blacksmith, and teachers.** suits, they shall be entitled to a farmer and blacksmith, at the expense of the Government, as also teachers, at the option of the Secretary of the Interior, whenever deemed necessary.

Amendments to be binding. ARTICLE 6. Any amendment or modification of this treaty by the Senate of the United States shall be considered final and binding upon the said band, represented in council, as a part of this treaty, in the same manner as if it had been subsequently presented and agreed to by the chiefs and head-men of said band.

Execution. In testimony whereof, the Commissioners on the part of the United States, and the chiefs and headmen of the said Onkpahpah band of Dakota or Sioux Indians, have hereunto set their hands this twentieth day of October, eighteen hundred and sixty-five, after the contents had previously been read, interpreted, and explained to the chiefs and headmen.

Newton Edmunds,
Edward B. Taylor,
S. R. Curtis, major-general,
H. H. Sibley, brigadier-general,
Henry W. Reed,
Orrin Guernsey.

Chiefs:
Ah-ke-tche-tah-hon-skah, The Tall Soldier, his x mark.
Mah-to-che-kah, The Little Bear, his x mark.
Muzzah-e-nom-pah, The Iron that Comes Out, his x mark.
Wak-ke-an-skah, The White Thunder, his x mark.
Chief Soldiers:
Mah-to-nom-pah, The Two Bears, his x mark.
Cha-tan-me-ne-o-me-nee, The Whirling Heart, his x mark.

Chiefs:
Ma-to-chewicksa, Bear's Rib, his x mark.
Running Antelope, Ta-to-kee-un, his x mark.
The Man that Has a Heart for All, O-en-e-chan-ta-u-can, his x mark.
Soldiers:
Thunder Hawk, Cha-ton-wa-ke-on, his x mark.
Iron Horn, Ha-ma-za, his x mark.
Plenty Crows, Con-ge-o-ta, his x mark.
The Man that Fears the Eagle, Wam-bel-le-co-ke-pa, his x mark.
Spotted Buffalo Bull, Ta-tanka-ge-lis-ka, his x mark.

Signed by the Commissioners on the part of the United States, and by the chiefs and headmen, after the treaty had been fully read, interpreted, and explained in our presence:—

Hez. L. Hosmer, chief justice of Montana Territory.
S. S. Curtis, brevet lieutenant colonel U. S. Volunteers.
E. F. Ruth, secretary of Commission.
W. S. Woods, surgeon U. S. Volunteers.
C. S. Morrison.
O. E. Guernsey.
Charles Degre, his x mark, interpreter.

TREATY WITH THE SIOUX—UPPER YANKTONAI BAND, 1865.

Articles of a treaty made and concluded at Fort Sully, in the Territory of Dakota, by and between Newton Edmunds, governor and ex-officio superintendent of Indian affairs of Dakota Territory, Edward B. Taylor, superintendent of Indian affairs for the northern superintendency, Major-General S. R. Curtis, Brigadier-General H. H. Sibley, Henry W. Reed, and Orrin Guernsey, commissioners on the part of the United States, duly appointed by the President, and the undersigned chiefs and head-men of the Upper Yanktonais band of Dakota or Sioux Indians.

Oct. 28, 1865.

14 Stats., 743.
Ratified Mar. 5, 1866.
Proclaimed, Mar.17, 1866.

ARTICLE 1. The Upper Yanktonais band of Dakota or Sioux Indians, represented in council, hereby acknowledge themselves to be subject to the exclusive jurisdiction and authority of the United States, and hereby obligate and bind themselves, individually and collectively, not only to cease all hostilities against the persons and property of its citizens, but to use their influence, and, if necessary, physical force, to prevent other bands of the Dakota Indians, or other adjacent tribes, from making hostile demonstrations against the Government or people of the United States. *(margin: Jurisdiction and authority of the United States acknowledged.)*

ARTICLE 2. Inasmuch as the Government of the United States is desirous to arrest the effusion of blood between the Indian tribes within its jurisdiction hitherto at war with each other, the Upper Yanktonais band of Dakota or Sioux Indians, represented in council, anxious to respect the wishes of the Government, hereby agree to discontinue for the future all attacks upon the persons or property of other tribes, unless first attacked by them, and to use their influence to promote peace everywhere in the region occupied or frequented by them. *(margin: Persons and property of other tribes not to be first attacked.)*

ARTICLE 3. All controversies or differences arising between the Upper Yanktonais band of Dakota or Sioux Indians, represented in council, and other tribes of Indians, involving the question of peace or war, shall be submitted for the abitrament of the President, or such person or persons as may be designated by him, and the decision or award faithfully observed by the said band represented in council. *(margin: Controversies to be submitted to the arbitrament of the President.)*

ARTICLE 4. The said band represented in council shall withdraw from the routes overland already established, or hereafter to be established, through their country; and in consideration thereof, and of their non-interference with the persons and property of citizens of the United States travelling thereon, the Government of the United States agree to pay the said band the sum of ten thousand dollars, annually, for twenty years, in such articles as the Secretary of the Interior may direct: *Provided*, That said band so represented in council shall faithfully conform to the requirements of this treaty. *(margin: Indians to withdraw from overland routes. Payments. Proviso.)*

ARTICLE 5. Should any individual or individuals, or portion of the band of the Upper Yanktonais band of Dakota or Sioux Indians, represented in council, desire hereafter to locate permanently upon any land claimed by said band for the purposes of agricultural or other similar pursuits, it is hereby agreed by the parties to this treaty that said individuals shall be protected in such location against any annoyance or molestation on the part of whites or Indians, and whenever twenty lodges or families of the Upper Yanktonais band shall have located on land for agricultural purposes, and signified the same to their agent or superintendent, they, as well as other families so locating, shall receive the sum of twenty-five dollars annually for five years, for each family, in agricultural implements and improvements; and when one hundred lodges or families shall have so engaged in agricultural pursuits they shall be entitled to a farmer and blacksmith at the expense of the Government, as also teachers, at the option of the Secretary of the Interior, whenever deemed necessary. *(margin: Individual Indians locating on lands to be protected. Payments for agricultural purposes. Farmer, blacksmith, and teachers.)*

Amendments to be binding. ARTICLE 6. Any amendment or modification of this treaty by the Senate of the United States shall be considered final and binding upon the said band, represented in council, as a part of this treaty, in the same manner as if it had been subsequently presented and agreed to by the chiefs and head-men of said band.

In testimony whereof, the Commissioners on the part of the United States, and the chiefs and headmen of the said Upper Yanktonais band of Dakota or Sioux Indians, have hereunto set their hands this twenty-eighth day of October, eighteen hundred and sixty-five, after the contents had previously been read, interpreted, and explained to the chiefs and headmen.

Newton Edmunds,
Edward B. Taylor,
S. R. Curtis, major-general,
H. H. Sibley, brigadier-general,
Henry W. Reed,
Orrin Guernsey.

The above signatures were made in our presence:—
Geo. D. Hill.
S. L. Spink.
A. W. Hubbard.
G. C. Moody.
Chief: Big Head, Na-su-la-tan-ka, his x mark.
Soldier: Big Hand, Na-pa-tan-ka, his x mark.
Soldier: Left-handed Bear, Ma-to-chat-ka, his x mark.
Soldier: The Fine Dressed Man, Wa-ich-co-ya-ka, his x mark.
The Man Covered with Lice, Ha-o-poo-za, his x mark.
Little Soldier, A-kich-it-a-chi-ki-la, his x mark.
The Spread Horn, Ha-ka-ti-na, his x mark.
Black Tiger, Ego-mo-sa-pa, his x mark.
The Man Afraid of his War-club, Cham-pi-co-qui-pa, his x mark.
The Big Shaved Head, Cosh-la-ton-ca, his x mark.
Lazy Bear, Ma-to-chick-pa-ne, his x mark.
The Man.
Rock Man, Ton-ka-wi-cha-sa, his x mark.
Chief: Black Catfish, O-wa-sa-pa, his x mark.
Chief: The Curley-headed Goose, Ma-ga-bo-ma-do, his x mark.

The above signatures in this handwriting (that of Gen'l Curtis) were made in presence of the undersigned, on the 28th and 29th Oct., 1865, at Fort Sully.
Maj. A. P. Shreve, Paymaster U. S. Army.
John Pattee, Lieutenant-Colonel Seventh Iowa Cavalry.

TREATY WITH THE SIOUX—OGLALA BAND, 1865.

Oct. 28, 1865.

14 Stats., 747.
Ratified, Mar. 5, 1866.
Proclaimed Mar. 17, 1866.

Articles of a treaty made and concluded at Fort Sully, in the Territory of Dakota, by and between Newton Edmunds, governor and ex-officio superintendent of Indian affairs of Dakota Territory, Edward B. Taylor, superintendent of Indian affairs for the northern superintendency, Major-General S. R. Curtis, Brigadier-General, H. H. Sibley, Henry W. Reed, and Orrin Guernsey, commissioners on the part of the United States, duly appointed by the President, and the undersigned chiefs and head-men of the O'Galla band of Dakota or Sioux Indians.

Jurisdiction and authority of the United States acknowledged. ARTICLE 1. The O'Gallala band of Dakota or Sioux Indians, represented in council, hereby acknowledge themselves to be subject to the exclusive jurisdiction and authority of the United States, and hereby obligate and bind themselves, individually and collectively, not only to cease all hostilities against the persons and property of its citizens, but to use their influence, and, if necessary, physical force, to prevent other bands of the Dakota Indians, or other adjacent tribes, from making hostile demonstrations against the Government or people of the United States.

ARTICLE 2. Inasmuch as the Government of the United States is desirous to arrest the effusion of blood between the Indian tribes within its jurisdiction hitherto at war with each other, the O'Gallala band of Dakota or Sioux Indians, represented in council, anxious to respect the wishes of the Government, hereby agree to discontinue for the future all attacks upon the persons or property of other tribes, unless first attacked by them, and to use their influence to promote peace everywhere in the region occupied or frequented by them. *Persons and property of other tribes not to be first attacked.*

ARTICLE 3. All controversies or differences arising between the O'Gallala band of Dakota or Sioux Indians, represented in council, and other tribes of Indians, involving the question of peace or war, shall be submitted *shall be submitted* for the arbitrament of the *arbitrament of the* President, or such person or persons as may be designated by him, and the decision or award faithfully observed by the said band represented in council. *Controversies to be submitted to the arbitrament of the President.*

ARTICLE 4. The said band represented in council shall withdraw from the routes overland already established or hereafter to be established through their country: and in consideration thereof, the Government of the United States agree to pay to the said band the sum of ten thousand dollars annually for twenty years, in such articles as the Secretary of the Interior may direct: *Provided*, That said band, so represented in council, shall faithfully conform to the requirements of this treaty. *Indians to withdraw from overland routes. Payments. Proviso.*

ARTICLE 5. Should any individual or individuals, or portion of the band of the [O'Gallala] band of Dakota or Sioux Indians, represented in council, desire hereafter to locate permanently upon any land claimed by said band for the purposes of agricultural or other similar pursuits, it is hereby agreed by the parties to this treaty, that such individuals shall be protected in such location against any annoyance or molestation on the part of whites or Indians; and whenever twenty lodges or families of the O'Gallala band shall have located on land for agricultural purposes, and signified the same to their agent or superintendent, they as well as other families so locating shall receive the sum of twenty-five dollars annually, for five years, for each family, in agricultural implements and improvements; and when one hundred lodges or families shall have so engaged in agricultural pursuits they shall be entitled to a farmer and blacksmith, at the expense of the Government, as also teachers, at the option of the Secretary of the Interior, whenever deemed necessary. *Individual Indians locating on lands to be protected. Payments for agricultural, etc., purposes. Farmers, blacksmith, and teachers.*

ARTICLE 6. Any amendment or modification of this treaty by the Senate of the United States shall be considered final and binding upon the said band, represented in council, as a part of this treaty, in the same manner as if it had been subsequently presented and agreed to by the chiefs and head-men of said band. *Amendments to be binding.*

In testimony whereof, the Commissioners on the part of the United States, and the chiefs and headmen of the said O'Gallala band of Dakota or Sioux Indians, have hereunto set their hands this twenty-sixth day of October, eighteen hundred and sixty-five after the contents had previously been read, interpreted, and explained to the chiefs and headmen.

> Newton Edmunds,
> Edward B. Taylor,
> S. R. Curtis, major-general,
> H. H. Sibley, brigadier-general,
> Henry W. Reed,
> Orrin Guernsey.

Signed on the part of the Commission, in our presence:—

    S. L. Spink,
    Geo. D. Hill,
    A. W. Hubbard,
    G. C. Moody.
    Chief Long Bull, Tan-tan-ka-has-ka, his x mark.
    The Charging Bear, Ma-lo-wa-ta-khe, his x mark.
    The Man that Stands on a Hill, Pa-ha-to-na-je, his x mark.

The foregoing signatures in this handwriting (that of General Curtis) were made in presence of the undersigned on the 28th and 29th Oct., 1865, at Fort Sully.

    Maj. A. P. Shreve,
        Paymaster U. S. Army.
    John Pattee,
        Lieutenant-Colonel Seventh Iowa Cavalry.

TREATY WITH THE MIDDLE OREGON TRIBES, 1865.

Nov. 15, 1865.

14 Stats., 751.
Ratified, Mar. 2, 1867.
Proclaimed Mar. 28, 1867.

Articles of agreement and convention entered into at the Warm Springs Agency, Oregon, by J. W. Perit Huntington, sup't Indian affairs for Oregon, on behalf of the United States, and the undersigned, chiefs and head-men of the confederated tribes and bands of Middle Oregon, the same being amendatory of and supplemental to the treaty negotiated with the aforesaid tribes on the twenty-fifth day of June, eighteen hundred and fifty-five, and ratified by the Senate of the United States on the eighteenth day of April, eighteen hundred and fifty-nine.

Certain rights granted by the former treaty relinquished hereby.

ARTICLE 1. It having become evident from experience that the provision of article 1 of the treaty of the twenty-fifth of June, A. D. eighteen hundred and fifty-five, which permits said confederated tribes to fish, hunt, gather berries and roots, pasture stock, and erect houses on lands outside the reservation, and which have been ceded to the United States, is often abused by the Indians to the extent of continuously residing away from the reservation, and is detrimental to the interests of both Indians and whites; therefore it is hereby stipulated and agreed that all the rights enumerated in the third proviso of the first section of the before-mentioned treaty of the twenty-fifth of June, eighteen hundred and fifty-five—that is to say, the right to take fish, erect houses, hunt game, gather roots and berries, and pasture animals upon lands without the reservation set apart by the treaty aforesaid—are hereby relinquished by the confederated Indian tribes and bands of Middle Oregon, parties to this treaty.

The tribes to remain upon their reservations.
Penalty for leaving, etc.

ARTICLE 2. The tribes aforesaid covenant and agree that they will hereafter remain upon said reservation, subject to the laws of the United States, the regulations of the Indian Department, and the control of the officers thereof; and they further stipulate that if any of the members of said tribes do leave, or attempt to leave, said reservation in violation of this treaty, they will assist in pursuing and returning them, when called upon to do so by the superintendent or agent in charge.

Permits to go without the boundaries of the reservation.

ARTICLE 3. In cases which may arise which make it necessary for any Indian to go without the boundaries of said reservation, the superintendent or agent in charge may, in his discretion, give to such Indian a written permit or pass, which shall always be for a short period and the expiration definitely fixed in said paper. Any Indian who, having gone out with a written pass, shall remain beyond the boundaries for a longer period than the time named in said pass, [shall] be deemed to have violated this treaty to the same extent as if he or she had gone without a pass.

ARTICLE 4. An infraction of this treaty shall subject the Indian guilty thereof to a deprivation of his or her share of the annuities, and to such other punishment as the President of the United States may direct. *Indians breaking this treaty to forfeit annuities.*

ARTICLE 5. It is stipulated and agreed on the part of the United States, as a consideration for the relinquishment of the rights herein enumerated, that the sum of three thousand five hundred dollars shall be expended in the purchase of teams, agricultural implements, seeds, and other articles calculated to advance said confederated tribes in agriculture and civilization. *Money for the purchase of teams, etc.*

ARTICLE 6. It is further agreed that the United States shall cause to be alloted to each head of a family in said confederated tribes and bands a tract of land sufficient for his or her use, the possession of which shall be guaranteed and secured to said family and the heirs thereof forever. *Allotment of land to each head of family.*

ARTICLE 7. To the end that the vice of intemperance among said tribes may be checked, it is hereby stipulated that when any members thereof shall be known to drink ardent spirits, or to have the same in possession, the facts shall be immediately reported to the agent or superintendent, with the name of the person or persons from whom the liquor was obtained; and the Indians agree to diligently use, under the direction of the superintendent or agent, all proper means to secure the identification and punishment of the persons unlawfully furnishing liquor as aforesaid. *Punishment of persons unlawfully furnishing ardent spirits to Indians.*

In testimony whereof, the said J. W. Perit Huntington, superintendent of Indian affairs, on the part of the United States, and the undersigned chiefs and head confederated tribes and bands aforesaid, have hereunto, in the presence of the subscribing witnesses and of each other, affixed our signatures and seals on this fifteenth day of November, in the year one thousand eight hundred and sixty-five. *Execution.*

J. W. Perit Huntington, [SEAL.]
Sup't Indian Affairs in Oregon, and acting Commissioner
on behalf of the United States.

Mark, head chief, his x mark.	[SEAL.]	Sin-ne-wah, his x mark.	[SEAL.]
Wm. Chinook, his x mark.	[SEAL.]	Ump-chil-le-poo, his x mark.	[SEAL.]
Kuck-up, his x mark.	[SEAL.]	Shooley, his x mark.	[SEAL.]
Ponst-am-i-ne, his x mark.	[SEAL.]	Tah-koo, his x mark.	[SEAL.]
Alex-zan, his x mark.	[SEAL.]	Tum-tsche-cus, his x mark.	[SEAL.]
Tas-simk, his x mark.	[SEAL.]	Tou-wacks, his x mark.	[SEAL.]
John Mission, his x mark.	[SEAL.]	Hul-le-quil-la, his x mark.	[SEAL.]
Lock-squis-squis-sa, his x mark.	[SEAL.]	Te-ah-ki-ak, his x mark.	[SEAL.]
Kuck-ups, his x mark.	[SEAL.]	Chok-te, his x mark.	[SEAL.]
Hote, his x mark.	[SEAL.]	Kootsh-ta, his x mark.	[SEAL.]
I-palt-pel, his x mark.	[SEAL.]		

Done in presence of—

Tallax, his x mark, interpreter.
Donald McKay, his x mark, interpreter.
Charles Lafollett, captain, First Oregon Infantry.
J. W. D. Gillett, school teacher.
Myron Reaves, superintendent farming operations.

TREATY WITH THE SEMINOLE, 1866.

Mar. 21, 1866.
————————
14 Stats., 755.
Ratified, July 19, 1866.
Proclamed, Aug. 16, 1866.

Articles of a treaty made and concluded at Washington, D. C., March 21, A. D., 1866, between the United States Government, by its commissioners, D. N. Cooley, Commissioner of Indian Affairs, Elijah Sells, superintendent of Indian affairs, and Ely S. Parker, and the Seminole Indians, by their chiefs, John Chup-co, or Long John, Cho-cote-harjo, Fos-ha[r]-jo, John F. Brown.

Preamble.

Whereas existing treaties between the United States and the Seminole Nation are insufficient to meet their mutual necessities; and

Whereas the Seminole Nation made a treaty with the so-called Confederate States, August 1st, 1861, whereby they threw off their allegiance to the United States, and unsettled their treaty relations with the United States, and thereby incurred the liability of forfeiture of all lands and other property held by grant or gift of the United States; and whereas a treaty of peace and amity was entered into between the United States and the Seminole and other tribes at Fort Smith, September *13* [10,] 1865,[a] whereby the Seminoles revoked, cancelled, and repudiated the said treaty with the so-called Confederate States; and whereas the United States, through its commissioners, in said treaty of peace promised to enter into treaty with the Seminole Nation to arrange and settle all questions relating to and growing out of said treaty with the so-called Confederate States; and whereas the United States, in view of said treaty of the Seminole Nation with the enemies of the Government of the United States, and the consequent liabilities of said Seminole Nation, and in view of its urgent necessities for more lands in the Indian Territory, requires a cession by said Seminole Nation of part of its present reservation, and is willing to pay therefor a reasonable price, while at the same time providing new and adequate lands for them:

Now, therefore, the United States, by its commissioners aforesaid, and the above-named delegates of the Seminole Nation, the day and year above written, mutually stipulate and agree, on behalf of the respective parties, as follows, to wit:

ARTICLE 1. There shall be perpetual peace between the United States and the Seminole Nation, and the Seminoles agree to be and remain firm allies of the United States, and always faithfully aid the Government thereof to suppress insurrection and put down its enemies.

Peace and friendship.

The Seminoles also agree to remain at peace with all other Indian tribes and with themselves. In return for these pledges of peace and friendship, the United States guarantee them quiet possession of their country, and protection against hostilities on the part of other tribes; and, in the event of such hostilities, that the tribe commencing and prosecuting the same shall make just reparation therefor. Therefore the Seminoles agree to a military occupation of their country at the option and expense of the United States.

Military occupation and protection by the United States.

A general amnesty of all past offences against the laws of the United States, committed by any member of the Seminole Nation, is hereby declared; and the Seminoles, anxious for the restoration of kind and friendly feelings among themselves, do hereby declare an amnesty for all past offenses against their government, and no Indian or Indians shall be proscribed or any act of forfeiture or confiscation passed against those who have remained friendly to or taken up arms against the United States, but they shall enjoy equal privileges with other members of said tribe, and all laws heretofore passed inconsistent herewith are hereby declared inoperative.

Amnesty.

_____

[a] A copy of this agreement, which has never been ratified, is found in an Appendix to the Report of the Commissioner of Indian Affairs for 1865, with the report of the negotiating commissioners, which copy has been reproduced in the Appendix to this compilation, *post*, p. 1050.

ARTICLE 2. The Seminole Nation covenant that henceforth in said nation slavery shall not exist, nor involuntary servitude, except for and in punishment of crime, whereof the offending party shall first have been duly convicted in accordance with law, applicable to all the members of said nation. And inasmuch as there are among the Seminoles many persons of African descent and blood, who have no interest or property in the soil, and no recognized civil rights, it is stipulated that hereafter these persons and their descendants, and such other of the same race as shall be permitted by said nation to settle there, shall have and enjoy all the rights of native citizens, and the laws of said nation shall be equally binding upon all persons of whatever race or color, who may be adopted as citizens or members of said tribe.

Slavery not to exist among the Seminoles.

Rights of those of African descent.

ARTICLE 3. In compliance with the desire of the United States to locate other Indians and freedmen thereon, the Seminoles cede and convey to the United States their entire domain, being the tract of land ceded to the Seminole Indians by the Creek Nation under the provisions of article first, (1st,) treaty of the United States with the Creeks and Seminoles, made and concluded at Washington, D. C., August 7, 1856. In consideration of said grant and cession of their lands, estimated at two million one hundred and sixty-nine thousand and eighty (2,169,080) acres, the United States agree to pay said Seminole Nation the sum of three hundred and twenty-five thousand three hundred and sixty-two ($325,362) dollars, said purchase being at the rate of fifteen cents per acre. The United States having obtained by grant of the Creek Nation the westerly half of their lands, hereby grant to the Seminole Nation the portion thereof hereafter described, which shall constitute the national domain of the Seminole Indians. Said lands so granted by the United States to the Seminole Nation are bounded and described as follows, to wit: Beginning on the Canadian River where the line dividing the Creek lands according to the terms of their sale to the United States by their treaty of February 6, 1866,[a] following said line due north to where said line crosses the north fork of the Canadian River; thence up said north fork of the Canadian River a distance sufficient to make two hundred thousand acres by running due south to the Canadian River; thence down said Canadian River to the place of beginning. In consideration of said cession of two hundred thousand acres of land described above, the Seminole Nation agrees to pay therefor the price of fifty cents per acre, amounting to the sum of one hundred thousand dollars, which amount shall be deducted from the sum paid by the United States for Seminole lands under the stipulations above written. The balance due the Seminole Nation after making said deduction, amounting to one hundred thousand dollars, the United States agree to pay in the following manner, to wit: Thirty thousand dollars shall be paid to enable the Seminoles to occupy, restore, and improve their farms, and to make their nation independent and self-sustaining, and shall be distributed for that purpose under the direction of the Secretary of the Interior; twenty thousand dollars shall be paid in like manner for the purpose of purchasing agricultural implements, seeds, cows, and other stock; fifteen thousand dollars shall be paid for the erection of a mill suitable to accommodate said nation of Indians; seventy thousand dollars to remain in the United States Treasury, upon which the United States shall pay an annual interest of five per cent.; fifty thousand of said sum of seventy thousand dollars shall be a permanent school-fund, the interest of which shall be paid annually and appropriated to the support of schools; the remainder of the seventy thousand dollars, being twenty thousand dollars, shall remain a permanent fund, the

Cession of lands to the United States.

Payments by the United States.

Grants to Seminoles.

Boundaries.

Payment therefor.

Balance due the Seminoles.

How to be paid.

a This refers to the Creek treaty of June 14, 1866, post, p. 931. See Annual Report of Commissioner of Indian Affairs, 1866, p. 10.

interest of which shall be paid annually for the support of the Seminole government; forty thousand three hundred and sixty-two dollars shall be appropriated and expended for subsisting said Indians, discriminating in favor of the destitute; all of which amounts, excepting the seventy thousand dollars, to remain in the Treasury as a permanent fund, shall be paid upon the ratification of said treaty, and disbursed in such manner as the Secretary of the Interior may direct. The balance, fifty thousand dollars, or so much thereof as may be necessary to pay the losses ascertained and awarded as hereinafter provided, shall be paid when said awards shall have been duly made and approved by the Secretary of the Interior. And in case said fifty thousand dollars shall be insufficient to pay all said awards, it shall be distributed *pro rata* to those whose claims are so allowed; and until said awards shall be thus paid, the United States agree to pay to said Indians, in such manner and for such purposes as the Secretary of the Interior may direct, interest at the rate of five per cent. per annum from the date of the ratification of this treaty.

Board of commissioners to determine losses sustained by loyal Seminoles. ARTICLE 4. To reimburse such members of the Seminole Nation as shall be duly adjudged to have remained loyal and faithful to their treaty relations to the United States, during the recent rebellion of the so-called Confederate States for the losses actually sustained by them thereby, after the ratification of this treaty, or so soon thereafter as the Secretary of the Interior shall direct, he shall appoint a board of commissioners, not to exceed three in number, who shall proceed to **Census of those loyal.** the Seminole country and investigate and determine said losses. Previous to said investigation the agent of the Seminole Nation shall prepare a census or enumeration of said tribe, and make a roll of all Seminoles who did in no manner aid or abet the enemies of the Government, but remained loyal during said rebellion; and no award shall **No compensation except to loyal Indians.** be made by said commissioners for such losses unless the name of the claimant appear on said roll, and no compensation shall be allowed any person for such losses whose name does not appear on said roll, unless said claimant, within six months from the date of the completion of said roll, furnishes proof satisfactory to said board, or to the Commissioner of Indian Affairs, that he has at all times remained loyal to the **Awards of commissioners.** United States, according to his treaty obligations. All evidence touching said claims shall be taken by said commissioners, or any of them, under oath, and their awards made, together with the evidence, shall be transmitted to the Commissioner of Indian Affairs, for his approval, **Pay.** and that of the Secretary of the Interior. Said commissioners shall be paid by the United States such compensation as the Secretary of the **What claims for losses included.** Interior may direct. The provisions of this article shall extend to and embrace the claims for losses sustained by loyal members of said tribe, irrespective of race or color, whether at the time of said losses the claimants shall have been in servitude or not; provided said claimants are made members of said tribe by the stipulations of this treaty.

Right of way for railroads granted through the lands of the Seminoles. ARTICLE 5. The Seminole Nation hereby grant a right of way through their lands to any company which shall be duly authorized by Congress, and shall, with the express consent and approbation of the Secretary of the Interior, undertake to construct a railroad from any point on their eastern to their western or southern boundary; but said railroad company, together with all its agents and employés, shall be subject to the laws of the United States relating to the intercourse with Indian tribes, and also to such rules and regulations as may be prescribed by the Secretary of the Interior for that purpose. **Lands will be sold.** And the Seminoles agree to sell to the United States, or any company duly authorized as aforesaid, such lands, not legally owned or occupied by a member or members of the Seminole Nation lying along the line of said contemplated railroad, not exceeding on each side thereof a belt or strip of land three miles in width, at such price per acre as may be eventually agreed upon between said Seminole Nation and the party or parties building said road—subject to the approval of the President of the United States: *Provided, however*, That said land thus sold shall not be reconveyed, leased, or rented to, or be occupied by, any one not a citizen of the Seminole Nation, according to its laws and recognized usages: *Provided also*, That officers, servants, and employés of said railroad necessary to its construction and management shall not be excluded from such necessary occupancy, they being subject to the provisions of the Indian-intercourse laws, and such rules and regulations as may be established by the Secretary of the Interior; nor shall any conveyance of said lands be made to the party building and managing said road, until its completion as a first-class railroad and its acceptance as such by the Secretary of the Interior.

Proviso.

ARTICLE 6. Inasmuch as there are no agency buildings upon the new Seminole reservation, it is therefore further agreed that the United States shall cause to be constructed, at an expense not exceeding ten thousand (10,000) dollars, suitable agency buildings, the site whereof shall be selected by the agent of said tribe, under the direction of the superintendent of Indian affairs; in consideration whereof, the Seminole Nation hereby relinquish and cede forever to the United States one section of their lands upon which said agency buildings shall be *directed*, [erected,] which land shall revert to said nation when no longer used by the United States, upon said nation paying a fair value for said buildings at the time vacated.

Agency buildings.

ARTICLE 7. The Seminole Nation agrees to such legislation as Congress and the President may deem necessary for the better administration of the rights of person and property within the Indian Territory: *Provided, however*, [That] said legislation shall not in any manner interfere with or annul their present tribal organization, rights, laws, privileges, and customs.

Seminoles agree to certain legislation.

Proviso.

The Seminole Nation also agree that a general council, consisting of delegates elected by each nation, a tribe lawfully resident within the Indian Territory, may be annually convened in said Territory, which council shall be organized in such manner and possess such powers as are hereinafter described:

General council.

1st. After the ratification of this treaty, and as soon as may be deemed practicable by the Secretary of the Interior, and prior to the first session of said council, a census or enumeration of each tribe lawfully resident in said Territory shall be taken, under the direction of the superintendent of Indian affairs, who, for that purpose, is hereby authorized to designate and appoint competent persons, whose compensation shall be fixed by the Secretary of the Interior and paid by the United States.

Census.

2d. The first general council shall consist of one member from each tribe, and an additional member for each one thousand Indians, or each fraction of a thousand greater than five hundred, being members of any tribe lawfully resident in said Territory, and shall be elected by said tribes, respectively, who may assent to the establishment of said general council; and if none should be thus formally selected by any nation or tribe, the said nation or tribe shall be represented in said general council by the chiefs and head-men of said tribes, to be taken in the order of their rank, in the same number and proportion as above indicated. After the said census shall have been taken and completed, the superintendent of Indian affairs shall publish and declare to each tribe the number of members of said council to which they shall be entitled under the provisions of this article; and the persons so entitled to represent said tribe shall meet at such time and place as he shall appoint; but thereafter the time and place of the sessions of said council shall be determined by its action: *Provided*, That no session in any one year shall exceed the term of thirty days, *And provided* That special sessions of said council may be called by

First council, how composed.

Time and place of meeting.

Session not to exceed thirty days.
Special sessions.

said superintendent whenever, in his judgment, or that of the Secretary of the Interior, the interest of said tribes shall require.

Powers of general council.

3d. Said general council shall have power to legislate upon all rightful subjects and matters pertaining to the intercourse and relations of the Indian tribes and nations resident in said Territory; the arrest and extradition of criminals and offenders escaping from one tribe to another; the administration of justice between members of the several tribes of said Territory, and persons other than Indians and members of said tribes or nations; the construction of works of internal improvement and the common defence and safety of the nation of said Territory. All laws enacted by said council shall take effect at such time as may therein be provided, unless suspended by direction of the Secretary of the Interior or the President of the United States. No law shall be enacted inconsistent with the Constitution of the United States, or the laws of Congress, or existing treaty stipulations with the United States; nor shall said council legislate upon matters pertaining to the organization, laws, or customs of the several tribes, except as herein provided for.

Who to preside over council.

4th. Said council shall be presided over by the superintendent of Indian affairs, or, in case of his absence for any cause, the duties of said superintendent enumerated in this article shall be performed by such person as the Secretary of the Interior may direct.

Secretary of council.

5th. The Secretary of the Interior shall appoint a secretary of said council, whose duty it shall be to keep an accurate record of all the proceedings of said council, and who shall transmit a true copy of all such proceedings, duly certified by the superintendent of Indian affairs, to the Secretary of the Interior immediately after the session of said council. He shall be paid out of the Treasury of the United States an annual salary of five hundred dollars.

Pay.

Pay of members.

6th. The members of said council shall be paid by the United States the sum of four dollars per diem during the time actually in attendance upon the sessions of said council, and at the rate of four dollars for every twenty miles necessarily travelled by them in going to said council and returning to their homes, respectively, to be certified by the secretary of the said council and the sup[erintenden]t of Indian affairs.

Courts.

7th. The Seminoles also agree that a court or courts may be established in said Territory, with such jurisdiction and organized in such manner as Congress may by law provide.

This treaty to be a full settlement of all claims.

ARTICLE 8. The stipulations of this treaty are to be a full settlement of all claims of said Seminole Nation for damages and losses of every kind growing out of the late rebellion, and all expenditures by the United States of annuities in clothing and feeding refugee and destitute Indians since the diversion of annuities for that purpose, con-

Diversions of annuities.

sequent upon the late war with the so-called Confederate States. And the Seminoles hereby ratify and confirm all such diversions of annuities heretofore made from the funds of the Seminole Nation by the United States. And the United States agree that no annuities shall be diverted from the object for which they were originally devoted by treaty stipulations, with the Seminoles, to the use of refugee and destitute Indians, other than the Seminoles or members of the Seminole Nation, after the close of the present fiscal year, June thirtieth, eighteen hundred and sixty-six.

Treaty obligations reaffirmed.

ARTICLE 9. The United States re-affirms and reassumes all obligations of treaty stipulations entered into before the treaty of said Seminole Nation with the so-called Confederate States, August first, eighteen hundred and sixty-one, not inconsistent herewith; and further agree to renew all payments of annuities accruing by force of said treaty stipulations, from and after the close of the present fiscal year, June thirtieth, in the year of our Lord one thousand eight hundred and sixty-six, except as is provided in article eight, (viii.)

ARTICLE 10. A quantity of land not exceeding six hundred and forty acres, to be selected according to legal subdivisions, in one body, and which shall include their improvements, is hereby granted to every religious society or denomination which has erected, or which, with the consent of the Indians, may hereafter erect, buildings within the Seminole country for missionary or educational purposes; but no land thus granted, nor the buildings which have been or may be erected thereon, shall ever be sold or otherwise disposed of except with the consent and approval of the Secretary of the Interior. And whenever any such land or buildings shall be so sold or disposed of, the proceeds thereof shall be applied, under the direction of the Secretary of the Interior, to the support and maintenance of other similar establishments for the benefit of the Seminoles and such other persons as may be, or may hereafter become, members of the tribe according to its laws, customs, and usages. *Lands granted for missionary or educational purposes.* *Not to be sold except, etc.* *When sold proceeds to be how applied.*

ARTICLE 11. It is further agreed that all treaties heretofore entered into between the United States and the Seminole Nation which are inconsistent with any of the articles or provisions of this treaty shall be, and are hereby, rescinded and annulled. *Inconsistent treaty provisions annulled.*

In testimony whereof, the said Dennis N. Cooley, Commissioner of Indian affairs, Elijah Sells, superintendent of Indian affairs, and Col. Ely S. Parker, as aforesaid, and the undersigned, persons representing the Seminole nation, have hereunto set their hands and seals the day and year first above written.

Dennis N. Cooley,   [SEAL.]
Commissioner of Indian Affairs.
Elijah Sells,   [SEAL.]
Superintendent Indian Affairs.
Col. Ely S. Parker,   [SEAL.]
Special commissioner.
John Chup-co, his x mark,   [SEAL.]
King or head chief.
Cho-cote-harjo, his x mark,   [SEAL.]
Counsellor.
Fos-harjo, his x mark, chief.   [SEAL.]
John F. Brown,   [SEAL.]
Special delegate for Southern Seminoles.

In presence of—

Robert Johnson, his x mark,
    United States interpreter for Seminole Indians.
Geo. A. Reynolds, United States Indian agent for Seminoles.
Ok-tus-sus-har-jo, his x mark, or Sands.
Cow-e-to-me-ko, his x mark.
Che-chu-chee, his x mark.
Harry Island, his x mark,
    United States interpreter for Creek Indians.
J. W. Dunn, United States Indian agent for the Creek Nation.
Perry Fuller.

Signed by John F. Brown, special delegate for the Southern Seminoles, in presence of, this June thirtieth, eighteen hundred and sixty-six—

W. R. Irwin.
J. M. Tebbetts.
Geo. A. Reynolds, United States Indian agent.
Robert Johnson, his x mark, United States interpreter.

TREATY WITH THE POTAWATOMI, 1866.

Mar. 29, 1866.

14 Stats., 763.
Ratified Apr. 26, 1866.
Proclaimed May 5, 1866.

Whereas certain amendments are desired by the Pottawatomie Indians to their treaty concluded at the Pottawatomie agency on the fifteenth day of November, A. D. 1861, and amended by resolution of the Senate of the United States dated April the fifteenth, A. D. 1862; and whereas the United States are willing to assent to such amendments, it is therefore agreed by and between Dennis N. Cooley, commissioner, on the part of the United States, thereunto duly authorized, and the undersigned business committee, acting on behalf of said tribe, and being thereunto duly authorized, in manner and form following, that is to say:

Provisions of third article of former treaty extended to all adult persons of the tribe.

ARTICLE 1. The beneficial provisions in behalf of the more prudent and intelligent members of said tribe, contained in the third article of the amended treaty above recited, shall not hereafter be confined to males and heads of families, but the same shall be and are hereby extended to all adult persons of said tribe, without distinction of sex, whether such persons are or shall be heads of families or otherwise, in the same manner, to the same extent, and upon the same terms, conditions, and stipulations as are contained in said third article of said treaty with reference to " males and heads of families."

In testimony whereof the said parties by their Commissioner and Business Committee aforesaid have hereunto set their hands and seals at Washington City, District of Columbia, this 29th day of March, in the year of our Lord one thousand eight hundred and sixty-six.

Dennis N. Cooley, [SEAL.]
    Commissioner.

J. N. Bourassa,   [SEAL.]
U. F. Navane,   [SEAL.]
B. N. Bertrand,   [SEAL.]
    Business Committee.

Signed in presence of—
  L. R. Palmer,
  James Steele.

TREATY WITH THE CHIPPEWA—BOIS FORT BAND, 1866.

Apr. 7, 1866.

14 Stats., 765.
Ratified Apr. 26, 1866.
Proclaimed May 5, 1866.

Articles of a treaty made and concluded at Washington, District of Columbia, this seventh day of April, in the year of our Lord one thousand eight hundred and sixty-six, by and between the United States, party of the first part, by their commissioners, D. N. Cooley, Commissioner of Indian Affairs, and E. E. L. Taylor, thereunto duly authorized, and the Bois Forte band of Chippewa Indians, parties of the second part, by the undersigned chiefs, head-men, and warriors of said bands, thereunto duly authorized.

Peace and friendship.

ARTICLE 1. The peace and friendship now existing between the United States and said Bois Forte bands of Indians shall be perpetual.

Cession of lands to the United States.

ARTICLE 2. In consideration of the agreements, stipulations, and undertakings to be performed by the United States, and hereinafter expressed, the Bois Forte bands of Chippewas have agreed to, and do hereby, cede and forever relinquish and surrender to the United States all their right, title, claim, and interest in and to all lands and territory heretofore claimed, held, or possessed by them, and lying east of the boundary line mentioned and established in and by the first article of the treaty made and concluded by and between the United States of the one part, and the Chippewas of Lake Superior and the Mississippi of the other part, on the 30th day of September, A. D. 1854, and more

Boundaries.

especially in and to all that portion of said territory heretofore claimed and occupied by them at and near Lake Vermillion as a reservation. The Bois Forte band of Chippewas in like manner cede and relinquish forever to the United States all their claim, right, title, and interest in and to all lands and territory lying westerly of said boundary line, or elsewhere within the limits of the United States.

ARTICLE 3. In consideration of the foregoing cession and relinquishment, the United States agree to and will perform the stipulations, undertakings, and agreements following, that is to say:— *The United States to set apart a reservation.*

1st. There shall be set apart within one year after the date of the ratification of this treaty, under the direction of the President of the United States, within the Chippewa country, for the perpetual use and occupancy of said Bois Forte band of Chippewas, a tract of land of not less than one hundred thousand acres, the said location to include a lake known by the name of Netor As-sab-a-co-na, if, upon examination of the country by the agent sent by the President of the United States to select the said reservation, it is found practicable to include the said lake therein, and also one township of land on the Grand Fork River, at the mouth of Deer Creek, if such location shall be found practicable.

2d. The United States will, as soon as practicable after the setting apart of the tract of country first above mentioned, erect thereon, without expense to said Indians, one blacksmith's shop, to cost not exceeding five hundred dollars; one school-house, to cost not exceeding five hundred dollars; and eight houses for their chiefs, to cost not exceeding four hundred dollars each; and a building for an agency house and storehouse for the storage of goods and provisions, to cost not exceeding two thousand dollars. *The United States to erect shop, school-house, houses for chiefs, and other buildings.*

3d. The United States will expend annually for and in behalf of said Bois Forte band of Chippewas, for and during the term of twenty years from and after the ratification of this treaty, the several sums and for the purposes following, to wit: For the support of one blacksmith and assistant, and for tools, iron, and steel, and other articles necessary for the blacksmith's shop, fifteen hundred dollars; for one school-teacher, and the necessary books and stationery for the school, eight hundred dollars, the chiefs in council to have the privilege of selecting, with the approval of the Secretary of the Interior, the religious denomination to which the said teacher shall belong; for instructions of the said Indians in farming, and the purchase of seeds, tools, &c., for that purpose, eight hundred dollars; and for annuity payments, the sum of eleven thousand dollars, three thousand five hundred dollars of which shall be paid to them in money per capita, one thousand dollars in provisions, ammunition, and tobacco, and six thousand five hundred dollars to be distributed to them in goods and other articles suited to their wants and condition. *To pay annuity for twenty years.* *Objects of annuities.*

ARTICLE 4. To enable the chiefs, head-men, and warriors now present to establish their people upon the new reservation, and to purchase useful articles and presents for their people, the United States agree to pay them, upon the ratification of this treaty, the sum of thirty thousand dollars, to be expended under the direction of the Secretary of the Interior. *Payment of $30,000 to Indians.*

ARTICLE 5. In consideration of the services heretofore rendered to the said Indians by Francis Roussaire, senior, Francis Roussaire, jr., and Peter E. Bradshaw, it is hereby agreed that the said persons shall each have the right to select one hundred and sixty acres of land, not mineral lands, and to receive patents therefor from the United States; and for the like services to the Indians, the following named persons, to wit: Peter Roy, Joseph Gurnoe, Francis Roy, Vincent Roy, Eustace Roussaire, and D. George Morrison shall each have the right to select eighty acres of land, not mineral lands, and to receive from the United States patents therefor. *Grant of lands to certain persons for services.*

Annuities to be paid upon the reservation if, etc.

ARTICLE 6. It is further agreed that all payments of annuities to the Bois Forte band of Chippewas shall be made upon their reservation if, upon examination, it shall be found practicable to do so.

Inconsistent provisions of former treaties abrogated.

Part of treaty of Sept. 30, 1854, to remain in full force.

ARTICLE 7. It is agreed by and between the parties hereto that, upon the ratification of this treaty, all former treaties existing between them inconsistent herewith shall be, and the same are hereby, abrogated and made void to all intents and purposes; and the said Indians hereby relinquish any and all claims for arrears of payments claimed to be due under such treaties, or that are hereafter to fall due under the provisions of the same; except that as to the third clause of the twelfth article of the treaty of September 30, 1854, providing for a blacksmith, smith-shop, supplies, and instructions in farming, the same shall continue in full force and effect, but the benefits thereof shall be transferred to the Chippewas of Lake Superior.

Payment of expenses of delegation to Washington.

ARTICLE 8. The United States also agree to pay the necessary expenses of transportation and subsistence of the delegates who have visited Washington for the purpose of negotiating this treaty, not exceeding the sum of ten thousand dollars.

In testimony whereof, the undersigned, Commissioners on behalf of the United States, and the delegates on behalf of the Bois Forte band of Chippewas, have hereunto set their hands and seals the day and year first above written.

D. N. Cooley, Commissioner of Indian Affairs. [L. S.]
E. E. L. Taylor, Special Commissioner. [L. S.]
Gabeshcodaway, or Going through the Prairie, his x mark. [L. S.]
Babawmadjeweshcang, or Mountain Traveller, his x mark. [L. S.]
Adawawnequabenace, or Twin-haired Bird, his x mark. [L. S.]
Sagwadacamegishcang, or He who Tries the Earth, his x mark. [L. S.]
Neoning, or The Four Fingers, his x mark. [L. S.]
Wabawgamawgau, or The Tomahawk, his x mark. [L. S.]
Ganawawbamina, or He who is Looked at, his x mark. [L. S.]
Gawnandawawinzo, or Berry Hunter, his x mark. [L. S.]
Abetang, or He who Inhabits, his x mark. [L. S.]

In presence of—

Luther E. Webb, [L. S.]
　　United States Indian agent for Chippewas, Lake Superior.
Joseph D. Gurnoe, [L. S.]
　　United States interpreter, Lake Superior.

J. C. Ramsey.
Benj'n Thompson.
Peter Roy.   } [L. S.]
D. Geo. Morrison.
Vincent Roy, jr.
W. H. Watson.

TREATY WITH THE CHOCTAW AND CHICKASAW, 1866.

Apr. 28, 1866.

14 Stats., 769.
Ratified June 28, 1866.
Proclaimed July 10, 1866.

Articles of agreement and convention between the United States and the Choctaw and Chickasaw Nations of Indians, made and concluded at the City of Washington the twenty-eighth day of April, in the year eighteen hundred and sixty-six, by Dennis N. Cooley, Elijah Sells, and E. S. Parker, special commissioners on the part of the United States, and Alfred Wade, Allen Wright, James Riley, and John Page, commissioners on the part of the Choctaws, and Winchester Colbert, Edmund Pickens, Holmes Colbert, Colbert Carter, and Robert H. Love, commissioners on the part of the Chickasaws.

Peace and friendship.

ARTICLE 1. Permanent peace and friendship are hereby established between the United States and said nations; and the Choctaws and Chickasaws do hereby bind themselves respectively to use their influence and to make every exertion to induce Indians of the plains to maintain peaceful relations with each other, with other Indians, and with the United States.

ARTICLE 2. The Choctaws and Chickasaws hereby covenant and agree that henceforth neither slavery nor involuntary servitude, otherwise than in punishment of crime whereof the parties shall have been duly convicted, in accordance with laws applicable to all members of the particular nation, shall ever exist in said nations. *Slavery and involuntary servitude to cease.*

ARTICLE 3. The Choctaws and Chickasaws, in consideration of the sum of three hundred thousand dollars, hereby cede to the United States the territory west of the 98° west longitude, known as the leased district, provided that the said sum shall be invested and held by the United States, at an interest not less than five per cent., in trust for the said nations, until the legislatures of the Choctaw and Chickasaw Nations respectively shall have made such laws, rules, and regulations as may be necessary to give all persons of African descent, resident in the said nation at the date of the treaty of Fort Smith, and their descendants, heretofore held in slavery among said nations, all the rights, privileges, and immunities, including the right of suffrage, of citizens of said nations, except in the annuities, moneys, and public domain claimed by, or belonging to, said nations respectively; and also to give to such persons who were residents as aforesaid, and their descendants, forty acres each of the land of said nations on the same terms as the Choctaws and Chickasaws, to be selected on the survey of said land, after the Choctaws and Chickasaws and Kansas Indians have made their selections as herein provided; and immediately on the enactment of such laws, rules, and regulations, the said sum of three hundred thousand dollars shall be paid to the said Choctaw and Chickasaw Nations in the proportion of three-fourths to the former and one-fourth to the latter,—less such sum, at the rate of one hundred dollars per capita, as shall be sufficient to pay such persons of African descent before referred to as within ninety days after the passage of such laws, rules, and regulations shall elect to remove and actually remove from the said nations respectively. And should the said laws, rules, and regulations not be made by the legislatures of the said nations respectively, within two years from the ratification of this treaty, then the said sum of three hundred thousand dollars shall cease to be held in trust for the said Choctaw and Chickasaw Nations, and be held for the use and benefit of such of said persons of African descent as the United States shall remove from the said Territory in such manner as the United States shall deem proper,—the United States agreeing, within ninety days from the expiration of the said two years, to remove from said nations all such persons of African descent as may be willing to remove; those remaining or returning after having been removed from said nations to have no benefit of said sum of three hundred thousand dollars, or any part thereof, but shall be upon the same footing as other citizens of the United States in the said nations. *Cession of the leased district to the United States.* *Purchase money to be invested by the United States and held in trust until, etc.*

ARTICLE 4. The said nations further agree that all negroes, not otherwise disqualified or disabled, shall be competent witnesses in all civil and criminal suits and proceedings in the Choctaw and Chickasaw courts, any law to the contrary notwithstanding; and they fully recognize the right of the freedmen to a fair remuneration·on reasonable and equitable contracts for their labor, which the law should aid them to enforce. And they agree, on the part of their respective nations, that all laws shall be equal in their operation upon Choctaws, Chickasaws, and negroes, and that no distinction affecting the latter shall at any time be made, and that they shall be treated with kindness and be protected against injury; and they further agree, that while the said freedmen, now in the Choctaw and Chickasaw Nations, remain in said nations, respectively, they shall be entitled to as much land as they *Rights of negroes and freedmen.*

may cultivate for the support of themselves and families, in cases where they do not support themselves and families by hiring, not interfering with existing improvements without the consent of the occupant, it being understood that in the event of the making of the laws, rules, and regulations aforesaid, the forty acres aforesaid shall stand in place of the land cultivated as last aforesaid.

Amnesty for past offenses.

ARTICLE 5. A general amnesty of all past offences against the laws of the United States, committed before the signing of this treaty by any member of the Choctaw or Chickasaw Nations, is hereby declared; and the United States will especially request the States of Missouri. Kansas, Arkansas, and Texas to grant the like amnesty as to all offences committed by any member of the Choctaw or Chickasaw Nation. And the Choctaws and Chickasaws, anxious for the restoration of kind and friendly feelings among themselves, do hereby declare an amnesty for all past offences against their respective governments, and no Indian or Indians shall be proscribed, or any act of forfeiture or confiscation passed against those who may have remained friendly to the United States, but they shall enjoy equal privileges with other members of said tribes, and all laws heretofore passed inconsistent herewith are hereby declared inoperative. The people of the Choctaw and Chickasaw Nations stipulate and agree to deliver up to any duly authorized agent of the United States all public property in their possession which belong to the late "so-called Confederate States of America," or the United States, without any reservation whatever; particularly ordnance, ordnance-stores, and arms of all kinds.

Right of way through their country for railroads.

ARTICLE 6. The Choctaws and Chickasaws hereby grant a right of way through their lands to any company or companies which shall be duly authorized by Congress, or by the legislatures of said nations, respectively, and which shall, with the express consent and approbation of the Secretary of the Interior, undertake to construct a railroad through the Choctaw and Chickasaw Nations from the north to the south thereof, and from the east to the west side thereof, in accordance with the provisions of the 18th article of the treaty of June twenty-second, one thousand eight hundred and fifty-five, which provides that for any property taken or destroyed in the construction

Damages.

thereof full compensation shall be made to the party or parties injured, to be ascertained and determined in such manner as the President of

Companies subject to laws, etc.

the United States shall direct. But such railroad company or companies, with all its or their agents and employés shall be subject to the laws of the United States relating to intercourse with Indian tribes, and also to such rules and regulations as may be prescribed by the Sec-

Indians may subscribe to stock.

retary of the Interior for that purpose. And it is also stipulated and agreed that the nation through which the road or roads aforesaid shall pass may subscribe to the stock of the particular company or companies such amount or amounts as they may be able to pay for in alternate sections of unoccupied lands for a space of six miles on each side of said road or roads, at a price per acre to be agreed upon between said Choctaw and Chickasaw Nations and the said company or companies, subject to the approval of the President of the United States:

Proviso.

Provided, however, That said land, thus subscribed, shall not be sold, or demised, or occupied by any one not a citizen of the Choctaw or Chickasaw Nations, according to their laws and recognized usages: *Provided*, That the officers, servants, and employés of such companies necessary to the construction and management of said road or roads shall not be excluded from such occupancy as their respective functions may require, they being subject to the provisions of the Indian intercourse law and such rules and regulations as may be established by the Secretary of the Interior: *And provided also*, That the stock thus subscribed by either of said nations shall have the force and effect of a first-mortgage bond on all that part of said road, appurtenances, and equipments situated and used within said nations respectively, and shall be a perpetual lien on the same, and the said nations shall have the right, from year to year, to elect to receive their equitable proportion of declared dividends of profits on their said stock, or interest on the par value at the rate of six per cent. per annum.

2. And it is further declared, in this connection, that as fast as sections of twenty miles in length are completed, with the rails laid ready for use, with all water and other stations necessary to the use thereof, as a first-class road, the said company or companies shall become entitled to patents for the alternate sections aforesaid, and may proceed to dispose thereof in the manner herein provided for, subject to the approval of the Secretary of the Interior. *When companies to be entitled to patents for the lands.*

3. And it is further declared, also, in case of one or more of said alternate sections being occupied by any member or members of said nations respectively, so that the same cannot be transferred to the said company or companies, that the said nation or nations, respectively, may select any unoccupied section or sections, as near as circumstances will permit, to the said width of six miles on each side of said road or roads, and convey the same as an equivalent for the section or sections so occupied as aforesaid. *Other lands may be selected in lieu of occupied sections.*

ARTICLE 7. The Choctaws and Chickasaws agree to such legislation as Congress and the President of the United States may deem necessary for the better administration of justice and the protection of the rights of person and property within the Indian Territory: *Provided, however,* Such legislation shall not in anywise interfere with or annul their present tribal organization, or their respective legislatures or judiciaries, or the rights, laws, privileges, or customs of the Choctaw and Chickasaw Nations respectively. *Legislation by Congress for rights of persons and property.*

ARTICLE 8. The Choctaws and Chickasaws also agree that a council, consisting of delegates elected by each nation or tribe lawfully resident within the Indian Territory, may be annually convened in said Territory, to be organized as follows: *A council to be convened annually.*

1. After the ratification of this treaty, and as soon as may be deemed practicable by the Secretary of the Interior, and prior to the first session of said assembly, a census of each tribe, lawfully resident in said Territory, shall be taken, under the direction of the Superintendent of Indian Affairs, by competent persons, to be appointed by him, whose compensation shall be fixed by the Secretary of the Interior and paid by the United States. *Census of the tribes to be taken.*

2. The council shall consist of one member from each tribe or nation whose population shall exceed five hundred, and an additional member for each one thousand Indians, native or adopted, or each fraction of a thousand greater than five hundred being members of any tribe lawfully resident in said Territory, and shall be selected by the tribes or nations respectively who may assent to the establishment of said general assembly; and if none should be thus formally selected by any nation or tribe, it shall be represented in said general assembly by the chief or chiefs and head-men of said tribes, to be taken in the order of their rank as recognized in tribal usage in the number and proportions above indicated. *Council to consist of whom.*

3. After the said census shall have been taken and completed, the superintendent of Indian affairs shall publish and declare to each tribe the number of members of said council to which they shall be entitled under the provisions of this article; and the persons so to represent the said tribes shall meet at such time and place as he shall designate, but thereafter the time and place of the sessions of the general assembly shall be determined by itself: *Provided,* That no session in any one year shall exceed the term of thirty days, and provided that the special sessions may be called whenever, in the judgment of the Secretary of the Interior, the interests of said tribes shall require it. *Members to which each tribe is entitled. Time and place of meeting. Length of session and special session.*

Powers of general assembly.

4. The general assembly shall have power to legislate upon all subjects and matters pertaining to the intercourse and relations of the Indian tribes and nations resident in the said Territory, the arrest and extradition of criminals escaping from one tribe to another, the administration of justice between members of the several tribes of the said Territory, and persons other than Indians and members of said tribes or nations, the construction of works of internal improvement, and the common defence and safety of the nations of the said Territory. All laws enacted by said council shall take effect at the times therein provided, unless suspended by the Secretary of the Interior or the President of the United States. No law shall be enacted inconsistent with the Constitution of the United States or the laws of Congress, or existing treaty stipulations with the United States; nor shall said council legislate upon matters pertaining to the legislative, judicial, or other organization, laws, or customs of the several tribes or nations, except as herein provided for.

President of council.

5. Said council shall be presided over by the superintendent of Indian affairs, or, in case of his absence from any cause, the duties of the superintendent enumerated in this article shall be performed by such person as the Secretary of the Interior shall indicate.

Secretary, duty and pay.

6. The Secretary of the Interior shall appoint a secretary of said council, whose duty it shall be to keep an accurate record of all the proceedings of said council, and to transmit a true copy thereof, duly certified by the superintendent of Indian affairs, to the Secretary of the Interior immediately after the sessions of said council shall terminate. He shall be paid five hundred dollars, as an annual salary, by the United States.

Pay and mileage of members.

7. The members of the said council shall be paid by the United States four dollars per diem while in actual attendance thereon, and four dollars mileage for every twenty miles going and returning therefrom by the most direct route, to be certified by the secretary of said council and the presiding officer.

Courts may be established.

8. The Choctaws and Chickasaws also agree that a court or courts may be established in said Territory with such jurisdiction and organization as Congress may prescribe: *Provided*, That the same shall not interfere with the local judiciary of either of said nations.

Delegates from the Territory.

9. Whenever Congress shall authorize the appointment of a Delegate from said Territory, it shall be the province of said council to elect one from among the nations represented in said council.

Superintendent of Indian affairs to be executive.
Title and duties.

10. And it is further agreed that the superintendent of Indian affairs shall be the executive of the said Territory, with the title of "governor of the Territory of Oklahoma," and that there shall be a secretary of the said Territory, to be appointed by the said superintendent; that the duty of the said governor, in addition to those already imposed on the superintendent of Indian affairs, shall be such as properly belong to an executive officer charged with the execution of the laws, which the said council is authorized to enact under the provisions of this treaty; and that for this purpose he shall have authority to appoint

Marshal.

a marshal of said Territory and an interpreter; the said marshal to appoint such deputies, to be paid by fees, as may be required to aid him in the execution of his proper functions, and be the marshal of the principal court of said Territory that may be established under the provisions of this treaty.

Salary of marshal and secretary.

11. And the said marshal and the said secretary shall each be entitled to a salary of five hundred dollars per annum, to be paid by the United States, and such fees in addition thereto as shall be established by said governor, with the approbation of the Secretary of the Interior, it being understood that the said fee-lists may at any time be corrected and altered by the Secretary of the Interior, as the experience of the system proposed herein to be established shall show to be necessary,

and shall in no case exceed the fees paid to marshals of the United States for similar services.

The salary of the interpreter shall be five hundred dollars, to be paid in like manner by the United States. Salary of interpreter.

12. And the United States agree that in the appointment of marshals and deputies, preference, qualifications being equal, shall be given to competent members of the said nations, the object being to create a laudable ambition to acquire the experience necessary for political offices of importance in the respective nations. Appointments of marshals and deputies.

13. And whereas it is desired by the said Choctaw and Chickasaw Nations that the said council should consist of an upper and lower house, it is hereby agreed that whenever a majority of the tribes or nations represented in said council shall desire the same, or the Congress of the United States shall so prescribe, there shall be, in addition to the council now provided for, and which shall then constitute the lower house, an upper house, consisting of one member from each tribe entitled to representation in the council now provided for—the relations of the two houses to each other being such as prevail in the States of the United States; each house being authorized to choose its presiding officer and clerk to perform the duties appropriate to such offices; and it being the duty, in addition, of the clerks of each house to make out and transmit to the territorial secretary fair copies of the proceedings of the respective houses immediately after their respective sessions, which copies shall be dealt with by said secretary as is now provided in the case of copies of the proceedings of the council mentioned in this act, and the said clerks shall each be entitled to the same per diem as members of the respective houses, and the presiding officers to doube that sum. Provision for an upper house of the council.

ARTICLE 9. Such sums of money as have, by virtue of treaties existing in the year eighteen hundred and sixty-one, been invested for the purposes of education, shall remain so invested, and the interest thereof shall be applied for the same purposes, in such manner as shall be designated by the legislative authorities of the Choctaw and Chickasaw Nations, respectively. Certain sums invested to remain so invested.

ARTICLE 10. The United States re-affirms all obligations arising out of treaty stipulations or acts of legislation with regard to the Choctaw and Chickasaw Nations, entered into prior to the late rebellion, and in force at that time, not inconsistent herewith; and further agrees to renew the payment of all annuities and others moneys accruing under such treaty stipulations and acts of legislation, from and after the close of the fiscal year ending on the thirtieth of June, in the year eighteen hundred and sixty-six. Treaty obligations, etc., reaffirmed, and payment of annuities to be renewed.

ARTICLE 11. Whereas the land occupied by the Choctaw and Chickasaw Nations, and described in the treaty between the United States and said nations, of June twenty-second, eighteen hundred and fifty-five, is now held by the members of said nations in common, under the provisions of the said treaty; and whereas it is believed that the holding of said land in severalty will promote the general civilization of said nations, and tend to advance their permanent welfare and the best interests of their individual members, it is hereby agreed that, should the Choctaw and the Chickasaw people, through their respective legislative councils, agree to the survey and dividing their land on the system of the United States, the land aforesaid east of the ninety-eighth degree of west longitude shall be, in view of the arrangements hereinafter mentioned, surveyed and laid off in ranges, townships, sections, and parts of sections; and that for the purpose of facilitating such surveys and for the settlement and distribution of said land as hereinafter provided, there shall be established at Boggy Depot, in the Choctaw Territory, a land-office; and that, in making the said surveys and conducting the business of the said office, including the appointment of all Survey and division of lands in severalty. Land office established at Boggy Depot.

necessary agents and surveyors, the same system shall be pursued which has heretofore governed in respect to the public lands of the United States, it being understood that the said surveys shall be made at the cost of the United States and by their agents and surveyors, as in the case of their own public lands, and that the officers and employés shall receive the same compensation as is paid to officers and employés in the land-offices of the United States in Kansas.

Maps of survey to exhibit actual occupancies, etc.

ARTICLE 12. The maps of said surveys shall exhibit, as far as practicable, the outlines of the actual occupancy of members of the said nations, respectively; and when they are completed, shall be returned to the said land-office at Boggy Depot for inspection by all parties interested, when notice for ninety days shall be given of such return, in such manner as the legislative authorities of the said nations, respectively, shall prescribe, or, in the event of said authorities failing to give such notice in a reasonable time, in such manner as the register of said land-office shall prescribe, calling upon all parties interested to examine said maps to the end that errors, if any, in the location of such occupancies, may be corrected.

Notice to parties interested to examine the maps.

ARTICLE 13. The notice required in the above article shall be given, not only in the Choctaw and Chicksaw Nations, but by publication in newspapers printed in the States of Mississippi and Tennessee, Louisiana, Texas, Arkansas, and Alabama, to the end that such Choctaws and Chickasaws as yet remain outside of the Choctaw and Chickasaw Nations, may be informed and have opportunity to exercise the rights hereby given to resident Choctaws and Chickasaws: *Provided*, That, before any such absent Choctaw or Chickasaw shall be permitted to select for him or herself, or others, as hereinafter provided, he or she shall satisfy the register of the land-office of his or her intention, or the intention of the party for whom the selection is to be made, to become bona-fide resident in the said nation within five years from the time of selection; and should the said absentee fail to remove into said nation, and occupy and commence an improvement on the land selected within the time aforesaid, the said selection shall be cancelled, and the land shall thereafter be discharged from all claim on account thereof.

Lands may be selected for seats of justice, for schools, seminaries, and colleges.

ARTICLE 14. At the expiration of the ninety days aforesaid the legislative authorities of the said nations, respectively, shall have the right to select one quarter-section of land in each of the counties of said nations respectively, in trust for the establishment of seats of justice therein, and also as many quarter-sections as the said legislative councils may deem proper for the permanent endowment of schools, seminaries, and colleges in said nation, provided such selection shall not embrace or interfere with any improvement in the actual occupation of any member of the particular nation without his consent; and provided the proceeds of sale of the quarter-sections selected for seats of justice shall be appropriated for the erection or improvement of public buildings in the county in which it is located.

Each Indian to have a right to one quarter section of land.

ARTICLE. 15. At the expiration of the ninety days' notice aforesaid, the selection which is to change the tenure of the land in the Choctaw and Chickasaw Nations from a holding in common to a holding in severalty shall take place, when every Choctaw and Chickasaw shall have the right to one quarter-section of land, whether male or female, adult or minor, and if in actual possession or occupancy of land improved or cultivated by him or her, shall have a prior right to the quarter-section in which his or her improvement lies; and every infant shall have selected for him or her a quarter-section of land in such location as the father of such infant, if there be a father living, and if no father living, then the mother or guardian, and should there be neither father, mother, nor guardian, then as the probate judge of the county, acting for the best interest of such infant, shall select.

Actual occupant.

Infants.

ARTICLE 16. Should an actual occupant of land desire, at any time prior to the commencement of the surveys aforesaid, to abandon his improvement, and select and improve other land, so as to obtain the prior right of selection thereof, he or she shall be at liberty to do so; in which event the improvement so abandoned shall be open to selection by other parties: *Provided*, That nothing herein contained shall authorize the multiplication of improvements so as to increase the quantity of land beyond what a party would be entitled to at the date of this treaty.

Actual occupant, prior to surveys, may abandon his improvements and select other land.

Proviso.

ARTICLE 17. No selection to be made under this treaty shall be permitted to deprive or interfere with the continued occupation, by the missionaries established in the respective nations, of their several missionary establishments; it being the wish of the parties hereto to promote and foster an influence so largely conducive to civilization and refinement. Should any missionary who has been engaged in missionary labor for five consecutive years before the date of this treaty in the said nations, or either of them, or three consecutive years prior to the late rebellion, and who, if absent from the said nations, may desire to return, wish to select a quarter-section of land with a view to a permanent home for himself and family, he shall have the privilege of doing so, provided no selection shall include any public buildings, schools or seminary; and a quantity of land not exceeding six hundred and forty acres, to be selected according to legal subdivisions in one body, and to include their improvements, is hereby granted to every religious society or denomination which has erected, or which, with the consent of the Indians, may hereafter erect buildings within the Choctaw and Chickasaw country for missionary or educational purposes; but no land thus granted, nor the buildings which have been or may be erected thereon, shall ever be sold or otherwise disposed of, except with the consent of the legislatures of said nations respectively and approval of the Secretary of the Interior; and whenever such lands or buildings shall be sold or disposed of, the proceeds thereof shall be applied, under the direction of the Secretary of the Interior, to the support and maintenance of other similar establishments for the benefit of the Choctaws and Chickasaws, and such other persons as may hereafter become members of their nations, according to their laws, customs, and usages.

Occupation by missionaries of missionary establishments not to be interfered with.

Rights of certain missionaries.

ARTICLE 18. In making a selection for children the parent shall have a prior right to select land adjacent to his own improvements or selection, provided such selection shall be made within thirty days from the time at which selections under this treaty commence.

Rights of parents in selecting land for children.

ARTICLE 19. The manner of selecting as aforesaid shall be by an entry with the register of the land-office, and all selections shall be made to conform to the legal subdivisions of the said lands as shown by the surveys aforesaid on the maps aforesaid; it being understood that nothing herein contained is to be construed to confine a party selecting to one section, but he may take contiguous parts of sections by legal subdivisions in different sections, not exceeding together a quarter-section.

Mode of selecting lands.

ARTICLE 20. Prior to any entries being made under the foregoing provisions, proof of improvements, or actual cultivation, as well as the number of persons for whom a parent or guardian, or probate judge of the county proposes to select, and of their right to select, and of his or her authority to select, for them, shall be made to the register and receiver of the land-office, under regulations to be prescribed by the Secretary of the Interior.

Proof of improvements to be made prior to entries.

ARTICLE 21. In every township the sections of land numbered sixteen and thirty-six shall be reserved for the support of schools in said township: *Provided*, That if the same has been already occupied by a party or parties having the right to select it, or it shall be so sterile as

Sections 16 and 36 to be reserved for schools.

Proviso

to be unavailable, the legislative authorities of the particular nations shall have the right to select such other unoccupied sections as they may think proper.

Military posts and Indian agencies.

ARTICLE 22. The right of selection hereby given shall not authorize the selection of any land required by the United States as a military post, or Indian agency, not exceeding one mile square, which, when abandoned, shall revert to the nation in which the land lies.

Names of persons for whom selections are made to be in books of register.

ARTICLE 23. The register of the land-office shall inscribe in a suitable book or books, in alphabetical order, the name of every individual for whom a selection shall be made, his or her age, and a description of the land selected.

Town lots.

ARTICLE 24. Whereas it may be difficult to give to each occupant of an improvement a quarter-section of land, or even a smaller subdivision, which shall include such improvement, in consequence of such improvements lying in towns, villages, or hamlets, the legislative authorities of the respective nations shall have power, where, in their discretion, they think it expedient, to lay off into town lots any section or part of a section so occupied, to which lots the actual occupants, being citizens of the respective nations, shall have pre-emptive right, and, upon paying into the treasury of the particular nation the price of the land, as fixed by the respective legislatures, exclusive of the value of said improvement, shall receive a conveyance thereof. Such occupant shall not be prejudiced thereby in his right to his selection elsewhere. The town lots which may be unoccupied shall be disposed of for the benefit of the particular nation, as the legislative authorities may direct from time to time. When the number of occupants of the same quarter-section shall not be such as to authorize the legislative authorities to lay out the same, or any part thereof, into town lots, they may make such regulations for the disposition thereof as they may deem proper, either by subdivision of the same, so as to accommodate the actual occupants, or by giving the right of prior choice to the first occupant in point of time, upon paying the others for their improvements, to be valued in such way as the legislative authorities shall prescribe, or otherwise. All occupants retaining their lots under this section, and desiring, in addition, to make a selection, must pay for the lots so retained, as in the case of town lots. And any Choctaw or Chickasaw who may desire to select a sectional division other than that on which his homestead is, without abandoning the latter, shall have the right to purchase the homestead sectional division at such price as the respective legislatures may prescribe.

When patents to issue for selected lands.

ARTICLE 25. During ninety days from the expiration of the ninety days' notice aforesaid, the Choctaws and Chickasaws shall have the exclusive right to make selections, as aforesaid, and at the end of that time the several parties shall be entitled to patents for their respective selections, to be issued by the President of the United States, and countersigned by the chief executive officer of the nation in which the land lies, and recorded in the records of the executive office of the particular nation; and copies of the said patents, under seal, shall be evidence in any court of law or equity.

Citizens by adoptions or intermarriage to have same rights.

ARTICLE 26. The right here given to the Choctaws and Chickasaws, respectively, shall extend to all persons who have become citizens by adoption or intermarriage of either of said nations, or who may hereafter become such.

Disputes as to selections of lands, how to be settled.

ARTICLE 27. In the event of disputes arising in regard to the rights of parties to select particular quarter-sections or other divisions of said land, or in regard to the adjustment of boundaries, so as to make them conform to legal divisions and subdivisions such disputes shall be settled by the register of the land-office and the chief executive officer of the nation in which the land lies, in a summary way, after hearing the parties; and if said register and chief officer cannot agree, the two to call in a third party, who shall constitute a third referee, the decision of any two of whom shall be final, without appeal.

ARTICLE 28. Nothing contained in any law of either of the said nations shall prevent parties entitled to make selections contiguous to each other; and the Choctaw and Chickasaw Nations hereby agree to repeal all laws inconsistent with this provision. *Contiguous selections.*

ARTICLE 29. Selections made under this treaty shall, to the extent of one quarter-section, including the homestead or dwelling, be inalienable for the period of twenty-one years from the date of such selection, and upon the death of the party in possession shall descend according to the laws of the nation where the land lies; and in the event of his or her death without heirs, the said quarter-section shall escheat to and become the property of the nation. *Selections to be inalienable, etc.*

ARTICLE 30. The Choctaw and Chickasaw Nations will receive into their respective districts east of the ninety-eighth degree of west longitude, in the proportion of one-fourth in the Chickasaw and three-fourths in the Choctaw Nation, civilized Indians from the tribes known by the general name of the Kansas Indians, being Indians to the north of the Indian Territory, not exceeding ten thousand in number, who shall have in the Choctaw and Chickasaw Nations, respectively, the same rights as the Choctaws and Chickasaws, of whom they shall be the fellow-citizens, governed by the same laws, and enjoying the same privileges, with the exception of the right to participate in the Choctaw and Chickasaw annuities and other moneys, and in the public domain, should the same, or the proceeds thereof, be divided per capita among the Choctaws and Chickasaws, and among others the right to select land as herein provided for Choctaws and Chickasaws, after the expiration of the ninety days during which the selections of land are to be made, as aforesaid, by said Choctaws and Chickasaws; and the Choctaw and Chickasaw Nations pledge themselves to treat the said Kansas Indians in all respects with kindness and forbearance, aiding them in good faith to establish themselves in their new homes, and to respect all their customs and usages not inconsistent with the constitution and laws of the Choctaw and Chickasaw Nations respectively. In making selections after the advent of the Indians and the actual occupancy of land in said nation, such occupancy shall have the same effect in their behalf as the occupancies of Choctaws and Chickasaws; and after the said Choctaws and Chickasaws have made their selections as aforesaid, the said persons of African descent mentioned in the third article of the treaty, shall make their selections as therein provided, in the event of the making of the laws, rules, and regulations aforesaid, after the expiration of ninety days from the date at which the Kansas Indians are to make their selections as therein provided, and the actual occupancy of such persons of African descent shall have the same effect in their behalf as the occupancies of the Choctaws and Chickasaws. *Not over 10,000 Kansas Indians will be received into districts, east of, etc., who shall have same rights, etc.*

ARTICLE 31. And whereas some time must necessarily elapse before the surveys, maps, and selections herein provided for can be completed so as to permit the said Kansas Indians to make their selections in their order, during which time the United States may desire to remove the said Indians from their present abiding places, it is hereby agreed that the said Indians may at once come into the Choctaw and Chickasaw Nations, settling themselves temporarily as citizens of the said nations, respectively, upon such land as suits them and is not already occupied. *Such Kansas Indians may come at once.*

ARTICLE 32. At the expiration of two years, or sooner, if the President of the United States shall so direct, from the completion of the surveys and maps aforesaid, the officers of the land-offices aforesaid *Documents in land offices to be given to the Choctaw and Chickasaw in two years.*

shall deliver to the executive departments of the Choctaw and Chickasaw Nations, respectively, all such documents as may be necessary to elucidate the land-title as settled according to this treaty, and forward copies thereof, with the field-notes, records, and other papers pertaining to said titles, to the Commissioner of the General Land Office; and thereafter grants of land and patents therefor shall be issued in such *Proceedings afterwards.* manner as the legislative authorities of said nations may provide for all the unselected portions of the Choctaw and Chickasaw districts as defined by the treaty of June twenty-second, eighteen hundred and fifty-five.

Selected lands to be held in severalty and unselected lands in common. ARTICLE 33. All lands selected as herein provided shall thereafter be held in severalty by the respective parties, and the unselected land shall be the common property of the Choctaw and Chickasaw Nations, in their corporate capacities, subject to the joint control of their legislative authorities.

Those prevented from selecting in ninety days may select afterwards. ARTICLE 34. Should any Choctaw or Chickasaw be prevented from selecting for him or herself during the *the* ninety days aforesaid, the failure to do so shall not authorize another to select the quarter-section containing his improvement, but he may at any time make his selection thereof, subject to having his boundaries made to conform to legal divisions as aforesaid.

Selection after transfer of land records. ARTICLE 35. Should the selections aforesaid not be made before the transfer of the land records to the executive authorities of said nations, respectively, they shall be made according to such regulations as the legislative authorities of the two nations, respectively, may prescribe, to the end that full justice and equity may be done to the citizens of the respective territories.

Selected lands abandoned for seven years, except, etc., may be rented, etc. ARTICLE 36. Should any land that has been selected under the provisions of this treaty be abandoned and left uncultivated for the space of seven years by the party selecting the same, or his heirs, except in the case of infants under the age of twenty-one years, or married women, or persons non compos mentis, the legislative authorities of the nation where such land lies may either rent the same for the benefit of those interested, or dispose of the same otherwise for their benefit, and may pass all laws necessary to give effect to this provision.

Payment by the United States for lands selected by the Indians. ARTICLE 37. In consideration of the right of selection hereinbefore accorded to certain Indians other than the Choctaws and Chickasaws, the United States agree to pay to the Choctaw and Chickasaw Nations, out of the funds of Indians removing into said nations respectively, under the provisions of this treaty, such sum as may be fixed by the legislatures of said nations, not exceeding one dollar per acre, to be divided between the said nations in the proportion of one-fourth to the Chickasaw Nation and three-fourths to the Choctaw Nation, with the understanding that at the expiration of twelve months the actual number of said immigrating Indians shall be ascertained, and the amount paid that may be actually due at the rate aforesaid; and should still further immigrations take place from among said Kansas Indians, still further payments shall be made accordingly from time to time.

White persons marrying Indians and residing in the nation, or adopted, to be members of the nation and subject to its laws. ARTICLE 38. Every white person who, having married a Choctaw or Chickasaw, resides in the said Choctaw or Chickasaw Nation, or who has been adopted by the legislative authorities, is to be deemed a member of said nation, and shall be subject to the laws of the Choctaw and Chickasaw Nations according to his domicile, and to prosecution and trial before their tribunals, and to punishment according to their laws in all respects as though he was a native Choctaw or Chickasaw.

Licenses to trade. ARTICLE 39. No person shall expose goods or other articles for sale as a trader without a permit of the legislative authorities of the nation he may propose to trade in; but no license shall be required to authorize any member of the Choctaw or Chickasaw Nations to trade in the

Choctaw or Chickasaw country who is authorized by the proper authority of the nation, nor to authorize Choctaws or Chickasaws to sell flour, meal, meat, fruit, and other provisions, stock, wagons, agricultural implements, or tools brought from the United States into the said country.

ARTICLE 40. All restrictions contained in any treaty heretofore made, or in any regulation of the United States upon the sale or other disposition of personal chattel property by Choctaws or Chickasaws are hereby removed.

Treaty restrictions upon sales of personal property removed.

ARTICLE 41. All persons who are members of the Choctaw or Chickasaw Nations, and are not otherwise disqualified or disabled, shall hereafter be competent witnesses in all civil and criminal suits and proceedings in any courts of the United States, any law to the contrary notwithstanding.

Witnesses.

ARTICLE 42. The Choctaw and Chickasaw Nations shall deliver up persons accused of crimes against the United States who may be found within their respective limits on the requisition of the governor of any State for a crime committed against the laws of said State, and upon the requisition of the judge of the district court of the United States for the district within which the crime was committed.

Surrender of fugitives from justice.

ARTICLE 43. The United States promise and agree that no white person, except officers, agents, and employés of the Government, and of any internal improvement company, or persons travelling through, or temporarily sojourning in, the said nations, or either of them, shall be permitted to go into said Territory, unless formally incorporated and naturalized by the joint action of the authorities of both nations into one of the said nations of Choctaws and Chickasaws, according to their laws, customs, or usages; but this article is not to be construed to affect parties heretofore adopted, or to prevent the employment temporarily of white persons who are teachers, mechanics, or skilled in agriculture, or to prevent the legislative authorities of the respective nations from authorizing such works of internal improvement as they may deem essential to the welfare and prosperity of the community, or be taken to interfere with or invalidate any action which has heretofore been had in this connection by either of the said nations.

No white persons, except, etc., to be permitted to go into said territory, unless, etc.

ARTICLE 44. Post-offices shall be established and maintained by the United States at convenient places in the Choctaw and Chickasaw Nations, to and from which the mails shall be carried at reasonable intervals, at the rates of postage prevailing in the United States.

Post-offices and mails.

ARTICLE 45. All the rights, privileges, and immunities heretofore possessed by said nations or individuals thereof, or to which they were entitled under the treaties and legislation heretofore made and had in connection with them, shall be, and are hereby declared to be, in full force, so far as they are consistent with the provisions of this treaty.

Former rights and immunities of the Indians to remain in force.

ARTICLE 46. Of the moneys stipulated to be paid to the Choctaws and Chickasaws under this treaty for the cession of the leased district, and the admission of the Kansas Indians among them, the sum of one hundred and fifty thousand dollars shall be advanced and paid to the Choctaws, and fifty thousand dollars to the Chickasaws, through their respective treasurers, as soon as practicable after the ratification of this treaty, to be repaid out of said moneys or any other moneys of said nations in the hands of the United States; the residue, not affected by any provisions of this treaty, to remain in the Treasury of the United States at an annual interest of five per cent., no part of which shall be paid out as annuity, but shall be annually paid to the treasurer of said nations, respectively, to be regularly and judiciously applied, under the direction of their respective legislative councils, to the support of their government, the purposes of education, and such other objects as may be best calculated to promote and advance the welfare and happiness of said nations and their people respectively.

Money due the Indians under this treaty; how to be paid.

ARTICLE 47. As soon as practicable after the lands shall have been surveyed and assigned to the Choctaws and Chickasaws in severalty as herein provided, upon application of their respective legislative councils, and with the assent of the President of the United States, all the annuities and funds invested and held in trust by the United States for the benefit of said nations respectively shall be capitalized or converted into money, as the case may be; and the aggregate amounts thereof belonging to each nation shall be equally divided and paid per capita to the individuals thereof respectively, to aid and assist them in improving their homesteads and increasing or acquiring flocks and herds, and thus encourage them to make proper efforts to maintain successfully the new relations which the holding of their lands in severalty will involve: *Provided, nevertheless,* That there shall be retained by the United States such sum as the President shall deem sufficient of the said moneys to be invested, that the interest thereon may be sufficient to defray the expenses of the government of said nations respectively, together with a judicious system of education, until these objects can be provided for by a proper system of taxation; and whenever this shall be done to the satisfaction of the President of the United States, the moneys so retained shall be divided in the manner and for the purpose above mentioned.

ARTICLE 48. Immediately after the ratification of this treaty there shall be paid, out of the funds of the Choctaws and Chickasaws in the hands of the United States, twenty-five thousand dollars to the Choctaw and twenty-five thousand dollars to the Chickasaw commissioners, to enable them to discharge obligations incurred by them for various incidental and other expenses to which they have been subjected, and for which they are now indebted.

ARTICLE 49. And it is further agreed that a commission, to consist of a person or persons to be appointed by the President of the United States, not exceeding three, shall be appointed immediately on the ratification of this treaty, who shall take into consideration and determine the claim of such Choctaws and Chickasaws as allege that they have been driven during the late rebellion from their homes in the Choctaw [and Chickasaw] Nations on account of their adhesion to the United States, for damages, with power to make such award as may be consistent with equity and good conscience, taking into view all circumstances, whose report, when ratified by the Secretary of the Interior, shall be final, and authorize the payment of the amount from any moneys of said nations in the hands of the United States as the said commission may award.

ARTICLE 50. Whereas Joseph G. Heald and Reuben Wright, of Massachusetts, were licensed traders in the Choctaw country at the commencement of the rebellion, and claim to have sustained large losses on account of said rebellion, by the use of their property by said nation, and that large sums of money are due them for goods and property taken, or sold to the members of said nation, and money advanced to said nation; and whereas other loyal citizens of the United States may have just claims of the same character: It is hereby agreed and stipulated that the commission provided for in the preceding article shall investigate said claims, and fully examine the same; and such sum or sums of money as shall by the report of said commission, approved by the Secretary of the Interior, be found due to such persons, not exceeding ninety thousand dollars, shall be paid by the United States to the persons entitled thereto, out of any money belonging to said nation in the possession of the United States: *Provided.* That no claim for goods or property of any kind shall be allowed or paid, in whole or part, which shall have been used by said nation or any member thereof in aid of the rebellion, with the consent of said claimants: *Provided also,* That if the aggregate of said claims thus

Marginal notes:

After survey and assignment of the lands in severalty, annuities and funds to be capitalized, etc.

To be divided per capita.

Certain sums may be retained.

Payment of $25,000 to commissioners of each nation for incidental expenses.

Commission to settle damages of loyal Indians driven from their homes.

Commission to determine the claims of loyal citizens of the United States for damages.

Provisos.

allowed and approved shall exceed said sum of ninety thousand dollars, then that sum shall be applied pro rata in payment of the claims so allowed.

ARTICLE 51. It is further agreed that all treaties and parts of treaties inconsistent herewith be, and the same are hereby, declared null and void.

Inconsistent treaty provisions declared null.

In testimony whereof, the said Dennis N. Cooley, Elijah Sells, and E. S. Parker, commissioners in behalf of the United States, and the said commissioners on behalf of the Choctaw and Chickasaw nations, have hereunto set their hands and seals the day and year first above written.

D. N. Cooley, Commissioner of Indian Affairs,	[SEAL.]
Elijah Sells, superintendent of Indian affairs,	[SEAL.]
E. S. Parker, special commissioner,	[SEAL.]

Commissioners for United States.

Alfred Wade,	[SEAL.]
Allen Wright,	[SEAL.]
James Riley,	[SEAL.]
John Page,	[SEAL.]

Choctaw commissioners.

Winchester Colbert,	[SEAL.]
Edmund (his x mark) Pickens,	[SEAL.]
Holmes Colbert,	[SEAL.]
Colbert Carter,	[SEAL.]
Robert H. Love,	[SEAL.]

Chickasaw commissioners.

Campbell Leflore,
      Secretary of Choctaw delegation.
E. S. Mitchell,
      Secretary of Chickasaw delegation.

In presence of—

Jno. H. B. Latrobe,
P. P. Pitchlynn,
      Principal chief Choctaws.
Douglas H. Cooper.
J. Harlan.
Charles E. Mix.

TREATY WITH THE CREEKS, 1866.

Treaty of cession and indemnity concluded at the city of Washington on the fourteenth day of June, in the year of our Lord one thousand eight hundred and sixty-six, by and between the United States, represented by Dennis N. Cooley, Commissioner of Indian Affairs, Elija Sells, superintendent of Indian affairs for the southern superintendency, and Col. Ely S. Parker, special commissioner, and the Creek Nation of Indians, represented by Ok-tars-sars-harjo, or Sands; Cow-e-to-me-co and Che-chu-chee, delegates at large, and D. N. McIntosh and James Smith, special delegates of the Southern Creeks.

June 14, 1866.
14 Stats., 785.
Ratified July 19, 1866.
Proclaimed Aug. 11, 1866.

PREAMBLE.

Whereas existing treaties between the United States and the Creek Nation have become insufficient to meet their mutual necessities; and whereas the Creeks made a treaty with the so-called Confederate States, on the tenth of July, one thousand eight hundred and sixty-one, whereby they ignored their allegiance to the United States, and unsettled the treaty relations existing between the Creeks and the United States, and did so render themselves liable to forfeit to the

Ante, p. 911, and note.

United States all benefits and advantages enjoyed by them in lands, annuities, protection, and immunities, including their lands and other property held by grant or gift from the United States; and whereas in view of said liabilities the United States require of the Creeks a portion of their land whereon to settle other Indians; and whereas a treaty of peace and amity was entered into between the United States and the Creeks and other tribes at Fort Smith, September *thirteenth* [tenth,] eighteen hundred and sixty-five,[a] whereby the Creeks revoked, cancelled, and repudiated the aforesaid treaty made with the so-called Confederate States; and whereas the United States, through its commissioners, in said treaty of peace and amity, promised to enter into treaty with the Creeks to arrange and settle all questions relating to and growing out of said treaty with the so-called Confederate States: Now, therefore, the United States, by its commissioners, and the above-named delegates of the Creek Nation, the day and year above mentioned, mutually stipulate and agree, on behalf of the respective parties, as follows, to wit:

Peace and friendship.
ARTICLE 1. There shall be perpetual peace and friendship between the parties to this treaty, and the Creeks bind themselves to remain firm allies and friends of the United States, and never to take up arms against the United States, but always faithfully to aid in putting down its enemies. They also agree to remain at peace with all other Indian tribes; and, in return, the United States guarantees them quiet possession of their country, and protection against hostilities on the part of other tribes. In the event of hostilities, the United States agree that the tribe commencing and prosecuting the same shall, as far as may be practicable, make just reparation therefor. To insure this protection, the Creeks agree to a military occupation of their country, at any time, by the United States, and the United States agree to station and continue in said country from time to time, at its own expense, *Military occupation and protection by the United States.* such force as may be necessary for that purpose. A general amnesty *Amnesty.* of all past offenses against the laws of the United States, committed by any member of the Creek Nation, is hereby declared. And the Creeks, anxious for the restoration of kind and friendly feelings among themselves, do hereby declare an amnesty for all past offenses against their government, and no Indian or Indians shall be proscribed, or any act of forfeiture or confiscation passed against those who have remained friendly to, or taken up arms against, the United States, but they shall enjoy equal privileges with other members of said tribe, and all laws heretofore passed inconsistent herewith are hereby declared inoperative.

ARTICLE 2. The Creeks hereby covenant and agree that henceforth neither slavery nor involuntary servitude, otherwise than in the punishment of crimes, whereof the parties shall have been duly convicted in accordance with laws applicable to all members of said tribe, shall *Slavery not to exist among the Creeks.* ever exist in said nation; and inasmuch as there are among the Creeks many persons of African descent, who have no interest in the soil, it is stipulated that hereafter these persons lawfully residing in said Creek country under their laws and usages, or who have been thus *Rights of those of African descent.* residing in said country, and may return within one year from the ratification of this treaty, and their descendants and such others of the same race as may be permitted by the laws of the said nation to settle within the limits of the jurisdiction of the Creek Nation as citizens [thereof,] shall have and enjoy all the rights and privileges of native citizens, including an equal interest in the soil and national funds, and the laws of the said nation shall be equally binding upon and give equal protection to all such persons, and all others, of what-

---

[a] This agreement, a copy of which has been obtained from the report of the negotiating commissioners, found accompanying the Report of the Commissioner of Indian Affairs for 1865, is set forth in the Appendix to this Compilation, post, p. 1050.

soever race or color, who may be adopted as citizens or members of said tribe.

ARTICLE 3. In compliance with the desire of the United States to locate other Indians and freedmen thereon, the Creeks hereby cede and convey to the United States, to be sold to and used as homes for such other civilized Indians as the United States may choose to settle thereon, the west half of their entire domain, to be divided by a line running north and south; the eastern half of said Creek lands, being retained by them, shall, except as herein otherwise stipulated, be forever set apart as a home for said Creek Nation; and in consideration of said cession of the west half of their lands, estimated to contain three millions two hundred and fifty thousand five hundred and sixty acres, the United States agree to pay the sum of thirty (30) cents per acre, amounting to nine hundred and seventy-five thousand one hundred and sixty-eight dollars, in the manner hereinafter provided, to wit: two hundred thousand dollars shall be paid per capita in money, unless otherwise directed by the President of the United States, upon the ratification of this treaty, to enable the Creeks to occupy, restore, and improve their farms, and to make their nation independent and self-sustaining, and to pay the damages sustained by the mission schools on the North Fork and the Arkansas Rivers, not to exceed two thousand dollars, and to pay the delegates such per diem as the agent and Creek council may agree upon, as a just and fair compensation, all of which shall be distributed for that purpose by the agent, with the advice of the Creek council, under the direction of the Secretary of the Interior. One hundred thousand dollars shall be paid in money and divided to soldiers that enlisted in the Federal Army and the loyal refugee Indians and freedmen who were driven from their homes by the rebel forces, to reimburse them in proportion to their respective losses; four hundred thousand dollars be paid in money and divided per capita to said Creek Nation, unless otherwise directed by the President of the United States, under the direction of the Secretary of the Interior, as the same may accrue from the sale of land to other Indians. The United States agree to pay to said Indians, in such manner and for such purposes as the Secretary of the Interior may direct, interest at the rate of five per cent. per annum from the date of the ratification of this treaty, on the amount hereinbefore agreed upon for said ceded lands, after deducting the said two hundred thousand dollars; the residue, two hundred and seventy-five thousand one hundred and sixty-eight dollars, shall remain in the Treasury of the United States, and the interest thereon, at the rate of five per centum per annum, be annually paid to said Creeks as above stipulated.

ARTICLE 4. Immediately after the ratification of this treaty the United States agree to ascertain the amount due the respective soldiers who enlisted in the Federal Army, loyal refugee Indians and freedmen, in proportion to their several losses, and to pay the amount awarded each, in the following manner, to wit: A census of the Creeks shall be taken by the agent of the United States for said nation, under the direction of the Secretary of the Interior, and a roll of the names of all soldiers that enlisted in the Federal Army, loyal refugee Indians, and freedmen, be made by him. The superintendent of Indian affairs for the Southern superintendency and the agent of the United States for the Creek Nation shall proceed to investigate and determine from said roll the amounts due the respective refugee Indians, and shall transmit to the Commissioner of Indian affairs for his approval, and that of the Secretary of the Interior, their awards, together with the reasons therefor. In case the awards so made shall be duly approved, said awards shall be paid from the proceeds of the sale of said lands within one year from the ratification of this treaty, or so soon as said

Cession of lands to the United States.

Payment therefor, and mode of payment.

Losses of loyal refugee Indians and freedmen, soldiers enlisted in Federal Army.

Census.

amount of one hundred thousand ($100,000) dollars can be raised from the sale of said land to other Indians.

Right of way granted for a railroad.
ARTICLE 5. The Creek Nation hereby grant a right of way through their lands, to the Choctaw and Chickasaw country, to any company which shall be duly authorized by Congress, and shall, with the express consent and approbation of the Secretary of the Interior, undertake to construct a railroad from any point north of to any point in or south of the Creek country, and likewise from any point on their eastern to their western or southern boundary, but said railroad company, together with all its agents and employés, shall be subject to the laws of the United States relating to intercourse with Indian tribes, and also to such rules and regulations as may be prescribed by the Secretary of the Interior for that purpose, and the Creeks agree to sell to the United States, or any company duly authorized as aforesaid, such lands not legally owned or occupied by a member or members of the Creek Nation, lying along the line of said contemplated railroad, not exceeding on each side thereof a belt or strip of land three miles in width, at such price per acre as may be eventually agreed upon between said Creek Nation and the party or parties building said road, subject to the approval of the President of the United States: *Provided, however,* That said land thus sold shall not be reconveyed, leased, or rented to, or be occupied by any one not a citizen of the Creek Nation, according to its laws and recognized usages: *Provided, also,* That officers, servants, and employés of said railroad necessary to its construction and management, shall not be excluded from such necessary occupancy, they being subject to the provisions of the Indian intercourse law and such rules and regulations as may be established by the Secretary of the Interior, nor shall any conveyance of any of said lands be made to the party building and managing said road until its completion as a first-class railroad, and its acceptance as such by the Secretary of the Interior.

ARTICLE 6. [Stricken out.]

Seminole may convey to the United States.
ARTICLE 7. The Creeks hereby agree that the Seminole tribe of Indians may sell and convey to the United States all or any portion of the Seminole lands, upon such terms as may be mutually agreed upon by and between the Seminoles and the United States.

Line dividing Creek country to be surveyed.
ARTICLE 8. It is agreed that the Secretary of the Interior forthwith cause the line dividing the Creek country, as provided for by the terms of the sale of Creek lands to the United States in article third of this treaty, to be accurately surveyed under the direction of the Commissioner of Indian Affairs, the expenses of which survey shall be paid by the United States.

Agency buildings.
ARTICLE 9. Inasmuch as the agency buildings of the Creek tribe have been destroyed during the late war, it is further agreed that the United States shall at their own expense, not exceeding ten thousand dollars, cause to be erected suitable agency buildings, the sites whereof shall be selected by the agent of said tribe, in the reduced Creek reservation, under the direction of the superintendent of Indian affairs.

In consideration whereof, the Creeks hereby cede and relinquish to the United States one section of their lands, to be designated and selected by their agent, under the direction of the superintendent of Indian affairs, upon which said agency buildings shall be erected, which section of land shall revert to the Creek nation when said agency buildings are no longer used by the United States, upon said nation paying a fair and reasonable value for said buildings at the time vacated.

Creeks agree to certain legislation.
ARTICLE 10. The Creeks agree to such legislation as Congress and the President of the United States may deem necessary for the better administration of justice and the protection of the rights of person and property within the Indian territory: *Provided, however,* [That] said

legislation shall not in any manner interfere with or annul their present tribal organization, rights, laws, privileges, and customs. The Creeks also agree that a general council, consisting of delegates elected by each nation or tribe lawfully resident within the Indian territory, may be annually convened in said territory, which council shall be organized in such manner and possess such powers as are hereinafter described.

General council.

First. After the ratification of this treaty, and as soon as may be deemed practicable by the Secretary of the Interior, and prior to the first session of said council, a census, or enumeration of each tribe lawfully resident in said territory, shall be taken under the direction of the superintendent of Indian affairs, who for that purpose is hereby authorized to designate and appoint competent persons, whose compensation shall be fixed by the Secretary of the Interior, and paid by the United States.

Census.

Second. The first general council shall consist of one member from each tribe, and an additional member from each one thousand Indians, or each fraction of a thousand greater than five hundred, being members of any tribe lawfully resident in said territory, and shall be selected by said tribes respectively, who may assent to the establishment of said general council, and if none should be thus formerly selected by any nation or tribe, the said nation or tribe shall be represented in said general council by the chief or chiefs and head men of said tribe, to be taken in the order of their rank as recognized in tribal usage, in the same number and proportion as above indicated. After the said census shall have been taken and completed, the superintendent of Indian affairs shall publish and declare to each tribe the number of members of said council to which they shall be entitled under the provisions of this article, and the persons entitled to so represent said tribes shall meet at such time and place as he shall appoint, but thereafter the time and place of the sessions of said council shall be determined by its action: *Provided*, That no session in any one year shall exceed the term of thirty days, and provided that special sessions of said council may be called whenever, in the judgment of the Secretary of the Interior, the interest of said tribe shall require.

First general council; how composed.

Time and place of meeting.
Sessions not to exceed thirty days.
Special session.

Third. Said general council shall have power to legislate upon all rightful subjects and matters pertaining to the intercourse and relations of the Indian tribes and nations resident in said territory, the arrest and extradition of criminals and offenders escaping from one tribe to another, the administration of justice between members of the several tribes of said territory, and persons other than Indians and members of said tribes or nations, the construction of works of internal improvement, and the common defence and safety of the nations of said territory. All laws enacted by said general council shall take effect at such time as may therein be provided, unless suspended by direction of the Secretary of the Interior or the President of the United States. No law shall be enacted inconsistent with the Constitution of the United States, or the laws of Congress, or existing treaty stipulations with the United States, nor shall said council legislate upon matters pertaining to the organization, laws, or customs of the several tribes, except as herein provided for.

Powers of general council.

Fourth. Said council shall be presided over by the superintendent of Indian affairs, or, in case of his absence from any cause, the duties of said superintendent enumerated in this article shall be performed by such person as the Secretary of the Interior may direct.

Who to preside over council.

Fifth. The Secretary of the Interior shall appoint a secretary of said council, whose duty it shall be to keep an accurate record of all the proceedings of said council, and who shall transmit a true copy of all such proceedings, duly certified by the superintendent of Indian affairs, to the Secretary of the Interior immediately after the sessions of said

Secretary of council.

Pay.

council shall terminate.   He shall be paid out of the Treasury of the United States an annual*ly* salary of five hundred dollars.

Pay of members.

Sixth. The members of said council shall be paid by the United States the sum of four dollars per diem during the time actually in attendance on the sessions of said council, and at the rate of four dollars for every twenty miles necessar[il]ly traveled by them in going to and returning to their homes respectively, from said council, to be certified by the secretary of said council and the superintendent of Indian affairs.

Courts.

Seventh. The Creeks also agree that a court or courts may be established in said territory, with such jurisdiction and organized in such manner as Congress may by law provide.

This treaty to be a full settlement of all claims.

ARTICLE 11. The stipulations of this treaty are to be a full settlement of all claims of said Creek Nation for damages and losses of every kind growing out of the late rebellion and all expenditures by the United States of annuities in clothing and feeding refugee and destitute Indians since the diversion of annuities for that purpose consequent

Diversion of annuities.

upon the late war with the so-called Confederate States; and the Creeks hereby ratify and confirm all such diversions of annuities heretofore made from the funds of the Creek Nation by the United States, and the United States agree that no annuities shall be diverted from the objects for which they were originally devoted by treaty stipulations with the Creeks, to the use of refugee and destitute Indians other than the Creeks or members of the Creek Nation after the close of the present fiscal year, June thirtieth, eighteen hundred and sixty-six.

Treaty obligations reaffirmed.

ARTICLE 12. The United States re-affirms and re-assumes all obligations of treaty stipulations with the Creek Nation entered into before the treaty of said Creek Nation with the so-called Confederate States, July tenth, eighteen hundred and sixty-one, not inconsistent herewith; and further agrees to renew all payments accruing by force of said treaty stipulations from and after the close of the present fiscal year, June thirtieth, eighteen hundred and sixty-six, except as is provided in article eleventh.

Lands granted for missionary and educational purposes.

ARTICLE 13. A quantity of land not exceeding one hundred and sixty acres, to be selected according to legal subdivision, in one body, and to include their improvements, is hereby granted to every religious society or denomination, which has erected, or which, with the consent of the Indians, may hereafter erect, buildings within the Creek

Not to be sold except, etc.

country for missionary or educational purposes; but no land thus granted, nor the buildings which have been or may be erected thereon, shall ever be sold or otherwise disposed of, except with the consent and approval of the Secretary of the Interior; and whenever any such

When sold, proceeds to be how applied.

lands or buildings shall be so sold or disposed of, the proceeds thereof shall be applied, under the direction of the Secretary of the Interior, to the support and maintenance of other similar establishments for the benefit of the Creeks and such other persons as may be or may hereafter become members of the tribe according to its laws, customs, and usages; and if at any time said improvements shall be abandoned for one year for missionary or educational purposes, all the rights herein granted for missionary and educational purposes shall revert to the said Creek Nation.

Inconsistent treaty provisions annulled.

ARTICLE 14. It is further agreed that all treaties heretofore entered into between the United States and the Creek Nation which are inconsistent with any of the articles or provisions of this treaty shall be, and are hereby, rescinded and annulled; and it is further agreed that ten thousand dollars shall be paid by the United States, or so much thereof as may be necessary, to pay the expenses incurred in negotiating the foregoing treaty.

Execution.

In testimony whereof, we, the commissioners representing the United States and the delegates representing the Creek nation, have hereunto set our hands and seals at the place and on the day and year above written.

D. N. Cooley, Commissioner Indian Affairs. [SEAL.]

Elijah Sells, Superintendent Indian Affairs. [SEAL.]

Ok-ta-has Harjo, his x mark. [SEAL.]

Cow Mikko, his x mark. [SEAL.]

Cotch-cho-chee, his x mark. [SEAL.]

D. N. McIntosh. [SEAL.]

James M. C. Smith. [SEAL.]

In the presence of—

J. W. Dunn, United States Indian agent.

J. Harlan, United States Indian agent.

Charles E. Mix.

J. M. Tebbetts.

Geo. A. Reynolds, United States Indian agent.

John B. Sanborn.

John F. Brown, Seminole delegate.

John Chupco, his x mark.

Fos-har-jo, his x mark.

Cho-cote-huga, his x mark.

R. Fields, Cherokee delegate.

Douglas H. Cooper.

Wm. Penn Adair.

Harry Island, his x mark, United States interpreter, Creek Nation.

Suludin Watie.

TREATY WITH THE DELAWARES, 1866.

Articles of agreement between the United States and the chiefs and councillors of the Delaware Indians, on behalf of said tribe, made at the Delaware Agency, Kansas, on the fourth day of July, eighteen hundred and sixty-six.

July 4, 1866.

14 Stats., 793.
Ratified July 26, 1866.
Proclaimed Aug. 10, 1866.

Whereas Congress has by law made it the duty of the President of the United States to provide by treaty for the removal of the Indian tribes from the State of Kansas; and whereas the Delaware Indians have expressed a wish to remove from their present reservation in said State to the Indian country, located between the States of Kansas and Texas; and whereas the United States have, by treaties negotiated with the Choctaws and Chickasaws, with the Creeks, and with the Seminoles, Indian tribes residing in said Indian country, acquired the right to locate other Indian tribes within the limits of the same; and whereas the Missouri River Railroad Company, a corporation existing in the State of Kansas by the laws thereof,—and which company has built a railroad connecting with the Pacific Railroad, from near the mouth of the Kaw River to Leavenworth, in aid of which road the Delawares, by treaty in eighteen hundred and sixty-four, agreed to dispose of their lands,--has expressed a desire to purchase the present Delaware Indian reservation in the said State, in a body, at a fair price:

It is hereby agreed between Thomas Murphy, superintendent of Indian affairs, John G. Pratt, agent for the Delawares, and William H. Watson, special commissioner, who are duly appointed to act for the United States; and Captain John Connor, Captain Sarcoxie, and Charles Journeycake, chiefs, and James Ketchum, James Connor, Andrew Miller, and John Sarcoxie, councillors, duly appointed and authorized by said Delaware Indians to act for them and in their behalf, viz:

ARTICLE 1. That the United States shall secure and cause to be paid to said Indians the full value of all that part of their reservation, with the improvements then existing on the same, heretofore sold to the Leavenworth, Pawnee, and Western Railroad Company, according to the terms of a treaty ratified August twenty-second, eighteen hundred and sixty, and supplemental treaties, and in accordance with the conditions, restrictions, and limitations thereof.

ARTICLE 2. That the Secretary of the Interior shall be, and he is, authorized to sell to said Missouri River Railroad Company, or to other responsible party or parties, in a body, all the remaining part of said reservation, being the lands conveyed to said Delaware Indians in pursuance of the provisions of the supplemental treaty of September twenty-fourth, eighteen hundred and twenty-nine, and all other lands owned by the said tribe in the State of Kansas not previously disposed

of, except as hereinafter provided, for a price not less than two dollars and fifty cents per acre, exclusive of improvements.

ARTICLE 3. It shall be the duty of the Secretary of the Interior to give each of all the adult Delaware Indians who have received their proportion of land in severalty an opportunity, free from all restraint, to elect whether they will dissolve their relations with their tribe and become citizens of the United States: and the lands of all such Indians as may elect so to become citizens, together with those of their minor children, held by them in severalty, shall be reserved from the sale

hereinbefore provided for. And the Secretary of the Interior shall cause any and all improvements made on any of the said lands, the sale of which is provided for, whether held in common or in severalty, to

be appraised, and the value thereof added to the price of said lands, to be paid for when payment is made for the lands upon which said improvements exist; and the money received for the improvements on the land of each Indian held in severalty shall be paid to him at any time after its payment to the Secretary of the Interior, when the Department shall be notified that said Indian is ready to remove to the Indian country, to provide for his removal to, and to enable him to

make improvements on his new home therein: *Provided*, That whenever it shall be ascertained under the registry above provided for what lands will be vacated, there shall be set apart from the lands held in common, for each child of Delaware blood, born since the allotment of land to said tribe in severalty was made under previous treaties, a quantity of land equal to the amount to which they would have been entitled had they been born before said allotment, provided that selections for children belonging to families whose head may elect to remain may be made from lands which are to be vacated by those who

elect to remove: *And provided further*, That in case there shall be improvements upon any heretofore allotted lands, so selected for children of the Delawares, payment shall be made for such improvements, at their appraised value, by the parents or guardians of said children, at the same time as if the said lands had been sold to the railroad company or other parties.

ARTICLE 4. The United States agree to sell to the said Delaware Indians a tract of land ceded to the Government by the Choctaws and Chickasaws, the Creeks, or the Seminoles, or which may be ceded by the Cherokees in the Indian country, to be selected by the Delawares in one body in as compact a form as practicable, so as to contain timber, water, and agricultural lands, to contain in the aggregate, if the said Delaware Indians shall so desire, a quantity equal to one hundred and sixty (160) acres for each man, woman, and child who

shall remove to said country, at the price per acre paid by the United States for the said lands, to be paid for by the Delawares out of the proceeds of sales of lands in Kansas, heretofore provided for. The said tract of country shall be set off with clearly and permanently marked boundaries by the United States; and also surveyed as public lands are surveyed, when the Delaware council shall so request, when the same may, in whole or in part, be allotted by said council to each member of said tribe residing in said country, said allotment being subject to the approval of the Secretary of the Interior.

ARTICLE 5. The United States guarantee to the said Delewares peace- able possession of their new home herein provided to be selected for them in the Indian country, and protection from hostile Indians and internal strife and civil war, and a full and just participation in any general council or territorial government that may be established for the nations and tribes residing in said Indian country.

ARTICLE 6. It is agreed that the proceeds of the sale of the Dela- ware lands herein provided for shall be paid to said Indians in the manner following, to wit: Whenever the Department of the Interior shall be notified by the council, through the agent, that any of the Delawares who hold land in severalty are ready to remove, at the same time describing their allotments, there shall be paid to each such person the value of his allotment, and that of his family, to enable him to remove to and improve his new home, provided the money for the said allotment shall have been paid to the Secretary of the Interior; and while said money, or any part thereof, shall remain in the Treasury of the United States, the Delawares shall be entitled to receive interest on the amount so retained, at the rate of five (5) per cent. per annum. And the residue of the proceeds of the sale of the Delaware lands, being those which have not been allotted, or which have once been allotted, but have been abandoned by the allottees, shall be added to the general fund of the Delawares, interest thereon to be paid to the Indians in the same manner as is now provided in regard to that fund.

ARTICLE 7. Within thirty days after the ratification of this treaty it shall be the duty of the Secretary of the Interior to give the said Missouri River Railroad Company notice that he is authorized to contract with them or other responsible party or parties for the sale of said lands on the terms specified in this treaty, indicating the approximate quantity thereof; and within twenty days after receiving said notice at their usual place of doing business in the State of Kansas it shall be competent for said company to elect to make the purchase, by filing with the said secretary their bond, with approved security, in double the amount proposed to be paid by them for the whole of said lands, guaranteeing that they will purchase all of the lands to be sold under the provisions of this treaty, and that they will pay for them in accordance with the terms thereof. And upon the filing of a satisfactory bond as above provided by said company, the contract for such purchase shall be concluded by the said secretary with said Missouri River Railroad Company, at not less than two dollars and fifty cents per acre for the whole of the lands herein provided to be sold: *Provided, however*, That if said railroad company shall not within the twenty days above limited file its bond for the purchase as herein prescribed, the Secretary of the Interior may at the expiration of that time accept any offer for the whole of said lands in one body, at not less than two dollars and fifty cents per acre, from any other responsible parties; but no offer shall be considered from other parties than said Missouri River Railroad Company, unless accompanied by a certificate of deposit in the First National Bank of the city of Washington, D. C., to the credit of the said secretary, for an amount equal to ten per cent. of the aggregate value of the land at the price proposed, to be forfeited for the use of the Delawares if the sale should be awarded to said person or corporation so proposing to purchase the lands, and said party should fail to make payment as hereinafter provided.

ARTICLE 8. That within sixty days after the sale of said land shall have been effected, the purchaser shall pay to the said Secretary, in trust for the Delawares, the stipulated price of said unallotted lands, with the appraised value of improvements thereon, excepting therefrom the mill reservation and the quarter sections upon which the council-house and blacksmith-shops are built, the use of which shall be retained until the final removal of the Delawares, and for which payment shall not be required from the purchaser until possession is delivered; and from time to time thereafter, as often as the Secretary of the Interior shall notify the said purchaser that ten thousand acres or more of said lands have been vacated by said Indians within three months thereafter, said purchaser shall pay to the Secretary of the Interior, in trust for the said Indians, the stipulated price for said lands, with the appraised value of the improvements; and so on until all are paid for, according to the true intent and meaning hereof; and as said lands shall be paid for, patents therefor, conveying the same in fee-simple, shall be from time to time issued to said purchaser, or to his or its assigns, by the President of the United States.

ARTICLE 9. It is also stipulated that the Secretary of the Interior shall cause a registry to be made of the names of all of said Delawares who have elected to dissolve their tribal relations and to become citizens of the United States, as provided in this treaty, with the names, ages, and sex of the members of the family of each of said Delawares, and present a certified copy of the same to the judge of the district court of the United States for the district of Kansas, and cause a copy to be filed in the office of the Commissioner of Indian Affairs, after which any of said Delawares, being adults, may appear before the said judge in open court, and make the same proof and take the same oath of allegiance as is provided by law for the naturalization of aliens, and also make proof, to the satisfaction of said court, that he is sufficiently intelligent and prudent to control his own affairs and interests, that he has adopted the habits of civilized life, and has been able to support, for at least five years, himself and family; when he shall receive a cer- tificate of the same under the seal of the said court; and on the filing of the said certificate in the office of the Commissioner of Indian Affairs, the said Delaware Indian shall be constituted a citizen of the United States, and be entitled to receive a patent, in fee-simple, with power of alienation, for the land heretofore allotted him, and his just proportion, in cash or in bonds, of the cash value of the credits of said tribe, principal and interest, then held in trust by the United States; and also, as the same may be received, his proportion of the proceeds of the sale of lands under the provisions of this treaty, when he shall cease to be a member of said tribe.   Whereupon all of the minor children of those who have become citizens shall be construed to have elected to sever their connection with said tribe for the time being, and be entitled to their just proportion of the annuities of the tribe, to be paid to the head of the family to be expended for their support and education until they shall attain the age of twenty-one years, after which each shall elect to remove to his tribe or to become a citizen of the United States, as hereinbefore provided, and if thus admitted to citizenship, shall be entitled to all the privileges and interests herein provided for the head of the family.   Should any minor as aforesaid, arriving at the age of twenty-one years, and electing to become a citizen of the United States, or any adult Indian having so elected, fail to be admitted, he shall not be compelled to remove, but the Secretary of the Interior shall provide proper guardianship for the protection of his rights and interests and those of his family.   There shall be granted to each of the Delawares who have thus become citizens, a patent, in fee-simple, for the lands heretofore allotted to them, and, if they do not remove with the nation, their *pro rata* share of all annuities and trust-property held by the United States for them, the division to be made under the direction of the President of the United States, after which such persons shall cease to be members of the Delaware tribe, and shall not further participate in their councils, nor share in their property or annuities.

ARTICLE 10. It is further agreed that the funds of the Delawares shall never be applied by the Government to the payment of the debt or debts of any individual member or members of the nation; nor shall any person be licensed to trade with the Delawares without the consent of the chiefs and council; and the salaries of the chiefs shall henceforward be four hundred dollars per annum. *Funds of the tribe not to pay debts of individual members.* *Licenses to trade.* *Salaries of chiefs.*

ARTICLE 11. The Delawares acknowledge their dependence upon the United States, and again renew their pledges of devotion to the Government thereof, and ask its protection; and the United States agree to protect, preserve, and defend them in all their just rights. *Dependence and protection.*

ARTICLE 12. It is also agreed that if the said Secretary should not be able to sell the said lands as hereinbefore provided, he may cause the same to be appraised, in separate tracts, at their fair cash value, no tract to be valued at less than two dollars and fifty cents per acre, and the same when appraised may be sold at not less than the appraised value, and for as much more as the same will bring, and the money arising from the sale to be applied and distributed as hereinbefore provided. *Sale of lands.*

ARTICLE 13. It is agreed by the Delawares that railroad companies engaged in building roads whose routes shall lie through their new reservation in the Indian country shall have a right of way through and over said lands, not exceeding two hundred feet in width for any such road, and also the right to enter on all lands and take and use such gravel, stone, and other material except timber as may be necessary for the construction of such roads, compensation to be made for any damages done in obtaining such material, and for any damages arising from the location or running of such roads to improvements which shall have been made before such road shall have been located, such damages to be ascertained under regulations to be prescribed by the Secretary of the Interior. *Right of way for railroads.*

ARTICLE 14. The United States further agree that, in accordance with the general provisions of the sixth article of the Delaware treaty of May thirty, eighteen hundred and sixty, which have not yet been fulfilled, there shall be credited to the Delawares, in the purchase of their new reservation in the Indian country, the sum of thirty thousand dollars, which credit by the United States shall be received by the Delawares as a full settlement of all claims against the Government for depredations upon timber to the date of the signing of this treaty; and the Delawares shall receive, without cost, from the United States, land included within their new reservation to the amount of twenty-three sections, in place of the twenty-three sections of half-breed Kaw lands referred to in said sixth section of the treaty of eighteen hundred and sixty; and inasmuch as the Delawares claim that a large amount of stock has been stolen from them by whites since the treaty of eighteen hundred and fifty-four, the United States agree to have a careful examination of such claims made under the direction of the Secretary of the Interior, and when the value of such stolen stock shall have been ascertained, the same shall be reported to Congress with a recommendation for an appropriation to pay for the same; and all moneys appropriated for such purpose shall be paid to the owners of said stock. *Settlement of all claims of the Delawares for depredations.*

ARTICLE 15. It is also agreed by the contracting parties that nothing contained in this treaty shall be so construed as to require the Delawares to remove from their present homes, until after they shall have selected and received title to lands for new homes elsewhere. *Delawares not to move until new homes are provided.*

Execution.

In testimony whereof, the said superintendent, agent, and special commissioner, on behalf of the United States, and the said chiefs and councillors on behalf of the Delawares, have hereunto set their hands and seals this fourth day of July, one thousand eight hundred and sixty-six.

Thos. Murphy,   [SEAL.]
      Superintendent.
John G. Pratt,   [SEAL.]
      Agent.
W. H. Watson,   [SEAL.]
      Special Commissioner.
John Connor, his x mark,   [SEAL.]
      Head Chief.
Captain Sarcoxie, his x mark,   [SEAL.]
      Assistant Chief.
Charles Journeycake,   [SEAL.]
      Assistant Chief.
James Ketch[u]m,   [SEAL.]
James Connor, his x mark,   [SEAL.]
Andrew Miller, his x mark,   [SEAL.]
John Sarcoxie, his x mark,   [SEAL.]
      Councillors.

Isaac Johnycake,
    United States interpreter.
In presence of—
    Henry S. Bulkley.
    Edward S. Menager.
    Louis A. Menager.

TREATY WITH THE CHEROKEE, 1866.

July 19, 1866.
_____
14 Stats., 799.
Ratified July 27, 1866.
Proclaimed Aug. 11, 1866.

Articles of agreement and convention at the city of Washington on the nineteenth day of July, in the year of our Lord one thousand eight hundred and sixty-six, between the United States, represented by Dennis N. Cooley, Commissioner of Indian Affairs, [and] Elijah Sells, superintendent of Indian affairs for the southern superintendency, and the Cherokee Nation of Indians, represented by its delegates, James McDaniel, Smith Christie, White Catcher, S. H. Benge, J. B. Jones, and Daniel H. Ross—John Ross, principal chief of the Cherokees, being too unwell to join in these negotiations.

PREAMBLE.

Whereas existing treaties between the United States and the Cherokee Nation are deemed to be insufficient, the said contracting parties agree as follows, viz:

Pretended treaty declared void.

ARTICLE 1..The pretended treaty made with the so-called Confederate States by the Cherokee Nation on the seventh day of October, eighteen hundred and sixty-one, and repudiated by the national council of the Cherokee Nation on the eighteenth day of February, eighteen hundred and sixty-three, is hereby declared to be void.

Amnesty.

ARTICLE 2. Amnesty is hereby declared by the United States and the Cherokee Nation for all crimes and misdemeanors committed by one Cherokee on the person or property of another Cherokee, or of a citizen of the United States, prior to the fourth day of July, eighteen hundred and sixty-six; and no right of action arising out of wrongs committed in aid or in the suppression of the rebellion shall be prosecuted or maintained in the courts of the United States or in the courts of the Cherokee Nation.

But the Cherokee Nation stipulate and agree to deliver up to the United States, or their duly authorized agent, any or all public property, particularly ordnance, ordnance stores, arms of all kinds, and quartermaster's stores, in their possession or control, which belonged to the United States or the so-called Confederate States, without any reservation.

ARTICLE 3. The confiscation laws of the Cherokee Nation shall be repealed, and the same, and all sales of farms, and improvements on real estate, made or pretended to be made in pursuance thereof, are hereby agreed and declared to be null and void, and the former owners of such property so sold, their heirs or assigns, shall have the right peaceably to re-occupy their homes, and the purchaser under the confiscation laws, or his heirs or assigns, shall be repaid by the treasurer of the Cherokee Nation from the national funds, the money paid for said property and the cost of permanent improvements on such real estate, made thereon since the confiscation sale; the cost of such improvements to be fixed by a commission, to be composed of one person designated by the Secretary of the Interior and one by the principal chief of the nation, which two may appoint a third in cases of disagreement, which cost so fixed shall be refunded to the national treasurer by the returning Cherokees within three years from the ratification hereof.

Confiscation laws repealed and former owners restored to their rights.

Improvements.

ARTICLE 4. All the Cherokees and freed persons who were formerly slaves to any Cherokee, and all free negroes not having been such slaves, who resided in the Cherokee Nation prior to June first, eighteen hundred and sixty-one, who may within two years elect not to reside northeast of the Arkansas River and southeast of Grand River, shall have the right to settle in and occupy the Canadian district southwest of the Arkansas River, and also all that tract of country lying northwest of Grand River, and bounded on the southeast by Grand River and west by the Creek reservation to the northeast corner thereof; from thence west on the north line of the Creek reservation to the ninety-sixth degree of west longitude; and thence north on said line of longitude so far that a line due east to Grand River will include a quantity of land equal to one hundred and sixty acres for each person who may so elect to reside in the territory above-described in this article: *Provided,* That that part of said district north of the Arkansas River shall not be set apart until it shall be found that the Canadian district is not sufficiently large to allow one hundred and sixty acres to each person desiring to obtain settlement under the provisions of this article.

Cherokees, freed persons, and free negroes may elect to reside where.

Proviso.

ARTICLE 5. The inhabitants electing to reside in the district described in the preceding article shall have the right to elect all their local officers and judges, and the number of delegates to which by their numbers they may be entitled in any general council to be established in the Indian Territory under the provisions of this treaty, as stated in Article XII, and to control all their local affairs, and to establish all necessary police regulations and rules for the administration of justice in said district, not inconsistent with the constitution of the Cherokee Nation or the laws of the United States; *Provided,* The Cherokees residing in said district shall enjoy all the rights and privileges of other Cherokees who may elect to settle in said district as hereinbefore provided, and shall hold the same rights and privileges and be subject to the same liabilities as those who elect to settle in said district under the provisions of this treaty; *Provided also,* That if any such police regulations or rules be adopted which, in the opinion of the President, bear oppressively on any citizen of the nation, he may suspend the same. And all rules or regulations in said district, or in any other district of the nation, discriminating against the citizens of other districts, are prohibited, and shall be void.

Those so electing to reside there may elect local officers, judges, etc.

Proviso.

Proviso.

Representation in national council.

ARTICLE 6. The inhabitants of the said district hereinbefore described shall be entitled to representation according to numbers in the national council, and all laws of the Cherokee Nation shall be uniform throughout said nation.

Unequal laws.

And should any such law, either in its provisions or in the manner of its enforcement, in the opinion of the President of the United States, operate unjustly or injuriously in said district, he is hereby authorized and empowered to correct such evil, and to adopt the means necessary to secure the impartial administration of justice, as well as a fair and equitable application and expenditure of the national funds as between the people of this and of every other district in said nation.

Courts.

ARTICLE 7. The United States court to be created in the Indian Territory; and until such court is created therein, the United States district court, the nearest to the Cherokee Nation, shall have exclusive original jurisdiction of all causes, civil and criminal, wherein an inhabitant of the district hereinbefore described shall be a party, and where an inhabitant outside of said district, in the Cherokee Nation, shall be the other party, as plaintiff or defendant in a civil cause, or shall be defendant or prosecutor in a criminal case, and all process issued in said district by any officer of the Cherokee Nation, to be executed on an inhabitant residing outside of said district, and all process issued

Process.

by any officer of the Cherokee Nation outside of said district, to be executed on an inhabitant residing in said district, shall be to all intents and purposes null and void, unless indorsed by the district judge for the district where such process is to be served, and said person, so arrested, shall be held in custody by the officer so arresting him, until he shall be delivered over to the United States marshal, or consent to be tried by the Cherokee court:

Proviso.

Provided, That any or all the provisions of this treaty, which make any distinction in rights and remedies between the citizens of any district and the citizens of the rest of the nation, shall be abrogated whenever the President shall have ascertained, by an election duly ordered by him, that a majority of the voters of such district desire them to be abrogated, and he shall

Proviso.

have declared such abrogation: *And provided further*, That no law or regulation, to be hereafter enacted within said Cherokee Nation or any district thereof, prescribing a penalty for its violation, shall take effect or be enforced until after ninety days from the date of its promulgation, either by publication in one or more newspapers of general circulation in said Cherokee Nation, or by posting up copies thereof in the Cherokee and English languages in each district where the same is to take effect, at the usual place of holding district courts.

Licenses to trade not to be granted unless, etc.

ARTICLE 8. No license to trade in goods, wares, or merchandise *merchandise* shall be granted by the United States to trade in the Cherokee Nation, unless approved by the Cherokee national council, except in the Canadian district, and such other district north of Arkansas River and west of Grand River occupied by the so-called southern Cherokees, as provided in Article 4 of this treaty.

Slavery, etc., not to exist.

ARTICLE 9. The Cherokee Nation having, voluntarily, in February, eighteen hundred and sixty-three, by an act of the national council, forever abolished slavery, hereby covenant and agree that never hereafter shall either slavery or involuntary servitude exist in their nation otherwise than in the punishment of crime, whereof the party shall have been duly convicted, in accordance with laws applicable to all the members of said tribe alike. They further agree that all freedmen who

Freedmen.

have been liberated by voluntary act of their former owners or by law, as well as all free colored persons who were in the country at the commencement of the rebellion, and are now residents therein, or who may return within six months, and their descendants, shall have all

No pay for emancipated slaves.

the rights of native Cherokees: *Provided*, That owners of slaves so emancipated in the Cherokee Nation shall never receive any compensation or pay for the slaves so emancipated.

ARTICLE 10. Every Cherokee and freed person resident in the Cherokee Nation shall have the right to sell any products of his farm, including his or her live stock, or any merchandise or manufactured products, and to ship and drive the same to market without restraint, paying any tax thereon which is now or may be levied by the United States on the quantity sold outside of the Indian Territory.

Farm products may be sold, etc.

ARTICLE 11. The Cherokee Nation hereby grant a right of way not exceeding two hundred feet wide, except at stations, switches, water-stations, or crossing of rivers, where more may be indispensable to the full enjoyment of the franchise herein granted, and then only two hundred additional feet shall be taken, and only for such length as may be absolutely necessary, through all their lands, to any company or corporation which shall be duly authorized by Congress to construct a railroad from any point north to any point south, and from any point east to any point west of, and which may pass through, the Cherokee Nation. Said company or corporation, and their employés and laborers, while constructing and repairing the same, and in operating said road or roads, including all necessary agents on the line, at stations, switches, water tanks, and all others necessary to the successful operation of a railroad, shall be protected in the discharge of their duties, and at all times subject to the Indian intercourse laws, now or which may hereafter be enacted and be in force in the Cherokee Nation.

Right of way of railroads.

ARTICLE 12. The Cherokees agree that a general council, consisting of delegates elected by each nation or tribe lawfully residing within the Indian Territory, may be annually convened in said Territory, which council shall be organized in such manner and possess such powers as hereinafter prescribed.

General council.

First. After the ratification of this treaty, and as soon as may be deemed practicable by the Secretary of the Interior, and prior to the first session of said council, a census or enumeration of each tribe lawfully resident in said Territory shall be taken under the direction of the Commissioner of Indian Affairs, who for that purpose is hereby authorized to designate and appoint competent persons, whose compensation shall be fixed by the Secretary of the Interior, and paid by the United States.

Census.

Second. The first general council shall consist of one member from each tribe, and an additional member for each one thousand Indians, or each fraction of a thousand greater than five hundred, being members of any tribe lawfully resident in said Territory, and shall be selected by said tribes respectively, who may assent to the establishment of said general council; and if none should be thus formally selected by any nation or tribe so assenting, the said nation or tribe shall be represented in said general council by the chief or chiefs and headmen of said tribes, to be taken in the order of their rank as recognized in tribal usage, in the same number and proportion as above indicated. After the said census shall have been taken and completed, the superintendent of Indian affairs shall publish and declare to each tribe assenting to the establishment of such council the number of members of such council to which they shall be entitled under the provisions of this article, and the persons entitled to represent said tribes shall meet at such time and place as he shall approve; but thereafter the time and place of the sessions of said council shall be determined by its action: *Provided*, That no session in any one year shall exceed the term of thirty days: *And provided*, That special sessions of said council may be called by the Secretary of the Interior whenever in his judgment the interest of said tribes shall require such special session.

First general council; how composed.

Time and place of first meeting.

Session not to exceed thirty days.
Special sessions.

Third. Said general council shall have power to legislate upon matters pertaining to the intercourse and relations of the Indian tribes and nations and colonies of freedmen resident in said Territory; the arrest and extradition of criminals and offenders escaping from one tribe to another, or into any community of freedmen; the administration of

Powers of general council.

justice between members of different tribes of said Territory and persons other than Indians and members of said tribes or nations; and the common defence and safety of the nations of said Territory.

Laws, when to take effect.

All laws enacted by such council shall take effect at such time as may therein be provided, unless suspended by direction of the President of the United States. No law shall be enacted inconsistent with the Constitution of the United States, or laws of Congress, or existing treaty stipulations with the United States. Nor shall said council legislate upon matters other than those above indicated: *Provided, however,* That the legislative power of such general council may be enlarged by the consent of the national council of each nation or tribe assenting to its establishment, with the approval of the President of the United States.

Legislative power may be enlarged.

President of council.

Fourth. Said council shall be presided over by such person as may be designated by the Secretary of the Interior.

Secretary of council.

Fifth. The council shall elect a secretary, whose duty it shall be to keep an accurate record of all the proceedings of said council, and who shall transmit a true copy of all such proceedings, duly certified by the presiding officer of such council, to the Secretary of the Interior, and to each tribe or nation represented in said council, immediately after the sessions of said council shall terminate. He shall be paid out of the Treasury of the United States an annual salary of five hundred dollars.

Pay.

Pay of members of council.

Sixth. The members of said council shall be paid by the United States the sum of four dollars per diem during the term actually in attendance on the sessions of said council, and at the rate of four dollars for every twenty miles necessarily traveled by them in going from and returning to their homes, respectively, from said council, to be certified by the secretary and president of the said council.

Courts.

ARTICLE 13. The Cherokees also agree that a court or courts may be established by the United States in said Territory, with such jurisdiction and organized in such manner as may be prescribed by law: *Provided,* That the judicial tribunals of the nation shall be allowed to retain exclusive jurisdiction in all civil and criminal cases arising within their country in which members of the nation, by nativity or adoption, shall be the only parties, or where the cause of action shall arise in the Cherokee Nation, except as otherwise provided in this treaty.

Lands for missionary or educational purposes.

ARTICLE 14. The right to the use and occupancy of a quantity of land not exceeding one hundred and sixty acres, to be selected according to legal subdivisions in one body, and to include their improvements, and not including the improvements of any member of the Cherokee Nation, is hereby granted to every society or denomination which has erected, or which with the consent of the national council may hereafter erect, buildings within the Cherokee country for missionary or educational purposes. But no land thus granted, nor buildings which have been or may be erected thereon, shall ever be sold or [o]therwise disposed of except with the consent and approval of the Cherokee national council and the Secretary of the Interior. And whenever any such lands or buildings shall be sold or disposed of, the proceeds thereof shall be applied by said society or societies for like purposes within said nation, subject to the approval of the Secretary of the Interior.

Not to be sold except for.

Proceeds of sale.

The United States may settle civilized Indians in the Cherokee country.

ARTICLE 15. The United States may settle any civilized Indians, friendly with the Cherokees and adjacent tribes, within the Cherokee country, on unoccupied lands east of 96°, on such terms as may be agreed upon by any such tribe and the Cherokees, subject to the approval of the President of the United States, which shall be consistent with the following provisions, viz: Should any such tribe or band of Indians settling in said country abandon their tribal organization, there being first paid into the Cherokee national fund a sum of money which shall sustain the same proportion to the then existing national fund that the number of Indians sustain to the whole number of Cherokees then residing in the Cherokee country, they shall be incorporated into and ever after remain a part of the Cherokee Nation, on equal terms in every respect with native citizens. And should any such tribe, thus settling in said country, decide to preserve their tribal organizations, and to maintain their tribal laws, customs, and usages, not inconsistent with the constitution and laws of the Cherokee Nation, they shall have a district of country set off for their use by metes and bounds equal to one hundred and sixty acres, if they should so decide, for each man, woman, and child of said tribe, and shall pay for the same into the national fund such price as may be agreed on by them and the Cherokee Nation, subject to the approval of the President of the United States, and in cases of disagreement the price to be fixed by the President.

How may be made part of Cherokee Nation.

Those wishing to preserve tribal organization to have land set off to them.

And the said tribe thus settled shall also pay into the national fund a sum of money, to be agreed on by the respective parties, not greater in proportion to the whole existing national fund and the probable proceeds of the lands herein ceded or authorized to be ceded or sold than their numbers bear to the whole number of Cherokees then residing in said country, and thence afterwards they shall enjoy all the rights of native Cherokees. But no Indians who have no tribal organizations, or who shall determine to abandon their tribal organizations, shall be permitted to settle east of the 96° of longitude without the consent of the Cherokee national council, or of a delegation duly appointed by it, being first obtained. And no Indians who have and determine to preserve the tribal organizations shall be permitted to settle, as herein provided, east of the 96° of longitude without such consent being first obtained, unless the President of the United States, after a full hearing of the objections offered by said council or delegation to such settlement, shall determine that the objections are insufficient, in which case he may authorize the settlement of such tribe east of the 96° of longitude.

To pay sum into national fund.

Limits of places of settlement

ARTICLE 16. The United States may settle friendly Indians in any part of the Cherokee country west of 96°, to be taken in a compact form in quantity not exceeding one hundred and sixty acres for each member of each of said tribes thus to be settled; the boundaries of each of said districts to be distinctly marked, and the land conveyed in fee-simple to each of said tribes to be held in common or by their members in severalty as the United States may decide.

Where the United States may settle friendly Indians.

Lands.

Said lands thus disposed of to be paid for to the Cherokee Nation at such price as may be agreed on between the said parties in interest, subject to the approval of the President; and if they should not agree, then the price to be fixed by the President.

The Cherokee Nation to retain the right of possession of and jurisdiction over all of said country west of 96° of longitude until thus sold and occupied, after which their jurisdiction and right of possession to terminate forever as to each of said districts thus sold and occupied.

Possession and jurisdiction over such lands.

ARTICLE 17. The Cherokee Nation hereby cedes, in trust to the United States, the tract of land in the State of Kansas which was sold to the Cherokees by the United States, under the provisions of the second article of the treaty of 1835; and also that strip of the land ceded to the nation by the fourth article of said treaty which is included in the State of Kansas, and the Cherokees consent that said lands may be included in the limits and jurisdiction of the said State.

Cession of lands to the United States in trust.

The lands herein ceded shall be surveyed as the public lands of the United States are surveyed, under the direction of the Commissioner of the General Land-Office, and shall be appraised by two disinterested persons, one to be designated by the Cherokee national council and one by the Secretary of the Interior, and, in case of disagreement,

Lands to be surveyed and appraised.

by a third person, to be mutually selected by the aforesaid appraisers. The appraisement to be not less than an average of one dollar and a quarter per acre, exclusive of improvements.

May be sold to highest bidder.

And the Secretary of the Interior shall, from time to time, as such surveys and appraisements are approved by him, after due advertisements for sealed bids, sell such lands to the highest bidders for cash, in parcels not exceeding one hundred and sixty acres, and at not less than the appraised value: *Provided,* That whenever there are improve-

Improvements.

ments of the value of fifty dollars made on the lands not being mineral, and owned and personally occupied by any person for agricultural purposes at the date of the signing hereof, such person so owning, and in person residing on such improvements, shall, after due proof, made under such regulations as the Secretary of the Interior may prescribe, be entitled to buy, at the appraised value, the smallest quantity of land in legal subdivisions which will include his improvements, not exceeding in the aggregate one hundred and sixty acres; the expenses of survey and appraisement to be paid by the Secretary out of the

Proviso.

proceeds of sale of said land: *Provided,* That nothing in this article shall prevent the Secretary of the Interior from selling the whole of said lands not occupied by actual settlers at the date of the ratification of this treaty, not exceeding one hundred and sixty acres to each person entitled to pre-emption under the pre-emption laws of the United States, in a body, to any responsible party, for cash, for a sum not less than one dollar per acre.

Sales by Cherokee of lands in Arkansas.

ARTICLE 18. That any lands owned by the Cherokees in the State of Arkansas and in States east of the Mississippi may be sold by the Cherokee Nation in such manner as their national council may prescribe, all such sales being first approved by the Secretary of the Interior.

Heads of families.

ARTICLE 19. All Cherokees being heads of families residing at the date of the ratification of this treaty on any of the lands herein ceded, or authorized to be sold, and desiring to remove to the reserved country, shall be paid by the purchasers of said lands the value of such improvements, to be ascertained and appraised by the commissioners who appraise the lands, subject to the approval of the Secretary of the Interior; and if he shall elect to remain on the land now occupied by him, shall be entitled to receive a patent from the United States in fee-simple for three hundred and twenty acres of land to include his improvements, and thereupon he and his family shall cease to be members of the nation.

And the Secretary of the Interior shall also be authorized to pay the reasonable costs and expenses of the delegates of the southern Cherokees.

The moneys to be paid under this article shall be paid out of the proceeds of the sales of the national lands in Kansas.

Lands reserved to be surveyed and allotted.

ARTICLE 20. Whenever the Cherokee national council shall request it, the Secretary of the Interior shall cause the country reserved for the Cherokees to be surveyed and allotted among them, at the expense of the United States.

Boundary line to be run and marked.

ARTICLE 21. It being difficult to learn the precise boundary line between the Cherokee country and the States of Arkansas, Missouri, and Kansas, it is agreed that the United States shall, at its own expense, cause the same to be run as far west as the Arkansas, and marked by permanent and conspicuous monuments, by two commissioners, one of whom shall be designated by the Cherokee national council.

Agent of Cherokees to examine accounts, books, etc.

ARTICLE 22. The Cherokee national council, or any duly appointed delegation thereof, shall have the privilege to appoint an agent to examine the accounts of the nation with the Government of the United States at such time as they may see proper, and to continue or discharge such agent, and to appoint another, as may be thought best by such council or delegation; and such agent shall have free access to all accounts and books in the executive departments relating to the business of said Cherokee Nation, and an opportunity to examine the same in the presence of the officer having such books and papers in charge.

ARTICLE 23. All funds now due the nation, or that may hereafter accrue from the sale of their lands by the United States, as hereinbefore provided for, shall be invested in the United States registered stocks at their current value, and the interest on all said funds shall be paid semi-annually on the order of the Cherokee Nation, and shall be applied to the following purposes, to wit: Thirty-five per cent. shall be applied for the support of the common-schools of the nation and educational purposes; fifteen per cent. for the orphan fund, and fifty per cent. for general purposes, including reasonable salaries of district officers; and the Secretary of the Interior, with the approval of the President of the United States, may pay out of the funds due the nation, on the order of the national council or a delegation duly authorized by it, such amount as he may deem necessary to meet outstanding obligations of the Cherokee Nation, caused by the suspension of the payment of their annuities, not to exceed the sum of one hundred and fifty thousand dollars. *Funds, how to be invested.* *Interest, how to be paid.*

ARTICLE 24. As a slight testimony for the useful and arduous services of the Rev. Evan Jones, for forty years a missionary in the Cherokee Nation, now a cripple, old and poor, it is agreed that the sum of three thousand dollars be paid to him, under the direction of the Secretary of the Interior, out of any Cherokee fund in or to come into his hands not otherwise appropriated. *Payment to Rev. Evan Jones.*

ARTICLE 25. A large number of the Cherokees who served in the Army of the United States having died, leaving no heirs entitled to receive bounties and arrears of pay on account of such service, it is agreed that all bounties and arrears for service in the regiments of Indian United States volunteers which shall remain unclaimed by any person legally entitled to receive the same for two years from the ratification of this treaty, shall be paid as the national council may direct, to be applied to the foundation and support of an asylum for the education of orphan children, which asylum shall be under the control of the national council, or of such benevolent society as said council may designate, subject to the approval of the Secretary of the Interior. *Bounties and arrears for services as Indian volunteers; how to be paid.*

ARTICLE 26. The United States guarantee to the people of the Cherokee Nation the quiet and peaceable possession of their country and protection against domestic feuds and insurrections, and against hostilities of other tribes. They shall also be protected against inter-[r]uptions or intrusion from all unauthorized citizens of the United States who may attempt to settle on their lands or reside in their territory. In case of hostilities among the Indian tribes, the United States agree that the party or parties commencing the same shall, so far as practicable, make reparation for the damages done. *Possession and protection guaranteed.*

ARTICLE 27. The United States shall have the right to establish one or more military posts or stations in the Cherokee Nation, as may be deemed necessary for the proper protection of the citizens of the United States lawfully residing therein and the Cherokee and other citizens of the Indian country. But no sutler or other person connected therewith, either in or out of the military organization, shall be permitted to introduce any spirit[u]ous, vinous, or malt liquors into the Cherokee Nation, except the medical department proper, and by them only for strictly medical purposes. And all persons not in the military service of the United States, not citizens of the Cherokee Nation, are to be prohibited from coming into the Cherokee Nation, or remaining in the same, except as herein otherwise provided; and *Military posts in Cherokee Nation.* *Spirituous, etc., liquors forbidden except, etc.* *Certain persons prohibited from coming into the nation.*

it is the duty of the United States Indian agent for the Cherokees to have such persons, not lawfully residing or sojourning therein, removed from the nation, as they now are, or hereafter may be, required by the Indian intercourse laws of the United States.

Payment for certain provisions and clothing.

ARTICLE 28. The United States hereby agree to pay for provisions and clothing furnished the army under Appotholehala in the winter of 1861 and 1862, not to exceed the sum of ten thousand dollars, the accounts to be ascertained and settled by the Secretary of the Interior.

Expenses of Cherokee delegations.

ARTICLE 29. The sum of ten thousand dollars or so much thereof as may be necessary to pay the expenses of the delegates and representatives of the Cherokees invited by the Government to visit Washington for the purposes of making this treaty, shall be paid by the United States on the ratification of this treaty.

Payment of certain losses by missionaries, etc.

ARTICLE 30. The United States agree to pay to the proper claimants all losses of property by missionaries or missionary societies, resulting from their being ordered or driven from the country by United States agents, and from their property being taken and occupied or destroyed by *by* United States troops, not exceeding in the aggregate twenty thousand dollars, to be ascertained by the Secretary of the Interior.

Inconsistent treaty provisions annulled.

ARTICLE 31. All provisions of treaties heretofore ratified and in force, and not inconsistent with the provisions of this treaty, are hereby re-affirmed and declared to be in full force; and nothin herein shall be construed as an acknowledgment by the United States, or as a relinquishment by the Cherokee Nation of any claims or demands under the guarantees of former treaties, except as herein expressly provided.

Execution.

In testimony whereof, the said commissioners on the part of the United States, and the said delegation on the part of the Cherokee Nation, have hereunto set their hands and seals at the city of Washington, this *ninth* [nineteenth] day of July, A. D. one thousand eight hundred and sixty-six.

> D. N. Cooley, Commissioner of Indian Affairs.
> Elijah Sells, Superintendent of Indian Affairs.
> Smith Christie,
> White Catcher,
> James McDaniel,
> S. H. Benge,
> Danl. H. Ross,
> J. B. Jones.

Delegates of the Cherokee Nation, appointed by Resolution of the National Council.

In presence of—
> W. H. Watson,
> J. W. Wright.

Signatures witnessed by the following-named persons, the following interlineations being made before signing: On page 1st the word "the" interlined, on page 11 the word "the" struck out, and to said page 11 sheet attached requiring publication of laws; and on page 34th the word "ceded" struck out and the words "neutral lands" inserted. Page 47½ added relating to expenses of treaty.

> Thomas Ewing, jr.
> Wm. A. Phillips,
> J. W. Wright.

TREATY WITH THE SAUK AND FOXES, 1867.

Articles of agreement made and concluded this eighteenth day of February, one thousand eight hundred and sixty-seven, between the United States, represented by Lewis V. Bogy, Commissioner of Indian Affairs; William H. Watson, special commissioner; Thomas Murphy, superintendent of Indian Affairs for Kansas; and Henry W. Martin, United States Indian agent, duly authorized, and the tribes of Sacs and Foxes of the Mississippi, represented by Keokuk, Che-kus-kuk, Uc-quaw-ho-ko, Mut-tut-tah, and Man-ah-to-wah, chiefs of said tribes.

Feb. 18, 1867.

15 Stat., 495.
Ratified July 25, 1868.
Proclaimed Oct. 14, 1868.

ARTICLE 1. The Sacs and Foxes of the Mississippi cede to the Government of the United States all the lands, with the improvements thereon, contained in their unsold portion of their diminished reserve defined in the first article of their treaty ratified July ninth, one thousand eight hundred and sixty, (the said tract containing about eighty-six thousand and four hundred acres, and being more particularly described by the survey and plats on file in the Department of the Interior,) except as reserved in previous treaties, or in this treaty.

Cession of lands to the United States.

ARTICLE 2. The said Indians also cede to the United States a full and complete title to the land, with the improvements thereon, now remaining unsold in that portion of their old reservation provided by article four of the treaty of July ninth, one thousand eight hundred and sixty, to be sold by the Government for their benefit, the cession herein made being subject to the exceptions defined in this treaty.

Additional cession.

ARTICLE 3. The United States agree to pay to the Sac and Fox Indians, parties to this treaty, at the rate of one dollar an acre for the whole of the land ceded in the two preceding sections, being about one hundred and fifty-seven thousand acres of land, less the amount of land set apart for individuals; and further agree to pay the outstanding indebtedness of the said tribe, now represented by scrip issued under the provisions of previous treaties, and amounting, on the first of November, eighteen hundred and sixty-five, to twenty-six thousand five hundred and seventy-four dollars, besides the interest thereon; out of the proceeds of the sale of lands ceded in this treaty, and the amount herein provided to be paid to said Indians, after deducting such sums as, under the provisions of this treaty, are to be expended for their removal, subsistence, and establishing them in their new country, shall be added to their invested funds, and five per cent. interest paid thereon in the same manner as the interest of their present funds is now paid.

Payments by the United States.

ARTICLE 4. At any time after the ratification of this treaty, the lands ceded in the first article shall be held and considered at the disposal of the United States, except that, until the time for the removal of the Indians is fixed by public notice, under the provisions of this treaty, no interference shall be made with the rights of the Indians as the occupants of the lands, but they shall remain in all respects without molestation, in the same manner as if this treaty had not been made: *And provided further*, That inasmuch as there are valuable improvements upon said reservation, such improvements shall be appraised under the direction of the Secretary of the Interior, and the appraised value of the same shall be paid to the United States, before title is given to any individual or corporation for the lands upon which such improvements are situated.

Lands ceded, when to be at the disposal of the United States.

Proviso.

ARTICLE 5. The lands ceded in the second article of this treaty, being the unsold remainder of the lands provided in the fourth article of the treaty of July ninth, one thousand eight hundred and sixty, to be sold in trust for said Indians, shall, immediately upon the ratification of this treaty, become the property of the United States, and

Same subject.

shall be open to entry and settlement, and the lands in the second article ceded, as well as those ceded in the first article, shall be subject to all the laws and regulations of the General Land-Office the same as other public lands, except as relates to the provisions in the next preceding article relating to the time when they shall be open for settlement, and the requirement of payment for the improvements; and should there be any improvements upon the land ceded in the second article, they shall be appraised, and payment shall be required therefor: *Provided*, That such lands shall be subject to sale, in tracts of not exceeding one hundred and sixty acres to any one person, and at a price not less than one dollar and fifty cents per acre.

New reservation for the Sacs and Foxes.

ARTICLE 6. The United States agree, in consideration of the improvements upon the said reservation, to give to the Sacs and Foxes for their future home a tract of land in the Indian country south of Kansas, and south of the Cherokee lands, not exceeding seven hundred and fifty square miles in extent.

How to be selected.

The selection of such new reservation shall be made under the direction of the Secretary of the Interior, and with his approval, by commissioners appointed by the said Secretary, who shall visit the Indian country, with delegations from all the tribes proposing to remove thereto, as soon as practicable after the ratification of this treaty; and said reservation shall be surveyed as to its exterior lines, at the cost of the United States, under the direction of the Commissioner of Indian Affairs, not to exceed three thousand dollars:

How surveyed.

Proviso.

Provided, That if it shall be found impracticable to select a suitable home for the tribe except by purchase from the Cherokees, the United States will pay toward the said purchase the same amount that would have been payable to the Creeks if the reservation had been selected upon the former Creek lands; and in that case the balance of the money payable to the Cherokees shall be deducted from the amount due the Sacs and Foxes under this treaty.

Buildings to be erected.

ARTICLE 7. As soon as practicable after the selection of the new reservation herein provided for, there shall be erected thereon, at the cost of the United States, a dwelling-house for the agent of the tribe, a house and shop for a blacksmith, and dwelling-house for a physician, the aggregate cost of which shall not exceed ten thousand dollars; and also, at the expense of the tribe, five dwelling-houses for the chiefs, to cost in all not more than five thousand dollars.

Removal of Indians to new reservation.

As soon as practicable after such selection of a reservation as it may, in the discretion of the Secretary of the Interior, be deemed advisable for the Indians to remove thereto, regard being had to the proper season of the year for such removal, notice shall be given to their agent, directing such removal; and whenever such time shall be fixed, public notice thereof shall be given in three leading newspapers of Kansas, and thereafter the land ceded to the United States by the first article of this treaty, shall be open to entry and settlement under the provisions of the fourth article.

Certain claims against the tribe, how to be paid.

ARTICLE 8. No part of the invested funds of the tribe, or of any moneys which may be due to them under the provisions of previous treaties, nor of any moneys provided to be paid to them by this treaty, shall be used in payment of any claims against the tribe accruing previous to the ratification of this treaty unless herein expressly provided for.

Manual-labor school, school buildings, etc.

ARTICLE 9. In order to promote the civilization of the tribe, one section of land, convenient to the residence of the agent, shall be selected by said agent, with the approval of the Commissioner of Indian Affairs, and set apart for a manual-labor school; and there shall also be set apart, from the money to be paid to the tribe under this treaty, the sum of ten thousand dollars for the erection of the necessary school-buildings and dwelling for teacher, and the annual amount of five thousand dollars shall be set apart from the income of their funds after the erection of such school-buildings, for the support of the school; and after settlement of the tribe upon their new reservation, the sum of five thousand dollars of the income of their funds may be annually used, under the direction of the chiefs, in the support of their national government, out of which last-mentioned amount the sum of five hundred dollars shall be annually paid to each of the chiefs.

ARTICLE 10. The United States agree to pay annually, for five years after the removal of the tribe, the sum of fifteen hundred dollars for the support of a physician and purchase of medicines, and also the sum of three hundred and fifty dollars annually for the same time, in order that the tribe may provide itself with tobacco and salt. *Physician, medicines, tobacco, and salt.*

ARTICLE 11. In consideration of certain improvements made by John Goodell upon the lands of the nation within their present reservation, and of his services as their interpreter, he shall be allowed to select therefrom a half section of land; and it is further provided that of said land, Sarah A. Whistler and Pash-e-ca-cah, or Amelia Mitchell, shall each be allowed to select a half section of land, the latter selection to include the house in which she lives; and Julia A. Goodell one quarter section, besides the land, not exceeding eight acres, upon which her house and improvements are situated; and Mary A. Means, one quarter section, to includ[e] the improvements occupied by her; and there shall also be allowed to Antoine Gokey and William Avery, each one hundred and sixty acres, to Leo Whistler and Gertrude Whistler, each three hundred and twenty acres, and to James Thorpe, Virginia Thorpe, and Cassandra Thorpe, Thomas J. Miles, Hattie Miles, Ema-Ke-O-Kuck, Hannie Ke-O-Kuck, Mo-Co-P-quah, each eighty acres; Man-a-tah, Pah-me-che-kaw-paw, Henry Jones, Wilson McKinney, and Carrie C. Capper, each one hundred and sixty acres, to be selected from unimproved lands: *Provided*, That the parties herein named shall pay to the Secretary of the Interior, within three months after the ratification of this treaty, the sum of one dollar per acre for said lands, the avails of which shall be used for the benefit of the Sacs and Foxes in the same manner as the other funds arising from the sales of their lands: *Provided also*, That George Powers, the present Government interpreter, for valuable services rendered and uniform kindness toward the nation, shall have patented to him, in fee-simple, three hundred and twenty acres of land, to be located by the agent: *Provided also*, That they may select from land upon which improvements exist, by paying the appraised value of such improvements; but no selection shall include the agency, mission, or mill buildings; and upon the approval by the Secretary of the Interior of such selections, and on payment therefor as hereinbefore provided, patents in fee-simple shall be issued to the respective parties, their heirs or assigns. *Grants of land to certain persons.*

ARTICLE 12. In consideration of the faithful services of Samuel Black in protecting their houses and timber from trespass and depredation, there shall be patented to him in fee-simple the tract of land upon which he lives, being the west half of the northwest quarter-section four, town[ship] seventeen, range sixteen. *Land to Samuel Black.*

ARTICLE 13. John K. Rankin, licensed traders, having erected valuable building at the agency, it is agreed that [he] may have a patent for the land, not exceeding eight acres, upon which such improvements are built, and not to include any other improvements, on the payment of two dollars and fifty cents per acre.

ARTICLE 14. The Sacs and Foxes, parties to this treaty, agree that the Sacs and Foxes of Missouri, if they shall so elect, with the approval of the Secretary of the Interior, may unite with them and become a *The Sauk and Foxes of Missouri may unite with, etc.*

part of their people, upon their contributing to the common fund such a portion of their funds as will place them on an equal footing in regard to annuities.

Certain claims against the United States to be paid.

ARTICLE 15. The claims of the Sacs and Foxes against the United States for stealing of stock, which have heretofore been adjusted, amounting to sixteen thousand four hundred dollars, shall be paid by the United States, and the amount disbursed and expended for the benefit of the tribe in such objects for their improvement and comfort upon the new reservation as the chiefs, through their agent, shall desire; and whereas the Indians claim that one full payment due under previous treaty has never been made to them, it is agreed that a careful examination of the books of the Commissioner of Indian Affairs shall be made, and if any sum is found to be still due and unpaid, the same shall be paid to them per capita in the same manner as their annuities are paid.

Advance to the Indians for subsistence and removal.

ARTICLE 16. The United States will advance to the said tribe of Indians the sum of twenty thousand dollars, or so much thereof as may be necessary, to pay the expenses of their subsistence for the first year after their arrival at their new home in the Indian country, and to pay the necessary expenses of removal, and furnish necessary rations for the journey during such removal; said removal to be made under direction of the superintendent or agent, to be designated by the Secretary of the Interior; the moneys thus expended to be deducted from the whole amount provided to be paid for their lands herein ceded.

Patents for lands heretofore selected and approved.

ARTICLE 17. It is hereby provided that the half-breeds and full-bloods of the tribe, who were entitled to selections of land under the Sac and Fox treaty, ratified July ninth, one thousand eight hundred and sixty, and which selections have been approved by the Secretary of the Interior, shall be entitled to patents in fee-simple for the lands heretofore selected, according to the schedule annexed to this treaty: *Provided,* That where such selections have been made and the allottees have sold their lands for a valuable consideration, not less than one dollar and twenty-five cents per acre, the Secretary of the Interior shall, upon full proof being made, cause patents to issue to the purchasers or their assigns.

Sales of land to be approved, etc.

ARTICLE 18. All sales hereafter made by or on behalf of persons to whom lands are assigned in this treaty shall receive the approval of the Secretary of the Interior before taking effect in conveying titles to lands so sold.

Expenses of treaty.

ARTICLE 19. The United States agree to pay the expenses of negotiating this treaty, not to exceed the sum of fifteen hundred dollars.

Provisions as to cultivated farms.

ARTICLE 20. The chiefs and head-men of the Sacs and Foxes having permitted their employees to cultivate farms, which, together with the farms of Ke-o-kuck and other chiefs, are embraced within an area two miles by four, and the said Sacs and Foxes believing that the lands comprising the said area having been made valuable by reason of said occupancy, and in order that they may receive a fair compensation for said area of land, bounded and described as follows, except as heretofore specially excepted, and the mill and mission building, to wit: commencing at the northwest corner of section thirty-three, township sixteen, range seventeen, thence east two and a quarter ($2\frac{1}{4}$) miles to the reservation line; thence south along said line four miles; thence west two and a fourth ($2\frac{1}{4}$) miles to the southwest corner of section sixteen, township seventeen, range seventeen; thence north along the section line to the place of beginning, are hereby withdrawn from sale, as is provided for the sale of their lands in this treaty, and the said area of land, as above described, shall be sold by the chiefs and agent for the tribe at the best price obtainable; and they are hereby empowered to make warrantee deeds for the same, subject to the approval of the Secretary of the Interior, at not less than two dollars per acre in addition to the appraised value of the improvements. The avails of said lands shall be expended by the agent, under the direction of the chiefs, for the benefit of the nation.

ARTICLE 21. The Sacs and Foxes of the Mississippi, parties to this agreement, being anxious that all the members of their tribe shall participate in the advantages to be derived from the investment of their national funds, sales of lands, and so forth, it is therefore agreed that, as soon as practicable, the Commissioner of Indian Affairs shall cause the necessary proceedings to be adopted, to have such members of the tribe as may be absent notified of this agreement and its advantages, and to induce them to come in and permanently unite with their brethren; and that no part of the funds arising from or due the nation under this or previous treaty stipulations shall be paid to any bands or parts of bands who do not permanently reside on the reservation set apart to them by the Government in the Indian Territory, as provided in this treaty, except those residing in the State of Iowa; and it is further agreed that all money accruing from this or former tribes, [treaties,] now due or to become due said nation, shall be paid them on their reservation in Kansas; and after their removal, as provided in this treaty, payments shall be made at their agency, on their lands as then located.

Absent members of the tribe to be notified of this treaty, etc.

List of Sac and Fox lands selected for individuals referred to in Article XVII of the above treaty, selected by Perry Fuller, agent.

Schedule annexed.

Names of persons.	Description of land.	Sec[tion.]	Town[ship.]	Range.
Alvira Connolly	S. ½ NW. ¼	5	17	18
Alvira Connolly	SW. ¼	5	17	18
Alvira Connolly	N. ½ NW. ¼	8	17	18
Alexander Connolly	E. ½	4	17	18
Cordelia Connolly	E. ½	35	16	17
Isaac Goodell	W. ½	3	17	18
Kish-Kah-Iwah	S. ½	16	17	18
Mary I. Thorp	E. ½	12	17	17
Hiram P. Thorp	E. ½	1	17	17
Francis A. Thorp	W. ½	6	17	18
Amelia McPherson	W. ½	1	17	17
Sarah A. Whistler	SW. ¼	34	16	18
Sarah A. Whistler	SW. ¼ SW. ¼	35	16	18
Sarah A. Whistler	W. ½ NW. ¼	2	17	18
Sarah A. Whistler	NW. ¼ SW. ¼	2	17	18
Julia A. Goodell	N. ½	21	17	18
Susan J. Goodell	E. ½	3	17	18
John Goodell, jr	E. ½	17	17	18
Jane Goodell	NE. ¼	10	17	18
Jane Goodell	NW. ¼ NW. ¼	10	17	18
Jane Goodell	E. ½ NW. ¼	10	17	18
Jane Goodell	NW. ¼ NW. ¼	11	17	18
Mary A. Byington	E. ½ NE. ¼	9	17	18
Mary A. Byington	E. ½ SE. ¼	9	17	18
Mary A. Byington	W. ½ SW. ¼	10	17	18
Mary A. Byington	SW. ¼ NW. ¼	10	17	18
Mary A. Byington	NE. ¼ NE. ¼	16	17	18
Margaret Miles	W. ½	4	17	18
Thomas J. Connolly	SW. ¼ SE. ¼	9	17	18
Thomas J. Connolly	SE. ¼ NE. ¼	16	17	18
Thomas J. Connolly	W. ½ NE. ¼	16	17	18
Thomas J. Connolly	NW. ¼	16	17	18
Charles T. Connolly	E. ½ NW. ¼	9	17	18
Charles T. Connolly	W. ½ NE. ¼	9	17	18
Charles T. Connolly	NW. ¼ SE. ¼	9	17	18
Charles T. Connolly	SE. ¼ SW. ¼	9	17	18
Charles T. Connolly	S. ½ SW. ¼	9	17	18

The following were selected by C. C. Hutchinson:

Names of persons.	Description.	Sec[tion.]	Town[ship.]	Range.
Kaw-Kol-we-nah	E. ½	2	17	17
George Powers	NE. ¼	8	17	18
George Powers	S. ½ NW. ¼	8	17	18
George Powers	N. ½ SW. ¼	8	17	18
Joseph Gokey	W. ½ SE. ¼	21	17	18
Joseph Gokey	N. ½ NW. ¼	28	17	18
Joseph Gokey	SW. ¼ NW. ¼	28	17	18
Joseph Gokey	NW. ¼ NE. ¼	28	17	18
Joseph Gokey	W. ½ SE. ¼	29	17	18
Met-tach-ah-pack-o tah	E. ½	7	17	18
Mack-oh-tach-o-quit	W. ½	7	17	18

In testimony whereof, the parties hereinbefore named have hereunto set their hands and seals the day and year first above mentioned.

Lewis V. Bogy,   [SEAL.]
   Commissioner of Indian Affairs.
W. H. Watson,   [SEAL.]
   Special Commissioner.
Thos. Murphy,   [SEAL.]
   Superintendent of Indian Affairs.
Henry W. Martin,   [SEAL.]
   United States Indian agent.
Keokuk, his x mark.   [SEAL.]
Chekuskuk, his x mark.   [SEAL.]
Uc-quaw-ho-ko, his x mark.   [SEAL.]
Mut-tut-tah, his x mark.   [SEAL.]
Man-ah-to-wah, his x mark.   [SEAL.]

In presence of—
   Antoine Gokey, his x mark,
      United States interpreter.
   Charles E. Mix.
   Thos. E. McGraw.
   Wm. Whistler.
   C. H. Norris.
   Vital Jarrot.
   G. P. Beauvais.
   H. W. Farnsworth.

TREATY WITH THE SIOUX—SISSETON AND WAHPETON BANDS, 1867.

Feb. 19, 1867.

15 Stats., 505.
Ratified April 15, 1867.
Proclaimed May 2, 1867.

Preamble.

Whereas it is understood that a portion of the Sissiton and Warpeton bands of Santee Sioux Indians, numbering from twelve hundred to fifteen hundred persons, not only preserved their obligations to the Government of the United States, during and since the outbreak of the Medewakantons and other bands of Sioux in 1862, but freely perilled their lives during that outbreak to rescue the residents on the Sioux reservation, and to obtain possession of white women and children made captives by the hostile bands; and that another portion of said Sissiton and Warpeton bands, numbering from one thousand to twelve hundred persons, who did not participate in the massacre of the whites in 1862, fearing the indiscriminate vengeance of the whites, fled to the great prairies of the Northwest, where they still remain; and

Whereas Congress, in confiscating the Sioux annuities and reservations, made no provision for the support of these, the friendly portion of the Sissiton and Warpeton bands, and it is believed [that] they have been suffered to remain homeless wanderers, frequently subject to intense sufferings from want of subsistence and clothing to protect them from the rigors of a high northern latitude, although at all times prompt in rendering service when called upon to repel hostile raids and to punish depredations committed by hostile Indians upon the persons and property of the whites; and

Whereas the several subdivisions of the friendly Sissitons and Warpeton bands ask, through their representatives, that their adherence to their former obligations of friendship to the Government and people of the United States be recognized, and that provision be made to enable them to return to an agricultural life and be relieved from a dependence upon the chase for a precarious subsistence: Therefore,

A treaty has been made and entered into, at Washington City, District of Columbia, this nineteenth day of February, A. D. 1867, by and between Lewis V. Bogy, Commissioner of Indian Affairs, and William H. Watson, commissioners, on the part of the United States, and the undersigned chiefs and head-men of the Sissiton and Warpeton bands of Dakota or Sioux Indians, as follows, to wit: *Contracting parties.*

ARTICLE 1. The Sissiton and Warpeton bands of Dakota Sioux Indians, represented in council, will continue their friendly relations with the Government and people of the United States, and bind themselves individually and collectively to use their influence to the extent of their ability to prevent other bands of Dakota or other adjacent tribes from making hostile demonstrations against the Government or people of the United States. *Friendly relations.*

ARTICLE 2. The said bands hereby cede to the United States the right to construct wagon-roads, railroads, mail stations, telegraph lines, and such other public improvements as the interest of the Government may require, over and across the lands claimed by said bands, (including their reservation as hereinafter designated) over any route or routes that *that* may be selected by the authority of the Government, said lands so claimed being bounded on the south and east by the treaty-line of 1851, and the Red River of the North to the mouth of Goose River; on the north by the Goose River and a line running from the source thereof by the most westerly point of Devil's Lake to the Chief's Bluff at the head of James River, and on the west by the James River to the mouth of Mocasin River, and thence to Kampeska Lake. *Cession of rights to construct wagon roads, railroads, mail stations, and telegraph lines.* *Boundaries.*

ARTICLE 3. For and in consideration of the cession above mentioned, and in consideration of the faithful and important services said to have been rendered by the friendly bands of Sissitons and Warpetons Sioux here represented, and also in consideration of the confiscation of all their annuities, reservations, and improvements, it is agreed that there shall be set apart for the members of said bands who have heretofore surrendered to the authorities of the Government, and were not sent to the Crow Creek reservation, and for the members of said bands who were released from prison in 1866, the following-described lands as a permanent reservation, viz: *Permanent reservation set apart.*

Beginning at the head of Lake Travers[e], and thence along the treaty-line of the treaty of 1851 to Kampeska Lake; thence in a direct line to Reipan or the northeast point of the Coteau des Prairie[s], and thence passing north of Skunk Lake, on the most direct line to the foot of Lake Traverse, and thence along the treaty-line of 1851 to the place of beginning. *Boundaries.*

ARTICLE 4. It is further agreed that a reservation be set apart for all other members of said bands who were not sent to the Crow Creek *Reservation.*

reservation, and also for the Cut-Head bands of Yanktonais Sioux, a reservation bounded as follows, viz:

Boundaries.

Beginning at the most easterly point of Devil's Lake; thence along the waters of said lake to the most westerly point of the same; thence on a direct line to the nearest point on the Cheyenne River; thence down said river to a point opposite the lower end of Aspen Island, and thence on a direct line to the place of beginning.

Reservations to be apportioned in tracts of 160 acres, to, etc.

ARTICLE 5. The said reservations shall be apportioned in tracts of (160) one hundred and sixty acres to each head of a family or single person over the age of (21) twenty-one years, belonging to said bands and entitled to locate thereon, who may desire to locate permanently and cultivate the soil as a means of subsistence: each (160) one hundred

Tracts to conform to legal subdivisions.

and sixty acres so allotted to be made to conform to the legal subdivisions of the Government surveys when such surveys shall have been made; and every person to whom lands may be allotted under the provisions of this article, who shall occupy and cultivate a portion thereof for five consecutive years shall thereafter be entitled to receive a patent for the same so soon as he shall have fifty acres of said tract

Patents; when to issue; effect of.

fenced, ploughed, and in crop: *Provided*, [That] said patent shall not authorize any transfer of said lands, or portions thereof, except to the United States, but said lands and the improvements thereon shall descend to the proper heirs of the persons obtaining a patent.

Congress will make appropriations to enable Indians to return to an agricultural life, etc.

ARTICLE 6. And, further, in consideration of the destitution of said bands of Sissiton and Warpeton Sioux, parties hereto, resulting from the confiscation of their annuities and improvements, it is agreed that Congress will, in its own discretion, from time to time make such appropriations as may be deemed requisite to enable said Indians to return to an agricultural life under the system in operation on the Sioux reservation in 1862; including, if thought advisable, the establishment and support of local and manual-labor schools; the employment of agricultural, mechanical, and other teachers; the opening and improvement of individual farms; and generally such objects as Congress in its wisdom shall deem necessary to promote the agricultural improvement and civilization of said bands.

Agents.

ARTICLE 7. An agent shall be appointed for said bands, who shall be located at Lake Traverse; and whenever there shall be five hundred (500) persons of said bands permanently located upon the Devil's Lake reservation there shall be an agent or other competent person appointed to superintend at that place the agricultural, educational, and mechanical interests of said bands.

Expenditures.

ARTICLE 8. All expenditures under the provisions of this treaty shall be made for the agricultural improvement and civilization of the members of said bands authorized to locate upon the respective reservations, as hereinbefore specified, in such manner as may be directed

Goods, provisions, etc., not to be issued to Indians, etc., unless.

by law; but no goods, provisions, groceries, or other articles—except materials for the erection of houses and articles to facilitate the operations of agriculture—shall be issued to Indians or mixed-bloods on either reservation unless it be in payment for labor performed or for

Proviso.

produce delivered: *Provided*, That when persons located on either reservation, by reason of age, sickness, or deformity, are unable to labor, the agent may issue clothing and subsistence to such persons from such supplies as may be provided for said bands.

No person to trade for furs and peltries.

ARTICLE 9. The withdrawal of the Indians from all dependence upon the chase as a means of subsistence being necessary to the adoption of civilized habits among them, it is desirable that no encouragement be afforded them to continue their hunting operations as means of support, and, therefore, it is agreed that no person will be authorized to trade for furs or peltries within the limits of the land claimed by said bands, as specified in the second article of this treaty, it being contemplated that the Indians will rely solely upon agricultural and mechanical labor for subsistence, and that the agent will supply the Indians and mixed-bloods on the respective reservations with clothing, provisions, &c., as set forth in article eight, so soon as the same shall be provided for that purpose. And it is further agreed that no person not a member of said bands, parties hereto whether white, mixed-blood, or Indian, except persons in the employ of the Government or located under its authority, shall be permitted to locate upon said lands, either for hunting, trapping, or agricultural purposes.

Members of bands only, except, etc., to locate on lands.

ARTICLE 10. The chiefs and head-men located upon either of the reservations set apart for said bands are authorized to adopt such rules, regulations, or laws for the security of life and property, the advancement of civilization, and the agricultural prosperity of the members of said bands upon the respective reservations, and shall have authority, under the direction of the agent, and without expense to the Government, to organize a force sufficient to carry out all such rules, regulations, or laws, and all rules and regulations for the government of said Indians, as may be prescribed by the Interior Department: *Provided,* That all rules, regulations, or laws adopted or amended by the chiefs and head-men on either reservation shall receive the sanction of the agent.

Chiefs and head men may adopt rules.

In testimony whereof, we, the commissioners representing the United States, and the delegates representing the Sissiton and Warpeton bands of Sioux Indians, have hereunto set our hands and seals, at the place and on the day and year above written.

Lewis V. Bogy,
Commissioner of Indian Affairs.
W. H. Watson.

Signed in the presence of—
    Charles E. Mix.

Gabriel Renville, head chief Siss(i)ton and Wa(r)peton bands.
Wamdiupiduta, his x mark, head Siss(i)ton chief.
Tacandupahotanka, his x mark, head Wa(r)peton chief.
Oyehduze, his x mark, chief Sissiton.
Umpehtutokca, his x mark, chief Wahpeton.
John Otherday.
Akicitananjin, his x mark, Sissiton soldier.
Waxicunmaza, his x mark, Sissiton soldier.
Wasukiye, his x mark, Sissiton soldier.
Wamdiduta, his x mark, Sissiton soldier.
Hokxidanwaxte, his x mark, Sissiton soldier.

Wakanto, his x mark, Sissiton soldier.
Ecanajinke, his x mark, Sissiton soldier.
Canteiyapa, his x mark, Sissiton soldier.
Tihdonica, his x mark, Sissiton soldier.
Tawapahamaza, his x mark, Sissiton soldier.
Wandiiyeza, his x mark, Sissiton soldier.
Tacunrpipeta, his x mark, Sissiton soldier.
Wicumrpinumpa, his x mark, Wa(r)peton soldier.
Xupehiyu, his x mark, Wa(r)peton soldier.
Ecetukiye, his x mark, Wa(r)peton soldier.
Kangiduta, his x mark, Wa(r)peton soldier.

Witnesses to signatures of above chiefs and soldiers:

Charles E. Mix.
Benj'n Thompson.
J. R. Brown.
Anexus M. A. Brown, Interpreter.
Chas. Crawford.

Thos. E. McGraw.
J. H. Leavenworth.
A. B. Norton.
Geo. B. Jonas.
Frank S. Mix.

TREATY WITH THE SENECA, MIXED SENECA AND SHAWNEE, QUAPAW, ETC., 1867.

Feb. 23, 1867.

15 Stats., 513.
Ratified June 18, 1868.
Proclaimed Oct. 14, 1868.

Articles of agreement, concluded at Washington, D. C., the twenty-third day of February, one thousand eight hundred and sixty-seven, between the United States, represented by Lewis V. Bogy, Commissioner of Indian Affairs, W. H. Watson, special commissioner. Thomas Murphy, superintendent of Indian Affairs, George C. Snow, and G. A. Colton, U. S. Indian agents, duly authorized, and the Senecas, represented by George Spicer and John Mush; the Mixed Senecas and Shawnees, by John Whitetree, John Young, and Lewis Davis; the Quapaws, by S. G. Vallier and Ka-zhe-cah; the Confederated Peorias, Kaskaskias, Weas, and Piankeshaws, by Baptiste Peoria, John Mitchell, and Edward Black; the Miamies, by Thomas Metosenyah and Thomas Richardville, and the Ottawas of Blanchard's Fork and Roche de Bœuf, by John White and J. T. Jones, and including certain Wyandott[e]s, represented by Tauromee, or John Hat, and John Karaho.

Preamble.

Whereas it is desirable that arrangements should be made by which portions of certain tribes, parties hereto, now residing in Kansas, should be enabled to remove to other lands in the Indian country south of that State, while other portions of said tribes desire to dissolve their tribal relations, and become citizens; and whereas it is necessary to provide certain tribes, parties hereto, now residing in the Indian country, with means of rebuilding their houses, re-opening their farms, and supporting their families, they having been driven from their reservations early in the late war, and suffered greatly for several years, and being willing to sell a portion of their lands to procure such relief; and whereas a portion of the Wyandottes, parties to the treaty of one thousand eight hundred and fifty-five, although taking lands in severalty, have sold said lands, and are still poor, and have not been compelled to become citizens, but have remained without clearly recognized organization, while others who did become citizens are unfitted for the responsibilities of citizenship; and whereas the Wyandottes, treated with in eighteen hundred and fifty-five, have just claims against the Government, which will enable the portion of their people herein referred to to begin anew a tribal existence: Therefore it is agreed:

Cession of lands to the United States by the Seneca.

ARTICLE 1. The Senecas cede to the United States a strip of land on the north side of their present reservation in the Indian country; the land so ceded to be bounded on the east by the State of Missouri, on the north by the north line of the reservation, on the west by the Neosho River, and running south for the necessary distance, to contain twenty thousand acres; for which the Government is to pay twenty thousand dollars upon the ratification of this treaty; the south line of said tract to be ascertained by survey, at the cost of the United States.

Further cession.

ARTICLE 2. The Senecas now confederated with the Shawnees, and owning an undivided half of a reservation in the Indian country immediately north of the Seneca reservation mentioned in the preceding article, cede to the United States one-half of said Seneca and Shawnee reserve, which it is mutually agreed shall be the north half, bounded on the east by the State of Missouri, north by the Quapaw reserve, west by the Neosho River, and south by an east and west line bisecting the present Seneca and Shawnee reserve into equal parts, the said line to be determined by survey, at the expense of the United States; for which tract of land, estimated to contain about thirty thousand acres, the United States will pay the sum of twenty-four thousand dollars.

ARTICLE 3. The Shawnees, heretofore confederated with the Senecas, cede to the United States that portion of their remaining lands, bounded as follows, beginning at a point where Spring River crosses the south line of the tract in the second article ceded to the United States, thence down said river to the south line of the Shawnee reserve, thence west to the Neosho River, thence up said river to the south line of the tract ceded in the second article, and thence east to the place of beginning; supposed to contain about twelve thousand acres, the area to be ascertained by survey, at the expense of the United States; the United States to pay for the same at the rate of one dollar per acre, as soon as the area shall be ascertained. *Cession of lands to the United States by the Shawnee.*

ARTICLE 4. The Quapaws cede to the United States that portion of their land lying in the State of Kansas, being a strip of land on the north line of their reservation, about one half mile in width, and containing about twelve sections in all, excepting therefrom one half section to be patented to Samuel G. Vallier, including his improvements. Also the further tract within their present reserve, bounded as follows: Beginning at a point in the Neosho River where the south line of the Quapaw reserve strikes that stream, thence east three miles, thence north to the Kansas boundary-line, thence west on said line to the Neosho River, thence down said river to the place of beginning; and the United States will pay to the Quapaws for the half-mile strip lying in Kansas at the rate of one dollar and twenty-five cents per acre, whenever the area of the same shall be ascertained; and for the other tract described in this article at the rate of one dollar and fifteen cents per acre, whenever the area of the same shall be ascertained by survey, said survey to be made at the cost of the tribe to which said tract is herein provided to be sold under the pre-emption laws of the United States; but all such pre-emption shall be paid in the money of the United States, at the proper land-office, within one year from the date of entry and settlement. *By the Quapaw.*

PROVISIONS RELATING TO THE SENECAS.

ARTICLE 5. The Senecas now confederated with the Shawnees, the said Shawnees thereto consenting, agree to dissolve their connection with the said Shawnees, and to unite with the Senecas, parties to the treaty of February twenty-eighth, one thousand eight hundred and thirty-one, upon their reservation described in article second of said treaty; and the several bands of Senecas will unite their funds into one common fund for the benefit of the whole tribe; and an equitable division shall be made of all funds or annuities now held in common by the Senecas and Shawnees. *Seneca to separate from the Shawnee.*

ARTICLE 6. Of the sum of twenty-four thousand dollars to be paid to the Senecas, as provided in the second article, the sum of four thousand dollars shall be paid to them immediately after the ratification of this treaty, to enable them to re-establish their homes and provide themselves with agricultural implements, seed, and provisions for themselves and their families; and the balance of the said first-mentioned sum, being twenty thousand dollars, shall be consolidated with the twenty thousand dollars in the first article provided to be paid, and invested for the tribe of Senecas, as constituted by this treaty, at five per cent. interest, to be paid per capita semi-annually; and their annuity of five hundred dollars in specie, provided by article four of the treaty of September twenty-ninth, one thousand eight hundred and seventeen, shall likewise become the property of the tribe. *Payments to the Seneca.*

ARTICLE 7. The amount annually due the Senecas under the provisions of article four of the treaty of February twenty-eight, one thousand eight hundred and thirty-one, for blacksmith, after their separation from the Shawnees, shall be annually paid to them as a *Payments for improvements in agriculture.*

national fund, to enable them to purchase such articles for their wants and improvements in agriculture as the chiefs, with the consent of their agent, may designate; and this provision shall apply also to the fund for support of a miller belonging to the Senecas heretofore occupying the southernmost reserve referred to in this treaty; and there shall be added to the said fund whatever amount belonging to either band of the Senecas shall be found due and unpaid upon an examination of their accounts with the Government, and particularly the amount of bonds and stocks invested in their name; and the interest thereon shall be annually paid to the said Senecas for the purposes mentioned in this article.

PROVISIONS RELATING TO THE SHAWNEES.

Payments to the Shawnee.

ARTICLE 8. Of the amount in the third article provided to be paid to the Shawnees by the United States for the lands therein ceded, the sum of two thousand dollars shall be advanced to them to be used in establishing their homes, and the balance of the said amount shall be invested for the said tribe, under the name of Eastern Shawnees, and five per cent. be paid semi-annually thereon; and the amount due and unpaid upon the bonds or stocks invested in their name shall be paid to them, as well as the interest thereon hereafter to become due, to be used under the direction of the chiefs, with the consent of the agent, for the purchase of agricultural implements or other articles necessary for the general welfare of the people; and the one-half of the black-smith fund remaining after the division to be made with the Senecas provided for in article five shall remain devoted to the same purpose, and the Government will add thereto the sum of five hundred dollars annually for five years.

PROVISIONS RELATING TO THE QUAPAWS.

Payment to the Quapaw.

ARTICLE 9. Of the amount to be paid to the Quapaws for the lands ceded by them in the fourth article of this treaty, the sum of five thousand dollars shall be paid to them upon the ratification of this treaty, to assist them in re-establishing themselves at their homes upon their remaining reservation; and the balance of said amount shall be invested as a permanent fund at five per cent. interest, payable per capita, semi-annually.

School fund.

ARTICLE 10. If the Osage mission school should be closed, so that the school fund of the Quapaws cannot be used for them to advantage at that institution, the said fund shall remain in the Treasury of the United States until such time as it can, under the direction of the Secretary of the Interior, with the consent of the chiefs, be used to advantage in establishing a school upon their reservation.

Aid in agriculture.

ARTICLE 11. The amount now due and unpaid for a farmer, under the provisions of the third article of their treaty of May thirteen one thousand eight hundred and thirty-*eight* [three], may be used by the chiefs and council for the purchase of provisions, farming-implements, seed, and otherwise for the purpose of assisting the people in agriculture; and their annual income now paid for farmer shall hereafter be set apart for the purposes of assistance and improvement in agriculture.

CLAIMS FOR LOSSES BY THE WAR.

Claims for losses by the war.

Commission to investigate claims.

ARTICLE 12. Whereas the aforesaid Senecas, Mixed Senecas and Shawnees, and Quapaws were driven from their homes during the late war, and their property destroyed, it is agreed that a commission of not to exceed two persons shall be appointed by the Secretary of the Interior, who shall proceed to their country and make careful investigation of their claims for losses, and make full report of the same to the Department; and the Secretary of the Interior shall report the same to Congress.

PROVISIONS IN RELATION TO THE WYANDOTTES.

ARTICLE 13. The United States will set apart for the Wyandottes for their future home the land ceded by the Senecas in the first article hereof, and described in said article, to be owned by the said Wyandottes in common; and the Secretary of the Interior is hereby authorized and required to appoint three persons whose duty it shall be to ascertain and report to the Department the amount of money, if any, due by the United States to the Wyandott[e] Indians under existing treaty stipulations, and the items mentioned in Schedule A, appended to this treaty, and the report of the persons so appointed, with the evidence taken, shall be submitted to Congress for action at its next session. A register of the whole people, resident in Kansas and elsewhere, shall be taken by the agent of the Delawares, under the direction of the Secretary of the Interior, on or before the first of July, one thousand eight hundred and sixty-seven, which shall show the names of all who declare their desire to be and remain Indians, and in a tribal condition, together with incompetents and orphans, as described in the treaty of one thousand eight hundred and fifty-five; and all such persons, and those only, shall hereafter constitute the tribe: *Provided,* That no one who has heretofore consented to become a citizen, nor the wife or children of any such person, shall be allowed to become members of the tribe, except by the free consent of the tribe after its new organization, and unless the agent shall certify that such party is, through poverty or incapacity, unfit to continue in the exercise of the responsibilities of citizenship of the United States, and likely to become a public charge.

Lands set apart for the Wyandot.

Payment.

Register to be taken.

Who to constitute the tribe.
Proviso.

ARTICLE 14. Whenever the register in the next preceding article shall have been completed and returned to the Commissioner of Indian Affairs, the amount of money in said article acknowledged to be due to the Wyandott[e]s shall be divided, and that portion equitably due to the citizens of said people shall be paid to them or their heirs, under the direction of the Secretary of the Interior; and the balance, after deducting the cost of the land purchased from the Senecas by the first article hereof, and the sum of five thousand dollars to enable the Wyandott[e]s to establish themselves in their new homes, shall be paid to the Wyandott[e] tribe per capita.

Upon completion of register amount to be divided.

Remainder, how to be applied.

ARTICLE 15. All restrictions upon the sale of lands assigned and patented to "incompetent" Wyandott[e]s under the fourth article of the treaty of one thousand eight hundred and fifty-five, shall be removed after the ratification of this treaty, but no sale of lands heretofore assigned to orphans or incompetents shall be made, under decree of any court, or otherwise, for or on account of any claim, judgment, execution, or order, or for taxes, until voluntarily sold by the patentee or his or her heirs, with the approval of the Secretary of the Interior; and whereas many sales of land belonging to this class have heretofore been made, contrary to the spirit and intent of the treaty of one thousand eight hundred and fifty-five, it is agreed that a thorough examination and report shall be made, under direction of the Secretary of the Interior, in order to ascertain the facts relating to all such cases, and, upon a full examination of such report, and hearings of the parties interested, the said Secretary may confirm the said sales, or require an additional amount to be paid, or declare such sales entirely void, as the very right of the several cases may require.

Certain restrictions upon sales of lands removed.

PROVISIONS RELATING TO THE OTTAWAS.

ARTICLE 16. The west part of the Shawnee reservation, ceded to the United States by the third article, is hereby sold to the Ottawas, at one dollar per acre; and for the purpose of paying for said reservation the United States shall take the necessary amount, whenever

Sale of land to the Ottawa.

Payment.

the area of such land shall be found by actual survey, from the funds in the hands of the Government arising from the sale of the Ottawa trust-lands, as provided in the ninth article of the treaty of one thousand eight hundred and sixty-two, and the balance of said fund, after the payment of accounts provided for in article five of the treaty of one thousand eight hundred and sixty-two, shall be paid to the tribe per capita.

Provisions of former treaty as to members of the tribe becoming citizens extended.

ARTICLE 17. The provisions of the Ottawa treaty of one thousand eight hundred and sixty-two, under which all the tribe were to become citizens upon the sixteenth of July, one thousand eight hundred and sixty-seven, are hereby extended for two years, or until July sixteenth, one thousand eight hundred and sixty-nine; but any time previous to that date any member of the tribe may appear before the United States district court for Kansas, and declare his intention to become a citizen, when he shall receive a certificate of citizenship, which shall include his family, and thereafter be disconnected with the tribe, and shall be entitled to his proportion of the tribal fund; and all who shall not have made such declaration previous to the last-mentioned date shall still be considered members of the tribe. In order to enable the tribe to dispose of their property in Kansas, and remove to their new homes and establish themselves thereon, patents in fee-simple shall be given to the heads of families and to all who have come of age among the allottees under the treaties of one thousand eight hundred and sixty-two, so that they may sell their lands without restriction; but the said lands shall remain exempt from taxation so long as they may be retained by members of the tribe down to the said sixteenth of July, one thousand eight hundred and sixty-nine; and the chiefs and council of the said tribe shall decide in the case of disputed heirship to real estate, taking as a rule the laws of inheritance of the State of Kansas.

Payment to individuals for losses.

ARTICLE 18. The United States agree to pay the claim of J. T. Jones, for which a bill of appropriation has passed one of the branches of Congress, but which has been withdrawn from before Congress, being for destruction by fire of his dwelling and other property by whites in one thousand eight hundred and fifty-six, shall be allowed and paid to him, amounting to six thousand seven hundred dollars.

Education and schools.

ARTICLE 19. The sixth article of the treaty of one thousand eight hundred and sixty-two shall remain unchanged, except as provided in this article. The children of the tribe between the ages of six and eighteen (6 and 18) shall be entitled to be received at said institution, and to be subsisted, clothed, educated, and attended in sickness, where the sickness is of such a nature that the patient promises a return to study within a reasonable period; the children to be taught and practised in industrial pursuits, suitable to their age and sex, and both sexes in such branches of learning, and to receive such advantages as the means of the institution will permit; these rights and privileges to continue so long as any children of the tribe shall present themselves for their exercise. And the Secretary of the Interior and the senior corresponding secretary of the American Baptist Home Mission Society shall be members *ex officio* of the board of trustees, with power to vote in person or by proxy, it being the special intention of this provision to furnish additional supervision of the institution, so that the provisions of this article may be carried into effect in their full spirit and intent.

Sale of lands to Ottawa University.

ARTICLE 20. It is further agreed that the remaining unsold portion of trust-lands of the Ottawas, amounting to seven thousand two hundred and twenty-one and twenty one-hundredths acres, shall be sold to the trustees of Ottawa University, to be disposed of for the benefit of said institution at the appraised value thereof, and that the said trustees shall have until July sixteenth, one thousand eight hundred and sixty-nine, to dispose of the same and pay to the Government the value of said lands: *Provided,* That the said trustees shall furnish, within thirty days after the ratification of this treaty, to the Secretary of the Interior, a satisfactory bond for the fulfilment of their obligations.

PROVISIONS RELATING TO THE PEORIAS, KASKASKIAS, WEAS, AND PIANKESHAWS.

ARTICLE 21. Whereas certain arrangements have been made by the chiefs of the confederated tribes of Peorias, Kaskaskias, Weas, and Piankeshaws, for the sale to actual settlers of the lands held by them in common, being nine and one-half sections, for a reasonable consideration, according to the terms of a certain petition of the said tribe, with schedule annexed, (which schedule is annexed to this treaty, and marked "B,") dated December twenty-sixth, one thousand eight hundred and sixty-six, filed in the office of the Commissioner of Indian Affairs, it is agreed that the said arrangements shall be carried into full effect, and the purchasers thereunder shall receive patents from the United States for the lands so purchased, upon making full payment for the same to the Secretary of the Interior, and the amount already paid by said purchasers, as appears from said schedule, and in the hands of the chiefs, shall be paid to the Secretary of the Interior, and the whole amount of the purchase-money shall also be paid to the said Secretary on or before the first day of June, one thousand eight hundred and sixty-seven, and shall be held by him for the benefit of the tribe, subject to the provisions of this treaty.

Purchasers of land from the Peoria, etc., to receive patents.

ARTICLE 22. The land in the second and fourth articles of this treaty proposed to be purchased from the Senecas and Quapaws, and lying south of Kansas, is hereby granted and sold to the Peorias, &c., and shall be paid for, at the rate paid for the same by the Government, out of the proceeds of the nine and a half sections referred to in the last preceding article, adding thereto whatever may be necessary out of other moneys in the hands of the United States belonging to said Peorias, &c.

Lands sold to the Peoria, etc.

ARTICLE 23. The said Indians agree to dispose of their allotments in Kansas and remove to their new homes in the Indian country within two years from the ratification of this treaty; and to that end the Secretary of the Interior is authorized to remove altogether the restrictions upon the sales of their lands, provided under authority of the third article of the treaty of May thirtieth, one thousand eight hundred and fifty-four, in such manner that adult Indians may sell their own lands, and that the lands of minors and incompetents may be sold by the chiefs, with the consent of the agent, certified to the Secretary of the Interior and approved by him. And if there should be any allotments for which no owner or heir thereof survives, the chiefs may convey the same by deed, the purchase-money thereof to be applied, under the direction of the Secretary, to the benefit of the tribe; and the guardianship of orphan children shall remain in the hands of the chiefs of the tribe, and the said chiefs shall have the exclusive right to determine who are members of the tribe and entitled to be placed upon the pay-rolls.

Indians to remove to new homes within, etc.

ARTICLE 24. An examination shall be made of the books of the Indian Office, and an account-current prepared, stating the condition of their funds, and the representations of the Indians for overcharges for sales of their lands in one thousand eight hundred and fifty-seven and one thousand eight hundred and fifty-eight shall be examined and reported to Congress; and in order further to assist them in preparing for removal and in paying their debts, the further amount of twenty-

Amounts due the Indians to be paid them.

Further allowances.

1862, ch. 156, 12 Stat., 539.

five thousand dollars shall be at the same time paid to them per capita from the sum of one hundred and sixty-nine thousand six hundred and eighty-six dollars and seventy-five cents, invested for said Indians under act of Congress of July twelfth, one thousand eight hundred and sixty-two; and the balance of said sum of one hundred and sixty-nine thousand six hundred and eighty-five dollars and seventy-five cents, together with the sum of ninety-eight thousand dollars now invested on behalf of the said Indians in State stocks of Southern States, and the sum of three thousand seven hundred dollars, being the balance of interest, at five per cent. per annum, on thirty-nine thousand nine hundred and fifty dollars held by the United States, from July, one thousand eight hundred and fifty-seven, till vested in Kansas bonds in December, one thousand eight hundred and sixty-one, after crediting five thousand dollars thereon heretofore receipted for by the chiefs of said Indians, shall be and remain as the permanent fund of the said tribe, and five per cent. be paid semi-annually thereon, per capita, to the tribe; and the interest due upon the sum of twenty-eight thousand five hundred dollars in Kansas bonds, and upon sixteen thousand two hundred dollars in United States stocks, now held for their benefit, shall be paid to the tribe semi-annually in two equal payments, as a permanent school-fund income: *Provided*, That there shall be taken from the said invested fund and paid to the said tribe, per capita, on the first of July, one thousand eight hundred and sixty-eight, the sum of thirty thousand dollars, to assist them in establishing themselves upon their new homes; and at any time thereafter, when the chiefs shall represent to the satisfaction of the Secretary of the Interior that an additional sum is necessary, such sum may be taken from their invested fund: *And provided also*, That the said invested fund shall be subject to such division and diminution as may be found necessary in order to pay those who may become citizens their share of the funds of the tribe.

Certain taxes to be refunded.

ARTICLE 25. Whereas taxes have been levied by the authority of the State of Kansas upon lands allotted to members of the tribe, the right and justice of which taxation is not acknowledged by the Indians, and on which account they have suffered great vexation and expense, and which is now a matter in question in the Supreme Court of the United States, it is agreed that, in case that court shall decide such taxes unlawful, the Government will take measures to secure the refunding of said taxes to such of the Indians as have paid them.

Miami may be united with the Peoria, etc.

ARTICLE 26. The Peorias, Kaskaskias, Weas, and Piankeshaws agree that the Miamies may be confederated with them upon their new reservation, and own an undivided right in said reservation in proportion to the sum paid, upon the payment by the said Miamies of an amount which, in proportion to the number of the Miamies who shall join them, will be equal to their share of the purchase-money in this treaty provided to be paid for the land, and also upon the payment into the common fund of such amount as shall make them equal in annuities to the said Peorias, &c., the said privilege to remain open to the Miamies two years from the ratification of this treaty.

Blacksmith's iron and steel.

ARTICLE 27. The United States agree to pay the said Indians the sum of one thousand five hundred dollars per year for six years for their blacksmith, and for necessary iron and steel and tools; in consideration of which payment the said tribe hereby relinquish all claims for damages and losses during the late war, and, at the end of the said six years, any tools or materials remaining shall be the property of the tribe.

Register to be taken.

ARTICLE 28. Inasmuch as there may be those among them who may desire to remain in Kansas and become citizens of the United States, it is hereby provided that, within six months after the ratification of this treaty, a register shall be taken by the agent, which shall show the names separately of all who voluntarily desire to remove, and all who desire to remain and become citizens; and those who shall elect to remain may appear before the judge of the United States district court for Kansas and make declaration of their intention to become citizens, and take the oath to support the Constitution of the United States; and upon filing of a certificate of such declaration and oath in the office of the Commissioner of Indian Affairs they shall be entitled to receive the proportionate share of themselves and their children in the invested funds and other common property of the tribe; and therefrom they and their children shall become citizens, and have no further rights in the tribe; and all the females who are heads of families, and single women of full age shall have the right to make such declaration and become disconnected from the tribe. Those wishing to remain may become citizens.

Articles 29 to 39, inclusive.   [Stricken out.]

ARTICLE 40. If any amendments shall be made to this treaty by the Senate, it shall only be necessary to submit the same for the assent of the particular tribe or tribes interested; and should any such amendments be made, and the assent of the tribe or tribes interested not be obtained, the remainder of the treaty not affected by such amendment shall nevertheless take effect and be in force. Amendments.

ARTICLE 41. [Stricken out.]

In testimony whereof, the before-named commissioners on behalf of the United States, and the before-named delegates on behalf of the Senecas, mixed Senecas and Shawnees, Quapaws, confederated Peorias, Kaskaskias, Weas, and Piankeshaws, Miamies, Ottawas, and Wyandottes have hereunto set our hands and seals the day and year first above written. Signature.

> Lewis V. Bogy,   [SEAL.]
> Commissioner of Indian Affairs.
> W. H. Watson,   [SEAL.]
> Special Commissioner.
> Thos. Murphy,   [SEAL.]
> Superintendent of Indian Affairs.
> G. C. Snow,   [SEAL.]
> United States Indian Agent, Neosho Agency.
> G. A. Colton,   [SEAL.]
> United States Indian Agent for Miamis, Peorias, &c.

George Spicer, his x mark,	[SEAL.]	Edward Black,	[SEAL.]
John Mush, his x mark,	[SEAL.]	Peorias, &c.	
Senecas.		Thomas Metosenyah, his x mark,	[SEAL.]
John Whitetree, his x mark,	[SEAL.]	Thos. F. Richardville,	[SEAL.]
John Young, his x mark,	[SEAL.]	Miamies.	
Lewis Davis, his x mark,	[SEAL.]	John Wilson, his x mark,	[SEAL.]
Senecas and Shawnees.		J. T. Jones,	[SEAL.]
S. G. Valier,	[SEAL.]	Ottawas.	
Ka-she-cah, his x mark,	[SEAL.]	Tauromee, his x mark,	[SEAL.]
Quapaws.		John Karaho, his x mark,	[SEAL.]
Baptiste Peoria, his x mark,	[SEAL.]	Wyandottes.	
John Mitchell, his x mark,	[SEAL.]		

In presence of—

Frank Valle, his x mark,	Geo. Wright, Interpreter for Wyandottes.
United States Interpreter	Abelard Guthrie.
for Osage River Agency.	George B. Jonas.
John B. Roubideau, his x mark,	Thos. E. McGraw.
United States Interpreter	Lewis S. Hayden.
for Miamis.	Charles Sims.
Wm. Hurr, Interpreter for Ottawas.	R. McBratney.

Witnesses to signature of Lewis Davis:

> G. L. Young.
> G. C. Snow,
> United States Indian Agent.

A.—Schedule showing the several items embraced in the sum agreed to be paid to the Wyandottes by the thirteenth article of the foregoing treaty.

1. Annuity due under the 6th article of the treaty of January 31, 1855.. $8,750.00
2. Amount discounted on $53,594.53 in State bonds on the 13th of May, 1859 .... 15,187.03
3. Interest on the above $15,787.03 [$15,187.03] from May 13th, 1859, to February, 1867, at 5 per cent 6,150.87
4. Amount discounted on $53,000 in State bonds, March 24, 1860........ 11,130.00
5. Interest on the above $11,130 from March 24, 1860, to February 24, 1867. 4,618.95
6. Moneys heretofore appropriated in fulfilment of treaty stipulations, but transferred to the surplus fund................................. 3,635.05
7. Amount for depredations on Wyandotte property, claim approved by Secretary of the Interior, March 21st, 1862 .... 34,342.50

Total amount... $83,814.40

The above-named total sum is designed to represent the full claim of the Wyandottes against the United States under former treaties.

The 1st, 2d, and 4th items, together with another named in the 14th article of the foregoing treaty, were examined and approved by the House Committee on Indian Affairs, and their payment recommended.—(See Congressional Globe, page 1037, part 2d, 2d session of 38th Congress.)

The 3d and 5th items constitute the interest on the moneys discounted on the bonds mentioned in items 2 and 4. Although the committee did not recommend the payment of this interest, they acknowledged its justice, but said that its allowance would possibly endanger the passage of the appropriation, as the general feeling was averse to paying interest on claims.

The 7th item embraces several small amounts for schools, blacksmith, &c., which were due and appropriated at the date of the treaty, but not paid, and were afterwards transferred to the surplus fund.

The 8th item is for depredations on Wyandotte property during the Kansas troubles and the entire emigration to California. It was examined and approved by the Secretary of the Interior, March 21, 1862.

B.—Names of settlers, Nos. of land and price thereof, together with the amount deposited by each settler on the ten-section reserve, in Miami County, Kansas.

Names.	Quarter.	Section.	Township.	Range.	Number of acres.	Price per acre.	Sum deposited.	Total.
Andrew J. Sinclair...	E. ½	23	16	24	320	$4 00	$426 66	$1,280 00
Zacheus Hays........	NW. and E. ½. SW. and SE. } of NW.	26 22	16	... ...	160 120	4 75 4 50	433 00	1,300 00
Randolph Boyd......	NE	26	...	...	160	4 75	253 33	760 00
John Nichols and William Gray.	W. ½ SE.......	...	...	...	80	3 75	100 00	300 00
John Martin........	SE	19	...	25	160	5 25		
Same...........	S. ½ SE........	18	...	...	80	5 00	500 00	1,240 00
David H. Banta......	SW	19	...	...	160	5 00	267 00	800 00
Reuben Fellows......	SW	27	...	24	160	4 00	214 00	640 00
J. T. Pifer..........	NW	...	...	...	160	3 50	186 00	560 00
Leroy W. Martin.....	NE	19	...	25	160	5 25	200 00	840 00
Charles Converse	E. ½ NW. and W. ½ and NE. ¼ of NE.	30	...	...	200	4 25		850 00
Benjamin Wingrove..	SE	31	...	...	160	4 25 }	226 66	840 00
Same............	SW. of SE.....	30	...	...	40	4 00		
Samuel McKinney ...	SW	31	...	...	160	4 00	213 33	640 00
Squire James Waller .	NE	6	17	...	160	3 30	165 00	528 00
George A. Whitaker..	E. ½	27	16	24	320	4 50	480 00	1,440 00
William Smith.......	E. ½ SE. and SE. of NE.	28	...	...	120	4 00	....	480 00
Edward Morgan	N. ½ and SW. ¼ of NW., and NW. ¼ of SW.	6	17	25	160	4 00	215 00	640 00
Albert Benndorf	S. ½ NE	22	16	24	80	3 50	95 00	280 00

B.—*Names of settlers, Nos. of land and price thereof, together with the amount deposited by each settler on the ten-section reserve, in Miami County, Kansas*—Continued.

Names.	Quarter.	Section.	Township.	Range.	Number of acres.	Price per acre.	Sum deposited.	Total.
Charles Martin	NW., S. ½, and NW. ¼ of SW.	†	16	25	280	3 50	....	980 00
Francis Hastings and William Morgan, jr.	Half	23	...	24	320	4 00	426 66	1,280 00
Joel O. Loveridge, Geo. W. Loveridge, Alfred Loveridge, jointly.	E. ½ and SW. ¼ of SW.	‡	...	...	760	4 00	1,013 33	3,040 00
Isaac Shaw	NE	1	17	24	160	5 00	250 00	800 00
Jacob Sims	SE	13	16	24	160	3 50	....	560 00
Zacheus Hays	SW	26	16	24	160	3 50	....	560 00
Town tract *	N. ½	31	...	25	320	4 00	....	1,280 00
Ambrose Shields	NE	34	16	24	160	3 50	....	560 00
Anthony Cott	SE	22	16	24	160	3 00	....	480 00
Edward Dagenett		...	17	25	80	4 00	....	320 00
Total					5,680	......	5,664 97	22,278 00

* This tract to be conveyed to David Perry and Chas. Sims, on payment of said one thousand two hundred and eighty dollars by June first.

† 19 and 18.   ‡ 24 and 13.

The three last-named are half-breed Indians, who will become citizens. Said Shields has 5 children, said Cott 3, and Dagenette 2. William Smith, the settler aforesaid, has a half-breed wife and 2 children. He takes said 120 acres in full of the interest of his family in net proceeds of the reserve, and is to pay one hundred and sixty dollars ($160) besides.

Said Shields, Cott, and Dagenett take their respective tracts at the price stated, in lieu of a like sum of the shares of themselves and families in the net proceeds of the reserve: *Provided*, That, should the share of either family in the net proceeds of the reserves be less than the price agreed for the land taken by the head of such family, then the deficit to be paid in money as by other settlers. The title in each of the four cases last mentioned to be made jointly to the various members of the family by name, whose shares in said proceeds pay for same.

Joshua Clayton takes SE. ¼ section 36, township 16, range 24, 160 acres, at $4 per acre, and deposits $213; total payment, $640.00.

Knoles Shaw, W. ½ of SE. ¼ section 6, town[ship] 17, range 25, 80 acres; has deposited $94; total payment, $280.00.

Thos. Morgan and John W. Majors take E. ½ of said quarter, at $3 per acre; deposited, $9; total, $240.00.

There *is* [are] 80 acres untaken, for which a purchaser will be named by the chiefs before 1st June next.

Total land disposed of, 6,000 acres.

Total money deposited, $5,970.00.

Total amount at prices agreed, 23,438.00.

The above lands to be patented to the persons aforesaid, or their representatives, on prompt payment of the price agreed, by 1st June, 1867: *Provided*, That if any settler refuse or neglect to pay as aforesaid, then the tract of land by him claimed to be sold under sealed bids.

TREATY WITH THE POTAWATOMI, 1867.

Feb. 27, 1867.

15 Stats., 531.
Ratified July 25, 1868.
Proclaimed, Aug. 7, 1868.

Articles of agreement concluded at Washington, D. C., on the twenty-seventh day of February, 1867, between the United States, represented by Lewis G. Bogy, Commissioner of Indian Affairs, W. H. Watson, special commissioner, Thos. Murphy, supt. of Indian affairs for Kansas, and Luther R. Palmer, U. S. Indian agent, duly authorized, and the Pottawatomie tribe of Indians, represented by their chiefs, braves, and head-men, to wit: Mazhee, Mianco, Shawgwe, B. H. Bertrand, J. N. Bourassa, M. B. Beaubien, L. H. Ogee, and G. L. Young.

Whereas the Pottawatomies believe that it is for the interest of their tribe that a home should be secured for them in the Indian country south of Kansas, while there is yet an opportunity for the selection of a suitable reservation; and whereas the tribe has the means of purchasing such reservation from funds to arise from the sale of lands under the provisions of this treaty, without interfering with the exclusive rights of those of their people who hold their lands in common to the ownership of their diminished reserve, held by them in common, or with their right to receive their just proportion of the moneys arising from the sale of unallotted lands, known as surplus lands: Now, therefore, it is agreed—

Commission to select a reservation.

ARTICLE 1. It being the intention of the Government that a commission shall visit the Indian country as soon as practicable after the ratification of the treaties contemplating the removal of certain tribes from Kansas, accompanied by delegates from the several tribes proposing to remove, it is agreed that a delegation of the Pottawatomies may accompany said commission in order to select, if possible, a suitable location for their people without interfering with the locations made for other Indians; and if such location shall be found satisfactory to the Pottawatomies, and approved by the Secretary of the Interior, such tract of land, not exceeding thirty miles square, shall be set apart as a reservation for the exclusive use and occupancy of that tribe; and upon the survey of its lines and boundaries, and ascertaining of its area, and payment to the United States for the same, as hereinafter mentioned and set forth, the said tract shall be patented to the Pottawatomie Nation: *Provided*, That if the said Pottawatomies shall prefer to select a new home among the Cherokees, by agreement with the said Cherokees, for a price within the means of the Pottawatomies, the Government will confirm such agreement.

Proviso.

Price to be paid for the reservation.

ARTICLE 2. In case the new reservation shall be selected upon the lands purchased by the Government from the Creeks, Seminoles, or Choctaws, the price to be paid for said reservation shall not exceed the cost of the same to the Government of the United States; and the sum to be paid by the tribe for said reservation shall be taken from the amount which may be received for the lands which were offered for sale to the Leavenworth, Pawnee, and Western Railroad Company, under the treaty dated November fifteen, eighteen hundred and sixty-one, which amount shall be the common property of the tribe, except the Prairie band, who shall have no interest in said reservation to be purchased as aforesaid, but in lieu thereof shall receive their pro rata share of the proceeds of the sale of said land in money, as the same may be received: *Provided*, That if the United States shall advance the amount necessary to purchase the said reservation, the interest due upon the deferred payments for said lands, sold as hereinafter provided, shall, when received by the United States, be retained and credited to said tribe interested in said reservation, or so much of said

Prairie band.

Proviso.

interest as may be due said tribe under this treaty: *And provided further*, That the Leavenworth, Pawnee and Western Railroad Company, their successors and assigns, having failed to purchase said lands, the Atchison, Topeka and Santa Fé Railroad Company may, within thirty days after the promulgation of this treaty, purchase of the said Pottawatomies their said unallotted lands, except as hereinafter provided, to St. Mary's Mission, at the price of one dollar per acre, lawful money of the United States, and upon filing their bond for the purchase and payment of said lands in due form, to be approved by the Secretary of the Interior within the time above named, the Secretary of the Interior shall issue to the last-named railroad company certificates of purchase, and such certificates of purchase shall be deemed and holden, in all courts, as evidence of title and possession in the said railroad company to all or any part of said lands, unless the same shall be forfeited as herein provided. The said purchase-money shall be paid to the Secretary of the Interior in trust for said Indians within five years from the date of such purchase, with interest at the rate of six per cent. per annum on all deferred payments, until the whole purchase-money shall have been paid; and before any patents shall issue for any part of said lands, one hundred thousand dollars shall be deposited with the Secretary of the Interior, to be forfeited in case the whole of the lands are not paid for as herein provided; (said money may be applied as the payment for the last one hundred thousand acres of said land;) payments shall also be made for at least one-fourth of said unallotted lands at the rate of one dollar per acre, and when so paid the President is authorized hereby to issue patents for the land so paid for; and then for every additional part of said land upon the payment of one dollar per acre. The interest on said purchase-money shall be paid annually to the Secretary of the Interior for the use of said Indians. If the said company shall fail to pay the principal when the same shall become due, or to pay all or any part of the interest upon such purchase-money within thirty (30) days after the time when such payment of interest shall fall due, then this contract shall be deemed and held absolutely null and void, and cease to be binding upon either of the parties thereto, and said company and its assigns shall forfeit all payments of principal and interest made on such purchase, and all right and title, legal and equitable, of any kind whatsoever, in and to all and every part of said lands which shall not have been, before the date of such forfeiture, paid for as herein provided: *Provided, however*, That in case any of said lands have been conveyed to bona-fide purchasers by said Atchison, Topeka and Santa Fé Railroad Company, such purchasers shall be entitled to patents for said land so purchased by them upon the payment of one dollar and twenty-five cents per acre therefor, under such rules and regulations as may be prescribed by the Secretary of the Interior.

ARTICLE 3. After such reservation shall have been selected and set apart for the Pottawatomies, it shall never be included within the jurisdiction of any State or Territory, unless an Indian Territory shall be organized, as provided for in certain treaties made in eighteen hundred and sixty-six with the Choctaws and other tribes occupying "Indian country;" in which case, or in case of the organization of a legislative council or other body, for the regulation of matters affecting the relations of the tribes to each other, the Pottawatomies resident thereon shall have the right to representation, according to their numbers, on equal terms with the other tribes.

ARTICLE 4. A register shall be made, under the direction of the agent and the business committee of the tribe, within two years after the ratification of this treaty, which shall show the names of all members of the tribe who declare their desire to remove to the new reser-

Atchison, etc., R. R. Co. may purchase the lands if, etc.

Conditions and terms of purchase and payment.

Reservation not to be included in any State, etc.

Register to be made of members of tribe who desire to remove or remain.

vation, and of all who desire to remain and to become citizens of the United States; and after the filing of such register in the office of the Commissioner of Indian Affairs, all existing restrictions shall be removed from the sale and alienation of lands by adults who shall have

Sale, etc., of lands. declared their intention to remove to the new reservation: But, *provided*, That no person shall be allowed to receive to his own use the avails of the sale of his land, unless he shall have received the certificate of the agent and business committee that he is fully competent to manage his own affairs; nor shall any person also be allowed to sell and receive the proceeds of the sale of the lands belonging to his family, unless the certificate of the agent and business committee shall declare him competent to take the charge of their property; but such persons may negotiate for the sales of their property and that of their families, and any contracts for sales so made, if certified by the agent and business committee to be at reasonable rates, shall be confirmed by the Secretary of the Interior, and patents shall issue to the purchaser upon full payment; and all payments for such land shall be made to the agent, and the funds by him deposited on the first of each month in some Government depository to be designated by the Secretary of the Treasury, and triplicate certificates of deposit taken therefor, one to be forwarded to the Commissioner of Indian Affairs, one to be retained at the agency, and the third to be sent to the superintendent of Indian affairs for Kansas; after which deposit the United States will be responsible for said funds until drawn out for use as hereinafter provided, and the bonds of the agent shall be increased to a sufficient amount to cover his increased liabilities under this section.

Moneys to be retained until, etc. ARTICLE 5. The moneys received and deposited as provided in the preceding article shall be retained until the party on whose behalf it is held shall be ready to remove to the new reservation, and shall then, or such part thereof as may from time to time be necessary, be drawn out, under the direction of the Commissioner of Indian Affairs, by the agent, and expended for the benefit of the owner in providing for his removal and that of his family to the new reservation, and in such articles and for such uses as may, with the advice of the business committee, be deemed for his best interest at his new home.

Provisions of Article III of former treaty to be in force. Ante, p. 825. ARTICLE 6. The provisions of article third of the treaty of *November fifteenth, eighteen hundred and sixty-one* [April nineteenth, eighteen hundred and sixty-two], relative to Pottawatomies who desire to Patents not to issue until, etc. become citizens, shall continue in force, with the additional provisions that, before patents shall issue and full payments be made to such persons, a certificate shall be necessary from the agent and business committee that the applicant is competent to manage his own affairs; and when computation is made to ascertain the amount of the funds to the tribe to which such applicants are entitled, the amounts invested in the new reservation provided for in the treaty shall not be taken into account; and where any member of the tribe shall become a citizen under the provisions of the said treaty of eighteen hundred and sixty-two, the families of said parties shall also be considered as citizens, and the head of the family shall be entitled to patents and the proportional share of funds belonging to his family; and women who are also heads of families, and single women of adult age, may become citizens in the same manner as males.

ARTICLE 7. [Stricken out.]

Settlement of estates of those deceased. ARTICLE 8. Where allottees under the treaty of eighteen hundred and sixty-one shall have died, or shall hereafter decease, such allottees shall be regarded, for the purpose of a careful and just settlement of their estates, as citizens of the United States, and of the State of Kansas, and it shall be competent for the proper courts to take charge of the settlement of their estates under all the forms and in accordance with the laws of the State, as in the case of other citizens deceased:

and in cases where there are children of allottees left orphans, guardians for such orphans may be appointed by the probate court of the county in which such orphans may reside, and such guardians shall give bonds, to be approved by the said court, for the proper care of the person and estate of such orphans, as provided by law.

ARTICLE 9. It is agreed that an examination shall be made of the books of the Indian Office in order to ascertain what amount is justly due to the Pottawatomies under the provisions of their treaties of eighteen hundred and eighteen and eighteen hundred and twenty-nine, providing for the payment of their annuities in coin, whereas they have been paid for several years in currency; and the result of such examination shall be reported to Congress, and the difference in amount due to said Indians shall be paid to them. *Amounts due the Potawatomi to be ascertained.*

ARTICLE 10. It is further agreed that, upon the presentation to the Department of the Interior of the claims of said tribe for depredations committed by others upon their stock, timber, or other property, accompanied by evidence thereof, examination and report shall be made to Congress of the amount found to be equitably due, in order that such action may be taken as shall be just in the premises. *Claims for depredations on the property of the Indians.*

And it is further agreed that the claims of the Pottawatomies heretofore examined and reported on by the Secretary of the Interior under the act of Congress of March two, eighteen hundred and sixty-one, shall be submitted to two commissioners, to be named by the President of the United States, for examination, and said commissioners, after being sworn impartially to decide on said claims, shall make report of their judgment in the premises, together with the evidence taken, to the Secretary of the Interior, and the same shall be communicated to Congress at its next session: *Provided,* That no part of the money reported due by the said commissioners shall be paid until the same shall be appropriated by Congress. *Proviso*

ARTICLE 11. The half sections of land heretofore set apart for the mission-schools, to wit, those of the St. Mary's mission, and the American Baptist mission, shall be granted in fee-simple, the former to John F. Diels, John Schoenmaker and M. Gillaud, and the latter to such party as the American Baptist Board of Missions shall designate. *Lands for school purposes.*

And the said John F. Deils, John Shoemaker, and M. Gillaud shall have the right to purchase in a compact body ten hundred and thirteen 54-100 acres of the unallotted lands at the price of one dollar per acre, to be paid to the Secretary of the Interior, for the use of said tribe, and when the consideration shall be paid as aforesaid the President shall issue patents to said purchasers therefor; and in selecting said ten hundred and thirteen 54-100 acres, said purchasers shall have the preference over all other parties. *Certain persons may purchase lands of the Indians.*

ARTICLE 12. No provisions of this treaty shall be held to apply in such manner as to authorize any interference with the exclusive rights in their own lands of those members of the tribe who hold their lands in common; but such Indians shall be entitled to their share in the ownership of the new reservation; and it shall not be necessary at any future time to treat with the representatives of the whole people for a cession of the lands of those who hold in common, but special treaty arrangements may be made at any time with the class of persons last named for the sale of their lands, and the disposition to be made of the proceeds thereof. *Rights of those members of the tribe who hold their lands in common.*

ARTICLE 13. All provisions of former treaties inconsistent with the provisions of this treaty shall be hereafter null and void. *Inconsistent provisions void.*

ARTICLE 14. The expenses of negotiating this treaty shall be paid by the United States, not to exceed six thousand dollars. *Expenses of this treaty.*

In testimony whereof, the aforenamed commissioners on behalf of the United States, and on behalf of the Pottawatomies the aforenamed *Execution.*

chiefs, braves, and headmen, have hereunto set their hands and seals the day and year first above mentioned.

Lewis V. Bogy, Commissioner of Indian Affairs. [SEAL.]
W. H. Watson, Special Commissioner. [SEAL.]
Thos. Murphy, Superintendent of Indian Affairs. [SEAL.]
L. R. Palmer, United States Indian agent. [SEAL.]
Mazhee, his x mark. [SEAL.]
Mianco, his x mark. [SEAL.]
Shawgwe, his x mark. [SEAL.]
B. H. Bertrand. [SEAL.]
J. N. Bourassa. [SEAL.]
M. B. Beaubien. [SEAL.]
L. H. Ogee. [SEAL.]
George L. Young. [SEAL.]

In presence of—

J. N. Bourassa, United States interpreter.
Lewis S. Hayden.
H. W. Farnsworth.
Vital Jarrot.
W. R. Irwin.

TREATY WITH THE CHIPPEWA OF THE MISSISSIPPI, 1867.

Mar. 19. 1867.

16 Stats., 719.
Ratified Apr. 8, 1867.
Proclaimed Apr. 18, 1867.

Articles of agreement made and concluded at Washington, D. C., this 19th day of March, A. D. 1867, between the United States represented by Louis V. Bogy, special commissioner thereto appointed, William H. Watson, and Joel B. Bassett, United States agent, and the Chippewas of the Mississippi, represented by Que-we-zance, or Hole-in-the-Day, Qui-we-shen-shish, Wau-bon-a-quot, Min-e-do-wob, Mijaw-ke-ke-shik, Shob-osk-kunk, Ka-gway-dosh, Me-no-ke-shick, Way-namee, and O-gub-ay-gwan-ay-aush.

Whereas, by a certain treaty ratified March 20, 1865, between the parties aforesaid, a certain tract of land was, by the second article thereof, reserved and set apart for a home for the said bands of Indians, and by other articles thereof provisions were made for certain moneys to be expended for agricultural improvements for the benefit of said bands; and whereas it has been found that the said reservation is not adapted for agricultural purposes for the use of such of the Indians as desire to devote themselves to such pursuits, while a portion of the bands desire to remain and occupy a part of the aforementioned reservation, and to sell the remainder thereof to the United States: Now, therefore, it is agreed—

Cession of lands.

ARTICLE 1. The Chippewas of the Mississippi hereby cede to the United States all their lands in the State of Minnesota, secured to them by the second article of their treaty of March 20, 1865,* excepting and reserving therefrom the tract bounded and described as follows, to wit: Commencing at a point on the Mississippi River, opposite the mouth of Wanoman River, as laid down on Sewall's map of Minnesota; thence

Reservation.
Boundaries.

due north to a point two miles further north than the most northerly point of Lake Winnebagoshish; thence due west to a point two miles west of the most westerly point of Cass Lake; thence south to Kabekona River; thence down said river to Leech Lake; thence along the north shore of Leech Lake to its outlet in Leech Lake River; thence down the main channel of said river to its junction with the Mississippi River, and thence down the Mississippi to the place of beginning.

---

*This refers to the treaty of May 7, 1864, proclaimed March 20, 1865, ante p. 862.

And there is further reserved for the said Chippewas out of the land now owned by them such portion of their western outlet as may upon location and survey be found to be within the reservation provided for in the next succeeding section.   *Further reservation.*

ARTICLE 2. In order to provide a suitable farming region for the said bands there is hereby set apart for their use a tract of land, to be located in a square form as nearly as possible, with lines corresponding to the Government surveys; which reservation shall include White Earth Lake and Rice Lake, and contain thirty-six townships of land: and such portions of the tract herein provided for as shall be found upon actual survey to lie outside of the reservation set apart for the Chippewas of the Mississippi by the second article of the treaty of March 20, 1865, shall be received by them in part consideration for the cession of lands made by this agreement.   *Land for farming.*

ARTICLE 3. In further consideration for the lands herein ceded, estimated to contain about two million of acres, the United States agree to pay the following sums, to wit: Five thousand dollars for the erection of school buildings upon the reservation provided for in the second article; four thousand dollars each year for ten years, and as long as the President may deem necessary after the ratification of this treaty, for the support of a school or schools upon said reservation; ten thousand dollars for the erection of a saw-mill, with grist-mill attached, on said reservation; five thousand dollars to be expended in assisting in the erection of houses for such of the Indians as shall remove to said reservation.   *Payments for lands ceded.*   *Schools.*   *Mills.*   *Houses.*

Five thousand dollars to be expended, with the advice of the chiefs, in the purchase of cattle, horses, and farming utensils, and in making such improvements as are necessary for opening farms upon said reservation.   *Cattle, etc.*

Six thousand dollars each year for ten years, and as long thereafter as the President may deem proper, to be expended in promoting the progress of the people in agriculture, and assisting them to become self-sustaining by giving aid to those who will labor.   *Agriculture, etc.*

Twelve hundred dollars each year for ten years for the support of a physician, and three hundred each year for ten years for necessary medicines.   *Physician, etc.*

Ten thousand dollars to pay for provisions, clothing, or such other articles as the President may determine, to be paid to them immediately on their removal to their new reservation.   *Provisions and clothing.*

ARTICLE 4. No part of the annuities provided for in this or any former treaty with the Chippewas of the Mississippi bands shall be paid to any half-breed or mixed-blood, except those who actually live with their people upon one of the reservations belonging to the Chippewa Indians.   *No part to any half-breed, etc., except, etc.*

ARTICLE 5. It is further agreed that the annuity of $1,000 a year which shall hereafter become due under the provisions of the third article of the treaty with the Chippewas of the Mississippi bands, of August 2, 1847, shall be paid to the chief, Hole-in-the-Day, and to his heirs; and there shall be set apart, by selections to be made in their behalf and reported to the Interior Department by the agent, one half section of land each, upon the Gulf Lake reservation, for Min-a-ge-shig and Truman A. Warren, who shall be entitled to patents for the same upon such selections being reported to the Department.   *Annuities.*   *Hole-in-the-Day and his heirs.*   *Land to Min-a-ge-shig and Truman A. Warren.*

ARTICLE 6. Upon the ratification of this treaty, the Secretary of the Interior shall designate one or more persons who shall, in connection with the agent for the Chippewas in Minnesota, and such of their chiefs, parties to this agreement, as he may deem sufficient, proceed to locate, as near as may be, the reservation set apart by the second article hereof, and designate the places where improvements shall be made, and such portion of the improvements provided for in the fourth   *Reservation to be located.*

article of the Chippewa treaty of May 7, 1864, as the agent may deem necessary and proper, with the approval of the Commissioner of Indian Affairs, may be made upon the new reservation, and the United States will pay the expenses of negotiating this treaty, not to exceed ten thousand dollars.

Survey.ARTICLE 7. As soon as the location of the reservation set apart by the second article hereof shall have been approximately ascertained, and reported to the office of Indian Affairs, the Secretary of the Interior shall cause the same to be surveyed in conformity to the system of Government surveys, and whenever, after such survey, any Indian,

Indians having ten acres under cultivation to be entitled to receive a certificate for 40 acres, etc. of the bands parties hereto, either male or female, shall have ten acres of land under cultivation, such Indian shall be entitled to receive a certificate, showing him to be entitled to the forty acres of land, according to legal subdivision, containing the said ten acres or the greater part thereof, and whenever such Indian shall have an additional ten acres under cultivation, he or she shall be entitled to a certificate for additional forty acres, and so on, until the full amount of one hundred and sixty acres may have been certified to any one Indian; and

Land exempt from taxation and not to be alienated, except, etc. the land so held by any Indian shall be exempt from taxation and sale for debt, and shall not be alienated except with the approval of the Secretary of the Interior, and in no case to any person not a member of the Chippewa tribe.

ARTICLE 8. For the purpose of protecting and encouraging the Indians, parties to this treaty, in their efforts to become self-sustaining by means of agriculture, and the adoption of the habits of civilized life, it is hereby agreed that, in case of the commission by any of the said Indians of crimes against life or property, the person charged

Arrest and punishment of Indians for crimes. with such crimes may be arrested, upon the demand of the agent, by the sheriff of the county of Minnesota in which said reservation may be located, and when so arrested may be tried, and if convicted, punished in the same manner as if he were not a member of an Indian tribe.

In testimony whereof, the parties aforementioned, respectively representing the United States and the said Chippewas of the Mississippi, have hereunto set their hands and seals the day and year first above written.

Lewis V. Bogy, special commissioner.	[SEAL.]
W. H. Watson.	[SEAL.]
Joel B. Bassett, U. S. Indian agent.	[SEAL.]
Que-we-zance, or Hole-in-the-Day, his x mark.	[SEAL.]
Qui-we-shen-shish, his x mark.	[SEAL.]
Wau-bon-a-quot, his x mark.	[SEAL.]
Min-e-do-wob, his x mark.	[SEAL.]
Mi-jaw-ke-ke-shik, his x mark.	[SEAL.]
Shob-osh-kunk, his x mark.	[SEAL.]
Ka-gway-dosh, his x mark.	[SEAL.]
Me-no-ke-shick, his x mark.	[SEAL.]
Way-na-mee, his x mark.	[SEAL.]
O-gub-ay-gwan-ay-aush, his x mark.	[SEAL.]

In presence of—

T. A. Warren, United States interpreter.
Charles E. Mix.
Lewis S. Hayden.
George B. Jonas.
Thos. E. McGraw.
John Johnson.
George Bonga.

TREATY WITH THE KIOWA AND COMANCHE, 1867.

[NOTE BY THE DEPARTMENT OF STATE.—The words of this treaty which are put in brackets with an asterisk are written in the original with black pencil, the rest of the original treaty being written with black ink.]

Oct. 21, 1867.

15 Stats., 581.
Ratified, July 25, 1868.
Proclaimed, Aug. 25, 1868.

Articles of a treaty and agreement made and entered into at the Council Camp, on Medicine Lodge Creek, seventy miles south of Fort Larned, in the State of Kansas, on the twenty-first day of October, one thousand eight hundred and sixty-seven, by and between the United States of America, represented by its commissioners duly appointed thereto, to wit, Nathaniel G. Taylor, William S. Harney, C. C. Augur, Alfred S. [H.] Terry, John B. Sanborn, Samuel F. Tappan, and J. B. Henderson, of the one part, and the confederated tribes of Kiowa and Comanche Indians, represented by their chiefs and head-men, duly authorized and empowered to act for the body of the people of said tribes, (the names of said chiefs and head-men being hereto subscribed,) of the other part, witness:

ARTICLE 1. From this day forward all war between the parties to this agreement shall forever cease.

The Government of the United States desires peace, and its honor is here pledged to keep it. The Indians desire peace, and they now pledge their honor to maintain it. If bad men among the whites, or among other people subject to the authority of the United States, shall commit any wrong upon the person or property of the Indians, the United States will, upon proof made to the agent and forwarded to the Commissioner of Indian Affairs at Washington City, proceed at once to cause the offender to be arrested and punished according to the laws of the United States, and also re-imburse the injured person for the loss sustained.

If bad men among the Indians shall commit a wrong or depredation upon the person or property of any one, white, black, or Indians, subject to the authority of the United States and at peace therewith, the tribes herein named solemnly agree that they will, on proof made to their agent and notice by him, deliver up the wrong-doer to the United States, to be tried and punished according to its laws, and in case they wilfully refuse so to do, the person injured shall be re-imbursed for his loss from the annuities or other moneys due or to become due to them under this or other treaties made with the United States. And the President, on advising with the Commissioner of Indian Affairs shall prescribe such rules and regulations for ascertaining damages under the provisions of this article as, in his judgment, may be proper; but no such damages shall be adjusted and paid until thoroughly examined and passed upon by the Commissioner of Indian Affairs and the Secretary of the Interior; and no one sustaining loss, while violating or because of his violating, the provisions of this treaty or the laws of the United States, shall be re-imbursed therefor.

ARTICLE 2. The United States agrees that [the*] following district of country, to wit: commencing at a point where the Washita River crosses the 98th meridian, west from Greenwich; thence up the Washita River, in the middle of the main channel thereof, to a point thirty miles, by river, west of Fort Cobb, as now established; thence, due west to the north fork of Red River, provided said line strikes said river east of the one hundredth meridian of west longitude; if not, then only to said meridian-line, and thence south, on said meridian-line, to the said north fork of Red River; thence down said north fork, in the middle of the main channel thereof, from the point where it may be first intersected by the lines above described, to the main Red

Marginal notes:
War to cease.

Peace to be kept.

Offenders against the Indians to be arrested, etc.

Wrongdoers against the whites to be punished.

Damages.

Reservation.
Boundaries.

River; thence down said river, in the middle of the main channel thereof to its intersection with the ninety-eighth meridian of longitude west from Greenwich; thence north, on said meridian-line, to the place of beginning, shall be and the same is hereby set apart for the absolute and undisturbed use and occupation of the tribes herein named, and for such other friendly tribes or individual Indians as, from time to time, they may be willing [with the consent of the United States*] to admit among them; and the United States now solemnly agrees that no persons except those herein authorized so to do and except such officers, agents, and employés of the Government as may be authorized to enter upon Indian reservation in discharge of duties enjoined by law, shall ever be permitted to pass over, settle upon, or reside in the territory described in this article, or in such territory as may be added to this reservation, for the use of said Indians.

Certain persons not to enter or reside thereon.

Additional arable land to be added, if, etc.

ARTICLE 3. If it should appear from actual survey or other satisfactory examination of said tract of land, that it contains less than one hundred and sixty acres of tillable land, for each person, who at the time may be authorized to reside on it under the provisions of this treaty, and a very considerable number of such persons shall be disposed to commence cultivating the soil as farmers, the United States agrees to set apart for the use of said Indians, as herein provided, such additional quantity of arable land adjoining to said reservation, or as near the same as it can be obtained, as may be required to provide the necessary amount.

Buildings on reservation.

ARTICLE 4. The United States agrees at its own proper expense to construct at some place, near the centre of said reservation, where timber and water may be convenient, the following buildings, to wit: A warehouse or store-room for the use of the agent, in storing goods belonging to the Indians, to cost not exceeding fifteen hundred dollars; an agency-building for the residence of the agent, to cost not exceeding three thousand dollars; a residence for the physician, to cost not more than three thousand dollars; and five other buildings, for a carpenter, farmer, blacksmith, miller, and engineer, each to cost not exceeding two thousand dollars; also a school-house or mission-building, so soon as a sufficient number of children can be induced by the agent to attend school, which shall not cost exceeding five thousand dollars.

The United States agrees further to cause to be erected on said reservation, near the other buildings herein authorized, a good steam circular saw mill, with a grist-mill and shingle-machine attached; the same to cost not exceeding eight thousand dollars.

Agent's residence, office, and duties.

ARTICLE 5. The United States agrees that the agent for the said Indians in the future shall make his home at the agency-building; that he shall reside among them, and keep an office open at all times, for the purpose of prompt and diligent inquiry into such matters of complaint by and against the Indians as may be presented for investigation under the provisions of their treaty stipulations, as also for the faithful discharge of other duties enjoined on him by law. In all cases of depredation on person or property, he shall cause the evidence to be taken in writing and forwarded, together with his findings to the Commissioner of Indian Affairs, whose decision, subject to the revision of the Secretary of the Interior, shall be binding on the parties to this treaty.

Head of family may select lands for farming.

ARTICLE 6. If any individual belonging to said tribes of Indians, or legally incorporated with them, being the head of a family, shall desire to commence farming, he shall have the privilege to select, in the presence and with the assistance of the agent then in charge, a tract of land within said reservation, not exceeding three hundred and twenty acres in extent, which tract, when so selected, certified, and recorded in the "land book" as herein directed, shall cease to be held in common.

but the same may be occupied and held in the exclusive possession of the person selecting it, and of his family so long as he or they may continue to cultivate it. Any person over eighteen years of age, not being the head of a family, may in like manner select and cause to be certified to him or her, for purposes of cultivation, a quantity of land not exceeding eighty acres in extent, and thereupon, be entitled to the exclusive possession of the same as above directed. For each tract of land so selected, a certificate, containing a description thereof and the name of the person selecting it, with a certificate indorsed thereon that the same has been recorded, shall be delivered to the party entitled to it, by the agent, after the same shall have been recorded by him in a book to be kept in his office, subject to inspection, which said book shall be known as the "Kiowa and Comanche land book." The President may, at any time, order a survey of the reservation, and, when so surveyed, Congress shall provide for protecting the rights of settlers, in their improvements, and may fix the character of the title held by each. The United States may pass such laws, on the subject of alienation and descent of property and on all subjects connected with the government of the said Indians on said reservations, and the internal police thereof, as may be thought proper. *Others may select land for cultivation.* *Surveys.* *Alienation and descent of property.*

ARTICLE 7. In order to insure the civilization of the tribes, entering into this treaty, the necessity of education is admitted, especially by such of them as are or may be settled on said agricultural reservations; and they therefore pledge themselves to compel their children, male and female, between the ages of six and sixteen years, to attend school; and it is hereby made the duty of the agent for said Indians to see that this stipulation is strictly complied with; and the United States agrees that for every thirty children between said ages, who can be induced or compelled to attend school, a house shall be provided, and a teacher competent to teach the elementary branches of an English education, shall be furnished, who will reside among said Indians, and faithfully discharge his or her duties as a teacher. The provisions of this article to continue for not less than twenty years. *Education.* *Children to attend school.* *Schoolhouses and teachers.*

ARTICLE 8. When the head of a family or lodge shall have selected lands and received his certificate as above directed, and the agent shall be satisfied that he intends in good faith to commence cultivating the soil for a living, he shall be entitled to receive seeds and agricultural implements for the first year not exceeding in value one hundred dollars, and for each succeeding year he shall continue to farm for a period of three years more, he shall be entitled to receive seeds and implements as aforesaid not exceeding in value twenty-five dollars. And it is further stipulated that such persons as commence farming shall receive instruction from the farmer herein provided for, and whenever more than one hundred persons shall enter upon the cultivation of the soil a second blacksmith shall be provided, together with such iron, steel, and other material as may be needed. *Seeds and agricultural implements to be furnished to whom.* *Instructions in farming.* *Blacksmith.*

ARTICLE 9. At any time after ten years from the making of this treaty the United States shall have the privilege of withdrawing the physician, farmer, blacksmiths, carpenter, engineer, and miller herein provided for; but, in case of such withdrawal, an additional sum thereafter of ten thousand dollars per annum shall be devoted to the education of said Indians, and the Commissioner of Indian Affairs shall, upon careful inquiry into the condition of said Indians, make such rules and regulations for the expenditure of said sum as will best promote the educational and moral improvement of said tribes. *Physician, farmer, etc., may be withdrawn.* *Additional appropriation in such cases.*

ARTICLE 10. In lieu of all sums of money or other annuities provided to be paid to the Indians, herein named, under the treaty of October eighteenth, one thousand eight hundred and sixty-five, made at the mouth of the "Little Arkansas," and under all treaties made *Delivery of goods in lieu of annuities.*

previous thereto, the United States agrees to deliver at the agency-house on the reservation herein named, on the fifteenth day of October of each year, for thirty years, the following articles, to wit:

Clothing.

For each male person over fourteen years of age, a suit of good substantial woollen clothing, consisting of coat, pantaloons, flannel shirt, hat, and a pair of home-made socks.   For each female over twelve years of age, a flannel skirt, or the goods necessary to make it, a pair of woolen hose, *and* twelve yards of calico, and twelve yards of "domestic."

For the boys and girls under the ages named, such flannel and cotton goods as may be needed, to make each a suit as aforesaid, together with a pair of woollen hose for each; and in order that the Commissioner of Indian Affairs may be able to estimate properly for the articles herein named, it shall be the duty of the agent, each year, to forward him a full and exact census of the Indians on which the estimates from year to year can be based; and, in addition to the clothing herein named, the sum of twenty-five thousand dollars shall be annually appropriated for a period of thirty years, to be used by the Secretary of the Interior in the purchase of such articles, upon the recommendation of the Commissioner of Indian Affairs, as from time to time the condition and necessities of the Indians may indicate to be proper; and if at any time within the thirty years it shall appear that the amount of money needed for clothing under this article can be appropriated to better uses for the tribes herein named, Congress may by law change the appropriation to other purposes, but in no event shall the amount of this appropriation be withdrawn or discontinued for the period named; and the President shall, annually, detail an officer of the Army to be present and attest the delivery of all the goods herein named to the Indians, and he shall inspect and report on the quantity and quality of the goods and the manner of their delivery.

Census.

Other necessary articles.

Army officer to attest the delivery.

Right to occupy territory outside of reservation surrendered.

ARTICLE 11. In consideration of the advantages and benefits conferred by this treaty and the many pledges of friendship by the United States, the tribes who are parties to this agreement hereby stipulate that they will relinquish all right to occupy permanently the territory outside of their reservation, as herein defined, but they yet reserve the right to hunt on any lands south of the Arkansas [River,*] so long as the buffalo may range thereon in such numbers as to justify the chase, [and no white settlements shall be permitted on any part of the lands contained in the old reservation as defined by the treaty made between the United States and the Cheyenne, Arapahoe, and Apache tribes of Indians at the mouth of the Little Arkansas, under date of October fourteenth, one thousand eight hundred and sixty-five, within three years from this date;*] and they, [the said tribes,*] further expressly agree—

Right to hunt reserved.

Agreements as to railroads.

1st. That they will withdraw all opposition to the construction of the railroad now being built on the Smoky Hill River, whether it be built to Colorado or New Mexico.

2d. That they will permit the peaceable construction of any railroad not passing over their reservation as herein defined.

Emigrants and emigrant travelers.

3d. That they will not attack any persons at home, nor travelling, nor molest or disturb any wagon-trains, coaches, mules, or cattle belonging to the people of the United States, or to persons friendly therewith.

Women and children.

4th. They will never capture or carry off from the settlements white women or children.

5th. They will never kill nor scalp white men nor attempt to do them harm.

Pacific railroad, wagon roads, etc.

6th. They withdraw all pretence of opposition to the construction of the railroad now being built along the Platte River and westward to the Pacific Ocean; and they will not, in future, object to the construction of railroads, wagon-roads, mail-stations, or other works of utility or necessity which may be ordered or permitted by the laws of the United States. But should such roads or other works be constructed on the lands of their reservation, the Government will pay the tribes whatever amount of damage may be assessed by three disinterested commissioners, to be appointed by the President for that purpose; one of said commissioners to be a chief or head-man of the tribes. *Damages for crossing these reservations.*

7th. They agree to withdraw all opposition to the military posts now established in the western Territories. *Military posts.*

ARTICLE 12. No treaty for the cession of any portion or part of the reservation herein described, which may be held in common, shall be of any validity or force as against the said Indians, unless executed and signed by at least three-fourths of all the adult male Indians occupying the same, and no cession by the tribe shall be understood or construed in such manner as to deprive, without his consent, any individual member of the tribe of his rights to any tract of land selected by him as provided in Article *III* [VI] of this treaty. *No treaty for cession of reservation to be valid unless, etc.*

ARTICLE 13. The Indian agent, in employing a farmer, blacksmith, miller, and other employés herein provided for, qualifications being equal, shall give the preference to Indians. *In employing farmers, etc., preference to be given to the Indians, if, etc.*

ARTICLE 14. The United States hereby agrees to furnish annually to the Indians the physician, teachers, carpenter, miller, engineer, farmer, and blacksmiths, as herein contemplated, and that such appropriations shall be made from time to time, on the estimates of the Secretary of the Interior, as will be sufficient to employ such persons. *United States to furnish physicians, teachers, etc.*

ARTICLE 15. It is agreed that the sum of seven hundred and fifty dollars be appropriated for the purpose of building a dwelling-house on the reservation for "Tosh-e-wa," (or the Silver Brooch,) the Comanche chief who has already commenced farming on the said reservation. And the sum of five hundred dollars annually, for three years from date, shall be expended in presents to the ten persons of said tribes who in the judgment of the agent may grow the most valuable crops for the period named. *House for Tosh-e-wa.* *Presents for best crops.*

ARTICLE 16. The tribes herein named agree, when the agency-house and other buildings shall be constructed on the reservation named, they will make said reservation their permanent home and they will make no permanent settlement elsewhere, but they shall have the right to hunt on the lands south of the Arkansas River, formerly called theirs, in the same manner, subject to the modifications named in this treaty, as agreed on by the treaty of the Little Arkansas, concluded the eighteenth day of October, one thousand eight hundred and sixty-five. *Reservation to be permanent home of tribes.*

In testimony of which, we have hereunto set our hands and seals on the day and year aforesaid.

N. G. Taylor, [SEAL.]
President of Indian Commission.
Wm. S. Harney, [SEAL.]
Brevet Major-General.
C. C. Augur, [SEAL.]
Brevet Major-General.
Alfred H. Terry, [SEAL.]
Brigadier and Brevet Major-General.
John B. Sanborn, [SEAL.]
Samuel F. Tappan, [SEAL.]
J. B. Henderson. [SEAL.]

Attest: Ashton S. H. White, secretary.

Kioways:

Satank, or Sitting Bear, his x mark. [SEAL.]

Sa-tan-ta, or White Bear, his x mark. [SEAL.]

Wa-toh-konk, or Black Eagle, his x mark. [SEAL.]

Ton-a-en-ko, or Kicking Eagle, his x mark. [SEAL.]

Fish-e-more, or Stinking Saddle, his x mark. [SEAL.]

Ma-ye-tin, or Woman's Heart, his x mark. [SEAL.]

Sa-tim-gear, or Stumbling Bear, his x mark. [SEAL.]

Sit-par-ga, or One Bear, his x mark. [SEAL.]

Corbeau, or The Crow, his x mark. [SEAL.]

Sa-ta-more, or Bear Lying Down. [SEAL.]

Comanches:

Parry-wah-say-men, or Ten Bears, his x mark. [SEAL.]

Tep-pe-navon, or Painted Lips, his x mark. [SEAL.]

To-sa-in, or Silver Brooch, his x mark. [SEAL.]

Cear-chi-neka, or Standing Feather, his x mark. [SEAL.]

Ho-we-ar, or Gap in the Woods, his x mark. [SEAL.]

Tir-ha-yah-guahip, or Horse's Back, his x mark. [SEAL.]

Es-a-nanaca, or Wolf's Name, his x mark. [SEAL.]

Ah-te-es-ta, or Little Horn, his x mark. [SEAL.]

Pooh-yah-to-yeh-be, or Iron Mountain, his x mark. [SEAL.]

Sad-dy-yo, or Dog Fat, his x mark. [SEAL.]

Attest:

Jas. A. Hardie. Inspector-General, U. S. Army.

Sam'l S. Smoot, U. S. surveyor.

Philip McCusker, interpreter.

J. H. Leavenworth, United States Indian agent.

Thos. Murphy, superintendent Indian affairs.

Henry Stanley, correspondent.

A. A. Taylor, assistant secretary.

Wm. Fayel, correspondent.

James O. Taylor, artist.

Geo. B. Willis, phonographer.

C. W. Whitraker, trader

TREATY WITH THE KIOWA, COMANCHE, AND APACHE, 1867.

Oct. 21, 1867.

15 Stats., 589.
Ratified, July 25, 1868.
Proclaimed Aug. 25 1868.

Articles of a treaty concluded at the Council Camp on Medicine Lodge Creek, seventy miles south of Fort Larned, in the State of Kansas, on the twenty-first day of October, eighteen hundred and sixty-seven, by and between the United States of America, represented by its commissioners duly appointed thereto to-wit: Nathaniel G. Taylor, William S. Harney, C. C. Augur, Alfred S. [H.] Terry, John B. Sanborn, Samuel F. Tappan, and J. B. Henderson, of the one part, and the Kiowa, Comanche, and Apache Indians, represented by their chiefs and headmen duly authorized and empowered to act for the body of the people of said tribes (the names of said chiefs and headmen being hereto subscribed) of the other part, witness:

Whereas, on the twenty-first day of October, eighteen hundred and sixty-seven, a treaty of peace was made and entered into at the Council Camp, on Medicine Lodge Creek, seventy miles south of Fort Larned, in the State of Kansas, by and between the United States of America, by its commissioners Nathaniel G. Taylor, William S. Harney, C. C. Augur, Alfred H. Terry, John B. Sanborn, Samuel F. Tappan, and J. B. Henderson, of the one part, and the Kiowa and Comanche tribes of Indians, of the Upper Arkansas, by and through their chiefs and headmen whose names are subscribed thereto, of the other part, reference being had to said treaty; and whereas, since the making and signing of said treaty, at a council held at said camp on this day, the chiefs and headmen of the Apache nation or tribe of Indians express to the commissioners on the part of the United States, as aforesaid, a wish to be confederated with the said Kiowa and Comanche tribes, and to be placed, in every respect, upon an equal footing with said tribes; and whereas, at a council held at the same place and on the same day, with the chiefs and headmen of the said Kiowa and Comanche Tribes, they consent to the confederation of the said Apache tribe, as desired by it, upon the terms and conditions hereinafter set forth in this supplementary treaty: Now, therefore, it is hereby stipulated and agreed by and between the aforesaid commissioners, on the part of the United States, and the chiefs and headmen of the Kiowa and Comanche tribes, and, also, the chiefs and headmen of the said Apache tribe, as follows, to-wit:

ARTICLE 1. The said Apache tribe of Indians agree to confederate and become incorporated with the said Kiowa and Comanche Indians, and to accept as their permanent home the reservation described in the aforesaid treaty with said Kiowa and Comanche tribes, concluded as aforesaid at this place, and they pledge themselves to make no permanent settlement at any place, nor on any lands, outside of said reservation. *The Apaches agree to become incorporated with the Kiowa and Comanche.*

ARTICLE 2. The Kiowa and Comanche tribes, on their part, agree that all the benefits and advantages arising from the employment of physicians, teachers, carpenters, millers, engineers, farmers, and blacksmiths, agreed to be furnished under the provisions of their said treaty, together with all the advantages to be derived from the construction of agency buildings, warehouses, mills, and other structures, and also from the establishment of schools upon their said reservation, shall be jointly and equally shared and enjoyed by the said Apache Indians, as though they had been originally a part of said tribes; and they further agree that all other benefits arising from said treaty shall be jointly and equally shared as aforesaid. *Advantages of former treaty to be shared by the Apaches.*

ARTICLE 3. The United States, on its part, agrees that clothing and other articles named in Article X. of said original treaty, together with all money or other annuities agreed to be furnished under any of the provisions of said treaty, to the Kiowa and Comanches, shall be shared equally by the Apaches. In all cases where specific articles of clothing are agreed to be furnished to the Kiowas and Comanches, similar articles shall be furnished to the Apaches, and a separate census of the Apaches shall be annually taken and returned by the agent, as provided for the other tribes. And the United States further agrees, in consideration of the incorporation of said Apaches, to increase the annual appropriation of money, as provided for in Article X. of said treaty, from twenty-five thousand to thirty thousand dollars; and the latter amount shall be annually appropriated, for the period therein named, for the use and benefit of said three tribes, confederated as herein declared; and the clothing and other annuities, which may from time to time be furnished to the Apaches, shall be based upon the census of the three tribes, annually to be taken by the agent, and shall be separately marked, forwarded, and delivered to them at the agency house, to be built under the provisions of said original treaty. *Annuities, etc., to be shared by the Apache.* *Census.* *Annual appropriation increased.*

ARTICLE 4. In consideration of the advantages conferred by this supplementary treaty upon the the Apache tribe of Indians, they agree to observe and faithfully comply with all the stipulations and agreements entered into by the Kiowas and Comanches in said original treaty. They agree, in the same manner, to keep the peace toward the whites and all other persons under the jurisdiction of the United States, and to do and perform all other things enjoined upon said tribes by the provisions of said treaty; and they hereby give up and forever relinquish to the United States all rights, privileges, and grants now vested in them, or intended to be transferred to them, by the treaty between the United States and the Cheyenne and Arapahoe tribes of Indians, concluded at the camp on the Little Arkansas River, in the State of Kansas, on the fourteenth day of October, one thousand eight hundred and sixty-five, and also by the supplementary treaty, concluded at the same place on the seventeenth day of the same month, between the United States, of the one part, and the Cheyenne, Arapahoe, and Apache tribes, of the other part. *Apaches to observe stipulations of original treaty.* *To keep the peace.* *To give up certain rights.*

Signature.

In testimony of all which, the said parties have hereunto set their hands and seals at the place and on the day hereinbefore stated.

N. G. Taylor,   [SEAL.]
President of Indian Commission.

Wm. S. Harney,   [SEAL.]
Brevet Major-General, Commissioner, &c.

C. C. Augur,   [SEAL.]
Brevet Major-General.

Alfred H. Terry,   [SEAL.]
Brevet Major-General and Brigadier-General.

John B. Sanborn.   [SEAL.]

Samuel F. Tappan.   [SEAL.]

J. B. Henderson.   [SEAL.]

On the part of the Kiowas:
Satanka, or Sitting Bear, his x mark,   [SEAL.]
Sa-tan-ta, or White Bear, his x mark,   [SEAL.]
Wah-toh-konk, or Black Eagle, his x mark,   [SEAL.]
Ton-a-en-ko, or Kicking Eagle, his x mark,   [SEAL.]
Fish-e-more, or Stinking Saddle, his x mark,   [SEAL.]
Ma-ye-tin, or Woman's Heart, his x mark,   [SEAL.]
Sa-tim-gear, or Stumbling Bear, his x mark,   [SEAL.]
Sa-pa-ga, or One Bear, his x mark,   [SEAL.]
Cor-beau, or The Crow, his x mark,   [SEAL.]
Sa-ta-more, or Bear Lying Down, his x mark,   [SEAL.]
On the part of the Comanches:
Parry-wah-say-men, or Ten Bears, his x mark,   [SEAL.]
Tep-pe-navon, or Painted Lips, his x mark,   [SEAL.]
To-she-wi, or Silver Brooch, his x mark,   [SEAL.]

Cear-chi-neka, or Standing Feather, his x mark,   [SEAL.]
Ho-we-ar, or Gap in the Woods, his x mark,   [SEAL.]
Tir-ha-yah-gua-hip, or Horse's Back, his x mark,   [SEAL.]
Es-a-man-a-ca, or Wolf's Name, his x mark,   [SEAL.]
Ah-te-es-ta, or Little Horn, his x mark,   [SEAL.]
Pooh-yah-to-yeh-be, or Iron Mountain, his x mark,   [SEAL.]
Sad-dy-yo, or Dog Fat, his x mark,   [SEAL.]
On the part of the Apaches:
Mah-vip-pah, Wolf's Sleeve, his x mark,   [SEAL.]
Kon-zhon-ta-co, Poor Bear, his x mark,   [SEAL.]
Cho-se-ta, or Bad Back, his x mark,   [SEAL.]
Nah-tan, or Brave Man, his x mark,   [SEAL.]
Ba-zhe-ech, Iron Shirt, his x mark,   [SEAL.]
Til-la-ka, or White Horn, his x mark,   [SEAL.]

Attest:

Ashton S. H. White, secretary.
Geo. B. Willis, reporter.
Philip McCusker, interpreter.
John D. Howland, clerk Indian Commission.
Sam'l S. Smoot, United States surveyor.

A. A. Taylor.
J. H. Leavenworth, United States Indian agent.
Thos. Murphy, superintendent Indian affairs.
Joel H. Elliott, major, Seventh U. S. Cavalry.

TREATY WITH THE CHEYENNE AND ARAPAHO, 1867.

Oct. 28, 1867.

15 Stats., 593.
Ratified July 25, 1868.
Proclaimed Aug. 19, 1868.

Articles of a treaty and agreement made and entered into at the Council Camp on Medicine Lodge Creek, seventy miles south of Fort Larned, in the State of Kansas, on the twenty-eighth day of October, eighteen hundred and sixty-seven, by and between the United States of America, represented by its commissioners duly appointed thereto, to wit: Nathaniel G. Taylor, William S. Harney, C. C. Augur, Alfred H. Terry, John B. Sanborn, Samuel F. Tappan and John B. Henderson, of the one part, and the Cheyenne and Arapahoe tribes of Indians, represented by their chiefs and head-men duly authorized and empowered to act for the body of the people of said tribes—the names of said chiefs and head-men being hereto subscribed—of the other part, witness:

Peace and friendship.

ARTICLE 1. From this day forward all war between the parties to this agreement shall forever cease. The Government of the United

States desires peace, and its honor is here pledged to keep it. The Indians desire peace, and they now pledge their honor to maintain it.

If bad men among the whites, or among other people subject to the authority of the United States, shall commit any wrong upon the person or property of the Indians, the United States will, upon proof made to the agent and forwarded to the Commissioner of Indian Affairs at Washington City, proceed at once to cause the offender to be arrested and punished according to the laws of the United States, and also reimburse the injured person for the loss sustained. *Offenders among the whites to be arrested and punished.*

If bad men among the Indians shall commit a wrong or depredation upon the person or property of any one, white, black, or Indian, subject to the authority of the United States and at peace therewith, the tribes herein named solemnly agree that they will, on proof made to their agent, and notice by him, deliver up the wrongdoer to the United States, to be tried and punished according to its laws; and in case they wilfully refuse so to do, the person injured shall be re-imbursed for his loss from the annuities or other moneys due or to become due to them under this or other treaties made with the United States. And the President, on advising with the Commissioner of Indian Affairs, shall prescribe such rules and regulations for ascertaining damages, under the provisions of this article, as in his judgment may be proper. But no such damages shall be adjusted and paid until thoroughly examined and passed upon by the Commissioner of Indian Affairs and the Secretary of the Interior, and no one sustaining loss, while violating, or because of his violating, the provisions of this treaty or the laws of the United States, shall be re-imbursed therefor. *Among the Indians, to be given up to the United States, etc.* *Rules for ascertaining damages.*

ARTICLE 2. The United States agrees that the following district of country, to wit: commencing at the point where the Arkansas River crosses the 37th parallel of north latitude, thence west on said parallel—the said line being the southern boundary of the State of Kansas—to the Cimarone River, (sometimes called the Red Fork of the Arkansas River), thence down said Cimarone River, in the middle of the main channel thereof, to the Arkansas River; thence up the Arkansas River, in the middle of the main channel thereof, to the place of beginning, shall be and the same is hereby set apart for the absolute and undisturbed use and occupation of the Indians herein named, and for such other friendly tribes or individual Indians, as from time to time they may be willing, with the consent of the United States, to admit among them; and the United States now solemnly agrees that no persons except those herein authorized so to do, and except such officers, agents, and employés of the Government as may be authorized to enter upon Indian reservations in discharge of duties enjoined by law, shall ever be permitted to pass over, settle upon, or reside in the territory described in this article, or in such territory as may be added to this reservation for the use of said Indians. *Reservation.* *Boundaries.* *Who not to reside thereon, etc.*

ARTICLE 3. If it should appear from actual survey or other examination of said tract of land, that it contains less than one hundred and sixty acres of tillable land for each person who at the time may be authorized to reside on it, under the provisions of this treaty, and a very considerable number of such persons shall be disposed to commence cultivating the soil as farmers, the United States agrees to set apart for the use of said Indians as herein provided, such additional quantity of arable land adjoining to said reservation, or as near the same as it can be obtained, as may be required to provide the necessary amount. *Reservation to be enlarged, if, etc.*

ARTICLE 4. The United States agrees at its own proper expense to construct at some place near the center of said reservation, where timber and water may be convenient, the following buildings, to wit: a warehouse or store-room for the use of the agent in storing goods belonging to the Indians, to cost not exceeding fifteen hundred dollars; *Buildings to be constructed*

an agency-building for the residence of the agent, to cost not exceeding three thousand dollars; a residence for the physician, to cost not
more than three thousand dollars; and five other buildings, for a carpenter, farmer, blacksmith, miller, and engineer, each to cost not
exceeding two thousand dollars; also a school-house or mission-building, so soon as a sufficient number of children can be induced by the
agent to attend school, which shall not cost exceeding five thousand
dollars. The United States agrees, further, to cause to be erected on
said reservation, near the other buildings herein authorized, a good
steam circular saw-mill, with a grist-mill and shingle machine attached;
the same to cost not exceeding eight thousand dollars.

Agent to make his home and reside where. ARTICLE 5. The United States agrees that the agent for said Indians
in the future shall make his home at the agency building; that he shall
reside among them, and keep an office open at all times for the purpose
of prompt and diligent inquiry into such matters of complaint by and
against the Indians as may be presented for investigation, under the
provisions of their treaty stipulations, as also for the faithful discharge
of other duties enjoined on him by law. In all cases of depredation
on person or property, he shall cause the evidence to be taken in writing and forwarded, together with his finding, to the Commissioner of
Indian Affairs, whose decision, subject to the revision of the Secretary
of the Interior, shall be binding on the parties to this treaty.

Heads of families desiring to commence farming may select land, etc. ARTICLE 6. If any individual, belonging to said tribes of Indians,
or legally incorporated with them, being the head of a family, shall
desire to commence farming, he shall have the privilege to select, in
the presence and with the assistance of the agent then in charge, a tract
of land within said reservation not exceeding three hundred and twenty
Effect of such selection. acres in extent, which tract when so selected, certified, and recorded
in the land-book as herein directed, shall cease to be held in common,
but the same may be occupied and held in the exclusive possession of
the person selecting it, and of his family, so long as he or they may
Persons not heads of families. continue to cultivate it. Any person over eighteen years of age, not
being the head of a family, may in like manner select and cause to be
certified to him, or her, for purposes of cultivation, a quantity of land
not exceeding eighty acres in extent, and thereupon be entitled to the
exclusive possession of the same as above directed.

Certificates of selection to be delivered, etc., to be recorded. For each tract of land so selected, a certificate containing a description thereof, and the name of the person selecting it, with a certificate
indorsed thereon, that the same has been recorded, shall be delivered
to the party entitled to it by the agent, after the same shall have been
recorded by him in a book to be kept in his office, subject to inspection, which said book shall be known as the "Cheyenne and Arapahoe
Survey. Land Book." The President may at any time order a survey of the
reservation, and, when so surveyed, Congress shall provide for protecting the rights of settlers in their improvements, and may fix the
character of the title held by each.

Alienation and descent of property. The United States may pass such laws on the subject of alienation
and descent of property, and on all subjects connected with the gov-
ernment of the Indians on said reservations, and the internal police
thereof as may be thought proper.

Children between 6 and 16 to attend school. ARTICLE 7. In order to insure the civilization of the tribes entering
into this treaty, the necessity of education is admitted, especially by such
of them as are or may be settled on said agricultural reservation, and
they therefore pledge themselves to compel their children, male and
female, between the ages of six and sixteen years, to attend school; and
Duty of agent. it is hereby made the duty of the agent for said Indians to see that this
stipulation is strictly complied with; and the United States agrees that
for every thirty children between said ages, who can be induced or
Schoolhouses and teachers. compelled to attend school, a house shall be provided, and a teacher
competent to teach the elementary branches of an English education

shall be furnished, who will reside among said Indians, and faithfully discharge his or her duties as a teacher. The provisions of this article to continue for not less than twenty years.

ARTICLE 8. When the head of a family or lodge shall have selected lands and received his certificate as above directed, and the agent shall be satisfied that he intends in good faith to commence cultivating the soil for a living, he shall be entitled to receive seeds and agricultural implements for the first year, not exceeding in value one hundred dollars; and for each succeeding year he shall continue to farm for a period of three years more, he shall be entitled to receive seeds and implements as aforesaid, not exceeding in value twenty-five dollars. *Seeds and agricultural implements.*

And it is further stipulated that such persons as commence farming shall receive instruction from the farmer herein provided for; and whenever more than one hundred persons shall enter upon the cultivation of the soil, a second blacksmith shall be provided, with such iron, steel, and other material as may be needed. *Instructions in farming.*

ARTICLE 9. At any time after ten years from the making of this treaty the United States shall have the privilege of withdrawing the physician, farmer, blacksmith, carpenter, engineer, and miller, herein provided for, but in case of such withdrawal, an additional sum, thereafter, of ten thousand dollars per annum shall be devoted to the education of said Indians, and the Commissioner of Indian Affairs shall upon careful inquiry into their condition make such rules and regulations for the expenditure of said sum as will best promote the educational and moral improvement of said tribes. *Physician, farmer, etc., may be withdrawn, etc.; and additional appropriation in such cases.*

ARTICLE 10. In lieu of all sums of money or other annuities provided to be paid to the Indians herein named, under the treaty of October fourteenth, eighteen hundred and sixty-five, made at the mouth of Little Arkansas, and under all treaties made previous thereto, the United States agrees to deliver at the agency house on the reservation herein named, on the fifteenth day of October, of each year, for thirty years, the following articles, to wit: *Articles in lieu of money and annuities.*

For each male person over fourteen years of age, a suit of good, substantial woolen clothing, consisting of coat, pantaloons, flannel shirt, hat, and a pair of home-made socks. *Clothing.*

For each female over twelve years of age, a flannel skirt, or the goods necessary to make it, a pair of woolen hose, twelve yards of calico and twelve yards of cotton domestics.

For the boys and girls under the ages named, such flannel and cotton goods as may be needed to make each a suit as aforesaid, together with a pair of woolen hose for each.

And in order that the Commissioner of Indian Affairs may be able to estimate properly for the articles herein named, it shall be the duty of the agent each year to forward to him a full and exact census of the Indians on which the estimate from year to year can be based. *Census annually.*

And, in addition to the clothing herein named, the sum of twenty thousand dollars shall be annually appropriated for a period of thirty years, to be used by the Secretary of the Interior in the purchase of such articles as, from time to time, the condition and necessities of the Indians may indicate to be proper. And if at any time, within the thirty years, it shall appear that the amount of money needed for clothing, under this article, can be appropriated to better uses for the tribe herein named, Congress may, by law, change the appropriation to other purposes; but, in no event, shall the amount of this appropriation be withdrawn or discontinued for the period named. And the President shall, annually, detail an officer of the Army to be present, and attest the delivery of all the goods herein named to the Indians, and he shall inspect and report on the quantity and quality of the goods and the manner of their delivery. *Annual appropriation of money for thirty years.* *Army officer to be present at delivery of goods.*

ARTICLE 11. In consideration of the advantages and benefits conferred by this treaty, and the many pledges of friendship by the United States, the tribes who are parties to this agreement hereby stipulate that they will relinquish all right to occupy permanently the territory outside of their reservation as herein defined, but they yet reserve the right to hunt on any lands south of the Arkansas so long as the buffalo may range thereon in such numbers as to justify the chase; and no white settlements shall be permitted on any part of the lands contained in the old reservation as defined by the treaty made between the United States and the Cheyenne, Arapahoe, and Apache tribes of Indians, at the mouth of the Little Arkansas, under date of October fourteenth, eighteen hundred and sixty-five, within three years from this date, and they, the said tribes, further expressly agree:

1st. That they will withdraw all opposition to the construction of the railroad now being built on the Smoky Hill River, whether it be built to Colorado or New Mexico.

2d. That they will permit the peaceable construction of any railroad not passing over their reservation, as herein defined.

3d. That they will not attack any persons at home or travelling, nor molest or disturb any wagon-trains, coaches, mules, or cattle belonging to the people of the United States or to persons friendly therewith.

4th. They will never capture or carry off from the settlements white women or children.

5th. They will never kill or scalp white men, nor attempt to do them harm.

6th. They withdraw all pretense of opposition to the construction of the railroad now being built along the Platte River, and westward to the Pacific Ocean; and they will not in future object to the construction of railroads, wagon-roads, mail-stations, or other works of utility or necessity, which may be ordered or permitted by the laws of the United States. But should such roads or other works be constructed on the lands of their reservation, the Government will pay the tribe whatever amount of damage may be assessed by three disinterested commissioners to be appointed by the President for that purpose, one of said commissioners to be a chief or head-man of the tribe.

7th. They agree to withdraw all opposition to the military posts or roads now established, or that may be established, not in violation of treaties heretofore made or hereafter to be made with any of the Indian tribes.

ARTICLE 12. No treaty for the cession of any portion or part of the reservation herein described, which may be held in common, shall be of any validity or force as against the said Indians unless executed and signed by at least three-fourths of all the adult male Indians occupying or interested in the same; and no cession by the tribe shall be understood or construed in such manner as to deprive without his consent any individual member of the tribe of his rights to any tract of land selected by him as provided in Article 6 of this treaty.

ARTICLE 13. The United States hereby agree to furnish annually to the Indians the physician, teachers, carpenter, miller, engineer, farmer, and blacksmiths, as herein contemplated, and that such appropriations shall be made from time to time, on the estimates of the Secretary of the Interior, as will be sufficient to employ such persons.

ARTICLE 14. It is agreed that the sum of five hundred dollars, annually, for three years from date, shall be expended in presents to the ten persons of said tribe who, in the judgment of the agent, may grow the most valuable crops for the respective year.

ARTICLE 15. The tribes herein named agree that when the agency-house and other buildings shall be constructed on the reservation

---

Marginal notes:

Lands outside the reservation to be relinquished to the United States.

Right to hunt reserved.

Limit to white settlements.

Express agreements as to railroads.

Wagon trains, coaches, etc.

White women and children.

White men.

Railroads and other roads.

Damage to their reservation.

Military posts and roads.

Cession of reservation not to be valid unless, etc.

Physicians, etc., to be furnished by the United States.

Annual presents for the most valuable crops.

Reservation to be permanent home, etc.

named, they will regard and make said reservation their permanent home, and they will make no permanent settlement elsewhere, but they shall have the right, subject to the conditions and modifications of this treaty, to hunt on the lands south of the Arkansas River, formerly called theirs, in the same manner as agreed on by the treaty of the " Little Arkansas," concluded the fourteenth day of October, eighteen hundred and sixty-five.

In testimony of which, we have hereunto set our hands and seals, on the day and year aforesaid.

N. G. Taylor,   [SEAL.]
President of Indn. Commission.
Wm. S. Harney,   [SEAL.]
Major-General, Brevet, &c.
C. C. Augur,   [SEAL.]
Brevet Major-General.
Alfred H. Terry,   [SEAL.]
Brevet Major-General.
John B. Sanborn,   [SEAL.]
Commissioner.
Samuel F. Tappan.   [SEAL.]
J. B. Henderson.   [SEAL.]

Attest:

Ashton S. H. White, secretary.
Geo. B. Willis, phonographer.

On the part of the Cheyennes:

O-to-ah-nac-co, Bull Bear, his x mark,   [SEAL.]
Moke-tav-a-to, Black Kettle, his x mark,   [SEAL.]
Nac-co-hah-ket, Little Bear, his x mark,   [SEAL.]
Mo-a-vo-va-ast, Spotted Elk, his x mark,   [SEAL.]
Is-se-von-ne-ve, Buffalo Chief, his x mark,   [SEAL.]
Vip-po-nah, Slim Face, his x mark, [SEAL.]
Wo-pah-ah, Gray Head, his x mark,   [SEAL.]
O-ni-hah-ket, Little Rock, his x mark,   [SEAL.]
Ma-mo-ki, or Curly Hair, his x mark,   [SEAL.]
O-to-ah-has-tis, Tall Bull, his x mark,   [SEAL.]

Wo-po-ham, or White Horse, his x mark,   [SEAL.]
Hah-ket-home-mah, Little Robe, his x mark,   [SEAL.]
Min-nin-ne-wah, Whirlwind, his x mark,   [SEAL.]
Mo-yan-histe-histow, Heap of Birds, his x mark,   [SEAL.]

On the part of the Arapahoes:

Little Raven, his x mark,   [SEAL.]
Yellow Bear, his x mark,   [SEAL.]
Storm, his x mark,   [SEAL.]
White Rabbit, his x mark,   [SEAL.]
Spotted Wolf, his x mark,   [SEAL.]
Little Big Mouth, his x mark,   [SEAL.]
Young Colt, his x mark,   [SEAL.]
Tall Bear, his x mark,   [SEAL.]

Attest:

C. W. Whitaker, interpreter.
H. Douglas, major, Third Infantry.
Jno. D. Howland, clerk Indian Commission.
Sam'l. S. Smoot, United States surveyor.
A. A. Taylor.

Henry Stanley, correspondent.
John S. Smith, United States interpreter.
George Bent, interpreter.
Thos. Murphy, superintendent Indian affairs.

TREATY WITH THE UTE, 1868.

Mar. 2, 1868.

15 Stats., 619.
Ratified, July 25, 1868.
Proclaimed, Nov. 6, 1868.

Articles of a treaty and agreement made and entered into at Washington City, D. C., on the second day of March, one thousand eight hundred and sixty-eight, by and between Nathaniel G. Taylor, Commissioner of Indian Affairs, Alexander C. Hunt, governor of Colorado Territory and ex-officio superintendent of Indian affairs, and Kit Carson, duly authorized to represent the United States, of the one part, and the representatives of the Tabaquache, Muache, Capote, Weeminuche, Yampa, Grand River, and Uintah bands of Ute Indians, (whose names are hereto subscribed,) duly authorized and empowered to act for the body of the people of said bands, of the other part, witness:

Certain provisions of former treaty re-affirmed.

ARTICLE 1. All of the provisions of the treaty concluded with the Tabequache band of Utah Indians October seventh, one thousand eight hundred and sixty-three, as amended by the Senate of the United States and proclaimed December fourteenth, one thousand eight hundred and sixty-four, which are not inconsistent with the provisions of this treaty, as hereinafter provided, are hereby re-affirmed and declared to be applicable and to continue in force as well to the other bands, respectively, parties to this treaty, as to the Tabequache band of Utah Indians.

Reservation.

Boundaries.

ARTICLE 2. The United States agree that the following district of country, to wit: Commencing at that point on the southern boundary-line of the Territory of Colorado where the meridian of longitude 107 west from Greenwich crosses the same; running thence north with said meridian to a point fifteen miles due north of where said meridian intersects the fortieth parallel of north latitude; thence due west to the western boundary-line of said Territory; thence south with said western boundary-line of said Territory to the southern boundary-line of said Territory; thence east with said southern boundary-line to the place of beginning, shall be, and the same is hereby, set apart for the absolute and undisturbed use and occupation of the Indians herein named, and for such other friendly tribes or individual Indians as from time to time they may be willing, with the consent of the United States, to admit among them; and the United States now solemnly agree that no persons, except those herein authorized so to do, and except such officers, agents, and employés of the Government as may be authorized to enter upon Indian reservations in discharge of duties enjoined by law shall ever be permitted to pass over, settle upon, or reside in the Territory described in this article, except as herein otherwise provided.

Only certain persons to reside thereon.

Claims to all other lands released.

ARTICLE 3. It is further agreed by the Indians, parties hereto, that henceforth they will and do hereby relinquish all claims and rights in and to any portion of the United States or Territories, except such as are embraced in the limits defined in the preceding article.

Two agencies on the reservation.

ARTICLE 4. The United States agree to establish two agencies on the reservation provided for in article two, one for the Grand River, Yampa, and Uintah bands, on White River, and the other for the Tabequache, Muache, Weeminuche, and Capote bands, on the Rio de los Pinos, on the reservation, and at its own proper expense to construct at each of said agencies a warehouse, or store-room, for the use of the agent in storing goods belonging to the Indians, to cost not exceeding fifteen hundred dollars; an agency-building for the residence of the agent, to cost not exceeding three thousand dollars; and four other buildings for a carpenter, farmer, blacksmith, and miller, each to cost not exceeding two thousand dollars; also a school-house or mission-building, so soon as a sufficient number of children can be induced by the agent to attend school, which shall not cost exceeding five thousand dollars.

Warehouse and other buildings.

Schoolhouse.

Water-power saw-mill.

The United States agree, further, to cause to be erected on said reservation, and near to each agency herein authorized, respectively, a good water-power saw-mill, with a grist-mill and a shingle-machine attached, the same to cost not exceeding eight thousand dollars each: *Provided*, The same shall not be erected until such time as the Secretary of the Interior may think it necessary to the wants of the Indians.

ARTICLE 5. The United States agree that the agents for said Indians, in the future, shall make their homes at the agency-buildings; that they shall reside among the Indians, and keep an office open at all times for the purpose of prompt and diligent inquiry into such matters of complaint by and against the Indians, as may be presented for investigation under the provisions of their treaty stipulations, as also for the faithful discharge of other duties enjoined on them by law. In all cases of depredation on person or property they shall cause the evidence to be taken in writing and forwarded, together with their finding, to the Commissioner of Indian Affairs, whose decision, subject to the revision of the Secretary of the Interior, shall be binding on the parties to this treaty. *Indian agents to make their homes and reside where.* *Depredations.*

ARTICLE 6. If bad men among the whites or among other people, subject to the authority of the United States, shall commit any wrong upon the person or property of the Indians, the United States will, upon proof made to the agent and forwarded to the Commissioner of Indian Affairs at Washington City, proceed at once to cause the offender to be arrested and punished according to the laws of the United States, and also re-imburse the injured person for the loss sustained. *Offenders among the whites.*

If bad men among the Indians shall commit a wrong or depredation upon the person or property of any one, white, black, or Indian, subject to the authority of the United States and at peace therewith, the tribes herein named solemnly agree that they will, on proof made to their agent and notice to him, deliver up the wrong-doer to the United States, to be tried and punished according to its laws, and in case they wilfully refuse so to do, the person injured shall be re-imbursed for his loss from the annuities or other moneys due or to become due to them under this or other treaties made with the United States. *Wrongdoers among the Indians.*

ARTICLE 7. If any individual belonging to said tribe of Indians or legally incorporated with them, being the head of a family, shall desire to commence farming, he shall have the privilege to select, in the presence and with the assistance of the agent then in charge, by metes and bounds, a tract of land within said reservation not exceeding one hundred and sixty acres in extent, which tract, when so selected, certified, and recorded in the land-book, as herein directed, shall cease to be held in common, but the same may be occupied and held in exclusive possession of the person selecting it and his family so long as he or they may continue to cultivate it. Any person over eighteen years of age, not being the head of a family may, in like manner, select and cause to be certified to him or her for purposes of cultivation, a quantity of land not exceeding eighty acres in extent, and thereupon be entitled to the exclusive possession of the same as above directed. *Indians, heads of families, desirous of commencing farming may select lands.* *Tract to be recorded and held in exclusive possession.* *Persons not heads of families.*

For each tract of land so selected a certificate containing a description thereof, and the name of the person selecting it, with a certificate endorsed thereon that the same has been recorded, shall be delivered to the party entitled to it, by the agent, after the same shall have been recorded by him in a book to be kept in his office, subject to inspection, which said book shall be known as the " Ute Land-Book." *Ute Land-Book.*

The President may at any time order a survey of the reservation; and when so surveyed Congress shall provide for protecting the rights of such Indian settlers in their improvements, and may fix the character of the title held by each. *Survey, etc.*

The United States may pass such laws on the subject of alienation and descent of property, and on all subjects connected with the government of the Indians on said reservation and the internal police thereof as may be thought proper. *Alienation and descent of property.*

Education.

ARTICLE 8. In order to insure the civilization of the bands entering into this treaty, the necessity of education is admitted, especially by such of them as are or may be engaged in either pastoral, agricultural, or other peaceful pursuits of civilized life on said reservation, and they therefore pledge themselves to induce their children, male and

Children to attend school.

female, between the age[s] of seven and eighteen years, to attend school; and it is hereby made the duty of the agent for said Indians to see that this stipulation is complied with to the greatest possible extent; and the United States agree that for every thirty children

Schoolhouses and teachers.

between said ages who can be induced to attend school a house shall be provided, and a teacher competent to teach the elementary branches of an English education shall be furnished, who will reside among said Indians, and faithfully discharge his or her duties as teacher, the provisions of this article to continue for not less than twenty years.

Seeds and agricultural implements.

ARTICLE 9. When the head of a family or lodge shall have selected lands, and received his certificate as above described, and the agent shall be satisfied that he intends, in good faith, to commence cultivating the soil for a living, he shall be entitled to receive seeds and agricultural implements for the first year, not exceeding in value one hundred dollars, and for each succeeding year he shall continue to farm, for a period of three years more, he shall be entitled to receive seeds and implements as aforesaid, not exceeding in value fifty dollars; and it is further stipulated that such persons as commence farming

Instructions from farmer.
Additional blacksmith.

shall receive instructions from the farmer herein provided for; and it is further stipulated that an additional blacksmith to the one provided for in the treaty of October seventh, one thousand eight hundred and sixty-three, referred to in article one of this treaty, shall be provided with such iron, steel, and other material as may be needed for the Uintah, Yampa, and Grand River agency.

United States may withdraw farmers, etc.

ARTICLE 10. At any time after ten years from the making of this treaty, the United States shall have the privilege of withdrawing the farmers, blacksmiths, carpenters, and millers herein, and in the treaty of October seventh, one thousand eight hundred and sixty-three, referred to in article one of this treaty, provided for, but in case of such withdrawal, an additional sum thereafter of ten thousand dollars per annum shall be devoted to the education of said Indians, and the Commissioner of Indian Affairs shall, upon careful inquiry into their condition, make such rules and regulations, subject to the approval of the Secretary of the Interior, for the expenditure of said sum as will best promote the educational and moral improvement of said Indians.

Clothing, blankets, etc.

ARTICLE 11. That a sum, sufficient in the discretion of Congress, for the absolute wants of said Indians, but not to exceed thirty thousand dollars per annum, for thirty years, shall be expended, under the direction of the Secretary of the Interior for clothing, blankets, and such other articles of utility as he may think proper and necessary upon full official reports of the condition and wants of said Indians.

Food, meat, and vegetables.

ARTICLE 12. That an additional sum sufficient, in the discretion of Congress, (but not to exceed thirty thousand dollars per annum,) to supply the wants of said Indians for food, shall be annually expended under the direction of the Secretary of the Interior, in supplying said Indians with beef, mutton, wheat, flour, beans, and potatoes, until such time as said Indians shall be found to be capable of sustaining themselves.

Cows and sheep.

ARTICLE 13. That for the purpose of inducing said Indians to adopt habits of civilized life and become self-sustaining, the sum of forty-five thousand dollars, for the first year, shall be expended, under the direction of the Secretary of the Interior, in providing each lodge or head of a family in said confederated bands with one gentle American cow, as distinguished from the ordinary Mexican or Texas breed, and five head of sheep.

ARTICLE 14. The said confederated bands agree that whensoever, in the opinion of the President of the United States, the public interest may require it, that all roads, highways, and railroads, authorized by law, shall have the right of way through the reservations herein designated. *(margin: Railways and highways to have right of way.)*

ARTICLE 15. The United States hereby agree to furnish the Indians the teachers, carpenters, millers, farmers, and blacksmiths, as herein contemplated, and that such appropriations shall be made from time to time, on the estimates of the Secretary of the Interior, as will be sufficient to employ such persons. *(margin: Teachers and mechanics and their support.)*

ARTICLE 16. No treaty for the cession of any portion or part of the reservation herein described, which may be held in common, shall be of any validity or force as against the said Indians, unless executed and signed by at least three-fourths of all the adult male Indians occupying or interested in the same; and no cession by the tribe shall be understood or construed in such manner as to deprive, without his consent, any individual member of the tribe of his right to any tract of land selected by him, as provided in article seven of this treaty. *(margin: Cession of reservation not to be valid unless, etc.)*

ARTICLE 17. All appropriations now made, or to be hereafter made, as well as goods and stock due these Indians under existing treaties, shall apply as if this treaty had not been made, and be divided proportionately among the seven bands named in this treaty, as also shall all annuities and allowances hereafter to be made: *Provided*, That if any chief of either of the confederated bands make war against the people of the United States, or in any manner violate this treaty in any essential part, said chief shall forfeit his position as chief and all rights to any of the benefits of this treaty: *But provided further*, Any Indian of either of these confederated bands who shall remain at peace, and abide by the terms of this treaty in all its essentials, shall be entitled to its benefits and provisions, notwithstanding his particular chief and band may have forfeited their rights thereto. *(margin: Appropriations, how to apply and be divided. Forfeitures by making war. Those at peace.)*

In testimony whereof, the commissioners as aforesaid on the part of the United States, and the undersigned representatives of the Tabequache, Muache, Capote, Weeminuche, Yampa, Grand River and Uintah bands of Ute Indians, duly authorized and empowered to act for the body of the people of said bands, have hereunto set their hands and seals, at the place and on the day, month and year first hereinbefore written.

N. G. Taylor, [SEAL.]
A. C. Hunt, governor, &c., [SEAL.]
Kit Carson, [SEAL.]
Commissioners on the part of the United States.
U-re, his x mark.
Ka-ni-ache, his x mark.
An-ka-tosh, his x mark.
Jose-Maria, his x mark.
Ni-ca-a-gat, or Greenleaf, his x mark.
Guero, his x mark.
Pa-ant, his x mark.
Pi-ah, his x mark.
Su-vi-ap, his x mark.
Pa-bu-sat, his x mark.

Witnesses:
Daniel C. Oakes, United States Indian agent.
Lafayette Head, United States Indian agent.
U. M. Curtis, interpreter.
H. P. Bennet.
Albert G. Boone.
E. H. Kellogg.
Wm. J. Godfroy.

We, the chiefs and headmen of the aforesaid named bands of Ute Indians, duly authorized by our people, do hereby assent and agree to the amendment of the Senate, the same having been interpreted to us, and being fully understood by us.

Witness our hands and seals on the days and dates set opposite our names respectively.

Date of signing.	Signatures.	Interpretation of names.	Band.
1868. Aug. 15	Sac-we-och, his x mark.	White Lock of Hair.	Grand River Ute Indians.
	Tah-nach, his x mark.	Granite Rock.	
	Pah-ah-pitch, his x mark.	Sweet Herb.	
	Tab-y-ou-souck-en, his x mark.	Sun Rise.	
	Shou-wach-a-wicket, his x mark.	Rain Bow.	
	Pe-ah, his x mark.	Black Tail Deer.	
	Ah-ump, his x mark.	Pine Tree.	
	An-tro, his x mark.	Rocking.	Uintah Ute Indians.
	Pah, his x mark.	Water.	
	Quir-nauch, his x mark.	Eagle.	
	Yah-mah-na, his x mark.	Briar.	

Signed in the presence of—

A. Sagendorf.

Uriah M. Curtis, special interpreter.

E. H. Kellogg, secretary Colorado Indian superintendency.

Daniel C. Oakes, United States Indian agent.

Louis O. Howell.

Date of signature.	Signature.	Interpretation of names.	Band.
Sept. 1	Sa-wa-wat-se-witch, his x mark.	Blue River.	Yampas.
	Colorado, his x mark.	Red. (Spanish.)	
	Pa-ant, his x mark.	Tall.	
	Su-ri-ap, his x mark.	Lodge Pole's Son.	
	Nick-a-a-gah, his x mark.	Green Leaf.	

Signed in the presence of—

E. H. Kellogg, secretary Indian superintendency Colorado Territory.

U. M. Curtis, special United States interpreter.

Daniel C. Oakes, United States Indian agent.

H. P. Bennet.

Louis O. Howell.

Date of signing.	Signatures.	Intrepetation of names.	Band.
Sept. 14	Ou-ray, his x mark.	Arrow.	Muaches.
	Sha-wa-na, his x mark.	Blue Flower.	
	Guero, his x mark.	Light Haired.	
	Tah-be-wah-che-kah, his x mark.	Sun Rise.	
	Ah-kan-ash, his x mark.	Red Cloud.	
	Ka-ni-ache, his x mark.	One who was taken down.	
	An-ka-tosh, his x mark.	Red. (Ute.)	
	Sap-po-wan-e-ri, his x mark.		Tabaguaches.
	Tu-sa-sa-ri-be, his x mark.		
	Na-ca-get, his x mark.	Son to Tu-sa-sa-ri-be.	
	Ya-ma-aj, his x mark.	or George.	

Signed in the presence of—

    Wm. J. Godfroy.
    Daniel C. Oakes, United States Indian agent.
    Edward R. Harris, special interpreter.
    E. H. Kellogg, secretary Colorado Indian superintendency.
    Louis O. Howell.
    Uriah M. Curtis, interpreter.

To the other copy of these instruments are signed as witnesses the following names: Juan Martine Martines, (friend of Indians,) Albert H. Pfeiffer, (their old agent,) Manuel Lusero.

Date of signing.	Signature.	Interpretation of names.	Band.
Sept. 24.	So-bo-ta, his x mark.	A Big Frock.	
	I-si-dro, his x mark.		
	Sow-wa-ch-wiche, his x mark.	A Green Herb.	
	Ba-bu-zat, his x mark.	A Crystal Drop Water.	
	Sab-ou-ichie, his x mark.	Wounded in the Abdomen.	
	Chu-i-wish, his x mark.	Long Tailed Deer.	
	I-ta-li-uh, his x mark.		
	E-ri-at-ow-up, his x mark.	Water Carrier.	Ca - po - tas Utes.
	Aa-ca-wa, his x mark.	Red Eyes.	
	Ac-i-apo-co-ego, his x mark.	Red Snake.	
	Martine, his x mark.	Named after a Mexican friend.	
	Ou-a-chee, his x mark.		
	Tap-ap-o-watie, his x mark.		
	Su-vi-ath, his x mark.	The Swoop of a Bird.	
	Wi-ar-ow, his x mark.		

Signed in the presence of—

    Lafayette Head.
    Alb. H. Pfeiffer.
    Manuel Lusero.
    E. H. Kellogg, secretary Colorado Indian superintendency.
    Uriah M. Curtis, interpreter.
    Daniel C. Oakes, United States Indian agent.

Date of signing.	Signatures.	Interpretation of names.	Band.
Sept. 25.	Pa-ja-cho-pe, his x mark.	A Claw.	
	Pa-no-ar, his x mark.	Broad Brow.	
	Su-bi-to-au, his x mark.	Ugly Man.	We - mi - nu- ches Utes.
	Te-sa-ga-ra-pou-it, his x mark.	White Eyes.	
	Sa-po-eu-a-wa, his x mark.	Big Belly.	
	Qu-er-a-ta, his x mark.	A Bear.	

Signed in the presence of—

    Lafayette Head.
    Manuel Lusero.
    Alb. H. Pfeiffer.
    E. H. Kellogg, secretary Colorado Indian superintendency.
    Juan Martine Martines, interpreter and Indian's friend.
    Daniel C. Oakes, United States Indian agent.
    Uriah M. Curtis, interpreter.

I hereby certify that, pursuant to the order from the Commissioner of Indian Affairs, dated August fourth, one thousand eight hundred and sixty-eight, I visited and held councils with the various bands of

Ute Indians, at the times and places named in this instrument; and to all those familiar with the provisions of the treaty referred to have had the Senate amendment fully interpreted to them, and to all those not familiar with the treaty itself I have had the same fully explained and interpreted; and the forty-seven chiefs whose names are hereunto subscribed, placed their names to this instrument with the full knowledge of its contents and likewise with the provisions of the treaty itself.

Given under my hand at Denver, this fourteenth day of October, one thousand eight hundred and sixty-eight.

A. C. Hunt,
Governor, Ex-officio Superintendent Indian Affairs.

TREATY WITH THE CHEROKEE, 1868.

Apr. 27, 1868.

16 Stats., 727.
Ratified June 6, 1868.
Proclaimed June 10, 1868.

Supplemental article to a treaty concluded at Washington City, July 19th, A. D. 1866; ratified with amendments, July 27th, A. D. 1866; amendments accepted, July 31st, A. D. 1866; and the whole proclaimed, August 11th, A. D. 1866, between the United States of America and the Cherokee Nation of Indians.

Contract by the Secretary of the Interior with the American Emigrant Company for the sale of Cherokee neutral lands.

Whereas under the provisions of the seventeenth article of a treaty and amendments thereto made between the United States and the Cherokee Nation of Indians, and proclaimed August 11th, A. D. 1866, a contract was made and entered into by James Harlan, Secretary of the Interior, on behalf of the United States, of the one part, and by the American Emigrant Company, a corporation chartered and existing under the laws of the State of Connecticut, of the other part, dated August 30th, A. D. 1866, for the sale of the so-called "Cherokee neutral lands," in the State of Kansas, containing eight hundred thousand acres, more or less, with the limitations and restrictions set forth in the said seventeenth article of said treaty as amended, on the terms and conditions therein mentioned, which contract is now on file in the Department of the Interior; and

Contract with James F. Joy for sale of same lands.

Whereas Orville H. Browning, Secretary of the Interior, regarding said sale as illegal and not in conformity with said treaty and amendments thereto, did, on the ninth day of October, A. D. 1867, for and in behalf of the United States, enter into a contract with James F. Joy, of the city of Detroit, Michigan, for the sale of the aforesaid lands on the terms and conditions in said contract set forth, and which is on file in the Department of the Interior; and

Whereas, for the purpose of enabling the Secretary of the Interior, as trustee for the Cherokee Nation of Indians, to collect the proceeds of sales of said lands and invest the same for the benefit of said Indians, and for the purpose of preventing litigation and of harmonizing the conflicting interests of the said American Emigrant Company and of the said James F. Joy, it is the desire of all the parties in interest that the said American Emigrant Company shall assign their said contract and all their right, title, claim, and interest in and to the said "Cherokee neutral lands" to the said James F. Joy, and that the said Joy shall

Contract with American Emigrant Company to be assigned to Joy.

assume and conform to all the obligations of said company under their said contract, as hereinafter modified:

It is, therefore, agreed, by and between Nathaniel G. Taylor, commissioner on the part of the United States of America, and Lewis Downing, H. D. Reese, Wm. P. Adair, Elias C. Boudinot, J. A. Scales, Archie Scraper, J. Porum Davis, and Samuel Smith, commissioners on the part of the Cherokee Nation of Indians, that an assignment of the contract made and entered into on the 30th day of August, A. D. 1866, by and between James Harlan, Secretary of the Interior, for and in behalf of the United States of America, of the one part, and the American Emigrant Company, a corporation chartered and existing under the laws of the State of Connecticut, of the other part, and now on file in the Department of the Interior, to James F. Joy, of the city of Detroit, Michigan, shall be made; and that said contract, as hereinafter modified, be and the same is hereby, with the consent of all parties, re-affirmed and declared valid; and that the contract entered into by and between Orville H. Browning, for and in behalf of the United States, of the one part, and James F. Joy, of the city of Detroit, Michigan, of the other part, on the 9th day of October, A. D. 1867, and now on file in the Department of the Interior, shall be relinquished and cancelled by the said James F. Joy, or his duly authorized agent or attorney; and the said first contract as hereinafter modified, and the assignment of the first contract, and the relinquishment of the second contract, are hereby ratified and confirmed, whenever said assignment of the first contract and the relinquishment of the second shall be entered of record in the Department of the Interior, and when the said James F. Joy shall have accepted said assignment and shall have entered into a contract with the Secretary of the Interior to assume and perform all obligations of the said American Emigrant Company under said first-named contract, as hereinafter modified.

Contracts with Joy to be canceled.

The modifications hereinbefore mentioned of said contract are hereby declared to be:—

Modifications of contract with American Emigrant Company assigned to Joy.

1. That within ten days from the ratification of this supplemental article the sum of seventy-five thousand dollars shall be paid to the Secretary of the Interior as trustee for the Cherokee Nation of Indians.

2. That the other deferred payments specified in said contract shall be paid when they respectively fall due, with interest only from the date of the ratification hereof.

It is further agreed and distinctly understood that, under the conveyance of the "Cherokee neutral lands" to the said American Emigrant Company, "with all beneficial interests therein," as set forth in said contract, the said company and their assignees shall take only the residue of said lands after securing to "actual settlers" the lands to which they are entitled under the provisions of the seventeenth article and amendments thereto of the said Cherokee treaty of August 11th, 1866; and that the proceeds of the sales of said lands, so occupied at the date of said treaty by "actual settlers," shall enure to the sole benefit of, and be retained by, the Secretary of the Interior as trustee for the said Cherokee Nation of Indians.

In testimony whereof, the said commissioners on the part of the United States, and on the part of the Cherokee nation of Indians, have hereunto set their hands and seals, at the city of Washington, this 27th day of April, A. D. 1868.

N. G. Taylor,
Commissioner in behalf of the United States.

Delegates of the Cherokee Nation:

Lewis Downing,
Chief of Cherokees.
H. D. Reese,
Chairman of Delegation.
Samuel Smith,
Wm. P. Adair,
J. P. Davis,
Elias C. Boudinot,
J. A. Scales,
Arch. Scraper,
Cherokee Delegates.

In presence of—
    H. M. Watterson.
    Charles E. Mix.

TREATY WITH THE SIOUX—BRULÉ, OGLALA, MINICONJOU, YANKTONAI, HUNKPAPA, BLACKFEET, CUTHEAD, TWO KETTLE, SANS ARCS, AND SANTEE—AND ARAPAHO, 1868.

Apr. 29, 1868.

15 Stats., 635.
Ratified, Feb. 16, 1869.
Proclaimed, Feb. 24, 1869.

Articles of a treaty made and concluded by and between Lieutenant-General William T. Sherman, General William S. Harney, General Alfred H. Terry, General C. C. Augur, J. B. Henderson, Nathaniel G. Taylor, John B. Sanborn, and Samuel F. Tappan, duly appointed commissioners on the part of the United States, and the different bands of the Sioux Nation of Indians, by their chiefs and head-men, whose names are hereto subscribed, they being duly authorized to act in the premises.

War to cease and peace to be kept.

ARTICLE 1. From this day forward all war between the parties to this agreement shall forever cease. The Government of the United States desires peace, and its honor is hereby pledged to keep it. The Indians desire peace, and they now pledge their honor to maintain it.

Offenders against the Indians to be arrested, etc.

If bad men among the whites, or among other people subject to the authority of the United States, shall commit any wrong upon the person or property of the Indians, the United States will, upon proof made to the agent and forwarded to the Commissioner of Indian Affairs at Washington City, proceed at once to cause the offender to be arrested and punished according to the laws of the United States, and also re-imburse the injured person for the loss sustained.

Wrongdoers against the whites to be punished.

If bad men among the Indians shall commit a wrong or depredation upon the person or property of any one, white, black, or Indian, subject to the authority of the United States, and at peace therewith, the Indians herein named solemnly agree that they will, upon proof made to their agent and notice by him, deliver up the wrong-doer to the United States, to be tried and punished according to its laws; and

Damages.

in case they wilfully refuse so to do, the person injured shall be re-imbursed for his loss from the annuities or other moneys due or to become due to them under this or other treaties made with the United States. And the President, on advising with the Commissioner of Indian Affairs, shall prescribe such rules and regulations for ascertaining damages under the provisions of this article as in his judgment may be proper. But no one sustaining loss while violating the provisions of this treaty or the laws of the United States shall be re-imbursed therefor.

Reservation boundaries.

ARTICLE 2. The United States agrees that the following district of country, to wit, viz: commencing on the east bank of the Missouri River where the forty-sixth parallel of north latitude crosses the same, thence along low-water mark down said east bank to a point opposite where the northern line of the State of Nebraska strikes the river, thence west across said river, and along the northern line of Nebraska to the one hundred and fourth degree of longitude west from Greenwich, thence north on said meridian to a point where the forty-sixth parallel of north latitude intercepts the same, thence due east along said parallel to the place of beginning; and in addition thereto, all existing reservations on the east bank of said river shall be, and the same is, set apart for the absolute and undisturbed use and occupation of the Indians herein named, and for such other friendly tribes or individual Indians as from time to time they may be willing, with the

Certain persons not to enter or reside thereon.

consent of the United States, to admit amongst them; and the United States now solemnly agrees that no persons except those herein designated and authorized so to do, and except such officers, agents, and employés of the Government as may be authorized to enter upon Indian reservations in discharge of duties enjoined by law, shall ever be permitted to pass over, settle upon, or reside in the territory described in this article, or in such territory as may be added to this reservation for the use of said Indians, and henceforth they will and do hereby relinquish all claims or right in and to any portion of the United States or Territories, except such as is embraced within the limits aforesaid, and except as hereinafter provided.

ARTICLE 3. If it should appear from actual survey or other satisfactory examination of said tract of land that it contains less than one hundred and sixty acres of tillable land for each person who, at the time, may be authorized to reside on it under the provisions of this treaty, and a very considerable number of such persons shall be disposed to commence cultivating the soil as farmers, the United States agrees to set apart, for the use of said Indians, as herein provided, such additional quantity of arable land, adjoining to said reservation, or as near to the same as it can be obtained, as may be required to provide the necessary amount. *Additional arable land to be added, if, etc.*

ARTICLE 4. The United States agrees, at its own proper expense, to construct at some place on the Missouri River, near the center of said reservation, where timber and water may be convenient, the following buildings, to wit: a warehouse, a store-room for the use of the agent in storing goods belonging to the Indians, to cost not less than twenty-five hundred dollars; an agency-building for the residence of the agent, to cost not exceeding three thousand dollars; a residence for the physician, to cost not more than three thousand dollars; and five other buildings, for a carpenter, farmer, blacksmith, miller, and engineer, each to cost not exceeding two thousand dollars; also a school-house or mission-building, so soon as a sufficient number of children can be induced by the agent to attend school, which shall not cost exceeding five thousand dollars. *Buildings on reservation.*

The United States agrees further to cause to be erected on said reservation, near the other buildings herein authorized, a good steam circular-saw mill, with a grist-mill and shingle-machine attached to the same, to cost not exceeding eight thousand dollars.

ARTICLE 5. The United States agrees that the agent for said Indians shall in the future make his home at the agency-building; that he shall reside among them, and keep an office open at all times for the purpose of prompt and diligent inquiry into such matters of complaint by and against the Indians as may be presented for investigation under the provisions of their treaty stipulations, as also for the faithful discharge of other duties enjoined on him by law. In all cases of depredation on person or property he shall cause the evidence to be taken in writing and forwarded, together with his findings, to the Commissioner of Indian Affairs, whose decision, subject to the revision of the Secretary of the Interior, shall be binding on the parties to this treaty. *Agent's residence, office, and duties.*

ARTICLE 6. If any individual belonging to said tribes of Indians, or legally incorporated with them, being the head of a family, shall desire to commence farming, he shall have the privilege to select, in the presence and with the assistance of the agent then in charge, a tract of land within said reservation, not exceeding three hundred and twenty acres in extent, which tract, when so selected, certified, and recorded in the "land-book," as herein directed, shall cease to be held in common, but the same may be occupied and held in the exclusive possession of the person selecting it, and of his family, so long as he or they may continue to cultivate it. *Heads of families may select lands for farming.*

Any person over eighteen years of age, not being the head of a family, may in like manner select and cause to be certified to him or her, for purposes of cultivation, a quantity of land not exceeding eighty acres in extent, and thereupon be entitled to the exclusive possession of the same as above directed. *Others may select land for cultivation.*

Certificates.

For each tract of land so selected a certificate, containing a description thereof and the name of the person selecting it, with a certificate endorsed thereon that the same has been recorded, shall be delivered to the party entitled to it, by the agent, after the same shall have been recorded by him in a book to be kept in his office, subject to inspection, which said book shall be known as the "Sioux Land-Book."

Surveys.

The President may, at any time, order a survey of the reservation, and, when so surveyed, Congress shall provide for protecting the rights of said settlers in their improvements, and may fix the character of the title held by each. The United States may pass such laws on the subject of alienation and descent of property between the Indians and their descendants as may be thought proper. And it is further stipulated that any male Indians, over eighteen years of age, of any band or tribe that is or shall hereafter become a party to this treaty, who now is or who shall hereafter become a resident or occupant of any reservation or Territory not included in the tract of country designated and described in this treaty for the permanent home of the Indians, which is not mineral land, nor reserved by the United States for special purposes other than Indian occupation, and who shall have made improvements thereon of the value of two hundred dollars or more, and continuously occupied the same as a homestead for the term of three years, shall be entitled to receive from the United States a patent for one hundred and sixty acres of land including his said improvements, the same to be in the form of the legal subdivisions of the surveys of the public lands. Upon application in writing, sustained by the proof of two disinterested witnesses, made to the register of the local land-office when the land sought to be entered is within a land district, and when the tract sought to be entered is not in any land district, then upon said application and proof being made to the Commissioner of the General Land-Office, and the right of such Indian or Indians to enter such tract or tracts of land shall accrue and be perfect from the date of his first improvements thereon, and shall continue as long as he continues his residence and improvements, and no longer. And any Indian or Indians receiving a patent for land under the foregoing provisions, shall thereby and from thenceforth become and be a citizen of the United States, and be entitled to all the privileges and immunities of such citizens, and shall, at the same time, retain all his rights to benefits accruing to Indians under this treaty.

Alienation and descent of property.

Certain Indians may receive patents for 160 acres of land.

Such Indians receiving patents to become citizens of the United States.

Education.

ARTICLE 7. In order to insure the civilization of the Indians entering into this treaty, the necessity of education is admitted, especially of such of them as are or may be settled on said agricultural reservations, and they therefore pledge themselves to compel their children, male and female, between the ages of six and sixteen years, to attend school; and it is hereby made the duty of the agent for said Indians to see that this stipulation is strictly complied with; and the United States agrees that for every thirty children between said ages who can be induced or compelled to attend school, a house shall be provided and a teacher competent to teach the elementary branches of an English education shall be furnished, who will reside among said Indians, and faithfully discharge his or her duties as a teacher. The provisions of this article to continue for not less than twenty years.

Children to attend school.

Schoolhouses and teachers.

ARTICLE 8. When the head of a family or lodge shall have selected lands and received his certificate as above directed, and the agent shall be satisfied that he intends in good faith to commence cultivating the soil for a living, he shall be entitled to receive seeds and agricultural implements for the first year, not exceeding in value one hundred dollars, and for each succeeding year he shall continue to farm, for a period of three years more, he shall be entitled to receive seeds and implements as aforesaid, not exceeding in value twenty-five dollars.

Seeds and agricultural implements.

And it is further stipulated that such persons as commence farming shall receive instruction from the farmer herein provided for, and

Instructions in farming.

whenever more than one hundred persons shall enter upon the cultivation of the soil, a second blacksmith shall be provided, with such iron, steel, and other material as may be needed.

Second blacksmith.

ARTICLE 9. At any time after ten years from the making of this treaty, the United States shall have the privilege of withdrawing the physician, farmer, blacksmith, carpenter, engineer, and miller herein provided for, but in case of such withdrawal, an additional sum thereafter of ten thousand dollars per annum shall be devoted to the education of said Indians, and the Commissioner of Indian Affairs shall, upon careful inquiry into their condition, make such rules and regulations for the expenditure of said sum as will best promote the educational and moral improvement of said tribes.

Physician, farmer, etc., may be withdrawn.

Additional appropriation in such cases.

ARTICLE 10. In lieu of all sums of money or other annuities provided to be paid to the Indians herein named, under any treaty or treaties heretofore made, the United States agrees to deliver at the agency-house on the reservation herein named, on or before the first day of August of each year, for thirty years, the following articles, to wit:

Delivery of goods in lieu of money or other annuities.

For each male person over fourteen years of age, a suit of good substantial woolen clothing, consisting of coat, pantaloons, flannel shirt, hat, and a pair of home-made socks.

Clothing.

For each female over twelve years of age, a flannel skirt, or the goods necessary to make it, a pair of woolen hose, twelve yards of calico, and twelve yards of cotton domestics.

For the boys and girls under the ages named, such flannel and cotton goods as may be needed to make each a suit as aforesaid, together with a pair of woolen hose for each.

And in order that the Commissioner of Indian Affairs may be able to estimate properly for the articles herein named, it shall be the duty of the agent each year to forward to him a full and exact census of the Indians, on which the estimate from year to year can be based.

Census.

And in addition to the clothing herein named, the sum of ten dollars for each person entitled to the beneficial effects of this treaty shall be annually appropriated for a period of thirty years, while such persons roam and hunt, and twenty dollars for each person who engages in farming, to be used by the Secretary of the Interior in the purchase of such articles as from time to time the condition and necessities of the Indians may indicate to be proper. And if within the thirty years, at any time, it shall appear that the amount of money needed for clothing under this article can be appropriated to better uses for the Indians named herein, Congress may, by law, change the appropriation to other purposes; but in no event shall the amount of this appropriation be withdrawn or discontinued for the period named. And the President shall annually detail an officer of the Army to be present and attest the delivery of all the goods herein named to the Indians, and he shall inspect and report on the quantity and quality of the goods and the manner of their delivery. And it is hereby expressly stipulated that each Indian over the age of four years, who shall have removed to and settled permanently upon said reservation and complied with the stipulations of this treaty, shall be entitled to receive from the United States, for the period of four years after he shall have settled upon said reservation, one pound of meat and one pound of flour per day, provided the Indians cannot furnish their own subsistence at an earlier date. And it is further stipulated that the United States will furnish and deliver to each lodge of Indians or family of persons legally incorporated with them, who shall remove to the reservation herein described and commence farming, one good American cow, and one good well-broken pair of American oxen within sixty days after such lodge or family shall have so settled upon said reservation.

Other necessary articles.

Appropriation to continue for thirty years.

Army officer to attend the delivery.

Meat and flour.

Cows and oxen.

ARTICLE 11. In consideration of the advantages and benefits conferred by this treaty, and the many pledges of friendship by the

Right to occupy territory outside of the reservation surrendered.

United States, the tribes who are parties to this agreement hereby stipulate that they will relinquish all right to occupy permanently the territory outside their reservation as herein defined, but yet reserve the right to hunt on any lands north of North Platte, and on the Republican Fork of the Smoky Hill River, so long as the buffalo may range thereon in such numbers as to justify the chase. And they, the said Indians, further expressly agree:

Right to hunt reserved.

1st. That they will withdraw all opposition to the construction of the railroads now being built on the plains.

Agreements as to railroads.

2d. That they will permit the peaceful construction of any railroad not passing over their reservation as herein defined.

3d. That they will not attack any persons at home, or travelling, nor molest or disturb any wagon-trains, coaches, mules, or cattle belonging to the people of the United States, or to persons friendly therewith.

Emigrants, etc.

4th. They will never capture, or carry off from the settlements, white women or children.

Women and children.

5th. They will never kill or scalp white men, nor attempt to do them harm.

White men.

6th. They withdraw all pretence of opposition to the construction of the railroad now being built along the Platte River and westward to the Pacific Ocean, and they will not in future object to the construction of railroads, wagon-roads, mail-stations, or other works of utility or necessity, which may be ordered or permitted by the laws of the United States. But should such roads or other works be constructed on the lands of their reservation, the Government will pay the tribe whatever amount of damage may be assessed by three disinterested commissioners to be appointed by the President for that purpose, one of said commissioners to be a chief or head-man of the tribe.

Pacific Railroad, wagon roads, etc.

Damages for crossing their reservation.

7th. They agree to withdraw all opposition to the military posts or roads now established south of the North Platte River, or that may be established, not in violation of treaties heretofore made or hereafter to be made with any of the Indian tribes.

Military posts and roads.

ARTICLE 12. No treaty for the cession of any portion or part of the reservation herein described which may be held in common shall be of any validity or force as against the said Indians, unless executed and signed by at least three-fourths of all the adult male Indians, occupying or interested in the same; and no cession by the tribe shall be understood or construed in such manner as to deprive, without his consent, any individual member of the tribe of his rights to any tract of land selected by him, as provided in article 6 of this treaty.

No treaty for cession of reservation to be valid unless, etc.

ARTICLE 13. The United States hereby agrees to furnish annually to the Indians the physician, teachers, carpenter, miller, engineer, farmer, and blacksmiths as herein contemplated, and that such appropriations shall be made from time to time, on the estimates of the Secretary of the Interior, as will be sufficient to employ such persons.

United States to furnish physician, teachers, etc.

ARTICLE 14. It is agreed that the sum of five hundred dollars annually, for three years from date, shall be expended in presents to the ten persons of said tribe who in the judgment of the agent may grow the most valuable crops for the respective year.

Presents for crops.

ARTICLE 15. The Indians herein named agree that when the agency-house or other buildings shall be constructed on the reservation named, they will regard said reservation their permanent home, and they will make no permanent settlement elsewhere; but they shall have the right, subject to the conditions and modifications of this treaty, to hunt, as stipulated in Article 11 hereof.

Reservation to be permanent home of tribes.

ARTICLE 16. The United States hereby agrees and stipulates that the country north of the North Platte River and east of the summits of the Big Horn Mountains shall be held and considered to be unceded Indian territory, and also stipulates and agrees that no white person or persons shall be permitted to settle upon or occupy any portion of

Unceded Indian territory.

Not to be occupied by whites, etc.

the same; or without the consent of the Indians first had and obtained, to pass through the same; and it is further agreed by the United States that within ninety days after the conclusion of peace with all the bands of the Sioux Nation, the military posts now established in the territory in this article named shall be abandoned, and that the road leading to them and by them to the settlements in the Territory of Montana shall be closed.

ARTICLE 17. It is hereby expressly understood and agreed by and between the respective parties to this treaty that the execution of this treaty and its ratification by the United States Senate shall have the effect, and shall be construed as abrogating and annulling all treaties and agreements heretofore entered into between the respective parties hereto, so far as such treaties and agreements obligate the United States to furnish and provide money, clothing, or other articles of property to such Indians and bands of Indians as become parties to this treaty, but no further.

Effect of this treaty upon former treaties.

In testimony of all which, we, the said commissioners, and we, the chiefs and headmen of the Brulé band of the Sioux nation, have hereunto set our hands and seals at Fort Laramie, Dakota Territory, this twenty-ninth day of April, in the year one thousand eight hundred and sixty-eight.

> N. G. Taylor,   [SEAL.]
> W. T. Sherman,   [SEAL.]
>   Lieutenant-General.
> Wm. S. Harney,   [SEAL.]
> Brevet Major-General U. S. Army.
> John B. Sanborn,   [SEAL.]
> S. F. Tappan,   [SEAL.]
> C. C. Augur,   [SEAL.]
>   Brevet Major-General.
> Alfred H. Terry,   [SEAL.]
> Brevet Major-General U. S. Army.

Attest:
    A. S. H. White, Secretary.

Executed on the part of the Brulé band of Sioux by the chiefs and headmen whose names are hereto annexed, they being thereunto duly authorized, at Fort Laramie, D. T., the twenty-ninth day of April, in the year A. D. 1868.

Ma-za-pon-kaska, his x mark, Iron Shell.   [SEAL.]

Wah-pat-shah, his x mark, Red Leaf.   [SEAL.]

Hah-sah-pah, his x mark, Black Horn.   [SEAL.]

Zin-tah-gah-lat-skah, his x mark, Spotted Tail.   [SEAL.]

Zin-tah-skah, his x mark, White Tail.   [SEAL.]

Me-wah-tah-ne-ho-skah, his x mark, Tall Mandas.   [SEAL.]

She-cha-chat-kah, his x mark, Bad Left Hand.   [SEAL.]

No-mah-no-pah, his x mark, Two and Two.   [SEAL.]

Tah-tonka-skah, his x mark, White Bull.   [SEAL.]

Con-ra-washta, his x mark, Pretty Coon.   [SEAL.]

Ha-cah-cah-she-chah, his x mark, Bad Elk.   [SEAL.]

Wa-ha-ka-zah-ish-tah, his x mark, Eye Lance.   [SEAL.]

Ma-to-ha-ke-tah, his x mark, Bear that looks behind.   [SEAL.]

Bella-tonka-tonka, his x mark, Big Partisan.   [SEAL.]

Mah-to-ho-honka, his x mark, Swift Bear.   [SEAL.]

To-wis-ne, his x mark, Cold Place.   [SEAL.]

Ish-tah-skah, his x mark, White Eyes.   [SEAL.]

Ma-ta-loo-zah, his x mark, Fast Bear.   [SEAL.]

As-hah-kah-nah-zhe, his x mark, Standing Elk.   [SEAL.]

Can-te-te-ki-ya, his x mark, The Brave Heart.   [SEAL.]

Shunka-shaton, his x mark, Day Hawk.   [SEAL.]

Tatanka-wakon, his x mark, Sacred Bull.   [SEAL.]

Mapia shaton, his x mark, Hawk Cloud.   [SEAL.]

Ma-sha-a-ow, his x mark, Stands and Comes.   [SEAL.]

Shon-ka-ton-ka, his x mark, Big Dog.   [SEAL.]

Attest:

Ashton S. H. White, secretary of commission.
George B. Withs, phonographer to commission.
Geo. H. Holtzman.

John D. Howlana.
James C. O'Connor.
Chas. E. Guern, interpreter.
Leon F. Pallardy, interpreter.
Nicholas Janis, interpreter.

Execution by the Ogallalah band.

Executed on the part of the Ogallalah band of Sioux by the chiefs and headmen whose names are hereto subscribed, they being thereunto duly authorized, at Fort Laramie, the twenty-fifth day of May, in the year A. D. 1868.

Tah-shun-ka-co-qui-pah, his x mark, Man-afraid-of-his-horses. [SEAL.]
Sha-ton-skah, his x mark, White Hawk. [SEAL.]
Sha-ton-sapah, his x mark, Black Hawk. [SEAL.]
E-ga-mon-ton-ka-sapah, his x mark, Black Tiger. [SEAL.]
Oh-wah-she-cha, his x mark, Bad Wound. [SEAL.]
Pah-gee, his x mark, Grass. [SEAL.]
Wah-non-reh-che-geh, his x mark, Ghost Heart. [SEAL.]
Con-reeh, his x mark, Crow. [SEAL.]
Oh-he-te-kah, his x mark, The Brave. [SEAL.]
Tah-ton-kah-he-yo-ta-kah, his x mark, Sitting Bull. [SEAL.]
Shon-ka-oh-wah-mon-ye, his x mark, Whirlwind Dog. [SEAL.]
Ha-hah-kah-tah-miech, his x mark, Poor Elk. [SEAL.]
Wam-bu-lee-wah-kon, his x mark, Medicine Eagle. [SEAL.]
Chon-gah-ma-he-to-hans-ka, his x mark, High Wolf. [SEAL.]
Wah-se-chun-ta-shun-kah, his x mark, American Horse. [SEAL.]
Mah-hah-mah-ha-mak-near, his x mark, Man that walks under the ground. [SEAL.]
Mah-to-tow-pah, his x mark, Four Bears. [SEAL.]
Ma-to-wee-sha-kta, his x mark, One that kills the bear. [SEAL.]
Oh-tah-kee-toka-wee-chakta, his x mark, One that kills in a hard place. [SEAL.]
Tah-ton-kah-ta-miech, his x mark, The poor Bull. [SEAL.]

Oh-huns-ee-ga-non-sken, his x mark, Mad Shade. [SEAL.]
Shah-ton-oh-nah-om-minne-ne-oh-minne, his x mark, Whirling Hawk. [SEAL.]
Mah-to-chun-ka-oh, his x mark, Bear's Back. [SEAL.]
Che-ton-wee-koh, his x mark, Fool Hawk. [SEAL.]
Wah-hoh-ke-za-ah-hah, his x mark, One that has the lance. [SEAL.]
Shon-gah-manni-toh-tan-ka-seh, his x mark, Big Wolf Foot. [SEAL.]
Eh-ton-kah, his x mark, Big Mouth. [SEAL.]
Ma-pah-che-tah, his x mark, Bad Hand. [SEAL.]
Wah-ke-yun-shah, his x mark, Red Thunder. [SEAL.]
Wak-sah, his x mark, One that Cuts Off. [SEAL.]
Cham-nom-qui-yah, his x mark, One that Presents the Pipe. [SEAL.]
Wah-ke-ke-yan-puh-tah, his x mark, Fire Thunder. [SEAL.]
Mah-to-nonk-pah-ze, his x mark, Bear with Yellow Ears. [SEAL.]
Con-ree-teh-ka, his x mark, The Little Crow. [SEAL.]
He-hup-pah-toh, his x mark, The Blue War Club. [SEAL.]
Shon-kee-toh, his x mark, The Blue Horse. [SEAL.]
Wam-Balla-oh-con-quo, his x mark, Quick Eagle. [SEAL.]
Ta-tonka-suppa, his x mark, Black Bull. [SEAL.]
Moh-to-ha-she-na, his x mark, The Bear Hide. [SEAL.]

Attest:

S. E. Ward.
Jas. C. O'Connor.
J. M. Sherwood.
W. C. Slicer.
Sam Deon.

H. M. Matthews.
Joseph Bissonette, interpreter.
Nicholas Janis, interpreter.
Lefroy Jott, interpreter.
Antoine Janis, interpreter.

Execution by the Minneconjon band.

Executed on the part of the Minneconjon band of Sioux by the chiefs and headmen whose names are hereto subscribed, they being thereunto duly authorized.

At Fort Laramie, D. T., May 26, '68, 13 names.

Heh-won-ge-chat, [SEAL.]
his x mark, One Horn.
Oh-pon-ah-tah-e-manne, [SEAL.]
his x mark, The Elk that bellows Walking.

At Fort Laramie, D. T., May 25, '68, 2 names.

Heh-ho-lah-reh-cha-skah,
his x mark, Young White Bull. [SEAL.]

Wah-chah-chum-kah-coh-kee-pah, his x mark, One that is afraid of Shield. [SEAL.]
He-hon-ne-shakta, his x mark, The Old Owl. [SEAL.]
Moc-pe-a-toh, his x mark, Blue Cloud. [SEAL.]
Oh-pong-ge-le-skah, his x mark, Spotted Elk. [SEAL.]
Tah-tonk-ka-hon-ke-schne, his x mark, Slow Bull. [SEAL.]
Shonk-a-nee-shah-shah-a-tah-pe, his x mark, The Dog Chief. [SEAL.]
Ma-to-tah-ta-tonk-ka, his x mark, Bull Bear. [SEAL.]

Wom-beh-le-ton-kah, his x mark, The Big Eagle. [SEAL.]
Ma-toh-eh-schne-lah, his x mark, The Lone Bear. [SEAL.]
Mah-toh-ke-su-yah, his x mark, The One who Remembers the Bear. [SEAL.]
Ma-toh-oh-he-to-keh, his x mark, The Brave Bear. [SEAL.]
Eh-che-ma-heh, his x mark, The Runner. [SEAL.]
Ti-ki-ya, his x mark, The Hard. [SEAL.]
He-ma-za, his x mark, Iron Horn. [SEAL.]

Attest:

Jas. C. O'Connor.
Wm. H. Brown.

Nicholas Janis, interpreter.
Antoine Janis, interpreter.

Executed on the part of the Yanctonais band of Sioux by the chiefs and headmen whose names are hereto subscribed, they being thereunto duly authorized. Execution by the Yanctonais band.

Mah-to-non-pah, his x mark, Two Bears. [SEAL.]
Ma-to-hna-skin-ya, his x mark, Mad Bear. [SEAL.]
He-o-pu-za, his x mark, Louzy. [SEAL.]
Ah-ke-che-tah-che-ca-dan, his x mark, Little Soldier. [SEAL.]
Mah-to-e-tan-chan, his x mark, Chief Bear. [SEAL.]
Cu-wi-h-win, his x mark, Rotten Stomach. [SEAL.]
Skun-ka-we-tko, his x mark, Fool Dog. [SEAL.]
Ish-ta-sap-pah, his x mark, Black Eye. [SEAL.]
Ih-tan-chan, his x mark, The Chief. [SEAL.]
I-a-wi-ca-ka, his x mark, The one who Tells the Truth. [SEAL.]
Ah-ke-che-tah, his x mark, The Soldier. [SEAL.]
Ta-shi-na-gi, his x mark, Yellow Robe. [SEAL.]
Nah-pe-ton-ka, his x mark, Big Hand. [SEAL.]
Chan-tee-we-kto, his x mark, Fool Heart. [SEAL.]
Hoh-gan-sah-pa, his x mark, Black Catfish. [SEAL.]
Mah-to-wah-kan, his x mark, Medicine Bear. [SEAL.]
Shun-ka-kan-sha, his x mark, Red Horse. [SEAL.]
Wan-rode, his x mark, The Eagle. [SEAL.]
Can-hpi-sa-pa, his x mark, Black Tomahawk. [SEAL.]
War-he-le-re, his x mark, Yellow Eagle. [SEAL.]

Cha-ton-che-ca, his x mark, Small Hawk, or Long Fare. [SEAL.]
Shu-ger-mon-e-too-ha-ska, his x mark, Tall Wolf. [SEAL.]
Ma-to-u-tah-kah, his x mark, Sitting Bear. [SEAL.]
Hi-ha-cah-ge-na-skene, his x mark, Mad Elk. [SEAL.]
Arapahoes:
Little Chief, his x mark. [SEAL.]
Tall Bear, his x mark. [SEAL.]
Top Man, his x mark. [SEAL.]
Neva, his x mark. [SEAL.]
The Wounded Bear, his x mark. [SEAL.]
Thirlwind, his x mark. [SEAL.]
The Fox, his x mark. [SEAL.]
The Dog Big Mouth, his x mark. [SEAL.]
Spotted Wolf, his x mark. [SEAL.]
Sorrel Horse, his x mark. [SEAL.]
Black Coal, his x mark. [SEAL.]
Big Wolf, his x mark. [SEAL.]
Knock-knee, his x mark. [SEAL.]
Black Crow, his x mark. [SEAL.]
The Lone Old Man, his x mark. [SEAL.]
Paul, his x mark. [SEAL.]
Black Bull, his x mark. [SEAL.]
Big Track, his x mark. [SEAL.]
The Foot, his x mark. [SEAL.]
Black White, his x mark. [SEAL.]
Yellow Hair, his x mark. [SEAL.]
Little Shield, his x mark. [SEAL.]
Black Bear, his x mark. [SEAL.]
Wolf Mocassin, his x mark. [SEAL.]
Big Robe, his x mark. [SEAL.]
Wolf Chief, his x mark. [SEAL.]

Witnesses:

Robt. P. McKibbin, captain, Fourth Infantry, brevet lieutenant-colonel, U. S. Army, commanding Fort Laramie.
Wm. H. Powell, brevet major, captain, Fourth Infantry.
Henry W. Patterson, captain, Fourth Infantry.

Theo. E. True, second lieutenant, Fourth Infantry.
W. G. Bullock.
Chas. E. Guern, special Indian interpreter for the peace commission.

FORT LARAMIE, WG. T., *Nov. 6, 1868.*

Makh-pi-ah-lu-tah, his x mark, Red Cloud. [SEAL.]

Wa-ki-ah-we-cha-shah, his x mark, Thunder Man. [SEAL.]

Ma-zah-zah-geh, his x mark, Iron Cane. [SEAL.]

Wa-umble-why-wa-ka-tuyah, his x mark, High Eagle. [SEAL.]

Ko-ke-pah, his x mark, Man Afraid. [SEAL.]

Wa-ki-ah-wa-kou-ah, his x mark, Thunder Flying Running. [SEAL.]

Witnesses:

W. McE. Dye, brevet colonel, U. S. Army, commanding.

A. B. Cain, captain, Fourth Infantry, brevet major, U. S. Army.

Robt. P. McKibbin, captain, Fourth Infantry, brevet lieutenant-colonel, U. S. Army.

Jno. Miller, captain, Fourth Infantry.

G. L. Luhn, first lieutenant, Fourth Infantry, brevet captain, U. S. Army.

H. C. Sloan, second lieutenant, Fourth Infantry.

Whittingham Cox, first lieutenant, Fourth Infantry.

A. W. Vogdes, first lieutenant, Fourth Infantry.

Butler D. Price, second lieutenant, Fourth Infantry.

HEADQRS., FORT LARAMIE, *Novr. 6, '68.*

Executed by the above on this date.

All of the Indians are Ogallalahs excepting Thunder Man and Thunder Flying Running, who are Brulés.

Wm. McE. Dye,

Major Fourth Infantry, and Brevet-Colonel

U. S. Army, Commanding.

Attest:

Jas. C. O'Connor.

Nicholas Janis, interpreter.

Franc. La Framboise, interpreter.

P. J. De Smet, S. J., missionary among the Indians.

Saml. D. Hinman, B. D., missionary.

Execution by the Uncpapa band. Executed on the part of the Uncpapa band of Sioux, by the chiefs and headmen whose names are hereto subscribed, they being thereunto duly authorized.

Co-kam-i-ya-ya, his x mark, The Man that Goes in the Middle. [SEAL.]

Ma-to-ca-wa-weksa, his x mark, Bear Rib. [SEAL.]

Ta-to-ka-in-yan-ke, his x mark, Running Antelope. [SEAL.]

Kan-gi-wa-ki-ta, his x mark, Looking Crow. [SEAL.]

A-ki-ci-ta-han-ska, his x mark, Long Soldier. [SEAL.]

Wa-ku-te-ma-ni, his x mark, The One who Shoots Walking. [SEAL.]

Un-kca-ki-ka, his x mark, The Magpie. [SEAL.]

Kan-gi-o-ta, his x mark, Plenty Crow. [SEAL.]

He-ma-za, his x mark, Iron Horn. [SEAL.]

Shun-ka-i-na-pin, his x mark, Wolf Necklace. [SEAL.]

I-we-hi-yu, his x mark, The Man who Bleeds from the Mouth. [SEAL.]

He-ha-ka-pa, his x mark, Elk Head. [SEAL.]

I-zu-za, his x mark, Grind Stone. [SEAL.]

Shun-ka-wi-tko, his x mark, Fool Dog. [SEAL.]

Ma-kpi-ya-po, his x mark, Blue Cloud. [SEAL.]

Wa-mln-pi-lu-ta, his x mark, Red Eagle. [SEAL.]

Ma-to-can-te, his x mark, Bear's Heart. [SEAL.]

A-ki-ci-ta-i-tau-can, his x mark, Chief Soldier. [SEAL.]

Attest:

Jas. C. O'Connor.

Nicholas Janis, interpreter.

Franc. La Frambois[e], interpreter.

P. J. De Smet, S. J., missionary among the Indians.

Saml. D. Hinman, missionary.

By the Blackfeet band Executed on the part of the Blackfeet band of Sioux by the chiefs and headmen whose names are hereto subscribed, they being thereunto duly authorized.

Can-te-pe-ta, his x mark, Fire Heart. [SEAL.]

Wan-mdi-kte, his x mark, The One who Kills Eagle. [SEAL.]

Sho-ta, his x mark, Smoke. [SEAL.]

Wan-mdi-ma-ni, his x mark, Walking Eagle. [SEAL.]

Wa-shi-cun-ya-ta-pi, his x mark, Chief White Man. [SEAL.]

Kan-gi-i-yo-tan-ke, his x mark, Sitting Crow. [SEAL.]

Pe-ji, his x mark, The Grass. [SEAL.]

Kda-ma-ni, his x mark, The One that Rattles as he Walks. [SEAL.]

Wah-han-ka-sa-pa, his x mark, Black Shield. [SEAL.]

Can-te-non-pa, his x mark, Two Hearts. [SEAL.]

Attest:

Jas. C. O'Connor.
Nicholas Janis, interpreter.
Franc. La Framboise, interpreter.
P. J. De Smet, S. J., missionary among the Indians.
Saml. D. Hinman, missionary.

Executed on the part of the Cutheads band of Sioux by the chiefs and headmen whose names are hereto subscribed, they being thereunto duly authorized. *Execution by the Cutheads band.*

To-ka-in-yan-ka, his x mark, The One who Goes Ahead Running.	[SEAL.]
Ta-tan-ka-wa-kin-yan, his x mark, Thunder Bull.	[SEAL.]
Sin-to-min-sa-pa, his x mark, All over Black.	[SEAL.]
Can-i-ca, his x mark, The One who Took the Stick.	[SEAL.]
Pa-tan-ka, his x mark, Big Head.	[SEAL.]

Attest:

Jas. C. O'Connor.
Nicholas Janis, interpreter.
Franc. La Frambois[e], interpreter.
P. J. De Smet, S. J., missionary among the Indians.
Saml. D. Hinman, missionary.

Executed on the part of the Two Kettle band of Sioux by the chiefs and headmen whose names are hereto subscribed, they being thereunto duly authorized. *By the Two Kettle band.*

Ma-wa-tan-ni-han-ska, his x mark, Long Mandan.	[SEAL.]
Can-kpe-du-ta, his x mark, Red War Club.	[SEAL.]
Can-ka-ga, his x mark, The Log.	[SEAL.]

Attest:

Jas. C. O'Connor.
Nicholas Janis, interpreter.
Franc. La Framboise, interpreter.
P. J. De Smet, S. J., missionary among the Indians.
Saml. D. Hinman, missionary to the Dakotas.

Executed on the part of the Sans Arch band of Sioux by the chiefs and headmen whose names are hereto annexed, they being thereunto duly authorized. *By the Sans Arch band.*

He-na-pin-wa-ni-ca, his x mark, The One that has Neither Horn.	[SEAL.]
Wa-inlu-pi-lu-ta, his x mark, Red Plume.	[SEAL.]
Ci-tan-gi, his x mark, Yellow Hawk.	[SEAL.]
He-na-pin-wa-ni-ca, his x mark, No Horn.	[SEAL.]

Attest:

Jas. C. O'Connor.
Nicholas Janis, interpreter.
Franc. La Frambois[e], interpreter.
P. J. De Smet, S. J., missionary among the Indians.
Saml. D. Hinman, missionary.

Executed on the part of the Santee band of Sioux by the chiefs and headmen whose names are hereto subscribed, they being thereunto duly authorized. *Execution by the Santee band.*

Wa-pah-shaw, his x mark, Red Ensign.	[SEAL.]
Wah-koo-tay, his x mark, Shooter.	[SEAL.]
Hoo-sha-sha, his x mark, Red Legs.	[SEAL.]
O-wan-cha-du-ta, his x mark, Scarlet all over.	[SEAL.]
Wau-mace-tan-ka, his mark x, Big Eagle.	[SEAL.]
Cho-tan-ka-e-na-pe, his x mark, Flute-player.	[SEAL.]
Ta-shun-ke-mo-za, his x mark, His Iron Dog.	[SEAL.]

Attest:

Saml. D. Hinman, B. D., missionary.
J. N. Chickering,
    Second lieutenant, Twenty-second Infantry, brevet captain, U. S. Army.
P. J. De Smet, S. J.
Nicholas Janis, interpreter.
Franc. La Framboise, interpreter.

TREATY WITH THE CROWS, 1868.

May 7, 1868.

15 Stats., 649.
Ratified, July 25, 1868.
Proclaimed, Aug. 12, 1868.

Articles of a treaty made and concluded at Fort Laramie, Dakota Territory, on the seventh day of May, in the year of our Lord one thousand eight hundred and sixty-eight, by and between the undersigned commissioners on the part of the United States, and the undersigned chiefs and head-men of and representing the Crow Indians, they being duly authorized to act in the premises.

Peace and friendship.

Offenders among the whites to be arrested and punished.

ARTICLE 1. From this day forward peace between the parties to this treaty shall forever continue. The Government of the United States desires peace, and its honor is hereby pledged to keep it. The Indians desire peace, and they hereby pledge their honor to maintain it. If bad men among the whites or among other people, subject to the authority of the United States, shall commit any wrong upon the person or property of the Indians, the United States will, upon proof made to the agent and forwarded to the Commissioner of Indian Affairs at Washington City, proceed at once to cause the offender to be arrested and punished according to the laws of the United States, and also re-imburse the injured person for the loss sustained.

Among the Indians, to be given up to the United States or, etc.

If bad men among the Indians shall commit a wrong or depredation upon the person or property of any one, white, black, or Indian, subject to the authority of the United States and at peace therewith, the Indians herein named solemnly agree that they will, on proof made to their agent and notice by him, deliver up the wrong-doer to the United States, to be tried and punished according to its laws; and in case they refuse willfully so to do the person injured shall be re-imbursed for his loss from the annuities or other moneys due or to become due to them under this or other treaties made with the United States.

Rules for ascertaining damages.

And the President, on advising with the Commissioner of Indian Affairs, shall prescribe such rules and regulations for ascertaining damages under the provisions of this article as in his judgment may be proper. But no such damages shall be adjusted and paid until thoroughly examined and passed upon by the Commissioner of Indian Affairs, and no one sustaining loss while violating, or because of his violating, the provisions of this treaty or the laws of the United States shall be re-imbursed therefor.

Reservation boundaries.

ARTICLE 2. The United States agrees that the following district of country, to wit: commencing where the 107th degree of longitude west of Greenwich crosses the south boundary of Montana Territory; thence north along said 107th meridian to the mid-channel of the Yellowstone River; thence up said mid-channel of the Yellowstone to the point where it crosses the said southern boundary of Montana, being the 45th degree of north latitude; and thence east along said parallel of latitude to the place of beginning, shall be, and the same is, set apart for the absolute and undisturbed use and occupation of the Indians herein named, and for such other friendly tribes or individual Indians as from to time they may be willing, with the consent of the United States, to admit amongst them; and the United States now solemnly

Who not to reside thereon.

agrees that no persons, except those herein designated and authorized so to do, and except such officers, agents, and employés of the Government as may be authorized to enter upon Indian reservations in discharge of duties enjoined by law, shall ever be permitted to pass over, settle upon, or reside in the territory described in this article for the use of said Indians, and henceforth they will, and do hereby, relinquish all title, claims, or rights in and to any portion of the territory of the United States, except such as is embraced within the limits aforesaid.

Buildings to be erected by the United States.

ARTICLE 3. The United States agrees, at its own proper expense, to construct on the south side of the Yellowstone, near Otter Creek, a warehouse or store-room for the use of the agent in storing goods belonging to the Indians, to cost not exceeding twenty-five hundred dollars; an agency-building for the residence of the agent, to cost not exceeding three thousand dollars; a residence for the physician, to cost not more than three thousand dollars; and five other buildings, for a carpenter, farmer, blacksmith, miller, and engineer, each to cost not exceeding two thousand dollars; also a school-house or mission-building, so soon as a sufficient number of children can be induced by the agent to attend school, which shall not cost exceeding twenty-five hundred dollars.

The United States agrees further to cause to be erected on said reservation, near the other buildings herein authorized, a good steam circular saw-mill, with a grist-mill and shingle-machine attached, the same to cost not exceeding eight thousand dollars.

ARTICLE 4. The Indians herein named agree, when the agency-house and other buildings shall be constructed on the reservation named, they will make said reservation their permanent home, and they will make no permanent settlement elsewhere, but they shall have the right to hunt on the unoccupied lands of the United States so long as game may be found thereon, and as long as peace subsists among the whites and Indians on the borders of the hunting districts. *Reservation to be the permanent home of the Indians.*

ARTICLE 5. The United States agrees that the agent for said Indians shall in the future make his home at the agency-building; that he shall reside among them, and keep an office open at all times for the purpose of prompt and diligent inquiry into such matters of complaint, by and against the Indians, as may be presented for investigation under the provisions of their treaty stipulations, as also for the faithful discharge of other duties enjoined on him by law. In all cases of depredation on person or property, he shall cause the evidence to be taken in writing and forwarded, together with his finding, to the Commissioner of Indian Affairs, whose decision shall be binding on the parties to this treaty. *Agent to make his home and reside where.* *His duties.*

ARTICLE 6. If any individual belonging to said tribes of Indians, or legally incorporated with them, being the head of a family, shall desire to commence farming, he shall have the privilege to select, in the presence and with the assistance of the agent then in charge, a tract of land within said reservation, not exceeding three hundred and twenty acres in extent, which tract, when so selected, certified, and recorded in the "land book," as herein directed, shall cease to be held in common, but the same may be occupied and held in the exclusive possession of the person selecting it, and of his family, so long as he or they may continue to cultivate it. *Heads of families desiring to commence farming may select lands, etc.* *Effect of such selection.*

Any person over eighteen years of age, not being the head of a family, may in like manner select and cause to be certified to him or her, for purposes of cultivation, a quantity of land not exceeding eighty acres in extent, and thereupon be entitled to the exclusive possession of the same as above directed. *Persons not heads of families.*

For each tract of land so selected a certificate, containing a description thereof and the name of the person selecting it, with a certificate endorsed thereon that the same has been recorded, shall be delivered to the party entitled to it by the agent, after the same shall have been recorded by him in a book to be kept in his office, subject to inspection, which said book shall be known as the "Crow land book." *Certificate of selection to be delivered, etc., to be recorded.*

The President may at any time order a survey of the reservation, and, when so surveyed, Congress shall provide for protecting the rights of settlers in their improvements, and may fix the character of the title held by each. The United States may pass such laws on the subject of alienation and descent of property as between Indians, and on all subjects connected with the government of the Indians on said reservations and the internal police thereof, as may be thought proper. *Survey.* *Alienation and descent of property.*

Children between
6 and 16 to attend
school.

ARTICLE 7. In order to insure the civilization of the tribe entering into this treaty, the necessity of education is admitted, especially by such of them as are, or may be, settled on said agricultural reservation; and they therefore pledge themselves to compel their children, male and female, between the ages of six and sixteen years, to attend school; and it is hereby made the duty of the agent for said Indians to see that this stipulation is strictly complied with; and the United States agrees that for every thirty children, between said ages, who can be induced or compelled to attend school, a house shall be provided, and a teacher, competent to teach the elementary branches of an English education, shall be furnished, who will reside among said Indians, and faithfully discharge his or her duties as a teacher. The provisions of this article to continue for twenty years.

Duty of agent.

Schoolhouses and teachers.

ARTICLE 8. When the head of a family or lodge shall have selected lands and received his certificate as above directed, and the agent shall be satisfied that he intends in good faith to commence cultivating the soil for a living, he shall be entitled to receive seed and agricultural implements for the first year in value one hundred dollars, and for each succeeding year he shall continue to farm, for a period of three years more, he shall be entitled to receive seed and implements as aforesaid in value twenty-five dollars per annum.

Seeds and agricultural implements.

And it is further stipulated that such persons as commence farming shall receive instructions from the farmer herein provided for, and whenever more than one hundred persons shall enter upon the cultivation of the soil, a second blacksmith shall be provided, with such iron, steel, and other material as may be required.

Instruction in farming.

ARTICLE 9. In lieu of all sums of money or other annuities provided to be paid to the Indians herein named, under any and all treaties heretofore made with them, the United States agrees to deliver at the agency house, on the reservation herein provided for, on the first day of September of each year for thirty years, the following articles, to wit:

Delivery of articles in lieu of money and annuities.

For each male person, over fourteen years of age, a suit of good substantial woolen clothing, consisting of coat, hat, pantaloons, flannel shirt, and a pair of woolen socks.

Clothing.

For each female, over twelve years of age, a flannel skirt, or the goods necessary to make it, a pair of woolen hose, twelve yards of calico, and twelve yards of cotton domestics.

For the boys and girls under the ages named, such flannel and cotton goods as may be needed to make each a suit as aforesaid, together with a pair of woollen hose for each.

And in order that the Commissioner of Indian Affairs may be able to estimate properly for the articles herein named, it shall be the duty of the agent, each year, to forward to him a full and exact census of the Indians, on which the estimate from year to year can be based.

Census.

And, in addition to the clothing herein named, the sum of ten dollars shall be annually appropriated for each Indian roaming, and twenty dollars for each Indian engaged in agriculture, for a period of ten years, to be used by the Secretary of the Interior in the purchase of such articles as, from time to time, the condition and necessities of the Indians may indicate to be proper. And if, at any time within the ten years, it shall appear that the amount of money needed for clothing, under this article, can be appropriated to better uses for the tribe herein named, Congress may, by law, change the appropriation to other purposes; but in no event shall the amount of this appropriation be withdrawn or discontinued for the period named. And the President shall annually detail an officer of the Army to be present and attest the delivery of all the goods herein named to the Indians, and he shall inspect and report on the quantity and quality of the goods and the manner of their delivery; and it is expressly stipulated that

Annual appropriation in money for ten years.

May be changed.

Army officer to attend delivery of goods.

Subsistence.

each Indian over the age of four years, who shall have removed to and settled permanently upon said reservation, and complied with the stipulations of this treaty, shall be entitled to receive from the United States, for the period of four years after he shall have settled upon said reservation, one pound of meat and one pound of flour per day, provided the Indians cannot furnish their own subsistence at an earlier date. And it is further stipulated that the United States will furnish and deliver to each lodge of Indians, or family of persons legally incorporated with them, who shall remove to the reservation herein described, and commence farming, one good American cow and one good, well-broken pair of American oxen, within sixty days after such lodge or family shall have so settled upon said reservation. *Cow and oxen to each family.*

ARTICLE 10. The United States hereby agrees to furnish annually *Physician and teachers, etc.* to the Indians the physician, teachers, carpenter, miller, engineer, farmer, and blacksmiths as herein contemplated, and that such appropriations shall be made from time to time, on the estimates of the Secretary of the Interior, as will be sufficient to employ such persons.

ARTICLE 11. No treaty for the cession of any portion of the reser- *Cession of reservation not to be valid, unless, etc.* vation herein described, which may be held in common, shall be of any force or validity as against the said Indians unless executed and signed by, at least, a majority of all the adult male Indians occupying or interested in the same, and no cession by the tribe shall be understood or construed in such a manner as to deprive, without his consent, any individual member of the tribe of his right to any tract of land selected by him as provided in Article 6 of this treaty.

ARTICLE 12. It is agreed that the sum of five hundred dollars *Annual presents for most valuable crops* annually, for three years from the date when they commence to cultivate a farm, shall be expended in presents to the ten persons of said tribe who, in the judgment of the agent, may grow the most valuable crops for the respective year.

W. T. Sherman,
Lieutenant-General.
Wm. S. Harney,
Brevet Major-General and Peace Commissioner.
Alfred H. Terry,
Brevet Major-General.
C. C. Augur,
Brevet Major-General.
John B. Sanborn.
S. F. Tappan.

Ashton S. H. White, Secretary.

Che-ra-pee-ish-ka-te, Pretty Bull, his x mark.	[SEAL.]
Chat-sta-he, Wolf Bow, his x mark.	[SEAL.]
Ah-be-che-se, Mountain Tail, his x mark.	[SEAL.]
Kam-ne-but-sa, Black Foot, his x mark.	[SEAL.]
De-sal-ze-cho-se, White Horse, his x mark.	[SEAL.]
Chin-ka-she-arache, Poor Elk, his x mark.	[SEAL.]
E-sa-woor, Shot in the Jaw, his x mark.	[SEAL.]
E-sha-chose, White Forehead, his x mark.	[SEAL.]
—— Roo-ka, Pounded Meat, his x mark.	[SEAL.]
De-ka-ke-up-se, Bird in the Neck, his x mark.	[SEAL.]
Me-na-che, The Swan, his x mark.	[SEAL.]

Attest:
George B. Willis, phonographer.
John D. Howland.
Alex. Gardner.
David Knox.
Chas. Freeman.
Jas. C. O'Connor.

TREATY WITH THE NORTHERN CHEYENNE AND NORTHERN ARAPAHO, 1868.

May 10, 1868,

15 Stats., 655.
Ratified July 25, 1868.
Proclaimed Aug. 25, 1868.

Articles of a treaty made and concluded at Fort Laramie, Dakota Territory, on the tenth day of May, in the year of our Lord one thousand eight hundred and sixty-eight, by and between the undersigned commissioners on the part of the United States, and the undersigned chiefs and head-men of and representing the Northern Cheyenne and Northern Arapahoe Indians, they being duly authorized to act in the premises.

Peace and friendship.

Offenders among the whites to be arrested and punished.

ARTICLE 1. From this day forward peace between the parties to this treaty shall forever continue. The Government of the United States desires peace, and its honor is hereby pledged to keep it. The Indians desire peace, and they hereby pledge their honor to maintain it. If bad men among the whites, or among other people subject to the authority of the United States, shall commit any wrong upon the person or property of the Indians, the United States will, upon proof made to the agent and forwarded to the Commissioner of Indian Affairs at Washington City, proceed at once to cause the offender to be arrested and punished according to the laws of the United States, and also reimburse the injured person for the loss sustained.

Among the Indians, to be given up to the United States, etc.

If bad men among the Indians shall commit a wrong or depredation upon the person or property of any one, white, black, or Indian, subject to the authority of the United States and at peace therewith, the Indians herein named solemnly agree that they will, on proof made to their agent and notice by him, deliver up the wrong-doer to the United States, to be tried and punished according to its laws; and in case they wilfully refuse so to do, the person injured shall be reimbursed for his loss from the annuities or other moneys due or to become due to them under this or other treaties made with the United States.

Rules for ascertaining damages.

And the President, on advising with the Commissioner of Indian Affairs, shall prescribe such rules and regulations for ascertaining damages under the provisions of this article as in his judgment may be proper. But no such damages shall be adjusted and paid until thoroughly examined and passed upon by the Commissioner of Indian Affairs, and no one sustaining loss while violating or because of his violating the provisions of this treaty or the laws of the United States shall be reimbursed therefor.

Reservation.

ARTICLE 2. The Indians, parties to this treaty, hereby agree to accept for their permanent home some portion of the tract of country set apart and designated as a permanent reservation for the Southern Cheyenne and Arapahoe Indians by a treaty entered into by and between them and the United States, at Medicine Lodge Creek, on the — day of October, eighteen hundred and sixty-seven, or some portion of the country and reservation set apart and designated as a permanent home for the Brulé and other bands of Sioux Indians, by a treaty entered into by and between said Indians and the United States, at Fort Laramie, D. T., on the twenty-ninth day of April, eighteen

Territory outside surrendered.

hundred and sixty-eight. And the Northern Cheyenne and Arapahoe Indians do hereby relinquish, release, and surrender to the United States, all right, claim, and interest in and to all territory outside the two reservations above mentioned, except the right to roam and hunt while game shall be found in sufficient quantities to justify the chase.

To belong to what agency.

And they do solemnly agree that they will not build any permanent homes outside of said reservations, and that within one year from this date they will attach themselves permanently either to the agency provided for near the mouth of Medicine Lodge Creek, or to the agency about to be established on the Missouri River, near Fort Randall, or to the Crow agency near Otter Creek, on the Yellowstone River, provided for by treaty of the seventh day of May, eighteen hundred and sixty-eight, entered into by and between the United States and said Crow Indians, at Fort Laramie, D. T.; and it is hereby expressly understood that one portion of said Indians may attach themselves to one of the afore-mentioned reservations, and another portion to another of said reservations, as each part or portion of said Indians may elect.

Selection of reservation.

ARTICLE 3. If any individual belonging to said tribes of Indians, or legally incorporated with them, being the head of a family, shall desire to commence farming, he shall have the privilege to select, in the presence and with the assistance of the agent then in charge, a tract of land within said reservations not exceeding three hundred and twenty acres in extent, which tract, when so selected, certified, and recorded in the "Land Book" as herein directed, shall cease to be held in common, but the same may be occupied and held in the exclusive possession of the person selecting it, and of his family, so long as he or they may continue to cultivate it.

Heads of families desiring to commence farming may select lands, etc.

Effect of such selection.

Any person over eighteen years of age, not being the head of a family, may in like manner select and cause to be certified to him or her, for purposes of cultivation, a quantity of land not exceeding eighty acres in extent, and thereupon be entitled to the exclusive possession of the same as above directed.

Persons not heads of families.

For each tract of land so selected a certificate containing a description thereof and the name of the person selecting it, with a certificate endorsed thereon that the same has been recorded, shall be delivered to the party entitled to it by the agent after the same shall have been recorded by him in a book to be kept in his office, subject to inspection, which said book shall be known as the "Northern Cheyenne and Arapahoe Land Book."

Certificates of selection to be delivered, etc.

To be recorded.

The President may, at any time, order a survey of the reservation; and when so surveyed, Congress shall provide for protecting the rights of settlers in their improvements, and may fix the character of the title held by each.

Survey

The United States may pass such laws on the subject of alienation and descent of property as between Indians and on all subjects connected with the government of the Indians on said reservations, and the internal police thereof, as may be thought proper.

Alienation and descent of property.

ARTICLE 4. In order to insure the civilization of the tribe entering into this treaty, the necessity of education is admitted, especially by such of them as are or may be settled on said agricultural reservation, and they therefore pledge themselves to compel their children, male and female, between the ages of six and sixteen years, to attend school; and it is hereby made the duty of the agent for said Indians to see that this stipulation is strictly complied with; and the United States agrees that for every thirty children, between said ages, who can be induced or compelled to attend school, a house shall be provided, and a teacher, competent to teach the elementary branches of an English education, shall be furnished, who will reside among said Indians, and faithfully discharge his or her duties as a teacher. The provisions of this article to continue for twenty years.

Children between 6 and 16 to attend school.

Duty of agent.
Schoolhouses and teachers.

ARTICLE 5. When the head of a family or lodge shall have selected lands, and received his certificate as above directed, and the agent shall be satisfied that he intends in good faith to commence cultivating the soil for a living, he shall be entitled to receive seeds and agricultural implements for the first year in value one hundred dollars, and for each succeeding year he shall continue to farm for a period of three years more he shall be entitled to receive seeds and implements as aforesaid in value twenty-five dollars per annum.

Seeds and agricultural implements.

Instructions in farming.

And it is further stipulated that such persons as commence farming shall receive instructions from the farmer herein provided for, and whenever more than one hundred persons shall enter upon the cultivation of the soil a second blacksmith shall be provided, with such iron, steel, and other material as may be needed.

Delivery of articles in lieu of money and annuities.

ARTICLE 6. In lieu of all sums of money or other annuities provided to be paid to the Indians herein named, under any and all treaties heretofore made with them, the United States agrees to deliver at the agency-house, on the reservations herein provided for, on the first day of September of each year, for thirty years, the following articles, to wit:

Clothing.

For each male person over fourteen years of age, a suit of good substantial woolen clothing, consisting of coat, hat, pantaloons, flannel shirt, and a pair of woolen socks.

For each female over twelve years of age, a flannel skirt, or the goods necessary to make it, a pair of woolen hose, twelve yards of calico, and twelve yards of cotton domestics.

For the boys and girls under the ages named, such flannel and cotton goods as may be needed to make each a suit, as aforesaid, together with a pair of woolen hose for each.

Census.

And in order that the Commissioner of Indian Affairs may be able to estimate properly for the articles herein named, it shall be the duty of the agent each year to forward to him a full and exact census of the Indians, on which the estimates from year to year can be based.

Annual appropriation in money for ten years.

And, in addition to the clothing herein named, the sum of ten dollars shall be annually appropriated for each Indian roaming, and twenty dollars for each Indian engaged in agriculture, for a period of ten years, to be used by the Secretary of the Interior in the purchase of such articles as from time to time the condition and necessities of the Indians may indicate to be proper.

May be changed.

And if, at any time within the ten years, it shall appear that the amount of money needed for clothing under this article can be appropriated to better uses for the tribes herein named, Congress may by law change the appropriation to other purposes; but in no event shall the amount of this appropriation be withdrawn or discontinued for the period named.

Army officer to attend the delivery of goods.

And the President shall annually detail an officer of the Army to be present and attest the delivery of all the goods, herein named, to the Indians, and he shall inspect and report on the quantity and quality of the goods and the manner of their delivery; and it is expressly stipulated that each Indian over the age of four years, who shall have removed to and settled permanently upon said reservation and complied with the stipulations of this treaty, shall be entitled to receive from the United States, for the period of four years after he shall have settled upon said reservation, one pound of meat and one pound of flour per day,

Subsistence.

provided that the Indians cannot furnish their own subsistence at an earlier date; and it is further stipulated that the United States will furnish and deliver to each lodge of Indians, or family of persons legally incorporated with them, who shall remove to the reservation

Cow and oxen to each family.

herein described and commence farming, one good American cow and one well-broken pair of American oxen, within sixty days after such lodge or family shall have so settled upon said reservation.

Physician, teachers, etc.

ARTICLE 7. The United States hereby agrees to furnish annually to the Indians who settle upon the reservation a physician, teachers, carpenter, miller, engineer, farmer, and blacksmiths, as herein contemplated, and that such appropriations shall be made from time to time on the estimates of the Secretary of the Interior as will be sufficient to employ such persons.

Cession of reservation not to be valid unless, etc.

ARTICLE 8. No treaty for the cession of any portion of the reservations herein described, which may be held in common, shall be of any force or validity as against the said Indians unless executed and signed by at least a majority of all the adult male Indians, occupying or interested in the same; and no cession by the tribe shall be understood or construed in such manner as to deprive, without his consent, any individual member of the tribe of his right to any tract of land selected by him, as hereinbefore provided.

ARTICLE 9. It is agreed that the sum of five hundred dollars annually for three years, from the date when they commenced to cultivate a farm, shall be expended in presents to the ten persons of said tribe who, in the judgment of the agent, may grow the most valuable crops for the respective year.

Annual presents for most valuable crops.

W. T. Sherman,
Lieutenant-General.

Wm. S. Harney,
Brevet Major-General, U. S. Army.

Alfred H. Terry,
Brevet Major-General.

C. C. Augur,
Brevet Major-General.

John B. Sanborn,
S. F. Tappan,
Commissioners.

Attest:
Ashton S. H. White, Secretary.

Wah-tah-nah, Black Bear, his x mark. [SEAL.]
Bah-ta-che, Medicine Man, his x mark. [SEAL.]
Oh-cum-ga-che, Little Wolf, his x mark. [SEAL.]
Ichs-tah-en, Short Hair, his x mark. [SEAL.]
Non-ne-se-be, Sorrel Horse, his x mark. [SEAL.]
Ka-te-u-nan, The Under Man, his x mark. [SEAL.]
Ah-che-e-wah, The Man in the Sky, his x mark. [SEAL.]

We-ah-se-vose, The Big Wolf, his x mark. [SEAL.]
Ches-ne-on-e-ah, The Beau, his x mark. [SEAL.]
Mat-ah-ne-we-tah, The Man that falls from his horse, his x mark. [SEAL.]
Oh-e-na-ku, White Crow, his x mark. [SEAL.]
A-che-kan-koo-eni, Little Shield, his x mark. [SEAL.]
Tah-me-la-pash-me, or Dull Knife, his x mark. [SEAL.]

Attest:
George B. Willis, Phonographer.   David Knox.
John D. Howland.   Chas. Freeman.
Alex. Gardner.   Jas. C. O'Connor.

TREATY WITH THE NAVAHO, 1868.

Articles of a treaty and agreement made and entered into at Fort Sumner, New Mexico, on the first day of June, one thousand eight hundred and sixty-eight, by and between the United States, represented by its commissioners, Lieutenant-General W. T. Sherman and Colonel Samuel F. Tappan, of the one part, and the Navajo Nation or tribe of Indians, represented by their chiefs and head-men, duly authorized and empowered to act for the whole people of said nation or tribe, (the names of said chiefs and head-men being hereto subscribed,) of the other part, witness:

June 1, 1868.

15 Stats., p. 667.
Ratified July 25, 1868.
Proclaimed Aug. 12, 1868.

ARTICLE 1. From this day forward all war between the parties to this agreement shall forever cease. The Government of the United States desires peace, and its honor is hereby pledged to keep it. The Indians desire peace, and they now pledge their honor to keep it.

Peace and friendship.

Offenders among the whites to be arrested and punished.

If bad men among the whites, or among other people subject to the authority of the United States, shall commit any wrong upon the person or property of the Indians, the United States will, upon proof made to the agent and forwarded to the Commissioner of Indian Affairs at Washington City, proceed at once to cause the offender to be arrested and punished according to the laws of the United States, and also to reimburse the injured persons for the loss sustained.

Among the Indians, to be given up to the United States.

If the bad men among the Indians shall commit a wrong or depredation upon the person or property of any one, white, black, or Indian, subject to the authority of the United States and at peace therewith, the Navajo tribe agree that they will, on proof made to their agent, and on notice by him, deliver up the wrongdoer to the United States, to be tried and punished according to its laws; and in case they wilfully refuse so to do, the person injured shall be reimbursed for his loss from the annuities or other moneys due or to become due to them under this treaty, or any others that may be made with the United States. And the President may prescribe such rules and regulations **Rules for ascertaining damages.** for ascertaining damages under this article as in his judgment may be proper; but no such damage shall be adjusted and paid until examined and passed upon by the Commissioner of Indian Affairs, and no one sustaining loss whilst violating, or because of his violating, the provisions of this treaty or the laws of the United States, shall be reimbursed therefor.

Reservation boundaries.

ARTICLE 2. The United States agrees that the following district of country, to wit: bounded on the north by the 37th degree of north latitude, south by an east and west line passing through the site of old Fort Defiance, in Cañon Bonito, east by the parallel of longitude which, if prolonged south, would pass through old Fort Lyon, or the Ojo-de-oso, Bear Spring, and west by a parallel of longitude about 109° 30' west of Greenwich, provided it embraces the outlet of the Cañon-de-Chilly, which cañon is to be all included in this reservation, shall be, and the same is hereby, set apart for the use and occupation of the Navajo tribe of Indians, and for such other friendly tribes or individual Indians as from time to time they may be willing, with the **Who not to reside thereon.** consent of the United States, to admit among them; and the United States agrees that no persons except those herein so authorized to do, and except such officers, soldiers, agents, and employés of the Government, or of the Indians, as may be authorized to enter upon Indian reservations in discharge of duties imposed by law, or the orders of the President, shall ever be permitted to pass over, settle upon, or reside in, the territory described in this article.

Buildings to be erected by the United States.

ARTICLE 3. The United States agrees to cause to be built, at some point within said reservation, where timber and water may be convenient, the following buildings: a warehouse, to cost not exceeding twenty-five hundred dollars; an agency building for the residence of the agent, not to cost exceeding three thousand dollars; a carpenter-shop and blacksmith-shop, not to cost exceeding one thousand dollars each; and a schoolhouse and chapel, so soon as a sufficient number of children can be induced to attend school, which shall not cost to exceed five thousand dollars.

Agent to make his home and reside where.

ARTICLE 4. The United States agrees that the agent for the Navajos shall make his home at the agency building; that he shall reside among them, and shall keep an office open at all times for the purpose of prompt and diligent inquiry into such matters of complaint by or against the Indians as may be presented for investigation, as also for the faithful discharge of other duties enjoined by law. In all cases of depredation on person or property he shall cause the evidence to be taken in writing and forwarded, together with his finding, to the Commissioner of Indian Affairs, whose decision shall be binding on the parties to this treaty.

ARTICLE 5. If any individual belonging to said tribe, or legally incorporated with it, being the head of a family, shall desire to commence farming, he shall have the privilege to select, in the presence and with the assistance of the agent then in charge, a tract of land within said reservation, not exceeding one hundred and sixty acres in extent, which tract, when so selected, certified, and recorded in the "land-book" as herein described, shall cease to be held in common, but the same may be occupied and held in the exclusive possession of the person selecting it, and of his family, so long as he or they may continue to cultivate it. *Heads of family desiring to commence farming may select lands, etc.* *Effect of such selection.*

Any person over eighteen years of age, not being the head of a family, may in like manner select, and cause to be certified to him or her for purposes of cultivation, a quantity of land, not exceeding eighty acres in extent, and thereupon be entitled to the exclusive possession of the same as above directed. *Persons not heads of families.*

For each tract of land so selected a certificate containing a description thereof, and the name of the person selecting it, with a certificate endorsed thereon, that the same has been recorded, shall be delivered to the party entitled to it by the agent, after the same shall have been recorded by him in a book to be kept in his office, subject to inspection, which said book shall be known as the "Navajo land-book." *Certificates of selection to be delivered, etc.* *To be recorded.*

The President may at any time order a survey of the reservation, and when so surveyed, Congress shall provide for protecting the rights of said settlers in their improvements, and may fix the character of the title held by each. *Survey.*

The United States may pass such laws on the subject of alienation and descent of property between the Indians and their descendants as may be thought proper. *Alienation and descent of property.*

ARTICLE 6. In order to insure the civilization of the Indians entering into this treaty, the necessity of education is admitted, especially of such of them as may be settled on said agricultural parts of this reservation, and they therefore pledge themselves to compel their children, male and female, between the ages of six and sixteen years, to attend school; and it is hereby made the duty of the agent for said Indians to see that this stipulation is strictly complied with; and the United States agrees that, for every thirty children between said ages who can be induced or compelled to attend school, a house shall be provided, and a teacher competent to teach the elementary branches of an English education shall be furnished, who will reside among said Indians, and faithfully discharge his or her duties as a teacher. *Children between 6 and 16 to attend school.* *Duty of agent,* *Schoolhouses and teachers.*

The provisions of this article to continue for not less than ten years.

ARTICLE 7. When the head of a family shall have selected lands and received his certificate as above directed, and the agent shall be satisfied that he intends in good faith to commence cultivating the soil for a living, he shall be entitled to receive seeds and agricultural implements for the first year, not exceeding in value one hundred dollars, and for each succeeding year he shall continue to farm, for a period of two years, he shall be entitled to receive seeds and implements to the value of twenty-five dollars. *Seeds and agricultural implements.*

ARTICLE 8. In lieu of all sums of money or other annuities provided to be paid to the Indians herein named under any treaty or treaties heretofore made, the United States agrees to deliver at the agency-house on the reservation herein named, on the first day of September of each year for ten years, the following articles, to wit: *Delivery of articles in lieu of money and annuities.*

Such articles of clothing, goods, or raw materials in lieu thereof, as the agent may make his estimate for, not exceeding in value five dollars per Indian—each Indian being encouraged to manufacture their own clothing, blankets, &c.; to be furnished with no article which they can manufacture themselves. And, in order that the Commissioner of Indian Affairs may be able to estimate properly for the articles herein *Clothing, etc.* *Indians to be furnished with no articles they can make.*

Census.

named, it shall be the duty of the agent each year to forward to him a full and exact census of the Indians, on which the estimate from year to year can be based.

Annual appropriation in money for ten years.

And in addition to the articles herein named, the sum of ten dollars for each person entitled to the beneficial effects of this treaty shall be annually appropriated for a period of ten years, for each person who engages in farming or mechanical pursuits, to be used by the Commissioner of Indian Affairs in the purchase of such articles as from time to time the condition and necessities of the Indians may indicate

May be changed.

to be proper; and if within the ten years at any time it shall appear that the amount of money needed for clothing, under the article, can be appropriated to better uses for the Indians named herein, the Commissioner of Indian Affairs may change the appropriation to other purposes, but in no event shall the amount of this appropriation be withdrawn or discontinued for the period named, provided they

Army officer to attend delivery of goods, etc.

remain at peace. And the President shall annually detail an officer of the Army to be present and attest the delivery of all the goods herein named to the Indians, and he shall inspect and report on the quantity and quality of the goods and the manner of their delivery.

Stipulations by the Indians as to outside territory.

ARTICLE 9. In consideration of the advantages and benefits conferred by this treaty, and the many pledges of friendship by the United States, the tribes who are parties to this agreement hereby stipulate that they will relinquish all right to occupy any territory outside their reservation, as herein defined, but retain the right to hunt on any unoccupied lands contiguous to their reservation, so long as the large game may range thereon in such numbers as to justify the chase; and they, the said Indians, further expressly agree:

Railroads.

1st. That they will make no opposition to the construction of railroads now being built or hereafter to be built across the continent.

2d. That they will not interfere with the peaceful construction of any railroad not passing over their reservation as herein defined.

Residents, travelers, wagon trains.

3d. That they will not attack any persons at home or travelling, nor molest or disturb any wagon-trains, coaches, mules, or cattle belonging to the people of the United States, or to persons friendly therewith.

Women and children.

4th. That they will never capture or carry off from the settlements women or children.

Scalping.

5th. They will never kill or scalp white men, nor attempt to do them harm.

Roads or stations.

6th. They will not in future oppose the construction of railroads, wagon-roads, mail stations, or other works of utility or necessity which

Damages.

may be ordered or permitted by the laws of the United States; but should such roads or other works be constructed on the lands of their reservation, the Government will pay the tribe whatever amount of damage may be assessed by three disinterested commissioners to be appointed by the President for that purpose, one of said commissioners to be a chief or head-man of the tribe.

Military posts and roads.

7th. They will make no opposition to the military posts or roads now established, or that may be established, not in violation of treaties heretofore made or hereafter to be made with any of the Indian tribes.

Cession of reservation not to be valid unless, etc.

ARTICLE 10. No future treaty for the cession of any portion or part of the reservation herein described, which may be held in common, shall be of any validity or force against said Indians unless agreed to and executed by at least three-fourths of all the adult male Indians occupying or interested in the same; and no cession by the tribe shall be understood or construed in such manner as to deprive, without his consent, any individual member of the tribe of his rights to any tract of land selected by him as provided in article [5] of this treaty.

Indians to go to reservation when required.

ARTICLE 11. The Navajos also hereby agree that at any time after the signing of these presents they will proceed in such manner as may be required of them by the agent, or by the officer charged with their removal, to the reservation herein provided for, the United States paying for their subsistence en route, and providing a reasonable amount of transportation for the sick and feeble.

ARTICLE 12. It is further agreed by and between the parties to this agreement that the sum of one hundred and fifty thousand dollars appropriated or to be appropriated shall be disbursed as follows, subject to any condition provided in the law, to wit:

Appropriations, how to be disbursed.

1st. The actual cost of the removal of the tribe from the Bosque Redondo reservation to the reservation, say fifty thousand dollars.

Removal.

2d. The purchase of fifteen thousand sheep and goats, at a cost not to exceed thirty thousand dollars.

Sheep and goats.

3d. The purchase of five hundred beef cattle and a million pounds of corn, to be collected and held at the military post nearest the reservation, subject to the orders of the agent, for the relief of the needy during the coming winter.

Cattle and corn.

4th. The balance, if any, of the appropriation to be invested for the maintenance of the Indians pending their removal, in such manner as the agent who is with them may determine.

Remainder.

5th. The removal of this tribe to be made under the supreme control and direction of the military commander of the Territory of New Mexico, and when completed, the management of the tribe to revert to the proper agent.

Removal, how made.

ARTICLE 13. The tribe herein named, by their representatives, parties to this treaty, agree to make the reservation herein described their permanent home, and they will not as a tribe make any permanent settlement elsewhere, reserving the right to hunt on the lands adjoining the said reservation formerly called theirs, subject to the modifications named in this treaty and the orders of the commander of the department in which said reservation may be for the time being; and it is further agreed and understood by the parties to this treaty, that if any Navajo Indian or Indians shall leave the reservation herein described to settle elsewhere, he or they shall forfeit all the rights, privileges, and annuities conferred by the terms of this treaty; and it is further agreed by the parties to this treaty, that they will do all they can to induce Indians now away from reservations set apart for the exclusive use and occupation of the Indians, leading a nomadic life, or engaged in war against the people of the United States, to abandon such a life and settle permanently in one of the territorial reservations set apart for the exclusive use and occupation of the Indians.

Reservation to be permanent home of Indians.

Penalty for leaving reservation.

In testimony of all which the said parties have hereunto, on this the first day of June, one thousand eight hundred and sixty-eight, at Fort Sumner, in the Territory of New Mexico, set their hands and seals.

W. T. Sherman,
Lieutenant-General, Indian Peace Commissioner.
S. F. Tappan,
Indian Peace Commissioner.

Barboncito, chief, his x mark.
Armijo, his x mark.
Delgado.
Manuelito, his x mark.
Largo, his x mark.
Herrero, his x mark.
Chiqueto, his x mark.
Muerto de Hombre, his x mark.
Hombro, his x mark.
Narbono, his x mark.
Narbono Segundo, his x mark.
Gañado Mucho, his x mark.
 Council:
Riquo, his x mark.
Juan Martin, his x mark.

Serginto, his x mark.
Grande, his x mark.
Inoetenito, his x mark.
Muchachos Mucho, his x mark.
Chiqueto Segundo, his x mark.
Cabello Amarillo, his x mark.
Francisco, his x mark.
Torivio, his x mark.
Desdendado, his x mark.
Juan, his x mark.
Guero, his x mark.
Gugadore, his x mark.
Cabason, his x mark.
Barbon Segundo, his x mark.
Cabares Colorados, his x mark.

Attest:

Geo. W. G. Getty, colonel Thirty-seventh Infantry, brevet major-general U. S. Army.

B. S. Roberts, brevet brigadier-general U. S. Army, lieutenant-colonel Third Cavalry.

J. Cooper McKee, brevet lieutenant-colonel, surgeon U. S. Army.

Theo. H. Dodd, United States Indian agent for Navajos.

Chas. McClure, brevet major and commissary of subsistence, U. S. Army.

James F. Weeds, brevet major and assistant surgeon, U. S. Army.

J. C. Sutherland, interpreter.

William Vaux, chaplain U. S. Army.

TREATY WITH THE EASTERN BAND SHOSHONI AND BANNOCK, 1868.

July 3, 1868.

15 Stat., 673.
Ratified Feb. 26, 1869.
Proclaimed Feb. 24, 1869.

Articles of a treaty made and concluded at Fort Bridger, Utah Territory, on the third day of July, in the year of our Lord one thousand eight hundred and sixty-eight, by and between the undersigned commissioners on the part of the United States, and the undersigned chiefs and head-men of and representing the Shoshonee (eastern band) and Bannack tribes of Indians, they being duly authorized to act in the premises:

Peace and friendship.

ARTICLE 1. From this day forward peace between the parties to this treaty shall forever continue. The Government of the United States desires peace, and its honor is hereby pledged to keep it. The Indians desire peace, and they hereby pledge their honor to maintain it.

Offenders among the whites to be arrested and punished.

If bad men among the whites, or among other people subject to the authority of the United States, shall commit any wrong upon the person or property of the Indians, the United States will, upon proof made to the agent and forwarded to the Commissioner of Indian Affairs, at Washington City, proceed at once to cause the offender to be arrested and punished according to the laws of the United States, and also re-imburse the injured person for the loss sustained.

Among the Indians to be given up to the United States, etc.

If bad men among the Indians shall commit a wrong or depredation upon the person or property of any one, white, black, or Indian, subject to the authority of the United States, and at peace therewith, the Indians herein named solemnly agree that they will, on proof made to their agent and notice by him, deliver up the wrong-doer to the United States, to be tried and punished according to the laws; and in case they wilfully refuse so to do, the person injured shall be re-imbursed for his loss from the annuities or other moneys due or to become due to them under this or other treaties made with the United States. And

Rules for ascertaining damages.

the President, on advising with the Commissioner of Indian Affairs, shall prescribe such rules and regulations for ascertaining damages under the provisions of this article as in his judgment may be proper. But no such damages shall be adjusted and paid until thoroughly examined and passed upon by the Commissioner of Indian Affairs, and no one sustaining loss while violating or because of his violating the provisions of this treaty or the laws of the United States, shall be reimbursed therefor.

Reservation.

ARTICLE 2. It is agreed that whenever the Bannacks desire a reservation to be set apart for their use, or whenever the President of the United States shall deem it advisable for them to be put upon a reservation, he shall cause a suitable one to be selected for them in their present country, which shall embrace reasonable portions of the "Port Neuf" and "Kansas Prairie" countries, and that, when this reservation is declared, the United States will secure to the Bannacks the same rights and privileges therein, and make the same and like expenditures therein for their benefit, except the agency-house and residence of agent, in proportion to their numbers, as herein provided for the Shoshonee reservation. The United States further agrees that the following district of country, to wit: Commencing at the mouth of Owl Creek and running due south to the crest of the divide between the Sweet-water and Papo Agie Rivers; thence along the crest of said divide and the summit of Wind River Mountains to the longitude of North Fork of Wind River; thence due north to mouth of said North Fork and up its channel to a point twenty miles above its mouth; thence in a straight line to head-waters of Owl Creek and along middle of channel of Owl Creek to place of beginning, shall be and the same is set apart for the absolute and undisturbed use and occupation of the Shoshonee Indians herein named, and for such other friendly tribes or individual Indians as from time to time they may be willing, with the consent of the United States, to admit amongst them; and the United States now solemnly agrees that no persons except those herein designated **Who not to reside thereon.** and authorized so to do, and except such officers, agents, and employés of the Government as may be authorized to enter upon Indian reservations in discharge of duties enjoined by law, shall ever be permitted to pass over, settle upon, or reside in the territory described in this article for the use of said Indians, and henceforth they will and do hereby relinquish all title, claims, or rights in and to any portion of the territory of the United States, except such as is embraced within the limits aforesaid.

ARTICLE 3. The United States agrees, at its own proper expense, to **Buildings to be erected by the United States.** construct at a suitable point of the Shoshonee reservation a warehouse or store-room for the use of the agent in storing goods belonging to the Indians, to cost not exceeding two thousand dollars; an agency building for the residence of the agent, to cost not exceeding three thousand; a residence for the physician, to cost not more than two thousand dollars; and five other buildings, for a carpenter, farmer, blacksmith, miller, and engineer, each to cost not exceeding two thousand dollars; also a school-house or mission building so soon as a sufficient number of children can be induced by the agent to attend school, which shall not cost exceeding twenty-five hundred dollars.

The United States agrees further to cause to be erected on said Sho- **Mills.** shonee reservation, near the other buildings herein authorized, a good steam circular-saw mill, with a grist-mill and shingle-machine attached, the same to cost not more than eight thousand dollars.

ARTICLE 4. The Indians herein named agree, when the agency house **Reservation to be permanent home of Indians.** and other buildings shall be constructed on their reservations named, they will make said reservations their permanent home, and they will make no permanent settlement elsewhere; but they shall have the right to hunt on the unoccupied lands of the United States so long as game may be found thereon, and so long as peace subsists among the whites and Indians on the borders of the hunting districts.

ARTICLE 5. The United States agrees that the agent for said Indians **Agent to make his home and reside where.** shall in the future make his home at the agency building on the Shoshonee reservation, but shall direct and supervise affairs on the Bannack reservation; and shall keep an office open at all times for the purpose of prompt and diligent inquiry into such matters of complaint by and against the Indians as may be presented for investigation under the provisions of their treaty stipulations, as also for the faithful discharge of other duties enjoined by law. In all cases of depredation on person or property he shall cause the evidence to be taken in writing and forwarded, together with his finding, to the Commissioner of Indian Affairs, whose decision shall be binding on the parties to this treaty.

ARTICLE 6. If any individual belonging to said tribes of Indians, or **Heads of families desiring to commence farming may select lands, etc.** legally incorporated with them, being the head of a family, shall desire to commence farming, he shall have the privilege to select, in the presence and with the assistance of the agent then in charge, a tract of land within the reservation of his tribe, not exceeding three hundred

and twenty acres in extent, which tract so selected, certified, and
recorded in the "land-book," as herein directed, shall cease to be held
in common, but the same may be occupied and held in the exclusive
possession of the person selecting it, and of his family, so long as he
or they may continue to cultivate it.

Any person over eighteen years of age, not being the head of a family, may in like manner select and cause to be certified to him or her,
for purposes of cultivation, a quantity of land not exceeding eighty
acres in extent, and thereupon be entitled to the exclusive possession
of the same as above described. For each tract of land so selected a
a certificate, containing a description thereof, and the name of the person selecting it, with a certificate indorsed thereon that the same has
been recorded, shall be delivered to the party entitled to it by the
agent, after the same shall have been recorded by him in a book to be
kept in his office subject to inspection, which said book shall be known
as the "Shoshone (eastern band) and Bannack land-book."

The President may at any time order a survey of these reservations,
and when so surveyed Congress shall provide for protecting the rights
of the Indian settlers in these improvements, and may fix the character of the title held by each. The United States may pass such laws
on the subject of alienation and descent of property as between Indians,
and on all subjects connected with the government of the Indians on
said reservations, and the internal police thereof, as may be thought
proper.

ARTICLE 7. In order to insure the civilization of the tribes entering
into this treaty, the necessity of education is admitted, especially of
such of them as are or may be settled on said agricultural reservations, and they therefore pledge themselves to compel their children,
male and female, between the ages of six and sixteen years, to attend
school; and it is hereby made the duty of the agent for said Indians
to see that this stipulation is strictly complied with; and the United
States agrees that for every thirty children between said ages who
can be induced or compelled to attend school, a house shall be provided and a teacher competent to teach the elementary branches of
an English education shall be furnished, who will reside among said
Indians and faithfully discharge his or her duties as a teacher. The
provisions af this article to continue for twenty years.

ARTICLE 8. When the head of a family or lodge shall have selected
lands and received his certificate as above directed, and the agent
shall be satisfied that he intends in good faith to commence cultivating
the soil for a living, he shall be entitled to receive seeds and agricultural implements for the first year, in value one hundred dollars, and
for each succeeding year he shall continue to farm, for a period of
three years more, he shall be entitled to receive seeds and implements
as aforesaid in value twenty-five dollars per annum.

And it is further stipulated that such persons as commence farming
shall receive instructions from the farmers herein provided for, and
whenever more than one hundred persons on either reservation shall
enter upon the cultivation of the soil, a second blacksmith shall be
provided, with such iron, steel, and other material as may be required.

ARTICLE 9. In lieu of all sums of money or other annuities provided
to be paid to the Indians herein named, under any and all treaties
heretofore made with them, the United States agrees to deliver at the
agency-house on the reservation herein provided for, on the first day
of September of each year, for thirty years, the following articles,
to wit:

For each male person over fourteen years of age, a suit of good
substantial woollen clothing, consisting of coat, hat, pantaloons, flannel shirt, and a pair of woollen socks; for each female over twelve
years of age, a flannel skirt, or the goods necessary to make it, a pair

of woollen hose, twelve yards of calico; and twelve yards of cotton domestics.

For the boys and girls under the ages named, such flannel and cotton goods as may be needed to make each a suit as aforesaid, together with a pair of woollen hose for each.

And in order that the Commissioner of Indian Affairs may be able to estimate properly for the articles herein named, it shall be the duty of the agent each year to forward to him a full and exact census of the Indians, on which the estimate from year to year can be based; and in addition to the clothing herein named, the sum of ten dollars shall be annually appropriated for each Indian roaming and twenty dollars for each Indian engaged in agriculture, for a period of ten years, to be used by the Secretary of the Interior in the purchase of such articles as from time to time the condition and necessities of the Indians may indicate to be proper. And if at any time within the ten years it shall appear that the amount of money needed for clothing under this article can be appropriated to better uses for the tribes herein named, Congress may by law change the appropriation to other purposes; but in no event shall the amount of this appropriation be withdrawn or discontinued for the period named. And the President shall annually detail an officer of the Army to be present and attest the delivery of all the goods herein named to the Indians, and he shall inspect and report on the quantity and quality of the goods and the manner of their delivery. *Census.* *May be changed.* *Army officer to attest delivery of goods, etc.*

ARTICLE 10. The United States hereby agrees to furnish annually to the Indians the physician, teachers, carpenter, miller, engineer, farmer, and blacksmith, as herein contemplated, and that such appropriations shall be made from time to time, on the estimates of the Secretary of the Interior, as will be sufficient to employ such persons. *Physician, teachers, carpenter, etc.*

ARTICLE 11. No treaty for the cession of any portion of the reservations herein described which may be held in common shall be of any force or validity as against the said Indians, unless executed and signed by at least a majority of all the adult male Indians occupying or interested in the same; and no cession by the tribe shall be understood or construed in such manner as to deprive without his consent, any individual member of the tribe of his right to any tract of land selected by him. as provided in Article 6 of this treaty. *Cession of reservation not to be valid unless, etc.*

ARTICLE 12. It is agreed that the sum of five hundred dollars annually, for three years from the date when they commence to cultivate a farm, shall be expended in presents to the ten persons of said tribe who, in the judgment of the agent, may grow the most valuable crops for the respective year. *Presents for most valuable crops.*

ARTICLE 13. It is further agreed that until such time as the agency-buildings are established on the Shoshonee reservation, their agent shall reside at Fort Bridger, U. T., and their annuities shall be delivered to them at the same place in June of each year.

> N. G. Taylor,   [SEAL.]
> W. T. Sherman,   [SEAL.]
>   Lieutenant-General.
> Wm. S. Harney,   [SEAL.]
> John B. Sanborn,   [SEAL.]
> S. F. Tappan,   [SEAL.]
> C. C. Augur,   [SEAL.]
> Brevet Major-General, U. S. Army, Commissioners.
> Alfred H. Terry,   [SEAL.]
> Brigadier-General and Brevet Major-General, U. S. Army.

Attest:

A. S. H. White, Secretary.

Shoshones:

Wash-a-kie,	his x mark.
Wau-ny-pitz,	his x mark.
Toop-se-po-wot,	his x mark.
Nar-kok,	his x mark.
Taboonshe-ya,	his x mark.
Bazeel,	his x mark.
Pan-to-she-ga,	his x mark.
Ninny-Bitse,	his x mark.

Bannacks:

Taggee,	his x mark.
Tay-to-ba,	his x mark.
We-rat-ze-won-a-gen,	his x mark.
Coo-sha-gan,	his x mark.
Pən-sook-a-motse,	his x mark.
A-wite-etse,	his x mark.

Witnesses:

Henry A. Morrow,
    Lieutenant-Colonel Thirty-sixth Infantry and
        Brevet Colonel U. S. Army, Commanding Fort Bridger.
Luther Manpa, United States Indian agent.
W. A. Carter.
J. Van Allen Carter, interpreter.

TREATY WITH THE NEZ PERCÉS, 1868.

Aug. 13, 1868.

15 Stats., 693.
Ratified Feb. 16, 1869.
Proclaimed Feb. 24, 1869.

Whereas certain amendments are desired by the Nez Percé tribe of Indians to their treaty concluded at the council ground in the valley of the Lapwai, in the Territory of Washington, on the ninth day of June, in the year of our Lord one thousand eight hundred and sixty-three; and whereas the United States are willing to assent to said amendments; it is therefore agreed by and between Nathaniel G. Taylor, commissioner, on the part of the United States, thereunto duly authorized, and Lawyer, Timothy, and Jason, chiefs of said tribe, also being thereunto duly authorized, in manner and form following, that is to say:

Reservation.

ARTICLE 1. That all lands embraced within the limits of the tract set apart for the exclusive use and benefit of said Indians by the 2d article of said treaty of June 9th, 1863, which are susceptible of cultivation and suitable for Indian farms, which are not now occupied by the United States for military purposes, or which are not required for agency or other buildings and purposes provided for by existing treaty stipulations, shall be surveyed as provided in the 3d article of said treaty of June 9th, 1863, and as soon as the allotments shall be plowed and fenced, and as soon as schools shall be established as provided by existing treaty stipulations, such Indians now residing outside the reservation as may be decided upon by the agent of the tribe and the Indians themselves, shall be removed to and located upon allotments within the reservation: *Provided, however,* That in case there should

Allotments.

not be a sufficient quantity of suitable land within the boundaries of the reservation to provide allotments for those now there and those residing outside the boundaries of the same, then those residing outside, or as many thereof as allotments cannot be provided for, may remain upon the lands now occupied and improved by them, provided, that the land so occupied does not exceed twenty acres for each and every male person who shall have attained the age of twenty-one years or is the head of a family, and the tenure of those remaining upon lands outside the reservation shall be the same as is provided in said 3d article of said treaty of June 9th, 1863, for those receiving allotments within the reservation; and it is further agreed that those now residing outside of the boundaries of the reservation and who may continue to so reside shall be protected by the military authorities in their rights upon the allotments occupied by them, and also in the privilege of grazing their animals upon surrounding unoccupied lands.

ARTICLE 2. It is further agreed between the parties hereto that the stipulations contained in the 8th article of the treaty of June 9th, 1863, relative to timber, are hereby annulled as far as the same provides that the United States shall be permitted to use thereof in the maintaining of forts or garrisons, and that the said Indians shall have the aid of the military authorities to protect the timber upon their reservation, and that none of the same shall be cut or removed without the consent of the head-chief of the tribe, together with the consent of the agent and superintendent of Indian affairs, first being given in writing, which written consent shall state the part of the reservation upon which the timber is to be cut, and also the quantity, and the price to be paid therefor.

Timber to be protected.

ARTICLE 3. It is further hereby stipulated and agreed that the amount due said tribe for school purposes and for the support of teachers that has not been expended for that purpose since the year 1864, but has been used for other purposes, shall be ascertained and the same shall be re-imbursed to said tribe by appropriation by Congress, and shall be set apart and invested in United States bonds and shall be held in trust by the United States, the interest on the same to be paid to said tribe annually for the support of teachers.

School moneys, etc.

In testimony whereof the said Commissioner on the part of the United States and the said chiefs representing said Nez Percé tribe of Indians have hereunto set their hands and seals this 13th day of August, in the year of our Lord one thousand eight hundred and sixty-eight, at the city of Washington, D. C.

N. G. Taylor,	[L. S.]
Commissioner Indian Affairs.	
Lawyer, Head Chief Nez Percés.	[L. S.]
Timothy, his x mark, Chief.	[L. S.]
Jason, his x mark, Chief.	[L. S.]

In presence of—

Charles E. Mix.
Robert Newell, United States Agent.
W. R. Irwin.

APPENDIX.

AGREEMENT WITH THE FIVE NATIONS OF INDIANS, 1792.

George Washington, President of the United States of America,
" To all who shall see these presents, greeting:

" Whereas an article has been stipulated with the Five Nations of April 23, 1792.
Indians, by, and with the advice and consent of the Senate of the United American State Papers. Indian Affairs. Vol. 1, p. 232.
States, which article is in the words following, to wit:

" 'The President of the United States, by Henry Knox, Secretary
for the Department of War, stipulates, in behalf of the United States,
the following article, with the Five Nations of Indians, so called, being
the Senecas, Oneidas, and the Stockbridge Indians, incorporated with
them the Tuscaroras, Cayugas, and Onondagas, to wit: the United
States, in order to promote the happiness of the Five Nations of Indians,
will cause to be expended, annually, the amount of one thousand five
hundred dollars, in purchasing for them clothing, domestic animals,
and implements of husbandry, and for encouraging useful artificers to
reside in their villages.

" ' In behalf of the United States: [L. S.]   H. Knox,
                           Secretary for the Department of War.

" ' Done in the presence of Tobias Lear,
      Nathan Jones.

" Now, know ye, That I, having seen and considered the said article,
do accept, ratify, and confirm the same.

" In testimony whereof, I have caused the seal of the United States
to be hereunto affixed, and signed the same with my hand.

" Given at the City of Philadelphia, the twenty-third day of April,
in the year of our Lord one thousand seven hundred and ninety-two,
and in the sixteenth year of the sovereignty and independence of the
United States.

                                        GEO. WASHINGTON.

  " By the President:
      THOMAS JEFFERSON."

AGREEMENT WITH THE SENECA, 1797.

Contract entered into, under the sanction of the United States of Sept. 15, 1797.
America, between Robert Morris and the Seneca nation of Indians. 7 Stat., 601.

This indenture, made the fifteenth day of September, in the year of our Contract between Robert Morris and the Senecas.
  Lord one thousand seven hundred and ninety-seven, between the
  sachems, chiefs, and warriors of the Seneca nation of Indians, of
  the first part, and Robert Morris, of the city of Philadelphia, Esquire,
  of the second part:
Whereas the Commonwealth of Massachusetts have granted, bargained, and sold unto the said Robert Morris, his heirs and assigns

forever, the pre-emptive right, and all other the right, title and interest which the said Commonwealth had to all the tract of land hereinafter particularly mentioned, being part of a tract of land lying within the State of New York, the right of pre-emption of the soil whereof, from the native Indians, was ceded and granted by the said State of New York, to the said Commonwealth: and whereas, at a treaty held under the authority of the United States, with the said Seneca nation of Indians, at Genesee, in the county of Ontario, and State of New York, on the day of the date of these presents, and on sundry days immediately prior thereto, by the Honorable Jeremiah Wadsworth, Esquire, a commissioner appointed by the President of the United States, to hold the same in pursuance of the constitution, and of the **Act of 1802, c. 13, § 12.** act of the Congress of the United States, in such case made and provided, it was agreed, in the presence and with the approbation of the said commissioner, by the sachems, chiefs and warriors of the said nations of Indians, for themselves and in behalf of their nation, to sell to the said Robert Morris, and to his heirs and assigns forever, all their right to all that tract of land above recited, and hereinafter particularly specified, for the sum of one hundred thousand dollars, to be by the said **Robert Morris to vest $100,000 in bank stock for use of the Senecas, etc.** Robert Morris vested in the stock of the bank of the United States, and held in the name of the President of the United States, for the use and behoof of the said nation of Indians, the said agreement and sale being also made in the presence, and with the approbation of the honorable William Shepard, Esquire, the superintendent appointed for such purpose, in pursuance of a resolve of the General Court of the Commonwealth of Massachusetts, passed the eleventh day of March, in the year of our Lord one thousand seven hundred and ninety-one; now this indenture witnesseth, that the said parties, of the first part, for and in consideration of the premises above recited, and for divers other good and valuable considerations them thereunto moving, have granted, bargained, sold, aliened, released, enfeoffed, and confirmed; and by these presents do grant, bargain, sell, alien, release, enfeoff, and confirm, unto the said party of the second part, his heirs and assigns forever, all that certain tract of land, except as is hereinafter excepted, lying within the county of Ontario and State of New York, being part of a tract of land, the right of pre-emption whereof was ceded by the state of New York to the Commonwealth of Massachusetts, by deed of cession executed at Hartford, on the sixteenth day of December, in the year of our Lord one thousand seven hundred and eighty-six, being all such part thereof as is not included in the Indian purchase made by Oliver **Boundary of the lands sold to Robert Morris.** Phelps and Nathaniel Gorham, and bounded as follows, to wit: easterly, by the land confirmed to Oliver Phelps and Nathaniel Gorham by the legislature of the Commonwealth of Massachusetts, by and act passed the twenty-first day of November, in the year of our Lord one thousand seven hundred and eighty-eight; southerly, by the north boundary line of the State of Pennsylvania; westerly, partly by a tract of land, part of the land ceded by the State of Massachusetts to the United States, and by them sold to Pennsylvania, being a righ' angled triangle, whose hypothenuse is in or along the shore of Lake Erie; partly by Lake Erie, from the northern point of that triangle to the Southern bounds of a **Reservations to the Senecas.** tract of land a mile in width, lying on and along the east side of the strait of Niagara, and partly by the said tract to lake Ontario; and on the north, by the boundary line between the United States and the King of Great Britain; excepting, nevertheless, and reserving always out of this grant and conveyance, all such pieces or parcels of the aforesaid tract, and such privileges thereunto belonging as are next hereinafter mentioned, which said pieces or parcels of land so excepted are, by the parties to these presents, clearly and fully understood to remain the property of the said parties of the first part, in as full and ample manner as if these presents had not been executed; that is to say, excepting and reserving to them, the said parties of the first part, and their nation, one piece or parcel of the aforesaid tract, at Canawaugas, of two square miles, to be laid out in such manner as to include the village extending in breadth one mile along the river; one other piece or parcel at Big Tree, of two square miles, to be laid out in such manner as to include the village, extending in breadth along the river one mile; one other piece or parcel of two square miles at Little Beard's town, extending one mile along the river, to be laid off in such manner as to include the village; one other tract of two square miles at Squawky Hill, to be laid off as follows, to wit: one square mile to be laid off along the river, in such manner as to include the village, the other directly west thereof and contiguo's thereto; one other piece or parcel at Gardeau, beginning at the mouth of Steep Hill creek, thence due east until it strikes the old path, thence south until a due west line will intersect with certain steep rocks on the west side of Genesee river, then extending due west, due north and due east, until it strikes the first mentiones bound, enclosing as much land on the west side as on the east side of the river.   One other piece or parcel at Kaounadeau extending in length eight miles along the river and two miles in breadth.   One other piece or parcel at Cataraugos, beginning at the mouth of the Eighteen mile or Koghquaugu creek, thence a line or line to be drawn parallel to lake Erie, at the distance of one mile from there, to the mouth of Cataraugos creek, thence a line or lines extending 12 miles up the north side of said creek at the distance of one mile therefrom, thence a direct line to the said creek, thence down the said creek to lake Erie, thence along the lake to the first mentioned creek, and thence to the place of beginning. Also one other piece at Cataraugos, beginning at the shore of lake Erie, on the south side of Cataraugos creek, at the distance of one mile from the mouth thereof, thence running one mile from the lake, thence on a line parallel thereto, to a point within one mile from the Connondauweyea creek, thence up the said creek one mile, on a line parallel thereto, thence on a direct line to the said creek, thence down the same to lake Erie, thence along the lake to the place of beginning.   Also one other piece or parcel of forty-two square miles, at or near the Allegenny river.   Also, two hundred square miles, to be laid off partly at the Buffalo and partly at the Tonnawanta creeks.   Also, excepting and reserving to them, the said parties of the first part and their heirs, the privilege of fishing and hunting on the said tract of land hereby intended to be conveyed.   And it is hereby understood by and between the parties to these presents, that all such pieces or parcels of land as are hereby reserved and are not particularly described as to the manner in which the same are to be laid off, shall be laid off in such manner as shall be determined by the sachems, chiefs, residing at or near the respective villages where such reservations are made, a particular note whereof to be indorsed on the back of this deed, and recorded therewith, together with all and singular the rights, privileges, hereditaments, and appurtenances thereunto belonging, or in anywise appertaining.   And all the estate, right, title, and interest, whatsoever, of them the said parties of the first part and their nation, of, in, and to the said tract of land above described, except as is above excepted, to gave and to hold all and singular the said granted premises, with the appurtenances to the said party of the second part, his heirs and assigns, to his and their proper use, benefit and behoof forever.

In witness whereof, the parties to these presents have hereunto interchangeably set their hands and seals, the day and year first above written.

Robert Morris, by his attorney, Thomas Morris, [L. S.]

Koyengquahtah, alias Young King, his x mark, [L. S.]

Soonookshewan, his x mark, [L. S.]

Konutaico, alias Handsome Lake, his x mark, [L. S.]

Sattakanguyase, alias Two Skies of a length, his x mark, [L. S.]

Onayawos, or Farmer's Brother, his x mark, [L. S.]

Soogooyawautau, alias Red Jacket, his x mark, [L. S.]

Gishkaka, alias Little Billy, his x mark, [L. S.]

Kaoundoowana, alias Pollard, his x mark, [L. S.]

Ouneashataikau, or Tall Chief, by his agent, Stevenson, his x mark, [L. S.]

Teahdowainggua, alias Thos. Jemison, his x mark, [L. S.]

Onnonggaiheko, alias Infant, his x mark, [L. S.]

Tekonnondee, his x mark, [L. S.]

Oneghtaugooau, his x mark, [L. S.]

Connawaudeau, his x mark, [L. S.]

Taosstaiefi, his x mark, [L. S.]

Koeentwahka, or Corn Planter, his x mark, [L. S.]

Oosaukaunendauki, alias to Destroy a Town, his x mark, [L. S.]

Sooeoowa, alias Parrot Nose, his x mark, [L. S.]

Toonahookahwa, his x mark, [L. S.]

Howwennounew, his x mark, [L. S.]

Kounahkaetoue, his x mark, [L. S.]

Taouyaukauna, his x mark, [L. S.]

Woudougoohkta, his x mark, [L. S.]

Sonauhquaukau, his x mark, [L. S.]

Twaunauiyana, his x mark, [L. S.]

Takaunoudea, his x mark, [L. S.]

Shequinedaughque, or Little Beard, his x mark, [L. S.]

Jowaa, his x mark, [L. S.]

Saunajee, his x mark, [L. S.]

Tauoiyuquatakausea, his x mark, [L. S.]

Taoundaudish, his x mark, [L. S.]

Tooauquinda, his x mark, [L. S.]

Ahtaou, his x mark, [L. S.]

Taukooshoondakoo, his x mark, [L. S.]

Kauneskanggo, his x mark, [L. S.]

Soononjuwau, his x mark, [L. S.]

Tonowauiya, or Captain Bullet, his x mark, [L. S.]

Jaahkaaeyas, his x mark, [L. S.]

Taugihshauta, his x mark, [L. S.]

Sukkenjoonau, his x mark, [L. S.]

Ahquatieya, or Hot Bread, his x mark, [L. S.]

Suggonundau, his x mark, [L. S.]

Taunowaintooh, his x mark, [L. S.]

Konnonjoowauna, his x mark, [L. S.]

Soogooeyandestak, his x mark, [L. S.]

Hautwanauekkau, by Young King, his x mark, [L. S.]

Sauwejuwan, his x mark, [L. S.]

Kaunoohshauwen, his x mark, [L. S.]

Taukonondaugekta, his x mark, [L. S.]

Kaouyanoughque, or John Jemison, his x mark, [L. S.]

Hoiegush, his x mark, [L. S.]

Taknaahquau, his x mark, [L. S.]

Sealed and delivered in presence of

Nat. W. Howell,
Joseph Ellicott,
Israel Chapin,
James Rees,

Henry Aaron Hills,
Henry Abeel,
Jaspar Parrish, } Interpreters.
Horatio Jones,

Done at a full and general treaty of the Seneka nation of Indians, held at Genesee, in the county of Ontario, and State of New York, on the fifteenth day of September, in the year of our Lord one thousand seven hundred and ninety-seven, under the authority of the United States.

In testimony whereof, I have hereunto set my hand and seal, the day and year aforesaid.

Jere. Wadsworth, [L. S.]

Pursuant to a resolution of the legislature of the Commonwealth of Massachusetts, passed the eleventh day of March, in the year of our Lord one thousand seven hundred and ninety-one, I have attended a full and general treaty of the Seneka nation of Indians, at Genesee, in the county of Ontario, when the within instrument was duly executed in my presence by the sachems, chiefs, and warriors of the said nation, being fairly and properly understood and transacted by all the parties of Indians concerned, and declared to be done to their universal satisfaction: I therefore certify and approve of the same.

William Shepard.

Subscribed in presence of
Nat. W. Howell.

TREATY WITH THE SIOUX, 1805.

Conference Between the United States of America and the Sioux Nation of Indians.

Whereas, a conference held between the United States of America and the Sioux Nation of Indians, Lieut. Z. M. Pike, of the Army of the United States, and the chiefs and warriors of the said tribe, have agreed to the following articles, which when ratified and approved of by the proper authority, shall be binding on both parties:

ARTICLE 1. That the Sioux Nation grants unto the United States for the purpose of the establishment of military posts, nine miles square at the mouth of the river St. Croix, also from below the confluence of the Mississippi and St. Peters, up the Mississippi, to include the falls of St. Anthony, extending nine miles on each side of the river. That the Sioux Nation grants to the United States, the full sovereignty and power over said districts forever, without any let or hindrance whatsoever.

ARTICLE 2. That in consideration of the above grants the United States (*shall, prior to taking possession thereof, pay to the Sioux two thousand dollars, or deliver the value thereof in such goods and merchandise as they shall choose*).

ARTICLE 3. The United States promise on their part to permit the Sioux to pass, repass, hunt or make other uses of the said districts, as they have formerly done, without any other exception, but those specified in article first.

In testimony hereof, we, the undersigned, have hereunto set our hands and seals, at the mouth of the river St. Peters, on the 23rd day of September, one thousand eight hundred and five.

Z. M. Pike, [SEAL.]

First Lieutenant and Agent at the above conference.

Le Petit Carbeau, his x mark. [SEAL.]
Way Aga Enogee, his x mark. [SEAL.]

Sept. 23, 1805.

Laws Relating to Indian Affairs, 1883, p. 316.
Ratified Apr. 16, 1808. Never proclaimed by the President.

AGREEMENT WITH THE PIANKESHAW, 1818.

Contract entered into under the authority of the United States, between governor Thomas Posey, superintendent of Indian affairs, and Chekommia or Big River, principal chief of the Piankeshaws.

This indenture, made this third day of January, 1818, between governor Thomas Posey, superintendent of Indian affairs, on the one part, and Chekommia or Big River, principal chief of the Piankeshaw tribe of Indians, acting as well in his own name, as in the name and

Jan. 3, 1818.

Unratified.
Indian Office Compilation of Treaties, 1837, p. 230.

---

*This treaty does not appear among those printed in the United States Statutes at Large. It was, however, submitted by the President to the Senate, March 29, 1808. The Senate committee reported favorably, on the 13th of April, with the following amendment to fill the blank in article 2, viz: "After the word 'States' in the second article insert the following words: 'shall, prior to taking possession thereof, pay to the Sioux two thousand dollars, or deliver the value thereof in such goods and merchandise as they shall choose.'" In this form the Senate, on the 16th of April, 1808, advised and consented to its ratification by a *unanimous* vote.

An examination of the records of the State Department fails to indicate any subsequent action by the President in proclaiming the ratification of this treaty; but more than twenty-five years subsequent to its approval by the Senate the correspondence of the War Department speaks of the cessions of land described therein as an accomplished fact.

behalf of the said Piankeshaw tribe of Indians, on the other part, witnesseth:

Whereas, at a treaty held under the authority of the United States, with the chiefs and head men of the said Piankeshaw nation of Indians, at Vincennes, in the Indiana territory, the 27th day of August, *1804,* [1084] and William Henry Harrison, governor of the Indiana territory, superintendent of Indian Affairs, and commissioner plenipotentiary of the United States, for concluding any treaty or treaties with said tribe, it was agreed by said William Henry Harrison, on the one part, and the chiefs and head men of said tribe, on the other; that the Piankeshaw tribe, for the consideration therein mentioned, should cede and relinquish to the United States forever, all that tract of country, which lies between the Wabash and the tract ceded by the Kaskaskia tribe, in the year one thousand eight hundred and three, and south of a line to be drawn from the northwest corner of Vincennes tract, northerly seventy-eight degrees west, until it intersects the boundary line which has heretofore separated the lands of the Piankeshaws from the said tract ceded by the Kaskaskia tribe.

And it was also further agreed by the chiefs of the said Piankeshaw tribe, on the one part, and the said William Henry Harrison, on the other part, that the said tribe should reserve to themselves, the right of locating a tract of two square miles, or twelve hundred and eighty acres: the fee of which is to remain with them forever.

And whereas the said Piankeshaw nation, being reduced in number, and being unable to occupy the land reserved to them, by the treaty concluded between the chiefs of said tribe, and William Henry Harrison as aforesaid: therefore be it known, to all to whom these presents shall come, greeting: That the said Chekommia, commonly called Big River, principal chief and head man of the Piankeshaw tribe of Indians, as well in his own name and behalf of the said Piankeshaw tribe, for the consideration of one thousand dollars received to our full satisfaction, of governor Thomas Posey, superintendent of Indian affairs, and with full power and authority from the President of the United States, to act concerning the within named premises, have relinquished, and do by these presents, cede and relinquish to the United States, all that tract of land two miles square, and containing twelve hundred and eighty acres, being the same tract which was reserved to us by the treaty concluded at Vincennes, as aforesaid, between governor William Henry Harrison, on the one part, and the chiefs and head men of the said Piankeshaw nation, on the other.

In testimony whereof, the said Thomas Posey, superintendent of Indian affairs, and Chekommia, principal chief, and representing the said Piankeshaw tribe, have hereunto set their hands and affixed their seals.

Done at Vincennes, this third day of January, in the year of our Lord one thousand eight hundred and eighteen, and of the independence of the United States the forty-second.

Th. Posey.   [L. s.]
Chekommia, or Big River, his x mark. [L. s.]

Signed, sealed, and executed, in presence of—
    John Law, attorney at law.
    H. Lasselle.
    Caleb Lownes.
    Joseph Barron, Indian interpreter.
    Macatamanguay, or Loon, a Wea chief, his x mark.

This may certify, that Chehommia, or Big River, who has signed the above, is principal chief and head man of the Piankeshaw tribe, and with full power and authority from said tribe, to sign and execute the above contract, on behalf of said tribe.

Macatamanguay, or Loon, a Wea chief, his x mark.   [L. s.]
Little Eyes, or Washington, a Wea chief, his x mark. [L. s.]

AGREEMENT WITH THE SENECA, 1823.

At a treaty held under the authority of the United States at Moscow, in the county of Livingston, in the State of New York, between the sachems, chiefs, and warriors of the Seneka nation of Indians in behalf of said nation, and John Greig and Henery B. Gibson of Canandaigua in the county of Ontario; in the presence of Charles Carroll, esquire, commissioner appointed by the United States for holding said treaty, and of Nathaniel Gorham, esquire, superintendent, in behalf of the State of Massachusetts.

Sept. 3, 1823.

Unratified.
Indian Office Compilation of Treaties, 1837, p. 305.

Know all men by these presents, that the said sachems, chiefs, and warriors, for and in consideration of the sum of four thousand two hundred and eighty-six dollars, lawful money of the United States, to them in hand paid by the said John Greig and Henry B. Gibson, at or immediately before the ensealing and delivery of these presents, the receipt whereof is hereby acknowledged, have granted, bargained, sold, aliened, released, quit claimed and confirmed unto the said John Greig and Henry B. Gibson, and by these presents do grant, bargain, sell, alien, release, quit claim, and confirm, unto the said John Greig and Henry B. Gibson, their heirs and assigns, forever, all that tract, piece or parcel of land commonly called and known by the name of the Gordeau reservation, situate, lying and being in the counties of Livingston and Genesee, in the State of New York, bounded as follows, that is to say: Beginning at the mouth of Steep Hill creek, thence due east, until it strikes the Old Path, thence south until a due west line will intersect with certain steep rocks on the west side of Genesee river, thence extending due west, due north, and due east, until it strikes the first mentioned bound, enclosing as much land on the west side as on the east side of the river, and containing according to the survey and measurement made of the same by Augustus Porter, surveyor, seventeen thousand nine hundred and twenty-seven 137-160 acres, be the same more or less: excepting nevertheless, and always reserving out of this grant and conveyance, twelve hundred and eighty acres of land, bounded as follows, that is to say; on the east by Genesee river, on the south by a line running due west from the centre of the Big Slide so called, on the north by a line parallel to the south line and two miles distant therefrom, and on the west by a line running due north and south, and at such a distance from the river as to include the said quantity of twelve hundred and eighty acres and no more; which said twelve hundred and eighty acres are fully and clearly understood, to remain the property of the said parties of the first part, and their nation, in as full and ample a manner, as if these presents had not been executed: together with all and singular the rights, privileges, hereditaments, and appurtenances, to the said hereby granted premises belonging or in anywise appertaining, and all the estate, right, title, and interest, whatsoever, of them the said parties of the first part, and of their nation, of, in, and to, the said tract of land above described, except as is above excepted. To have and to hold all and singular the above granted premises with the appurtenances, unto the said John Greig and Henry B. Gibson, their heirs and assigns, to the sole and only proper use, benefit, and behoof, of the said John Greig and Henry B. Gibson, their heirs and assigns forever.

In testimony whereof, the parties to these presents have hereunto, and to three other instruments of the same tenor and date, one to remain with the United States, one to remain with the State of Massachusetts, one to remain with the Senaka nation of Indians, and one to remain with the said John Greig and Henry B. Gibson, interchangeably set their hands and seals, the third day of September, in the year of our Lord one thousand eight hundred and twenty three.

Saquiungarluchta, or Young King, his x mark.	[L. S.]	Genuchsckada, or Stevenson, his x mark.	[L. S.]
Karlundawana, or Pollard, his x mark.	[L. S.]	Mary Jamieson, her x mark.	[L. S.]
Sagouata, or Red Jacket, his x mark.	[L. S.]	Talwinaha, or Little Johnson, his x mark.	[L. S.]
Tishkaaga, or Little Billy, his x mark.	[L. S.]	Atachsagu, or John Big Tree, his x mark.	[L. S.]
Tywaneash, or Black Snake, his x mark.	[L. S.]	Teskaiy, or John Pierce, his x mark.	[L. S.]
Kahalsta, or Strong, his x mark.	[L. S.]	Teaslaegee, or Charles Cornplanter, his x mark.	[L. S.]
Chequinduchque, or Little Beard, his x mark.	[L. S.]	Teoncukaweh, or Bob Stevens, his x mark.	[L. S.]
Tuyongo, or Seneka White, his x mark.	[L. S.]	Checanadughtwo, or Little Beard, his x mark.	[L. S.]
Onondaki, or Destroy Town, his x mark.	[L. S.]	Canada, his x mark.	[L. S.]
Lunuchshewa, or War Chief, his x mark.	[L. S.]		

Sealed and delivered in the presence of

Nat. W. Howell.
Ch. Carroll.

Jasper Parrish.
Horatio Jones.

Done at a treaty held with the sachems, chiefs, and warriors of the Seneka nation of Indians at Moscow, in the county of Livingston and State of New York, on the third day of September, one thousand eight hundred and twenty-three, under the authority of the United States. In testimony whereof, I have hereunto set my hand and seal, the day and year aforesaid, by virtue of a commission issued under the seal of the commonwealth of Massachusetts, bearing date the 31st day of August, A. D. 1815, pursuant to a resolution of the legislature of the said commonwealth, passed the eleventh day of March, one thousand seven hundred and ninety-one.

N. Gorham, Superintendent.

I have attended a treaty of the Seneka nation of Indians held at Moscow in the county of Livingston and State of New York, on the third day of September, in the year of our Lord one thousand eight hundred and twenty-three, when the within instrument was duly executed in my presence, by the sachems, chiefs, and warriors of the said nation, being fairly and properly understood and transacted by all the parties of Indians concerned, and declared to be done to their full satisfaction. I do therefore certify and approve the same.

Ch. Carroll, Commissioner.

AGREEMENT WITH THE CREEKS, 1825.

Council House, Broken Arrow, Creek Nation, 29 June, 1825.

June 29, 1825.

Unratified. Indian office—General Files, Creek, 1825–26, E. P. Gaines. See note, ante p. 266, and H. R. Ex. Doc. 17, 19th Cong., 1st sess.

Resolved by the Chiefs and Warriors in Council assembled that after a suitable consideration which the nature of the case demands, they solemnly and strictly declare for themselves and for the whole Muscogee Nation, that all of the late General McIntosh's party who have opposed the Laws of the Nation, are hereby pardoned to all intents and purposes, and they are hereby invited to return to their usual places of abode or elsewhere, and their to dwell in the full enjoyment of peace & security and of all their rights and privileges guaranteed to them by our Laws.

The property which they have with them, & that which is in the Nation owned by them when they left it is theirs. Such of their property as may have been lost or destroyed contrary to the known laws of the Nation which once belonged to General McIntosh & Samuel Hawkins or others shall be restored or paid for to the proper owners by the Nation whenever it shall appear to the satisfaction of the United States Agent after hearing both parties in Council that it was or any part of it taken or destroyed contrary to the Laws of the Nation. Either party may appeal from the decision of the Agent to the Secretary of War, whose decision in the case shall be final.

Some individuals of the pardoned party are justly indebted to the Nation for monies borrowed in different amounts and otherwise, for which the Nation expect to be paid.—But the authorities of the Nation will wait patiently a reasonable time until these debtors can be prepared to reimburse the National Treasury. In every case, at all times these misguided and unfortunate people are required to conform to the Laws of the Nation and to obey and respect the proper authorities, and conduct themselves as good citizens of the Nation. A general talk shall be given in public and observed by the whole Nation, that these people shall be secure in their persons and property. Any person or persons who shall kill any of the pardoned party on any pretence for past offences shall suffer Death. And it is clearly to be understood that they are to be in no respect punished or held accountable for the past, but are in future subject to all the restraints of the Law and entitled to the privileges of good citizens.

Done in Council and subscribed in behalf of the whole Nation.

> Tustinuggee Hopor (his x mark).
> Tuskeneehuk (his x mark).
> Opothee Yoholo (his x mark).
> Yoholo Mico (his x mark).
> Tustenuggee Mald (his x mark).
> Oftfuskee Yoholo (his x mark).
> Mad Wolf (his x mark).
> Enedhlah Toholo (his x mark).
> Hopoi Hajo (his x mark).
> Mad Tiger (his x mark).
> Tuskenuhuh of Caseteck (his x mark).

TREATY WITH THE CHICKASAW, 1830.

Aug. 31, 1830.

Unratified.
Indian Office, box 1,
Treaties, 1802–1853.
See note, ante, p. 360.

Articles of a treaty, entered into at Franklin, Tennessee, this 31st day of August, 1830, by John H. Eaton, Secretary of War, and General John Coffee, commissioners appointed by the President, on the part of the United States, and the chiefs and head men of the Chickasaw Nation of Indians, duly authorized, by the whole nation, to conclude a treaty.

ARTICLE 1. The Chickasaw Nation hereby cede to the United States all the lands owned and possessed by them, on the East side of the Mississippi River, where they at present reside, and which lie north of the following boundary, viz: beginning at the mouth of the Oacktibbyhaw (or Tibbee) creek; thence, up the same, to a point, being a marked tree, on the old Natchez road, about one mile Southwardly from Wall's old place; thence, with the Choctaw boundary, and along it, Westwardly, through the Tunicha old fields, to a point on the Mississippe river, about twenty-eight miles, by water, below where the

St. Francis river enters said stream, on the West side. All the lands North, and North-East of said boundary, to latitute thirty-five North the South boundary of the State of Tennessee, being owned by the Chickasaws, are hereby ceded to the United States.

ART. 2. In consideration of said cession, the United States agree to furnish to the Chickasaw Nation of Indians, a country, West of the territory of Arkansaw, to lie South of latitude thirty-six degrees and a half, and of equal extent with the one ceded; and in all respects as to timber, water and soil, it shall be suited to the wants and condition of said Chickasaw people. It is agreed further, that the United States will send one or more commissioners to examine and select a country of the description stated, who shall be accompanied by an interpreter and not more than twelve persons of the Chickasaws, to be chosen by the nation, to examine said country; and who, for their expenses and services, shall be allowed two dollars a day each, while so engaged. If, after proper examination, a country suitable to their wants and condition can not be found; then, it is stipulated and agreed, that this treaty, and all its provisions, shall be considered null and void. But, if a country shall be found and approved, the President of the United States shall cause a grant in fee simple to be made out, to be signed by him as other grants are usually signed, conveying the country to the Chickasaw people, and to their children, so long as they shall continue to exist as a nation, and shall reside upon the same.

ART. 3. The Chickasaws being a weak tribe, it is stipulated that the United States will, at all times, extend to them their protection and care against enemies of every description, but it is, at the same time, agreed, that they shall act peacably, and never make war, nor resort to arms, except with the consent and approval of the President, unless in cases where they may be invaded by some hostile power or tribe.

ART. 4. As further consideration, the United States agree, that each warrior and widow having a family, and each white man, having an Indian family, shall be entitled to a half section of land, and if they have no family, to half that quantity. The delegation present, having full knowledge of the population of their country, stipulate, that the first class of cases (those with families), shall not exceed five hundred, and that the other class shall not exceed one hundred persons. The reservations secured under this article, shall be granted in *fee simple*, to those who choose to remain, and become subject to the laws of the whites; and who, having recorded such intention with the agent, before the time of the first removal, shall continue to reside upon, and cultivate the same, for five years; at the expiration of which time, a grant shall be issued. But should they prefer to remove, and actually remove, then the United States, in lieu of such reservations, will pay for the same, at the rate of one dollar and a half per acre; the same to be paid in ten equal, annual instalments, to commence after the period of the ratification of this treaty, if, at that time, they shall have removed.

ART. 5. It is agreed, that the United States, as further consideration, will pay to said Nation of Indians, fifteen thousand dollars annually, for twenty years; the first payment to be made after their removal shall take place, and they be settled at their new homes, West of the Mississippi.

ART. 6. Whereas Levi Clolbert, George Colbert, Tessemingo, William McGilvery and Saml. Seeley Senr, have been long known, as faithful and steady friends of the United States, and regardless of the interest of their own people; to afford them an earnest of our good feeling, now that they are about to seek a new home; the commissioners, of their own accord, and without any thing of solicitation or request, on the part of said persons, have proposed, and do agree, that they have reservations of four sections each, to include their present improvements, as nearly as may be; or, if they have improvements at any other place than one, then, equally to divide said reservations, so that two sections may be laid off at one place of improvement, and two at another; or, the whole at one place, as the party entitled may choose. They shall be entitled to the same in fee simple, to be resided upon; or, if they prefer it, they may, with the consent of the President, sell and convey the same, in fee. And it is further agreed, that upon the same terms and conditions, a reservation of two sections, to be surveyed together, and to include the improvements of the party entitled, shall and the same is hereby declared to be, secured to Capt. James Brown, James Colbert, John McLish & Isaac Alberson.

ART. 7. The delegation having selected the following persons, as worthy their regard and confidence, to wit;—Ish to yo to pe, To pul ka, Ish te ke yo ka tubbe, Ish te ke cha, E le paum be, Pis te la tubbe, Ish tim mo lat ka, Pis ta tubbe, Im mo hoal te tubbe, Ba ka tubbe, Ish to ye tubbe, Ah to ko wa, Pak la na ya ubbe, In hie yo che tubbe, Thomas Seally, Tum ma sheck ah, Im mo la subbe, Am le mi ya tubbe; Benjamin Love and Malcomb McGee;—it is consented that each of said persons shall be entitled to a reservation of one section of land, to be located in a body, to include their present improvement, and upon which, intending to become resident citizens of the country, they may continue, and at the end of five years, shall receive a grant for the same; or, should they prefer to remove, they shall be entitled, in lieu thereof, to receive from the United States, one dollar and twenty-five cents per acre for the same, to be paid in two equal, annual instalments, to commence after the ratification of this treaty, and after the nation shall have removed.

ART. 8. No person receiving a special reservation, shall be entitled to claim any further reservation, under the provisions of the fourth article of this treaty.

ART. 9. At the request of the delegation, it is agreed that Levi Colbert shall have an additional section of land, to that granted him in the 6th article, to be located where he may prefer, and subject to the conditions contained in said sixth article.

ART. 10. All the reservations made by this treaty, shall be in sections, half sections, or quarter sections, agreeably to the legal surveys made, and shall include the present houses and improvements of the reservees, as nearly as may be.

ART. 11. It is agreed that the Chickasaw people, in removing to their new homes, shall go there at the expense of the United States; and that when they shall have arrived at their new homes, the United States will furnish to each one, for the space of one year, meat and corn rations, for himself and his family; that thereby, time may be afforded to clear the ground, and prepare a crop. And the better to effect this object, it is agreed that one-half the nation shall remove in the fall of 1831, and the other half the following fall. The supplies to be furnished by the United States, are to be delivered at one or two places in the nation, which shall be as convenient to the body of the people as may be practicable; having regard to the position or places, where the supplies may be had or deposited, with the greatest convenience, and least expense to the United States.

ART. 12. The United States, at the time of the removal of each portion of the nation, at the valuation of some respectable person, to be appointed by the President, agree to purchase all the stock they may desire to part with, (except horses), and to pay them therefor, at their new homes, as early as practicable after the ratification of this treaty. Also, to receive their agricultural and farming utencils, and to furnish them, at the West, with axes, hoes and ploughs, suited to their wants respectively. Also, to furnish each family with a spinning wheel and cards, and a loom to every six families.

ART. 13. A council house, and two houses of public worship, which may be used for the purposes of schools, shall be built by the United States; and the sum of four thousand dollars shall be appropriated for that purpose. Also, one blacksmith, and no more, shall be employed at the expense of the government, for twenty years, for the use of the Indians; and a mill-wright for five years, to aid them in erecting their saw and grist-mills.

ART. 14. The sum of two thousand dollars a year, shall be paid for ten years, for the purpose of employing suitable teachers of the Christian religion, and superintending common schools in the nation. And it is further consented, that twenty Chickasaw boys of promise, from time to time, for the period of twenty years, shall be selected from the nation by the chiefs, to be educated within the States at the expense of the United States, under the direction of the Secretary of War.

ART. 15. A desire having been expressed by Levi Colbert, that two of his younger sons, Abijah Jackson Colbert, and Andrew Morgan Colbert, aged seven and five years, might be educated under the direction and care of the President of the United States;—and George Colbert having also expressed a wish that his grand-son, Andrew J. Frazier, aged about twelve years, might have a similar attention: It is consented, that at a proper age, as far as they may be found to have capacity, they shall receive a liberal education, at the expense of the United States, under the direction and control of the President.

ART. 16. The United States shall have authority, after the ratification of this treaty by the Senate, to survey and prepare the country for sale; but no sale shall take place before the fall of 1832, or until they shall remove. And that every clause and article herein contained may be strictfully fulfilled;—it is stipulated and agreed, that the lands herein ceded shall be, and the same are hereby pledged, for the payment of the several sums which are secured and directed to be paid, under the several provisions of this treaty.

ART. 17. The United States, and the Chickasaw nation of Indians herein stipulate, that perpetual peace, and unaltered and lasting friendship, shall be maintained between them.

It is agreed, that the President of the United States will use his good offices, and kind mediation, and make a request of the governor and legislature of the State of Mississippi, not to extend their laws over the Chickasaws; or to suspend their operation, until they shall have time to remove, as limited in this treaty.

In witness of all and every thing herein determined, between the United States, and the delegation representing the whole Chickasaw nation, the parties have hereunto set their hands and seals, at Franklin, Tennessee, within the United States, this thirty-first day of August, one thousand, eight hundred and thirty.

Jn H Eaton,
Secr. of War.
Jno. Coffee.

Levi Colbert, his x mark.
George Colbert, his x mark.
James Colbert, his x mark.
Wm. McGilvery, his x mark.
James Brown, his x mark.
Isaac Alberson, his x mark.
To pul ka, his x mark.
Ish te ke yo ka tubbe, his x mark.
Ish te ke cha, his x mark.
Im me houl te tubbe, his x mark.

In ha yo chet tubbe, his x mark.
Ish te ya tubbe, his x mark.
Ah to ko wa, his x mark.
Ook la na ya ubbe, his x mark.
Im mo la subbe, his x mark.
Hush ta ta be, his x mark.
In no wa ke che, his x mark.
Oh he cubbe, his x mark.
Kin hi che, his x mark.
J. W. Lish.

Signed in presence of us,

Preston Hay, Secretary.
Benj. Reynolds, U. S. agent.
Benjamin Love, interpreter.
R. M. Gavock.
R. P. Currin.

Lemuel Smith.
Leml. Donelson.
Jos. H. Fry.
James H. Wilson.
J. R. Davis.

———

Articles, supplementary to a treaty this day entered into, between John H. Eaton and John Coffee, on the part of the United States, and the Chiefs of the Chickasaw nation.

1. It is agreed that the United States will furnish the Chickasaw nation, to be distributed by the agent, under the direction of the chiefs, at or before the time of their removal West of the Mississippi river, three hundred rifles, with moulds and wipers; also, three hundred pounds of good powder, and twelve hundred pounds of lead. They will also furnish as aforesaid, three hundred copper or brass kettles, and six hundred blankets. Likewise three thousand weight of leaf tobacco.

2. Colbert's Island, in the Tennessee river, just below the mouth of Caney Creek, supposed to contain five hundred acres, has always been in the use and occupancy of George Colbert, and has been admitted by the nation, to be his individual property. It is agreed now, that he shall be recognized, as having a title to the same, and that he shall receive from the United States, in consideration of it, one thousand dollars, to be paid in one year after the Chickasaws shall remove to their new homes.

3. James Colbert has represented, that he has a claim of thirteen hundred dollars, of money due from a citizen of the United States;— that he has become insolvent, and is unable to pay it. It is further represented, that by the rule of the Chickasaw people, where an Indian cannot pay a debt due to a white man, the nation assumes it. Also, Levi Colbert shews, that some time since, he purchased of a white citizen, a horse which was stolen, and proven and taken out of his possession, as stolen property, for which he has not, and cannot, obtain remuneration. Being now about to leave their ancient homes, for a new one, too distant to attend to their business here;—it is agreed that a section of land may be located and reserved, to be bound by sectional lines; which land, with the consent of the President, they may sell.

4. The Chickasaw delegation request, that a reservation of land may be made in favor of their excellent agent, Col. Benjamin Reynolds, who, since he has been among them, has acted uprightly and faithfully, and of their sub-agent, Major John L. Allen, who also, has been of much service:—The commissioners accordingly consent thereto; and it is stipulated that Col. Reynolds shall have a reservation of five quarter sections of land, to be bounded by sectional lines, or quarter sectional lines, and to lie together, in a body; and in further consideration, it is stipulated, with the consent of said Reynolds, that his pension of two hundred and forty dollars a year, granted to him by the United States, shall thereafter cease and determine. The application in favor of the sub-agent, Maj. Allen, is also recognized, and a reservation of a quarter section is admitted to his wife, to whom and for whose benefit a grant shall issue. But said reservations shall not be located, so as to interfere with other claims to reservations, secured under this treaty, nor shall this treaty be affected if this article is not ratified.

5. The 4th article of the treaty of 19th October 1818, which reserves a salt lick, and authorizes Levi Colbert and James Brown to lease the same for a reasonable quantity of salt, is hereby changed;—And with

the consent of the commissioners present, the following agreement, made by Robert P. Currin, for himself and William B. Lewis, is entered as part of this treaty, to wit;

Whereas a lease of land, of four miles square, was secured under the fourth article of a treaty, concluded on the 19th day of October 1818, between the United States and the Chickasaw nation of Indians; and Levi Colbert and James Brown, under the same treaty, were appointed agents and trustees by the Chickasaw nation to make said lease. And whereas William B. Lewis, a citizen of the United States afterwards procured from said trustees, Colbert and Brown, a lease for the same, on condition of his paying annually, a certain amount of salt to said nation, provided he should succeed in finding salt water. And whereas the said William B. Lewis and Robert P. Currin, who subsequently became interested with him, have, as is shown, expended about the sum of three thousand dollars, in endeavoring to find salt water, but without success. And the Indians, who are about to leave their ancient country, being desirous to have this land and lease placed in such a condition, as that some benefit may result to their nation, They do hereby agree with said Robert P. Currin, a citizen of the United States, for himself, and as the agent and attorney in fact of the said William B. Lewis (John H. Eaton and John Coffee, the United States commissioners, to treat with said Chickasaw nation being present and assenting thereto); that the lease heretofore made, be so changed, that the rent therein agreed to be paid is entirely released and discharged, from the date of said lease, together with all claim arising on account of the same.

And it is now agreed, that said lease shall remain, as heretofore made, with this alteration: that two thousand dollars shall be paid to said Colbert and Brown, trustees as aforesaid, for the Chickasaw nation: to wit: five hundred dollars now in hand; five hundred dollars on the first day of October one thousand eight hundred and thirty-one; and one thousand dollars on the first day of October one thousand eight hundred and thirty-two. And it is further agreed, in consideration of said alteration of said original contract and lease, herein made and agreed upon; and the said Robert P. Currin, for himself and the said William B. Lewis, for each and for both, he having full authority to act in the premises, will annually pay to said trustees, four bushels of salt, or the value thereof, as they and the nation may agree to and direct.

In testimony whereof, and in the presence of the commissioners, appointed to treat with the Chickasaw nation of people, on the part of the United States, the parties respectively have hereto set their hands and affixed their seals, this first day of September, one thousand eight hundred and thirty.

Jn. H. Eaton, Secty. of War.	Im me houl te tubbe, his x mark.
Jno. Coffee.	In hei yo chit tubbe, his x mark.
Levi Colbert, his x mark.	Ish te ya tubbe, his x mark.
George Colbert, his x mark.	Ah to ko wa, his x mark.
James Colbert, his x mark.	Ook la na ya ubbe, his x mark.
Wm. McGilvery, his x mark.	Im mo la tubbe, his x mark.
Isaac Alberson, his x mark.	Hush ta ta be, his x mark.
James Bown, his x mark.	In no wa ke che, his x mark.
To pul ka, his x mark.	Oh he cubbe, his x mark.
Ish te ki yo ka tubbe, his x mark.	Kin hu che, his x mark.
Ish te he cha, his x mark.	J. W. Lish.

Signed in presence of us,

Preston Hay, secretary.	Leml. Smith.
Benj. Reynolds, U. S. agent.	R. P. Currin.
Benjamin Love, as interpreter.	Jos. H. Fry.
R. M. Gavock.	James H. Wilson.
Leml. Donelson.	J. R. Davis.

AGREEMENT WITH THE CHEROKEE, 1835.

Articles of a Treaty agreed upon at the City of Washington, March 14th, 1835, between J. F. Schermerhorn, on the part of the United States, and a Delegation of the Cherokee Tribe of Indians, which, by the President of the United States, is directed to be submitted to the Cherokee Nation of Indians, for their consideration and approbation.

March 14, 1835.

Unratified.
Indian Office, box 1, Treaties 1802–1853.
See Senate Doc. No. 120, 25th Congress, 2d session, p. 459.

Whereas, several persons of the Cherokee Nation of Indians, east of the Mississippi river, have visited the City of Washington, as delegates from that part of their Nation, in favor of emigration, with a hope and desire of making some arrangements which might be acceptable to the Government of the United States, and to their Nation generally, and thereby terminating the difficulties which they have experienced during a residence within the settled portion of the United States, under the jurisdiction and laws of the State Governments, and with a view of re-uniting their people in one body, and securing to themselves and their descendents the country selected by their forefathers, and sufficient for all their wants, and whereon they can establish and perpetuate such a state of society as may be most consonant with their habits and views, and as may tend to their individual comfort and their advancement in civilization:

And whereas, the President of the United States, animated with a sincere desire to relieve them from their embarrassments, and to provide for them a permanent establishment; and being willing, as far as his Constitutional power extends, to use all his efforts to accomplish these objects, has yielded to the wishes thus expressed to him in behalf of the Cherokees, and has authorized John F. Schermerhorn to meet the said members of the Cherokee Nation, and to arrange with them such terms as may be just and proper, between the parties:

And whereas, the said John F. Schermerhorn and the said Delegation of the Cherokee Nation of Indians, have met together and have taken the whole matter into consideration, and have agreed upon certain articles, which are to be considered merely as propositions to be made to the Cherokee people, on behalf of the United States, and to be utterly invalid until approved by them; it being distinctly understood that the said Cherokee people are not in the slightest manner committed by the formation of this provisional arrangement—

Now, therefore, in consideration of the premises, and with a view to the final adjustment of all claims, and demands of every kind, of the Cherokees east of the Mississippi river, upon the United States, it is agreed as follows:

ARTICLE 1. This treaty shall be submitted to the people of the Cherokee Nation, for that purpose, to be assembled at New Echota, after due notice being given of the time of meeting by the Commissioner appointed by the President of the United States, whose duty it shall be fully to explain all its contents to them, and the views of the Government in regard to it, for their concurrence and adoption; and if it shall appear, after a fair, free, and full expression of their sentiments, that a majority of the people are in favor of the treaty, it shall be considered as approved and confirmed by the Nation; and their whole country shall be deemed to be ceded, and their claim and title to it to cease. But it is always understood that the treaty stipulations in former treaties, that have not been annulled or superseded by this, shall continue in full force.

ART. 2. The Cherokee Nation of Indians, for and in consideration of the additional quantity of land guarantied and secured to them by the third article of this treaty, and of the fulfilment of the covenants and stipulations hereinafter mentioned, and also of the sum of four millions five hundred thousand dollars, to be expended, paid, and invested, as agreed in the following articles, do hereby cede, relinquish, and convey to the United States, all their right and title to all the lands owned, claimed, and possessed by them, including the lands reserved by them for a school fund, east of the Mississippi river.

ART. 3. Whereas, by the treaty of May 6th, 1828, and the supplementary treaty thereto, of February 14th, 1833, with the Cherokees west of the Mississippi, the United States guarantied and secured, to be conveyed by patent, to the Cherokee Nation of Indians, the following tract of country: "Beginning at a point on the old western territorial line of Arkansas territory, being twenty-five miles north from the point where the territorial line crosses Arkansas river; thence running from said north point south on the said territorial line to the place where the said territorial line crosses Verdegris river; thence down said Verdegris river, to the Arkansas river; thence down said Arkansas to a point where a stone is placed, opposite to the east or lower bank of Grand river, at its junction with the Arkansas; thence running south forty-four degrees west, one mile; thence in a straight line to a point four miles northerly, from the mouth of the north fork of the Canadian; thence along the said four miles line to, the Canadian; thence down the Canadian to the Arkansas; thence down the Arkansas to that point on the Arkansas where the eastern Choctaw boundary strikes said river, and running thence with the western line of Arkansas territory, as now defined, to the southwest corner of Missouri; thence along the western Missouri line to the land assigned the Senecas; thence on the south line of the Senecas to Grand river; thence up said Grand river as far as the south line of the Osage reservation, extended if necessary; thence up and between said south Osage line, extended west if necessary, and a line drawn due west from the point of beginning to a certain distance west, at which a line running north and south from said Osage line to said due west line, will make seven millions of acres within the whole described boundaries. In addition to the seven millions of acres of land thus provided for and bounded, the United States further guaranty to the Cherokee Nation a perpetual outlet west, and a free and unmolested use of all the country lying west of the western boundary of said seven millions of acres, as far west as the sovereignty of the United States and their right of soil extend: *Provided however*, that if the saline or salt plain on the western prairie shall fall within said limits prescribed for said outlet, the right is reserved to the United States to permit other tribes of red men to get salt on said plain, in common with the Cherokees; and letters patent shall be issued by the United States, as soon as practicable, for the land hereby guarantied."

And whereas it is apprehended by the Cherokees, that in the above cession there is not contained a sufficient quantity of land for the accommodation of the whole nation, on their removal west of the Mississippi, the United States, therefore, hereby covenant and agree to convey to the said Indians, and their descendants, by patent, in fee simple, the following additional tract of country, situated between the west line of the State of Missouri and the Osage reservation, beginning at the southeast corner of the same, and runs north along the east line of the Osage lands, fifty miles, to the northeast corner thereof; and thence east to the west line of the State of Missouri; thence with said line, south fifty miles; thence west to the place of beginning; estimated to contain 800,000 acres of land; but it is expressly understood, that if any of the lands assigned the Quapaws shall fall within the aforesaid bounds, the same shall be reserved and excepted out of the lands above granted.

ART. 4. The United States also agree that the lands above ceded by the treaty of February 14, 1833, including the outlet and those ceded by this treaty, shall all be included in one patent, to be executed to the Cherokee Nation of Indians, by the President of the United States, according to the provisions of the act of May 28, 1830. It is, however, understood and agreed that the Union Missionary Station shall be held by the American Board for Foreign Missions, and the Military Reservation at Fort Gibson shall be held by the United States. But should the United States abandon said post, and have no further use for the same, it shall revert to the Cherokee nation. The United States shall always have the right to make and establish such post and military roads, and forts, in any part of the Cherokee country, as they may deem proper for the interest and protection of the same, and the free use of as much land, timber, fuel, and materials of all kinds for the construction and support of the same as may be necessary; provided, that if the private rights of individuals are interfered with, a just compensation therefor shall be made. With regard to the Union Missionary Reservation, it is understood that the American Board of Foreign Missions will continue to occupy the same, for the benefit of the Cherokee nation; and if, at any time hereafter, they shall abandon the same, upon payment for their improvements by the United States, it shall revert to the Cherokee Nation.

ART. 5. The United States also stipulate and agree to extinguish, for the benefit of the Cherokees, the title to the reservations within their country, made in the Osage treaty of 1825, to certain half breeds, and for this purpose they hereby agree to pay to the persons to whom the same belong or have been assigned, or to their agents or guardians, whenever they shall execute, after the ratification of this treaty, a satisfactory conveyance for the same, to the United States, the sum of fifteen thousand dollars, according to a schedule accompanying this treaty, of the relative value of the several reservations.

ART. 6. The United States hereby covenant and agree, that the lands ceded to the Cherokee nation, in the foregoing article, shall, in no future time, without their consent, be included within the territorial limits or jurisdiction of any State or Territory; but they shall secure to the Cherokee Nation the right, by their National Councils, to make and carry into effect all such laws as they may deem necessary for the government and protection of the persons and property within their own country, belonging to their people, or such persons as have connected themselves with them: *Provided always*, That they shall not be inconsistent with the Constitution of the United States, and such acts of Congress as have been or may be passed for the regulation of Indian affairs; and also, that they shall not be considered as extending to such citizens and army of the United States, as may travel or reside in the Indian country, according to the laws and regulations established by the government of the same.

ART. 7. Perpetual peace and friendship shall exist between the citizens of the United States and the Cherokee Indians. The United States agree to protect the Cherokee Nation from domestic strife and foreign enemies, and against intestine wars between the several tribes. They shall endeavor to preserve and maintain the peace of the country, and not make war upon their neighhors; and should hostilities commence by one or more tribes, upon another, the Cherokee Council of the Nation, when called upon by the authority of the President of the United States, shall aid the United States with as many warriors as may be deemed necessary to protect and restore peace in the Indian country; and while in service, they shall be entitled to the pay and rations of the army of the United States. They shall also be protected against all interruption and intrusion from citizens of the United

States, who may attempt to settle in the country without their consent; and all such persons shall be removed from the same by order of the President of the United States. But this is not intended to prevent the residence among them of useful farmers, mechanics, and teachers, for the instruction of the Indians, according to the treaty stipulations, and the regulations of the Government of the United States.

ART. 8. The Cherokee Nation, having already made great progress in civilization, and deeming it important that every proper and laudable inducement should be offered to their people to improve their condition, as well as to guard and secure, in the most effectual manner, the rights guarantied to them in this treaty, and with a view to illustrate the liberal and enlarged policy of the Government of the United States towards the Indians, in their removal beyond the territorial limits of the States, it is stipulated that they shall be entitled to a delegate in the House of Representatives of the United States, whenever Congress shall make provision for the same.

ART. 9. The United States also agree and stipulate to remove the Cherokees to their new homes, and to subsist them one year after their arrival there, and that a sufficient number of steamboats and baggage-wagons shall be furnished to remove them comfortably, and so as not to endanger their health; and that a physician, well supplied with medicines, shall accompany each detachment of emigrants removed by the Government. They shall also be furnished with blankets, kettles, and rifles, as stipulated in the treaty of 1828. The blankets shall be delivered before their removal, and the kettles and rifles after their removal in their new country. Such persons and families as, in the opinion of the Emigrating Agent, are capable of subsisting and removing themselves, shall be permitted to do so; and they shall be allowed in full for all claims for the same, twenty-five dollars for each member of their family, slaves excepted, for whom (those now owned in the nation,) they shall be allowed eighteen dollars each; and in lieu of their one year's rations, they shall be paid the sum of thirty-three dollars, thirty-three cents, if they prefer it. And, in order to encourage immediate removal, and with a view to benefitting the poorer class of their people, the United States agree and promise to pay each member of the Cherokee Nation one hundred and fifty dollars on his removal, at the Cherokee Agency West, provided they enrol and remove within one year from the ratification of this treaty; and one hundred dollars to each person that removes within two years; and after this no *per capita* allowance whatever will be made; and it is expressly understood, that the whole Nation shall remove within two years from the ratification of the treaty. There shall also be paid to each emigrant since June 1833, one hundred and fifty dollars, according to the assurances given them by the Secretary of War, that they should be entitled to all the advantages and provisions of the treaty which should be finally concluded with their Nation. They shall also be paid for the improvements, according to their appraised value before they removed, where fraud has not already been shown in the valuation.

Such Cherokees, also, as reside at present out of the Nation, and shall remove with them, in two years, west of the Mississippi, shall be entitled to *per capita* allowance, removal, and subsistence, as above provided.

ART. 10. The United States agree to appoint suitable agents, who shall make a just and fair valuation of all such improvements now in the possession of the Cherokees, as add any value to the lands; and, also, of the ferries owned by them, according to their nett income; and such improvements and ferries from which they have been dispossessed in a lawless manner, or under any existing laws of the State where the same may be situated. The just debts of the Indians shall be paid out of any moneys due them for their improvements and claims; and they shall also be furnished, at the discretion of the President, with a sufficient sum to enable them to obtain the necessary means to remove themselves to their new homes, and the balance of their dues shall be paid them at the Cherokee Agency west of the Mississippi. The Missionary establishments shall also be valued and appraised in like manner, and the amount of them paid over by the United States to the treasurers of the respective Missionary Societies by whom they have been established and improved, in order to enable them to erect such buildings, and make such improvements, among the Cherokees west of the Mississippi, as they may deem necessary for their benefit. Such teachers at present among the Cherokees as their Council shall select and designate, shall be removed west of the Mississippi with the Cherokee Nation, and on the same terms allowed to them. It is, however, understood, that from the valuation of the Missionary establishments shall be deducted the *pro rata* amount advanced and expended for the same by the United States.

ART. 11. The President of the United States shall invest in some safe and most productive public stocks of the country, for the benefit of the whole Cherokee Nation, who have removed or shall remove to the lands assigned by this treaty to the Cherokee Nation west of the Mississippi, the following sums, as a permanent fund, for purposes hereinafter specified, and pay over the nett income of the same annually, to such person or persons as shall be authorized or appointed by the Cherokee Nation to receive the same, and their receipt shall be a full discharge for the amount paid to them, viz.: The sum of four hundred thousand dollars, to constitute a general fund, the interest of which shall be applied annually by the Council of the Nation to such purposes as they may deem best for the general interest of their people. The sum of fifty thousand dollars, to constitute an orphans' fund, the annual income of which shall be expended towards the support and education of such orphan children as are destitute of the means of subsistence. The sum of one hundred and sixty thousand dollars, to constitute a permanent school fund, the interest of which shall be applied annually by the Council of the Nation for the support of common schools, and such a literary institution of a higher order as may be established in the Indian country, and in order to secure, as far as possible, the true and beneficial application of the orphans' and school fund, the Council of the Cherokee Nation, when required by the President of the United States, shall make a report of the application of those funds; and he shall at all times have the right, if the funds have been misapplied, to correct any abuses of them, and to direct the manner of their application, for the purposes for which they were intended. The Council of the Nation may, by giving two years' notice of their intention, withdraw their funds, by and with the consent of the President and Senate of the United States, and invest them in such a manner as they may deem most proper for their interest. The United States also agree and stipulate to pay to the Cherokee Council East, sixty thousand dollars, and to expend thirty thousand dollars in the erection of such mills, council and school-houses in their country west of the Mississippi as their Council shall designate. The sum of ten thousand dollars shall be expended for the introduction of improved breeds of the different domestic animals, as horses, hogs, cattle, and sheep, which shall be placed under the direction of the Agent of the Tribe; and who, by and with the advice of the Council, shall distribute them to the best advantage for the general benefit of the whole people. They shall also pay to the Council five thousand dollars towards procuring materials for a printing press, to enable them to print a public newspaper, and books in the Cherokee language for gratuitous distribution.

ART. 12. The sum of two hundred and fifty thousand dollars is hereby set apart to satisfy and liquidate all claims of every kind and nature whatever of the Cherokees, upon the United States, and such claims of the citizens of the United States against the Cherokees as come within the provisions of the intercourse act of 1802, and as existed in either of the States of Georgia, Alabama, North Carolina, and Tennessee, prior to the extension of the laws of either such States over them. All claims of the Indians shall first be examined by the Council of the Nation, and then reported to the Commissioner appointed to adjudicate the same; and the claims of the United States shall first be examined by the Agent and Council of the Nation, and then referred to the Commissioner, who shall finally decide upon them; and on his certificate of the amount due in favor of the several claimants, they shall be paid. If the above claims do not amount to the sum of two hundred and fifty thousand dollars, the amount unexpended shall be added to the orphans' and school funds.

ART. 13. The Cherokee Nation of Indians, believing it will be for the interest of their people to have all their funds and annuities under their own direction and future disposition, hereby agree to commute their permanent annuity of ten thousand dollars for the sum of two hundred and fourteen thousand dollars, the same to be invested by the President of the United States as a part of the general fund of the Nation; and their present school fund, amounting to forty-eight thousand two hundred and fifty-one dollars and seventy-six cents, shall be invested in the same manner as the school fund provided in this treaty, and constitute a part of the same; and both of them to be subject to the same disposal as the other part of these funds by their National Council.

ART. 14. Those individuals and families of the Cherokee Nation that are averse to a removal to the Cherokee country west of the Mississippi, and are desirous to become citizens of the States, where they reside, and such as, in the opinion of the Agent, are qualified to take care of themselves and their property, shall be entitled to receive their due portion of all the personal benefits accruing under this treaty, for their claims, improvements, ferries, removal, and subsistence; but they shall not be entitled to any share or portion of the funds vested or to be expended for the common benefit of the Nation.

ART. 15. It is also agreed on the part of the United States, that such warriors of the Cherokee Nation as were engaged on the side of the United States, in the late wars with Great Britain and the southern tribes of Indians, and who were wounded in such service, shall be entitled to such pensions as shall be allowed them by the Congress of the United States, to commence from the period of their disability.

ART. 16. The United States hereby agree to protect and defend the Cherokees in their possessions and property, by all legal and proper means, after their enrolment, or the ratification of this treaty, until the time fixed upon for their removal; and if they are left unprotected, the United States shall pay the Cherokees for the losses and damages sustained by them in consequence thereof.

ART. 17. The expenditures, payments and investments, agreed to be made by the United States, in the foregoing articles of this treaty, it is understood, are to be paid out of the sum of four millions five hundred thousand dollars, agreed to be given to the Cherokee Nation for the cession of their lands, and in full for all their claims, of every kind, now existing against the United States.

ART. 18. The annexed schedule contains the estimate for carrying into effect the several pecuniary stipulations and agreements contained in this treaty; and if the sums affixed for any specific object shall be more or less than is requisite to carry the same into effect, the excess for such estimate shall be applied to make up the deficiency, if any occur, for the other objects of expenditure; and if, in the aggregate, the payments and expenditures shall exceed or fall short of the several sums appropriated for them, the same shall be taken from or added to, (as the case may be,) the funds to be vested for the benefit of the Cherokee Nation, according to the relative amounts intended to be invested for each specific fund, by this treaty; but the sum of two hundred and fourteen thousand dollars commuted for their permanent annuity, and their present school fund, already invested, shall not be considered as any part of the above sum of four millions and five hundred thousand dollars, the full amount agreed to be paid by the United States for all claims and demands against the same, and for the cession of their lands; and in no case shall the amount agreed to be paid and invested in the aforesaid articles of this treaty exceed this sum.

SCHEDULE.

For Removal	$255,000.00
Subsistence	400,000.00
Improvements and ferries	1,000,000.00
Claims and spoliations	250,000.00
Domestic animals	10,000.00
National debts	60,000.00
Public buildings	30,000.00
Printing press, &c	5,000.00
Blankets	36,000.00
Rifles	37,000.00
Kettles	7,000.00
Per capita allowance	1,800,000.00
General fund	400,000.00
School fund	160,000.00
Orphan's fund	50,000.00
Additional territory	500,000.00
	5,000,000.00
School fund already invested	48,251.76
Commutation of perpetual annuity	214,000.00
	5,262,251.76

ART. 19. This treaty, when it shall have been approved and signed by a majority of the Chiefs, Headmen, and Warriors, of the Cherokee Nation of Indians, and ratified by the President, by and with the advice and consent of the Senate of the United States, shall be binding on the contracting parties.

In testimony whereof the said John F. Schermerhorn, authorized as aforesaid, and the said Cherokee Delegation, have set their hands and seals the day and year above written.

John F. Schermerhorn.	[SEAL.]
John Ridge.	[SEAL.]
Archilla Smith.	[SEAL.]
Elias Boudinot.	[SEAL.]
S. W. Bell,	[SEAL.]
John West.	[SEAL.]
Wm. A. Davis.	[SEAL.]
Ezekiel West.	[SEAL.]

Witness present,

Alex. Macomb, Major General U. S. Army.
Geo. Gibson, Commissary-General.
William Allen.
Hudson M. Garland.
Sherman Page.
John Garland, Major U. S. Army.
Ben. F. Currey, Sup. Cher. remov. &c.
A. Van Buren, U. S. Army.
Dyer Castor.

AGREEMENT WITH THE DELAWARES AND WYANDOT, 1843.

Agreement between the Delaware and Wyandot nations of Indians, concluded on the 14th day of December, 1843.

Dec. 14, 1843.

9 Stat., 337.
Ratified July 25, 1848, with the proviso: "That the Wyandot Indian Nation shall take no better right or interest in and to said lands than is now vested in the Delaware Nation of Indians."

Whereas from a long and intimate acquaintance, and the ardent friendship which has for a great many years existed between the Delawares and Wyandots, and from a mutual desire that the same feeling shall continue and be more strengthened by becoming near neighbors to each other; therefore the said parties, the Delawares on one side, and the Wyandots on the other, in full council assembled, have agreed, and do agree, to the following stipulations, to wit:—

ARTICLE 1. The Delaware nation of Indians, residing between the Missouri and Kansas rivers, being very anxious to have their uncles, the Wyandots, to settle and reside near them, do hereby donate, grant and quitclaim forever, to the Wyandot nation, three sections of land, containing six hundred and forty acres each, lying and being situated at the point of the junction of the Missouri and Kansas Rivers.

ARTICLE 2. The Delaware chiefs, for themselves, and by the unanimous consent of their people; do hereby cede, grant, quitclaim to the Wyandot nation and their heirs forever, thirty-six sections of land, each containing six hundred and forty acres, situated between the aforesaid Missouri and Kansas rivers, and adjoining on the west the aforesaid three donated sections, making in all thirty-nine sections of land, bounded as follows, viz.: Commencing at the point at the junction of the aforesaid Missouri and Kansas rivers, running west along the Kansas river sufficiently far to include the aforesaid thirty-nine sections; thence running north to the Missouri river; thence down the said river with its meanders to the place of beginning; to be surveyed in as near a square form as the rivers and territory ceded will admit of.

ARTICLE 3. In consideration of the foregoing donation and cession of land, the Wyandot chiefs bind themselves, successors in office, and their people to pay to the Delaware nation of Indians, forty-six thousand and eighty dollars, as follows, viz: six thousand and eighty dollars to be paid the year eighteen hundred and forty-four, and four thousand dollars annually thereafter for ten years.

ARTICLE 4. It is hereby distinctly understood, between the contracting parties, that the aforesaid agreement shall not be binding or obligatory until the President of the United States shall have approved the same and caused it to be recorded in the War Department.

In testimony whereof, we, the chiefs and headmen of the Delaware nation, and the chiefs and headmen of the Wyandott nation, have, this fourteenth day of December, eighteen hundred and forty-three, set our signatures.

Nah-koo-mer, his x mark.		Henry Jacquis, his x mark.	
Captain Ketchum, his x mark.		James Washington, his x mark.	
Captain Suavec, his x mark,		Matthew Peacock, his x mark.	Wyandotts.
Jackenduthen, his x mark.	Delaware chiefs.	James Bigtree, his x mark.	
San-kock-sa, his x mark.		George Armstrong, his x mark.	
Cock-i-to-wa, his x mark,		Tan-roo-mie, his x mark.	
Sa-sar-sit-tona, his x mark,		T. A. Hicks.	
Pemp-scah, his x mark,			
Nah-que-non, his x mark,			

Signed in open council in presence of
　　Jonathan Phillips, Sub-agent for the Wyandotts.
　　Richard W. Cummins, Indian Agent.
　　James M. Simpson.
　　Charles Graham.
　　Joel Walker, Secretary of the Wyandott Council.
　　Henry Tiblow, Indian Interpreter, Delaware."

AGREEMENT WITH THE ROGUE RIVER, 1853.

Stipulations of a treaty of peace made and entered into by Joseph Lane Commanding forces of Oregon Territory, and Joe, principal Chief of the Rogue River tribe of Indians, Sam, Subordinate Chief and Jim, Subordinate Chief, on the part of the tribes under their jurisdiction.

Sept. 8, 1853.

Unratified. Indian Office—Oregon, 1844–1858, Ore. Supt. L., 323.

ARTICLE 1. A treaty of peace having this day been entered into between the above named parties whereby it is agreed that all the bands of Indians living within the following boundaries to wit, commencing just below the mouth of Applegate Creek, on Rogue River, thence to the highlands which divide Applegate from Althouse creek, thence with said highlands Southeasterly to the summit of the Siskiou mountains, thence easterly along said range to the Pilot Rock, thence northeasterly following the range of mountains to Mount Pitt, thence northerly to Rogue River, thence northwesterly to the head waters of Jump-off-Joe, thence down this stream to a point due north from the mouth of Applegate Creek, thence to the mouth of Applegate Creek shall cease hostilities, and that all the property taken by them from the whites, in battle or otherwise shall be given up either to Genl. Lane or the Indian Agent.   The Chiefs further stipulate to maintain peace and promptly deliver up to the Indian Agent for trial and punishment any one of their people who may in any way disturb the friendly relations this day entered into, by stealing property of any description or in any way interfering with the persons or property of the whites, and shall also be responsible for the amount of the property so destroyed   .   .   .

See ante, p. 603.

ART. 2. It is stipulated by the Chiefs that all the different bands of Indians now residing in the Territory above described shall hereafter reside in the place to be set apart for them.

ART. 3. It is further stipulated that all fire arms belonging to the Indians of the above named bands, shall be delivered to Gen. Lane, or to the Agent, for a fair consideration to be paid in blankets, clothing, &c., except Joe, principal Chief, seven guns, for hunting purposes, Sam, Subordinate Chief, five guns, Jim Subordinate Chief five guns.

ART. 4. It is further stipulated, that when their right to the above described country is purchased from the Indians by the United States, a portion of the purchase money shall be reserved to pay for the property of the whites destroyed by them during the war, not exceeding fifteen thousand dollars.

ART. 5. It is further stipulated that in case the above named Indians shall hereafter make war upon the whites, they shall forfeit all right to the annuities or money to be paid for the right to their lands.

ART. 6. It is further stipulated, that whenever any Indians shall enter the Territory above described for the purpose of committing hostilities against the whites the chiefs above named shall immediately give information to the Agent, and shall render such other assistance as may be in their power.

ART. 7. An Agent shall reside near the above named Indians to enforce the above stipulations, to whom all complaints of injuries to the Indians shall be made through their Chiefs.

Signed this 8th day of September 1853.

Joseph Lane   [L. s.]
Joe (his x mark) Aps-er-ka-har   [L. s.]
Principal Chief.
Sam (his x mark) To-qua-he-ar   [L. s.]
Subordinate Chief.
Jim (his x mark) Ana-chak-a-rah   [L. s.]
Subordinate Chief.

Witnesses,
    C. B. Gray, interpreter
    R. B. Metcalf
    Y. Y. Turney, Sec.

The above stipulations of treaty were entered into and signed by the respective parties in my presence, and with my approval.

Joel Palmer,
Superintendent Indian Affairs Oregon Territory.

AGREEMENT WITH THE CHEROKEE AND OTHER TRIBES IN THE INDIAN TERRITORY, 1865.

FORT SMITH, ARKANSAS, *September 13, 1865.*

Sept. 13, 1865.

Unratified.
See note, post 1051, ante p. 910, 931.
For the proceedings relative to the negotiation of this agreement, see Ann. Rep. Commr. Ind. Aff.,1865, pp. 34, 312–353.
Also House Ex. Doc. No. 1, 1st sess. 39th Cong., vol. 2, 1865–66, pp. 480 to 542.

Articles of agreement entered into this thirteenth day of September, 1865, between the commissioners designated by the President of the United States and the persons here present representing or connected with the following named nations and tribes of Indians located within the Indian country, viz: Cherokees, Creeks, Choctaws, Chickasaws, Osages, Seminoles, Senecas, Senecas and Shawnees, and Quapaws.

Whereas the aforesaid nations and tribes, or bands of Indians, or portions thereof, were induced by the machinations of the emissaries of the so-called Confederate States to throw off their allegiance to the government of the United States, and to enter into treaty stipulations with said so-called Confederate States, whereby they have made themselves liable to a forfeiture of all rights of every kind, character, and description which had been promised and guaranteed to them by the United States; and whereas the government of the United States has maintained its supremacy and authority within its limits; and whereas it is the desire of the government to act with magnanimity with all parties deserving its clemency, and to re-establish order and legitimate authority among the Indian tribes; and whereas the undersigned representatives or parties connected with said nations or tribes of Indians have become satisfied that it is for the general good of the people to reunite with and be restored to the relations which formerly existed between them and the United States, and as indicative of our personal feelings in the premises, and of our several nations and tribes, so far as we are authorized and empowered to speak for them; and whereas questions have arisen as to the status of the nations, tribes, and bands that have made treaties with the enemies of the United States, which are now being discussed, and our relations settled by treaty with the United States commissioners now at Fort Smith for that purpose:

The undersigned do hereby acknowledge themselves to be under the protection of the United States of America, and covenant and agree, that hereafter they will in all things recognize the government of the United States as exercising exclusive jurisdiction over them, and will not enter into any allegiance or conventional arrangement with any state, nation, power or sovereign whatsoever; that any treaty of alliance for cession of land, or any act heretofore done by them, or any of their people, by which they renounce their allegiance to the United States, is hereby revoked, cancelled, and repudiated.

In consideration of the foregoing stipulations, made by the members of the respective nations and tribes of Indians present, the United States, through its commissioners, promises that it will re-establish peace and friendship with all the nations and tribes of Indians within the limits of the so-called Indian country; that it will afford ample protection for the security of the persons and property of the respective nations or tribes, and declares its willingness to enter into treaties to arrange and settle all questions relating to and growing out of former treaties with said nations, as affected by any treaty made by said nations with the so-called Confederate States, at this council now convened for that purpose, or at such time in the future as may be appointed.*

In testimony whereof, the said commissioners on the part of the United States, and the said Indians of the several nations and tribes, as respectively hereafter enumerated, have hereunto subscribed their names, and affixed their seals, on the day and year first above written.

(Note.—This treaty is presumed to have been signed, as indicated by the report of the proceedings at Fort Smith, by the commissioners of the United States and the delegations of Indians represented in the Council.   Their names follow:)

> Hon. D. N. Cooley, president,
> Hon. Elijah Sells,
> Thomas Wistar,
> Brig. Gen. W. S. Harney, U. S. Army,
> Col. Ely S. Parker,
> > Commissioners.

> Charles E. Mix,
> George L. Cook,
> W. R. Irwin,
> John B. Garrett,
> > Secretaries.

Creeks:
Ock-tar-sars-ha-jo, head chief.
Mik-ko-hut-kee, little white chief.
Cow-we-ta-mik-ko.
Cah-cho-she.
Thlo-cos-ya-lo.
Loch-er-ha-jo.
Co-me-ha-jo.
Tul-wah-mik-ko-che.
Tul-wah-mik-ko.
David Grayson.
David Field.
Tuka-basha-ha-jo.
Captain Johnneh.
Cap-tah-ka-na.
Passa.
Sa-to-wee.
Co-lo-ma-ha-jo.
Tul-me-mek-ko.

Jacob Conal.
David Berryhill.
Sanford Berryman.
Co-nip Fix-i-co, and others.
Wm. F. Brown, clerk.
Harry Island, interpreter for Creeks.
John Marshal, interpreter for Euchees.
Delegates for the black population living among the Creeks and Euchees:
Ketch Barnett.
John McIntosh.
Scipio Barnett.
Jack Brown.
Cow Tom.
Osages:
White Hair, principal chief.
Po-ne-no-pah-she, second chief Big Hill band.
Wah-dah-ne-gah, counsellor.

---

* This document is claimed by the Indian Office not to be a treaty, but simply an agreement which formed the bases for the treaty with the Seminole of May 21, 1866, (ante p. 910) and of the treaty with the Creeks of June 14, 1866, (ante p. 931). It is not on file in the Indian Office and is found only in the Report of the Commissioner of Indian Affairs for 1865.

In the Seminole and Creek treaties mention is made of the treaty of peace and amity at Fort Smith September 10, 1865.   This date is evidently erroneous, as no treaty was made at Fort Smith on that date.   The agreement of September 13, 1865, must have been the one referred to.

As to the signatories of the agreement the Commissioner of Indian Affairs, in his annual report for 1865, page 35, says:

"All of the delegates representing the following tribes and sections of tribes, in the order given, had signed treaties, (some of them holding out for several days until they could agree among themselves:) Senecas, Senecas and Shawnees, Quapaws, loyal Seminoles, loyal Chickasaws, loyal Creeks, Kansas, Shawnees (uncalled for, but asking to be permitted again to testify their allegiance,) loyal Osages, tribes of the Wichita agency, loyal Cherokees, disloyal Seminoles, disloyal Creeks, disloyal Cherokees, disloyal Osages, Comanches, disloyal Choctaws, and Chickasaws.

"Friendly relations were established between the members of the various tribes hitherto at variance, except in the case of the Cherokees.   The ancient feuds among this people are remembered still."

For the full proceedings at Fort Smith see Annual Report of the Commissioner of Indian Affairs for 1865, pp. 312–353.

Me-lo-tah-mo-ne, "Twelve o'clock."
Ko-she-ce-gla.
Ge-ne-o-ne-gla, (brave,) "Catch Alive."
Mah-ha-ah-ba-so, (brave,) "Sky-reaching man."
Shar-ba-no-sha, (brave,) "Done brown."
　Interpreters:
Alexander Bayette.
Augustus Captain.
　Cowskin Senecas:
Isaac Warrior, chief.
　Senecas and Shawnees:
Lewis Davis, chief.
A. McDonald.
Goodhunt.
Jas. Tallchief.
Lewis Denny.
　Interpreter, Lewis Davis.
　Cherokees:
Kah-sah-nie, Smith Christie.
Ah-yes-takie, Thomas Pegg.
Oo-nee-na-kah-ah-nah-ee, White Catcher.
Cha-loo-kie, Fox Flute.
Da-wee-oo-sal-chut-tee, David Rowe.
Ah-tah-lah-ka-no-skee-skee, Nathan Fish.
Koo-nah-vah, W. B. Downing.
Ta-la-la.
Oo-too-lah, ta-neh, Charles Conrad.
Oo-la-what-tee, Samuel Smith.
Tah-skee-kee-tee-hee, Jesse Baldridge.
Suu-kee, Mink Downing.
Chee-chee.
Tee-coo-le-to-ske, H. D. Reese.
Colonel Lewis Downing, acting and assistant principal chief.
　Seminoles:
John Shup-co.
Pascofa.
Fo-hut-she.
Fos-har-go.
Chut-cote-har-go.
　Interpreters: Robert Johnson, Cesar Bruner.

Shawnees:
Charles Blue Jacket, first chief.
Graham Rogers, second chief.
Moses Silverheels.
Solomon Madden.
Eli Blackhoof.
　Interpreter, Matthew King.
　Wyandotts:
Silas Armstrong, first chief.
Matthew Mud-eater, second chief.
　Quapaws:
George Wa-te-sha.
Ca-ha-she-ka.
Wa-she-hon-ca.
　S. G. Valier, interpreter.
　Chickasaws:
Et Tor Lutkee,
Louis Johnson,
Esh Ma Tubba,
A. G. Griffith,
Maharda Colbert, headmen.
Frazier McCrean.
Benjamin Colbert.
Ed Colbert.
———— Jackson.
Jim Doctor.
Simpson Killcrease.
A. B. Johnson.
———— Corman.
George Jonson.
———— Wolburn.
　Choctaws:
William S. Patton.
Robert B. Patton.
A. J. Stanton.
Jeremiah Ward.
　Indian agents:
Major G. C. Snow, for Osages.
George A. Reynolds, for Seminoles.
Isaac Coleman, for Choctaws and Chickasaws.
Justin Harlan, for Cherokees.
J. W. Dunn, for Creeks.
Milo Gookins, for Wichitas.
J. B. Abbott, for Shawnees.

AGREEMENT AT FORT BERTHOLD, 1866.

July 27, 1866.

Unratified.
Indian Office, "Treaties, box 3, 1864–1866."

Agreement with Arikara, Grosventres, and Mandan.

Articles of agreement and convention made and concluded at Fort Berthold in the Territory of Dakota, on the twenty-seventh day of July, in the year of our Lord one thousand eight hundred and sixty-six, by and between Newton Edmunds, governor and *ex-officio* superintendent of Indian affairs of Dakota Territory; Major General S. R. Curtis, Orrin Guernsey and Henry W. Reed, commissioners appointed on the part of the United States to make treaties with the Indians of the Upper Missouri; and the chiefs and headmen of the Arickaree tribe of Indians, Witnesseth as follows:

ARTICLE 1ST. Perpetual peace, friendship, and amity shall hereafter exist between the United States and the said Arickaree Indians.

ARTICLE 2D. The said Arickaree tribe of Indians promise and agree that they will maintain peaceful and friendly relations toward the whites; that they will in future, abstain from all hostilities against each other, and cultivate mutual good will and friendship, not only among themselves, but toward all other friendly tribes of Indians.

ARTICLE 3. The chiefs and headmen aforesaid acting as the representatives of the tribe aforesaid and being duly authorized and hereunto directed, in consideration of the payments and privileges hereinafter stated, do hereby grant and convey to the United States the right to lay out and construct roads, highways, and telegraphs through their country, and to use their efforts to prevent them from annoyance or interruption by their own or other tribes of Indians.

ARTICLE 4. No white person, unless in the employ of the United States, or duly licensed to trade with said Indians, or members of the families of such persons shall be permitted to reside or make settlement upon any part of the country belonging to said Indians, not included or described herein; nor shall said Indians sell, alienate, or in any manner dispose of any portion thereof, except to the United States.

ARTICLE 5. The said Aricara tribe of Indians hereby acknowledge their dependence on the United States and their obligation to obey the laws thereof; and they further agree and obligate themselves to submit to and obey such laws as may be made by Congress for their government and the punishment of offenders; and they agree to exert themselves to the utmost of their ability in enforcing all the laws under the superintendent of Indian affairs, or agent; and they pledge and bind themselves to preserve friendly relations with the citizens of the United States, and commit no injuries to, or depredations upon, their persons or property. They also agree to deliver to the proper officer or officers of the United States, all offenders against the treaties, laws, or regulations of the United States, and to assist in discovering, pursuing and capturing all such offenders who may be within the limits of the country claimed by them, whenever required so to do by such officer or officers. And the said Aricara tribe of Indians further agree that they will not make war upon any other tribe or band of Indians, except in self-defence, but will submit all matters of difference between themselves and other Indians to the Government of the United States for adjustment, and will abide thereby; and if any of the Indians, party to this treaty, commit depredations upon any other Indians within the jurisdiction of the United States, the same rule shall prevail with regard to compensation and punishment as in cases of depredations against citizens of the United States.

ARTICLE 6. In consideration of the great evil of intemperance among some of the Indian tribes, and in order to prevent such consequences among ourselves, we, the said Aricara tribe of Indians agree to do all in our power to prevent the introduction or use of spirituous liquors among our people, and to this end we agree that should any of the members of our tribe encourage the use of spirituous liquors, either by using it themselves, or buying and selling it, whosoever shall do so shall forfeit his claim to any annuities paid by the Government for the current year; or should they be aware of such use or sale or introduction of liquor into their country, either by whites or by persons of Indian blood and not aid by all proper means to effect its extermination and the prosecution of offenders, shall be liable to the forfeiture above mentioned.

ARTICLE 7. In consideration of the foregoing agreements, stipulations, cessions, and undertakings and of their faithful observance by the said Aricara tribe of Indians, the United States agree to expend for the said Indians, in addition to the goods and provisions distributed at the time of signing this treaty, the sum of ten thousand dollars annually for twenty years, after the ratification of this treaty by the President and Senate of the United States, to be expended in such goods, provisions, and other articles as the President may in his discretion, from time to time determine; provided, and it is hereby agreed that the President may, at his discretion, annually expend so much of the sum of three thousand dollars as he shall deem proper, in the purchase of stock, animals, agricultural implements, in establishing and instructing in agricultural and mechanical pursuits, such of said Indians as shall be disposed thereto; and in the employment of mechanics for them, in educating their children, in providing necessary and proper medicines, medical attendance, care for and support of the aged, sick, and infirm of their number, for the helpless orphans of said Indians, and in any other respect promoting their civilization, comfort, and improvement; provided further, that the President of the United States may, at his discretion determine in what proportion the said annuities shall be distributed among said Indians; and the United States further agree that out of the sum above stipulated to be paid to said Indians, there shall be set apart and paid to the head-chief, the sum of two hundred dollars annually, and to the soldier-chiefs, fifty dollars annually in money or supplies, so long as they and their bands remain faithful to their treaty obligations; and for and in consideration of the long continued and faithful services of *Pierre Garreau* to the Indians of the aforesaid tribe, and his efforts for their benefit, the United States agree to give him, out of the annuities to said tribe, the sum of two hundred dollars annually, being the same amount as is paid the head chiefs as aforesaid; and also to the eight leading men presented by the said tribe as the headmen and advisers of the principal chiefs, and to their successors in office, the sum of fifty dollars per annum, so long as they remain faithful to their treaty obligations; and *provided* that the President may, at his discretion, vary the amount paid to the chiefs, if in his judgment there may be either by the fidelity or efficiency of any of said chiefs sufficient cause; yet not so as to change the aggregate amount.

ARTICLE 8. It is understood and agreed by the parties to this treaty, that if any of the bands of Indians, parties hereto, shall violate any of the agreements, stipulations, or obligations herein contained, the United States may withhold, for such length of time as the President may determine, any portion or all the annuities agreed to be paid to said Indians under the provisions of this treaty.

ARTICLE 9. The annuities of the aforesaid Indians shall not be taken to pay the debts of individuals, but satisfaction for depredations committed by them shall be made in such manner as the President may direct.

ARTICLE 10. This treaty shall be obligatory upon the aforesaid tribe of Indians from the date hereof, and upon the United States so soon as the same shall be ratified by the President and Senate.

ARTICLE 11. Any amendment or modification of this treaty by the Senate of the United States, not materially changing the nature or obligation of the same, shall be considered final and binding on said bands the same as if it had been subsequently presented and agreed to by the said chiefs and headmen, in open council.

In testimony whereof the aforesaid commissioners on the part of the United States, and the chiefs and headmen of the aforementioned tribe of Indians, have hereunto set their hands this twenty-seventh day of July, in the year of our Lord one thousand eight hundred and sixty-six, after the contents thereof had been previously read, interpreted, and explained.

NEWTON EDMUNDS.
S. R. CURTIS.
ORRIN GUERNSEY.
HENRY W. REED.

White Shield, his x mark.
Iron Bear, his x mark.
The Son of the Star, or Rushing Bear, his
   x mark.
The Black Trail, his x mark.
The Wolf Necklace, his x mark.
The one that comes out first, his x mark.
The Whistling Bear, his x mark.
The Yellow Knife, his x mark.
The Bear of the Woods, his x mark.
The Dog Chief, his x mark.
  Headmen:
White Cow Chief, his x mark.
The Walking Wolf, his x mark.
The White Bear, his x mark.
The Bully Head, his mark.
The Young Wolf, his x mark.
The Short Tail Bull, his x mark.

The Lone Horse, his x mark.
The War Eagle Cap, his x mark.
The Sitting Night, his x mark.
The Yellow Wolf, his x mark.
The Old Bear, his x mark.
The Brave, his x mark.
The Big Head, his x mark.
The Elk River, his x mark.
Mahlon Wilkinson, agent.
Reuben S. Pike.
Jos. La Burg, jr.
Charles Reader.
Chas. F. Picotte.
  U. S. Interpreters:
Pierre Garreau, his x mark.
Charles Papin.
Charles Larpenteur.

Signed by the commissioners on the part of the United States, and by the chiefs and headmen, after the treaty had been fully read, interpreted, and explained in our presence.

                     Chas. A. Reed,
                       Secy. of Commission.
                M. K. Armstrong,
                       Assist. Secty.

ADDENDA.

The chiefs and headmen of the Gros Ventres and Mandan tribes, heretofore long associated with the Arickarees named in the foregoing treaty, and anxious to continue their residence in the same community and perpetuate their friendly relations with the Arickarees and the United States, do concur in, and become parties and participants in and to all the stipulations of the foregoing treaty.

Supplement, whereby Gros Ventre and Mandan tribes become parties to the foregoing treaty.

And it being made known to all the tribes thus associated that the United States may desire to connect a line of stages with the river, at the salient angle thereof about thirty miles below this point, and may desire to establish settlements and convenient supplies and mechanical structures to accommodate the growing commerce and travel, by land and river, the chiefs and headmen of the Arickarees, Gros Ventres, and Mandans, acting and uniting also with the commissioners of the United States aforesaid, do hereby convey to the United States all their right and title to the following lands, situated on the northeast side of the Missouri River, to wit: Beginning on the Missouri River at the mouth of Snake River, about thirty miles below Ft. Berthold; thence up Snake River and in a northeast direction twenty-five miles; thence southwardly parallel to the Missouri River to a point opposite and twenty-five miles east of old Ft. Clarke; thence west to a point on the Missouri River opposite to old Ft. Clarke; thence up the Missouri River to the place of beginning: *Provided*, That the premises here named shall not be a harbor for Sioux or other Indians when they are hostile to the tribes, parties to this treaty; but it shall be the duty of the United States to protect and defend these tribes in the lawful occupation of their homes, and in the enjoyment of their civil rights, as the white people are protected in theirs.

ARTICLE 2. It is also agreed by the three tribes aforesaid, now united in this treaty as aforesaid, that in consideration of the premises named in the aforesaid treaty, and the further consideration of the cession of lands at Snake River, in addition to the payments by the United States of annuities there named to the Arickarees, there shall be paid five thousand dollars to the Gros Ventres, and five thousand dollars to the

Mandans, annually, in goods, at the discretion of the President.   And for the Gros Ventres and Mandan tribes twenty per cent. of their annuity may be expended for agricultural, mechanical, and other purposes as specified in the latter clause of Article Seven of the aforesaid treaty.

And also out of the aforesaid annuity to the Gros Ventres there shall be paid to the first, or principal chief, the sum of two hundred dollars each, annually, and to the six soldier chiefs the sum of fifty dollars each, annually.

There shall also be paid to the head, or principal chief, of the Mandans, out of the annuities of said tribe, the sum of two hundred dollars, annually, and to each of the nine soldier chiefs the sum of fifty dollars, annually.

In testimony whereof the aforesaid commissioners on the part of the United States, and the chiefs and headmen of the aforementioned tribes of Indians, have hereunto set their hands this twenty-seventh day of July, in the year of our Lord one thousand eight hundred and sixty-six, after the contents thereof had been previously read, interpreted, and explained to the chiefs and headmen of the aforementioned tribes.

NEWTON EDMUNDS.   [SEAL.]
S. R. CURTIS.   [SEAL.]
ORRIN GUERNSEY.   [SEAL.]
HERNY W. REED.   [SEAL.]

Signatures of Arickarees:
White Shield, Head Chief, his x mark.
Rushing Bear, Second Chief, his x mark.
Wolf Necklace, Chief, his x mark.
Bear of the woods, Chief, his x mark.
Whistling Bear, Chief, his x mark.
Iron Bear, Soldier C., his x mark.
Black trail, Second Chief, his x mark.
The Two Bears, Chief, his x mark.
The Yellow Knife, Chief, his x mark.
The Crow Chief, Chief, his x mark.
  Gros Ventres Chiefs:
Crow Breast, Head Chief, his x mark.
Poor Wolf, Second Chief, his x mark.
Red Tail, his x mark.
The War Chief, his x mark.
Short Tail Bull, his x mark.

One whose mouth rubbed with cherries, his x mark.
The Yellow Shirt, his x mark,
  Chief Soldiers:
The Flying Crow, his x mark.
The Many Antelope, his x mark.
One who eats no marrow, his x mark.
  Mandan Chiefs:
The Red Cow, his x mark.
The Running Eagle, his x mark.
The Big Turtle, his x mark.
The Scabby Wolf, his x mark.
The Crazy Chief, his x mark.
The Crow Chief, his x mark.
  Chief Soldiers:
One who strikes in the back, his x mark.

Signed by the commissioners on the part of the United States, and by the chiefs and headmen after the treaty had been fully read, interpreted and explained in our presence.
  Witnesses to the above signatures:
      Chas. A. Reed, Secty. of Commission.
      Mahlon Wilkinson, Agent.
      M. K. Armstrong, Asst. Secy.
      Reuben S. Pike.

  U. S. interpreters:
      Charles Reader.
      C. F. Picotte.
      Charles Larpenteur.
      Pierre Garreau, his x mark.
      Charles Papin.

AGREEMENT WITH THE SISSETON AND WAHPETON BANDS OF SIOUX INDIANS, 1872.

Whereas, the Sisseton and Wahpeton bands of Dakota or Sioux Indians made and concluded a treaty with the United States, at the city of Washington, D. C., on the 19th day of February, A. D. 1867, which was ratified, with certain amendments, by the Senate of the United States on the 15th day of April, 1868, and finally promulgated by the President of the United States on the 2d day of May, in the year aforesaid, by which the Sisseton and Wahpeton bands of Sioux Indians ceded to the United States certain privileges and rights supposed to belong to said bands in the territory described in article two (2) of said treaty, and

Whereas, it is desirable that all said territory, except the portion thereof comprised in what is termed the permanent reservations, particularly described in articles three (3) and four (4) of said treaty, shall be ceded absolutely to the United States, upon such consideration as in justice and equity should be paid therefor by the United States; and,

Whereas, said territory, now proposed to be ceded, is no longer available to said Indians for the purposes of the chase, and such value or consideration is essentially necessary in order to enable said bands interested therein to cultivate portions of said permanent reservations, and become wholly self-supporting by the cultivation of the soil and other pursuits of husbandry: therefore, the said bands, represented in said treaty, and parties thereto, by their chiefs and head-men, now assembled in council, do propose to M. N. Adams, William H. Forbes, and James Smith, jr., commissioners on behalf of the United States, as follows:

First. To cede, sell, and relinquish to the United States all their right, title, and interest in and to all lands and territory, particularly described in article two (2) of said treaty, as well as all lands in the Territory of Dakota to which they have title or interest, excepting the said tracts particularly described and bounded in articles three (3) and four (4) of said treaty, which last-named tracts and territory are expressly reserved as permanent reservations for occupancy and cultivation, as contemplated by articles eight, (8,) nine, (9,) and ten (10) of said treaty.

Second. That, in consideration of said cession and relinquishment, the United States shall advance and pay, annually, for the term of ten (10) years from and after the acceptance by the United States of the proposition herein submitted, eighty thousand (80,000) dollars, to be expended under the direction of the President of the United States, on the plan and in accordance with the provisions of the treaty aforesaid, dated February 19, 1867, for goods and provisions, for the erection of manual-labor and public school-houses, and for the support of manual-labor and public schools, and in the erection of mills, blacksmiths-shops, and other workshops, and to aid in opening farms, breaking land, and fencing the same, and in furnishing agricultural implements, oxen, and milch-cows, and such other beneficial objects as may be deemed most conducive to the prosperity and happiness of the Sisseton and Wahpeton bands of Dakota or Sioux Indians entitled thereto according to the said treaty of February 19, 1867. Such annual appropriation or consideration to be apportioned to the Sisseton and Devil's Lake agencies, in proportion to the number of Indians of the said bands located upon the Lake Traverse and Devil's Lake reservations respectively. Such apportionment to be made upon the basis of the annual reports or returns of the agents in charge. Said consider-

September 20, 1872.

Unratified.
Indian Office, Sisseton, S. 247 (1872).

See 1874, c. 389, 18 Stat., 167.

Sections 3 to 9 inclusive stricken out by amended agreement following.

ation, amounting, in the aggregate, to eight hundred thousand (800,000) dollars, payable as aforesaid, without interest.

Third. As soon as may be, the said territory embraced within said reservation described in article four, (4,) (Devil's Lake reservation,) shall be surveyed, as Government lands are surveyed, for the purpose of enabling the Indians entitled to acquire permanent rights in the soil, as contemplated by article five (5) of said treaty.

Fourth. We respectfully request that, in case the foregoing propositions are favorably entertained by the United States, the sale of spirituous liquors upon the territory ceded may be wholly prohibited by the United States Government.

Fifth. The provisions of article five (5) of the treaty of February 19, 1867, to be modified as follows: An occupancy and cultivation of five (5) acres, upon any particular location, for a term of (5) consecutive years shall entitle the party to a patent for forty acres; a like occupancy and cultivation of ten (10) acres, to entitle the party to a patent to eighty acres; and a like occupancy and cultivation of any tract, to the extent of twenty acres, shall entitle the party so occupying and cultivating to a patent for 160 acres of land. Parties who have already selected farms and cultivated the same may be entitled to the benefit of this modification. Patents so issued (as hereinbefore set forth) shall authorize a transfer or alienation of such lands situate within the Sisseton agency, after the expiration of ten (10) years from this date, and within the Devil's lake reservation after the expiration of fifteen (15) years, but not sooner.

Sixth. The consideration to be paid, as hereinbefore proposed, is in addition to the provision of article 6 (6) of the treaty of February 19, 1867, under which Congress shall appropriate, from time to time, such an amount as may be required to meet the necessities of said Indians, to enable them to become civilized.

Seventh. Sections sixteen (16) and thirty-six (36) within the reservations shall be set apart for educational purposes, and all children of a suitable age within either reservation shall be compelled to attend school at the discretion of the agents.

Eighth. At the expiration of ten (10) years, from this date, all members of said bands under the age of twenty-one years shall receive forty acres of land from said permanent reservations in fee simple.

Ninth. At the expiration of ten (10) years, the President of the United States shall sell or dispose of all the remaining or unoccupied lands in the lake Traverse reservation, (excepting that which may hereafter be set apart for school purposes;) the proceeds of the sale of such lands to be expended for the benefit of the members of said bands located on said lake Traverse reservation; and, at the expiration of fifteen (15) years, the President shall sell or dispose of all the remaining unoccupied lands (excepting that which may be hereafter set apart for school purposes) in the Devil's Lake reservation; the proceeds of the sale of such land shall be expended for the benefit of all members of said bands who may be located on the said Devil's Lake reservation.

Executed at Sisseton agency, Dakota territory, Lake Traverse reservation, this 20th day of September, A. D. 1872.

MOSES N. ADAMS,
WM. H. FORBES,
JAMES SMITH, JR.,
Commissioners.

Gabriel Renville, head chief of Sissetons and Wahpetons.

Wicanipinonpa, chief councilor Wahpetons and Sissetons.

Wasuiciyapi, chief Sisseton band Swantain, his x mark.

Hokxidanwaxte, chief councilor Sissetons, his x mark.

Wasukiye, chief councilor Sissetons, his x mark.

Peter Tapatatonka, hereditary chief Wahpetons.

Magaiyahe, chief councilor, a soldier, Sissetons, his x mark.

Waxicunmaza, chief councilor Sissetons, his x mark.

Wakanto, chief councilor or soldier, his x mark.

Ecetukiye.

Ampetuxa, Wahpeton councilor, his x mark.

Rupacokamaza, Wahpeton soldier, his x mark.

Itojanjan, Sisseton soldier, his x mark.

Inihan, Sisseton soldier, his x mark.

Michael Renville, chief councilor or soldier.

Ixakiya, Sesseton soldier, his x mark.

Paul Mazakutemani, chief councilor.

Edwin Phelps, chief councilor.

Elias Oranwayakapi, chief councilor.

Aojanjanna, second soldier and councilor, his x mark.

Wasincaga, second soldier and councilor, his x mark.

Kampeska, chief soldier Wahpeton, his x mark.

Marpiyakudan, chief Sissetons, his x mark.

Matocatka, Wahpeton soldier, his x mark.

Wamdiokiya, Wahpeton soldier, his x mark.

Tanwannonpa, Wahpeton soldier, his x mark.

Hinhanxunna, Sisseton soldier, his x mark.

Tamazakanna, Sisseton soldier, his x mark.

Akacitamane, Sisseton soldier, his x mark.

Wamdiupiduta, chief Sissetons, his x mark.

Tacandupahotanka, chief Wahpetons, his x mark.

Tacaurpipeta, soldier or councilor, his x mark.

Tamniyage, head chief Sissetons, his x mark.

Wamdiduta, chief soldier Sissetons, his x mark.

Canteryapa, soldier Sissetons, his x mark.

Xupehiyu, Wahpeton soldier, his x mark.

Chadoze, Sisseton soldier, his x mark.

Wakinyanrota, Sisseton soldier, his x mark.

Cantemaza, Wahpeton chief.

Ecanaginka, Sisseton soldier, his x mark.

Inimusapa, Sisseton soldier, his x mark.

Icartaka, Sisseton soldier, his x mark.

Ximto, Sisseton soldier, his x mark.

Rdohinhda, Sisseton soldier, his x mark.

Wicastawakan, Sisseton soldier, his x mark.

Makaideya, Sisseton soldier, his x mark.

Mniyatohonaxte, Sisseton soldier, his x mark.

Akicitaduta, Sisseton soldier, his x mark.

Cagewanica, Sisseton soldier, his x mark.

Wanaita, hereditary chief of Sissetons and Cut-Heads, his x mark.

Towaxte, head chief Sissetons, his x mark.

Makanahuza, Sisseton soldier, his x mark.

Mazakahomni, Sisseton soldier, his x mark.

Ousepekaga, Sisseton soldier, his x mark.

Tate, Sisseton soldier, his x mark.

Cokahdi, Sisseton soldier, his x mark.

Rupaicasna, Sisseton soldier, his x mark.

Ixkiya, chief soldier, Wahpetons, his x mark.

Witnesses to signatures of above chiefs and soldiers:

    H. T. Lovett.
    G. H. Hawes.
    T. A. Robertson.
    G. H. Faribault.
    C. P. La Grange.

We hereby certify, on honor, that we have fully explained to the Indians the above instrument, and that the Indians acknowledge the same to be well understood by them.

                                            T. A. Robertson,
                                            G. H. Faribault,
                                                    Interpreters.

AMENDED AGREEMENT WITH CERTAIN SIOUX INDIANS, 1873.

WHEREAS, the *Sisseton* and *Wahpeton Bands of Dakota* or *Sioux Indians,* on the 20th day of September A. D. 1872 made and entered into an agreement in writing, signed on one part by the Chiefs and headmen of said bands, with the assent and approval of the members of [said] bands, and upon the other part by *Moses N. Adams, James Smith, jr.,* and *William H. Forbes,* commissioners on the part of the *United States;* which said agreement is as follows, to wit:

"*Whereas,* the Sisseton and Wahpeton bands of Dakota or Sioux Indians made and concluded a treaty with the United States, at the city

May 2, 1873.

Ratified by acts of Feb. 14, 1873 (17 Stat., 456), and June 24, 1874 (18 Stat., 167).

Indian office, Sisseton S. 128, and I. 355 (1873).

of Washington, D. C., on the 19th day of February, A. D. 1867, which was ratified, with certain amendments, by the Senate of the United States on the 15th day of April, 1867, and finally promulgated by the President of the United States on the 2d day of May, in the year aforesaid, by which the Sisseton and Wahpeton bands of Sioux Indians ceded to the United States certain privileges and rights supposed to belong to said bands in the territory described in article II of said treaty, and

" *Whereas*, it is desirable that all said territory, except the portion thereof comprised in what is termed the permanent reservations, particularly described in articles III and IV of said treaty, shall be ceded absolutely to the United States, upon such consideration as in justice and equity should be paid therefor by the United States; and

" *Whereas*, said territory, now proposed to be ceded, is no longer available to said Indians for the purposes of the chase, and such value or consideration is essentially necessary in order to enable said bands interested therein to cultivate portions of said permanent reservations, and become wholly self-supporting by the cultivation of the soil and other pursuits of husbandry; *therefore*, the said bands, represented in said treaty, and parties thereto, by their chiefs and head-men, now assembled in council, do propose to M. N. Adams, William H. Forbes, and James Smith, jr., commissioners on behalf of the United States, as follows:

"*First*. To cede, sell, and relinquish to the United States all their right, title, and interest in and to all lands and territory, particularly described in article II of said treaty, as well as all lands in the Territory of Dakota to which they have title or interest, excepting the said tracts particularly described and bounded in articles III and IV of said treaty, which last named tracts and territory are expressly reserved as permanent reservations for occupancy and cultivation, as contemplated by articles VIII, IX, and X of said treaty.

"*Second*. That, in consideration of said cession and relinquishment, the United States shall advance and pay, annually, for the term of ten years from and after the acceptance by the United States of the proposition herein submitted, eighty thousand (80,000) dollars, to be expended under the direction of the President of the United States, on the plan and in accordance with the provisions of the treaty aforesaid, dated February 19, 1867, for goods and provisions, for the erection of manual-labor and public school-houses, and for the support of manual-labor and public schools, and in the erection of mills, blacksmith-shops, and other work-shops, and to aid in opening farms, breaking land, and fencing the same, and in furnishing agricultural implements, oxen, and milch-cows, and such other beneficial objects as may be deemed most conducive to the prosperity and happiness of the Sisseton and Wahpeton bands of Dakota or Sioux Indians entitled thereto according to the said treaty of February 19, 1867. Such annual appropriation or consideration to be apportioned to the Sisseton and Devil's Lake agencies, in proportion to the number of Indians of the said bands located upon the Lake Traverse and Devil's Lake reservations respectively. Such apportionment to be made upon the basis of the annual reports or returns of the agents in charge. Said consideration, amounting, in the aggregate, to eight hundred thousand (800,000) dollars, payable as aforesaid, without interest.

Third to ninth sections stricken out by amendment.

"*Third*. As soon as may be, the said territory embraced within said reservation described in article IV, (Devil's Lake reservation,) shall be surveyed, as Government lands are surveyed, for the purpose of enabling the Indians entitled to acquire permanent rights in the soil, as contemplated by article V of said treaty.

"*Fourth*. We respectfully request that, in case the foregoing propositions are favorably entertained by the United States, the sale of spirituous liquors upon the territory ceded may be wholly prohibited by the United States Government.

"*Fifth*. The provisions of article V of the treaty of February 19, 1867, to be modified as follows: An occupancy and cultivation of five acres, upon any particular location, for a term of five consecutive years, shall entitle the party to a patent for forty acres; a like occupancy and cultivation of ten acres, to entitle the party to eighty acres; and a like occupancy and cultivation of any tract, to the extent of twenty acres, shall entitle the party so occupying and cultivating to a patent for 160 acres of land. Parties who have already selected farms and cultivated the same, may be entitled to the benefit of this modification. Patents so issued, (as hereinbefore set forth) shall authorize a transfer or alienation of such lands situate within the Sisseton agency, after the expiration of ten years from this date, and within the Devil's Lake reservation after the expiration of fifteen years, but not sooner.

"*Fifth (sixth)*. The consideration to be paid, as hereinbefore proposed, is in addition to the provisions of Article VI of the treaty of February 19, 1867, under which Congress shall appropriate from time to time, such an amount as may be required to meet the necessities of said Indians to enable them to become civilized.

"*Sixth (seventh)*. Sections sixteen and thirty-six within the reservations shall be set apart for educational purposes, and all children of a suitable age within either reservation shall be compelled to attend school at the discretion of the agents.

"*Seventh (eighth)*. At the expiration of ten years from this date, all members of said bands, under the age of twenty-one years shall receibe forty acres of land from said permanent reservations in fee simple.

"*Eighth (ninth)*. At the expiration of ten years, the President of the United States shall sell or dispose of all the remaining or unoccupied lands in the lake Traverse reservation, (excepting that which may hereafter be set apart for school purposes;) the proceeds of the sale of such lands to be expended for the benefit of the members of said bands located on said Lake Traverse; and, at the expiration of fifteen years, the President shall sell or dispose of all the remaining unoccupied lands (excepting that which may hereafter be set apart for school purposes) in the Devil's Lake reservation; the proceeds of the sales of such lands shall be expended for the benefit of all members of said bands who may be located on the said Devil's Lake reservation.

"Executed at Sisseton Agency, Dakota Territory, Lake Traverse reservation, this 20th day of September, A. D. 1872.

And whereas, the Congress of the United States, upon consideration of the provisions of said agreement hereinbefore recited, did, by the act making appropriations for the current and contingent expenses of the Indian department, and for fulfilling treaty stipulations with various Indian tribes, for the year ending June thirtieth, eighteen hundred and seventy-four, and for other purposes, approved February 14th, 1873, provide as follows, to wit: "For this amount, being the first of ten installments of the sum of eight hundred thousand dollars named in a certain agreement made by the commissioners appointed by the Secretary of the Interior, under the provisions of the act of June seventh, eighteen hundred and seventy-two, with the Sisseton and Wahpeton bands of Sioux Indians for the relinquishment by said Indians of their claim to, or interest in, the lands described in the second article of the treaty made with them February nineteenth, eighteen hundred and sixty-seven: the same to be expended under the direction of the President, for the benefit of said Indians, in the manner prescribed in said treaty of eighteen hundred and sixty-seven, as amended by the Senate, eighty thousand dollars. And the said agreement is hereby confirmed, excepting so much thereof as is included in paragraphs numbered respectively, third, fourth, fifth, sixth, seventh, eighth, and ninth: *Provided*, That no part of this amount shall be expended until after the ratification, by said Indians, of said agreement as hereby amended."

And whereas, the said Bands of Dakota or Sioux Indians have been duly assembled in council, and therein represented by the chiefs and head-men, and the provisions of said act of Congress, and amendments thereby made to the said above recited agreement, having been fully explained by the commissioners on the part of the United States, and the said agreement as amended having been fully interpreted, and now being understood, we the said chiefs and head-men of the said Sisseton and Wahpeton Bands, duly authorized by our people so to do, do hereby accept, assent to, confirm, ratify and agree to the said amendments, and to the said agreement as amended, and declare that the same is, and shall hereafter be binding upon us and the members of said Bands.

Witness our hands and seals at the Lac Traverse agency, Dakota Territory, this second day of May, A. D. 1873.

Gabriell Renville.	Itojanjan, his x mark.
Wamdienpiduta, his x mark.	Inihan, his x mark.
Tacandupahotanka, his x mark.	Michel Renvill.
Wicanspinupa.	Ixakiye, his x mark.
Eutinkiya.	Paul Mazawakutemani, his x mark.
Hokxidannaxte, his x mark.	Elias Oranwayakapi.
Wakanto, his x mark.	Kampeska, his x mark.
Wamdiduta, his x mark.	Simon Anawagmani, his x mark.
Waxicunmaza, his x mark.	John R. Renvill.
Wasukiye, his x mark.	Daniel Renville.
Tacaurpipeta, his x mark.	Taokiyeota, his x mark.
Akicitanajin, his x mark.	Mechael Paul.
Xupehiyu, his x mark.	John Waniyarpeya, his x mark.
Magaiyahe, his x mark.	Robert Hopkins.
Peter Tapetatonka.	Alex. La Framboise.
Tamniyage, his x mark.	

We certify, on honor, that we were present and witnessed the signatures of the Indians as above.

> G. H. HAWES.
> H. T. LOVETT.
> JNO. L. HODGMAN.
> CHARLES P. LA GRANGE.

I hereby certify, on honor, that I have fully explained to the Indians in council, the above instrument, and that the Indians acknowledged the same to be well understood by them.

> THOS. A. ROBERTSON,
> Interpreter.

Executed at Sisseton agency, Lake Traverse Reservation, D. T., this second day of May, 1873.

> MOSES N. ADAMS,
> JAMES SMITH, JR.,
> Commissioners.

Devil's Lake Reservation, Fort Totten agency, D. T., May 19, 1873.

Wah-na-ta, his x mark.	Ca-do-ze, his x mark.
Tee-oh-wash-tag, his x mark.	Wa-kin-yan-ro-ta, his x mark.
Mah-pee-ah-keo-den, his x mark.	I-car-ta-ke, his x mark.
E-chah-na-gee-kah, his x mark.	In-im-u-sa-pa, his x mark.
Mat-te-o-he-chat-kah, his x mark.	Mu-i-ya-to-ho-nax-te, his x mark.
Ou-s(e)-pe-ka-ge, his x mark.	Ton-wau-non-pa, his x mark.
Chan-te-ma-za, his x mark.	We-i-za-ka-ma-za.

Ma-ka-na-hu-hu-za.
Ma-ka-i-de-ya, his x mark.
Xip-to, his x mark.
Wa-ka-no-ki-ta, his x mark.
Ta-te-o-pax-im-a-ni, his x mark.
Ru-pahn-wa-kam-a, his x mark.
A-ki-ci-ta-du-ta, his x mark.
Ta-wa-cin-ha, his x mark.
Ru-pahu-wax-te, his x mark.
Ri-o-in-yan-i-yan-ke, his x mark.
Ran-in-wan-ke, his x mark.
A-ki-ci-tam-a-ne, his x mark.
Maza-ka-hom-ni.
Wam-di-hi-ye-ya, his x mark.
Wi-cer-pi-wa-kan-na, his x mark.
Wax-i-em-u-nape-wu-az-u-za, his x mark.

Ha-oih-da, his x mark.
Wam-di-o-ki-ga, his x mark.
Wa-kan-hoi-ma-za, his x mark.
He-wa-kan-na, his x mark.
I-han-gi, his x mark.
Ma-koi-ya-te, his x mark.
Ta-rin-ca-sin-te, his x mark.
Na-gi-wa-kan, his x mark.
We-ci-ni-han, his x mark.
Ca-je-wan-i-ca, his x mark.
Wan-di-cax-kpi, his x mark.
Tate, his x mark.
U-jin-pi, his x mark.
Hint-ka-ro-ta, his x mark.
Hin-han-xo-na, his x mark.

Witnesses to signatures of above chiefs and soldiers,

LEWIS CASS HUNT,
Lieut. Col. 20th Infantry.
JAMES B. FERGUSON,
Act. Asst. Surgeon, U. S. A.

I hereby certify, upon honor, that I have fully explained to the Indians the above instrument and that the Indians acknowledge the same to be well understood by them.

GEORGE H. FARIBAULT,
Interpreter.

Executed at the Fort Totten agency, "Devil's Lake" reservation, this 19th day of May, 1873, in open council, by the Sisseton and Wahpeton and "Cut-Head" bands of Sioux not included in the Sisseton and Wahpeton bands of Sioux of "Lac Travers" reservation, who signed this, on the 2nd of May, 1873, as above written.

JAMES SMITH, JR.,
WM. H. FORBES,
MOSES N. ADAMS,
Commissioners.

AGREEMENT WITH THE CROWS, 1880.

The chiefs of the Crow tribe of Indians now present in Washington hereby give their own consent and promise to use their best endeavors to procure the consent of the adult male members of said tribe to cede to the United States all that part of the present Crow reservation in the Territory of Montana described as follows, to wit:

May 14, 1880.

Unratified.*
Indian Office, Montana C. 839 (1880).
See note a, Vol. 1, p. 195.

Beginning in mid-channel of the Yellowstone River, at a point opposite the mouth of Boulder Creek; thence up the mid-channel of said river to the point where it crosses the southern boundary of Montana, being the forty-fifth degree of north latitude; thence east along said parallel of latitude to the one hundred and ninth meridian of longitude; thence north on said meridian, to a point six miles south of the first standard parallel south, being on the township-line between townships six and seven south; thence west on said township-line to the one hundred and tenth meridian of longitude; thence north along said meridian to a point either west or east of the source of the Eastern Branch of Boulder Creek; thence in a straight line to the source of the Eastern Branch of Boulder Creek; thence down said Eastern Branch to Boulder Creek; thence down Boulder Creek, and to the place of beginning.

The said chiefs of the Crow tribe of Indians promise to obtain the consent of their people as aforesaid to the cession of the territory of their reserve as above, on the following express conditions:

First. That the Government of the United States cause the agricultural lands remaining in their reservation to be properly surveyed and divided among the said Indians in severalty in the proportions hereinafter mentioned, and to issue patents to them respectively therefor, so soon as the necessary laws are passed by Congress. Allotments in severalty of said surveyed lands shall be made as follows: To each head of a family not more than one-quarter of a section, with an additional quantity of grazing-land, not exceeding one-quarter of a section. To each single person over eighteen years of age not more than one-eighth of a section, with an additional quantity of grazing-land not exceeding one-eighth of a section. To each orphan child under eighteen years of age not more than one-eighth of a section, with an additional quantity of grazing land not exceeding one-eighth of a section, and to each other person, under eighteen years, or who may be born prior to said allotments, one-eighth of a section, with a like quantity of grazing land. All allotments to be made with the advice of the Agent for said Indians, or such other person as the Secretary of the Interior may designate for that purpose, upon the selection of the Indians, heads of families selecting for their minor children, and the agent making the allotment for each orphan child.

The title to be acquired by the Indians shall not be subject to alienation, lease, or incumbrance, either by voluntary conveyance of the grantee or his heirs, or by the judgment, order, or decree of any court, or subject to taxation of any character, but shall be and remain inalienable, and not subject to taxation for the period of twenty-five years, and until such time thereafter as the President may see fit to remove the restriction, which shall be incorporated in the patents.

Second. That in consideration of the cession of territory to be made by the said Crow tribe, the United States, in addition to the annuities and sums for provisions and clothing stipulated and provided for in existing treaties and laws, agrees to appropriate annually for twenty-five years, the sum of thirty thousand dollars, to be expended under the direction of the President for the benefit of the said Indians, in assisting them to erect houses, to procure seeds, farming implements, stock, or in cash, as the President may direct.

Third. That if at any time hereafter the Crow Indians shall consent to permit cattle to be driven across their reservation or grazed on the same, the Secretary of the Interior shall fix the amount to be paid by parties desiring to so drive or graze cattle; all moneys arising from this source to be paid to the Indians under such rules and regulations as the Secretary of the Interior may prescribe.

Fourth. All the existing provisions of the treaty of May seventh, 1868, shall continue in force.

Done at Washington, this fourteenth day of May, anno Domini, eighteen hundred and eighty.

                                 Plenty Coos, his x mark.
                                   Old Crow, his x mark
                                   Two Belly, his x mark
                                   Long Elk, his x mark
                                   Pretty Eagle, his x mark
                                   Medicine Crow, his x mark.

Witnesses:
     A. M. Quivly, Interpreter.
     E. J. Brooks
     J. F. Stoek
     A. R. Keller, United States Indian Agent.

NOTE.—This agreement was not ratified, but substituted by that of June 12, 1880, which was ratified April 11, 1882 (22 Stat., 42.)

AGREEMENT WITH THE SIOUX OF VARIOUS TRIBES, 1882–83.

This agreement made pursuant to an item in the sundry civil act of Congress, approved August 7, 1882, by Newton Edmunds, Peter C. Shannon, and James H. Teller, duly appointed commissioners on the part of the United States, and the different bands of the Sioux Indians by their chiefs and headmen whose names are hereto subscribed, they being duly authorized to act in the premises, witnesseth that— *Oct. 17, 1882, to Jan. 3, 1883.*

Unratified. See H. R. Ex. Doc. 68, 47th Congress, 2d session.

ARTICLE I.

Whereas it is the policy of the Government of the United States to provide for said Indians a permanent home where they may live after the manner of white men, and be protected in their rights of property, person and life, therefore to carry out such policy it is agreed that hereafter the permanent of the various bands of said Indians shall be upon the separate reservations hereinafter described and set apart. Said Indians, acknowledging the right of the chiefs and headmen of the various bands at each agency to determine for themselves and for their several bands, with the Government of the United States, the boundaries of their separate reservations, hereby agree to accept and abide by such agreements and conditions as to the location and boundaries of such reservations as may be made and agreed upon by the United States and the band or bands for which such separate reservation may be made, and as the said separate boundaries may be herein set forth.

ARTICLE II.

The said Indians do hereby relinquish and cede to the United States all of the Great Sioux Reservation—as reserved to them by the treaty of 1868, and modified by the agreement of 1876—not herein specifically reserved and set apart as separate reservations for them. The said bands do severally agree to accept and occupy the separate reservations to which they are herein assigned as their permanent homes, and they do hereby severally relinquish to the other bands respectively occupying the other separate reservations, all right, title, and interest in and to the same reserving to themselves only the reservation herein set apart for their separate use and occupation. *Great Sioux Reservation—Indians cede title to.*

ARTICLE III.

In consideration of the cession of territory and rights, as herein made, and upon compliance with each and every obligation assumed by the said Indians, the United States hereby agrees that each head of a family entitled to select three hundred and twenty acres of land, under Article 6, of the treaty of 1868, may, in the manner and form therein prescribed, select and secure for purposes of cultivation, in addition to said three hundred and twenty acres, a tract of land not exceeding eighty (80) acres within his reservation, for each of his children, living at the ratification of this agreement, under the age of eighteen (18) years; and such child, upon arriving at the age of eighteen years shall have such selection certified to him or her in lieu of the selection granted in the second clause of said Article 6; but no right of alienation or encumbrance is acquired by such selection and occupation; unless hereafter authorized by act of Congress. *Allotments in severalty.*

ARTICLE IV.

The United States further agrees to furnish and deliver to the said Indians twenty-five thousand cows, and one thousand bulls, of which *Cattle to be furnished Indians.*

the occupants of each of said separate reservations shall receive such proportion as the number of Indians thereon bears to the whole number of Indian parties to this agreement. All of the said cattle and their progeny shall bear the brand of the Indian department, and shall be held subject to the disposal of said department, and shall not be sold, exchanged or slaughtered, except by consent or order of the agent in charge, until such time as this restriction shall be removed by the Cmmissioner of Indian Affairs.

ARTICLE V.

Oxen to be furnished Indian allottees. It is also agreed that the United States will furnish and deliver to each lodge of said Indians or family of persons legally incorporated with them, who shall, in good faith, select land within the reservation to which such lodge or family belongs, and begin the cultivation thereof, one good cow, and one well broken pair of oxen, with yoke and chain, within reasonable time after making such selection and settlement.

ARTICLE VI.

Physician, farmer, etc. The United States will also furnish to each reservation herein made and described, a physician, carpenter, miller, engineer, farmer, and blacksmith, for a period of ten years from the date of this agreement.

ARTICLE VII.

Reservations for school purposes. It is hereby agreed that the sixteenth and thirty-sixth sections of each township in said separate reservations shall be reserved for school purposes, for the use of the inhabitants of said reservations, as provided in sections 1946 and 1947 of the revised statutes of the United States.

Education annuity. It is also agreed that the provisions of Article VII of the treaty of 1868, securing to said Indians the benefits of education, shall be continued in force for not less than twenty (20) years, from and after the ratification of this agreement.

ARTICLE VIII.

The provisions of the treaty of 1868, and the agreement of 1876, except as herein modified, shall continue in full force.

This agreement shall not be binding upon either party until it shall have received the approval of the President and Congress of the United States.

Dated and signed at Santee Agency, Nebraska, October 17th, 1882.

NEWTON EDMUNDS.   [SEAL.]
PETER C. SHANNON.   [SEAL.]
JAMES H. TELLER.   [SEAL.]

The foregoing articles of agreement, having been fully explained to us in open council, we the undersigned chiefs and head-men of the Sioux Indians receiving rations and annuities at the Santee Agency, in Knox County, in the State of Nebraska, do hereby consent and agree to all the stipulations therein contained, saving and reserving all our rights, both collective and individual, in and to the Santee Reservation, in said Knox County and State of Nebraska, upon which we and our people are residing.

Witness our hands and seals at Santee Agency this 17th day of October, 1882.

Robert Hakewaste, his x mark. Seal.	Napoleon Wabashaw. Seal.
John Buoy. Seal.	Thomas Wakute. Seal.
Joseph Rouillard. Seal.	A. J. Campbell. Seal.
Solomon Jones. Seal.	Daniel Graham. Seal.
William Dick, his x mark. Seal.	Star Frazier. Seal.
Samuel Hawley. Seal.	Albert E. Frazier. Seal.
Eli Abraham. Seal.	John White. Seal.
Iron Elk, his x mark. Seal.	Henry Jones. Seal.
Husasa, his x mark. Seal.	Louis Frenier. Seal.
Harpi yaduta. Seal.	John Reibe. Seal.

Attest:
Alfred L. Riggs, Missionary to the Dakotas.
W. W. Fowler, Missionary to·Santee Sioux.
Isaiah Lightner, U. S. Indian Agent.
Charles Mitchell, U. S. Interpreter.
C. L. Austin, Agency Clerk.
Geo. W. Ira, Agency Physician.

I certify that the foregoing agreement was read and explained by me, and was fully understood by the above-named Sioux Indians, before signing, and that the same was executed by said Sioux Indians, at Santee Agency, county of Knox, and State of Nebraska, on the 17th day of October, 1882.

Sam'l D. Hinman,
Official Interpreter.

It is hereby agreed that the separate reservation for the Indians receiving rations and annuities at Pine Ridge Agency, Dakota, shall be bounded and described as follows, to wit:

Separate reservation for Pine Ridge Agency Indians.

Beginning at the intersection of the one hundred and third meridian of longitude with the northern boundary of the state of Nebraska, thence north along said meridian to the south fork of Cheyenne river, and down said stream to a point due west from the intersection of White River with the one hundred and second meridian; thence due east to said point of intersection and down said White River to a point in longitude one hundred and one degrees and twenty minutes west, thence due south to said north line of the State of Nebraska, thence west on said north line to the place of beginning.

Dated and signed at Pine Ridge Agency, Dakota, October 28th, 1882.

NEWTON EDMUNDS.   [SEAL.]
PETER C. SHANNON.   [SEAL.]
JAMES H. TELLER.   [SEAL.]

The foregoing articles of agreement having been fully explained to us in open council, we, the undersigned chiefs and headmen of the Sioux Indians receiving rations and annuities at Pine Ridge Agency in the Territory of Dakota, do hereby consent and agree to all the stipulations therein contained.

Witness our hands and seals at Pine Ridge Agency, Dakota, this 28th day of October, 1882.

Mahpiya-luta, his x mark. Seal.	Owa-sica-hoksila, his x mark. Seal.
Taopicikala, his x mark. Seal.	Toicuwa, his x mark. Seal.
Simka-luta, his x mark. Seal.	Sunmanito-isnala, his x mark. Seal.
Simka-wakan-hin-to, his x mark. Seal.	Kisun-sni, his x mark. Seal.
Tatanka-hunka-sni, his x mark. Seal.	Hehaka-sapa, his x mark. Seal.
Mato-sapa, his x mark. Seal.	Zitkala-ska, his x mark. Seal.
Sunanito-wankantuya, his x mark. Seal.	Ogle-sa, his x mark. Seal.
Pehinzizi, his x mark. Seal.	Sunmanito-wakpa, his x mark. Seal.
Canker-tanka, his x mark. Seal.	Wasicum-tasunke, his x mark. Seal.
Sunka-bloka, his x mark. Seal.	Egeonge-word, Captain Polo. Seal.
Wapaha-sapa, his x mark. Seal.	Akicita-injin, his x mark. Seal.
Mim-wanica, his x mark. Seal.	Tasunko-inyauko, his x mark. Seal.

Wagmu-su, his x mark. Seal.	Sunka-himka-sni, his x mark. Seal.
Wamli-heton, his x mark. Seal.	Manka-tamahica, his x mark. Seal.
Kangi-maza, his x mark. Seal.	Cotan-cikala, his x mark. Seal.
Sunmanito-ska, his x mark. Seal.	John Jangrau, his x mark. Seal.
Sunka-unzica, his x mark. Seal.	Charles Jamis, his x mark. Seal.
Mato-sapa, his x mark. Seal.	Richard Hunter, his x mark. Seal.
Hinho-kinyau, his x mark. Seal.	David Gallineau. Seal.
Tasunka-kokipapi, sr., his x mark. Seal.	Thomas Toion, his x mark. Seal.
Hazska-mlaska, his x mark. Seal.	James Richard, his x mark. Seal.
Tasunke-maza, his x mark. Seal.	Opauingowica-kte, his x mark. Seal
Okiksahe, his x mark. Seal.	Hogan, his x mark. Seal.
Mato-nasula, his x mark. Seal.	Antoine Provost. Seal.
Kangi-cikala, his x mark. Seal.	Benj. Claymore. Seal.
Wicahhpi-yamin, his x mark. Seal.	Soldier Storr. Seal.
Wasicun-waukautuya, his x mark. Seal.	Sili-kte, his x mark. Seal.
Antoine Leiddeau, his x mark. Seal.	Petaga, his x mark. Seal.
Beaver Morto, his x mark. Seal.	Talo-kakse, his x mark. Seal.
Sam Daon. Seal.	Wiyaka-wicasa, his x mark. Seal.
Edward Larramie. Seal.	Akicita, his x mark. Seal.
Wakinyan-peta, his x mark. Seal.	Zitkala-napin, his x mark. Seal.
Pehan-luta, his x mark. Seal.	Leon F. Pallardy, his x mark. Seal.
Tasunka-kokipapi, his x mark. Seal.	J. C. Whelan. Seal.
Conica-wanica, his x mark. Seal.	Sunka-cikala, his x mark. Seal.
Suniska-yaha, his x mark. Seal.	Pehin-zizi-si-ca, his x mark. Seal.
Wahanka-wakuwa, his x mark. Seal.	Mato-akisya, his x mark. Seal.
Si-tanka, his x mark. Seal.	Wasicun-mato, his x mark. Seal.
Wahukeza-wompa, his x mark. Seal.	Wi-cikala, his x mark. Seal.
Mato-hi, his x mark. Seal.	Taku-kokipa-sni, his x mark. Seal.
Wicasa-tankala, his x mark. Seal.	Mato-can-wegna-eya, his x mark. Seal.
Mato-witkotkoka, his x mark. Seal.	Mato-Wakuya, his x mark. Seal.
Wankan-mato, his x mark. Seal.	

Attest:

S. S. Benedict, U. S. Indian Interpreter.
V. T. McGellycuddy, U. S. Ind. Ag't.
J. W. Alder, Agency Clerk.
William Garnett, Agency Interpreter.

I hereby certify that the foregoing agreement was read and explained by me and was fully understood by the above named Sioux Indians, before signing, and that the same was executed by said Indians at Pine Ridge Agency, Dakota, on the 29th day of October, 1882.

Sam'l D. Hinman,
Official Interpreter.

Separate reservation for Rosebud Agency Indians.

It is hereby agreed that the separate reservation for the Indians receiving rations and annuities at Rosebud Agency, Dakota, shall be bounded and described as follows, to wit:—

Beginning on the north boundary of the State of Nebraska, at a point in longitude one hundred and one degrees and twenty minutes west, and running thence due north to White River, thence down said White River to a point in longitude ninety-nine degrees and thirty minutes west, thence due south to said north boundary of the state of Nebraska, and thence west on said north boundary to the place of beginning. If any of said Indians belonging to the Rosebud agency have permanently located east of longitude ninety-nine degrees and thirty minutes, they may hold the lands so located, and have the same certified to them in accordance with the provisions of Article 6, of the treaty of 1868 and Article III of this agreement, or they may return to the separate reservation above described, in which case they shall be entitled to receive from the government the actual value of all improvements made on such locations.

Dated and signed at Rosebud Agency, Dakota, this 6th day of November, 1882.

NEWTON EDWARDS.   [SEAL.]
JAMES H. TELLER.   [SEAL.]
PETER C. SHANNON.   [SEAL.]

The foregoing articles of agreement having been fully explained to us in open council, we, the undersigned chiefs and headmen of the Sioux Indians receiving rations and annuities at Rosebud Agency in, the Territory of Dakota, do hereby consent and agree to all the stipulations therein contained.

Witness our hands and seals at Rosebud Agency, Dakota, this 6th day of November, 1882.

Sinto-gleska, his x mark. Seal.
Mato-luzaham, his x mark. Seal.
Wakinyau-ska, his x mark. Seal.
Kangi-sapa, his x mark. Seal.
Mato-ohanka, his x mark. Seal.
Wakinyau-ska, 2nd, his x mark. Seal.
Tasunke-tokeca, his x mark. Seal.
Asampi, his x mark. Seal.
Mahpiya-inazin, his x mark. Seal.
He-to-pa, his x mark. Seal.
Tasimke-wakita, his x mark. Seal.
Sunka-bloka, his x mark. Seal.
Caugleska-wakinyin, his x mark. Seal.
Wamniomni-akicita, his x mark. Seal.
Wanmli-cikala, his x mark. Seal.
Wamli-waste, his x mark. Seal.
Mahpiya-tatanka, his x mark. Seal.
Wapashupi, his x mark. Seal.
Mato-wankantuya, his x mark. Seal.
Igmu-wakute, his x mark. Seal.
Hohaka-gloska, his x mark. Seal.
Mato-ska, his x mark. Capt. Police. Seal.
Pehan-san-mani, his x mark. Seal.
Okise-wakan, his x mark. Seal.
Getau-wakimyau, his x mark. Seal.
Wakinyau-tomaheca, his x mark. Seal.
Mloka-cikala, his x mark. Seal.
Toka-kte, his x mark. Seal.
Mato-wakan, his x mark. Seal.
Tacauhpi-to, his x mark. Seal.
Ho-waste, his x mark. Seal.
Ito-cantkoze, his x mark. Seal.
Kutepi, his x mark. Seal.
Zaya-hiyaya, his x mark. Seal.
Mato-glakinyau, his x mark. Seal.
Mato-cante, his x mark. Seal.
Cecala, his x mark. Seal.
Pehin-zi-sica, his x mark. Seal.
Pte-he-napin, his x mark. Seal.
Sunsun-pa, his x mark. Seal.
Tasunke-wamli, his x mark. Seal.
Louis Richard. Seal.
Louis Bordeax. Seal.
Tasunke-hin-zi, his x mark. Seal.
Itoga-otanka, his x mark. Seal.
Tunkan-sila, his x mark. Seal.
Wagleksun-tanka, his x mark. Seal.
Caugleska-sapa, his x mark. Seal.
Wospi-gli, his x mark. Seal.
Naca-cikala, his x mark. Seal.
Cante-maza, his x mark. Seal.
Tatanka-kucila, his x mark. Seal.
Mato-wakuwa, his x mark. Seal.
Si-hauska, his x mark. Seal.
Kinyau-mani, his x mark. Seal.
Tatanka, his x mark. Seal.
Hehaka-wanapoya, his x mark. Seal.
Taspan, his x mark. Seal.
Tasunke-hin-zi, his x mark. Seal.
Wicauhpi-cikala, his x mark. Seal.
Wohela, his x mark. Seal.

Jack Stead. Seal.
Joseph Schweigman. Seal.
Zitkala-sapa, his x mark. Seal.
Mato-najin, his x mark. Seal.
Yahota, his x mark. Seal.
Hunku, his x mark. Seal.
Sunka-wanmli, his x mark. Seal.
Pte-san-wanmli, his x mark. Seal.
Tatanka-ho-waste, his x mark. Seal.
Tasunke-hin-zi, his x mark. Seal.
Tasunke-luzahan, his x mark. Seal.
Kangi-sapa, his x mark. Seal.
Sunka-ha, his x mark. Seal.
Cikala, his x mark. Seal.
Si-husakpe, his x mark. Seal.
Thomas Dorion, his x mark. Seal.
Tacannonpe-waukantuya, his x mark. Seal.
Caza, his x mark. Seal.
Wagluhe, his x mark. Seal.
Ista-toto, his x mark. Seal.
Wahacauka-hinapa, his x mark. Seal.
Mle-wakan, his x mark. Seal.
Hehaka-wanmli, his x mark. Seal.
Si-tompi-ska, his x mark. Seal.
Hehaka-witko, his x mark. Seal.
Sinte-ska, his x mark. Seal.
Wahacauka-waste, his x mark. Seal.
Mato-kinajin, his x mark. Seal.
Mawatani-hanska, his x mark. Seal.
Wanmli-wicasa, his x mark. Seal.
Henry Clairmont, his x mark. Seal.
Cecil Iron-wing. Seal.
Mato-maka-kicum, his x mark. Seal.
Kiyetehan, his x mark. Seal.
Mato-wanmli, his x mark. Seal.
Ite-cihila, his x mark. Seal.
Cante-peta, his x mark. Seal.
William Bordeau. Seal.
Wanmlisun-maza, his x mark. Seal.
Louis Moran, his x mark. Seal.
William Redmond. Seal.
Tatanka-taninyau-mani, his x mark. Seal.
Mato-ite-wanagi, his x mark. Seal.
Wanagi pa, his x mark. Seal.
Baptiste McKinzy, his x mark. Seal.
John Cordier, his x mark. Seal.
Akan-yanka-kte, his x mark. Seal.
Maza-wicasa, his x mark. Seal.
Ipiyaka, his x mark. Seal.
Tunka-yuha, his x mark. Seal.
Tawahacanka-sna, his x mark. Seal.
Cetan-nonpa, his x mark. Seal.
Zuya-hanska, his x mark. Seal.
Mato-wakau, his x mark. Seal.
Wanmli-mani, his x mark. Seal.
Keya-tucuhu, his x mark. Seal.
Cega, his x mark. Seal.
Ohan-ota, his x mark. Seal.
Sunka-wananon, his x mark. Seal.
Dominick Brey. Seal.

Attest:

Jas. G. Wright, U. S. Ind. Ag't.
Chas. P. Jordan, Clerk.
Chas. R. Corey, Physician.
Louis Raulindeane, Agency Interpreter.

I hereby certify that the foregoing agreement was read and explained by me and was fully understood by the above-named Sioux Indians before signing, and that the same was executed by said Indians at Rosebud Agency, Dakota, on the 6th day of November, 1882.

Sam'l D. Hinman,
Official Interpreter.

Separate reservation for Standing Rock Agency Indians. It is hereby agreed that the separate reservations for the Indians receiving rations and annuities at Standing Rock Agency, Dakota, shall be bounded and described as follows, to wit:—

Beginning at a point at low-water mark, on the east bank of the Missouri River, opposite the mouth of cannon ball river; thence down said east bank along said low-water mark to a point opposite the mouth of Grand River, thence westerly to said Grand River, and up and along the middle channel of the same to its intersection with the one hundred and second meridian of longitude; thence north along said meridian to its intersection with the south branch of Cannon Ball River—also known as Cedar Creek; thence down said south branch of Cannon Ball River to its intersection with the main Cannon Ball River, and down said main Cannon Ball River to the Missouri River at the place of beginning.

Dated and signed at Standing Rock Agency, Dakota, this 30th day of November, 1882.

NEWTON EDMUNDS.   [SEAL.]
JAMES H. TELLER.   [SEAL.]
PETER C. SHANNON.   [SEAL.]

The foregoing articles of agreement having been fully explained to us in open council, we, the undersigned chiefs and head-men of the Sioux Indians, receiving rations and annuities at Standing Rock Agency, in the Territory of Dakota, do hereby consent and agree to all the stipulations therein contained. We also agree that the Lower Yanktonais Indians at Crow Creek, and the Indians now with Sitting Bull, may share with us the above-described separate reservation, if assigned thereto by the United States, with consent of said Indians.

Witness our hands and seals at Standing Rock Agency, Dakota, this 30th day of November, 1882.

Akicita-hauska, his x mark. Seal.	Taloka-inyauke, his x mark. Seal.
Mato-gnaskinyan, his x mark. Seal.	Mato-wapostan, his x mark. Seal.
Mato-nonpa, his x mark. Seal.	Heton-yuha, his x mark. Seal.
Ista-sapa, his x mark. Seal.	Sungila-luta, his x mark. Seal.
Wanmli-waukautuya, his x mark. Seal.	Mastinca, his x mark. Seal.
Wakute-mani, his x mark. Seal.	Sunka-maza, his x mark. Seal.
Wiyaka-hanska, his x mark. Seal.	Wanmli-cikala, his x mark. Seal.
Cante-peta, his x mark. Seal.	Kangi-mato, his x mark. Seal.
John Grass, his x mark. Seal.	Mato-wankantuya, his x mark. Seal.
Sasunke-luta, his x mark. Seal.	Ite-glaga, his x mark. Seal.
Owape, his x mark. Seal.	Cetan-unzica, his x mark. Seal.
Cante-peta, sr., his x mark. Seal.	Mato-luta, his x mark. Seal.
Mato-wayuhi, his x mark. Seal.	Pizi, his x mark. Seal.
Pahin-ska, his x mark. Seal.	Kangi-wanagi, his x mark. Seal.
Kangi-atoyapi, his x mark. Seal.	Wanmdi-mani, his x mark. Seal.
Mato-kawinge, his x mark. Seal.	Mato-ska, his x mark. Seal.
Wakinyan-watakope, his x mark. Seal.	Tacanhpi-kokipapi, his x mark. Seal.
Tasina-luta, his x mark. Seal.	Tatanka-cikida, his x mark. Seal.
Tasunke-hin-zi, his x mark. Seal.	Wahacanka-sapa, his x mark. Seal.
Hehaka-okan-nazin, his x mark. Seal.	Sna-waknya, his x mark. Seal.
Maga, his x mark. Seal.	Cante-tchiya, his x mark. Seal.

Wan-awega, his x mark. Seal.
Wakankdi-sapa, his x mark. Seal.
Ingang-mani, his x mark. Seal.
Wanmdi-sake, his x mark. Seal.
Nakata-wakinyan, his x mark. Seal.
Wanmli-watakpe, his x mark. Seal.
Hato-sabiciya, his x mark. Seal.
Baptiste Rondeau, his x mark. Seal.
Tacanhpi-sapa, his x mark. Seal.
Hato-ite-wakan, his x mark. Seal.
Wakinyan-ska, his x mark. Seal.
Hakikta-nazin, his x mark. Seal.
Hitonkala-ista, his x mark. Seal.
Hanpa-napin, his x mark. Seal.
Waumdi-yuha, his x mark. Seal.
Hinto-kdeska, his x mark. Seal.
Candi-ynta, his x mark. Seal.
Zitka-mani, his x mark. Seal.
Nasula-tonka, his x mark. Seal.
Hohaka-ho-waste, his x mark. Seal.
Sunk-sapa-wicasa, his x mark. Seal.
Mastinca, his x mark. Seal.
Thomas C. Fly. Seal.
Joseph Primeau. Seal.
Leon Primeau. Seal.
Matilda Galpin, her x mark. Seal.
John Pleets. Seal.
Tasumke-ska, his x mark. Seal.
Kangi-maza, his x mark. Seal.
Ota-inyanke, his x mark. Seal.
Wahascanka, his x mark. Seal.
Anoka-sau, his x mark. Seal.
Mato-hota, his x mark. Seal.
Hehakato-tamahoca, his x mark. Seal.
Tamina-wewe, his x mark. Seal.
Waga, his x mark. Seal.
Tatanka-duta, his x mark. Seal.
Mato-wankantuya, his x mark. Seal.
Iyayung-mani, his x mark. Seal.
Magi-wakau, his x mark. Seal.
Wamli-wanapeya, his x mark. Seal.
Can-ica, his x mark. Seal.
Tahinca-ska, his x mark. Seal.
Hogan-duta, his x mark. Seal.
Sunka-wanzila, his x mark. Seal.
Ite-wakan, his x mark. Seal.
Sunka-wawapin, his x mark. Seal.
Cetau-to, his x mark. Seal.
Inyan-knwapi, his x mark. Seal.
Waukau-inyanka, his x mark. Seal.
Sunka-duta, his x mark. Seal.

Pehin-jasa, his x mark. Seal.
Waumdi-watakpe, his x mark. Seal.
Wapata, his x mark. Seal.
Taopi, his x mark. Seal.
Mato-unzinca, his x mark. Seal.
Zitkadan-maza, his x mark. Seal.
Cetau-iyotanka, his x mark. Seal.
Kangi-napin, his x mark. Seal.
Tatanka-hanska, his x mark. Seal.
Kaddy, his x mark. Seal.
Wanmdi-konza, his x mark. Seal.
Mini-aku, his x mark. Seal.
Mato-sapa, his x mark. Seal.
Makoyate-duta, his x mark. Seal.
Pa-inyankana, his x mark. Seal.
Mato-zina, his x mark. Seal.
Isanati-win-yuza, his x mark. Seal.
Mato-wastedan, his x mark. Seal.
Hehaka-ho-waste, his x mark. Seal.
Gan-waste, his x mark. Seal.
Itohega-tate, his x mark. Seal.
Hi-seca, his x mark. Seal.
Hunke-sni, his x mark. Seal.
Gilciya, his x mark. Seal.
Owe-nakebeza, his x mark. Seal.
Mato-ho-tanka, his x mark. Seal.
Henry Agard, his x mark. Seal.
Hitonka-sau-sinte, his x mark. Seal.
Antoine Claymore, his x mark. Seal.
Benedict Cihila. Seal.
Charles Marshall, his x mark. Seal.
Tatanka-wanzila, his x mark. Seal.
Tatanka-hauska, his x mark. Seal.
Tatanka-himke-sni, his x mark. Seal.
Kankeca-duta, his x mark. Seal.
Hehaka-cante, his x mark. Seal.
Sna-wakuya, his x mark. Seal.
Citan-pegnaka, his x mark. Seal.
Wasu-mato, his x mark. Seal.
Mato-kawinge, his x mark. Seal.
Nig-woku, his x mark. Seal.
Maza-kan-wicaki, his x mark. Seal.
Waniyutu-wakuya, his x mark. Seal.
Waumdi-wicasa, his x mark. Seal.
Putin-hanska, his x mark. Seal.
Hoksina-waste, his x mark. Seal.
Sam-iyeiciya, his x mark. Seal.
Wahacanka-maza, his x mark. Seal.
Tatanke-ehanna, his x mark. Seal.
Tawacanka-wakinyan, his x mark. Seal.

Attest:

James McLaughlin, U. S. Indian Agent.
James H. Stewart, Agency Clerk.
Thomas H. Miller, Issue Clerk.
Charles Primeau, Interpreter.
Philip L. Wells, Interpreter.
Joseph Primeau, Interpreter.
M. L. McLaughlin, Agency Interpreter.

I hereby certify that the foregoing agreement was read and explained by me and was fully understood by the above-named Sioux Indians before signing, and that the same was executed by said Indians at Standing Rock Agency, Dakota, on the 30th day of November, 1882.

Sam'l D. Hinman, Official Interpreter.

It is hereby agreed that the separate reservation for the Indians receiving rations and annuities at Cheyenne River Agency, Dakota, and for such other Indians as may hereafter be assigned thereto, shall be bounded and described as follows, to wit:— *Separate reservation for Cheyenne River Agency Indians.*

Beginning at a point at low-water mark on the east bank of the Missouri River opposite the mouth of Grand River said point being the south-easterly corner of the Standing-Rock Reservation; thence down said east bank of the Missouri River along said low-water mark to a point opposite the mouth of the Cheyenne river; thence west to said Cheyenne River and up the same to its intersection with the one hundred and second meridian of longitude; thence north along said meridian to its intersection with the Grand River; thence down said Grand River, along the middle channel thereof, to the Missouri River, at the place of beginning.

It is also agreed that said Indians shall receive all necessary aid from the government in their removal to said reservation, and when so removed, each of said Indians shall be entitled to receive from the government the full value of all improvements in buildings or on lands owned by him at the time of such removal and lost to him thereby. Said compensation shall be given in such manner and on such appraisements as shall be ordered by the Secretary of the Interior.

Dated and signed at Cheyenne River Agency, Dakota, this 21st day of December.

NEWTON EDMUNDS.   [SEAL.]
PETER C. SHANNON.   [SEAL.]
JAMES H. TELLER.   [SEAL.]

The foregoing articles of agreement having been fully explained to us in open council, we, the undersigned chiefs and headmen of the Sioux Indians receiving rations and annuities at the Cheyenne River Agency, in the Territory of Dakota, do hereby consent and agree to all the stipulations therein contained.

Witness our hands and seals at Cheyenne River Agency, Dakota, this 21st day of December, 1882.

Zitkala-kinyan, his x mark. Seal.	Cetan-tokapa, his x mark. Seal.
Cuwi-hda-mani, his x mark. Seal.	Waumli-ohitika, his x mark. Seal.
Mato-wanmli, his x mark. Seal.	Wagmasa, his x mark. Seal.
Toicuwa, his x mark. Seal.	Cuwila, his x mark. Seal.
Waumli-gleska, his x mark. Seal.	Mato-nakpa, his x mark. Seal.
Mato-luta, his x mark. Seal.	Maste-au, his x mark. Seal.
Waunatan, his x mark. Seal.	Nape-wanmiomin, his x mark. Seal.
Cante-wanica, his x mark. Seal.	Sunka-ha-oin, his x mark. Seal.
Wokai, his x mark. Seal.	Tacauhpi-maza, his x mark. Seal.
Wankan-mato, his x mark. Seal.	Nato-cikala, his x mark. Seal.
Cetan, his x mark. Seal.	Nahpiya-watakpe, his x mark. Seal.
Maza-hanpa, his x mark. Seal.	Louis Benoist, his x mark. Seal.
Maga-ska, his x mark. Seal.	Wahacauka-cikala, his x mark. Seal.
Kangi-wakuya, his x mark. Seal.	Sunk-ska, his x mark. Seal.
Pte-san-wicasa, his x mark. Seal.	Wanmli-main, his x mark. Seal.
Mahpiya-iyapata, his x mark. Seal.	Wicasa-itancan, his x mark. Seal.
Mato-topa, his x mark. Seal.	Siha-sapa-cikala, his x mark. Seal.
Cawhpi-sapa, his x mark. Seal.	Eugene Bruguier. Seal.
Tatanke-paha-akan-nazin, his x mark. Seal.	

Attest:

Wm. A. Swan, United States Indian Agent.
Rob't V. Levers, Agency Clerk.
N. G. Landmepe, Issue Clerk.
Narcisse Narcello, his x mark, Agency Interpreter.
Mark Wells, Interpreter.

Separate reservation for Lower Brulés.

It having been understood and agreed by the undersigned commissioners and the Brule Indians at Rosebud Agency, parties to this agreement, that the reservation for the Lower Brule Indians shall be located between the Rosebud Reservation and the Missouri River, it is hereby agreed that the reservation for the said Brule Indians, now at Lower Brule Agency, Dakota, and for such other Indians as may be assigned thereto, shall consist of all that part of township No. 103, range 72, west of the 5th principal meridian, in the Territory of Dakota, lying on the north bank of the White River, together with the tract of land bounded and described as follows, to wit:

Beginning at a point at low-water mark on the east bank of the Missouri River opposite the mouth of the said White River; thence down said east bank of the Missouri River along said low-water mark to a point opposite the mouth of Pratt Creek; thence due south to the forty-third parallel of latitude; thence west along said parallel to a point in longitude ninety-nine degrees and thirty minutes west; thence due north along the eastern boundary of Rosebud Reservation to the White River, and thence down said White River to the Missouri River, at the place of beginning. It is also agreed that said Indians shall receive all necessary aid from the government in their removal to said reservation, and when so removed each of said Indians shall be entitled to receive from the government the full value of all improvements, in buildings or on lands, owned by him at the time of such removal and lost to him thereby. Said compensation shall be made in such manner and on such appraisement as shall be ordered by the Secretary of the Interior.

Witness our hands and seals this 23rd day of January, 1883.

NEWTON EDMUNDS. [SEAL.]
PETER C. SHANNON. [SEAL.]
JAMES H. TELLER. [SEAL.]

AGREEMENT WITH THE COLUMBIA AND COLVILLE, 1883.

In the conference with chief Moses and Sar-sarp-kin, of the Columbia reservation, and Tonaskat and Lot, of the Colville reservation, had this day, the following was substantially what was asked for by the Indians:

July 7, 1883.

Ratified July 4, 1884, 23 Stat., 79. Vol. 1, p. 224.

Tonasket asked for a saw and grist mill, a boarding school to be established at Bonaparte Creek to accommodate one hundred pupils (100), and a physician to reside with them, and $100. (one hundred) to himself each year.

See report of Commissioner of Indian Affairs for 1882, p. lxx.

Sar-sarp-kin asked to be allowed to remain on the Columbia reservation with his people, where they now live, and to be protected in their rights as settlers, and in addition to the ground they now have under cultivation within the limit of the fifteen mile strip cut off from the northern portion of the Columbia Reservation, to be allowed to select enough more unoccupied land in Severalty to make a total to Sar-sarp-kin of four square miles, being 2,560 acres of land, and each head of a family or male adult one square mile; or to move on to the Colville Reservation, if they so desire, and in case they so remove, and relinquish all their claims to the Columbia Reservation, he is to receive one hundred (100) head of cows for himself and people, and such farming implements as may be necessary.

All of which the Secretary agrees they should have, and that he will ask Congress to make an appropriation to enable him to perform.

The Secretary also agrees to ask Congress to make an appropriation to enable him to purchase for Chief Moses a sufficient number of cows to furnish each one of his band with two cows; also to give Moses one thousand dollars ($1,000) for the purpose of erecting a dwelling-house for himself; also to construct a saw mill and grist-mill as soon as the same shall be required for use; also that each head of a family or each male adult person shall be furnished with one wagon, one double set of harness, one grain cradle, one plow, one harrow, one scythe, one hoe, and such other agricultural implements as may be necessary.

And on condition that Chief Moses and his people keep this agreement faithfully, he is to be paid in cash, in addition to all of the above, one thousand dollars ($1,000) per annum during his life.

All this on condition that Chief Moses shall remove to the Colville Reservation and relinquish all claim upon the Government for any land situate elsewhere.

Further, that the Government will secure to Chief Moses and his people, as well as to all other Indians who may go on to the Colville Reservation, and engage in farming, equal rights and protection alike with all other Indians now on the Colville Reservation, and will afford him any assistance necessary to enable him to carry out the terms of this agreement on the part of himself and his people. That until he and his people are located permanently on the Colville Reservation, his status shall remain as now, and the police over his people shall be vested in the military, and all money or articles to be furnished him and his people shall be sent to some point in the locality of his people, there to be distributed as provided. All other Indians now living on the Columbia Reservation shall be entitled to 640 acres, or one square mile of land, to each head of family or male adult, in the possession and ownership of which they shall be guaranteed and protected. Or should they move on to the Colville Reservation within two years, they will be provided with such farming implements as may be required, provided they surrender all rights to the Columbia Reservation.

All of the foregoing is upon the condition that Congress will make an appropriation of funds necessary to accomplish the foregoing, and confirm this agreement; and also, with the understanding that Chief Moses or any of the Indians heretofore mentioned shall not be required to remove to the Colville Reservation until Congress does make such appropriation, etc.

> H. M. TELLER,
> Secretary of Interior.
> H. PRICE,
> Commissioner of Indian Affairs.
> MOSES (his x mark),
> TONASKET (his x mark),
> SAR-SARP-KIN (his x mark).

INDEX.

A.

C.

P.

O

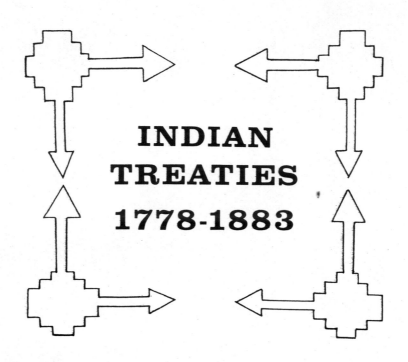

INDIAN
TREATIES
1778-1883

Private Hermann Stieffel, present at the signing of the treaty at Medicine Lodge Creek, Kansas, in

Second printing 1973

Foreword and Introduction © 1972 by Interland Publishing, Inc.
Originally published as Indian Affairs: Laws and Treaties, Volume 2 (Treaties)
Reprinted from the edition of 1904, Washington, D.C.
First Interland Edition Published 1972
Manufactured in the United States of America

International Standard Book Number: 0-87989-025-8
Library of Congress Catalog Card Number: 72-75770

The illustration on the endpaper is used courtesy of The National Collection
of Fine Arts, Smithsonian Institution.

Frontispiece illustration reproduced from the original copyrighted by
Nick Eggenhofer, and used for this edition only, by permission of the artist.
The illustration on the last page is reproduced from the original drawing by
Brummett Echohawk, a Pawnee Indian, and used in this edition only,
by permission of the artist.

Map by courtesy of Sol Tax for Bruce Mac Lachlan, Samuel Stanley,
Robert K. Thomas, and the Smithsonian Institution.

The ornaments used on the binding and the Title Page are taken from
Decorative Art of the Southwestern Indians by Dorothy Smith Sides and
American Indian Design and Decoration by Le Roy H. Appleton and are
used with the permission of Dover Publications, Inc.

Binding design by Joan Stoliar

INTERLAND PUBLISHING, INC.
799 Broadway
New York, N.Y. 10003

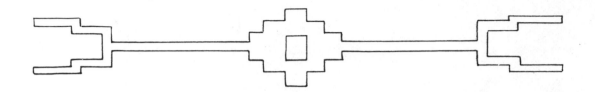

Indian Treaties
1778-1883

COMPILED AND EDITED BY Charles J. Kappler

WITH A NEW FOREWORD BY Brantley Blue
Indian Claims Commissioner

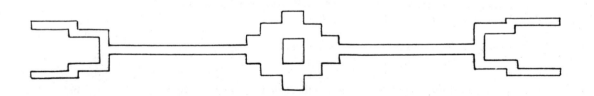

INTERLAND PUBLISHING INC.
NEW YORK, N.Y.

N. EGGENHOFER.